MIDDLE AND JUNIOR HIGH SCHOOL LIBRARY CATALOG

EIGHTH EDITION

STANDARD CATALOG SERIES

JULIETTE YAAKOV, GENERAL EDITOR

CHILDREN'S CATALOG

FICTION CATALOG

MIDDLE AND JUNIOR HIGH SCHOOL
LIBRARY CATALOG

PUBLIC LIBRARY CATALOG

SENIOR HIGH SCHOOL LIBRARY CATALOG

MIDDLE AND JUNIOR HIGH SCHOOL LIBRARY CATALOG

EIGHTH EDITION

EDITED BY

ANNE PRICE AND JULIETTE YAAKOV

MANAGING EDITOR

ZAIDA NIDZA PADRÓ

NEW YORK • DUBLIN

THE H. W. WILSON COMPANY

2000

Printed in the United States of America

Abridged Dewey Decimal Classification and Relative Index, Edition 13 is © 1997-2000 OCLC Online Computer Library Center, Incorporated. Portions Reprinted with Permission. DDC, Dewey, Dewey Decimal Classification, and Forest Press are registered trademarks of OCLC.

Library of Congress Cataloging-in-Publication Data

Middle and junior high school library catalog / edited by Anne Price and Juliette Yaakov; managing editor, Zaida Nidza Padró. – 8th ed.
   p. cm. – (Standard catalog series)
  Includes index.
  ISBN 0-8242-0996-6 (alk. paper)
   1. Young adult literature—Bibliography. 2. Junior high school libraries—United States—Book lists. I. Price, Anne, 1946- II. Yaakov, Juliette. III. Series.

Z1037.J854 2000   00-063316
011.62´5—dc21

CONTENTS

CONTENTS

PREFACE

Middle and Junior High School Library Catalog is a selective list of fiction and nonfiction books recommended for young people in grades five through nine. In addition to this volume, the service unit comprises annual supplements for 2001, 2002, 2003, and 2004 without further charge.

History

Junior High School Library Catalog, first published in 1965, was developed to address the unique needs of early adolescents. It developed from the *Standard Catalog for High School Libraries*, which was subsequently modified in scope and retitled *Senior High School Library Catalog*. Since its inception the Catalog has been published regularly every five years with annual supplements. With the seventh edition the title of the Catalog was changed from *Junior High School Library Catalog* to *Middle and Junior High School Library Catalog* to reflect the prevalence of middle school programs and the extension of coverage to grades five and six.

Preparation

An advisory committee of distinguished librarians assisted in the compilation of the voting list. The committee reaffirmed the selection policy, reevaluated titles from the previous edition of the Catalog and its supplements, and proposed many new titles. The list that resulted from the committee's deliberations was then submitted to a group of experienced librarians familiar with the needs of young people. This group, representing diverse geographical areas, elected the titles included. In most cases their vote represents the composite judgment of a number of their colleagues.

Scope and Purpose

Middle and Junior High School Library Catalog lists books for youth in grades five through nine, along with review sources and other professional aids for the librarian or school media specialist. This edition includes 4,520 book titles and 4,492 analytical entries for parts of books. Entries for works other than reference works that are most likely to be of interest to young people in grades seven and higher are given the notation "7 and up." In a special section there are entries for a selection of CD-ROMs devoted to reference and educational materials. Libraries and media centers serving large systems and those with special curriculum needs will wish to supplement this Catalog.

Books listed were published in the United States, or published in Canada or the United Kingdom and distributed in the United States. A small number of out-of-print titles that are considered essential to a well-rounded collection have been included at the suggestion of the advisory committee. They are noted as o.p.

All other titles were in print at the time of listing. For some books, paper is the only available binding. If a book has been deleted from the catalog in this edition because it is no longer in print, that deletion is not intended as a sign that the book is no longer valuable or that it should necessarily be weeded from the collection.

Because of the lack of uniform national standards and the movement away from a set curriculum, the Catalog does not aim to support any particular middle level curriculum but rather to cover a broad spectrum of topics. In the nonfiction section special importance is given to works devoted to technology, personal values, and current social and political issues, with special emphasis on ethnic diversity and minorities. Topics of particular importance are the World Wide Web, virtual reality and other new technologies, environmental problems, animal ecology, and the protection of endangered species. The fiction section contains a wide range of literary works that are of interest to youth and many that are frequently included in the school curriculum—classics as well as contemporary fiction and genre literature. Among the works for the librarian or media specialist are bibliographies, professional journals, and other resources for the selection and evaluation of print and nonprint materials and the use of the internet in instruction. The CD-ROM section is devoted primarily to reference works and interactive educational materials in support of the curriculum in the areas of science, social studies, geography, and mathematics. The items in this section were chosen on the basis of accuracy of content, scope of coverage, quality of multimedia elements, ease of navigation, and usefulness of supporting documentation. It is not intended to be a comprehensive list and can be augmented according to the needs of individual collections. The availability of a CD-ROM version of a print equivalent is indicated at the entry for the book version. Upon the recommendation of the advisory committee, the Catalog lists professional journals that review, evaluate, and recommend educational Web sites rather than listing Web sites themselves.

The Catalog excludes the following: nonprint materials other than CD-ROMs; non-English-language materials, with the exception of dictionaries and similar items; periodicals, except for professional review media; works of adult fiction, except for books originally written for adults but read by young people or books widely used in the curriculum; textbooks; and books about specific vocations, individual computer programs or versions of programs, and other topics that quickly become outdated.

Organization

The Catalog consists of four parts.

Part 1, the Classified Catalog, is arranged according to the Dewey Decimal Classification for nonfiction, followed by sections for fiction and story collections. The information supplied for each book includes bibliographic description, suggested subject headings, an annotation, and an evaluation, frequently from a quoted source.

Part 2, the Author, Title, Subject, and Analytical Index, serves as a comprehensive key to Part 1. Analytical entries provide indexing for parts of works and are an important feature of the Catalog in that they maximize use of the library's holdings. Subject analytics afford access to parts of books not covered by the subject headings for the whole, while author and title analytics provide an approach to anthologies and collections, especially of plays and short stories.

Part 3, a Select List of Recommended CD-ROMs, includes reference works, source material, periodical indexes and abstracts, and interactive educational software. Many of these materials are not available in print format. Title and subject access to this section is included in the Index.

Part 4, the Directory of Publishers and Distributors, includes name, address, telephone number, and other pertinent information about the publishers of the works listed in the Catalog.

The section that follows, Directions for Use of the Catalog, contains more detailed information about the uses and content of the Catalog.

Acknowledgments

This Catalog could not have been published without the cooperative efforts of publishers and the library community. The H.W. Wilson Company is indebted to the publishers who generously supplied copies of their books, as well as information about editions and prices. The Company also acknowledges its gratitude to the two groups of librarians who gave so generously of their time and expertise: the advisory committee and the consultants. Their names appear below.

The advisory committee comprised:

Raymond W. Barber, Chair
Director of Libraries
The William Penn Charter School
Philadelphia, Pa.

Tracie Hall
Formerly Young Adult Services Specialist
Seattle Public Library
Seattle, Wash.

Curtis L. Kiefer
Youth Services Supervisor
Corvallis-Benton County Public Library
Corvallis, Or.

Suzanne Manczuk
Library Consultant
Pennington, N.J.

Mary Ann Paulin, Director
Superiorland Library Cooperative
    Preview Center
Marquette, Mich.

Susan Rosenzweig, Adjunct Professor
Graduate School of Library and
    Information Studies
University of Rhode Island
Kingston, R.I.

Gerry Solomon, Assistant Section Chief
N.C. Dept. of Public Instruction Evaluation Center
Raleigh, N.C.

The following consultants participated in the voting:

Ginger Armstrong, Library Associate
Chesterfield County Central Library
Chesterfield, Va.

Donna Bessant, Librarian
Monterey Peninsula Unified School District
Monterey, Calif.

Claudine Jackson
Young Adult Specialist
Kansas City Public Library
Kansas City, Mo.

Linda Jordan, Director of Library Services
Waco Independent School District
Waco, Tex.

Ann Roush, Children's Librarian
Redmond Regional Library
Redmond, Wash.

Patricia Scales, Library Media Specialist
Greenville Middle School
Greenville, S.C.

MaryKay Schnare
Strategic Planning Specialist
Providence School Board
Providence, R.I

Betsy Shorb
Young Adult Age Level Specialist
Prince George's County Memorial
   Library System
Bowie, Md.

DIRECTIONS FOR USE OF THE CATALOG

USES OF THE CATALOG

Middle and Junior High School Library Catalog is designed to serve these purposes:

As an aid in purchasing. The Catalog is designed to assist in the selection and ordering of titles. Annotations are provided for each title along with information concerning publisher, ISBN, price, and availability. Since Part 1, the Classified Catalog, is arranged according to the Dewey Decimal Classification, the Catalog may be used to identify elements of the library collection that should be updated or strengthened. In evaluating the suitability of a work each library will want to consider the special character of the school and community it serves. It would be inadvisable, of course, to depend upon a single source for book selection.

As an aid to the reader's advisor. The work of the reader's advisor is furthered by the information about sequels and companion volumes and the descriptive and critical annotations in the Classified Catalog, and by the subject access in the Index. The analytical entries in the Index augment the library's catalog by providing access to parts of composite works.

As an aid in verification of information. For this purpose full bibliographical data are provided in the Classified Catalog. Entries also include recommended subject headings based upon *Sears List of Subject Headings* and a suggested classification derived from the *Abridged Dewey Decimal Classification and Relative Index*. Notes describe editions available, awards, publication history, and other titles in the series.

As an aid in curriculum support. The classified approach, subject indexing, and annotations are helpful in identifying materials appropriate for classroom use.

As an aid in collection maintenance. Information about the titles available on a subject facilitates decisions to rebind, replace, or discard items.

As an instructional aid. The Catalog is useful in courses that deal with literature and book selection for young people.

THE CLASSIFIED CATALOG

The Classified Catalog is arranged with the nonfiction books first, classified by the Dewey Decimal Classification in numerical order from 000 to 999. Individual biographies are classed at 92 and follow the 920's (collective biography). Fiction books, denoted by the symbol "Fic," follow the nonfiction. Short story collections, denoted by "S C," follow fiction.

An Outline of Classification, which serves as a table of contents to the Classified Catalog, is reproduced on page 2. It should be remembered that many subjects are treated in more than one discipline and so are found in various parts of the classification. If a particular title is not found where it might be expected, the Index should be consulted to determine if the work is classified elsewhere.

Within classes, books are arranged alphabetically under main entry, usually the author. An exception is made for works of individual biography, classed at 92, which are arranged alphabetically under the name of the person written about. The following is an example of a typical entry and a description of its components:

> **Bolden, Tonya**
> And not afraid to dare. Scholastic 1998 216p
> il $16.95   **920**
> 1. African American women
> ISBN 0-590-48080-4   LC 96-7320
> Biographical portraits of ten African-American women including Leontyne Price, Toni Morrison, and Jackie Joyner-Kersee
> "The writing is clear and compelling. While these biographical sketches are interesting and provocative enough to attract recreational readers, the primary use for such a title would be research." SLJ
> Includes bibliographical references

The name of the author, Tonya Bolden, is given in conformity with *Anglo-American Cataloguing Rules*, 2nd edition, 1998 revision. It is inverted and printed in dark or bold face type.

The title of the book is *And not afraid to dare*. The book was published by Scholastic. Reference to the Directory of Publishers and Distributors will provide this publisher's address and other pertinent ordering information.

The date the book was published is 1998. It has 216 pages, contains illustrations, and sells for $16.95. (Prices given were current when the Catalog went to press; as time passes they should be rechecked with the publisher for possible changes.)

At the end of the last line of type in the body of the entry is the figure 920 in bold face type. This is the classification number derived from the thirteenth edition of the *Abridged Dewey Decimal Classification*. The number 920 is the classification number for "Biography."

The numbered term "1. African American women" is the recommended subject heading for this book based on *Sears List of Subject Heading*. In some cases the subjects assigned to the entire book will not show that there are portions of the book dealing with more specific topics. In such cases subject analytic entries are made. The book listed above contains sections dealing with Leontyne Price, Toni Morrison, Jackie Joyner-Kersee, and seven other African American women. Separate entries for these ten portions of the book appear in the Index under the names of the women included.

The ISBN (International Standard Book Number) is included to facilitate ordering. The Library of Congress control number (also called the LC card number) is provided when available.

Following are three notes supplying additional information about the book. The first is a description of the book's content. The second is a critical note from *School Library Journal*. Such annotations are useful in evaluating books for selection and in determining which of several books on the same subject is best suited for the individual reader. The final note describes special features, in this case a bibliography. Notes are also made to describe sequels and companion volumes, editions available, awards, and publication history.

AUTHOR, TITLE, SUBJECT, AND ANALYTICAL INDEX

This section is an alphabetical index of all the works in the Classified Catalog and in the list of recommended CD-ROMs. Each of the books in the Classified Catalog is entered under author; title, if distinctive; series; subject; and other added entries as necessary. Following the name of the series all the titles in that series are listed. Also included are subject, author, and title analytics for parts of composite works. The classification number in bold face type is the key to the location of the main entry of the book in the Classified Catalog. Works classed at 92, individual biography, will be found under the name of the person written about. The index includes title and subject entries for the CD-ROMs listed in Part 3, the Select List of Recommended CD-ROMs, with the indication, "See entry in CD-ROM section, Part 3."

Cross-references are made in the index from variant forms of names, from terms not used as subject headings to the term that is used, and from terms used as subject headings to related or more specific headings.

The following are examples of Index entries for the book cited above:

Author	**Bolden, Tonya**	
	And not afraid to dare	**920**
Title	**And** not afraid to dare. Bolden, T.	**920**
Subject	**African American women**	
	Bolden, T. And not afraid to dare	**920**

Subject Analytic
> **Price, Leontyne**
> *See/See also pages in the following book(s):*
> Bolden, T. And not afraid to dare **920**

Examples of other types of entries:

Joint Author **Levine, Alan H.**
> (jt. auth) Cary, E. The rights of students
>
> **344**

Author Analytic
> **Cortázar, Julio, 1914-1984**
> The bear's speech
> *In* Where angels glide at dawn p3-5
>
> **S C**

Title Analytic
> The **bear's** speech. Cortázar, J.
> *In* Where angels glide at dawn p3-5 **S C**

SELECT LIST OF RECOMMENDED CD-ROMs

The Select List of Recommended CD-ROMs is arranged alphabetically by title. The entry for a CD-ROM in this list consists of the title; the publisher; the publisher's address, when it is not included in Part 4, the Directory of Publishers and Distributors; the year of publication, when it can be established; the number of discs; the price; a suggested Dewey Classification number; one or more suggested subject headings, based on the *Sears List of Subject Headings*; a platform note; and an annotation, in some cases including a quotation from a review. The price given is for a single copy in a stand-alone situation. Prices for networking situations should be requested from the publisher. Version numbers and hardware requirements, because they so frequently change, should also be requested from the producer of the item.

PART 1

CLASSIFIED CATALOG

Outline of Classification

Reproduced below is the Second Summary of the Dewey Decimal Classification.* It will serve as a table of contents for the nonfiction section of the Classified Catalog. (Fiction and Story Collections follow the nonfiction.) Note that the inclusion of this outline is not considered a substitute for consulting the Dewey Decimal Classification itself.

*Reprinted from Edition 13 of the Abridged Dewey Decimal Classification, copyright 1997-2000 OCLC Online Computer Library Center, Incorporated, with permission of OCLC Forest Press, a division of OCLC.

MIDDLE AND JUNIOR HIGH SCHOOL LIBRARY CATALOG

EIGHTH EDITION

CLASSIFIED CATALOG

000 GENERALITIES

001.4 Research; statistical methods

Markle, Sandra, 1946-
Discovering graph secrets; experiments, puzzles, and games exploring graphs. Atheneum Bks. for Young Readers 1997 36p il $17   **001.4**
1. Graphic methods
ISBN 0-689-31942-8   LC 96-15435
Contains activities dealing with charts and graphs, showing how to construct them, what can be plotted, and how they illustrate mathematical concepts
"This slim volume could be a dream come true for students looking for math projects or teachers looking for enrichment activities." Bull Cent Child Books

Smoothey, Marion, 1943-
Graphs; illustrated by Ann Baum. Marshall Cavendish 1995 64p il $17.95   **001.4**
1. Graphic methods
ISBN 1-85435-775-1   LC 94-13133
Explores basic concepts of graphing through investigation, hands-on activity, and theory. Includes practical projects and encourages problem-solving strategies utilizing graphic methods

001.9 Controversial knowledge

Blackwood, Gary L.
Alien astronauts. Benchmark Bks. (Tarrytown) 1999 80p il (Secrets of the unexplained) lib bdg $28.50   **001.9**
1. Unidentified flying objects
ISBN 0-7614-0469-4   LC 97-13
This book "takes a historical look at UFO sightings and aboriginal beliefs in creatures from space. Following a description of the most common varieties of sightings, types of encounters are each presented in a separate chapter." SLJ
"A young reader is likely to get a well-balanced and accurate view of the subject of UFOs from this book." Sci Books Films
Includes glossary and bibliographical references

Extraordinary events and oddball occurrences. Benchmark Bks. (Tarrytown) 1999 80p il (Secrets of the unexplained) lib bdg $28.50   **001.9**
1. Parapsychology 2. Curiosities and wonders
ISBN 0-7614-0748-0   LC 98-30261

Discusses the details and possible explanations of mysterious events throughout human history, including strange things falling out of the sky, the teleportation of objects, and unexplained appearances and disappearances
Includes bibliographical references

Cohen, Daniel, 1936-
Great conspiracies and elaborate cover-ups. Millbrook Press 1997 128p il lib bdg $22.40 (7 and up)   **001.9**
1. Conspiracies
ISBN 0-7613-0010-4   LC 96-36483
"Cohen introduces readers to the often-bizarre world of conspiracy theories by examining a number of them. Some, such as the Lincoln and JFK assassination plots and the Jack the Ripper murder theories, will be familiar to most students; others, such as the Illuminati group, Lyndon LaRouche's theories, and the Cold War rantings of Joseph McCarthy, will be new to many readers. . . . This book is a calm, well-balanced introduction to this subject." SLJ
Includes bibliographical references

Floyd, E. Randall
Great American mysteries; raining snakes, fabled cities of gold, strange disappearances, and other baffling tales. August House 1991 190p hardcover o.p. paperback available $9.95 (7 and up)   **001.9**
1. Curiosities and wonders
ISBN 0-87483-170-9 (pa)   LC 91-6566
A collection of "legends of the weird and bizarre in American life. Unsolved murders, buildings with no exits, tales from the Bermuda Triangle, and the mysterious moving rocks of Death Valley . . . make for absorbing, sometimes spooky, reading. Great for browsers." Booklist
Includes bibliographical references

Kettelkamp, Larry, 1933-
ETs and UFOs; are they real? Morrow Junior Bks. 1996 86p il lib bdg $16   **001.9**
1. Unidentified flying objects 2. Extraterrestrial beings
ISBN 0-688-12868-8   LC 96-6825
An overview of reported sightings of UFOs and reports of encounters with aliens as well as the agencies whose work is to monitor and investigate such claims
"Kettelkamp clearly believes that something is going on. In a straightforward, nonhysterical manner, he presents a litany of evidence. . . . Solid, well-researched material that readers can use for reports or for their own enlightenment." Booklist
Includes bibliographical references

Netzley, Patricia D.
Alien abductions: opposing viewpoints. Greenhaven Press 1996 128p il (Great mysteries) lib bdg $22.45 (7 and up)   **001.9**
1. Unidentified flying objects 2. Extraterrestrial beings
ISBN 1-56510-352-1   LC 95-25106
Explores reports of UFO sightings and alleged kidnapping of humans by extraterrestrials
Includes bibliographical references

Rovin, Jeff
The encyclopedia of monsters. Facts on File 1989 390p il $35; pa $19.95 (7 and up)   **001.9**
1. Monsters
ISBN 0-8160-1824-3; 0-8160-2303-4 (pa)
   LC 89-30417
This work "covers a variety of fiends, specters, werewolves, mummies, and other creatures and demons. . . . Information includes: the common name or nickname; where and when the monster first appeared; its size, gender and species; its distinguishing features and powers; a biographical sketch, from origin to demise; and a bibliography or filmography." SLJ

Simon, Seymour, 1931-
Strange mysteries from around the world. Morrow Junior Bks. 1997 58p il $16; pa $6.95
   001.9
1. Curiosities and wonders
ISBN 0-688-14636-8; 0-688-14637-6 (pa)
   LC 96-2693
A revised edition of the title first published 1980 by Four Winds Press
Describes ten strange natural phenomena and possible explanations for them, including the day it rained frogs, an atomic explosion that occurred forty years before the atom bomb, and an eerie crystal skull
"Simon's enticingly simple and clear descriptions make the subjects accessible with no unsubstantiated speculations. Worn-out copies of the 1980 edition can be safely replaced with this updated version." SLJ

Wilson, Colin, 1931-
Mysteries of the universe. DK Pub. 1997 37p il (Unexplained) $14.95   **001.9**
1. Curiosities and wonders
ISBN 0-7894-2165-8   LC 97-15424
Explores such mysteries as Bigfoot, the Loch Ness Monster, weird weather, and black holes
This book "has a few tantalizing words to say about everything from the Turin shroud to showers of fish to life on Mars." Booklist

UFOs and aliens. DK Pub. 1997 37p il (Unexplained) $14.95   **001.9**
1. Unidentified flying objects 2. Extraterrestrial beings
ISBN 0-7894-2166-6   LC 97-15425
Examines various explanations and evidence related to UFO sightings and alien encounters throughout history
"The photographs, often in color, are a browser's

dream come true. . . . [This book] doesn't get into the scientific pros and cons, focusing instead on the occurrences that suggest alien visitations, including stories of abduction and UFO sightings, and a few headline-making hoaxes." Booklist

004   Data processing. Computer science

Spencer, Donald D., 1931-
Illustrated computer dictionary for young people. 2nd ed. Camelot 1999 117p il $16.95   **004**
1. Computers—Dictionaries 2. Electronic data processing—Dictionaries
ISBN 0-89218-323-3   LC 98-47643
First published 1995
This dictionary contains over 700 entries covering various aspects of computer science, including artificial intelligence, computer graphics, networks, and desktop publishing

004.6   Interfacing and communications. Networks

Barron, Ann E.
The Internet and instruction; activities and ideas; [by] Ann E. Barron, Karen S. Ivers. 2nd ed. Libraries Unlimited 1998 244p il pa $28.50
   004.6
1. Internet 2. Computer assisted instruction
ISBN 1-56308-613-1   LC 98-15021
First published 1996
"The first section gives a general overview of the Internet; how to get connected; and descriptions of its many forms including e-mail, World Wide Web, FTP, and Gopher. . . . The second section provides a breakdown of Web sites by subject. Each subject area has a number of Web sites previewed and annotated." Voice Youth Advocates
Includes bibliographical references

Benson, Allen C.
Connecting kids and the Internet; a handbook for librarians, teachers, and parents; [by] Allen C. Benson, Linda M. Fodemski. 2nd ed. Neal-Schuman 1999 398p (Neal-Schuman net-guide series) pa $49.95   **004.6**
1. Internet 2. Computer assisted instruction
ISBN 1-55570-348-8   LC 99-16424
First published 1996
This is a "resource for questions about browsers, search engines, e-mail, news groups, Web pages, virtual field trips, and filters. Fourteen lesson plans suggest practical ideas for teaching students to become skilled, savvy Internet users. Packed with information and ideas, the book is accompanied by a useful CD-ROM. . . . A useful addition to school and public libraries." Booklist
Includes bibliographical references

Benson, Allen C.—*Continued*

Neal-Schuman complete Internet companion for librarians. new ed. Neal-Schuman 1997 xxx, 513p il (Neal-Schuman net-guide series) pa $65 **004.6**
1. Internet
ISBN 1-55570-317-8   LC 97-29536
First published 1995 with title: The complete Internet companion for librarians
This book "covers information ranging from basic definitions to practical instructions for using a wide variety of online sources. Especially useful for library media specialists are sections devoted to justifying the need for the Internet in libraries, a list of library school Web sites, and job hunting via the Internet for library professionals. In addition to the chapters on software, hardware, security, and e-mail, there is information about online library catalogs, tips on keeping up with new developments, contact information for Internet service providers, technical support, and discussion groups." Book Rep

Berger, Pam

Internet for active learners; curriculum-based strategies for K.12. American Lib. Assn. 1998 189p il pa $35   **004.6**
1. Internet 2. Computer assisted instruction
ISBN 0-8389-3487-0   LC 98-23102
The author "starts by discussing the different roles school librarians will have to play in the 21st century. She then shows readers how the Internet can help them meet these challenges successfully. . . . A useful chapter covers creating a home page for the library, and the book ends with ideas for teaching the Internet to faculty and parents." SLJ
"If you can afford only one Internet manual for your school library, this one should fill the spot." Book Rep
Includes bibliographical references

Henderson, Harry, 1951-

The Internet. Lucent Bks. 1998 96p il (Lucent overview series) lib bdg $17.96 (7 and up) **004.6**
1. Internet
ISBN 1-56006-215-0   LC 97-39314
This is a "survey of how the Net got started and its many uses, now and in the future. . . . All the glories of the new technology are lauded, but its pitfalls are also pointed out. The threats of swindlers, hackers, and abuses of privacy are addressed, as well as issues concerning children on the Net and censorship." Booklist
"A well-written overview on a timely subject. . . . Useful for reports." SLJ
Includes glossary and bibliographical references

The **Internet**; edited by Gray Young. Wilson, H.W. 1998 215p (Reference shelf, v70 no5) pa $25 (7 and up)   **004.6**
1. Internet
ISBN 0-8242-0945-1   LC 98-48498
The editor has collected "short, newsy pieces . . . that offer intelligent and timely reviews of both sides of some of today's hottest Internet-related topics." Voice Youth Advocates
Includes bibliographical references

Jefferis, David

Cyberspace; virtual reality and the World Wide Web. Crabtree 1999 32p il (Megatech) $14.97; pa $8.06   **004.6**
1. Computers 2. Computer simulation 3. Virtual reality 4. World Wide Web
ISBN 0-7787-0047-X; 0-7787-0057-7 (pa)
LC 98-48512
Surveys digital technology from the early days of computers to virtual reality and the World Wide Web, describing the uses of computer simulation in flight, battle, hazardous environments, and entertainment

Kalbag, Asha

Build your own Web site. EDC 1999 48p (Usborne computer guides series) pa $8.95 **004.6**
1. Internet
ISBN 0-7460-3293-5
This book "focuses not only on the hows but also on the whys, whens, and wheres of creating Web pages. It explains how to create a Web site with a text editor, but the aesthetic and content advice hold true no matter what program is being used." SLJ

Kyker, Keith

Wading the World Wide Web; Internet activities for beginners. Libraries Unlimited 1998 170p il pa $18   **004.6**
1. Internet 2. World Wide Web
ISBN 1-56308-605-0   LC 98-18615
Designed to give students entry-level Internet experience, this book provides reproducible activities based on educationally oriented World Wide Web sites. Each project contains Web addresses, guidelines for instructors, step-by-step instructions for students, and 10 to 15 related questions

Lampton, Christopher

The World Wide Web. Watts 1997 63p il maps lib bdg $22; pa $6.95   **004.6**
1. World Wide Web
ISBN 0-531-20262-3; 0-531-15842-X (pa)
LC 96-36145
"A First book"
A description of the World Wide Web, including the history of its development and details on how to use it
"Lampton has carefully thought through his subject to figure out what children will really want and need to know, and he explains each term with precision and clarity." Booklist
Includes glossary

Mambretti, Catherine, 1950-

Internet technology for schools; foreword by Joel J. Mambretti. McFarland & Co. 1999 303p pa $39.95   **004.6**
1. Internet 2. Computer assisted instruction
ISBN 0-7864-0727-1   LC 99-17284
The author presents a "guide to designing and using an Internet network. She begins with suggestions for planning, funding, and implementing a network, aimed at

Mambretti, Catherine, 1950——*Continued*
the district's decision makers and technical experts. The second part, intended for those with little computer experience, provides a history of the Internet and an overview of the kinds of materials available there. A final section explains the technical details of network infrastructures."
Booklist
Includes bibliographical references

McCormick, Anita Louise
The Internet; surfing the issues. Enslow Pubs. 1998 128p il (Issues in focus) lib bdg $19.95 (7 and up)   **004.6**
1. Internet
ISBN 0-89490-956-8   LC 98-12673
"Organized around the major issues of control, security, equity, and access, the book addresses such topics as filters, pornography, viruses, encryption, Web TV, and Internet2. Although none are examined in depth, enough information is provided to allow readers to begin to form opinions or launch further research." Booklist
Includes bibliographical references

Miller, Elizabeth B.
The Internet resource directory for K-12 teachers and librarians. Libraries Unlimited pa $27.50   **004.6**
1. Internet 2. Information systems—Directories

Annual. First published 1994 for 1994-1995
This directory "provides details on accessing more than 400 discussion groups, electronic books and newspapers, lesson plans, and a variety of other teaching resources by E-mail, gopher, telnet, and FTP. . . . The directory proper is arranged under broad curricular areas plus resources for educators, reference, and school library media applications. Each of these is further divided by narrower disciplines. . . . Recommended for all school library media centers." Booklist

Murray, Laura K.
Basic Internet for busy librarians; a quick course for catching up. American Lib. Assn. 1998 137p il pa $26   **004.6**
1. Internet 2. Library information networks
ISBN 0-8389-0725-3   LC 98-14067
The author "presents step-by-step exercises on accessing the Internet, working with the World Wide Web, creating Web pages, and using such other Internet aspects as electronic lists, e-mail, telnet, and FTP. One chapter is devoted to searching. All exercises are accompanied by screen images." Booklist
"If you are still looking for an on-ramp to the information superhighway, this is the book for you." SLJ

Reese, Jean
Internet books for educators, parents, and students. Libraries Unlimited 1999 299p pa $32.50   **004.6**
1. Internet 2. Computer assisted instruction
ISBN 1-56308-697-2   LC 99-26463

"The author describes a variety of general handbooks and guides, lesson plans, guides for teaching with the Internet and curriculum-related books, Web design and publishing and children's fiction that incorporates the Internet into its storyline. . . . Annotations cite purpose, presentation, target audience, practical applications, and educational possibilities of each work." Publisher's note
Includes bibliographical references

Simpson, Carol Mann, 1949-
Internet for schools. 2nd ed, by Carol Namm Simpson and Sharron L. McElmeel. Linworth Pub. 1997 256p il (Professional growth series) pa $29.95   **004.6**
1. Internet
ISBN 0-938865-59-5   LC 97-6448
First published 1995
"The authors explain Internet history and operation, electronic mail, telnet, file transfer protocol, and the World Wide Web as well as search techniques, acceptable use policies, and training for students and staff. They also include extensive listings of useful Internet sites, arranged by subject and content area. . . . An excellent manual for Internet trainers or reference for school personnel." Booklist
Includes bibliographical references

Wallace, M. (Mark), 1955-
101 things to do on the Internet; illustrated by Isaac Quaye & Zoe Wray. EDC 1999 64p (Usborne computer guides series) pa $9.95 **004.6**
1. Internet
ISBN 0-7460-3294-3
This illustrated guide focuses on activities surrounding a theme, such as space, sports, music, games, movies, or weather. Includes safety and security information

005   Computer programming, programs, data

The **Software** encyclopedia. Bowker 2v pa set $265   **005**
1. Computer software

Annual. First published 1985
Contents: v1 Titles, publishers; v2 System compatibility/applications
"This item is a software-in-print source, but it does not include specifically scholastic educational software. It does include more than 20,000 titles of application, library and home educational programs that may be of interest in schools. It also includes CD-ROM products. . . . Recommended for large district professional collections." Safford. Guide to Ref Books for Sch Libr Media Cent. 5th edition

005.7   Data in computer systems

Jacsó, Péter
Build your own database; [by] Péter Jacsó and F.W. Lancaster. American Lib. Assn. 1999 163p il pa $34   **005.7**
1. Database management
ISBN 0-8389-0750-4   LC 98-41983

Jacsó, Péter—*Continued*

The authors "show you how to create quality in databases with advice in such areas as: designing content while considering domain of coverage, accessibility, and other criteria; constructing databases that facilitate retrieval of useful information; selecting the best software tools for your needs; indexing your data; determining how software features affect database capabilities." Publisher's note

006 Special computer methods

Grady, Sean M., 1965-

Virtual reality; computers mimic the physical world. Facts on File 1998 170p il (Facts on File science sourcebooks) $19.95 (7 and up)   **006**

1. Virtual reality

ISBN 0-8160-3605-5   LC 97-15813

This describes the history and technology of virtual reality and its applications in architecture, engineering, medicine, business, education, and the military, and outlines some of its drawbacks

Includes glossary and bibliographical references

Pascoe, Elaine

Virtual reality; beyond the looking glass; adapted by Elaine Pascoe. Blackbirch Press 1998 48p il (New explorers) lib bdg $16.95   **006**

1. Virtual reality

ISBN 1-56711-228-5   LC 96-42984

Discusses in general terms the computer technology involved in virtual reality and how it has been used and will be used in the future

"The book is well written and easy to follow, and gives readers a good understanding of the subject. . . . Full color photos and/or illustrations appear on every double-page spread and help to clarify the concepts." SLJ

Includes bibliographical references

Weiss, Ann E., 1943-

Virtual reality; a door to cyberspace. 21st Cent. Bks. (NY) 1996 128p il lib bdg $23.90 (7 and up)   **006**

1. Virtual reality

ISBN 0-8050-3722-5   LC 95-34444

The author "provides examples of current applications of virtual reality in fields from medicine to the military and the predominance of entertainment-related research and development. She also probes the dark side of virtual reality raising questions about its possible promotion of violence, mind control, and threat to social interaction." Voice Youth Advocates

"This title is useful and interesting for both reports and general reading." SLJ

Includes bibliographical references

011 Bibliographies

Recommended reference books for small and medium-sized libraries and media centers. Libraries Unlimited $55   **011**

1. Reference books—Bibliography 2. Reference books—Reviews

ISSN 0277-5948

Annual. First published 1981

Editor: 1981- Bohdan S. Wynar

Each annual volume includes reviews of about 550 titles chosen by the editor as the most valuable reference titles published during the previous year

"Where budget restrictions are a consideration, this is an invaluable asset; for all small libraries, a superior selection/acquisitions tool." Voice Youth Advocates

011.6 General bibliographies of works for specific kinds of users

Best books for young adult readers; Stephen J. Calvert, editor. Bowker 1997 xx, 744p $59.95   **011.6**

1. Best books 2. Young adult literature—Bibliography

ISBN 0-8352-3832-6   LC 97-478

Combines and updates Best books for Junior high readers and Best books for senior high readers

This volume lists and annotates about 6,500 titles for grades 7-12 published between 1990 and 1996. Each entry provides bibliographic information, awards, review citations, etc.

Children's catalog; edited by Anne Price and Juliette Yaakov. 17th ed. Wilson, H.W. 1996 1373p $105   **011.6**

1. Classified catalogs 2. Children's literature—Bibliography 3. School libraries—Catalogs

ISBN 0-8242-0893-5   LC 96-34846

"Standard catalog series"

First published 1909

Kept up to date by annual supplements included in price of main volume

This collection of recommended materials includes 6,971 titles and 6,732 analytical entries of books for children from preschool to grade six. Entries contain full bibliographic information, Dewey Decimal classification number, subject headings, reading level, descriptive, and when possible, critical annotations

"The most comprehensive bibliography in its field." Guide to Ref Books. 11th edition

Denman-West, Margaret W., 1926-

Children's literature: a guide to information sources. Libraries Unlimited 1998 187p (Reference sources in the humanities series) $38.50   **011.6**

1. Books and reading—Bibliography 2. Teenagers—Books and reading—Bibliography 3. Young adults' library services—Bibliography

ISBN 1-56308-448-1   LC 98-10177

This "is an annotated bibliography of more than 400 bibliographies and other reference works published from

Denman-West, Margaret W., 1926——*Continued*
1985 to 1997. Young-adult-related resources are included despite the book's title. It is arranged in chapters on subjects such as award-winning books, multicultural literature, core periodicals, reference books, nonprint media, special collections, professional associations, and the Internet." Booklist

Gillespie, John Thomas, 1928-
Guides to collection development for children and young adults; [by] John T. Gillespie, Ralph J. Folcarelli. Libraries Unlimited 1998 191p pa $23
                                        011.6
1. Children's literature—Bibliography 2. Young adult literature—Bibliography
ISBN 1-56308-532-1   LC 98-12944
Based in part upon sections of Guides to library collection development (1994), this "provides in-depth annotations for more than 800 books and periodicals about children's and young adult materials, print and nonprint, including CD-ROMs and online services. From preschool read-alouds to YA genre fiction and self-help, this will help librarians find resources for programming, readers' advisory, and selection." Booklist

Latino periodicals; a selection guide; Salvador Güereña and Vivian M. Pisano, editors. McFarland & Co. 1998 147p pa $30   **011.6**
1. Hispanic Americans—Periodicals—Bibliography
ISBN 0-7864-0540-6   LC 98-16582
An annotated list of 300 Spanish-and English-language publications. "It is organized by type of magazine (general interest, parenting, focus on teens, etc.), includes other types of periodicals (*fotonovelas*, newspapers, etc.), and is indexed by topic and title. The book covers titles ranging from professional journals and fashion magazines to comic books and computer magazines." SLJ

Matulka, Denise I.
Picture this; picture books for young adults: a curriculum-related annotated bibliography. Greenwood Press 1997 xx, 267p $39.95   **011.6**
1. Picture books for children—Bibliography 2. Teenagers—Books and reading—Bibliography 3. Young adult literature—Bibliography
ISBN 0-313-30182-4   LC 97-2234
"This bibliography introduces 424 titlies. . . . It is organized according to curriculum-content areas—the arts, health, literature, mathematics, science, and social sciences and history. Each annotation lists bibliographic information, summarizes the book, discusses artistic style and mediums employed, suggests companion titles, and provides ideas for classroom use." SLJ
For a fuller review see: Booklist, April 15, 1998

National Council of Teachers of English. Committee on the Junior High and Middle School Booklist
Your reading; a booklist for junior high and middle school; C. Anne Webb, editor; Paul Hirth, associate editor, and the Committee on the Junior High and Middle School Booklist of the National Council of Teachers of English. 9th ed. National Council of Teachers of English 1993 250p (NCTE bibliography series) o.p.   **011.6**
1. Children's literature—Bibliography 2. Young adult literature—Bibliography 3. Best books
                                   LC 93-8652
First published 1954
New edition in preparation
"Nearly 600 fiction and nonfiction books appropriate for middle school readers are arranged in 26 categories and annotated. . . . The list covers 1991, 1992, and a few 1993 titles. A 150-title recommended list of classics published from 1940 to 1990 is included at the end. Author, title, and subject indexes are provided. . . . Recommended for librarians, teachers, and parents of the younger teen set." Am Ref Books Annu, 1994

New York Public Library
Books for the teen age. New York Public Lib. pa $6   **011.6**
1. Young adult literature—Bibliography 2. Best books

Annual
"This annual list has been published since 1929, and contains about 1,000 titles in 70 subject areas such as AIDS, horror, science fiction and fantasy and young love. The list is designed to be attractive to young people, and the brief annotations are intended to motivate readers. Its comprehensive and quality listings plus the low price make it a best buy for both middle and high school collections." Safford. Guide to Ref Books for Sch Libr Media Cent. 5th edition

Newbery and Caldecott medalists and honor book winners; bibliographies and resource material through 1991; [compiled by] Muriel W. Brown, Rita Schoch Foudray; edited by Jim Roginski. 2nd ed. Neal-Schuman 1992 511p $65   **011.6**
1. Caldecott Medal 2. Newbery Medal 3. Children's literature—Bibliography
ISBN 1-55570-118-3   LC 92-14324
Also available Newbery and Caldecott medal and honor books in other media $35 (ISBN 1-55570-119-1)
First published 1977
"The medalists and honorees are arranged in alphabetical order. Each entry includes the recipient's name and dates, award(s), a bibliography of his or her published works, a listing of pertinent library collections, and a bibliography of background readings. Other features include separate chronological lists of award-winning books through 1992 and updated bibliographies of collections and background readings. A combined author-illustrator-title index is also provided." Booklist

Rochman, Hazel
Against borders; promoting books for a multicultural world. American Lib. Assn. 1993 288p il pa $25　　　　　　　　　　**011.6**
1. Young adult literature—Bibliography 2. Books and reading 3. Minorities—Bibliography
ISBN 0-8389-0601-X　　　　　　LC 93-17840
"Starting with her personal immigrant's journey from South Africa to the U.S., Rochman's essays focus on using books across cultures. The second part of the book is made up of bibliographies—many of them updated and expanded from *Booklist*—on specific ethnic groups and cultural issues." Booklist
"The subject access by ethnic group and nationality will prove useful for doing reader's advisory work as well as developing units on ethnic and cultural identity." SLJ

Rosenberg, Judith K.
Young people's books in series: fiction and non-fiction, 1975-1991; [by] Judith K. Rosenberg with the assistance of C. Allen Nichols. Libraries Unlimited 1992 424p o.p.　　　　**011.6**
1. Children's literature—Bibliography 2. Young adult literature—Bibliography
　　　　　　　　　　　　　LC 91-36646
Originally published 1972 and 1973 with titles: Young people's literature in series: fiction and Young people's literature in series: publishers' and non-fiction series; supplementary volume combining fiction and non-fiction published 1977
This reference work lists and describes "series published for young people from early elementary grades through high school. . . . Fiction series from 1976 through 1990 (and new titles in existing series through 1991) are included as well as nonfiction series, which are limited to in-print items only. Each entry includes the publisher, a brief description of the series, a list of books and their publication dates, and recommended grade level." Publisher's note

Rosow, La Vergne
Light 'n lively reads for ESL, adult, and teen readers; a thematic bibliography. Libraries Unlimited 1996 xxxvii, 343p il pa $40　　**011.6**
1. English as a second language—Bibliography 2. High interest-low vocabulary books—Bibliography 3. Young adult literature—Bibliography
ISBN 1-56308-365-5　　　　　　LC 96-7084
"This bibliography is arranged by themes such as arts, sports and science. Within each theme, recommended books are listed in order of difficulty with easier titles first. Each entry includes a thoughtful and motivating annotation. . . . An author, illustrator, title and subject index adds further access. Recommended for all levels to support reading guidance." Safford. Guide to Ref Materials for Sch Libr Media Cent. 5th edition

Safford, Barbara Ripp
Guide to reference materials for school media centers. 5th ed. Libraries Unlimited 1998 353p $45
　　　　　　　　　　　　　　　　011.6
1. Reference books—Bibliography 2. School libraries—Catalogs 3. Instructional materials centers
ISBN 1-56308-545-3　　　　　　LC 98-29867

First edition by Christine Gehrt Wynar published 1973 with title: Guide to reference books for school media centers
"This guide contains critical annotations with full bibliographical information for 1,672 reference materials that are currently available and appropriate for elementary, middle, and senior high schools. Entries include titles published between 1992 and 1997 and older titles that still contain accurate information. Materials focus on the United States and include print, CD-ROM, and on-line resources. Criteria for inclusion are usefulness for curricular applications, interest for students, readability, clarity, accuracy, and currency of information." Voice Youth Advocates

Schon, Isabel
The best of the Latino heritage; a guide to the best juvenile books about Latino people and cultures. Scarecrow Press 1997 285p $37.50
　　　　　　　　　　　　　　　　011.6
1. Children's literature—Bibliography 2. Latin America—Bibliography 3. Spain—Bibliography
ISBN 0-8108-3221-6　　　　　　LC 96-24249
"This volume acts as a cumulation of the other Schon bibliographies, and includes new titles. Arranged by countries, it includes the United States as well as the Spanish-speaking countries of Central and South America. The brief annotations include grade level indications. There are author, title and subject indexes." Safford. Guide to Ref Materials for Sch Libr Media Cent. 5th edition

Recommended books in Spanish for children and young adults, 1991-1995. Scarecrow Press 1997 327p $42.50　　　　　　**011.6**
1. Latin American literature—Bibliography 2. Spanish literature—Bibliography 3. Children's literature—Bibliography 4. Young adult literature—Bibliography
ISBN 0-8108-3235-6　　　　　　LC 96-32447
This resource contains "1,055 annotations of fiction and nonfiction books written in or translated into Spanish. All entries were in print as of May 1996 and are organized into four sections: reference, nonfiction, publishers' series, and fiction. . . . Schon recommends grade levels for the books but warns readers that these levels are subjective." SLJ

Senior high school library catalog; edited by Juliette Yaakov. 15th ed. Wilson, H.W. 1997 1312p $130　　　　　　　　　　**011.6**
1. Classified catalogs 2. High school libraries—Catalogs 3. Young adult literature—Bibliography
ISBN 0-8242-0921-4
"Standard catalog series"
First published 1926-28 with title: Standard catalog for high school libraries
Kept up to date by annual supplements included in price of main volume
This edition includes 5,432 titles and 10,344 analytical entries of books for grades nine through twelve. Entries contain full bibliographic information, Abridged Dewey Decimal Classification number, subject headings, descriptive, and when available, critical annotations. Includes a select list of recommended CD-ROM reference works

Totten, Herman L., 1938-
Culturally diverse library collections for youth;
[by] Herman L. Totten, Carolyn Garner, Risa W.
Brown. Neal-Schuman 1996 220p pa $38.50
011.6
1. Minorities—Bibliography 2. Young adult literature—Bibliography
ISBN 1-55570-141-8   LC 96-1020
This volume includes "books and videos about African
American, Hispanic, Asian, and Native American cultures. Nonfiction, biography, folk tales, reference books,
and scholarly works are covered. Each title is annotated
with full bibliographic data and suggested ages and
grades. Relevant adult ethnic books are also evaluated
for use in school." Publisher's note
For a review see: Booklist, Oct. 15, 1996

Wright, Cora M.
Hot links; literature links for the middle school
curriculum; Marilyn Wright, illustrator. Libraries
Unlimited 1998 173p il pa $30   **011.6**
1. Children's literature—Bibliography 2. Books and
reading
ISBN 1-56308-587-9   LC 98-36039
"Wright has selected approximately 300 contemporary
and classic fiction and nonfiction titles. . . . Chapters
cover science, history (ancient cultures and U.S.), English language (classic literature and usage), mathematics,
fine arts, and sports and games. The book also contains
selections of biographies, multicultural literature, poetry,
read-alouds, recent releases, high-interest/low-reading
level material, myths and legends, and unique reads."
Publisher's note

Zvirin, Stephanie
The best years of their lives; a resource guide
for teenagers in crisis. 2nd ed. American Lib.
Assn. 1996 154p pa $26   **011.6**
1. Adolescence—Bibliography
ISBN 0-8389-0686-9   LC 96-14446
First published 1992
A selective, annotated bibliography of fiction, nonfiction and video self-help works for teenagers. Topics
addressed include: pregnancy, suicide, sexual abuse,
learning disabilities, sexuality, violence, safety and health
"Highly recommended; an essential purchase for all
public libraries and school libraries serving youth aged
ten to eighteen." J Youth Serv Libr
Includes filmography

015.73 Bibliographies and catalogs of works issued or printed in the United States

Books in print. Bowker 9v set $595   **015.73**
1. Bibliography
ISSN 0068-0214

Also available CD-ROM version
Annual. First published 1948
Updated by Books in print Supplement (3v) published
annually in Spring, available at $279 (ISSN 0000-0310)

v1-4: Authors; v5-8 Titles; v9:Publishers
Lists titles available during the current year from
American publishers, supplying such information as authors, co-authors, title, price, publisher, year of publication, and International Standard Book Numbers of coop-
erating publishers

Hoffmann, Frank W. (Frank William), 1949-
Guide to popular U.S. government publications;
[by] Frank W. Hoffmann, Richard J. Wood. 5th
ed. Libraries Unlimited 1998 xxvi, 300p $38.50
015.73
1. Government publications—United States—Bibliography
ISBN 1-56308-607-7   LC 98-29868
First edition compiled by LeRoy C. Schwarzkopf published 1986
This is a guide to 1,500 federal documents in print,
microfiche, CD-ROM and electronic formats arranged by
subject. Includes title and subject indexes. Most of the
documents cited were published or printed during the
1995 and 1996 calendar years

Subject guide to Books in print. Bowker 7v set
$399   **015.73**
1. Subject catalogs 2. Bibliography
ISSN 0000-0159

Also available CD-ROM version
Annual. First published 1957
This companion publication to Books in print lists titles currently available from United States publishers indexing them under LC subject headings

Subject guide to Children's books in print.
Bowker $179.95   **015.73**
1. Children's literature—Bibliography 2. Subject catalogs
ISSN 0000-0167

Also available CD-ROM version
Annual. First published 1970
This publication provides a subject approach to its
companion work: Children's books in print. The headings
used are based on the Sears list of subject headings supplemented by headings from LC. Entries include author,
title, publisher, year of publication, binding, price, ISBN,
and, in some cases, grade level. A directory of publishers
and distributors is included

Vertical file index; guide to pamphlets and
references to current topics. Wilson, H.W. pa
$65 per year   **015.73**
1. Pamphlets—Bibliography 2. Pamphlets—Indexes
ISSN 0042-4439

First published 1932. Issued monthly except August
"A list of free and inexpensive pamphlets, booklets,
leaflets, and similar material considered to be of interest
to general libraries. Subjects range from those suitable
for school libraries to specialized technical reports. Arranged alphabetically by subject headings (deemed suitable for vertical file use) with title index." Guide to Ref
Books. 11th edition

016.3 Bibliographies of the social sciences

Notable children's trade books in the field of social studies. Children's Bk. Council pa $2
016.3
1. Social sciences—Bibliography 2. Best books

An annual annotated list, reprinted from an issue of the periodical Social Education, of the preceding year's best trade books in the field of social studies of interest to children in grades K-8. Prepared by the Book Review Panel of the National Council for the Social Studies—Children's Book Council Joint Committee. Titles are selected for emphasis on human relations, originality, readability and, when appropriate, illustrations. General reading levels (primary, intermediate, advanced) are indicated

016.3637 Bibliographies of environmental problems and services

Dwyer, James R., 1949-
Earth works; recommended fiction and nonfiction about nature and the environment for adults and young adults; [by] Jim Dwyer. Neal-Schuman 1996 507p pa $49.95
016.3637
1. Environmental protection—Bibliography
ISBN 1-55570-194-9
LC 94-36284
Dwyer "lists 2600 entries, including about 1000 fiction titles, that were in print as of March 1995. The nonfiction titles are arranged into seven chapters by such topics as specific environments (deserts, rainforests), activities and issues (water supply, energy), and, in the largest section, environmental action (deep ecology, green business). The fiction titles are arranged by such topics as animals, ecofeminism, and the New West. . . . Entries offer standard bibliographic information . . . a two- to three-sentence annotation discussing the scope of the work, and reading level for young adult titles." Libr J

016.3713 Bibliographies of instructional materials

El-hi textbooks and serials in print. Bowker 2v
$175
016.3713
1. Textbooks—Bibliography 2. Periodicals—Bibliography
ISSN 0000-0825

Annual. Title varies
"Index to textbooks, dictionaries, encyclopedias, maps, atlases, professional books, teaching aids and auxiliary AV materials for grades K-12, plus adult and special education. Subject index contains grade and reading level; also author and title indexes and series index. Lists information not in 'Books in Print.'" N Y Public Libr. Ref Books for Child Collect. 2d edition

Media review digest; the only complete guide to reviews of non-book media. Pierian Press $255 per year
016.3713
1. Audiovisual materials—Reviews 2. Audiovisual materials—Bibliography
ISSN 0363-7778

Annual. First published 1971 with title: Multi media reviews index
"Indexes and digests reviews, evaluations, and descriptions of nonbook media (films and filmstrips, records and tapes, miscellaneous media). Includes cataloging information, subject indexing, and review ratings assigned by the *Digest* staff." Ref Sources for Small & Medium-sized Libr. 6th edition

016.4 Bibliographies of language

McCaffery, Laura Hibbets
Building an ESL collection for young adults; a bibliography of recommended fiction and nonfiction for schools and public libraries. Greenwood Press 1998 182p $39.95
016.4
1. English as a second language—Bibliography
2. Young adult literature—Bibliography
ISBN 0-313-29937-4
LC 98-5271
"This annotated bibliography offers more than 500 titles for grades 5 through adult. The entries are organized by genre or topic and arranged alphabetically by author. They include complete bibliographic information, ISBN, price, Fry Reading Level, interest level, and possible uses in and out of the classroom. An introduction outlines the changing need for ESL materials in the United States and explains McCaffery's selection criteria." Libr J

For a fuller review see: Booklist, Feb. 15, 1999

016.5 Bibliographies of science

Appraisal; science books for young people. Children's Science Bk. Review Com. $46 per year
016.5
1. Science—Bibliography—Periodicals 2. Books—Reviews
ISSN 0003-7052
Quarterly. First published 1967
This periodical "reviews almost all science and math books published each year that are written for children and young adults. . . . Some 70 trade books and series are reviewed in each quarterly issue; two signed reviews, 100-200 words each, by two reviewers, a librarian and a subject specialist; complete bibliographic and order information and grade level; five rating codes." Safford. Guide to Ref Materials for Sch Libr Media Cent. 5th edition

Outstanding science trade books for children. Children's Bk. Council pa $2
016.5
1. Science—Bibliography 2. Best books

An annual annotated list, reprinted from an issue of the periodical Science and Children, of the preceding

Outstanding science trade books for children—
Continued

year's best trade books in the field of science of interest to children in grades K-8. Prepared by a Book Review Committee appointed by the National Science Teachers Association in cooperation with the Children's Book Council. Titles are selected for accuracy, readability and pleasing format. General reading levels (primary, intermediate, advanced) are indicated

Science Books & Films. American Assn. for the Advancement of Science $40 per year **016.5**
1. Science—Bibliography—Periodicals 2. Books—Reviews 3. Audiovisual materials—Reviews
ISSN 0098-342X
Nine issues a year. First published 1965 with title: Science Books, a quarterly review
"This magazine is an indispensable tool for librarians in all types of libraries who wish to make informed collection development decisions in the area of science. . . . Arranged by Dewey decimal class numbers, the reviews cover books, audiovisual (AV) materials, even software." Katz. Mag for Libr. 9th edition

016.7 Bibliographies of the arts

Rodgers, Marie E.
The Harlem Renaissance; an annotated reference guide for student research. Libraries Unlimited 1998 139p il $28 **016.7**
1. Harlem Renaissance—Bibliography 2. African American arts—Bibliography
ISBN 1-56308-580-1   LC 97-46660
This is a "listing of over 200 resources about the flowering of African-American culture in New York City during the 1920s. In short chapters, Rodgers explains various social and historical aspects of this era and then presents an annotated list of print and non-print sources. Topics include literature, photography, music, and dance along with biographical information on many figures such as Marian Anderson, Langston Hughes, Zora Neale Hurston, Marcus Garvey, and Josephine Baker." SLJ

016.8 Bibliographies of literature

Anderson, Vicki, 1928-
Fiction sequels for readers 10 to 16; an annotated bibliography of books in succession. 2nd ed. McFarland & Co. 1998 176p pa $29.95
016.8
1. Children's literature—Bibliography 2. Young adult literature—Bibliography 3. Fiction—Bibliography
ISBN 0-7864-0185-0   LC 98-5236
First published 1990
This list contains about 3000 titles that are part of a series. "The entries are arranged by author and provide title, publisher and date of publication along with a brief annotation." Publisher's note

From biography to history; best books for children's entertainment and education; edited by Catherine Barr; foreword by James Cross Giblin; contributors, Rebecca L. Thomas, Deanna McDaniel. Bowker 1998 508p il $59.95
016.8
1. Biography—Bibliography 2. History—Bibliography
ISBN 0-8352-4012-6   LC 98-23147
"This annotated bibliography recommends biographies and related books that provide information about nearly 300 people of historical interest and the time periods in which they lived. The entries are arranged alphabetically; a brief paragraph about the individual is followed by suggested titles for 'Older Readers' (grades six to nine) and 'Younger Readers' (grades three to five). The bibliographic information is complete and most of the titles have been published in the last 10 years." SLJ

Herald, Diana Tixier
Teen genreflecting. Libraries Unlimited 1997 134p $23.50 **016.8**
1. Young adult literature—Bibliography 2. Teenagers—Books and reading
ISBN 1-56308-287-X   LC 96-29139
"The first chapter discusses teen reading habits and ways in which libraries can market to teens. It also provides a selection of resources for librarians, including online resources. The chapters that follow deal with specific genres: historical novels; science fiction; fantasy; mystery, suspense, and horror; adventure; contemporary (which includes problem novels and sports); and romance. . . . As a collection-development and reader's-advisory tool, as well as a way to educate oneself about genre fiction for teens, *Teen Genreflecting* is highly recommended for school and public libraries." Booklist

Holsinger, M. Paul, 1938-
The ways of war; the era of World War II in children's and young adult fiction: an annotated bibliography. Scarecrow Press 1995 487p $60.50
016.8
1. World War, 1939-1945—Literature and the war—Bibliography 2. Young adult literature—Bibliography 3. Children's literature—Bibliography 4. War stories—Bibliography
ISBN 0-8108-2925-X   LC 94-20484
This annotated bibliography analyzes 750 fiction books that deal with World War II. Entries are arranged alphabetically by author and include reading level as well as quality rating. There is a title index and a geographical and thematic index
"Teachers and students have a valuable resource here in finding specific books to help with their understanding of a complex period in world history." Voice Youth Advocates

Kennemer, Phyllis K.
Using literature to teach middle grades about war. Oryx Press 1993 xxiii, 209p pa $29.95
016.8
1. War in literature 2. Children's literature—Bibliography
ISBN 0-89774-778-X   LC 92-31932

Kennemer, Phyllis K.—*Continued*
The author combines "annotated bibliographies with lesson plans and activities. She includes chapters on the Revolution, the Civil War, World War I, World War II, the Vietnam War, and the Gulf War. In each case there's a chronology, an annotated list—picture books, factual books, biography, and fiction—a sample lesson plan, and suggested questions and activities." Booklist

Makowski, Silk, 1940-
Serious about series; evaluations and annotations of teen fiction in paperback series; edited by Dorothy M. Broderick. Scarecrow Press 1998 291p pa $26.50   **016.8**
1. Young adult literature—Bibliography 2. Fiction—Bibliography
ISBN 0-8108-3304-2   LC 97-48913
"Following introductory material on the genre, each chapter cites a series, explains and evaluates it, and provides an annotated title list with ISBNs and publication dates. Makowski covers more than 50 series of all types, including romance, horror, sci-fi, 'Tom Swift,' and the 'Hardy Boys.' Comparisons between series of similar nature are helpful." SLJ
Includes bibliographical references

016.80881   Bibliographies of poetry collections

Katz, William A., 1924-
The Columbia Granger's guide to poetry anthologies; [by] William Katz, Linda Sternberg Katz, Esther Crain. 2nd enl ed. Columbia Univ. Press 1995 c1994 xxxiv, 440p $75   **016.80881**
1. Poetry—Collections—Bibliography
ISBN 0-231-10104-X   LC 94-6482
Also available as part of Columbia Granger's world of poetry on CD-ROM, which also includes Granger's index to poetry and the Columbia Granger's index to poetry
First published 1990
The authors provide critical annotations for all 800 anthologies indexed in the seventh and eighth editions of Granger's index to poetry and the ninth and tenth editions of Columbia Granger's index to poetry

016.813   Bibliographies of American fiction

Adamson, Lynda G.
American historical fiction; an annotated guide to novels for adults and young adults. Oryx Press 1999 405p $49.95   **016.813**
1. Historical fiction—Bibliography 2. American fiction—Bibliography 3. United States—History—Fiction—Bibliography
ISBN 1-57356-067-7   LC 98-38044
Based on Dickinson's American historical fiction, 5th edition published 1986 by Scarecrow Press

"Organized by time period, the entries include author, title, date of publication, number of pages, content notes, setting, main characters, and, where applicable, genres, awards, and series/sequel information. . . . This work should be a boon to reader's advisory and collection development librarians needing to build specific areas of the collection." Libr J
For a fuller review see: Booklist, April 1, 1999

Coffey, Rosemary K.
America as story; historical fiction for middle and secondary schools; [by] Rosemary K. Coffey, Elizabeth F. Howard. 2nd ed. American Lib. Assn. 1997 xxi, 216p pa $25   **016.813**
1. Historical fiction—Bibliography 2. American fiction—Bibliography 3. United States—History—Fiction—Bibliography
ISBN 0-8389-0702-4   LC 96-43453
First published 1988 under the authorship of Elizabeth F. Howard
"This is an annotated bibliography of approximately 200 recommended titles arranged by historical period. Coded according to appropriate reading levels, the entries include annotations, comments on what readers will learn about historical events, and suggestions for reports and activities." Publisher's note

VanMeter, Vandelia
America in historical fiction; a bibliographic guide; [by] Vandelia L. VanMeter. Libraries Unlimited 1997 280p $38.50   **016.813**
1. Historical fiction—Bibliography 2. American fiction—Bibliography 3. United States—History—Fiction—Bibliography
ISBN 1-56308-496-1   LC 96-34745
"Arranged in major chronological divisions of U.S. history, the annotated entries include standard bibliographic information, time period, subject, location, research base (if known), and whether the title is more appropriate for mature students or younger secondary students." Publisher's note

016.9   Bibliographies of geography and history

Adamson, Lynda G.
Literature connections to world history, 7-12; resources to enhance and entice. Libraries Unlimited 1998 511p pa $32.50   **016.9**
1. History—Bibliography 2. Audiovisual materials—Catalogs 3. CD-ROMs—Reviews
ISBN 1-56308-505-4   LC 97-35953
Also available: Literature connections to world history, K-6
This resource is divided "into two main sections. The first section lists authors and book titles in the categories of historical fiction, biography, collective biography, history trade book, CD-ROM, and videotape within specific time periods according to grade levels. The second section contains annotated bibliographies of titles listed in the first part: books, CD-ROMs, and videotapes." Introduction

016.94053   Bibliographies of World War II, 1939-1945

Sullivan, Edward T.
The Holocaust in literature for youth; a guide and resource book. Scarecrow Press 1999 259p $29.50   **016.94053**
1. Holocaust, 1933-1945—Bibliography
ISBN 0-8108-3607-6   LC 98-48768
A "guide to literature of the Holocaust for youth ages ten to seventeen. . . . Each entry contains a synopsis, evaluation of the work's quality, grade level, and notes on special features such as indexes. . . . Fully one-half of the book is devoted to appendixes that include lists of professional resources for the teaching of the Holocaust (including ERIC citations), electronic resources, Holocaust museums and organizations, and a section of booktalks and classroom activities related to the books." Voice Youth Advocates

016.973   Bibliographies of United States history

Adamson, Lynda G.
Literature connections to American history, 7-12; resources to enhance and entice. Libraries Unlimited 1997 624p pa $34.50   **016.973**
1. United States—History—Bibliography 2. Audiovisual materials—Catalogs 3. CD-ROMS—Reviews
ISBN 1-56308-503-8   LC 97-19560
Also available: Literature connections to American history, K-6
"The first part of the book is divided into 13 time periods or topics, each of which is subdivided by grade level for grades 7-12. . . . The books, identified only by author and title, are listed according to genre, including historical fiction, biography, collective biography, and history trade books. Multimedia listings include CD-ROMs and videos. The bulk of the volume contains short annotated bibliographies of the nearly 3,000 books, CD-ROMs, and videos." Book Rep
"This comprehensive title should be valuable as a reader's advisory tool, a purchasing guide, and a resource for curriculum enrichment." Bull Cent Child Books

Stephens, Elaine C., 1943-
Learning about—the Civil War; literature and other resources for young people; [by] Elaine C. Stephens and Jean E. Brown. Linnet Professional Publs. 1998 259p $32; pa $22.50   **016.973**
1. United States—History—1861-1865, Civil War—Bibliography
ISBN 0-208-02464-6; 0-208-02449-2 (pa)
                                      LC 98-14569
"First discussing separately both the Civil War and the role of literature in the curriculum, the authors then discuss how literature can be used to teach about the Civil War. . . . Each of the following chapters focuses on one aspect of the Civil War, providing basic information and the significance of that aspect for those with little background. 'Focus Books' directly relating to that specific aspect are then listed. Each book is briefly summarized, then fully annotated with the appropriate grade level indicated." Voice Youth Advocates

020   Library and information sciences

Crawford, Walt
Being analog; creating tomorrow's libraries. American Lib. Assn. 1999 245p pa $28   **020**
1. Library science 2. Libraries—Data processing
ISBN 0-8389-0754-7   LC 98-40764
The author explores digital technology, media and cataloging. He argues that a sensible combination of human intelligence and computer power will be necessary to face the bibliographical future
Includes bibliographical references

021.7   Promotion of libraries, information centers

Flowers, Helen F., 1931-
Public relations for school library media programs; 500 ways to influence people and win friends for your school library media center. Neal-Schuman 1998 158p pa $38.50   **021.7**
1. Public relations—Libraries 2. School libraries
ISBN 1-55570-320-8   LC 98-11470
The author recommends "techniques for promoting the use of the library media services by students, faculty, building administrators, and school support staff. Readers will also learn how to target administrators, the board of education, parents, community, and legislators to maintain and increase support for staff, materials, equipment, and space." Publisher's note
"Writing with a sense both of purpose and of humor, Flowers turns a book of excellent lists into a good, entertaining read." Voice Youth Advocates
Includes bibliographical references

025   Operations of libraries, information centers

Mambretti, Catherine, 1950-
CD-ROM technology; a manual for librarians and educators. McFarland & Co. 1998 299p pa $39.95   **025**
1. School libraries 2. Computer assisted instruction 3. CD-ROMs
ISBN 0-7864-0501-5   LC 98-10321
Part 1 provides information on "designing your CD-ROM system and developing acquisition strategies. Such topics as hardware requirements, financial planning, compatibility between systems, copyright issues, and licensing are covered here. Part 2 is a practical guide to managing the CD-ROM system, including details on installation of the titles, maintaining hardware and software, and troubleshooting. Technical information is provided in Part 3." Publisher's note
Includes bibliographical references

Smith, Mark, 1956-
Neal-Schuman Internet policy handbook for libraries. Neal-Schuman 1999 219p il (Neal-Schuman net-guide series) $55   **025**
1. Internet
ISBN 1-55570-345-3   LC 98-49487
"In seven sections, the handbook covers physical considerations like privacy screens, access issues such as restricting Internet terminals to library card holders, acceptable and unacceptable uses, formal Internet Use Policies, filtering, and staff responsibility for training. . . . Additional material is provided for measuring Internet use and handling challenges to Internet-related policies and procedures." Publisher's note
Includes bibliographical references

025.04   Automated information storage and retrieval systems

Minkel, Walter
Delivering Web reference services to young people; [by] Walter Minkel and Roxanne Hsu Feldman. American Lib. Assn. 1998 121p il $49.95   **025.04**
1. Children's libraries 2. World Wide Web 3. Library information networks
ISBN 0-8389-0743-1   LC 98-26112
"Minkel and Feldman have written a book designed to guide both school and public librarians through using, teaching, and developing the Web for youth. . . . Descriptions of search tools are given in a manner that anyone trained in research will be able to understand and use easily." J Youth Serv Libr
Includes bibliographical references

Pappas, Marjorie L.
Searching electronic resources; by Marjorie L. Pappas, Gayle A. Geitgey, Cathy A. Jefferson. 2nd ed. Linworth Pub. 1999 105p (Professional growth series) $34.95   **025.04**
1. Information systems 2. Research
ISBN 0-938865-67-6   LC 98-54104
First published 1976
This book presents techniques for a four-step search process: browse, hypertext, hierarchical and analytical. Search strategy forms are included for 60 CD-ROMs and on-line electronic resources
Includes bibliographical references

025.1   Library administration

Woolls, E. Blanche
The school library media manager. 2nd ed. Libraries Unlimited 1999 340p $48.50; pa $38.50   **025.1**
1. School libraries 2. Instructional materials centers
ISBN 1-56308-772-3; 1-56308-702-2 (pa)
LC 99-11493
First published 1994
Incorporating the new AASL guidelines this guide discusses staffing, facilities, collection development, budget, marketing, evaluation, and planning for the future
Includes bibliographical references

025.2   Acquisitions and collection development

Slote, Stanley J.
Weeding library collections; library weeding methods. 4th ed. Libraries Unlimited 1997 xxi, 240p $55   **025.2**
1. Libraries—Collection development
ISBN 1-56308-511-9   LC 96-54865
First published 1975
"The author demonstrates how weeding strengthens a collection and increases circulation. . . . Four weeding methods are presented: the book care method, the spine-marking method, the historical reconstruction method, and the computer-assisted method. Slote gives precise instructions for each method, enhanced with illustrations." Book Rep
Includes glossary and bibliographical references

Walker, Barbara J.
Developing Christian fiction collections for children and adults; selection criteria and a core collection. Neal-Schuman 1998 224p pa $38.50   **025.2**
1. Christian fiction—Bibliography
ISBN 1-55570-292-9   LC 98-5881
"Areas covered include an overview of Christian fiction, establishing a solid selection process, and promoting this category in your library. Detailed appendixes feature annotated bibliographies of recommended books for children, adults, and young adults; listings of the Gold Medallion Fiction award winners from 1978 to present; biographies of prominent authors; and a selected, annotated videography on the best Christian videos." Publisher's note
Includes bibliographical references

025.3   Bibliographic analysis and control

Anglo-American cataloguing rules; prepared under the direction of the Joint Steering Committee for Revision of AACR, a committee of: the American Library Association, the Australian Committee on Cataloguing, the British Library, the Canadian Committee on Cataloguing, the Library Association, the Library of Congress. 2nd ed, 1998 revision. American Lib. Assn. 1998 676p $80; pa $55   **025.3**
1. Cataloging
ISBN 0-8389-3486-2; 0-8389-3485-4 (pa)
LC 98-8479
Also available CD-ROM version
First published 1967
This volume provides rules that cover the description of, and the provision of access points for, library materials. Included are all changes and corrections authorized by the Joint Steering Committee for Revision of AACR since 1988

Cataloging correctly for kids; an introduction to the tools; Sharon Zuiderveld, editor. 3rd ed. American Lib. Assn. 1998 116p pa $20   **025.3**
1. Cataloging
ISBN 0-8389-3476-5   LC 97-41145
First published 1989 by the Cataloging of Children's Materials Committee
Among the topics discussed are: cataloging nonbook materials; authority control; cataloging Internet cources; curriculum-enhanced MARC; search and retrieval strategies; vendors of cataloging for children's materials
Includes bibliographical references

Gorman, Michael, 1941-
The concise AACR2, 1998 revision; prepared by Michael Gorman. American Lib. Assn. 1999 168p pa $32   **025.3**
1. Anglo-American cataloguing rules 2. Cataloging
ISBN 0-8389-3494-3   LC 98-55150
First published 1988
This practical guide for beginning catalogers incorporates the 1993-1997 Amendments to the Anglo-American cataloguing rules

Intner, Sheila S., 1935-
Standard cataloging for school and public libraries; [by] Sheila S. Intner and Jean Weihs. 2nd ed. Libraries Unlimited 1996 278p il lib bdg $32.50   **025.3**
1. Cataloging 2. Books—Classification
ISBN 1-56308-349-3   LC 95-53186
First published 1990
This explains the Anglo-American Cataloging Rules (AACR2), Sears and Library of Congress subject headings, Dewey decimal and Library of Congress classification systems, MARC format, large computer networks, policy manuals, and how to manage a cataloging department
"The beauty of this manual is in clear discussions and backgrounds for every major area, phase, rule, and detail." Book Rep
Includes glossary and bibliographical references

025.4   Subject analysis and control

Dewey, Melvil, 1851-1931
Abridged Dewey decimal classification and relative index; devised by Melvil Dewey. ed 13, edited by Joan S. Mitchell, Julianne Beall, Winton E. Matthews, Jr., Gregory R. New. Forest Press (Albany) 1997 1023p $90   **025.4**
1. Dewey Decimal Classification
ISBN 0-910608-59-8   LC 97-10791
First abridged edition published 1894
The 13th Abridged Edition is an abridgement of the four volume 21st Edition. Adapted to the needs of small and growing libraries, the 13th Abridged Edition is designed primarily for school and public libraries with collections of up to 20,000 titles

Scott, Mona L.
Dewey decimal classification, 21st edition: a study manual and number building guide. Libraries Unlimited 1998 198p $47.50   **025.4**
1. Dewey Decimal Classification
ISBN 1-56308-598-4   LC 98-6948
"Ten chapters cover the ten main classes, 000s-900s, and include exercises, preceded by four chapters on history and current status, general aspects, principles of number building, and the tables. A final chapter explaining book numbers is very useful. . . . Scott highlights features of the 21st edition that differ from previous ones." Libr J

Sears list of subject headings. 17th ed, edited by Joseph Miller. Wilson, H.W. 2000 xlvi, 770p $65   **025.4**
1. Subject headings
ISBN 0-8242-0989-3
New edition of Canadian companion in preparation
First published 1923 with title: List of subject headings for small libraries, by Minnie Earl Sears
"A major feature of this seventeenth edition of the Sears List is the revision of the headings for the native peoples of the Western Hemisphere. . . . Also in this edition many new subdivisions have been added to those provided for in the List. . . . The new terms in the present edition represent developments in many different areas, especially computers, personal relations, politics, and popular culture." Preface

025.5   Services to users

Developing an information literacy program K-12; a how-to-do-it manual and CD-ROM package; developed by the Iowa City Community School District and edited by Mary Jo Langhorne. Neal-Schuman 1998 292p il (How-to-do-it manuals for librarians) pa $75   **025.5**
1. Bibliographic instruction 2. School libraries 3. Library information networks
ISBN 1-55570-332-1   LC 98-7714
This manual "equips students with the means to optimize their searches, evaluate located information, and effectively communicate their findings via graphics and databases. Throughout the text, information problem solving activities are integrated with classroom subjects. . . . The accompanying CD-ROM, formated in Microsoft Word 6.0 (in both Mac and IBM-compatible versions), enables the user to print out forms, handouts, and transparencies from the text as needed." J Youth Serv Libr
Includes bibliographical references

Heiligman, Deborah
The New York Public Library kid's guide to research. Scholastic Ref. 1998 134p il $14.95   **025.5**
1. Research 2. Libraries
ISBN 0-590-30715-0   LC 97-28939
Provides guidance on how to do research, including how to use libraries and their resources, the Internet, and other sources such as interviews and surveys
"Short and complete, this book contains a wealth of

Heiligman, Deborah—*Continued*
material for young researchers. . . . A book that is appealing and informative, with content appeal across the grades." SLJ

Volkman, John D.
Cruising through research; library skills for young adults. Libraries Unlimited 1998 207p il pa $25   **025.5**
1. Research 2. Bibliographic instruction
ISBN 1-56308-536-4   LC 97-40408
"The author uses the 'cruise' theme throughout the book calling each assignment an 'excursion.'. . . The first two excursions cover the use of reference materials that most students will need to use. . . . Other excursions guide students through the process of writing a term paper by identifying a topic, taking notes, outlining, and writing the paper and the bibliography." Voice Youth Advocates
This book "would be an asset to any professional collection and is an excellent personal choice for librarians looking for new ideas." Book Rep
Includes bibliographical references

Yucht, Alice H.
Flip it! an information skills strategy for student researchers. Linworth Pub. 1997 105p il (Professional growth series) $27.95   **025.5**
1. Bibliographic instruction 2. School libraries
ISBN 0-938865-62-5   LC 97-3887
The author "presents a new information skills strategy for librarians and teachers to use with students. . . . FLIP IT is a mnemonic for research processes: Focus—on the topic; Link—new information to what is already known; Input—implement the information; Payoff—put it all together (finished product)." Voice Youth Advocates
Includes bibliographical references

025.7 Physical preparation for storage of library materials

Greenfield, Jane
Books: their care and repair. Wilson, H.W. 1984 204p il $42   **025.7**
1. Books—Conservation and restoration
ISBN 0-8242-0695-9   LC 83-25926
"Geared to librarians, this useful handbook explains in clear, precise language how major and minor book repairs can be performed in-house without costly materials. . . . [The author] also furnishes basic background material on the structure of books and how proper care prevents deterioration. Simple line drawings supplement the text." Booklist
Includes glossary and bibliographical references

027.62 Libraries for children and young people

Jones, Patrick
Connecting young adults and libraries; a how-to-do-it manual. 2nd ed. Neal-Schuman 1998 xxii, 460p (How-to-do-it manuals for librarians) pa $59.95   **027.62**
1. Young adults' library services 2. Young adult literature—Bibliography 3. Books and reading
ISBN 1-55570-315-1   LC 97-37124
First published 1992
This volume includes information about young adult internet use in libraries, librarian's internet resources, reading research and collection development lists, a discussion of intellectual freedom issues, lists of young adult publishers, magazines, and professional periodicals
Includes bibliographical references

Kan, Katharine
Sizzling summer reading programs for young adults; [by] Katherine L. Kan for the Young Adult Library Services Association. American Lib. Assn. 1998 60p il pa $25   **027.62**
1. Young adults' library services 2. Teenagers—Books and reading
ISBN 0-8389-3480-3   LC 97-52973
This "book is divided by subject: type of program (general incentive or thematic); participation opportunities (volunteers, teen advisory board, etc.); programs for teens with special needs. A solid introduction explains how to connect with YAs. Each program is thoroughly described and includes graphics of such things as giveaways and posters. Some of the programs give insights into difficulties other libraries might run up against." Booklist

Rankin, Virginia
The thoughtful researcher; teaching the research process to middle school students. Libraries Unlimited 1999 211p il (Information literacy series) $27   **027.62**
1. School libraries 2. Bibliographic instruction 3. Research
ISBN 1-56308-698-0   LC 98-55916
Rankin "offers concrete suggestions (and 16 reproducible handouts) for researching a topic, generating questions, planning a project, managing time, searching for information, evaluating sources, note taking, mastering thinking skills, selecting a presentation format, and assessing the product and the process. . . . A must-have resource for school libraries serving grades 5-9, this will be welcomed by classroom teachers and teacher-librarians." Booklist
Includes bibliographical references

Young adults and public libraries; a handbook of materials and services; edited by Mary Anne Nichols and C. Allen Nichols. Greenwood Press 1998 283p (Greenwood library management collection) $75   **027.62**
1. Public libraries 2. Young adults' library services
ISBN 0-313-30003-8   LC 97-45649

Young adults and public libraries—*Continued*

A "collection of articles by 24 leading experts in the field of YA services. The authors speak with authority and commitment about important current issues: from balancing popularity and quality in collection building and readers' advisory to training YA staff, providing homework assistance programs, and confronting challenges of intellectual freedom." Booklist

Includes bibliographical references

027.6205   Libraries for children and young people—Serial publications

Journal of Youth Services in Libraries. American Lib. Assn. $40 per year   **027.6205**
1. Young adults' library services—Periodicals 2. Children's libraries—Periodicals 3. Books—Reviews
ISSN 0894-2498

Quarterly. Formerly Top of the News
"This publication includes news, columns, bibliographic essays, refereed feature articles, and reviews of professional reading. . . . Typical of ALA divisional journals, this is of high quality and highly recommended for school and public library professional collections." Katz. Mag for Libr. 9th edition

VOYA: Voice of Youth Advocates. Scarecrow Press $42 per year   **027.6205**
1. Young adults' library services—Periodicals 2. Young adult literature—Periodicals 3. Books—Reviews
ISSN 0160-4201

Bimonthly. First published 1978
This "continues to be an attractive journal devoted to library service to young adults. . . . Each issue includes four or five feature articles, as well as a large number of concise reviews of materials for young adults. VOYA regularly takes on controversial issues, providing a forum for practitioners working with young people." Katz. Mag for Libr. 9th edition

027.8   School libraries

American Association of School Librarians
Information power; building partnerships for learning; prepared by the American Association of School Librarians [and] Association for Educational Communications and Technology. American Lib. Assn. 1998 205p il pa $35   **027.8**
1. School libraries 2. Instructional materials centers
ISBN 0-8389-3470-6   LC 98-23291
First published 1988 as replacement for: Media programs: district and school (1975)
This work "is intended to be a persuasive and fundamental statement about school library media programs. . . . Chapters on information literacy, technology, and collaboration suggest a scope that relates the library-media program to the entire educational infrastructure. The authors explicate their themes in terms of standards, indicators, levels of proficiency, goals, principles, and examples of student activities." Libr J
Includes bibliographical references

Bard, Therese Bissen
Student assistants in the school library media center. Libraries Unlimited 1999 226p pa $30
          027.8
1. School libraries 2. Instructional materials centers
ISBN 1-56308-406-6   LC 98-49267
The author "provides job descriptions for various kinds of assistants (elementary, middle school, and high school as well as informal library clubs) and offers advice for recruitment and program evaluation. . . . Appended with sample application forms, teacher recommendations, responsibilities, and bylaws, this will be useful in any library that uses volunteers." Booklist
Includes bibliographical references

Bradburn, Frances Bryant
Output measures for school library media programs. Neal-Schuman 1999 95p pa $49.95
          027.8
1. School libraries 2. Instructional materials centers
ISBN 1-55570-326-7   LC 98-45557
"Bradburn's handbook is intended to guide school library specialists in collecting data on budgets, staff, and services and in using the data to evaluate programs and argue for increased funding. Forms and work sheets as well as three case studies are included." Booklist
Includes bibliographical references

Doiron, Ray
Partners in learning; students, teachers, and the school library; [by] Ray Doiron and Judy Davies; foreword by Ken Haycock. Libraries Unlimited 1998 182p il pa $24   **027.8**
1. School libraries 2. Bibliographic instruction
ISBN 1-56308-552-6   LC 97-30591
"The authors spell out the need for a more integrated approach to teaching skills necessary for finding, accessing, evaluating, using, and sharing information. Strategies for building the partnership and involving students more fully in their learning are included along with planning guides, sample research projects, and evaluation tools. The advice given is practical and the projects are easy to replicate." SLJ
Includes bibliographical references

The **Emerging** school library media center; historical issues and perspectives; Kathy Howard Latrobe, editor. Libraries Unlimited 1998 288p $42   **027.8**
1. School libraries 2. Instructional materials centers
ISBN 1-56308-389-2   LC 98-43715
"Designed to give a history of the development of school library media centers (SLMC) and the key issues surrounding them, the readings in this volume cover a broad range of topics, including the education, certification, and licensure of school librarians; standards and guidelines; intellectual freedom; collection development; the role of technology; and the emergence of professional organizations." Booklist
Includes bibliographical references

Wasman, Ann—*Continued*

This work "provides basic information on establishing and maintaining a quality school library media center. Beginning with ideas for developing a mind-set and surviving the first week, Wasman offers practical, detailed suggestions for circulation, collection development, budgeting, and facilities management, as well as tips for handling the various personalities within a school system." SLJ

Yesner, Bernice L.

Operating and evaluating school library media programs; a handbook for administrators and librarians; [by] Bernice L. Yesner and Hilda L. Jay. Neal-Schuman 1998 xxi, 424p pa $49.95

027.8

1. School libraries 2. Instructional materials centers
ISBN 1-55570-250-3   LC 98-11469

"Yesner and Jay attempt to clarify for school administrators everything a school librarian should be doing in an exemplary school library media program. They cover staffing, programming, collection management, instructional strategies, and technology use. . . . For each topic, they provide a brief philosophy of current practices followed by checklists of positive, negative, and missing elements and possible solutions." Booklist

027.805 School libraries—Serial publications

The **Book** Report; the journal for junior and senior high school librarians. Linworth Pub. $49 per year   **027.805**

1. School libraries—Periodicals 2. Books—Reviews
ISSN 0731-4388

Five issues per year. First published 1982

"Aimed at the school library professional, the pages are filled with ideas for providing more effective library service. The book reviews are plentiful and critical and provide a very useful selection tool." Katz. Mag for Libr. 9th edition

School Library Journal; the magazine of children's, young adult, and school libraries. Bowker $97.50 per year   **027.805**

1. School libraries—Periodicals 2. Books—Reviews
ISSN 0362-8930

Monthly. First published 1954 with title: Junior Libraries

In addition to the feature articles this journal includes "a calendar of events, news from the field, notes on people, columns . . . as well as many reviews—of professional reading, books for children and young adults, audiovisuals, and computer software. The annual *SLJ* 'Reference Books Roundup' is a very useful selection tool. This is an essential professional journal for school and public librarians." Katz. Mag for Libr. 9th edition

028 Reading and use of other information media

Krashen, Stephen D.

The power of reading; insights from the research; [by] Stephen Krashen. Libraries Unlimited 1993 119p pa $15   **028**

1. Reading 2. Literacy
ISBN 1-56308-006-0   LC 92-15096

The author "outlines and 'proves' via . . . research reports how Free Voluntary Reading (FVR), the use of in-school free reading programs, is beneficial to children's reading comprehension, writing style, vocabulary, spelling, and grammatical development. . . . This book will be useful for teachers and librarians (media specialists) who need solid data and numbers to take to their library directors or principals." Voice Youth Advocates

Includes bibliographical references

028.1 Reviews of books and other media

AudioFile; the audiobook review. AudioFile Pubs. $48 per year   **028.1**

1. Audiobooks—Reviews
ISSN 1063-0244

Bimonthly. First published 1992 as monthly

Price of subscription includes *AudioFile* issues, the *Audiobook Reference Guide* and the *Annual Index of Titles* (published in May)

"AudioFile reviews unabridged and abridged audiobooks, original audio programs, commentary and dramatizations in the spoken-word format. Our focus is the audio presentation, not the critique of the written material." Publisher's note

Bauermeister, Erica

Let's hear it for the girls; 375 great books for readers 2-14; [by] Erica Bauermeister and Holly Smith. Penguin Bks. 1997 224p pa $10.95   **028.1**

1. Girls—Books and reading 2. Children's literature—Bibliography
ISBN 0-14-025732-2   LC 96-9791

This bibliography attempts to address "the need to provide children with strong female role models. . . . [This guide] is organized by reading level and includes fiction, nonfiction, biography, poetry, and picture books by both women and men writers from all over the world. Cross-referenced indexes by author, title, date, country, genre, and subject." Publisher's note

Booklist. American Lib. Assn. $74.50 per year   **028.1**

1. Books—Reviews 2. Books and reading—Best books
ISSN 0006-7385

Semimonthly September through June; monthly July and August. First published 1905 with title: A.L.A. Booklist. Merged with Subscription Books Bulletin in 1956

The Reference Books Bulletin section is also available separately in an annual cumulation for $28.50

Booklist—*Continued*

"Intended chiefly as a guide for librarians in public and school libraries, each issue covers titles in five major areas: forthcoming titles, adult books, books for youth, audiovisual media, and reference books. . . . Because of its selectivity, its early reviews, and its broad coverage of popular non-print media, *Booklist* is essential reading for public, school, and many academic libraries." Katz. Mag for Libr. 9th edition

Bulletin of the Center for Children's Books. University of Ill. Press $40 per year   **028.1**
1. Books—Reviews 2. Children's literature—Reviews—Periodicals
ISSN 0008-9036

Monthly except August. First published 1945 for the University of Chicago, Graduate Library School

"This highly regarded reviewing source covers selected titles from the thousands of children's books published each year. In addition to complete bibliographic information, the critical annotations are supplemented by an indication of suitable age and/or grade level, a shorthand code noting a range of quality, from 'books of special distinction' to 'NR' for not recommended. . . . Librarians in schools, public libraries, and academic libraries with children's literature collections will find this an indispensable guide." Katz. Mag for Libr. 9th edition

Carter, Betty, 1944-
Best books for young adults; the selections, the history, the romance. American Lib. Assn. 1994 214p il pa $25   **028.1**
1. Young adult literature—Bibliography 2. Best books
ISBN 0-8389-3439-0   LC 94-2640
New edition in preparation

"In this overview of the annual Best Books for Young Adults lists chosen by a committee of the Young Adult Library Services Association of the ALA, Carter discusses the history of the list and addresses such issues as . . . how the list should be used in schools and libraries. A final section includes annotated bibliographies of titles chosen from 1966-93." Booklist

"A valuable resource for any middle school, junior high, high school, or public library." Voice Youth Advocates

Children's book review index. Gale Res. $145
        028.1
1. Books—Reviews—Indexes 2. Children's literature—Reviews—Indexes
ISSN 0147-5681

Previous cumulations available. Contact publisher for prices

Annual. First published 1975

"Each annual cites more than 17,700 reviews of more than 10,000 children's books, preschool through grade 10. The same citations also appear in *Book Review Index,* of which this is a spinoff. Reviews cited can be found in the 470 periodicals indexed in *BRI.* It is arranged in a single alphabet by author." Nichols. Guide to Ref Books for Sch Media Cent. 4th edtion

Cooper-Mullin, Alison, 1954-
Once upon a heroine; 400 books for girls to love; [by] Alison Cooper-Mullin and Jennifer Marmaduke Coye. Contemporary Bks. 1998 349p pa $14.95   **028.1**
1. Girls—Books and reading 2. Children's literature—Bibliography 3. Young adult literature—Bibliography
ISBN 0-8092-3020-8   LC 97-32121

The authors "have gathered books whose heroines are smart and strong-willed. Nontraditional roles, interesting plots, meaningful character development, and rich language were some of their criteria for inclusion. Organized from 'early readers' to 'young adults,' their book includes a resource list for finding the books mentioned." SLJ

Dodson, Shireen
100 books for girls to grow on; lively descriptions of the most inspiring books for girls, terrific discussion questions to spark conversation, great ideas for book-inspired activities, crafts, and field trips. HarperCollins Pubs. 1998 334p pa $14
        028.1
1. Girls—Books and reading 2. Children's literature—Bibliography 3. Young adult literature—Bibliography
ISBN 0-06-095718-2   LC 98-27606

The author summarizes "books that girls ages nine to thirteen might enjoy reading on their own or sharing in a book discussion group. . . . Organized alphabetically by title, each book is broken down into several categories including the summary, reading time, themes, discussion questions, information about the author, activities to do beyond the book, and recommended further reading." Voice Youth Advocates

Horning, Kathleen T.
From cover to cover; evaluating and reviewing children's books. HarperCollins Pubs. 1997 230p $24.95; pa $12.95   **028.1**
1. Books—Reviews 2. Children's literature—History and criticism
ISBN 0-06-024519-0; 0-06-446167-X (pa)
        LC 96-27281

The author "begins with an overview of how children's books are published in the United States, the physical parts of the book, and categories of children's books. The next six chapters are devoted to the definition and scope of those categories." Bull Cent Child Books

"Anyone entering the field of children's book reviewing, or indeed, the wider field of children's literature, will find *From Cover to Cover* an excellent guide to analyzing books and presenting clear, useful reviews." Booklist

Includes bibliographical references

Into focus; understanding and creating middle school readers; editors: Kylene Beers, Barbara G. Samuels. Christopher-Gordon Pubs. 1998 xx, 490p il pa $46.95   **028.1**
1. Reading 2. Literature—Study and teaching
ISBN 0-926842-64-1

In this "handbook, 24 experts from the fields of reading theory, library science, response theory, children's lit-

Into focus—*Continued*

erature, and middle school philosophy present strategies, describe programs, and provide lists that foster academic success and a lifelong love of reading." SLJ

Kliatt; reviews of selected paperback books, educational software and audiobooks. , 33 Bay State Rd., Wellesley, Mass. 02181 $39 per year
028.1
1. Paperback books—Reviews 2. Young adult literature—Periodicals
ISSN 1065-8602

Six issues per year. First published 1967. Former titles: Kliatt Young Adult Paperback Book Guide; Kliatt Paperback Book Guide

This is "a review service devoted chiefly to paperback books, whether reprints, reissues, or originals. Reference books suitable for high school libraries, audiobooks, and educational software are also included. Each review is coded for reading level and difficulty. . . . A recommended selection tool for junior high, high school and YA librarians." Katz. Mag for Libr. 8th edition

Odean, Kathleen
Great books for boys; more than 600 books for boys 2 to 14. Ballantine Bks. 1998 384p pa $12.95
028.1
1. Boys—Books and reading 2. Children's literature—Bibliography 3. Young adult literature—Bibliography
ISBN 0-345-42083-7   LC 97-45926

This annotated bibliography offers recommended titles and strategies for parents, teachers, and librarians to promote reading among boys
"An excellent resource." SLJ

Great books for girls; over 600 books to inspire today's girls and tomorrow's women. Ballantine Bks. 1997 420p pa $12.95   **028.1**
1. Girls—Books and reading 2. Children's literature—Bibliography 3. Young adult literature—Bibliography
ISBN 0-345-40484-X   LC 96-44392

This bibliography "introduces 600 titles, ranging from picture-story books for toddlers to biographies and novels for adolescents that depict girls and women who are self-sufficient, decisive, and assertive. . . . Odean's background as a children's book expert is apparent in her well-crafted, descriptive annotations. . . . The introduction and last chapter provide advice about locating good children's books, reading aloud, etc." Libr J

Toussaint, Pamela
Great books for African-American children. New Am. Lib. 1999 278p $12.95   **028.1**
1. African American children—Books and reading 2. Children's literature—Bibliography
ISBN 0-452-28044-3   LC 98-31519

"Toussaint has collected poetry, fiction, and nonfiction that reflect a wide range of black experience. . . . Entries suggest ways to explore a story further. An author-devised code helps the user determine what values the story reflects. . . . Helpful extras include a list of out-of-print titles, a bookstore directory, and a section listing magazines, television shows, web sites, videos, and other sources that promote reading, and regularly include African Americans." Libr J

028.5 Reading and use of other information media by children and young people

Ammon, Bette D.
More rip-roaring reads for reluctant teen readers; [by] Bette D. Ammon, Gale W. Sherman. Libraries Unlimited 1999 161p il pa $26.50
028.5
1. Books and reading 2. Young adult literature—Bibliography
ISBN 1-56308-571-2   LC 98-37150

Companion volume to Rip-roaring reads for reluctant teen readers, entered under Sherman, Gale W.

This volume "is divided into two parts—20 books for middle-grade readers and the same for high-school students. Each book gets one page that contains such information as genre, themes, reading and interest levels, author information, plot summary, and ways to introduce the book. . . . The titles recommended are appealing, and librarians on the lookout for books to hand reluctant readers will find many suggestions here in an easy-to-use format." Booklist

Barker, Keith, d. 1998
Outstanding books for children and young people; the LA guide to Carnegie/Greenaway winners 1937-1997. Library Assn. Pub.; distributed by Bernan Assocs. 1998 135p il pa $35   **028.5**
1. Children's literature—Bibliography 2. Carnegie medal 3. Kate Greenaway medal
ISBN 1-85604-287-1

An annotated list of the prestigious British book awards winners

"The gossip and strong opinions (Barker makes no bones about which books he thinks were good choices and which books he thinks were inferior) makes this survey informative as well as readable, and it's fascinating to see the trends both in awards and in responses." Bull Cent Child Books

Children's books and their creators; Anita Silvey, editor. Houghton Mifflin 1995 800p il $40
028.5
1. Children's literature—Bio-bibliography 2. Children's literature—History and criticism
ISBN 0-395-65380-0   LC 95-19049

This volume "compiles, in alphabetical order, 823 articles, most of them essays on contemporary creators of children's books. Writers as early as Aesop and as varied as Anna Sewell and Mark Twain are also included. . . . Each essay focuses on the subject's importance to the field of children's books and notes major contributions. . . . Silvey's editorial judgment is sound, and the entries, although varying in quality and depth, are usually well done." SLJ

Children's books: awards & prizes; includes prizes and awards for young adult books; compiled & edited by the Children's Book Council. Children's Bk. Council $60   **028.5**
1. Literary prizes 2. Children's literature—Bibliography 3. Young adult literature—Bibliography
ISSN 0069-3472

Children's books: awards & prizes—*Continued*
First published 1969. (1996 edition) Periodically revised

This publication lists over 200 awards divided as follows: Part I: United States awards selected by adults; Part II: United States awards selected by young readers; Part III: Australian, Canadian, New Zealand, and United Kingdom (UK) awards; Part IV: Selected international and multinational awards; Part V: Awards classified; Part VI: Publications and lists for selecting U. S. children's and young adult books. A brief history of each award precedes the list of winners

"Libraries that can afford only one dictionary of children's literature awards should have this one." Choice

Children's books from other countries; [sponsored by] United States Board on Books for Young People; Carl M. Tomlinson, editor. Scarecrow Press 1998 304p il pa $24   **028.5**
1. Books and reading 2. Children's literature—Bibliography
ISBN 0-8108-3447-2   LC 97-41768

This is a "reference guide to children's titles originally published outside of the U.S. and translated into English. This resource is divided into three sections, containing a broad overview of the field, advice on how to use the books, and signed evaluative annotations for over 700 titles, arranged by genre." SLJ

"An excellent tool that shows and tells the importance of global reach." Booklist

Includes bibliographical references

Children's books in children's hands; an introduction to their literature; [by] Charles Temple [et al.]; with contributions by Evelyn Freeman, Joy Moss. Allyn & Bacon 1998 xxvii, 580p il $65   **028.5**
1. Children's literature—History and criticism
2. Books and reading
ISBN 0-205-16995-3   LC 97-9950

Part I covers the intellectual development of children, literary elements of children's literature, and reader response criticism. Part II surveys the literature by genre. Part III shows how to create a literature-based classroom through activities, classroom libraries, and book discussions. Appendices list award-winning titles, professional organizations, publishers, children's periodicals and Web sites

Includes bibliographical references

Closter, Kathryn, 1950-
Fiction, food, and fun; the original recipe for the Read 'n' Feed Program; [by] Kathryn Closer, Karen L. Sipes, and Vickie Thomas; foreword by Caroline B. Cooney. Libraries Unlimited 1998 xx, 224p il pa $24.50   **028.5**
1. Books and reading
ISBN 1-56308-519-4   LC 98-9511

This "resource provides detailed information—activities, publicity, discussion questions, author background, and more—for 10 titles. . . . The program is designed to introduce young people to quality literature, actively involve them in discussion, and encourage them to become lifelong readers. Each chapter includes bibliographic information, suggested interest level, plot summary, and a booktalk." SLJ

The **Coretta** Scott King Awards book, 1970-1999; edited by Henrietta M. Smith. American Lib. Assn. 1999 135p pa $32   **028.5**
1. Children's literature—History and criticism
2. American literature—African American authors
3. African Americans in literature
ISBN 0-8389-3496-X   LC 99-25046
First published 1994

This work begins with discussions of the 1994-1999 award winners and honor books and then goes back year by year to 1969

"The text is broken up with quotes from the winning titles, and the book ends with photos and biographies of the authors and artists. An essential resource." Booklist

Dear author; students write about the books that changed their lives; collected by Weekly reader's Read magazine; introduction by Lois Lowry. Conari Press 1995 186p pa $9.95   **028.5**
1. Letters 2. Books and reading
ISBN 1-57324-003-6   LC 95-14455

A collection of letters from students to an assortment of authors both past and present about the impact of their work on the lives of their readers

"The letters themselves are well written, thought-provoking, and likely to stimulate curiosity about the titles mentioned. Teachers could use this collection to help motivate their students or to use as examples of letter-writing." SLJ

Donelson, Kenneth L.
Literature for today's young adults; [by] Kenneth L. Donelson, Aileen Pace Nilsen. 5th ed. Longman 1997 486p il $51.95   **028.5**
1. Young adult literature—History and criticism
2. Books and reading
ISBN 0-673-99737-5   LC 95-26604
First published 1980

"The work begins with an introductory section about the young adult and young adult books and then discusses the body of work by genre. A final section discusses evaluating and promoting books, censorship and the history of young adult literature from 1800 to the present. Features such as author profiles and comments and boxed bibliographies add interest to the text. . . . Middle and high school collections will find this source essential." Safford. Guide to Ref Materials for Sch Libr Media Cent. 5th edition

Includes bibliographical references

Dresang, Eliza T.
Radical change; books for youth in a digital age. Wilson, H.W. 1999 xxiv, 344p il $50   **028.5**
1. Children's literature—History and criticism
2. Youth—Books and reading 3. Literature and technology 4. Publishers and publishing
ISBN 0-8242-0953-2   LC 98-34791

The author offers a "look at YA and children's contemporary literature that shows how 'handheld' books are changing in today's digital world. . . . She addresses how today's youth, the Net Generation, thinks and learns; the types of handheld books they are reading;

Dresang, Eliza T.—*Continued*
their access to the digital world. . . . Each chapter closes with valuable lists: one of books for youth, the other, professional resources. . . . Professionals who work with youth will come away from this with a new understanding of contemporary youth literature and how to evaluate it." Booklist

Gillespie, John Thomas, 1928-
Juniorplots 4; a book talk guide for use with readers ages 12-16; by John T. Gillespie and Corinne J. Naden. Bowker 1993 450p $42   **028.5**
1. Books—Reviews 2. Literature—Stories, plots, etc. 3. Books and reading
ISBN 0-8352-3167-4   LC 92-35670
This volume provides entries for 81 contemporary fiction and nonfiction titles arranged by genre. Cumulative author, title and subject indexes for the earlier Juniorplots volumes are included in this volume

Middleplots 4; a book talk guide for use with readers ages 8-12; by John T. Gillespie and Corinne J. Naden. Bowker 1994 434p $45   **028.5**
1. Books—Reviews 2. Young adult literature—Stories, plots, etc. 3. Books and reading
ISBN 0-8352-3446-0   LC 93-21146
Continues Gillespie's Introducing books (1970), Introducing more books, by D.L. Spirt (1978), and Introducing bookplots 3, by D.L. Spirt (1988)
"The selections are organized thematically in eight interest categories such as 'Adventure and Mystery' and 'Other Lands and Times.' Each selection is organized under six sections: plot summary, thematic material, booktalk suggestions, similar books, review citations, and books and articles about the author. . . . Author, title, and subject indexes for this volume are followed by cumulative author, title, and subject indexes to the series." Booklist

The Newbery companion; booktalk and related materials for Newbery medal and honor books; [by] John T. Gillespie, Corinne J. Naden. Libraries Unlimited 1996 406p $48   **028.5**
1. Newbery Medal 2. Children's literature—History and criticism 3. Authors
ISBN 1-56308-356-6   LC 96-23699
"For each winning title there is a detailed plot summary, a discussion of themes and subjects, passages for booktalking and reading aloud, related children's books for follow-up reading, biographical references about the author, and sources for the acceptance speech. For each Honor book there is a brief plot summary. An introductory essay covers the history of the award, and there's a final general bibliography. This will be a much used reference by teachers, librarians, and students." Booklist

Jay, M. Ellen
Ready-to-go reading incentive programs for schools and libraries; [by] M. Ellen Jay and Hilda L. Jay. Neal-Schuman 1998 299p il pa $45
028.5
1. Children's libraries 2. Books and reading
ISBN 1-55570-330-5   LC 98-15210

A discussion of the elements of a well-designed reading incentive program are followed by descriptions of programs available from commercial sources and associations. The authors then introduce 16 ready-to-go thematic programs of their own. Outlines and handouts are provided
"School library media specialists and public librarians should take a look at this refreshingly diverse and stimulating book." SLJ
Includes bibliographical references

Newbery and Caldecott Medal books, 1966-1975; with acceptance papers, biographies and related material chiefly from The Horn Book magazine; edited by Lee Kingman. Horn Bk. 1975 xx, 321p il $22.95   **028.5**
1. Newbery Medal 2. Caldecott Medal 3. Children's literature—History and criticism 4. Authors 5. Illustrators
ISBN 0-87675-003-X
Combines Newbery Medal books, 1922-1955, Caldecott Medal books, 1938-1957, and Newbery and Caldecott Medal books, 1956-1965 (o.p.)
"Gives for each Newbery or Caldecott award winner his acceptance speech, a biographical note, and a book note. An excerpt from each Newbery book gives an example of the writer's style; a sample illustration from each Caldecott book is supplemented by notes on size, medium, printing process, number of illustrations and type used." Choice

Newbery and Caldecott medal books, 1976-1985; with acceptance papers, biographies, and related material chiefly from the Horn book magazine; edited by Lee Kingman. Horn Bk. 1986 358p il $24.95   **028.5**
1. Newbery Medal 2. Caldecott Medal 3. Children's literature—History and criticism 4. Authors 5. Illustrators
ISBN 0-87675-004-8   LC 86-15223
This volume "compiles the winning speeches, biographies and book notes for the 1976 through 1985 awards. It includes essays by Barbara Bader, Ethel Heins and Zena Sutherland." Bookbird

Newbery Medal books, 1922-1955; with their authors' acceptance papers & related material chiefly from The Horn Book magazine; edited by Bertha Mahony Miller and Elinor Whitney Field. Horn Bk. 1955 458p il $22.95   **028.5**
1. Newbery Medal 2. Children's literature—History and criticism 3. Authors
ISBN 0-87675-000-5
Companion volume to Caldecott Medal books, 1938-1957
"Largely biographical notes about award recipients and the acceptance papers." Ref Sources for Small & Medium-sized Libr. 5th edition

Pauses; autobiographical reflections of 101 creators of children's books; [compiled by] Lee Bennett Hopkins. HarperCollins Pubs. 1995 233p $23   **028.5**
1. Children's literature—History and criticism 2. Authors 3. Illustrators
ISBN 0-06-024748-7   LC 94-14641

Pauses—*Continued*

"This is a compilation of Hopkins' interviews with authors and illustrators, conducted primarily in the '60s and '70s. Each figure gets a paragraph of updated biography and a two or three-page edited version of the interviews; while topics addressed vary, the interviews all tend to describe growing up, beginnings as a children's author or illustrator, and the creative process." Bull Cent Child Books

Sutherland, Zena, 1915-
Children & books; [by] Zena Sutherland.
Addison Wesley Longman il $78   **028.5**
1. Children's literature—History and criticism

First edition by May Hill Arbuthnot published 1947 by Scott, Foresman. (9th edition, 1997) Periodically revised

"This children's literature textbook emphasizes the best books and authors. The introductory sections about children and books in general are followed by genre overviews which emphasize the major authors in each category. A third section discusses ways to bring children and books together, while a final section covers issues such as censorship. Lavish color illustrations, viewpoint boxes, extensive bibliographies and useful appendices make this an attractive and stimulating work." Safford. Guide to Ref Materials for Sch Libr Media Cent. 5th edition

Trelease, Jim
The read-aloud handbook. 4th ed. Penguin Bks.
1995 xxvi, 387p pa $13.95   **028.5**
1. Books and reading 2. Children's literature—Bibliography
ISBN 0-14-046971-0   LC 95-2269
First published 1982

"Trelease shares his firm belief in books. A pep talk, with new research on the value of reading aloud and new methods for its encouragement, is followed by the 'Treasury of Read-Alouds,' featuring 300 children's books . . . all nicely annotated and with notes leading to even more titles. An essential library book, of value to parents and professionals." Booklist [review of 1989 edition]

028.505 Children and young people's reading—Serial publications

The **ALAN** Review. National Council of Teachers of English $15 per year   **028.505**
1. Books—Reviews 2. Young adult literature—Periodicals
ISSN 0882-2840
Three issues per year. First published 1973
Published by the Assembly on Literature for Adolescents, National Council of Teachers of English
This publication "is unique in being devoted entirely to adolescent literature. Each issue contains 'Clip and File' reviews of approximately twenty new hardbacks or paperbacks and includes [several] feature articles, news announcements, and occasional in-depth reviews of professional books." Donelson. Literature for Today's Young Adults

Book Links. American Lib. Assn. $22   **028.505**
1. Children's literature—Periodicals 2. Best books
ISSN 1055-4742
Bimonthly. First issued as an insert in Booklist, Nov. 15, 1990
This periodical "offers feature articles on children's books (e.g., best books of the year, a Newbery/Caldecott retrospective) and regular columns that suggest ways to incorporate fine children's literature into the curriculum. Background information on special topics . . . is accompanied by an annotated bibliography, complete with appropriate grade level. Columns devoted to specific children's books and interviews with authors and illustrators are a plus for the adult who wants to read to or select books for children." Katz. Mag for Libr. 9th edition

The **Horn** Book Guide to Children's and Young Adult Books. Horn Bk. $50 per year   **028.505**
1. Children's literature—Periodicals 2. Books—Reviews
ISSN 1044-405X
Biannual. First published 1990
"This offshoot of *The Horn Book Magazine* provides critical annotations on all hardcover trade children's and young adult books published in the United States during the previous six months. Fiction is arranged by grade level and genre (e.g., picture books, readers); nonfiction by the ten broad Dewey classes and then narrower topics. . . . Numerous indexes (author, illustrator, title, series, subject, and new editions and reissues) help the librarian track down particular titles." Katz. Mag for Libr. 9th edition

The **Horn** Book Magazine. Horn Bk. $50 per year   **028.505**
1. Children's literature—Periodicals 2. Best books
3. Books—Reviews
ISSN 0018-5078
Bimonthly. First published 1924 with title: The Horn Book
"One of the first magazines to treat children's literature as serious material for discussion and review. . . . The book reviews, most of which are for recommended titles, are grouped by age level and/or format (picture books, folklore, etc.). Other sections of the magazine include lists of new paperbacks, reissues, books in Spanish, and audiobooks." Katz. Mag for Libr. 9th edition

031 American encyclopedias

Additional encyclopedias are listed in CD-ROM section, Part 3

Academic American encyclopedia. Grolier Educ.
21v il maps apply to publisher for price   **031**
1. Encyclopedias and dictionaries

Also available CD-ROM version The Grolier multimedia encyclopedia

First published 1980 by Aretê Publishing Company. Frequently revised

This encyclopedia's "coverage is based on American curriculum. Articles are clear, accurate and objective. Emphasis is on the arts and humanities and science and technology and about 35% of the articles are biographical. There are good bibliographies and an outstanding index." Safford. Guide to Ref Materials for Sch Libr Media Cent. 5th edition

Children's illustrated encyclopedia. 2nd rev ed. DK Pub. 1998 644p il maps $39.95　　**031**
1. Encyclopedias and dictionaries
ISBN 0-7894-2787-7　　LC 97-52096
Includes CD-ROM
First published 1991 in the United Kingdom with title: Dorling Kindersley children's illustrated encyclopedia and in the United States with title: The Random House children's encyclopedia
"Each topic is presented on one to six pages. About half the space on a page consists of full-color photographs and drawings. Most topic pages include a 'find out more' box that directs the reader to related entries. A 21-page reference section makes known such facts as what is the world's largest animal and on what date the world's first printed book appeared." Sci Books Films
For a fuller review see: Booklist, Nov. 1, 1998

Compton's encyclopedia & fact-index. Compton's Learning, P.O. Box 1167, Elmhurst, Il 60126 26v il maps set $599　　**031**
1. Encyclopedias and dictionaries

Also available Compton's interactive encyclopedia
First published 1922 with title: Compton's pictured encyclopedia. Frequently revised
Accompanied by two CD-ROMs
Supplemented by: Compton yearbook
"Recommended for home and school use by young people ages nine through eighteen. The main text, consisting of more than 5,000 articles, is supported by the nearly 30,000 brief articles among the 70,000 entries in the 'fact-index.' This volume presents brief dictionary entries, biographical sketches, statistics, and capsule treatments of topics not considered in the main text." Ref Sources for Small & Medium-sized Libr. 6th edition

The **Encyclopedia** Americana. Grolier Educ. 30v il maps apply to publisher for price　　**031**
1. Encyclopedias and dictionaries

Also available CD-ROM version
First published 1829. Frequently revised
Supplemented by: The Americana annual
This encyclopedia contains approximately 52,000 articles. "The index is comprehensive and analytical. *Americana* contains an exceptionally large number of U.S. place-names and biographies. The sciences, mathematics, American history, and the social sciences are particularly well developed. There are bibliographies at the end of major articles." Safford. Guide to Ref Materials for Sch Libr Media Cent. 5th edition

Hirsch, E. D. (Eric Donald), 1928-
The dictionary of cultural literacy; [by] E. D. Hirsch, Jr., Joseph F. Kett, James Trefil. 2nd ed, rev and updated. Houghton Mifflin 1993 619p il maps $27.50　　**031**
1. Civilization—Dictionaries 2. English language—Dictionaries 3. United States—Civilization—Dictionaries
ISBN 0-395-65597-8　　LC 93-19568
First published 1988

"This dictionary contains the body of information a literate American of the late 20th century should have absorbed by the senior year of high school. The content of the list includes phrases, terms, people, events, and dates and is arranged by broad areas of knowledge." Safford. Guide to Ref Materials for Sch Libr Media Cent. 5th edition

The **New** Grolier children's encyclopedia. Grolier Educ. 1999 10v il $225　　**031**
1. Encyclopedias and dictionaries
ISBN 0-7172-9373-4　　LC 98-7378
First published 1994 with title: The Grolier children's encyclopedia
Topics range "from science-related areas such as astronomy and wolves to social studies considerations such as geographic information and historical milestones. Each topic is clearly defined initially, and then subtopics are identified and described in the text. . . . Information is vibrantly enhanced through an effective display of illustrations, charts, and graphics." Sci Books Films

Oxford American children's encyclopedia. Oxford Univ. Press 1998 9v il $300　　**031**
1. Encyclopedias and dictionaries
ISBN 0-19-511081-1　　LC 97-40343
"The first seven volumes consist of alphabetically arranged entries that reflect the historical, cultural, social, and scientific topics taught in American classrooms. . . . Volume eight consists of short biographical sketches of more than 500 noted individuals. . . . Volume nine begins with a double-page map, four pages of flags, and a brief time line of world history. An easy-to-use index completes the set." SLJ
For a fuller review see: Booklist, April 15, 1999

The **World** Book encyclopedia. World Bk. 22v il maps apply to publisher for price　　**031**
1. Encyclopedias and dictionaries

Also available CD-ROM version, The World Book multimedia encyclopedia
First published 1917-1918 by Field Enterprises. Frequently revised
Supplemented by: The World Book year book; another available supplement is Science year
"Curriculum-oriented, this superior encyclopedia is well-edited and produced to meet the reference and informational needs of students from grade four through high school. Long standing tradition of excellence for readability, accuracy, authoritativeness, objectivity, judicious and extensive use of outstanding graphics and timeliness." N Y Public Libr. Ref Books for Child Collect

031.02　American books of miscellaneous facts

Amazing facts; written by Ned Halley. DK Pub. 1997 44p il $9.95　　**031.02**
1. Curiosities and wonders
ISBN 0-7894-2023-6　　LC 97-15214
A collection of facts about history, medicine, sports, nature, inventions, and other topics

Ash, Russell
Fantastic book of 1001 lists. DK Pub. 1999
208p il $19.95; pa $14.95   **031.02**
1. Curiosities and wonders
ISBN 0-7894-3769-4; 0-7894-3412-1 (pa)
                LC 98-7701
A "smorgasbord of fantastic facts, from the essential
to the bizarre, organized into 12 subject areas such as
'Space,' 'The Earth,' 'Science,' 'Countries,' 'The Arts',
and 'World Sports'. . . . Lists are organized in neat columns with succinct headings. The index is not very detailed, but suffices in identifying key subjects. A fun, visually appealing, and informative title." SLJ

Incredible comparisons; written by Russell Ash.
DK Pub. 1996 63p il $19.95   **031.02**
1. Measurement 2. Size 3. Shape
ISBN 0-7894-1009-5   LC 96-13875
Offers a visual guide, with brief explanatory text, to
comparative sizes, heights, weights, and numbers in such
areas as capacity, population, growth, weather, disasters,
speed, and others
"An incredible and fascinating book. . . . Brilliant illustrations, sometimes to scale, and succinct text demonstrate unique characteristics of thousands of facts." Sci
Child

The top 10 of everything 2000. DK Pub. 1999
288p il $24.95; pa $17.95   **031.02**
1. Curiosities and wonders 2. World records—Miscel-
lanea
ISBN 0-7894-4892-0; 0-7894-4632-4 (pa)
               LC 99-23292
This illustrated collection of facts and trivia features
1,000 lists encompassing human achievements and the
natural world. Features a section on how the world has
changed over the last millennium

The world in one day; written by Russell Ash.
DK Pub. 1997 32p il $15.95   **031.02**
1. Curiosities and wonders
ISBN 0-7894-2028-7   LC 97-16465
Provides illustrations and statistics on what happens to
the world in a single day, in such areas as geology, biology, technology, and culture

The **Guinness** book of records 1492; the world
five hundred years ago; editor, Deborah Manley;
editorial consultant, Geoffrey Scammell. Facts
on File 1992 192p il maps $24.95   **031.02**
1. Curiosities and wonders 2. World records 3. Fifteenth century
ISBN 0-8160-2772-2   LC 91-58588
"Grouped by eleven broad subjects, the thousands of
factual tidbits presented here bring the world of Columbus to life for researchers and browsers. Topics range
from the academic, such as science, architecture, and religion to such informal activities as sports, the arts, and
entertainment. . . . Numerous, outstanding full-color illustrations depict the period's artwork and inventions."
SLJ

Information please almanac, atlas & yearbook.
Houghton Mifflin $24.95; pa $10.95   **031.02**
1. Almanacs 2. Statistics 3. United States—Statistics

Annual. First published 1947 by Doubleday. Publisher
varies
"Statistical and factual material organized by subject
area; contains special articles by experts. Illustrated, with
a color map section and detailed index." N Y Public
Libr. Book of How & Where to Look It Up

Kane, Joseph Nathan, 1899-
Famous first facts; a record of first happenings,
discoveries, and inventions in American history;
by Joseph Nathan Kane, Steven Anzovin, Janet
Podell. Wilson, H.W. $95   **031.02**
1. Encyclopedias and dictionaries 2. United States—
History—Dictionaries

Also available CD-ROM version and Famous first
facts, international edition by Steven Anzovin and Janet
Podell (2000) $95 (ISBN 0-8242-0958-3)
First published 1933. (5th edition 1997) Periodically
revised
"Aims to establish the earliest date of various occurrences, achievements, inventions, etc. Dictionary arrangement with many cross-references. Gives brief description
or explanation together with the date; some references to
sources." Guide to Ref Books. 11th edition

The **New** York Times almanac. Penguin Ref.;
distributed by Penguin Putnam il maps $27.95;
pa $10.95   **031.02**
1. Almanacs 2. Statistics 3. United States—Statistics

Annual. First published 1997
Edited by John W. Wright
This almanac contains a "chronology of the year; major news stories of the year; U.S. history; U.S. presidential biographies; world history; world geography; economic and climate data; major awards in the arts, sciences, and sports; and a wide variety of U.S. demographic information. . . . It is well organized, the table layout
is easy to read, and the typeface does not invite eye
strain." Am Ref Books Annu, 1998

The **World** almanac and book of facts. World
Almanac il maps $29.95; pa $10.95   **031.02**
1. Almanacs 2. Statistics 3. United States—Statistics
ISSN 0084-1382

Annual. First published 1868. Publisher varies
"This is the most comprehensive and well-known of
almanacs. . . . Contains a chronology of the year's
events, consumer information, historical anniversaries,
annual climatological data, and forecasts. Color section
has flags and maps. Includes detailed index." N Y Public
Libr. Book of How & Where to Look It Up

The **World** almanac for kids. World Almanac il
maps $18.95; pa $10.95   **031.02**
1. Almanacs

Annual. First published 1995 for 1996
This volume contains information on animals, art, religion, sports, books, law, language, science and computers. Includes a section of full-color maps and flags. Illustrated throughout with pictures, diagrams, and charts

032.02 English books of miscellaneous facts

Guinness book of records. Guinness Media Inc.; distributed by Mint Pubs. il $26.95   **032.02**
1. Curiosities and wonders
ISSN 1057-4557

Annual. First published 1955 in the United Kingdom; in the United States 1962. Variant title: Guinness book of world records
Editors vary
"Ready reference for current record holders in all fields, some esoteric. Index provides access to information arranged in broad subject categories. Must be replaced annually." N Y Public Libr. Ref Books for Child Collect

051 American general serial publications and their indexes

Abridged readers' guide to periodical literature. Wilson, H.W. $170 per year   **051**
1. Periodicals—Indexes
ISSN 0001-334X

Also available CD-ROM version
First published July 1935. Monthly except June, July, and August (the indexing for these months is included in the September issue). Permanent bound annual cumulations
An index to over 80 periodicals of general interest which have been chosen by the subscribers to the index from the approximately 200 periodicals covered by the unabridged Readers' guide to periodical literature. The form of indexing is the same as that used in the unabridged Readers' guide
"Designed especially for school and small public libraries unable to afford the regular Readers' guide." Guide to Ref Books. 11th edition

Readers' guide to periodical literature. Wilson, H.W. $290 per year   **051**
1. Periodicals—Indexes
ISSN 0034-0464

Also available CD-ROM version
First published 1900. Monthly. Permanent bound annual cumulations
A free pamphlet How to use the Reader's guide to periodical literature, is available upon request
A cumulative author and subject index to over 200 periodicals. Coverage includes computers, business, health, fashion, politics, education, science, sports, arts and literature with criticism of individual dramatic works, videodiscs and videotapes, operas, ballets, musicals, movies, phonograph records, dance, and television and radio programs
"This is a modern index of the best type." Guide to Ref Books. 11th edition

060.4 General rules of order (Parliamentary procedure)

Riddick, Floyd M. (Floyd Millard), 1908-
Riddick's Rules of procedure; a modern guide to faster and more efficient meetings; [by] Floyd M. Riddick & Miriam H. Butcher. Scribner 1985 224p o.p.; Madison Bks. paperback available $14.95   **060.4**
1. Parliamentary practice
ISBN 0-8191-8064-5 (pa)   LC 85-18470
"Since most people find *Robert's Rules of Order* difficult to use, this simplified guide to parliamentary procedure is recommended. It discusses various processes alphabetically, making it easier to locate a specific rule. . . . The work is authoritative." Safford. Guide to Ref Materials for Sch Libr Media Cent. 5th edition

Robert, Henry Martyn, 1837-1923
The Scott, Foresman Robert's Rules of order newly revised. a new and enl ed, by Sarah Corbin Robert, with the assistance of Henry M. Robert III, William J. Evans. Scott, Foresman $18.95 **060.4**
1. Parliamentary practice

A simplified paperback version with title: The new Robert's Rules of order, by Mary A. De Vries, is available from New Am. Lib.
First published 1876 as: Pocket manual of rules of order for deliberate assemblies. Later editions have title: Robert's Rules of order
"Long the standard compendium of parliamentary law, explaining methods of organizing and conducting the business of societies, conventions, and other assemblies. Includes convenient charts and tables." Ref Sources for Small & Medium-sized Libr. 6th edition

070.1 News media

Bentley, Nancy
The young journalist's book; how to write and produce your own newspaper; [by] Nancy Bentley and Donna Guthrie; illustrated by Katy Keck Arnsteen. Millbrook Press 1998 64p il lib bdg $23.40   **070.1**
1. Journalism 2. Newspapers
ISBN 0-7613-0360-X   LC 97-43692
Describes the various functions and elements of a newspaper, giving practical advice on writing, producing, and distributing
"The full-color cartoons are appealing. Inspirational, practical fare for writers and would-be reporters." SLJ

Garner, Joe
We interrupt this broadcast; relive the events that stopped our lives—from the Hindenburg to the death of Princess Diana. Sourcebooks 1998 154p il $45 (7 and up)   **070.1**
1. Television broadcasting of news 2. Broadcast journalism 3. Disasters
ISBN 1-57071-328-6   LC 98-17236

Garner, Joe—*Continued*

This work "recounts the details of the events and spot-lights the photographs that tell the stories. Accompanying the book, two digitally mastered compact discs contain over two hours of audio from the events, narrated by award-winning journalist Bill Kurtis." Publisher's note

"Garner has done a masterful job of collecting these moments." Booklist

Wakin, Edward

How TV changed America's mind. Lothrop, Lee & Shepard Bks. 1996 248p il $15 (7 and up)
070.1

1. Broadcast journalism
ISBN 0-688-13482-3   LC 94-22542

This book surveys television "news and documentary reports—decade by decade from the '50s through the '90s, examining ways in which the medium changed history or affected Americans' views of themselves. . . . This is a clear, persuasive, and useful synthesis of the immense significance of television in recent history." Bull Cent Child Books

Includes bibliography

070.4   Journalism

Flash!: the Associated Press covers the world; introduction by Peter Arnett; edited by Vincent Alabiso, Kelly Smith Tunney, and Chuck Zoeller. Abrams 1998 200p il $39.95 (7 and up)
070.4

1. Associated Press 2. Journalism 3. Photojournalism
ISBN 0-8109-1974-5   LC 97-40307

"A collection of notable news photos 'from the AP wire' marks the 150th anniversary of the news cooperative begun in 1848, which was the first wire service to provide photographs. . . . The text here includes Peter Arnett's appreciation of the AP's ethos and achievements and a history of the service by Charles J. Hanley." Booklist

"The human side of history is especially evident in this book in the faces of refugees, movie stars, soldiers, athletes, and politicians. . . . This outstanding work will be eagerly pored over in all libraries." Voice Youth Advocates

070.5   Publishing

Brookfield, Karen

Book; written by Karen Brookfield; photographed by Laurence Pordes. Knopf 1993 63p il (Eyewitness books) $19; lib bdg $20.99
070.5

1. Books
ISBN 0-679-84012-5; 0-679-94012-X (lib bdg)
LC 93-18833

"A Dorling Kindersley book"

Text and photographs trace the evolution of the written word, how the alphabet grew out of pictures, the development of papermaking, bookbinding, children's books, and more

"The text is augmented heavily with numerous high-quality photographs, which are, perhaps, the crowning touch. They make the text come alive." Sci Books Films

071   Journalism and newspapers—North America

Senna, Carl, 1944-

The black press and the struggle for civil rights. Watts 1993 160p il (African-American experience) lib bdg $24; pa $6.95 (7 and up)
071

1. African American newspapers 2. African Americans—Civil rights 3. United States—Race relations
ISBN 0-531-11036-2 (lib bdg); 0-531-15693-1 (pa)
LC 93-17558

"Senna traces the evolution of the black press from 1827 to the present with specific and detailed attention to its role in African Americans' struggle for civil rights. The book is a solid, academic contribution for students of history and journalism. Especially interesting are the chapters that deal with slavery, the Civil War, and Reconstruction." SLJ

Includes bibliographical references

100   PHILOSOPHY & PSYCHOLOGY

Weate, Jeremy

A young person's guide to philosophy; "I think, therefore I am". DK Pub. 1998 64p il $16.95
100

1. Philosophy 2. Philosophers
ISBN 0-7894-3074-6   LC 97-33454

Socrates, Aquinas, Descartes, Nietzsche, Simone de Beauvoir and Herbert Marcuse are among the thinkers discussed. Schools of thought and philosophical concepts are covered

"Teens who have thought about and questioned the hows, whats, and whys of human existence will find this introduction fascinating." Booklist

128   Humankind

Human nature: opposing viewpoints; Mark Ray Schmidt, book editor. Greenhaven Press 1999 154p lib bdg $20.96; pa $12.96 (7 and up)
128

1. Human beings
ISBN 0-7377-0073-4 (lib bdg); 0-7377-0072-6 (pa)
LC 98-31859

"Opposing viewpoints series"

"Renowned thinkers such as Freud, Pascal, Rousseau, Sartre, Darwin, and even Apostle Paul offer not only divergent assessments of human behavior, gender roles, and socialization but also impressively deep explorations for essays so brief. Sections from this book will provide useful curriculum support in many disciplines." Booklist

Includes bibliographical references

133 Parapsychology and occultism

Duncan, Lois, 1934-
Psychic connections; a journey into the mysterious world of psi; [by] Lois Duncan and William Roll. Delacorte Press 1995 264p il pa $12.95 (7 and up)   **133**
1. Parapsychology
ISBN 0-385-32072-8   LC 95-175641
The authors "cover the range of psychic phenomenon: ESP, out-of-body and near-death experiences, apparitions, channeling, telepathy and clairvoyance, precognition, psychokinesis, psychic detectives and healers, and frauds. The last chapter is devoted to Duncan's own journey into parapsychology as a result of her daughter's slaying." Book Rep
Includes glossary and bibliographical references

Gardner, Robert, 1929-
What's super about the supernatural? 21st Cent. Bks. (Brookfield) 1998 80p il lib bdg $20.40
                    133
1. Parapsychology 2. Supernatural
ISBN 0-7613-3228-6   LC 98-27062
Discusses ESP, psychokinesis, ghosts and apparitions, UFOs and extraterrestrials and other paranormal phenomena, as well as some of the hoaxes that have been perpetrated involving the supernatural
"Fun as well as thought-provoking, the selection can't miss with readers, particularly reluctant ones." Booklist
Includes bibliographical references

Paranormal phenomena: opposing viewpoints; Paul A. Winters, book editor. Greenhaven Press 1997 200p lib bdg $26.20; pa $16.20 (7 and up)
                    133
1. Parapsychology
ISBN 1-56510-558-3 (lib bdg); 1-56510-557-5 (pa)
                    LC 96-49921
"Opposing viewpoints series"
Presents differing opinions about whether or not belief in paranormal phenomena is unscientific, and divergent opinions about UFOs, extrasensory perception, and life after death
Includes bibliographical references

133.1 Apparitions

Cohen, Daniel, 1936-
Dangerous ghosts. Putnam 1995 85p $14.95
                    133.1
1. Ghosts 2. Parapsychology
ISBN 0-399-22913-2   LC 95-45439
A collection of seventeen tales about ghosts drawn from a wide variety of sources from psychical research to pure legend and folklore
"These selections are not for those who enjoy a slight thrill. For readers who find other ghost stories much too tame and are not prone to nightmares, however, this collection will be just the thing for which they've been searching the shadows." SLJ

Ghostly warnings; illustrated by David Linn. Cobblehill Bks. 1996 64p il $14.99   **133.1**
1. Ghosts 2. Parapsychology
ISBN 0-525-65227-2   LC 96-17111
"Cohen recounts 10 tales of ghostly appearances that warned of impending doom. Some of these ghosts are legendary, such as the White Lady who foretold death to members of the powerful Hohenzollern family of Germany, or ghostly doubles, such as 'the fetch.'. . . The stories are well told. Skeptical readers may dismiss these tales as coincidence. However, there are enough unexplained aspects to foster belief." Book Rep

Ghosts of the deep. Putnam 1993 103p $14.95
                    133.1
1. Ghosts
ISBN 0-399-22435-1   LC 92-34669
"These accounts of ocean-going specters—from sailing ship days to World War II—are dramatically written, and many include corroborating historical detail, heightening the impression of authenticity. . . . The book reflects Cohen's open-minded attitude toward the uncanny—neither credulous nor scornful. Sure to be welcomed by fans of the supernatural." SLJ

Wilson, Colin, 1931-
Ghosts and the supernatural. DK Pub. 1998 37p il (Unexplained) $12.95   **133.1**
1. Ghosts 2. Supernatural
ISBN 0-7894-2819-9   LC 97-32448
Relates purportedly true accounts of ghosts, poltergeists, phantom animals, and other supernatural wonders and discusses research on such phenomena

Wood, Ted
Ghosts of the West Coast; the lost souls of the Queen Mary and other real-life hauntings. Walker & Co. 1999 48p il (Haunted America) $16.95; lib bdg $17.85   **133.1**
1. Ghosts
ISBN 0-8027-8668-5; 0-8027-8669-3 (lib bdg)
                    LC 98-26718
Chronicles true ghost stories from Washington State, Oregon, and California, including those about the gold miners of Bodie State Historic Park, the Whaley House in San Diego, and the Heceta Head Lighthouse
"This is a wonderful combination of guidebook and chilling ghost stories that provides thrills to be savored many times over." SLJ

Woog, Adam, 1953-
Poltergeists: opposing viewpoints. Greenhaven Press 1995 128p il (Great mysteries) lib bdg $22.45 (7 and up)   **133.1**
1. Ghosts
ISBN 1-56510-261-4   LC 94-30708
"What constitutes poltergeist activity, how it differs from ghostly hauntings and apparitions, and investigators' suggestions as to possible causes are explored at length. One chapter centers on psychic investigators of the past 100 years, such as Harry Price, J. B. Rhine, and William G. Roll." SLJ
Includes bibliographical references

133.3 Divinatory arts

Cohen, Daniel, 1936-
Prophets of doom. millennium ed. Millbrook
Press 1999 160p il lib bdg $20.90 (7 and up)
                                                133.3
1. End of the world 2. Prophecies
ISBN 0-7613-1317-6   LC 98-38462
First published 1992
This "survey of doomsayers touches on Bible prophe-
cy, the oracles of ancient Greece, and the predictions of
Nostradamus. . . . [Cohen discusses] apocalyptic groups
such as the Branch Davidians, the portentous nature of
the Hale-Bopp comet, and the millennial madness that
has fueled terrorist groups." Horn Book Guide
A "nonsensational book about a topic that's a perennial favorite." Booklist
Includes bibliographical references

Krull, Kathleen, 1952-
They saw the future; oracles, psychics,
scientists, great thinkers, and pretty good guessers;
illustrated by Kyrsten Brooker. Atheneum Bks. for
Young Readers 1999 108p il $19.99   **133.3**
1. Prophets 2. Prophecies
ISBN 0-689-81295-7   LC 97-51705
"An Anne Schwartz book"
Discusses the work and predictions of those who have
speculated about or claimed to see the future, from the
oracles of ancient Greece to such modern figures as Edgar Cayce and Jeane Dixon
"Krull's sweeping chronicle of people reputed to have
personal pipelines to the future . . . makes fascinating,
illuminating reading." Booklist
Includes bibliographical references

Schwartz, Alvin, 1927-1992
Telling fortunes; love magic, dream signs, and
other ways to learn the future; illustrations by
Tracey Cameron. Lippincott 1987 128p il lib bdg
$13.89; pa $4.50   **133.3**
1. Divination 2. Fortune telling 3. Astrology
ISBN 0-397-32133-3 (lib bdg); 0-06-446094-0 (pa)
                                   LC 85-45174
This is a "compilation of fortune-telling beliefs, traditions, and folklore which emphasizes the fun to be had
in trying each method. With his customary thoroughness,
Schwartz has amassed an amusing catalog of both familiar and little-known methods of fortune-telling. . . . Procedures and step-by-step directions are included when
necessary, enabling readers of all ages to become amateur fortune-tellers." SLJ
Includes bibliographical references

133.4 Demonology and witchcraft

Fremon, David K.
The Salem witchcraft trials in American history.
Enslow Pubs. 1999 128p il maps (In American
history) lib bdg $19.95   **133.4**
1. Witchcraft 2. Salem (Mass.)—History
ISBN 0-7660-1125-9   LC 98-6240

Discusses the issues and controversy surrounding the
trials, highlighting possible causes and the key figures
Includes bibliographical references

Kallen, Stuart A., 1955-
The Salem witch trials. Lucent Bks. 1999 96p il
(World history series) $23.70 (7 and up)   **133.4**
1. Witchcraft 2. Salem (Mass.)—History
ISBN 1-56006-544-3   LC 98-52010
Discusses the Salem witch trials, including their Puritan background, the accusations made, and the outcome
of the social hysteria that produced the situation
"Kallen borrows heavily from firsthand accounts such
as trial notes and diary excerpts to provide a real sense
of these chaotic times. With its exceptional organization
and ample background information, this is an excellent
resource." SLJ
Includes bibliographical references

Roach, Marilynne K.
In the days of the Salem witchcraft trials.
Houghton Mifflin 1996 92p il maps $14.95 **133.4**
1. Witchcraft 2. Salem (Mass.)—History
ISBN 0-395-69704-2   LC 94-32383
After a short discussion of the trials this "volume explores the social history of the times to show the context
that made such events possible. Topics include the law
and punishment, magic, social status, clothing, food,
household goods, occupations, recreation, common activities, government, and the political troubles leading to
widespread tension and unrest. Readers will come away
with a much fuller picture of who lived in Salem and
how they lived. Small ink drawings decorate the pages."
Booklist
Includes bibliographical references

Wilson, Lori Lee
The Salem witch trials. Lerner Publs. 1997 112p
il map (How history is invented) lib bdg $23.93
                                      133.4
1. Witchcraft 2. Salem (Mass.)—History
ISBN 0-8225-4889-5   LC 96-21371
Discusses the witchcraft trials in Salem in 1692, the
events leading up to them, and how the trials have been
viewed by different historians since then
"The full-color and black-and-white illustrations complement and balance the text. . . . The writing is accessible and the text provides a great deal of interesting information in a palatable format. . . . This is truly historical
research at its best." SLJ
Includes bibliographical references

133.5 Astrology

Royer, Mary-Paige, 1955-
Astrology: opposing viewpoints. Greenhaven
Press 1991 112p il maps (Great mysteries) lib bdg
$22.45   **133.5**
1. Astrology
ISBN 0-89908-090-1   LC 91-21657
Discusses the history and uses of astrology and
presents opposing viewpoints on its validity
Includes bibliographical references

133.6 Palmistry

Reid, Lori
The art of hand reading. DK Pub. 1996 120p il
$24.95 (7 and up)   **133.6**
1. Palmistry
ISBN 0-7894-1060-5   LC 96-15506
This volume uses color photographs of hands and
handprints to analyze all the significant lines, mounts,
and markings on hands. It shows how the different areas
of the palm reveal the balance between instinctive desires
and powers of intellect and reason

133.8 Psychic phenomena

Wilson, Colin, 1931-
Psychic powers. DK Pub. 1998 37p il
(Unexplained) $12.95   **133.8**
1. Parapsychology
ISBN 0-7894-2820-2   LC 97-44359
Explores such subjects as levitation, psychokinesis,
mind control, psychic abilities, and other powers of the
mind
"Fascinating photographs and tantalizing tidbits intro-
duce puzzling mysteries of human experience." SLJ

152.14 Visual perception

Jennings, Terry, 1938-
101 amazing optical illusions; fantastic visual
tricks; illustrated by Alex Pang. Sterling 1996 87p
il $17.95   **152.14**
1. Optical illusions
ISBN 0-8069-9462-2   LC 96-37628
"The illusions are divided into three sections that deal
with sight . . . perception . . . and movement." SLJ
"Familiar and lesser-known optical illusions are featured in an attractive, informative book. . . . The easy-
to-follow instructions and large format make the book a
noteworthy choice for the curious minded." Booklist
Includes glossary

Joyce, Katherine
Astounding optical illusions. Sterling 1994 96p
il hardcover o.p. paperback available $5.95
                                                152.14
1. Optical illusions
ISBN 0-8069-0432-1 (pa)   LC 93-43911
"Joyce includes not only interesting optical designs
and explanations of how the eyes and brain perceive
them, but also information on visual aberrations readers
may not automatically associate with illusions—for example, mirages and hidden pictures. . . . The explanations are clear and concise, as are the illustrations. . . .
An entertaining, informative book." Booklist

Simon, Seymour, 1931-
Now you see it, now you don't; the amazing
world of optical illusions; drawings by Constance
Ftera. rev ed. Morrow Junior Bks. 1998 64p il $15
                                                152.14
1. Optical illusions
ISBN 0-688-16152-9   LC 97-49855
First published 1976 by Four Winds Press with title:
The optical illusion book
The author explains optical illusions involving lines
and spaces, changeable figures, depth and distance,
brightness and contrast, and color
"One of the clearest and most interesting discussions
of optical illusions ever written for children." Booklist

Wick, Walter
Walter Wick's optical tricks. Cartwheel Bks.
1998 43p il $13.95   **152.14**
1. Optical illusions
ISBN 0-590-22227-9   LC 97-35672
Presents a series of optical illusions and explains
what is seen
The author "has produced a stunnng picture book of
optical illusions. With crystal-clear photographs, he
creates a series of scenes that fool the eye and the
brain." Booklist

152.4 Emotions and feelings

Dentemaro, Christine
Straight talk about anger; [by] Christine
Dentemaro and Rachel Kranz. Facts on File 1995
148p $19.95; pa $9.95 (7 and up)   **152.4**
1. Anger
ISBN 0-8160-3079-0; 0-8160-3551-2 (pa)
                                 LC 94-34591
"The authors probe biological reactions associated
with anger and present situations that may serve as prov-
ocations. There are excellent discussions of hidden anger
and passive-aggressive behavior, strategies for construc-
tive release of anger, and valuable suggestions for using
it as an ally to correct injustice." SLJ
Includes bibliographical references

Fisher, Enid
Emotional ups and downs. Stevens, G. 1998 32p
il (Good health guides) lib bdg $14.95   **152.4**
1. Emotions 2. Human relations
ISBN 0-8368-2179-3   LC 98-24235
Discusses feelings such as shyness, embarrassment,
and anger and examines specific situations such as the
death of a loved one and fighting with family members
Fisher's "advice is clear and compassionate in helping
young readers to see beyond the immediate crisis to the
bigger picture of life." SLJ
Includes bibliographical references

153 Imagination, imagery, creativity

The **Human** mind explained; an owner's guide to the mysteries of the mind; Susan A. Greenfield, general editor. Holt & Co. 1996 192p il (Henry Holt reference book) $40 (7 and up)   **153**
1. Intellect 2. Brain 3. Comparative psychology
ISBN 0-8050-4499-X   LC 96-6139
"Exploring both the anatomy and physiology of the brain, the text surveys . . . [such subjects as] the role of neurotransmitters, brain mapping, sensory and motor functions, brain development, and the neurobiology of memory." Sci Books Films
"The book is lavishly illustrated with pictures, drawings, charts, and other visuals. An excellent resource." SLJ
Includes bibliographical references

155.9 Environmental psychology

Cobain, Bev, 1940-
When nothing matters anymore; a survival guide for depressed teens; edited by Elizabeth Verdick. Free Spirit 1998 165p il pa $13.95 (7 and up)   **155.9**
1. Depression (Psychology)
ISBN 1-575-42036-8   LC 98-24911
A guide to understanding and coping with depression, discussing the different types, how and why the condition begins, how it may be linked to substance abuse or suicide, and how to get help
"Cobain has written a book that ought to be on every teacher's desk and in every place teens gather." Book Rep
Includes bibliographical references

Death and dying: opposing viewpoints; Paul A. Winters, book editor. Greenhaven Press 1998 191p il lib bdg $26.20; pa $16.20 (7 and up)   **155.9**
1. Death
ISBN 1-56510-671-7 (lib bdg); 1-56510-670-9 (pa)
          LC 97-21804
Replaces the edition published 1992 under the editorship of William Dudley
"Opposing viewpoints series"
A collection of essays which "debate a variety of death-related issues, including appropriate treatment for terminally ill or severely disabled patients and the right to specify the manner and timing of one's death, . . . arguments for and against cryogenic preservation of dead humans are included with discussions of the meaning of near-death experiences. . . . A rich resource for debates as well as opinion." SLJ
Includes bibliographical references

Death is hard to live with; teenagers and how they cope with loss; [compiled by] Janet Bode; art by Stan Mack. Delacorte Press 1993 178p il $16.95; pa $4.50 (7 and up)   **155.9**
1. Death 2. Bereavement
ISBN 0-385-31041-2; 0-440-21929-9 (pa)
          LC 92-32409

This book explores death "from both the cultural and the emotional perspective. Viewpoints of therapists and representatives from religious communities, as well as insights from specialists (a forensic expert, a funeral director, and so on), entwine with teenagers' moving personal stories." Booklist
"A sane, sensitive exploration of a difficult subject." Horn Book
Includes bibliographical references

DiGiulio, Robert C., 1949-
Straight talk about death and dying; [by] Robert DiGiulio, Rachel Kranz. Facts on File 1995 134p $19.95; pa $9.95 (7 and up)   **155.9**
1. Death 2. Bereavement
ISBN 0-8160-3078-2; 0-8160-3553-9 (pa)
          LC 95-2488
The authors "utilize three fictionalized situations in which adolescents deal with death, grief, and mourning. These continuing scenarios serve as introductions to each chapter and act as guides through the bereavement process." SLJ
"The clear, cogent text is accessible to a range of readers, and its potential audience extends to any adult who deals with teenagers on a regular basis." Voice Youth Advocates

Fry, Virginia Lynn, 1952-
Part of me died, too; stories of creative survival among bereaved children and teenagers; illustrated with the children's own artwork, with a foreword by Katherine Paterson. Dutton Children's Bks. 1995 xx, 218p il $19.99   **155.9**
1. Death 2. Bereavement
ISBN 0-525-45068-8   LC 94-36536
The author "tells stories of children and teenagers who have lost a loved one and how they coped. The types of death experienced are on all levels from that of a beloved pet to the death of parents, siblings and friends. Suicide, murder and AIDs-related deaths are included. Each story is resolved through therapy involving people close to the youngsters and art activities that help them cope with the pain." Book Rep
"Highly compelling, compassionate and comforting, this powerful book should be part of libraries, counseling centers and anywhere else where adults help those who deal with death." Child Book Rev Serv

Gellman, Marc
Lost & found; a kid's book for living through loss; [by] Marc Gellman and Thomas Hartman; illustrated by Debbie Tilley. Morrow Junior Bks. 1999 176p il $15   **155.9**
1. Loss (Psychology)
ISBN 0-688-15752-1   LC 98-27779
Describes different kinds of losses—losing possessions, competitions, health, trust, and the permanent loss because of death—and discusses how to handle these situations
The authors' "informal text is aimed straight at kids and incorporates lots of examples children can relate to. . . . A practical, heartfelt exploration." Booklist
Includes bibliographical references

Gootman, Marilyn E., 1944-
When a friend dies; a book for teens about grieving & healing. Free Spirit 1994 107p pa $7.95 (7 and up)   **155.9**
1. Death 2. Bereavement
ISBN 0-915793-66-0   LC 93-37992
This book "aids teenagers who are grieving the loss of a friend, someone of their own generation. The reader is addressed alternately by the author and by teenagers who have experienced such a loss. . . . The young mourner accesses what he or she needs from the book through the questions that are the table of contents." Voice Youth Advocates
Includes bibliographical references

Grollman, Earl A.
Straight talk about death for teenagers; how to cope with losing someone you love. Beacon Press 1993 146p hardcover o.p. paperback available $7.95 (7 and up)   **155.9**
1. Death 2. Bereavement
ISBN 0-8070-2501-1 (pa)   LC 92-34540
"Grollman explains the grieving process to teenagers in a poetic, reflective way, gently, but firmly guiding his readers through the painful process of dealing with loss of a parent, sibling, or friend. He suggests survival techniques that emphasize self-understanding and use of whatever support services are available in their communities." Book Rep

Grosshandler, Janet
Coping when a parent dies; [by] Janet Grosshandler-Smith. Rosen Pub. Group 1995 136p $17.95 (7 and up)   **155.9**
1. Death 2. Bereavement
ISBN 0-8239-1514-X   LC 94-23310
"The book covers a range of topics, from emotional responses to grief, to funeral services, to coping with the surviving parent. . . . Included are a 'Help List' and a summary of brief suggestions for dealing with the grief process, as well as a glossary and a list for further reading." Booklist

Hyde, Margaret Oldroyd, 1917-
Meeting death; [by] Margaret O. Hyde and Lawrence E. Hyde. Walker & Co. 1989 129p il $14.95; lib bdg $15.85   **155.9**
1. Death 2. Bereavement
ISBN 0-8027-6873-3; 0-8027-6874-1 (lib bdg)
    LC 88-27933
Provides information to promote the acceptance of the concept of death, discussing such aspects as the terminally ill, suicide, grief and mourning, and the treatment of death in various cultures
"This offers thought-provoking material that will be useful to students or those simply interested in a topic that's often tough to talk about." Booklist
Includes bibliographical references

Krementz, Jill
How it feels when a parent dies. Knopf 1981 110p il hardcover o.p. paperback available $15
   155.9
1. Death 2. Bereavement
ISBN 0-394-75854-4 (pa)   LC 80-8808
Also available in hardcover from P. Smith
This book is "a hopeful tribute to the healing power sustained by young survivors, who are competently interviewed and photographed in their widely varied reactions and situations. The subjects range in age from 7 to 16 and cope with a variety of deaths by suicide, accident, and illness. Adults helping children through a hard time will better understand their charges' problems through the honest opinions expressed here, and young readers might feel less alone." Booklist

Packard, Gwen K.
Coping with stress. Rosen Pub. Group 1997 154p lib bdg $17.95 (7 and up)   **155.9**
1. Stress (Psychology)
ISBN 0-8239-2081-X   LC 96-52137
A discussion of why teenagers may face stress and what they can do about it, suggesting techniques for dealing with situations such as school difficulties, relationships, and natural disasters
Includes glossary and bibliographical references

Schleifer, Jay
Everything you need to know when someone you know has been killed. Rosen Pub. Group 1998 64p il (Need to know library) lib bdg $16.95 (7 and up)   **155.9**
1. Death 2. Bereavement
ISBN 0-8239-2779-2   LC 98-16193
Discusses death and the fear of death, explains the emotions experienced when someone you know is killed, and gives strategies to cope with them
"For students seeking help for themselves or others, this resource offers a valuable first step toward identifying emotional reactions to untimely death and taking action to begin healing." Booklist
Includes bibliographical references

Sneddon, Pamela Shires
Body image; a reality check. Enslow Pubs. 1999 112p il (Issues in focus) lib bdg $19.95 (7 and up)
   155.9
1. Self-acceptance 2. Self-perception
ISBN 0-89490-960-6   LC 98-35120
"Sneddon discusses what factors contribute to a person's perception of self and the pressure to conform to idealized images. She identifies television, newspapers, magazines, movies, music videos, and advertisements as having the greatest negative impact on a teen's self-image today. The author discusses the effects of such influences and the problems and issues associated with them, such as eating disorders, steroid use, cosmetic surgery, and body decoration." SLJ
Includes bibliographical references

Weiss, Stefanie
Everything you need to know about dealing with losses. Rosen Pub. Group 1998 64p il (Need to know library) lib bdg $16.95 (7 and up) **155.9**
1. Loss (Psychology) 2. Bereavement
ISBN 0-8239-2780-6   LC 98-29092
Describes different kinds of losses, including the death of a loved one, the end of a love affair, and the loss of virginity, and suggests such coping mechanisms as the natural grieving process, the finding of a creative outlet, and getting help from others
Includes bibliographical references

158 Applied psychology

Bode, Janet
Trust & betrayal; real life stories of friends and enemies. Delacorte Press 1995 161p hardcover o.p. paperback available $4.99 (7 and up)   **158**
1. Friendship 2. Human relations
ISBN 0-440-22035-1 (pa)   LC 94-21415
"Through group and individual conversations, Bode lets teens tell their own stories about their experiences with and concerns about peer relationships. Topics include sexual harassment, attention deficit disorder, computer bulletin board dating, homosexuality, gangs, handicapped accessibility, suicide, teen pregnancy, and abusive relationships." Book Rep
"This title gives today's YAs . . . [a] realistic, up-to-date book that speaks to their needs." SLJ

Cann, Kate, 1954-
Living in the world; illustrated by Derek Matthews. Watts 1997 32p il (Life education) $19
        158
1. Human relations 2. Conduct of life
ISBN 0-531-14430-5   LC 96-11877
An anecdotal exploration of group and interpersonal interactions. Racism, prejudice and social activism are among the issues discussed. Illustrated with photographs and cartoon drawings

Chicken soup for the kid's soul; 101 stories of courage, hope, and laughter; [compiled by] Jack Canfield [et al.] Health Communications 1998 xxv, 398p il $24; pa $12.95   **158**
1. Human relations 2. Emotions
ISBN 1-55874-608-0; 1-55874-609-9 (pa)
                                LC 98-16871
A collection of short stories, anecdotes, poems, and cartoons which present a positive outlook on life

Chicken soup for the teenage soul; 101 stories of life, love, and learning; [compiled by] Jack Canfield, Mark Victor Hansen, Kimberly Kirberger. Health Communications 1997 354p il $24; pa $12.95 (7 and up)   **158**
1. Human relations 2. Emotions
ISBN 1-55874-468-1; 1-55874-463-0 (pa)
                                LC 97-5378
This book covers "subjects running the gamut from love, family ties, and self-esteem to developing values

and life crises, such as a death in the family. . . . Teenagers not only helped select the poems, stories, and accounts that have been included but also have written some of them . . . with a few contributions by well-known people, including Sandra Cisneros, Helen Keller, and Robert Fulghum. . . . This isn't a religious book, but it is an inspirational and motivational one, sometimes funny, sometimes poignant." Booklist
Includes bibliographical references

Jamiolkowski, Raymond M., 1953-
Coping with an emotionally distant father. Rosen Pub. Group 1994 146p $17.95 (7 and up)
        158
1. Fathers 2. Parent and child 3. Emotions
ISBN 0-8239-1966-8   LC 94-21679
The author suggests strategies for dealing with a father's inability to express tenderness, sympathy, or compassion
Includes bibliographical references

Kreiner, Anna
Everything you need to know about creating your own support system. Rosen Pub. Group 1996 64p il (Need to know library) lib bdg $17.95 (7 and up)   **158**
1. Human relations
ISBN 0-8239-2215-4   LC 95-10753
Discusses how teenagers can create their own support system, a group of people in their lives to whom they feel connected and who can help them build skills and solve problems
This offers "valuable information in easily understood language, illustrated with appealing black-and-white and full-color photographs with a nice mix of genders and ethnic groups." SLJ
Includes glossary and bibliographical references

Nathan, Amy
Everything you need to know about conflict resolution. Rosen Pub. Group 1996 64p il (Need to know library) lib bdg $17.95 (7 and up)   **158**
1. Peer counseling 2. Human relations 3. Problem solving
ISBN 0-8239-2058-5   LC 95-40195
This title "presents ways to solve disagreements through words and mediation instead of force. Different kinds of conflict are described and its inevitability in life is emphasized. Skills, such as active listening, brainstorming, and seeing the other side of an argument, are presented." SLJ
Includes glossary and bibliographical references

Romain, Trevor
Cliques, phonies & other baloney. Free Spirit 1998 129p il pa $9.95   **158**
1. Social groups 2. Human relations 3. Friendship
ISBN 1-57542-045-7   LC 98-36248
Discusses cliques, what they are and their negative aspects, and gives advice on forming healthier relationships and friendships
"With a sense of ease and lighthearted humor. . . the author serves up solid advice in friendly, reassuring prose." SLJ
Includes bibliographical references

170 Ethics (Moral philosophy)

Lewis, Barbara A., 1943-
What do you stand for? a kid's guide to building character; edited by Pamela Espeland. Free Spirit 1998 277p il $18.95 **170**
1. Character 2. Values 3. Conduct of life
ISBN 1-57542-029-5 LC 97-13952
Text, anecdotes, and activities direct the reader to explore and practice honesty, kindness, empathy, integrity, tolerance, and more
"This well-organized, factual compendium provides a marvelous approach to character development. . . . Excellent indexes provide easy access to subjects, reproducible pages, and Web sites." Voice Youth Advocates

174 Occupational ethics

Bioethics for students; how do we know what's right?: issues in medicine, animal rights, and the environment; edited by Stephen G. Post. Macmillan Lib. Ref. USA 1999 4v il set $325 (7 and up) **174**
1. Medical ethics 2. Bioethics 3. Science—Ethical aspects
ISBN 0-02-864940-0 LC 98-29518
Based on Encyclopedia of bioethics (1995)
This "set examines issues in medicine, animal rights and the environment, along with the associated public debates and court cases. . . . The set provides historical and social context, creating a framework for ethical consideration of these and other related issues in the future." Publisher's note
For a review see: Booklist, May 1, 1999

Biomedical ethics: opposing viewpoints; Tamara L. Roleff, book editor. Greenhaven Press 1998 252p lib bdg $26.20; pa $16.20 (7 and up) **174**
1. Medical ethics 2. Bioethics
ISBN 1-56510-793-4 (lib bdg); 1-56510-792-6 (pa) LC 97-51374
Replaces the edition published 1994 under the editorship of Terry O'Neill
"Opposing viewpoints series"
Presents opposing viewpoints on biomedical ethics issues such as human cloning, genetic research and engineering, organ transplants and reproductive technologies
Includes glossary and bibliographical references

Cloning; Paul A. Winters, book editor. Greenhaven Press 1998 89p (At issue) lib bdg $18.70; pa $11.20 (7 and up) **174**
1. Cloning
ISBN 1-56510-753-5 (lib bdg); 1-56510-752-7 (pa) LC 97-28560
"Opposing viewpoints series"
Scientists, theologians and philosophers debate the cloning of animals and humans. Included is an interview with Ian Wilmut, who cloned Dolly the sheep
Includes bibliographical references

Genetic engineering: opposing viewpoints; Carol Wekesser, book editor. Greenhaven Press 1995 240p lib bdg $27.45; pa $17.95 (7 and up) **174**
1. Genetic engineering 2. Bioethics
ISBN 1-56510-359-9 (lib bdg); 1-56510-358-0 (pa) LC 95-241
Replaces the edition published 1990 under the editorship of William Dudley
"Opposing viewpoints series"
This collection of articles presents various points of view about genetic engineering including whether or not it benefits society, its effects on agriculture and health care, whether or not it should be regulated, and the accuracy of DNA fingerprinting
Includes bibliographical references

O'Neill, Terry, 1944-
Biomedical ethics. Greenhaven Press 1999 144p il (Opposing viewpoints digests) ilb bdg $23.70; pa $14.95 (7 and up) **174**
1. Medical ethics 2. Bioethics
ISBN 1-56510-875-2 (lib bdg); 1-56510-874-4 (pa) LC 98-37239
Presents opposing viewpoints on various issues of biomedical ethics, including animal testing, human testing, organ transplants, genetic testing, gene therapy, and cloning
Includes bibliographical references

Sherrow, Victoria
Bioethics and high-tech medicine. 21st Cent. Bks. (NY) 1996 144p $21.40 (7 and up) **174**
1. Medical ethics 2. Bioethics
ISBN 0-8050-3832-9 LC 95-34222
An exploration of "issues surrounding high-tech medicine. Sherrow discusses both medical users' and providers' rights and responsibilities and deals with social and moral aspects of medical practices and developments in both present and future tense. Topics include genetic engineering, cloning, cell engineering, and pregnancy at any cost." Book Rep
"Sherrow does an admirable job of putting complex science into layman's terms, without speaking down to her audience. She is also careful to provide real-life illustrations of what could otherwise become academic discussions." Voice Youth Advocates
Includes bibliographical references

Yount, Lisa
Issues in biomedical ethics. Lucent Bks. 1998 128p il (Contemporary issues) $22.45 (7 and up) **174**
1. Medical ethics 2. Bioethics
ISBN 1-56006-476-5 LC 97-30784
Yount "explores the pros and cons of several controversial biomedical ethics issues including assisted suicide, the use of animals in medical research, genetic engineering, and cloning." Booklist
"While no one book can provide the last word on such volatile issues, Yount's inclusion of an annotated list of organizations to contact and lengthy bibliography offer a number of extended research suggestions." SLJ

179 Other ethical norms

Animal rights: opposing viewpoints; Andrew Harnack, book editor. Greenhaven Press 1996 240p lib bdg $27.45; pa $17.45 (7 and up)
179
1. Animal rights
ISBN 1-56510-399-8 (lib bdg); 1-56510-398-X (pa)
LC 95-52147
Replaces the edition published 1990 under the editorship of Janelle Rohr
"Opposing viewpoints series"
This collection of articles presents varying viewpoints regarding animal rights, animal experimentation, using animals for food, genetic engineering of farm animals, protection of wildlife, and disagreements within the animal rights movement
Includes bibliographical references

Catalano, Julie
Animal welfare; introduction by Russell E. Train. Chelsea House 1994 111p il (Earth at risk) $19.95
179
1. Animal welfare 2. Animal rights
ISBN 0-7910-1591-2
LC 93-26841
The author "presents a short history of man's highly ambivalent relationship with animals both wild and domestic from the Stone Age to the present. . . . The subject spawning the most controversy is the use of animals in various forms of scientific research. . . .The pros and cons of factory farming are presented, as well as the ramifications of a population explosion among pet animals in the United States." Voice Youth Advocates
Includes bibliographical references

Cohen, Daniel, 1936-
Animal rights; a handbook for young adults. Millbrook Press 1993 128p il lib bdg $22.40 (7 and up)
179
1. Animal rights
ISBN 1-56294-219-0
LC 92-40875
Among the issues explored are: agribusiness practices, vegetarianism, medical research, zoos, and hunting
"Cohen does an admirable job of presenting all sides of this issue fairly and without prejudice. . . . A valuable, informative volume." SLJ
Includes bibliographical references

Day, Nancy
Animal experimentation; cruelty or science? rev ed. Enslow Pubs. 2000 128p il (Issues in focus) lib bdg $19.95
179
1. Animal experimentation 2. Animal rights
ISBN 0-7660-1244-1
LC 99-49334
First published 1994
Discusses issues surrounding animal experimentation, including animal rights, medical breakthroughs, and alternatives to animal experimentaion
"Great for reports or debates." Voice Youth Advocates
Includes glossary and bibliographical references

Hurley, Jennifer A., 1973-
Animal rights. Greenhaven Press 1999 110p il (Opposing viewpoints digests) lib bdg $23.70; pa $14.95 (7 and up)
179
1. Animal rights
ISBN 1-56510-869-8 (lib bdg); 1-56510-868-X (pa)
LC 98-42321
Presents opposing viewpoints about animal rights, discussing their capacity to suffer, the question of whether they can be the property of people, whether they should be used as food, and animal experimentation
Includes bibliographical references

James, Barbara, 1953-
Animal rights. Raintree Steck-Vaughn Pubs. 1999 64p il (Talking points) $27.11
179
1. Animal rights
ISBN 0-8172-5317-3
LC 98-8199
Discusses the animal rights movement, including the difference between animal rights and animal welfare, using animals for experiments, animals as entertainment, keeping pets, and hunting
"Balance is provided by the differing views that are presented of experts, public figures, and people with personal experiences." Sci Books Films
Includes glossary and bibliographical references

Levine, Herbert M.
Animal rights. Raintree Steck-Vaughn Pubs. 1998 128p il (American issues debated) lib bdg $19.98 (7 and up)
179
1. Animal rights
ISBN 0-8172-4350-X
LC 97-1223
Debates topics such as banning the use of animals in scientific testing, the wearing of fur, and whether or not the modern animal rights movement is good for America
"Levine provides detailed, in-depth arguments from many sides. . . . There are excellent chapter bibliographies." Booklist

The **Rights** of animals; Tamara L. Roleff, book editor; Jennifer A. Hurley, assistant editor. Greenhaven Press 1999 223p (Current controversies) lib bdg $20.96; pa $12.96 (7 and up)
179
1. Animal rights
ISBN 0-7377-0069-6 (lib bdg); 0-7377-0068-8 (pa)
LC 98-45934
Includes chapters on animal experimentation, the breeding of animals for human consumption, the ethics of hunting, and animal use in the entertainment industry
"The essays, footnoted and subdivided for easy reference use, provide impassioned, balanced arguments from scientific, religious, and social viewpoints. Bibliography; list of organizations to contact." Booklist

Sateren, Shelley Swanson
The humane societies; a voice for the animals. Dillon Press 1997 80p il lib bdg $14.95; pa $7.95
179
1. Animal welfare
ISBN 0-87518-622-X (lib bdg); 0-382-39309-0 (pa)
LC 95-35445

Sateren, Shelley Swanson—*Continued*
Explains how members of humane societies use methods such as adoption to deal with problems including animal overpopulation and abandonment

Young, Ed
Voices of the heart. Scholastic 1997 unp il $22.99 **179**
1. Ethics 2. Emotions 3. Chinese language
ISBN 0-590-50199-2   LC 96-7595
"Young lists 26 emotions with their modern Chinese characters. He then devotes a page to each emotion, breaking each character into its parts and creating a collage out of the parts and the figure of a heart to express the feeling of the emotion. . . . Emotions include panic, rudeness, mercy and loyalty." Booklist
"This is a powerful combination of words and imagery that lends itself to a number of uses both in the library and the classroom, but it will need the intercession of a knowledgeable adult to make this a part of a language, art, or religion curriculum." Bull Cent Child Books

179.7 Respect and disrespect for human life

Assisted suicide; Laura K. Egendorf, book editor. Greenhaven Press 1998 221p (Current controversies) lib bdg $26.20; pa $16.20 (7 and up) **179.7**
1. Euthanasia
ISBN 1-56510-807-8 (lib bdg); 1-56510-806-X (pa)
LC 97-52277
"Individual chapters address both sides of legalization, ethics, constitutional rights, and the influence of assisted suicide on society as a whole. Each one includes at least four commentaries on each position. This well-balanced presentation provides points of consideration that require sophisticated readers." SLJ
Includes bibliographical references

Euthanasia: opposing viewpoints; Carol Wekesser, book editor. Greenhaven Press 1995 214p il lib bdg $26.20; pa $16.20 (7 and up) **179.7**
1. Euthanasia
ISBN 1-565-10244-4 (lib bdg); 1-565-10243-6 (pa)
LC 94-41046
"Opposing viewpoints series"
Replaces the edition published 1989 under the editorship of Neal Bernards
Dr. Jack Kevorkian is among the contributors to this collection of articles which debate ethical and legal aspects of euthanasia, including such issues as physician-assisted euthanasia and treatment of severely handicapped newborns
Includes bibliographical references

Torr, James D., 1974-
Euthanasia. Greenhaven Press 1999 143p il (Opposing viewpoints digests) lib bdg $23.70; pa $14.95 (7 and up) **179.7**
1. Euthanasia
ISBN 1-56510-871-X (lib bdg); 1-56510-870-1 (pa)
LC 98-42321

Presents opposing views on the ethical issues related to euthanasia, physician participation, and legalization of voluntary euthanasia
Includes bibliographical references

Walker, Richard
A right to die? Watts 1997 32p il (Viewpoints) lib bdg $22 **179.7**
1. Right to die 2. Euthanasia
ISBN 0-531-14413-5   LC 96-24439
Discusses the moral and ethical aspects of euthanasia and related topics
"Numerous quotations and photographs complement the text. A glossary, a list of useful addresses, facts to think about, and an index complete this well-balanced little book. . . . Teachers and parents should find this . . . volume very useful." Sci Books Films

200 RELIGION

Birdseye, Debbie Holsclaw
What I believe; kids talk about faith; by Debbie Holsclaw Birdseye and Tom Birdseye; photographs by Robert Crum. Holiday House 1996 32p il $15.95 **200**
1. Religions
ISBN 0-8234-1268-7   LC 96-11240
Six children of different religious backgrounds tell about their faith and what it means to them; includes background information on each religious tradition
"These simple personal portraits show kids who have made a strong place for religion in their everyday world. . . . An affirmation of faith that goes beyond any single faith." Booklist
Includes bibliographical references

Gellman, Marc
How do you spell God? answers to the big questions from around the world; [by] Marc Gellman & Thomas Hartman; illustrated by Jos. A. Smith; with a foreword by his Holiness the Dalai Lama. Morrow Junior Bks. 1995 206p il $16; pa $6.95 **200**
1. Religions
ISBN 0-688-13041-0; 0-688-15296-1 (pa)
LC 94-28770
The authors "show how the various religions—Judaism, Christianity, Islam, Buddhism, and Hinduism—deal with the soul-searching questions central to all people. . . . There is also information on each religion's teachers, holy days and places, sanctuaries, and prayers, among other topics." Booklist
This book "is warm, friendly and, most of all, respectful of the importance and variety of belief." Book Rep

Langley, Myrtle
Religion; written by Myrtle Langley. Knopf 1996 59p il (Eyewitness books) $19; lib bdg $20.99 **200**
1. Religion
ISBN 0-679-88123-9; 0-679-98123-3 (lib bdg)
LC 96-12236

Langley, Myrtle—*Continued*
"A Dorling Kindersley book"
Each "illustrated double-page spread in this volume addresses either a different religion or a significant facet of a religion. Egyptian, Greek, Primitive, Hindu, Buddhist, Confucian, Taoist, Jainist, Sikh, Zoroastrian, Judaic, Christian, and Islamic faiths are included. The essence of each belief is stated clearly in an introductory paragraph. The remaining text consists of comprehensive, elucidative captions for the eye-catching, full-color photographs, drawings, and reproductions of paintings clustered on the pages. . . . The information given is accurate and unbiased." SLJ

Logan, John, 1923-1987
Christianity. Thomson Learning; distributed by Raintree Steck-Vaughn Pubs. 1995 48p il (World religions) lib bdg $24.26   **200**
1. Christianity
ISBN 1-56847-374-5   LC 95-8282
An illustrated history and explanation of some of the beliefs and practices of Christianity around the world
Includes glossary and bibliographical references

Lynch, Patricia Ann
Christianity. Facts on File 1991 128p (World religions) $26.95 (7 and up)   **200**
1. Christianity
ISBN 0-8160-2441-3   LC 90-25325
"The story of the world's most widespread religion, beginning with its history and customs, and tracing its historical spread. Includes an overview of how Christianity is practiced throughout the world." Publisher's note
Includes bibliographical references

200.3   Religion—Encyclopedias and dictionaries

The **Encyclopedia** of world religions; Robert S. Ellwood, general editor; Gregory D. Alles, associate editor. Facts on File 1998 390p il maps $29.95 (7 and up)   **200.3**
1. Religions
ISBN 0-8160-3504-0   LC 97-39529
"Nearly 500 entries cover topics from prehistoric and ancient religions, major contemporary world religions, concepts, symbols, and personages." Booklist
"This encyclopedia presents discussions that are unbiased and succinct, reflects modern scholarship and current problems, and includes areas related to religious practices as well as definitions of the religions themselves. And it's interesting to read." SLJ

215   Science and religion

Science & religion: opposing viewpoints; Janelle Rohr, book editor; Bonnie Szumski, assistant editor. Greenhaven Press 1988 233p hardcover o.p. paperback available $16.20 (7 and up)
     215
1. Religion and science
ISBN 8-89908-406-0 (pa)   LC 87-38066

"Opposing viewpoints series"
Replaces the edition published 1981 under the editorship of David L. Bender and Bruno Leone
"After presenting some debates from past history, [this book] covers four major questions: the compatibility of science and religion, the origin of the universe, the origin of life, and whether ethical values should limit scientific research." SLJ
Includes bibliographical references

220.3   Bible—Encyclopedias and topical dictionaries

The **Oxford** companion to the Bible; edited by Bruce M. Metzger, Michael D. Coogan. Oxford Univ. Press 1993 xxi, 874p il maps $55   **220.3**
1. Bible—Dictionaries
ISBN 0-19-504645-5   LC 93-19315
This volume "contains more than 700 signed entries treating the formation, transmission, circulation, sociohistorical situation, interpretation, theology, uses, and influence of the Bible." Libr J
"The many contributors read as a veritable who's who among biblical scholars. Although this companion is not meant to be an exhaustive reference, it is a highly reliable guide." Booklist

220.5   Bible—Modern versions

Bible
Good news Bible; today's English version. American Bible Soc. prices vary   **220.5**

Available in various bindings and editions
"Begun in 1964 with the Gospel of Mark, The New Testament was completed in 1966, with rev. eds. in 1971 and 1976. The whole Bible was published in 1976. An extremely popular, inexpensive translation using contemporary American English. . . . Especially useful for youth or lay Bible study as well as for private reading." Bollier. Lit of Theol

The Holy Bible; containing the Old and New Testaments; translated out of the original tongues; and with the former translations diligently compared and revised by King James's special command, 1611. Oxford Univ. Press prices vary
     220.5

Available in various bindings and editions
The authorized or King James Version originally published 1611

The Holy Bible: new revised standard version; containing the Old and New Testaments with the Apocryphal/Deuterocanonical books. Nelson, T. maps prices vary   **220.5**

Available in various bindings and editions
This version first published 1989

Bible—*Continued*

This version "attempts to be as literal as possible while following standard American English usage. It uses inclusive language 'as far as this can be done without altering passages that reflect the historical situation of ancient patriarchal culture.'" Guide to Ref Books. 11th edition

Holy Bible: the new King James Version; containing the Old and New Testaments. Nelson, T. prices vary **220.5**

Available in various bindings and editions including large print edition

This version first published 1982

"Protestant. This edition replaces 17th Century verb forms and second person pronouns. Updates archaic terms. Psalms and Job appear as poetry." N Y Public Libr. Ref Books for Child Collect. 2d edition

The new American Bible; with revised New Testament; translated from the original languages, with critical use of all the ancient sources by members of the Catholic Biblical Association of America; sponsored by the Bishops' Committee of the Confraternity of Christian Doctrine maps **220.5**

Available in various bindings and editions from various publishers

First published 1970 by Kenedy

"Roman Catholic version based on modern English translations; replaces the Douay edition." N Y Public Libr. Book of How & Where to Look It Up

The new Jerusalem Bible. Doubleday maps prices vary **220.5**

Available in various bindings and editions

First published in this format 1966 with title: The Jerusalem Bible

General editor: Henry Wansbrough

"Derives from the French version edited at the Dominican Ecole Biblique de Jerusalem and known as 'La Bible de Jerusalem.' The introductions and notes are 'a direct translation from the French, though revised and brought up to date in some places' but translation of the Biblical text goes back to the original languages." Guide to Ref Books. 11th edition

The **Illustrated** children's Bible; paintings by Bill Farnsworth. Harcourt Brace & Co. 1993 300p il $19.95 **220.5**

1. Bible—Paraphrases 2. Bible stories

ISBN 0-15-232876-9   LC 93-16222

"Episodes from the Bible are told in a narrative style that draws on several traditional translations, particularly the King James Version. . . . Valuable for the supplemental maps, notes, glossaries and sections on geography, plants and animals, and ancient Egypt." Horn Book Guide

220.7   Bible—Commentaries

Asimov, Isaac, 1920-1992

Asimov's guide to the Bible; maps by Rafael Palacios. Doubleday 1968-1969 2v maps o.p.; Random House Value Pub. reprint available $16.99 **220.7**

1. Bible—Commentaries

ISBN 0-517-34582-X

Also available in paperback from Avon Bks.

Contents: v1 The Old Testament; v2 The New Testament

The author discusses the Bible book by book, verse by verse, letting us in on the actual historical, geographical, and biographical aspects of Biblical history

"Asimov is relaxed, down-to-earth, calmly analytical, not irreverent but also not 'pious' in his approach." Publ Wkly

220.9   Bible—Geography, history, biography, stories

Armstrong, Carole

Women of the Bible; with paintings from the great art museums of the world. Simon & Schuster Bks. for Young Readers 1998 45p il $18 **220.9**

1. Women in the Bible 2. Bible stories

ISBN 0-689-81728-2   LC 97-17059

Presents several prominent women from the Bible, including Eve, Sarah, Bathsheba, Ruth, Mary, Elizabeth, and Martha

"Gracefully written. . . . Grandly illustrated with large, full-page reproductions of appropriate Renaissance paintings by artists such as Giorgione, Filippo Lippi, Cranach, Poussin, and Caravaggio, as well as one more recent work by Dante Gabriel Rossetti." SLJ

Hunter, Elrose

The story atlas of the Bible. Silver Burdett Press 1996 64p il maps $15.95; pa $8.95 **220.9**

1. Bible—History of Biblical events 2. Bible—Geography

ISBN 0-382-39102-0; 0-382-39103-9 (pa)

LC 94-40789

First published 1994 in the United Kingdom

This work summarizes Bible passages from Genesis in the Old Testament to Paul's travels in the New Testament, and provides a map and illustrated cultural information for each passage

Motyer, Stephen, 1950-

Who's who in the Bible. DK Pub. 1998 64p il $14.95 **220.9**

1. Bible—Biography

ISBN 0-7894-2837-7   LC 97-44747

An introduction, arranged thematically, to three hundred people from both the Old and New Testaments

Tubb, Jonathan N.
Bible lands; written by Jonathan N. Tubb. Knopf 1991 63p il map (Eyewitness books) $19; lib bdg $20.99   **220.9**
1. Bible—Antiquities
ISBN 0-679-81457-4; 0-679-91457-9 (lib bdg)
LC 91-2388
Photographs and text document life in Biblical times, surveying the clothing, food, and civilizations of a wide variety of cultures, including the Israelites, Babylonians, Persians, and Romans
"This is an excellent resource on the civilizations that existed in the Fertile Crescent 10 millennia before the Christian Era. With a minimum of text, it is primarily a book of illustrations." Sci Books Films

221.5   Bible. Old Testament— Modern versions

Stories from the Old Testament; with masterwork paintings inspired by the stories. Simon & Schuster Bks. for Young Readers 1996 45p il $18   **221.5**
1. Bible stories 2. Religious art and symbolism
ISBN 0-689-80955-7   LC 95-48105
A collection of 17 well-known stories from the Old Testament, including the story of The Creation, Noah's Ark, Joseph and his Brothers, and The Ten Commandments, with illustrations by such artists as Raphael, Bruegel, and Rosselli
"A good resource for any student doing a report on religious painting, not only to discover the story that inspired the artist but also for thumbnail sketches about the artists and the paintings, which are found in the appendix." Booklist

221.9   Bible. Old Testament— Geography, history, biography, stories

Bach, Alice
Miriam's well; stories about women in the Bible; [by] Alice Bach and J. Cheryl Exum; with a frontispiece and decorations by Leo and Diane Dillon. Delacorte Press 1991 171p $16   **221.9**
1. Bible stories 2. Women in the Bible
ISBN 0-385-30435-8   LC 90-48099
A retelling of Old Testament stories focusing on women including Naomi and Ruth, Miriam, Hagar, Judith, Esther, and others
"The tales are gracefully told, enlivened by plausible and vivid details and an informative introduction and notes." SLJ
Includes bibliographical references

Gellman, Marc
Does God have a big toe? stories about stories in the Bible; paintings by Oscar de Mejo. Harper & Row 1989 88p il $16.95; pa $7.95   **221.9**
1. Bible stories
ISBN 0-06-022432-0; 0-06-440453-6 (pa)
LC 89-1893

This is a collection of twenty "tales that use familiar characters and situations from the Bible, but which imagine events and feelings and consequences the Bible never recorded. . . . Oscar de Mejo's primitive-style paintings suit the text exactly. Adam and Eve, for example, pop up behind the bushes in the Garden of Eden, just as a child might imagine them. These tales have the ring of genuine folk-fables and the wit of a single, affectionate heart." N Y Times Book Rev

Kimmel, Eric A.
Be not far from me; the oldest love story: legends from the Bible; retold by Eric A. Kimmel; illustrated by David Diaz. Simon & Schuster Bks. for Young Readers 1998 256p il maps $25 **221.9**
1. Bible stories
ISBN 0-689-81088-1   LC 97-24543
A collection of stories drawn from the Bible and the Midrash telling of twenty heroes and heroines including Abraham, Moses, Samson, Deborah, Elijah, and six other prophets
"The retellings of the stories . . . are quite wonderful. . . . The collage-style art, featuring cut silhouettes of black and light papers set against softer backgrounds, is dynamic." Booklist
Includes bibliographical references

McKissack, Patricia C., 1944-
Let my people go; Bible stories told by a freeman of color to his daughter, Charlotte, in Charleston, South Carolina, 1806-16; by Patricia and Fredrick McKissack; illustrated by James Ransome. Atheneum Bks. for Young Readers 1998 134p il $20   **221.9**
1. African Americans—Fiction 2. Bible stories 3. Slavery—Fiction
ISBN 0-689-80856-9   LC 97-19983
"An Anne Schwartz book"
Charlotte, the daughter of a free black man who worked as a blacksmith in Charleston, South Carolina, in the early 1800s recalls the stories from the Bible that her father shared with her, relating them to the experiences of African Americans
"The poignant juxtaposition of the Biblical characters and Charlotte's personal narrative is authentic and moving. . . . The occasional illustrations are powerful oil paintings in rich colors, emotional and evocative." SLJ
Includes bibliographical references

222   Historical books of Old Testament

Goldin, Barbara Diamond
Journeys with Elijah; eight tales of the Prophet; retold by Barbara Diamond Goldin; paintings by Jerry Pinkney. Harcourt Brace & Co. 1999 77p il $20   **222**
1. Elijah (Biblical figure) 2. Jewish legends 3. Bible stories
ISBN 0-15-200445-9   LC 96-9278
"Gulliver books"

Goldin, Barbara Diamond—*Continued*
Presents eight stories about the Old Testament prophet Elijah, set in a variety of time periods and in places all over the world where Jews have lived
"Goldin's storytelling is every bit as colorful as Pinkney's radiant, masterfully composed paintings, and both text and art testify to careful historical research." Publ Wkly
Includes bibliographical references

223   Poetic books of Old Testament

Bible. O.T. Ecclesiastes
To every thing there is a season; verses from Ecclesiastes; illustrations by Leo and Diane Dillon. Blue Sky Press (NY) 1998 unp il $15.95   **223**
ISBN 0-590-47887-7   LC 97-35124
Presents that selection from Ecclesiastes which relates that everything in life has its own time and season
"The Dillons compellingly convey the relevance of the Ecclesiastes verse throughout history, via a stunning array of artwork that embraces motifs from cultures the world over." Publ Wkly

Eisler, Colin T.
David's songs; his Psalms and their story; selected, edited, and with an introduction by Colin Eisler; illustrations by Jerry Pinkney. Dial Bks. for Young Readers 1992 57p il $17; lib bdg $16.89
                                                            223
1. David, King of Israel 2. Bible. O.T. Psalms
ISBN 0-8037-1058-5; 0-8037-1059-3 (lib bdg)
                                            LC 90-25459
Eisler presents forty-six versions of passages from the Book of Psalms that he believes reflect King David's "life and faith. They are presented to re-create a self-portrait in poetry." Preface
"The excerpts are slightly 'retold,' but the results are close to (and often better than) the New English Bible." SLJ

231.7   God's relation to the world

Arvey, Michael
Miracles: opposing viewpoints. Greenhaven Press 1990 112p il (Great mysteries) lib bdg $22.45 (7 and up)   **231.7**
1. Miracles
ISBN 0-89908-084-7   LC 90-39156
Presents opposing views of the experts about unusual events such as apparitions of saints, the stigmata, miracles, healings, miraculous images, etc.
Includes bibliographical references

232.9   Family and life of Jesus

Bible. N.T. Selections
The Christmas story; according to the Gospels of Matthew and Luke from the King James Bible; paintings by Gennady Spirin. Holt & Co. 1998 32p il $19.95   **232.9**
1. Jesus Christ—Nativity
ISBN 0-8050-5292-5   LC 97-50417
Presents the story of the birth of Christ, from Mary's meeting with the angel Gabriel to the birth of baby Jesus in a stable and the visit of the shepherds and three Wise Men
"The beautiful illustrations, with angels everywhere and Christian symbols such as lilies, are illuminated by an appropriate golden glow that gives an air of religiosity and holiness to the art." Booklist

L'Engle, Madeleine, 1918-
The glorious impossible; illustrated with frescoes from the Scrovegni Chapel by Giotto; afterword by A. Richard Turner. Simon & Schuster Bks. for Young Readers 1990 unp il $22
                                                            232.9
1. Jesus Christ
ISBN 0-671-68690-9   LC 89-6104
Describes the life of Jesus Christ and presents twenty-four paintings showing scenes from the life of Christ by the fourteenth-century Italian artist Giotto

235   Spiritual beings

Durrett, Deanne, 1940-
Angels: opposing viewpoints. Greenhaven Press 1996 96p il (Great mysteries) lib bdg $22.45 (7 and up)   **235**
1. Angels
ISBN 1-56510 353 X   LC 95-35981
The author discusses belief in angels in Christian, Jewish, and Islamic traditions from ancient times to the present
Includes bibliographical references

270   History of Christianity and Christian church

The **Oxford** dictionary of the Christian Church; edited by F. L. Cross and E. A. Livingstone. Oxford Univ. Press 1997 3rd ed xxxvii, 1786p $125   **270**
1. Christianity—Dictionaries 2. Church history—Dictionaries
ISBN 0-19-211655-X
First published 1957
"Indispensable reference work. . . . The dictionary is designed to serve both general readers and those of a scholarly bent. And while its primary use will be for one-stop reference, the volume is also eminently browsable." Guide to Ref Books. 11th edition

The **Rise** of Christianity; Don Nardo, book editor. Greenhaven Press 1999 224p (Turning points in world history) lib bdg $20.96; pa $13.96 (7 and up)   **270**
1. Church history
ISBN 1-56510-963-5 (lib bdg); 1-56510-962-7 (pa)
    LC 98-17499
"Among the topics covered are the Jewish background of Christianity; the life of Jesus; the growth of Christianity, with emphasis on the work of the apostles; Roman persecution of Christians and the impact of rival religions on the early church; and the spread of Christianity across Europe and the role of Christianity as the official religion of Rome. The lucid and thought-provoking essays are presented in a crisply designed format." Booklist
Includes bibliographical references

289 Other denominations and sects

Williams, Jean Kinney
The Shakers. Watts 1997 111p il (American religious experience) lib bdg $21.50 (7 and up)
    289
1. Shakers
ISBN 0-531-11342-6   LC 96-51498
Examines the history, beliefs, way of life, and current status of this devout Christian group
"Williams gives a lucid account of the movement's history and beliefs. . . . An accessible and interesting introduction." Booklist
Includes bibliographical references

289.3 Latter-Day Saints (Mormons)

Book of Mormon
The Book of Mormon. Herald House prices vary
    289.3
1. Mormons

Available in various bindings and editions
First published 1830
"Based on golden plates which Joseph Smith claimed were revealed to him, and which he unearthed from Cumorah Hill, New York, this book is roughly similar in structure to the *Bible*. . . . Emphasized are the doctrines of pre-existence, perfection, the after-life, and Christ's second coming." Haydn. Thesaurus of Book Dig

Bushman, Claudia L.
Mormons in America; [by] Claudia Lauper Bushman and Richard Lyman Bushman. Oxford Univ. Press 1998 142p il (Religion in American life) $22 (7 and up)   **289.3**
1. Church of Jesus Christ of Latter-day Saints
ISBN 0-19-510677-6   LC 98-18605
Chronicles the history of the Church of Jesus Christ of Latter-Day Saints beginning in America in the early 1800s and continuing to the present day throughout the world
"A solid resource for libraries. Illustrated with historical material and black-and-white photos. Time line and bibliography appended." Booklist

Nash, Carol Rust
The Mormon Trail and the Latter-Day Saints in American history. Enslow Pubs. 1999 128p il (In American history) lib bdg $19.95   **289.3**
1. Church of Jesus Christ of Latter-day Saints
ISBN 0-89490-988-6   LC 98-35588
Explores the founding of the Latter-Day Saints by Joseph Smith, their persecution, the migration west led by Brigham Young, the church's legacy, and its present role in society
Includes bibliographical references

Williams, Jean Kinney
The Mormons. Watts 1996 111p il map (American religious experience) lib bdg $21.50 (7 and up)   **289.3**
1. Church of Jesus Christ of Latter-day Saints
ISBN 0-531-11276-4   LC 96-33829
This history of the Mormon Church includes discussions of its general doctrines, practices, social structure, evolution of beliefs, and its place in and conflicts with American society
The author "does not shy away from a discussion of the polygamy issue but gives only a sentence or two to the controversy over the place of blacks in the church. The book is at its best when describing how the Church of Jesus Christ of Latter-day Saints came into existence. . . . This is a fine introduction to the faith." Booklist

289.5 Church of Christ, Scientist (Christian Science)

Williams, Jean Kinney
The Christian Scientists. Watts 1997 109p il (American religious experience) lib bdg $21.50 (7 and up)   **289.5**
1. Eddy, Mary Baker, 1821-1910 2. Christian Science
ISBN 0-531-11309-4   LC 96-9878
Provides a history of Christian Scientists, covering their doctrines and practices, organization, place in American society, and changes in beliefs, as well as discussing the work of Mary Baker Eddy
"Large black-and-white photographs and art reproductions appear throughout. The author's research is thorough, and her prose style is straightforward and skilled." SLJ
Includes bibliographical references

289.6 Society of Friends (Quakers)

Williams, Jean Kinney
The Quakers. Watts 1998 110p il (American religious experience) $21.50 (7 and up)   **289.6**
1. Society of Friends
ISBN 0-531-11377-9   LC 97-35133
Examines the history, notable individuals, beliefs, way of life, and current status of this longstanding Christian group
"Those studying William Penn will find an insightful chapter on his 'Holy Experiment.'. . . The research in this well-documented title is sound." SLJ
Includes bibliographical references

289.7 Mennonite churches

Kenna, Kathleen
A people apart; photographs by Andrew Stawicki. Somerville House Pub.; Houghton Mifflin 1995 64p il $17.95   **289.7**
1. Mennonites
ISBN 0-395-67344-5   LC 94-18545
"A Nick Harris book"
This photo-essay "shows various aspects of life in Old Order Mennonite communities, including home, work, education, and worship. The well-written text does a good job of explaining the Mennonites' lifestyle and the reasons they choose to live as they do. It also explains how groups splinter off or individuals leave or are expelled because of disagreements about what is acceptable and unacceptable. . . . The full-page black-and-white photographs are marvelous and reflect the same respect for the way of life expressed in the narrative." SLJ
Includes bibliographical references

Williams, Jean Kinney
The Amish. Watts 1996 111p il (American religious experience) lib bdg $21.50 (7 and up)   **289.7**
1. Amish
ISBN 0-531-11275-6   LC 96-33830
Includes a history of the Amish, their general doctrines, practices, social structure, place in American society, changes in beliefs, and issues facing them in modern society
"Students working on reports will be well served by the thorough discussion of the key players and precepts, as well as by the endnotes, lists of further reading, indexes, and Internet sites. . . . Large, well-reproduced black-and-white captioned photographs and prints are attractive and informative." SLJ

291 Comparative religion and religious mythology

Breuilly, Elizabeth
Religions of the world; the illustrated guide to origins, beliefs, traditions & festivals; [by] Elizabeth Breuilly, Joanne O'Brien, Martin Palmer; consultant editor, Martin E. Marty. Facts on File 1997 160p il maps $29.95 (7 and up)   **291**
1. Religions
ISBN 0-8160-3723-X   LC 97-22829
This "overview of 10 major faiths is divided into three sections: the Abrahamic faiths (Judaism, Christianity, and Islam), the Vedic faiths (Hinduism, Buddhism, and Jainism), and the other major traditions (Shinto, Taoism, Sikhism, and Baha'i). The history, development, ways of worship, and celebrations are given for each. The material is particularly well arranged in a large, handsome format and lavishly illustrated. . . . The writing is scholarly, lucid, and nonpartisan." SLJ
Includes glossary and bibliographical references

Osborne, Mary Pope, 1949-
One world, many religions; the ways we worship. Knopf 1996 86p il map $25; lib bdg $26.99   **291**
1. Religions
ISBN 0-679-83930-5; 0-679-93930-X (lib bdg)
          LC 96-836
This is an "overview of major world religions—Judaism, Christianity, Islam, Hinduism, Buddhism, Confucianism, and Taoism. . . . Each of six essay-styled chapters addresses themes of religious tenets, deities, morality, and ritual only as they are pertinent to a particular faith." Bull Cent Child Books
"The presentation is notable for its respect to each group, succinctness, and clarity. . . . The artful, full-page, color and black-and-white photographs tell much of the story." SLJ
Includes glossary and bibliographical references

291.1 Religious mythology

Bulfinch, Thomas, 1796-1867
Bulfinch's Mythology   **291.1**
1. Mythology 2. Folklore—Europe 3. Chivalry

Hardcover and paperback editions available from various publishers
First combined edition published 1913 by Crowell. First published in three separate volumes 1855, 1858 and 1862 respectively
Contents: The age of fable; The age of chivalry; Legends of Charlemagne
"The basic work on classical mythology. Includes information on Greek, Roman, Norse, Egyptian, Asian, Germanic myths, as well as the Arthurian cycle and other heroic epics." N Y Public Libr. Ref Books for Child Collect

Goddesses, heroes and shamans; the young people's guide to world mythology. Kingfisher (NY) 1994 159p il maps $22.95   **291.1**
1. Mythology 2. Legends 3. Folklore
ISBN 1-85697-999-7   LC 94-1374
In this volume an "introductory essay is followed by six geographically divided sections. More than half of the volume focuses on the familiar mythology of the Northern and Mediterranean lands. Each part opens with an overview of the region's culture and the themes of its myths, a map, and a timeline. The entries do not contain the stories themselves, although some are briefly described, but instead present limited biographical sketches of the characters." SLJ

Hamilton, Virginia, 1936-
In the beginning: creation stories from around the world; told by Virginia Hamilton; illustrated by Barry Moser. Harcourt Brace Jovanovich 1988 161p il lib bdg $25; pa $18   **291.1**
1. Creation 2. Mythology
ISBN 0-15-238740-4; 0-15-238742-0 (pa)
          LC 88-6211
A Newbery Medal honor book, 1989

Hamilton, Virginia, 1936-—*Continued*
"Hamilton has gathered 25 creation myths from various cultures and retold them in language true to the original. . . . Included in the collection are the familiar stories (biblical creation stories, Greek and Roman myths), and some that are not so familiar (tales from the Australian aborigines, various African and native American tribes, as well as from countries like Russia, China, and Iceland). At the end of each tale, Hamilton provides a brief commentary on the story's origin and originators." Booklist
Includes bibliographical references

Philip, Neil
The illustrated book of myths; tales & legends of the world; retold by Neil Philip; illustrated by Nilesh Mistry. Dorling Kindersley 1995 192p il $19.95   **291.1**
1. Mythology
ISBN 0-7894-0202-5   LC 95-2156
"This collection represents a wide variety of world cultures and stories. Selections are grouped by type (creation myths, fertility and cultivation, visions of the end), which helps readers understand the commonality of the tales. The standard Greek and Norse myths are here, but what makes this volume special is its inclusion of less frequently anthologized stories of the Aztecs, Haitians, Africans, and Japanese, to name a few." SLJ

Mythology. Knopf 1999 59p il (Eyewitness books) $19; lib bdg $20.99   **291.1**
1. Mythology 2. Religions
ISBN 0-375-80135-9; 0-375-90135-3 (lib bdg)
    LC 98-32234
"A Dorling Kindersley book"
Surveys the treatment of gods, goddesses, the heavens, creation, death, and evil as expressed in various mythologies around the world
"Collected from museums worldwide, lavish photos of figurines, paintings, mosaics, masks, textiles, and other treasures display a veritable gallery of culture within these pages." SLJ

World mythology; Roy Willis, general editor; foreword by Robert Walter. Holt & Co. 1993 311p il maps (Henry Holt reference book) $45; pa $22.50   **291.1**
1. Mythology
ISBN 0-8050-2701-7; 0-8050-4913-4 (pa)
    LC 93-3045
This book describes "the myths of Egypt, the Middle East, India, China, Tibet, Mongolia, Japan, Greece, Rome, the Celtic lands, Northern and Eastern Europe, the Arctic, North and South America, Mesoamerica, Africa, Australia, Oceania, and Southeast Asia." Libr J

291.103   Religious mythology— Encyclopedias and dictionaries

Wilkinson, Philip, 1955-
Illustrated dictionary of mythology; heroes, heroines, gods, and goddesses from around the world; written by Philip Wilkinson; consultant, Neil Philip. DK Pub. 1998 128p il maps $24.95   **291.103**
1. Mythology—Dictionaries
ISBN 0-7894-3413-X   LC 98-22992
This volume describes myths and deities from cultures around the world divided into nine geographic regions including Japan, North America, Australia, Greece and Rome. 2000 illustrations accompany the text

291.9   Sects and reform movements

Barghusen, Joan D., 1935-
Cults. Lucent Bks. 1998 96p il (Lucent overview series) lib bdg $22.45 (7 and up) **291.9**
1. Cults
ISBN 1-56006-199-5   LC 97-26652
Describes the nature and history of cults and the different aspects of living in a cult, including the difficulty of leaving it
"A balanced and informative look at the subject. . . . A smooth prose style and careful use of transitions contribute to the book's readability. . . . Detailed notes and a list of works consulted reflect the breadth of the author's research." SLJ

Cohen, Daniel, 1936-
Cults. Millbrook Press 1994 144p il $22.40 (7 and up)   **291.9**
1. Cults 2. United States—Religion
ISBN 1-56294-324-3   LC 94-966
"Cohen leads off with a demonstration of the power of cults and cult leaders by discussing the tragedies that took place in Waco, Texas, and in Jonestown, Guyana. He then takes a look at the definition of cults and pinpoints several in America's early history—the Pilgrims, Quakers, and Shakers, for example—that actually helped shape the country. Turning next to modern times, he looks at other kinds of cults, including the LaRouchies, Satanists, and Moonies." Booklist
"The book has the credibility of investigative reporting, is easy-to-read, and pragmatic." Child Book Rev Serv
Includes bibliographical references

Gay, Kathlyn
Communes and cults. 21st Cent. Bks. (NY) 1997 125p lib bdg $21.40 (7 and up)   **291.9**
1. Cults
ISBN 0-8050-3803-5   LC 96-47842
The author "recounts her own experiences growing up in Zion City, a religious commune in Illinois. She then describes different types of communes and cults, tracing

Gay, Kathlyn—*Continued*
the histories of significant communities, including the Rappists, the Shakers, and the Mormons. Doomsday cults and destructive communes, such as Jones-town, are also discussed." Booklist
"This is a valuable title, clearly written, and informative." SLJ
Includes bibliographical references

Porterfield, Kay Marie
Straight talk about cults. Facts on File 1995 151p $19.95; pa $9.95 (7 and up)   **291.9**
1. Cults
ISBN 0-8160-3115-0; 0-8160-3750-7 (pa)
LC 94-37296
"Porterfield defines cults, distinguishes between those that are dangerous and those that are nonthreatening, and looks at their special appeal to teens. She combines vignettes of impressionable young people joining cults with a detailed and fair analysis of what makes them vulnerable to the groups' enticements, how they become entrapped, and how new recruits are molded into obedient members." SLJ
Includes bibliographical references

Zeinert, Karen
Cults. Enslow Pubs. 1997 128p il (Issues in focus) lib bdg $19.95 (7 and up)   **291.9**
1. Cults
ISBN 0-89490-900-2   LC 96-40886
Describes various types of cults including their history, characteristics, and danger to American society
"This is a thought-provoking title with an engaging narrative on a fascinating subject." Booklist
Includes bibliographical references

292 Classical religion and religious mythology

Craft, Marie
Cupid and Psyche; as told by M. Charlotte Craft; illustrated by K. Y. Craft. Morrow Junior Bks. 1996 unp il $16; lib bdg $15.93   **292**
1. Eros (Greek deity) 2. Psyche (Greek deity) 3. Classical mythology
ISBN 0-688-13163-8; 0-688-13164-6 (lib bdg)
LC 95-14895
"In this Greek myth, Cupid falls in love with Psyche and treats her royally but does not reveal himself. When Psyche tries to discover his identity, Cupid leaves her, but she wins him back by accomplishing three difficult tasks. Recalling an earlier artistic era, the occasionally ornate romantic paintings—some of them quite dramatic—feature detailed landscapes and beautiful figures in flowing drapery." Horn Book Guide

Daly, Kathleen N.
Greek and Roman mythology A to Z; a young reader's companion. Facts on File 1992 132p il map lib bdg $19.95   **292**
1. Classical mythology—Dictionaries
ISBN 0-8160-2151-1   LC 91-43037

"Over 400 entries explore the characters, places, legends, and epics of Greek and Roman mythology. The format is accessible, making the book useful for school assignments, as well as enjoyable for general reading. Each entry provides a clear definition, and retells the stories associated with the character or place. The broad coverage, ample cross-references, and extensive index enable readers to recognize the many connections and interrelationships between characters and myths." SLJ
Includes bibliographical references

Fisher, Leonard Everett, 1924-
Cyclops; written and illustrated by Leonard Everett Fisher. Holiday House 1991 unp il map lib bdg $15.95; pa $5.95   **292**
1. Cyclopes (Greek mythology) 2. Odysseus (Greek mythology) 3. Classical mythology
ISBN 0-8234-0891-4 (lib bdg); 0-8234-1062-5 (pa)
LC 90-29317
Describes the encounter between the Cyclops Polyphemus and Odysseus and his men after the end of the Trojan War
"Fisher's narrative is compressed and direct; the illustrations, in rich, saturated oils complement its simplified and dramatic qualities." SLJ
Includes bibliographical references

Fleischman, Paul
Dateline: Troy; collages by Gwen Frankfeldt & Glenn Morrow. Candlewick Press 1996 79p il $15.99 (7 and up)   **292**
1. Trojan War 2. Classical mythology
ISBN 1-56402-469-5   LC 95-36356
The author juxtaposes a "redaction of the legendary conflagration at Troy with newspaper clippings that report events ranging from World War I to sociological experiments on babies' reactions to unattractive women. Each page of text faces such clippings, selected to highlight relevant themes." Publ Wkly
"Fleischman's precision of language reflects the stately perspective of a Homeric story but also, ironically, the distance of modern news reporting styles, which makes the parallels of content even more uncanny. A thought-provoking book, classically austere in design, with a partnership of text and illustration unusual in young adult [literature]." Bull Cent Child Books

Hamilton, Edith, 1867-1963
Mythology; illustrated by Steele Savage. Little, Brown 1942 497p il $27.50   **292**
1. Classical mythology 2. Norse mythology
ISBN 0-316-34114-2
Also available in paperback from New Am. Lib.
Contents: The gods, the creation and the earliest heroes; Stories of love and adventure; Great heroes before the Trojan War; Heroes of the Trojan War; Great families of mythology; Less important myths; Mythology of the Norsemen; Genealogical tables

McCaughrean, Geraldine, 1951-
Greek gods and goddesses; retold by Geraldine
McCaughrean; illustrated by Emma Chichester
Clark. Margaret K. McElderry Bks. 1998 108p il
$20   **292**
1. Classical mythology
ISBN 0-689-82084-4
"McCaughrean uses the literary device of a story within a story to relate tales of Greek gods and goddesses.
. . . The lively narrative offers accurate accounts of Ar-
temis, Apollo, Demeter, Hephaestus, Aphrodite, and others. Chichester Clark has incorporated stylistic Greek art
into her bright watercolor interpretations of the Olympi-
ans as they frolic on nearly every page." SLJ

Morley, Jacqueline
Greek myths; retold by Jacqueline Morley;
illustrated by Giovanni Caselli. Bedrick Bks. 1998
96p il $22.50   **292**
1. Classical mythology
ISBN 0-87226-560-9   LC 97-45899
An illustrated collection of twenty Greek myths
including "Prometheus and Pandora," "Theseus and the
Minotaur," "Meleager and the blazing logs," and "The
story of Phaeton"
"In well-written prose, Morley preserves the essence
of the myths and adds just enough dialogue to help
younger readers with the complexities of the stories."
SLJ

293 Germanic religion and religious mythology

Branston, Brian, 1914-
Gods and heroes from Viking mythology; text
by Brian Branston; illustrations by Giovanni
Caselli. Bedrick Bks. 1994 c1978 156p il (World
mythology series) $24.95; pa $14.95   **293**
1. Norse mythology
ISBN 0-87226-905-1; 0-87226-906-X (pa)
                                          LC 92-29705
A reissue of the title first published 1978 in the United Kingdom; first United States edition published 1982
by Schocken Bks.
A collection of myths about Thor, Balder, King Gylfi,
and other Nordic gods and goddesses

Osborne, Mary Pope, 1949-
Favorite Norse myths; retold by Mary Pope
Osborne; illustrated by Troy Howell. Scholastic
1996 87p il $17.95   **293**
1. Norse mythology
ISBN 0-590-48046-4   LC 94-34222
A collection of rarely retold tales from the "Elder
Edda" and the "Younger Edda," two six-hundred-year-
old Norse manuscripts
The tales are "retold with clarity and grace. The unusual artwork combines acrylic paintings with line drawings reminiscent of Norse carvings in their simplicity and
vigor. . . . The informative appendixes include glossaries
of the gods, goddesses, giants, giantesses, dwarves,
worlds, events, places, and things as well as discussions
of symbols and runes." Booklist
Includes bibliographical references

Philip, Neil
Odin's family; myths of the Vikings; retold by
Neil Philip; illustrated by Maryclare Foa. Orchard
Bks. 1996 124p il $19.95   **293**
1. Norse mythology
ISBN 0-531-09531-2   LC 96-1965
"Philip tells the stories of the origin of the gods and
frost giants, how Odin got his wisdom, the death of
Baldur, the coming of Ragnarok, and eleven other Norse
myths. What distinguishes Philip's anthology is its design: large print, a generous amount of white space, and
full-page color art make this an eminently accessible,
easily promoted collection. Foa's oil paintings (with a
preponderance of red, gold and blue) have a primitive
vigor." Bull Cent Child Books
Includes bibliographical references

294.3 Buddhism

Demi, 1942-
Buddha. Holt & Co. 1996 unp il $18.95   **294.3**
1. Gautama Buddha
ISBN 0-8050-4203-2   LC 95-16906
The author "tells the story of Siddhartha's birth and
the prophecies surrounding it, touches upon his childhood, and then follows his path to enlightenment." Booklist
Demi "uses clear, uncomplicated storytelling to
present complex philosophical concepts. . . . The gilded
illustrations (based, according to the jacket, on "Indian,
Chinese, Japanese, Burmese, and Indonesian paintings,
sculptures, and sutra illustrations") are delicate, yet the
colors and composition are bold, with central figures and
action cascading beyond the careful borders." Bull Cent
Child Books

Ganeri, Anita, 1961-
Buddhist. Childrens Press 1997 c1996 32p il
map (Beliefs and cultures) lib bdg $21   **294.3**
1. Buddhism
ISBN 0-516-08086-5   LC 96-4409
First published 1996 in the United Kingdom
Introduces the religion of Buddhism, describing its or-
igins and traditions. Includes related crafts and activities
Includes glossary

Hewitt, Catherine
Buddhism. Thomson Learning; distributed by
Raintree Steck-Vaughn Pubs. 1995 48p il maps
(World religions) lib bdg $24.26   **294.3**
1. Buddhism
ISBN 1-56847-375-3   LC 95-1942
The author "presents the story of Prince Siddhartha,
who became the Buddha, and traces the spread of Bud-
dhism from its Indian origins. Surveys of the sacred
scriptures, home and family practices, life-cycle events,
and festivals are highly informative." SLJ
Includes glossary and bibliographical references

Pandell, Karen
Learning from the Dalai Lama; secrets of the wheel of time; [by] Karen Pandell with Barry Bryant; photographs by John B. Taylor; concept by Manuel C. Menendez; with a foreword by Richard Gere. Dutton Children's Bks. 1995 40p il $16.99 **294.3**
    1. Dalai Lama XIV, 1935- 2. Buddhism
    ISBN 0-525-45063-7   LC 95-6984
This "photo-essay describes a Tibetan Buddhist ceremony in which the Dalai Lama constructs a wheel of time made out of sand. Facts about Buddhism expand the text." Booklist
"What makes the book exceptional is not only the clarity of the writing and organization, but also the incredibly rich photographs, inextricably linked to the descriptive text." SLJ
Includes glossary

Wangu, Madhu Bazaz
Buddhism. Facts on File 1993 128p il (World religions) $26.95 (7 and up) **294.3**
    1. Buddhism
    ISBN 0-8160-2442-1   LC 92-33177
Presents the story of Buddhism's origins and growth through the centuries, discussing its basic philosophy and the evolution of the three major schools of Buddhist thought
Includes glossary and bibliographical references

294.5 Hinduism

Kadodwala, Dilip
Hinduism. Thomson Learning; distributed by Raintree Steck-Vaughn Pubs. 1995 48p il (World religions) lib bdg $24.26 **294.5**
    1. Hinduism
    ISBN 1-56847-377-X   LC 95-14422
An overview of the Hindu religion, including its history, scriptures, ceremonies, and customs
Includes glossary and bibliographical references

Wangu, Madhu Bazaz
Hinduism. Facts on File 1991 128p il (World religions) $26.95 (7 and up) **294.5**
    1. Hinduism
    ISBN 0-8160-2447-2   LC 90-25431
Presents the history, customs, and beliefs of Hinduism, describing the mysteries and myths that sustained its growth over the centuries
"A detailed, complex look at a major religion. . . . Black-and-white photographs and drawings with excellent captions accompany the well-written analysis. . . . This is a good choice for advanced students seeking an in-depth approach." SLJ
Includes glossary and bibliographical references

294.6 Sikhism

Kaur-Singh, Kanwaljit
Sikhism. Thomson Learning; distributed by Raintree Steck-Vaughn Pubs. 1995 48p il (World religions) lib bdg $24.26 **294.6**
    1. Sikhism
    ISBN 1-56847-379-6   LC 95-4711
This describes the Sikh religion including its history, home, family and community life, ceremonies and festivals
Includes glossary and bibliographical references

296 Judaism

Fisher, Leonard Everett, 1924-
To bigotry, no sanction; the story of the oldest synagogue in America. Holiday House 1998 64p il $16.95 **296**
    1. Touro Synagogue (Newport, R.I.) 2. Jews—United States
    ISBN 0-8234-1401-9   LC 98-12834
The author discusses "the history of the Jews in America in general and the building of the Touro Synagogue, the oldest in the U.S. in particular. Fisher does his usual excellent job of bringing history to life." Booklist
Includes bibliographical references

Gates, Fay Carol
Judaism. Facts on File 1991 128p il (World religions) $26.95 (7 and up) **296**
    1. Judaism
    ISBN 0-8160-2444-8   LC 90-25436
An account of the history and rituals of Judaism, examining such areas as sacred use of the Hebrew language and the role of the faith in establishing the contemporary nation of Israel
Includes glossary and bibliographical references

296.03 Judaism—Encyclopedias and dictionaries

The **Oxford** dictionary of the Jewish religion; editors in chief, R.J. Zwi Werblowsky, Geoffrey Wigoder. Oxford Univ. Press 1997 764p $95 **296.03**
    1. Judaism—Dictionaries
    ISBN 0-19-508605-8   LC 96-45517
"The 2400 entries in this dictionary include unsigned but revised articles from the editors' Encyclopedia of the Jewish Religion (1966), as well as . . . new signed articles covering [topics] . . . and biographies related to the Jewish religion and interfaith relations." Libr J
For a fuller review see: Booklist, July, 1997

296.1   Judaism—Sources

Chaikin, Miriam, 1928-
Clouds of glory; legends and stories about Bible times; illustrations by David Frampton. Clarion Bks. 1997 118p il $19   **296.1**
1. Jewish legends 2. Bible stories
ISBN 0-395-74654-X   LC 97-5042
"The stories in this book are largely based on Rashi's commentary on the book of Genesis, and on midrashic threads found in Louis Ginzberg's Legends of the Bible and in Raphael Patai's Gates to the Old City." Acknowledgments
Presents twenty-one stories, in a single narrative, about God's relationship with His creation, from creating angels on the second day to testing Abraham's love
"The stories are told in an involving narrative style and the book lends itself to discussions about values and historical development. The woodcuts are few in number, but provide authenticity to the stories." Child Book Rev Serv
Includes bibliographical references

Cooper, Ilene
The Dead Sea scrolls; illustrated by John Thompson. Morrow Junior Bks. 1997 58p il $15
296.1
1. Dead Sea scrolls
ISBN 0-688-14300-8   LC 96-21983
Details the important archaeological discovery of the ancient manuscripts known as the Dead Sea Scrolls and discusses efforts to translate them, the battle over their possession, and the people who have figured in their history
"The text's seven brief chapters are clear and accessible. In covering the events from 1947 to the present, Cooper also manages to get in a good bit of the ancient history relevant to readers' understanding of the whole picture, all the while conveying the intrigue of the many questions that still mystify scholars." Horn Book
Includes glossary and bibliographical references

Lester, Julius
When the beginning began; stories about God, the creatures, and us; illustrations by Emily Lisker. Silver Whistle Bks. 1999 100p il $17   **296.1**
1. Creation 2. Bible stories 3. Jewish legends
ISBN 0-15-201238-9   LC 97-37352
A collection of traditional and original Jewish tales interpreting the Biblical story of the creation of the world
"Lester fuses two traditions here—the 'loving irreverence' of African-American storytelling and the imaginative inquiry of midrashim. . . . Lisker's paintings capture the stories' primal essence (and a bit of their playfulness) in bold, archetypal forms. A reverent, wise, witty, and wonderfully entertaining book." Horn Book Guide
Includes bibliographical references

Patterson, José
Angels, prophets, rabbis & kings from the stories of the Jewish people; text by José Patterson; colour illustrations by Claire Bushe. Bedrick Bks. 1991 144p il (World mythology series) $24.95   **296.1**
1. Jewish legends 2. Bible stories
ISBN 0-87226-912-4   LC 90-23469
A collection of traditional Jewish legends from the earliest times, stories of the rabbis, and tales from the communities of medieval Europe

Schwartz, Howard, 1945-
Next year in Jerusalem; 3,000 years of Jewish stories; retold by Howard Schwartz; illustrated by Neil Waldman. Viking 1996 56p il $16.99; pa $6.95   **296.1**
1. Jewish legends 2. Jerusalem
ISBN 0-670-86110-3; 0-14-056438-1 (pa)
LC 95-31213
"A collection of 11 Jewish folktales and legends from around the world, all centering on the city of Jerusalem. Stories are taken from the Talmud and Midrash, from folklore, or from mystical or Hasidic sources." SLJ
"Sidebars set the tales in a factual framework, and all are lovingly illustrated by Waldman in a dreamy style colored with the golds, pinks, and blues that shine from the real city of Jerusalem." Booklist
Includes glossary and bibliographical references

Sobel, Ileene
Moses and the angels; by Ileene Smith Sobel; paintings by Mark Podwal; with an introduction by Elie Wiesel. Delacorte Press 1998 64p il $16.95
296.1
1. Moses (Biblical figure) 2. Jewish legends 3. Bible stories
ISBN 0-385-32612-2   LC 98-5125
"Drawn from Jewish folklore, midrash, and the five books of Moses, these ten stories remind us that the Hebrews' journey from Egyptian bondage to the promised land was indeed an epic. . . . Many of the legendary details here may need some cultural context, but the basic structure is biblical." Bull Cent Child Books
Includes bibliographical references

296.4   Judaism—Traditions, rites, public services

Adler, David A., 1947-
The kids' catalog of Jewish holidays. Jewish Publ. Soc. 1996 283p il pa $15.95   **296.4**
1. Jewish holidays
ISBN 0-8276-0581-1   LC 96-17784
Presents stories, poems, songs, recipes, crafts, and other activities for special days that are significant to Jews

Berger, Gilda
Celebrate! stories of the Jewish holidays; paintings by Peter Catalanotto. Scholastic 1998 114p il $17.95   **296.4**
1. Jewish holidays
ISBN 0-590-93503-8   LC 97-40150

Berger, Gilda—*Continued*

"Berger examines the history of the major holidays of the Jewish faith and the Bible story that lies behind the celebration of each, as well as the customs that make these special days. The lively writing coupled with Catalanotto's dramatic watercolors ensure that this volume will become a treasured family favorite." Publ Wkly

Goldin, Barbara Diamond

Bat mitzvah; a Jewish girl's coming of age; illustrated by Erika Weihs. Viking 1995 139p il $14.99 **296.4**

1. Bat mitzvah 2. Women in Judaism

ISBN 0-670-86034-4 LC 95-22100

The author "cameos courageous females from biblical to modern times who wielded behind-the-scenes power to affect the fate of the Jewish people. She describes how women's roles in many congregations are still evolving as are the ways in which a young woman fulfills her responsibilities as a bat mitzvah. The variety of ways some girls have chosen to celebrate their bat mitzvah are sampled as are several young women's reflections on the highlights of their preparation and ceremony." Booklist

Includes glossary and bibliographical references

The Passover journey; a Seder companion; illustrated by Neil Waldman. Viking 1994 56p il $15.99; pa $7.99 **296.4**

1. Passover

ISBN 0-670-82421-6; 0-14-056131-5 (pa)

LC 93-5133

Retells the story of the Israelites' fight for liberation from slavery in Egypt and explains the traditions of the Passover Seder

"Goldin speaks simply, warmly, and directly throughout the book and lets her own love of the holiday shine through." Booklist

Includes glossary and bibliographical references

Kimmel, Eric A.

Bar mitzvah; a Jewish boy's coming of age; illustrated by Erika Weihs. Viking 1995 143p il $15 **296.4**

1. Bar mitzvah

ISBN 0-670-85540-5 LC 94-34956

"Kimmel imparts basic information about Judaism, including some comparisons between Judaism and Catholicism and Islam, and discusses ritual objects, important texts, the Shabbat service, and the actual responsibilities of the bar mitzvah child. The vivid impact traditionally left by the ceremony is made clear through several short interviews." Booklist

"Children with no previous exposure to Jewish beliefs and rituals will find the explanations here both clear and enticing, respectful of different religious traditions. . . . Kimmel also accommodates Jewish readers from a variety of backgrounds, from Reform to Orthodox." Publ Wkly

Includes glossary

Schecter, Ellen

The family Haggadah; illustrated by Neil Waldman. Viking 1999 66p il music pa $12.99 **296.4**

1. Passover

ISBN 0-670-88341-7 LC 98-28597

"This book interweaves original writing with traditional Haggadah, prayer book, and biblical texts, as well as with midrash (rabbinic stories and commentaries)." Verso of title page

"Although really intended for parents to use with their children at a family Passover seder, this attractive book may also be useful to children wanting to plan their own model celebration." Booklist

Yolen, Jane

Milk and honey; a year of Jewish holidays; illustrations by Louise August; musical arrangements by Adam Stemple. Putnam 1996 80p il music $21.95 **296.4**

1. Jewish holidays 2. Jews—Folklore

ISBN 0-399-22652-4 LC 93-44474

"Beginning with Rosh Hashanah, Yolen outlines the history and practice of the eight most celebrated holidays on the Jewish calendar, then gives readers a taste of the literature. She includes original as well as traditional selections carefully keyed to the celebration—folk tales, poems, plays, and songs, with music scored for guitar and piano. The combination makes her book wonderful for introducing the Jewish holidays." Booklist

297 Islam, Babism, Bahai Faith

Banks, William, 1946-

The Black Muslims; [by] William H. Banks. Chelsea House 1997 127p il (African-American achievers) lib bdg $19.95; pa $8.95 **297**

1. Black Muslims

ISBN 0-7910-2593-4 (lib bdg); 0-7910-2594-2 (pa)

LC 96-31055

A history of the Nation of Islam, from its founding to the present day with emphasis on the leadership roles of Elijah Muhammad, Malcolm X, and Louis Farrakhan

Includes bibliographical references

Child, John, 1951-

The rise of Islam. Bedrick Bks. 1995 64p il maps (Biographical history) pa $17.95 **297**

1. Islam

ISBN 0-87226-116-6 LC 94-37633

This historical survey provides a look at the events and major figures that gave rise to Islamic religion and civilization. Includes original primary and secondary source material. Illustrations and photographs accompany the text

Includes bibliographical references

Gordon, Matthew

Islam; by Matthew S. Gordon. Facts on File 1991 128p il (World religions) $22.95 (7 and up) **297**

1. Islam

ISBN 0-8160-2443-X LC 90-24830

Gordon, Matthew—*Continued*

An overview of Islam chronicling the religion's impact historically and in the modern world and discussing its origins, basic beliefs, structure, places of worship, and rites of passage

Includes glossary and bibliographical references

Koran

The Koran   **297**

Available in various bindings and editions

"The sacred scripture of Islam, regarded by Muslims as the Word of God, and except in sūra I.—which is a prayer to God—and some few passages in which Muhammad or the angels speak in the first person, the speaker throughout is God." Ency Britannica

Macdonald, Fiona

A 16th century mosque; [by] Fiona Macdonald, Mark Bergin. Bedrick Bks. 1994 48p il (Inside story) $18.95   **297**

1. Mosques 2. Islam

ISBN 0-87226-310-X   LC 94-20008

The author describes "the construction of the great Süleymaniye Mosque in Istanbul, built in the mid-16th century by the Ottoman Turkish imperial architect Sinan. . . . The text is much enhanced by numerous attractive and informative illustrations." Sci Books Films

Includes glossary

The **Muslim** almanac; a reference work on the history, faith, culture, and peoples of Islam; Azim A. Nanji, editor. Gale Res. 1996 xxxv, 581p il map $110   **297**

1. Islam 2. Islamic countries

ISBN 0-8103-8924-X   LC 95-17324

This "basic reference on Islam contains 39 chapters, each contributed by a recognized scholar and each discussing a broad topic area of Islamic history, belief, or culture. Chapters conclude with useful topical bibliographies. A general bibliography, a chronology of Islamic history, and a glossary of Islamic terms also appear." Libr J

Shahrukh Husain, 1950-

What do we know about Islam? Bedrick Bks. 1996 45p il maps lib bdg $18.95   **297**

1. Islam

ISBN 0-87226-388-6   LC 96-30873

An illustrated guide to the origins, history, practices, and beliefs of Islam

"This book provides concise information in digestible bites. . . . The many full-color photos and illustrations are attractive. . . . This title should be a useful addition to other materials on the subject, especially for school reports." SLJ

Includes glossary

The **Spread** of Islam; Clarice Swisher, book editor. Greenhaven Press 1999 240p maps (Turning points in world history) lib bdg $20.96; pa $12.96 (7 and up)   **297**

1. Islam

ISBN 1-56510-967-8 (lib bdg); 1-56510-966-X (pa)

LC 98-16517

Following an introductory overview of Islamic beliefs and practices, contributors focus primarily on the major turning points in Islamic expansion. An appendix contains primary documents discussed in the essays. A glossary of Arabic words and a chronology of significant events are appended

Includes bibliographical references

Wormser, Richard, 1933-

American Islam; growing up Muslim in America. Walker & Co. 1994 130p il $16.95; lib bdg $16.85 (7 and up)   **297**

1. Islam

ISBN 0-8027-8343-0; 0-8027-8344-9 (lib bdg)

LC 94-12335

"A portrait of Muslim American youth and their faith. Wormser describes the cultural, literary, and scientific heritage of Islamic civilization; their traditional tolerance of unbelievers; and the history of Muslim settlement in the Christian West. He also offers a concise summary of the religion's origins, its Sunni and Shia branches, and its basic beliefs." SLJ

"Although historical background is interlaced within the text, much of the information comes from interviews. This anecdotal method lends an immediacy that will appeal to young people." Book Rep

Includes bibliographical references

299   Other religions

Bierhorst, John

The mythology of Mexico and Central America. Morrow 1990 239p il maps $17; pa $10 (7 and up)   **299**

1. Indians of Mexico—Religion 2. Indians of Central America—Religion

ISBN 0-688-06721-2; 0-688-11280-3 (pa)

LC 90-5879

The author collects twenty basic myths of the Aztec and Mayan people and examines their influence on the culture and political life of the region

Includes glossary and bibliographical references

The mythology of North America. Morrow 1985 259p il maps hardcover o.p. paperback available $13 (7 and up)   **299**

1. Indians of North America—Religion

ISBN 0-688-06666-6 (pa)   LC 85-281

"In an overview of native American mythology, . . . Bierhorst first discusses characteristic patterns and themes, then defines 11 mythological regions, and examines the sacred stories of each. He shows what unifies the North American myths . . . and identifies elements they have in common with other world mythologies." Booklist

"The description, history, and recounting of tales flow together smoothly. Bierhorst's usual fine scholarship and meticulous attention to sources are evident in the extensive notes section and introduction." Horn Book

The mythology of South America. Morrow 1988 269p il maps o.p. (7 and up)   **299**

1. Indians of South America—Religion

LC 87-26237

Bierhorst, John—*Continued*

"While providing samples of the stories themselves, Bierhorst concentrates on the themes and motifs of the principal myths, the variants of them among the tribes, and on legends unique to individual tribes. He divides South America into seven regions, summarizing the great mythological themes of each." SLJ

"This handsome book lends itself to browsing and reference use, but reading straight through allows the great themes and patterns to emerge more clearly. Extensive source notes and a scholarly bibliography are included, and they enhance the pleasure of a good read." N Y Times Book Rev

Gifford, Douglas

Warriors, gods & spirits from Central & South American mythology; text by Douglas Gifford; illustrations by John Sibbick. Bedrick Bks. 1993 c1983 132p il (World mythology series) $24.95; pa $14.95   299
1. Indians of Central America—Religion 2. Indians of South America—Religion
ISBN 0-87226-914-0; 0-87226-915-9 (pa)
LC 93-1013
A reissue of the title first published 1983 by Schocken Bks.
This study of the myths and legends from Central and South America "begins with a history of the area's inhabitants and a description of the terrain that nurtured them. There is also information about recurring themes and symbolism as well as the purpose of the myths. . . . More than a book on mythology for literature classes, this will be useful to students of history and anthropology as well." Booklist
Includes bibliographical references

Gill, Sam D., 1943-

Dictionary of Native American mythology; [by] Sam D. Gill, Irene F. Sullivan. ABC-CLIO 1992 xxx, 425p il maps lib bdg $69.50   299
1. Indians of North America—Religion—Dictionaries
ISBN 0-87436-621-6   LC 92-27053
Also available in paperback from Oxford Univ. Press
"The authors have included entries representing more than 150 Native American language groups. . . . For each of the alphabetically arranged entries, tribal source and culture area are included. A collection of vivid black-and-white illustrations is reprinted. A comprehensive bibliography and index by tribe complete this excellent reference work." Libr J

Harris, Geraldine, 1951-

Gods & pharaohs from Egyptian mythology; text by Geraldine Harris; colour illustrations by David O'Connor; line drawings by John Sibbick. Bedrick Bks. 1991 c1982 132p il (World mythology series) $24.50; pa $17.95   299
1. Egyptian mythology
ISBN 0-87226-907-8; 0-87226-908-6 (pa)
LC 90-23455
A reissue of the title first published 1982 in the United Kingdom; first United States edition published 1983 by Schocken Bks.

Presents the myths of the ancient Egyptians and a glimpse of the civilization that created them

Hartz, Paula

Native American religions; by Paula R. Hartz. Facts on File 1997 128p il maps (World religions) $26.95 (7 and up)   299
1. Indians of North America—Religion 2. Indians of North America—Rites and ceremonies
ISBN 0-8160-3578-4   LC 96-39201
Surveys the history and basic beliefs of Native American religions
Includes bibliographical references

Taoism; [by] Paula R. Hartz. Facts on File 1993 128p il (World religions) $26.95 (7 and up)   299
1. Taoism
ISBN 0-8160-2448-0   LC 91-43018
This is a "survey of one of China's three great religious traditions, offering [an] explanation of Taoism's basic outlook and [an] account of its metamorphosis from a mystical way of life to a religion of monastic orders and secular hierarchies." Publisher's note
Includes glossary and bibliographical references

Hoobler, Thomas

Confucianism; by Thomas and Dorothy Hoobler. Facts on File 1993 128p il (World religions) $26.95 (7 and up)   299
1. Confucianism
ISBN 0-8160-2445-6   LC 92-33178
Describes how the teachings of Confucius evolved from a social order to a religion, infusing all phases of Chinese life for 2000 years
Includes glossary and bibliographical references

Knappert, Jan

Kings, gods & spirits from African mythology; text by Jan Knappert; illustrations by Francesca Pelizzoli. Bedrick Bks. 1993 c1986 92p il (World mythology series) $24.95; pa $12.95   299
1. African mythology
ISBN 0-87226-916-7; 0-87226-917-5 (pa)
LC 93-12903
A reissue of the title first published 1986 by Schocken Bks.
These myths and legends of Africa "include tales of gods, ghosts and spirits, sagas about famous heroes, fables about magical animals and stories of the powerful kingdoms of the past." Publisher's note
Includes bibliographical references

Martin, Joel

Native American religion. Oxford Univ. Press 1999 157p il (Religion in American life) $22 (7 and up)   299
1. Indians of North America—Religion
ISBN 0-19-511035-8   LC 98-50155
An "examination of religious life and practices from ancient times through the Colonial period and the Western Expansion, and into the 20th century. Martin ac-

Martin, Joel—*Continued*
knowledges the importance of religion in all aspects of Native American daily life and explores some of the differences among the various cultures. He also addresses the impact of the arrival of Europeans on spiritual life." SLJ
Includes bibliographical references

Ross, Anne
Druids, gods & heroes from Celtic mythology; text by Anne Ross; illustrations by Roger Garland; line illustrations by John Sibbick. Bedrick Bks. 1994 c1986 132p il (World mythology series) $24.95; pa $14.95   **299**
1. Celtic mythology
ISBN 0-87226-918-3; 0-87226-919-1 (pa)
                                                    LC 93-31615
A reissue of the title first published 1986 in the United Kingdom; first United States edition published 1986 by Schocken Bks.
Presents a collection of myths about Fionn, Cu Chuliann, and other Celtic heros and briefly describes the civilization that created them
Includes bibliographical references

Sita, Lisa, 1962-
The rattle and the drum; Native American rituals and celebrations; illustrated by James Watling. Millbrook Press 1994 71p il lib bdg $25.90   **299**
1. Indians of North America—Rites and ceremonies
ISBN 1-56294-420-7   LC 93-27209
This "work covers eight celebrations of Native American life: the girls' puberty rite of the Apache, the Hamatsa Society of the Kwakiutl, tobacco offerings and sweat rituals of the Lakota, the Green Corn Dance of the Creek, the Snake Ceremony of the Hopi, healing chants of the Navajo, the False Face Society of the Iroquois, and modern powwows. The brief description of each ceremony is laced with attention-grabbing details." SLJ
Includes glossary and bibliographical references

300 SOCIAL SCIENCES

302 Social interaction

Erlbach, Arlene
The kids' volunteering book. Lerner Publs. 1998 64p il lib bdg $23.54; pa $9.95   **302**
1. Volunteer work
ISBN 0-8225-2415-5 (lib bdg); 0-8225-9820-5 (pa)
                                                    LC 97-23356
Presents some opportunities for young people to perform volunteer service, and briefly profiles some children who are volunteers
"The profiles are interesting and inspiring, and substantial information is provided on the practical details of . . . a volunteer enterprise." Horn Book Guide
Includes glossary and bibliographical references

Worth the risk; true stories about risk takers plus how you can be one, too. Free Spirit 1999 127p il pa $12.95   **302**
1. Risk-taking (Psychology)
ISBN 1-57542-051-1   LC 98-38615
Discusses the value of taking risks and different kinds of risk-taking, both good and bad, and offers advice on and examples of this type of behavior and how to learn from both successes and mistakes
"The narratives are sure to provoke discussion about various types of behavior." SLJ
Includes bibliographical references

Kids explore kids who make a difference; [by] Westridge Young Writers Workshop. Muir Publs. 1997 117p il pa $9.95   **302**
1. Volunteer work
ISBN 1-56261-354-5   LC 97-5616
Features young people who have made a difference in their own lives and in the lives of those around them

302.2 Communication

Bruce-Mitford, Miranda
The illustrated book of signs & symbols. DK Pub. 1996 128p il $24.95 (7 and up)   **302.2**
1. Signs and symbols
ISBN 0-7894-1000-1   LC 96-14202
The symbols included range "from ancient times to modern fictitious characters that reflect characteristics of ancient gods and goddesses. The entries are grouped into four major categories: mythologies and religions; nature; people; and symbol systems." Booklist
Includes bibliographical references

Liungman, Carl G., 1938-
Dictionary of symbols. ABC-CLIO 1991 596p il lib bdg $67.50 (7 and up)   **302.2**
1. Signs and symbols 2. Picture writing
ISBN 0-87436-610-0   LC 91-36657
Also available in paperback from Norton
Original Swedish edition, 1974
This book "allows students to locate a symbol by defining just four of its visual characteristics from a set of common descriptors. Included are symbols used in design, decoration, architecture, logos, and more. Extensive cross-references for meanings, words, names of sign systems, and names of symbols are included." SLJ
Includes bibliographical references

302.23 Media (Means of communication)

Mass media: opposing viewpoints; Byron L. Stay, book editor. Greenhaven Press 1999 203p il lib bdg $26.20; pa $17.45 (7 and up)   **302.23**
1. Mass media
ISBN 0-7377-0055-6 (lib bdg); 0-7377-0054-8 (pa)
                                                    LC 98-47722
"Opposing viewpoints series"
Replaces the edition published 1994 under the editorship of William Barbour

Mass media: opposing viewpoints—*Continued*
Presents opposing viewpoints on various aspects of mass media including television's affect on society, whether or not advertising is harmful, the influence of media on politics, whether or not pornography on the internet should be regulated, and the regulation of television for children
Includes bibliographical references

302.3 Social interaction within groups

Hinojosa, Maria, 1961-
Crews; gang members talk to Maria Hinojosa; photographs by German Perez. Harcourt Brace & Co. 1995 168p il $17; pa $9 (7 and up)   **302.3**
1. Gangs
ISBN 0-15-292873-1; 0-15-200283-4 (pa)
LC 94-12173
A "look at Latino gang members in New York City. Shank, Coki, Cindy, Tre, Smooth b, and their friends answer the interviewer's questions to reveal lives driven overwhelmingly by some common threads: the need for acceptance, suppressed anger, dysfunctional families, poverty, violence, and drugs. . . . Hinojosa's open-ended questioning style encourages young men and women to tell their own stories." SLJ

303.4 Social change

Henderson, Harry, 1951-
Issues in the information age. Lucent Bks. 1999 112p il (Contemporary issues) lib bdg $22.45 (7 and up)   **303.4**
1. Information technology
ISBN 1-56006-365-3   LC 98-36765
Explores the controversies surrounding the impact of information technology on society such as possible censorship of the Internet, privacy concerns, and education issues
Includes bibliographical references

The **Information** revolution: opposing viewpoints; Paul A. Winters, book editor. Greenhaven Press 1998 202p il lib bdg $26.50; pa $16.20 (7 and up)   **303.4**
1. Information technology 2. Information society
ISBN 1-56510-801-9 (lib bdg); 1-56510-800-0 (pa)
LC 98-5038
"Opposing viewpoints series"
This collection of articles is divided into chapters which address the following questions: "Will the information revolution benefit society? Will the information revolution transform education? Will the information revolution transform work? Are rights threatened in the information age?" Publisher's note
Includes bibliographical references

Kronenwetter, Michael
Protest! 21st Cent. Bks. (NY) 1996 126p il lib bdg $21.40 (7 and up)   **303.4**
1. Dissent 2. Demonstrations
ISBN 0-8050-4103-6   LC 96-9866

This is an "introduction to and overview of the history of protest in the U.S. and elsewhere. . . . Particularly attention-getting are the chapters on the birth of the women's rights movement and the persistence of the suffragists; on the heroism of Gandhi and his consistent practice of nonviolent protest throughout his long life; and on the role of unions and strikes within the labor movement." SLJ
Includes glossary and bibliographical references

Seo, Danny
Generation react; activism for beginners. Ballantine Bks. 1997 183p pa $10.95 (7 and up)   **303.4**
1. Politics 2. Lobbying
ISBN 0-345-41242-7   LC 97-16733
This guide to political activism "provides step-by-step directions for starting groups, fund-raising, protesting and boycotting, gaining exposure . . . and lobbying. A 'Tools of the Trade' section in each chapter suggests helpful resources or organizations to contact for further information. An incredibly useful manual for student organizers and their advisers." Booklist

303.49 Social forecasts

21st century earth: opposing viewpoints; Oliver W. Markley and Walter R. McCuan, editors. Greenhaven Press 1996 288p il lib bdg $26.20; pa $16.20 (7 and up)   **303.49**
1. Twenty-first century 2. Human ecology 3. Forecasting
ISBN 1-56510-415-3 (lib bdg); 1-56510-414-5 (pa)
LC 95-39051
"Opposing viewpoints series"
This book "deals with an assortment of forecasts for the near future. The first section, 'How will demographic trends affect humanity?' includes discussion of overpopulation, the gap between haves and have-nots, and teens vs. senior citizen as the dominant age-group. The impacts of new technologies and trends that might affect the global ecology are addressed." SLJ
"Students researching topics for speeches, science, social studies, and persuasive essay assignments on futuristic topics will find the readings and their supplemental bibliographies invaluable." Booklist

303.6 Conflict

Altman, Linda Jacobs, 1943-
Genocide; the systematic killing of a people. Enslow Pubs. 1995 112p il (Issues in focus) $19.95 (7 and up)   **303.6**
1. Genocide
ISBN 0-89490-664-X   LC 95-6941
The author "devotes a chapter each to the war against the Native Americans, the Armenian massacre, the Soviet genocide in the Ukraine, the Holocaust of the Jews, Hitler's 'other' victims, the killing fields of Cambodia, and contemporary ethnic warfare, from Bosnia to Rwanda. Occasional black-and-white photographs bear eloquent witness to the quiet, terrible narrative." Booklist
Includes bibliographical references

Edgar, Kathleen J.
Everything you need to know about media violence. Rosen Pub. Group 1998 64p il (Need to know library) lib bdg $16.95   **303.6**
1. Violence 2. Mass media
ISBN 0-8239-2568-4   LC 97-32823
"This volume suggests that media violence is . . . mirrored in today's world. Edgar explores its use in film, television, radio, music, and the Internet." SLJ
Includes bibliographical references

Grant, R. G. (Reg G.)
Genocide. Raintree Steck-Vaughn Pubs. 1999 64p il (Talking points) $27.12   **303.6**
1. Genocide
ISBN 0-8172-5314-9   LC 98-38347
Explains the nature, history, effects, and various causes of genocide
The author "uses facts, statistics, and case studies to examine the phenomenon of cultural and racial extermination. His concluding section suggests a realistic view of this issue." Sci Books Films
Includes glossary and bibliographical references

Media violence: opposing viewpoints; William Dudley, book editor. Greenhaven Press 1999 186p il lib bdg $26.20; pa $16.20 (7 and up)   **303.6**
1. Violence 2. Mass media
ISBN 1-56510-945-7 (lib bdg); 1-56510-944-9 (pa)   LC 98-22828
"Opposing viewpoints series"
Articles explore the political, social, legal, and ethical issues raised by the depiction of violence in mass media. John Leo, Joseph Lieberman, James Bowman and Bob Dole are among the contributors
Includes bibliographical references

Violence: opposing viewpoints; Scott Barbour, book editor, Karin L. Swisher, book editor. Greenhaven Press 1996 306p lib bdg $26.20; pa $16.20 (7 and up)   **303.6**
1. Violence 2. Family violence
ISBN 1-56510-355-6 (lib bdg); 1-56510-354-8 (pa)   LC 95-35628
"Opposing viewpoints series"
This "book begins by examining both sides of the question, 'Is violence a serious problem in America?' It discusses some of the possible causes and devotes particular attention to the problems of domestic and youth violence. The final section includes debates on policies to reduce violence, the use of anti-crime measures, increased gun control, and increased incarceration." SLJ
Includes bibliographical references

304.6   Population

Fyson, Nance Lui
World population; [by] Nance Fyson. Watts 1998 32p il (Living for the future) lib bdg $18.50   **304.6**
1. Population 2. Human ecology
ISBN 0-531-14479-8   LC 97-7787

Examines the growth of the world's population over time, its responses to agricultural, industrial, and medical factors, and the effects of overpopulation

304.8   Movement of people

Flanders, Stephen A.
Atlas of American migration. Facts on File 1998 214p il maps $85 (7 and up)   **304.8**
1. Internal migration
ISBN 0-8160-3158-4
This source "is divided into 10 thematic chapters, from 'A Shifting Mosaic: America and Migration,' to 'The Suburban Frontier: Migration since 1945.' Intervening chapters cover such topics as slavery, Native American migration, the settlement of the West, and the move to the cities after 1890. . . . The most important features of the atlas are the many tables, graphs, and maps." Booklist

305   Social groups

Inequality: opposing viewpoints in social problems; Lori Shein, book editor. Greenhaven Press 1998 448p lib bdg $26.20; pa $16.20 (7 and up)   **305**
1. Equality 2. United States—Social conditions 3. United States—Economic conditions
ISBN 1-56510-737-3 (lib bdg); 1-56510-736-5 (pa)   LC 97-40016
"Opposing viewpoints series"
Beginning with an "exchange concerning inequality in this country, the book addresses racism in the criminal-justice system, gender bias, ageism, environmental discrimination, social inequity, and the role of government as equalizer. . . . [This book presents] multiple and conflicting perspectives on a variety of related issues. The result is a compelling juxtaposition of ideas and arguments designed to encourage critical thinking and analysis." SLJ
Includes bibliographical references

305.23   Young people

Allison, Anthony
Hear these voices; youth at the edge of the millennium. Dutton Children's Bks. 1999 169p il $22.99 (7 and up)   **305.23**
1. Youth
ISBN 0-525-45353-9   LC 98-38464
Presents case studies of teenagers living with homelessness, prostitution, alcoholism, and neighborhood violence and interviews with staff members from organizations committed to helping teenagers in crisis
"Allison lets his subjects speak for themselves: the interviews are authentic and credible. . . . The terrain is unquestionably bleak, but the lives of these teens still reflect hope." Booklist

Benson, Peter L.

What teens need to succeed; proven, practical ways to shape your own future; [by] Peter L. Benson, Judy Galbraith, and Pamela Espeland. Free Spirit 1998 361p il pa $14.95 (7 and up)

305.23

1. Life skills 2. Conduct of life
ISBN 1-57542-027-9 LC 98-6036
Describes forty "developmental assets" that teenagers need to succeed in life, such as family support, positive peer influences, and religious community, and suggests ways to acquire these assets
"A useful resource for teens and those who work with them." SLJ
Includes bibliographical references

Daldry, Jeremy, 1969-

The teenage guy's survival guide. Little, Brown 1999 136p il pa $8.95 (7 and up) 305.23
1. Boys 2. Adolescence 3. Sex education
ISBN 0-316-17824-1 LC 98-40816
First published 1997 in the United Kingdom with title: Boys behaving badly
This book is "designed to answer questions . . . about dating, physical changes, emotional problems, and social survival. The author's style—breezy, humorous, and hip—should attract his intended audience. . . . Other concerns addressed include safe sex, being gay, pornography, alcohol, drugs, tobacco, and fighting. That is a lot of information packed into these pages, but that information, while not exhaustive, is certainly sound and clearly presented." Voice Youth Advocates
Includes bibliographical references

Girls know best; advice from girls for girls on just about everything! written by girls just like you!; compiled by Michelle Roehm; designed and illustrated by Marci Doane Roth. Beyond Words Pub. 1997 160p il pa $8.95 305.23
1. Girls 2. Human relations
ISBN 1-88522-363-3 LC 97-19942
Thirty-eight different girls respond to questions on specific issues including siblings, school, homework, parents, divorce, stepfamilies, boys, race, religion, and personal appearance
The "advice is on-target and mature, and the perspective is fresh and welcome." SLJ
Includes bibliographical references

Gray, Heather M.

Real girl/real world; tools for finding your true self; by Heather M. Gray & Samantha Phillips. Seal Press 1998 221p il pa $14.95 (7 and up)

305.23

1. Girls 2. Adolescence 3. Sex education
ISBN 1-58005 005-0 LC 98-8612
Provides information for teenage girls about sexuality, birth control, health, body image, eating disorders, and feminism
This is a "highly recommended resource book that belongs in every young adult collection. . . . Fun and readable, this is a highly accessible discussion of the issues." Voice Youth Advocates
Includes bibliographical references

Gurian, Michael

From boys to men; all about adolescence and you; illustrated by Brian Floca. Price/Stern/Sloan 1999 86p il (Plugged in) $13.89; pa $5.99

305.23

1. Boys 2. Adolescence 3. Sex education
ISBN 0-8431-7474-9; 0-8431-7483-8 (pa)
LC 98-37025
This offers "advice for preteens on how to cope with the emotional and physical changes that typically accompany adolescence. Gurian . . . addresses such subjects as developing romantic and sexual relationships, friendships, peer pressure, and even nutrition and wellness. The writing is direct, personal, and conversational. The tone is always positive and empathetic." SLJ

Jukes, Mavis

It's a girl thing; how to stay healthy, safe, and in charge; illustrations by Debbie Tilley. Knopf 1996 135p il $12; lib bdg $16.99; pa $5.99

305.23

1. Adolescence 2. Girls 3. Sex education
ISBN 0-679-87392-9; 0-679-94325-0 (lib bdg); 0-679-88771-7 (pa) LC 93-40296
"Jukes discusses a wide variety of subjects from buying a bra to sexual harassment and abuse. In a warm, conversational style, she covers body changes in both boys and girls, menstruation, general health, drinking and drugs, sexual feelings, pregnancy, contraceptives, and sexually transmitted diseases including AIDS. The text is sometimes humorous, but always conveys caring, respect, and concern." SLJ
Includes bibliographical references

Malaspina, Ann, 1957-

Children's rights. Lucent Bks. 1998 112p il (Lucent overview series) lib bdg $22.45 (7 and up)

305.23

1. Children—Civil rights 2. Children—Law and legislation
ISBN 1-56006-175-8 LC 97-35064
Discusses issues relating to children's rights such as equal access to education, health care, rights in schools, and the juvenile justice system
"An informative survey. . . . The balanced text is strengthened by appropriate citations of court decisions. Editorial cartoons and black-and-white photographs illustrate the volume." Horn Book Guide
Includes bibliographical references

Parks, Rosa, 1913-

Dear Mrs. Parks; a dialogue with today's youth; by Rosa Parks, with Gregory J. Reed. Lee & Low Bks. 1996 111p il $16.95; pa $8.95 305.23
1. African American children
ISBN 1-880000-45-8; 1-880000-61-X (pa)
LC 96-18389
Presents correspondence between Rosa Parks and various children in which the "Mother of the Modern Day Civil Rights Movement" answers questions and encourages young people to reach their highest potential
"Parks responds to young people with boundless compassion, respect, and hope." Booklist

Shandler, Sara
Ophelia speaks; adolescent girls write about their search for self. HarperPerennial 1999 285p pa $12.95 (7 and up)   **305.23**
1. Girls 2. Adolescence
ISBN 0-06-095297-0   LC 99-13534
"Shandler collected writings from adolescent girls all over the country on topics that include sexuality, eating disorders, feminism, family dynamics, and friendship; their words, framed by Shandler's own reflections, are riveting and revealing." Libr J

305.3   Men and women

Male/female roles: opposing viewpoints; Laura K. Egendorf, book editor. Greenhaven Press 2000 186p $21.96; pa $13.96 (7 and up)   **305.3**
1. Sex role
ISBN 0-7377-0131-5; 0-7377-0130-7 (pa)
                                      LC 99-25743
"Opposing viewpoints series"
Replaces the 1995 edition under the editorship of Jonathan S. Petrikin
"The essays cover such cultural and biological determinants for gender identification as the controversial concept of multiple genders. . . . Other sections tackle the oppression of women on the job, at home, and in the military, and the notion of traditional masculinity. Most interesting is the final section, which . . . [suggests] what will improve relationships between men and women." Booklist
Includes bibliographical references

McGowan, Keith, 1968-
Sexual harassment. Lucent Bks. 1999 112p il (Lucent overview series) lib bdg $22.45 (7 and up)
                                      305.3
1. Sexual harassment
ISBN 1-56006-507-9   LC 98-14683
An overview of sexual harassment, including its aspects in the law, the workplace, education, and the military
"McGowan does a steady job of defining and differentiating complex and weighted terms. . . . Quick, basic, informative, and detailed enough without being overwhelming." SLJ
Includes bibliographical references

305.4   Women

Cullen-DuPont, Kathryn
The encyclopedia of women's history in America. Facts on File 1995 339p $48 (7 and up)
                                      305.4
1. Women—United States—History 2. Feminism—Encyclopedias
ISBN 0-8160-2625-4   LC 95-4308
Also available in paperback from Da Capo Press
This reference work "covers people, significant events, organizations, legislation, court cases, and issues affecting women. . . . Rounding out the more than 500 entries are appendixes containing the complete texts of 34 documents ranging from a 1647 request for suffrage to a 1992 court case." Booklist

Franck, Irene M.
The Wilson chronology of women's achievements; a record of women's achievements from ancient times to present; by Irene M. Franck and David M. Brownstone. Wilson, H.W. 1998 507p $60 (7 and up)   **305.4**
1. Women—History
ISBN 0-8242-0936-2   LC 97-34394
First published 1995 by HarperPerennial with title: Women's world
This chronicle of women's history ranges "from the Egyptian queen Nefertiti and the Greek poet Sappho to Susan B. Anthony, Marie Curie, Eleanor Roosevelt, and Janet Reno." Publisher's note
Includes bibliographical references

Heinemann, Sue, 1948-
The New York Public Library amazing women in American history; a book of answers for kids. Wiley 1998 192p (New York Public Library answer books for kids series) pa $12.95   **305.4**
1. Women—United States—History
ISBN 0-471-19216-3   LC 97-18465
"A Stonesong Press book"
Consists of short answers to questions about the roles and achievements of women in America from prehistory to the end of the twentieth century
"The text is succinct, easy to read, and informative. . . . Pertinent black-and-white photos appear throughout." SLJ
Includes glossary and bibliographical references

Macdonald, Fiona
Women in 19th-century America. Bedrick Bks. 1999 48p il (Other half of history) $17.95 **305.4**
1. Women—United States—History 2. Women—Social conditions
ISBN 0-87226-566-8   LC 98-42644
Examines the everyday life of women in the United States during the 1800s, contrasting society's ideal view of women with their real lives
Includes glossary and bibliographical references

Women in 19th-century Europe. Bedrick Bks. 1999 48p il (Other half of history) $17.95 **305.4**
1. Women—Europe 2. Women—Social conditions
ISBN 0-87226-565-X   LC 98-42170
Examines the reality of women's lives in Europe during the 1800s and how change slowly occurred
"The pages are a panorama of illustrations from black-and-white woodcuts to line drawings and full-color reproductions, each accompanied by a succinct caption. . . . A delight to browse, and should lead readers to more extensive exploration." SLJ
Includes glossary and bibliographical references

Moss, Kary L.
The rights of women and girls; with an introduction by Norman Dorsen. Puffin Bks. 1998 132p (ACLU handbooks for young Americans) pa $9.99 (7 and up)   **305.4**
1. Women's rights 2. Sex role 3. Women—Social conditions
ISBN 0-14-037782-4   LC 97-36596

Moss, Kary L.—*Continued*

Presents a historical overview of the status of women in society and discusses the evolution of rights for women and the relevant court decisions that made those rights possible

"A good source of legal information for students of either gender." SLJ

Includes bibliographical references

Sullivan, George

The day the women got the vote; a photo history of the women's rights movement. Scholastic 1994 96p il pa $6.95   305.4

1. Women's rights 2. Feminism 3. Women—Suffrage

ISBN 0-590-47560-6   LC 94-188990

"Beginning with the early suffragists, Sullivan tells the story in a series of 24 short photo-essays on subjects including 'Anti-slavery Women,' 'Dress Reform,' 'Women at War,' and 'Fighting for Civil Rights.' He shows that the struggle for equality involved much more than the right to vote, and he devotes several chapters to the new feminism and the women's movement that started in the 1960s." Booklist

"A refreshing change from more scholarly treatments of the topic, and yet informative enough to warrant a second flip through." SLJ

Includes bibliographical references

Women's almanac; edited by Linda Schmittroth & Mary Reilly McCall. U.X.L 1997 3v il set $89   305.4

1. Women 2. Almanacs

ISBN 0-7876-0656-1   LC 96-25681

Contents: v1 History; v2 Society; v3 Culture

This almanac focuses on "women throughout history—their social concerns and cultural contributions. . . . Twenty-five chapters examine topics such as 'Civil Rights and Legal Status,' 'Women in Developing Countries,' 'Women's Movements,' 'Jobs and Money,' 'Education,' 'Health, ' 'Family,' 'Literature,' 'Music,' and 'Science and Exploration.' Each chapter presents a historical overview and current information on women's roles, achievements, and influences in these areas." SLJ

For a fuller review see: Booklist, April 15, 1997

305.8   Racial, ethnic, national groups

The **African-American** almanac. Gale Res. il $170   305.8

ISSN 1071-8710

First edition published 1967 by Bellwether with title: The Negro almanac. (8th edition 1999) Periodically revised

"Reference covering the cultural and political history of Black Americans. Includes generous amount of statistical information and biographies of Black Americans, both historical and contemporary." N Y Public Libr. Book of How & Where to Look It Up

African American breakthroughs; 500 years of black firsts; Jay P. Pederson and Jessie Carney Smith, editors. U.X.L 1995 280p il (African American reference library) $39   305.8

1. African Americans—History

ISBN 0-8103-9496-0   LC 95-122049

Also available adult version entitled Black firsts (1994) published by Visible Ink Press

"Organized by subject, events are then listed chronologically. Subjects include *Business and Labor*; *Justice, Law Enforcement, and Public Safety*; *Religion*; and *Science, Medicine, and Invention*. . . . Each of the 500 entries consists of three or four sentences on the person or event with the original source or sources cited." Booklist

The **African** American encyclopedia; editor: Michael W. Williams. Marshall Cavendish 1993 6v il maps set $449.95; pa set $149.95   305.8

1. African Americans—Encyclopedias

ISBN 1-85435-545-7; 0-7614-0563-1 (pa)

LC 93-141

"Entries are arranged alphabetically in two columns per page and range from *A. Philip Randolph Institute* to *Zydeco*. Coverage includes individuals, institutions, literary works, films, plays, television series, musical groups and styles, sports, legal decisions, events, places, movements, and organizations." Booklist

The **African-American** experience on file. Facts on File 1999 various paging il maps loose-leaf $125   305.8

1. African Americans—History

ISBN 0-8160-3697-7   LC 98-29845

Executive editor, Carter Smith

A collection of over 300 maps, charts, graphs, and illustrations with explanatory text covering African American history from ancient Africa to the present

Includes bibliographical references

African Americans: opposing viewpoints; William Dudley, book editor. Greenhaven Press 1997 320p (American history series) lib bdg $26.20; pa $16.20 (7 and up)   305.8

1. African Americans—History

ISBN 1-565-10522-2 (lib bdg); 1-565-10521-4 (pa)

LC 96-18328

This "anthology documents the history of African Americans from the time of slavery to recent controversies over affirmative action. The views of black nationalists, white supremacists, civil rights activists, and others are featured." Publisher's note

"This is an informative compilation that skillfully uses a number of primary sources to examine African-American issues." SLJ

Includes bibliographical references

Altman, Susan
The encyclopedia of African-American heritage; special writing and research by Joel Kemelhor; consultants: Arnold H. Taylor, Debra Newman Ham, Arthur Bust. Facts on File 1997 308p il $37.95; pa $18.95   **305.8**
1. African Americans—Encyclopedias 2. Africa—Encyclopedias
ISBN 0-8160-3289-0; 0-8160-3824-4 (pa)
    LC 96-15459
This reference provides "information on the Africans who remained on their ancestral continent, those who were forced to move, and their progeny who matured in a new land. Entries on people, places, culture, politics, and history are complete enough to whet a student's interest." Booklist
"A welcome addition to any collection or classroom." SLJ

Ashabranner, Brent K., 1921-
To seek a better world; the Haitian minority in America; [by] Brent Ashabranner; photographs by Paul Conklin. Cobblehill Bks. 1997 88p il $16.99
    305.8
1. Haitian Americans
ISBN 0-525-65219-1   LC 96-42967
"Containing some background information on Haiti's troubled political and economic past, the focus is on the half-million Haitians who have immigrated to the United States. . . . The book puts a human face on the culture by profiling long-term and recent immigrants, many of whom have achieved success in the fields of art, medicine, and civil service." Horn Book Guide
Includes bibliographical references

The **Asian-American** experience on file. Facts on File 1998 various paging il maps loose-leaf $125   **305.8**
1. Asian Americans
ISBN 0-8160-3696-9   LC 98-33466
Executive editor, Carter Smith
A collection of over 300 maps, charts, graphs, and illustrations with explanatory text covering Asian American history and cultures from China, South and Southeast Asia, Hawaii and the Pacific Islands, Japan, and Korea
"Upper-elementary and secondary teachers and students looking for supplementary materials for units on diversity, the California Gold Rush, Hawaii, and Chinese history will certainly find it here." Booklist
Includes bibliographical references

Asian Americans: opposing viewpoints; William Dudley, book editor. Greenhaven Press 1997 240p (American history series) lib bdg $26.20; pa $16.20 (7 and up)   **305.8**
1. Asian Americans—History
ISBN 1-56510-524-9 (lib bdg); 1-565-10523-0 (pa)
    LC 96-30439
"This collection of speeches and articles . . . provides in-depth primary material about how this country has looked on Asian immigrants. There are arguments from the 1850s onward about whether Chinese immigration should be restricted, whether Japanese residents can be

assimilated, whether Asian Americans have been accepted in Hawaii. Policy makers in the 1940s argue for and against the internment of Japanese Americans during World War II. A final section looks at Asian Americans in the years after 1965." Booklist
Includes bibliographical references

Bair, Barbara
Though justice sleeps; African Americans, 1880-1900. Oxford Univ. Press 1997 142p il (Young Oxford history of African Americans) lib bdg $21 (7 and up)   **305.8**
1. African Americans—History 2. United States—History—1865-1898
ISBN 0-19-509343-7   LC 96-8472
Chronicles the lives of African Americans during the late 1800's
This book "gives a detailed account of how blacks coped with racism; terrorism; and the gradual stripping away of hard-won economic, political, and social gains. Illustrations are copious, consisting of period photographs, documents, and drawings." SLJ
Includes bibliographical references

Birdseye, Debbie Holsclaw
Under our skin; kids talk about race; by Debbie Holsclaw Birdseye and Tom Birdseye; photographs by Robert Crum. Holiday House 1997 30p il $15.95   **305.8**
1. United States—Race relations 2. Ethnic relations
ISBN 0-8234-1325-X   LC 97-9395
Six young people discuss their feelings about their own ethnic backgrounds and about their experiences with people of different races
"This book provides an excellent starting point for discussion. It gives readers a chance to see what life is like through someone else's eyes, and in someone else's skin." SLJ
Includes bibliographical references

Cooper, Michael L., 1950-
Bound for the promised land; the great black migration. Lodestar Bks. 1995 85p il $15.99
    305.8
1. African Americans—History
ISBN 0-525-67476-4   LC 95-2611
"About one million African Americans left the South from 1915 to 1930 in search of better lives in the cities of the North. This short history of what is called the Great Migration discusses why black people left, what they hoped for, what they found, and how they changed America. . . . Fascinating archival black-and-white photographs add interest throughout the text." Booklist
Includes bibliographical references

Diner, Hasia R.
Jews in America. Oxford Univ. Press 1999 158p il (Religion in American life) lib bdg $22 (7 and up)   **305.8**
1. Jews—United States
ISBN 0-19-510678-4   LC 98-17645

Diner, Hasia R.—*Continued*

Examines the migration and background of those Jews who came to America, their adaptations to their new life, the rituals, traditions, and organizations of Jewish Americans, and their contemporary situation

"The coverage is brief, but the text is clear and lively. A host of archival photos and reproductions enhance the presentation." SLJ

Includes glossary and bibliographical references

Discrimination: opposing viewpoints; Mary E. Williams, book editor. Greenhaven Press 1997 223p il lib bdg $26.20; pa $16.20 (7 and up)
305.8

1. Discrimination 2. Minorities
ISBN 1-56510-657-1 (lib bdg); 1-56510-656-3 (pa)
LC 96-49920

"Opposing viewpoints series"

"The extent to which discrimination is a national problem, its causes, the validity of claims of reverse discrimination, and ways society can fight to end it are addressed by writers, scholars, and media personalities. . . . The collection offers an evenhanded overview. . . . A solid choice for students doing research, preparing for debates, or those simply interested in the many aspects of this complex issue." SLJ

Includes bibliographical references

Dornfeld, Margaret

The turning tide; from the desegregation of the armed forces to the Montgomery bus boycott (1948-1956). Chelsea House 1995 119p il (Milestones in black American history) lib bdg $19.95; pa $7.95 (7 and up)
305.8

1. African Americans—History 2. African Americans—Civil rights 3. United States—Race relations
ISBN 0-7910-2255-2 (lib bdg); 0-7910-2681-7 (pa)
LC 94-48331

This illustrated history covers the rise of the civil rights movement, including the desegregation of the armed forces, public schools, and professional baseball. The Montgomery bus boycott and the increase in popularity of rhythm and blues are also featured

Includes bibliographical references

Douglass, Frederick, 1817?-1895

Frederick Douglass, in his own words; edited by Milton Meltzer; illustrated by Stephen Alcorn. Harcourt Brace & Co. 1995 220p il $22 (7 and up)
305.8

1. Slavery—United States 2. African Americans—History
ISBN 0-15-229492-9
LC 94-14524

"Sixty-six speeches, encompassing a span of 40 years, are chronologically divided into sections devoted to before, during, and after the Civil War. A brief descriptive annotation introduces each speech, noting its date, place delivered, and circumstances surrounding its presentation. The selections, mainly two to three pages in length, afford a rich resource for report writers, orators, and debaters." SLJ

Includes bibliographical references

Encyclopedia of African-American culture and history; edited by Jack Salzman, David Lionel Smith, Cornel West. Macmillan Lib. Ref. USA 1996 5v il set $495
305.8

1. African Americans—Encyclopedias
ISBN 0-02-897345-3
LC 95-33607

Also available: The African-American experience: selections from the five-volume Macmillan Encyclopedia of African-American culture and history $39.95 (ISBN-02-865017-4)

With coverage beginning with the arrival in 1619 of the first slaves from Africa, this set provides a "survey of both the contributions to and the problems of blacks in American society. The 2,300 signed entries treat North America only. . . . Two-thirds of the entries are biographies treating such important historical figures as Sojourner Truth and Frederick Douglass and such contemporary people as Marian Wright Edelman and Colin Powell. . . . Many well-known scholars are contributors: James Cone, John Hope Franklin, David Levering Lewis, C. Eric Lincoln, and Eric Foner, for example." Booklist

Frankel, Noralee, 1950-

Break those chains at last: African Americans, 1860-1880. Oxford Univ. Press 1996 143p il maps (Young Oxford history of African Americans) lib bdg $22 (7 and up)
305.8

1. African Americans—History 2. Slavery—United States
ISBN 0-19-508798-4
LC 95-1848

After a chapter on the Civil War, this volume addresses such topics as suffrage and political participation; economic and educational opportunities; and marriage and family life of the newly freed slaves

"Frankel makes especially good use of quotations from interviews with former slaves done in the 1930s; Reconstruction Era pension examiners' interviews with Black Civil War widows; Freedmen's Bureau records, etc." SLJ

Includes bibliographical references

Golay, Michael, 1951-

Reconstruction and reaction; the emancipation of slaves, 1861-1913. Facts on File 1996 158p il (Library of African-American history) $19.95 (7 and up)
305.8

1. African Americans—History 2. Reconstruction (1865-1876) 3. Slavery—United States
ISBN 0-8160-3318-8
LC 96-1881

This "explores how former slaves struggled to find their place in American society as free people following the Civil War. Author Golay relates the advancements of African Americans immediately following the war. . . . The book concludes with a brief discussion of the Civil Rights Movement." Publisher's note

Includes bibliographical references

Grossman, James R.

A chance to make good; African Americans, 1900-1929. Oxford Univ. Press 1997 157p (Young Oxford history of African Americans) lib bdg $21 (7 and up)
305.8

1. African Americans—History
ISBN 0-19-508770-4
LC 96-8471

Grossman, James R.—*Continued*

Chronicles the lives of African Americans from the turn of the twentieth century to the Great Depression
Includes bibliographical references

Hamanaka, Sheila

The journey; Japanese Americans, racism, and renewal; painting and text by Sheila Hamanaka; book design by Steve Frederick. Orchard Bks. 1990 39p il $19.95; lib bdg $20.99; pa $8.95
  305.8
1. World War, 1939-1945—United States 2. Japanese Americans—Evacuation and relocation, 1942-1945
ISBN 0-531-05849-2; 0-531-08449-3 (lib bdg); 0-531-07060-3 (pa)   LC 89-22877
"A Richard Jackson book"
"Hamanaka has created a five-panel mural depicting the Japanese-American experience with particular emphasis on the watershed of that experience, the concentration camps. Here the mural is reproduced detail by detail with amplifying text. . . . There are other books on this subject . . . but none with the punch and universality of this one." SLJ

Hispanic American almanac; Bryan Ryan and Nicolás Kanellos, editors. U.X.L 1995 213p il maps $39   **305.8**
1. Hispanic Americans
ISBN 0-8103-9823-0   LC 95-196496
Also available adult version with title: The Hispanic-American almanac (1993) published by Gale Res.
This volume "provides information about 'the heritage, the communities and the growing influence of hispanics on U.S. culture.'. . . Fourteen chapters cover Spanish exploration, immigration to the U.S. from Mexico, Puerto Rico, and Cuba; family structure and the role of religion; the workplace and education; and contributions in the arts and sports." Booklist

Hoobler, Dorothy

The African American family album; [by] Dorothy and Thomas Hoobler; introduction by Phylicia Rashad. Oxford Univ. Press 1995 127p il (American family albums) $19.95; lib bdg $25; pa $12.95   **305.8**
1. African Americans
ISBN 0-19-509460-3; 0-19-508128-5 (lib bdg); 0-19-512419-7 (pa)   LC 94-34697
"Beginning with life in pre-colonial Africa, the Hooblers make superb use of personal histories, autobiographies, slave narratives, and other original documents to paint a vivid picture of life in medieval Africa, in Africa during the slave trade, and of the lives of slaves and former slaves in the U.S. Readers are introduced to a complex set of historical events, presented in a simple, yet moving manner. . . . An excellent addition to any collection." SLJ
Includes bibliographical references

The Chinese American family album; [by] Dorothy and Thomas Hoobler; introduction by Bette Bao Lord. Oxford Univ. Press 1994 128p il map (American family albums) $19.95; lib bdg $25; pa $12.95   **305.8**
1. Chinese Americans
ISBN 0-19-509123-X; 0-19-508130-7 (lib bdg); 0-19-512421-9 (pa)   LC 93-11873
"This sourcebook on the Chinese immigrant experience is divided into six topics: the homeland, the voyage to America, arrival in America, first-generation life, the integration of . . . generations, and Chinese Americans today. The authors introduce each chapter with a summary essay, then let the immigrants and their descendents speak for themselves in excerpts from oral reminiscences, written histories, and fiction spanning the years from the Gold Rush to the 1980s. Period photographs and drawings, maps, and sidebars enhance the text. The result resembles a well-organized, handsomely designed scrapbook. . . . A valuable resource." SLJ
Includes bibliographical references

The Cuban American family album; [by] Dorothy and Thomas Hoobler; introduction by Oscar Hijuelos. Oxford Univ. Press 1996 127p il (American family albums) $19.95; lib bdg $25; pa $12.95   **305.8**
1. Cuban Americans
ISBN 0-19-510340-8; 0-19-508132-3 (lib bdg); 0-19-512425-1 (pa)   LC 95-38103
Interviews, excerpts from diaries and letters, newspaper accounts, profiles of famous individuals, and pictures from family albums portray the Cuban American experience
Includes bibliographical references

The German American family album; [by] Dorothy and Thomas Hoobler; introductions by Werner Klemperer. Oxford Univ. Press 1996 127p il (American family albums) $19.95; lib bdg $25; pa $12.95   **305.8**
1. German Americans
ISBN 0-19-510341-6; 0-19-508133-1 (lib bdg); 0-19-512422-7 (pa)   LC 95-14448
Traces the history of German immigrants to the United States through letters, diaries and newspaper accounts
Includes bibliographical references

The Irish American family album; [by] Dorothy and Thomas Hoobler; introduction by Joseph P. Kennedy II. Oxford Univ. Press 1995 128p il (American family albums) $19.95; lib bdg $25; pa $12.95   **305.8**
1. Irish Americans
ISBN 0-19-509461-1; 0-19-508127-7 (lib bdg); 0-19-512418-9 (pa)   LC 94-19569
"Selections from diaries, letters, interviews, newspaper and magazine articles, and books provide an arresting picture of what it has meant to be of Irish heritage in America. . . . Topics such as prejudice, working conditions and labor unions; politics; and the importance of family, friends, and the Catholic Church are touched upon." SLJ
Includes bibliographical references

Hoobler, Dorothy—*Continued*

The Italian American family album; [by] Dorothy and Thomas Hoobler; introduction by Governor Mario M. Cuomo. Oxford Univ. Press 1994 127p il map (American family albums) $19.95; lib bdg $25; pa $12.95   **305.8**
   1. Italian Americans
   ISBN 0-19-509124-8; 0-19-508126-9 (lib bdg);
   0-19-512420-0 (pa)   LC 93-46918
This volume includes selections from "diaries, letters, and oral histories. . . . Each of the six chapters begins with background information and then goes on to discuss life in the old country, coming to America, first impressions, working, forming a new life, and becoming a part of America." SLJ
Includes bibliographical references

The Japanese American family album; [by] Dorothy and Thomas Hoobler. Oxford Univ. Press 1996 127p il map (American family albums) $19.95; lib bdg $25; pa $12.95   **305.8**
   1. Japanese Americans
   ISBN 0-19-509934-6; 0-19-508131-5 (lib bdg);
   0-19-512423-5 (pa)   LC 94-43466
This book describes "the Japanese-American experience. Each of the six chapters offers a succinct historical presentation followed by first-person accounts. Relying on oral histories and original documents, both pictorial and written, the Hooblers have truly humanized historical events. . . . Like a family album, the pages of the book are filled with fine quality archival black-and white photographs that tell a story." SLJ
Includes bibliographical references

The Jewish American family album; [by] Dorothy and Thomas Hoobler; introduction by Mandy Patinkin. Oxford Univ. Press 1995 127p il (American family albums) $19.95; lib bdg $25; pa $12.95   **305.8**
   1. Jews—United States
   ISBN 0-19-509935-4; 0-19-508135-8 (lib bdg);
   0-19-512417-0 (pa)   LC 94-43460
This volume "begins with a five-page thumbnail sketch of Jewish history from Abraham to the rise of the State of Israel. Successive chapters detail Jewish life in 'the old country', immigration to America, and the contributions Jews have made to their new homeland." Book Rep
"What makes this title unique is the high quality of the carefully researched and varied historical information and the Hooblers' judicious selection of primary-source excerpts, many of which are by well-known writers, politicians, and celebrities." SLJ
Includes bibliographical references

The Mexican American family album; [by] Dorothy and Thomas Hoobler; introduction by Henry G. Cisneros. Oxford Univ. Press 1994 127p il (American family albums) $19.95; lib bdg $25; pa $12.95   **305.8**
   1. Mexican Americans
   ISBN 0-19-509459-X; 0-19-508129-3 (lib bdg);
   0-19-512426-X (pa)   LC 94-7785

"Using almost exclusively first-person accounts, the Hooblers present vignettes of history, culture, and experience from the first Mexican American settlers to the Chicano Movement. . . . Gathered together, these accounts present a powerful portrait of a strong people, rich in history and culture. A must for multicultural studies." Book Rep
Includes bibliographical references

Hornsby, Alton, Jr.

Chronology of African American history; from 1492 to the present; [by] Alton Hornsby, Jr. 2nd ed. Gale Res. 1997 720p il $68 (7 and up)
          305.8
   1. African Americans—History—Chronology
   ISBN 0-8103-8573-2   LC 97-10558
First published 1991
This is a "chronological guide to the people, places and events significant to African American history. . . . [It] includes details on important births and deaths, legislation and court decisions, rebellions and demonstrations, awards and honors, elections and appointment. . . . Brief biographies on many noteworthy individuals are also included. Excerpts from significant speeches, legislation, publications and other documents are reprinted in an appendix." Publisher's note
Includes bibliographical references

Hull, Mary

Ethnic violence. Lucent Bks. 1997 112p il (Lucent overview series) $22.45 (7 and up) **305.8**
   1. Ethnic relations 2. Violence 3. Culture conflict
   ISBN 1-56006-184-7   LC 96-40128
Examines some of the causes of conflict between ethnic groups, the impact of such conflicts, instances of violence in various countries, and efforts to prevent it
"Focusing on countries such as Ireland, Bosnia, and Sudan as examples of ethnically conflicted lands, Hull discusses the subject from a variety of perspectives. . . . Hull provides a good overview of a complex topic." SLJ
Includes glossary and bibliographical references

Struggle and love, 1972-1997; from the Gary Convention to the aftermath of the Million Man March. Chelsea House 1997 118p il (Milestones in black American history) $19.95; pa $8.95 (7 and up)   **305.8**
   1. African Americans—Civil rights 2. African Americans—History
   ISBN 0-7910-2262-5; 0-7910-2688-4 (pa)
          LC 96-30513
Discusses the efforts of African Americans to achieve equality in education, employment, politics, and other areas, from the 1970s into the 1990s
Includes bibliographical references

Isserman, Maurice

Journey to freedom; the African-American great migration. Facts on File 1997 131p il maps (Library of African-American history) $19.95 (7 and up)   **305.8**
   1. African Americans—History 2. United States—Race relations
   ISBN 0-8160-3413-3   LC 96-52160

Isserman, Maurice—*Continued*

Discusses the northward journey of Black southerners, the greatest internal mass migration of people in American history

"This book uses primary source material copiously. . . . The black and white photographs are clearly reproduced. . . . [The book] is well-written and the historical detail is fascinating." Book Rep

Includes bibliographical references

Katz, William Loren

Black Indians: a hidden heritage. Atheneum Pubs. 1986 198p il $17; pa $10   **305.8**

1. African Americans 2. Indians of North America

ISBN 0-689-31196-6; 0-689-80901-8 (pa)

         LC 85-28770

Traces the history of relations between blacks and American Indians, and the existence of black Indians, from the earliest foreign landings through pioneer days

"Katz gives a full and impassioned account of the ways in which black and red peoples united as warriors, settlers, and family members to produce a history that has been largely ignored in books about the history of the Americas. The material is inherently dramatic, moving, and absorbing." Bull Cent Child Books

Includes bibliographical references

King, Wilma, 1942-

Toward the promised land; from Uncle Tom's cabin to the onset of the Civil War (1851-1861). Chelsea House 1995 111p il maps (Milestones in black American history) lib bdg $19.95; pa $8.95 (7 and up)   **305.8**

1. African Americans—History 2. Slavery—United States

ISBN 0-7910-2265-X (lib bdg); 0-7910-2691-4 (pa)

         LC 94-42109

This book "sets the stage for the Civil War, bringing a new perspective to the period by detailing the role blacks played in the abolitionist and human rights movements. Familiar leaders such as Sojourner Truth, Harriet Tubman, and Frederick Douglass are included, but so are lesser known figures like Martin R. Delany, Mary Ann Shadd Cary, Henry Bibb, and Henry Highland Garnett. King presents a detailed, but simple and clear, description of the events that led to war, ending with John Brown's execution and Abraham Lincoln's election." SLJ

Includes bibliographical references

Littlefield, Daniel C.

Revolutionary citizens; African Americans, 1776-1804. Oxford Univ. Press 1997 141p (Young Oxford history of African Americans) lib bdg $21 (7 and up)   **305.8**

1. African Americans—History 2. United States—History—1775-1783, Revolution 3. United States—History—1783-1865

ISBN 0-19-508715-1   LC 96-8470

Chronicles the lives of African Americans during the Revolutionary War and the early years of the nation

Includes bibliographical references

Myers, Walter Dean, 1937-

Now is your time! the African-American struggle for freedom. HarperCollins Pubs. 1991 292p il lib bdg $17.89; pa $10.95   **305.8**

1. African Americans—History

ISBN 0-06-024371-6 (lib bdg); 0-06-446120-3 (pa)

         LC 91-314

Coretta Scott King Award for text, 1992

A history of the African-American struggle for freedom and equality, beginning with the capture of Africans in 1619, continuing through the American Revolution, the Civil War, and into contemporary times

"Myers's unique episodic approach makes this history a compelling exploration of the African-American experience. . . . This fascinating book will engender pride in heritage for young African Americans and provide insight into American history for all of us." Horn Book

Includes bibliographical references

Nardo, Don, 1947-

Braving the New World, 1619-1784; from the arrival of the enslaved Africans to the end of the American Revolution. Chelsea House 1995 117p il (Milestones in black American history) $19.95; pa $8.95 (7 and up)   **305.8**

1. Slavery—United States 2. African Americans—History

ISBN 0-7910-2259-5; 0-7910-2685-X (pa)

         LC 94-2963

This book provides "explanations of how and why the slave trade became established in North America and a flowing, interesting narrative on slave life and the strength and legacy of slave culture." Booklist

Includes bibliographical references

Nash, Gary B.

Forbidden love; the secret history of mixed-race America. Holt & Co. 1999 214p il $21.95 (7 and up)   **305.8**

1. Racially mixed people 2. Interracial marriage 3. United States—Race relations

ISBN 0-8050-4953-3   LC 98-12154

Presents accounts of how mainly anonymous Americans have defied the official racial ideology and points out how guardians of the past have written that side of our history out of the record

"Nash dispels myths and misconceptions to fight prejudice as he reflects on a difficult subject. An intriguing topic, well handled." SLJ

Includes bibliographical references

Ochoa, George

The New York Public Library amazing Hispanic American history; a book of answers for kids. Wiley 1998 192p il maps pa $12.95   **305.8**

1. Hispanic Americans

ISBN 0-471-19204-X   LC 98-23797

"A Stonesong Press book"

Consists of questions and answers about Latinos, revealing the common history which unites them while also showing how they differ depending upon their country of origin

Ochoa, George—*Continued*
"Recommended for purchase as a bargain buy and extremely handy source for frequently requested and sometimes hard-to-find information about Hispanic Americans." Booklist
Includes glossary and bibliographical references

Pascoe, Elaine
Racial prejudice; why can't we overcome? rev ed. Watts 1997 128p il $24   **305.8**
1. United States—Race relations 2. Prejudices 3. Minorities
ISBN 0-531-11402-3   LC 96-36913
First published 1985
Discusses the causes and history of prejudice against minority groups in the United States, reviewing the damaging effects of prejudice and suggesting ways to eliminate it
This offers "valuable information and perspective." Voice Youth Advocates
Includes bibliographical references

Patrick, Diane, 1955-
The New York Public Library amazing African American history; a book of answers for kids. Wiley 1998 170p il (New York Public Library answer books for kids series) pa $12.95   **305.8**
1. African Americans—History
ISBN 0-471-19217-1   LC 97-16938
"A Stonesong Press book"
Presents questions and answers relating to important periods in African American history including the Revolution, Civil War, Reconstruction, Migration, and the Civil Rights Movement
"Enhanced by black-and-white photographs, this useful resource provides information in a formal but readable style. . . . A well-organized, objective, accessible guide for students." SLJ
Includes glossary and bibliographical references

Rasmussen, R. Kent
Farewell to Jim Crow; the rise and fall of segregation in America. Facts on File 1997 168p il maps (Library of African-American history) $19.95 (7 and up)   **305.8**
1. African Americans—Segregation 2. African Americans—Civil rights 3. United States—Race relations
ISBN 0-8160-3248-3   LC 96-48329
This book "deals with the origins and causes of segregation in America. There is a chapter devoted to the definition of Jim Crow and how the unjust practice affected African Americans' lives from housing to entertainment to education. The author then begins the history of segregation in colonial times and covers the slavery issue in the South. . . . He also covers the blacks and their part in the Civil War, the Reconstruction period, and the beginnings of segregation in the South." Book Rep
"This is a solidly written and thoroughly researched book that inspires the reader to learn more." Voice Youth Advocates
Includes bibliographical references

Reef, Catherine
Africans in America; the spread of people and culture. Facts on File 1999 136p il (Library of African-American history) lib bdg $19.95 (7 and up)   **305.8**
1. African Americans—History
ISBN 0-8160-3772-8   LC 98-11793
Describes the spread of Africans to the western hemisphere and the influences and development of their culture
"Written with clarity and depth, this is an excellent account of the 'African diaspora.'" Booklist
Includes bibliographical references

Takaki, Ronald T., 1939-
Strangers at the gates again; Asian American immigration after 1965; [by] Ronald Takaki; adapted by Rebecca Stefoff with Carol Takaki. Chelsea House 1995 124p il map (Asian American experience) lib bdg $19.95 (7 and up)   **305.8**
1. Asian Americans
ISBN 0-7910-2190-4   LC 94-21105
Adapted from the author's adult title, Strangers from a different shore, published 1989 by Little, Brown
This book "examines the 'second wave' of Asian immigration after the passing of the 1965 Immigration Act. . . . The particular history of each Asian group (Chinese, Japanese, Koreans, Filipinos, Asian Indians, Southeast Asians) is examined, as well as how those circumstances shaped their lives in the United States. Anecdotes and thoughtful reflections personalize the facts." Voice Youth Advocates
Includes bibliographical references

Trotter, Joe William, 1945-
From a raw deal to a New Deal? African Americans, 1929-1945; [by] Joe William Trotter, Jr. Oxford Univ. Press 1995 125p il (Young Oxford history of African Americans) lib bdg $22 (7 and up)   **305.8**
1. African Americans—History 2. United States—Race relations
ISBN 0-19-508771-2   LC 95-17348
The author "examines the important events and major forces of 1929-1945 in the U.S. from the perspective of African Americans. He notes that while they made sociopolitical, economic, and cultural advancements through a plethora of New Deal-created opportunities, many blacks were concurrently being treated as second-class citizens and suffering racial violence at the hands of disgruntled, fearful working-class whites. He concludes that it wasn't until 1935 that the 'raw deal' began to be transformed into a 'new deal.'" SLJ
"A concise, well-researched, readable account of African American life. . . . The text is amply illustrated with excellent photographs, documents, and political cartoons." Booklist
Includes bibliographical references

What are you? voices of mixed-race young people; [edited by] Pearl Fuyo Gaskins. Holt & Co. 1999 273p il $18.95 (7 and up)   **305.8**
1. Racially mixed people 2. Teenagers 3. United States—Race relations
ISBN 0-8050-5968-7   LC 98-37381

What are you?—*Continued*

Many young people of racially mixed backgrounds discuss their feelings about family relationships, prejudice, dating, personal identity, and other issues

"While underscoring the complexity of the mixed-race experience, these unadorned voices offer a genuine, poignant, enlightening and empowering message to all readers." SLJ

Includes bibliographical references

White, Deborah Gray

Let my people go: African Americans, 1804-1860. Oxford Univ. Press 1996 141p il (Young Oxford history of African Americans) lib bdg $22 (7 and up)   **305.8**

1. African Americans—History 2. Slavery—United States

ISBN 0-19-508769-0   LC 95-38104

Discusses the lives of African Americans from the early years of the nineteenth century to the start of the Civil War

"History comes alive for students when reading the words of the people who lived it. This volume does just that and is recommended for all American history students." Voice Youth Advocates

Includes bibliographical references

Wu, Dana Ying-hui, 1969-

The Chinese-American experience; by Dana Ying-hui Wu and Jeffrey Dao-sheng Tung. Millbrook Press 1993 61p il (Coming to America) lib bdg $22.40   **305.8**

1. Chinese Americans

ISBN 1-56294-271-9   LC 92-15649

Traces the history of Chinese immigration to the United States, discussing why they emigrated, their problems in a new land, and their contributions to American culture

Includes bibliographical references

305.9   Occupational and miscellaneous groups

Homosexuality: opposing viewpoints; Mary E. Williams, book editor. Greenhaven Press 1999 218p il lib bdg $26.20; pa $16.20 (7 and up)   **305.9**

1. Homosexuality

ISBN 0-7377-0053-X (lib bdg); 0-7377-0052-1 (pa)   LC 98-32020

"Opposing viewpoints series"

Replaces the edition published 1993 under the editorship of William Dudley

Presents opposing viewpoints on such aspects of homosexuality as what causes it, discrimination against homosexuals, whether or not society should encourage increased acceptance of homosexuals, and whether or not to sanction gay and lesbian families

Includes bibliographical references

Mastoon, Adam

The shared heart; portraits and stories celebrating lesbian, gay, and bisexual young people; photographs by Adam Mastoon. Morrow 1997 87p il $24.50 (7 and up)   **305.9**

1. Homosexuality 2. Lesbians 3. Bisexuality

ISBN 0-688-14931-6   LC 97-3276

This is a "collection of 40 narratives and photographs of gay, lesbian, and bisexual young adults. . . . Mastoon does a wonderful job of capturing the personalities of these young people. . . . Young adult readers, gay and straight, will find these passionate, life-affirming testimonies memorable and moving." SLJ

Includes bibliographical references

Oliver, Marilyn Tower, 1935-

Gay and lesbian rights; a struggle. Enslow Pubs. 1998 128p il maps lib bdg $19.95 (7 and up)   **305.9**

1. Gay liberation movement 2. Homosexuality

ISBN 0-89490-958-4   LC 98-21258

Examines the issue of gay and lesbian rights in the United States, covering the history of the gay rights movement, the current struggles it faces, and arguments both for and against it

The author "presents a broad spectrum of valuable information with diplomacy. . . . This resource should prove useful to students researching the topic for class assignments as well as to those engaged in personal-interest reading." Booklist

Includes bibliographical references

306   Culture and institutions

America's victims: opposing viewpoints; Paul A. Winters, book editor. Greenhaven Press 1996 185p il lib bdg $26.20; pa $16.20 (7 and up)   **306**

1. United States—Moral conditions 2. United States—Social policy

ISBN 1-56510-401-3 (lib bdg); 1-56510-400-5 (pa)   LC 95-49648

"Opposing viewpoints series"

This volume "discusses the issue of 'victimhood' and its influence on American society, the civil rights movement, the recovery movement, and the justice system. . . . The essays are well organized, and the summary paragraphs and questions for consideration at the beginning of each article are especially helpful." SLJ

Includes bibliographical references

Culture wars: opposing viewpoints; Mary E. Williams, book editor. Greenhaven Press 1999 208p lib bdg $26.20; pa $16.20 (7 and up)   **306**

1. Popular culture—United States

ISBN 1-56510-939-2 (lib bdg); 1-56510-938-4 (pa)   LC 98-28276

"Opposing viewpoints series"

Replaces the edition published 1994 under the editorship of Fred Whitehead

In this collection of articles "scholars, political activists, and religious leaders focus on social issues of diver-

Culture wars: opposing viewpoints—*Continued*
sity, including abortion, homosexuality, welfare reform, and school prayer, as well as bilingual education and funding for the National Endowment for the Arts." Booklist
Includes bibliographical references

Junior Worldmark encyclopedia of world cultures. U.X.L 1999 9v il maps set $225   **306**
1. Ethnology—Encyclopedias 2. Human geography—Encyclopedias
ISBN 0-7876-1756-3   LC 98-13810
Timothy L. Gall and Susan Bevans Gall, editors
Arranges countries around the world alphabetically, subdivides these countries into 250 culture groups, and provides information about the ethnology and human geography of each group
"The short and engaging articles are based on entries in the *Worldmark Encyclopedia of Cultures and Daily Life* . . . and targeted to appeal to a younger audience. . . . This is a valuable and timely resource." SLJ

Peoples of the world; customs and cultures; editor, Amiram Gonen; educational editor, Barbara P. Sutnick. Grolier Educ. 1998 10v il maps set $249 (7 and up)   **306**
1. Ethnology—Encyclopedias
ISBN 0-7172-9236-3   LC 97-32980
An encyclopedia of world peoples combining anthropological and social information, both historical and current, on the status of ethnic groups worldwide
"The information on peoples of the world is accurate in a broad sense and is presented clearly enough to provide inquiring young minds with a place to begin a research project or simply satisfy their curiosity." Sci Books Films

Worldmark encyclopedia of cultures and daily life. Gale Res. 1997 4v il maps set $299   **306**
1. Ethnology—Encyclopedias 2. Manners and customs—Encyclopedias
ISBN 0-7876-0552-2   LC 97-3278
Contents: v1 Africa; v2 Americas; v3 Asia & Oceania; v4 Europe
Provides information on 500 cultures of the world, covering twenty different areas of daily life including clothing, food, language, and religion
For a review see: Booklist, May 1, 1998

306.4   Specific aspects of culture

Lakin, Pat
Everything you need to know when a parent doesn't speak English; [by] Patricia Lakin. Rosen Pub. Group 1994 64p (Need to know library) lib bdg $16.95 (7 and up)   **306.4**
1. Immigrants 2. United States—Immigration and emigration 3. Parent and child 4. English language—Study and teaching
ISBN 0-8239-1691-X   LC 94-1905
The author "offers some reasons why parents may not have learned the new language, shows practical ways for readers to help them become proficient, and deals realistically with their own feelings and the stress that results from the situation." SLJ
Includes bibliographical references

306.8   Marriage and family

The **Family:** opposing viewpoints; Mary E. Williams, book editor. Greenhaven Press 1998 224p il lib bdg $26.20; pa $16.20 (7 and up)
                                   306.8
1. Family
ISBN 1-56510-669-5 (lib bdg); 1-56510-668-7 (pa)
                                   LC 97-19211
"Opposing viewpoints series"
Replaces The Family in America published 1992 under the editorship of Viqi Wagner
The articles and essays in this volume "examine the state of the family, how divorce-law reforms and work-related policies have affected it, adoption policies, and how public policy and values impact upon it. . . . The selections are well chosen, clearly written, and thought-provoking." SLJ
Includes bibliographical references

Marriage and divorce; Tamara L. Roleff, Mary E. Williams, book editors. Greenhaven Press 1997 190p (Current controversies) lib bdg $26.20; pa $16.20 (7 and up)   **306.8**
1. Marriage 2. Divorce
ISBN 1-56510-568-0 (lib bdg); 1-56510-567-2 (pa)
                                   LC 97-4941
This title "addresses several issues: premarital cohabitation, divorce's effect upon children, child custody, and same-sex marriage. The 32 reprinted articles present several sides of the issues, including Andrew Sullivan's piece on gay marriage from the New Republic, and an argument made by Commonweal, a Catholic magazine, that marriage is for procreation. . . . The book ends with an annotated list of organizations dealing with marriage and divorce." SLJ
Includes bibliographical references

Presma, Frances
Straight talk about today's families; [by] Frances Presma and Paula Edelson. Facts on File 1999 136p $19.95 (7 and up)   **306.8**
1. Family
ISBN 0-8160-3905-4   LC 98-44901
Discusses the nature, importance, and challenges of being part of a family and explains ways to deal with family stress and dysfunction
Includes bibliographical references

Schultz, Margaret A.
Teens with single parents; why me? Enslow Pubs. 1997 128p (Teen issues) lib bdg $17.95 (7 and up)   **306.8**
1. Single parent family 2. Children of divorced parents
ISBN 0-89490-913-4   LC 96-39439
Examines the effects of living in a single-parent family, discussing such topics as emotional aspects and economic factors
"Interviews with teens, parents, and psychologists offer young people excellent coping strategies and a chance to see that their anger and frustration are hardly unique." Booklist
Includes bibliographical references

Trapani, Margi
Listen up! teenage mothers speak out. Rosen
Pub. Group 1997 64p il (Teen pregnancy
prevention library) lib bdg $16.95 (7 and up)
306.8
1. Teenage mothers 2. Teenage pregnancy
ISBN 0-8239-2254-5   LC 95-42449
"Seven young mothers describe the reality of their
lives before and since the birth of their babies. None of
them have maintained a relationship with their child's father. They all voice regret for lost youth and forgone opportunities." SLJ
Includes glossary and bibliographical references

Reality check; teenage fathers speak out. Rosen
Pub. Group 1997 64p il (Teen pregnancy
prevention library) lib bdg $16.95 (7 and up)
306.8
1. Teenage fathers 2. Parenting
ISBN 0-8239-2255-3   LC 95-42450
Teenage fathers highlight the challenges of being a
teen parent, discussing responsibility, economic hardship,
and emotional issues involved in parenting at a young
age
This book presents "a true picture of the hardships of
being a teenage parent." Voice Youth Advocates
Includes glossary and bibliographical references

306.89   Separation and divorce

Goldentyer, Debra
Divorce. Raintree Steck-Vaughn Pubs. 1998 48p
il (Preteen pressures) $24.26   **306.89**
1. Divorce
ISBN 0-8172-5030-1   LC 97-17930
Describes divorce and explains how to deal with the
breaking up of your parents' marriage
"Informative as well as objective. . . . Full-color photographs and an attractive format [makes this title] accessible to the intended audience." SLJ
Includes bibliographical references

Porterfield, Kay Marie
Straight talk about divorce. Facts on File 1999
148p $19.95 (7 and up)   **306.89**
1. Divorce
ISBN 0-8160-3725-6   LC 98-45473
Discusses the legal, financial, and emotional aspects of
the divorce process, examining the impact of divorce on
the lives of young people and providing resources for
more information and for help
Includes bibliographical references

Sanders, Pete
Divorce and separation; [by] Pete Sanders and
Steve Myers. Copper Beech Bks. 1997 32p il
(What do you know about) lib bdg $20.90
306.89
1. Divorce
ISBN 0-7613-0574-2   LC 96-35822

Discusses the meaning of separation and divorce and
some of the reasons that relationships come to an end.
Also examines the effects that divorce and separation can
have on people's lives
"The clear writing style and open format [makes this]
useful for reports and for general interest reading." SLJ

310.5   General statistics—Serial publications

Rand McNally world facts & maps. Rand
McNally maps pa $10.95   **310.5**
1. Almanacs 2. Statistics
ISSN 1057-9834

Annual. First published 1989
"The first section of this guide gives an overview of
the current areas of conflict in the world, with backgrounds, chronologies, and issues. The following section
lists every country in the world with brief facts, locator
maps, and data about the people, languages, government,
economics and history. Maps are in gray tones rather
than in color, but are sufficient for their purpose in this
volume." Safford. Guide to Ref Materials for Sch Libr
Media Cent. 5th edition

The **Statesman's** yearbook; the politics, cultures,
and economies of the world. St. Martin's Press
$120   **310.5**
1. Statistics 2. Political science
ISSN 0081-4601

Annual. First published 1864
"Descriptive and statistical information about international organizations and countries of the world—brief
history, area, political status, economy, etc." N Y Public
Libr. Ref Books for Child Collect. 2d edition

317.3   General statistics of the United States

United States. Bureau of the Census
Statistical abstract of the United States. U.S.
Govt. Ptg. Office $39   **317.3**
1. United States—Statistics 2. Statistics

Annual. First published for the year 1878
"Compendium of statistics on the social, political and
economic organization of the U.S. presented in tables.
Lists other sources of such information." N Y Public
Libr. Ref Books for Child Collect. 2d edition

320.03   Political science— Encyclopedias and dictionaries

Encyclopedia of American government; consulting
editor, Joseph M. Bessette; project editor, R.
Kent Rasmussen. Salem Press 1998 4v il maps
set $210   **320.03**
1. United States—Politics and government—Encyclopedias
ISBN 0-89356-117-7   LC 98-28986

Encyclopedia of American government—*Continued*

"Two hundred alphabetically arranged essays make up this. . . set that covers the basics of American government. Well-written, illuminating articles range from broad subjects such as Federalism to more specific topics such as 'Iron Triangles' and reflect an awareness for gender and minority issues." SLJ

For a fuller review see: Booklist, April 1, 1999

320.3   Comparative government

Pious, Richard M., 1944-
Governments of the world; a student companion. Oxford Univ. Press 1998 3v il maps set $120 (7 and up)   **320.3**
1. Comparative government 2. World politics
ISBN 0-19-508486-1   LC 95-36684
Includes over 700 articles with information on the politics and government of every country in the world, on political systems, movements, and leaders, and on human rights, wars, international organizations, and related topics

For a review see: Booklist, June 1 & 15, 1998

320.4   Structure and functions of government

Tomaselli-Moschovitis, Valerie
Government on file. Facts on File 1998 various paging il maps loose-leaf $165   **320.4**
1. United States—Politics and government
ISBN 0-8160-3560-1   LC 97-45171
This offers "explanations of how U.S. government is structured and operates. . . . Information is clearly presented. Among the topics are how a bill becomes a law, the electoral college, the organization of the federal court system, the history of immigration and immigration policy, and foreign exchange and balance of trade." Booklist
Includes bibliographical references

322   Relation of the state to organized groups and their members

Gaustad, Edwin Scott
Church and state in America; [by] Edwin S. Gaustad. Oxford Univ. Press 1999 157p il (Religion in American life) $21 (7 and up)   **322**
1. Church and state 2. United States—Church history 3. United States—Religion
ISBN 0-19-510679-2   LC 98-18001
Examines the different roles played by church and state in considerations of religion throughout the history of the United States, beginning with concerns of the original colonists through the current debate about religion in schools
The author "presents the issues clearly, without distracting details, in a lively style that is thoroughly consistent with the topic." SLJ
Includes bibliographical references

Gay, Kathlyn
Who's running the nation? how corporate power threatens democracy. Watts 1998 128p il lib bdg $24 (7 and up)   **322**
1. Business and politics 2. Corporations
ISBN 0-531-11489-9   LC 97-37186
Examines how large U.S. corporations can influence the activities of federal, state, and local governments. Coverage includes: monopolies, New Deal reforms, corporate welfare, and the rise of multinational corporations
"Gay delivers an insightful analysis of current social trends in this well-documented account. . . . Her writing style is clear and lively, with many direct quotations and attributions to lend immediacy to the presentation." SLJ
Includes bibliographical references

Stewart, Gail, 1949-
Militias. Lucent Bks. 1998 96p il (Lucent overview series) lib bdg $22.45 (7 and up)   **322**
1. Militia movements 2. Political crimes and offenses
ISBN 1-56006-501-X   LC 97-23362
Discusses the rise of the anti-government militia movement in the United States, the involvement of militias with white supremacists and other hate groups, and the connections between these groups and such events as the Oklahoma City bombing
Includes bibliographical references

323   Civil and political rights

Civil liberties: opposing viewpoints; Tamara L. Roleff, book editor. Greenhaven Press 1999 208p lib bdg $26.20; pa $16.20 (7 and up)   **323**
1. Civil rights
ISBN 1-565-10937-6 (lib bdg); 1-565-10936-8 (pa)
                                      LC 98-11808
"Opposing viewpoints series"
Replaces the edition published 1994 under the editorship of Charles P. Cozic
This collection of articles explores "issues related to freedom of expression, the right to privacy, separation of church and state, and the Internet and civil liberties. . . . This title will be helpful for reports or debates." SLJ
Includes bibliographical references

Human rights: opposing viewpoints; Mary E. Williams, book editor. Greenhaven Press 1998 218p il lib bdg $26.20; pa $16.20 (7 and up)   **323**
1. Human rights
ISBN 1-56510-797-7 (lib bdg); 1-56510-796-9 (pa)
                                      LC 97-51706
"Opposing viewpoints series"
"The rights of women, refugees, child laborers, and political prisoners are among the issues debated in this collection of articles and essays. . . . Contributors from many sides include Hillary Rodham Clinton, Midge Decter, Katha Pollitt, Jimmy Carter, Amnesty International, and the China Internet Information Center. . . . There are fine bibliographies to stimulate students' further reading." Booklist

O'Connor, Maureen
Equal rights. Watts 1998 46p il (What do we mean by human rights?) $22   **323**
1. Human rights
ISBN 0-531-14448-8   LC 96-53582
Considers equal rights issues, including those that involve race, religion, gender, sexual orientation, and physical disabilities, with reference to the universal declaration of human rights
This book "will draw readers into discussing big political issues." Booklist

323.1   Civil and political rights of nondominant groups

Allen, Zita
Black women leaders of the civil rights movement. Watts 1996 128p il (African-American experience) lib bdg $24 (7 and up)   **323.1**
1. African American women 2. African Americans—Civil rights
ISBN 0-531-11271-3   LC 96-26134
This volume includes stories of women who participated in the desegregation of schools, buses, lunch counters, and other public facilities
"The brief, but detailed text captures the spirit of the movement. . . . Libraries would do well to add this book to the many other titles available on the movement because of its central focus and perspectives." SLJ
Includes bibliographical references

Alonso, Karen
Korematsu v. United States; Japanese-American internment camps. Enslow Pubs. 1998 128p il (Landmark Supreme Court cases) lib bdg $19.95 (7 and up)   **323.1**
1. Korematsu, Fred, 1919- 2. Japanese Americans—Evacuation and relocation, 1942-1945 3. World War, 1939-1945—Reparations
ISBN 0-89490-966-5   LC 97-29582
Profiles the case of Fred Korematsu, who sought compensation from the American government for his time spent in a Japanese-American internment camp during World War II
"The book makes the operations of the judicial branch intelligible. . . . It offers many possible topics for classroom discussion." SLJ
Includes glossary and bibliographical references

Andryszewski, Tricia, 1956-
The March on Washington, 1963; gathering to be heard. Millbrook Press 1996 64p il (Spotlight on American history) lib bdg $21.90   **323.1**
1. Demonstrations 2. African Americans—Civil rights
ISBN 0-7613-0009-0   LC 96-1217
Recounts the historical antecedents and events leading up to the March on Washington in 1963, led by Martin Luther King, Jr., and other prominent African American leaders in their quest for equal civil rights
"Both the immediate drama and the lasting importance of the 1963 March on Washington are captured in this title. . . . [Written] in a clear, direct style, and with many photographs, some in color." Booklist
Includes bibliographical references

Bullard, Sara
Free at last; a history of the Civil Rights Movement and those who died in the struggle; introduction by Julian Bond. Oxford Univ. Press 1993 112p il map lib bdg $25; pa $12.95 (7 and up)   **323.1**
1. African Americans—Civil rights 2. United States—Race relations
ISBN 0-19-508381-4 (lib bdg); 0-19-509450-6 (pa)   LC 92-38174
An illustrated history of the civil rights movement, including a timeline and profiles of forty people who gave their lives in the movement
Includes bibliographical references

Dear Dr. King; letters from today's children to Dr. Martin Luther King, Jr.; edited by Jan Colbert and Ann McMillan Harms; with photographs by Ernest C. Withers and Roy Cajero. Hyperion Bks. for Children 1998 59p il $14.95   **323.1**
1. King, Martin Luther, 1929-1968 2. Children's writings 3. United States—Race relations
ISBN 0-7868-0417-3   LC 97-32031
"Contemporary Memphis schoolchildren, ages seven to thirteen, wrote these letters to offer their thoughts and questions to Dr. King." Bull Cent Child Books
This is "both poignant and witty. The young writers speak of fears and hatreds, hopes and dreams." SLJ

Dunn, John M., 1949-
The civil rights movement. Lucent Bks. 1998 128p il (World history series) lib bdg $22.45 (7 and up)   **323.1**
1. African Americans—Civil rights 2. United States—Race relations
ISBN 1-56006-310-6   LC 97-27443
A historical overview of the movement for freedom and equality for blacks in the United States
"Well-written, well-organized. . . . Dunn deftly brings to life all of the drama and personalities involved." SLJ
Includes bibliographical references

Haskins, James, 1941-
Freedom Rides; journey for justice. Hyperion Bks. for Children 1995 99p il $15.49; lib bdg $14.89   **323.1**
1. African Americans—Civil rights 2. Southern States—Race relations
ISBN 0-7868-0048-8; 0-7868-2037-3 (lib bdg)   LC 94-7996
The author discusses the efforts of the people who tested the series of court decisions aimed at desegregating buses and trains in the United States. The story begins in the 1850's with a New York City incident and trial, but the focus is mainly on the events of the 1940's, 1950's and 1960's and the freedom riders of those years
"Good-quality black-and-white photographs are scattered throughout. Haskins has . . . given YAs an important source of information on African American history with this well-researched, well-documented book." SLJ
Includes bibliographical references

King, Casey

Oh, freedom! kids talk about the Civil Rights Movement with the people who made it happen; illustrated with photographs; by Casey King and Linda Barrett Osborne; foreword by Rosa Parks; portraits by Joe Brooks. Knopf 1997 137p il $18; lib bdg $19.99; pa $10.99 **323.1**

1. African Americans—Civil rights 2. United States—Race relations

ISBN 0-679-85856-3; 0-679-95856-8 (lib bdg); 0-679-89005-X (pa) LC 96-13014

Interviews between young people and people who took part in the civil rights movement accompany essays that describe the history of efforts to make equality a reality for African Americans

"King and Osborne present a carefully unbiased overview of the civil rights movement. . . . But most impressive is the way the authors use interesting interviews by students . . . [that] humanize history and add depth to the bare facts of the historical account." Book Rep

Includes bibliographical references

King, Martin Luther, 1929-1968

The words of Martin Luther King, Jr.; selected by Coretta Scott King. Newmarket Press 1983 112p il $14.95; pa $10 **323.1**

1. African Americans—Civil rights 2. United States—Race relations

ISBN 0-937858-28-5; 0-937858-79-X (pa) LC 83-17306

This "volume of selections from Dr. King's speeches and writings, . . . focuses on seven areas of his concerns: 'The Community of Man, Racism, Civil Rights, Justice and Freedom, Faith and Religion, Nonviolence, and Peace.'" Publisher's note

"This work will be useful only for general readers, since individual quotations are not documented by citations." Libr J

Includes bibliographical references

Levine, Ellen

Freedom's children; young civil rights activists tell their own stories. Putnam 1993 167p il $16.95 **323.1**

1. African Americans—Civil rights 2. United States—Race relations

ISBN 0-399-21893-9 LC 92-1358

Also available Thorndike Press large print edition and in paperback from Avon Bks.

Southern blacks who were young and involved in the civil rights movement during the 1950s and 1960s describe their experiences

"*Freedom's Children* belongs in every school library and should quickly take its place as an invaluable resource for teachers planning thematic units on prejudice or American minorities. Powerful, readable, authentic." ALAN

Includes bibliographical references

Lusane, Clarence, 1953-

No easy victories; Black Americans and the vote. Watts 1996 160p il (African-American experience) lib bdg $24 (7 and up) **323.1**

1. African Americans—Suffrage

ISBN 0-531-11270-5 (lib bdg) LC 96-21469

"Starting with colonial history and moving forward through the 1994 elections, Lusane offers a comprehensive overview of the drive for African Americans to attain the vote and then to use it. He includes primary-source materials and biographical sketches of many of the early Congressional leaders as well as others who made things happen." SLJ

"This thoroughly documented title is replete with the names and statistics kids need to satisfy curricular demands." Booklist

Includes bibliographical references

McKissack, Patricia C., 1944-

The civil rights movement in America from 1865 to the present; by Patricia and Fredrick McKissack. 2nd ed. Children's Press 1991 351p il $45.80 **323.1**

1. African Americans—Civil rights 2. African Americans—History

ISBN 0-516-00579-0 LC 91-4103

First published 1987

From the beginning of Reconstruction to the present, this book traces the struggle of blacks to gain their civil rights in America, with a brief comparison of their problems to those of other minorities

"The biographical sketches of civil rights personalities and short explanations of particular events make this an effective ready reference tool." SLJ

Includes bibliographical references

Powledge, Fred

We shall overcome; heroes of the civil rights movement; photographs by the author. Scribner 1993 214p il $17 **323.1**

1. African Americans—Civil rights 2. United States—Race relations

ISBN 0-684-19362-0 LC 92-25184

"Following an overview of the early history of slavery in the U.S. through the major civil rights events of the 1960s, Powledge introduces readers to 10 remarkable participants in that movement, none of whose name is a household word." SLJ

"The author's grasp of his topic is commendable. . . . His passionate involvement in the issues always comes through." Booklist

Rochelle, Belinda

Witnesses to freedom; young people who fought for civil rights. Lodestar Bks. 1993 97p il $15.99; pa $5.99 **323.1**

1. African Americans—Civil rights 2. United States—Race relations

ISBN 0-525-67377-6; 0-14-038432-4 (pa) LC 93-16165

Describes the experiences of young Blacks who were involved in significant events in the civil rights move-

Rochelle, Belinda—*Continued*
ment, including Brown vs. Board of Education, the
Montgomery bus boycott, and the sit-in movement

"Some of the individuals portrayed may not be well
known, but their stories are inspiring and touching. Rochelle does a commendable job of explaining issues and
relating events in an understandable manner." SLJ
Includes bibliographical references

Walter, Mildred Pitts, 1922-
Mississippi challenge. Bradbury Press 1992
205p il $18.95; pa $6.95   **323.1**
1. African Americans—Civil rights 2. Mississippi—
Race relations
ISBN 0-02-792301-0; 0-02-045641-7 (pa)
LC 92-6718
Describes the struggle for civil rights for the blacks in
Mississippi, from the time of slavery to the signing of
the Voting Rights Act in 1965
This is "a history book that will make readers think
carefully about the democratic process as a whole. . . .
It represents a stern and important synthesis." Bull Cent
Child Books
Includes bibliographical references

Wexler, Sanford
The civil rights movement; an eyewitness
history; introduction by Julian Bond. Facts on File
1993 356p il maps (Eyewitness history series) $50;
pa $21.95 (7 and up)   **323.1**
1. African Americans—Civil rights 2. United States—
Race relations
ISBN 0-8160-2748-X; 0-8160-4102-4 (pa)
LC 92-28674
Uses speeches, articles, and other writings of those involved to trace the history of the civil rights movement
in the United States, primarily from 1954 to 1965
"This very readable source deserves a place in every
public and middle and high school library." Booklist
Includes bibliographical references

Williams, Juan
Eyes on the prize: America's civil rights years,
1954-1965; [by] Juan Williams with the Eyes on
the prize production team; introduction by Julian
Bond. Viking 1987 300p il hardcover o.p.
paperback available $15.95 (7 and up)   **323.1**
1. African Americans—Civil rights 2. United States—
Race relations
ISBN 0-14-009653-1 (pa)   LC 86-40271
"A Robert Lavelle book"
"This companion volume to the PBS TV series of the
same name is an . . . account of black America's struggle for social and political equality, covering the civil
rights battle from the landmark Brown v. Board of Education decision in 1954 to the Selma protest marches,
and Voting Rights Act of 1965." Libr J
"Highly recommended both as a socio-historical document and as a heartfelt, poignant remembrance of a
movement and its activists." Booklist
Includes bibliographical references

323.44   Freedom of action (Liberty)

Intellectual freedom manual; compiled by the
Office for Intellectual Freedom of the American
Library Association. American Lib. Assn. il pa
$38   **323.44**
1. Intellectual freedom 2. Libraries—Censorship

First published 1974. (5th edition 1996) Periodically
revised
This guide to preserving intellectual freedom includes:
ALA interpretations to the Library Bill of Rights; recommendations for special libraries and specific situations;
information about legal decisions affecting school and
public libraries; a section on the ALA's Intellectual Freedom Action Network
Includes bibliographical references

King, David C.
The right to speak out. Millbrook Press 1997
47p il (Land of the free) lib bdg $19.90   **323.44**
1. Freedom of speech 2. Freedom of the press
ISBN 0-7613-0063-5   LC 96-21966
Focuses on freedom of speech and of the press while
discussing freedom of expression as guaranteed by the
Bill of Rights
Students will "appreciate the straightforward style and
the excellent examples used to explain the principles be-
hind our essential rights and freedoms." Booklist
Includes glossary and bibliographical references

Steffens, Bradley, 1956-
Free speech; identifying propaganda techniques;
curriculum consultant, JoAnne Buggey.
Greenhaven Press 1992 36p il lib bdg $10.95 (7
and up)   **323.44**
1. Freedom of speech 2. Propaganda
ISBN 0-89908-098-7   LC 92-23594
"Opposing viewpoints juniors"
Presents opposing viewpoints on topics related to free
speech, accompanied by critical thinking activities to
help the reader discern fact from opinion and recognize
propaganda techniques
Includes bibliographical references

Symons, Ann K.
Protecting the right to read; a how-to-do-it
manual for school and public librarians; [by] Ann
K. Symons, Charles Harmon; illustrations by Pat
Race. Neal-Schuman 1995 211p il (How-to-do-it
manuals for librarians) pa $45   **323.44**
1. Libraries—Censorship 2. Intellectual freedom
ISBN 1-55570-216-3   LC 95-42444
"The authors take readers from discussion of the policies and principles of intellectual freedom to considerations specific to school and public libraries to the protection of freedom on the Internet. . . . Appendixes consist of reprints of documents put out by the ALA and the
Minnesota Coalition Against Censorship." Book Rep
"Intellectual freedom issues and guiding principles get
a thorough and comprehensive treatment. . . . An essential book." Voice Youth Advocates
Includes bibliographical references

324 The political process

Archer, Jules

Special interests; how lobbyists influence legislation. Millbrook Press 1997 144p il lib bdg $23.90 (7 and up) **324**
1. Lobbying
ISBN 0-7613-0060-0 LC 96-27076
"A Lucas-Evans book"

Describes the concept of lobbying, the history of its development, and the efforts of present-day lobbyists to influence state and federal legislators in such areas as tobacco, oil, and firearms

"Archer enlivens what could have been a dull read with clear, concise writing, well-placed political cartoons, and intriguing examples of dirty politics from the birth of the U.S. to the present." Booklist

Includes bibliographical references

324.6 Election systems and procedures; suffrage

Frost-Knappman, Elizabeth

Women's suffrage in America; an eyewitness history; [by] Elizabeth Frost and Kathryn Cullen-DuPont. Facts on File 1992 452p il (Eyewitness history series) lib bdg $45 (7 and up) **324.6**
1. Women—Suffrage 2. Women—United States—History—Sources
ISBN 0-8160-2309-3 LC 91-31177

Chronicles the struggle of American women for the right to vote, from 1800 to their victory in 1920. Includes quotations from contemporary witnesses through memoirs, letters, and other documents of the period

This is "a lively and important sourcebook for students of American political and cultural history." SLJ

Includes bibliographical references

325.73 Immigration to the United States

American immigration. Grolier Educ. 1999 10v il set $325 **325.73**
1. United States—Immigration and emigration—Encyclopedias
ISBN 0-7172-9283-5 LC 98-18077

An alphabetical reference work examining the background, statistics, reception, and current status of those groups who have immigrated to America throughout history

"This set does a nice job of bringing to life the experiences of different immigrant groups and providing balanced coverage of various issues related to immigration." Booklist

Ashabranner, Brent K., 1921-

Our beckoning borders; illegal immigration to America; [by] Brent Ashabranner; photographs by Paul Conklin. Cobblehill Bks. 1996 99p il $15.99 **325.73**
1. Illegal aliens 2. United States—Immigration and emigration
ISBN 0-525-65223-X LC 95-45584

Examines the problems connected with illegal immigration in the United States, from the perspectives of the immigrants themselves as well as from that of law enforcement officials

"The compassion and understanding of the author are apparent throughout. Photographs and life stories of illegal immigrants personalize the situation so that the reader realizes that this is a complex issue without easy answers. Interesting and easy to read with just enough statistical data on this important issue." Book Rep

Includes bibliographical references

Still a nation of immigrants; [by] Brent Ashabranner; photographs by Jennifer Ashabranner. Cobblehill Bks. 1993 131p il $15.99 **325.73**
1. United States—Immigration and emigration
ISBN 0-525-65130-6 LC 92-44335

Identifies who today's immigrants to the United States are, describes their experiences, contributions, and impact on society, and discusses how an immigrant becomes a citizen

"Engaging contemporary photographs, in addition to archival prints from the Library of Congress . . . personalize the commentary and add to the book's appeal. A carefully thought-out presentation." SLJ

Includes bibliographical references

Coan, Peter M.

Ellis Island interviews; in their own words; [by] Peter Morton Coan. Facts on File 1997 xxxii, 432p il $29.95; pa $16.95 (7 and up) **325.73**
1. Ellis Island Immigration Station 2. United States—Immigration and emigration
ISBN 0-8160-3414-1; 0-8160-3548-2 (pa) LC 97-2892

This "volume culls interviews with men and women . . . from Europe and the Middle East who passed through Ellis Island on their way to America." Horn Book Guide

"Coan provides a brisk but effective history of Ellis Island, then yields the stage to these brave travelers whose memories of the their arduous journeys remain so sharp, so precious." Booklist

Hauser, Pierre

Illegal aliens; Sandra Stotsky, general editor. Chelsea House 1997 142p il (Immigrant experience) $19.95 **325.73**
1. Illegal aliens 2. United States—Immigration and emigration
ISBN 0-7910-3363-5 LC 95-23636

Examines the history of undocumented immigration to the United States, the hardships endured by illegal aliens, their motives in immigrating, and current efforts to control this situation

"An up-to-date, evenhanded look at the subject." SLJ

Includes bibliographical references

I was dreaming to come to America; memories from the Ellis Island Oral History Project; selected and illustrated by Veronica Lawlor; foreword by Rudolph W. Giuliani. Viking 1995 38p il $15.99; pa $5.99   **325.73**
1. Ellis Island Immigration Station 2. United States—Immigration and emigration
ISBN 0-670-86164-2; 0-14-055622-2 (pa)
LC 95-1281
In their own words, coupled with hand-painted collage illustrations, immigrants recall their arrival in the United States. Includes brief biographies and facts about the Ellis Island Oral History Project
"There is a flavor of Chagall in the peasant figures dancing above the ship or hopping ashore near the turreted towers of the huge building on Ellis Island. The elegant rendering offers a timeless view of this significant journey that is at once personal and universal." Horn Book

Immigration: opposing viewpoints; Tamara L. Roleff, book editor. Greenhaven Press 1998 218p il lib bdg $26.20; pa $16.20 (7 and up)
325.73
1. United States—Immigration and emigration
ISBN 1-56510-799-3 (lib bdg); 1-56510-798-5 (pa)
LC 98-5034
"Opposing viewpoints series"
Replaces the edition published 1992 under the editorship of Teresa O'Neill
This collection of articles addresses such questions as "Should immigration be restricted? How do immigrants affect America? How should U.S. immigration policy be reformed? Is illegal immigration a serious problem?" Publisher's note
Includes bibliographical references

Kosof, Anna
Living in two worlds; the immigrant children's experience. 21st Cent. Bks. (NY) 1996 112p il lib bdg $22.40 (7 and up)   **325.73**
1. United States—Immigration and emigration 2. Children of immigrants
ISBN 0-8050-4083-8   LC 96-13004
After a brief history of immigration, the author "introduces teen immigrants that she interviewed in schools around the country. Cultural differences, from food, to dress, to ways to show respect are easily understood from these vignettes about young people who came here from around the world." SLJ
Includes bibliographical references

326   Slavery and emancipation

Bial, Raymond
The strength of these arms; life in the slave quarters. Houghton Mifflin 1997 40p il $16   **326**
1. Slavery—United States 2. Plantation life 3. African Americans—Social life and customs
ISBN 0-395-77394-6   LC 96-39860
Describes how slaves were able to preserve some elements of their African heritage despite the often brutal treatment they experienced on Southern plantations
"This volume features clear, color photographs of plantation sites and artifacts, as well as a few early photos of people living under slavery. . . . This makes slavery in America more concrete than many other books on the subject." Booklist
Includes bibliographical references

The underground railroad. Houghton Mifflin 1995 48p il map $16; pa $5.95   **326**
1. Underground railroad 2. Slavery—United States
ISBN 0-395-69937-1; 0-395-97915-3 (pa)
LC 94-19614
Using first-person accounts, historical documents, and his own photographs, the author "focuses on the history of the Underground Railroad, building on the experiences of both riders and conductors as he outlines the political climate and the moral beliefs that allowed slavery to thrive and those that helped bring about its downfall." Publ Wkly
"Although the text covers ground often trodden by other works on this popular subject, Bial's shoots of places and things which now appear tidy and innocent conjure spirits of desperate freedom-seekers as handily as do more detailed narratives." Bull Cent Child Books
Includes bibliographical references

Currie, Stephen, 1960-
Slavery. Greenhaven Press 1999 111p il (Opposing viewpoints digests) lib bdg $17.96; pa $11.96 (7 and up)   **326**
1. Slavery—United States
ISBN 1-56510-881-7 (lib bdg); 1-56510-880-9 (pa)
LC 98-36198
Contributors discuss slavery in the United States from historical, political, economic and sociological perspectives
Includes bibliographical references

Gorrell, Gena K. (Gena Kinton), 1946-
North star to freedom; the story of the Underground railroad; foreword by Rosemary Brown. Delacorte Press 1997 c1996 168p il $17.95
326
1. Underground railroad 2. Slavery—United States 3. Abolitionists
ISBN 0-385-32319-0   LC 96-8552
First published 1996 in Canada
Details the history of the Underground Railroad from the roots of slavery through the post-Emancipation era by focusing on the lives of the participants
"Told from the British and British-Canadian viewpoint, this history adds a new dimension and perspective to the story of the Underground Railroad. . . . It is clearly written and will be useful both as an introduction to the subject and as a supplement to other titles about the period." SLJ
Includes bibliographical references

Hamilton, Virginia, 1936-
Many thousand gone; African Americans from slavery to freedom; illustrated by Leo and Diane Dillon. Knopf 1993 151p il $18; lib bdg $18.99
326
1. Underground railroad 2. Slavery—United States
ISBN 0-394-82873-9; 0-394-92873-3 (lib bdg);
2-679-87936-6   LC 89-19988
Companion volume to The people could fly
In this book the author tells "the story of slavery through a series of dramatic biographical vignettes. . . . Her book includes such famous historical figures as Frederick Douglass, Sojourner Truth and Harriet Tubman. She also presents some more obscure individuals. . . . All of these profiles drive home the sickening realities of slavery in a personal way. . . . These are powerful stories eloquently told." N Y Times Book Rev
Includes bibliographical references

Haskins, James, 1941-
Bound for America; the forced migration of Africans to the New World; [by] James Haskins & Kathleen Benson; illustrated by Floyd Cooper. Lothrop, Lee & Shepard Bks. 1999 48p il $18; lib bdg $17.93   **326**
1. Slave trade 2. Slavery—History
ISBN 0-688-10258-1; 0-688-10259-X (lib bdg)
LC 98-24101
Discusses the European enslavement of Africans, including their capture, branding, conditions on slave ships, shipboard mutinies, and arrival in the Americas
"This combination of clear text and judicious use of primary-source material makes crystalline the inhumanity and commercialism that kept the trade in slaves alive for 350 years." SLJ
Includes bibliographical references

Get on board: the story of the Underground Railroad. Scholastic 1993 152p il map hardcover o.p. paperback available $3.50   **326**
1. Underground railroad 2. Slavery—United States
ISBN 0-590-45419-6 (pa)   LC 92-13247
The author "relates the history of the Underground Railroad in the U.S., and introduces those who made it a success." SLJ
"Weaving together poignant personal stories and carefully researched historical data, Haskins has produced a stirring account of the founding and the workings of the Underground Railroad." Publ Wkly
Includes bibliographical references

Jurmain, Suzanne
Freedom's sons; the true story of the Amistad mutiny. Lothrop, Lee & Shepard Bks. 1998 128p il $15   **326**
1. Amistad (Schooner) 2. Slavery—United States
ISBN 0-688-11072-X   LC 97-37258
This is an "account of the 1839 *Amistad* mutiny and the trial that followed. . . . [The author] places the event in the historical context of a pre-Civil War United States." SLJ
"With meticulous research and a storyteller's knack for pace and well-placed detail, Jurmain re-creates a fascinating chapter in American history." Booklist
Includes bibliographical references

Katz, William Loren
Breaking the chains: African-American slave resistance. Atheneum Pubs. 1990 194p il $16; pa $10 (7 and up)   **326**
1. Slavery—United States
ISBN 0-689-31493-0; 0-689-81919-6 (pa)
LC 89-36355
The author "debunks myths and corrects misconceptions about black slavery in the U.S. Basing his text largely on slave testimony, the recollections of white slaveowners, and public records, he supplies a comprehensive study that details the harshness of slave life and the many forms of slave resistance, including military involvement during the Civil War." Booklist
Includes bibliographical references

Lester, Julius
From slave ship to freedom road; paintings by Rod Brown. Dial Bks. 1998 40p il $17.99   **326**
1. Slavery—United States
ISBN 0-8037-1893-4   LC 96-44422
"Lester uses empathy-provoking exercises, open-ended questions, and the paintings of Rod Brown to help readers understand the experience of African-American slaves." Bull Cent Child Books
"Lester's impassioned questions grow from his visceral response to Brown's narrative paintings. . . . The combination of history, art, and commentary demands interaction." Booklist

To be a slave; illustrated by Tom Feelings. Dial Bks. for Young Readers 1968 160p il $16.99
326
1. Slavery—United States
ISBN 0-8037-8955-6   LC 68-28738
Also available in paperback from Scholastic
"Through the words of the slave, interwoven with strongly sympathetic commentary, the reader learns what it is to be another man's property; how the slave feels about himself; and how he feels about others. Every aspect of slavery, regardless of how grim, has been painfully and unrelentingly described." Read Ladders for Hum Relat. 6th edition
Includes bibliographical references

McKissack, Patricia C., 1944-
Rebels against slavery; by Patricia C. McKissack and Fredrick McKissack. Scholastic 1996 181p il $14.95; pa $5.99   **326**
1. Slavery—United States
ISBN 0-590-45735-7; 0-590-66259-7 (pa)
LC 94-41089
The authors "explore slave revolts and the men and women who led them, weaving a tale of courage and defiance in the face of tremendous odds. Readers learn not only about Nat Turner and Denmark Vesey, but also about Cato, Gabriel Prosser, the maroons, and the relationship between escaped slaves and Seminole Indians. The activities of abolitionists are described as well. The authors' careful research, sensitivity, and evenhanded style reveal a sad, yet inspiring story of the will to be free." SLJ

Myers, Walter Dean, 1937-
Amistad: a long road to freedom. Dutton Children's Bks. 1998 99p il maps $16.99   **326**
1. Amistad (Schooner) 2. Slavery—United States
ISBN 0-525-45970-7
This is an "account of the capture in West Africa, the hellish journey aboard the slave ship on the Middle Passage, the sale in Cuba, the mutiny led by Sengbe on the *Amistad* as it sailed from Cuba, the forced landing in Connecticut, the subsequent court trials in the U.S., and the final struggle to return home. The design is clear and readable. . . . Myers includes considerable detail drawn from primary reports. . . . The narrative is exciting, not only the account of the uprising but also the tension of the court arguments." Booklist
Includes bibliographical references

Palmer, Colin A., 1942-
The first passage; blacks in the Americas, 1502-1617. Oxford Univ. Press 1994 126p il maps (Young Oxford history of African Americans) $22 (7 and up)   **326**
1. Slavery—History 2. Blacks—History
ISBN 0-19-508699-6   LC 94-17355
"Palmer's text ranges from detailing differences among African cultures to providing precise information on the changes traditional customs and religions underwent as a result of diaspora and enslavement. Much of the book focuses on the experiences of slaves in Mexico, Brazil, and Peru; this sets it apart from many other works that deal mainly with slavery in the U.S." SLJ
Includes bibliographical references

Rappaport, Doreen
Escape from slavery; five journeys to freedom; illustrated by Charles Lilly. HarperCollins Pubs. 1991 117p il $14.95; pa $4.95   **326**
1. Underground railroad 2. Slavery—United States
ISBN 0-06-021631-X; 0-06-446169-6 (pa)
LC 90-38170
Five accounts of black slaves who managed to escape to freedom during the period preceding the Civil War
"These accounts of a courageous and daring people deserve a wide readership. Readable, clear and precise, the book shows evidence of careful research and is an excellent addition to books on Black History." Child Book Rev Serv
Includes bibliographical references

Sawyer, Kem Knapp
The underground railroad in American history. Enslow Pubs. 1997 128p il maps (In American history) lib bdg $19.95   **326**
1. Underground railroad 2. Slavery—United States
ISBN 0-89490-885-5   LC 96-30901
Describes the Underground Railroad and the historical events surrounding it and presents the stories of some of its conductors
Includes bibliographical references

Thomas, Velma Maia
Lest we forget; the passage from Africa to slavery and emancipation. Crown 1997 32p il $29.95 (7 and up)   **326**
1. Slavery—United States 2. African Americans—History 3. Slave trade
ISBN 0-609-60030-3   LC 96-54240
"A three-dimensional interactive book with photographs and documents from the Black Holocaust Exhibit" Title page
"By combining highly effective and readable text with photographs, news clippings, drawings, and facsimilies of documents, Thomas shares with her readers the details of virtually every aspect of slave life. . . . Throughout the assortment of pop-out and pull-out replicas, points are raised that will lead to classroom discussion." SLJ

327.1   Foreign policy and international relations

Carter, Jimmy, 1924-
Talking peace; a vision for the next generation. rev ed. Dutton Children's Bks. 1995 205p il maps $18.99; pa $5.99 (7 and up)   **327.1**
1. Peace 2. International relations 3. United States—Foreign relations
ISBN 0-525-45517-5; 0-14-037440-X (pa)
LC 95-40247
A revised and updated edition of the title first published 1993
Carter discusses the various factors involved in peace negotiations and conflict resolution, examining such elements as the living conditions of citizens in peacetime and wartime and the effect of international relations on innocent citizens. The former president writes in detail about Camp David, his work in Atlanta and his peace missions to Korea, Haiti, Bosnia, and Sudan
Includes bibliographical references

Cheney, Glenn Alan
Nuclear proliferation; the problems and possibilities. Watts 1999 144p il (Impact books) lib bdg $24 (7 and up)   **327.1**
1. Arms control 2. Nuclear weapons
ISBN 0-531-11431-7   LC 98-4526
Discusses current policies governing the spread of nuclear weapons along with potential problems and possible outcomes
"The writing is clear and straightforward. . . . Cheney's overview . . . will be especially useful for debaters and speech or report writers." SLJ
Includes glossary and bibliographical references

327.12   Espionage and subversion

Platt, Richard, 1953-
Spy; written by Richard Platt; photographed by Geoff Dann and Steve Gorton. Knopf 1996 59p il (Eyewitness books) $19; lib bdg $20.99   **327.12**
1. Espionage 2. Intelligence service
ISBN 0-679-88122-0; 0-679-98122-5 (lib bdg)
LC 96-11003

Platt, Richard, 1953-—_Continued_
"A Dorling Kindersley book"
Numerous photos, drawings and maps illustrate this history of espionage. "Every aspect of spy culture is examined, including equipment and its concealment, methods of bugging and tapping, codes and ciphers, double agents and defectors, and industrial espionage and surveillance. Famous past and present spy personalities, as well as fictional spies, are discussed. The book is eye-catching." Booklist

327.73 United States—Foreign relations

Dolan, Edward F., 1924-
Shaping U.S. foreign policy; profiles of twelve secretaries of state; [by] Edward F. Dolan, Margaret M. Scariano. Watts 1996 128p il (Democracy in action) lib bdg $24 (7 and up) **327.73**
1. Cabinet officers 2. Statesmen 3. United States—Foreign relations
ISBN 0-531-11264-0 LC 95-49390
"This book examines the contributions of 12 Secretaries of State ranging from James Madison, who arranged the Louisiana Purchase, to Henry Kissinger. . . . Dolan and Scariano begin each chapter with a brief biographical introduction and then describe how the Secretary made some change in either the size of the country or its relations with other nations. The authors are positive about the men and their accomplishments and do not discuss more critical interpretations of their actions." SLJ
Includes bibliographical references

Lindop, Edmund
Panama and the United States; divided by the Canal. 21st Cent. Bks. (NY) 1997 127p il maps lib bdg $22.40 (7 and up) **327.73**
1. United States—Foreign relations—Panama 2. Panama—Foreign relations—United States 3. Panama Canal
ISBN 0-8050-4768-9 LC 96-40948
Discusses foreign policy issues between the United States and Panama, specifically regarding the Canal
"A well-written, balanced survey of the often turbulent relationship between the two countries." SLJ
Includes bibliographical references

Pascoe, Elaine
Mexico and the United States; cooperation and conflict. 21st Cent. Bks. (NY) 1996 126p il map lib bdg $22.40 (7 and up) **327.73**
1. United States—Foreign relations—Mexico 2. Mexico—Foreign relations—United States
ISBN 0-8050-4180-X LC 96-11430
This discussion of the relationship between the two nations focuses on political, economic and environmental issues as well as immigration and drug trafficking
"The strong narrative and balanced point of view recommend the text to students needing more information about Mexico-U.S. relations than textbooks normally can supply." Booklist
Includes bibliographical references

Warren, James A.
Cold War; the American crusade against world communism, 1945-1991. Lothrop, Lee & Shepard Bks. 1996 288p il $16 (7 and up) **327.73**
1. Cold war 2. World politics—1945-1991 3. United States—Foreign relations—Soviet Union 4. Soviet Union—Foreign relations—United States
ISBN 0-688-10596-3 LC 94-24554
This overview of the cold war both at home and abroad covers topics ranging from the Truman Doctrine and the Korean War to the destruction of the Berlin Wall in 1989
"An exceptionally intelligent and measured look at the forces driving American foreign policy during the latter half of the 20th century." SLJ
Includes bibliographical references

328.73 The legislative process in the United States

Christianson, Stephen G.
Facts about the Congress; with an introduction by Richard Allan Baker. Wilson, H.W. 1996 xxvii, 635p il $65 (7 and up) **328.73**
1. United States. Congress 2. United States—Politics and government
ISBN 0-8242-0883-8 LC 95-53691
This volume describes "the structure, function, and history of both houses of the U.S. Congress. An opening section discusses how the Congress operates in the passage of legislation, including the details of its committee and subcommittee structure, leadership and seniority, and relations with the President. The main part of the book consists of chapters devoted to the activities of every Congress, from the First (1789-1791) to the One Hundred Fourth (1995)." Publisher's note
Includes glossary and bibliographical references

Pollack, Jill S.
Women on the Hill; a history of women in Congress. Watts 1996 207p il (Women then—women now) lib bdg $24 (7 and up) **328.73**
1. United States. Congress 2. Women in politics
ISBN 0-531-11306-X LC 96-33831
Describes the historic, ongoing struggle of women to find equal representation in national politics, including short biographies of prominent Congresswomen, an analysis of special roles of women in Congress, and a summary of how that legislative body works
This is "well documented and thorough in scope." Booklist
Includes bibliographical references

330.973 United States—Economic conditions

The **Industrial** revolution: opposing viewpoints; William Dudley, editor. Greenhaven Press 1998 282p il (American history series) lib bdg $26.20; pa $16.20 (7 and up) **330.973**
1. Industrial revolution 2. United States—Economic conditions
ISBN 1-56510-707-1 (lib bdg); 1-56510-706-3 (pa) LC 97-48274

The Industrial revolution: opposing viewpoints—*Continued*

"This anthology traces the evolution of the United States from a collection of small agricultural colonies to an industrial giant—a development that radically changed how Americans worked and lived. The views of industrialists, labor organizers, and social critics of industrialism are featured." Publisher's note

Includes bibliographical references

Meltzer, Milton, 1915-

Brother, can you spare a dime? the Great Depression, 1929-1933; illustrated with contemporary prints & photographs. Facts on File 1991 130p il maps (Library of American history) $19.95 (7 and up)   **330.973**

1. United States—Economic conditions—1919-1933 2. Great Depression, 1929-1939 3. United States—Social conditions

ISBN 0-8160-2372-7   LC 90-39760

First published 1969 by Knopf

"Meltzer focuses on the human reactions to the events of the Great Depression, and as such, draws heavily on first-hand accounts of those who experienced them." SLJ

"Young people reading the narratives and essays here can begin to understand the importance and relevance of this time in history." Voice Youth Advocates

Includes bibliographical references

331.2 Conditions of employment

Prior, Katherine

Workers' rights. Watts 1997 46p il (What do we mean by human rights?) lib bdg $22   **331.2**

1. Employees—Civil rights

ISBN 0-531-14434-8   LC 96-42445

Focuses on this one area of human rights, and considers how employee rights have been established, and how they work, or are overlooked, in societies around the world

This offers "thought-provoking examples, drawn from a broad international and historical spectrum." Horn Book Guide

Includes glossary

331.3 Workers by age group

Bartoletti, Susan Campbell, 1958-

Growing up in coal country. Houghton Mifflin 1996 127p il $16.95; pa $7.95   **331.3**

1. Children—Employment 2. Coal mines and mining

ISBN 0-395-77847-6; 0-395-97914-5 (pa)

LC 96-3142

This is an "account of working and living conditions in Pennsylvania coal towns. The first half of the volume details various duties in the mines, from jobs performed by the youngest boys to the tasks of adult miners, while the second half describes the company village, common customs and recreational activities, and the accidents and diseases that frequently beset the workers." Horn Book

"With compelling black-and-white photographs of children at work in the coal mines of northeastern Pennsylvania about 100 years ago, this handsome, spacious photo-essay will draw browsers as well as students doing research on labor and immigrant history." Booklist

Includes bibliographical references

Freedman, Russell

Kids at work; Lewis Hine and the crusade against child labor; with photographs by Lewis Hine. Clarion Bks. 1994 104p il $18; pa $9.95

331.3

1. Hine, Lewis Wickes, 1874-1940 2. Children—Employment

ISBN 0-395-58703-4; 0-395-79726-8 (pa)

LC 93-5989

"Using the photographer's work throughout, Freedman provides a documentary account of child labor in America during the early 1900s and the role Lewis Hine played in the crusade against it. He offers a look at the man behind the camera, his involvement with the National Child Labor Committee, and the dangers he faced trying to document unjust labor conditions." SLJ

Freedman "does an outstanding job of integrating historical photographs with meticulously researched and highly readable prose." Publ Wkly

Includes bibliographical references

Gay, Kathlyn

Child labor; a global crisis. Millbrook Press 1998 128p il lib bdg $21.40 (7 and up)   **331.3**

1. Children—Employment

ISBN 0-7613-0368-5   LC 98-17670

Examines child-labor practices throughout the world within a historical context and discusses ways of dealing with the problem

"As chapter after chapter describes cruelty, deception, and greed, it becomes clear that exploiters prey on the poorest people, particularly in poor countries. . . . Gay's treatment is balanced in its historical and economic perspectives and reasoned in its approach to solutions." SLJ

Includes bibliographical references

Gourley, Catherine, 1950-

Good girl work; factories, sweatshops, and how women changed their role in the American workforce. Millbrook Press 1999 96p il lib bdg $22.40   **331.3**

1. Children—Employment 2. Women—Employment

ISBN 0-7613-0951-9   LC 98-35529

Discusses the girls and women in the industrial workforce of the nineteenth and early twentieth centuries, and the reforms and movements that changed their working conditions and the nature of the work itself

"A well-organized overview of girls' and women's struggles in the workplace." Bull Cent Child Books

Includes bibliographical references

Kuklin, Susan

Iqbal Masih and the crusaders against child slavery. Holt & Co. 1998 133p il $16.95 (7 and up)   **331.3**

1. Masih, Iqbal, d. 1995 2. Children—Employment

ISBN 0-8050-5459-6   LC 98-5100

Kuklin, Susan—*Continued*

An account of the former Pakistani child labor activist whose life and unexplained murder has brought to the attention of the world the evil of child bondage

"Kuklin's thorough research makes this an excellent resource for anyone interested in child welfare issues. The names, addresses, and Web sites of many child labor information sources are provided, along with how to contact various activists groups and heads of state. . . . This book belongs in every library." Voice Youth Advocates

Includes glossary and bibliographical references

Meltzer, Milton, 1915-

Cheap raw material. Viking 1994 167p il $15.99 (7 and up)   **331.3**

1. Children—Employment

ISBN 0-670-83128-X   LC 93-31478

A "discourse on child labor which starts with a history of practices including slavery, servitude, apprenticeship, and the early period of industrialization. [The author] moves next to the recent child labor abuses cited in fast-food chains, farming, and industrial home work. . . . Although Meltzer tries to prove, through example, systemic and systematic abuse and exploitation of child workers in this country and worldwide, he succeeds primarily when he talks of farm laborers and children in less regulated countries such as India and Mexico. . . . Meltzer's research is commendable and his sources are well documented." Bull Cent Child Books

Parker, David L., 1951-

Stolen dreams; portraits of working children; by David L. Parker with Lee Engfer and Robert Conrow; photographs by David L. Parker. Lerner Publs. 1998 112p il map lib bdg $14.95   **331.3**

1. Children—Employment

ISBN 0-8225-2960-2   LC 97-4939

Photographs and text document working children especially in Nepal, India, Bangladesh, and Mexico. Includes a chapter on Iqbal Masih, the child labor activist from Pakistan

"This hard-hitting exploration, set in a handsome volume, is a sobering reflection on contemporary childhood." Horn Book Guide

Includes bibliographical references

Springer, Jane

Listen to us; the world's working children. Douglas & McIntyre; distributed by Publishers Group West 1997 96p il $24.95; pa $16.95 (7 and up)   **331.3**

1. Children—Employment

ISBN 0-88899-291-2; 0-88899-307-2 (pa)

This "photo-essay looks at the hazardous work children do in developing and industrialized countries, in agriculture, industry, the home, the military, on the street, and in sex work. . . . There are easy-to-read sidebars, charts, and maps, but it is the personal accounts that have the most authority. The pictures of small brickmakers, garbage pickers, migrant workers, and bonded laborers are heartbreaking, and the voices are authentic." Booklist

Includes glossary and bibliographical references

331.4 Women workers

Colman, Penny

Rosie the riveter; women working on the home front in World War II. Crown 1995 120p il $19; lib bdg $20.99; pa $10.99   **331.4**

1. Women—Employment 2. World War, 1939-1945—United States

ISBN 0-517-59790-X; 0-517-59791-8 (lib bdg); 0-517-88567-0 (pa)   LC 94-3614

"Setting her study in the context of political events and using as her focus a real person—a young girl named Dot Chastney—Colman evokes the lifestyle of the era from a child's perspective. Black-and-white photographs of women in traditional male occupations, from assembly-line worker to physicist, underscore the diversity of opportunities that were made available. A thoughtfully prepared look at women's history and wartime society." Horn Book Guide

Includes bibliographical references

Dash, Joan

We shall not be moved; the women's factory strike of 1909. Scholastic 1996 165p il $15.95; pa $5.99 (7 and up)   **331.4**

1. Women—Employment 2. Labor unions 3. Strikes

ISBN 0-590-48409-5; 0-590-48410-9 (pa)

LC 95-19404

Describes the conditions that gave rise to efforts to secure better working conditions for the women working in the garment industry in early twentieth-century New York and led to the formation of the Women's Trade Union League and the first women's strike in 1909

"Dash brings a novelist's skill to her descriptions of Lower East Side streets, and she conveys the general excitement of the movement by focusing on key individuals, memorably presenting them as impassioned agents for social change." Publ Wkly

Includes bibliographical references

Working women: opposing viewpoints; Mary E. Williams, book editor; Brenda Stalcup, Karin L. Swisher, assistant editors. Greenhaven Press 1998 186p il lib bdg $26.20; pa $16.20 (7 and up)   **331.4**

1. Women—Employment

ISBN 1-56510-677-6 (lib bdg); 1-56510-676-8 (pa)

LC 97-27517

"Opposing viewpoints series"

A collection of essays discussing opposing viewpoints on such issues as the effects of women's increased participation in the work force, discrimination against female workers, sexual harassment, and women in the military

Includes bibliographical references

331.5　Special categories of workers other than by age or sex

Atkin, S. Beth
Voices from the fields; children of migrant farmworkers tell their stories; interviews and photographs by S. Beth Atkin. Little, Brown 1993 96p il $17.95; pa $12.95　　**331.5**
1. Migrant labor 2. Agricultural laborers 3. Mexican Americans 4. Children's writings
ISBN 0-316-05633-2; 0-316-05620-0 (pa)
　　　　　　　　　　　　　　　　LC 92-32248
"Joy Street books"
Photographs, poems in Spanish and English, and interviews with children reveal the hardships and hopes of Mexican American migrant farm workers and their families
"Accessible and revealing, the oral histories will have an immediate and profound impact. Illustrated with black-and-white photographs, the book, which will fill both curriculum and current information needs, gives a voice to children who are rarely acknowledged and even more rarely heard." Booklist
Includes bibliographical references

331.7　Labor by industry and occupation

Career discovery encyclopedia. Ferguson, J.G. 8v set $139.95　　**331.7**
1. Vocational guidance 2. Occupations

Also available CD-ROM version
First published 1990. (4th edition 2000) periodically revised
"The entries for occupations in this set are two pages in length and describe the work, preparation, current salaries and demand. There is a picture of a person engaged in the occupation and a list of addresses to write to for more information. There is a general index and an index to skill requirements. The information is presented clearly and is appropriate for upper elementary and middle school students." Safford. Guide to Ref Materials for Sch Libr Media Cent. 5th edition

The **Encyclopedia** of careers and vocational guidance; William E. Hopke, editor-in-chief. Ferguson, J.G. 4v il set $159.95　　**331.7**
1. Occupations 2. Vocational guidance

Also available CD-ROM version
First published 1967. (11th edition 1999) Periodically revised
"Entries describe educational and training requirements, duties, salaries, and prospects. Each volume contains a complete index of the job titles in all four volumes; v. 4 has an index of jobs by *Dictionary of occupational titles* number. . . . Appendixes list organizations that assist in training and job placement for disabled and other special groups and provide information on internships, apprenticeships, and special training programs." Guide to Ref Books. 11th edition

Professional & technical careers; a guide from World Book. World Bk. 1998 496p il $35 (7 and up)　　**331.7**
1. Vocational guidance 2. Occupations
ISBN 0-7166-3311-6　　　　　　　　LC 97-20404
Includes advice on identifying personal skills and goals, an overview of career families such as Accountancy and Audit, and an A-Z section on main careers
"The information is valuable. . . . The extensive index is helpful." SLJ
Includes bibliographical references

Unger, Harlow G., 1931-
But what if I don't want to go to college; a guide to success through alternative education. rev ed. Facts on File 1998 216p il $22.95; pa $12.95 (7 and up)　　**331.7**
1. Occupational training 2. Vocational education 3. Vocational guidance
ISBN 0-8160-3793-0; 0-8160-3861-9 (pa)
　　　　　　　　　　　　　　　　LC 97-50278
First published 1992
The author describes "opportunities available to young adults through alternative and vocational education. . . . [This] discusses the kinds of positions available; explores the minimum education needed to land that first, most important job; and examines positions available for those with special skills and abilities." Publisher's note

United States. Bureau of Labor Statistics
Occupational outlook handbook. U.S. Govt. Ptg. Office il $22.95; pa $18.95　　**331.7**
1. Occupations 2. Vocational guidance
　　　　　　　　　　　　　　　　LC 49-6
Biennial. First published 1949. Supplemented by Occupational Outlook Quarterly, subscription $9.50
"Gives information on employment trends and outlook in more than 800 occupations. Indicates nature of work, qualifications, earnings and working conditions, how to enter, where to go for more information, etc." Guide to Ref Books. 11th edition

331.8　Labor unions and labor-management relations

Bartoletti, Susan Campbell, 1958-
Kids on strike! Houghton Mifflin 1999 208p il $20　　**331.8**
1. Strikes 2. Children—Employment
ISBN 0-395-88892-1　　　　　　　　LC 98-50575
Describes the conditions and treatment that drove workers, including many children, to various strikes, from the mill workers strikes in 1828 and 1836 and the coal strikes at the turn of the century to the work of Mother Jones on behalf of child workers
"This well-researched and well-illustrated account creates a vivid portrait of the working conditions of many American children in the 19th and early 20th centuries." SLJ
Includes bibliographical references

Stanley, Jerry, 1941-
Big Annie of Calumet; a true story of the Industrial Revolution. Crown 1996 102p il maps $19; lib bdg $19.99 **331.8**
1. Clemenc, Ana K., 1888-1956 2. Labor movement 3. Strikes
ISBN 0-517-70097-2; 0-517-70098-0 (lib bdg)
LC 95-18856
"This is the story of the copper miners of Calumet, Michigan, and their bloody strike against the C & H Mining Company in 1913. Stanley . . . provides background with a discussion of the Industrial Revolution and exploitation of working people and immigrants. The workers in Calumet finally opted for defiance when the company instituted the one-man drill, known as the 'widow maker,' in the mines. Annie Clemenc, daughter and wife of miners, was the leader of the feminine opposition." Book Rep
"The documentary evidence and numerous archival photographs of places, people, and events support the readable presentation." SLJ
Includes bibliographical references

332.024 Personal finance

Godfrey, Neale S.
Neale S. Godfrey's ultimate kids' money book; illustrated by Randy Verougstraete. Simon & Schuster Bks. for Young Readers 1998 122p il $18
332.024
1. Personal finance 2. Money
ISBN 0-689-81717-7 LC 97-35433
Provides an overview of economics and money, including earning, spending, saving, checks and credit cards, banks, and the history of money
"Facts, fables, advice, strategies, games, history, vocabulary, and more are energetically packaged with cartoon art, photos, and archival documents in this exciting treatment of money and economics for kids. The eye-catching pages playfully combine bold colors and varied sizes of print with lighthearted illustrations and commendably cogent text." Booklist
Includes glossary

Guthrie, Donna, 1946-
Real world math; money, credit, & other numbers in your life; [by] Donna Guthrie and Jan Stiles; illustrations by Robyn Kline. Millbrook Press 1997 128p il lib bdg $24.40 (7 and up)
332.024
1. Personal finance
ISBN 0-7613-0251-4 LC 97-1092
A guide outlining how math is used in everyday situations such as banking, using credit, and buying a car. Offers tips on ways to avoid problems with money
This book "is filled with sound advice, fun tips, and important and accurate information." Voice Youth Advocates
Includes bibliographical references

Otfinoski, Steven, 1949-
The kid's guide to money; earning it, saving it, spending it, growing it, sharing it. Scholastic 1996 128p il $12.95; pa $4.95 **332.024**
1. Personal finance
ISBN 0-590-53850-0; 0-590-53853-5 (pa)
LC 95-38767
After presenting "moneymaking ideas, Otfinoski covers budgeting and standard consumer advice. Other useful information includes the difference between simple and compound interest; a succinct explanation of stocks, bonds, and mutual funds; and the three golden rules of using a credit card. A chapter on sharing encourages charitable giving of both cash and personal effort." SLJ
"A concise, very useful and accessible guide to handling personal finances that covers a lot of ground." Voice Youth Advocates
Includes glossary and bibliographical references

332.4 Money

Cribb, Joe
Money. Knopf 1990 63p il (Eyewitness books) $19; lib bdg $20.99 **332.4**
1. Money
ISBN 0-679-80438-2; 0-679-90438-7 (lib bdg)
LC 89-15589
Examines, in text and photographs, the symbolic and material meaning of money, from shekels, shells, and beads to gold, silver, checks, and credit cards. Also discusses how coins and banknotes are made, the value of money during wartime, and how to collect coins

333.7 Natural resources and energy

Conserving the environment; Laura K. Egendorf, book editor. Greenhaven Press 1999 208p (Current controversies) lib bdg $26.20; pa $16.20 (7 and up) **333.7**
1. Environmental protection
ISBN 1-56510-951-1 (lib bdg); 1-56510-950-3 (pa)
LC 98-35009
This offers opposing viewpoints on such issues as whether or not an environmental crisis exists, preserving biodiversity, reducing pollution, and whether or not free-market solutions are effective in protecting the environment
Includes bibliographical references

Macmillan encyclopedia of the environment; general editor, Stephen R. Kellert; associate editors, Matthew Black, Richard Haley. Macmillan Lib. Ref. USA; Prentice-Hall Int. 1997 6v il maps set $300 **333.7**
1. Environmental protection—Encyclopedias 2. Ecology—Encyclopedias
ISBN 0-02-897381-X LC 96-29045
"These volumes provide a snapshot of the current state of the environment and human efforts to exploit or protect it. Types of pollution, environmental law and regulation, and the interaction of human populations with the environment are just some of the topics covered in this

Macmillan encyclopedia of the environment—
Continued
excellent set. Useful appendixes list major environmental legislation, organizations, and U.S. governmental agencies with environmental responsibilities, while outstanding indexing facilitates access. Lavishly illustrated, the encyclopedia will appeal to students and laypersons interested in environmental topics, legislation, ecology, and evolution." Am Libr

Malaspina, Ann, 1957-
Saving the American wilderness. Lucent Bks. 1999 96p il (Our endangered planet) lib bdg $35.92   **333.7**
1. Wilderness areas 2. Conservation of natural resources
ISBN 1-56006-505-2   LC 98-31959
Discusses saving the American wilderness, including preservation and conservation, environmental activism, recreation in the wilderness, and the future of wilderness management
Includes bibliographical references

Netzley, Patricia D.
Issues in the environment. Lucent Bks. 1998 95p il (Contemporary issues) lib bdg $22.45 (7 and up)   **333.7**
1. Environmental protection 2. Environmental policy—United States
ISBN 1-56006-475-7   LC 97-25894
"This book looks at our government's environmental policies regarding the protection of endangered species, management of federal wilderness areas, and the disposal of garbage. . . . Netzley concludes with a short discussion of the ozone layer. . . . This title could be useful for balance and support in libraries serving students researching these controversial questions." SLJ
Includes bibliographical references

333.79   Energy

Parker, Steve
Fuels for the future. Raintree Steck-Vaughn Pubs. 1998 48p il maps (Protecting our planet) $25.68   **333.79**
1. Fuel 2. Energy resources
ISBN 0-8172-4937-0   LC 97-17983
First published 1997 in the United Kingdom
Describes the availability and uses of various fuels including petrol, diesel, gas, wood, and coal, and discusses the future prospects of these as power resources
This book "is loaded with a wealth of information, wonderful color photographs, and easy-to-read charts, graphs, and maps. The information is clear and concise." Voice Youth Advocates
Includes glossary and bibliographical references

333.95   Biological resources

The **Atlas** of endangered species; editor, John A. Burton; pictures supplied by Bruce Coleman Ltd. 2nd ed. Macmillan Lib. Ref. USA 1999 272p il maps $125   **333.95**
1. Endangered species 2. Wildlife conservation 3. Environmental protection
ISBN 0-02-865034-4   LC 98-44328
First published 1991
Describes the various animals and plants throughout the world whose survival is being threatened and the steps being taken to save them from extinction
Includes bibliographical references

Nagel, Rob
Endangered species. U.X.L 1999 3v il set $84
                                                          333.95
1. Endangered species—Encyclopedias
ISBN 0-7876-1875-6   LC 98-34259
Contents: v1 Mammals; v2 Arachnids, birds, crustaceans, insects, and mollusks; v3 Amphibians, fish, plants, and reptiles
Entries on 200 extinct, endangered, vulnerable, and threatened animals and plants describe the individual species, its habitat and current distribution, and efforts to protect and preserve it
"This reference set is easy to use, pleasant to look at, and comprehensive in its coverage of the subject." Voice Youth Advocates

Patent, Dorothy Hinshaw
Biodiversity; photographs by William Muñoz. Clarion Bks. 1996 109p il $17.95   **333.95**
1. Biological diversity 2. Nature conservation
ISBN 0-395-68704-7   LC 95-49982
Provides a global perspective on environmental issues while demonstrating the concept which encompasses the many forms of life on earth and their interdependence on one another for survival
"Patent imbues her lucid scientific discussion with many examples of her personal experience both in childhood and as an adult, and she employs a wide array of examples from many parts of the world to demonstrate current problems and scientific and conservation activity. Illustrated with plentiful and helpful photos." Horn Book
Includes glossary

Roberts, Russell, 1953-
Endangered species. Lucent Bks. 1999 95p il maps (Our endangered planet) $22.45   **333.95**
1. Endangered species 2. Wildlife conservation 3. Human influence on nature
ISBN 1-56006-191-X   LC 98-15038
Discusses various aspects of endangered species, including causes of extinction, land use, protection laws, and the race to prevent more extinctions
Includes bibliographical references

Swinburne, Stephen R.
Once a wolf; how wildlife biologists fought to bring back the gray wolf; with photographs by Jim Brandenburg. Houghton Mifflin 1999 48p il $16
333.95
1. Wolves 2. Wildlife conservation
ISBN 0-395-89827-7   LC 98-16865
Surveys the history of the troubled relationship between wolves and humans, examines the view that these predators are a valuable part of the ecosystem, and describes the conservation movement to restore them to the wild
The "crisp color photographs showing wolves in their natural environment are exceptional. Swinburne's text adds suspense and excitement to the story. . . . This is an involving study of an attempt to restore an altered ecosystem, an ongoing experiment the description of which makes fascinating reading." Bull Cent Child Books
Includes bibliographical references

336.3 Public borrowing, debt, expenditure

Sandak, Cass R., 1950-
The national debt. 21st Cent. Bks. (NY) 1996 63p il (Inside government) lib bdg $18.90 **336.3**
1. Public debts 2. United States—Economic policy
ISBN 0-8050-3423-4   LC 95-40737
Examines the budget process, government spending, tax system, and other aspects of the current federal debt problems in the United States
This is "clear, concise, and readable." SLJ
Includes glossary and bibliographical references

338 Production

McCormick, Anita Louise
The industrial revolution in American history. Enslow Pubs. 1998 128p il (In American history) lib bdg $19.95   **338**
1. Industrial revolution
ISBN 0-89490-985-1   LC 97-23479
Traces the history of the industrial revolution from its roots in eighteenth-century England, through its beginnings in the United States, to its decline in the twentieth-century
"This book competently surveys the topic. . . . The illustrations include black-and-white reproductions of period photos, portraits, and documents." Booklist
Includes bibliographical references

338.5 General production economics

Fremon, David K.
The Great Depression in American history. Enslow Pubs. 1997 128p il (In American history) lib bdg $19.95   **338.5**
1. Great Depression, 1929-1939 2. United States—Economic conditions—1933-1945
ISBN 0-89490-881-2   LC 96-34289

Describes the history surrounding the Great Depression, highlighting the causes and key figures
Includes bibliographical references

Ross, Stewart
Causes and consequences of the Great Depression. Raintree Steck-Vaughn Pubs. 1998 80p il (Causes and consequences) lib bdg $27.11 (7 and up)   **338.5**
1. Great Depression, 1929-1939
ISBN 0-8172-4059-4   LC 97-26532
Examines the reasons for the Great Depression, the events that happened during that period, and some of its tragic consequences
This offers an "attractive, well-organized layout, crisp prose, and informative, captioned archival illustrations." SLJ
Includes glossary and bibliographical references

342 Constitutional and administrative law

Alonso, Karen
Schenck v. United States; restrictions on free speech. Enslow Pubs. 1999 128p il (Landmark Supreme Court cases) lib bdg $19.95 (7 and up)
342
1. Schenck, Charles 2. Freedom of speech
ISBN 0-7660-1089-9   LC 98-34010
Describes the landmark case which limited free speech in cases of "clear and present danger" to national security, as well as later cases which continued working out the limits of freedom of speech
Includes glossary and bibliographical references

Cate, Fred H.
The Internet and the First Amendment; schools and sexually explicit expression. Phi Delta Kappa Educ. Foundation 1998 103p pa $12   **342**
1. Freedom of speech 2. Internet 3. Computer networks
ISBN 0-87367-398-0   LC 97-75653
The author provides "a legal history of First Amendment rights, particularly as pertaining to the Internet and minors. He identifies the legal issues surrounding minors' access to sexually explicit material and discusses the ramifications of controlling and regulating that access, citing many court rulings and statutes." SLJ

Collier, Christopher, 1930-
Creating the Constitution, 1787; [by] Christopher Collier, James Lincoln Collier. Benchmark Bks. (Tarrytown) 1999 95p il maps (Drama of American history) $28.50   **342**
1. United States. Constitutional Convention (1787) 2. Constitutional history—United States 3. United States—Politics and government—1783-1809
ISBN 0-7614-0776-6   LC 97-1788

Collier, Christopher, 1930-—*Continued*

Examines the events and personalities involved in creating the Constitution of the United States in 1787

"Most spreads are brightened by at least one illustration, a painting or print from the period, a photo of a site or artifact, or a map. Useful for school reports and surprisingly readable." Booklist

Includes bibliographical references

The **Constitution** and its amendments; Roger K. Newman, editor in chief. Macmillan Lib. Ref. USA 1998 4v set $225   342

1. United States. Constitution 2. Constitutional history—United States 3. Constitutional law—United States

ISBN 0-02-864858-7   LC 98-8570

Provides a chronological history of the Constitution's seven articles and twenty-seven amendments to date, placing them in the context of the social, political, and judicial events that formed them, and examining contemporary issues and court cases where constitutional interpretation plays a key role

"This will be a useful addition to school and public libraries serving students at the middle-school level and up." Booklist

Farish, Leah

Tinker v. Des Moines; student protest. Enslow Pubs. 1997 128p il (Landmark Supreme Court cases) lib bdg $19.95 (7 and up)   342

1. Tinker, John Frederick 2. Des Moines Independent Community School District 3. Freedom of speech 4. Vietnam War, 1961-1975—Protest movements

ISBN 0-89490-859-6   LC 96-25704

Considers the landmark case that dealt with the rights of students to wear arm bands to protest U.S. involvement in the Vietnam War

Includes glossary and bibliographical references

Fireside, Harvey, 1929-

New York Times v. Sullivan; affirming freedom of the press. Enslow Pubs. 1999 128p il (Landmark Supreme Court cases) lib bdg $19.95 (7 and up)   342

1. Sullivan, L. B. 2. New York Times Company 3. Freedom of the press

ISBN 0-7660-1085-6   LC 98-36959

Describes the Supreme Court decision in the case of New York Times v. Sullivan, preventing public officials from receiving damages for false statements unless they can prove actual malice

Includes glossary and bibliographical references

Plessy v. Ferguson; separate but equal? Enslow Pubs. 1997 128p il (Landmark Supreme Court cases) lib bdg $19.95 (7 and up)   342

1. Plessy, Homer 2. Discrimination in public accommodations 3. Segregation—Law and legislation 4. United States—Race relations

ISBN 0-89490-860-X   LC 96-53651

Examines the people, events, and legal issues involved in the Supreme Court case that challenged a state's right to allow separate but equal railroad accommodations for different races

"This is the most accessible and detailed treatment of this important milestone in the African-Americans' fight for civil and social equality currently available for young people." SLJ

Includes glossary and bibliographical references

Fleischner, Jennifer

The Dred Scott case; testing the right to live free. Millbrook Press 1997 64p il map (Spotlight on American history) lib bdg $21.90   342

1. Scott, Dred, ca. 1795-1858 2. Slavery—United States

ISBN 0-7613-0005-8   LC 96-17034

This case "deals with a slave suing for his and his family's freedom based on the fact that they had been taken to live for a time in free territories. . . . In this tightly and vibrantly written volume, Fleischner clearly presents the economic and political ramifications of the legal action." SLJ

Includes bibliographical references

Herda, D. J., 1948-

The Dred Scott case; slavery and citizenship. Enslow Pubs. 1994 104p il (Landmark Supreme Court cases) lib bdg $19.95 (7 and up)   342

1. Scott, Dred, ca. 1795-1858 2. Slavery—United States

ISBN 0-89490-460-4   LC 93-22402

This volume "examines the pivotal pre-Civil War case in which a slave was denied his freedom and the Missouri Compromise was deemed unconstitutional, and it also shows the personal and historical consequences of the Supreme Court decision." Booklist

Includes bibliographical references

New York Times v. United States; national security and censorship. Enslow Pubs. 1994 104p il (Landmark Supreme Court cases) lib bdg $19.95 (7 and up)   342

1. New York Times Company v. United States 2. Pentagon Papers 3. Freedom of the press

ISBN 0-89490-490-6   LC 93-32156

This examination of the conflict between the public's right to information and the government's desire to maintain national security focuses on the New York Times decision to publish articles about the United States government's "secret war" in Cambodia and Vietnam. The author follows the case through the Supreme Court

Includes bibliographical references

January, Brendan, 1972-

The Dred Scott decision. Children's Press 1998 30p il maps (Cornerstones of freedom) lib bdg $19.50; pa $5.95   342

1. Scott, Dred, ca. 1795-1858 2. Slavery—United States

ISBN 0-516-20833-0 (lib bdg); 0-516-26457-5 (pa)
                                       LC 97-11713

Places the events relating to the 1857 Supreme Court decision regarding rights of slaves into the larger context of the conflict about slavery among the states

"Those with an interest in the case will be captivated by the account and researchers will find more than enough information for a report." SLJ

Johnson, Linda Carlson, 1949-
Our Constitution. Millbrook Press 1992 48p il (I know America) lib bdg $20.90; pa $8.95 **342**
1. Constitutional history—United States
ISBN 1-56294-090-2 (lib bdg); 1-56294-813-X (pa)
LC 91-43232
Describes the creation of the document which sets out the rules of government for our country
"This basic introduction will capture the interest of readers who may wish to pursue further related topics, such as women's suffrage and the Indian Civil Rights Act." SLJ
Includes bibliographical references

King, David C.
Freedom of assembly. Millbrook Press 1997 47p il (Land of the free) lib bdg $19.90 **342**
1. Freedom of assembly 2. Freedom of speech
ISBN 0-7613-0064-3 LC 96-21960
Focuses on freedom of assembly and its close link to freedom of expression as guaranteed by the Bill of Rights
Includes bibliographical references

McDonald, Laughlin
The rights of racial minorities; [by] Laughlin McDonald and John A. Powell; with an introduction by Norman Dorsen. Puffin Bks. 1998 185p (ACLU handbooks for young Americans) pa $9.99 (7 and up) **342**
1. Minorities—Law and legislation 2. Race discrimination—Law and legislation
ISBN 0-14-037785-9 LC 97-36594
Discussion and analysis of the rights of racial minorities, including historical perspective and relevant court decisions
"A comprehensive, informative handbook. Written in an unintimidating question-and-answer format." SLJ
Includes bibliographical references

Miller, J. Anthony
Texas v. Johnson; the flag burning case. Enslow Pubs. 1997 112p il (Landmark Supreme Court cases) lib bdg $19.95 (7 and up) **342**
1. Johnson, Gregory Lee 2. Freedom of speech
ISBN 0-89490-858-8 LC 96-34850
Covers the case of Texas v. Johnson, in which the question before the court was whether flag burning is an activity protected by the Bill of Rights
Includes glossary and bibliographical references

Morin, Isobel V., 1928-
Our changing Constitution; how and why we have amended it. Millbrook Press 1998 176p il lib bdg $22.90 (7 and up) **342**
1. Constitutional history—United States 2. Constitutional law—United States
ISBN 0-7613-0222-0 LC 97-26909
Explores the amendments that have been made to the Constitution, as well as the proposed amendments that were not passed, detailing the controversies and Supreme

Court cases that surrounded them
"Solid and readable, the text provides a surprisingly good overview of American history from a constitutional point of view." Booklist
Includes glossary and bibliographical references

Nardo, Don, 1947-
The Bill of Rights. Greenhaven Press 1998 128p il (Opposing viewpoints digests) lib bdg $22.45; pa $13.70 (7 and up) **342**
1. United States. Constitution. 1st-10th amendments 2. Civil rights
ISBN 1-56510-741-1 (lib bdg); 1-56510-740-3 (pa)
LC 97-27519
Includes an overview of the original debate over the need for a bill of rights, an exploration of some later debates about rights issues, and an appendix of original documents
Includes bibliographical references

Pevar, Stephen L.
The rights of American Indians and their tribes. Puffin Bks. 1997 225p map (ACLU handbooks for young Americans) pa $8.99 (7 and up) **342**
1. Indians of North America—Government relations
ISBN 0-14-037783-2 LC 97-20124
A history of Federal Indian policy precedes discussion of topics related to the legal rights of American Indians, including treaties; tribal self-government; hunting, fishing, and gathering rights; civil rights; and criminal jurisdiction in Indian country
"The writing is clear and straightforward, even though many of the concepts are convoluted and potentially confusing. . . . A worthwhile purchase." SLJ
Includes bibliographical references

Schleichert, Elizabeth, 1945-
The Thirteenth Amendment; ending slavery. Enslow Pubs. 1998 128p il (Constitution) lib bdg $19.95 (7 and up) **342**
1. Slavery—United States
ISBN 0-89490-923-1 LC 97-34082
Presents an overview of the history of slavery in the United States, its abolition by constitutional amendment in 1865, and the Reconstruction and its aftermath
"A title that will shed light on the efforts to reconcile past inequities in our government." SLJ
Includes bibliographical references

Vile, John R.
The United States Constitution; questions and answers. Greenwood Press 1998 316p il $39.95 (7 and up) **342**
1. United States. Constitution 2. Constitutional law—United States
ISBN 0-313-30643-5 LC 97-32008
The author examines each section of the U.S. Constitution "and provides a question-and-answer format that allows for easy explanation of a complicated document. The amendments are addressed in detail. . . . The book is easy to read and well laid out." Book Rep
Includes bibliographical references

343   Military, tax, trade, industrial law

Freedman, Suzanne, 1932-
Clay v. United States; Muhammad Ali objects to war. Enslow Pubs. 1997 112p il (Landmark Supreme Court cases) lib bdg $19.95 (7 and up)   **343**
1. Ali, Muhammad, 1942- 2. Conscientious objectors
ISBN 0-89490-855-3   LC 97-9985
Describes the trial of Muhammad Ali, the first three-time boxing Heavyweight Champion of the world, for refusing to serve in the Vietnam War
Includes bibliographical references

Levinson, Isabel Simone
Gibbons v. Ogden; controlling trade between states. Enslow Pubs. 1999 112p il (Landmark Supreme Court cases) lib bdg $19.95 (7 and up)   **343**
1. Gibbons, Thomas, 1757-1826 2. Ogden, Aaron, 1756-1839 3. Interstate commerce
ISBN 0-7660-1086-4   LC 98-34011
Describes the Supreme Court case concerning the steamboat monopoly between New York State and New Jersey, which established the right of Congress to regulate interstate commerce
Includes glossary and bibliographical references

344   Labor, social service, education, cultural law

Andryszewski, Tricia, 1956-
School prayer; a history of the debate. Enslow Pubs. 1997 104p il (Issues in focus) lib bdg $19.95 (7 and up)   **344**
1. Religion in the public schools 2. Church and state
ISBN 0-89490-904-5   LC 96-51951
"Beginning with a discussion of the concept of separation of church and state, the author discusses the Supreme Court cases and laws dealing with school prayer." Horn Book Guide
"With clear, concise language, difficult and often ambiguous concepts, such as tolerance, equal access, and separation of church and state, are delineated and elucidated." Voice Youth Advocates
Includes bibliographical references

Banfield, Susan
The Bakke case; quotas in college admissions. Enslow Pubs. 1998 128p il (Landmark Supreme Court cases) lib bdg $19.95 (7 and up)   **344**
1. Bakke, Allan Paul 2. Discrimination in education—Law and legislation
ISBN 0-89490-968-1   LC 97-21309
Provides background and discussion of the case brought by a white male student who challenged the affirmative action policy used in admitting students to the University of California medical school
Includes glossary and bibliographical references

Cary, Eve
The rights of students; [by] Eve Cary, Alan H. Levine, Janet Price. Puffin Bks. 1997 166p (ACLU handbooks for young Americans) pa $8.99 (7 and up)   **344**
1. Students—Civil rights
ISBN 0-14-037784-0   LC 97-18976
First published 1973
Explains the legal rights and obligations that pertain to students, including such topics as free public education, freedom of expression, personal appearance, corporal punishment, grades, school records, and more
Includes bibliographical references

Dudley, Mark E.
Brown v. Board of Education (1954); school desegregation. 21st Cent. Bks. (NY) 1994 96p il (Supreme Court decisions) $18.90 (7 and up)   **344**
1. Brown, Oliver 2. Topeka (Kan.). Board of Education 3. Segregation in education
ISBN 0-8050-3657-1   LC 94-21862
This is a discussion of the Supreme Court decision which ended racial segregation in public schools
"Informative, objective, well-researched." SLJ
Includes bibliographical references

Engel v. Vitale (1962); religion in the schools. 21st Cent. Bks. (NY) 1995 96p il (Supreme Court decisions) $18.90 (7 and up)   **344**
1. Engel, Stephen 2. Vitale, William J. 3. Religion in the public schools 4. Church and state
ISBN 0-8050-3916-3   LC 95-19435
The author points out that although a 1962 Supreme Court case decided that official prayers in public schools are unconstitutional, the issue of separation of church and state remains
This volume is "clearly written and well organized." SLJ
Includes bibliographical references

Fuller, Sarah Betsy
Hazelwood v. Kuhlmeier; censorship in school newspapers. Enslow Pubs. 1998 128p il (Landmark Supreme Court cases) lib bdg $19.95 (7 and up)   **344**
1. Censorship 2. Freedom of the press 3. Students—Law and legislation
ISBN 0-89490-971-1   LC 98-13336
Examines the 1988 Supreme Court case which dealt with the question of whether the censorship of student newspapers by school administrators violated the students' first amendment rights to freedom of speech and freedom of the press
"Fuller offers thought-provoking ideas. . . . Sections devoted to the Supreme Court case and residual effects of the decision are balanced, compelling, and relevant." Booklist
Includes bibliographical references

Gold, John C.
Board of Education v. Pico (1982); book banning. 21st Cent. Bks. (NY) 1994 93p il (Supreme Court decisions) $18.90 (7 and up)
344
1. Pico, Steven A. 2. Island Trees Public Schools (Levittown, N.Y.) 3. Censorship
ISBN 0-8050-3660-1   LC 94-21861
This discusses the Supreme Court decision "ensuring students the right to read what they choose. . . . [It] presents the pivotal issue and then reviews the historical context and complicated chain of legal decisions leading up to the ultimate ruling. . . . [It adds] depth and perspective to the current literature." SLJ
Includes bibliographical references

Gold, Susan Dudley
Roe v. Wade (1973); abortion. 21st Cent. Bks. (NY) 1994 95p il (Supreme Court decisions) $18.90 (7 and up)
344
1. McCorvey, Norma 2. Wade, Henry, 1914- 3. Abortion—Law and legislation
ISBN 0-8050-3659-8   LC 94-21860
"Focusing on the 1973 case of *Roe v. Wade,* this volume . . . discusses the constitutional right to abortion. Gold shows the climate of opinion in the country at the time and then traces the case from its beginnings in Texas to its argument before the U.S. Supreme Court and the written opinions of the justices to the continuing conflict in the wake of the Court's decision." Booklist
Includes bibliographical references

Hanson, Freya Ottem, 1949-
The Second Amendment; the right to own guns. Enslow Pubs. 1998 128p il (Constitution) lib bdg $18.95 (7 and up)
344
1. Firearms—Law and legislation
ISBN 0-89490-925-8   LC 97-30805
Presents an overview of the Second Amendment of the United States Constitution and examines the debate which has surrounded the right to bear arms
The author "presents an intelligent and studied case for a wide debate of the issue, and includes accounts of both sides of the argument. . . . The text is logically arranged and the illustrations add interest." SLJ
Includes glossary and bibliographical references

Romaine, Deborah S., 1956-
Roe v. Wade; abortion and the Supreme Court. Lucent Bks. 1998 112p il (Famous trials) lib bdg $22.45 (7 and up)
344
1. McCorvey, Norma 2. Wade, Henry, 1914- 3. Abortion—Law and legislation
ISBN 1-56006-274-6   LC 98-2540
A "look at the watershed case that legalized abortion. . . . While sharing a great deal of legal and historical information, Romaine manages to examine the people, events, and stories connected to the case in a way that makes the story read like a gripping courtroom drama." SLJ
Includes glossary and bibliographical references

Stevens, Leonard A., 1920-
The case of Roe v. Wade. Putnam 1996 188p $16.99 (7 and up)
344
1. McCorvey, Norma 2. Wade, Henry, 1914- 3. Abortion—Law and legislation
ISBN 0-399-22812-8   LC 96-11286
This is an "account of the events and issues surrounding, the Supreme Court's decision. Stevens's sociological and legal history of reproductive issues in this country includes the early efforts of Margaret Sanger to bring legal information about contraception to women, efforts to overturn early legislation in regard to the private behaviors of married couples, and, ultimately, the *Roe v. Wade* case, as well as its future implications." SLJ
"This is an exceptional book, replete with the names and stories of the many people associated with the landmark court decision." Booklist
Includes glossary and bibliographical references

Tackach, James
Brown v. Board of Education. Lucent Bks. 1998 111p il (Famous trials) lib bdg $22.45 (7 and up)
344
1. Brown, Oliver 2. Topeka (Kan.). Board of Education 3. Segregation in education
ISBN 1-560-06273-8   LC 97-7482
Provides a historical overview of the case that desegregated public education in the United States
"Tackach gives a compelling account of the Brown decision. . . . Enhanced by black-and-white photos and reproductions and makes good use of sidebars to present additional background." Booklist
Includes bibliographical references

Trespacz, Karen L.
Ferrell v. Dallas I.S.D.; hairstyles in schools. Enslow Pubs. 1998 128p il (Landmark Supreme Court cases) lib bdg $19.95 (7 and up)
344
1. Ferrell, L. W. 2. Dallas Independent School District (Tex.) 3. Students—Law and legislation
ISBN 0-7660-1054-6   LC 97-28930
Discusses the case in which three students in the Dallas Independent School District were suspended from school in 1966 because of their hairstyles
"Trespacz presents a highly readable account of the issues surrounding this landmark case." SLJ
Includes glossary and bibliographical references

345   Criminal law

Aaseng, Nathan, 1953-
You are the juror. Oliver Press (Minneapolis) 1997 160p (Great decisions) lib bdg $18.95   **345**
1. Trials 2. Jury
ISBN 1-88150-840-4   LC 96-53046
The reader assumes the role of a juror in eight famous trials of the twentieth century: the Lindbergh kidnapping, Sullivan v. New York Times, the Chicago Seven, Patty Hearst's trial for armed robbery, and others
"For each case, the author presents just enough information for readers to assume the role of juror, with three

Aaseng, Nathan, 1953-—*Continued*
options from which to choose. He then reveals the actual
results and analyzes the consequences. This format balances the passions of those on all sides of these cases
and allows Aaseng to present controversial views in a
palatable way." SLJ
Includes bibliographical references

Blake, Arthur
The Scopes trial; defending the right to teach.
Millbrook Press 1994 64p (Spotlight on American
history) lib bdg $21.90   **345**
1. Scopes, John Thomas 2. Evolution—Study and
teaching
ISBN 1-56294-407-X   LC 93-37018
An illustrated look at the personalities, issues and legal maneuvering involved in the 1925 trial of Tennessee
teacher John Scopes, Darwin's theory of evolution and
the argument for divine creation are discussed
Includes bibliographical references

Criminal justice: opposing viewpoints; Jill
Karson, book editor. Greenhaven Press 1998
208p il lib bdg $26.20; pa $16.20 (7 and up)
    345
1. Administration of criminal justice
ISBN 1-56510-795-0 (lib bdg); 1-56510-794-2 (pa)
     LC 98-4778
"Opposing viewpoints series"
Replaces the edition published 1993 under the
editorship of Michael D. Biskup
This collection of articles addresses such questions as
"What reforms would improve the criminal justice system? Do the rights of the accused undermine the criminal
justice system? How do sentencing laws affect the criminal justice system? How does the legal system affect the
criminal justice system?" Publisher's note
Includes bibliographical references

Gold, Susan Dudley
In re Gault (1967); juvenile justice. 21st Cent.
Bks. (NY) 1995 96p il (Supreme Court decisions)
lib bdg $18.90 (7 and up)   **345**
1. Gault, Gerald 2. Juvenile courts 3. Children—Law
and legislation
ISBN 0-8050-3917-1   LC 95-19446
Discusses the case involving fifteen-year-old Gerald
Gault and its impact on children's rights and due process
of law for juveniles
This is "clearly written and well organized." SLJ
Includes bibliographical references

Miranda v. Arizona (1966); suspects' rights.
21st Cent. Bks. (NY) 1995 96p il (Supreme Court
decisions) lib bdg $18.90 (7 and up)   **345**
1. Miranda, Ernesto
ISBN 0-8050-3915-5   LC 94-45045
On June 13, 1966, a divided Supreme Court ruled that
suspects must be informed of their rights, including the
right to remain silent and the right to counsel, before
they are questioned by the police
"Carefully detailed background notes and quotations
from lawyers, suspects, and judges are included. In a
straightforward text, the entire process is explained, as
well as the workings of the Supreme Court itself." SLJ
Includes bibliographical references

Herda, D. J., 1948-
Furman v. Georgia; the death penalty case.
Enslow Pubs. 1994 104p il (Landmark Supreme
Court cases) lib bdg $17.95 (7 and up)   **345**
1. Furman, William Henry 2. Capital punishment
ISBN 0-89490-489-2   LC 93-37512
Herda presents "the account of William Furman—con-
victed in 1967 and sentenced with the death penalty—
and his legal attempts to appeal. The story highlights the
author's goal of dealing with the issue of capital punish-
ment in the United States, including the history of capital
punishment and suspected bias according to race." Sci
Books Films
Includes bibliographical references

Hogrogian, John G.
Miranda v. Arizona; the rights of the accused;
by John Hogrogian. Lucent Bks. 1999 111p il
(Famous trials) $22.45 (7 and up)   **345**
1. Miranda, Ernesto
ISBN 1-56006-471-4   LC 98-50357
Discusses the trial Miranda v. Arizona, including the
crime, the state appeal, the Supreme Court decision, and
its lasting effects
Includes bibliographical references

Horne, Gerald
Powell v. Alabama; the Scottsboro boys and
American justice. Watts 1997 128p il (Historic
Supreme Court cases) lib bdg $24 (7 and up)
    345
1. Powell, Ozie 2. Scottsboro case
ISBN 0-531-11314-0   LC 96-33602
"Horne retells the facts of the 1932 case in which nine
young black men, some only boys, were accused by two
white women of rape, though one later recanted. . . .
The decision served as the foundation for the principle
that everyone charged with a crime in the United States
has the right to effective legal counsel. Readable and fascinating excerpts from briefs of both sides are presented,
as is the discussion of how difficult it is to establish
standards to assure the effectiveness of counsel." SLJ
Includes bibliographical references

Nardo, Don, 1947-
The Scopes trial. Lucent Bks. 1997 96p il
(Famous trials) lib bdg $22.45 (7 and up)   **345**
1. Scopes, John Thomas 2. Evolution—Study and
teaching
ISBN 1-56006-268-1   LC 96-34421
Examines the Scopes trial concerning the teaching of
evolution in public schools
This book "presents the 'trial of the century' in a
readable format with interesting archival photographs and
useful sidebars." SLJ
Includes bibliographical references

Persico, Deborah
Mapp v. Ohio; evidence and search warrants;
[by] Deborah A. Persico. Enslow Pubs. 1997 128p
il (Landmark Supreme Court cases) lib bdg $19.95
(7 and up)   **345**
1. Mapp, Dollree 2. Right of privacy
ISBN 0-89490-857-X   LC 96-21295

Persico, Deborah—*Continued*
The landmark Supreme Court case that dealt with drawing the line between legal and illegal searches of private residences and what evidence obtained from such searches is admissible in court
This "contains information useful for reports and questions for subsequent discussion." SLJ
Includes bibliographical references

New Jersey v. T.L.O.; drug searches in schools; [by] Deborah A. Persico. Enslow Pubs. 1998 128p il (Landmark Supreme Court cases) lib bdg $19.95 (7 and up)   345
1. Students—Law and legislation 2. Right of privacy
ISBN 0-89490-969-X   LC 97-38667
Details the Supreme Court case which dealt with drug searches by public school employees and debated the Fourth Amendment rights of students
"Persico's endeavor is characterized by scholarship, clarity of exposition, and succinctness." SLJ
Includes glossary and bibliographical references

Sherrow, Victoria
Gideon v. Wainwright; free legal counsel. Enslow Pubs. 1995 104p il (Landmark Supreme Court cases) lib bdg $18.95 (7 and up)   345
1. Gideon, Clarence Earl 2. Wainwright, Louie L. 3. Legal aid
ISBN 0-89490-507-4   LC 93-45981
This "volume details the genesis of the case that established the right to free legal counsel, the Supreme Court decision, and the arguments presented by the lawyers for each side. A fine addition to the thought-provoking series." Horn Book Guide
Includes bibliographical references

Tackach, James
The trial of John Brown, radical abolitionist. Lucent Bks. 1998 112p il maps (Famous trials) lib bdg $22.45 (7 and up)   345
1. Brown, John, 1800-1859 2. Abolitionists
ISBN 1-56006-468-4   LC 97-39780
Focuses on the trial of the abolitionist who was hanged for treason and murder following his attempt to capture a military arsenal and arm the slaves for revolt
"A concise, organized look at the events that led up to the raid on Harpers Ferry, John Brown's trial, and his execution." SLJ
Includes bibliographical references

Thorndike, Jonathan L., 1959-
Epperson v. Arkansas; the evolution-creationism debate. Enslow Pubs. 1999 128p il (Landmark Supreme Court cases) lib bdg $19.95 (7 and up)   345
1. Epperson, Susan 2. Evolution—Study and teaching
ISBN 0-7660-1084-8   LC 98-21605
Examines the 1968 Supreme Court case which dealt with the question of whether teaching creationism rather than evolution in schools in Arkansas was acceptable
Includes bibliographical references

Wetterer, Charles M.
The Fourth Amendment; search and seizure. Enslow Pubs. 1998 128p il (Constitution) lib bdg $19.95 (7 and up)   345
1. Right of privacy
ISBN 0-89490-924-X   LC 97-29946
Shows how the Fourth Amendment of the United States Constitution has been historically interpreted by the judicial system and presents cases which illustrate how it is currently being applied
This volume is "clearly written [and] evenhanded." Horn Book Guide
Includes glossary and bibliographical references

Wice, Paul B.
Miranda v. Arizona; "You have the right to remain silent—". Watts 1996 158p il (Historic Supreme Court cases) lib bdg $24 (7 and up)
                                                        345
1. Miranda, Ernesto
ISBN 0-531-11250-0   LC 95-45284
Wice "begins with the crime for which a young man named Ernest Miranda was accused, the rape and kidnapping of a young woman. . . . He confessed and was eventually tried and convicted. The Supreme Court ruled that since he had not been informed of his rights against self-incrimination and to have a lawyer present, the confession was invalid. The author discusses other aspects of the case, including other court cases involving self-incrimination, the opinions of the Supreme Court justices who overturned the conviction, and the interpretation of the fifth amendment of the U.S. Constitution." SLJ
Includes bibliographical references

346   Private law

Frost-Knappman, Elizabeth
Women's rights on trial; 101 historic trials from Anne Hutchinson to the Virginia Military Institute cadets; [by] Elizabeth Frost-Knappman and Kathryn Cullen-DuPont. Gale Res. 1997 xxxi, 478p il $49.95 (7 and up)   346
1. Trials 2. Women—Law and legislation
ISBN 0-7876-0384-8   LC 96-43656
"A New England Publishing Associates book"
This describes legal cases relating to women's rights from colonial times to the present. Each entry lists major facts of the trial and includes an essay discussing the case's historical significance and legal issues
"This outstanding resource will give any student of this country's judicial system or the profound changes in the legal status of American women a strong, up-to-date foundation." SLJ
Includes glossary and bibliographical references

Greenberg, Keith Elliot, 1959-
Adolescent rights; are young people equal under the law? [by] Keith Greenberg. 21st Cent. Bks. (NY) 1995 64p il (Issues of our time) $18.90 (7 and up)   346
1. Youth—Law and legislation 2. Children—Law and legislation
ISBN 0-8050-3877-9   LC 94-41753

Greenberg, Keith Elliot, 1959-—*Continued*
An illustrated overview of how the legal system has treated children in the past and discusses the rights young people have today
This is "clearly written and well rounded." SLJ
Includes glossary and bibliographical references

Jacobs, Thomas A.
What are my rights? 95 questions and answers about teens and the law. Free Spirit 1997 199p il pa $14.95 (7 and up)   **346**
1. Youth—Law and legislation
ISBN 1-57542-028-7   LC 97-8599
Provides information to help the reader understand laws, recognize responsibilities, and appreciate rights especially in relation to parents, school, job, and personal matters
"In clear, everyday language, with just a sprinkling of legal terms, Jacobs presents useful guidelines and background on a variety of topically organized concerns related to teens' rights." Booklist
Includes glossary and bibliographical references

Landau, Elaine
Your legal rights; from custody battles to school searches, the headline-making cases that affect your life. Walker & Co. 1995 84p $13.95; lib bdg $14.85 (7 and up)   **346**
1. Children—Law and legislation
ISBN 0-8027-8359-7; 0-8027-8360-0 (lib bdg)
LC 94-42718
"Beginning with the history of the treatment of children from ancient times through today, Landau goes on to discuss court cases that made headlines: the adoption of baby Jessica, the murder of Lisa Steinberg, Michael Fay's caning in Singapore, Gregory Kingsley's attempt to divorce his mother, and Kimberly May's effort to sever her ties with her biological parents." Book Rep
Includes bibliographical references

Nunez, Sandra Joseph
And justice for all; the legal rights of young people; by Sandra Joseph Nunez and Trish Marx. Millbrook Press 1997 174p il lib bdg $22.40 (7 and up)   **346**
1. Children—Law and legislation
ISBN 0-7613-0068-6   LC 96-40523
Examines various legal issues, including free speech, privacy, child labor, and discrimination, as they apply to minors
"A well-written and thoroughly researched account of the constitutional rights of young people in America." SLJ
Includes bibliographical references

Sherrow, Victoria
Cherokee Nation v. Georgia; Native American rights. Enslow Pubs. 1997 128p il (Landmark Supreme Court cases) lib bdg $19.95 (7 and up)
346
1. Indians of North America—Government relations
ISBN 0-89490-856-1   LC 96-39651

Discusses the cases brought by the Cherokee Nation and its supporters against the state of Georgia beginning in the 1830s to protect the rights of the Cherokee living there
This offers "cogently written prose." Horn Book Guide
Includes bibliographical references

346.04   Property law

Talab, Rosemary Sturdevant
Commonsense copyright; a guide for educators and librarians; by R. S. Talab. 2nd ed. McFarland & Co. 1999 292p pa $39.95   **346.04**
1. Copyright
ISBN 0-7864-0675-5   LC 99-12915
First published 1986
This volume "highlights recent copyright legislation and the impact of current copyright protection on new technologies. The text includes an entire section on 'Computer-Based Systems' detailing copyright and electronic publishing, educational multimedia, distance learning, and the Internet and World Wide Web. The accurate, well-organized guide describes the legal and ethical 'fair use' of copyrighted materials and provides the librarian and the educator with an excellent resource for dealing with current copyright issues." Libr J

347   Civil procedure and courts

Courtroom drama; 120 of the world's most notable trials; Elizabeth Frost-Knappman, Edward W. Knappman, and Lisa Paddock, editors. U.X.L 1998 3v il set $84 (7 and up)
347
1. Trials
ISBN 0-7876-1735-0   LC 97-23014
Covers 120 notable trials that occurred around the world, from Socrates to Timothy McVeigh
"The authors have done an excellent job of identifying relevant information and describing the significance of the legal process. What makes this resource so useful is the broad coverage that spans many countries and historical periods." SLJ
Includes glossary and bibliographical references

DeVillers, David
Marbury v. Madison; powers of the Supreme Court. Enslow Pubs. 1998 112p il (Landmark Supreme Court cases) lib bdg $19.95 (7 and up)
347
1. Marbury, William, 1761?-1835 2. Madison, James, 1751-1836 3. United States. Supreme Court
ISBN 0-89490-967-3   LC 97-24865
Discusses the case Marbury v. Madison in which the idea of judicial review became part of the federal government's system of checks and balances
Includes glossary and bibliographical references

Fireside, Harvey, 1929-
The Fifth Amendment; the right to remain silent. Enslow Pubs. 1998 128p il (Constitution) lib bdg $19.95 (7 and up) **347**
1. Criminal procedure
ISBN 0-89490-894-4   LC 97-33476
An overview of the Fifth Amendment of the United States Constitution, which defines and protects a citizen's rights within the legal system
Includes glossary and bibliographical references

Kraft, Betsy Harvey
Sensational trials of the 20th century. Scholastic 1998 216p il $16.95 (7 and up) **347**
1. Trials
ISBN 0-590-37205-X   LC 97-49432
Presents accounts of eight significant trials in the twentieth century, including the Scopes trial, Watergate, Brown v. the Board of Education, the Hinckley trial, and the O.J. Simpson trial
"Kraft has created a rich social, historical, and literary work neither the curious reader nor the researcher will want to put down." Booklist
Includes bibliographical references

The **Supreme** Court, A to Z; Kenneth Jost, editor. 2nd ed. Congressional Quarterly 1998 584p il (CQ's ready reference encyclopedia of American government) $95 (7 and up) **347**
1. United States. Supreme Court
ISBN 1-568-02357-X   LC 98-38585
First published 1993
"Topics covered range from abortion to zoning. Historic cases are explored and the evolution of constitutional intepretation is examined. Includes articles on the Internet and gay rights. There is also a section on how to obtain Supreme Court information online." Booklist

352.23   Chief executives

The **Presidency** A to Z; a ready reference encyclopedia; Michael Nelson, advisory editor. 2nd ed. Congressional Quarterly 1998 650p (CQ's encyclopedia of American government) $95 **352.23**
1. Presidents—United States—Encyclopedias
ISBN 1-56802-359-6   LC 98-26632
First published 1992
This reference covers such topics as the presidents' constitutional powers and elections, and describes the presidents through the Clinton administration including their backgrounds, public experiences, family lives, and lives in the White House

352.24   Cabinets and cabinet-level committees

Feinberg, Barbara Silberdick, 1938-
The cabinet. 21st Cent. Bks. (NY) 1995 64p il (Inside government) $18.90 **352.24**
1. Cabinet officers
ISBN 0-8050-3421-8   LC 94-41760

Provides a historical perspective for the development of the cabinet with heads of executive departments of government as advisers to the president
"Excellent-quality black-and-white and full-color photographs and reproductions accompany the interesting and lively text." SLJ
Includes bibliographical references

353   Specific fields of public administration

The **United** States government manual; Office of the Federal Register, National Archives and Records Administration. Superintendent of Docs. pa $45 **353**
1. United States—Politics and government—Handbooks, manuals, etc.

Annual. First published 1935. Variant title: United States government organization manual
"Official handbook of the Federal government describing the purposes and programs of most Government agencies and listing the top personnel." N Y Pub Libr. Ref Books for Child Collect. 2d edition

355   Military science

Gay, Kathlyn
After the shooting stops; the aftermath of war; [by] Kathlyn Gay and Martin Gay. Millbrook Press 1998 128p il lib bdg $21.40 (7 and up) **355**
1. War and civilization 2. United States—Military history
ISBN 0-7613-3006-2   LC 98-11387
Discusses the major social, political, and technological changes that occured in the United States as a result of various wars from the Revolution to the Gulf War
This is "an insightful, balanced, and impressively comprehensive overview of U.S. history." Booklist
Includes bibliographical references

Meltzer, Milton, 1915-
Weapons & warfare; from the stone age to the space age; illustrated by Sergio Martinez. HarperCollins Pubs. 1996 85p il lib bdg $16.89 **355**
1. Weapons 2. Military art and science
ISBN 0-06-024876-9   LC 95-48464
Highlights some weapons of war explaining how and why they were developed, various responses people have had to them, and the impact they have had upon society
"A concise, tautly written, introductory survey of an ever-popular subject. In straightforward, seemingly effortless prose, Meltzer presents readers with essential facts and figures." SLJ
Includes bibliographical references

Robertshaw, Andrew
A soldier's life; a visual history of soldiers through the ages. Lodestar Bks. 1997 48p il $16.99; pa $7.99   **355**
1. Soldiers—History
ISBN 0-525-67550-7; 0-14-130076-0 (pa)
LC 96-44309
This "photo history of soldiering features contemporary models posed in the historic garb of those who fought in the Crusades, the Civil War, the two world wars, and several other conflicts. A concise text accompanies the clear color photographs and explains the details of the various uniforms, weapons, and equipment used in each war. A time line and list of battle sites and museums are included." Horn Book Guide
Includes glossary

War: opposing viewpoints; book editor, Tamara L. Roleff. Greenhaven Press 1999 206p lib bdg $27.45; pa $17.45 (7 and up)   **355**
1. War
ISBN 0-7377-0061-0 (lib bdg); 0-7377-0060-2 (pa)
LC 98-32019
"Opposing viewpoints series"
Presents opposing viewpoints on what causes war, whether or not the international community should intervene in the world's conflicts, the role the U.S. should play in maintaining peace, and how war can be prevented
Includes bibliographical references

Worth, Richard, 1945-
Women in combat; the battle for equality. Enslow Pubs. 1999 112p il maps (Issues in focus) lib bdg $19.95 (7 and up)   **355**
1. Women in the armed forces
ISBN 0-7660-1103-8   LC 98-35034
Discusses women's changing role in the military and examines the issues related to whether or not women should be allowed to serve in combat
This "title is sure to generate much discussion and thought. . . . Reader-friendly prose makes the arguments easy to follow." Booklist
Includes glossary and bibliographical references

355.1   Military life and customs

The **Visual** dictionary of military uniforms. Dorling Kindersley 1992 64p il (Eyewitness visual dictionaries) $18.95; lib bdg $15.99
355.1
1. Military uniforms
ISBN 1-56458-010-5; 1-56458-011-3 (lib bdg)
LC 91-58206
Labeled illustrations with explanatory text show the parts of various military uniforms that have been used from ancient Roman times to the twentieth century
"The book uses beautiful color photographs of actual or reproduced military uniforms. Each uniform has been taken apart in minute detail, and all relevant parts are labeled clearly and accurately." Sci Books Films

355.7   Military installations

Day, Malcolm
The world of castles and forts. Bedrick Bks. 1996 c1995 45p il lib bdg $19.95   **355.7**
1. Castles 2. Fortification
ISBN 0-87226-278-2   LC 96-31619
First published 1995 by MacDonald Young Bks. with title: Keep out!
An illustrated history of castles and forts through the ages, from Mycenaean citadels to bomb shelters
"Fascinating reading. . . . Each chapter or subject is handled on a double-page spread with brief text and numerous colorful drawings partnered with informative captions." SLJ

Macdonald, Fiona
A Roman fort; illustrated by Gerald Wood. Bedrick Bks. 1993 48p il maps (Inside story) $18.95; pa $9.95   **355.7**
1. Fortification 2. Rome—Antiquities
ISBN 0-87226-370-3; 0-87226-259-6 (pa)
LC 93-16397
Text and illustrations describe the construction of an ancient Roman fort and the lives of the soldiers who manned it in defense of the Empire
"Full-color, detailed drawings and diagrams are an integral part of the presentation. A wealth of information can be obtained from the blocks of text and numerous cutaways showing the inside and outside of buildings." SLJ
Includes glossary

355.8   Military equipment and supplies. Weapons

Byam, Michèle
Arms & armor. Knopf 1988 63p il (Eyewitness books) $19   **355.8**
1. Weapons 2. Armor
ISBN 0-394-89622-X   LC 87-26449
A photo essay examining the design, construction, and uses of hand weapons and armor from a Stone Age axe to the revolvers and rifles of the Wild West

358   Air and other specialized forces and warfare

Weapons of mass destruction: opposing viewpoints; Jennifer A. Hurley, book editor. Greenhaven Press 1999 176p il $27.45; pa $17.45 (7 and up)   **358**
1. Weapons
ISBN 0-7377-0059-9; 0-7377-0058-0 (pa)
LC 98-43910
"Opposing viewpoints series"
Presents differing viewpoints on nuclear, chemical, and biological weapons and their possible uses by terrorists, U.S policy toward them, their use in defense, and the effectiveness of international treaties in controlling them
Includes glossary and bibliographical references

359.1   Naval life and customs

Biesty, Stephen
Stephen Biesty's cross-sections: Man-of-war; illustrated by Stephen Biesty; written by Richard Platt. Dorling Kindersley 1993 27p il $16.95
359.1
1. Great Britain. Royal Navy 2. Seafaring life 3. Ships
ISBN 1-56458-321-X   LC 92-21227
Text and cutaway illustrations depict life aboard a British warship of the Napoleonic era, covering such topics as work, leisure, discipline, navigating, and fighting
"The intriguing text, presented in brief, anecdotal notes, is accompanied by smaller drawings, making this meticulously presented book a treasure of factual content and visual imagery." Booklist
Includes glossary

361.3   Social work

Duper, Linda Leeb
160 ways to help the world; community service projects for young people. Facts on File 1996 136p lib bdg $19.95; pa $9.95   **361.3**
1. Social action 2. Volunteer work
ISBN 0-8160-3324-2; 0-8160-3503-2 (pa)
LC 95-34223
"In the nine brief chapters the author extols the virtues of community service, how young people can become involved in community projects, and gives specific examples of projects. . . . A prominent feature of this book is the helpful hints on dealing with sensitive issues, community standards, and dealing with bureaucracies." Voice Youth Advocates
Includes bibliographical references

361.6   Governmental action

Welfare reform; Charles P. Cozic, book editor. Greenhaven Press 1997 112p il (At issue) lib bdg $18.70; pa $11.20 (7 and up)   **361.6**
1. Public welfare 2. United States—Social policy
ISBN 1-56510-546-X (lib bdg); 1-56510-545-1 (pa)
LC 96-33567
"This book presents a collection of essays that juxtapose opinions of various experts in the field. A selection by The Women's Alliance entitled 'Welfare Reform is a Mistake' is opposed by Robert Rector in 'Welfare Reform is Necessary' and Michael Tanner's 'Welfare Should Be Eliminated.' Other essays deal with women and children, illegitimacy, and immigrants as recipients of welfare benefits." SLJ
Includes bibliographical references

362.1   Physical illness

Landau, Elaine
Alzheimer's disease. Watts 1996 112p il lib bdg $24 (7 and up)   **362.1**
1. Alzheimer's disease
ISBN 0-531-11268-3   LC 95-48848

"A Venture book"
"The author opens with true stories, some ending tragically, and continues with questions and answers and descriptions of the stages of the progressive disease—loss of memory, panic, paranoia, and decline in physical condition. Landau also describes treatment currently used. . . . A major part of the book discusses research concerning the cause of the illness and treatments that may help to retard its progress." Booklist
"The writing is crisp and well organized. . . . The material will be useful for reports as well as for families touched by the disease." SLJ
Includes bibliographical references

Wolf, Bernard, 1930-
HIV positive. Dutton Children's Bks. 1997 unp il $16.99   **362.1**
1. AIDS (Disease)
ISBN 0-525-45459-4   LC 96-20974
"This photo-essay describes how Sara, a 29-year-old single mother, bravely faces full-blown AIDS on a daily basis. . . . Wolf is never melodramatic or maudlin, but there are deeply affecting sections. . . . Wolf's talent and experience as a photojournalist are evident in handsome, full-color photographs and readable text." SLJ

362.28   Suicide

Suicide: opposing viewpoints; Tamara L. Roleff, book editor. Greenhaven Press 1998 192p lib bdg $26.20; pa $16.20 (7 and up)   **362.28**
1. Suicide
ISBN 1-56510-665-2 (lib bdg); 1-56510-664-4 (pa)
LC 97-6697

"Opposing viewpoints series"
Replaces the edition published 1992 under the editorship of Michael D. Biskup and Carol Wekesser
Sections of this collection of articles deal with "individual rights in regard to suicide, including the influence that Christianity has had on such thinking and actions, the causes of teen suicide, the issue of assisted suicide. . . . [The book] examines whether suicide prevention is, in fact, always appropriate. . . . The juxtaposition of popular and unpopular opinions is particularly helpful for students preparing to debate." SLJ
Includes bibliographical references

362.29   Substance abuse

Ayer, Eleanor H.
Teen smoking. Lucent Bks. 1999 112p il (Teen issues) lib bdg $22.45 (7 and up)   **362.29**
1. Tobacco habit 2. Smoking
ISBN 1-56006-442-0   LC 98-25983
This book focuses on tobacco advertising and peer influences as major causes of teen smoking and offers strategies for quitting the tobacco habit
"Peppered with insightful quotes from young smokers and nonsmokers that humanize the issue. . . . [This] will easily satisfy class assignments." Booklist
Includes glossary and bibliographical references

Chemical dependency: opposing viewpoints; Carol Wekesser, book editor. Greenhaven Press 1997 192p lib bdg $26.20; pa $16.20 (7 and up)
362.29
1. Drug abuse 2. Alcoholism
ISBN 1-56510-552-4 (lib bdg); 1-56510-551-6 (pa)
LC 96-48030
"Opposing viewpoints series"
Replaces the edition published 1991 under the editorship of Charles P. Cozic and Karin Swisher
Articles debate the following issues: How great a problem is chemical dependency? What causes chemical dependency? What treatments are effective for chemical dependency? Should drug laws be reformed?
Includes bibliographical references

Connelly, Elizabeth Russell
Through a glass darkly; the psychological effects of marijuana and hashish. Chelsea House 1999 88p il (Encyclopedia of psychological disorders) lib bdg $24.95 (7 and up) **362.29**
1. Marijuana 2. Drug abuse
ISBN 0-7910-4897-7
LC 98-34150
Examines the history, use, and mental and psychological effects of marijuana and hashish, as well as their impact on society and current treatment for their abuse
This offers "a clear presentation and description of the malady, providing a good starting point for student researchers and general information seekers." Voice Youth Advocates
Includes glossary and bibliographical references

Drug abuse: opposing viewpoints; James D. Torr, book editor; Scott Barbour, assistant editor; Jennifer A. Hurley, assistant editor. Greenhaven Press 1999 176p il lib bdg $26.20; pa $16.20 (7 and up) **362.29**
1. Drug abuse
ISBN 0-7377-0051-3 (lib bdg); 0-7377-0050-5 (pa)
LC 98-32056
"Opposing viewpoints series"
Replaces the edition published 1994 under the editorship of Karin L. Swisher
A collection of articles and speeches, book excerpts and quotations on various aspects of the drug abuse problem
Includes bibliographical references

Hanan, Jessica
When someone you love is addicted. Rosen Pub. Group 1999 64p il (Drug abuse prevention library) lib bdg $17.95 (7 and up) **362.29**
1. Alcoholism 2. Drug abuse
ISBN 0-8239-2831-4
LC 98-39622
Discusses how and why people may become addicted to drugs or alcohol, the effects such addictions can have on family members and friends, and ways to get help
This book "has a sensitive, empathetic tone without negating the harsh realities of the situation." SLJ
Includes glossary and bibliographical references

Holmes, Ann
Psychological effects of cocaine and crack addiction. Chelsea House 1999 96p il (Encyclopedia of psychological disorders) $22.95 (7 and up) **362.29**
1. Crack (Drug) 2. Cocaine 3. Drug abuse
ISBN 0-7910-4898-5
LC 98-30975
Examines the problems associated with the use of crack and other forms of cocaine, focusing on the mental and psychological disorders that can occur
Includes bibliographical references

Klein, Wendy
Drugs and denial. Rosen Pub. Group 1998 64p il (Drug abuse prevention library) lib bdg $17.95 (7 and up) **362.29**
1. Drug abuse
ISBN 0-8239-2773-3
LC 98-14709
"Focusing on the signs of addiction, the four stages of adolescent drug use, and the three components of denial, Klein suggests that teens also consider the codependency and enabling behaviors of people surrounding a drug abuser as well as methods of prevention and intervention." Booklist
Includes glossary and bibliographical references

Littell, Mary Ann
Heroin drug dangers. Enslow Pubs. 1999 64p il (Drug dangers) lib bdg $19.95 **362.29**
1. Heroin 2. Drug abuse
ISBN 0-7660-1156-9
LC 98-30743
Discusses the dangers of using heroin, its resurgence in popularity in the 1990s, some famous people who have died from heroin overdoses, and how to get help if you have a problem
Includes bibliographical references

Mass, Wendy, 1967-
Teen drug abuse. Lucent Bks. 1998 112p il (Teen issues) lib bdg $22.45 (7 and up) **362.29**
1. Drug abuse
ISBN 1-56006-196-0
LC 97-23361
Examines the problem of drug abuse among young people in the United States, discussing the various drugs that are used and why, consequences of drug use, and ways to prevent and treat this problem
Includes bibliographical references

McMillan, Daniel
Teen smoking; understanding the risks. Enslow Pubs. 1998 128p il (Issues in focus) lib bdg $18.95 (7 and up) **362.29**
1. Tobacco habit 2. Smoking
ISBN 0-89490-722-0
LC 96-36323
Focuses on the health risks associated with tobacco use, tactics employed by tobacco manufacturers, social consequences of smoking, prevention efforts, and treatment options
"The organization and presentation of material is interesting and informative without being preachy." Voice Youth Advocates
Includes bibliographical references

Monroe, Judy
Inhalant drug dangers. Enslow Pubs. 1999 64p
il (Drug dangers) lib bdg $19.95   **362.29**
1. Solvent abuse
ISBN 0-7660-1153-4   LC 98-33668
Describes the dangers of inhaling all kinds of chemical products, including paints, gasoline, aerosols, glues,
and more, and discusses the signs of inhalant abuse and
where to go for help
This offers "enough information and enough cautionary material to be worth purchasing." Booklist
Includes glossary and bibliographical references

Steroid drug dangers. Enslow Pubs. 1999 64p il
(Drug dangers) lib bdg $19.95   **362.29**
1. Steroids 2. Athletes—Drug use 3. Drug abuse
ISBN 0-7660-1154-2   LC 98-39942
Discusses the short-term and long-term effects and
dangers of steroid drug use, recounts the stories of various people who have abused them, and explains how to
get help with this problem
Includes glossary and bibliographical references

Pringle, Laurence P.
Smoking; a risky business. Morrow Junior Bks.
1996 124p il $16   **362.29**
1. Smoking 2. Tobacco habit
ISBN 0-688-13039-9   LC 96-5359
The author describes "the harmful effects of smoking
and then takes on the advertising strategies used to dis-
credit such claims. . . . The involvement of the federal
government in agricultural subsidies, and interest in tobacco as a growth industry are laid out, as well as FDA
regulations, congressional bills, and class-action suits."
SLJ
"Condemnatory but still restrained and with an excellent array of illustrations, this well-researched volume
will satisfy curiosity and be a good source for reports."
Booklist
Includes glossary and bibliographical references

Robbins, Paul R. (Paul Richard)
Crack and cocaine drug dangers. Enslow Pubs.
1999 64p il (Drug dangers) lib bdg $19.95
          362.29
1. Crack (Drug) 2. Cocaine 3. Drug abuse
ISBN 0-7660-1155-0   LC 98-30271
Examines the social, medical, and legal aspects of
crack and cocaine, the effects of their abuse, and different treatment programs
Includes glossary and bibliographical references

Schleifer, Jay
Methamphetamine; speed kills. Rosen Pub.
Group 1999 64p il (Drug abuse prevention library)
lib bdg $17.95 (7 and up)   **362.29**
1. Methamphetamine 2. Amphetamines 3. Drug abuse
ISBN 0-8239-2512-9   LC 98-45096
Discusses the drug methamphetamine, how it is used
and abused, its effects, ways to avoid drug addiction, and
how to get help for an addiction
This "has solid information." SLJ
Includes glossary and bibliographical references

Smoking; Carol Wekesser, book editor.
Greenhaven Press 1997 192p (Current
controversies) lib bdg $26.20; pa $16.20 (7 and
up)   **362.29**
1. Smoking 2. Tobacco habit
ISBN 1-56510-534-6 (lib bdg); 1-56510-533-8 (pa)
          LC 96-36098
This is a compilation of articles regarding such questions as "'Are the health risks of smoking exaggerated?';
'Is the tobacco industry to blame for leading people to
smoke?'; 'How can smoking be reduced?'; 'Are increased measures needed to combat teen smoking?'; and
'Should government regulation of smoking be increased?'
. . . A fascinating and authoritative debate on many as-
pects of a complicated subject." SLJ
Includes bibliographical references

Stewart, Gail, 1949-
Drugs and sports; [by] Gail B. Stewart.
Greenhaven Press 1998 111p il (Opposing
viewpoints digests) lib bdg $22.45; pa $13.70 (7
and up)   **362.29**
1. Athletes—Drug use
ISBN 1-56510-749-7 (lib bdg); 1-56510-748-9 (pa)
          LC 98-14610
Addresses opposing views on drugs and sports, including whether drug use is a serious problem in sports,
whether drug use should be banned, why athletes take
drugs, and if they should be tested for them
"This is a brief, lively, and informative examination of
the basic issues involving drugs and sports. It should be
especially useful to young writers of term papers." Booklist
Includes bibliographical references

Teen addicts; by Gail B. Stewart; photographs
by Carl Franzen. Lucent Bks. 2000 112p il (Other
America) lib bdg $18.96 (7 and up)   **362.29**
1. Drug abuse
ISBN 1-56006-574-5   LC 99-20820
Provides an overview of drug addiction, describes the
lives of four teenage drug addicts, and suggests ways to
get involved in fighting this social problem
"A personal look at addiction in which teens speak
powerfully for themselves. Several black-and-white photos enhance the text." Booklist
Includes bibliographical references

Tobacco and smoking: opposing viewpoints;
Tamara L. Roleff, book editor; Mary E.
Williams, book editor; Charles P. Cozic,
assistant editor. Greenhaven Press 1998 192p il
lib bdg $26.20; pa $16.20 (7 and up)   **362.29**
1. Tobacco habit 2. Smoking 3. Tobacco industry
ISBN 1-56510-803-5 (lib bdg); 1-56510-802-7 (pa)
          LC 97-51730
"Opposing viewpoints series"
"Authors in this anthology discuss the health effects of
smoking, the influence of tobacco advertising, and other
related issues." Publisher's note
Includes bibliographical references

The **War** on drugs: opposing viewpoints; Stephen P. Thompson, book editor. Greenhaven Press 1998 223p il lib bdg $26.20; pa $16.20 (7 and up)   362.29
1. Drug abuse
ISBN 1-56510-805-1 (lib bdg); 1-56510-804-3 (pa)
LC 97-52384
"Opposing viewpoints series"
Replaces the edition published 1990 under the editorship of Neal Bernards
Presents differing opinions on a range of social, political, and legal issues associated with the war on drugs including the merits of incarceration, treatment programs, drug education programs, and legalization
Includes bibliographical references

362.292   Alcoholism

Alcohol: opposing viewpoints; Scott Barbour, senior editor, book editor. Greenhaven Press 1998 218p lib bdg $26.20; pa $16.20 (7 and up)   362.292
1. Drinking of alcoholic beverages
ISBN 1-56510-675-X (lib bdg); 1-56510-674-1 (pa)
LC 97-14487
"Opposing viewpoints series"
"The four areas debated are health, industry responsibility, alcoholism treatment, and what can be done about alcohol-related problems. The previously published material taken from a variety of sources has been edited for length and accessibility. . . . A fine vehicle to help young people evaluate sources of information and hone critical-thinking skills." SLJ
Includes bibliographical references

Chiu, Christina
Teen guide to staying sober. Rosen Pub. Group 1998 64p il (Drug abuse prevention library) $16.95 (7 and up)   362.292
1. Alcoholism
ISBN 0-8239-2765-2   LC 98-16213
Discusses the social and physical effects of alcohol, the reasons teenagers drink, the problems caused by teenage alcoholism, and possible preventive measures and treatments
Includes bibliographical references

Clayton, L. (Lawrence)
Alcohol drug dangers. Enslow Pubs. 1999 64p il (Drug dangers) lib bdg $19.95   362.292
1. Alcoholism
ISBN 0-7660-1159-3   LC 98-35776
Examines the popularity and social impact of alcohol, discusses the dangers of alcohol abuse, and offers suggestions on how to get help for those with a drinking problem
"A colorful, informative guide." BAYA Book Rev
Includes bibliographical references

Miner, Jane Claypool, 1933-
Alcohol and you; [by] Jane Claypool. 3rd ed. Watts 1997 143p il (Impact books) $24 (7 and up)   362.292
1. Alcoholism
ISBN 0-531-11351-5   LC 96-49943
First published 1981
Examines the causes and consequences of use of alcohol by teenagers, problems of teenage alcoholism, and sources of help
"The text is readable, logical, and a good choice for reports." SLJ
Includes bibliographical references

Mitchell, Hayley R., 1968-
Teen alcoholism. Lucent Bks. 1998 96p il (Teen issues) lib bdg $22.45 (7 and up)   362.292
1. Alcoholism
ISBN 1-56006-514-1   LC 97-27500
Discusses the effects of alcohol on the body, the reasons teenagers drink, the problems caused by teenage alcoholism, and possible preventive measures and treatments
"Much interesting data . . . make this a multifaceted resource that students could use for personal information as well as persuasive reports." Booklist
Includes glossary and bibliographical references

Pringle, Laurence P.
Drinking; a risky business; [by] Laurence Pringle. Morrow Junior Bks. 1997 112p il $16   362.292
1. Alcoholism 2. Drinking of alcoholic beverages
ISBN 0-688-15044-6   LC 97-7807
Describes the history of alcohol, its effects on the body and personality, how to deal with peer pressure to drink, and how to get help for alcoholism
"Pringle's chapters on the history of the U.S. temperance movement and the economic side of the alcohol industry set his book apart. . . . Readable and well organized." SLJ
Includes glossary and bibliographical references

362.5   Problems of and services to the poor

Criswell, Sara Dixon, 1945-
Homelessness. Lucent Bks. 1998 112p il (Lucent overview series) lib bdg $22.45 (7 and up)   362.5
1. Homeless persons
ISBN 1-56006-180-4   LC 97-42439
Discusses the causes of homelessness, life on the streets, homeless children, the shelter system, and help for the homeless
"Criswell does justice to the complexity of the problem. . . . Well-chosen black-and-white photographs complement the text." Booklist
Includes bibliographical references

Gottfried, Ted, 1928-
Homelessness: whose problem is it? Millbrook Press 1999 128p il (Issue and debate) lib bdg $21.90 (7 and up)   **362.5**
1. Homeless persons
ISBN 0-7613-0953-5   LC 98-22484
Discusses the issue of homelessness, examining who the homeless are, how they become that way, and differing views on how to deal with the problem
"This utilitarian collection builder does what it sets out to do, giving readers a framework for developing either (or, ideally, both) written assignments or personal opinions." Booklist
Includes bibliographical references

Poverty: opposing viewpoints; Laura K. Egendorf, book editor. Greenhaven Press 1999 224p il lib bdg $26.20; pa $16.20 (7 and up)   **362.5**
1. Poverty 2. United States—Economic conditions 3. Public welfare
ISBN 1-56510-947-3 (lib bdg); 1-56510-946-5 (pa)
                                    LC 98-17866
"Opposing viewpoints series"
Replaces the edition published 1994 under the editorship of Katie de Koster
A collection of articles which present differing viewpoints on the problem of poverty in America, its causes, and possible remedies
Includes bibliographical references

Stearman, Kaye
Homelessness. Raintree Steck-Vaughn Pubs. 1999 64p il (Talking points) lib bdg $27   **362.5**
1. Homeless persons
ISBN 0-8172-5312-2   LC 98-6039
Looks at some of the causes and experiences of homelessness throughout the world and considers how societies might solve the problem and ensure every person a safe place to live
This "is distinguished by easy-to-read texts and full-color photographs laid out in an appealing format. Bold headings divide each chapter into easy-to-browse sections." SLJ
Includes glossary and bibliographical references

Stewart, Gail, 1949-
Homeless teens; by Gail B. Stewart; photographs by Carl Franzén. Lucent Bks. 1999 112p il (Other America) lib bdg $22.45 (7 and up)
                                        362.5
1. Homeless persons
ISBN 1-56006-398-X   LC 98-37997
Discusses the numbers of homeless teenagers, their situation and behavior, and looks at the lives of four of them
"The attention-grabbing stories highlight a variety of scenarios and readers are likely to develop a new understanding about the unfortunate situations that dominate the lives of these young people." SLJ
Includes bibliographical references

Welfare: opposing viewpoints; Charles P. Cozic, Paul A. Winters, book editors. Greenhaven Press 1997 208p il lib bdg $26.20; pa $16.20 (7 and up)   **362.5**
1. Public welfare 2. United States—Social policy 3. United States—Economic policy
ISBN 1-56510-520-6 (lib bdg); 1-56510-519-2 (pa)
                                    LC 96-31261
"Opposing viewpoints series"
This "book addresses whether welfare is necessary, whether it encourages dependency, if abuse of the system is a serious problem, and the question of reform. Entries include excerpts from speeches by elected officials and articles by journalists, economists, and former welfare recipients." SLJ
Includes bibliographical references

362.7 Problems of and services to young people

Blue, Rose
Staying out of trouble in a troubled family; [by] Rose Blue and Corinne J. Naden. 21st Cent. Bks. (Brookfield) 1998 112p lib bdg $21.40 (7 and up)
                                        362.7
1. Family
ISBN 0-7613-0365-0   LC 98-15625
Case studies and interviews present ways to cope with life in a troubled family, including such problems as drug abuse, divorce, child abuse, alcoholism, disability, and adoption
"Interspersed within each story are analyses by trained professionals who dignify and make comprehensible to teens the reactions of each study's central character. The comments are articulated simply but effectively." Booklist

Bode, Janet
Kids still having kids; talking about teen pregnancy; art by Stan Mack and Ida Marx Blue Spruce. rev ed. Watts 1999 159p il lib bdg $22.50
                                        362.7
1. Teenage pregnancy 2. Teenage mothers
ISBN 0-531-11588-7   LC 98-45477
First published 1992
Presents interviews with teenage mothers and provides information about adoption, parenting, abortion, and foster care
"Bode provides a valuable resource for young adults making decisions about pregnancy, as well as those researching the issue for school projects. . . . A lively design, which includes cartoon strips and snippets from current newspaper and magazine articles, adds to the dynamic presentation." Horn Book Guide
Includes bibliographical references

Child abuse: opposing viewpoints; Jennifer Hurley, book editor. Greenhaven Press 1999 206p lib bdg $26.20; pa $16.20 (7 and up)
                                        362.7
1. Child abuse
ISBN 1-56510-935-X (lib bdg); 1-56510-173-1 (pa)
                                    LC 98-16387

Child abuse: opposing viewpoints—*Continued*
"Opposing viewpoints series"
Replaces the edition published 1994 under the editorship of Katie de Koster
A collection of articles which present differing viewpoints about the causes of child abuse, false allegations of child abuse, how the legal system should deal with child molesters, and how to reduce child abuse
Includes bibliographical references

Child welfare: opposing viewpoints; Carol Wekesser, book editor. Greenhaven Press 1998 192p il lib bdg $26.20; pa $16.20 (7 and up)
                             362.7
1. Child welfare 2. Children—United States—Social conditions
ISBN 1-56510-679-2 (lib bdg); 1-56510-678-4 (pa)
                             LC 97-27518
"Opposing viewpoints series"
This collection of essays offers opposing viewpoints on such issues as illegitmacy, divorce, child support, welfare reform, parental rights, orphanages, adoption, child abuse, and role models
Includes bibliographical references

Connelly, Elizabeth Russell
Child abuse and neglect; examining the psychological components. Chelsea House 2000 93p il (Encyclopedia of psychological disorders) $24.95 (7 and up)   **362.7**
1. Child abuse
ISBN 0-7910-4955-8   LC 98-53702
Discusses the nature, history, and causes of child abuse and neglect and the impact of this problem on society
A "well-designed monograph. . . . [The] . . . narrative is supported by 20 gripping photos taken from various news and case files." Sci Books Films
Includes glossary and bibliographical references

Dean, Ruth, 1947-
Teen prostitution; by Ruth Dean and Melissa Thomson. Lucent Bks. 1998 96p il (Teen issues) lib bdg $22.45 (7 and up)   **362.7**
1. Juvenile prostitution
ISBN 1-56006-512-5   LC 97-27452
Presents an overview of the problem of teenage prostitutes, including some of the causes and consequences of this phenomenon and what can be done to prevent it
Includes glossary and bibliographical references

Edelson, Paula
Straight talk about teenage pregnancy. Facts on File 1999 136p il lib bdg $19.95 (7 and up)
                             362.7
1. Teenage pregnancy 2. Teenage mothers
ISBN 0-8160-3717-5   LC 98-7268
Explains responsible sexual behavior, the ramifications of teenage pregnancy, ways to avoid it, and methods for coping with it, including various options
"This short, easy-to-read self-help book . . . is a useful, nonjudgmental source of information for young adults. . . . The information is clear, concise, and up to date." Booklist
Includes bibliographical references

Hyde, Margaret Oldroyd, 1917-
Missing and murdered children; by Margaret O. Hyde. Watts 1998 112p il lib bdg $24 (7 and up)
                             362.7
1. Missing children
ISBN 0-531-11384-1   LC 97-23355
Discusses missing and abducted children, abused children, and murder victims, and outlines ways to prevent and cope with these increasing problems
"By blending real-life scenarios with generally well documented data, this volume employs a format that helps advance its purpose: to stir the emotions of readers who have been numbed by the overwhelming vastness of the problem." Booklist
Includes bibliographical references

The sexual abuse of children and adolescents; [by] Margaret O. Hyde and Elizabeth H. Forsyth. Millbrook Press 1997 96p lib bdg $22.40 (7 and up)   **362.7**
1. Child sexual abuse
ISBN 0-7613-0058-9   LC 96-36366
Covers the history of sexual abuse of children, effects on children, profiles of abusers, controversies surrounding the internet, Megan's law, and repressed and false memories
"Both students doing reports and victims of abuse will find this book to be highly readable, comprehensive, and useful." SLJ
Includes glossary and bibliographical references

Kaminker, Laura
Everything you need to know about being adopted. Rosen Pub. Group 1999 64p il (Need to know library) $17.95 (7 and up)   **362.7**
1. Adoption
ISBN 0-8239-2834-9   LC 98-45629
"Kaminker gives legal facts about adoption and brings up many of the problems adolescent adoptees face. . . . The author's suggestions are sensible." SLJ
Includes glossary and bibliographical references

Kuklin, Susan
After a suicide; young people speak up. Putnam 1994 121p il $16.95; pa $9.95 (7 and up)   **362.7**
1. Suicide
ISBN 0-399-22605-2; 0-399-22801-2 (pa)
                             LC 93-33141
"The book is divided into two parts. Part I is concerned with survivors who are family members, friends, and schoolmates, while Part II focuses on a person who attempted suicide and another who considered it. The addendum is comprised of two composites created from hotline calls by people who threatened suicide." Voice Youth Advocates
"With their indepth view of the cycle of events leading to suicide and the recovery, these poignant stories can move any reader toward greater understanding of the suicidal person." Libr J
Includes bibliographical references

Rue, Nancy N., 1951-
Everything you need to know about abusive relationships. Rosen Pub. Group 1996 64p il (Need to know library) lib bdg $17.95 (7 and up) **362.7**
1. Dating (Social customs)
ISBN 0-8239-2216-2   LC 95-24743
This "covers emotional, physical, and sexual abuse, with some emphasis on date rape. Advice is given to teens on how to get help, whether they are being abused or inflicting abuse." SLJ
Includes glossary and bibliographical references

Stewart, Gail, 1949-
Teen dropouts; photographs by Carl Franzén. Lucent Bks. 1999 112p il (Other America) lib bdg $17.96 (7 and up)   **362.7**
1. Dropouts
ISBN 1-56006-399-8   LC 98-27051
Uses four case studies of teenagers who dropped out of high school to explain who drops out and why and to examine the economic and social consequences of such a decision
"The teens' stories are moving, sad, and realistic. . . . Stewart's narrative is appropriate and nonjudgmental; she does an excellent job of letting the teen voices shine through." SLJ
Includes bibliographical references

Teenage pregnancy: opposing viewpoints; Stephen P. Thompson, book editor. Greenhaven Press 1997 190p lib bdg $26.20; pa $16.20 (7 and up) **362.7**
1. Teenage pregnancy 2. Teenage mothers
ISBN 1-56510-562-1 (lib bdg); 1-56510-561-3 (pa)
LC 96-48031
"Opposing viewpoints series"
A collection of articles representing varying opinions about teenage pregnancy including whether or not it is a serious problem, its causes and prevention, and possible new solutions
Includes bibliographical references

Teens at risk: opposing viewpoints; Laura K. Egendorf, book editor; Jennifer A. Hurley, book editor. Greenhaven Press 1999 190p il lib bdg $26.20; pa $16.20 (7 and up)   **362.7**
1. Teenagers
ISBN 1-56510-949-X (lib bdg); 1-56510-948-1 (pa)
LC 98-23191
"Opposing viewpoints series"
This collection of articles presents differing viewpoints about the causes, possible prevention, and remedies for such problems as teenage crime, pregnancy, and drug use
Includes bibliographical references

Warren, Andrea
Orphan train rider; one boy's true story. Houghton Mifflin 1996 80p il $16; pa $7.95
362.7
1. Nailling, Lee, 1917- 2. Orphans 3. Abandoned children
ISBN 0-395-69822-7; 0-395-91362-4 (pa)
LC 94-43688

"From 1854 to 1930, the orphan trains took homeless children from cities in the East to new homes in the West, the Midwest, and the South. In Warren's book, one man's memories of his childhood abandonment and adoption give a personal slant on the subject. Chapters telling the story of Lee Nailing, who took an orphan train west in 1926, alternate with chapters filling in background information about the trains and the experiences of other children who rode them to their destinies." Booklist
"An excellent introduction to researching or discussing children-at-risk in an earlier generation. The book is clearly written and illustrated with numerous black-and-white photographs and reproductions." SLJ
Includes bibliographical references

362.82 Problems of and services to families

Battered women; Louise Gerdes, book editor. Greenhaven Press 1999 144p (Contemporary issues companion) lib bdg $20.96; pa $12.96 (7 and up)   **362.82**
1. Abused women
ISBN 1-56510-897-3 (lib bdg); 1-56510-896-5 (pa)
LC 98-27299
The reprints and articles in this volume are "organized into four categories: the nature of violence against women, help for victims, legal issues, and personal stories of abuse and survival. . . . The personal narratives will grip readers. . . . A powerful and affecting treatment that will be of use to researching students and anyone interested in the issue." Booklist
Includes bibliographical references

Hong, Maria
Family abuse; a national epidemic. Enslow Pubs. 1997 128p (Issues in focus) lib bdg $17.95 (7 and up)   **362.82**
1. Family violence
ISBN 0-89490-720-4   LC 97-7906
Discusses many forms of family abuse, including child abuse, sexual abuse, and domestic violence
"Hong's well-written book dispels myths about the perpetrators and the victims of abuse and takes a thorough look at this disturbing national epidemic. . . . With a selection of quotes from abuse survivors making the material even more compelling, this book is far more than just 'good report material.'" Booklist
Includes bibliographical references

362.83 Problems of and services to women

Stewart, Gail, 1949-
Mothers on welfare; by Gail B. Stewart; photographs by Theodore E. Roseen. Lucent Bks. 1998 112p il (Other America) lib bdg $22.45 (7 and up)   **362.83**
1. Public welfare 2. Unmarried mothers
ISBN 1-56006-576-1   LC 97-43223

Stewart, Gail, 1949-—*Continued*
Uses first-person accounts of four women who are raising children on welfare to provide a look at the problems and concerns involved in this system
"The author does no editorializing, but allows readers to draw their own conclusions from the representative voices." Voice Youth Advocates
Includes bibliographical references

362.88   Problems of and services to victims of crimes

Faherty, Sara
Victims and victims' rights. Chelsea House 1999 111p il (Crime, justice, and punishment) lib bdg $19.95 (7 and up)   **362.88**
1. Victims of crimes
ISBN 0-7910-4308-8   LC 98-36531
Explores victims and victims' rights from various perspectives, including the psychological consequences of victimization, the divergent responses of victims seeking justice and emotional healing, and the tension between granting the wishes of victims and protecting the rights of criminal defendants
Includes bibliographical references

Zeinert, Karen
Victims of teen violence. Enslow Pubs. 1996 128p il (Issues in focus) lib bdg $19.95 (7 and up)   **362.88**
1. Victims of crimes 2. Juvenile delinquency 3. Violence
ISBN 0-89490-737-9   LC 95-42133
Relates accounts of teen violence in school, at home, among friends, and in public places, and offers information for victims about what to do and where to get help
This provides "accessible, definitive information complemented by numerous statistics, as well as actual, often harrowing, examples." SLJ
Includes bibliographical references

362.883   Problems of and services to victims of rape

Bode, Janet
Voices of rape. rev ed. Watts 1998 160p il lib bdg $22.50; pa $9.95 (7 and up)   **362.883**
1. Rape
ISBN 0-531-11518-6 (lib bdg); 0-531-15932-9 (pa)
LC 97-41225
First published 1990
This volume uses first-person accounts of both rape victims and offenders to depict the physical, psychological and legal aspects of rape and gives advice on what can be done in various situations
"A fine book." Booklist
Includes bibliographical references

Kaminker, Laura
Everything you need to know about dealing with sexual assault. Rosen Pub. Group 1998 64p il (Need to know library) lib bdg $17.95 (7 and up)   **362.883**
1. Rape
ISBN 0-8239-2837-3   LC 98-7048
Discusses the myths and facts surrounding sexual assault and rape, the physical and psychological consequences, suggests ways to stay safe, and explains what to do if sexually assaulted
Includes glossary and bibliographical references

363.1   Public safety programs

Cole, Michael D.
TWA flight 800; explosion in midair. Enslow Pubs. 1999 48p il (American disasters) lib bdg $18.95   **363.1**
1. Aircraft accidents
ISBN 0-7660-1217-4   LC 98-30265
Describes the explosion that caused TWA Flight 800 to break apart in midair, killing 230 people on July 17, 1996, and examines some possible causes for the disaster
Includes bibliographical references

363.2   Police services

Campbell, Andrea
Forensic science; evidence, clues, and investigation. Chelsea House 2000 135p il (Crime, justice, and punishment) lib bdg $19.95 (7 and up)   **363.2**
1. Forensic sciences 2. Criminal investigation
ISBN 0-7910-4950-7   LC 99-19454
Examines forensic science and how it can be used to apprehend criminals by finding clues in rug fibers, the way a bone is broken, DNA "fingerprints," and more
"A rich compilation of current criminal-investigation techniques." SLJ
Includes bibliographical references

Gaines, Ann
Private investigators and bounty hunters; [by] Ann G. Gaines; Austin Sarat, general editor. Chelsea House 1999 96p il (Crime, justice, and punishment) lib bdg $19.95 (7 and up)   **363.2**
1. Detectives 2. Crime
ISBN 0-7910-4285-5   LC 98-56198
Details the history and cases of private investigators and bounty hunters and discusses their fictional representations in novels, short stories, motion pictures, and television shows
Includes bibliographical references

Jones, Charlotte Foltz, 1945-
Fingerprints and talking bones; how real-life crimes are solved; illustrated by David G. Klein. Delacorte Press 1997 131p il $16.95   **363.2**
1. Forensic sciences 2. Criminal investigation
ISBN 0-385-32299-2   LC 96-41277

Jones, Charlotte Foltz, 1945—*Continued*
Describes the many different methods used to solve crimes including skeletal and facial reconstruction, botanical or geological information, voiceprints, and hypnosis

This book "offers concise, straightforward explanations and simple, nonsensationalized examples of how forensic techniques have been used in real cases. It is also very comprehensive." Booklist

Includes glossary and bibliographical references

Kronenwetter, Michael
The FBI and law enforcement agencies of the United States. Enslow Pubs. 1997 112p il (American government in action) lib bdg $19.95 (7 and up)   **363.2**
1. United States. Federal Bureau of Investigation
2. Law enforcement
ISBN 0-89490-746-8   LC 96-30468
Explores the diverse responsibilities and powers of various law enforcement agencies in the United States, including the FBI, the DEA, and the United States Marshals

Includes bibliographical references

Silverstein, Herma
Threads of evidence; using forensic science to solve crimes. 21st Cent. Bks. (NY) 1996 128p lib bdg $21.40 (7 and up)   **363.2**
1. Forensic sciences 2. Criminal investigation
ISBN 0-8050-4370-5   LC 96-32701
Examines ways in which science helps solve crimes using blood, teeth, teethmarks, fingerprints, eye prints, DNA, hairs, fibers, and corpses

This book "stands out for its effective writing, up-to-date coverage, and gory details." SLJ

Includes bibliographical references

Wiese, Jim, 1948-
Spy science; 40 secret-sleuthing, code-cracking, spy-catching activities for kids; illustrations by Ed Shems. Wiley 1996 120p il pa $12.95   **363.2**
1. Espionage 2. Intelligence service
ISBN 0-471-14620-X   LC 96-7019
Describes the skills, equipment, and techniques that spies use. Includes activities and experiments

Includes glossary

Wirths, Claudine G.
Coping with confrontations and encounters with the police; [by] Claudine G. Wirths, Mary Bowman-Kruhm. Rosen Pub. Group 1998 155p lib bdg $17.95 (7 and up)   **363.2**
1. Police 2. Law enforcement
ISBN 0-8239-2431-9   LC 97-19059
A practical guide to minimize risks when dealing with police officers and law enforcement procedures

This book "is well written and easy to read, and the real-life examples feel authentic." Voice Youth Advocates

Includes glossary and bibliographical references

363.3   Other aspects of public safety

Gun control: opposing viewpoints; Tamara L. Roleff, book editor. Greenhaven Press 1997 185p lib bdg $26.20; pa $16.20 (7 and up)   **363.3**
1. Gun control
ISBN 1-565-10663-6 (lib bdg); 1-565-10662-8 (pa)
    LC 96-48029
"Opposing viewpoints series"
A collection of articles representing varying viewpoints about such issues as whether or not private gun ownship is a serious threat to society, whether the constitution protects private gun ownership, whether gun ownership is an effective means of self-defense, and what measures would reduce gun violence

Includes bibliographical references

Guns and violence; Henny H. Kim, book editor. Greenhaven Press 1999 219p (Current controversies) lib bdg $27.45; pa $17.45 (7 and up)   **363.3**
1. Gun control 2. Violence
ISBN 0-7377-0065-3 (lib bdg); 0-7377-0064-5 (pa)
    LC 98-56515
Presents differing viewpoints on the seriousness of gun violence, whether or not gun control reduces crime and its constitutionality, the effectiveness of gun ownership as self defense, and what measures would reduce gun violence

Includes bibliographical references

Schwarz, Ted, 1945-
Kids and guns; the history, the present, the dangers, and the remedies. Watts 1999 128p il lib bdg $22.50 (7 and up)   **363.3**
1. Gun control 2. Violence
ISBN 0-531-11723-5   LC 98-47197
Examines the history of guns and gun use, issues of gun ownership and control, and the relationship between guns and violence involving young people

"In clear, easy-to-read language that will hold readers' attention . . . [the author] provides a solid case for gun-control legislation and what teens can and must do to help make their schools safer." Booklist

Includes bibliographical references

363.34   Disasters

Bonson, Richard
Disaster! illustrated by Richard Bonson; written by Richard Platt. DK Pub. 1997 31p il maps $15.95   **363.34**
1. Natural disasters
ISBN 0-7894-2034-1   LC 97-15423
Captioned illustrations and brief text describe such disasters as the eruption of Mount Vesuvius, the Black Death, the New York blizzard of 1888, the San Franciso earthquake of 1906, the Dust Bowl, the Sinking of The Titanic, and other natural disasters and accidents

363.4 Controversies related to public morals and customs

Hjelmeland, Andy
Legalized gambling; solution or illusion? Lerner Publs. 1998 128p il (Pro/Con) lib bdg $21.27 (7 and up)   **363.4**
1. Gambling
ISBN 0-8225-2615-8   LC 97-10336
Examines the arguments in favor of and opposed to legalized gambling, looking at various types of gambling, problems of compulsive gamblers, the lure of this activity, and more
"With impressive documentation of sources and a simple, straightforward style, this title is a model of nonfiction writing for this age group." SLJ
Includes glossary and bibliographical references

Newton, David E.
Drug testing; an issue for school, sports, and work. Enslow Pubs. 1999 128p il (Issues in focus) lib bdg $19.95 (7 and up)   **363.4**
1. Drug testing
ISBN 0-89490-954-1   LC 98-21607
Examines differing opinions on the topic of drug testing by employers, in schools, and in sports as a means of curbing drug abuse
"The writing is clear, succinct, and objective. The text is well organized." SLJ
Includes bibliographical references

Pornography: opposing viewpoints; Carol Wekesser, book editor. Greenhaven Press 1997 202p il lib bdg $27.45; pa $17.45 (7 and up)   **363.4**
1. Pornography
ISBN 1-56510-518-4 (lib bdg); 1-56510-517-6 (pa)   LC 96-28268
"Opposing viewpoints series"
"This volume is a legalistic study dealing with violence, censorship, and sexual exploitation of women. It covers international laws and which countries observe them, which do not. . . . The articles deal with obscenity, personal reactions to it, and why pornography is controversial." Book Rep
Includes bibliographical references

Saunders, Carol Silverman
Straight talk about teenage gambling. Facts on File 1999 115p il lib bdg $19.95 (7 and up)   **363.4**
1. Gambling
ISBN 0-8160-3718-3   LC 98-25719
Explores the issue of teenage gambling, discussing its addictive nature, effects on the individual and the family, and place in society
"In a well-rounded presentation, rife with fascinating facts [the author] convincingly depicts the pitfalls of gambling without histrionics or condemnation . . . . The book includes helpful Web sites, hotlines, and state-by-state phone numbers for Gamblers Anonymous." Booklist
Includes bibliographical references

363.46 Abortion

Abortion: opposing viewpoints; Tamara L. Roleff, book editor. Greenhaven Press 1997 216p lib bdg $26.20; pa $16.20 (7 and up)   **363.46**
1. Abortion
ISBN 1-565-10506-0 (lib bdg); 1-565-10505-2 (pa)   LC 96-17342
"Opposing viewpoints series"
Replaces the edition published 1991 under the editorship of Charles Cozic and Stacey L. Tipp
This collection of articles "not only looks at moral, ethical, and safety issues but also considers justification and whether abortion rights should be restricted." Booklist
Includes bibliographical references

Lowenstein, Felicia
The abortion battle; looking at both sides. Enslow Pubs. 1996 128p il (Issues in focus) lib bdg $19.95 (7 and up)   **363.46**
1. Abortion
ISBN 0-89490-724-7   LC 95-42448
This book "defines abortion from the medical and philosophical perspectives; presents the history of its practice; discusses the right-to-life view and the pro-choice stance; and tells readers where to go for more information. Lowenstein does a commendable job of presenting facts and balancing the pros and cons of both sides of the emotionally charged issue." SLJ
Includes bibliographical references

363.7 Environmental problems

Baines, John D. (John David), 1943-
Keeping the air clean; [by] John Baines. Raintree Steck-Vaughn Pubs. 1998 48p il (Protecting our planet) lib bdg $25.68   **363.7**
1. Air pollution
ISBN 0-8172-4936-2   LC 97-17980
Explains the phenomenon of air pollution and discusses the importance of preserving clean air
This book "offers young readers a realistic view of the serious problems facing the planet and concrete suggestions for things they can do to make a difference. . . . The photographs are well chosen." Booklist
Includes glossary and bibliographical references

Chandler, Gary
Kids who make a difference; by Gary Chandler and Kevin Graham. 21st Cent. Bks. (NY) 1996 64p il (Making a better world) lib bdg $16.98   **363.7**
1. Environmental protection 2. Social action
ISBN 0-8050-4625-9   LC 96-23067
Focuses on some of the innovative environmental programs that kids have founded and run
This is "clear, concise, and certainly inspiring. Useful for assignments and for recreational reading." SLJ
Includes glossary and bibliographical references

Davis, Lee Allyn
Environmental disasters; a chronicle of individual, industrial, and governmental carelessness; [by] Lee Davis. Facts on File 1998 246p il $45 (7 and up)   **363.7**
1. Pollution 2. Human influence on nature 3. Industrial accidents 4. Disasters
ISBN 0-8160-3265-3   LC 98-29134
"This volume chronicles nearly 100 different environmental tragedies. Although the concentration is on the twentieth century, Davis has also included some events, such as deforestation, that began earlier. . . . The strength of this work is in its coverage of events that did not have the international impact of Chernobyl or Bhopal. Davis makes a strong effort to include the underlying causes of these disasters." Booklist
Includes bibliographical references

Dolan, Edward F., 1924-
Our poisoned waters. Cobblehill Bks. 1997 122p $14.99 (7 and up)   **363.7**
1. Water pollution
ISBN 0-525-65220-5   LC 96-47175
Examines the serious problem of water pollution in both fresh and salt water bodies throughout the world and describes what is being done about it
"This is an admirably objective treatment of the issue, one that is careful to note that we must balance our use of resources, neither plundering nor preserving them at the cost of our own lives." Booklist
Includes bibliographical references

DuTemple, Lesley A., 1952-
Oil spills. Lucent Bks. 1999 96p il (Our endangered planet) lib bdg $35.95 (7 and up)   **363.7**
1. Oil spills
ISBN 1-56006-524-9   LC 99-21614
Examines the causes and some specific occurrences of oil spills and leaks and discusses the environmental issues and efforts to prevent future spills
Includes glossary and bibliographical references

Gardner, Robert, 1929-
Science projects about the environment and ecology. Enslow Pubs. 1999 112p il (Science projects) lib bdg $19.95 (7 and up)   **363.7**
1. Environmental protection 2. Ecology 3. Science—Experiments 4. Science projects
ISBN 0-89490-951-7   LC 98-35049
Presents experiments and projects suitable for science fairs, dealing with such aspects of the environment and ecology as the atmosphere, soil, water, plants, animals, and climate
"Each project is clearly outlined with a list of generally available supplies. The text [is] concise and informative." SLJ
Includes bibliographical references

Global warming: opposing viewpoints; Tamara L. Roleff, book editor, Scott Barbour and Karin L. Swisher, assistant editors. Greenhaven Press 1997 192p il map lib bdg $27.45; pa $17.45 (7 and up)   **363.7**
1. Greenhouse effect
ISBN 1-565-10512-5 (lib bdg); 1-565-10511-7 (pa)
LC 96-25705
"Opposing viewpoints series"
A collection of articles exploring the scientific evidence for global warming and what, if any, measures should be taken to combat it. Preservation of the world's rain forests is also discussed
Includes bibliographical references

Kidd, J. S. (Jerry S.)
Into thin air; the problem of air pollution; [by] J.S. Kidd and Renee A. Kidd. Facts on File 1998 134p il maps (Science and society) $19.95 (7 and up)   **363.7**
1. Air pollution
ISBN 0-8160-3585-7   LC 98-9886
Examines the causes of atmospheric pollution, acid rain, ozone depletion, and global warming and explains how these conditions affect our health and economic prosperity
"The complexity of issues is not glossed over. Students will find the book . . . accessible and useful for research." Booklist
Includes glossary and bibliographical references

Shades of green; the clash of agricultural science and environmental science; [by] J.S. Kidd and Renee A. Kidd. Facts on File 1998 136p il (Science and society) lib bdg $19.95 (7 and up)   **363.7**
1. Agriculture 2. Environmental movement
ISBN 0-8160-3583-0   LC 97-15968
This book "examines the struggle between agriculture and the environment. In addition to offering readers a historical perspective of this social conflict, the authors also introduce some of the scientists responsible for the growth in agricultural technology, and individuals, such as Rachel Carson, who have struggled to preserve an uncontaminated environment. . . . Designed for curricular use, this concise overview is a solid supplement and reference source." Booklist
Includes glossary and bibliographical references

Markle, Sandra, 1946-
After the spill; the Exxon Valdez disaster, then and now. Walker & Co. 1999 30p il $16.95; lib bdg $17.85   **363.7**
1. Exxon Valdez (Ship) 2. Oil spills
ISBN 0-8027-8610-3; 0-8027-8611-1 (lib bdg)
LC 98-38550
Examines the impact of the 1989 Exxon Valdez oil spill on the environment and people of Prince William Sound and describes the steps taken to minimize the damage and prevent a recurrence
"The easy-to-read text, child-friendly format, and attractive photos will appeal to students writing reports and to teachers looking for material on environmental issues." SLJ
Includes glossary

McLeish, Ewan, 1950-
Keeping water clean. Raintree Steck-Vaughn Pubs. 1998 48p il maps (Protecting our planet) $25.68   **363.7**
1. Water pollution 2. Water supply
ISBN 0-8172-4935-4   LC 97-1257
This is a "review of the global problems associated with sources, pollution, purification, and maintenance of clean water for human, agricultural, and industrial needs." Sci Books Films
"The prose is aided by color photographs and clear, interesting graphics." Horn Book Guide
Includes glossary and bibliographical references

Miller, Christina G.
Air alert; rescuing the earth's atmosphere; [by] Christina G. Miller and Louise A. Berry. Atheneum Bks. for Young Readers 1996 118p il $16   **363.7**
1. Air pollution
ISBN 0-689-31792-1   LC 95-21295
The authors "analyze the effects of smog, acid rain, and the thinning ozone layer, and present ways to ameliorate these human-caused problems. Without presuming that readers have a lot of background knowledge, they strike an excellent balance between basic explanations and interesting technical information." SLJ
Includes glossary and bibliographical references

Paladino, Catherine
One good apple; growing our food for the sake of the earth. Houghton Mifflin 1999 48p il $15   **363.7**
1. Pesticides 2. Organic farming
ISBN 0-395-85009-6   LC 97-45866
Discusses the problems created by the use of pesticides to grow food crops and the benefits of organic farming
The author's "information is well organized and her message is straightforward and accessible. . . . This is nonfiction writing at its best." SLJ
Includes bibliographical references

Pringle, Laurence P.
Vanishing ozone; protecting earth from ultraviolet radiation; [by] Laurence Pringle. Morrow Junior Bks. 1995 64p il $16; lib bdg $15.93   **363.7**
1. Ozone layer
ISBN 0-688-04157-4; 0-688-04158-2 (lib bdg)
     LC 94-25928
"A Save-the-earth book"
This is an "introduction to the science and politics of the ozone layer. A history of the scientific study of ozone includes names of major scientists and the titles of their published articles. The political side of the debate includes reactions of elected officials and members of the chemical industry." Horn Book Guide
"The organization is excellent. . . . Technical terms are well balanced. . . . Crisp black-and-white photographs, diagrams, and maps illustrate the text. Concluding chapters offer suggestions for taking action and include addresses for government agencies and environmental groups." SLJ
Includes glossary and bibliographical references

Sherrow, Victoria
The Exxon Valdez; tragic oil spill. Enslow Pubs. 1998 48p il (American disasters) lib bdg $18.95   **363.7**
1. Exxon Valdez (Ship) 2. Oil spills
ISBN 0-7660-1058-9   LC 97-39182
Details the grounding of the Exxon Valdez oil tanker in Prince William Sound, discusses why this disaster happened, describes the cleanup effort, and suggests lessons learned from the event
This "is well documented with citations for all of the statistics and quotes. . . . Reluctant readers will be drawn to . . . [this title] for the simplicity of language and the full-color photos." SLJ
Includes glossary and bibliographical references

Simon, Seymour, 1931-
Earth words; a dictionary of the environment; illustrated by Mark Kaplan. HarperCollins Pubs. 1995 48p il maps lib bdg $15.89   **363.7**
1. Pollution—Dictionaries 2. Ecology—Dictionaries
ISBN 0-06-020234-3   LC 92-34005
Simon defines "66 essential environmental terms: words that explain how the Earth works and describe the forces that threaten to upset the delicate balance of our global ecosystem." Publisher's note
"Less space is devoted to text than to the unusual and sometimes striking illustrations, which vary from the diagrammatic to the impressionistic to the hyperrealistic." Booklist

364   Criminology

Lane, Brian
Crime & detection; written by Brian Lane; photographed by Andy Crawford. Knopf 1998 59p il (Eyewitness books) $19; lib bdg $20.99   **364**
1. Crime 2. Forensic sciences 3. Criminal investigation
ISBN 0-679-89117-X; 0-679-99117-4 (lib bdg)
     LC 97-32376
Explores the many different methods used to solves crimes, covering such topics as criminal, detectives, and forensics

364.1   Criminal offenses

D'Angelo, Laura
Hate crimes. Chelsea House 1998 95p il (Crime, justice, and punishment) lib bdg $19.95 (7 and up)   **364.1**
1. Hate crimes 2. Prejudices
ISBN 0-7910-4266-9   LC 97-39090
Discusses the increasing incidence of crimes that are motivated by bias against another person or group, examining the causes and occurrences of such hate crimes and the psychology of those who commit them
"Frequent, captioned black-and-white photos help bring these crimes out of abstraction and into reality. . . . This will make a useful introduction for report writers and debaters." Booklist
Includes glossary and bibliographical references

DeAngelis, Gina
Cyber crimes; [by] Gina De Angelis; Austin Sarat, general editor. Chelsea House 2000 101p il (Crime, justice, and punishment) lib bdg $19.95 (7 and up) **364.1**
1. Computer crimes
ISBN 0-7910-4936-1 LC 99-25797
Discusses the high tech crimes committed by hackers, crackers, and phone phreaks using computers, including fraud, embezzlement, and espionage, as well as the best ways to minimize the occurrence of such crimes
"Clear, [and] informative." SLJ
Includes bibliographical references

White-collar crime. Chelsea House 1999 81p (Crime, justice, and punishment) $19.95 (7 and up) **364.1**
1. White collar crimes
ISBN 0-7910-4279-0 LC 99-26299
Discusses such white-collar crimes as fraud, computer crimes, and insider stock trading and how these crimes should be deterred and punished
"The direct text argues that betraying the public trust is as much a crime as cold-blooded murder. Appropriate photos give face to these often victimless crimes." Booklist
Includes bibliographical references

Gaines, Ann
Terrorism; Austin Sarat, general editor. Chelsea House 1999 117p il (Crime, justice, and punishment) lib bdg $19.95 (7 and up) **364.1**
1. Terrorism
ISBN 0-7910-4596-X LC 98-20190
Examines the history, mentality, goals, and acts of terrorists and discusses what a free society can do to protect itself against them
"An important examination of an escalating threat to peace and peace of mind." SLJ
Includes bibliographical references

Hate groups: opposing viewpoints; Tamara L. Roleff, book editor; Brenda Stalcup, assistant editor; Mary E. Williams, assistant editor. Greenhaven Press 1999 192p il lib bdg $26.20; pa $16.20 (7 and up) **364.1**
1. Hate crimes 2. Militia movements
ISBN 1-56510-943-0 (lib bdg); 1-56510-942-2 (pa) LC 98-36586
"Opposing viewpoints series"
This collection of articles is divided in four chapters titled: Are hate crimes a serious problem? Do certain groups promote hate and violence? Does the militia movement present a serious threat? and How can hate crimes and terrorism be reduced?
Includes bibliographical references

Illegal drugs; Charles P. Cozic, book editor. Greenhaven Press 1998 173p (Current controversies) lib bdg $26.20; pa $16.20 (7 and up) **364.1**
1. Drug abuse
ISBN 1-56510-683-0 (lib bdg); 1-56510-682-2 (pa) LC 97-29281

A collection of essays providing varying viewpoints on drug abuse, drug testing, antidrug programs, and drug legalization
Includes bibliographical references

Jones, Rebecca C., 1947-
The president has been shot! true stories of the attacks on ten U.S. presidents. Dutton Children's Bks. 1996 134p il $15.99; pa $7.99 **364.1**
1. Presidents—United States—Assassination
ISBN 0-525-45333-4; 0-14-038505-3 (pa) LC 96-162584
The author presents a "history of attacks on 10 U.S. presidents, 4 of which have been fatal. She describes each incident in a clear narrative style and in considerable detail, explaining the motivations of the assailant, the particulars of the attack, and the immediate and far-reaching effects of it. . . . The well-written text informs readers without resorting to sensationalism." SLJ

Powell, Phelan
Major unsolved crimes; Austin Sarat, general editor. Chelsea House 2000 93p il (Crime, justice, and punishment) lib bdg $19.95 (7 and up) **364.1**
1. Crime
ISBN 0-7910-4277-4 LC 99-24140
Discusses six criminal cases in which there was no completely satisfactory conclusion reached, including the case of the Zodiac killer, the Tylenol murderer, the assassination of President Kennedy, and an unusual skyjacking in 1971
"Each murder is recounted along with an insightful consideration of the sociopathic context in which it took place; each is presented in a captivating journalistic style. . . . The book is a fascinating read." Sci Books Films
Includes bibliographical references

Sherrow, Victoria
The Oklahoma City bombing; terror in the heartland. Enslow Pubs. 1998 48p il (American disasters) lib bdg $18.95 **364.1**
1. Oklahoma City (Okla.) bombing, 1995 2. Terrorism
ISBN 0-7660-1061-9 LC 97-45750
Details the events surrounding the 1995 terrorist bombing of the federal building in Oklahoma City, as well as the investigation and trial of those responsible for the blast
"A vivid accounting. . . . Chapters are brief and punctuated with photographs, which, though not gory, bring the disaster to life in horrifying color." Booklist
Includes glossary and bibliographical references

The World Trade Center bombing; terror in the towers. Enslow Pubs. 1998 48p il (American disasters) lib bdg $18.95 **364.1**
1. World Trade Center Bombing, New York, N.Y., 1993 2. Terrorism
ISBN 0-7660-1056-2 LC 97-45769
Details the events surrounding the 1993 bombing of the World Trade Center as well as the investigation and trial of those responsible for the terrorist attack
"Dramatic photographs are included with lively captions." Voice Youth Advocates
Includes glossary and bibliographical references

Silverstein, Herma
Kids who kill. 21st Cent. Bks. (NY) 1997 128p
il lib bdg $22.40 (7 and up)   **364.1**
1. Homicide 2. Juvenile delinquency
ISBN 0-8050-4369-1   LC 97-8706
Examines the causes, cases, and social and personal
impact of the increasing incidence of murders being
committed by children and teenagers
"A thoroughly researched, insightful look at the histories, motives, and tragic results of juvenile murders in
our society." SLJ
Includes bibliographical references

St. George, Judith, 1931-
In the line of fire; presidents' lives at stake.
Holiday House 1999 144p il lib bdg $18.95
                                        364.1
1. Presidents—United States—Assassination
ISBN 0-8234-1428-0   LC 98-39030
"The first of the two main sections concerns the four
slain U.S. presidents as well as their respective assassins,
and also discusses the effects of these fatal events on the
country. Each chapter preface relays the day's events
preceding the murder in a dramatic fashion. The second
half concerns the assassination attempts on six presidents
and their would-be assassins. St. George includes intriguing anecdotes. . . . Nicely placed illustrations and photos
add power to the text." SLJ
Includes bibliographical references

Wilker, Josh
Organized crime; Austin Sarat, general editor.
Chelsea House 1999 95p il (Crime, justice, and
punishment) lib bdg $19.95 (7 and up)   **364.1**
1. Organized crime
ISBN 0-7910-4271-5   LC 98-47954
Recounts the history of organized crime from the Cosa
Nostra to Al Capone to recent global criminal organiza-
tions
Includes bibliographical references

364.36   Juvenile delinquents

Barr, Roger, 1951-
Juvenile crime. Lucent Bks. 1998 112p il
(Lucent overview series) $22.45 (7 and up)
                                        364.36
1. Juvenile delinquency 2. Administration of criminal
justice
ISBN 1-56006-198-7   LC 97-27336
Defines juvenile crime and its causes and discusses
both punishment and prevention
Includes bibliographical references

Bode, Janet
Hard time; a real life look at juvenile crime and
violence; [by] Janet Bode and Stan Mack.
Delacorte Press 1996 218p il $16.95; pa $4.99 (7
and up)   **364.36**
1. Juvenile delinquency 2. Crime 3. Violence
ISBN 0-385-32186-4; 0-440-21953-1 (pa)
                                        LC 95-40598

Young people whose lives have been impacted by violence and crime, either as perpetrators or as victims, tell
their stories. Also includes comments from concerned
adults who work with these teens
This volume "is well organized, engrossing, and informative, and it provides glimpses of hope for those wishing to leave violence behind." SLJ
Includes glossary and bibliographical references

Goodwin, William, 1943-
Teen violence. Lucent Bks. 1998 128p il (Teen
issues) lib bdg $22.45 (7 and up)   **364.36**
1. Juvenile delinquency 2. Violence 3. Administration
of criminal justice
ISBN 1-56006-511-7   LC 97-37741
An overview of violence by teenagers, examining its
causes, prevention, and handling by the juvenile justice
system
This book is "very readable, clearly organized. . . .
Provides solid information." Booklist
Includes glossary and bibliographical references

Stewart, Gail, 1949-
Gangs; [by] Gail B. Stewart. Greenhaven Press
1998 112p il (Opposing viewpoints digests) lib
bdg $22.45; pa $13.70 (7 and up)   **364.36**
1. Gangs
ISBN 1-56510-751-9 (lib bdg); 1-56510-750-0 (pa)
                                        LC 97-40096
Presents contrasting viewpoints on the following ques-
tions: "How serious a problem are gangs in the United
States?" "What factors encourage gang behavior?" and
"How can gangs be eliminated?"
Includes bibliographical references

Voices from the streets; young former gang
members tell their stories; interviews and
photographs by S. Beth Atkin. Little, Brown
1996 131p il $17.95 (7 and up)   **364.36**
1. Gangs
ISBN 0-316-05634-0   LC 95-26757
"Atkin shares interviews with former gang members
she met, photographed, and interviewed in a two-year
odyssey to document why young people join gangs and
how they terminate memberships and reenter society's
mainstream. . . . The young people's comments are
largely unedited, which means there is plenty of street
language in the narratives. Nothing in them offends as
much, however, as the horrors of their lives. . . . An extremely powerful and revealing book." SLJ
Includes glossary and bibliographical references

Youth violence; Henny H. Kim, book editor.
Greenhaven Press 1998 204p (Current
controversies) lib bdg $26.20; pa $16.20 (7 and
up)   **364.36**
1. Juvenile delinquency 2. Violence
ISBN 1-56510-811-6 (lib bdg); 1-56510-810-8 (pa)
                                        LC 98-5784
Replaces the edition published 1992 under the
editorship of Michael D. Biskup and Charles P. Cozic
This collection of articles "examines the problem of
violence among the nation's young people. Chapters in-

Youth violence—*Continued*
clude: Is youth violence a serious problem? What causes youth violence? How can youth violence be reduced? Should violent youths receive harsh punishment?" Publisher's note

Includes bibliographical references

364.66 Capital punishment

The **Death** penalty: opposing viewpoints; Paul A. Winters, book editor. Greenhaven Press 1997 192p il lib bdg $19.95; pa $11.95 (7 and up)
364.66
1. Capital punishment
ISBN 1-56510-510-9 (lib bdg); 1-56510-509-5 (pa)
LC 96-22575
"Opposing viewpoints series"
Replaces the edition published 1991 under the editorship of Carol Wekesser
"This book is a constitutional study, reporting and discussing court cases. The sections considered are: Three centuries of debate on the death penalty. Is the death penalty just? Is the death penalty an effective punishment? Is the death penalty applied unfairly?" Book Rep
Includes bibliographical references

Does capital punishment deter crime? Stephen E. Schonebaum, book editor. Greenhaven Press 1998 95p il (At issue) lib bdg $21.20; pa $13.70 (7 and up)
364.66
1. Capital punishment
ISBN 1-56510-791-8 (lib bdg); 1-56510-091-3 (pa)
LC 98-9752
"Opposing viewpoints series"
"This collection includes 10 articles by politicians, lawyers, and human rights activists, who debate the relative power of the death penalty versus life in prison. . . . This volume provides a serious introduction to one aspect of a crucial controversial issue." Booklist
Includes bibliographical references

Stewart, Gail, 1949-
The death penalty; [by] Gail B. Stewart. Greenhaven Press 1998 96p il (Opposing viewpoints digests) lib bdg $22.45; pa $13.70 (7 and up)
364.66
1. Capital punishment
ISBN 1-56510-745-4 (lib bdg); 1-56510-744-6 (pa)
LC 97-47685
Reviews opposing arguments regarding the death penalty, including whether or not it is just, deters murder, and is applied fairly
Includes bibliographical references

Wolf, Robert V.
Capital punishment. Chelsea House 1997 85p il (Crime, justice, and punishment) $19.95 (7 and up)
364.66
1. Capital punishment
ISBN 0-7910-4311-8
LC 97-12035

Surveys the history of the death penalty, describes different methods of execution, and discusses the legal and ethical ramifications using case histories
"The evenhanded, readable text is broken up with good-quality black-and-white photos and reproductions and quotations." SLJ
Includes bibliographical references

365 Penal and related institutions

America's prisons: opposing viewpoints; Charles P. Cozic, book editor. Greenhaven Press 1997 199p lib bdg $27.45; pa $17.45 (7 and up)
365
1. Prisons—United States
ISBN 1-56510-550-8 (lib bdg); 1-56510-549-4 (pa)
LC 96-47990
"Opposing viewpoints series"
Replaces the edition published 1991 under the editorship of Stacey L. Tipp
Articles "discuss the growth of America's prisons and debate the treatment and punishment of criminal offenders. Contributors examine questions regarding prison conditions, prison sentences, and prisoner rights." Publisher's note
Includes bibliographical references

369.43 Boy Scouts

Boy Scouts of America
Boy Scout handbook. Boy Scouts of Am. pa $12.95
369.43
1. Boy Scouts—Handbooks, manuals, etc.

First published 1910 with title: Official handbook for boys. Periodically revised with varying titles. Eleventh edition (1998) by Robert Birkby
Provides information and instruction in the four skill areas in scouting: camping and hiking, communication, nature, and citizenship. Illustrated with full-color drawings

Fieldbook. 3rd ed. Boy Scouts of Am. 1984 630p il maps pa $16.25
369.43
1. Boy Scouts—Handbooks, manuals, etc. 2. Outdoor life
ISBN 0-8395-3200-8
LC 84-72053
First edition by James E. West and William Hillcourt published 1944 with title: Scout field book
This "is a worthwhile guide for those involved in outdoor activities as well as Boy Scouts. The volume addresses hiking, camping, mountaineering, horseback riding, cross-country skiing, swimming, orienteering, canoeing, fitness conditioning, first aid, and outdoor safety. The concise text is supplemented by clear black-and-white and color photographs." Nichols. Guide to Ref Books for Sch Media Cent. 4th edition

369.463 Girl Scouts and Girl Guides

Girl Scouts of the United States of America
Girl Scout badges and signs. Girl Scouts of the
U.S.A. pa $6   **369.463**
1. Awards 2. Insignia

First published 1980. Periodically revised
This handbook describes the activities required to earn
various Girl Scout badges and insignia

370.25 Education—Directories

The **Handbook** of private schools; an annual
descriptive survey of independent education.
Sargent Pubs. il maps $93   **370.25**
1. Private schools—Directories 2. Education—United
States—Directories
ISSN 0072-9884

Annual. First published 1915 with title: Handbook of
the best private schools of the United States and Canada
"Describes more than 1,700 boarding and day schools,
providing information on age and grade ranges, whether
co-educational or for boys or girls, enrollment, faculty
size and background, academic orientation and curriculum, and where graduates attend college. 'Features
classifield' section lists institutions offering military programs, elementary boarding divisions, programs for students with learning differences, international and bilingual schools, and schools with more than 500 or fewer
than 100 students." Guide to Ref Books. 11th edition

370.9 Education—Historical and geographic treatment

Loeper, John J.
Going to school in 1776. Atheneum Pubs. 1973
79p il $16   **370.9**
1. Education—United States—History 2. Schools—
United States—History 3. United States—Social life
and customs—1600-1775, Colonial period
ISBN 0-689-30089-1
The author tells what it was like to be a child and to
go to school in America in 1776. He describes children's
dress, schools, teachers, school books, lessons, discipline
and after-school recreation
Includes bibliographical references

371.2 School administration

Gilbert, Sara D.
How to do your best on tests; [by] Sara Dulaney
Gilbert. rev ed. Morrow Junior Bks. 1998 128p il
(School survival guide) $15; pa $4.95 (7 and up)
                                        371.2
1. Examinations 2. Study skills
ISBN 0-688-16089-1; 0-688-16090-5 (pa)
                                  LC 98-14297

First published 1983 with title: How to take tests
Discusses effective ways to successfully study for and
take tests, including quizzes, final exams, and standard-
ized tests, emphasizing the methods of preview, view, review

371.3 Methods of instruction and study

Wood, Gail
How to study; use your personal learning style
to help you succeed when it counts.
LearningExpress 1998 172p pa $13.95 (7 and up)
                                        371.3
1. Study skills
ISBN 1-57685-084-6   LC 97-44967
This offers advice on developing such skills as overcoming procrastination, time management, reading comprehension, listening and note-taking, class participation
and discussion, and preparing for tests

371.305 Methods of instruction and study—Serial publications

Media & Methods; multimedia products,
technologies & programs for K-12 school
districts. American Soc. of Educators $33.50 per
year   **371.305**
1. Teaching—Aids and devices—Periodicals 2. Computer assisted instruction—Periodicals 3. Computer
software—Reviews
ISSN 0025-6897
Five issues per year. First published 1964; subtitle
varies
"Practical application of instructional technology and
media management; innovative projects; reviews and pre-
views of instructional media products and equipment."
Safford. Guide to Ref Materials for Sch Libr Media
Cent. 5th edition

MultiMedia schools; a practical journey of
technology for education, including multimedia,
CD-ROM, online, internet, & hardware in k-12.
Information Today $39.95 per year   **371.305**
1. Teaching—Aids and devices—Periodicals
ISSN 1075-0479
6 issues per year. First published 1994
"Professional materials reviewed in a column called
'Reference Shelf.' Items may be in any format, but
books predominate; there are 8-10 critical annotations per
issue. Entries include bibliographic information and features. 'Title Watch' lists new products by curriculum
area. 'Product Reviews in Brief' are original reviews of
CD-ROMs, videodiscs, magnetic media and Web sites
written by practicing educators. Reviews are long and
cover the company, price, audience, format, system requirements, a description, comments about installation,
contents and features, ease of use, and product support,
and a final recommendation." Safford. Guide to Ref Materials for Sch Libr Media Cent. 5th edition

Technology and Learning; the leading magazine of electronic education. Miller Freeman $29.95 per year **371.305**
1. Teaching—Aids and devices—Periodicals 2. Computer assisted instruction—Periodicals 3. Computer software—Reviews
ISSN 1053-6728

Eight issues per year. First published 1980. Former titles Classroom Computer Learning; Classroom Computer News

"'What's New,' 'Industry News,' and 'Newsline' departments highlight important information related to education and technology, while the cover story explores software related to a specific topic. . . . 'Picks of the Month' evaluates two or three software programs. The 'Help file' and 'Grants, Contests, Etc.' are useful items for seeking funding, while 'What Works' looks at projects schools have had success with and 'Update' offers new technology on the market. . . . An invaluable resource." Katz. Mag for Libr. 9th edition

TechTrends; for leaders in education and training. Association for Educ. Communications & Technology $40 per year **371.305**
1. Teaching—Aids and devices—Periodicals 2. Computer assisted instruction—Periodicals
ISSN 8756-3894

6 issues a year. Continues Instructional innovator (until 1985)

"Columns and departments about technology issues, copyright, and related matters." Safford. Guide to Ref Materials for Sch Libr Media Cent. 5th edition

371.9 Special education

Stanley, Jerry, 1941-
Children of the Dust Bowl; the true story of the school at Weedpatch Camp. Crown 1992 85p il maps $15; lib bdg $15.99; pa $7.99 **371.9**
1. Migrant labor 2. Great Depression, 1929-1939 3. Education—Social aspects
ISBN 0-517-58781-5; 0-517-58782-3 (lib hdg); 0-517-88094-6 (pa) LC 92-393

Describes the plight of the migrant workers who traveled from the Dust Bowl to California during the Depression and were forced to live in a federal labor camp and discusses the school that was built for their children

This "is a compelling document. . . . The story is inspiring and disturbing, and Stanley has recorded the details with passion and dignity." Booklist
Includes bibliographical references

372.6 Language arts (Communication skills)

Hopkins, Lee Bennett, 1938-
Pass the poetry, please! 3rd ed. HarperCollins Pubs. 1998 277p $25 **372.6**
1. Poetry—Study and teaching
ISBN 0-06-027746-7 LC 98-19617
First published 1972

"Written for teachers and librarians seeking ways of getting poetry into the lives of children. . . . Throughout, many poets are cited, from Langston Hughes to Nikki Giovanni and from Jack Prelutsky to Robert Frost." Booklist
This is "a must-purchase." SLJ
Includes bibliographical references

Pellowski, Anne, 1933-
The storytelling handbook; a young people's collection of unusual tales and helpful hints on how to tell them; illustrated by Martha Stoberock. Simon & Schuster 1995 129p il $16 **372.6**
1. Storytelling
ISBN 0-689-80311-7 LC 95-2991

This work "addresses the young person who wants to tell stories in a public setting. It is similar in format to many adult books on storytelling how-tos, with sections on getting started and selecting and preparing stories, as well as a selection of sample tales. Pellowski's notes are extensive and will be very useful to novices looking for ways to research stories." Booklist
Includes bibliographical references

373 Secondary education

Lieberman, Susan Abel
The real high school handbook; how to survive, thrive, and prepare for what's next. Houghton Mifflin 1997 130p pa $9.95 (7 and up) **373**
1. High schools
ISBN 0-395-79760-8 LC 97-26558
"A Mariner original"

This book provides information about courses, grades, testing, communicating with teachers, and postgraduation options

"The book is chockablock with information. . . . A good book that does exactly what it sets out to do: help YAs start thinking clearly about school as it impacts on the rest of their lives." Booklist

373.1 Organization and activities in secondary education

Peters, Max, 1906-
How to prepare for the SSAT, ISEE high school entrance examinations; by Max Peters, Jerome Shostak. Barron's Educ. Ser. il pa $13.95 **373.1**
1. High schools—Entrance requirements

First published 1961 with title: Barron's how to prepare for high school entrance examinations, SSAT, ISEE. (8th edition 1997) Periodically revised

This book attempts to prepare students for qualifying exams required by prep schools, parochial high schools and specialized public high schools. It reviews basic verbal and mathematical skills as well as abstract reasoning. Answers are provided for all questions, and step-by-step solutions are demonstrated for mathematics problems

379   Public policy issues in education

Haskins, James, 1941-
Separate, but not equal; the dream and the struggle. Scholastic 1998 184p il $15.95   **379**
1. African Americans—Education 2. School integration 3. Segregation in education
ISBN 0-590-45910-4   LC 96-51507
The author traces "the history of the African American struggle for equal rights to education, from the enforced illiteracy of slavery times to the present debate about affirmative action." Booklist
"With his knack for blending historical facts and thoughtful interpretation, Haskins offers an informative, closeup look at the course of black education in America." SLJ
Includes bibliographical references

384   Communications. Telecommunication

Ganeri, Anita, 1961-
The story of communications. Oxford Univ. Press 1997 30p il (Signs of the times) $14.95
384
1. Communication—History
ISBN 0-19-521411-0   LC 97-30691
Surveys the history of communication throughout the ages, including signs and symbols, letter writing, the telegraph, the telephone, radio, television, and computers
This combines "beautiful, full-color photographs and reproductions with easy-to-read, large-print text." SLJ
Includes glossary

Henderson, Harry, 1951-
Communications and broadcasting. Facts on File 1997 136p il (Milestones in science and discovery) $19.95 (7 and up)   **384**
1. Telecommunication
ISBN 0-8160-3565-2   LC 96-48633
Presents the history of modern communications and broadcasting through an overview of key inventions and their inventors including, among others, the telegraph and Samuel Morse, sound recording and Thomas Edison, and television and Philo Farnsworth
"Students interested in the history of communications and broadcasting will find plenty of information here." Book Rep
Includes bibliographical references

385.09   Railroad transportation— Historical and geographic treatment

Blumberg, Rhoda, 1917-
Full steam ahead; the race to build a transcontinental railroad. National Geographic Soc. 1996 159p il maps $18.95   **385.09**
1. Union Pacific Railroad Company 2. Central Pacific Railroad 3. Railroads—History 4. Frontier and pioneer life—West (U.S.)
ISBN 0-7922-2715-8   LC 94-34979

The author "offers not only an assiduously documented, spikes-and-bolts chronicle of the 'great race' to create the first cross-country railroad by laying track between Sacramento and Omaha, but an absorbing panorama of the project's dramatic effect on the American frontier. Lacing her narrative with often amusing anecdotes and ample quotes, Blumberg spins a tale thick with intrigue and controversy. . . . Attractively designed, the volume contains numerous period illustrations and on-site photos of the mammoth undertaking." Publ Wkly
Includes bibliographical references

Stein, R. Conrad, 1937-
The Transcontinental Railroad in American history. Enslow Pubs. 1997 128p il maps (In American history) lib bdg $19.95   **385.09**
1. Railroads—History
ISBN 0-89490-882-0   LC 96-45525
Describes the building of the first railroad to join the eastern and western part of the United States and the effect of this transcontinental link on the future development of the country
"An interesting and well-balanced view of the building of the transcontinental railroad." SLJ
Includes bibliographical references

386   Inland waterway and ferry transportation

McNeese, Tim
The Panama Canal. Lucent Bks. 1997 96p il maps (Building history series) lib bdg $22.45 (7 and up)   **386**
1. Panama Canal
ISBN 1-56006-425-0   LC 96-45623
Describes the planning and building of the Panama Canal
"McNeese describes in detail the great effort that was required to complete this project, from the political conniving to the physical construction of the canal itself. Historical black-and-white photographs illustrate this monumental venture. . . . A solid choice for libraries wanting to provide support for research reports." SLJ
Includes bibliographical references

387.2   Ships

Kentley, Eric
Boat; written by Eric Kentley. Knopf 1992 63p il (Eyewitness books) $19; lib bdg $20.99   **387.2**
1. Ships 2. Boats and boating
ISBN 0-679-81678-X; 0-679-91678-4 (lib bdg)
LC 91-53136
"A Dorling Kindersley book"
A history of the development and uses of boats, ships, and rafts, from birch-bark canoes to luxury liners

Macaulay, David, 1946-
Ship. Houghton Mifflin 1993 96p il $19.95; pa $8.95 **387.2**
1. Shipwrecks 2. Underwater exploration 3. Caribbean region—Antiquities
ISBN 0-395-52439-3; 0-395-74518-7 (pa)
LC 92-1346
This book "opens with an underwater find in the Caribbean and, in story and illustration, follows the work of marine archeologists in studying the wreck. As part of the background research in Spain, one of the team finds a diary recording the building of a caravel in 1504. The rest of the book contains a 'translation' of the diary with accompanying illustrations. Though a fictional account, the narrative gives a good feel for the maritime technology of the early 16th century." Sci Books Films

The **Visual** dictionary of ships and sailing. Dorling Kindersley 1991 64p il (Eyewitness visual dictionaries) $18.95 **387.2**
1. Boats and boating 2. Ships
ISBN 1-879431-20-3
LC 91-60900
This is a visual guide to nautical terminology with brief text describing ships and boats from ancient times to the present
"*Ships and Sailing* is intriguing. The pages proceed from the ships of Greece, Rome, and the Vikings through wooden and iron ships of all kinds to knots, signals, flags, and gear used and worn by sailors. The detailed cutaways are works of art." Booklist

391 Costume and personal appearance

Baker, Patricia
Fashions of a decade, The 1940s; original illustrations by Robert Price. Facts on File 1992 64p il $19.95 **391**
1. Costume
ISBN 0-8160-2467-7
LC 91-10326
Chronicles clothing trends of the 1940s and the influence of World War II on styles of dress, availability of many fabrics, and the new ideas of "designers at war"
Includes glossary and bibliographical references

Fashions of a decade, The 1950s; original illustrations by Robert Price. Facts on File 1991 64p il $19.95 **391**
1. Costume
ISBN 0-8160-2468-5
LC 90-46333
Surveys the fads, fashions, trends, and cultural and intellectual preoccupations of the 1950s
Includes glossary and bibliographical references

Carnegy, Vicky
Fashions of a decade, The 1980s; original illustrations by Robert Price. Facts on File 1990 64p il $19.95 **391**
1. Costume
ISBN 0-8160-2471-5
LC 90-30895

A pictorial survey chronicling the international clothing fashions of the 1980s
This "provides an accessible overview of [the] decade, placing fashion trends within their appropriate political and historical contexts. . . . Browsers and fashion design students alike will be intrigued." Booklist
Includes glossary and bibliographical references

Connikie, Yvonne
Fashions of a decade, The 1960s; original illustrations by Robert Price. Facts on File 1990 64p il $19.95 **391**
1. Costume
ISBN 0-8160-2469-3
LC 90-30896
A pictorial survey chronicling how the fashions of the 1960s reflected the political, social, and cultural changes in society
This is "not for serious students of fashion, but will be fun for browsers and those interested in an introduction to the concept of clothing design in the context of contemporary events." SLJ
Includes glossary and bibliographical references

Costantino, Maria
Fashions of a decade, The 1930s; original illustrations by Robert Price. Facts on File 1992 64p il $19.95 **391**
1. Costume
ISBN 0-8160-2466-9
LC 91-10327
Chronicles trends in 1930s styles such as lower hemlines and broader shoulders; the introduction of synthetic fabrics; and new views of fitness, health, and personal beauty
Includes glossary and bibliographical references

Feldman, Elane
Fashions of a decade, The 1990s; original illustrations by Robert Price. Facts on File 1992 64p il $19.95 **391**
1. Costume
ISBN 0-8160-2472-3
A pictorial survey chronicling the international fashions of the 1990s
"The major flaw is that the book understandably includes only two years' worth of information; certainly the years 1992-1999 deserve treatment before a volume may purport to be about the entire decade." SLJ
Includes glossary and bibliographical references

Finley, Carol
The art of African masks; exploring cultural traditions. Lerner Publs. 1999 64p il map (Art around the world) $22.60 **391**
1. Masks (Facial) 2. African art
ISBN 0-8225-2078-8
LC 98-10570
Describes how different types of masks are made and used in Africa and how they reflect the culture of their ethnic groups
Includes bibliographical references

Herald, Jacqueline
Fashions of a decade, The 1920s; original illustrations by Robert Price. Facts on File 1991 64p il $19.95   **391**
1. Costume
ISBN 0-8160-2465-0   LC 90-46334
Surveys the fads, fashions, trends, and cultural and intellectual preoccupations of the 1920s
"Students interested in fashion and societal changes, as well as those in need of a good outline reference, will find [this volume] . . . helpful." Booklist
Includes glossary and bibliographical references

Fashions of a decade, The 1970s. Facts on File 1992 64p il $19.95   **391**
1. Costume
ISBN 0-8160-2470-7   LC 91-44209
This volume in the series looks at how the fashions of the 1970s reflected the social, historical and cultural events of that decade
This "includes chapters on 'Black is Beautiful,' 'Dressed to Clash,' 'Trash Culture,' etc. . . . An abundance of full-color and black-and-white illustrations and photographs amplify the text with generally appropriate placement and captions." SLJ
Includes glossary and bibliographical references

Knight, Margaret
Fashion through the ages; from overcoats to petticoats; illustrated by Kim Dalziel. Viking 1998 unp il $19.99   **391**
1. Costume
ISBN 0-670-86521-4   LC 98-60152
This book illustrates and describes "Western clothing styles from the Roman Empire through the 1960s. Twelve colorful two-page spreads are each introduced with a double-sided gatefold that gives historical background on the era and descriptions of its clothing. . . . When lifted, the flaps depicting the garments reveal the next layer of clothing, often down to the underwear. . . . The only drawback to this unique and fascinating book is its fragile design." SLJ

Lawlor, Laurie
Where will this shoe take you? a walk through the history of footwear. Walker & Co. 1996 132p il $17.95; lib bdg $18.85   **391**
1. Shoes
ISBN 0-8027-8434-8; 0-8027-8435-6 (lib bdg)
    LC 96-3718
The author "traces footwear from the Ice Age to Air Jordans. . . . An initial chapter chronicling the early development of footwear is followed by thematic chapters on topics such as shoes as protection, status symbol, fashion statement, play equipment, and shoes in literature." Horn Book Guide
"Sketches and photos enhance the book throughout. . . . This is a rich, in-depth study of a simple topic." Booklist
Includes bibliographical references

Miller, Brandon Marie
Dressed for the occasion; what Americans wore 1620-1970. Lerner Publs. 1999 96p il $22.60
    391
1. Costume
ISBN 0-8225-1738-8   LC 98-22668
Examines the history, manufacture, and care of American clothing from colonial times to the 1970s and discusses its relationship to the social milieu
"An excellent overview. . . . Interesting tidbits, such as what was under those hoop skirts, enliven the presentation. The text is highlighted with sepia-toned reproductions and photographs." SLJ
Includes bibliographical references

Rowland-Warne, L.
Costume; written by L. Rowland-Warne. Knopf 1992 63p il (Eyewitness books) $19   **391**
1. Costume
ISBN 0-679-81680-1   LC 91-53135
"A Dorling Kindersley book"
Photographs and text document the history and meaning of clothing, from loincloths to modern children's clothes
This "fascinating historical overview . . . blends close-up, full-color photographs of period clothing and accessories with brief snippets of text that explain the item's significance and purpose." SLJ

392   Customs of life cycle and domestic life

King, Elizabeth, 1953-
Quinceañera; celebrating fifteen. Dutton Children's Bks. 1998 40p il $15.99   **392**
1. Quinceañera (Social custom) 2. Mexican Americans—Social life and customs
ISBN 0-525-45638-4   LC 97-44539
Also available Spanish language edition
Focuses on describing the celebration of this rite of passage in the life of a specific Mexican American girl, while also presenting historical background for the occasion
"The photographs are so full of spectacle and genuine warmth that we feel as though we have been invited, too." Booklist

393   Death customs

Bendick, Jeanne, 1919-
Tombs of the ancient Americas; written and illustrated by Jeanne Bendick. Watts 1993 64p il maps lib bdg $13.93   **393**
1. Funeral rites and ceremonies 2. Indians 3. America—Antiquities 4. Tombs
ISBN 0-531-20148-1   LC 92-24546
"A First book"
"Bendick introduces the reader to a number of archeological questions based on the mysteries surrounding the tombs discovered throughout the Americas. The material

Bendick, Jeanne, 1919-—*Continued*
is divided geographically into South American, Mesoamerican, and North American tombs." Sci Books Films
This is an "attractive volume, written in a style that will appeal to browsers more than information seekers. . . . Illustrating the book is a combination of color photos and color pencil drawings executed in an appealing folk-art style." Booklist
Includes glossary and bibliographical references

Colman, Penny
Corpses, coffins, and crypts; a history of burial. Holt & Co. 1997 212p il $17.95 (7 and up) **393**
1. Funeral rites and ceremonies 2. Burial
ISBN 0-8050-5066-3 LC 97-7842
Documents the burial process throughout the centuries and in different cultures
The author "is both candid and detailed in her handling of the gruesome nitty-gritty, whether it concerns determination of death, corpse disposal, burial practices, or burial containers. Many of the photographs in the liberally illustrated text are from her own explorations, and all are captioned, some in great detail. . . . She's filled her sensitive, solid book with answers to questions people often need and want to know but are too reluctant to ask." Booklist
Includes glossary and bibliographical references

Ganeri, Anita, 1961-
The search for tombs. Raintree Steck-Vaughn Pubs. 1998 46p il (Treasure hunters) lib bdg $25.69 **393**
1. Tombs 2. Archeology
ISBN 0-8172-4839-0 LC 96 51660
Discusses the discovery of notable tombs around the world, including the pyramid chamber of the Egyptian boy king Tutankhamen, the royal tombs of China, and the burial ships of Vikings
This features "evocative illustrations and finely reproduced full-color photographs." SLJ
Includes glossary and bibliographical references

Perl, Lila
Mummies, tombs, and treasure: secrets of ancient Egypt; drawings by Erika Weihs. Clarion Bks. 1987 120p il lib bdg $16; pa $7.95 **393**
1. Mummies 2. Funeral rites and ceremonies 3. Egypt—Antiquities
ISBN 0-89919-407-9 (lib bdg); 0-395-54796-2 (pa)
LC 86-17646
The author incorporates "information on burial customs, religious beliefs, and historical background along with specifics of the mummification process and the archeological finds that have kept the study of the dead a dynamic one." Bull Cent Child Books
"A thorough, interesting history with fascinating, black-and-white photographs." Sci Child
Includes bibliographical references

Putnam, James
Mummy; written by James Putnam; photographed by Peter Hayman. Knopf 1993 c1992 63p il (Eyewitness books) $17; lib bdg $20.99 **393**
1. Mummies 2. Funeral rites and ceremonies
ISBN 0-679-83881-3; 0-679-93881-8 (lib bdg)
LC 92-1591
"A Dorling Kindersley book"
First published 1992 in the United Kingdom
Documents the history and significance of mummies, both natural and man-made, and describes the principles and ceremonies associated with them
"A great collection of mummy information and specimens. . . . The full-color photographs and illustrations are well lit, and captions add additional information." SLJ

394.1 Eating, drinking; using drugs

Giblin, James, 1933-
From hand to mouth; or, How we invented knives, forks, spoons, and chopsticks & the table manners to go with them; [by] James Cross Giblin. Crowell 1987 86p il lib bdg $16.89 **394.1**
1. Tableware 2. Table etiquette
ISBN 0-690-04662-6 LC 86-29341
The author "traces the history of eating utensils and customs from the ancient world to the present. Beginning with the use of small spears to pick meat out of the fire and spoons made of curved goat horns, he follows the development to the controversial introduction of forks, the invention of stainless steel, and the return to casual eating practices with the popularity of fast foods. Readers will be especially interested in the information on eating customs and table manners in different eras and cultures." SLJ
Includes bibliographical references

394.2 Customs—Special occasions

The **American** book of days; compiled and edited by Jane M. Hatch. 3d ed. Wilson, H.W. 1978 xxvi, 1214p o.p. **394.2**
1. Holidays 2. Festivals—United States
LC 78-16239
First edition, by George W. Douglas, published 1937
New edition in preparation
"Emphasis is on historical events relating to the founding and development of the U.S. and major religious and public holidays; descriptive articles; chronological order with detailed index by topic, key people and events." N Y Public Libr. Ref Books for Child Collect. 2d edition

Heath, Alan
Windows on the world; multicultural festivals for schools and libraries. Scarecrow Press 1995 392p il $52 **394.2**
1. Festivals 2. Multiculturalism
ISBN 0-8108-2880-4 LC 94-10032

Heath, Alan—Continued

This guide "promotes reading through thematic festive activities centered around diverse cultural celebrations. Students explore varied art forms, from sculpture, printmaking, batik, and puppetry to drama, music, dancing, cooking, and writing. . . . The book is profusely illustrated with photographs, diagrams, activity sheets, maps, bulletin board ideas, and . . . instructions for arts and crafts projects." Publisher's note

Includes bibliographical references

Ingpen, Robert R.

A celebration of customs & rituals of the world; [by] Robert Ingpen & Philip Wilkinson. Facts on File 1996 224p il $35   **394.2**
1. Manners and customs 2. Rites and ceremonies 3. Festivals

ISBN 0-8160-3479-6   LC 95-33420

First published 1994 in the United Kingdom

Explores initiation rites, wedding feasts, harvest celebrations, religious rituals, and many other customs used around the world to mark all kinds of special occasions

"Rich full-color illustrations, some of them showing partial nudity, and detailed captions help bring more meaning to these sometimes complex ceremonies." Booklist

394.26 Holidays

Branch, Muriel Miller

Juneteenth; freedom day; photographs by Willis Branch. Cobblehill Bks. 1998 54p il $15.99
                                            394.26
1. African Americans—History

ISBN 0-525-65222-1   LC 97-9656

Discusses the origin and present-day celebration of Juneteenth, a holiday marking the day Texan slaves realized they were free

"Branch provides a lengthy bibliography for further research, as well as a wealth of holiday enthusiasm that is hard to ignore." Booklist

Christmas in colonial and early America. World Bk. 1996 80p il $19   **394.26**
1. Christmas 2. United States—Social life and customs

ISBN 0-7166-0875-8

Describes the celebration of Christmas in America from colonial times to the nineteenth century and includes directions for making gifts and holiday dinners

The **Folklore** of American holidays; Hennig Cohen and Tristram Potter Coffin, editors. 3rd ed. Gale Res. 1998 c1999 573p $99   **394.26**
1. Holidays 2. Festivals—United States 3. Folklore—United States

ISBN 0-8138-8642-2   LC 98-37035

First published 1987

"A compilation of more than 600 beliefs, legends, superstitions, proverbs, riddles, poems, songs, dances, games, plays, pageants, fairs, foods, and processions associated with over 140 American calendar customs and festivals." Title page

The **Folklore** of world holidays; Robert Griffin and Ann H. Shurgin, editors. 2nd ed. Gale Res. 1998 c1999 841p $99   **394.26**
1. Holidays 2. Festivals 3. Folklore

ISBN 0-8103-8901-0   LC 98-37030

First published 1992 under the editorship of Margaret Read MacDonald

This includes holidays celebrated in more than 150 countries with "descriptive information on nearly 2,000 beliefs, stories, superstitions, proverbs, recipes, games, pageants, fairs, processions and other lore related to more than 350 special dates. Arranged chronologically." Publisher's note

Holidays, festivals, and celebrations of the world dictionary; detailing more than 2,000 observances from all 50 states and more than 100 nations; edited by Helene Henderson and Sue Ellen Thompson. 2nd ed. Omnigraphics 1997 822p $84   **394.26**
1. Holidays 2. Festivals

ISBN 0-7808-0074-5   LC 97-9160

First published 1994 compiled by Sue Ellen Thompson and Barbara W. Carlson

"The alphabetically arranged entries . . . include holidays of national or religious importance, as well as colorful local observances. . . . A worthwhile purchase for libraries developing a comprehensive holiday reference collection." Libr J

Lizon, Karen Helene

Colonial American holidays and entertainment. Watts 1993 111p il (Colonial America) lib bdg $22   **394.26**
1. Holidays 2. United States—Social life and customs—1600-1775, Colonial period

ISBN 0-531-12546-7   LC 92-40262

Surveys the different holidays celebrated throughout the year by the early settlers in America and describes some of the various activities, sports, and toys with which they amused themselves

Includes glossary and bibliographical references

Marks, Diana F.

Let's celebrate today; calendars, events, and holidays; illustrated by Donna L. Farrell. Libraries Unlimited 1998 337p il pa $35   **394.26**
1. Holidays 2. Festivals 3. Calendars

ISBN 1-56308-558-5   LC 98-26745

This begins "with a chapter on calendars that recognizes religious and cultural holidays with dates that vary (Easter, Hanukkah, Ramadan). . . . The remainder of the book, which includes celebrations around the globe, is organized by month. Month-long celebrations lead off each chapter, followed by 'special days,' such as Martin Luther King Jr. Day, and notations of historical events, holidays, and special birthdays. Keyed to the text are a scattering of ideas that can be used to prompt class discussion and research. . . . Teachers and librarians . . . will find this chockablock with useful stuff, and the book is entertaining enough to attract children who like to browse." Booklist

Includes bibliographical references

McKissack, Patricia C., 1944-

Christmas in the big house, Christmas in the quarters; by Patricia C. McKissack and Fredrick L. McKissack; illustrated by John Thompson. Scholastic 1994 68p il $17.95   **394.26**

1. Plantation life 2. Christmas 3. Slavery—United States

ISBN 0-590-43027-0   LC 92-33831

Coretta Scott King award for text, 1995

This is a "description of a traditional Christmas on a Virginia plantation in 1859. . . . The authors view the holiday from the perspectives of both slaveholder and his household in the 'Big House' and the slaves in the 'Quarters.' Rich descriptions of preparations fill the text—recipes and menus from both groups are provided—and colorful paintings reflect the antebellum period. Sprinkled throughout the book are lyrics of traditional spirituals, carols, and poetry. . . . Use of authentic language of the time helps the narrative flow, and carefully documented notes illuminate the interesting text." Horn Book

Includes bibliographical references

Walter, Mildred Pitts, 1922-

Kwanzaa: a family affair. Lothrop, Lee & Shepard Bks. 1995 95p il $15   **394.26**

1. Kwanzaa

ISBN 0-688-11553-5

Also available in paprback from Avon Bks.

This is a "guide to preparing for and celebrating Kwanzaa that encourages early planning and the sharing of family histories. The principles and symbols are clearly explained, and the directions for making simple gifts are accompanied by adequate line drawings. Walter's enthusiasm for her subject brightens this modest effort." Booklist

Includes glossary and bibliographical references

395   Etiquette (Manners)

James, Elizabeth

Social smarts; manners for today's kids; by Elizabeth James and Carol Barkin; illustrated by Martha Weston. Clarion Bks. 1996 103p il $15; pa $6.95   **395**

1. Etiquette 2. Conduct of life

ISBN 0-395-66585-X; 0-395-81312-3 (pa)

LC 95-35613

Offers advice on how to handle all kinds of social situations and personal interactions, presented with letters from two eighth graders to an etiquette advice columnist, K. T. Answers

"The writing throughout is clear; and it's noteworthy that the authors do more than simply tell readers how to behave—they usually explain why." Booklist

Packer, Alex J., 1951-

How rude! the teenagers' guide to good manners, proper behavior, and not grossing people out. Free Spirit 1997 465p il pa $19.95 (7 and up)   **395**

1. Etiquette

ISBN 1-57542-024-4   LC 97-13015

This guide to etiquette for teenagers discusses such topics as "'Sex-Ediquette' (realistic rules for relationships with the opposite sex), Toiletiquette, (polite bathroom-sharing), and Netiquette (cyberspace behavior codes). The correct way to answer an invitation, which fork to use at a formal dinner, and all of the standard protocols for life in what once was called a 'proper' environment are included." SLJ

"This volume not only uses humor to make the subject palatable but also makes good sense in terms of most young people's everyday lives." Booklist

Includes bibliographical references

Post, Elizabeth L.

Emily Post's etiquette. HarperCollins Pubs. il $28; Thumb indexed $35 (7 and up)   **395**

1. Etiquette

First published 1922 under the authorship of Emily Post with title: Etiquette in society, in business, in politics and at home. (16th edition 1997) Periodically revised and updated. Title varies. Current editor: Elizabeth Post

"The classic reference for which fork to use has been expanded to include such modern situations as dating, living together, second marriages, and co-ed business traveling." N Y Public Libr. Book of How & Where to Look It Up

"Long a standard work." Guide to Ref Books. 11th edition

Emily Post's teen etiquette; [by] Elizabeth L. Post and Joan M. Coles. HarperPerennial 1995 177p il pa $12.50 (7 and up)   **395**

1. Etiquette

ISBN 0-06-273337-0   LC 95-18503

Replaces Emily Post talks with teens about manners and etiquette published 1986

"Practical, commonsense advice on dealing with your family, communicating with others, mealtime manners, your appearance, social survival (friendship and dating), money, and getting a job. The basics of how to write a thank you note and which fork to use are covered as well as dealing with call waiting and beepers. The family section recognizes divorce and stepfamilies as well as situations involving abuse." Voice Youth Advocates

398   Folklore

Cohen, Daniel, 1936-

Real vampires. Cobblehill Bks. 1995 114p $13.99   **398**

1. Vampires

ISBN 0-525-65189-6   LC 94-22028

Also available in papervack from Scholastic

"Spurning the image of the vampire as popularized in literature and film, Cohen relates gruesome legends from history and folklore about 'real' vampires in Europe, China, and even the United States, where many early New Englanders feared the undead creatures." Horn Book Guide

Includes bibliographical references

Werewolves. Cobblehill Bks. 1996 117p $14.99   **398**

1. Werewolves

ISBN 0-525-65207-8   LC 95-34934

Cohen, Daniel, 1936-—*Continued*
The author recounts the history of the belief in werewolves from 16th century France to the present, retells werewolf legends and stories, and includes a critical guide to ten werewolf films and information about an Internet news group
"Cohen has digested a great deal of research and put it in clear and readable prose. . . . This is a fascinating book." Book Rep
Includes bibliographical references

Hughes, Mary
Popular superstitions. Chelsea House 1999 64p il (Costume, tradition and culture) lib bdg $16.95
398
1. Superstition 2. Folklore
ISBN 0-7910-5172-2   LC 98-36081
Explores twenty-five superstitions and how they may have started, including those about walking under a ladder, breaking a mirror, and opening an umbrella indoors
Includes bibliographical references

Nigg, Joe
Wonder beasts; tales and lore of the phoenix, the griffin, the unicorn, and the dragon. Libraries Unlimited 1995 160p il $26 (7 and up)   **398**
1. Animals—Folklore
ISBN 1-56308-242-X   LC 94-46797
The author "has compiled material ranging from Herodotus, Ovid, Pliny the Elder, to Chinese and Native American folk tales, and fantasies by Edith Nesbit. Each entry is carefully documented and a reference list at the end provides dozens of full citations for those who'd like to delve deeper. Wonder Beasts will be useful to students who are researching myth and folklore, and to librarians and scholars who are looking for a comprehensive source list on the topic." Voice Youth Advocates

Rose, Carol, 1943-
Spirits, fairies, gnomes, goblins; an encyclopedia of the little people. ABC-CLIO 1996 369p il $49.50 (7 and up)   **398**
1. Fairies—Encyclopedias 2. Folklore—Encyclopedias 3. Supernatural—Encyclopedias
ISBN 0-87436-811-1   LC 96-8460
This reference describes over 2,000 supernatural beings from a variety of sources including folklore, mythology, religions, and literature
For a review see: Booklist, May 1, 1997

Van Laan, Nancy
With a whoop and a holler; a bushel of lore from way down south; illustrated by Scott Cook. Atheneum Bks. for Young Readers 1998 102p il map $19.95   **398**
1. Folklore—Southern States
ISBN 0-689-81061-X   LC 96-24336
"An Anne Schwartz book"
A collection of tales, rhymes, riddles, superstitions, and sayings organized around the three distinct regions of the South: the Bayou, the Deep South, and Appalachia
"Cook's caricature-like illustrations draw out the fun-loving humor with an affectionate wink-and-a-nod style." Horn Book Guide

398.2   Folk literature

Sagas, romances, legends, ballads, and fables in prose form, and fairy tales, folk tales, and tall tales are included here, instead of with the literature of the country of origin, to keep the traditional material together and to make it more readily accessible. Modern fairy tales are classified with Fiction, Story collections (SC)

African folktales; traditional stories of the black world; selected and retold by Roger D. Abrahams. Pantheon Bks. 1983 354p il hardcover o.p. paperback available $17   **398.2**
1. Folklore—Africa
ISBN 0-394-72117-9 (pa)   LC 83-2474
"The Pantheon fairy tale and folklore library"
"From across sub-Saharan Africa, Abrahams has collected a wealth of creation myths, ghosts stories, trickster tales, riddles, and more, and he retells them in many different voices that capture the storytelling tradition." Rochman. Against borders
Includes bibliographical references

American Indian myths and legends; selected and edited by Richard Erdoes and Alfonso Ortiz. Pantheon Bks. 1984 527p il hardcover o.p. paperback available $18   **398.2**
1. Indians of North America—Folklore 2. Indians of North America—Religion
ISBN 0-394-74018-1 (pa)   LC 84-42669
"This volume comprises 160 tales of native folklore and myth ranging from one geographical end of our continent to the other. The book is organized according to type of myth. . . . Erdoes and Ortiz seek to keep Indian myth intact and pure through their retellings, using, as often as possible, primary sources." Booklist
Includes bibliographical references

Brown, Dee Alexander
Dee Brown's folktales of the Native American; retold for our times; illustrated by Louis Mofsie. Holt & Co. 1993 174p il pa $9.95   **398.2**
1. Indians of North America—Folklore
ISBN 0-8050-2607-X   LC 93-12449
"An Owl book"
First published 1979 by Holt, Rinehart & Winston with title: Teepee tales of the American Indian
This is a collection of 36 folktales from Native American tribes, including the Seneca, Hopi, Navaho, Creek, Cheyenne, Cherokee, and Blackfoot, grouped by themes such as tricksters and magicians, heroes and heroines, and ghost stories
Includes bibliographical references

Bruchac, Joseph, 1942-
Four ancestors; stories, songs, and poems from Native North America; told by Joseph Bruchac; pictures by S.S. Burrus [et al.] BridgeWater Bks. 1996 96p il lib bdg $18.95   **398.2**
1. Indians of North America—Folklore
ISBN 0-8167-3843-2   LC 95-15250
A collection of traditional Native American tales celebrating the wonder and mystery of the natural world, ar-

Bruchac, Joseph, 1942—_Continued_
ranged under the categories "Fire," "Earth," "Water," and "Air"

"This handsome volume will enhance any folklore collection and enliven programs and lessons on Native American lore and ecology." SLJ

Includes bibliographical references

The girl who married the Moon: tales from Native North America; told by Joseph Bruchac and Gayle Ross. BridgeWater Bks. 1994 127p il $13.95; pa $5.95 **398.2**
  1. Indians of North America—Folklore
  ISBN 0-8167-3480-1; 0-8167-3481-X (pa)
                                 LC 93-43824
Companion volume Flying with the eagle, racing the great bear (1993)

"This anthology focuses on the role of women in traditional Indian cultures. The 16 stories, collected from tribes representing all areas of North America, range from female rites of passage to cautionary and _pourquoi_ tales. . . . Striking black-and-white stylized drawings as well as background information about the region and the stories introduce each section. . . . An excellent addition for storytelling collections." Booklist

Includes bibliographical references

When the Chenoo howls; native American tales of terror; [by] Joseph and James Bruchac; illustrations by William Sauts Netamux̂we Bock. Walker & Co. 1998 136p il $16.95; lib bdg $17.85; pa $7.95 **398.2**
  1. Indians of North America—Folklore
  ISBN 0-8027-8638-3; 0-8027-8639-1 (lib bdg); 0-8027-7576-4 (pa)   LC 97-48715

"Twelve monster tales from a variety of American Indian tribes. . . . These pithily retold tales are short enough for reading aloud and easy enough to learn to tell quickly. Brief notes at the end of each tale give cultural context as well as specific written and oral sources. Full-page black-and-white pen and ink drawings and spot art effectively evoke the spooky but concrete creepiness of the tales. . . . A successful, accessible collection." Bull Cent Child Books

Includes bibliographical references

Bryan, Ashley, 1923-
Ashley Bryan's African tales, uh-huh; retold and illustrated by Ashley Bryan. Atheneum Bks. for Young Readers 1998 198p il $22 **398.2**
  1. Folklore—Africa
  ISBN 0-689-82076-3
This edition combines three previously published titles: The ox of the wonderful horns and other African folktales (1971), Beat the story-drum, pum-pum (1980) and Lion and the ostrich chicks and other African folktales (1986)

Climo, Shirley, 1928-
Magic & mischief; tales from Cornwall; retold by Shirley Climo; illustrated by Anthony Bacon Venti. Clarion Bks. 1999 127p il $17 **398.2**
  1. Folklore—Great Britain
  ISBN 0-395-86968-4   LC 97-34091

"Ten tales of Cornwall featuring supernatural beings (giants, piskies, spriggans, knackers, changelings, etc.) are accompanied by explanatory bits of traditional lore (how to please piskies, ways to scare spriggans, etc.) in this handsomely presented volume. . . . Climo's style is polished and literary, and her selection of tales to retell from detailed sources leans toward the humorous happy ending with just the occasional creepy shiver." Bull Cent Child Books

The **Dancing** fox: Arctic folktales; edited by John Bierhorst; illustrated by Mary K. Okheena. Morrow 1997 141p il $15 **398.2**
  1. Inuit—Folklore
  ISBN 0-688-14406-3   LC 96-17146
A description of Inuit culture accompanies a collection of eighteen Inuit folktales from an ancient oral tradition in which animals could take human form and in which magic usually had a part

"For folklore, the book is an essential; for storytelling, a source; for readers, a new place to look." Horn Book Guide

Includes bibliographical references

Delacre, Lulu, 1957-
Golden tales; myths, legends, and folktales from Latin America; retold and illustrated by Lulu Delacre. Scholastic Press 1996 73p il maps $18.95 **398.2**
  1. Folklore—Latin America
  ISBN 0-590-48186-X   LC 94-36724
This includes 12 "stories from four native cultures (Taino, Zapotec, Muisca, and Quechua), including _pourquio_ tales, legends of the conquistadores, and folktales from before and after the age of Columbus. . . . [The author's] . . . retellings are done in a clear and confident voice and are accompanied by her robust, colorful oil paintings. . . . This impressively presented and referenced collection will inspire readers and tellers alike." Booklist

Includes bibliographical references

Early, Margaret, 1951-
William Tell; retold and illustrated by Margaret Early. Abrams 1991 unp il $17.95 **398.2**
  1. Tell, William 2. Legends—Switzerland
  ISBN 0-8109-3854-5
This is a retelling of the legend of the Swiss archer who saved his country from the oppressive Austrian emperor Gessler

"Early's illustrations, lavishly embellished with gold, reflect the medieval period in which the events took place. A unique border decorates each page, framing the elaborate paintings with elegant repetitive designs, lending a fittingly mannered feeling to the art. Even the skies, the water, and the trees are made up of minutely executed patterns. A welcome new retelling that makes this inspiring story of freedom accessible to a new generation of young people." Horn Book

Fairman, Tony

Bury my bones but keep my words; African tales for retelling; retold by Tony Fairman; illustrated by Meshack Asare. Holt & Co. 1992 c1991 192p il music $15.95　　　**398.2**

1. Folklore—Africa

ISBN 0-8050-2333-X　　　LC 92-25014

Also available in paperback from Penguin Bks.

First published 1991 in the United Kingdom

A collection of traditional African tales from Kenya, Gambia, Egypt, Botswana, Nigeria, South Africa, and Namibia

"Asare, a Ghanian artist, contributes lively ink drawings." Booklist

Includes bibliographical references

Forest, Heather

Wisdom tales from around the world; retold by Heather Forest. August House 1996 156p $27.95; pa $17.95　　　**398.2**

1. Folklore

ISBN 0-87483-478-3; 0-87483-479-1 (pa)

LC 96-31141

A collection of traditional stories from around the world, reflecting the cumulative wisdom of Sufi, Zen, Taoist, Buddhist, Jewish, Christian, African, and Native American cultures

"Forest retells folktales, proverbs, and parables in a thoughtful and satisfying style that amuses as it deftly imparts lessons for living." SLJ

Includes bibliographical references

Hamilton, Virginia, 1936-

The dark way; stories from the spirit world; told by Virginia Hamilton; illustrated by Lambert Davis. Harcourt Brace Jovanovich 1990 154p il $19.95　　　**398.2**

1. Supernatural—Fiction 2. Folklore

ISBN 0-15-222340-1　　　LC 90-36251

A collection of folk tales, legends, and myths involving the supernatural, from cultures around the world

"Hamilton breathes life into the tales with her highly personal and intelligent brand of storytelling, and Lambert Davis's grisly monsters are appropriately horrific." Horn Book Guide

Includes bibliographical references

Her stories; African American folktales, fairy tales, and true tales; told by Virginia Hamilton; illustrated by Leo & Diane Dillon. Blue Sky Press (NY) 1995 112p il $19.95　　　**398.2**

1. African American women—Folklore

ISBN 0-590-47370-0　　　LC 94-33055

Coretta Scott King award for text, 1996

"Nineteen African-American fairy tales, animal stories, supernatural tales, legends and true narratives of a female kind are presented in this single volume." Child Book Rev Serv

"Retold from a variety of sources, the stories flow smoothly in Hamilton's expertly measured prose. The full-color illustrations, one per story, are lush and detailed. . . . These are tales to be read over and over again." Publ Wkly

Includes bibliographical references

The people could fly: American black folktales; told by Virginia Hamilton; illustrated by Leo and Diane Dillon. Knopf 1985 178p il $18; lib bdg $18.99; pa $13　　　**398.2**

1. African Americans—Folklore

ISBN 0-394-86925-7; 0-394-96925-1 (lib bdg); 0-679-84336-1 (pa)　　　LC 84-25020

Coretta Scott King Award for text, 1986

Companion volume to Many thousand gone

"An extraordinary collection of 24 tales that depict the black slaves' struggles for survival. Includes animal tales, stories of fantasy and the supernatural, and spirited tales of freedom. The use of black English lends authenticity, keeping the flavor of the slave storyteller alive." Soc Educ

Hearne, Betsy Gould

Beauties and beasts; by Betsy Hearne; illustrated by Joanne Caroselli. Oryx Press 1993 179p il (Oryx multicultural folktale series) pa $24.95　　　**398.2**

1. Fairy tales 2. Folklore 3. Mythology

ISBN 0-89774-729-1　　　LC 93-16

"The theme of a lonely beast who is transformed by the magic of human love is threaded throughout worldwide variations of the 'Beauty and the Beast' folktale. Author Betsy G. Hearne presents 28 versions of the beloved fable with minimal adaptations from around the world." Publisher's note

"Professionals will be very grateful for this sensitively written, thoughtful, and accessible interpretive collection." J Youth Serv Libr

Includes bibliographical references

Helbig, Alethea

Myths and hero tales; a cross-cultural guide to literature for children and young adults; [by] Alethea K. Helbig and Agnes Regan Perkins. Greenwood Press 1997 288p $49.95　　　**398.2**

1. Mythology—Bibliography

ISBN 0-313-29935-8　　　LC 97-8778

"Brief, incisive critical reviews of 189 books, published between 1985 and 1996, that contain 1455 myths and hero tales form the heart of this . . . sourcebook. Scholarly accuracy and literary quality are the authors' chief criteria for inclusion, but they also comment trenchantly on illustrations. Indexes list stories by writer, tale type, culture, character and place name, grade level, title, or illustrator." SLJ

For a fuller review see: Booklist, March 1, 1998

Index to fairy tales; including folklore, legends, and myths in collections. Scarecrow Press 1985-1994 4v　　　**398.2**

1. Folklore—Indexes 2. Fairy tales—Indexes 3. Legends—Indexes 4. Mythology—Indexes

Volumes covering 1949-1972 and 1973-1977 first published by Faxon 1973 and 1979 respectively

A continuation of Index to fairy tales, myths and legends and its two supplements, compiled by Mary Huse Eastman, published 1926-1952 by Faxon (o.p.)

Index to fairy tales—*Continued*

Volume covering 1949-1972 compiled by Norma Olin Ireland $55.50 (ISBN 0-8108-2011-0); volume covering 1973-1977 compiled by Norma Olin Ireland $37 (ISBN 0-8108-1855-8); volume covering 1978-1986 compiled by Norma Olin Ireland and Joseph W. Sprug $58 (ISBN 0-8108-2194-X); volume covering 1987-1992 compiled by Joseph W. Sprug $62.50 (ISBN 0-8108-2750-6)

"An invaluable reference source for locating specific tales in collections." Peterson. Ref Books for Child. 4th edition

Jaffe, Nina

The cow of no color: riddle stories and justice tales from around the world; [by] Nina Jaffe and Steve Zeitlin; pictures by Whitney Sherman. Holt & Co. 1998 159p il $15.95   **398.2**

1. Folklore
ISBN 0-8050-3736-5   LC 98-14167

In each of these stories, collected from around the world, a character faces a problem situation which requires that he make a decision about what is fair or just

"Sherman's black-and-white line drawings have a stark gracefulness that complements the tales' form and structure; the tales themselves are simply told with little embellishment." Bull Cent Child Books

Includes bibliographical references

Krishnaswami, Uma, 1956-

Shower of gold: girls and women in the stories of India; retold by Uma Krishnaswami; with illustrations by Maniam Selven. Linnet Bks. 1999 125p il $19.95   **398.2**

1. Folklore—India
ISBN 0-208-02484-0   LC 98-43142

A collection of stories featuring strong female figures from Hindu mythology, Buddhist tales, and others from the history and folklore of the Indian subcontinent. Each piece is accompanied by background information

"Retold with immediacy and verve. . . . Krishnaswami's informal introduction is eloquent about themes, ideas, women's roles, and cultural traditions in the stories she has chosen, and also about the way all stories move through time and place." Booklist

Lelooska, Don

Echoes of the elders; the stories and paintings of Chief Lelooska; edited by Christine Normandin. DK Pub.; Callaway Eds. 1997 38p il $24.95

398.2

1. Indians of North America—Folklore
ISBN 0-7894-2455-X

This "compendium showcases five traditional legends of the Kwakiutl people, one of the Northwest Coast Peoples." Publ Wkly

"Lelooska's paintings command as much attention as his words. The images, rendered in the flat colors and bold patterns familiar from coastal masks and totem poles, are placed for maximum impact. . . . A CD featuring Lelooska's animated tellings accompanies the book. A celebration of centuries of culture that will delight and give pause for generations to come." SLJ

Lester, Julius

The last tales of Uncle Remus; as told by Julius Lester; illustrated by Jerry Pinkney. Dial Bks. 1994 156p il $18.99; lib bdg $18.89   **398.2**

1. African Americans—Folklore 2. Animals—Fiction
ISBN 0-8037-1303-7; 0-8037-1304-5 (lib bdg)
                    LC 93-7531

Also available omnibus edition of all four titles in this series Uncle Remus: the complete tales $30 (ISBN 0-8037-2451-9)

"Thirty-nine selections—from tall tales and ghost stories to trickster tales—drawn from the African American tradition are reclaimed and retold in this . . . volume." Booklist

Other available titles about Uncle Remus are:
Further tales of Uncle Remus (1989)
More tales of Uncle Remus (1988)
The tales of Uncle Remus (1987)

Livo, Norma J., 1929-

Folk stories of the Hmong; peoples of Laos, Thailand, and Vietnam; [by] Norma J. Livo and Dia Cha. Libraries Unlimited 1991 135p il $22
                    398.2

1. Hmong (Asian people)
ISBN 0-87287-854-6   LC 91-370

This is a collection of folktales of the Hmong people of Asia which also includes a description of Hmong history and culture, with 16 pages of color photographs of Hmong dress and needlework

Includes bibliographical references

Martin, Rafe, 1946-

Mysterious tales of Japan; illustrated by Tatsuro Kiuchi. Putnam 1996 74p il $18.95   **398.2**

1. Folklore—Japan
ISBN 0-399-22677-X   LC 94-43464

"Some of these 10 stories, such as 'The Boy Who Drew Cats,' will be familiar to readers; others will not. . . . Most of the tales focus on the spiritual powers within nature. A woman falls in love with a pine tree; a man marries a dangerous snow maiden; a priest is granted a wish to live three days as a carp." Booklist

The author retells these "well-chosen tales in the lively voice of a talented storyteller. . . . Shivery, mysterious, and cool as moonlight, these retellings respect both their sources and their audience, while doing what stories do best—entertain." SLJ

Includes bibliographical references

Mayo, Margaret, 1935-

Mythical birds & beasts from many lands; retold by Margaret Mayo; illustrated by Jane Ray. Dutton Children's Bks. 1997 c1996 108p il $19.99 **398.2**

1. Animals—Fiction 2. Folklore 3. Mythology
ISBN 0-525-45788-7   LC 96-36798

First published 1996 in the United Kingdom with title: The Orchard book of mythical birds & beasts

"Mayo retells ten stories, among them tales of Pegasus and the Chimera, the Thunderbird, Quetzalcoatl, and the Nagini, a Burmese Cobra-Woman." Bull Cent Child Books

Mayo, Margaret, 1935-—*Continued*
The "stories are from a variety of cultures and are narrated in an informal yet smooth storytelling style, often with light, effective touches of humor. . . . Ray's distinctive textured paintings are lush and full paged. . . . The earthy palette adds mystery and magic to the text, and her restrained use of gold highlighting is . . . highly effective." SLJ
Includes bibliographical references

McCaughrean, Geraldine, 1951-
The bronze cauldron: myths and legends of the world; illustrated by Bee Willey. Margaret K. McElderry Bks. 1998 c1997 130p il $19.95
                                                        398.2
1. Folklore
ISBN 0-689-81758-4   LC 97-72081
First published 1997 in the United Kingdom
"This collection presents twenty-seven elegantly retold stories, gleaned from sources as diverse as the Mayan *Popul Vuh,* French *Chansons de geste,* Russian *byliny,* as well as Greek, Indian, Chinese, Polynesian, Australian, and Inuit folklore. Willey's playful, brightly colored illustrations are a perfect match for this celebration of story around the world." Horn Book Guide

The crystal pool: myths and legends of the world; illustrated by Bee Willey. Margaret K. McElderry Bks. 1999 C1998 138p il $20   **398.2**
1. Folklore
ISBN 0-689-82266-9
First published 1998 in the United Kingdom
This is a "collection of twenty-eight legends, myths, and stories from a variety of cultures including Inuit, Maori, Sumerian, Egyptian, Hindu, and Bantu." Bull Cent Child Books
"Bee Willey's stylized paintings seem lit from within, intensifying the sense of mystery that underlies even the jocular tales. Unsurpassed for range, language, and presentation." Booklist

The golden hoard: myths and legends of the world; illustrated by Bee Willey. Margaret K. McElderry Bks. 1996 c1995 130p il $19.95
                                                        398.2
1. Folklore
ISBN 0-689-80741-4
First published 1995 in the United Kingdom
This collection of 22 tales includes the story of King Midas, an Anansi story, Polynesian, Mexican, and Native American myths and a Robin Hood story
"This is a resource anthology for reading aloud or storytelling and for readers to dip into for themselves, one story at a time. Mixed media illustrations in brilliantly colored folk-art style extend the action, romance, and magic of the stories." Booklist

The silver treasure: myths and legends of the world; illustrated by Bee Willey. Margaret K. McElderry Bks. 1997 c1996 130p il $19.95
                                                        398.2
1. Folklore
ISBN 0-689-81322-8   LC 96-76845
First published 1996 in the United Kingdom

"In this collection of 23 myths and legends, some stories are as familiar as Rip Van Winkle and the Tower of Babel, whereas others may be new to most readers." Booklist
"These tales are truly marvels—in both their meaningful content and in the teller's lyrical mastery of language." SLJ

McKinley, Robin
The outlaws of Sherwood. Greenwillow Bks. 1988 282p $17   **398.2**
1. Robin Hood (Legendary character)
ISBN 0-688-07178-3   LC 88-45227
Also available in paperback from Ace Bks.
"McKinley takes a fresh look at a classic, changing some of the events or deviating from standard characterization to gain new dimensions. Her afterword explains her artistic compromise with myth and history, her wish to write a version that is 'historically unembarrassing.' With a few exceptions, she has done that admirably, creating a story that has pace and substance and style, and that is given nuance and depth by the characterization." Bull Cent Child Books

Myths, legends, and folktales of America; an anthology; [edited by] David Leeming and Jake Page. Oxford Univ. Press 1999 221p il $25; pa $15.95 (7 and up)   **398.2**
1. Folklore—United States 2. United States—Social life and customs
ISBN 0-19-511783-2; 0-19-511784-0 (pa)
                                     LC 97-48607
This presents "beliefs, myths, sketches, and tall tales that reflect the American experience. Though modest in length, it effectively covers America's polyglot society. . . . Deftly arranged and clearly written." Libr J
Includes bibliographical references

Norman, Howard
The girl who dreamed only geese, and other tales of the Far North; told by Howard Norman; illustrated by Leo & Diane Dillon. Harcourt Brace & Co. 1997 147p il $22   **398.2**
1. Inuit—Folklore
ISBN 0-15-230979-9   LC 96-20880
"Gulliver books"
A collection of stories retold from Inuit folklore
"The narratives have a marvelous vitality and excitement. They capture the sound and cadence of the spoken word. . . . The plots reflect the diversity and humor of Inuit culture. . . . Each tale is accompanied by several large, full-color acrylic illustrations in addition to outstanding black-and-white friezes that run across the top of each page." SLJ

Olson, Arielle North, 1932-
Ask the bones: scary stories from around the world; selected and retold by Arielle North Olson and Howard Schwartz; illustrated by David Linn. Viking 1999 145p il $15.99   **398.2**
1. Folklore
ISBN 0-670-87581-3   LC 98-19108

Olson, Arielle North, 1932-—*Continued*
A collection of scary folktales from countries around the world including China, Russia, Spain, and the United States
"David Linn's bone-chilling black-and-white illustrations . . . will stay with the reader long after the book is closed. Excellent for reading aloud, this collection will satisfy even jaded genre fans." Booklist
Includes bibliographical references

Oodgeroo, 1920-1993
Dreamtime; aboriginal stories; illustrated by Bronwyn Bancroft. Lothrop, Lee & Shepard Bks. 1994 c1972 95p il $16   398.2
1. Australian aborigines—Folklore 2. Folklore—Australia
ISBN 0-688-13296-0   LC 93-79375
First published 1972 in Australia with title: Stradbroke dreamtime
"A combination of traditional and autobiographical tales, this title is divided into two sections. 'Stories from Stradbroke' comprises family stories from the author's life on Stradbroke Island off the Queensland coast and reflects the hardships and joys of Aboriginal living under encroaching white civilization. The second section is called 'Stories from the Old and New Dreamtime' and includes traditional stories recalled by the author from her youth as well as some new stories written in the traditional format." Booklist
"This generous collection provides a fascinating and personal introduction to Aboriginal culture." Publ Wkly

Osborne, Mary Pope, 1949-
Favorite medieval tales; retold by Mary Pope Osborne; illustrated by Troy Howell. Scholastic 1998 86p il $17.95   398.2
1. Folklore—Europe
ISBN 0-590-60042-7   LC 96-17285
A collection of well-known tales from medieval Europe, including "Beowulf," "The Sword in the Stone," "The Song of Roland," and "Gudren and the Island of the Lost Children"
"Inspired by medieval art and illuminated manuscripts, Howell's paintings complement the well-researched text." Horn Book Guide
Includes bibliographical references

Mermaid tales from around the world; retold by Mary Pope Osborne; illustrated by Troy Howell. Scholastic 1993 84p il $16.95; pa $7.99   398.2
1. Mermaids and mermen 2. Folklore
ISBN 0-590-44377-1; 0-439-04781-1 (pa)
LC 92-30527
A collection of twelve mermaid tales from around the world, featuring such sources as France, Greece, and North Africa
"Howell's noteworthy illustrations render each painting in a style reflective of the traditional artwork from the tale's place of origin. . . . Both author and illustrator provide extensive source notes for their work. A great choice for primary read-alouds and a welcome compilation for folk-tale units." Booklist

Paterson, Katherine
Parzival; the quest of the Grail Knight; retold by Katherine Paterson. Lodestar Bks. 1998 127p $15.99   398.2
1. Arthurian romances
ISBN 0-525-67579-5   LC 97-23891
A retelling of the Arthurian legend in which Parzival, unaware of his noble birth, comes of age through his quest for the Holy Grail
"Nearly 800 years old, the story has freshness, humor, grace, and depth. . . . Paterson clarifies much of the Christian doctrine that is the basis of the story, but she is never dull or pedantic." SLJ

Philip, Neil
The Arabian nights; retold by Neil Philip; illustrated by Sheila Moxley. Orchard Bks. 1994 157p il $19.95   398.2
1. Fairy tales 2. Arabs—Folklore
ISBN 0-531-06868-4   LC 94-9137
"Sixteen of the classic stories are retold, each accompanied by one full-page and several smaller illustrations rendered in jewel-toned acrylics. A worthy addition to any collection, the volume includes a helpful explanation of the origins of the tales." Horn Book Guide

Myths & legends. DK Pub. 1999 128p il (Annotated guides) $24.95 (7 and up)   398.2
1. Mythology 2. Legends
ISBN 0-7894-4117-9   LC 98-48836
"Philip uses art in various forms—from Chinese plates to Norwegian wooden church doors to the paintings of Raphael—to illustrate and illuminate 56 myths and legends. . . . Each page is colorful and informative, with details of the artwork sidebarred for further explanation and arrows with captions pointing out details relevant to the myths." Libr J

The story of Robin Hood; illustrated by Nick Harris. DK Pub. 1997 64p il maps (Eyewitness classics) $14.95   398.2
1. Robin Hood (Legendary character)
ISBN 0-7894-1490-2   LC 96-39117
Recounts the life and adventures of Robin Hood, who, with his band of followers, lived in Sherwood Forest as an outlaw dedicated to fighting tyranny. Illustrated notes throughout the text explain the historical background of the story
"This retelling stays true to the tale of Robin Hood, handed down through 14th-century ballads. Philip's version is fast-moving, readable, and child-friendly without becoming inane." SLJ

The tale of Sir Gawain; illustrated by Charles Keeping. Philomel Bks. 1987 102p il $14.95
398.2
1. Arthur, King 2. Gawain (Legendary character) 3. Arthurian romances
ISBN 0-399-21488-7   LC 87-6997
The knight Gawain recounts the adventures of King Arthur and his fellow members of the Round Table, his own battle with the Green Knight, his marriage, and the final days before the fall of Camelot
"Gawain's narration is, appropriately, that of an elder-

Philip, Neil—*Continued*

ly person—he is garrulous, colloquial, articulate, heart-sick at the breach with his best friend and the disintegration of the Round Table company. Philip has linked episodes and characters in the Arthurian cycle in a way that clarifies loyalties and relationships." Bull Cent Child Books

Includes bibliographical references

Pyle, Howard, 1853-1911

The merry adventures of Robin Hood of great renown in Notinghamshire; as written and illustrated by Howard Pyle (7 and up)   **398.2**
1. Robin Hood (Legendary character)

Available from various publishers
First published 1883
Twenty-two stories of Robin Hood and his adventures with the King's foresters in Sherwood Forest. This band of outlaws made a practice of robbing the rich to help the poor. Set during the reign of Henry II of England
"Of all the books of Robin Hood this is best for literary style, adherence to the spirit and events of the old ballads and wealth of historical background." Toronto Public Libr

The story of King Arthur and his knights; written and illustrated by Howard Pyle. Scribner 1984 312p il $21 (7 and up)   **398.2**
1. Arthur, King 2. Arthurian romances
ISBN 0-684-14814-5

Also available in paperback from Dover Publs. and New Am. Lib.
A reissue of the title first published 1903
The first of a four-volume series retelling the Arthurian legends
"An introduction to the loftiest of medieval romances, worthy in style and illustrations of its noble theme." Hodges. Books for Elem Sch Libr

The story of Sir Launcelot and his companions 340p il (7 and up)   **398.2**
1. Lancelot (Legendary character) 2. Arthurian romances

Dover Publs. paperback available
First published 1907
This third book of the series follows "Sir Launcelot's adventures as he rescues Queen Guinevere from the clutches of Sir Mellegrans, does battle with the Worm of Corbin, wanders as a madman in the forest and is finally returned to health by the Lady Elaine." Best Sellers

The story of the champions of the Round Table; written and illustrated by Howard Pyle (7 and up)   **398.2**
1. Arthurian romances

Dover Publs. paperback available
First published 1905
Contents: The story of Launcelot; The book of Sir Tristram; The book of Sir Percival

"Pyle's second volume of Arthurian legends will be of interest to motivated students of literature and history, as well as useful in professional collections for comparisons and source work. In spite of the archaic language . . . the narrative depth and graphic force . . . will draw in readers." Booklist

The story of the Grail and the passing of Arthur (7 and up)   **398.2**
1. Arthur, King 2. Arthurian romances 3. Grail—Fiction

Dover Publs. paperback available
First published 1910
This volume follows the adventures of Sir Geraint, Galahad's quest for the holy Grail, the battle between Launcelot and Gawaine, and the slaying of Mordred

Rogasky, Barbara

The golem; a version; illustrated by Trina Schart Hyman. Holiday House 1996 96p il $18.95 **398.2**
1. Jewish legends
ISBN 0-8234-0964-3   LC 94-13040
This is "the legend of the golem—a monster created of clay—who, under the guidance of the chief rabbi of Prague, rescued the Jews from persecution by anti-Semitic Christians in the late 16th century. Rogasky's strong storytelling skills are evident. . . . Hyman's colorful, fairy tale-like illustrations bring the story to life." SLJ

San Souci, Robert, 1946-

Cut from the same cloth; American women of myth, legend, and tall tale; collected and told by Robert D. San Souci; illustrated by Brian Pinkney; introduction by Jane Yolen. Philomel Bks. 1993 140p il $19.99   **398.2**
1. Folklore—United States 2. Tall tales 3. Women—Folklore
ISBN 0-399-21987-0   LC 92-5233
A collection of fifteen stories about legendary American women from Anglo-American, African American, and Native American folklore
"San Souci's language is vigorous and action verbs abound; Pinkney's black-and-white block prints match the strength of the telling. The inclusion of notes on the sources and a general bibliography make this an academic resource as well as a good collection of rolicking stories." Child Book Rev Serv

A terrifying taste of short & shivery; thirty creepy tales; retold by Robert D. San Souci; illustrated by Lenny Wooden. Delacorte Press 1998 159p il $14.95   **398.2**
1. Ghost stories 2. Folklore
ISBN 0-385-32635-1   LC 98-5551
Also available: Short & shivery (1987); More short & shivery (1994); and Even more short & shivery (1997)
"Drawing on urban legends, myths, folktales, and ghost stories from around the world and across time, the reteller serves up 30 tales of the supernatural that range from eerie to downright scary. . . . Suspenseful, accessible, and energetic, the tales are uniformly brief and gripping." SLJ

Includes bibliographical references

Schwartz, Alvin, 1927-1992
More scary stories to tell in the dark; collected & retold from folklore by Alvin Schwartz; drawings by Stephen Gammell. Lippincott 1984 100p il $14.95; lib bdg $14.89; pa $4.95　**398.2**
1. Ghost stories 2. Horror fiction 3. Folklore—United States
ISBN 0-397-32081-7; 0-397-32082-5 (lib bdg); 0-06-440177-4 (pa)　　LC 83-49494
This volume contains additional stories of ghosts, murders, graveyards and other horrors

Scary stories 3; more tales to chill your bones; collected from folklore and retold by Alvin Schwartz; drawings by Stephen Gammell. HarperCollins Pubs. 1991 115p il $14.95; lib bdg $14.89; pa $4.95　**398.2**
1. Ghost stories 2. Horror fiction 3. Folklore—United States
ISBN 0-06-021794-4; 0-06-021795-2 (lib bdg); 0-06-440418-8 (pa)　　LC 90-47474
More traditional and modern-day stories of ghosts, haunts, superstitions, monsters, and horrible scary things
"The book is well paced and continually captivates, surprises, and entices audiences into reading just one more page. Gammell's gauzy, cobwebby, black-and-white pen-and-ink drawings help to sustain the overall creepy mood." SLJ
Includes bibliographical references

Scary stories to tell in the dark; collected from American folklore by Alvin Schwartz; with drawings by Stephen Gammell. Lippincott 1981 111p il $14.95; lib bdg $14.89; pa $4.95　**398.2**
1. Ghost stories 2. Horror fiction 3. Folklore—United States
ISBN 0-397-31926-6; 0-397-31927-4 (lib bdg); 0-397-31970-3 (pa)　　LC 80-8728
Also available in paperback boxed set with More scary stories to tell in the dark and Scary stories 3 for $14.85 (ISBN 0-06-440465-X)
"A collection of scary, semi-scary, and humorous stories about ghosts and witches collected from American folklore. Most of the stories (poems and songs also) are very short and range from the traditional to the modern. The author includes suggestions on how to tell scary stories effectively." Bull Cent Child Books
"The scholarship in the source notes and bibliography will be useful to serious literature students." SLJ

The **Seven** voyages of Sinbad the Sailor; illustrated by Quentin Blake; retold by John Yeoman. Margaret K. McElderry Bks. 1997 c1996 119p il $19.95　**398.2**
1. Fairy tales 2. Arabs—Folklore
ISBN 0-689-81368-6
First published 1996 in the United Kingdom
"Yeoman's first-person narration . . . leads readers through Sinbad's seven shipwrecks while introducing them to the amazing inhabitants of the islands on which the sailor is inevitably stranded." SLJ
"Blake's ink drawings with watercolors . . . illustrate the story with style and grace. A handsome edition in every way, this book features good storytelling, lively illustrations, and excellent design." Booklist

Sherman, Josepha
Merlin's kin; world tales of the hero magician. August House 1998 192p $21.95; pa $11.95
　　398.2
1. Folklore 2. Magicians—Folklore
ISBN 0-87483-523-2; 0-87483-519-4 (pa)
　　LC 98-24524
"Sherman presents 30 international folktales that feature heroic magicians. Among her sorcerers are Gwydion of Wales, King Solomon of ancient Israel, Clever Aja of the Ashante in Ghana, and Glooscap of the Wabanaki of New England and Canada." Booklist
"This is a good book for collections of folklore, or for fantasy readers who love classic tales of magic." Voice Youth Advocates
Includes bibliographical references

Sutcliff, Rosemary, 1920-1992
The light beyond the forest; the quest for the Holy Grail; decorations by Shirley Felts. Dutton 1980 143p il o.p.; Viking paperback available $4.99 (7 and up)　**398.2**
1. Arthur, King 2. Grail—Fiction 3. Arthurian romances
ISBN 0-14-037150-8 (pa)　　LC 79-23396
First published 1979 in the United Kingdom
This is a retelling of the adventures of King Arthur's knights as they search for the Holy Grail. "After a vision of the Cup from the Last Supper appears, Sir Lancelot, Sir Galahad, Sir Bors, and Sir Percival quit Camelot to look for the Grail, knowing that only the world's most perfect knight will succeed. The individual adventures, which take on a loftier meaning as the journeys also become the knights' personal searches for God, will be most appreciated by special readers interested in King Arthur and his time." Booklist
Followed by The sword and the circle

The road to Camlann; decorations by Shirley Felts. Dutton 1982 142p il o.p.; Viking paperback available $4.99 (7 and up)　**398.2**
1. Arthur, King 2. Arthurian romances
ISBN 0-14-037147-8 (pa)　　LC 82-9481
First published 1981 in the United Kingdom
"This book completes Rosemary Sutcliff's Arthurian trilogy, begun with 'The Light Beyond the Forest' and 'The Sword and the Circle'. Here Sutcliff describes the events from the coming of Mordred to the death of Lancelot. The title refers to The Last Battle, in which Arthur and his civilization perish. Sutcliff writes with her usual economy and rich prose, with a touch of archaic diction in the speeches. . . . Other than Malory, I can think of no better introduction to the whole sweep of Arthurian stories and values." SLJ

The sword and the circle; King Arthur and the Knights of the Round Table. Dutton 1981 260p o.p.; Penguin Bks. paperback available $4.99 (7 and up)　**398.2**
1. Arthur, King 2. Arthurian romances
ISBN 0-14-037149-4 (pa)　　LC 81-9759
The second volume in the author's Arthurian trilogy, begun with: The light beyond the forest. The events in this volume precede those in the earlier volume

Sutcliff, Rosemary, 1920-1992—_Continued_
"The author has brought together thirteen stories associated with the Arthurian cycle, beginning with 'The Coming of Arthur' and concluding not with the passing of Arthur but with 'The Coming of Perceval.' Although she has relied on Malory's 'Morte d'Arthur' for most of her material, she has drawn upon other medieval sources for some of her best storytelling: For example 'Sir Gawain and the Green Knight' comes from a Middle English poem, and the twenty-nine-page 'Tristan and Iseult' is indebted to Godfrey of Strasburg's version." Horn Book
Followed by The road to Camlann

Talk that talk: an anthology of African-American storytelling; edited by Linda Goss & Marian E. Barnes. Simon & Schuster 1989 521p hardcover o.p. paperback available $14 (7 and up)   **398.2**
1. African Americans—Folklore
ISBN 0-671-67168-5 (pa)   LC 89-10582
The selections included range "from slave stories and the animal legends of Brer Rabbit and Brer Fox to the comedy monologues of Dick Gregory and rap routines. . . . Interspersed throughout are brief sections of commentary and analysis." Booklist
Includes bibliographical references

Willard, Nancy
Beauty and the beast; wood engravings by Barry Moser. Harcourt Brace Jovanovich 1992 67p il hardcover o.p. paperback available $7   **398.2**
1. Folklore—France 2. Fairy tales
ISBN 0-15-201549-3 (pa)   LC 91-28398
Through her great capacity to love, a kind and beautiful young woman releases a handsome young man from the spell which has made him into an ugly beast
"This elegant, handsomely packaged retelling, set in turn-of-the-century New York, is graced by Moser's quietly dramatic woodcuts and Willard's sure command of language." Publ Wkly

Yep, Laurence
The rainbow people; [retold by] Lawrence Yep; illustrated by David Wiesner. Harper & Row 1989 194p il $16; pa $4.95   **398.2**
1. Folklore—China
ISBN 0-06-026760-7; 0-06-440441-2 (pa)
LC 88-21203
"Twenty Chinese folktales, selected and retold by Yep from those collected in the 1930s in the Oakland Chinatown as part of a WPA project. . . . The tales, while drawn from and depicting Chinese culture, present a variety of familiar motifs and types: wizards and saints, shape changing and magical objects, pourquoi tales and lessons. An 'Afterword' provides suggestions for further reading on Chinese folktales. This is an excellent introduction to Chinese and Chinese-American folklore." SLJ

The tree of dreams; ten tales from the garden of night; pictures by Isadore Seltzer. BridgeWater Bks. 1995 93p il $13.95   **398.2**
1. Folklore 2. Dreams—Fiction
ISBN 0-8167-3498-4   LC 94-11250

"Yep retells 10 stories from Japan, India, China, Greece, Brazil, and Senegal in lively prose, shaping plot and point of view to emphasize each tale's dream aspect. . . . Seltzer offers one illustration per tale in a brash, deliberately rough-hewn style emphasizing the tales' strangeness." SLJ
Includes bibliographical references

398.9 Proverbs

Titelman, Gregory Y.
Random House dictionary of America's popular proverbs and sayings; [by] Gregory Titelman. 2nd ed. Random House 2000 480p pa $16.95   **398.9**
1. Proverbs
ISBN 0-375-70584-8   LC 99-21554
First published 1996
This dictionary contains over 1,500 expressions. Each proverb or saying is given a definition; a discussion of its origins; a list of variants, and examples from a variety of sources
Includes bibliographical references

400 LANGUAGE

411 Writing systems

Samoyault, Tiphaine
Alphabetical order; how the alphabet began. Viking 1998 unp il $14.99   **411**
1. Alphabet 2. Writing—History
ISBN 0-670-87808-1   LC 97-61745
"Explains how the alphabet began and traces the history of writing from cuneiform to modern-day languages." Booklist
"The text is greatly augmented by luminous paintings of nearly 20 alphabets, including Braille, Morse code and United States Navy semaphore arm positions. As a visual catalogue, the book succeeds handsomely." N Y Times Book Rev

419 Verbal language not spoken and written

Butterworth, Rod R.
The Perigee visual dictionary of signing; an A-to-Z guide to over 1,350 signs of American Sign Language; [by] Rod R. Butterworth and Mickey Flodin. rev & expanded 3rd ed. Berkley Pub. Group 1995 478p il pa $15   **419**
1. Sign language
ISBN 0-399-51952-1   LC 95-1380
"A Perigee book"
First published 1983
This guide to American Sign Language features more than 1,350 alphabetically arranged signs with directions on how to form them. Illustrations show precise hand positions and movements. Includes memory aids

The **Comprehensive** signed English dictionary; edited by Harry Bornstein, Karen L. Saulnier, Lillian B. Hamilton; illustrated by Ralph R. Miller, Sr. Gallaudet College Press 1983 456p il $35 **419**

1. Sign language
ISBN 0-913580-81-3 LC 82-82830

"An introductory essay about learning Signed English is followed by 3,100 words and 14 markers representing English usage. The words are arranged in alphabetical order with illustrations and descriptions." Safford. Guide to Ref Materials for Sch Libr Media Cent. 5th edition

Costello, Elaine
Random House American sign language dictionary; illustrated by Lois Lenderman, Paul M. Setzer, Linda C. Tom. Random House 1994 xxxiv, 1067p il $55; pa $20 **419**

1. Sign language
ISBN 0-394-58580-1; 0-679-78011-4 (pa)

Costello "has compiled over 5000 signs in this massive dictionary. Each sign is illustrated with a full-torso picture showing hand configuration and movement, and both the common and alternate meanings are given where necessary. Arranged like a typical dictionary, this work is easy to use and very detailed." Libr J

Kelly, Michael
Native American talking signs. Chelsea House 1997 64p il (Looking into the past: people, places, and customs) $16.95 **419**

1. Indians of North America—Sign language 2. Indians of North America—Social life and customs
ISBN 0-7910-4681-8 LC 97-26194

Directions for the signs for twenty-five words used by various Native Americans accompanies information about the customs, daily life, religious beliefs, and history of these peoples
Includes bibliographical references

Riekehof, Lottie L.
The joy of signing; the illustrated guide for mastering sign language and the manual alphabet. 2nd ed. Gospel Pub. House 1987 352p il $21.95 **419**

1. Sign language
ISBN 0-88243-520-5 LC 86-80173

First published 1963 with title: Talk to the deaf
This manual presents over 1300 signs used for communicating with deaf adults, and provides basic vocabulary needed for entering interpreter training programs. Signs are arranged in 25 categories with an alphabetical index. For each sign there is a line drawing, description of how to make the sign, origin (concept) and notes on usage
Includes bibliographical references

Sternberg, Martin L. A.
American Sign Language; a comprehensive dictionary; illustrated by Herbert Rogoff. Unabridged. HarperCollins Pubs. 1998 xxi, 983p il pa $22 **419**

1. Sign language
ISBN 0-06-271608-5 LC 98-26649

Also available CD-ROM version; and American Sign Language concise dictionary pa $11 (ISBN 0-06-274010-5)

First published 1981
This dictionary contains more than 7,000 signs and 12,000 illustrations

"The strengths of this work lie not only in its breadth of coverage . . . but also in the 'sign rationale' and 'verbal description' given for each term. These explanations help the reader remember the sign and its meaning. . . . For those who learn via visuals rather than text, the illustrations provided are simple outlines of the hand gestures and help with the physical execution of each sign. Another useful feature for the novice are the synonyms given after each word indicating that the sign has multiple meanings." Am Ref Books Annu, 1995

422.03 Etymology of standard English—Dictionaries

The **Barnhart** dictionary of etymology; Robert K. Barnhart, editor; Sol Steinmetz, managing editor. Wilson, H.W. 1988 xxvii, 1284p $85 **422.03**

1. English language—Etymology—Dictionaries
ISBN 0-8242-0745-9 LC 87-27994

"The 30,000 entries focus on current U.S. English and provide spelling variations, pronunciation, part of speech, a short definition, date of first recorded use in English, information about the language from which the word evolved, and (in some cases) comments on the word's history. Words of U.S. origin are so indicated. The work includes scientific and technical words, regional English, slang, product names, and recent words." Safford. Guide to Ref Materials for Sch Libr Media Cent. 5th edition

Morris, William, 1913-1994
Morris dictionary of word and phrase origins; [by] William and Mary Morris; foreword by Isaac Asimov. 2nd ed. Harper & Row 1988 669p $38 **422.03**

1. English language—Etymology—Dictionaries 2. English language—Terms and phrases
ISBN 0-06-015862-X LC 87-45651

Original three volume edition published 1962-1971; one volume edition first published 1977

"Traces the origins of several thousand words and phrases in the English language, including slang terms and clichés not usually found in more formal works. Entries are listed alphabetically by the first word in the phrase, with an index at the end." Ref Sources for Small & Medium-sized Libr. 5th edition

423 English language—Dictionaries

The **American** Heritage children's dictionary; by the editors of the American heritage dictionaries. Houghton Mifflin 1998 856p il maps $17 **423**

1. English language—Dictionaries
ISBN 0-395-85739-2 LC 98-21414

First published 1986
Also available CD-ROM version

This illustrated reference includes an A-Z vocabulary listing, a thesaurus, and special sections on synonyms, word histories, vocabulary builders, and phonics

The **American** Heritage student dictionary. Houghton Mifflin $18   **423**
1. English language—Dictionaries

First published 1977 with title: The American Heritage school dictionary (1998 edition). Periodically revised

The more than 65,000 entries are accompanied by over 2000 photographs and illustrations. Includes geographical and biographical entries, usage notes, word histories, synonym paragraphs, and regionalisms. Computer and Internet terms are featured

Bartlett's Roget's thesaurus. Little, Brown 1996 xxxii, 1415p $19.95   **423**
1. English language—Synonyms and antonyms
ISBN 0-316-10138-9   LC 96-18343
This includes "more than 350,000 terms and phrases in an easy-to-use format. . . . A thesaurus that reflects the current state of American English, including terminology from the worlds of computers and television, with such sub-categories as 'Living Things,' 'The Arts,' 'Feelings.' But what really makes the book a joy to use is the tremendously useful lists—everything from phobias to styles and periods of furniture." Am Libr

Corbeil, Jean-Claude
The Facts on File visual dictionary. Facts on File 1986 797p il $29.95   **423**
1. Picture dictionaries
ISBN 0-8160-1544-9   LC 86-6261
"Thousands of objects and their parts are labeled in this graphic presentation. . . . Each page is captioned, and each item and its parts is clearly labeled. The table of contents lists over 40 topical sections with their subsections. There are general, topical, and specialized (e.g., athletics, automobile, baseball, bicycle, camping) indexes." Nichols. Guide to Ref Books for Sch Media Cent. 4th edition

DK dictionary/thesaurus. DK Pub. 1999 512p $9.95   **423**
1. English language—Dictionaries 2. English language—Synonyms and antonyms
ISBN 0-7894-3949-2   LC 98-52899
This combined dictionary and thesaurus for school-aged children is alphabetically arranged with more than 20,000 dictionary entries and 50,000 synonyms

DK ultimate visual dictionary 2000. DK Pub. 1999 640p il $39.95   **423**
1. Picture dictionaries 2. English language—Dictionaries
ISBN 0-7894-4619-7
First published 1994 with title: Dorling Kindersley ultimate visual dictionary
This work, "covering over 30,000 terms in 270 major entries, . . . is divided into 14 sections, ranging from prehistoric life to architecture to music. A detailed index provides access to the entries, and the book's beautiful photographs and illustrations make it an enjoyable as well as an educational resource." Libr J

The **Doubleday** Roget's thesaurus in dictionary form; Sidney I. Landau, editor in chief; Ronald J. Bogus, managing editor. rev ed. Doubleday 1987 804p thumb-indexed $14.95   **423**
1. English language—Synonyms and antonyms
2. Americanisms
ISBN 0-385-23997-1   LC 86-24184
First published 1977
"Despite the words 'Roget' and 'thesaurus' in the title, which may imply a classified arrangement, the entry words in this volume are listed in alphabetical order. Some 250,000 synonyms and antonyms, including slang, are provided, but with little guidance in word selection. This work's arrangement will appeal to those who find *Roget's International Thesaurus* awkward to use." Safford. Guide to Ref Materials for Sch Libr Media Cent. 5th edition

Hellweg, Paul
The American Heritage children's thesaurus; by Paul Hellweg with the editors of the American Heritage dictionaries. Houghton Mifflin 1997 279p il $17   **423**
1. English language—Synonyms and antonyms
ISBN 0-395-84977-2   LC 97-12396
Presents over 4000 alphabetically arranged words with several synonyms and an illustrative sentence for each
"Each entry word is printed in dark purple, followed by part of speech. Best choices are listed first, followed by other choices. . . . Homographs are entered separately and are numbered. . . . Recommended for breadth, attractiveness, and usefulness." Booklist

Merriam-Webster's dictionary of synonyms. Merriam-Webster thumb-indexed $21.95   **423**
1. English language—Synonyms and antonyms

First published 1942 with title: Webster's dictionary of synonyms. (1993 edition) Periodically revised
"This synonym dictionary is an outstanding work. . . . Synonyms and similar words, alphabetically arranged, are carefully defined, discriminated, and illustrated with thousands of quotations. The entries also include antonyms and analogous words." Nichols. Guide to Ref Books for Sch Media Cent. 4th edition

Merriam-Webster's school thesaurus. Merriam-Webster 1994 690p $15.95   **423**
1. English language—Synonyms and antonyms
ISBN 0-87779-178-3
First published 1978 with title: Webster's student thesaurus
This alphabetically arranged volume includes more than 43,000 synonyms, antonyms, idiomatic phrases, related words, and contrasted words

Random House Webster's unabridged dictionary. 2nd ed. Random House 1998 xxvi, 2230p il maps $100   **423**
1. English language—Dictionaries
ISBN 0-679-40383-3   LC 97-17702
First published 1966 with title: Random House dictionary of the English language
Also available CD-ROM version

Random House Webster's unabridged dictionary—*Continued*

This dictionary contains over 315,000 entries. A new-words section and an essay on the growth of English are included. 2,400 spot maps and illustrations complement the text

Roget's II; the new thesaurus; by the editors of The American heritage dictionaries. 3rd ed. Houghton Mifflin 1995 1200p $16.95 (7 and up) **423**

1. English language—Synonyms and antonyms
ISBN 0-395-68722-5   LC 94-42879
First published 1980

This work's "alphabetical sequence of headwords supplemented by a category index and plentiful cross-references supplies an array of colorful and vivid synonyms that will be helpful for writers who do not have the time to engage in the long process of using a classified or category-indexed thesaurus." Booklist

Roget's international thesaurus. 5th ed, edited by Robert L. Chapman. HarperCollins Pubs. 1992 1139p $18.95; thumb indexed $21   **423**

1. English language—Synonyms and antonyms
ISBN 0-06-270046-4; 0-06-270014-6 (thumb indexed)
LC 92-7615

First copyright edition published 1911 with title: The standard thesaurus of English words and phrases classified and arranged so as to facilitate the expression of ideas and assist in literary composition

"Roget's 150-year-old plan of organizing words within eight broad classes has been revised by Chapman to create a simpler, more natural, and contemporary arrangement of 15 new classes." Libr J

Roget's student thesaurus. rev ed. Scott Foresman-Addison Wesley 1994 536p il $16   **423**

1. English language—Synonyms and antonyms
ISBN 0-673-12437-1

Replaces the edition published 1991 under the authorship of Andrew Schiller and William A. Jenkins

"This book also appears under the title Writer's Thesaurus." Verso of title page

An illustrated alphabetical list of words, their synonyms, antonyms, and the shades of meaning between them. Also includes quotations from historical figures; examples from literature, and writing tips

Terban, Marvin
Scholastic dictionary of idioms. Scholastic 1996 245p il $15.95; pa $8.95   **423**

1. English language—Idioms
ISBN 0-590-27549-6; 0-590-38157-1 (pa)
LC 95-16593

"Terban explains the meanings and origins (if known) of more than 600 idioms and proverbs. . . . Each page includes one lightly comical line drawing of a child expressing feelings such as quizzical, annoyed, amused, or distressed. Not only is this a good resource for teachers who discuss idioms in the classroom but it also has some appeal for browsers." Booklist

Webster's third new international dictionary of the English language, unabridged. Merriam-Webster il   **423**

1. English language—Dictionaries

Prices vary according to binding

Original edition by Noah Webster published 1828 with title: An American dictionary of the English language. Has also appeared under various other titles. First published with present title 1961. (1993 edition) Frequently reprinted with additions and changes to keep it up to date

"First choice unabridged dictionary." N Y Public Libr. Ref Books for Child Collect. 2d edition

Young, Sue
The new comprehensive American rhyming dictionary. Morrow 1991 622p o.p.; Avon Bks. paperback available $14   **423**

1. English language—Rhyme 2. Americanisms
ISBN 0-380-71392-6 (pa)   LC 90-19165

This book contains over 65,000 words and phrases categorized by sound, rather than spelling. It includes many colloquialisms and slang expressions

427   English language variations

Dictionary of American slang; edited by Robert L. Chapman. 3rd ed. HarperCollins Pubs. 1995 xxii, 617p $40   **427**

1. English language—Slang 2. Americanisms
ISBN 0-06-270107-X   LC 97-2771

First published 1960 by Crowell. Variant title: New dictionary of American slang

This dictionary defines over 17,000 terms. Examples of usage are provided and derivations noted. Particular emphasis has been placed on language pertaining to technology, business and the media

428   Standard English usage

Terban, Marvin
Scholastic dictionary of spelling; over 15,000 words. Scholastic Ref. 1998 223p il $16.95   **428**

1. Spellers
ISBN 0-590-30697-9   LC 97-18020

The words in this speller are "arranged alphabetically (i.e., ladies comes before lady) broken into syllables with the accented syllables in boldface, on attractively laid-out pages, with occasional cartoonish illustrations. Homophones include pronunciation help, and a parenthetical sentence illustrates proper use. The first 26 pages are a treasure trove of helpful hints. . . . The book concludes with the 'Misspeller's Dictionary,' 600 words with tricky beginnngs listed in matched pairs of the common misspelling and the correct one." Book Rep

433 German language—Dictionaries

Cassell's German-English, English-German dictionary; completely revised by Harold T. Betteridge. Macmillan 2v in 1 $25; thumb-indexed $27   **433**
1. German language—Dictionaries (thumb-indexed)
Also available in a concise edition for $13.95 (ISBN 0-02-522650-9)
First compiled 1888 by Elizabeth Weir and published by Heath. Peridically revised. Previous American editions published by Funk & Wagnalls with title: The New Cassell's German dictionary
This dictionary incorporates "many new words and usages. Gives phonetic transcriptions of headwords. One of the most useful bilingual dictionaries." Guide to Ref Books. 11th edition

443 French language—Dictionaries

Cassell's French dictionary: French-English, English-French; completely revised by Denis Girard with the assistance of Gaston Dulong, Oliver Van Oss, and Charles Guinness. Macmillan 1977 762, 655p $25; thumb-indexed $27   **443**
1. French language—Dictionaries
ISBN 0-02-522610-X; 0-02-522620-7 (thumb-indexed)
LC 77-7669
Also available in a concise edition for $12.95 (ISBN 0-02-522670-3)
First published 1920 with title: Cassell's French-English, English-French dictionary. Previous American editions published by Funk & Wagnalls with title: The New Cassell's French dictionary
"New words including colloquialisms, slangs, American English and French-Canadian terms [are included]. . . . There are also sections on French verbs and French and English abbreviations. Reliable, standard dictionary. A first choice." N Y Public Libr. Ref Books for Child Collect. 2d edition

453 Italian language—Dictionaries

Cassell's Italian dictionary: Italian-English, English-Italian; compiled by Piero Rebora with the assistance of Francis M. Guercio and Arthur L. Hayward. Macmillan $21; thumb-indexed $24.95   **453**
1. Italian language—Dictionaries

First published 1958 in the United Kingdom with title: Cassell's Italian-English, English-Italian dictionary. Periodically revised. Previous United States editions published by Funk & Wagnalls
"A general dictionary of the Italian language as currently written and spoken." Ref Sources for Small & Medium-sized Libr. 5th edition

463 Spanish language—Dictionaries

Cassell's Spanish-English, English-Spanish dictionary. Completely rev and reset ed, completely rev by Anthony Gooch, Angel García de Paredes. Macmillan 1978 $19.95; thumb-indexed $22.95   **463**
1. Spanish language—Dictionaries
ISBN 0-02-522900-1; 0-02-522910-9 (thumb-indexed)
LC 77-18453
Also available in a concise edition for $13 (ISBN 0-02-522660-6)
First published 1959 in the United Kingdom. First American edition published 1960 by Funk & Wagnalls with title: Cassell's Spanish dictionary
This dictionary emphasizes the Spanish of Latin America, and includes both classical and literary Spanish as well as the language of the modern Spanish-speaking world

473 Latin language—Dictionaries

Cassell's Latin dictionary: Latin-English, English-Latin; by D. P. Simpson. Macmillan 1977 c1959 883p thumb-indexed $24.95   **473**
1. Latin language—Dictionaries
ISBN 0-02-522580-4
Also available in a concise edition for $12.95 (ISBN 0-02-522630-4)
First published 1854. This edition first published 1959. Previous United States editions published by Funk & Wagnalls with title: Cassell's new Latin dictionary
"This remains a standard work and the best choice of an inexpensive, one-volume Latin dictionary. The 30,000 entries include geographical and proper names, etymological notes, and illustrative quotations." Safford. Guide to Ref Materials for Sch Libr Media Cent. 5th edition

491.7 East Slavic languages. Russian

English-Russian dictionary; compiled by V. K. Müller. 7th ed, new rev ed completely reset. Dutton 1965 1192p o.p.   **491.7**
1. Russian language—Dictionaries

Available only from Saphrograph for $40.95
First published 1944 in the United States
This dictionary is arranged alphabetically by the English word. Russian translations are derived from the actual literary, conversational, and specialized vocabularies of English, American and Australian works. Separate lists of names, geographical terms, initials

493 Non-Semitic Afro-Asiatic languages

Giblin, James, 1933-
The riddle of the Rosetta Stone; key to ancient Egypt; [by] James Cross Giblin. Crowell 1990 85p il lib bdg $15.89; pa $6.95 **493**
1. Rosetta stone 2. Egyptian language 3. Hieroglyphics
ISBN 0-690-04799-1 (lib bdg); 0-06-446137-8 (pa)
LC 89-29289
Describes how the discovery and deciphering of the Rosetta Stone unlocked the secret of Egyptian hieroglyphics
"Suspense keeps the reader glued to this fine piece of nonfiction as the mystery of hieroglyphs is slowly unraveled. . . . The author has done a masterful job of distilling information, citing the highlights, and fitting it all together in an interesting and enlightening look at a puzzling subject." Horn Book
Includes bibliographical references

Katan, Norma Jean
Hieroglyphs, the writing of ancient Egypt; by Norma Jean Katan with Barbara Mintz. Atheneum Pubs. 1981 96p il map $16 **493**
1. Egyptian language 2. Hieroglyphics
ISBN 0-689-50176-5 LC 80-13576
"A Margaret K. McElderry book"
Explains the origins of hieroglyphics and what they mean, tells how this ancient form of writing was decoded, and describes the training and importance of scribes

495.6 Japanese language

Basic Japanese-English dictionary; Kiso Nihongo gakushū jiten; [by] The Japan Foundation. Paperback ed. Oxford Univ. Press 1993 958p pa $18.95 **495.6**
1. Japanese language—Dictionaries
ISBN 0-19-864328-4 LC 92-38748
First published 1986 in Japan; 1989 by Oxford University Press
"This desk dictionary provides basic vocabulary for the daily use of those learning Japanese. The nearly 2,900 entries are written in Roman letters followed by Kanji and/or Kana. Example sentences are included." Guide to Ref Books. 11th edition

Merriam-Webster's Japanese-English learner's dictionary. Merriam-Webster 1993 1121p il $27.95 **495.6**
1. Japanese language—Dictionaries
ISBN 0-87779-164-3 LC 93-27294
Published in collaboration with Kenkyusha Limited
"This dictionary is designed for use by students at all levels and by business professionals who intend to master practical modern Japanese. Each Japanese entry, which [has] accent marks, is shown in roman letters, then by the standard writing in *hiragana* or *katakana*; this is followed, where appropriate, by another writing in parentheses that contains *kanji*, and then the English equivalent is given. Model sentences and phrases are provided for most entries." Am Ref Books Annu, 1994

The **Oxford-Duden** pictorial Japanese and English dictionary. Oxford Univ. Press 1997 880p il pa $21.95 **495.6**
1. Japanese language—Dictionaries 2. Picture dictionaries
ISBN 0-19-860119-0
First published 1983 with title: The Oxford-Duden pictorial English-Japanese dictionary
"Pictures of hospitals and doctor's and dentist's offices, clothing, houses and furniture, supermarkets, airports and libraries (and about 380 more items) are labeled with numbers which are keys for the terms printed below in each language. Complete indexes in each language provide quick access." Safford. Guide to Ref Materials for Sch Libr Media Cent. 5th edition

500 NATURAL SCIENCES & MATHEMATICS

Barnes-Svarney, Patricia
The New York Public Library science desk reference. Macmillan 1995 668p il maps $39.95 **500**
1. Science 2. Technology
ISBN 0-02-860403-2 LC 94-40445
"A Stonesong Press book"
"Thirteen chapters cover major divisions of science (e.g., astronomy, biology, chemistry, computer and environmental sciences, technology) listing basic facts, formulas, terms, and processes. One additional chapter lists 'useful resources' such as books, organizations, museums, zoos, national parks, and planetariums." Libr J

Graham, Ian, 1953-
Questions & answers book of science facts; written by Ian Graham & Paul Sterry. Facts on File 1997 80p il maps $19.95 **500**
1. Science 2. Technology
ISBN 0-8160-3655-1 LC 97-8725
This book answers questions in science and technology such as "Is there life on other planets? How did ancient people use stone? What is inside an earthworm? How does a doorbell work?" Publisher's note
"Large typeface, nice color illustrations and interesting information make this a great browsing book for a middle school-age student. . . . Each question has a clear, understandable answer to a child with good reading skills and basic science background." Am Ref Books Annu, 1998

U.X.L science fact finder; Phillis Engelbert, editor. U.X.L 1997 3v il set $95 **500**
1. Science 2. Technology
ISBN 0-7876-1727-X LC 97-24046
Adapted from The handy science answer book, 2nd edition, published 1996 by Visible Ink Press
Contents: v1 The natural world; v2 The physical world; v3 The technological world
This set "answers more than 750 FAQs (frequently asked questions) from all areas of science: natural, physical, and technological. The three volumes are arranged

U.X.L science fact finder—*Continued*
by subject, with numerous sidebars, photos, diagrams, and charts. There is a further reading list repeated at the beginning of each volume, divided into books, journals and periodicals, online sources, and CD-ROMs. . . . A fun, interesting, and helpful resource." Booklist

502   Science—Miscellany

Ochoa, George
The Wilson chronology of science and technology; [by] George Ochoa and Melinda Corey. Wilson, H.W. 1997 440p $60   **502**
1. Science—History 2. Technology—History
ISBN 0-8242-0933-8   LC 97-22060
This chronology begins in 2,500,000 B.C. and continues into 1997. "Within each year, entries are arranged alphabetically according to one of 13 categories: archaeology; astronomy, space science, and space exploration; biology, biochemistry, agriculture, and ecology; chemistry; earth sciences (geology, oceanography, meteorology) and earth exploration; mathematics; medicine; miscellaneous; paleontology; physics; psychology, neuroscience, and artificial intelligence; social sciences (anthropology, sociology, economics, political science) and linguistics; and technology and engineering." Publisher's note
Includes bibliographical references

502.8   Science—Auxiliary techniques and procedures; apparatus, equipment, materials

Levine, Shar
Fun with your microscope; [by] Shar Levine & Leslie Johnstone; illustrations by Jason Coons; photomicrographs by James Humphreys & the authors. Sterling 1998 80p il $19.95; pa $9.95   **502.8**
1. Microscopes 2. Science—Experiments
ISBN 0-8069-9945-4; 0-8069-9946-2 (pa)
          LC 97-27609
Presents basic techniques for using a microscope to observe and investigate a variety of materials that might be found around the house. Also includes experiments and ideas for science fair projects
"A very interesting, scientifically accurate, and stimulating book." Appraisal

The microscope book; [by] Shar Levine & Leslie Johnstone; illustrations by David Sovka. Sterling 1996 80p il $19.95; pa $9.95   **502.8**
1. Microscopes 2. Science—Experiments
ISBN 0-8069-4898-1; 0-8069-4899-X (pa)
          LC 95-43239
An introduction to microscopes and magnification with experiments using such easily obtained materials as comic books, leaves, hair, and potatoes
"An excellent introduction. . . . The attractive, well-designed format features colorful drawings and full-color microscopic photographs that are helpful in illustrating and explaining projects." SLJ

Tomb, Howard, 1959-
Microaliens; dazzling journeys with an electron microscope; [by] Howard Tomb and Dennis Kunkel; with drawings by Tracy Dockray. Farrar, Straus & Giroux 1993 79p il $16   **502.8**
1. Electron microscopes 2. Science—Pictorial works
ISBN 0-374-34960-6   LC 93-1403
Text and photographs taken with an electron microscope examine such items as bird feathers, fleas, skin, mold, and blood
"Tomb's short introduction is a good overview of the history of the electron microscope and how it works. . . . [This is] a fascinating look at a relatively unknown world." Booklist
Includes bibliographical references

503   Science—Encyclopedias and dictionaries

The **DK** science encyclopedia. new rev ed. DK Pub. 1998 448p il maps $39.95   **503**
1. Science—Encyclopedias
ISBN 0-7894-2190-9   LC 97-20881
First published 1993 with title: The Dorling Kindersley science encyclopedia
This work "features more than 280 main entries and 1,900 subentries grouped under subjects such as matter, materials, weather, and space." Booklist
"An outstanding, comprehensive reference work. That so much can be packed into one volume and still maintain clarity, organization, and scope is a tribute to the efforts of the exceptional team of science writers and specialists." Am Ref Books Annu, 1999

Macmillan encyclopedia of science. rev ed. Macmillan Lib. Ref. USA 1997 12v il maps set $375   **503**
1. Science—Encyclopedias 2. Technology—Encyclopedias
ISBN 0-02-864556-1   LC 96-36597
First published 1991
An encyclopedia of science and technology, covering such areas as the Earth, astronomy, plants and animals, medicine, the environment, manufacturing, communication, and transportation
For a review see: Booklist, Aug. 1, 1997

Ultimate visual dictionary of science. DK Pub. 1998 448p il $29.95   **503**
1. Science—Dictionaries
ISBN 0-7894-3512-8   LC 98-11900
At head of title: Dorling Kindersley
"Much of this title is a compilation of several previously published volumes. *The Visual Dictionary of Physics* (1995), *The Visual Dictonary of Chemistry* (1996), and *The Visual Dictionary of Human Anatomy* (1996, all DK) have been virtually reprinted page by page, illustration by illustration, and shrunk to fit a smaller format . . . . Other sections include medical science, life sciences and ecology, earth sciences, astronomy and astrophysics, electronics and computer science, and mathematics. Here, the information has been synthesized from earlier books and updated." SLJ

The **World** Book encyclopedia of science. World Bk. 8v il set $209 **503**
1. Science—Encyclopedias

Based on a German encyclopedia copyright 1984; this title was first published in 1985 in seven volumes. (2000 edition) Periodically revised

Contents: v1 Astronomy; v2 Physics; v3 Chemistry; v4 The planet earth; v5 The plant world; v6 The animal world; v7 The human body; v8 Men and women of science. Index

"This set was last published by World Book in 1986. It is based on a German work but has been revised for an American audience. Its intent is 'to explain for adults and children alike the many aspects of science that are not only fascinating in themselves but are also vitally important to an understanding of the world today." Booklist

"An overall excellent and affordable effort to present science clearly to a wide range of ages and abilities." Am Ref Books Annu, 1998

507.05 Science—Education and related topics—Serial publications

The **Science** Teacher. National Science Teachers Assn. $72 per year **507.05**
1. Science—Study and teaching—Periodicals
ISSN 0036-8555

Nine issues per year. First published 1934

"Most of the contributors of this journal are high school science teachers, and they deal quite specifically with teaching techniques and problems in the areas of biology, chemistry, physics, astronomy, and physical and earth sciences in grades 7-12. In addition to the usual features, the May issue contains a special section of articles entitled 'Student/Teacher Success Stories.' Recommended for high school and science education collections." Katz. Mag for Libr. 10th edition

507.8 Science—Use of apparatus and equipment in study and teaching

Adams, Richard C., 1945-
More ideas for science projects; [by] Richard Adams and Robert Gardner. rev. Watts 1998 128p il (Experimental science series) lib bdg $24 (7 and up) **507.8**
1. Science projects
ISBN 0-531-11380-9   LC 97-5792
First published 1989

This "offers over 100 ideas in a variety of scientific disciplines. In some cases, detailed instructions are given for projects; in others, an idea is presented with a number of questions to be considered. . . . [It includes] suggestions for using computers to collect and analyze data. . . . This is a good resource for class assignments and science-fair projects." SLJ
Includes glossary and bibliographical references

Bochinski, Julianne Blair, 1966-
The complete handbook of science fair projects; illustrations by Judy J. Bochinski-DiBiase. rev ed. Wiley 1996 221p il $29.95; pa $14.95 (7 and up) **507.8**
1. Science projects
ISBN 0-471-12378-1; 0-471-12377-3 (pa)
LC 95-22791
First published 1991

"The book starts with a section on how to conduct an experiment, record and evaluate results, and then put it all together in an informative and appealing display. . . . Besides the 50 experiments described, an additional 400 ideas are suggested in Appendix A. Other appendices list suppliers of scientific materials and science fairs on a state-by-state and country basis. This inexpensive and useful collection is highly recommended." Sci Books Films
Includes glossary

Bombaugh, Ruth J.
Science fair success; [by] Ruth Bombaugh. rev & expanded. Enslow Pubs. 1999 128p il lib bdg $19.95 (7 and up) **507.8**
1. Science projects
ISBN 0-7660-1163-1   LC 98-3297
First published 1989

A guide for choosing, designing, and completing an investigative science fair project, with an appendix listing prize winning projects by students
Includes bibliographical references

Cash, Terry
175 more science experiments to amuse and amaze your friends; experiments! tricks! things to make! by Terry Cash, Steve Parker, and Barbara Taylor; illustrated by Kuo Kang Chen and Peter Bull. Random House 1991 172p il pa $14.99 **507.8**
1. Science—Experiments 2. Scientific recreations
ISBN 0-679-80390-4   LC 90-39250
Companion volume to 175 science experiments to amuse and amaze your friends, by B. Walpole (1988)

This volume provides step-by-step instructions for 175 experiments, tricks, and things to make that illustrate the principles of sound, electricity, simple chemistry, and weather

"This book will be useful for the varied activities and for its general clarity in explanations and descriptions." SLJ
Includes glossary

Cobb, Vicki, 1938-
Don't try this at home! science fun for kids on the go; [by] Vicki Cobb and Kathy Darling; illustrated by True Kelley. Morrow Junior Bks. 1998 175p il lib bdg $15 **507.8**
1. Science—Experiments 2. Scientific recreations
ISBN 0-688-14856-5   LC 97-20481
Also available in paperback from Avon Bks.

Provides instructions for a variety of science activities outside, arranged by such categories as school, parks, and vehicles

"Good ideas and good presentation combine for an appealing book of hands-on science." Booklist

Cobb, Vicki, 1938—*Continued*

Science experiments you can eat; illustrated by David Cain. rev & updated. HarperCollins Pubs. 1994 214p il $14.89; pa $5.95   **507.8**
1. Science—Experiments 2. Cooking
ISBN 0-06-023534-9; 0-06-446002-9 (pa)
                     LC 93-13679
First published 1972
Experiments with food demonstrate various scientific principles and produce an eatable result. Includes rock candy, grape jelly, cupcakes, and popcorn
Includes glossary

You gotta try this! absolutely irresistible science; by Vicki Cobb and Kathy Darling; illustrated by True Kelly. Morrow Junior Bks. 1999 144p il $15   **507.8**
1. Science—Experiments 2. Scientific recreations
ISBN 0-688-15740-8   LC 98-29556
A collection of science experiments and activities, arranged in such categories as "Physical Attractions," "Curious Chemistry," and "Freaky Fluids"
"True Kelley's line-and-gray-wash illustrations clarify the directions and add their own good-natured visual appeal. A fine addition to science collections." Booklist

Friedhoffer, Robert
Science lab in a supermarket; by Bob Friedhoffer; illustrated by Joe Hosking. Watts 1998 95p il (Physical science labs) lib bdg $24
                              507.8
1. Science—Experiments
ISBN 0-531-11335-3   LC 96-37285
Presents a variety of experiments using items you can buy in the supermarket. Also explains the scientific basis for such things as the flexible plastic strips that cover doorways leading into the meat departments in many large markets
"Explanations are clear and thought provoking, and the writing style is lively and humorous." SLJ
Includes glossary and bibliographical references

Gardner, Robert, 1929-
Science fair projects—planning, presenting, succeeding. Enslow Pubs. 1999 104p il (Science projects) lib bdg $19.95 (7 and up)   **507.8**
1. Science projects
ISBN 0-89490-949-5   LC 98-8667
Provides information on choosing and planning a science fair project, carrying it out, recording your findings, writing a report, and exhibiting the project
Includes bibliographical references

Science projects about physics in the home. Enslow Pubs. 1999 112p il (Science projects) lib bdg $19.95 (7 and up)   **507.8**
1. Physics 2. Science—Experiments 3. Science projects
ISBN 0-89490-948-7   LC 98-6822
Presents instructions for physics projects and experiments that can be done at home and exhibited at science fairs
"This volume is well organized with lots of hands-on activities that use relatively simple pieces of equipment. . . . A good starting point in the understanding of the physics of objects and events in our daily life." Sci Books Films
Includes bibliographical references

Krieger, Melanie Jacobs
How to excel in science competitions. rev and updated ed. Enslow Pubs. 1999 128p il (Science fair success) lib bdg $19.95   **507.8**
1. Science projects
ISBN 0-7660-1292-1   LC 98-31754
First published 1991
This is a "resource for preparing for science competitions. Students are guided from start to finish, including beginning a project, writing and presenting a paper, and answering judges' questions. . . . This well-researched, clearly written book will encourage exploration and experimentation." SLJ
Includes bibliographical references

Parker, Steve
Science experiments. Sterling 1998 96p il $19.95   **507.8**
1. Science—Experiments
ISBN 0-8069-6295-X   LC 99-162341
"A Quarto children's book"
Cover title: Shocking, slimy, stinky, shiny science experiments
"A collection of 73 . . . projects. Each chapter begins with a brief introduction followed by a number of experiments. The first chapter, 'Shiny Science,' covers light and sight, including reflections, lenses, and rainbows. 'Shocking Science' begins with static electricity and progresses to electromagnetism. The last two chapters, 'Slimy Science' and 'Stinky Science,' invite children to create, observe, and analyze a variety of slimes and smells." SLJ
Includes glossary

Rosner, Marc Alan
Science fair success using the Internet. Enslow Pubs. 1999 112p il (Science fair success) lib bdg $19.95 (7 and up)   **507.8**
1. Science projects 2. Internet
ISBN 0-7660-1172-0   LC 98-25945
Explains how to use Internet resources, including emailing experts and using search engines, to enhance science projects, with sample projects in biology, chemistry, physics, environment and earth science, and astronomy
Includes bibliographical references

Science experiments on file; experiments, demonstrations, and projects for school and home; edited by Judith A. Bazler. rev ed. Facts on File 2000 2v il loose-leaf set $300   **507.8**
1. Science—Experiments
ISBN 0-8160-3998-4   LC 99-52951
First published 1988
Contents: v1 Earth science; weather; space; biology; v2 Chemistry; physics

Science experiments on file—*Continued*

This offers 200 science experiments, listing time required, safety precautions, materials, procedure, principles illustrated, data tables, connections, and additional activities, which may be reproduced for classroom use

Science fairs: ideas and activities. World Bk. 1997 80p il $15; pa $11   **507.8**
1. Science projects
ISBN 0-7166-4498-3; 0-7166-4497-5 (pa)
LC 97-29786
Ideas for hands-on science fair projects in the areas of space, earth, machines, plants, and time
"Great care has been taken to make the experiments attractive and accessible." SLJ
Includes bibliographical references

Tocci, Salvatore

How to do a science fair project. rev ed. Watts 1997 127p il (Experimental science series) lib bdg $22.30; pa $9.95   **507.8**
1. Science projects 2. Science—Experiments
ISBN 0-531-11346-9 (lib bdg); 0-531-15881-0 (pa)
LC 96-50019
First published 1986
A step-by-step guide for creating a variety of projects suitable for entry in a science fair with suggestions for choosing a subject, performing the experiment, and polishing the presentation
"The author provides sage advice on how to select a project, conduct the research, and present the results. A good list of dos and don'ts includes a nice discussion of what works as a project topic and what doesn't. . . . The author also provides a good list of science supply companies." SLJ
Includes glossary and bibliographical references

VanCleave, Janice Pratt

Janice VanCleave's guide to the best science fair projects; [by] Janice VanCleave. Wiley 1997 156p il pa 14.95   **507.8**
1. Science projects 2. Science—Experiments
ISBN 0-471-14802-4   LC 96-27512
"In the first section, VanCleave discusses scientific methodology: how to organize a project from selecting a topic through the investigatory process, the importance of keeping records, writing a final report, and the value of a nicely crafted presentation. . . . The next section—the largest by far—presents a number of double-page projects in a variety of fields. . . . A clear and informative addition." SLJ
Includes glossary and bibliographical references

Voth, Danna

Kidsource; science fair handbook; illustrated by Mike Moran. Lowell House Juvenile 1998 112p il pa $9.95   **507.8**
1. Science projects
ISBN 1-56565-514-1   LC 98-25059
Provides information on choosing and planning a science fair project, finding and using resources, applying scientific principles, and delivering the final project
"Lively, accurate, and thorough information is presented in an attractive format." SLJ
Includes glossary and bibliographical references

508 Natural history

DK nature encyclopedia. DK Pub. 1998 304p il maps $29.95   **508**
1. Natural history—Encyclopedias
ISBN 0-7894-3411-3   LC 98-16657
"The book is divided into six sections. 'The Natural World' describes the origins and evolution of life on earth. 'How Living Things Work' examines the basic characteristics shared by all living things—respiration, reproduction, life cycles, etc. 'Ecology' surveys the major types of habitats around the world and discusses topics such as food chains and endangered species. A short section explains 'How Living Things Are Classified,' while the final chapters look at specific groups of plants. . . . Well organized, clearly written, and with an amazing scope, this encyclopedia makes a valuable guide to nature." SLJ

Gates, Phillip

Nature got there first. Kingfisher (NY) 1995 80p il $17.95   **508**
1. Nature 2. Technology 3. Inventions
ISBN 1-85697-587-8   LC 94-42784
"Inventions from eight categories of technology, including building materials and building designs, and the shape of tools, are presented and contrasted with nature's designs." Sci Child
"The color pictures, a mix of original artwork and photographs, will intrigue kids, who may want to pursue in more depth elsewhere the connections Gates introduces." Booklist
Includes glossary

Myers, Lynne Born

Galápagos: islands of change; text by Lynne Born Myers and Christopher A. Myers; photographs by Nathan Farb. Hyperion Bks. for Children 1995 48p il maps $16.95; lib bdg $17.49
508
1. Natural history—Galapagos Islands 2. Galapagos Islands
ISBN 0-7868-0074-7; 0-7868-2061-6 (lib bdg)
LC 94-26173
This tells the "story of the Galápagos—the formation of the islands, how they came to be inhabited, and the amazing evolutionary changes taking place there. Difficult concepts, such as plate tectonics and Darwin's theory of evolution, are explained in simple-to-understand terms and accompanied by appropriate examples. . . . Covering subjects as varied as volcanoes, plant and animal life, evolution, erosion, and human exploitation of the environment, this will be a useful research tool as well as a rich supplement for the science curriculum." Booklist
Includes glossary

509 Science—Historical and geographic treatment

Asimov, Isaac, 1920-1992
Asimov's chronology of science and discovery. updated and illustrated. HarperCollins Pubs. 1994 790p il $37.50   **509**
1. Science—History 2. Inventions—History
ISBN 0-06-270113-4   LC 94-2504
First published 1989
This volume "includes major political leaders and discoverers in addition to the major developments in science, math, and technology. The range of topics is vast, from Homo habilis of 2,000,000 B.C. to Fermat's Last Theorem in 1993. This book is a 'must have' for any library serving youth." Voice Youth Advocates

Beshore, George W.
Science in ancient China; [by] George Beshore. Watts 1998 63p il map (Science of the past) lib bdg $25; pa $8.95   **509**
1. Science—China—History 2. Science and civilization
ISBN 0-531-11334-5 (lib bdg); 0-531-15914-0 (pa)
LC 97-3519
First published 1988 in the First book series
Surveys the achievements of the ancient Chinese in science, medicine, astronomy, and cosmology, and describes such innovations as rockets, wells, the compass, water wheels, and movable type
Includes glossary and bibliographical references

Science in early Islamic culture; [by] George Beshore. Watts 1998 64p il maps (Science of the past) lib bdg $25; pa $8.95   **509**
1. Science—History 2. Science and civilization 3. Islamic countries—Civilization
ISBN 0-531-20355-7 (lib bdg); 0-531-15917-5 (pa)
LC 97-5012
First published 1988 in the First book series
Discusses the extraordinary scientific discoveries and advancements in the Islamic world after the birth of Mohammed in 570 and their impact on Western civilization in subsequent centuries and today
"The writing is crisp and lively. . . . Numerous full-color and black-and-white photographs, reproductions, and drawings illuminate the text." SLJ
Includes glossary and bibliographical references

Gay, Kathlyn
Science in ancient Greece. Watts 1998 64p il (Science of the past) lib bdg $25; pa $8.95   **509**
1. Science—Greece—History 2. Science and civilization
ISBN 0-531-20357-3 (lib bdg); 0-531-15929-9 (pa)
LC 97-24029
First published 1988 in the First book series
Discusses the theories of ancient Greek philosopher-scientists such as Ptolemy, Pythagoras, Hippocrates, and Aristotle, and describes some of the scientific discoveries attributed to the Greeks and their impact on modern science

"Useful for reports, and there's also much to interest science students." SLJ
Includes glossary and bibliographical references

Harris, Jacqueline L., 1929-
Science in ancient Rome. Watts 1998 64p il map (Science of the past) lib bdg $25; pa $8.95   **509**
1. Science—Rome—History 2. Science and civilization
ISBN 0-531-20354-9 (lib bdg); 0-531-15916-7 (pa)
LC 97-1901
First published 1988 in the First book series
Describes how the Romans put to use and expanded the scientific achievements of earlier civilizations
This "includes clear, easy-to-read text; simple yet effective topic headings; excellent-quality, full-color photographs and reproductions; and Internet sites." SLJ
Includes glossary and bibliographical references

January, Brendan, 1972-
Science in colonial America. Watts 1999 64p il (Science of the past) lib bdg $25; pa $8.95   **509**
1. Science—United States—History 2. Science and civilization
ISBN 0-531-11525-9 (lib bdg); 0-531-15940-X (pa)
LC 98-10450
Describes the scientific contributions made by people in colonial America, including natural history, medicine, astronomy, and electricity
"Attractive and accessible. . . . Plentiful, accurate material." SLJ
Includes glossary and bibliographical references

Science in the Renaissance. Watts 1999 64p il (Science of the past) lib bdg $25   **509**
1. Science—History 2. Science and civilization 3. Renaissance
ISBN 0-531-11526-7   LC 97-38633
Describes advances in scientific knowledge that occurred during the Renaissance in Europe during the 15th and 16th centuries
"Many colorful photographs as well as reproductions of period art illustrate [this] attractive and interesting book." Booklist
Includes glossary and bibliographical references

Moss, Carol (Carol Marie)
Science in ancient Mesopotamia. Watts 1998 63p il (Science of the past) lib bdg $25; pa $8.95   **509**
1. Science—Iraq—History 2. Science and civilization
ISBN 0-531-20364-6 (lib bdg); 0-531-15930-2 (pa)
LC 97-24030
First published 1988 in the First book series
Describes the enormous accomplishments of the Sumerians and Babylonians of ancient Mesopotamia in every scientific area, a heritage which affects our own everyday lives
"Clearly written. . . . Black-and-white and full-color photographs and reproductions . . . are well captioned." SLJ
Includes glossary and bibliographical references

Mount, Ellis, 1921-
Milestones in science and technology; the ready reference guide to discoveries, inventions, and facts; by Ellis Mount and Barbara A. List. 2nd ed. Oryx Press 1994 206p il $34.50 **509**
1. Science 2. Technology 3. Inventions
ISBN 0-89774-671-6   LC 93-25679
First published 1987
This is a "guide to who invented or discovered what and to where and when the invention or discovery took place. It's 1,250 entries vary from 2 to 12 sentences in length and usually take a historical and social bent, rather than defining or explaining the process of invention or the invention itself." Sci Books Films
"This well-planned and well-researched volume will complement basic science dictionaries and encyclopedias." SLJ
Includes bibliographical references

Nardo, Don, 1947-
Greek and Roman science. Lucent Bks. 1998 128p il (World history series) lib bdg $22.45 (7 and up) **509**
1. Science—Greece—History 2. Science—Rome—History 3. Science and civilization
ISBN 1-56006-317-3   LC 97-22336
Examines the efforts of Greeks and Romans to study and understand the underlying principles of nature and discusses their development of a more systematic approach to science
"Clearly and concisely written. Black-and-white illustrations enhance the text, and the sidebars are informative and interesting." SLJ
Includes bibliographical references

Spangenburg, Ray, 1939-
The history of science from the ancient Greeks to the scientific revolution; [by] Ray Spangenburg and Diane K. Moser. Facts on File 1993 166p il $19.95 (7 and up) **509**
1. Science—History
ISBN 0-8160-2739-0   LC 92-33180
Surveys the early history of science, discussing the philosophical underpinnings developed by Greek thinkers, continuing through the developments of the Middle Ages and the Renaissance, and concluding with the discoveries of the seventeenth century
"Very well written and thoroughly understandable, the book succeeds hugely in its objective to introduce the development of science in an interesting fashion to the intended audience without patronizing or oversimplifying." Sci Books Films
Includes bibliographical references

The history of science in the eighteenth century; [by] Ray Spangenburg and Diane K. Moser. Facts on File 1993 xx, 156p $19.95 (7 and up) **509**
1. Science—History
ISBN 0-8160-2740-4   LC 92-41500
"Astronomy, geology, chemistry, electricity, natural history, and the life sciences are discussed in the context of social and political developments and the industrial revolution. From the vast scope of scientific activity that this century offers, the authors have chosen judiciously and fairly. The vignettes present enough biographical and contextual information to make them interesting and colorful, yet convey the important contributions of the men and women discussed." Sci Books Films
Includes bibliographical references

The history of science in the nineteenth century; by Ray Spangenburg and Diane K. Moser. Facts on File 1994 142p il $19.95 (7 and up) **509**
1. Science—History
ISBN 0-8160-2741-2   LC 93-10576
Examines the role of science in the Industrial Revolution, its establishment as a popular discipline, and discoveries in the areas of atoms and the elements, chemistry, evolution, and energy
This "is a valuable resource." Voice Youth Advocates
Includes bibliographical references

The history of science from 1895 to 1945; [by] Ray Spangenburg and Diane K. Moser. Facts on File 1994 xi, 164p il $19.95 (7 and up) **509**
1. Science—History
ISBN 0-8160-2742-0   LC 93-26820
The first part of this "science survey covers developments in the physical sciences in the first half of the twentieth century. . . . The second part of the book deals with the life sciences: microbiology, biochemistry, genetics, and archaeology, with each science linked with the lives of scientists studying it." Booklist
Includes bibliographical references

The history of science from 1946 to the 1990s; [by] Ray Spangenburg and Diane K. Moser. Facts on File 1994 176p il $19.95 (7 and up) **509**
1. Science—History
ISBN 0-8160-2743-9   LC 93-46058
The authors provide "descriptions of complex scientific theories and lines of research in the latter part of the 20th century—but only in the natural sciences: physics (new particles, lasers, and superconductors), astronomy (quasars, black holes, cosmology, dark matter, planetary geology, and SETI), geology (evolution, plate tectonics, and environmental change), and biology (DNA, biotechnology, the human genome, and retroviruses)." Sci Books Films
Includes bibliographical references

Stefoff, Rebecca, 1951-
Scientific explorers; travels in search of knowledge. Oxford Univ. Press 1992 151p il maps (Extraordinary explorers) $26 **509**
1. Scientific expeditions 2. Explorers
ISBN 0-19-507689-3   LC 92-7947
This illustrated survey discusses the history of scientific exploration with emphasis on the discoveries of Charles Darwin and Alexander von Humboldt
This book "should be attractive to faculty and students alike." Book Rep
Includes bibliographical references

Stewart, Melissa, 1968-
Science in ancient India. Watts 1999 64p il map
(Science of the past) lib bdg $25   **509**
1. Science—India—History 2. Science and civiliza-
tion
ISBN 0-531-11626-3   LC 98-18536
An overview of the scientific contributions of ancient
India including Arabic numerals, ayurveda, basic chemis-
try and physics, and celestial observations
"A useful and unique resource." SLJ
Includes glossary and bibliographical references

Woods, Geraldine, 1948-
Science in ancient Egypt. Watts 1998 64p il
(Science of the past) lib bdg $25; pa $8.95   **509**
1. Science—Egypt—History 2. Science and civiliza-
tion
ISBN 0-531-20341-7 (lib bdg); 0-531-15915-9 (pa)
LC 97-649
First published 1988 in the First book series
Discusses the achievements of the ancient Egyptians
in science, mathematics, astronomy, medicine, agricul-
ture, and technology
"Well-researched and easy-to-understand. . . . Woods
offers a fascinating look at the ancient Egyptians' accom-
plishments." SLJ
Includes glossary and bibliographical references

Science of the early Americas. Watts 1999 64p
(Science of the past) lib bdg $25; pa $8.95   **509**
1. Science—History 2. Science and civilization 3. In-
dians
ISBN 0-531-11524-0 (lib bdg); 0-531-15941-8 (pa)
LC 97-44047
Discusses the scientific accomplishments in such fields
as medicine, mathematics, engineering, and astronomy of
various groups of American Indians
Includes glossary and bibliographical references

510.7   Mathematics—Education and related topics

Lobosco, Michael L.
Mental math workout. Sterling 1998 80p il
$16.95   **510.7**
1. Mathematics—Study and teaching
ISBN 1-895569-27-3   LC 97-44396
"A Sterling/Tamos book"
"The 34 projects are divided into categories such as
symmetry, magical mind reading, solitaire, instant calculations, 3-D math models, gamesmanship, and real-life
experiments. . . . Printed instructions are clear and concise, supplemented by sharp, full-color photographs and
well-labeled diagrams." SLJ

Maganzini, Christy
Cool math; math tricks, amazing math activities,
cool calculations, awesome math factoids and
more; written by Christy Maganzini; illustrated by
Ruta Daugavietis. Price/Stern/Sloan 1997 96p il pa
$6.95   **510.7**
1. Mathematics
ISBN 0-8431-7857-4   LC 96-40484

Describes mathematics from zero to infinity with stops
along the way for ancient puzzles, awesome math tricks,
tantalizing math trivia, incredible shortcuts, and mysterious number magic

Salvadori, Mario George, 1907-1997
Math games for middle school; challenges and
skill-builders for students at every level; [by]
Mario Salvadori and Joseph P. Wright. Chicago
Review Press 1998 168p il pa $14.95   **510.7**
1. Mathematics—Study and teaching
ISBN 1-55652-288-6   LC 97-51422
Uses explanations, word problems, and games to cover
some mathematical topics that middle school students
need to know, including the invention of numerical notations, basic arithmatical operations, measurements, geometry, graphs, and probability

513   Arithmetic

Fisher, Leonard Everett, 1924-
Number art: thirteen 1 2 3s from around the
world; written and illustrated by Leonard Everett
Fisher. Four Winds Press 1982 61p il $16.95
513
1. Numerals
ISBN 0-02-735240-4   LC 82-5050
"Traces the history and design of 13 systems of numerical notation—Arabic, Armenian, Brahmi, Chinese,
Egyptian, Gothic, Greek, Mayan, Roman, Runes, Sanskrit, Thai and Tibetan. Beautifully designed, this book
will be useful as an introduction to the different number
systems." N Y Public Libr. Ref Books for Child Collect.
2d edition

Julius, Edward H., 1952-
Arithmetricks; 50 easy ways to add, subtract,
multiply, and divide without a calculator;
illustrations by Dale M. Gladstone. Wiley 1995
142p il pa $10.95   **513**
1. Arithmetic
ISBN 0-471-10639-9   LC 94-41836
This book "offers fifty ways to do simple arithmetic
calculations in one's head. . . . Each trick is covered on
two facing pages. The first page presents the problem
and gives two examples of how to use the trick. The facing page has a black and white cartoon and extra exercises to practice. The correct answers are given at the
end of the book. This would be a fun book for mathe-
matically inclined Middle-Schoolers and up. Math teachers will enjoy using this book for extra-curricular activities." Appraisal

519.5   Statistical mathematics

Krieger, Melanie Jacobs
Means and probabilities; using statistics in
science projects. Watts 1996 144p il (Experimental
science series) lib bdg $24 (7 and up)   **519.5**
1. Statistics 2. Science projects
ISBN 0-531-11225-X   LC 95-49013

Krieger, Melanie Jacobs—*Continued*

An introduction to statistics with emphasis on their use in science projects. Explains averages, frequency distribution, range, percentile, probability, standard diviation, and more

"This is an excellent introduction to elementary statistics and statistical methodology." Sci Books Films

Includes glossary and bibliographical references

520 Astronomy and allied sciences

Astronomy. Reader's Digest Assn. 1998 159p il (Reader's digest explores) $24.95 (7 and up)
520

1. Astronomy 2. Outer space—Exploration
ISBN 0-7621-0042-7   LC 97-46925

This illustrated volume discusses such topics as space exploration, moon landings, space probes, shuttles, and space stations

Bond, Peter, 1948-

DK guide to space. DK Pub. 1999 63p il $19.95
520

1. Astronomy
ISBN 0-7894-3946-8   LC 98-42054

Presents discoveries, observations, and theories about the planets and other phenomena in our solar system as well as in outer space, using text, illustrations, and photographs from NASA

"This book demonstrates both the author's enthusiasm and his knowledge of astronomy. The photographs are beautiful, well chosen, and up to date." Sci Books Films

Bramwell, Martyn

Mapping the planets and space; illustrated by George Fryer. Lerner Publs. 1998 48p il (Maps & mapmakers) lib bdg $22.60   520

1. Astronomy 2. Planets 3. Outer space
ISBN 0-8225-2922-X   LC 97-12188

Explains what our study of outer space has revealed to us about the planets and other heavenly bodies

Includes glossary

Campbell, Ann

The New York Public Library amazing space; a book of answers for kids; [by] Ann-Jeanette Campbell; illustrated by Jessica Wolk-Stanley. Wiley 1997 186p il pa $12.95   520

1. Astronomy 2. Outer space
ISBN 0-471-14498-3   LC 96-29785

"A Stonesong Press book"

"Arranged in chapters by major topics, the author states and then addresses questions on general astronomy, celestial objects, our solar system, and space exploration. . . . The material is up to date and presented clearly." Sci Books Films

Includes glossary and bibliographical references

Dickinson, Terence

NightWatch; a practical guide to viewing the universe; foreword by Timothy Ferris; illustrations by Adolf Schaller, Victor Costanzo and Roberta Cooke; principal photography by Terrance Dickinson. 3rd ed, rev and expanded. Firefly Bks. (Buffalo) 1998 176p il $45; pa $29.95 (7 and up)
520

1. Astronomy
ISBN 1-55209-300-X; 1-55209-302-6 (pa)

First published 1983

This "handbook for amateur astronomers combines a text both meaty and hard to put down with a great array of charts, boxes, tables, and dazzling full-color photos of the sky." SLJ

Includes bibliographical references

Ford, Harry

The young astronomer. DK Pub. 1998 37p il $15.95   520

1. Astronomy
ISBN 0-7894-2061-9   LC 97-39623

Introduces the basics of astronomy through a variety of projects, including a model of a lunar eclipse and a chart of a comet's path

"Outstanding charts listing a variety of useful information are included. . . . Both browsers and astronomy buffs will find something of interest." Booklist

Includes glossary

Lippincott, Kristen, 1954-

Astronomy; written by Kristen Lippincott. Dorling Kindersley 1994 64p il (Eyewitness science) $15.95   520

1. Astronomy
ISBN 1-56458-680-4   LC 94-18479

The author "defines basic terms and concepts of astronomy. . . . Information ranges from ancient discoveries and scientists to the most modern equipment and advances. Many colorful photographs and diagrams are scattered throughout the book." Appraisal

Mitton, Simon, 1946-

The young Oxford book of astronomy; [by] Simon and Jacqueline Mitton. Oxford Univ. Press 1995 160p il lib bdg $30; pa $16.90   520

1. Astronomy
ISBN 0-19-521168-5 (lib bdg); 0-19-521445-5 (pa)
LC 95-7015

First published 1994 in the United Kingdom

The authors "set out the aims and methods of astronomy, such as how astronomers map and measure the universe. Then they turn to our own solar system, detailing vital statistics in 'Fact Files' for each planet and highlighting important discoveries or remarkable characteristics. Finally, they move to the stars and . . . galaxies." Publisher's note

Includes glossary

Outer space. Grolier Educ. 1998 12v il maps set $269   520

1. Astronomy 2. Outer space
ISBN 0-7172-9179-0   LC 97-49010

Outer space—*Continued*

Contents: v1 The sun's family, by R. Hitt, Jr.; v2 The moon, by R. Hitt, Jr.; v3 The inner planets, by A. Gallagher; v4 The outer planets, by F. Jackson; v5 The night sky, by A. Gallagher; v6 Stars and galaxies, by C. Hatchett; v7 Astronomy, by F. Jackson; v8 Space travel, by C. Hatchett; v9 Space shuttle, by F. Jackson; v10 Astronauts and cosmonauts, by A. Evans; v11 Space stations, by B. Wetterau; v12 Satellites and probes, by B. Bunch and C. Hatchett

"Each of the 12 volumes in this set contains a table of contents, a short introduction and conclusion, a glossary unique to that volume, and an index to the entire set. . . . The text is printed in two columns, and items printed in bold typeface are explained in the glossary. Explanations of more complex concepts, such as parallax or the Apollo Lunar Launch System are given in large sidebars. Cross-references are also shown in bold print. The text is well-supplemented with color and black-and-white photographs, drawings, and data tables." Am Ref Books Annu, 1999

For a fuller review see: Booklist, Dec. 1, 1998

Redfern, Martin

The Kingfisher young people's book of space. Kingfisher (NY) 1998 95p il $19.95   **520**

1. Astronomy 2. Outer space—Exploration

ISBN 0-7534-5136-0   LC 97-51122

Examines our exploration of outer space and discusses the solar system, stars, galaxies, and the universe in general

"The book's layout, with outstanding pictures and text, complements this engaging journey through our space." Sci Child

Includes glossary

Ridpath, Ian

Facts on File stars & planets atlas. 2nd ed. Facts on File 1997 80p il $18.95   **520**

1. Astronomy 2. Stars 3. Planets

ISBN 0-8160-3716-7   LC 97-15966

First published 1993 with title: The Facts on File atlas of stars and planets

This covers the solar system, stars and constellations, star families and galaxies, comets, asteroids, meteors and other space debris, supernovae, quasars, and neutron stars and black holes and includes images from space probes, The Hubble Space Telescope and earthbound observatories

Stott, Carole

New astronomer; editorial consultant, Amie Gallagher. DK Pub. 1999 144p il maps $25.95 (7 and up)   **520**

1. Astronomy

ISBN 0-7894-4175-6   LC 98-45283

Planisphere in pocket

This introduces astronomical tools and techniques, combines photographs from the Hubble Space Telescope with surface-contour maps from space probes, and includes charts and advice for observing planets and stars and other astronomical phenomena

"Beautifully illustrated with clear photographs and dia-

grams. . . . Cross-referencing within the text is excellent, explanations are in-depth, and the sky maps in the Star section are exemplary." Voice Youth Advocates

Includes glossary

The **Universe**. Time-Life Bks. 1998 127p il (Time-Life student library) $18.95 (7 and up)   **520**

1. Cosmology 2. Astronomy

LC 98-16907

Examines the origin, structure, and workings of the universe, including galaxies, stars, dark matter, light years, black holes, and other aspects, and describes space exploration from ancient astronomy to modern probes

"Whether the reader is interested in Mayans, Miranda, or moon rocks, there's enough in these jam-packed pages for him or her to become conversant about these topics. Interest is increased by an attractive multicolored collage of articles, headlines, and illustrations." Sci Books Films

Includes glossary

522   Techniques, equipment, materials of astronomy

Cole, Michael D.

Hubble Space Telescope; exploring the universe. Enslow Pubs. 1999 48p il (Countdown to space) lib bdg $18.95   **522**

1. Astronomy 2. Hubble Space Telescope 3. Astronautics

ISBN 0-7660-1120-8   LC 98-3298

Details the initiation of the Hubble Space Telescope in April 1990 and the repair and servicing missions which followed; explains the telescope's role in answering questions about the universe

"Illustrated with color photographs, the book provides solid basic information." Horn Book

Includes glossary and bibliographical references

523   Specific celestial bodies and phenomena

Chartrand, Mark R.

The Audubon Society field guide to the night sky; astronomical charts by Wil Tirion. Knopf 1991 714p il maps $18   **523**

1. Astronomy

ISBN 0-679-40852-5   LC 91-52708

"A Chanticleer Press edition. The Audubon Society field guide series"

"This is a comprehensive guide to the night sky useful for students and amateur astronomers." Voice Youth Advocates

Includes bibliographical references

Pasachoff, Jay M.
A field guide to the stars and planets. 4th ed,
Jay M. Pasachoff ; with monthly star maps and
atlas charts by Wil Tirion. Houghton Mifflin 2000
578p il maps (The Peterson field guide series)
$30; pa $19 **523**
1. Astronomy
ISBN 0-395-93432-X; 0-395-93431-1 (pa)
LC 99-27354
First published 1964 under the authorship of Donald
H. Menzel and Jay M. Pasachoff
This guide contains star maps and atlas charts in color
with close-up of areas of special interest such as the Ple-
iades and the Orion Nebula
Includes bibliographical references

Scott, Elaine, 1940-
Close encounters; exploring the universe with
the Hubble Space Telescope. Hyperion Bks. for
Children 1998 64p il $16.95; lib bdg $17.49
523
1. Outer space—Exploration 2. Hubble Space Telescope
ISBN 0-7868-0147-6; 0-7868-2120-5 (lib bdg)
LC 96-39104
Describes what scientists have been able to deduce
about the nature of our solar system and the universe
based on data collected by the Hubble Telescope
"The striking photos are explained in captions and
text, and the magnitude of time and distance conveyed
by these images truly inspires wonder." Horn Book
Guide

523.1 The universe, galaxies, quasars

Couper, Heather
Big bang; [by] Heather Couper and Nigel
Henbest; illustrated by Luciano Corbella. DK Pub.
1997 45p il $16.95 **523.1**
1. Big bang theory
ISBN 0-7894-1484-8 LC 96-30995
Explores the Big Bang theory of how the universe
may have begun
"The pictures, the text, and, above all, the science
combine to make this book an exciting adventure. The
authors have done an outstanding job in describing the
big bang model at a child's level." Sci Child
Includes glossary

523.2 Solar system

Vogt, Gregory
The solar system; facts and exploration; [by]
Gregory L. Vogt. 21st Cent. Bks. (NY) 1995 96p
il (Scientific American sourcebooks) lib bdg
$22.40; pa $8.95 **523.2**
1. Solar system 2. Outer space—Exploration
ISBN 0-8050-3249-5 (lib bdg); 0-8050-3248-7 (pa)
LC 95-941

This book serves as a "guide to the planets and moons
as well as an introduction to asteroids, comets, and mete-
oroids. Accounts of discoveries and disappointments in
the space program give readers a feel for the ongoing
challenge of understanding the solar system. The excellent full-color illustrations include many recent images
from the Hubble space telescope." Booklist
Includes bibliographical references

523.3 Moon

Bredeson, Carmen
The moon. Watts 1998 63p il lib bdg $22; pa
$6.95 **523.3**
1. Project Apollo 2. Moon
ISBN 0-531-20308-5 (lib bdg); 0-531-15911-6 (pa)
LC 96-40226
"A First book"
Describes what people have believed about the moon
and what has been learned over time and presents an
overview of the Apollo space program
"Clear, effective illustrations, most in color, appear
throughout the book. . . . A good resource for science
collections." Booklist
Includes glossary and bibliographical references

Gardner, Robert, 1929-
Science project ideas about the moon. Enslow
Pubs. 1997 96p il (Science project ideas) lib bdg
$18.95 **523.3**
1. Moon 2. Science projects 3. Science—Experiments
ISBN 0-89490-844-8 LC 97-6486
Introduces the phases and other characteristics of the
moon through a series of experiments, most of which can
be used to start a science fair project
"Includes a wealth of information about the moon, as
well as telescopes." Sci Books Films
Includes bibliographical references

523.4 Planets

Fradin, Dennis B.
The planet hunters; the search for other worlds;
[by] Dennis Brindell Fradin; illustrated with
full-color and black-and-white prints and
photographs. Margaret K. McElderry Bks. 1997
148p il $19.95 **523.4**
1. Astronomers 2. Astronomy 3. Planets
ISBN 0-689-81323-6 LC 96-29721
Provides historical information on astronomy, the discovery of the planets, and the people who have made
such discoveries
This is "a well-researched book. . . . Black-and-white
photographs appear throughout the book, with a section
of color plates inserted in the middle. . . . The immediacy of the writing will carry readers along in the narrative
flow of this often dramatic story." Booklist
Includes bibliographical references

Kraske, Robert
Asteroids; invaders from space. Atheneum Pubs.
1995 90p il maps $15; pa $5.99   **523.4**
1. Asteroids
ISBN 0-689-31860-X; 0-689-82456-4 (pa)
                                    LC 94-8072
"Readers will learn about land formations caused by
asteroids, how future collisions might be averted, the solar system, comets, meteors, and more. Featuring highly
readable prose, strong visual aids, and vivid description,
this title makes the mindboggling accessible." Booklist
Includes bibliographical references

Skurzynski, Gloria
Discover Mars. National Geographic Soc. 1998
44p il $17.95   **523.4**
1. Mars (Planet)
ISBN 0-7922-7099-1   LC 98-13190
Includes two pairs of 3-D glasses
Reviews results from the study of Mars, from Copernicus through the Viking and Pathfinder missions, and
speculates on a future human landing
"Scattered throughout this thoroughly illustrated report
are specially printed photos that, when viewed through
cardboard 'anaglyph' glasses, appear as 3-D. . . . The
book makes an inviting package, with plenty of big,
bright photographs and artists' conceptions for standard
illustrations, a concise but specific summary of what is
now known about Mars, and a generous selection of
Web sites at the end." SLJ

523.5 Meteoroids, solar wind, zodiacal light

Aronson, Billy
Meteors; the truth behind shooting stars. Watts
1996 63p il lib bdg $22.50; pa $6.95   **523.5**
1. Meteors
ISBN 0-531-20242-9 (lib bdg); 0-531-15813-6 (pa)
                                    LC 95-48846
"A First book"
Explains such things as the difference between a mete-
or, a meteoroid, and a meteorite and what happens when
an asteroid or comet gets too close to the earth
"Offers a clear and concise explanation of a . . . common phenomenon. . . . The well-chosen photographs of
assorted meteorites and their effects will appeal to readers." SLJ
Includes glossary and bibliographical references

523.6 Comets

Bonar, Samantha
Comets. Watts 1998 63p il lib bdg $22; pa
$6.95   **523.6**
1. Comets
ISBN 0-531-20301-8 (lib bdg); 0-531-15907-8 (pa)
                                    LC 96-53502
"A First book"

Describes what has been learned about the composition, orbits, and the existence of several well-known
comets
"Attractive, colorful illustrations are numerous and
complement the text. . . . An excellent reference book
for young readers." Sci Books Films
Includes glossary and bibliographical references

523.7 Sun

Gallant, Roy A.
When the sun dies. Marshall Cavendish 1999
128p il $14.95   **523.7**
1. Stars 2. Sun
ISBN 0-7614-5036-X   LC 98-9430
Discusses what is known about the sun in particular
and stars in general and describes some possible effects
of the sun's gradual demise on life on earth
"Serious students of astrophysics, stellar evolution, cli-
matology, the search for extra-solar planets, and other related topics will be well served by this title." SLJ
Includes glossary and bibliographical references

Gardner, Robert, 1929-
Science project ideas about the sun. Enslow
Pubs. 1997 96p il (Science project ideas) lib bdg
$18.95   **523.7**
1. Sun 2. Science projects 3. Science—Experiments
ISBN 0-89490-845-6   LC 96-42693
Uses experiments to illustrate the phases and patterns
of the sun as well as the reasons for its importance as
an energy source
"A mixture of mostly simple experiments, facts, and
activities that utilize easy-to-find objects. . . . The dia-
grams and drawings are clear and helpful." SLJ
Includes bibliographical references

523.8 Stars

Couper, Heather
Black holes; [by] Heather Couper and Nigel
Henbest; illustrated by Luciano Corbella. DK Pub.
1996 45p il $16.95   **523.8**
1. Black holes (Astronomy)
ISBN 0-7894-0451-6   LC 95-44391
"The authors cover such topics as the discovery of
black holes, Einstein's theory of relativity, gravitation,
time travel and wormholes." Book Rep
"Deftly distilled brief blocks of text and captions accompany technically sophisticated photographs and painstakingly detailed, realistic art, while diagrams further
clarify the concepts introduced." Publ Wkly
Includes glossary

Rükl, Antonín
Constellation guidebook. Sterling 1998 223p il
$17.95 (7 and up)   **523.8**
1. Constellations
ISBN 0-8069-4299-1   LC 98-22850

Rükl, Antonín—*Continued*

"After a brief introduction and detailed directions on how to find constellations, Rukl begins his celestial guide. The guide explains what stars are and how scientists measure their brightness, luminosity and temperature. Maps of the whole sky and of individual constellations are provided. With each constellation map there is the story of how the constellation was named, where to look for the constellation and information about the stars that make up the constellation. . . . This book will be useful to budding astronomers and students seeking information on a specific constellation." Appraisal

Includes glossary

525 Earth (Astronomical geography)

Lauber, Patricia, 1924-

Seeing Earth from space. Orchard Bks. 1990 80p il maps lib bdg $22.99; pa $9.95 **525**
1. Earth sciences 2. Earth
ISBN 0-531-08502-3 (lib bdg); 0-531-07057-3 (pa)
LC 89-77523

"This book uses photographs taken in space by astronauts and man-made satellites to describe Earth. It also discusses remote sensors and how they are used to study our planet." Voice Youth Advocates

"Well researched, clearly written, and beautifully made, this eye-opening book represents non-fiction at its best." Booklist

Includes bibliographical references

529 Chronology

Gardner, Robert, 1929-

Experimenting with time. Watts 1995 160p il maps lib bdg $24 (7 and up) **529**
1. Time 2. Science projects
ISBN 0-531-12554-8
LC 95-1471

"A Venture book"

"This volume contains a challenging combination of the history of human concepts of time and experiments or projects that investigate ways of understanding and measuring time. The book explores how scientists view time and how they apply their concepts in many situations." Sci Books Films

Includes bibliographical references

Mandell, Muriel, 1921-

Simple experiments in time with everyday materials; illustrated by Frances Zweifel. Sterling 1997 96p il maps $14.95; pa $4.95 **529**
1. Time 2. Science projects
ISBN 0-8069-3803-X; 0-8069-4298-3 (pa)
LC 97-992

"How we measure time—both when and how long—is the subject of the many experiments in this small, lively, information-packed volume. . . . The focus is on basic discoveries and applied science, from constructing a perpetual calendar or an hourglass to telling time by the stars. . . . The style is clear and informal." Booklist

530 Physics

Challoner, Jack

The visual dictionary of physics; written by Jack Challoner. Dorling Kindersley 1995 64p il (Eyewitness visual dictionaries) $18.95 **530**
1. Physics
ISBN 0-7894-0239-4
LC 95-11937

"This book offers a bit about a wide variety of topics, from Newton's Laws to Feynman diagrams. It is an enticing choice for browsing that may inspire further research, or that might possibly supply just the information needed for an assignment." SLJ

Includes glossary

Cooper, Chris

Matter; written by Christopher Cooper. Dorling Kindersley 1992 64p il (Eyewitness science) $15.95 **530**
1. Matter 2. Atoms 3. Molecules
ISBN 1-87943-188-2
LC 92-6928

Examines the elements that make up the physical world and the properties and behavior of different kinds of matter

This book features "lavish full-color photographs and drawings. . . . Many are of items rarely seen in science books—historic equipment from museum collections. . . . Because the art dominates, the text is limited." SLJ

Friedhoffer, Robert

Physics lab in a hardware store; illustrated by Joe Hosking. Watts 1996 112p il (Physical science labs) lib bdg $24; pa $6.95 **530**
1. Physics 2. Science—Experiments
ISBN 0-531-11292-6 (lib bdg); 0-531-15824-1 (pa)
LC 96-15828

Examines such topics in physics as mass, weight, gravity, buoyancy, and pressure with experiments using common household tools

"Clearly written and illustrated with line drawings [this makes] scientific principles understandable by providing hands-on experiences related to familiar phenomena." Booklist

Includes glossary and bibliographical references

Physics lab in the housewares store; illustrated by Joe Hosking. Watts 1996 95p il (Physical science labs) lib bdg $24; pa $6.95 **530**
1. Physics 2. Science—Experiments
ISBN 0-531-11293-4 (lib bdg); 0-531-15824-1 (pa)
LC 95-49012

Explores such topics in physics as levers, friction, heat transmission, and density with experiments using common household utensils

"Explanations are clear and simple. Black-and-white drawings accompany most of the devices and, in the lever and screws section, aid significantly in explaining the physics. . . . A lively and informative presentation." SLJ

Includes glossary and bibliographical references

530.1   Physics—Theories and mathematical physics

Gribbin, John R.
Time & space; written by John and Mary Gribbin. Dorling Kindersley 1994 64p il maps (Eyewitness science) lib bdg $15.95   **530.1**
1. Space and time
ISBN 1-56458-619-7   LC 93-44285
This book "shows how the concepts of time and space enter into the description and discussion of an amazingly large number of aspects of nature and human affairs, from archaeological discoveries to current scientific theory and practice." Appraisal
"Highly 'browsable' and captivating with its captioned color photos and charts." BAYA Book Rev

530.4   States of matter

Mebane, Robert C.
Air & other gases; [by] Robert C. Mebane, Thomas R. Rybolt; illustrations by Anni Matsick. 21st Cent. Bks. (NY) 1995 63p il (Everyday material science experiments) lib bdg $18.90   **530.4**
1. Gases 2. Air 3. Science—Experiments
ISBN 0-8050-2839-0   LC 94-24959
This book includes instructions for 16 science experiments
"The use of everyday material makes the experiments attractive to children. . . . The level of the discussion is outstanding. Here the authors exhibit their breadth of knowledge and their ability to communicate it simply and clearly." Appraisal
Includes bibliographical references

Salts & solids; [by] Robert C. Mebane, Thomas R. Rybolt; illustrations by Anni Matsick. 21st Cent. Bks. (NY) 1995 64p il (Everyday material science experiments) lib bdg $18.90   **530.4**
1. Matter 2. Solids 3. Science—Experiments
ISBN 0-8050-2841-2   LC 94-25201
In addition to the 16 science experiments, this book offers "clear instructions for materials needed, set up, what to observe, and a brief and clear explanation of what occurred." Appraisal
Includes bibliographical references

Water & other liquids; [by] Robert C. Mebane, Thomas R. Rybolt; illustrations by Anni Matsick. 21st Cent. Bks. (NY) 1995 64p il (Everyday material science experiments) lib bdg $18.90   **530.4**
1. Liquids 2. Water 3. Science—Experiments
ISBN 0-8050-2840-4   LC 94-43154
This book includes illustrated instructions for 16 science experiments that demonstrate various properties of liquids
Includes bibliographical references

531   Classical mechanics. Solid mechanics

Gardner, Robert, 1929-
Experiments with motion. Enslow Pubs. 1995 112p il (Getting started in science) lib bdg $18.95   **531**
1. Motion 2. Science—Experiments
ISBN 0-89490-667-4   LC 95-8543
This book "includes numerous experiments dealing with motion. Newton's laws of motion are carefully discussed, and experiments illustrate how they explain the movement of objects subject to friction and gravity, as well as in space. . . . Experimental procedures are well organized and supplemented with helpful illustrations." Voice Youth Advocates
Includes bibliographical references

Lafferty, Peter
Force & motion; written by Peter Lafferty. Dorling Kindersley 1992 64p il (Eyewitness science) $15.95   **531**
1. Force and energy 2. Motion
ISBN 1-87943-185-8   LC 92-6927
Explores the principles of force and motion, describing how they have been applied from ancient to modern times
This book features "lavish full-color photographs and drawings. . . . *Force & Motion* is well written, featuring standard subjects (friction and gravity) mixed with unusual ones (the science of cannonballs and hoists)." SLJ

532   Fluid mechanics

Williams, John
Water projects. Raintree Steck-Vaughn Pubs. 1998 32p il (Design and create) lib bdg $22.12   **532**
1. Water 2. Science—Experiments
ISBN 0-8172-4890-0   LC 97-20320
Provides instructions for a variety of projects involving water, including a water clock, a flood alarm, and a dredger
"The full-color photos enhance the step-by-step instructions. . . . The book presents material not readily found in any other single source." SLJ
Includes glossary and bibliographical references

Zubrowski, Bernie, 1939-
Making waves; finding out about rhythmic motion; illustrated by Roy Doty. Morrow Junior Bks. 1994 96p il lib bdg $14.93; pa $6.95   **532**
1. Waves 2. Science—Experiments
ISBN 0-688-11787-2 (lib bdg); 0-688-11788-0 (pa)
LC 93-35455
"A Boston Children's Museum activity book"
"Zubrowski shows readers how to build equipment and observe waves in water, soap film, plastic and cloth materials, string, and a 'wave machine' constructed with

Zubrowski, Bernie, 1939-—*Continued*

dowels, nails, masking tape, and rubber bands. The step-by-step directions and the use of everyday objects for apparatus make this book useful for students preparing for science fairs as well as for teachers who want to demonstrate waves in their classrooms." Booklist

533 Gas mechanics (Pneumatics)

Gardner, Robert, 1929-
Science project ideas about air. Enslow Pubs. 1997 96p il (Science project ideas) lib bdg $18.95
533
1. Air 2. Science projects 3. Science—Experiments
ISBN 0-89490-838-3   LC 97-7389
Presents experiments that reveal the properties of air, with special attention to those that would make good science fair projects
"The author does a nice job of choosing materials that will be readily accessible to most readers or that can be made at home; however, some adult assistance will be necessary. 'Did you know' fact boxes offer informative tidbits." SLJ
Includes bibliographical references

535 Light and paraphotic phenomena

Burnie, David
Light. Dorling Kindersley 1992 64p il (Eyewitness science) lib bdg $13.95   **535**
1. Light
ISBN 1-879431-79-3   LC 92-7661
A guide to the origins, principles, and historical study of light
"Each double-page spread is lavishly illustrated with full-color photographs and diagrams, and each contains a wealth of information. For example, the pages on refraction feature a brief history of the study of the subject, portraits of Ptolemy and Willebrord Snell and summaries of their work, drawings of how mirages are created, and photographs illustrating light being bent through a glass block and concentrated by a lacemaker's condensers." Booklist

Cobb, Vicki, 1938-
Light action! amazing experiments with optics; [by] Vicki Cobb and Josh Cobb; illustrated by Theo Cobb. HarperCollins Pubs. 1993 198p il lib bdg $15.89   **535**
1. Optics 2. Light 3. Science—Experiments
ISBN 0-06-021437-6   LC 92-25528
Explains what light is and explores the basic principles of optics through experiments
"The activities are simple and well designed and will give students basic knowledge. Cheerful line drawings and diagrams illustrate the text." Booklist

Zubrowski, Bernie, 1939-
Mirrors; finding out about the properties of light; illustrated by Roy Doty. Morrow Junior Bks. 1992 96p il $13.93; pa $6.95   **535**
1. Mirrors 2. Light 3. Science—Experiments
ISBN 0-688-10592-0; 0-688-10591-2 (pa)
          LC 91-29142
"A Boston Children's Museum activity book"
Suggested activities explore how mirrors work and how they demonstrate the properties of light
"The activities, many of which use household materials, range in scope from forming funny reflections to making a stage illusion of a ghost. . . . The best thing about this book is that it makes learning science fun." Sci Books Films

535.6 Color

Nassau, Kurt
Experimenting with color. Watts 1997 128p il lib bdg $24 (7 and up)   **535.6**
1. Color 2. Science—Experiments
ISBN 0-531-11327-2   LC 96-25865
Experiments and activities reinforce a general discussion of the properties of light, the electromagnetic spectrum, and color vision, that also outlines the fifteen ways in which electron interactions result in color
"A well-written, informative book. . . . Excellent-quality, full-color photographs and captioned and labeled diagrams and tables supplement the text. Most of the 17 suggested projects can be done with readily available materials and with minimum adult supervision." SLJ
Includes glossary and bibliographical references

536 Heat

Gardner, Robert, 1929-
Science projects about temperature and heat; [by] Robert Gardner and Eric Kemer. Enslow Pubs. 1994 128p il lib bdg $19.95 (7 and up)
536
1. Temperature 2. Heat 3. Science—Experiments
ISBN 0-89490-534-1   LC 93-48800
The authors suggest "investigations about heat and how it is measured as temperature. Some of the experiments cover the rules of temperature change, how different materials conduct heat, and how heat is made by friction." Publisher's note
Includes bibliographical references

537 Electricity and electronics

Parker, Steve
Electricity; written by Steve Parker. Dorling Kindersley 1992 64p il (Eyewitness science) $15.95   **537**
1. Electricity
ISBN 1-87943-182-3   LC 92-6926
Discusses the properties of electricity and describes how it is made and used
"Pictures and text work together to offer a lucid chronicle of pertinent experiments, discoveries and inventions from ancient times to the present." Publ Wkly

539.7 Atomic and nuclear physics

Henderson, Harry, 1951-
Nuclear physics. Facts on File 1998 132p il (Milestones in discovery and invention) $19.95 (7 and up)   **539.7**
1. Nuclear physics 2. Physicists
ISBN 0-8160-3567-9   LC 97-17380
This book profiles physicists Marie and Pierre Curie, Ernest Rutherford, Niels Bohr, Lise Meitner, Richard Feynman, and Murray Gell-Mann, explains their scientific discoveries, and outlines questions in current physics research
Includes bibliographical references

540 Chemistry & allied sciences

Challoner, Jack
The visual dictionary of chemistry; written by Jack Challoner. DK Pub. 1996 64p il (Eyewitness visual dictionaries) $18.95   **540**
1. Chemistry
ISBN 0-7894-0444-3   LC 95-52796
Text and illustrations present the fundamentals of chemistry, including such topics as atomic bonds, catalysts, chemical reactions, and various elements
"This book succeeds in making the non-visual perceivable and easy to understand. . . . The pages are well organized and illustrated with brightly colored, labeled photographs and diagrams." SLJ
Includes glossary

540.7 Chemistry—Education and related topics

Gardner, Robert, 1929-
Science projects about kitchen chemistry. Enslow Pubs. 1999 128p il (Science projects) lib bdg $19.95 (7 and up)   **540.7**
1. Chemistry 2. Science projects 3. Science—Experiments
ISBN 0-89490-953-3   LC 98-35050
Presents experiments suitable for science fair projects, dealing with the chemistry involved with foods and activities related to the kitchen
"The author has assembled some very engaging and safe experiments for middle-school-aged children." Sci Books Films
Includes bibliographical references

Oxlade, Chris
Chemistry; photography by Chris Fairclough. Raintree Steck-Vaughn Pubs. 1999 48p il (Science projects) $24.26   **540.7**
1. Chemistry 2. Science projects 3. Science—Experiments
ISBN 0-8172-4948-6   LC 97-46796

Introduces basic concepts of chemistry through a variety of experiments, exploring such topics as changes of state, distillation, and catalysts
"A colorful and commonsensical introduction to major topics in chemistry." Sci Books Films
Includes glossary and bibliographical references

546 Inorganic chemistry

Blashfield, Jean F.
Sparks of life; chemical elements that make life possible. Raintree Steck-Vaughn Pubs. 1999 6v il ea $27.12; set $162.72   **546**
ISBN 0-8172-5043-3 (set)
Contents: Calcium; Carbon; Hydrogen; Nitrogen; Oxygen; Sodium
"Each volume begins with the complete periodic table of elements, with that volume's element highlighted, and discusses such topics as atomic weight and element groups. The following chapters focus on the element's history. . . . The way the element reacts with other elements, how and where it is found in the world and in outer space, and how it is used in industry." Booklist

Elements. Grolier Educ. 1996 15v set $269 **546**
1. Chemical elements
ISBN 0-7172-7572-8   LC 95-82222
Contents: v1 Hydrogen and the noble gases; v2 Sodium and potassium; v3 Calcium and magnesium; v4 Iron, chromium, and manganese; v5 Copper, silver, and gold; v6 Zinc, cadmium, and mercury v7 Aluminum; v8 Carbon; v9 Silicon; v10 Lead and tin; v11 Nitrogen and phosphorus; v12 Oxygen; v13 Sulfur; v14 Chlorine, fluorine, bromine, and iodine; v15 Uranium and other radioactive elements
This set "discusses each element's discovery, forms, extraction, industrial uses, and unique character. In a one-topic-per-spread format, text blocks surround several large, clear, full-color photos or, more rarely, schematics. . . . This resource will strengthen both school labs and library collections." SLJ
For a fuller review see: Booklist, January 15, 1997

The **Elements**. Benchmark Bks. (Tarrytown) 1999-2000 8v il lib bdg ea $22.79   **546**
1. Chemical elements

Contents: Calcium, by J. Farndon; Carbon, by G. Sparrow; Gold, by S. Angliss; Hydrogen, by J. Farndon; Iron, by G. Sparrow; Magnesium, by C. Uttley; Nitrogen, by J. Farndon; Oxygen, by J. Farndon
These "titles cover where these substances are found, how they were discovered, their characteristics and reactions, and their importance in the human body and the environment. Each volume includes a double-page spread on the element's position in the periodic table. The captioned, full-color drawings, photographs, and diagrams clarify the text while boxed 'Did you Know?' items offer interesting extensions to it. . . . Informative, accessible science books that will be of interest for both general reading and report writing." SLJ
Includes glossaries

Fitzgerald, Karen
The story of oxygen. Watts 1996 63p il lib bdg
$22   **546**
1. Oxygen
ISBN 0-531-20225-9   LC 96-6202
"A First book"
Explores the history of the chemical element oxygen
and explains its chemistry, how it works in the body, and
its importance in our lives
"Colorful illustrations, photographs, diagrams, and
charts support and enhance the text. All in all, this is a
complete and informative overview." SLJ
Includes glossary and bibliographical references

Newton, David E.
Chemical elements; from carbon to krypton;
Lawrence W. Baker, editor. U.X.L 1999 3v set
$84   **546**
1. Chemical elements
ISBN 0-7876-2844-1   LC 98-31207
In this reference "the 112 elements of the periodic table are arranged alphabetically by chemical name, with
the exception of elements 101-112, which are discussed
under the entry *transfermium elements*. . . . [Each entry
includes] 'basic information about the chemical element:
its chemical symbol, atomic number, atomic mass, family
and pronunciation.'. . . The entry then discusses the element's discovery and naming, physical and chemical
properties, occurrence in nature, isotopes, methods of extraction, important compounds and uses, and health effects. Sidebars within the entries highlight commonly
used terms, well-known products, interesting facts, and
scientists." Booklist
Includes bibliographical references

547   Organic chemistry

Mebane, Robert C.
Plastics & polymers; [by] Robert C. Mebane,
Thomas R. Rybolt; illustrations by Anni Matsick.
21st Cent. Bks. (NY) 1995 64p il (Everyday
material science experiments) lib bdg $18.90
                                                 547
1. Plastics 2. Polymers 3. Science—Experiments
ISBN 0-8050-2843-9   LC 94-24963
This book includes instructions for 16 science experiments involving plastics and polymers
This "is good for children and educators who are
looking for new science activities or for new versions of
older ones. It may also help the serious students to combine facts taught in school with everyday experience."
Appraisal
Includes bibliographical references

548   Crystallography

Symes, R. F.
Crystal & gem; written by R.F. Symes and R.R.
Harding. Knopf 1991 63p il (Eyewitness books)
$19; lib bdg $20.99   **548**
1. Crystals 2. Precious stones
ISBN 0-679-80781-0; 0-679-90781-5 (lib bdg)
                                       LC 90-4930

Describes how crystals form in nature, how crystals
are grown artificially, and how crystals are used in industry. Numerous color photos with text identify the various gemstones
"The color photographs and drawings are dazzling and
show care in selection and positioning. . . . The text is
lucid, readable, and informative." Appraisal

549   Mineralogy

Chesterman, Charles W.
The Audubon Society field guide to North
American rocks and minerals; scientific consultant,
Kurt E. Lowe. Knopf 1979 c1978 850p il $19
                                                 549
1. Minerals 2. Rocks
ISBN 0-394-50269-8   LC 78-54893
"Pocket guide providing color photos and descriptions
of some 232 mineral species and forty types of rocks. Includes guide to mineral environments, glossary, bibliography, and indexes by name and locality." Ref Sources
for Small & Medium-sized Libr. 5th edition

Pellant, Chris
Rocks and minerals; Helen Pellant, editorial
consultant; photography by Harry Taylor. Dorling
Kindersley 1992 256p il (Eyewitness handbooks)
$29.95; pa $18.95   **549**
1. Minerals 2. Rocks
ISBN 1-56458-033-4; 1-56458-061-X (pa)
                                       LC 91-58222
This field guide to identification of rocks and minerals
includes techniques for collection and classification and
facts about physical and chemical composition and formation
"Visually attractive, with many color photographs [this
provides] detail and information that would benefit either
new or experienced naturalists." SLJ

Pough, Frederick H. (Frederick Harvey), 1906-
A field guide to rocks and minerals;
photographs by Jeffrey Scovil. Houghton Mifflin
$27.95; pa $17.95   **549**
1. Minerals 2. Rocks
                                       LC 94-49005
"The Peterson field guide series"
First published 1953. (5th edition 1996) Periodically
revised
"Sponsored by the National Audubon Society, the National Wildlife Federation, and the Roger Tory Peterson
Institute"
This illustrated guide utilizes traditional identification
methods and includes discussions of crystallography,
mineralogy and home laboratory techniques
Includes bibliographical references

Simon and Schuster's guide to rocks and minerals;
edited by Martin Prinz, George Harlow, and
Joseph Peters. Simon & Schuster 1978 607p il
hardcover o.p. paperback available $15   **549**
1. Minerals 2. Rocks
ISBN 0-671-24417-5 (pa)   LC 78-8610

Simon and Schuster's guide to rocks and minerals—*Continued*

Original Italian edition, 1977

"Half of this book consists of color plates; the other half is an authoritative text which describes the elements of mineralogy and petrology. Crystal system or family, physical and chemical properties, occurrence, uses, and rarity are included for each species." Libr J

Symes, R. F.

Rocks & minerals; written by R.F. Symes and the staff of the Natural History Museum, London. Knopf 1988 63p il (Eyewitness books) $19; lib bdg $20.99   **549**

1. Minerals 2. Rocks

ISBN 0-394-89621-1; 0-394-99621-6 (lib bdg)
LC 87-26514

Text and photographs examine the creation, importance, erosion, mining, and uses of rocks and minerals

"The material presented is technically sound and well and appropriately condensed. . . . It provides, through the use of visual aids and associated text, useful information for individuals with no formal training in geology." Sci Books Films

Zim, Herbert S.

Rocks and minerals; a guide to familiar minerals, gems, ores and rocks; by Herbert S. Zim and Paul R. Shaffer; illustrated by Raymond Perlman. Golden Bks. (NY) 1957 160p il maps (Golden nature guide) hardcover o.p. paperback available $5.95   **549**

1. Minerals 2. Rocks

ISBN 0-307-24499-7 (pa)

"Introductory material on the earth and its rocks gives basic geological information, and activities for amateurs are suggested in identifying, collecting and studying rocks and minerals. Colored diagrams and pictures of specimens aid in identification. Descriptions [of over 400 specimens] include information on formation, structure, use and importance." Bull Cent Child Books

550 Earth sciences

Campbell, Ann

The New York Public Library incredible Earth; a book of answers for kids; [by] Ann-Jeanette Campbell and Ronald Rood; illustrated by Jessica Wolk-Stanley. Wiley 1996 186p il maps pa $12.95
550

1. Earth sciences

ISBN 0-471-14497-5   LC 96-22112

"A Stonesong Press book"

Presents 1000 questions and answers on such topics as rocks and minerals, fossils, oceans, seasons, earthquakes, and volcanoes

This is an "accessible, fact-rich book for the science-minded." Booklist

Includes glossary and bibliographical references

Daniels, Patricia, 1955-

Earth. National Geographic Soc. 1998 60p il (National Geographic nature library) $12.95   **550**

1. Earth sciences

ISBN 0-7922-7046-0   LC 97-27748

Examines the composition and surface characteristics of the Earth, describing such features as rivers, mountains and other land formations, and various vegetation regions

Earth science on file; [by] the Diagram Group. rev ed. Facts on File 1999 various paging il maps loose-leaf $165   **550**

1. Earth sciences

ISBN 0-8160-3873-2   LC 98-55739

First published 1988

A looseleaf "compilation of 300 charts, all intended to be copied, covering the earth, astronomy, geology, tectonics, earthquakes, the atmosphere, oceans, weather, climate, erosion processes, paleontology, evolution, and earth resources. The pages are on heavy card-stock to withstand repeated copying." Malinowsky. Best Sci & Technol Ref Books for Young People [entry for 1988 edition]

English, June, 1955-

Mission: Earth; voyage to the home planet; [by] June A. English, Thomas D. Jones. Scholastic 1996 40p il $16.95   **550**

1. Earth sciences 2. Astronautics

ISBN 0-590-48571-7   LC 95-17474

The authors "explain the international Mission to Planet Earth program, which involved the use of space radar and an air-pollution sensor flown aboard the space shuttle Endeavor in April and September 1994. . . . The account is interesting, and the many high-quality, often breathtaking color photographs and radar images complement the text nicely." Booklist

Gallant, Roy A.

Earth; the making of a planet; by Roy A. Gallant and Christopher J. Schuberth. Marshall Cavendish 1998 160p il maps $14.95 (7 and up)
550

1. Earth

ISBN 0-7614-5012-2   LC 97-13224

Examines the formation, size, rocks and minerals, crust, mantle, climate, oceans, and other features of our planet

"Purchase is recommended to accompany middle or high school earth science courses especially for research purposes." Appraisal

Includes glossary and bibliographical references

Rocks & fossils; [by] Arthur B. Busbey III [et al.] Time-Life Bks. 1996 288p il (Nature Company guide) $29.95   **550**

1. Geology 2. Rocks 3. Fossils

LC 95-47661

This volume explores the "clues that rocks and minerals provide in deciphering the Earth's complex past. . . . [It addresses] topics in geology and paleontology. . . . The presentation emphasizes the collection of specimens; it includes descriptions of their appearances, physical attributes, locations, and chemical compositions." SLJ

Includes bibliographical references

Taylor, Barbara, 1954-
Earth explained; a beginner's guide to our planet. Holt & Co. 1997 69p il maps (Your world explained series) $18.95 **550**
1. Earth
ISBN 0-8050-4873-1 LC 96-41139
This book discusses "Earth's place in space, its surface structures, its changing features, its climates, and its future. Within each section, two-page chapters focus on subjects such as plate tectonics or caves." Booklist
This offers "excellent organization and graphics. Although the text is brief, it is up-to-date." SLJ

Van Rose, Susanna
The earth atlas; illustrated by Richard Bonson. Dorling Kindersley 1994 63p il maps $19.95 **550**
1. Geology
ISBN 1-56458-626-X LC 94-8765
"This very oversize volume looks at the geography of the earth, including the earth's crust, the ocean floor, and various kinds of rocks as well as the history of the earth." Booklist
"What is unique and fascinating about this book is its format: Each topic appears on a double page and consists of a brief introduction to major ideas, photographs, illustrations, maps, charts, and captions. The one-paragraph captions are crisp and informative. The full-color illustrations . . . are outstanding, and most portray geologic features in three dimensional blocks." Sci Books Films

VanCleave, Janice Pratt
Janice VanCleave's A+ projects in earth science; winning experiments for science fairs and extra credit. Wiley 1999 234p il $27.95; pa $12.95 (7 and up) **550**
1. Earth sciences 2. Science projects 3. Science—Experiments
ISBN 0-471-17769-5; 0-471-17770-9 (pa)
LC 98-14795
Presents thirty sample science projects as well as ideas for small changes to the original experiments thereby encouraging creativity and increased learning
"Students will appreciate the clear, organized instructions and the fact that most of the projects use such ordinary household items as soda bottles, kitchen utensils, rulers, and strings. . . . A rock-solid addition to library collections." SLJ
Includes glossary

The **Visual** dictionary of the earth. Dorling Kindersley 1993 64p il maps (Eyewitness visual dictionaries) $18.95 **550**
1. Earth sciences
ISBN 1-56458-335-X LC 93-18571
This volume provides an "overview of the Earth and all its systems. Included among its 25 two-page topical sections are coverage of geological time; the rock cycle; mineral resources; and processes such as faulting and folding, mountain building, and weathering and erosion. In addition, the Earth's waters (rivers, lakes and groundwater, coastlines, oceans, and seas) are addressed, as well as the atmosphere and weather." Am Ref Books Annu, 1994

550.3 Earth sciences— Encyclopedias and dictionaries

Farndon, John
Dictionary of the earth. Dorling Kindersley 1994 192p il $19.95 **550.3**
1. Earth sciences—Dictionaries 2. Geology—Dictionaries
ISBN 0-7894-0049-9 LC 94-35497
This work, which defines 2000 terms, is "arranged by themes such as 'Soil' and 'Seas & Oceans.' One section treats the human impact on the earth (i.e., pollution, flood management). Biographies of more than 70 earth science pioneers precede the index." Booklist

551 Geology, hydrology, meteorology

Lambert, David, 1932-
The field guide to geology; [by] David Lambert and the Diagram Group. updated ed. Facts on File 1998 256p il $27.95; pa $14.95 **551**
1. Geology
ISBN 0-8160-3840-6; 0-8160-3823-6 (pa)
LC 98-168173
First published 1988
This "introductory field guide to geology for students and the general public is well-illustrated, depicting all aspects of geology." Malinowsky. Best Sci & Technol Ref Books for Young People [entry for 1988 edition]

551.1 Gross structure and properties of the earth

Clifford, Nick
Incredible earth. DK Pub. 1996 44p il (Inside guides) $15.95 **551.1**
1. Earth—Internal structure 2. Geology
ISBN 0-7894-1013-3
This book introduces "a variety of the earth's geological features and phenomena in summary fashion. Each double-page spread is a grab bag of information about a subject: 'Crust to Core,' for example, briefly explores the earth's structure and introduces the theory of continental drift. . . . Volcanoes, Antarctica, and geysers are among other topics. . . . Color photos are dynamic; organization is clear; and charts will be helpful, but this is more for science-minded browsers than for children needing report material." Booklist

Sattler, Helen Roney
Our patchwork planet; the story of plate tectonics; illustrated by Giulio Maestro, and with photographs. Lothrop, Lee & Shepard Bks. 1995 48p il maps $16; lib bdg $15.93 **551.1**
1. Plate tectonics 2. Continental drift 3. Geology
ISBN 0-688-09312-4; 0-688-09313-2 (lib bdg)
LC 90-32623

Sattler, Helen Roney—*Continued*
"Sattler discusses the formation of the Earth's plates, their locations, and how their movements affect what happens on our planet's surface. She explains how earthquakes and volcanoes occur, and gives detailed descriptions of 'hot spots' in the world." SLJ
"Report writers and students seeking material to supplement textbook lessons will particularly appreciate Maestro's comprehensible diagrams and maps. . . . This title will claim a place even in basic science collections and will be useful to readers well into junior high." Bull Cent Child Books
Includes bibliographical references

Silverstein, Alvin
Plate tectonics; [by] Alvin Silverstein, Virginia Silverstein [and] Laura Silverstein Nunn. 21st Cent. Bks. (Brookfield) 1998 64p il maps (Science concepts) lib bdg $23.40   **551.1**
1. Plate tectonics 2. Earthquakes 3. Volcanoes
ISBN 0-7613-3225-1   LC 98-24934
Discusses plate tectonics, the theory that the surface of the earth is always moving, and the connection of this phenomenon to earthquakes and volcanoes
"The inviting layout includes many colorful photographs, maps, and diagrams, as well as some interesting informational sidebars." Booklist
Includes glossary and bibliographical references

551.2 Volcanoes, earthquakes, thermal waters and gases

Christian, Spencer
Shake, rattle, and roll; the world's most amazing volcanoes, earthquakes, and other forces; [by] Spencer Christian and Antonia Felix. Wiley 1997 122p il pa $12.95   **551.2**
1. Earthquakes 2. Volcanoes
ISBN 0-471-15291-9   LC 97-5541
The author "covers technical details such as plate tectonics, P and S seismic waves, and types of volcanic eruptions. There is . . . a section on volcanoes on other planets and moons, and another linking geologic activity to geysers and hot springs." SLJ
"Everything young readers want to know about . . . the movements of the earth is explained clearly and with a sense of humor." Appraisal
Includes glossary

Lauber, Patricia, 1924-
Volcano: the eruption and healing of Mount St. Helens. Bradbury Press 1986 60p il $16.95; pa $8.99   **551.2**
1. Mount Saint Helens (Wash.) 2. Volcanoes
ISBN 0-02-754500-8; 0-689-71679-6 (pa)
          LC 85-22442
A Newbery Medal honor book, 1987
"An account of the volcano's 1980 eruption in Washington State, with handsome color photographs of every phase of the eruption and its aftermath. Perhaps most interesting is the detailed description of the healing process—what flora and fauna survived and how." N Y Times Book Rev

Levy, Matthys
Earthquake games; earthquakes and volcanoes explained by 32 games and experiments; [by] Matthys Levy and Mario Salvadori; illustrated by Christina C. Blatt. Margaret K. McElderry Bks. 1997 116p il $16   **551.2**
1. Earthquakes 2. Volcanoes
ISBN 0-689-81367-8   LC 96-48157
Uses numerous activities and experiments to explain the forces and phenomena connected with earthquakes and volcanoes
"An informative tool that effectively uses hands-on techniques to teach kids about geologic wonders." Booklist

Thro, Ellen
Volcanoes of the United States. Watts 1992 112p il maps lib bdg $24 (7 and up)   **551.2**
1. Volcanoes
ISBN 0-531-12522-X   LC 91-36002
"A Venture book"
Explores volcanoes and volcanic activity in the United States, discussing the study of volcanoes, their effect on the environment, and volcanic hazards and risks
"Thro is a fine writer—her enticing and simple style will appeal to all age levels. Her introductory description of the 1980 eruption of Mount St. Helens has a captivating journalistic flair. Comments on the role of humans and technology in volcano-related research and a section called 'How to Become a Volcanologist' are perceptive and innovative." Sci Books Films
Includes glossary and bibliographical references

Walker, Sally M.
Earthquakes. Carolrhoda Bks. 1996 48p il (Carolrhoda earth watch book) lib bdg $19.93
          551.2
1. Earthquakes
ISBN 0-87614-888-7   LC 94-36178
The author offers "explanations for how and where earthquakes occur, how scientists are working to predict them, and how to survive if one strikes. In addition to photographs, a number of informative charts and graphs extend the text. . . . This book is informative enough for reports, yet readable and visually appealing to browsers." SLJ
Includes glossary

Volcanoes: earth's inner fire. Carolrhoda Bks. 1994 56p il maps (Carolrhoda earth watch book) lib bdg $14.96   **551.2**
1. Volcanoes
ISBN 0-87614-812-7   LC 93-23172
Describes volcanoes, where they form, the kinds of lava and landforms they create, and how volcanologists are learning to predict eruptions
Includes glossary

551.3 Surface and exogenous processes and their agents

Winner, Cherie
Erosion; written and photographed by Cherie Winner. Carolrhoda Bks. 1999 48p il (Carolrhoda earth watch book) $21.27 **551.3**
1. Erosion
ISBN 1-57505-223-7 LC 98-16456
Describes the forces of erosion as caused by glaciers, water, and wind, how they affect the earth's surface, and how their destructive effects can be prevented

551.4 Geomorphology and hydrosphere

Gallant, Roy A.
Limestone caves. Watts 1998 63p il lib bdg $22; pa $6.95 **551.4**
1. Caves
ISBN 0-531-20293-3 (lib bdg); 0-531-15910-8 (pa) LC 97-3467
"A First book"
Describes types of caves, particularly the formation and physical features of limestone caves, and provides information about the animal and plant life found in caves, as well as about human cave dwellers and their paintings
"Color photographs and their captions are well matched to the informative text. A helpful internet site index can assist readers in finding a nearby cave to visit." Horn Book Guide
Includes glossary and bibliographical references

Kaplan, Elizabeth, 1956-
The tundra. Marshall Cavendish 1995 64p il (Biomes of the world) lib bdg $25.64 **551.4**
1. Tundra ecology 2. Arctic regions
ISBN 0-7614-0080-X LC 95-2192
This book "concerns life in 'the earth's coldest biome,' including seasonal changes in the arctic tundra, the fragile ecosystem of the alpine tundra, wildlife from algae to musk oxen, and environmental hazards." Booklist
Includes bibliographical references

Simon, Seymour, 1931-
Mountains. Morrow Junior Bks. 1994 il $15; lib bdg $14.93; pa $5.95 **551.4**
1. Mountains
ISBN 0-688-11040-1; 0-688-11041-X (lib bdg); 0-688-15477-8 (pa) LC 93-11398
Introduces various mountain ranges, how they are formed and shaped, and how they affect vegetation and animals, including humans
"This book's spectacular full-color photographs will capture readers' attention and the text and well-designed diagrams will hold it." SLJ

551.46 Hydrosphere. Oceanography

Carson, Rachel, 1907-1964
The sea around us; [by] Rachel L. Carson; introduction by Ann H. Zwinger; afterword by Jeffrey S. Levinton. Oxford Univ. Press 1989 xxvii, 250p hardcover o.p. paperback available $13.95 (7 and up) **551.46**
1. Ocean
ISBN 0-19-506997-8 (pa) LC 89-16333
First published 1951; revised edition published 1961; this is a reissue of the 1979 edition which added the introduction and afterword
Beginning with a description of how the earth acquired its oceans, the book covers such topics as how life began in the primeval sea, the hidden lands, the life discovered in the abyss by highly delicate sounding apparatus, currents and tides, the formation of volcanic islands, and mineral resources
Includes bibliographical references

Day, Trevor
Oceans. Facts on File 1999 216p il maps (Ecosystem) $45 (7 and up) **551.46**
1. Oceanography
ISBN 0-8160-3647-0 LC 98-18110
This volume describes the oceans of the world with regard to their geography, geology, history, chemistry, exploration, relationship to the atmosphere, economic resources, and management
Includes bibliographical references

Erickson, Jon, 1948-
Marine geology; undersea landforms and life forms. Facts on File 1996 243p il maps (Changing earth) $26.95 (7 and up) **551.46**
1. Submarine geology 2. Marine biology
ISBN 0-8160-3354-4 LC 95-22109
"Erickson explains how the ocean's dynamics affect and are affected by the extravagantly sculptured ocean floor as he describes this vast, mysterious, and decidedly inhuman realm within the context of geologic history as well as the history of deep-sea research and exploration." Booklist
Includes bibliographical references

Fredericks, Anthony D.
Exploring the oceans; science activities for kids; illustrated by Shawn Shea. Fulcrum Resources 1998 118p il pa $16.95 **551.46**
1. Ocean 2. Marine ecology 3. Ecology
ISBN 1-55591-379-2 LC 98-15688
Presents information about the oceans of the world, the life they support, their importance as an ecosystem, and the threats they face. Includes related activities
"This volume is an excellent resource book for teachers and students. . . . The book is easily adapted to Internet applications due to its exhaustive listing of Web sites throughout the continental United States having to do with aquariums, environmental groups, and other information and resources." Sci Books Films
Includes glossary and bibliographical references

Library of the oceans. Grolier Educ. 1998 12v il
lib bdg set $289   **551.46**
1. Ocean 2. Oceanography
ISBN 0-7172-9180-4   LC 97-42835
Contents: v1 The shape of the oceans; v2 The restless
waters; v3 The prehistoric ocean; v4 Life in the ocean;
v5 Hunters and monsters; v6 The cold seas; v7 The
warm seas; v8 The shallow seas; v9 Exploring the
oceans; V10 The world's oceans; v11 Coasts and islands;
v12 The future of the ocean
This "is a feast for the eyes and mind. It is chock full
of beautiful and educational illustrations, charts, and
graphs. . . . Together, these books present a
comprehensive view of the ocean, while each volume
stands alone as an excellent reference." Sci Books Films

Sayre, April Pulley
Ocean. 21st Cent. Bks. (NY) 1996 80p il
(Exploring Earth's biomes) lib bdg $20.40 **551.46**
1. Ocean
ISBN 0-8050-4084-6   LC 96-2419
Describes the physical features of the ocean biome, as
well as ocean life, human use, and conservation efforts
"Presents clear, accurate information. Almost every
page has a small color picture or color diagram, nicely
captioned, to augment the text." Voice Youth Advocates

Sullivan, George
To the bottom of the sea; the exploration of
exotic life, the Titanic, and other secrets of the
oceans. 21st Cent. Bks. (Brookfield) 1999 80p il
lib bdg $24.90   **551.46**
1. Underwater exploration 2. Shipwrecks
ISBN 0-7613-0352-9   LC 98-41263
Examines different methods and technologies of undersea exploration, both past and present, the scientific
discoveries that have been made, and the shipwrecks that
have been explored
"Black-and-white and full-color photographs accompany the text. . . . Interesting and readable, this title is also
useful for homework support." SLJ
Includes bibliographical references

551.48 Hydrology

Allaby, Michael, 1933-
Floods. Facts on File 1998 135p il maps
(Dangerous weather) $24.95 (7 and up)   **551.48**
1. Floods
ISBN 0-8160-3520-2   LC 97-18374
The author describes: floodplains and meanders; aqui-
fers, springs, and wells; natural drainage; floods and agriculture; latent heat and dewpoint; tsunamis; tidal surges;
coastal erosion; prevention, warning, and survival. Illustrated with black-and-white photographs, drawings, charts
and graphs

551.5 Meteorology

Dunn, Andrew
Fog, mist, and smog. Raintree Steck-Vaughn
Pubs. 1998 48p il maps (Living with the weather)
$25.69   **551.5**
1. Fog 2. Weather 3. Air pollution
ISBN 0-8172-5053-0   LC 97-22354
This "volume includes discussions not only on the nature of fog, mist, and smog, but also on the causes of the
weather, the nature of clouds, temperature inversions,
coping with foggy conditions, the health effects of smog,
ways to reduce the pollution that produces smog, and
even the use of fog for special effects in movies." Sci
Books Films
Includes glossary and bibliographical references

Elsom, Derek M.
Weather explained; a beginner's guide to the
elements; [by] Derek Elsom. Holt & Co. 1997 69p
il maps (Your world explained series) $18.95
                                                  551.5
1. Weather 2. Meteorology
ISBN 0-8050-4875-8   LC 97-11968
This book describes the way weather works, storms,
extreme weather, and forecasting
"The information and the inviting format of this book
make it required reading for anyone curious about the
weather. The author has taken complex phenomena and
described them with words and pictures in a very understandable way." Sci Child
Includes glossary

Engelbert, Phillis
The complete weather resource. U.X.L 1997 3v
il set $84   **551.5**
1. Weather 2. Meteorology
ISBN 0-8103-9787-0   LC 97-6930
Contents: v1 Understanding weather; v2 Weather phe-
nomenas; v3 Forecasting & climate
"Front matter in each volume—table of contents to the
set, introduction, and glossary—is identical, as are the
bibliography and cumulative index at the end. Sidebars
enrich the text. These include biographies and pictures of
weather researchers; 'Key References,' which are scientific laws that apply to weather science experiments, such
as how to make fog. . . . There are charts and graphs
throughout. The few pronunciation guides are in the text
rather than the glossary. . . . *The Complete Weather Resource* makes weather and forecasting understandable.
The price is right, and the information is fascinating,
readable, and accessible for young adults." Booklist

Gardner, Robert, 1929-
Science projects about weather; by Robert
Gardner and David Webster. Enslow Pubs. 1994
128p il (Science projects) lib bdg $19.95 (7 and
up)   **551.5**
1. Weather 2. Science projects 3. Science—Experiments
ISBN 0-89490-533-3   LC 93-48720

Gardner, Robert, 1929-—*Continued*
Black-and-white line drawings accompany instructions on how to make weather stations and to do experiments with wind speed, precipitation and temperature
"This title will not disappoint students and teachers looking for interesting, challenging projects on an ever-fascinating subject." SLJ
Includes bibliographical references

Kahl, Jonathan D.
National Audubon Society first field guide: weather. Scholastic 1998 159p il $17.95; pa $10.95   **551.5**
1. Weather 2. Meteorology
ISBN 0-590-05469-4; 0-590-05488-0 (pa)
                                       LC 98-2938
Provides an overview of various weather conditions, how they develop, and how they are studied
Includes glossary and bibliographical references

Oxlade, Chris
Weather; photography by Chris Fairclough. Raintree Steck-Vaughn Pubs. 1999 48p il (Science projects) $24.26   **551.5**
1. Weather 2. Science projects 3. Science—Experiments
ISBN 0-8172-4949-4   LC 97-41171
Introduces basic concepts of weather, discussing such topics as atmospheric pressure, clouds, rain, and wind and includes experiments
This is "a colorful and commonsensical introduction." Sci Books Films
Includes glossary and bibliographical references

Silverstein, Alvin
Weather and climate; [by] Alvin Silverstein, Virginia Silverstein, and Laura Silverstein Nunn. 21st Cent. Bks. (Brookfield) 1998 64p il maps $23.40   **551.5**
1. Weather 2. Meteorology
ISBN 0-7613-3223-5   LC 98-24932
Examines the changes in the atmosphere that produce various weather phenomena and how weather patterns over a period of time determine the climates of the Earth's various regions
Includes bibliographical references

551.55   Atmospheric disturbances and formations

Lauber, Patricia, 1924-
Hurricanes; Earth's mightiest storms. Scholastic 1996 64p il maps $16.95   **551.55**
1. Hurricanes
ISBN 0-590-47406-5   LC 95-25788
Tells how hurricanes form, how scientists study them, and how they have affected the United States throughout this century
"The simple, dramatic prose communicates the rising tension and the terrifying facts. . . . Browsers will start

with the clearly captioned photos of pounding seas, wrecked neighborhoods, and flattened trees. The spacious book design, with large type, thick paper, wide margins, and clear maps and diagrams, will keep them reading." Booklist
Includes bibliographical references

Longshore, David
Encyclopedia of hurricanes, typhoons and cyclones. Facts on File 1998 372p il maps $45 (7 and up)   **551.55**
1. Hurricanes 2. Typhoons 3. Cyclones
ISBN 0-8160-3398-6   LC 97-20860
This encyclopedia describes named hurricanes, typhoons and cyclones, explains meteorological terms and instruments, includes biographical data, a chronology, and a list of hurricane safety procedures

Sherrow, Victoria
Hurricane Andrew; nature's rage. Enslow Pubs. 1998 48p il (American disasters) lib bdg $18.95
                                       551.55
1. Hurricanes
ISBN 0-7660-1057-0   LC 97-39193
Details the course of Hurricane Andrew, which hit the southeastern United States in 1992, and describes the recovery efforts that followed the storm
"Quotes from individuals who survived the hurricane add credence to the descriptions of its destructiveness. Numerous colored photos vividly portray the damage inflicted by the storm." Sci Books Films
Includes glossary and bibliographical references

551.56   Atmospheric electricity and optics

Simon, Seymour, 1931-
Lightning. Morrow Junior Bks. 1997 unp il $16; lib bdg $15.93; pa $5.95   **551.56**
1. Lightning
ISBN 0-688-14638-4; 0-688-14639-2 (lib bdg); 0-688-16706-3 (pa)   LC 96-16962
Photographs and text explore the natural phenomenon of lightning
"The subject is exciting, the information is amazing, and the full-color photographs are riveting. . . . Simon's explanations are concise but thorough." Booklist

551.57   Hydrometeorology

Allaby, Michael, 1933-
Droughts. Facts on File 1997 135p il (Dangerous weather) $26.95 (7 and up)   **551.57**
1. Droughts
ISBN 0-8160-3519-9   LC 97-9544
This book "examines droughts and their global and domestic impact. Offering readable explanations of scientific concepts and clearly defined terms, the book provides the reader with an understanding of rain—how it forms, why it falls, and what happens when it doesn't." Booklist

Gardner, Robert, 1929-
Science project ideas about rain. Enslow Pubs.
1997 96p il (Science project ideas) lib bdg $19.95
551.57
1. Rain 2. Clouds 3. Science projects 4. Science—
Experiments
ISBN 0-89490-843-X   LC 96-42411
Uses experiments to illustrate the properties of rain as
well as the reasons that water is such an important part
of life
"This useful collection of demonstrations, experiments,
and information . . . is clearly written and well illustrated with charts and diagrams that assist in the understanding of the text." Voice Youth Advocates
Includes bibliographical references

551.6   Climatology and weather

Arnold, Caroline, 1944-
El Niño; stormy weather for people and wildlife.
Clarion Bks. 1998 48p il $16   **551.6**
1. El Niño (Ocean current) 2. Climate
ISBN 0-395-77602-3   LC 98-4826
Explores the nature of the El Niño current and its ef-
fects on people and wildlife
This book has a "readable, informative text. . . . Full-
color photos, a computer-image series, diagrams, and
Internet sources bolster the narrative." SLJ
Includes glossary and bibliographical references

Encyclopedia of climate and weather; Stephen H.
Schneider, editor in chief. Oxford Univ. Press
1996 2v il maps set $275   **551.6**
1. Climate 2. Weather
ISBN 0-19-509485-9   LC 95-31019
This "is an alphabetical arrangement of over 300 short
articles . . . on everything from clouds and tornadoes to
human influences on weather and climate (e.g., acid rain,
deforestation, and effects of aerosols on the ozone layer).
. . . The set contains over 400 black-and-white line
drawings, photographs, charts, and maps, as well as a
glossary." Libr J

Weather almanac. Gale Res. il maps $145 **551.6**
1. United States—Climate—Statistics 2. Weather—
Statistics
ISSN 0731-5627

First published 1974. (9th edition 2000) Periodically
revised
Editors vary
"Definitions and articles on major weather events and
meteorological issues. Includes layperson's guide to
'weather fundamentals' and a glossary. Provides meteorological and climatological information and statistics for
major U.S. and world cities." N Y Public Libr. Book of
How & Where to Look It Up

551.7   Historical geology

The **Historical** atlas of the earth; a visual
exploration of the earth's physical past; general
editors, Roger Osborne and Donald Tarling;
consultant editor, Stephen Jay Gould; additional
contributions by G.A.L. Johnson. Holt & Co.
1996 192p il maps (Henry Holt reference book)
$45   **551.7**
1. Stratigraphic geology 2. Fossils
ISBN 0-8050-4552-X   LC 95-79328
Organized around the "divisions of geologic time [this
volume] tracks continental drift as inferred from fossils,
paleomagnetism, radioactive dating, or glaciation. The
editors portray the evidence in two-page color spreads
devoted to a specific topic, for instance, rocks such as
coal or limestone that characterize ancient epochs. . . .
[This is an] excellent info-jammed atlas." Booklist
Includes bibliographical references

552   Petrology

Ricciuti, Edward R.
National Audubon Society first field guide:
rocks and minerals; written by Edward Ricciuti,
Margaret W. Carruthers. Scholastic 1998 159p il
$17.95; pa $10.95   **552**
1. Rocks 2. Minerals
ISBN 0-590-05463-5; 0-590-05484-8 (pa)
LC 97-17991
This aims to help beginning naturalists observe and
understand over 150 types of rocks and minerals
This is "illustrated with vibrant, full-color photo-
graphs. . . . Attractive and useful." SLJ
Includes glossary and bibliographical references

553.8   Gems

Hall, Cally
Gemstones; photography by Harry Taylor;
editorial consultant, Joseph J. Peters. Dorling
Kindersley 1994 160p il (Eyewitness handbooks)
hardcover o.p. flexible bdg available $18.95 (7 and
up)   **553.8**
1. Precious stones 2. Gems
ISBN 1-56458-498-4   LC 93-28348
A visual guide to over 130 gemstone varieties. Each
entry includes a description with annotated photographs
to identify the gemstone's characteristics

560   Paleontology. Paleozoology

Benton, Michael, 1939-
Dinosaur and other prehistoric animal factfinder.
Kingfisher (NY) 1992 256p il maps pa $14.95
560
1. Dinosaurs—Dictionaries 2. Prehistoric animals—
Dictionaries
ISBN 1-85697-802-8

Benton, Michael, 1939-—*Continued*
"Dinosaurs and other prehistoric animals are arranged alphabetically within their scientifically recognized orders in this fact finder. Information boxes at the top of each page provide the name of the animal and an explanation of its meaning, a pronunciation guide, the individual who named the animal, and the year in which it was discovered. Geographical sites are indicated on an outline map of the continents." Recomm Ref Books for Small & Medium-sized Libr & Media Cent, 1994

Lindsay, William, 1956-
Prehistoric life; photographed by Harry Taylor. Knopf 1994 63p il maps (Eyewitness books) $19; lib bdg $20.99   **560**
1. Fossils 2. Evolution
ISBN 0-679-86001-0; 0-679-96001-5 (lib bdg)
                                                LC 93-32076
"A Dorling Kindersley book"
The author discusses "the fossil record and its evolutionary implications. . . . The information presented with the excellent photos of fossils and reconstructions is fact focused and generally accurate. In addition to presentations on various early life forms, there are pages devoted to the ice ages, fossil hunting, and extinctions." Sci Books Films

Taylor, Paul D., 1953-
Fossil. Knopf 1990 63p il (Eyewitness books) $19; lib bdg $20.99   **560**
1. Fossils
ISBN 0-679-80440-4; 0-679-90440-9 (lib bdg)
                                                LC 89-36444
This book "details how fossils are formed and what man has learned about life on Earth from discovering them. The sections on early paleontology, fossil folklore, and the tools of paleontology are particularly well done." SLJ

The **Visual** dictionary of prehistoric life. Dorling Kindersley 1995 64p il (Eyewitness visual dictionaries) $15.95   **560**
1. Fossil hominids 2. Fossils 3. Dinosaurs
ISBN 1-56458-859-9   LC 94-30705
This volume presents a "history of the development of life on earth through skillful integration of text, diagrams, and color photographs of fossils. Representations of biological development are divided into sections on plants and animals, introduced by text that sets the time frame and evolutionary frame. Useful charts allow readers to compare population growth and extinction over time." Horn Book Guide

567.9 Fossil reptiles. Dinosaurs

Benton, M. J. (Michael J.), 1956-
Dinosaurs; [by] Michael Benton. Kingfisher (NY) 1998 63p il $15.95   **567.9**
1. Dinosaurs
ISBN 0-7534-5131-X   LC 97-51121

Illustrations and text look at how dinosaur remains have been excavated and studied, what we know about how dinosaurs lived, about related prehistoric creatures, and about why dinosaurs are extinct
"The up-to-date text includes some intriguing minutiae; color illustrations and photographs add interest to the oversized volume." Horn Book Guide
Includes glossary

Dingus, Lowell
The tiniest giants; discovering dinosaur eggs; [by] Lowell Dingus and Luis Chiappe. Doubleday Bks. for Young Readers 1999 42p il $17.95
                                                567.9
1. Dinosaurs 2. Fossils
ISBN 0-385-32642-4   LC 98-28886
"Two paleontologists recount their expedition to Patagonia, where they discovered a nesting ground that included eggs containing sauropod embryos. . . . The book, illustrated with color photos, is a significant primary resource providing a firsthand description of how a dinosaur hunt is planned and performed and the post-expedition lab research that must be done." Horn Book Guide
Includes glossary and bibliographical references

Dinosaurs of the world; with an introduction by Mark Norell; consultants, Michael Benton, Tom Holtz; edited by Chris Marshall. Marshall Cavendish 1998 11v il maps set $329.95 **567.9**
1. Dinosaurs—Encyclopedias
ISBN 0-7614-7072-7   LC 97-43365
"The first 10 volumes contain more than 200 articles on dinosaurs and related topics. Volume 11 has been designated the 'reference' volume, and features a brief history of the earth, time lines, a list of famous fossil sites and digs, dinosaur family trees, brief biographies of 24 dinosaur hunters, museums with pertinent collections, and a section called 'Things to Do,' which lists resources and activities." Booklist
"This superb set is current, well organized, and provides interesting and comprehensive coverage of life in prehistoric times." SLJ

Facklam, Margery, 1927-
Tracking dinosaurs in the Gobi. 21st Cent. Bks. (NY) 1997 79p il map lib bdg $21.40   **567.9**
1. Andrews, Roy Chapman, 1884-1960 2. Dinosaurs 3. Fossils 4. Gobi Desert (Mongolia and China)
ISBN 0-8050-5165-1   LC 97-8070
Describes the work of paleontologists, beginning with Roy Chapman Andrews in the 1920s, who have searched in the Gobi Desert for evidence of dinosaurs
"Facklam's superb text keeps readers involved throughout. . . . The excellent-quality photos, both archival black-and-white and full-color modern shots, show specimens and scenes of the scientists at work, and act as a window to help readers visualize the expeditions." SLJ
Includes glossary and bibliographical references

Lambert, David, 1932-
The ultimate dinosaur book; foreword by John H. Ostrom. Dorling Kindersley 1993 192p il maps $29.95   **567.9**
1. Dinosaurs
ISBN 1-56458-304-X   LC 93-21885
Published in association with The Natural History Museum, London
"The opening section defines dinosaurs, describes the world they lived in, how they lived, and possible reasons for their extinction. . . . Profiles of 55 representative genera are illustrated with skeletons and museum models, plus a Fact File for each showing location, diet, classification, size and geologic era in which they lived. An A to Z of Dinosaurs (with pronunciation of names) includes 638 genera. Every page of this book includes color photos and detailed drawings." Book Rep
This "is a remarkable book, filled with information and high-quality illustrations." Sci Books Films

Lessem, Don
Dinosaur worlds; new dinosaurs, new discoveries. Boyds Mills Press 1996 192p il $19.95   **567.9**
1. Dinosaurs 2. Fossils
ISBN 1-56397-597-1   LC 95-83194
"This book tracks the evolution and extinction of dinosaurs and includes new information gleaned from the latest diggings." Book Rep
"Careful comparisons with places and animals known today help link the past to the present, and full-color artists' renderings, maps, and photos, all nicely captioned, jam the pages." Booklist
Includes glossary and bibliographical references

Lindsay, William, 1956-
Tyrannosaurus. Dorling Kindersley 1993 29p il map hardcover o.p. paperback available $7.95
                                              567.9
1. Dinosaurs 2. Fossil reptiles
ISBN 0-789-44272-8 (pa)   LC 92-52820
First published in the United Kingdom
At head of title: American Museum of Natural History
This focuses on the tyrannosaurus skeleton in the American Museum of Natural History. . . . The colorful, large-format [book [is] profusely illustrated with cartoons of fossil preservation, archival photos, photos of whole skeletons and of anatomical details, and reconstructions of muscles, whole bodies, the environment in which the dinosaur lived, and modern animals that provide anatomical or ecological analogies." Sci Books Films

Patent, Dorothy Hinshaw
In search of the maiasaurs. Benchmark Bks. (Tarrytown) 1999 64p il (Frozen in time) lib bdg $27.07   **567.9**
1. Horner, John R. 2. Dinosaurs 3. Fossils
ISBN 0-7614-0787-1   LC 97-46733
Describes John R. Horner's discovery and study of fossil records revealing the herding and nesting behavior of the dinosaur known as Maiasaura
This offers clear expository style, accuracy, informa-

tive sidebars, time lines, [and] maps. . . . [It is] heavily illustrated with crisp full-color photos and a few paintings." SLJ
Includes glossary and bibliographical references

Tanaka, Shelley
Graveyards of the dinosaurs; what it's like to discover prehistoric creatures; paleontological consultation by Philip J. Currie, Mark Norell, and Paul Sereno; featuring illustrations by Alan Barnard. Hyperion Bks. for Children 1998 48p il maps $16.95   **567.9**
1. Fossils 2. Dinosaurs
ISBN 0-7868-0375-4   LC 97-31286
"An I was there book"
Discusses the work of paleontologists who have found dinosaur bones and fossils in Canada, Argentina, and the Gobi Desert
"Full-color photos of the sites and of important finds and dramatic re-creations of dinosaurs in action enhance the readable text." Horn Book Guide
Includes glossary and bibliographical references

The **Visual** dictionary of dinosaurs. Dorling Kindersley 1993 64p il (Eyewitness visual dictionaries) $16.95   **567.9**
1. Dinosaurs
ISBN 1-56458-188-8   LC 92-53446
Text and labeled illustrations present the different types of dinosaurs, their anatomy, behavior, and the physical environments in which they lived
"A remarkable resource for the study of these creatures and, in fact, for the study of the entire Mesozoic era (the 'Age of the Reptiles'). It is well written, authoritative, and superbly illustrated." Sci Books Films

Zallinger, Peter, 1943-
Dinosaurs and other archosaurs; written and illustrated by Peter Zallinger. new ed. Random House 1999 96p il (Random House library of knowledge) lib bdg $15.99; pa $12.99   **567.9**
1. Dinosaurs 2. Prehistoric animals 3. Fossils
ISBN 0-394-94421-6 (lib bdg); 0-394-84421-1 (pa)
                                        LC 85-42930
First published 1986
Surveys the dinosaurs and other smaller prehistoric reptiles and describes many individual species
Includes glossary

569   Fossil mammals

Giblin, James, 1933-
The mystery of the mammoth bones; and how it was solved. HarperCollins Pubs. 1999 97p il $14.95; lib bdg $14.89   **569**
1. Peale, Charles Willson, 1741-1827 2. Mastodon 3. Fossil mammals
ISBN 0-06-027493-X; 0-06-027494-8 (lib bdg)
                                        LC 98-6701
Describes the efforts of the artist, museum curator, and self-taught paleontologist, Charles Willson Peale, to

Giblin, James, 1933-—*Continued*
excavate, study, and display the bones of a prehistoric creature that is later named "mastodon"
"Giblin's research is superb, and he turns to Peale's actual notes for details. He also includes recent information about the mammoth (and mastodon)." SLJ
Includes bibliographical references

570.3 Life sciences—Encyclopedias and dictionaries

Burnie, David
Dictionary of nature. Dorling Kindersley 1994 192p il $19.95 **570.3**
1. Biology—Dictionaries
ISBN 1-56458-473-9 LC 93-30696
"Arranged thematically rather than alphabetically, the dictionary takes readers through topics such as cells, evolution, plants, animals, and ecology, covering more than 2,000 concepts. Each main heading consists of one to two pages of information, including a broad introduction and a series of definitions and explanations. . . . If applicable, a brief biography of a scientist linked to that subject is included. Topics are illustrated with three dimensional models, diagrams, and photographs." Am Ref Books Annu, 1995

571.3 Anatomy and morphology

Animal anatomy on file; [by] the Diagram Group. Rev ed. Facts on File 1999 unp $165 **571.3**
1. Comparative anatomy
ISBN 0-8160-3875-9 LC 98-55740
First published 1990
This looseleaf volume "contains 250 photocopiable charts and diagrams of the major divisions of the animal kingdom. . . . The diagramatic plates illustrate the external form, the skeleton, various body systems, muscles, and major organs. . . . Almost 50 species of animals are illustrated, including the bat, cat, dog, dolphin, pigeon, kangaroo, and pig. Biology students doing reports will find the book useful. Art students also may find it helpful when they need a really clear external view of a particular animal." SLJ [review of 1990 edition]

Parker, Steve
The beginner's guide to animal autopsy; a "hands-in" approach to zoology, the world of creatures and what's inside them; written by Steve Parker; illustrated by Rob Shone. Copper Beech Bks. 1997 48p il lib bdg $23.90; pa $8.95 **571.3**
1. Anatomy 2. Dissection
ISBN 0-7613-0702-8 (lib bdg); 0-7613-0627-7 (pa)
LC 97-10032
Investigates the internal workings of animals, with drawings of dissections and cartoons illustrating how the animals' bodies work, including chapters on invertebrates, insects, fish, amphibians, birds, and mammals
"The text is easy to read. . . . Humor is used for emphasis, in both the illustrations and the text, and sidebars offer interesting trivia." Sci Books Films

571.7 Biological control and secretions

Silverstein, Alvin
Clocks and rhythms; [by] Alvin Silverstein, Virginia Silverstein, Laura Silverstein Nunn. 21st Cent. Bks. (Brookfield) 1999 64p il (Science concepts) lib bdg $23.40 **571.7**
1. Biological rhythms
ISBN 0-7613-3224-3 LC 98-26058
Discusses the concepts of time and biological cycles, including the phases of the moon, the internal clocks of plants and animals, seasonal rhythms, and the aging process
"The text, which will require a capable reader, is well organized and the explanations are clear; boxed facts and diagrams add interesting bits." Booklist
Includes glossary and bibliographical references

571.8 Reproduction, development, growth

Cohen, Daniel, 1936-
Cloning. Millbrook Press 1998 128p il lib bdg $22.90 (7 and up) **571.8**
1. Cloning 2. Genetic engineering
ISBN 0-7613-0356-1 LC 98-7015
Examines the history, current developments, future, and ethical ramifications of cloning, recombinant DNA, and gene therapy
"Cohen succeeds in covering the ethical questions and social ramifications surrounding this issue." SLJ
Includes bibliographical references

572 Biochemistry

Silverstein, Alvin
Photosynthesis; [by] Alvin Silverstein, Virginia Silverstein, Laura Silverstein Nunn. 21st Cent. Bks. (Brookfield) 1998 63p il lib bdg $23.40
572
1. Photosynthesis
ISBN 0-7613-3000-3 LC 98-9279
Explains photosynthesis, the process responsible for providing the material and energy for all living things, and discusses such related issues as respiration, the carbon cycle, acid rain, and the greenhouse effect
This book is "well researched and interesting and the format is inviting for both general-interest reading and research." SLJ
Includes glossary and bibliographical references

573.7 Musculoskeletal system

Parker, Steve
Skeleton; written by Steve Parker. Knopf 1988 63p il (Eyewitness books) $19; lib bdg $20.99
573.7
1. Skeleton 2. Bones
ISBN 0-394-89620-3; 0-394-99620-8 (lib bdg)
LC 87-26314

Parker, Steve—*Continued*
"An introduction to the structure and evolution of human and animal skeletal systems. Photographs of actual bones are used with some drawings to illustrate the book. There is a brief text, but the bulk of the book is the illustrations and their captions." BAYA Book Rev

The **Visual** dictionary of the skeleton. Dorling Kindersley 1995 64p il (Eyewitness visual dictionaries) $18.95   **573.7**
1. Skeleton 2. Bones
ISBN 0-7894-0135-5   LC 95-11936
"This comprehensive and exquisitely illustrated treasure trove of anatomical terms provides clear and instant access to the skeletons of humans, trees, amphibians, sea mammals, and others." Sci Child

576.5   Genetics

Kidd, J. S. (Jerry S.)
Life lines; the story of the new genetics; [by] J.S. Kidd and Renee A. Kidd. Facts on File 1999 152p il (Science and society) $19.95 (7 and up)   **576.5**
1. Genetics
ISBN 0-8160-3586-5   LC 98-22219
Surveys the field of genetics, discussing genetic analysis, cloning, other new research and developments, and their ethical aspects
Includes glossary and bibliographical references

Tagliaferro, Linda
Genetic engineering; progress or peril? Lerner Publs. 1997 128p il (Pro/Con) lib bdg $21.27 (7 and up)   **576.5**
1. Genetic engineering 2. Bioethics
ISBN 0-8225-2610-7   LC 95-25667
Discusses current and potential uses of genetic engineering in fields such as medicine, criminal investigation, and agriculture and examines some of the ethical questions involved
"Tagliaferro makes a complex, difficult subject understandable without oversimplification." Booklist
Includes glossary and bibliographical references

Yount, Lisa
Genetics and genetic engineering. Facts on File 1997 147p il (Milestones in discovery and invention) $19.95 (7 and up)   **576.5**
1. Genetics 2. Genetic engineering
ISBN 0-8160-3566-0   LC 97-8891
Profiles geneticists and highlights discoveries they have made; includes Gregor Mendel and the laws of inheritance, James Watson and the structure of DNA, and Stanley Cohen and genetic engineering
"This book is an outstanding, readable resource for basic information on heredity, gene mapping, the structure of DNA, disease-causing genes, and gene therapy." Booklist
Includes bibliographical references

576.8   Evolution

Couper, Heather
Is anybody out there? [by] Heather Couper and Nigel Henbest; illustrated by Luciano Corbella. DK Pub. 1998 45p il $16.95   **576.8**
1. Life on other planets
ISBN 0-7894-2798-2   LC 97-35398
Explores the possibility of life on other planets from both scientific and mythological perspectives
"The brief text is extended by the lengthy captions accompanying the many color photos and drawings. Despite the crowded format, readers will find solid discussions of astronomy and chemistry." Horn Book Guide
Includes glossary

Fradin, Dennis B.
Searching for alien life; is anyone out there? 21st Cent. Bks. (NY) 1997 80p il lib bdg $20.40   **576.8**
1. Life on other planets 2. Outer space—Exploration
ISBN 0-8050-4573-2   LC 97-12794
Examines the history of our beliefs regarding extraterrestrial life and our continuing efforts to explore outer space
"This title includes impressive, current photographs, such as those of possible Martian fossil life-forms in a meteorite found on Earth and of the sensational *Mars Pathfinder* that landed on the Red Planet in 1997. . . . This is a fine and sensible adjunct to the myriad UFO and alien-abduction accounts." SLJ
Includes bibliographical references

Gamblin, Linda
Evolution; written by Linda Gamblin. Dorling Kindersley 1993 64p il map (Eyewitness science) $15.95   **576.8**
1. Evolution
ISBN 1-56458-233-7   LC 92-54478
An illustrated examination of the ideas and fossil discoveries that have led to modern views of evolution
This offers "a wealth of outstanding color photographs and drawings and interesting information in a format that is particularly attractive for browsing." SLJ

Silverstein, Alvin
Evolution; [by] Alvin Silverstein, Virginia Silverstein, Laura Silverstein Nunn. 21st Cent. Bks. (Brookfield) 1998 64p il lib bdg $23.40   **576.8**
1. Evolution
ISBN 0-7613-3003-8   LC 98-9278
Discusses early theories of evolution, the work of Darwin, fossil and other evidence, and the effects of evolution on us and the future
This book "will be welcomed by students and teachers who are looking for clearly written, dependable material." SLJ
Includes glossary and bibliographical references

577 Ecology

Allaby, Michael, 1933-
Biomes of the world. Grolier Educ. 1999 9v il
maps lib bdg set $249   577
1. Ecology
ISBN 0-7172-9341-6   LC 98-37524
Contents: v1 The Polar regions; v2 Deserts; v3
Oceans; v4 Wetlands; v5 Mountains; v6 Temperate forests; v7 Tropical forests; v8 Temperate grasslands; v9
Tropical grasslands
In nine volumes, explores each of the earth's major
ecological regions, defining important features, animals,
and environmental issues
This "is a well designed nine-volume set of books
providing an excellent introduction to the principal
biomes of planet Earth. The books are an outstanding resource for students and teachers." Sci Books Films

Guiberson, Brenda Z.
Exotic species; invaders in paradise. 21st Cent.
Bks. (Brookfield) 1999 80p il lib bdg $23.90
577
1. Biological invasions 2. Ecology
ISBN 0-7613-1319-2   LC 98-41508
The author discusses species that have been introduced
into a new environment and have subsequently harmed
the established species. Included are starlings, zebra mus-
sels, kudzu, and mountain goats
"The text is well written in clear, lively language. The
accompanying color photos help to illustrate the subject
under discussion." SLJ
Includes glossary and bibliographical references

Orr, Richard
Nature cross-sections; illustrated by Richard Orr;
written by Moira Butterfield. Dorling Kindersley
1995 30p il $17.95   577
1. Habitat (Ecology) 2. Ecology
ISBN 0-7894-0147-9   LC 94-44798
"Orr's colorful paintings show cutaway views of ecosystems such as a rain forest, a tidal pool, and an
American desert, as well as structures such as a beaver
lodge and a beehive. . . . In addition to the brief introduction to each subject, short paragraphs identify and
discuss portions of the illustrations." Booklist
"The large pages will captivate readers of all ages,
kindling a long-lasting interest in the natural world." Sci
Child

Scott, Michael M.
The young Oxford book of ecology; [by]
Michael Scott. Oxford Univ. Press 1995 159p il
lib bdg $30; pa $16.90   577
1. Ecology
ISBN 0-19-521166-9 (lib bdg); 0-19-521428-5 (pa)
LC 95-7012
After explaining basic processes such as photosynthesis, food webs, and migration the author examines the
earth's habitats and ecosystems. Extinction, conservation,
pollution and habitat loss are also explored

This book is "not only lavishly illustrated with photographs, maps, diagrams, and drawings, but [it is] also
packed with the kind of in-depth, interesting information
students need for reports." Booklist
Includes glossary

Silverstein, Alvin
Food chains; [by] Alvin Silverstein, Virginia
Silverstein, Laura Silverstein Nunn. 21st Cent.
Bks. (Brookfield) 1998 63p il lib bdg $23.40
577
1. Food chains (Ecology)
ISBN 0-7613-3002-X   LC 97-52147
Explains various components of a food chain and dis-
cusses the concepts of food webs, umbrella species,
biogeochemical cycles, and more
"Clearly written, dependable material. Utilitarian. Use-
ful." SLJ
Includes glossary and bibliographical references

Snedden, Robert
The environment; photography by Chris
Fairclough. Raintree Steck-Vaughn Pubs. 1999 48p
il (Science projects) $24.26   577
1. Ecology 2. Science projects 3. Science—Experiments
ISBN 0-8172-4964-8   LC 97-46789
Describes the various elements that make up an environment, including the carbon cycle, the water cycle, and
food chains. Experiments are included
Includes glossary and bibliographical references

VanCleave, Janice Pratt
Janice Vancleave's ecology for every kid; easy
activities that make learning science fun. Wiley
1996 219p il maps (Science for every kid series)
$24.95; pa $10.95   577
1. Ecology 2. Habitat (Ecology) 3. Science—Experiments
ISBN 0-471-10100-1; 0-471-10086-2 (pa)
LC 95-6112
This book of science activities covers "25 topics,
ranging from plant and animal food chains to the effect
of plastics on the environment. Subjects are introduced in
a 'What You Need to Know' section that gives explanation of the scientific principles, plus plenty of everyday
examples. A brief preparatory exercise follows, usually
in the form of an imaginative game. . . . Simple black-
line drawings are crisp, uncluttered, and well placed.
. . . Solid information and a generous portion of fun are
combined to elevate this selection above the standard
collection of experiments." SLJ
Includes glossary

577.2 Specific factors affecting ecology

Patent, Dorothy Hinshaw
Fire: friend or foe; photographs by William
Muñoz. Clarion Bks. 1998 80p il $16   577.2
1. Forest fires 2. Ecology
ISBN 0-395-73081-3   LC 98-11754

Patent, Dorothy Hinshaw—*Continued*
Discusses forest fires and the effect that they have on both people and the natural world
"The text offers rich science support. . . . Muñoz's full-color photographs are a nice complement to the text." Booklist

Yellowstone fires; flames and rebirth; photos by William Muñoz and others. Holiday House 1990 40p il $14.95   **577.2**
1. Forest fires 2. Yellowstone National Park 3. Forest ecology
ISBN 0-8234-0807-8   LC 89-24544
This account of the 1988 forest fire in Yellowstone National Park discusses some financial issues, the media depiction of the fire, and the animals and birds disturbed or killed by firefighters
"Clear, colorful photos illustrate points covered in the text." SLJ

Pringle, Laurence P.
Fire in the forest; a cycle of growth and renewal; by Laurence Pringle; paintings by Bob Marstall. Atheneum Pubs. 1995 32p il $16 **577.2**
1. Forest fires 2. Forest ecology 3. Yellowstone National Park
ISBN 0-689-80394-X   LC 92-32257
Depicts, in text and illustrations, the stages of fire and regrowth in a Western lodgepole pine forest over a period of three hundred years. Also discusses the fire cycle and the role of fire in forest ecology
"This book presents fire as a natural phenomenon necessary for the health of the forest. Pringle urges readers to look beyond the media presentation of fire as a destroyer, using the northern Rocky Mountain landscape to show the forest ecosystem before, during, and after a fire, and regrowth over two centuries. Small, labeled pictures identify plants and animals in the side margins." Sci Child
Includes bibliographical references

Simon, Seymour, 1931-
Wildfires. Morrow Junior Bks. 1996 unp il $15; lib bdg $14.93   **577.2**
1. Forest fires 2. Forest ecology
ISBN 0-688-13935-3; 0-688-13936-1 (lib bdg)
                                            LC 95-12653
"Exploring the place of fire in nature, Simon explains that . . . forest fires have important functions in the ecosystem. With a brilliantly clear and colorful photograph facing each page of text, the book describes the causes and the progression of the wildfires that burned areas of Yellowstone National Park in 1988, explains how the fires were beneficial in many ways. . . . Lucid writing and excellent book design." Booklist

577.3 Forest ecology

Allaby, Michael, 1933-
Temperate forests. Facts on File 1999 216p il maps (Ecosystem) $45 (7 and up)   **577.3**
1. Forest ecology 2. Forests and forestry
ISBN 0-8160-3678-0   LC 98-23458

This book "explores the ecology, biology, chemistry, history, and economics of the forest." Publisher's note
Includes bibliographical references

Fielding, Eileen
The Eastern forest. Benchmark Bks. (Tarrytown) 1999 64p il (Ecosystems of North America) lib bdg $18.95   **577.3**
1. Forest ecology
ISBN 0-7614-0895-9   LC 97-33115
Examines the forests of eastern North America, their ecosystems, and their responses to temperature and weather
Includes glossary and bibliographical references

Goodman, Susan, 1952-
Bats, bugs, and biodiversity; adventures in the Amazonian rain forest; photographs by Michael J. Doolittle. Atheneum Bks. for Young Readers 1995 45p il (Ultimate field trip 1) hardcover o.p. paperback available $5.99   **577.3**
1. Rain forest ecology 2. Amazon River valley
ISBN 0-689-82870-5 (pa)   LC 94-35029
Title of paperback Ultimate field trip 1
This book provides a "description of the Peruvian rain forest as told through the eyes of seventh and eighth graders from Michigan. . . . The 74 middle school students spent one week living lives similar to those of the inhabitants of the region. . . . They explored the jungle's canopy, climbed trees, walked on rope bridges, and identified many of the plants and animals they had studied in the classroom." Sci Books Films
"There is enough factual material to tie in with more thorough studies of rain forests, but the real value of this book is the opportunity it offers children to relate to an exotic environment by seeing it through the eyes of their peers. A real plus to any collection." SLJ
Includes glossary and bibliographical references

Greenaway, Theresa, 1947-
Jungle; written by Theresa Greenaway; photographed by Geoff Dann. Knopf 1994 63p il (Eyewitness books) $19; lib bdg $20.99   **577.3**
1. Rain forest ecology
ISBN 0-679-86168-8; 0-679-96168-2 (lib bdg)
                                             LC 94-7948
"A Dorling Kindersley book"
Color photographs, drawings, and brief text describe the animals, plants, and ecology of tropical forests of the world
The author "presents a clear understanding of the composition, similarities and differences among rain forests around the world. A good addition to the book lies in the explanation of the value of this type of ecosystem and, sadly, how jungles are being destroyed at a rapid rate on a daily basis." Appraisal

Johnson, Darv, 1971-
The Amazon rainforest. Lucent Bks. 1999 96p il maps (Endangered animals & habitats) lib bdg $22.45 (7 and up)   **577.3**
1. Rain forest ecology 2. Amazon River valley
ISBN 1-56006-369-6   LC 98-35272

Johnson, Darv, 1971—*Continued*
Discusses the destruction of the Amazon rainforest and details the efforts to save it
Includes glossary and bibliographical references

Kaplan, Elizabeth, 1956-
Temperate forest. Marshall Cavendish 1996 64p il (Biomes of the world) lib bdg $25.64   **577.3**
1. Forest ecology
ISBN 0-7614-0082-6   LC 95-4065
The author "discusses the four types of temperate forests, where they occur, and how they differ from one another as well as how they change through the seasons. Diagrams show the forest layers, the stages of primary succession, and a typical food web in the biome. The final chapter focuses on problems threatening temperate forests." Booklist
Includes bibliographical references

Lasky, Kathryn
The most beautiful roof in the world; exploring the rainforest canopy; photographs by Christopher G. Knight. Harcourt Brace & Co. 1997 unp il $18; pa $8   **577.3**
1. Lowman, Margaret 2. Rain forest ecology
ISBN 0-15-200893-4; 0-15-200897-7 (pa)
                              LC 95-48193
"Gulliver Green"
Describes the work of Meg Lowman in the rainforest canopy, an area unexplored until the last ten years and home to previously unknown species of plants and animals
"Fresh in out-look and intriguing in details, this memorable book features colorful photographs that reflect the you-are-there quality of the text." Booklist
Includes glossary

Lewington, Anna
People of the rain forests; [by] Anna Lewington and Edward Parker. Raintree Steck-Vaughn Pubs. 1999 48p il maps (Wide world) $25.69   **577.3**
1. Rain forest ecology 2. Human ecology
ISBN 0-8172-5061-1   LC 97-38626
Describes the geography, plant and animal life, mineral resources, destruction, and environmental protection of the world's rain forests and how people live in this ecosystem
"Lewington and Parker offer a broad and well-balanced perspective of people's interactions with this environment." SLJ
Includes glossary and bibliographical references

Pipes, Rose
Rain forests. Raintree Steck-Vaughn Pubs. 1998 32p il map (World habitats) $22.83   **577.3**
1. Rain forest ecology
ISBN 0-8172-5003-4   LC 97-9070
"A Zoe book"
Introduces some notable rain forests around the world, including those of South America, Congo, and Central America

Sayre, April Pulley
Taiga. 21st Cent. Bks. (NY) 1994 64p il maps (Exploring Earth's biomes) lib bdg $18.90   **577.3**
1. Forest ecology
ISBN 0-8050-2830-7   LC 94-19388
The author describes the taiga environments of open lichen woodland and closed forests, including weather and climate, geology, plants and animals, and the effects of human habitation. Includes experiments
"An excellent resource book. . . . Appropriately illustrated with color photos and sketches and written in a refreshing style, the pages are loaded with information about the taiga biome." Sci Books Films
Includes glossary and bibliographical references

Temperate deciduous forest. 21st Cent. Bks. (NY) 1994 64p il maps (Exploring Earth's biomes) lib bdg $18.90   **577.3**
1. Forest ecology
ISBN 0-8050-2828-5   LC 94-25425
This locates temperate deciduous forests geographically "giving an overall description and treating the plants, animals, and people found there. Individual chapters, which are broken into small units, are brief and well illustrated and include suggestions for experiments using easily obtainable materials." Booklist
Includes glossary and bibliographical references

Tropical rain forest. 21st Cent. Bks. (NY) 1994 64p il maps (Exploring Earth's biomes) lib bdg $18.90   **577.3**
1. Rain forest ecology
ISBN 0-8050-2826-9   LC 94-25427
This geographically locates and describes tropical rain forests of the world and their plants and animals, and the effects of human habitation on the flora and fauna
"Filled with facts and interesting science projects. . . . Most illustrations are in full color, and the many charts and graphs add to the presentation." SLJ
Includes glossary and bibliographical references

Staub, Frank J.
America's forests; written and photographed by Frank Staub. Carolrhoda Bks. 1998 48p il map (Carolrhoda earth watch book) lib bdg $19.93
                                    577.3
1. Forests and forestry 2. Forest ecology
ISBN 1-57505-265-2   LC 98-7291
Examines the growth and changing nature of forests, the plants and animals living there, and the uses to which these lands are put
"Solid, accessible information presented in an attractive format. . . . Even students with little interest in nature will be drawn to the numerous full-color photographs that depict the beauty and variety of our country's woodlands." SLJ
Includes glossary

577.4   Grassland ecology

Ormsby, Alison
The prairie. Benchmark Bks. (Tarrytown) 1999
64p il (Ecosystems of North America) lib bdg
$18.95   **577.4**
1. Prairie ecology
ISBN 0-7614-0897-5   LC 97-39444
Examines the prairies of central North America, their
ecosystems, and their responses to temperature, weather,
and agriculture
This title is "well-written [and] well-organized." SLJ
Includes glossary and bibliographical references

Sayre, April Pulley
Grassland. 21st Cent. Bks. (NY) 1994 64p il
maps (Exploring Earth's biomes) lib bdg $18.90
                                            577.4
1. Grassland ecology 2. Prairie ecology
ISBN 0-8050-2827-7   LC 94-19389
This book "reviews the similarities and differences in
the grasslands that occur on every continent except Antarctica. The author examines the impact of the unique
combination of the abiotic factors of weather, climate,
and geology on the creation of conditions conducive for
the various types of grasslands." Sci Books Films
"The experiments and observations noted are interesting and within the range of most students' understanding.
. . . Full-color photos are scattered throughout." SLJ
Includes glossary and bibliographical references

Staub, Frank J.
America's prairies; written and photographed by
Frank Staub. Carolrhoda Bks. 1994 47p il maps
(Carolrhoda earth watch book) lib bdg $19.95
                                            577.4
1. Prairie ecology
ISBN 0-87614-781-3   LC 93-7841
Describes the ecology and biology of the three different types of North American prairie—tallgrass, mixed-
grass, and shortgrass
"A fact-filled trip from Indiana through the tallgrass
prairie and the Great Plains to eastern Colorado. Discover ongoing changes through colorful photographs and informative text, and learn about plants that made travel
difficult for previous generations." Sci Child
Includes glossary

Waterlow, Julia
Grasslands. Raintree Steck-Vaughn Pubs. 1997
48p il maps (Habitats) $24.26   **577.4**
1. Grassland ecology
ISBN 0-81724-518-9   LC 95-46356
Explains how grasslands are formed, the wildlife that
inhabits them, and the impact man has on the grassland
environment
This book "contains wonderful color photographs and
illustrations . . . and would make a wonderful resource
for a unit on the environment." Sci Books Films
Includes glossary and bibliographical references

577.5   Ecology of miscellaneous environments

Macquitty, Miranda
Desert; photographed by Alan Hills and Frank
Greenway. Knopf 1994 63p il map (Eyewitness
books) $19; lib bdg $20.99   **577.5**
1. Deserts 2. Human influence on nature
ISBN 0-679-86003-7; 0-679-96003-1 (lib bdg)
                                     LC 93-21068
"A Dorling Kindersley book"
This book "features photographs and drawings of flora
and fauna, mainly of the deserts of northern Africa and
the Middle East. Examples from the American Southwest
and Australia are included, but not Arctic, Antarctic, or
high-elevation regions. Brief explanatory paragraphs accompany the illustrations. . . . A browser's delight." SLJ

Mudd-Ruth, Maria
The deserts of the Southwest. Benchmark Bks.
(Tarrytown) 1999 64p il (Ecosystems of North
America) lib bdg $18.95   **577.5**
1. Desert ecology
ISBN 0-7614-0899-1   LC 97-49842
Examines the deserts of the Southwest, their eco-
systems, and their responses to temperature and weather
Includes glossary and bibliographical references

Sayre, April Pulley
Desert. 21st Cent. Bks. (NY) 1994 64p il maps
(Exploring Earth's biomes) lib bdg $18.90 **577.5**
1. Desert ecology
ISBN 0-8050-2825-0   LC 94-21427
This describes deserts of the world, their plants and
animals, and the effects of human habitation
"Lively and interesting. . . . Adept and well present-
ed." Booklist
Includes glossary and bibliographical references

Tundra. 21st Cent. Bks. (NY) 1994 64p il maps
(Exploring Earth's biomes) lib bdg $18.90 **577.5**
1. Tundra ecology 2. Arctic regions
ISBN 0-8050-2829-3   LC 94-19385
This book "presents an overview of the land of the
midnight sun—the Arctic tundra biome—with its unique
plants, animals, and ecosystems. . . . The book is filled
with interesting information. . . . Appropriately illustrated with photos and illustrations. . . . A superior resource
book." Sci Books Films

577.6   Aquatic ecology. Freshwater ecology

Bredeson, Carmen
Tide pools. Watts 1999 61p il lib bdg $22; pa
$6.95   **577.6**
1. Seashore ecology 2. Marine biology
ISBN 0-531-20368-9 (lib bdg); 0-531-15958-2 (pa)
                                     LC 97-41630
"A First book"

Bredeson, Carmen—*Continued*
Describes the physical characteristics of tide pools and the organisms that inhabit them
"Illustrated with many full-color photographs, this book presents basic information in an accessible format." Booklist
Includes glossary and bibliographical references

Goodman, Susan, 1952-
Ultimate field trip 3; Wading into marine biology; photographs by Michael J. Doolittle. Atheneum Bks. for Young Readers 1999 46p il map $17　　　　**577.6**
1. Seashore ecology 2. Marine biology 3. Natural history—Maine
ISBN 0-689-81963-3　　　　LC 98-13985
A middle school class from Boston visits Cobscook Bay, Maine, to learn about the marine biology of the Bay's tidal zone
"This celebrates the pleasures of hands-on, outdoor science with an inviting mix of fact and frolic." Booklist
Includes glossary and bibliographical references

Katz, Sharon
The Great Lakes. Benchmark Bks. (Tarrytown) 1999 64p il (Ecosystems of North America) $18.95　　　　**577.6**
1. Lake ecology
ISBN 0-7614-0898-3　　　　LC 97-32693
Describes the formation of the Great Lakes, the varied life forms that are part of this ecosystem, the interactions among the plants and animals that live there, and threats to this environment
Includes glossary and bibliographical references

Martin, Patricia A. Fink, 1955-
Rivers and streams. Watts 1999 143p il maps (Exploring ecosystems) lib bdg $23 (7 and up)　　　　**577.6**
1. River ecology 2. Science—Experiments
ISBN 0-531-11523-2　　　　LC 98-10117
Provides instructions for projects and activities that explore river and stream habitats and explains why these environments should be preserved and protected
"The well-written, generally well illustrated text provides abundant information beyond the activities." Booklist
Includes glossary and bibliographical references

Sayre, April Pulley
Lake and pond. 21st Cent. Bks. (NY) 1996 78p il (Exploring Earth's biomes) lib bdg $20.40　　　　**577.6**
1. Lake ecology 2. Pond ecology
ISBN 0-8050-4089-7　　　　LC 95-36228
Discusses the lake and pond biomes and how each is affected by the environment and people
"The writing style, lively and precise, makes this . . . unusually readable." Booklist
Includes glossary

River and stream. 21st Cent. Bks. (NY) 1996 80p il (Exploring Earth's biomes) lib bdg $20.40　　　　**577.6**
1. River ecology
ISBN 0-8050-4088-9　　　　LC 95-34458
Describes aquatic biomes, focusing on life in rivers and streams, and explains the effect of pollution on these biotic communities and on the lives of people everywhere
"Exceptionally well-focused, well-organized." SLJ
Includes glossary

Wetland. 21st Cent. Bks. (NY) 1996 78p il (Exploring Earth's biomes) lib bdg $20.40　**577.6**
1. Wetlands 2. Ecology
ISBN 0-8050-4086-2　　　　LC 95-36227
This describes the characteristics of wetlands, the plants and animals that inhabit it, and the effects of human use
"Engrossing, highly usable, and useful." SLJ
Includes glossary

577.7　Marine ecology

Carson, Rachel, 1907-1964
The edge of the sea; with illustrations by Bob Hines. Houghton Mifflin 1955 276p il hardcover o.p. paperback available $14 (7 and up)　　　**577.7**
1. Marine biology 2. Seashore
ISBN 0-395-92496-0 (pa)
"The seashores of the world may be divided into three basic types: the rugged shores of rock, the sand beaches, and the coral reefs and all their associated features. Each has its typical community of plants and animals. The Atlantic coast of the United States [provides] clear examples of each of these types. I have chosen it as the setting for my pictures of shore life." Preface

Cerullo, Mary M.
Coral reef; a city that never sleeps; text by Mary M. Cerullo; photographs by Jeffrey L. Rotman. Cobblehill Bks. 1996 58p il $17.99
　　　577.7
1. Coral reefs and islands 2. Marine ecology
ISBN 0-525-65193-4　　　　LC 95-6635
This describes the ecosystem of coral reefs and their inhabitants
"As fascinatingly fact-filled as the text is, it's even more outstanding because of Rotman's spectacular, full-color photographs." SLJ
Includes glossary and bibliographical references

Endangered oceans: opposing viewpoints; William Dudley, book editor. Greenhaven Press 1999 208p il lib bdg $20.96; pa $12.96 (7 and up)　　　**577.7**
1. Marine ecology 2. Environmental policy 3. Marine pollution
ISBN 0-7377-0063-7 (lib bdg); 0-7377-0062-9 (pa)
　　　　LC 98-45933
"Opposing viewpoints series"

Endangered oceans: opposing viewpoints—*Continued*

"This volume addresses how endangered the world's oceans and coastlines are, potential management and conservation practices, how the world's fisheries can be protected, and how whales can be protected. . . . A welcome addition." SLJ

Includes bibliographical references

Gowell, Elizabeth Tayntor
Fountains of life; the story of deep sea vents. Watts 1998 63p il $21; pa $6.95   **577.7**
1. Ocean bottom 2. Marine ecology
ISBN 0-531-20369-7; 0-531-15908-6 (pa)
          LC 97-10924
"A First book"
Discusses the formation and discovery of hydrothermal vents and the unusual animals and plants that can be found near them
"Color diagrams of the formation of new sea floor and tectonic plates are clear and understandable, and the computer-generated map of the ocean floor pulsates in vibrant color. Full-color illustrations amplify the descriptions, definitions, and explanations." SLJ
Includes glossary and bibliographical references

Kricher, John C.
Peterson first guide to seashores; [by] John Kricher; illustrated by Gordon Morrison. Houghton Mifflin 1992 128p il   **577.7**
1. Seashore 2. Marine biology
          LC 91-38829
Available 1998 edition with title: Peterson first guide to the seashore $5.95 (ISBN 0-395-91180-X)
This is a guide to identification of plants and animals found at the seashore
This is "sure to satisfy the curiosity of novices and inspire a deeper interest in nature. . . . The selections, grouped geographically and by habitat, are limited to those most commonly discovered by hikers or beachcombers. The clear, full-color pictures are simply labeled for easy identification." SLJ

Macquitty, Miranda
Ocean; written by Miranda Macquitty; photographed by Frank Greenaway. Knopf 1995 63p il (Eyewitness books) $19; lib bdg $20.99
          577.7
1. Marine animals 2. Ocean
ISBN 0-679-87331-7; 0-679-97331-1 (lib bdg)
          LC 95-1477
"A Dorling Kindersley book"
This illustrated introduction to underwater life briefly describes animals which live in various ocean environments including coastal waters, coral reefs, rocky seabeds, and the ocean bottom
This offers "two-page entries illustrated with bright, full-color photographs. . . . Browsing through these fully packed pages and dipping here and there into the text can be fun." SLJ

Parker, Steve
Seashore; written by Steve Parker. Knopf 1989 63p il (Eyewitness books) $19; lib bdg $20.99
          577.7
1. Seashore 2. Marine animals 3. Marine plants
ISBN 0-394-82254-4; 0-394-92254-9 (lib bdg)
          LC 88-27173
A photo essay introduces the animal inhabitants of the seashore, including fish, crustaceans, snails, and shorebirds
This book "contains . . . exquisite, three dimensional photographs and a myriad of easily digested facts about life where land and sea meet. . . . Better for browsing than in-depth research." BAYA Book Rev

Pringle, Laurence P.
Coral reefs; earth's undersea treasures; [by] Laurence Pringle. Simon & Schuster Bks. for Young Readers 1995 45p il map $16   **577.7**
1. Coral reefs and islands 2. Marine ecology
ISBN 0-689-80286-2   LC 94-5875
"Pringle describes the physical conditions and biological partnerships that contribute to this rich, complex ecosystem. He compares the coral reef to the rain forest in terms of its diversity of life, potential benefits to humankind, and ongoing destruction of habitat. Clearly written and well illustrated, the book provides close-up views of many reef animals as well as a wider perspective on this beautiful, vulnerable ecosystem." Booklist
Includes bibliographical references

Ricciuti, Edward R.
Ocean. Marshall Cavendish 1996 64p il maps (Biomes of the world) lib bdg $25.64   **577.7**
1. Marine biology 2. Ocean
ISBN 0-7614-0079-6   LC 95-4064
This describes ocean environments, including rocky tide pools, sandy beaches, and off-shore waters, and the plants and animals that inhabit them
Includes bibliographical references

Sayre, April Pulley
Coral reef. 21st Cent. Bks. (NY) 1996 80p il (Exploring Earth's biomes) lib bdg $16.98   **577.7**
1. Coral reefs and islands 2. Marine ecology
ISBN 0-8050-4087-0   LC 96-2838
This describes the physical features, plants and animals, and ecology of coral reefs
"The small full-color photographs and drawings in this book clearly portray reef inhabitants and structure." SLJ
Includes glossary

Sea searcher's handbook; activities from the Monterey Bay Aquarium; editor, Pam Armstrong. Monterey Bay Aquarium 1996 224p il pa $16.95   **577.7**
1. Marine ecology 2. Marine animals
ISBN 1-87824-415-9   LC 96-27100
Surveys kelp forests, wetlands, the open ocean, and other aquatic environments, encountering otters, sharks, and many more creatures

Sea searcher's handbook—*Continued*
This "is a treasury of information, activities and illustrations designed to help young people know, love and take care of the sea." Sci Child
Includes bibliographical references

World Book looks at the sea and its marvels. World Bk. 1997 64p il (World Book looks at) $11; pa $8 **577.7**
1. Marine biology
ISBN 0-7166-1803-6; 0-7166-1811-7 (pa)
LC 96-61142
This look at the ocean and marine life is based on information and illustrations contained in the World Book encyclopedia

Wroble, Lisa A.
The oceans. Lucent Bks. 1998 96p il maps (Endangered animals & habitats) lib bdg $22.45 (7 and up) **577.7**
1. Marine pollution 2. Marine ecology
ISBN 1-56006-464-1
LC 97-27275
Discusses the world's oceans as habitats endangered by human pollution and examines efforts to counter the damage and conserve them
"Packed with facts and statistics . . . well-researched." Horn Book Guide
Includes glossary and bibliographical references

577.8 Synecology and population biology

Silverstein, Alvin
Symbiosis; [by] Alvin Silverstein, Virginia Silverstein, Laura Silverstein Nunn. 21st Cent. Bks. (Brookfield) 1998 64p il lib bdg $23.40 **577.8**
1. Symbiosis
ISBN 0-7613-3001-1
LC 97-52149
Discusses the three kinds of symbiosis: mutualism, commensalism, and parasitism and describes examples of these relationships
"Well researched and interesting and the format is inviting for both general-interest reading and research." SLJ
Includes glossary and bibliographical references

578 Natural history of organisms and related subjects

Kerrod, Robin, 1938-
Facts on File wildlife atlas; [by] Robin Kerrod and John Stidworthy. 2nd ed. Facts on File 1997 80p il maps $18.95 **578**
1. Habitat (Ecology) 2. Animals 3. Plants 4. Ecology
ISBN 0-8160-3714-0
LC 97-15967
First published 1992 in the United Kingdom with title: Philip's wildlife atlas

Describes the different types of wild animals and plants in the world and explains how and why each region has its own unique mix of creatures. Habitats, evolution, migratory patterns, and danger of extinction are discussed
This volume "offers an attractive, informal introduction." Booklist

Wildlife and plants of the world. Marshall Cavendish 1998 17v set $329.95 **578**
1. Animals 2. Plants
ISBN 0-7614-7099-9
LC 97-32139
First published 1994 with title: Wildlife of the world
Edited by Deborah Evans and Leon Gray
Alphabetically-arranged illustrated articles introduce nerly 400 animals, plants and habitats
"The books are easy to use. . . . The set will be useful for research by upper-elementary and middle-school students." Booklist

578.7 Organisms characteristic of specific kinds of environments

Taylor, L. R. (Leighton R.)
Creeps from the deep; text by Leighton Taylor; photographed by Norbert Wu. Chronicle Bks. 1997 45p il $12.95 **578.7**
1. Marine biology 2. Marine animals 3. Ocean bottom
ISBN 0-8118-1297-9
LC 97-4081
In text and photographs, presents what is known about the deep ocean and the exotic creatures that live there
"The informative text is complemented by colorful photos. . . . Taylor makes this fascinating world very accessible." SLJ
Includes glossary

579 Microorganisms, fungi, algae

Silverstein, Alvin
Monerans & protists; [by] Alvin, Virginia, and Robert Silverstein. 21st Cent. Bks. (NY) 1996 64p il (Kingdoms of life) lib bdg $21.40 **579**
1. Microbiology
ISBN 0-8050-3521-4
LC 95-42322
This describes protists, a classification of single-celled organisms which includes amoebas, sporozoans, and diatoms, and monerans, a classification which includes bacteria and cyanobacteria. Viruses are also discussed
"The lucid text conveys well the need for . . . classifying the moneran and protist kingdoms. It is illustrated with color photos and includes 'boxes' with fascinating asides or amplifications of the main text." Sci Books Films
Includes glossary

579.2   Viruses and subviral organisms

Facklam, Howard
Viruses; [by] Howard and Margery Facklam. 21st Cent. Bks. (NY) 1994 64p il (Invaders) lib bdg $18.90   **579.2**
1. Viruses
ISBN 0-8050-2856-0   LC 94-25429
"In the first two chapters, the authors describe the nature of viruses and trace the work of scientists that went into the final identification of the organisms. . . . The next three chapters describe some specific diseases for which vaccines were made and take the reader through the history of smallpox, rabies, yellow fever, polio, HIV, and other flu viruses. The last two chapters touch upon the impact of viruses on plants and upon emerging viruses." Sci Books Films
Includes glossary and bibliographical references

579.3   Prokaryotes (Bacteria)

Facklam, Howard
Bacteria; [by] Howard and Margery Facklam. 21st Cent. Bks. (NY) 1994 64p il (Invaders) lib bdg $18.90   **579.3**
1. Bacteria 2. Microbiology
ISBN 0-8050-2857-9   LC 94-25430
This book "consists of six chapters that tell the reader where bacteria are located, who first discovered bacteria, ways to kill bacteria, how bacteria interact with the environment, how scientists have changed bacteria so the bacteria do things the scientists want them to do, and how scientists are using bacteria to introduce genetic materials into other organisms. The illustrations and the examples used in the text complement each other well." Sci Books Films
Includes glossary and bibliographical references

579.5   Fungi

Lincoff, Gary
The Audubon Society field guide to North American mushrooms; [by] Gary H. Lincoff; visual key by Carol Nehring. Knopf 1981 926p il flexible bdg $19   **579.5**
1. Mushrooms
ISBN 0-394-51992-2   LC 81-80827
"A Chanticleer Press edition. The Audubon Society field guide series"
This guide to 703 species of common mushrooms provides 762 color photographs and descriptions as keys to identifying these plants
This book "very successfully uses the three-part Audubon series format (key, color photos, text) which, at its best, provides browsing pleasure, effective field identification and full reference information. . . . The author is an expert on mushroom toxins and instills responsible cautions. The photos are uncommonly beautiful." SLJ

Pascoe, Elaine
Slime, molds, and fungi; text by Elaine Pascoe; photographs by Dwight Kuhn. Blackbirch Press 1999 48p il (Nature close-up) lib bdg $16.95
                                          579.5
1. Fungi
ISBN 1-56711-182-3   LC 97-36751
Using hands-on natural science projects, explores and explains different types and characteristics of fungi
This is "clearly written and well organized, and the photographs are outstanding in their clarity and composition." SLJ
Includes glossary and bibliographical references

Silverstein, Alvin
Fungi; [by] Alvin, Virginia, and Robert Silverstein. 21st Cent. Bks. (NY) 1996 64p il (Kingdoms of life) lib bdg $21.40   **579.5**
1. Fungi
ISBN 0-8050-3520-6   LC 95-42326
Introduces fungi, discussing their varieties, physical structure, reproduction, role in the ecosystem, and uses
This will be "very helpful for young scientists or anyone else interested in biological classification." Booklist
Includes glossary

580   Plants

Burnie, David
Plant; written by David Burnie. Knopf 1989 63p il (Eyewitness books) $19; lib bdg $20.99   **580**
1. Plants
ISBN 0-394-82252-8; 0-394-92252-2 (lib bdg)
                                        LC 88-27172
A photo essay introduces the world of plants, including the germination of seeds, plant defenses, and uses of plants
"Plant is the sort of book that makes botany exciting." Sci Books Films

Ross, Bill
Straight from the bear's mouth; the story of photosynthesis; written and illustrated by Bill Ross. Atheneum Pubs. 1995 32p il $16   **580**
1. Photosynthesis
ISBN 0-689-31726-3   LC 95-60387
Mr. Mildew, an eccentric scientist, helps Dana and Jake set up a science project on photosynthesis
"Set up like a mystery and employing the scientific method, the book slings lots of biology and chemistry in a painless manner. The story will tickle the funny bones of most readers, while the information is presented in colorful and clear charts and graphs." SLJ
Includes glossary

Silverstein, Alvin
Plants; [by] Alvin, Virginia, and Robert Silverstein. 21st Cent. Bks. (NY) 1996 64p il (Kingdoms of life) lib bdg $21.40   **580**
1. Plants 2. Botany
ISBN 0-8050-3519-2   LC 95-45673

Silverstein, Alvin—*Continued*

Begins with a general description of the plant kingdom and its classification before going on to discuss specific kinds of plants

"This easy-to-read and-understand book containing accurate information will be of interest to children at the junior high school level." Sci Books Films

Includes glossary

Taylor, Barbara, 1954-

Incredible plants. DK Pub. 1997 44p il (Inside guides) $15.95   **580**

1. Botany 2. Plants

ISBN 0-7894-1505-4   LC 96-45925

Describes in words and exposes through close-up photographs the anatomy of a variety of plants

"Captions for the photographs are unusually clear and concise. . . . Compelling for browsing or gaining an overview." SLJ

VanCleave, Janice Pratt

Janice VanCleave's plants; mind-boggling experiments you can turn into science fair projects. Wiley 1997 90p il (Spectacular science projects series) pa $10.95   **580**

1. Botany 2. Plants 3. Science projects 4. Science—Experiments

ISBN 0-471-14687-0   LC 96-2744

Presents facts about plants and includes experiments, projects, and activities related to each topic

This book "is inspiring without being flashy. . . . The black-and-white line drawings are sketchy but helpful. . . . This is a fine example of helpful information that is neither academically dry nor ingratiatingly slangy." SLJ

Includes glossary

The **Visual** dictionary of plants. Dorling Kindersley 1992 64p il (Eyewitness visual dictionaries) $15.95   **580**

1. Plants

ISBN 1-56458-016-4   LC 91-58208

Text and labeled illustrations depict a variety of plants and their parts, including woody, flowering, desert, and tropical plants

"Excellent photographs and clear illustrations depict a large sampling of plants. The text includes both scientific and common names and is filled with detailed labels and a brief, informative introduction for each ecosystem. This is an important reference for the classroom library or for the plant enthusiast." Sci Child

580.7 Plants—Education, research, related topics

Gardner, Robert, 1929-

Science projects about plants. Enslow Pubs. 1999 112p il (Science projects) lib bdg $19.95 (7 and up)   **580.7**

1. Plants 2. Science projects 3. Science—Experiments

ISBN 0-89490-952-5   LC 98-6821

Provides instructions for over thirty experiments appropriate for science fairs, involving plant physiology, reproduction, and growth

"The book offers solid ideas for projects." Booklist

Includes bibliographical references

Hershey, David R.

Plant biology science projects. Wiley 1995 165p il (Best science projects for young adults) pa $12.95 (7 and up)   **580.7**

1. Botany 2. Plants 3. Science projects 4. Science—Experiments

ISBN 0-471-04983-2   LC 94-12934

"The introduction provides a guide to scientific experimentation with explanations of the metric system, descriptions of instruments and equipment, and excellent planning guidelines. The activities are divided into five broad areas—seeds, plants and water, light and photosynthesis, soils and fertilizers, and hydroponics; the author provides background information, sources for further research, and a bibliography for each section." SLJ

Perry, Phyllis J., 1933-

Science fair success with plants. Enslow Pubs. 1999 104p il (Science fair success) lib bdg $19.95 (7 and up)   **580.7**

1. Botany 2. Plants 3. Science projects 4. Science—Experiments

ISBN 0-7660-1170-4   LC 98-25944

Details twenty-five experiments demonstrating the structure, environmental needs, and life processes of plants

Includes glossary and bibliographical references

581.6 Miscellaneous nontaxonomic kinds of plants

Dowden, Anne Ophelia Todd, 1907-

Poisons in our path; plants that harm and heal; [by] Anne Ophelia Dowden. HarperCollins Pubs. 1994 61p il lib bdg $17.89   **581.6**

1. Poisonous plants 2. Medical botany

ISBN 0-06-020862-7   LC 92-9518

Describes the physical characteristics and natural habitats of several varieties of plants, as well as their poisonous, medical, and magical properties

This "is a useful reference book of poisonous plants, with all plants indexed and pictured, but it is also a captivating narrative on the influence of poisonous plants in history and medicine." Sci Books Films

582 Plants notable for specific vegetative characteristics and flowers

Pascoe, Elaine

Seeds and seedlings; text by Elaine Pascoe; photographs by Dwight Kuhn. Blackbirch Press 1997 48p il (Nature close up) lib bdg $16.95   **582**

1. Seeds

ISBN 1-56711-178-5   LC 95-25178

Pascoe, Elaine—*Continued*
Describes how seeds are formed, how they grow, what they look like, how they reproduce, and how they make food. Instructions for related hands-on science projects is included
"The clearly written, interesting text is enhanced by numerous high-quality, full-color photographs." SLJ
Includes glossary and bibliographical references

582.13   Plants noted for their flowers

Hood, Susan
National Audubon Society first field guide: wildflowers. Scholastic 1998 159p il $17.95; pa $10.95   **582.13**
1. Wild flowers
ISBN 0-590-05464-3; 0-590-05486-4 (pa)
LC 97-17992
Provides an overview of wildflowers and where they grow, with specific information about individual species
"Illustrated with vibrant, full-color photographs. . . . Attractive and useful." SLJ
Includes glossary and bibliographical references

Landau, Elaine
State flowers; including the Commonwealth of Puerto Rico. Watts 1992 64p il (Our state symbols) lib bdg $24   **582.13**
1. State flowers
ISBN 0-531-20059-0 (lib bdg)   LC 92-8950
Describes each state's official flower and tells of legends associated with the flower
Includes bibliographical references

Niehaus, Theodore F.
A field guide to Pacific states wildflowers; illus. by Charles L. Ripper. Houghton Mifflin 1976 xxxii, 432p il map hardcover o.p. paperback available $18   **582.13**
1. Wild flowers
ISBN 0-395-91095-1 (pa)
"The Peterson field guide series"
Sponsored by the National Audubon Society and National Wildlife Federation
"Field marks of species found in Washington, Oregon, California and adjacent areas; a visual approach arranged by color, form, and detail." Title page
"This offering identifies 1492 common wildflowers. . . . An unusual and highly useful feature is a key to plant families that leads the user to a general description of the family with page references to the genus. . . . Common and scientific name, habitat, and recognition features are given for each plant." Libr J

Niering, William A.
The Audubon Society field guide to North American wildflowers: eastern region; [by] William A. Niering and Nancy C. Olmstead; visual key by Susan Rayfield and Carol Nehring. Knopf 1979 863p il $19   **582.13**
1. Wild flowers
ISBN 0-394-50432-1   LC 78-20383

"A Chanticleer Press edition"
"Covers the area east of the Rockies and east of the Big Bend area of Texas to the Atlantic. Color photographs together with family and species descriptions make this a most useful field guide." Sci News

Peterson, Roger Tory, 1908-1996
A field guide to wildflowers of northeastern and north-central North America; a visual approach arranged by color, form, and detail; by Roger Tory Peterson and Margaret McKenny. Houghton Mifflin 1968 xxviii, 420p il map hardcover o.p. paperback available $18   **582.13**
1. Wild flowers
ISBN 0-395-1172-9 (pa)
Also available in abridged form with title: Peterson first guide to wildflowers of northeastern and north-central North America, by Roger Tory Peterson pa $5.95
"The Peterson field guide series"
A "guide to the most frequently encountered flowering plants of Northeastern and North-central North America. There are 1344 illustrations, many in color, of nearly 1300 species. . . . The material is accurate and the authors have used only a small number of technical terms. This guide is invaluable to those interested in the natural history of eastern North America." Sci Books Films
Includes glossary

Spellenberg, Richard
The Audubon Society field guide to North American wildflowers: western region; visual key by Susan Rayfield and Carol Nehring. Knopf 1979 862p il $19   **582.13**
1. Wild flowers
ISBN 0-394-50431-3   LC 78-20384
"A Chanticleer Press edition"
This is an illustrated guide to wildflowers found from Alaska through California. Subjects are arranged by color and shape to facilitate identification. More than 600 species are covered in detail with notes on 400 others

582.16   Trees

Brandt, Sue R., 1916-
State trees; including the Commonwealth of Puerto Rico. Watts 1992 63p il (Our state symbols) lib bdg $24   **582.16**
1. State trees
ISBN 0-531-20000-0 (lib bdg)   LC 92-8946
Describes each state's official tree and how it was chosen
Includes bibliographical references

Brockman, C. Frank (Christian Frank), 1902-
Trees of North America; a field guide to the major native and introduced species north of Mexico; illus. by Rebecca Merrilees; under the editorship of Herbert S. Zim. Golden Bks. (NY) 1968 280p il hardcover o.p. paperback available $13.95   **582.16**
1. Trees—North America
ISBN 0-307-13658-2 (pa)

Brockman, C. Frank (Christian Frank), 1902—
Continued
"A Golden field guide"
This book identifies 594 species of trees "native to North America north of Mexico, plus some important foreign species that have become naturalized, and some that are grown commercially or as ornamentals. Each of the 730 species is illustrated and described briefly. Technical terms are held to a minimum and the brief descriptions emphasize only the most obvious field characteristics that may not be apparent in the illustrations." Appraisal

Burnie, David
Tree; written by David Burnie. Knopf 1988 63p il (Eyewitness books) $19; lib bdg $20.99 **582.16**
1. Trees
ISBN 0-394-89617-3; 0-394-99617-8 (lib bdg)
LC 88-1572
"Every imaginable aspect of the life of a tree is examined in a series of 2-page poster-format chapters, from 'The Birth of a Tree' to 'The Death of a Tree.' Anatomy, physiology, reproduction, growth and development are described using the best photographs I have seen in botanical literature and succinct, lively captions. Each page is a delight to the eye. . . . Of particular note is the coverage of tree diseases and pollution including acid rain, and the practical, amateur study of trees." Sci Books Films

Cassie, Brian, 1953-
National Audubon Society first field guide: trees; written by Brian Cassie. Scholastic 1999 159p il $17.95; pa $11.95 **582.16**
1. Trees
ISBN 0-590-05472-4; 0-590-05490-2 (pa)
LC 98-21855
A visual guide to the natural science of trees as well as a field guide to the trees found in the United States and Canada
Includes glossary and bibliographical references

Gardner, Robert, 1929-
Science project ideas about trees. Enslow Pubs. 1997 96p il (Science project ideas) lib bdg $19.95
582.16
1. Trees 2. Science projects 3. Science—Experiments
ISBN 0-89490-846-4
LC 97-6515
Contains many experiments introducing the processes that take place in plants and trees
The directions "are easy to understand, and the vocabulary is fairly accessible. The accompanying diagrams are particularly sharp and clear." SLJ
Includes bibliographical references

Petrides, George A.
A field guide to trees and shrubs; illus. by George A. Petrides, Roger Tory Peterson. 2nd. Houghton Mifflin 1972 xxxii, 428p il hardcover o.p. paperback available $18 **582.16**
1. Trees—North America 2. Shrubs 3. Climbing plants
ISBN 0-395-35370-X (pa)

Also available in abridged form with title: Peterson first guide to trees by George A. Petrides and Roger Tory Peterson pa $5.95
"The Peterson field guide series"
First published 1958
"Field marks of all trees, shrubs, and woody vines that grow wild in the northeastern and north-central United States and in southeastern and south-central Canada." Title page
"Descriptions and clear drawings compare similar species. Includes silhouettes showing typical branching of many of the trees." AAAS. Sci Book List. 3d edition

583 Dicotyledons

Wexler, Jerome
Sundew stranglers; plants that eat insects. Dutton Children's Bks. 1995 unp il $15.99 **583**
1. Carnivorous plants
ISBN 0-525-45208-7
LC 94-24188
The author "first gives a brief overview of insect-eating plants in general. . . . He then zeroes in on the sundew, discussing its range, size, carnivorous method, and suitability for home cultivation." Bull Cent Child Books
"Fascinating photographs, dramatic book design, and a straightforward text combine to produce an excellent book." Horn Book

590 Animals

Myers, Jack
On the trail of the Komodo dragon and other explorations of science in action; scientists probe 11 animal mysteries; illustrated by John Rice. Boyds Mills Press 1999 63p il $17.95 **590**
1. Animals
ISBN 1-56397-761-3
Based on science reporting columns published in Highlights for Children
"Each article answers an intriguing question about a particular animal: How do horses sleep? Why do snakes flick their tongues? What helps cats fall safely? Information is clearly presented in succinct chapters; frequent illustrations, sidebars, and section titles further break up the text." Booklist
Includes bibliographical references

590.3 Animals—Encyclopedias and dictionaries

The **Kingfisher** illustrated encyclopedia of animals; from aardvark to zorille—and 2,000 other animals; consultant editor: Michael Chinery. rev & enl ed. Kingfisher (NY) 1992 379p il $22.95 **590.3**
1. Animals—Encyclopedias
ISBN 1-85697-801-X
LC 92-053113
First published 1984 by Arco with title: Dictionary of animals

The Kingfisher illustrated encyclopedia of animals—*Continued*

Alphabetical entries provide information on over 2,000 animals. "Each brief description is from a paragraph to a column in length and includes information on the size, habitat, and behavior of the animal. At the end of each description, the names of the order, family, genus and species of the animal are provided. Short articles on selected topics, such as animal language and parental care, are also included. Full-color photographs and drawings of selected animals are featured on every page." Recomm Ref Books for Small & Medium-sized Libr & Media Cent, 1994

The **Simon** & Schuster encyclopedia of animals; a visual who's who of the world's creatures; consultant editor Philip Whitfield. Simon & Schuster 1998 616p il $50   **590.3**
1. Vertebrates—Encyclopedias 2. Animals—Encyclopedias
ISBN 0-684-85237-3   LC 98-31177
"A look at birds, mammals, fish, reptiles, and amphibians that represent the diversity of the vertebrate kingdom. . . . Names (both common and scientific), range, habitat, and size are provided for each of the nearly 2000 animals included. Descriptions of their appearances, adaptations, habits, and habitats flow around clear, colorful drawings, creating appealing pages. . . . An authoritative and interesting introduction to the animal world." SLJ
For a fuller review see: Booklist, Oct. 15, 1998

590.7 Animals—Education, research, related topics

Sayre, April Pulley
Put on some antlers and walk like a moose; how scientists find, follow, and study wild animals. 21st Cent. Bks. (NY) 1997 79p il lib bdg $20.40   **590.7**
1. Zoologists 2. Zoology
ISBN 0-8050-5182-1   LC 97-8072
Describes the work of field scientists who study animals in their natural habitats, discussing the challenges of finding the animals, tracking them, and recording data about them
"The well-organized text is enhanced by clear, full-color photos. . . . This lively and informative book will be an excellent resource for budding naturalists, but it should also be of interest to more casual browsers and students seeking information for reports on careers." SLJ
Includes glossary and bibliographical references

591.4 Physical adaptation

The **Visual** dictionary of animals. Dorling Kindersley 1991 64p il (Eyewitness visual dictionaries) $18.95   **591.4**
1. Animals
ISBN 1-879431-19-X   LC 91-60901
This volume "begins with introductory pages on animal bodies and animal heads. . . . The book then proceeds from butterflies and moths through mammals. Al-

most every page shows a skeleton and often a photograph or diagram of a dissected animal. . . . The book closes with animal tracks and a chart of animal classification." Booklist

591.47 Protective and locomotor adaptations

Perry, Phyllis J., 1933-
Armor to venom; animal defenses. Watts 1997 63p il lib bdg $22; pa $6.95   **591.47**
1. Animal defenses
ISBN 0-531-20299-2; 0-531-15884-5 (pa)
          LC 96-37289
"A First book"
Describes how animals survive by using their armor, camouflage, horns, stings, and other natural protective devices and strategies
"A readable compendium. . . . Six well-organized chapters are interspersed with captioned, full-color photographs. . . . Useful for report writers and browsers, this is a book that most libraries will want to stock." SLJ
Includes glossary and bibliographical references

Hide and seek; creatures in camouflage. Watts 1997 63p il lib bdg $22   **591.47**
1. Camouflage (Biology) 2. Animal defenses
ISBN 0-531-20306-9   LC 96-37290
"A First book"
Discusses the importance of camouflage in the animal kingdom, describing different types of disguise including disruptive coloration, countershading, mimicry, and masking
"This informative overview . . . will be of interest to report writers and browsers alike. . . . The full-color photographs are clear and eye-catching." SLJ
Includes glossary and bibliographical references

591.5 Behavior

Gardner, Robert, 1929-
Science project ideas about animal behavior; [by] Robert Gardner and David Webster. Enslow Pubs. 1997 96p il (Science project ideas) lib bdg $18.95   **591.5**
1. Animal behavior 2. Science projects 3. Science—Experiments
ISBN 0-89490-842-1   LC 97-13136
Presents facts about animal behavior and includes related experiments, projects, and activities
"The authors provide a well-written and -illustrated guide to experiments in animal behavior with just enough original science to give background and pique interest." Sci Books Films
Includes bibliographical references

Lavies, Bianca
Compost critters; text and photographs by Bianca Lavies. Dutton Children's Bks. 1993 unp il $14.99   **591.5**
1. Compost 2. Soil ecology
ISBN 0-525-44763-6   LC 92-35651

Lavies, Bianca—*Continued*

Examines how creatures, from bacteria and mites to millipedes and earthworms, aid in the process of turning compost into humus

"The author is to be commended for her excellent use of basic taxonomy in reference to animals. . . . The writing is very well done, and almost every page has a beautiful full-color photograph." Sci Books Films

Settel, Joanne

Exploding ants; amazing facts about how animals adapt. Atheneum Bks. for Young Readers 1999 40p il $16   **591.5**

1. Animal behavior

ISBN 0-689-81739-8   LC 97-35395

Describes examples of animal behavior that may strike humans as disgusting, including the "gross" ways animals find food, shelter, and safety in the natural world

"This attractive volume presents its material as wondrous science instead of sensational effect." Booklist

Includes glossary and bibliographical references

Taylor, Barbara, 1954-

Animal homes; written by Barbara Taylor. DK Pub. 1996 44p il (Inside guides) $15.95   **591.5**

1. Animals—Habitations

ISBN 0-7894-1012-5   LC 96-201950

"A variety of animal homes, including those of ants, termites, birds, and small mammals are depicted in this book. Beautiful illustrations show the complexities of many animal homes. These pictures are embellished with interesting and accurate information." Sci Child

Includes glossary

591.6 Miscellaneous nontaxonomic kinds of animals

Aaseng, Nathan, 1953-

Poisonous creatures. 21st Cent. Bks. (NY) 1997 95p il map (Scientific American sourcebooks) lib bdg $22.40; pa $8.95   **591.6**

1. Poisonous animals

ISBN 0-8050-4690-9; 0-8050-4689-5 (pa)

     LC 97-8728

Describes various species from every animal family that use some kind of venom to protect themselves or as a means of acquiring food

"The crisply written text is matched by a clean format enhanced by lots of intriguing color photos." Booklist

Includes bibliographical references

591.68 Rare and endangered animals

The **Grolier** student encyclopedia of endangered species. Grolier Educ. 1995 10v il maps set $299   **591.68**

1. Endangered species—Encyclopedias 2. Wildlife conservation

ISBN 0-7172-7385-7

"The 400 entries are organized alphabetically by common name. . . . Each begins with a colorful graphic that serves as a summary of the animal's vital statistics: common name, Latin name, endangerment code, a small map with the animal's habitat marked in red, and a color code that identifies the animal as a mammal, bird, reptile, or amphibian. The entry contains a description of the animal, its size, habitat, diet, breeding habits, young, and interesting facts. It also notes the estimated remaining populations, the reasons for endangerment, and whether any conservation measures are being employed. . . . The easy-to-use format coupled with the beautifully reproduced photographs mean that it will be used for more than just reports. Students and teachers will love it." Booklist

591.7 Animals characteristic of specific environments, animal ecology

Johnson, Jinny

Simon & Schuster children's guide to sea creatures. Simon & Schuster Bks. for Young Readers 1998 80p il $19.95   **591.7**

1. Marine animals

ISBN 0-689-81534-4   LC 97-8227

Describes the major groups of marine animals, including fish, birds, mammals, and crustaceans

"A beautifully illustrated guide, with a full-color drawing of each animal. . . . The book has enough information to be a useful research tool in the library. The organization, by habitat, is outstanding." Book Rep

Includes glossary

Lauber, Patricia, 1924-

Fur, feathers, and flippers; how animals live where they do. Scholastic 1994 48p il maps $16.95   **591.7**

1. Habitat (Ecology) 2. Biogeography

ISBN 0-590-45071-9   LC 93-40915

The author "looks at five widely differing habitats: the seas of Antarctica, the grasslands of East Africa, the forests of New England, the desert of the southwestern U.S., and the tundra of the Far North. In each case, she shows with vivid examples how the plants and animals 'fit together' to help each other survive through the day and through the seasons. . . . Each chapter includes a small map and splendid color photographs from a variety of sources." Booklist

592 Invertebrates

Aaseng, Nathan, 1953-

Invertebrates. Watts 1993 110p il lib bdg $24 (7 and up)   **592**

1. Invertebrates

ISBN 0-531-12550-5   LC 93-4093

"A Venture book"

Discusses animals with no backbones, including protozoans, sponges, worms, mollusks, arachnids, and arthro-

Aaseng, Nathan, 1953-—Continued
pods
"Each chapter contains interesting, pertinent information describing the animals presented and emphasizing the similarities and differences among the species." Book Rep
Includes glossary and bibliographical references

Meinkoth, Norman August, 1913-
The Audubon Society field guide to North American seashore creatures; [by] Norman A. Meinkoth. Knopf 1981 799p il maps flexible bdg $19   **592**
1. Invertebrates 2. Marine biology
ISBN 0-394-51993-0   LC 81-80828
"A Chanticleer Press edition. The Audubon Society field guide series"
This "unique field guide covers some 850 marine invertebrate animals living in or around the shallow waters of the temperate seacoasts of the United States and Canada. Excellent color photographs are grouped at the beginning of the book, followed by text that gives, for each animal, a short description, common and scientific names, habitat, range, and comments." Malinowsky. Best Sci & Technol Ref Books for Young People

Pascoe, Elaine
Earthworms; text by Elaine Pascoe; photographs by Dwight Kuhn. Blackbirch Press 1997 48p il (Nature close up) lib bdg $16.95   **592**
1. Worms
ISBN 1-56711-177-7   LC 95-25177
Describes the digging habits, physical characteristics, reproduction process, and habitat of the earthworm and provides instructions for related hands-on science projects
Written "in a chatty, enthusiastic style and with extraordinary close-up color photographs and clear instructions for activities and experiments." Booklist
Includes glossary and bibliographical references

Silverstein, Alvin
Invertebrates; [by] Alvin, Virginia, and Robert Silverstein. 21st Cent. Bks. (NY) 1996 64p il (Kingdoms of life) lib bdg $20.40   **592**
1. Invertebrates
ISBN 0-8050-3518-4   LC 95-45725
This "book describes the characteristics and origins of animal life and the evolutionary advance from simple to more complex organisms, illustrated by reference to several of the larger, generally more visible groups, including sponges, cnidarians, worms, arthropods, molluscs, and echinoderms. Major group divisions are indicated, along with physical characteristics, habitat, lifestyle, economic importance, etc." Sci Books Films
Includes glossary

594 Mollusks and mollusk-like animals

Arthur, Alex
Shell; written by Alex Arthur. Knopf 1989 62p il (Eyewitness books) $19; lib bdg $19.99   **594**
1. Shells
ISBN 0-394-82256-0; 0-394-92256-5 (lib bdg)
LC 88-13449
"Arthur showcases varieties of shelled mollusks, echinoderms, crustaceans, turtles, tortoises, and terrapins, illustrating how shells and pearls form and comparing species that inhabit such different environments as freshwater bodies and coral reefs." Booklist

Douglass, Jackie Leatherbury
Peterson first guide to shells of North America; illustrations by John Douglass. Houghton Mifflin 1989 128p il pa $5.95   **594**
1. Shells
ISBN 0-395-48297-6   LC 88-32884
"Shell collectors will enjoy the basic descriptions of shell types. Douglass has included the 'most colorful, not necessarily the most common, shells.' . . . Filled with precise color drawings and concise identification information." Booklist

Pascoe, Elaine
Snails and slugs; text by Elaine Pascoe; photographs by Dwight Kuhn. Blackbirch Press 1999 48p il (Nature close-up) lib bdg $16.95
594
1. Snails 2. Slugs (Mollusks)
ISBN 1-56711-181-5   LC 97-29159
Describes the physical characteristics, reproduction processes, habitats, and metamorphoses of snails and slugs and provides instructions for related hands-on science projects
"The interesting, clearly written [text is] enhanced by numerous high-quality, full-color photographs." Sci Books Films
Includes glossary and bibliographical references

Rehder, Harald Alfred, 1907-1996
The Audubon Society field guide to North American seashells; [by] Harald A. Rehder; with photographs by James H. Carmichael, Jr.; visual key by Carol Nehring and Mary Beth Brewer. Knopf 1981 894p il flexible bdg $19   **594**
1. Shells 2. Mollusks
ISBN 0-394-51913-2   LC 80-84239
"A Chanticleer Press edition. The Audubon Society field guide series"
"The more than 700 color plates are arranged according to shape and color rather than family or genus, making identification very simple for even the rankest amateur. . . . The text gives the common name, scientific name, description, habitat, range, and comments for each species. This is the most comprehensive field guide to North American seashells." Libr J

595.7 Insects

Burnie, David
Insects & spiders; text by David Burnie. Time-Life Bks. 1997 64p il (Discoveries library) $16   **595.7**
1. Insects 2. Spiders
LC 96-28417
An introduction to the physical characteristics, habits, and habitats of different types of insects and spiders
"Illustrated with large, detailed drawings and numerous color photos, this introduction is fairly complete and well organized." Horn Book Guide

Lasky, Kathryn
Monarchs; photographs by Christopher G. Knight. Harcourt Brace & Co. 1993 63p il $16.95; pa $105   **595.7**
1. Butterflies 2. Wildlife conservation
ISBN 0-15-255296-0; 0-15-255297-9 (pa)
LC 92-33972
"A Gulliver Green book"
Describes the life cycle and winter migrations of the eastern and western monarch butterflies and towns that protect their winter habitats including Pacific Grove, California and El Rosario, Mexico
"Vibrant description melds with fascinating full-color photographs in a book that strikes a perfect balance between science and humanity." SLJ

Lavies, Bianca
Killer bees; text and photographs by Bianca Lavies. Dutton Children's Bks. 1994 unp il maps $15.99   **595.7**
1. Bees
ISBN 0-525-45243-5
LC 94-18581
"Drawing on conversations with honey hunters, beekeepers, and scientists, this book explores life in the nests of killer bees, how climate has shaped their behavior, and the current breeding experiments to create a milder but equally productive bee." Publisher's note

Macquitty, Miranda
Amazing bugs. DK Pub. 1996 44p il (Inside guides) $15.95   **595.7**
1. Insects
ISBN 0-7894-1010-9
LC 96-214874
This "looks at such diverse insects as the mosquito, wasp, and bee by literally dissecting them. Other sections focus on how insects breathe, see, and mate. . . . Some of the pictures are fascinating." SLJ

Milne, Lorus Johnson, 1912-
The Audubon Society field guide to North American insects and spiders; [by] Lorus and Margery Milne; visual key by Susan Rayfield. Knopf 1980 989p il flexible bdg $19   **595.7**
1. Insects 2. Spiders
ISBN 0-394-50763-0
LC 80-7620
"A Chanticleer Press edition. The Audubon Society field guide series"

The authors "have based their field guide on 702 excellent color photographs (75 of which are of spiders and other arachnids). In addition to some general information, the text (two thirds of the book) is made up of brief comments on each kind of arthropod pictured. . . . The aim of this book is to enable one with little or no knowledge of insects to flip through the photographs and perhaps find one that looks similar to what he wants to identify." Choice
Includes glossary

Pascoe, Elaine
Ants; text by Elaine Pascoe; photographs by Dwight Kuhn. Blackbirch Press 1999 48p il (Nature close-up) lib bdg $16.95   **595.7**
1. Ants
ISBN 1-56711-183-1
LC 97-43571
Describes the physical characteristics, habitats, and life cycle of ants
"With its excellent visuals and simple experiments, *Ants* will be a useful supplement to other material about the topic." SLJ
Includes glossary and bibliographical references

Butterflies and moths; text by Elaine Pascoe; photographs by Dwight Kuhn. Blackbirch Press 1997 48p il lib bdg $16.95   **595.7**
1. Butterflies 2. Moths
ISBN 1-56711-180-7
LC 95-42704
Investigates the physical characteristics, reproductive processes, habitats, and metamorphoses of butterflies and moths through hands-on projects
This volume is "attractively designed and heavily illlustrated with bright, full-color, close-up photos." SLJ
Includes glossary and bibliographical references

Crickets and grasshoppers; text by Elaine Pascoe; photographs by Dwight Kuhn. Blackbirch Press 1999 48p il (Nature close-up) lib bdg $16.95   **595.7**
1. Crickets 2. Grasshoppers
ISBN 1-56711-176-9
LC 97-43572
Describes the physical characteristics, habitats, and life cycle of crickets and grasshoppers. Includes related activities
This offers "clear, readable text and striking close-up photos." Horn Book Guide
Includes glossary and bibliographical references

Pringle, Laurence P.
An extraordinary life; the story of a monarch butterfly; by Laurence Pringle; paintings by Bob Marstall. Orchard Bks. 1997 64p il $18.95; lib bdg $19.99   **595.7**
1. Butterflies
ISBN 0-531-30002-1; 0-531-33002-8 (lib bdg)
LC 96-31482
Introduces the life cycle, feeding habits, migration, predators, and mating of the monarch butterfly through the observation of one particular monarch named Danaus
"The narrative is scientifically sound and includes information from the most recent research. . . . The attractive, oversized book is lavished with realistic, full-color paintings." SLJ
Includes bibliographical references

Pyle, Robert Michael
The Audubon Society field guide to North American butterflies; visual key by Carol Nehring and Jane Opper. Knopf 1981 916p il $19   **595.7**
1. Butterflies
ISBN 0-394-51914-0   LC 80-84240
"A Chanticleer Press edition. The Audubon Society field guide series"
This guide "introduces more than 600 species of North American butterfly, including those native to the Hawaiian Islands. A section of brilliant color plates (more than 1,000 of them) featuring butterflies in their natural habitats, follows a general introduction and notes on text organization and use." Booklist
Includes glossary

Whalley, Paul Ernest Sutton
Butterfly & moth; written by Paul Whalley. Knopf 1988 63p il (Eyewitness books) $19; lib bdg $20.99   **595.7**
1. Butterflies 2. Moths
ISBN 0-394-89618-1; 0-394-99618-6 (lib bdg)
                        LC 88-1574
This book "explores the changes that occur at each stage of the life cycles of these insects. Temperate, mountain, and exotic species are described as are shapes, camouflage, and mimicry." Sci Teach
"This is an impressive, informative, and high-quality book." Sci Books Films

Wilsdon, Christina
National Audubon Society first field guide: insects; written by Christina Wilsdon. Scholastic 1998 159p il $17.95; pa $10.95   **595.7**
1. Insects
ISBN 0-590-05447-3; 0-590-05483-X (pa)
                        LC 97-17990
A visual guide to the natural science of insects which includes information on the ten most common orders, pollination, and life-cycles; also works as a field guide
This offers "sharp, clear full-color photos. . . . inviting and easy-to-use." SLJ
Includes glossary and bibliographical references

596   Chordates

Aaseng, Nathan, 1953-
Vertebrates. Watts 1993 112p il lib bdg $22.50
                              596
1. Vertebrates
ISBN 0-531-12551-3   LC 93-13391
"A Venture book"
Examines fish, reptiles, mammals, and other animals with backbones, noting both their similarities and their differences
"Well written and readable." SLJ
Includes glossary and bibliographical references

Silverstein, Alvin
Vertebrates; [by] Alvin, Virginia, and Robert Silverstein. 21st Cent. Bks. (NY) 1996 64p il (Kingdoms of life) lib bdg $21.40   **596**
1. Vertebrates
ISBN 0-8050-3517-6   LC 95-45672

"Using a minimal amount of scientific terminology, the authors . . . provide a successful introduction for young readers to the basic principles of the taxonomy of vertebrates. . . . Color photographs that are suitably placed throughout the text aid in making the subject matter clear." Sci Books Films
Includes glossary

597   Cold-blooded vertebrates. Fishes

The **Audubon** Society field guide to North American fishes, whales, and dolphins; [by] Herbert T. Boschung, Jr. [et al.]; visual key by Carol Nehring and Jordan Verner. Knopf 1983 848p il flexible bdg $19   **597**
1. Fishes—North America 2. Whales 3. Dolphins
ISBN 0-394-53405-0   LC 83-47962
"A Chanticleer Press edition. The Audubon Society field guide series"
This guide has "a first section containing excellent photographs of 529 marine and freshwater fishes and 45 cetacean species found in or near North America north of Mexico, and a second section giving brief descriptions of each species. . . . The well-organized and well-written text includes descriptions of physical features, habitat, range (generally with a small map), and related or similar species." Choice
Includes glossary

Macquitty, Miranda
Shark; written by Miranda MacQuitty. Knopf 1992 62p il maps (Eyewitness books) $19; lib bdg $20.99   **597**
1. Sharks
ISBN 0-679-81683-6; 0-679-91683-0 (lib bdg)
                        LC 92-4712
"A Dorling Kindersley book"
Describes, in text and photographs, the physical characteristics, behavior, and life cycle of various types of sharks
This "concentrates on the unusual, the strange, the odd, and the frightening with minimal text and clear, bright illustrations. . . . This is clearly a book for dipping in and out of, and not for reference." SLJ

Page, Lawrence M.
A field guide to freshwater fishes: North America north of Mexico; [by] Lawrence M. Page, Brooks M. Burr; illustrations by Eugene C. Beckham III, John Parker Sherrod, Craig W. Ronto. Houghton Mifflin 1991 432p il maps hardcover o.p. paperback available $19 (7 and up)
                              597
1. Fishes—North America
ISBN 0-395-91091-9 (pa)   LC 90-42049
"The Peterson field guide series"
"Sponsored by the National Audubon Society, the National Wildlife Federation, and the Roger Tory Peterson Institute"

Page, Lawrence M.—*Continued*
This guide "covers all 790 species known in North America north of Mexico. Over 700 illustrations, most in color, show identifying marks. Also includes 377 distribution maps and additional line drawings of key details." Publisher's note
Includes bibliographical references

Robins, C. Richard
A field guide to Atlantic coast fishes of North America; [by] C. Richard Robins, G. Carleton Ray; illustrations by John Douglass and Rudolf Freund. Houghton Mifflin 1986 354p il hardcover o.p. paperback available $19   **597**
1. Fishes—North America
ISBN 0-395-97515-8 (pa)   LC 85-18144
"The Peterson field guide series"
"Sponsored by the National Audubon Society and the National Wildlife Federation"
This guide describes and illustrates 1,100 species that inhabit the waters between the Canadian Arctic and the Gulf of Mexico
Includes bibliographical reference

Woog, Adam, 1953-
The shark. Lucent Bks. 1998 96p il (Endangered animals & habitats) lib bdg $23.70 (7 and up)
597
1. Sharks 2. Endangered species
ISBN 1-56006-462-5   LC 97-21348
Presents an overview of various species of shark, how they have become endangered, and what is being done to protect them from extinction
Includes glossary and bibliographical references

597.8 Amphibians

Clarke, Barry
Amphibian; written by Barry Clarke; photographed by Geoff Brightling and Frank Greenaway. Knopf 1993 63p il (Eyewitness books) $19; lib bdg $20.99   **597.8**
1. Amphibians
ISBN 0-679-83879-1; 0-679-93879-6 (lib bdg)
LC 92-1589
"A Dorling Kindersley book"
Photographs and text examine the evolution, behavior, physical characteristics, and life cycle of all kinds of amphibians

Cole, Joanna
A frog's body; with photographs by Jerome Wexler. Morrow 1980 47p il lib bdg $15.93
597.8
1. Frogs
ISBN 0-688-32228-X   LC 80-10705
"Cole and Wexler have constructed a superb introduction to the life processes and anatomy of the adult bullfrog. The author is exceptionally skillful at selecting interesting bits of information . . . and deftly combining

explanations of fact and concepts in a simple, lucid text. Wexler's photographs, in color and black-and-white, include almost uncanny shots of the frog in motion. . . . The photographs are complemented by clear drawings of the frog's internal organs." SLJ

Pascoe, Elaine
Tadpoles; text by Elaine Pascoe; photographs by Dwight Kuhn. Blackbirch Press 1997 48p il (Nature close-up) lib bdg $17.95   **597.8**
1. Frogs
ISBN 1-56711-179-3   LC 95-40848
Explores the physical characteristics, reproduction, habitat, and metamorphosis of tadpoles. Includes hands-on activities
"The full-color photographs are of excellent quality." SLJ
Includes glossary and bibliographical references

597.9 Reptiles

Behler, John L.
The Audubon Society field guide to North American reptiles and amphibians; [by] John L. Behler, F. Wayne King. Knopf 1979 743p il flexible bdg $19   **597.9**
1. Reptiles 2. Amphibians
ISBN 0-394-50824-6   LC 79-2217
"A Chanticleer Press edition. The Audubon Society field guide series"
"Photographs of the reptiles and amphibians are arranged in six main groups: salamanders, frogs and toads, crocodilians, turtles, lizards, and snakes, then sub-arranged by color. The marine turtles of coastal waters are also included. The text describes each of the species and gives common and scientific names, description, voice, breeding, habitat, subspecies, range, and descriptive comments." Malinowsky. Best Sci & Technol Ref Books for Young People

National Audubon Society first field guide: reptiles; written by John L. Behler. Scholastic 1999 160p il maps $17.95; pa $11.95   **597.9**
1. Reptiles
ISBN 0-590-05467-8; 0-590-05487-2 (pa)
LC 98-8332
Explores the world of reptiles, discussing their subspecies and races, anatomy, behavior, and habitat, and providing photographs and detailed descriptions of individual species
"Clear, full-color photographs and short capsules of information make it easy to identify each animal and its relatives." SLJ
Includes glossary and bibliographical references

Darling, Kathy
Chameleons on location; photographs by Tara Darling. Lothrop, Lee & Shepard Bks. 1997 40p il $16; lib bdg $15.93   **597.9**
1. Chameleons
ISBN 0-688-12537-9; 0-688-12538-7 (lib bdg)
LC 94-14584

Darling, Kathy—*Continued*
This book describes "a variety of chameleons and their lives, including their diets, mating, young, and changeable skin color. The chameleons' habitats and the creatures' value in the ecosystem are also discussed." Booklist
"Chock-full of interesting facts, this friendly book features a lively text and a stunning selection of sharply focused, full-color photographs." SLJ

Dow, Lesley
Alligators and crocodiles. Facts on File 1990 68p il maps (Great creatures of the world) $17.95 (7 and up)   **597.9**
1. Alligators 2. Crocodiles
ISBN 0-8160-2273-9   LC 90-31570
Discusses the biological features of alligators and crocodiles, their habitats, lifestyles, and history
The book is "highlighted by abundant clear, full-color (and, at times, full-page) photographs and excellent drawings, interspersed with diagrams and maps." SLJ

Mattison, Christopher
Snake; by Chris Mattison. DK Pub. 1999 192p il $29.95   **597.9**
1. Snakes
ISBN 0-7894-4660-X   LC 99-19957
An illustrated guide to "more than 60 types of snakes, ranging from adders to yellow anacondas. This richly formatted book features each snake in detailed entries with informative, readable text." Sci Child
Includes glossary

McCarthy, Colin, 1951-
Reptile; written by Colin McCarthy. Knopf 1991 63p il (Eyewitness books) $19; lib bdg $20.99
    597.9
1. Reptiles
ISBN 0-679-80783-7; 0-679-90783-1 (lib bdg)
    LC 90-4890
Photographs and text depict the many different kinds of reptiles, their similarities and differences, habitats, and behavior
This book "stands out because of the fascinating photographs, which are brilliantly lifelike and well-chosen to demonstrate concepts discussed. . . . The text is nicely balanced between straightforward factual data and intriguing bits of trivia." SLJ

McDonald, Mary Ann, 1956-
Pythons; by Mary Ann and Joe McDonald; illustrated with photographs by the authors. Capstone Press 1996 48p il (Animals & the environment) lib bdg $19   **597.9**
1. Pythons
ISBN 1-56065-296-9   LC 95-438
Describes the physical characteristics, habitat, and different varieties of pythons
Includes bibliographical references

Rattlesnakes; by Mary Ann and Joe McDonald; illustrated with photographs by the authors. Capstone Press 1996 48p il (Animals & the environment) lib bdg $19   **597.9**
1. Rattlesnakes
ISBN 1-56065-294-2   LC 95-436
Describes the physical characteristics, behavior, and different varieties of rattlesnakes
Includes bibliographical references

Montgomery, Sy
The snake scientist; photographs by Nic Bishop. Houghton Mifflin 1999 48p il map $16   **597.9**
1. Mason, Bob 2. Snakes
ISBN 0-395-87169-7   LC 98-6124
Discusses the work of Bob Mason and his efforts to study and protect snakes, particularly red-sided garter snakes
"The lively text communicates both the meticulous measurements required in this kind of work and the thrill of new discoveries. Large, full-color photos of the zoologist and young students at work, and lots of wriggly snakes, pull readers into the presentation." SLJ
Includes bibliographical references

Patent, Dorothy Hinshaw
The American alligator; photographs by William Muñoz. Clarion Bks. 1994 77p il $15.95   **597.9**
1. Alligators
ISBN 0-395-63392-3   LC 93-37704
This "book offers an overview of the facts and folklore surrounding alligators and their family, the crocodilians. The informative text, which discusses the habits and life cycle of the cold-blooded animals, is complemented by the well-chosen full-color photographs that appear on almost every page." Booklist
Includes bibliographical references

Ripple, Jeff, 1963-
Sea turtles. Voyageur Press 1996 85p il (World life library) pa $16.95 (7 and up)   **597.9**
1. Sea turtles
ISBN 0-89658-315-5   LC 95-22059
This book covers sea turtle distribution, biology, behavior, historical background and conservation techniques. The text is "lavishly illustrated with more than 50 full-color photographs that bring these animals to vibrant life." SLJ
Includes bibliographical references

Simon, Seymour, 1931-
Snakes. HarperCollins Pubs. 1992 unp il $16; pa $6.95   **597.9**
1. Snakes
ISBN 0-06-022529-7; 0-06-446165-3 (pa)
    LC 91-15948
Describes, in text and photographs, the physical characteristics, habits, and natural environment of various species of snakes
"Once again Simon demonstrates his skill in molding a lucid discussion and striking photographs into a compelling, informative overview." Horn Book

The **Snake** book; photography by Frank Greenaway and Dave King. DK Pub. 1997 unp il $12.95   **597.9**
1. Snakes
ISBN 0-7894-1526-7   LC 96-38294
Written and edited by Mary Ling and Mary Atkinson
The "creators of the book have used a stark white box as a background for some spectacular life-size photographs of 12 varieties of snakes. . . . Text containing very basic information about each snake sweeps around and inside the reptiles' coils, with the font varying in size from large to very small." Booklist

Stebbins, Robert C. (Robert Cyril), 1915-
A field guide to western reptiles and amphibians; text and illustrations by Robert C. Stebbins. 2nd ed rev. Houghton Mifflin 1985 336p il hardcover o.p. paperback available $19   **597.9**
1. Reptiles 2. Amphibians
ISBN 0-395-93611-X (pa)   LC 84-25125
Also available in abridged form with title: Peterson first guide to reptiles and amphibians $5.95
"The Peterson field guide series"
First published 1966
Sponsored by the National Audubon Society and National Wildlife Federation
"Field marks of all species in western North America, including Baja California." Title page
This field guide features over 240 species, most accompanied by illustration and distribution map. Coverage includes Baja California and information on reptile reproduction
Includes bibliographical references

598 Birds

Arnold, Caroline, 1944-
Hawk highway in the sky; watching raptor migration; photographs by Robert Kruidenier. Harcourt Brace & Co. 1997 48p il $18; pa $8   **598**
1. Hawks 2. Eagles 3. Falcons 4. Birds—Migration
ISBN 0-15-200868-3; 0-15-200040-2 (pa)
LC 95-51213
"A Gulliver Green book"
Provides information about hawks, eagles, and falcons and efforts to study them, especially the HawkWatch International Raptor Migration Project in the Goshute Mountains in Nevada
"Robert Kruidenier's sharply shot full-color photographs (many of them close-ups) work well with Arnold's clear, well-organized text, capturing the fierce beauty of the birds as well as the scientists' painstaking work." Booklist

On the brink of extinction; the California condor; photographs by Michael Wallace. Harcourt Brace Jovanovich 1993 48p il $17.95   **598**
1. Condors 2. Endangered species 3. Wildlife conservation
ISBN 0-15-257990-7   LC 92-14914
"A Gulliver Green book"

Describes the history of the condor in North America and the efforts to capture and breed the few remaining California condors to save them from extinction
"Author and photographer have collaborated to describe, with a clearly written text and outstanding, informative photographs, the efforts to save the condor." Sci Books Films

Bailey, Jill
Birds of prey. Facts on File 1988 61p il (Nature watch series) $15.95   **598**
1. Birds of prey
ISBN 0-8160-1655-0   LC 88-45088
This book "covers birds of all continents, dealing with topics such as the differences between owls and other raptors, beak and feet adaptations, migration, vision, nesting and mating behavior, and endangered species. A quick check list helps distinguish between the various raptors, and a good bibliography is included." Sci Books Films

Barghusen, Joan D., 1935-
The bald eagle. Lucent Bks. 1999 96p il maps (Endangered animals & habitats) lib bdg $23.70 (7 and up)   **598**
1. Bald eagle 2. Endangered species
ISBN 1-56006-254-1   LC 98-19034
Describes the physical characteristics and habits of bald eagles, threats to their existence, changes in their habitats, and efforts to protect these birds
Includes glossary and bibliographical references

Bull, John L.
National Audubon Society field guide to North American birds, Eastern region; [by] John Bull and John Farrand, Jr.; revised by John Farrand, Jr.; visual key by Amanda Wilson and Lori Hogan. rev ed. Knopf 1994 797p il maps pa $19   **598**
1. Birds—North America
ISBN 0-679-42852-6   LC 94-7768
Companion volume National Audubon Society field guide to North American birds, Western region, by Miklos D. F. Udvardy
"A Chanticleer Press edition"
First published 1977
This pictorial guide to 508 eastern species arranges birds by color and shape to simplify identification. It also includes information on bird-watching and conservation status
Includes glossary

Burnie, David
Bird; written by David Burnie. Knopf 1988 63p il (Eyewitness books) $19; lib bdg $20.99   **598**
1. Birds
ISBN 0-394-89619-X; 0-394-99619-4 (lib bdg)
LC 87-26441
A photo essay on the world of birds examining such topics as body construction, feathers and flight, the adaptation of beaks and feet, feeding habits, courtship, nests and eggs, and bird watching

Burnie, David—Continued
"From first impression to final reading, this photographic encyclopedia on the world of birds is an inviting pleasure. . . . *Bird* has a distinctly British tone, and many of the illustrative species are not native to the United States, but since they are each selected as examples of various adaptations, this should cause no problems." Sci Books Films

DuTemple, Lesley A., 1952-
North American cranes. Carolrhoda Bks. 1999 48p il (Carolrhoda nature watch book) $22.60
598
1. Cranes (Birds)
ISBN 1-57505-302-0   LC 98-4519
Describes the physical characteristics, diet, natural habitat, and life cycle of these large wading birds, and tells about the efforts of scientists to establish resident flocks
"Colorful and informative. . . . Illustrated with many excellent, full-color photos." Booklist

Griggs, Jack L.
All the birds of North America; American Bird Conservancy's field guide; concept and design by Jack L. Griggs. HarperPerennial 1997 172p il maps pa $19.95   **598**
1. Birds—North America
ISBN 0-06-273028-2   LC 96-49679
This identification guide to North American birds uses a system based on how and where birds collect food, with icons, color bars, key numbers, and color illustrations

Harrison, Colin
Birds of the world; by Colin Harrison and Alan Greensmith. Dorling Kindersley 1993 416p il maps (Eyewitness handbooks) $29.95; flexible bdg $19.95 (7 and up)   **598**
1. Birds
ISBN 1-56458-296-5; 1-56458-295-7 (flexible bdg)
LC 93-7065
This book "starts with a how-to-section, then discusses anatomy, variations within species, watching birds, flight patterns, and, finally, presents a user-friendly identification key. . . . In addition, there are very readable range maps, pictures of alternative plumages, and scale drawings of each bird." Sci Books Films

Kaufman, Kenn
Lives of North American birds. Houghton Mifflin 1996 xxv, 675p il maps (Peterson natural history companions) $35 (7 and up)   **598**
1. Birds—North America
ISBN 0-395-77017-3   LC 96-20285
This "is the print version of the previously issued CD-ROM, *Peterson Mulimedia Guides: North American Birds*. Organized like the CD-ROM, the book presents 600 species of birds in taxonomic order and groups them by family. Small color photographs and range maps accompany concise, plain-language information regarding

nesting, feeding, migration, courtship, habitat, clutch size, and conservation status. Upping the included species to 900 are brief descriptions of nonendemic vagrant birds." Libr J
For a fuller review see: Booklist, April 15, 1997
Includes bibliographical references

Landau, Elaine
State birds; including the Commonwealth of Puerto Rico. Watts 1992 63p il (Our state symbols) lib bdg $24   **598**
1. State birds
ISBN 0-531-20058-2   LC 92-8949
Describes each state's official bird and how it was chosen
Includes bibliographical references

Latimer, Jonathan P.
Backyard birds; [by] Jonathan P. Latimer, Karen Stray Nolting; illustrations by Roger Tory Peterson; foreword by Virginia Marie Peterson. Houghton Mifflin 1999 48p il (Peterson field guides for young naturalists) $15; pa $5.95   **598**
1. Birds
ISBN 0-395-95210-7; 0-395-92276-3 (pa)
LC 98-35509

Birds of prey; [by] Jonathan P. Latimer, Karen Stray Nolting; illustrations by Roger Tory Peterson; foreword by Virginia Marie Peterson. Houghton Mifflin 1999 48p il (Peterson field guides for young naturalists) $15; pa $5.95   **598**
1. Birds of prey
ISBN 0-395-95211-5; 0-395-92277-1 (pa)
LC 98-35516

Bizarre birds; [by] Jonathan P. Latimer, Karen Stray Nolting; illustrations by Roger Tory Peterson; foreword by Virginia Marie Peterson. Houghton Mifflin 1999 48p il (Peterson field guides for young naturalists) $15; pa $5.95   **598**
1. Birds
ISBN 0-395-95213-1; 0-395-92279-8 (pa)
LC 98-35512

Shorebirds; [by] Jonathan P. Latimer, Karen Stray Nolting; illustrations by Roger Tory Peterson; foreword by Virginia Marie Peterson. Houghton Mifflin 1999 48p il (Peterson field guides for young naturalists) $15; pa $5.95   **598**
1. Birds
ISBN 0-395-95212-3; 0-395-92278-X (pa)
LC 98-35510
"Each guidebook includes a rather subjective selection of about 20 creatures. The organization of material is different in each title: the backyard birds are grouped by color, the raptors by size, and the bizarre birds by such characteristics as odd bills. The shorebirds are arranged by where they are likely to be seen—the air, water, ground, or grass. A two-page entry for each creature instructs readers on how to recognize it and provides a solid introduction to individual characteristics." SLJ

Patent, Dorothy Hinshaw
Eagles of America; photographs by William Muñoz. Holiday House 1995 40p il $15.95   **598**
1. Eagles
ISBN 0-8234-1198-2   LC 95-6083
"The only two native species of North American eagles, the bald and golden, are treated in this comparative presentation. Patent describes how their numbers declined dramatically during the 19th and 20th centuries. . . . She also discusses the work of wildlife rehabilitators and conservation efforts. Splendid full-color photographs illustrate the lively text and clarify descriptions." SLJ

Peterson, Roger Tory, 1908-1996
A field guide to the birds; a completely new guide to all the birds of eastern and central North America; text and illustrations by Roger Tory Peterson; maps by Virginia Marie Peterson. 4th ed, completely rev and enl. Houghton Mifflin 1980 384p il maps 1998 reissue available $27; pa $18
598
1. Birds—North America
ISBN 0-395-91173-3; 0-395-91176-1 (pa)
LC 80-14304
Also available large format edition
"The Peterson field guide series"
First published 1934
Sponsored by the National Audubon Society and National Wildlife Federation
This guide to birds found east of the Rocky Mountains contains colored illustrations painted by the author, with description of each species on the facing page. Views of young birds and seasonal variations in plumage are included. Birds are arranged in eight major groups of body shape. There are also 390 colored maps showing summer and winter range

A field guide to western birds; text and illustrations by Roger Tory Peterson; maps by Virginia Marie Peterson. 3rd ed, completely rev and enl. Houghton Mifflin 1989 432p il maps 1998 reissue available $27; pa $18   **598**
1. Birds—West (U.S.)
ISBN 0-395-91174-5; 0-395-91173-7 (pa)
LC 89-31517
"The Peterson field guide series"
First published 1941
"A completely new guide to field marks of all species found in North America west of the 100th meridian and north of Mexico." Title page
Sponsored by the National Audubon Society, the National Wildlife Federation, and the Roger Tory Peterson Institute
This guide illustrates over 1,000 birds (700 species) on 165 color plates. In addition, over 400 distribution maps are included

Quinlan, Susan E., 1954-
Puffins; photographs by Bud Lehnhausen. Carolrhoda Bks. 1999 48p il (Carolrhoda nature watch book) lib bdg $22.60   **598**
1. Puffins
ISBN 1-57505-090-0   LC 97-38983

Discusses the physical characteristics, life cycle, and ecology of Atlantic puffins, tufted puffins, and horned puffins
"A solid introduction to this seabird. . . . The large, clear, full-color photographs with their informative captions add to the book's appeal and make it a good choice for recreational reading and reports." SLJ
Includes glossary

Rauzon, Mark J.
Hummingbirds. Watts 1997 63p il lib bdg $22; pa $6.95   **598**
1. Hummingbirds
ISBN 0-531-20260-7 (lib bdg); 0-531-15849-7 (pa)
LC 96-36156
"A First book"
Describes the physical characteristics, behavior, and habitat of the smallest bird in the world
"The book is scientifically accurate, well written, and well illustrated." Sci Books Films
Includes glossary and bibliographical references

Vultures. Watts 1997 63p il lib bdg $22; pa $6.95   **598**
1. Vultures
ISBN 0-531-20271-2 (lib bdg); 0-531-15853-5 (pa)
LC 96-31019
"A First book"
Describes the physical characteristics, behavior, and different species of these scavenger birds
This "is well written and illustrated and contains much good science." Sci Books Films
Includes glossary and bibliographical references

Robbins, Chandler S., 1918-
Birds of North America; a guide to field identification; by Chandler S. Robbins, Bertel Bruun, and Herbert S. Zim; illustrated by Arthur Singer. expanded rev ed. Golden Bks. (NY) 1983 360p il maps $14.50; pa $13.95   **598**
1. Birds—North America
ISBN 0-307-37002-X; 0-307-33656-5 (pa)
LC 83-60422
"A Golden field guide"
First published 1966
"Water birds are presented first, followed by land birds; within each of these two main divisions, arrangement is by related groups of species. Featured are carefully made, full-color illustrations, clear textual descriptions, and detailed range maps." Booklist

Sattler, Helen Roney
The book of North American owls; illustrated by Jean Day Zallinger. Clarion Bks. 1995 64p il maps $15.95; pa $6.95   **598**
1. Owls
ISBN 0-395-60524-5; 0-395-90017-4 (pa)
LC 91-43626
This volume "includes owl classification and history, hunting and habitat, courtship and nesting, and the complex relationship between owls and humans. The comprehensive glossary includes all of the 21 North

Sattler, Helen Roney—*Continued*
American species." Sci Child
This "is a superb ornithological primer. . . . The book is lavishly illustrated." Appraisal
Includes bibliographical references

Sayre, April Pulley
Endangered birds of North America. 21st Cent. Bks. (NY) 1997 95p il maps (Scientific American sourcebooks) $22.40; pa $8.95   **598**
1. Birds—Protection 2. Rare animals 3. Endangered species
ISBN 0-8050-4549-X; 0-8050-4548-1 (pa)
LC 97-12793
Discusses why certain bird species are endangered and examines such examples as the snail kite, piping plover, and whooping crane
"The text is clear, readable, and larded with bright-color photos and habitat maps." SLJ
Includes bibliographical references

Silverstein, Alvin
The California condor; [by] Alvin and Virginia Silverstein and Laura Silverstein Nunn. Millbrook Press 1998 64p il (Endangered in America) lib bdg $22.40   **598**
1. Condors 2. Wildlife conservation
ISBN 0-7613-0264-6   LC 97-45025
Describes the physical characteristics and behavior of the California condor, its decline in numbers due to human population growth and activities, and the efforts being made to maintain its population
"Clearly reproduced color photographs enhance the readable text." Horn Book Guide
Includes bibliographical references

Udvardy, Miklos D. F., 1919-1998
National Audubon Society field guide to North American birds, Western region; revised by John Farrand, Jr.; visual key by Amanda Wilson and Lori Hogan. rev ed. Knopf 1994 822p il maps pa $19   **598**
1. Birds—West (U.S.) 2. Birds—North America
ISBN 0-679-42851-8   LC 94-7415
Companion volume National Audubon Society field guide to North American birds, Eastern region by John L. Bull
"A Chanticleer Press edition"
First published 1977
This pictorial guide to 544 western species arranges birds by color and shape to simplify identification. It also includes information on bird-watching and conservation status
Includes glossary

Walters, Michael
Birds' eggs; photography by Harry Taylor; editorial consultant, Mark Robbins. Dorling Kindersley 1994 256p il (Eyewitness handbooks) $29.95; flexible bdg $17.95 (7 and up)   **598**
1. Birds—Eggs
ISBN 1-56458-178-0; 1-56458-175-6 (flexible bdg)
LC 92-53468

This book "describes the eggs of 500 species. For each bird, one or more eggs are shown in actual size and color. Each entry has a small drawing of the bird and egg in correct proportion. . . . Information is also given about nest building or other breeding activity and the geographic range in which the bird is found. . . . Since many widely held general reference books on birds have little information about eggs, many academic and public libraries will find this book a useful supplement." Booklist

Weidensaul, Scott
National Audubon Society first field guide: birds; [writer, Scott Weidensaul] Scholastic 1998 159p il maps $17.95; pa $10.95   **598**
1. Birds
ISBN 0-590-05446-5; 0-590-05482-1 (pa)
LC 97-17989
A visual guide to the natural science of birds as well as a field guide to over 150 species found in North America
This offers "a great deal of information in a handy format . . . [and] large, beautifully colored photos of each bird." Booklist
Includes glossary and bibliographical references

599   Mammals

Bateman, Robert, 1930-
Safari; [by] Robert Bateman and Rick Archbold. Little, Brown 1998 unp il $17.95   **599**
1. Animals—Africa
ISBN 0-316-08265-1   LC 98-6139
"A Madison Press book"
Paintings and brief text present some of the animals found in Africa, including elephants, giraffes, cheetahs, wildebeests, lions, ostriches, and zebras
"At least one full page per spread is devoted to Bateman's spectacular oil paintings that are photographic in detail and perfectly capture the essence and beauty of their subjects. These illustrations combined with the text create a sort of travel diary that clearly conveys the artist's love of wildlife." SLJ

Burt, William Henry, 1903-1987
A field guide to the mammals; text and maps by William Henry Burt; illus. by Richard Philip Grossenheider. 3d ed. Houghton Mifflin 1976 xxv, 289p il maps $24.95; pa $16.95   **599**
1. Mammals
ISBN 0-395-24082-4; 0-395-24084-0 (pa)
Also available paperback abridgement with title: Peterson first guide to mammals of North America, by Peter Alden $5.95
"The Peterson field guide series"
First published 1952
Sponsored by the National Audubon Society and National Wildlife Federation
"Field marks of all North American species found north of Mexico." Title page
"This field guide covers 380 species of mammals, including whales, dolphins, and porpoises. Each one is

Burt, William Henry, 1903-1987—*Continued*
described in detail and most are depicted in color photographs and additional black-and-white sketches. Range maps are included. The description includes information on distinguishing marks, habitat, litter size, appearance of young, specimen tracks, and representations of nests." Malinowsky. Best Sci & Technol Ref Books for Young People

Encyclopedia of mammals. Marshall Cavendish
    1996 17v set $459.95   **599**
    1. Mammals—Encyclopedias
    ISBN 0-7614-0575-5   LC 96-17736
    "The world's living mammals are covered in 95 essays, each divided into three broad sections: profile, behavior, and survival. The profile includes information on anatomy, evolution, and classification. Diet, habitat, reproduction, and other topics are presented in the behavior section." Libr J
    This encyclopedia "is a treat to browse, with its high-quality photographs, drawings and graphics, and its lively informational style. . . . The format, quality and depth of information . . . will make this set popular and useful in any school or public library." Am Ref Books Annu, 1998

Grassy, John
    National Audubon Society first field guide: mammals; written by John Grassy and Chuck Keene. Scholastic 1998 159p il maps $17.95; pa $10.95   **599**
    1. Mammals
    ISBN 0-590-05471-6; 0-590-05489-9 (pa)
                                     LC 98-2939
    Explores the world of mammals, identifying their characteristics and describing individual species
    Includes glossary and bibliographical references

Hare, Tony
    Animal fact-file; head-to-tail profiles of more than 100 mammals. Facts on File 1999 191p il $35   **599**
    1. Mammals
    ISBN 0-8160-3921-6   LC 98-42092
    This is "an alphabetical guide to mammals from aardvarks to wombats. The full-color illustrations are excellent. Pictures show external and internal views of the animals as a whole and highlight distinctive body parts. Interesting comparison drawings abound. . . . And there is, for every entry, an easy reference chart giving the mammal's classification, size, coloration, and features. . . . The book provides a lot of easily accessed information in digestible bits." SLJ

Mammals. Time-Life Bks. 1997 127p il maps
    (Time-Life student library) $18.95   **599**
    1. Mammals
                                     LC 97-28565
    Describes the eating habits, defenses, parenting, and social behavior of mammals

National Geographic book of mammals; prepared by the Book Division, National Geographic Society. National Geographic Soc. 1998 607p il $34.95   **599**
    1. Mammals—Encyclopedias
    ISBN 0-7922-7141-6   LC 98-160028
    First published 1981 in two volumes
    Provides an illustrated introduction to the world's mammals, arranged alphabetically from aardvark to zorilla, describing their physical characteristics, habits, and natural environment
    This "would be a good starting place for research or for browsing." Book Rep
    Includes glossary

Parker, Steve
    Mammal; written by Steve Parker. Knopf 1989 63p il (Eyewitness books) $19; lib bdg $20.99
                                              599
    1. Mammals
    ISBN 0-394-82258-7; 0-394-92258-1 (lib bdg)
                                     LC 88-22656
    Photographs and text examine the world of mammals, depicting their development, feeding habits, courtship rituals, protective behavior, and physical adaptation to their various ways of life
    This book takes a "comprehensive yet detailed look at members of the class that includes humans. Filled with color photographs keyed to the text, the book provides ample illustrations of a variety of mammals and their unique traits." Sci Books Films

Sherrow, Victoria
    Endangered mammals of North America. 21st Cent. Bks. (NY) 1995 96p il maps (Scientific American sourcebooks) lib bdg $22.40; pa $8.95
                                              599
    1. Endangered species 2. Mammals 3. Wildlife conservation
    ISBN 0-8050-3253-3 (lib bdg); 0-8050-3252-5 (pa)
                                     LC 95-940
    "Sherrow presents a clear and reasoned look at Caribbean manatees, bowhead whales, Mount Graham squirrels, long-nosed bats, gray and red wolves, black-footed ferrets and black-tailed prairie dogs, and Florida panthers. She discusses the animals' physical features, behavior, the history of their decline in numbers, and efforts being made on their behalf." SLJ
    Includes bibliographical references

Whitaker, John O., Jr.
    National Audubon Society field guide to North American mammals. rev ed. Knopf 1996 937p il maps flexible bdg $19   **599**
    1. Mammals
    ISBN 0-679-44631-1   LC 95-81456
    "A Chanticleer Press edition. The Audubon Society field guide series"
    First published 1980
    This field guide describes 390 species of mammals of North America and includes keys for identification, range maps, information on tracks and anatomy, and 375 color photos

599.3   Miscellaneous orders of placental mammals

Alderton, David
Rodents of the world; photographs by Bruce Tanner. Facts on File 1996 192p il maps $29.95 (7 and up)   **599.3**
1. Rodents
ISBN 0-8160-3229-7   LC 96-15285
"This volume describes the biology of this populous species, their feeding habits, their senses, their defenses against predators, and their breeding cycles."
Includes bibliographical references

Patent, Dorothy Hinshaw
Prairie dogs; photographs by William Muñoz. Clarion Bks. 1993 63p il lib bdg $15.95   **599.3**
1. Prairie dogs 2. Prairie ecology
ISBN 0-395-56572-3   LC 92-34724
Discusses the habits and life cycle of prairie dogs and examines their place in the ecology of their grassland environment
"The text and illustrations work together, each enlarging the other and both enlightening the reader. Appearing on nearly every page, the full-color photographs take readers out to the prairie to see its plants and animals clearly." Booklist
Includes bibliographical references

599.4   Bats

Perry, Phyllis J., 1933-
Bats; the amazing upside-downers. Watts 1998 63p il lib bdg $22; pa $6.95   **599.4**
1. Bats
ISBN 0-531-20342-5 (lib bdg); 0-531-15903-5 (pa)
                                              LC 97-4048
"A First book"
Discusses the evolution, physiology, conservation, habits, and habitats of the only mammals that fly
"Illustrating the text are many full-color photographs, including some excellent stop-motion shots of bats in flight. . . . Well-organized and clearly written, this offers plenty of intriguing information as well as useful facts for school reports." Booklist
Includes glossary and bibliographical references

599.5   Cetaceans and sea cows

Carwardine, Mark
Whales, dolphins, and porpoises; illustrated by Martin Camm; editorial consultants: Peter Evans, Mason Weinrich. Dorling Kindersley 1995 256p il maps (Eyewitness handbooks) $29.95; flexible bdg $18.95 (7 and up)   **599.5**
1. Whales 2. Dolphins 3. Porpoises
ISBN 1-56458-621-9; 1-56458-620-0 (flexible bdg)
                                              LC 94-33301

This book is "arranged by species. Each entry has a drawing of the animal; drawings of body parts, such as teeth and fins; and a map showing the distribution of the species. Information is given on status, population size, threats to survival, birth and adult weight, and diet. The introduction discusses cetacean behavior and where and how to observe the animals. An identification key helps in distinguishing among various species." Booklist
"A book with efficient organization, concise information, and loads of illustrations." SLJ
Includes bibliographical references

Cerullo, Mary M.
Dolphins; what they can teach us; text by Mary M. Cerullo; photographs by Jeffrey L. Rotman. Dutton Children's Bks. 1998 42p il $16.99 **599.5**
1. Dolphins
ISBN 0-525-65263-9   LC 97-34424
Focuses on the behavior of these large sea animals, their interactions with humans, and ways in which dolphins and people can benefit each other
"Eye-catching full-color photos, many of dolphins and humans together do much to add to the book's appeal. . . . This title is a good supplemental source. It has lots of appeal for casual readers and fans of this popular animal." SLJ
Includes glossary and bibliographical references

Price-Groff, Claire
The manatee. Lucent Bks. 1999 112p il (Endangered animals & habitats) lib bdg $23.70 (7 and up)   **599.5**
1. Manatees 2. Endangered species
ISBN 1-56006-445-5   LC 98-53230
Discusses the physical characteristics, behavior, habitats, and endangered status of the manatee and the closely related dugong
Includes glossary and bibliographical references

Woog, Adam, 1953-
The whale. Lucent Bks. 1998 112p il (Endangered animals & habitats) lib bdg $23.70 (7 and up)   **599.5**
1. Whales 2. Endangered species
ISBN 1-56006-460-9   LC 97-21349
Presents an overview of various species of whale, how they have become endangered, and what is being done to protect them from extinction
This book is "packed with facts and statistics [and] . . . well-researched. . . . Illustrated with dark black-and-white photos, editorial cartoons, diagrams, maps, and reproductions." Horn Book Guide
Includes glossary and bibliographical references

599.64   Bovids

Lindblad, Lisa
The Serengeti migration; photographs by Sven-Olof Lindblad. Hyperion Bks. for Children 1994 40p il maps $15.95; lib bdg $16.49 **599.64**
1. Gnus 2. Zebras 3. Serengeti National Park (Tanzania)
ISBN 1-56282-668-9; 1-56282-669-7 (lib bdg)
                                              LC 93-26338

Lindblad, Lisa—*Continued*

"As the seasons change and food supplies dwindle, vast herds of wildebeests and zebras cross seven hundred miles of the Serengeti National Park to find food. Their journey, along with many other animals, across the varied and changing landscape is beautifully illustrated with dramatic color photographs. The narrative and photographs evoke the drama of the age-old migration." Horn Book Guide

Includes glossary

Patent, Dorothy Hinshaw

Deer and elk; photographs by William Muñoz. Clarion Bks. 1994 77p il maps $15.95   **599.64**

1. Deer 2. Elk

ISBN 0-395-52003-7   LC 93-25894

"The text describes in detail the lives, enemies, and survival of North American whitetail deer, mule deer, and elk, among others." Horn Book Guide

"Numerous full-color photographs enhance the presentation; each includes a caption. A great addition to the animal science section of any library." SLJ

Includes bibliographical references

599.66   Odd-toed ungulates

Hull, Mary

The rhinoceros. Lucent Bks. 1998 96p il maps (Endangered animals & habitats) lib bdg $23.70 (7 and up)   **599.66**

1. Rhinoceros 2. Endangered species

ISBN 1-56006-461-7   LC 97-46766

Presents an overview of various species of rhinoceroses, how they have become endangered, and what is being done to protect them from extinction

Includes glossary and bibliographical references

Ryden, Hope

Wild horses I have known. Clarion Bks. 1999 90p il $18   **599.66**

1. Horses

ISBN 0-395-77520-5   LC 97-49021

Text and photographs depict mustang social behavior observed by the author, as well as an account of how the mustang established itself and adapted to being a wild horse in the American West

"A carefully crafted book that features abundant use of strikingly beautiful photographs. . . . A nice combination of elegance and sound information." Horn Book

Silverstein, Alvin

The mustang; by Alvin and Virginia Silverstein and Laura Silverstein Nunn. Millbrook Press 1997 64p il (Endangered in America) $22.40   **599.66**

1. Horses 2. Wildlife conservation

ISBN 0-7613-0048-1   LC 96-42682

Describes the habits and habitats of wild mustangs and the efforts being made to save these horses from extinction

This is a "solid, accurate book illustrated with color photographs." Horn Book Guide

Includes bibliographical references

599.67   Elephants

Caras, Roger A.

A most dangerous journey; the life of an African elephant; with photographs by the author. Dial Bks. 1995 189p il $15.99; pa $4.99 (7 and up)   **599.67**

1. Elephants

ISBN 0-8037-1880-2; 0-14-038227-5 (pa)

LC 95-2548

The author "follows the elephant Ndovu, a composite based on Caras' own observations and the research of others, from birth to adulthood—depicting a life filled with natural disasters and deadly encounters with human beings. An ardent conservationist, Caras harshly criticizes poachers and condemns corrupt officials and military officers who profit from ivory." Booklist

"This is a touching and rewarding work that can be read not only for information but also as a great story." SLJ

Levine, Stuart P., 1968-

The elephant. Lucent Bks. 1998 96p il maps (Endangered animals & habitats) lib bdg $23.70 (7 and up)   **599.67**

1. Elephants 2. Endangered species

ISBN 1-56006-522-2   LC 97-28532

Presents an overview of elephants, how they have become endangered, and what is being done to protect them from extinction

Includes glossary and bibliographical references

Pringle, Laurence P.

Elephant woman; Cynthia Moss explores the world of elephants; [by] Laurence Pringle; photographs by Cynthia Moss. Atheneum Bks. for Young Readers 1997 42p il $16   **599.67**

1. Moss, Cynthia 2. Elephants 3. Amboseli National Park (Kenya)

ISBN 0-689-80142-4   LC 96-40241

Pringle recounts the work of Cynthia Moss, world-renowned elephant researcher, in Kenya's Amboseli National Park

"Excellent photos, most in color, appear on nearly every page, providing an intriguing look at the elephants' world as they illustrate the well-written text." Booklist

Includes bibliographical references

Redmond, Ian

Elephant; photographed by Dave King. Knopf 1993 63p il (Eyewitness books) $19; lib bdg $20.99   **599.67**

1. Elephants

ISBN 0-679-83880-5; 0-679-93880-X (lib bdg)

LC 92-20855

"A Dorling Kindersley book"

Text and numerous illustrations portray elephants, their physiology, behavior, evolution, relatives, uses by humans, and conservation

"The photography is excellent with pictures that are exciting to the eye. The information, while not definitive, is interesting." Appraisal

Smith, Roland, 1951-
In the forest with the elephants; [by] Roland Smith and Michael J. Schmidt. Harcourt Brace & Co. 1998 unp il $18; pa $9   **599.67**
1. Elephants 2. Myanmar 3. Lumber and lumbering
ISBN 0-15-201289-3; 0-15-201290-7 (pa)
LC 97-6638
"A Gulliver Green book"
Describes how elephants are trained to help in the timber camps of Myanmar, formerly known as Burma, and their important contribution to the selective and sustainable harvesting of teak there
"An informative and rich cultural experience." SLJ

599.7   Carnivores. Land carnivores

North, Sterling, 1906-1974
Rascal; illustrated by John Schoenherr. Dutton 1984 c1963 189p il $14.99   **599.7**
1. Raccoons
ISBN 0-525-18839-8   LC 84-10292
Also available in paperback from Puffin Bks.
A Newbery Award honor book, 1964
First published 1963 with subtitle: A memoir of a better era
A book about Rascal "a young raccoon, Sterling North's pet the year he was eleven, in rural Wisconsin. . . . The book calls up a series of marvelous pictures; boy fishing in peaceful company of raccoon, boy riding on bike with raccoon (a demon for speed) standing up in the bike basket, raccoon with friend, a prize trotting horse, raccoon helping boy to win a pie-eating contest. A central episode is about an idyllic camping trip." Publ Wkly

Silverstein, Alvin
The sea otter; [by] Alvin, Virginia, and Robert Silverstein. Millbrook Press 1995 64p il maps (Endangered in America) lib bdg $22.40; pa $6.95
599.7
1. Otters 2. Endangered species
ISBN 1-56294-418-5 (lib bdg); 0-7613-0165-8 (pa)
LC 94-17998
"The sea otter's behavior is described, including swimming, hunting, feeding, reproducing, and growing. Its main physical features are detailed, including those especially important to its lifestyle. . . . With color photographs, reading and organizations lists, a factual summary, and an index, this book is very suitable for use as a reference, in classrooms, and for general awareness." Sci Books Films
Includes bibliographical references

599.75   Cat family

Adamson, Joy, 1910-1980
Born free: a lioness of two worlds. Pantheon Bks. 1987 c1960 220p il hardcover o.p. paperback available $15   **599.75**
1. Lions 2. Kenya—Description
ISBN 0-394-74635-X (pa)   LC 86-42972

A reissue of the title first published 1960
The "story of a lioness who bridged the gulf between two worlds, that of the jungle and of man. The author and her husband, a Kenya game warden, reared a cub to kill and fend for herself when she was returned to the jungle. At the same time they were able to preserve the bond of confidence and affection established with her as a pet." Cincinnati Public Libr

Alderton, David
Wild cats of the world; photographs by Bruce Tanner. Facts on File 1993 192p il maps $29.95 (7 and up)   **599.75**
1. Wild cats
ISBN 0-8160-2736-6   LC 92-38774
"A broad, comprehensive overview of the world's wild felines. The first half of the book covers the animals' anatomy, way of life, and interaction with humans. The second half is a species-by-species look at the specific cats. A map and a description indicates where they can be found. The author's ecological concerns are evident throughout. The full-color photographs are detailed and intriguing and amount to perhaps a third of the book." SLJ
Includes bibliographical references

Clutton-Brock, Juliet
Cat; written by Juliet Clutton-Brock. Knopf 1991 63p il (Eyewitness books) $19; lib bdg $20.99   **599.75**
1. Wild cats 2. Cats
ISBN 0-679-81458-2; 0-679-91458-7 (lib bdg)
LC 91-9399
Text and photographs present the anatomy, behavior, habitats, and other aspects of wild and domestic cats
"The information is generally well written and well presented. . . . This is a browser's delight that will also appeal to the serious reader seeking facts about cats." Sci Books Films

Levine, Stuart P., 1968-
The tiger. Lucent Bks. 1999 96p il (Endangered animals & habitats) lib bdg $23.70 (7 and up)
599.75
1. Tigers 2. Endangered species
ISBN 1-56006-465-X   LC 98-27237
Discusses the various species of tigers and their behavior and examines how they have become endangered through habitat loss, hunting, research, and captivity
Includes glossary and bibliographical references

MacMillan, Dianne M., 1943-
Cheetahs; photographs by Gerry Ellis. Carolrhoda Bks. 1997 48p il (Carolrhoda nature watch book) lib bdg $19.93; pa $7.95   **599.75**
1. Cheetahs
ISBN 1-575-05044-7 (lib bdg); 1-575-05225-3 (pa)
LC 96-28554
Describes the physical characteristics, life cycle, behavior, and conservation of cheetahs
This is an "informative and attractively illustrated book. . . . Includes many clear full-color photographs of cheetahs in the wild." Booklist
Includes glossary

Saign, Geoffrey, 1955-
The African cats. Watts 1999 64p il lib bdg $22
599.75
1. Wild cats 2. Animals—Africa
ISBN 0-531-20365-4   LC 97-41629
"A First book"
Describes the physical characteristics and behavior
patterns of ten types of cats found in Africa
"This combines dramatic wildlife color photographs
with a lively, informative text." Booklist
Includes glossary and bibliographical references

Thompson, Sharon Elaine, 1952-
Built for speed; the extraordinary, enigmatic
cheetah. Lerner Publs. 1998 88p il lib bdg $23.93
599.75
1. Cheetahs
ISBN 0-8225-2854-1   LC 96-51094
Describes the habitat, physical characteristics, and behavior of the cheetah, as well as efforts to ensure the
continued existence of this fastest land mammal
This "includes and explains many fascinating details
of the animals' lives in a comprehensive, well-organized,
and attractive way." Sci Books Films
Includes glossary and bibliographical references

599.77 Dog family

Mitchell, Hayley R., 1968-
The wolf. Lucent Bks. 1998 96p il (Endangered
animals & habitats) lib bdg $23.70 (7 and up)
599.77
1. Wolves 2. Endangered species
ISBN 1-56006-252-5   LC 97-51586
Discusses the habits, habitat, and endangered status of
the wolf, as well as its place in human society
Includes glossary and bibliographical references

Smith, Roland, 1951-
Journey of the red wolf; photographs by the
author. Cobblehill Bks. 1996 60p il $16.99
599.77
1. Wolves 2. Wildlife conservation
ISBN 0-525-65162-4   LC 95-10641
In 1971, when red wolves were near extinction, seventeen of the wolves "were taken into captivity and became
a part of the Red Wolf Captive Breeding Facility. *Journey of the Red Wolf* is the story of how this facility grew
from 17 to almost 300 red wolves. . . . This is a well-
written book, with many good color photographs illustrative of both the red wolf and the work of the captive
breeding program." Sci Books Films

599.78 Bears

Barghusen, Laura, 1964-
The bear. Lucent Bks. 1999 96p il (Endangered
animals & habitats) lib bdg $23.70 (7 and up)
599.78
1. Bears 2. Endangered species
ISBN 1-56006-394-7   LC 98-50214

Discusses the bears of the world and threats to their
existence, such as hunting and international trade, habitat
destruction, and captivity, as well as the future of bears
Includes glossary and bibliographical references

Ovsyanikov, Nikita
Polar bears. Voyageur Press 1998 72p il maps
(World life library) pa $16.95 (7 and up) **599.78**
1. Polar bear
ISBN 0-89658-358-9   LC 98-3431
This describes the polar bear's habits, behavior, and
biology
"Approachable. . . . Written by an expert on the spe-
cies. . . . Well illustrated with many excellent photos."
Booklist
Includes bibliographical references

Patent, Dorothy Hinshaw
The way of the grizzly; photographs by William
Muñoz. Clarion Bks. 1987 65p il hardcover o.p.
paperback available $5.95   **599.78**
1. Grizzly bear
ISBN 0-395-58112-5 (pa)   LC 86-17562
Describes, in text and illustrations, the physical characteristics, habits, and natural environment of the grizzly
bear and discusses the threats that humans pose to their
survival
"Clear black-and-white photos appear on almost every
page and show grizzlies in their daily life and being examined by environmentalists. This will certainly be useful to report writers." SLJ

Presnall, Judith Janda
The giant panda. Lucent Bks. 1998 96p il maps
(Endangered animals & habitats) lib bdg $23.70 (7
and up)   **599.78**
1. Giant panda 2. Endangered species
ISBN 1-56006-463-3   LC 97-27276
Discusses the forces pushing the giant panda toward
extinction and the efforts being made to counter those
forces
This book is "packed with facts and statistics [and]
. . . well-researched." Horn Book Guide
Includes glossary and bibliographical references

Silverstein, Alvin
The grizzly bear; [by] Alvin and Virginia
Silverstein and Laura Silverstein Nunn. Millbrook
Press 1998 64p il (Endangered in America) lib bdg
$22.40   **599.78**
1. Grizzly bear 2. Endangered species
ISBN 0-7613-0265-4   LC 97-45026
Describes the physical characteristics and behavior of
the grizzly bear, its decline in numbers due to human
population growth and activities, and the efforts being
made to maintain its population
"Large color photographs and a highly readable text
characterize this presentation of the once-feared
American ursine." Horn Book Guide
Includes bibliographical references

Stonehouse, Bernard
Bears; a visual introduction; illustrated by
Martin Camm. Checkmark Bks. 1998 46p il maps
(Animal watch) $16.95   **599.78**
  1. Bears
  ISBN 0-8160-3923-2   LC 98-25083
This describes 10 types of bears throughout the world,
as well as pandas and prehistoric cave bears, with color
illustrations, facts about classification, size, and range,
environment, and behavior, endangered species and con-
servation efforts
  Includes glossary

Ward, Paul, 1959-
Wild bears of the world; [by] Paul Ward and
Suzanne Kynaston. Facts on File 1995 191p il
maps $25.95 (7 and up)   **599.78**
  1. Bears
  ISBN 0-8160-3245-9   LC 95-12487
This book "starts by explaining how and why bears
have meant so much from early in our evolutionary history. . . . It then describes the bears' position and
uniqueness among carnivores, introduces the living species, charts their evolutionary history, tells how they live,
what they eat, how they cope with their habitats, and
looks at their behavior. It concludes with a re-
examination of the interrelationship they have with us."
Publisher's note
  Includes glossary and bibliographical references

599.79   Marine carnivores

DuTemple, Lesley A., 1952-
Seals and sea lions. Lucent Bks. 1999 112p il
maps (Endangered animals & habitats) lib bdg
$23.70 (7 and up)   **599.79**
  1. Seals (Animals) 2. Endangered species
  ISBN 1-56006-473-0   LC 98-30303
Describes the physical characteristics and behavior of
seals and sea lions, how they differ from each other, how
they relate to humans, how they have become endangered, and what is being done to protect them
  Includes glossary and bibliographical references

Patent, Dorothy Hinshaw
Seals, sea lions, and walruses. Holiday House
1990 88p il lib bdg $14.95   **599.79**
  1. Seals (Animals) 2. Walruses
  ISBN 0-8234-0834-5   LC 90-55101
"A competent, well-organized look at the lives of
three mammals called pinnipeds because of their unique,
finlike feet. Clear photographs enrich informative, accurate text. Includes a list of scientific names." Sci Child
  Includes glossary

599.8   Primates

Ake, Anne, 1943-
The gorilla. Lucent Bks. 1999 112p il
(Endangered animals & habitats) lib bdg $23.70 (7
and up)   **599.8**
  1. Gorillas 2. Endangered species
  ISBN 1-56006-492-7   LC 98-53231

Discusses the physical characteristics, behavior, habitats, and endangered status of the gorilla
  Includes glossary and bibliographical references

Goodall, Jane, 1934-
With love; illustrated by Alan Marks.
North-South Bks. 1998 c1994 unp il $15.95; lib
bdg $15.88   **599.8**
  1. Chimpanzees
  ISBN 1-55858-911-2; 1-55858-912-0 (lib bdg)
                                     LC 97-49948
First published 1994 by the Jane Goodall Institute
A collection of stories based on the author's experiences with chimpanzees in Gombe Stream National Park
in Tanzania over a period of almost forty years
  "Children will love these stories because they are
sometimes silly or gross and because they are always
tender, and young humans will recognize aspects of
themselves in the younger chimps. . . . Marks' watercol-
or-and-ink paintings capture both action and stasis beautifully and without affectation or sentimentality." Booklist

Redmond, Ian
Gorilla; written by Ian Redmond; photographed
by Peter Anderson & Geoff Brightling. Knopf
1995 63p il maps (Eyewitness books) $19; lib bdg
$20.99   **599.8**
  1. Primates
  ISBN 0-679-87332-5; 0-679-97332-X (lib bdg)
                                     LC 95-3241
"A Dorling Kindersley book"
An illustrated look at primates, including lemurs, monkeys, and apes
  This offers "the same fabulous layout, interesting photographs, and fascinating facts that have made the series
so popular. . . . Fun to browse through." SLJ

Saign, Geoffrey, 1955-
The great apes; [by] Geoffrey C. Saign. Watts
1998 63p il lib bdg $22   **599.8**
  1. Apes
  ISBN 0-531-20361-1   LC 97-1189
"A First book"
Describes and compares the four great apes: chimpanzees, bonobos, orangutans, and gorillas through a discussion of their physical, intellectual, emotional, and social
characteristics
  This is an "appealing, involving introduction. . . . The
many color photographs are well chosen for their clarity
and sensitivity as well as for their clear illustration of the
text." Booklist
  Includes glossary and bibliographical references

599.93   Genetics, sex and age
characteristics, evolution

Gallant, Roy A.
Early humans. Benchmark Bks. (Tarrytown)
1999 c2000 80p il maps (Story of science) lib bdg
$19.95   **599.93**
  1. Fossil hominids 2. Human origins 3. Evolution
  ISBN 0-7614-0960-2   LC 98-28037

Gallant, Roy A.—*Continued*

Discusses human evolution and the search for the earliest forms of humans, examining the Neanderthals, Homo erectus, the variety of fossils found in Africa, and the early apelike hominids

"Richly illustrated with color photos, drawings, and charts. . . . Gallant writes clearly and provides readers with balanced, informative discussions." Booklist

Includes glossary and bibliographical references

Gardner, Robert, 1929-

Human evolution. Watts 1999 144p il $24 (7 and up)   **599.93**

1. Human origins 2. Evolution
ISBN 0-531-11528-3   LC 98-20859

"Historical charts show what is known of hominid lineage, geologic periods, and human cultural development. Early chapters describe eight different methods used to date fossils, Darwin's and Lamarck's evolution theories, genetic structures, functions and mutations, and how fossil bones are judged to be ape or hominid. Descriptions of significant hominid fossil finds, who made them, and where and when they were found lead to questions concerning the age of humans." SLJ

The "author makes the subject fascinating. . . . A wonderful text for the classroom, but the curious general reader will learn plenty by thumbing through its pages." Voice Youth Advocates

Includes glossary and bibliographical references

600 TECHNOLOGY (APPLIED SCIENCES)

Graham, Ian, 1953-

How things work. Time-Life Bks. 1996 64p il (Discoveries library) $16   **600**

1. Technology
LC 95-32819

Text and drawings explain the workings of certain everyday items including bicycles, traffic lights, computers, fax machines, and microwave ovens

Macaulay, David, 1946-

The new way things work; by David Macaulay with Neil Ardley. Houghton Mifflin 1998 400p il $35   **600**

1. Technology 2. Machinery 3. Inventions
ISBN 0-395-93847-3   LC 98-14224

First published 1988 with title: The way things work

Arranged in five sections this volume provides information on "the workings of hundreds of machines and devices—holograms, helicopters, airplanes, mobile phones, compact disks, hard disks, bits and bytes, cash machines. . . . Explanations [are also given] of the scientific principles behind each machine—how gears make work easier, why jumbo jets are able to fly, how computers actually compute." Publisher's note

Tambini, Michael

Future; written by Michael Tambini. Knopf 1998 59p il (Eyewitness books) $19; lib bdg $20.99   **600**

1. Technology 2. Forecasting
ISBN 0-679-89317-2; 0-679-99317-7 (lib bdg)
LC 98-16440

"A Dorling Kindersley book"

Provides a speculative look ahead to the technological, environmental, and biological developments of the twenty-first century

603 Technology—Encyclopedias and dictionaries

Engelbert, Phillis

Technology in action; science applied to everyday life; edited by Jane Hoehner. U.X.L 1999 3v set $79.95   **603**

1. Technology—Encyclopedias
ISBN 0-7876-2809-3   LC 98-15377

Contents: v1. Communications, electronics & computers; v2. Energy, food & agriculture, health & medicine; v3. Civil engineering, manufacturing & materials, transportation

Contains information on approximately 120 technological terms such as computers, fiberoptics, and biochemistry. Includes sidebars and inserts of famous firsts, trivia items, and unusual facts

"Technology is explained in terms that any middle- or junior-high-school student will understand and most adults will appreciate. An excellent resource." Booklist

608 Inventions and patents

Brown, Travis, 1926-

Historical first patents; the first United States patent for many everyday things. Scarecrow Press 1994 216p il $41.50 (7 and up)   **608**

1. Patents—History 2. Inventions—History
ISBN 0-8108-2898-7   LC 94-14814

This "is an overview of over 80 granted U.S. patent applications, with emphasis on the familiar: Howe, Whitney, Bell, and others whose names are closely associated with a specific device. Each entry consists of the historical developments leading to the invention, a biographical description of the inventor, and the story of the creation of the invention itself. A patent drawing accompanies most entries." Libr J

Includes bibliographical references

Erlbach, Arlene

The kids' invention book. Lerner Publs. 1997 64p il $22.60; pa $9.95   **608**

1. Inventions
ISBN 0-8225-2414-7; 0-8225-9844-2 (pa)
LC 96-27105

Profiles eleven inventors between the ages of eight and fourteen, describes the steps involved in inventing a new product, and discusses contests, patents, lawyers,

Erlbach, Arlene—Continued
and clubs
"Readers will enjoy the stories behind such clever creations as an edible pet-food spoon, an adjustable jump-rope belt, and a portable wheelchair ramp; and the accounts serve as wonderful encouragement for kids who want to pursue ideas of their own." Booklist
Includes bibliographical references

Karnes, Frances A.
Girls & young women inventing; twenty true stories about inventors plus how you can be one yourself; [by] Frances A. Karnes and Suzanne M. Bean; edited by Rosemary Wallner. Free Spirit 1995 168p il pa $12.95   **608**
1. Women inventors 2. Inventions
ISBN 0-915793-89-X   LC 95-16300
"Part one relates in first-person narrative the development of inventions in such diverse areas as conservation, safety, convenience, and fun. . . . Part two focuses on how to be an inventor with practical advice on getting started, developing sketches, and patenting and marketing ideas. The final part contains resource information about organizations and associations, a bibliography, inspiring quotes, and a chronological listing of female inventors. Illustrated with photos and diagrams, this book will be useful for any would-be inventor." Voice Youth Advocates

609   Technology—Historical and geographic treatment

Bender, Lionel
Invention; written by Lionel Bender. Knopf 1991 63p il (Eyewitness books) $19   **609**
1. Inventions
ISBN 0-679-80782-9   LC 90-4888
Photographs and text explore such inventions as the wheel, gears, levers, clocks, telephones, and rocket engines
"The photographs are . . . stunning, the information served up in tiny but fascinating bites." BAYA Book Rev

Crosher, Judith
Technology in the time of ancient Egypt. Raintree Steck-Vaughn Pubs. 1998 48p il $25.69   **609**
1. Technology—History 2. Egypt—Civilization
ISBN 0-8172-4875-7   LC 97-13922
Describes many of the innovative inventions that the Egyptians incorporated into their daily life, including ground looms, glass pots, and wooden sledges
Includes bibliographical references

Technology in the time of ancient Greece. Raintree Steck-Vaughn Pubs. 1998 48p il $25.69   **609**
1. Technology—History 2. Greece—Civilization
ISBN 0-8172-4877-3   LC 97-19067

Describes many of the innovative discoveries that the ancient Greeks incorporated into their daily lives, including the tools and technology they used to produce their clothes, food, pottery, statues, and temples
Includes bibliographical references

Technology in the time of the Maya. Raintree Steck-Vaughn Pubs. 1998 48p il $25.69   **609**
1. Technology—History 2. Mayas
ISBN 0-8172-4881-1   LC 97-24119
Explores innovative tools and methods used by the Maya in the areas of food production, building, metalwork, and transportation, among others. Illustrations include photographs of artifacts and line drawings
Includes bibliographical references

Haskins, James, 1941-
Outward dreams; black inventors and their inventions. Walker & Co. 1991 101p il $13.95; lib bdg $14.85   **609**
1. African American inventors 2. Inventions—History
ISBN 0-8027-6993-4; 0-8027-6994-2 (lib bdg)
    LC 90-12973
Also available in paperback from Bantam Bks.
"Haskins describes some of the uncredited inventions of blacks and concisely examines the lives and contributions of inventors whose names have been recorded. . . . He also devotes a chapter exclusively to women inventors. . . . An inspiring work, this will enhance science, black history, and women's studies courses." Booklist
Includes bibliographical references

Hicks, Peter, 1952-
Technology in the time of the Vikings. Raintree Steck-Vaughn Pubs. 1998 48p il $25.69   **609**
1. Technology—History 2. Vikings
ISBN 0-8172-4880-3   LC 97-28053
Examines many of the technological innovations that the Vikings incorporated into their daily lives in such areas as weapons and armor, transportation, and jewelery-making
Includes bibliographical references

Historical inventions on file; [by] the Diagram Group. Facts on File 1994 various paging il loose-leaf $165   **609**
1. Inventions—History
ISBN 0-8160-2911-3   LC 94-7098
This work contains "65 experiments re-creating famous inventions. The purpose of these re-creations is to assist students in understanding important concepts and innovations in science. Intended for grades 6-12, the work is multidisciplinary in approach, making use of history, science, mathematics, and abstract and applied thinking. . . . This will be a useful source for middle- and high-school students and teachers doing science projects and experiments." Booklist

James, Portia P.
The real McCoy; African-American invention and innovation, 1619-1930. Smithsonian Institution Press 1990 c1989 110p il o.p. (7 and up)   **609**
1. African American inventors 2. Inventions—History
    LC 89-21837

James, Portia P.—*Continued*

"Published for the Anacostia Museum of the Smithsonian Institution"

Spine title: African-American invention and innovation, 1619-1930

This book explores "the contributions of creative African-American inventors to the technological culture of the United States." SLJ

"This book is a valuable contribution to the story of intellectual contributions to US technology." Choice

Includes bibliographical references

Platt, Richard, 1953-

Inventions explained; a beginner's guide to technological breakthroughs. Holt & Co. 1997 69p il (Your world explained series) $18.95   **609**

1. Inventions—History

ISBN 0-8050-4876-6   LC 97-11969

This "is a history of technology, from the tools and weapons of the earliest humans to the Apple computer and the space shuttle. There is also a detailed three-page time line of inventions by date." Booklist

This title offers "concise, accurate facts." SLJ

Includes glossary

Smithsonian visual timeline of inventions; foreword by Steven Lubar. Dorling Kindersley 1994 64p il $16.95   **609**

1. Inventions—History

ISBN 1-56458-675-8   LC 94-21429

"The timeline begins at 600,000 B.C. with the use of fire and ends with predictions of future trends and inventions, such as zero-emission vehicles. Each page of the timeline is divided into four main sections: Counting and Communication, Daily Life and Health, Agriculture and Industry, and Travel and Conquest." Voice Youth Advocates

This book is "not only a visual treat and browser's delight, but also has reference value." Book Rep

Sandler, Martin W.

Inventors; a Library of Congress book; introduction by James H. Billington. HarperCollins Pubs. 1996 93p il $21.95; pa $10.95   **609**

1. Inventions—History 2. Inventors

ISBN 0-06-024923-4; 0-06-446746-5 (pa)

LC 95-944

"Composed mainly of historical photographs, reproductions, and period writing culled from the Library of Congress archives, the volume presents an intriguing montage of the inventors, technology, and ingenuity that flourished around the turn of the twentieth century. The brief present tense narrative is informative; the illustrative material is hugely appealing." Horn Book

Snedden, Robert

Technology in the time of ancient Rome. Raintree Steck-Vaughn Pubs. 1998 48p il $25.69   **609**

1. Technology—History 2. Rome—Civilization

ISBN 0-8172-4876-5   LC 97-13924

Describes many of the innovative inventions that the Romans incorporated into their daily lives, including aqueducts, hot baths, and central heating

Includes bibliographical references

Tucker, Tom, 1944-

Brainstorm! the stories of twenty American kid inventors; with drawings by Richard Loehle. Farrar, Straus & Giroux 1995 148p il $15; pa $6.95   **609**

1. Inventors 2. Inventions

ISBN 0-374-30944-2; 0-374-40928-5 (pa)

LC 94-38780

The author looks at inventions devised by children since the 18th century. Ear muffs, water skis, the popsicle, colored car wax and the electronic television are among the products discussed. Includes a discussion of how the Patent Office works

Includes glossary and bibliographical references

Wood, Richard, 1949-

Great inventions. Time-Life Bks. 1995 64p il (Discoveries library) $16   **609**

1. Inventions

LC 95-12947

Describes the invention of common items such as thimbles, sugar cubes, paper handkerchiefs, ice cream cones as well as inventions in transportation, communication, medicine, and other fields

"This book is a delightful read and would be very interesting to young readers." Sci Books Films

Includes glossary

Wulffson, Don L., 1943-

The kid who invented the popsicle and other surprising stories about inventions. Cobblehill Bks. 1997 114p $13.99   **609**

1. Inventions—History

ISBN 0-525-65221-3   LC 96-31148

"Beginning with animal crackers and ending with the zipper, this book alphabetically lists a number of 'inventions' and briefly describes how they came into being. Among the items noted are blue jeans, doughnuts, matches, miniature golf, and Scrabble." Booklist

This book is "very entertaining. . . . It would be a useful starting point for class projects." Sci Books Films

610   Medical sciences. Medicine

Parker, Steve

Medicine; written by Steve Parker. Dorling Kindersley 1995 64p il (Eyewitness science) $15.95   **610**

1. Medicine

ISBN 1-56458-882-3   LC 94-34860

This book "travels from ancient times to the future, addressing alternative treatments, modern drugs, fads in health care, diagnostic techniques, etc. What really stands out are the numerous examples of tools of the trade, like the 18th-century brass enema syringe and the 20th-century electronic hand." SLJ

"Many readers will enjoy just browsing through the volume, looking at the numerous excellent illustrations and reading the text more closely if they are interested. The author makes a concerted effort to avoid controversial questions." Sci Books Films

610.69   Medical personnel

Storring, Rod
A doctor's life; a visual history of doctors and nurses through the ages. Dutton Children's Bks. 1998 48p il $17.99   **610.69**
1. Medical personnel 2. Medicine—History
ISBN 0-525-67577-9
This "book uses profiles of real doctors and nurses to describe the development of medicine from the ancient Romans to the present. Each two-page spread introduces a practitioner, tells about his or her practice, and discusses the prevailing beliefs and treatments of the time." SLJ
Includes glossary

610.9   Medical sciences—Historical and geographic treatment

Gates, Phil
Medicine. Candlewick Press 1997 32p il $15.99
                                                610.9
1. Medicine—History
ISBN 0-7636-0316-3   LC 97-14668
At head of title: The history news
Presents in newspaper format the stories of breakthroughs in medicine in many different cultures and lands from the year 8000 B.C. to the 1990s
This book offers "a fresh and lively presentation of information children ask for year after year. . . . Colorful illustrations in a variety of styles add to the child appeal." Booklist
Includes bibliographical references

Terkel, Susan Neiburg, 1948-
Colonial American medicine. Watts 1993 111p il (Colonial America) lib bdg $22   **610.9**
1. Medicine—History 2. United States—History—1600-1775, Colonial period
ISBN 0-531-12539-4   LC 92-43988
This illustrated survey "addresses the colonists' problems with illness and the risks of seeking help from medical practitioners. . . . In addition to a lively account of traditional medicine, Terkel contrasts the colonists' medical beliefs and practices with those of Native Americans and devotes chapters to the development of hospitals, illness among the troops in the Revolutionary War, and the widespread mistrust of smallpox inoculation in the colonies." Booklist
Includes glossary and bibliographical references

611   Human anatomy, cytology, histology

Biesty, Stephen
Stephen Biesty's incredible body; illustrated by Stephen Biesty; written by Richard Platt. DK Pub. 1998 32p il $19.95   **611**
1. Human anatomy
ISBN 0-7894-3424-5   LC 98-16806

Uses the perspective of tiny people traveling through a man's body to present its various systems and organs and how they work
"The pen-and-ink and color drawings are nothing short of amazing." SLJ

Ganeri, Anita, 1961-
Funny bones; illustrated by Steve Ficker and John Holder. Simon & Schuster Bks. for Young Readers 1997 29p il (How it works) $14   **611**
1. Human anatomy
ISBN 0-689-81187-X   LC 96-38844
Describes various parts of the human body—including skin and hair, lungs, bones, nerves, heart, and stomach—and the functions of each

Human body on file: anatomy; [by] The Diagram Group. Facts on File 1996 unp il $165   **611**
1. Human anatomy
ISBN 0-8160-3527-X
Companion volume to Human body on file: physiology
First published 1983 with title: The human body. Present edition incorporates the original material plus the images in the update volume (available separately $60 ISBN 0-8160-5528-8)
"The work consists of black-and-white line drawings of the various systems/parts of the human body. All are clearly labeled with numbers keyed to terms which appear below each drawing. . . . Purchasers may make copies of any part by any means for nonprofit educational or private use without obtaining any further permission or payment of fees. This is an excellent source for anyone studying or teaching anatomy at any basic level, particularly in K-12 and junior colleges." Booklist [review of 1983 edition]

Parker, Steve
The body atlas; illustrated by Giuliano Fornari. Dorling Kindersley 1993 63p il $19.95   **611**
1. Human anatomy
ISBN 1-56458-224-8   LC 92-54307
"The human body is mapped here in detail from head to toe, and in that order. Sections entitled 'Head and Neck,' 'Upper Torso,' 'Arm and Hand,' 'Lower Torso,' and 'Leg and Foot' neatly group a huge amount of information into meaningful, manageable units. Throughout, various organs are illustrated from both the outside and the inside. . . . In all sections, scientific photographs have been included to supplement Fornari's interesting medical illustrations." Booklist

Rowan, Peter
Some body! illustrations by John Temperton. Knopf 1995 44p il $20   **611**
1. Human anatomy
ISBN 0-679-87043-1   LC 94-20402
"Covering the brain; sense organs; circulatory and immune systems; and skeletal, muscular, digestive, urinary, and reproductive systems, the book serves as an introduction to the basic makeup of the human body." Sci Books Films

Rowan, Peter—*Continued*

"Temperton's meticulous, lifelike renderings range from elaborate cross-sections to detailed spot art, while complete or partial fold-outs on 10 pages afford a more realistic scale and show precisely what lies beneath specific body parts." Publ Wkly

The **Visual** dictionary of human anatomy. DK Pub. 1996 64p il (Eyewitness visual dictionaries) $18.95   **611**
1. Human anatomy
ISBN 0-7894-0445-1   LC 95-52789
"This guide details the physical structure of the human body, naming its parts and providing basic information on how the systems function. The first section describes the skeletal, muscular, nervous, endocrine, circulatory, lymphatic, respiratory, digestive, urinary, and reproductive systems. . . . The second part of the book describes the detailed structure of body areas. . . . This organization clarifies the interrelationship of systems in each area. . . . Overall, it is a clear, informative reference source that should get heavy use." SLJ

Williams, Frances

Human body; written by Frances Williams. DK Pub. 1997 44p il (Inside guides) $15.95   **611**
1. Human anatomy
ISBN 0-7894-1506-2   LC 96-44243
In this book of human anatomy "Williams covers the skeletal, nervous, circulatory, respiratory, excretory, and reproductive systems, as well as the sense organs." SLJ

"Carefully constructed, consistently oriented models of organ systems open in layers in precise, full-color photos. Small drawings and highly magnified photos of cells add information to the brief text and extensive captions." Horn Book Guide
Includes glossary

612 Human physiology

Beckelman, Laurie

The human body. Reader's Digest Children's Bks. 1999 64p il (Reader's Digest pathfinders) $16.99; lib bdg $18.99   **612**
1. Human anatomy
ISBN 1-57584-289-0; 1-57584-297-1 (lib bdg)
     LC 98-53122
Examines the structure and function of various parts of the human body, including skin, hair, muscles, and bones, and describes how the various parts of the brain sense our environment and coordinate our actions

Burnie, David

The concise encyclopedia of the human body. Dorling Kindersley 1995 160p il $19.95   **612**
1. Human anatomy 2. Physiology
ISBN 0-7894-0204-1   LC 95-15134
"Arranged thematically by major body systems, this volume succinctly explains and illustrates over 2000 basic terms and concepts in human biology and physiology. . . . A final chapter gives brief biographical information

on over 100 doctors and biologists, and some individuals are highlighted within relevant subject areas. Full-color drawings, diagrams, models, photographs, and electron micrographs are clearly labeled and add to the textual information." SLJ

Glover, David M.

The young Oxford book of the human being; [by] David Glover. Oxford Univ. Press 1997 160p il $25; lib bdg $27   **612**
1. Human beings
ISBN 0-19-521375-0; 0-19-521374-2 (lib bdg)
     LC 97-11922
Explores the way the human body works, the origins of human beings, and the various ways that humans live and organize themselves socially and culturally
"The author tackles all of this material in direct, uncomplicated sentences." SLJ
Includes glossary

Human body. Time-Life Bks. 1999 128p (Time-Life student library) $24.95 (7 and up)   **612**
1. Physiology 2. Human anatomy
ISBN 0-7835-1353-4   LC 98-53020
Examines the structure and function of various parts of the human body, including bones, muscles, heart, lungs, brain, nervous system, digestive system, immune system, and reproductive organs

Human body on file: physiology; [by] The Diagram Group. Facts on File 1996 unp il $165   **612**
1. Physiology 2. Human anatomy
ISBN 0-8160-3415-X   LC 95-42852
This companion volume to Human body on file: anatomy presents the physiological processes of the body and shows how the body's systems and components function when healthy or when experiencing problems

Parker, Steve

Human body. Dorling Kindersley 1993 64p il (Eyewitness science) $15.95; pa $9.95   **612**
1. Human anatomy 2. Physiology
ISBN 1-56458-325-2; 1-56458-322-8 (pa)
     LC 93-7752
This work "serves as an interesting overview of the fields of anatomy and physiology as well as a visual guide to the structure and physiology of the body. The full-color photographs of well-crafted museum models are outstanding." SLJ

The human body. Time-Life Bks. 1997 64p il (Discoveries library) $16   **612**
1. Human anatomy 2. Physiology
     LC 95-53787
This illustrates and describes the various systems of the human body using drawings, microphotography, and brief text, and mentions artificial body parts
Includes glossary

Under the microscope; the human body; [by] Richard Walker [et al.] Grolier Educ. 1998 8v il set $219   **612**
1. Physiology 2. Human anatomy
ISBN 0-7172-9265-7   LC 97-38977

Under the microscope—*Continued*
Contents: v1 Heart; v2 Skeleton; v3 Digesting; v4 Making life; v5 Breathing; v6 Senses; v7 Muscles; v8 Brain

"A one-page introduction to the body system begins each volume. This is followed by double-page spreads presenting information on the system as a whole, and on its various components. For example, the skeleton volume not only covers the entire human skeleton but also the ankle, elbow, leg, and arm bones. The concise text is fitted in among the many drawings (including diagrams and cutaways), photographs, and examples of microphotography. . . . The illustrations are beautifully detailed and clearly labeled. The set is well done. Information is logically organized, and the vocabulary is accessible." Booklist

612.1 Blood and circulation

Ballard, Carol
The heart and circulatory system. Raintree Steck-Vaughn Pubs. 1997 48p il (Human body) lib bdg $25.68   **612.1**
1. Blood 2. Heart 3. Cardiovascular system
ISBN 0-8172-4800-5   LC 96-31764
Describes the parts of the circulatory system and how they function
"Organs and other components that contribute to the proper functioning of [the] system are illustrated with diagrams, colored drawings, photographs, X rays, and electron micrographs, and are described in easy-to-read text." Sci Books Films
Includes glossary and bibliographical references

Silverstein, Alvin
The circulatory system; [by] Alvin, Virginia and Robert Silverstein. 21st Cent. Bks. (NY) 1994 96p il (Human body systems) lib bdg $20.40   **612.1**
1. Heart 2. Blood—Circulation
ISBN 0-8050-2833-1   LC 94-21426
This illustrated introduction to the circulatory system "briefly discusses related systems in plants and animals and the history of our knowledge of the human heart and blood vessels, then focuses on the various parts of the human circulatory system." Booklist
Includes glossary

Simon, Seymour, 1931-
The heart. Morrow Junior Bks. 1996 unp $16; lib bdg $15.93   **612.1**
1. Cardiovascular system 2. Heart
ISBN 0-688-11407-5; 0-688-11408-3 (lib bdg)
                               LC 95-38021
The author "explains the system of blood vessels; the role of blood, lungs, and the heart; and a few of the problems that can develop in the circulatory system. The text, layout, diagrams, and color photographs work together to make an eye-catching and useful book." Horn Book Guide

612.2 Respiration

Parker, Steve
The lungs and respiratory system. Raintree Steck-Vaughn Pubs. 1997 48p il (Human body) lib bdg $25.68   **612.2**
1. Lungs 2. Respiratory system
ISBN 0-8172-4803-X   LC 96-43516
Examines the different parts and functions of the lungs and respiratory system
The information in this book "is especially well organized and well coordinated with colorful illustrations and photographs." SLJ
Includes glossary and bibliographical references

Silverstein, Alvin
The respiratory system; [by] Alvin, Virginia and Robert Silverstein. 21st Cent. Bks. (NY) 1994 96p il (Human body systems) lib bdg $20.40   **612.2**
1. Respiratory system
ISBN 0-8050-2831-5   LC 94-21422
This illustrated introduction to the morphology and physiology of the respiratory system also discusses respiratory diseases and their treatments
Includes glossary

612.3 Digestion

Ballard, Carol
The stomach and digestive system. Raintree Steck-Vaughn Pubs. 1997 48p il (Human body) lib bdg $25.68   **612.3**
1. Digestion 2. Stomach
ISBN 0-8172-4801-3   LC 96-31769
Describes the appearance, characteristics, and function of each part of the digestive system
This is "easy-to-read and will attract reluctant readers because of the short chapters, 'Fact Boxes,' and many colorful photographs and illustrations." SLJ
Includes glossary and bibliographical references

612.6 Reproduction, development, maturation

Flanagan, Geraldine Lux
Beginning life. DK Pub. 1996 120p il $19.95
                               612.6
1. Embryology 2. Pregnancy 3. Childbirth
ISBN 0-7894-0609-8   LC 95-52790
The author "describes pregnancy month by month from conception through birth. The detailed text of this oversize book is enhanced by magnified photographs, ultrasound images, and color video sequences of the baby's development in the womb." Book Rep

Gravelle, Karen

The period book; everything you don't want to ask (but need to know); by Karen Gravelle & Jennifer Gravelle; illustrations by Debbie Palen. Walker & Co. 1996 117p il $15.95; pa $8.95

612.6

1. Menstruation

ISBN 0-8027-8420-8; 0-8027-7478-4 (pa)

LC 95-31101

"An aunt and her fifteen-year-old niece provide forthright information about tampon insertion, pelvic exams, body changes during puberty, and other topics adolescent girls might feel uncomfortable discussing with parents and friends. The cartoonlike illustrations and conversational tone make this a friendly, reassuring resource as well as a thorough one." Horn Book Guide

What's going on down there? answers to questions boys find hard to ask; [by] Karen Gravelle, with Nick and Chava Castro; illustrations by Robert Leighton. Walker & Co. 1998 150p il $15.95; pa $8.95

612.6

1. Adolescence 2. Boys 3. Sex education

ISBN 0-8027-8671-5; 0-8027-7540-3 (pa)

LC 98-3686

This title "covers physical changes, sexual intercourse, peer pressure, and pregnancy and birth. Gravelle reassures readers that there are a lot of different ways to describe normal when discussing puberty, and that each person will experience changes on his own timetable. The book balances information about being a sexual person with that of being a responsible person." SLJ

Jukes, Mavis

Growing up: it's a girl thing; straight talk about first bras, first periods, and your changing body; illustrations by Debbie Tilley. Knopf 1998 72p il lib bdg $16.99; pa $10

612.6

1. Adolescence 2. Girls 3. Menstruation

ISBN 0-679-99027-5 (lib bdg); 0-679-89027-0 (pa)

LC 98-18113

This is a slightly revised version of chapters from the author's It's a girl thing

This "covers body hair and shaving, perspiration and deodorant, and how to buy your first bra. The second half of the book is devoted to what to expect and how to plan for your first period. . . . The narration has an easy, comfortable voice and imparts accurate and important information." SLJ

Parker, Steve

Reproduction and growth; illustrated by Peter Bull Associates, Aziz Khan, and Ian Thompson. Millbrook Press 1998 31p il (Look at your body) $20.90

612.6

1. Reproduction 2. Growth

ISBN 0-7613-0813-X

LC 97-43128

Presents an overview of the human life cycle, with information about reproduction, heredity, child development, and aging

The reproductive system. Raintree Steck-Vaughn Pubs. 1998 48p il (Human body) lib bdg $25.68

612.6

1. Reproduction 2. Growth

ISBN 0-8172-4806-4

LC 96-29685

Explains the parts of the reproductive system and their functions and provides an overview of human development from birth through adolescence

The text is "succinct but complete, and include[s] plenty of detail without being overwhelming." SLJ

Includes glossary and bibliographical references

612.7 Musculoskeletal system, integument

Ballard, Carol

The skeleton and muscular system. Raintree Steck-Vaughn Pubs. 1998 48p il (Human body) lib bdg $25.68

612.7

1. Musculoskeletal system 2. Skeleton

ISBN 0-8172-4805-6

LC 96-29688

Explains the various parts of the human skeleton and different types of muscles and their functions

The text is "well organized and well written. The full-color photos, diagrams, and illustrations are clear and complement the text." SLJ

Includes glossary and bibliographical references

Simon, Seymour, 1931-

Bones; our skeletal system. Morrow Junior Bks. 1998 unp il $16; lib bdg $15.93

612.7

1. Bones 2. Skeleton

ISBN 0-688-14644-9; 0-688-14645-7 (lib bdg)

LC 97-44751

Describes the skeletal system and outlines the many important roles that bones play in the healthy functioning of the human body

"Simon once again proves his remarkable facility for making complicated science clear and understandable." Booklist

Muscles; our muscular system. Morrow Junior Bks. 1998 unp il $16; lib bdg $15.93

612.7

1. Muscles

ISBN 0-688-14642-2; 0-688-14643-0 (lib bdg)

LC 97-44758

Describes the nature and work of muscles, the different kinds, and the effects of exercise and other activities on them

"The full-paged illustrations are great and include full-color photographs, MRI scans, X rays, and excellent drawings." SLJ

612.8 Nervous functions. Sensory functions

Barmeier, Jim

The brain. Lucent Bks. 1996 128p il (Lucent overview series) $22.45 (7 and up)

612.8

1. Brain

ISBN 1-56006-107-3

LC 95-25183

Barmeier, Jim—*Continued*
Explores how the human brain works, covering such topics as memory, sleep, dreaming, dysfunctions, and new technology used to learn more about it
Includes bibliographical references

Brynie, Faith Hickman, 1946-
101 questions your brain has asked about itself but couldn't answer . . . until now. Millbrook Press 1998 176p il lib bdg $23.90   **612.8**
1. Brain
ISBN 0-7613-0400-2   LC 98-9797
Provides information about the physical aspects of the brain and how it functions, effects of diseases and drugs on the brain, memory, senses, and more in question and answer format
"Clear and helpful monochromatic diagrams punctuate the text, along with a few decorative black-and-white photos. A clear and lively addition that incorporates much of what scientists have learned about the brain in the last 10 years." SLJ
Includes bibliographical references

Simon, Seymour, 1931-
The brain; our nervous system. Morrow Junior Bks. 1997 unp il $16; lib bdg $15.93   **612.8**
1. Brain 2. Nervous system
ISBN 0-688-14640-6; 0-688-14641-4 (lib bdg)
                                     LC 96-36801
Describes the various parts of the brain and the nervous system and how they function to enable us to think, feel, move, and remember
Simon's "clear, concise writing style is complemented by stunning color images taken with radiological scanners, such as CAT scans, MRIs, and SEMs (scanning electron microscopes.)" SLJ

613   Promotion of health

Folkers, Gladys, 1947-
Taking charge of my mind & body; a girls' guide to outsmarting alcohol, drugs, smoking, and eating problems; [by] Gladys Folkers and Jeanne Engelmann. Free Spirit 1997 199p il pa $13.95 (7 and up)   **613**
1. Health
ISBN 1-57542-015-5   LC 96-46732
Offers advice, with quotes from teenagers, on making appropriate choices about using alcohol and other drugs, smoking, dealing with body image and eating disorders, and other adolescent concerns
"Readers will appreciate the straightforward approach the authors take in discussing these issues and the realistic techniques they suggest to avoid trouble. . . . Cool graphics, hot line information, and Internet resources complete this up-to-date and readable work." Voice Youth Advocates
Includes glossary and bibliographical references

Health on file; [by] Victoria Chapman & Associates. Facts on File 1995 various paging il loose-leaf $165   **613**
1. Health
ISBN 0-8160-2993-8   LC 94-7097

"Presented on heavy paper stock in a three-ring binder, all the materials in this excellent resource are copyright free and can be reproduced and distributed as classroom materials. Topics include: mental health; social & family health; growth & development; food & nutrition; personal health; substance abuse; diseases & disorders; consumer health; and environmental health. Current issues such as AIDS, wellness, refusal skills and conflict resolution are covered." Book Rep

613.6   Special topics of health and safety

Chaiet, Donna
The safe zone; a kid's guide to personal safety; by Donna Chaiet and Francine Russell; photographs by Lillian Gee. Beech Tree Bks. 1998 160p il $15; pa $5.95   **613.6**
1. Safety education
ISBN 0-688-15307-0; 0-688-15308-9 (pa)
                                     LC 97-36309
Discusses various self-defense options which may be used when in an uncomfortable or unsafe situation and suggests what solutions might work in real life
"The frank discussions and on-target advice may go a long way toward making young people less vulnerable to those who prey upon them." SLJ
Includes bibliographical references

Wiloch, Thomas
Everything you need to know about protecting yourself and others from abduction. Rosen Pub. Group 1998 64p il (Need to know library) $17.95
                                       613.6
1. Kidnapping 2. Safety education
ISBN 0-8239-2553-6   LC 97-44784
"This title calls attention to the increasing number of abductions of teens and children. While it categorizes the different types of abductions, it focuses on those committed by strangers. . . . Preventive measures as well as strategies for escaping attempted kidnappings are described. Chapters are devoted to precautions to take at home, and while babysitting, jogging, bicycling, using the Internet, etc. The author addresses teens although there is some discussion of the vulnerability of children. Most suggestions are intelligent, practical, and easy to follow." SLJ
Includes bibliographical references

613.7   Physical fitness

Savage, Jeff, 1961-
Fundamental strength training; photographs by Jimmy Clarke. Lerner Publs. 1998 64p il (Fundamental sports) lib bdg $22.60   **613.7**
1. Weight lifting 2. Bodybuilding
ISBN 0-8225-3461-4   LC 97-44292
An introduction to the sport of strength training, with and without weights, including its history, equipment, techniques, and variations
The exercises "are explained simply and clearly and are demonstrated with beautifully reproduced, full-color photographs." SLJ
Includes glossary and bibliographical references

Schwager, Tina, 1964-
The right moves; a girl's guide to getting fit and feeling good; by Tina Schwager and Michele Schuerger; edited by Elizabeth Verdick. Free Spirit 1998 273p il pa $14.95 (7 and up)   **613.7**
   1. Women—Health and hygiene 2. Physical fitness
   ISBN 1-57542-035-X   LC 98-9851
Explains how girls can achieve total fitness by focusing on three broad areas: developing a positive self-image, choosing nutritious foods, and exercising regularly
  "This useful addition to the self-help genre is both cheerleader and resource, providing valuable advice and information." Booklist
  Includes bibliographical references

Stiefer, Sandy
A risky prescription; sports and health. Lerner Publs. 1997 96p il (Sports issues) lib bdg $22.60
                  613.7
   1. Sports medicine
   ISBN 0-8225-3304-9   LC 96-48340
Discusses athletes and sports in today's society, focusing on mental and physical health aspects, including the use of drugs, the stress placed on professional athletes, and the pressure to win at any cost
  "Full-color photos add action to the text, and boxed sidebars add additional information. The author writes clearly and without sensationalism, calmly conveying her message of caution and common sense." SLJ
  Includes bibliographical references

613.9 Birth control, reproductive technology, sex hygiene

Bell, Ruth
Changing bodies, changing lives; a book for teens on sex and relationships; [by] Ruth Bell and other co-authors of Our bodies, ourselves and Ourselves and our children, together with members of the Teen Book Project. expanded 3rd ed. Times Bks. 1998 411p il pa $23 (7 and up)   **613.9**
   1. Sex education
   ISBN 0-8129-2990-X   LC 97-29249
   First published 1980
This work discusses teenage sexuality and the physical and emotional changes that occur during adolescence. Eating disorders, AIDS, drugs, sexual harassment, and rape are among the topics discussed

Fenwick, Elizabeth, 1935-
How sex works; a clear, comprehensive guide for teenagers to emotional, physical, and sexual maturity; [by] Elizabeth Fenwick & Richard Walker. Dorling Kindersley 1994 96p il hardcover o.p. paperback available $9.95 (7 and up)   **613.9**
   1. Sex education
   ISBN 0-7894-0634-9 (pa)   LC 93-37638
The authors give an "explanation of the body changes, feelings, and decisions that all young people face during the teen years. Issues such as sexual abuse, AIDS, pregnancy, contraception, and sexual preference are clearly addressed with enough information for teens to make their own decisions as to how to deal with them. The book is illustrated throughout with photos, drawings, and diagrams that help to clarify and explain the subject." Voice Youth Advocates

Harris, Robie H.
It's perfectly normal; a book about changing bodies, growing up, sex, and sexual health; illustrated by Michael Emberley. Candlewick Press 1994 89p il $19.95; pa $9.99   **613.9**
   1. Sex education
   ISBN 1-56402-199-8; 1-56402-159-9 (pa)
                 LC 93-48365
The author "explains the physical, psychological, emotional and social changes that occur during puberty—and the implications of these changes." Publ Wkly
  "This caring, conscientious, and well-crafted book will be a fine library resource as well as a marvelous adjunct to the middle-school sex-education curriculum. . . . The bold color cartoon drawings are very candid: a double-page spread of nudes, which beautifully demonstrates the varied shapes and sizes humans come in; a picture of a couple making love; one of a boy masturbating as he sits on his bed; another of a girl examining her genitals with a mirror. . . . Harris' text, as forthright as Emberley's art, encompasses . . . (the structure of the reproductive system and puberty) . . . intercourse, birth, abortion, sexual health, abuse, and issues of responsibility and respect." Booklist

Stoppard, Miriam
Sex ed; illustrated by Sally Artz. DK Pub. 1997 96p il $14.95; pa $9.95 (7 and up)   **613.9**
   1. Sex education
   ISBN 0-7894-2385-5; 0-7894-1751-0 (pa)
                 LC 97-14341
A guide to growing up, relationships, and sex, discussing such topics as male and female anatomy, petting, intercourse, different kinds of sexual activities, contraception, and safe sex
  "The text is clearly written and acceptably detailed, the exceptions being rather skimpy sections on birth control methods and STDs. . . . Diagrams are excellent, and the cartoons supply helpful emotional subtext and lighten the tone." Booklist

614 Forensic medicine, incidence & prevention of disease

Jackson, Donna, 1958-
The bone detectives; how forensic anthropologists solve crimes and uncover mysteries of the dead; by Donna M. Jackson; photographs by Charlie Fellenbaum. Little, Brown 1996 48p il lib bdg $16.95   **614**
   1. Forensic anthropology 2. Criminal investigation
   ISBN 0-316-82935-8   LC 95-19051
  "Jackson follows forensic anthropologist Dr. Michael Charney and his colleagues as they solve an actual case

Jackson, Donna, 1958-—*Continued*
by developing a physical profile from bones and teeth,
reconstructing the victim's skull, and using clues from fibers and other material to make further identification."
Booklist

"Laced with eye-catching full-color photos, this readable book is a fine example of the application of scientific knowledge to the 'real' world." SLJ
Includes glossary

Thomas, Peggy
Talking bones; the science of forensic
anthropology. Facts on File 1995 136p il (Facts on
File science sourcebooks) $19.95 (7 and up) **614**
1. Forensic anthropology
ISBN 0-8160-3114-2   LC 94-44110
Introduces the history, technology, and importance of
the science of using human remains to solve crimes and
includes actual forensic cases

"Not only does this book give interesting and somewhat gory facts about forensics, it provides students with
an understanding of how this science benefits our society." Book Rep
Includes glossary and bibliographical references

614.4 Incidence of and public measures to prevent disease

Altman, Linda Jacobs, 1943-
Plague and pestilence; a history of infectious
disease. Enslow Pubs. 1998 128p il (Issues in
focus) lib bdg $19.95   **614.4**
1. Communicable diseases
ISBN 0-89490-957-6   LC 98-12677
Traces the battles that societies have waged against infectious diseases from the Black Death of the fourteenth
century to the Ebola virus of more recent times

"The inclusion of large numbers of references, including Internet Web sites, will encourage further reading."
Sci Books Films

Epidemics: opposing viewpoints; William Dudley,
book editor. Greenhaven Press 1999 188p lib
bdg $26.20; pa $16.20 (7 and up)   **614.4**
1. Epidemics
ISBN 1-56510-941-4 (lib bdg); 1-56510-940-6 (pa)
LC 98-28458
"Opposing viewpoints series"

This collection of articles presents varying viewpoints
on the following questions: Do infectious diseases pose
a significant threat to humanity? What can be done to
curtail the AIDS epidemic? Are government vaccination
programs beneficial? How can food-borne illnesses be
prevented?
Includes glossary and bibliographical references

Farrell, Jeanette
Invisible enemies; stories of infectious disease.
Farrar, Straus & Giroux 1998 246p il $17 (7 and
up)   **614.4**
1. Communicable diseases
ISBN 0-374-33637-7   LC 96-53247

A history of the fight against seven major diseases:
smallpox, leprosy, plague, tuberculosis, malaria, cholera,
and AIDS

"The anecdotal style is accessible; the tone, conversational; the whole, informative, with ample documentation." Horn Book Guide
Includes glossary and bibliographical references

614.5 Incidence & prevention of specific diseases

The **Black** Death; Don Nardo, book editor.
Greenhaven Press 1999 173p (Turning points in
world history) $20.96; pa $12.96 (7 and up)
614.5
1. Plague 2. Epidemics
ISBN 1-56510-995-3; 1-56510-994-5 (pa)
LC 98-44752
"The two major sections, 'The Black Death Ravages
Europe' and 'The Economic and Cultural Impact of the
Black Death,' illustrate the focus of the text. Students are
given a clear explanation of the disease and how it may
have spread and some coverage of its social, economic,
and cultural repercussions. The essays each speak to a
specific issue. An appendix that includes 16 primary documents, a concise chronology, lists for further reading divided by content, and an index complete this valuable research tool." SLJ

Corzine, Phyllis
The Black Death. Lucent Bks. 1997 112p il
maps (World history series) lib bdg $22.45 (7 and
up)   **614.5**
1. Plague
ISBN 1-56006-299-1   LC 96-19441
Examines the causes, effects, and legacy of the epidemic that killed millions of people in Europe during the
fourteenth century

"Students will find answers to homework questions in
[this] clearly written volume." SLJ
Includes bibliographical references

615 Pharmacology and therapeutics

Barrett, Cece
The dangers of diet drugs and other weight-loss
products. Rosen Pub. Group 1999 64p il (Teen
health library of eating disorder prevention) $17.95
615
1. Appetite depressants 2. Eating disorders
ISBN 0-8239-2768-7   LC 98-29712
Discusses the use of over-the-counter, prescription,
and herbal diet drugs as well as liquid and prepackaged
diet foods and explains their relation to eating disorders
and proper nutrition

Clayton, L. (Lawrence)
Diet pill drug dangers. Enslow Pubs. 1999 64p
il (Drug dangers) lib bdg $19.95   **615**
1. Appetite depressants 2. Eating disorders
ISBN 0-7660-1158-5   LC 98-20514

Clayton, L. (Lawrence)—*Continued*
Examines the history of diet pill use, focusing on society's obsession with weight loss and the dangers of abusing these drugs
Includes bibliographical references

Gordon, Melanie Apel
Drug interactions; protecting yourself from dangerous drug, medication, and food combinations; [by] Melanie Gordon. Rosen Pub. Group 1999 63p il (Drug abuse prevention library) $17.95   **615**
1. Drugs
ISBN 0-8239-2825-X   LC 98-44974
Discusses illegal and legal drugs (both over-the-counter and prescription), alcohol, and food and explains how to prevent dangerous interactions among these substances
Includes bibliographical references

Kidd, J. S. (Jerry S.)
Mother Nature's pharmacy; potent medicines from plants; [by] J.S. Kidd and Renee A. Kidd. Facts on File 1998 134p il maps (Science and society) $19.95 (7 and up)   **615**
1. Pharmacology 2. Medical botany
ISBN 0-8160-3584-9   LC 97-37925
"The Kidds guide the reader through a general history of medicine and medical care, the nature of folk medicine, the growth of government regulation, and the role of the South American rain forests as a source of new drugs. They include biographical sketches of medical pioneers and brief histories of several significant plant-derived drugs, such as quinine, curare, ephedrine, and cortisone." Book Rep
"Well-organized and well-researched, the book is a good introduction to the history of traditional medicine, from Hippocrates to modern times." Booklist
Includes glossary and bibliographical references

Powledge, Fred
Pharmacy in the forest; how medicines are found in the natural world. Atheneum Bks. for Young Readers 1998 47p il $17   **615**
1. Medical botany 2. Drugs
ISBN 0-689-80863-1   LC 97-6938
Identifies medicinal plants and their natural habitats while also explaining how these plants are found and tested for medical value
"With large, attractive, full-color pictures (some uncaptioned) and readable text, this book will make a solid addition to most collections." SLJ
Includes glossary

Thomas, Peggy
Medicines from nature. 21st Cent. Bks. (NY) 1997 128p il lib bdg $21.40 (7 and up)   **615**
1. Medical botany 2. Drugs
ISBN 0-8050-4168-0   LC 96-47686
Discusses how we have learned from traditional healers around the world about the medicinal value of substances from nature
"Thomas' detailed description of the process of searching for, mixing up, and testing the various medicines and treatments; her evenhanded discussion of the threats to biodiversity and its consequences; and her obvious knowledge of a too-seldom-discussed topic all make for a book that should be read from cover to cover by teens—and adults as well." Booklist
Includes glossary and bibliographical references

615.5 Therapeutics

Facklam, Howard
Alternative medicine; cures or myths? 21st Cent. Bks. (NY) 1996 126p $21.40 (7 and up)   **615.5**
1. Alternative medicine
ISBN 0-8050-4169-9   LC 96-32699
Discusses various kinds of non-traditional methods of medical treatment, including acupuncture, herbal medicine, massage, and meditation
"This excellent volume is useful for research, but is just as appealing as a good nonfiction read." SLJ
Includes glossary and bibliographical references

Kowalski, Kathiann M., 1955-
Alternative medicine; is it for you? Enslow Pubs. 1998 128p il (Issues in focus) $19.95 (7 and up)   **615.5**
1. Alternative medicine
ISBN 0-89490-955-X   LC 98-12676
Analyzes different types of alternative medicine practiced today, such as homeopathy, chiropractic, herbal, and nutritional therapies, and discusses how to make an informed decision about medical care
"Kowalski writes clearly and directly, maintaining both respect for the reader's intelligence and an objective attitude toward the material." Booklist
Includes bibliographical references

Rattenbury, Jeanne
Understanding alternative medicine. Watts 1999 128p il $24 (7 and up)   **615.5**
1. Alternative medicine
ISBN 0-531-11413-9   LC 98-15669
Introduces five alternative medical systems and five major alternative treatments, including osteopathy, traditional Chinese medicine, acupuncture, herbal medicine, and massage therapy
"The history, effectiveness, and variations of therapies are clearly detailed. An extensive glossary, solid bibliography, and listing of 16 organizations related to alternative-medical systems add to the usefulness of this volume." SLJ

615.9 Toxicology

Goldish, Meish
The dangers of herbal stimulants. Rosen Pub. Group 1998 64p il (Drug abuse prevention library) $17.95   **615.9**
1. Herbs 2. Stimulants
ISBN 0-8239-2555-2   LC 97-6986

Goldish, Meish—*Continued*
Explains the different types of herbal stimulants as well as dangers and benefits associated with their use
Includes bibliographical references

Latta, Sara L.
Food poisoning and foodborne diseases. Enslow Pubs. 1999 128p il (Diseases and people) lib bdg $19.95 (7 and up)   **615.9**
1. Food poisoning
ISBN 0-7660-1183-6   LC 98-36134
"The eight chapters include the history of foodborne diseases, the various microbes involved and how they are toxic to our bodies, diagnosis and treatment of illnesses, the social costs of food poisoning, and methods of prevention on both a personal and societal level. . . . Appendixes include a question-and-answer section; a list of contact organizations; extensive chapter notes; recommended books, articles, videos, and Web sites; and a helpful index." SLJ
Includes bibliographical references

616   Diseases

Hyde, Margaret Oldroyd, 1917-
The disease book; a kid's guide; [by] Margaret O. Hyde and Elizabeth H. Forsyth; illustrations by Bari Weissman. Walker & Co. 1997 147p il $16.95; lib bdg $17.85   **616**
1. Diseases 2. Medical care
ISBN 0-8027-8497-6; 0-8027-8498-4 (lib bdg)
LC 97-155
Discusses the causes, symptoms, effects, and treatment of a variety of diseases and disorders arranged under such categories as "Disorders of the Lungs," "Mental Illness," and "Disorders of the Digestive System"
"An interesting and useful guide. . . . This unique volume provides age-appropriate, thorough coverage of many major diseases and disorders, including those that are rare or historically significant." SLJ
Includes bibliographical references

Jacobs, Marian B.
Coping with hereditary diseases. Rosen Pub. Group 1999 152p il $17.95 (7 and up)   **616**
1. Medical genetics 2. Diseases
ISBN 0-8239-2823-3   LC 98-48064
Examines common hereditary diseases and ways of avoiding them, discussing diabetes, heart disease, cancer, alcoholism, and the exploration of one's family medical tree
Includes bibliographical references

Landau, Elaine
Joined at birth; the lives of conjoined twins. Watts 1997 64p il $22   **616**
1. Siamese twins
ISBN 0-531-20331-X   LC 96-38707
"A First book"
Explores the issue of conjoined twins, including a discussion of the difficult decision regarding physical separation that parents must face
Includes bibliographical references

616.02   Domestic medicine and medical emergencies

Masoff, Joy, 1951-
Emergency! principal photography by Brian Michaud and Peter Escobedo. Scholastic Ref. 1999 48p il $16.95   **616.02**
1. Emergency medicine
ISBN 0-590-97898-5   LC 97-26995
Discusses all aspects of emergency medicine including the medical personnel and equipment needed to successfully help the patient
"A colorful, information-packed volume. Each double-page spread features lots of excellent full-color photographs, a large heading, and sidebars." SLJ
Includes bibliographical references

616.07   Pathology

Friedlander, Mark P.
The immune system; your body's disease-fighting army; [by] Mark P. Friedlander, Jr. & Terry M. Phillips. Lerner Publs. 1998 112p il $23.93 (7 and up)   **616.07**
1. Immune system
ISBN 0-8225-2858-4   LC 97-10711
Describes the immune system, its major components, and such related topics as bacteria, viruses, parasites, vaccines, and current research in immunology
"This surprisingly readable book presents the complex processes of the immune system through precise explanations and lively imagery. . . . The clear, colorful illustrations include diagrams, photographs, and excellent, highly magnified images of cells, viruses, bacteria, and allergens such as pollen grains and dander." Booklist
Includes glossary

616.1   Diseases of the cardiovascular system

Johansson, Philip
Heart disease. Enslow Pubs. 1998 128p il (Diseases and people) lib bdg $18.95   **616.1**
1. Heart diseases 2. Cardiovascular system
ISBN 0-7660-1051-1   LC 97-30804
Describes the workings of the heart and the circulatory system and the array of ailments that can affect them, discussing symptoms, diagnosis, prevention, and treatment
Includes bibliographical references

Silverstein, Alvin
Sickle cell anemia; [by] Alvin and Virginia Silverstein and Laura Silverstein Nunn. Enslow Pubs. 1997 112p il (Diseases and people) lib bdg $18.95 (7 and up)   **616.1**
1. Sickle cell anemia
ISBN 0-89490-711-5   LC 96-22643

Silverstein, Alvin—*Continued*
  Explores the history of sickle cell anemia, discussing
its symptoms, diagnosis, and treatment
  "The text is clear and well organized, with sections on
gene therapy, diagnostic techniques, research, and even
ethical concerns about the possible use of fetal tissue in
treatment. Informative black-and-white photos and graphics complement the presentation." SLJ
  Includes glossary and bibliographical references

616.2 Diseases of the respiratory system

Murphy, Wendy B.
  Asthma. Millbrook Press 1998 112p il
(Millbrook medical library) lib bdg $23.90 (7 and
up)   **616.2**
    1. Asthma
    ISBN 0-7613-0364-2   LC 97-52128
  Examines the various causes of asthma, what happens
during an attack, how the disease can be controlled, and
theories of treatment
  "Asthma sufferers, their families and friends, and students researching the disease will make good use of this
informative title." Booklist
  Includes glossary and bibliographical references

Silverstein, Alvin
  Asthma; [by] Alvin and Virginia Silverstein and
Laura Silverstein Nunn. Enslow Pubs. 1997 128p
il (Diseases and people) lib bdg $18.95 (7 and up)
                                                        616.2
    1. Asthma
    ISBN 0-89490-712-3   LC 96-29095
  "Beginning with a brief outline of its characteristics
and effects, the authors then trace the history of asthma,
its treatments, and theories about its causes." SLJ
  "This well-researched and well-written book balances
clear scientific thought and progression with anecdotal
examples of celebrities and historical figures who have
overcome the constraints of the disease." Sci Books
Films
  Includes glossary and bibliographical references

616.4 Diabetes

Ferber, Elizabeth, 1967-
  Diabetes. Millbrook Press 1996 96p il
(Millbrook medical library) lib bdg $23.90 (7 and
up)   **616.4**
    1. Diabetes
    ISBN 1-56294-655-2   LC 96-5173
  The author "describes the disease, its diagnosis and
treatment, how it's complicated by the hormonal and
emotional changes of adolescence, and how it affects relationships with friends and family members. She also
provides information on detection, prevention, and management of the illness. . . . Young people diagnosed
with diabetes, as well as their family and friends, will
find this a matter-of-fact presentation." Booklist
  Includes glossary and bibliographical references

Kelly, Pat
  Coping with diabetes. Rosen Pub. Group 1998
145p $17.95 (7 and up)   **616.4**
    1. Diabetes
    ISBN 0-8239-2549-8   LC 97-49084
  Discusses the types and causes of diabetes, how the
disease is diagnosed and treated, and ways of managing
this condition and its impact on your life
  "Addressing the teen reader, the author provides clear-
cut, concise information about the disease and how to
handle it. Teens with diabetes share their stories of problems faced and overcome." Voice Youth Advocates
  Includes bibliographical references

Stewart, Gail, 1949-
  Diabetes. Lucent Bks. 1999 95p il $17.95 (7 and
up)   **616.4**
    1. Diabetes
    ISBN 1-56006-527-3   LC 98-31963
  Discusses the history, nature, causes, symptoms, diagnosis, treatment, emergencies, and complications of diabetes and explains ways to live with it
  "The well-organized and well-paced text is suitable for
research or for personal information." SLJ
  Includes bibliographical references

616.5 Diseases of integument, hair, nails

Landau, Elaine
  Living with albinism. Watts 1997 63p il $22
                                                        616.5
    1. Albinos and albinism
    ISBN 0-531-20296-8   LC 97-1771
  "A First book"
  Describes albinism, the inherited condition in which
the individual lacks or has a shortage of melanin, the
substance responsible for the body's coloring
  "A concise consideration of a medical condition and
its consequences on personal health. . . . This is a positive book, written without sensationalism and illustrated
with full-color and black-and-white photographs that support this approach." SLJ

616.7 Diseases of the musculoskeletal system

Eisenpreis, Bettijane
  Coping with scoliosis. Rosen Pub. Group 1998
164p il $17.95 (7 and up)   **616.7**
    1. Scoliosis
    ISBN 0-8239-2557-9   LC 98-37198
  The author "explores the physical and emotional is-
sues involved in the diagnosis and treatment of scoliosis.
Pencil drawings include illustrations of the spine and the
types of orthopedic braces patients wear." SLJ
  Includes bibliographical references

616.8   Diseases of the nervous system and mental disorders

Carson, Mary Kay
Epilepsy. Enslow Pubs. 1998 112p il (Diseases and people) lib bdg $18.95 (7 and up)   **616.8**
1. Epilepsy
ISBN 0-7660-1049-X   LC 97-34160
Explores the topic of epilepsy, discussing its history, symptoms, diagnosis, treatment, and possible ways to prevent some forms of the disease
Includes bibliographical references

Harmon, Dan
Life out of focus; Alzheimer's disease and related disorders. Chelsea House 1999 104p il $24.95 (7 and up)   **616.8**
1. Alzheimer's disease
ISBN 0-7910-4896-9   LC 98-26537
Discusses the nature, possible causes, effects on the patient as well as family and friends, and treatment options of this deteriorative disease
Includes bibliographical references

Johansson, Philip
Carpal tunnel syndrome and other repetitive strain injuries. Enslow Pubs. 1999 128p il (Diseases and people) lib bdg $19.95 (7 and up)   **616.8**
1. Wounds and injuries
ISBN 0-7660-1184-4   LC 98-30305
"This general discussion examines the causes, symptoms, diagnosis, treatment, and prevention of some of the most common repetitive strain injuries (RSIs) such as carpal tunnel syndrome and tennis elbow. Many of the chapters begin with individual case studies that will engage readers' interest and sympathy." SLJ
Includes bibliographical references

Landau, Elaine
Epilepsy. 21st Cent. Bks. (NY) 1994 64p il (Understanding illness) lib bdg $18.90   **616.8**
1. Epilepsy
ISBN 0-8050-2991-5   LC 94-13833
In this book "personal case histories highlight important background information about . . . epilepsy. This is followed by chapters on diagnosis and treatment (both medical and surgical), facts about epilepsy presented in a question-and-answer format, and a brief discussion of famous individuals who had epilepsy. The material is accurate and easy to follow." Sci Books Films

Parkinson's disease. Watts 1999 112p il $24 (7 and up)   **616.8**
1. Parkinsonism
ISBN 0-531-11423-6   LC 98-22450
"A Venture book"
The author "explains the symptoms of Parkinson's disease, from tremors and rigidity to emotional changes and speech problems, and discusses the difficulty of diagnosing it. Although its cause is not known, researchers speculate that it could be environmental, viral, or even a result of the aging process. Treatment options range from medication to brain surgery to the controversial fetal tissue transplant, and Landau carefully explains both sides of that issue." SLJ
Includes bibliographical references

Tourette syndrome. Watts 1998 95p il lib bdg $24 (7 and up)   **616.8**
1. Tourette syndrome
ISBN 0-531-11399-X   LC 97-48736
Describes the causes, symptoms, and treatment of Tourette Syndrome and explains the challenges faced by people with the disorder
"The attractive format and accessible reading level make this an effective guide for a young person facing the symptoms, a student needing report information, or an adult needing a concise overview." Voice Youth Advocates
Includes bibliography

SPINAbilities; a young person's guide to spina bifida; edited by Marlene Lutkenhoff and Sonya G. Oppenheimer. Woodbine House 1996 138p il pa $16.95   **616.8**
1. Spina bifida
ISBN 0-933149-86-7   LC 96-42056
A guide to coping with the medical, self-care, and emotional issues of spinal bifida, with an emphasis on becoming as independent as possible

Votava, Andrea
Coping with migraines and other headaches. Rosen Pub. Group 1997 162p il $17.95 (7 and up)   **616.8**
1. Headache
ISBN 0-8239-2566-8   LC 97-31918
The author "covers different kinds of headaches and migraines, including their symptoms, causes, triggers, and prevention. Medication and alternative treatments such as yoga, meditation, massage, and acupuncture are discussed, as are recommendations relating to sleep and exercise. Personal stories are included. . . . Web sites and e-mail addresses of organizations to contact for further information are listed." SLJ
Includes bibliographical references

Willett, Edward, 1959-
Meningitis. Enslow Pubs. 1999 112p il (Diseases and people) lib bdg $19.95 (7 and up)   **616.8**
1. Meningitis
ISBN 0-7660-1187-9   LC 99-12279
Discusses the history, symptoms, diagnosis, and treatment of meningitis and examines ongoing research and its effect on the future treatment of this disease
"The material is presented in an easy-to-read style." Sci Books Films
Includes glossary and bibliographical references

616.85 Neuroses; speech and language disorders; disorders of personality, intellect, impulse control

Beal, Eileen
Everything you need to know about ADD/ADHD. Rosen Pub. Group 1998 64p il (Need to know library) $25.45 (7 and up) **616.85**
1. Attention deficit disorder
ISBN 0-8239-2748-2   LC 97-45149
Defines both attention deficit disorder and attention deficit hyperactivity disorder and discusses what can be done to treat these conditions, including medication, behavior modification, and counseling
Includes bibliographical references

Ritalin; its use and abuse. Rosen Pub. Group 1999 64p il (Drug abuse prevention library) lib bdg $16.95; pa $6.95 (7 and up)   **616.85**
1. Ritalin
ISBN 0-8239-2775-X (lib bdg); 1-56838-248-0 (pa)
LC 98-27089
Describes the medical uses of the prescription drug Ritalin, the problems presented by overprescribing it, its potential for abuse, and ways to prevent such abuse
"Parents, students, and educators may find the book helpful for addressing the potential pressure, social stigma, and recreational Ritalin abuse that may result from listening to uninformed classmates." Booklist
Includes glossary and bibliographical references

Bode, Janet
Food fight; a guide to eating disorders for preteens and their parents. Simon & Schuster Bks. for Young Readers 1997 154p $16   **616.85**
1. Eating disorders
ISBN 0-689-80272-2   LC 96-29186
"This book defines eating disorders and discusses why they occur, who gets them, and what to do to help. Nutrition facts are also provided. A section for adults tells how to recognize eating disorders in children, how to get professional help, and what parents can do. . . . Bode includes numerous personal stories from preteens and adults. A list of organizations is appended." Horn Book Guide
"Bode's approach is highly readable and her tone is conversational. . . . Solid information is presented." SLJ
Includes bibliographical references

Burby, Liza N.
Bulimia nervosa; the secret cycle of bingeing and purging. Rosen Pub. Group 1998 64p il (Teen health library of eating disorder prevention) $17.95 (7 and up)   **616.85**
1. Bulimia
ISBN 0-8239-2762-8   LC 98-16888
Introduces the eating disorder known as bulimia nervosa, including its development, its prevention, and sources of help
Includes bibliographical references

Clarke, Alicia
Coping with self-mutilation; a helping book for teens who hurt themselves. Rosen Pub. Group 1999 104p $17.95 (7 and up)   **616.85**
1. Self-mutilation
ISBN 0-8239-2559-5   LC 98-54123
Discusses self-mutilating behavior in teens, including possible causes and avenues for recovery
"Emphasis is placed on self-help measures and available treatment. Brief, personal stories and profiles illustrate the author's points." SLJ
Includes bibliographical references

Davis, Brangien
What's real, what's ideal; overcoming a negative body image. Rosen Pub. Group 1999 64p il (Teen health library of eating disorder prevention) $17.95 (7 and up)   **616.85**
1. Eating disorders 2. Self-perception
ISBN 0-8239-2771-7   LC 98-29941
The author "defines for readers what it means to have a negative body image, what some of the causes might be, and suggestions for overcoming self-defeating perceptions and finding peace within one's own skin. This title also discusses the practice of self-mutilation, which is closely tied to eating disorders and too often not mentioned." Voice Youth Advocates
Includes bibliographical references

Depression; Henny H. Kim, editor. Greenhaven Press 1999 186p (Contemporary issues companion) lib bdg $20.96; pa $12.96 (7 and up)   **616.85**
1. Depression (Psychology)
ISBN 1-56510-889-2 (lib bdg); 1-56510-888-4 (pa)
LC 98-21728
"The essays included in this volume present a general introduction to the various types of depression, current and potential treatments for the disorder, and the way in which depression affects the lives of those afflicted with it." Publishers's note
Includes bibliographical references

Drohan, Michele Ingber
Weight-loss programs; weighing the risks and realities. Rosen Pub. Group 1998 64p il (Teen health library of eating disorder prevention) $17.95 (7 and up)   **616.85**
1. Eating disorders 2. Weight loss
ISBN 0-8239-2770-9   LC 98-4418
Discusses the relationship between health and diet and examines a variety of commercial weight-loss programs and the health risks that they pose to their members
"The book may not find favor with national weight-loss chains, but it provides youth with important information regarding weight-loss programs and alternatives." Booklist
Includes glossary and bibliographical references

Eating disorders; Myra H. Immell, book editor. Greenhaven Press 1999 191p (Contemporary issues companion) lib bdg $20.96; pa $12.96 (7 and up)   **616.85**
1. Eating disorders
ISBN 1-56510-895-7 (lib bdg); 1-56510-894-9 (pa)
    LC 98-35418
"In this anthology, contributing authors explore issues related to anorexia nervosa, bulimia, compulsive overeating, and other eating disorders. Through . . . essays and personal narratives, readers gain insight into the causes, effects, and treatments of the different types of eating disorders." Publisher's note
Includes bibliographical references

Frankenberger, Elizabeth
Food and love; dealing with family attitudes about weight. Rosen Pub. Group 1998 64p il (Teen health library of eating disorder prevention) $17.95 (7 and up)   **616.85**
1. Eating disorders 2. Food—Psychological aspects
ISBN 0-8239-2760-1   LC 98-16922
Examines the role that food plays in the home and how the family affects self-image, and provides suggestions for healthy living to protect against eating disorders
"This is an excellent title for someone who may have food issues but needs a gentle introduction to the topic." Voice Youth Advocates
Includes bibliographical references

Frissell, Susan
Eating disorders and weight control; [by] Susan Frissell & Paula Harney. Enslow Pubs. 1998 128p (Teen issues) lib bdg $18.95 (7 and up)   **616.85**
1. Eating disorders 2. Weight loss
ISBN 0-89490-919-3   LC 97-12489
Discusses weight control, body image, and eating disorders including the social pressures which may cause them; presents information about diet, nutrition, and exercise
The authors "offer information about symptoms as well as organizations that give treatment and support. Chapter notes, a glossary, and an extensive bibliography round out an excellent resource." Booklist

Harmon, Dan
Anorexia nervosa; starving for attention. Chelsea House 1998 87p il (Encyclopedia of psychological disorders) $24.95 (7 and up)   **616.85**
1. Anorexia nervosa 2. Bulimia
ISBN 0-7910-4901-9   LC 98-25197
Explores the truth and misconceptions regarding anorexia nervosa by examining its history, causes, considerations, treatment, and related eating disorders
"The special articles found within the text offer chilling case studies of anorexia victims such as actress Tracey Gold, gymnast Christy Henrich, and author Marya Hornbacher. The photographs of these young women are startling testaments to anorexia's effects." Voice Youth Advocates
Includes glossary and bibliographical references

Klebanoff, Susan, 1955-
Ups & downs; how to beat the blues and teen depression; written by Susan Klebanoff and Ellen Luborsky; illustrated by Andy Cooke. Price/Stern/Sloan 1999 90p il $13.89; pa $4.99   **616.85**
1. Depression (Psychology)
ISBN 0-8431-7460-9; 0-8431-7450-1 (pa)
    LC 98-46802
Examines the nature, causes, and effects of depression, where to turn for help, and ways to cope with it
This is a "remarkably complete resource written in a clear, down-to-earth style that is accessible to reluctant readers." SLJ

Moragne, Wendy
Dyslexia. Millbrook Press 1997 96p il (Millbrook medical library) lib bdg $23.90 (7 and up)   **616.85**
1. Dyslexia
ISBN 0-7613-0206-9   LC 96-31119
Explains the nature of dyslexia, the various forms of treatment, and the many challenges faced by those living with this condition. Includes case studies and interviews
"This is an excellent source for term papers." BAYA Book Rev
Includes glossary and bibliographical references

Ng, Gina
Everything you need to know about self-mutilation; a helping book for teens who hurt themselves. Rosen Pub. Group 1998 64p il (Need to know library) lib bdg $16.95 (7 and up)   **616.85**
1. Self-mutilation 2. Adolescent psychology
ISBN 0-8239-2758-X   LC 98-20115
Explores ways of dealing with the anger and emotional pain that may cause teens to mutilate themselves
Includes bibliographical references

O'Brien, Eileen, 1955-
Starving to win; athletes and eating disorders. Rosen Pub. Group 1998 64p il (Teen health library of eating disorder prevention) lib bdg $17.95 (7 and up)   **616.85**
1. Eating disorders 2. Athletes
ISBN 0-8239-2764-4   LC 98-16884
Explains why many young athletes are vulnerable to eating disorders and what they can do to prevent them
Includes bibliographical references

Sanders, Pete
Anorexia and bulimia; by Pete Sanders and Steve Myers; illustrated by Mike Lacy and Liz Sawyer. Copper Beech Bks. 1999 32p il (What do you know about) lib bdg $21.90   **616.85**
1. Anorexia nervosa 2. Bulimia
ISBN 0-7613-0914-4   LC 98-47318
First published 1995 in the United Kingdom with title: Anorexia, bulimia, and other eating disorders

Sanders, Pete—*Continued*

This look at the nature, causes, and effects of anorexia and bulimia focuses on "Nicky, who looks about 12 or 13, decides she's too fat and stops eating on a regular basis. In addition to her self-image problem, the girl misses her father after her parents' recent divorce. She resorts to lying about when and where she eats and finally gets caught. Her mother eventually seeks professional help for her daughter." SLJ

Silverstein, Alvin

Depression; [by] Alvin and Virginia Silverstein and Laura Silverstein Nunn. Enslow Pubs. 1997 128p il (Diseases and people) lib bdg $18.95 (7 and up)   **616.85**

1. Depression (Psychology)
ISBN 0-89490-713-1   LC 97-1789

Discusses the causes, symptoms, and treatments of depression, examining the different types of depression and their effects on the individual and on society

This "is an exceptional treatment of a difficult and sometimes controversial subject. . . . The authors do a splendid job of avoiding tediousness and complication. . . . At the same time, they avoid oversimplification." Sci Books Films

Includes glossary and bibliographical references

Smith, Erica

Anorexia nervosa; when food is the enemy. Rosen Pub. Group 1999 64p il (Teen health library of eating disorder prevention) lib bdg $17.95 (7 and up)   **616.85**

1. Anorexia nervosa
ISBN 0-8239-2766-0   LC 98-29713

Describes the origins and symptoms of anorexia nervosa, who is at risk, why it develops in certain individuals, and how it can be controlled by healthy eating habits

Includes bibliographical references

Vollstadt, Elizabeth Weiss, 1942-

Teen eating disorders. Lucent Bks. 1999 112p il (Teen issues) lib bdg $17.96 (7 and up)   **616.85**

1. Eating disorders
ISBN 1-56006-516-8   LC 99-10031

"After defining eating disorders, Vollstadt discusses possible causes and physical consequences (there's a separate section on eating disorders among males), and clearly explains current treatments. She integrates many anecdotal stories, but the tone of text remains detached and objective. Black-and-white photos, . . . charts, and cartoons are scattered through the book." Booklist

Includes bibliographical references

Weaver, Robyn M.

Depression. Lucent Bks. 1999 96p il (Lucent overview series) lib bdg $17.96 (7 and up)

                                            616.85

1. Depression (Psychology)
ISBN 1-56006-437-4   LC 98-8464

"Weaver concisely defines depression, looks at the three forms it can take and who is at risk, and provides a clear discussion of the causes and current recommended and alternative treatments. He also explains how to obtain help." Booklist

Includes glossary and bibliographical references

Wolff, Lisa, 1954-

Teen depression. Lucent Bks. 1999 112p il (Teen issues) lib bdg $22.45 (7 and up)   **616.85**

1. Depression (Psychology)
ISBN 1-56006-519-2   LC 98-16379

Discusses the nature, possible causes, special problems, and both conventional and alternative treatments of depression

"Wolff's prose is clear. . . . [This] will easily satisfy class assignments." Booklist

Includes bibliographical references

616.86   Substance abuse (Drug abuse)

Banfield, Susan

Inside recovery; how the twelve step program can work for you. Rosen Pub. Group 1998 64p il (Drug abuse prevention library) $16.95   **616.86**

1. Twelve-step programs 2. Alcoholism 3. Drug abuse
ISBN 0-8239-2634-6   LC 98-11797

Describes the practices and principles of twelve-step programs, how they can be used in dealing with such problems as alcoholism and drug addiction, and how to get involved in them

"Includes a glossary, a listing of various twelve step programs, a further reading list, and an index. The book is packed with information that should be valuable to the curious, those needing help, and the researcher." Book Rep

Bridgers, Jay

Everything you need to know about having an addictive personality. Rosen Pub. Group 1998 64p il (Need to know library) lib bdg $17.95 (7 and up)   **616.86**

1. Compulsive behavior 2. Drug abuse
ISBN 0-8239-2777-6   LC 98-8496

Discusses the nature of addictions to gambling, food, sex, alcohol, and other drugs, how they form and develop, their negative effects, and how to deal with them

Includes bibliographical references

Hyde, Margaret Oldroyd, 1917-

Mind drugs; by Margaret O. Hyde with Duke D. Fisher, Elizabeth Forsyth, Allan Y. Cohen. 6th ed. Millbrook Press 1998 128p lib bdg $23.90 (7 and up)   **616.86**

1. Drugs 2. Drug abuse
ISBN 0-7613-0970-5   LC 98-20392

First published 1968 by McGraw-Hill

Hyde, Margaret Oldroyd, 1917——*Continued*
A "survey of and current attitudes toward the use and abuse of mind-altering substances, including LSD, uppers, downers, marijuana, and legal drugs. Also included are chapters on the legalization controversy and alternatives to drugs. Lists of organizations, hotlines, and websites are appended." Horn Book Guide
Includes bibliographical references

Shepherd, K. R. (Kenneth Ronald)
Drugs and low self-esteem; [by] Kenneth R. Shepherd. Rosen Pub. Group 1998 64p il (Drug abuse prevention library) $17.95 (7 and up)
                                                616.86
1. Drug abuse 2. Self-esteem
ISBN 0-8239-2826-8   LC 98-8497
Discusses various aspects of low self-esteem, how it can lead to drug abuse, the negative consequences, and where to get help for such a problem
Includes bibliographical references

616.9   Other diseases

Landau, Elaine
Tuberculosis. Watts 1995 96p il lib bdg $22 (7 and up)   **616.9**
1. Tuberculosis
ISBN 0-531-12555-6   LC 94-39305
"A Venture book"
"Explains tuberculosis and its method of transmission, traces its etiology, and explains why it is presently resurfacing globally. In conclusion, she counters the belief of middle-class Americans that TB only affects the poor, the homeless, and AIDS patients." Booklist
"A well-organized, well-written look at the resurgence of this deadly disease that offers an extensive appendix for further information." SLJ
Includes bibliographical references

Silverstein, Alvin
Chickenpox and shingles; [by] Alvin and Virginia Silverstein and Laura Silverstein Nunn. Enslow Pubs. 1998 128p il (Diseases and people) lib bdg $18.95 (7 and up)   **616.9**
1. Chickenpox 2. Shingles (Disease)
ISBN 0-89490-715-8   LC 97-34041
"The book begins with a general profile of the two diseases mentioned in the title—their causes, transmission, symptoms, treatment, and prevention. In subsequent chapters, each disease is described in greater detail. The relationship between these two viral infections is discussed, and how one may develop immunity to them is examined." Sci Books Films
Includes bibliographical references

Measles and rubella; [by] Alvin, Virginia, and Robert Silverstein. Enslow Pubs. 1997 128p il (Diseases and people) lib bdg $18.95 (7 and up)
                                                616.9
1. Measles 2. Rubella
ISBN 0-89490-714-X   LC 97-3785

Tracing the medical history of measles and rubella "from ancient to modern times, this solid work considers symptoms and transmission, including discussion about outbreaks on college campuses and among preschool children that have forced the medical community to reexamine how and when immunizations should be given. The authors also explore the development of the measles vaccine and explain why the diseases continue to pose a health problem. An outstanding curricular supplement . . . as well as a handy, readable reference source." Booklist
Includes glossary and bibliographical references

Smart, P. (Paul), 1957-
Everything you need to know about mononucleosis. Rosen Pub. Group 1998 63p il (Need to know library) lib bdg $16.95 (7 and up)
                                                616.9
1. Mononucleosis
ISBN 0-8239-2550-1   LC 98-10119
Discusses the nature and diagnosis of mononucleosis and how to protect against it or cope with having it
Includes bibliographical references

Veggeberg, Scott
Lyme disease. Enslow Pubs. 1998 104p il (Diseases and people) lib bdg $18.95 (7 and up)
                                                616.9
1. Lyme disease
ISBN 0-7660-1052-X   LC 97-34042
Explores the history of Lyme disease and discusses its symptoms, diagnosis, prevention, and treatment
"This book covers a wide range of information about Lyme disease. The information, accurate and up to date, is presented in ways that are clear, interesting, and imaginative." Sci Books Films
Includes glossary and bibliographical references

616.95   Sexually transmitted diseases

Curran, Christine Perdan
Sexually transmitted diseases. Enslow Pubs. 1998 128p il (Diseases and people) lib bdg $19.95 (7 and up)   **616.95**
1. Sexually transmitted diseases
ISBN 0-7660-1050-3   LC 97-44140
Examines the history, symptoms, treatment, and prevention of such sexually transmitted diseases as syphilis, gonorrhea, herpes, AIDS, and hepatitis
Includes glossary and bibliographical references

Little, Marjorie
Sexually transmitted diseases. Chelsea House 1999 110p il (21st century health and wellness) lib bdg $24.95 (7 and up)   **616.95**
1. Sexually transmitted diseases
ISBN 0-7910-5528-0
First published 1991 in the Encyclopedic of health series
Discusses the symptoms, diagnosis, treatment, and complications of such diseases as syphilis, gonorrhea, herpes, and HIV

616.97 Diseases of the immune system

AIDS: opposing viewpoints; Tamara L. Roleff, Charles P. Cozic, book editors. Greenhaven Press 1998 203p il lib bdg $26.20; pa $16.20 (7 and up) **616.97**
1. AIDS (Disease)
ISBN 1-56510-667-9 (lib bdg); 1-56510-666-0 (pa)
LC 97-28424
"Opposing viewpoints series"
Replaces the edition published 1988 under the editorship of Lynn Hall and Thomas Modl
"This examines the many aspects of the disease, its controversial prevention strategies, and its treatments. . . . The currency and the wide-ranging articles from both mainstream and less well known sources, juxtaposed to invite thought and debate, are especially valuable." Booklist
Includes bibliographical references

Check, William A.
AIDS; introduction by C. Everett Koop. rev ed. Chelsea House 1998 c1999 128p il (Encyclopedia of health) $19.95 (7 and up) **616.97**
1. AIDS (Disease)
ISBN 0-7910-4885-3 LC 98-195764
First published 1988
"Each chapter follows an AIDS-related issue from its late 1970s—early 1980s identification and discusses the social and medical changes in information, attitude, and treatment to the present. . . . The book does an excellent job of updating YA collections with current AIDS/HIV information while integrating the disease's history appropriately throughout the text." Booklist

Latta, Sara L.
Allergies. Enslow Pubs. 1998 128p (Diseases and people) lib bdg $18.95 (7 and up) **616.97**
1. Allergy
ISBN 0-7660-1048-1 LC 97-34156
Explores the history of information about allergies and discusses symptoms, diagnosis, prevention, and treatments
"Fictional case histories and true anecdotes add interest. Black-and-white photos and information boxes are included." Horn Book Guide
Includes glossary and bibliographical references

Majure, Janet, 1954-
AIDS. Enslow Pubs. 1998 128p il (Diseases and people) lib bdg $19.95 (7 and up) **616.97**
1. AIDS (Disease)
ISBN 0-7660-1182-8 LC 97-44139
Discusses the history, diagnosis, causes, prevention, and treatment of a disease that has affected more people over a wider geographic range than any other epidemic
Includes glossary and bibliographical references

Packer, Kenneth L.
HIV infection; the facts you need to know. Watts 1998 160p il lib bdg $24; pa $9.95 (7 and up) **616.97**
1. AIDS (Disease)
ISBN 0-531-11333-7 (lib bdg); 0-531-15899-3 (pa)
LC 97-13755
Explains HIV, how infection with it can lead to AIDS, how it is transmitted, and what is being done to prevent and cure the disease
"The depth of information and attention to detail make this book unique. . . . Packer provides a thorough, concise examination of the biology of the HIV virus and its effects on the immune system. . . . Readers will find vital information appropriate both for reports and personal elucidation." SLJ
Includes glossary and bibliographical references

Shein, Lori, 1957-
AIDS. Lucent Bks. 1998 112p il (Lucent overview series) lib bdg $22.45 (7 and up) **616.97**
1. AIDS (Disease)
ISBN 1-56006-193-6 LC 98-9461
An overview of AIDS including information about its discovery, methods of prevention, testing for HIV infection, the global epidemic, and what the future holds
Includes bibliographical references

Silverstein, Alvin
AIDS; an all-about guide for young adults; [by] Alvin and Virginia Silverstein, and Laura Silverstein Nunn. Enslow Pubs. 1999 160p il (Issues in focus) lib bdg $19.95 (7 and up) **616.97**
1. AIDS (Disease)
ISBN 0-89490-716-6 LC 98-37988
"Eight chapters provide detailed information about the history of the disease; current methods for diagnosis, treatment, and prevention; and the global public-health impacts. Numerous personal profiles effectively illustrate various aspects of the disease and both patients' and societal reactions to it. The writing is crisp and professional. . . . Black-and-white photos, diagrams, and graphs add clarity and impact, and frequent text boxes punctuate the often-complex wording with interesting highlights." SLJ
Includes glossary and bibliographical references

616.99 Tumors

Benowitz, Steven I.
Cancer. Enslow Pubs. 1999 128p il (Diseases and people) lib bdg $19.95 (7 and up) **616.99**
1. Cancer
ISBN 0-7660-1181-X LC 98-36123
Discusses the history, symptoms, diagnosis, treatment, prevention, and different kinds of cancer, as well as the possible impact of research on the future
Includes bibliographical references

Yount, Lisa
Cancer. Lucent Bks. 1999 111p il (Lucent overview series) lib bdg $17.96 (7 and up)
                                                            616.99
1. Cancer
ISBN 1-56006-363-7   LC 98-54797
First published 1991
Yount presents a discussion of how "cancer cells develop and the different types of the disease. While offering information on the possible carcinogenic effects of food additives, smoking, pesticides, and even electromagnetic fields, she explains difficult concepts in simple terms. Diagnostic techniques and traditional and alternative treatment options are presented including chemotherapy, radiation, gene therapy, biofeedback, and reflexology." SLJ
Includes bibliographical references

617.6   Dentistry

Lee, Jordan
Coping with braces and other orthodontic work. Rosen Pub. Group 1998 95p il lib bdg $17.95
                                                            617.6
1. Orthodontics
ISBN 0-8239-2721-0   LC 98-9276
"Lee describes various procedures involved in orthodontic care from the taking of impressions to the removal of the hardware. Discussions about the assorted accidents that can happen, how various appliances work, and how the doctor develops a plan of treatment are also included. The text is well written and reassuring, reminding readers that treatments are available to reduce or eliminate pain." SLJ
Includes bibliographical references

Rourke, Arlene C., 1944-
Teeth and braces. Rourke Publs. 1989 32p il (Looking good) lib bdg $19.93   **617.6**
1. Teeth 2. Orthodontics
ISBN 0-86625-282-7   LC 88-11642
Discusses the function, anatomy, and care of teeth, dental problems, and how orthodontists straighten teeth using braces and other appliances
This is "short, to the point, well-illustrated, and can supplement what's on the shelf." SLJ
Includes bibliographical references

Siegel, Dorothy Schainman
Dental health; [by] Dorothy Siegel; introduction by C. Everett Koop. Chelsea House 1993 111p il (Encyclopedia of health) lib bdg $19.95 (7 and up)
                                                            617.6
1. Dentistry 2. Teeth
ISBN 0-7910-0014-1   LC 92-45205
This overview of dental care includes a discussion of the basic anatomy of the teeth, jaws and gums. Oral hygiene and advances in dental technology are reviewed
Includes glossary and bibliographical references

617.8   Otology and audiology

Landau, Elaine
Deafness. 21st Cent. Bks. (NY) 1994 64p il (Understanding illness) lib bdg $18.90   **617.8**
1. Deaf
ISBN 0-8050-2993-1   LC 94-13843
"The text opens with a series of vignettes about the varying presentations of deafness and then moves on to a discussion of the causes of hearing loss. Case histories are also used to highlight issues concerning the acceptance of individuals with deafness in our society; this is followed by a recounting of achievements of other individuals with impaired hearing. The material is clear and easy to read. . . . The book is a useful introduction to the issues presented by impaired hearing." Sci Books Films
Includes glossary and bibliographical references

617.9   Transplantation of tissue and organs

Fradin, Dennis B.
"We have conquered pain"; the discovery of anesthesia; [by] Dennis Brindell Fradin. Margaret K. McElderry Bks. 1996 148p il $16   **617.9**
1. Anesthetics
ISBN 0-689-50587-6   LC 95-35538
"Fradin relates the story of four men, each of whom claimed to have discovered the use of anesthesia for medical purposes. . . . The author examines the lives of Crawford Long, Horace Wells, William Morton, and Charles Jackson, and interprets the role each man played in the great discovery and the battle over recognition that ensued. . . . It's a fascinating and objectively presented piece of medical history. Good-quality photographs and reproductions expand and extend interest and information." SLJ
Includes bibliographical references

Wilkinson, Beth
Coping with the dangers of tattooing, body piercing, and branding. Rosen Pub. Group 1998 126p il lib bdg $18.95 (7 and up)   **617.9**
1. Tattooing 2. Body piercing
ISBN 0-8239-2717-2   LC 97-45683
Gives information needed to make an informed decision about body modification including the laws and safety regulations surrounding this business
"A clearly written look at body-making arts. . . . The dangers are explained and strongly emphasized throughout the book, and readers are cautioned against making decisions in haste, at too early an age, or otherwise ill-advisedly." SLJ
Includes glossary and bibliographical references

618.1 Gynecology

Diamond, Shifra N.
Everything you need to know about going to the gynecologist. Rosen Pub. Group 1999 64p il (Need to know library) lib bdg $17.95 (7 and up) **618.1**
1. Gynecologists 2. Sex education 3. Women—Health and hygiene
ISBN 0-8239-2839-X LC 98-40929
Describes what to expect in a gynecological examination, discusses birth control methods, the female reproductive system, and possible health problems and treatment
"An appendix of organization contact information, including some Web sites, may help readers find more detailed information." SLJ
Includes bibliographical references

618.2 Obstetrics

Landau, Elaine
Multiple births. Watts 1998 64p il $22 **618.2**
1. Multiple birth
ISBN 0-531-20309-3 LC 96-40224
"A First book"
Explores the phenomenon of multiple births, including those of twins, triplets, and larger groupings, discussing possible causes, medical issues, effects on the families, and other moral and practical concerns
Includes bibliographical references

620.1 Engineering mechanics and materials

Graham, Ian, 1953-
Water power. Raintree Steck-Vaughn Pubs. 1999 48p il (Energy forever?) $25.69 **620.1**
1. Water power
ISBN 0-8172-5363-7 LC 98-13438
Examines the historical uses of water as a source of energy, the advantages and disadvantages, and new advances in harnessing water power
Includes bibliographical references

621 Applied physics

Challoner, Jack
Energy. Dorling Kindersley 1993 64p il (Eyewitness science) $15.95 **621**
1. Energy resources 2. Force and energy
ISBN 1-56458-232-9 LC 92-54479
Surveys various sources of energy and the ways in which they have been harnessed
This "serves well as a first exploration of its topic, emphasizing historical connections but also considering technological and societal aspects. [This book's] striking visual impact will draw in even the most casual readers." SLJ

Silverstein, Alvin
Energy; [by] Alvin Silverstein, Virginia Silverstein, Laura Silverstein Nunn. 21st Cent. Bks. (Brookfield) 1998 64p il $23.40 **621**
1. Energy resources
ISBN 0-7613-3222-7 LC 98-41915
Discusses the sources and uses of different types of energy, both natural and man-made, including electrical, magnetic, light, heat, sound, and nuclear energy
Includes bibliographical references

621.3 Electrical engineering; superconductivity; electronics; communication engineering; computers

Pinna, Simon de
Electricity; photography by Chris Fairclough. Raintree Steck-Vaughn Pubs. 1998 48p il (Science projects) $24.26 **621.3**
1. Electricity 2. Science—Experiments
ISBN 0-8172-4945-1 LC 97-24637
Introduces the basic concept of electricity through simple experiments that can be performed at home or at school
Includes bibliographical references

Pollard, Michael, 1931-
The light bulb and how it changed the world. Facts on File 1995 46p il $16.95 **621.3**
1. Electricity 2. Inventions
ISBN 0-8160-3145-0 LC 94-15226
"This volume first reviews the electric inventions that preceded Edison's light bulb—the battery, the telegraph, and the telephone—and then explains how electricity has been generated, supplied, and used ever since." Publisher's note
Includes bibliographical references

621.36 Applied optics and paraphotic technology

Morgan, Nina
Lasers. Raintree Steck-Vaughn Pubs. 1997 48p il (20th century inventions) $24.26 **621.36**
1. Lasers
ISBN 0-8172-4812-9 LC 96-44293
Explains what lasers are and how they are used in communications, medicine, industry, and warfare, as well as possible future uses
Includes glossary

621.381 Electronics

Hoare, Stephen
Digital revolution. Raintree Steck-Vaughn Pubs. 1999 48p il (20th century inventions) $24.26 **621.381**
1. Electronics
ISBN 0-8172-4897-8 LC 97-32063

Hoare, Stephen—*Continued*

"The book is organized by category—entertainment, communications, work, home, and cars. The technologies covered include compact discs (all varieties), telephones, televisions, watches, and cameras. Cutting-edge technology such as DVD (digital videodiscs), HDTV (high-definition television), and global-positioning systems are included as well." SLJ

Includes bibliographical references

621.383 Telegraphy

Coe, Lewis, 1911-

The telegraph; a history of Morse's invention and its predecessors in the United States. McFarland & Co. 1993 184p il $28.50 **621.383**

1. Morse, Samuel Finley Breese, 1791-1872 2. Telegraph

ISBN 0-89950-736-0   LC 92-53597

This study of the development of the telegraph includes brief biographical sketches of Samuel Morse and other inventors

Includes bibliographical references

621.4 Heat engineering and prime movers

Graham, Ian, 1953-

Wind power. Raintree Steck-Vaughn Pubs. 1999 48p il (Energy forever?) $25.69 **621.4**

1. Wind power

ISBN 0-8172-5364-5   LC 98-25665

Discusses traditional and developing ways of using wind power as a source of energy

Includes bibliographical references

621.43 Internal-combustion engines

Maurer, Richard, 1950-

Rocket! how a toy launched the space age. Crown 1995 64p il lib bdg $17.99 **621.43**

1. Rocketry

ISBN 0-517-59629-6   LC 94-19243

"Maurer guides readers from early science fiction speculations of rocket travel to the scientific trials and errors of three important scientists—Robert Goddard, Hermann Oberth, and Konstantin Tsiolkovsky—and to the U.S.-Soviet space race." Booklist

"An interesting and informative introduction to the history of modern rocketry. . . . Well-captioned black-and-white and full-color photographs, diagrams, and reproductions add interest." SLJ

Includes bibliographical references

Miller, Ron, 1947-

The history of rockets. Watts 1999 128p il lib bdg $24 **621.43**

1. Rocketry

ISBN 0-531-11430-9   LC 97-49808

"A Venture book"

"Miller opens with homespun demonstrations of Isaac Newton's relevant principles, then retraces the chain of experiments, disasters, and refinements that began with Archytas of Tarentum's steam-driven wooden pigeon and culminated in the mighty Saturn 5. . . . Taking pains to point out how many uses rockets have beyond carrying weapons, Miller brings readers into the present era of active space exploration and space-plane designs that look beyond the shuttle, then closes with both a page of recommended books and two pages of Web sites." SLJ

621.47 Solar-energy engineering

Graham, Ian, 1953-

Solar power. Raintree Steck-Vaughn Pubs. 1999 48p il (Energy forever?) $25.69 **621.47**

1. Solar energy

ISBN 0-8172-5362-9   LC 98-5839

Examines solar energy, its history, uses, advantages and disadvantages, and new developments in the field

Includes bibliographical references

621.48 Nuclear engineering

Kidd, J. S. (Jerry S.)

Quarks and sparks; the story of nuclear power; [by] J.S. Kidd and Renee A. Kidd. Facts on File 1999 146p il (Science and society) $19.95 (7 and up) **621.48**

1. Nuclear energy

ISBN 0-8160-3587-3   LC 98-44389

Examines the people, events, and motivations leading up to modern-day discoveries and advances in nuclear physics

"Extensive scientific explanations are kept manageable, thanks to consistent references to their historical context; and descriptions of the nuclear race during the Second World War are especially riveting." Booklist

Includes bibliographical references

621.8 Machine engineering

Locke, Ian

The wheel and how it changed the world. Facts on File 1995 46p il maps $16.95 **621.8**

1. Wheels

ISBN 0-8160-3143-6   LC 94-15228

This history of the wheel's impact on society ranges from discussion of the earliest potter's wheel to the nineteenth-century flywheel and beyond

Includes bibliographical references

623.4 Ordnance

Cohen, Daniel, 1936-

The Manhattan Project. 21st Cent. Bks. (Brookfield) 1999 128p il lib bdg $22.90 (7 and up) **623.4**

1. Manhattan Project 2. Atomic bomb

ISBN 0-7613-0359-6   LC 98-44499

Cohen, Daniel, 1936-—*Continued*
Discusses the personalities and events involved in the research, development and detonation of the atomic bombs built by the United States in the 1940s
"Historically and scientifically illuminating, this well-written, dramatic story of political intrigue and the birth of the arms race conveys the magnitude of one of the twentieth century's most profoundly defining events." Booklist
Includes bibliographical references

Weapons; an international encyclopedia from 5000 B.C. to 2000 A.D; [by] the Diagram Group. St. Martin's Press 1990 336p il $29.95; pa $19.95
623.4
1. Weapons—History
ISBN 0-312-03951-4; 0-312-03950-6 (pa)
LC 90-28498
First published 1980
This "is a visual display of combat weapons of every century and culture. It is not, however, arranged alphabetically or chronologically. Instead, chapters are ordered by function. . . . The historical and regional indexes will be useful to readers who want to focus on weapons of a particular time or place. . . . The quality of illustrations is what distinguishes Diagram Group publications, and these are up to the usual standards. More than 2,500 black-and-white drawings are included." Booklist

623.7 Military vehicles

Harvey, Ian
Tanks; illustrated by Richard Chasemore; written by Ian Harvey. DK Pub. 1996 30p il (Look inside cross-sections) pa $8.95
623.7
1. Military tanks
ISBN 0-7894-0768-X
LC 96-13961
Takes a look at the construction and inner workings of a variety of military tanks

623.8 Nautical engineering and seamanship

Butterfield, Moira
Ships; illustrated by Jonathan Potter; written by Moira Butterfield. Dorling Kindersley 1994 32p il (Look inside cross-sections) pa $5.95
623.8
1. Ships 2. Seafaring life
ISBN 1-56458-521-2
LC 93-46382
"Ten ships are presented, each in a two-page spread (except for the *USS Lexington*, which gets four) that contains on average six sentences of facts and a box entitled 'Technical Data,' which lists length, beam, and other details. Children will probably be more interested in the clear, detailed, well-labeled drawings." SLJ
Includes glossary

Graham, Ian, 1953-
Boats. Raintree Steck-Vaughn Pubs. 1999 32p il (Built for speed) $22.83; pa $7.95
623.8
1. Motorboats
ISBN 0-8172-4221-X; 0-8172-8071-5 (pa)
LC 97-48416

Describes how various kinds of boats are designed and constructed for speed

Boats, ships, submarines, and other floating machines. Kingfisher (NY) 1993 40p il (How things work) hardcover o.p. paperback available $6.95
623.8
1. Ships 2. Boats and boating
ISBN 1-85697-867-2 (pa)
LC 92-33588
Text, illustrations, and diagrams examine different kinds of boats and how they work. Includes simple experiments and activities
"The pages are busy but well planned. . . . The information is introductory at best. . . . But what's here is nicely presented; the drawings are colorful, clear, and adequately labeled." Booklist

Paine, Lincoln P.
Ships of the world; an historical encyclopedia; with contributions by James H. Terry and Hal Fessenden. Houghton Mifflin 1997 680p il maps $50
623.8
1. Ships—Encyclopedias
ISBN 0-395-71556-3
LC 97-12872
This work contains "the stories of more than 1000 of the most important or well-known vessels throughout history. Each entry contains basic specifications, narrative history, and a source note. . . . Along with the real stories of *Titanic* and *Amistad*, there are listings for historically important ships like the *Mayflower* and the *Nina, Pinta,* and *Santa Maria* as well the *Lusitania* and the *Bismarck.* There are even entries for literary ships like the *African Queen.* Various chronologies describe archaeological sites, maritime technology, voyages of discovery, naval history, and disasters." Libr J

624 Civil engineering

Macaulay, David, 1946-
Underground. Houghton Mifflin 1976 109p il $18; pa $9.95
624
1. Civil engineering 2. Building 3. Public utilities
ISBN 0-395-24739-X; 0-395-34065-9 (pa)
LC 76-13688
In this "examination of the intricate support systems that lie beneath the street levels of our cities, Macaulay explains the ways in which foundations for buildings are laid or reinforced, and how the various utilities or transportation services are constructed." Bull Cent Child Books
"Introduced by a visual index—a bird's eye view of a busy, hypothetical intersection with colored indicators marking the specific locations analyzed in subsequent pages—detailed illustrations are combined with a clear, precise narrative to make the subject comprehensible and fascinating." Horn Book
Includes glossary

Wilkinson, Philip, 1955-
Super structures; written by Philip Wilkinson. DK Pub. 1996 44p il (Inside guides) $15.95 **624**
1. Civil engineering 2. Architecture 3. Buildings
ISBN 0-7894-1011-7

Wilkinson, Philip, 1955-—*Continued*
"Wilkinson explains the construction of *Super Structures* such as a skyscraper, a theater complex, the Chunnel, a 2808-foot bridge, a dam, a roller coaster, a super airport, a multilayer freeway, a nuclear reactor, and an ocean-based oil drilling rig." SLJ
Includes glossary

625.1   Railroads

Johnstone, Michael
Trains; written by Michael Johnstone. Dorling Kindersley 1995 32p il (Look inside cross-sections) pa $6.95   **625.1**
1. Railroads
ISBN 0-7894-0319-6   LC 95-15135
This volume includes labeled cross-section drawings of 10 history-making trains, beginning with the 1829 'Rocket' steam engine and ending with 'Le Shuttle' which traverses the English Channel Tunnel
Includes glossary

628.9   Fire-fighting technology

Beil, Karen Magnuson
Fire in their eyes; wildfires and the people who fight them. Harcourt Brace & Co. 1999 64p il $18; pa $10   **628.9**
1. Fire fighters 2. Forest fires 3. Forest ecology
ISBN 0-15-201043-2; 0-15-201042-4 (pa)
                    LC 98-6378
Depicts in text and photographs the training, equipment, and real-life experiences of people who risk their lives to battle wildfires, as well as people who use fire for ecological reasons
"The ferocity of fire is forcefully depicted in both narrative and well-chosen photographs." Horn Book Guide

Gorrell, Gena K. (Gena Kinton), 1946-
Catching fire; the story of firefighting. Tundra Bks. 1999 152p il $16.95   **628.9**
1. Fire fighting
ISBN 0-88776-430-4   LC 98-61435
"Beginning with fire fighting through history, the discussion turns to modern techniques, equipment, and the rescue function of fire fighting teams as well as special circumstances such as fires in forests and on ships, planes, subways. The book closes with an informative chapter on how to prevent fires and what to do when there is a fire. Full of pertinent information and intriguing anecdotes." Booklist

Masoff, Joy, 1951-
Fire! principal photography by Jack Reznicki and Barry D. Smith. Scholastic Ref. 1998 48p il $16.95   **628.9**
1. Fire fighters
ISBN 0-590-97872-1   LC 97-10928

Presents the work done by fire fighters, including the equipment they use, the fires they fight, the rescues and investigations they perform, and the history and future of fire fighting
"Masoff's personal enthusiasm for her subject along with her attention to detail and clear, lively writing set this far above the common run of razzle-dazzle, photo-filled compendia." Horn Book Guide
Includes bibliographical references

629.04   Transportation engineering

Somerville, Louisa
Rescue vehicles; illustrated by Hans Jenssen; written by Louisa Somerville. Dorling Kindersley 1995 32p il (Look inside cross-sections) pa $6.95
                    629.04
1. Vehicles
ISBN 1-56458-879-3   LC 94-23756
This volume includes labeled cross-section drawings of 12 rescue vehicles, including a police car, fire engine, lifeboat, ambulance, and helicopter, with brief text
Includes glossary

Wilson, Anthony, 1939-
Dorling Kindersley visual timeline of transportation. Dorling Kindersley 1995 48p il $16.95 (7 and up)   **629.04**
1. Transportation
ISBN 1-56458-880-7   LC 94-48714
"From transportation on land and water in 10,000 B.C. to future trends [the author] documents innovations and milestones throughout the world (natives in Hawaii were using surfboards when Cook arrived in 1778), as well as related technological developments (fuels, materials) and advances in scientific knowledge. The book is a browser's delight, but there's enough solid information for reports." Booklist

629.13   Aeronautics

Hart, Philip S.
Flying free; America's first black aviators; foreword by Reeve Lindbergh. Lerner Publs. 1992 64p il lib bdg $22.60; pa $6.95   **629.13**
1. African American pilots
ISBN 0-8225-1598-9 (lib bdg); 0-8225-9727-6 (pa)
                    LC 91-21433
Surveys the history of black aviators, from the early black aviation community in Chicago in the 1920s through World War II to modern times
"Hart eloquently documents the lives of America's pioneer black aviators. . . . This well-written account, with quotes from personal and newspaper interviews and historic photographs, brings these inspiring stories to life." SLJ
Includes bibliographical references

Haskins, James, 1941-
Black eagles; African Americans in aviation. Scholastic 1995 196p il $14.95; pa $4.95 **629.13**
1. African American pilots
ISBN 0-590-45912-0; 0-590-45913-9 (pa)
LC 94-18623
"Haskins presents the . . . achievements of African-American aviators from the beginning of the twentieth century to the present." Horn Book Guide
"In addition to introducing the people involved, Haskins ably sets the background scene, revealing a social context of discrimination. . . . An excellent job of dealing with the particular and the more general aspects of 'what it was like'." Booklist
Includes bibliographical references

Taylor, Richard L., 1933-
The first solo flight around the world; the story of Wiley Post and his airplane, the Winnie Mae. Watts 1993 64p il lib bdg $21 **629.13**
1. Post, Wiley, 1898-1935 2. Winnie Mae (Airplane) 3. Air pilots 4. Aeronautics—Flights
ISBN 0-531-20160-0
LC 93-6880
"A First book"
This is "an account of Wiley Post and his *Winnie Mae*, a Lockheed Vega monoplane. Post took off from New York City, headed in a nor'westerly direction on July 5, 1933, returning on July 22. Howard Hughes called this achievement 'the greatest of all time.'" SLJ
Includes bibliographical references

Weiss, Harvey, 1922-
Strange and wonderful aircraft. Houghton Mifflin 1995 64p il $15.95 **629.13**
1. Flight
ISBN 0-395-68716-0
LC 94-3788
"From fables and myths about flying through the Wright brothers' first brief but successful flight, Weiss details humankind's efforts to fly." Booklist
"There are a couple of airplane model instructions in the book, which go along with the explanation of aerodynamics. The materials are easily obtainable and young people should enjoy making the models and testing them out." Appraisal

629.133 Aircraft types

Johnstone, Michael
Planes; illustrated by Hans Jenssen; written by Michael Johnstone. Dorling Kindersley 1994 32p il (Look inside cross-sections) pa $6.95 **629.133**
1. Airplanes
ISBN 1-56458-520-4
LC 93-46373
"Each of the 10 planes featured in this book is drawn in colorful cross sections. Clear labels and narrative texts, coupled with authentic figures, heighten interest and provide information." Sci Books Films
Includes bibliographical references

Nahum, Andrew
Flying machine; written by Andrew Nahum. Knopf 1990 62p il (Eyewitness books) $19; lib bdg $20.99 **629.133**
1. Aeronautics—History
ISBN 0-679-80744-6; 0-679-90744-0 (lib bdg)
LC 90-4007
A photo essay tracing the history and development of aircraft from hot-air balloons to jetliners. Includes information on the principles of flight and the inner workings of various flying machines
"Strikingly clear images leap from a white background; numerous captions and brief text encourage browsing over methodical exploration. The whole effect is made orderly by careful layout and unobtrusive black outlines around each spread." SLJ

The **Visual** dictionary of flight. Dorling Kindersley 1992 64p il (Eyewitness visual dictionaries) $16.95 **629.133**
1. Airplanes 2. Aeronautics
ISBN 1-56458-101-2
LC 92-7670
Text and labeled illustrations depict a variety of historic and modern aircraft and their components, as well as aviation-related equipment
This "offers strikingly visual and comprehensively informative material to provide instant access to the specialized vocabulary of its topic. . . . [It is] eye-catching from cover to cover and [includes] a detailed general index. While simple in presentation [it is] rich in visual splendor." Booklist

629.22 Types of vehicles

Carroll, John, 1943-
4 x 4 vehicles. Chelsea House 1998 80p il $24.95 **629.22**
1. Off-road vehicles
ISBN 0-7910-5004-1
LC 98-18098
Describes the history and development of four-wheel drive vehicles and some of the models manufactured around the world. Also discusses the increasingly popular sport of off-road racing

629.222 Passenger automobiles

Dale, Rodney, 1933-
Early cars. Oxford Univ. Press 1994 64p il (Discoveries and inventions) lib bdg $20 **629.222**
1. Automobiles—History
ISBN 0-19-521002-6
LC 93-3660
Examines the invention, development, and technology of the earliest automobiles, discussing their vital components and how they were refined over the years
Includes bibliographical references

Johnstone, Michael
Cars; illustrated by Alan Austin; written by Michael Johnstone. Dorling Kindersley 1994 32p il (Look inside cross-sections) pa $6.95 **629.222**
1. Automobiles
ISBN 1-56458-681-2
LC 94-18481

Johnstone, Michael—*Continued*
This volume includes labeled cross-section drawings of 11 automobiles with brief text
Includes glossary

Willson, Quentin
Classic American cars; photography by Matthew Ward. DK Pub. 1997 192p il $29.95 (7 and up)
629.222
1. Automobiles
ISBN 0-7894-2083-X   LC 97-16172
This is an illustrated history of American cars from post-World War II to the 1970s
"In this homage to the boldness and beauty of the best, or at least the most legendary, makes and models, 60 are featured in beguiling graphics: front, back, and side shots that capture both sweep and detail. . . . Textual accompaniment highlights production, sales, and design background." Booklist

The ultimate classic car book; [by] Quentin Willson with David Selby. Dorling Kindersley 1995 224p il $29.95 (7 and up)   **629.222**
1. Automobiles
ISBN 0-7894-0159-2   LC 95-11903
"An introduction covers what the term 'classic car' means, goes on to discuss such models by decade, and has a section on the purchase of such a vehicle. One-paragraph profiles of innovators such as Andre Citrone, Ferdinand Porsche, and Lee Iacocca are included. But the drawing card here is the cars. There are more than 90 of them, all displayed in splendid full-color photographs." SLJ

629.228   Racing cars

Hodges, David W.
Classic racing cars; Grand Prix and Indy. Chelsea House 1998 78p il $24.95   **629.228**
1. Automobile racing 2. Automobiles
ISBN 0-7910-4999-X   LC 98-18188
Text and photographs present different kinds of racing cars and explore their history and future

629.4   Astronautics

Cole, Michael D.
Living on Mars; mission to the Red Planet. Enslow Pubs. 1999 48p il (Countdown to space) lib bdg $18.95   **629.4**
1. Space flight to Mars 2. Mars (Planet)—Exploration
ISBN 0-7660-1121-6   LC 98-13125
"Half summary account of what we know about Mars from observations and space probes, and half a speculative mission profile for the first crewed expedition that will be sent there, this book sets the stage for one of our space program's next big objectives. The text is backed by endnotes citing almost as many Web sites as print sources." SLJ

Moon base; first colony in space. Enslow Pubs. 1999 48p il (Countdown to space) lib bdg $18.95
629.4
1. Lunar bases 2. Moon—Exploration
ISBN 0-7660-1118-6   LC 98-13126
Describes the Apollo 11 mission to the moon, explains the need for establishing a moon base, and speculates about future situations in which the base would be used

Johnstone, Michael
The history news in space; author, Michael Johnstone. Candlewick Press 1999 32p il $16.99
629.4
1. Astronautics 2. Outer space—Exploration
ISBN 0-7636-0490-9   LC 98-38682
Uses a newspaper format to take a look at developments that led from the ideas of Copernicus and other early scientists to the technological advances that enabled man to venture to the moon and beyond
"This breezy overview gives readers tantalizing glimpses of the history of space science." SLJ

Stott, Carole
Space exploration; written by Carole Stott; photographed by Steve Gorton. Knopf 1997 59p il (Eyewitness books) $19   **629.4**
1. Astronautics 2. Outer space—Exploration
ISBN 0-679-88563-3   LC 97-9546
"A Dorling Kindersley book"
This survey "touches on an array of space-exploration topics, from the early history of rocketry to animals in orbit, space stations, astronaut underwear, and probes to the outer planets." SLJ
"The book is extensively and very well illustrated, and its images significantly add to the information being presented." Sci Books Films

629.43   Unmanned flight

Cole, Michael D.
Galileo spacecraft; mission to Jupiter. Enslow Pubs. 1999 48p il (Countdown to space) lib bdg $18.95   **629.43**
1. Galileo Project 2. Jupiter (Planet)—Exploration
ISBN 0-7660-1119-4   LC 98-3627
Discusses the travel of the Galileo spacecraft from its launch to its orbit around Jupiter, explaining the goals and accomplishments of the mission
Includes bibliographical references

Wunsch, Susi Trautmann
The adventures of Sojourner; the mission to Mars that thrilled the world. Mikaya Press 1998 60p il $22.95; pa $9.95   **629.43**
1. Space flight to Mars 2. Mars (Planet)—Exploration
ISBN 0-9650493-5-3; 0-9650493-6-1 (pa)
LC 98-7660
Tells the story of the mission that placed the Sojourner remote-control rover on Mars on July 4, 1997
"The photographs not only cover *Sojourner's* movements about the surface of Mars, but also track the entire Mars project from its inception. In addition to an index, there is a time line of all the Mars voyages and a page of astronomical facts." Sci Books Films

629.45 Manned space flight

Baird, Anne

The U.S. Space Camp book of astronauts; foreword by N. Jan Davis; introduction by James B. Odom. Morrow Junior Bks. 1996 48p $16; lib bdg $15.93 **629.45**

1. Astronauts 2. Astronautics

ISBN 0-688-12226-4; 0-688-12227-2 (lib bdg)

LC 95-10634

"An Official U.S. Space Camp book"

"Presented as a narrative told by a U.S. Space Camp counselor to a group of campers, this brightly illustrated book is a collection of brief biographical sketches of 14 astronauts from Project Mercury to the present." Sci Books Films

Includes bibliographical references

Cole, Michael D.

Astronauts; training for space. Enslow Pubs. 1999 48p il (Countdown to space) lib bdg $18.95 **629.45**

1. Astronauts

ISBN 0-7660-1116-X

LC 98-3299

Describes the qualities needed to be part of the space program and various aspects of the training that astronaut candidates receive to prepare them for their first flight

This title should "be commended for presenting female as well as male role models for the budding astronaut." Sci Books Films

Includes bibliographical references

Collins, Michael, 1930-

Flying to the moon; an astronaut's story. 2nd ed, with a preface & a revised final chapter. Farrar, Straus & Giroux 1994 162p il pa $4.50 **629.45**

1. Space flight to the moon 2. Astronauts

ISBN 0-374-42356-3

LC 93-42001

"A Sunburst book"

First published 1976 with title: Flying to the moon, and other strange places

Based in part on author's Carrying the fire (1974)

The author recounts his early days as an Air Force test pilot, his NASA training and his experiences aboard Gemini 10 and the Apollo 11 mission to the moon. Collins also advocates continued exploration of the universe

"A well told tale, which includes a lot of easily explained science." BAYA Book Rev

Green, Jen

Race to the moon; the story of Apollo 11; written by Jen Green; illustrated by Mark Bergin; created and designed by David Salariya. Watts 1998 32p il (Expedition) $21; pa $7.95 **629.45**

1. Project Apollo 2. Apollo 11 (Spacecraft) 3. Space flight to the moon

ISBN 0-531-14456-9; 0-531-15343-6 (pa)

LC 97-34691

Describes the events leading up to the Apollo 11 flight that put the first man on the moon and the technological advances that made this and later flights possible

Ride, Sally K.

To space & back; by Sally Ride with Susan Okie. Lothrop, Lee & Shepard Bks. 1986 96p il $19; pa $12.95 **629.45**

1. Space flight 2. Space shuttles

ISBN 0-688-06159-1; 0-688-09112-1 (pa)

LC 85-23757

This "account of a space journey, from blastoff to landing, gives . . . details of adjusting to weightlessness, preparing and eating meals, going to the bathroom, sleeping, washing, dressing, and working on scientific projects or up-keep technology on board the shuttle. Ride gives plenty of examples from her own experience but keeps the focus generalized enough to be broadly informative." Bull Cent Child Books

Includes glossary

Stott, Carole

Moon landing; the race for the moon; illustrated by Richard Bonson. DK Pub. 1999 48p il (DK discoveries) $14.95 **629.45**

1. Space flight to the moon

ISBN 0-7894-3958-1

LC 99-11937

An illustrated account of humanity's exploration of the moon, from our first observations and attempts to the first landing and later expeditions

629.8 Automatic control engineering

Jefferis, David

Artificial intelligence; robotics and machine evolution. Crabtree 1999 32p il (Megatech) lib bdg $14.37; pa $8.06 **629.8**

1. Robots 2. Artificial intelligence

ISBN 0-7787-0046-1 (lib bdg); 0-7787-0056-9 (pa)

LC 98-44481

An introduction to the past, present, and future of artificial intelligence and robotics, discussing early science fiction predictions, the dawn of AI, and today's use of robots in factories and space exploration

This book has "bright, full-color photographs on nearly every page." SLJ

Includes glossary

630.1 Agriculture—Philosophy and theory. Country and farm life

Bial, Raymond

Portrait of a farm family. Houghton Mifflin 1995 48p il $15.95 **630.1**

1. Farm life 2. Agriculture

ISBN 0-395-69936-3

LC 94-38201

In this photo essay about the Steidinger family farm in Illinois "Bial explores the specifics of milking, raising feed-lot calves, and cutting silage and discusses the factors to be weighed before buying expensive equipment or choosing a particular kind of animal to raise. . . . Bial brings the Steidingers' everyday world to life, fitting it neatly into an excellent discussion of family-farm-based agriculture and the U.S. economy." Booklist

Includes bibliographical references

Halley, Ned
Farm; written by Ned Halley; photographed by Geoff Brightling. Knopf 1996 63p il (Eyewitness books) $19; lib bdg $20.99   **630.1**
1. Agriculture 2. Farms
ISBN 0-679-88078-X; 0-679-98078-4 (lib bdg)
LC 95-37053
"A Dorling Kindersley book"
Text and photographs depict different aspects of farming through the ages including the equipment, domestic animals, crops, and the future of farming
"Probably one of the better entries in the ever-growing series. . . . Lengthy captions describe the many detailed full-color illustrations, photographs, reproductions, and artifacts that are scattered around the pages." SLJ

635   Garden crops (Horticulture)

Hughes, Meredith Sayles
Buried treasure; roots & tubers; [by] Meredith Sayles Hughes and Tom Hughes. Lerner Publs. 1998 80p il lib bdg $25.26   **635**
1. Root crops 2. Potatoes
ISBN 0-8225-2830-4   LC 97-28436
Relates the history and describes the use and production of such roots and tubers as potatoes, yams, cassava, carrots, beets, turnips, radishes, and parsnips. Includes recipes
"This book combines thorough research with a lively presenation. . . . Not only does this book give readers facts about foods that they eat, but it also widens their awareness of how these vegetables are viewed in other countries." SLJ
Includes bibliographical references

636   Animal husbandry

Silverstein, Alvin
A pet or not? [by] Alvin Silverstein, Virginia Silverstein, Laura Silverstein Nunn. 21st Cent. Bks. (Brookfield) 1999 48p il lib bdg $21.40   **636**
1. Pets
ISBN 0-7613-3230-8   LC 98-46358
Discusses the pros and cons of owning exotic pets such as armadillos, llamas, monkeys, potbellied pigs, and sugar gliders, and offers advice on their care, feeding, and emotional support
"The authors present the facts in an orderly, informative, and dispassionate manner, devoting four pages to each pet." SLJ

636.1   Equines. Horses

Edwards, Elwyn Hartley
The encyclopedia of the horse; photographs by Bob Langrish, Kit Houghton; foreword by Sharon Ralls Lemon. Dorling Kindersley 1994 400p il maps $39.95   **636.1**
1. Horses
ISBN 1-56458-614-6   LC 94-644

"Over 150 breeds of horses and ponies are featured in this work. . . . Arranged chronologically, chapters trace the horse from its evolution and early use to classical riding, its influence in different areas of the world, and the horse at work, in sports, and in war. Within each chapter are highlighted breeds associated with the period, geographic area, or activity." Am Libr

Horses; photographs by Bob Langrish. Dorling Kindersley 1993 256p il (Eyewitness handbooks) $29.95; pa $18.95   **636.1**
1. Horses
ISBN 1-56458-180-2; 1-56458-177-2 (pa)
LC 92-53469
Illustrated with full-color photographs, this guide begins with a general overview of horses and then presents the histories and characteristics of various breeds
This "is a compact, handy, easy-to-use guide with excellent illustrations." Recomm Ref Books for Small & Medium-sized Libr & Media Cent, 1994
Includes glosssary

Henderson, Carolyn
Horse & pony breeds. DK Pub. 1999 48p il (DK riding club) pa $7.95   **636.1**
1. Horses 2. Ponies
ISBN 0-7894-4267-1   LC 98-50742
An illustrated guide to horse and pony breeds, their history, physical characteristics, and uses

Horse & pony care. DK Pub. 1999 48p il (DK riding club) $12.95; pa $7.95   **636.1**
1. Horses 2. Ponies
ISBN 0-7894-4270-1; 0-7894-4269-8 (pa)
LC 98-49618
This book "provides an overview of the many facets of caring for a horse or pony, including tips on handling, health, and feeding. . . . Sure to be popular in areas where youngsters have access to stables." Booklist
Includes glossary

Meltzer, Milton, 1915-
Hold your horses; a feedbag full of fact and fable. HarperCollins Pubs. 1995 133p il lib bdg $14.89   **636.1**
1. Horses
ISBN 0-06-024478-X   LC 95-2983
The author "examines equines' uses and contributions throughout history, starting with charioteers' steeds, through knights' chargers, military mounts, cowponies, farm horses, and racetrack Thoroughbreds." Bull Cent Child Books
"A well-researched, concisely written, and thought-provoking book that's as fascinating as the subject itself. Black-and-white reproductions and photographs appear throughout. An excellent choice for recreational reading or reports." SLJ
Includes bibliographical references

Pritchard, Louise
My pony book; written by Louise Pritchard. DK Pub. 1998 61p il $15.95   **636.1**
1. Ponies
ISBN 0-7894-2810-5   LC 97-34425

Pritchard, Louise—*Continued*

Describes the characteristics, origins, and history of ponies, from the powerful Fjord to the minute, hardy Shetland, and provides tips on their care and development

"The presentation is accurate. . . . The book contains just the right amount of information for its intended audience." Horn Book Guide

Includes glossary

The **Visual** dictionary of the horse. Dorling Kindersley 1994 64p il (Eyewitness visual dictionaries) $18.95   **636.1**
1. Horses
ISBN 1-56458-504-2   LC 93-20819

"Along with spreads detailing the animal's anatomy, there are two double-page spreads illustrated with full-color photographs of the various breeds, divided into light and heavy horses. Following this overview, the guide briefly focuses on the care and activities of equines today, including grooming, shoeing, racing, jumping, and equipment." SLJ

"In this visually spectacular introduction to horses and equine and equestrian terms, the information is complete and concise; color photographs and diagrams extend the text. The anatomical drawings, with detailed labeling, are particularly instructive and useful." Horn Book Guide

636.5   Poultry. Chickens

Zeaman, John

Birds; from forest to family room. Watts 1999 63p il $24   **636.5**
1. Birds 2. Cage birds
ISBN 0-531-20351-4   LC 98-2706

The author presents a "look at bird domestication, including information on bird evolution, the first human attempts at taming (including geese and jungle fowl for food, doves and pigeons for communication, and raptors for hunting), and the history of domestication of birds for pleasure. Reproductions and color photos add to the liveliness of the presentation." Horn Book Guide

Includes bibliographical references

636.7   Dogs

Alderton, David

Dogs; photography by Tracy Morgan. Dorling Kindersley 1993 304p il (Eyewitness handbooks) $29.95; pa $18.95 (7 and up)   **636.7**
1. Dogs
ISBN 1-56458-179-9; 1-56458-176-4 (pa)
                    LC 92-53450

This is a "descriptive and pictorial guide to more than 300 breeds of dogs, from the most recognizable to the lesser known . . . Following a history of the domestic dog, the introduction includes a guide to the use of the book and sections on choosing and caring for a dog and showing dogs competitively. A well-arranged pictorial identification chart helps to identify a breed by size and other key characteristics, such as shape of head and hair type." Recomm Ref Books for Small & Medium-sized Libr & Media Cent, 1994

Allan, Ross

Dog obedience training; a complete and up-to-date guide. Chelsea House 1997 64p il $19.95   **636.7**
1. Dogs—Training
ISBN 0-7910-4605-2   LC 97-4185

Full color photographs accompany step-by-step instructions for basic dog training techniques

American Kennel Club

The complete dog book. Howell Bk. House il $32.95   **636.7**
1. Dogs

First published 1935. (19th edition 1997) Frequently revised

"The official guide to 124 AKC registered breeds and their history, appearance, selection, training, care and feeding, and first aid. Some color plates." N Y Public Libr. Ref Books for Child Collect. 2d edition

The **Complete** dog book for kids; official publication of the American Kennel Club. Howell Bk. House 1996 274p il maps $34.95; pa $22.95   **636.7**
1. Dogs
ISBN 0-87605-458-0; 0-87605-460-2 (pa)
                    LC 96-29228

This "begins with a general section that advises readers on buying a dog, responsibilities, rewards, and how to match a dog with one's situation. . . . More than 100 dogs are profiled, with information on history, appearance, health, and 'fun facts.' Crisp color photographs accompany each article. . . . A final section gives good advice about nutrition and health issues." Booklist

636.8   Cats

Alderton, David

Cats; photography by Marc Henrie. Dorling Kindersley 1992 256p il (Eyewitness handbooks) $29.95; pa $18.95 (7 and up)   **636.8**
1. Cats
ISBN 1-56458-073-3; 1-56458-070-9 (pa)
                    LC 92-7611

This illustrated identification guide to more than 250 types of cats "traces the evolution of the domestic cat, looks at how cats are classified, and examines feline anatomy in detail. Tips are provided on choosing the right cat, sexing kittens, grooming, and handling and showing. Visual identification keys help one recognize the different types of cats. Each entry combines a precise description with annotated photographs to highlight the main characteristics and distinguishing features." Recomm Ref Books for Small & Medium-sized Libr & Media Cent, 1994

Includes glossary

Edney, A. T. B.

ASPCA complete cat care manual; [by] Andrew Edney; foreword by Roger Caras. Dorling Kindersley 1992 192p il $24.95   **636.8**
1. Cats
ISBN 1-56458-064-4   LC 92-52783

Edney, A. T. B.—*Continued*
"Cat care is made easy through step-by-step photographs that illustrate grooming, handling, detecting illness, first aid, and other concerns. Difficult-to-explain procedures, such as how to administer medication or transport an injured cat, are clearly understandable." Libr J

Includes bibliographical references

639   Hunting, fishing, conservation, related technologies

Coborn, John
Snakes. Chelsea House 1999 64p il $17.95
639
1. Snakes
ISBN 0-7910-5085-8   LC 98-7659
Discusses the physical characteristics, health, and behavior of snakes and provides information on keeping these animals as pets

Silverstein, Alvin
Snakes & such; [by] Alvin Silverstein, Virginia Silverstein, Laura Silverstein Nunn. 21st Cent. Bks. (Brookfield) 1999 48p il lib bdg $21.40
639
1. Reptiles 2. Amphibians
ISBN 0-7613-3229-4   LC 98-41305
Discusses the positive and negative aspects of keeping such creatures as boas and pythons, chameleons, iguanas, turtles, frogs, and salamanders as pets
"The authors present the facts in an orderly, informative, and dispassionate manner, devoting four pages to each pet. A 'Fast Facts' box, imposed on a full-color photo of the creature, gives its scientific name along with cost, food, housing, and training requirements." SLJ
Includes bibliographical references

639.2   Commercial fishing, whaling, sealing

McKissack, Patricia C., 1944-
Black hands, white sails; the story of African-American whalers; [by] Patricia C. McKissack & Fredrick L. McKissack. Scholastic Press 1999 xxiv, 152p il $15.95   **639.2**
1. Whaling—History 2. African Americans
ISBN 0-590-48313-7   LC 99-11439
A Coretta Scott King honor book for text, 2000
A history of African-American whalers between 1730 and 1880, describing their contributions to the whaling industry and their role in the abolitionist movement
"A well-researched and detailed book." SLJ
Includes bibliographical references

Murphy, Jim, 1947-
Gone a-whaling; the lure of the sea and the hunt for the great whale. Clarion Bks. 1998 208p il $18 (7 and up)   **639.2**
1. Whaling—History
ISBN 0-395-69847-2   LC 97-13051

Surveys the history of the whaling industry from its earliest days to the present, focusing on the young boys who managed to sign on for whaling voyages
"Murphy makes history fascinating and immediate with a lively, engrossing narrative that both informs and entertains." Voice Youth Advocates
Includes glossary and bibliographical references

639.34   Aquariums

Burgess, Warren
Dr. Burgess's atlas of marine aquarium fishes; [by] Warren E. Burgess, Herbert R. Axelrod, Raymond E. Hunziker III. T.F.H. Publs. 1988 736p il $79.95   **639.34**
1. Marine aquariums 2. Tropical fish
ISBN 0-86622-896-9   LC 89-121239
"A pictorial aid to fish identification. Included are over 4,000 photographs, 560 colorplates, and an aquaristic section on marine fish aquarium maintenance. Drs. Burgess and Axelrod are recognized as 'the' names in aquarium fish books, and the availability of this new marine fish identification guide is good news indeed." Am Libr

Mills, Dick
Aquarium fish. DK Pub. 1996 72p il (101 essential tips) pa $6.95   **639.34**
1. Aquariums 2. Fishes
ISBN 0-7894-1074-5
This book offers advice on choosing fish for aquariums, aquarium equipment, decoration, feeding, and health care, and describes various species of tropical, coldwater, freshwater, and marine fishes
"Accurate, clear, and concise writing is enhanced with wonderful color photographs on each page." Voice Youth Advocates

639.9   Conservation of biological resources

Patent, Dorothy Hinshaw
Back to the wild; photos by William Muñoz. Harcourt Brace & Co. 1997 69p il $18   **639.9**
1. Wildlife conservation 2. Endangered species
ISBN 0-15-200280-4   LC 95-43254
"A Gulliver Green book"
"Examining the reintroduction of captive-bred endangered species into the wild, Patent discusses the issue generally and focuses specifically on reintroduction programs for the red wolf, the black-footed ferret, the golden lion tamarin, and several species of lemur." Bull Cent Child Books
This offers "striking color photos and an authoritative text." Horn Book Guide

The whooping crane; a comeback story; photographs by William Muñoz. Clarion Bks. 1988 88p il hardcover o.p. paperback available $6.95
639.9
1. Cranes (Birds) 2. Birds—Protection 3. Wildlife conservation
ISBN 0-395-66505-1 (pa)   LC 88-2871

Patent, Dorothy Hinshaw—*Continued*
"The graceful whooping crane, native to the United States and Canada, was threatened by the encroachment of civilization. A captive breeding program and wildlife refuges are examined in an exciting, heartening story of the rescue of an endangered species. Stunning full-color and black-and-white photographs." Sci Child

641.3 Food

Johnson, Sylvia A.
Tomatoes, potatoes, corn, and beans; how the foods of the Americas changed eating around the world. Atheneum Bks. for Young Readers 1997 138p $16   **641.3**
1. Food 2. Vegetables
ISBN 0-689-80141-6   LC 96-7207
Describes many foods native to the Americas, including corn, peppers, peanuts, and chocolate, which were taken to Europe and used in new ways around the world
"This well-documented book is a treasure of information presented in a clear, interesting style. . . . There are b&w photos or drawings on nearly every page. The layout is attractive and well spaced for easy reading." Book Rep
Includes bibliography

Jones, Charlotte Foltz, 1945-
Eat your words; a fascinating look at the language of food; illustrated by John O'Brien. Delacorte Press 1999 87p il $16.95   **641.3**
1. Food 2. English language—Terms and phrases
ISBN 0-385-32575-4   LC 98-27748
Discusses the history and meaning of all kinds of food-related words and phrases and describes customs and beliefs about various foods
"The layout and accessible writing style make this book easy to understand and interesting to read. It is filled with anecdotes and amusing illustrations." SLJ
Includes bibliographical references

Marshall, Elizabeth L.
High-tech harvest; a look at genetically engineered foods. Watts 1999 144p il lib bdg $24 (7 and up)   **641.3**
1. Agriculture 2. Food 3. Biotechnology
ISBN 0-531-11434-1   LC 98-8203
An overview of recombined DNA technology, or genetic engineering, techniques used to create crop plants and farm animals with characteristics that are attractive to farmers, food processors, and consumers
"Students looking for a discussion of the techniques and implications of gene-splicing to create new types of food plants and animals will find this just the ticket. . . . The notes, plus generous lists of books, articles and URL's, at the end will facilitate further inquiry." Booklist

Solheim, James
It's disgusting—and we ate it! true food facts from around the world—and throughout history! illustrated by Eric Brace. Simon & Schuster Bks. for Young Readers 1998 37p il $16   **641.3**
1. Food—History 2. Eating customs
ISBN 0-689-80675-2   LC 96-7406
This "look at culinary culture is divided into three sections, the first discussing the global breadth of tastes, the second describing some startling dishes of history, and the third revealing some of the colorful truths behind contemporary American favorites." Bull Cent Child Books
Includes bibliographical references

Ventura, Piero
Food; its evolution through the ages; [by] Piero Ventura, with the collaboration of Max Casalini [et al.] Houghton Mifflin 1994 64p il $16.95   **641.3**
1. Food—History
ISBN 0-395-66790-9   LC 94-14419
This illustrated book explores how people have nourished themselves "from the paleolithic era, when bows and arrows were first used for hunting, to the age of exploration, when new foods were brought from newfound lands, to the Industrial Revolution, when advances were made in farming equipment, and onward." Publisher's note

641.5 Cooking

Albyn, Carole Lisa, 1955-
The multicultural cookbook for students; by Carole Lisa Albyn and Lois Sinaiko Webb. Oryx Press 1993 xxii, 287p maps pa $26.95   **641.5**
1. Cooking
ISBN 0-89774-735-6   LC 92-41634
Presents a collection of recipes from over 120 countries and briefly discusses the culture and culinary habits of each country

Cook, Deanna F., 1965-
The kids' multicultural cookbook; food & fun around the world; illustrated by Michael P. Kline. Williamson 1995 159p il $12.95   **641.5**
1. Cooking 2. Manners and customs
ISBN 0-913589-91-8   LC 94-44231
"A Williamson kids can! book"
In this "tour of 41 countries, readers are given a quick dose of culture from each one. There are one or two recipes (their difficulty is rated by one, two, or three spoons) for each place and an introduction to a child who lives there. Occasional riddles and 'fun facts' are inserted, such as the world record for watermelon-seed spitting. Foreign words are included with pronunciations." SLJ

Copage, Eric V.
Kwanzaa; a celebration of culture and cooking. Morrow 1991 xxvii, 356p il pa $15 (7 and up)
                                             641.5
1. African American cooking 2. Kwanzaa
ISBN 0-688-10939-X   LC 91-4112

Copage, Eric V.—*Continued*
In addition to providing information on the seven principles of Kwanzaa, this volume focuses on holiday food preparation with over 125 recipes

D'Amico, Joan, 1957-
The healthy body cookbook; over 50 fun activities and delicious recipes for kids; [by] Joan D'Amico, Karen Eich Drummond; illustrations by Tina Cash-Walsh. Wiley 1999 184p il pa $12.95
641.5
1. Cooking 2. Nutrition
ISBN 0-471-18888-3   LC 98-2776
Discusses the various parts of the human body and what to eat to keep them healthy. Includes recipes that contain nutrients important for the heart, muscles, teeth, skin, nerves, and other parts of the body
"The recipes are clear, thoroughly explained, and tasty; level of difficulty is indicated by number of chef's hats. Important information related in an encouraging way." SLJ

Erdosh, George, 1935-
The African American kitchen; food for body and soul. Rosen Pub. Group 1999 64p il (Library of African American arts and culture) lib bdg $17.95 (7 and up)   **641.5**
1. African American cooking
ISBN 0-8239-1850-5   LC 98-51814
Describes the influences on and the evolution of African-American cooking. Includes recipes and suggestions for healthy cooking
Includes bibliographical references

Fisher, Teresa
France. Raintree Steck-Vaughn Pubs. 1999 32p il (Food and festivals) lib bdg $22.83   **641.5**
1. French cooking 2. France—Social life and customs
ISBN 0-8172-5550-8   LC 98-15671
Discusses some of the foods enjoyed in France and describes special foods that are part of such specific celebrations as Christmas, Mardi Gras, and Menton's Lemon Festival. Includes recipes
Includes bibliographical references

Holiday cooking around the world; photographs by Robert L. and Diane Wolfe. Lerner Publs. 1988 51p il (Easy menu ethnic cookbooks) lib bdg $19.93; pa $5.95   **641.5**
1. Cooking
ISBN 0-8225-0922-9 (lib bdg); 0-8225-9573-7 (pa)
LC 88-8876
A collection of holiday recipes from fifteen different countries including a variety of dishes such as Thai egg rolls, Passover layer cake, paella, and Danish rice pudding
"Lacking background information on each country's customs and culture, the book may not be as useful as others in the series. There is, however, an overview of the holidays mentioned in the menus, and the finished products, shown in attractive color photographs, may intrigue young chefs." Booklist

Krizmanic, Judy
A teen's vegetarian cookbook; illustrations by Matthew Wawiorka. Viking 1999 186p il $15.99; pa $9.99 (7 and up)   **641.5**
1. Vegetarian cooking
ISBN 0-670-87426-4; 0-14-038506-1 (pa)
LC 98-21856
Recipes for all types of vegetarian dishes are accompanied by information and advice on vegetarian diet and quotes from teenage vegetarians
"Recipes are laid out nicely, with ingredients listed first, followed by a numbered sequence of clear instructions. Boxed insets in Krizmanic's strong, clear voice add background on vegetarianism, and there's a helpful food chart to remind readers about nutritional values. Teens new to vegetarian cooking will find the glossary of 'unusual' foods helpful, as well." Booklist

Medearis, Angela Shelf, 1956-
Cooking; [by] Angela Shelf Medearis, Michael R. Medearis. 21st Cent. Bks. (NY) 1997 80p il (African-American arts) lib bdg $20.40   **641.5**
1. African American cooking
ISBN 0-8050-4484-1   LC 97-8071
Introduces the influence of African-based foods, cooking techniques, and traditions to American culinary history
"Students will find this useful for projects on black-American contributions, history, culture, and cuisine." Book Rep
Includes bibliographical references

Perl, Lila
Hunter's stew and hangtown fry: what pioneer America ate and why; pictures by Richard Cuffari. Clarion Bks. 1977 156p il $16.95   **641.5**
1. Cooking 2. United States—Social life and customs
ISBN 0-395-28922-X   LC 77-5366
First published by Seabury Press
"This is a culinary cultural history of the growing United States during the 19th Century. The author divides the country into five sections and, in a readable style, describes the people, the food, and the ambience of the times. There are 20 choice and representative recipes, a few at the end of each chapter." SLJ
Includes bibliographical references

Slumps, grunts, and snickerdoodles: what Colonial America ate and why; drawings by Richard Cuffari. Clarion Bks. 1975 125p il $14.95
641.5
1. Cooking 2. United States—Social life and customs—1600-1775, Colonial period
ISBN 0-395-28923-8   LC 75-4894
First published by Seabury Press
"In three major chapters dividing the pre-Revolutionary colonies into regions—New England, Middle Atlantic, Southern—the author explains ' . . . not only "what" the colonists ate and "why," but . . . the geographical and historical background as well as the intimate domestic surroundings.' . . . Emphasis is on foods grown in different areas and how traditional recipes developed from the materials available, but local manners and mores are also skillfully woven into the narrative." SLJ

Vezza, Diane Simone

Passport on a plate; a round-the-world cookbook for children; illustrated by Susan Greenstein. Simon & Schuster Bks. for Young Readers 1997 150p il $19.95 **641.5**

1. Cooking

ISBN 0-689-80155-6 LC 96-50409

"This international cookbook contains 100 recipes from Africa, the Caribbean, China, France, Germany, India, Italy, Japan, Mexico, the Middle East, Russia, and Vietnam. Each place is introduced in a one-and-a-half-page explanation of the area's foods and eating habits. . . . They are clearly written and carefully chosen to represent the locale and the foods that are grown there." SLJ

Webb, Lois Sinaiko, 1922-

Holidays of the world cookbook for students. Oryx Press 1995 xxxiv, 297p il maps pa $26.95 **641.5**

1. Cooking 2. Holidays

ISBN 0-89774-884-0 LC 95-26019

In this cookbook "more than 136 countries are represented, with 388 recipes. The U.S. is divided into six sections with 10 recipes for regional celebrations. History behind the holiday is included where possible, as is pertinent background information on the culture represented. . . . A discussion of different calendars used around the world is an interesting inclusion. The recipes' directions are clear and include equipment lists." SLJ

Includes glossary and bibliographical references

Wilder, Laura Ingalls, 1867-1957

The Laura Ingalls Wilder country cookbook; compiled by Laura Ingalls Wilder; commentary by William Anderson; photographs by Leslie A. Kelly. HarperCollins Pubs. 1995 152p il $24.95; pa $12.95 **641.5**

1. Wilder, Laura Ingalls, 1867-1957 2. Cooking

ISBN 0-06-024917-X; 0-06-446196-3 (pa)

LC 94-42326

"A recently discovered recipe collection compiled during the author's life with Almanzo at Rocky Ridge Farm in Mansfield, MI. The 73 recipes are good, honest fare from the 1930s and '40s for everyday and special occasions. At least as interesting as the recipes is the glimpse into Wilder's happy and productive adult life as a farmer, friend, and writer. This large format book is full of black-and-white photographs of her family and friends, and full-color photos of Rocky Ridge Farm, inside and out." SLJ

Wilkes, Angela

Children's quick & easy cookbook; 101 delicious step-by-step recipes. DK Pub. 1997 96p il $16.95 **641.5**

1. Cooking

ISBN 0-7894-2026-0 LC 97-15422

Discusses cooking techniques, food hygiene, and kitchen safety, and presents step-by-step instructions for all types of dishes

This is a "beautiful cookbook, full of eye-catching photographs. . . . The recipes . . . are inviting and are composed of real ingredients rather than mixes." SLJ

641.6 Cooking specific materials

George, Jean Craighead, 1919-

Acorn pancakes, dandelion salad and 38 other wild recipes; illustrated by Paul Mirocha. HarperCollins Pubs. 1995 63p il $14.95 **641.6**

1. Cooking 2. Edible plants

ISBN 0-06-021549-6 LC 93-42490

Based on the author's The wild, wild cookbook, published 1982 by Crowell

"After a short introduction to the joys and ways of food gathering, George concentrates on 15 wild edibles such as acorns, berries, plantains, cacti, and day lilies. Each section introduces a plant, including a beautifully accurate gouache and colored-pencil illustration; discusses its preparation; and offers a couple of recipes. . . . The writing reflects both the author's love of nature and her attention to scientific clarity and detail." SLJ

643 Housing and household equipment

Colman, Penny

Toilets, bathtubs, sinks, and sewers; a history of the bathroom. Atheneum Pubs. 1994 70p il $16 **643**

1. Bathrooms 2. Sanitation—History

ISBN 0-689-31894-4 LC 93-48413

"The author relates the history of our efforts to deal with human waste. . . . The book is packed with facts succinctly delivered in a crisp writing style with sufficient explanation to clearly place the material in historic context. Neatly inserted asides are used to lighten the tone. The author has chosen appropriate vintage prints and photographs to illustrate the evolution of fixtures." Horn Book

Includes bibliographical references

Plante, Ellen M.

The American kitchen, 1700 to the present; from hearth to highrise. Facts on File 1995 340p il $29.95 (7 and up) **643**

1. Kitchens 2. Cooking 3. United States—Social life and customs

ISBN 0-8160-3038-3 LC 94-33235

This is a "history of the evolution of the focal point of the American home, beginning with the colonial kitchen and traveling to the present. Plante gives readers not only a clear view of how the room has changed, but also of how the family itself has changed. The illustrations and reproductions of advertisements make visualizing the text interesting and easy. The 'Household Hints and Recipes' are outstanding, each worthy of the era they reflect." SLJ

Includes glossary and bibliographical references

650.14   Success in obtaining jobs and promotions

Pervola, Cindy, 1956-
How to get a job if you're a teenager; [by] Cindy Pervola and Debby Hobgood. Alleyside Press 1998 62p il pa $12.95 (7 and up)   **650.14**
1. Job hunting 2. Vocational guidance
ISBN 1-57950-013-7   LC 97-45843
This book provides "information on how to select the best job, where to look, how to apply, how best to prepare for the interview, how to get the job, what to expect on the first day, and what to do when leaving a job. It offers various resources like job web sites and Internet guides, and tells how to create your own job." Book Rep
"An excellent addition to career collections." SLJ
Includes bibliographical references

652   Processes of written communication

Ganeri, Anita, 1961-
The story of writing and printing. Oxford Univ. Press 1996 c1995 30p (Signs of the times) lib bdg $14.95   **652**
1. Writing—History 2. Printing—History
ISBN 0-19-521256-8   LC 96-14232
Presents an overview, from ancient times to the present, of the evolution of writing including the development of alphabets, writing instruments, inks and papers, and printing methods
"The style is lively and immediate, and the snippets of information will stimulate kids to find out more." Booklist
Includes glossary

Huckle, Helen
The secret code book. Dial Bks. 1995 57p il $14.99   **652**
1. Cryptography 2. Ciphers
ISBN 0-8037-1725-3   LC 94-30019
This "book features one- to four-page sections explaining 19 codes, many of them significant in history, as well as methods for encoding and deciphering messages using the codes. Full-color photographs, diagrams, and reproductions of period artwork and documents illustrate the text. . . . The codes will intrigue and challenge readers. Tipped into the back endcovers is a heavy paper sheet with press-out pieces for making two cipher disks." Booklist
Includes glossary

658   General management

Karnes, Frances A.
Girls and young women entrepreneurs; true stories about starting and running a business, plus how you can do it yourself; [by] Frances A. Karnes and Suzanne M. Bean; edited by Elizabeth Verdick. Free Spirit 1997 189p il pa $12.95 (7 and up)   **658**
1. Entrepreneurship 2. Businesswomen 3. Business enterprises
ISBN 1-57542-022-8   LC 97-13535
This "book introduces dozens of young female entrepreneurs ranging in age from 9 to 25, and offers advice and instruction for others wishing to start a business. In addition to the personal narratives, a detailed and current annotated list for further reading, a glossary of business terms, and contact information (including Internet addresses) for organizations relevant to young people in business are appended." SLJ

659.1   Advertising

Day, Nancy L.
Advertising; information or manipulation? Enslow Pubs. 1999 128p il (Issues in focus) lib bdg $19.95   **659.1**
1. Advertising
ISBN 0-7660-1106-2   LC 98-35032
Discusses how advertising has developed, how companies use it to entice consumers, and the impact of advertising on people, particularly young people
"The book includes tips for critically evaluating advertising, which are useful for classroom discussion on media influence, and stresses the importance of being informed before buying. . . . Readers and educators will find the book fascinating, thought-provoking, and educational, inside and outside the classroom. All in all, a top-notch culture-consumerism book, comprehensive and easy to follow." Booklist
Includes glossary and bibliographical references

Dunn, John M., 1949-
Advertising. Lucent Bks. 1997 112p il (Lucent overview series) lib bdg $22.45 (7 and up) **659.1**
1. Advertising
ISBN 1-560-06182-0   LC 96-35920
Discusses the functions, goals, and methods of advertising and examines such issues as targeting the youth market, political ads, and the right of free speech
This "offers lots of information in an attractive, well-organized, and readable format. . . . This book will be useful for school reports, and will attract interested browsers." SLJ
Includes bibliographical references

664 Food technology

Busenberg, Bonnie
Vanilla, chocolate, & strawberry; the story of your favorite flavors. Lerner Publs. 1994 112p il maps lib bdg $23.95 **664**
1. Flavoring essences
ISBN 0-8225-1573-3 LC 93-15101
Describes how vanilla, chocolate, and strawberry came to become popular flavorings, how they were originally used, how they're used today, and what makes them taste the way they do. Includes recipes
"This book truly has something for everyone. It is genuinely fun to read, fascinating, and well illustrated." Sci Books Films
Includes glossary

669 Metallurgy

Fitzgerald, Karen
The story of iron. Watts 1997 64p il lib bdg $22 **669**
1. Iron
ISBN 0-531-20270-4 LC 96-31541
"A First book"
Explores the history of the chemical element iron and explains its chemistry and its importance in our lives
Includes glossary and bibliographical references

Mebane, Robert C.
Metals; [by] Robert C. Mebane, Thomas R. Rybolt; illustrations by Anni Matsick. 21st Cent. Bks. (NY) 1995 64p il (Everyday material science experiments) lib bdg $18.90 **669**
1. Metals 2. Science—Experiments
ISBN 0-8050-2842-0 LC 94-43110
This book includes instructions for 16 science experiments involving metals
"The experiments are workable and demonstrate important ideas." Booklist
Includes bibliographical references

670 Manufacturing

Biesty, Stephen
Stephen Biesty's incredible everything; illustrated by Stephen Biesty; written by Richard Platt. DK Pub. 1997 32p il $19.95 **670**
1. Manufactures
ISBN 0-7894-2049-X LC 97-15426
Cut-away illustrations and explanatory captions explain how such diverse objects as chocolate bars and cathedrals, false teeth and tanks are made
Biesty "manages to combine simplicity and fine detail in his drawings. . . . The authors convey to the reader the awe-inspiring technology and attention to detail that go into many of the everyday products we take for granted." Voice Youth Advocates

CD's, superglue, and salsa [series 2]; how everyday products are made; edited by Kathleen L. Witman, Kyung Lim Kalasky, & Neil Schlager. U.X.L 1996 2v il set $55 **670**
1. Manufactures
ISBN 0-8103-9791-9 LC 96-12523
Also available CDs, super glue, and salsa [series 1] edited by Sharon Rose & Neil Schlager 2v set $55 (ISBN 0-7876-0870-9)
This book describes "30 household or high-interest products, including bungee cords, bicycles, chewing gum, perfume, sunscreen, violins and 24 others." Publisher's note
Includes bibliographical references

681.1 Instruments for measuring time

Pollard, Michael, 1931-
The clock and how it changed the world. Facts on File 1995 46p il maps (History and invention) $16.95 **681.1**
1. Clocks and watches 2. Time
ISBN 0-8160-3142-8 LC 94-15225
Traces the historical development and societal impact of time measuring devices. Color photos, drawings and maps illustrate the text
Includes bibliographical references

683 Hardware and household appliances

Rubin, Susan Goldman, 1939-
Toilets, toasters & telephones; the how and why of everyday objects; illustrated with photographs and with illustrations by Elsa Warnick. Browndeer Press 1998 132p il $20 **683**
1. Industrial design 2. Inventions 3. Household equipment and supplies
ISBN 0-15-201421-7 LC 97-28650
"In addition to the three objects mentioned in the title, the lively text discusses the history and development of many familiar conveniences from refrigerators to paper clips. The book is readable, with solid grounding in research, and the appeal of the amusing trivia is well supported by the historical underpinnings." Horn Book Guide
Includes bibliographical references

690 Buildings

Giblin, James, 1933-
Let there be light: a book about windows; [by] James Cross Giblin; illustrated with photographs and prints. Crowell 1988 162p il $16 **690**
1. Windows
ISBN 0-690-04693-6 LC 87-35052

Giblin, James, 1933-—*Continued*
Surveys the development of windows from prehistory to the modern era. The author discusses shapes, sizes, materials used, as well as social and political influences
"Splendid illustrations abound in this fascinating history of windows. Much information is also included about making stained glass in this highly recommended book." Child Book Rev Serv
Includes bibliographical references

Macaulay, David, 1946-
Mill. Houghton Mifflin 1983 128p il $18; pa $8.95   **690**
1. Mills 2. Textile industry—History
ISBN 0-395-34830-7; 0-395-52019-3 (pa)
                                                    LC 83-10652
This is an "account of the development of four fictional 19th-Century Rhode Island cotton mills. In explaining the construction and operation of a simple water-wheel powered wooden mill, as well as the more complex stone, turbine and steam mills to follow, the author also describes the rise and decline of New England's textile industry." SLJ

Unbuilding. Houghton Mifflin 1980 78p il $18; pa $8.95   **690**
1. Empire State Building (New York, N.Y.) 2. Building 3. Skyscrapers
ISBN 0-395-29457-6; 0-395-45360-7 (pa)
                                                    LC 80-15491
This fictional account of the dismantling and removal of the Empire State Building describes the structure of a skyscraper and explains how such an edifice would be demolished
"Save for the fact that one particularly stunning double-page spread is marred by tight binding, the book is a joy: accurate, informative, handsome, and eminently readable." Bull Cent Child Books

Wilkinson, Philip, 1955-
Building; written by Philip Wilkinson; photographed by Dave King & Geoff Dann. Knopf 1995 61p il (Eyewitness books) $19   **690**
1. Structural engineering 2. House construction 3. Building materials
ISBN 0-679-87256-6   LC 94-37733
"A Dorling Kindersley book"
First published 1994 in the United Kingdom
This covers "the history of building techniques, materials, and philosophy from earth-and-thatch houses to cathedrals and skyscrappers." SLJ
An "extremely handsome volume. . . . This is an informative book, fascinating for study or browsing." Sci Books Films

700 THE ARTS. FINE & DECORATIVE ARTS

Aronson, Marc
Art attack; a short cultural history of the avant-garde. Clarion Bks. 1998 192p il $20 (7 and up)   **700**
1. Modern art 2. Art appreciation 3. Art and society
ISBN 0-395-79729-2   LC 97-22372

Discusses the arts, life styles, politics, and fashions while tracing the story of bohemians, radicals, hipsters, and hippies from Paris in the nineteenth century to contemporary America
"*Art Attack* would make an excellent resource for the secondary level student who might be interested in exploring some creative outlets or as a catalyst for discussions about aesthetics, expression, or contemporary lifestyles." ALAN
Includes bibliographical references

Chambers, Veronica
The Harlem Renaissance. Chelsea House 1997 128p il (African-American achievers) $19.95; pa $8.95   **700**
1. Harlem Renaissance 2. African American arts
ISBN 0-7910-2597-7; 0-7910-2598-5 (pa)
                                                    LC 97-20585
Recounts the vibrant personalities and remarkable cultural movements that flourished in America's leading Black community during the 1920s and 1930s
This is a "sophisticated, in-depth history." Booklist
Includes bibliographical references

Creative fire; by the editors of Time-Life Books. Time-Life Bks. 1994 256p il (African Americans: voices of triumph) $29.95 (7 and up)   **700**
1. African American arts
                                                    LC 93-31616
This book "begins with a look at the creative arts in ancient Africa, and then traces the development of film-making, music, writing, and the visual arts from their beginnings here in America to the present time. Excellent-quality fine-art reproductions appear throughout. What sets this book apart, however, is the scope and variety of the full-color and black-and-white archival photographs. . . . This treatment makes the subject accessible to a wide range of readers." SLJ
Includes bibliographical references

Haskins, James, 1941-
The Harlem Renaissance. Millbrook Press 1996 192p lib bdg $30.90 (7 and up)   **700**
1. Harlem Renaissance 2. African American arts
ISBN 1-56294-565-3   LC 96-4608
This introduction to the Harlem Renaissance discusses "the music, art, and literature that were produced by African Americans in that time and place. Notables such as Duke Ellington, Zora Neale Hurston, Ethel Waters, Langston Hughes, Bill Robinson, Aaron Douglas, and Augusta Savage are included." SLJ
This "is a beautiful piece of bookmaking that is filled with photographs and portraits. The extensive source notes and a bibliography that includes books for adults and youngsters makes this a book that will appeal to adults as well as teens." Child Book Rev Serv

Isaacson, Philip M., 1924-
A short walk around the Pyramids & through the world of art. Knopf 1993 120p il $25; lib bdg $20.99   **700**
1. Art
ISBN 0-679-81523-6; 0-679-91523-0 (lib bdg)
                                                    LC 91-8854

Isaacson, Philip M., 1924-—*Continued*

Introduces tangible and abstract components of art, and the many forms art can take including sculpture, pottery, painting, photographs, and even furniture and cities

"A handsomely designed book with spacious margins and brilliantly clear full-color photographs. . . . Isaacson conducts his tour with a gentle, conversational style, surprising readers with fascinating juxtapositions." SLJ

Ochoa, George

The Wilson chronology of the arts; [by] George Ochoa and Melinda Corey. Wilson, H.W. 1998 476p $60 (7 and up)   **700**

1. Arts—History

ISBN 0-8242-0934-6   LC 97-23541

Replaces The timeline book of the arts, published 1995 by Ballantine Bks.

"The authors provide a timeline detailing human creativity that progresses from ca. 43,000 B.C.E. to 1997, with 4,000 entries spread over 13 categories of artistic endeavor. . . . The chronology is global in scope and comprehensive in coverage, emphasizing well-established art forms without neglecting the oral traditions and decorative art forms of nonliterate societies and currently emerging art forms. . . . The straightforward organization of this work makes it suitable for many different uses." Recomm Ref Books for Small & Medium-sized Libr & Media Cent, 1999

Includes bibliographical references

701 Art—Philosophy and theory

Hughes, Langston, 1902-1967

The book of rhythms; illustrations by Matt Wawiorka; introduction by Wynton Marsalis; afterword by Robert G. O'Meally. Oxford Univ. Press 1995 55p il (Iona and Peter Opie library of children's literature) $16.95   **701**

1. Rhythm

ISBN 0-19-509856-0   LC 94-41270

A newly illustrated reissue of The first book of rhythms published 1954 by Watts

The author describes the concept of rhythm in such things as musical notes, patterns in a shell, the ebb and flow of water, or a child spinning a top, and shows how rhythms connect humans with each other and nature

703 Art—Encyclopedias and dictionaries

International encyclopedia of art. Facts on File 1996-1997 8v set $175   **703**

1. Art—Encyclopedias

ISBN 0-8160-3327-7

Contents: African art, by W. Rea; Art of the ancient Mediterranean world, by B. Wilson; European art to 1850, by T. Lucchesi; European art since 1850, by N. Malloy; Far Eastern art, by C. Doherty; Mexican Central and South American art, by J. F. Scott; North American art to 1900, by A. Pancza-Graham; North American art since 1900, by C. M. E. P. Turner

"This set introduces world art, including both folk and fine art. . . . Arrangement is roughly chronological with 40 color and 60 black and white photographs in each volume. Sidebars and boxes are used for biographical and background information. . . . The easy reading level and attractive layout make this set useful as a basic guide to world art for all collections." Safford. Guide to Ref Materials for Sch Libr Media Cent. 5th edition

The **Oxford** dictionary of art; edited by Ian Chilvers and Harold Osborne; consultant editor, Dennis Farr. new ed. Oxford Univ. Press 1997 647p $49.95 (7 and up)   **703**

1. Art—Dictionaries

ISBN 0-19-860084-4   LC 97-200771

First published 1988

"This work contains over, 3,000 articles on Western painting, sculpture, drawing, graphic arts, and applied arts. Artists, schools, periods, techniques, and critical terms are also included."

"Lastingly useful and very readable." Booklist

704 Art—Special topics

Butler, Jerry, 1947-

A drawing in the sand; a story of African American art; written and illustrated by Jerry Butler. Zino Press Children's Bks. 1998 64p il $24.95   **704**

1. African American art 2. African American artists

ISBN 1-55933-216-6   LC 98-4139

The author "brings together his memories of growing up a fledgling artist in Magnolia, Miss., with brief biographies of 15 African-American artists (an additional 17 are listed at the end) who overcame racial and economic barriers to pursue their art." Publ Wkly

Butler's "discovery of African American art becomes an eye-opening journey of discovery for readers as well. An original and personal introduction to the field." Booklist

Includes bibliographical references

Finley, Carol

Art of the Far North; Inuit sculpture, drawing, and printmaking. Lerner Publs. 1998 56p il map (Art around the world) lib bdg $22.60   **704**

1. Inuit—Art 2. Inuit—Social life and customs

ISBN 0-8225-2075-3   LC 97-28375

Provides a brief history of the Inuit people and discusses their customs as a background for understanding their sculpture, drawing, and printmaking

The "text is accurate and informative. The full-color photographs are sharp and clear and the art itself is marvelous." SLJ

Includes bibliographical references

708 Art—Galleries, museums private collections

Thomson, Peggy, 1922-
The nine-ton cat: behind the scenes at an art museum; by Peggy Thomson and Barbara Moore; edited by Carol Eron. Houghton Mifflin 1997 96p il $21.95; pa $14.95　　　　**708**
　1. National Gallery of Art (U.S.) 2. Art museums
　ISBN 0-395-82655-1; 0-395-82683-7 (pa)
　　　　　　　　　　　　　　　LC 96-18809
　A behind-the-scenes look at the National Gallery of Art including its private spaces, workshops, offices, and labs where visitors rarely enter
　"This fascinating look at what goes on behind the scenes is as appealing to look at as it is informative. The unsung heroes of the institution—curators, conservators, gardeners, security personnel—get their due in short, intriguing chapters. . . . Photos, all nicely captioned, are a careful, very successful mix of color and black-and-white shots, including pictures of some of the museum's treasures." Booklist

709 Art—Historical and geographic treatment

Art: a world history. DK Pub. 1998 720p il $59.95 (7 and up)　　　　**709**
　1. Art—History
　ISBN 0-7894-2382-0　　　　LC 97-20234
　Original Italian edition, 1997
　This survey consists of "brief 50- to 500-word discussions of artists, topics, styles, and historic moments, presented via multiple columns, text boxes, time lines, and the like." Libr J
　Includes bibliographical references

Gardner's art through the ages. Harcourt Brace Jovanovich il maps $84 (7 and up)　　　**709**
　1. Art—History

　First published 1926 under the authorship of Helen Gardner. Starting with 5th edition, 1970, revised by Horst De La Croix and Richard G. Tansey. (10th edition 1996) Periodically revised by Richard G. Tansey and Fred S. Kleiner
　This book surveys world art from prehistoric times to the present day. Painting, sculpture, architecture and some decorative arts are considered. Although the focus is on European art, there are also chapters on ancient Near Eastern, Asian, pre-Columbian, American Indian, African and Oceanic art

Janson, H. W. (Horst Woldemar), 1913-1982
History of art for young people; [by] H.W. Janson and Anthony F. Janson. 5th ed. Abrams 1997 632p il maps $49.50 (7 and up)　　　**709**
　1. Art—History
　ISBN 0-8109-4150-3　　　　LC 96-22361
　First published 1972

Surveys the history of art, including painting, sculpture, architecture, and photography, from cave paintings to modern art. Included are "boxed essays . . . that comment on music, theater, and poetry through the ages." Booklist
Includes glossary and bibliographical references

709.01 Arts of nonliterate peoples, and earliest times to 499

Arnold, Caroline, 1944-
Stories in stone; rock art pictures by early Americans; photographs by Richard Hewett. Clarion Bks. 1996 48p il map $15.95　　　**709.01**
　1. Indians of North America—Antiquities 2. Rock drawings, paintings, and engravings
　ISBN 0-395-72092-3　　　　LC 96-387
　This focuses "on the rock art found in the Coso Range of eastern California. . . . Arnold describes the various methods that were used to create the designs. She also discusses climatic changes in the area, beginning with the last Ice Age, and surmises what life might have been like for those ancient people." Booklist
　"This is a crisply written, richly photographed account of the oldest known art in the world. . . . Hewett's color photographs are finely detailed, clear, and well composed, and they enrich the text enormously." Bull Cent Child Books
　Includes glossary

709.02 Art—500-1499

Cole, Alison
The Renaissance. Dorling Kindersley 1994 64p il (Eyewitness art) $16.95 (7 and up)　　**709.02**
　1. Renaissance art
　ISBN 1-56458-493-3　　　　LC 93-21264
　A guide to the art of Northern Europe and Italy from the 14th to the 16th century. Color photographs of paintings, sculpture and architecture representative of the period include the works of Giotto, Leonardo, Dürer, Titian, Raphael and Michelangelo. Features include detailed close-ups, diagrams and charts
　Includes glossary

Corrain, Lucia
The art of the Renaissance; illustrated by L.R. Galante, Simone Boni. Bedrick Bks. 1997 64p il maps (Masters of art) $22.50　　　**709.02**
　1. Renaissance art 2. Art appreciation
　ISBN 0-87226-526-9　　　　LC 97-19338
　An illustrated survey of the art and culture of Renaissance Europe
　"Despite the brevity of each entry, a surprising amount of solid information is conveyed. A typical entry consists of an introductory paragraph; a large illustration; and three-to-eight smaller illustrations, photographs, and full-color reproductions. . . . This title does a fine job of introducing young readers to this period in art history." SLJ

711 Area planning

Macaulay, David, 1946-
City: a story of Roman planning and construction. Houghton Mifflin 1974 112p il $18; pa $7.95 **711**
1. City planning—Rome 2. Civil engineering 3. Roman architecture
ISBN 0-395-19492-X; 0-395-34922-2 (pa)
"By following the inception, construction, and development of an imaginary Roman city, the account traces the evolution of Verbonia from the selection of its site under religious auspices in 26 B.C. to its completion in 100 A.D." Horn Book
Includes glossary

720 Architecture

Corbishley, Mike
The world of architectural wonders. Bedrick Bks. 1997 c1996 45p il maps $19.95 **720**
1. Structural engineering 2. Architecture
ISBN 0-87226-279-0 LC 96-47596
First published 1996 in the United Kingdom with title: Superstructures
Examines the stories behind such wonders of the world's architecture as the pyramids of Giza, the Great Wall of China, Chartes Cathedral, the city of Venice, and Hoover Dam
"Color photographs are paired with detailed drawings. Together, the text and illustrations capture the awe and spectacle of humankind's greatest building achievements." Booklist
Includes glossary

Isaacson, Philip M., 1924-
Round buildings, square buildings, & buildings that wiggle like a fish; with photographs by the author. Knopf 1988 121p il $22; pa $13 **720**
1. Architecture
ISBN 0 394-89382-4; 0-679-80649-0 (pa)
LC 87-16967
This discussion of architecture presents ninety-three buildings and structures from various times and places, including Stonehenge, Chartres, the Taj Mahal, the Great Mosque in Córdoba, the Parthenon, and the Brooklyn Bridge
"Beautifully composed and reproduced color photographs are numbered for reference in the text, which describes almost poetically the effects of contrasting architectural elements, styles, shapes, materials, and functions. . . . The writing is lyrical without abandoning fact, and the photographic perspectives are arresting." Bull Cent Child Books

Jessop, Joanne
The X-ray picture book of big buildings of the ancient world; written by Joanne Jessop; created and designed by David Salariya. Watts 1993 c1992 48p il lib bdg $24; pa $8.95 **720**
1. Ancient architecture
ISBN 0-531-14286-8 (lib bdg); 0-531-15709-1 (pa)
LC 93-36704

First published 1992 in the United Kingdom
"A pyramid at Giza, Abu Simbel, the Parthenon, the Colosseum, Notre Dame, Bodiam Castle, Mont St. Michel, the Basilica of St. Peter, the Taj Mahal, and the Forbidden City are all shown in marvelous full-color drawings in this oversize book. The many cutaway (not X-ray) and construction-in-action views are augmented with lucid explanations of each main, two-page diagram. . . . This book is not just for children; anyone interested in history, art, world culture, or travel will enjoy it." Sci Books Films
Includes glossary

The X-ray picture book of big buildings of the modern world; written by Joanne Jessop; created and designed by David Salariya. Watts 1994 c1993 48p il maps lib bdg $24; pa $8.95 **720**
1. Modern architecture
ISBN 0-531-14307-4 (lib bdg); 0-531-15716-4 (pa)
LC 93-40315
First published 1993 in the United Kingdom
This book presents cutaway views and discusses the construction of the Royal Pavilion, the Eiffel Tower, the Empire State Building, Sagrada Familia, Pompidou Center, the Sydney Opera House and other modern structures
Includes glossary

Lynch, Anne, 1941-
Great buildings; [text and] consulting editor, Anne Lynch. Time-Life Bks. 1996 64p il (Discoveries library) $24.95 **720**
1. Historic buildings 2. Architecture—History
LC 95-32821
Examines the history of some of the world's great buildings and describes the different architectural elements and styles that have been used throughout history in countries around the world
"This is a book that will intrigue the reader, primarily because of the quality of the illustrations." Sci Books Films
Includes glossary

The **Visual** dictionary of buildings. Dorling Kindersley 1992 64p il (Eyewitness visual dictionaries) $16.95 **720**
1. Architecture
ISBN 1-56458-102-0 LC 92-7673
Labeled illustrations with explanatory text depict historical and contemporary structures, architectural elements, and building components from ancient times to the present
This "is a splendidly visual architectural journey through time. . . . This visual dictionary easily stands tall as an art history source as well as a reference for the structures, forms, and components of buildings." Booklist

725 Public structures

Nardo, Don, 1947-
The Roman Colosseum. Lucent Bks. 1998 96p il maps (Building history series) lib bdg $22.45 (7 and up) **725**
1. Colosseum (Rome, Italy) 2. Rome—Antiquities
ISBN 1-56006-429-3 LC 97-2839

Nardo, Don, 1947-—*Continued*
Describes the planning and construction of the Colosseum in ancient Rome and traces its history through subsequent centuries
This is "thorough and well-written. . . . This book's numerous black-and-white photos, reproductions, diagrams, and maps enhance and extend the information. Sidebars provide primary-source materials and interesting quotations from writers and visitors throughout the ages." SLJ
Includes glossary and bibliographical references

726   Buildings for religious and related purposes

Macaulay, David, 1946-
Cathedral: the story of its construction. Houghton Mifflin 1973 77p il $18; pa $7.95
726
1. Cathedrals 2. Gothic architecture
ISBN 0-395-17513-5; 0-395-31668-5 (pa)
This is a description, illustrated with black-and-white line drawings, of the construction of an imagined representative Gothic cathedral "in southern France from its conception in 1252 to its completion in 1338. The spirit that motivated the people, the tools and materials they used, the steps and methods of constructions, all receive . . . attention." Booklist
Includes glossary

Pyramid. Houghton Mifflin 1975 80p il $18; pa $8.95
726
1. Pyramids 2. Egypt—Civilization
ISBN 0-395-21407-6; 0-395-32121-2 (pa)
The construction of a pyramid in 25th century B.C. Egypt is described. "Information about selection of the site, drawing of the plans, calculating compass directions, clearing and leveling the ground, and quarrying and hauling the tremendous blocks of granite and limestone is conveyed as much by pictures as by text." Horn Book
Includes glossary

Moorcroft, Christine
The Taj Mahal. Raintree Steck-Vaughn Pubs. 1998 48p il (Great buildings) lib bdg $25.69
726
1. Taj Mahal (Agra, India) 2. India
ISBN 0-8172-4920-6   LC 97-15619
Examines the design and construction of the architectural masterpiece that was built during the Mughal rule of India
"Undying love, tragedy, murder, and betrayal make the story of the building of the Taj Mahal one of the world's great romantic tales. Along with the fascinating history behind the creation of this architectural wonder, Moorcroft describes how the building was constructed and the reasoning behind some of its features. . . . An excellent source for reports as well as interesting reading for budding architecture buffs." Booklist
Includes bibliographical references

728   Residential and related buildings

Yue, Charlotte
The igloo; [by] Charlotte and David Yue. Houghton Mifflin 1988 117p il $16; pa $6.95
728
1. Igloos 2. Inuit
ISBN 0-395-44613-9; 0-395-62986-1 (pa)
LC 88-6154
Describes how an igloo is constructed and the role it plays in the lives of the Eskimo people. Also discusses many other aspects of Eskimo culture that have helped them adapt to life in the Arctic
"This book is a tidy source of reference information, curriculum support, and just plain compelling reading." SLJ
Includes bibliographical references

728.8   Large and elaborate private dwellings

Cairns, Conrad
Medieval castles. Cambridge Univ. Press 1987 48p il (Cambridge introduction to world history) pa $12 (7 and up)
728.8
1. Castles 2. Medieval civilization
ISBN 0-521-31589-1   LC 85-366
A history and discussion of those fortified private dwellings, known as castles, which were built in Europe only during the Middle Ages, with particular attention to those of Britain

Gravett, Christopher
Castle; written by Christopher Gravett; photographed by Geoff Dann. Knopf 1994 63p il (Eyewitness books) $19; lib bdg $20.99   **728.8**
1. Castles 2. Fortification
ISBN 0-679-86000-2; 0-679-96000-7 (lib bdg)
LC 93-32594
"A Dorling Kindersley book"
"*Castle* looks at European fortifications, Byzantine and Muslim-influenced constructions of the Crusades, and Japanese strongholds and defense strategies through photographs of architectural features, designs, and weapons. Everyday life is also documented with pictures of artifacts and people in period costumes." SLJ
"This book offers page after page of excellent photographs. . . . Each photo is clearly described in language concise enough that the reader understands the functioning of obscure implements and features of castles. The information presented is generally accurate." Sci Books Films

Macaulay, David, 1946-
Castle. Houghton Mifflin 1977 74p il $18; pa $8.95
728.8
1. Castles 2. Fortification
ISBN 0-395-25784-0; 0-395-32920-5 (pa)
LC 77-7159

Macaulay, David, 1946-—_Continued_
Macaulay depicts "the history of an imaginary thirteenth-century castle—built to subdue the Welsh hordes—from the age of construction to the age of neglect, when the town of Aberwyfern no longer needs a fortified stronghold." Economist
Includes glossary

Steele, Philip
Castles. Kingfisher (NY) 1995 63p il $15.95
728.8
1. Castles
ISBN 1-85697-547-9   LC 94-29366
An "overview of medieval European (and a few Near Eastern) castles. The book's strengths are its well-organized format and careful balance of text and illustrations. Steele touches on almost every facet of castle construction, inhabitants, celebrations, and rituals, as well as more mundane topics such as sanitation and the kitchen." SLJ
Includes glossary

730.9 Sculpture—Historical and geographic treatment

Curlee, Lynn, 1947-
Rushmore. Scholastic Press 1999 48p il $17.95
730.9
1. Borglum, Gutzon, 1867-1941 2. Mount Rushmore National Memorial (S.D.)
ISBN 0-590-22573-1   LC 98-16891
Describes how this patriotic shrine and tourist attraction was conceived, designed, and created by the dedicated artist Gutzon Borglum
The text "is straightforward and readable, giving a sense of the creator and the difficult project. The layout is spacious and pleasing, as are the large, carefully executed paintings." Booklist
Includes bibliographical references

Greenberg, Jan, 1942-
The sculptor's eye; looking at contemporary American art; [by] Jan Greenberg and Sandra Jordan. Delacorte Press 1993 128p il $19.95
730.9
1. American sculpture 2. Modern sculpture—1900-1999 (20th century) 3. Art appreciation
ISBN 0-385-30902-3   LC 92-16323
Discusses the nature, subject matter, and techniques of modern American sculpture and presents such contemporary artists as Red Grooms, Viola Frey, and George Segal
"The sculptures are presented in glorious, full color, but the artists are pictured in candid black-and-white shots." Booklist
Includes glossary and bibliographical references

Opie, Mary-Jane
Sculpture. Dorling Kindersley 1994 64p il maps (Eyewitness art) $16.95 (7 and up)
730.9
1. Sculpture
ISBN 1-56458-495-X   LC 94-2593

"This book surveys the history of sculpture. Each two-page section introduces a new topic, from 'Eastern deities' to 'Carving a totem pole' to 'The High Renaissance' to 'New materials.' Several full-color illustrations appear on each page. . . . Text consists of a short introduction to each double-page spread and, for each example of sculpture, fairly detailed captions." Booklist

736 Carving and carvings. Paper cutting and folding

Diehn, Gwen, 1943-
Making books that fly, fold, wrap, hide, pop up, twist, and turn; books for kids to make. Lark Bks. 1998 96p il $19.95
736
1. Paper crafts 2. Handicraft
ISBN 1-57990-023-2   LC 97-41037
Presents instructions for making various kinds of books including those that carry messages across space and time as well as those that save words, ideas, and pictures
"Clear directions and diagrams and attractive full-color photographs of completed projects will make it easy for readers to duplicate 18 different folded, wrapped, and pop-up books." Booklist
Includes glossary

Rich, Chris, 1949-
The book of papercutting; a complete guide to all the techniques with more than 100 project ideas. Sterling 1993 128p il hardcover o.p. paperback available $14.95
736
1. Paper crafts
ISBN 0-8069-0286-8 (pa)   LC 92-21536
This guide presents "the technical information and tools necessary to complete projects ranging from the very simple to the extremely challenging. Examples include German- and Swiss-style works, folk art from Poland and China, projects with religious themes, and contemporary designs." Booklist
"Beginning and experienced paper cutters will treasure this book. . . . Students will find ideas here to enhance social studies as well as art assignments." SLJ
Includes bibliographical references

737.4 Coins

Hughes, Roderick P.
Fell's official know-it-all guide: coins; your absolute, quintessential, all you wanted to know, complete guide to United States coins. Fell 1999 309p $16.95
737.4
1. Coins
ISBN 0-88391-006-3   LC 99-34275
Replaces Fell's United States coin book
This guide to United States coins includes hundreds of photos and thousands of prices and lists names and addresses of coin publications, professional organizations, and grading and authentication services

741.2 Drawing—Techniques, equipment, materials

Ames, Lee J., 1921-
Drawing with Lee Ames; from the bestselling, award-winning creator of the Draw 50 series, a proven step-by-step guide to the fundamentals of drawing for all ages. Doubleday 1990 262p il pa $21   741.2
1. Drawing
ISBN 0-385-23701-4   LC 90-31436
The author "offers a compendium of samples for beginning artists. Ames explains his approach to beginning art instruction as a form of mimicry, where students copy samples in order to get a feel for the process of drawing. . . . This is definitely for the beginning student who possesses very little to no drawing experience. . . . Ames's approach offers a good base from which students can then move on to more in-depth instruction." Voice Youth Advocates
Includes bibliographical references

Welton, Jude, 1955-
Drawing; a young artist's guide; Tate Gallery consultant, Colin Grigg. Dorling Kindersley 1994 45p il (Eyewitness art) $14.95 (7 and up) 741.2
1. Drawing
ISBN 1-56458-676-6   LC 94-13103
"This is not a traditional 'how to' book that instructs youngsters in copying an existing drawing; instead, it suggests techniques and encourages them to use their own imaginations. Brief paragraphs written in a conversational tone and attractive, full-color photographs should spark an appreciation for art." SLJ

741.5 Cartoons, caricatures, comics

Bohl, Al
Guide to cartooning. Pelican 1997 176p il pa $13.95   741.5
1. Cartoons and caricatures
ISBN 1-56554-177-4   LC 96-44340
Provides instructions for drawing different styles of cartooning, including political, strips, books, and illustration, and gives advice on how to get a job in the field
This "is so chockablock with information that any teen interested in cartooning will come away with a multitude of tips and tricks." Booklist
Includes bibliographical references

Bulloch, Ivan
Cartoons & animation. Children's Press 1998 31p il (Arts and crafts skills) $20.50; pa $6.95   741.5
1. Cartoons and caricatures 2. Animated films
ISBN 0-516-21194-3; 0-516-26342-0 (pa)
LC 97-51969
Provides information about different kinds of cartoons and how to create them, including a simple look at the process of animation

Hart, Christopher
How to draw comic book bad guys and gals. Watson-Guptill 1998 64p il pa $9.95   741.5
1. Comic books, strips, etc. 2. Cartoons and caricatures
ISBN 0-8230-2372-9   LC 98-6411
This guide to drawing comic book villains covers such topics as head tilts, facial expressions, hands and muscle groups, the body in action, using light and shadow, composition, and storytelling
"Not for beginners, but for those who already have some knowledge of drawing and ability. . . . Boldly colored illustrations combined with the line drawings add to the professional look of the book." Voice Youth Advocates

Mind riot; coming of age in comix; edited and with an introduction by Karen D. Hirsch; foreword by Peter Bagge. Aladdin Paperbacks 1997 127p il pa $9.99 (7 and up)   741.5
1. Comic books, strips, etc.
ISBN 0-689-80622-1   LC 96-48073
"Hirsch has assembled 16 previously unpublished coming-of-age stories from the realm of 'underground comix,' with themes as diverse as the artists and their illustration styles. Subjects include self-esteem, aging, body image, skateboarding, sexuality, self-acceptance, computer dating, compassion, sexual abuse, gangs, friendship, etc. The book has a particularly helpful introduction to the genre, a foreword, names of mail-order catalogs, and a list of related Internet sites." SLJ
Includes bibliographical references

Pellowski, Michael, 1949-
The art of making comic books; [by] Michael Morgan Pellowski; with illustrations by Howard Bender. Lerner Publs. 1995 80p il (Media workshop) $21.27; pa $8.95   741.5
1. Comic books, strips, etc. 2. Cartoons and caricatures
ISBN 0-8225-2304-3; 0-8225-9672-5 (pa)
LC 94-27589
"After a brief overview of comic-book history, the text describes the making of a comic book, explaining the various jobs people hold and the various stages books must go through. . . . Serious comic fans will relish Pellowski's detail-oriented and knowledgeable pragmatism." Bull Cent Child Books
Includes glossary and bibliographical references

Sanderson, Peter
Marvel universe. Abrams 1996 256p il $49.95 (7 and up)   741.5
1. Marvel Comics Group 2. Comic books, strips, etc.
ISBN 0-8109-4285-2   LC 95-7151
"Sanderson traces the evolution of the Marvel superheroes from their conception in 1939 to the present day. . . . The history and contributions of Marvel artists and writers such as Jack Kirby and Stan Lee are highlighted throughout the text and numerous illustrations." SLJ
"Featuring 400 color illustrations, the book is a visual knockout." Publ Wkly

The **World** encyclopedia of comics; edited by Maurice Horn. [rev & updated] Chelsea House 1999 7v il set $245 **741.5**
1. Comic books, strips, etc.
ISBN 0-7910-4854-3   LC 97-50448
Also available single volume version $59.95 (ISBN 0-7910-4856-X)
First published 1976
Containing some 1400 signed entries, this reference work opens with historical and analytical essays and a chronology. "Then the listings begin, reporting on writers, artists, publishers, and characters galore, all mixed together alphabetically and covering information up to December 1997." Libr J
For a fuller review see: Booklist, April 1, 1999

741.6 Graphic design, illustration and commercial art

Biesty, Stephen
Stephen Biesty's incredible explosions; illustrated by Stephen Biesty; written by Richard Platt. DK Pub. 1996 32p il $19.95 **741.6**
1. Illustration of books
ISBN 0-7894-1024-9   LC 96-13948
This book includes cross-section and other inside-view illustrations of twelve diverse subjects, including the Grand Canyon, an airport, a city block, a space station, a windmill, the human body, and the Tower Bridge
"Painstakingly crafted and filled with mind-boggling detail, [Biesty's] artwork invites close, repeated viewing; combined with Platt's brisk text, it is guaranteed to both educate and entertain." Publ Wkly

Marcus, Leonard S., 1950-
A Caldecott celebration; six artists and their paths to the Caldecott medal. Walker & Co. 1998 49p il $18.95; lib bdg $19.95 **741.6**
1. Caldecott Medal 2. Illustrators 3. Illustration of books
ISBN 0-8027-8656-1; 0-8027-8658-8 (lib bdg)
     LC 98-6616
Profiles six Caldecott award winning books and their authors, including Robert McCloskey's "Make Way for Ducklings," Marcia Brown's "Cinderella," Maurice Sendak's "Where the Wild Things Are," William Steig's "Sylvester and the Magic Pebble," Chris Van Allsburg's "Jumanji," and David Wiesner's "Tuesday"
"Marcus, who interviewed each artist, provides a lively, informative introduction to each book and its maker. A beautifully made book, this will serve as a fine resource for children interested in illustration and for teachers researching author/illustrator studies." Booklist
Includes glossary

Talking with artists [I-III]; compiled and edited by Pat Cummings. Bradbury Press 1992-1999 3v il $22; $19.95; $20 **741.6**
1. Illustrators 2. Illustration of books
ISBN 0-02-724245-5 (v1); 0-689-80310-9 (v2 Simon & Schuster); 0-395-89132-9 (v3 Clarion Bks.)
     LC 91-9982
Volume two published by Simon & Schuster Bks. for Young Readers; volume three published by Clarion Bks.

Each volume presents interviews with illustrators, who discuss their lives and works. Among the 14 artists in the first volume are Victoria Chess, Leo and Diane Dillon, Amy Schwartz, Tom Feelings, and Steven Kellogg. The 13 artists represented in the second volume include Brian Pinkney, Denise Fleming, Floyd Cooper, Maira Kalman, and David Wisniewski. Among the 13 illustrators profiled in the third volume are Raul Colon, Lisa Desimini, G. Brian Karas, Peter Sis, and Paul Zelinsky. Samples of each illustrator's work are included

741.9 Collections of drawings

—**I** never saw another butterfly—; children's drawings and poems from Terezin concentration camp, 1942-1944; edited by Hana Volavková; foreword by Chaim Potok; afterword by Vaclav Havel. expanded 2nd ed, by U.S. Holocaust Memorial Mus. Schocken Bks. 1993 xxii, 106p il $26; pa $16 **741.9**
1. Child artists 2. Child authors 3. Terezin (Czechoslovakia: Concentration camp)
ISBN 0-8052-4115-9; 0-8052-1015-6 (pa)
     LC 92-50477
Original Czech edition, 1959; first American edition published 1964 by McGraw-Hill
"Of the 15,000 children who passed through Terezin before going to Auschwitz, only 100 lived. This book is a collection of poems and drawings by some of them. . . . This touching book adds another facet to library collections on the Holocaust." SLJ

742 Perspective in drawing

DuBosque, Doug
Draw 3-D; a step-by-step guide to perspective drawing. Peel Productions 1999 63p il pa $8.95 **742**
1. Perspective 2. Drawing
ISBN 0-939217-14-7   LC 98-42174
"Using easy-to-follow, step-by-step sketches, DuBosque introduces readers to the techniques of three-dimensional drawing. Beginning with such elementary concepts as depth, he progresses logically through shading, reflections, and multiple vanishing points. The supportive tone encourages novices to keep trying and not become discouraged." SLJ

743 Drawing and drawings by subject

Ames, Lee J., 1921-
[Draw 50 series] Doubleday 1974-1998 25v pa ea $8.95 **743**
1. Drawing

Most titles available in both hardcover and paperback
Available titles are: Draw 50 animals (1974); Draw 50 boats, ships, trucks, & trains (1976); Draw 50 airplanes, aircraft, & spacecraft (1977); Draw 50 dinosaurs and oth-

Ames, Lee J., 1921——Continued

er prehistoric animals (1977); Draw 50 famous faces (1978); Draw 50 vehicles (1978); Draw 50 famous cartoons (1979); Draw 50 buildings and other structures (1980); Draw 50 dogs (1981); Draw 50 monsters, creeps, superheroes, demons, dragons, nerds, dirts, ghouls, giants, vampires, zombies, and other curiosa (1983); Draw 50 horses (1984); Draw 50 athletes (1985); Draw 50 cats (1986); Draw 50 cars, trucks, and motorcycles (1986); Draw 50 holiday decorations (1987); Draw 50 beasties and yugglies and turnover uglies and things that go bump in the night (1988); Draw 50 sharks, whales, and other sea creatures (1989); Draw 50 famous faces (1990); Draw 50 creepy crawlies (1991); Draw 50 endangered animals (1992); Draw 50 people (1993); Draw 50 flowers, trees, and other plants (1994); Draw 50 people of the Bible (1995); Draw 50 birds (1996); Draw 50 aliens, UFO's galaxy ghouls, milky way marauders, and other extra terrestrial creatures (1998)

Each volume presents step-by-step instructions for drawing a variety of animals, people, or objects

Arnosky, Jim

Sketching outdoors in spring. Lothrop, Lee & Shepard Bks. 1987 48p il $12.95   **743**
1. Drawing 2. Landscape drawing 3. Animal painting and illustration
ISBN 0-688-06284-9   LC 86-21308

Provides drawings of landscapes, plants, animals, and other aspects of nature in spring, accompanied by comments from the artist on how and why he drew them

"An enchanting, delightful, and succinct appetizer, this book will appeal to artist and naturalist alike." Sci Books Films

Sketching outdoors in summer. Lothrop, Lee & Shepard Bks. 1988 47p il $12.95   **743**
1. Drawing 2. Landscape drawing 3. Animal painting and illustration
ISBN 0-688-06286-5   LC 87-29728

The author "shares some of the sources of his artistic inspiration by taking readers on a guided tour through a summer of sketching his home, his garden, the surrounding woods and ponds complete with wildlife, and a few boats that he favored during the summer months." Sci Books Films

This "is a wonderful book, effectively integrating science and art. . . . The author's text and black-and-white illustrations are full of interesting and useful information." Appraisal

DuBosque, Doug

Draw insects. Peel Productions 1997 63p il pa $8.95   **743**
1. Insects in art 2. Drawing
ISBN 0-939217-28-7   LC 97-44401

Provides step-by-step instructions for drawing insects, including the bumblebee, giant beetle, and yellow jacket

This is a "carefully constructed drawing book. . . . Basic information such as the order and family of each creature and where it may be found is provided. This additional material makes this book more useful for both observations of insects and for report writing than other titles currently available." SLJ

Tallarico, Tony

Drawing and cartooning monsters; a step-by-step guide for the aspiring monster-maker. Putnam 1993 92p pa $10.95   **743**
1. Monsters in art 2. Drawing 3. Cartoons and caricatures
ISBN 0-399-51785-5   LC 92-19060
"A Perigee book"

Provides step-by-step instructions for making drawings and cartoons of monsters, both simple and sophisticated

745.2 Industrial art and design

Tambini, Michael

The look of the century. DK Pub. 1996 288p il $39.95 (7 and up)   **745.2**
1. Industrial design
ISBN 0-7894-0950-X   LC 96-11806
"In association with Cooper-Hewitt, National Design Museum, Smithsonian Institution." Cover

"Form and function are showcased as to their design elements in the products of the 1900-1990's. A wonderful browsing book! Highly illustrative with full-color photos and drawings. . . . Concludes with a pictorial summary of posters, advertising and short biographies of designers." BAYA Book Rev

Includes bibliographical references

745.5 Handicrafts

Chapman, Gillian

The Egyptians. Heinemann Interactive Lib. 1997 37p il (Crafts from the past) lib bdg $24.22   **745.5**
1. Handicraft 2. Egypt—Civilization 3. Egypt—Antiquities
ISBN 1-57572-556-8   LC 97-29172

Describes various aspects of life in ancient Egypt and provides instructions for creating hieroglyphic messages, mummy cases, reed boats, board games, pharoah's jewels, and more

"The colorful crafts are attractive, often ambitious, and generally reflective of the culture." SLJ

Includes glossary

The Greeks. Heinemann Lib. 1998 39p il (Crafts from the past) lib bdg $19.92   **745.5**
1. Handicraft 2. Greece—Civilization
ISBN 1-57572-733-1   LC 98-15668

Describes various aspects of life in ancient Greece and provides instructions for creating related crafts, including labyrinths, a bronze helmet, and a Trojan horse

This offers "sophisticated-looking crafts that children will want to try." SLJ

Includes glossary

The Romans. Heinemann Lib. 1998 39p il (Crafts from the past) lib bdg $19.92   **745.5**
1. Handicraft 2. Rome—Civilization
ISBN 1-57572-734-X   LC 98-15666

Describes various aspects of life in ancient Rome and provides instructions for creating related crafts, including scrolls, temples, statues, and terracotta lamps

Includes glossary

Doney, Meryl
Festivals. Watts 1997 32p il (World crafts) $21; pa $6.95   **745.5**
1. Festivals 2. Handicraft
ISBN 0-531-14431-3; 0-531-15329-0 (pa)
LC 96-15838
Introduces a variety of well known festivals from around the world and provides instructions for related crafts, including a dragon toy for the Chinese New Year, dancing wings for Mardi Gras, and a sugar skull for Halloween
Includes bibliographical references

Engelbreit, Mary
Hey, kids! Come craft with me. Meredith Bks. 1999 112p il $19.95   **745.5**
1. Handicraft
ISBN 0-696-20906-3   LC 98-68022
This describes "crafts such as twig picture frames, costumes and accessories, patterns for tea-party place settings, paper crafts such as greeting cards and stationery, and dozens more. The book is loaded with ideas." SLJ

Hendry, Linda
Making picture frames; written by Linda Hendry and Lisa Rebnord; illustrated by Linda Hendry. Kids Can Press 1999 c1998 40p il (Kids Can do it) pa $5.95   **745.5**
1. Handicraft 2. Picture frames and framing
ISBN 1-55074-505-0
First published 1998 in Canada
This offers directions and ideas for creating and decorating picture frames using materials such as cardboard, paper maché, stones, sticks, hardware, foil, paper, and ribbons
"Lots of fun and creative ideas are presented in this clearly illustrated book. . . . A good choice for experienced young crafters and teachers and librarians looking for new ideas." SLJ

Holtschlag, Margaret
Button crafts; by Margaret Holtschlag and Carol Trojanowski; illustrated by Lynne Woodcock Cravath. Random House 1999 il pa $3.25   **745.5**
1. Handicraft 2. Buttons
ISBN 0-679-88646-X   LC 98-17177
Provides instructions for using buttons to make a variety of crafts, including picture frames, gift boxes, and necklaces

Needham, Bobbe
Ecology crafts for kids; 50 great ways to make friends with planet earth. Sterling 1998 144p il $24.95; pa $14.95   **745.5**
1. Handicraft   2. Environmental   protection
3. Recycling
ISBN 0-8069-0685-5; 0-8069-2024-6 (pa)
LC 98-3565
"A Sterling/Lark book"
This "contains more than fifty projects that utilize the recycling of selected materials (i.e, twigs, gourds, used furniture, eggshells, newspapers, and rocks). . . . The text is supported by a very large number of high quality photographs. . . . One of the best publications of its kind." Appraisal

Stevens, Bernardine S.
Colonial American craftspeople. Watts 1993 128p il (Colonial America) lib bdg $22   **745.5**
1. Handicraft 2. United States—Social life and customs—1600-1775, Colonial period
ISBN 0-531-12536-X   LC 93-19323
The author describes the training and work of such craftspeople as carpenters, masons, silversmiths, wigmakers, and leatherworkers living in the American colonies
"Informative and readable." SLJ
Includes glossary and bibliographical references

Temko, Florence
Traditional crafts from Africa; with illustrations by Randall Gooch; and photographs by Robert L. and Diane Wolfe. Lerner Publs. 1996 64p il maps (Culture crafts) lib bdg $22.60   **745.5**
1. Handicraft
ISBN 0-8225-2936-X   LC 95-8109
"Each chapter focuses on one craft technique and includes a project from a specific African region. Vivid maps of each region show its climate and the culture of its people. . . . Bright, full-color photographs accompany descriptions of technique. Clear diagrams demonstrate how to make reproductions of the crafts with readily available materials." SLJ
Includes glossary and bibliographical references

Traditional crafts from Mexico and Central America; with illustrations by Randall Gooch and photographs by Robert L. and Diane Wolfe. Lerner Publs. 1996 63p il (Culture crafts) lib bdg $22.60   **745.5**
1. Handicraft
ISBN 0-8225-2935-1   LC 95-46583
Provides instructions on how to make traditional Mexican and Central American handicraft such as metal ornaments, tissue paper banners, and Guatemalan worry dolls
"The directions and pictures are clear and enticing; there are full-color photographs of the completed projects as well as of the original handiwork that inspired them." SLJ
Includes glossary and bibliographical references

745.59   Making specific objects

Doney, Meryl
Masks. Watts 1995 32p il maps (World crafts) lib bdg $22; pa $6.95   **745.59**
1. Masks (Facial) 2. Handicraft
ISBN 0-531-14397-X (lib bdg); 0-531-15870-5 (pa)
LC 96-112757
The author presents instructions for making various masks from around the world
"Every project is presented clearly on a two-page spread along with information; a map of the country of origin; a fine, full-color photograph of the original artifact; and step-by-step illustrations that explain how to make a similar item." SLJ

745.592   Toys, models, miniatures, related objects

Doney, Meryl
Puppets. Watts 1995 32p il (World crafts) lib bdg $22; pa $6.95   **745.592**
1. Puppets and puppet plays 2. Handicraft
ISBN 0-531-14399-6 (lib bdg); 0-531-15872-1 (pa)
                                                    LC 95-11433
Color photographs and diagrams accompany step-by-step instructions for constructing a variety of puppets
Includes bibliographical references

Schmidt, Norman
Super paper airplanes; biplanes to space planes. Sterling 1995 96p il $19.95   **745.592**
1. Airplanes—Models 2. Paper crafts
ISBN 1-895569-30-3   LC 94-35543
Provides instructions for creating 28 airplane models using paper, ruler, pencil, scissors, and glue, and includes historical, technical, and scientific information about each airplane

Temko, Florence
Planes and other flying things. Millbrook Press 1996 45p il (Paper magic) lib bdg $20.90; pa $7.95   **745.592**
1. Airplanes—Models 2. Paper crafts
ISBN 0-7613-0041-4 (lib bdg); 0-7613-0082-1 (pa)
                                                    LC 96-4545
Presents simple instructions for folding paper to make airplanes and other flying things including the glider, star ship, helicopter, pterosaur, and even the Concorde
"This nice-looking, simply written guide will fill a need. . . . The format is appealingly crisp, with color diagrams set against lots of white space." Booklist

745.6   Calligraphy, illumination, heraldic design

Fisher, Leonard Everett, 1924-
Alphabet art: thirteen ABCs from around the world; written and illustrated by Leonard Everett Fisher. Four Winds Press 1985 c1978 61p il lib bdg $16.95   **745.6**
1. Alphabets 2. Lettering
ISBN 0-02-735230-7   LC 84-28752
Companion volume to Number art (1982) and Symbol art (1985)
A reissue of the title first published 1978
"Well written and beautifully designed book. Provides brief information on the people and background for each of the following alphabets in use around the world today—Arabic, Cherokee, Chinese, Cyrillic, Eskimo, Gaelic, German, Greek, Hebrew, Japanese, Sanskrit, Thai and Tibetan." N Y Public Libr. Ref Books for Child Collect. 2d edition

Wilson, Elizabeth B.
Bibles and bestiaries; a guide to illuminated manuscripts. Farrar, Straus & Giroux 1994 64p il $25   **745.6**
1. Bible—Pictorial works 2. Illumination of books and manuscripts
ISBN 0-374-30685-0   LC 94-6687
"Using examples of illuminated manuscripts from the Pierpont Morgan Library as illustrations, Wilson describes how a book was crafted in the Middle Ages. . . . A beautiful adjunct to studies of the Middle Ages, the volume is as elegant and special as its subject." Booklist
Includes glossary and bibliographical references

746.46   Patchwork and quilting

Bial, Raymond
With needle and thread; a book about quilts. Houghton Mifflin 1996 48p il $14.95   **746.46**
1. Quilting 2. Quilts
ISBN 0-395-73568-8   LC 95-16416
The author "describes the processes of marking, piecing, and quilting. An historical overview ranges from the Colonial period to the famous AIDS Memorial Quilt. . . . Bial shows work by Amish, African-American, and Hmong quilters. The narrative is accessibly simple, the photography is clear and colorful." Bull Cent Child Books
Includes bibliographical references

Wilson, Sule Greg
African American quilting; the warmth of tradition; [by] Sule Greg C. Wilson. Rosen Pub. Group; PowerKids Press 1999 64p il map (Library of African American arts and culture) $17.95
                                                    746.46
1. Quilting 2. African American art
ISBN 0-8239-1854-8   LC 99-18290
Explains the art and craft of quilting among Afro-Americans and describes its roots in African textiles and traditions
"A delightful treasure trove of information." SLJ
Includes glossary and bibliographical references

747   Interior decoration

Bull, Jane, 1957-
Change your room. DK Pub. 1999 96p il $14.95
                                                    747
1. Interior design
ISBN 0-7894-3956-5   LC 99-11936
Presents ideas and techniques to help create a personal space that reflects one's own style
"A creative, thematic approach to decorating using basic craft techniques and materials. . . . The title, the cover, and the brightly colored photography will attract youngsters." SLJ

748.2 Glassware

Houston, James A., 1921-
Fire into ice; adventures in glass making; by James Houston. Tundra Bks. 1998 unp il $15.95
748.2
1. Steuben Glass 2. Glassware
ISBN 0-88776-459-2   LC 98-60387
The author describes how his experiences living among the Inuit influenced his work as a designer for the Steuben glass company

750 Painting and paintings

Richardson, Joy
Looking at pictures; an introduction to art for young people; with illustrations by Charlotte Voake. Abrams 1997 80p il $17.95   **750**
1. National Gallery (Great Britain) 2. Painting 3. Art appreciation 4. Art museums
ISBN 0-8109-4252-6   LC 96-86476
This "art-appreciation book delves into the world of painting using works from London's National Gallery that span 700 years. First, the author takes readers behind the scenes, focusing on how paintings are selected and hung as well as the detailed labor of restoration. The remaining chapters present major themes in the study of art including color, light, subject matter, and perspective." SLJ
"This large-size volume makes art appreciation accessible to middle-grade readers. The text is chatty and direct. . . . [It includes] beautiful full-color pictures on every page." Booklist

750.1 Painting—Philosophy and theory

Sturgis, Alexander
Optical illusions in art. Sterling 1996 32p il $14.95   **750.1**
1. Art appreciation 2. Optical illusions
ISBN 0-8069-6135-X   LC 95-46740
This volume includes "chapters on trompe l'oeil, surrealism, perspective, anamorphosis (distortions corrected by use of mirrors or acute viewing angles), reversible images and op art." Publ Wkly

Welton, Jude, 1955-
Looking at paintings. Dorling Kindersley 1994 64p il (Eyewitness art) $16.95 (7 and up) **750.1**
1. Art appreciation
ISBN 1-56458-494-1   LC 93-38299
Featuring examples of paintings from all periods, each two-page spread discusses a different topic. Headings included are Composition; Using color; Light, shade, and space; Illusion and reality; Fresco, tempera, and oil; Watercolor and pastel; Portraits; The nude; Landscapes, and Still lifes.
Includes glossary

751 Painting—Techniques, procedures, apparatus, equipment, materials

The **DK** art school series. Dorling Kindersley 1993-1995 12v il Prices range from $8.95 for paperback editions to $15.25 for hardcover (7 and up)   **751**
1. Painting—Technique

Titles published in 1993: An introduction to acrylics, by R. Smith; An introduction to oil painting, by R. Smith; An introduction to pastels, by M. Wright; An introduction to watercolor, by R. Smith; Watercolor color, by R. Smith; Watercolor landscape, by R. Smith
Titles published in 1994: Drawing figures, by R. Smith; An introduction to drawing, by J. Horton; Oil painting portraits, by R. Smith; Watercolor still life, by L. E. Lloyd
Titles published in 1995: An introduction to mixed media, by M. Wright; An introduction to perspective, by R. Smith
"Each book begins with a very brief history of the medium specific to that volume. The best uses for each medium are introduced along with choices of tools, brushes, papers and canvas. Little prior knowledge is assumed; the reader is taken step-by-step through the techniques possible for each medium. . . . Each book is lavishly illustrated. A few photos are used, but the dominant look is that of the medium being discussed. . . . Examples of well-known art in each medium are also included. This series would serve as a good introduction that would not overwhelm beginners." Book Rep

751.7 Paintings—Specific forms

Capek, Michael, 1947-
Murals; cave, cathedral, to street. Lerner Publs. 1996 80p il maps lib bdg $23.93   **751.7**
1. Mural painting and decoration
ISBN 0-8225-2065-6   LC 95-346
This "survey covers murals in the United States, Mexico, Europe, ancient Egypt, and prehistory. Capek discusses what these paintings teach about their respective cultures and the influence they have had on society." Horn Book Guide
"Photographs of painters and many full-color reproductions of murals illustrate the text effectively. The book is both attractive and well written." Booklist
Includes glossary and bibliographical references

759.01 Painting of nonliterate peoples, and earliest times to 499

Finley, Carol
Aboriginal art of Australia; exploring cultural traditions. Lerner Publs. 1998 56p il maps (Art around the world) $23.93   **759.01**
1. Australian painting 2. Australian aborigines
ISBN 0-8225-2076-1   LC 97-28467

Finley, Carol—*Continued*
Describes the art of the Australian Aborigines including rock painting and engraving as well as sand and bark painting; also discusses the symbolism found in these works
"Clear, full-color photographs of the art, people, and landscape illustrate the text." SLJ
Includes bibliographical references

Lauber, Patricia, 1924-
Painters of the caves. National Geographic Soc. 1998 48p il map $17.95 **759.01**
1. Prehistoric art 2. Prehistoric peoples
ISBN 0-7922-7095-9 LC 97-24172
Describes the 1994 discovery made in Chauvet, France, of a cave with Stone Age rock paintings, and discusses the significance of cave art to people living in prehistoric as well as modern times
"This impressive work is rich in both its artwork and its text." Booklist
Includes bibliographical references

Patent, Dorothy Hinshaw
Mystery of the Lascaux Cave. Benchmark Bks. (Tarrytown) 1999 64p il (Frozen in time) $27.07 **759.01**
1. Prehistoric art 2. Prehistoric peoples
ISBN 0-7614-0784-7 LC 97-48276
Discusses the paintings on the walls of Lascaux Cave in France including the cave's discovery, its significance, and the efforts to preserve the paintings themselves
This title will be welcomed for its "clear expository style, accuracy, [and] informative sidebars. . . . [It is] heavily illustrated with crisp full-color photos and a few paintings." SLJ
Includes glossary and bibliographical references

759.13 American painting

Feelings, Tom, 1933-
The middle passage; white ships/black cargo; introduction by John Henrik Clarke. Dial Bks. 1995 unp il map $45 (7 and up) **759.13**
1. Blacks in art 2. Slavery—Pictorial works
ISBN 0-8037-1804-7 LC 95-13866
"Consisting entirely of Feeling's uncaptioned black-and white illustrations, this . . . picture book chronicles the inhumane conditions endured by enslaved Africans during 'four centuries of the slave trade.'" Booklist
"A book for careful study and discussion, both at home and in the classroom." N Y Times Book Rev
Includes bibliographical references

Lawrence, Jacob
The great migration; an American story; paintings by Jacob Lawrence; with a poem in appreciation by Walter Dean Myers. Museum of Modern Art 1993 unp il hardcover o.p. paperback available $7.95 **759.13**
1. African Americans in art
ISBN 0-06-443428-1 (pa) LC 93-16788

"A noted African-American artist chronicles the 1916-1919 migration of blacks from the South through a sequence of 60 paintings and accompanying narrative captions." SLJ
"Lawrence is a storyteller with words as well as pictures: his captions and his own 1992 introduction to this book are the best commentary on his work." Booklist

769 Prints

Owens, Tom, 1960-
Collecting baseball cards; by Thomas S. Owens. Millbrook Press 1993 80p il lib bdg $22.40 **769**
1. Baseball cards
ISBN 1-56294-254-9 LC 92-18166
Provides practical advice on building a baseball card collection, covering such topics as trading cards, preserving them, and finding rookie cards, errors, and other specialities
"The serious minded, YA card collector could profit from and enjoy the book." Voice Youth Advocates
Includes glossary

Collecting basketball cards. Millbrook Press 1998 78p il lib bdg $23.90 **769**
1. Basketball cards
ISBN 0-7613-0418-5 LC 98-4432
Provides practical advice on building a basketball card collection, covering such topics as buying and trading cards, as well as grading and preserving them
"A title sure to get an enthusiastic response from the ever-expanding fraternity of card collectors." SLJ

769.56 Postage stamps

Postal Service guide to U.S. stamps. U.S. Postal Service il pa $14.95 **769.56**
1. Postage stamps

First published 1974 with title: United States stamps and stories. Revised annually
Contains reproductions and histories of U.S. postage stamps

Scott standard postage stamp catalogue. Scott Pub. Co. (Sidney) 5v il pa ea $35 **769.56**
1. Postage stamps—Catalogs

Annual. First published 1868. Title, publisher's name and number of volumes vary
"International multi-volume catalog; lists all stamps issued by the various governments and provides date of issue and value." N Y Public Libr. Ref Books for Child Collect. 2d edition

770.9 Photography—Historical and geographic treatment

Czech, Kenneth P.
Snapshot; America discovers the camera. Lerner Publs. 1996 88p il $22.60 **770.9**
1. Photography—History
ISBN 0-8225-1736-1 LC 95-51136

Czech, Kenneth P.—*Continued*
"A history of photography from its inception to its many influences in American history. . . . The author explains complex photographic inventions and processes in easy-to-understand language. . . . A profusion of excellent black-and-white photographs are distributed throughout and complement the text. Well-placed quotes, historical diagrams, anecdotes, and advertisements enhance and accent topics discussed." SLJ
Includes bibliographical references

771 Photography—Techniques, equipment, materials

King, Dave
My first photography book. Dorling Kindersley 1994 48p il $12.95   **771**
1. Photography
ISBN 1-56458-673-1   LC 94-7359
This "handbook . . . offers advice and creative projects for beginning photographers. . . . Materials and equipment are inexpensive and readily available, e.g, colored, transparent candy wrappers are used as filters, and magnifying glasses are used as close-up lenses. . . . Vivid, well-labeled illustrations in primary colors are attractive and informative." SLJ
Includes glossary

Langford, Michael John, 1933-
Photography. Dorling Kindersley 1995 72p il pa $4.95 (7 and up)   **771**
1. Photography
ISBN 0-7894-0174-6
At head of title: 101 essential tips
This work covers camera choice, use and accessories. Suggestions on how to better compose and expose photographs are included

Price, Susanna
Click! fun with photography; [by] Susanna Price & Tim Stephens. Sterling 1997 48p il $14.95; pa $7.95   **771**
1. Photography 2. Cameras
ISBN 0-8069-9541-6; 0-8069-9652-8 (pa)
LC 96-37211
First published 1995 in the United Kingdom
Presents the basics of photography, from choosing a camera to making the most of the flash
"With numerous full-color photos and a brief, clearly written text, this book exposes more than just the basics. The authors include frequent checklists that summarize major points and an extensive glossary. . . . A multitude of activities complete this useful introduction." SLJ

778.5 Cinematography, video production, related activities

Baker, Christopher W., 1956-
Let there be life! animating with the computer. Walker & Co. 1997 49p il $16.95; lib bdg $17.85
778.5
1. Animation (Cinematography)
ISBN 0-8027-8472-0; 0-8027-8473-9 (lib bdg)
LC 96-23289
Explains how the computer is used to create animation and compares the approach to traditional animation
"Many interesting examples from short and feature films illustrate the stages of story boarding, modeling, refining, and rendering." Horn Book Guide

778.59 Video production (Television photography)

Lewis, Roland
Video. Dorling Kindersley 1995 72p il pa $4.95 (7 and up)   **778.59**
1. Video recording—Handbooks, manuals, etc.
ISBN 0-7894-0183-5
At head of title: 101 essential tips
In this guide "colored photographs accompany text explaining equipment, techniques, composition, lighting, editing, audio, and so forth. Additional tips are provided for shooting weddings, vacations, sporting events, and animals." Voice Youth Advocates

778.9 Photography of specific subjects

Kramer, Stephen P.
Eye of the storm; chasing storms with Warren Faidley; [by] Stephen Kramer; photographs by Warren Faidley. Putnam 1997 48p il $18.95
778.9
1. Faidley, Warren 2. Photography—Scientific applications 3. Storms
ISBN 0-399-23029-7   LC 96-19296
Storm chaser Warren Faidley discusses the techniques, dangers, and difficulties of photographing lightning, tornadoes, and hurricanes
This book offers "dramatic full-color photos [and]. . . readable, exciting text. . . . This eye-catching book will undoubtedly be utilized by nonfiction lovers hungry for a good read." SLJ
Includes glossary and bibliographical references

779 Photographs

Myers, Walter Dean, 1937-
One more river to cross; an African American photograph album. Harcourt Brace & Co. 1995 166p il $40 (7 and up)   **779**
1. African Americans—Pictorial works
ISBN 0-15-200089-5   LC 95-3839

Myers, Walter Dean, 1937-—*Continued*
"This collection of period photography documents the African-American struggle from captivity to freedom." Book Rep

"This oversized, superbly produced album is dramatic, with spare, almost poetic narration by Myers. . . . Although there are some photos of well-known individuals, the strength of this book is the pictures of ordinary people, engaged in the everyday tasks and enjoyments of life. . . . In his introduction, Myers tells us he has set out to show the fullness of black life, not to portray African American people as simply victims. And in this, he amply succeeds." Voice Youth Advocates

780   Music

Ardley, Neil, 1937-
A young person's guide to music; with music by Poul Ruders. Dorling Kindersley 1995 80p il $24.95   **780**
1. Music 2. Orchestra
ISBN 0-7894-0313-7   LC 95-19595
"In association with the BBC Symphony Orchestra conducted by Andrew Davis." Title page
This "interactive guide to the orchestra is a combination of book and compact disk. The CD features a new work by the Dutch composer Poul Ruders. . . . The text itself has facts on the orchestra as a whole, the conductor, composer, and each instrument. . . . A history section features a timeline, names of musicians and composers, definitions of musical forms with examples, and a glossary." SLJ
"A rich resource for young people who want to understand orchestral music." Booklist

780.3   Music—Encyclopedias and dictionaries

Kennedy, Michael, 1926-
The concise Oxford dictionary of music; associate editor, Joyce Bourne. 4th ed. Oxford Univ. Press 1996 780p il pa $16.95   **780.3**
1. Music—Dictionaries 2. Musicians—Dictionaries
ISBN 0-19-280037-X
First published 1952 as a condensation of The Oxford companion to music
This volume "contains a medley of information on composers, individual works, musical theory and terminology, instruments, forms and genres, performers, orchestras, and ensembles. The articles on major composers are of particular value. . . . Many will find this tool handy for a quick lookup of instantly needed information, such as dates and places of birth and death, middle names, and so forth." Am Ref Books Annu, 1997

780.89   Music of racial, ethnic, national groups

Igus, Toyomi, 1953-
I see the rhythm; paintings by Michele Wood; text by Toyomi Igus. Children's Bk. Press 1998 32p il $15.95   **780.89**
1. African American music
ISBN 0-89239-151-0   LC 97-29310
Coretta Scott King award for illustration, 1999
Chronicles and captures poetically the history, mood, and movement of African American music
"The text, made up of free verse and music lyrics, incorporates different font sizes, shapes, and colors to underline the mood of each genre. . . . The colors of each full-page scenario underline the mood. . . This book celebrates music with art and words and successfully blends all three." SLJ

Medearis, Angela Shelf, 1956-
Music; [by] Angela Medearis, Michael Medearis. 21st Cent. Bks. (NY) 1997 80p il (African-American arts) lib bdg $20.40   **780.89**
1. African American music—History and criticism
ISBN 0-8050-4482-5   LC 96-47276
Discusses the evolution of African-American music from its roots in the rhythms and instruments from Africa through the development of the blues, gospel, and soul to modern rock and rap
"Photographs, both full-color and black-and-white, complement the readable text." Booklist
Includes bibliographical references

780.9   Music—Historical and geographical treatment

The **Kingfisher** young people's book of music. Kingfisher (NY) 1996 127p il maps $19.95
                                            780.9
1. Music—History and criticism
ISBN 1-85697-586-X   LC 96-3532
An introduction to musical periods and styles from ancient times to the present day
"With a brief text and attractive full-color photographs and drawings on each page, the format will appeal to youngsters." SLJ
Includes glossary and discography

Ventura, Piero
Great composers. Putnam 1989 124p il $25.95
                                            780.9
1. Composers 2. Music—History and criticism
ISBN 0-399-21746-0   LC 89-32861
"Early segments are devoted to the Chinese, Indians, Egyptians, and Greeks and Romans, but the majority of the book focuses on individual figures, from Vivaldi, Handel, Beethoven, Chopin, and Debussy, to Gershwin, Louis Armstrong, and Duke Ellington. Ventura stresses their artistic personalities and talks about their talents in the context of the time in which they lived. . . . A highly pleasurable invitation to the world of music." Booklist

781 Music—General principles and musical forms

Sabbeth, Alex, 1950-
Rubber-band banjos and a java jive bass; projects and activities on the science of music and sound; project illustrations by Laurel Aiello. Wiley 1997 102p il pa $12.95   **781**
1. Music 2. Sound 3. Musical instruments
ISBN 0-471-15675-2   LC 96-22144
An exploration of the world of sound with instructions for making musical instruments. Famous scientists with musical inclinations are mentioned
"Numerous, clear, pen-and-ink drawings illustrate the construction of instruments from a glass harmonica, to a violin, drums, and a foot-powered organ. . . . The scientific principles behind the creation of all the wonderful noises are explained, as is basic music notation." SLJ
Includes glossary

781.64 Western popular music

Jones, K. Maurice
Say it loud! the story of rap music. Millbrook Press 1994 128p il lib bdg $27.40; pa $12.95 (7 and up)   **781.64**
1. Rap music
ISBN 1-56294-386-3 (lib bdg); 1-56294-724-9 (pa)
LC 93-1939
A survey of rap music tracing "its origins back to the oratory tradition of the *griots* of West African societies. . . . Quotes and the use of lyrics (fully documented) by a variety of rappers and other recording artists effectively enhance and expand the discussion." SLJ
Includes glossary, discography and bibliographical references

Press, David Paul, 1949-
A multicultural portrait of America's music; by David P. Press. Marshall Cavendish 1994 80p il (Perspectives) lib bdg $28.50 (7 and up)   **781.64**
1. Popular music
ISBN 1-85435-666-6   LC 93-48847
This book covers the various forms of American popular music, including Native American traditional music, Cajun and zydeco, country, blues, ragtime, jazz, rock 'n' roll, doo-wop, R & B, soul and rap. Many individual artists are featured
Includes glossary and bibliographical references

781.643 Blues music

Elmer, Howard
Blues; its birth and growth. Rosen Pub. Group 1999 64p il (Library of African American arts and culture) $17.95 (7 and up)   **781.643**
1. Blues music
ISBN 0-8239-1853-X   LC 98-43705

Traces the origins of blues music, its evolution in the United States, and its influence on jazz and rock and roll
This is "informative and interesting. . . . The artistic photographs and reproductions, in color and in black and white, appear on almost every page and enliven the text." SLJ
Includes discography and bibliographical references

781.65 Jazz music

Collier, James Lincoln, 1928-
Jazz; an American saga. Holt & Co. 1997 104p il $16.95 (7 and up)   **781.65**
1. Jazz music
ISBN 0-8050-4121-4   LC 97-3004
Examines the possible origins of jazz, its variety, greatness, and individual artists
"Written in a crisp, enthusiastic style. . . . The information presented will be helpful for reports, but the book lends itself to a good nonfiction read as well." SLJ
Includes discography

Gourse, Leslie
Striders to beboppers and beyond; the art of jazz piano. Watts 1997 144p il (Art of jazz) lib bdg $25; pa $8.95 (7 and up)   **781.65**
1. Jazz music 2. Jazz musicians 3. Pianists
ISBN 0-531-11320-5 (lib bdg); 0-531-15836-5 (pa)
LC 96-31530
Describes the lives and artistry of some of the best-known jazz pianists, traces their influence on one another, and investigates the impact of different innovators on the development of jazz music
"The book contains some lively writing, accurate information, and carefully footnoted dialogue, but the main value of Gourse's overview is the biographical information it provides." SLJ
Includes discography and bibliographical references

Swingers and crooners; the art of jazz singing. Watts 1997 144p il (Art of jazz) lib bdg $25; pa $8.95 (7 and up)   **781.65**
1. Singers 2. Jazz music
ISBN 0-531-11321-3 (lib bdg); 0-531-15837-3 (pa)
LC 96-31529
Describes the lives of notable jazz singers, traces their influence on one another, and investigates the impact of different innovators on the development of jazz music
This provides "biographical information on some fairly obscure people. . . . There are a few excellent-quality archival photos." SLJ
Includes discography and bibliographical references

Lee, Jeanne
Jam! the story of jazz music. Rosen Pub. Group 1999 64p il (Library of African American arts and culture) $17.95 (7 and up)   **781.65**
1. Jazz music
ISBN 0-8239-1852-1   LC 99-10973
Describes the history and development of jazz music in America from its roots in Africa to the contemporary music scene
Includes glossary and bibliographical references

781.66   Rock (Rock 'n' roll)

The **New** Rolling Stone encyclopedia of rock & roll; edited by Patricia Romanowski and Holly George-Warren; consulting editor, Jon Pareles. completely rev and updated. Fireside Bks. 1995 1120p il pa $27 (7 and up)   **781.66**
1. Rock music—Encyclopedias
ISBN 0-684-81044-1   LC 95-35045
"A Rolling Stone Press book"
First published 1983 with title: The Rolling Stone encyclopedia of rock & roll
This volume includes 2200 "entries describing rock figures from the famous to the all but forgotten. A typical entry for a band gives the year and date the group formed, the members and their birth dates and places, their instruments, and a discography followed by an essay. The essays range from 100 words (Mungo Jerry) to four-plus pages (Elvis) and deal noncritically with the artists' work, history, and influence." Libr J

The **Rolling** Stone illustrated history of rock & roll; the definitive history of the most important artists and their music; edited by Anthony DeCurtis and James Henke with Holly George-Warren; original editor: Jim Miller. 3rd ed. Random House 1992 710p il pa $29.95 (7 and up)   **781.66**
1. Rock music
ISBN 0-679-73728-6   LC 92-6339
First published 1976
This volume presents biographical information; definitions of rock styles and terms; and select discographies
"The essays are lucid, fun to read, and, for the most part, respectful toward the subjects. . . . With photos complementing the text, readers will dip into any part of this book and be hooked. Highly recommended as a historical view of the enduring aspects of rock music." Voice Youth Advocates

Woog, Adam, 1953-
The history of rock and roll. Lucent Bks. 1999 112p il (World history series) lib bdg $17.96 (7 and up)   **781.66**
1. Rock music
ISBN 1-56006-498-6   LC 98-53048
Traces the history and evolution of rock music from the early days of rock and roll through the present day
Includes bibliographical references

782.42   Songs

Johnson, James Weldon, 1871-1938
Lift every voice and sing; illustrations by Elizabeth Catlett; introduction by Jim Haskins. Walker & Co. 1993 unp il music $14.95; lib bdg $15.85; pa $6.95   **782.42**
1. African American music 2. Songs
ISBN 0-8027-8250-7; 0-8027-8251-5 (lib bdg); 0-8027-7442-3 (pa)   LC 92-27333

"Widely known as the African American national anthem, Johnson's song is combined here with dramatic linocut prints by the celebrated artist Elizabeth Catlett. The song was originally written for schoolchildren at an Abraham Lincoln birthday celebration in 1900. The pictures were originally created in the 1940s as part of Catlett's series on black women through history. Together they make not a literal matching of words and illustrations but a powerful image of ordinary people enduring through hard times. . . . At the end of the book is the full sheet music." Booklist

National anthems of the world; edited by W.L. Reed and M.J. Bristow. Blandford Press; distributed by Sterling music $95 (7 and up)   **782.42**

1. National songs

First published 1943 in the United Kingdom with title: National anthems of the United Nations and France. (9th edition 1997) Periodically revised
This volume contains national anthems of 182 nations, including melody and accompaniment. Words are presented in the native language with transliteration provided where necessary. English translations follow. Brief historical notes on the adoption of each anthem are included and the book concludes with a list of national holidays

Silverman, Jerry
African roots; [arranged and compiled by] Jerry Silverman. Chelsea House 1994 64p il music (Traditional black music) lib bdg $18.95; pa $9.95   **782.42**
1. African music 2. Songs
ISBN 0-7910-1828-8 (lib bdg); 0-7910-1844-X (pa)

Presented here is a "collection of twenty-eight [African] folk songs with short text giving insight into the origin and history of the song. English translations also show how closely many of the songs compare to our own folk music. An index to titles as well as an index to first lines makes it easy to find a particular song. . . . This slim volume presents some of the richness of the African heritage." Voice Youth Advocates

Just listen to this song I'm singing; African-American history through song. Millbrook Press 1996 95p il music lib bdg $30.90   **782.42**
1. African American music 2. Songs
ISBN 1-56294-673-0   LC 95-22307
"Three to five pages of text precede each of the thirteen well-known African-American songs of freedom, from the old Gullah song 'Michael Row the Boat Ashore' to 'We Shall Overcome,' written in the 1960s. The text and music provide a moving history of perseverance in the face of dire conditions. Piano accompaniments and guitar chords are provided." Horn Book Guide
Includes bibliographical references

Songs and stories from the American Revolution. Millbrook Press 1994 71p il music lib bdg $27.90   **782.42**
1. United States—History—1775-1783, Revolution—Songs
ISBN 1-56294-429-0   LC 94-10658

Silverman, Jerry—*Continued*
"This book presents 10 broadside ballads of the 1770s and 1780s, with piano and chord notations and the story behind each song. . . . An interesting combination of music and history." Booklist

Songs of protest and civil rights; [compiled by] Jerry Silverman. Chelsea House 1992 64p il music (Traditional black music) o.p.   **782.42**
1. African American music 2. Songs

An illustrated songbook of the black music that was sung during civil rights protests of the 1960s

Songs of the Wild West; commentary by Alan Axelrod; arrangements by Dan Fox. Metropolitan Mus. of Art; Simon & Schuster Bks. for Young Readers 1991 128p il music $19.95   **782.42**
1. Cowhands—Songs 2. Folk songs—United States
ISBN 0-671-74775-4   LC 91-751467
At head of title: The Metropolitan Museum of Art, in association with the Buffalo Bill Historical Center
"Axelrod combines 45 songs of the Old West with works of art from the Metropolitan Museum of Art and the Buffalo Bill Historical Center to create a nostalgic picture of cowboys and western settlers. . . . Each score is lavishly illustrated with memorable western art and introduced by a brief essay linking the song with art and history. A beautifully designed book that will appeal to armchair browsers as well as students researching the westward movement through its music and art." Booklist

784.19 Musical instruments

Baines, Anthony
The Oxford companion to musical instruments; written and edited by Anthony Baines. Oxford Univ. Press 1992 404p il $55 (7 and up) **784.19**
1. Musical instruments—Dictionaries
ISBN 0-19-311334-1   LC 92-8635
Based on The New Oxford companion to music (1983)
This volume presents alphabetically arranged entries for musical instruments. "The individual entries cover specific instruments and families thereof (e.g., Wind Instruments) as well as their representation in different countries (e.g., Africa) and time periods (e.g., Baroque). . . . Playing techniques, a brief history, and a list of the major repertory are [discussed]." Booklist

Hasday, Judy L., 1957-
Musical instruments from around the world. Chelsea House 1999 64p il (Costume, tradition, and culture) lib bdg $16.95   **784.19**
1. Musical instruments
ISBN 0-7910-5168-4   LC 98-36094
Highlights twenty-five musical instruments from around the world, arranged according to the way in which they produce sound, including aerophones, chordophones, electrophones, idiophones, and membranophones
Includes bibliographical references

784.2 Symphony orchestra

Ganeri, Anita, 1961-
The young person's guide to the orchestra; Benjamin Britten's composition on CD narrated by Ben Kingsley; book written by Anita Ganeri. Harcourt Brace & Co. 1996 56p il $25   **784.2**
1. Orchestra 2. Musical instruments 3. Music appreciation
ISBN 0-15-201304-0   LC 95-41478
"Accompanying this book on orchestral music is a CD featuring Britten's *A Young Person's Guide to the Orchestra* . . . as well as Dukas' *The Sorcerer's Apprentice*. The book begins with an overview of the orchestra and then centers around groups of instruments, explaining a bit of their history and their sound's distinctive quality. . . . The book also introduces eight famous composers, world music, Benjamin Britten, and the background of *The Young Person's Guide to the Orchestra*. . . . Handsome and useful." Booklist
Includes glossary

790.1 Recreational activities

Owens, Tom, 1960-
Collecting baseball memorabilia; [by] Thomas S. Owens. Millbrook Press 1996 96p il lib bdg $23.40   **790.1**
1. Collectors and collecting 2. Baseball
ISBN 1-56294-579-3   LC 95-19827
"This introduction delves into a wide array of baseball collectibles including tickets stubs, team schedules, autographs, and other items that can be obtained at little or no cost. . . . This book has a crisp layout with full-color photos or reproductions on nearly every page. While not a price guide, this title will be of interest to young baseball enthusiasts." SLJ
Includes glossary

Peterson's summer opportunities for kids and teenagers. Peterson's Guides pa $26.95   **790.1**
1. Recreation—Directories 2. Camps—Directories
ISSN 0894-9417

Annual. First published 1984
This guide profiles more than 1600 summer programs offered by camps, independent secondary schools, colleges and universities, and private organizations. Arranged alphabetically by state, country, and travel program, each entry provides general information, principal activities, program information including dates, costs and age range, and winter contact. Other features include quick-reference charts and listings divided by activities

791.3 Circuses

Granfield, Linda
Circus; an album. DK Ink 1998 96p il $19.95
791.3
1. Circus
ISBN 0-7894-2453-3   LC 97-33523

Granfield, Linda—*Continued*

First published 1997 in Canada

Traces the history of circuses from the time of ancient Egypt and Greece through their evolution in eighteenth-century Europe to the spectacles created by P.T. Barnum and other modern-day showmen

"Each page is a colorful montage of old photographs, postcards, period illustrations, posters, ticket stubs, rhymes and the like. Difficult to put down." Publ Wkly

791.43   Motion pictures

Finch, Christopher, 1939-

The art of Walt Disney; from Mickey Mouse to the Magic Kingdoms. Abrams 1995 451p il $60

791.43

1. Disney, Walt, 1901-1966 2. Walt Disney Company

ISBN 0-8109-1962-1   LC 95-1746

Also available concise edition $19.95 (ISBN 0-8109-2702-0)

First published 1973

This describes the history of Walt Disney motion pictures and theme parks with over 600 illustrations including concept art, background paintings, and animation cels

Hahn, Don

Animation magic; a behind-the-scenes look at how an animated film is made. Disney Press 1996 95p il lib bdg $16.95   **791.43**

1. Walt Disney Company 2. Animated films 3. Animation (Cinematography)

ISBN 0-7868-3072-7   LC 95-50050

New edition in preparation

Discusses the techniques and people involved in creating Disney's animated films, from the first story idea to opening night

"The text is informative, entertaining, and easy to follow. . . . This title focuses soley on traditional Disney cell animation, rather than on stop-motion or computer techniques. With this limitation in mind, it is of interest both to fans of animation and to budding animators." SLJ

Includes glossary and bibliographical references

Hamilton, Jake

Special effects in film and television; written by Jake Hamilton. DK Pub. 1998 63p il $17.95

791.43

1. Cinematography 2. Animation (Cinematography)

ISBN 0-7894-2813-X   LC 97-43121

Presents a behind-the-scenes look at some of the magic of the movies including the puppetry techniques used in ET, the animation in Toy Story, and much more

"Packed with lots of great movie stills, this introduction is a dazzling, but cursory, look behind the scenes. . . . Readers will be informed and possibly inspired." SLJ

O'Brien, Lisa, 1963-

Lights, camera, action! making movies and TV from the inside out; illustrated by Stephen MacEachern. Owl Bks. (Toronto); distributed by Firefly Bks. (Buffalo) 1998 64p il $19.95; pa $12.95   **791.43**

1. Motion pictures—Production and direction 2. Acting

ISBN 1-895688-75-2; 1-895688-76-0 (pa)

"Youngsters interested in a career in the television or film industry will find this a helpful introduction. Using a fictional character named Johnny who wants to be an actor, O'Brien reveals how to break into the business, giving tips on everything from finding an agent to creating a character and preparing for an audition. . . . O'Brien . . . [takes] readers through every facet of a production." Booklist

Includes glossary

Parkinson, David

The young Oxford book of the movies. Oxford Univ. Press 1996 161p il $25; lib bdg $30

791.43

1. Motion pictures—History and criticism

ISBN 0-19-521244-4; 0-19-521243-6 (lib bdg)

LC 96-4684

Explores the history of film around the world, from the earliest shadow show to the blockbusters of today, discussing the transition from the silent era to "talkies" and examining specific genres such as comedy, cowboy pictures, and horror movies

"The work is fully illustrated with photographs, drawings, and reprints of posters and movie stills. Parkinson includes many sidebars with assorted cinematic information, such as how film projectors work, lists of recommended films on a variety of subjects, movie trivia, etc." Voice Youth Advocates

Includes glossary

Reynolds, David West

Star Wars: episode I: incredible cross-sections; illustrated by Hans Jenssen & Richard Chasemore. Lucas Bks.; DK Pub. 1999 32p il $19.95 **791.43**

1. Star Wars films

ISBN 0-7894-3962-X (DK Pub.)   LC 99-10178

Presents detailed labeled drawings, with background text, of the various spacecraft in the Star Wars movie, "The Phantom Menace."

Star Wars: incredible cross sections; illustrated by Hans Jenssen & Richard Chasemore. DK Pub. 1998 32p il $19.95   **791.43**

1. Star Wars films

ISBN 0-7894-3480-6   LC 98-22878

This book "includes diagrams for the *Millennium Falcon,* T-65 X-wing, Blockade Runner, Tie Fighters, Sandcrawler, and BLT-A4 Y-wing, among others. An elaborate four-page fold-out analyzes the Death Star in minute detail. . . . AT-AT Walkers, AT-STs, snowspeeders, and speeder bikes are also included. Diagrams are surrounded by inserts of fascinating trivia, history, and technical notes." Voice Youth Advocates

Reynolds, David West—*Continued*
Star Wars: the visual dictionary; written by David West Reynolds; special fabrications by Don Bies and Nelson Hall; new photography by Alexander Ivanov. DK Pub. 1998 64p il $19.95
791.43
1. Star Wars films
ISBN 0-7894-3481-4   LC 98-22877
"This oversized volume is packed with full-color photographs of the characters and costumes, equipment, weaponry, mechanical droids, and assorted creatures from the *Star Wars* universe. . . . 'Data Files' provide additional, often fascinating, and personal tidbits about the inhabitants of this fantasy world. . . . It is a visual treat." SLJ

792   Stage presentations

Cummings, Richard, 1931-
Simple makeup for young actors; illustrations by Melanie Carter. Plays 1990 128p il pa $14.95
792
1. Theatrical makeup
ISBN 0-8238-0290-6   LC 89-23118
Discusses basic theatrical makeup and how it can be used to transform the actor into many different characters

Jackson, Sheila, 1956-
Costumes for the stage: a complete handbook for every kind of play. Dutton 1978 144p il o.p.; New Amsterdam Bks. paperback available $14.95
792
1. Costume
ISBN 0-941533-36-0 (pa)   LC 77-93888
Provides practical costume ideas for use in summer camp and school productions. Choosing materials, colors, and accessories for their stage effect is discussed
Includes bibliographical references

792.09   Theater—Historical and geographic treatment

Aliki
William Shakespeare & the Globe; written & illustrated by Aliki. HarperCollins Pubs. 1999 48p il $15.95; lib bdg $15.89   **792.09**
1. Shakespeare, William, 1564-1616 2. Globe Theatre (London, England) 3. Shakespeare's Globe (London, England)
ISBN 0-06-027820-X; 0-06-027821-8 (lib bdg)
LC 98-7903
The "text describes Shakespeare's life, the Elizabethan world and entertainments, and the ups and downs of the theatrical industry . . . including tidbits such as the Burbage brothers' piece-by-piece theft of the original Globe Theatre. A fast-forward to the twentieth century then treats Sam Wanamaker's dream of making the Globe rise again." Bull Cent Child Books
"A logically organized and engaging text, plenty of detailed illustrations with informative captions, and a clean design provide a fine introduction to both hard and theater." Horn Book Guide

Morley, Jacqueline
Shakespeare's theater; [illustrated by] John James. Bedrick Bks. 1994 48p il (Inside story) $17.95   **792.09**
1. Shakespeare, William, 1564-1616 2. Globe Theatre (London, England)
ISBN 0-87226-309-6   LC 94-16386
"A brief history of European theater precedes information on theater during Shakespeare's lifetime. While actors' roles, costumes, and audiences are discussed, the focus is on the Globe playhouse and the performances that took place there. Profuse illustrations, many of which allow cutaway views of the various structures, accompany a solid, detailed volume for budding thespians." Horn Book
Includes glossary

792.5   Opera

Geras, Adèle
The Random House book of opera stories; retold by Adèle Geras; illustrations by Ian Beck [et al.]; costume designs by Rosemary Vercoe. Random House 1998 127p il $29.99; lib bdg $31.99   **792.5**
1. Opera—Stories, plots, etc.
ISBN 0-679-89315-6; 0-679-99315-0 (lib bdg)
LC 97-51795
First published 1997 in the United Kingdom with title: The Orchard book of opera stories
This "book presents the stories of eight operas: *The Magic Flute, Aida, Carmen, The Cunning Little Vixen, Turandot, Cinderella, Hansel and Gretel,* and *The Love for Three Oranges.* . . . Each opera story is illustrated by a different artist, such as Emma Chichester Clark and Jane Ray. A colorful painting, border, or costume design appears on nearly every page, giving the pages an appealing look. A useful and attractive book." Booklist

792.6   Musical plays

Ross, Beverly B., 1931-
Junior Broadway; how to produce musicals with children 9 to 13; by Beverly B. Ross and Jean P. Durgin. 2nd ed. McFarland & Co. 1998 215p il $28.50   **792.6**
1. Musicals 2. Amateur theater 3. Children's plays
ISBN 0-7864-0341-1   LC 97-47309
First published 1983
Areas covered include choosing and adapting a script, getting financing, meeting parents, auditions and casting, rehearsals, directing, voice coaching, dance, costumes, makeup, scenery, stage managing, cast parties, and assessing musical productions
"Ross has done a great service for other teachers and youth workers by sharing her expertise in producing versions of Broadway musicals performed by fifth graders. . . . The author's enthusiasm for working with children is evident, and contagious. Highly recommended." Libr J [review of 1983 edition]

792.8　Ballet and modern dance

Balanchine, George, 1904-1983
101 stories of the great ballets; [by] George
Balanchine and Francis Mason. Dolphin Bks. (NY)
1975 541p pa $14　　　　　　　　　**792.8**
1. Ballet—Stories, plots, etc.
ISBN 0-385-03398-2
"A Doubleday Dolphin book"
This collection contains the stories of well-known 19th
and 20th century ballets

Bussell, Darcey
The young dancer; [by] Darcey Bussell with
Patricia Linton. Dorling Kindersley 1994 64p il
$15.95　　　　　　　　　　　　**792.8**
1. Ballet
ISBN 1-56458-468-2　　　　　　LC 93-36790
Published in association with Royal Ballet School
This "book introduces children to the positions, move-
ments, traditions, and history of ballet. Both the text and
the illustrations are unusually clear and precise. . . .
Dorling Kindersley's signature visual style works quite
effectively here, with full-color photographs throughout.
. . . Appendixes include an address list of American
dance companies and a glossary of ballet terms." Booklist

Castle, Kate
Ballet. Kingfisher (NY) 1996 64p il $15.95
　　　　　　　　　　　　　　　792.8
1. Ballet
ISBN 0-7534-5001-1　　　　　　LC 96-5986
An introduction to ballet, discussing its history, costumes, steps, performances, and other aspects
"Featuring colorful, accurate, and sometimes very detailed illustrations, this introduction to the world of ballet
provides a wealth of information." SLJ
Includes glossary

My ballet book; written by Kate Castle. DK
Pub. 1998 61p il $15.95　　　　　　**792.8**
1. Ballet
ISBN 0-7894-3432-6　　　　　　LC 98-22803
Introduces the world of ballet and presents its notable
stories, dancers, techniques, and routines
"Young balletomanes will pore over every detail of
this colorful volume. . . . This book is copiously illustrated with photographs reflecting all manner of details
about the art form." SLJ
Includes glossary

Grau, Andrée
Dance; written by Andrée Grau. Knopf 1998
59p il (Eyewitness books) $19; lib bdg $20.99
　　　　　　　　　　　　　　　792.8
1. Dance
ISBN 0-679-89316-4; 0-679-99316-9 (lib bdg)
　　　　　　　　　　　　　　LC 98-17269
Surveys all forms of dance throughout the world, discussing its cultural and social significance, its costume,
its history, and noted dancers and choreographers

McCaughrean, Geraldine, 1951-
The Random House book of stories from the
ballet; retold by Geraldine McCaughrean;
illustrated by Angela Barrett. Random House 1995
c1994 112p il $20; lib bdg $19.99　　　**792.8**
1. Ballet—Stories, plots, etc.
ISBN 0-679-87125-X; 0-679-97125-4 (lib bdg)
　　　　　　　　　　　　　　LC 94-22640
First published 1994 in the United Kingdom with title:
The Orchard book of stories from the ballet
"Dramatic plots, unusual characters, and magical
spells are interwoven into each of the well-written retellings. The essence of a ballet production is successfully
captured by the full-color illustrations." Booklist

Mitchell, Jack
Alvin Ailey American Dance Theater: Jack
Mitchell photographs; foreword by Judith Jamison;
introduction by Richard Philp. Andrews &
McMeel 1993 129p il $29.95; pa $19.95 (7 and
up)　　　　　　　　　　　　　**792.8**
1. Alvin Ailey American Dance Theater
ISBN 0-8362-4509-1; 0-8362-4508-3 (pa)
　　　　　　　　　　　　　　LC 93-13582
"A Donna Martin book"
This collection of black-and-white photographs traces
the work of choreographer Alvin Ailey over a thirty-year
period, arranged chronologically from 1961 to 1993
"Mitchell has done us all a great service by preserving
these otherwise ephemeral creations." Booklist

Newman, Barbara
The illustrated book of ballet stories; written by
Barbara Newman; illustrated by Gill Tomblin; with
an introduction by Darcy Bussell. DK Pub. 1997
64p il $19.95　　　　　　　　　　**792.8**
1. Ballet—Stories, plots, etc.
ISBN 0-7894-2024-4　　　　　　LC 97-15462
Also available without CD for $15.95 (ISBN 0-7894-
2225-5)
In story and illustrations, presents five classic ballets:
Giselle, Coppelia, Sleeping Beauty, The Nutcracker, and
Swan Lake. Includes photographs from Royal Ballet pro-
ductions, and is accompanied by an audio CD
"The storytelling is lively, the comments are
insightful. . . . Featuring 18 selections from the five ballets, the CD provides an excellent recording of the mu-
sic." Booklist
Includes glossary

793　Indoor games and amusements

Loeffelbein, Robert L.
The recreation handbook; 342 games and other
activities for teams and individuals. McFarland &
Co. 1992 237p il pa $27.50　　　　　　**793**
1. Games 2. Sports
ISBN 0-89950-744-1　　　　　　LC 92-50310
"This volume briefly describes hundreds of games and
activities for teams and individuals. The author includes
many traditional games along with modern variations and

Loeffelbein, Robert L.—*Continued*
some newer pastimes for players age six and up. Games are arranged under basic themes. . . . Most entries note age level, organizational level, number of players, supervision (referee, scorekeeper, or none), playing time, space, and equipment. Directions for playing, scoring, and variations complete each entry." Booklist

793.3 Social, folk, national dancing

Medearis, Angela Shelf, 1956-
Dance; [by] Angela Shelf Medearis, Michael R. Medearis. 21st Cent. Bks. (NY) 1997 80p il (African-American arts) lib bdg $20.40   **793.3**
1. African American dancers 2. Dance—History
ISBN 0-8050-4481-7   LC 96-45198
Explores the dance traditions of African Americans, from their origins in the expressive dances that the slaves brought from Africa through the development of jazz and tap to modern dance and ballet
This is a "well-written volume, profusely illustrated with high-quality black-and-white and full-color photos." SLJ
Includes bibliographical references

793.7 Games not characterized by action

Kenda, Margaret
Math wizardry for kids; [by] Margaret Kenda and Phyllis S. Williams; illustrated by Tim Robinson. Barron's Educ. Ser. 1995 324p il pa $13.95   **793.7**
1. Mathematical recreations
ISBN 0-8120-1809-5   LC 94-31243
This includes over 200 mathematical puzzles and games plus a 180-degree protractor, 30-, 45-, and 60-degree triangles, a 6″ ruler, compass, pencil sharpener, and eraser
Includes glossary

793.73 Puzzles and puzzle games

Agee, Jon
Go hang a salami! I'm a lasagna hog! and other palindromes. Farrar, Straus & Giroux 1992 unp il $12.21; pa $5.95   **793.73**
1. Word games
ISBN 0-374-33473-0; 0-374-44473-0 (pa)
                                      LC 91-31319
A collection of palindromes, sentences that read the same forward and backward
"Agee offers a humorous look at the concept, using more than 50 wacky alphabetic examples. . . . Cartoon sketches extend and often clarify the meaning of the crazy phrases." Booklist

Sit on a potato pan, Otis! more palindromes. Farrar, Straus & Giroux 1999 unp il $14.41
                                      793.73
1. Word games
ISBN 0-374-31808-5   LC 98-31783

"This volume collects more than sixty palindromes and displays them in witty cartoon drawings, notable for their off-center deadpan humor. Most of the entries will have readers chuckling aloud and trying to concoct their own palindromes." Horn Book Guide

Who ordered the jumbo shrimp? and other oxymorons. HarperCollins Pubs. 1998 unp il $12.95   **793.73**
1. Word games
ISBN 0-06-205159-8   LC 97-78386
"Michael Di Capua books"
"This collection of oxymorons, illustrated with spirited black-and-white cartoons, offers readers a great way to understand the concepts while giving them a good laugh." SLJ

793.8 Magic and related activities

Eldin, Peter
Magic. Kingfisher (NY) 1997 64p il $15.95
                                      793.8
1. Magic tricks 2. Magicians
ISBN 0-7534-5084-4   LC 97-1424
Discusses the history of magic from around the world, the classics of the repertoire, great masters of magic, and how magicians learn their craft

Friedhoffer, Robert
Magic and perception; the art and science of fooling the senses; by Bob Friedhoffer; illustrations by Linda Eisenberg. Watts 1996 109p il lib bdg $25; pa $6.95   **793.8**
1. Magic tricks 2. Optical illusions
ISBN 0-531-11254-3 (lib bdg); 0-531-15803-9 (pa)
                                      LC 95-51214
Presents step-by-step instructions for a variety of magic tricks, explaining how the tricks work by affecting people's perceptions
"A good introduction to magic, presented with a new twist. . . . Most of the tricks are easy to master with practice. Simple black-and-white line drawings add clarity." SLJ
Includes bibliographical references

Mitchelson, Mitch, 1950-
The most excellent book of how to be a juggler; illustrated by Rob Shone and Peter Harper. Copper Beech Bks. 1997 32p il lib bdg $19.90; pa $6.95
                                      793.8
1. Juggling
ISBN 0-7613-0618-8 (lib bdg); 0-7613-0632-3 (pa)
                                      LC 97-8012
This is an illustrated guide to juggling techniques, routines, and performances

Oxlade, Chris
Science magic with magnets. Barron's Educ. Ser. 1995 29p il (Science magic) $10.95; pa $4.95
                                      793.8
1. Magic tricks 2. Magnets 3. Scientific recreations
ISBN 0-8120-6501-8; 0-8120-9190-6 (pa)
                                      LC 94-32055

Oxlade, Chris—*Continued*
First published 1994 in the United Kingdom
This describes ten magic tricks using simple magnets, batteries, wire, and common household items
This book is "colorful and energetic." Horn Book
Includes glossary

Severn, Bill
Bill Severn's best magic; 50 top tricks to entertain and amaze your friends on all occasions; illustrated by Timothy Wenk. Stackpole Bks. 1990 210p il $14.95   **793.8**
1. Magic tricks
ISBN 0-8117-2229-5   LC 89-11569
"Instructions for performing more than 50 simple magic tricks using cards, paper, and coins, etc., are presented in a logically structured manual that will be a good starting point for teens who want to learn magic without investing heavily in props and equipment." Booklist

794.1   Chess

Keene, Raymond D., 1948-
The Simon & Schuster pocket book of chess; [by] Raymond Keene. Simon & Schuster Bks. for Young Readers 1989 192p il hardcover o.p. paperback available $8.95 (7 and up)   **794.1**
1. Chess
ISBN 0-671-67924-4 (pa)   LC 88-30555
Describes the game of chess, from the basic moves to strategies for attack and defense, with chapters on the history of the game, great champions, competitions, and computer chess
"Those new to the game of chess and established players as well will find something of interest here." Booklist
Includes glossary and bibliographical references

796   Athletic and outdoor sports and games

Brown, Fern, 1918-
Special Olympics. Watts 1992 64p il lib bdg $22   **796**
1. Special Olympics
ISBN 0-531-20062-0   LC 91-31661
"A First book"
Describes the history and organization of the Special Olympics and explains how athletes and volunteers can get involved
"Page after page of full-color photographs show athletes training and competing. Individual events are described, with the emphasis not on winning, but on the joy of competing. Specialized programs within the organization are also covered. The text is clearly written; the glossary includes terms as varied as 'Down syndrome' and 'slalom.' Informative and inspirational." SLJ

Currie, Stephen, 1960-
Issues in sports. Lucent Bks. 1998 96p il (Contemporary issues) lib bdg $22.45 (7 and up)   **796**
1. Sports
ISBN 1-56006-477-3   LC 97-27451
Explores the controversies about how closely the reality of sport matches the ideal and presents debates about what sport is, what it can be, and what it should be
This "will be a useful resource for students' 'I-Search' papers and for informative and persuasive speeches." Booklist
Includes bibliographical references

Encyclopedia of women and sport in America; edited by Carole A. Oglesby; with [contributions by] Doreen L. Greenberg [et al.] Oryx Press 1998 xxiii, 360p il $65   **796**
1. Women athletes—Encyclopedias 2. Sports—Encyclopedias
ISBN 0-89774-993-6   LC 97-52787
"This encyclopedia provides short biographical entries with time and place of birth and then spells out the women's athletic accomplishments. It also includes historical articles, such as 'Badminton and Women' and sociological/psychological entries, such as 'Goal Setting and Women'." Voice Youth Advocates
"This clearly written book offers more information about American female athletes than any other single source." SLJ

The **Information** please sports almanac; edited by Mike Meserole. Houghton Mifflin pa $10.95   **796**
1. Sports
ISSN 1046-4980

Annual. First published 1989
Covers the major sports events of the previous year and presents facts and records

Margolis, Jeffrey A., 1948-
Violence in sports; victory at what price? Enslow Pubs. 1999 128p il (Issues in focus) lib bdg $19.95 (7 and up)   **796**
1. Sports 2. Violence
ISBN 0-89490-961-4   LC 98-35031
Discusses the issues related to manifestations of violent behavior in sports at all levels of competition and the effect of this violence on society in general
"This well-documented, clearly written book examines a topic that is a perennial favorite for term papers." SLJ
Includes glossary and bibliographical references

McComb, David G.
Sports; an illustrated history. Oxford Univ. Press 1998 139p il map (Illustrated histories) $25 (7 and up)   **796**
1. Sports—History
ISBN 0-19-510097-2   LC 98-15133
Surveys the history of athletic competition from the time of ancient civilizations through the twentieth century

McComb, David G.—*Continued*
The book "examines the ways in which sport has, at various times, intermingled with religion, politics, nationalism, and terrorism and warfare. . . . McComb examines these issues in a thoughtful, balanced manner, eschewing easy, conventional interpretation." SLJ
Includes bibliographical references

Meserole, Mike
DK ultimate sports lists. DK Pub. il $24.95; pa $17.95 **796**
1. Sports

First published 1997 with title: The ultimate book of sports lists (1999 edition). Frequently revised
This "is less a compilation of sports lists than of sports records—and some unexpected ones at that. . . . You will find some unique material . . . extensive coverage of women's sports, and a section of miscellaneous information not found in other sports references. The material is organized by sport, with particularly strong coverage of the major sports." Libr J

Nardo, Don, 1947-
Greek and Roman sport. Lucent Bks. 1999 112p il maps (World history series) lib bdg $17.96 (7 and up) **796**
1. Sports—History   2. Rome—Civilization
3. Greece—Civilization
ISBN 1-56006-436-6   LC 98-39636
Discusses the role of sports in the ancient Greek and Roman world, covering the Olympics, the glories of physical achievement, spectacle sports, horse and chariot racing, and leisure sports
This book "will prove invaluable for research and reports. . . . Numerous black-and-white drawings and photos are a fine addition to the text." SLJ
Includes bibliographical references

Play like a girl; a celebration of women in sports; edited by Sue Macy and Jane Gottesman. Holt & Co. 1999 32p il $15.95 **796**
1. Women athletes
ISBN 0-8050-6071-5   LC 98-47754
"This photographic celebration of women in sport captures professional, college, Olympic, and amateur athletes doing what they love best. Excellent-quality, full and double-page action photographs are accompanied by excerpts from magazine articles, short stories, and fiction and nonfiction books." SLJ

Rules of the game; the complete illustrated encyclopedia of all the sports of the world. [rev ed] St. Martin's Press 1990 320p il hardcover o.p. paperback available $15.95 (7 and up) **796**
1. Sports
ISBN 0-312-11940-2 (pa)   LC 90-37196
First published 1974
This volume covers 150 sports "grouped under 13 headings such as water, court, team, wheels, and air. Each article contains a detailed discussion of major objectives, playing area and equipment, rules, timing and scoring, and participants and officials." Booklist

Sports and athletes: opposing viewpoints; Laura K. Egendorf, book editor. Greenhaven Press 1999 203p il lib bdg $20.96; pa $16.20 (7 and up) **796**
1. Sports
ISBN 0-7377-0057-2 (lib bdg); 0-7377-0056-4 (pa)
LC 98-32022
"Opposing viewpoints series"
"The 30 point and counterpoint essays cover five general areas: children and sports, college athletic reform, racial discrimination, gender inequality, and drugs. . . . Writers from many different fields are included, all of whom share strong opinions and usually present compelling, thought-provoking arguments." Booklist
Includes bibliographical references

Sports Illustrated . . . sports almanac; by the editors of Sports Illustrated. Little, Brown il pa $12.95 **796**
1. Sports

Annual. First published 1991
"Provides team and individual records and highlights for all major sports. . . . A brief essay opens the section on each sport, followed by page upon page of records, both current and retrospective. Interspersed throughout . . . are black-and-white and color photographs and notable quotations by sports figures." Am Ref Books Annu, 1993

796.21 Roller skating

Edwards, Chris
The young inline skater. DK Pub. 1996 37p il $15.95 **796.21**
1. In-line skating
ISBN 0-7894-1124-5   LC 96-13031
Text and color photographs explain "the essentials—warming up, proper stances, strokes and glides, stopping, and falling safely. The instructions then graduate to proper turns, maneuvering hills, and 'extreme' jumping. Written by a world champion skater, the book is an intelligent and thorough guide to safe skating." Horn Book Guide
Includes glossary

796.22 Skateboarding

Ryan, Pat
Extreme skateboarding. Capstone Press 1998 48p il (Extreme sports) lib bdg $19 **796.22**
1. Skateboards and skateboarding
ISBN 1-560-65535-6   LC 97-9396
Describes the history, equipment, and contemporary practice of extreme skateboarding
Includes glossary and bibliographical references

796.323 Basketball

Bayne, Bijan C.
Sky kings; black pioneers of professional basketball. Watts 1997 144p il (African-American experience) lib bdg $24; pa $9.95 (7 and up)
796.323
1. Basketball 2. African American athletes
ISBN 0-531-11308-6 (lib bdg); 0-531-15900-0 (pa)
LC 96-38708
The author presents "the history of black professional basketball, from James Naismith's invention of the game in 1890 to the great basketball players of the 1960s and early 1970s. Significant early players are spotlighted with several pages, and there is a brief section dealing with early black women's teams. However, the majority of the book is devoted to four major players—Elgin Baylor, Wilt Chamberlain, Oscar Robertson, and Bill Russell." Booklist
Includes bibliographical references

Gutman, Bill
Shooting stars; the women of pro basketball. Random House 1998 120p il lib bdg $11.99; pa $3.99
796.323
1. Women's National Basketball Association 2. Women athletes 3. Basketball
ISBN 0-679-99196-4 (lib bdg); 0-679-89196-X (pa)
LC 97-44054
Traces women's participation in basketball from the early days of this sport to the recent establishment of professional women's teams and profiles some of the players who have had key roles in advancing this sport

Layden, Joseph, 1959-
NBA game day; by Joe Layden and James Preller. Scholastic 1997 64p il $10.95 **796.323**
1. National Basketball Association 2. Basketball
ISBN 0-590-89799-3 LC 97-19257
Photographs and text present an up-close look at varied aspects of the lives of professional basketball players, from pre-game preparations, practice, game action, signing autographs, and more
"Twenty-six fine sports photographers are represented in this glossy, close-up collection. . . . Worthwhile text simply outlines each of the activities." Voice Youth Advocates

McKissack, Fredrick, 1939-
Black hoops; the history of African Americans in basketball; [by] Fredrick McKissack, Jr. Scholastic Press 1999 154p il $15.95 **796.323**
1. Basketball 2. African American athletes
ISBN 0-590-48712-4 LC 98-14107
Surveys the history of African Americans in basketball, from the beginning of the sport to the present, discussing individual teams and players and the integration of the National Basketball Association
"This book makes a unique and important contribution for this age range and should not be missed." SLJ
Includes glossary and bibliographical references

Stewart, Mark
Basketball; a history of hoops. Watts 1998 160p il (Watts history of sports) lib bdg $32 (7 and up)
796.323
1. Basketball
ISBN 0-531-11492-9 LC 98-25040
Discusses the origins and evolution of the sport of basketball, as well as important events and key personalities in both college and professional versions of the game
Includes bibliographical references

796.325 Volleyball

Crisfield, Deborah
Winning volleyball for girls; [by] Deborah W. Crisfield; foreword by Jerry Sherman. Facts on File 1994 149p il $24.95; pa $12.95 **796.325**
1. Volleyball
ISBN 0-8160-3033-2; 0-8160-3034-0 (pa)
LC 94-27344
"A Mountain Lion book"
"Everything a prospective player wants to know is included here: rules, techniques, and strategies, with plenty of diagrams so that readers can get a visual image of what is being described. The black-and-white photos are occasionally grainy and/or dark, but in the main, they support the text." Booklist
Includes bibliographical references

796.332 American football

Anderson, Dave
The story of football; foreword by Troy Aikman. rev ed. Morrow 1997 160p il $16; pa $9.95
796.332
1. Football
ISBN 0-688-14314-8; 0-688-14315-6 (pa)
LC 96-46539
First published 1985
Traces the history of this American sport from the first college game at Rutgers in 1869 to the present
"The book is fast-paced, well-written, and entertaining." Book Rep

Buckley, James, Jr.
America's greatest game; the real story of football and the NFL; foreword by Jerry Rice. Hyperion Bks. for Children 1998 64p il $16.95
796.332
1. National Football League 2. Football
ISBN 0-7868-0433-5 LC 97-47744
A historical overview of how the game of football has evolved through the years and how the National Football League began
"This book consists mainly of outstanding full-color photographs of players at various levels of proficiency from peewee to pro. . . . Certain to be a popular browsing item for young football fans." SLJ

Owens, Tom, 1960-
Football; [by] Thomas S. Owens, Diana Star Helmer. 21st Cent. Bks. (Brookfield) 1998 64p il lib bdg $23.40   **796.332**
1. Football
ISBN 0-7613-3233-2   LC 98-26711
Describes how professional football teams prepare for games, analyze the games afterwards for improvement, develop strategies, and build themselves through player selection
"A lively and informative look at professional football that offers the kind of inside information young fans crave. . . . Appealing full-color photographs appear on nearly every other page." SLJ
Includes glossary and bibliographical references

Stewart, Mark
Football; a history of the gridiron game. Watts 1998 144p il (Watts history of sports) lib bdg $32 (7 and up)   **796.332**
1. Football
ISBN 0-531-11493-7   LC 98-25038
Discusses the origins and evolution of the game of football, as well as memorable events and key personalities in the game's history
Includes bibliographical references

796.334   Soccer

Baddiel, Ivor
Ultimate soccer. DK Pub. 1998 96p il $16.95; pa $12.95   **796.334**
1. Soccer
ISBN 0-7894-2795-8; 0-7894-3071-1 (pa)
    LC 97-36602
Cover title: Soccer: the ultimate World Cup companion
"Baddiel begins with a history of soccer and then moves on to rules and techniques. Great teams and players from the various countries competing are highlighted. The concluding chapters cover World Cup games from 1930 to the present." SLJ
"An excellent resource for young soccer enthusiasts eager to know more about this international sport." Booklist

Coleman, Lori
Fundamental soccer; photographs by Andy King. Lerner Publs. 1995 64p il (Fundamental sports) lib bdg $21.27   **796.334**
1. Soccer
ISBN 0-8225-3451-7   LC 94-11907
This "book covers the history of the sport, positions, equipment, basic and more advanced moves, rules, the merits of practice, and variations in the game. . . . King's colorful, clear, informative photographs enhance the text." SLJ
Includes glossary and bibliographical references

Hamm, Mia, 1972-
Go for the goal; a champion's guide to winning in soccer and life; [by] Mia Hamm with Aaron Heifetz. HarperCollins Pubs. 1999 222p il $20 (7 and up)   **796.334**
1. Soccer
ISBN 0-06-019342-5   LC 99-19592
Personal anecdotes and both action and instructional photos illustrate soccer skills and techniques

Scott, Nina Savin
The thinking kid's guide to successful soccer; illustrations by Anne Canevari Green. Millbrook Press 1999 96p il lib bdg $18.90   **796.334**
1. Soccer
ISBN 0-7613-0324-3   LC 98-17201
Presents strategies for playing soccer under pressure, dealing with various situations during a game, setting goals, playing with teammates, coping with coaches, and dealing with doubts and fears
"This well-designed book, with genuinely funny cartoon illustrations, deserves a space on the shelf right next to those books on rules and techniques." Booklist
Includes bibliographical references

Stewart, Mark
Soccer; a history of the world's most popular game. Watts 1998 128p il (Watts history of sports) lib bdg $32 (7 and up)   **796.334**
1. Soccer
ISBN 0-531-11456-2   LC 97-17201
A comprehensive history of soccer, focusing on its evolution, momentous events, and key personalities
This book is "chock full of outstanding full-color and black-and-white photos. There is strong coverage of memorable contests and individuals and the statistical appendix [is] useful." SLJ
Includes bibliographical references

796.34   Racket games

Nicholson, Lois, 1949-
The composite guide to lacrosse. Chelsea House 1999 64p il (Composite guide) $15.95   **796.34**
1. Lacrosse 2. Indians of North America—Games
ISBN 0-7910-4719-9   LC 98-13891
Traces the history of lacrosse from the time it was played by North American Indians to its current popularity in elementary schools and up to professional and international levels
This is "a good basic book." SLJ
Includes bibliographical references

796.342   Tennis

Douglas, Paul
Tennis. Dorling Kindersley 1995 72p il pa $4.95 (7 and up)   **796.342**
1. Tennis
ISBN 0-7894-0182-7

Douglas, Paul—*Continued*
At head of title: 101 essential tips
Aspects covered include strokes, positions, playing surfaces, dress and equipment
"This is a good text for those just picking up the sport, as well as for those seasoned players who want to brush up on their game or improve their strategy." Voice Youth Advocates

796.352 Golf

Anderson, Dave
The story of golf; foreword by Jack Nicklaus. Morrow 1998 159p il $16; pa $7.95   **796.352**
1. Golf—History
ISBN 0-688-15796-3; 0-688-15797-1 (pa)
LC 97-44097
Traces the development of the game of golf from its modern-day origins in fifteenth-century Scotland, highlighting key players, courses and tournaments
"Anderson skillfully interweaves anecdotes with straight narrative in this highly readable and engaging book, which features plenty of photos." Horn Book Guide
Includes glossary

796.357 Baseball

Aylesworth, Thomas G.
The kids' world almanac of baseball; introduction by Cal Ripken, Jr. rev ed. World Almanac 1996 284p il hardcover o.p. paperback available $8.95 (7 and up)   **796.357**
1. Baseball
ISBN 0-88687-787-3 (pa)   LC 95-62358
First published 1990
This collection of baseball records and facts includes a history of the game, players profiles, statistics, trivia, quotes, and anecdotes

Brashler, William
The story of Negro league baseball. Ticknor & Fields 1994 166p il $15.95; pa $10.95   **796.357**
1. Baseball 2. African American athletes
ISBN 0-395-67169-8; 0-395-69721-2 (pa)
LC 93-36547
"This book intersperses chapters on such black stars as Satchel Paige, Josh Gibson, and Jackie Robinson among the accounts of the various Negro Leagues. Archival and scrapbook black-and-white photographs . . . appear throughout. A list of Negro League all-star teams chosen by a variety of groups and individuals is appended." SLJ
"The author brings to life some of the finest players and most interesting men who ever chose the career of baseball." Horn Book
Includes bibliographical references

Gardner, Robert, 1929-
The forgotten players; the story of black baseball in America; [by] Robert Gardner and Dennis Shortelle. Walker & Co. 1993 120p il $12.95; lib bdg $13.85   **796.357**
1. Baseball 2. African American athletes
ISBN 0-8027-8248-5; 0-8027-8249-3 (lib bdg)
LC 92-29618
Traces the history of the Negro leagues that evolved due to segregation in professional baseball and the experiences of black players from the late nineteenth through the early twentieth century
"Sports fans who are used to being fed statistics, game accounts, and biographical information will get some of this, but more significantly will be exposed to an insightful look at social history. Both the black-and-white photographs and the text are fully documented with the inclusion of over 125 endnotes." SLJ

Gilbert, Thomas W.
Damn Yankees; Casey, Whitey, Yogi, and the Mick; [by] Thomas Gilbert. Watts 1997 143p il $24; pa $9.95 (7 and up)   **796.357**
1. New York Yankees (Baseball team) 2. Baseball
ISBN 0-531-11338-8; 0-531-15879-9 (pa)
LC 97-3492
A history of baseball from 1949-1964, focusing on the incredible New York Yankees who won fourteen of sixteen American League pennants and became champions of the world nine times
This "narrative is driven largely by statistics and exciting action, and personalized by black-and-white photos of many players. . . . A partisan portrait of a memorable team and an authoritative account of an exciting era of baseball history." SLJ
Includes bibliographical references

Gutman, Dan
Baseball's greatest games. Viking 1994 212p il hardcover o.p. paperback available $4.99 (7 and up)   **796.357**
1. Baseball
ISBN 0-14-037933-9 (pa)   LC 93-31504
"Gutman introduces young fans to nine of the greatest baseball games ever played, starting in 1886 and ending in 1988. Rather than going into batter-by-batter detail, he summarizes most of each game, then zeros in on moments of *tension*, the quality that Gutman thinks defines a great game." Booklist
"This book is a lot of fun to read, Gutman's descriptions of the games don't get bogged down in too many details, and he has an old-fashioned, snappy, sportswriter's style that's just right for this type of presentation." SLJ
Includes bibliographical references

McKissack, Patricia C., 1944-
Black diamond; the story of the Negro baseball leagues; [by] Patricia C. McKissack and Fredrick McKissack, Jr. Scholastic 1994 184p il $14.95; pa $3.99   **796.357**
1. Baseball 2. African American athletes
ISBN 0-590-45809-4; 0-590-45810-8 (pa)
LC 93-22691

McKissack, Patricia C., 1944—_Continued_
Traces the history of baseball in the Negro Leagues and its great heroes, including Monte Irwin, Buck Leonard, and Cool Papa Bell
This is "an engaging account. . . . It includes a chronology, player profiles and wonderful photographs from the Negro Leagues." N Y Times Book Rev
Includes bibliographical references

Neft, David S.
The sports encyclopedia: baseball; [by] David S. Neft, Richard M. Cohen. St. Martin's Press pa $19.99   **796.357**
1. Baseball—Statistics

First published 1974 by Grosset & Dunlap. (2000 edition) Periodically revised
Covers baseball from 1876 to the present and contains team statistics, alphabetical registers of batters and pitchers, and summaries of each season

Nitz, Kristin Wolden
Fundamental softball; photographs by Andy King. Lerner Publs. 1997 80p il (Fundamental sports) lib bdg $21.27   **796.357**
1. Softball
ISBN 0-8225-3460-6   LC 96-34258
Introduces the history, equipment, skills, and strategies of softball
"Clear color photographs and helpful diagrams aid in the initial instruction of softball fundamentals. . . . The informative book provides an adequate source for more mature beginners." Horn Book Guide
Includes glossary and bibliographical references

Ritter, Lawrence S.
The story of baseball; foreword by Ted Williams. 3rd rev & expanded ed. Morrow Junior Bks. 1999 205p il $16   **796.357**
1. Baseball
ISBN 0-688-16264-9   LC 98-35456
First published 1983
Traces the history of baseball, which was first played in a form resembling the modern game in Hoboken, New Jersey, in 1846, and first played by professional players in 1869
"This edition of _the_ classic baseball book covers quite recent events, including Cal Ripken, Jr.'s amazing 1995 breaking of Lou Gehrig's record for consecutive games played as well as the spectacular 1998 season (in which Mark McGwire hit seventy home runs to overtake Roger Maris's sixty-one in 1961)." Horn Book Guide

Smyth, Ian
The young baseball player; written by Ian Smyth; with a foreword by Eduardo Perez. DK Pub. 1998 37p il (Young enthusiast) $15.95
                                             796.357
1. Baseball
ISBN 0-7894-2825-3   LC 97-41728

Provides information on the offensive and defensive techniques of baseball as well as on the history and equipment of the game, with step-by-step instructions on individual positions
This is "filled with beautifully-reproduced full-color photos. . . . Smyth provides solid, basic information in an attractive format." SLJ
Includes glossary

Stewart, Mark
Baseball; a history of the national pastime. Watts 1998 159p il (Watts history of sports) lib bdg $32 (7 and up)   **796.357**
1. Baseball
ISBN 0-531-11455-4   LC 97-18066
A comprehensive history of baseball focusing on its evolution, momentous events, and key personalities
This "book offers a wealth of information for even the most knowledgeable fans, especially about the game's early days. Stewart does an excellent job of demonstrating how social, financial, and organizational issues influence sports." SLJ
Includes bibliographical references

Ward, Geoffrey C.
Shadow ball; the history of the Negro leagues; by Geoffrey C. Ward and Ken Burns, with Jim O'Connor. Knopf 1994 79p il (Baseball, the American epic) $15; lib bdg $16.99   **796.357**
1. Baseball 2. African American athletes
ISBN 0-679-86749-X; 0-679-96749-4 (lib bdg)
                                             LC 94-5552
"Based on the Public Television series." Title page
"_Shadow Ball_ focuses on the Negro leagues, from their formation after a 'gentleman's' agreement effectively barred black players from professional baseball through the breakthrough of players to the major leagues. . . . It tells the story well, and the excellent photos and quotations help make the players memorable." Booklist

796.42   Track and field

Jackson, Colin
The young track and field athlete; with a foreword by Gwen Torence. DK Pub. 1996 32p il $15.95; pa $9.95   **796.42**
1. Track athletics
ISBN 0-7894-0855-4; 0-7894-0474-5 (pa)
                                             LC 95-44331
This describes "the preparation for and execution of a number of track-and-field events. The descriptions are clear and accurate with step-by-step diagrams of youngsters performing the skills. . . . World record holders are shown competing in heptathlon and decathlon events. Vocabulary terms are defined within the text. This attractive, oversized title can be enjoyed for the pictures or for the information." SLJ

Macht, Norman L. (Norman Lee), 1929-
The composite guide to track & field. Chelsea House 1999 64p il (Composite guide) $15.95
                                             796.42
1. Track athletics
ISBN 0-7910-4720-2   LC 97-47684

Macht, Norman L. (Norman Lee), 1929——_Continued_

Surveys the history of track and field competitions from their origins in ancient Greece to the accomplishments of top athletes in the twentieth century

Includes bibliographical references

796.44 Sports gymnastics

Bragg, Linda Wallenberg

Fundamental gymnastics; photographs by Andy King. Lerner Publs. 1995 80p il (Fundamental sports) lib bdg $19.93   **796.44**

1. Gymnastics

ISBN 0-8225-3453-3   LC 94-40770

"Four chapters provide a brief history of gymnastics, descriptions of the six events for boys and the four events for girls, the basic moves, the general workout, and competition. The events and some of the skills are shown in excellent-quality full-color photographs on each page. Interesting facts in orange boxes appear throughout." SLJ

Includes glossary and bibliographical references

Gutman, Dan

Gymnastics. Viking 1996 187p il $14.99

                    796.44

1. Gymnastics

ISBN 0-670-86949-X   LC 95-50420

Discusses the history, competitive events, and some superstars of gymnastics, as well as problems and miscellaneous facts related to the sport

"Gutman's tone throughout is breezy and enthusiastic, and . . . he is truly bedazzled by the athletes and their skill. But he also examines the dark side of the sport: serious injuries, eating disorders, abusive coaches, and the competitive system." Booklist

Includes glossary and bibliographical references

Jackman, Joan

The young gymnast; foreword by Shannon Miller. Dorling Kindersley 1995 45p il $15.95

                    796.44

1. Gymnastics

ISBN 1-56458-677-4   LC 94-36256

"The author differentiates between events such as vaulting, the balance beam, rhythmic gymnastics, sports acrobatics, and tumbling. The many full-color photographs reflect the descriptive text as well as add information." SLJ

796.48 Olympic games

Currie, Stephen, 1960-

The Olympic games. Lucent Bks. 1999 111p il (Lucent overview series) lib bdg $17.96 (7 and up)

                    796.48

1. Olympic games

ISBN 1-56006-395-5   LC 98-50360

Discusses various aspects of the Olympic games, including their history, politics, commercialization, size, participation, and drug use

"Well written, well argued, and extremely well documented." SLJ

Includes bibliographical references

Glubok, Shirley, 1933-

Olympic games in ancient Greece; by Shirley Glubok and Alfred Tamarin. Harper & Row 1976 116p il lib bdg $16.89   **796.48**

1. Olympic games 2. Greece—Civilization

ISBN 0-06-022048-1

"The authors take a systematic look at the ancient Greek Olympics around 400 B.C. . . . The subsequent narrative describes the pageantry and the competitions, many of which have come down to us in modern form while others, such as chariot races and the race in armor, have passed out of existence. Bits of Greek history influencing the games, recorded anecdotes, and legends add color to the account." Booklist

796.5 Outdoor life

Paulsen, Gary

Woodsong. Bradbury Press 1990 132p map $16 (7 and up)   **796.5**

1. Sled dog racing 2. Outdoor life 3. Minnesota

ISBN 0-02-770221-9   LC 89-70835

Also available in paperback from Viking

For the author and his family, life in northern Minnesota is a wild experience involving wolves, deer, and the sled dogs that make their way of life possible. Includes an account of Paulsen's first Iditarod, a dogsled race across Alaska

"The book is packed with vignettes that range among various shades of terror and lyrical beauty that beg for a booktalking introduction to lure students into reading the entire work." Voice Youth Advocates

796.51 Walking

Andryszewski, Tricia, 1956-

Step by step along the Appalachian Trail. 21st Cent. Bks. (Brookfield) 1998 64p il lib bdg $23.90

                    796.51

1. Hiking 2. Nature study 3. Appalachian Trail

ISBN 0-7613-0273-5   LC 98-7304

An overview of the natural history of the Appalachian Trail and of historical events related to the route, an imaginary hike up the trail, and a description of what can be seen and experienced along the way

"Clear, full-color photographs give readers a sense of 'you are there' immediacy. Students using [this book] for reports are sure to get wrapped up in the vivid descriptions, while nature lovers and budding adventurers will want to pack up and start walking." SLJ

Includes bibliographical references

Step by step along the Pacific Crest Trail. 21st Cent. Bks. (Brookfield) 1998 63p il lib bdg $23.90

                    796.51

1. Hiking 2. Nature study 3. Pacific Crest Trail

ISBN 0-7613-0274-3   LC 98-7303

Andryszewski, Tricia, 1956-—*Continued*
An overview of the natural history of the Pacific Crest Trail and of historical events related to the route, an imaginary hike up the trail, and a description of what can be seen and experienced along the way
Includes bibliographical references

Hart, John, 1948-
Walking softly in the wilderness; the Sierra Club guide to backpacking. completely rev & updated. Sierra Club Bks. 1998 478p il maps pa $16 (7 and up) **796.51**
1. Backpacking
ISBN 0-87156-392-4
First published 1977
This guide for both the novice and experienced hiker reflects the environmental concerns of the Sierra Club. Among topics covered are: clothing and equipment; making and breaking camp; problem animals and plants; hiking and camping with kids. Listings of conservation and wilderness travel organizations, map and equipment sources, land management agencies, and Internet contacts are appended

796.52 Walking and exploring by kind of terrain

Brimner, Larry Dane, 1949-
Rock climbing. Watts 1997 unp il lib bdg $22; pa $6.95 **796.52**
1. Mountaineering
ISBN 0-531-20269-0 (lib bdg); 0-531-15860-8 (pa)
LC 96-28943
"A First book"
Presents a brief description of rock climbing, a sport that requires little equipment, appeals to all ages, and is considered to be mental as well as physical
"The beautiful color photos in this brief description of rock climbing will inspire any novice." Booklist
Includes bibliographical references

Pfetzer, Mark
Within reach: my Everest story; [by] Mark Pfetzer and Jack Galvin. Dutton 1998 224p il $16.95; pa $6.99 (7 and up) **796.52**
1. Mountaineering 2. Mount Everest (China and Nepal)
ISBN 0-525-46089-6; 0-14-130497-9 (pa)
LC 98-29215
Mark Pfetzer describes how he spent his teenage years climbing mountains in the United States, South America, Africa, and Asia, with an emphasis on his two expeditions up Mount Everest
"Throughout the detail-rich, briskly paced account, Pfetzer is psychologically challenging, yet always emotionally within reach." Booklist
Includes glossary

796.72 Automobile racing

Burgess Wise, David
The ultimate race car. DK Pub. 1999 168p il $29.95 (7 and up) **796.72**
1. Automobile racing
ISBN 0-7894-4182-9
LC 98-32294
"Following the opening chapter, which gives an overview of the history of car racing, in which all developmental highlights are discussed, the author focuses on specific makes of cars and famous racing circuits. . . . The third part is a gallery of profiles of 'racing personalities.'" Booklist

796.8 Combat sports

Blot, Pierre
Karate for beginners; foreword by J. Allen Queen; illustrated by Christophe Heymann. Sterling 1996 144p il $19.95; pa $12.95 **796.8**
1. Karate
ISBN 0-8069-3874-9; 0-8069-3873-0 (pa)
LC 95-40698
The author "explains the different blocks, punches, kicks, and stances. Almost all of the Japanese terms are translated, sparring competitions are explained in detail, and a short history of karate is included. Readers are taken through the forms and self-defense techniques that must be mastered at each belt level for seven different ranks." SLJ

Dallas, Kim
Fundamental karate; photographs by Andy King. Lerner Publs. 1998 64p il (Fundamental sports) lib bdg $22.60 **796.8**
1. Karate
ISBN 0-8225-3462-2
LC 97-29623
An introduction to the history, skills, and techniques of karate
Includes bibliographical references

Gallagher, Jim, 1969-
The composite guide to wrestling. Chelsea House 1999 64p il (Composite guide) lib bdg $16.95 **796.8**
1. Wrestling
ISBN 0-7910-4721-0
LC 98-5610
Explores the world of wrestling and how competitors practice it as a time-honored sport
Includes bibliographical references

Goedecke, Christopher J., 1951-
Smart moves; a kid's guide to self-defense; [photographs by] Rosmarie Hausherr. Simon & Schuster Bks. for Young Readers 1995 96p il $16 **796.8**
1. Self-defense
ISBN 0-689-80294-3
LC 94-36863

Goedecke, Christopher J., 1951——*Continued*
The authors "describe specific self-defense maneuvers, which range from achieving a stable stance to blocking punches and escaping choke holds. . . . Eleven authentic, progressively more menacing conflict scenarios, which beg for classroom discussion, are presented, along with suggestions for appropriate responses." Booklist

Gutman, Bill
Tae kwon do; illustrated with photographs by Peter Ford. Capstone Press 1995 48p il (Action sports) lib bdg $19   **796.8**
1. Karate
ISBN 1-56065-266-7   LC 95-7809
Describes the kicking and striking techniques of tae kwon do, originally a Korean art, now a worldwide sport
Includes glossary and bibliographical references

Queen, J. Allen
Learn karate. Sterling 1998 80p il $17.95
                                       796.8
1. Karate
ISBN 0-8069-8136-9   LC 98-26367
Introduces the philosophy, uniform, stances, kicks, punches, strikes, and sparring and competition techniques of karate
"Clear, full-color photos place this instruction manual a notch above the others available. . . . For self-instruction, or as an adjunct to karate classes, this book will do the trick." SLJ

Santoro, Laura
Aikido for kids; by Laura Santoro & Jennifer Corso; photographs by Gerald F. Penca. Sterling 1998 96p il $14.95; pa $5.95   **796.8**
1. Aikido
ISBN 0-8069-9405-3; 0-8069-9425-8 (pa)
                                       LC 98-44563
An introduction to the martial art of aikido which comes from Japan and which demonstrates how one's spirit can be brought into harmony with the world

796.9   Ice and snow sports

Brimner, Larry Dane, 1949-
Snowboarding. Watts 1997 63p il lib bdg $21; pa $6.95   **796.9**
1. Snowboarding
ISBN 0-531-20313-1 (lib bdg); 0-531-15890-X (pa)
                                       LC 97-8962
"A First book"
A revised edition of the title first published 1989
Traces the history of this recreational activity, describes the required equipment and basic techniques, concludes with a discussion of safety issues and competitive aspects of the sport
"Well-reproduced, full-color photographs, listings of organizations, magazines, books, and Internet resources round out this solid effort." SLJ

Lurie, Jon
Fundamental snowboarding; photographs by Jimmy Clarke. Lerner Publs. 1996 64p il (Fundamental sports) lib bdg $21.27   **796.9**
1. Snowboarding
ISBN 0-8225-3457-6   LC 95-11721
Introduces the history and techniques of snowboarding
"The information is solid, and the clear photographs are eye-catching." SLJ
Includes glossary and bibliographical references

McKenna, Lesley
The fantastic book of snow-boarding. Copper Beech Bks. 1998 40p il $10; lib bdg $22.40
                                       796.9
1. Snowboarding
ISBN 0-7613-0649-8; 0-7613-0717-6 (lib bdg)
                                       LC 97-35115
This introduction to snowboarding covers "clothing, equipment, instruction for beginners, and a discussion of advanced techniques. There are some nice bonuses including illustrations of how to get on and off a T-bar, an informative examination of snowboard care and repair, and an eight-page fold-out. . . . This is a solid effort." SLJ
Includes glossary

796.91   Ice skating

Boo, Michael
The story of figure skating. Morrow Junior Bks. 1998 224p il $16; pa $7.95   **796.91**
1. Ice skating
ISBN 0-688-15820-X; 0-688-15821-8 (pa)
                                       LC 98-13569
Surveys the history of figure skating and examines some of its notable performers
"From axel to Zamboni, from Jackson Haines to Tara Lipinski—its's all here. Boo has done a superb job." SLJ
Includes bibliographical references

Morrissey, Peter, 1953-
The young ice skater; written by Peter Morrissey; with a foreword by Todd Eldredge. DK Pub. 1998 37p il (Young enthusiast) $15.95
                                       796.91
1. Ice skating
ISBN 0-7894-3422-9   LC 98-11936
Introduces the history, equipment, and techniques of ice skating
"The photographs are wonderful. . . . Young skaters will relish this book, while nonathletes may find it interesting enough to read or browse through." SLJ
Includes glossary

796.962   Ice hockey

Foley, Mike
Fundamental hockey; photographs by Andy King. Lerner Publs. 1996 80p il (Fundamental sports) lib bdg $22.60   **796.962**
1. Hockey
ISBN 0-8225-3456-8   LC 95-7077

Foley, Mike—*Continued*
"A brief history of the sport is followed by an explanation of what players do during hockey practice and what occurs during a game. Finally, readers see some of the drills and variations of the game, such as broomball and sledge hockey, which is played by players with lower-body disabilities. A substantial glossary and list of places to write for more information are appended." SLJ
Includes bibliographical references

Owens, Tom, 1960-
Hockey; [by] Thomas S. Owens, Diana Star Helmer. 21st Cent. Bks. (Brookfield) 1999 64p il lib bdg $23.40   **796.962**
1. Hockey
ISBN 0-7613-3236-7   LC 98-40624
Describes how professional hockey teams prepare for games, analyze the games afterwards for improvement, develop strategies, and build themselves through player selection
Includes glossary and bibliographical references

Stewart, Mark
Hockey; a history of the fastest game on ice. Watts 1998 127p il (Watts history of sports) lib bdg $32 (7 and up)   **796.962**
1. Hockey
ISBN 0-531-11494-5   LC 98-25039
Discusses the origins and evolution of the game of hockey, as well as memorable events and key personalities in this sport
Includes bibliographical references

Sullivan, George
All about hockey; illustrated with photographs and diagrams. Putnam 1998 159p il $15.99; pa $9.99   **796.962**
1. Hockey
ISBN 0-399-23172-2; 0-399-23173 0 (pa)
                    LC 97-38125
An introduction to the sport of ice hockey, including its history, equipment, techniques, terminology, rules, and players
"This clearly written guide provides a good, solid introduction to the sport." Booklist
Includes glossary and bibliographical references

796.98 Winter Olympic games

Wallechinsky, David, 1948-
The complete book of the Winter Olympics. Overlook Press $27.95; pa $14.95   **796.98**
1. Olympic games

First published 1984. (1998 edition) Periodically revised
"Contains national medal totals in each Olympics, and a brief history of the Winter Games. Sports are considered in separate sections, with full information on each event, lists winners (with times, scores, etc.) by year, usually with commentary on specific contests and notes on the contestants. Some sections include a glossary of terms for the particular sport. Includes discontinued events." Guide to Ref Books. 11th edition

797.1 Boating

Conner, Dennis
Learn to sail; [by] Dennis Conner and Michael Levitt; illustrations by Chris Lloyd. St. Martin's Press 1994 240p il $22.95 (7 and up)   **797.1**
1. Sailing
ISBN 0-312-11020-0   LC 94-2611
In this beginner's guide "Conner recommends boats on which to learn, defines sailing etiquette, offers weather analysis, and discusses sailing under adverse conditions and coping with emergencies. . . . This is an excellent introduction to the principles of the sport." Booklist
Includes bibliographical references

George, Charles, 1949-
White-water rafting; by Charles and Linda George. Riverfront Bks. 1999 48p il (Sports alive!) $19; lib bdg $19.93   **797.1**
1. Rafting (Sports)
ISBN 0-531-11619-0; 0-7368-0055-7 (lib bdg)
                    LC 98-7188
Describes the history, equipment, and techniques of white water rafting
Includes bibliographical references

797.2 Swimming and diving

Holbrook, Mike
Snorkeling. Crestwood House 1993 48p il (Adventurers) lib bdg $13.95   **797.2**
1. Skin diving
ISBN 0-89686-823-0   LC 92-45219
This introduction to snorkeling discusses basic equipment, basic techniques, clothing and accessories, hand signals, safety and basic rescue, marine life, and where to receive instruction
Includes glossary

Rouse, Jeff, 1970-
The young swimmer. DK Pub. 1997 37p il $15.95   **797.2**
1. Swimming
ISBN 0-7894-1533-X
This volume "explores what to wear, where to swim, and the basic rules of water safety. It introduces the four main strokes of crawl, backstroke, breaststroke, and butterfly, using young swimmers to demonstrate the proper techniques in step-by-step photos." Publisher's note
"Most of the text appears in the captions that accompany the many small photos of swimmers in action. Young swimmers should find the sequences of pictures helpful." Booklist
Includes glossary

797.5   Air sports

Perry, Phyllis J., 1933-
Soaring. Watts 1997 63p il lib bdg $22; pa
$6.95   **797.5**
1. Gliding and soaring 2. Gliders (Aeronautics)
ISBN 0-531-20258-5 (lib bdg); 0-531-15852-7 (pa)
                                         LC 96-41075
"A First book"
This introduction to the sport of soaring defines terms
and gives a brief history and description of gliders and
their recreational uses
Includes glossary and bibliographical references

798.2   Horsemanship

Green, Lucinda
The young rider. Dorling Kindersley 1993 64p
il $15.95   **798.2**
1. Horsemanship
ISBN 1-56458-320-1   LC 93-22103
Covers how to choose, care for, and train a pony, basic and more advanced riding skills, and necessary equipment
"Green's style is breezy and encouraging, and the text
is concise and easy to read, all of which should make the
book popular with young readers." Booklist
Includes glossary

Henderson, Carolyn
Horse & pony shows & events; foreword by
Carl Hester. DK Pub. 1999 48p il (DK riding
club) $12.95; pa $7.95   **798.2**
1. Horsemanship
ISBN 0-7894-4266-3; 0-7894-4265-5 (pa)
                                         LC 98-50743
An illustrated guide to horse and pony shows, compe-
titions, and other events
Includes glossary

Improve your riding skills; foreword by Lynn
Russell. DK Pub. 1999 48p il (DK riding club)
$12.95; pa $7.95   **798.2**
1. Horsemanship
ISBN 0-7894-4264-7; 0-7894-4263-9 (pa)
                                         LC 98-50744
This illustrated guide to horseback riding describes
such skills as mounting and dismounting, exercises in the
saddle, trotting, cantering and galloping, jumping and
trail riding
Includes glossary

798.8   Dog racing

Crisman, Ruth, 1914-
Racing the Iditarod Trail. Dillon Press 1993 72p
il $14.95; pa $7.95   **798.8**
1. Iditarod Trail Sled Dog Race, Alaska
ISBN 0-87518-523-1; 0-382-39229-9 (pa)
                                         LC 92-25870

This book describes the annual 1049 mile sled dog
race in Alaska and the dramatic life-or-death event that
prompted the Iditarod
"By focusing on the 1991 race, the author takes readers along on the suspenseful journey from start to finish.
. . . A few anecdotes from earlier races plus many good-
quality, full-color photos provide a lively and clear account of the challenging contest." SLJ
Includes bibliographical references

Dolan, Ellen M., 1943-
Susan Butcher and the Iditarod Trail. Walker &
Co. 1993 103p il $14.95; lib bdg $15.85; pa $7.95
                                                 798.8
1. Butcher, Susan 2. Iditarod Trail Sled Dog Race,
Alaska
ISBN 0-8027-8211-6; 0-8027-8212-4 (lib bdg);
0-8027-7496-2 (pa)   LC 92-36837
Describes the annual dog sled race from Anchorage to
Nome, Alaska, and the life of the woman who was the
first person to win it for three consecutive years

Paulsen, Gary
Puppies, dogs, and blue northers; reflections on
being raised by a pack of sled dogs. Harcourt
Brace & Co. 1996 81p il $16   **798.8**
1. Sled dog racing 2. Dogs
ISBN 0-15-292881-2   LC 95-18981
Also available in paperback from Delacorte Press
Illustrated by Ruth Wright Paulsen
"In seven vignettes, Paulsen recounts the story of his
lead dog, Cookie, as she mates and gives birth, and her
puppies mature toward their destiny—to race and pull
sleds. Readers are drawn into that special bond between
driver and lead dog through Paulsen's real-life experiences racing in Minnesota. . . . Ruth Wright Paulsen's
occasional paintings add warmth and charm to the book."
SLJ

Winterdance; the fine madness of running the
Iditarod. Harcourt Brace & Co. 1994 256p il
$21.95; pa $15   **798.8**
1. Iditarod Trail Sled Dog Race, Alaska
ISBN 0-15-126227-6; 0-15-600145-4 (pa)
                                         LC 93-42096
"This book is primarily an account of Paulsen's first
Iditarod and its frequent life-threatening disasters. . . .
However, the book is more than a tabulation of tribula-
tions; it is a meditation on the extraordinary attraction
this race holds for some men and women." Libr J

Shahan, Sherry, 1949-
Dashing through the snow; the story of the Jr.
Iditarod. Millbrook Press 1997 47p il lib bdg
$22.40; pa $9.95   **798.8**
1. Sled dog racing
ISBN 0-761300208-5 (lib bdg); 0-7613-0143-7 (pa)
                                         LC 96-27075
Presents the history and action of the Junior Iditarod,
the annual dogsled race for young people in Alaska, discussing such related topics as dog care, equipment, and
technique
"Each page is lavishly illustrated with color photographs that complement the wealth of information giv-
en." Child Book Rev Serv
Includes glossary

Wood, Ted, 1965-
Iditarod dream; Dusty and his sled dogs compete in Alaska's Jr. Iditarod. Walker & Co. 1996 48p il map $16.95; lib bdg $17.85 **798.8**
1. Sled dog racing
ISBN 0-8027-8406-2; 0-8027-8407-0 (lib bdg)
LC 95-31084
This "photo essay follows 15-year-old Dusty Whittemore of Cantwell, AK, through the 1995 Jr. Iditarod Sled Dog Race—158 miles from Lake Lucille to Yentna and back." SLJ
"Clear, close-up color photographs portray every stage of the event and offer interesting information about the difficulties and hazards of this two-day competition." Booklist

799.1 Fishing

Bailey, John
The young fishing enthusiast. DK Pub. 1999 48p il (Young enthusiast) $15.95 **799.1**
1. Fishing
ISBN 0-7894-3965-4
LC 99-10042
An introduction to the basic techniques of fishing, including advice on tackle, bait, and clothing
"Excellent full-color photographs, especially the how-to and underwater shots, would be enough reason to add this book to any collection." SLJ
Includes glossary

Schmidt, Gerald D., 1934-1990
Let's go fishing! a book for beginners; illustrated by Brian W. Payne. Roberts Rinehart Pubs.; distributed by Court Wayne Press 1990 85p il pa $11.95 **799.1**
1. Fishing
ISBN 0-911797-84-X
LC 90-62933
This book "explores all aspects of freshwater fishing. The types of fish and fishing, how to locate them, equipment, cleaning and cooking, and ethics are among the topics discussed. Line drawings are informative. . . . Safety is strongly emphasized in both text and illustrations." SLJ

800 LITERATURE & RHETORIC

803 Literature—Encyclopedias and dictionaries

Benet's reader's encyclopedia. HarperCollins Pubs. 1996 $50 **803**
1. Literature—Dictionaries
LC 96-217151
First published 1948 under the editorship of William Rose Benet. (4th edition 1996). Periodically revised
Current editor: Bruce Murphy
This encyclopedia contains over 10,000 entries and covers world literature from early times to the present. Includes entries on authors, literary movements, principal characters, plot synopses, terms, awards, myths and legends, etc.

Brewer's dictionary of phrase and fable. Harper & Row $45 **803**
1. Literature—Dictionaries 2. Allusions

First published 1870. (15th edition 1995) Periodically revised
Current editor: Ivor H. Evans
"Over 15,000 brief entries give the meanings and origins of a broad range of terms, expressions, and names of real, fictitious and mythical characters from world history, science, the arts and literature." N Y Public Libr. Ref Books for Child Collect. 2d edition

808 Rhetoric

Dragisic, Patricia
How to write a letter. Watts 1998 127p (Speak out, write on! book) lib bdg $24; pa $7.95 (7 and up) **808**
1. Letter writing
ISBN 0-531-11391-4 (lib bdg); 0-531-15931-0 (pa)
LC 97-35265
Describes the basic parts of many types of business and personal letters, offers examples of each kind, and suggests ways to write effectively for particular situations
This "is filled with easy-to-understand, useful information. . . . There is a definite need for this book in most collections." SLJ
Includes bibliographical references

Henderson, Kathy
The market guide for young writers; where and how to sell what you write. Writer's Digest Bks. pa $16.99 **808**
1. Authorship—Handbooks, manuals, etc.

First published 1986 by Savage Pub. (5th edition 1996) Periodically revised
Provides publishing information for the young writer including tips on preparing a manuscript, profiles of published young writers, opportunities online, and market and contest listings
Includes bibliographical references

James, Elizabeth
How to write super school reports; [by] Elizabeth James and Carol Barkin. rev ed. Lothrop, Lee & Shepard Bks. 1998 90p (School survival guide) $15 **808**
1. Report writing 2. Research
ISBN 0-688-16132-4
LC 98-13767
First published 1983 with title: How to write a great school report
This guide "offers suggestions for choosing a topic, finding facts, using the library, organizing notes, and, finally, putting the report together. . . . Advice on how to conduct searches, cite sources, and validate information found on the Internet." SLJ

James, Elizabeth—*Continued*
How to write terrific book reports; [by] Elizabeth James and Carol Barkin. rev ed. Lothrop, Lee & Shepard Bks. 1998 80p (School survival guide) $15   **808**
1. Report writing 2. Books—Reviews
ISBN 0-688-16131-6   LC 98-9198
First published 1986 with title: How to write your best book report
"The authors explore what a book report is, how to choose a title, writing preliminary and final drafts, giving an oral presentation, the importance of the library in finding material, and other aspects of this common assignment." SLJ

Sincerely yours; how to write great letters; by Elizabeth James & Carol Barkin. Clarion Bks. 1993 166p $14.95   **808**
1. Letter writing
ISBN 0-395-58831-6   LC 91-42374
Discusses the general purposes of writing letters and outlines the elements of different types of personal and business letters. Includes information on state abbreviations, forms of address, and pen pals

Seuling, Barbara
To be a writer; a guide for young people who want to write and publish. 21st Cent. Bks. (NY) 1997 110p il lib bdg $16.98   **808**
1. Authorship 2. Creative writing
ISBN 0-8050-4692-5   LC 96-47653
"The main body of the book covers the how and what of writing: how writers get their ideas and what they do about them. . . . Seuling offers a list of publishers (including those that put out E-zines) that accept the work of young writers. There is also information about contests and prizes, and even writers' camps. A fine, information-packed piece." Booklist
Includes glossary and bibliographical references

Shields, Nancy E., 1928-
Where credit is due; a guide to proper citing of sources, print and nonprint; [by] Nancy E. Shields, with the assistance of Mary E. Uhle. 2nd ed. Scarecrow Press 1997 189p $32.50 (7 and up)
                                           808
1. Bibliographical citations 2. Research
ISBN 0-8108-3211-9   LC 96-6523
First published 1985
"This book is a style guide for students to properly document the vast array of sources for the research paper. It includes every possible source that could be used as a reference with examples of footnotes and bibliography entries. . . . This book is exactly what the librarian needs to provide students with up-to-date styles for documentation in their writing." Book Rep

Stevens, Carla
A book of your own; keeping a diary or journal. Clarion Bks. 1993 100p $16; pa $7.95   **808**
1. Authorship 2. Diaries
ISBN 0-89919-256-4; 0-395-67887-0 (pa)
                                          LC 92-33818

"The author offers advice on getting started, selecting tools to use, maintaining privacy, and overcoming writer's block. . . . Stevens includes excerpts from the diaries of personal friends and historical figures. Among the famous diarists quoted are Anne Frank, Anais Nin, Theodore Roosevelt, Beatrix Potter, and Louisa May Alcott." Voice Youth Advocates
"A very useful book; libraries where journal writing is in the curriculum may want more than one copy." Booklist
Includes bibliographical references

Sullivan, Helen
Research reports; a guide for middle and high school students; by Helen Sullivan and Linda Sernoff. Millbrook Press 1996 127p lib bdg $24.90 (7 and up)   **808**
1. Report writing 2. Research
ISBN 1-56294-694-3   LC 95-21489
Also available in paperback from Copper Beech Books
This guide to report writing takes "students step by step through the process, from selecting a topic to researching, note-taking, interviewing, writing and editing, using graphics, and compiling a bibliography. Chapters are clear, short, readable, and sprinkled with examples of interest to teens." SLJ
Includes glossary and bibliographical references

Young, Sue
Writing with style. Scholastic Ref. 1997 143p (Scholastic guides) $12.95; pa $8.95   **808**
1. Authorship 2. Creative writing
ISBN 0-590-50977-2; 0-590-25424-3 (pa)
                                          LC 96-8772
Presents tips for writing interesting stories, passionate essays, and exciting reports, focusing on the elements of sentence structure, paragraph organization, grammar, usage, punctuation, and footnotes
"The book is easy to comprehend, upbeat, and relevant. A must for library shelves and classrooms." SLJ
Includes bibliographical references

808.1   Rhetoric of poetry

Hulme, Joy N., 1922-
How to write, recite, and delight in all kinds of poetry; [by] Joy N. Hulme and Donna W. Guthrie. Millbrook Press 1996 96p il lib bdg $24.90
                                         808.1
1. Poetics
ISBN 1-562-94576-9   LC 95-12607
This is a "guide to the tools and techniques of writing verse—including rap poetry—featuring more than 70 original poems by children ages 10-14 and illustrated with paintings and well-known artwork." Publisher's note
Includes bibliographical references

Janeczko, Paul B., 1945-
How to write poetry. Scholastic Ref. 1999 117p il (Scholastic guides) $12.95   **808.1**
1. Poetics
ISBN 0-590-10077-7   LC 98-26866

Janeczko, Paul B., 1945-—*Continued*
Provides practical advice with checklists on the art of writing poetry
"A friendly, accessible, and highly usable primer." Horn Book Guide
Includes glossary and bibliographical references

Poetry from A to Z; a guide for young writers; compiled by Paul B. Janeczko; illustrated by Cathy Bobak. Bradbury Press 1994 131p il $15.95   **808.1**
1. Poetics 2. American poetry—Collections
ISBN 0-02-747672-3   LC 94-10528
"In his guide, Janeczko gives many examples and ideas to get young writers started writing poetry. The book is organized alphabetically with seventy-two poems on almost any topic you could imagine. In addition, fourteen exercises labeled 'Try This' explain how to write different types of poems and help a young writer get started." Voice Youth Advocates
Includes bibliographical references

808.3   Rhetoric of fiction

Bauer, Marion Dane, 1938-
Our stories; a fiction workshop for young authors; compiled and with commentary by Marion Dane Bauer. Clarion Bks. 1996 195p $13.95; pa $6.95   **808.3**
1. Authorship 2. Creative writing
ISBN 0-395-69719-0; 0-395-81599-1 (pa)
    LC 95-51091
The author presents a selection of short fiction written by students in grades four through twelve and then critiques each piece
"This book would be an excellent resource for teachers looking for a new approach to the writing process. . . . Anyone who enjoys writing cannot help but be inspired by the remarkable talent of these young authors, and by Bauer's friendly, encouraging and helpful advice." Voice Youth Advocates

What's your story? a young person's guide to writing fiction. Clarion Bks. 1992 134p $14.95; pa $6.95   **808.3**
1. Authorship 2. Creative writing
ISBN 0-395-57781-0; 0-395-57780-2 (pa)
    LC 91-3816
Discusses how to write fiction, exploring such aspects as character, plot, point of view, dialogue, endings, and revising
"Bauer reveals the somber reality that writing can be hard work, though worth the effort for those who persevere. What follows is a clear, concise elucidation on the elements of fiction. . . . Bauer has taken a thorough, clear, and functional approach to this topic." Horn Book

Kerr, M. E., 1927-
Blood on the forehead; what I know about writing. HarperCollins Pubs. 1998 262p $21.95; pa $12.95 (7 and up)   **808.3**
1. Authorship
ISBN 0-06-027996-6; 0-06-446207-2 (pa)
    LC 97-41953

Using examples from five novels and five short stories, young adult writer M. E. Kerr offers insights into ways writers can get ideas and create successful stories
"The autobiographical tidbits and writer's tips are interesting, but the book best serves as a writing sampler (and exemplar) of one of today's finest authors for young adults." Horn Book Guide

808.5   Rhetoric of speech

Detz, Joan
You mean I have to stand up and say something? illustrated by David Marshall. Atheneum Pubs. 1986 86p il $13.95   **808.5**
1. Public speaking
ISBN 0-689-31221-0   LC 86-3611
In this guide to speech making the author "shows readers how to judge an audience, figure out what to say, track down facts and information, and organize such material into a coherent whole. There are also discussions of humor . . . visual aids, and techniques for taming the jitters. The presentation is well organized and buttressed with concrete examples and lists of sources for quotes, jokes, facts and statistics, and general information." Booklist

Otfinoski, Steven, 1949-
Speaking up, speaking out; a kid's guide to making speeches, oral reports, and conversation; illustrated by Carol Nicklaus. Millbrook Press 1996 79p il lib bdg $23.90; pa $8.95   **808.5**
1. Public speaking
ISBN 1-56294-345-6; 0-7613-0138-0 (pa)
    LC 96-509
Provides strategies and encouraging tips for speaking in social situations, reading aloud, presenting oral reports, and making speeches of all kinds
"This appealing handbook provides youngsters with just about everything they need to know about oral communication. . . . Nicklaus's cartoon illustrations are appropriately lighthearted, adding touches of humor to the text." SLJ
Includes glossary and bibliographical references

808.8   Literature—Collections

Anthology for the earth; edited by Judy Allen. Candlewick Press 1998 96p il $21.99   **808.8**
1. Literature—Collections 2. Nature
ISBN 0-7636-0301-5   LC 97-674
An illustrated anthology of poetry and prose about the natural world, by such authors as Rudyard Kipling, Ovid, and Tolstoy
This "is a handsome volume, a picture book for older readers, as suitable for dipping as for reading straight through. Allen's selections range in length from a few lines to several pages. . . . The quotations are set in varying type styles mostly on two-page spreads with illustrations concretely connected to the subject." SLJ

Bearing witness; stories of the Holocaust; selected by Hazel Rochman and Darlene Z. McCampbell. Orchard Bks. 1995 135p il map $15.95; lib bdg $16.99; pa $8.95 (7 and up)   **808.8**
1. Holocaust, 1933-1945 2. Literature—Collections
ISBN 0-531-09488-X; 0-531-08788-3 (lib bdg); 0-531-07115-4 (pa)   LC 95-13352
A "selection of prose about aspects of the Holocaust by writers for adults who were themselves witnesses or brought the stories of participants to public attention, including Primo Levi, Art Spiegelman and Carl Friedman." N Y Times Book Rev
"The editors have included their personal connections to the Holocaust in their introduction. A bibliography of books at the end of the anthology is annotated and will serve as a helpful reference for young adult readers." Voice Youth Advocates

Leaving home: stories; selected by Hazel Rochman and Darlene Z. McCampbell. HarperCollins Pubs. 1997 231p $16.95; lib bdg $16.89 (7 and up)   **808.8**
1. Youth—Fiction 2. Short stories
ISBN 0-06-024873-4; 0-06-024874-2 (lib bdg)
LC 96-28979
An international anthology that reflects the thoughts and feelings of young people as they make their own ways into the world, including such authors as Amy Tan, Sandra Cisneros, Tim Wynne-Jones, and Toni Morrison
"The editors have varied the tones, the music, the voices, and the meanings of the pieces, which provide both humorous and heartbreaking stories of the meaning of adolescence." ALAN

The **Necessary** cat; a celebration of cats in picture and word; [compiled by] Nicola Bayley. Candlewick Press 1998 77p il $17.99   **808.8**
1. Literature—Collections 2. Cats
ISBN 0-7636-0571-9   LC 97-46491
A collection of poems, stories, facts, and illustrations about all kinds of cats
"What appears at first to be just a vehicle for Bayley's artwork is truly a finely crafted tribute to the cat with a strong focus on verse." SLJ

The **Oxford** book of scary tales; [edited by] Dennis Pepper. Oxford Univ. Press 1992 155p il $20   **808.8**
1. Literature—Collections 2. Supernatural—Fiction
ISBN 0-19-278131-6
"The 35 stories and poems (half of them written for this book) vary in scariness, eschew the gruesome, and some—like that of the gravedigging great-grandfather—share a laugh. Although mostly British, there are retellings from Africa, India, Japan, and the United States." SLJ
"The poems here are as good as the tales, direct in voice and domestic in detail. The whole collection is clearly meant for reading aloud and sharing." Booklist

Read all about it! great read-aloud stories, poems, and newspaper pieces for preteens and teens; edited by Jim Trelease. Penguin Bks. 1993 489p il pa $13.95   **808.8**
1. Young adult literature 2. Literature—Collections 3. Authors
ISBN 0-14-014655-5   LC 93-21781

This is a collection of 52 selections of fiction, poetry, and nonfiction from newspapers, magazines, and books by such authors as Cynthia Rylant, Jerry Spinelli, Howard Pyle, Rudyard Kipling, Robert W. Service, Maya Angelou, Moss Hart, Pete Hamill, and Leon Garfield. Includes biographical informaton about the authors

808.81   Poetry—Collections

The **Columbia** Granger's Index to poetry in anthologies; indexing anthologies published through Jan. 31, 1997; edited by Nicholas Frankovich. 11th ed completely rev. Columbia Univ. Press 1997 xxvii, 2299p $275   **808.81**
1. Poetry—Indexes
ISBN 0-231-10130-9   LC 97-18668
Also available as part of Columbia Granger's world of poetry on CD-ROM
First edition, edited by Edith Granger, published 1904 by A. C. McClurg with title: Index to poetry and recitations. Fifth through eighth editions have title: Granger's index to poetry
This work is organized into title and first line index, author index, subject index, and a list of anthologies with their symbols. Coverage includes poetry translated into English

A **Compilation** of works listed in Granger's Index to poetry, 1904-1978; prepared by the Editorial Board, Granger Book Co., Inc. Granger 1980 217p lib bdg $49.95   **808.81**
1. Poetry—Indexes
ISBN 0-89609-201-1   LC 80-65559
"A cumulative and complete listing by Granger Symbol, title, and Author of over 1500 works analyzed and indexed in 'Granger's Index to Poetry' from the First Edition of 1904 to the Edition of 1978." Title page

I feel a little jumpy around you; a book of her poems & his poems collected in pairs; [by] Naomi Shihab Nye and Paul B. Janeczko. Simon & Schuster Bks. for Young Readers 1996 256p $18 (7 and up)   **808.81**
1. Poetry—Collections
ISBN 0-689-80518-7   LC 95-44904
A collection of poems, by male and female authors, presented in pairings that offer insight into how men and women look at the world, both separately and together
"Though the gender counterpoint really plays little part in the juxtaposition, the pairings are piquant and provide a manageable way to start talking about a very large collection of poetry. . . . Highly readable notes from contributors are included, as is an index of poems and a gender-segregated index of poets." Bull Cent Child Books

I like you, if you like me: poems of friendship; selected and edited by Myra Cohn Livingston. Margaret K. McElderry Bks. 1987 144p $14.95   **808.81**
1. Friendship—Poetry 2. Poetry—Collections
ISBN 0-689-50408-X   LC 86-21108
"A collection of 90 poems and verses from as far away as China and sources as unusual as autograph col-

I like you, if you like me: poems of friendship—
Continued

lections, on the subject of friendship. The poets represented include Langston Hughes, Carl Sandburg, Randall Jarrell, Lucille Clifton and Yevgeny Yevtushenko. The selections are mostly short and good for reading aloud." N Y Times Book Rev

I wouldn't thank you for a valentine; poems for young feminists; edited by Carol Ann Duffy; illustrated by Trisha Rafferty. Holt & Co. 1993 104p il $14.95; pa $6.95 **808.81**
1. Feminism—Poetry 2. Poetry—Collections
ISBN 0-8050-2756-4; 0-8050-5545-2 (pa)
LC 93-3172

First published 1992 in the United Kingdom

A collection of poems by women from different cultures and backgrounds, portraying the varied facets of the female experience from childhood to old age

"The anthology draws on poets from many cultures and includes well-known poets, such as Nikki Giovanni, Sharon Olds, and Mary Oliver, as well as several new voices. . . . These poems open up the range of love and family." Booklist

Index to children's poetry; a title, subject, author, and first line index to poetry in collections for children and youth; compiled by John E. and Sara W. Brewton. Wilson, H.W. 1942-1965 3v **808.81**
1. Poetry—Indexes
LC 42-20148

Basic volume published 1942 $63 (ISBN 0-8242-0021-7); first supplement published 1954 $40 (ISBN 0-8242-0022-5); second supplement published 1965 $40 (ISBN 0-8242-0023-3)

The main volume indexes 15,000 poems by 2,500 authors in 130 collections. The two supplements analyze another 15,000 poems by 2700 authors in 151 collections

"This tool is an invaluable reference source." Peterson. Ref Books for Child

Continued by: Index to poetry for children and young people

Index to poetry for children and young people; a title, subject, author, and first line index to poetry in collections for children and young people. Wilson, H.W. 1972-1994 5v **808.81**
1. Poetry—Indexes

A continuation of: Index to children's poetry. The volume published 1972 covering 1964-1969 compiled by John E. and Sara W. Brewton and G. Meredith Blackburn III $65 (ISBN 0-8242-0435-2); 1970-1975 published 1978 compiled by John E. Brewton, G. Meredith Blackburn III and Lorraine A. Blackburn $65 (ISBN 0-8242-0621-5); 1976-1981 published 1984 compiled by John E. Brewton, G. Meredith Blackburn III and Lorraine A. Blackburn $65 (ISBN 0-8242-0681-9); 1982-1987 published 1989 compiled by G. Meredith Blackburn III and Lorraine A. Blackburn $70 (ISBN 0-8242-0773-4); 1988-1992 published 1994 compiled by G. Meredith Blackburn III $70 (ISBN 0-8242-0861-7); 1993-1997 published 1999 compiled by G. Meredith Blackburn III $75 (ISBN 0-8242-0939-7)

Each volume analyzes approximately 10,000 poems by some 2,000 authors in more than 110 collections. Over 2,000 subject headings are used in each volume

The Oxford book of war poetry; chosen and edited by John Stallworthy. Oxford Univ. Press 1984 xxxi, 358p $30 (7 and up) **808.81**
1. War poetry 2. Poetry—Collections
ISBN 0-19-214125-2
LC 83-19303

"This comprehensive anthology focuses on poetic treatment of warfare ranging from the battlefields of ancient history to the conflicts in Vietnam, Northern Ireland, and El Salvador." Univ Press Books for Second Sch Libr

This collection "reminds one of the large numbers and great variety of war poems from many centuries that are very good poems. Mr. Stallworthy's selections include most of the best, at least the best in English." N Y Times Book Rev

Includes bibliographical references

Peeling the onion; an anthology of poems; selected by Ruth Gordon. HarperCollins Pubs. 1993 94p lib bdg $14.89 **808.81**
1. Poetry—Collections
ISBN 0-06-021728-6
LC 92-571

"A Charlotte Zolotow book"

An international anthology of poems about animals, seasons, games, and other topics, by such authors as Octavio Paz, Boris Pasternak, and Walt Whitman

"This is a particularly useful collection for schools and libraries in which young people and their teachers are taking time to look at poetry that is more challenging than popular, humorous verse." SLJ

Pierced by a ray of sun; poems about the times we feel alone; selected by Ruth Gordon. HarperCollins Pubs. 1995 105p $16; lib bdg $15.89 (7 and up) **808.81**
1. Poetry—Collections
ISBN 0-06-023613-2; 0-06-023614-0 (lib bdg)
LC 94-3757

"Gordon has gathered poems reflecting that feeling of alienation that crosses all cultures and time periods. The collection includes a wide array of poetry from anonymous poets and from renowned Western poets such as Keats and Yeats, as well as translations of poems from poets around the globe." Book Rep

"Poetry, with its tendency towards private observation, is peculiarly suited to this theme, and young adults, who are struggling to find their place in the world, will find it particularly relevant, especially when they encounter it in such a fine poetic assortment." Bull Cent Child Books

The Space between our footsteps; poems and paintings from the Middle East; selected by Naomi Shihab Nye. Simon & Schuster Bks. for Young Readers 1998 144p il maps $19.95 (7 and up) **808.81**
1. Poetry—Collections 2. Middle East—Poetry
ISBN 0-689-81233-7
LC 97-18622

"Lyrical verse about family, friendship, nature, and daily life makes up this collection of poems from 19 countries in the Middle East, with gloriously colored paintings in a wide range of styles." Booklist

Step lightly; poems for the journey; collected by Nancy Willard. Harcourt Brace & Co. 1998 99p $18; pa $12 (7 and up)   **808.81**
1. Poetry—Collections
ISBN 0-15-201849-2; 0-15-202052-7 (pa)
LC 98-5228
A collection of poems celebrating the ordinary in an unordinary way, by such authors as Emily Dickinson, Theodore Roethke, and D. H. Lawrence
"Willard weaves an anthology in which readers can find happiness, insight, inspiration, and wisdom." SLJ

Stopping for death; poems of death and loss; edited by Carol Ann Duffy; illustrated by Trisha Rafferty. Holt & Co. 1996 134p il $14.95 (7 and up)   **808.81**
1. Death—Poetry 2. Poetry—Collections
ISBN 0-8050-4717-4   LC 95-52423
A collection of poems about death, loss, and mourning written by poets from all over the world including Janet Frame, Alice Walker, and Seamus Heaney
"The collection is not all grim; there are evocations of paradise, hope, and memory here. Duffy's anthology addresses an often-avoided subject in a conscientious way, and readers will gain from it a healthy understanding of the ways to deal with and move on from loss." SLJ

Time is the longest distance; an anthology of poems; selected by Ruth Gordon. HarperCollins Pubs. 1991 74p $13.95 (7 and up)   **808.81**
1. Time—Poetry 2. Poetry—Collections
ISBN 0-06-022297-2   LC 90-4947
"A Charlotte Zolotow book"
An international anthology of poetry about the timelessness of time. Includes works by such poets as Emily Dickinson, Rumi, Salvatore Quasimodo and Ono no Komachi
"A quality collection, selected with integrity and arranged with intelligence." Horn Book

A **Time** to talk; poems of friendship; selected by Myra Cohn Livingston. Margaret K. McElderry Bks. 1992 115p $13.95 (7 and up)   **808.81**
1. Friendship—Poetry 2. Poetry—Collections
ISBN 0-689-50558-2   LC 91-42234
A collection of poems about friendship, by poets ranging from ancient China to the present
"A variety of poetic forms are represented including a concrete poem by Lillian Morrison. The breadth of the collection is excellent. Since the popularity of the theme will assure continual use, readers will be exposed to a richly diverse assortment of poets and their works." Voice Youth Advocates

War and the pity of war; edited by Neil Philip; illustrated by Michael McCurdy. Clarion Bks. 1998 96p il $20   **808.81**
1. War poetry 2. Poetry—Collections
ISBN 0-395-84982-9   LC 97-32897
Presents an illustrated collection of poems about the waste, horror, and futility of war as well as the nobility, courage, and sacrifice of individuals in wartime
"The selections, covering conflicts from ancient Persia to modern-day Bosnia, are by a wide variety of poets, from the well known (Tennyson, Whitman, Sandburg,

Auden), to the obscure (Anakreon from ancient Greece and 11th-century Chinese poet Bunno). . . . The stark and simple scratchboard drawings are reminiscent of the Ernie Pyle illustrations from World War II and are as memorable as the best propaganda." SLJ

What have you lost? poems; selected by Naomi Shihab Nye; photographs by Michael Nye. Greenwillow Bks. 1999 $19 (7 and up) **808.81**
1. Loss (Psychology) 2. Poetry—Collections
ISBN 0-688-16184-7   LC 98-26674
In her "introduction, the anthologist-poet considers loss—its certainty, scope, and effect, and its ability to give rise to art. The topic is thoroughly explored by the one hundred and forty poets whose work is collected here in twenty-two unlabeled, thematically arranged sections. . . . The poets are all contemporary, with a dozen or so hailing from outside the United States." Horn Book

808.82   Drama—Collections

The **Book** of monologues for aspiring actors; [edited by] Marsh Cassady. NTC Pub. Group 1995 212p il pa $18 (7 and up)   **808.82**
1. Monologues 2. Acting
ISBN 0-8442-5771-0   LC 94-66239
"The selections range from the classical Greeks to Sam Shepard and Oscar Wilde; they give YA's the opportunity to develop characters of like ages in many different settings. Several questions to probe the actors' imaginations appear at the end of each monologue." SLJ

Great monologues for young actors; Craig Slaight, Jack Sharrar, editors. Smith & Kraus 1992-1999 2v v1 pa $11.95; v2 pa $14.95   **808.82**
1. Monologues 2. Acting
ISBN 1-880399-03-2 (v1); 1-57525-106-X (v2)
These volumes provide an introduction and acting notes for monologues for men and women drawn from contemporary and classic works

Great scenes and monologues for children; Craig Slaight and Jack Sharrar, editors. Smith & Kraus 1993 175p (Young actor series) pa $11.95
808.82
1. Monologues 2. Acting
ISBN 1-880399-15-6   LC 93-15723
"Offering scenes and monologues from children's novels and fairy tales, the editors also provide an eclectic mix of 'adult' drama and short story. The inclusion of mature selections, such as Lillian Hellman's *The Children's Hour* and Thornton Wilder's *The Skin of Our Teeth*, makes the collection appealing to young adults for speech and drama study. . . . Teachers seeking resources and activities to extend or enrich classroom literature units will find this a handy tool for readers' theater or booktalks. Providing a broad range of material with a wide spectrum of uses, this practical compilation is a must buy." Booklist

Great scenes for young actors; Craig Slaight and Jack Sharrar, editors. Smith & Kraus 1991-1998 2v v1 pa $11.95; v2 pa $14.95   **808.82**
1. Drama—Collections 2. Acting
ISBN 0-9622722-6-4 (v1); 1-57525-107-8 (v2)
LC 91-60869

Great scenes for young actors—*Continued*
v2 has title: Great scenes for young actors from the stage

Contains scenes from classic and contemporary plays. The selections, graded according to ability level, include a range of roles for men, women, and groups. Includes a brief synopsis of each play along with special notes

Karp, Rashelle Schlessinger
Plays for children and young adults; an evaluative index and guide; [by] Rashelle S. Karp, June H. Schlessinger; editorial staff, Bernard S. Schlessinger [et al.] Garland 1991 580p (Garland reference library of social science) o.p.   **808.82**
1. Drama—Indexes
LC 90-44195
Available: Plays for children and young adults, Supplement 1, 1989-1994 $83 (ISBN 0-8153-1493-0)

Provides evaluative information about plays that may be produced by or for young people, ages 5 to 18. Coverage includes plays, choral readings, scenes, musical reviews, readers' theater, and skits published either separately or in collections

808.83   Fiction—Collections

Short story index. Wilson, H.W. $165   **808.83**
1. Short stories—Indexes
ISSN 0360-9774
LC 75-649762
Also available CD-Rom version
Also available: Short story index: collections indexed 1900-1978 $90 (ISBN 0-8242-0643-6)

Basic volume edited by Dorothy E. Cook and Isabel S. Monro published 1953 $70 (ISBN 0-8242-0384-4); Supplementary volumes: 1950-1954 edited by Dorothy E. Cook and Estelle A. Fidell $80 (ISBN 0-8242-0385-2); 1955-1958 edited by Estelle A. Fidell and Esther V. Flory $80 (ISBN 0-8242-0386-0); 1959-1963 edited by Estelle A. Fidell $80 (ISBN 0-8242-0387-9); 1964-1968 edited by Estelle A. Fidell $80 (ISBN 0-8242-0399-2); 1969-1973 edited by Estelle A. Fidell $80 (ISBN 0-8242-0497-2); 1974-1978 edited by Gary L. Bogart $115; 1979-1983 edited by Juliette Yaakov $120; 1984-1988 edited by Juliette Yaakov $155; 1989-1993 edited by John Greenfieldt and Juliette Yaakov $155; 1994-1998 edited by John Greenfieldt and Juliette Yaakov $165. Beginning 1974 issued annually with five-year cumulations

"These indexes provide valuable access to short stories in collections published since 1900. The original volume indexes more than 60,000 stories published in 4,320 collections between 1900 and 1949. Indexing is by author, title, and subject of the short story. A list of collections indexed provides a useful buying guide for the library." Ref Sources for Small & Medium-sized Libr. 6th edition

808.85   Speeches—Collections

Lend me your ears; great speeches in history; selected and introduced by William Safire. rev and expanded ed. Norton 1997 1,055p $39.95
808.85
1. Speeches
ISBN 0-393-04005-4   LC 96-43423

First published 1992
Pope Urban II, Bob Dole, Cicero, Jesus, Boris Yeltsin, Richard Nixon and Colin Powell are among the orators represented in this anthology of over 200 speeches grouped chronologically into thematic categories

808.88   Collections of miscellaneous writings

Bartlett, John, 1820-1905
Familiar quotations. Little, Brown $40   **808.88**
1. Quotations

Also available CD-ROM version
First published 1855. (16th edition 1992) Periodically revised. Editors vary

"Arranged chronologically by author, with exact references. Includes many interesting footnotes, tracing history or usage of analogous thoughts, the circumstances under which a particular remark was made, etc. Author and keyword indexes. One of the best books of quotations with a long history." Guide to Ref Books. 11th edition

Burleigh, Robert, 1936-
Who said that? famous Americans speak; illustrated by David Catrow. Holt & Co. 1997 45p il $15.95   **808.88**
1. Quotations
ISBN 0-8050-4394-2   LC 96-19985
"Brief quotations from famous Americans are accompanied by satirical pen-and-ink caricatures and a short explanation of the subject's place in history. . . . Burleigh has assembled a multicultural group of men and women from the 18th through the 20th centuries, such as Benjamin Franklin, Daniel Boone, Abigail Adams, Mother Jones, Groucho Marx, Louis Armstrong, Marilyn Monroe, and Babe Ruth. . . . The humor is akin to the style of *Mad* magazine and appealing to middle-grade sensibilities." SLJ

My soul looks back, 'less I forget; a collection of quotations by people of color; Dorothy Winbush Riley, editor. HarperCollins Pubs. 1993 498p hardcover o.p. paperback available $20   **808.88**
1. Quotations 2. Blacks—Quotations
ISBN 0-06-272057-0 (pa)   LC 92-25754
First published privately in 1991 by Winbush Pub. Co.

"Included are over 7000 quotes from 700 speakers that range from such early historical figures as Aesop and Amenemope to familiar contemporaries like Colin Powell and Clarence Thomas. Quotes are chronological within 450 alphabetically arranged topics. An index by speaker, contents by topics, and comprehensive bibliography of 400 sources used for this solidly researched work add to its usefulness." Libr J

Quotations for kids; compiled and edited by J.A. Senn; illustrations by Steve Pica. Millbrook Press 1999 256p il lib bdg $37.90   **808.88**
1. Quotations
ISBN 0-7613-0267-0   LC 98-40310
Includes bibliographical references

Quotations for kids—*Continued*

An illustrated reference work offering more than 2000 quotations ranging from the Bible to folklore to children's literature

"Lively cartoonlike illustrations by Steve Pica and excellent cross-references enhance the volume. . . . The compendium will have enormous appeal to all ages: it will be useful for reports, creative writing, and discussion, as well as being a delightfully entertaining book to browse." Booklist

Scholastic treasury of quotations for children; [compiled by] Adrienne Betz. Scholastic Ref. 1998 254p $16.95   **808.88**
1. Quotations
ISBN 0-590-27146-6   LC 97-34153
Presents 1,200 quotations from ancient to modern times on topics such as cooperation, growing up, nature, success, and faith

"A comprehensive and accessible compendium. . . . An excellent introduction explains how to use the book, guides readers on including quotations in their own speaking and writing, and discusses sources consulted." SLJ

809 Literary history and criticism

Masterpieces of world literature; edited by Frank N. Magill. Harper & Row 1989 957p $50 **809**
1. Literature—Stories, plots, etc. 2. Literature—History and criticism
ISBN 0-06-016144-2   LC 89-45052
"While this volume gives plot information, character descriptions, and critical evaluation of 204 works (novels, plays, stories, and poems), plus analysis of 66 others (mostly essays), the information is straight from the *Critical Surveys* series, the *Masterplots* series, and the *Cyclopedia of Literary Characters*. . . . The unsigned articles are clearly written, objective, accurate, and informative. Arrangement is alphabetical by the best-known English title. . . . Two indexes provide access to authors and original titles." Booklist

809.3 Fiction—History and criticism

The **Encyclopedia** of fantasy; edited by John Clute and John Grant; contributing editors: Mike Ashley et al.; consultant editors: David G. Hartwell, Gary Westfahl. St. Martin's Press 1997 1049p $75   **809.3**
1. Fantasy fiction—Encyclopedias
ISBN 0-312-14594-2   LC 96-37472
With more than 4,000 signed entries, this volume "documents and surveys the writers, artists, literatures, and media that have used fantasy themes or have fantasy content, from the form's earliest days until the present. Numerous terms and concepts relevant to fantasy are also defined. Entries are clear and well-written and contain bibliographies when appropriate." Am Libr

Short stories for students. Gale Res. il   **809.3**
1. Short stories—History and criticism
LC 98-153009

Irregular. Started publication 1997
Volumes 1 to 9 available at $60 each
"Presenting analysis, context, and criticism on commonly studied short stories." Title page
"Each volume contains entries for 20 stories arranged alphabetically by title. . . . Each entry includes a brief biographical sketch of the writer; a plot summary; descriptions of characters; a discussion of the major themes and style (use of irony, symbolism, points of view, etc.); an introduction to the historical and cultural period during which the story was written; a critical overview; and an essay written for this resource along with excerpts from the work of other critics." SLJ

The **Ultimate** encyclopedia of fantasy; the definitive illustrated guide; general editor, David Pringle. Overlook Press 1999 256p il $35
809.3
1. Fantasy fiction—Encyclopedias 2. Fantasy films—Encyclopedias
ISBN 0-87951-937-1   LC 99-10503
This reference presents an overview of the genre, identifies major sub-genres, and reviews literary works, films, and television shows. Coverage also includes a listing of famous fantasy characters, descriptions of fantasy worlds, and information on games

810.3 American literature— Encyclopedias and dictionaries

Lives and works: young adult authors. Grolier Educ. 1999 8v il   **810.3**
1. Young adult literature—Bio-bibliography 2. Authors—Dictionaries
ISBN 0-7172-9227-4 (set $255)   LC 98-4339
"From Douglas Adams to Paul Zindel, this set provides information designed to meet the needs of middle-school students. . . . More than 250 writers are covered, the classic (Louisa May Alcott, Edgar Allan Poe, William Shakespeare), as well as the modern. Arranged alphabetically by writer, each entry averages three pages and describes the writer's life and works. A quotation from one of the works and a black-and-white photograph accompany the text. At the end of each entry, one finds a selected list of the writer's works and, in some cases, a few titles about the writer and a Web site address for further information." Booklist

McElmeel, Sharron L.
100 most popular children's authors; biographical sketches and bibliographies. Libraries Unlimited 1999 xxxi, 493p il (Popular authors series) $48   **810.3**
1. Children's literature—Bio-bibliography
ISBN 1-56308-646-8   LC 98-41942
"Based on a 1997 survey of both teachers and students, this volume includes such well-known authors as Beverly Cleary (most recognized by the survey respondents) and classic writers like Lewis Carroll and C. S. Lewis. Each entry provides several pages about the author and his or her writings followed by a section called 'Books and Notes,' which has details about specific books and their themes, including bibliographic information. A list of additional material about or by the author completes each entry." Booklist

810.8 American literature—Collections

33 things every girl should know; stories, songs, poems, and smart talk by 33 extraordinary women; edited by Tonya Bolden. Crown 1998 159p il lib bdg $17.99; pa $13 (7 and up) **810.8**

1. Girls 2. American literature—Collections
ISBN 0-517-70999-6 (lib bdg); 0-517-70936-8 (pa)
LC 97-29431

A mix of short stories, essays, a comic strip, a speech, an interview, poems, and more which offer insights and advice for girls

"Astute, compassionate, sometimes witty, sometimes painfully honest, the pieces are highly readable, entertaining, and educational." Booklist

American dragons; twenty-five Asian American voices; edited by Laurence Yep. HarperCollins Pubs. 1993 237p hardcover o.p. paperback available $4.95 (7 and up) **810.8**
1. American literature—Asian American authors—Collections
ISBN 0-06-440603-2 (pa)
LC 92-28489

These "short stories, poems, and other selections are written by a cross section of Asian Americans, with roots in China, Vietnam, Japan, Korea, Tibet, and Thailand. The book is organized by theme, covering such issues of interest to adolescents as identity, family relationships, generational and cultural conflicts, and love." Horn Book
"A kaleidoscopic, occasionally brilliant, illumination of the Asian-American experience." SLJ
Includes bibliographical references

Christmas gif', an anthology of Christmas poems, songs, and stories, written by and about African-Americans; compiled by Charlemae Rollins; illustrated by Ashley Bryan; with a new introduction by Augusta Baker. Morrow Junior Bks. 1993 xxii, 106p il $14 **810.8**
1. Christmas—Collections 2. American literature—African American authors—Collections
ISBN 0-688-11667-1
LC 92-18976
First published 1963 by Follett

A collection of Christmas poems, songs, and stories relating to African Americans by such authors as Langston Hughes, Frederick Douglass, Countee Cullen, and Zora Neale Hurston. Includes holiday recipes
This edition "has been newly illustrated by Bryan with linocuts that express the joy and reverence, the mystery and dailiness, of the collection." Booklist

From sea to shining sea; a treasury of American folklore and folk songs; illustrated by eleven Caldecott Medal and four Caldecott honor book artists: Molly Bang [et al.]; compiled by Amy L. Cohn. Scholastic 1993 399p il music $29.95 **810.8**
1. American literature—Collections 2. Folklore—United States 3. Folk songs—United States
ISBN 0-590-42868-3
LC 92-30598

A compilation of more than 140 folk songs, tales, poems, non-fiction, and stories telling the history of America and reflecting its multicultural society
This is "a treasure chest that will be dipped into year after year and generation after generation. The attention to detail and love that each illustrator brought to their section is evident as is the research Ms. Cohn did before making her choices. A masterpiece that is also a gorgeous piece of book making." Child Book Rev Serv
Includes glossary and bibliographical references

Grand fathers; reminiscences, poems, recipes and photos of the keepers of our traditions; edited by Nikki Giovanni. Holt & Co. 1999 242p il music $18.95 **810.8**
1. Grandfathers 2. American literature—Collections
ISBN 0-8050-5484-7
LC 98-38463

This "is primarily a collection of reminiscences and poems about grandfathers and great-grandfathers. Some well-known authors have contributed, including Pearl Cleage and Rita Dove, and there are lesser-known writers, from teenagers to grandparents themselves." Voice Youth Advocates
"With assistance, this anthology of individual voices . . . may provide a useful variety of models for young readers and writers." Bull Cent Child Books

Grand mothers; poems, reminiscences, and short stories about the keepers of our traditions; edited by Nikki Giovanni. Holt & Co. 1994 xxi, 168p $15.95; pa $7.95 **810.8**
1. Grandmothers 2. American literature—Women authors—Collections
ISBN 0-8050-2766-1; 0-8050-4903-7 (pa)
LC 94-6144

"This anthology brings together writings about grandmothers. . . . Though the topic of grandmothers might be expected to bring out a certain sentimentality, the writers cut through the clichés to the basic human needs that grandmothers fill and the fundamental questions their lives and their memories raise in those who know them, remember them, or pass down their stories. Varied in quality, but still a unique collection of writings." Booklist

Growing up Latino; memoirs and stories; edited with an introduction by Harold Augenbraum and Ilan Stavans; foreword by Ilan Stavans. Houghton Mifflin 1993 xxix, 344p hardcover o.p. paperback available $13.95 **810.8**
1. American literature—Hispanic American authors—Collections 2. Hispanic American authors
ISBN 0-395-66124-2 (pa)
LC 92-32624
"A Marc Jaffe book"

A collection of short stories and excerpts from novels and memoirs written by twenty-five Latino authors. Among the contributors are Julia Alvarez, Oscar Hijuelos, Denise Chávez, Rolando Hinojosa, and Sandra Cisneros
Includes bibliographical references

Here is my kingdom; Hispanic-American literature and art for young people; edited by Charles Sullivan; foreword by Luis R. Cancel. Abrams 1994 119p il $24.95   **810.8**
1. American literature—Hispanic American authors—Collections 2. Hispanic American art
ISBN 0-8109-3422-1   LC 93-37412
The editor "combines poetry and short prose works with art to introduce young people to selected aspects of various Hispanic cultures. More than 118 writers and artists from countries such as Mexico, Puerto Rico, Cuba, Peru and Chile are represented. A wide spectrum of history is covered, from early explorers to contemporary issues such as the Vietnam War. The works of art, reproduced in color and b&w, are skillfully combined with thematically related text." Book Rep

A Way out of no way; writing about growing up Black in America; edited by Jacqueline Woodson. Holt & Co. 1996 172p (Edge books) $15.95 (7 and up)   **810.8**
1. American literature—African American authors—Collections
ISBN 0-8050-4570-8   LC 96-7891
Also available in paperback from Fawcett Bks.
A collection of stories and poems about coming of age written by African American authors such as James Baldwin, Langston Hughes, Jamaica Kincaid, Toni Morrison, and Rosa Guy
"A distinguished anthology of excerpts from some fine modern writing." N Y Times Book Rev

Yolen, Jane
Here there be ghosts; illustrated by David Wilgus. Harcourt Brace & Co. 1998 121p il $19   **810.8**
1. Ghost stories 2. Ghosts—Poetry 3. American literature—Collections
ISBN 0-15-201566-3   LC 98-13732
An illustrated collection of short stories and poems about ghosts
"Readers will do some serious thinking about topics such as God, souls, and the supernatural while devouring these creepy tales." SLJ

810.9   American literature—History and criticism

Drew, Bernard A. (Bernard Alger), 1950-
The 100 most popular young adult authors; biographical sketches and bibliographies. rev 1st ed. Libraries Unlimited 1997 xxviii, 531p $55   **810.9**
1. Young adult literature—Bio-bibliography
ISBN 1-56308-615-8   LC 97-25882
First published 1996
A "tool for brief biographical information about authors writing books from upper elementary to adult levels which are of interest to young adults. Coverage is of mostly contemporary American authors, but other nationalities and classic writers are included as well. Arranged

alphabetically, each entry gives biographical data, the types of books written and some critical analysis. Lists for further reading are appended." Safford. Guide to Ref Materials for Sch Libr Media Cent. 5th edition
Includes bibliographical references

Susag, Dorothea M.
Roots and branches; a resource of Native American literature: themes, lessons, and bibliographies. National Council of Teachers of English 1998 310p il maps pa $25.95   **810.9**
1. American literature—American Indian authors—Bibliography
ISBN 0-8141-4195-1   LC 98-45105
This resource situates the study of Native American literature in its historical context and provides annotated bibliographies of primary and secondary source materials. Includes lessons, units, and activities keyed to grade levels

811   American poetry

Asch, Frank
Sawgrass poems; a view of the Everglades : poems; photographs by Ted Levin. Harcourt Brace & Co. 1996 unp il $18   **811**
1. Everglades (Fla.)—Poetry
ISBN 0-15-200180-8   LC 95-22762
"A Gulliver green book"
"Beginning with an . . . introduction to the Everglades, this collection of 20 illustrated poems transports readers to that unique place and challenges them to look at it intently, often through the eyes of those who live there. The many striking, full-color photographs provide glimpses of a wide variety of animals, plants, and landscapes." Booklist

Begay, Shonto
Navajo; visions and voices across the Mesa. Scholastic 1995 48p il $15.95   **811**
1. Navajo Indians—Poetry
ISBN 0-590-46153-2   LC 93-31610
The author "presents a very personal view of contemporary Navajo life in this picture-book collection for older readers. Pairing 20 of his paintings with original poetry, Begay moves from the spiritual aspects of Navajo life through personal childhood memories into striking present-day images, concluding with an affirmation of continuing life and rebirth." Booklist

Benét, Rosemary
A book of Americans; by Rosemary and Stephen Vincent Benét; illustrated by Charles Child. Holt & Co. 1986 c1933 114p il hardcover o.p. paperback available $5.95   **811**
1. United States—Biography—Poetry 2. United States—History—Poetry
ISBN 0-8050-0284-7 (pa)
A reissue of the title first published 1933 by Farrar and Rinehart
A collection of poems portraying 56 famous historical figures from Columbus to Woodrow Wilson

Burleigh, Robert, 1936-

Hoops; illustrated by Stephen T. Johnson. Harcourt Brace & Co. 1997 unp il $16   **811**

1. Basketball—Poetry

ISBN 0-15-201450-0   LC 96-18440

"Silver Whistle"

Illustrations and poetic text describe the movement and feel of the game of basketball

"Burleigh's staccato text is well matched by Johnson's dynamic pastels. Muted colors and a strong sense of motion as bodies leap and lift, pounce and poke, aptly complement the words." SLJ

Dunbar, Paul Laurence, 1872-1906

The collected poetry of Paul Laurence Dunbar; edited and with an introduction by Joanne M. Braxton. University Press of Va. 1993 xxxvi, 396p $40; pa $14.95   **811**

ISBN 0-8139-1454-X; 0-8139-1438-8 (pa)

LC 92-37190

This volume contains the entire text of The complete poems of Paul Laurence Dunbar published 1913 by Dodd, Mead, and an additional sixty poems, sixteen of which were found in manuscript form

"The poet's predecessors in the use of African-American dialect were white writers, such as Irwin Russell, Stephen Collins Foster, Joel Chandler Harris, and Thomas Nelson Page, but they were unable to portray African American life with Dunbar's personal insights." Benet's Reader's Ency of Am Lit

Fleischman, Paul

I am phoenix: poems for two voices; illustrated by Ken Nutt. Harper & Row 1985 51p il hardcover o.p. paperback available $4.95   **811**

1. Birds—Poetry

ISBN 0-06-446092-4 (pa)   LC 85-42615

"A Charlotte Zolotow book"

A collection of poems about birds to be read aloud by two voices

"Devotés of the almost lost art of choral reading should be among the first to appreciate this collection. . . . Printed in script form, the selections . . . have a cadenced pace and dignified flow." Bull Cent Child Books

Joyful noise: poems for two voices; illustrated by Eric Beddows. Harper & Row 1988 44p il $14.95; lib bdg $14.89; pa $4.95   **811**

1. Insects—Poetry

ISBN 0-06-021852-5; 0-06-021853-3 (lib bdg); 0-06-446093-2 (pa)   LC 87-45280

Awarded the Newbery Medal, 1989

"A Charlotte Zolotow book"

"This collection of poems for two voices explores the lives of insects. Designed to be read aloud, the phrases of the poems are spaced vertically on the page in two columns, one for each reader. The voices sometimes alternate, sometimes speak in chorus, and sometimes echo each other." Booklist

"The imagery throughout the volume is as remarkable as the technique. . . . Each selection is a gem, polished perfection." Horn Book

Fletcher, Ralph J.

Buried alive; the elements of love; poems by Ralph Fletcher; photographs by Andrew Moore. Atheneum Bks. for Young Readers 1996 46p il $14   **811**

1. Love poetry

ISBN 0-689-80593-4   LC 95-30856

A collection of poems exploring the mysteries and wonders of love, arranged in the categories "Earth," "Water," "Air," and "Fire."

"This volume should intrigue YA readers. They will enjoy discovering stories of requited and unrequited love, puzzling over the gender of certain narrators, and pondering the added dimension each element gives to the poetry." SLJ

I am wings; poems about love; photographs by Joe Baker. Bradbury Press 1994 48p il $14   **811**

1. Love poetry

ISBN 0-02-735395-8   LC 93-40259

"These thirty-one poems about love are arranged into two sections, 'Falling In' and 'Falling Out'; the volume is as brief as the typical crush of a young adolescent, the intended audience for this book. Length of time should not be equated with depth of feeling, however. These short, unrhymed verses speak with the touching intensity of untutored, hard-felt emotions." Horn Book

Ordinary things; poems from a walk in early spring; by Ralph Fletcher; drawings by Walter Lyon Krudop. Atheneum Bks. for Young Readers 1997 48p il $15   **811**

1. Nature—Poetry 2. Spring—Poetry

ISBN 0-689-81035-0   LC 96-3393

A collection of poems recall the sights and feelings experienced on a springtime walk—from home, through the woods, and back again

"Simple, well-chosen language and careful observations make his early spring walk fresh and vivid." Horn Book Guide

Relatively speaking; poems about family; by Ralph Fletcher; drawings by Walter Lyon Krudop. Orchard Bks. 1999 42p il $14.95; lib bdg $15.99   **811**

1. Family life—Poetry

ISBN 0-531-30141-9; 0-531-33141-5 (lib bdg)

LC 98-30238

"These poems come together to form a picture of one family. Narrated by the youngest member, each poem highlights a different person or event. . . . The selections are striking in their simplicity, universal themes, and realistic voice. Pen-and-ink line drawings detail items ranging from a favorite quilt to a water bucket and sponge used to wash the car." SLJ

Frost, Robert, 1874-1963

The road not taken; illustrated by John O'Hara Cosgrave II. Holt & Co. 1951 xxxvii, 282p il $25; pa $13.95   **811**

ISBN 0-8050-0529-3; 0-8050-0528-5 (pa)

"An introduction to Robert Frost; a selection of Robert Frost's poems; with a biographical preface and running commentary by Louis Untermeyer." Title page

Frost, Robert, 1874-1963—*Continued*
You come too: favorite poems for young readers; with wood engravings by Thomas W. Nason. Holt & Co. 1959 94p il $14.95; pa $6.95
811

ISBN 0-8050-0299-5; 0-8050-0316-9 (pa)
LC 59-12940
Frost's "simplicity, wisdom, and humanity, as well as his craftsmanship, come clear in some half-hundred poems, among them 'Mending Wall,' 'The Death of the Hired Man,' and 'Tree at My Window.'" Libr J

Giovanni, Nikki
Ego-tripping and other poems for young people; illustrations by George Ford; foreword by Virginia Hamilton. 2nd ed. Hill Bks. 1993 52p il $14.95; pa $9.95
811
ISBN 1-55652-188-X; 1-55652-189-8 (pa)
LC 93-29578
First published 1974
Giovanni has added 10 new poems to her earlier "collection of 23 poems for young people. Ford's illustrations in sepia shades are bold and full of character and dreaming. As Virginia Hamilton says in her foreword, Giovanni's voice is personal and warm, she 'celebrates ordinary folks' and writes of struggle and liberation. She's upbeat and celebratory without minimizing hard times." Booklist

Glenn, Mel, 1943-
Foreign exchange; a mystery in poems. Morrow Junior Bks. 1999 159p $15 (7 and up)
811
ISBN 0-688-16472-2
LC 98-40551
A series of poems reflect the thoughts of various people—town residents young and old, teachers, and some students visiting from the city—caught up in the events surrounding the murder of a beautiful high school student who had recently moved to the small lake-side community of Hudson Landing
"The characters are solidly evoked and their voices are distinct." Bull Cent Child Books

The taking of Room 114; a hostage drama in poems. Lodestar Bks. 1997 182p $16.99 (7 and up)
811
ISBN 0-525-67548-5
LC 96-45545
A series of poems reflect the thoughts of school officials, parents, police, and especially a class of seniors who have been taken hostage by their high school history teacher
"The selections lack the conceits that heighten the enjoyment of traditional poetry—metaphor, simile, alliteration, onomatopoeia. But they're never boring and often very clever. YAs will find their interest piqued and reluctant readers particularly will be drawn to the excitement of design and content." SLJ

Granfield, Linda
In Flanders fields; the story of the poem by John McCrae; illustrated by Janet Wilson. Doubleday Bks. for Young Readers 1996 il $15.95
811
1. McCrae, John, 1872-1918. In Flanders fields
2. World War, 1914-1918—Poetry 3. War poetry
ISBN 0-385-32228-3
LC 95-52386

"Within a framework of the basic historical facts of World War I, John McCrae's famous poem is juxtaposed with paintings and a biography of the poet. Vivid descriptions of the life of a soldier and an explanation of the powerful influence the poem had on society at the time are also included. Black-and-white sketches, photographs of the subject, and memorabilia (e.g., war posters and medals) add to the visual appeal created by Wilson's artwork." SLJ

Grimes, Nikki
A dime a dozen; pictures by Angelo. Dial Bks. for Young Readers 1998 54p $15.99
811
1. African Americans—Poetry
ISBN 0-8037-2227-3
LC 97-5798
A collection of poems about an African-American girl growing up in New York
"Free-flowing and very accessible, the poetry may inspire readers to distill their own life experiences into precise, imaginative words and phrases." Booklist

Hopscotch love; a family treasury of love poems; illustrated by Melodye Benson Rosales. Lothrop, Lee & Shepard Bks. 1999 39p il $14.95
811
1. Love poetry
ISBN 0-688-15667-3
LC 98-21310
A collection of more than twenty poems speaking of different kinds of love
"All of the poetry is simple, written with everyday language in a straightforward style that needs no analysis or search for symbolism. . . . This small treasury will lift readers' spirits and touch their hearts." SLJ

Hearne, Betsy Gould
Polaroid and other poems of view; [by] Betsy Hearne; illustrated with photographs by Peter Kiar. Margaret K. McElderry Bks. 1991 68p il $13.95
811
ISBN 0-689-50530-2
LC 90-45577
A collection of forty-six of the author's poems about people, places, and rites of passage
"While an occasional line is lifeless and prose-like, overall Hearne crafts often-magical portraits of the commonplace through her artful use of imagery, sound devices, and arresting metaphors." Voice Youth Advocates

Herrera, Juan Felipe, 1948-
Laughing out loud, I fly; poems in English and Spanish; drawings by Karen Barbour. HarperCollins Pubs. 1998 unp il $14.95
811
1. Bilingual books—English-Spanish
ISBN 0-06-027604-5
LC 96-45476
"Joanna Cotler books"
A collection of poems in Spanish and English about childhood, place, and identity
"Barbour's black-and-white drawings accompany each poem, delicately underlining its images but allowing the strong sensuality of the words to seep into readers' minds." SLJ

Hopkins, Lee Bennett, 1938-
Been to yesterdays: poems of a life; illustrations
by Charlene Rendeiro. Wordsong 1995 64p il
$14.95   **811**
ISBN 1-56397-467-3   LC 94-73320
Autobiographical poems capture a thirteen-year old
boy's feelings, experiences, and aspirations in one tumultuous year of his life

Hughes, Langston, 1902-1967
The block; collage by Romare Bearden; poems
by Langston Hughes; selected by Lowery S. Sims
and Daisy Murray Voigt; introduction by Bill
Cosby. Metropolitan Mus. of Art; Viking 1995
32p il $15.99   **811**
ISBN 0-670-86501-X (Viking)   LC 95-12336
"Romare Bearden's six-panel collage *The Block*
(1971), serves, in small selections, big chunks, and the
whole scene, as illustrations for thirteen Langston
Hughes poems. The poems are lesser-known verses, pos-
sessing Hughes' unstudied deftness with language and
aptness of phrase, plus a certain freshness that overexpo-
sure has unfortunately dimmed in his more famous poetry. Bearden's collage offers a rainbow palette of geometric buildings standing vigil over a gray street." Bull Cent
Child Books

The collected poems of Langston Hughes;
Arnold Rampersad, editor; David Roessel,
associate editor. Knopf 1994 708p $35   **811**
ISBN 0-679-42631-0   LC 94-14509
"The editors have attempted to collect every poem
(860 in all) published by the writer in his lifetime, and
have also provided a brief but informative introduction,
a detailed chronology and extensive textual notes that include the original date and place of publication for each
poem. . . . Although Hughes is best known for his poems celebrating African American life, he was also a
passionately political poet." Publ Wkly

The dream keeper and other poems; including
seven additional poems; illustrated by Brian
Pinkney. Knopf 1994 83p il $14.99; lib bdg
$12.99; pa $7.99   **811**
ISBN 0-679-84421-X; 0-679-94421-4 (lib bdg);
0-679-88347-9 (pa)   LC 92-10240
First published 1932
"Langston Hughes's poems range from the romantic to
the poignant, from the spiritual to the challenging. His
lyrical voice asks for recognition of the Negro, offers encouragement, and reminds his African-American brothers
of their glorious past. Although the pieces in *The Dream
Keeper* were written over a half-century ago . . . the
words have the same strength of meaning and power as
if they had been written today." Horn Book

Janeczko, Paul B., 1945-
Stardust hotel; poems; illustrated by Dorothy
Leech. Orchard Bks. 1993 64p il $15.95 (7 and
up)   **811**
ISBN 0-531-05498-5   LC 92-44514
"A Richard Jackson book"

A series of free-verse poems in which 15-year-old
Leary describes his life with his flower children parents,
his friends, and neighbors
"Even students who think they hate poetry will delight
in the quirky, but very human, characters who people the
pages and poems of this volume." Book Rep

That sweet diamond; baseball poems; illustrated
by Carole Katchen. Atheneum Bks. for Young
Readers 1998 unp il $16   **811**
1. Baseball—Poetry
ISBN 0-689-80735-X   LC 97-5044
"Nineteen free-verse poems about baseball describe
the game from many angles—bases covered include an
elderly fan's devotion, how to spit, and a curse for the
pitcher. . . . Janeczko's love of baseball is infectious,
and Katchen's illustrations capture the taut energy of
both players and fans in thick smears of pastels." Horn
Book Guide

Johnson, Angela, 1961-
The other side; Shorter poems. Orchard Bks.
1998 44p il $15.95; lib bdg $16.99   **811**
1. African Americans—Poetry
ISBN 0-531-30114-1; 0-531-33114-8 (lib bdg)
                                LC 98-13736
A Coretta Scott King honor book for text, 1999
A collection of poems reminiscent of growing up as
an African-American girl in Shorter, Alabama
"Photographs of the author as a child emphasize the
personal nature of this captivating narrative." Horn Book

Lewis, J. Patrick
Boshblobberbosh; runcible poems for Edward
Lear; illustrations by Gary Kelley. Harcourt Brace
& Co. 1998 unp il $18   **811**
1. Lear, Edward, 1812-1888—Poetry 2. Nonsense
verses
ISBN 0-15-201949-9   LC 98-84158
"In this tribute to the 'King of High Bosh,' Lewis
draws on actual instances in Edward Lear's unusual life
to create some entertaining and informative poems. . . .
Detailed endnotes cite the source of his inspiration for
each poem. . . . Kelley's illustrations have a surreal
quality that will appeal to older readers." SLJ

Livingston, Myra Cohn
Cricket never does; a collection of haiku and
tanka; illustrations by Kees de Kiefte. Margaret K.
McElderry Bks. 1997 42p il $15   **811**
1. Seasons—Poetry 2. Haiku
ISBN 0-689-81123-3   LC 96-30528
A collection of more than fifty original haiku and tan-
ka verses about the four seasons
"Livingston's skillful use of simple language . . .
creates fresh images of the everyday world." Horn Book
Guide

Longfellow, Henry Wadsworth, 1807-1882
Henry Wadsworth Longfellow; edited by
Frances Schoonmaker; illustrated by Chad
Wallace. Sterling 1998 48p il (Poetry for young
people) $14.95   **811**
ISBN 0-8069-9417-7   LC 98-14833

Longfellow, Henry Wadsworth, 1807-1882—
Continued

A collection of 27 poems, "among them, 'The Village Blacksmith,' 'The Wreck of the Hesperus.' 'The Children's Hour,' 'Paul Revere's Ride,' and 'Hiawatha's Childhood' from 'The Song of Hiawatha.' A several-page introduction to Longfellow's life also includes some of the stories behind the poems." Booklist

Mora, Pat
The desert is my mother. El desierto es mi madre; art by Daniel Lechon. Piñata Bks. 1994 il $14.95   **811**
1. Deserts—Poetry 2. Bilingual books—English-Spanish
ISBN 1-55885-121-6   LC 94-20047
A poetic depiction of the desert as the provider of comfort, food, spirit, and life
"Presented in both English and Spanish, the text's short verses provide opportunities for children to use their senses to explore and learn about their environment." Kaleidoscope. 2nd edition

Myers, Walter Dean, 1937-
Harlem; a poem; pictures by Christopher Myers. Scholastic 1997 unp il $16.95   **811**
1. African Americans—Poetry 2. Harlem (New York, N.Y.)—Poetry
ISBN 0-590-54340-7   LC 96-8108
A Caldecott Medal honor book, 1998
A poem celebrating the people, sights, and sounds of Harlem
"Myers's paean to Harlem sings, dances, and swaggers across the pages, conveying the myriad sounds on the streets. . . . Christopher Myers's collages add an edge to his father's words, vividly bringing to life the sights and scenes of Lenox Avenue." Horn Book Guide

Nash, Ogden, 1902-1971
I wouldn't have missed it: selected poems of Ogden Nash; selected by Linell Smith and Isabel Eberstadt; introduction by Archibald MacLeish. Little, Brown 1975 xxiii, 407p il $33   **811**
ISBN 0-316-59830-5
This "is a collection of poems by Ogden Nash covering a period of more than forty years, from his early days at the 'New Yorker' until his death in 1971. The collection of more than four hundred poems was selected by his daughters. Interspersed throughout the book are sixteen line drawings by Nash, very much in the Thurber style. The book also contains a useful double index of poems by first and last lines." Best Sellers

Poe, Edgar Allan, 1809-1849
Annabel Lee; illustrated by Gilles Tibo. Tundra Bks. of Northern N.Y. 1987 unp il $19.95; pa $7.95   **811**
1. Death—Poetry 2. Friendship—Poetry
ISBN 0-88776-200-X; 0-88776-230-1 (pa)
An illustrated "interpretation of Poe's well-known poem portrays a fisherman's son sharing the joys of the coast with a playmate who dies and is borne away by a ghostly schooner." Publ Wkly

Rylant, Cynthia
Something permanent; photographs by Walker Evans; poetry by Cynthia Rylant. Harcourt Brace & Co. 1994 61p il $18 (7 and up)   **811**
ISBN 0-15-277090-9   LC 93-3861
"Nearly 60 years ago, Walker Evans and James Agee documented the lives of poor Southern sharecroppers. Their efforts resulted in a devastating, legendary account of the Depression, *Let Us Now Praise Famous Men.* Here, Rylant pairs Evans's photographs with 29 short, lyrical poems." SLJ
"For students in junior high and high school, the juxtaposition of Evans' photos and Rylant's poems will demonstrate how emotions can be rooted in objects and how, to dig them out, you need to use strong, sturdy words." Booklist

Sandburg, Carl, 1878-1967
Early moon; illustrated by James Daugherty. Harcourt Brace Jovanovich 1930 136p il hardcover o.p. paperback available $1.95   **811**
ISBN 0-15-627326-8 (pa)
"A selection of seventy stimulating poems for young people by a . . . poet whose work they admire and understand. The selection is prefaced by a short talk on poetry." Cleveland Public Libr

Service, Robert W., 1874-1958
The cremation of Sam McGee; paintings by Ted Harrison; introduction by Pierre Berton. Greenwillow Bks. 1987 c1986 unp il $18   **811**
1. Yukon Territory—Poetry
ISBN 0-688-06903-7   LC 86-14971
Text first published 1907; this newly illustrated edition first published 1986 in Canada
"In the tradition of tall tales, the story of Sam McGee is told here in Service's original rollicking verses. Pledged to cremate his friend Sam, the narrator tells how, after carting the frozen body for miles, he stuffs it into a ship's roaring furnace. To his surprise, when he later opens the door he discovers Sam alive . . . and warm for the first time 'since he left Tennessee.'" Publ Wkly
"A fine example of a 20th-Century regional ballad." SLJ

The shooting of Dan McGrew; paintings by Ted Harrison. Godine 1988 unp il $14.95   **811**
1. Yukon Territory—Poetry
ISBN 0-87923-748-1   LC 88-6124
Text first published 1907
A narrative poem set in the Yukon describing the shoot-out in a saloon between a trapper and the man who stole his girl
"While the action of the poem is intense and demanding, the painterly illustrations by Harrison are overwhelmingly powerful." Publ Wkly

Silverstein, Shel
Falling up; poems and drawings by Shel Silverstein. HarperCollins Pubs. 1996 171p il $16.95; lib bdg $17.89   **811**
1. Humorous poetry 2. Nonsense verses
ISBN 0-06-024802-5; 0-06-024803-3 (lib bdg)
LC 96-75736

Silverstein, Shel—*Continued*

This "collection includes more than 150 poems. . . . As always, Silverstein has a direct line to what kids like, and he gives them poems celebrating the gross, the scary, the absurd, and the comical. The drawings are much more than decoration. They often extend a poem's meaning and, in many cases, add some great comedy." Booklist

A light in the attic. Harper & Row 1981 167p il $16.95; lib bdg $16.89 **811**
1. Humorous poetry 2. Nonsense verses
ISBN 0-06-025673-7; 0-06-025674-5 (lib bdg)
LC 80-8453

This collection of more than one hundred poems "will delight lovers of Silverstein's raucous, rollicking verse and his often tender, whimsical, philosophical advice. . . . The poems are tuned in to kids' most hidden feelings, dark wishes and enjoyment of the silly. . . . The witty line drawings are a full half of the treat of this wholly satisfying anthology by the modern successor to Edward Lear and Hilaire Belloc." SLJ

Where the sidewalk ends; the poems & drawings of Shel Silverstein. Harper & Row 1974 166p il $16.95; lib bdg $16.89 **811**
1. Humorous poetry 2. Nonsense verses
ISBN 0-06-025667-2; 0-06-025668-0 (lib bdg)
LC 70-105486

"There are skillful, sometimes grotesque line drawings with each of the 127 poems, which run in length from a few lines to a couple of pages. The poems are tender, funny, sentimental, philosophical, and ridiculous in turn, and they're for all ages." Saturday Rev

Soto, Gary

Canto familiar; [illustrated by Annika Nelson] Harcourt Brace & Co. 1995 79p il $17 **811**
ISBN 0-15-200067-4 LC 94-24218

"This collection of simple free verse captures common childhood moments at home, at school, and in the street. Many of the experiences are Mexican American . . . and occasional Spanish words are part of the easy, colloquial, short lines. . . . The occasional full-page, richly colored woodcuts by Annika Nelson capture the child's imaginative take on ordinary things." Booklist

Neighborhood odes; illustrated by David Diaz. Harcourt Brace Jovanovich 1992 68p il $15.95 **811**
ISBN 0-15-256879-4 LC 91-20710

Also available in paperback from Scholastic

"Twenty-one poems, all odes, celebrate life in a Hispanic neighborhood. Other than the small details of daily life—peoples' names or the foods they eat—these poems could be about any neighborhood. With humor, sensitivity, and insight, Soto explores the lives of children. . . . David Diaz's contemporary black-and-white illustrations, which often resemble cut paper, effortlessly capture the varied moods—happiness, fear, longing, shame, and greed—of this remarkable collection. With a glossary of thirty Spanish words and phrases." Horn Book

New and selected poems. Chronicle Bks. 1995 177p $22.95; pa $12.95 (7 and up) **811**
ISBN 0-8118-0758-4; 0-8118-0761-4 (pa)
LC 94-27081

"In one of his more striking poems, Soto stares longingly at the unkempt lot in the California slum where his family's house used to be. Elsewhere, a Mexican American simply jogs and laughs after he has been ushered out the back door when immigration officials show up at his workplace. With rare lyricism, gentleness, and a touch of humor, Soto covers the ground that leads many highly touted poets to erupt in pulsating anger. Soto has it all—the learned craft, the intrinsic abilities with language, a fascinating autobiography, and the storyteller's ability to manipulate memories into folklore." Libr J

Turner, Ann Warren, 1945-

A lion's hunger; poems of first love; by Ann Turner; illustrations by Maria Jimenez. Marshall Cavendish 1998 47p il $15.95 (7 and up) **811**
1. Dating (Social customs)—Poetry 2. Love poetry
ISBN 0-7614-5035-1 LC 98-10865

Poems follow a year in a girl's life as she meets a boy, starts dating him, falls in love, and sees their special relationship come to an end

"These poems effectively snap-shot the fragile highs and dangerous lows of love. The shape, style, and language of the poems are quite accessible." Voice Youth Advocates

Whitman, Walt, 1819-1892

Leaves of grass (7 and up) **811**

Hardcover and paperback editions available from various publishers

First published 1855

"The book, radical in form and content, takes its title from the themes of fertility, universality, and cyclical life. . . . As he revised and added to the original edition, Whitman arranged the poems in a significant autobiographical order." Reader's Ency. 4th edition

Walt Whitman; edited by Jonathan Levin; illustrated by Jim Burke. Sterling 1997 48p il (Poetry for young people) $14.95 (7 and up) **811**
ISBN 0-8069-9530-0 LC 97-433

An illustrated collection of twenty-six poems and excerpts from longer poems by the renowned nineteenth-century poet

"An outstanding introduction to Whitman's life and work. . . . This superb volume can be used to teach literature or to show a variety of poetic devices and style." SLJ

Wood, Nancy C.

Sacred fire; poetry and prose; by Nancy Wood; paintings by Frank Howell. Doubleday 1998 73p il lib bdg $25 (7 and up) **811**
ISBN 0-385-32515-0 LC 97-39414

The author's "poetry and prose tell of the Old Man of Pueblo lore who keeps the sacred fire burning. The sacred fire keeps the contemporary Indians connected to their history and ancestors." Book Rep

"Matching Wood's words in intensity and imagination are breathtakingly beautiful paintings. . . . As much lamentation as celebration, *Sacred Fire* is haunting in its evocation of the past and of memories that indict the poverty of the present." Booklist

Yolen, Jane

O Jerusalem; illustrated by John Thompson. Blue Sky Press (NY) 1996 unp il lib bdg $15.95 **811**

1. Jerusalem—Poetry 2. Religious poetry

ISBN 0-590-48426-5   LC 95-6013

A poetic tribute to Jerusalem, in honor of the 3000th anniversary of its founding, celebrating its history as a holy city for three major religions

"Yolen captures the feelings of Judaism, Christianity, and Islam toward Jerusalem in her poetry, and Thompson brings her words to life in exquisite paintings." Booklist

Sacred places; illustrated by David Shannon. Harcourt Brace & Co. 1996 38p il $16 **811**

1. Religious poetry

ISBN 0-15-269953-8   LC 92-30323

A collection of poems about different places around the world that are considered sacred by various cultures, including Mecca, the Ganges River, and Christian cathedrals

"The hazy moodiness of Shannon's paintings capture the mystery Yolen explores in her text, while his dense figures and literal interpretations of a passage from each poem draw Yolen's mystical flights back down to solid ground. Appended notes offer historical information on each sacred place." Bull Cent Child Books

811.008   American poetry—Collections

American sports poems; selected by R.R. Knudson and May Swenson. Orchard Bks. 1988 226p $18.95; lib bdg $19.99 **811.008**

1. Sports—Poetry 2. American poetry—Collections

ISBN 0-531-05753-4; 0-531-08353-5 (lib bdg)

LC 87-24384

"Beginning with poetic tributes to sports greats like Babe Ruth, Vince Lombardi and Joan Benoit, this anthology moves through baseball . . . football, soccer, hockey, basketball, swimming, skating. . . . With more than 150 selections that include Updike, Sexton and Nemerov (as well as Runyon, Nash, and Cole Porter), this is an all-star lineup. Notes on the poems and poets, title and author index, and a valuable subject index are included." Bull Cent Child Books

Book poems; poems from National Children's Book Week, 1959-1998; introduction by Lee Bennett Hopkins; [ed., Mary Perrotta Rich] Children's Bk. Council 1998 95p il pa $20

811.008

1. American poetry—Collections 2. Books and reading—Poetry

ISBN 0-933633-05-X   LC 99-158017

This anthology contains four decades of poems about the importance of books and reading. Includes biographies and bibliographies of the contributiing poets

Includes bibliographical references

Celebrate America in poetry and art; paintings, sculpture, drawings, photographs, and other works of art from the National Museum of American Art, Smithsonian Institution; edited by Nora Panzer. Hyperion Bks. for Children 1994 96p il $18.95; lib bdg $18.89 **811.008**

1. American poetry—Collections 2. American art 3. United States—Poetry

ISBN 1-56282-664-6; 1-56282-665-4 (lib bdg)

LC 93-32336

"Published in association with the National Museum of American Art, Smithsonian Institution"

A collection of American poetry that celebrates over 200 years of American life and history as illustrated by fine art from the collection of the National Museum of American Art

"There's a terrific cross-section of writers and illustrators—Maya Angelou, Robert Frost, Winslow Homer, Thomas Hart Benton—and there is special pleasure in the pairings. . . . Combined, the art and words are exhilaratingly more than the sum of their parts." Booklist

Celebrating America; a collection of poems and images of the American spirit; poetry compiled by Laura Whipple; art provided by the Art Institute of Chicago. Philomel Bks. 1994 79p il $19.95 **811.008**

1. American poetry—Collections

ISBN 0-399-22036-4   LC 92-26197

Whipple "includes work by modern writers well known to children (Myra Cohn Livingston and Robert Newton Peck, for example) as well as poetry by individuals better known to adults. Both the art, which was provided by the Art Institute of Chicago, and the poetry reflect a diversity of American styles, periods, and cultures—from poetry by a Toltec writer and by Langston Hughes to art by Frederic Church and Edward Hopper." Booklist

Includes bibliographical references

Cool salsa; bilingual poems on growing up Latino in the United States; edited by Lori M. Carlson; introduction by Oscar Hijuelos. Holt & Co. 1994 xx, 123p il $14.95 **811.008**

1. American poetry—Hispanic American authors—Collections 2. Bilingual books—English-Spanish

ISBN 0-8050-3135-9   LC 93-45798

Also available in paperback from Fawcett Books

"This collection presents poems by 29 Mexican-American, Cuban-American, Puerto Rican, and other Central and South American poets, including Sandra Cisneros, Luis J. Rodriguez, Pat Mora, Gary Soto, Ana Castillo, Oscar Hijuelos, Ed J. Vega, Judith Ortiz-Cofer, and other Latino writers both contemporary and historical. Brief biographical notes on the authors are provided. All the poems deal with experiences of teenagers." Book Rep

Hand in hand; an American history through poetry; collected by Lee Bennett Hopkins; illustrated by Peter M. Fiore. Simon & Schuster Bks. for Young Readers 1994 144p il $19.95

811.008

1. United States—History—Poetry 2. American poetry—Collections

ISBN 0-671-73315-X   LC 92-24230

Hand in hand—*Continued*

"Hopkins divides the country's past into nine arbitrary eras and presents 5-10 selections as representative of each period or theme. He includes patriotic songs, speeches, and individual anthems by a veritable feast of American poets, such as Walt Whitman, Carl Sandburg, Langston Hughes, and Robert Frost. . . . Fiore's bold impressionistic oil paintings, in the form of expansive tableaus and cameo vignettes, provide vivid visuals to go along with the poetic imagery." SLJ

I am the darker brother; an anthology of modern poems by African Americans; edited and with an afterword by Arnold Adoff; drawings by Benny Andrews; introduction by Rudine Sims Bishop; foreword by Nikki Giovanni. rev ed. Simon & Schuster Bks. for Young Readers 1997 208p il $16; pa $4.99   **811.008**
1. American poetry—African American authors—Collections
ISBN 0-689-81241-8; 0-689-80869-0 (pa)
LC 97-144181
First published 1968
This anthology presents "the African-American experience through poetry that speaks for itself without the distraction of artwork or the need to trumpet itself as being multicultural. . . . Because of the historical context of many of the poems, the book will be much in demand during Black History Month, but it should be used and treasured as part of the larger canon of literature to be enjoyed by all Americans at all times of the year. An indispensable addition to library collections." SLJ

I am writing a poem about—a game of poetry; edited by Myra Cohn Livingston. Margaret K. McElderry Bks. 1997 54p $15   **811.008**
1. American poetry—Collections
ISBN 0-689-81156-X
LC 97-4098
"Livingston devised a series of exercises to be used in her master poetry class at UCLA. Some of the poetry that was produced by her students from those exercises has been gathered here. . . . The poems are remarkably diverse in meter, length, and mood. . . . This small volume would be a wonderful addition to a classroom, school, or public library as an inspiration for students to try writing poems." Voice Youth Advocates

I, too, sing America; three centuries of African American poetry; [selected and annotated by] Catherine Clinton; illustrated by Stephen Alcorn. Houghton Mifflin 1998 128p il $20   **811.008**
1. American poetry—African American authors—Collections
ISBN 0-395-89599-5
LC 97-46137
A collection of poems by African-American writers, including Lucy Terry, Gwendolyn Bennett, and Alice Walker
"For each poet, Clinton provides a biography and a brief, insightful commentary on the poem(s) she has chosen, including a discussion of political as well as literary connections. Alcorn's dramatic, full-page, full-color illustrations opposite each poem evoke the quiltlike patterns and rhythmic figures of folk art." Booklist

In search of color everywhere; a collection of African-American poetry; edited by E. Ethelbert Miller; illustrated by Terrance Cummings. Stewart, Tabori & Chang 1994 255p il $24.95
811.008
1. American poetry—African American authors—Collections
ISBN 1-55670-339-2
LC 94-4395
This "anthology gathers a generous range of work, from anonymous spirituals to Langston Hughes's classic 'Mother to Son.' It also includes poetry by Pulitzer Prize-winning Yusef Komunyakaa, Poet Laureate Rita Dove, Lucille Clifton, June Jordan, the gifted young Elizabeth Alexander and many others. The editorial choices are imaginative, and not all of the writers will be immediately or widely familiar—a boon for any reader looking to make discoveries." Publ Wkly
Includes bibliographical references

The **Invisible** ladder; an anthology of contemporary American poems for young readers with the poets' own photos and commentary; edited by Liz Rosenberg. Holt & Co. 1996 210p il $16.95 (7 and up)   **811.008**
1. American poetry—Collections 2. Poets, American
ISBN 0-8050-3836-1
LC 96-12361
Features such poets as Robert Bly, Allen Ginsberg, Nikki Giovanni, and Galway Kinnell by including photos, selections of their work, and comments on their poetry
Rosenberg "introduces many exciting new adult voices to young people. Some of the poets' commentaries are sophisticated, some are pretentious; but most are immediate and extraordinarily moving, nearly as powerful as the poetry they lead into." Booklist

A **Jar** of tiny stars: poems by NCTE award-winning poets; Bernice E. Cullinan, editor; illustrations by Andi MacLeod; portraits by Marc Nadel. Wordsong 1996 94p il $16.95
811.008
1. American poetry—Collections
ISBN 1-56397-087-2
LC 93-60466
"Each poet who has won the NCTE Poetry Award—David McCord, Aileen Fisher, Karla Kuskin, Myra Cohn Livingston, Eve Merriam, John Ciardi, Lilian Moore, Arnold Adoff, Valerie Worth, and Barbara Esbensen—is pictured at the beginning of a section that includes several representative poems and a significant quote. The portraits are watercolor renditions from photographs, with cheerful pen-and-ink sketches accompanying the verse; all are in black and white." Bull Cent Child Books

Lives: poems about famous Americans; selected by Lee Bennett Hopkins; illustrated by Leslie Staub. HarperCollins Pubs. 1999 31p il $15.95; lib bdg $15.89   **811.008**
1. United States—Biography—Poetry 2. American poetry—Collections
ISBN 0-06-027767-X; 0-06-027768-8 (lib bdg)
LC 98-29851
A collection of poetic portraits of sixteen famous Americans from Paul Revere to Neil Armstrong, by such authors as Jane Yolen, Nikki Grimes, and X. J. Kennedy
"Hopkins's eloquent introduction praises the power of

Lives: poems about famous Americans—*Continued*

poetry. Concluding 'Notes on the Lives' give readers useful biographical information. Full-page portraits feature Staub's distinctive, flat, primitive style, and their backgrounds have details particular to the subject. . . . A winning combination of poems and illustrations." SLJ

Marvelous math; a book of poems; selected by Lee Bennett Hopkins; illustrated by Karen Barbour. Simon & Schuster Bks. for Young Readers 1997 31p il $17   **811.008**
1. Mathematics—Poetry 2. American poetry—Collections
ISBN 0-689-80658-2   LC 96-21597
Presents such poems as "Math Makes Me Feel Safe," "Fractions," "Pythagoras," and "Time Passes," by such writers as Janet S. Wong, Lee Bennett Hopkins, and Ilo Orleans
"Rhymed and open verse styles are represented, as are a variety of tones. . . . Barbour's lively illustrations dance and play around the poems. Her boldly outlined watercolor figures, often wearing ill-fitting hats, fill the pages with childlike whimsy." SLJ

The **Music** of what happens; poems that tell stories; selected by Paul B. Janeczko. Orchard Bks. 1988 188p $17.95   **811.008**
1. American poetry—Collections
ISBN 0-531-05757-7   LC 87-30791
Among the poets included in this collection of narrative verse are: Ann Stafford, Paul Zimmer, Norman Dubie, Erika Mumford and Robert Morgan
"Janeczko has played these poems like a piano, combining themes, tones, and even sounds for a true composition that will take young readers beyond the usual dose of Henry Wadsworth Longfellow or Rudyard Kipling." Bull Cent Child Books

My black me; a beginning book of black poetry; edited by Arnold Adoff. [rev ed] Dutton Children's Bks. 1994 83p $14.99; pa $4.99
811.008
1. American poetry—African American authors—Collections
ISBN 0-525-45216-8; 0-14-037443-4 (pa)
First published 1974
A compilation of poems reflecting thoughts on being black by such authors as Langston Hughes, Lucille Clifton, Nikki Giovanni, and Imamu AmiriBaraka

The **New** Oxford book of American verse; chosen and edited by Richard Ellmann. Oxford Univ. Press 1976 liv, 1076p $45 (7 and up) **811.008**
1. American poetry—Collections
ISBN 0-19-502058-8
Replaces The Oxford book of American verse, edited by F. D. Matthiessen (1950)
"This volume begins with Anne Bradstreet, who died in 1672, and ends with Imamu Amiri Baraka (LeRoy Jones), born in 1934. . . . A few ballads and folk songs, and one hymn, are . . . included. Most of the poets are represented with some amplitude so as to give a sense of their range and variety." Introduction

The **Oxford** book of children's verse in America; edited by Donald Hall. Oxford Univ. Press 1985 xxxviii, 319p $35; pa $15.95   **811.008**
1. American poetry—Collections
ISBN 0-19-503539-9; 0-19-506761-4 (pa)
LC 84-20755
"Hall's intention, expressed in the introduction, is to create an anthology of American poetry actually written for or adopted by children during a particular historical period. The emphasis is on authenticity rather than personal taste." SLJ
"A fine and carefully winnowed collection of American poetry is gathered in a book that will interest students of children's literature and young people who simply enjoy browsing." Horn Book

The **Place** my words are looking for; what poets say about and through their work; selected by Paul B. Janeczko. Bradbury Press 1990 150p il $16   **811.008**
1. American poetry—Collections 2. Poetics
ISBN 0-02-747671-5   LC 89-39331
"More than forty contemporary poets are included: Eve Merriam, X. J. Kennedy, Felice Holman, Gary Soto, Mark Vinz, Karla Kuskin, and John Updike, among others. Their contributions vary widely in theme and mood and style, though the preponderance of the pieces are written in modern idiom and unrhymed meter. The accompanying comments frequently are as insightful and eloquent as the poems themselves." Horn Book

Poetspeak: in their work, about their work; a selection by Paul B. Janeczko. Bradbury Press 1983 238p il $15.95; pa $9.95 (7 and up)
811.008
1. American poetry—Collections
ISBN 0-02-747770-3; 0-02-043850-8 (pa)
LC 83-2715
"In an anthology that includes the work of sixty contemporary poets, Janeczko includes comments by the poets about themselves, their writing, and at times about the particular poem that precedes the comment. The contributors include such well-known writers as William Dickey, Nikki Giovanni, X. J. Kennedy, Howard Nemerov, Joyce Carol Oates, and John Updike, as well as others, and many poets, who are less well-known. The book has variety in mood, style, theme, and subject, and the poems reflect many of the interests of adolescents." Bull Cent Child Books

Quiet storm; voices of young black poets; selected by Lydia Omolola Okutoro. Jump at the Sun 1999 102p $16.99 (7 and up)   **811.008**
1. American poetry—African American authors—Collections
ISBN 0-7868-0461-0   LC 98-30346
"An anthology that celebrates the African Diaspora. The selections were written by teenagers. . . . Individual chapters include selections about Black pride, the '. . . Poets as Keeper of the Oral Tradition,' home and homelessness, spirituality, love, freedom, the future, and '. . . Our Elders.' Many of the poems will have relevance to their audience and the book could be a helpful tool when approaching the genre thematically." SLJ

Reflections on a gift of watermelon pickle . . . and other modern verse; [compiled by] Stephen Dunning, Edward Lueders, Hugh Smith. Lothrop, Lee & Shepard Bks. 1967 c1966 139p il $20 **811.008**
1. American poetry—Collections
ISBN 0-688-41231-9
First published 1966 by Scott, Foresman in a text edition

"Although some of the [114] selections are by recognized modern writers, many are by minor or unknown poets, and few will be familiar to the reader. Nearly all are fresh in approach and contemporary in expression. . . . Striking photographs complementing or illuminating many of the poems enhance the attractiveness of the volume." Booklist

Shimmy shimmy shimmy like my sister Kate; looking at the Harlem Renaissance through poems; [edited by] Nikki Giovanni. Holt & Co. 1995 186p $16.95 **811.008**
1. American poetry—African American authors—Collections 2. Harlem Renaissance
ISBN 0-8050-3494-3 LC 95-38617
This anthology includes poems by such authors as Paul Laurence Dunbar, Langston Hughes, Countee Cullen, Gwendolyn Brooks, and Amiri Baraka. Commentary and a discussion of the development of African American arts known as the Harlem Renaissance is provided by editor Giovanni
Includes bibliographical references

Singing America; selected with an introduction by Neil Philip; illustrated by Michael McCurdy. Viking 1995 160p il o.p. **811.008**
1. American poetry—Collections

This "collection of poems includes traditional songs and poetry from the eighteenth century through the twentieth century. . . . The voices of poetry represent Native Americans, African Americans, Asian Americans, Hispanic Americans, and European immigrants." Voice Youth Advocates
"McCurdy's bold, beautiful woodcuts, many depicting people at work, extend the energy and individuality of the words." Booklist

Slam dunk: basketball poems; compiled by Lillian Morrison; illustrated by Bill James. Hyperion Bks. for Children 1995 64p il $15.95; lib bdg $15.89 **811.008**
1. Basketball—Poetry 2. American poetry—Collections
ISBN 0-7868-0054-2; 0-7868-2042-X (lib bdg)
LC 94-14620
"Complete with odes to Patrick Ewing, Magic Johnson, and Michael Jordan, the sport and its stars are celebrated by such varied writers as Jerry Spinelli, Jack Prelutsky, Walter Dean Myers, and Myra Cohn Livingston." SLJ
"Bill James' black-and-white, shaded pencil drawings and color-shot pastels capture movement as well as subject and composition. The lively lines and vibrant colors reflect the quickness of the game and the many moods of the verse." Booklist

Soul looks back in wonder; [illustrated by] Tom Feelings. Dial Bks. 1993 unp il o.p.; Puffin Bks. paperback available $6.99 **811.008**
1. African Americans—Poetry 2. American poetry—African American authors—Collections
ISBN 0-14-056501-9 (pa) LC 93-824
Artwork and poems by such writers as Maya Angelou, Langston Hughes, and Askia Toure portray the creativity, strength, and beauty of their African American heritage
"This thoughtful collection of poetry is unique. . . . Feelings selected sketches done while he was in West Africa, South America, and at home in America." Horn Book

Three centuries of American poetry, 1623-1923; edited by Allen Mandelbaum and Robert D. Richardson, Jr. Bantam Bks. 1999 733p $35; pa $20 (7 and up) **811.008**
1. American poetry—Collections
ISBN 0-553-10250-8; 0-553-37518-0 (pa)
LC 98-31408
This anthology contains works by well-known poets (Bradstreet, Whitman, Dickinson, Stevens) as well as obscure names such as Ellen Sturgis Hooper and Lucretia Davidson. Spirituals, popular song lyrics and Native American poems are included

812 American drama

Shepard, Aaron
Stories on stage; scripts for reader's theater. Wilson, H.W. 1993 162p $40 **812**
1. Readers' theater 2. Drama in education
ISBN 0-8242-0851-X LC 91-42236
A collection of twenty-two plays adapted from folk tales, short stories, myths, and novels and intended for use in reader's theater programs with middle grade and junior high school students. For each script, information provided includes: genre; culture of origin or setting; theme; grade-level recommendation; number of roles; approximate reading time

Soto, Gary
Novio boy; a play. Harcourt Brace & Co. 1997 78p pa $7 (7 and up) **812**
1. Dating (Social customs)—Drama 2. Mexican Americans—Drama
ISBN 0-15-201531-0 LC 96-32605
Rudy anxiously prepares for and then goes out on a first date with an attractive girl who is older than he is
"A hip, funny play. . . . Since the Mexican-American cast spouts frequent Spanish words, several lines of dialogue could be lost on an audience unfamiliar with the language. The visual clues of a live performance might serve to clarify some unfamiliar words. . . . Young actors should be able to perform this entertaining play with or without adult assistance." SLJ

Winther, Barbara
Plays from Hispanic tales; one-act, royalty-free dramatizations for young people, from Hispanic stories and folktales. Plays 1998 149p pa $13.95
812
1. Folklore—Latin America—Drama 2. Folklore—Spain—Drama
ISBN 0-8238-0307-4   LC 97-51973
"Winther has adapted 11 traditional folktales and legends from Spain, South and Central America, and the Caribbean for presentation on a stage or in a classroom. The collection is nicely balanced, including amusing trickster tales, a *pourquoi* story, a ghost tale, and folktales that explore themes of honor and honesty." Booklist
Includes glossary

812.008 American drama— Collections

The **Big** book of holiday plays; 31 one-act plays, curtain raisers, and adaptations for the celebration of holidays and special occasions round the year; edited by Sylvia E. Kamerman. Plays 1990 339p $18.95   **812.008**
1. Holidays—Drama 2. One act plays
ISBN 0-8238-0291-4   LC 90-7615
This "book features 31 one-act plays and adaptations, both dramas and comedies, geared to 14 holidays. . . . Production notes for each play appended." Booklist

Center stage; one-act plays for teenage readers and actors; edited by Donald R. Gallo. Harper & Row 1990 361p lib bdg $17; pa $5.95 (7 and up)   **812.008**
1. One act plays
ISBN 0-06-022171-2 (lib bdg); 0-06-447078-4 (pa)
LC 90-4050
This collection of ten "plays are appropriate for individual reading, but equally well suited for performance. Some are serious, some comic. Robin Brancato creates a gang verbal warfare in 'War of the Words,' wherein one gang speaks in monosyllables and cliches, the other in iambic pentameter; Walter Dean Myers, in a good versus possible evil drama, creates a metaphor for freedom in 'Cages.' Other equally provocative plays have been written by Susan Beth Pfeffer, Dallin Malmgren, Jean Davies Okimoto, Sandy Asher, and Lensey Namioka. *Center Stage* should attract adolescent readers into the readability of drama and, perhaps, its performance." ALAN

Plays of black Americans; the black experience in America, dramatized for young people; edited by Sylvia E. Kamerman. new expanded ed. Plays 1994 154p pa $13.95   **812.008**
1. One act plays 2. African Americans—Drama
ISBN 0-8238-0301-5   LC 94-9314
First published 1987
A collection of 10 plays and a choral reading reflecting the black experience in America. "Selections revolve around George Washington Carver, Mary McLeod Bethune, Dr. Daniel Hale Williams, Dr. Martin Luther King, Jr., John Henry, Abraham Lincoln, and the abolitionist movement. . . . Most of the theater pieces do not require elaborate sets or costumes, and the performance times average 30 minutes." SLJ

Theatre for young audiences; 20 great plays for children; edited by Coleman A. Jennings; foreword by Maurice Sendak. St. Martin's Press 1998 604p il $35   **812.008**
1. Drama—Collections
ISBN 0-312-18194-9   LC 97-36542
A collection of plays, many of which are based on favorite children's tales, including such titles as: "Charlotte's Web," "Really Rosie," "Wiley and the Hairy Man," "Wise Men of Chelm," and "The Crane Wife"
"Highly recommended for school and public libraries and anyone interested in a substantial collection of plays for children." Booklist

813.009   American fiction—History and criticism

Bloom, Susan P.
Presenting Avi; [by] Susan P. Bloom, Cathryn M. Mercier. Twayne Pubs. 1997 206p il (Twayne's young adult authors series) $28 (7 and up)   **813.009**
1. Avi, 1937-
ISBN 0-8057-4569-6   LC 96-53878
A critical introduction to the life and work of the prolific writer of young adult and children's books
"The text shows painstakingly careful reading of Avi's work." SLJ
Includes bibliographical references

Brown, Joanne, 1933-
Presenting Kathryn Lasky. Twayne Pubs. 1998 173p il (Twayne's young adult authors series) $28 (7 and up)   **813.009**
1. Lasky, Kathryn
ISBN 0-8057-1677-7   LC 98-35177
A critical introduction to the life and work of the author of such novels as The bone wars, The night journey, and Memoirs of a bookbat and of nonfiction works
Includes bibliographical references

Campbell, Patricia J., 1930-
Presenting Robert Cormier. Updated ed. Twayne Pubs. 1989 152p (Twayne's young adult authors series) $28 (7 and up)   **813.009**
1. Cormier, Robert
ISBN 0-8057-8212-5   LC 89-33707
First published 1985
A discussion of the life and work of the controversial YA author of The chocolate war, I am the cheese and After the first death
Includes bibliographical references

Crowe, Chris
Presenting Mildred D. Taylor. Twayne Pubs. 1999 162p il (Twayne's United States authors series) $28 (7 and up)   **813.009**
1. Taylor, Mildred D.
ISBN 0-8057-1687-4   LC 99-25527

Crowe, Chris—*Continued*

Crowe "shows how much of Taylor's fiction is rooted in her extended family's storytelling tradition and in her personal experience growing up with racism and violence, sustained by her family's loving support and pride. He discusses her books in their historical context, including her Newbery award winner, *Roll of Thunder, Hear My Cry* (1976), and provides a background chapter on the civil rights movement in Mississippi." Booklist

Includes bibliographical references

Daly, Jay

Presenting S.E. Hinton. Updated ed. Twayne Pubs. 1989 148p (Twayne's young adult authors series) $28 (7 and up) **813.009**

1. Hinton, S. E.
ISBN 0-8057-8211-7   LC 89-32347
First published 1987
An introductory look at the life and work of the author of The outsiders, Tex, and Rumble fish
Includes bibliographical references

Davis, Terry

Presenting Chris Crutcher. Twayne Pubs. 1997 xxvi, 144p il (Twayne's young adult authors series) $28 (7 and up) **813.009**

1. Crutcher, Chris, 1946-
ISBN 0-8057-8223-0   LC 97-14505
A critical introduction to the life and work of the author of such novels as Staying fat for Sarah Byrnes, Running loose, The Crazy Horse Electric game
"Davis's insights illuminate the complexity of Crutcher's philosophy. . . . Fascinating reading." Voice Youth Advocates
Includes bibliographical references

Gallo, Donald R.

Presenting Richard Peck. Twayne Pubs. 1989 154p (Twayne's young adult authors series) $28 (7 and up) **813.009**

1. Peck, Richard, 1934-
ISBN 0-8057-8209-5   LC 89-32346
Discusses the life and work of Richard Peck, examining his essays, poetry, and novels for children, young adults, and adults
The author "provides background on Peck's career, but he lets his subject do most of the talking, smoothly interweaving Peck's remarks throughout the text." Booklist
Includes bibliographical references

Jones, Patrick

What's so scary about R.L. Stine? Scarecrow Press 1998 xxvii, 249p il $32.50 (7 and up) **813.009**

1. Stine, R. L., 1943-
ISBN 0-8108-3468-5   LC 98-8374
"Based on interviews and articles by experts in the fields of literature and psychology, this book includes Jones's own viewpoint to build a powerful argument for appreciating and evaluating Stine's style, popularity, and contribution to young adult literature. . . . This is a sure bet for reports." SLJ
Includes bibliographical references

Kies, Cosette N., 1936-

Presenting young adult horror fiction; [by] Cosette Kies. Twayne Pubs. 1992 203p (Twayne's young adult authors series) $28 (7 and up) **813.009**

1. Horror fiction—History and criticism 2. American fiction—History and criticism
ISBN 0-8057-8217-6   LC 91-27002
"A look at the history of the genre; an analysis of select elements (traditional Gothic, satanism, true crime, splatterpunk, and dark fantasy); criticism of popular authors (V. C. Andrews, Dean R. Koontz, John Saul, Robert R. McCammon, Anne Rice, Chelsea Quinn Yarbro, Robert Bloch, and Stephen King); and projections for the future are all here. Students interested in horror and/or individual authors, curious about critical analysis, or seeking information for English papers will find a place to begin within these pages." SLJ

Krull, Kathleen, 1952-

Presenting Paula Danziger. Twayne Pubs. 1995 109p il (Twayne's young adult authors series) $28 (7 and up) **813.009**

1. Danziger, Paula, 1944-
ISBN 0-8057-4153-4   LC 94-42014
"Open about her personal problems, Danziger told Krull about her battles with bulimia and the problems of a difficult early family life. Her humorous experiences as a teacher are chronicled, as is her success as a funny and sought-after speaker. Krull groups her discussions of Danziger's books into six thematic chapters, covering a total of 15 novels." Booklist
Includes bibliographical references

MacRae, Cathi Dunn

Presenting young adult fantasy fiction. Twayne Pubs. 1998 xxx, 464p (Twayne's young adult authors series) $28 (7 and up) **813.009**

1. Fantasy fiction—History and criticism
ISBN 0-8057-8220-6   LC 98-12896
MacRae "examines alternate worlds, magic realism, myth, legend, magic bestiary, and time fantasy. She includes in-depth critical analysis and interviews with four authors: Terry Brooks, Barbara Hambly, Jane Yolen, and Meredith Anne Pierce." Booklist
The author "is obviously enamored of her subject and its writers; her enthusiasm is contagious, and her research outstandingly useful." Bull Cent Child Books
Includes bibliographical references

Monseau, Virginia R., 1941-

Presenting Ouida Sebestyen. Twayne Pubs. 1995 130p il (Twayne's young adult authors series) $28 (7 and up) **813.009**

1. Sebestyen, Ouida, 1924-
ISBN 0-8057-8224-9   LC 94-3681
Monseau "unveils Sebestyen's unorthodox writing habits (she writes outdoors, in longhand) and life. The body of her work includes six novels—each of which is given a detailed and thorough analysis—short fiction, and drama." Booklist
Includes bibliographical references

Nilsen, Alleen Pace
Presenting M.E. Kerr. updated ed. Twayne Pubs. 1997 173p il (Twayne's young adult authors series) $28 (7 and up)   **813.009**
1. Kerr, M. E., 1927-
ISBN 0-8057-9248-1   LC 96-39134
First published 1986
A critical introduction to the life and work of the young adult novelist M. E. Kerr
"The book is well researched and includes numerous quotes from two lengthy interviews. Nilsen skillfully combines biographical information and literary criticism in an inviting manner, creating a professional resource that can be enjoyed for personal reading and utilized for research." Voice Youth Advocates
Includes bibliographical references

Norris, Jerrie
Presenting Rosa Guy. Twayne Pubs. 1988 111p (Twayne's young adult authors series) $28 (7 and up)   **813.009**
1. Guy, Rosa
ISBN 0-8057-8207-9   LC 88-5369
Examines the life and works of the author, born in Trinidad and raised in Harlem, of such young adult fiction as Ruby and The friends
"Each chapter begins with one or two well-chosen passages from Guy effectively conveying her philosophy and style. A chronology including personal and publishing events precedes the first chapter. . . . Jerrie Norris is admiring and enthusiastic but also critical in her discussion." Horn Book
Includes bibliographical references

Reid, Suzanne Elizabeth
Presenting Cynthia Voigt. Twayne Pubs. 1995 133p il (Twayne's young adult authors series) $28 (7 and up)   **813.009**
1. Voigt, Cynthia
ISBN 0-8057-8219-2   LC 94-44197
This work "provides a brief biography and then comprehensive, in-depth analysis of each of Voigt's novels. . . . Reid quotes from a range of critical reviews, but her own literary analysis is almost entirely positive. The focus is on interpretation, and she does a fine job of identifying Voigt's dominant themes—the challenge to traditional gender roles, the emphasis on work, etc.—in a style that's both scholarly and stimulating." Booklist
Includes bibliographical references

Presenting Ursula Le Guin. Twayne Pubs. 1997 121p (Twayne's young adult authors series) $28 (7 and up)   **813.009**
1. Le Guin, Ursula K., 1929-
ISBN 0-8057-4609-9   LC 96-38622
A critical introduction to the life and work of the science fiction novelist Ursula K. Le Guin
Includes bibliographical references

Presenting young adult science fiction. Twayne Pubs. 1998 230p (Twayne's young adult authors series) $28 (7 and up)   **813.009**
1. Science fiction—History and criticism
ISBN 0-8057-1653-X   LC 98-35178

A critical introduction to science fiction authors Orson Scott Card, Douglas Hill, H. M. Hoover, Pamela Sargent, Octavia Butler, Pamela Service, Piers Anthony, and Douglas Adams, with chapters discussing the classical masters of science fiction, cyberpunk, Star trek, and new themes and trends
Includes filmography and bibliographical references

Stover, Lois T.
Presenting Phyllis Reynolds Naylor; [by] Lois Thomas Stover. Twayne Pubs. 1997 187p il (Twayne's young adult authors series) $28 (7 and up)   **813.009**
1. Naylor, Phyllis Reynolds, 1933-
ISBN 0-8057-7805-5   LC 96-36022
Examines the major works of the author of the Newbery Award-winning "Shiloh," provides biographical background, and discusses some of the efforts to censor her work
"A scholarly work that provides fascinating insights into Naylor's writing." Voice Youth Advocates
Includes bibliographical references

815   American speeches

Asian American voices; Deborah Gillan Straub, editor. U.X.L 1997 240p $39   **815**
1. Asian Americans 2. Speeches
ISBN 0-8103-9676-9   LC 97-6449
This book "presents full or excerpted speeches of 15 Asian Americans. Accompanying the speeches are brief biographies, definitions of terms, historical background, illustrations, and short lists of sources." Booklist

Historic speeches of African Americans; introduced and selected by Warren J. Halliburton. Watts 1993 192p il (African-American experience) $24; pa $6.95   **815**
1. African Americans—History—Sources 2. Speeches
ISBN 0-531-11034-6; 0-531-15677-X (pa)
                LC 92-39318
Presents speeches by various African American religious and political leaders from the days of slavery to the present, along with biographical information and historical background
"Kids will dip into this for personal reading, and for curriculum research; they'll also find stirring pieces to read aloud and think about. The detailed sources at the end of the book make it easy to find out more about the individuals and their ideas." Booklist

821   English poetry

Cohen, Barbara, 1932-1992
Canterbury tales; [by] Geoffrey Chaucer; selected, translated, and adapted by Barbara Cohen; illustrated by Trina Schart Hyman. Lothrop, Lee & Shepard Bks. 1988 87p il $17.95   **821**
ISBN 0-688-06201-6   LC 86-21045
Contents: The nun's priest's tale; The pardoner's tale; The wife of Bath's tale; The franklin's tale

Cohen, Barbara, 1932-1992—*Continued*

"Cohen's evident love and respect for Chaucer's writing keep her close to the text. Her writing retains the flavor of the times and the spirit of Chaucer's words while her prose retelling, enriched by Hyman's lively full-color paintings, enhances the book's appeal to young people. . . . An excellent introduction to *The Canterbury Tales* for young readers." Booklist

821.008 English poetry—Collections

Committed to memory; 100 best poems to memorize; edited, with an introduction, by John Hollander. Academy of American Poets 1996 196p **821.008**
1. English poetry—Collections 2. American poetry—Collections

Available in hardcover from Turtle Point Press $24.95 (ISBN 1-885983-15-8) and in paperback from Riverhead Bks. $12 (ISBN 1-57322-646-7)

Hollander "has selected 100 poems by poets-including lyrics and narratives, meditations and counsels-ranging from Blake and Hughes, Bishop and Thomas, to Yeats and Hayden. These are classics that lend themselves to memory, being short; often in form, or at least metrical; always rhythmic; and delightful." Libr J

The **Norton** anthology of modern poetry; edited by Richard Ellmann and Robert O'Clair. 2nd ed. Norton 1988 xlix, 1865p pa $50 (7 and up) **821.008**
1. English poetry—Collections 2. American poetry—Collections
ISBN 0-393-95636-9   LC 87-28310
First published 1973

An anthology of English and American verse from Whitman to the present day
Includes bibliographical references

The **Oxford** book of story poems; [compiled by] Michael Harrison and Christopher Stuart-Clark. Oxford Univ. Press 1990 175p il $25; pa $14.95 **821.008**
1. English poetry—Collections 2. American poetry—Collections
ISBN 0-19-276087-4; 0-19-276212-5 (pa)
LC 89-043715

This anthology contains "narrative verse by British and American poets, from traditional ballads such as 'Sir Patrick Spens' to contemporary poems such as Judith Nicholls' 'Storytime.' . . . [The poets include] Carroll, Keats, de la Mare, Kennedy, Lear, Lindsay, Longfellow, Noyes, Poe, Southey, and Tolkien. . . . A handy collection of story poems for reading aloud or alone." Booklist

The **Oxford** book of twentieth-century English verse; chosen by Phillip Larkin. Oxford Univ. Press 1973 l, 641p $35 (7 and up)   **821.008**
1. English poetry—Collections
ISBN 0-19-812137-7

This anthology of more than 600 poems by more than 200 twentieth-century British writers includes works by John Masefield, T. S. Eliot, W. B. Yeats, W. H. Auden, Dylan Thomas and Alan Sillitoe

The **Oxford** treasury of classic poems; [compiled by] Michael Harrison and Christopher Stuart-Clark. Oxford Univ. Press 1996 159p il hardcover o.p. paperback available $15.95 (7 and up)   **821.008**
1. English poetry—Collections 2. American poetry—Collections
ISBN 0-19-276187-0 (pa)   LC 95-52205

"Ninety-three poems by William Blake, John Keats, Dylan Thomas, Walt Whitman, and other . . . versifiers include sonnets and story poems as well as a smattering of nonsense verse. Various artists have illuminated the verse in styles ranging from loose-lined watercolors to precise pen-and-ink drawings." Horn Book Guide

The "poems in this glorious collection have thrilled readers and performers for years, and the lines still sing to kids today." Booklist

The **Oxford** treasury of time poems; [edited by] Michael Harrison and Christopher Stuart-Clark. Oxford Univ. Press 1999 155p il $25 **821.008**
1. Time—Poetry 2. English poetry—Collections 3. American poetry—Collections
ISBN 0-19-276175-7   LC 98-5382

A collection of poems about the many aspects of time, by such authors as Emily Dickinson, David McCord, and D.H. Lawrence

"Appropriately accompanying the varied types of poems are a variety of art styles, including black-and-white sketches, woodcuts, lighthearted watercolors, rich landscapes, detailed portraits, and abstract modern paintings, all from 10 different artists." SLJ

The **Random** House book of poetry for children; selected and introduced by Jack Prelutsky; illustrated by Arnold Lobel. Random House 1983 248p il $19; lib bdg $21.99 **821.008**
1. American poetry—Collections 2. English poetry—Collections
ISBN 0-394-85010-6; 0-394-95010-0 (lib bdg)
LC 83-2990

Opening poems for each section especially written for this anthology by Jack Prelutsky

In this anthology emphasis "is placed on humor and light verse; but serious and thoughtful poems are also included. . . . Approximately two thirds of the selections were written within the past forty years—the splendid contributions of such writers as John Ciardi, Aileen Fisher, Dennis Lee, Myra Cohn Livingston, David McCord, Eve Merriam, and Lilian Moore. [There are] . . . samplings of earlier poets from Shakespeare and Blake to Emily Dickinson and Walter de la Mare." Horn Book

822.3 William Shakespeare

Coville, Bruce

William Shakespeare's A midsummer night's dream; retold by Bruce Coville; pictures by Dennis Nolan. Dial Bks. 1996 unp il $16.99; lib bdg $16.89 **822.3**
ISBN 0-8037-1784-9; 0-8037-1785-7 (lib bdg)
LC 94-12600

Coville, Bruce—*Continued*

A simplified prose retelling of Shakespeare's play about the strange events that take place in a forest inhabited by fairies who magically transform the romantic fate of two young couples

"Coville introduces the story and also conveys something of the poetry and drama. Nolan's framed graphite and watercolor paintings express the dreaminess and absurdity of the play, and the pictures have a theatrical flair." Booklist

William Shakespeare's Macbeth; retold by Bruce Coville; pictures by Gary Kelley. Dial Bks. 1997 unp il $16.99; lib bdg $16.89   822.3
ISBN 0-8037-1899-3; 0-8037-1900-0 (lib bdg)
LC 97-7582

A simplified prose retelling of Shakespeare's play about a man who kills his king after hearing the prophesies of three witches

"Kelley's framed pastel illustrations of the hideous hags will hold kids from the start, and Coville's dramatic narrative will keep them reading. . . . Words and pictures are true to the dark, brooding spirit of the play." Booklist

Garfield, Leon, 1921-1996

Shakespeare stories [I]-II; illustrated by Michael Foreman. Houghton Mifflin 1991-1995 c1985-c1994 2v il v1 $26; pa $16; v2 $24.95
822.3
1. Shakespeare, William, 1564-1616—Adaptations
ISBN 0-395-56397-6 (v1); 0-395-86140-3 (pa); 0-395-70893-1 (v2)
Original volume first published 1985 by Schocken Bks.

In these volumes Garfield has rewritten twenty-one of Shakespeare's plays in narrative form, retaining much of the original language

Lamb, Charles, 1775-1834

Tales from Shakespeare; by Charles & Mary Lamb   822.3
1. Shakespeare, William, 1564-1616—Adaptations

Hardcover and paperback editions available from various publishers
First published 1807

"The *Tales* were the first version of 'Shakespeare' to be published specifically for children. They are written in a clear, vigorous style, not often encumbered by the attempt to make the language resemble that of the original. A lot is left out. . . . But the literary quality of the *Tales* makes them outshine almost every other English children's book of this period, and they proved an immediate and lasting success." Oxford Companion to Child Lit

Nesbit, E. (Edith), 1858-1924

The best of Shakespeare; introduction by Iona Opie; afterword by Peter Hunt. Oxford Univ. Press 1997 110p il (Iona and Peter Opie library of children's literature) $16.95   822.3
1. Shakespeare, William, 1564-1616—Adaptations
ISBN 0-19-511689-5   LC 97-15223

Simplified prose retellings of Romeo and Juliet, Hamlet, The Merchant of Venice, Othello, The Tempest, King Lear, Macbeth, As You Like It, Twelfth Night, and The Winter's Tale

"These stories don't recapitulate every subplot but capture the essential events and retain a little of the original wording. . . . This volume features photographs from productions by the Royal Shakespeare Company in Stratford-upon-Avon, as well as several North American companies." Booklist

Shellard, Dominic

William Shakespeare. Oxford Univ. Press 1998 120p il (British Library writers' lives) $22 (7 and up)   822.3
1. Shakespeare, William, 1564-1616
ISBN 0-19-521442-0   LC 99-206199

Shellard "weaves the known facts of Shakespeare's life and times with archival fragments and the conjectures that have grown from them. The difference between fact and speculation is always clearly presented. . . . The information is enhanced by excellent-quality full-color and black-and-white photograhps, period reproductions, and drawings." SLJ

Includes bibliographical references

Williams, Marcia, 1945-

Tales from Shakespeare; seven plays; presented and illustrated by Marcia Williams. Candlewick Press 1998 unp il $16.99   822.3
1. Shakespeare, William, 1564-1616—Adaptations
ISBN 0-7636-0441-0   LC 97-42165

"Each of the seven selections, *Hamlet, Romeo and Juliet, Macbeth, The Winter's Tale, Julius Caesar, Midsummer Night's Dream*, and *The Tempest*, is told as if it were on a stage, with cartoon panels carrying the actions and direct quotations from the play. The author's narration appears below the panels." SLJ

Williams "offers an inviting taste of the Shakespearean buffet, as well as a rare glimpse into the character of Elizabethan theater." Booklist

823.009   English fiction—History and criticism

Blishen, Edward, 1920-1996

Stand up Mr. Dickens; a Dickens anthology; presented by Edward Blishen; illustrated by Jill Bennett. Houghton Mifflin 1996 87p il $16.95 (7 and up)   823.009
1. Dickens, Charles, 1812-1870
ISBN 0-395-75656-1   LC 95-18237

Portrays the life of the famed English novelist and describes how he entertained audiences by reading his stories aloud. Includes excerpts from "The Pickwick Papers," "Oliver Twist," "A Christmas Carol," "Dombey and Son," "David Copperfield," and "Great Expectations"

"Blishen includes selections that are still great for acting and reading aloud; they will also make kids want to read more of Dickens. . . . Jill Bennett's watercolor-and-crayon full-page art and small pen-and-ink sketches on every page are done in a comic, theatrical style that connects the characters in the stories with the people in the audience." Booklist

860.8 Spanish literature—Collections

Latino voices; edited by Frances R. Aparicio. Millbrook Press 1994 143p il (Writers of America) $23.90 (7 and up)   **860.8**
1. American literature—Hispanic American authors—Collections 2. Hispanic Americans
ISBN 1-56294-388-X   LC 93-42893

An anthology of Latino fiction, poetry, biography, and other writings which describe the experiences of Hispanic Americans

This book "is an excellent way to help youngsters understand another culture or begin to make sense of living in two cultures. The book will enhance bi-cultural education, stimulate discussions, and help students learn what it means to be an American." Child Book Rev Serv

Includes bibliographical references

The **Tree** is older than you are; a bilingual gathering of poems & stories from Mexico with paintings by Mexican artists; selected by Naomi Shihab Nye. Simon & Schuster Bks. for Young Readers 1995 111p il $19.95; pa $12 (7 and up)   **860.8**
1. Mexican literature—Collections 2. Bilingual books—English-Spanish
ISBN 0-689-80297-8; 0-689-82087-9 (pa)
                LC 95-1565

"This bilingual anthology of poems, stories, and paintings by Mexican writers and artists brims over with a sense of wonder and playful exuberance, its themes as varied and inventive as a child's imagination." Voice Youth Advocates

860.9 Spanish literature—History and criticism

Shirey, Lynn
Latin American writers. Facts on File 1997 134p il (Global profiles) $19.95 (7 and up)   **860.9**
1. Authors, Latin American 2. Latin American literature—Bio-bibliography
ISBN 0-8160-3202-5   LC 96-18378

An introduction to the lives and works of eight Latin American writers, including Jorge Luis Borges, Gabriel García Márquez, Jorge Amado, and Isabel Allende

"Ideal for researching students and others needing general background on the profiled authors." Booklist

Includes bibliographical references

883 Classical Greek epic poetry and fiction

Sutcliff, Rosemary, 1920-1992
Black ships before Troy; the story of the Iliad; illustrated by Alan Lee. Delacorte Press 1993 128p il $24.95   **883**
1. Trojan War
ISBN 0-385-31069-2   LC 92-38782

Retells the story of the Trojan War, from the quarrel for the golden apple, and the flight of Helen with Paris, to the destruction of Troy

"Sutcliff's strong rhythms and Lee's misty watercolors in shades of brown, blue, and silvergray make this large-size volume great for reading aloud." Booklist

Includes bibliographical references

The wanderings of Odysseus; the story of the Odyssey; illustrated by Alan Lee. Delacorte Press 1996 119p il map $24.95   **883**
1. Homer—Adaptations 2. Odysseus (Greek mythology)
ISBN 0-385-32205-4   LC 95-15518

Companion volume to Black ships before Troy

A retelling of the adventures of Odysseus on his long voyage home from the Trojan War

"Poetic without being self-conscious, cadenced without seeming artificial, this prose retelling of Homer's great work retains the epic grandeur of the original, yet addresses the comprehension of contemporary listeners. Spectacular watercolors incorporate motifs from Greek art in this handsome volume." Horn Book Guide

896 African literatures

The **Penguin** book of modern African poetry; edited by Gerald Moore and Ulli Beier. 4th ed. Penguin Bks. 1998 xxvi, 448p pa $15.95   **896**
1. African poetry—Collections
ISBN 0-14-118100-1

First published 1963 in the United Kingdom with title: Modern poetry from Africa

This anthology includes over 200 poems by 67 poets from 23 countries

897 North American native literatures

Dancing teepees; poems of American Indian youth; selected by Virginia Driving Hawk Sneve, with art by Stephen Gammell. Holiday House 1989 32p il $16.95; pa $8.95   **897**
1. Indians of North America—Poetry
ISBN 0-8234-0724-1; 0-8234-0879-5 (pa)
                LC 88-11075

An illustrated collection of poems from the oral tradition of Native Americans

This is an "eclectic collection, drawn from a variety of tribal traditions. Printed on heavy paper, the book is illustrated with a catalogue of marvelously rendered designs and motifs, ranging from those of the Northwest Coast to the intricate beadwork patterns of the Great Lakes and the zigzag geometric borders of Southwestern pottery." N Y Times Book Rev

Earth always endures; Native American poems; selected by Neil Philip; illustrated with photographs by Edward S. Curtis. Viking 1996 93p il $19.99 (7 and up)   **897**
1. Indians of North America—Poetry
ISBN 0-670-86873-6   LC 95-62372

Earth always endures—*Continued*
This collection of poetry includes prayers, lullabies, and chants of the Sioux, Chippewa, Zuni, Navajo and other tribes
"The honesty of spirit reflected in this collection is intimately enhanced by stunning sepia-tone photographs." SLJ

Gleason, Katherine, 1960-
Native American literature. Chelsea House 1996 79p il (Junior library of American Indians) $25.43; pa $14.93   **897**
1. American literature—American Indian authors
2. Indians of North America in literature
ISBN 0-7910-2477-6; 0-7910-2478-4 (pa)
    LC 95-40562
Introduces Native American authors and provides a glimpse into their culture, historical perspective and world-view
"This fine introduction to the long history of Native American oral and written literature includes authors of books for children and adults." SLJ

900 GEOGRAPHY & HISTORY

902 History—Miscellany. Chronologies

Tomaselli-Moschovitis, Valerie
Junior timelines on file. Facts on File 1997 various paging il loose-leaf $165   **902**
1. Historical chronology 2. World history
ISBN 0-8160-3444-3   LC 96-53364
This loose-leaf binder provides "coverage of religion, worship, philosophy, art, education, exploration, colonialism, revolution, and impact of technological advances, both on a country-by-country basis and from a world history perspective." Book Rep
For a fuller review see: Booklist, Feb. 1, 1998

Wetterau, Bruce
World history; a dictionary of important people, places, and events from ancient times to the present. Holt & Co. 1994 1173p (Henry Holt reference book) $60   **902**
1. Historical chronology 2. History—Dictionaries
ISBN 0-8050-2350-X   LC 93-38510
Revised edition of Macmillan concise dictionary of world history, published 1983
Alphabetically arranged entries focusing mainly on political history but also covering the arts, religion, intellectual life, science and technology. Chronologies are provided for some countries, periods and wars

904 Collected accounts of events

Newson, Lesley
Devastation! the world's worst natural disasters. DK Pub. 1998 159p il maps $24.95 (7 and up)   **904**
1. Natural disasters
ISBN 0-7894-3518-7   LC 98-2567

Text and numerous illustrations explore the destructive power of nature from violent volcanic eruptions and earthquakes to fires, floods and disease-causing viruses and bacteria. A gazetteer section lists and locates various types of disasters throughout the world
Includes glossary

909 World history. Civilization

Altman, Linda Jacobs, 1943-
Forever outsiders; Jews and history from ancient times to August 1935. Blackbirch Press 1998 80p il maps (Holocaust) lib bdg $19.45   **909**
1. Jews—History
ISBN 1-567-11200-5   LC 96-48179
Book 1 in the Holocaust series, other volumes entered in class 940.53. This volume "provides a social and economic history of the Jews, shaped and punctuated by repeated acts of persecution, actions that in modern times lead to the growth of Zionism and the Holocaust." SLJ
"Authoritative, readable." Booklist
Includes glossary and bibliographical references

Burrell, R. E. C. (Roy Eric Charles), 1923-
Oxford first ancient history; [by] Roy Burrell; with many illustrations by Peter Connolly. Oxford Univ. Press 1994 c1991 320p il maps (Rebuilding the past) hardcover o.p. paperback available $22.95   **909**
1. Ancient history
ISBN 0-19-521373-4 (pa)
First published 1991 in the United Kingdom
"Beginning with prehistory, this book surveys ancient civilizations, primarily in the Mediterranean region. . . . Every page includes at least one full-color illustration, a map, a cutaway drawing, a painting re-creating the times, or a photograph of a wall painting, sculpture, artifact, site, or explorer. Not only is the format inviting, but the text is also quite readable. . . . A lively, helpful resource." Booklist

Mann, Kenny, 1946-
The ancient Hebrews. Benchmark Bks. (Tarrytown) 1999 80p il (Cultures of the past) $19.95   **909**
1. Jews—History
ISBN 0-7614-0302-7   LC 97-6551
This illustrated work "discusses the social and religious history of the Jewish people and its influence on modern Judaism, and touches on the relationship between present-day Israel and Arab countries." SLJ
Includes bibliographical references

Millard, Anne
Pyramids. Kingfisher (NY) 1996 63p il maps $15.95   **909**
1. Pyramids
ISBN 1-85697-674-2   LC 95-39660
Describes the pyramids of Egypt and the Americas and their significance in the social, political, and reli-

Millard, Anne—*Continued*
gious life of long-vanished civilizations
"By combining well-captioned, clear, full-color illustrations and an engrossing narrative, this book teaches in the best way—by showing and explaining." SLJ
Includes glossary

Ochoa, George
The Wilson chronology of ideas; [by] George Ochoa and Melinda Corey. Wilson, H.W. 1998 431p $60 **909**
1. Civilization—History 2. Philosophy
ISBN 0-8242-0935-4   LC 97-17591
A chronological presentation of influential philosophical, political, theological and social thought from ancient times to the late 20th century. Sidebars feature profiles of celebrated thinkers

Putnam, James
Pyramid; written by James Putnam; photographed by Geoff Brightling & Peter Hayman. Knopf 1994 63p il $19; lib bdg $20.99
909
1. Pyramids
ISBN 0-679-86170-X; 0-679-96170-4 (lib bdg)
LC 94-8804
"A Dorling Kindersley book"
This introduction to pyramids of the world features "full-color photographs. The best coverage is given to Egyptian tombs, but pyramids in Nubia, Mexico, and Central America are also described. In addition to sharing information on what is known about the Egyptian pyramids, Putnam also mentions unsolved riddles about them, such as how many workers built them, how the stones were moved, etc." SLJ

World history on file. Facts on File 1999 4v il maps loose-leaf set $500 **909**
1. World history
ISBN 0-8160-3938-0
Produced by the Diagram Group/Victoria L. Chapman & David Lindroth
Contents: v1 Early civilizations (prehistory to 300 C.E.); v2 The expanding world (300 to 1750); v3 The age of revolution (1750 to 1914); v4 The 20th century
Each volume includes approximately 500 maps, charts, timelines, and line drawings with explanatory text regarding a period of world history

The **World** in 1492; by Jean Fritz [et al.]; with illustrations by Stefano Vitale. Holt & Co. 1992 168p il maps $19.95 **909**
1. Fifteenth century 2. World history
ISBN 0-8050-1674-0   LC 92-5434
A collection of essays on 15th century life divided by continent. "Jean Fritz writes of Europe; Katherine Paterson, Asia; the McKissacks, Africa; Margaret Mahy, Australia and Oceania; and Jamake Highwater, the Americas." SLJ
Includes bibliographical references

The **Young** reader's encyclopedia of Jewish history; Ilana Shamir, general editor; Shlomo Shavit, editor. Viking Kestrel 1987 125p il maps lib bdg $17.95 **909**
1. Jews—History
ISBN 0-670-81738-4   LC 87-10599
This volume "is organized into 28 chapters. Each is about four pages long, from a discussion of early nomadic tribes to an assessment of contemporary international Jewry. Examples of other topics include the Babylonian exile, Jewish life in early Christian Europe and in the Ottoman Empire, Messianism during the Middle Ages, the rise of Zionism, the Holocaust, the Sinai Campaign and Yom Kippur War, and problems of Jews in the Eastern Bloc." Bull Cent Child Books
"The format is excellent; the text is concise and well organized; and the supplemental graphic material . . . is superb and is consistently clearly labeled and well integrated into the text." SLJ

909.07 World history — ca. 500-1450/1500

Cox, Reginald H. W.
The seven wonders of the historic world; [by] Reg Cox & Neil Morris; illustrated by James Field. Silver Burdett Press 1996 c1995 32p il (Wonders of the world) $14.95; pa $7.95 **909.07**
1. Middle Ages
ISBN 0-382-39269-8; 0-382-39270-1 (pa)
LC 95-40993
First published 1995 in the United Kingdom
Features seven wonders of the Middle Ages including the Krak des Chevaliers in Syria, the Alhambra citadel in southern Spain, and the Aztec city of Tenochtitlán
Includes glossary

Gregory, Tony
The Dark Ages. Facts on File 1993 79p il maps (Illustrated history of the world) lib bdg $19.95
909.07
1. Middle Ages
ISBN 0-8160-2787-0   LC 91-43093
First published 1991 in the United Kingdom
Explores the history of the world, from the fall of Rome to the rise of Islam, discussing such areas as Europe, the Mediterranean, the Far East, and the Americas
This is "clearly written, culturally well balanced, and logically organized. Perhaps most importantly, [it is] visually appealing and likely to attract even the most reluctant reader." SLJ
Includes glossary and bibliographical references

Hanawalt, Barbara
The Middle Ages; an illustrated history; [by] Barbara A. Hanawalt. Oxford Univ. Press 1998 158p il maps $29.95 (7 and up) **909.07**
1. Middle Ages
ISBN 0-19-510359-9   LC 98-5889
A history of the Middle Ages, including the merger of Roman, Christian, and Germanic cultures; the transforma-

Hanawalt, Barbara—*Continued*
tion of the Roman Empire; and social, economic, religious, and cultural aspects of medieval life
"This is a valuable supplement for students researching medieval topics. Amply and well illustrated, the handsome, oversize volume includes engaging sidebars and captions, an extensive bibliography, a glossary, and a chronology." Booklist

Macdonald, Fiona
The Middle Ages. Facts on File 1993 79p il maps (Illustrated history of the world) lib bdg $21.95   **909.07**
1. Middle Ages
ISBN 0-8160-2788-9   LC 91-43094
First published 1991 in the United Kingdom
Text and illustrations explore the history of the world from the Mongol invasions through the voyages of Christopher Columbus
This work contains "abundant full-color illustrations and detailed maps and charts. . . . An excellent source of introductory information." Book Rep
Includes glossary and bibliographical references

McNeill, Sarah
The Middle Ages. Oxford Univ. Press 1998 46p il (Spotlights) $10.95   **909.07**
1. Middle Ages
ISBN 0-19-521394-7   LC 97-38864
Describes various aspects of life in the Middle Ages, including religion and monastic life, feudalism, homes and families, education, trade, art and architecture, and more. Also presents captioned pictures of related artifacts

909.08   Modern history, 1450/1500-

Martell, Hazel Mary
The age of discovery. Facts on File 1993 79p il maps (Illustrated history of the world) lib bdg $17.95   **909.08**
1. Modern history
ISBN 0-8160-2789-7   LC 92-18621
Explores the history of the world from 1500 to 1650, an active period which included the Renaissance in Europe, European explorations among the ancient empires of Africa and South America, and the decline of the Mogul Empire in India
Includes glossary and bibliographical references

909.7   World history—18th century, 1700-1799

Reynoldson, Fiona
Conflict and change. Facts on File 1993 79p il maps (Illustrated history of the world) lib bdg $21.95   **909.7**
1. Modern history
ISBN 0-8160-2790-0   LC 92-20460
First published 1991 in the United Kingdom

Explores the history of the world from 1650 to 1800 with emphasis on the agricultural revolution, the Enlightenment, the Industrial Revolution, the American and French Revolutions, Manchu China, and Shogunate Japan
Includes glossary and bibliographical references

909.81   World history—19th century, 1800-1899

Corrick, James A.
The Industrial Revolution. Lucent Bks. 1998 112p il maps (World history series) lib bdg $22.45 (7 and up)   **909.81**
1. Industrial revolution
ISBN 1-56006-318-1   LC 98-6922
Discusses the Industrial Revolution, including its birth in England, its spread to Europe and America, and its effects on society
"This book tells its story concisely and illustrates it with black-and-white photos, engravings, diagrams, and maps. Looking beyond the expected topics of the steam engine, cotton gin, and electric power, Corrick discusses the history, changing technology, and social impact of computers." Booklist
Includes bibliographical references

909.82   World history—20th century, 1900-1999

Adams, Simon
The DK visual timeline of the 20th century. DK Pub. 1996 48p il $15.95   **909.82**
1. Modern history—1900-1999 (20th century)
ISBN 0-7894-0997-6   LC 96-13171
This volume covers notable events "in the areas of arts and entertainment, science and discovery, everyday life, and world history." SLJ
"This book uses an attractive, easily accessible format as a tool to help children begin to understand the significance of what came before they did. Adams does a good job of covering the century." Booklist

Children's history of the 20th century. DK Pub. 1999 352p il $29.95   **909.82**
1. Modern history—1900-1999 (20th century)
ISBN 0-7894-4722-3
This illustrated, chronological look at the century features special sections on the U.S. government, sports, music and theater

Jennings, Peter, 1938-
The century for young people; [by] Peter Jennings, Todd Brewster; adapted by Jennifer Armstrong; photographs edited by Katherine Bourbeau. Random House 1999 245p il $29.95   **909.82**
1. Modern history—1900-1999 (20th century)
ISBN 0-385-32708-0
An adaptation of the authors' The century published 1998 by Doubleday

Jennings, Peter, 1938-—*Continued*
The "authors use primary sources throughout the narrative to highlight the events and people of the 1900s. . . . Excellent-quality, archival photos capture the moments on almost every page. This is a unique and valuable book." SLJ

Junior chronicle of the 20th century. DK Pub. 1997 336p il $39.95   **909.82**
1. Modern history—1900-1999 (20th century)
ISBN 0-7894-2033-3   LC 97-5212
A visual history covering personalities and topics of the twentieth-century and including key events in the fields of international politics, entertainment, and science
"Plenty of trivia tidbits make this an excellent choice for browsers, and the information can be used in timeline reports, as well." Voice Youth Advocates

Leonard, Thomas M., 1937-
Day by day: the seventies; by Thomas Leonard, Cynthia Crippen, and Marc Aronson. Facts on File 1988 2v il set $195 (7 and up)   **909.82**
1. Modern history—1900-1999 (20th century)
ISBN 0-8160-1020-X   LC 83-11520
This title "will be useful in . . . libraries needing a summary of events of the decade that brought us the end of U.S. military involvement in Vietnam, the resignation of a president, and the world's first test-tube baby." Booklist

Meltzer, Ellen
Day by day: the eighties; [by] Ellen Meltzer and Marc Aronson. Facts on File 1995 2v il set $195 (7 and up)   **909.82**
1. Modern history—1900-1999 (20th century)
ISBN 0-8160-1592-9   LC 94-26632
Entries addressing politics, economics, culture and recreation are presented in a day by day chronological order

Parker, Thomas, 1947-
Day by day: the sixties; by Thomas Parker and Douglas Nelson. Facts on File 1983 2v il set $195 (7 and up)   **909.82**
1. Modern history—1900-1999 (20th century)
ISBN 0-87196-648-4   LC 80-22432
This volume traces events of the 1960s in a day by day chronological order

910 Geography and travel

The **DK** geography of the world. DK Pub. 1996 304p il maps $39.95   **910**
1. Geography
ISBN 0-7894-1004-4   LC 96-15129
This work provides basic facts about "each country in the world, from Vatican City to the Russian Federation. Each region has a detailed map with an insert suggesting things to look for on the map, weather information, colored pictures of the flag, life style information and fact boxes with statistics i.e. population, religion, type of government, currency etc." BAYA Book Rev
Includes glossary

Platt, Richard, 1953-
DK illustrated book of great adventurers; written by Richard Platt; illustrated by George Sharp [et al.] DK Pub. 1999 96p il maps $15.95   **910**
1. Adventure and adventurers
ISBN 0-7894-4461-5   LC 98-49574
Presents the activities and accomplishments of great adventurers throughout history, including the Viking explorer Leif Eriksson, the glamorous female spy Mata Hari, and astronaut Neil Armstrong

910.2 Geography—Miscellany. Travel guides

Countries of the world and their leaders yearbook. Gale Res. 2v il maps $225   **910.2**
1. Geography 2. Politicians 3. Political science
ISSN 0196-2809

First published 1974 with title: Countries of the world; issued annually since 1980 with slight variations in title. Supplementary volume published at mid-year available at $105
A compilation of U.S. Department of State Background Notes and other government reports, this two-volume yearbook offers geographical, social, political, and economic data on about 170 nations. In addition, it provides information on: overseas business services from the Departments of State and Commerce, U.S. embassies and consulates, travel warnings, world health, and climate

910.3 Geography—Dictionaries, encyclopedias, gazetteers

Lands and peoples. Grolier Educ. 6v il maps lib bdg set $269   **910.3**
1. Geography—Dictionaries 2. World history—Dictionaries 3. Civilization—Dictionaries

Biennial. First published 1929-1930
Contents: v 1 Africa; v2 Asia, Australia, New Zealand, Oceania; v3-4 Europe; v5 North America; v6 South and Central America, Antarctica, Facts and figures, Selected readings, Index
This is "a standard social studies reference tool for school and public libraries. . . . [Articles] . . . include detailed information on geography and climate, people (ethnic groups, language, religion), culture (customs, arts and literature), economy, and history. . . . Positive aspects of this work, such as the up-to-date coverage, the accessibility of the information, and the attractive format, make it an extremely useful research tool." Booklist

Merriam-Webster's geographical dictionary. 3rd ed. Merriam-Webster 1997 26a, 1361p maps $29.95   **910.3**
1. Geography—Dictionaries
ISBN 0-87779-546-0   LC 96-52365
First published 1949 with title: Webster's geographical dictionary

Merriam-Webster's geographical dictionary—
Continued

"There are about 50,000 entries which describe, locate, and give pronunciation of cities, towns, counties, countries, and geographical features. Over 250 maps help identification. Each entry has population, area, and brief facts about the economy and history where appropriate." Safford. Guide to Ref Materials for Sch Libr Media Cent. 5th edition

Worldmark encyclopedia of the nations. Gale Res.; distributed by Wiley 5v il maps set $345
910.3
1. Geography—Encyclopedias 2. World history—Encyclopedias 3. World politics—Encyclopedias

First published 1960. (9th edition 1998) Periodically revised

"Separate volumes on the United Nations, the Americas, Europe, Asia and Oceania, and Africa contain factual information on 176 countries. Fifty different subjects are examined for each country—flags, currency, armed forces, ethnic groups, languages, famous persons, environment, transportation, resources, government, travel and recreation, etc. Volume on the United Nations treats its organization, operation, membership, departments, agencies, committees and commissions. Supplements encyclopedias." N Y Public Libr. Ref Books for Child Collect. 2d edition

910.4   Accounts of travel. Seafaring life. Buried treasure

Aaseng, Nathan, 1953-
The Titanic. Lucent Bks. 1999 96p il (Building history series) $22.45 (7 and up)   **910.4**
1. Titanic (Steamship) 2. Shipwrecks
ISBN 1-56006-569-9   LC 98-31964
Discusses the design and building of the monster ship the Titanic, its maiden voyage, and what went wrong on the fateful night when it struck an iceberg and sank
Includes bibliographical references

Adams, Simon
Titanic. DK Pub. 1999 64p il (Eyewitness books) $15.95   **910.4**
1. Titanic (Steamship) 2. Shipwrecks
ISBN 0-7894-4724-X   LC 99-32241
Detailed descriptions of the Titanic, including its accommodations, and a retelling of its sinking in the North Atlantic in April, 1912

Ballard, Robert D.
The discovery of the Titanic; [by] Robert D. Ballard, with Rick Archbold; introduction by Walter Lord; illustrations of the Titanic by Ken Marschall. new & updated [ed] Madison Press Bks. 1995 287, liiip il pa $13.99 (7 and up)
910.4
1. Titanic (Steamship) 2. Shipwrecks 3. Underwater exploration
ISBN 0-446-67174-6   LC 95-226990

"A Warner/Madison Press book"
First published 1987 by Warner Bks.
An account of the discovery and exploration of the sunken ocean liner by the leader of the joint French/American expedition

Exploring the Titanic; edited by Patrick Crean; illustrations by Ken Marschall. Scholastic 1988 64p il maps $14.95; pa $6.95   **910.4**
1. Titanic (Steamship) 2. Shipwrecks 3. Underwater exploration
ISBN 0-590-41953-6; 0-590-41952-8 (pa)
LC 88-6478
"A Scholastic/Madison Press book"
A narrative for young readers based on the author's The discovery of the Titanic
"The technically accurate and lucid explanations are greatly enchanced by Marshall's stunning paintings, as well as by diagrams and current and period photographs." SLJ
Includes glossary and bibliographical references

Ghost liners; exploring the world's greatest lost ships; by Robert D. Ballard and Rick Archbold; illustrations by Ken Marschall. Little, Brown 1998 64p il $18.95   **910.4**
1. Shipwrecks
ISBN 0-316-08020-9   LC 98-3412
"A Madison Press book"
Depicts five famous ships that have been lost at sea in modern times, the Empress of Ireland, the Lusitania, the Andrea Doria, the Brittanic, and the Titanic
"The large, attractive format and informative text combine to make this an appealing book on a subject that continues to fascinate young people." Booklist
Includes glossary and bibliographical references

Lost liners; by Robert D. Ballard and Rick Archbold; paintings by Ken Marschall; historical consultation by Eric Sauder. Hyperion 1997 223p il maps $60 (7 and up)   **910.4**
1. Shipwrecks 2. Ocean travel 3. Ships
ISBN 0-7868-6296-3   LC 97-15270
In an "illustrated introduction that chronicles the history of the transatlantic ocean liner . . . the authors affirm that the 'truly 'lost' liners that sank at sea form the real legacy of this vanished age.' Then the authors profile the major ocean queens that sank (among them, the *Lusitania,* the *Titanic,* and the *Andrea Doria*) and show what is left of them below the waves." Booklist
Includes bibliographical references

Brewster, Hugh
882 ½ amazing answers to your questions about the Titanic; by Hugh Brewster and Laurie Coulter; text research by Greg Curtis; historical consultation by Don Lynch paintings by Ken Marschall. Scholastic 1998 96p il $16.95; pa $9.99
910.4
1. Titanic (Steamship) 2. Shipwrecks
ISBN 0-590-18730-9; 0-439-04296-8 (pa)
LC 98-27558
"A Scholastic/Madison Press book"

Brewster, Hugh—Continued
Questions and answers present information about the building, passengers, launching, sailing, sinking, and re-discovery of the Titanic. Includes illustrations, archival images, and step-by-step diagrams

Fritz, Jean
Around the world in a hundred years; from Henry the Navigator to Magellan; illustrated by Anthony Bacon Venti. Putnam 1994 128p il maps $18.95; pa $6.99 **910.4**
  1. Explorers
  ISBN 0-399-22527-7; 0-698-11638-0 (pa)
  LC 92-27042
"Fritz examines the voyages of ten explorers, acknowledging that their contributions, though deserving of recognition, were dearly bought. Opening and closing chapters summarize the fourteenth-century world view and indicate later expansion of geographic understanding. As always, Fritz tempers scholarship with humor in this brief volume—illustrated with drawings in pencil—which reads like an adventure story." Horn Book Guide
Includes bibliographical references

Grolier student library of explorers and exploration. Grolier Educ. 1998 10v il maps set $299 **910.4**
  1. Exploration 2. Explorers
  ISBN 0-7172-9135-9
  LC 97-27683
This set "begins with Australopithecus and concludes with the exploration of space and the ocean. Each volume concentrates on a specific region or aspect of discovery, such as European imperial expansion in the seventeenth and eighteenth centuries (volume 3,) voyages to Asia and Australia (volume 7), and exploration of the North and South Poles (volume 9). . . . Highly recommended for the school and public library where students are searching for material beyond what they can find in a general encyclopedia." Booklist

Johnstone, Michael
Explorers; author: Michael Johnstone; consultant: Shane Winser. Candlewick Press 1997 32p il (History news) $15.99 **910.4**
  1. Explorers
  ISBN 0-7636-0314-7
  LC 96-52758
Uses a newspaper format to present the adventures and accomplishments of such explorers as Columbus, Cortes, and Cook
This is "colorfully illustrated throughout. . . . Lively headlines . . . entice readers into the articles." SLJ

Macdonald, Fiona
Magellan; a voyage around the world; written by Fiona MacDonald; illustrated by Mark Bergin; created and designed by David Salariya. Watts 1998 32p il maps (Expedition) hardcover o.p. paperback available $7.95 **910.4**
  1. Magellan, Ferdinand, 1480?-1521 2. Explorers
  3. Voyages around the world
  ISBN 0-531-15341-X (pa)
  LC 97-13836

Follows Magellan's expedition, the first voyage around the world, and describes the adventures that ensued
"The appealing format lends itself to easy use by student researchers, particularily reluctant readers. . . . Detailed, full-color pen-and-watercolor illustrations and small text bits provide lifestyle and cultural details." SLJ

Marschall, Ken
Inside the Titanic; illustrated by Ken Marschall; text by Hugh Brewster. Little, Brown 1997 32p il $18.95 **910.4**
  1. Titanic (Steamship) 2. Shipwrecks
  ISBN 0-316-55716-1
  LC 97-382
"A Madison Press book"
"Color cutaway paintings of the *Titanic* in this over-size book allow readers to view every deck as they follow two 12-year-old boys exploring the vessel, and to see how the liner struck the iceberg and sank." Booklist
Includes glossary and bibliographical references

Matthews, Rupert
Explorer; written by Rupert Matthews. Knopf 1991 63p il (Eyewitness books) $16; lib bdg $20.99 **910.4**
  1. Exploration 2. Explorers
  ISBN 0-679-81460-4; 0-679-91460-9 (lib bdg)
  LC 91 8428
This "is the story of travel and discovery, from the journeys of the Egyptians and Vikings, to the North and South Poles, underwater, and space." Voice Youth Advocates
"The illustrations are accurate and fascinating and include the best examples from each period discussed." Sci Books Films

Pickford, Nigel
The atlas of shipwrecks & treasure; the history, location, and treasures of ships lost at sea. Dorling Kindersley 1994 200p il maps $29.95 (7 and up) **910.4**
  1. Buried treasure 2. Shipwrecks
  ISBN 1-56458-599-9
  LC 93-48856
The author "chronicles shipwrecks from the Bronze Age to the Vikings, then moves on to Chinese junks, the Levantine trade, the Portuguese and Spanish plate fleets, pirates, gold rush paddle-steamers, and, finally, to the *Titanic* and other modern ships. To be included, wrecks must have been laden with treasure. Colorful maps detail the historical trade routes and pinpoint the wrecks." Libr J
"Recommended as a seaworthy addition to public, academic, and elementary and secondary school libraries for both reference and browsing." Booklist

Platt, Richard, 1953-
Pirate; photographed by Tina Chambers. Knopf 1994 63p il maps (Eyewitness books) $19; lib bdg $20.99 **910.4**
  1. Pirates
  ISBN 0-679-87255-8; 0-679-97255-2 (lib bdg)
  LC 94-37732

Platt, Richard, 1953-—*Continued*
"A Dorling Kindersley book"
"Platt looks at the subject of piracy from the time of
ancient Greece to the 19th century. . . . Readers are introduced to privateers, buccaneers, and corsairs, and told
how they differ. Illustrations of various types of pirate
ships, and the merchant vessels that were most often
their targets, are particularly effective." SLJ

Shipwreck; written by Richard Platt;
photographed by Alex Wilson and Tina Chambers.
Knopf 1997 59p il (Eyewitness books) $19; lib
bdg $20.99   **910.4**
1. Shipwrecks
ISBN 0-679-88562-5; 0-679-98562-X (lib bdg)
                                          LC 97-9278
"A Dorling Kindersley book"
"In 26 sections Platt covers ancient wrecks, British
wrecks, the *Titanic*, shipwreck survivors, guiding lights,
navigation, wreck recovery, and reconstruction and preservation. This book would be a nice addition to any lesson plan on exploring ships and weather, and it makes
for just informative pleasure reading." Book Rep

Sherrow, Victoria
The Titanic. Lucent Bks. 1999 112p il (World
history series) lib bdg $22.45 (7 and up)   **910.4**
1. Titanic (Steamship) 2. Shipwrecks
ISBN 1-56006-472-2   LC 98-43466
Describes the planning and building of the Titanic, its
departure and passengers, its fatal collision with an iceberg and sinking, and the fascination with this disaster
held by so many people
Includes bibliographical references

911 Historical geography

Atlas of American history. 2nd rev ed. Scribner
1985 c1984 306p maps lib bdg $85   **911**
1. United States—Historical geography—Maps
ISBN 0-684-18411-7   LC 84-675413
First published 1943 under the editorship of James
Truslow Adams
"Development of the United States illustrated by
maps. Provides coverage through the Vietnam War. In-
cludes some demographic maps. Indexed." N Y Public
Libr. Book of How & Where to Look It Up

Ferrell, Robert H.
Atlas of American history; [by] Robert H.
Ferrell, Richard Natkiel. rev and updated. Facts on
File 1995 192p il maps $35; pa $19.95   **911**
1. United States—Historical geography—Maps
ISBN 0-8160-3441-9; 0-8160-3702-7 (pa)
                                          LC 95-24122
First published 1987
This work incorporates 250 maps and charts along
with archival photographs, drawings and paintings to
cover American history from Columbus' voyages up to
the conflicts of 1995. Geography, politics, economics and
social conditions are surveyed but the emphasis is primarily on warfare, both foreign and domestic

Historical atlas of the United States. rev ed.
National Geographic Soc. 1993 289p il maps
$100   **911**
1. United States—Historical geography—Maps
ISBN 0-87044-970-2   LC 93-32201
First published 1988
This oversize volume contains maps, timelines, historical charts, photographs and other illustrations. It is divided into six thematic sections covering the land, people,
boundaries, economy, networks of transportation, and
communities, alternating with five chronological chapters
that highlight changes from 1400 to the 1990s

The **Times** atlas of world history; edited by
Geoffrey Barraclough. 4th ed, edited by
Geoffrey Parker. Hammond 1993 360p il maps
$95   **911**
1. Historical atlases
ISBN 0-7230-0534-6   LC 93-23944
First published 1978
"Plates, with accompanying text by contributing scholars, are grouped in seven main sections: (1) The world
of early man; (2) The first civilizations; (3) The classical
civilizations of Eurasia; (4) The world of divided regions; (5) The world of the emerging West; (6) The age
of European dominance; (7) The age of global
civilisation." Guide to Ref Books. 11th edition

912 Atlases. Maps

Atlas of the world. Oxford Univ. Press il maps
$75   **912**
1. Atlases

First published 1992. (6th edition 1998) Frequently revised
"The quality and color of the maps and the 75,000 entry index make this atlas a good choice for schools. An
introduction to world geography with both narrative and
maps covers the earth, people, production and quality of
life. There is a section of 66 city maps with its own index, followed by the world maps arranged by continent
and country." Safford. Guide to Ref Materials for Sch
Libr Media Cent. 5th edition [entry for 5th edition]

DK student atlas. DK Pub. 1998 160p il maps
$19.95   **912**
1. Atlases
ISBN 0-7894-2399-5
This atlas features "multi-colored maps, scenic photos,
and topographical keys. . . . For school reports, the elevation maps, climate details, industry, farming, and land
use charts, and landscape discussions will be invaluable.
. . . An exciting, non-intimidating, yet factual resource
for teaching basic world geography and map/chart reading skills." Sci Books Films

Europe on file; Ireland & United Kingdom;
France, Spain & Portugal; Germany, Austria &
Switzerland; Italy & Greece; Scandinavia. Facts
on File 1997 2v loose-leaf set $185   **912**
1. Europe—Maps
ISBN 0-8160-3508-3

Europe on file—*Continued*
This two volume looseleaf compilation of maps, graphs and charts "is divided into 11 sections: one for each of 9 European regions . . . one for the 6 microstates (e.g., Liechtenstein, Malta, Vatican City), and one for specialized regional maps of Europe and the former Soviet Union that cover topics such as languages, deforestation, education expenditures, religions, ethnic minorities, rainfall, and energy consumption. . . . Readers will find this an accessible resource useful for locating facts quickly." SLJ
For a fuller review see: Booklist, Jan. 15, 1998

Explorer atlas of the world. Hammond 120p il maps pa $11.95 **912**
1. Atlases

First published 1993. (1999 edition) Periodically revised
This atlas features computer-generated area maps, detailed political world maps and a color section on flags of the world. An index to over 12,000 places and geographic features is included

Geography on file. Facts on File various paging il maps loose-leaf $165 **912**
1. Atlases 2. Geography

Annual updates available for $45
First published 1991. Periodically revised
A collection of more than 250 maps, graphs, and statistical charts on both human and physical geography. Topics covered include demographic shifts, economic growth, language distribution, and political institutions

Goode's world atlas; editor, Edward B. Espenshade, Jr. Rand McNally il maps $34.95 **912**
1. Atlases

First published 1922 with title: Goode's school atlas. (19th edition 1996) Periodically revised
"Contains thematic maps and tables showing distribution of population, minerals, manufacturing, and other subjects. Also included are metropolitan-area maps, physical-political maps of regions, geographic tables, and ocean-floor maps showing earth movement. Pronouncing index included." N Y Public Libr. Book of How & Where to Look It Up

Maps on file. Facts on File 2v maps loose-leaf $195 **912**
1. Atlases

Annual updates available for $45
First published 1981. Periodically revised
Maps copyrighted by Martin Greenwald Associates
A collection of approximately 500 black-and-white maps covering countries, every U.S. state, Canadian provinces, oceans, and continents

Millennium world atlas. DK Pub. 1999 xxxvi, 492p il maps $87.45 **912**
1. Atlases
ISBN 0-7894-4604-9
Accompanied by CD-ROM featuring satellite images of earth

This atlas contains 96 large-scale regional maps, 320 high-resolution satellite images, 180 at-a-glance maps, 200 terrain models, and more than 750 photographs. Accompanying texts describe the landscape, the political and cultural make-up of each region and the distribution of resources and economic activity. Includes glossary and 80,000 item Index-gazetteer

National Geographic atlas of the world. National Geographic Soc. il maps $100 **912**
1. Atlases

First published 1963. (7th edition, 1999) Periodically revised
"Well balanced in coverage between the U.S. and the rest of the world, with maps by area rather than by state or country. While some maps have a crowded appearance, they are legible and generally up-to-date. Includes a fold-out map of the world using the recently adopted Robinson projection, and a number of spacecraft images of the earth and the planets. Indexes more than 150,000 place names." Guide to Ref Books. 11th edition [entry for 6th edition]

917.3 Geography of and travel in the United States

The **Cambridge** gazetteer of the United States and Canada; a dictionary of places; edited by Archie Hobson. Cambridge Univ. Press 1995 743p maps $54.95 **917.3**
1. United States—Gazetteers 2. Canada—Gazetteers
ISBN 0-521-41579-9 LC 95-8898
"This is a comprehensive guide to both geographic glossary terms and place names which are interfiled in alphabetical order. Included are such expected entries as states, provinces, territories, capitals, and municipalities. . . . Also included are places in the news, of historical or cultural interest, likely travel destinations, generic or metaphorical places, neighborhoods, extinct cities and towns, regional names, military installations, industrial locations, national forests, and legendary places." Safford. Guide to Ref Materials for Sch Libr Media Cent. 5th edition

Our national parks; America's spectacular wilderness heritage. Reader's Digest Assn. il maps $30 **917.3**
1. National parks and reserves—United States

First published 1985. (1997 edition) Periodically revised
This volume covers the histories, geological features, and wildlife of America's 52 national parks. Illustrated with over 350 color photographs, illustrations, and paintings

Spangenburg, Ray, 1939-
The African-American experience; by Ray Spangenburg and Diane K. Moser. Facts on File 1996 142p il maps (American historic places) $19.95 (7 and up) **917.3**
1. Historic sites 2. African Americans—History
ISBN 0-8160-3400-1 LC 96-27992

Spangenburg, Ray, 1939-—*Continued*
Explores locations that have had significant impact on
the African-American experience including the homes of
Harriet Tubman, Maggie Lena Walker, Mary McCloud
Bethune, and Frederick Douglass; Boston's African
Meeting House; the Nicodemus Historic District in Kan-
sas, Little Rock High School, and the Martin Luther
King historic district in Atlanta
Includes bibliographical references

The American Indian experience; [by] Ray
Spangenburg and Diane K. Moser. Facts on File
1997 128p il maps (American historic places)
$19.95 (7 and up)   **917.3**
1. Historic sites 2. Indians of North America 3. Unit-
ed States—Description
ISBN 0-8160-3403-6   LC 97-8387
Describes historic places in the United States associat-
ed with Native American history and culture, including
Little Big Horn Battlefield, Alcatraz Island, and Nez
Perce National Historic Park
Includes bibliographical references

Early settlements; [by]Ray Spangenburg and
Diane K. Moser. Facts on File 1998 143p
(American historic places) $19.95 (7 and up)
                                                     917.3
1. Historic sites 2. United States—Local history
3. United States—Description
ISBN 0-8160-3405-2   LC 97-27453
This is a guide to the homes and villages of Ameri-
ca's earliest inhabitants. Aztec Ruin National Monument,
St. Augustine and Castillo de San Marcos, Colonial
Pemaquid, San Antonio Missions National Historic Park,
Grand Portage National Monument, Fort Clatsop, Fort
Ross State Historic Park, Fort Larned, Bodie State His-
toric Park, and Fruita Orchards are described
Includes bibliographical references

Literature and the arts; [by] Ray Spangenburg
and Diane K. Moser. Facts on File 1997 163p il
maps (American historic places) $19.95 (7 and up)
                                                     917.3
1. Historic sites 2. Literary landmarks—United States
3. United States—Description
ISBN 0-8160-3401-X   LC 96-25939
A guidebook to the homes of writers and artists Loui-
sa May Alcott, Charles Wilson Peale, Winslow Homer,
Mark Twain, WIlla Cather, Augustus St. Gaudes, Charles
M. Russell, Tom Wolfe, Frank Lloyd Wright, Edith
Wharton, and William Faulkner
Includes bibliographical references

Political and social movements; [by] Ray
Spangenburg and Diane K. Moser. Facts on File
1998 130p il maps (American historic places)
$19.95 (7 and up)   **917.3**
1. Historic sites 2. United States—Politics and gov-
ernment
ISBN 0-8160-3404-4   LC 97-28096
This guide "focuses on 10 sites that are associated
with American political and social movements. Valley
Forge, Hancock Shaker Village, The Women's Rights
National Historic Park, The Jane Addams Hull-House
Museum, Wounded Knee, and the Ellis Island Immigra-

tion Center are a sampling of the places included. . . .
For each site, the authors discuss the associated movement and give a brief account of how the site was preserved, a list for further reading, and related sites." SLJ
Includes bibliographical references

Science and invention; [by] Ray Spangenburg
and Diane K. Moser. Facts on File 1997 158p il
maps (American historic places) $19.95 (7 and up)
                                                     917.3
1. Historic sites 2. Inventions—History 3. Science—
History 4. United States—Description
ISBN 0-8160-3402-8   LC 97-9873
This describes historic places in the United States associated with science and invention such as the Joseph
Priestley House, McDowell House and Apothecary shop,
Thomas Edison's Menlo Park Laboratory, George Washington Carver National Monument, Wright Brothers Na-
tional Memorial, Rachel Carson Homestead, Hopewell
Furnace, and the US Space and Rocket Center
"In addition to curricular value as a jumping-off place
for research, this . . . will appeal to biography readers
and parents (and teens) who are planning a vacation car
trip." Booklist
Includes bibliographical references

920   Biography

Books of biography are arranged as follows: 1. Biographical
collections (920) 2. Biographies of individuals alphabetically by
name of biographee (92)

Aaseng, Nathan, 1953-
Black inventors. Facts on File 1997 128p il
(American profiles) $19.95 (7 and up)   **920**
1. African American inventors 2. Inventions
ISBN 0-8160-3407-9   LC 96-40486
"Aaseng tells of 10 black inventors, the problems they
overcame, and the often slow, frustrating road to ingenious achievement. A bibliography, a chronology, and
photographs supplement each chapter as do patent drawings where appropriate." Booklist

Twentieth-century inventors. Facts on File 1991
132p il (American profiles) $19.95 (7 and up)
                                                      920
1. Inventors
ISBN 0-8160-2485-5   LC 90-46547
Provides accounts of ten significant twentieth-century
inventions and the people behind them, including the
Wright brothers and their airplane, Robert Goddard and
his rocket, and Gordon Gould and his laser
"The 10-to-12 page chapter entries are informative,
well-balanced, and clearly written." SLJ
Includes bibliographical references

Altman, Linda Jacobs, 1943-
Women inventors. Facts on File 1997 118p
(American profiles) $19.95 (7 and up)   **920**
1. Women inventors
ISBN 0-8160-3385-4   LC 96-20460

Altman, Linda Jacobs, 1943——*Continued*

This profiles ten women who invented such things as "vacuum canning, ore separation, brown paper bags, maritime signal flares, baby clothes, the eyedropper, hair straightener, brassier, Nysating, Barbie, mastectomy prosthesis, Liquid Paper, nonreflecting glass, and Kevlar." Publisher's note

Includes bibliographical references

Altman, Susan

Extraordinary black Americans: from colonial to contemporary times. Children's Press 1988 240p il lib bdg $37; pa $16.95   **920**

1. African Americans—Biography

ISBN 0-516-00581-2; 0-516-40581-0 (pa)

LC 88-11977

Among those profiled in this collection of 85 short biographies are Harriet Tubman, George Washington Carver, Jesse Jackson and Louis Armstrong

"The scope is wide ranging: Altman's subjects are men and women recognized for their achievements in exploration, invention, literature, theater, the military, education, politics, science, medicine, music, and sports. . . . A priority choice for black-studies collections." Booklist

Includes bibliographical references

American Indian biographies; edited by Harvey Markowitz; project editor, McCrea Adams. Salem Press 1999 436p il (Magill's choice) $55 **920**

1. Indians of North America—Biography

ISBN 0-89356-972-0   LC 98-41126

Chiefly articles published 1987-1995 in the publisher's American Indians; Great lives from history, American series; and Great lives from history, American women series, with 22 new articles written for this volume

"Some 329 individuals are given brief personal sketches, a significant number of which are also accompanied by illustrations or photographs of the subject. The entries include information on tribal affiliation, historical significance, and any other names associated with the individual, and those on better-known personalities also provide a short bibliography for further reading." Libr J

Archer, Jules

They had a dream; the civil rights struggle from Frederick Douglass to Marcus Garvey to Martin Luther King and Malcolm X. Viking 1993 258p il (Epoch biographies) hardcover o.p. paperback available $5.99   **920**

1. African Americans—Biography 2. African Americans—Civil rights

ISBN 0-14-034954-5 (pa)   LC 92-40071

Traces the progression of the civil rights movement and its effect on history through biographical sketches of four prominent and influential African Americans: Frederick Douglass, Marcus Garvey, Martin Luther King, Jr., and Malcolm X

"This discussion of the contributions of four pivotal civil rights activists is balanced and substantive." Publ Wkly

Includes bibliographical references

To save the earth; the American environmental movement. Viking 1998 198p il $17.99 (7 and up) **920**

1. Environmentalists

ISBN 0-670-87121-4   LC 97-35373

Presents a brief history of the environmental movement and accounts of the work of four environmental activists: John Muir, Rachel Carson, David McTaggart, and Dave Foreman

"Archer's work will appeal strongly to recreational readers interested in environmental issues and to fans of biography." Booklist

Includes bibliographical references

Armstrong, Carole

Lives and legends of the saints; with paintings from the great art museums of the world. Simon & Schuster 1995 45p il $17   **920**

1. Christian saints

ISBN 0-689-80277-3   LC 94-43009

"The 20 saints and martyrs gathered here are, with few exceptions, either biblical figures central to the Christian story (John the Baptist, Joseph, Peter, Paul, Mary Magdalene) or heroes of the early church. The biographies are brief—two or three paragraphs at most. . . . The emphasis, both in text and in the artistic renderings, is on legend and miracle; the stories are drawn from church tradition and hagiology. The volume concludes with an index of the paintings and a complete calendar of the saints venerated on each day of the year." SLJ

Avery, Susan, 1949-

Extraordinary American Indians; by Susan Avery and Linda Skinner. Children's Press 1992 xx, 252p il lib bdg $37; pa $16.95   **920**

1. Indians of North America—Biography

ISBN 0-516-00583-9; 0-516-40583-7 (pa)

LC 92-11358

This work discusses the lives and accomplishments of outstanding Native Americans from the eighteenth century to the present, including Wilma Mankiller, Billy Mills, Sacagawea, Louis Ballard, and Will Rogers

"More than a recitation of famous chiefs and war leaders from past centuries, [the book] offers students a much-needed, well-rounded look at the diversity of Indian talents and achievements." SLJ

Includes bibliographical references

Biography index; a cumulative index to biographical material in books and magazines. Wilson, H.W. annual subscription $220 **920**

1. Biography—Indexes 2. Biography—Bibliography

ISSN 0006-3053

Also available CD-ROM version

First issued September 1946

Published quarterly, November, February, May, and August, with bound annual and permanent two-year cumulations. Permanent volumes $245 each

"This is a guide to material appearing in the more than 2,800 periodicals indexed in Wilson publications, other biographical periodicals, approximately 2,000 cur-

Biography index—*Continued*

rent books of individual and collective biography and as incidental biographical materials in other books. It covers biographies and autobiographies, fiction, obituaries, collections of letters, diaries, memoirs, juvenile literature and book reviews. It is international in scope and covers all subject areas." Safford. Guide to Ref Materials for Sch Libr Media Cent. 5th edition

Blassingame, Wyatt

The look-it-up book of presidents. Random House il $14.99, pa $8.99   **920**
1. Presidents—United States

First published 1968 and periodically revised to include new Presidents and administrations

"Brief biographies of the presidents are arranged chronologically in this easy-to-read source. Entries are from two to six pages and are accompanied by cleverly selected portraits, photographs, maps, cartoons, and other illustrations. There is an achievement chart also arranged chronologically. Recommended for elementary and middle school collections." Safford. Guide to Ref Materials for Sch Libr media Cent. 5th edition

Bolden, Tonya

And not afraid to dare. Scholastic 1998 216p il $16.95   **920**
1. African American women
ISBN 0-590-48080-4   LC 96-7320

Biographical portraits of ten African-American women including Leontyne Price, Toni Morrison, and Jackie Joyner-Kersee

"The writing is clear and compelling. While these biographical sketches are interesting and provocative enough to attract recreational readers, the primary use for such a title would be research." SLJ

Includes bibliographical references

Breen, Karen, 1943-

Index to collective biographies for young readers. 4th ed. Bowker 1988 xxxiii, 494p $48   **920**
1. Biography—Indexes 2. Biography—Bibliography
ISBN 0-8352-2348-5   LC 88-19410

First edition edited by Judith Silverman published 1970 with title: An index to young readers' collective biographies

This "book indexes approximately 9,773 people representing the contents of 1,129 collective biographies. The fourth edition retains most of the titles indexed in the preceding editions and notes out-of-print titles by an 'o.p.' . . . This index and a sizeable collection of the titles included are essential for all libraries serving children." Peterson. Ref Books for Child

Briggs, Carole S., 1950-

Women in space. rev ed. Lerner Publs. 1999 112p il (A & E biography) $25.26   **920**
1. Women astronauts 2. Astronautics
ISBN 0-8225-4937-9   LC 98-2916

First published 1988

Profiles some of the women, including two Russians, who have had important roles in space exploration and provides a brief history of the U.S. space program

Includes glossary and bibliographical references

Brooks, Philip, 1963-

Extraordinary Jewish Americans. Children's Press 1998 288p il (Extraordinary people) lib bdg $37; pa $16.95   **920**
1. Jews—United States—Biography
ISBN 0-516-20609-5 (lib bdg); 0-516-26350-1 (pa)
     LC 97-37535

Presents short biographies of more than sixty Jewish Americans who have flourished in careers including law, finance, entertainment, writing, politics, and science

Includes bibliographical references

Bruno, Leonard C.

Math and mathematicians; the history of math discoveries around the world; Lawrence W. Baker, editor. U.X.L 1999 2v set $79   **920**
1. Mathematicians 2. Mathematics
ISBN 0-7876-3812-9   LC 99-32424

Compilation of fifty biographies of mathematicians from throughout history and approximately thirty-five articles describing math concepts and principles

"This effective resource is marked by its attention to detail and variety of information. Readers can readily cross-reference concepts, people, and discoveries. Easy to use, this wonderful reference will be appropriate for middle, high school, and public libraries." Voice Youth Advocates

Includes glossary and bibliographical references

Burns, Khephra

Black stars in orbit; NASA's African-American astronauts; [by] Khephra Burns and William Miles. Harcourt Brace & Co. 1995 72p il $18.95; pa $8.95   **920**
1. Astronauts 2. African Americans—Biography 3. African American pilots
ISBN 0-15-200432-7; 0-15-200276-6 (pa)
     LC 93-44624

"Gulliver books"

Based on a 1990 television documentary, this book begins "with a chapter on the African American pilots of World War II, the Tuskegee Airmen, and [continues] with the experience of Ed Dwight, a Korean War era pilot who was recommended for the Astronaut Training Program by President Kennedy. . . . The contributions of African American scientists and physicians who worked behind the scenes are documented, as is NASA's campaign, with the advent of the Space Shuttle Program, to recruit minority trainees. The authors use quotations from the television documentary to tell the compelling and at times horrifying story in a full and lively manner." SLJ

Byrnes, Patricia, 1942-

Environmental pioneers. Oliver Press (Minneapolis) 1998 160p il (Profiles) lib bdg $16.95 (7 and up)   **920**
1. Environmentalists
ISBN 1-88150-845-5   LC 97-30233

Byrnes, Patricia, 1942-—*Continued*
Profiles people who have been influential in the environmental movement: John Muir, Jay Norwood "Ding" Darling, Rosalie Edge, Aldo Leopold, Olaus and Margaret Murie, Rachel Carson, David Brower, and Gaylord Nelson
"Unlike most authors of books on this topic for a young audience, Byrnes is an experienced environmental writer, and takes an affectionate tone in describing her subjects." SLJ
Includes bibliographical references

Calvert, Patricia, 1931-
Great lives: the American frontier. Atheneum Bks. for Young Readers 1997 388p il $25   **920**
1. West (U.S.)—Biography 2. Frontier and pioneer life—West (U.S.)
ISBN 0-689-80640-X   LC 96-48519
A collective biography of great figures in the history of the American frontier
"Calvert's writing style is consistently readable and succinct. . . . In addition, the author maintains a balanced treatment of ethnic roles within their proper historical context. The brutality of both white men and Indians during this era is honestly depicted. This fascinating array of individuals will inspire and educate readers." SLJ
Includes bibliographical references

Camp, Carole Ann
American astronomers; searchers and wonderers. Enslow Pubs. 1996 104p il (Collective biographies) lib bdg $19.95   **920**
1. Astronomers
ISBN 0-89490-631-3   LC 95-14472
This "profiles Maria Mitchell, Percival Lowell, Williamina Fleming, Annie Jump Cannon, George Ellery Hale, Harlow Shapley, Edwin Hubble, Cecilia Payne-Gaposchkin, and Carl Sagan." Booklist
"A good research source for middle school students. . . . The writing style is clear and concise in highlighting the person's life and accomplishments." BAYA Book Rev
Includes bibliographical references

Celebrating women in mathematics and science; edited by Miriam P. Cooney. National Council of Teachers of Mathematics 1996 223p il pa $22.50   **920**
1. Women mathematicians 2. Women scientists
ISBN 0-87353-425-5   LC 96-14119
"A collective biography detailing the struggles and triumphs of women in the fields of mathematics and sciences from ancient times to the present. . . . While most of the women are mathematicians, health-care professionals, biologists, and naturalists are also represented. . . . *Celebrating Women* is a useful chronological history, ideal for short reports." SLJ
Includes bibliographical references

Chiu, Christina
Lives of notable Asian Americans: literature and education. Chelsea House 1996 125p il (Asian American experience) $19.95 (7 and up)   **920**
1. Asian Americans—Biography 2. American literature—Asian American authors
ISBN 0-7910-2182-3   LC 94-45842
Discusses the lives of some Asian Americans primarily known for their writing, including Amy Tan, David Henry Hwang, Bharati Mukherjee, Jessica Hagedorn, and Laurence Yep
Includes bibliographical references

DeAngelis, Gina
Science & medicine; introduction by Roslyn Rosen. Chelsea House 1999 64p il (Female firsts in their fields) lib bdg $16.95   **920**
1. Women scientists 2. Women in medicine
ISBN 0-7910-5143-9   LC 98-31676
Chronicles the lives and accomplishments of notable women working in the fields of medicine and science in general, including Marie Curie, Rachel Carson, Margaret Mead, Elizabeth Blackwell, Clara Barton, and Antonia Novello are profiled
Includes bibliographical references

Distinguished African American scientists of the 20th century; [by] James H. Kessler [et al.]; with Sigrid Berge, portrait artist, and Alyce Neukirk, computer graphics artist. Oryx Press 1996 382p il $59.95 (7 and up)   **920**
1. Scientists 2. African Americans—Biography
ISBN 0-89774-955-3   LC 95-43880
"One hundred famous and not-so-famous African American scientists (both living and dead) are covered in this biographical reference. . . . Men and women accomplished in anthropology, biology, chemistry, engineering, geology, mathematics, medicine, and physics are included." Libr J

Drimmer, Frederick
Incredible people; five stories of extraordinary lives. Atheneum Bks. for Young Readers 1997 182p il $16   **920**
1. Curiosities and wonders
ISBN 0-689-31921-5   LC 96-9082
Presents the stories of six people whose lives were shaped by their physical and cultural differences from the rest of Western society: Jack Erlich, the Hilton Siamese twins, Ota Benga, Ishi, and the "Wild Boy" of France
"Drimmer is sympathetic but not condescending as he clearly explains each of his subject's differences." SLJ
Includes bibliographical references

Dubovoy, Sina
Civil rights leaders. Facts on File 1997 136p il (American profiles) $19.95 (7 and up)   **920**
1. African Americans—Civil rights
ISBN 0-8160-3363-3   LC 96-2920
Profiles the lives and achievements of nine civil rights leaders, including Ida B. Wells, A. Philip Randolph, Thurgood Marshall, Rosa Parks, and Fannie Lou Hamer
Includes bibliographical references

Faber, Doris, 1924-
Great lives: American literature; [by] Doris
Faber and Harold Faber. Atheneum Bks. for
Young Readers 1995 313p il $24   **920**
1. Authors, American
ISBN 0-684-19448-1   LC 94-10866
"The lives of thirty American literary figures whose
major work was completed by 1960 are covered in this
collection. Novelists, poets and playwrights are included.
. . . The 1960 parameter for inclusion limits the cover-
age of many women and minority writers but as a collec-
tive biography of major American literary figures, this
does a more than adequate job of gathering the type of
information needed by middle and junior high students."
Voice Youth Advocates
Includes bibliographical references

Freedman, Russell
Indian chiefs. Holiday House 1987 151p il map
lib bdg $19.95; pa $9.95   **920**
1. Indians of North America—Biography
ISBN 0-8234-0625-3 (lib bdg); 0-8234-0971-6 (pa)
    LC 86-46198
This "book chronicles the lives of six renowned Indian
chiefs, each of whom served as a leader during a critical
period in his tribe's history. . . . The text relates information about the lives of each chief and aspects of Indi-
an/white relationships that illuminate his actions. Interesting vignettes and quotations are well integrated into the
narrative as are dramatic accounts of battles. While the
tone of the text is nonjudgmental, an underlying sympathy for the Indians' situation is apparent." Horn Book
Includes bibliographical references

Gaines, Ann
Entertainment & performing arts; introduction
by Roslyn Rosen. Chelsea House 1998 64p il
(Female firsts in their fields) $16.95   **920**
1. Actors 2. Women—Biography
ISBN 0-7910-5145-5   LC 98-47614
Chronicles the lives of Mary Pickford, Lucille Ball,
Katharine Hepburn, Marlee Matlin, Rita Moreno, and
Jodie Foster
Includes bibliographical references

Sports & athletics; [by] Ann Graham Gaines;
introduction by Roslyn Rosen. Chelsea House
1999 64p il (Female firsts in their fields) $16.95
    920
1. Women athletes
ISBN 0-7910-5144-7   LC 98-46775
Discusses the lives and athletic accomplishments of
six women: Althea Gibson, Wilma Rudolph, Janet
Guthrie, Debi Thomas, Sheryl Swoopes, and Pat Head
Summitt
Includes bibliographical references

Glass, Andrew
Bad guys; true stories of legendary gunslingers,
sidewinders, fourflushers, drygulchers,
bushwhackers, freebooters, and downright bad
guys and gals of the Wild West. Doubleday Bks.
for Young Readers 1998 unp il $16.95   **920**
1. Criminals 2. West (U.S.)—History
ISBN 0-385-32310-7   LC 97-31408

This collective biography includes the exploits of
"Wild Bill Hickok, Calamity Jane, Doc Holliday, Jesse
James, Belle Starr, Billy the Kid, Black Bart, and Joa-
quin Murietta." SLJ
"Glass's yarn-spinning prowess is at its peak in these
eight accounts of the VIPs of the lawless West." Bull
Cent Child Books

Glubok, Shirley, 1933-
Great lives: painting. Scribner 1994 246p il
$24.95   **920**
1. Painters—Biography
ISBN 0-684-19052-4   LC 93-8319
"Glubok provides brief introductions to the lives and
works of 23 European and American painters. Students
will have encountered most of the artists during the
course of social-studies research projects . . . but Glubok
also includes a few surprises—among them, Vermeer,
Chagall, Titian, and Velázquez." Booklist
Includes bibliographical references

Graham, Kevin, 1959-
Contemporary environmentalists. Facts on File
1996 178p il (Global profiles) $19.95 (7 and up)
    920
1. Environmentalists 2. Environmental protection
ISBN 0-8160-3222-X   LC 95-35266
Profiles ten environmentalists including Jacques
Cousteau, David Ross Brower, Vo Quy, Thomas
Odhiambo, Gro Harlem Brundtland, Anita Roddick,
Randy Hayes, Joseph Krecek, Michael Bloomfield and
Neca Marcovaldi
Includes bibliographical references

Graham, Paula W.
Speaking of journals; children's book writers
talk about their diaries, notebooks and
sketchbooks. Boyds Mills Press 1999 226p il pa
$14.95   **920**
1. Authors, American
ISBN 1-56397-741-9   LC 98-88261
"This collection of essays by and interviews with writers for children and young adults is a rich source of material for teachers who want to expose their students to
a variety of diary, journal, and notebook-keeping practices." SLJ

Greenberg, Jan, 1942-
The American eye; eleven artists of the
twentieth century; [by] Jan Greenberg and Sandra
Jordan. Delacorte Press 1995 120p il $22.50   **920**
1. Artists, American
ISBN 0-385-32173-2   LC 94-30625
"This book examines American impulses in twentieth-
century art by giving a chapter to each of eleven
American artists. Figures included range from the ubiqui-
tous (Georgia O'Keeffe, Jackson Pollock, Edward Hopper) to the less popularized (Arthur Dove, Eva Hesse,
Romare Bearden), and their works (four or five pictured
per artist) include a variety of painting and sculpture
styles with a broad range of influences (kids will particu-

Greenberg, Jan, 1942—_Continued_
larly enjoy the pop-culture homages of Stuart Davis and
Andy Warhol)." Bull Cent Child Books
"The writing is insightful and the prose accessible and
authoritative without being mired in pedantic scholarship." SLJ
Includes bibliographical references

Growing up black; from slave days to the present:
25 African-Americans reveal the trials and
triumphs of their childhoods; edited by Jay
David. [rev ed] Avon Bks. 1992 276p pa $12
                                                        920
1. African Americans—Biography
ISBN 0-380-76632-9   LC 92-135054
First published 1968 by Morrow
"This compelling collection of autobiographical accounts of 25 African Americans will introduce readers to
some of the best black writers—from Frederick Douglass
to Audre Lorde, Claude Brown, John Wideman, and
Lorene Cary—and will help students write with candor
and control about their own memories." Rochman.
Against borders

Gulotta, Charles
Extraordinary women in politics. Children's
Press 1998 288p il (Extraordinary people) lib bdg
$37; pa $16.95   **920**
1. Women in politics
ISBN 0 516 20610 9; 0-516-26399-4 (pa)
                                      LC 97-38230
This book "profiles 55 women who have been active
in politics or influential in the political climate of their
times. Spanning history from 69 B.C.E. to the present,
the chronological coverage is international and
multicultural, though women from the U.S. make up
more than half of the entries." SLJ
"A good introduction to a topic seldom addressed in
books for young teens." Booklist
Includes bibliographical references

Hacker, Carlotta
Great African Americans in history. Crabtree
1997 64p il (Outstanding African Americans) lib
bdg $21.28; pa $8.95   **920**
1. African Americans—Biography
ISBN 0-86505-805-9 (lib bdg); 0-86505-819-9 (pa)
                                      LC 96-38690
Profiles thirteen African Americans who have excelled
in various fields, including medicine, science, civil rights,
and exploration. Harriet Tubman, W.E.B. Du Bois, Sojourner Truth, and Matthew Henson are among those
profiled

Nobel Prize winners. Crabtree 1998 48p il maps
(Women in profile) $15.96; pa $8.06   **920**
1. Nobel Prizes 2. Women—Biography
ISBN 0-7787-0007-0; 0-7787-0029-1 (pa)
                                      LC 97-53222
Chronicles the lives and achievements of women who
have received Nobel Prizes in a variety of fields, includ-
ing Aung San Suu Kyi, Barbara McClintock, and Nadine
Gordimer
Includes glossary and bibliographical references

Hamanaka, Sheila
In search of the spirit; the Living National
Treasures of Japan; by Sheila Hamanaka and
Ayano Ohmi; illustrations by Sheila Hamanaka;
calligraphy by Ayano Ohmi. Morrow Junior Bks.
1999 48p il $16; lib bdg $15.93   **920**
1. Japan—Biography
ISBN 0-688-14607-4; 0-688-14608-2 (lib bdg)
                                      LC 98-23051
This book "introduces six individuals (including a
bamboo weaver, a puppet master, and a sword maker)
honored in Japan for having 'devoted their lives to traditional crafts and performing arts'." Horn Book Guide
"Bold, red calligraphy and a large, full-color photo of
the craft or performer at work open several pages of lyrical, informative text about each artist." SLJ

Hansen, Joyce
Women of hope; African Americans who made
a difference; foreword by Moe Foner. Scholastic
1998 31p il $22.99   **920**
1. African American women
ISBN 0-590-93973-4   LC 96-32117
Features photographs and biographies of thirteen
African-American women, including Maya Angelou,
Ruby Dee, and Alice Walker
"The book developed from a series of posters issued
by the Bread and Roses Cultural Project of the National
Health and Human Service Employees Union. . . .
Hansen has added a clear, readable, and informative sin-
gle-page commentary for each of the striking black-and-
white portraits." SLJ
Includes bibliographical references

Haskins, James, 1941-
African American entrepreneurs. Wiley 1998
184p il (Black stars) $19.95   **920**
1. African American business people 2. African
Americans—Biography
ISBN 0-471-14576-9   LC 97-37389
Profiles 31 African American entrepreneurs, from the
early years, through the Civil War and Reconstruction, to
modern times
The author "has chosen his subjects well. . . .
Haskins has done a good job of individualizing his sub-
jects and catching a sense of the enormous obstacles they
had to overcome to succeed." Booklist
Includes bibliographical references

African American military heroes; [by] Jim
Haskins. Wiley 1998 182p il (Black stars) $19.95
                                                        920
1. African American soldiers 2. United States—
Armed forces 3. United States—Military history
ISBN 0-471-14577-7   LC 98-14312
This "volume highlights the lives and contributions of
30 individuals who served in the military from the Revolutionary War to the present day. Well-known figures
such as Private Peter Salem, Scout Harriet Tubman,
Lieutenant Henry O. Flipper, and General Colin Powell
are here as well as others who deserve recognition." SLJ
"The broad coverage makes this an unusual resource
for teachers and researchers; there's enough information
for middle-graders, and older students can use it as a
jumping-off point for deeper studies." Booklist
Includes bibliographical references

Haskins, James, 1941-—*Continued*

Against all opposition; black explorers in America; [by] Jim Haskins. Walker & Co. 1992 86p il $13.95; lib bdg $14.85   **920**
1. African Americans—Biography 2. Explorers 3. America—Exploration
ISBN 0-8027-8137-3; 0-8027-8138-1 (lib bdg)
LC 91-30203
Surveys the lives and adventures of black explorers who helped discover new worlds
This is "a readable, informative collective biography. . . . [The author offers] crisp, flowing prose that incorporates telling details and cogent quotations, bringing his subjects to life and giving their toils meaning and relevance." SLJ
Includes bibliographical references

One more river to cross; the stories of twelve black Americans; by Jim Haskins. Scholastic 1992 215p il $13.95; pa $4.50   **920**
1. African Americans—Biography
ISBN 0-590-42896-9; 0-590-42897-7 (pa)
LC 91-8817
This book presents biographical sketches of twelve African Americans who courageously fought against racism to become leaders in their fields, including Marian Anderson, Ralph Bunche, Fannie Lou Hamer, and Malcolm X
"Through clear and dramatic writing, Haskins helps readers to understand the impact of institutional racism. . . . A valuable compilation for reading aloud, for independent recreational reading, and for reports." SLJ
Includes bibliographical references

Haven, Kendall F.
100 most popular scientists for young adults; biographical sketches and professional paths; by Kendall Haven and Donna Clark. Libraries Unlimited 1999 526p il (Profiles and pathways series) $56 (7 and up)   **920**
1. Scientists
ISBN 1-56308-674-3   LC 99-13755
"Well-known individuals such as Jacques Cousteau, Sally Ride, and Carl Sagan are assembled here along with unheralded newcomers to the field. One third of the entries are about women and many ethnic groups are represented. . . . A bibliography concludes each entry. Valuable appendixes include an extensive list of Web sites and lists of scientists by their field of specialization. The clear type and attractive layout combined with lively writing, good organization, and curriculum-related content will make the book a useful reference source." SLJ

Helmer, Diana Star, 1962-
Women suffragists. Facts on File 1998 146p il (American profiles) $19.95 (7 and up)   **920**
1. Suffragists 2. Women—Suffrage
ISBN 0-8160-3579-2   LC 97-32374
A collective biography of important American women who fought for the female right to vote, including Elizabeth Cady Stanton, Susan B. Anthony, and Sojourner Truth
"This book will be mostly used for reports, but the narrative is interesting enough for general reading." SLJ
Includes bibliographical references

Henderson, Harry, 1951-
Modern mathematicians. Facts on File 1996 139p il (Global profiles) $19.95 (7 and up)   **920**
1. Mathematicians
ISBN 0-8160-3235-1   LC 95-18363
This book "includes thirteen brief biographies of men and women who, through achievements in the field of mathematics, advanced modern science. . . . The biographies are arranged chronologically. . . . The coverage of women scientists and the demonstrations of how discoveries in the fields of logic, algebra, and chaos have led to a greater understanding in other scientific fields make this book a valuable resource." Voice Youth Advocates
Includes bibliographical references

Herstory: women who changed the world; edited by Ruth Ashby and Dobrorah Gore Ohrn; introduction by Gloria Steinem. Viking 1995 304p il $22.95 (7 and up)   **920**
1. Women—Biography
ISBN 0-670-85434-4   LC 94-61492
"A Byron Preiss book"
"Here are 120 biographical sketches of women from around the world, from ancient times to the present, ranging from Queen Hatshepsut to Rigoberta Menchú. Helpful introductory material, bibliography and indexes. A great book for browsing." N Y Times Book Rev

Jeffrey, Laura S.
Great American businesswomen. Enslow Pubs. 1996 112p il (Collective biographies) lib bdg $19.95   **920**
1. Businesswomen 2. Women executives
ISBN 0-89490-706-9   LC 96-1009
This "profiles of 10 20th century American women who have achieved success in the male-dominated world of business. Some are relatively unknown, such as Maggie L. Walker, an African American who was the first female banker, and Ruth Handler, who created the Barbie doll. Others, such as television-personality Oprah Winfrey and cookie-maker Debbie Fields, are well known. The other figures, Olive Ann Beech, Madam C.J. Walker, Katharine Graham, Eileen Ford, Alice Rivlin, and Elaine Garzarelli, excelled in a wide variety of fields. . . . This title would be a good choice for reports or for special units on women's history." SLJ
Includes bibliographical references

Jones, Veda Boyd
Government & politics. Chelsea House 1999 64p il (Female firsts in their fields) lib bdg $16.95   **920**
1. Women in politics 2. Women—Biography
ISBN 0-7910-5140-4   LC 98-45391
Profiles women who have been active in politics and government, including Barbara Jordan, Geraldine Ferraro, Sandra Day O'Connor, and Madeleine Albright
Includes bibliographical references

Kallen, Stuart A., 1955-
Native American chiefs and warriors. Lucent Bks. 1999 112p il maps (History makers) $22.45 (7 and up)   **920**
1. Indians of North America—Biography
ISBN 1-56006-364-5   LC 99-13227

Kallen, Stuart A., 1955——*Continued*
Discusses the lives and achievements of five famous and influential Native American chiefs: King Philip, Chief Pontiac, Geronimo, Crazy Horse, and Wilma Mankiller
Includes bibliographical references

Kane, Joseph Nathan, 1899-
Facts about the presidents; a compilation of biographical and historical information. 6th ed. Wilson, H.W. 1993 433p il $85   **920**
1. Presidents—United States
ISBN 0-8242-0845-5   LC 93-9207
First published 1959
The main part of this work provides an individual chapter on each President, from Washington through Clinton, presenting such information as family, education, election, Vice President, main events and accomplishments of his administration, and First Lady. Part two contains tables and lists presenting comparative data on all the Presidents

Katz, William Loren
Black pioneers; an untold story. Atheneum Bks. for Young Readers 1999 193p il maps $17 (7 and up)   **920**
1. African Americans—History 2. Frontier and pioneer life 3. Abolitionists
ISBN 0-689-81410-0   LC 98-19104
A biographical history of influential African American pioneers and freedom fighters in the Midwest, including Sara Jane Woodson, Peter Clark, and Henry Clay Bruce
"The narration is clear, fluid, and enlivened with quotes from the pioneers themselves." Horn Book Guide
Includes bibliographical references

Proudly red and black; stories of African and Native Americans; [by] William Loren Katz and Paula A. Franklin. Atheneum Pubs. 1993 88p il $15   **920**
1. Blacks—Biography 2. Indians of North America—Biography
ISBN 0-689-31801-4   LC 92-36119
Companion volume to Katz's Black Indians: a hidden heritage
Brief biographies of people of mixed Native American and African ancestry who, despite barriers, made their mark on history, including trader Paul Cuffe, frontiersman Edward Rose, Seminole leader John Horse, and sculptress Edmonia Lewis
"Clearly written, lively." SLJ
Includes bibliographical references

Kennedy, John F. (John Fitzgerald), 1917-1963
Profiles in courage; special foreword by Robert F. Kennedy. Commemorative ed. Perennial Lib. 1988 c1964 282p pa $7 (7 and up)   **920**
1. Politicians—United States 2. Courage
ISBN 0-06-080698-2
Also available G.K. Hall large print edition
First published 1956 by Harper & Brothers

This series of profiles of Americans who took courageous stands at crucial moments in public life includes John Quincy Adams, Daniel Webster, Thomas Hart Benton, Sam Houston, Edmund G. Ross, Lucius Q. C. Lamar, George Norris, Robert A. Taft and others
Includes bibliographical references

Kent, Deborah, 1948-
Extraordinary people with disabilities; by Deborah Kent & Kathryn A. Quinlan. Children's Press 1996 288p il (Extraordinary people) $37; pa $16.95   **920**
1. Handicapped
ISBN 0-516-20021-6; 0-516-26074-X (pa)
          LC 96-11895
Profiles seven dozen people throughout history with various physical or mental disabilities. Additional articles provide historical background on the disability rights movement
"Many of the names are obvious, such as Beethoven, Helen Keller, FDR; others are not usually associated with a disability, such as Tom Cruise (dyslexia). . . . A fine combination of biography and the history of the disability-rights movement." SLJ
Includes bibliographical references

Kozar, Richard
Inventors and their discoveries. Chelsea House 1999 64p il (Costume, tradition, and culture) $16.95   **920**
1. Scientists 2. Inventors
ISBN 0-7910-5163-3   LC 98-33701
Highlights twenty-five notable achievements in science, medicine, and industry and the individuals responsible, including Alexander Graham Bell, Madame Curie, and Samuel F. B. Morse
Includes bibliographical references

Krull, Kathleen, 1952-
Lives of the presidents; fame, shame (and what the neighbors thought); written by Kathleen Krull; illustrated by Kathryn Hewitt. Harcourt Brace & Co. 1998 96p il $20   **920**
1. Presidents—United States
ISBN 0-8172-4049-7   LC 97-33069
Focuses on the lives of presidents as parents, husbands, pet-owners, and neighbors while also including humorous anecdotes about hairstyles, attitudes, diets, fears, and sleep patterns
"Packed with enough detail for brief reports, these articles are also just plain entertaining. . . . Hewitt's spirited watercolor cartoons add to the presentation immensely." SLJ
Includes bibliographical references

Leadership; by the editors of Time-Life Books. Time-Life Bks. 1994 256p il (African Americans: voices of triumph) $29.95   **920**
1. African Americans—Biography
          LC 93-21147
This volume "discusses African-Americans who have excelled in science, business, religion, education, and politics. It is immensely informative, well organized, and clearly written." SLJ
Includes bibliographical references

Lilley, Stephen R., 1950-
Fighters against American slavery. Lucent Bks. 1999 128p (History makers) lib bdg $7.95 (7 and up)   **920**
   1. Abolitionists
   ISBN 1-56006-036-0   LC 98-18281
Highlights the careers of leading abolitionists including Benjamin Lundy, William Lloyd Garrison, Frederick Douglass, Harriet Tubman, Nat Turner, and John Brown
"The black-and-white drawings and reproductions are well chosen and, along with the many maps, greatly enhance the presentation. The suggestions for further reading and the works cited will be helpful for research." SLJ

Lindop, Edmund
George Washington, Thomas Jefferson, Andrew Jackson. 21st Cent. Bks. (NY) 1995 64p il (Presidents who dared) $18.90   **920**
   1. Presidents—United States 2. United States—Politics and government—1783-1865
   ISBN 0-8050-3401-3   LC 95-18345

James K. Polk, Abraham Lincoln, Theodore Roosevelt. 21st Cent. Bks. (NY) 1995 64p il (Presidents who dared) $18.90   **920**
   1. Presidents—United States 2. United States—Politics and government—1815-1861 3. United States—Politics and government—1861-1865 4. United States—Politics and government—1898-1919
   ISBN 0-8050-3402-1   LC 95-18344

Woodrow Wilson, Franklin D. Roosevelt, Harry S. Truman. 21st Cent. Bks. (NY) 1995 64p il (Presidents who dared) $18.90   **920**
   1. Presidents—United States 2. United States—Politics and government—1900-1999 (20th century)
   ISBN 0-8050-3403-X   LC 95-19526
"Within each of these interesting books, three presidents are linked by the circumstances in which he held office. For example, Polk, Lincoln and Theodore Roosevelt held the nation together by acquiring territories and maintaining the state of the union. The rest of each book is divided into three chapters in which a short biographical sketch is given, outlining the presidents' early years and careers leading up to the presidency. History is brought into understandable terms with this introductory source. Color photos; index; suggested readings." Book Rep

Lindop, Laurie
Champions of equality. 21st Cent. Bks. (NY) 1997 125p il (Dynamic modern women) lib bdg $21.40 (7 and up)   **920**
   1. Women—Biography
   ISBN 0-8050-4165-6   LC 96-39557
Biographies of the following women who have made contributions toward furthering equality: Margarethe Cammermeyer, Marian Wright Edelman, Myrlie Evers-Williams, Elizabeth Glaser, Delores Huerta, Patricia Ireland, Maggie Kuhn, Wilma Mankiller, Vilma Martinez, and Eleanor Holmes Norton
"By going beyond the standard biographical information into discussions of politics, history, and social issues, this valuable resource increases students' understanding of these individuals." SLJ
Includes bibliographical references

Political leaders. 21st Cent. Bks. (NY) 1996 128p il (Dynamic modern women) lib bdg $21.40 (7 and up)   **920**
   1. Women in politics
   ISBN 0-8050-4164-8   LC 96-11431
"This collective biography presents 10 women who are or have been prominent in American politics: Elizabeth Dole, Dianne Feinstein, Geraldine Ferraro, Ruth Bader Ginsburg, Barbara Jordan, Jeane Kirkpatrick, Peggy Noonan, Janet Reno, Ann Richards, and Christine Todd Whitman. . . . Though the portraits are admiring, they mention controversies, weaknesses, and defeats. A full-color photo appears at the beginning of each profile. The writing style is fairly lively and clear, and a few humanizing anecdotes are provided." SLJ
Includes bibliographical references

Scientists and doctors. 21st Cent. Bks. (NY) 1997 128p il (Dynamic modern women) lib bdg $21.40 (7 and up)   **920**
   1. Women scientists 2. Women in medicine
   ISBN 0-8050-4166-4   LC 96-41923
Biographies of ten women in the fields of medicine and science including "Biruté Galdikas . . . Mae Jemison . . . Mildred Dresselhaus, Mary-Claire King, Mary Leakey, Rita Levi-Montalcini, Susan Love, Helen Taussig, Chien-Shiung Wu, and Rosalyn Yalow. . . . The subjects are presented in a lively, entertaining manner and are accompanied by a full-page photograph." SLJ
Includes bibliographical references

Lomask, Milton
Great lives: exploration. Scribner 1988 258p il maps lib bdg $22.95   **920**
   1. Explorers
   ISBN 0-684-18511-3   LC 88-15744
The author "focuses upon 25 significant geographical explorers arranged alphabetically from Roald Amundsen to Amerigo Vespucci, covering a time span from the Fourth Century to 1957. . . . Most subjects are well known, although Lomask has also included less-noted individuals such as Francisco de Orellana and Hoei-shin." SLJ
"Writing style varies, but as a supplementary resource for both familiar and less-known subjects, this is a useful compendium." Booklist
Includes bibliographical references

Lucas, Eileen
Contemporary human rights activists. Facts on File 1997 125p il (Global profiles) lib bdg $19.95 (7 and up)   **920**
   1. Human rights
   ISBN 0-8160-3298-X   LC 96-41253
Profiles ten significant figures in the world-wide struggle for human rights, including Mother Teresa, Archbishop Desmond Tutu, Joan Baez, Jimmy Carter, and Fang

Lucas, Eileen—*Continued*

Lizhi

"Middle-and junior-high-school students will find this work highly useful as a jumping-off point for report research." Booklist

Includes bibliographical references

Lutz, Norma Jean

Business & industry. Chelsea House 1999 64p il (Female firsts in their fields) lib bdg $16.95

920

1. Businesswomen

ISBN 0-7910-5142-0   LC 98-40821

Discusses the lives and business careers of six women: Madam C.J. Walker, Katharine Graham, Mary Kay Ash, Martha Stewart, Oprah Winfrey, and Sherry Lansing

Includes bibliographical references

Lyman, Darryl, 1944-

Holocaust rescuers; ten stories of courage. Enslow Pubs. 1999 128p il (Collective biographies) lib bdg $19.95   **920**

1. World War, 1939-1945—Jews 2. Holocaust, 1933-1945

ISBN 0-7660-1114-3   LC 98-21584

Discusses the efforts of ten individuals who did what they could to save Jews from the Nazis, including Anna Borkowska, Varian Fry, Irene Gut Opdyke, Mustafa Hardaga, Jorgen Kieler, Oskar Schindler, Andrew Sheptitsky, Sempo Sugihara, Marion van Binsbergen Pritchard, and Raoul Wallenberg

Includes bibliographical references

Lyons, Mary E.

Keeping secrets; the girlhood diaries of seven women writers. Holt & Co. 1995 180p il $15.95 (7 and up)   **920**

1. Authors, American 2. Women authors

ISBN 0-8050-3065-4   LC 94-36139

This is a "collection of seven literary biographies liberally sprinkled with brief quotations from the subjects' diaries, written when they were young adults. It is Lyons intention to show how each of them developed as individuals and as writers by keeping them. . . . Louisa May Alcott, Charlotte Forten, Sarah Jane Foster, Kate Chopin, Alice Dunbar-Nelson, Ida B. Wells, and Charlotte Perkins Gilman are featured women. Their stories are interesting, well told, and extensively documented." SLJ

Includes bibliographical references

McKissack, Patricia C., 1944-

African-American inventors; by Patricia and Fredrick McKissack. Millbrook Press 1994 96p il (Proud heritage) lib bdg $25.90   **920**

1. African American inventors 2. Inventions

ISBN 1-56294-468-1   LC 93-42625

"After presenting a brief history of the patent process and the law, the McKissacks provide an overview of African American inventors throughout the 19th and 20th centuries, including those who were free born and those who were slaves. . . . Good-quality black-and-white pho-

tographs and reproductions, along with the drawings that accompanied the original patent applications, appear throughout. This title fills a real need; its readable text gives information not often found in books on inventions or on U.S. history." SLJ

Includes bibliographical references

African-American scientists; by Patricia and Fredrick McKissack. Millbrook Press 1994 96p il (Proud heritage) lib bdg $25.90   **920**

1. Scientists 2. African Americans—Biography

ISBN 1-56294-372-3   LC 93-11226

Examines the lives and achievements of African-American scientists from colonial days to the present

"Not only do the McKissacks provide documented, fascinating portraits of well-known figures such as Benjamin Banneker and George Washington Carver, but they also consider the remarkable contributions of persons rarely written about, including outstanding women scientists." Horn Book Guide

Includes bibliographical references

Meltzer, Milton, 1915-

Ten queens; portraits of women of power; illustrated by Bethanne Andersen. Dutton Children's Bks. 1998 134p il maps $24.99   **920**

1. Queens

ISBN 0-525-45643-0   LC 97-36428

"The 10 women Meltzer showcases are Esther, Cleopatra, Boudicca, Zenobia, Eleanor of Aquitaine, Isabella of Spain, Elizabeth I, Christine of Sweden, Maria Theresa, and Catherine the Great." Booklist

Meltzer "has a storyteller's flair and an eye for the small details and anecdotes that bring these queens to life. . . . Colorful expressionistic paintings, boldly stroked onto unframed panels, enrich the pages." SLJ

Includes bibliographical references

Mendoza, Patrick M.

Extraordinary people in extraordinary times; heroes, sheroes, and villains. Libraries Unlimited 1999 142p il pa $18 (7 and up)   **920**

1. Heroes and heroines 2. United States—Biography

ISBN 1-56308-611-5   LC 99-14238

Stories of little-known historical characters from American history. Subjects range from that of the first woman to receive the Congressional Medal of Honor to the first woman to be hanged in the United States. Jeanette Rankin, Jose Marti and two survivors of the Sand Creek Massacre are among those profiled

Morey, Janet

Famous Hispanic Americans; [by] Janet Nomura Morey and Wendy Dunn. Cobblehill Bks. 1996 190p il $15.99; pa $5.99   **920**

1. Hispanic Americans

ISBN 0-525-65190-X; 0-14-038436-7

LC 95-10670

"This book presents portraits of fourteen Hispanic (Latino) Americans from varying fields of endeavor: the arts (Gloria Estefan, Andy Garcia, Lourdes Lopez, Paul Rodriguez), sports (Felipe Alou, Gigi Fernandez), the

Morey, Janet—*Continued*
professions and business (Jaime Escalante, Roberto Goizueta, Carolina Herrera, Antonia Novella), politics (Frederico Pena, Matt Rodriguez, Ileana Ros-Lehtinen), and NASA (Ellen Ocha)." ALAN
Includes bibliographical references

Famous Mexican Americans; [by] Janet Morey & Wendy Dunn. Cobblehill Bks. 1989 176p il hardcover o.p. paperback available $5.99   **920**
1. Mexican Americans
ISBN 0-14-038437-5 (pa)   LC 89-7218
This collection "gives sketches of the lives of fourteen contemporary Mexican Americans; the men and women who are discussed represent such diverse fields as the law, sports, entertainment, business, and public service at the local or federal level." Bull Cent Child Books
"While the intent of the book is to showcase the outstanding contributions of the selected Mexican Americans, the book also provides young readers with role models to be admired and emulated." SLJ
Includes bibliographical references

Mour, Stanley I.
American jazz musicians. Enslow Pubs. 1998 128p il (Collective biographies) lib bdg $19.95   **920**
1. Jazz musicians 2. Jazz music
ISBN 0-7660-1027-9   LC 97-27173
Profiles ten notable jazz musicians, including Louis Armstrong, John Coltrane, Miles Davis, Duke Ellington and Wynton Marsalis
Includes discography and bibliographical references

Nardo, Don, 1947-
Leaders of ancient Greece. Lucent Bks. 1999 128p il maps (History makers) $17.96 (7 and up)   **920**
1. Greece—Biography 2. Kings and rulers
ISBN 1-56006-543-5   LC 99-18176
"Nardo profiles eight political and military leaders from Greece's Classic Age and describes the historical events and forces that brought them to power. . . . Solon, Themistocles, Pericles, and Alcibiades are the Athenians featured, followed by Epaminondas, Philip, Alexander, and Pyrrhus. The thorough documentation, lists of ancient and modern works consulted, and recommendations for further reading make this book ideal for reports." SLJ

Rulers of ancient Rome. Lucent Bks. 1999 128p il maps (History makers) lib bdg $22.45 (7 and up)   **920**
1. Nero, Emperor of Rome, 37-68 2. Rome—Biography 3. Rome—History
ISBN 1-56006-356-4   LC 98-3841
Discusses the contributions of various rulers of ancient Rome, including Fabius, Marius, Caesar, Cicero, Augustus, Nero, Constantine, and Justinian
This is "well written, logically organized, and lucid." SLJ
Includes bibliographical references

Scientists of Ancient Greece. Lucent Bks. 1999 128p il maps (History makers) lib bdg $17.96 (7 and up)   **920**
1. Science—Greece—History 2. Scientists
ISBN 1-56006-362-9   LC 98-3842
Discusses the life and work of the seven Greek thinkers considered to be the first true scientists of the western world. Included are Democritus, Plato, Aristotle, Theophrastus, Archimedes, Ptolemy, and Galen
"Well written, logically organized, and lucid." SLJ
Includes bibliographical references

Northrup, Mary
American computer pioneers. Enslow Pubs. 1998 112p il (Collective biographies) lib bdg $19.95   **920**
1. Computers 2. Inventors
ISBN 0-7660-1053-8   LC 97-24155
Profiles some of the people who have made contributions to the computer industry including Herman Hollerith, Johnny von Neumann, Grace Hopper, John W. Mauchly, J. Presper Eckert, Jr., and An Wang
"Students will find the text easy to read, nontechnical, and filled with enough information for reports and enough appeal to spark further investigation." SLJ
Includes bibliographical references

Notable mathematicians; from ancient times to the present; Robyn V. Young, editor; Zoran Minderovic, associate editor. Gale Res. 1998 xxi, 612p il $85 (7 and up)   **920**
1. Mathematicians
ISBN 0-7876-3071-3   LC 97-33662
This work profiles "300 mathematicians chosen for their historical importance, discoveries, familiarity to the public, awards and prizes, and involvement in mathematics education. . . . Female and minority mathematicians have been expressly represented." Libr J
For a fuller review see: Booklist, Aug. 1998
Includes bibliographical references

Oleksy, Walter G., 1930-
Hispanic-American scientists; [by] Walter Oleksy. Facts on File 1998 120p il (American profiles) $19.95 (7 and up)   **920**
1. Hispanic Americans 2. Scientists 3. Engineers
ISBN 0-8160-3704-3   LC 98-6558
"A look at 10 Hispanic Americans who have made important contributions in various fields of science since the end of World War II. Luis Alvarez, Francisco Dallmeier, Adriana Ocampo, Margarita Colmenares, and Ellen Ochoa are among the individuals profiled." SLJ
This "book provides a useful general introduction to many interesting areas of scientific study and what they entail, via the often-overlooked contributions of an important ethnic group." Booklist
Includes bibliographical references

Polking, Kirk
Oceanographers and explorers of the sea. Enslow Pubs. 1999 128p il (Collective biographies) lib bdg $19.95   **920**
1. Oceanography—Biography 2. Explorers 3. Scientists
ISBN 0-7660-1113-5   LC 98-36135

Polking, Kirk—*Continued*
The author "introduces 10 20th-century American oceanographers. Some are well known (Sylvia Earle, Eugenie Clark, Robert Ballard), while others are not so familiar (Henry Stommel, Ernest Everett Just). The brief biographies examine how these individuals became involved in their fields of study, where they studied and worked, and their accomplishments or discoveries." SLJ
Includes bibliographical references

Poynter, Margaret
Top 10 American women's figure skaters. Enslow Pubs. 1998 48p il (Sports top 10) lib bdg $18.95   **920**
1. Ice skating—Biography 2. Women athletes
ISBN 0-7660-1075-9   LC 97-27217
Profiles ten notable women figure skaters in American history, including Peggy Fleming, Dorothy Hamill, and Kristi Yamaguchi
Includes bibliographical references

Presidents in a time of change; a sourcebook on the U.S. presidency; edited by Carter Smith. Millbrook Press 1993 96p il map (American albums from the collections of the Library of Congress) hardcover o.p. paperback available $8.95   **920**
1. Presidents—United States 2. United States—Politics and government—1900-1999 (20th century)
ISBN 1-56294-877-6 (pa)   LC 93-15092
This overview uses a variety of contemporary materials to describe and illustrate the political and personal lives of the United States presidents from Harry Truman to Bill Clinton
Includes bibliographical references

Presidents of a divided nation; a sourcebook on the U.S. presidency; edited by Carter Smith. Millbrook Press 1993 96p il map (American albums from the collections of the Library of Congress) lib bdg $25.90   **920**
1. Presidents—United States 2. United States—Politics and government—1861-1865 3. Reconstruction (1865-1876)
ISBN 1-56294-360-X   LC 93-12753
An illustrated look at the political and personal lives of Abraham Lincoln, Andrew Johnson, and Ulysses S. Grant
Includes bibliographical references

Presidents of a growing country; a sourcebook on the U.S. presidency; edited by Carter Smith. Millbrook Press 1993 96p il maps (American albums from the collections of the Library of Congress) lib bdg $25.90; pa $8.95   **920**
1. Presidents—United States 2. United States—Politics and government—1865-1898
ISBN 1-56294-358-8; 1-56294-875-X (pa)
                    LC 93-15090
A variety of contemporary materials are used to describe and illustrate the political and personal lives of United States presidents from Rutherford Hayes to William McKinley
Includes bibliographical references

Presidents of a world power; a sourcebook on the U.S. presidency; edited by Carter Smith. Millbrook Press 1993 96p il maps (American albums from the collections of the Library of Congress) lib bdg $25.90   **920**
1. Presidents—United States 2. United States—Politics and government—1900-1999 (20th century)
ISBN 1-56294-361-8   LC 93-15091
An illustrated look at the political and personal lives of the United States presidents from Theodore Roosevelt to Franklin Delano Roosevelt
Includes bibliographical references

Presidents of a young republic; a sourcebook on the U.S. presidency; edited by Carter Smith. Millbrook Press 1993 96p il maps (American albums from the collections of the Library of Congress) lib bdg $25.90; pa $8.95   **920**
1. Presidents—United States 2. United States—Politics and government—1815-1861
ISBN 1-56294-359-6; 1-56294-873-3 (pa)
                    LC 93-12752
Materials from the collections of the Library of Congress are used to describe and illustrate the political and personal lives of the United States presidents from John Quincy Adams to James Buchanan
Includes bibliographical references

Price-Groff, Claire
Extraordinary women journalists. Childrens Press 1997 272p il (Extraordinary people) lib bdg $37   **920**
1. Women journalists
ISBN 0-516-20474-2   LC 96-50341
Profiles the life and work of notable women journalists, including Sarah Hale, Margaret Fuller, and Nellie Bly
"Chapters are short but full of useful information and are accompanied by large black-and-white photos. Because these women's chosen field intersects with so many other subjects, students learn about American and world history, politics, and culture as they read these short biographies. . . . Good for reports or leisure reading." SLJ
Includes glossary and bibliographical references

Twentieth-century women political leaders. Facts on File 1998 142p il (Global profiles) $19.95 (7 and up)   **920**
1. Women politicians 2. Women in politics
ISBN 0-8160-3672-1   LC 97-32373
Presents biographies of twelve women who have held positions of political leadership around the world, including Golda Meir, Margaret Thatcher, Winnie Mandela, Corazon Aquino, Wilma Mankiller, and Benazir Bhutto
"The detailed index provides easy points of access for students doing research, and the variety of women included make this title a useful reference resource." SLJ
Includes bibliographical references

Rappoport, Ken
Guts and glory; making it in the NBA. Walker & Co. 1997 147p il $15.95; lib bdg $16.84   **920**
1. National Basketball Association 2. Basketball—Biography
ISBN 0-8027-8430-5; 0-8027-8431-3 (lib bdg)
                                            LC 96-48212
Examines the lives of ten professional basketball players, including Muggsy Bogues, Bobby Hurley, John Lucas, Hakeem Olajuwon, and Buck Williams, who overcame various obstacles on their way to success in the NBA
Includes bibliographical references

Rasmussen, R. Kent
Modern African political leaders. Facts on File 1998 130p il (Global profiles) $19.95 (7 and up)
                                                  920
1. Kings and rulers 2. Africa—Politics and government
ISBN 0-8160-3277-7   LC 97-31162
Profiles eight modern African political leaders, including Nelson Mandela and Haile Selassie
Includes bibliographical references

Reef, Catherine
Black fighting men; a proud history. 21st Cent. Bks. (NY) 1994 80p il (African-American soldiers) $17.90   **920**
1. African American soldiers
ISBN 0-8050-3106-5   LC 93-44279
"Reef chronicles the heroism of individual black soldiers and airmen in the major wars of the U.S., beginning with the American Revolution. Reef's approach is straightforward; the heroic action of each soldier is examined, as well as his life before and—for those who survived—after the conflict." SLJ
Includes bibliographical references

Reger, James P., 1952-
Civil War generals of the Confederacy. Lucent Bks. 1999 144p il maps (History makers) $22.45 (7 and up)   **920**
1. Confederate States of America. Army 2. Generals 3. United States—History—1861-1865, Civil War—Biography
ISBN 1-56006-359-9   LC 98-36191
Focuses on the military careers of influential generals of the Confederacy during the Civil War. Robert E. Lee, Stonewall Jackson, James Longstreet, Jeb Stuart, and Nathan Bedford Forrest are profiled

Reynolds, Moira Davison
American women scientists; 23 inspiring biographies, 1900-2000. McFarland & Co. 1999 149p il $33.50 (7 and up)   **920**
1. Women scientists
ISBN 0-7864-0649-6   LC 99-14603
"Four-to-six page profiles of 23 of the century's premier women scientists, representing a wide variety of disciplines. The entries are arranged chronologically beginning with Cornelia Clapp (1849-1934) and ending with Mary Good (1931-). . . . Each entry includes a black-and-white portrait." SLJ
Includes bibliographical references

Rutledge, Rachel
The best of the best in gymnastics. Millbrook Press 1999 64p il (Women of sports) lib bdg $22.90; pa $6.95   **920**
1. Gymnastics 2. Women athletes
ISBN 0-7613-1321-4 (lib bdg); 0-7613-0784-2 (pa)
                                            LC 98-51657
Discusses the past and future of women's gymnastics and presents biographies of eight of the sport's most famous players: Simona Amanar, Vanessa Atler, Dominique Dawes, Ling Jie, Svetlana Khorkina, Kris Maloney, Shannon Miller, and Dominique Moceanu
"The book does not shy away from controversial issues, addressing eating disorders, injury and sometimes even death, pushing young girls too hard, and Moceanu's legal separation from her parents due to financial matters. . . . [This is an] attractive book." SLJ

The best of the best in track & field. Millbrook Press 1999 64p il (Women of sports) lib bdg $22.90; pa $6.95   **920**
1. Track athletics 2. Women athletes
ISBN 0-7613-1300-1 (lib bdg); 0-7613-0446-0 (pa)
                                            LC 98-51645
Discusses the past and present of women's track and field and presents biographies of eight notable competitors, including Sally Barsosio, Cathy Freeman, and Angela Williams
"A great resource for any public or school library." SLJ

Savage, Jeff, 1961-
Top 10 Heisman trophy winners. Enslow Pubs. 1999 48p il (Sports top 10) lib bdg $18.95   **920**
1. Football—Biography 2. Heisman Trophy
ISBN 0-7660-1072-4   LC 98-12023
Highlights the lives and careers of ten winners of the Heisman trophy: Marcus Allen, Tim Brown, Ernie Davis, Tony Dorsett, Doug Flutie, Eddie George, Archie Griffin, Paul Hornung, Barry Sanders, and Roger Staubach
Includes bibliographical references

Sills, Leslie
Inspirations; stories about women artists: Georgia O'Keeffe, Frida Kahlo, Alice Neel, Faith Ringgold. Whitman, A. 1989 49p il lib bdg $17.95
                                                  920
1. Women artists
ISBN 0-8075-3649-0   LC 88-80
A look at the lives and works of "four 20th-century women artists of great talent. There are photographs of the artists as children and adults, and well-chosen examples of their work reproduced in full color." N Y Times Book Rev
Includes bibliographical references

Visions; stories about women artists: Mary Cassatt, Betye Saar, Leonora Carrington, Mary Frank. Whitman, A. 1993 58p il lib bdg $18.95
                                                  920
1. Women artists
ISBN 0-8075-8491-6   LC 92-32909

Sills, Leslie—*Continued*

This volume presents the lives and works of four pioneering women artists

"Written with clarity, simplicity, and insight. . . . Full-color reproductions of each artist's work are included. The text is further broken up by black-and-white photos of the subjects. Design and layout are carefully planned, resulting in a beautiful book worth sharing with many readers." SLJ

Includes bibliographical references

Sinnott, Susan

Extraordinary Hispanic Americans. Childrens Press 1991 277p il lib bdg $37   **920**

1. Hispanic Americans

ISBN 0-516-00582-0   LC 91-13909

Profiles the lives of Hispanics who helped shape the history of the United States beginning with the age of exploration and leading into the 20th century. Among those profiled are: Hernando de Soto, Father Junípero Serra, Francisco Ramírez, Desi Arnaz, Roberto Clemente and Joan Baez

"The volume is a substantial resource that should be on all library reference shelves." Booklist

Includes bibliographical references

The **Smithsonian** book of the First Ladies; their lives, times, and issues; Edith P. Mayo, general editor; foreword by Hillary Rodham Clinton. Holt & Co. 1996 302p il $24.95 (7 and up)   **920**

1. Presidents' spouses—United States

ISBN 0-8030-1751-8   LC 94-6147

This "book gives a brief account of the life and White House doings of first ladies from Martha Washington to Hillary Rodham Clinton; it also mentions White House hostesses who were not presidential wives (such as James Buchanan's niece) and gives a quick précis of those women who didn't live long enough to see their husbands attain the highest office in the land." Bull Cent Child Books

"Well illustrated and punctuated with tidbits of useful information, this is both an excellent reference book for studying American's First Ladies and an informative look at women's history." Voice Youth Advocates

Includes bibliographical references

Stille, Darlene R.

Extraordinary women of medicine. Childrens Press 1997 288p il (Extraordinary people) lib bdg $37   **920**

1. Women physicians 2. Women in medicine

ISBN 0-516-20307-X   LC 96-43196

Presents biographical sketches highlighting the contributions of women, mostly American, to the field of medicine in the nineteenth and twentieth centuries

"The thick volume, which spans two centuries of history, is made user-friendly by large type, occasional black-and-white photographs, and short biographical chapters." Booklist

Includes glossary and bibliographical references

Streissguth, Thomas

Legendary labor leaders. Oliver Press (Minneapolis) 1998 160p il (Profiles) $16.95 (7 and up)   **920**

1. Labor movement

ISBN 1-88150-844-7   LC 97-29017

Traces the history of the labor movement in the United States through brief biographies of labor leaders: Samuel Gompers, Eugene Debs, William Haywood, "Mother" Jones, John Lewis, A. Philip Randolph, Jimmy Hoffa, and Cesar Chavez

Includes bibliographical references

Strickland, Michael R., 1965-

African-American poets. Enslow Pubs. 1996 112p il (Collective biographies) lib bdg $19.95   **920**

1. Poets, American 2. African American authors 3. American poetry—African American authors

ISBN 0-89490-774-3   LC 96-2016

Profiles the lives and work of ten African American poets: Phillis Wheatley, Gwendolyn Brooks, Haki R. Madhubuti, Rita Dove, Eloise Greenfield, Langston Hughes, Imamu Amiri Baraka, Maya Angelou, Paul Laurence Dunbar, and Nikki Giovanni

"The clear, focused writing makes this a solid choice for reports, especially in multicultural units." SLJ

Includes bibliographical references

Sullivan, George

Glovemen; twenty-seven of baseball's greatest. Atheneum Bks. for Young Readers 1996 72p il $18   **920**

1. Baseball—Biography

ISBN 0-689-31991-6   LC 95-24749

Profiles twenty-seven talented fielders in the history of baseball, including Barry Bonds, Nap Lajoie, and Joe DiMaggio

"Both full-color and black-and-white photos contribute to the presentation and capture the action. An attractive, useful addition." SLJ

In the line of fire; eight women war spies. Scholastic 1996 118p il pa $3.99   **920**

1. Spies 2. Women—Biography

ISBN 0-590-48294-7

The author "recounts the stories of eight female war spies who risked their lives to obtain information for the military. Some, such as Lydia Darraugh (who warned George Washington about an imminent British attack), were ordinary wives and mothers who found themselves privy to secrets, which they relayed to the proper authorities. Others, such as Betty Pack (who stole a secret code book for the Allies during World War II), relished the thrill and adventure their espionage careers afforded them. . . . A section of period photos and an appended bibliography will assist young report writers." Booklist

Quarterbacks! eighteen of football's greatest. Atheneum Bks. for Young Readers 1998 60p il $18   **920**

1. Football—Biography

ISBN 0-689-81334-1   LC 97-34167

Sullivan, George—*Continued*
Profiles some of the top-rated quarterbacks of all time, including Sammy Baugh, Bart Starr, Fran Tarkenton, Dan Marino, Steve Young, and Troy Aikman
"Each athlete is described in a two-to-four page entry complete with action photographs, many in full color. The excellent introduction includes a good description of the quarterback's importance to the game and the qualities and skills required for the job." SLJ

Sullivan, Otha Richard, 1941-
African American inventors; Jim Haskins, general editor. Wiley 1998 164p il (Black stars) $22.95   **920**
1. African American inventors
ISBN 0-471-14804-0   LC 97-46932
Profiles the lives of twenty-five African American inventors who made significant scientific contributions from the eighteenth century to modern times
This is "a particularly engaging book to read; Sullivan highlights those aspects of the subjects' lives that will interest readers the most and writes about them with insight. The book is attractive, too, with lots of historical engravings and photographs." Booklist
Includes bibliographical references

Taitz, Emily
Remarkable Jewish women; rebels, rabbis, and other women from biblical times to the present; by Emily Taitz and Sondra Henry. Jewish Publ. Soc. 1996 219p il maps $29.95; pa $19.95 (7 and up)   **920**
1. Jewish women—Biography
ISBN 0-8276-0573-0; 0-8276-0643-5 (pa)
LC 95-51989
Based on the authors' Written out of history (1978)
Presents brief portraits of more than eighty Jewish women and introduces the historical, social, and cultural backgrounds of the periods during which they lived
"Coverage is impressively wide-ranging. . . . Many of the biographies offer role models, although the authors point out that some of the women listed rejected Judaism as a religion and the Jewish community. An excellent and much-needed reference tool." SLJ
Includes glossary and bibliographical references

Wakin, Eric
Asian independence leaders. Facts on File 1997 160p il map (Global profiles) $19.95 (7 and up)   **920**
1. Asia—Biography 2. Heads of state
ISBN 0-8160-3320-X   LC 96-31505
Profiles nine men, including Sun Yat-sen of China, Gandhi of India, Ho Chi Minh of Vietnam, and Emilio Aguinaldo of the Philippines, who struggled to free their respective countries from colonial rule or monarchy
Includes bibliographical references

Weitzman, David L.
Great lives: theater; [by] David Weitzman. Atheneum Bks. for Young Readers 1996 311p il $24 (7 and up)   **920**
1. Dramatists 2. Actors
ISBN 0-689-80579-9   LC 95-25994

Presents biographies of more than twenty actors and playwrights who have left their mark on the theater, including Anton Chekhov, Edwin Booth, Sarah Bernhardt, George Bernard Shaw, and Paul Robeson
"Theater enthusiasts will enjoy this as pleasure reading. Students needing information on the playwrights and actors will find the text most accessible. A strong addition to the theater and collective biography shelves." Booklist
Includes bibliographical references

World Book of America's presidents. World Bk. 2v il lib bdg set $69   **920**
1. Presidents—United States

First published 1982. (5th edition 1999) Periodically revised
Contents: v1 The President's world; v2 Portraits of the Presidents
Volume one describes the duties, privileges, and power of the chief executive. The second volume offers profiles of the presidents and their administrations

Yount, Lisa
Asian-American scientists. Facts on File 1998 112p il (American profiles) lib bdg $19.95 (7 and up)   **920**
1. Scientists 2. Asian Americans—Biography
ISBN 0-8160-3756-6   LC 98-10804
Profiles twelve Asian-American scientists, including Subrahmanyan Chandrasekhar, Paul Chung-wu Chu, and Constance Tom Noguchi
The author writes "succinctly, developing a series of interesting narratives highlighting scientific accomplishments." Booklist
Includes bibliographical references

Contemporary women scientists. Facts on File 1994 124p il (American profiles) lib bdg $16.95 (7 and up)   **920**
1. Women scientists
ISBN 0-8160-2895-8   LC 93-26821
An introduction to the life and work of 10 women prominent in the natural sciences. "Each chapter teaches some of the science relevant to that woman's career and contributions in an exceptionally clear way, defining terms and giving enough background so that the content is understandable to those with little scientific background." Sci Books Films
Includes bibliographical references

920.003   Biographical reference works

African American biography. U.X.L 1994-2000 7v (African American reference library) v1-4 set $125; ea $42   **920.003**
1. African Americans—Biography
ISBN   0-8103-9234-8;   0-7876-3562-6   (v5); 0-7876-3563-4 (v6); 0-7876-3564-2 (v7)
LC 93-45651
"Individuals were selected from sports, entertainment, politics, literature, religion, and science areas as well as

African American biography—*Continued*
from history. For each person there is a picture, a quote, a summary significance, a life history which emphasizes their career. Controversy is not ignored. . . . A classified index to all volumes is in each volume. This is an attractive and useful set." Safford. Guide to Ref Materials for Sch Libr Media Cent. 5th edition

African biography; Virginia Curtin Knight, editor. U.X.L 1998 3v il set $95   **920.003**
1. Africa—Biography—Dictionaries
ISBN 0-7876-2823-9   LC 98-14069
Presents biographical entries on seventy-five noteworthy Africans, historical and contemporary, in a variety of fields, from a wide range of sub-Saharan countries
"A well-researched resource that is inviting and easy to use." SLJ
Includes bibliographical references

Almanac of famous people. Gale Res. 2v set $115
    920.003
1. Biography

First published 1981 with title: Biography almanac. (6th edition 1997) Periodically revised
"A comprehensive reference guide to more than 27,000 famous and infamous newsmakers from Biblical times to the present." Title page
Contents: v1 Biographies; v2 Indexes, chronological by year, chronological by date, geographic, occupation

American authors, 1600-1900; a biographical dictionary of American literature; edited by Stanley J. Kunitz and Howard Haycraft. Wilson, H.W. 1938 846p il (Authors series) $90
    920.003
1. Authors, American—Dictionaries 2. American literature—Bio-bibliography
ISBN 0-8242-0001-2
"Complete in one volume with 1300 biographies and 400 portraits." Title page
"This volume contains biographies of 1,300 authors who contributed to the development of American literature, from the founding of Jamestown (1607) to the end of the nineteenth century. Each essay describes the author's life, discusses past and present significance, and evaluates principal works." Safford. Guide to Ref Materials for Sch Libr Media Cent. 5th edition

American men & women of science; a biographical directory of today's leaders in physical, biological and related sciences. Bowker 8v set $900   **920.003**
1. Scientists—Dictionaries
ISSN 0192-8570

Also available CD-ROM version
Irregular. First published 1906 by Science Press with title: American men of science. Some editions were divided into two sections: Physical and biological sciences and Social sciences (20th edition 1998-99)
"Brief biographical sketches of about 124,000 scientists and engineers active in the United States and Canada. Arranged alphabetically, with discipline index." Safford. Guide to Ref Materials for Sch Libr Media Cent. 5th edition

Authors & artists for young adults. Gale Res. il ea $85   **920.003**
1. Authors—Dictionaries 2. Artists—Dictionaries 3. Literature—Bio-bibliography
ISSN 1040-5682

Semi-annual. First published 1988
Editors vary
"Each volume contains 20-25 entries offering personal, behind-the-scenes information, . . . sidelights, portraits, movie stills, bibliographies, cumulative index and much more. Its international scope ranges from contemporary to classic, fantasy to nonfiction." Publisher's note

A **Biographical** dictionary of artists; general editor, Sir Lawrence Gowing. rev ed. Facts on File 1995 784p il $50   **920.003**
1. Artists—Dictionaries
ISBN 0-8160-3252-1   LC 94-38801
"An Andromeda book"
First published 1983 by Prentice-Hall as volume two of the Encyclopedia of visual art
"Architects, painters, sculptors, stage designers, landscape designers and book illuminators are all represented. An extensive chronology divided into three major periods: Romanesque to Baroque, Baroque to Realism and Impressionism to the present, is further classified by country. The artists are then listed in alphabetical order with articles varying from about one paragraph to two pages for Picasso. . . . Highly recommended for middle school and high school." Safford. Guide to Ref Materials for Sch Libr Media Cent. 5th edition

Biographical encyclopedia of mathematicians; editor, Donald R. Franceschetti. Marshall Cavendish 1999 2v set $149.95   **920.003**
1. Mathematicians—Biography—Encyclopedias
ISBN 0-7614-7069-7   LC 98-25846
"Written by academicians and researchers, this set introduces the people behind mathematical equations and theorems. Clearly written articles present 25 women and 153 men." SLJ
For a fuller review see: Booklist, Dec. 15, 1998

Biography today; profiles of people of interest to young readers. Omnigraphics apply to publisher for subscription options   **920.003**
1. Biography—Periodicals
ISSN 1058-2347

Three issues a year with bound annual cumulations. First published 1992
"This periodical provides short, biographical profiles of people of current interest. Four-to-six page entries are arranged alphabetically. . . . There is at least one photograph of the subject, a contact address, and a bibliography of accessible books and articles. . . . Useful name, subject, and place of birth indexes will cumulate with each new issue. Written in a friendly, almost chatty tone, the profiles offer quick and objective information." SLJ

The **Cambridge** biographical encyclopedia; edited by David Crystal. 2nd ed. Cambridge Univ. Press 1998 1179p $54.95   **920.003**
1. Biography—Dictionaries
ISBN 0-521-63099-1   LC 97-34577

The Cambridge biographical encyclopedia—
Continued

First published 1994

This biographical dictionary presents "an A-Z section of around 16,000 entries. . . . The Ready Reference section is a 150-page presentation of over 10,000 people in tabular form, . . . in such domains as history, politics, sport, and the arts. . . . Compared with other works within the genre, [this title] pays proportionately more attention in its A-Z section to 20th-[century] personalities . . . in subject areas which biographical dictionaries often neglect, such as television, the cinema, sport, science and popular music." Booklist

Cassutt, Michael

Who's who in space; the international space station edition. 3rd ed. Macmillan Lib. Ref. USA 1999 xxi, 665p il $115   **920.003**

1. Astronauts—Dictionaries 2. Space flight

ISBN 0-02-864965-6   LC 98-35587

First published 1987

Includes biographies of every U.S. astronaut, Russian cosmonaut, and international astronaut who has flown or trained for space missions. Illustrated with black-and-white photographs along with full-color section of NASA mission crew patches

"Comprehensive, international in scope, and refreshingly frank in its presentation of careers and events, this unique resource belongs in every reference collection." SLJ

Current biography yearbook. Wilson, H.W. il $115   **920.003**

1. Biography—Periodicals

ISSN 0084-9499

Also available CD-ROM version

Annual. First published 1940 with title: Current biography

Also issued monthly except December at a subscription price of $115 per year (ISSN 0011-3344). Yearbooks 1940-date ea $115

"Biographies of prominent people written in lively, popular prose. Emphasis is on entertainers, star athletes, politicians, and other celebrities. Series is cumulative, with biographies revised and updated occasionally. Each volume has seven-year index." N Y Public Libr. Book of How & Where to Look It Up

Current biography: cumulated index, 1940-1995 available $35 (ISBN 0-8242-0892-7)

Encyclopedia of biography; edited by Christine Nicholls. St. Martin's Press 1997 1046p il $80   **920.003**

1. Biography—Dictionaries

ISBN 0-312-17568-X   LC 97-12316

First published 1996 in the United Kingdom with title: The Hutchinson encyclopedia of biography

This biographical dictionary has 10,000 entries, "2,000 quotations, 1,200 bibliographies, and 400 illustrations. . . . [It] bristles with appendixes, from Academy Award winners to Princes of Wales; and also provides a chronological index." Booklist

Encyclopedia of world biography. 2nd ed. Gale Res. 1998 17v il set $975   **920.003**

1. Biography—Dictionaries

ISBN 0-7876-2221-4   LC 97-42327

Also available CD-ROM version

Supplementary volume designated v18 $105 (ISBN 0-7876-2945-6)

Abridged six volume edition also available $495 (ISBN 0-7876-3904-4)

First published 1973 with title: McGraw-Hill encyclopedia of world biography

Presents brief biographical sketches which provide vital statistics as well as information on the importance of the person listed. Volumes 1-16 are arranged alphabetically; volume 17 is the index

For a review see: Booklist, May 1, 1998

Ergas, G. Aimée

Artists: from Michelangelo to Maya Lin. U.X.L 1995 2v il set $49   **920.003**

1. Artists—Biography

ISBN 0-8103-9862-1   LC 95-186053

"Biographies of 62 artists, arranged alphabetically in 2 volumes. The scope of the work concentrates on North America and Europe from the Renaissance to the present. Each 5-10 page entry contains a portrait of the artist, birth and death dates, and a quote by or about the subject. There are nearly 140 black-and-white illustrations throughout. Each volume begins with an index of artists by field and media (architecture, cartoons, ceramics, etc.); a timeline; and a glossary of key art terms. As an introductory text, this title is useful for students since the focus is on the individual rather than an artistic movement or period." SLJ

Explorers; from ancient times to the space age; consulting editors, John Logan Allen, E. Julius Dasch, Barry M. Gough. Macmillan Lib. Ref. USA 1999 3v il maps set $275   **920.003**

1. Explorers—Dictionaries

ISBN 0-02-864893-5   LC 98-8809

"This set profiles 333 world explorers, including cartographers, merchants, navigators, botanists, archaeologists, treasure hunters, and astronauts. . . . Well-selected, high-quality black-and-white portraits and maps abound. . . . This is a solid resource with considerable browsing appeal." SLJ

For a fuller review see: Booklist, March 15, 1999

Explorers & discoverers; from Alexander the Great to Sally Ride; [edited by] Peggy Saari, Daniel B. Baker. Gale Res. 1995-1999 7v il maps v1-4 set $98; v5-7 ea $42   **920.003**

1. Explorers—Dictionaries 2. Adventure and adventurers

ISBN 0-8103-9787-8 (set); 0-7876-1990-6 (v5); 0-7876-2946-4 (v6); 0-7876-3681-9 (v7)

LC 95-166826

Volumes 5-7 edited by Nancy Pear and Daniel B. Baker

Profiles men and women explorers from ancient Greek scholars and travelers to contemporary astronauts and oceanographers

The **Grolier** library of women's biographies. Grolier Educ. 1998 10v unp set $319 **920.003**
1. Women—Biography—Dictionaries
ISBN 0-7172-9124-3   LC 97-25792
This "set presents over 1800 biographies of women largely from North America, Europe, and Asia, ranging from Queen Hatshepsut to Steffi Graf. Egypt and South Africa are represented, but most African countries are not. The entries are alphabetically arranged and most include black-and-white photos or reproductions. Ranging from a paragraph to three pages, the articles list birth and death years, provide quick descriptions . . ., and offer highlights on each woman's life." SLJ
For a fuller review see: Booklist, March 15, 1998

Keenan, Sheila, 1953-
Scholastic encyclopedia of women in the United States. Scholastic Ref. 1996 206p il $17.95
920.003
1. Women—Biography—Dictionaries
ISBN 0-590-22792-0   LC 95-26236
"Keenan includes 217 biographical entries and brief cameos of 43 more subjects in sidebars. Each of the six chronological chapters begins with an essay, and more sidebars provide further cultural context, plus quotations and definitions for words like 'suffrage' and 'bra-burners.'" Publ Wkly
For a fuller review see: Booklist, Nov. 15, 1996

Keene, Ann T.
Peacemakers; winners of the Nobel Peace Prize. Oxford Univ. Press 1998 303p il (Oxford profiles) lib bdg $35   **920.003**
1. Nobel Prizes 2. Pacifism
ISBN 0-19-510316-5   LC 98-13522
An essay describing the establishment of the Nobel Peace Prize precedes chronologically organized profiles of all the individuals and organizations that have received the award since 1901
Includes bibliographical references

Kranz, Rachel
The biographical dictionary of African Americans; [by] Rachel Kranz and Philip Jo Koslow. Facts on File 1999 310p il $35; pa $18.95
920.003
1. African Americans—Biography—Dictionaries
ISBN 0-8160-3903-8; 0-8160-3904-6 (pa)
LC 98-12355
First published 1992 with title: The biographical dictionary of black Americans
This work "covers 230 individuals and ranges chronologically from Colonial times to the present and represents many fields of endeavor. . . . The black-and-white photographs and drawings are well chosen. All entries include books for further reading, and an extensive list of recommended resources is appended. Indexes organize the listings by area of activity, year of birth, and subject. A worthwhile purchase." SLJ

MacNee, Marie J.
Outlaws, mobsters & crooks; from the Old West to the Internet; edited by Jane Hoehner. U.X.L 1998 3v il set $84   **920.003**
1. Criminals—Dictionaries
ISBN 0-7876-2803-4   LC 98-14861
Contents: v1 Mobsters, racketeers & gamblers, robbers; v2 Computer criminals, spies, swindlers, terrorists; v3 Bandits & gunslingers, bootleggers, pirates
Presents the lives of seventy-five North American criminals including the nature of their crimes, their motivations, and information relating to the law officers who challenged them
"Browsers and researchers alike will make good use of this enjoyable reference set due to its fact-filled content and peek into the lives of such a wide variety of outlaws." Voice Youth Advocates

Meyer, Nicholas E.
The biographical dictionary of Hispanic Americans. Facts on File 1997 242p il $26.95
920.003
1. Hispanic Americans—Dictionaries
ISBN 0-8160-3280-7   LC 95-36140
This work "provides articles on 200 Hispanic Americans in a variety of fields of endeavor beginning with early explorers such as Juan Ponce de León. . . . Entries are readable and entertaining. Each begins with a statement giving the subject's claim to fame, then traces their life from birth to death or to current times. . . . Each entry offers a source or sources for further reading. Some include a photograph of the subject. A bibliography of fairly current titles and a general index conclude the book." Booklist

O'Brien, Steven
American political leaders; from colonial times to the present; editor, Paula McGuire; consulting editors, James M. McPherson, Gary Gerstle. ABC-CLIO 1991 473p il $65   **920.003**
1. Politicians—United States—Dictionaries 2. United States—Biography—Dictionaries
ISBN 0-87436-570-8   LC 91-30755
This work presents "profiles of over 400 national political leaders who have had a substantial impact on the political affairs of the United States. . . . Every president, vice president, speaker of the House, and chief justice is included in addition to cabinet officials, presidential advisors, and government agency directors. The profiles are factual and well-written. . . . This is a well done one-volume work that students can use as a starting point for research or simply to identify a political figure." SLJ

People of the Holocaust; [edited by] Linda Schmittroth and Mary Kay Rosteck. U.X.L 1998 2v il set $55   **920.003**
1. Holocaust, 1933-1945 2. Jews—Biography
ISBN 0-7876-1743-1   LC 98-4988
Profiles sixty women and men who were caught up in the Holocaust, including Nazi perpetrators and their victims, world leaders and policy makers, and those who showed their humanity and courage by resisting Hitler's reign of genocidal terror
"This unique resource will be in constant demand." SLJ

Podell, Janet

Old worlds to new; the age of exploration and discovery; [by] Janet Podell and Steven Anzovin. Wilson, H.W. 1993 286p il maps (They changed the world) $55   **920.003**

1. Explorers—Dictionaries 2. Scientists—Dictionaries

ISBN 0-8242-0838-2   LC 92-19264

This "compilation of important discoveries begins with approximately 1000 and continues through 1800. The book is divided into logical areas of discovery with individual explorers covered in chronological order within the division. Section topics include the empires of Spain and Portugal, mariners and pirates, the exploration of Africa, and the age of scientific discovery. Individuals are treated in articles of two to four pages. Portraits, maps and period art are included." Book Rep

Scientists; the lives and works of 150 scientists; Peggy Saari and Stephen Allison, editors. U.X.L 1996 6v il v1-3 set $115; v4-6 ea $42
    920.003

1. Scientists—Dictionaries

ISBN 0-7876-0959-5 (set); 0-7876-1874-8 (v4); 0-7876-2797-6 (v5); 0-7876-3682-7 (v6)

    LC 96-25579

Volume 4-5 edited by Marie C. Ellavich

"The alphabetically arranged volumes profile figures . . . ranging from the Industrial Revolution to the present. Each entry lists birth and death dates and birthplace, followed by an accessible, fact-filled text that accurately chronicles the subject's early life, educational background, career milestones, discoveries, and awards." SLJ [review of original 3 volume set]

Scientists and inventors. Macmillan Lib. Ref. USA 1998 389p il (Macmillan profiles) $75 **920.003**

1. Scientists—Dictionaries 2. Inventors—Dictionaries

ISBN 0-02-864983-4   LC 98-28744

Alphabetical articles profile the life and work of notable scientists and inventors from antiquity to the present, beginning with Jean Louis Rodolphe Agassiz and concluding with the Wright Brothers

Seventh book of junior authors & illustrators; edited by Sally Holmes Holtze. Wilson, H.W. 1996 371p il $60   **920.003**

1. Authors—Dictionaries 2. Illustrators—Dictionaries
3. Children's literature—Bio-bibliography

ISBN 0-8242-0873-0   LC 95-47983

Previous volumes only available as part of Junior authors and illustrators electronic edition

Provides biographical or autobiographical sketches of 235 noted children's authors and illustrators who have come into prominence since 1989

Something about the author; facts and pictures about authors and illustrators of books for young people. Gale Res. il ea $108   **920.003**

1. Authors—Dictionaries 2. Illustrators—Dictionaries
3. Children's literature—Bio-bibliography

ISSN 0276-816X

First published 1971. Frequency varies

Editors vary

"This important series gives comprehensive coverage of the individuals who write and illustrate books for children. Each new volume adds about 100 profiles. Entries include career and personal data, a bibliography of the author's works, information on works in progress and references to further information." Safford. Guide to Ref Materials for Sch Libr Media Cent. 5th edition

Something about the author: autobiography series. Gale Res. il ea $108   **920.003**

1. Authors—Dictionaries 2. Illustrators—Dictionaries
3. Children's literature—Bio-bibliography

First published 1986

Editors vary

An "ongoing series in which juvenile authors discuss their lives, careers, and published works. Each volume contains essays by 20 established writers or illustrators (e.g., Evaline Ness, Nonny Hogrogian, Betsy Byars, Jean Fritz) who represent all types of literature, preschool to young adult. . . . Some articles focus on biographical information, while others emphasize the writing career. Most, however, address young readers and provide family background, discuss the writing experience, and cite some factors that influenced it. Illustrations include portraits of the authors as children and more recent action pictures and portraits. There are cumulative indexes by authors, important published works, and geographical locations mentioned in the essays." Safford. Guide to Ref Materials for Sch Libr Media Cent. 5th edition

Sonneborn, Liz

A to Z of Native American women. Facts on File 1998 228p il (Encyclopedia of women) $27.95
    920.003

1. Indians of North America—Women

ISBN 0-8160-3580-6   LC 97-36674

This "reference source features more than 100 fascinating profiles of notable Native American women from the 1500s to the present. Detailed entries include biographical sketches, photographs, descriptions of individual challenges and accomplishments, and recommended reading for each woman profiled." Libr J

For a fuller review see: Booklist, Aug. 1998

The **Supreme** Court justices; illustrated biographies, 1789-1995; edited by Clare Cushman; foreword by William H. Rehnquist. 2nd ed. Congressional Quarterly 1995 xxi, 588p il $59.95; pa $36.95   **920.003**

1. United States. Supreme Court 2. Judges

ISBN 1-56802-127-5; 1-56802-126-7 (pa)

    LC 95-32634

First published 1993 covering the years 1789-1993

A collection of biographies of the 108 Supreme Court justices from John Jay through Ruth Bader Ginsburg and Stephen Breyer. They describe each justice's background, career and major cases

Twentieth-century young adult writers; with an introductory essay by Robert Cormier; editor, Laura Standley Berger. St. James Press 1994 xxiii, 830p $140   **920.003**

1. Authors—Dictionaries 2. Young adult literature—Bio-bibliography

ISBN 1-55862-202-0   LC 93-42870

Twentieth-century young adult writers—*Continued*

"Biographies of 400 young adult authors, bibliographies of their works and signed critical essays about their writing make this reference a useful tool for middle and high school collections." Safford. Guide to Ref Materials for Sch Libr Media Cent. 5th edition

Waldman, Carl
Who was who in world exploration; [by] Carl Waldman and Alan Wexler. Facts on File 1992 712p il maps $65   920.003
1. Explorers—Dictionaries
ISBN 0-8160-2172-4   LC 91-21277
This work "includes information on more than 800 explorers from ancient times up to the 20th century. Each entry begins with a chronology of an explorer's accomplishments and concludes with a discussion of his or her place in world exploration. . . . Two excellent appendixes and an extensive bibliography enhance the usefulness of this essential reference work." Libr J

Welch, Rosanne
Encyclopedia of women in aviation and space. ABC-CLIO 1998 286p il $65   920.003
1. Women air pilots 2. Women astronauts
ISBN 0-87436-958-4   LC 98-8042
"Most entries treat people, but many organizations, places, and events are also covered. The nearly 200 entries range in length from brief paragraphs to two pages and include extensive bibliographies. Well known aviators and astronauts are covered (e.g., Amelia Earhart, Sally Ride), but lesser known women are included as well. Page design is attractive, more than 50 photographs are interspersed throughout, and there is an excellent index." Choice

Woolum, Janet, 1955-
Outstanding women athletes; who they are and how they influenced sports in America. 2nd ed. Oryx Press 1998 412p $49.95   920.003
1. Women athletes—Dictionaries
ISBN 1-57356-120-7   LC 98-17076
First published 1992
This resource is "organized into three parts: history, biographies of individual athletes and teams, and resources/appendixes. . . . An excellent reference for students, middle school through college, that would prove useful and enjoyable for general readers as well." Libr J

World authors, 1900-1950; editors, Martin Seymour-Smith and Andrew Kimmens. Wilson, H.W. 1996 4v il (Authors series) set $395
920.003
1. Authors—Dictionaries
ISBN 0-8242-0899-4   LC 96-16380
Replaces Twentieth century authors (1942) and its First supplement (1955)
Contents: v1 Abbot-Doyle; v2 Dreiser-Ledwidge; v3 Lee-Saintsbury; v4 Saki-Zweig
Provides almost 2700 articles on twentieth-century authors from all over the world who wrote in English or whose works are available in English translation

World authors, 1950-1970; a companion volume to Twentieth century authors; edited by John Wakeman; editorial consultant: Stanley J. Kunitz. Wilson, H.W. 1975 1594p il (Authors series) $95   920.003
1. Authors—Dictionaries   2. Literature—Biobibliography
ISBN 0-8242-0419-0
This volume includes 959 "authors who came into prominence between 1950 and 1970. . . . Authors were chosen for literary importance or outstanding popularity." Wilson Libr Bull

World authors, 1970-1975; editor, John Wakeman; editorial consultant, Stanley J. Kunitz. Wilson, H.W. 1980 894p il (Authors series) $85
920.003
1. Authors—Dictionaries   2. Literature—Biobibliography
ISBN 0-8242-0641-X   LC 79-21874
This volume provides biographical or autobiographical sketches for 348 of the most influential and popular men and women of letters who have come into prominence between 1970 and 1975

World authors, 1975-1980; editor, Vineta Colby. Wilson, H.W. 1985 829p il (Authors series) $85
920.003
1. Authors—Dictionaries   2. Literature—Biobibliography
ISBN 0-8242-0715-7   LC 85-10045
This work profiles the lives and works of 379 writers

World authors, 1980-1985; editor, Vineta Colby. Wilson, H.W. 1990 938p il (Authors series) $85
920.003
1. Authors—Dictionaries   2. Literature—Biobibliography
ISBN 0-8242-0797-1   LC 90-49782
This volume covers 320 contemporary writers

World authors, 1985-1990; a volume in the Wilson authors series; editor, Vineta Colby. Wilson, H.W. 1995 970p il (Authors series) $85
920.003
1. Authors—Dictionaries   2. Literature—Biobibliography
ISBN 0-8242-0875-7   LC 95-41656
This volume covers 345 novelists, playwrights, poets, and other authors who have risen to prominence in the late 1980s

World authors 1990-1995; editor, Clifford Thompson. Wilson, H.W. 1999 863p il (Authors series) $100   920.003
1. Authors—Dictionaries   2. Literature—Biobibliography
ISBN 0-8242-0956-7   LC 99-48161
The 317 authors treated in this volume include novelists, playwrights, and poets who have published significant work in the early 1990s. Also covers essayists, historians, biographers, critics, philosophers, and social scientists who have made exceptional contributions to the literature of our time

Writers for young adults; Ted Hipple, editor.
Scribner 1997 3v il set $195   **920.003**
1. Authors, American 2. Authors, English 3. Young
adult literature
ISBN 0-684-80474-3   LC 97-6890
Contains articles on writers whose works are popular
with young adults, including contemporary authors, such
as Francesca Lia Block and Maya Angelou, and classic
authors, such as Sir Arthur Conan Doyle and Louisa
May Alcott
"This set is an extremely valuable tool for every reference librarian serving young adults or those who teach
and care for them." Libr J

Yount, Lisa
A to Z of women in science and math. Facts on
File 1999 254p il (Encyclopedia of women) $30
920.003
1. Women scientists 2. Women mathematicians
ISBN 0-8160-3797-3   LC 98-46093
Profiles over 150 women "who have made contributions in a wide range of fields—medicine, genetics, ecology, archaeology, astronomy, botany, mathematics, physics, computer science, zoology, chemistry, and related
scientific fields. The selections cover women from antiquity to the present. . . . Essays on each woman are generally 300 to 1000 words, recounting essential biographical information: education, career, contributions to the
field, and, perhaps most interestingly, obstacles they
faced in male-dominated careers." Libr J

92 Individual biography

Lives of individuals are arranged alphabetically under the
name of the person written about. Some subject headings have
been added to aid in curriculum work.

Adams, Abigail, 1744-1818
Bober, Natalie. Abigail Adams; witness to a
revolution. Atheneum Bks. for Young Readers
1995 248p il maps $18; pa $8.99 (7 and up)
92
1. Presidents' spouses—United States
ISBN 0-689-31760-3; 0-689-81916-1 (pa)
LC 94-19259
"By interweaving excerpts from Adams's correspondence into a coherent biography, Bober creates a vibrant,
three-dimensional portrait of a fascinating person whose
comments on women's place have reverberated throughout history. This scholarly, thoroughly documented study
will appeal to more mature readers, but it is more formi-
dable in appearance than in presentation. Black-and-white
reproductions are included." Horn Book Guide
Includes bibliographical references

Adams, Samuel, 1722-1803
Fradin, Dennis B. Samuel Adams; the father of
American Independence; [by] Dennis Brindell
Fradin. Clarion Bks. 1998 182p il $18   **92**
1. United States—History—1775-1783, Revolution
ISBN 0-395-82510-5   LC 97-20027

Presents the life and accomplishments of the colonist
and patriot who was involved in virtually every major
event that resulted in the birth of the United States
"Archival reproductions effectively complement a descriptive and accurate narrative that imaginatively integrates details of Adams's life with the social and political milieu of the time." Horn Book Guide
Includes bibliographical references

Adamson, Joy, 1910-1980
Neimark, Anne E. Wild heart: the story of Joy
Adamson, author of Born free. Harcourt Brace &
Co. 1999 118p il $17 (7 and up)   **92**
1. Zoologists 2. Wildlife conservation
ISBN 0-15-201368-7   LC 98-26097
Discusses the life and work of the woman best known
for relationship with a lion cub, described in her book
"Born Free."
This is "an insightful look at one of the world's pio-
neers in wildlife conservation." SLJ
Includes bibliographical references

Addams, Jane, 1860-1935
Harvey, Bonnie C. Jane Addams; Nobel Prize
winner and founder of Hull House; [by] Bonnie
Carman Harvey. Enslow Pubs. 1999 128p il
(Historical American biographies) lib bdg $19.95
92
1. Hull House (Chicago, Ill.) 2. Chicago (Ill.)—Social
conditions
ISBN 0-7660-1094-5   LC 98-35589
Describes the life of the woman whose devotion to social work led to her establishing Hull House in Chicago
and who was awarded the Nobel Peace Prize in 1931
This is "a good, basic introductory biography of the
author, social reformer, and humanitarian. . . . Black-
and-white photographs, maps, and quotes enliven the presentation." SLJ
Includes bibliographical references

Aguirre, Hank, 1932-1994
Copley, Bob. The tall Mexican: the life of Hank
Aguirre, all-star pitcher, businessman,
humanitarian; with a foreword by Jośe F. Niño.
Piñata Bks. 1998 159p il $16.95 (7 and up)   **92**
1. Baseball—Biography 2. Businessmen
ISBN 1-55885-225-5   LC 98-3185
A biography of the All-Star major-league pitcher
whose commitment to his Hispanic heritage led him to
found Mexican Industries to help provide economic opportunities to the inner-city Detroit community
"Myriad reminiscences from friends, family, employees, colleagues, and fellow athletes provide readers with
the sense of true admiration felt for the subject." SLJ

Ailey, Alvin
Lewis-Ferguson, Julinda. Alvin Ailey, Jr.: a life
in dance. Walker & Co. 1994 84p il $14.95; lib
bdg $15.85   **92**
1. African American dancers 2. Choreographers
ISBN 0-8027-8239-6; 0-8027-8241-8 (lib bdg)
LC 93-17906

Ailey, Alvin—*Continued*
"The author traces Ailey's involvement with the dance from his work with Lester Horton to the formation of his own ballet company with its attendant trials and triumphs." Bull Cent Child Books
"A wonderful book for readers deeply interested in modern dance, it should prove to be interesting to others as well." SLJ
Includes bibliographical references

Albright, Madeleine Korbel, 1937-
Hasday, Judy L. Madeleine Albright. Chelsea House 1999 134p il (Women of achievement) lib bdg $19.95; pa $9.95   92
1. Women politicians 2. Cabinet officers
ISBN 0-7910-4708-3 (lib bdg); 0-7910-4709-1 (pa)
LC 98-14110
Focuses on the accomplishments of the former United States ambassador to the United Nations who became the first woman to serve as Secretary of State
"Good for assignments year-round, and especially valuable for women's history month." SLJ
Includes bibliographical references

Howard, Megan. Madeleine Albright. Lerner Publs. 1998 128p il (A & E biography) $25.26
92
1. Women politicians 2. Cabinet officers
ISBN 0-8225-4935-2   LC 97-27450
This biography traces the life and career of the first woman appointed U.S. Secretary of State, from her childhood in Czechoslovakia to her role in the Middle East peace talks
Includes bibliographical references

Alcott, Louisa May, 1832-1888
Meigs, Cornelia Lynde. Invincible Louisa; the story of the author of Little Women; with a new introduction by the author. Little, Brown 1968 195p il hardcover o.p. paperback available $5.95
92
1. Authors, American 2. Women authors
ISBN 0-316-56594-6 (pa)
Awarded the Newbery Medal, 1934
"Alcott Centennial edition"
First published 1933
This biography "is to be praised still for its straightforward account of a life of struggle and success. . . . If you want to know about Louisa's external life, and trace there the events which gave rise to the internal urges and passions that produced 'Little Women,' this book will serve well." N Y Times Book Rev

Ruth, Amy. Louisa May Alcott. Lerner Publs. 1999 128p il (A & E biography) $25.26   92
1. Authors, American 2. Women authors
ISBN 0-8225-4938-7   LC 97-47283
Discusses the life of the popular nineteenth-century author of "Little Women"
This is a "well-written, highly readable biography. . . . Both Alcott's personal life and writing career are effectively explored. Like the TV biographies, this is a lucid and inspirational production." SLJ
Includes bibliographical references

Ali, Muhammad, 1942-
Tessitore, John. Muhammed Ali; the world's champion. Watts 1998 143p il (Impact biography) lib bdg $24 (7 and up)   92
1. Boxing—Biography 2. African American athletes
ISBN 0-531-11437-6   LC 97-31204
A biography of the only boxer crowned Heavyweight Champion of the World three times
"In this well-documented biography, Tessitore details not only the fights Ali faced in the ring, but the battles fought throughout his life. The comprehensive account covers Ali's controversial involvement in boxing, the civil rights movement, Vietnam protests, the Islamic faith, and international humanitarian efforts. Black-and-white photographs accompany the informative text." Horn Book Guide
Includes bibliographical references

Alomar, Roberto, 1968-
Macht, Norman L. (Norman Lee). Roberto Alomar; an authorized biography. Mitchell Lane Pubs. 1999 64p il (Latinos in baseball) $18.95
92
1. Baseball—Biography
ISBN 1-883845-84-X   LC 98-48048
Discusses the personal life and professional career of the talented Puerto Rican-born baseball player, Roberto Alomar

Alou, Moises, 1966-
Muskat, Carrie. Moises Alou; an authorized biography. Mitchell Lane Pubs. 1999 64p il (Latinos in baseball) $18.95   92
1. Baseball—Biography
ISBN 1-883845-86-6   LC 98-48046
Presents a biography of the son of baseball great Felipe Alou who grew up to lead the Florida Marlins to victory in the 1997 World Series
The author uses "an accessible, conversational style that smoothly blends factual text with meaningful quotations." Booklist

Anastasii͡a Nikolaevna, Grand Duchess, daughter of Nicholas II, Emperor of Russia, 1901-1918
Brewster, Hugh. Anastasia's album. Hyperion Bks. for Children 1996 64p il $17.95   92
1. Russia—Kings and rulers
ISBN 0-7868-0292-8   LC 96-18417
"The book spans the tragically brief life of Grand Duchess Anastasia Romanov, the youngest daughter of Tsar Nicholas II, from her birth in 1901 to the execution of her entire family in 1918. Many of Anastasia's own black-and-white photographs, often hand-colored, along with other family photos, depict a close-knit family at home and at play." Horn Book
Includes glossary and bibliographical references

Anderson, Marian, 1897-1993

Ferris, Jeri. What I had was singing: the story of Marian Anderson. Carolrhoda Bks. 1994 96p il (Trailblazers) lib bdg $23.93; pa $6.95   **92**

1. African American singers 2. African American women

ISBN 0-87614-818-6 (lib bdg); 0-87614-634-5 (pa)
                LC 93-28502

The author "tracks Anderson's life and career as a singer, from her youth in Philadelphia to her debut at the Metropolitan Opera. Warm and informative, the biography shows how the accomplished contralto, who at first received more recognition in Europe than in her own country because of racism, paved the way for the careers of future African-American singers." Horn Book Guide
Includes bibliographical references

Angelou, Maya

Cuffie, Terrasita A. Maya Angelou. Lucent Bks. 1999 80p il (Importance of) $22.45 (7 and up)
                92

1. African American authors 2. Women authors

ISBN 1-56006-532-X   LC 99-20045

Discusses the life and work of the well-known writer, entertainer, and political activist

"Referenced quotes and sidebars paint an inspirational picture of a woman who has succeeded in so many areas. . . . This volume will work best for those who need an overview of how [Angelou] began her career and why she is important." SLJ
Includes bibliographical references

Harper, Judith E. Maya Angelou. Child's World 1999 39p il (Journey to freedom) lib bdg $24.21
                92

1. African American authors 2. Women authors

ISBN 1-56766-570-5   LC 98-45559

Examines the life and accomplishments of the African American writer, performer, and teacher, as well as her impact on literature and black culture

This biography is "attractively formatted with lots of white space, print size that is easy on the eyes, and one or two clear sepia-toned or full-color photographs or reproductions per spread. Boxed captions for each picture add to the information found in the text." SLJ
Includes bibliographical references

Kite, L. Patricia. Maya Angelou. Lerner Publs. 1999 112p il (A & E biography) $25.26   **92**

1. African American authors 2. Women authors

ISBN 0-8225-4944-1   LC 98-15763

A biography of the multi-faceted African-American woman, Maya Angelou, tracing her life from her childhood in the segregated South to her prominence as a well-known writer
Includes bibliographical references

Anthony, Susan B., 1820-1906

Weisberg, Barbara. Susan B. Anthony. Chelsea House 1988 111p il (American women of achievement) lib bdg $19.95; pa $8.95   **92**

1. Feminism 2. Women—Suffrage

ISBN 1-55546-639-7 (lib bdg); 0-7910-0408-2 (pa)
                LC 87-35528

A biography of an early leader in the campaign for women's rights, particularly in getting women the right to vote
Includes bibliographical references

Appleseed, Johnny, 1774-1845

Lawlor, Laurie. The real Johnny Appleseed; wood engravings by Mary Thompson. Whitman, A. 1995 63p il map lib bdg $13.95   **92**

1. Frontier and pioneer life

ISBN 0-8075-6909-7   LC 94-22010

"Lawlor's clear narrative style and impeccable scholarship combine to make this biography of John Chapman an outstanding choice. In four short chapters, her subject's adventures, the exciting period of frontier expansion during which he lived, and the northern area of the country through which he traveled come alive. . . . The author cites . . . his business acumen, his fondness for children and books, his friendly co-existence with several tribes of Native Americans, and his zeal in spreading the ideas of Emmanuel Swedenborg (e.g., 'every person must be a help to others in need'). . . . This attractive title belongs in every collection." SLJ

Arafat, Yasir, 1929-

Ferber, Elizabeth. Yasir Arafat; the battle for peace in Palestine. Millbrook Press 1995 144p lib bdg $23.90   **92**

1. Palestine Liberation Organization

ISBN 1-56294-585-8   LC 94-48285

The author offers an "account of Arafat's life, neither condoning his past violence nor praising his recent peace efforts. Readers are encouraged to draw personal conclusions about this man who rarely explains his life choices, and are challenged to pause and reflect on the issues involved. All questions are not answered; instead, facts are presented." SLJ
Includes bibliographical references

Armstrong, Louis, 1900-1971

Old, Wendie. Louis Armstrong; king of jazz. Enslow Pubs. 1998 128p il (African-American biographies) lib bdg $19.95   **92**

1. Jazz musicians 2. African American musicians

ISBN 0-89490-997-5   LC 97-35860

Explores the life and career of the renowned trumpeter and bandleader of the jazz era

This book is "eye-catching and highly readable." SLJ
Includes bibliographical references

Armstrong, Neil, 1930-

Bredeson, Carmen. Neil Armstrong; a space biography. Enslow Pubs. 1998 48p il (Countdown to space) lib bdg $18.95   **92**

1. Astronauts

ISBN 0-89490-973-8   LC 97-25449

A biography of the first man on the moon, covering his youth, his career as an astronaut, and his life after NASA

"The clear, concise [text is] enhanced by full-color and black-and-white photos throughout. The information is well organized and the rigors of training and space flight are clearly explained." SLJ
Includes bibliographical references

Arnold, Benedict, 1741-1801

Fritz, Jean. Traitor: the case of Benedict Arnold. Putnam 1981 191p il $16.95; pa $5.99   **92**
   1. Generals 2. United States—History—1775-1783, Revolution—Biography
   ISBN 0-399-20834-8; 0-698-11553-8 (pa)
                          LC 81-10584
A study of the life and character of the brilliant Revolutionary War general who deserted to the British for money
"The writing is smooth, the material carefully organized and used in the best of biographical style—that is, Arnold is presented accurately and the reader is left to judge the strength and weaknesses of his character rather than being told by the author." Bull Cent Child Books
Includes bibliographical references

King, David C. Benedict Arnold and the American Revolution. Blackbirch Press 1999 80p il (Notorious Americans and their times) lib bdg $19.95   **92**
   1. Generals 2. United States—History—1775-1783, Revolution—Biography
   ISBN 1-56711-221-8   LC 98-11580
Examines the life of the brilliant general who became America's most infamous Revolutionary War traitor
"A humanized portrayal of Arnold emerges from the pages. Interesting details about Arnold in his youth will keep students reading." Book Rep
Includes glossary and bibliographical references

Ashe, Arthur

Lazo, Caroline Evensen. Arthur Ashe; [by] Caroline Lazo. Lerner Publs. 1999 128p il (A & E biography) $25.26   **92**
   1. Tennis—Biography 2. African American athletes
   ISBN 0-8225-4932-8   LC 97-38737
Traces the tennis career of Arthur Ashe and describes the discrimination he faced as he worked to master "the white man's game."
Includes bibliographical references

Martin, Marvin. Arthur Ashe; of tennis & the human spirit. Watts 1999 176p il (Impact biography) lib bdg $24 (7 and up)   **92**
   1. Tennis—Biography 2. African American athletes
   ISBN 0-531-11432-5   LC 98-8535
Discusses the personal life and sports career of the African-American tennis champion, Arthur Ashe, as well as his struggles with racism and AIDS
"This book is well documented. . . . The black-and-white photographs are well chosen and support the written text." SLJ
Includes bibliographical references

Aung San Suu Kyi

Stewart, Whitney. Aung San Suu Kyi; fearless voice of Burma. Lerner Publs. 1997 128p il lib bdg $23.93 (7 and up)   **92**
   1. Myanmar—Politics and government
   ISBN 0-8225-4931-X   LC 96-41812
A biography of the Burmese leader who won the Nobel Peace Prize in 1991 while under house arrest
"A thorough, well-documented effort." Booklist
Includes bibliographical references

Babbage, Charles, 1792-1871

Collier, Bruce. Charles Babbage and the engines of perfection; [by] Bruce Collier and James MacLachlan. Oxford Univ. Press 1998 123p il (Oxford portraits in science) $21 (7 and up)   **92**
   1. Mathematicians 2. Computers—History
   ISBN 0-19-508997-9   LC 98-17054
Traces the life and work of the man whose nineteenth century inventions led to the development of the computer
"This is a fascinating portrait of Charles Babbage. . . . Generous b&w illustrations enliven the work." Book Rep
Includes bibliographical references

Baiul, Oksana

Baiul, Oksana. Oksana: my own story; as told to Heather Alexander. Random House 1997 46p il $16.99   **92**
   1. Ice skating—Biography 2. Women athletes
   ISBN 0-679-88382-7   LC 96-69537
"While coping with the deaths of her mother and grandparents, Baiul pursued her dream of becoming a 'great skater' in Ukraine. The hard work this sport demands comes across in spite of Baiul's bubbly accounts of her performances at competitions. . . . [This] will interest fans and anyone looking to relive her gold-medal performance at the 1994 Olympics." Horn Book Guide

DuPont, Lonnie Hull. Oksana Baiul. Chelsea House 1999 64p il (Female figure skating legends) lib bdg $16.95   **92**
   1. Ice skating—Biography 2. Women athletes
   ISBN 0-7910-4201-4   LC 98-21901
A biography of the young Ukrainian figure skater who won a gold medal at the 1994 Winter Olympics
Includes bibliographical references

Baldwin, James, 1924-1987

Gottfried, Ted. James Baldwin; voice from Harlem. Watts 1997 112p il (Impact biography) lib bdg $24; pa $9.95 (7 and up)   **92**
   1. African American authors
   ISBN 0-531-11318-3 (lib bdg); 0-531-15863-2 (pa)
                          LC 96-43381
This "biography of a great American writer discusses his childhood, his politics, his gay identity, and his influential books." Booklist
This is an "involving piece of nonfiction. . . . This biography carefully blends Baldwin's life with the volatile political events that surrounded it, and the result is an intriguing synthesis." Bull Cent Child Books
Includes bibliographical references

Ballard, Robert D.

Archbold, Rick. Deep-Sea explorer: the story of Robert Ballard, discoverer of the Titanic. Scholastic 1994 144p il maps   **92**
   1. Oceanography—Biography   LC 93-1983
Available from Houghton Mifflin $9.60 (ISBN 0-395-73272-7)

Ballard, Robert D.—*Continued*

This is a biography "of the scientist/explorer who discovered the *Titanic*, the *Bismarck*, and shipwrecks from the Battle of Guadalcanal." Booklist

"This is an engaging narrative of a sometimes controversial figure, providing a glimpse of the public frustrations and personal disappointments that pioneers often face." SLJ

Includes glossary and bibliographical references

Banneker, Benjamin, 1731-1806

Litwin, Laura Baskes. Benjamin Banneker; astronomer and mathematician. Enslow Pubs. 1999 112p il (African-American biographies) lib bdg $19.95   92

1. Astronomers 2. African Americans—Biography
ISBN 0-7660-1208-5   LC 98-34913

A biography of the eighteenth-century African-American who taught himself mathematics and astronomy and helped survey what would become Washington, D.C

Includes bibliographical references

Barnum, P. T. (Phineas Taylor), 1810-1891

Andronik, Catherine M. Prince of Humbugs: a life of P.T. Barnum. Atheneum Pubs. 1994 136p il $15.95   92

1. Circus
ISBN 0-689-31796-4   LC 93-36724

A "biography of the great 19th-century showman who dubbed himself the Prince of Humbugs. Most readers will associate his name with the Barnum and Bailey Circus, but that venture was preceded by a long life of selling and promoting. Barnum started museums, brought Jenny Lind to America, exhibited Tom Thumb and other incredible human curiosities, and showcased Jumbo the elephant." SLJ

"Although she starts out a bit slowly, Andronik does a good job of evoking the drive and imagination of the man, and she displays a healthy skepticism for the veracity of many Barnum anecdotes while using his autobiography to set the record straight on others." Bull Cent Child Books

Includes bibliographical references

Barton, Clara, 1821-1912

Whitelaw, Nancy. Clara Barton; Civil War nurse. Enslow Pubs. 1997 128p il maps (Historical American biographies) lib bdg $19.95   92

1. Nurses
ISBN 0-89490-778-6   LC 97-7270

Traces the life of the Civil War nurse who cared for wounded soldiers and earned the title, "Angel of the Battlefield"

"Whitelaw makes use of her subject's original diaries from the Library of Congress, along with her published work. The chapters consist of easy, short sentences, lots of footnotes, and some direct quotes. Occasionally a box offers interesting incidental information." SLJ

Includes glossary and bibliographical references

Bauer, Marion Dane, 1938-

Bauer, Marion Dane. A writer's story; from life to fiction. Clarion Bks. 1995 134p $14.95; pa $6.95 (7 and up)   92

1. Authors, American 2. Women authors
ISBN 0-395-72094-X; 0-395-75053-9 (pa)
LC 94-48800

"Drawing on her own experiences, the novelist examines the origins of inspiration and the subconscious drives that compel authors to write. She points out that many components of fiction—characters, settings, plot details—need not be autobiographical, yet the text does suggest that a story's meaning is directly linked to the unique experiences of its creator. . . . Bauer provides invaluable information for both writers and readers of fiction." Publ Wkly

Baum, L. Frank (Lyman Frank), 1856-1919

Carpenter, Angelica Shirley. L. Frank Baum; royal historian of Oz; [by] Angelica Shirley Carpenter and Jean Shirley. Lerner Publs. 1992 144p il maps lib bdg $21.50; pa $7.95   92

1. Authors, American
ISBN 0-8225-4910-7 (lib bdg); 0-8225-9617-2 (pa)
LC 90-27436

A biography of the author of "The Wizard of Oz," who invented a new kind of fairy tale, uniquely modern and American

"The authors offer an entertaining and informative look at the vicissitudinous life of Baum, born in 1856, setting him squarely within his time. . . . Kids who have loved the Oz series will enjoy reading about its creator." Booklist

Includes bibliographical references

Beiderbecke, Bix, 1903-1931

Collins, David R. Bix Beiderbecke; jazz age genius. Morgan Reynolds 1998 112p il (Notable Americans) $18.95 (7 and up)   92

1. Jazz musicians
ISBN 1-88384-636-6   LC 98-19824

A biography of the cornet player from Davenport, Iowa, who helped raise jazz to a respected musical form and who was inducted into the International Jazz Hall of Fame in 1997

"With well selected details, Collins depicts the bright and the dark elements of Bix's character in crisp, concise language." Booklist

Includes bibliographical references

Bell, Alexander Graham, 1847-1922

Fisher, Leonard Everett. Alexander Graham Bell. Atheneum Pubs. 1999 unp il $16   92

1. Inventors
ISBN 0-689-81607-3   LC 97-32217

A biography of the prolific inventor who had a keen interest in voice and sound and who worked tirelessly on behalf of deaf people

"Well-composed acrylic paintings in black, white, and many shades of gray include scenes from the inventor's life as well as a full-page portrait. . . . Written with dignity and without concessions to limited vocabulary, this clear, concise biography will appeal to readers of any age." Booklist

Bell, Alexander Graham, 1847-1922—*Continued*

Matthews, Tom L. Always inventing: a photobiography of Alexander Graham Bell. National Geographic Soc. 1999 64p il $16.95
    92
1. Inventors
ISBN 0-7922-7391-5   LC 98-27209
A biography, with photographs and quotes from Bell himself, which follows this well known inventor from his childhood in Scotland through his life-long efforts to come up with ideas that would improve people's lives
"Succinct, lively, and readable, the text is illustrated with many well-captioned period photographs of Bell, his family, his associate, and his inventions as well as a host of diagrams." Booklist
Includes bibliographical references
St. George, Judith. Dear Dr. Bell—your friend, Helen Keller. See entry under Keller, Helen, 1880-1968

Bethune, Mary Jane McLeod, 1875-1955

Meltzer, Milton. Mary McLeod Bethune; voice of black hope; illustrated by Stephen Marchesi. Viking Kestrel 1987 58p il (Women of our time) hardcover o.p. paperback available $4.99   **92**
1. African American educators 2. African American women
ISBN 0-14-032219-1 (pa)   LC 86-15923
This profile of the African American educator describes "not only her accomplishments but also the context in which those achievements occurred." Booklist
"The book offers a well-researched, non-fictionalized account that's not hard to read and offers an introduction to more multi-dimensional coverage." Bull Cent Child Books

Bitton-Jackson, Livia

Bitton-Jackson, Livia. My bridges of hope; searching for life and love after Auschwitz. Simon & Schuster Bks. for Young Readers 1999 258p $17 (7 and up)   **92**
1. Holocaust survivors
ISBN 0-689-82026-7   LC 98-8046
Sequel to I have lived a thousand years
In 1945, after surviving a harrowing year in Auschwitz, fourteen-year-old Elli returns, along with her mother and brother, to the family home, now part of Slovakia, where they try to find a way to rebuild their shattered lives
The author's "story is utterly involving, and adds an important chapter to the ongoing attempt to understand the Holocaust and its consequences." Publ Wkly
Includes glossary

Bly, Nellie, 1864-1922

Davidson, Sue. Getting the real story: Nellie Bly and Ida B. Wells. Seal Press 1992 152p il (Women who dared series) pa $8.95   **92**
1. Wells-Barnett, Ida B., 1862-1931 2. Women journalists
ISBN 1-87806-716-8   LC 91-38041

Parallel biographies of two women who used their journalistic skills to fight against unjust treatment based on sex and race in late nineteenth- and early twentieth-century America
"The readable and interesting stories focus on their personal and professional failures and achievements. . . . Davidson's work, although a good blending of fact and fiction, will be most useful as a smooth-flowing introduction to the lives of these two 19th-century crusaders." SLJ

Boitano, Brian

Boitano, Brian. Boitano's edge; inside the real world of figure skating; written by Brian Boitano with Suzanne Harper; introduction by Peggy Fleming. Simon & Schuster 1997 144p il $25
    92
1. Ice skating—Biography
ISBN 0-689-81915-3   LC 97-29498
Olympic ice skating champion Brian Boitano describes the sport of figure skating and his own experiences as a skater
"The myriad crisp, clear photos will attract browsers, but fascinating, behind-the-scenes details will keep them reading from cover to cover." Booklist
Includes glossary and bibliographical references

Bonetta, Sarah Forbes, b. 1843?

Myers, Walter Dean. At her majesty's request; an African princess in Victorian England. Scholastic Press 1999 146p il maps $15.95   **92**
ISBN 0-590-48669-1   LC 98-7217
Biography of the African princess saved from execution and taken to England where Queen Victoria oversaw her upbringing and where she lived for a time before marrying an African missionary
"Myers tells an extraordinary tale which will intrigue young readers. . . . A fascinating narrative of a little-known facet of Victorian history, this book is rich with illustrations, including photographs, sketches, portraits, and maps." ALAN
Includes bibliographical references

Booth, John Wilkes, 1838-1865

Otfinoski, Steven. John Wilkes Booth and the Civil War; by Steve Otfinoski. Blackbirch Press 1999 80p il (Notorious Americans and their times) lib bdg $19.95   **92**
1. Lincoln, Abraham, 1809-1865—Assassination 2. United States—History—1861-1865, Civil War
ISBN 1-56711-222-6   LC 98-11571
Sets the life story of the man who assassinated Abraham Lincoln against the backdrop of the Civil War
Includes glossary and bibliographical references

Borges, Jorge Luis, 1899-1986

Lennon, Adrian. Jorge Luis Borges. Chelsea House 1992 111p il (Hispanics of achievement) lib bdg $19.95   **92**
1. Authors, Latin American
ISBN 0-7910-1236-0   LC 91-17667

Borges, Jorge Luis, 1899-1986—*Continued*
Presents the life and times of the Argentine writer in text and photos
"Lennon does a commendable job of defining Borges as a man of remarkable achievements. His multicultural heritage is positively portrayed, as is his political and cultural involvement in Argentinian affairs." SLJ
Includes bibliographical references

Bosch, Hieronymus, d. 1516
Schwartz, Gary. Hieronymus Bosch. Abrams 1997 92p il (First impressions) $19.95 (7 and up)
92
1. Artists, Dutch 2. Middle Ages
ISBN 0-8109-3138-9   LC 95-34369
Discusses the life of the fifteenth-century Dutch artist and explores his complex works
"Although little is known of the artist's life, Schwartz does a good job of communicating how his society differed from the present and what scholars know and surmise about him based on historical records and the work he left behind. The full-color reproductions of Bosch's paintings give readers many opportunities to view the faces of his beautifully painted yet frequently disturbing visions." Booklist

Bourke-White, Margaret, 1904-1971
Rubin, Susan Goldman. Margaret Bourke-White; her pictures were her life; photographs by Margaret Bourke-White. Abrams 1999 96p il $19.95 (7 and up)   **92**
1. Women photographers
ISBN 0-8109-4381-6   LC 98-53967
"Rubin traces the celebrated photographer's life." SLJ
"Filled with Bourke-White's marvelous photographs, this stellar biography seamlessly blends the personal and the professional." Booklist
Includes bibliographical references

Welch, Catherine A. Margaret Bourke-White; racing with a dream. Carolrhoda Bks. 1998 104p il $23.93   **92**
1. Women photographers
ISBN 1-57505-049-8   LC 97-37939
Examines the personal life and photographic career of the woman who served as a photojournalist for the magazine "Life" during World War II and the Korean War
"While Welch presents the drama of Bourke-White's assignments. . . . She does not gloss over the personal tradeoffs resulting from her career choices, including her battle with Parkinson's disease. Crisp black-and-white photographs capture the progression of both her vision and visage." SLJ
Includes bibliographical references

Brady, Mathew B., ca. 1823-1896
Sullivan, George. Mathew Brady: his life and photographs. Cobblehill Bks. 1994 136p il $15.99
92
1. Photographers 2. United States—History—1861-1865, Civil War
ISBN 0-525-65186-1   LC 93-28354

This "biography of the man credited with documenting the American Civil War focuses on Brady's professional life as a photographer." SLJ
"The beauty of the photographs—all taken more than a hundred years ago—eloquently conveys the truth of Brady's insight into the power and dramatic possibilities of the medium. The well-written book is interesting as a history of photography, of the man, and of the nation." Horn Book
Includes bibliographical references

Van Steenwyk, Elizabeth. Mathew Brady; Civil War photographer. Watts 1997 64p il lib bdg $22
92
1. Photographers 2. United States—History—1861-1865, Civil War
ISBN 0-531-20264-X   LC 96-35102
"A First book"
A biography of the pioneering photographer, who is known for his unique portrayal of the Civil War, as well as for portraits of such personalities as Lincoln, Grant, Lee, and others
"Besides biography, Van Steenwyk also fills readers in on the course of the war, a surprise given the brevity of the text. Illustrated with many reproductions of Brady's photos." Booklist
Includes bibliographical references

Braille, Louis, 1809-1852
Freedman, Russell. Out of darkness: the story of Louis Braille; illustrated by Kate Kiesler. Clarion Bks. 1997 81p il $16; pa $7.95   **92**
1. Blind
ISBN 0-395-77516-7; 0-395-96888-7 (pa)
LC 95-52353
This biography "tells about Braille's life and the development of his alphabet system for the blind." SLJ
"Without melodrama, Freedman tells the momentous story in quiet chapters in his best plain style, making the facts immediate and personal. . . . A diagram explains how the Braille alphabet works." Booklist

Brant, Joseph, 1742-1807
Bolton, Jonathan. Joseph Brant; Mohawk chief; [by] Jonathan Bolton and Claire Wilson; senior consulting editor, W. David Baird. Chelsea House 1992 111p il maps (North American Indians of achievement) lib bdg $19.95   **92**
1. Mohawk Indians
ISBN 0-7910-1709-5   LC 91-38917
Examines the life of the Mohawk chief, missionary, and statesman who led his people on the side of the British in the Revolutionary War
Includes bibliographical references

Brave Bird, Mary
Brave Bird, Mary. Lakota woman; by Mary Crow Dog and Richard Erdoes. Grove Weidenfeld 1990 263p il o.p.; HarperCollins Pubs. paperback available $13 (7 and up)   **92**
1. Dakota Indians
ISBN 0-06-097389-7 (pa)   LC 89-24862

Brave Bird, Mary—*Continued*

"Born in 1955 and raised in poverty on the Rosebud Reservation, Mary Crow Dog escaped an oppressive Catholic boarding school but fell into a marginal life of urban shoplifting and barhopping. A 1971 encounter with AIM (the American Indian Movement), participation in the 1972 Trail of Broken Treaties march on Washington, and giving birth to her first child while under fire at the 1973 siege of Wounded Knee radicalized her." Libr J

"The story of Mary Crow Dog's coming of age in the Indian civil rights movement is simply told—and, at times, simply horrifying." N Y Times Book Rev

Breckinridge, Mary, 1881-1965

Wells, Rosemary. Mary on horseback; three mountain stories; pictures by Peter McCarty. Dial Bks. for Young Readers 1998 53p il $16.99; lib bdg $16.89   **92**
1. Nurses
ISBN 0-8037-2154-4; 0-8037-2155-2 (lib bdg)
                                        LC 97-43409
Tells the stories of three families who were helped by the work of Mary Breckinridge, the first nurse to go into the Appalachian Mountains and give medical care to the isolated inhabitants. Includes an afterword with facts about Breckinridge and the Frontier Nursing Service she founded

"These beautifully written stories will remain with the reader long after the book is closed." Booklist

Bridges, Ruby

Bridges, Ruby. Through my eyes: the autobiography of Ruby Bridges; articles and interviews compiled and edited by Margo Lundell. Scholastic Press 1999 63p il $16.95   **92**
1. African Americans—Civil rights 2. New Orleans (La.)—Race relations
ISBN 0-590-18923-9   LC 98-49242
Ruby Bridges recounts the story of her involvement, as a six-year-old, in the integration of her school in New Orleans in 1960

"Profusely illustrated with sepia photos—including many gritty journalistic reproductions—this memoir brings some of the raw emotions of a tumultuous period into sharp focus. . . . A powerful personal narrative that every collection will want to own." SLJ

Brooks, Garth

Howey, Paul. Garth Brooks; chart bustin' country. Lerner Pubs. 1998 64p il lib bdg $19.93; pa $6.95   **92**
1. Country musicians 2. Singers
ISBN 0-8225-2898-3 (lib bdg); 0-8225-9809-4 (pa)
                                        LC 97-6888
Follows the life and work of the popular singer-songwriter who went from struggling musician to multi-millionaire

"Howey paints a picture of the person behind the phenomenon, incorporating interviews with Brooks and family members as well as an abundance of interesting photos into the accessible narrative." Booklist

Brown, John, 1800-1859

Cox, Clinton. Fiery vision: the life and death of John Brown. Scholastic 1997 230p il $15.95 (7 and up)   **92**
1. Abolitionists
ISBN 0-590-47574-6   LC 96-21368
A biography of the abolitionist who led the raid on the United States arsenal at Harpers Ferry

"Cox's research traces Brown's controversial life, weaving the historical, political, and social events of an often brutal time into a riveting narrative that will galvanize readers." Bull Cent Child Books

Includes bibliographical references

Bruchac, Joseph, 1942-

Bruchac, Joseph. Bowman's store; a journey to myself. Dial Bks. 1997 311p il $17.99 (7 and up)   **92**
1. Abnaki Indians 2. Authors, American
ISBN 0-8037-1997-3   LC 96-33708
"Combining Native American stories with personal memories and dreams, Bruchac crafts a memoir of his childhood growing up with his grandparents in upstate New York." Horn Book Guide

"Each episode is constructed with a true storyteller's attention to language and plot development. Students of modern Native American cultures will find plenty of food for thought." Booklist

Bunche, Ralph J. (Ralph Johnson), 1904-1971

Schraff, Anne E. Ralph Bunche; winner of the Nobel Peace Prize; [by] Anne Schraff. Enslow Pubs. 1999 128p il (African-American biographies) lib bdg $19.95   **92**
1. African Americans—Biography
ISBN 0-7660-1203-4   LC 98-26886
Discusses the personal and professional life of the statesman and diplomat who was one of the founders of the United Nations and who received the Nobel Prize for his peacemaking efforts

"A solid introduction to a man who devoted his career to fighting war and intolerance." SLJ

Includes bibliographical references

Burns, Anthony, 1834-1862

Hamilton, Virginia. Anthony Burns; the defeat and triumph of a fugitive slave. Knopf 1988 193p lib bdg $14.99; pa $4.99   **92**
1. Slavery—United States 2. African Americans—Biography
ISBN 0-394-98185-5 (lib bdg); 0-679-83997-6 (pa)
                                        LC 87-38063
A biography of the slave who escaped to Boston in 1854, was arrested at the instigation of his owner, and whose trial caused a furor between abolitionists and those determined to enforce the Fugitive Slave Act

"This book does exactly what good biography for children ought to do: takes readers directly into the life of the subject and makes them feel what it was like to be that person in those times." Horn Book

Includes bibliographical references

Burroughs, John, 1837-1921
Wadsworth, Ginger. John Burroughs; the sage of Slabsides. Clarion Bks. 1997 95p il $16.95   92
1. Naturalists
ISBN 0-395-77830-1   LC 95-48400
A photobiography of the naturalist, ornithologist, author, poet, teacher, and pioneer of the conservation movement who lived and worked in his rustic cabin in the Catskill Mountains
"The pictures are mostly informal and candid, taken from personal collections, with a few studio portraits interspersed. Written with a familiar, almost intimate tone, the text is liberally sprinkled with quotes from Burroughs's publications." SLJ
Includes bibliographical references

Bush, Barbara, 1925-
Greenberg, Judith E. Barbara Pierce Bush, 1925-. Children's Press 1999 110p il (Encyclopedia of first ladies) $32   92
1. Presidents' spouses—United States
ISBN 0-516-20475-0   LC 98-45255
A biography of the wife of the forty-first president, describing her childhood, marriage, family life, political activities, and volunteer work for such causes as literacy and AIDS
Includes bibliographical references

Byars, Betsy Cromer, 1928-
Byars, Betsy Cromer. The moon and I; [by] Betsy Byars. Messner 1991 96p il o.p.; Beech Tree Bks. paperback available $4.95   92
1. Authors, American 2. Women authors
ISBN 0-688-13704-0 (pa)   LC 91-15000
"Weaving back and forth between her recent experiences with snake-watching and her childhood and career, Byars eschews the usual chronology in favor of a more freely associated sequence of episodes that all bear, ultimately, on her writing. . . . Byars uses the element of surprise, injects it with humor, and blends in information at the same time." Bull Cent Child Books

Caesar, Julius, 100-44 B.C.
Bruns, Roger. Julius Caesar. Chelsea House 1987 112p il (World leaders past & present) lib bdg $19.95   92
1. Emperors—Rome 2. Rome—History
ISBN 0-87754-514-6   LC 87-6339
"Drawing in part upon writings of the Greek historian Plutarch, the Roman historian Suetonius, and Shakespeare, [the author] tells the story of Caesar. . . . Bruns' well-paced analytical text points out the many facets of this complex man." Booklist
Includes bibliographical references

Calamity Jane, 1852-1903
Faber, Doris. Calamity Jane; her life and her legend. Houghton Mifflin 1992 62p il $16; pa $6.95   92
1. Cowhands
ISBN 0-395-56396-8; 0-395-86539-5 (pa)
                                      LC 91-40050

Examines the life of the Wild West heroine, born Mary Jane Cannary, who was transformed into a legendary figure in the public mind
"With little reliable fact to go on, Faber's portrait of Cannary remains elusive, but the legend of Calamity Jane comes through strong and clear. . . . The book is spaciously and cleanly designed, with reproductions of old photos and dime novel covers . . . that further the evidence of both life and myth." Bull Cent Child Books
Includes bibliographical references

Sanford, William R. Calamity Jane: frontier original; [by] William R. Sanford & Carl R. Green. Enslow Pubs. 1996 48p il (Legendary heroes of the Wild West) lib bdg $15.95   92
1. Cowhands
ISBN 0-89490-647-X   LC 95-41420
"*Calamity Jane* focuses on uncovering the truth about this unusual woman who dressed like a man, could do a man's job, and could outshoot, outdrink, and outcuss most men. . . . The authors have done a fine job of sorting fact from fiction, giving a well-rounded picture of this woman's life." SLJ

Campbell, Ben Nighthorse
Henry, Christopher E. Ben Nighthorse Campbell; Cheyenne chief and U.S. senator; [by] Christopher Henry. Chelsea House 1994 101p il (North American Indians of achievement) lib bdg $19.95   92
1. Cheyenne Indians 2. Indians of North America
ISBN 0-7910-2046-0   LC 93-27063
A biography of the Senator from Colorado and tribal chief of the Cheyenne Indians
"This is a clear, informative, balanced account of this often controversial, 'maverick' senator. . . . Campbell is an intriguing figure, especially for young adults who may identify with Campbell's quest for meaning, and his desire to experiment." Voice Youth Advocates
Includes bibliographical references

Capone, Al, 1899-1947
King, David C. Al Capone and the roaring twenties. Blackbirch Press 1999 80p il (Notorious Americans and their times) lib bdg $19.95   92
1. Criminals
ISBN 1-56711-218-8   LC 98-14591
The life of one of America's most infamous and powerful gangsters set in 1920s Chicago during the Prohibition
"Important information is here, supplemented by black-and-white photographs and some particularly interesting Web-site references. . . . The introduction to organized crime makes this a worthy addition to most collections." SLJ
Includes bibliographical references

Carnegie, Andrew, 1835-1919
Kent, Zachary. Andrew Carnegie; steel king and friend to libraries. Enslow Pubs. 1999 128p il maps (Historical American biographies) lib bdg $19.95   92
1. Capitalists and financiers 2. Philanthropists
ISBN 0-7660-1212-3   LC 98-3160

Carnegie, Andrew, 1835-1919—*Continued*

A biography of the Scottish immigrant who made a fortune in the steel industry and used much of it for philanthropic causes

Includes glossary and bibliographical references

Meltzer, Milton. The many lives of Andrew Carnegie. Watts 1997 159p il lib bdg $28 (7 and up) **92**

1. Capitalists and financiers 2. Philanthropists

ISBN 0-531-11427-9   LC 96-40144

A biography of the steel industry capitalist and philanthropist

"This fascinating portrait makes a lively read, with no attempt to gloss over or excuse the steelmaker's hard-driving tactics. Readers also get a good look at the times." Booklist

Includes bibliographical references

Carrey, Jim

Wukovits, John F. Jim Carrey. Lucent Bks. 1999 112p il (People in the news) lib bdg $23.70 (7 and up) **92**

1. Actors

ISBN 1-56006-561-3   LC 99-20366

Discusses the life and career of the comedian who has starred in such movies as "The Mask," "Dumb and Dumber," and "The Truman Show"

Includes bibliographical references

Carson, Rachel, 1907-1964

Presnall, Judith Janda. Rachel Carson. Lucent Bks. 1995 96p il (Importance of) $22.45 (7 and up) **92**

1. Women scientists

ISBN 1-56006-052-2   LC 93-49487

This is a "biography of biologist-writer Rachel Carson, whose pioneering book *Silent Spring* called attention to dangers to the environment. . . . As well as providing some information in ecology and related areas, it contains examples of how science publishing and science policy function. It also shows a strong instance of non-traditional family life. . . . This book could be a particularly good choice for students who like both science and writing." Appraisal

Includes bibliographical references

Carver, George Washington, 1864?-1943

Adair, Gene. George Washington Carver. Chelsea House 1989 110p il (Black Americans of achievement) lib bdg $19.95; pa $8.95 **92**

1. Scientists 2. African Americans—Biography

ISBN 1-55546-577-3 (lib bdg); 0-7910-0234-9 (pa)
          LC 89-770

A biography of the African American whose scientific research revolutionized the economy of the South

"Carver's great accomplishments, as this book demonstrates, lay less in his inventions than in his teaching and in his efforts to help the poorest black and white farmers manage on what little they had." Sci Books Films

Includes bibliographical references

Casals, Pablo, 1876-1973

Garza, Hedda. Pablo Casals. Chelsea House 1993 111p il (Hispanics of achievement) lib bdg $19.95; pa $7.95 **92**

1. Violoncellists 2. Hispanic Americans

ISBN 0-7910-1237-9 (lib bdg); 0-7910-1261-1 (pa)
          LC 92-13091

Presents the life and times of the celebrated cellist who modernized cello technique and firmly established the cello as a concert instrument

Includes bibliographical references

Cervantes Saavedra, Miguel de, 1547-1616

Goldberg, Jake. Miguel de Cervantes. Chelsea House 1993 111p il maps (Hispanics of achievement) lib bdg $19.95 **92**

1. Authors, Spanish

ISBN 0-7910-1238-7   LC 92-32543

Describes the life and career of the noted Spanish writer, including the creation of his masterpiece "Don Quixote"

Includes bibliographical references

Chagall, Marc, 1887-1985

Pozzi, Gianni. Chagall; illustrated by Claudia Saraceni, L.R. Galante. Bedrick Bks. 1997 64p il (Masters of art) $22.50 **92**

1. Artists, Russian

ISBN 0-87226-527-7   LC 97-7330

A "look at Chagall's life, art, and times. Not a standard biography, this visually stunning, oversized volume looks at where the artist came from; the influences in his life; and the people, places, and artistic and cultural developments that took place during his 97 years. . . . A visual gallery complemented by an intelligent and far-ranging text." SLJ

Chaka, Zulu Chief, 1787?-1828

Stanley, Diane. Shaka, king of the Zulus; [by] Diane Stanley and Peter Vennema; illustrated by Diane Stanley. Morrow Junior Bks. 1988 unp il $15.93; lib bdg $14.88; pa $5.95 **92**

1. Zulu (African people)

ISBN 0-688-07342-5; 0-688-07343-3 (lib bdg); 0-688-13114-X (pa)   LC 87-27376

A biography of the nineteenth-century military genius and Zulu chief

"Diane Stanley and Peter Vennema have culled the massive amount of historical material that exists about this strange and fascinating figure. Their text is lucid; the incidents are tactfully within the scope and decorum of a children's book but representative and true to the facts." N Y Times Book Rev

Includes bibliographical references

Charles, Ray

Turk, Ruth. Ray Charles: soul man. Lerner Publs. 1996 112p il (Newsmakers) lib bdg $23.93 **92**

1. African American singers

ISBN 0-8225-4928-X   LC 95-20953

Charles, Ray—_Continued_
A biography of the African American popular singer, who became blind as a young boy
"The material about Charles's childhood is compelling. Turk includes the unpleasant aspects of his subject's life—his failed marriages and drug addiction." SLJ
Includes discography and bibliographical references

Chavez, Cesar, 1927-1993
Cedeño, Maria E. Cesar Chavez; labor leader; consultants: Julian Nava, Yolanda Quintanilla-Finley. Millbrook Press 1993 32p il (Hispanic heritage) lib bdg $19.90; pa $4.95   92
1. United Farm Workers of America 2. Migrant labor 3. Mexican Americans
ISBN 1-56294-280-8 (lib bdg); 1-56294-808-3 (pa)
LC 92-22620
Traces the accomplishments of the labor leader who fought to improve the lives of Mexican American farm workers in California
"There is enough information for reports, and the scope is a bit greater than encyclopedia entries. . . . Although the literary quality is not high, the information is correct and the nonthreatening look may appeal to students." SLJ
Includes bibliographical references

Collins, David R. Farmworker's friend: the story of Cesar Chavez. Carolrhoda Bks. 1996 80p il (Trailblazers) lib bdg $22.60   92
1. United Farm Workers of America 2. Migrant labor 3. Mexican Americans
ISBN 0-87614-982-4   LC 95-42759
Examines the life and accomplishments of the Mexican American labor activist who helped organize migrant farm workers and establish a union to fight for their rights
"Set against the backdrop of turbulent times aspects of Chavez' personal life are smoothly blended with his continued struggles to improve the plight of his fellow man. The book is enriched by black-and-white photographs and authenticated by the inclusion of a notes section providing additional information on incidents mentioned in the text." Booklist
Includes bibliographical references

Churchill, Sir Winston, 1874-1965
Severance, John B. Winston Churchill; soldier, statesman, artist. Clarion Bks. 1996 144p il map $17.95   92
1. Great Britain—Politics and government—1900-1999 (20th century)
ISBN 0-395-69853-7   LC 94-25129
This "biography presents an affectionate portrait of Britain's renowned Prime Minister. Although Severance focuses on Churchill's contributions during World War II, he also describes the statesman's boyhood, Boer War adventures, and political ascendancy." SLJ
"This fair, balanced, and duly appreciative biography is handsomely produced and illustrated with a fine collection of photographs." Horn Book Guide
Includes bibliographical references

Cisneros, Henry
Bredeson, Carmen. Henry Cisneros; building a better America. Enslow Pubs. 1995 128p il (People to know) lib bdg $19.95   92
1. Mexican Americans 2. Cabinet officers
ISBN 0-89490-546-5   LC 94-41906
This is a biography of the Secretary of the Department of Housing and Urban Development during the Clinton administration and the first Hispanic American mayor of a major U.S. city, San Antonio, Texas
Includes bibliographical references

Cisneros, Sandra
Mirriam-Goldberg, Caryn. Sandra Cisneros; Latina writer and activist. Enslow Pubs. 1998 112p il maps (Hispanic biographies) lib bdg $19.95
92
1. Authors, American 2. Mexican Americans 3. Women authors
ISBN 0-7660-1045-7   LC 98-20828
Surveys the life and work of this award-winning Latina author
"An inspirational portrait of a Latina woman who showed perseverance and grit, overcoming poverty and cultural biases to become a noted writer and activist. . . . A valuable title, especially where the writer's books are studied." SLJ
Includes bibliographical references

Cleary, Beverly
Cleary, Beverly. A girl from Yamhill: a memoir. Morrow 1988 279p il $19.95   92
1. Authors, American 2. Women authors
ISBN 0-688-07800-1   LC 87-31554
Also available in paperback from Avon Camelot Bks.
Follows the popular children's author from her childhood years in Oregon through high school and into young adulthood, highlighting her family life and her growing interest in writing
"The author sees her child self with the same clarity and objectivity as she has seen her fictional characters, and her reminiscences have a resultant integrity and candor." Bull Cent Child Books

Cleary, Beverly. My own two feet. Morrow Junior Bks. 1995 261p il $16   92
1. Authors, American 2. Women authors
ISBN 0-688-14267-2   LC 95-1764
Also available in paperback from Avon Camelot Bks.
This second installment in the author's autobiography "begins during the '30s, with the young Cleary leaving her home state of Oregon to attend junior college in California. The volume ends in 1949, with Morrow's acceptance of Cleary's first novel, the now-classic _Henry Huggins_." Publ Wkly
"Cleary recalls the past with humor, affection, and insight. Those who have always admired her books will, after reading this memoir, have an even greater admiration for the author." Horn Book

Clemens, Roger

Macht, Norman L. (Norman Lee). Roger Clemens; introduction by Jim Murray. Chelsea House 1999 63p il (Baseball legends) $16.95
92

1. Baseball—Biography
ISBN 0-7910-5156-0 LC 98-51064
A biography of the pitcher for the Boston Red Sox, Toronto Blue Jays, and New York Yankees who won his fourth Cy Young award in 1997
Includes bibliographical references

Cleopatra, Queen of Egypt, d. 30 B.C.

Brooks, Polly Schoyer. Cleopatra; goddess of Egypt, enemy of Rome. HarperCollins Pubs. 1995 151p il maps $15.95; lib bdg $15.89 (7 and up)
92

1. Queens 2. Egypt—History
ISBN 0-06-023607-8; 0-06-023608-6 (lib bdg)
LC 95-10688
The "portrait that emerges here of the last Ptolomeic ruler of Egypt is an admiring one: she is charming and erudite, multilingual, a brave warrior, a savvy politician and, above all, a beloved queen dedicated to maintaining Egypt's independence from Rome. Her relationship with Julius Caesar is portrayed as motivated by personal attraction, not political expediency; with Mark Antony, mutual need is said to have led to affection. Avoiding the temptation to tell too much, Brooks demonstrates a keen eye for recognizing the essential components of a compelling narrative." Publ Wkly
Includes bibliographical references

Stanley, Diane. Cleopatra; [by] Diane Stanley, Peter Vennema; illustrated by Diane Stanley. Morrow Junior Bks. 1994 unp il maps $16; lib bdg $15.93; pa $5.95
92
1. Queens 2. Egypt—History
ISBN 0-688-10413-4; 0-688-10414-2 (lib bdg); 0-688-15480-8 (pa) LC 93-27032
Using a "picture book biography format . . . Stanley and Vennema present the life of a legend, Cleopatra. . . . The story concerns Cleopatra's life from the age of 18, when she became the queen of Egypt (51 B.C.), through her liaisons with Julius Caesar and Mark Antony, and her struggle to bring back Egypt's former glory, to her death at the age of 39. . . . An intriguing portrait." Booklist
Includes bibliographical references

Clinton, Bill, 1946-

Cwiklik, Robert. Bill Clinton; president of the 90s. Millbrook Press 1997 48p il (Gateway biography) lib bdg $21.90; pa $8.95 **92**
1. Presidents—United States
ISBN 0-7613-0129-1; 0-7613-0146-1 (pa)
LC 97-797
First published 1993
Covers the Clinton presidency through his 1996 re-election campaign

Kelly, Michael. Bill Clinton. Chelsea House 1999 112p il (Overcoming adversity) lib bdg $19.95; pa $8.95 (7 and up) **92**
1. Presidents—United States
ISBN 0-7910-4700-8 (lib bdg); 0-7910-4701-6 (pa)
LC 98-13775
Presents a biography of the forty-second president, who survived a difficult childhood with an abusive stepfather to become the youngest governor of Arkansas and serve two terms as American president
"The author provides a good balance between coverage of Clinton's achievements and problems. . . . A useful book for reports." SLJ
Includes bibliographical references

Landau, Elaine. Bill Clinton and his presidency. Watts 1997 63p il lib bdg $22; pa $6.95 **92**
1. Presidents—United States
ISBN 0-531-20295-X; 0-531-15841-1 (pa)
LC 96-37870
"A First book"
Examines Bill Clinton's first four years in office as president, including his work on domestic affairs and foreign relations
"A straightforward, workmanlike biography of the president." SLJ
Includes glossary and bibliographical references

Clinton, Hillary Rodham, 1947-

Kozar, Richard. Hillary Rodham Clinton. Chelsea House 1998 112p il (Women of achievement) lib bdg $19.95; pa $9.95 **92**
1. Presidents' spouses—United States
ISBN 0-7910-4712-1 (lib bdg); 0-7910-4713-X (pa)
LC 97-45702
Examines the childhood, family life, and social and political activities of this powerful and important First Lady
"With an engaging narrative style marked by frequent quotations and occasional humor, the author paints a portrait of this talented, ambitious woman." SLJ
Includes bibliographical references

Close, Chuck, 1940-

Greenberg, Jan. Chuck Close, up close; [by] Jan Greenberg and Sandra Jordan. DK Ink 1998 48p il $19.95 **92**
1. Artists, American
ISBN 0-7894-2486-X LC 97-31076
A biography of the revisionist artist who achieved prominence in the late 1960s for enormous, photographically realistic, black and white portraits of himself and his friends
"In this moving account of the acclaimed portraitist's triumph over a severe learning disorder and physical disabilities, handsome reproductions, photos and Close's own observations illuminate the sources of his innovative artistic approach." Publ Wkly
Includes glossary and bibliographical references

Cochise, Apache Chief, d. 1874
Schwarz, Melissa. Cochise, Apache chief. Chelsea House 1992 119p il maps (North American Indians of achievement) lib bdg $19.95; pa $9.95 **92**
1. Apache Indians
ISBN 0-7910-1706-0; 0-7910-1694-3 (pa)
LC 91-23495
Examines the life and career of the noted Apache warrior chief
"This sympathetic profile of a strong Native American leader, illustrated with many black-and-white museum maps, reproductions, and photographs, would be best read along with a book on Apache history." SLJ
Includes bibliographical references

Coleman, Bessie, 1896?-1926
Hart, Philip S. Up in the air: the story of Bessie Coleman. Carolrhoda Bks. 1996 80p il (Trailblazers) lib bdg $16.96; pa $6.95 **92**
1. Women air pilots 2. African American pilots
ISBN 0-87614-949-2 (lib bdg); 0-87614-978-6 (pa)
LC 95-32906
Presents the story of Bessie Coleman, an American, who in 1920 traveled to France to become the first black woman to earn a pilot's license
This "will be useful for research and recreational reading." SLJ
Includes bibliographical references

Columbus, Christopher
Meltzer, Milton. Columbus and the world around him. Watts 1990 192p il maps lib bdg $28
92
1. Explorers 2. America—Exploration
ISBN 0-531-10899-6 LC 89-24764
Describes the voyages of Columbus, the terrible impact of the Spaniards on the Indians, and the ultimate cultural influence of the Native Americans on their white conquerors
"Meltzer excels in a candid and graphic exposé of the Spaniards' behaviors and attitudes, including enormous cruelty and greed. . . . This thought-provoking book includes handsome and profuse reproductions of historical maps, artwork, manuscripts, and letters." Booklist
Includes bibliographical references

Confucius
Wilker, Josh. Confucius; philosopher and teacher. Watts 1999 111p il (Book report biography) lib bdg $22 **92**
1. Philosophers
ISBN 0-531-11436-8 LC 97-18362
A biography of the Chinese teacher and sage whose teachings influenced all aspects of Chinese life for many centuries after his death
Includes bibliographical references

Cosby, Bill, 1937-
Schuman, Michael. Bill Cosby; actor and comedian; [by] Michael A. Schuman. Enslow Pubs. 1995 128p il (People to know) lib bdg $19.95 **92**
1. African American entertainers 2. Comedians
ISBN 0-89490-548-1 LC 95-9811
Describes the life of Bill Cosby from his childhood in Philadelphia through his successful career as a comedian
Includes bibliographical references

Crazy Horse, Sioux Chief, ca. 1842-1877
Freedman, Russell. The life and death of Crazy Horse; drawings by Amos Bad Heart Bull. Holiday House 1996 166p il maps $21.95 **92**
1. Oglala Indians
ISBN 0-8234-1219-9 LC 95-33303
A biography of the Oglala leader who relentlessly resisted the white man's attempt to take over Indian lands
This is "a compelling biography that is based on primary source documents and illustrated with pictographs by a Sioux band historian." Voice Youth Advocates
Includes bibliographical references

Crick, Francis, 1916-
Edelson, Edward. James Watson and Francis Crick and the building blocks of life. See entry under Watson, James D., 1928-

Cruise, Tom
Powell, Phelan. Tom Cruise; introduction by James Scott Brady. Chelsea House 1999 110p il (Overcoming adversity) $19.95; pa $9.95 **92**
1. Actors
ISBN 0-7910-4940-X; 0-7910-4941-8 (pa)
LC 98-47621
Follows the life and career of the popular actor, focusing on his struggle with dyslexia, his starring roles in such movies as "Risky Business," "Top Gun," and "Jerry Maguire," and his involvement in the Church of Scientology
Includes filmography and bibliographical references

Curie, Marie, 1867-1934
Pasachoff, Naomi E. Marie Curie and the science of radioactivity; [by] Naomi Pasachoff. Oxford Univ. Press 1996 109p il (Oxford portraits in science) lib bdg $21; pa $11.95 (7 and up)
92
1. Chemists 2. Women scientists
ISBN 0-19-509214-7; 0-19-512011-6 (pa)
LC 95-13639
"The book discusses the lack of recognition accorded the Curies by the French scientific community, the personal attacks Curie experienced because of her friendship with Paul Langevin, and professional criticisms of her work. Boxed sections provide related information on such topics as radioactivity, radon, and Mendeleyev's organization of the periodic table." Booklist
"This is a thorough biography, particularly useful for reports." SLJ
Includes bibliographical references

Curie, Marie, 1867-1934—*Continued*

Poynter, Margaret. Marie Curie: discoverer of radium. Enslow Pubs. 1994 128p il maps (Great minds of science) lib bdg $19.95 **92**
1. Chemists 2. Women scientists
ISBN 0-89490-477-9 LC 93-21224
This "biography emphasizes Marie Curie's early life of poverty, desire to study, and contributions to the fields of chemistry, physics, and medicine." Horn Book Guide
"The writing style is straightforward, with a combination of personal detail and scientific explanation. . . . Sure to be in demand for those middle-grade biography and science assignments." Booklist
Includes glossary and bibliographical references

Dahl, Roald

Dahl, Roald. Boy: tales of childhood. Farrar, Straus & Giroux 1984 160p il $16 **92**
1. Authors, English
ISBN 0-374-37374-4 LC 84-48462
Also available in paperback from Viking
"In these memoirs, Dahl reminisces about growing up in a large Norwegian family living in Wales during the 1920s and 1930s. The text is illustrated with sketches, old photographs and excerpts of letters he wrote as a boy." SLJ
"This should be of particular interest to Dahl's fans, but it should also appeal to anyone who likes writing that is direct, candid, and free-flowing." Bull Cent Child Books

Dahl, Roald. Going solo. Farrar, Straus & Giroux 1986 207p il $14.95 **92**
1. Authors, English 2. World War, 1939-1945—Personal narratives
ISBN 0-374-16503-3 LC 86-12022
Also available in paperback from Viking
Continuing his autobiography, the author presents his impressions of Tanzania, where he worked for the Shell Oil Company prior to World War II, and describes his later experiences as a RAF fighter pilot
"A brief, masterly remembrance of the gifts of youth and good luck." Time

Dalai Lama XIV, 1935-

Demi. The Dalai Lama; a biography of the Tibetan spiritual and political leader. Holt & Co. 1998 unp il $16.95 **92**
1. Buddhism 2. Tibet (China)
ISBN 0-8050-5443-X LC 97-30654
In this biography of the Buddhist spiritual leader, Demi "uses straightforward prose and fluid, eastern-influenced art—small pen-and-ink and watercolor images with fine, intricate detail. . . . Told with respect and devotion, this is an inspirational picture-book biography." Horn Book

Darwin, Charles, 1809-1882

Parker, Steve. Charles Darwin and evolution. Chelsea House 1995 c1992 32p il (Science discoveries) lib bdg $15.95 **92**
1. Naturalists 2. Evolution
ISBN 0-7910-3007-5 LC 94-20656

Also available Spanish language edition
First published 1992 by HarperCollins Pubs.
Traces the life of the English naturalist from his early years through his expedition aboard the H.M.S. Beagle and the development of his theory of evolution by natural selection
Includes glossary and bibliographical references

Stefoff, Rebecca. Charles Darwin and the evolution revolution. Oxford Univ. Press 1996 126p il (Oxford portraits in science) lib bdg $21; pa $11.95 (7 and up) **92**
1. Naturalists 2. Evolution
ISBN 0-19-508996-0 (lib bdg); 0-19-512028-0 (pa)
LC 95-35802
Examines the personality as well as the thought process which led this naturalist to his discoveries which have helped shape our understanding of the natural world
"Extensive photos of Darwin and his family, friends, and colleagues, as well as reproductions of public notices and cartoons, are handsome additions to the nicely laid-out text. . . . It offers generally thorough, clear explanations of Darwin's scientific theories and sheds light on his personality." Booklist
Includes glossary and bibliographical references

Davis, Jefferson, 1808-1889

Burch, Joann Johansen. Jefferson Davis; president of the Confederacy. Enslow Pubs. 1998 128p il maps (Historical American biographies) lib bdg $19.95 **92**
1. United States—History—1861-1865, Civil War 2. Confederate States of America
ISBN 0-7660-1064-3 LC 97-18046
Traces the life of the president of the Confederacy from his childhood, through his rise in Southern politics, and to his role as leader of the South during the Civil War
"The well-organized text is clear and readable, with short, simply constructed sentences. Well-designed half-page sidebars explain important terms or events." SLJ
Includes bibliographical references

Degas, Edgar, 1834-1917

Skira-Venturi, Rosabianca. A weekend with Degas. Rizzoli Int. Publs. 1992 c1991 63p il $19.95 **92**
1. Artists, French
ISBN 0-8478-1439-4 LC 91-38364
The nineteenth-century French artist talks about his life and work as if entertaining the reader for the weekend. Includes reproductions of the artist's work and a list of museums where works are on display
This is a "beautiful, informative book." Soc Educ

Diana, Princess of Wales, 1961-1997

Krohn, Katherine E. Princess Diana; [by] Katherine Krohn. Lerner Publs. 1999 112p il (A & E biography) $25.26 **92**
ISBN 0-8225-4941-7 LC 98-27491
A biography of the young woman who married Britain's Prince Charles in 1981 and lived in the public eye until her tragic death in 1997
Includes bibliographical references

Dickinson, Emily, 1830-1886

Dommermuth-Costa, Carol. Emily Dickinson; singular poet. Lerner Publs. 1998 112p il $25.26   **92**

1. Poets, American 2. Women poets
ISBN 0-8225-4958-1   LC 97-40081
Examines the life, work, and significance of the visionary poet from Amherst, Massachusetts
"Extensive quotations from poems and letters help bring the major figures to life and offer a period flavor as well. A solid addition to biography collections." Booklist
Includes bibliographical references

Disney, Walt, 1901-1966

Walt Disney: his life in pictures; edited by Russell Schroeder; photographs from the Walt Disney Archives; quoted material drawn from interviews with Walt Disney; introduction by Diane Disney Miller. Disney Press 1996 64p il $15.95; lib bdg $15.89   **92**

1. Animation (Cinematography) 2. Motion pictures—Biography
ISBN 0-7868-3116-2; 0-7868-5043-4 (lib bdg)
    LC 96-17248
"Schroeder has compiled a scrapbook of 178 photos, many never before published, from the company archives. Focusing on Walt Disney's (1901-1966) private life, as well as his career as animator, film producer and television personality, the chronologically arranged shots are accompanied by extended captions and quotations from interviews and films." Publ Wkly
"This is not an in-depth study, but it is an appealing tribute to a creative individual." SLJ
Includes bibliographical references

Domingo, Placido

Stefoff, Rebecca. Plácido Domingo. Chelsea House 1992 111p il (Hispanics of achievement) lib bdg $19.95; pa $8.95   **92**

1. Singers
ISBN 0-7910-1563-7 (lib bdg); 0-7910-1692-7 (pa)
    LC 91-32358
Profiles the life and career of the Spanish opera singer who is also known in the world of popular music
Includes discography and videography

Douglass, Frederick, 1817?-1895

Douglass, Frederick. Escape from slavery; the boyhood of Frederick Douglass in his own words; edited and illustrated by Michael McCurdy; foreword by Coretta Scott King. Knopf 1994 63p il $15; pa $6.99   **92**

1. Abolitionists 2. African Americans—Biography
ISBN 0-679-84652-2; 0-679-84651-4 (pa)
    LC 93-19239
A shortened autobiography presenting the early life of the slave who became an abolitionist, journalist, and statesman
"McCurdy has done a splendid job of bringing the *Narrative of the Life of Frederick Douglass* to middle-grade readers. There are brief introductory notes about

what's been left out in each chapter; otherwise, the voice is Douglass' own, in all its simplicity, lyricism, and fury." Booklist
Includes bibliographical references

Drake, Sir Francis, 1540?-1596

Marrin, Albert. The sea king: Sir Francis Drake and his times. Atheneum Bks. for Young Readers 1995 168p il maps $20 (7 and up)   **92**

1. Explorers
ISBN 0-689-31887-1   LC 95-60386
"Sir Francis Drake is seen variously as explorer, naval military genius, and pirate; Marrin paints a picture including all those characteristics and more, tracing Drake's life from his early days on the sea, through his unsuccessful and successful quests for Central American gold and his global circumnavigation, to his unofficial spearheading of the defeat of the Spanish Armada." Bull Cent Child Books
"Marrin does an exemplary job of defining words in context, incorporating quotations, explaining both sides of a conflict, all while retaining the essential drama of Britain's most famous sailor. Marrin's Drake is not just a swashbuckling hero, but a complex character." Voice Youth Advocates
Includes bibliographical references

Drew, Charles Richard, 1904-1950

Talmadge, Katherine S. The life of Charles Drew; illustrated by Antonio Castro. 21st Cent. Bks. (NY) 1992 84p il (Pioneers in health and medicine) lib bdg $13.95   **92**

1. Surgeons 2. African Americans—Biography
ISBN 0-941477-65-7   LC 91-29854
A biography of the black surgeon who was noted for his research on blood plasma
The life of the medical researcher is "recounted in clear, lively detail and the importance of [his] work is placed in historical perspective without unnecessarily weighing down the [text]." SLJ
Includes bibliographical references

Du Bois, W. E. B. (William Edward Burghardt), 1868-1963

McDaniel, Melissa. W.E.B. DuBois; scholar and civil rights activist. Watts 1999 96p il (Book report biography) lib bdg $22   **92**

1. African Americans—Biography
ISBN 0-531-11433-3   LC 98-8718
Examines the life of the African American scholar and leader who helped establish the NAACP and devoted his life to gaining equality for his people
Includes bibliographical references

McKissack, Patricia C. W.E.B. DuBois; [by] Patricia and Fredrick McKissack. Watts 1990 143p il (Impact biography) lib bdg $23.60   **92**

1. African Americans—Biography
ISBN 0-531-10939-9   LC 90-37823
"William Edward Burghardt DuBois (1868-1963) is acknowledged as the great African-American journalist, author, educator, historian, and as one of the most impor-

Du Bois, W. E. B. (William Edward Burghardt), 1868-1963—*Continued*
tant civil rights leaders of the 20th century. This is a biography that emphasizes his dedication, determination, disappointment, and triumph in the continuing struggle for worldwide human rights." Voice Youth Advocates
Includes bibliographical references

Troy, Don. W.E.B. DuBois. Child's World 1999 39p il (Journey to freedom) lib bdg $16.95   **92**
1. African Americans—Biography
ISBN 1-56766-555-1   LC 98-4328
A brief biography of the African American educator and activist who helped found the NAACP and worked much of his life to gain equitable treatment for his people
"Attractive and clearly written. . . . The large, beautifully reproduced sepia-toned photographs on almost every page help personalize the text." SLJ
Includes glossary and bibliographical references

Dunbar, Paul Laurence, 1872-1906
Gentry, Tony. Paul Laurence Dunbar. Chelsea House 1989 110p il (Black Americans of achievement) $19.95; pa $8.95   **92**
1. Poets, American 2. African American authors
ISBN 1-55546-583-8; 0-7910-0223-3 (pa)
                                       LC 88-16140
An examination of the life of the black poet and novelist
"The book is skillfully crafted, with a smooth and flowing prose which belies the junior high reading level, and is filled with high quality, intriguing, black and white photos which enhance the text." Voice Youth Advocates
Includes bibliographical references

Duncan, Isadora, 1878-1927
O'Connor, Barbara. Barefoot dancer: the story of Isadora Duncan. Carolrhoda Bks. 1994 95p il (Trailblazers) lib bdg $22.60   **92**
1. Dancers
ISBN 0-87614-807-0   LC 93-14312
Describes the life of the modern dancer who created a spontaneous, free-form dance style accompanied by literary readings and non-dance music
This is "a competent and easy-reading survey of a glamorous life." Bull Cent Child Books
Includes bibliographical references

Earhart, Amelia, 1898-1937
Szabo, Corinne. Sky pioneer: a photobiography of Amelia Earhart. National Geographic Soc. 1997 63p il maps $16   **92**
1. Women air pilots
ISBN 0-7922-3737-4   LC 96-32763
A biography, with numerous photographs and quotes from Earhart herself, tracing this determined woman's life and interest in flying
"Readers will find the anecdotal text, captioned black-and-white photographs, and philosophical quotes from Earhart engrossing and motivating." SLJ
Includes bibliographical references

Earp, Wyatt, 1848-1929
Wukovits, John F. Wyatt Earp. Chelsea House 1997 61p il (Legends of the West) lib bdg $15.95 (7 and up)   **92**
1. Frontier and pioneer life—West (U.S.)
ISBN 0-7910-3852-1   LC 97-3941
Examines the personal life and career of the Western lawman
Includes bibliographical references

Eastman, Charles Alexander, 1858-1939
Badt, Karin Luisa. Charles Eastman; Sioux physician and author. Chelsea House 1995 127p il (North American Indians of achievement) $19.95   **92**
1. Dakota Indians 2. Physicians
ISBN 0-7910-2048-7   LC 94-34896
This is a biography of the Sioux physician, writer, athlete and activist for Native American rights. Illustrated with black-and-white photographs and drawings; a chronology is included
Includes bibliographical references

Edelman, Marian Wright
Old, Wendie. Marian Wright Edelman; fighting for children's rights. Enslow Pubs. 1995 128p il (People to know) lib bdg $19.95 (7 and up)   **92**
1. African American women
ISBN 0-89490-623-2   LC 95-7508
A biography of the African American lawyer and social reformer who is known for her work on behalf of children's rights
Includes bibliographical references

Siegel, Beatrice. Marian Wright Edelman; the making of a crusader. Simon & Schuster Bks. for Young Readers 1995 159p il $15   **92**
1. African American women
ISBN 0-02-782629-5   LC 94-41245
This is a biography of the "advocate for children and civil rights. . . . Siegel focuses mainly on Edelman's political work and her involvement in the civil rights movement." Voice Youth Advocates
This book "has the advantage of using primary sources, including an interview with the subject herself. . . . An unusually good example of contemporary biography." Booklist
Includes bibliographical references

Edison, Thomas A. (Thomas Alva), 1847-1931
Parker, Steve. Thomas Edison and electricity. Chelsea House 1995 32p il (Science discoveries) lib bdg $15.95   **92**
1. Inventors
ISBN 0-7910-3012-1   LC 94-20658
First published 1992 by HarperCollins
Details the life and work of Thomas Edison, who developed such inventions as the stock ticker, the lightbulb, and the phonograph
Includes glossary

Einstein, Albert, 1879-1955

Bernstein, Jeremy. Albert Einstein and the frontiers of physics. Oxford Univ. Press 1996 189p il (Oxford portraits in science) lib bdg $20 (7 and up)   **92**
1. Physicists
ISBN 0-19-509275-9   LC 95-37500
"Bernstein devotes considerable space in this . . . biography to explanations of relativity, quantum mechanics, gravitation, and the relevant mathematical formulas, and to the various scientists whose theories influenced Einstein in some way." SLJ
"Einstein's personal life, his political and religious beliefs, and his work for control of nuclear arms are well covered. . . . Recommended for those who want to know as much about Einstein's science as about his life." Voice Youth Advocates
Includes bibliographical references

Goldberg, Jacob. Albert Einstein. Watts 1996 128p il (Impact biography) lib bdg $24 (7 and up)   **92**
1. Physicists
ISBN 0-531-11251-9   LC 95-48768
Describes the life and work of the scientist whose theory of relativity revolutionized scientific thinking
"Goldberg's well-written summary of biographical information provides a well-organized and quite readable account of Einstein's life story." Booklist
Includes glossary and bibliographical references

Elizabeth I, Queen of England, 1533-1603

Stanley, Diane. Good Queen Bess: the story of Elizabeth I of England; by Diane Stanley and Peter Vennema; illustrated by Diane Stanley. Four Winds Press 1990 unp il $16.95   **92**
1. Queens 2. Great Britain—Kings and rulers 3. Great Britain—History—1485-1603, Tudors
ISBN 0-02-786810-9   LC 88-37501
Follows the life of the strong-willed queen who ruled England in the time of Shakespeare and the defeat of the Spanish Armada
"The handsome illustrations . . . are worthy of their subject. Although the format suggests a picture-book audience, this biography needs to be introduced to older readers who have the background to appreciate and understand this woman who dominated and named an age." SLJ
Includes bibliographical references

Thomas, Jane Resh. Behind the mask: the life of Queen Elizabeth I. Clarion Bks. 1998 196p il maps $19 (7 and up)   **92**
1. Queens 2. Great Britain—Kings and rulers 3. Great Britain—History—1485-1603, Tudors
ISBN 0-395-69120-6   LC 94-31975
This biography "begins with Elizabeth's father, King Henry VIII. . . . Thomas then covers the Tudor queen's life from her negotiation of pre-accession pitfalls to the major aspects of her tenure, both political and personal." Bull Cent Child Books
This is a "vital and intelligent biography. Throughout, Thomas has a good story to tell—one full of intrigue, passion, and larger-than-life characters—and her docu-

mentation backs it up. This handsome book, filled with black-and-white photographs, contains a stunning eight-page color insert of the queen's life in portraits." Horn Book Guide
Includes bibiographical references

Ellington, Duke, 1899-1974

Old, Wendie. Duke Ellington: giant of jazz; [by] Wendie C. Old. Enslow Pubs. 1996 128p il (African-American biographies) lib bdg $19.95   **92**
1. Jazz musicians 2. African American musicians
ISBN 0-89490-691-7   LC 96-3279
Examines the life and career of the talented jazz composer, bandleader, and pianist, from his childhood in Washington, D.C., through his battle against racism, to his influence on the world of jazz
"This biography will send young jazz enthusiasts back to their CD players or even to the piano to find out for themselves just what was that great Ellington sound." BAYA Book Rev
Includes bibliographical references

Elway, John

Christopher, Matt. In the huddle with—John Elway. Little, Brown 1999 109p il pa $4.50   **92**
1. Denver Broncos (Football team) 2. Football—Biography
ISBN 0-316-13355-8   LC 98-45549
Examines the personal life and football career of the quarterback for the Denver Broncos

Equiano, Olaudah, b. 1745

Cameron, Ann. The kidnapped prince: the life of Olaudah Equiano; by Olaudah Equiano; adapted by Ann Cameron; with an introduction by Henry Louis Gates, Jr. Knopf 1995 133p il $16; pa $4.99   **92**
1. Slavery 2. Blacks—Biography
ISBN 0-679-85619-6; 0-375-80346-7 (pa)
LC 93-29914
Adaptation of The interesting narrative of the life of Olaudah Equiano
This is an "adaptation of an influential slave narrative by an African prince who was kidnapped as a child and later freed from slavery; first published in 1789." N Y Times Book Rev
"The inspired simplicity of Cameron's adaptation quickly allows Equiano's gifted voice to establish a compelling relationship between himself and young readers. Well sculpted with detail." SLJ
Includes glossary and bibliographical references

Estefan, Gloria

Gonzales, Doreen. Gloria Estefan; singer and entertainer. Enslow Pubs. 1998 128p il maps (Hispanic biographies) lib bdg $19.95   **92**
1. Singers 2. Hispanic Americans
ISBN 0-89490-890-1   LC 97-42787
"Estefan is presented as a talented teenager who was able to achieve more than she could have dreamed de-

Estefan, Gloria—*Continued*

spite tragic setbacks in her career. It shows what can be accomplished with a will to persevere. Estefan is portrayed as more than an entertainer. She is devoted to family, social and political concerns. . . . This book highlights the integrity of a positive role model for youth today." Book Rep

Includes discography and bibliographical references

Evans, Minnie, 1892-1987

Lyons, Mary E. Painting dreams: Minnie Evans, visionary artist. Houghton Mifflin 1995 47p il $14.95   **92**

1. African American artists 2. Women artists

ISBN 0-395-72032-X   LC 95-3994

A biography of the North Carolina painter whose art had its origins in her religious visions and the African traditions of her slave ancestors

"A readable, interesting, and well-documented title." SLJ

Includes bibliographical references

Farmer, James

Jakoubek, Robert E. James Farmer and the freedom rides. Millbrook Press 1994 32p il (Gateway civil rights) lib bdg $20.90; pa $4.95
                                                              92

1. African Americans—Biography 2. African Americans—Civil rights

ISBN 1-56294-381-2; 1-56294-860-1 (pa)

                                        LC 93-24143

Presents the life and times of the black civil rights activist who was one of the founders of the Congress of Racial Equality (CORE) and an organizer of the Freedom Rides

Includes bibliographical references

Farnsworth, Philo T., 1906-1971

McPherson, Stephanie Sammartino. TV's forgotten hero: the story of Philo Farnsworth. Carolrhoda Bks. 1996 96p il (Trailblazers) $16.95
                                                              92

1. Inventors 2. Television

ISBN 1-57505-017-X   LC 95-26383

A biography of the persistent experimenter whose interest in electricity led him to develop an electronic television system in the 1920s

This is a "well-researched and accurate biography. . . . There is enough drama and suspense to stimulate readers' interest. Good, clear diagrams explain concepts and theory." SLJ

Includes bibliographical references

Farrakhan, Louis

De Angelis, Therese. Louis Farrakhan. Chelsea House 1998 112p il (Black Americans of achievement) $19.95; pa $8.95   **92**

1. Black Muslims

ISBN 0-7910-4688-5; 0-7910-4689-3 (pa)

                                        LC 98-6101

"De Angelis recounts the life of the . . . leader of the Nation of Islam. . . . The author reveals some pertinent facts about Farrakhan, clearly explains the evolution of his leadership, and clarifies the reasons for the controversy that surrounds him." SLJ

Includes bibliographical references

Haskins, James. Louis Farrakhan and the Nation of Islam; [by] Jim Haskins. Walker & Co. 1996 152p il $15.95; lib bdg $16.85   **92**

1. Black Muslims

ISBN 0-8027-8422-4; 0-8027-8423-2 (lib bdg)

                                        LC 96-3607

A biography of the Afro-American who dreamed of a career as a violinist before joining the Nation of Islam and rising in its ranks, eventually becoming its leader

"A good use of primary source material and quotes, relevant footnoting, and a solid bibliography enhance this well-organized book." Booklist

Favre, Brett

Gutman, Bill. Brett Favre; leader of the pack. Millbrook Press 1998 48p il (Millbrook sports world) lib bdg $19.90; pa $6.95   **92**

1. Green Bay Packers (Football team) 2. Football—Biography

ISBN 0-7613-0310-3 (lib bdg); 0-7613-0328-6 (pa)

                                        LC 97-25905

A biography of the star quarterback, from his childhood in small-town Mississippi, through his college days, to his professional career with the Atlanta Falcons and Super Bowl champion Green Bay Packers

This book "will be useful for reports and popular with young sports fans." Booklist

Includes bibliographical references

Fermi, Enrico, 1901-1954

Cooper, Dan. Enrico Fermi and the revolutions in modern physics. Oxford Univ. Press 1999 117p il (Oxford portraits in science) lib bdg $21 (7 and up)   **92**

1. Physicists

ISBN 0-19-511762-X   LC 98-34471

A biography of the Nobel Prize-winning physicist whose work led to the discovery of nuclear fission, the basis of nuclear power and the atom bomb

"This book will be useful for reports. . . . The extensive list for further reading includes biographies of Fermi, books on both scientific and political aspects of the atomic-bomb project, and information on tours of laboratories involved in nuclear research today." SLJ

Filipovic, Zlata

Filipovic, Zlata. Zlata's diary; a child's life in Sarajevo; with an introduction by Janine Di Giovanni; translated with notes by Christina Pribichevich-Zorić. Viking 1994 200p il hardcover o.p. paperback available $8.95 (7 and up)   **92**

1. Sarajevo (Bosnia and Hercegovina)

ISBN 0-14-024205-8 (pa)

"In September 1991, at the beginning of a new school year and while war was already as close as Croatia,

Filipovic, Zlata—*Continued*

Filipovic, a ten-year-old girl in Sarajevo began keeping a diary about her school friends, her classes, and her after-school activities. The following spring that childhood world disappeared when the war moved to Sarajevo." Libr J

"Filipovic's diary personalizes the tragedy in war-torn Sarajevo. A must for YA collections." Booklist

Fleischman, Sid, 1920-

Fleischman, Sid. The abracadabra kid; a writer's life. Greenwillow Bks. 1996 198p il $16; pa $4.95
92

1. Authors, American
ISBN 0-688-14859-X; 0-688-15855-2 (pa)
LC 95-47382

This autobiography, "turns real life into a story complete with cliffhangers. And it's a classic *boy's* story, from card tricks and traveling magic shows to World War II naval experiences and screen-writing gigs for John Wayne movies. En route, we learn how Fleischman learned the craft of writing." Bull Cent Child Books
Includes bibliographical references

Fleming, Alexander, 1881-1955

Gottfried, Ted. Alexander Fleming; discoverer of penicillin. Watts 1997 112p il (Book report biography) lib bdg $21.50
92

1. Bacteriologists 2. Penicillin
ISBN 0-531-11370-1
LC 97-7671

Also available in paperback from Scholastic Bks.
A biography of the British bacteriologist, born in Scotland, who was knighted and awarded the 1945 Nobel Prize in medicine for discovering penicillin

"The easy reading and simple explanations of the medical procedures being developed and practiced make this a good choice for readers looking for a short biography of an interesting scientist." SLJ
Includes glossary and bibliographical references

Fluek, Toby Knobel

Fluek, Toby Knobel. Memories of my life in a Polish village, 1930-1949; paintings, drawings, and text by Toby Knobel Fluek. Knopf 1990 110p il $19.95 (7 and up)
92

1. Jews—Poland 2. Holocaust, 1933-1945—Personal narratives 3. World War, 1939-1945—Jews
ISBN 0-394-58617-4
LC 90-32320

In this "memoir composed equally of text and . . . paintings and drawings, Fluek moves with powerful simplicity through the details of Jewish pre-war life, her struggle to survive the Nazi occupation, and her eventual emigration. Beauty and warmth of illustration combine with clarity of prose to make this a recommendation for readers from middle school on up." Booklist

Fortune, Amos, 1709 or 10-1801

Yates, Elizabeth. Amos Fortune, free man; illustrations by Nora S. Unwin. Dutton 1950 181p il $15.99; pa $4.99
92

1. African Americans—Biography 2. Slavery—United States
ISBN 0-525-25570-2; 0-14-034158-7

Awarded the Newbery Medal, 1951

"Born free in Africa, Amos Fortune was sold into slavery in America in 1725. After more than 40 years of servitude Amos was able to purchase his freedom and, in time, that of several others. He died a tanner of enviable reputation, a landowner, and a respected citizen of his community. Based on fact, this is a . . . story of a life dedicated to the fight for freedom and service to others." Booklist

Fossey, Dian

Matthews, Tom L. Light shining through the mist: a photobiography of Dian Fossey. National Geographic Soc. 1998 64p il $17.95
92

1. Gorillas 2. Women scientists
ISBN 0-7922-7300-1
LC 97-34084

Traces the adventurous life of the American woman who worked as a zoologist among the mountain gorillas of the Virunga area of central Africa

"Gorgeous color photographs will be the main draw to this biography of the controversial primatologist, but Matthews's text also does a fine job." Horn Book
Includes bibliographical references

Frank, Anne, 1929-1945

Frank, Anne. The diary of a young girl; translated from the Dutch by B. M. Mooyaart-Doubleday
92

1. Jews—Netherlands 2. Holocaust, 1933-1945—Personal narratives
Available in various bindings and editions

This is the diary of a "German-Jewish girl who hid from the Nazis with her parents, their friends, and some other fugitives in an Amsterdam warehouse from 1942 to 1944. Her diary, covering the years of hiding, was found by friends and published as *Het achterhus* (1947); it was later published in English as *The Diary of a Young Girl* (1952). . . . Written with humor as well as insight, it shows a growing girl with all the preoccupations of adolescence and first love. The diary ends three days before the Franks and their group were discovered by the Nazis." Reader's Ency. 4th edition

Frank, Anne. The diary of a young girl: the definitive edition; edited by Otto H. Frank and Mirjam Pressler; translated by Susan Massotty. Doubleday 1995 340p $25
92

1. Jews—Netherlands 2. Holocaust, 1933-1945—Personal narratives
ISBN 0-385-47378-8
LC 94-41379

"This new translation of Frank's famous diary includes material about her emerging sexuality and her relationship with her mother that was originally excised by Frank's father, the only family member to survive the Holocaust." Libr J

Gold, Alison Leslie. Memories of Anne Frank; reflections of a childhood friend. Scholastic 1997 135p il $16.95
92

1. Pick-Goslar, Hannah 2. Jews—Netherlands 3. Holocaust, 1933-1945
ISBN 0-590-90722-0
LC 96-41185

Frank, Anne, 1929-1945—*Continued*

This "story of Anne Frank's neighbor and friend, Hannah Elizabeth Pick-Goslar, recounts the tragedy of World War II through a young girl's eyes. . . . The account traces the childhood friendship of the two girls from the time Anne disappeared to the removal of Hannah and her family to concentration camps. The narrative also tells of the brief meeting between Anne and Hannah at Bergen-Belsen shortly before Anne's death." SLJ

"Gold uses carefully chosen details and specific incidents to communicate the horrors of the Holocaust. . . . Readers drawn to Anne Frank's diary will be grateful for the fuller picture rendered here." Publ Wkly

Müller, Melissa. Anne Frank; the biography; translated by Rita and Robert Kimber. Holt & Co. 1998 330p $23; pa $14 (7 and up)   **92**

   1. Jews—Netherlands 2. Holocaust, 1933-1945

   ISBN 0-8050-5996-2; 0-8050-5997-0 (pa)

                  LC 98-22923

This biography covers Anne Frank's life from her childhood to her last days in Bergen-Belsen concentration camp

"Müller includes a family tree; a family history; and considerable insight into the character, personality, and quality of life of Anne's parents, relatives, and friends. Interviews with many of these surviving people give a clearer idea of the situation and Anne's reactions to it." SLJ

Rol, Ruud van der. Anne Frank, beyond the diary; a photographic remembrance; by Ruud van der Rol and Rian Verhoeven; in association with the Anne Frank House; translated by Tony Langham and Plym Peters; with an introduction by Anna Quindlen. Viking 1993 113p il maps $17; pa $8.99   **92**

   1. Jews—Netherlands 2. Holocaust, 1933-1945

   ISBN 0-670-84932-4; 0-14-036926-0 (pa)

                  LC 92-41528

Original Dutch edition, 1992

Photographs, illustrations, and maps accompany historical essays, diary excerpts, and interviews, providing an insight to Anne Frank and the massive upheaval which tore apart her world

"Readers will become absorbed in the richness of the detail and careful explanation which revisit and expand the familiar, well-loved story." Horn Book

Wukovits, John F. Anne Frank. Lucent Bks. 1999 96p il maps (Importance of) $22.45 (7 and up)   **92**

   1. Jews—Netherlands 2. Holocaust, 1933-1945

   ISBN 1-56006-353-X   LC 98-4327

Discusses the life of Anne Frank, focusing on the years she and her family spent in hiding and the impact of her story upon the world

"Do we need yet another book about Anne Frank? The answer is yes, if junior-high and high-school readers want a context for the diary. . . . This combines biography, history, and commentary, in a highly readable format, with photos and boxed quotes from the diary and from other sources." Booklist

Includes bibliographical references

Franklin, Benjamin, 1706-1790

Parker, Steve. Benjamin Franklin and electricity. Chelsea House 1995 32p il (Science discoveries) lib bdg $15.95   **92**

   ISBN 0-7910-3006-7   LC 94-25255

Discusses the life and times of the 18th century statesman, scientist, and inventor

Includes glossary

Freud, Sigmund, 1856-1939

Muckenhoupt, Margaret. Sigmund Freud; explorer of the unconscious. Oxford Univ. Press 1997 157p il (Oxford portraits in science) lib bdg $21; pa $11.95 (7 and up)   **92**

   1. Psychiatrists

   ISBN 0-19-509933-8; 0-19-513212-2 (pa)

                  LC 95-42340

The author discusses "Freud's groundbreaking work in psychoanalysis and includes examples of some of his actual cases to illustrate his theories. His personal life, from his struggle with his Jewish identity to family relationships is explored and related to developments in his work. . . . The writing is clear and concise; terms of psychoanalysis are defined and explained." SLJ

Includes bibliographical references

Fritz, Jean

Fritz, Jean. Homesick: my own story; illustrated with drawings by Margot Tomes and photographs. Putnam 1982 163p il $15.99   **92**

   1. China

   ISBN 0-399-20933-6   LC 82-7646

Also available in paperback from Dell

Companion volume to China homecoming

This is a somewhat fictionalized memoir of the author's childhood in China. "Born in Hankow, where her father was director of the YMCA, Jean loved the city. . . . But she knew she 'belonged on the other side of the world'—in Pennsylvania with her grandmother and her other relations." Horn Book

"The descriptions of places and the times are vivid in a book that brings to the reader, with sharp clarity and candor, the yearnings and fears and ambivalent loyalties of a young girl." Bull Cent Child Books

Fulton, Robert, 1765-1815

Kroll, Steven. Robert Fulton; from submarine to steamboat; illustrated by Bill Farnsworth. Holiday House 1999 il $16.95   **92**

   1. Inventors 2. Steamboats

   ISBN 0-8234-1433-7   LC 98-29944

Describes the life and work of the inventor who developed the steamboat and made it a commercial success

"Report writers will find most of what they need to know about Fulton's early career as a painter of miniatures and panoramas, his later business ventures into marine engineering, and his eventual perfection of the commercially viable steamship which plied the Hudson River." Bull Cent Child Books

Galilei, Galileo, 1564-1642

Fisher, Leonard Everett. Galileo. Macmillan 1992 unp il $15.95   **92**
1. Astronomers
ISBN 0-02-735235-8   LC 91-31146
Examines the life and discoveries of the noted mathematician, physicist, and astronomer, whose work changed the course of science
"The fact-filled yet graceful narrative places Galileo within the continuum of scientific inquiry even as it reveals considerable information about his valuable discoveries." Publ Wkly

Gandhi, Mahatma, 1869-1948

Mitchell, Pratima. Gandhi; the father of modern India; illustrated by Mrinal Mitra. Oxford Univ. Press 1998 31p il (What's their story?) $12.95   **92**
1. India—Politics and government 2. Passive resistance
ISBN 0-19-521434-X   LC 97-38799
A biography of Mahatma Gandhi, the Indian statesman who led his country to freedom from British rule through his policy of nonviolent resistance
"A serviceable, simple biography. . . . The format will appeal to upper-primary or less-competent intermediate readers: one half-page of text and a watercolor drawing on each page." SLJ

Severance, John B. Gandhi, great soul. Clarion Bks. 1997 143p il map $15.95   **92**
1. India—Politics and government 2. Passive resistance
ISBN 0-395-77179-X   LC 95-20887
Severance "begins with an introduction to Gandhi's message and gives a brief overview of the mahatma's personal evolution as well as India's external and internal struggles. He then chronicles Gandhi's life. . . . Severance details Gandhi's philosophy of *satyagraha*, or peaceful resistance." Booklist
"It is not only Gandhi who comes alive in this considered, well-documented biography but the multifarious personalities and politics of his world." Horn Book Guide
Includes bibliographical references

García Márquez, Gabriel, 1928-

Dolan, Sean. Gabriel García Márquez. Chelsea House 1994 127p il (Hispanics of achievement) lib bdg $19.95   **92**
1. Authors, Colombian
ISBN 0-7910-1243-3   LC 93-9478
Discusses the life and career of the Colombian novelist who achieved fame in a genre known as magical realism and who won the 1982 Nobel Prize for literature
Includes bibliographical references

Garvey, Marcus, 1887-1940

Lawler, Mary. Marcus Garvey. Chelsea House 1988 110p il (Black Americans of achievement) lib bdg $19.95; pa $9.95   **92**
1. Universal Negro Improvement Association 2. African Americans—Biography
ISBN 1-55546-587-0 (lib bdg); 0-7910-0203-9 (pa)
LC 87-14593

The author "traces Garvey's life from his birth in Jamaica to his founding of the Universal Negro Improvement Association (UNIA) and his lifelong efforts to secure an independent African homeland for all the world's blacks." Booklist
Includes bibliographical references

Gates, Bill, 1955-

Woog, Adam. Bill Gates. Lucent Bks. 1999 127p il (People in the news) $22.45 (7 and up)   **92**
1. Microsoft Corporation 2. Businessmen
ISBN 1-56006-256-8   LC 98-18162
A biography of Bill Gates including his childhood, his early work in computers, the founding of Microsoft and the expansion of the company, his private life, and future prospects
"Although not an extensive biography, it hits the high points and portrays Gates's family, his successes, and his shortcomings. This book will suit assignment needs." SLJ
Includes bibliographical references

Gauguin, Paul, 1848-1903

Greenfeld, Howard. Paul Gauguin. Abrams 1993 92p il (First impressions) $19.95 (7 and up)   **92**
1. Artists, French
ISBN 0-8109-3376-4   LC 93-9454
Examines the life and work of the nineteenth-century post-Impressionist painter known for his use of bright colors and his depiction of South Seas scenes
This is "written in a conversational tone that will hold readers' interest. . . . The format is an open and inviting one, and the numerous full-color reproductions are of excellent quality. Engaging and informative." SLJ

Genghis Khan, 1162-1227

Humphrey, Judy. Genghis Khan. Chelsea House 1987 111p il (World leaders past & present) lib bdg $19.95   **92**
1. Kings and rulers
ISBN 0-87754-527-8   LC 87-5194
Traces the life of the chief of a small Mongol tribe who established a vast empire from Peking to the Black Sea in the twelfth century
"The author succeeds admirably in presenting 800-year-old history in a powerful present tense. An era that will be unfamiliar to many, Humphrey's view of the culture and time is well balanced." Booklist
Includes bibliographical references

George, Jean Craighead, 1919-

George, Jean Craighead. A tarantula in my purse; and 172 other wild pets; written and illustrated by Jean Craighead George. HarperCollins Pubs. 1996 134p il $14.95; lib bdg $14.89; pa $4.95   **92**
1. Women authors 2. Authors, American 3. Naturalists 4. Pets
ISBN 0-06-023626-4; 0-06-023627-2 (lib bdg); 0-06-446201-3 (pa)   LC 95-54151

George, Jean Craighead, 1919-—*Continued*

"George tells of the many wild pets that lived with her family, particularly while her children were growing up. Each chapter describes a different animal or incident." Booklist

"Told in a casual and thoroughly engaging manner, the stories will enchant all animal lovers and even those who aren't." SLJ

Geronimo, Apache Chief, 1829-1909

Schwarz, Melissa. Geronimo, Apache warrior. Chelsea House 1992 127p il maps (North American Indians of achievement) lib bdg $19.95; pa $9.95 **92**

1. Apache Indians

ISBN 0-7910-1701-X (lib bdg); 0-7910-1691-9 (pa)

LC 91-12691

Examines the life and career of the Apache warrior chief

"This is an eye-opening account." SLJ

Includes bibliographical references

Glenn, John, 1921-

Kramer, Barbara. John Glenn; a space biography. Enslow Pubs. 1998 48p il (Countdown to space) lib bdg $18.95 **92**

1. Astronauts

ISBN 0-89490-964-9

LC 97-17978

A biography of the first American to orbit the earth. Covering his youth, his career as an astronaut, and his life after NASA

"The information is well organized and the rigors of training and space flight are clearly explained." SLJ

Includes glossary and bibliographical references

Goddard, Robert Hutchings, 1882-1945

Coil, Suzanne M. Robert Hutchings Goddard; pioneer of rocketry and space flight. Facts on File 1992 134p il (Makers of modern science) lib bdg $19.95 (7 and up) **92**

1. Scientists

ISBN 0-8160-2591-6

LC 91-47503

Discusses the life and achievements of a pioneer in the fields of rocketry and space flight

Includes bibliographical references

Gogh, Vincent van, 1853-1890

Skira-Venturi, Rosabianca. A weekend with Van Gogh; text by Rosabianca Skira-Venturi; translated by Ann Keay Beneduce. Rizzoli Int. Publs. 1994 62p il $19.95 **92**

1. Artists, Dutch

ISBN 0-8478-1836-5

LC 94-16262

The author "has designed the narrative as a letter from the artist to the son of his beloved brother, Theo. . . . Within this framework, Skira-Venturi integrates art history and analysis with biographical detail to place the subject's work in an understandable context, particularly in relation to the Impressionists." Horn Book

Goldberg, Whoopi

Caper, William. Whoopi Goldberg; comedian and movie star. Enslow Pubs. 1999 128p il (African-American biographies) lib bdg $19.95 **92**

1. African American entertainers

ISBN 0-7660-1205-0

LC 98-30306

Examines the life and career of the versatile actress and comedian who overcame a drug addiction and became the first black female Academy Award winner since 1939

"The facts of Goldberg's life make for an inspirational story, but the biography will be more useful as a reference than as a motivational tool. A chronology, a filmography, suggested readings, notes, and an adequate number of black-and-white photos are provided." Booklist

Gaines, Ann. Whoopi Goldberg; introduction by James Scott Brady. Chelsea House 1999 112p il (Overcoming adversity) $19.95; pa $9.95 **92**

1. African American entertainers

ISBN 0-7910-4938-8; 0-7910-4939-6 (pa)

LC 98-41265

A biography of the single mother, former welfare recipient, and one-time drug addict whose determination helped her become a successful actress and television personality

This book is "generally well-written. . . . The series layout is clean and the typeface easy to read. There are many clear black-and-white photos." Booklist

Includes filmography and bibliographical references

Gordeeva, Ekaterina

Shea, Pegi Deitz. Ekaterina Gordeeva. Chelsea House 1999 64p il $19.95; pa $9.95 **92**

1. Ice skating—Biography 2. Women athletes

ISBN 0-7910-5027-0; 0-7910-4949-3 (pa)

LC 98-25571

A biography of skating star Ekaterina Gordeeva who, with her husband Sergei Grinkov, won two Olympic gold medals, and who, since his untimely death in 1995, skates alone

Gordeeva "story offers readers hope that although tragic things happen, life goes on. Skating terminology used in the text is explained in the glossary. The black-and-white photographs depict both happy and sad times in the skaters' lives." SLJ

Includes bibliographical references

Gore, Tipper, 1948-

Kramer, Barbara. Tipper Gore; activist, author, photographer. Enslow Pubs. 1999 112p il (People to know) lib bdg $19.95 **92**

1. Vice-presidents—United States—Spouses

ISBN 0-7660-1142-9

LC 98-26888

Chronicles the political and personal life of the wife of Vice President Al Gore, focusing on her work with the Parents Music Resource Center and the National Mental Health Association, the books she has written, and her duties as "Second Lady" of the United States

"This well-written, useful biography . . . captures some of the spontaneity that is one of Mrs. Gore's hallmarks." Booklist

Gorman, R. C. (Rudolph Carl), 1933-

Hermann, Spring. R.C. Gorman; Navajo artist. Enslow Pubs. 1995 104p il (Multicultural junior biographies) lib bdg $19.95   92
1. American Indian artists
ISBN 0-89490-638-0   LC 95-8807
Covers the life and work of the contemporary Navajo artist, R. C. Gorman, from his childhood days on an Arizona reservation to his commercial success and the recognition of his artistic achievements
Includes bibliographical references

Goya, Francisco, 1746-1828

Richardson, Martha. Francisco Goya. Chelsea House 1994 111p il (Hispanics of achievement) lib bdg $19.95   92
1. Artists, Spanish
ISBN 0-7910-1780-X   LC 93-2326
Presents the life and career of the famous Spanish painter
Includes bibliographical references

Graham, Martha

Freedman, Russell. Martha Graham, a dancer's life. Clarion Bks. 1998 175p il $18 (7 and up)
                92
1. Dancers 2. Choreographers 3. Modern dance
ISBN 0-395-74655-8   LC 97-15832
A photo-biography of the American dancer, teacher, and choreographer who was born in Pittsburgh in 1895 and who became a leading figure in the world of modern dance
"A showstopping biography that captures its dynamic subject's personality, vision, and artistry." SLJ
Includes bibliographical references

Gretzky, Wayne

Santella, Andrew. Wayne Gretzky; the great one. Watts 1998 112p il (Book report biography) $22; pa $6.95   92
1. Hockey—Biography
ISBN 0-531-11567-4; 0-531-15954-X (pa)
                LC 98-17976
Describes the personal life and hockey career of one of the greatest players in the NHL
Includes bibliographical references

Griffey, Ken, Jr.

Gutman, Bill. Ken Griffey, Jr.; baseball's best. Millbrook Press 1998 48p il (Millbrook sports world) lib bdg $19.90; pa $6.95   92
1. Seattle Mariners (Baseball team) 2. Baseball—Biography
ISBN 0-7613-0415-0 (lib bdg); 0-7613-0381-2 (pa)
                LC 97-51679
Highlights the life and career of baseball player Ken Griffey, Jr., centerfielder for the Seattle Mariners
Includes bibliographical references

Grimké, Angelina Emily, 1805-1879

Todras, Ellen H. Angelina Grimké; voice of abolition. Linnet Bks. 1999 178p il $25 (7 and up)
                92
1. Abolitionists 2. Feminism
ISBN 0-208-02485-9   LC 98-42931
This "illustrated biography of the Quaker abolitionist includes the famous 1838 address, delivered in Philadelphia, that made her the first Southern woman to speak publicly against slavery. A helpful chronology places her life against other events in American history." N Y Times Book Rev
Includes bibliographical references

Grisham, John

Weaver, Robyn M. John Grisham. Lucent Bks. 1999 80p il (People in the news) lib bdg $17.96 (7 and up)   92
1. Authors, American
ISBN 1-56006-530-3   LC 99-14325
Discusses the life, career, and influence of the popular writer of legal thrillers
"This accessible, laudatory biography will fill the bill for young Grisham fans curious about a favorite author or in need of background information for reports. Black-and-white photos throughout." Booklist
Includes bibliographical references

Grove, Andrew S.

Byman, Jeremy. Andrew Grove and the Intel Corporation. Morgan Reynolds 1999 112p il (Notable Americans) $18.95 (7 and up)   92
1. Intel Corp. 2. Semiconductor industry
ISBN 1-88384-638-2   LC 98-49120
Describes the life of Andrew Grove, the head of the world's leading producer of microprocessors, which provide the "brains" for the computers in cell phones, cars, coffeepots, and cameras, as well as personal computers
"The detailed but comprehensible analysis of Intel's intricate journey through the past three decades will interest computer enthusiasts and should prove an excellent resource for business students." Booklist
Includes glossary and bibliographical references

Gunther, John, 1929-1947

Gunther, John. Death be not proud; a memoir. Harper & Row 1949 261p il hardcover o.p. paperback available $10 (7 and up)   92
ISBN 0-06-092989-8 (pa)
Also available in hardcover from Buccaneer Bks.
A memoir of John Gunther's seventeen-year-old son, who died after a series of operations for a brain tumor. Not only a tribute to a remarkable boy but an account of a brave fight against disease

Hansberry, Lorraine, 1930-1965

McKissack, Patricia C. Young, black, and determined: a biography of Lorraine Hansberry; by Patricia C. McKissack and Fredrick L. McKissack. Holiday House 1998 152p il $18.95   92
1. Dramatists, American 2. African American women
ISBN 0-8234-1300-4   LC 97-2084

Hansberry, Lorraine, 1930-1965—*Continued*
A biography of the black playwright who received great recognition for her work at an early age
"The McKissacks' biography sparkles with the energy and passion that characterize their subject." Booklist
Includes bibliographical references

Hautzig, Esther Rudomin, 1930-
Hautzig, Esther Rudomin. The endless steppe: growing up in Siberia; by Esther Hautzig. Crowell 1968 243p $15; pa $4.95   **92**
  1. World War, 1939-1945—Personal narratives 2. Siberia (Russia)
ISBN 0-690-26371-6; 0-06-447027-X (pa)
"When the Russians invaded Poland in 1941, Esther, her parents and grandmother were exiled to Siberia. In her very personal narrative about this little-known aspect of World War II, the author recalls four years of hardship, challenge and, miraculously, survival of the family." Cincinnati Public Libr
"This is a magnificent book. Amazingly free of bitterness and hate, it radiates the optimism, the resilience of the human spirit as typified in its vital young author." Book World

Hawking, S. W. (Stephen W.)
McDaniel, Melissa. Stephen Hawking; revolutionary physicist. Chelsea House 1994 111p il (Great achievers: lives of the physically challenged) lib bdg $19.95 (7 and up)   **92**
  1. Physicists 2. Physically handicapped
ISBN 0-7910-2078-9   LC 93-4832
"Hawking, who suffers from amyotrophic lateral sclerosis (Lou Gehrig's disease), is one of the century's great scientific theorists. [His] physical challenges are neither over- nor underemphasized in the clearly written, well-rounded, and inspiring [biography]." Horn Book Guide
Includes bibliographical references

Hayden, Lewis, 1815-1889
Strangis, Joel. Lewis Hayden and the war against slavery. Linnet Bks. 1999 167p il $23.50 (7 and up)   **92**
  1. African Americans—Biography 2. Abolitionists
ISBN 0-208-02430-1   LC 98-29406
A biography of a former slave who was active in the anti-slavery movement, as a fugitive in Canada, a "stationmaster" on the Underground Railroad, a supporter of John Brown, and a recruiter for "black regiments"
"Strangis acknowledges the difficulties involved in conveying this man's life, as there were few written records about him. The book is well researched and has a detailed bibliographical essay." SLJ

Hemingway, Ernest, 1899-1961
Pratt, Paula. Ernest Hemingway; by Paula Bryant Pratt. Lucent Bks. 1999 108p il maps (Importance of) lib bdg $22.45 (7 and up)   **92**
  1. Authors, American
ISBN 1-56006-358-0   LC 98-37073
Discusses the life, work, and significance of the noted American writer, author of such works as "For Whom the Bell Tolls" and "The Old Man and the Sea"
Includes bibliographical references

Yannuzzi, Della A. Ernest Hemingway; writer and adventurer. Enslow Pubs. 1998 112p il (People to know) lib bdg $19.95   **92**
  1. Authors, American
ISBN 0-89490-979-7   LC 97-33351
Describes the life and career of the Pulitzer and Nobel prize winner whose accounts of his adventures and new style of writing brought him worldwide recognition
"After reading this biography, even those unfamiliar with Hemingway will discover how his vivid and adventurous life impacted his writing." SLJ
Includes bibliographical references

Henry VIII, King of England, 1491-1547
Green, Robert. King Henry VIII. Watts 1998 59p il lib bdg $21   **92**
  1. Great Britain—Kings and rulers 2. Great Britain—History—1485-1603, Tudors
ISBN 0-531-20305-0   LC 97-10988
"A First book"
A biography of the English monarch who challenged the Pope's authority, established a state religion, married six wives, and presided over the beginnings of the Renaissance in England
The book includes "many full-color reproductions of period paintings and engravings, as well as photographs of sites . . . giving the pages a lively, engaging look." Booklist
Includes bibliographical references

Hensel, Fanny Cécile Mendelssohn, 1805-1847
Kamen, Gloria. Hidden music; the life of Fanny Mendelssohn. Atheneum Bks. for Young Readers 1996 82p il $15   **92**
  1. Women composers
ISBN 0-689-31714-X   LC 95-15215
This biography offers a portrait of Fanny Mendelssohn Hensel, "a talented pianist and composer who was never accorded the recognition given her brother, Felix. Kamen describes the social milieu into which Fanny was born, conveying a feeling of frustration bordering on tragedy. An epilogue relates Fanny's story to the larger question of women's place in the world of music by outlining the accomplishments of later pioneers such as Nadia Boulanger, Sarah Caldwell, and Wanda Landowska." Horn Book Guide
Includes glossary and bibliographical references

Henson, Matthew Alexander, 1866-1955
Williams, Jean Kinney. Matthew Henson, polar adventurer. Watts 1994 63p il map lib bdg $22; pa $5.95   **92**
  1. Explorers 2. North Pole 3. African Americans—Biography
ISBN 0-531-20006-X (lib bdg); 0-531-15724-5 (pa)
      LC 93-6101
"A First book"
This is a biography of the African American explorer who, with Admiral Peary, was co-discoverer of the North Pole
Includes bibliographical references

Hickam, Homer H., 1943-

Hickam, Homer H. Rocket boys; a memoir; [by] Homer H. Hickam, Jr. Delacorte Press 1998 368p $23.95 (7 and up)   **92**

    ISBN 0-385-33320-X   LC 98-19304

"Raised in Appalachian coal country, Homer H. Hickam, Jr., might well have followed his father and grandfather into the mine. But when he was 14, his life was changed by a space launch on the other side of the world. Hickam's story of how a teenage boy's handmade rockets lifted the hopes of a hardscrabble town is told in his [memoir]." Smithsonian

"Even if Hickam stretched the strict truth to metamorphose his memories into Stand By Me-like material for Hollywood . . . the embellishing only converts what is a good story into an absorbing, rapidly readable one that is unsentimental but artful about adolescence, high school, and family life." Booklist

Holiday, Billie, 1915-1959

Kliment, Bud. Billie Holiday. Chelsea House 1990 111p il (Black Americans of achievement) lib bdg $19.95; pa $8.95   **92**

    1. African American singers 2. African American women

    ISBN 1-55546-592-7 (lib bdg); 0-7910-0241-1 (pa)
       LC 89-30450

"Neither sentimental nor exploitative, [the author] describes Holiday's life of bitter struggle—against poverty, prostitution, prejudice, heroin, prison—and shows how her art grew from and transcended her pain. He places her blues-inspired jazz singing in the black music tradition." Booklist

Includes discography and bibliographical references

Homer, Winslow, 1836-1910

Beneduce, Ann. A weekend with Winslow Homer; by Ann Keay Beneduce. Rizzoli Int. Publs. 1993 64p il $19.95; pa $9.95   **92**

    1. Artists, American

    ISBN 0-8478-1622-2; 0-8478-1919-1 (pa)
       LC 93-12189

American painter Winslow Homer talks about his life and work as if entertaining the reader for the weekend. Includes reproductions of the artist's works and a list of museums where they are on display

Hoover, Herbert, 1874-1964

Holford, David M. Herbert Hoover. Enslow Pubs. 1999 128p il (United States presidents) lib bdg $19.95   **92**

    1. Presidents—United States

    ISBN 0-7660-1035-X   LC 98-11688

A biography of Herbert Hoover, thirty-first president of the United States, describing his career as mining engineer, businessman, and president during the Great Depression

"This biography is insightful. . . . The writing is lucid, and the information is not overwhelming." SLJ

Includes bibliographical references

Hopkins, Sarah Winnemucca, 1844?-1891

Scordato, Ellen. Sarah Winnemucca; northern Paiute writer and diplomat. Chelsea House 1992 127p il (North American Indians of achievement) lib bdg $19.95; pa $9.95   **92**

    1. Paiute Indians

    ISBN 0-7910-1710-9 (lib bdg); 0-7910-1696-X (pa)
       LC 92-2910

Discusses the life of the Paiute woman who became known for her outspoken criticism of the government's mistreatment of her people in the late nineteenth century

"This very detailed biography, illustrated with black-and-white period photographs, gives a wealth of information on a dedicated woman who valiantly struggled her entire life for the benefit of her people." SLJ

Includes bibliographical references

Horne, Lena

Palmer, Leslie. Lena Horne. Chelsea House 1989 127p il (Black Americans of achievement) lib bdg $19.95   **92**

    1. African American singers 2. African American women

    ISBN 1-55546-594-3   LC 88-30248

A look at the black singer's successful musical career and her active participation in the civil rights movement

Horner, John R.

Lessem, Don. Jack Horner: living with dinosaurs; illustrated by Janet Hamlin. Scientific Am. Bks. for Young Readers 1994 47p il (Science superstars) $14.95; pa $4.95   **92**

    1. Scientists 2. Fossils 3. Dinosaurs

    ISBN 0-7167-6546-2; 0-7167-6549-7 (pa)
       LC 94-17993

This is the biography of the paleontologist who, despite dyslexia and several unsuccessful years in school, has gone on to become one of the world's leading dinosaur experts

The author "writes with zest, showing the determination and excitement that accompanied Horner's explorations. . . . Chapters are short, with many pencil illustrations that add interest and help clarify the science, making the book a good choice for reluctant readers." Bull Cent Child Books

Includes bibliographical references

Houston, Samuel, 1793-1863

Fritz, Jean. Make way for Sam Houston; illustrations by Elise Primavera. Putnam 1986 109p il map $14.95; pa $7.95   **92**

    ISBN 0-399-21303-1; 0-399-21304-X (pa)
       LC 85-25601

This is a biography of the "lawyer, governor of Tennessee, general in the wars against Santa Anna, president of the Republic of Texas, and finally U.S. senator and governor of the state of Texas." Horn Book

"Artfully weaving the threads of fact, Fritz creates a biography that is both interesting and informative. Developing Houston as a human character that readers can identify with as well as admire, and drawing him against the scene of America's own political turmoil, Fritz gives us a book to be read and to be felt." Voice Youth Advocates

Includes bibliographical references

Howard, Ron

Kramer, Barbara. Ron Howard; child star & Hollywood director. Enslow Pubs. 1998 112p il (People to know) lib bdg $19.95   **92**

1. Motion picture producers and directors 2. Actors

ISBN 0-89490-981-9   LC 97-43577

Presents the life and career of Ron Howard who gained fame as a young actor starring in television shows and went on to become a film director and producer

This is a "fast-paced, easy to understand book. Any terms that the reader may not be familiar with are explained. . . . Reviews of Howard's movies are cited, presenting both the positive and negative. Overall, this is a very informative and interesting book." Book Rep

Includes bibliographical references

Hubble, Edwin Powell, 1889-1953

Datnow, Claire L. Edwin Hubble; discoverer of galaxies. Enslow Pubs. 1997 128p il (Great minds of science) lib bdg $18.95   **92**

1. Astronomers

ISBN 0-89490-934-7   LC 96-37095

Traces the life and work of the man whose study of galaxies led to a new understanding of the universe

"There is a good balance between the presentation of the scientist's personal life . . . and his achievements. Good-quality black-and-white photos appear throughout. A highly readable biography." SLJ

Includes bibliographical references

Hughes, Langston, 1902-1967

Hill, Christine M. Langston Hughes; poet of the Harlem Renaissance. Enslow Pubs. 1997 128p il (African-American biographies) lib bdg $19.95   **92**

1. Poets, American 2. African American authors

ISBN 0-89490-815-4   LC 97-10991

Surveys the private life and literary accomplishments of the writer whose varied works reflect the traditions, feelings, and experiences of African Americans

"The text flows smoothly and is written in an engaging style that will hold students' interest." SLJ

Includes bibliographical references

Meltzer, Milton. Langston Hughes; illustrated by Stephen Alcorn. Millbrook Press 1997 239p il lib bdg $39.40; pa $16.95   **92**

1. Poets, American 2. African American authors

ISBN 0-7613-0205-0 (lib bdg); 0-7613-0372-8 (pa)

LC 97-1403

A revised and newly illustrated edition of the title first published 1968 by Crowell

Tells the story of a leading poet of the Harlem Renaissance during the 1920s who devoted his life to writing about the black experience in America

"Alcorn's stylized, two-toned prints pique excitement and interest and invite repeated viewings. . . . Only slight, subtle changes have been made in the well-written text. . . . An author's note precedes the text. The bibliography has been updated and includes audio and video recordings. The compelling artistry of this edition makes it a first-purchase consideration even for libraries that own the older title." SLJ

Hunter, Clementine, 1886?-1988

Hunter, Clementine. Talking with Tebé: Clementine Hunter, memory artist; edited by Mary Lyons. Houghton Mifflin 1998 48p il $16   **92**

1. African American artists 2. Women artists

ISBN 0-395-72031-1   LC 97-42253

"Clementine Hunter was an African-American primitive painter who lived all of her 101 years in Louisiana as a manual laborer. . . . The story of her life and art is fascinating, and Lyons has let Tebé, as she was called, tell it in her own words. . . . Hunter's bright, colorful, childlike paintings and a handful of black-and-white photographs decorate the book and illuminate her words." SLJ

Includes bibliographical references

Hurston, Zora Neale, 1891-1960

Lyons, Mary E. Sorrow's kitchen: the life and folklore of Zora Neale Hurston. Scribner 1990 144p il $14.95; pa $7.99   **92**

1. African American authors 2. Women authors

ISBN 0-684-19198-9; 0-02-044445-1 (pa)

LC 90-8058

This biography details "Hurston's migration from Florida to Baltimore, Washington, D.C., and finally Harlem as well as her travels through the West Indies to collect folklore. The text contains eleven excerpts from Hurston's books. . . . Lyons has created a prime example of biography—fascinating, enlightening, stimulating, and satisfying." Horn Book

Includes bibliographical references

Hutchinson, Anne Marbury, 1591-1643

IlgenFritz, Elizabeth. Anne Hutchinson. Chelsea House 1991 111p il maps (American women of achievement) lib bdg $19.95   **92**

1. Puritans

ISBN 1-55546-660-5   LC 90-33748

Recounts the story of the Puritan woman who was banished from her colony for being outspoken against the religious leaders there

"Through its balanced scope and historic documentation, this title exemplifies the fierce struggle Reformists like Hutchinson faced. Numerous quality black-and-white illustrations, an extensive index, and an outstanding text offer readers a solid background on this important religious leader." SLJ

Includes bibliographical references

Huynh, Quang Nhuong

Huynh, Quang Nhuong. The land I lost: adventures of a boy in Vietnam; with pictures by Vo-Dinh Mai. Harper & Row 1982 115p il hardcover o.p. paperback available $4.95   **92**

1. Vietnam—Social life and customs

ISBN 0-06-440183-9 (pa)   LC 80-8437

"Each chapter in this book of reminiscence about the author's boyhood in a hamlet in the Vietnamese highlands, is a separate episode, although the same characters appear in many of the episodes. . . . The writing has an ingenuous quality that adds to the appeal of the strong sense of familial and communal ties that pervades the story." Bull Cent Child Books

Jackson, Andrew, 1767-1845

Meltzer, Milton. Andrew Jackson and his America. Watts 1993 207p il maps lib bdg $28 (7 and up)   **92**

1. Presidents—United States 2. United States—Politics and government—1815-1861

ISBN 0-531-11157-1   LC 93-3947

"Jackson's life is covered from his birth, poor beginnings and numerous scuffles, through his apprenticeship in the study of law, to his political career. The author tries to show Jackson in the context of his time." Book Rep

"Besides providing the young adult reader with an enjoyable biography, the author has succeeded in creating a critical survey of Jackson's life that is useful and credible as a piece of historical research." Voice Youth Advocates

Includes bibliographical references

Jackson, Mahalia, 1911-1972

Gourse, Leslie. Mahalia Jackson: queen of gospel song. Watts 1996 128p il (Impact biography) lib bdg $23.60 (7 and up)   **92**

1. African American singers 2. African American women

ISBN 0-531-11228-4   LC 95-49845

Traces the rise of the famous gospel singer from her early youth in New Orleans to her Chicago-based musical career

"Gourse has penned a lively and balanced portrait of the ebullient, warm, and ever down-to-earth singer. And because Jackson was active in the civil rights movement, her story is a fascinating piece of American social as well as musical history." Booklist

Includes discography and bibliographical references

Jackson, Stonewall, 1824-1863

Fritz, Jean. Stonewall; with drawings by Stephen Gammell. Putnam 1979 152p il map $15.95; pa $5.95   **92**

1. Generals 2. United States—History—1861-1865, Civil War

ISBN 0-399-20698-1; 0-698-11552-X (pa)

LC 79-12506

A biography of the southern general who gained the nickname Stonewall by his stand at Bull Run during the Civil War

"Fritz's trenchant, compassionate life of General Thomas Jonathan Jackson grips the reader and makes one understand why Stonewall is an honored legend in American history. . . . The tragic irony of his death at age 39 is movingly described." Publ Wkly

Includes bibliographical references

Pflueger, Lynda. Stonewall Jackson; Confederate general. Enslow Pubs. 1997 128p il (Historical American biographies) lib bdg $19.95   **92**

1. Generals 2. United States—History—1861-1865, Civil War

ISBN 0-89490-781-6   LC 96-8827

A biography of the Confederate general who gained the nickname Stonewall for his stand at the first battle of Bull Run during the Civil War

"The content is thorough and includes valuable historical background." Horn Book Guide

Includes glossary and bibliographical references

Jacobs, Harriet A. (Harriet Ann), 1813-1896 or 7

Fleischner, Jennifer. I was born a slave: the story of Harriet Jacobs; with illustrations by Melanie K. Reim. Millbrook Press 1997 93p il lib bdg $24.90   **92**

1. Slavery—United States 2. African American women

ISBN 0-7613-0111-9   LC 96-44350

Traces the life of a slave who suffered mistreatment from her master, spent years as a fugitive from slavery in North Carolina, and was eventually released to freedom with her children

"Basing her account on Jacobs's autobiography written in 1861, Fleischner presents a moving and readable record of one woman's experiences. . . . Reim's powerful, full-page woodcut prints illustrate incidents from Jacobs's life." SLJ

Includes bibliographical references

James, Jesse, 1847-1882

Bruns, Roger. Jesse James; legendary outlaw. Enslow Pubs. 1998 128p il maps (Historical American biographies) lib bdg $19.95   **92**

1. Thieves

ISBN 0-7660-1055-4   LC 97-24615

Traces the life of the renowned bandit, from his childhood in Missouri, through his years as guerilla fighter and outlaw, exploring the development of his legend and the romanticization of his illegal deeds

"The book is heavily footnoted, thus providing not only avenues for further research, but also a more authoritative tone than many biographies for this age group. Even so, the scholarship does not impede the flow of the narrative or the clear analysis of events." SLJ

Includes bibliographical references

Jefferson, Thomas, 1743-1826

Meltzer, Milton. Thomas Jefferson; the revolutionary aristocrat. Watts 1991 255p il maps lib bdg $28 (7 and up)   **92**

1. Presidents—United States

ISBN 0-531-11069-9   LC 91-15943

An "examination of Jefferson's brilliant and complex life, detailing his successes and failures. Meltzer writes with his usual lively style and clarity and provides plenty of historical background and detail." SLJ

Includes bibliographical references

Severance, John B. Thomas Jefferson; architect of democracy. Clarion Bks. 1998 192p il maps $18 (7 and up)   **92**

1. Presidents—United States

ISBN 0-395-84513-0   LC 97-31010

Explores the life of the third president, from his childhood in Virginia, through his involvement in the Revolutionary War, to his years in office

"In this respectful, literate, and handsomely illustrated biography, Severance focuses equally on Jefferson's remarkable accomplishments and the beliefs behind them." Booklist

Includes bibliographical references

Jemison, Mae C.

Yannuzzi, Della A. Mae Jemison; a space biography. Enslow Pubs. 1998 48p il (Countdown to space) lib bdg $18.95   92

1. Women astronauts 2. African American women

ISBN 0-89490-813-8   LC 97-34159

Traces the life of the first African-American woman to go into space, from her childhood in Chicago through her astronaut training and first spaceflight to life after working with NASA

The text is "readable and interesting. . . . Many colorful photographs illustrate the [book]." Booklist

Includes glossary and bibliographical references

Joan, of Arc, Saint, 1412-1431

Stanley, Diane. Joan of Arc. Morrow Junior Bks. 1998 unp il $16; lib bdg $15.93   92

1. Christian saints 2. France—History—1328-1589, House of Valois

ISBN 0-688-14329-6; 0-688-14330-X (lib bdg)
                LC 97-45652

A biography of the fifteenth-century peasant girl who led a French army to victory against the English and was burned at the stake for witchcraft

Stanley "orchestrates the complexities of history into a gripping, unusually challenging story in this exemplary biography. . . . Judiciously chosen details build atmosphere in both the text and the artwork—painstakingly wrought, gilded paintings modeled after the illuminated manuscripts of Joan's day." Publ Wkly

Includes bibliographical references

Johnson, Isaac, 1844-1905

Marston, Hope Irvin. Isaac Johnson; from slave to stonecutter; illustrated by Maria Magdalena Brown. Cobblehill Bks. 1995 80p il $14.99   92

1. Slavery—United States 2. African Americans—Biography

ISBN 0-525-65165-9   LC 94-32671

"Based on Johnson's own Slavery Days in Old Kentucky, this readable biography begins in 1851 when seven-year-old Isaac was sold into slavery by his white father. It briefly recounts his 10 years of labor as a slave and how he ran away to join the Union Army. Marston's account of Johnson's life after the war is documented and enlivened by primary-source material. She avoids sensationalism, but depicts slavery and her subject's consequent career as a stonecutter and stonemason in Ontario and in New York in a spare and poignant manner." SLJ

Includes bibliographical references

Jones, Mother, 1830-1930

Josephson, Judith Pinkerton. Mother Jones; fierce fighter for workers' rights. Lerner Publs. 1997 144p il lib bdg $25.26   92

1. Reformers

ISBN 0-8225-4924-7   LC 96-11802

A biography of Mary Harris Jones, the union organizer who worked tirelessly for the rights of workers

"Josephson brings this remarkable woman to life through well-documented sources and photographs of Jones and the environs in which she worked." SLJ

Includes bibliographical references

Jones, James Earl

Hasday, Judy L. James Earl Jones. Chelsea House 1998 127p il (Overcoming adversity) lib bdg $19.95; pa $9.95   92

1. African American actors

ISBN 0-7910-4702-4 (lib bdg); 0-7910-4703-2 (pa)
                LC 97-31919

Examines the life and career of the successful actor, James Earl Jones, who overcame a severe problem as a stutterer to become one of the most recognizable voices in entertainment

This book is "well written [and] thoroughly researched. . . . [It] could be used for class reports, but even reluctant readers will also read [it] simply for information and pleasure." Voice Youth Advocates

Includes filmography and bibliographical references

Jones, Quincy

Kavanaugh, Lee Hill. Quincy Jones; musician, composer, producer. Enslow Pubs. 1997 128p il (African-American biographies) lib bdg $19.95
                92

1. Jazz musicians 2. African American musicians

ISBN 0-89490-814-6   LC 97-21958

Discusses the life and accomplishments of the jazz musician, record producer, and composer of movie scores and television themes

Includes discography and bibliographical references

Joplin, Scott, 1868-1917

Otfinoski, Steven. Scott Joplin; a life in ragtime. Watts 1995 143p il (Impact biography) lib bdg $24 (7 and up)   92

1. Composers, American 2. African American musicians

ISBN 0-531-11244-6   LC 95-8526

The story of one of America's most famous composers of ragtime music

Includes discography and bibliographical references

Preston, Katherine K. Scott Joplin; [by] Katherine Preston. Chelsea House 1988 110p il (Black Americans of achievement) lib bdg $19.95; pa $9.95   92

1. Composers, American 2. African American musicians

ISBN 1-55546-598-6 (lib bdg); 0-7910-0205-5 (pa)
                LC 87-21218

The author "describes the musician's Texas upbringing and his development as a talented composer of ragtime. Woven through the account is a social history of the time that underscores the racial prejudice that hindered Joplin in pursuing his livelihood." Booklist

Includes bibliographical references

Jordan, Barbara, 1936-1996

Rhodes, Lisa Renee. Barbara Jordan; voice of democracy; by Lisa R. Rhodes. Watts 1998 112p il (Book report biography) $22   92

1. Women politicians 2. African American women

ISBN 0-531-11450-3   LC 98-24134

Jordan, Barbara, 1936-1996—_Continued_

Traces the life and work of this African-American woman who was a respected politician, teacher, and spokeswoman for democracy

"The book is well organized and competently written. There are frequent quotes from Jordan's autobiography as well as other primary sources. Well-chosen black-and-white photos enhance the narrative." SLJ

Includes bibliographical references

Jordan, Michael

Halberstam, David. Playing for keeps: Michael Jordan and the world he made. Random House 1999 426p $25.90 (7 and up)   **92**

1. Basketball—Biography 2. African American athletes

ISBN 0-679-41562-9   LC 98-49964

Also available in paperback from Broadway Bks.

Halberstam presents a biography of basketball player Michael Jordan

"What's particularly effective about Halberstam's storytelling is that he follows Jordan's athletic trajectory, not in chronological order but through juxtaposed images of a hot-blooded college player with an as-yet unpolished game and an even-tempered 30-year-old at the height of his career. Jordan was not born a flawless pro, but developed his gifts by working tirelessly and intensely." Natl Rev

Lipsyte, Robert. Michael Jordan; a life above the rim. HarperCollins Pubs. 1994 106p il (Superstar lineup) lib bdg $14.89   **92**

1. Basketball—Biography 2. African American athletes

ISBN 0-06-024235-3   LC 93-50561

"Rather than focusing solely on the subject's life on and off the court, Lipsyte examines M.J. the multimillion dollar commodity. He puts the Jordan phenomenon into historical perceptive, correlating the man's success with the rise in popularity of the N.B.A. and the changes in the style of the game over the years. In addition, he explores the relationship between athletics and the marketing of products." SLJ

Includes bibliographical references

Pietrusza, David. Michael Jordan. Lucent Bks. 1999 112p il (People in the news) lib bdg $22.45 (7 and up)   **92**

1. Basketball—Biography 2. African American athletes

ISBN 1-56006-350-5   LC 98-22485

Describes the life and career of Michael Jordan, including his childhood in North Carolina, involvement in sports, success with the Chicago Bulls, retirement from basketball, second career in baseball, and triumphant return to the Bulls

Includes bibliographical references

Joseph, Nez Percé Chief, 1840-1904

Scott, Robert Alan. Chief Joseph and the Nez Percés; [by] Robert A. Scott. Facts on File 1993 134p il maps (Makers of America) lib bdg $19.95   **92**

1. Nez Percé Indians

ISBN 0-8160-2475-8   LC 92-15885

A biography of the nineteenth-century Nez Percé chief, concentrating on his unending struggle to win peace and equality for his people

Includes bibliographical references

Taylor, M. W. (Marian W.). Chief Joseph; Nez Perce leader; [by] Marian W. Taylor. Chelsea House 1993 110p il (North American Indians of achievement) lib bdg $19.95   **92**

1. Nez Percé Indians

ISBN 0-7910-1708-7   LC 92-31311

Presents the life and times of the Nez Percé Indian chief who led his people on a great trek to escape the injustices of the American government

Includes bibliographical references

Kahlo, Frida, 1907-1954

Turner, Robyn Montana. Frida Kahlo. Little, Brown 1993 32p il (Portraits of women artists for children) $16.95   **92**

1. Artists, Mexican 2. Women artists

ISBN 0-316-85651-7   LC 91-29556

"Turner introduces Kahlo's life and work in this attractive biography. . . . Black-and-white photos offer glimpses of this Mexican painter and her world, but the full-color reproductions of her paintings will intrigue kids more." Booklist

Kaiulani, Princess of Hawaii, 1875-1899

Linnea, Sharon. Princess Ka'iulani; hope of a nation, heart of a people. Eerdmans Bks. for Young Readers 1999 234p il $18; pa $10   **92**

1. Princesses 2. Hawaii—History

ISBN 0-8028-5145-2; 0-8028-5088-X (pa)

     LC 97-14260

"This biography describes the life of Hawaiian crown princess Ka'iulani. Born in 1875, Ka'iulani was raised in Hawaii, educated in England, and remained in Europe until the overthrow of her aunt Queen Lili'uokalani in 1893 when she traveled to America." Booklist

"Linnéa presents a thorough and detailed account of her subject's life. . . . This is an interesting, accessible book about an intriguing individual. Black-and-white photos and reproductions add visual interest." SLJ

Includes bibliographical references

Stanley, Fay. The last princess: the story of Princess Ka'iulani of Hawai'i; illustrated by Diane Stanley. Four Winds Press 1991 40p il map $18; pa $5.95   **92**

1. Princesses 2. Hawaii—History

ISBN 0-02-786785-4; 0-689-71829-2 (pa)

     LC 89-71445

Recounts the story of Hawaii's last heir to the throne, who was denied her right to rule when the monarchy was abolished

"This bittersweet drama will certainly capture the reader's imagination. . . . Biography that tells its story and touches the heart." Booklist

Includes bibliographical references

Keckley, Elizabeth, ca. 1818-1907

Rutberg, Becky. Mary Lincoln's dressmaker; Elizabeth Keckley's remarkable rise from slave to White House confidante. Walker & Co. 1995 166p il $15.95; lib bdg $15.89   **92**
1. African American women
ISBN 0-8027-8224-8; 0-8027-8225-6 (lib bdg)
    LC 94-45839
This is a biography of Elizabeth Keckley, who was born a slave in 1818. Keckley was eventually able to buy her freedom and went on to become Mary Todd Lincoln's dressmaker
"Libraries with a high demand for multicultural material or women's history should find this a useful, readable purchase." SLJ
Includes bibliographical references

Keller, Helen, 1880-1968

Keller, Helen. The story of my life. Doubleday 1954 382p il   **92**
1. Blind 2. Deaf
Various editions available
First published 1903
This biography of the inspirational Keller contains accounts of her home life and her relationship with her devoted teacher Anne Sullivan

St. George, Judith. Dear Dr. Bell—your friend, Helen Keller. Putnam 1992 95p il hardcover o.p. paperback available $4.95   **92**
1. Bell, Alexander Graham, 1847-1922 2. Blind 3. Deaf
ISBN 0-688-12814-9 (pa)   LC 91-37327
Follows the parallel lives of Helen Keller and Alexander Graham Bell, who continued to encounter and support each other from that eventful meeting when he recommended she be given a teacher and thus led her to Annie Sullivan
"A lively style and plenty of quotes from each person's writing and letters show the feelings and thoughts behind the friendship. Black-and-white photographs show scenes from both of their lives as well as of their times together." SLJ
Includes bibliographical references

Kennedy, John F. (John Fitzgerald), 1917-1963

Uschan, Michael V. John F. Kennedy. Lucent Bks. 1999 120p il (Importance of) lib bdg $22.45 (7 and up)   **92**
1. Presidents—United States
ISBN 1-56006-482-X   LC 98-36402
A biography of the thirty-fifth president of the United States who served from 1961 until his assassination in 1963
"Objective, well-chosen primary-source material includes many quotes from Kennedy's speeches and books. Chapter endnotes and familiar black-and-white archival photos and maps contribute to the title's usefulness for reports." SLJ
Includes bibliographical references

Kennedy, Robert F., 1925-1968

Schulman, Arlene. Robert F. Kennedy; promise for the future. Facts on File 1998 128p il (Makers of America) $19.95 (7 and up)   **92**
1. Politicians—United States 2. United States—Politics and government—1900-1999 (20th century)
ISBN 0-8160-3674-8   LC 97-20610
"This volume traces Kennedy's early rise through politics, his role in his brother's presidential election, and his appointment to attorney general of the United States, culminating with the tragic assassination that ended his . . . pursuit of the presidency." Publisher's note
Includes bibliographical references

Kherdian, Veron, 1907-

Kherdian, David. The road from home; the story of an Armenian girl. Greenwillow Bks. 1979 238p il map lib bdg $15.93; pa $4.95   **92**
1. Armenians—Turkey 2. Armenian massacres, 1915-1923
ISBN 0-688-84205-4 (lib bdg); 0-688-14425-X (pa)
    LC 78-72511
A Newbery Medal honor book, 1980
The author presents a "biography of his mother's early life as a young Armenian girl. Veron Dumehjian was part of a prosperous Armenian family in Turkey, but the Armenian minority undergoes a holocaust when the Turkish government persecutes its Christian minorities. In 1915 Veron and her family are deported and, as refugees, live through hardships of disease, starvation, bombing, and fire until, at sixteen, Veron is able to go to America as a 'mail-order' bride." Babbling Bookworm

King, B. B.

Shirley, David. Everyday I sing the blues: the story of B.B. King. Watts 1995 127p il (Impact biography) $24; pa $8 (7 and up)   **92**
1. Blues music 2. African American musicians
ISBN 0-531-11229-2, 0-531-15752-0 (pa)
    LC 95-16151
Traces the life of the influential African American blues musician, from his birth in the Mississippi Delta in 1925 to the present
Includes bibliographical references

King, Coretta Scott, 1927-

Klingel, Cynthia Fitterer. Coretta Scott King; by Cynthia Klingel. Child's World 1999 39p il (Journey to freedom) lib bdg $16.95   **92**
1. King, Martin Luther, 1929-1968 2. African American women 3. African Americans—Civil rights
ISBN 1-56766-567-5   LC 98-27012
A brief biography of the wife of the Reverend Martin Luther King, Jr., who shared his dedication to working peaceably to achieve equality for all Americans
"The clean, uncluttered book design features framed photographs meant to look like snapshots, with handsomely boxed captions. Heartbreaking, difficult subjects such as segregation, lynching (including photographs), the Ku Klux Klan, and assassination are lucidly explained." Booklist
Includes bibliographical references

King, Coretta Scott, 1927——*Continued*

Rhodes, Lisa Renee. Coretta Scott King. Chelsea House 1997 143p il (Black Americans of achievement) lib bdg $19.95; pa $9.95   **92**
1. King, Martin Luther, 1929-1968 2. African American women 3. African Americans—Civil rights
ISBN 0-7910-4690-7 (lib bdg); 0-7910-4691-5 (pa)
    LC 97-36364
Biography of Martin Luther King's widow, from her childhood in rural Alabama to her crusade to keep her husband's message of peace and equality alive after his murder in 1968
"The chapters are well organized and the clear, well-chosen black-and-white photographs are attractively presented." SLJ
Includes bibliographical references

King, Martin Luther, 1929-1968

Haskins, James. I have a dream: the life and words of Martin Luther King, Jr.; by Jim Haskins. Millbrook Press 1992 111p il lib bdg $27.40; pa $8.95   **92**
1. African Americans—Biography 2. African Americans—Civil rights
ISBN 1-56294-087-2 (lib bdg); 1-56294-837-7 (pa)
    LC 91-42528
Presents the life, words, and principles of the noted civil rights worker through extensive quotations from his speeches and writings
"All quotations are sourced, and Haskins includes a time line of important events in King's life as well as suggestions for further reading. A serviceable, practical biography, this will be a good addition to any size collection." Booklist

Haskins, James. The life and death of Martin Luther King, Jr. Lothrop, Lee & Shepard Bks. 1977 176p il hardcover o.p. paperback available $5.95   **92**
1. African Americans—Biography 2. African Americans—Civil rights
ISBN 0-688-11690-6 (pa)   LC 77-3157
The author "writes about the civil rights leader in a simple, readable manner. Part one describes the development of the civil rights movement; part two describes the assassination, and an inordinate amount of space is given to James Earl Ray and the theory of a conspiracy behind the murder." Horn Book

King, Coretta Scott. My life with Martin Luther King, Jr; introduction by Bernice, Dexter, Martin, and Yolanda King. rev ed. Holt & Co. 1993 335p il $17.95   **92**
1. African Americans—Biography 2. African Americans—Civil rights
ISBN 0-8050-2445-X   LC 92-23525
First published 1969
An inside look at the life and work of the noted civil rights leader, from the viewpoint of his wife Coretta Scott King
"King's voice comes through clearly, as does her personality. At times, though, she sounds old-fashioned, particularly when she makes an appeal to today's teenagers.

Her view of her husband is naturally an uncritical one, and it is but one perspective in a many-sided and often acrimonious debate." SLJ
Klingel, Cynthia Fitterer. Coretta Scott King. See entry under King, Coretta Scott, 1927-

Wukovits, John F. Martin Luther King, Jr. Lucent Bks. 1999 112p il (Importance of) lib bdg $22.45 (7 and up)   **92**
1. African Americans—Biography 2. African Americans—Civil rights
ISBN 1-56006-483-8   LC 98-36197
Discusses the childhood, education, social activism, and assassination of the noted civil rights leader
Includes bibliographical references

King, Stephen, 1947-
Wukovits, John F. Stephen King. Lucent Bks. 1999 96p il (People in the news) $22.45 (7 and up)   **92**
1. Authors, American
ISBN 1-56006-562-1   LC 99-20085
Discusses the life, career, and influence of the popular horror writer Stephen King
"Librarians and teachers may not be thrilled with King's books, but middle-school and high-school students certainly are. They will read this biography for pleasure and use it for the 'read a biography or autobiography' assignment, if they can. Black-and-white photos are scattered throughout, as are boxed insets and numerous quotes from the author, his friends, associates, and rivals." Booklist
Includes bibliographical references

Koehn, Ilse, 1929-1991
Koehn, Ilse. Mischling, second degree: my childhood in Nazi Germany; with a foreword by Harrison E. Salisbury. Greenwillow Bks. 1977 240p o.p.; Puffin Bks. paperback available $5.99   **92**
1. World War, 1939-1945—Jews 2. Germany—History—1933-1945 3. Jews—Germany
ISBN 0-14-034290-7 (pa)   LC 77-6189
This story "is told in retrospect by an author who did not know why her loving parents separated until after the war, when she learned that it had helped her and her mother avoid the consequences of the fact that her father had one Jewish parent. Liberals and intellectuals, the Koehns coped, as many did, with a government and a philosophy they detested. And Ilse, a young adolescent, was drafted into the Hitler Youth, forced to go through the motions of devotion." Bull Cent Child Books

Kublai Khan, 1216-1294
Dramer, Kim. Kublai Khan. Chelsea House 1990 111p il maps (World leaders past & present) lib bdg $19.95   **92**
1. Kings and rulers 2. China—History
ISBN 1-55546-812-8   LC 89-48915
A biography of the founder of the Mongol dynasty
The author "has done an excellent job of informing the reader about the rise of a Mongol leader from the

Kublai Khan, 1216-1294—*Continued*
harsh nomadic life to the opulent life of a Chinese emperor. There are many details about the daily military life, battles, court intrigues, and home life of the Mongols." Voice Youth Advocates
Includes bibliographical references

Kwan, Michelle
Gatto, Kimberly. Michelle Kwan; champion on ice. Lerner Publs. 1998 64p il (Sports achievers biographies) $19.93; pa $5.95   **92**
1. Ice skating—Biography 2. Women athletes
ISBN 0-8225-3669-2; 0-8225-9830-2 (pa)
LC 98-16846
A biography of the young Chinese-American figure skater who won National and World Championships in 1996 and a silver medal at the 1998 Winter Olympics
Includes bibliographical references

Kwan, Michelle. Michelle Kwan, heart of a champion; an autobiography; as told to Laura James. Scholastic 1997 151p il $14.95; pa $4.99   **92**
1. Ice skating—Biography 2. Women athletes
ISBN 0-590-76340-7; 0-590-76356-3 (pa)
LC 97-30183
The 1996 World Figure Skating Champion discusses the rigors of competition, the importance of a strong support group, her love of ice skating, and her Olympic dream
This is "refreshingly frank. . . . The style is informal and chatty. . . . Kwan comes across as a talented, hardworking, and remarkably well adjusted young woman." Booklist
Includes glossary

Lange, Dorothea, 1895-1965
Partridge, Elizabeth. Restless spirit: the life and work of Dorothea Lange. Viking 1998 122p il $19.99   **92**
1. Women photographers
ISBN 0-670-87888-X   LC 98-9807
A biography of Dorothea Lange, whose photographs of migrant workers, Japanese American internees, and rural poverty helped bring about important social reforms
"Generously placed throughout this accessibly written biography are the photographic images that make Lange a pre-eminent artist of the century. The book is elegantly designed and the photographic reproductions are excellent." Bull Cent Child Books

Latimer, Lewis Howard, 1848-1928
Norman, Winifred Latimer. Lewis Latimer; [by] Winifred Latimer Norman and Lily Patterson. Chelsea House 1994 101p il (Black Americans of achievement) lib bdg $19.95   **92**
1. African American inventors
ISBN 0-7910-1977-2   LC 93-185
This book "tells the story of a man who lived in the early days of the electrification of America. That he worked with Alexander Graham Bell and Thomas Edison and contributed to their achievements of fame is remarkable when one finds out that he had no formal education or training in what he did. Along the way, he received several patents on inventions of his own. . . . The book . . . is interesting in the perspective it gives of the slavery and postslavery eras." Sci Books Films
Includes bibliographical references

Lawrence, Jacob
Duggleby, John. Story painter: the life of Jacob Lawrence. Chronicle Bks. 1998 55p il $16.95   **92**
1. African American artists
ISBN 0-8118-2082-3   LC 98-4513
A biography of the African American artist who grew up in the midst of the Harlem Renaissance and became one of the most renowned painters of the life of his people
"Lawrence's expressionistic, stark paintings, in excellent full-page color reproduction . . . nicely complement Duggleby's measured account of a materially poor but culturally rich childhood and Lawrence's subsequent struggles and successes." Publ Wkly
Includes bibliographical references

Leakey, Louis Seymour Bazett, 1903-1972
Poynter, Margaret. The Leakeys; uncovering the origins of humankind. Enslow Pubs. 1997 128p il maps (Great minds of science) lib bdg $19.95   **92**
1. Leakey, Mary D., 1913-1996 2. Anthropologists 3. Human origins
ISBN 0-89490-788-3   LC 96-40899
Profiles the lives of Louis and Mary Leakey and their dedication to the study of human evolution
Includes bibliographical references

Leakey, Mary D., 1913-1996
Poynter, Margaret. The Leakeys. See entry under Leakey, Louis Seymour Bazett, 1903-1972

Lee, Robert E. (Robert Edward), 1807-1870
Kerby, Mona. Robert E. Lee; Southern hero of the Civil War. Enslow Pubs. 1997 128p il (Historical American biographies) lib bdg $19.95   **92**
1. Generals 2. United States—History—1861-1865, Civil War
ISBN 0-89490-782-4   LC 96-31432
Describes the life of the famous Confederate general of the Civil War
"This objective and personal biography . . . is well written and interesting and will give readers a closer look at the man behind the reputation." SLJ
Includes glossary and bibliographical references

Marrin, Albert. Virginia's general: Robert E. Lee and the Civil War. Atheneum Pubs. 1994 218p il maps $22 (7 and up)   **92**
1. Generals 2. United States—History—1861-1865, Civil War
ISBN 0-689-31838-3   LC 94-13353

Lee, Robert E. (Robert Edward), 1807-1870—
Continued
"Beginning with Lee's pivotal decision to refuse command of the U.S. Army, the book fills in the details of his childhood, education, marriage, and career, and then concentrates on the Civil War years. Quotations from Lee, his generals, and particularly his soldiers offer insight into the times. Source notes are appended. Period photographs and prints of people and battles illustrate the book, and maps show the location of significant places and battlefield positions." Booklist
Includes bibliographical references

Lee, Spike
Haskins, James. Spike Lee; by any means necessary; [by] Jim Haskins. Walker & Co. 1997 124p il $15.95; lib bdg $16.85 (7 and up)   **92**
1. Motion picture producers and directors 2. African Americans—Biography
ISBN 0-8027-8494-1; 0-8027-8496-8 (lib bdg)
LC 96-41774
Examines the life and works of the filmmaker who has chosen to explore the many dimensions of the black American experience
"This well-rounded, informative portrait of the filmmaker is appealing and engaging to read." SLJ
Includes bibliographical references

McDaniel, Melissa. Spike Lee; on his own terms. Watts 1998 96p il (Book report biography) lib bdg $22   **92**
1. Motion picture producers and directors 2. African Americans—Biography
ISBN 0-531-11460-0   LC 98-10449
"This title examines the career of the talented director, writer, and promoter who has challenged and changed the way blacks are portrayed on screen. McDaniel presents an objective and interesting overview without glossing over the controversies that have surrounded her subject's actions." SLJ
Includes bibliographical references

Leeuwenhoek, Antoni van, 1632-1723
Yount, Lisa. Antoni van Leeuwenhoek; first to see microscopic life. Enslow Pubs. 1996 128p il (Great minds of science) lib bdg $19.95   **92**
1. Biologists 2. Microscopes
ISBN 0-89490-680-1   LC 96-6057
A biography of the cloth merchant-turned-scientist who made many discoveries examining microsopic life
"The book ends with experiments the reader can do, a chronology of van Leeuwenhoek's life, and chapter notes. These are useful additions for a reader or teacher who wants to delve more deeply into the science aspects of the book." Sci Books Films
Includes bibliographical references

Lenin, Vladimir Il´ich, 1870-1924
Haney, John. Vladimir Ilich Lenin. Chelsea House 1988 112p il (World leaders past & present) lib bdg $19.95   **92**
1. Russia—History
ISBN 0-87754-570-7   LC 87-26584

This biography follows the life of the leader of the Bolshevik Revolution, who became the first head of the Soviet state
"Readers will find this a full account of both Lenin and the Russian revolution. Numerous black-and-white photographs, extensively captioned, add to the discussion. A thoughtful, well-written piece." Booklist
Includes bibliographical references

Leonardo, da Vinci, 1452-1519
Herbert, Janis. Leonardo da Vinci for kids; his life and ideas: 21 activities. Chicago Review Press 1998 90p il $16.95   **92**
1. Artists, Italian
ISBN 1-55652-298-3   LC 98-25690
Presents a biography of this prolific artist and inventor through projects in cartography, animal art, bird observation, and mask making
"Herbert describes Leonardo's life while also providing a good deal of historical information about Italy and background about art. . . . The high-quality reproductions of the artist's sketches and paintings coupled with an interesting text give readers a full picture of this truly amazing man." SLJ
Includes bibliographical references

Lewin, Ted, 1935-
Lewin, Ted. Touch and go; travels of a children's book illustrator. Lothrop, Lee & Shepard Bks. 1999 67p il $15   **92**
1. Illustrators
ISBN 0-688-14109-9   LC 98-40548
"Perhaps best known as an award-winning illustrator, Lewin has also written several fine picture books. Research for his various projects has taken him around the globe, and this book, which is targeted to an older audience than his usual one, recalls in nicely polished, descriptive chapters some of the people he has met and the experiences he has had during his far-flung travels." Booklist

Lewis, C. S. (Clive Staples), 1898-1963
Gormley, Beatrice. C.S. Lewis; Christian and storyteller. Eerdmans Bks. for Young Readers 1998 182p il hardcover o.p. paperback available $8   **92**
1. Authors, English
ISBN 0-8028-5069-3 (pa)   LC 97-7860
This "is a clearly written, solidly researched, and insightful picture of the popular author. Gormley weaves human texture into the book by layering the threads of Lewis' life whether trivial, tragic, literary, or spiritual into a highly readable exposition of a warm, amiable, and brilliant man." Bull Cent Child Books

Lin, Maya Ying
Malone, Mary. Maya Lin; architect and artist. Enslow Pubs. 1995 112p il (People to know) lib bdg $19.95   **92**
1. Architects
ISBN 0-89490-499-X   LC 94-5333

Lin, Maya Ying—*Continued*
A "look into the background and life of Maya Lin, who at age twenty-one won the design contest for the proposed Vietnam Veteran's Memorial in Washington, D.C. Lin's family roots in China, the family's move to the United States in the late 1940s, Maya's childhood, and her career are all covered here. Since designing the Vietnam Veteran's Memorial, Lin has gained renown around the world for her art work, including sculptures." Kaleidoscope. 2nd edition
Includes bibliographical references

Lincoln, Abraham, 1809-1865
Burchard, Peter. Lincoln and slavery. Atheneum Bks. for Young Readers 1999 196p $17 (7 and up) **92**
1. Presidents—United States 2. Slavery—United States
ISBN 0-689-81570-0   LC 98-12464
A biography of the sixteenth president which focuses on the issue of slavery and the importance it had throughout Lincoln's life from his early days as a lawyer through his presidency
"Fluent and engaging language, historical anecdotes, excerpts from primary sources, and unfamiliar information . . . maintain interest, and the glimpses of the men and women of Lincoln's day . . . are especially compelling. The book gives a balanced presentation of Lincoln's strenghts and flaws." Bull Cent Child Books
Includes bibliographical references

Freedman, Russell. Lincoln: a photobiography. Clarion Bks. 1987 149p il $16.95; pa $7.95 **92**
1. Presidents—United States
ISBN 0-89919-380-3; 0-395-51848-2 (pa)
LC 86-33379
Awarded the Newbery Medal, 1988
The author "begins by contrasting the Lincoln of legend to the Lincoln of fact. His childhood, self-education, early business ventures, and entry into politics comprise the first half of the book, with the rest of the text covering his presidency and assassination." SLJ
This is "a balanced work, elegantly designed and enhanced by dozens of period photographs and drawings, some familiar, some refreshingly unfamiliar." Publ Wkly
Includes bibliographical references

Lincoln, in his own words; edited by Milton Meltzer; illustrated by Stephen Alcorn. Harcourt Brace & Co. 1993 226p il $22.95 **92**
1. Presidents—United States 2. United States—History—1861-1865, Civil War
ISBN 0-15-245437-3   LC 92-17431
Combines background commentary with quotes from Lincoln's letters, speeches, and public papers to provide a personal view of his life, thoughts, and actions
"Meltzer gives Lincoln's words rich historical context by framing them with the facts of his life. Alcorn's powerful black-and-white and color linoleum block prints have impact and majesty." Booklist
Includes bibliographical references

Lincoln, Mary Todd, 1818-1882
Santow, Dan. Mary Todd Lincoln, 1818-1882. Children's Press 1999 111p il (Encyclopedia of first ladies) $33 **92**
1. Presidents' spouses—United States
ISBN 0-516-20481-5   LC 98-45254
A biography of the wife of the sixteenth president of the United States, discussing her upbringing, marriage, and the tragedies that marred her life
Includes bibliographical references

Lindbergh, Charles, 1902-1974
Denenberg, Barry. An American hero: the true story of Charles A. Lindbergh. Scholastic 1996 255p il maps $16.95; pa $5.99 (7 and up) **92**
1. Air pilots
ISBN 0-590-46923-1; 0-590-46955-X (pa)
LC 95-24628
Dividing "Lindbergh's life into two parts, 'Ascent' and 'Descent,' Denenberg charts his subject's course from childhood and adolescence through his historic transatlantic flight and marriage to Anne Morrow." Bull Cent Child Books
"Denenberg delivers a fascinating, evenhanded, and carefully researched examination of the aviator. . . . Well-placed excerpts from Lindbergh's own writings and from those of Anne Morrow Lindbergh effectively position the reader in the excitement of the moment." Booklist
Includes bibliographical references

Giblin, James. Charles A. Lindbergh; a human hero; [by] James Cross Giblin. Clarion Bks. 1997 212p il $20 **92**
1. Air pilots
ISBN 0-395-63389-3   LC 96-9501
A biography of the pilot whose life was full of controversy and tragedy, but also fulfilling achievements
"This sympathetic and informed account (beautifully illustrated with contemporary photographs) is an excellent introduction to Lindbergh and also to the early years of the celebrity society in which we live now." N Y Times Book Rev
Includes bibliographical references

Linné, Carl von, 1707-1778
Anderson, Margaret Jean. Carl Linnaeus; father of classification. Enslow Pubs. 1997 128p il maps (Great minds of science) lib bdg $18.95 **92**
1. Naturalists
ISBN 0-89490-786-7   LC 96-48900
Profiles the life of the eighteenth-century Swedish naturalist whose scientific naming of plants and animals provided an international language of nature
"Well organized and clearly written. . . . This sound chronological study provides useful report material." SLJ
Includes bibliographical references

Lipinski, Tara
Christopher, Matt. On the ice with—Tara Lipinski. Little, Brown 1999 110p il pa $4.50 **92**
1. Ice skating—Biography 2. Women athletes
ISBN 0-316-14257-3   LC 98-36098

Lipinski, Tara—*Continued*
Describes the life and skating career of the young woman who won a gold medal in figure skating at the 1998 Olympics

Liuzzo, Viola, 1925-1965
Siegel, Beatrice. Murder on the highway: the Viola Liuzzo story; foreword by Rosa Parks. Four Winds Press 1993 125p il maps $19.95   92
1. African Americans—Civil rights
ISBN 0-02-782632-5   LC 93-7148
"Viola Liuzzo was an Italian American living in Detroit, Michigan, when she learned that hundreds of marchers for civil rights had been attacked in Selma, Alabama. She went to Selma to lend her support and was murdered in her car by gunmen. Beatrice Siegel's eloquent account begins with the march and Liuzzo's murder, then retraces the events in Liuzzo's life that brought her to Selma. The book includes excellent maps, stirring photographs, a bibliography, and a fine index." Kaleidoscope. 2nd edition

Lobel, Anita, 1934-
Lobel, Anita. No pretty pictures; a child of war. Greenwillow Bks. 1998 193p il $16 (7 and up)   92
1. Jews—Poland 2. Holocaust, 1933-1945—Personal narratives
ISBN 0-688-15935-4   LC 97-48392
The author, known as an illustrator of children's books, describes her experiences as a Polish Jew during World War II and for years in Sweden afterwards
"Lobel brings to these dramatic experiences an artist's sensibility for the telling detail, a seemingly unvarnished memory and heartstopping candor." Publ Wkly

London, Jack, 1876-1916
Dyer, Daniel. Jack London; a biography. Scholastic 1997 221p il $17.95 (7 and up)   92
1. Authors, American
ISBN 0-590-22216-3   LC 96-29910
Biography of the colorful American writer who had been an oyster pirate, a seal hunter, a mill worker, a hobo, and a political activist before becoming a popular author at the age of twenty-nine
"This is a superior biography that is likely to inspire YAs to read London's novels and stories." SLJ
Includes bibliographical references

Louis, Joe, 1914-1981
Jakoubek, Robert E. Joe Louis; [by] Robert Jakoubek. Chelsea House 1990 127p il (Black Americans of achievement) lib bdg $19.95   92
1. Boxing—Biography 2. African American athletes
ISBN 1-55546-599-4   LC 89-48677
A biography of Joe Louis describing his youth in a Detroit ghetto, his rise to heavyweight champion and major sports hero, and his role in destroying the myth of racial inferiority
Includes bibliographical references

Lowry, Lois
Lowry, Lois. Looking back; a book of memories. Houghton Mifflin 1998 181p il $16   92
1. Authors, American 2. Women authors
ISBN 0-395-89543-X   LC 98-11376
"Walter Lorraine books"
Using family photographs and quotes from her books, the author provides glimpses into her life
"A compelling and inspirational portrait of the author emerges from these vivid snapshots of life's joyful, sad and surprising moments." Publ Wkly

Markham, Lois. Lois Lowry. Learning Works 1995 128p il (Learning Works meet the author series) pa $6.95   92
1. Authors, American 2. Women authors
ISBN 0-88160-278-7   LC 95-77388
A look at the life and career of the noted children's author
"Some anecdotes provide insight into the influences that led her to write, while others reveal personal experiences that have been woven into her stories." SLJ
Includes bibliographical references

Lucas, George
Rau, Dana Meachen. George Lucas; creator of Star wars; by Dana Meachen Rau and Christopher Rau. Watts 1999 112p il (Book report biography) $22   92
1. Motion picture producers and directors
ISBN 0-531-11457-0   LC 98-17938
A biography of the director of the Star Wars films
This is a "book that recounts the requisite facts and figures of the popular filmmaker's life in a fairly entertaining style." SLJ
Includes bibliographical references

Lucid, Shannon
Bredeson, Carmen. Shannon Lucid; space ambassador. Millbrook Press 1998 48p il (Gateway biography) lib bdg $20.90   92
1. Women astronauts
ISBN 0-7613-0406-1   LC 97-47147
Chronicles the life of the astronaut from her childhood in Oklahoma through her various space shuttle missions to her six months aboard the Mir space station
"Full-color photographs are a bonus, as are fun facts about life in space. A chronology and a bibliography are also included." Booklist

Luther, Martin, 1483-1546
Booth, Edwin P. Martin Luther; the great reformer; edited and abridged by Dan Harmon. Chelsea House 1998 207p (Heroes of the faith) $17.95 (7 and up)   92
1. Reformation
ISBN 0-7910-5037-8   LC 98-24325
An abridged version of an adult title published 1933; this edition was first published 1995 in paperback by Barbour
A biography of the German monk who led the Protestant Reformation in Europe from its beginning in 1517 until his death in 1546

Lyon, Mary, 1797-1849

Rosen, Dorothy. A fire in her bones: the story of Mary Lyon; [by] Dorothy Schack Rosen. Carolrhoda Bks. 1995 88p il map (Trailblazers) lib bdg $22.60   **92**
1. Mount Holyoke College 2. Women teachers 3. Educators
ISBN 0-87614-840-2   LC 94-1978
Presents "the story of Mary Lyon, a farm girl who loved education and went on to start Mount Holyoke Female Seminary." Booklist
"Rosen presents her subject's story in an easy-to-understand, straightforward manner that emphasizes Lyon's earnest and persevering drive to establish the first college for women in America. . . . The text is augmented with many period black-and-white reproductions." SLJ
Includes bibliographical references

MacArthur, Douglas, 1880-1964

Feinberg, Barbara Silberdick. Douglas MacArthur; an American hero. Watts 1999 128p il (Book report biography) lib bdg $22   **92**
1. Generals
ISBN 0-531-11562-3   LC 98-29755
Examines the childhood, training, and career of the man known for his military leadership during World War II, the administration of occupied Japan after the war, and the Korean War
"The exciting and controversial life of this famous general is told in easy-to-read prose, with plenty of black-and-white photos. Readers get a feel for MacArthur's flair and style and a sense of his personal life." SLJ
Includes bibliographical references

Fox, Mary Virginia. Douglas MacArthur. Lucent Bks. 1999 96p il (Importance of) $22.45 (7 and up)   **92**
1. Generals
ISBN 1-56006-545-1   LC 98-49749
Describes the childhood, training, career, and contributions of the man known for his military leadership during World War II
"There are many evocative black-and-white photos taken from various periods of MacArthur's life. . . . The book gives a good historical overview of much of America's 20th-century military action." SLJ
Includes bibliographical references

Madison, Dolley, 1768-1849

Pflueger, Lynda. Dolley Madison; courageous first lady. Enslow Pubs. 1999 128p il maps (Historical American biographies) lib bdg $19.95   **92**
1. Presidents' spouses—United States
ISBN 0-7660-1092-9   LC 98-5811
"Pflueger recounts her subject's strict Quaker upbringing, family circumstances, her first marriage, and her marriage to James Madison. The author explains that Madison became known for her political acumen and her ability to smooth ruffled feathers and deal with politicians of both parties, that she defined the role of First Lady for future administrations, and that she inspired many with her gracious manners and patriotism." SLJ
Includes bibliographical references

Madison, James, 1751-1836

Fritz, Jean. The great little Madison. Putnam 1989 159p il $15.95; pa $4.99   **92**
1. Presidents—United States
ISBN 0-399-21768-1; 0-698-11621-6 (pa)
                                      LC 88-31584
"Small, soft-spoken, and by nature diffident, James Madison found it difficult to speak in the midst of controversy, but his zeal and his convictions in the struggle between Republicans and Federalists gave him confidence, and his successes brought him to the presidency. Fritz has given a vivid picture of the man and an equally vivid picture of the problems—especially the internal dissension—that faced the leaders of the new nation. . . . Notes by the author and a bibliography are appended." Bull Cent Child Books

Malone, Mary. James Madison. Enslow Pubs. 1997 128p il (United States presidents) lib bdg $19.95   **92**
1. Presidents—United States
ISBN 0-89490-834-0   LC 96-39133
Chronicles the life and career of the fourth President with emphasis on his many contributions to the government of the United States including his role in writing the Constitution and the Bill of Rights
This "is a well-researched, smoothly written biography." Booklist
Includes bibliographical references

Malcolm X, 1925-1965

Myers, Walter Dean. Malcolm X; by any means necessary; a biography. Scholastic 1993 210p il $13.95; pa $5.99 (7 and up)   **92**
1. African Americans—Biography 2. Black Muslims
ISBN 0-590-46484-1; 0-590-98759-3 (pa)
                                      LC 92-13480
"Myers organizes Malcolm X's life into four stages: his childhood; his adolescence; his period of working under Elijah Mohammad; and his life after breaking with the Nation of Islam. Throughout, his experiences and actions are presented in a broader social context." SLJ
"If you can choose only one book about Malcolm X this is the book of choice. . . . Myers respects his subject and his teenage audience." Voice Youth Advocates
Includes bibliographical references

Malone, Karl

Schnakenberg, Robert. Teammates: Karl Malone and John Stockton. Millbrook Press 1998 96p il lib bdg $20.90   **92**
1. Stockton, John 2. Basketball—Biography
ISBN 0-7613-0300-6   LC 97-19765
A dual biography that emphasizes how greatly two Utah Jazz basketball stars rely on each other on and off the court and the extent to which their careers have intertwined
"Using vivid descriptions of games as well as anecdotes about the two's personal relationship, Schnakenberg gives readers insight into the duo's special bond." Booklist

Mandela, Nelson

Finlayson, Reggie. Nelson Mandela. Lerner Publs. 1999 112p il (A & E biography) $25.26 **92**

1. South Africa—Race relations 2. South Africa—Politics and government

ISBN 0-8225-4936-0   LC 97-50167

"This overview concentrates on Mandela's childhood in the Xhosa nation, his training as a lawyer, and his rise through the ranks of the ANC, and includes ample black-and-white and full-color photographs. His actual imprisonment, release, and election to the presidency of South Africa are confined to the last 15 pages. His divorce from Winnie Mandela and marriage to Graca Machel are not mentioned." SLJ

Includes bibliographical references

Mankiller, Wilma

Schwarz, Melissa. Wilma Mankiller; principal chief of the Cherokees. Chelsea House 1994 111p il (North American Indians of achievement) lib bdg $19.95 **92**

1. Cherokee Indians

ISBN 0-7910-1715-X   LC 93-44435

This is a biography of "the first female Principal Chief of the Cherokee Nation. Schwarz has captured not only Mankiller's struggles both politically and physically, (she was the victim in a serious car accident and struggled with a kidney disease), but also that of the entire Cherokee Nation. The book is easy to read and also will work well for reports. A good purchase for any library." Voice Youth Advocates

Includes bibliographical references

Marley, Bob

Dolan, Sean. Bob Marley. Chelsea House 1997 119p il (Black Americans of achievement) lib bdg $19.95; pa $9.95 **92**

1. Singers 2. Reggae music 3. Blacks—Biography

ISBN 0-7910-2041-X (lib bdg); 0-7910-3255-8 (pa)   LC 95-35932

Traces the life of the Jamaican musician who helped popularize reggae before his untimely death

"The book is fascinating reading: it brings its subject alive, and inspires readers to listen to Marley's music. The text is filled with details that keep readers' interest." SLJ

Includes bibliographical references

Marshall, Thurgood

Kent, Deborah. Thurgood Marshall and the Supreme Court. Children's Press 1997 30p il (Cornerstones of freedom) lib bdg $19.50; pa $5.95 **92**

1. United States. Supreme Court 2. Judges 3. African Americans—Biography

ISBN 0-516-20297-9 (lib bdg); 0-516-26139-8 (pa)   LC 96-9865

Narrates the life of the first African-American to serve as a judge on the United States Supreme Court

"Kent's clear and simple text adequately covers the noted Justice. . . . Color and black-and-white photographs and a time line are included." Horn Book Guide

Includes glossary

Martínez, María Montoya, 1887-1980

Morris, Juddi. Tending the fire: the story of Maria Martinez. Rising Moon Bks. for Young Readers 1997 113p map $12.95; pa $6.95 **92**

1. Pueblo Indians 2. Women artists

ISBN 0-87358-665-4; 0-87358-654-9 (pa)   LC 97-12009

A biography of the Tewa Indian woman who revived the dying art of her people, ceramic pottery, and shared her knowledge of pottery-making with others

"Maria Martinez . . . is given her due in this straightforward, chronological biography. . . . A welcome book about a little-known American artist." Booklist

Includes glossary and bibliographical references

Martinez, Pedro, 1971-

Gallagher, Jim. Pedro Martinez. Mitchell Lane Pubs. 1999 64p il (Latinos in baseball) $18.95 **92**

1. Baseball—Biography

ISBN 1-883845-85-8   LC 98-48047

Presents a biography of the professional baseball pitcher from the Dominican Republic who won the National League's Cy Young Award in 1997 and currently pitches for the Boston Red Sox

Includes bibliographical references

Matisse, Henri

Kostenevich, A. G. (Al´bert Grigor´evich). Henri Matisse; [by] Albert Kostenevich; in collaboration with Lory Frankel. Abrams 1998 92p il (First impressions) $19.95 (7 and up) **92**

1. Artists, French

ISBN 0-8109-4296-8   LC 96-34076

Discusses the life of the French artist and makes observations about his work

"Throughout the book, reproductions of paintings, drawings, and cut-paper collages appear, some in color, some in black and white. In addition, photographs record Matisse with family, with friends, and at work. . . . A handsome resource for art students." Booklist

McAuliffe, Christa

Jeffrey, Laura S. Christa McAuliffe; a space biography. Enslow Pubs. 1998 48p il (Countdown to space) lib bdg $18.95 **92**

1. Challenger (Spacecraft) 2. Women astronauts

ISBN 0-89490-976-2   LC 97-22114

A biography of the school teacher turned astronaut whose life was tragically ended when the space shuttle Challenger exploded just after liftoff

"An accurate, well-researched . . . biography." SLJ

Includes glossary and bibliographical references

McCarthy, Joseph, 1908-1957

Sherrow, Victoria. Joseph McCarthy and the Cold War. Blackbirch Press 1998 80p il (Notorious Americans and their times) lib bdg $18.95 **92**

1. United States—Politics and government—1945-1953 2. United States—Politics and government—1953-1961

ISBN 1-56711-219-6   LC 98-15559

McCarthy, Joseph, 1908-1957—*Continued*
A biography of the unknown first-term senator from Wisconsin who gained notoriety by stirring up anti-Communist fears in the years after World War II
"Interesting sidebars introduce some of McCarthy's contemporaries such as 'The Hollywood Ten,' Alger Hiss, and Robert Oppenheimer. . . . As many history books at this level contain surprisingly scant information about the father of McCarthyism, this title is a worthwhile addition for most libraries." SLJ
Includes bibliographical references

McClintock, Barbara
Fine, Edith Hope. Barbara McClintock; Nobel Prize geneticist. Enslow Pubs. 1998 128p il (People to know) lib bdg $19.95 (7 and up)   92
    1. Women scientists 2. Genetics
    ISBN 0-89490-983-5   LC 97-43754
Presents the life and career of the geneticist who spent many years studying the cells of maize and in 1983 was awarded the Nobel Prize in Physiology or Medicine
"This book is what every good biography should be. . . . Throughout the narrative, McClintock's lively personality and dedication to her work shine through." SLJ
Includes glossary and bibliographical references

McGwire, Mark
Muskat, Carrie. Mark McGwire; introduction by Jim Murray. Chelsea House 1999 64p il (Baseball legends) $16.95; pa $7.95   92
    1. Baseball—Biography
    ISBN 0-7910-5155-2; 0-7910-5491-8 (pa)
                                LC 98-51065
Presents a biography of the St. Louis Cardinal power hitter who broke Roger Maris' single-season home run record in 1998
Includes bibliographical references

Stewart, Mark. Home run heroes: McGwire and Sosa. Millbrook Press 1999 64p il lib bdg $22.90; pa $6.95   92
    1. Sosa, Sammy 2. Baseball—Biography
    ISBN 0-7613-1559-4 (lib bdg); 0-7613-1045-2 (pa)
                                LC 98-50292
Presents the lives, on and off the baseball field, of two athletes whose battle for the home run record dominated sports headlines in 1998
"Includes all sorts of action packed color pictures and provides a fast-moving account of the home-run battle between Sosa and McGwire. . . . The colorful layout, sprinkled with quotes and statistics, is sure to spark interest." SLJ

Stewart, Mark. Mark McGwire; home-run king. Children's Press 1999 48p il (Sports stars) lib bdg $18; pa $5.95   92
    1. Baseball—Biography
    ISBN 0-516-21612-0 (lib bdg); 0-516-26512-1 (pa)
                                LC 98-48386
A look at the life and playing career of the St. Louis Cardinal slugger who, since 1998, holds baseball's single-season home run record
"Adding interest are several clear, color action photographs." Horn Book

Thornley, Stew. Mark McGwire; star home run hitter. Enslow Pubs. 1999 104p il (Sports reports) lib bdg $19.95   92
    1. Baseball—Biography
    ISBN 0-7660-1329-4   LC 98-33313
Examines the life and career of baseball superstar Mark McGwire, from his earliest playing days to his record-breaking 1998 season
Includes bibliographical references

Mead, Margaret, 1901-1978
Mark, Joan T. Margaret Mead; coming of age in America; [by] Joan Mark. Oxford Univ. Press 1998 110p il (Oxford portraits in science) $21 (7 and up)   92
    1. Anthropologists
    ISBN 0-19-511679-8   LC 98-18604
An "account of the life and works of the influential, pioneering anthropologist. . . . Mark does a fine job of abstracting Mead's research and published works and showing why they were both critically acclaimed and criticized. The reader-friendly prose is peppered with fascinating anecdotes and photos. Mead herself is presented as a complex, intriguing figure, with fascinating, often contradictory, public and private lives." Booklist
Includes bibliographical references

Meir, Golda, 1898-1978
Hitzeroth, Deborah. Golda Meir. Lucent Bks. 1998 111p il maps (Importance of) lib bdg $22.45 (7 and up)   92
    1. Israel—Politics and government 2. Zionism
    ISBN 1-56006-090-5   LC 97-36465
A biography of the woman who dedicated her life to the creation and preservation of a Jewish state
"This admiring and informative portrait emphasizes Meir's lasting contributions to the development of the state of Israel and communicates to young readers the heroic dimensions of her rich and full life." SLJ
Includes bibliographical references

Mendel, Gregor, 1822-1884
Edelson, Edward. Gregor Mendel, and the roots of genetics. Oxford Univ. Press 1999 105p il (Oxford portraits in science) lib bdg $21 (7 and up)   92
    1. Genetics
    ISBN 0-19-512226-7   LC 98-37541
"This biography provides details of the scientist's life and his experiments as well as the political and social context of his times. . . . A two-page chronology tracks important events in his life and the vital contributions he made to the study of genetics. Black-and-white photographs, reproductions of artwork, and pages from the scientist's notebooks and manuscripts accompany the text." SLJ
Includes bibliographical references

Klare, Roger. Gregor Mendel; father of genetics. Enslow Pubs. 1997 128p il (Great minds of science) lib bdg $19.95   92
    1. Genetics
    ISBN 0-89490-789-1   LC 96-35791

Mendel, Gregor, 1822-1884—*Continued*
Examines the life and work of the nineteenth-century Austrian monk who discovered the laws of genetics
"Easy-to-understand explanations of groundbreaking discoveries. . . . An activity section encourages readers to try their hands at the techniques and principles under discussion. Black-and-white photos, reproductions, and diagrams enhance the [presentation]. Useful . . . especially for reports." SLJ
Includes bibliographical references

Meredith, James
Elish, Dan. James Meredith and school desegregation. Millbrook Press 1994 32p il (Gateway civil rights) lib bdg $21.90; pa $7.95
92
1. African Americans—Biography 2. African Americans—Civil rights 3. Mississippi—Race relations
ISBN 1-56294-379-0; 1-56294-861-X (pa)
LC 93-9383
Focuses on the events surrounding James Meredith's efforts to be allowed to attend the University of Mississippi in 1962
This book gives "readers a look at the era of legal segregation in the U.S. and its injustices. . . . The historical black-and-white photographs are compelling and chilling." SLJ
Includes bibliographical references

Michelangelo Buonarroti, 1475-1564
Pettit, Jayne. Michelangelo; genius of the Renaissance. Watts 1998 128p il (Book report biography) lib bdg $22
92
1. Artists, Italian
ISBN 0-531-11490-2
LC 97-26724
Recounts the life of the famous sculptor, painter, poet, and architect who flourished during the Italian Renaissance
"Though at times the narrative meanders and gives extraneous information . . . the fascinating details revealed about Michelangelo's life and art overshadow this minor shortcoming." SLJ
Includes bibliographical references

Mitchell, Maria, 1818-1889
Gormley, Beatrice. Maria Mitchell; the soul of an astronomer. Eerdmans 1995 123p il hardcover o.p. paperback available $8 (7 and up)
92
1. Women astronomers
ISBN 0-8028-5099-5 (pa)
LC 95-21980
A biography of the first female science professor at Vassar College and the first American woman astronomer
"With a smoothly flowing and lively style, this biography introduces readers to the 19th-century astronomer. Well-chosen, primary-source quotations and quality black-and-white photos add authenticity to the text, and contribute greatly to the author's objective and comprehensive description of Mitchell's accomplishments." SLJ
Includes bibliographical references

Moceanu, Dominique
Durrett, Deanne. Dominique Moceanu. Lucent Bks. 1999 111p il (People in the news) lib bdg $17.96 (7 and up)
92
1. Gymnastics 2. Women athletes
ISBN 1-56006-099-9
LC 98-17195
Discusses the personal life and gymnastics career of the youngest member of the U.S. women's gymnastics team that won a gold medal at the 1996 Olympics in Atlanta
"Those interested in gymnastics will enjoy the detailed account of competitions, routines, scoring, etc., and may glean an appreciation for what it takes to become an Olympic champion." SLJ
Includes bibliographical references

Montgomery, L. M. (Lucy Maud), 1874-1942
Andronik, Catherine M. Kindred spirit: a biography of L. M. Montgomery, creator of Anne of Green Gables. Atheneum Pubs. 1993 160p il $16
92
1. Authors, Canadian 2. Women authors
ISBN 0-689-31671-2
LC 92-25869
Covers the personal life and literary career of the Canadian writer best known for her novels about Anne, a girl from Prince Edward Island
Andronik "offers fascinating insight into this popular author's life." Booklist
Includes bibliographical references

Morgan, Sir Henry, 1635?-1688
Marrin, Albert. Terror of the Spanish Main: Sir Henry Morgan and his buccaneers. Dutton 1998 240p il maps $19.99 (7 and up)
92
1. Pirates
ISBN 0-525-45942-1
LC 98-7819
An account of the life and times of the English buccaneer, Henry Morgan, from his birth in Wales through his daring exploits in the Spanish Main to his later years in Jamaica
"Although Marrin's often gory account is not for the weak of stomach, most readers will find this gripping and complex historical drama impossible to put down." Publ Wkly
Includes bibliographical references

Mowat, Farley
Mowat, Farley. Born naked. Houghton Mifflin 1994 c1993 256p il maps hardcover o.p. paperback available $12 (7 and up)
92
1. Authors, Canadian
ISBN 0-395-73528-9 (pa)
LC 93-23702
"A Peter Davison book"
First published 1993 in Canada
The "renowned naturalist and writer gives us a glimpse of his parents, his growing up in Canada, and the roots of his love for animals." Booklist
"There are no dull pages here; every man, woman, child, and animal mentioned even casually makes an impression. . . . Highly recommended to all those who like good writing." Libr J

Muir, John, 1838-1914

Naden, Corinne J. John Muir, saving the wilderness; [by] Corinne J. Naden and Rose Blue. Millbrook Press 1992 48p il (Gateway biography) lib bdg $19.90; pa $5.95   **92**
1. Naturalists 2. Nature conservation
ISBN 1-56294-110-0 (lib bdg); 1-56294-797-4 (pa)
LC 91-18106
This book profiles the life and times of naturalist John Muir
"Attractively designed with clear framed text and lots of photographs. . . . Kids will be intrigued by Muir's work for conservation, especially his role in founding the national parks." Booklist
Includes bibliographical references

Murrow, Edward R.

Finkelstein, Norman H. With heroic truth: the life of Edward R. Murrow. Clarion Bks. 1997 175p il $17.95 (7 and up)   **92**
1. Journalists
ISBN 0-395-67891-9   LC 94-25128
A biography of the early radio and television journalist who reported on World War II and opposed Joseph McCarthy in the 1950s
"Drawing heavily upon primary-source materials, including transcripts of many of Murrow's radio and television broadcasts, Finkelstein presents a sharp, clear portrait of one of the 20th-century's great journalists. . . . A fine selection of black-and-white photographs appears throughout." SLJ
Includes bibliographical references

Neruda, Pablo, 1904-1973

Goodnough, David. Pablo Neruda; Nobel prize-winning poet. Enslow Pubs. 1998 128p il maps (Hispanic biographies) lib bdg $19.95   **92**
1. Poets, Chilean
ISBN 0-7660-1042-2   LC 97-32888
Traces the life and career, including the political activities, of the famous Chilean poet
"The fact that students are introduced to political issues is itself something of a real plus in this age of homogenized education. Ending with a chronology, chapter notes, and a list of suggested reading, this slender volume satisfies the needs of beginning report writers and provides a springboard to further research for more experienced students." SLJ

Newton, Sir Isaac, 1642-1727

Anderson, Margaret Jean. Isaac Newton; the greatest scientist of all time; [by] Margaret J. Anderson. Enslow Pubs. 1996 128p il (Great minds of science) lib bdg $19.95   **92**
1. Scientists
ISBN 0-89490-681-X   LC 96-4958
"The life, work, and goals of the brilliant scientist Isaac Newton are described in this very readable book about perhaps 'the greatest scientist of all time.' A descriptive chapter of experiments on color, paddle wheels, and gravity motivates childen to think and explore, as Newton did." Sci Child
Includes glossary and bibliographical references

Christianson, Gale E. Isaac Newton and the scientific revolution. Oxford Univ. Press 1996 155p il (Oxford portraits in science) lib bdg $21; pa $11.95 (7 and up)   **92**
1. Scientists
ISBN 0-19-509224-4 (lib bdg); 0-19-512080-9 (pa)
LC 96-13179
Explores the life and scientific contributions of the famed English mathematician and natural philosopher
This book "reads easily and with a pleasant and comfortable flow. Structured around pivotal moments in Newton's life, the book is an excellent reference for biographical data on the great English scientist; in addition, it affords a fine historical perspective of the scientific revolution." Sci Books Films
Includes bibliographical references

Nixon, Richard M. (Richard Milhous), 1913-1994

Barron, Rachel. Richard Nixon; American politician. Morgan Reynolds 1998 112p il (Notable Americans) $18.95 (7 and up)   **92**
1. Presidents—United States
ISBN 1-88384-633-1   LC 98-29836
"A comprehensive portrait of the statesman's political career and personal life. . . . Barron is objective about her subject, giving him credit for his considerable successes and holding him responsible for his failures." SLJ
Includes bibliographical references

Goldman, Martin S. Richard M. Nixon; a complex legacy. Facts on File 1998 146p il (Makers of America) $19.95 (7 and up)   **92**
1. Presidents—United States
ISBN 0-8160-3397-8   LC 97-19928
A biography of the controversial president which covers his early life and political career, the presidential elections of 1960 and 1968, his roles in the Vietnam War and Watergate scandal, and his retirement
Includes bibliographical references

Larsen, Rebecca. Richard Nixon; rise and fall of a president. Watts 1991 189p il lib bdg $24 (7 and up)   **92**
1. Presidents—United States
ISBN 0-531-10997-6   LC 90-23828
Traces the life and political career of the thirty-seventh president, from his student days, through the Watergate scandal which cost him the presidency, to his retirement and new career as a writer
"Larsen writes well and is quite objective about her subject. . . . This is interesting enough to recommend to students for both general reading and reports." SLJ
Includes bibliographical references

Oakley, Annie, 1860-1926

Flynn, Jean. Annie Oakley; legendary sharpshooter. Enslow Pubs. 1998 128p il (Historical American biographies) lib bdg $19.95
92
ISBN 0-7660-1012-0   LC 97-25394

Oakley, Annie, 1860-1926—*Continued*
Recounts the life of the markswoman and performer who achieved fame with Buffalo Bill Cody's Wild West Show
"With sensitivity, the author relates the facts as well as some of the stories that have created the legend. The book has a good index and interesting black-and-white archival photographs." SLJ
Includes bibliographical references

O'Connor, Sandra Day
Huber, Peter W. Sandra Day O'Connor; [by] Peter Huber. Chelsea House 1990 111p il (American women of achievement) lib bdg $19.95; pa $9.95   92
1. United States. Supreme Court 2. Women judges
ISBN 1-55546-672-9 (lib bdg); 0-7910-0448-1 (pa)
LC 89-13902
Examines the life of the first woman Supreme Court justice, including her childhood, early career, and work as a judge
"Successfully interwoven into the biography is a basic introduction to the U.S. judiciary system and O'Connor's stands on important and controversial issues. The portrayal of her efforts to overcome obstacles faced because she was female and her abilities to balance a high-power career and a family life will set a positive example for all young women in similar situations." SLJ
Includes bibliographical references

O'Donnell, Rosie
Kallen, Stuart A. Rosie O'Donnell. Lucent Bks. 1999 96p il (People in the news) lib bdg $17.96 (7 and up)   92
1. Entertainers
ISBN 1-56006-546-X   LC 98-52126
Follows the life and career of popular comedienne Rosie O'Donnell
"Unlike many talk show hosts, Rosie O'Donnell has a strong following among kids. Her young fans will appreciate this look at her life. . . . Thoroughly sourced, the book also features a time line and bibliography." Booklist

Krohn, Katherine E. Rosie O'Donnell; [by] Katherine Krohn. Lerner Publs. 1999 112p il (A & E biography) $25.26; pa $7.95   92
1. Entertainers
ISBN 0-8225-4939-5; 0-8225-9681-4 (pa)
LC 97-49015
Discusses the childhood, young adulthood, career, and parenthood of an entertainer known as "the Queen of Nice"
This "is a breezy, interesting look at a pop-culture icon. . . . The book is well documented with extensive source notes, including a personal interview with O'Donnell, giving it a veracity and immediacy lacking in most biographies for young people." SLJ
Includes filmography and bibliographical references

Onassis, Jacqueline Kennedy
Santow, Dan. Jacqueline Bouvier Kennedy Onassis, 1929-1994. Children's Press 1998 111p il (Encyclopedia of first ladies) $32.50   92
1. Presidents' spouses—United States
ISBN 0-516-20477-7   LC 97-47280
Presents a biography of the wife of the thirty-fifth president of the United States, an elegant and fashionable First Lady who helped Washington become the social and cultural center of the country
Includes bibliographical references

O'Neal, Shaquille
Ungs, Tim. Shaquille O'Neal; introduction by Chuck Daly. Chelsea House 1996 64p il (Basketball legends) $15.95   92
1. Basketball—Biography 2. African American athletes
ISBN 0-7910-2437-7   LC 95-9263
This biography of the African American basketball star discusses O'Neal's athletic development from childhood to professional success, and includes black-and-white photographs and career statistics
Includes bibliographical references

Orozco, José Clemente, 1883-1949
Cruz, Bárbara. José Clemente Orozco; Mexican artist. Enslow Pubs. 1998 128p il (Hispanic biographies) lib bdg $19.95   92
1. Artists, Mexican
ISBN 0-7660-1041-4   LC 98-26414
Discusses the life and times of Jose Clemente Orozco, who has been called "the most original and powerful mural painter" in Mexico despite having been badly injured in an explosion as a teenager
"The author clearly explains the controversial themes of Orozco's works, which often dealt with sensitive political and social issues. There are many black-and-white photos. . . . The book has extensive chapter notes and a list for further reading, both evidence of its scholarly format that nevertheless remains approachable." SLJ

Owens, Jesse, 1913-1980
Nuwer, Hank. The legend of Jesse Owens. Watts 1998 176p il lib bdg $24 (7 and up)   92
1. African American athletes 2. Track athletics
ISBN 0-531-11356-6   LC 96-51188
Explores the personal life, athletic accomplishments, and career of Jesse Owens
"This is a good source of information about the legendary Olympic sprinter." Horn Book Guide
Includes bibliographical references

Paderewski, Ignace Jan, 1860-1941
Lisandrelli, Elaine Slivinski. Ignacy Jan Paderewski; Polish pianist and patriot. Morgan Reynolds 1998 112p il (Champions of freedom) $18.95 (7 and up)   92
1. Pianists 2. Statesmen—Poland
ISBN 1-88384-629-3   LC 98-37784

Paderewski, Ignace Jan, 1860-1941—*Continued*
A biography of the Polish piano virtuoso who became the first prime minister of a united Poland after World War I
"An engaging look at a loyal Polish citizen who used his musical talent and oratory skills to advance the ideals of his country." SLJ
Includes bibliographical references

Paine, Thomas, 1737-1809
Meltzer, Milton. Tom Paine: voice of revolution. Watts 1996 175p il lib bdg $28 (7 and up) **92**
ISBN 0-531-11291-8   LC 96-11956
The story of the self-educated craftsman who earned a place in history as the voice of the American Revolution
"The author succeeds in creating a biography that is replete with the rich details of the man's life as well as conveying the exciting times in which he lived." SLJ
Includes bibliographical references

Parker, Charlie, 1920-1955
Frankl, Ron. Charlie Parker, musician. Chelsea House 1992 127p il (Black Americans of achievement) lib bdg $19.95   **92**
1. Jazz musicians 2. African American musicians
ISBN 0-7910-1134-8   LC 92-12126
Introduces the life and times of the noted jazz musician Charlie Parker
"In this brief, authoritative, and well-written biography of the greatest saxophonist in jazz history, Frankl conveys both the brilliance of Bird's music and the tragedy of his short life." SLJ
Includes discography and bibliographical references

Parker, Quanah, Comanche Chief, 1854?-1911
Marrin, Albert. Plains warrior: Chief Quanah Parker and the Comanches. Atheneum Bks. for Young Readers 1996 200p il map $18 (7 and up)   **92**
1. Comanche Indians
ISBN 0-689-80081-9   LC 95-23048
This biography of the Comanche chief "focuses on the Comanche and their losing nineteenth-century battle for their traditional life and lands on the Great Plains." Bull Cent Child Books
"Vivid descriptions of life on the Great Plains, compelling anecdotes, and lavish use of black-and-white photographs provide a strong sense of time and place as well as the personalities involved in the struggle to settle the Southwest." Booklist
Includes bibliographical references

Parks, Rosa, 1913-
Parks, Rosa. Rosa Parks: my story; by Rosa Parks with Jim Haskins. Dial Bks. 1992 192p il $17; pa $4.99   **92**
1. African American women 2. African Americans—Civil rights
ISBN 0-8037-0673-1; 0-14-130120-1 (pa)
LC 89-1124

Rosa Parks describes her early life and experiences with race discrimination, and her participation in the Montgomery bus boycott and the civil rights movement
"A remarkable story, a record of quiet bravery and modesty, a document of social significance, a taut drama told with candor." Bull Cent Child Books

Pasteur, Louis, 1822-1895
Smith, Linda Wasmer. Louis Pasteur; disease fighter. Enslow Pubs. 1997 128p il (Great minds of science) lib bdg $19.95   **92**
1. Scientists
ISBN 0-89490-790-5   LC 96-38082
A biography of the noted French scientist whose discoveries, including a rabies vaccine and the process of pasteurization, had important practical applications in both medicine and industry
"This well-rounded biography gives enough information about Pasteur's childhood and private life to be interesting but devotes most of the pages to the world-altering discoveries that put Pasteur solidly at the forefront of scientists in history." Booklist
Includes glossary and bibliographical references

Pauling, Linus C., 1901-1994
Hager, Thomas. Linus Pauling and the chemistry of life. Oxford Univ. Press 1998 142p il (Oxford portraits in science) $21 (7 and up)   **92**
1. Chemists
ISBN 0-19-510853-1   LC 97-43403
Profiles the Nobel Prize-winning chemist who described the nature of chemical bonds, made important discoveries in the fields of quantum mechanics, immunology, and evolution, and used his scientific fame to help advance political causes
"Students with a strong science background will get the most out of this biography, but even young people who don't like science will be able to identify with a man whose scientific curiosity and political principles led him to try to change the world. Chronology and recommended readings." Booklist

Paulsen, Gary
Paulsen, Gary. My life in dog years; with drawings by Ruth Wright Paulsen. Delacorte Press 1998 137p il $15.95; pa $4.99   **92**
1. Authors, American 2. Dogs
ISBN 0-385-32570-3; 0-440-41471-7 (pa)
LC 97-40254
The author describes some of the dogs that have had special places in his life, including his first dog, Snowball, in the Philippines; Dirk, who protected him from bullies; and Cookie, who saved his life
"Paulsen differentiates his canine friends beautifully, as only a keen observer and lover of dogs can. At the same time, he presents an intimate glimpse of himself, a lonely child of alcoholic parents, who drew strength and solace from his four-legged companions and a love of the great outdoors. Poignant but never saccharine, honest, and open." Booklist

Peters, Stephanie True. Gary Paulsen. Learning Works 1999 112p il (Learning Works meet the author series) pa $6.95   **92**
1. Authors, American
ISBN 0-88160-324-4   LC 98-54725

Paulsen, Gary—Continued

"Arranged in chronological order, each chapter begins with a quote from one of Paulsen's books, connecting his writings with his own life experiences. Peters addresses difficult issues forthrightly, including Paulsen's own alcoholism and continuing health problems. A straightforward, concise biography of a favorite author." Booklist

Pavlova, Anna, 1881-1931

Levine, Ellen. Anna Pavlova, genius of the dance. Scholastic 1995 132p il $14.95   **92**

1. Ballet dancers

ISBN 0-590-44304-6   LC 94-7310

This biography of the ballerina covers "Pavlova's early years in Russia, her later settling in England, and then her extensive touring through Europe, the United States, South America, and Asia." Bull Cent Child Books

"Short chapters with lots of dialogue and anecdotes create a lively tension that pulls the reader through the book. Pavlova's sparkling personality is evident at every turn. . . . Ideal for middle grades, Levine's writing style is also interesting enough to capture older reluctant readers." Voice Youth Advocates

Includes glossary and bibliographical references

Peale, Charles Willson, 1741-1827

Wilson, Janet. The ingenious Mr. Peale; painter, patriot, and man of science; illustrated with paintings by Charles Willson Peale. Atheneum Bks. for Young Readers 1996 122p il $16   **92**

1. Artists, American

ISBN 0-689-31884-7   LC 95-30818

Narrates the life of the early American portrait painter who established the first public picture gallery in America and who pursued numerous other interests including natural history

"Quotations from Peale's diary and letters offer a sense of the man's personality. Reproductions of his paintings and sketches appear throughout the book. This readable biography offers an intriguing portrait of Peale as well as a fresh perspective on a significant period in American history." Booklist

Includes bibliographical references

Peary, Robert Edwin, 1856-1920

Dwyer, Christopher. Robert Peary and the quest for the North Pole; introductory essay by Michael Collins. Chelsea House 1992 111p il maps (World explorers) lib bdg $19.95   **92**

1. Explorers 2. North Pole

ISBN 0-7910-1316-2   LC 92-8446

Describes the history of Admiral Robert Peary's expeditions to the North Pole, which he reached in 1909

Includes bibliographical references

Peck, Richard, 1934-

Peck, Richard. Anonymously yours. Messner 1991 122p il (In my own words) o.p.; Morrow paperback available $4.95   **92**

1. Authors, American

ISBN 0-688-13702-4 (pa)   LC 91-10067

The popular author describes how he grew up in Decatur, Illinois, went into teaching, and eventually became a writer, incorporating his earlier experiences into novels intended to reach and change young readers

"This memoir is . . . engaging and filled with insight into Peck's creative processes." SLJ

Includes bibliographical references

Peet, Bill

Peet, Bill. Bill Peet: an autobiography. Houghton Mifflin 1989 190p il $20; pa $12   **92**

1. Walt Disney Productions 2. Authors, American 3. Illustrators

ISBN 0-395-50932-7; 0-395-68982-1 (pa)   LC 88-37067

A Caldecott Medal honor book, 1990

This memoir "describes the life of the well-known children's book author who worked as an illustrator for Walt Disney from the making of 'Dumbo' until 'Mary Poppins.'" N Y Times Book Rev

"Every page of this oversized book is illustrated with Peet's unmistakable black-and-white drawings of himself and the people, places, and events described in the text. Familiar characters from his books and movies appear often." SLJ

Pelé, 1940-

Arnold, Caroline. Pelé: the king of soccer. Watts 1992 64p il lib bdg $22   **92**

1. Soccer—Biography

ISBN 0-531-20077-9   LC 91-33557

"A First book"

Examines the life and career of the renowned soccer player from Brazil

"Arnold does a good job of tracing Pelé's soccer career from early promise through young star to international superstar." Booklist

Includes bibliographical references

Penn, William, 1644-1718

Doherty, Kieran. William Penn; Quaker colonist. Millbrook Press 1998 192p il lib bdg $22.40   **92**

1. Society of Friends 2. Pennsylvania—History

ISBN 0-7613-0355-3   LC 97-48504

A biography of William Penn, founder of the Quaker colony of Pennsylvania, who struggled throughout his life for the freedom to practice his religion

"An excellent account of an extraordinary life. Doherty . . . tells the story of Penn's life in an interesting and compelling manner that reads almost like a good adventure novel." SLJ

Includes bibliographical references

Picasso, Pablo, 1881-1973

Beardsley, John. Pablo Picasso. Abrams 1991 92p il (First impressions) $19.95 (7 and up)   **92**

1. Artists, Spanish

ISBN 0-8109-3713-1   LC 91-7741

Examines the life and work of Picasso, discussing how and why his art looks the way it does and how it relates to the artist

This is a "readable and informative study. . . . This book is as much a series of marvelous lessons in 'reading' art as it is a tribute to a unique artist." Horn Book

Picasso, Pablo, 1881-1973—*Continued*

Loria, Stephano. Pablo Picasso; illustrated by Simone Boni, L.R. Galante. Bedrick Bks. 1995 64p il (Masters of art) $22.50　　　　**92**
1. Artists, Spanish
ISBN 0-87226-318-5　　　　LC 95-31830
The author examines periods of the artists work through full-color reproductions of major paintings. Picasso's political views, friendships, and relationships with women are discussed

Rodari, Florian. A weekend with Picasso. Rizzoli Int. Publs. 1991 64p il $19.95; pa $9.95
92
1. Artists, Spanish
ISBN 0-8478-1437-8; 0-8478-1920-5 (pa)
　　　　LC 91-12427
The twentieth century artist talks about his life and work as if entertaining the reader for a weekend
"What could have sounded forced or contrived becomes instead an inviting and lively romp. The author not only succeeds in providing solid information and astute commentary but also seems to capture . . . the childlike exuberance of Picasso." Horn Book
Includes bibliographical references

Pick-Goslar, Hannah
Gold, Alison Leslie. Memories of Anne Frank. See entry under Frank, Anne, 1929-1945

Pickett, Bill, ca. 1860-1932
Sanford, William R. Bill Pickett: African-American rodeo star; [by] William R. Sanford & Carl R. Green. Enslow Pubs. 1997 48p il (Legendary heroes of the Wild West) lib bdg $15.95　　　　**92**
1. Cowhands 2. African Americans—Biography
ISBN 0-89490-676-3　　　　LC 96-1891
Describes the life and accomplishments of the son of a former slave whose unusual bulldogging style made him a rodeo star
Includes glossary and bibliographical references

Pippen, Scottie
McMane, Fred. Scottie Pippen; introduction by Chuck Daly. Chelsea House 1996 63p il (Basketball legends) $15.95　　　　**92**
1. Basketball—Biography
ISBN 0-7910-2498-9　　　　LC 95-18518
Examines the life and basketball career of a member of the 1992 Olympics "Dream Team" and one of the key players for the Chicago Bulls
Includes bibliographical references

Pippin, Horace, 1888-1946
Lyons, Mary E. Starting home: the story of Horace Pippin, painter. Scribner 1993 42p il (African-American artists and artisans) $15.95
92
1. Artists, American 2. African American artists
ISBN 0-684-19534-8　　　　LC 92-26990

"Horace Pippin was a self-taught painter whose work reflects his personal story. Haunted by his experience as a soldier in World War I, he painted scenes from the trenches years after he returned. . . . The paintings are haunting, and Lyons speaks about them with warm appreciation." Booklist

Poe, Edgar Allan, 1809-1849
Anderson, Madelyn Klein. Edgar Allan Poe; a mystery. Watts 1993 158p il (Impact biography) lib bdg $24 (7 and up)　　　　**92**
1. Authors, American
ISBN 0-531-13012-6　　　　LC 92-43935
This biography traces "Poe's history from his childhood with his foster family, his mercurial relations with friends and enemies (particularly female friends and enemies), and his professional life as an editor and writer for various periodicals." Bull Cent Child Books
The author "includes a useful chronology of composition and publication dates for all the poems and tales and a rather unique bibliography in which she states 'not all the books . . . are recommended.' She explains that many are inaccessible for a variety of reasons and then tells which are good for young readers." Voice Youth Advocates

Polo, Marco, 1254-1323?
Macdonald, Fiona. Marco Polo; a journey through China; written by Fiona Macdonald; Illustrated by Mark Bergin; created and designed by David Salariya. Watts 1998 32p il maps (Expedition) $21; pa $7.95　　　　**92**
1. Voyages and travels 2. Explorers 3. China—Description
ISBN 0-531-14453-4; 0-531-15340-1 (pa)
　　　　LC 97-7533
Describes Marco Polo's travels through Asia, and discusses the people and cultures he encountered
"The appealing format lends itself to easy use by student researchers, particularly reluctant readers. . . . Detailed, full-color pen-and-watercolor illustrations and small text bits provide lifestyle and cultural details about the areas traveled." SLJ

Stefoff, Rebecca. Marco Polo and the medieval explorers. Chelsea House 1992 111p il maps (World explorers) lib bdg $19.95　　　　**92**
1. Voyages and travels 2. Explorers 3. China—Description
ISBN 0-7910-1294-8　　　　LC 91-14049
Examines the life and travels of the medieval explorer
This "is an immensely fascinating contemporary geography/medieval history book. . . . The style of writing and the sentence structure are as if the author is in conversation with the reader. It is this feature that places the reader back in the medieval time frame." Voice Youth Advocates
Includes bibliographical references

Powell, Colin L.
Haskins, James. Colin Powell; a biography; [by] Jim Haskins. Scholastic 1992 101p il (Scholastic biography) pa $3.50　　　　**92**
1. Generals 2. African American soldiers
ISBN 0-590-45243-6　　　　LC 92-201957

Powell, Colin L.—*Continued*
"From Haskins's biography of Powell, we learn . . . about the subject's feelings, his motivations, and his relationships with his family, his handling of conflicts, and his responses to lines of authority. The person, more than the military leader, emerges from the portrait Haskins paints." Voice Youth Advocates
Includes glossary and bibliographical references

Hughes, Libby. Colin Powell: a man of quality. Dillon Press 1996 171p il (People in focus) lib bdg $13.95; pa $7.95 (7 and up)   **92**
1. Generals 2. African American soldiers
ISBN 0-382-39260-4 (lib bdg); 0-382-39261-2 (pa)
LC 95-44435
Examines the life and career of the African American four-star general
The author "draws on both published accounts for adults and on her own interview with Powell, an approach that allows readers to appreciate both his philosophy of hard work and education and his many achievements, and also understand how his values have contributed to his enormous popularity." SLJ
Includes bibliographical references

Powers, Harriet, 1837-1911
Lyons, Mary E. Stitching stars: the story quilts of Harriet Powers. Scribner 1993 41p il (African-American artists and artisans) $17; pa $6.99   **92**
1. Quilts 2. Artists, American 3. Women artists 4. African American artists
ISBN 0-684-19576-3; 0-689-81707-X (pa)
LC 92-38561
"Harriet Powers was born in slavery and lived in poverty, with few records of her life except her richly imaginative story quilts. In this brief artistic biography, Lyons openly surmises or fictionalizes where the bitter obscurity of slavery and poverty has resulted in an absence of records, but Harriet speaks eloquently through her handiwork depicting Bible stories and natural phenomena. . . . Lyons' lively writing stitches concepts together with smoothness and clarity." Bull Cent Child Books
Includes bibliographical references

Presley, Elvis, 1935-1977
Daily, Robert. Elvis Presley: the king of rock 'n' roll. Watts 1996 144p il (Impact biography) lib bdg $24; pa $9.95 (7 and up)   **92**
1. Rock musicians
ISBN 0-531-11288-8; 0-531-15821-7 (pa)
LC 96-5942
Examines the rock star's childhood, family life, musical career, films, and legacy
"An upbeat but honest look at the man who changed (some would say invented) the face of rock and roll. . . . This biography of the musician is filled with the kind of detail that will make the cultural icon a little more real to readers who weren't even born at the time of his death in 1977. . . . Good-quality, black-and-white photos appear throughout." SLJ
Includes discography and bibliographical references

Price, Leontyne
Steins, Richard. Leontyne Price, opera superstar. Blackbirch Press 1993 64p il (Library of famous women) lib bdg $17.95   **92**
1. African American singers 2. African American women
ISBN 1-56711-009-6   LC 92-40333
A biography of the renowned soprano who helped break the color barrier in professional opera during the 1960s
"Readers will get a real feel for Price and a clearer understanding of opera." Booklist
Includes glossary and bibliographical references

Pulitzer, Joseph, 1847-1911
Whitelaw, Nancy. Joseph Pulitzer and the New York World. Morgan Reynolds 1999 112p il (Makers of the media) $18.95   **92**
1. Journalists
ISBN 1-88384-644-7   LC 99-14132
A biography of the newspaper editor who crusaded against corruption, established the Pulitzer Prize, and founded the Columbia School of Journalism
"Complemented by period photographs, the profile also illustrates how the newspaper industry has changed since the early days. Appendixes include Pulitzer's advice to his writers, facts about the Pulitzer Prize and how it's awarded, and some of its recipients." Booklist
Includes bibliographical references

Pyle, Ernie, 1900-1945
O'Connor, Barbara. The soldiers' voice: the story of Ernie Pyle. Carolrhoda Bks. 1996 80p il (Trailblazers) lib bdg $16.95   **92**
1. Journalists 2. World War, 1939-1945
ISBN 0-87614-942-5   LC 94-44283
This is a biography of the Pulitzer Prize winning journalist renowned for his battle front coverage of World War II from a soldiers' perspective
"O'Connor has created a fine, well-written introduction to the man, complete with a selection of black-and-white photographs that elucidate the text." SLJ
Includes bibliographical references

Randolph, Asa Philip, 1889-1979
Hanley, Sally. A. Philip Randolph. Chelsea House 1989 110p il (Black Americans of achievement) lib bdg $19.95; pa $9.95   **92**
1. African Americans—Biography
ISBN 1-55546-607-9 (lib bdg); 0-7910-0222-5 (pa)
LC 87-34118
A biography of the civil rights activist who organized the Brotherhood of Sleeping Car Porters, which acted as a labor union for Pullman car porters
Includes bibliographical references

Reeve, Christopher
Howard, Megan. Christopher Reeve. Lerner Publs. 1999 128p il (A & E biography) $25.26   **92**
1. Actors 2. Physically handicapped
ISBN 0-8225-4945-X   LC 98-8200

Reeve, Christopher—*Continued*

A biography of the actor who became well known for his movie portrayal of Superman and for his activities in support of nerve damage research since the riding accident that left him a quadriplegic

"In friendly, accessible prose, Howard offers an intimate portrait of the actor. . . . Readers may find the detailed description of Reeve's accident and physical repercussions painful to read, but will gain perspective on the daily challenges facing quadriplegics." Booklist

Includes bibliographical references

Wren, Laura Lee. Christopher Reeve; Hollywood's man of courage. Enslow Pubs. 1999 112p (People to know) lib bdg $19.95   **92**
1. Actors 2. Physically handicapped
ISBN 0-7660-1149-6   LC 98-29493

A biography of the actor famous for playing Superman, discussing his activities before and after the accident that paralyzed him and focusing on his determination to go on with his life despite his problems

Includes bibliographical references

Reiss, Johanna

Reiss, Johanna. The journey back. Crowell 1976 212p hardcover o.p. paperback available $4.95
                                          92
1. Jews—Netherlands
ISBN 0-06-447042-3 (pa)

Sequel to The upstairs room

"The journey is the return home in the spring of 1945 for thirteen-year-old Annie and her older sister Sini. . . . The background of the early years is recapitulated. . . . The book offers an intensely provocative story, recalling many personal crises and tests of human nature cruelly beset by the dangers and deprivations of war." Horn Book

Reiss, Johanna. The upstairs room. Crowell 1972 $15; pa $4.95   **92**
1. World War, 1939-1945—Jews 2. Netherlands—History—1940-1945, German occupation 3. Jews—Netherlands
ISBN 0-690-85127-8; 0-06-440370-X (pa)

A Newbery Medal honor book, 1973

"In a vital, moving account the author recalls her experiences as a Jewish child hiding from the Germans occupying her native Holland during World War II. . . . Ten-year-old Annie and her twenty-year-old sister Sini, . . . are taken in by a Dutch farmer, his wife, and mother who hide the girls in an upstairs room of the farm house. Written from the perspective of a child the story affords a child's-eye-view of the war." Booklist

Followed by The journey back

Rembrandt Harmenszoon van Rijn, 1606-1669

Bonafoux, Pascal. A weekend with Rembrandt. Skira/Rizzoli 1992 64p il $19.95   **92**
1. Artists, Dutch
ISBN 0-8478-1441-6   LC 91-40507

The seventeenth-century Dutch painter talks about his life and work as if entertaining the reader for the weekend. Includes reproductions of the artist's works and a list of museums where works are on display

"Immediate, vivid, and enticing, this examination of Rembrandt's life and work suggests the intensity of the man. . . . The narrative, printed in two typefaces, separates commentary from the carefully crafted soliloquies, thus providing insight into Rembrandt's personal and artistic life." Horn Book

Renoir, Auguste, 1841-1919

Rayfield, Susan. Pierre-Auguste Renoir. Abrams 1998 92p il (First impressions) $19.95 (7 and up)
                                          92
1. Artists, French
ISBN 0-8109-3795-6   LC 98-12988

Examines the life and work of this French impressionist painter and sculptor whose work reflects his joy in life

"The author writes in a clear, informative, easy-to-read, well-organized style. The collection of 55 illustrations, 37 in full color, celebrates Renoir's artistic development." Book Rep

Skira-Venturi, Rosabianca. A weekend with Renoir. Rizzoli Int. Publs. 1991 61p il hardcover o.p. paperback available $9.95   **92**
1. Artists, French
ISBN 0-8478-1921-3 (pa)   LC 91-12426

The nineteenth century artist talks about his life and work as if entertaining the reader for a weekend

"The author not only succeeds in providing solid information and astute commentary but also seems to capture the individual personality of [the painter]." Horn Book

Includes bibliographical references

Ride, Sally K.

Hurwitz, Jane. Sally Ride; shooting for the stars; [by] Jane Hurwitz and Sue Hurwitz. Fawcett Columbine 1989 115p il (Great lives) pa $4.99
                                          92
1. Women astronauts
ISBN 0-449-90394-X   LC 89-90821

A biography of the California astrophysicist who became, with the second mission of the Challenger spacecraft in June 1983, the first American woman and the youngest American astronaut to orbit earth

Includes bibliographical references

Ripken, Cal, Jr.

Ripken, Cal, Jr. Cal Ripken, Jr., my story; by Cal Ripken, Jr. and Mike Bryan; adapted by Dan Gutman. Dial Bks. for Young Readers 1999 113p $16.99   **92**
1. Baltimore Orioles (Baseball team) 2. Baseball—Biography
ISBN 0-8037-2348-2   LC 98-7799

"In this adaptation of Ripken's autobiography, *The Only Way I Know* (1997), Ripken recounts events from his childhood, his years in the minors, and his career as a major league shortstop and third baseman for the Baltimore Orioles. . . . Illustrated with two sections of clear, mostly color photos . . . this should appeal to a wide range of readers." Booklist

Robeson, Paul, 1898-1976

Wright, David K. Paul Robeson; actor, singer, political activist. Enslow Pubs. 1998 128p il (African-American biographies) $19.95   **92**
1. African Americans—Biography
ISBN 0-89490-944-4   LC 97-34194
"This book chronicles the life of 'actor, singer, political activist' Paul Robeson, and the times and country that shaped him. While style and format are targeted at young YAs, older teens doing reports will find much of value here. In addition to the index, further reading and notes on each chapter, there is also a discography, filmography and chronology of Robeson's life." BAYA Book Rev

Robinson, Jackie, 1919-1972

Dingle, Derek T. First in the field: baseball hero Jackie Robinson. Hyperion Bks. for Children 1998 48p il $16.95; lib bdg $17.49; pa $5.99   **92**
1. Baseball—Biography 2. African American athletes
ISBN 0-7868-0348-7; 0-7868-2289-9 (lib bdg); 0-7868-1230-3 (pa)   LC 97-41333
A biography which discusses the discrimination faced by Jackie Robinson, the baseball legend who became the first African American to play Major League baseball for the Brooklyn Dodgers
"The narrative is written in a clear, matter-of-fact style. The archival black-and-white photographs are well chosen and of excellent quality." SLJ
Includes bibliographical references

Weidhorn, Manfred. Jackie Robinson. Atheneum Pubs. 1993 207p il $15.95   **92**
1. Baseball—Biography 2. African American athletes
ISBN 0-689-31644-5   LC 92-15248
A biography of the African American who fought racial injustice both during and after his celebrated baseball career
"A creditable and highly readable account of one of the most popular sports figures of the twentieth century." Horn Book
Includes bibliographical references

Rogers, Will, 1879-1935

Sonneborn, Liz. Will Rogers, Cherokee entertainer. Chelsea House 1993 110p il (North American Indians of achievement) lib bdg $19.95; pa $9.95   **92**
1. Entertainers 2. Cherokee Indians
ISBN 0-7910-1719-2 (lib bdg); 0-7910-1988-8 (pa)   LC 92-45050
"Sonneborn presents a brief overview of the Cherokee nation prior to and during the subject's lifetime. His childhood is recounted, as is his career as a cowboy, actor, public speaker, philosopher, and all-around nice guy. Although larded with some academic vocabulary, the exposition is readable and informative." SLJ
Includes bibliographical references

Roosevelt, Eleanor, 1884-1962

Freedman, Russell. Eleanor Roosevelt; a life of discovery. Clarion Bks. 1993 198p il $17.95   **92**
1. Presidents' spouses—United States
ISBN 0-89919-862-7   LC 92-25024

A Newbery Medal honor book, 1994
"Readers are made privy to the telling details of a full life through numerous quotes from Roosevelt and her wide inner circle in this frank, well-documented portrait of the 'First Lady of the World.' A superlative biography." SLJ
Includes bibliographical references

Spangenburg, Ray. Eleanor Roosevelt: a passion to improve; [by] Ray Spangenburg & Diane K. Moser. Facts on File 1997 114p il (Makers of America) $19.95 (7 and up)   **92**
1. Presidents' spouses—United States
ISBN 0-8160-3371-4   LC 96-16381
Describes the life and significant achievements of the woman who helped transform the role of first lady
Includes bibliographical references

Westervelt, Virginia Veeder. Here comes Eleanor; a new biography of Eleanor Roosevelt for young people. Avisson Press 1998 142p il (Avisson young adult series) pa $16   **92**
1. Presidents' spouses—United States
ISBN 1-888105-33-X   LC 98-38556
A biography of the first wife of a president to have a public life and career of her own, devoted to helping others and working for peace
"Westervelt's direct writing, supported by quotes and excerpts from Eleanor's own works, provides an intriguing portrait of an important American." Voice Youth Advocates
Includes bibliographical references

Roosevelt, Franklin D. (Franklin Delano), 1882-1945

Freedman, Russell. Franklin Delano Roosevelt. Clarion Bks. 1990 200p il $18; pa $8.95   **92**
1. Presidents—United States
ISBN 0-89919-379-X; 0-395-62978-0 (pa)
LC 89-34986
The author "traces the personal and public events in a life that led to the formation of one of the most influential and magnetic leaders of the twentieth century." Horn Book
"The carefully researched, highly readable text and extremely effective coordination of black-and-white photographs chronicle Roosevelt's priviledged youth, his early influences, and his maturation. . . . Even students with little or no background in American history will find this an intriguing and inspirational human portrait." SLJ
Includes bibliographical references

Morris, Jeffrey Brandon. The FDR way; [by] Jeffrey Morris. Lerner Pubs. 1996 136p il maps (Great presidential decisions) lib bdg $23.93   **92**
1. Presidents—United States
ISBN 0-8225-2929-7   LC 95-12575
Discusses the life and presidency of Franklin Delano Roosevelt, with an emphasis on the important decisions he made in that office regarding the American banking system, social security, the Supreme Court, World War II, and the United Nations, among others

Roosevelt, Franklin D. (Franklin Delano), 1882-1945—*Continued*

Spies, Karen Bornemann. Franklin D. Roosevelt. Enslow Pubs. 1999 128p il (United States presidents) lib bdg $19.95   **92**

1. Presidents—United States

ISBN 0-7660-1038-4   LC 98-19645

A biography of the thirty-second president of the United States, the only man to be elected president four times

Includes bibliographical references

Roosevelt, Theodore, 1858-1919

Fritz, Jean. Bully for you, Teddy Roosevelt! illustrations by Mike Wimmer. Putnam 1991 127p il $15.95; pa $5.99   **92**

1. Presidents—United States

ISBN 0-399-21769-X; 0-698-11609-7 (pa)

LC 90-8142

Follows the life of the twenty-sixth president, discussing his conservation work, hunting expeditions, family life, and political career

"Jean Fritz gives a rounded picture of her subject and deftly blends the story of a person and a picture of an era." Bull Cent Child Books

Includes bibliographical references

Meltzer, Milton. Theodore Roosevelt and his America. Watts 1994 191p il $28 (7 and up)

92

1. Presidents—United States

ISBN 0-531-11192-X   LC 94-17369

"Both critical and appreciative, Meltzer's biography conveys a sense of the complexities and contradictions in the president who led his country during the tumultuous first years of the twentieth century. . . . There's no direct documentation, even for quotes, but a fine bibliographic note discusses TR's own writings, what various people have written about him, and how Meltzer's personal values must inevitably come into play in how he selects his material." Booklist

Rousseau, Henri Julien Félix, 1844-1910

Plazy, Gilles. A weekend with Rousseau. Rizzoli Int. Publs. 1993 63p il $19.95   **92**

1. Artists, French

ISBN 0-8478-1717-2   LC 93-12187

The nineteenth-century French painter who captured the sights of Paris talks about his life and work as if entertaining the reader for the weekend. Includes reproductions of the artist's work and a list of museums where they are on display

"Although many are familiar with [Rousseau's] best-known works, it is likely that they may not be as conversant with his life and times. This approachable biography offers insight into both." Horn Book

Rudolph, Wilma, 1940-1994

Biracree, Tom. Wilma Rudolph. Chelsea House 1988 111p il (American women of achievement) lib bdg $19.95; pa $9.95   **92**

1. African American athletes 2. Women athletes

ISBN 1-55546-675-3 (lib bdg); 0-7910-0217-9 (pa)

LC 87-15138

A biography of the woman who overcame crippling polio as a child to become the first woman to win three gold medals in track in a single Olympics

"This warmly adulatory biography gives a strong sense of Rudolph's struggle. . . . The profusion of black-and-white photographs extends and enlivens the text, which focuses on the athletics." Booklist

Includes bibliographical references

Rustin, Bayard, 1910-1987

Haskins, James. Bayard Rustin: behind the scenes of the civil rights movement. Hyperion Bks. for Children 1997 121p il $14.95; lib bdg $15.49   **92**

1. African Americans—Civil rights 2. African Americans—Biography

ISBN 0-7868-0168-9; 0-7868-2140-X (lib bdg)

LC 96-1256

A biography of Bayard Rustin, a skillful organizer behind the scenes of the American civil rights movement whose ideas stongly influenced Martin Luther King, Jr

"Haskins not only gives enough personal information to flesh out his subject . . . but also presents each historical event with nuance, fairness, and clarity. Obviously an excellent resource for reports, this is also a moving, inspirational story." Booklist

Includes bibliographical references

Rylant, Cynthia

Rylant, Cynthia. But I'll be back again; an album. Orchard Bks. 1989 54p il o.p.; Beech Tree Bks. paperback available $4.95   **92**

1. Authors, American 2. Women authors

ISBN 0-688-12653-7 (pa)   LC 88-17860

"A Richard Jackson book"

"In this autobiographical essay, Rylant recounts the formative events of her childhood." Publ Wkly

"Not everyone will care about what happened to Rylant's childhood friends, but the description of the first kiss, and later ones as well, will have inherent appeal. Verses from the Beatles are somewhat irrelevantly interspersed, and snapshots of Rylant growing up are appended. Honest and heartfelt." Bull Cent Child Books

Sabin, Florence Rena, 1871-1953

Kaye, Judith. The life of Florence Sabin. 21st Cent. Bks. (NY) 1993 80p il (Pioneers in health and medicine) lib bdg $13.95   **92**

1. Women physicians

ISBN 0-8050-2299-6   LC 92-34419

A biography of the physician who made significant contributions to the field of medicine as a researcher, professor, and public health advocate and who became the first woman ever to be elected to the National Academy of Sciences

"This well written, short biography of Dr. Florence Sabin is interesting not only from a scientific point of view, but also from historical, sociological, and political perspectives." Sci Books Films

Includes bibliographical references

Sacagawea, b. 1786

St. George, Judith. Sacagawea. Putnam 1997 115p maps $16.95   **92**
1. Lewis and Clark Expedition (1804-1806) 2. Shoshoni Indians
ISBN 0-399-23161-7   LC 96-49311
Tells the story of the Shoshoni Indian girl who served as interpreter, peacemaker, and guide for the Lewis and Clark Expedition to the Northwest in 1805-1806
"In a well-written and well-researched account, St. George humanizes her subject. . . . Adventure lovers will find much to like in the book." Booklist
Includes bibliographical references

Salk, Jonas, 1914-1995

Sherrow, Victoria. Jonas Salk. Facts on File 1993 134p il (Makers of modern science) lib bdg $16.95   **92**
1. Scientists
ISBN 0-8160-2805-2   LC 92-32302
This "biography of the scientist credited with developing a successful polio vaccine begins with some history of the disease and then follows Salk through his schooling and into the scientific laboratory. Salk's years of research and laboratory work, described in some detail, are the subject of several chapters. The last section explains the Salk Institute's . . . work in researching cancer and AIDS. . . . A readable, inspiring portrait of a hero in the field of medical research." Booklist
Includes glossary and bibliographical references

San Martín, José de, 1778?-1850

Fernández, José B. José de San Martín; Latin America's quiet hero. Millbrook Press 1994 32p il map (Hispanic heritage) lib bdg $19.90   **92**
1. Generals 2. South America—History
ISBN 1-56294-383-9   LC 93-9735
A biography of the Argentinian general who was instrumental in liberating South America from Spanish rule in the early nineteenth century
This is "written in a clear, easy-to-read style, and [includes] interesting tidbits of trivia that will attract readers." SLJ
Includes bibliographical references

Santa Anna, Antonio López de, 1794?-1876

O'Brien, Steven. Antonio López de Santa Anna. Chelsea House 1992 102p il (Hispanics of achievement) lib bdg $19.95   **92**
1. Presidents—Mexico 2. Mexico—History
ISBN 0-7910-1245-X   LC 91-37815
Examines the life and times of the Mexican general and politician and his role in his country's politics and movement for independence
Includes bibliographical references

Schubert, Franz, 1797-1828

Thompson, Wendy. Franz Schubert. Viking 1991 48p il map music (Composer's world) $17.95   **92**
1. Composers
ISBN 0-670-84172-2   LC 91-50213

The composer's life, work, and times are described, with musical excerpts, and illustrated with historical paintings and drawings
Includes glossary

Schumann, Clara, 1819-1896

Reich, Susanna. Clara Schumann; piano virtuoso. Clarion Bks. 1999 118p il $18   **92**
1. Pianists
ISBN 0-395-89119-1   LC 98-24510
Describes the life of the German pianist and composer who made her professional debut at age nine and who devoted her life to music and to her family
"This thoroughly researched book draws on primary sources, both Clara's own diaries and her voluminous correspondence with her husband. . . . Reich's lucid, quietly passionate biography is liberally illustrated with photographs and reproductions." Horn Book Guide

Sequoyah, 1770?-1843

Klausner, Janet. Sequoyah's gift; a portrait of the Cherokee leader; with an afterword by Duane H. King. HarperCollins Pubs. 1993 111p il $15; lib bdg $14.89   **92**
1. Cherokee Indians
ISBN 0-06-021235-7; 0-06-021236-5 (lib bdg)
          LC 92-24939
A biography of the Cherokee Indian who created a method for his people to write and read their own language
"This is a solid work with many applications for study." Booklist
Includes bibliographical references

Shumate, Jane. Sequoyah; inventor of the Cherokee alphabet. Chelsea House 1994 111p il (North American Indians of achievement) lib bdg $19.95   **92**
1. Cherokee Indians
ISBN 0-7910-1720-6   LC 93-18107
This book "stresses Cherokee history and Sequoyah's place in it. . . . Interesting and informative." Horn Book Guide
Includes bibliographical references

Serra, Junípero, 1713-1784

Dolan, Sean. Junípero Serra. Chelsea House 1991 111p il (Hispanics of achievement) lib bdg $19.95; pa $9.95   **92**
1. Explorers 2. Christian missionaries
ISBN 0-7910-1255-7 (lib bdg); 0-7910-1282-4 (pa)
          LC 91-6863
Focuses on the achievements of the eighteenth-century Spanish missionary who was one of the early explorers of California
"Clearly written and objective, the text presents an intriguing picture of the man's life." SLJ
Includes bibliographical references

Shakespeare, William, 1564-1616

Stanley, Diane. Bard of Avon: the story of William Shakespeare; by Diane Stanley and Peter Vennema; illustrated by Diane Stanley. Morrow Junior Bks. 1992 unp il $16; lib bdg $15.93; pa $5.95 **92**

1. Dramatists, English

ISBN 0-688-09108-3; 0-688-09109-1 (lib bdg); 0-688-16294-0 (pa)   LC 90-46564

This "picture of Shakespeare's life and the period in which he lived includes a thoughtful attempt to relate circumstances in his personal life to the content of his plays. Splendidly supported by stylized illustrations, the discerning, knowledgeable biography rises far above the ordinary." Horn Book Guide

Includes bibliographical references

Shaw, Robert Gould, 1837-1863

Burchard, Peter. "We'll stand by the Union": Robert Gould Shaw and the Black 54th Massachusetts Regiment. Facts on File 1993 132p il (Makers of America) $19.95 (7 and up) **92**

1. United States. Army. Massachusetts Infantry Regiment, 54th (1863-1865) 2. African American soldiers 3. United States—History—1861-1865, Civil War

ISBN 0-8160-2609-2   LC 92-37132

"The son of wealthy abolitionists, Shaw grew up in Boston, went to Harvard, traveled in Europe, and when war broke out, joined the Union army, and eventually was charged with training and leading Massachusetts' first black regiment. Although the book focuses mainly on Shaw, it includes a history of the regiment after his death and assesses the impact of black soldiers on the course of the war." Booklist

Includes bibliographical references

Siegal, Aranka

Siegal, Aranka. Upon the head of the goat: a childhood in Hungary, 1939-1944. Farrar, Straus & Giroux 1981 213p $16 **92**

1. World War, 1939-1945—Jews 2. Jews—Hungary 3. Holocaust, 1933-1945—Personal narratives

ISBN 0-374-38059-7   LC 81-12642

Also available in paperback from Viking

The author "recalls her childhood in Hungary at the time of Hitler's rise to power. As the book opens, she is nine years old and is trapped in the Ukraine at her grandmother's as the border is temporarily closed. When she returns to Hungary, she begins to feel more acutely the impact of the war on her life. . . . As the story ends the author and her family are boarded on a train for Auschwitz." Voice Youth Advocates

"The story is familiar . . . but a few pages into Aranka Siegal's fine memoir . . . you feel the power and interest of her particular experience and remember that this story cannot be told too often." Newsweek

Simmons, Philip

Lyons, Mary E. Catching the fire: Philip Simmons, blacksmith; with photographs by Mannie Garcia. Houghton Mifflin 1997 47p il $16 **92**

1. African American artists

ISBN 0-395-72033-8   LC 96-38643

Tells the story of this African American artist, the great-grandson of slaves, who has achieved fame and admiration for his ornamental wrought-iron creations

"The narrative, based on Simmons' memories and words, involves readers through its lively presentation of an intriguing subject. . . . Photographs appear on every spread, with black-and-white pictures of Simmons' early days and beautifully lit and composed color shots of the man today." Booklist

Includes bibliographical references

Sitting Bull, Dakota Chief, 1831-1890

St. George, Judith. To see with the heart: the life of Sitting Bull. Putnam 1996 182p il maps $17.95 **92**

1. Dakota Indians

ISBN 0-399-22930-2   LC 95-458

This is a "portrait of Sitting Bull as son, husband, father, friend, holy man, hunter, and war chief of the Sioux Nation. The author has thoroughly researched her subject. Her use of transcripts of interviews with Sitting Bull's contemporaries . . . and visits to battlefields and camping grounds in the northern United States and Canada give *To See with the Heart* an attention to detail and a richness that are not found in other accounts of this man's life." SLJ

Includes bibliographical references

Smith, Will

Stauffer, Stacey. Will Smith. Chelsea House 1998 96p il (Black Americans of achievement) lib bdg $19.95; pa $9.95 **92**

1. African American actors

ISBN 0-7910-4914-0 (lib bdg); 0-7910-4915-9 (pa)   LC 98-18551

A biography of the African American rap singer who became the acting star of such popular motion pictures as Independence Day and Men in Black

Includes discography, filmography and bibliographical references

Sosa, Sammy

Muskat, Carrie. Sammy Sosa; an authorized biography. Mitchell Lane Pubs. 1999 64p il (Latinos in baseball) $18.95 **92**

1. Baseball—Biography

ISBN 1-883845-92-0   LC 98-54377

This account "of Sosa's rise from extreme poverty . . . emphasizes his strong family relationships and love for his homeland, the Dominican Republic. Career highlights and statistics bring the coverage up-to-date including a chapter on Sosa's amazing 1998 home-run season and how it fits into baseball history." SLJ

Stewart, Mark. Home run heroes: McGwire and Sosa. See entry under McGwire, Mark

Spielberg, Steven, 1947-

Woog, Adam. Steven Spielberg. Lucent Bks. 1999 112p il (People in the news) $22.45 **92**

1. Motion picture producers and directors

ISBN 1-56006-361-0   LC 98-7463

Spielberg, Steven, 1947-—*Continued*
Explores the public and private lives of Steven Spielberg, who has combined popular storytelling with artistic creativity to become hailed as the most successful film director in the world
Includes filmography and bibliographical references

Spinelli, Jerry, 1941-
Spinelli, Jerry. Knots in my yo-yo string; the autobiography of a kid. Knopf 1998 148p il lib bdg $15.99; pa $9.99   **92**
1. Authors, American
ISBN 0-679-98791-6 (lib bdg); 0-679-88791-1 (pa)
LC 97-30827
This Italian-American Newbery Medalist presents a humorous account of his childhood and youth in Norristown, Pennsylvania
"There is an 'everyboy' universality to Spinelli's experiences, but his keen powers of observation and recall turn the story into a richly rewarding personal history." Horn Book Guide

Stanton, Elizabeth Cady, 1815-1902
Cullen-DuPont, Kathryn. Elizabeth Cady Stanton and women's liberty. Facts on File 1992 133p il (Makers of America) lib bdg $19.95 (7 and up)   **92**
1. Feminism
ISBN 0-8160-2413-8   LC 91-21781
A biography of one of the first leaders of the women's rights movement, whose work led to the adoption of the nineteenth amendment that ensured women's right to vote
"The presentation is superb, relying on original sources and written in a style that is both accessible to young readers and sophisticated enough to do justice to its subject matter. The text is supplemented by archival photographs and reproductions of Cady Stanton and her family that capture the character of the woman and her times." SLJ
Includes bibliographical references

Steinbeck, John, 1902-1968
Reef, Catherine. John Steinbeck. Clarion Bks. 1996 163p il $17.95 (7 and up)   **92**
1. Authors, American
ISBN 0-395-71278-5   LC 95-11500
"The book traces Steinbeck's life from his childhood in California, to his burgeoning writing career and his passion for social justice, to his worldwide recognition. Reef does an excellent job of synthesizing Steinbeck's work, his private life, and his politics and philosophy." Bull Cent Child Books
Includes bibliographical references

Steinem, Gloria
Lazo, Caroline Evensen. Gloria Steinem; feminist extraordinaire. Lerner Publs. 1998 128p il $25.26 (7 and up)   **92**
1. Feminism
ISBN 0-8225-4934-4   LC 97-16831

"Looking at Steinem's difficult childhood, her experiences in India, her career as a journalist, and her role as an advocate for women's rights and a cofounder of *Ms.* magazine, this biography presents a thorough picture of an influential leader of the modern women's movement." Horn Book Guide
Includes bibliographical references

Stevenson, Robert Louis, 1850-1894
Gherman, Beverly. Robert Louis Stevenson, teller of tales. Atheneum Bks. for Young Readers 1996 136p il $16   **92**
1. Authors, Scottish
ISBN 0-689-31985-1   LC 95-52448
This biography of the Scottish author of Treasure Island and The strange case of Dr. Jekyll and Mr. Hyde recounts "his childhood, marriage, and . . . travels. There are occasional black-and-white photos, unobtrusive chapter notes at the back, and a bibliography. A wonderful extra bonus is the brief stanza of Stevenson's singing poetry at the head of each chapter." Booklist

Murphy, Jim. Across America on an emigrant train. Clarion Bks. 1993 150p il $17   **92**
1. Railroads—History 2. United States—Description
ISBN 0-395-63390-7   LC 92-38650
"Murphy presents a forthright and thoroughly engrossing history of the transcontinental railway, with entries from Robert Louis Stevenson's 1879 journal as he rode cross country. It's also an inviting introduction to Stevenson, with a romance in the bargain." SLJ
Includes bibliographical references

Stine, R. L., 1943-
Stine, R. L. It came from Ohio!: my life as a writer; [by] R. L. Stine as told to Joe Arthur. Scholastic 1997 140p il $9.95   **92**
1. Authors, American
ISBN 0-590-36674-2
The "popular author shares his life as a self-avowed shy person, his writing secrets, and the bumps (and 'Bumps!) in his career in this light autobiography related with attractively understated candor. The fast-pace text is straightforward . . . and the book is illustrated with grayish family snapshots." Horn Book

Stockton, John
Schnakenberg, Robert. Teammates: Karl Malone and John Stockton. See entry under Malone, Karl

Stowe, Harriet Beecher, 1811-1896
Coil, Suzanne M. Harriet Beecher Stowe. Watts 1993 173p il (Impact biography) lib bdg $24 (7 and up)   **92**
1. Authors, American 2. Women authors 3. Abolitionists
ISBN 0-531-13006-1   LC 93-13710
A biography of the nineteenth-century author whose anti-slavery novel "Uncle Tom's Cabin" helped intensify the disagreement between North and South
"This is an excellent biography for any collection. Coil has gone beyond a mere recounting of the facts to paint an excellent picture of life in the United States in the middle of the 19th century." Voice Youth Advocates
Includes bibliographical references

Stowe, Harriet Beecher, 1811-1896—*Continued*

Fritz, Jean. Harriet Beecher Stowe and the Beecher preachers. Putnam 1994 144p il $16.95; pa $5.99 **92**
1. Beecher family 2. Women authors 3. Authors, American 4. Abolitionists
ISBN 0-399-22666-4; 0-698-11660-7 (pa)
LC 93-6408

This is a biography of the abolitionist author of "Uncle Tom's Cabin," with an emphasis on the influence of her preacher father and her family on her life and work
"Written with vivacity and insight, this readable and engrossing biography is an important contribution to women's history as well as to the history of American letters." Horn Book
Includes bibliographical references

Stuart, Jeb, 1833-1864

Pflueger, Lynda. Jeb Stuart; Confederate cavalry general. Enslow Pubs. 1998 128p il maps (Historical American biographies) lib bdg $19.95 **92**
1. Generals 2. United States—History—1861-1865, Civil War
ISBN 0-7660-1013-9
LC 97-4367

Traces the life of the famous Confederate general from his childhood in Virginia through his West Point education and brilliant military career to his death following the Battle of Yellow Tavern
"Black-and-white period photographs and maps provide additional historical information, as do sidebars that present prose snapshots related to topics under discussion. A readable resource especially for report writers." SLJ
Includes bibliographical references

Tecumseh, Shawnee Chief, 1768-1813

Cwiklik, Robert. Tecumseh, Shawnee rebel. Chelsea House 1993 110p il (North American Indians of achievement) lib bdg $19.95 **92**
1. Shawnee Indians
ISBN 0-7910-1721-4
LC 92-21656

A biography of the Shawnee warrior, orator, and leader who united a confederacy of Indians in an effort to save Indian land from the advance of white soldiers and settlers
"The writing is admirable; it flows forward and carries readers with it, without puzzles to impede them. It is handsomely complemented by many black-and-white period prints and paintings, each of which seems chosen to give visual imagery to the words." SLJ
Includes bibliographical references

Stefoff, Rebecca. Tecumseh and the Shawnee confederation. Facts on File 1998 138p il maps (Library of American Indian history) $19.95 (7 and up) **92**
1. Shawnee Indians
ISBN 0-8160-3648-9
LC 97-22773

A biography of the Shawnee Indian leader who united various Indian nations and cultures in opposition to white settlement of Indian lands
Includes bibliographical references

Teresa, Mother, 1910-1997

Morgan, Nina. Mother Teresa: saint of the poor. Raintree Steck-Vaughn Pubs. 1998 48p il lib bdg $25.68; pa $7.95 **92**
1. Missionaries of Charity 2. Nuns
ISBN 0-8172-3997-9 (lib bdg); 0-8172-7848-6 (pa)
LC 97-45165

A biography of Mother Teresa, the Albanian nun who founded the Order of the Missionaries of Charity in Calcutta, won the Nobel Peace Prize, and dedicated her life to helping the destitute
"The information provided is accurate and useful." SLJ
Includes glossary and bibliographical references

Ruth, Amy. Mother Teresa. Lerner Publs. 1999 112p il (A & E biography) $25.26 **92**
1. Missionaries of Charity 2. Nuns
ISBN 0-8225-4943-3
LC 98-23315

A biography of the nun who founded the order known as the Missionaries of Charity to work with the sick and destitute in Calcutta and other places and who was awarded the Nobel Peace Prize in 1979
Includes bibliographical references

Thoreau, Henry David, 1817-1862

Reef, Catherine. Henry David Thoreau; a neighbor to nature; illustrated by Larry Raymond. 21st Cent. Bks. (NY) 1992 72p il (Earth keepers) lib bdg $14.95 **92**
1. Authors, American 2. Naturalists
ISBN 0-941477-39-8
LC 91-19779

Describes the life of the author who came to value the natural world and whose writings have influenced and inspired others concerning nature
This is "nicely drawn and organized. . . . Highly readable." SLJ
Includes glossary

Thorpe, Jim, 1888-1953

Lipsyte, Robert. Jim Thorpe; 20th-century jock. HarperCollins Pubs. 1993 103p il (Superstar lineup) hardcover o.p. paperback available $3.95 **92**
1. Athletes
ISBN 0-06-446141-6 (pa)
LC 92-44069

A biography of the American Indian known as one of the best all-round athletes for his accomplishments as an Olympic medal winner and as an outstanding professional football and baseball player
"Involving and thought provoking, the account has wide applicability across curriculum lines, and it will fill a number of current information needs in the areas of biography, sports, Native Americans, and race relations." Booklist
Includes bibliographical references

Tillage, Leon, 1936-

Tillage, Leon. Leon's story; [by] Leon Walter Tillage; collage art by Susan L. Roth. Farrar, Straus & Giroux 1997 107p il $14 **92**
1. African Americans—Biography 2. North Carolina—Race relations
ISBN 0-374-34379-9
LC 96-43544

Tillage, Leon, 1936-—_Continued_

The son of a North Carolina sharecropper recalls the hard times faced by his family and other African Americans in the first half of the twentieth century and the changes that the civil rights movement helped bring about

The author's "voice is direct, the words are simple. There is no rhetoric, no commentary, no bitterness. . . . This quiet drama will move readers of all ages . . . and may encourage them to record their own family stories." Booklist

Tiulana, Paul, 1921-1994

Tiulana, Paul. Wise words of Paul Tiulana; an Inupiat Alaskan's life; [edited] by Vivian Senungetuk. Watts 1998 80p il maps (In their own voices) $22   92

1. Inuit

ISBN 0-531-11448-1   LC 97-51859

"An earlier version of the book was published as A place for winter: Paul Tiulana's story, by the CIRI foundation in 1987" verso of title page

Presents the life of an Alaskan hunter, storyteller, craftsman, and traditional leader who grew up on King Island, Alaska, in the 1920s

"The text is taken from interviews with Tiulana in 1987 and has been updated since his death in 1994. Added are a note about the Jesuit whose contemporary photos illustrate the story, and a brief outline of how one might go about writing the stories of one's own elders." Booklist

Includes bibliographical references

Tolkien, J. R. R. (John Ronald Reuel), 1892-1973

Neimark, Anne E. Myth maker: J.R.R. Tolkien; illustrated by Brad Weinman. Harcourt Brace & Co. 1996 118p il $17   92

1. Authors, English

ISBN 0-15-298847-5   LC 96-4196

Also available in paperback from Beech Tree Bks.

Follows the life and work of the renowned fantasy writer, creator of hobbits and Middle Earth and "The Lord of the Rings."

Toussaint Louverture, 1743?-1803

Myers, Walter Dean. Toussaint L'Ouverture; the fight for Haiti's freedom; paintings by Jacob Lawrence; written by Walter Dean Myers. Simon & Schuster Bks. for Young Readers 1996 unp il $16   92

1. Generals 2. Haiti 3. Blacks—Biography

ISBN 0-689-80126-2   LC 95-30046

"In the late 1930s, Lawrence painted a series of pictures that documented the oppression of the Haitian people at the end of the 18th century and their eventual liberation in 1804. The paintings are used here to tell readers about the man who lead that revolution. . . . The artist's muted colors and stylized figures show the pain of the oppressed people and the glory of their fight. Myers's understated text is elegantly written, letting the brilliant artwork take center stage." SLJ

Truman, Harry S., 1884-1972

Hargrove, Jim. Harry S. Truman. Children's Press 1987 98p il (Encyclopedia of presidents) lib bdg $24   92

1. Presidents—United States

ISBN 0-516-01388-2   LC 87-11797

Traces the life and political career of the statesman from Missouri who became president of the United States following the death of Franklin D. Roosevelt in 1945

"An abundance of illustrations adds support to the well-rounded [text], documenting the strengths and successes of [the] man as well as his difficulties and failures." Booklist

Truth, Sojourner, d. 1883

Krass, Peter. Sojourner Truth. Chelsea House 1988 110p il (Black Americans of achievement) lib bdg $19.95; pa $9.95   92

1. African American women 2. Feminism 3. Abolitionists

ISBN 1-55546-611-7 (lib bdg); 0-7910-0215-2 (pa)

                                       LC 88-6107

Traces the life of the former slave who could neither read nor write, yet earned a reputation as one of the most articulate and outspoken antislavery and women's rights activists in the United States

Includes bibliographical references

McKissack, Patricia C. Sojourner Truth: ain't I a woman? [by] Patricia C. McKissack and Fredrick McKissack. Scholastic 1992 186p il $13.95; pa $3.50   92

1. African American women 2. Feminism 3. Abolitionists

ISBN 0-590-44690-8; 0-590-44691-6 (pa)

                                       LC 91-45988

This "is a great deal more than a biography of a remarkable woman. The forceful narrative also offers a startling portrayal of a pivotal yet appalling era in American history." Publ Wkly

Includes bibliographical references

Tubman, Harriet, 1815?-1913

Elish, Dan. Harriet Tubman and the underground railroad. Millbrook Press 1993 32p il (Gateway civil rights) lib bdg $20.90; pa $4.95

                                              92

1. African American women 2. Underground railroad

ISBN 1-56294-273-5 (lib bdg); 1-56294-791-5 (pa)

                                       LC 92-9562

A biography of the African American woman who escaped from slavery, led slaves to freedom on the Underground Railroad, aided Northern troops during the Civil War, and worked for women's suffrage

Includes bibliographical references

Taylor, M. W. (Marian W.). Harriet Tubman. Chelsea House 1991 111p il (Black Americans of achievement) lib bdg $19.95; pa $9.95   92

1. African American women 2. Underground railroad

ISBN 1-55546-612-5 (lib bdg); 0-7910-0249-7 (pa)

                                       LC 89-77281

Tubman, Harriet, 1815?-1913—_Continued_
"Beginning with her tough and often brutal treatment as a young child in slavery, Taylor traces the development of an unconventional and heroic woman. . . . A good, solid biography." SLJ
Includes bibliographical references

Turner, Nat, 1800?-1831
Barrett, Tracy. Nat Turner and the slave revolt. Millbrook Press 1993 32p il (Gateway civil rights) hardcover o.p. paperback available $4.95   92
1. African Americans—Biography 2. Slavery—United States
ISBN 1-56294-792-3 (pa)   LC 92-12086
This book "recounts Turner's life as slave-turned-revolutionary. . . . Barrett attempts to place the event in its historical context in a concise, noninflammatory text." Booklist
Includes bibliographical references

Bisson, Terry. Nat Turner. Chelsea House 1988 111p il (Black Americans of achievement) lib bdg $19.95; pa $9.95   92
1. African Americans—Biography 2. Slavery—United States
ISBN 1-55546-613-3 (lib bdg); 0-7910-0214-4 (pa)   LC 87-37559
A biography of the slave and preacher who, believing that God wanted him to free the slaves, led a major revolt in 1831
"A well-written, sympathetic biography. . . . Bisson creates an excellent background to Turner's life, describing not only the daily life of a slave, but also how it felt to have no control over one's destiny. The violence of Turner's revolt is toned down a bit for the younger audience, without losing the chaotic emotions behind it." SLJ
Includes bibliographical references

Turner, Tina
Hasday, Judy L. Tina Turner. Chelsea House 1999 104p il (Black Americans of achievement) $19.95; pa $9.95   92
1. African American singers 2. African American women
ISBN 0-7910-4967-1; 0-7910-4968-X (pa)   LC 99-13359
Traces the life and career of Tina Turner, from the early days of the Ike and Tina Revue, through the years of spousal abuse, to the success of Grammy Awards and film work
Includes bibliographical references

Twain, Mark, 1835-1910
Cox, Clinton. Mark Twain; America's humorist, dreamer, prophet. Scholastic 1995 234p il $14.95; pa $4.50   92
1. Authors, American
ISBN 0-590-45642-3; 0-590-45641-5 (pa)   LC 94-18624
"Laced with quotes from Twain's letters, journals, and memoirs, this readable biography presents the humorist's personal life, literary accomplishments, and role as a social critic." SLJ
Includes bibliographical references

Lasky, Kathryn. A brilliant streak: the making of Mark Twain; illustrated by Barry Moser. Harcourt Brace & Co. 1998 41p il $18   92
1. Authors, American
ISBN 0-15-252110-0   LC 95-18479
An illustrated biography of young Samuel Clemens, who grew up to be the writer known as Mark Twain
"An obvious delight in her subject makes Lasky's biography an appealing choice, and a similar enthusiasm invests Moser's illustrations." Horn Book Guide
Includes bibliographical references

Meltzer, Milton. Mark Twain himself; produced by Milton Meltzer. Wings Bks. 1993 303p il map $12.99   92
1. Authors, American
ISBN 0-517-01248-0   LC 92-42530
A reissue of the title first published 1960 by Crowell
This pictorial biography combines photographs, drawings, cartoons and other illustrations with selections from Twain's autobiography, letters, notebooks, fiction and other writings
Includes bibliographical references

Ross, Stewart. Mark Twain and Huckleberry Finn; illustrated by Ronald Himler. Viking 1998 43p il $16.99   92
1. Authors, American
ISBN 0-670-88181-3   LC 98-29892
Examines the personal life and literary career of the American author of many well known books, including the somewhat controversial title, "The Adventures of Huckleberry Finn."
"The information here will be helpful for students and language-arts teachers seeking background information for research and reports." SLJ

Uchida, Yoshiko, 1921-1992
Uchida, Yoshiko. The invisible thread. Messner 1991 136p il (In my own words) hardcover o.p. paperback available $4.95   92
1. Authors, American 2. Japanese Americans 3. Women authors
ISBN 0-688-13703-2 (pa)   LC 91-12398
Children's author Uchida describes growing up in Berkeley, California, as a Nisei (second generation Japanese American) and her family's internment in a Nevada concentration camp during World War II
The author "writes with mastery of style and an implicit respect for her readers." Bull Cent Child Books
Includes bibliographical references

Ungerer, Tomi, 1931-
Ungerer, Tomi. Tomi: a childhood under the Nazis. Roberts Rinehart Pubs.; distributed by Court Wayne Press 1998 175p il $29.95 (7 and up)   92
1. France—History—1940-1945, German occupation
ISBN 1-57098-163-9
"Rewritten and enlarged from a book published in 1991 in French, this episodic and reflective autobiography reveals memorable incidents in the childhood of the

Ungerer, Tomi, 1931——*Continued*
well-known artist and author. When Ungerer was eight, the Nazis invaded and occupied his homeland in the Alsace region of France and displaced many of the region's residents. Ungerer intersperses family photos, vivid paintings and drawings he did as a child, and excerpts from his well-kept diary with his well-written narrative." SLJ

Victoria, Queen of Great Britain, 1819-1901
Green, Robert. Queen Victoria. Watts 1998 64p il lib bdg $22   **92**
1. Queens 2. Great Britain—Kings and rulers 3. Great Britain—History—1800-1899 (19th century)
ISBN 0-531-20330-1   LC 97-10990
"A First book"
A biography of the nineteenth-century queen who ruled Britain longer than any other monarch
"A clear, well-written presentation. . . . This is an approachable introduction to this queen's life and times." SLJ
Includes bibliographical references

Villa, Pancho, 1878-1923
O'Brien, Steven. Pancho Villa. Chelsea House 1994 111p il (Hispanics of achievement) lib bdg $19.95   **92**
1. Mexico—History
ISBN 0-7910-1257-3   LC 93-37890
The author "handles the life and lifestyle of Villa, one of Mexico's controversial, legendary heroes, in a candid and unbiased manner. Illustrated with black-and-white photographs, the biography of this revolutionary is an enjoyable, readable, welcome addition." Horn Book Guide
Includes bibliographical references

Walker, C. J., Madame, 1867-1919
Colman, Penny. Madam C.J. Walker; building a business empire. Millbrook Press 1994 48p il (Gateway biography) lib bdg $21.90   **92**
1. African American women 2. African American business people
ISBN 1-56294-338-3   LC 93-13824
A biography of the businesswoman who was born in poverty on a Louisiana plantation, founded her own hair care business, and made more money than any woman, black or white, had ever made before in America
This is "an interesting portrait of a little-known African-American entrepreneur. . . . Colman vividly describes the social conditions of the late-19th century, making Walker's triumphs over numerous hardships come alive for young readers." SLJ
Includes bibliographical references

Wallenberg, Raoul
Bierman, John. Righteous gentile; the story of Raoul Wallenberg, missing hero of the Holocaust. Viking 1981 218p il hardcover o.p. paperback available $11.95 (7 and up)   **92**
1. Holocaust, 1933-1945 2. Jews—Hungary 3. World War, 1939-1945—Jews—Rescue
ISBN 0-14-024664-9 (pa)   LC 80-52465

"The horrors of the Holocaust as well as the courageous humanitarianism and appalling fate of one man are vividly evoked in an account recommended for older teenagers." Booklist
Includes bibliographical references

Walters, Barbara, 1931-
Remstein, Henna. Barbara Walters. Chelsea House 1999 104p il (Women of achievement) $19.95; pa $9.95   **92**
1. Women journalists
ISBN 0-7910-4716-4; 0-7910-4717-2 (pa)
    LC 98-2789
A biography of the television journalist whose interviewing skills have won her seven Emmy Awards in her thirty-year career
"Wonderful photographs enhance the text. . . . [This] volume provides excellent coverage for the middle schooler or the high school reader in search of pertinent information." Voice Youth Advocates
Includes bibliographical references

Wang, Ya-ni, 1975-
Cheng, Chen-sun. A young painter; the life and paintings of Wang Yani—China's extraordinary young artist; by Zheng Zhensun and Alice Low; photographs by Zheng Zhensun; introduction by Jan Stuart. Scholastic 1991 80p il map $17.95
    92
1. Child artists 2. Artists, Chinese
ISBN 0-590-44906-0   LC 90-29319
"A Byron Preiss/New China Pictures book"
Examines the life and works of the young Chinese artist who started painting animals at the age of three and in her teens became the youngest artist to have a one-person show at the Smithsonian Institution
"Admiring but not hyperbolic, the text gives a rounded picture of the artist as a person and discusses her work in great detail; it is illustrated by color photographs of Yani and myriad reproductions of her paintings." Bull Cent Child Books
Includes glossary

Washington, Booker T., 1856-1915
Nicholson, Lois. Booker T. Washington; [by] Lois P. Nicholson. Chelsea Jrs. 1997 86p il (Junior world biographies) lib bdg $16.95; pa $6.95   **92**
1. African American educators
ISBN 0-7910-2388-5 (lib bdg); 0-7910-4461-0 (pa)
    LC 96-52428
"A Junior black Americans of achievement book"
Covers the life of Booker T. Washington from his early childhood as a Virginia slave through his rise to founder of the Tuskegee Institute
"Nicholson's straightforward, chronological narrative is divided into six brief chapters, each illustrated with archival photographs. . . . A readable introduction to a notable figure." SLJ
Includes glossary and bibliographical references

Washington, Booker T. Up from slavery: an autobiography   **92**
1. Tuskegee Institute 2. African American educators

Washington, Booker T., 1856-1915—*Continued*
Various editions available
First published 1901
"The classic autobiography of the man who, though
born in slavery, educated himself and went on to found
Tuskegee Institute." N Y Public Libr

Washington, Denzel
Hill, Anne E. Denzel Washington. Chelsea
House 1999 96p il (Black Americans of
achievement) $19.95; pa $9.95 (7 and up)   **92**
1. African American actors
ISBN 0-7910-4692-3; 0-7910-4693-1 (pa)
                                              LC 98-15401
"Hill traces the meteoric rise of this media star
through stage and television roles to feature films. In his
career, Washington has avoided typecasting; instead, he
has exhibited chameleonlike versatility in playing a variety of figures. . . . Stock black-and-white photographs,
mostly of the actor in his various roles, appear throughout." SLJ
Includes filmography and bibliographical references

Washington, George, 1732-1799
Meltzer, Milton. George Washington and the
birth of our nation. Watts 1986 188p il maps lib
bdg $26.80   **92**
1. Presidents—United States
ISBN 0-531-10253-X   LC 86-9222
A biography of our first President, from his growing-
up years in Virginia to his death at Mount Vernon
This "is a competently written and carefully documented book, well illustrated with reproductions of historic art, manuscript pages, and maps." Bull Cent Child
Books
Includes bibliographical references

Osborne, Mary Pope. George Washington;
leader of a new nation. Dial Bks. for Young
Readers 1991 117p il map lib bdg $13.89   **92**
1. Presidents—United States
ISBN 0-8037-0949-8   LC 90-42601
This "biography of Washington gives a clear picture
of the man and his achievements. Osborne covers both
his personal and public life in straightforward, easy-to-
understand chronological order, and providing plenty of
background information. . . . The real strength of this
book, however, is its excellent use of primary sources."
SLJ
Includes bibliographical references

Rosenburg, John M. First in peace: George
Washington, the Constitution, and the presidency;
[by] John Rosenburg. Millbrook Press 1998 256p
il lib bdg $23.40 (7 and up)   **92**
1. Presidents—United States
ISBN 0-7613-0422-3   LC 98-18631
First volume in the author's biographical trilogy begun
with: First in war (1998) and Young George Washington
(1997)
"Rosenburg opens the book with Washington's resignation as commander in chief of the Continental Army
and goes on to outline significant events such as the

Constitutional Convention, the Whiskey Rebellion, and
debates concerning controversial issuses like slavery and
taxation. The author's straightforward, factual narrative
contains a painstaking amount of detail sprinkled with dialogue and primary-source material." SLJ

Washington, Martha, 1731-1802
McPherson, Stephanie Sammartino. Martha
Washington; first lady. Enslow Pubs. 1998 128p il
(Historical American biographies) lib bdg $19.95
                                              92
1. Presidents' spouses—United States
ISBN 0-7660-1017-1   LC 97-23478
Traces the life of the wife of the first president of the
United States, from her childhood in Virginia through
her marriage to George Washington to her role in the
American Revolution and the early years of the new
country's history
"The author describes the historical events of the time
to set the scene, but does not let George Washington
overshadow Martha's story. The facts are accurate and
sidebars add anecdotal information about this period in
American history." SLJ
Includes bibliographical references

Watson, James D., 1928-
Edelson, Edward. James Watson and Francis
Crick and the building blocks of life. Oxford Univ.
Press 1998 110p il (Oxford portraits in science)
$21 (7 and up)   **92**
1. Crick, Francis, 1916- 2. Scientists
ISBN 0-19-511451-5   LC 97-42791
Describes the collaboration of Watson and Crick in
the effort to discover DNA
This dual biography is "also a history of the develop-
ment of modern molecular biology. . . . The science is
well presented and quite current." Sci Books Films
Includes bibliographical references

Wells-Barnett, Ida B., 1862-1931
Davidson, Sue. Getting the real story: Nellie Bly
and Ida B. Wells. See entry under Bly, Nellie,
1864-1922

Haynes, Richard M. Ida B. Wells, antilynching
crusader; with an introduction by James P.
Shenton. Raintree Steck-Vaughn Pubs. 1994 128p
il (American troublemakers) lib bdg $25.26   **92**
1. African American women 2. African Americans—
Civil rights
ISBN 0-8114-2325-5   LC 92-22192
"A Gallin House Press book"
This biography of Ida B. Wells "chronicles her youth
and her initial involvement in the cause that was to dom-
inate her life—eradicating the practice of lynching. . . .
This biography will make a good addition to public and
school libraries. There is much good information and
Wells was certainly a remarkable woman." Voice Youth
Advocates
Includes glossary and bibliographical references

Wells-Barnett, Ida B., 1862-1931—*Continued*
Lisandrelli, Elaine Slivinski. Ida B.
Wells-Barnett; crusader against lynching. Enslow
Pubs. 1998 128p il (African-American biographies)
lib bdg $19.95 (7 and up)   **92**
1. African American women 2. African Americans—
Civil rights
ISBN 0-89490-947-9   LC 97-34253
Traces the life and career of the African American
journalist and social activist who spoke out against the
lynching of blacks in the South
"Students looking for material on this well-known cru-
sader will appreciate this clearly written biography." SLJ
Includes bibliographical references

Wesley, John, 1703-1791
Wellman, Sam. John Wesley; founder of the
Methodist Church. Chelsea House 1998 207p
(Heroes of the faith) $17.95 (7 and up)   **92**
1. Methodist Church
ISBN 0-7910-5036-X   LC 98-7107
Describes the life of John Wesley, the Anglican minis-
ter who founded the Methodist Church

Wheatley, Phillis, 1753-1784
Richmond, M. A. (Merle A.). Phillis Wheatley;
[by] Merle Richmond. Chelsea House 1987 111p
il (American women of achievement) lib bdg
$19.95; pa $9.95   **92**
1. Poets, American 2. African American authors
3. Women poets
ISBN 1-55546-683-4 (lib bdg); 0-7910-0218-7 (pa)
LC 87-6626
Traces the life of the black American poet who was
born in Africa, brought over to New England as a slave,
and published her first poem while still a teenager
"The biographer indulges in much drumbeating and
grandiose foreshadowing . . . and provides no footnotes,
but she is careful to distinguish fact from surmise, making this a readable introduction to a remarkable woman."
Booklist
Includes bibliographical references

Whistler, James McNeill, 1834-1903
Berman, Avis. James McNeill Whistler. Abrams
1993 92p il (First impressions) $19.95 (7 and up)
    92
1. Artists, American
ISBN 0-8109-3968-1   LC 93-9453
A biography of the nineteenth-century American artist
who spent most of his life in Europe and is known for
his flamboyant personality, as well as his innovative
painting and printmaking techniques and famous portrait
of his mother
The text "is chatty and readable, fleshing out the character of Whistler as well as describing in clear and concise terms his techniques and philosophies." Bull Cent
Child Books

Whitman, Walt, 1819-1892
Reef, Catherine. Walt Whitman. Clarion Bks.
1995 148p il $16.95 (7 and up)   **92**
1. Poets, American
ISBN 0-395-68705-5   LC 94-7405

"Here is a biography of Whitman that presents the life
of the subject, the world in which he lived, and representative passages from his writings." Voice Youth Advocates
"This is not a biography for pleasure reading, but it
could be a source for those interested in historical events
of 19th century America. It also would be a good resource for students doing a critique of Whitman's work
for an American literature course." Book Rep
Includes bibliographical references

Wilder, Laura Ingalls, 1867-1957
Anderson, William T. Laura Ingalls Wilder; a
biography; by William Anderson. HarperCollins
Pubs. 1992 240p il $16; pa $5.95   **92**
1. Authors, American 2. Frontier and pioneer life
3. Women authors
ISBN 0-06-020113-4; 0-06-446103-3 (pa)
LC 91-33805
A biography of the writer whose pioneer life on the
American prairie became the basis for her "Little House"
books
"A readable biography that is easily accessible to mid-
dle grade children who are likely to read the Little
House books. Particularly interesting are the sections that
fill in the gaps in Wilder's stories." Booklist

**William I, the Conqueror, King of England,
1027 or 8-1087**
Green, Robert. William the Conqueror. Watts
1998 64p il lib bdg $22   **92**
1. Great Britain—Kings and rulers 2. Great Britain—
History—1066-1154, Norman period
ISBN 0-531-20353-0   LC 97-10985
"A First book"
Profiles the Duke of Normandy whose victory at Has-
tings in 1066 established him as the English king respon-
sible for unifying the system of government and law
The life of the monarch is "surveyed in an interesting
manner." Horn Book Guide
Includes bibliographical references

Williams, Daniel Hale, 1856-1931
Kaye, Judith. The life of Daniel Hale Williams.
21st Cent. Bks. (NY) 1993 80p il (Pioneers in
health and medicine) lib bdg $13.95   **92**
1. Physicians 2. African Americans—Biography
ISBN 0-8050-2302-X   LC 93-7986
A biography of the African American doctor who performed the first surgery on the human heart in the nineteenth century and who founded the first interracial hospital in the United States
This volume "will prove useful to middle-grade report
writers." SLJ
Includes bibliographical references

Williams, Venus
Aronson, Virginia. Venus Williams. Chelsea
House 1999 64p il (Galaxy of superstars) $16.95;
pa $9.95   **92**
1. Tennis—Biography 2. Women athletes 3. African
American athletes
ISBN 0-7910-5153-6; 0-7910-5153-6 (pa)
LC 98-37650

Williams, Venus—*Continued*
A biography of the teenage tennis player who is consistently ranked among the top ten women players in the world
"In this well-written book, Aronson describes how Williams' father took control of her career, making sure that her education and life came before tennis. Interwoven with her story is a history of women's tennis and a frank discussion of how players' lives have unraveled by becoming pros too early." Booklist
Includes bibliographical references

Wilson, Edith Bolling Galt, 1872-1961
Flanagan, Alice K. Edith Bolling Galt Wilson, 1872-1961. Children's Press 1998 111p il (Encyclopedia of first ladies) $33   92
1. Presidents' spouses—United States
ISBN 0-516-20596-X   LC 98-7893
Presents a biography of the wife of the twenty-eighth president of the United States, a woman who helped her husband manage the affairs of his office after he suffered a stroke
Includes bibliographical references

Giblin, James. Edith Wilson: the woman who ran the United States; by James Cross Giblin; illustrated by Michele Laporte. Viking 1992 52p il (Women of our time) $11; pa $3.99   92
1. Wilson, Woodrow, 1856-1924 2. Presidents' spouses—United States
ISBN 0-670-83005-4; 0-14-034249-4 (pa)
LC 91-42265
A biography of the First Lady who gave vital support to her husband, President Woodrow Wilson, and to the nation during and after World War I
"For reports or pleasure reading, this simply written, well-organized volume captures this remarkable woman's personality and contributions to society." SLJ

Wilson, Woodrow, 1856-1924
Schraff, Anne E. Woodrow Wilson. Enslow Pubs. 1998 112p il (United States presidents) lib bdg $18.95   92
1. Presidents—United States
ISBN 0-89490-936-3   LC 97-4372
Traces the life of the twenty-eighth president, from his childhood, through his years of extensive writing, to his terms as president and his involvement in the end of World War I and the founding of the League of Nations
"Readers will not only learn about our 28th president, but they will also come away with a clear picture of the early 20th century here and around the world." SLJ
Includes bibliographical references

Winfrey, Oprah
Presnall, Judith Janda. Oprah Winfrey. Lucent Bks. 1999 111p il (People in the news) lib bdg $22.45 (7 and up)   92
1. African American actors 2. African American women
ISBN 1-56006-360-2   LC 98-23237

Discusses the life of actress and talk show host Oprah Winfrey, her early years, life in Baltimore and Chicago, the evolution of her television show, and her charity work
Includes bibliographical references

Wooten, Sara McIntosh. Oprah Winfrey; talk show legend. Enslow Pubs. 1999 128p il (African-American biographies) lib bdg $19.95
92
1. African American actors 2. African American women
ISBN 0-7660-1207-7   LC 98-27770
A biography of the performer and talk show host, discussing her childhood of neglect and her rise to the top of the entertainment world
Includes bibliographical references

Wollstonecraft, Mary, 1759-1797
Miller, Calvin Craig. Mary Wollstonecraft and the rights of women. Morgan Reynolds 1999 112p il (World writers) $18.95 (7 and up)   92
1. Authors, English 2. Women authors 3. Feminism
ISBN 1-88384-641-2   LC 99-13519
A "anecdotal portrait of a founding member of the women's rights movement. Victimized by a father whose 'bad habits' eroded family finances, and exposed to the gender inequities of 18th-century British society, Wollstonecraft sought independence through work as a lady's companion, a school teacher, and a governess. . . . She found her voice at last, however, in writing and published several works, including *Thoughts on the Education of Daughters* (1786) and *A Vindication of the Rights of Woman* (1792)." SLJ
"Miller's lively biography of this most interesting woman makes an excellent resource for students studying the women's movement or modern history." Booklist
Includes bibliographical references

Woods, Tiger
Lace, William W. Tiger Woods; star golfer. Enslow Pubs. 1999 104p il (Sports reports) $19.95
92
1. Golf—Biography
ISBN 0-7660-1081-3   LC 98-36958
A biography of the youngest golfer to win the Masters Tournament, from his childhood in California to his development as one of the most highly recognized players of the game
Includes bibliographical references

Uschan, Michael V. Tiger Woods. Lucent Bks. 1999 112p il (People in the news) $22.45 (7 and up)   92
1. Golf—Biography
ISBN 1-56006-528-1   LC 98-50295
Discusses the life and career of Tiger Woods, including his childhood, early fame, success as the greatest amateur golfer ever, and achievements as a professional player
Includes bibliographical references

Woodson, Carter Godwin, 1875-1950

Durden, Robert Franklin. Carter G. Woodson; father of African-American history. Enslow Pubs. 1998 128p il (African-American biographies) lib bdg $18.95 (7 and up)   **92**
1. Historians 2. African Americans—Biography
ISBN 0-89490-946-0   LC 97-30243
A biography of the son of former slaves who received a Ph.D. in history from Harvard and devoted his life to bringing the achievements of his race to the world's attention
"This balanced and documented account focuses on the historian's successes and failures (his prickly personality alienated many would-be supporters). Black-and-white photographs appear throughout." SLJ
Includes bibliographical references

Wozniak, Stephen

Kendall, Martha E. Steve Wozniak; inventor of the Apple computer. Walker & Co. 1994 104p il $14.95; lib bdg $15.85 (7 and up)   **92**
1. Apple Computer Inc.
ISBN 0-8027-8341-4; 0-8027-8342-2 (lib bdg)   LC 94-38804
"The story of the whiz kid of the Silicon Valley who built a computer when he was 11 and developed the revolutionary Apple just 15 years later. Today, the man is a multimillionaire, volunteer computer teacher, and doting father. This biography, written with the cooperation of Wozniak and family, paints a positive picture of the electronics genius, although unflattering characteristics surface from time to time." SLJ

Wright, Frank Lloyd, 1867-1959

Boulton, Alexander O. Frank Lloyd Wright, architect; an illustrated biography; introduction by Bruce Brooks Pfeiffer. Rizzoli Int. Publs. 1993 128p il $24.95 (7 and up)   **92**
1. Architects
ISBN 0-8478-1683-4   LC 93-12188
The author "shows how Wright changed forever contemporary architecture with his radical approach to creating a uniquely American design for homes and buildings. . . . This is also an art book; interspersed throughout the spacious text are many fine reproductions of Wright's drawings and color photographs of his famous homes and buildings. His life story, including the scandal that surrounded his private life, is presented in a straightforward style." Booklist
Includes glossary and bibliographical references

Rubin, Susan Goldman. Frank Lloyd Wright. Abrams 1994 92p il (First impressions) $19.95 (7 and up)   **92**
1. Architects
ISBN 0-8109-3974-6   LC 93-48523
"Rubin integrates Wright's life story with a detailed focus on his development as an architect and on his wide and lasting influence." Booklist
"Lots of photographs and illustrations, many in full color, provide a look at many interesting projects, including the only dog house Wright ever designed." SLJ

Wright, David K. Frank Lloyd Wright; visionary architect. Enslow Pubs. 1999 128p il (People to know) lib bdg $19.95   **92**
1. Architects
ISBN 0-7660-1032-5   LC 97-29056
Examines the life and career of the American architect, detailing the evolution of his innovative design and the structures which won him fame around the world
Includes bibliographical references

Wright, Orville, 1871-1948

Freedman, Russell. The Wright brothers: how they invented the airplane; with original photographs by Wilbur and Orville Wright. Holiday House 1991 129p il $19.95; pa $12.95   **92**
1. Wright, Wilbur, 1867-1912 2. Aeronautics—History
ISBN 0-8234-0875-2; 0-8234-1082-X (pa)   LC 90-48440
A Newbery Medal honor book, 1992
In this "combination of photography and text, Freedman reveals the frustrating, exciting, and ultimately successful journey of these two brothers from their bicycle shop in Dayton, Ohio, to their Kitty Hawk flights and beyond. . . . An essential purchase for younger YAs." Voice Youth Advocates
Includes bibliographical references

Wright, Richard, 1908-1960

Urban, Joan. Richard Wright. Chelsea House 1989 111p il (Black Americans of achievement) lib bdg $19.95   **92**
1. Authors, American 2. African American authors
ISBN 1-55546-618-4   LC 88-34614
This is a biography of the author of Native son and Black boy
"The discussion of books like . . . Native Son, with some well-chosen quotations, will be a stimulus to seek out [Wright's] works. There is also some brisk discussion of the crucial social and political issues of the times." Booklist
Includes bibliographical references

Wright, Wilbur, 1867-1912

Freedman, Russell. The Wright brothers: how they invented the airplane. See entry under Wright, Orville, 1871-1948

Wyeth, Andrew, 1917-

Meryman, Richard. Andrew Wyeth. Abrams 1991 92p il (First impressions) $19.95 (7 and up)   **92**
1. Artists, American
ISBN 0-8109-3956-8   LC 90-47605
The author "provides in-depth coverage of the painter's formative years. . . . The book contains a number of black-and-white photographs and 28 full-color plates that complement the text nicely. Although the book presents paintings created as recently as 1988, the biography ends in the late 1940s. . . . This is a beautiful, powerful book that stresses the significance of childhood." SLJ

Yep, Laurence

Yep, Laurence. The lost garden. Messner 1991 117p il (In my own words) o.p.; Smith, P. reprint available $19   **92**

1. Authors, American 2. Chinese Americans—Biography

ISBN 0-8446-6980-6 (pa)   LC 90-40647

The author describes how he grew up as a Chinese American in San Francisco and how he came to use his writing to celebrate his family and his ethnic heritage

"The writing is warm, wry, and humorous. . . . *The Lost Garden* will be welcomed as a literary autobiography for children and, more, a thoughtful probing into what it means to be an American." SLJ

Zaharias, Babe Didrikson, 1911-1956

Freedman, Russell. Babe Didrikson Zaharias; the making of a champion. Clarion Bks. 1999 192p il $18   **92**

1. Women athletes

ISBN 0-395-63367-2   LC 98-50208

A biography of Babe Didrikson, who broke records in golf, track and field, and other sports, at a time when there were few opportunities for female athletes

"Freedman's measured yet lively style captures the spirit of the great athlete. . . . Plenty of black-and-white photos capture Babe's spirit and dashing good looks; the documentation . . . is impeccable." Horn Book

Includes bibliographical references

Zhang, Song Nan

Zhang, Song Nan. A little tiger in the Chinese night; an autobiography in art. Tundra Bks. 1993 48p il $19.95   **92**

1. Artists, Chinese

ISBN 0-88776-320-0

"Song Nan Zhang traces his life in China, describing an idyllic childhood after World War II; his youthful idealism during the 'Great Leap Forward,' which entailed years of hard work under harsh conditions; and the even more horrible Cultural Revolution." SLJ

"The writing is so vivid and the story so involving that it is hard to put down. Best of all, colorful, well-composed illustrations appear on nearly every spread, bringing Zhang's experiences more sharply into focus." Booklist

Zitkala-Ša, 1876-1938

Rappaport, Doreen. The flight of Red Bird; the life of Zitkala-Ša; re-created from the writings of Zitkala-Ša and the research of Doreen Rappaport. Dial Bks. 1997 186p il $15.99 (7 and up)   **92**

1. Yankton Indians

ISBN 0-8037-1438-6   LC 96-18339

"Gertrude Bonnin, a Yankton Indian educated in white society, worked as a teacher and a writer. In the early part of the century, she reclaimed her heritage, named herself Zitkala-Sa, and became an advocate for Native Americans. This involving biography is composed primarily of extended quotations from her writings; Rappaport's accompanying third-person text documents events that Zitkala-Sa did not record herself." Horn Book Guide

Includes glossary and bibliographical references

929   Genealogy, names, insignia

Douglas, Ann, 1942-

The family tree detective; cracking the case of your family's story; illustrated by Stephen MacEachern. Owl Bks. (Toronto); distributed by Firefly Bks. (Buffalo) 1999 48p il $15.95; pa $9.95   **929**

1. Genealogy

ISBN 1-895688-88-4; 1-895688-89-2 (pa)

"In 16 brief chapters, a . . . method for conducting genealogical research is outlined. General background predominates in the first four sections, which cover rationale, basic Mendelian genetics, and degrees of relatedness. The rest of the book introduces various interviewing techniques, data collection and storage, and ways to present the story of a family once it is together. . . . MacEachern's cartoon illustrations are bright and energetic enough to carry readers through the more nuts-and-bolts portions. A brief glossary and short but accurate index round out this useful resource." SLJ

Perl, Lila

The great ancestor hunt; the fun of finding out who you are; drawings by Erika Weihs; illustrated with photographs. Clarion Bks. 1989 104p il $16; pa $7.95   **929**

1. Genealogy

ISBN 0-89919-745-0; 0-395-54790-3 (pa)
                              LC 88-36211

The author "weaves the how-to of genealogy with a historical perspective on immigration. All the basics are covered: drawing an ancestry chart, conducting interviews with relatives, finding family memorabilia, and, for those who wish to continue their quest, writing away for documentation. The format is also a plus. Interesting black-and-white photos alternate with charts, diagrams, and a few (softly executed) drawings by Erika Weihs." Booklist

Includes bibliographical references

Taylor, Maureen, 1955-

Through the eyes of your ancestors. Houghton Mifflin 1999 86p il $16; pa $8.95   **929**

1. Genealogy

ISBN 0-395-86980-3; 0-395-86982-X (pa)
                              LC 98-8776

Discusses genealogy, the study of one's family, examining how such an interest develops, how to get started, how to use family stories and keepsakes, where to get help, and the positive effects of such study

"Motivated young researchers with adult help will find the book a good starting place." SLJ

Includes bibliographical references

Wolfman, Ira

Do people grow on family trees? genealogy for kids & other beginners: the official Ellis Island handbook; foreword by Alex Haley; illustrations by Michael Klein. Workman 1990 179p il pa $10.95   **929**

1. Genealogy

ISBN 0-89480-348-4   LC 88-51586

Wolfman, Ira—*Continued*

A guide to finding out one's own family history and how to formally record it

"Readable and interesting, full of intriguing stories, this guide is also visually attractive, with large print and many photographs and sidebars." SLJ

Includes bibliographical references

929.9   Flags

Armbruster, Ann

The American flag. Watts 1991 63p il lib bdg $22   **929.9**

1. Flags—United States

ISBN 0-531-20045-0   LC 91-3771

"A First book"

"A look at the fact and the legend behind the evolution of the familiar Stars and Stripes leads into discussion of modern flag manufacture and how the flag has been used to symbolize both patriotism and protest. Armbruster also summarizes the legal battles related to the flag salute." Booklist

Includes bibliographical references

Brandt, Sue R., 1916-

State flags; including the Commonwealth of Puerto Rico. Watts 1992 63p il lib bdg $24

929.9

1. Flags—United States

ISBN 0-531-20001-9   LC 92-8948

Describes the history, design, and significance of the fifty state flags

Includes bibliographical references

Flags of the world. Grolier Educ. 1997 9v il maps set $255   **929.9**

1. Flags

ISBN 0-7172-9159-6   LC 97-24204

Depicts the flags of every independent nation, as well as the flags of the U.S. states and territories and those of Canadian provinces and territories

"Arrangement is attractive and accessible. . . . *Flags of the World* is an impressive, comprehensive, and useful compilation, bound to receive heavy use in school and public library environments." Booklist

Shearer, Benjamin F.

State names, seals, flags, and symbols; a historical guide; [by] Benjamin F. Shearer and Barbara S. Shearer; illustrations by Jerrie Yehling Smith. rev and expanded. Greenwood Press 1994 438p il $49.95   **929.9**

1. Geographic names—United States 2. Seals (Numismatics) 3. Flags—United States

ISBN 0-313-28862-3   LC 93-49552

First published 1987

"Chapters on mottoes, flowers, trees, birds, songs, holidays, and license plates are just a sampling of what is covered, and the format is such that the concisely written material can be found as expeditiously as possible. Even though the book is touted predominantly as a reference tool, the information provided makes fascinating and enlightening reading." Libr J

Includes bibliographical references

Ultimate pocket flags of the world. DK Pub. 1997 240p il $12.95   **929.9**

1. Flags 2. National emblems

ISBN 0-7894-2085-6   LC 97-13688

This profiles over 300 national, state, and provincial flags, national emblems, historical flags, international flags, and signal flags, with color illustrations and a brief history of each, and describes types and parts of flags and heraldic terms

930   History of ancient world to ca.499

Corbishley, Mike

Rome and the ancient world. Facts on File 1993 78p il (Illustrated history of the world) $19.95

930

1. Ancient history 2. Rome—History

ISBN 0-8160-2786-2   LC 91-43789

This work explores the history of the Roman Empire and the world outside the Empire, including ancient China, ancient India, and the empires of Africa

This is "an excellent source of introductory information." Book Rep

Includes glossary and bibliographical references

Pickels, Dwayne E.

Egyptian kings and queens and classical deities. Chelsea House 1997 64p il (Looking into the past: people, places, and customs) lib bdg $16.95 **930**

1. Kings and rulers 2. Egypt—Civilization 3. Classical mythology

ISBN 0-7910-4677-X   LC 97-25504

Introduces a dozen kings and queens of ancient Egypt and relates the often amazing exploits of other figures from the classical age of Greek and Roman mythology

Includes bibliographical references

Smithsonian timelines of the ancient world; [editor-in-chief] Chris Scarre. Dorling Kindersley 1993 256p il maps $49.95   **930**

1. Historical chronology 2. Ancient history—Pictorial works 3. Middle Ages—Pictorial works

ISBN 1-56458-305-8   LC 93-18480

Published in the United Kingdom with title: Timelines of the ancient world

"Information is displayed across 18 broad time periods utilizing [a] . . . grid that allows the user to look up a specific time period and region and discover facts about food and environment, shelter, technology, art, and ritual, for a specific location and time. Each time period is illustrated with characteristic artifacts of each period and region." Am Libr

"This beautiful reference book . . . should be a part of reference sections in every public library and all school libraries." Booklist

The **Visual** dictionary of ancient civilizations. Dorling Kindersley 1994 64p il (Eyewitness visual dictionaries) $18.95   **930**

1. Ancient civilization

ISBN 1-56458-701-0   LC 94-8395

Labeled illustrations and text briefly describe ancient artifacts and civilizations of the world. Timelines are included

930.1 Archaeology

Deem, James M.
Bodies from the bog. Houghton Mifflin 1998
42p il $16   **930.1**
1. Archeology 2. Prehistoric peoples 3. Mummies
ISBN 0-395-85784-8   LC 97-12010
Describes the discovery of bog bodies in northern Europe and the evidence which their remains reveal about themselves and the civilizations in which they lived
"The text is engaging and accessible, and the starkly dramatic photos are given dignity by the spacious and understated page design." Horn Book Guide

Early humans. Knopf 1989 63p il maps (Eyewitness books) $16; lib bdg $16.99   **930.1**
1. Prehistoric peoples 2. Ancient civilization
ISBN 0-394-82257-9; 0-394-92257-3 (lib bdg)
LC 88-13431

Text and photographs present a description of early humans: their origins; their tools and weapons; how they hunted and foraged for food; and the role of family life, money, religion, and magic
"The book is beautifully illustrated, with a paragraph of text at the beginning of each two-page section and an explanatory caption for each artifact pictured. The 25 sections range in topic from the toolmakers to the first artists to bronzeworking." Sci Books Films

Getz, David, 1957-
Frozen man; illustrated by Peter McCarty. Holt & Co. 1994 68p il maps $14.95; pa $6.95 **930.1**
1. Archeology 2. Prehistoric peoples 3. Mummies
ISBN 0-8050-3261-4; 0-8050-4645-3 (pa)
LC 94-9109
"A Redfeather book"
"This is an account of the mummified stone-age corpse who was found in Austria in 1991. . . . Getz's generally well-organized information and smooth exposition makes the effort to understand the Iceman, as this book calls him, into an intriguing detective story. This could well stimulate the interest of kids who didn't think they liked science or archeology. Black and white drawings include useful maps and diagrams." Bull Cent Child Books
Includes glossary and bibliographical references

Goodman, Susan, 1952-
Stones, bones, and petroglyphs; digging into Southwest archaeology; by Susan E. Goodman; photographs by Michael J. Doolittle. Atheneum Bks. for Young Readers 1998 48p il (Ultimate field trip 2) $17   **930.1**
1. Pueblo Indians—Antiquities 2. Excavations (Archeology)
ISBN 0-689-81121-7   LC 97-6501
"Modern eighth graders experience the long-ago habitations of the Pueblo people as they work side-by-side with archaeologists in this account of a week-long field trip to Crow Canyon Archaeological Center in Colorado and Mesa Verde National Park." Horn Book Guide
The author and illustrator "have combined clear, informative, color photographs with simply stated, easy-to-comprehend prose." SLJ
Includes glossary and bibliographical references

Jespersen, James
Mummies, dinosaurs, moon rocks; how we know how old things are; by James Jespersen and Jane Fitz-Randolph; illustrated by Bruce Hiscock and with photographs. Atheneum Bks. for Young Readers 1996 92p il $16   **930.1**
1. Radiocarbon dating
ISBN 0-689-31848-0   LC 96-5170
"This book follows scientists as they examine old things including mummies, the Dead Sea Scrolls, violins, and even stars, and then use everything from hunches to highly scientific techniques to place these items on a time line." SLJ
"It's not easy to present sophisticated scientific principles in a manner that will be accessible to students with limited knowledge of biochemistry and physics, but Jespersen and Fitz-Randolph have done an admirable job." Booklist
Includes glossary and bibliographical references

Lauber, Patricia, 1924-
Tales mummies tell. Crowell 1985 118p il lib bdg $15.89   **930.1**
1. Mummies 2. Archeology
ISBN 0-690-04389-9   LC 83-46172
"Lauber describes the various ways, intentional or accidental, that animals and human beings have become mummies, and she discusses the various ways (carbon-14 dating, x-rays, analysis of body tissue and stomach contents) that scientists use to establish facts about the individual or the culture or changes over the centuries. Clearly written and well-organized, this is an informative and eminently readable text." Bull Cent Child Books
Includes bibliographical references

Lessem, Don
The iceman. Crown 1994 32p il maps $16; lib bdg $14.99   **930.1**
1. Archeology 2. Prehistoric peoples 3. Mummies
ISBN 0-517-59596-6; 0-517-59597-4 (lib bdg)
LC 93-31534
"This is a story of the remarkable discovery of a man who, more than 5,000 years ago, was frozen in an Alpine glacier along with his tools and weapons. Full-page, color photographs accompany a high-interest narrative that will surely captivate even the most reluctant readers." Sci Child

Macdonald, Fiona
The Stone Age news. Candlewick Press 1998 32p il maps $16.99   **930.1**
1. Stone Age 2. Prehistoric peoples
ISBN 0-7636-0451-8   LC 97-41255
Uses a newspaper format to present the inventions, lifestyles, climate changes, and progress in hunting and farming of the Stone Age
"The layout is impressive, yielding copious amounts of information while remaining easy on the eye. . . . Enjoyable and useful in the classroom, with endless possibilities for discussion and tie-in projects." Booklist

McGowen, Tom
Adventures in archaeology. 21st Cent. Bks. (NY) 1997 95p il map (Scientific American sourcebooks) $22.40   **930.1**
1. Archeology 2. Antiquities 3. Ancient civilization
ISBN 0-8050-4688-7   LC 97-9755
Discusses some of the discoveries made by archeologists around the world, including mummies found in Denmark and the sophisticated ancient city of Mohenjodaro in Pakistan
This is an "attractive and accessible book. . . . Excellent-quality full-color photographs, reproductions, and drawings add to readers' understanding." SLJ
Includes glossary and bibliographical references

McIntosh, Jane
Archeology; written by Jane McIntosh. Knopf 1994 63p il (Eyewitness books) $19; lib bdg $20.99   **930.1**
1. Archeology
ISBN 0-679-86572-1; 0-679-96572-6 (lib bdg)
                    LC 94-9378
"A Dorling Kindersley Book"
This volume "touches on aspects of archaeology in many locations around the world. Each double-page spread examines one or two concepts: preservation and decay, excavation, clues to the past, human remains, fakes and forgeries, etc. . . . Readers are not likely to use this book for research, but will want to make repeated short visits." SLJ

Moloney, N. (Norah)
The young Oxford book of archaeology; [by] Norah Moloney. Oxford Univ. Press 1997 160p il maps $25; lib bdg $30 (7 and up)   **930.1**
1. Archeology 2. Antiquities
ISBN 0-19-910067-5; 0-19-521248-7 (lib bdg)
                    LC 97-16096
Defines archaeology, examines how archaeologists work, surveys excavation methods, and visits archaeology sites—from Olduvai Gorge in Tanzania to the Garbage Project in America
"For anyone looking for report topics covering the most significant finds of the 19th and 20th centuries, this will be the place to start. . . . The stunning full-color photographs and illustrations found on every page will entice browsers of a wide age group, but the text is sophisticated." SLJ
Includes glossary

Patent, Dorothy Hinshaw
Secrets of the ice man. Benchmark Bks. (Tarrytown) 1999 72p il (Frozen in time) $27.07
                    930.1
1. Archeology 2. Prehistoric peoples 3. Mummies
ISBN 0-7614-0782-0   LC 97-49512
Describes the examination of the Ice Man, his clothing and equipment, found in the Alps near the Austrian-Italian border in September 1991 and thought to be more than 4000 years old
This book is "well researched." Book Rep
Includes glossary and bibliographical references

Reinhard, Johan
Discovering the Inca Ice Maiden; my adventures on Ampato. National Geographic Soc. 1998 48p il $17.95   **930.1**
1. Archeology 2. Mummies 3. Peru—Antiquities 4. Incas
ISBN 0-7922-7142-4   LC 97-31291
A first-person account of the 1995 discovery of the over 500-year-old Peruvian ice mummy on Mount Ampato and a description of the subsequent retrieval and scientific study
"Vibrant color photographs of the mummy and Incan artifacts found on the expedition illustrate the engrossing text." Horn Book Guide
Includes glossary

Stefoff, Rebecca, 1951-
Finding the lost cities. Oxford Univ. Press 1997 191p il maps $30; pa $15.95 (7 and up)   **930.1**
1. Extinct cities 2. Ancient civilization 3. Archeology
ISBN 0-19-509248-1; 0-19-512541-X (pa)
                    LC 96-9802
Explores twelve archeological "lost cities," with accounts of site discovery and investigation of the meaning of recovered objects
"This stunning, oversized book has 13 maps, 130 illustrations and reproductions (30 in color), and a chronology from before 4000 B.C. to 1995. A title that's certain to spark interest in vanished civilizations and in archaeology, with its mix of dramatic discoveries and careful deductions." SLJ
Includes bibliographical references

Tanaka, Shelley
Discovering the Iceman; what was it like to find a 5,300-year-old mummy? illustrations by Laurie McGaw; historical consultants, Janet E. Levy, Walter Leitner, Konrad Spindler. Hyperion Bks. for Children 1996 48p il $16.95   **930.1**
1. Archeology 2. Prehistoric peoples 3. Mummies
ISBN 0-7868-0284-7   LC 96-28986
"An I was there book"
Recounts the discovery and examination of a 5,300-year-old man whose remains were found by hikers in the Alps in 1991 and explores how this discovery provides clues about the everyday life of our ancestors
"The cornucopia of facts, combined with the gruesome appeal of Otzi's decomposing visage, makes this an enticing dip into history." Bull Cent Child Books
Includes glossary and bibliographical references

Wood, Tim
Ancient wonders. Viking 1997 48p il maps (See through history) $17.99   **930.1**
1. Antiquities 2. Curiosities and wonders
ISBN 0-670-87468-X   LC 96-61598
This offers a "glance at some of the major wonders of the ancient world. . . . Sites surveyed include Egypt's pyramids, sphinxes, and tombs; the City of Troy; the Palace of Knossos; and Stonehenge. . . . Four overlays allow readers to look at several structures from both inside and out." SLJ

931 China to 420 A.D.

Cotterell, Arthur
Ancient China; written by Arthur Cotterell; photographed by Alan Hills & Geoff Brightling. Knopf 1994 63p il maps (Eyewitness books) $19; lib bdg $20.99 **931**
1. China—Civilization
ISBN 0-679-86167-X; 0-679-96167-4 (lib bdg)
LC 94-9319
"A Dorling Kindersley book"
"This volume touches upon such topics as Chinese history, the first emperor, inventions, health and medicine, waterways, food and drink, clothing, the Silk Road, and arts and crafts. . . . The book will . . . be popular for browsing." SLJ

932 Egypt to 640 A.D.

Baines, John, 1946-
Atlas of ancient Egypt; by John Baines and Jaromír Málek. Facts on File 1980 240p il maps $45 **932**
1. Egypt—Antiquities 2. Egypt—Civilization
3. Egypt—Maps
ISBN 0-87196-334-5 LC 80-132792
"A historical atlas with maps, plans and illustrations . . . presented in conjunction with the text. In three sections: (1) The cultural setting; (2) A journey down the Nile; (3) Aspects of Egyptian society. Includes a list of museums with Egyptian collections, a glossary, bibliography, gazetteer, and index." Guide to Ref Books. 11th edition

Caselli, Giovanni
In search of Tutankhamun; the discovery of a king's tomb; written and illustrated by Giovanni Caselli. Bedrick Bks. 1999 44p il maps lib bdg $18.95 **932**
1. Tutankhamen, King of Egypt 2. Egypt—Antiquities
ISBN 0-87226-543-9 LC 98-44348
Describes the discovery of the tomb of the Egyptian king Tutankhamun and what it revealed about everyday life in his time
This work is "attractively illustrated and thoughtfully arranged." SLJ
Includes glossary

Green, Robert, 1969-
Tutankhamun. Watts 1996 64p il map lib bdg $22; pa $6.95 **932**
1. Tutankhamen, King of Egypt 2. Egypt—Antiquities
ISBN 0-531-20233-X (lib bdg); 0-531-15802-0 (pa)
LC 95-46150
"A First book"
Tells the story of the discovery of Tutankhamen's tomb by Howard Carter and Lord Carnarvon and the supposed curse connected with it, as well as information on the life and dynasty of the pharaoh
"This account nicely intermingles details of what is known about the pharaoh and his reign with Howard Carter's amazing rediscovery. . . . Full-color and black-and-white photographs show objects described in the text, and a timeline and list of Internet sites provide backup information." SLJ
Includes bibliographical references

Hart, George, 1945-
Ancient Egypt; written by George Hart. Knopf 1990 63p il (Eyewitness books) $19; lib bdg $20.99 **932**
1. Egypt—Antiquities 2. Egypt—Civilization
ISBN 0-679-80742-X; 0-679-90742-4 (lib bdg)
LC 90-4106
A photo essay on ancient Egypt and the people who lived there, documented through the mummies, pottery, weapons, and other objects they left behind. Describes their society, religion, obsession with the afterlife, and methods of mummification
"Dazzles the eye with hundreds of color photographs and illustrations. Each two-page spread treats one particular aspect of the civilization. . . . All items pictured are identified with brief captions and clear definitions." SLJ

Haynes, Joyce
Egyptian dynasties. Watts 1998 64p il (African civilizations) lib bdg $22 **932**
1. Egypt—Civilization
ISBN 0-531-20280-1 LC 97-29390
"A First book"
A survey of the history and culture of the North African Egyptian dynasties
This book is "clearly written. . . . Captioned color photographs . . . archival portraits, maps, and time lines are included." Horn Book
Includes glossary and bibliographical references

Murdoch, David Hamilton, 1937-
Tutankhamun; the life and death of a pharaoh; written by David Murdoch. DK Pub. 1998 47p il maps (DK discoveries) $14.95 **932**
1. Tutankhamen, King of Egypt 2. Egypt—Antiquities
ISBN 0-7894-3420-2 LC 98-23088
Relates the story of the discovery of Tutankhamun's tomb by Howard Carter and Lord Carnarvon and what it revealed about the funeral rites of the pharaoh

Steedman, Scott
The Egyptian news; consultant, James Putnam. Candlewick Press 1997 32p il maps $15.99 **932**
1. Egypt—Civilization
ISBN 1-56402-873-9 LC 96-30842
Uses a newspaper format to present articles about the history, politics, fashion, food, daily life, and afterlife of the ancient Egyptians
This book brings "readers a wealth of information in colorful pictures, short articles, and witty 'ads.'" SLJ

933   Palestine to 70 A.D.

Waldman, Neil, 1947-
Masada; written and illustrated by Neil
Waldman. Morrow Junior Bks. 1998 64p il maps
$16   **933**
1. Jews—History 2. Excavations (Archeology) 3. Masada Site (Israel)
ISBN 0-688-14481-0   LC 97-32912
Discusses the history of Masada, from the building of
Herod's Temple through its use by Zealots as a refuge
from the Romans to its rediscovery in the mid-20th
century
"Dramatic illustrations and two large maps, all in
charcoal shades of acrylic and India ink, show realistic
scenes, many of them painted from photos, relief sculptures, and artifacts found during the excavation of Masada." SLJ
Includes glossary and bibliographical references

936   Europe north and west of Italian peninsula to ca. 499 A.D.

Millard, Anne
A street through time; written by Anne Millard;
illustrated by Steve Noon. DK Pub. 1998 32p il
$16.95   **936**
1. Cities and towns
ISBN 0-7894-3426-1   LC 98-3226
Traces the development of one street from the Stone
Age to the present day, from dirt track to the rebuilding
of inns as wine bars, showing how people lived and what
they did all day
"The time-line construct is a useful demonstration for
children, and the busy vistas would make a fine springboard for encouraging students to create scenes of local
history." Horn Book Guide
Includes glossary

936.2   England to 410 A.D.

Mass, Wendy, 1967-
Stonehenge. Lucent Bks. 1998 96p il maps
(Building history series) lib bdg $22.45 (7 and up)
                                                936.2
1. Stonehenge (England) 2. Great Britain—Antiquities
ISBN 1-56006-432-3   LC 97-47569
Discusses the history, construction, and possible purposes of Stonehenge
Includes bibliographical references

937   Roman Empire

Connolly, Peter, 1935-
Pompeii; written and illustrated by Peter
Connolly. Oxford Univ. Press 1990 77p il maps
hardcover o.p. paperback available $12.95   **937**
1. Pompeii (Extinct city) 2. Excavations (Archeology)—Italy
ISBN 0-19-917158-0 (pa)

Presents archeological information about Pompeii
through text, photographs, and reconstructive drawings
"This is as complete and thorough a documentation of
the story of Pompeii as any that can currently be found
in children's collections." SLJ
Includes glossary

Corbishley, Mike
Ancient Rome; [by] Michael Corbishley. Facts
on File 1989 96p il maps (Cultural atlas for young
people) $19.95   **937**
1. Rome—Antiquities 2. Rome—Civilization
ISBN 0-8160-1970-3   LC 88-31687
"An Equinox book"
This topical atlas "begins with a 'Table of Dates,' a
chronology of the history, arts, and literature of [Roman]
culture. The remainder of [the] book is made up of double-page spreads, each covering a different subject."
Booklist
Includes glossary and bibliographical references

James, Simon, 1957-
Ancient Rome; written by Simon James. Knopf
1990 62p il (Eyewitness books) $19; lib bdg
$20.99   **937**
1. Rome—Antiquities 2. Rome—Civilization
ISBN 0-679-80741-1; 0-679-90741-6 (lib bdg)
                                         LC 90-4111
A photo essay documenting ancient Rome and the
people who lived there as revealed through the many artifacts they left behind, including shields, swords, tools,
toys, cosmetics, and jewelry

Langley, Andrew
The Roman news; [by] Andrew Langley &
Philip De Souza. Candlewick Press 1996 32p il
maps lib bdg $15.99; pa $6.99   **937**
1. Rome—Civilization
ISBN 0-7636-0055-5 (lib bdg); 0-7636-0341-4 (pa)
                                         LC 96-3584
Uses a newspaper format to present Roman history,
politics, religion, fashion, food, and daily life, spanning
the years of the Roman Empire from 753 B.C. to 476
A.D
"Each page presents readable articles complete with
headlines, boldface, column breaks, illustrations, and, often classifieds. . . . The facts . . . are accurate." SLJ

Mann, Elizabeth, 1948-
The Roman Colosseum; with illustrations by
Michael Racz. Mikaya Press 1998 45p (Wonders
of the world book) $19.95   **937**
1. Colosseum (Rome, Italy) 2. Rome—Antiquities
ISBN 0-9650493-3-7   LC 98-20060
Describes the building of the Colosseum in ancient
Rome, and tells how it was used
This offers "a clear, well-written text and full-color
drawings and paintings." SLJ
Includes glossary

Morley, Jacqueline
A Roman villa; [by] Jacqueline Morley, John James. Bedrick Bks. 1992 48p il (Inside story) lib bdg $18.95 **937**
1. Rome—Social life and customs 2. Domestic architecture
ISBN 0-87226-360-6 LC 92-15279
Illustrations and text describe life in the villa of a wealthy family situated in the countryside outside Rome during the first century A.D.

Nardo, Don, 1947-
Life of a Roman slave. Lucent Bks. 1998 111p il (Way people live) lib bdg $22.45 (7 and up) **937**
1. Slavery—Rome 2. Rome—Civilization
ISBN 1-56006-388-2 LC 97-46715
Discusses aspects of slavery in ancient Rome, including becoming a slave, its privileges and perils, and the use of slaves in farming, business, and public service
"This is an excellent choice for specific information on this . . . topic." SLJ
Includes glossary and bibliographical references

Rice, Melanie
Pompeii; the day a city was buried; written by Melanie and Christopher Rice; illustrated by Richard Bonson. DK Pub. 1998 48p il (DK discoveries) $14.95 **937**
1. Pompeii (Extinct city)
ISBN 0-7894-3419-9 LC 98-20336
Describes the life and people of Pompeii, a city in southern Italy destroyed during the eruption of Mount Vesuvius in A.D. 79

938 Greece to 323 A.D.

Ancient Greece and Rome; an encyclopedia for students; Carroll Moulton, editor in chief. Scribner 1998 4v il maps set $350 **938**
1. Classical civilization—Encyclopedias
ISBN 0-684-80507-3 LC 98-13728
Presents a history of ancient Greece and Rome as well as information about the literature and daily life of these early civilizations
"The articles are readable and direct, and topics include those that students typically investigate such as food, alphabets, burial customs, festivals, and weapons. . . . Articles are of an appropriate length for the importance of each topic, with long entries about historic events, famous individuals, religion, and the arts. Some articles about Greece are followed by a similar article about Rome." Voice Youth Advocates
For a fuller review see: Booklist, Oct. 1, 1998

Baker, Rosalie F.
Ancient Greeks; creating the classical tradition; [by] Rosalie F. Baker and Charles F. Baker. Oxford Univ. Press 1997 254p il maps (Oxford profiles) $35 (7 and up) **938**
1. Greece—Biography 2. Greece—Civilization
ISBN 0-19-509940-0 LC 95-26637

"The influence of ancient Greek civilization is chronicled in concise biographies of over 37 Greek statesmen, playwrights, artists, mathematicians, philosophers, and military leaders." Book Rep
"Students looking for biographical or historical information on ancient Greece will find it valuable, as will teachers seeking to integrate the classics into other disciplines." Booklist
Includes glossary and bibliographical references

Bardi, Piero
The atlas of the classical world; ancient Greece and ancient Rome; illustrations by Matteo Chesi [et al.] Bedrick Bks. 1997 61p il maps $19.95 **938**
1. Greece—Civilization 2. Rome—Civilization
ISBN 0-87226-369-X LC 97-41581
"This chronological, largely pictorial history of the classical world includes maps and diagrams that depict layouts of cities, military campaigns, trade routes, etc. Double-page spreads devoted to aspects of ancient Greek and Roman life, culture, and history also provide graphs and full-color photographs and drawings of artifacts, archeological sites, and scenes from everyday life. . . . The text is brief, informative, well written, and logically organized." SLJ

Hart, Avery
Ancient Greece! 40 hands-on activities to experience this wondrous age; [by] Avery Hart & Paul Mantell; illustrations by Michael Kline. Williamson 1999 104p il pa $10.95 **938**
1. Greece—Civilization 2. Handicraft
ISBN 1-885593-25-2 LC 98-35762
"A Kaleidoscope Kids book"
Introduces the places, people, historical events, myths, culture, and philosophy of ancient Greece. Includes forty hands-on activities, such as making an early Greek theater, building an Ionic temple, and pressing olives for oil
This is "a clever title that encourages learning and creativity." SLJ
Includes bibliographical references

Macdonald, Fiona
A Greek temple; [by] Fiona Macdonald, Mark Bergin. Bedrick Bks. 1992 48p il (Inside story) $18.95 **938**
1. Parthenon (Athens, Greece) 2. Athens (Greece)—Antiquities
ISBN 0-87226-361-4 LC 92-10712
"While focusing on the Parthenon, Macdonald discusses the religious customs, sacrifices, games, and gods all of which had some bearing on the purpose, uses, and decorations of Greek temples. Two chapters focus on the people: those who visited the temples, the workers who built them, and the craftsmen who provided the designs and skilled labor." SLJ

Powell, Anton
The Greek news; [by] Anton Powell & Philip Steele. Candlewick Press 1996 32p il maps lib bdg $15.99; pa $6.99 **938**
1. Greece—Civilization
ISBN 1-56402-874-7 (lib bdg); 0-7636-0340-6 (pa)
LC 95-48489

Powell, Anton—*Continued*
Uses an newspaper format to present Greek civilization from the years 1500 to 146 B.C. and contains articles about history, politics, feasts, fashions, theater, gods, and wars
This book is "entertaining [and] deftly organized." Publ Wkly

938.003 Classical dictionaries

The **Oxford** companion to classical civilization; edited by Simon Hornblower and Antony Spawforth. Oxford Univ. Press 1998 xxiv, 793p il maps $49.95   **938.003**
1. Classical dictionaries
ISBN 0-19-860165-4   LC 99-191129
An abridgement of the third edition of the Oxford classical dictionary
This guide to ancient Greece and Rome covers such topics as military history, architecture, law, mythology, sciences, and the arts and includes essay length articles as well as short reference entries arranged alphabetically, cross referenced and illustrated with color plates
Includes bibliographical references

939 Other parts of ancient world to ca. 640

Caselli, Giovanni
In search of Troy; one man's quest for Homer's fabled city; written and illustrated by Giovanni Caselli. Bedrick Bks. 1999 44p il lib bdg $18.95
                                                        939
1. Schliemann, Heinrich, 1822-1890 2. Troy (Extinct city)
ISBN 0-87226-542-0   LC 98-42579
Discusses the efforts of Heinrich Schliemann to uncover the ancient city of Troy and what his archeological finds revealed about life in this legendary location
"Each spread features a well-written paragraph or two on the topic, supported by nicely drawn artwork, with captions giving extra information." Booklist
Includes glossary

940.1 Europe—Early history to 1453

Biesty, Stephen
Stephen Biesty's cross-sections: Castle; illustrated by Stephen Biesty; written by Richard Platt. Dorling Kindersley 1994 27p il $16.95
                                                        940.1
1. Castles 2. Medieval civilization
ISBN 1-56458-467-4   LC 93-30158
This "volume displays pictures of a cutaway medieval castle, revealing how the castle was constructed for protection and showing the way of life shared by those inside its walls." Horn Book Guide
"The duo's trademark humor is evident throughout. . . . Not only is the book guaranteed to attract browsers but it will also make fun and fruitful work of report research." Booklist

Corbishley, Mike
The Middle Ages. Facts on File 1989 96p il maps (Cultural atlas for young people) $17.95
                                                        940.1
1. Medieval civilization 2. Middle Ages
ISBN 0-8160-1973-8   LC 88-31692
"An Equinox book"
Maps, charts, illustrations, and text explore the history and culture of the Middle Ages
Includes bibliographical references

Gravett, Christopher
Knight; written by Christopher Gravett; photographed by Geoff Dann. Knopf 1993 63p il (Eyewitness books) $19; lib bdg $20.99   **940.1**
1. Knights and knighthood 2. Medieval civilization
ISBN 0-679-83882-1; 0-679-93882-6 (lib bdg)
                                            LC 92-1590
"A Dorling Kindersley book"
Discusses the age of knighthood, covering such aspects as arms, armor, training, ceremonies, tournaments, the code of chivalry, and the Crusades
"The strength of the 'Eyewitness' title is, of course, the wonderful full-color photographs." SLJ

The world of the medieval knight; illustrations by Brett Breckon. Bedrick Bks. 1996 64p il map lib bdg $19.95   **940.1**
1. Knights and knighthood 2. Medieval civilization
ISBN 0-87226-277-4   LC 96-32958
"Gravett introduces knights and medieval European civilization through a series of more specific topics such as castles, jousting, battles, sieges, crusades, chivalry, armor, and weapons. Each spread includes several attractive paintings illustrating knights in action as well as labeled and captioned details of their world, all attractively framed by narrow, decorated borders." Booklist
Includes glossary

Hart, Avery
Knights & castles; 50 hands-on activities to experience the Middle Ages; [by] Avery Hart & Paul Mantell. Williamson 1998 96p il pa $10.95
                                                        940.1
1. Medieval civilization 2. Middle Ages 3. Knights and knighthood 4. Handicraft
ISBN 1-885593-17-1   LC 97-32863
"A Kaleidoscope Kids book"
Introduces the Middle Ages, including activities and crafts that are representative of medieval life, for example creating an hour glass, a catapult, a coat of arms, and a code of honor
"The text is written in a breezy tone and illustrated with a combination of line drawings and blue-or purple-ink reproductions of medieval art and woodcuts." SLJ
Includes bibliographical references

Howarth, Sarah
The Middle Ages. Viking 1993 48p il maps (See through history) $14.99   **940.1**
1. Middle Ages 2. Medieval civilization
ISBN 0-670-85098-5   LC 92-56930

Howarth, Sarah—*Continued*

This volume "includes information on family organization, clothing, and food, with the differences in the status and lifestyle of peasant, noble, and cleric clearly depicted . . . . Each topic is briefly presented in its own two-page spread, extensively illustrated with paintings, charts, examples of objects from the period, and original artwork." Booklist

Includes glossary

Langley, Andrew

Castle at war; the story of a siege; written by Andrew Langley; illustrated by Peter Dennis. DK Pub. 1998 47p il (DK discoveries) $14.95 **940.1**

1. Castles 2. Medieval civilization

ISBN 0-7894-3418-0 LC 98-20907

Describes, in brief text and illustrations, how the inhabitants of a medieval castle prepared for war and endured a siege

"A good choice for recreational reading and reports." SLJ

Medieval life; written by Andrew Langley; photographed by Geoff Dann & Geoff Brightling. Knopf 1996 63p il (Eyewitness books) $19; lib bdg $20.99 **940.1**

1. Medievcal civilization

ISBN 0-679-88077-1; 0-679-98077-6 (lib bdg)
LC 95-25064

"A Dorling Kindersley book"

An illustrated look at various aspects of life in medieval Europe, covering everyday life, religion, royalty, and more

This "gives a clear picture of life and the times through a combination of brief text and an abundance of high-quality pictures with descriptive and informative captions." SLJ

Macdonald, Fiona

A medieval castle; [illustrated by] Mark Bergin. Bedrick Bks. 1990 48p il (Inside story) $18.95; pa $10.95 **940.1**

1. Castles 2. Medieval civilization

ISBN 0-87226-340-1; 0-87226-258-8 (pa)
LC 90-36253

Text and cutaway illustrations depict how people lived and worked inside a medieval castle

Includes glossary

Nardo, Don, 1947-

The medieval castle. Lucent Bks. 1998 96p il (Building history series) lib bdg $22.45 (7 and up) **940.1**

1. Castles 2. Medieval civilization

ISBN 1-56006-430-7 LC 97-34638

Describes how medieval castles were built and examines the daily lives of those inhabiting them

"A well-written, thorough study. . . . Black-and-white diagrams, drawings, and reproductions are effectively used to further inform readers about castle life." SLJ

Includes bibliographical references

Nicolle, David, 1944-

Medieval knights. Viking 1997 48p il maps (See through history) $17.99 **940.1**

1. Knights and knighthood 2. Medieval civilization

ISBN 0-670-87463-9 LC 96-61599

This introduction to knights and medieval civilization covers such topics as "myths and legends, the feudal system, the tournament, the Crusades, and the decline of the knight. . . . A welcome addition." SLJ

940.2 Europe—1453-

Corrick, James A.

The Renaissance. Lucent Bks. 1998 112p il maps (World history series) lib bdg $22.45 (7 and up) **940.2**

1. Renaissance

ISBN 1-56006-311-4 LC 97-27261

Traces developments in European art, architecture, music, literature, philosophy, science, and exploration between 1300 and 1600

This book "has a wealth of black-and-white illustrative material that is as informative as it is attractive. Boxed primary-source quotations appear throughout the clear, explanatory text." SLJ

Includes bibliographical references

Dunn, John M., 1949-

The Enlightenment. Lucent Bks. 1999 108p il (World history series) lib bdg $17.96 (7 and up) **940.2**

1. Enlightenment 2. Eighteenth century

ISBN 1-56006-242-8 LC 98-8373

Discusses various aspects of the Enlightenment including its roots, philosophies, attacks on Christianity, revolt against reason, campaigns to reform society, and legacy

Includes bibliographical references

Langley, Andrew

Renaissance. Knopf 1999 59p il (Eyewitness books) $19; lib bdg $20.99 **940.2**

1. Renaissance

ISBN 0-375-80136-7; 0-375-90136-1 (lib bdg)
LC 98-49766

"A Dorling Kindersley book"

An overview of the philosophy, inventions, art, government, religion, and daily life of the Renaissance

"Langley has combined in-depth research with the arresting, trademark photographs of the series to showcase a complex period in European history." SLJ

Netzley, Patricia D.

Life during the Renaissance. Lucent Bks. 1998 96p il maps (Way people live) lib bdg $22.45 (7 and up) **940.2**

1. Renaissance

ISBN 1-56006-375-0 LC 97-39781

Describes the history, culture, and life of people living during the Renaissance addressing such topics as the distribution of wealth and the rise of the middle class, education and humanism, religious reforms and conflicts, exploration and conquest as sources of wealth, and the arts and sciences

Includes bibliographical references

Wood, Tim
The Renaissance. Viking 1993 48p il maps (See through history) $17.99   **940.2**
1. Renaissance
ISBN 0-670-85149-3   LC 93-60028
Drawings, photographs, and text describe 15th and 16th century European civilization. Four see-through acetate pages lift to reveal the inner structures of three buildings and Columbus' ship, the Santa Maria
Includes glossary

940.3   World War I, 1914-1918

Bosco, Peter I.
World War I; John Bowman, general editor. Facts on File 1991 124p il maps (America at war) $19.95 (7 and up)   **940.3**
1. World War, 1914-1918—United States
ISBN 0-8160-2460-X   LC 90-49086
Tells why America abandoned its isolationism to participate in World War I, and its significance for America
"The text . . . is nicely balanced. Bosco concisely discusses all aspects of the war, from military logistics and political maneuvering to the horrors of the battlefield." SLJ
Includes bibliographical references

Dolan, Edward F., 1924-
America in World War I. Millbrook Press 1996 96p il maps lib bdg $27.40   **940.3**
1. World War, 1914-1918—United States
ISBN 1-56294-522-X   LC 95-35487
Explains the roots of World War I and shows how the United States was drawn in despite strong sentiment for remaining uninvolved. Actions of U.S. troops ˝over there,˝ new weapons such as the tank and airplane, the home front, and the peace that ended the war are covered
"The author's prose is taut and seemingly effortless, but he wisely never overwhelms or dazzles young readers with extraneous facts and figures. . . . Maps and black-and-white reproductions of period photographs and graphics with informative captions augment the volume's general attractiveness and usefulness." SLJ
Includes bibliographical references

Gay, Kathlyn
World War I; [by] Kathlyn Gay, Martin Gay. 21st Cent. Bks. (NY) 1995 64p il maps (Voices from the past) lib bdg $18.90   **940.3**
1. World War, 1914-1918
ISBN 0-8050-2848-X   LC 95-12300
An illustrated look at America's role in World War I on the battlefield and on the home front. Includes excerpts from letters, diaries and newspaper accounts
Includes bibliographical references

Kirchberger, Joe H.
The First World War; an eyewitness history. Facts on File 1992 402p il maps (Eyewitness history series) $50 (7 and up)   **940.3**
1. World War, 1914-1918—Personal narratives
ISBN 0-8160-2552-5   LC 91-19970

The author bases this narrative history of World War I on eyewitness accounts from personalitites such as Rudyard Kipling, Theodore Roosevelt, Alexandra Feodorovna and Austrian empress Zita
Includes bibliographical references

940.4   World War I, 1914-1918 (Military conduct of the war)

Cooper, Michael L., 1950-
Hell Fighters; African American soldiers in World War I. Lodestar Bks. 1997 72p il $16.99   **940.4**
1. World War, 1914-1918 2. African American soldiers
ISBN 0-525-67534-5   LC 96-29082
Describes the experiences of African Americans who joined the military during World War I. Racism within the ranks is discussed
"In highly readable prose, Cooper tells the story of the mostly black Fifteenth New York Voluntary Infantry of the National Guard from its formation in 1916 through its transformation into the 369th regiment, its service in France, and its return to a triumphal parade down New York City's Fifth Avenue." SLJ
Includes bibliographical references

Uschan, Michael V., 1948-
A multicultural portrait of World War I. Benchmark Bks. (Tarrytown) 1996 80p il (Perspectives) lib bdg $28.50 (7 and up)   **940.4**
1. World War, 1914-1918
ISBN 0-7614-0054-0   LC 95-11035
This traces the history of the First World War with emphasis on the roles of ethnic minorities and women and issues of prejudice. Illustrated with color and black-and-white photographs
Includes glossary and bibliographical references

940.53   World War II, 1939-1945

Adler, David A., 1947-
We remember the Holocaust. Holt & Co. 1989 147p il $18.95; pa $9.95   **940.53**
1. Holocaust, 1933-1945—Personal narratives 2. World War, 1939-1945—Jews
ISBN 0-8050-0434-3; 0-8050-3715-2 (pa)
                    LC 87-21139
"Survivors of the Holocaust share their unique stories in an informative, moving account that serves to remind readers of the terrible effects of hatred." Soc Educ
Includes glossary and bibliographical references

Ayer, Eleanor H.
A firestorm unleashed; January 1942—June 1943. Blackbirch Press 1998 80p il map (Holocaust) lib bdg $19.45   **940.53**
1. Holocaust, 1933-1945 2. Genocide
ISBN 1-567-11204-8   LC 96-44430

Ayer, Eleanor H.—*Continued*

Book 4 in the series explores the unique aspects and events in the period of the Holocaust between January 1942 and June 1943, blending historical narrative and primary sources

This "is impeccably researched and well presented. . . . [It] records the full fury of the Holocaust as Germany implemented the genocide of the Jews." SLJ

Includes glossary and bibliographical references

In the ghettos; teens who survived the ghettos of the Holocaust. Rosen Pub. Group 1998 64p il map (Teen witnesses to the Holocaust) $17.95 (7 and up) **940.53**

1. Holocaust, 1933-1945—Personal narratives

ISBN 0-8239-2845-4   LC 98-43859

Chronicles the deportation of Jews into ghettos during Hitler's Third Reich and presents the narratives of three individuals who, as teenagers, lived in the ghettos of Lodz, Theresienstadt, and Warsaw and survived physical deprivations, abuse, and deportation to the death camps

Includes bibliographical references

Inferno; June 1943—May 1945. Blackbirch Press 1998 80p il maps (Holocaust) lib bdg $19.45 **940.53**

1. Holocaust, 1933-1945 2. Holocaust survivors

ISBN 1-56711-205-6   LC 96-48528

Book 5 in the series "chronicles the last battles, resistance, rescue, and liberation. It includes a discussion of the plight of the Displaced Persons (DPs) and of U.S. President Harry Truman's efforts on their behalf." SLJ

Includes glossary and bibliographical references

Parallel journeys; [by] Eleanor H. Ayer with Helen Waterford and Alfons Heck. Atheneum Bks. for Young Readers 1995 244p il $16; pa $5.99 (7 and up) **940.53**

1. Holocaust, 1933-1945 2. Germany—History—1933-1945 3. Jews—Germany

ISBN 0-689-31830-8; 0-689-83236-2 (pa)

LC 94-23277

"Alternating chapters contrast the wartime experiences of two young Germans—Waterford, who was interned in a Nazi concentration camp, and Heck, a member of the Hitler Youth. The volume is composed mainly of excerpts from their published autobiographies, connected by Ayer's overall account of the era. A powerful and painful picture emerges, vividly describing life before, during, and, most impressively, after the Holocaust." Horn Book Guide

Includes bibliographical references

The survivors. Lucent Bks. 1998 96p il maps (Holocaust library) lib bdg $22.45 **940.53**

1. Holocaust survivors 2. Jewish refugees

ISBN 1-56006-096-4   LC 97-27260

Describes the conditions of Holocaust survivors when they were liberated as well as their struggle as they attempt to rebuild their lives

Includes glossary and bibliographical references

Bachrach, Susan D., 1948-

Tell them we remember; the story of the Holocaust. Little, Brown 1994 109p il maps $21.95; pa $14.95 **940.53**

1. United States Holocaust Memorial Museum 2. Holocaust, 1933-1945

ISBN 0-316-69264-6; 0-316-07484-5 (pa)

LC 93-40090

"Intended to extend the experience of the United States Holocaust Memorial Museum beyond its walls, this book reproduces some of its artifacts, photographs, maps, and taped oral and video histories. . . . Bachrach makes the victims of Hitler's cruelty immediate to readers, showing that, like readers, they were individuals with hobbies and desires, friends and families. . . . This is a very personal approach to Holocaust history and a very effective one." SLJ

Includes glossary and bibliographical references

Bitton-Jackson, Livia

I have lived a thousand years; growing up in the Holocaust; by Livia E. Bitton-Jackson. Simon & Schuster Bks. for Young Readers 1997 224p $17 (7 and up) **940.53**

1. Holocaust, 1933-1945—Personal narratives 2. Jews—Hungary

ISBN 0-689-81022-9   LC 96-19971

Based on the author's book for adults, Elli: coming of age in the Holocaust (1980)

"This memoir covers the last fourteen months of World War II, during which thirteen-year-old Elli Friedmann (as the author was then named) and members of her family are deported from their home . . . to two ghettos and several camps, including Auschwitz." Bull Cent Child Books

"This is a memorable addition to the searing accounts of Holocaust survivors." Horn Book

Includes glossary

Followed by My bridges of hope

Boas, Jacob

We are witnesses; five diaries of teenagers who died in the Holocaust. Holt & Co. 1995 196p $15.95 (7 and up) **940.53**

1. Holocaust, 1933-1945—Personal narratives 2. World War, 1939-1945—Jews 3. Jews—Europe

ISBN 0-8050-3702-0   LC 94-43889

Also available in paperback from Scholastic

"Narrative accounts of five young Jews, including Anne Frank, whose diaries hold their observations and emotions, give immediacy to the horrors of the Holocaust. The text provides historical information and compares the experiences of the diarists, quoting liberally from the teenagers' writings. Although these condensed versions lack the impact of a complete diary, the cumulative effect of the five journals is overwhelming." Horn Book Guide

Includes bibliographical references

Brimner, Larry Dane, 1949-
Voices from the camps; internment of Japanese Americans during World War II. Watts 1994 110p il $24 (7 and up)   **940.53**
1. Japanese Americans—Evacuation and relocation, 1942-1945 2. World War, 1939-1945—United States
ISBN 0-531-11179-2   LC 93-30201
This is "an account of the effect of American policy during World War II on Japanese Americans in California. The internment in prison camps is described through interviews with the survivors and their children." Publisher's note
"Brimner has done an effective job relating the various kinds of experiences that occurred as the Japanese Americans were forced to leave their homes and businesses, often selling them at a mere fraction of their worth, and journey to the various camps for their incarceration. . . . In addition, he has included a number of black and white photos that help to document the events." Voice Youth Advocates
Includes glossary and bibliographical references

Byers, Ann
The Holocaust overview. Enslow Pubs. 1998 128p il maps (Holocaust remembered series) lib bdg $19.95 (7 and up)   **940.53**
1. Holocaust, 1933-1945 2. Germany—Politics and government—1933-1945
ISBN 0-7660-1062-7   LC 97-37637
Examines Hitler's treatment of the Jews, before and during World War II, from their early exclusion from German society to the later policy of extermination
"Life in the concentration camps, liberation, and subsequent war-crimes trials are vividly described. This is a thorough and accurate book." SLJ
Includes glossary and bibliographical references

Chicoine, Stephen
From the ashes; June 1945 and after; by Stephen D. Chicoine and Eleanor H. Ayer. Blackbirch Press 1998 80p il map (Holocaust) lib bdg $19.45   **940.53**
1. Holocaust survivors 2. Jews—Europe
ISBN 1-56711-206-4   LC 96-47707
Book 6 in the series discusses the fate of those Jews who survived annihilation by the Nazis: their further persecution, search for a homeland in Palestine, and hunt for war criminals. Also examines other cases of genocide in Bosnia, Rwanda, and elsewhere
Includes glossary and bibliographical references

Feldman, George
Understanding the Holocaust. U.X.L 1998 2v il maps set $49   **940.53**
1. Holocaust, 1933-1945 2. Germany—Politics and government—1933-1945 3. Germany—History—1933-1945
ISBN 0-7876-1740-7   LC 97-26864
"This overview describes the Holocaust, the events that led up to it, and how the Nazis attempted to eradicate an entire people while fighting a war on two fronts. Sidebars provide information on related individuals,

events, and policies. Black-and-white photographs help clarify the text." SLJ
For a fuller review see: Booklist, Sept. 15, 1998
Includes bibliographical references

Finkelstein, Norman H., 1941-
Remember not to forget; a memory of the Holocaust; illustrations by Lois and Lars Hokanson. Watts 1985 31p il o.p.; Morrow paperback available $4.95   **940.53**
1. Holocaust, 1933-1945
ISBN 0-688-11802-X (pa)   LC 84-17315
"This spare, starkly illustrated book explains what the Holocaust was and how it is remembered on Yom Hashoa, Holocaust Remembrance Day. The explanation reaches back to the explusion of the Jews from Jerusalem in A.D. 70 and describes how Jews, strangers in many lands became targets of anti-Semitism, which culminated in the systematic murder of six million by the Nazis in World War II. The tone is straightforward and matter-of-fact. Black-and-white woodcuts accompany the text with somber scenes reflective of the narrative." Booklist

Fox, Anne L., 1926-
Ten thousand children; true stories told by children who escaped the Holocaust on the Kindertransport; by Anne L. Fox and Eva Abraham-Podietz. Behrman House 1998 128p il pa $12.95   **940.53**
1. Holocaust, 1933-1945—Personal narratives 2. Jewish refugees
ISBN 0-87441-648-5   LC 98-33600
Tells the true stories of children who escaped Nazi Germany on the Kindertransport, a rescue mission led by concerned British to save Jewish children from the Holocaust
"The design is like an open scrapbook, with different size typefaces, snapshots, news photos, and marginal notes; and the combination of the general overview with personal memories will bring readers, from middle grades through adult, close to the experience." Booklist

Friedman, Ina R.
The other victims; first-person stories of non-Jews persecuted by the Nazis. Houghton Mifflin 1990 214p hardcover o.p. paperback available $5.95   **940.53**
1. Persecution 2. World War, 1939-1945—Personal narratives
ISBN 0-395-74515-2 (pa)   LC 89-27036
Personal narratives of Christians, Gypsies, deaf people, homosexuals, and blacks who suffered at the hands of the Nazis before and during World War II
"Well organized and edited, the tales are harrowing, though they all end happily, often with escape or immigration to America and highly successful careers. Friedman points out that these were the lucky ones, and her book serves as a much-needed reminder that the Nazi nightmare extended far beyond Europe's Jewish population." Bull Cent Child Books
Includes bibliographical references

Gay, Kathlyn
World War II; [by] Kathlyn Gay, Martin Gay.
21st Cent. Bks. (NY) 1995 64p il maps (Voices
from the past) lib bdg $18.90 **940.53**
1. World War, 1939-1945
ISBN 0-8050-2849-8 LC 95-12301
An illustrated look at the battles, campaigns and
weapons of World War II. Military and political leaders
are profiled
"What enlivens the facts are the individual eye-witness
stories of ordinary people who were there. The excerpts
from letters, memoirs, and interviews make immediate
the American experience, at the battle front and at
home." Booklist
Includes bibliographical references

The Holocaust; editor, Geoffrey Wigoder. Grolier
Educ. 1997 4v il maps set $169 **940.53**
1. Holocaust, 1933-1945—Encyclopedias
ISBN 0-7172-7637-6 LC 96-9566
"A Grolier student library"
Contents: v1 Abwehr to extermination camps; v2
Family camps to Lvov; v3 Macedonia to Szenes; v4 Teh-
ran children to Zyklon B
Articles identify and describe individuals and events
connected with the persecution of Jews and others across
Europe in the 1930s and 1940s
"Essential for middle-school libraries and useful wher-
ever a basic guide on the Holocaust is required." Libr J

Houston, Jeanne Wakatsuki, 1933-
Farewell to Manzanar; a true story of Japanese
American experience during and after World War
II internment; [by] Jeanne Wakatsuki Houston &
James D. Houston. Houghton Mifflin 1973 177p
o.p.; Bantam Bks. paperback available $5.99 (7
and up) **940.53**
1. Japanese Americans—Evacuation and relocation,
1942-1945 2. World War, 1939-1945—United States
ISBN 0-553-27258-6 (pa)
"The author tells of the three years she and her family
spent at Manzanar, a Japanese internment camp. . . .
The last part of the book deals with her post-war adolescence and re-entry into American life." Libr J
"A spare, powerful memoir." Rochman. Against borders

Isserman, Maurice
World War II. Facts on File 1991 184p il maps
(America at war) lib bdg $19.95 (7 and up)
940.53
1. World War, 1939-1945—United States 2. United
States—History—1933-1945
ISBN 0-8160-2374-3 LC 90-25840
This history of the American experience in World War
II "provides a broad, well-organized overview. Chapters
on specific aspects, such as the effect of the war on
women and minorities, are smoothly interspersed into the
narrative." SLJ
Includes bibliographical references

Kinderlager; an oral history of young Holocaust
survivors; edited by Milton J. Nieuwsma.
Holiday House 1998 161p il map $18.95 (7 and
up) **940.53**
1. Holocaust, 1933-1945—Personal narratives
2. Holocaust survivors 3. Auschwitz (Poland: Concentration camp)
ISBN 0-8234-1358-6 LC 97-34959
Draws on interviews with three women who recount
their experiences as child survivors of Auschwitz-
Birkenau, the Nazi death camp
These "accounts combine the immediacy of the child's
experience with the sophistication of adult hindsight. The
occasional haunting family photographs document all that
is lost, but contemporary photos show each survivor with
her children and grandchildren." Booklist
Includes glossary and bibliographical references

Kustanowitz, Esther
The hidden children of the Holocaust; teens who
hid from the Nazis. Rosen Pub. Group 1998 64p
il map (Teen witnesses to the Holocaust) $17.95 (7
and up) **940.53**
1. Holocaust, 1933-1945—Personal narratives
2. World War, 1939-1945—Jews—Rescue
ISBN 0-8239-2562-5 LC 98-32072
In their own words, details the experiences of Jewish
teenagers hiding from the Nazis
Includes bibliographical references

Lace, William W.
The death camps. Lucent Bks. 1998 112p il
(Holocaust library) lib bdg $22.45 (7 and up)
940.53
1. Holocaust, 1933-1945 2. Concentration camps
ISBN 1-56006-094-8 LC 97-36192
Describes the establishment of concentration camps
throughout Nazi-occupied territory whose sole purpose
was to exterminate Jews and other people considered un-
desirable by Hitler and his followers
Includes bibliographical references

Leapman, Michael, 1938-
Witnesses to war; eight true-life stories of Nazi
persecution. Viking 1998 127p il maps $16.99
940.53
1. Holocaust, 1933-1945 2. World War, 1939-1945—
Children
ISBN 0-670-87386-1 LC 98-208868
The author "suggests the far reaches of Nazi terror by
focusing on the experiences of eight children, each victimized during WWII." Publ Wkly
"Leapman presents an authoritative, informative, and
attractive work. . . . The narrative is riveting." Voice
Youth Advocates

Levine, Ellen
A fence away from freedom;
Japanese-Americans and World War II. Putnam
1995 260p il map $18.95 (7 and up) **940.53**
1. Japanese Americans—Evacuation and relocation,
1942-1945 2. World War, 1939-1945—United States
ISBN 0-399-22638-9 LC 95-13357

Levine, Ellen—*Continued*

This book "reveals little known facts about the internment of Japanese-Americans during World War II and its aftermath. Levine interviewed evacuees who were children and teenagers at the time and who were interned in all the states in which camps were established. She intersperses their stories with her narrative of the 'relocation.'" Book Rep

"This is an excellent source of information about a period of our history that is just beginning to be fully examined." SLJ

Includes bibliographical references

Mandell, Sherri Lederman

Writers of the Holocaust. Facts on File 1999 xxvi, 132p il maps (Global profiles) $19.95 (7 and up)   **940.53**

1. Holocaust, 1933-1945—Personal narratives
2. Jews—Biography

ISBN 0-8160-3729-9   LC 98-23601

Profiles ten men and women who have written about or whose writings were influenced by their experiences during the Holocaust

"There's a general historical overview; and then, with each writer's profile, Mandell weaves in general facts and statistics. She ends each chapter with a briefly annotated bibliography. . . . This is an excellent Holocaust curriculum resource for students and teachers who want to know what to read." Booklist

McGowen, Tom

World War II. Watts 1993 64p il maps lib bdg $22; pa $6.95   **940.53**

1. World War, 1939-1945

ISBN 0-531-20150-3 (lib bdg); 0-531-15661-3 (pa)   LC 92-28328

"A First book"

Provides an overview of the military battles and political changes that occurred during World War II

Includes bibliographical references

Meltzer, Milton, 1915-

Never to forget: the Jews of the Holocaust. Harper & Row 1976 217p maps lib bdg $15.89; pa $6.95   **940.53**

1. Holocaust, 1933-1945

ISBN 0-06-024175-6 (lib bdg); 0-06-446118-1 (pa)   LC 75-25409

"The mass murder of six million Jews by the Nazis during World War II is the subject of this compelling history. Interweaving background information, chilling statistics, individual accounts and newspaper reports, it provides an excellent introduction to its subject." Interracial Books Child Bull

Includes bibliographical references

Rescue: the story of how Gentiles saved Jews in the Holocaust. Harper & Row 1988 168p il maps $16.89; lib bdg $15.89; pa $6.95   **940.53**

1. World War, 1939-1945—Jews—Rescue 2. Holocaust, 1933-1945

ISBN 0-06-024209-4; 0-06-024210-8 (lib bdg); 0-06-446117-3 (pa)   LC 87-47816

A recounting drawn from historic source material of the many individual acts of heroism performed by righteous gentiles who sought to thwart the extermination of the Jews during the Holocaust

"This is an excellent portrayal of a difficult topic. Meltzer manages to both explain without accusing, and to laud without glorifying. . . . The discussion of the complicated relations between countries are clear, but not simplistic. An impressive aspect of this book is its lack of didacticism." Voice Youth Advocates

Includes bibliographical references

O'Neill, William L.

World War II: a student companion. Oxford Univ. Press 1999 384p il (Oxford student companions to American history) lib bdg $40 (7 and up)   **940.53**

1. World War, 1939-1945

ISBN 0-19-510800-0   LC 98-54918

In this volume "the war is covered on all fronts, with entries on individuals, battles, military organizations, theaters, origins, weapon systems, and countries. . . . Articles vary in length from two or three paragraphs to several pages. . . . *Literature* and *motion pictures* have brief lists of classic World War II novels and films, respectively. A chronology, a list of museums and historic sites, and a general bibliography that includes Web sites give students additional tools to expand their original search." Booklist

"A readable, concise, and informative book." SLJ

Opdyke, Irene Gut, 1921-

In my hands; memories of a Holocaust rescuer; [by] Irene Gut Opdyke with Jennifer Armstrong. Knopf 1999 276p il $18; lib bdg $19.99 (7 and up)   **940.53**

1. World War, 1939-1945—Jews—Rescue 2. World War, 1939-1945—Personal narratives 3. Holocaust, 1933-1945 4. World War, 1939-1945—Poland

ISBN 0-679-89181-1; 0-679-99181-6 (lib bdg)   LC 98-54095

Recounts the experiences of the author who, as a young Polish girl, hid and saved Jews during the Holocaust

"No matter how many Holocaust stories one has read, this one is a must, for its impact is so powerful. . . . Opdyke's remarkable story is simply told, with clarity and feeling." SLJ

Perl, Lila

Four perfect pebbles; a Holocaust story; by Lila Perl and Marion Blumenthal Lazan. Greenwillow Bks. 1996 130p il $15 (7 and up)   **940.53**

1. Holocaust, 1933-1945—Personal narratives
2. Jews—Germany

ISBN 0-688-14294-X   LC 95-9752

"Starting with a description of one of the days that Marion Blumenthal Lazan survived in Bergen-Belsen, this chronicle of her experiences during the Holocaust then goes further back for a look at her family's secure prewar life in Germany. . . . Hitler's policies cut off their living and endanger their lives as they move to

Perl, Lila—_Continued_

Hanover, flee to Holland, are deported from Westerbork to Bergen-Belsen, and finally are shipped on a death train toward Auschwitz before the Russians liberate them." Bull Cent Child Books

"This book warrants attention both for the uncommon experiences it records and for the fullness of that record. . . . Quotes from Lazan's 87-year-old mother are invaluable—her memories of the family's experiences afford Marion's story a precision and wholeness rarely available to child survivors." Publ Wkly

Includes bibliographical references

Rogasky, Barbara

Smoke and ashes: the story of the Holocaust. Holiday House 1988 187p il maps $19.95; pa $12.95 **940.53**
1. Holocaust, 1933-1945
ISBN 0-8234-0697-0; 0-8234-0878-7 (pa)
LC 87-28617

The author "details the dark horror of Nazism—from the beginning pogroms the Nazis organized against German Jews to the setting up of concentration camps and death factories. She utilizes many primary sources . . . to tell the story of mass murder. In clear and simple prose, she relates how the Jews lived and died in the camps, how they fought and prayed, how a few escaped, and how a small number of non-Jews helped them in their struggle. She concludes with an account of the Nuremburg Trials and the many instances of contemporary anti-Semitism that have outlived Hitler." SLJ

Includes bibliographical references

Rosenberg, Maxine B., 1939-

Hiding to survive; stories of Jewish children rescued from the Holocaust. Clarion Bks. 1994 166p il $16; pa $8.95 **940.53**
1. Holocaust, 1933-1945—Personal narratives
2. Holocaust survivors
ISBN 0-395-65014-3; 0-395-90020-4 (pa)
LC 93-28328

First person accounts of fourteen Holocaust survivors who as children were hidden from the Nazis by non-Jews

"Told in plain, unvarnished language of childhood memories, these harrowing first-person accounts are particularly moving in their straightforward simplicity, and all are accompanied by photos of the survivors as children and as they are today." Voice Youth Advocates

Includes glossary and bibliographical references

Sender, Ruth Minsky, 1926-

The cage. Macmillan 1986 245p o.p.; Simon & Schuster paperback available $4.50 (7 and up) **940.53**
1. Holocaust, 1933-1945—Personal narratives
ISBN 0-689-81321-X (pa)
LC 86-8562

"In the first section of the book, [the author] recalls her widowed mother's deportation and her attempts to support three younger brothers through the hunger, illness, and persecution that plagued residents of the Lodz ghetto in Nazi-occupied Poland. The second half relates her experiences in the Auschwitz death camp and, later, the work camp at Mitelsteine, where she had the strength

and luck to survive, barely." Bull Cent Child Books

"Hers is an unsparing and pain-filled record that some teenagers will surely find too harrowing and too disjointed to pursue. Yet its very explicitness makes it important documentary material." Booklist

To life. Macmillan 1988 229p $14.95 (7 and up) **940.53**
1. Holocaust, 1933-1945—Personal narratives
2. Holocaust survivors
ISBN 0-02-781831-4
LC 88-9312

In this continuation of her memoirs, Holocaust survivor Sender recounts her liberation from a Nazi concentration camp, search for surviving family members, and long and difficult ordeal of trying to immigrate with her husband and two children to America

"A powerful, poetic account of the problems and terrors faced by Jewish survivors of World War II." Soc Educ

Sherrow, Victoria

The blaze engulfs; January 1939—December 1941. Blackbirch Press 1998 80p il map (Holocaust) lib bdg $19.45 **940.53**
1. Holocaust, 1933-1945
ISBN 1-56711-202-1
LC 96-37216

Book 3 in the series "begins with Germany's invasion of Poland and Czechoslovakia, and ends with the forming of the Axis partners. . . . Those who helped the Jews are not neglected, nor are the complex relations between Poles and Jews. The presence of little known information and quotes throughout reveal the depth of the author's research." SLJ

Includes glossary and bibliographical references

The righteous gentiles. Lucent Bks. 1998 112p il (Holocaust library) lib bdg $22.45 (7 and up) **940.53**
1. Holocaust, 1933-1945 2. World War, 1939-1945—Jews—Rescue
ISBN 1-56006-093-X
LC 97-36191

Presents an overview of non-Jews throughout Europe who tried to save Jews from persecution and extermination by the Nazis

Includes bibliographical references

Smoke to flame; September 1935 - December 1938. Blackbirch Press 1998 80p il maps (Holocaust) lib bdg $19.45 **940.53**
1. Holocaust, 1933-1945 2. Jews—Persecutions
ISBN 1-567-11201-3
LC 96-52206

Book 2 in the Holocaust series. This volume provides "a description of and commentary on the increasing anti-Semitism and restrictions upon the Jews, first in Germany and then in other countries as conditions deteriorated and panic escalated throughout Europe." SLJ

Includes glossary and bibliographical references

Shulman, William L.

Resource guide; a comprehensive listing of media for further study; compiled by William L. Shulman. Blackbirch Press 1998 80p il (Holocaust) lib bdg $19.45 **940.53**
1. Holocaust, 1933-1945—Bibliography
ISBN 1-567-11208-0
LC 97-19132

Shulman, William L.—Continued
Book 8 in this series, this volume lists sources of information about the Holocaust including books, CD-ROMs, videos, Web sites, museums, and resource centers
This "will be invaluable for librarians and educators."
Booklist

Spiegelman, Art
Maus; a survivor's tale. Pantheon Bks. 1996 2v in 1 il $35 (7 and up)   **940.53**
1. Spiegelman, Vladek 2. Holocaust, 1933-1945
ISBN 0-679-40641-7   LC 96-32796
A combined edition of Maus (1986) and Maus II (1991)
Contents: My father bleeds history; And here my troubles began
In this work "Spiegelman takes the comic book to a new level of seriousness, portraying Jews as mice and Nazis as cats. Depicting himself being told about the Holocaust by his Polish survivor father, Spiegelman not only explores the concentration-camp experience, but also the guilt, love, and anger between father and son." Rochman. Against borders

Stanley, Jerry, 1941-
I am an American; a true story of Japanese internment. Crown 1994 102p il $18; lib bdg $17.99; pa $9.99   **940.53**
1. Japanese Americans—Evacuation and relocation, 1942-1945 2. World War, 1939-1945—United States
ISBN 0-517-59786-1; 0-517-59787-X (lib bdg); 0-517-88551-4 (pa)   LC 93-41330
The author discusses "the internment of Japanese-Americans during World War II. He has spun a cogent narrative of the shameful events, focusing them through the experiences of Shi Nomura, a high school student sent with his family to Manzanar in 1942. . . . This is a first-rate, readable introduction to this particular part of history, and it's complemented by a spacious page design, numerous black-and-white photos, an exemplary bibliographic note, and an index." Bull Cent Child Books

Strahinich, Helen, 1949-
The Holocaust; understanding and remembering. Enslow Pubs. 1996 112p il map (Issues in focus) lib bdg $19.95 (7 and up)   **940.53**
1. Holocaust, 1933-1945
ISBN 0-89490-725-5   LC 96-1889
This book "leads readers chronologically from Hitler's rise to power, through the devastation of the Holocaust, to its aftermath. The text consistently examines hard-to-answer questions such as: Why did so many Jewish people remain in Germany? Why didn't the German people do anything to save their Jewish citizens? What were the roots of anti-Semitism? The clean layout helps make difficult ideas and information comprehensible, and includes clear maps, appropriate black-and-white photographs, and crisp charts. . . . In addition, this book discusses other groups of people whom the Nazis persecuted: the Gypsies, the Polish elite, homosexuals, etc." SLJ
Includes glossary and bibliographical references

Tunnell, Michael O.
The children of Topaz; the story of a Japanese-American internment camp; based on a classroom diary; by Michael O. Tunnell and George W. Chilcoat. Holiday House 1996 74p il $16.95   **940.53**
1. Central Utah Relocation Center 2. Japanese Americans—Evacuation and relocation, 1942-1945 3. World War, 1939-1945—Children
ISBN 0-8234-1239-3   LC 95-49360
"Interned behind barbed wire in a desert relocation camp in Topaz, Utah, Japanese American teacher Lillian 'Anne' Yamauchi Hori kept a classroom diary with her third-grade class from May to August 1943. . . . Twenty of the small diary entries appear in this book, together with several black-and-white archival photos of the camps. Tunnell and Chilcoat provide a long historical introduction and then detailed commentary that puts each diary entry in the context of what was happening in the camp and in the country at war. . . . The primary sources have a stark authority; it's the very ordinariness of the children's concerns that grabs you." Booklist
Includes bibliographical references

Voices and visions; a collection of primary sources; compiled by William L. Shulman. Blackbirch Press 1998 80p il (Holocaust) lib bdg $19.45   **940.53**
1. Holocaust, 1933-1945—Personal narratives 2. Holocaust survivors
ISBN 1-567-11207-2   LC 97-2578
Book 7 in the series is a compilation of personal narratives of people who survived the Holocaust
This "is especially well designed for classroom and group discussion as well as for personal reading." Booklist
Includes glossary and bibliographical references

We survived the Holocaust; [edited] by Elaine Landau. Watts 1991 144p il lib bdg $24   **940.53**
1. Holocaust, 1933-1945—Personal narratives 2. Holocaust survivors
ISBN 0-531-11115-6   LC 91-16982
"This book consists of brief (three-to-eight page) accounts by 16 survivors of the Nazi persecution of the Jews during World War II." Voice Youth Advocates
"Poignant and moving memories, presented in a straightforward manner." SLJ
Includes glossary and bibliographical references

940.54 World War II, 1939-1945
(Military conduct of the war)

Aaseng, Nathan, 1953-
Navajo code talkers. Walker & Co. 1992 114p il map $15.95; lib bdg $16.85   **940.54**
1. World War, 1939-1945 2. Navajo Indians 3. Cryptography
ISBN 0-8027-8182-9; 0-8027-8183-7 (lib bdg)
          LC 92-11408

Aaseng, Nathan, 1953-—*Continued*
Describes how the American military in World War II used a group of Navajo Indians to create an indecipherable code based on their native language
"A good choice for an offbeat 'war book,' this would also make an unusual complement for both history and language arts classes. Historical photos of the code-talkers in action are included." Bull Cent Child Books
Includes bibliographical references

Anderson, Madelyn Klein
So proudly they served; American military women in World War II. Watts 1995 63p il lib bdg $22   **940.54**
1. Women in the armed forces 2. World War, 1939-1945—Women
ISBN 0-531-20197-X   LC 94-39907
"A First book"
This outlines the role of women in the armed forces during World War II, and traces the history of discrimination against women in the military from the American Revolution to the present
Includes bibliographical references

Cooper, Michael L., 1950-
The double V campaign; African Americans and World War II. Lodestar Bks. 1998 86p il maps $16.99   **940.54**
1. World War, 1939-1945—African Americans 2. African American soldiers 3. United States—Race relations
ISBN 0-525-67562-0   LC 97-28229
Recounts how African Americans fought two wars during World War II, one against enemy dictators abroad and the other against racial discrimination at home
"Numerous black-and-white photographs show the participation of these men and women in all aspects of the war effort. This book will draw both report writers and general readers." SLJ
Includes bibliographical references

Durrett, Deanne, 1940-
Unsung heroes of World War II; the story of the Navajo code talkers. Facts on File 1998 122p il (Library of American Indian history) $19.95 (7 and up)   **940.54**
1. World War, 1939-1945 2. Navajo Indians 3. Cryptography
ISBN 0-8160-3603-9   LC 97-50083
Describes the role of a select group of Navajo Marines who developed a code based on their own native language that provided a means for secure communications among American forces in the Pacific during World War II
"Astounding facts, as well as stirring personal accounts of battle, make for fascinating, educational reading." Booklist
Includes bibliographical references

Grant, R. G. (Reg G.)
Hiroshima and Nagasaki. Raintree Steck-Vaughn Pubs. 1998 64p il (New perspectives) lib bdg $27.12 (7 and up)   **940.54**
1. Atomic bomb 2. Hiroshima (Japan)—Bombardment, 1945 3. Nagasaki (Japan)—Bombardment, 1945
ISBN 0-8172-5013-1   LC 97-3250
Describes the causes and horrible effects of the 1945 bombing of Hiroshima and Nagasaki
This combines "a clear historical perspective, vivid personal accounts, and contemporary viewpoints from all sides. The writing is direct and detailed." Booklist
Includes glossary and bibliographical references

Harris, Jacqueline L., 1929-
The Tuskegee airmen; black heroes of World War II. Dillon Press 1996 144p il maps $13.95; pa $7.95   **940.54**
1. World War, 1939-1945—Aerial operations 2. African American pilots 3. World War, 1939-1945—African Americans
ISBN 0-382-39215-9; 0-382-39217-5 (pa)
    LC 95-14366
"Harris recounts the story of African American aviators who fought against prejudice in the U.S. in order to become fighter pilots during World War II. She discusses early black fliers and their difficulties recruiting others, which eventually led to the formation of the all-black Ninety-ninth Fighter Squadron. . . . This will make an excellent introduction to a frequently neglected chapter in American history." Booklist
Includes bibliographical references

Maruki, Toshi, 1912-
Hiroshima no pika; words and pictures by Toshi Maruki. Lothrop, Lee & Shepard Bks. 1982 c1980 unp il $16   **940.54**
1. Hiroshima (Japan)—Bombardment, 1945 2. World War, 1939-1945—Japan
ISBN 0-688-01297-3   LC 82-15365
First published 1980 in Japan
Focusing on the experiences of a real family "the horrifying story of the atomic bombing or 'flash' of Hiroshima is told here with a remarkable eloquence, including many poignant details. The story is terribly disturbing and painful to read, but the narrative is at the same time so spare and compelling one must go on. . . . Although it is in picture book format, this is *definitely* not a book for elementary school children. Young people twelve and over, as well as adults, should know this terrible story. This superb book can begin to tell it to them." Appraisal

McGowen, Tom
Germany's lightning war; Panzer divisions of World War II. 21st Cent. Bks. (Brookfield) 1999 64p il (Military might) lib bdg $23.90   **940.54**
1. World War, 1939-1945—Germany 2. Military tanks
ISBN 0-7613-1511-X   LC 98-44009
Discusses the development and actions of German tank units in World War II, covering specific battles and the changes that tanks brought to warfare in general
This book "should inspire youngsters to pursue their interest in the subject." SLJ

McGowen, Tom—*Continued*

Sink the Bismarck; Germany's super-battleship of World War II. 21st Cent. Bks. (Brookfield) 1999 64p il (Military might) lib bdg $23.90
940.54
1. Bismarck (Battleship) 2. World War, 1939-1945—Naval operations
ISBN 0-7613-1510-1   LC 98-48500
Describes the actions of the German battleship "Bismarck" during World War II and the operations of the British navy to destroy this ship
The presentation is "straightforward, simple. . . . The writing is . . . easy to follow." SLJ

McKissack, Patricia C., 1944-
Red-tail angels: the story of the Tuskegee airmen of World War II; [by] Patricia and Fredrick McKissack. Walker & Co. 1995 136p il maps $19.95; lib bdg $20.85   **940.54**
1. African American pilots 2. World War, 1939-1945—Aerial operations 3. World War, 1939-1945—African Americans
ISBN 0-8027-8292-2; 0-8027-8293-0 (lib bdg)
LC 95-15223
"After a brief account of African American aviation pioneers, [the authors] focus on the formation and training of the 332nd Fighter Group and its exploits in the North African and European campaigns of World War II." Booklist
"This attractive book has a wonderful collection of seldom-seen historical photos and an extensive bibliography of secondary and primary sources (interviews)." SLJ

Rice, Earle
The attack on Pearl Harbor. Lucent Bks. 1998 111p il maps (Battles of World War II) lib bdg $26.20 (7 and up)   **940.54**
1. Pearl Harbor (Oahu, Hawaii), Attack on, 1941
ISBN 1-56006-421-8   LC 95-35504
This "account gives readers sufficient background information concerning the Japanese and American roles in the Pacific and Far East from the opening of trade with Japan in 1853 to 1941. This discussion leads to the conclusion that the events of December 7, 1941, were almost inevitable and the lack of preparedness on the part of the U.S. was a 'seeming invitation to disaster. The author covers in great detail the plans for the Japanese attack and descriptions of what occurred on the fateful day itself. . . . The extensive use of primary-source material makes history come alive." SLJ
Includes glossary and bibliographical references

Stein, R. Conrad, 1937-
World War II in Europe; "America goes to war". Enslow Pubs. 1994 128p il maps (American war series) lib bdg $19.95   **940.54**
1. World War, 1939-1945—Campaigns
ISBN 0-89490-525-2   LC 93-47396
"Stein commences with a reprise of the opening shots on the Polish frontier in 1939 and takes a quick look at Nazi Germany's origins and subsequent 'lightning war'

across Europe. Coverage moves quickly onward to the attack on Pearl Harbor, Germany's declaration of war on America, through V-E Day and the conclusion of hostilities with Japan. . . . [This offers] the interest-holding and informative prose befitting such an introductory title. Furthermore, Stein has appended a useful chronology, detailed chapter notes, a short list of books for further reading, and a helpful index; these features add greatly to the book's value." SLJ

World War II in the Pacific; "remember Pearl Harbor". Enslow Pubs. 1994 128p il maps (American war series) lib bdg $19.95   **940.54**
1. World War, 1939-1945—Campaigns—Pacific Ocean
ISBN 0-89490-524-4   LC 93-33623
This is an "overview of U.S. participation in the Pacific war. . . . Stein packs a great deal of information into this slim volume and manages to do so without oversimplification. The narrative is arranged in basic chronological order . . . and is enlivened by direct, nononsense prose, the prudent use of quotations, black-and-white archival photographs, and helpful maps." SLJ
Includes bibliographical references

941   British Isles

Fuller, Barbara, 1961-
Britain. Reference ed. Marshall Cavendish 1994 128p il map (Cultures of the world) lib bdg $24.95
941
1. Great Britain
ISBN 1-85435-587-2   LC 93-45745
An introduction to Great Britain's "history, current economic and governmental systems, religion, language, arts, and lifestyles." Horn Book Guide
This is "attractive, readable, and current." SLJ
Includes glossary and bibliographical references

The **Young** Oxford history of Britain & Ireland; [by] Mike Corbishley [et al.]; general editor, Kenneth O. Morgan. Oxford Univ. Press 1997 415p il $39.95 (7 and up)   **941**
1. Great Britain—History 2. Ireland—History
ISBN 0-19-910035-7   LC 97-19451
Surveys the social, economic, cultural, and technological developments in Great Britain and Ireland from the time of the first inhabitants through the twentieth century
"The value of this title is in pulling together so much information into one well-organized and readable volume." SLJ

941.6   Ulster. Northern Ireland

McMahon, Patricia
One Belfast boy; photographs by Alan O'Connor. Houghton Mifflin 1999 54p il maps $16   **941.6**
1. Belfast (Northern Ireland)—Social life and customs
ISBN 0-395-68620-2   LC 98-28568

McMahon, Patricia—*Continued*
Describes the life of Liam Leatham, a young Catholic boy, and his family as he prepares for a boxing match that he sees as the first step out of violence-plagued Belfast
"A fine balance of hard-hitting facts and lyrical passages. . . . A preface cogently sorts out Ireland's complex, strife-torn history." Publ Wkly

Meyer, Carolyn
Voices of Northern Ireland; growing up in a troubled land. Harcourt Brace Jovanovich 1987 212p maps $15.95; pa $9.95 (7 and up)   **941.6**
1. Northern Ireland—Social conditions 2. Northern Ireland—Description
ISBN 0-15-200635-4; 0-15-200638-9 (pa)
LC 87-199
"Gulliver books"
This book is a "first hand account of the 'Troubles' in Northern Ireland that have made that country a political hotspot. For six weeks during the summer of 1986, [the author] traveled throughout the country's six counties while interviewing people from all walks of life, both Protestant and Catholic. Her candid narratives reveal centuries old bigotries fostered by a narrow educational system and a socio-economic order based on privilege and power." Voice Youth Advocates
Includes bibliographical references

942 England and Wales

Lace, William W.
England. Lucent Bks. 1997 128p il maps (Modern nations of the world) lib bdg $22.45 (7 and up)   **942**
1. England
ISBN 1-56006-194-4
LC 96-40121
Examines the land, people, and history of England and discusses its state of affairs and place in the world today
This "is full of reliable facts packaged in a compact and easily accessible format." SLJ
Includes bibliographical references

Lister, Maree
England. Stevens, G. 1998 96p il (Countries of the world) lib bdg $26.20   **942**
1. England
ISBN 0-8368-2125-4
LC 98-13067
Introduces the geography, history, economy, government, culture, food, and people of England
This book "will provide students with a solid introduction." SLJ
Includes glossary and bibliographical references

942.03 England—Period of House of Plantagenet, 1154-1399

Sancha, Sheila, 1924-
The Luttrell village; country life in the Middle Ages. Crowell 1983 c1982 64p il $13.95; lib bdg $13.89   **942.03**
1. England—Social life and customs 2. Country life—England 3. Medieval civilization
ISBN 0-690-04323-6; 0-690-04324-4 (lib bdg)
LC 82-45588
First published 1982 in Scotland
"Between 1320 and 1340 Sir Geoffrey Luttrell commissioned an artist to make drawings of daily life in his village; it is from this psalter . . . as well as other sources, that Sancha has created this book. . . . She introduces children to a typical year in 14th-Century Gerneham." SLJ
"Elaborate ink-and wash illustrations—many clearly labeled—fill the pages, showing countryside panoramas, cutaway buildings and the countryfolk themselves working at various tasks. . . . The book presents an exceptionally fine portrait of medieval life." Horn Book
Includes glossary

942.05 England—Tudor period, 1485-1603

Ashby, Ruth
Elizabethan England. Benchmark Bks. (Tarrytown) 1999 80p il (Cultures of the past) lib bdg $19.95   **942.05**
1. Great Britain—History—1485-1603, Tudors 2. England—Social life and customs 3. Sixteenth century
ISBN 0-7614-0269-1
LC 96-43868
Examines the history, culture, religion, and social conditions of sixteenth-century England, during the reign of Queen Elizabeth I
This is "an effective presentation, enhanced by colorful illustrations and graphics." SLJ
Includes glossary and bibliographical references

943 Central Europe. Germany

Ayer, Eleanor H.
Germany. Lucent Bks. 1999 112p il maps (Modern nations of the world) lib bdg $22.45 (7 and up)   **943**
1. Germany
ISBN 1-56006-355-6
LC 98-15471
Examines the land, people, and history of Germany and discusses its state of affairs and place in the world today
"A volume that stands on its own as a fine little history book. . . . Rich in sharp, interesting details. . . . Interspersed throughout each section are well-chosen black-and-white illustrations." Booklist
Includes bibliographical references

943.086   Germany—Period of Third Reich, 1933-1945

Lace, William W.
The Nazis. Lucent Bks. 1998 111p il (Holocaust library) lib bdg $22.45 (7 and up)   **943.086**
1. Hitler, Adolf, 1889-1945 2. National socialism 3. Germany—History—1933-1945
ISBN 1-56006-091-3   LC 97-21376
A history of the Nazi movement in Germany beginning in 1919 with the German Workers' Party and including discussion of Adolf Hitler, anti-Semitism, and World War II
This offers "an excellent selection of period photographs and salted with pithy quotations." SLJ
Includes bibliographical references

The **Rise** of Nazi Germany; Don Nardo, book editor. Greenhaven Press 1999 240p (Turning points in world history) lib bdg $20.96; pa $12.96 (7 and up)   **943.086**
1. Hitler, Adolf, 1889-1945 2. National socialism 3. Germany—Politics and government—1933-1945
ISBN 1-56510-965-1 (lib bdg); 1-56510-964-3 (pa)
          LC 98-8404
"This book contains well-chosen excerpts of essays and books written by historians. They describe Hitler's roots, his rise to power, why Germany succumbed to the dictator's diabolical politics, how he remade German society, how and why Hitler so easily conquered established European countries, and, finally, what led to the fall of the Nazi empire. . . . An appendix with excerpts of primary documents written by Hitler and his supporters and opponents further illuminate the issues addressed in the main body of the book. A useful overview and cogent analysis." SLJ
Includes bibliographical references

943.087   Germany—1945-1999

Grant, R. G. (Reg G.)
The Berlin Wall. Raintree Steck-Vaughn Pubs. 1999 64p il maps (New perspectives) $27.12
          943.087
1. Berlin Wall (1961-1989) 2. Germany—Politics and government—1945-1990
ISBN 0-8172-5017-4   LC 97-51149
Discusses the history of the Berlin Wall from its building, through life with tensions this barrier created, to the destruction of the wall and life afterwards
Includes glossary and bibliographical references

Westerfeld, Scott
The Berlin airlift. Silver Burdett Press 1989 64p il maps (Turning points in American history) lib bdg $14.95; pa $7.95   **943.087**
1. Berlin (Germany)—History
ISBN 0-382-09833-1 (lib bdg); 0-382-09852-8 (pa)
          LC 89-6173

The author "gives solid background on the causes and conditions that lead the Soviets to blockade West Berlin. . . . The last quarter of the book outlines the beginnings of the cold war and both the United States' and the USSR's involvement in the foreign affairs of other countries." SLJ
Includes bibliographical references

943.7   Czech Republic and Slovakia

Sioras, Efstathia
Czech Republic. Marshall Cavendish 1999 128p il maps (Cultures of the world) lib bdg $35.64
          943.7
1. Czech Republic
ISBN 0-7614-0870-3   LC 98-30290
Describes the geography, history, government, economy, people, lifestyle, religion, language, arts, leisure, festivals, and food of the Czech Republic
Includes glossary and bibliographical references

943.8   Poland

Hintz, Martin, 1945-
Poland. Children's Press 1998 144p il (Enchantment of the world, second series) lib bdg $32   **943.8**
1. Poland
ISBN 0-516-20605-2   LC 97-25559
Describes the history, geography, economy, plants and animals, language, religion, sports, arts, and people of this central European country which has ties to both East and West
Includes bibliographical references

943.9   Hungary

Steins, Richard
Hungary; crossroads of Europe. Benchmark Bks. (Tarrytown) 1997 64p il (Exploring cultures of the world) $27.07   **943.9**
1. Hungary
ISBN 0-7614-0141-5   LC 96-51582
Describes the geography, history, culture, and people of Hungary
"Color photographs and easy-to-read [text makes the book] accessible and appealing." Horn Book
Includes glossary and bibliographical references

944   France and Monaco

NgCheong-Lum, Roseline, 1962-
France. Stevens, G. 1999 96p il (Countries of the world) lib bdg $18.95   **944**
1. France
ISBN 0-8368-2260-9   LC 98-33770
An overview of France, discussing its history, geography, government, economy, culture, and relations with North America
"The full-color photos on every page are outstanding and the style of writing is graceful." SLJ
Includes glossary and bibliographical references

944.04 France—Revolutionary period, 1789-1804

Banfield, Susan
The rights of man, the reign of terror: the story of the French Revolution. Lippincott 1989 213p il $15; lib bdg $14.89 (7 and up) **944.04**
1. France—History—1789-1799, Revolution
ISBN 0-397-32353-0; 0-397-32354-9 (lib bdg)
LC 89-2742
Recounts the political, social, and economic turmoil that took place during the French Revolution
"Each chapter begins with a calendar of main events and has many subheadings which explain in detail what happened and exactly why. The impartial view of the events is Banfield's best feature." Voice Youth Advocates
Includes bibliographical references

The **French** Revolution; Don Nardo, book editor. Greenhaven Press 1999 223p (Turning points in world history) lib bdg $20.96; pa $12.96 (7 and up) **944.04**
1. France—History—1789-1799, Revolution
ISBN 1-56510-934-1 (lib bdg); 1-56510-933-3 (pa)
LC 98-16604
"After a historical summary, 19 essays are presented in four sections, covering causes, significant events, social and cultural aspects, and the impact and legacy of the Revolution. An appendix contains excerpts from 26 original documents relevant to the topic. . . . The book is thorough and thought-provoking." SLJ
Includes bibliographical references

944.05 France—Period of First Empire, 1804-1815

Henderson, Harry, 1951-
The age of Napoleon. Lucent Bks. 1999 112p il maps (World history series) lib bdg $18.96 (7 and up) **944.05**
1. Napoleon I, Emperor of the French, 1769-1821
2. France—History—1799-1815
ISBN 1-56006-319-X
LC 98-8372
Discusses French history under the influence of Napoleon Bonaparte's rise from lowly origins to military and political power, ending with his defeat and the legacy he left to Europe
Includes bibliographical references

945 Italian Peninsula and adjacent islands. Italy

Foster, Leila Merrell
Italy. Lucent Bks. 1999 112p il (Modern nations of the world) lib bdg $22.45 (7 and up) **945**
1. Italy
ISBN 1-56006-481-1
LC 98-36878

Examines the land, people, and history of Italy and discusses its state of affairs and place in the world today
"Collapsing several millennia into a survey that is both succinct and readable is a daunting task, but Foster succeeds admirably." SLJ
Includes bibliographical references

King, David C.
Italy; gem of the Mediterranean. Benchmark Bks. (Tarrytown) 1998 64p il maps (Exploring cultures of the world) lib bdg $25.64 **945**
1. Italy
ISBN 0-7614-0394-9
LC 97-6452
Discusses the geography, history, economy, culture, and people of Italy
"The accessible text . . . include[s] engaging topics about everyday life, such as school, sports, entertainment, and food." Horn Book Guide
Includes glossary and bibliographical references

946 Iberian Peninsula and adjacent islands. Spain

Chicoine, Stephen
Spain; bridge between continents. Benchmark Bks. (Tarrytown) 1997 64p il maps (Exploring cultures of the world) lib bdg $25.64 **946**
1. Spain
ISBN 0-7614-0143-1
LC 96-45498
Examines the geography, people, customs, and history of one of the largest countries on the continent of Europe
"Color photographs and easy-to-read text make the book . . . accessible and appealing, as do the inclusion of traditional recipes and lists of common Spanish . . . phrases. Chapters devoted to festivals, foods, and the arts are especially entertaining." Horn Book Guide
Includes glossary and bibliographical references

Millar, Heather, 1963-
Spain in the age of exploration. Benchmark Bks. (Tarrytown) 1999 80p il maps (Cultures of the past) $20.95 **946**
1. Spain—Civilization
ISBN 0-7614-0303-5
LC 97-2090
Surveys the important events in the history of Spain between the voyages of Columbus and the defeat of the Spanish Armada and examines the role of the arts and religion during these two centuries
This title offers "very good writing, colorful graphics, well-chosen pictures, and excellent design work." Booklist
Includes glossary and bibliographical references

947 Eastern Europe. Russia

Bachrach, Deborah, 1943-
The Crimean War. Lucent Bks. 1998 112p il maps (World history series) lib bdg $22.45 (7 and up) **947**
1. Crimean War, 1853-1856
ISBN 1-56006-315-7
LC 97-34045

Bachrach, Deborah, 1943-—*Continued*
A historical overview of the events leading up to, during, and after the Crimean War
"The prose is lean and engaging. The author's writing and the well-chosen quotes, maps, and black-and-white photographs and illustrations bring the story to life." SLJ
Includes bibliographical references

Clay, Rebecca
Ukraine; a new independence. Benchmark Bks. (Tarrytown) 1997 64p il maps (Exploring cultures of the world) lib bdg $25.64   **947**
1. Ukraine
ISBN 0-7614-0334-5   LC 96-19002
Discusses the geography, history, people, and culture of this rich and fertile nation, which struggled for centuries to be independent and now faces the challenges of its freedom
Includes glossary and bibliographical references

Fader, Kim Brown, 1956-
Russia. Lucent Bks. 1998 144p il maps (Modern nations of the world) lib bdg $22.45 (7 and up)
          947
1. Russia—History 2. Soviet Union—History 3. Russia (Federation)—History
ISBN 1-56006-521-4   LC 97-29557
Examines the history of the country now known as the Russian Federation, from its earliest days through its role as part of the Soviet Union to its current place in the world
"Textural sidebars and good historical maps enrich this gracefully written history." SLJ
Includes bibliographical references

Murrell, Kathleen Berton
Russia; written by Kathleen Berton Murrell; photographed by Andy Crawford. Knopf 1998 59p il (Eyewitness books) $19; lib bdg $20.99   **947**
1. Russia—History 2. Soviet Union—History
ISBN 0-679-89118-8; 0-679-99118-2 (lib bdg)
          LC 97-38878
An overview of the land, people, history, and culture of Russia from its earliest days to the present
"Teachers will appreciate the many images and fascinating details available in one volume. . . . While this title does not present in-depth information on any one aspect of Russian culture, it does offer an abundance of topics for further research." SLJ

Rice, T. M.
Russia. Stevens, G. 1999 96p il (Countries of the world) lib bdg $18.95   **947**
1. Russia (Federation)
ISBN 0-8368-2263-3   LC 98-8858
Surveys the history, geography, government, economy, culture, people, and foreign relations of Russia
"The full-color photos on every page are outstanding and the style of writing is graceful." SLJ
Includes glossary and bibliographical references

947.085   Russia (Soviet Union)— 1953-1991

The **Collapse** of the Soviet Union; Paul A. Winters, book editor. Greenhaven Press 1999 288p (Turning points in world history) lib bdg $20.96; pa $13.96 (7 and up)   **947.085**
1. Soviet Union—Politics and government 2. Russia (Federation)—Politics and government
ISBN 1-56510-997-X (lib bdg); 1-56510-996-1 (pa)
          LC 98-17506
"A chapter summarizing the history of the Soviet Union from the end of the Brezhnev era to the collapse of the government introduces a compilation of excerpts from articles organized into five topical chapters. . . . The compendium includes short questions about each essay; excerpts from reports, speeches, and interviews; a chronology; suggestions for further research." SLJ
"Sophisticated reading, the book will nicely support a modern history curriculum." Booklist
Includes glossary and bibliographical references

Kort, Michael
Russia. rev ed. Facts on File 1998 200p il maps (Nations in transition) lib bdg $19.95 (7 and up)
          947.085
1. Russia (Federation)
ISBN 0-8160-3776-0   LC 98-10751
First published 1995
Examines the people, religion, daily life, politics, culture, history, and geography of Russia, emphasizing its transition, since 1991, from a communist to a free nation
This "lucid narrative recounts events clearly. . . . [It] will be helpful to students doing reports." SLJ
Includes bibliographical references

947.5   Caucasus

Dhilawala, Sakina, 1964-
Armenia. Marshall Cavendish 1997 128p il maps (Cultures of the world) lib bdg $34.21
          947.5
1. Armenia
ISBN 0-7614-0683-2   LC 96-30046
Discusses the geography, history, government, economy, culture, and religion of the republic atop the Armenian Plateau in the Caucausus Mountains
Includes glossary and bibliographical references

Spilling, Michael
Georgia. Marshall Cavendish 1998 128p il maps (Cultures of the world) lib bdg $34.21   **947.5**
1. Georgia (Republic)
ISBN 0-7614-0691-3   LC 97-16570
Describes the geography, history, government, economy, people, lifestyle, religion, language, arts, leisure, festivals, and food of a Caucasian republic with a turbulent past
Includes glossary and bibliographical references

947.7 Ukraine

Bassis, Volodymyr
Ukraine. Marshall Cavendish 1997 128p il maps (Cultures of the world) lib bdg $34.21 **947.7**
1. Ukraine
ISBN 0-7614-0684-0 LC 96-40207
Examines the geography, history, government, economy, and customs of Ukraine, formerly part of the Union of Soviet Socialist Republics
Includes glossary and bibliographical references

Otfinoski, Steven, 1949-
Ukraine. Facts on File 1999 122p il map (Nations in transition) lib bdg $19.95 (7 and up) **947.7**
1. Ukraine
ISBN 0-8160-3757-4 LC 98-7988
Gives a historical and cultural overview of the country of Ukraine with particular emphasis on changes that have occurred since the collapse of the Soviet Union
"Well-chosen, fine-quality black-and-white photos enhance a . . . text that . . . is up to date and packed with information of use to students." Booklist
Includes bibliographical references

947.8 Belarus

Levy, Patricia Marjorie, 1951-
Belarus. Marshall Cavendish 1998 128p il maps (Cultures of the world) $34.21 **947.8**
1. Belarus
ISBN 0-7614-0811-8 LC 97-48562
This describes the geography, history, government, economy, people, lifestyle, religion, language, arts, leisure, festivals, and food of Belarus
Includes glossary and bibliographical references

947.9 Lithuania, Latvia, Estonia

Kagda, Sakina, 1939-
Lithuania. Marshall Cavendish 1997 128p il maps (Cultures of the world) lib bdg $34.21 **947.9**
1. Lithuania
ISBN 0-7614-0681-6 LC 96-29460
Examines the geography, history, government, economy, and customs of the Baltic state
"Kagda manages to tell an interesting story in *Lithuania*, by writing gracefully and eschewing the use of too much detail." SLJ
Includes glossary and bibliographical references

Spilling, Michael
Estonia. Marshall Cavendish 1999 128p il (Cultures of the world) lib bdg $35.64 **947.9**
1. Estonia
ISBN 0-7614-0951-3 LC 98-43682

Introduces the geography, history, government, economy, culture, and people of Estonia, the most northerly and least populated of the three Baltic states
Includes glossary and bibliographical references

948 Scandinavia

Margeson, Susan M.
Viking; photographed by Peter Anderson. Knopf 1994 63p il maps (Eyewitness books) $19; lib bdg $20.99 **948**
1. Vikings
ISBN 0-679-86002-9; 0-679-96002-3 (lib bdg)
LC 93-32593
"A Dorling Kindersley book"
This overview of Viking culture ranges from domestic life and social structure "to the more violent aspects of their explorations and expansions into new territories." SLJ
"This book is a very fine supplement to texts dealing with the history of Europe and with the Vikings." Sci Books Films

Trent, Lynda
The Viking longship. Lucent Bks. 1999 112p il maps (Building history series) lib bdg $22.45 (7 and up) **948**
1. Vikings 2. Ships
ISBN 1-56006-443-9 LC 98-30360
Describes the history and culture of the Vikings and attributes much of their exploring and raiding success to the well-designed longship
Includes glossary and bibliographical references

Wright, Rachel
The Viking news; consultant, Richard Hall. Candlewick Press 1998 32p il maps $16.99 **948**
1. Vikings
ISBN 0-7636-0450-X LC 97-35634
Uses a newspaper format to present information about the explorations, heroes, battles, and traditions of the Vikings
"Colorful pages with informative articles, advertising, and heavy use of illustrations result in a wonderful way to introduce readers to Viking . . . life, as well as to interest students in journalism. [This text is] easy to understand, light, and breezy." SLJ

948.5 Sweden

McNair, Sylvia, 1924-
Sweden. Children's Press 1998 143p il maps (Enchantment of the world, second series) lib bdg $32 **948.5**
1. Sweden
ISBN 0-516-20607-9 LC 97-26886
Describes the history, geography, economy, culture, religion, language, sports, arts, and people of this northern European country
Includes bibliographical references

949.3 Southern Low Countries. Belgium

Pateman, Robert, 1954-
Belgium. Marshall Cavendish 1995 128p il maps (Cultures of the world) lib bdg $34.21
949.3
1. Belgium
ISBN 0-7614-0176-8   LC 95-14900
Introduces the geography, history, government, economy, culture, and people of the small European country of Belgium
"Organization is clear and user friendly. Fine-quality, full-color photographs and reproductions draw readers in and help to hold their interest." SLJ
Includes glossary and bibliographical references

949.35 Luxembourg

Sheehan, Patricia, 1954-
Luxembourg. Marshall Cavendish 1997 128p il maps (Cultures of the world) lib bdg $34.21
949.35
1. Luxembourg
ISBN 0-7614-0685-9   LC 96-53367
Discusses the geography, history, government, economy, and customs of the smallest of the Benelux countries
This is "lucidly written. . . . Informative chapters include discussion about body language, religion, education, and women." Horn Book Guide
Includes glossary and bibliographical references

949.7 Yugoslavia, Croatia, Slovenia, Bosnia and Hercegovina, Macedonia

Black, Eric
Bosnia; fractured region. Lerner Publs. 1999 96p il maps (World in conflict) lib bdg $18.95 (7 and up)
949.7
1. Yugoslav War, 1991- 2. Bosnia and Hercegovina
ISBN 0-8225-3553-X   LC 96-24951
Describes the history of the ethnic conflict in Bosnia, including current issues
"A book that attempts to explain the history of the Balkans in a way that is clear, concise, fair, and thorough is taking on a huge burden. This title succeeds and then some, for it is also interestingly written and engaging." Booklist
Includes bibliographical references

Milivojevic, JoAnn
Serbia. Children's Press 1999 144p il maps (Enchantment of the world, second series) $32
949.7
1. Serbia
ISBN 0-516-21196-X   LC 98-19256
An introduction to the geography, history, natural resources, economy, culture, and people of Serbia, the larger of the two republics that make up the country of Yugoslavia
"An accessible, well-illustrated overview." SLJ
Includes bibliographical references

O'Grady, Scott F.
Basher five-two; the true story of F-16 fighter pilot Captain Scott O'Grady; [by] Scott O'Grady with Michael French. Doubleday 1997 133p il map $16.95
949.7
1. Yugoslav War, 1991-
ISBN 0-385-32300-X   LC 96-51181
"O'Grady writes about being shot down, escaping capture, and surviving in enemy territory in Bosnia in 1995." Book Rep
This account "is smartly paced, with care taken over the particulars young readers will want to know. An insert of photos is included." Horn Book Guide

949.9 Bulgaria

Otfinoski, Steven, 1949-
Bulgaria. Facts on File 1998 118p (Nations in transition) $19.95 (7 and up)
949.9
1. Bulgaria
ISBN 0-8160-3705-1   LC 98-10577
Examines the people, religion, daily life, politics, culture, history, and geography of Bulgaria, emphasizing its transition from a communist to a free nation
"Educators and students will find the book useful for learning about a variety of governments, the challenging process of political transitions, and the intriguing history of a country still trying to find its identity. Pronunciation guide; chronology; further reading." Booklist

950 Asia. Orient. Far East

Major, John S., 1942-
The Silk Route; 7,000 miles of history; illustrated by Stephen Fieser. HarperCollins Pubs. 1995 32p il maps hardcover o.p. paperback available $5.95
950
1. Trade routes 2. China—History
ISBN 0-06-443468-0 (pa)   LC 92-38169
"Major traces the journey of a caravan as it leaves Chang'an, China, in A.D.700, travels along the established silk traders' route, and finally arrives at its destination in Byzantium several months later. The 7,000-mile trek crosses cities, deserts, mountains, and the Mediterranean Sea." SLJ
"The pictures and short segments make the book a teaching tool as well as a resource when learning about China and its silk industry." Child Book Rev Serv

Pascoe, Elaine
The Pacific rim; East Asia at the dawn of a new century. 21st Cent. Bks. (Brookfield) 1999 128p il lib bdg $24.90 (7 and up)
950
1. Pacific rim
ISBN 0-7613-3015-1   LC 98-28556
Examines the history and current economic and political importance of Japan, China, Taiwan, the Koreas, Southeast Asia, Indonesia, and Malaysia
"Teenagers investigating the current economic crisis in the Pacific Rim will benefit from the encapsulated histories and the relative currency of the text." Booklist
Includes bibliographical references

951 China and adjacent areas

Green, Robert, 1969-
China. Lucent Bks. 1999 128p il maps (Modern nations of the world) lib bdg $22.45 (7 and up)
951
1. China
ISBN 1-56006-440-4   LC 98-30578
Discusses the history, geography, culture, and current conditions in the People's Republic of China
This is a "well-written overview. . . . Organization is a key asset of the book and the narrative is smooth flowing and chock-full of information, with many textual sidebars to catch readers' interest." SLJ
Includes bibliographical references

Sis, Peter
Tibet; through the red box. Farrar, Straus & Giroux 1998 unp il maps $25   **951**
1. Tibet (China)
ISBN 0-374-37552-6   LC 97-50175
A Caldecott Medal honor book, 1999
"Frances Foster books"
"When Sis opens the red lacquered box that has sat on his father's table for decades, he finds the diary his father kept when he was lost in Tibet in the mid-1950s. The text replicates the diary's spidery handwriting, while the illustrations depict elaborate mazes and mandalas, along with dreamlike spreads that are filled with fragmented details of the father's and son's lives. . . . Impeccably designed and beautifully made, the book has a dreamlike quality that will keep readers of many ages coming back to find more in its pages." Booklist

951.04 China—Period of Republic, 1912-1949

Fritz, Jean
China's Long March; 6,000 miles of danger; with illustrations by Yang Zhr Cheng. Putnam 1988 124p il maps $16.95   **951.04**
1. China—History—1912-1949
ISBN 0-399-21512-3   LC 87-31171
Describes the events of the 6,000 mile march undertaken by Mao Zedong and his Communist followers as they retreated before the forces of Chiang Kai-shek
"Because Fritz is adept at gauging her intended audience, and because most of her material is based on interviews with survivors, the writing has an easy flow and an immediacy that make the ordeal vivid and personal." Bull Cent Child Books
Includes bibliographical references

951.05 China—Period of People's Republic, 1949-

Fritz, Jean
China homecoming; with photographs by Michael Fritz. Putnam 1985 145p il $16.95
951.05
1. China
ISBN 0-399-21182-9   LC 84-24775

Companion volume to Homesick: my own story
This account of the author's return to Hankow after four decades "is intended for a slightly older readership than 'Homesick' . . . as it is not only an autobiography, but also a glimpse of Chinese history and a social commentary. It is, however, a book to be read and reread." SLJ
Includes bibliographical references

Jiang, Ji-li
Red scarf girl; a memoir of the Cultural Revolution; foreword by David Henry Hwang. HarperCollins Pubs. 1997 285p $15.95; pa $4.95
951.05
1. China—History—1949-1976
ISBN 0-06-027585-5; 0-06-446208-0 (pa)
    LC 97-5089
"This is an autobiographical account of growing up during Mao's Cultural Revolution in China in 1966. . . . Jiang describes in terrifying detail the ordeals of her family and those like them, including unauthorized search and seizure, persecution, arrest and torture, hunger, and public humiliation. . . . Her voice is that of an intelligent, confused adolescent, and her focus on the effects of the revolution on herself, her family, and her friends provides an emotional focal point for the book, and will allow even those with limited knowledge of Chinese history to access the text." Bull Cent Child Books

951.24 Taiwan

Wee, Jessie
Taiwan. Chelsea House 1999 104p il maps (Major world nations) lib bdg $19.95   **951.24**
1. Taiwan
ISBN 0-7910 4986 8   LC 98-4308
First published 1987 in the Let's visit series
Explores the people, history, climate, economy, and topography of Taiwan, the island province of China that continues to resist communism

951.25 Hong Kong

Kagda, Falaq
Hong Kong. ref ed. Marshall Cavendish 1998 128p il maps (Cultures of the world) lib bdg $34.21   **951.25**
1. Hong Kong (China)
ISBN 0-7614-0692-1   LC 97-15885
Surveys the geography, history, government, economy, and culture of this territory on China's southeastern coast, made up of a section of the mainland and 235 islands of various sizes
Includes glossary and bibliographical references

Lyle, Garry
Hong Kong. Chelsea House 1999 104p il (Major world nations) lib bdg $19.95   **951.25**
1. Hong Kong (China)
ISBN 0-7910-4990-6   LC 98-15073

Lyle, Garry—*Continued*
Describes the history, geography, economy, daily life, and people of Hong Kong

951.7 Mongolia

Cheng, Pang Guek, 1950-
Mongolia. Marshall Cavendish 1999 128p il maps (Cultures of the world) lib bdg $35.64

951.7

1. Mongolia
ISBN 0-7614-0954-8   LC 98-31897
Describes the geography, history, government, economy, people, lifestyle, religion, language, arts, leisure, festivals, and food of Mongolia
"High quality, full-color photography combines with clearly written text and meaningful sidebars." SLJ
Includes glossary and bibliographical references

951.9 Korea

Dolan, Edward F., 1924-
America in the Korean War. Millbrook Press 1998 112p il maps lib bdg $28.90 (7 and up)

951.9

1. Korean War, 1950-1953
ISBN 0-7613-0361-8   LC 97-50460
In this history of the Korean War the author concentrates "on the military action of the conflict itself and describing the campaigns and the strategies behind them. . . . He also profiles many of the commanders and discusses the Truman-MacArthur confrontation." SLJ
"Readers interested in battlefield strategies will relish this account. . . . The book will provide good curriculum support for history classes, but it will need to be supplemented by other books." Booklist
Includes bibliographical references

Isserman, Maurice
The Korean War. Facts on File 1992 117p il maps (America at war) lib bdg $19.95 (7 and up)

951.9

1. Korean War, 1950-1953
ISBN 0-8160-2688-2   LC 92-10201
Examines the political climate and military situation that led to the Korean War and discusses the key people and events involved in the conflict itself
This combines "a well-written and well-researched account of what some have termed America's 'forgotten war'. . . . The book is thought-provoking as well as informative and entertaining." SLJ
Includes bibliographical references

McGowen, Tom
The Korean War. Watts 1992 63p il maps lib bdg $22; pa $6.95

951.9

1. Korean War, 1950-1953
ISBN 0-531-20040-X; 0-531-15655-9 (pa)

LC 91-14747

An overview of the three-year war that took over two million lives and resolved none of the conflicts that split Korea into two irreconcilable nations
This work combines "interest-holding prose with full-color maps and informative photographs." SLJ
Includes bibliographical references

Smith, Carter, 1962-
The Korean War. Silver Burdett Press 1990 64p il maps (Turning points in American history) lib bdg $14.95; pa $7.95 (7 and up)

951.9

1. Korean War, 1950-1953
ISBN 0-382-09953-2 (lib bdg); 0-382-09949-4 (pa)

LC 90-8421

Following a brief overview of Korea's geography, government, and military history, this book covers the Korean War, concluding with a description of present day relations between North and South Korea
Includes bibliographical references

951.95 South Korea (Republic of Korea)

Williams, Jean Kinney
South Korea. Lucent Bks. 1999 111p il maps (Modern nations of the world) lib bdg $22.45 (7 and up)

951.95

1. Korea (South)
ISBN 1-56006-446-3   LC 98-34605
Discusses the history, geography, culture, and current state of South Korea, a land of both tradition and modern development
Includes bibliographical references

952 Japan

Blumberg, Rhoda, 1917-
Commodore Perry in the land of the Shogun. Lothrop, Lee & Shepard Bks. 1985 144p il map lib bdg $17

952

1. Perry, Matthew Calbraith, 1794-1858 2. United States Naval Expedition to Japan (1852-1854) 3. United States—Foreign relations—Japan 4. Japan—Foreign relations—United States
ISBN 0-688-03723-2   LC 84-21800
A Newbery Medal honor book, 1986
"The diplomatic expeditions of Commodore Mathew C. Perry to secure a treaty to provide for U.S. trade with Japan are described. The black-and-white period illustrations and informative text provide an in-depth and intimate view of nineteenth century Japan, Japanese and U.S. values and attitudes, and treaty negotiations." Soc Educ
Includes bibliographical references

Galvin, Irene Flum
Japan; a modern land with ancient roots. Benchmark Bks. (Tarrytown) 1996 64p il maps (Exploring cultures of the world) lib bdg $25.64

952

1. Japan
ISBN 0-7614-0188-1   LC 95-15321

Galvin, Irene Flum—*Continued*
This "survey of Japan touches on the country's history, geography, people, and culture. Colorful details abound, and young readers will be especially interested in learning about Japan's long school year and the games and hobbies Japanese children enjoy. Most of the color photographs are clear and appealing." Horn Book Guide
Includes glossary and bibliographical references

Heinrichs, Ann
Japan. Children's Press 1998 143p il (Enchantment of the world, second series) lib bdg $32   **952**
1. Japan
ISBN 0-516-20649-4   LC 97-38771
Describes the history, geography, plants and animals, economy, language, people and culture of the island nation of Japan
"The writing is clear . . . the topics covered are broad in scope and will be suitable for assignments. Good-quality, full-color photographs, reproductions, and maps are interspersed throughout." SLJ
Includes bibliographical references

Roberson, John R., 1930-
Japan meets the world; the birth of a super power. Millbrook Press 1998 208p il maps $24.90 (7 and up)   **952**
1. Japan—History
ISBN 0-7613-0407-X   LC 98-6071
First published 1985 with title: Japan from Shogun to Sony, 1543-1984
Examines the history of Japan through various stages of progress and isolationism, including its rise to world power, up to the present day and the current Asian economic crisis
"This is an accessible, must-have resource for students needing detailed information about the history and current status of Japan. Glossary; bibliography; well-chosen but average-quality black-and white-photos." Booklist

952.04   Japan—1945-

Stefoff, Rebecca, 1951-
Japan. Chelsea House 1999 112p il maps (Major world nations) $19.95   **952.04**
1. Japan
ISBN 0-7910-4761-X   LC 87-18322
An overview of the history, geography, economy, government, people, and culture of Japan
This is "readable, informative, current, and fair, with lots of good photos and up-to-date maps." Booklist

953.3   Yemen

Hestler, Anna
Yemen. Marshall Cavendish 1999 128p il maps (Cultures of the world) lib bdg $35.64   **953.3**
1. Yemen
ISBN 0-7614-0956-4   LC 98-53993

Presents information about the geography, history, government, and economy of this country located on the southwestern tip of the Arabian Peninsula and describes many aspects of the lifestyle of its people
Includes glossary and bibliographical references

953.67   Kuwait

Foster, Leila Merrell
Kuwait. Children's Press 1998 143p il (Enchantment of the world, second series) lib bdg $32   **953.67**
1. Kuwait
ISBN 0-516-20604-4   LC 97-23845
Describes the history, geography, economy, language, religion, sports, arts, and people of this oil-rich country located on the northwestern shore of the Persian Gulf
Includes bibliographical references

O'Shea, Maria
Kuwait. Marshall Cavendish 1999 128p il maps (Cultures of the world) lib bdg $24.95   **953.67**
1. Kuwait
ISBN 0-7614-0871-1   LC 98-25833
Introduces the geography, history, religious beliefs, government, and people of Kuwait, a small country on the Persian Gulf
Includes glossary and bibliographical references

954   South Asia. India

Brace, Steve
India. Heinemann Lib. 1999 64p il maps (Country studies) lib bdg $27.07   **954**
1. India
ISBN 1-575-72893-1   LC 98-52758
Describes the history, geography, population, economic development, natural resources, and future of India
Includes bibliographical references

954.02   India—647-1785

Rothfarb, Ed
In the land of the Taj Mahal; the world of the fabulous Mughals. Holt & Co. 1998 243p il $21.95 (7 and up)   **954.02**
1. Mogul Empire
ISBN 0-8050-5299-2   LC 97-8281
Describes the history and accomplishments of the Mughal dynasty, with an emphasis on the period from Babur to Shah Jahan
"There are few titles for young adults on the Mughal empire, and this is a superb choice to fill that void." SLJ

954.92   Bangladesh

Whyte, Mariam
Bangladesh. Marshall Cavendish 1999 128p il
maps (Cultures of the world) lib bdg $23.95
                                        954.92
1. Bangladesh
ISBN 0-7614-0869-X   LC 98-22428
Describes the geography, history, government, economy, people, religion, language, arts, leisure, festivals, and
food of Bangladesh
Includes glossary and bibliographical references

956.7   Iraq

Foster, Leila Merrell
Iraq. Children's Press 1997 144p il
(Enchantment of the world, second series) lib bdg
$36   **956.7**
1. Iraq
ISBN 0-516-20584-6   LC 97-2005
Describes the geography, history, culture, industry,
and people of Iraq, formerly known as Mesopotamia
Includes bibliographical references

Gay, Kathlyn
Persian Gulf War; [by] Kathlyn Gay and Martin
Gay. 21st Cent. Bks. (NY) 1996 63p il map
(Voices from the past) lib bdg $18.90   **956.7**
1. Persian Gulf War, 1991
ISBN 0-8050-4102-8   LC 96-15579
Describes the circumstances leading up to Iran's invasion of Kuwait and the political and military events of
the Persian Gulf War
"A clearly written, objective overview. . . . First-
person quotes from television reporters, journalists, political leaders, military correspondents, pilots, and ground
soldiers add immediacy to the text. A map of the conflict
and small full-color and black-and-white photos further
enhance the presentation." SLJ
Includes bibliographical references

956.92   Lebanon

Sheehan, Sean, 1951-
Lebanon. ref ed. Marshall Cavendish 1997 128p
il maps (Cultures of the world) lib bdg $34.21
                                        956.92
1. Lebanon
ISBN 0-7614-0283-7   LC 96-22480
This describes the geography, history, government,
economy and culture of Lebanon
Includes glossary and bibliographical references

956.94   Palestine. Israel

Altman, Linda Jacobs, 1943-
The creation of Israel. Lucent Bks. 1998 112p
il maps (World history series) $22.45 (7 and up)
                                        956.94
1. Zionism 2. Israel—History
ISBN 1-56006-288-6   LC 97-46033
Provides a historical overview of the treatment of
Jews and discusses the role of various individuals and
specific events in leading to the creation of the state of
Israel in 1948
Includes bibliographical references

Blumberg, Arnold, 1925-
The history of Israel. Greenwood Press 1998
218p (Greenwood histories of the modern nations)
$35 (7 and up)   **956.94**
1. Israel—History 2. Palestine—History 3. Zionism
ISBN 0-313-30224-3   LC 97-45659
"Starting with a description of life in modern Israel,
Blumberg . . . quickly covers Israel's early history, from
3,500 years ago to World War I. . . . The battles leading
to independence, the isolation of Israel, conflicts within
Israel, the Suez Crisis and subsequent wars, the *Intifada,*
the development of the PLO, and the Peace Process are
described in a manner that enables readers to have a
much better understanding of the events happening in Israel now." Voice Youth Advocates
Includes bibliographical references

Corzine, Phyllis
The Palestinian-Israeli accord. Lucent Bks. 1997
112p il (Lucent overview series) $22.45 (7 and up)
                                        956.94
1. Israel-Arab conflicts
ISBN 1-56006-181-2   LC 96-34886
Presents an historical overview of the events leading
up to the 1993 peace treaty between the state of Israel
and the PLO
"The historical information and the generally objective
tone of [the author's] text provide readers with an accurate and understandable introduction to this complex
world problem." SLJ
Includes bibliographical references

Jerusalem and the Holy Land; chronicles from
National Geographic; Arthur M. Schlesinger, Jr.,
senior consulting editor; Fred L. Israel, general
editor. Chelsea House 1999 131p il (Cultural
and geographical exploration) $24.95   **956.94**
1. Israel—Social life and customs
ISBN 0-7910-5101-3   LC 98-44248
Articles from National Geographic present an account
of Muslim village life, the travel impressions of a British
historian, and a description of the Passover celebration of
a small group of Orthodox Jews known as Samaritans
Includes bibliographical references

Schroeter, Daniel J.
Israel; an illustrated history. Oxford Univ. Press 1998 157p il maps (Illustrated histories) $24.95 (7 and up) **956.94**
1. Israel—History 2. Palestine—History 3. Zionism
ISBN 0-19-510885-X LC 98-15915
Presents information on ancient Israel while focusing on the modern nation with both religious and secular history including the roles of Romans, Muslims, and Palestinians as well as Jews
The author's "insights into modern Israeli life are abundant and honestly address the social and economic tensions and the pressing security concerns of the culturally diverse nation." Booklist
Includes glossary and bibliographical references

Wolf, Bernard, 1930-
If I forget Thee, O Jerusalem; written and photographed by Bernard Wolf. Dutton Children's Bks. 1998 64p il $17.99 **956.94**
1. Jerusalem
ISBN 0-525-45738-0 LC 98-11106
Surveys the history of the city of Jerusalem and its importance to three of the world's major religions: Judaism, Christianity, and Islam
"An involving photo essay." Booklist

956.95 West Bank and Jordan

South, Coleman
Jordan. Marshall Cavendish 1997 128p il maps (Cultures of the world) lib bdg $34.21 **956.95**
1. Jordan
ISBN 0-7614-0287-X LC 96-18307
Examines the geography, history, government, economy, and culture of Jordan
Includes glossary and bibliographical references

Stefoff, Rebecca, 1951-
West Bank/Gaza Strip. Chelsea House 1999 104p il maps (Major world nations) $19.95 **956.95**
1. West Bank 2. Gaza Strip
ISBN 0-7910-4771-7 LC 87-18243
First published 1988 in the Places and peoples of the world series
Surveys the history, topography, people, and culture of the West Bank and the Gaza Strip, with an emphasis on current economy, industry, and place in the political world
This is "clearly presented and straightforward. . . . Useful report material." SLJ
Includes glossary

959.3 Thailand

McNair, Sylvia, 1924-
Thailand. Children's Press 1998 144p (Enchantment of the world, second series) $32 **959.3**
1. Thailand
ISBN 0-516-21100-5 LC 98-16319

Explores the geography, history, arts, religion, and everyday life of Thailand
Includes bibliographical references

959.4 Laos

Mansfield, Stephen
Laos. Marshall Cavendish 1998 128p il maps (Cultures of the world) lib bdg $34.21 **959.4**
1. Laos
ISBN 0-7614-0689-1 LC 97-16568
Introduces the geography, history, religious beliefs, government, and people of Laos
Includes glossary and bibliographical references

Zickgraf, Ralph
Laos. Chelsea House 1999 110p il (Major world nations) $19.95 **959.4**
1. Laos
ISBN 0-7910-4743-1
First published 1990 in the Places and peoples of the world series
This examines the land, plant and animal life, people, history, and future of Laos

959.7 Vietnam

Skelton, Olivia
Vietnam; still struggling, still spirited. Benchmark Bks. (Tarrytown) 1998 64p il maps (Exploring cultures of the world) lib bdg $25.64 **959.7**
1. Vietnam
ISBN 0-7614-0395-7 LC 97-8802
Describes the geography, history, climate, government, people, and culture of this small country in the southeastern corner of Asia
"An accessible introduction to Vietnam is especially good at exploring the human side of the country—including work and school customs, cultural traditions, food, and celebrations." Horn Book Guide
Includes glossary and bibliographical references

959.704 Vietnam—1949-

Ashabranner, Brent K., 1921-
Their names to live; what the Vietnam Veterans Memorial means to America; [by] Brent Ashabranner; photographs by Jennifer Ashabranner. Millbrook Press 1998 64p il lib bdg $23.90 **959.704**
1. Vietnam Veterans Memorial (Washington, D.C.)
ISBN 0-7613-3235-9 LC 98-21004
Describes the planning and creation of the Vietnam Veterans Memorial and how it came to be a symbol for the dead of all American wars
"A simple, often-moving book of information, photographs, and reflections on the Memorial." Booklist
Includes bibliographical references

Denenberg, Barry
Voices from Vietnam. Scholastic 1995 249p
$16.95; pa $4.99 (7 and up)   **959.704**
1. Vietnam War, 1961-1975
ISBN 0-590-44267-8; 0-590-44267-8 (pa)
LC 93-44886
"Tracing the history of the Vietnam War in chronological sequence, the volume contains personal narratives of
those who were involved—from presidents and generals
to soldiers, nurses, and Vietnamese citizens. The dispa-
rate voices speak with insight, passion, and occasional
graphic language to create a picture of war gone wrong,
in this extremely powerful book." Horn Book Guide
Includes glossary and bibliographical references

Devaney, John
The Vietnam War. Watts 1992 63p il maps lib
bdg $22; pa $6.95   **959.704**
1. Vietnam War, 1961-1975
ISBN 0-531-20046-9 (lib bdg); 0-531-15658-3 (pa)
LC 91-14755
A look at the politics of this controversial war, from
the French withdrawal after the Battle of Dien Bien Phu
to the fall of Saigon in 1975

Gay, Kathlyn
Vietnam war; [by] Kathlyn Gay and Martin
Gay. 21st Cent. Bks. (NY) 1996 64p il (Voices
from the past) lib bdg $18.90   **959.704**
1. Vietnam War, 1961-1975
ISBN 0-8050-4101-X   LC 96-15578
Provides an overview of the history of the Vietnam
War and U.S. involvement
This "presents a concise, comprehensive, clear and un-
biased overview of the Vietnam War. . . . An excellent
choice for middle or junior-high school and public librar-
ies." Voice Youth Advocates
Includes bibliographical references

Super, Neil
Vietnam War soldiers. 21st Cent. Bks. (NY)
1993 80p il (African-American soldiers) lib bdg
$17.90   **959.704**
1. Vietnam War, 1961-1975 2. African American sol-
diers
ISBN 0-8050-2307-0   LC 93-10626
This work focuses on the experiences of African-
American soldiers in the Vietnam War, experiences that
reflected and amplified the struggle for civil rights in
America during this same time period
Includes bibliographical references

The **Vietnam** War: opposing viewpoints; William
Dudley, book editor. Greenhaven Press 1998
284p (American history series) lib bdg $26.20;
pa $16.20 (7 and up)   **959.704**
1. Vietnam War, 1961-1975
ISBN 1-56510-701-2 (lib bdg); 1-56510-700-4 (pa)
LC 97-9448
Replaces the edition published 1990
This collection of essays presents varying viewpoints
on such issues as the wisdom and morality of U.S. military intervention in Vietnam, Vietnamization of the war,
the antiwar movement, and media coverage of the war
Includes bibliographical references

Wills, Charles A.
The Tet offensive; by Charles Wills. Silver
Burdett Press 1989 64p il maps (Turning points in
American history) lib bdg $14.95; pa $7.95
959.704
1. Vietnam War, 1961-1975 2. Tet Offensive, 1968
ISBN 0-382-09849-8 (lib bdg); 0-382-09855-2 (pa)
LC 89-6186
Describes the massive offensive launched by the Viet
Cong during the Tet holiday in 1968 and places it in the
context of the entire Vietnamese conflict
Includes bibliographical references

959.8 Indonesia

Lyle, Garry
Indonesia. Chelsea House 1999 104p il (Major
world nations) lib bdg $19.95   **959.8**
1. Indonesia
ISBN 0-7910-4987-6   LC 98-15072
Published 1984 by Burke with title: Let's visit Indonesia
Describes the geography, history, government, culture,
and daily life of the country that is comprised of 13,000
islands

959.9 Philippines

Wee, Jessie
The Philippines. Chelsea House 1998 104p il
(Major world nations) lib bdg $19.95   **959.9**
1. Philippines
ISBN 0-7910-4984-1   LC 98-4314
First published 1988
Explores the people, history, culture, land, climate,
and economy of the Philippines, the only Christian na-
tion in Asia

960 Africa

Haskins, James, 1941-
African beginnings; [by] James Haskins &
Kathleen Benson; paintings by Floyd Cooper.
Lothrop, Lee & Shepard Bks. 1998 48p il map
$18; lib bdg $17.93   **960**
1. Africa—History
ISBN 0-688-10256-5; 0-688-10257-3 (lib bdg)
LC 94-9848
This is an "overview of the great African kingdoms
between 3800 B.C. and A.D. 1800. Sections on the king-
doms of Nubia, Egypt, Jenne-Jeno, Ghana, Mao,
Songhay, etc., briefly discuss trade, education, art, agri-
culture, and other practices." Bull Cent Child Books
Cooper "fills in the geographical and cultural details
with soft-edged, luminous oil paintings." Publ Wkly
Includes bibliographical references

Haskins, James, 1941-—Continued

From Afar to Zulu; a dictionary of African cultures; [by] Jim Haskins, and Joann Biondi. Walker & Co. 1995 212p il maps $18.95; lib bdg $19.85; pa $10.95 **960**

1. Africa—Social life and customs—Dictionaries

ISBN 0-8027-8290-6; 0-8027-8291-4 (lib bdg); 0-8027-7550-0 (pa) LC 94-11545

This volume describes "more than 30 major and 200 smaller ethnic groups on the African continent. History, social customs, religions, political issues and contemporary events are discussed in each entry." BAYA Book Rev

This "fulfills its intent as a concise, clear source of information on the peoples of Africa for upper-elementary and middle-school students." Booklist

Includes glossary and bibliographical references

Jones, Constance, 1961-

Africa, 1500-1900. Facts on File 1993 140p il maps (World history library) $19.95 (7 and up) **960**

1. Africa—History

ISBN 0-8160-2774-9 LC 92-22677

Examines the history of Africa from the sixteenth through the nineteenth century, discussing such topics as the different cultures that existed on the continent, the importance of Islam, European colonization, and the slave trade

"Clear, uncluttered black-and-white maps and historical photographs are interspersed throughout. The book is nicely laid out, with lots of boldface type to break up the text. There is an excellent chronology, and the list for further reading includes both fiction and nonfiction titles." SLJ

Peoples of Africa; by the Diagram Group. Facts on File 1997 6v maps set $102.75 **960**

1. Africa

ISBN 0-8160-3482-6

Contents: Nations of Africa; Peoples of Central Africa; Peoples of East Africa; Peoples of Northern Africa; Peoples of Southern Africa; Peoples of West Africa

"The first five volumes each cover a different region of Africa, describing the climate, wildlife, and ecology found in that particular area, as well as detailing the history and life-styles of nearly twenty present-day ethnic groups with information about languages, religion, trade, social mores, history, art, and warfare. The last volume in the series explores the individual nations of Africa." Publisher's note

961.1 Tunisia

Brown, Roslind Varghese

Tunisia. Marshall Cavendish 1998 128p il maps (Cultures of the world) lib bdg $34.21 **961.1**

1. Tunisia

ISBN 0-7614-0690-5 LC 97-15883

Examines the history, economy, people, lifestyles, and culture of this Arab country in northern Africa

Includes glossary and bibliographical references

962 Egypt and Sudan

Kallen, Stuart A., 1955-

Egypt. Lucent Bks. 1999 111p il maps (Modern nations of the world) lib bdg $17.96 (7 and up) **962**

1. Egypt

ISBN 1-56006-535-4 LC 98-43851

Discusses the history, geography, people, and culture of Egypt and its significance in the world today

"The strength of this volume is its carefully developed history of Egypt from ancient times to the present." SLJ

Includes bibliographical references

King, David C.

Egypt; ancient traditions, modern hopes. Benchmark Bks. (Tarrytown) 1997 64p il map (Exploring cultures of the world) lib bdg $25.64 **962**

1. Egypt

ISBN 0-7614-0142-3 LC 96-49588

Discusses the geography, history, culture, daily life, and people of the North African country of Egypt

"Illustrated with color photographs. . . . A sampling of Arabic phrases and a traditional recipe add to the book's appeal." Horn Book

Includes glossary and bibliographical references

Wilkens, Frances

Egypt. Chelsea House 1998 104p il (Major world nations) lib bdg $19.95 **962**

1. Egypt

ISBN 0-7910-4989-2 LC 98-15075

Describes the history, geography, economy, culture, and people of the North African nation of Egypt

962.4 Sudan

Levy, Patricia Marjorie, 1951-

Sudan. Marshall Cavendish 1997 128p il maps (Cultures of the world) $23.95 **962.4**

1. Sudan

ISBN 0-7614-0284-5 LC 96-20493

Examines the geography, history, government, economy, and culture of the war-torn country where the African and Arab worlds mingle

Includes glossary and bibliographical references

963 Ethiopia and Eritrea

Peffer-Engels, John, 1966-

States of Ethiopia. Watts 1998 64p il (African civilizations) $22 **963**

1. Ethiopia—History

ISBN 0-531-20278-X LC 97-37354

"A First book"

Surveys the history and culture of the states of Ethiopia in northeast Africa

Includes bibliographical references

964   Northwest African coast and offshore islands. Morocco

Blauer, Ettagale
Morocco; by Ettagale Blauer and Jason Lauré. Children's Press 1999 144p il maps (Enchantment of the world, second series) lib bdg $32   **964**
1. Morocco
ISBN 0-516-20961-2   LC 98-17644
Describes the geography, plants and animals, history, economy, language, religions, culture, and people of Morocco, a unique northern African nation surrounded by both water and desert
Includes bibliographical references

965   Algeria

Kagda, Falaq
Algeria. Marshall Cavendish 1997 128p il maps (Cultures of the world) lib bdg $34.21   **965**
1. Algeria
ISBN 0-7614-0680-8   LC 96-40373
Examines the geography, history, government, economy, people, and culture of Algeria
Includes glossary and bibliographical references

966.1   Mauritania

Green, Rebecca L.
The empire of Ghana. Watts 1998 64p il (African civilizations) $22   **966.1**
1. Ghana Empire
ISBN 0-531-20276-3   LC 97-37574
"A First book"
A survey of the history and culture of the West African Empire of Ghana that, flourishing from about 750 until 1076, is not related to modern Ghana
Includes glossary and bibliographical references

966.2   Mali, Burkina Faso, Niger

Conrad, David C.
The Songhay Empire; [by] David Conrad. Watts 1998 64p il maps (African civilizations) $22
   966.2
1. Songhai Empire
ISBN 0-531-20284-4   LC 97-31288
A First book
A survey of the history and culture of the West African Songhai Empire that flourished from the 1460s until the 1590s, when it was conquered by Morocco
Includes glossary and bibliographical references

McKissack, Patricia C., 1944-
The royal kingdoms of Ghana, Mali, and Songhay; life in medieval Africa; [by] Patricia and Fredrick McKissack. Holt & Co. 1993 142p il maps hardcover o.p. paperback available $7.95
   966.2
1. Ghana Empire 2. Mali—History 3. Songhai Empire
ISBN 0-8050-4259-8 (pa)   LC 93-4838
Examines the civilizations of the Western Sudan which flourished from 700 to 1700 A.D., acquiring such vast wealth that they became centers of trade and culture for a continent
"The McKissacks are careful to distinguish what is known from what is surmised; they draw on the oral tradition, eyewitness accounts, and contemporary scholarship; and chapter source notes discuss various conflicting views of events." Booklist
Includes bibliographical references

966.3   Senegal

Berg, Elizabeth, 1953-
Senegal; [by] Elizabeth L. Berg. Marshall Cavendish 1999 128p il maps (Cultures of the world) lib bdg $35.64   **966.3**
1. Senegal
ISBN 0-7614-0872-X   LC 98-7790
Describes the geography, history, economy, lifestyle, and religion of Senegal, as well as its people, languages, and festivals
Includes glossary and bibliographical references

966.62   Liberia

Levy, Patricia Marjorie, 1951-
Liberia; [by] Patricia Levy. Marshall Cavendish 1998 128p il maps (Cultures of the world) lib bdg $34.21   **966.62**
1. Liberia
ISBN 0-7614-0810-X   LC 97-43613
Describes the geography, history, government, economy, people, lifestyle, religion, language, arts, leisure, festivals, and food of the West African nation of Liberia
Includes glossary and bibliographical references

966.68   Ivory Coast

Kummer, Patricia K.
Côte d'Ivoire (Ivory Coast). Children's Press 1996 128p il maps (Enchantment of the world) lib bdg $32   **966.68**
1. Ivory Coast
ISBN 0-516-02641-0   LC 95-33594
Describes the geography, history, culture, economy, people, and cities of the West African country of Côte d'Ivoire

966.7 Ghana

Levy, Patricia Marjorie, 1951-
Ghana. Marshall Cavendish 1999 128p il map
(Cultures of the world) lib bdg $35.64   **966.7**
1. Ghana
ISBN 0-7614-0952-1   LC 98-49004
Describes the geography, history, government, econo-
my, people, lifestyle, religion, language, arts, leisure, fes-
tivals, and food of Ghana
This offers "a readable text along with plenty of clear
photos." Horn Book Guide
Includes glossary and bibliographical references

966.9 Nigeria

Nnoromele, Salome, 1967-
Life among the Ibo women of Nigeria. Lucent
Bks. 1998 96p il maps (Way people live) lib bdg
$17.96 (7 and up)   **966.9**
1. Igbo (African people) 2. Nigeria—Social life and
customs 3. Women—Nigeria
ISBN 1-56006-344-0   LC 97-45172
Examines the traditional role of Ibo women as equal
participants in the social, economic, religious, and political lives of their communities and how this role has been
influenced and changed by centuries of colonization and
the pressures of modern society
"Nnoromele's clear language will make research a
pleasure and understanding a given." Booklist
Includes bibliographical references

967.51 Zaire

Heale, Jay
Democratic Republic of the Congo. Marshall
Cavendish 1999 128p il maps (Cultures of the
world) lib bdg $35.64   **967.51**
1. Congo (Republic)
ISBN 0-7614-0874-6   LC 98-28538
Describes the geography, history, government, economy, people, lifestyle, religion, languages, arts, leisure,
festivals, and food of the third largest country in Africa,
a former colony of Belgium
Includes glossary and bibliographical references

967.6 Uganda and Kenya

Wilson, Thomas H.
City states of the Swahili coast. Watts 1998 64p
il maps (African civilizations) $22   **967.6**
1. East Africa—History
ISBN 0-531-20281-X   LC 97-37569
"A First book"
Discusses the history and culture of the Swahili peo-
ples living along the eastern coast of Africa, from
present-day Somalia to Mozambique
Includes glossary and bibliographical references

967.61 Uganda

Creed, Alexander
Uganda. Chelsea House 1999 96p il (Major
world nations) $19.95   **967.61**
1. Uganda
ISBN 0-7910-4770-9   LC 87-11710
First published 1988 in the Places and peoples of the
world series
Surveys the history, topography, people, and culture of
Uganda with an emphasis on its current economy, indus-
try, and place in the political world
Includes glossary

967.62 Kenya

King, David C.
Kenya; let's all pull together! Benchmark Bks.
(Tarrytown) 1998 64p il maps (Exploring cultures
of the world) lib bdg $25.64   **967.62**
1. Kenya
ISBN 0-7614-0393-0   LC 97-14448
Describes the geography, history, language, people,
and culture of this country on the east coast of Africa
Includes glossary and bibliographical references

967.73 Somalia

Hassig, Susan M., 1969-
Somalia. Marshall Cavendish 1997 128p il maps
(Cultures of the world) $34.21   **967.73**
1. Somalia
ISBN 0-7614-0288-8   LC 96-20492
Discusses the geography, history, government, econo-
my, people, and culture of this peninsular African nation
on the Indian Ocean
Includes glossary and bibliographical references

967.8 Tanzania

Heale, Jay
Tanzania. Marshall Cavendish 1998 128p il
maps (Cultures of the world) lib bdg $34.21
                                      967.8
1. Tanzania
ISBN 0-7614-0809-6   LC 97-42180
Describes the geography, history, government, economy, ethnic groups, lifestyle, religion, language, arts, leisure, festivals, and food of this Eastern African nation
This offers "a clear and informative text [and] . . .
captioned color photographs." Horn Book Guide
Includes glossary and bibliographical references

McCulla, Patricia E.
Tanzania. Chelsea House 1999 112p il map
(Major world nations) lib bdg $19.95   **967.8**
1. Tanzania
ISBN 0-7910-4768-7

McCulla, Patricia E.—*Continued*
First published 1989 in the Places and peoples of the
world series
Discusses the history, geography, industry, culture and
people of Tanzania
Includes glossary

967.9   Mozambique

James, R. S.
Mozambique. Chelsea House 1999 103p il
(Major world nations) lib bdg $19.95 (7 and up)
                                                    967.9
1. Mozambique
ISBN 0-7910-4744-X
First published 1988 in the Places and peoples of the
world series
Surveys the history, topography, people, and culture of
Mozambique
Includes glossary

968   Southern Africa. Republic of South Africa

Blauer, Ettagale
South Africa; by Ettagale Blauer and Jason
Lauré. Children's Press 1998 144p il (Enchantment
of the world, second series) lib bdg $32   **968**
1. South Africa
ISBN 0-516-20606-0   LC 97-26014
Describes the geography, plants, animals, history,
economy, languages, religions, sports, arts, and people of
a country that shares land borders with six nations and
surrounds one of them
Includes bibliographical references

Stein, R. Conrad, 1937-
Cape Town. Children's Press 1998 64p il maps
(Cities of the world) $26   **968**
1. Cape Town (South Africa)
ISBN 0-516-20781-4   LC 98-22246
Describes the history, culture, daily life, people,
sports, and points of interest of the legislative capital of
South Africa
Includes bibliographical references

968.06   Period as Republic, 1961-

Canesso, Claudia
South Africa. Chelsea House 1999 120p il
(Major world nations) $19.95   **968.06**
1. South Africa
ISBN 0-7910-4766-0   LC 87-18273
First published 1989 in the Places and peoples of the
world series
Surveys the history, topography, people, and culture of
South Africa, with emphasis on its current economy, in-
dustry, and place in the political world
This is "readable, informative, current, and fair, with
lots of good photos and up-to-date maps." Booklist
Includes glossary

No more strangers now; young voices from a new
South Africa; interviews by Tim McKee;
photographs by Anne Blackshaw; foreword by
Archbishop Desmond Tutu. DK Ink 1998 107p
il $19.95   **968.06**
1. South Africa
ISBN 0-7894-2524-6   LC 97-47293
"A Melanie Kroupa book"
In their own words, a variety of teenagers from South
Africa talk about their years growing up under apartheid,
and about the changes now occuring in their country
"Anne Blackshaw's engaging photographs . . . and
their captions extend the narrative with a focus on the
personal details of the individual teens' everyday life. A
wonderful book." Booklist

968.91   Zimbabwe

Barnes-Svarney, Patricia
Zimbabwe. Chelsea House 1997 128p il (Major
world nations) $19.95   **968.91**
1. Zimbabwe
ISBN 0-7910-4753-9   LC 97-18122
First published 1989 in Places and peoples of the
world series
This book about Zimbabwe presents "basic facts on
history, geography, politics, government, economy, natural resources, education, people, and culture. . . . [This
title] would be useful for reports and general background
information." SLJ
Includes glossary

968.94   Zambia

Holmes, Timothy
Zambia. Marshall Cavendish 1998 128p il maps
(Cultures of the world) lib bdg $34.21   **968.94**
1. Zambia
ISBN 0-7614-0694-8   LC 97-22298
Describes the geography, history, government, econo-
my, people, lifestyle, religion, language, arts, leisure, fes-
tivals, and food of this high plateau country in the interi-
or of Africa
Includes glossary and bibliographical references

969.1   Madagascar

Heale, Jay
Madagascar. Marshall Cavendish 1998 128p il
maps (Cultures of the world) lib bdg $34.21
                                              969.1
1. Madagascar
ISBN 0-7614-0693-X   LC 97-16569
Introduces the geography, history, religious beliefs,
government, and people of Madagascar
This offers a "lucidly written text. . . . Informative
chapters include discussion about ethnic groups, rites of
passage, family life, sports, etiquette, and human rights."
Horn Book Guide
Includes glossary and bibliographical references

Stevens, Rita
Madagascar. Chelsea House 1999 111p il map (Major world nations) $19.95 **969.1**
1. Madagascar
ISBN 0-7910-4762-8
First published 1988 in the Places and peoples of the world series
Surveys the history, topography, people, and culture of Madagascar
Includes glossary

970 North America

Peoples of the Americas. Marshall Cavendish 1999 11v set $329.95 **970**
1. Ethnology—America
ISBN 0-7614-7050-6 LC 98-2801
Contents: v1 Anguilla-Belize; v2 Bermuda-Brazil; v3 Canada-Cayman Islands; v4 Chile-Costa Rica; v5 Cuba-French Guiana; v6 Greenland-Jamaica; v7 Martinique-Paraguay; v8 Peru-Turks and Caicos Islands; v9 United States of America; v10 United States of America-Virgin Islands
"The 50 entries, arranged alphabetically by country, vary in length from 2 to 74 pages and focus on native, ethnic, and immigrant groups in these nations. Discussions center on their way of life; on their contributions, both cultural and political; and often, on their struggle for survival." SLJ
"The amount of information, logical organization, multiple access points, and attractive layout combine to create a reference tool that most school and public libraries will want in their collections." Booklist

970.004 North American native peoples

Bial, Raymond
The Cherokee. Benchmark Bks. (Tarrytown) 1999 127p il maps (Lifeways) $32.79 **970.004**
1. Cherokee Indians
ISBN 0-7614-0801-0 LC 97-26574

The Iroquois. Benchmark Bks. (Tarrytown) 1999 127p il (Lifeways) $32.79 **970.004**
1. Iroquois Indians
ISBN 0-7614-0802-9 LC 97-26573

The Navajo. Benchmark Bks. (Tarrytown) 1999 127p il maps (Lifeways) $32.79 **970.004**
1. Navajo Indians
ISBN 0-7614-0803-7 LC 97-53248

The Sioux. Benchmark Bks. (Tarrytown) 1999 127p il (Lifeways) $32.79 **970.004**
1. Dakota Indians
ISBN 0-7614-0804-5 LC 98-2915
"This series represents the social and cultural heritage of four major nations of Native Americans. Beginning with the nation's creation story and continuing through modern times, emphasis is placed on each group's struggle to survive with dignity in the modern world. Infor-

mation such as hunting, warfare, language, etc., is included. Illustrations are a blend of color photography, artwork and maps. Each book contains a time line, biographies of notables, a glossary, bibliography, index, and list of web sites and organizations. These books would be valuable resources for students doing reports." Book Rep

Brown, Dee Alexander
Bury my heart at Wounded Knee; an Indian history of the American West. Holt & Co. 1970 487p il $27.50; pa $14.95 (7 and up) **970.004**
1. Indians of North America—West (U.S.) 2. West (U.S.)—History 3. Indians of North America—Wars
ISBN 0-8050-1045-9; 0-8050-1730-5 (pa)
This is an account of the experience of the American Indian during the white man's expansion westward
"A gripping chronicle of 30 years of conflict between Native Americans and whites." Rochman. Against borders
Includes bibliographical references

Bruchac, Joseph, 1942-
Lasting echoes; an oral history of native American people. Harcourt Brace & Co. 1997 xx, 148p il $16 (7 and up) **970.004**
1. Indians of North America
ISBN 0-15-201327-X LC 97-11884
"Bruchac uses the words of American Indians (including songs and poetry) from a wide variety of tribes and sources to bring the history and plight of American Indians after their initial encounter with European explorers to life. . . . This is a well-constructed, involving presentation of an integral part of American history." Bull Cent Child Books

Ciment, James
Scholastic encyclopedia of the American Indian; [by] James Ciment with Ronald LaFrance. Scholastic Ref. 1996 224p il maps $17.95 **970.004**
1. Indians of North America—Encyclopedias
ISBN 0-590-22790-4 LC 95-26171
This is an "introduction to the history and cultures of nearly 150 tribes and groups, from Inuit to Maya. . . . Each entry contains a fact box and map, followed by a simply written narrative adorned with a plethora of cross references and plenty of small, sepia-toned photos." SLJ

Collier, Christopher, 1930-
Clash of cultures, prehistory-1638; [by] Christopher Collier, James Lincoln Collier. Benchmark Bks. (Tarrytown) 1998 95p il maps (Drama of American history) lib bdg $28.50 **970.004**
1. Indians of North America 2. United States—History—1600-1775, Colonial period 3. Culture conflict
ISBN 0-7614-0436-8 LC 96-31859
This volume "examines the civilizations on both sides of the Atlantic in the years before and during European settlement in North America. . . . While consistently

Collier, Christopher, 1930——*Continued*
presenting the big picture, the Colliers paint their
American portrait 'warts and all,' caring less about ideal-
izing our history than increasing understanding of it."
Booklist
Includes bibliographical references

Ehrlich, Amy, 1942-
Wounded Knee: an Indian history of the
American West; adapted for young readers by
Amy Ehrlich from Dee Brown's Bury my heart at
Wounded Knee. Holt & Co. 1974 202p il maps
hardcover o.p. paperback available $9.95 **970.004**
    1. Indians of North America—West (U.S.) 2. Indians
of North America—Wars 3. West (U.S.)—History
ISBN 0-8050-2700-9 (pa)
This book traces the plight of the Navaho, Apache,
Cheyenne and Sioux Indians in their struggles against the
white man in the West between 1860 and 1890. It re-
counts battles and their causes, participants, and conse-
quences during this era
"The editing is good, and this version is interesting,
readable, and smooth. A good choice for junior high students who may find the 470-page original tough going."
SLJ
Includes bibliographical references

The **Encyclopedia** of North American Indians;
general editor, D.L. Birchfield. Marshall
Cavendish 1997 11v il maps set $459.95
                                           970.004
    1. Indians of North America—Encyclopedias
ISBN 0-7614-0227-6   LC 96-7700
A comprehensive reference work on the culture and
history of Native Americans
This "is a lavishly illustrated encyclopedia providing
a multicultural perspective that will enhance the juvenile
or general reference collections of any library." Libr J
Includes bibliographical references

The **Gale** encyclopedia of Native American tribes;
edited by Sharon Malinowski [et al.] Gale Res.
1998 4v il maps set $349   **970.004**
    1. Indians of North America—Encyclopedias
ISBN 0-7876-1085-2   LC 97-36848
Contents: v1 Northeast, Southeast Caribbean; v2 Great
Basin, Southwest Middle America; v3 Arctic, Subarctic,
Great Plains, Plateau; v4 California, Pacific Northwest,
Pacific Islands
Divided by regions this set provides historical, cultural
and current information on Native American tribes
For a review see: Booklist, Sept. 1, 1998

Golston, Sydele E.
Changing woman of the Apache; women's lives
in past and present. Watts 1996 144p il map
(American Indian experience) lib bdg $24 (7 and
up)   **970.004**
    1. Apache Indians 2. Indians of North America—
Women
ISBN 0-531-11255-1   LC 95-36349

This "explores the lives of Apache women in past and
present times. Golston begins with a lengthy, detailed description of the traditional Apache ceremony marking a
young woman's passage into adulthood as that ceremony
is still practiced today. Subsequent chapters focus on the
four stages of an Apache woman's life." Booklist
    "The technique of using actual biographies as the core
of the narrative brings a refreshing immediacy and authenticity to the text." Voice Youth Advocates
Includes bibliographical references

Hazen-Hammond, Susan
Thunder Bear and Ko; the Buffalo nation and
Nambe Pueblo; text and photographs by Susan
Hazen-Hammond. Dutton Children's Bks. 1999
unp il $16.99   **970.004**
    1. Pueblo Indians
ISBN 0-525-46013-6   LC 98-22402
Describes the life of Thunder Bear Yates and his family in Nambe Pueblo, where they are trying to preserve
the traditions of their ancestors as well as the buffalo
that are sacred to their people
    "Thunder Bear's story is nicely told, and the attractive
volume will easily fit into a multicultural collection and
be a useful supplement to the study of New Mexico or
the Pueblo Indians." Booklist

Indians of North America series. Chelsea House
1987-1997 67v il maps apply to publisher for
price and availability   **970.004**
    1. Indians of North America

Volumes published in series include: The Abenaki, by
C. G. Calloway; The Apache, by M. E. Melody; The
Arapaho, by L. Fowler; The archaeology of North Amer-
ica, by D. R. Snow; The Aztecs, by F. Berdan; The
Blackfeet, by T. J. Lacey; The Cahuilla, by L. J. Bean;
The Catawbas, by J. H. Merrell; The Cherokee, by T.
Perdue; The Cheyenne, by S. Hoig; The Chicasaw, by D.
K. Hale; The Chinook, by C. E. Trafzer; The Choctaw,
by J. O. McKee; The Chumash, by R. O. Gibson; The
Coast Salish peoples, by F. W. Porter; The Comanche,
by W. H. Rollings; The Creeks, by M. D. Green; The
Crow, by F. E. Hoxie; Federal Indian policy, by L. C.
Kelly; The Hidatsa, by M. J. Schneider; The Hopi, by N.
Bonvillain; The Huron, by N. Bonvillain; The Innu (The
Montagnais-Naskapi), by P. Armitage; The Inuit, by N.
Bonvillain; The Iroquois, by B. Graymont; The Kiowa,
by J. R. Wunder; The Kwakiutl, by S. Walens; The
Lenapes, by R. S. Grumet; Literatures of the American
Indian, by A. L. Ruoff; The Lumbee, by A. L. Dial; The
Maya, by L. Trout; The Menominee, by P. K. Ourada;
The Modoc, by O. B. Faulk; The Mohawk, by N.
Bonvillain; The Nanticoke, by F. W. Porter; The Narra-
gansett, by W. S. Simmons; Native American medicine,
by N. Bonvillain; Native American religion, by N.
Bonvillain; Native Americans and Black Americans, by
K. Dramer; Native Americans and Christianity, by S.
Klots; Native Americans and the Spanish, by T. De
Angelis; The Navajos, by P. Iverson; The Nez Perce, by
C. E. Trafzer; The Ojibwa, by H. H. Tanner; The Osage,
by T. P. Wilson; The Paiute, by R. J. Franklin; The Paw-
nee, by T. J. Lacey; The Pima-Maricopa, by H. F.
Dobyns; The Potawatomi, by J. A. Clifton; The Powha-
tan tribes, by C. F. Feest; The Pueblo, by A. Ortiz; The

Indians of North America series—*Continued*
Quapaws, by W. D. Baird; The Sac and Fox, by N. Bonvillain; The Santee Sioux, by N. Bonvillain; The Seminole, by M. S. Garbarino; The Shawnee, by J. Hubbard-Brown; The Shoshone, by K. Draper; The Tarahumara, by J. G. Kennedy; The Teton Sioux, by N. Bonvillain; Urban Indians, by D. L. Fixico; The Wampanoag, by L. Weinstein-Farson; Women in American Indian society, by R. Green; The Yakima, by H. H. Schuster; The Yankton Sioux, by H. T. Hoover; The Yuma, by R. L. Bee; The Zuni, by N. Bonvillain

"The books cover all aspects of the various tribes' life-styles, including their histories, religions, relationships with white explorers and settlers, and present situation. Solidly written and fully illustrated with black-and-white photographs and historical documents, these titles will be well received as curriculum supplements, though some libraries may not want or need each book. Glossaries and short bibliographies are appended." Booklist

Krull, Kathleen, 1952-
One nation, many tribes; how kids live in Milwaukee's Indian community; photographs by David Hautzig. Lodestar Bks. 1995 48p il map (World of my own) o.p.; Penguin Bks. paperback available $5.99   **970.004**
1. Indians of North America—Wisconsin
ISBN 0-14-036522-2 (pa)   LC 93-39538
This book "introduces an Oneida/Ojibwa girl who is a talented solo hoop dancer and an Ojibwa/Comanche/Mexican boy. They are both students at the Milwaukee Indian Community School, which incorporates Native American cultures into every aspect of its curriculum. . . . Large, full color photographs, one or more on almost every page, and the use of the subjects' own words bring these children to life." SLJ
Includes bibliographical references

Lassieur, Allison
Before the storm; American Indians before the Europeans. Facts on File 1998 150p il maps (Library of American Indian history) $19.95 (7 and up)   **970.004**
1. Indians of North America
ISBN 0-8160-3651-9   LC 97-50072
A narrative history about the various Indian people of North America and their way of life before contact with Europeans
"Archaeological evidence and the science of ethnographic and historical research are utilized throughout the book. Numerous side-bars enliven the text. . . . A well-researched account." SLJ
Includes bibliographical references

Lavender, David Sievert, 1910-
Mother Earth, Father Sky; Pueblo Indians of the American Southwest; [by] David Lavender. Holiday House 1998 117p il $16.95   **970.004**
1. Pueblo Indians 2. Southwestern States—Antiquities
ISBN 0-8234-1365-9   LC 97-38119
"Lavender has combined a study of the Anasazi with a general overview of recorded Pueblo Indian history and

culture. . . . This is a lively, intriguing exploration into the archaeological study of the Anasazi culture. . . . The last three chapters sum up Pueblo peoples from the Spanish invaders to education efforts today." SLJ
Includes glossary and bibliographical references

Monroe, Jean Guard
First houses; Native American homes and sacred structures; [by] Jean Guard Monroe and Ray A. Williamson; illustrated by Susan Johnston Carlson. Houghton Mifflin 1993 147p il $16   **970.004**
1. Indians of North America—Dwellings 2. Indians of North America—Rites and ceremonies 3. Indians of North America—Folklore
ISBN 0-395-51081-3   LC 92-34900
Presents a variety of North American Indian creation myths and discusses how the "first houses" described in these myths set the pattern used by the tribes for their own homes and ritual structures
"A well-researched and documented book that takes a unique approach to its topic." SLJ
Includes glossary and bibliographical references

Murdoch, David Hamilton, 1937-
North American Indian; written by David Murdoch; photographed by Lynton Gardiner. Knopf 1995 62p il (Eyewitness books) $19; lib bdg $20.99   **970.004**
1. Indians of North America
ISBN 0-679-86169-6; 0-679-96169-0 (lib bdg)
                                                LC 94-36193
"A Dorling Kindersley book"
Published in association with the American Museum of Natural History
"Brief, scattered information concerning the history and culture of a variety of Native-American peoples is accompanied by sharp color photographs of clothing, tools, weapons, and many other antiquities. Although far from comprehensive, the book is a fine photographic resource on historical and contemporary native artifacts." Horn Book Guide

Native Americans: opposing viewpoints; William Dudley, book editor. Greenhaven Press 1998 320p il (American history series) lib bdg $26.20; pa $16.20 (7 and up)   **970.004**
1. Indians of North America
ISBN 1-56510-705-5 (lib bdg); 1-56510-704-7 (pa)
                                                LC 97-38334
A collection of primary sources documenting the history of European-Indian relations. Culture conflict, land tenure, forced removal, and assimilation are among the topics debated
Includes bibliographical references

Native North American almanac; Cynthia Rose and Duane Champagne, editors. U.X.L 1994 2v il maps set $67   **970.004**
1. Indians of North America
ISBN 0-8103-9820-6
Also available one volume adult version with same title from Gale Res.

Native North American almanac—*Continued*

"This work opens with a glossary of terms that relate to the history and culture of native peoples, followed by essays on their history and demography. Chapters then treat major cultures in the various geographic regions. Volume 2 has chapters on religion, languages, education, health, art, literature, media, and activism. Interlaced throughout the volumes are black-and-white photographs and maps. Each volume concludes with an index to the set. A good overview of contemporary Native Americans for public and middle-school libraries." Booklist

Pritzker, Barry

Native Americans; an encyclopedia of history, culture, and peoples; [by] Barry M. Pritzker. ABC-CLIO 1998 2v il maps set $150   **970.004**

1. Indians of North America—Encyclopedias

ISBN 0-87436-836-7   LC 98-21718

"Organized geographically, each section begins with an introduction to the area and its original inhabitants. Tribal entries follow, with some smaller related groups discussed together. Each article includes sections on location, population, language, history, religion, government, customs, dwellings, diet, key technology, trade, notable arts, transportation, dress, and war/weapons. A contemporary section follows, with information on government/reservations, economy, legal status, and daily life." Libr J

For a fuller review see: Booklist, Dec. 1, 1998

The **Serpent's** tongue; prose, poetry, and art of the New Mexico pueblos; edited by Nancy Wood. Dutton 1997 xxv, 230p il $35 (7 and up)
                                        970.004

1. Pueblo Indians 2. Indians of North America—Literature—Collections 3. Indians of North America—Art

ISBN 0-525-45514-0   LC 97-26295

For this collection Wood has compiled "prose, poetry, art, legends, recipes, drawings, and photographs on the Pueblos from the 1500s to the present." Book Rep

"A dynamic and haunting portrait of the daily and spiritual life of the Pueblos through time." Booklist

Includes bibliographical references

Waldman, Carl

Encyclopedia of Native American tribes; illustrations by Molly Braun. rev ed. Facts on File 1999 xxiii, 312p $65; pa $19.95   **970.004**

1. Indians of North America—Encyclopedias

ISBN 0-8160-3963-1; 0-8160-3964-X (pa)
                                        LC 98-50263

First published 1988

This "gives an overview of the history and culture of tribes and peoples from Abenaki to Zuni. Focus is on U.S. North American tribes, but there is also coverage of cultural groupings in Canada and Central America. The volume is notable for its ease of use, its wonderful illustrations, and the great starting point it provides." Booklist

Wolfson, Evelyn

From Abenaki to Zuni; a dictionary of native American tribes; illustrated by William Sauts Bock. Walker & Co. 1988 215p il maps $20.95; lib bdg $18.85; pa $11.95   **970.004**

1. Indians of North America—Dictionaries

ISBN 0-8027-6789-3; 0-8027-6790-7 (lib bdg); 0-8027-7445-8 (pa)   LC 87-27875

An alphabetical identification of sixty-eight of the larger North American Indian tribes, describing their habitats, social life and customs, food, means of travel, and modern descendants

"Although, as the author notes, the book is not exhaustive in terms of tribes covered, Wolfson has provided help for researchers by pulling together data on so many native peoples in such a handy format. Students will be pleased with the concise summaries of information needed for school reports." Booklist

Includes bibliographical references

From the earth to beyond the sky; Native American medicine; illustrated by Jennifer Hewitson. Houghton Mifflin 1993 96p il $16
                                        970.004

1. Indians of North America—Medicine 2. Shamanism 3. Indians of North America—Religion

ISBN 0-395-55009-2   LC 92-46035

An illustrated account of the traditions and customs of Native American medicine men

"Clearly written and spiced with anecdotes, this provides a view of another way of thinking as well as concrete information about medical practices." Booklist

Includes glossary and bibliographical references

Yue, Charlotte

The Pueblo; [by] Charlotte and David Yue. Houghton Mifflin 1986 117p il hardcover o.p. paperback available $6.95   **970.004**

1. Pueblo Indians

ISBN 0-395-54961-2 (pa)   LC 85-27087

"A look at the many facets of Pueblo life, not often covered in the many books on Native Americans. Filled with illustrations and diagrams that expand and clarify, it emphasizes the relationship between the people and the land. Superb nonfiction and a boon to report writers." SLJ

Includes bibliographical references

The wigwam and the longhouse; [by] Charlotte and David Yue. Houghton Mifflin 2000 118p il $15   **970.004**

1. Woodland Indians

ISBN 0-395-84169-0   LC 98-28971

Describes the history, customs, religion, government, homes, and present-day status of the various native peoples that inhabited the eastern woodlands since before the coming of the Europeans

Includes bibliographical references

970.01 North America—Early history to 1599

West, Delno C., 1936-
Braving the North Atlantic; the Vikings, the Cabots, and Jacques Cartier voyage to America; by Delno C. West and Jean M. West. Atheneum Bks. for Young Readers 1996 86p il maps $16 **970.01**
1. America—Exploration 2. Explorers
ISBN 0-689-31822-7   LC 95-43140
"Beginning with the sometimes accidental exploration of the Vikings, the Wests touch on Columbus, and then take a detailed look at John Cabot's voyages. A final section discusses Verrazano and Cartier and mentions Frobisher and Hudson's searches for the Northwest Passage. With lively discussion of cartography, ethnic populations, archaeological evidence, and the uses and limitations of primary-source material, this is a compact, accurate resource." SLJ
Includes glossary and bibliographical references

971 Canada

Grabowski, John F.
Canada. Lucent Bks. 1998 112p il maps (Modern nations of the world) lib bdg $22.45 (7 and up)   **971**
1. Canada
ISBN 1-56006-520-6   LC 97-40226
Examines the land, people, and history of Canada and discusses its state of affairs and place in the world today
"A mature and intelligent treatment of a complex nation." SLJ
Includes bibliographical references

Junior Worldmark encyclopedia of the Canadian provinces. U.X.L 1997 225p il maps $39   **971**
1. Canada—Encyclopedias
ISBN 0-7876-1490-4   LC 96-34240
"Arranged alphabetically, each article begins with an overview that includes such information as the origins of the province or territory's name, the flag, and the coat of arms. The scope of the detailed entries is extensive, presenting information under 40 numbered headings, such as topography, environmental protection, industry, and public finance. . . . The numerous black-and-white photographs are appropriately placed. For each province or territory, there is a clear gray-tone map, a population chart, and a chronological list of the premiers or territorial leaders." SLJ
Includes glossary and bibliographical references

971.3 Ontario

Fisher, Leonard Everett, 1924-
Niagara Falls; nature's wonder. Holiday House 1996 63p il $16.95   **971.3**
1. Niagara Falls (N.Y. and Ont.)
ISBN 0-8234-1240-7   LC 95-42740

"Among the topics covered are the Maid of the Mist ferry, the construction of suspension bridges over the Niagara River, the impact of the Falls on painters and writers, and the persistent attempt to conquer them via tightrope, raft, and barrel. The many black-and-white illustrations include nineteenth-century paintings, engravings, and broadsides as well as nineteenth- and twentieth-century photographs." Booklist

971.9 Northern territories of Canada

Jones, Charlotte Foltz, 1945-
Yukon gold; the story of the Klondike Gold Rush. Holiday House 1999 99p il $18.95   **971.9**
1. Klondike River valley (Yukon)—Gold discoveries
ISBN 0-8234-1403-5   LC 98-20977
Recounts the quest for gold that took place in the late 1890s in the Klondike region of the Yukon Territory of northwestern Canada
"Historical photographs, posters and newspaper headlines give readers a flavor of the times. This is a solid resource for information about the period." Publ Wkly
Includes glossary and bibliographical references

Walsh Shepherd, Donna, 1948-
The Klondike gold rush. Watts 1998 64p il maps lib bdg $22.50; pa $6.95   **971.9**
1. Klondike River valley (Yukon)—Gold discoveries
ISBN 0-531-20360-3 (lib bdg); 0-531-15909-4 (pa)
                                   LC 97-38340
"A First book"
Describes the adventures of those who flocked to the Klondike after gold was discovered there in 1896
"Short enough to appeal to reluctant researchers and long enough to provide a basic grasp of the events, the book succeeds admirably." SLJ
Includes bibliographical references

972 Middle America. Mexico

Arnold, Caroline, 1944-
City of the Gods; Mexico's ancient city of Teotihuacán; photographs by Richard Hewitt. Clarion Bks. 1994 49p il map $14.95   **972**
1. Indians of Mexico 2. Teotihuacán site (San Juan Teotihuacán, Mexico)
ISBN 0-395-66584-1   LC 93-40811
In text and photographs, this book examines the ancient city of Teotihuacán in Mexico
"Students doing reports will find this a good resource, but the arresting photographs will draw browsers in as well." Booklist
Includes glossary

Building the Panama Canal; chronicles from National Geographic; Arthur M. Schlesinger, Jr., senior consulting editor; Fred L. Israel, general editor. Chelsea House 1999 131p il (Cultural and geographical exploration) lib bdg $19.95 (7 and up)   **972**
1. Panama Canal
ISBN 0-7910-5102-1   LC 98-44479

Building the Panama Canal—*Continued*
"Four articles reprinted from *National Geographic* magazine between 1904-1914. Two of them were written by George Goethals, the chief engineer of the project. They provide an insider's look at the many human and technological problems that had to be overcome to complete the canal. . . . [This] title is useful in providing a unique look at the building of what U.S. Secretary of War Lindley Garrison in 1914 called, 'a perpetual memorial to the genius and enterprise of our people.' It is an excellent supplemental purchase." SLJ
Includes bibliographical references

Goodwin, William, 1943-
Mexico. Lucent Bks. 1999 128p il maps (Modern nations of the world) lib bdg $22.45 (7 and up)   972
1. Mexico
ISBN 1-56006-351-3   LC 98-29730
Discusses the history, geography, climate, government, culture, people, and modern aspects of Mexico
"The information is thorough and clear, with well-researched detail." Booklist
Includes bibliographical references

Greene, Jacqueline Dembar
The Maya. Watts 1992 63p il lib bdg $22; pa $6.95   972
1. Mayas
ISBN 0-531-20067-1 (lib bdg); 0-531-15638-9 (pa)
LC 91-29433
"A First book"
Describes life in this ancient civilization, including farming techniques, rulers, priests, gods, markets, courts, palaces, science, letters, and art
Includes bibliographical references

Meyer, Carolyn
The mystery of the ancient Maya; [by] Carolyn Meyer and Charles Gallenkamp. rev ed. Margaret K. McElderry Bks. 1995 159p $15 (7 and up)
972
1. Mayas
ISBN 0-689-50619-8   LC 94-18274
First published 1985
This overview of Mayan culture examines the discovery of ancient ruins in the mid-1800s and follows modern scientists and archaeologists as they seek an explanation for the civilization's abrupt end

Platt, Richard, 1953-
Aztecs; the fall of the Aztec capital; written by Richard Platt; illustrated by Peter Dennis. DK Pub. 1999 48p il (DK discoveries) $14.95   972
1. Aztecs
ISBN 0-7894-3957-3   LC 99-12002
A brief history of the Aztec Indians including their way of life, religion, and rulers

Rummel, Jack
Mexico. Chelsea House 1999 128p il map (Major world nations) $19.95   972
1. Mexico
ISBN 0-7910-4763-6   LC 89-28261

First published 1990 in Places and peoples of the world series
Surveys the history, topography, economy, peoples, and government of Mexico
This "is a worthy purchase." SLJ
Includes glossary

Steele, Philip
The Aztec news; consultants: Penny Bateman & Norma Rosso. Candlewick Press 1997 32p il $15.99; pa $6.99   972
1. Aztecs
ISBN 0-7636-0115-2; 0-7636-0427-5 (pa)
LC 96-31655
Uses a newspaper format to present articles about Aztec history, politics, religion, trading and farming, sports, the military and other aspects of daily life
"An alternative way of writing nonfiction that will attract those who are turned off by traditional nonfiction or are looking for something fresh." Booklist

Stefoff, Rebecca, 1951-
Independence and revolution in Mexico; 1810-1940. Facts on File 1993 150p il maps (World history library) $19.95 (7 and up)   972
1. Mexico—History
ISBN 0-8160-2841-9   LC 92-37380
An "account of 130 years in Mexico's struggle for independence—from the insurrection led by Father Miguel Hidalgo in 1810, through revolutions led by Pancho Villa and Emiliano Zapata, to the term of President Lazaro Cardenas (1936-40). . . . Stefoff writes about the political events and the people in an immediate, absorbing fashion that successfully engages the reader." Booklist
Includes glossary and bibliographical references

Stein, R. Conrad, 1937-
Mexico. Children's Press 1998 144p il maps (Enchantment of the world, second series) lib bdg $32   972
1. Mexico
ISBN 0-516-20650-8   LC 97-40708
This describes the geography, history, government, economy and culture of Mexico
"For the most part, the writing and presentation of information are of high quality." SLJ
Includes bibliographical references

Tanaka, Shelley
Lost temple of the Aztecs; what it was like when the Spaniards invaded Mexico; illustrations by Greg Ruhl; diagrams and maps by Jack McMaster; historical consultation by Eduardo Matos Moctezuma. Hyperion Bks. for Children; Madison Press Bks. 1998 48p il maps $16.95
972
1. Aztecs 2. Mexico—History
ISBN 0-7868-0441-6   LC 98-10986
"I was there books"
Uses the discovery of the temple in Mexico City, what was the Aztec city of Tenochtitlan, to introduce the story

Tanaka, Shelley—*Continued*
of the Spanish conquest of Moctezuma and his empire in
the sixteenth century
"Lavishly illustrated with full-color photos, period artwork, and dramatic full-page paintings, the book is handsome and eye-catching." SLJ
Includes glossary and bibliographical references

972.81   Guatemala

Sheehan, Sean, 1951-
Guatemala. Marshall Cavendish 1998 128p il
maps (Cultures of the world) lib bdg $34.21
972.81
1. Guatemala
ISBN 0-7614-0812-6   LC 97-44619
Introduces the geography, history, religion, government, economy, and culture of one of the poorest countries in the western hemisphere
"A good-quality full-color photograph, reproduction,
or map appears on most pages. This [is a] solid volume."
SLJ
Includes glossary and bibliographical references

972.83   Honduras

McGaffey, Leta
Honduras. Marshall Cavendish 1999 128p il
maps (Cultures of the world) lib bdg $35.64
972.83
1. Honduras
ISBN 0-7614-0955-6   LC 98-54908
This is a look at the Central American nation. "Following introductory chapters on the geography, history,
and government, the clearly written book focuses on contemporary life. The economy, population, religion, leisure
activities, holidays, indigenous and ethnic groups, and rural and urban lifestyles are all covered. . . . A quality,
full-color photograph appears on almost every page." SLJ
Includes glossary and bibliographical references

972.86   Costa Rica

Foley, Erin, 1967-
Costa Rica. Marshall Cavendish 1997 128p il
maps (Cultures of the world) lib bdg $34.21
972.86
1. Costa Rica
ISBN 0-7614-0285-3   LC 96-17309
Surveys the geography, history, government, and culture of Costa Rica
Includes glossary and bibliographical references

Morrison, Marion
Costa Rica. Children's Press 1998 144p il maps
(Enchantment of the world, second series) lib bdg
$32   **972.86**
1. Costa Rica
ISBN 0-516-20469-6   LC 97-40665

Describes the geography, history, culture, religion, and
people of the small Central American nation of Costa
Rica
Includes bibliographical references

972.9   West Indies and Bermuda

Anthony, Suzanne
West Indies. Chelsea House 1999 127p il maps
(Major world nations) $19.95   **972.9**
1. West Indies
ISBN 0-7910-4772-5   LC 88-30434
An overview of the history, geography, economy, gov-
ernment, people, and culture of the West Indies
Includes glossary

Hodge, Alison
The West Indies. Raintree Steck-Vaughn Pubs.
1998 47p il maps (Country fact files) lib bdg
$24.25   **972.9**
1. West Indies
ISBN 0-8172-5402-1   LC 97-34953
First published 1996 in the United Kingdom with title:
The Caribbean
Presents an overview of the geography, climate, econ-
omy, government, people, and culture of the West Indies
"Photographs, charts, graphs, and maps augment de-
tailed textual information . . . making the volume a use-
ful tool for school reports." Horn Book Guide
Includes glossary and bibliographical references

972.94   Haiti

Hintz, Martin, 1945-
Haiti. Children's Press 1998 143p il maps
(Enchantment of the world, second series) lib bdg
$32   **972.94**
1. Haiti
ISBN 0-516-20603-6   LC 97-25518
Describes the geography, history, government, people,
and culture of the second oldest republic in the Western
Hemisphere
Includes bibliographical references

973   United States

America the beautiful, second series. Children's
Press 1998-2000 38v il maps lib bdg ea $32
973

Replaces titles in the original series published 1987-
1992
Volumes available are: Alabama, by L. Davis; Alaska,
by D. Walsh Shepherd; California, by A. Heinrichs; Colorado, by J. F. Blashfield; Connecticut, by S. McNair;
Florida, by A. Heinrichs; Georgia, by N. Robinson Masters; Hawaii, by M. Hintz; Illinois, by A. Santella; Indiana, by A. Heinrichs; Iowa, by M. Hintz; Kansas, by N.
Robinson Masters; Kentucky, by R. C. Stein; Louisiana,

America the beautiful, second series—*Continued*
by M. Hintz; Maine, by D. Kent; Massachusetts, by S. McNair; Michigan, by M. Hintz; Minnesota, by M. Hintz; Mississippi, by C. George; Missouri, by M. Hintz; Nebraska, by S. McNair; Nevada, by R. C. Stein; New Jersey, by R. C. Stein; New Mexico, by D. Kent; New York, by A. Heinrichs; North Carolina, by M. Hintz; Ohio, by A. Heinrichs; Oklahoma, by J. Reedy; Oregon, by S. Ingram; Puerto Rico, by L. Davis; Rhode Island, by S. McNair; South Carolina, by R. C. Stein; Texas, by A. Heinrichs; Virginia, by J. F. Blashfield; Washington, D.C., by R. C. Stein; Wisconsin, by J. F. Blashfield

"Several chapters on the history of the state begin each book; sections on geography, government and politics, the economy, diversity of the population, education, arts and leisure, famous citizens, and museums and historical sites follow." SLJ

These books "are solid purchases for many libraries. They feature clear, lively writing with considerable amounts of information. . . . Maps are a particularly strong feature." Booklist

Celebrate the states. Benchmark Bks. (Tarrytown) 1996-2000 40v il maps music lib bdg ea $35.64
                                  973

Volumes available are: Alabama, by D. Shirley; Alaska, by R. Stefoff; Arkansas, by L. Altman; Arizona, by M. McDaniel; California, by L. Altman; Colorado, by E. H. Ayer; Connecticut by V. Sherrow; Delaware, by M. Schuman; Florida, by P. Chang; Hawaii, by J. Goldberg; Idaho, by R. Stefoff; Illinois, by M. T. Brill; Indiana, by M. T. Brill; Iowa, by P. Morice; Kansas, by R. Bjorkland; Kentucky, by T. Barrett; Louisiana, by S. LeVert; Maryland, by L. Pietrzyk; Massachusetts, by S. LeVert; Michigan, by M. T. Brill; Minnesota, by M. Schwabacher; Mississippi, by D. Shirley; New Hampshire, by S. Otfinoski; New Jersey, by W. Moragne; New Mexico, by M. McDaniel; New York, by V. Schomp; Ohio, by V. Sherrow; Oregon, by R. Stefoff; Pennsylvania, by S. Peters; Rhode Island, by T. Klein; South Dakota, by M. McDaniel; Tennessee, by T. Barrett; Texas, by C. Bredeson; Vermont, by D. Elish; Virginia, by T. Barrett; Washington,, by R. Steffof; Washington, D.C., by D. Elish; West Virginia, by N. Hoffman; Wisconsin, by K. Zeinert; Wyoming, by G. Baldwin

"These books each contain six chapters devoted to the state's geography, history, government and economy, people, achievements, and landmarks. A section of reference facts and figures is also included. Competently written, the books serve as attractive and accessible introductions to the . . . states." Horn Book Guide

Documents of American history; edited by Henry Steele Commager and Milton Cantor. Prentice-Hall 2v il o.p.   973
1. United States—History—Sources

First published 1934 by Crofts
"Compilation of official and archival documents that illustrate American history. All constitutional amendments, important Supreme Court decisions, and many presidential addresses are included. Useful for beginning documentary research." N Y Public Libr. Book of How & Where to Look It Up

Facts about the states; editors, Joseph Nathan Kane, Janet Podell, Steven Anzovin. 2nd ed. Wilson, H.W. 1994 c1993 624p il $60   973
1. United States—Local history 2. State governments
ISBN 0-8242-0849-8   LC 93-30328
First published 1989
Provides geographic, demographic, economic, political, and cultural facts about the fifty states, Puerto Rico, and the District of Columbia. Part I presents state entries in alphabetical order. Part II provides comparative tables that rank states in categories such as population, geography, education, and finance

Greenberg, Judith E.
Young people's letters to the president. Watts 1998 96p il (In their own voices) $22   973
1. Presidents—United States 2. Children—United States 3. United States—Politics and government—1900-1999 (20th century)
ISBN 0-531-11435-X   LC 97-51202
A selection of letters written to United States presidents by young people is accompanied by information providing historical context for the writers' concerns and ideas
"This is a worthwhile purchase for those interested in a look at letters to presidents over time." SLJ
Includes bibliographical references

Hakim, Joy
A history of US. 2nd ed. Oxford Univ. Press 1999 11v il maps set $219.45; pa $153.45   973
1. United States—History
ISBN 0-19-512773-0; 0-19-512774-9 (pa)
                      LC 98-180015
First published 1993-1995
Contents: bk 1 The first Americans; bk 2 Making thirteen colonies; bk 3 From colonies to country; bk 4 The new nation; bk 5 Liberty for all?; bk 6 War, terrible war; bk 7 Reconstruction and reform; bk 8 An age of extremes; bk 9 War, peace, and all that jazz; bk 10 All the people; bk 11 Sourcebook and index
Presents the history of America from the earliest times of the Native Americans to the Clinton administration
This is an "inviting American history series that has proved useful in the circulating collection as well as on the reference shelf." Booklist
Includes bibliographical references

Moss, Joyce, 1951-
Profiles in American history; significant events and the people who shaped them; [by] Joyce Moss and George Wilson. U.X.L 1994 8v il maps set $265   973
1. United States—History 2. United States—Biography
ISBN 0-8103-9207-0
v1 Exploration to Revolution; v2 Constitutional convention to the War of 1812; v3 Indian removal to the antislavery movement; v4 Westward movement to the Civil War; v5 Reconstruction to the Spanish-American War; v6 Immigration to women's rights and roles; v7 Great Depression to the Cuban Missile Crisis; v8 Civil rights movement to the present

Moss, Joyce, 1951-—*Continued*
In this "eight-volume set, each volume encompasses a specific time period, focusing on 5 to 7 events and 20 people who helped shape those events. The intent of the series is to expose middle-school and high-school readers to the diversity of personalities who left their mark on America. The use of portraits, maps, excerpts from primary sources, and sidebars containing related information is intended not only to increase the research value of the series, but also to make history more relevant to readers." Booklist

973.02   United States—History—Miscellany. Chronologies

Carruth, Gorton
The encyclopedia of American facts and dates. HarperCollins Pubs. $45   **973.02**
1. United States—History—Chronology 2. Historical chronology

Also available from New Am. Lib. in a paperback abridged edition with title: What happened when
Companion volume to The encyclopedia of world facts and dates (1993)
First published 1956 by Crowell. (10th edition 1997) Periodically revised
Entries that deal with a variety of topics are chronologically arranged in parallel columns to show concurrent events in American life, from around 1000 A.D. to the present

973.03   United States—History—Encyclopedias and dictionaries

The **American** Heritage encyclopedia of American history; general editor, John Mack Faragher. Holt & Co. 1998 1106p il $45   **973.03**
1. United States—History—Encyclopedias
ISBN 0-8050-4438-8   LC 97-19097
Covering American history from pre-Columbian times to the 1990s this reference comprises some 3000 entries each averaging "about a paragraph, with broader topics covered in several paragraphs. Most entries have *See* references, and larger subjects conclude with a bibliography. State entries have a chronology detailing their exploration and development." Libr J
For a fuller review see: Booklist, Nov. 15, 1998

Bock, Judy
Scholastic encyclopedia of the United States; [by] Judy Bock, Rachel Kranz; [pub. in assn. with] Bascom Communications. Scholastic Ref. 1997 140p il maps $17.95   **973.03**
1. United States—Encyclopedias
ISBN 0-590-94747-8   LC 96-39774
Presents historical, geographical, and miscellaneous information about each of the fifty states
For a review see: Booklist, Nov. 15, 1997

English, June, 1955-
Scholastic encyclopedia of the United States at war; [by] June A. English, Thomas D. Jones. Scholastic Ref. 1998 188p il maps $18.95 **973.03**
1. United States—Military history—Encyclopedias
ISBN 0-590-59959-3   LC 97-46492
Discusses all of the major wars in which the United States has participated beginning with the American Revolution and concluding with the Gulf War of 1991
"The use of color throughout the book is especially effective in keeping readers focused on the different areas under discussion. This would be a good choice for middle school students." Book Rep

Junior Worldmark encyclopedia of the states. U.X.L 1996 4v il maps lib bdg set $105
973.03
1. United States—Dictionaries
ISBN 0-7876-0736-3   LC 95-36740
Based on Worldmark encyclopedia of the States
This encyclopedia "includes the District of Columbia and Caribbean and Pacific dependencies, and provides an overview of the United States. Each state entry begins with a black-and-white illustration of the seal and flag and capsule information. . . . More detailed information follows under 40 numbered subject areas (simplifying comparison) and includes history, local government, industry, ethnic groups, environmental protection, economy, religion, migration, and famous natives." SLJ
"This set will be heavily used because it has most of the important information that teachers request for reports and much more. It is highly recommended for elementary, middle-school, and public libraries." Booklist

Worldmark encyclopedia of the states. Gale Res. maps $145   **973.03**
1. United States—Encyclopedias

First published 1981 by Harper & Row (4th edition 1998) Periodically revised
"Comprehensive examination of each state within the framework of 50 standard subject headings. Includes economic policy, energy and power, resources, education, the press, famous persons, etc." N Y Public Libr. Ref Books for Child Collect. 2d edition

973.2   United States—Colonial period, 1607-1775

Collier, Christopher, 1930-
The French and Indian War, 1660-1763; [by] Christopher Collier, James Lincoln Collier. Benchmark Bks. (Tarrytown) 1998 94p il maps (Drama of American history) lib bdg $28.50
973.2
1. United States—History—1755-1763, French and Indian War 2. United States—History—1600-1775, Colonial period
ISBN 0-7614-0439-2   LC 96-44063
This volume "explains what was happening in Europe as well as in North America during the conflict, giving the broad perspective necessary for understanding the events." Booklist
Includes bibliographical references

Colonial America. Grolier Educ. 1998 10v il set $299   **973.2**
1. United States—History—1600-1775, Colonial period
ISBN 0-7172-9193-6   LC 97-44595
Contents: v1 Arcadia-Byrd II, William; v2 Cabot-Detroit; v3 Disease-Games and sports; v4 George III-Indentured servants; v5 Indigo-Marquette, Jacques; v6 Marriage-Navigation acts; v7 New France-Pennsylvania; v8 Philadelphia-Revere; v9 Rhode Island-Stamp Act; v10 Stono Rebellion-Zenger
"Topics and items related to Colonial America are arranged alphabetically throughout this set. . . . The more than 250 entries are generally one to six pages long. . . . The numerous illustrations include photographs, drawings, diagrams, and maps—all fully captioned, many in color." Booklist
"An accessible, eye-catching, and valuable resource." SLJ
Includes bibliographical references

Dean, Ruth, 1947-
Life in the American colonies; by Ruth Dean and Melissa Thomson. Lucent Bks. 1999 96p il maps (Way people live) lib bdg $17.96 (7 and up)   **973.2**
1. United States—Social life and customs—1600-1775, Colonial period 2. United States—History—1600-1775, Colonial period
ISBN 1-56006-376-9   LC 98-28726
Discusses the day-to-day aspects of country and city life in the American colonies for a variety of people including members of different professions, specific immigrant groups, and slaves
Includes bibliographical references

Howarth, Sarah
Colonial people. Millbrook Press 1994 47p il (People and places) lib bdg $21.90   **973.2**
1. United States—Social life and customs—1600-1775, Colonial period
ISBN 1-56294-512-2   LC 94-20608
"Provides brief portraits of the life styles and work of Native Americans, governor, goodwife, apprentice, Puritan, servant, planter, slave, fur trader, constable, smuggler, and patriot. . . . Brief quotations and black-and-white and full-color illustrations and reproductions are interspersed throughout. . . . The material is well organized." SLJ
Includes glossary and bibliographical references

Colonial places. Millbrook Press 1994 46p il (People and places) lib bdg $21.90   **973.2**
1. United States—Social life and customs—1600-1775, Colonial period
ISBN 1-56294-513-0   LC 94-25754
This "describes several sites around which life in early America revolved, including the governor's house, the meetinghouse, the tobacco field, the church, the post office, the harbor, and the fort. . . . Topics [are] presented in short, well-outlined chapters. Large print and numerous photographic reproductions and drawings (some in color) add to the . . . appeal. Chapters also include quotations from period writings." Booklist
Includes glossary and bibliographical references

Warner, J. F. (John F.), 1929-
Colonial American home life; by John F. Warner. Watts 1993 127p il (Colonial America) lib bdg $22   **973.2**
1. United States—Social life and customs—1600-1775, Colonial period
ISBN 0-531-12541-6   LC 93-3963
Discusses why people settled in the American colonies and describes aspects of their daily lives, including homes, clothing, food, work, school, and amusements
This is "informative and readable." SLJ
Includes glossary and bibliographical references

Washburne, Carolyn Kott, 1944-
A multicultural portrait of colonial life. Marshall Cavendish 1994 80p il (Perspectives) lib bdg $28.50   **973.2**
1. Minorities 2. United States—History—1600-1775, Colonial period 3. United States—Social life and customs—1600-1775, Colonial period
ISBN 1-85435-657-7   LC 93-10320
"Washburne examines the influences of African Americans, women, and Native Americans on U.S. colonial life. Individuals such as Abigail Adams, Mary Katherine Goddard, James Forten, Pontiac, and Phillis Wheatley are briefly profiled and placed in a historical context. Each group's form of governance; work, trade, and manufacturing; home and family life; alliances and conflicts; and enduring legacies are related. . . . An attractive resource." SLJ
Includes glossary and bibliographical references

973.3 United States—Periods of Revolution and Confederation, 1775-1789

The **American** revolutionaries: a history in their own words, 1750-1800; edited by Milton Meltzer. Crowell 1987 210p il hardcover o.p. paperback available $6.95   **973.3**
1. United States—History—1775-1783, Revolution 2. United States—History—1755-1763, French and Indian War
ISBN 0-06-446145-9 (pa)   LC 86-47846
"Meltzer has assembled a collage of eyewitness accounts, speech and diary excerpts, letters, and other documents for a chronological account of the half century that included the American Revolution. . . . The voices of women who accompanied the troops and of blacks who fought with the army are both represented." Bull Cent Child Books

Brenner, Barbara
If you were there in 1776. Bradbury Press 1994 136p il $17   **973.3**
1. United States. Declaration of Independence 2. United States—Social life and customs—1600-1775, Colonial period
ISBN 0-02-712322-7   LC 93-24060
Demonstrates how the concepts and principles expressed in the Declaration of Independence were drawn

Brenner, Barbara—*Continued*
from the experiences of living in America in the late eighteenth century, with emphasis given to how children lived on a New England farm, a Southern plantation, and the frontier

"The author's inclusion of details of how peoples' lives began to change as a result of the Revolution and her accessible style are the selling points here. Both budding historians and report writers will find this title worth their time." SLJ

Includes bibliographical references

Collier, Christopher, 1930-
The American Revolution, 1763-1783; [by] Christopher Collier, James Lincoln Collier. Benchmark Bks. (Tarrytown) 1998 95p il maps (Drama of American history) lib bdg $28.50
973.3
1. United States—History—1775-1783, Revolution
ISBN 0-7614-0440-6   LC 96-45440
Examines the people and events involved in the significant war by which the thirteen original colonies broke away from England
Includes bibliographical references

Cox, Clinton
Come all you brave soldiers; blacks in the Revolutionary War. Scholastic 1999 182p il $15.95
973.3
1. African American soldiers 2. United States—History—1775-1783, Revolution
ISBN 0-590-47576-2   LC 97-44198
Tells the story of the thousands of black men who served as soldiers fighting for independence from England during the American Revolutionary War

"An interesting and informative survey. . . . Black-and-white reproductions of period prints, documents, and paintings are included." SLJ

Includes bibliographical references

Gay, Kathlyn
Revolutionary War; [by] Kathlyn Gay, Martin Gay. 21st Cent. Bks. (NY) 1995 64p il map (Voices from the past) lib bdg $18.90   **973.3**
1. United States—History—1775-1783, Revolution
ISBN 0-8050-2844-7   LC 95-13415
An illustrated look at the causes, battles and personalities of the American Revolution
Includes bibliographical references

Hull, Mary
The Boston Tea Party in American history. Enslow Pubs. 1999 128p il (In American history) lib bdg $19.95   **973.3**
1. Boston Tea Party, 1773 2. United States—History—1775-1783, Revolution—Causes
ISBN 0-7660-1139-9   LC 98-5798
Presents the people and events connected with the dynamic episode called the Boston Tea Party, which helped to spawn the American Revolution

"The writing is clear, and the pages are enlivened by black-and-white illustrations, including photos of source documents." Booklist

Includes bibliographical references

Jaffe, Steven H.
Who were the founding fathers? two hundred years of reinventing American history. Holt & Co. 1996 227p il $16.95 (7 and up)   **973.3**
1. United States—History—1775-1783, Revolution
2. Historiography
ISBN 0-8050-3102-2   LC 95-42581
"Beginning with the Founding Fathers as seen in their own time, by contemporary reporters and historians, Jaffe shows how we have reinterpreted our early leaders with each new historical era." Book Rep

"The text clips along at a lively pace, accompanied by interesting, seldom-seen archival cartoons and reproductions that illustrate the points. A fine way to encourage critical thinking and get young people to examine the societal values that we all take so much for granted." SLJ

Includes bibliographical references

Lukes, Bonnie L.
The Boston Massacre. Lucent Bks. 1998 111p il (Famous trials) lib bdg $17.96 (7 and up) **973.3**
1. Boston Massacre, 1770
ISBN 1-56006-467-6   LC 97-27445
"This book describes the Boston Massacre of March 5, 1770, as well as the laws, events, and public sentiments leading up to it, and the trials of the British soldiers accused of killing civilians that evening." Booklist

"A well-researched, readable book. Lukes presents a fair and detailed look at the many facets of the Boston Massacre." SLJ

Includes bibliographical references

Murphy, Jim, 1947-
A young patriot; the American Revolution as experienced by one boy. Clarion Bks. 1996 101p il maps $16; pa $6.95   **973.3**
1. Martin, Joseph Plumb, 1760-1850 2. United States—History—1775-1783, Revolution
ISBN 0-395-60523-7; 0-395-90019-0 (pa)
LC 93-38789
"Using Joseph Plumb Martin's first person account of his participation in the Revolutionary War as primary source material, Murphy intertwines this story of one teenager's life as a soldier with broader information about the Revolution, to put Martin's story in context. The handsome, informative, and fascinating look at American history is illustrated with many period reproductions." Horn Book Guide

Includes bibliographical references

Peacock, Louise
Crossing the Delaware; a history in many voices; illustrated by Walter Lyon Krudop. Atheneum Bks. for Young Readers 1998 40p il $17   **973.3**
1. Washington, George, 1732-1799 2. Trenton (N.J.), Battle of, 1776
ISBN 0-689-80994-8   LC 97-12431
Examines the events leading up to the Battle of Trenton, the battle itself, and its aftermath, as told through historical excerpts, a tour of Washington's crossing, and a series of fictionalized letters

"The shifts in voice work effectively, creating an unusually personal look at a historical event." SLJ

Zeinert, Karen
Those remarkable women of the American revolution. Millbrook Press 1996 96p il lib bdg $27.40 (7 and up)   **973.3**
1. Women—United States—History 2. United States—History—1775-1783, Revolution
ISBN 1-56294-657-9   LC 95-47609
"Zeinert chronicles the many contributions made by women during the Revolutionary War. She describes the role of both patriots and loyalists; black and Indian women; Northern women as well as those on Southern plantations, showing how the war forced them to assume nontraditional roles." SLJ
Students "will be well-served by Zeinert's work. . . . The book's format is friendly, and the pages have a crisp, clean look that young adults will find appealing. Illustrations and captions are well-chosen, adding to the reader's understanding of the material. The bibliography, index, and further reading sections make this a helpful resource for students doing more in-depth research on a particular woman or event." Voice Youth Advocates

Zell, Fran, 1947-
A multicultural portrait of the American Revolution. Benchmark Bks. (Tarrytown) 1996 80p il (Perspectives) lib bdg $28.50   **973.3**
1. United States—History—1775-1783, Revolution
ISBN 0-7614-0051-6   LC 95-11032
Describes the history of the American Revolution, focusing on the lives of African Americans, Native Americans, and women
This is "well-researched. . . . Illustrated with black-and-white and color photographs and historical reproductions." Horn Book Guide
Includes glossary and bibliographical references

973.4   United States—Constitutional period, 1789-1809

Blumberg, Rhoda, 1917-
What's the deal? Jefferson, Napoleon and the Louisiana Purchase. National Geographic Soc. 1998 144p il maps $18.95 (7 and up)   **973.4**
1. Napoleon I, Emperor of the French, 1769-1821 2. Jefferson, Thomas, 1743-1826 3. Louisiana Purchase 4. United States—History—1783-1809
ISBN 0-7922-7013-4   LC 97-43679
Discusses the Louisiana Purchase of 1803 and the political maneuverings of Napoleon and Jefferson that made it possible. Includes information on the people involved
"This is a straightforward, well-researched, and smoothly written book of political history." SLJ
Includes bibliographical references

Collier, Christopher, 1930-
Building a new nation: the Federalist era, 1789-1801; [by] Christopher Collier, James Lincoln Collier. Benchmark Bks. (Tarrytown) 1999 95p il (Drama of American history) lib bdg $28.50   **973.4**
1. United States—Politics and government—1783-1809 2. United States—History—1783-1809
ISBN 0-7614-0777-4   LC 97-26491

Examines the events and personalities involved in the political development of the United States in the period following the creation of the Constitution
Includes bibliographical references

The Jeffersonian Republicans: the Louisiana Purchase and the war of 1812; 1800-1823; [by] Christopher Collier, James Lincoln Collier. Benchmark Bks. (Tarrytown) 1999 93p il maps (Drama of American history) lib bdg $28.50   **973.4**
1. Republican Party (U.S.)—History 2. United States—Politics and government—1783-1865 3. United States—History—1812-1815, War of 1812
ISBN 0-7614-0778-2   LC 97-35909
Discusses the events and personalities that shaped this country, from the hotly contested election of 1800 which brought Thomas Jefferson into office through the westward expansion to the War of 1812 and James Madison's presidency
Includes bibliographical references

Our country's founders; a book of advice for young people; edited with commentary by William J. Bennett. Simon & Schuster 1998 314p il $17 (7 and up)   **973.4**
1. United States—History—Sources 2. Social ethics
ISBN 0-689-82106-9   LC 98-6592
Based on Our sacred honor (1997)
A book of advice from our nation's founders on how to be a good citizen and a worthy member of civil society
Bennett "draws on a wide variety of primary, secondary, and tertiary sources, ranging from the love letters of John and Abigail Adams to Mason Weems' apocryphal tale of George Washington and the cherry tree. Few young adults are likely to pick this up on their own, but teachers will find it a valuable resource." Booklist
Includes bibliographical references

973.5   United States—1809-1845

Collier, Christopher, 1930-
Andrew Jackson's America, 1824-1850; [by] Christopher Collier, James Lincoln Collier. Benchmark Bks. (Tarrytown) 1999 95p il maps (Drama of American history) lib bdg $28.50   **973.5**
1. Jackson, Andrew, 1767-1845 2. United States—History—1815-1861 3. United States—Politics and government—1815-1861
ISBN 0-7614-0779-0   LC 97-30546
Examines the events and personalities, particularly President Andrew Jackson, that shaped the development of the United States during the first half of the nineteenth century
Includes bibliographical references

Greenblatt, Miriam
The War of 1812. Facts on File 1994 124p il maps (America at war) $19.95   **973.5**
1. United States—History—1812-1815, War of 1812
ISBN 0-8160-2879-6   LC 93-42887

Greenblatt, Miriam—*Continued*

"The first three chapters describe the political climate of the time and examine the weak peace agreement that marked the end of the American Revolution. The author notes that the controversy over the Canadian border and the issue of free trade were the primary reasons for the War of 1812. He also discusses daily life during this period and the sentiments of Americans. . . . The last four chapters cover the principal leaders, the major battles, and the turbulent peace process. While the book will primarily be utilized for school assignments, the inclusion of personal narratives makes for lively reading." SLJ

Includes bibliographical references

Katz, William Loren

The Civil War to the last frontier, 1850-1880s. Raintree Steck-Vaughn Pubs. 1993 96p il (History of multicultural America) lib bdg $27.11; pa $6.95

973.5

1. Minorities 2. United States—History—1800-1899 (19th century)

ISBN 0-8114-6277-3 (lib bdg); 0-8114-2914-8 (pa)

LC 92-17924

A multicultural history of the United States, from 1850 to 1880, focusing on the events before, during, and after the Civil War and discussing the experiences of various ethnic groups, notably blacks, Native Americans, and Chinese immigrants, during this period

This "title is well written, and extremely informative." Voice Youth Advocates

Includes bibliographical references

The westward movement and abolitionism, 1815-1850. Raintree Steck-Vaughn Pubs. 1993 96p il (History of multicultural America) $27.11; pa $6.95

973.5

1. Minorities 2. United States—History—1815-1861

ISBN 0-8114-6276-5; 0-8114-2913-X (pa)

LC 92-14965

A multicultural history of the United States, from 1815 to 1850, focusing on the first wave of immigration and the abolitionist and feminist movements

The author "places events clearly within the context of the times, explaining but never excusing." Booklist

Includes bibliographical references

Marrin, Albert, 1936-

1812: the war nobody won; illustrated with old prints & engravings, and diagrams & maps by Patricia A. Tobin. Atheneum Pubs. 1985 175p il maps o.p.

973.5

1. United States—History—1812-1815, War of 1812

LC 84-21623

Describes the causes and leading events of the early nineteenth-century conflict between Great Britain and the United States

"A good introduction and overview of this often confusing chapter in American history." SLJ

Includes bibliographical references

973.6 United States—1845-1861

Collier, Christopher, 1930-

Hispanic America, Texas, and the Mexican War, 1835-1850; [by] Christopher Collier, James Lincoln Collier. Benchmark Bks. (Tarrytown) 1999 94p il maps (Drama of American history) lib bdg $28.50

973.6

1. Mexican War, 1846-1848 2. Southwestern States—History

ISBN 0-7614-0780-4

LC 97-34962

Examines the settlement of the area that became the southwestern portion of the United States, detailing how it evolved from land settled by Native Americans, to Spanish territory, to states that were pawns between the North and South prior to the Civil War

Includes bibliographical references

Nardo, Don, 1947-

The Mexican-American War. Lucent Bks. 1999 112p il (World history series) lib bdg $23.70 (7 and up)

973.6

1. Mexican War, 1846-1848

ISBN 1-56006-495-1

LC 99-14263

Examines the Mexican-American War, discussing American expansion, the fall of Mexico City, the conclusion of the war, the peace treaty, and the legacy of a "dirty" war

"A clear and concise look at a largely forgotten but extremely important part of American history. . . . Numerous black-and-white photos and reproductions enliven the presentation." SLJ

Includes bibliographical references

973.7 United States— Administration of Abraham Lincoln, 1861-1865. Civil War

Altman, Linda Jacobs, 1943-

Slavery and abolition in American history. Enslow Pubs. 1999 128p il maps (In American history) lib bdg $19.95

973.7

1. Slavery—United States 2. Abolitionists

ISBN 0-7660-1124-0

LC 99-19885

Traces the history of slavery in the United States, focusing on the abolition movement and the final steps that freed an enslaved people

Includes bibliographical references

Atlanta; by the editors of Time-Life Books. Time-Life Bks. 1996 168p il maps (Voices of the Civil War) $29.95 (7 and up)

973.7

1. Atlanta Campaign, 1864

LC 95-42425

"Chronicles the events leading up to and including the Atlanta battle; focusing on the condition and the morale of both the Union and Confederate armies, a look at generals Sherman and Johnston, the new Federal strategy, and the attitudes of civilians impacted by the war." Publisher's note

Atlanta—*Continued*
"After a brief overview of the topic, the author makes extensive use of diaries, memoirs, and letters of the participants to further illustrate the narrative. . . . Photographs of the people quoted are often included. This combination of letters and pictures brings a human touch to the series." SLJ
Includes glossary and bibliographical references

Behind the lines; a sourcebook on the Civil War; edited by Carter Smith. Millbrook Press 1993 95p il (American albums from the collections of the Library of Congress) lib bdg $25.90; pa $8.95   **973.7**
1. United States—History—1861-1865, Civil War
ISBN 1-56294-265-4 (lib bdg); 1-56294-882-2 (pa)
LC 92-16662
This book "focuses on life away from the battlefields during the Civil War; readers meet politicians, civilians, ordinary soldiers in their camps, and see the effect of war on cities in the North and South." SLJ
"A browser's delight, this is an excellent visual portrayal and overview of life during the years of the Civil War. Provides enough information to pique interest, this resource can be utilized as an impetus to explore further research on the subject." Voice Youth Advocates
Includes bibliographical references

Beller, Susan Provost, 1949-
To hold this ground; a desperate battle at Gettysburg. Margaret K. McElderry Bks. 1995 95p il maps $15   **973.7**
1. Gettysburg (Pa.), Battle of, 1863
ISBN 0-689-50621-X   LC 94-12775
"Beller examines the battle for Little Round Top and the two colonels who faced each other on that fateful July day. William Calvin Oates fought for the confederacy, and Joshua Lawrence Chamberlain commanded the 20th Maine. While this book tells the story of the battle that day, it focuses on the two men and the role they played not only in this battle but in the history of this country after the war was over." Book Rep
Includes bibliographical references

Black, Wallace B.
Slaves to soldiers; African-American fighting men in the Civil War. Watts 1998 63p il lib bdg $22   **973.7**
1. African American soldiers 2. United States—History—1861-1865, Civil War
ISBN 0-531-20252-6   LC 96-31630
"A First book"
Explores the circumstances of African-Americans who fought in the Civil War, including slaves, free southerners, and northerners
Includes bibliographical references

Chattanooga; by the editors of Time-Life Books. Time-Life Bks. 1998 168p il maps (Voices of the Civil War) $29.95 (7 and up)   **973.7**
1. Chattanooga, Battle of, 1863
LC 97-43712
A collection of primary source materials, including letters, journals, photographs, and drawings, of individuals involved in the 1863 Battle of Chattanooga
Includes glossary and bibliographical references

Chickamauga; by the editors of Time-Life Books. Time-Life Bks. 1997 168p il maps (Voices of the Civil War) $29.95 (7 and up)   **973.7**
1. Chickamauga, Battle of, 1863
LC 96-48665
A collection of primary source materials, including letters, journals, photographs and drawings, of individuals involved in the 1863 Battle of Chickamauga
Includes glossary and bibliographical references

The **Civil** War: opposing viewpoints; William Dudley, book editor. Greenhaven Press 1995 310p il (American history series) lib bdg $21.96 (7 and up)   **973.7**
1. United States—History—1861-1865, Civil War
ISBN 1-56510-225-8   LC 94-9510
"Dudley has arranged primary source, documentary evidence into six chapters that present differing views of issues and events surrounding the Civil War. For example, in the first chapter, which examines the roots of the war, two significant politicians of the time, Daniel Webster and John C. Calhoun, debate the preservation of the Union. . . . A valuable one-stop source of primary information." SLJ
Includes bibliographical references

Cox, Clinton
Undying glory; the story of the Massachusetts 54th Regiment. Scholastic 1991 167p il hardcover o.p. paperback available $3.25   **973.7**
1. United States. Army. Massachusetts Infantry Regiment, 54th (1863-1865) 2. United States—History—1861-1865, Civil War 3. African American soldiers
ISBN 0-590-44171-X (pa)   LC 90-22303
"This book discusses the history of the formation of the African-American Fifty-fourth Massachusetts Regiment and its battles from 1863 to 1865. The regiment's unsung heroes found an enemy in both the Confederate army and the Union government, both of which treated them as second-class soldiers." Soc Educ
Includes bibliographical references

Dolan, Edward F., 1924-
The American Civil War; a house divided. Millbrook Press 1997 96p il maps lib bdg $28.90   **973.7**
1. United States—History—1861-1865, Civil War
ISBN 0-7613-0255-7   LC 97-6995
An account of the Civil War from its causes to its final battles including discussions of dominant figures of the era, strategies of major battles, and brutal sieges which marked this conflict
"This is a good acquisition for libraries that need a simple introduction to this oft-confusing episode in American history." SLJ
Includes bibliographical references

First Manassas; by the editors of Time-Life Books. Time-Life Bks. 1997 168p il maps (Voices of the Civil War) $29.95 (7 and up)   **973.7**
1. Bull Run, 1st Battle of, 1861
LC 97-19101

First Manassas—*Continued*

An album of personal recollections about the Civil War Battle of First Manassas in Virginia, taken from letters, diaries, photographs, sketches, and artifacts of soldiers and civilians who experienced the campaign

Includes bibliographical references

Gettysburg; by the editors of Time-Life Books. Time-Life Bks. 1995 180p il maps (Voices of the Civil War) $29.95 (7 and up)   **973.7**
1. Gettysburg (Pa.), Battle of, 1863
LC 94-42303

"The story of the Battle of Gettysburg is told through the eyewitness accounts of the people who were at the scene. Diaries and letters of soldiers, officers, nurses and Gettysburg civilians are used. The book is well researched and . . . contains many excellent photos and maps as well as drawings and paintings done by the people who were in Gettysburg during the battle." Book Rep

Includes bibliographical references

Golay, Michael, 1951-

The Civil War. Facts on File 1992 180p il (America at war) lib bdg $19.95   **973.7**
1. United States—History—1861-1865, Civil War
ISBN 0-8160 2514-2   LC 91-25646

An account of the Civil War, discussing political background, military strategy, and battles

Includes bibliographical references

Haskins, James, 1941-

Black, blue, & gray; African Americans in the Civil War. Simon & Schuster Bks. for Young Readers 1998 154p $16   **973.7**
1. United States—History—1861-1865, Civil War 2. African American soldiers
ISBN 0-689-80655-8   LC 97-25414

An historical account of the role of African-American soldiers in the Civil War

"This tightly organized book is packed with facts and meticulously footnoted, yet it reads like a novel, thanks to the author's stylistic skills." SLJ

Includes bibliographical references

The day Fort Sumter was fired on; a photo history of the Civil War; by Jim Haskins. Scholastic 1995 96p il pa $6.95   **973.7**
1. United States—History—1861-1865, Civil War—Pictorial works
ISBN 0-590-46397-7   LC 95-193186

The course of the Civil War from Bull Run and on to Reconstruction is documented with photographs in this book which considers not just military maneuvers and politics but also the war's effect on women, blacks, and children

"This attractive book opens a valuable window on the period. A chronology and bibliography help make the volume perfect for students." Booklist

Haugen, David, 1969-

The Civil War; [by] David M. Haugen and Lori Shein. Greenhaven Press 1999 141p il maps (Opposing viewpoints digests) lib bdg $17.96; pa $10.96 (7 and up)   **973.7**
1. United States—History—1861-1865, Civil War
ISBN 1-56510-887-6 (lib bdg); 1-56510-886-8 (pa)
LC 98-46105

Offers opposing viewpoints on issues associated with the Civil War including secession, slavery, the Emancipation Proclamation, and the President's right to suspend civil liberties

Includes bibliographical references

January, Brendan, 1972-

The assassination of Abraham Lincoln. Children's Press 1998 30p il (Cornerstones of freedom) $19.50; pa $5.95   **973.7**
1. Lincoln, Abraham, 1809-1865—Assassination
ISBN 0-516-20947-7; 0-516-26394-3 (pa)
LC 97-34997

Chronicles the events leading to the murder of President Lincoln by John Wilkes Booth in April 1865

The Lincoln-Douglas debates. Children's Press 1998 30p il maps (Cornerstones of freedom) $19.50; pa $5.95   **973.7**
1. Lincoln, Abraham, 1809-1865 2. Douglas, Stephen Arnold, 1813-1861 3. Lincoln-Douglas debates, 1858
ISBN 0-516-20844-6; 0-516-26335-8 (pa)
LC 97-9302

Describes the seven debates held from August to October 1858 between Stephen Douglas and Abraham Lincoln who were campaigning for election as Illinois Senator

Kirchberger, Joe H.

The Civil War and Reconstruction; an eyewitness history; [by] Joe Kirchberger. Facts on File 1991 389p il maps (Eyewitness history series) $50 (7 and up)   **973.7**
1. United States—History—1861-1865, Civil War—Sources 2. Reconstruction (1865-1876)
ISBN 0-8160-2171-6   LC 90-40852

This work contains "quotations from eyewitnesses' memoirs, letters, diaries, newspapers, and official documents. Those quoted come from all walks of life. . . . Thirty-three documents are excerpted. Four appendixes contain valuable primary-source and reference materials. . . . Interspersed throughout are political cartoons, photographs, and paintings. . . . An excellent reference tool." SLJ

Includes bibliographical references

Marrin, Albert, 1936-

Commander in Chief Abraham Lincoln and the Civil War. Dutton Children's Bks. 1997 246p il maps $25 (7 and up)   **973.7**
1. Lincoln, Abraham, 1809-1865 2. United States—History—1861-1865, Civil War
ISBN 0-525-45822-0   LC 97-8518

Marrin, Albert, 1936— *Continued*

The author places Lincoln in the context of his own personal background and the larger circumstances of the Civil War

"The narrative is skillfully constructed and expressed in a strong, compelling style." SLJ

Includes bibliographical references

Unconditional surrender; U.S. Grant and the Civil War. Atheneum Pubs. 1994 200p il maps $21 (7 and up)   **973.7**
    1. Grant, Ulysses S. (Ulysses Simpson), 1822-1885
    2. United States—History—1861-1865, Civil War
    ISBN 0-689-31837-5   LC 93-20041

"Although this book tells of the early and post-war life of Ulysses Grant, it's not a biography so much as a Civil War chronicle that very successfully uses General Grant as a focus. . . . Using extensive eyewitness accounts, Marrin has distilled copious research into a history of living men and women who are complete with faults and contradictions (the racism of many of the Northern commanders, including Grant, is made clear); Grant seems here to be a man splendid in wartime and floundering in peace, except in his happy family life." Bull Cent Child Books

Includes bibliographical references

McPherson, James M.

Marching toward freedom; Blacks in the Civil War, 1861-1865. Facts on File 1991 142p il music (Library of American history) $16.95; pa $8.95 (7 and up)   **973.7**
    1. United States—History—1861-1865, Civil War
    2. African Americans—History
    ISBN 0-8160-2337-9; 0-8160-3092-8 (pa)
                         LC 90-13918

First published 1968 by Knopf in a different form

This book examines the Afro-Americans' role in the contribution to the Union and Confederacy during the Civil War, and the resulting change in their position as citizens

The author "does an excellent job of incorporating primary-source material and first-person accounts by both black participants and contemporary white observers. The coverage is quite fair and impartial. . . . This is sure to be a well-used addition to any collection." SLJ

Includes bibliographical references

Mettger, Zak

Till victory is won; black soldiers in the Civil War. Lodestar Bks. 1994 118p il (Young readers' history of the Civil War) $16.99; pa $8.99 **973.7**
    1. African American soldiers 2. United States—History—1861-1865, Civil War
    ISBN 0-525-67412-8; 0-14-038727-7 (pa)
                         LC 93-44154

"The two hundred thousand African Americans who fought in the Civil War proved their equality on the battlefield and helped to earn freedom for their families yet also continued to face racism and prejudice. The clear text is highlighted by the soldiers' letters and diary entries and is accompanied by archival illustrations and photographs in black and white." Horn Book Guide

Includes glossary and bibliographical references

Murphy, Jim, 1947-

The boys' war; Confederate and Union soldiers talk about the Civil War. Clarion Bks. 1990 110p il $17; pa $7.70   **973.7**
    1. United States—History—1861-1865, Civil War
    ISBN 0-89919-893-7; 0-395-66412-8 (pa)
                         LC 89-23959

This book includes diary entries, personal letters, and archival photographs to describe the experiences of boys, sixteen years old or younger, who fought in the Civil War

"An excellent selection of more than 45 sepia-toned contemporary photographs augment the text of this informative, moving work." SLJ

Includes bibliographical references

The long road to Gettysburg. Clarion Bks. 1992 116p il maps $17   **973.7**
    1. Gettysburg (Pa.), Battle of, 1863
    ISBN 0-395-55965-0   LC 90-21881

Describes the events of the Battle of Gettysburg in 1863 as seen through the eyes of two actual participants, nineteen-year-old Confederate lieutenant John Dooley and seventeen-year-old Union soldier Thomas Galway. Also discusses Lincoln's famous speech delivered at the dedication of the National Cemetery at Gettysburg

The author "uses all of his fine skills as an information writer—clarity of detail, conciseness, understanding of his age group, and ability to find the drama appealing to readers—to frame a well-crafted account of a single battle in the war." Horn Book

Includes bibliographical references

Piggins, Carol Ann

A multicultural portrait of the Civil War. Marshall Cavendish 1993 80p il (Perspectives) $28.50 (7 and up)   **973.7**
    1. United States—History—1861-1865, Civil War
    2. Minorities
    ISBN 1-85435-660-7   LC 93-10319

Using primary-source material and numerous illustrations the author looks at the events leading up to the Civil War and its aftermath from the perspective of Afro-Americans and women

"The book will be an excellent addition to most collections. It is balanced and well written." SLJ

Includes glossary and bibliographical references

Ray, Delia

Behind the Blue and Gray; the soldier's life in the Civil War. Lodestar Bks. 1991 102p il (Young readers' history of the Civil War) $17.99; pa $6.99   **973.7**
    1. United States—History—1861-1865, Civil War
    ISBN 0-525-67333-4; 0-14-038304-2 (pa)
                         LC 90-46412

This book traces the events of the Civil War from the first battle to the surrender with emphasis on the experiences of the individual soldier

The author "has chosen many informative, perceptive personal accounts upon which to base her work. The fears, horrors, boredom, and simple, transitory pleasures of these young men are brought into sharp focus by the

Ray, Delia—*Continued*

many first-person writings. . . . Black-and-white historical photographs and reproductions flesh out this highly readable volume." SLJ

Includes glossary and bibliographical references

A nation torn; the story of how the Civil War began. Lodestar Bks. 1990 102p il maps (Young readers' history of the Civil War) $18; pa $8.99
973.7

1. United States—History—1861-1865, Civil War 2. United States—Politics and government—1815-1861

ISBN 0-525-67308-3; 0-14-038105-8 (pa)

LC 90-5533

The author "probes the causes of the Civil War, tracing key movements and events that culminated in the Confederate attack on Fort Sumter." Booklist

"Ms. Ray provides a superb introduction to the events that plunged this country into the Civil War." Child Book Rev Serv

Includes glossary and bibliographical references

Reef, Catherine

Civil War soldiers. 21st Cent. Bks. (NY) 1993 80p il (African-American soldiers) lib bdg $17.90
973.7

1. African American soldiers 2. United States—History—1861-1865, Civil War

ISBN 0-8050-2371-2   LC 92-34412

Describes the crucial role played by African-American soldiers in securing victory for the Union in the Civil War

This work is "written in clear, interest-holding prose and plentifully illustrated with period black-and-white photographs and reproductions." SLJ

Includes bibliographical references

The **Road** to Appomattox; a sourcebook on the Civil War; edited by Carter Smith. Millbrook Press 1993 96p il (American albums from the collections of the Library of Congress) lib bdg $25.90; pa $8.95   **973.7**

1. Appomattox Campaign, 1865 2. United States—History—1861-1865, Civil War—Campaigns

ISBN 1-56294-264-6 (lib bdg); 1-56294-881-4 (pa)

LC 92-16546

This book "covers the last year of the war, from the appointment of Grant as Commander of the Union forces in 1864 through the Confederate surrender in 1865. The illustrations of the battles and various participants, and . . . the maps, will add to students' understanding." SLJ

Includes bibliographical references

Second Manassas; by the editors of Time-Life Books. Time-Life Bks. 1995 168p il maps (Voices of the Civil War) $29.95 (7 and up)
973.7

1. Bull Run, 2nd Battle of, 1862

LC 94-48737

This illustrated look at the Second Battle of Bull Run is based on primary source material and details the assault on federal troops by Jackson and Longstreet and the ensuing Union retreat

Includes bibliographical references

Shenandoah, 1862; by the editors of Time-Life Books. Time-Life Bks. 1997 168p il maps (Voices of the Civil War) $29.95 (7 and up)
973.7

1. Shenandoah Valley Campaign, 1862

LC 97-3198

Describes the Shenandoah Valley Civil War campaign of 1862 through over one hundred personal recollections taken from letters, diaries, and journals. Also includes photographs of military artifacts, soldiers, and civilians as well as sketches and maps

Includes bibliographical references

Shenandoah, 1864; by the editors of Time-Life Books. Time-Life Bks. 1998 168p il maps (Voices of the Civil War) $29.95 (7 and up)
973.7

1. Shenandoah Valley Campaign, 1864 (May-August)

LC 97-43711

An album of personal recollections from the letters, diaries, photographs, sketches, and artifacts of the soldiers and civilians who experienced the 1864 Shenandoah Valley campaign of the Civil War

Includes bibliographical references

Shiloh; by the editors of Time-Life Books. Time-Life Bks. 1996 168p il maps (Voices of the Civil War) $29.95 (7 and up)   **973.7**

1. Shiloh (Tenn.), Battle of, 1862

LC 96-33040

This covers the 1862 Civil War battle of Shiloh "primarily through excerpted regimental histories, letters, diaries, and memoirs written by participants and civilians on both sides. The interspersing text that sets the scene is clear and informative and places the personal accounts in context. . . . The layout is spacious, and the profusion of maps and period illustrations lends even more authenticity to the whole." Booklist

Includes glossary and bibliographical references

Soldier life; by the editors of Time-Life Books. Time-Life Bks. 1996 168p il (Voices of the Civil War) $29.95 (7 and up)   **973.7**

1. United States—History—1861-1865, Civil War—Personal narratives 2. United States—Armed forces—Military life

LC 96-2415

"In *Soldier Life,* the words of the soldiers themselves tell how they lived during the Civil War. The book is divided into five chapters, each on a separate aspect of soldier life and each beginning with a short overview of the chapter's focus followed by excerpts from diaries, letters, reminiscences, newspaper and magazine articles, and other primary sources." Book Rep

Includes glossary and bibliographical references

Stein, R. Conrad, 1937-

John Brown's Raid on Harpers Ferry in American history. Enslow Pubs. 1999 128p il (In American history) lib bdg $19.95   **973.7**

1. Brown, John, 1800-1859 2. Harpers Ferry (W. Va.)—History—John Brown's Raid, 1859 3. Abolitionists

ISBN 0-7660-1123-2   LC 98-35950

Stein, R. Conrad, 1937-—*Continued*
Explores the people and events connected with John Brown's attempted slave uprising in Harpers Ferry in 1859
Includes bibliographical references

Steins, Richard
The nation divides; the Civil War (1820-1880). 21st Cent. Bks. (NY) 1993 64p il (First person America) $18.90   **973.7**
1. Slavery—United States 2. United States—History—1861-1865, Civil War
ISBN 0-8050-2583-9   LC 93-24993
Primary source materials present different aspects of the Civil War, including the debate over slavery, secession of the Confederate States, the war itself, and life for the slaves after emancipation
This informs "without overwhelming by presenting not just dates and data, but also a snapshot of life in early America through the words of a cross section of its residents. Succinct introductions assist understanding of idiomatic or dated phrases." SLJ
Includes bibliographical references

Tackach, James
The Emancipation Proclamation; abolishing slavery in the South. Lucent Bks. 1999 112p il (Words that changed history) lib bdg $17.96 (7 and up)   **973.7**
1. United States. President (1861-1865: Lincoln). Emancipation Proclamation 2. Slavery—United States
ISBN 1-56006-370-X   LC 98-49678
Discusses slavery as a cause of the American Civil War and examines the events surrounding Lincoln's Emancipation Proclamation and the impact of this declaration on the course of the war and the institution of slavery
This is "presented in a well-organized and readable style. Frequent sidebars feature excerpts from the original sources and present supplemental information." SLJ
Includes bibliographical references

Trudeau, Noah Andre, 1949-
Like men of war; Black troops in the Civil War, 1862-1865. Little, Brown 1998 xxii, 548p il maps $29.95; pa $18 (7 and up)   **973.7**
1. African American soldiers 2. United States—History—1861-1865, Civil War
ISBN 0-316-85325-9; 0-316-85344-5 (pa)
LC 97-15380
A "study of the battlefield experiences of black Union regiments. Some 60 maps help the reader make sense of famous engagements (Fort Wagner and the Crater) and notorious incidents (Fort Pillow) in which black soldiers fought, as well as scores of lesser-known clashes. Rich archival research is integrated into a lively narrative that places the raising and deployment of black regiments in broader contexts. This book will become a basic source of information on the subject." Libr J
Includes bibliographical references

Zeinert, Karen
Those courageous women of the Civil War. Millbrook Press 1998 96p il map lib bdg $27.40 (7 and up)   **973.7**
1. Women—United States—History 2. United States—History—1861-1865, Civil War
ISBN 0-7613-0212-3   LC 97-21485
Examines the important contributions of various women, Northern, Southern, and slave, to the American Civil War, on the battlefield, in print, on the home front, and in other areas where they challenged traditional female roles
"A solid work that is sure to open the eyes of many readers and add a different dimension to studies about this era." SLJ
Includes bibliographical references

973.8   United States—Reconstruction period, 1865-1901

Aleshire, Peter
Reaping the whirlwind; the Apache wars. Facts on File 1998 152p il maps (Library of American Indian history) $19.95 (7 and up)   **973.8**
1. Apache Indians—Wars
ISBN 0-8160-3602-0   LC 97-22772
Examines the question of why policy makers and leaders on both sides of the Apache conflict sowed winds of injustice, hatred, and violence throughout the Southwest for three decades
"Aleshire presents a lucid, detailed account of the violent conflicts between the Apaches and the Europeans determined to settle on their lands. Extensive quotations from original sources on both sides add immediacy." Horn Book Guide
Includes bibliographical references

Brown, Gene
The struggle to grow; expansionism and industrialization (1880-1913). 21st Cent. Bks. (NY) 1993 64p il (First person America) lib bdg $18.90
973.8
1. United States—History—1865-1898 2. United States—History—1898-1919
ISBN 0-8050-2584-7   LC 93-24992
Primary source materials present life on the Western frontier, urbanization, immigration, social reformers, and contemporary technology
"Brown's text provides background information on the era, while photos, engravings, and paintings from the period offer vivid windows into the past." Booklist
Includes bibliographical references

Carter, Alden R.
The Spanish-American War; imperial ambitions. Watts 1992 64p il maps lib bdg $22; pa $6.95
973.8
1. Spanish-American War, 1898
ISBN 0-531-20078-7 (lib bdg); 0-531-15657-5 (pa)
LC 91-14753
"A First book"

Carter, Alden R.—*Continued*
Chronicles the ten-week war in 1898 between the United States and Spain over the liberation of Cuba, the outcome of which ended the Spanish colonial empire and elevated the United States to a world power
"Report writers will find plenty of well-organized, attractively presented information." SLJ
Includes bibliographical references

Ferrell, Nancy Warren
The Battle of the Little Bighorn in American history. Enslow Pubs. 1996 128p il maps (In American history) lib bdg $19.95   **973.8**
1. Little Bighorn, Battle of the, 1876
ISBN 0-89490-768-9   LC 96-11592
Describes the Battle of Little Bighorn and the events that led up to it
"The coverage is balanced and well documented. . . . With plenty of information, well supported by quotations and excerpts from firsthand accounts, this is a good resource." SLJ
Includes bibliographical references

January, Brendan, 1972-
Reconstruction. Children's Press 1999 30p il maps (Cornerstones of freedom) lib bdg $20; pa $5.95   **973.8**
1. Reconstruction (1865-1876) 2. United States—Politics and government—1865-1898
ISBN 0-516-21143-9 (lib bdg); 0-516-26461-3 (pa)
          LC 98-3492
A history of Reconstruction, the period after the Civil War during which programs were implemented to bring the Confederate States back to the Union
"The design is attractive, with clear type, photographs or prints on every page (some in color)." Booklist
Includes glossary

Mettger, Zak
Reconstruction; America after the Civil War. Lodestar Bks. 1994 122p il (Young readers' history of the Civil War) $16.99   **973.8**
1. Reconstruction (1865-1876) 2. United States—Politics and government—1865-1898
ISBN 0-525-67490-X   LC 93-44665
The author explains the "post-Civil War era, a time she defines as 'a period of great hope and crushing disappointment.' She accomplishes her goal with a clearly written, well-explained history. Unflinching in the details about lynchings, the Ku Klux Klan, and corrupt governments, she manages to put a human face on the times." SLJ
Includes glossary and bibliographical references

One nation again; a sourcebook on the Civil War; edited by Carter Smith. Millbrook Press 1993 96p il (American albums from the collections of the Library of Congress) lib bdg $25.90 **973.8**
1. Reconstruction (1865-1876) 2. United States—Politics and government—1865-1898
ISBN 1-56294-266-2   LC 92-16661

This volume "covers the Reconstruction period, and tells what happened to some of the major figures in the war. Those who became politicians are highlighted. The quality of illustrations is excellent." SLJ
Includes bibliographical references

Streissguth, Thomas
Wounded Knee, 1890; the end of the Plains Indian wars; [by] Tom Streissguth. Facts on File 1998 110p il maps (Library of American Indian history) $19.95 (7 and up)   **973.8**
1. Wounded Knee Creek, Battle of, 1890 2. Dakota Indians—Wars
ISBN 0-8160-3600-4   LC 97-43530
Narrates the events leading up to the massacre which marked the end of a long succession of wars between whites and Indians, and concludes with a description of the battle itself
"Amid the quotation-heavy narrative are inset articles and testimonials that provide variant points of view and create a balanced perspective on related incidents. Best of all, every element—text, photographs, art, maps—avoids melodrama." Booklist
Includes bibliographical references

Viola, Herman J.
It is a good day to die; Indian eyewitnesses tell the story of the Battle of the Little Bighorn. Crown 1998 101p il maps $18; lib bdg $19.99
          973.8
1. Custer, George Armstrong, 1839-1876 2. Little Bighorn, Battle of the, 1876 3. Dakota Indians—Wars 4. Cheyenne Indians
ISBN 0-517-70912-0; 0-517-70913-9 (lib bdg)
          LC 98-16477
A series of eyewitness accounts of the 1876 Battle of Little Bighorn and the defeat of General Custer as told by Native American participants in the war
"This is a thought-provoking, accessible compilation that will give new insight to the study of American history." Bull Cent Child Books
Includes bibliographical references

973.9   United States—1901-

Brown, Gene
Conflict in Europe and the Great Depression; World War I (1914-1940). 21st Cent. Bks. (NY) 1994 c1993 64p il (First person America) $18.90
          973.9
1. United States—History—1900-1999 (20th century) 2. World War, 1914-1918—United States
ISBN 0-8050-2585-5   LC 93-24998
First published 1993 in Canada
Primary source materials present such topics as U.S. involvement in World War I, the Great Depression, Prohibition, the growth of mass media, and the New Deal
"The writing is clear, the full-color and black-and-white photographs are plentiful, and the limited information is sound." SLJ
Includes bibliographical references

Wakin, Edward
Photos that made U.S. history; [by] Edward
Wakin with Daniel Wakin. Walker & Co. 1993 2v
il ea $12.95, lib bdg $13.85   **973.9**
1. United States—History—Pictorial works 2. Photography—History
                                                LC 93-12096
Contents: v1 From the Civil War era to the atomic
age (ISBN 0-8027-8230-2; 0-8027-8231-0); v2 From the
Cold War to the space age (ISBN 0-8027-8270-1; 0-
8027-8272-8)
"In each book, Wakin looks at seven well-known photographs that capture a significant event, individual, or
episode in U.S. history. Accompanying each picture is a
four-to-five page summary that sets the scene, discusses
the picture's effect on the public, and provides information on the photographer." SLJ
"Middle school students will find these books to be an
accessible introduction to many eras of American history.
The books would also be useful in high school journalism or photography classes." Book Rep

973.91   United States—1901-1953

Burg, David F.
The Great Depression; an eyewitness history.
Facts on File 1996 390p il (Eyewitness history
series) $50 (7 and up)   **973.91**
1. Great Depression, 1929-1939 2. United States—
Economic conditions—1933-1945 3. United States—
Economic conditions—1919-1933
ISBN 0-8160-3095-2   LC 95-15830
The author "delivers a narrative summary and chronology of major events in the United States and throughout
the world during the Depression. He offers seven chapters, each covering one or more years; brief contemporary quotations from politicians, journalists, authors, and
advertisements; and 80 black-and-white photographs. The
appendixes contain a selection of primary sources, mainly New Deal statutes and other documents, and capsule
biographies." Libr J

Katz, William Loren
The new freedom to the New Deal, 1913-1939.
Raintree Steck-Vaughn Pubs. 1993 96p il (History
of multicultural America) lib bdg $27.11; pa $6.95
                                                973.91
1. Minorities 2. United States—History—1900-1999
(20th century)
ISBN 0-8114-6279-X (lib bdg); 0-8114-2916-4 (pa)
                                                LC 92-39948
A multicultural history of the United States, from
1913 to 1939, focusing on the experiences of women and
minorities
This volume "successfully melds crisp, well-written
text with captions for interesting, informative, historical
black-and-white photographs." SLJ
Includes bibliographical references

Nishi, Dennis, 1967-
Life during the Great Depression. Lucent Bks.
1998 96p il maps (Way people live) lib bdg
$22.45 (7 and up)   **973.91**
1. Great Depression, 1929-1939 2. United States—Social life and customs
ISBN 1-56006-381-5   LC 97-33030
Describes daily life for Americans during the Great
Depression, as well as some of the lasting changes that
occurred such as the increased power of the federal government and technological and cultural innovations
"Nishi presents a well-crafted fusion of information,
statistics, and apt quotations that have been thoughtfully
selected from primary and secondary sources. The concise text is straightforward, objective, and lively." SLJ
Includes bibliographical references

Pietrusza, David, 1949-
The roaring twenties. Lucent Bks. 1998 96p il
(World history series) lib bdg $22.45 (7 and up)
                                                973.91
1. United States—History—1919-1933
ISBN 1-56006-309-2   LC 97-29771
This examination of the 1920s discusses "the economy, Prohibition, controversial issues and scandals, culture, professional sports, and the causes for the Great Depression." SLJ
Includes bibliographical references

Rensberger, Susan, 1953-
A multicultural portrait of the Great Depression.
Benchmark Bks. (Tarrytown) 1996 80p il
(Perspectives) lib bdg $28.50   **973.91**
1. Great Depression, 1929-1939
ISBN 0-7614-0053-2   LC 95-11029
Describes the history of the Great Depression from the
vantage point of minorities and women
This book is "well-researched [and] . . . illustrated
with black-and-white and color photographs and historical reproductions." Horn Book
Includes glossary and bibliographical references

Rock & roll generation; teen life in the 50s; by
the editors of Time-Life Books; with a foreword
by Dick Clark. Time-Life Bks. 1998 152p il
(Our American century) $29.95 (7 and up)
                                                973.91
1. Popular culture—United States 2. United States—
Social life and customs
                                                LC 97-32609
This overview of 1950s youth culture is illustrated
with photographs, cartoons, paintings and ads. The beat
generation, the rise of rock music, and the social role of
the automobile are covered
"The text is brief, concise, and engaging, and serves
exclusively to place the photographs in context. There is
an extensive list of suggestions for further reading and a
good subject index." SLJ

Watkins, T. H. (Tom H.), 1936-2000
The Great Depression; America in the 1930s.
Little, Brown 1993 375p il $24.95; pa $14.95 (7
and up)   **973.91**
1. United States—Economic conditions—1919-1933
2. United States—Economic conditions—1933-1945
3. Great Depression, 1929-1939
ISBN 0-316-92453-9; 0-316-92454-7 (pa)
LC 93-1332
In this companion to the PBS series Watkins "documents the devastating financial collapse that left an indelible imprint on the nation's collective cultural psyche and evokes that provocative combination of fear, desperation, and hope that characterized the 1930s. . . . More than 100 heartrending black-and-white photographs vivify the sensitive narrative." Booklist

Wormser, Richard, 1933-
Growing up in the Great Depression. Atheneum
Pubs. 1994 124p il $15.95 (7 and up)   **973.91**
1. Great Depression, 1929-1939 2. United States—
Economic conditions—1933-1945
ISBN 0-689-31711-5   LC 93-20686
Historical background, interviews, and photographs combine to provide an impression of childhood during the Great Depression
"Wormser does an excellent job of providing the flavor of the Great Depression, making good use of oral histories by people who were young back then. . . . This book goes a long way toward presenting a sense of the deprivation which many people experienced." Voice Youth Advocates
Includes bibliographical references

973.92 United States—1953-

The **1960s:** opposing viewpoints; William Dudley,
book editor. Greenhaven Press 1997 268p
(American history series) lib bdg $26.20; pa
$16.20 (7 and up)   **973.92**
1. United States—History—1961-1974 2. United
States—Social conditions
ISBN 1-56510-526-5 (lib bdg); 1-56510-525-7 (pa)
LC 96-49282
This collection of articles presents varying viewpoints about the New Frontier and the Great Society, the Vietnam War, the youth revolt and counter culture, the civil rights movement, the women's movement, and 1960s activism
Includes bibliographical references

Finkelstein, Norman H., 1941-
The way things never were; the truth about the
"good old days". Atheneum Bks. for Young
Readers 1999 104p il $16   **973.92**
1. United States—Social conditions 2. United
States—History—1945-
ISBN 0-689-81412-7   LC 98-15412
A history of the United States during the 1950s and 1960s including sections on health care, eating habits, family life, environmental issues, and the condition of the elderly

"This excellent source would promote discussion in social studies and history classes and stimulate intergenerational dialogue with family and friends." Voice Youth Advocates
Includes bibliographical references

Kronenwetter, Michael
America in the 1960s. Lucent Bks. 1998 112p
il maps (World history series) lib bdg $22.45 (7
and up)   **973.92**
1. United States—History—1961-1974
ISBN 1-56006-294-0   LC 97-34055
Discusses a decade of enormous change and conflict in all areas of life including science, civil rights, social welfare, national defense, politics, and the arts
"Kronenwetter has synthesized solid research with considerable skill to create a panoramic picture of the stormy decade that literally changed America. His prose is taut and straightforward but readable and scrupulously objective." SLJ
Includes bibliographical references

973.922 United States—Administration of John F. Kennedy, 1961-1963

Hampton, Wilborn
Kennedy assassinated! the world mourns: a
reporter's story. Candlewick Press 1997 96p il
$17.99   **973.922**
1. Kennedy, John F. (John Fitzgerald), 1917-1963—
Assassination 2. Journalism
ISBN 1-56402-811-9   LC 96-25801
This is the author's "account of November 22, 1963, when, as a cub reporter for UPI in Dallas, he was drafted to cover JFK's assassination. His personal response to the tragedy is fluidly juxtaposed with the nuts and bolts of scooping the story in this insider's view of one of the most pivotal events of our nation's recent history." Publ Wkly
Includes bibliographical references

974 Northeastern United States

Rylant, Cynthia
Appalachia; the voices of sleeping birds;
illustrated by Barry Moser. Harcourt Brace
Jovanovich 1991 21p il $16; pa $6   **974**
1. Appalachian region
ISBN 0-15-201605-8; 0-15-201893-X (pa)
LC 90-36798
"This is a running narrative description of the dogs, people, houses, seasons, and lifestyles of Appalachia." Bull Cent Child Books
"Taking her subtitle from a passage by James Agee, the author conveys with a marvelous economy of words the essence of the very special part of America where she was raised. A poetic text projects emotion as well as information." Horn Book

974.1 Maine

Murphy, Jim, 1947-
Into the deep forest with Henry David Thoreau;
illustrated by Kate A. Kiesler. Clarion Bks. 1995
39p il $14.95   **974.1**
1. Thoreau, Henry David, 1817-1862 2. Maine—Description
ISBN 0-395-60522-9   LC 94-11791
This "introduction to the naturalist/writer, written as a
third-person narrative, has been adapted from Thoreau's
own journal entries and an article he wrote about his
1857 trip into the Maine wilderness, during which he
climbed Mount Katahdin. Although Thoreau's entries
have been condensed, the text is liberally sprinkled with
quotes. Traveling with a friend and a Native American
guide, he noted his observations of plants and trees, animals and birds." SLJ

974.4 Massachusetts

Bowen, Gary
Stranded at Plimoth Plantation, 1626; words and
woodcuts by Gary Bowen; introduction by David
Freeman Hawke. HarperCollins Pubs. 1994 81p il
map $19.95; pa $9.95   **974.4**
1. Pilgrims (New England colonists) 2. Massachusetts—History—1600-1775, Colonial period
ISBN 0-06-022541-6; 0-06-440719-5 (pa)
                                          LC 93-31016
The author "gives an account of the year 1626 at the
by-then-well-established Pilgrim colony, rendered in the
form of a journal kept by an orphaned 13-year-old. Shipwrecked on the way to Jamestown, taken in by the settlers at Plimoth, Christopher Sears observes their customs, planting, harvesting, home tutoring, the eight-hour
Sabbath meeting, court day, the use of the stocks, etc."
Publ Wkly
"The youthful voice and observations, in language that
is a remarkable blend of clarity and period flavor, provide a more intimate and involving picture of the period
than more straightforward factual accounts." SLJ

Collier, Christopher, 1930-
Pilgrims and Puritans, 1620-1676; [by]
Christopher Collier, James Lincoln Collier.
Benchmark Bks. (Tarrytown) 1998 94p il maps
(Drama of American history) lib bdg $28.50
                                                 974.4
1. Pilgrims (New England colonists) 2. Puritans
3. Massachusetts—History—1600-1775, Colonial peri-
od
ISBN 0-7614-0438-4   LC 96-49382
Recounts the religious, political, and social history of
the Massachusetts Bay Colony, and its influence on our
lives today
Includes bibliographical references

Pilgrim voices; our first year in the New World;
edited by Connie and Peter Roop; illustrations
by Shelley Pritchett. Walker & Co. 1995 48p il
$16.95; lib bdg $17.85; pa $7.95   **974.4**
1. Pilgrims (New England colonists) 2. Massachusetts—History—1600-1775, Colonial period
ISBN 0-8027-8314-7; 0-8027-8315-5 (lib bdg);
0-8027-7530-6 (pa)   LC 95-10114
Drawing on diaries and journals, the editors "use the
Pilgrims' own words to describe the voyage on the *Mayflower*; exploring the land and meeting the Indians; the
hardships, illnesses, and hunger during the first winter;
and the harvest festival. The diary format and first-
person voice contribute authenticity and vitality to the
text, with colorful paintings by Shelley Pritchett adding
interest." Booklist
Includes bibliographical references

974.6 Connecticut

Fradin, Dennis B.
The Connecticut colony; by Dennis Brindell
Fradin. Children's Press 1990 159p il maps lib bdg
$30   **974.6**
1. Connecticut—History—1600-1775, Colonial period
ISBN 0-516-00393-3   LC 89-29205
Surveys the history of the colony of Connecticut from
its early days up through the American Revolution. Includes biographical sketches of prominent individuals
"Thorough and appealing with large print. . . . Despite a huge amount of factual information, Fradin injects
a degree of drama, especially with regard to the politics
of the times." Booklist

974.7 New York

Hansen, Joyce
Breaking ground, breaking silence; the story of
New York's African burial ground; by Joyce
Hansen and Gary McGowan. Holt & Co. 1998
130p il maps $17.95   **974.7**
1. African Americans—History 2. Cemeteries 3. Excavations (Archeology) 4. New York (N.Y.)—Antiquities
ISBN 0-8050-5012-4   LC 97-19105
Describes the discovery and study of the African burial site found in Manhattan in 1991, while excavating for
a new building, and what it reveals about the lives of
black people in Colonial times
"This book is well written and attractively designed,
and readers should have access to it in social studies
classrooms as well as in libraries. It will generate lots of
class discussion and writing projects." Voice Youth Advocates

975 Southeastern United States. Southern States

Erickson, Paul, 1976-
Daily life on a Southern plantation, 1853.
Lodestar Bks. 1998 c1997 48p il $16.99   **975**
1. Plantation life 2. Slavery—United States
ISBN 0-525-67547-7   LC 97-22540

Erickson, Paul, 1976—*Continued*
First published 1997 in the United Kingdom
Recreates a southern plantation of 1853 and describes the daily lives of its owners and of the slaves who worked there
"Erickson uses a family to make the information in the text accessible. This book follows two families . . . one living in the 'Big House'; and the other a slave family, through a typical day—a technique that provides a personal, well-informed view of slavery." Horn Book Guide
Includes glossary

975.3　District of Columbia (Washington)

Quiri, Patricia Ryon
The White House. Watts 1996 61p il maps lib bdg $22　　　　　**975.3**
1. White House (Washington, D.C.)
ISBN 0-531-20221-6　　　　LC 95-44444
"A First book"
"A brief overview of the White House from the planning of the capital city to the closing of Pennsylvania Avenue in 1995." SLJ
"Report writers needing information on the White House will find this competent introduction helpful. . . . One nice bonus is a page listing the White House sites on the World Wide Web." Booklist
Includes bibliographical references

975.5　Virginia

Collier, Christopher, 1930-
The paradox of Jamestown, 1585-1700; [by] Christopher Collier, James Lincoln Collier. Benchmark Bks. (Tarrytown) 1998 93p il maps (Drama of American history) lib bdg $28.50
　　　　　975.5
1. Slavery—United States 2. Jamestown (Va.)—History 3. United States—History—1600-1775, Colonial period
ISBN 0-7614-0437-6　　　　LC 96-34998
Discusses the circumstances surrounding English colonization of Virginia and the evolution of slavery in that colony
Includes bibliographical references

976.4　Texas

Carter, Alden R.
Last stand at the Alamo. Watts 1990 64p il maps lib bdg $22　　　　　**976.4**
1. Alamo (San Antonio, Tex.) 2. Texas—History
ISBN 0-531-10888-0　　　　LC 89-22688
"A First book"
A brief look at the battle of the Alamo, an event which was instrumental in procuring Texas's independence from Mexico
This book is "lucid and straightforward, giving background on key individuals involved." SLJ
Includes bibliographical references

Turner, Robyn Montana
Texas traditions; the culture of the Lone Star state. Little, Brown 1996 96p il $19.95; pa $12.95
　　　　　976.4
1. Texas
ISBN 0-316-85675-4; 0-316-85639-8 (pa)
　　　　　LC 95-34360
Discusses the history, geography, industry, and arts of Texas and includes such topics as folk medicine, home schooling, cowboy poets, the original rodeo, and contributions of Texas women
"Diversity is the theme of this carefully written, intelligent, and timely study. . . . The book is handsomely illustrated with full-color reproductions of paintings, photographs, posters, and maps, many from archival sources." Booklist
Includes bibliographical references

977.3　Illinois

Murphy, Jim, 1947-
The great fire. Scholastic 1995 144p il maps $16.95　　　　　**977.3**
1. Fires—Chicago (Ill.)
ISBN 0-590-47267-4　　　　LC 94-9963
A Newbery Medal honor book, 1996
"Firsthand descriptions by persons who lived through the 1871 Chicago fire are woven into a gripping account of this famous disaster. Murphy also examines the origins of the fire, the errors of judgment that delayed effective response, the organizational problems of the city's firefighters, and the post-fire efforts to rebuild the city. Newspaper lithographs and a few historical photographs convey the magnitude of human suffering and confusion." Horn Book Guide
Includes bibliographical references

978　Western United States

Alter, Judy
The Santa Fe Trail. Children's Press 1998 30p il maps (Cornerstones of freedom) $19.50; pa $5.95　　　　　**978**
1. Santa Fe Trail
ISBN 0-516-21145-5; 0-516-26396-X (pa)
　　　　　LC 97-32710
Presents a history of the trail that became an important commercial route to the southwestern United States during the 1800s

Bentley, Judith, 1945-
Brides, midwives, and widows. 21st Cent. Bks. (NY) 1995 96p il maps (Settling the West) $20.40
　　　　　978
1. Women—West (U.S.) 2. West (U.S.)—History 3. Frontier and pioneer life—West (U.S.)
ISBN 0-8050-2994-X　　　　LC 94-39897
The author "tells the often neglected story of the women who helped settle the West. Making use of diaries and other primary sources, she does an excellent job of introducing these women as well as the ups and downs (often downs) of their lives." Booklist
Includes bibliographical references

Blumberg, Rhoda, 1917-
The incredible journey of Lewis and Clark. Lothrop, Lee & Shepard Bks. 1987 143p il maps hardcover o.p. paperback available $9.95   **978**
1. Lewis, Meriwether, 1774-1809 2. Clark, William, 1770-1838 3. Lewis and Clark Expedition (1804-1806) 4. West (U.S.)—Exploration
ISBN 0-688-14421-7 (pa)   LC 87-4235
Describes the expedition led by Lewis and Clark to explore the unknown western regions of America at the beginning of the nineteenth century
"Blumberg's writing is dignified but never dry, and her sense of narrative makes familiar history an exciting story." Bull Cent Child Books
Includes bibliographical references

Calabro, Marian
The perilous journey of the Donner Party. Clarion Bks. 1999 192p il maps $20   **978**
1. Donner party 2. Frontier and pioneer life—West (U.S.) 3. Overland journeys to the Pacific
ISBN 0-395-86610-3   LC 98-29610
Uses materials from letters and diaries written by survivors of the Donner Party to relate the experiences of that ill-fated group as they endured horrific circumstances on their way to California in 1846-47
"Calabro's offering is a fine addition to the Donner Party canon and particularly well suited to its young audience, for whom the story of hardship and survival will be nothing short of riveting. . . . From the haunting cover with its lonely campfire to the recounting of a survivors' reunion, this is a page-turner." Booklist
Includes bibliographical references

Clark, William, 1770-1838
Off the map; the journals of Lewis and Clark; edited by Peter and Connie Roop; illustrations by Tim Tanner. Walker & Co. 1993 40p il $14.95; lib bdg $15.85; pa $8.95   **978**
1. Lewis and Clark Expedition (1804-1806) 2. West (U.S.)—Exploration
ISBN 0-8027-8207-8; 0-8027-8208-6 (lib bdg); 0-8027-7546-2 (pa)   LC 92-18340
A compilation of entries and excerpts from the journals of William Clark and Meriwether Lewis, describing their historic expedition
"The full-color illustrations, mainly in warm earth tones, give the pages an attractive look, but the most vivid pictures come from the journals themselves. . . . This vivid source material would be a welcome part of any classroom study of the subject." Booklist

Cox, Clinton
The forgotten heroes; the story of the Buffalo Soldiers. Scholastic 1993 174p il hardcover o.p. paperback available $4.50   **978**
1. African American soldiers 2. West (U.S.)—History
ISBN 0-590-45122-7 (pa)   LC 92-36622
"'Buffalo Soldiers' was the name Native Americans gave to the African-American soldiers posted in the American West in the years following the Civil War. . . . Their job: to clear the way for settlement of the

West." Voice Youth Advocates
"A thoroughly researched, well-written account. . . . The narrative is enlivened by dialogue taken from primary sources." SLJ
Includes bibliographical references

DeAngelis, Gina
The black cowboys. Chelsea House 1997 104p il maps (African-American achievers) $19.95; pa $8.95   **978**
1. Cowhands 2. African Americans—History 3. West (U.S.)—History
ISBN 0-7910-2589-6; 0-7910-2590-X (pa)
LC 97-24823
An account of the adventurous African Americans whose exploits contributed to the legends of the Wild West
This "will be useful for young report writers." Booklist
Includes bibliographical references

Duncan, Dayton
People of the West; with an introduction by Stephen Ives and Ken Burns. Little, Brown 1996 120p il $19.95; pa $10.95   **978**
1. West (U.S.)—History 2. Frontier and pioneer life—West (U.S.)
ISBN 0-316-19627-4; 0-316-19633-9 (pa)
LC 95-41641
"Based on the public television series The West"
Tells the stories of men and women whose individual experiences provide a representative picture of life during the formative years of the American West
Includes bibliographical references

The West; an illustrated history for children; with an introduction by Stephen Ives and Ken Burns. Little, Brown 1996 136p il hardcover o.p. paperback available $10.95   **978**
1. West (U.S.)—History 2. Frontier and pioneer life—West (U.S.)
ISBN 0-316-19632-0 (pa)   LC 95-26722
"Based on the public television series The West"
This history focuses "on individual people, both the famous and the little known, many of whom tell their stories in their own words, from the Native Americans who lost their land, to the cowboys and prospectors who came to pursue their dreams. With a detailed text and black-and-white photos on every page . . . [this volume] will attract browsers as well as students doing research." Booklist
Includes bibliographical references

Freedman, Russell
Cowboys of the wild West. Clarion Bks. 1985 103p il map lib bdg $15.95; pa $9.95   **978**
1. Cowhands 2. Frontier and pioneer life—West (U.S.) 3. West (U.S.)—History
ISBN 0-89919-301-3 (lib bdg); 0-395-54800-4 (pa)
LC 85-4200
"Freedman describes the herders' duties on the open range roundups and trail rides, their ranch and line-camp

Freedman, Russell—*Continued*
life, the clothes and equipment dictated by their work, and the economic necessities that defined the job in its heyday, from the 1860s to the 1890s." Bull Cent Child Books
"The author does a fine job of presenting us with information without belittling the real place the cowboy has in both history and fiction." Horn Book
Includes bibliographical references

Jones, Mary Ellen, 1937-
Daily life on the nineteenth century American frontier. Greenwood Press 1998 269p il $45 (7 and up) **978**
1. Frontier and pioneer life—West (U.S.) 2. West (U.S.)—History
ISBN 0-313-29634-0   LC 98-12149
This book attempts to counter stereotypes about the American frontier, and describes the lives of fur traders, explorers, miners, cowboys and settlers, the army and the Great Plains Indians
Includes bibliographical references

Katz, William Loren
Black women of the Old West. Atheneum Bks. for Young Readers 1995 84p il $18 **978**
1. African American women 2. Frontier and pioneer life—West (U.S.) 3. West (U.S.)—History
ISBN 0-689-31944-4   LC 95-9969
This work contains "vignettes and photographs of dozens of women, some famous, others unknown outside their own family circles, who lived across the West in the 19th and early 20th centuries." N Y Times Book Rev
"Katz succeeds in establishing that women of color were an important, if unsung, presence on the westward-shifting frontier." Bull Cent Child Books

Lavender, David Sievert, 1910-
Snowbound; the tragic story of the Donner Party; by David Lavender. Holiday House 1996 87p il maps $18.95 **978**
1. Donner party 2. Frontier and pioneer life—West (U.S.) 3. Overland journeys to the Pacific
ISBN 0-8234-1231-8   LC 95-41266
Relates the ordeals faced by a group of pioneers on their journey from Illinois to California in 1846
The author "draws on authentic primary documents, combining a vivid narrative with his analysis of what happened and why. His handsomely designed, slightly oversize volume has lots of photos of the places and people." Booklist
Includes bibliographical references

Marrin, Albert, 1936-
Cowboys, Indians, and gunfighters; the story of the cattle kingdom. Atheneum Pubs. 1993 196p il maps $22.95 **978**
1. West (U.S.)—History 2. Frontier and pioneer life—West (U.S.)
ISBN 0-689-31774-3   LC 92-5727

Describes life in the American West and the growth of the cattle industry, from the introduction of horses and cattle by the Spanish through the reign of the cattle barons in the late nineteenth century
"Prints by such notable artists as Frederic Remington and Charles M. Russell, as well as poignant period photographs bring the era to life." SLJ
Includes bibliographical references

McGowen, Tom
African-Americans in the Old West. Children's Press 1998 30p il map (Cornerstones of freedom) $20; pa $5.95 **978**
1. African Americans—History 2. Frontier and pioneer life—West (U.S.) 3. West (U.S.)—History
ISBN 0-516-20835-7; 0-516-26348-X (pa)
                               LC 97-26583
Describes the important role of freed slaves and other African-Americans in the settlement of the West

Murdoch, David Hamilton, 1937-
Cowboy; written by David H. Murdoch; photographed by Geoff Brightling. Knopf 1993 63p il (Eyewitness books) $19; lib bdg $20.99 **978**
1. Cowhands
ISBN 0-679-84014-1; 0-679-94014-6 (lib bdg)
                               LC 93-12768
"A Dorling Kindersley book"
Text and photographs trace the history and lore of cowboys around the globe
"Each chapter has excellent illustrations, primarily photographs taken from a variety of museums and photo collections from throughout the world. This book gives a good overview of cowboy culture." Sci Books Films

Patent, Dorothy Hinshaw
Homesteading; settling America's heartland; photographs by William Muñoz. Walker & Co. 1998 32p il maps $16.95; lib bdg $17.85 **978**
1. Frontier and pioneer life—West (U.S.) 2. West (U.S.)—Social life and customs
ISBN 0-8027-8664-2; 0-8027-8665-0 (lib bdg)
                               LC 98-12463
Chronicles the activities of the homesteaders who settled the vast American prairies during the late nineteenth and early twentieth centuries
"An attractive, informative, and well-written guide." Booklist

Schlissel, Lillian
Black frontiers; a history of African American heroes in the Old West. Simon & Schuster Bks. for Young Readers 1995 80p il $18 **978**
1. African Americans—History 2. Frontier and pioneer life—West (U.S.) 3. West (U.S.)—History
ISBN 0-689-80285-4   LC 92-120
Focuses on the experiences of blacks as mountain men, soldiers, homesteaders, and scouts on the frontiers of the American West
"Good-quality period photos and black-and-white reproductions appear on nearly every page, adding human interest and realism to the text. An excellent addition to black history or westward movement units." Booklist
Includes bibliographical references

Stovall, TaRessa

The Buffalo Soldiers. Chelsea House 1997 104p
il (African-American achievers) $19.95; pa $8.95
978

1. African American soldiers 2. West (U.S.)—History
ISBN 0-7910-2595-0; 0-7910-2596-9 (pa)
LC 97-14568

An account of the achievements of the Afro-American
Army regiments that distinguished themselves during numerous campaigns and played a vital role in the settlement of the American West

"A well-written, eye-opening account of a shamefully
obscure aspect of African American and U.S. armed
forces history." Booklist

Includes bibliographical references

Tunis, Edwin, 1897-1973

Frontier living; written and illustrated by Edwin
Tunis. Crowell 1976 c1961 165p il maps o.p.
978

1. Frontier and pioneer life—West (U.S.) 2. West
(U.S.)—History
LC 75-29639

Companion volume Colonial living (1957)
First published 1961 by World Publishing Company

This volume "portrays the manners and customs of the
frontiersman and his family from the beginning of the
westward movement through the 19th century in . . .
text and more than 200 drawings." Wis Libr Bull

Westward expansion; an eyewitness history;
[edited by] Sanford Wexler. Facts on File 1991
418p il maps (Eyewitness history series) $55
978

1. Frontier and pioneer life—West (U.S.) 2. West
(U.S.)—History 3. United States—Territorial expan-
sion
ISBN 0-8160-2407-3
LC 90-42599

This work "includes primary-source material from various points of view, arranged chronologically from the
French and Indian War through the settlement of the
Great Plains. It presents stories of exploration, Indian-
white relations, war and diplomacy, and settlers' experiences." Booklist

The accounts "are well chosen to portray the promises
and realities of the frontier. Strongly recommended as a
good introduction to source material." Libr J

Includes bibliographical references

Yount, Lisa

Frontiers of freedom; African Americans in the
West. Facts on File 1997 140p il maps (Library of
African-American history) $19.95 (7 and up)
978

1. African Americans—History 2. Frontier and pioneer life—West (U.S.) 3. United States—Race relations
ISBN 0-8160-3372-2
LC 96-46863

This "chronicles the important contributions African
Americans made to the explorations of the West, often
under difficult and dangerous situations." Horn Book
Guide

"Quotes from primary sources punctuate the text and

are documented in the chapter notes. The author presents
factual information about the political and sociological
situations of the era, and then uses vivid examples from
the lives of the people during the time period to show
what was happening." Book Rep

Includes bibliographical references

979   Great Basin and Pacific Coast states

Marrin, Albert, 1936-

Empires lost and won; the Spanish heritage in
the Southwest. Atheneum Bks. for Young Readers
1997 216p il maps $19 (7 and up)
979

1. Southwestern States—History 2. Spaniards—United
States
ISBN 0-689-80414-8
LC 96-20851

Discusses the history of the southwestern region of the
United States from the sixteenth century to the Mexican
War, examining the interactions between the Spanish, In-
dians, and American pioneers

"The powerful text, written by a gifted storyteller, is
beautifully blended with vivid, carefully placed, firsthand
accounts." SLJ

Includes bibliographical references

979.1   Arizona

Maurer, Richard, 1950-

The wild Colorado; the true adventures of Fred
Dellenbaugh, age 17, on the second Powell
Expedition into the Grand Canyon. Crown 1999
120p il $18; lib bdg $19.99 (7 and up)
979.1

1. Dellenbaugh, Frederick Samuel, 1853-1935
2. Powell, John Wesley, 1834-1902 3. Colorado River
(Colo.-Mexico) 4. Grand Canyon (Ariz.)
ISBN 0-517-70945-7; 0-517-70946-5 (lib bdg)
LC 98-33892

Recounts the adventures of seventeen-year-old Fred
Dellenbaugh, the youngest member of the second Powell
expedition, which explored the Colorado River and the
Grand Canyon in 1871-2

This is "a well-crafted, exciting book about exploration and adventure." SLJ

Includes bibliographical references

979.5   Oregon. Pacific Northwest

Blackwood, Gary L.

Life on the Oregon Trail. Lucent Bks. 1999
111p il maps (Way people live) lib bdg $23.70 (7
and up)
979.5

1. Oregon Trail 2. Overland journeys to the Pacific
3. Frontier and pioneer life—West (U.S.)
ISBN 1-56006-540-0
LC 98-48958

Describes how people traveling on the Oregon Trail
lived, discussing their reasons for going west, modes of
transportation, interaction with the Indians, and activities
on the Trail

Blackwood, Gary L.—*Continued*

"Inserts, maps, and black-and-white reproductions effectively augment the narrative. Well organized and extremely informative, this book is well suited for reports." SLJ

Includes bibliographical references

Fisher, Leonard Everett, 1924-

The Oregon Trail. Holiday House 1990 64p il maps $16.95 **979.5**

1. Oregon Trail 2. Overland journeys to the Pacific

ISBN 0-8234-0833-7 LC 90-55103

Charts the journey of those who followed the Oregon Trail in the first half of the nineteenth century

"Fisher brings this migration to life with a clear, readable text that makes generous use of the emigrants' own journal entries. . . . The illustrations are many and varied, including maps, photographs, drawings, documents, and paintings." Booklist

981 Brazil

Bender, Evelyn, 1936-

Brazil. Chelsea House 1999 112p il maps (Major world nations) $19.95 **981**

1. Brazil

ISBN 0-7910-4758-X LC 89-28262

Surveys the history, topography, people, and culture of Brazil, with emphasis on its current economy, industry, and place in the political world

Includes glossary

Kallen, Stuart A., 1955-

Life in the Amazon rainforest. Lucent Bks. 1999 96p il maps (Way people live) lib bdg $17.96 (7 and up) **981**

1. Yanoama Indians 2. Indians of South America—Brazil 3. Amazon River valley

ISBN 1-56006-387-4 LC 98-43616

Describes the history, life, and culture of the Yanomami, an indigenous tribe still living a primitive existence in the Amazon rainforest

Includes bibliographical references

982 Argentina

Dwyer, Christopher

Chile. Chelsea House 1999 128p il map (Major world nations) lib bdg $19.95 **982**

1. Chile

ISBN 0-7910-4734-2

First published 1990 in Places and peoples of the world series

An introduction to the geography, history, government, economy, people, and culture of Chile

Hintz, Martin, 1945-

Argentina. Children's Press 1998 144p il (Enchantment of the world, second series) $32 **982**

1. Argentina

ISBN 0-516-20647-8 LC 97-40666

Describes the geography, history, culture, religion, and people of the environmentally diverse South American country of Argentina

Includes bibliographical references

985 Peru

Bingham, Hiram, 1875-1956

The ancient Incas; chronicles from National geographic; Arthur M. Schlesinger, Jr., senior consulting editor; Fred L. Israel, general editor. Chelsea House 1999 133p il (Cultural and geographical exploration) lib bdg $19.95 **985**

1. Peruvian Expeditions (1912-1915) 2. Incas 3. Machu Picchu (Peru)

ISBN 0-7910-5104-8 LC 98-45472

"Examines the 1911 discovery of the lost city of Machu Picchu, an Inca city perched between two sharp mountain peaks in modern-day Peru whose ruins were found nearly intact. Led by Hiram Bigham, this exploration uncovered a city that had gone undetected for hundreds of years." Publisher's note

Includes bibliographical references

Falconer, Kieran, 1970-

Peru. Marshall Cavendish 1995 128p il maps (Cultures of the world) lib bdg $25.64 **985**

1. Peru

ISBN 0-7614-0179-2 LC 95-14898

Full-color photographs accompany information on many aspects of this South American country beginning with its geography and history and including government, religion, arts, and food

Includes glossary and bibliographical references

Hinds, Kathryn, 1962-

The Incas. Benchmark Bks. (Tarrytown) 1998 80p il map (Cultures of the past) lib bdg $28.50 **985**

1. Incas

ISBN 0-7614-0270-5 LC 96-30799

Examines the history, culture, religion, and social structure of the ancient Incas

Includes glossary and bibliographical references

King, David C.

Peru; lost cities, found hopes. Benchmark Bks. (Tarrytown) 1998 64p il maps (Exploring cultures of the world) lib bdg $34.21 **985**

1. Peru

ISBN 0-7614-0396-5 LC 97-2722

Examines the geography, history, government, people, and culture of Peru

"An accessible introduction to the South American country. . . . Kid-friendly topics such as school, holidays, and food are also discussed." Horn Book Guide

Includes glossary and bibliographical references

986.1   Colombia

Haynes, Tricia
 Colombia. Chelsea House 1999 102p il maps
(Major world nations) $19.95   **986.1**
 1. Colombia
 ISBN 0-7910-4969-8   LC 98-17466
 Examines the history, people, geography, economy,
climate, and culture of the South American nation of Co-
lombia
 Includes glossary

986.6   Ecuador

Foley, Erin, 1967-
 Ecuador; [by] Erin L. Foley. Marshall
Cavendish 1995 128p il maps (Cultures of the
world) $35.64   **986.6**
 1. Ecuador
 ISBN 0-7614-0173-3   LC 94-45266
 This introduction to the history and culture of Ecuador
"is especially successful in explaining social and economic hierarchies within the country. The cultures of the
indigenous populations, blacks, mestizos, Hispanics, and
other immigrants are discussed. The author describes
how members within each group relate to one another
and how these diverse cultures create the 'hierarchical
pyramid' that is Ecuadorian society." SLJ
 Includes glossary and bibliographical references

989.5   Uruguay

Jermyn, Leslie
 Uruguay. Marshall Cavendish 1999 128p il
maps (Cultures of the world) lib bdg $35.64
          989.5
 1. Uruguay
 ISBN 0-7614-0873-8   LC 98-27375
 Describes the geography, history, government, economy, people, lifestyle, religion, language, arts, leisure, festivals, and food of the smallest country in South America
 Includes glossary and bibliographical references

993   New Zealand

Smelt, Roselynn
 New Zealand. Marshall Cavendish 1998 128p il
maps (Cultures of the world) lib bdg $35.64
          993
 1. New Zealand
 ISBN 0-7614-0808-8   LC 97-42179
 Introduces the geography, history, religion, government, economy, and culture of a Pacific-island country
first populated by the Maori, to whom it was the "Land
of the Long White Cloud"
 Includes glossary and bibliographical references

994   Australia

Heinrichs, Ann
 Australia. Children's Press 1998 144p il
(Enchantment of the world, second series) $32
          994
 1. Australia
 ISBN 0-516-20648-6   LC 98-15780
 Explores the geography, history, arts, religions, and
everyday life of the Land Down Under, also called the
Lucky Country
 Includes bibliographical references

995.3   Papua New Guinea. New Guinea region

Gascoigne, Ingrid
 Papua New Guinea. Marshall Cavendish 1998
128p il maps (Cultures of the world) $35.64
          995.3
 1. Papua New Guinea
 ISBN 0-7614-0813-4   LC 97-43611
 Discusses the geography, history, economy, government, varied culture and peoples of the country made up
of more than 600 islands and archipelagos
 Includes glossary and bibliographical references

996   Polynesia and Micronesia

NgCheong-Lum, Roseline, 1962-
 Tahiti. Marshall Cavendish 1997 128p il maps
(Cultures of the world) lib bdg $35.64   **996**
 1. Tahiti (French Polynesia)
 ISBN 0-7614-0682-4   LC 96-40213
 Discusses the geography, history, government, econo-
my, people, and culture of the largest island in French
Polynesia
 This offers "lucidly written text. . . . Chapters include
discussion of nuclear testing in the Pacific, the Tahitian
language, and nationalism in the French territory. Maps
and a page of basic facts about Tahiti round out the useful book." Horn Book Guide
 Includes glossary and bibliographical references

998   Arctic islands and Antarctica

Armstrong, Jennifer, 1961-
 Shipwreck at the bottom of the world; the
extraordinary true story of Shackleton and the
Endurance. Crown 1998 134p il maps $18; lib bdg
$19.99 (7 and up)   **998**
 1. Shackleton, Sir Ernest Henry, 1874-1922 2. Endurance (Ship) 3. Imperial Trans-Antarctic Expedition
(1914-1917) 4. Antarctica
 ISBN 0-517-80013-6; 0-517-80014-4 (lib bdg)
          LC 97-52063

Armstrong, Jennifer, 1961——*Continued*

Describes the events of the 1914 Shackleton Antarctic expedition when, after being trapped in a frozen sea for nine months, their ship, Endurance, was finally crushed, forcing Shackleton and his men to make a very long and perilous journey across ice and stormy seas to reach inhabited land

"Excellent black-and-white photographs taken during the journey document the entire adventure story. . . . A book that will capture the attention and imagination of any reader." SLJ

Includes bibliographical references

Beattie, Owen

Buried in ice; by Owen Beattie and John Geiger with Shelley Tanaka. Scholastic 1992 64p il maps (Time quest book) hardcover o.p. paperback available $6.95　　　　**998**

1. Franklin, Sir John, 1786-1847 2. Arctic regions
ISBN 0-590-43839-2 (pa)　　　　LC 91-23897

"A Scholastic/Madison Press book"

Probes the tragic and mysterious fate of Sir John Franklin's failed expedition to the Arctic to find the Northwest Passage in 1845

"The narrative is interspersed with an imaginative section that relates the story of the expedition from the point of view of 19-year-old Luke, a member of the crew. While the text is exciting, the book's greatest strength is its superb illustrations: drawings, paintings, and historic and present day photographs are used to enrich each page." SLJ

Includes glossary and bibliographical references

Bramwell, Martyn

Polar exploration; journeys to the Arctic and the Antarctic; written by Martyn Bramwell, illustrated by Marjorie Crosby-Fairall and Ann Winterbotham. DK Pub. 1998 48p il (DK discoveries) $14.95　　　　**998**

1. Explorers 2. Polar regions
ISBN 0-7894-3421-0　　　　LC 98-4221

Describes some of the many explorations made to both the North and South Poles

Kimmel, Elizabeth Cody

Ice story; Shackleton's lost expedition. Clarion Bks. 1999 120p il maps $18　　　　**998**

1. Shackleton, Sir Ernest Henry, 1874-1922 2. Endurance (Ship) 3. Imperial Trans-Antarctic Expedition (1914-1917) 4. Antarctica
ISBN 0-395-91524-4　　　　LC 98-29956

Describes the events of the 1914 Shackleton Antarctic expedition, when the ship the Endurance was crushed in a frozen sea and the men made the perilous journey across ice and stormy seas to reach inhabited land

"The amazing story is well served in this account, which includes photos by expedition photographer Frank Hurley." Horn Book Guide

Includes bibliographical references

Robert E. Peary and the rush to the North Pole; chronicles from National Geographic; Arthur M. Schlesinger, senior consulting editor, Fred L. Israel, general editor. Chelsea House 1999 131p il (Cultural and geographical exploration) lib bdg $19.95 (7 and up)　　　　**998**

1. Peary, Robert Edwin, 1856-1920 2. Explorers 3. North Pole
ISBN 0-7910-5099-8　　　　LC 98-32303

Articles originally published in "National Geographic" present the life and accomplishments of Robert E. Peary, focusing on his explorations of the North Pole

This offers a "convenient [collection] of mostly primary sources, indexed and with original archival photographs." SLJ

Includes bibliographical references

Steger, Will

Over the top of the world; explorer Will Steger's trek across the Arctic; [by] Will Steger and Jon Bowermaster; sidebars by Barbara Horlbeck. Scholastic 1997 63p il $17.95　　　　**998**

1. Arctic regions 2. North Pole
ISBN 0-590-84860-7　　　　LC 96-6913

An account of explorer Will Steger's expedition from Russia to Canada by way of the North Pole, traveling by dog sled and canoe

"Written with a crispness and an immediacy, the narrative reads like an adventure story, with dramatic, compelling photographs." Booklist

Taylor, Barbara, 1954-

Arctic & Antarctic; written by Barbara Taylor; photographed by Geoff Brightling. Knopf 1995 63p il maps (Eyewitness books) $19; lib bdg $20.99　　　　**998**

1. Polar regions
ISBN 0-679-87257-4; 0-679-97257-9 (lib bdg)
　　　　LC 94-37730

"A Dorling Kindersley book"

This overview "features a series of two-page spreads focusing on the history, geology, plant life, wildlife and ecology of the polar regions. Each two-page topic is given a paragraph of explanatory text surrounded by diagrams, maps, charts and photographs with lengthy captions." Appraisal

Fic　Fiction

Abelove, Joan

Go and come back; a novel. DK Ink 1998 176p $16.95 (7 and up)　　　　**Fic**

1. Anthropologists—Fiction 2. Peru—Fiction 3. Indians of South America—Fiction
ISBN 0-7894-2476-2　　　　LC 97-36070

"A Richard Jackson book"

Alicia, a young tribeswoman living in a Amazonian village in the Andes, tells about the two American women anthropologists who arrive to study the way of life of her people

"By juxtaposing two radically different cultures (with attitudes toward sexuality prominent), Abelove provides humorous yet respectful insight into both." Horn Book Guide

Adams, Douglas, 1952-

The Hitchhiker's Guide to the Galaxy. Harmony Bks. 1980 215p $15 (7 and up)   **Fic**
1. Science fiction
ISBN 0-517-54209-9   LC 80-14572
Also available in paperback from Pocket Bks.

"Based on a BBC radio series, . . . this is the episodic story of Arthur Dent, a contemporary Englishman who discovers first that his unpretentious house is about to be demolished to make way for a bypass, and second that a good friend is actually an alien galactic hitchhiker who announces that Earth itself will soon be demolished to make way for an intergalactic speedway. A suitably bewildered Dent soon finds himself hitching . . . rides throughout space, aided by a . . . reference book, The Hitchhiker's Guide to the Galaxy, a compendium of 'facts,' philosophies, and wild advice." Libr J

Other titles featuring Arthur Dent are:
Life, the universe and everything (1982)
Mostly harmless (1992)
The restaurant at the end of the universe (1981)
So long, and thanks for all the fish (1984)

Adams, Richard, 1920-

Watership down. Macmillan 1974 c1972 429p $40   **Fic**
1. Rabbits—Fiction 2. Allegories
ISBN 0-02-700030-3   LC 73-6044
Also available G.K. Hall large print edition and in paperback from Avon Bks.

First published 1972 in the United Kingdom

"Faced with the annihilation of its warren, a small group of male rabbits sets out across the English downs in search of a new home. Internal struggles for power surface in this intricately woven, realistically told adult adventure when the protagonists must coordinate tactics in order to defeat an enemy rabbit fortress. It is clear that the author has done research on rabbit behavior, for this tale is truly authentic." Shapiro. Fic for Youth. 3d edition

Adler, C. S. (Carole S.), 1932-

Not just a summer crush. Clarion Bks. 1998 117p $15   **Fic**
1. Teachers—Fiction   2. Family life—Fiction 3. Beaches—Fiction
ISBN 0-395-88532-9   LC 98-11358
A twelve-year-old girl develops a crush on her English teacher when he spends a week at a beach near her family's cottage

"Adler's bittersweet narrative shrewdly captures the wretchedness of feeling completely misunderstood and of being neither a child nor an adult." Horn Book Guide

Aiken, Joan, 1924-

The wolves of Willoughby Chase; illustrated by Pat Marriott. Doubleday 1963 c1962 168p il hardcover o.p. paperback available $4.99   **Fic**
1. Great Britain—Fiction
ISBN 0-440-49603-9 (pa)   LC 63-18034
First published 1962 in the United Kingdom

"In this burlesque of a Victorian melodrama, two London children [Dido Twite and Simon] are sent to a country estate while their parents are away. Here they outwit a wicked governess, escape from packs of hungry wolves, and restore the estate to its rightful owner." Hodges. Books for Elem Sch Libr

"Plot, characterization, and background blend perfectly into an amazing whole." SLJ

Other available titles about Dido Twite and Simon are:
Black hearts in Battersea (1964)
Cold Shoulder Road (1996)
Dangerous games (1999)
Is underground (1993)
Nightbirds on Nantucket (1996)

Alder, Elizabeth

The king's shadow. Farrar, Straus & Giroux 1995 259p $17 (7 and up)   **Fic**
1. Harold, King of England, 1022?-1066—Fiction 2. Orphans—Fiction 3. Great Britain—History—0-1066—Fiction
ISBN 0-374-34182-6   LC 93-34159
Also available in paperback from Dell

After he is orphaned and has his tongue cut out in a clash with the bullying sons of a Welsh noble, Evyn is sold as a slave and serves many masters, from the gracious Lady Swan Neck to the valiant Harold Godwinson, England's last Saxon king

"Readers will get their history almost without noticing it, but will come to understand the complex society and world within which these individuals functioned easily. Evyn is easy to identify with as both a victim and an outcast." Voice Youth Advocates

Alexander, Lloyd

The Arkadians. Dutton Children's Bks. 1995 272p $16.99; pa $4.99   **Fic**
1. Fantasy fiction
ISBN 0-525-45415-2; 0-14-038073-6 (pa)
     LC 94-35025
To escape the wrath of the king and his wicked soothsayers, Lucian joins with Fronto, a poet-turned-jackass, and Joy-in-the-Dance, a young girl with mystical powers, on a series of epic adventures

"On one level, this is a rousing adventure complete with cliffhangers and do-or-die situations. On another, readers familiar with Greek mythology will find clever hints at the myths' purpose and genesis." SLJ

The Beggar Queen. Dutton 1984 221p hardcover o.p. paperback available $4.99   **Fic**
1. Adventure fiction
ISBN 0-440-90548-6 (pa)   LC 83-25502
The concluding volume in the author's Westmark trilogy

"Since the end of the war with Regia, Theo has become a consul to Mickle, now Queen Augusta. However, peace lasts only two years, when Cabbarus invades the country to wrest the kingdom back from Mickle. Theo is forced to take up arms again to help his beloved queen and country." Roman. Sequences

The book of three. rev ed. Holt & Co. 1999 190p (Chronicles of Prydain, 1) $17.95   **Fic**
1. Fantasy fiction
ISBN 0-8050-6132-0   LC 98-40901
Also available in paperback from Dell
First published 1964

Alexander, Lloyd—*Continued*

"The first of five books about the mythical land of Prydain finds Taran, an assistant pig keeper, fighting with Prince Gwydion against the evil which theatens the kingdom." Hodges. Books for Elem Sch Libr

"Related in a simple, direct style, this fast-paced tale of high adventure has a well-balanced blend of fantasy, realism, and humor." SLJ

Other available titles about the mythical land of Prydain are:

The black cauldron (1965)
The castle of Llyr (1966)
The foundling and other tales of Prydain, entered in short story collections section
The high king, entered separately
Taran Wanderer (1967)

Gypsy Rizka. Dutton Children's Bks. 1999 195p $16.99   **Fic**
  1. Gypsies—Fiction 2. Fantasy fiction
  ISBN 0-525-46121-3   LC 98-41399

Living alone in her wagon on the outskirts of a Greater Dunitsa while waiting for her father's return, Rizka, a Gypsy and a trickster, exposes the ridiculous foibles of some of the townspeople

"Scenes of broad slapstick effervesce with mind-tickling repartee in this book that is . . . lively, satirical, and with a core of pure gold." Horn Book Guide

The high king. rev ed. Holt & Co. 1999 c1968 253p (Chronicles of Prydain) $17.95   **Fic**
  1. Fantasy fiction
  ISBN 0-8050-6135-5   LC 98-40900

Also available in paperback from Dell

Awarded The Newbery Medal, 1969

Concluding title in the chronicles of Prydain which include: The book of three, The black cauldron, The castle of Llyr, and Taran Wanderer

First published 1968

This edition includes a pronunciation guide

In this final volume Taran, the assistant pig-keeper "becomes High King of Prydain, Princess Eilonwy becomes his queen, the predictions of Taran's wizard guardian Dallben are fulfilled, and the forces of black magic led by Arawn, Lord of Annuvin, Land of the Dead, are vanquished forever." SLJ

"The fantasy has the depth and richness of a medieval tapestry, infinitely detailed and imaginative." Saturday Rev

The Illyrian adventure. Dutton 1986 132p hardcover o.p. paperback available $4.50   **Fic**
  1. Adventure fiction
  ISBN 0-440-80161-3 (pa)   LC 85-30762

"Sixteen-year-old Vesper Holly drags her long-suffering guardian, Brinnie, off to Illyria to vindicate her late father's reputation as a scholar. With humor, beguiling charm, and intelligence she manages to find a treasure, thwart a conspiracy to murder Illyria's King Osman, and guide two rival factions to the peace table." Wilson Libr Bull

"Alexander's archeological mystery has intricate plotting and witty wording—a romp of a read-aloud for Raiders of the Lost Ark fans." Bull Cent Child Books

Other available adventure titles featuring Vesper Holly are:

The Drackenberg adventure (1988)
The El Dorado adventure (1987)
The Jedera adventure (1989)
The Philadelphia adventure (1990)

The iron ring. Dutton Children's Bks. 1997 283p $16.99; pa $4.99   **Fic**
  1. Adventure fiction 2. India—Fiction
  ISBN 0-525-45597-3; 0-14-130348-4 (pa)
                LC 96-29730

"Young Tamar, ruler of a small Indian kingdom, wagers with a visiting king and loses his kingdom and his freedom. Traveling to the king's land to make good on his debt, he collects quite an entourage and eventually overcomes his enemies with his friends' help. This tale offers delightful characters, a philosophical interest in the meaning of life, a thoughtful look at the caste system, and a clever use of Indian animal folktales." Horn Book Guide

The Kestrel. Dutton 1982 244p o.p.   **Fic**
  1. Adventure fiction
                LC 81-15290

"The second in Alexander's . . . Westmark trilogy follows the fates of Mickle, 'the Beggar Queen,' and her friend Theo, whom the cruelties of war transform into an uncharacteristically aggressive fighter facing despair even in victory." Booklist

Followed by The Beggar Queen

The remarkable journey of Prince Jen. Dutton Children's Bks. 1991 273p $15.99; pa $3.99 **Fic**
  1. Adventure fiction 2. China—Fiction
  ISBN 0-525-44826-8; 0-440-40890-3 (pa)
                LC 91-13720

Bearing six unusual gifts, young Prince Jen in Tang Dynasty China embarks on a perilous quest and emerges triumphantly into manhood

"Alexander satisfies the taste for excitement, but his vivid characters and the food for thought he offers will nourish long after the last page is turned." SLJ

Westmark. Dutton 1981 184p hardcover o.p. paperback available $4.50   **Fic**
  1. Adventure fiction
  ISBN 0-440-99731-3 (pa)   LC 80-22242

In this first volume of the Westmark trilogy, "Theo embarks on an adventure when, as a printer's apprentice, he assaults one of the king's men. Fleeing through the backwoods to save his life, he meets a variety of people including Mickle, who is in disguise. Theo becomes involved in the political scene and is torn because of his conflict between loyalty to the king and his sense that the revolutionaries are right. Characters are interesting because they are fully developed and unique, and the corruption of the ruling party is well portrayed." Roman. Sequences

Followed by The Kestrel

Almond, David, 1951-

Skellig. Delacorte Press 1999 c1998 182p $15.95   **Fic**
  1. Fantasy fiction
  ISBN 0-385-32653-X   LC 98-23121

Almond, David, 1951-—*Continued*
First published 1998 in the United Kingdom
Unhappy about his baby sister's illness and the chaos of moving into a dilapidated old house, Michael retreats to the garage and finds a mysterious stranger who is something like a bird and something like an angel
"The plot is beautifully paced and the characters are drawn with a graceful, careful hand. . . . A lovingly done, thought-provoking novel." SLJ

Armstrong, Jennifer, 1961-
The dreams of Mairhe Mehan. Knopf 1996 119p il $18; pa $4.99 (7 and up)   Fic
1. United States—History—1861-1865, Civil War—Fiction 2. Irish Americans—Fiction 3. Washington (D.C.)—Fiction
ISBN 0-679-88152-2; 0-679-88557-9 (pa)
                                                     LC 96-4153
Mairhe, who lives in an Irish slum in Washington, D.C. in the 1860s, struggles to come to grips with the impact of the Civil War on her family
"Richly textured and written in a lyrical style full of Irish storytelling and myth, this is a work to be savored." SLJ

Mary Mehan awake. Knopf 1997 119p il $18; pa $4.99 (7 and up)   Fic
1. Irish Americans—Fiction 2. Deaf—Fiction 3. New York (State)—Fiction
ISBN 0-679-88276-6; 0-679-89265-6 (pa)
                                                     LC 97-6465
Sequel to The dreams of Mairhe Mehan
While working as a servant in the home of a naturalist, Mary Mehan gradually recovers from the numbing effects of her experience as a Civil War nurse and falls in love with a man who had lost his hearing
"The beautiful writing captures personalities deftly and fully evokes Mary's internal suffering and quietude." Booklist

Steal away. Orchard Bks. 1992 206p o.p.; Scholastic paperback available $3.99   Fic
1. Slavery—Fiction 2. African Americans—Fiction 3. Underground railroad—Fiction
ISBN 0-590-46921-5 (pa)   LC 91-18504
"A Richard Jackson book"
In 1855 two thirteen-year-old girls, one white and one black, run away from a southern farm and make the difficult journey north to freedom, living to recount their story forty-one years later to two similar young girls
"Armstrong's novel has pace and suspense, characterization that is solid and consistent, and a crescendo that builds to a logical yet dramatic climax." Bull Cent Child Books

Armstrong, William Howard, 1914-1999
Sounder; [by] William H. Armstrong; illustrations by James Barkley. Harper & Row 1969 $14.95; lib bdg $14.89; pa $6   Fic
1. Dogs—Fiction 2. African Americans—Fiction 3. Family life—Fiction
ISBN 0-06-020143-6; 0-06-020144-4 (lib bdg); 0-06-080975-2 (pa)
Awarded the Newbery Medal, 1970

"Set in the South in the era of sharecropping and segregation, this succinctly told tale poignantly describes the courage of a father who steals a ham in order to feed his undernourished family; the determination of the eldest son, who searches for his father despite the apathy of prison authorities; and the devotion of a coon dog named Sounder." Shapiro. Fic for Youth. 3d edition

Auch, Mary Jane
Frozen summer. Holt & Co. 1998 202p $15.95
                                                     Fic
1. Frontier and pioneer life—Fiction 2. Mentally ill—Fiction 3. New York (State)—Fiction
ISBN 0-8050-4923-1   LC 98-23485
Sequel to Journey to nowhere
In this second title in the Genesee trilogy, twelve-year-old Mem's new home in the wilderness of western New York is disrupted when the birth of another baby sends her mother into "spells" that disconnect her from reality
"A thoughtful novel for readers ready to move beyond stories of idealized pioneers." Booklist

Journey to nowhere. Holt & Co. 1997 202p $15.95   Fic
1. Frontier and pioneer life—Fiction 2. New York (State)—Fiction
ISBN 0-8050-4922-3   LC 96-42249
This is the first title in the Genesee trilogy. In 1815, while traveling by covered wagon to settle in the wilderness of western New York, eleven-year-old Mem experiences a flood and separation from her family
"A well-written, realistic, and thoroughly researched novel." Booklist

Avi, 1937-
The barn. Orchard Bks. 1994 106p $14.95; lib bdg $15.99   Fic
1. Fathers and sons—Fiction 2. Farm life—Fiction 3. Frontier and pioneer life—Fiction
ISBN 0-531-06861-7; 0-531-08711-5 (lib bdg)
                                                     LC 94-6920
Also available in paperback from Avon Bks.
"A Richard Jackson book"
In an effort to fulfill their dying father's last request, nine-year-old Ben and his brother and sister construct a barn on their land in the Oregon Territory in the 1850s
"While focusing mainly on his characters, Avi presents a vivid picture of the time and place, including fairly involved details about how the barn is constructed. This novel . . . is a thought-provoking and engaging piece of historical fiction." SLJ

Beyond the western sea. Orchard Bks. 1996 2v ea $18.95; lib bdg $19.99   Fic
1. Immigration and emigration—Fiction 2. Brothers and sisters—Fiction
                                                     LC 95-36058
Also available boxed set $34.95 (ISBN 0-531-09547-9) and in paperback from Avon Bks.
"A Richard Jackson book"
Contents: bk 1 The escape from home (ISBN 0-531-09513-4; 0-531-08863-4); bk 2 Lord Kirkle's money (ISBN 0-531-09520-7; 0-531-08870-7)

Avi, 1937——*Continued*

Driven from their impoverished Irish village, fifteen-year-old Maura and her younger brother meet their landlord's runaway son in Liverpool while all three wait for a ship to America; their fates continue to intertwine on board ship and in the New World

"Beyond the Western Sea offers readers a terrific adventure tale, patterned on serialized Victorian novels. Avi creates vivid characters and an engrossing story." Christ Sci Monit

Blue heron. Bradbury Press 1992 186p $15
Fic
1. Family life—Fiction 2. Herons—Fiction
ISBN 0-02-707751-9   LC 91-4308
Also available in paperback from Avon Bks.

While spending the month of August on the Massachusetts shore with her father, stepmother, and their new baby, almost thirteen-year-old Maggie finds beauty in and draws strength from a great blue heron, even as the family around her unravels

"A wonderful story about growing up and accepting change." BAYA Book Rev

The fighting ground. Lippincott 1984 157p $12.95; lib bdg $14.89; pa $4.95   Fic
1. United States—History—1775-1783, Revolution—Fiction
ISBN 0-397-32073-6; 0-397-32074-4 (lib bdg); 0-06-440185-5 (pa)   LC 82-47719

"It's April 1776, and the fighting ground is both the farm country of Pennsylvania and the heart of a boy which is 'wonderful ripe for war.' Twenty-four hours transform Jonathan from a cocky 13-year-old, eager to take on the British, into a young man who now knows the horror, the pathos, the ambiguities of war." Voice Youth Advocates

The author "has written a taut, fast-paced novel that builds to a shattering climax. His protagonist's painful, inner struggle to understand the intense and conflicting emotions brought on by a war that spares no one is central to this finely crafted novel." ALAN

The man who was Poe; a novel. Orchard Bks. 1989 208p o.p.; Avon Bks. paperback available $4.99   Fic
1. Poe, Edgar Allan, 1809-1849—Fiction 2. Mystery fiction
ISBN 0-380-73022-7 (pa)   LC 89-42537
"A Richard Jackson book"

In Providence, R.I., in 1848, Edgar Allan Poe reluctantly investigates the problems of eleven-year-old Edmund, whose family has mysteriously disappeared and whose story suggests a new Poe tale with a ghastly final twist

Avi blends "drama, history, and mystery without a hint of pastiche or calculation. And, as in the best mystery stories, readers will be left in the end with both the comfort of puzzles solved and the unease of mysteries remaining." Bull Cent Child Books

Nothing but the truth; a documentary novel. Orchard Bks. 1991 177p $16.95; lib bdg $17.99
Fic
1. School stories
ISBN 0-531-05959-6; 0-531-08559-7 (lib bdg)
LC 91-9200

Also available Thorndike Press large print edition and in paperback from Avon Bks.

A Newbery Medal honor book, 1992

"A Richard Jackson book"

A ninth-grader's suspension for humming "The Star-Spangled Banner" during homeroom becomes a national news story

"The book is effectively set entirely in monologue or dialogue; conversations, memos, letters, diary entries, talk-radio transcripts, and newspaper articles are all interwoven to present an uninterrupted plot. The construction is nearly flawless; the characters seem painfully human and typically ordinary. . . . A powerful, explosive novel that involves the reader from start to finish." Horn Book

Perloo the bold. Scholastic 1998 225p $16.95
Fic
1. Fantasy fiction
ISBN 0-590-11002-0   LC 97-10681
Perloo, a peaceful scholar who has been chosen to succeed Jolaine as leader of the furry underground people called the Montmers, finds himself in danger when Jolaine dies and her evil son seizes control of the burrow

"Avi has brought these creatures and their world to life in a fast-paced, compelling read." Voice Youth Advocates

S.O.R. losers. Bradbury Press 1984 90p $15
Fic
1. Soccer—Fiction 2. School stories
ISBN 0-02-793410-1   LC 84-11022
Also available in paperback from Avon Bks.

Each member of the South Orange River eighth-grade soccer team has qualities of excellence, but not on the soccer field

"Short, pithy chapters highlighting key events maintain the pace necessary for successful comedy. . . . The style is vivid, believably articulate, for the narrator and his teammates may be deficient athletically but not intellectually. Certainly, the team manifesto 'People have a right to be losers' is as refreshing as it is iconoclastic." Horn Book

Something upstairs: a tale of ghosts. Orchard Bks. 1988 120p $15.95; lib bdg $16.99   Fic
1. Ghost stories
ISBN 0-531-05782-8; 0-531-08382-9 (lib bdg)
LC 88-60094
Also available in paperback from Avon Bks.

"A Richard Jackson book"

"When 12-year-old Kenny Huldorf moves with his family to Providence, Rhode Island, he finds himself embroiled in the century-old murder of a teenage slave named Caleb. Not only is Kenny haunted by the injustice of the murder, but also by the ghost of Caleb himself, who summons Kenny back in time to the early 19th Century, where the boy must solve Caleb's murder to return to his own century." SLJ

"This ghostly tale is exciting and well-written." Child Book Rev Serv

The true confessions of Charlotte Doyle; decorations by Ruth E. Murray. Orchard Bks. 1990 215p o.p.; Avon Bks. paperback available $4.99
Fic
1. Sea stories
ISBN 0-380-72885-0 (pa)   LC 90-30624

Avi, 1937——*Continued*

Also available Thorndike Press large print edition

A Newbery Medal honor book, 1991

"A Richard Jackson book"

This is a "seafaring adventure, set in 1832. Charlotte Doyle, 13, returning from school in England to join her family in Rhode Island, is deposited on a seedy ship with a ruthless, mad captain and a mutinous crew. Refusing to heed warnings about Captain Jaggery's brutality, Charlotte seeks his guidance and approval only to become his victim, a pariah to the entire crew, and a convicted felon for the murder of the first mate." SLJ

The author has "fashioned an intriguing, suspenseful, carefully crafted tale, with nonstop action on the high seas." Booklist

Wolf rider: a tale of terror. Bradbury Press 1986 202p $17; pa $4.50   **Fic**
1. Mystery fiction

ISBN 0-02-707760-8; 0-02-041513-3 (pa)

           LC 86-13607

"Fifteen-year-old Andrew Zadinsky receives a call from a mysterious man named Zeke, who says he has just killed a woman named Nina. Everyone Andy talks to, including his father, the school counselor, the police, his friends, and even the girl herself (once Andy finds her alive) believes the call is a crank, but Andy is convinced the caller is a dangerous psychotic and becomes obsessed with identifying and exposing him. . . . Perhaps just a touch too cold and calculating, this is nevertheless a gripping and above-average YA thriller." Bull Cent Child Books

Ayres, Katherine

North by night; a story of the Underground Railroad. Delacorte Press 1998 176p $15.95   **Fic**
1. Underground railroad—Fiction 2. Slavery—Fiction

ISBN 0-385-32564-9   LC 98-10039

Presents the journal of Lucinda, a sixteen-year-old girl whose family operates a stop on the Underground Railroad

This "is an absorbing tale. Ayres slips in a lot of evocative detail about the hard work of running a farm and a household before the Civil War, as well as some rather charming musing about kissing and its myriad effects on the psyche." Booklist

Baillie, Allan, 1943-

Secrets of Walden rising. Viking 1997 167p $13.99   **Fic**
1. Ghost stories 2. Australia—Fiction 3. Droughts—Fiction

ISBN 0-670-87351-9

"The new kid in an isolated Australian community parched by drought, Brendan feels unwelcome. After the school yard bully pummels him, Brendan takes off on his bicycle and finds Walden, a ghost town gradually rising from the bed of a reservoir as the water level falls." Booklist

This is a "powerfully written, gripping novel." SLJ

Baldwin, James, 1924-1987

Go tell it on the mountain. Knopf 1953 303p $14.95 (7 and up)   **Fic**
1. African Americans—Fiction 2. Harlem (New York, N.Y.)—Fiction

ISBN 0-679-60154-6

Also available in paperback from Dell

"During his early adolescence John Grimes confronts all of the psychological traumas of growing up, plus the impact of being part of a strict black God-fearing family. Under these conditions John makes his rite of passage into young adulthood. Interwoven with his story are the reflections of his parents and his aunt as they cope with the pressures of their own lives." Shapiro. Fic for Youth. 3d edition

Banks, Lynne Reid, 1929-

Broken bridge. Morrow Junior Bks. 1995 c1994 320p il $16   **Fic**
1. Jewish-Arab relations—Fiction 2. Israel—Fiction

ISBN 0-688-13595-1   LC 94-26636

Also available in paperback from Avon Bks.

First published 1994 in the United Kingdom

"In this sequel to *One More River* (1973), Lesley is a grown woman and still living in the kibbutz. Her young nephew is killed by an Arab terrorist the day he arrives for a visit, and her daughter, Nili, is the only witness. As a result of Glen's death and the uproar it causes, these complex characters engage in a reevaluation of their relationships to one another and to the kibbutz. . . . Thoughtful reading for young adults who aren't looking for pat endings and easy answers." Booklist

Maura's angel. Avon Bks. 1998 150p $14; pa $4.99   **Fic**
1. Angels—Fiction 2. Belfast (Northern Ireland)—Fiction

ISBN 0-380-97590-4; 0-380-79514-0 (pa)

           LC 97-50350

Just when her home life and the circumstances in violence-plagued Belfast seem more than she can bear, eleven-year-old Maura encounters an unusual person whose name, Angela, gives a clue to her real identity

"The author's skillful balancing of the magical elements and often grim reality that life holds will ring true for many young readers." Publ Wkly

Banks, Sara H., 1942-

Abraham's battle; a novel of Gettysburg; [by] Sara Harrell Banks. Atheneum Bks. for Young Readers 1999 88p $15   **Fic**
1. Gettysburg (Pa.), Battle of, 1863—Fiction 2. United States—History—1861-1865, Civil War—Fiction 3. African Americans—Fiction

ISBN 0-689-81779-7   LC 98-21108

"An Anne Schwartz book"

In 1863, as the Civil War approaches his home in Gettysburg and he realizes that a big battle is about to begin, a freed slave named Abraham decides to join the ambulance corps of the Union Army

"This very personal account, well-written and filled with Southern expressions and historical details, focuses on the common humanity that survives despite political differences and the horrors of war." Booklist

Barrett, Tracy, 1955-
Anna of Byzantium. Delacorte Press 1999 209p
map $14.95   **Fic**
1. Comnena, Anna, 1083-1148—Fiction 2. Middle
Ages—Fiction 3. Sex role—Fiction
ISBN 0-385-32626-2   LC 98-47457
Based on The Alexiad by Anna Comnena
In the eleventh century the teenage princess Anna
Comnena fights for her birthright, the throne to the Byz-
antine Empire, which she fears will be taken from her by
her younger brother John because he is a boy
"The book is a fascinating mix of history, mystery,
and intrigue." Horn Book Guide

Barron, T. A.
The lost years of Merlin. Philomel Bks. 1996
326p $19.99 (7 and up)   **Fic**
1. Merlin (Legendary character)—Fiction 2. Fantasy
fiction
ISBN 0-399-23018-1   LC 96-33920
Also available in paperback from Ace Bks.
"A boy, hurled on the rocks by the sea, regains consciousness unable to remember anything—not his parents, not his own name. He is sure that the secretive
Branwen is not his mother, despite her claims, and that
Emrys is not his real name. The two soon find them-
selves feared because of Branwen's healing abilities and
Emrys' growing powers. . . . Barron has created not
only a magical land populated by remarkable beings but
also a completely magical tale, filled with ancient Celtic
and Druidic lore, that will enchant readers." Booklist
 Other available titles about young Merlin are:
The fires of Merlin (1998)
The mirror of Merlin (1999)
The seven songs of Merlin (1997)

The Merlin effect. Philomel Bks. 1994 254p
$19.95   **Fic**
1. Merlin (Legendary character)—Fiction 2. Buried
treasure—Fiction 3. Fantasy fiction
ISBN 0-399-22689-3   LC 93-36234
Also available in paperback from TOR Bks.
When she joins her father and several others investigating a strange whirlpool and possible sunken treasure
ship off the coast of Baja California, thirteen-year-old
Kate, featured in Heartlight (1990) and The Ancient One
(1992), is drawn into a centuries-old conflict between
Merlin and the evil Vagar
The author "blends a wealth of sea lore with ancient
myth and fast-paced adventure." Libr J

Bartoletti, Susan Campbell, 1958-
No man's land; a young soldier's story. Blue
Sky Press (NY) 1999 168p $15.95   **Fic**
1. Fathers and sons—Fiction 2. United States—History—1861-1865, Civil War—Fiction
ISBN 0-590-38371-X   LC 98-24714
Because he had been unable to fight off the gator
which injured his father, fourteen-year-old Thrasher joins
the Confederate Army hoping to prove his manhood
"Bartoletti grounds her story in careful historical research, and in an afterword she talks about her union of
fact and imagination." Booklist

Bat-Ami, Miriam, 1950-
Two suns in the sky. Front St./Cricket Bks.
1999 223p $15.95 (7 and up)   **Fic**
1. Jewish refugees—Fiction 2. World War, 1939-
1945—Fiction 3. New York (State)—Fiction
ISBN 0-8126-2900-0   LC 98-88522
"Chris Cook is a Catholic American teenager who
feels stuck in her hometown of Oswego, New York, in
1944. Adam Bornstein is a young, Jewish Holocaust survivor from Yugoslavia living in the fenced-off Emergency Refugee Camp in Oswego. Their passionate love story
is woven into a docunovel that gives a strong sense of
the times." Booklist

Bauer, Joan
Backwater. Putnam 1999 185p $16.99 (7 and
up)   **Fic**
1. Genealogy—Fiction 2. Aunts—Fiction 3. Adirondack Mountains (N.Y.)—Fiction
ISBN 0-399-23141-2   LC 98-50729
While compiling a genealogy of her family of successful attorneys, sixteen-year-old history buff Ivy Breedlove
treks into the mountain wilderness to interview a reclu-
sive aunt with whom she identifies and who in turn helps
her to truly know herself and her family
"This warm, funny, patchwork quilt of a book offers
a sturdy heroine, vivid characters, a touch of romance,
and a final survival adventure that will keep readers turning the pages to the last." Booklist

Rules of the road. Putnam 1998 201p $15.99 (7
and up)   **Fic**
1. Automobile drivers—Fiction 2. Old age—Fiction
3. Alcoholism—Fiction
ISBN 0-399-23140-4   LC 97-32198
Sixteen-year-old Jenna gets a job driving the elderly
owner of a chain of successful shoe stores from Chicago
to Texas to confront the son who is trying to force her
to retire, and along the way Jenna hones her talents as
a saleswoman and finds the strength to face her alcoholic
father
"The author creates some fabulous and sometimes
flamboyant characters, witty dialogue, and memorable
scenes." SLJ

Squashed. Delacorte Press 1992 194p $15.95 (7
and up)   **Fic**
1. Country life—Fiction
ISBN 0-385-30793-4   LC 91-44905
Also available Thorndike Press large print edition and
in paperback from Dell
As sixteen-year-old Ellie pursues her two goals--
growing the biggest pumpkin in Iowa and losing twenty
pounds herself--she strengthens her relationship with her
father and meets a young man with interests similar to
her own
"Skillful plot development and strong characterization
are real strengths here. Ellie's perceptive, intelligent, and
funny narrative keeps the story lively right up to its satisfying conclusion." SLJ

Sticks. Delacorte Press 1996 182p $15.95; pa
$3.99   **Fic**
1. Pool (Game)—Fiction
ISBN 0-385-32165-1; 0-440-41387-7 (pa)
                                      LC 95-45483

Bauer, Joan—*Continued*

"Ten-year-old Mickey Vernon wants to win the Pool Hall Youth Championship more than anything, but his chances of beating the competition—obnoxious 13-year-old Buck Pender—are slim until Joseph Alvarez, an old friend of the family, comes back to town and agrees to be Mickey's pool coach. . . . Good characters, humor, and an engaging plot make this a solid piece of middle-grade fiction." Booklist

Thwonk. Delacorte Press 1995 215p hardcover o.p. paperback available $4.50 (7 and up)   **Fic**
1. Photography—Fiction
ISBN 0-440-21980-9 (pa)   LC 94-20293
"A.J. McCreary, photographer extraordinaire, lovelorn, and invisible to school hunk, Peter Terris, is unable to capture a fitting cover shot for the school paper's special Valentine's Day edition. Then, she stumbles upon a stuffed cupid who comes to life and offers her one of three alluring choices: artistic, academic, or romantic assistance." SLJ
"Bauer offers readers more than boy-meets-girl romance fare. Here are likable, rounded characters brought to life by gentle humor and realistic dialogue." ALAN

Bauer, Marion Dane, 1938-

Face to face; a novel. Clarion Bks. 1991 176p o.p.; Dell paperback available $3.99   **Fic**
1. Fathers and sons—Fiction 2. Rafting (Sports)—Fiction
ISBN 0-440-40791-5 (pa)   LC 90-49608
Picked on at school by bullies, thirteen-year-old Michael confronts his fears during a trip to Colorado to see his father, who works as a whitewater rafting guide and whom Michael has not seen in eight years
"Bauer remains true to Michael's perspective, portraying characters as the boy sees them but painstakingly revealing the flaws in his vision as well. Her handling of the psychological aspects of Michael's coming-of-age is deft and strong." Horn Book

On my honor. Clarion Bks. 1986 90p $15

    Fic
1. Accidents—Fiction
ISBN 0-89919-439-7   LC 86-2679
Also available in paperback from Dell
A Newbery Medal honor book, 1987
When his best friend drowns while they are both swimming in a treacherous river that they had promised never to go near, Joel is devastated and terrified at having to tell both sets of parents the terrible consequences of their disobedience
"Bauer's association of Joel's guilt with the smell of the polluted river on his skin is particularly noteworthy. Its miasma almost rises off the pages. Descriptions are vivid, characterization and dialogue natural, and the style taut but unforced. A powerful, moving book." SLJ

A question of trust. Scholastic 1994 130p $14.95   **Fic**
1. Mothers and sons—Fiction 2. Cats—Fiction
ISBN 0-590-47915-6   LC 93-4611
After his mother leaves the family, Brian copes with his feelings of rejection by secretly taking care of a stray

cat and her two newborn kittens
"The coming-of-age novel has powerful scenes, memorable characters, vivid dialogue, and palpable emotions." Horn Book Guide

A taste of smoke. Clarion Bks. 1993 106p $14.95   **Fic**
1. Sisters—Fiction 2. Ghost stories 3. Camping—Fiction
ISBN 0-395-64341-4   LC 92-32585
Also available in paperback from Dell
Thirteen-year-old Caitlan looks forward to the camping trip with her older sister in the woods of northern Minnesota, but she doesn't count on the intrusion of her sister's boyfriend or the ghost of a boy who died in the fire that destroyed the forest a century before
"Readers will enjoy the camping setting and the mixture of mystery, the supernatural, and a hint of romance." SLJ

Bawden, Nina, 1925-

Granny the Pag. Clarion Bks. 1996 c1995 184p $14.95   **Fic**
1. Grandmothers—Fiction 2. Parent and child—Fiction
ISBN 0-395-77604-X   LC 95-38191
Also available in paperback from Puffin Bks.
First published 1995 in the United Kingdom
Originally abandoned by her actor parents who later attempt to gain custody, Cat wages a spirited campaign to decide her own fate and remain with her grandmother
"Bawden has created some enormously appealing characters in this funny and very touching novel." SLJ

Off the road. Clarion Bks. 1998 192p $16

    Fic
1. Grandfathers—Fiction 2. Science fiction
ISBN 0-395-91321-7   LC 97-42576
In 2040, eleven-year-old Tom follows his grandfather through the Wall and into the forbidden Wild, where they seek to find his grandfather's boyhood home
"The characters will make readers think about ideas. . . . The great surprise ending shouts for a sequel." Booklist

The outside child. Lothrop, Lee & Shepard Bks. 1989 232p o.p.; Puffin Bks. paperback available $3.99   **Fic**
1. Brothers and sisters—Fiction
ISBN 0-14-036858-2 (pa)   LC 88-27349
"Suddenly and accidentally, thirteen-year-old Jane Tucker learns that her widowed father—a ship's engineer whom she rarely sees—is remarried and has two younger children. Inevitably, she defies her adoptive aunts to locate her half-sister and brother. What she doesn't expect to find is a dark secret that seems to spark violent hostility from her stepmother." Bull Cent Child Books
"Superb characterizations, the interplay of human relationships, and powerful emotions that lie beneath the surface of everyday life are presented wholly from the girl's ingenuous perspective." Horn Book

Beatty, Patricia, 1922-1991

Jayhawker. Morrow Junior Bks. 1991 214p
hardcover o.p. paperback available $4.95   **Fic**
1. United States—History—1861-1865, Civil War—
Fiction 2. Underground railroad—Fiction
ISBN 0-688-14422-5 (pa)   LC 91-17890
In the early years of the Civil War, teenage Kansan
farm boy Lije Tulley becomes a Jayhawker, an abolitionist raider freeing slaves from the neighboring state of
Missouri, and then goes undercover there as a spy
"Peppered with fascinating historical figures, vivid
with drama and action, Beatty's story has an accuracy
and a realism that are both addictive and illuminating."
Booklist

Bechard, Margaret, 1953-

If it doesn't kill you. Viking 1999 156p $15.99
(7 and up)   **Fic**
1. Homosexuality—Fiction 2. Fathers and sons—Fiction
ISBN 0-670-88547-9   LC 98-49553
High school freshman Ben should be enjoying playing
football, meeting girls, and going to parties, but he's too
busy trying to cope with his father's moving out to live
with another man
"Subtle, plausible, and convincing. Bechard, has done
a remarkable job of taking a sensitive issue and making
it comfortable for a wide audience. The absence of melodrama and the healthy doses of humor make this a winning and realistic novel." SLJ

Bell, Clare, 1952-

Ratha's challenge. Margaret K. McElderry Bks.
1994 231p $16.95 (7 and up)   **Fic**
1. Fantasy fiction 2. Cats—Fiction
ISBN 0-689-50586-8   LC 94-29209
An encounter with a group of unusual cats helps bring
Ratha, leader of the prehistoric cat clan called the
Named, and her estranged daughter Thistle to a better
understanding of each other
"Bell explores themes of culture, politics, individua-
tion, and family relations, all through the eyes of a riveting set of characters." SLJ

Bell, William

Zack. Simon & Schuster 1999 c1998 192p
$16.95 (7 and up)   **Fic**
1. Racially mixed people—Fiction 2. Prejudices—Fiction 3. Blacks—Fiction 4. Canada—Fiction
ISBN 0-689-82248-0   LC 98-6690
First published 1998 in Canada
The son of a Jewish father and black mother, high
school senior Zack has never been allowed to meet his
mother's family, but after doing a research project on a
former slave, he travels from his home in Canada to
Natchez, Mississippi to find his grandfather
"Zack's character is drawn with depth and dimension-
ality, and his relationship with his parents, paternal
grandparents, girlfriend, and the grandfather he meets on
his journey are realistic and profound." SLJ

Bellairs, John

The curse of the blue figurine. Dial Bks. for
Young Readers 1983 200p o.p.; Penguin Bks.
paperback available $3.99   **Fic**
1. Mystery fiction
ISBN 0-14-038005-1 (pa)   LC 82-73217
Also available Brad Strickland's titles based on John
Bellair's characters
"The terror for young Johnny Dixon begins when
cranky eccentric Professor Childermass tells him that St.
Michael's Church is haunted by Father Baart, an evil
sorcerer who mysteriously disappeared years ago. When
Johnny finds a blue Egyptian figurine hidden in the
church basement, he takes it home in spite of the warn-
ing note from Father Baart threatening harm to anyone
who removes it from the church." SLJ
The author "intertwines real concerns with sorcery in
a seamless fashion, bringing dimension to his characters
and events with expert timing and sharply honed atmo-
sphere." Booklist
Other available titles about Johnny Dixon and Professor
Childermass are:
The chessmen of doom (1989)
The drum, the doll and the zombie (1994)
The eyes of the killer robot (1986)
The mummy, the will and the crypt (1983)
The revenge of the wizard's ghost (1985)
The secret of the underground room (1990)
The spell of the sorcerer's skull (1984)
The trolley to yesterday (1989)

The dark secret of Weatherend; jacket and
frontispiece by Edward Gorey. Dial Bks. for
Young Readers 1984 180p o.p.; Penguin Bks.
paperback available $3.99   **Fic**
1. Supernatural—Fiction 2. Librarians—Fiction
3. Minnesota—Fiction
ISBN 0-14-038006-X (pa)   LC 83-24043
Fourteen-year-old Anthony Monday of Hoosac, Min-
nesota, and his friend Miss Eells, the Hoosac librarian,
try to stop an evil wizard from turning the world into an
icy wasteland
Other available titles about Anthony Monday and Miss
Eells are:
The lamp from the warlock's tomb (1988)
The mansion in the mist (1992)
The treasure of Alpheus Winter (1978)

Bennett, Cherie

Life in the fat lane. Delacorte Press 1998 260p
$15.95 (7 and up)   **Fic**
1. Obesity—Fiction
ISBN 0-385-32274-7   LC 97-24072
Also available in paperback from Dell
Sixteen-year-old Lara, winner of beauty pageants and
Homecoming Queen, is distressed and bewildered when
she starts gaining weight and becomes a fat girl
"A fast-paced story about compelling teen issues."
Child Book Rev Serv

Bennett, Jay, 1912-

Coverup; a novel. Watts 1991 144p o.p.;
Fawcett Bks. paperback available $4.50 (7 and up)
Fic
1. Mystery fiction
ISBN 0-449-70409-2 (pa)   LC 91-18506

Bennett, Jay, 1912-—*Continued*

Teenage Brad is tormented by confused memories of a drunken ride with his best friend Alden, during which they may have hit and killed a man

"Bennett has created another suspenseful mystery that is sure to please his confirmed fans and attract new ones." Booklist

Sing me a death song; a novel. Watts 1990 160p o.p.; Fawcett Bks. paperback available $4.50 (7 and up)   **Fic**

1. Mystery fiction 2. Mothers and sons—Fiction

ISBN 0-449-70369-X (pa)   LC 89-24812

Jason risks his life to find evidence that his mother, a convicted murderer facing execution, was framed

"Taut, spare, poignant, this mystery offers both a gripping plot and a convincing argument against capital punishment." Voice Youth Advocates

Skinhead; a novel. Watts 1991 139p o.p.; Fawcett Bks. paperback available $4.50 (7 and up)   **Fic**

1. Mystery fiction

ISBN 0-449-70397-5 (pa)   LC 90-13087

"Jonathan, a wealthy college student, receives a call to go cross country to see a dying man who seems to know all about him. The man dies before Jonathan gets there, but he is persuaded to stay and help find his killers. Jonathan becomes involved with skinheads, discovers the dead man was his real father, and that he is half-Jewish." Child Book Rev Serv

"A contemporary mystery that reads fast and easy. And by focusing on Skinheads and the racist, superior attitudes held by some 'respectable' citizens and leaders, Bennett makes this quick, attractive read food for additional thought." Voice Youth Advocates

Berry, James

Ajeemah and his son. Perlman Bks. 1992 c1991 83p hardcover o.p. paperback available $4.50   **Fic**

1. Slavery—Fiction 2. Fathers and sons—Fiction 3. Jamaica—Fiction

ISBN 0-06-440523-0 (pa)   LC 92-6615

First published 1991 in the United Kingdom in a collection entitled The Future-telling lady

"Ajeemah and his son Atu are kidnapped and sold in West Africa, never to see home or family again. After the bitter journey to Jamaica, they are separated forever, sold off to plantations 20 miles apart. . . . The son's rebellion ends in heartbreak, flogging, suicide. The father is betrayed, but he survives to marry, sire a daughter, and celebrate when freedom comes." Booklist

"The power of Berry's writing places us in the story, confronted by the feelings of Ajeemah and Atu—and the author keeps us there until the last word." Horn Book

Blackwood, Gary L.

The Shakespeare stealer; [by] Gary Blackwood. Dutton Children's Bks. 1998 216p $15.99   **Fic**

1. Shakespeare, William, 1564-1616—Fiction 2. Theater—Fiction 3. Orphans—Fiction 4. Great Britain—History—1485-1603, Tudors—Fiction

ISBN 0-525-45863-8   LC 97-42987

A young orphan boy is ordered by his master to infiltrate Shakespeare's acting troupe in order to steal the script of "Hamlet," but he discovers instead the meaning of friendship and loyalty

"Wry humor, cliffhanger chapter endings, and a plucky protagonist make this a fitting introduction to Shakespeare's world." Horn Book

Blakeslee, Ann R.

A different kind of hero. Marshall Cavendish 1997 143p $14.95   **Fic**

1. Frontier and pioneer life—Fiction 2. Prejudices—Fiction 3. West (U.S.)—Fiction

ISBN 0-7614-5000-9   LC 96-32786

In 1881 twelve-year-old Renny, who resists his father's efforts to turn him into a rough, tough, brawling boy, earns the disapproval of the entire mining camp when he befriends a newly arrived Chinese boy

"This story of friendship, hardship, and many forms of prejudice has a well-drawn main character and realistic conflict rooted in historic detail." SLJ

Block, Francesca Lia

I was a teenage fairy. HarperCollins Pubs. 1998 186p $14.95; lib bdg $14.89 (7 and up)   **Fic**

1. Fairies—Fiction 2. Child sexual abuse—Fiction 3. Los Angeles (Calif.)—Fiction 4. Fashion models—Fiction

ISBN 0-06-027747-5; 0-06-027748-3 (lib bdg)

                                      LC 98-14598

"Joanna Cotler books"

"When eleven-year-old Barbie, a child model, is molested by a photographer, her mother tells her 'life is full of problems.' In the second part of the book, sixteen-year-old Barbie meets Griffin, another model assaulted by the same photographer. Throughout, a petulant fairy named Mab serves as Barbie's surrogate mother, sister, and friend." Horn Book Guide

"Block's descriptions are stunning. . . . The teen dialogue rings absolutely true, filled with sarcastic humor, puns, and double meanings." Voice Youth Advocates

Bloor, Edward, 1950-

Tangerine. Harcourt Brace & Co. 1997 294p $17 (7 and up)   **Fic**

1. Soccer—Fiction 2. Brothers—Fiction 3. Florida—Fiction

ISBN 0-15-201246-X   LC 96-34182

Also available in paperback from Scholastic

Twelve-year-old Paul, who lives in the shadow of his football hero brother Erik, fights for the right to play soccer despite his near blindness and slowly begins to remember the incident that damaged his eyesight

"Readers will cheer for this bright, funny, decent kid." Horn Book Guide

Blume, Judy

Are you there God? it's me, Margaret. Twentieth anniversary ed. Bradbury Press 1990 c1970 149p $16   **Fic**

1. Religions—Fiction

ISBN 0-02-710991-7   LC 90-44484

Blume, Judy—*Continued*

Also available in paperback from Dell

First published 1970

"A perceptive story about the emotional, physical, and spiritual ups and downs experienced by 12-year-old Margaret, child of a Jewish-Protestant union." Adventuring with Books. 2d edition

"The writing style is lively, the concerns natural, and the problems are treated with both humor and sympathy, but the story is intense in its emphasis on the four girls' absorption in, and discussions of, menstruation and brassieres." Bull Cent Child Books

Here's to you, Rachel Robinson. Orchard Bks. 1993 196p $15.95 **Fic**
1. Brothers and sisters—Fiction 2. Gifted children—Fiction 3. Friendship—Fiction
ISBN 0-531-06801-3 LC 93-9631
Also available in paperback from Dell
Companion volume to the author's Just as long as we're together
"A Richard Jackson book"
Expelled from boarding school, Charles' presence at home proves disruptive, especially for sister Rachel, a gifted seventh grader juggling friendships and school activities
"Blume once again demonstrates her ability to shape multidimensional characters and to explore—often through very convincing dialogue—the tangled interactions of believable, complex people." Publ Wkly

Just as long as we're together. Orchard Bks. 1987 296p o.p.; Dell paperback available $4.99 **Fic**
1. Friendship—Fiction 2. Family life—Fiction
ISBN 0-440-21094-1 (pa) LC 87-7980
"The narrator is Stephanie, who's in her first year of junior high, who's distressed by her parents' trial separation (and, when she visits Dad, by his friend Iris), and who finds that best friends are not infallibly understanding or tolerant. Rachel has always been her friend, but both of them like a newcomer (Alison, a Vietnamese adoptee) enough to make it a triumvirate." Bull Cent Child Books
"As usual, Blume addresses many issues about growing up that make some adults nervous and ill at ease: menstruation, budding sexuality, and that inevitable first kiss. But she offers more: a family in a painful state of flux that can still function effectively." Wilson Libr Bull

Tiger eyes; a novel. Bradbury Press 1981 206p $16 (7 and up) **Fic**
1. Death—Fiction
ISBN 0-02-711080-X LC 81-6152
Also available in paperback from Dell
Resettled in Los Alamos with her mother and brother, Davey Wexler recovers from the shock of her father's death during a holdup of his 7-Eleven store in Atlantic City
"The plot is strong, interesting and believable. . . . The story though intense and complicated flows smoothly and easily." Voice Youth Advocates

Borland, Hal, 1900-1978

When the legends die. Lippincott 1963 288p o.p.; Bantam Bks. paperback available $5.50 **Fic**
1. Ute Indians—Fiction
ISBN 0-553-25738-2 (pa)
"Thomas Black Bull, a Ute Indian, is being reared in the traditional Native American way when his parents are forced to flee from the world of the white man. After the death of his parents Tom is returned to the white world, where he suffers the disintegration of his native heritage and traditions as he experiences school, sheep herding, and rodeo life. Following a serious accident at a rodeo he returns to the mountains and is drawn back into his past." Shapiro. Fic for Youth. 3d edition

Bosse, Malcolm J., 1934-

The examination. Farrar, Straus & Giroux 1994 296p $17; pa $7.50 (7 and up) **Fic**
1. Brothers—Fiction 2. China—Fiction
ISBN 0-374-32234-1; 0-374-42223-0 (pa)
LC 93-50955
Fifteen-year-old Hong and his older brother Chen face famine, flood, pirates, and jealous rivals on their journey through fifteenth century China as Chen pursues his calling as a scholar and Hong becomes involved with a secret society known as the White Lotus
"Bosse has constructed a compelling, picaresque novel which blends adventure and history into a seamless fabric." Horn Book

Bowler, Tim

Midget. Margaret K. McElderry Bks. 1995 159p $15 (7 and up) **Fic**
1. Physically handicapped—Fiction 2. Brothers—Fiction 3. Extrasensory perception—Fiction
ISBN 0-689-80115-7 LC 94-46963
First published 1994 in the United Kingdom
Subject to strange fits, physically abnormal, and psychologically disturbed from the constant torment and abuse of his older brother, fifteen-year-old Midget finds himself in control of his life for the first time when he gets his own sailboat and discovers untapped mental powers
"The tightly scripted plot, with its steadily building tension, will keep readers spellbound to the end." Horn Book Guide

Bradbury, Ray, 1920-

The Halloween tree; illustrated by Joseph Mugnaini. Knopf 1988 c1972 145p $19.95; lib bdg $15.99; pa $4.99 **Fic**
1. Halloween—Fiction 2. Fantasy fiction
ISBN 0-394-82409-1; 0-394-92409-6 (lib bdg); 0-375-80301-7 (pa)
A reissue of the title first published 1972
A group of boys meet a spirit-being and are carried back in time to the origins of Halloween celebrations
This is "fast-moving, genuinely eerie" Booklist

Something wicked this way comes. Avon Bks. 1999 293p $15; pa $5.99 (7 and up) **Fic**
ISBN 0-380-97727-3; 0-380-72940-7 (pa)
A reissue of the title first published 1962 by Simon and Schuster

Bradbury, Ray, 1920—*Continued*

"We read here of the loss of innocence, the recognition of evil, the bond between generations, and the purely fantastic. These forces enter Green Town, Illinois, on the wheels of Cooger and Dark's Pandemonium Shadow Show. Will Halloway and Jim Nightshade, two thirteen-year-olds, explore the sinister carnival for excitement, which becomes desperation as the forces of the dark threaten to engulf them. Bradbury's gentle humanism and lyric style serve this fantasy well." Shapiro. Fic for Youth. 3d edition

Brittain, Bill

Shape-changer. HarperCollins Pubs. 1994 108p hardcover o.p. paperback available $4.50   **Fic**
1. Science fiction 2. Extraterrestrial beings—Fiction
ISBN 0-06-440514-1 (pa)   LC 93-27268
Two seventh-grade friends help a shape-changing policeman from the planet Rodinam as he tries to recapture an alien master criminal who can also change form
"Funny scenes abound in the fast-paced, enthralling adventure." Horn Book Guide

The wish giver; three tales of Coven Tree; drawings by Andrew Glass. Harper & Row 1983 181p il $14; pa $4.95   **Fic**
1. Wishes—Fiction 2. Magic—Fiction
ISBN 0-06-020686-1; 0-06-440168-5 (pa)
LC 82-48264
A Newbery Medal honor book, 1984
"Witchy and devilish things happen in Coven Tree, New England, and their chronicler is Stew Meat, proprietor of the Coven Tree store. . . . Stew relates the King Midas luck that came to three young people, each of whom had a wish fulfilled, and each of whom rued that fulfillment." SLJ
"Captivating, fresh, and infused with homespun humor." Horn Book
Other available titles about Coven Tree are:
Dr. Dredd's wagon of wonders (1987)
Professor Popkin's prodigious polish (1990)

Brokaw, Nancy Steele

Leaving Emma. Clarion Bks. 1999 137p $15
Fic
1. Friendship—Fiction 2. Aunts—Fiction
ISBN 0-395-90699-7   LC 98-22688
Fifth-grader Emma faces many unpleasant changes as her best friend prepares to move away, her father goes to Turkey for five months, and her mother starts college, but with the help of her great-aunt Grace, Emma becomes a lot more independent and self-reliant
"A sympathetic heroine, Emma experiences personal growth that is believable and satisfying." Horn Book Guide

Brooks, Bruce, 1950-

Asylum for Nightface. HarperCollins Pubs. 1996 137p $13.95; lib bdg $13.89; pa $4.95 (7 and up)
Fic
1. Fanaticism—Fiction 2. Family life—Fiction
3. Christian life—Fiction
ISBN 0-06-027060-8; 0-06-027061-6 (lib bdg); 0-06-447214-0 (pa)   LC 95-40645

"A Laura Geringer Book"
"To the distress of his sophisticated, self-indulgent parents, 14 year-old Zimmerman has 'fallen in love with God.' But when the adults undergo their own religious conversion, it's time for an attitude about-face. . . . They now decide that he is 'marked by God for a holy purpose' and must become a poster boy for their own sect. . . . The boy's resistance to these designs will ultimately drive him to make a difficult moral decision." Booklist
"Brooks gives much to consider in this slim, thought-provoking novel." Voice Youth Advocates

Midnight hour encores. Harper & Row 1986 263p $14; pa $4.50 (7 and up)   **Fic**
1. Musicians—Fiction 2. Fathers and daughters—Fiction 3. Mothers and daughters—Fiction
ISBN 0-06-020709-4; 0-06-447021-0 (pa)
LC 86-45035
"A cello prodigy and her father take both a literal cross-country journey to meet the mother who gave her up at birth and a figurative trip through the 1960s to understand the woman." SLJ
"This is a rich and delightful book that holds up well for a second or even third reading. For teens, in addition to being an entertaining story about selfishness and devotion, *Midnight Hour Encores* can serve as an affectionate introduction to the essence of the era of peace and love." Wilson Libr Bull

The moves make the man; a novel. Harper & Row 1984 280p $15; lib bdg $15.89; pa $4.95 (7 and up)   **Fic**
1. African Americans—Fiction 2. Friendship—Fiction
ISBN 0-06-020679-9; 0-06-020698-5 (lib bdg); 0-06-447022-9 (pa)   LC 83-49476
"Jerome, the narrator, is very bright, very perceptive and articulate, and the only black student in a newly-integrated junior high school in a southern town. This is . . . [a book] about the white boy, Bix, who becomes a best friend—and at times an enemy." Bull Cent Child Books
This is an "excellent novel about values and the way people relate to one another. It is entertaining and accessible; the chapters in which Jerome teaches Bix how to play basketball could serve as a primer for any young athlete." N Y Times Book Rev

No kidding. Harper & Row 1989 207p $14; pa $4.95 (7 and up)   **Fic**
1. Alcoholism—Fiction 2. Family life—Fiction
ISBN 0-06-020722-1; 0-06-447051-2 (pa)
LC 88-22057
In his twenty-first century society, fourteen-year-old Sam is allowed to decide the fate of his family after his mother is released from an alcohol rehabilitation center
"Brooks is a fine writer: the structure is taut; the rhythm pulsing; narrative and dialogue are crisp. The point of view changes constantly, which makes for a fast pace but is confusing at first. . . . Brooks has created a wonderful vehicle for discussion in advanced middle school and high school classes." Horn Book

Vanishing. HarperCollins Pubs. 1999 103p $14.95; lib bdg $14.89   **Fic**
1. Death—Fiction 2. Hospitals—Fiction
ISBN 0-06-028236-3; 0-06-028237-1 (lib bdg)
LC 99-11743

Brooks, Bruce, 1950——*Continued*
"A Laura Geringer book"
"Hospitalized with bronchitis and not wanting to go home to her self-absorbed mother and racist stepfather, Alice goes on a hunger strike that keeps her in the hospital, where she shares space with Rex, who has cancer." Horn Book Guide
"This is a deeply felt, unusual, and absorbing story." SLJ

Zip. HarperCollins Pubs. 1997 106p (Wolfbay Wings) $14.89; pa $4.50   **Fic**
1. Hockey—Fiction 2. Friendship—Fiction
ISBN 0-06-927350-X; 0-06-440598-2 (pa)
LC 97-2049
"A Laura Geringer book"
Zip struggles to deal with his best friend's defection to a rival hockey team, a move that will test their friendship and leave them face to face on opposite sides in a close game
"While this series is aimed at hockey fans, readers unfamiliar with the intricacies of the sport will find themselves involved in the lives of these 11 year olds. Brooks successfully brings the boys into sharp focus." SLJ
Other available titles about the Wolfbay Wings hockey team are:
Billy (1998)
Boot (1998)
Cody (1997)
Dooby (1998)
Prince (1998)
Reed (1998)
Shark (1998)
Woodsie (1997)
Woodsie, again (1999)

Brooks, Martha, 1944-
Bone dance. Orchard Bks. 1997 179p $16.95; lib bdg $17.99 (7 and up)   **Fic**
1. Supernatural—Fiction 2. Indians of North America—Fiction 3. Canada Fiction
ISBN 0-531-30021-8; 0-531-33021-4 (lib bdg)
LC 97-10230
Also available in paperback from Bantam Bks.
When her father wills her a cabin on land in rural Manitoba, Alexandra meets a young man who shares her Indian heritage and her experience of being haunted by spirits
"Natural-sounding dialogue and a descriptive yet compact writing style mark this unconventional love story." Horn Book Guide

Bruchac, Joseph, 1942-
The heart of a chief; a novel. Dial Bks. for Young Readers 1998 153p $15.99   **Fic**
1. Indians of North America—Fiction 2. Alcoholism—Fiction
ISBN 0-8037-2276-1   LC 97-49248
Chris, an eleven-year-old Penacook Indian boy living on a reservation, faces his father's alcoholism, a controversy surrounding plans for a casino on a tribal island, and insensitivity toward Native Americans in his school and nearby town
"The story's themes are universal and Chris's compelling voyage of self-discovery is grounded in everyday events that middle-graders will recognize." Publ Wkly

Bunting, Eve, 1928-
The hideout. Harcourt Brace Jovanovich 1991 133p $14.95; pa $6   **Fic**
1. Runaway children—Fiction 2. Kidnapping—Fiction 3. Parent and child—Fiction
ISBN 0-15-233990-6; 0-15-233991-4 (pa)
LC 90-45515
Feeling unloved by his mother and new stepfather, Andy hides out in a luxurious San Francisco hotel and stages his own kidnapping in order to obtain ransom money to pay for a trip to England to see his father
"The involving first-person narrative and the mounting tension offset the unlikely events. Andy's character . . . is vividly portrayed." SLJ

Jumping the Nail. Harcourt Brace Jovanovich 1991 148p $15.95; pa $6 (7 and up)   **Fic**
ISBN 0-15-241357-X; 0-15-241358-8 (pa)
LC 91-11090
When teenagers in a California coastal community challenge each other to "jump the Nail"—leap from dangerous cliffs into the ocean—group pressure and manipulative relationships quickly drive the game out of control
"Characters and plot are simply but effectively sketched. It's Bunting's acknowledgment of the allure of danger and the power that comes from facing it, as well as her on-target depiction of how easy it is to lose perspective when you fall in love, that makes her novel more than just a good, fast read." Booklist

Someone is hiding on Alcatraz Island. Clarion Bks. 1984 136p o.p.; Berkley Pub. Group paperback available $4.99   **Fic**
1. Alcatraz Island (Calif.)—Fiction 2. Juvenile delinquency—Fiction
ISBN 0-425-10294-7 (pa)   LC 84-5019
"The Outlaws, the toughest gang in school, follow Danny Sullivan to Alcatraz Island after he unintentionally thwarts one member's attempt to mug an old woman. There he is trapped as they plot their revenge." Publ Wkly
The author "builds suspense and sustains it with brisk dialogue and taut scenes. Characters aren't given much depth, and the ending is fairly predictable, but the swiftly unfolding events are sure to keep kids turning pages. The story's content, simple style, and fast pace also target this as a good selection for reluctant readers." Booklist

SOS Titanic. Harcourt Brace & Co. 1996 240p $13; pa $6 (7 and up)   **Fic**
1. Titanic (Steamship)—Fiction 2. Shipwrecks—Fiction
ISBN 0-15-200271-5; 0-15-201305-9 (pa)
LC 95-10712
Fifteen-year-old Barry O'Neill, traveling from Ireland to America on the maiden voyage of the Titanic, finds his life endangered when the ship hits an iceberg and begins to sink
"Bunting accurately and dramatically describes the ship's sinking and, at the same time, immerses readers in the many human tragedies. . . . This fast-paced story will satisfy readers looking for the human element in the *Titanic's* history." Booklist

Bunting, Eve, 1928——_Continued_
Spying on Miss Müller. Clarion Bks. 1995 179p
$15   **Fic**
1. World War, 1939-1945—Fiction 2. School stories
3. Fathers and daughters—Fiction 4. Ireland—Fiction
ISBN 0-395-69172-9   LC 94-15003
Also available in paperback from Fawcett Bk. Group
At Alveara boarding school in Belfast at the start of
World War II, thirteen-year-old Jessie must deal with her
suspicions about a teacher whose father was German and
with her worries about her own father's drinking problem
"A thoughtful, moving coming-of-age novel, Jessie
and her world . . . are portrayed with page-turning immediacy." Horn Book

Burks, Brian
Soldier boy. Harcourt Brace & Co. 1997 151p
$12; pa $5   **Fic**
1. Custer, George Armstrong, 1839-1876—Fiction
2. Frontier and pioneer life—Fiction
ISBN 0-15-201218-4; 0-15-201219-2 (pa)
                                   LC 96-30289
A boy who grew up in the slums of late nineteenth-
century Chicago runs away, joins the cavalry, and fights
with General Custer in the battle of Little Big Horn
"Burks can write gripping, thoroughly researched historical fiction. Here, he mixes humor with the day-to-day
detail of a soldier's life in a fort, and he shows his character maturing into a thoughtful man." Booklist

Walks Alone. Harcourt Brace & Co. 1998 115p
$16   **Fic**
1. Apache Indians—Fiction
ISBN 0-15-201612-0   LC 97-14738
After a surprise attack leaves many of her people
dead, fifteen-year-old Walks Alone, an Apache girl
wounded in the massacre, struggles to survive and rejoin
the refugee band
"Fascinating details of Apache life are woven into a
novel that remains powerful even through a fatalistic
conclusion." Horn Book Guide

Burnford, Sheila, 1918-1984
The incredible journey. Little, Brown 1961 145p
o.p.; Amereon reprint available $18.95   **Fic**
1. Cats—Fiction 2. Dogs—Fiction 3. Canada—Fiction
ISBN 0-88410-099-0
Also available in paperback from Bantam Bks.
"A half-blind English bull terrier, a sprightly yellow
Labrador retriever, and a feisty Siamese cat have resided
for eight months with a friend of their owners, who are
away on a trip. Then their temporary caretaker leaves
them behind in order to take a short vacation. The lonely
trio decides to tackle the harsh 250-mile hike across the
Canadian wilderness in search of home, despite the human and wild obstacles the group will encounter." Shapiro. Fic for Youth. 3d edition

Byars, Betsy Cromer, 1928-
The burning questions of Bingo Brown; [by]
Betsy Byars. Viking Kestrel 1988 166p il
hardcover o.p. paperback available $4.50   **Fic**
1. School stories
ISBN 0-14-032479-8 (pa)   LC 87-21022

Also available G.K. Hall large print edition
A boy is puzzled by the comic and confusing questions of youth and worried by disturbing insights into
adult conflicts
"A fully worked out novel. . . . Readers will recognize the pitfalls, agonies, and joys of elementary school
life in this book. . . . The short chapters and comic style
are designed to appeal to young readers and to move
them right into other books." Christ Sci Monit
Other available titles about Bingo Brown are:
Bingo Brown and the language of love (1989)
Bingo Brown, gypsy lover (1990)
Bingo Brown's guide to romance (1992)

Cracker Jackson; by Betsy Byars. Viking
Kestrel 1985 147p hardcover o.p. paperback
available $4.50   **Fic**
1. Wife abuse—Fiction 2. Child abuse—Fiction
ISBN 0-14-031881-X (pa)   LC 84-24684
"Young Jackson discovers that his ex-baby sitter has
been beaten by her husband; and, spurred by affection
for her, the boy enlists his friend Goat to help drive her
to a home for battered women. The pathetic story of
Alma, with her adored baby, tidy home, and treasured
collection of Barbie dolls, is relieved by flashbacks to
the two boys' antics at school and by their hilarious, if
potentially lethal, attempt to drive her to safety." Horn
Book
"Suspense, danger, near-tragedy, heartbreak and ten-
sion-relieving, unwittingly comic efforts at seriously heroic action mark this as the best of middle-grade fiction
to highlight the problems of wife-battering and child
abuse." SLJ

The dark stairs; a Herculeah Jones mystery; by
Betsy Byars. Viking 1994 130p $13.99; pa $3.99
                                              Fic
1. Mystery fiction
ISBN 0-670-85487-5; 0-14-036996-1 (pa)
                                   LC 94-14012
The intrepid Herculeah Jones helps her mother, a pri-
vate investigator, solve a puzzling and frightening case
"There is plenty to laugh at in this book, including
classic chapter headings guaranteed to cause shivers for
the uninitiated; practiced mystery readers may feel that
they are in on a bit of a joke and appreciate the hint of
parody. This is a page-turner that is sure to entice the
most reluctant readers." SLJ
Other available titles about Herculeah Jones are:
Dead letter (1996)
Death's door (1997)
Disappearing acts (1998)
Tarot says beware (1995)

The night swimmers; by Betsy Byars; illustrated
by Troy Howell. Delacorte Press 1980 o.p.; Dell
paperback available $3.99   **Fic**
1. Single parent family—Fiction 2. Brothers and sisters—Fiction
ISBN 0-440-45857-9 (pa)
With their mother dead and their father working
nights, Retta tries to be mother to her two younger brothers but somehow things just don't seem to be working
right
"The plot moves a little slowly but characterization is
good. The ending presents a happy solution for this single parent family situation." Voice Youth Advocates

Byars, Betsy Cromer, 1928-—*Continued*

The not-just-anybody family; [by] Betsy Byars; illustrated by Jacqueline Rogers. Delacorte Press 1986 149p il o.p.; Dell paperback available $3.50
Fic
1. Brothers and sisters—Fiction 2. Family life—Fiction
ISBN 0-440-45951-6 (pa)   LC 85-16184
"It's an ordinary day in the Blossom family: Junior, with Maggie and Vernon watching, is poised to fly off the barn in homemade wings; Mom's on the rodeo circuit; and Pap and his dog, Mud, are in town. By evening, Pap's in jail; Junior's in the hospital; Mud is gone; and Maggie helps Vernon break into jail to be with their grandfather." Publisher's note
"The story of the pathetically self-reliant, eccentric, but deeply loving family makes a book that is funny and sad, warm and wonderful." Horn Book
Other available titles about the Blossom family are:
A Blossom promise (1987)
The Blossoms and the Green Phantom (1987)
The Blossoms meet the Vulture Lady (1986)
Wanted—Mud Blossom (1991)

The pinballs; [by] Betsy Byars. Harper & Row 1977 lib bdg $14.89; pa $4.95   **Fic**
1. Foster home care—Fiction 2. Friendship—Fiction
ISBN 0-06-020918-6 (lib bdg); 0-06-440198-7 (pa)

"Pinballs go where they're pushed—and life's 'tilts' have thrown together three misfits. Suddenly finding themselves in a warm, loving foster home are Thomas J, eight, who is homeless now that his octogenarian twin guardians are hospitalized; Harvey, 13, whose mother ran off to a commune and whose hard drinking father ran over him in a car; and Carlie, 15, who cannot get along with a succession of step-fathers—or the rest of the world, for that matter." SLJ
"A deceptively simple, eloquent story, its pain and acrimony constantly mitigated by the author's light, off-hand style and by Carlie's wryly comic view of life." Horn Book

The summer of the swans; [by] Betsy Byars; illustrated by Ted CoConis. Viking 1970 185p il $15.99; pa $4.50   **Fic**
1. Mentally handicapped children—Fiction 2. Brothers and sisters—Fiction
ISBN 0-670-68190-3; 0-14-031420-2 (pa)
LC 72-106919
Awarded the Newbery Medal, 1971
"Sara is jolted out of her self-pitying absorption with her own inadequacies by the disappearance of her ten-year-old retarded brother who gets lost while trying to find the swans he had previously seen on a nearby lake. Her agonizing, albeit ultimately successful, search for Charlie and the reactions of others to this traumatic event help Sara gain a new perspective on herself and life." Booklist

Cadnum, Michael

Edge. Viking 1997 215p $15.99; pa $3.99 (7 and up)   **Fic**
1. Violence—Fiction 2. Crime—Fiction 3. California—Fiction
ISBN 0-670-87335-7; 0-14-038714-5 (pa)
LC 96-44561
Zachary, living with his divorced mother in California, finds violence gradually invading his life and making significant changes in his day-to-day existence
"Cadnum tells a thought-provoking story full of rich, well-developed characters. He immediately engages readers' attention and brilliantly maintains the pacing." SLJ

Heat. Viking 1998 196p $15.99 (7 and up)
Fic
1. Diving—Fiction 2. Accidents—Fiction 3. Fathers and daughters—Fiction
ISBN 0-670-87886-3   LC 97-40938
Sixteen-year-old Bonnie, a diving champion, must deal with the aftermath of a diving accident and her attorney father's remarriage and subsequent arrest for fraud
"Tension and emotion bubble underneath the surface of the coolly introspective prose." Horn Book Guide

In a dark wood. Orchard Bks. 1998 246p $17.95; lib bdg $18.99 (7 and up)   **Fic**
1. Robin Hood (Legendary character)—Fiction 2. Great Britain—History—1154-1399, Plantagenets—Fiction 3. Middle Ages—Fiction
ISBN 0-531-30071-4; 0-531-33071-0 (lib bdg)
LC 97-24780
On orders from the King, the Sheriff of Nottingham seeks to capture the outlaw Robin Hood, but he finds him to be a tricky and elusive foe
"This complex, many-layered novel, which does not shirk in its descriptions of filth, violence, and sexual desire, offers an unusually subtle character study and a plot full of surprises." Horn Book Guide

Rundown. Viking 1999 168p $15.99 (7 and up)
Fic
1. Truthfulness and falsehood—Fiction 2. Rape—Fiction
ISBN 0-670-88377-8   LC 98-49554
As a game, sixteen-year-old Jennifer pretends that she has been attacked by a serial rapist, but then she finds herself getting more attention than she wanted, from the police and her parents
"Deft characterization and adroit descriptions of setting and motivation raise Cadnum's writing above the commonplace." SLJ

Zero at the bone. Viking 1996 218p $14.99; pa $4.99 (7 and up)   **Fic**
1. Family life—Fiction 2. Missing persons—Fiction
ISBN 0-670-86725-X; 0-14-038628-9 (pa)
LC 95-50145
When eighteen-year-old Anita fails to return home from work, her parents and younger brother try to understand and cope with her disappearance
"Taut, tense, and tightly plotted, this intimate portrayal of a contemporary nightmare is much more frightening than a generic horror tale." Booklist

Calvert, Patricia, 1931-

Bigger. Scribner 1994 137p $16   **Fic**
1. Frontier and pioneer life—Fiction 2. Fathers and sons—Fiction 3. Dogs—Fiction
ISBN 0-684-19685-9   LC 93-14415
Also available in paperback from Troll Communications

When his father disappears near the Mexican border at the end of the Civil War, twelve-year-old Tyler decides to go after him and bring him home, acquiring on the journey a strange dog which he names Bigger

"Calvert's story has many tantalizing elements: Tyler is likable and realistically portrayed, the book raises some provocative issues, and the ending is sad but satisfying. . . . This is an entertaining story even reluctant readers will relish." Booklist

Followed by Sooner

Glennis, before and after. Atheneum Bks. for Young Readers 1996 150p $16   **Fic**
1. Fathers and daughters—Fiction 2. Prisoners—Fiction
ISBN 0-689-80641-8   LC 96-2017
Also available in paperback from Avon Bks.

While her father serves his term in a detention center, twelve-year-old Glennis learns that "not all prisons are made out of stone, and spiders aren't the only ones who can weave webs"

"Throughout this poignant novel, readers will recognize Glennis's inner strength as she learns to accept and forgive human failings." Publ Wkly

Picking up the pieces. Scribner 1993 166p $15; pa $4.50 (7 and up)   **Fic**
1. Physically handicapped—Fiction
ISBN 0-684-19558-5; 0-689-82451-3 (pa)
          LC 92-27909

"We enter Megan's life eight months after a motorcycle accident has left her paralyzed from the waist down. She and her family have had time to recover from the shock and grief—but now what? Adjusting to the physical limitations of a wheelchair is one thing, but Megan must now deal with adjusting her dreams of competing in the Olympics, going to college and having a 'normal' family. . . . Calvert constructs Megan's journey back to independence as an organic, self-taught process that relies not at all on tempting deus ex machina." Publ Wkly

Sooner. Atheneum Bks. for Young Readers 1998 166p $16   **Fic**
1. Frontier and pioneer life—Fiction 2. Dogs—Fiction
ISBN 0-689-81114-4   LC 97-28007
Sequel to Bigger

With the realization that his father may not return now that the Civil War is over, thirteen-year-old Tyler finds himself the man of their Missouri farm and the master of a new dog, the strikingly colored Sooner

"The novel is more smoothly paced, more plausible, and more engaging than its prequel, *Bigger*." Booklist

Campbell, Eric

The Shark Callers. Harcourt Brace & Co. 1994 232p $10.95; pa $4.95 (7 and up)   **Fic**
1. Sharks—Fiction 2. Volcanoes—Fiction 3. New Guinea—Fiction 4. Adventure fiction
ISBN 0-15-200007-0; 0-15-200010-0 (pa)
          LC 93-44881
First published 1993 in the United Kingdom

Two teenage boys, one on a shark hunt and the other traveling with his family, face the challenge of their lives when a volcano erupts causing a massive tidal wave in the South Seas

"Campbell does a fine job of building suspense, skillfully describing violent and intense moments, and neatly integrates background information about geology and sailing into the story." SLJ

Cannon, A. E. (Ann Edwards)

The shadow brothers. Delacorte Press 1990 179p hardcover o.p. paperback available $3.99 (7 and up)   **Fic**
1. Navajo Indians—Fiction 2. Brothers—Fiction
ISBN 0-440-21167-0 (pa)   LC 89-37779

High school junior Marcus feels his entire world changing around him as Henry, the Navajo foster brother who has lived with him since the age of seven, starts to change his personality and wonder if he should return to his family's reservation in another state

"The plot unfolds believably, and there's a good cast of secondary characters. . . . The narrative is economical and well paced with touches of humor." Horn Book

Capote, Truman, 1924-1984

The Thanksgiving visitor. Random House 1968 c1967 63p $19.95   **Fic**
1. Alabama—Fiction
ISBN 0-394-44824-3

This autobiographical story is about Buddy who was being raised by elderly relatives, and by his spinster cousin, Miss Sook Faulk. When Buddy is persecuted by a bully, Odd Henderson, Miss Sook invites him to their Thanksgiving dinner and precipitates the incident to teach Buddy compassion

"If this volume seems thin . . . Capote has told his story with such precise economy that once inside the covers readers will no longer question the format. This is storytelling in the classic tradition." Times Lit Suppl

Carbone, Elisa Lynn, 1954-

Stealing freedom; [by] Elisa Carbone. Knopf 1998 258p $17; lib bdg $18.99   **Fic**
1. Weems, Anne-Marie—Fiction 2. Slavery—Fiction 3. Underground railroad—Fiction 4. African Americans—Fiction
ISBN 0-679-89307-5; 0-679-99307-X (lib bdg)
          LC 98-36929

A novel based on the events in the life of Anne-Marie Weems, a young slave girl from Maryland who endures all kinds of mistreatment and cruelty, including being separated from her family, but who eventually escapes to freedom in Canada

"This is a fine piece of historical fiction with a strong, appealing heroine." SLJ

Card, Orson Scott

Ender's game. TOR Bks. 1985 357p hardcover o.p. paperback available $12.95 (7 and up) **Fic**
1. Science fiction
ISBN 0-312-85323-8 (pa)   LC 85-136148
"A Tom Doherty Associates book"

"Chosen as a six-year-old for his potential military genius, Ender Wiggin spends his childhood in outer space at the Battle School of the Belt. Severed from his family, isolated from his peers, and rigorously tested and trained, Ender pours all his talent into the war games that will one day repel the coming alien invasion." Libr J

"The key, of course, is Ender Wiggin himself. Mr. Card never makes the mistake of patronizing or sentimentalizing his hero. Alternately likable and insufferable, he is a convincing little Napoleon in short pants." N Y Times Book Rev

Other available titles in the author's distant future series about Ender Wiggin are:
Children of the mind (1996)
Speaker for the Dead (1986)
Xenocide (1991)

Carter, Alden R.

Bull catcher. Scholastic 1997 279p $15.95 (7 and up) **Fic**
1. Baseball—Fiction 2. Friendship—Fiction
ISBN 0-590-50958-6   LC 95-39538

Pete and Jeff continue their friendship and love of baseball as they progress from ninth grade through high school in their small Wisconsin town

"Carter traces a boy's growth from baseball fanaticism to athletic wisdom in a gritty story of teenage love and loss." ALAN

Caseley, Judith, 1951-

Losing Louisa. Foster Bks. 1999 235p $17 (7 and up) **Fic**
1. Divorce—Fiction 2. Family life—Fiction 3. Pregnancy—Fiction
ISBN 0-374-34665-8   LC 98-19501

Sixteen-year-old Lacey worries about the effect of her parents' divorce on her family, especially her mother, and about her older sister's sexual activity, which may have made her pregnant

"Never maudlin or didactic, Caseley's novel is a story of love, family, and the resilience of the spirit." SLJ

Childress, Alice, 1920-1994

A hero ain't nothin' but a sandwich. Coward-McCann 1973 126p $15.95 **Fic**
1. Drug abuse—Fiction 2. African Americans—Fiction 3. Harlem (New York, N.Y.)—Fiction
ISBN 0-698-20278-3
Also available in paperback from Avon Bks.

"At the age of 13 Benjie Johnson is hooked on 'horse.' He believes that he can break the habit whenever he is ready. When two of Benjie's teachers realize that he is on drugs, they report him to the principal of the school. Then begins his seesaw battle to break his addiction. Using Black English, the author draws a picture of the urban drug scene." Shapiro. Fic for Youth. 3d edition

Rainbow Jordan. Coward, McCann & Geoghegan 1981 142p o.p.; Avon Bks. paperback available $3.99 (7 and up) **Fic**
1. Foster home care—Fiction 2. Mothers and daughters—Fiction 3. African Americans—Fiction
ISBN 0-380-58974-5 (pa)   LC 81-596

The author "examines the relationships among three women—Rainbow, a teenage child becoming a woman, her errant mother Kathie and Josephine, the foster mother who provides an anchor for Rainbow when Kathie can't or won't keep her stuff together. The reader also gets a few glimpses of Mayola, the Black social worker, who works conscientiously on Rainbow's behalf." Interracial Books Child Bull

"The handling of sex is tasteful, and positive social values are gently presented without moralizing. Race relations, crimes, aging, and drugs are also well handled." Voice Youth Advocates

Those other people. Putnam 1989 186p $14.95 (7 and up) **Fic**
1. Prejudices—Fiction 2. Rape—Fiction 3. School stories
ISBN 0-399-21510-7   LC 88-10309

Bigotry surfaces at Minitown High when a popular male teacher sexually assaults a delinquent fifteen-year-old girl and the only witnesses are a black boy and a gay student teacher

"The author treats her subject with sensitivity, compassion, and understanding." Horn Book

Choi, Sook Nyul

Year of impossible goodbyes. Houghton Mifflin 1991 171p $16 **Fic**
1. Korea—Fiction
ISBN 0-395-57419-6   LC 91-10502
Also available in paperback from Dell

Sookan, a young Korean girl, survives the oppressive Japanese and Russian occupation of North Korea during the 1940s, to later escape to freedom in South Korea

"Tragedies are not masked here, but neither are they overdramatized. . . . The observations are honest, the details authentic, the characterizations vividly developed." Bull Cent Child Books

Other available titles about Sookan are:
Echoes of the white giraffe (1993)
Gathering of pearls (1994)

Christie, Agatha, 1890-1976

The mirror crack'd. Dodd, Mead 1962 246p o.p.; HarperCollins Pubs. paperback available $4.99 (7 and up) **Fic**
1. Mystery fiction
ISBN 0-06-100285-2 (pa)

First published 1962 in the United Kingdom with title: The mirror crack'd from side to side

Miss Jane Marple, whose house in St. Mary Mead is close to the scene of the crime "gives Scotland Yard her gracious cooperation in solving a poisoning that takes place at a village reception where the hostess is a lovely film star. The murder puzzle is a good one, the village people and their gossip are acute and interesting." Publ Wkly

Christie, Agatha, 1890-1976—*Continued*
Murder on the Orient Express. Dodd, Mead 1985 c1933 263p il o.p.; HarperCollins Pubs. paperback available $5.99 (7 and up)   **Fic**
1. Mystery fiction
ISBN 0-06-100274-7 (pa)   LC 84-72783
First United States edition published 1934 with title: Murder on the Calais Coach
A man is murdered on a train going from Istanbul to Calais. The famous detective Hercule Poirot happens to be on board and unravels the mystery
"This is the tour de force in which Agatha makes conspiracy believable and enlivens it by a really satisfying description of the Taurus Express (part of the Orient system)." Barzun. Cat of Crime. Rev and enl edition

Christopher, John, 1922-
The White Mountains. Macmillan 1967 184p $16; pa $3.95   **Fic**
1. Science fiction
ISBN 0-02-718360-2; 0-02-042711-5 (pa)   LC 67-1262
Also available paperback boxed set with title: The Tripods. Includes The White Mountains and the three additional titles listed below $17.95 (ISBN 0-689-00852-X)
The world of the future is "ruled by Tripods, machine-like creatures who can control humanity. Will Parker tells of his and his companions' escapes to the White Mountains, Switzerland, where the few still free people dwell. The future world is believably developed, with traces of the past well integrated. The suspense is maintained as the reader follows Will's adventures. We are reminded that there may be evil present even in an apparently peaceful world." Roman. Sequences
Other available titles about the Tripods are:
The city of gold and lead (1967)
The pool of fire (1968)
When the Tripods came (1988)

Christopher, Matt, 1917-1997
Olympic dream; illustrated by Karen Meyer. Little, Brown 1996 171p il $15.95; pa $3.95
Fic
1. Bicycle racing—Fiction 2. Weight loss—Fiction
ISBN 0-316-14048-1; 0-316-14163-1 (pa)
LC 95-45653
When overweight fourteen-year-old video whiz Doug Cannon is introduced to the sport of cycling he begins a transformation that leads him to health and self-respect
"Christopher does a good job of presenting the main character's early self-consciousness and eventual pride and confidence." SLJ

Ciencin, Scott
Dinoverse; illustrations by Mike Fredericks. Random House 1999 282p il $18   **Fic**
1. Science fiction
ISBN 0-679-88842-X   LC 98-41377
When thirteen-year-old Bertram and three friends find themselves living in dinosaur bodies sixty-seven million years ago, they discover new ways to think about their lives
"Ciencin blends fantasy and scientific fact for a fresh, fun, and informative read. Distinctive characters, slapstick humor, snappy dialogue, and fast-paced suspense add to the book's appeal." Booklist

Cisneros, Sandra
The house on Mango Street. Knopf 1994 134p $23; pa $9.95 (7 and up)   **Fic**
1. Chicago (Ill.)—Fiction 2. Mexican Americans—Fiction
ISBN 0-679-43335-X; 0-679-73477-5 (pa)
LC 93-43564
"Originally published by Arte Público Press in 1984." Verso of title page
Composed of a series of interconnected vignettes, this "is the story of Esperanza Cordero, a young girl growing up in the Hispanic quarter of Chicago. For Esperanza, Mango Street is a desolate landscape of concrete and run-down tenements, where she discovers the hard realities of life—the fetters of class and gender, the specter of racial enmity, the mysteries of sexuality, and more." Publisher's note
This is "a composite of evocative snapshots that manages to passionately recreate the milieu of the poor quarters of Chicago." Commonweal

Clapp, Patricia, 1912-
The tamarack tree; a novel of the Siege of Vicksburg. Lothrop, Lee & Shepard Bks. 1986 214p $16 (7 and up)   **Fic**
1. Vicksburg (Miss.)—Siege, 1863—Fiction 2. United States—History—1861-1865, Civil War—Fiction
ISBN 0-688-02852-7   LC 86-108
An eighteen-year-old English girl finds her loyalties divided and all her resources tested as she and her friends experience the terrible physical and emotional hardships of the forty-seven day siege of Vicksburg in the spring of 1863
"There is a romantic element, but this is primarily a record of the long siege of the city and it gives, through its British narrator, a good perspective of the tragic division and of the conflicting viewpoints of North and South." Bull Cent Child Books

Clark, Clara Gillow, 1951-
Nellie Bishop. Boyds Mills Press 1996 128p $14.95; pa $7.95   **Fic**
1. Pennsylvania—Fiction 2. Irish Americans—Fiction 3. United States—History—1865-1898—Fiction
ISBN 1-56397-491-6; 1-56397-642-0 (pa)
LC 95-76355
"At 13, Nellie Bishop fights her parents' plan to marry her off for money to the highest bidder among the workmen in their Pennsylvania canal town. This . . . historical novel, set in the 1880s, dramatizes the hardship among the laboring Irish at the time and shows a young girl trapped in a family brutalized by poverty." Booklist

Clarke, Arthur C., 1917-
2001: a space odyssey. New Am. Lib. 1968 221p hardcover o.p. paperback available $3.95 (7 and up)   **Fic**
1. Science fiction
ISBN 0-451-15580-7 (pa)   LC 68-29754
Also available G.K. Hall large print edition
"Based on a screenplay by Stanley Kubrick and Arthur C. Clarke." Title page

Clarke, Arthur C., 1917-—*Continued*

Astronauts of the spaceship Discovery, aided by their computer, HAL, blast off in search of proof that extraterrestrial beings had a part in the development of intelligent life forms on Earth millions of years ago

"By standing the universe on its head, the author makes us see the ordinary universe in a different light." New Yorker

Followed by 2010: odyssey two (1982) and 2061: odyssey three (1987)

Cleary, Beverly

Dear Mr. Henshaw; illustrated by Paul O. Zelinsky. Morrow 1983 133p il $16; lib bdg $15.93 **Fic**

1. Divorce—Fiction 2. Parent and child—Fiction 3. School stories

ISBN 0-688-02405-X; 0-688-02406-8 (lib bdg)

LC 83-5372

Also available in paperback from Dell and Avon Bks.

Awarded the Newbery Medal, 1984

"Leigh Botts started writing letters to his favorite author, Boyd Henshaw, in the second grade. Now, Leigh is in the sixth grade, in a new school, and his parents are recently divorced. This year he writes many letters to Mr. Henshaw, and also keeps a journal. Through these the reader learns how Leigh adjusts to new situations, and of his triumphs." Child Book Rev Serv

"The story is by no means one of unrelieved gloom, for there are deft touches of humor in the sentient, subtly wrought account of the small triumphs and tragedies in the life of an ordinary boy." Horn Book

Strider; illustrated by Paul O. Zelinsky. Morrow Junior Bks. 1991 179p il $16; lib bdg $15.93 **Fic**

1. Dogs—Fiction 2. Divorce—Fiction

ISBN 0-688-09900-9; 0-688-09901-7 (lib bdg)

LC 90-6608

Also available in paperback from Avon Bks.

Sequel to Dear Mr. Henshaw

In a series of diary entries, Leigh Botts, now fourteen and beginning high school, tells how he comes to terms with his parents' divorce, acquires joint custody of an abandoned dog, and joins the track team at school

"The development of the narrative is vintage Beverly Cleary, an inimitable blend of comic and poignant moments." Horn Book

Cleaver, Vera

Where the lilies bloom; [by] Vera and Bill Cleaver; illus. by Jim Spanfeller. Lippincott 1969 174p il o.p.; HarperCollins Pubs. paperback available $4.95 **Fic**

1. Brothers and sisters—Fiction 2. Orphans—Fiction 3. Appalachian region—Fiction

ISBN 0-06-447005-9 (pa)

Mary Call Luther is "fourteen years old and made of granite. When her sharecropper father dies, Mary Call becomes head of the household, responsible for a boy of ten and a retarded, gentle older sister. Mary and her brother secretly bury their father so they can retain their home [in the Appalachian hills]; tenaciously she fights to keep the family afloat by selling medicinal plants and keep them together by fending off [Kiser Pease, their landlord], who wants to marry her sister." Saturday Rev

"The setting is fascinating, the characterization good, and the style of the first-person story distinctive." Bull Cent Child Books

Followed by Trial Valley (1977)

Cochran, Thomas, 1955-

Roughnecks. Harcourt Brace & Co. 1997 248p $15; pa $6 (7 and up) **Fic**

1. Football—Fiction

ISBN 0-15-201433-0; 0-15-201432-2 (pa)

LC 96-43939

"Gulliver books"

Travis Cody prepares for the final game of his high school football career, a rematch with his school's chief rival

"Travis is an appealing, positive character. . . . Football descriptions are authentic, intense, even lyrical at times." Booklist

Cole, Brock, 1938-

Celine. Farrar, Straus & Giroux 1989 216p $15; pa $3.95 (7 and up) **Fic**

1. Divorce—Fiction 2. Remarriage—Fiction

ISBN 0-374-31234-6; 0-374-41083-6 (pa)

LC 89-45614

A "first-person narrative about a sixteen-year-old artist and her irresolute yearnings to find a center to her life. Living with her new stepmother while her father is on a lecture tour in Europe and her mother is trying to find herself, Celine has vague ambitions of finishing high school a year early so that she can join an older woman friend in Florence." Horn Book

"Here's a rare pleasure: Brock Cole's 'Celine' is a novel that doesn't set out deliberately to instruct, uplift, comfort, amuse or expand the horizons of those readers known . . . as 'young adults.' Yet it manages to accomplish all this and much more simply by telling a fine story about an unforgettable character." N Y Times Book Rev

The facts speak for themselves. Front St. 1997 184p $15.95 (7 and up) **Fic**

1. Mothers and daughters—Fiction 2. Rape—Fiction

ISBN 1-88691-014-6 LC 97-4250

At the request of her social worker, thirteen-year-old Linda gradually reveals how her life with her unstable mother and her younger brother led to her rape and the murder she witnessed

"A complex character of great emotional subtlety, Linda is caught up in the uncontrollable facts of her life, powerless yet capable, battered yet loving, and disturbingly unforgettable." Bull Cent Child Books

The goats; written and illustrated by Brock Cole. Farrar, Straus & Giroux 1987 184p il $15; pa $3.95 **Fic**

1. Camps—Fiction 2. Friendship—Fiction

ISBN 0-374-32678-9; 0-374-42576-0 (pa)

LC 87-45362

"A boy and the girl have been chosen as 'the goats' at summer camp. Stripped naked, they are marooned on

Cole, Brock, 1938——*Continued*
Goat Island, as part of an annual prank played on campers who don't fit in. But the goats have much more spirit
than their fellow campers expect, and they decide to disappear completely." Publ Wkly
"This is an unflinching book, and there is a quality of
raw emotion that may score some discomfort among
adults. Such a first novel restores faith in the cultivation
of children's literature." Bull Cent Child Books

Coleman, Michael
Weirdo's war. Orchard Bks. 1998 c1996 184p
$16.95; lib bdg $17.99   **Fic**
1. School stories 2. Caves—Fiction
ISBN 0-531-30103-6; 0-531-33103-2 (lib bdg)
LC 98-10482
First published 1996 in the United Kingdom
While trapped in a cave with one of his fellow stu-
dents, a longtime enemy, Daniel relives his troubled rela-
tionship with his schoolmates
"Edge-of-the-seat pacing makes this a gripping adven-
ture, and Daniel's first-person narrative achieves a depth
of characterization unusual for a thriller." Horn Book
Guide

Collier, James Lincoln, 1928-
The bloody country; by James Lincoln Collier
and Christopher Collier. Four Winds Press 1976
183p o.p.; Scholastic paperback available $4.50
Fic
1. Pennsylvania—Fiction
ISBN 0-590-43126-9 (pa)   LC 75-34461
"An engrossing story which is based on historical
facts of a Connecticut man, Daniel Buck and his family,
who settled near the banks of the Susquehanna in Wyoming Valley [Pennsylvania] in the 1750's, survived the
Wyoming Massacre, suffered disastrous losses in a flood,
and struggled against the injustice of the Penamites' legal
maneuvers to wrest their land from them. Told by young
Ben, . . . he is first seen as a youngster of seven though
we share his thoughts and actions as he matures to a boy
of fifteen." Child Book Rev Serv
"The story is dramatic and convincing, the characters
drawn with depth and vigor." Bull Cent Child Books

Jump ship to freedom; [by] James Lincoln
Collier, Christopher Collier. Delacorte Press 1981
198p hardcover o.p. paperback available $5.99
Fic
1. United States—History—1783-1809—Fiction
2. Slavery—Fiction 3. African Americans—Fiction
ISBN 0-440-91158-3 (pa)   LC 81-65492
Companion volume to War comes to Willie Freeman
and Who is Carrie?
In 1787 Dan Arabus, a fourteen-year-old slave, anxious to buy freedom for himself and his mother, escapes
from his dishonest master and tries to find help in cash-
ing the soldier's notes received by his father, Jack
Arabus, for fighting in the Revolution
"The period seems well researched, and the speech
has an authentic ring without trying to imitate a dialect."
SLJ

My brother Sam is dead; by James Lincoln
Collier and Christopher Collier. Four Winds Press
1985 c1974 216p il $17   **Fic**
1. United States—History—1775-1783, Revolution—
Fiction
ISBN 0-02-722980-7   LC 84-28787
Also available in paperback from Scholastic
A reissue of the title first published 1974
"In 1775 the Meeker family lived in Redding, Connecticut, a Tory community. Sam, the eldest son, allied
himself with the Patriots. The youngest son, Tim,
watched a rift in the family grow because of his brother's decision. Before the war was over the Meeker family had suffered at the hands of both the British and the
Patriots." Shapiro. Fic for Youth. 3d edition

War comes to Willy Freeman; [by] James
Lincoln Collier, Christopher Collier. Delacorte
Press 1983 178p $12.95; pa $4.99   **Fic**
1. United States—History—1775-1783, Revolution—
Fiction 2. African Americans—Fiction 3. Slavery—
Fiction
ISBN 0-385-29235-X; 0-440-49504-0 (pa)
LC 82-70317
This deals with events prior to those in Jump ship to
freedom, and involves members of the same family.
"Willy is thirteen when she begins her story, which takes
place during the last two years of the Revolutionary war;
her father, a free man, has been killed fighting against
the British, her mother has disappeared. Willy makes her
danger-fraught way to Fraunces Tavern in New York,
her uncle, Jack Arabus, having told her that Mr.
Fraunces may be able to help her. She works at the tavern until the war is over, goes to the Arabus home to
find her mother dying, and participates in the trial (historically accurate save for the fictional addition of Willy)
in which her uncle sues for his freedom and wins." Bull
Cent Child Books

Who is Carrie? by James Lincoln Collier and
Christopher Collier. Delacorte Press 1984 158p
hardcover o.p. paperback available $4.99   **Fic**
1. United States—History—1783-1809—Fiction
2. Slavery—Fiction 3. African Americans—Fiction
ISBN 0-440-49536-9 (pa)   LC 83-23947
Companion volume to Jump ship to freedom, and War
comes to Willy Freeman
Carrie "is a kitchen slave in Samuel Fraunces Tavern.
. . . She keeps in touch with her special friend, Dan
Arabus, and he enlists Carrie's help in finding out if the
new government will honor the notes with which Dan
hopes to purchase his mother's freedom. In so doing,
Carrie finds out the truth about herself." Child Book Rev
Serv
"This is historical fiction at its best. The Collier's familiar 'How Much of This Book is True' addendum fills
readers in on the essentials concerning fictional and factual elements of the plot, as well as the research involved
in its composition." SLJ

Collier, James Lincoln, 1928-—*Continued*
With every drop of blood; [by] James Lincoln
Collier, Christopher Collier. Delacorte Press 1994
235p hardcover o.p. paperback available $4.99
                                                    Fic
1. United States—History—1861-1865, Civil War—
Fiction 2. Race relations—Fiction 3. African Americans—Fiction
ISBN 0-440-21983-3 (pa)   LC 93-37655
This is a "docu-novel of the Civil War. Johnny, 14, a
young, white rebel soldier, is captured by a black Union
soldier, Cush, a runaway slave. As they get to know each
other in the mess and slaughteer of battle and retreat, the
two boys gradually lose their mutual distrust, and each
risks his life to save the other. . . . A preface entitled
'About the Use of the Word Nigger in This Book' explains that historical accuracy requires the use of the
term." Booklist
"The relationship of Cush and Johnny and the convincingly conversational tone of Johnny's voice make
this book an effectively immediate evocation of a distant
and sometimes difficult-to-understand time." Horn Book

Coman, Carolyn
Tell me everything. Farrar, Straus & Giroux
1993 156p $15   **Fic**
1. Death—Fiction 2. Mothers and daughters—Fiction
3. Christian life—Fiction
ISBN 0-374-37390-6   LC 92-7969
Also available in paperback from Puffin Bks.
After her mother, Ellie, dies in a rescue mission on a
snowy mountain, twelve-year-old Roz wonders if talking
to God, and to the boy for whom her mother died, can
help her understand what happened
"Coman portrays both Roz and Ellie with fresh and
real poeticism, lending dignity and gravity to this spell
binding story." Publ Wkly

What Jamie saw. Front St. 1995 126p $13.95
                                                    Fic
1. Child abuse—Fiction
ISBN 1-886910-02-2   LC 95-23545
Also available in paperback from Penguin Bks.
A Newbery Medal honor book, 1996
Having fled to a family friend's hillside trailer after
his mother's boyfriend tried to throw his baby sister
against a wall, nine-year-old Jamie finds himself living
an existence full of uncertainty and fear
"Shocking in its simple narration and child's-eye
view, *What Jamie Saw* is a bittersweet miracle in understated language and forthright hopefulness." SLJ

Conly, Jane Leslie
Crazy lady! HarperCollins Pubs. 1993 180p lib
bdg $13.89; pa $4.95   **Fic**
1. Prejudices—Fiction 2. Death—Fiction 3. Alcohol-
ism—Fiction 4. Mentally handicapped—Fiction
ISBN 0-06-021360-4 (lib bdg); 0-06-440571-0 (pa)
                                                    LC 92-18348
A Newbery Medal honor book, 1994
"A Laura Geringer book"
As he tries to come to terms with his mother's death,
Vernon finds solace in his growing relationship with the
neighborhood outcasts, an alcoholic and her retarded son
The author is "fast and blunt, and the conversations
are lively and true." Bull Cent Child Books

R-T, Margaret, and the rats of NIMH;
illustrations by Leonard Lubin. Harper & Row
1990 260p il lib bdg $15.89; pa $4.95   **Fic**
1. Mice—Fiction 2. Rats—Fiction
ISBN 0-06-021364-7 (lib bdg); 0-06-440387-4 (pa)
                                                    LC 89-19968
Sequel to Racso and the rats of NIMH
The intelligent young rat Racso and his friends Christopher and Isabella try to ensure the survival of their secret community in Thorn Valley after its accidental discovery by two human children
"The novel proves enjoyable for its excitement and
believably drawn characterizations of the children and
their amazing rodent friends." Publ Wkly

Racso and the rats of NIMH; illustrations by
Leonard Lubin. Harper & Row 1986 278p il
hardcover o.p. paperback available $4.95   **Fic**
1. Mice—Fiction 2. Rats—Fiction
ISBN 0-06-440245-2 (pa)   LC 85-42634
Sequel to Mrs. Frisby and the rats of NIMH by Robert
C. O'Brien
This book "continues the NIMH saga with a focus on
the second rodent generation: Timothy, Mrs. Frisby's
son, and Racso, son of the rebel rat Jenner. On his way
to classes at Thorn Valley, Timothy saves Racso's life
but is himself severely injured. Both reach the Utopian
colony only to discover that the valley and surrounding
farms are to be turned into a tourist lake and camp-
grounds." SLJ
"The book is cleverly and gracefully built upon both
the philosophy of self-sufficiency and the details of the
plot of its predecessor. Given the difficulty of writing
good sequels, *Racso and the Rats of NIMH* is an outstanding success." Horn Book
Followed by R-T, Margaret, and the rats of NIMH

Trout summer. Holt & Co. 1995 234p $15.95
                                                    Fic
1. Brothers and sisters—Fiction 2. Canoes and canoc-
ing—Fiction 3. Summer—Fiction
ISBN 0-8050-3933-3   LC 95-16381
Also available in paperback from Scholastic
"When their father leaves them, Shana, 13, and Cody,
12, move with their mother to Maryland. . . . The kids
convince Mama that they should stay in an abandoned
cabin along the Leanna River for the summer. There they
meet Henry, an irascible old man who professes to be a
ranger. Ill and difficult but an excellent canoeist, he
teaches Cody his skills. . . . Shana's fast-paced, first-
person narrative is enhanced by Henry's quirky character
and revealing dialogue." SLJ

While no one was watching. Holt & Co. 1998
233p $16.95   **Fic**
1. Poverty—Fiction
ISBN 0-8050-3934-1   LC 97-48718
This "story is told from the point of view of five characters: siblings Earl, Frankie, and Angela (on their own
after their aunt disappears on a drinking binge) and, from
a very different part of the city, Maynard and Addie
(whose pet rabbit has been stolen by affection-starved,
seven-year-old Frankie). Conly writes convincingly and
unsentimentally about the working class poor in an urban
setting." Horn Book Guide

Conrad, Pam, 1947-1996

My Daniel. Harper & Row 1989 137p $13.95; lib bdg $15.89; pa $4.95   **Fic**
1. Brothers and sisters—Fiction 2. Nebraska—Fiction
ISBN 0-06-021313-2; 0-06-021314-0 (lib bdg); 0-06-440309-2 (pa)   LC 88-19850

"When she's 80 years old, Julia Summerwaithe decides to visit her grandchildren, Ellie and Stevie, in New York City, for the first time. She has something important to show them; in the Natural History Museum is the dinosaur she and her brother discovered on their farm in Nebraska when they were young. But even more important to Julia than seeing the dinosaur is sharing her memories of the discovery and excavation with her grandchildren." SLJ

"Rendering scenes from both the past and the present with equal skill, Conrad is at the peak of her storytelling powers." Publ Wkly

Prairie songs; illustrations by Darryl S. Zudeck. Harper & Row 1985 167p il $14; lib bdg $14.89; pa $4.95   **Fic**
1. Frontier and pioneer life—Fiction 2. Nebraska—Fiction
ISBN 0-06-021336-1; 0-06-021337-X (il bdg); 0-06-440206-1 (pa)   LC 85-42633

"The deterioration of the frail, young wife of a doctor who is unable to adapt to the harshness of prairie life is made more vivid because the reader views it through the eyes of an adolescent girl who lives nearby. Set in Nebraska at the turn of the century, this story is rich with detail about the beauty and hardships of pioneer life in the American West." Soc Educ

Stonewords; a ghost story. Harper & Row 1990 130p $14.89; lib bdg $13.89; pa $4.95   **Fic**
1. Ghost stories 2. Space and time—Fiction
ISBN 0-06-021315-9; 0-06-021316-7 (lib bdg); 0-06-440354-8 (pa)   LC 89-36382

Zoe discovers that her house is occupied by the ghost of an eleven-year-old girl, who carries her back to the day of her death in 1870 to try to alter that tragic event

"The supernatural and time-travel elements of the book are viscerally convincing, and the desperate neediness of both girls is fierce and real. The disquieting ending is in the richest gothic tradition, resolving one mystery only to reveal another even more frightening. This is a very scary book." Bull Cent Child Books

Zoe rising. HarperCollins Pubs. 1996 131p lib bdg $14.89; pa $4.95   **Fic**
1. Space and time—Fiction 2. Mothers and daughters—Fiction
ISBN 0-06-027218-X (lib bdg); 0-06-440687-3 (pa)   LC 95-42663

Companion volume to Stonewords
"A Laura Geringer book"

Zoe, traveling back to the time when her mother was a child, intervenes in the past in order to save the future

"The writing is splendidly atmospheric, with Conrad beautifully guiding readers through Zoe's misty corporeal changes and into a riveting, terrifying climax." Booklist

Cooney, Caroline B., 1947-

Burning up. Delacorte Press 1999 230p $15.95 (7 and up)   **Fic**
1. Race relations—Fiction
ISBN 0-385-32318-2   LC 98-19343

When a girl she had met at an innercity church is murdered, fifteen-year-old Macey channels her grief into a school project that leads her to uncover prejudice she had not imagined in her grandparents and their wealthy Connecticut community

"The plot moves along and stays right on track in this complex and thought-provoking novel." Voice Youth Advocates

Driver's Ed. Delacorte Press 1994 184p $16.95; pa $4.99 (7 and up)   **Fic**
1. School stories 2. Death—Fiction
ISBN 0-385-32087-6; 0-440-21981-7 (pa)   LC 94-445

Remy, Morgan, and Nickie's lives are changed forever when they thoughtlessly steal a stop sign from a dangerous intersection and a young mother is killed in an automobile accident there

"Given Cooney's vigorous, evocative prose and her carefully individuated characters, this modern-day morality tale is as convincing as it is irresistible." Publ Wkly

The face on the milk carton. Bantam Bks. 1990 184p o.p.; Delacorte Press reissue available $15.95; pa $5.50 (7 and up)   **Fic**
1. Kidnapping—Fiction
ISBN 0-385-32328-X; pa 0-440-22065-3   LC 89-18311

"Up to her fifteenth year, the most Jane Johnson had to worry about was her boring name. . . . Then the picture of a missing child on a school milk carton triggers flashbacks to long-buried memories of Jane as a child—the milk carton child, in fact. Is she the missing Jennie Spring, snatched from her family years before? Or is she simply Jane, who doesn't like her name?" Booklist

"Cooney again demonstrates an excellent ear for dialogue and a gift for portraying responsible middle-class teenagers trying to come to terms with very real concerns." SLJ

Followed by Whatever happened to Janie?

Flash fire. Scholastic 1995 198p $14.95; pa $4.50 (7 and up)   **Fic**
1. Fires—Fiction 2. Brothers and sisters—Fiction 3. California—Fiction
ISBN 0-590-25253-4; 0-590-48496-6 (pa)   LC 94-43805

As fire sweeps through a canyon near Los Angeles, teenagers Danna and Hall Press and other children whose parents are not around must work together to save themselves

This offers "thorough research, a humorously ironic tone, and page-turning action. . . . A high-quality offering that will appeal to reluctant readers as well as to teens who relish adventure stories." Booklist

Followed by Out of time (1996)

Flight #116 is down. Scholastic 1992 201p $14.95; pa $4.50 (7 and up)   **Fic**
1. Aircraft accidents—Fiction
ISBN 0-590-44465-4; 0-590-44479-4 (pa)   LC 91-9796

Cooney, Caroline B., 1947-—*Continued*

Teenager Heidi Landseth helps rescue people from a plane crash on her family's property, and the experience changes her life forever

"Using her trademark lightning pace, Cooney depicts the drama and human interest inherent in disaster. . . . This story will keep even the least bookish readers glued to their seats." Publ Wkly

Prisoner of time. Delacorte Press 1998 200p $15.95; pa $4.99 (7 and up) **Fic**
1. Space and time—Fiction
ISBN 0-385-32244-5; 0-440-22019-X (pa)
LC 97-24073

Previous titles in This series are: Both sides of time (1995) and Out of time (1996)

In the author's third time travel novel "the focus is on Strat's younger sister, Devonny, and Annie's younger brother, Tod, who rescues Devonny from a marriage with a young British lord. . . . The ironic ending is a treasure, as a woman in the male-dominated society of 1898 has her way with both her father and her future husband, ensuring herself a happy marriage." Booklist

The terrorist. Scholastic 1997 198p $15.95; pa $4.50 (7 and up) **Fic**
1. Terrorism—Fiction 2. Mystery fiction 3. London (England)—Fiction
ISBN 0-590-22853-6; 0-590-22854-4 (pa)
LC 96-42352

Sixteen-year-old Laura, an American living in London, tries to find the person responsible for the death of her younger brother Billy, who has been killed by a terrorist bomb

"Tension builds expertly in Cooney's latest thriller, which is sure to hook fans early on with its breezy dialogue, believable characters, and . . . interesting global perspective." Booklist

The voice on the radio. Delacorte Press 1996 183p $15.95; pa $4.99 (7 and up) **Fic**
1. Radio programs—Fiction
ISBN 0-385-32213-5; 0-440-21977-9 (pa)
LC 96-3688

Sequel to Whatever happened to Janie?

"Janie is a high-school junior and in love with Reeve. She finally feels that her life is somewhat normal and begins to reconcile with her biological family, but the voice on the radio destroys her trust. Cooney plots an engaging and realistic picture of betrayal, commitment, unconditional love, and forgiveness." ALAN

What child is this? a Christmas story. Delacorte Press 1997 150p $14.95 (7 and up) **Fic**
1. Christmas—Fiction 2. Foster home care—Fiction
ISBN 0-385-32317-4
LC 96-54891

When seventeen-year-old Matt tries to find a family for an eight-year-old foster child, his attempt backfires and both of them need a Christmas miracle

"Cooney weaves the threads of these young and fragile lives together in an involving, emotionally moving novel." Bull Cent Child Books

Whatever happened to Janie? Delacorte Press 1993 199p $15.95; pa $4.99 (7 and up) **Fic**
1. Kidnapping—Fiction 2. Parent and child—Fiction
ISBN 0-385-31035-8; 0-440-21924-8 (pa)
LC 92-32334

Sequel to The face on the milk carton

The members of two families have their lives disrupted when Jane who had been kidnapped twelve years earlier discovers that the people who raised her are not her biological parents

"However strange the events of this book, the emotions of its characters remain excruciatingly real." Publ Wkly

Followed by The voice on the radio

Cooper, Susan, 1935-

The Boggart. Margaret K. McElderry Bks. 1993 196p $15; pa $3.95 **Fic**
1. Supernatural—Fiction 2. Scotland—Fiction 3. Canada—Fiction
ISBN 0-689-50576-0; 0-689-80173-4 (pa)
LC 92-15527

After visiting the castle in Scotland which her family has inherited and returning home to Canada, twelve-year-old Emily finds that she has accidentally brought back with her a boggart, an invisible and mischievous spirit with a fondness for practical jokes

"Using both electronics and theater as metaphors for magic, Cooper has extended the world of high fantasy into contemporary children's lives through scenes superimposing the ordinary and the extraordinary." Bull Cent Child Books

Another available title about the Boggart is:
The Boggart and the monster (1997)

Over sea, under stone; illustrated by Margery Gill. Harcourt Brace & World 1966 c1965 252p il $17; pa $3.95 **Fic**
1. Fantasy fiction 2. Great Britain—Fiction
ISBN 0-15-259034-X; 0-02-042785-9 (pa)
First published 1965 in the United Kingdom

In this series, The Dark Is Rising, about the "conflict between the good of the Servants of Light and the evil of the Powers of Dark, Cooper has created an intricate fantasy. Ancient lore and mythology are believably interwoven into a modern setting. Ostensibly, the three Drew children, on a holiday in Cornwall, find an old map and, aided by their uncle, they begin a search for an ancient treasure linked with King Arthur. With each book, more reliance is placed on folklore and legend. There is much action and excitement included in the carefully wrought stories." Roman. Sequences

Other available titles in the Dark is rising series are:
The dark is rising (1973)
Greenwitch (1974)
The grey king (1975)
Silver on the tree (1977)

Cormier, Robert

After the first death. Pantheon Bks. 1979 233p lib bdg $14.99 (7 and up) **Fic**
1. Terrorism—Fiction
ISBN 0-394-94122-5
LC 78-11770

Also available in paperback from Dell

"A busload of children is hijacked by a band of terrorists whose demands include the exposure of a military brainwashing project. The narrative line moves from the teenage terrorist Milo to Kate the bus driver and the involvement of Ben, whose father is the head of the military operation, in this confrontation. The conclusion has a shocking twist." Shapiro. Fic for Youth. 3d edition

Cormier, Robert—*Continued*

Beyond the chocolate war; a novel. Knopf 1985 278p o.p.; Dell paperback available $4.99 (7 and up)   **Fic**
1. School stories
ISBN 0-440-90580-X (pa)   LC 84-22865
Sequel to The chocolate war
This "continues the chronicle of the school year at Trinity after the chocolate sale. Jerry Renault has returned to town after recovering at his aunt and uncle's home in Canada but is not attending school. Archie Costello is still controlling the Vigils, but his right-hand man, Obie, is more interested in his new girlfriend, Laurie Gundarson, a senior at Monument High, and later avenging her attempted rape. Bunting, a sophomore, is desperately trying to replace Obie so that he can become the assigner after Archie graduates." Voice Youth Advocates
"Some readers may find the story depressingly somber; for others it may have the catharic effect of Greek tragedy, evoking pity and fear." Bull Cent Child Books

The bumblebee flies anyway. Pantheon Bks. 1983 241p o.p.; Dell paperback available $4.99 (7 and up)   **Fic**
1. Death—Fiction   2. Terminal   care—Fiction
3. Friendship—Fiction
ISBN 0-440-90871-X (pa)   LC 83-2458
"Sixteen-year-old Barney is a patient in a hospital wing where terminally ill youngsters are being treated with experimental drugs. He believes he is the only one not terminal because they are treating him with drugs that have destroyed his memory. Thus he is relatively happy and even 'falls for' the twin sister of a fellow patient. He eventually does find out the truth and can no longer pretend he isn't in pain and dying." Child Book Rev Serv
"In a story that is as trenchant as it is poignant, Cormier shows the courage and desperation of adolescents who know that their deaths are imminent. . . . Although it is tragic, [it is] a stunning book." Bull Cent Child Books

The chocolate war; a novel. Pantheon Bks. 1974 253p $20 (7 and up)   **Fic**
1. School stories
ISBN 0-394-82805-4
Also available in hardcover from Buccaneer Bks. and in paperback from Dell
"In the Trinity School for Boys the environment is completely dominated by an underground gang, the Vigils. During a chocolate candy sale Brother Leon, the acting headmaster of the school, defers to the Vigils, who reign with terror in the school. Jerry Renault is first a pawn for the Vigils' evil deeds and finally their victim." Shapiro. Fic for Youth. 3d edition
Followed by Beyond the chocolate war

Heroes; a novel. Delacorte Press 1998 135p $15.95 (7 and up)   **Fic**
1. World War, 1939-1945—Fiction 2. Veterans—Fiction
ISBN 0-385-32590-8   LC 97-40326

After joining the army at fifteen and having his face blown away by a grenade in a battle in France, Francis returns home to Frenchtown hoping to find—and kill—the former childhood hero he feels betrayed him
"This lean, compelling read . . . is a powerful and thought-provoking study." SLJ

I am the cheese; a novel. Pantheon Bks. 1977 233p $20 (7 and up)   **Fic**
1. Intelligence service—Fiction 2. Organized crime—Fiction
ISBN 0-394-83462-3   LC 76-55948
Also available in paperback from Dell
"In a compellingly mysterious journey, Adam finds himself pedaling furiously on an old-fashioned bike, trying to get from Massachusetts to Vermont. He is not sure how much of the journey is real, for he is searching through snatches of memories to try to find a key to his past. He remembers a happy childhood that was jarred from time to time by a nagging mystery involving his father. He struggles to recall some terrible truth that is just outside his consciousness but that must not be remembered if he is to survive. The shattering climax leaves the reader wondering what is reality and what is illusion." Shapiro. Fic for Youth. 3d edition

In the middle of the night. Delacorte Press 1995 182p $15.95; pa $4.99 (7 and up)   **Fic**
1. Fathers and sons—Fiction 2. Guilt—Fiction
ISBN 0-385-32158-9; 0-440-22686-4 (pa)
                                          LC 94-38894
"In three narrative threads that twist into each other, a woman nurses her rage over a childhood accident that 'killed' her many years ago, a man still wrestles with his guilt over that tragic event, and his son Denny finds himself drawn into the pain of them both." Bull Cent Child Books
"Cormier's chilling tale of revenge and remorse is told by several narrators: the tormenter as well as the tormented father and son. Suspense and horror build as the harassment worsens for the family. This psychological thriller draws the reader deeper in to discover the truth." Book Rep

Tunes for bears to dance to. Delacorte Press 1992 101p hardcover o.p. paperback available $4.50 (7 and up)   **Fic**
1. Prejudices—Fiction 2. Jews—Fiction
ISBN 0-440-21903-5 (pa)   LC 92-2734
Eleven-year-old Henry escapes his family's problems by watching the woodcarving of Mr. Levine, an elderly Holocaust survivor, but when Henry is manipulated by his employer, Mr. Hairston, into betraying his friend he comes to know true evil
"A powerful book for discussion with readers of all ages. Henry's loss of innocence is a dramatic event, but how he reacts to this event is thought-provoking." Voice Youth Advocates

We all fall down. Delacorte Press 1991 193p hardcover o.p. paperback available $4.99 (7 and up)   **Fic**
1. Juvenile delinquency—Fiction
ISBN 0-440-21556-0 (pa)   LC 91-12190
Also available Thorndike Press large print edition

Cormier, Robert—*Continued*

"Four teen vandals trash a home. Into the melee steps the unsuspecting fourteen-year-old Karen Jerome. Forty-nine minutes later the invaders depart, leaving a battered Karen sprawled at the foot of the basement steps. The Jerome family is changed forever, especially Karen's sister, Jane. She falls in love with Buddy, never dreaming that he was one of the trashers." Child Book Rev Serv

"Signature Cormier, with calculated impact, sinister implications, and inevitable appeal." Bull Cent Child Books

Cottonwood, Joe

Quake! a novel. Scholastic 1995 146p $13.95; pa $3.50   **Fic**

1. Earthquakes—Fiction 2. Brothers and sisters—Fiction 3. California—Fiction

ISBN 0-590-22232-5; 0-590-22233-3 (pa)

LC 94-18193

With their parents away at the 1989 World Series, fourteen-year-old Franny, her younger brother, and their cousin try to cope with the frightening events following an earthquake that destroys their home on Loma Prieta mountain

"The experiences the youngsters have on their own and later when they are reunited with the parents are believable and vivid. The book is written in an easy style that will be appreciated by middle school readers." Book Rep

Couloumbis, Audrey

Getting near to baby. Putnam 1999 211p $17.99   **Fic**

1. Sisters—Fiction 2. Death—Fiction 3. Aunts—Fiction

ISBN 0-399-23389-X   LC 99-18191

A Newbery Medal honor book, 2000

Although thirteen-year-old Willa Jo and her Aunt Patty seem to be constantly at odds, staying with her and Uncle Hob helps Willa Jo and her younger sister come to terms with the death of their family's baby

"Couloumbis's writing is strong; she captures wonderfully the Southern voices of her characters and conveys with great depth powerful emotions. . . . A compelling novel." SLJ

Coville, Bruce

Aliens ate my homework; interior illustrations by Katherine Coville. Pocket Bks. 1993 179p il $14; pa $3.99   **Fic**

1. Science fiction 2. Extraterrestrial beings—Fiction

ISBN 0-671-87249-4; 0-671-72712-5 (pa)

LC 93-3945

"A Minstrel book"

Rod is surprised when a miniature spaceship lands in his school science project and reveals five tiny aliens, who ask his help in apprehending an interstellar criminal

"A funny and suspenseful romp, with appealing illustrations throughout." Horn Book Guide

Other available titles about Rod in the Aliens Adventures series are:

Aliens stole my body (1998)

I left my sneakers in dimension X (1994)

The search for Snout (1995)

Into the land of the unicorns. Scholastic 1994 159p (Unicorn chronicles) $12.95; pa $4.50   **Fic**

1. Unicorns—Fiction 2. Fantasy fiction

ISBN 0-590-45955-4; 0-439-10838-1 (pa)

LC 94-16892

Having jumped into the fantasy land of Luster, Cara joins Lightfoot the unicorn in the search for Queen Arabella Skydancer

"Coville weaves traditional unicorn myths into his light, accessible fantasy and provides a neatly contrived ending that hints at the next adventure." Booklist

The skull of truth; a magic shop book; illustrated by Gary A. Lippincott. Harcourt Brace & Co. 1997 195p il $17   **Fic**

1. Truthfulness and falsehood—Fiction 2. Fantasy fiction

ISBN 0-15-275457-1   LC 97-9264

Also available in paperback from Simon & Schuster

Charlie, a sixth-grader with a compulsion to tell lies, acquires a mysterious skull that forces its owner to tell only the truth, causing some awkward moments before he understands its power

"Coville has structured the story very carefully, with a great deal of sensitivity to children's thought processes and emotions. The mood shifts from scary to funny to serious are fused with understandable language and sentence structures." SLJ

Crane, Stephen, 1871-1900

The red badge of courage (7 and up)   **Fic**

1. Chancellorsville (Va.), Battle of, 1863—Fiction 2. United States—History—1861-1865, Civil War—Fiction

Hardcover and paperback editions available from various publishers

First published 1894

"An extraordinary example of psychological portraiture—subject, the state of mind of the soldier in action; the brilliant work of an inexperienced youth who studies the phenomena at second-hand. Consists virtually of one episode, the protracted battle of Chancellorsville, 1863." Baker. Guide to the Best Fic

Craven, Margaret

I heard the owl call my name. Doubleday 1973 166p o.p.; Dell paperback available $6.50 (7 and up)   **Fic**

1. Kwakiutl Indians—Fiction 2. Clergy—Fiction 3. Death—Fiction

ISBN 0-440-34369-0 (pa)

Also available in hardcover from Buccaneer Bks.

Not knowing that he has a fatal illness, a young Anglican priest is assigned to serve a parish of Kwakiutl Indians in the seacoast wilds of British Columbia. Among these vanishing Indians, Mark Brian learns enough of the meaning of life not to fear death

The author's "writing glows with delicate, fleeting images and a sense of peace. Her characters' hearts are bared by a few words—or by the fact that nothing is said at all." Christ Sci Monit

Creech, Sharon

Absolutely normal chaos. HarperCollins Pubs. 1995 c1990 230p $14.95; lib bdg $14.89; pa $4.95
Fic

1. Family life—Fiction
ISBN 0-06-026989-8; 0-06-026992-8 (lib bdg); 0-06-440632-6 (pa)   LC 95-22448
First published 1990 in the United Kingdom

"Mary Lou Finney's summer journal describes family life in a high-spirited household in Ohio that includes five children." N Y Times Book Rev

"Those in search of a light, humorous read will find it; those in search of something a little deeper will also be rewarded." SLJ

Bloomability. HarperCollins Pubs. 1998 273p $14.95; lib bdg $14.89; pa $5.95   **Fic**
1. School stories 2. Switzerland—Fiction
ISBN 0-06-026993-6; 0-06-026994-4 (lib bdg); 0-06-440823-X (pa)   LC 98-14601
"Joanna Cotler books"

When her aunt and uncle take her from New Mexico to Lugano, Switzerland, to attend an international school, thirteen-year-old Dinnie discovers her world expanding

"As if fresh, smart characters in a picturesque setting weren't engaging enough, Creech also poses an array of knotty questions, both personal and philosophical. . . . A story to stimulate both head and heart." Booklist

Chasing Redbird. HarperCollins Pubs. 1997 261p $14.95; lib bdg $15.89; pa $4.95   **Fic**
1. Family life—Fiction 2. Kentucky—Fiction
ISBN 0-06-026987-1; 0-06-026988-X (lib bdg); 0-06-440696-2 (pa)   LC 96-44128
"Joanna Cotler books"

Thirteen-year-old Zinnia Taylor uncovers family secrets and self truths while clearing a mysterious settler trail that begins on her family's farm in Kentucky

"With frequent flashbacks, the narrative makes clear the complexities of the story, while the unsolved puzzles lead the reader on to the end. The writing is laced with figurative language and folksy comments that intensify both atmosphere and emotion." Horn Book Guide

Walk two moons. HarperCollins Pubs. 1994 280p $15.95; lib bdg $15.89; pa $4.95   **Fic**
1. Death—Fiction 2. Grandparents—Fiction 3. Family life—Fiction 4. Friendship—Fiction
ISBN 0-06-023334-6; 0-06-023337-0 (lib bdg); 0-06-440517-6 (pa)   LC 93-31277
Awarded the Newbery Medal, 1995

After her mother leaves home suddenly, thirteen-year-old Sal and her grandparents take a car trip retracing her mother's route. Along the way, Sal recounts the story of her friend Phoebe, whose mother also left

"An engaging story of love and loss, told with humor and suspense. . . . A richly layered novel about real and metaphorical journeys." SLJ

Crew, Linda

Children of the river. Delacorte Press 1989 213p $14.95; pa $4.99 (7 and up)   **Fic**
1. Asian Americans—Fiction 2. Refugees—Fiction
ISBN 0-440-50122-9; 0-440-21022-4 (pa)
LC 88-20401

Having fled Cambodia four years earlier to escape the Khmer Rouge army, seventeen-year-old Sundara is torn between remaining faithful to her own people and enjoying life in her Oregon high school as a "regular" American

"Crew's characterization is excellent. . . . The plot is well-structured, allowing profound concepts to be simply and beautifully presented. . . . Crew entertains without trivializing and instructs without sermonizing." SLJ

Fire on the wind. Delacorte Press 1995 198p maps $14.95; pa $3.99   **Fic**
1. Forest fires—Fiction 2. Oregon—Fiction 3. Lumber and lumbering—Fiction
ISBN 0-385-32185-6; 0-440-21916-2 (pa)
LC 95-7092

The summer before her fourteenth birthday in 1933, a fierce forest fire rages throughout northwestern Oregon and threatens the logging camp where Storie and her family live

"An enlightening, quick read that infuses an interesting coming-of-age subplot into a larger tale of disaster and heroism." SLJ

Crichton, Michael, 1942-

Jurassic Park; a novel. Knopf 1990 399p $25 (7 and up)   **Fic**
1. Science fiction 2. Dinosaurs—Fiction 3. Genetic engineering—Fiction
ISBN 0-394-58816-9   LC 90-52960
Also available in paperback from Ballantine Bks.

This novel "tells of a modern-day scientist bringing to life a horde of prehistoric animals." N Y Times Book Rev

"Crichton is a master at blending technology with fiction. . . . Suspense, excitement, and good adventure pervade this book." SLJ

Crist-Evans, Craig

Moon over Tennessee; a boy's Civil War journal; wood engravings by Bonnie Christensen. Houghton Mifflin 1999 60p il $15   **Fic**
1. Fathers and sons—Fiction 2. Diaries—Fiction 3. United States—History—1861-1865, Civil War—Fiction
ISBN 0-395-91208-3   LC 98-11912

A thirteen-year-old boy sets off with his father from their farm in Tennessee to join the Confederate forces on their way to fight at Gettysburg. Told in the form of diary entries in free verse

An "evocative book, written with language so vibrant it begs to be read aloud." Booklist

Cross, Gillian, 1945-

The great American elephant chase. Holiday House 1993 c1992 193p $15.95   **Fic**
1. Elephants—Fiction 2. Adventure fiction
ISBN 0-8234-1016-1   LC 92-54492
First published 1992 in the United Kingdom with title: The great elephant chase

"Pursued by the villainous Hannibal Jackson, Tad and Cissie trek from Pennsylvania to Nebraska to bring Khush, a prized Indian elephant, to safety." Horn Book

Cross, Gillian, 1945-—_Continued_
Guide
"The chase is thrilling, the landscape brilliant and sprawling, the characters thoughtfully drawn; these elements alone provide uncommonly thrilling reading. But this novel offers more than mere adventure; along with rescuing the great elephant, Tad saves something just as important—his sense of self." Publ Wkly

New World. Holiday House 1995 c1994 171p
$15.95   Fic
1. Computer games—Fiction 2. Virtual reality—Fiction
ISBN 0-8234-1166-4   LC 94-29448
Also available in paperback from Penguin Bks.
First published 1994 in the United Kingdom
"Miriam and Stuart, both 14, have been chosen to participate in secret trials of a breakthrough virtual-reality game called New World. Will a third teen who is trying separately to hack into the game and discover its secrets before it goes on the market. Excitement gradually turns into terror as Miriam and Stuart realize that New World involves their innermost fears. . . . This is a cleverly plotted, suspenseful mystery." SLJ

Crutcher, Chris, 1946-
The Crazy Horse Electric game. Greenwillow
Bks. 1987 215p $14 (7 and up)   Fic
1. Handicapped—Fiction 2. Runaway children—Fiction
ISBN 0-688-06683-6   LC 86-14592
Also available in paperback from Dell
"Willie, a sixteen-year-old from a Montana town, is a star athlete until a freak accident causes brain damage. Unable to watch himself and his family deteriorate because of it, Willie runs away, ending up in Oakland, CA. With the help of the phys ed teacher at One More Last Chance High School, a black pimp friend, and other street people, Willie begins to put his life and body back together again." Child Book Rev Serv
"Although sometimes marred by plot problems—the details about the pimp and his prostitute seem quite unnecessary—the book magnificently portrays the thoughts and feelings of a crippled athlete and is a testimony to the indomitability of the human spirit." Horn Book

Ironman; a novel. Greenwillow Bks. 1995 181p
$16 (7 and up)   Fic
1. Fathers and sons—Fiction 2. School stories
3. Triathlon—Fiction
ISBN 0-688-13503-X   LC 94-1657
Also available in paperback from Dell
While training for a triathlon, seventeen-year-old Bo attends Mr. Nak's anger management group at school which leads him to examine his relationship with his father
"Through Crutcher's masterful character development, readers will believe in Bo, empathize with the other members of the anger-management group, absorb the wisdom of Mr. Nak and despise, yet at times pity, the boy's father. This is not a light read, as many serious issues surface, though the author's trademark dark humor (and colorful use of street language) is abundant." SLJ

Running loose. Greenwillow Bks. 1983 190p
$17.95 (7 and up)   Fic
1. School stories
ISBN 0-688-02002-X   LC 82-20935
Also available in paperback from Dell
"Louie Banks tells what happened to him in his senior year in a small town Idaho high school. Besides falling in love with Becky and losing her in a senseless accident, Louie takes a stand against the coach when he sets the team up to injure a black player on an opposing team, and learns that you can't be honorable with dishonorable men." Voice Youth Advocates
"This is a story of honor and principles, messages that are achieved without preaching. An unusually fine first novel." Bull Cent Child Books

Staying fat for Sarah Byrnes. Greenwillow Bks.
1993 216p $16   Fic
1. Obesity—Fiction 2. Child abuse—Fiction
3. Friendship—Fiction
ISBN 0-688-11552-7   LC 91-40097
Also available Thorndike Press large print edition and in paperback from Dell
"An obese boy and a disfigured girl suffer the emotional scars of years of mockery at the hands of their peers. They share a hard-boiled view of the world until events in their senior year hurl them in very different directions. A story about a friendship with staying power, written with pathos and pointed humor." SLJ

Stotan! Greenwillow Bks. 1986 183p lib bdg
$16 (7 and up)   Fic
1. Swimming—Fiction 2. School stories
ISBN 0-688-05715-2   LC 85-12712
Also available in paperback from Dell
A high school coach invites members of his swimming team to a memorable week of rigorous training that tests their moral fiber as well as their physical stamina
"A subplot involving the boys' fight against local Neo-Nazi activists provides some immediate action, while the various characters' conflicts tighten the middle and ending. The pace lags through the story's introductions; nevertheless, this is a searching sports novel, with a tone varying from macho-tough to sensitive." Bull Cent Child Books

Curry, Jane Louise, 1932-
Dark Shade. Margaret K. McElderry Bks. 1998
168p $16 (7 and up)   Fic
1. Space and time—Fiction 2. Delaware Indians—Fiction 3. Pennsylvania—Fiction
ISBN 0-689-81812-2   LC 97-30238
Sixteen-year-old Maggie attempts to save recently orphaned Kip from permanently going back in time to 1758 as an adopted Lenape in the primeval forests of western Pennsylvania
"Skillfully weaving history, time travel, and a hint of romance, Curry creates a page-turner with lots to explore." Booklist

Curtis, Christopher Paul
Bud, not Buddy. Delacorte Press 1999 245p
$15.95   Fic
1. Orphans—Fiction 2. African Americans—Fiction
3. Great Depression, 1929-1939—Fiction
ISBN 0-385-32306-9   LC 99-10614

Curtis, Christopher Paul—*Continued*

Awarded the Newbery Medal, 2000; Coretta Scott King Award for text, 2000

Ten-year-old Bud, a motherless boy living in Flint, Michigan, during the Great Depression, escapes a bad foster home and sets out in search of the man he believes to be his father—the renowned bandleader, H. E. Calloway of Grand Rapids

"Curtis says in a afterword that some of the characters are based on real people, including his own grandfathers, so it's not surprising that the rich blend of tall tale, slapstick, sorrow, and sweetness has the wry, teasing warmth of family folklore." Booklist

The Watsons go to Birmingham—1963; a novel. Delacorte Press 1995 210p $15.95; pa $5.50   **Fic**
1. African Americans—Fiction 2. Family life—Fiction 3. Prejudices—Fiction
ISBN 0-385-32175-9; 0-440-41412-1 (pa)
                   LC 95-7091

A Newbery Medal honor book, 1996

The ordinary interactions and everyday routines of the Watsons, an African American family living in Flint, Michigan, are drastically changed after they go to visit Grandma in Alabama in the summer of 1963

"Curtis's ability to switch from fun and funky to pinpoint-accurate psychological imagery works unusually well. . . . Ribald humor, sly sibling digs, and a totally believable child's view of the world will make this book an instant hit." SLJ

Cushman, Karen

The ballad of Lucy Whipple. Clarion Bks. 1996 195p $15   **Fic**
1. Frontier and pioneer life—Fiction 2. Family life—Fiction 3. California—Gold discoveries—Fiction
ISBN 0-395-72806-1   LC 95-45257
Also available in paperback from HarperCollins

In 1849, twelve-year-old California Morning Whipple, who renames herself Lucy, is distraught when her mother moves the family from Massachusetts to a rough California mining town

"Cushman's heroine is a delightful character, and the historical setting is authentically portrayed." SLJ

Catherine, called Birdy. Clarion Bks. 1994 169p $14.95   **Fic**
1. Middle Ages—Fiction 2. Great Britain—Fiction
ISBN 0-395-68186-3   LC 93-23333
Also available in paperback from HarperCollins

A Newbery Medal honor book, 1995

The fourteen-year-old daughter of an English country knight keeps a journal in which she records the events of her life, particularly her longing for adventures beyond the usual role of women and her efforts to avoid being married off

"In the process of telling the routines of her young life, Birdy lays before readers a feast of details about medieval England. . . . Superb historical fiction." SLJ

The midwife's apprentice. Clarion Bks. 1995 122p $10.95   **Fic**
1. Middle Ages—Fiction 2. Midwives—Fiction 3. Great Britain—Fiction
ISBN 0-395-69229-6   LC 94-13792
Also available in paperback from HarperCollins

Awarded the Newbery Medal, 1996

In medieval England, a nameless, homeless girl is taken in by a sharp-tempered midwife, and in spite of obstacles and hardship, eventually gains the three things she most wants: a full belly, a contented heart, and a place in this world

"Earthy humor, the foibles of humans both high and low, and a fascinating mix of superstition and genuinely helpful herbal remedies attached to childbirth make this a truly delightful introduction to a world seldom seen in children's literature." SLJ

Danziger, Paula, 1944-

The cat ate my gymsuit. Delacorte Press 1974 147p o.p.; Putnam Pub. Group paperback available $3.99   **Fic**
1. School stories 2. Teachers—Fiction
ISBN 0-698-11684-4 (pa)

Marcy Lewis is bored by school and tyrannized by her father. With the help of an unconventional teacher, she conquers many of her feelings of insecurity and, in turn, rallies the student body in support of the teacher who was fired because of her behavior

"A sad-funny novel. . . . Ms. Danziger has an attractive style; her prose sparkles with wit and originality." Publ Wkly

Followed by There's a bat in bunk five

The Divorce Express. Delacorte Press 1982 148p il o.p.; Putnam Pub. Group paperback available $3.99   **Fic**
1. Divorce—Fiction 2. Parent and child—Fiction
ISBN 0-698-11685-2 (pa)   LC 82-70318

The protagonist, fourteen year old Phoebe, shuttles "back and forth between her father's home in Woodstock and her mother's apartment in Manhattan via the bus she calls 'The Divorce Express' because there are so many children like her who ride it. She has not become adjusted to the man her mother is planning to marry, and feels more and more at home in Woodstock, especially when she makes a new friend, Rosie, whose parents . . . are also divorced." Bull Cent Child Books

This is "a warm, tender book for adolescents who must deal with the complexities of growing up." Child Book Rev Serv

P.S. Longer letter later; [by] Paula Danziger & Ann M. Martin. Scholastic 1998 234p $15.95; pa $4.99   **Fic**
1. Friendship—Fiction 2. Letters—Fiction
ISBN 0-590-21310-5; 0-590-21311-3 (pa)
                 LC 97-19120

Twelve-year-old best friends Elizabeth and Tara-Starr continue their friendship through letter-writing after Tara-Starr's family moves to another state

"The authenticity of the well-drawn characters gives life and vitality to the story. . . . Readers will thoroughly enjoy this fast-paced read." SLJ

The pistachio prescription; a novel. Delacorte Press 1978 154p o.p.; Putnam Pub. Group paperback available $3.99   **Fic**
1. Family life—Fiction 2. School stories
ISBN 0-698-11690-9 (pa)   LC 77-86330

Danziger, Paula, 1944-—_Continued_

"Thirteen-year-old Cassie, who tells the story, has asthma, is a hypochondriac, and eats pistachio nuts compulsively when anything goes wrong. And almost everything does, she thinks. But Cassie's elected president of the freshman class, she acquires Bernie, she has the stalwart support of her friend Vickie, who won't let Cassie retreat into coddling fears, and she manages to cope with a nagging mother, parental quarrels, and a hostile, competitive sister. . . . The characterization and dialogue are strong, the relationships depicted with perception, and the writing style vigorous." Bull Cent Child Books

There's a bat in bunk five. Delacorte Press 1980 150p il o.p.; Putnam Pub. Group paperback available $3.99 **Fic**
1. Camps—Fiction
ISBN 0-698-11687-5 (pa) LC 80-15581

"A thinner Marcy than appeared in 'The Cat Ate My Gymsuit' here eagerly accepts an invitation from Ms. Finney, her favorite teacher, to work as a counselor-in-training at a summer camp. Though wanting to do a good job, particularly in reaching the abrasive and uncooperative Ginger, Marcy also indulges in a romance with fellow camper Ted and spends time sorting out her own inner conflicts." Booklist

"In some ways this is the usual camping story of pranks, bunkmates, adjustment to separation from parents, etc. This doesn't, however, follow a formula plot; it has depth in the relationships and characterizations; and it's written with vigor and humor." Bull Cent Child Books

Deaver, Julie Reece

Chicago blues. HarperCollins Pubs. 1995 170p $14.95 (7 and up) **Fic**
1. Sisters—Fiction 2. Mothers and daughters—Fiction 3. Alcoholism—Fiction
ISBN 0-06-024675-8 LC 94-38195

Lissa, a seventeen-year-old art student living on her own in Chicago, must raise her eleven-year-old sister when their alcoholic mother becomes incapable of caring for her

"This is an unusual story that will be a hit with a wide variety of readers." Voice Youth Advocates

Say goodnight, Gracie. Harper & Row 1988 214p $15; pa $4.95 (7 and up) **Fic**
1. Death—Fiction 2. Friendship—Fiction 3. Actors—Fiction 4. Chicago (Ill.)—Fiction
ISBN 0-06-021418-X; 0-06-447004-5 (pa) LC 87-45278

"A Charlotte Zolotow book"

When a car accident kills her best friend Jimmy, with whom she has shared everything from childhood escapades to breaking into the professional theater scene in Chicago, seventeen-year-old Morgan must find her own way of coping with his death

"This is impressive in style (particularly dialogue) and narrative flow; while the pace is uneven and the focus narrow, the characters are strongly drawn and the protagonist is convincing and sympathetic." Bull Cent Child Books

DeClements, Barthe, 1920-

6th grade can really kill you. Viking Kestrel 1985 146p hardcover o.p. paperback available $3.99 **Fic**
1. Learning disabilities—Fiction
ISBN 0-14-037130-3 (pa) LC 85-40382

"Helen dreads the first day in sixth grade. Good in math and gifted on the pitcher's mound, she is a nonreader diagnosed as a behavior problem. Against the slice-of-life background of a skating party, pierced ears and overnights at friend Louise's, Helen loses the battle with the printed word." SLJ

This is "a story that amply compensates for its uneven pace by the natural quality of the relationships and the dialogue in the classroom environment and by the insight gained through the first person treatment of a learning disability." Bull Cent Child Books

Liar, liar. Marshall Cavendish 1998 144p $14.95 **Fic**
1. Truthfulness and falsehood—Fiction 2. School stories 3. Friendship—Fiction
ISBN 0-7614-5021-1 LC 97-17716

Sixth-grader Gretchen and her friends begin to have problems when a new girl starts telling some very believable, but untrue, stories

"DeClements knows this world well, and her readers will recognize it as their own." Horn Book Guide

DeFelice, Cynthia C.

The apprenticeship of Lucas Whitaker; [by] Cynthia DeFelice. Farrar, Straus & Giroux 1996 151p $15 **Fic**
1. Apprentices—Fiction 2. Orphans—Fiction 3. Physicians—Fiction
ISBN 0-374-34669-0 LC 95-26728

Also available in paperback from Avon Bks.

"Orphaned Lucas Whitaker has lost all his family to consumption, the scourge of the mid-nineteenth century. His grief leads him away from the family's marginal hill farm, and he stumbles into an apprenticeship with Doc Beecher, a rare college-trained physician. The pace of this fine piece of historical fiction is brisk in spite of a wealth of detail that not only establishes the setting but exposes beliefs and attitudes of the day regarding health, hygiene, and witchcraft." Horn Book

The ghost of Fossil Glen; [by] Cynthia DeFelice. Farrar, Straus & Giroux 1998 167p $16 **Fic**
1. Ghost stories
ISBN 0-374-31787-9 LC 97-33230

Also available in paperback from Avon Bks.

"Sixth-grader Allie Nichols encounters the ghost of Lucy Stiles and becomes involved with Lucy's unsolved death, eventually finding proof that Lucy was murdered." Horn Book Guide

"A supernatural cliff-hanger with breathless chases and riveting suspense." SLJ

Lostman's River; [by] Cynthia DeFelice. Macmillan 1994 160p $15 **Fic**
1. Environmental protection—Fiction 2. Everglades (Fla.)—Fiction
ISBN 0-02-726466-1 LC 93-40857

DeFelice, Cynthia C.—*Continued*

Also available in paperback from Avon Bks.

In the early 1900s, thirteen-year-old Tyler encounters vicious hunters whose actions threaten to destroy the Everglades ecosystem, and as a result joins the battle to protect that fragile environment

"This well-constructed novel has several elements going for it: an appealing cover; a believable story line; and a likable, gritty protagonist. The author has provided a vivid sense of place, and there is gripping action." Voice Youth Advocates

Nowhere to call home; [by] Cynthia DeFelice. Farrar, Straus & Giroux 1999 199p $16   **Fic**
1. Great Depression, 1929-1939—Fiction 2. Orphans—Fiction 3. Tramps—Fiction
ISBN 0-374-35552-5   LC 98-36602

When her father kills himself after losing his money in the stock market crash, twelve-year-old Frances, now a penniless orphan, decides to hop aboard a freight train and live the life of a hobo

"The dialogue rings true, and the fast pace of the narrative will keep readers turning pages until the poignant resolution." Voice Youth Advocates

Defoe, Daniel, 1661?-1731

Robinson Crusoe (7 and up)   **Fic**
1. Survival after airplane accidents, shipwrecks, etc.—Fiction

Hardcover and paperback editions available from various publishers

First published 1719

"A minutely circumstantial account of the hero's shipwreck and escape to an uninhabited island, and the methodical industry whereby he makes himself a comfortable home. The story is founded on the actual experiences of Alexander Selkirk, who spent four years on the island of Juan Fernandez in the early 18th century." Lenrow. Reader's Guide to Prose Fic

A "world-famous tale of adventure. . . . The simplicity of style, and the realistic atmosphere which pervades the narrative, have caused the popularity of this book to remain unimpaired." Keller. Reader's Dig of Books

Denenberg, Barry

When will this cruel war be over? the Civil War diary of Emma Simpson. Scholastic 1996 156p il maps (Dear America) $9.95   **Fic**
1. United States—History—1861-1865, Civil War—Fiction
ISBN 0-590-22862-5   LC 95-25540

The diary of a fictional fourteen-year-old girl living in Virginia, in which she describes the hardships endured by her family and friends during one year of the Civil War

"The book is filled with kindling for class discussion. . . . It is both informative and a good read." Voice Youth Advocates

Dessen, Sarah

Someone like you. Viking 1998 281p $15.99 (7 and up)   **Fic**
1. Pregnancy—Fiction 2. Unmarried mothers—Fiction 3. Friendship—Fiction
ISBN 0-670-87778-6   LC 97-36437

Halley's junior year of high school includes the death of her best friend Scarlett's boyfriend, the discovery that Scarlett is pregnant, and Halley's own first serious relationship

"Sparkling dialogue and incisive characterization illuminate this special novel." SLJ

That summer. Orchard Bks. 1996 198p $17.99; lib bdg $16.95 (7 and up)   **Fic**
1. Sisters—Fiction 2. Weddings—Fiction
ISBN 0-531-09538-X; 0-531-08888-X (lib bdg)
     LC 96-7643

Also available in paperback from Puffin Bks.

During the summer of her divorced father's remarriage and her sister's wedding, fifteen-year-old Haven comes into her own by letting go of the myths of the past

"Dessen writes in a fresh, unselfconscious style. . . . This is a wise book about growing up that won't give readers the feeling that they are being preached at." Horn Book Guide

Deuker, Carl, 1950-

Heart of a champion. Little, Brown 1993 199p o.p.; Avon Bks. paperback available $4.50 (7 and up)   **Fic**
1. Baseball—Fiction   2. Friendship—Fiction 3. Death—Fiction 4. Fathers and sons—Fiction
ISBN 0-380-72269-0 (pa)   LC 92-37231

"Joy Street books"

"Baseball has been the basis for Seth and Jimmy's friendship, from their first meeting on a practice field when they were 12 through their time together in summer leagues and on high school teams. Jimmy taught Seth how to play the game, encouraged him to excel, pushed him to his limits, and taught him to love the sport. The game also bridged the problems and differences in their lives: Seth's father's death, Jimmy's father's alcoholism and Jimmy's own drinking problem." Booklist

This is a "heartbreakingly beautiful book; it is everything that art should be: it instructs, communicates a human condition, and elicits emotion." Voice Youth Advocates

On the Devil's court. Little, Brown 1988 252p o.p.; Avon Bks. paperback available $4.50 (7 and up)   **Fic**
1. Basketball—Fiction
ISBN 0-380-70879-5 (pa)   LC 88-13432

"Joy Street books"

Struggling with his feelings of inadequacy and his failure to make the basketball team in his new school, seventeen-year-old Joe Faust finds himself willing to trade his soul for one perfect season of basketball

"This is a rare sports novel, with complex plot and characterization as well as gripping game play." Bull Cent Child Books

Painting the black. Houghton Mifflin 1997 248p $14.95 (7 and up)   **Fic**
1. Baseball—Fiction 2. School stories
ISBN 0-395-82848-1   LC 96-23763

Also available in paperback from Avon Bks.

Deuker, Carl, 1950——*Continued*

"After a disastrous fall from a tree, senior Ryan Ward wrote off baseball. But he is swept back into the game when cocky, charismatic Josh Daniels—a star quarterback with the perfect spiral pass as well as a pitcher with a mean slider—moves into the neighborhood. . . . The well-written sports scenes—baseball and football—will draw reluctant readers, but it is Ryan's moral courage that will linger when the reading is done." Booklist

Dexter, Catherine

Alien game. Morrow Junior Bks. 1995 204p hardcover o.p. paperback available $4.95   **Fic**
1. Extraterrestrial beings—Fiction 2. School stories 3. Science fiction
ISBN 0-688-15290-2 (pa)   LC 94-33240
As the students at her school become increasingly caught up in the annual game of Elimination, Zoe grows more and more convinced that the new girl in her eighth grade class is not what she seems
"This tale of an alien being and the eventual thwarting of her evil plan is told with increasing drama, drawing the reader to a heart-racing conclusion." Horn Book

Dickens, Charles, 1812-1870

A Christmas carol (7 and up)   **Fic**
1. Christmas—Fiction 2. Ghost stories 3. Great Britain—Fiction

Hardcover and paperback editions available from various publishers
Written in 1843
"This Christmas story of nineteenth century England has delighted young and old for generations. In it, a miser, Scrooge, through a series of dreams, finds the true Christmas spirit." Haydn. Thesaurus of Book Dig
"There is perhaps no story in English literature better known and loved, or one that carries a more potent appeal to the Christmas sentiment." Springfield Repub

Oliver Twist (7 and up)   **Fic**
1. Great Britain—Fiction

Hardcover and paperback editions available from various publishers
First published 1837-1838
"A boy from an English workhouse falls into the hands of rogues who train him to be a pickpocket. The story of his struggles to escape from an environment of crime is one of hardship, danger and the severe obstacles overcome." Natl Counc of Teachers of Engl

Dickinson, Peter, 1927-

AK. Delacorte Press 1992 c1990 229p hardcover o.p. paperback available $3.99 (7 and up)   **Fic**
1. Africa—Fiction
ISBN 0-440-21897-7 (pa)   LC 91-25628
Also available in paperback from Dell
First published 1990 in the United Kingdom
When a military coup occurs in the constantly war-torn African country of Nagala, teenage Paul is forced to flee into the open countryside to avoid enemy soldiers who seek his life
"This exceedingly ambitious novel succeeds at everything it attempts. . . . It is a thorough examination of the nature of both democracy and war; it explores the legacy of imperialism; and it provides the reader with an exceptionally vivid picture of an African country and a handful of memorable citizens. . . . But best of all, AK is a simply rip-roaring adventure story." Publ Wkly

A bone from a dry sea. Delacorte Press 1993 199p hardcover o.p. paperback available $4.99 (7 and up)   **Fic**
1. Fossil hominids—Fiction 2. Fossils—Fiction
ISBN 0-440-21928-0 (pa)   LC 92-20491
Also available Thorndike Press large print edition
"Li, a female child in a tribe of 'sea-apes' living some four million years ago, and Vinny, teenage daughter of a modern-day paleontologist, are the protagonists of alternating third-person stories, one extrapolating what life might have been like for an intelligent youngster in prehistoric times and the other demonstrating the difficulty of interpreting ancient shards." Booklist
"Basing his account of Li's people on an intriguing recent theory that we evolved from a semi-aquatic, ape-like mammal, the author brilliantly suggests how we might have started along the road to what we are today." SLJ

Eva. Delacorte Press 1989 219p hardcover o.p. paperback available $4.99 (7 and up)   **Fic**
1. Chimpanzees—Fiction 2. Science fiction
ISBN 0-440-20766-5 (pa)   LC 88-29435
"Eva wakes up from a deep coma that was the result of a terrible car accident and finds herself drastically altered. The accident leaves her so badly injured that her parents consent to a radical experiment to transplant her brain and memory into the body of a research chimpanzee. With the aid of a computer for communication, Eva slowly adjusts to her new existence while scientists monitor her progress, feelings, and insight into the animal world." Voice Youth Advocates
"Raising ethical and moral questions, Dickinson creates a vision both profound and chilling." SLJ

Shadow of a hero. Delacorte Press 1994 294p hardcover o.p. paperback available $3.99 (7 and up)   **Fic**
1. Grandfathers—Fiction 2. Eastern Europe—Fiction
ISBN 0-440-21963-9 (pa)   LC 94-8667
"Letta's grandfather, Restaur Vax, lives in the shadow of a legendary hero, his great-grandfather of the same name. Soon, Letta is in the shadow, also, as she learns that her grandfather is a hero to the people of Varina, a tiny country that has always struggled for autonomy. In exile in England, Letta's grandfather is fighting the same battle his ancestors had fought two centuries before." Book Rep
The author "creates a believable country and cause in Varina. . . . The not-unexpected but bittersweet conclusion is realistic, and Dickinson's device of alternating chapters of contemporary narrative with Varinian legend is brilliant. A tour de force of a novel, perhaps not to every reader's taste, but intelligent, complex, and as up-to-date as today's headlines." Horn Book

Dickinson, Peter, 1927——*Continued*

Suth's story. Grosset & Dunlap 1998 211p
$14.99; pa $3.99   **Fic**
1. Prehistoric peoples—Fiction 2. Orphans—Fiction
ISBN 0-399-23327-X; 0-448-41709-X (pa)
     LC 98-14226

"Suth and Noli are children belonging to the Kin, a
two-hundred-thousand-year-old human society. When
their group of Kin abandons four recently orphaned
young children, Suth and Noli decide to go back and rescue them." Horn Book Guide

"Dickinson develops distinct personalities and inner
conflicts in each of his characters. . . . Less a self-
contained story than an intriguing lead-in, this novel will
prepare middle readers for the subsequent adventures of
a young but resourceful band in a world 200 millennia
agone." SLJ

Other available titles about the Kin are:
Mana's story (1999)
Noli's story (1998)
Po's story (1998)

Dorris, Michael

Guests. Hyperion Bks. for Children 1994 119p
$13.45; pa $4.50   **Fic**
1. Algonquian Indians—Fiction 2. America—Exploration—Fiction
ISBN 0-7868-0047-X; 0-7868-1108-0 (pa)
     LC 94-26057

Moss and Trouble, an Algonquin boy and girl, struggle with the problems of growing up in the Massachusetts area during the time of the first Thanksgiving

"Dorris's writing is elegant, full of evocative images
and lush metaphors. He develops his intriguing characters
in a leisurely way." SLJ

Morning Girl. Hyperion Bks. for Children 1992
74p $12.45; pa $3.95   **Fic**
1. Taino Indians—Fiction 2. Brothers and sisters—
Fiction 3. America—Exploration—Fiction
ISBN 1-56282-284-5; 1-56282-661-1 (pa)
     LC 92-52989

Also available Spanish language edition

Twelve year old Morning Girl, a Taino Indian who
loves the day, and her younger brother Star Boy, who
loves the night, take turns describing their life on a Ba-
hamian island in 1492; in Morning Girl's last narrative,
she witnesses the arrival of the first Europeans to her
world

"The author uses a lyrical, yet easy-to-follow, style to
place these compelling characters in historical context.
. . . Dorris does a superb job of showing that family dynamics are complicated, regardless of time and place."
Horn Book

Sees Behind Trees. Hyperion Bks. for Children
1996 104p $14.95; lib bdg $15.49; pa $4.95 **Fic**
1. Indians of North America—Fiction 2. Vision disorders—Fiction
ISBN 0-7868-0224-3; 0-7868-2215-5 (lib bdg);
0-7868-1252-4 (pa)   LC 96-15859

"For the partially sighted Walnut, it is impossible to
prove his right to a grown-up name by hitting a target
with his bow and arrow. With his highly developed
senses, however, he demonstrates that he can do something even better: he can see 'what cannot be seen,'
which earns him the name Sees Behind Trees. . . . Set
in sixteenth-century America, this richly imagined and
gorgeously written rite-of-passage story has the gravity
of legend. Moreover, it has buoyant humor and the immediacy of a compelling story that is peopled with multidimensional characters." Booklist

The window. Hyperion 1997 106p $16.45; lib
bdg $17.49; pa $4.99   **Fic**
1. Family life—Fiction 2. Interracial marriage—Fiction 3. Racially mixed people—Fiction
ISBN 0-7868-0301-0; 0-7868-2240-6 (lib bdg);
0-7868-1373-3 (pa)   LC 97-2822

When Rayona's Native American mother enters an alcoholic treatment facility, her estranged father, a Black
man, finally introduces her to his side of the family, who
are not at all what she expected

"Rayona, the heroine of Dorris' adult novels *Yellow
Raft in Blue Water* and *Cloud Chamber*, is eleven years
old in this prequel. . . . Rayona is beautifully realized,
her emotional complexity combining with her self-
awareness and generosity of heart to make her a three-
dimensional character that reaches out from the page."
Bull Cent Child Books

Draanen, Wendelin van

Sammy Keyes and the hotel thief. Knopf 1998
163p il $15; lib bdg $16.99; pa $4.99   **Fic**
1. Mystery fiction
ISBN 0-679-88839-X; 0-679-98839-4 (lib bdg);
0-679-89264-8 (pa)   LC 97-40776

Thirteen-year-old Sammy's penchant for speaking her
mind gets her in trouble when she involves herself in the
investigation of a robbery at the "seedy" hotel across the
street from the seniors' building where she is living with
her grandmother

"This is a breezy novel with vivid characters." Bull
Cent Child Books

Other available titles about Sammy Keyes are:
Sammy Keyes and the curse of Moustache Mary (2000)
Sammy Keyes and the runaway elf (1999)
Sammy Keyes and the Sisters of Mercy (1999)
Sammy Keyes and the skeleton man (1998)

Draper, Sharon M. (Sharon Mills)

Forged by fire. Atheneum Bks. for Young
Readers 1997 151p $16; pa $3.99 (7 and up)
     Fic
1. Child abuse—Fiction 2. Brothers and sisters—Fiction 3. African Americans—Fiction
ISBN 0-689-80699-X; 0-689-81851-3 (pa)
     LC 96-2763

Companion volume to Tears of a tiger

Teenage Gerald, who has spent years protecting his
fragile half-sister from their abusive father, faces the
prospect of one final confrontation before the problem
can be solved

"What started out as an award-winning short story in
Ebony magazine was expanded into this sad but inspirational story. . . . With non-stop excitement, this is well-
written, easy to read, and possibly an inspiration for anyone trapped in family situations involving child abuse or
domestic violence." Voice Youth Advocates

Draper, Sharon M. (Sharon Mills)—*Continued*
Tears of a tiger. Atheneum Pubs. 1994 162p
$16; pa $3.95 (7 and up)   **Fic**
1. Death—Fiction 2. African Americans—Fiction
3. Suicide—Fiction
ISBN 0-689-31878-2; 0-689-80698-1 (pa)
LC 94-10278
The death of African American high school basketball
star Rob Washington in a drunk driving accident leads to
the suicide of his friend Andy, who was driving the car
"The story emerges through newspaper articles, journal entries, homework assignments, letters, and conversations that give the book immediacy; the teenage conversational idiom is contemporary and well written. Andy's
perceptions of the racism directed toward young black
males . . . will be recognized by African American
YAs." Booklist

Drucker, Malka, 1945-
Jacob's rescue; a Holocaust story; by Malka
Drucker and Michael Halperin. Bantam Bks. 1993
117p il $15.95; pa $4.50   **Fic**
1. Holocaust, 1933-1945—Fiction 2. Poland—Fiction
3. Jews—Poland—Fiction
ISBN 0-385-32519-3; 0-440-40965-9 (pa)
LC 92-30523
"At her family's traditional Passover seder in Israel,
eight-year-old Marissa hears the story of her father Jacob
and her Uncle David's experiences as children in Warsaw during the Holocaust. Alex and Mela hide the boys
in their home. After the war, the authorities insist that
Jacob and David must leave the people they now regard
as their parents, and it is sixteen years before the boys
locate them again. A heartening novel, based on a true
story, of great courage in the midst of the madness of
war." Horn Book Guide

Duane, Diane, 1952-
A wizard abroad. Harcourt Brace & Co. 1997
342p $15; pa $6   **Fic**
1. Fantasy fiction 2. Ireland—Fiction
ISBN 0-15-201209-5; 0-15-201207-9 (pa)
LC 96-45406
Sent on vacation to her aunt's home in Ireland,
teenage wizard Nita becomes entangled in a magic battle
to save the country from the ghosts of its past
"Moving easily between light, everyday language and
the sonorous formality of high fantasy, Duane seamlessly
interweaves encounters with creatures from legend with
glimpses of modern Irish life and teen culture. . . . An
unusually consistent fantasy, rich in details, subplots, and
Irish lore." SLJ
Other available titles about Nita are:
Deep wizardry (1996)
High wizardry (1997)
So you want to be a wizard (1996)

Dumas, Alexandre, 1802-1870
The three musketeers (7 and up)   **Fic**
1. France—History—1589-1789, Bourbons—Fiction

Hardcover and paperback editions available from various publishers
Original French edition, 1844

"D'Artagnan arrives in Paris one day in 1625 and
manages to be involved in three duels with three musketeers . . . Athos, Porthos and Aramis. They become
d'Artagnan's best friends. The account of their adventures from 1625 on develops against the rich historical
background of the reign of Louis XIII and the early part
of that of Louis XIV, the main plot being furnished by
the antagonism between Cardinal de Richelieu and
Queen Anne d'Autriche." Haydn. Thesaurus of Book Dig

Duncan, Lois, 1934-
Don't look behind you. Delacorte Press 1989
180p hardcover o.p. paperback available $4.99 (7
and up)   **Fic**
1. Mystery fiction
ISBN 0-440-20729-0 (pa)   LC 88-30045
Seventeen-year-old April finds her comfortable life
changed forever when death threats to her father, a witness in a federal case, force her family to go into hiding
under assumed names and flee the pursuit of a hired killer
"Though April's petulance may grate, her behavior
rings true enough, and teens who relish the trappings of
thrillers can immerse themselves in FBI agents, murder,
and secrets galore." Booklist

I know what you did last summer. Little, Brown
1973 199p o.p.; Dell paperback available $4.99 (7
and up)   **Fic**
1. Mystery fiction
ISBN 0-440-22844-1 (pa)   LC 73-8829
"Julie, Barry, Helen, and Ray have almost made themselves forget the terrible night when their joyriding had
ended in tragedy. Barry hit and killed a young cyclist on
the road and kept on going; they all swear to keep the
accident a secret. A year passes and they all believe they
are safe, but one day Julie gets a note in the mail which
says, 'I know what you did last summer.' Barry is shot
and lying paralyzed in the hospital when Helen is attacked and their silent menace goes about completing his
scheme to exact revenge." Publ Wkly
This book "has vivid characterization, good balance,
and the boding sense of impending danger that adds excitement to the best mystery stories." Bull Cent Child
Books

Killing Mr. Griffin. Little, Brown 1978 243p
o.p.; Dell paperback available $4.99 (7 and up)
Fic
1. School stories 2. Kidnapping—Fiction
ISBN 0-440-94515-1 (pa)   LC 77-27658
"Mr. Griffin, the stern high-school English teacher, is
loathed by those who should appreciate his determination
to educate them. Mark, a student, uses his cool glamour
and cleverness to mesmerize classmates Jeff, David,
Betsy and Sue, persuading them to kidnap Mr. Griffin,
with the idea of scaring the teacher into handing out high
grades for inferior work. They leave the man trussed and
gagged in a remote spot, where he dies. Sue wants to go
to the police with a confession, but Mark masterminds a
frantic coverup." Publ Wkly
The author's "skillful plotting builds layers of tension
that draws readers into the eye of the conflict. The ending is nicely handled in a manner which provides relief
without removing any of the chilling implications." SLJ

Duncan, Lois, 1934-—*Continued*

Locked in time. Little, Brown 1985 210p o.p.;
Dell paperback available $4.99 (7 and up)   **Fic**
1. Mystery fiction 2. Louisiana—Fiction
ISBN 0-440-94942-4 (pa)   LC 85-23

"Shortly after arriving at her strangely youthful step-
mother's isolated Louisiana mansion, Nore realizes that
Lisette and her two children—handsome, 17-year-old
Gabe and moody 13-year-old Josie—hide a sinister,
century-old secret, a secret that threatens the lives of
Nore and her infatuated father." Booklist

"The writing style is smooth, the characters strongly
developed, and the plot, which has excellent pace and
momentum, is an adroit blending of fantasy and realism."
Bull Cent Child Books

Stranger with my face. Little, Brown 1981 250p
o.p.; Dell paperback available $4.99 (7 and up)
                                            Fic
1. Supernatural—Fiction 2. Twins—Fiction
ISBN 0-440-98356-8 (pa)   LC 81-8299

"There are small things, at first—a face in the mirror,
a presence in an empty room, a beckoning figure on
treacherous rocks—that portend 17-year-old Laurie's confrontation with the astral projection of her previously unknown, malevolent identical twin. . . . The jealous twin,
Lia, pursues her, prodding her to explore astral projection
so that Lia may enter Laurie's body." SLJ

"The ghostly Lia is deliciously evil; the idea of astral
projection—Lia's method of travel—is novel; the island
setting is vivid; and the relationships among the young
people are realistic in the smoothly written supernatural
tale." Horn Book

Summer of fear. Little, Brown 1976 217p o.p.;
Dell paperback available $4.99 (7 and up)   **Fic**
1. Witchcraft—Fiction
ISBN 0-440-98324-X (pa)

"When Rachel's orphaned cousin comes to live with
the Bryants, 17-year-old Julia, whom the family had never seen before, charms everybody: Rachel's parents, her
brothers, her best friend, and worst of all, her steady
boyfriend. . . . Mysteriously, Rachel's little dog sickens
and dies after biting Julia; and on the day of a dance Rachel inexplicably comes down with a case of hives that
leaves her housebound and lets Julia borrow her cousin's
new dress. Sweet, lovely Julia, it turns out, is a witch:
how Rachel finally uncovers the truth and saves her family from the ruthless sorceress makes for a sensational
climax." SLJ

The third eye. Little, Brown 1984 220p $15.95
(7 and up)   **Fic**
1. Extrasensory perception—Fiction
ISBN 0-316-19553-7   LC 83-26777
Also available in paperback from Dell

"Despite her mother's efforts to persuade her otherwise, Karen Connors knows she's different, but she
doesn't understand how until she discovers, by chance,
that she has psychic talent—in particular, the intuitive
ability to locate missing children. . . . The unraveling of
the origins of Karen's special talent comes as no real
surprise, but Duncan still turns out plenty of page-turning
suspense, expertly blending realistic background with the
allure of the paranormal." Booklist

The twisted window. Delacorte Press 1987 183p
hardcover o.p. paperback available $4.99 (7 and
up)   **Fic**
1. Kidnapping—Fiction 2. Mystery fiction
ISBN 0-440-20184-5 (pa)   LC 86-29054

"When Brad tells Tracy that his little sister Mindy has
been kidnapped by his stepfather, she promises to help
him locate the child. Tracy is moved by Brad's story and
defiant of the aunt and uncle she has lived with ever
since her mother was stabbed to death. They find the
toddler Brad is searching for, and Tracy arranges to
baby-sit for Mindy, then turn her over to Brad. But the
situation turns dangerous when Brad shows up with a
gun, and Tracy realizes that the story he told was far
from the truth." Publ Wkly

"The plot and characterization have substance and nuance, and the author deftly builds tension and leads the
reader to an expectation (amply fulfilled) of an ending
that at first seems surprising—until the reader sees that
Duncan has carefully led to its dramatic twist." Bull Cent
Child Books

Durbin, William, 1951-

The broken blade. Delacorte Press 1997 163p
$14.95; pa $4.50   **Fic**
1. Fur trade—Fiction 2. Canada—Fiction
ISBN 0-385-32224-0; 0-440-41184-X (pa)
                                  LC 96-22114

When an injury prevents his father from going into
northern Canada with fur traders, thirteen-year-old Pierre
decides to take his father's place as a voyageur

"This look at the early nineteenth-century Canadian
fur trade should appeal to reluctant readers as well as adventure buffs, and it may be a welcome suggestion for
middle-school historical fiction reports." Bull Cent Child
Books

Wintering. Delacorte Press 1999 191p $14.95
                                              Fic
ISBN 0-385-32598-3   LC 98-25546
Companion to The broken blade

In 1801, fourteen-year-old Pierre returns to work for
the North West Fur Company and makes the long and
difficult journey to a winter camp, where he learns from
both the other voyageurs and from the Ojibwa Indians
whose land they share

This offers "adventure, surprises, humor, and a touching conclusion." Booklist

Durrant, Lynda, 1956-

The beaded moccasins; the story of Mary
Campbell. Clarion Bks. 1998 183p $15   **Fic**
1. Campbell, Mary, fl. 1764—Fiction 2. Delaware Indians—Fiction
ISBN 0-395-85398-2   LC 97-16288

After being captured by a group of Delaware Indians
and given to their leader as a replacement for his dead
granddaughter, twelve-year-old Mary Campbell is forced
to travel west with them to Ohio

"Based on a 1759 historical incident. . . . Thoughtful
characterizations, a strong sense of place, and an involving present tense narration make this a solid historical
novel." Horn Book Guide

Durrant, Lynda, 1956——*Continued*
Echohawk. Clarion Bks. 1996 181p $14.95
Fic
1. Mohegan Indians—Fiction 2. Brothers—Fiction
ISBN 0-395-74430-X   LC 96-2113
Also available in paperback from Dell
A twelve-year-old white boy, adopted and raised by Mohicans in the Hudson River Valley during the 1730's, is sent with his younger brother to an English settlement for schooling
"Durrant presents rich history, vast cultural information, and a story that will trigger discussion. An extensive bibliography demonstrates the author's depth of research." SLJ

Turtle clan journey. Clarion Bks. 1999 180p $15
Fic
1. Mohegan Indians—Fiction
ISBN 0-395-90369-6   LC 98-22710
Sequel to Echohawk
As the captive white boy Echohawk and his Mohican father and brother make a perilous journey from the Hudson River Valley to a settlement on the Ohio River, Echohawk feels the conflicting pulls of his dual heritage
"In this well-researched novel, the author gives life to the prejudices and fears of the time while offering a look into the culture and traditions of the Mohicans and the conflict resulting from the colonists' usurping of Native American lands." SLJ

Dygard, Thomas J., 1931-1996
Game plan. Morrow Junior Bks. 1993 220p $14 (7 and up)
Fic
1. Football—Fiction 2. School stories
ISBN 0-688-12007-5   LC 92-47252
Also available in paperback from Penguin Bks.
When the Barton High football coach's hospitalization forces skinny student manager Beano Hatton to take over coaching the team, he must deal with a rebellious quarterback and his own lack of confidence
"Dygard's competent storytelling and effective characterization make the book a pleasurable read. Beano is likable and his dilemma compelling, and while there are few surprises, this is a satisfying title to offer sportsminded readers." Booklist

River danger. Morrow 1998 151p $15 (7 and up)
Fic
1. Brothers—Fiction 2. Canoes and canoeing—Fiction
ISBN 0-688-14852-2   LC 97-36362
Although he reluctantly agrees to accompany his little brother on a canoe trip, eighteen-year-old Eric finally gains new respect for this younger sibling whose ingenuity rescues him
"Several unexpected plot twists keep the reader engaged. . . . Dygard proves once again that appealing, believable characters in any context are the strength of good fiction." Booklist

The rookie arrives. Morrow Junior Bks. 1988 197p o.p.; Penguin Bks. paperback available $4.99 (7 and up)
Fic
1. Baseball—Fiction
ISBN 0-14-034112-9 (pa)   LC 87-26238

Cocky Ted Bell moves from being star of his high school baseball team directly into playing in the major leagues and finds that he has a lot to learn before becoming the world's greatest third baseman
"This is a formula sports fiction (brash rookie makes good), but it's capably written, with game sequences that baseball buffs will enjoy, and it gives a realistic picture of major league ball as big business, as the coaches, owners, and managers of the team make their decisions about hiring, trading, and playing or benching men on their roster." Bull Cent Child Books

Running wild. Morrow Junior Bks. 1996 172p $15 (7 and up)
Fic
1. Football—Fiction 2. Friendship—Fiction 3. School stories
ISBN 0-688-14853-0   LC 96-10182
Also available in paperback from Penguin Bks.
"Arrested after a joyriding accident, Pete Holman is annoyed and confused when he's released to his high school's football coach on condition that he report to practice for the rest of the season. . . . He's stunned, however, to discover that he has natural athletic ability, and he loves the thrill of success on the field and the attention it brings. . . . A fast-paced story that skillfully blends exciting sports action with a realistic portrayal of the dynamics of high-school friendships." Booklist

Second stringer. Morrow Junior Bks. 1998 174p $15 (7 and up)
Fic
1. Football—Fiction
ISBN 0-688-15981-8   LC 98-11361
When Kevin replaces the quarterback and football hero who suffers a knee injury, the second stringer needs to prove that he can do the job and is not just a substitute
"Dygard offers just enough conflict and character development to add texture to the fast-paced plot." Booklist

Tournament upstart. Morrow 1984 200p o.p.; Penguin Bks. paperback available $4.99 (7 and up)
Fic
1. Basketball—Fiction
ISBN 0-14-034114-5 (pa)   LC 83-25039
Under the leadership of their new young coach, a Class B high school basketball team from the Ozark foothills challenges big-city schools for the state championship
The author "gives the reader exciting play-by-play reporting along with a reasonable story. It can even appeal to those who are not interested in basketball. The reader won't learn to be a better player, but he will learn the necessity of teamwork." Best Sellers

English, Karen
Francie. Farrar, Straus & Giroux 1999 199p $16
Fic
1. African Americans—Fiction 2. Race relations—Fiction 3. Alabama—Fiction
ISBN 0-374-32456-5   LC 98-53047
Coretta Scott King honor book for text, 2000
"The best student in her small, all-black school in preintegration Alabama, 12-year-old Francie hopes for a better life. . . . When Jessie, an older school friend who is without family, is forced on the run by a racist em-

English, Karen—*Continued*

ployer, Francie leaves her mother's labeled canned food for him in the woods. Only when the sheriff begins searching their woods . . . does she realize the depth of the danger she may have brought to her family. Francie's smooth-flowing, well-paced narration is gently assisted by just the right touch of the vernacular. Characterization is evenhanded and believable, while place and time envelop readers." SLJ

Erdrich, Louise

The birchbark house. Hyperion Bks. for Children 1999 244p il $14.99; lib bdg $15.49

Fic

1. Ojibwa Indians—Fiction
ISBN 0-7868-0300-2; 0-7868-2241-4 (lib bdg)

LC 98-46366

Omakayas, a seven-year-old Native American girl of the Ojibwa tribe, lives through the joys of summer and the perils of winter on an island in Lake Superior in 1847

"Erdrich crafts images of tender beauty while weaving Ojibwa words seamlessly into the text. Her gentle spot art throughout complements this first of several projected stories that will 'attempt to retrace [her] own family's history.'" Horn Book Guide

Farmer, Nancy, 1941-

The Ear, the Eye, and the Arm; a novel. Orchard Bks. 1994 311p $18.95; lib bdg $19.99

Fic

1. Science fiction 2. Zimbabwe—Fiction
ISBN 0-531-06829-3; 0-531-08679-8 (lib bdg)

LC 93-11814

Also available in paperback from Penguin Bks.
A Newbery Medal honor book, 1995
"A Richard Jackson Book"

In 2194 in Zimbabwe, General Matsika's three children Tendai, Rita, and Kuda, are kidnapped and put to work in a plastic mine, while three mutant detectives named The Ear, the Eye and the Arm use their special powers to search for them

"Throughout the story, it's the thrilling adventure that will grab readers, who will also like the comic, tender characterizations." Booklist

A girl named Disaster. Orchard Bks. 1996 309p $19.95; lib bdg $20.99   Fic

1. Shona (African people)—Fiction 2. Supernatural—Fiction 3. Mozambique—Fiction 4. Zimbabwe—Fiction
ISBN 0-531-09539-8; 0-531-08889-8 (lib bdg)

LC 96-15141

Also available in paperback from Penguin Bks.
A Newbery Medal honor book, 1997
"A Richard Jackson book"

While journeying from Mozambique to Zimbabwe to escape an arranged marriage, eleven-year-old Nhamo struggles to escape drowning and starvation and in so doing comes close to the luminous world of the African spirits

"This story is humorous and heartwrenching, complex and multilayered." SLJ

The warm place. Orchard Bks. 1995 152p $15.95; lib bdg $16.99   Fic

1. Giraffes—Fiction 2. Animals—Fiction 3. Fantasy fiction
ISBN 0-531-06888-9; 0-531-08738-7 (lib bdg)

LC 94-21984

Also available in paperback from Penguin Bks.
"A Richard Jackson book"

When Ruva, a young giraffe, is captured and sent to a zoo in San Francisco, she calls upon two rats, a streetsmart chameleon, a runaway boy, and all the magical powers of the animal world to return to the warm place that is home

"Farmer keeps her story fresh through lots of action and snappy dialogue." Bull Cent Child Books

Farmer, Penelope, 1939-

Penelope; a novel. Margaret K. McElderry Bks. 1996 184p $16   Fic

1. Reincarnation—Fiction 2. Supernatural—Fiction
ISBN 0-689-80121-1   LC 95-18801

"Did 12-year-old Flora live as someone else in an earlier time? Why does she remember words she's never learned? Why does she have memories of things that never happened to her? Flora's mother is dead; her father has left, and Flora is being raised by her aunt's loving working-class family in London. Is she Penelope, an eighteenth-century lord's daughter, come to life again?" Booklist

"This novel differs from run-of-the-mill supernatural tales not only for the expert quality of its prose but in the way the reincarnation story line serves the larger tale of Flora's coming of age and discovery of her family history." Publ Wkly

Fast, Howard, 1914-

April morning; a novel. Crown 1961 184p o.p.; Bantam Bks. paperback available $5.99 (7 and up)

Fic

1. United States—History—1775-1783, Revolution—Fiction 2. Lexington (Mass.), Battle of, 1775—Fiction
ISBN 0-553-27322-1 (pa)   LC 61-10306

"The spirit of the Revolutionary War, a country coming of age, and the life of a boy passing into manhood are captured in this historical novel. Fast focuses on one day in the life of Adam Cooper as his family and the community of Lexington rise to the events of April 19, 1775. Adam at first is caught up in the excitement, but by the end of the first skirmish the death of his father has brought home the horror and reality of war." Shapiro. Fic for Youth. 3d edition

Feiffer, Jules

The man in the ceiling; entirely written and illustrated by Jules Feiffer. HarperCollins Pubs. 1993 185p il $15; pa $6.95   Fic

1. Artists—Fiction
ISBN 0-06-205035-4; 0-06-205907-6 (pa)

LC 92-59953

"Michael Di Capua books"

"With his quest to invent the best-ever superhero, 10-year-old cartoonist Jimmy Jiggett bids for immortality—

Feiffer, Jules—*Continued*

or at least some attention from his type-A father." Publ Wkly

"Feiffer's deft depiction of moments of family dysfunction are wickedly funny. His rough-drawn, signature cartoon illustrations are charged with an energy that matches the briskly paced text." Booklist

Fenner, Carol

The king of dragons. Margaret K. McElderry Bks. 1998 216p $17   **Fic**
1. Homeless persons—Fiction 2. Fathers and sons—Fiction
ISBN 0-689-82217-0   LC 98-15434

Having lost access to the old railroad station where they had been staying, homeless Ian and his father move into an unused city courthouse and try to avoid being discovered by the authorities

"The characters are sharply etched, and the narrative moves swiftly, with moments of poignancy and suspense." Horn Book Guide

Randall's wall. Margaret K. McElderry Bks. 1991 85p $15   **Fic**
1. Poverty—Fiction 2. Friendship—Fiction 3. School stories
ISBN 0-689-50518-3   LC 90-46490

Also available in paperback from Dell Bks.

"Fifth grader Randall Lord is filthy. He smells. No one in his small Midwest school sits near him. . . . There's no water in his rundown shack. His abusive father hasn't been around for months; his mother is crumpled with suffering, both physically and mentally ill. . . . Behind his wall Randall keeps secret the fact that he loves to draw, and no one knows that he has a shining artistic gift. Then his feeling for Jean, a cheerful, bold girl in his class, makes him reach out." Booklist

"Fenner presents a disturbing yet believable story. . . . The serious and sometimes tragic tone is tempered by some touches of real humor. A well-written, compassionate story." SLJ

Yolonda's genius. Margaret K. McElderry Bks. 1995 211p $17; pa $4.50   **Fic**
1. Brothers and sisters—Fiction 2. Musicians—Fiction 3. African Americans—Fiction
ISBN 0-689-80001-0; 0-689-81327-9 (pa)
                                            LC 94-46962

A Newbery Medal honor book, 1996

After moving from Chicago to Grand River, Michigan, fifth grader Yolonda, big and strong for her age, determines to prove that her younger brother is not a slow learner but a true musical genius

"In this brisk and appealing narrative, readers are introduced to a close-knit, middle-class African-American family. . . . [This novel] is suffused with humor and spirit." Horn Book

Ferris, Jean, 1939-

All that glitters. Farrar, Straus & Giroux 1996 183p $16 (7 and up)   **Fic**
1. Buried treasure—Fiction 2. Fathers and sons—Fiction 3. Florida—Fiction
ISBN 0-374-30204-9   LC 95-590

Also available in paperback from Scholastic

"Brian, 16, is in Florida to spend part of another summer with his uncommunicative father, Leo. . . . The visit looks better after Brian meets beautiful Tia, also 16, learns to snorkel, and improves his scuba diving enough to help look for a sunken Spanish galleon. . . . An exciting story and unusual but realistic characters that teen readers will care about." Book Rep

Love among the walnuts. Harcourt Brace & Co. 1998 216p $16 (7 and up)   **Fic**
1. Crime—Fiction 2. Wealth—Fiction 3. Uncles—Fiction
ISBN 0-15-201590-6   LC 97-50291

Born and raised in isolation in a wealthy, eccentric family, Sandy is shocked when he, his parents, and their servants become victims of a vicious plot by his greedy uncles to incapacitate them and take their money

"This book is intentionally melodramatic, coincidental, improbable, and hilarious. The restrained, tongue-in-cheek tone heightens the humor of this spoof." SLJ

Fine, Anne

Flour babies. Little, Brown 1994 c1992 178p o.p.; Dell paperback available $4.50   **Fic**
1. School stories 2. Parent and child—Fiction
ISBN 0-440-21941-8 (pa)   LC 93-35698

First published 1992 in the United Kingdom

When his class of underachievers is assigned to spend three torturous weeks taking care of their own "babies" in the form of bags of flour, Simon makes amazing discoveries about himself while coming to terms with his long-absent father

"There's no mistaking Fine's underlying theme (she's not a bit subtle), but its couched in such splendid, trenchant humor—spiffy one-liners, funny, well-devised characters, and hilarious situations—that the story simply flies along." Booklist

Step by wicked step; a novel. Little, Brown 1996 138p $15.95   **Fic**
1. Divorce—Fiction 2. Stepfamily—Fiction
ISBN 0-316-28345-2   LC 95-43251

Also available in paperback from Dell

"Five children, all part of stepfamilies, spend the night in an old mansion as part of a class trip and read a journal they discover, written generations earlier by a boy their age. The diary inspires them to tell their own stories about struggling with change and shifting family conditions. The stories are wise and powerful, together composing an affecting and honest novel." Horn Book Guide

The Tulip touch; a novel. Little, Brown 1997 149p $15.95   **Fic**
1. Friendship—Fiction
ISBN 0-316-28325-8   LC 96-47185

Also available in paperback from Dell

Natalie, who lives in the large hotel managed by her father, has a dangerous friendship with Tulip, the wildly uncontrollable girl on a neighboring farm

"A provocative, disturbing novel. . . . This deeply felt, convincingly described examination of a complicated relationship leaves many issues properly unresolved. It would be a wonderful spring-board for discussions. . . . It is also a very good read." SLJ

Fisher, Leonard Everett, 1924-

The jetty chronicles. Marshall Cavendish 1997
96p $15.95   **Fic**

ISBN 0-7614-5017-3   LC 97-6451

"Fisher returns to his boyhood home in this novel based on his reminiscences from 1934 to 1939, set in the wake of a manmade jetty in southwestern Brooklyn. . . . Colorful fictional characters include an elderly geologist; a nameless ex-convict; an artist; and a radical newspaper vendor hell-bent on getting into the exclusive Sea Gate with his message of miracles, salvation, and eternal damnation. . . . This is a piece of Americana . . . portraying a real place and time that no longer exists. A place of power and majesty reclaimed by nature." SLJ

Flake, Sharon G.

The skin I'm in. Jump at the Sun; Hyperion Bks. for Children 1998 171p $14.95   **Fic**
1. African Americans—Fiction 2. Teachers—Fiction 3. School stories
ISBN 0-7868-0444-0   LC 98-19615

Thirteen-year-old Maleeka, uncomfortable because her skin is extremely dark, meets a new teacher with a birthmark on her face and makes some discoveries about how to love who she is and what she looks like

This "novel is fast-paced and realistic." Horn Book Guide

Fleischman, Paul

The borning room. HarperCollins Pubs. 1991
101p hardcover o.p. paperback available $4.95
Fic
1. Frontier and pioneer life—Fiction 2. Ohio—Fiction
ISBN 0-06-447099-7 (pa)   LC 91-4432
"A Charlotte Zolotow book"

Lying at the end of her life in the room where she was born in 1851, Georgina remembers what it was like to grow up on the Ohio frontier

"Fleischman successfully tackles many important themes and once again gifts readers with writing lush with similes, metaphors, and allusions, so subtly woven into the mesh of the narrative that they enrich without distracting. A memorable novel, rich and resonant in familial love and the strength of connection and tradition." SLJ

Bull Run; woodcuts by David Frampton. HarperCollins Pubs. 1993 104p il $14.95; lib bdg $14.89; pa $4.95   **Fic**
1. Bull Run, 1st Battle of, 1861—Fiction 2. United States—History—1861-1865, Civil War—Fiction
ISBN 0-06-021446-5; 0-06-021447-3 (lib bdg); 0-06-440588-5 (pa)   LC 92-14745
"A Laura Geringer book"

"In a sequence of sixty one- to two-page narratives, fifteen fictional characters (and one real general) recount their experiences during the Civil War. A few encounter each other, most meet unawares or not at all, but they have in common a battle, Bull Run, that affects—and sometimes ends—their lives." Bull Cent Child Books

"Abandoning the conventions of narrative fiction, Fleischman tells a vivid, many-sided story in this original and moving book. An excellent choice for readers' theater in the classroom or on stage." Booklist

A fate totally worse than death. Candlewick Press 1995 124p $15.99; pa $4.99 (7 and up)
Fic
1. School stories
ISBN 1-56402-627-2; 0-7636-0242-6 (pa)
LC 94-48433

In this horror novel parody, three self-centered members of Cliffside High School's ruling clique, who are beginning to age rapidly, become convinced that the beautiful new exchange student is the ghost of the girl whose death they caused the year before

"The fun is in the vapid thinking of the girls, the trendy teen scenes, and the parody of YA actions and dialogue. This hilarious farce should have teen-horror fans screaming with laughter." SLJ

Mind's eye. Holt & Co. 1999 108p $15.95 (7 and up)   **Fic**
ISBN 0-8050-6314-5   LC 99-20844

A novel in play form in which sixteen-year-old Courtney, paralyzed in an accident, learns about the power of the mind from an elderly blind woman who takes Courtney on an imaginary journey to Italy using a 1910 guidebook

"Fleischman's gift for language and dialogue vividly brings to life the distinctive characters and drama." Booklist

Saturnalia. Harper & Row 1990 113p lib bdg $14.89; pa $4.95   **Fic**
1. Narraganset Indians—Fiction 2. Apprentices—Fiction 3. Prejudices—Fiction 4. Boston (Mass.)—Fiction
ISBN 0-06-021913-0 (lib bdg); 0-06-447089-X (pa)
LC 89-36380
"A Charlotte Zolotow book"

This novel is set in Boston in 1681. Fourteen-year-old William, a Narraganset Indian captured six years earlier in a raid, is apprenticed to Mr. Currie, a printer. "William's accomplishments enrage Mr. Baggot, the tithingman whose grandsons were killed by Indians. . . . William often wanders the streets after curfew playing an Indian melody on a small bone flute in the hope of finding his lost brother." Horn Book

"While William is the main focus of the story, there are several bubbling subplots that illuminate the texture of Puritan colonial life. . . . Especially welcome as a support for history units, this absorbing story exemplifies Fleischman's graceful, finely honed use of the English language." Booklist

Seedfolks; illustrations by Judy Pedersen. HarperCollins Pubs. 1997 69p $13.95; lib bdg $13.89; pa $4.95   **Fic**
1. Gardens—Fiction 2. City life—Fiction
ISBN 0-06-027471-9; 0-06-027472-7 (lib bdg); 0-06-447207-8 (pa)   LC 96-26696
"Joanna Cotler books"

This "novel tells about an urban garden started by a child and nurtured by people of all ages and ethnic and economic backgrounds. Each of the thirteen chapters is narrated by a different character, allowing the reader to watch as a community develops out of disconnected lives and prior suspicions." Horn Book Guide

"The characters' vitality and the sharply delineated details of the neighborhood make this not merely an exer-

Fleischman, Paul—*Continued*
cise in craftsmanship or morality but an engaging, entertaining novel as well." Booklist

Whirligig. Holt & Co. 1998 133p $16.95 (7 and up) **Fic**
1. Guilt—Fiction
ISBN 0-8050-5582-7 LC 97-24429
"Humiliated at a party, Brent tries to commit suicide while driving home but instead kills a seventeen-year-old girl. Desperate to atone, Brent agrees to the victim's mother's request that he build four whirligigs and set them up in the four corners of the United States as monuments to her daughter." Horn Book Guide
"Mystical, powerful, and transcendent." SLJ

Fleischman, Sid, 1920-
The 13th floor; a ghost story; illustrations by Peter Sis. Greenwillow Bks. 1995 134p il $15 **Fic**
1. Fantasy fiction 2. Pirates—Fiction 3. Brothers and sisters—Fiction
ISBN 0-688-14216-8 LC 94-42806
Also available in paperback from Dell
When his older sister disappears, twelve-year-old Buddy Stebbins follows her back in time and finds himself aboard a seventeenth-century pirate ship captained by a distant relative
"Liberally laced with dry wit and thoroughly satisfying . . . readers could hardly ask for more." Publ Wkly

Bandit's moon; illustrations by Jos. A. Smith. Greenwillow Bks. 1998 136p $15 **Fic**
1. Murieta, Joaquín, d. 1853—Fiction 2. Thieves—Fiction 3. California—Gold discoveries—Fiction 4. Adventure fiction
ISBN 0-688-15830-7 LC 97-36197
Twelve-year-old Annyrose relates her adventures with Joaquín Murieta and his band of outlaws in the California gold-mining region during the mid-1800s
"A quick read, with lots of twists, wonderful phrasing, historical integrity, and a bit of the tall tale thrown in." SLJ

Jim Ugly; illustrations by Jos. A. Smith. Greenwillow Bks. 1992 130p il $16 **Fic**
1. Dogs—Fiction 2. West (U.S.)—Fiction
ISBN 0-688-10886-5 LC 91-14392
Also available in paperback from Dell
The adventures of twelve-year-old Jake and Jim Ugly, his father's part-mongrel, part-wolf dog, as they travel through the Old West trying to find out what really happened to Jake's actor father
"Fleischman wields his magic pen once again in a fast-moving, picaresque adventure with memorable characters, a well-honed descriptive style—perfectly suited to tone, time, and place—and a sure sense of story." Horn Book

The whipping boy; illustrations by Peter Sis. Greenwillow Bks. 1986 90p il $16 **Fic**
1. Thieves—Fiction 2. Adventure fiction
ISBN 0-688-06216-4 LC 85-17555
Also available in paperback from Troll
Awarded the Newbery Medal, 1987

"A round tale of adventure and humor, this follows the fortunes of Prince Roland (better known as Prince Brat) and his whipping boy, Jemmy, who has received all the hard knocks for the prince's mischief. . . . There's not a moment's lag in pace, and the stock characters, from Hold-Your-Nose Billy to Betsy's dancing bear Petunia, have enough inventive twists to project a lively air to it all." Bull Cent Child Books

Fletcher, Ralph J.
Flying solo; [by] Ralph Fletcher. Clarion Bks. 1998 138p $15 **Fic**
1. School stories 2. Death—Fiction
ISBN 0-395-87323-1 LC 98-10775
Rachel, having chosen to be mute following the sudden death of a classmate, shares responsibility with the other sixth-graders who decide not to report that the substitute teacher failed to show up
"Fletcher expertly balances a wide variety of emotions, giving readers a story that is by turns sad, poignant, and funny." Booklist

Spider Boy; by Ralph Fletcher. Clarion Bks. 1997 180p $15 **Fic**
1. Moving—Fiction 2. Honesty—Fiction 3. Spiders—Fiction
ISBN 0-395-77606-6 LC 96-31464
Also available in paperback from Dell
After moving to another state, seventh grader Bobby deals with the change by telling people at school made-up stories and then retreating into his world of pet spiders and books about spiders
"A sensitively written novel. . . . While accessible and fast-moving, the book is not lightweight; it deals head on with problems such as the bully who deliberately kills one of Bobby's pet tarantulas." Horn Book Guide

Fletcher, Susan, 1951-
Dragon's milk. Atheneum Pubs. 1989 242p $15.95; pa $4.50 (7 and up) **Fic**
1. Dragons—Fiction 2. Fantasy fiction
ISBN 0-689-31579-1; 0-689-71623-0 (pa)
LC 88-35059
First title in the author's series set in Elythia
"A Jean Karl book"
Kaeldra, an outsider adopted by an Elythian family as a baby, possesses the power to understand dragons and uses this power to try to save her younger sister who needs dragon's milk to recover from an illness
"High-fantasy fans will delight in the clash of swords, the flash of magic, the many escape-and-rescue scenes." Booklist

Flight of the Dragon Kyn. Atheneum Pubs. 1993 213p $17; pa $4.50 (7 and up) **Fic**
1. Fantasy fiction 2. Dragons—Fiction
ISBN 0-689-31880-4; 0-689-81515-8 (pa)
LC 92-44787
Second title in the author's series set in Elythia; a prequel to Dragon's milk
"A Jean Karl book"
Fifteen-year-old Kara is summoned by King Orrik, who believes she has the power to call down the dragons

Fletcher, Susan, 1951-—*Continued*
that have been plundering his realm, and she is caught
up in the fierce rivalry between Orrik and his jealous
brother Rog
"This is a solid fantasy in a medieval Scandinavian-
like setting, and there's plenty of drama, romance, and
knavery to keep genre fans happy." Bull Cent Child
Books

Shadow spinner. Atheneum Bks. for Young
Readers 1998 219p $17   **Fic**
1. Storytelling—Fiction 2. Physically handicapped—
Fiction 3. Iran—Fiction
ISBN 0-689-81852-1   LC 97-37346
"A Jean Karl book"
When Marjan, a thirteen-year-old crippled girl, joins
the Sultan's harem in ancient Persia, she gathers for
Shahrazad the stories which will save the queen's life
"An elegantly written novel that will delight and en-
tertain even as it teaches." SLJ

Sign of the dove. Atheneum Bks. for Young
Readers 1996 214p $17; pa $4.50 (7 and up)
                                                        Fic
1. Fantasy fiction 2. Dragons—Fiction
ISBN 0-689-80460-1; 0-689-82449-1 (pa)
                                          LC 95-584
Third title in the author's series set in Elythia
"A Jean Karl book"
As the last of the dragon eggs, laid long ago, begin
to hatch, Lyf becomes a reluctant friend who tries to
save both the dragon mothers and their newly born chil-
dren from their enemies
The author "offers a stalwart heroine in a rousing story filled with well-realized dragon lore." Booklist

Forbes, Esther, 1891-1967
Johnny Tremain; a novel for old & young; with
illustrations by Lynd Ward. Houghton Mifflin
1943 256p il $15   **Fic**
1. United States—History—1775-1783, Revolution—
Fiction 2. Boston (Mass.)—Fiction
ISBN 0-395-06766-9
Also available in paperback from Dell
Awarded the Newbery Medal, 1944
"Johnny, an orphan, works as a favored apprentice to
an aging silversmith until he burns his hand severely
while working on an important project. During the Revolutionary War he serves as a dispatch rider for the Committee on Public Safety, meeting such men as Paul Revere and John Hancock. An outcast for a time, he finally
learns on the battlefield of Lexington that his crippled
hand can be put to use." Shapiro. Fic for Youth. 3d edition

Forman, James D., 1932-
Becca's story. Scribner 1992 180p $15 (7 and
up)   **Fic**
1. United States—History—1861-1865, Civil War—
Fiction
ISBN 0-684-19332-9   LC 92-1375
"Using his grandmother's letters and diary, the author
recreates Becca Case's youth. The story takes place dur-

ing the Civil War and emphasizes Becca's relationships
with two suitors and how they competed for her love."
Soc Educ
"This tender story of friendship and love is one that
will endure. . . . The characters are strong and true, the
conclusion stirring and poignant." SLJ

Forrester, Sandra, 1949-
My home is over Jordan. Lodestar Bks. 1997
163p $15.99   **Fic**
1. African Americans—Fiction 2. United States—History—1865-1898—Fiction 3. North Carolina—Fiction
ISBN 0-525-67568-X   LC 97-15591
Sequel to Sound the jubilee
No longer a slave now that the Civil War is over, fifteen-year-old Maddie dreams of getting an education and
becoming a teacher, but she finds the reality of freedom
harsh
"Forrester writes with a sure touch, working the historical threads neatly into her story and making Maddie
come alive for readers." SLJ

Sound the jubilee. Lodestar Bks. 1995 183p
$15.99   **Fic**
1. Slavery—Fiction 2. Roanoke Island (N.C.)—Fiction 3. United States—History—1861-1865, Civil
War—Fiction
ISBN 0-525-67486-1   LC 94-32664
Also available in paperback from Penguin Bks.
"In 1861, strong-willed Maddie is an eleven-year-old
slave. Through her eyes, readers view the life of a family
and community that gain economic security in the North
Carolina settlement of Roanoke Island after being freed
from slavery. Depicting tragic and triumphant episodes
during a turbulent time in American history, the novel,
which follows the family for four years, is compelling
and informative." Horn Book Guide

Foster, Alan Dean, 1946-
The Hand of Dinotopia; illustrations by James
Gurney. HarperCollins Pubs. 1999 407p il $22.95
                                                        Fic
1. Dinosaurs—Fiction 2. Fantasy fiction
ISBN 0-06-028005-0   LC 98-27814
Based on the Dinotopia books by James Gurney
Will and Sylvia search for the mysterious Hand of
Dinotopia, which will supposedly lead to a safe sea route
to and from the hidden island where people and dino-
saurs live together peacefully
"A smoothly crafted tale with an entertainingly
contentious supporting cast, grandly formal language . . .
and replete with jawbreaking dinosaur nomenclature and
a plot urged along at a steady, if deliberate, pace." SLJ
Another available title about Dinotopia by this author
is:
Dinotopia lost (1996)

Fox, Paula
The eagle kite; a novel. Orchard Bks. 1995
127p $15.95; lib bdg $16.99   **Fic**
1. Homosexuality—Fiction 2. Fathers and sons—Fiction 3. AIDS (Disease)—Fiction 4. Death—Fiction
ISBN 0-531-06892-7; 0-531-08742-5 (lib bdg)
                                          LC 94-26415

Fox, Paula—*Continued*

Also available in paperback from Dell

"A Richard Jackson book"

Liam's father has AIDS, and his family cannot talk about it until Liam reveals a secret that he has tried to deny ever since he saw his father embracing another man at the beach

"The author's refusal to diminish the tangled emotional issues that underlie her story quietly challenges all preconceptions, and readers cannot help but be deeply affected." Publ Wkly

Monkey island. Orchard Bks. 1991 151p $15.95; lib bdg $16.99   **Fic**

1. Homeless persons—Fiction 2. New York (N.Y.)—Fiction

ISBN 0-531-05962-6; 0-531-08562-7 (lib bdg)

LC 91-7460

Also available in paperback from Dell

"A Richard Jackson book"

Forced to live on the streets of New York after his mother disappears from their hotel room, eleven-year-old Clay is befriended by two men who help him survive

"This is a carefully crafted, thoughtful book, and one in which the flow of language both sustains a mood of apprehension and encourages readers to consider carefully the plight of the homeless." SLJ

One-eyed cat; a novel. Bradbury Press 1984 216p $14.95   **Fic**

1. Firearms—Fiction 2. Cats—Fiction

ISBN 0-02-735540-3   LC 84-10964

Also available in paperback from Dell

"Told by his father that he's too young for the air rifle an uncle gives him as a birthday present, Ned sneaks the gun out one night and takes a shot at a shadowy creature. He is subsequently smitten with guilt when he sees a one-eyed feral cat, and the knowledge that he may have been responsible." Bull Cent Child Books

The author's "writing is sure. Her characterization is outstanding, and she creates a strong sense of place and mood. The relationships among the characters are complex and ring true." SLJ

The slave dancer; a novel; with illustrations by Eros Keith. Bradbury Press 1973 176p il $16

Fic

1. Slave trade—Fiction 2. Sea stories

ISBN 0-02-735560-8   LC 73-80642

Also available in paperback from Dell

Awarded the Newbery Medal, 1974

"Thirteen-year-old Jessie Bollier is kidnapped from New Orleans and taken aboard a slave ship. Cruelly tyrannized by the ship's captain, Jessie is made to play his fife for the slaves during the exercise period into which they are forced in order to keep them fit for sale. When a hurricane destroys the ship, Jessie and Ras, a young slave, survive. They are helped by an old black man who finds them, spirits Ras north to freedom, and assists Jessie to return to his family." Shapiro. Fic for Youth. 3d edition

Frank, Lucy K.

I am an artichoke; [by] Lucy Frank. Holiday House 1995 187p $14.95 (7 and up)   **Fic**

1. Anorexia nervosa—Fiction 2. Mothers and daughters—Fiction 3. New York (N.Y.)—Fiction

ISBN 0-8234-1150-8   LC 94-12315

Also available in paperback from Dell

"Sarah, 15, takes a summer job as a mother's helper in New York City. . . . She quickly realizes that she is in over her head at the Friedman's, with 12-year-old Emily suffering from a serious eating disorder and her divorced parents pitted against one another over her treatment." SLJ

"The pace of the first-person narrative is smooth and swift; the characters are consistently developed. An engrossing novel that will provide discussion material about friendship, self-esteem, and families." Horn Book

Will you be my Brussels sprout? Holiday House 1996 152p $15.95 (7 and up)   **Fic**

1. Musicians—Fiction 2. New York (N.Y.)—Fiction

ISBN 0-8234-1220-2   LC 95-34385

Companion volume to I am an artichoke

"Sarah, 16 and an aspiring cellist, begins taking lessons at the New York Conservatory of Music, meets Emily's older brother, David, and falls in love for the first time. Sarah and David connect on many levels, but the inexperienced Sarah faces a dilemma when David starts pressuring her to become intimate. Frank resolves the conflict in a believable, satisfying, and responsible manner. . . . Punctuated with humor and witty dialogue." Booklist

Franklin, Kristine L.

Dove song. Candlewick Press 1999 190p $16.99

Fic

1. Mental illness—Fiction 2. Brothers and sisters—Fiction 3. Vietnam War, 1961-1975—Fiction

ISBN 0-7636-0409-7   LC 98-37621

When eleven-year-old Bobbie Lynn's father is reported missing in action in Vietnam, she and her thirteen-year-old brother must learn to cope with their own despair, as well as their mother's breakdown

"This is both a sensitive story of friendship and family problems and solid historical fiction." SLJ

Nerd no more. Candlewick Press 1996 143p $15.99; pa $4.99   **Fic**

1. School stories 2. Friendship—Fiction

ISBN 1-56402-674-4; 0-7636-0487-9 (pa)

LC 96-7472

"Sixth-grader Wiggie is befriended by a new girl, Callie, who unlike Wiggie doesn't seem to mind being smart or unpopular." Horn Book Guide

"This realistic contemporary story told from Wiggie's point of view is humorous and fast paced." SLJ

Freeman, Suzanne T.

The cuckoo's child; by Suzanne Freeman. Greenwillow Bks. 1996 249p $15   **Fic**

ISBN 0-688-14290-7   LC 95-8385

Also available in paperback from Hyperion Bks.

Freeman, Suzanne T.—*Continued*

"Mia, who has grown up in Beirut but longs to be a 'normal' American, gets her wish under tragic circumstances when her parents are apparently lost at sea. Transported with disorienting suddenness to live with her aunt in . . . America, Mia struggles to fit into her new world. . . . This novel is emotionally intense and very real." Horn Book Guide

Gaeddert, LouAnn Bigge

Hope; [by] LouAnn Gaeddert. Atheneum Bks. for Young Readers 1995 165p $14; pa $4.50   **Fic**

1. Shakers—Fiction
ISBN 0-689-80128-9; 0-614-29085-6 (pa)
      LC 95-2704

"A Jean Karl book"

In this story set in 1851, "Hope's mother has died and it's been more than a year since anyone has heard from her father, prospecting for gold out West. A callous uncle deposits Hope and her younger brother, John, with the Shakers, who welcome orphans and abandoned children. . . . When they at last hear from their father . . . Hope chooses to join him while John stays with the Shakers." Publ Wkly

"The descriptions of Shaker life and customs are vivid and accurate, but not sentimentalized." Voice Youth Advocates

Gaines, Ernest J., 1933-

The autobiography of Miss Jane Pittman. Dial Press (NY) 1971 245p o.p.; Bantam Bks. paperback available $5.50 (7 and up)   **Fic**

1. African Americans—Fiction 2. Louisiana—Fiction
ISBN 0-553-26357-9 (pa)   LC 77-144380

"In the epic of Miss Jane Pittman, a 110-year-old exslave, the action begins at the time she is a small child watching both Union and Confederate troops come into the plantation on which she lives. It closes with the demonstrations of the sixties and the freedom walk she decides to make. This is a log of trials, heartaches, joys, love—but mostly of endurance." Shapiro. Fic for Youth. 3d edition

Gantos, Jack

Joey Pigza swallowed the key. Farrar, Straus & Giroux 1998 153p $16   **Fic**

1. Attention deficit disorder—Fiction 2. School stories
ISBN 0-374-33664-4   LC 98-24264
Also available in paperback from HarperCollins

To the constant disappointment of his mother and his teachers, Joey has trouble paying attention or controlling his mood swings when his prescription meds wear off and he starts getting worked up and acting wired

This "frenetic narrative pulls at heartstrings and tickles funny bones." SLJ

Garden, Nancy

Dove and sword; a novel of Joan of Arc. Farrar, Straus & Giroux 1995 237p $17 (7 and up)   **Fic**

1. Joan, of Arc, Saint, 1412-1431—Fiction
2. France—History—1328-1589, House of Valois—Fiction
ISBN 0-374-34476-0   LC 95-920

Also available in paperback from Scholastic

In 1455 in France, Gabrielle is visited by Pierre d'Arc, a brother of Joan of Arc, and with him reminisces about their childhood together in Domremy and Joan's subsequent trial and burning at the stake at Rouen twenty-four years before

"This is a fascinating and well-written historical novel, filled with rich details, evocative descriptions, and interesting characters." SLJ

Garland, Sherry, 1948-

Shadow of the dragon. Harcourt Brace & Co. 1993 314p $10.95; pa $3.95   **Fic**

1. Vietnamese Americans—Fiction 2. Family life—Fiction
ISBN 0-15-273530-5; 0-15-273532-1 (pa)
      LC 93-17258

"Danny Vo's attempts to meld his responsibilities as the oldest son in a traditional Vietnamese family and his desire to be part of the mainstream of American life are complicated by a runaway younger sister; a newly arrived cousin who becomes involved with a dangerous gang; and Tiffany, the girl he loves. Rich characterization and an earthy view of hte Vietnamese immigrant experience distinguish the coming-of-age novel." Horn Book Guide

The silent storm. Harcourt Brace Jovanovich 1993 240p $14.95; pa $5   **Fic**

1. Orphans—Fiction 2. Grandfathers—Fiction 3. Hurricanes—Fiction
ISBN 0-15-274170-4; 0-15-201336-9 (pa)
      LC 92-33690

Thirteen-year-old Alyssa has not spoken since seeing her parents die in a hurricane, and now, three years later, another storm threatens the home she shares with her grandfather on Galveston Island

"Garland writes evocatively of her coastal setting, developing a solid sense of place. . . . The characterizations of family members made fearful by previous losses are well developed. . . . This book will have appeal for lovers of the outdoors as well as anyone who appreciates an exciting, atmospheric story." SLJ

Song of the buffalo boy. Harcourt Brace Jovanovich 1992 249p $16; pa $6   **Fic**

1. Amerasians—Fiction 2. Vietnam—Fiction
ISBN 0-15-277107-7; 0-15-200098-4 (pa)
      LC 91-31872

Shunned and mistreated because of her mixed heritage and determined to avoid an arranged marriage, seventeen-year-old Loi runs away to Ho Chi Minh City with the hope that she and the boy she loves will be able to go to the United States to find her American father

"This is a poignant and illuminating story drawn from a sorrowful chapter in American history. . . . Without becoming preachy or overbearing, this is a quietly effective story." Voice Youth Advocates

Garner, Alan, 1934-

The owl service. Walck, H. Z. 1968 c1967 202p o.p.; Magic Carpet Bks. paperback available $6
      Fic

1. Wales—Fiction
ISBN 0-15-201798-4 (pa)

Garner, Alan, 1934——*Continued*
First published 1967 in the United Kingdom
"The discovery of a strangely patterned set of plates in the attic loft of an old Welsh house where Alison, daughter of the deceased owner of the house, her step-brother Roger, and the housekeeper's son Gwyn are spending the summer marks the beginning of ominous events which embitter relationships among the three and endanger the life of Alison." Booklist
"It is hard to write with restraint about Alan Garner's talent, so deftly does he build his story with laminations of bright fantasy and somber Welsh legend, of romantic adventure and acid realism." N Y Times Book Rev

George, Jean Craighead, 1919-
Julie; illustrated by Wendell Minor. HarperCollins Pubs. 1994 226p il $15; lib bdg $14.89; pa $4.95   **Fic**
1. Inuit—Fiction   2. Arctic   regions—Fiction
3. Wolves—Fiction
ISBN 0-06-023528-4; 0-06-023529-2 (lib bdg); 0-06-440573-7 (pa)   LC 93-27738
This continuation of the story of Julie of the wolves "details Julie's adjustment to family and modernization after returning home. Her father's musk oxen enterprise depicts the problems inherent to environment-versus-economics issues as Julie struggles to save her wolf friends." Sci Child

Julie of the wolves; pictures by John Schoenherr. Harper & Row 1972 170p il $15.95; lib bdg $15.89; pa $4.95   **Fic**
1. Inuit—Fiction 2. Wolves—Fiction 3. Arctic regions—Fiction
ISBN 0-06-021943-2; 0-06-021944-0 (lib bdg); 0-06-440058-1 (pa)   LC 72-76509
Awarded the Newbery Medal, 1973
"In a modern classic on survival, Jean George tells the story of Miyax, an Eskimo, who is Julie in the white world. At thirteen she is forced into an arranged marriage with a young Eskimo named Daniel. Finding the experience intolerable, Julie runs away and survives for many months on the Arctic tundra with a pack of wolves, staying alive through her knowledge of old Eskimo customs." Shapiro. Fic for Youth. 3d edition

Julie's wolf pack; illustrated by Wendell Minor. HarperCollins Pubs. 1997 192p il $15.95; lib bdg $15.89; pa $4.95   **Fic**
1. Wolves—Fiction 2. Arctic regions—Fiction
ISBN 0-06-027406-9; 0-06-027407-7 (lib bdg); 0-06-440721-7 (pa)   LC 96-54858
This focuses "primarily on the wolf pack led by Kapu, son of Amaroq, hero of *Julie of the Wolves.* Kapu's leadership is not as absolute as his father's and he must constantly fight off challenges from a new member of the pack, and the appearance of rabies in the territory means that his leadership is all that stands between the pack and destruction. . . . Though Julie appears occasionally, what's really absorbing here are the pack dramas and adventures, and kids will relish slipping into the four-footed world." Bull Cent Child Books

My side of the mountain; written and illustrated by Jean Craighead George. Dutton 1988 177p il $15.99; pa $4.95   **Fic**
1. Outdoor life—Fiction 2. Catskill Mountains (N.Y.)—Fiction
ISBN 0-525-44392-4; 0-525-44395-9 (pa)
LC 87-27556
Also available in paperback from Penguin Bks.
A reissue of the title first published 1959
"Sam Gribley feels closed in by the city and his large family so he runs away to the Catskills and the land that had belonged to his grandfather. He tells the story of his year in the wilderness—the loneliness, the struggle to survive, and the need for companionship." Read Ladders for Hum Relat. 6th edition
"The book is all the more convincing for the excellence of style, the subtlety of humor, aptness of phrases, and touches of poetry." Horn Book
Followed by On the far side of the mountain (1990)

The talking earth. Harper & Row 1983 151p $14; $15.89; pa $4.95   **Fic**
1. Seminole Indians—Fiction 2. Everglades (Fla.)—Fiction 3. Wilderness survival—Fiction
ISBN 0-06-021975-0; 0-06-021976-9; 0-06-440212-6 (pa)   LC 82-48850
"Billie Wind, a Seminole girl, has been going to school at the Kennedy Space Center and has lost faith in her people's legends. For not believing in talking animals and earth, she is sent into the Everglades to find her roots. What was to be several days becomes months as fire and other events force her to survive with only the animals and earth to help her." Child Book Rev Serv
This story, "imbued with Seminole lore, is appealing because of the pitting of one human being against the elements, and is . . . convincing in its plot development and impressive in its descriptions of natural phenomena." Bull Cent Child Books

Water sky. Harper & Row 1987 208p $13; lib bdg $14.89; pa $4.95   **Fic**
1. Inuit—Fiction 2. Whaling—Fiction 3. Alaska—Fiction
ISBN 0-06-022198-4; 0-06-022199-2 (lib bdg); 0-06-440202-9 (pa)   LC 86-45496
"Because his father had so enjoyed his own stay, when young, with an Eskimo family, he has sent Lincoln to Alaska. Caught up in the beauty of Eskimo culture, the excitement of whale hunting (Eskimo style) and a first shy love affair, Lincoln almost forgets that he is determined to find the beloved uncle who had disappeared in the vicinity. The characters are strong, the plot is smoothly developed, and the setting vividly drawn in a novel imbued with understanding and respect for the rich traditions of Eskimo life." Bull Cent Child Books

Giberga, Jane Sughrue
Friends to die for. Dial Bks. 1997 231p $15.99 (7 and up)   **Fic**
1. Homicide—Fiction 2. Wealth—Fiction 3. New York (N.Y.)—Fiction
ISBN 0-8037-2094-7   LC 96-32146
Also available in paperback from Penguin Bks.

Giberga, Jane Sughrue—*Continued*
Sixteen-year-old Cristina is forced to evaluate her sophisticated world of elegant New York apartments, private schools, and rich friends when a girl she knows is murdered after a party they both attended
"The writing is good, the characters fully developed, the plot tight, and the climax dramatic. This is an engrossing story that will have the readers thinking about their priorities." Book Rep

Giff, Patricia Reilly
Lily's crossing. Delacorte Press 1997 180p $15.95; pa $4.99 Fic
1. World War, 1939-1945—Fiction 2. Friendship—Fiction
ISBN 0-385-32142-2; 0-440-41453-9 (pa)
LC 96-23021
A Newbery honor book, 1998
During a summer spent at Rockaway Beach in 1944, Lily's friendship with a young Hungarian refugee causes her to see the war and her own world differently
"Gentle elements of danger and suspense . . . keep the plot moving forward, while the delicate balance of characters and setting gently coalesces into an emotional whole that is fully satisfying." Bull Cent Child Books

Gilbert, Barbara Snow, 1954-
Stone water. Front St. 1996 169p $15.95 (7 and up) Fic
1. Grandfathers—Fiction 2. Death—Fiction 3. Euthanasia—Fiction
ISBN 1-886910-11-1 LC 95-50378
Also available in paperback from Dell
Fifteen-year-old Grant confronts the difficult decision of whether or not to cooperate with his grandfather's wish that he not be placed on life-support systems
"The handling of this difficult subject is thoughtful, poignant, respectful, and honest." SLJ

Gipson, Frederick Benjamin, 1903-1973
Old Yeller; [by] Fred Gipson; drawings by Carl Burger. Harper & Row 1956 158p il $23; pa $5.50 Fic
1. Dogs—Fiction 2. Texas—Fiction 3. Frontier and pioneer life—Fiction
ISBN 0-06-011545-9; 0-06-080002-X (pa)
"Travis at fourteen was the man of the family during the hard summer of 1860 when his father drove his herd of cattle from Texas to the Kansas market. It was the summer when an old yellow dog attached himself to the family and won Travis' reluctant friendship. Before the summer was over, Old Yeller proved more than a match for thieving raccoons, fighting bulls, grizzly bears, and mad wolves. This is a skillful tale of a boy's love for a dog as well as a description of a pioneer boyhood and it can't miss with any dog lover." Horn Book

Golding, William, 1911-1993
Lord of the Flies; introduction by E.M. Forster. Coward-McCann 1962 243p hardcover o.p. paperback available $6.95 (7 and up) Fic
1. Allegories 2. Boys—Fiction 3. Survival after airplane accidents, shipwrecks, etc.—Fiction
ISBN 0-399-50148-7 (pa)

First published 1954 in the United Kingdom; first United States edition, 1955
"Stranded on an island, a group of English schoolboys leave innocence behind in a struggle for survival. A political structure modeled after English government is set up and a hierarchy develops, but forces of anarchy and aggression surface. The boys' existence begins to degenerate into a savage one. They are rescued from their microcosmic society to return to an adult, stylized milieu filled with the same psychological tensions and moral voids. Adventure and allegory are brilliantly combined in this novel." Shapiro. Fic for Youth. 3d edition

Goldman, E. M.
Getting Lincoln's goat; an Elliot Armbruster mystery. Delacorte Press 1995 216p hardcover o.p. paperback available $3.99 (7 and up) Fic
1. Mystery fiction
ISBN 0-440-41332-X (pa) LC 94-20291
Tenth-grader Elliot wants to be a detective when he grows up, and when he discovers that Lincoln the goat, the school mascot, is missing, he and some of his classmates get a taste of what their chosen careers would really be like
"The story is humorous and fast-paced, and the characters develop in surprising but satisfying ways." Horn Book Guide

The night room. Viking 1995 216p $14.99; pa $4.95 (7 and up) Fic
1. Virtual reality—Fiction 2. School stories
ISBN 0-670-85838-2; 0-14-037253-9 (pa)
LC 94-30727
"Ira participates in a virtual reality experiment that predicts that one of his classmates will die before their tenth high school reunion. Though seduced by the computer's visions of their future, Ira and the other participants must try to keep the predictions from coming true. Readers will be drawn in by Goldman's exciting story about a mad scientist who abuses her subjects' natural curiosity." Horn Book Guide

Goodman, Joan E., 1950-
Hope's crossing; [by] Joan Elizabeth Goodman. Houghton Mifflin 1998 212p $15 Fic
1. United States—History—1775-1783, Revolution—Fiction
ISBN 0-395-86195-0 LC 97-2796
When kidnapped by English Loyalists during the Revolutionary War, thirteen-year-old Hope draws on every ounce of courage within her to respond to the ordeal
A "gripping historical novel." Booklist

Greenberg, Joanne, 1932-
I never promised you a rose garden; a novel; [by] Hannah Green. Holt, Rinehart & Winston 1964 300p o.p.; NAL/Dutton paperback available $5.99 (7 and up) Fic
1. Schizophrenia—Fiction 2. Mentally ill—Fiction 3. Antisemitism—Fiction
ISBN 0-451-16031-2 (pa)

Greenberg, Joanne, 1932-—*Continued*

"The 16-year-old girl who is ill, Deborah, is sick of rebelling against the lies she hears, the hatred she feels, and, at a summer camp, the anti-Semitism she suffers. She is schizophrenic: She has invented for herself a mythical kingdom into which she retreats and only when her parents reluctantly commit her to an asylum does she begin with difficulty to face reality." Publ Wkly

"The hospital world and Deborah's fantasy world are strikingly portrayed, as is the girl's violent struggle between sickness and health, a struggle given added poignancy by youth, wit, and courage." Libr J

Greene, Bette, 1934-

Summer of my German soldier. Dial Press (NY) 1973 230p hardcover o.p. paperback available $5.50   **Fic**

1. World War, 1939-1945—Fiction 2. German prisoners of war—Fiction 3. Arkansas—Fiction

ISBN 0-440-21892-6 (pa)   LC 73-6025

"Patty knows the pain of loneliness, rejection, and even beatings in a family where she is the ugly duckling, unable to gain her parents' love. This is in contrast to the affection shown to her beautiful and submissive sister. Anton Reiker is a German prisoner-of-war in a camp outside of Jenkinsville, Arkansas, and when he escapes, Patty helps him. Because her family is Jewish, she pays dearly for this intervention." Shapiro. Fic for Youth. 3d edition

Followed by Morning is a long time coming (1978)

Gregory, Kristiana

Orphan runaways. Scholastic 1998 151p $15.95   **Fic**

1. Brothers—Fiction 2. Orphans—Fiction 3. Gold mines and mining—Fiction

ISBN 0-590-60366-3   LC 97-4345

Harrowing adventures accompany twelve-year-old Danny and his younger brother Judd when they run away from a San Francisco orphanage and search for their uncle in a gold rush boom town

"The adventures of the two boys will intrigue reluctant readers of historical fiction. . . . Gregory strikes a balance between fine character development, action, and adventure." Book Rep

The winter of red snow; the Revolutionary War diary of Abigail Jane Stewart. Scholastic 1996 173p il maps (Dear America) $9.95   **Fic**

1. United States—History—1775-1783, Revolution—Fiction

ISBN 0-590-22653-3   LC 95-44052

Eleven-year-old Abigail presents a diary account of life in Valley Forge from December 1777 to July 1778 as General Washington prepares his troops to fight the British

"*The Winter of Red Snow* gives readers an interesting and realistic look at the Revolutionary War." SLJ

Griffin, Adele

The other Shepards. Hyperion Bks. for Children 1998 218p $14.95; lib bdg $15.49; pa $5.99 **Fic**

1. Sisters—Fiction 2. New York (N.Y.)—Fiction

ISBN 0-7868-0423-8; 0-7868-2370-4 (lib bdg); 0-7868-1333-4 (pa)   LC 98-12609

Teenage Holland and her younger sister Geneva, having always lived under the shadow of siblings who died before they were born, struggle to establish separate identities and escape from the oppressive weight of their parents' continuing grief

"Both life-affirming and wise, this extraordinary tale will haunt readers as surely as the 'other Shepards' haunt the waking and sleeping dreams of these unforgettable sisters." N Y Times Book Rev

Sons of liberty. Hyperion Bks. for Children 1997 230p $14.45; lib bdg $15.49; pa $4.95   **Fic**

1. Runaway teenagers—Fiction 2. Fathers and sons—Fiction

ISBN 0-7868-0351-7; 0-7868-2292-9 (lib bdg); 0-7868-1300-8 (pa)   LC 97-2729

When thirteen-year-old Rock helps his friend Liza run away from home, he wonders whether escaping from his own troubled family would be an act of patriotism or of treason

The author's "pointedly jarring dialogue and keen ear for adolescent jargon have a magnetic quality few readers will be able to resist." Publ Wkly

Split just right. Hyperion Bks. for Children 1997 176p $14.45; lib bdg $15.49; pa $5.95   **Fic**

1. Mothers and daughters—Fiction 2. Single parent family—Fiction 3. Actors—Fiction

ISBN 0-7868-0347-9; 0-7868-2288-0 (lib bdg); 0-7868-1295-8 (pa)   LC 96-45403

After living her life in her actress mother's world of make-believe, ninth-grader Dandelion comes to realize that it is better to face reality

"The pacing is smooth and the tone is light, and Danny is a sunny, solid character." Horn Book Guide

Grimes, Nikki

Jazmin's notebook. Dial Bks. 1998 102p $15.99   **Fic**

1. African Americans—Fiction 2. Authorship—Fiction 3. Harlem (New York, N.Y.)—Fiction

ISBN 0-8037-2224-9   LC 97-5850

A Coretta Scott King honor book for text, 1999

Jazmin, an Afro-American fourteen-year-old who lives with her older sister in a small Harlem apartment in the 1960s, finds strength in writing poetry and keeping a record of the events in her sometimes difficult life

"An articulate, admirable heroine, Jazmin leaps over life's hurdles with agility and integrity." Publ Wkly

Grove, Vicki

The crystal garden. Putnam 1995 217p $15.95; pa $5.99   **Fic**

1. Friendship—Fiction 2. School stories 3. Mothers and daughters—Fiction

ISBN 0-399-21813-0; 0-698-11432-9 (pa)

LC 94-32702

Looking for a new beginning after her father's death, Eliza and her mother move to a backwater town in Missouri where Eliza's desperate attempts to be popular in her new school are thwarted by her growing friendship with the eccentric girl next door

"A multilayered book with memorable characters and humorous as well as poignant situations." Horn Book Guide

Grove, Vicki—*Continued*

Reaching Dustin. Putnam 1998 199p $16.99
                              Fic
1. School stories
ISBN 0-399-23008-4   LC 97-8181
"An interview assignment forces Carly to get to know Dustin Groat, the most unpopular member of her sixth-grade class. Dustin's unsociable behavior began at school in third grade, just after his mother died, and Carly and her friends have looked down upon him ever since. . . . Carly's inner development is convincingly painful as she realizes the part she played in creating Dustin's problems." SLJ

The starplace. Putnam 1999 214p $17.99   **Fic**
1. Prejudices—Fiction 2. African Americans—Fiction 3. Oklahoma—Fiction
ISBN 0-399-23207-9   LC 98-40894
Thirteen-year-old Frannie learns hard lessons about prejudice and segregation when she becomes friends with Celeste, a young black girl who moves into her small Oklahoma town in 1961
"The characterizations, particularly of Frannie and Celeste, are strong and memorable. . . . A wonderful, well-written, multilayered novel with lots of appeal." SLJ

Gurney, James, 1958-
Dinotopia: a land apart from time; written and illustrated by James Gurney. HarperCollins Pubs. 1998 159p il $35   **Fic**
1. Fantasy fiction 2. Dinosaurs—Fiction
ISBN 0-06-028003-4   LC 98-10961
A reissue of the title first published 1992 by Turner Pub.
Other titles about Dinotopia entered under Alan Dean Foster
In 1862, after being shipwrecked in uncharted seas, Professor Arthur Denison and his twelve-year-old son Will find themselves washed up on a strange island where people and dinosaurs live together peacefully
"This fairytale will capture the interests of older fantasy readers. . . . Younger readers, too, will be enticed by the dramatic, full-color illustrations." SLJ
Other available titles about Dinotopia by James Gurney are:
Dinotopia: first flight (1999)
Dinotopia: the world beneath (1995)

Gutman, Dan
Jackie and me; a baseball card adventure. Avon Bks. 1999 145p il $15   **Fic**
1. Robinson, Jackie, 1919-1972—Fiction
ISBN 0-380-97685-4   LC 98-53347
Companion volume to Honus and me (1997)
With his ability to travel through time by using baseball cards, Joe goes back to 1947 to meet Jackie Robinson, turning into a black boy in the process
"Full of action, this title will spark history discussions and be a good choice for book reports and leisure reading." SLJ

The million dollar shot. Hyperion Bks. for Children 1997 114p $13.95; lib bdg $13.89; pa $4.95   **Fic**
1. Basketball—Fiction 2. Contests—Fiction
ISBN 0-7868-0334-7; 0-7868-2275-9 (lib bdg); 0-7868-1220-6 (pa)   LC 97-6461
Eleven-year-old Eddie gets a chance to win a million dollars by sinking a foul shot at the National Basketball Association finals
This "will appeal to both sports readers and general audiences. Gutman's subtle humor, exciting sports action, and excruciating suspense make this title an outstanding choice for reluctant readers." SLJ

Virtually perfect. Hyperion Bks. for Children 1998 123p $13.95; lib bdg $14.49; pa $4.95 **Fic**
1. Computers—Fiction 2. Science fiction
ISBN 0-7868-0394-0; 0-7868-2344-5 (lib bdg); 0-7868-1316-4 (pa)   LC 97-34849
When twelve-year-old Yip uses his father's new software to make a computer simulation of a boy his age, the creation breaks out of cyberspace into the real world and begins to complicate Yip's life
"Gutman has created an amusing and thoughtful novel." SLJ

Guy, Rosa
The disappearance. Delacorte Press 1979 246p hardcover o.p. paperback available $3.99   **Fic**
1. Foster home care—Fiction 2. Mystery fiction 3. African Americans—Fiction
ISBN 0-440-92064-7 (pa)   LC 79-50672
The disappearance of the seven-year-old daughter of a Brooklyn family casts suspicion on a juvenile offender from Harlem who has recently come to live with them
"Some readers might have difficulty with the Black and West Indian speech; others may not appreciate the 'down' ending. But, by story's close, each character has touched us and the fine delineation of all of them stands out as Guy's greatest strength." SLJ
Followed by New guys around the block (1983)

The friends. Holt & Co. 1973 203p $13.95
                                  Fic
1. West Indians—New York (N.Y.)—Fiction 2. Harlem (New York, N.Y.)—Fiction 3. Friendship—Fiction
ISBN 0-8050-1742-9
Also available in paperback from Bantam Bks.
"During early adolescence, friendship can be painful as well as joyful. Phyllisia learns this in her relationship with Edith Jackson. Having just arrived in Harlem from the West Indies, Phyllisia finds life difficult because she is new to the urban scene and because her father is a very strict disciplinarian. Because her accent marks her as different, she is treated with hostility by her classmates, and only Edith befriends her when she is involved in a fight. Phyllisia resists her father's authority when he forbids her to maintain her friendship with poor and slovenly Edith." Shapiro. Fic for Youth. 3d edition
Followed by Ruby, an adult novel, and Edith Jackson (1978)

Haas, Jessie

Unbroken. Greenwillow Bks. 1999 185p $15
Fic
1. Death—Fiction 2. Orphans—Fiction 3. Horses—Fiction
ISBN 0-688-16260-6 LC 98-10485

Following her mother's death in the early 1900s, thirteen-year-old Harry lives on Aunt Sarah's farm where an accident with her spirited colt leaves her a changed young woman

"The quiet novel moves quickly and is enriched by genuine dialogue, realistic portrayals of grief, and careful observations in the first-person narrative." Horn Book Guide

Haddix, Margaret Peterson, 1964-

Among the hidden. Simon & Schuster Bks. for Young Readers 1998 153p $16 **Fic**
1. Science fiction
ISBN 0-689-81700-2 LC 97-33052

In a future where the Population Police enforce the law limiting a family to only two children, Luke has lived all his twelve years in isolation and fear on his family's farm, until another 'third' convinces him that the government is wrong

"The fully realized setting, honest characters, and fast paced plot combine for a suspenseful tale." ALAN

Don't you dare read this, Mrs. Dunphrey; [by] Margaret Peterson. Simon & Schuster Bks. for Young Readers 1996 108p $16 (7 and up) **Fic**
1. Family violence—Fiction 2. Parent and child—Fiction
ISBN 0-689-80097-5 LC 95-43200

"Tish Bonner is required to keep a journal for sophomore English class but is allowed to mark those entries she wants unread. . . . Tish is an underachieving 'big hair girl,' who cracks gum in class and works after school because her mother, severely depressed, is barely able to pay the bills. When her abusive father returns after a two-year absence, Tish records many family crises, ending with an account of the abandonment of herself and her little brother by both parents." Booklist

"This contemporary story realistically depicts the sad home life of a dysfunctional family and the burden put on young people to cope with adult problems." SLJ

Leaving Fishers. Simon & Schuster Bks. for Young Readers 1997 211p $17 (7 and up) **Fic**
1. Cults—Fiction
ISBN 0-689-81125-X LC 96-47857

After joining her new friends in the religious group called Fishers of Men, Dorry finds herself immersed in a cult from which she must struggle to extricate herself

"The novel does a credible job of showing the effect of a cult on a vulnerable person, without disavowing strong religious beliefs." Child Book Rev Serv

Running out of time. Simon & Schuster Bks. for Young Readers 1995 184p $16; pa $3.99 **Fic**
1. Diphtheria—Fiction 2. Space and time—Fiction
ISBN 0-689-80084-3; 0-689-81236-1 (pa)
LC 95-8459

When a diphtheria epidemic hits her 1840 village, thirteen-year-old Jessie discovers it is actually a 1995 tourist site under unseen observation by heartless scientists, and it's up to Jessie to escape the village and save the lives of the dying children

"This absorbing novel develops an unusual premise into the gripping story. . . . This book will appeal to fans of time-travel or historical novels as well as those who prefer realistic contemporary fiction." SLJ

Hahn, Mary Downing, 1937-

As ever, Gordy. Clarion Bks. 1998 184p $15
Fic
1. Brothers and sisters—Fiction
ISBN 0-395-83627-1 LC 97-18913
Sequel to Following my own footsteps

When he and his younger sister move in with their older brother after their grandmother dies, thirteen-year-old Gordy finds himself caught between the boy he was when he lived with his abusive father and the boy his grandmother was helping him become

"Played against a well-rendered post-World War II setting, Gordy's recidivism into his previously wild ways is presented with emotional complexity, as is his love/hate relationship with a female classmate." Horn Book Guide

Daphne's book. Clarion Bks. 1983 177p $15
Fic
1. School stories 2. Friendship—Fiction 3. Authorship—Fiction 4. Family life—Fiction
ISBN 0-89919-183-5 LC 83-7348
Also available in paperback from Avon Bks.

As author Jessica and artist Daphne collaborate on a picture book for a seventh-grade English class contest, Jessica becomes aware of conditions in Daphne's home life that seem to threaten her health and safety

"Characterizations are strong and the situations pressing, so that although the development has a weak spot or two, the story's capacity to move a reader is strong." Booklist

Following my own footsteps. Clarion Bks. 1996 186p $15 **Fic**
1. Family violence—Fiction 2. Fathers and sons—Fiction 3. Grandmothers—Fiction
ISBN 0-395-76477-7 LC 95-50144
Also available in paperback from Avon Bks.

In 1945, Gordy's grandmother takes him and his family into her North Carolina home after his abusive father is arrested, and he just begins to respond to his grandmother's loving discipline when his father returns

"Hahn gets us inside her character so quickly and skillfully that she maintains our sympathy for William without ever resorting to the sentimental. . . . Sometimes heartrending, sometimes funny, Gordy Smith will prove memorable to all who meet him." Booklist

Followed by As ever, Gordy

Stepping on the cracks. Clarion Bks. 1991 216p $16 **Fic**
1. World War, 1939-1945—Fiction
ISBN 0-395-58507-4 LC 91-7706
Also available in paperback from Avon Bks.

Hahn, Mary Downing, 1937—*Continued*

In 1944, while her brother is overseas fighting in World War II, eleven-year-old Margaret gets a new view of the school bully Gordy when she finds him hiding his own brother, an army deserter, and decides to help him

"Well-drawn characters and a satisfying plot. . . . There is plenty of action and page-turning suspense to please those who want a quick read, but there is much to ponder and reflect on as well." SLJ

Hall, Lynn, 1937-

If winter comes. Scribner 1986 119p $16 (7 and up)   **Fic**
1. Nuclear warfare—Fiction
ISBN 0-684-18575-X   LC 85-43348
"It is Friday afternoon, and high school sweethearts Meredith and Barry have just learned that their lives may end, along with everyone else's, on Sunday evening. A small island nation is threatening the United States with nuclear missiles. During that very long all-too-short, weekend, the two teens interact with their families and each other in ways new to them." Voice Youth Advocates

"This thought-provoking novel is a useful addition to nuclear-disaster fiction. The anti-nuclear message is obvious but not overwhelming, and readers who would otherwise avoid this depressing topic may be attracted by Hall's comparatively light touch." SLJ

Hamilton, Virginia, 1936-

Cousins. Philomel Bks. 1990 125p $15.95   **Fic**
1. Death—Fiction 2. Cousins—Fiction 3. Grandmothers—Fiction 4. African Americans—Fiction
ISBN 0-399-22164-6   LC 90-31451
Also available in paperback from Scholastic
"Cammy feels things strongly, whether it's the immeasurable love she has for her Gram Tut, or the jealousy and anger she feels for her perfect, sometimes patronizing cousin Patty Ann. But while those intense emotions make her a strong-willed, feisty girl, they also cause her a great deal of pain when Patty Ann drowns saving another cousin." SLJ

"The writing reverberates with honesty and truth. Virginia Hamilton encases the story in family tradition, which offsets the instabilities of contemporary life, and she beautifully counterposes superstition and rationality, separation and reconciliation, love and death." Horn Book

Followed by Second cousins

The house of Dies Drear; illustrated by Eros Keith. Macmillan 1968 246p il $17; pa $4.50
Fic
1. African Americans—Fiction 2. Mystery fiction 3. Ohio—Fiction
ISBN 0-02-742500-2; 0-02-043520-7 (pa)
LC 68-23059
"A hundred years ago, Dies Drear and two slaves he was hiding in his house, an Underground Railroad station in Ohio, had been murdered. The house, huge and isolated, was fascinating, Thomas thought, but he wasn't sure he was glad Papa had bought it—funny things kept happening, frightening things. The caretaker was forbidding, the neighbors unfriendly." Bull Cent Child Books

"The answer to the mystery comes in a startling dramatic dénouement that is pure theater. This is gifted writing; the characterization is unforgettable, the plot imbued with mounting tension." Saturday Rev

Followed by The mystery of Drear House

The mystery of Drear House; the conclusion of the Dies Drear chronicle. Greenwillow Bks. 1987 217p $15.95   **Fic**
1. African Americans—Fiction 2. Buried treasure—Fiction 3. Mystery fiction
ISBN 0-688-04026-8   LC 86-9829
Also available in paperback from Scholastic
Sequel to The house of Dies Drear
"Ingredients such as secret rooms and passages, moving walls, and awesome treasure will play well to a popular audience; yet substantive portrayals of characters and relationships provide the depth one associates with Hamilton. This solid tale displays a sensitivity toward feelings, emotions, and conflicting values—all in the context of a fantastic mystery laid to rest." Booklist

Plain City. Blue Sky Press (NY) 1993 194p $13.95; pa $4.50   **Fic**
1. Fathers and daughters—Fiction 2. African Americans—Fiction 3. Racially mixed people—Fiction
ISBN 0-590-47364-6; 0-590-47365-4 (pa)
LC 93-19910
Twelve-year-old Buhlaire, a "mixed" child who feels out of place in her community, struggles to unearth her past and her family history as she gradually discovers more and more about her long-missing father

"Richly textured with a cast of unforgettable characters, this extraordinary novel offers a rare glimpse of unconditional love, family loyalty and compassion." Publ Wkly

The planet of Junior Brown. Macmillan 1971 210p $17; pa $3.95   **Fic**
1. Friendship—Fiction 2. African Americans—Fiction
ISBN 0-02-742510-X; 0-02-043540-1 (pa)
"This is the story of a crucial week in the lives of two black, eighth-grade dropouts who have been spending their time with the school janitor. Each boy is presented as a distinct individual. Jr. is a three-hundred pound musical prodigy as neurotic as his overprotective mother. Buddy has learned to live by his wits in a world of homeless children. Buddy becomes Jr. Brown's protector and says to the other boys, 'We are together because we have to learn to live for each other.'" Read Ladders for Hum Relat. 6th edition

Second cousins. Blue Sky Press (NY) 1998 168p $14.95   **Fic**
1. Cousins—Fiction 2. African Americans—Fiction
ISBN 0-590-47368-9   LC 98-12859
Sequel to Cousins
The friendship of twelve-year-old cousins Cammy and Elodie is threatened when the family reunion includes two other cousins near their age and Elodie is tempted to drop Cammy for a new companion

"The author's on-target dialogue and skillfully drawn characterizations compensate for the book's uneven pacing." Publ Wkly

Hamilton, Virginia, 1936-—*Continued*
Sweet whispers, Brother Rush. Philomel Bks.
1982 215p $17.95   **Fic**
   1. Single parent family—Fiction 2. African Americans—Fiction 3. Ghost stories
   ISBN 0-399-20894-1   LC 81-22745
Also available in paperback from Avon Bks.
A Newbery Medal honor book, 1983. Coretta Scott
King award for text, 1983
"Teresa (Tree) is black and responsible for more than
a young teenager should have to manage. Because the father deserted the family long ago, M'Vy, the mother, has
had to work at exhausting jobs that kept her away from
home much of the time. Tree's responsibilities include
caring for her retarded older brother, Dab, who also—unknown to Tree—suffers a blood disease. An element of
mystic fantasy in the form of the ghost of Tree's uncle,
Brother Rush, heightens the tension in the story." Shapiro. Fic for Youth. 3d edition

Hansen, Joyce
The captive. Scholastic 1994 195p $13.95; pa
$3.50   **Fic**
   1. Slavery—Fiction
   ISBN 0-590-41625-1; 0-590-41624-3 (pa)
"Modeled after an actual slave narrative, this moving
first-person tale follows twelve-year-old Kofi from his
kidnapping in West Africa to his cruel enslavement in
Massachusetts and his subsequent freedom and career as
a sailor. The well-crafted and compelling survival story
juxtaposes two cultures and gives a unique account of
slavery from the sufferer's perspective." Horn Book
Guide

Which way freedom? Walker & Co. 1986 120p
$18.75   **Fic**
   1. African Americans—Fiction 2. United States—History—1861-1865, Civil War—Fiction
   ISBN 0-8027-6623-4   LC 85-29547
Also available in paperback from Avon Bks.
"Walker's American history series for young readers"
The author "describes the way in which one young
black man, Obi, struggles over a period of three years
(1861-1864) politically and ideologically toward the goal
of being a free man. . . . [He] eventually joins a Union
regiment and is one of the few to escape from the
bloody battle at Fort Pillow, Tennessee." Bull Cent Child
Books
"There is sufficient action to sustain readers' interest,
but it is in the book's characterization that the chief
strength lies. . . . A sensitive, thought-provoking historical novel." SLJ
   Followed by Out from this place (1988)

Harrell, Beatrice Orcutt, 1943-
Longwalker's journey; a novel of the Choctaw
trail of tears; [by] Beatrice O. Harrell; illustrated
by Tony Meers. Dial Bks. for Young Readers
1999 133p il $15.99   **Fic**
   1. Choctaw Indians—Fiction 2. Frontier and pioneer
life—Fiction
   ISBN 0-8037-2380-6   LC 98-9754

When the government removes their tribe from their
sacred homeland in 1831, ten-year-old Minko and his father endure terrible hardships on their journey from Mississippi to Oklahoma where Minko receives the name
Longwalker
"Simple text and straightforward narrative incorporate
aspects of Indian culture and lifestyle. . . . Based on
Harrell's family's experiences, this age-appropriate story
provides a good starting point for learning about an important chapter in American history." Booklist

Hautman, Pete, 1952-
Stone cold. Simon & Schuster Bks. for Young
Readers 1998 163p $16 (7 and up)   **Fic**
   1. Gambling—Fiction
   ISBN 0-689-81759-2   LC 97-48360
Sixteen-year-old Denn finds himself alienating both
friends and family when he becomes obsessed with play-
ing high-stakes poker with adult gamblers
"Fast paced and powerfully delivered, this novel is as
taut and suspenseful as a high-stakes game." SLJ

Hayes, Daniel, 1952-
Flyers. Simon & Schuster Bks. for Young
Readers 1996 203p $16; pa $4.50 (7 and up)
                                                    Fic
   ISBN 0-689-80372-9; 0-689-80373-7 (pa)
                                        LC 96-10568
"Fifteen-year-old Gabe and his friends are making a
film, Green Guy Gets Therapy, for their summer Gifted
and Talented class project. . . . The filming of the elaborate spoof is interrupted by a series of odd, seemingly
unrelated events, which cleverly build to a wholly believable and strangely moving climax involving death, redemption, forgiveness, and love. . . . Funny, sardonic,
clever, and ultimately uplifting, the story will appeal to
teens who love words and ideas." Booklist

No effect. Godine 1993 212p o.p.; Avon Bks.
paperback available $3.99   **Fic**
   1. School stories 2. Wrestling—Fiction
   ISBN 0-380-72392-1 (pa)   LC 93-29329
This novel about Tyler and Lyme "has the eighth-
grade boys trying out for the varsity wrestling team. Tyler's desire to be a wrestler stems less from any intrinsic
interest in the sport than from his belief that it will attract girls. . . . When a pretty young instructor takes
over their science classes after Mrs. Waverly is overcome by a fatal stroke, Tyler is helplessly smitten." Horn
Book
"The dialogue rings true to the age group, and Tyler's
feelings, which range from euphoria to depression, are
thoughtfully drawn." SLJ

Hearne, Betsy Gould
Listening for Leroy; [by] Betsy Hearne.
Margaret K. McElderry Bks. 1998 210p $16 **Fic**
   1. Fathers and daughters—Fiction 2. Race relations—
Fiction 3. Southern States—Fiction
   ISBN 0-689-82218-9   LC 98-4495
Growing up in rural Alabama in the 1950s, ten-year-
old Alice has no one to talk to but Leroy, the black farm
hand, but when Alice's doctor father moves the family

Hearne, Betsy Gould—*Continued*

to Tennessee, she has trouble fitting in and she sorely misses Leroy

"Realistic dialogue, well-defined characters, and fairly presented complex issues combine for a heartfelt look at the growing pains of an idealistic girl experiencing a less than ideal reality." Booklist

Heisel, Sharon E.

Eyes of a stranger. Delacorte Press 1996 168p hardcover o.p. paperback available $4.50 (7 and up)   **Fic**

1. Mystery fiction 2. Physically handicapped—Fiction

ISBN 0-440-21993-0 (pa)   LC 95-43571

Marissa, a shy self-conscious girl with a twisted leg, is attracted to a strikingly handsome visitor to her uncle's carousel but begins to suspect that he is a psychotic serial killer

"This page-turner combines suspenseful action with rich character development in a fluid and natural style." ALAN

Henkes, Kevin, 1960-

The birthday room. Greenwillow Bks. 1999 152p $16   **Fic**

1. Family life—Fiction 2. Uncles—Fiction

ISBN 0-688-16733-0   LC 98-39887

"For his twelfth birthday, Ben Hunter receives a room that he can use as an art studio and a letter from his uncle—the one responsible for the loss of Ben's little finger when Ben was a toddler. . . . Mrs. Hunter, who has been angry at her brother since the accident, reluctantly agrees to go to Oregon with Ben." Booklist

"Told in spare, unobtrusive prose, a story that helps us see our own chances for benefiting from mutual tolerance, creative conflict resolution, and other forms of good will." Horn Book

Protecting Marie. Greenwillow Bks. 1995 195p $15   **Fic**

1. Fathers and daughters—Fiction 2. Dogs—Fiction

ISBN 0-688-13958-2   LC 94-16387

Also available in paperback from Penguin Bks.

Relates twelve-year-old Fanny's love-hate relationship with her father, a temperamental artist, who has given Fanny a new dog

"The characters ring heartbreakingly true in this quiet, wise story; they are complex and difficult—like all of us—and worthy of our attention." Horn Book

Sun & spoon. Greenwillow Bks. 1997 135p $15   **Fic**

1. Grandmothers—Fiction 2. Death—Fiction

ISBN 0-688-15232-5   LC 96-46259

Also available in paperback from Penguin Bks.

"Spoon, 10, spends his summer trying to reconfigure his world, which seems strangely out of kilter since his grandmother's death." SLJ

"Sensitively placed metaphors enrich the narrative, embuing its perceptive depictions of grief with a powerful message of affirmation." Publ Wkly

Hentoff, Nat

The day they came to arrest the book; a novel. Delacorte Press 1982 169p o.p.; Dell paperback available $4.99 (7 and up)   **Fic**

1. Censorship—Fiction 2. School stories

ISBN 0-440-91814-6 (pa)   LC 82-71100

"Barney Roth, editor of the high school newspaper, believes he must take a stand when a group of students and parents decide that 'The Adventures of Huckleberry Finn' should be removed from the school library. The group finds the book offensive to blacks and insists that it be omitted from school reading lists. The question is, where does censorship end? What stops the next group from finding another book offensive to someone else's sensibilities?" Books for You

Hermes, Patricia, 1936-

Calling me home. Avon Bks. 1998 440p $15   **Fic**

1. Frontier and pioneer life—Fiction 2. Family life—Fiction 3. Nebraska—Fiction

ISBN 0-380-97451-7   LC 98-7909

"Abbie and her family have moved from St. Joseph, Missouri, to a sod house in Nebraska during the 1850s. Unhappy about the move, Abbie can't help complaining and feeling sorry for herself—until sickness brings tragedy to her family." Horn Book Guide

"A solid story, neatly told." Publ Wkly

Cheat the moon; a novel. Little, Brown 1998 167p $15.95   **Fic**

1. Fathers—Fiction   2. Alcoholism—Fiction 3. Death—Fiction

ISBN 0-316-35929-7   LC 97-34369

With her mother dead and her father an alcoholic who disappears for days at a time, Gabrielle must assume responsibility for her younger brother Will and herself, barely making ends meet and afraid to put her trust in anyone

"While the story and family relationships will hook readers, it is Gabby's voice—so clear, touching, and astute—that is most powerful in this novel." SLJ

Mama, let's dance; a novel. Little, Brown 1991 168p o.p.; Scholastic paperback available $2.99   **Fic**

1. Abandoned children—Fiction 2. Brothers and sisters—Fiction

ISBN 0-590-46633-X (pa)   LC 91-11988

"When their mother abandons them, eleven-year-old Mary Belle, seven-year-old Callie, and their older brother, Ariel, conspire to keep her absence a secret so that they will not be placed in separate foster homes by the county officials." Horn Book

The author "writes a moving expression of love and loyalty while carefully balancing faith with despair." Child Book Rev Serv

Someone to count on; a novel. Little, Brown 1993 184p o.p.; Scholastic paperback available $3.50   **Fic**

1. Mothers and daughters—Fiction 2. Grandfathers—Fiction 3. Ranch life—Fiction

ISBN 0-590-22275-9 (pa)   LC 93-13502

Hermes, Patricia, 1936-—*Continued*
When eleven-year-old Sam visits her grandfather's ranch for the first time, she finds a new life very different from the one she has known with her vagabond mother and discovers what really matters most to her

"The Colorado ranch setting will attract the horsey set and fans of family stories will be drawn to [the author's] quirky, distinctive characters." Voice Youth Advocates

Hesse, Karen
Letters from Rifka. Holt & Co. 1992 148p $14.95   **Fic**
1. Immigration and emigration—Fiction 2. Jews—Fiction
ISBN 0-8050-1964-2   LC 91-48007
Also available in paperback from Penguin Bks.

In letters to her cousin, Rifka, a young Jewish girl, chronicles her family's flight from Russia in 1919 and her own experiences when she must be left in Belgium for a while when the others emigrate to America

"Based on the true story of the author's great-aunt, the moving account of a brave young girl's story brings to life the day-to-day trials and horrors experienced by many immigrants as well as the resourcefulness and strength they found within themselves." Horn Book

The music of dolphins. Scholastic 1996 181p $14.95; pa $4.50   **Fic**
1. Wild children—Fiction 2. Dolphins—Fiction
ISBN 0-590-89797-7; 0-590-89798-5 (pa)
     LC 96-3494

Using sophisticated computer technology, Mila, a fifteen-year-old girl who has been raised by dolphins, records her thoughts about her reintroduction to the human world

"Deceptively easy in format, this is a complex and demanding book. . . . This powerful exploration of how we become human and how the soul endures is a song of beauty and sorrow, haunting and unforgettable." SLJ

Out of the dust. Scholastic 1997 227p $15.95; pa $4.99   **Fic**
1. Dust storms—Fiction 2. Farm life—Fiction 3. Great Depression, 1929-1939—Fiction 4. Oklahoma—Fiction
ISBN 0-590-36080-9; 0-590-37125-8 (pa)
     LC 96-40344
Awarded the Newbery Medal, 1998

"After facing loss after loss during the Oklahoma Dust Bowl, Billie Jo begins to reconstruct her life." SLJ

"Hesse's writing transcends the gloom and transforms it into a powerfully compelling tale of a girl with enormous strength, courage, and love. The entire novel is written in very readable blank verse." Booklist

Phoenix rising. Holt & Co. 1994 182p $15.95
     Fic
1. Nuclear power plants—Fiction 2. Death—Fiction 3. Friendship—Fiction
ISBN 0-8050-3108-1   LC 93-47301
Also available in paperback from Penguin Bks.

Thirteen-year-old Nyle learns about relationships and death when fifteen-year-old Ezra, who was exposed to radiation leaked from a nearby nuclear plant, comes to stay at her grandmother's Vermont farmhouse

"The author's under-stated approach heightens the emotional impact of her searching and memorable tale." Publ Wkly

Hesser, Terry Spencer
Kissing doorknobs. Delacorte Press 1998 149p $15.95; pa $4.99 (7 and up)   **Fic**
1. Obsessive-compulsive neurosis—Fiction
ISBN 0-385-32329-8; 0-440-41314-1 (pa)
     LC 97-26937
Fourteen-year-old Tara describes how her increasingly strange compulsions begin to take over her life and affect her relationships with her family and friends

"An honest, fresh, and multilayered story to which readers will instantly relate. . . . The prose is forthright, economical, and peppered with wry humor." SLJ

Hewett, Lorri
Dancer. Dutton Children's Bks. 1999 214p $15.99 (7 and up)   **Fic**
1. Ballet—Fiction 2. African Americans—Fiction
ISBN 0-525-45968-5   LC 98-55501
"Sixteen-year-old Stephanie works hard toward her goal of becoming a professional ballerina, but there are complications. Her father feels that her career choice is unrealistic, particularly for an African American girl. . . . Readers familiar with ballet will find the dance background vivid and convincing, but the strength of the book comes from the carefully drawn characters and relationships." Booklist

Hickman, Janet
Jericho; a novel. Greenwillow Bks. 1994 135p $15   **Fic**
1. Grandmothers—Fiction 2. Family life—Fiction 3. Old age—Fiction
ISBN 0-688-13398-3   LC 93-37309
Also available in paperback from Avon Bks.

An account of twelve-year-old Angela's visit to help take care of her great-grandmother alternates with the story of the old woman's life

"The author's unsentimental narrative reveals a sharp eye for detail, a profound understanding of the aging process and a deep love for humanity." Publ Wkly

Hinton, S. E.
The outsiders. Viking 1967 188p $15.99; pa $4.99 (7 and up)   **Fic**
1. Juvenile delinquency—Fiction
ISBN 0-670-53257-6; 0-14-038572-X (pa)
"From the perspective of Ponyboy Curtis, the author relates the story of the Greasers, who are from the lower class, and their conflict with the Socs, who are their middle-class opposite number. For the Greasers, the gang comprises their street family, all the family that some of them have. In the collision between the two social factions, two buddies die, one as a hood, the other, a hero." Shapiro. Fic for Youth. 3d edition

Rumble fish. Delacorte Press 1975 132p $13.95; pa $4.99 (7 and up)   **Fic**
1. Brothers—Fiction 2. Juvenile delinquency—Fiction
ISBN 0-385-28675-9; 0-440-07534-4 (pa)

Hinton, S. E.—*Continued*

"Young Rusty-James rapidly loses everything meaningful to him—his girl, his 'rep' as number one tough guy, and, most important, his idolized older brother—a James Dean look- and act-alike known only as the Motorcycle Boy. And, although it is the Motorcycle Boy who is gunned down at the end after breaking into a pet store, it is Rusty-James, emotionally burnt out at 14, who is the ultimate victim." SLJ

"Believable, written convincingly in first person, the story line is less a plot than a picture of personality disintegration. Memorable, but with no relief from depression, no note of hope." Bull Cent Child Books

Taming the Star Runner. Delacorte Press 1988 181p hardcover o.p. paperback available $4.99 (7 and up)   **Fic**
1. Authorship—Fiction 2. Horses—Fiction
ISBN 0-440-20479-8 (pa)   LC 88-7065

The author "centers her story around sixteen-year-old Travis Harris, a confused, angry, and withdrawn teenager who just happens to have written his first book. When Travis seriously wounds his stepfather in a fight, he is sent to live with his uncle on his Oklahoma ranch. There a whole new world opens up for him when he forms an uneasy friendship with Casey, the manager of the ranch's riding school. Travis is especially fascinated by and feels a strong bond with Star Runner, the beautiful, volatile horse Casey is struggling to tame." Child Book Rev Serv

"This is far from a formula horse story; it has depth, pattern, perception, and a communicable empathy for its protagonist." Bull Cent Child Books

Tex. Delacorte Press 1979 194p hardcover o.p. paperback available $4.99 (7 and up)   **Fic**
1. Brothers—Fiction
ISBN 0-440-97850-5 (pa)   LC 78-50448

"Fourteen-year-old Tex lives with his 17-year-old brother Mason in a rural area. Their father hasn't been home in five months, and the relationship between the two boys is tense. Each has his own problems, fears, and growing pains which keep him alienated from his brother, until a dramatic and terrifying experience forces them to seek comfort and support from each other." SLJ

"The novel is marked by Hinton's superb character development and realistic dialogue. . . . Tex is an appealing, likable anti-hero who just seems to attract trouble and danger." Child Book Rev Serv

That was then, this is now. Viking 1971 159p $15.99; pa $4.99 (7 and up)   **Fic**
1. Drug abuse—Fiction 2. Juvenile delinquency—Fiction
ISBN 0-670-69798-2; 0-14-038966-0 (pa)

"Mark had lived with Byron's family since he was nine (his parents had shot each other) and the two boys were like brothers. Now they are adolescent, skirmishing on the edge of delinquency. Bryon, who tells the story, is in love with a girl whose younger brother is a gentle, candid thirteen-year-old; when he and Cathy find that the boy has taken drugs and is on a bad trip, Bryon is deeply upset. Then he finds a cache of pills in Mark's room and realizes that Mark is a pusher. . . . The book has a bitter realism . . . it is distinguished by percipience in characterization, natural dialogue, and a sensitivity toward the complexity of human relationships." Sutherland. The Best in Child Books

Hite, Sid, 1954-

Answer my prayer. Holt & Co. 1995 182p $15.95 (7 and up)   **Fic**
1. Fantasy fiction 2. Angels—Fiction
ISBN 0-8050-3406-4   LC 94-39235
Also available in paperback from Dell

When the angel Ebol comes down to the land of Korasan to help the forester's sixteen-year-old daughter, Lydia, he finds himself involved in romance, political intrigues, and other escapades

"Lydia is an appealing, lovelorn heroine, modest but brave, and Ebol's humorous intervention and the happy solutions to both personal and national conflicts make a charmingly fresh and unusual novel." Horn Book

Cecil in space. Holt & Co. 1999 150p $15.95 (7 and up)   **Fic**
1. Friendship—Fiction 2. Virginia—Fiction
ISBN 0-8050-5055-8   LC 98-36948

Seventeen-year-old Cecil tries to help his best friend Isaac, who is under suspicion of having vandalized the welcome sign at the edge of their small Virginia town, and pursues his interest in Isaac's sister Isabel

"What YAs will enjoy is the relaxed summer story, the nervy flirting and kissing, the hip dialogue, and the funny, awkward, smart narrator." Booklist

Those darn Dithers. Holt & Co. 1996 184p $15.95   **Fic**
1. Family life—Fiction 2. Country life—Fiction 3. Virginia—Fiction
ISBN 0-8050-3838-8   LC 96-22400
Also available in paperback from Dell

In this book about the eccentric Dither family of rural Virginia "nine-year-old Archibald Dither helps former government operative and parapsychologist Aunt Bean build an astral projector, a vaudeville show features Porcellina the dancing pig, and a trip to the beach ends when elderly eccentric Leopold Hillacre falls asleep on a rubber raft and drifts out into the shipping lanes. . . . The pace is as leisurely as a stroll on a hot summer day, and the story is really character driven, with Hite managing to breathe life into a host of major and minor players." Booklist

Another available title about the Dither family is:
Dither farm (1992)

Hobbs, Valerie

How far would you have gotten if I hadn't called you back? a novel. Orchard Bks. 1995 306p $19.95; lib bdg $20.99 (7 and up)   **Fic**
1. Automobile racing—Fiction 2. California—Fiction
ISBN 0-531-09480-4; 0-531-08780-8 (lib bdg)
     LC 94-48799
Also available in paperback from Penguin Bks.

"A Richard Jackson book"

"Sixteen-year-old Brownwyn Lewis is sure that the only way a displaced New Jersey person like herself will make it in rural California is to own a car. It will be her ticket to acceptance and excitement—and to boys—as well as a way of acting out against her father, whose alcoholism and attempted suicide she's unwilling to forgive or forget. Although a car does enable her to find a group, it can't help her choose between two boys: solid, sensitive outsider Will Harding and cool, sexy bad boy

Hobbs, Valerie—*Continued*

JC. . . . Hobbs manipulates the elements (including the sex) with energy, confidence, and surprise. . . . An enticing coming-of-age story, unerringly accurate in both its passions and its scenery."

Hobbs, Will

Beardance. Atheneum Pubs. 1993 197p il $16 (7 and up)   **Fic**
   1. Ute Indians—Fiction 2. Bears—Fiction
   ISBN 0-689-31867-7   LC 92-44874
   Also available in paperback from Avon Bks.
   Sequel to Bearstone
   While accompanying an elderly rancher on a trip into the San Juan Mountains, Cloyd, a Ute Indian boy, tries to help two orphaned grizzly cubs survive the winter and, at the same time, completes his spirit mission
   "The story offers plenty of action and memorable characters, and the descriptions of Ute rituals and legends, the setting, and Cloyd's first experiences with spirit dreams are particularly well done." Horn Book Guide

Bearstone. Atheneum Pubs. 1989 154p $17 (7 and up)   **Fic**
   1. Ute Indians—Fiction
   ISBN 0-689-31496-5   LC 89-6641
   Also available in paperback from Avon Bks.
   "Rebellious at being forced to abandon his family and his Ute Indian heritage to attend high school, Cloyd is sent to spend a summer with a lonely old rancher in Colorado. Upon arriving, Cloyd accidentally finds a turquoise bear totem in an Anasazi grave site, which serves as a touchstone between his cultural roots and his feelings. As time goes by, he also develops a mutual respect and friendship for the old man." ALAN
   "The growth and maturity that Cloyd acquires as the summer progresses is juxtaposed poetically against the majestic Colorado landscape. Hobbs has creatively blended myth and reality as Cloyd forges a new identity for himself." Voice Youth Advocates
   Followed by Beardance

The Big Wander. Atheneum Pubs. 1992 181p $17 (7 and up)   **Fic**
   1. Uncles—Fiction 2. Navajo Indians—Fiction 3. Horses—Fiction
   ISBN 0-689-31767-0   LC 92-825
   Also available in paperback from Avon Bks.
   As he searches for his uncle through the rugged Southwest canyon country, fourteen-year-old Clay becomes involved with a group of Navajo Indians who are trying to save some of the last wild mustangs
   "Hobbs skillfully blends action scenes (flash flood, quicksand, and wild chases) with moments of humor and insight." SLJ

Downriver. Atheneum Pubs. 1991 204p $17 (7 and up)   **Fic**
   1. Rafting (Sports)—Fiction 2. Wilderness survival—Fiction
   ISBN 0-689-31690-9   LC 90-1044
   Also available in paperback from Bantam Bks.
   Fifteen-year-old Jessie and the other rebellious teenage members of a wilderness survival school team abandon their adult leader, hijack his boats, and try to run the dangerous white water at the bottom of the Grand Canyon
   "Will Hobbs has written a wonderful book. The reader vicariously lives through a trip through the Grand Canyon and at the same time watches a group of rebellious teenagers transformed into self-reliant adults." BAYA Book Rev

Far North. Morrow Junior Bks. 1996 226p $15 (7 and up)   **Fic**
   1. Wilderness survival—Fiction 2. Northwest Territories—Fiction
   ISBN 0-688-14192-7   LC 95-42686
   Also available in paperback from Avon Bks.
   After the destruction of their floatplane, sixteen-year-old Gabe and his Dene friend, Raymond, struggle to survive a winter in the wilderness of the Northwest Territories
   This "delivers breathless action and an inspiring sense of Canada's vast landscape." Publ Wkly

Ghost canoe. Morrow Junior Bks. 1997 195p $15   **Fic**
   1. Buried treasure—Fiction 2. Adventure fiction 3. Pacific Northwest—Fiction
   ISBN 0-688-14193-5   LC 96-34417
   Also available in paperback from Avon Bks.
   Fourteen-year-old Nathan, fishing with the Makah in the Pacific Northwest, finds himself holding a vital clue when a mysterious stranger comes to town looking for Spanish treasure
   "Hobbs blends together a number of elements to create an exciting adventure set in 1874. . . . A winning tale that artfully combines history, nature, and suspense." SLJ

Kokopelli's flute. Atheneum Bks. for Young Readers 1995 148p $16   **Fic**
   1. Flutes—Fiction 2. Magic—Fiction 3. Indians of North America—Fiction 4. New Mexico—Fiction
   ISBN 0-689-31974-6   LC 95-8422
   Also available in paperback from Avon Bks.
   Thirteen-year-old Tepary discovers an old flute in a cliff dwelling in New Mexico, and through its power he learns about ancient Native American magic
   "Outstanding characters, plot, mood, and setting combine in this satisfying and memorable book." SLJ

The maze. Morrow Junior Bks. 1998 198p $15 (7 and up)   **Fic**
   1. Runaway teenagers—Fiction 2. Foster home care—Fiction 3. Condors—Fiction 4. Wildlife conservation—Fiction
   ISBN 0-688-15092-6   LC 98-10791
   Also available in paperback from Avon Bks.
   Rick, a fourteen-year-old foster child, escapes from a juvenile detention facility near Las Vegas and travels to Canyonlands National Park in Utah where he meets a bird biologist working on a project to reintroduce condors to the wild
   "Hobbs spins an engrossing yarn, blending adventure with a strong theme, advocating the need for developing personal values." Horn Book Guide

Hodges, Margaret

Don Quíxote and Sancho Panza; adapted by Margaret Hodges from Don Quixote of La Mancha, by Miguel DeCervantes Saavedra; illustrated by Stephen Marchesi. Scribner 1992 72p il $16.95   **Fic**

1. Knights and knighthood—Fiction 2. Spain—Fiction
ISBN 0-684-19235-7   LC 90-24098

"Hodges abridges several episodes from Cervantes' famous novel, making them accessible to younger readers. Leading off with the tale in which Don Quixote first puts on armor and concluding with the story of his death. Hodges' selections include Quixote's battle with the windmills, the adventure involving the bearded duennas and the flying horse, and the story of Sancho Panza's island 'governorship.'" Booklist

Holland, Isabelle

Behind the lines. Scholastic 1994 194p $13.95   **Fic**

1. United States—History—1861-1865, Civil War—Fiction 2. New York (N.Y.)—Fiction 3. African Americans—Fiction 4. Irish Americans—Fiction
ISBN 0-590-45113-8   LC 93-2576

During the New York Draft Riot of 1863, 14 year-old Katie O'Farrell helps an African American make a daring escape from an angry mob

"Young readers 'will get a sense of history through this beautiful, well-written, action filled story." Child Book Rev Serv

The man without a face. Harper & Row 1987 c1972 159p lib bdg $12.89; pa $3.95   **Fic**

1. Homosexuality—Fiction
ISBN 0-397-32264-X (lib bdg); 0-06-447028-8 (pa)
                        LC 88-140924

Reissue of the title first published 1972

"From his tutor, the badly scarred recluse Justice McLeod, 14-year-old Charles Norstadt learns much more than the meaning of homosexuality." Booklist

"The author handles the homosexual experience with taste and discretion; the act of love between Justin and Charles is a necessary emotional catharsis for the boy within the context of his story, and is developed with perception and restraint. . . . A highly moral book, powerfully and sensitively written; a book that never loses sight of the humor and pain inherent in the human condition." Horn Book

Holm, Jennifer L.

Our only May Amelia. HarperCollins Pubs. 1999 253p il $15.95   **Fic**

1. Frontier and pioneer life—Fiction 2. Family life—Fiction 3. Finnish Americans—Fiction 4. Washington (State)—Fiction
ISBN 0-06-027822-6   LC 98-47504

A Newbery Medal honor book, 2000

As the only girl in a Finnish American family of seven brothers, May Amelia Jackson resents being expected to act like a lady while growing up in Washington state in 1899

"The voice of the colloquial first-person narrative rings true and provides a vivid picture of frontier and pioneer life. . . . An afterword discusses Holm's research into her own family's history and that of other Finnish immigrants." Horn Book Guide

Holman, Felice

Real. Atheneum Bks. for Young Readers 1997 176p $16   **Fic**

1. Space and time—Fiction 2. Indians of North America—Fiction 3. California—Fiction
ISBN 0-689-80772-4   LC 96-47457

In 1932, while exploring the California desert, Colly finds a Cahuilla Indian boy and his grandmother, who are trapped in a Forever Day that they are constantly repeating from their lives in 1774

"Holman does a nice job of combining a supernatural story with early Hollywood movie history, Cahuilla Indian traditions, and Indian heritage preservation. This is an easy read and will keep most middle schoolers interested." Voice Youth Advocates

Slake's limbo. Scribner 1974 117p $14.95; pa $3.95   **Fic**

1. Runaway children—Fiction 2. Subways—Fiction 3. New York (N.Y.)—Fiction
ISBN 0-684-13926-X; 0-689-71066-6 (pa)
                        LC 74-11675

Aremis Slake, at the age of thirteen, takes to the New York City subways as a refuge from an abusive home life and oppressive school system

"The economically told chronicle of Slake's adventures is more than a survival saga: it is also an eloquent study of poverty, of fear, and finally of hope." Horn Book

Holt, Kimberly Willis

My Louisiana sky. Holt & Co. 1998 200p $15.95   **Fic**

1. Parent and child—Fiction 2. Mentally handicapped—Fiction 3. Louisiana—Fiction
ISBN 0-8050-5251-8   LC 98-12345

Growing up in Saitter, Louisiana, in the 1950s, twelve-year-old Tiger Ann struggles with her feelings about her stern, but loving grandmother, her mentally slow parents, and her good friend and neighbor, Jesse

"Holt never resorts to over-dramatization or sentimentality in developing her uncannily credible characters." Horn Book Guide

Hoobler, Dorothy

The ghost in the Tokaido Inn; [by] Dorothy and Thomas Hoobler. Philomel Bks. 1999 214p $17.99   **Fic**

1. Japan—Fiction 2. Mystery fiction
ISBN 0-399-23330-X   LC 98-14089

While attempting to solve the mystery of a stolen jewel, Seikei, a merchant's son who longs to be a samurai, joins a group of kabuki actors in eighteenth-century Japan

"Precise characterization, suspenseful plot twists, and a pace defined by swift and sometimes violent action make this a lively period thriller." Bull Cent Child Books

Horvath, Betty F.

Sir Galahad, Mr. Longfellow, and me; [by] Betty Horvath. Atheneum Pubs. 1998 137p $15   **Fic**

1. School stories 2. Family life—Fiction
ISBN 0-689-81470-4   LC 96-43460

Horvath, Betty F.—*Continued*

"A Jean Karl book"

In 1938, encouraged by her sixth-grade teacher, Emily taps an unsuspected talent for writing poetry and makes many discoveries about friends, family, and life

"An engaging, humorous account of the joys and sorrows of early adolescence." Horn Book Guide

Hotze, Sollace

A circle unbroken. Clarion Bks. 1988 202p hardcover o.p. paperback available $5.95　　**Fic**

1. Dakota Indians—Fiction 2. Indians of North America—Fiction

ISBN 0-395-59702-1 (pa)　　　　LC 88-2569

Captured by a roving band of Sioux Indians and brought up as the chief's daughter, Rachel is recaptured by her white family and finds it difficult to adjust, as she longs to return to the tribe

"Rachel-Kata Wi is an extremely likable heroine. Her story moves quickly, filled more with people and their relationship than great detail of place or time, and is always grounded in her own growth and feelings. Involving historical fiction, with powerful emotional impact." SLJ

Houston, Gloria

Bright Freedom's song; a story of the Underground Railroad. Harcourt Brace & Co. 1998 145p $16　　**Fic**

1. Underground railroad—Fiction 2. Slavery—Fiction 3. African Americans—Fiction

ISBN 0-15-201812-3　　　　LC 98-13756

In the years before the Civil War, Bright discovers that her parents are providing a safehouse for the Underground Railroad and helps to save a runaway slave named Marcus

"Readable and well-researched historical fiction." SLJ

Houston, James A., 1921-

Frozen fire; a tale of courage; by James Houston; drawings by the author. Atheneum Pubs. 1977 149p il $15; pa $4.95　　**Fic**

1. Wilderness survival—Fiction 2. Arctic regions—Fiction 3. Inuit—Fiction

ISBN 0-689-50083-1; 0-689-71612-5 (pa)

　　　　LC 77-6366

"A Margaret K. McElderry book"

"Based on the true and dramatic ordeal of an Eskimo boy in the 1960's, this adventure story is set . . . in the far north. Kayak, a classmate of Matthew Morgan's in their Baffin Island school, suggests to his new friend Mattoosie (Matthew) that they take a snowmobile and go to the rescue of Mattoosie's father when the latter, a prospector, disappears. The spare can of gasoline leaks, and the two boys face a homeward trek through seventy-five miles of whirling snow and bitter cold." Bull Cent Child Books

"Convincing dialogue, good pace, and lean style mark this as first-class adventure." SLJ

Followed by Black diamonds (1982)

Howe, James, 1946-

The watcher. Atheneum Bks. for Young Readers 1997 167p $16; pa $7.99 (7 and up)　　**Fic**

1. Child abuse—Fiction 2. Beaches—Fiction

ISBN 0-689-80186-6; 0-689-82662-1 (pa)

　　　　LC 96-43045

"Margaret thinks that the families she observes on her summer vacation at the beach are happier than her own, but Howe slowly and skillfully reveals the truth—about those Margaret observes and about Margaret herself. While the book provides some small hope that Margaret—a victim of child abuse—will find a better life, the overall outlook is bleak. Somber but honest." Horn Book Guide

Howe, Norma

The adventures of Blue Avenger; a novel. Holt & Co. 1999 230p $15.95 (7 and up)　　**Fic**

ISBN 0-8050-6062-6　　　　LC 98-29788

On his sixteenth birthday, still trying to cope with the unexpected death of his father, David Schumacher decides—or does he—to change his name to Blue Avenger, hoping to find a way to make a difference in his Oakland neighborhood and in the world

"This is at once ingeniously plotted and howlingly funny." Bull Cent Child Books

Hughes, Dean, 1943-

Team picture. Atheneum Bks. for Young Readers 1996 155p $16; pa $3.99　　**Fic**

1. Foster home care—Fiction 2. Baseball—Fiction

ISBN 0-689-31924-X; 0-689-81990-0 (pa)

　　　　LC 95-52172

Sequel to Family pose (1989)

Trying to hold onto the newfound stability of his life in a foster home, thirteen-year-old David worries about the growing moodiness of his guardian Paul and the fluctuating fortunes of his Pony League baseball team

"No ordinary sports story, this novel is an absorbing psychological study, in which a boy's passion for baseball is a metaphor for his emotional problems." SLJ

Hughes, Monica

The Golden Aquarians. Simon & Schuster Bks. for Young Readers 1995 182p $15　　**Fic**

1. Science fiction 2. Fathers and sons—Fiction

ISBN 0-671-50543-2　　　　LC 94-12980

Walt Elliot goes with the father he hasn't seen for years to the planet Aqua, where he discovers that his father's project threatens the existence of a highly intelligent native species

"The watery planet and its frog-like creatures are inventive, and Walt is an extremely sympathetic character in a novel that explores the possible environmental issues of the future." Horn Book

Hunter in the dark. Atheneum Pubs. 1983 c1982 131p o.p.; Avon Bks. paperback available $2.95 (7 and up)　　**Fic**

1. Hunting—Fiction 2. Leukemia—Fiction

ISBN 0-380-67702-4 (pa)　　　　LC 82-13807

Hughes, Monica—_Continued_
"Sensitive story of sixteen-year-old Mike's lone hunt for his trophy white-tail buck. During the days he spends camping and tracking his deer, Mike reflects on his last year's struggle with leukemia and his relationship with his parents and his best friend, Doug. A thoughful, well-realized story of a boy's coming of age in painful circumstances." Soc Educ

Invitation to the game. Simon & Schuster Bks. for Young Readers 1991 183p hardcover o.p. paperback available $3.95 (7 and up)   **Fic**
1. Science fiction
ISBN 0-671-86692-3 (pa)   LC 90-22832
"The graduates of 2154 find a bleak and dangerous world with no jobs. Home for Lisse and friends is an abandoned warehouse, and they must scrounge for necessities. To their delight, they are asked to join The Game, which transports them to a paradise. Is this beautiful world real—or a computer simulation?" Publisher's note
"This bold and incisive parable for the future will by turns terrify and enchant both science fiction enthusiasts and readers concerned about the earth's fate." Publ Wkly

Hunt, Irene, 1907-
Across five Aprils. Silver Burdett Press 1993 c1964 212p hardcover o.p. paperback available $5.45   **Fic**
1. United States—History—1861-1865, Civil War—Fiction 2. Farm life—Fiction 3. Illinois—Fiction
ISBN 0-8136-7202-3 (pa)   LC 92-46736
Also available in paperback from Berkley Bks.
A reissue of the title first published 1964 by Follett
Young Jethro Creighton grows from a boy to a man when he is left to take care of the family farm in Illinois during the difficult years of the Civil War
"Authentic background, a feeling for the people of that time, and a story that never loses the reader's interest." Wilson Libr Bull

Up a road slowly; cover painting by Don Bolognese. Modern Curriculum Press c1966 192p $10.95   **Fic**
ISBN 0-382-24366-8
Also available in paperback from Scholastic
Awarded the Newbery Medal, 1967
First published 1966 by Follett
After her mother's death, Julie goes to live with Aunt Cordelia, a spinster schoolteacher, where she experiences many emotions and changes as she grows from seven to eighteen
"The problems of jealousy, first love, parental relations, and snobbishness are handled with ease and honesty; the more serious problems of alcoholism and of emotional disturbance in adult characters are handled with dignity. A moving and beautifully written book." Sutherland. The Best in Child Books

Hunter, Mollie, 1922-
The king's swift rider; a novel on Robert the Bruce. HarperCollins Pubs. 1998 241p $16.95; pa $5.95 (7 and up)   **Fic**
1. Robert I, King of Scotland, 1274-1329—Fiction 2. Scotland—Fiction
ISBN 0-06-027186-8; 0-06-447216-7 (pa)
     LC 98-10633

Unwilling to fight but feeling a sense of duty, sixteen-year-old Martin joins Scotland's rebel army as a swift rider and master of espionage for the leader, Robert the Bruce
"With its inherent drama, vivid descriptions, and compelling language, Hunter's marvelous blend of research and the oral tradition puts the story back in history." Horn Book Guide

Huxley, Aldous, 1894-1963
Brave new world. Harper & Row 1946 xx, 311p hardcover o.p. paperback available $10 (7 and up)
     Fic
1. Utopias—Fiction 2. Technology and civilization—Fiction
ISBN 0-06-092987-1 (pa)
First published 1932 by Doubleday, Doran & Company
"The ironic title, which Huxley has taken from Shakespeare's 'The Tempest,' describes a world in which science has taken control over morality and humaneness. In this utopia humans emerge from test tubes, families are obsolete, and even pleasure is regulated. When a so-called savage who believes in spirituality is found and is imported to the community, he cannot accomodate himself to this world and ends his life." Shapiro. Fic for Youth. 3d edition

Ibbotson, Eva
Which witch? illustrated by Annabel Large. Dutton Children's Bks. 1999 c1979 231p il $15.99
     Fic
1. Witchcraft—Fiction 2. Magic—Fiction 3. Fantasy fiction
ISBN 0-525-46164-7   LC 99-10199
First published 1979 in the United Kingdom
Deciding that he must sire a child to carry on his tradition of Loathing Light and Blighting the Beautiful, the Great Wizard Arriman announces a competition among the witches of Todcaster, one of whom will marry him
"The story's strength lies in its witty, satirical twists on beauty pageants and the Cinderella story, and its dimensional, generally comedic characters. . . . However, the Roald Dahl-esque humor is overshadowed by a particularly macabre scenario involving rats. . . . This one is not for the faint of heart or stomach." Booklist

Irving, Washington, 1783-1859
Rip Van Winkle and The legend of Sleepy Hollow; with a preface by Andrew Breen Myers, including an introduction by Haskell Springer; and illustrations based on those designed and etched by Felix O. C. Darley. 2d ed. Sleepy Hollow Press 1980 128p il $19.95   **Fic**
1. New York (State)—Fiction
ISBN 0-912882-42-5   LC 80-36844
These two stories first appeared 1819-1820 in Irving's: The sketch book of Geoffrey Crayon, Gent.
Rip Van Winkle "is based on a folk tale. Henpecked Rip and his dog Wolf wander into the Catskill mountains before the Revolutionary War. There they meet a dwarf, whom Rip helps to carry a keg. They join a group of

Irving, Washington, 1783-1859—*Continued*

dwarfs playing ninepins. When Rip drinks from the keg, he falls asleep and wakes 20 years later, an old man. Returning to his town, he discovers his termagant wife dead, his daughter married, and the portrait of King George replaced by one of George Washington. Irving uses the folk tale to present the contrast between the new and old societies." Reader's Ency. 3d edition

Set in Sleepy Hollow, New York, the second story tells how Ichabod Crane, a superstitious school teacher who is courting the beautiful daughter of a wealthy farmer, is scared off by his rival Brom Bones, masquerading as a legendary headless horseman

Irwin, Hadley

The original Freddie Ackerman. Margaret K. McElderry Bks. 1992 183p $15; pa $3.99 **Fic**
1. Aunts—Fiction 2. Islands—Fiction 3. Maine—Fiction
ISBN 0-689-50562-0; 0-689-80389-3 (pa)
LC 91-43145

Twelve-year-old Trevor Frederick Ackerman refuses to spend another summer with his extended family of divorced parents, step-parents, and step-brothers and step-sisters, so he is sent up to Maine to stay with two eccentric great aunts and there gets involved in a series of adventures

"This is a beautiful coming-of-age story with wonderful characterizations. Trevor's loneliness and low self-esteem are palpable as he escapes painful realities through a series of fantasies of himself as a war hero. . . . A fine book with a winning combination of humor and poignancy." SLJ

Sarah with an H. Margaret K. McElderry Bks. 1996 134p $16 **Fic**
1. Antisemitism—Fiction 2. Prejudices—Fiction 3. Jews—Fiction
ISBN 0-689-80949-2
LC 95-52559

"The opening of a chain hardware store owned by the Irvines, a Jewish family from Chicago, awakens the ignorance and ugliness of prejudice in the small farm town of LaMond, Iowa. Caught in the middle is Marti Sullivan, a hometown girl afraid of opening her mind, but even more afraid of keeping it closed. Her friendship grows with Sarah Irvine as they play basketball together and find their worlds mixing outside school." Voice Youth Advocates

"An action-packed, tightly woven story." SLJ

Jacobs, Paul Samuel

James Printer; a novel of rebellion. Scholastic 1997 220p $15.95 **Fic**
1. Printer, James—Fiction 2. King Philip's War, 1675-1676—Fiction 3. Massachusetts—History—1600-1775, Colonial period—Fiction 4. Indians of North America—Fiction
ISBN 0-590-16381-7
LC 96-25937

"Through the eyes of eleven-year-old Bartholomew, Jacobs tells the story of the historical figure James Printer of the Nipmuk tribe and his role in King Phillip's war. The courage, pain, and horrors of cultural conflict and warfare as experienced by both the Native people in New England and the colonists are skillfully presented." Horn Book Guide

Jacques, Brian

Redwall; illustrated by Troy Howell. anniversary ed. Philomel Bks. 1997 351p il $22.95 **Fic**
1. Mice—Fiction 2. Animals—Fiction 3. Fantasy fiction
ISBN 0-399-23160-9
LC 97-226680

Also available in paperback from Ace Bks.

First published 1986

When the peaceful life of ancient Redwall Abbey is shattered by the arrival of the evil rat Cluny and his villainous hordes, Matthias, a young mouse, determines to find the legendary sword of Martin the Warrior which, he is convinced, will help Redwall's inhabitants destroy the enemy

"Thoroughly engrossing . . . despite its length. . . . The theme will linger long after the story is finished." Booklist

Other available titles about Redwall Abbey are:
The Bellmaker (1995)
The legend of Luke (2000)
The long patrol (1998)
Mariel of Redwall (1992)
Marlfox (1998)
Martin the Warrior (1994)
Mattimeo (1990)
Mossflower (1998)
The outcast of Redwall (1996)
Pearls of Lutra (1997)
Salamandastron (1993)

Johnson, Angela, 1961-

Heaven. Simon & Schuster Bks. for Young Readers 1998 138p $16 **Fic**
1. Adoption—Fiction 2. African Americans—Fiction
ISBN 0-689-82229-4
LC 98-3291

Coretta Scott King Award for text, 1999

Fourteen-year-old Marley's seemingly perfect life in the small town of Heaven is disrupted when she discovers that her father and mother are not her real parents

"In spare, often poetic prose . . . Johnson relates Marley's insightful quest into what makes a family." SLJ

Humming whispers. Orchard Bks. 1995 121p $15.95; lib bdg $16.99 (7 and up) **Fic**
1. Schizophrenia—Fiction 2. Mentally ill—Fiction 3. Sisters—Fiction
ISBN 0-531-06898-6; 0-531-08748-4 (lib bdg)
LC 94-24223

Also available in paperback from Scholastic

"A Richard Jackson book"

"Her older sister's schizophrenia frightens and fascinates fourteen-year-old Sophy. . . . Afraid that she too might be similarly afflicted, she begins to shoplift compulsively. Johnson's beautifully crafted stream-of-consciousness novel is brief and atmospheric." Horn Book Guide

Songs of faith. Orchard Bks. 1998 103p $15.95; lib bdg $16.99 **Fic**
1. Divorce—Fiction 2. African Americans—Fiction
ISBN 0-531-30023-4; 0-531-33023-0 (lib bdg)
LC 97-40216

Also available in paperback from Knopf

Living in a small town in Ohio in 1975 and desperately missing her divorced father, thirteen-year-old Doreen

Johnson, Angela, 1961-—*Continued*

comes to terms with disturbing changes in her family life

"Johnson has set attractive and realistic African-American characters in situations in which race is not the focus. This short, sensitive book will appeal most to reflective readers." SLJ

Toning the sweep. Orchard Bks. 1993 103p
$15.95   **Fic**
1. Grandmothers—Fiction 2. Family life—Fiction
3. Death—Fiction 4. African Americans—Fiction
ISBN 0-531-05476-4   LC 92-34062
Also available in paperback from Scholastic
Coretta Scott King award for text, 1994
"A Richard Jackson book"
On a visit to her grandmother Ola, who is dying of cancer in her house in the desert, fourteen-year-old Emmie hears many stories about the past and her family history and comes to a better understanding of relatives both dead and living

"Full of subtle nuance, the novel is overlaid with meaning about the connections of family and the power of friendship; memorable scenes touch the heart and engage the imagination but never overpower this affecting story." SLJ

Johnston, Julie

Adam and Eve and Pinch-me. Little, Brown 1994 180p o.p.; Puffin Bks. paperback available $4.99 (7 and up)   **Fic**
1. Foster home care—Fiction
ISBN 0-14-037588-0 (pa)   LC 93-21023
Fifteen-year-old Sara Moone, abandoned at birth and shunted from one foster home to another, finds that she cannot remain aloof from her latest family

"Sara is a frequently unlikable but completely real character that young adult readers will understand, respect, and ultimately admire. . . . Other characters are equally unique and credible in this well-written novel." Voice Youth Advocates

Jones, Diana Wynne

Cart and cwidder. Greenwillow Bks. 1995 214p $15; pa $4.95 (7 and up)   **Fic**
1. Fantasy fiction
ISBN 0-688-13360-6; 0-688-13399-1 (pa)
                                        LC 94-1512
First published 1975 in the United Kingdom; first United States edition, 1977 by Atheneum

"Accompanying their gregarious father, Clennen the Singer, on panhorns and cwidders (a lute-like instrument) and traversing the earldoms of Dalemark in their gaily decorated cart make up the only life 11-year-old Moril and his brother and sister have ever known. . . . When his father is suddenly killed, Moril becomes heir to the large, ancient cwidder supposedly owned once by an old bard and having mystical powers. . . . Jones strikes a note of timelessness and universality in her forest setting and her theme of the struggle against oppressive forces, developing her characters in depth." Booklist

Followed by Drowned Ammet

Castle in the air. Greenwillow Bks. 1991 199p $16   **Fic**
1. Fantasy fiction
ISBN 0-688-09686-7   LC 90-30266

In this "follow-up to *Howl's Moving Castle* . . . the protagonist is a young carpet merchant called Abdullah, who spends much of his time creating a richly developed daydream in which he is the long-lost son of a great prince, kidnapped as a child by a villainous bandit. . . . Feisty Sophie and the Wizard Howl (from *Howl's Moving Castle*) do not become apparent till late in the story, but their fortunes do link up with those of Abdullah and his love. Jones maintains both suspense and wit throughout, demonstrating once again that frequently nothing is what it seems to be." Booklist

The crown of Dalemark. Greenwillow Bks. 1995 471p $17; pa $4.95 (7 and up)   **Fic**
1. Fantasy fiction
ISBN 0-688-13363-0; 0-688-13402-5 (pa)
                                        LC 94-17936
First published 1993 in the United Kingdom
This is the fourth title in the Dalemark quartet. The Countess and Lord Keril send Mitt to kill Noreth, who claims to know where the lost crown is hidden

"This volume contains 'A Guide to Dalemark,' with entries on the places and characters of all the books. A complex, engrossing fantasy by a master of the genre." Horn Book

Dark Lord of Derkholm. Greenwillow Bks. 1998 345p $16 (7 and up)   **Fic**
1. Fantasy fiction
ISBN 0-688-16004-2   LC 97-32661
Derk, an unconventional wizard, and his magical family become involved in a plan to put a stop to the devastating tours of their world arranged by the tyrannical Mr. Chesney

"This is a fine-tuned, intelligently funny fantasy." Bull Cent Child Books

Drowned Ammet. Greenwillow Bks. 1995 312p $15; pa $4.95 (7 and up)   **Fic**
1. Fantasy fiction
ISBN 0-688-13361-4; 0-688-13400-9 (pa)
                                        LC 94-1513
First published 1977 in the United Kingdom; first United States edition, 1978 by Atheneum
This is the second title in the Dalemark quartet. When his protest against the tyrannical government fails, Mitt escapes, with two other children, to the mysterious Holy Islands where they learn the identity and the power of two folk figures celebrated by their countrymen

"Jones' imaginative writing is rich with imagery and detail." Booklist

Followed by The spellcoats

Hexwood. Greenwillow Bks. 1994 c1993 295p $16 (7 and up)   **Fic**
1. Science fiction
ISBN 0-688-12488-7   LC 93-18172
Also available in paperback from Puffin Bks.
First published 1993 in the United Kingdom
Ann discovers that the wood near her village is under the control of a Bannus, a machine that manipulates reality, placed there many years ago by powerful extraterrestrial beings called Reigners

"The action is fast paced, the mysterious circumstances are compelling, and there's even a nice bit of humor. Readers who like conundrums will particularly enjoy this." Booklist

Jones, Diana Wynne—*Continued*

Howl's moving castle. Greenwillow Bks. 1986
212p $16   **Fic**
1. Fantasy fiction
ISBN 0-688-06233-4   LC 85-21981
"When the wicked Witch of the Waste turns Sophie
Hatter into an ugly crone, the girl seeks refuge in Wizard
Howl's moving castle. To her surprise and dismay, she
finds herself embroiled in a contest between the witch
and the wizard, in the tangled love affairs of the wizard,
and in a perplexing mystery." Child Book Rev Serv
"Satisfyingly, Sophie meets a fate far exceeding her
dreary expectations. This novel is an exciting, multi-
faceted puzzle, peopled with vibrant, captivating characters. A generous sprinkling of humor adds potency to
this skillful author's spell." Voice Youth Advocates
Followed by Castle in the air

The lives of Christopher Chant. Greenwillow
Bks. 1988 230p hardcover o.p. paperback available
$5.95   **Fic**
1. Fantasy fiction
ISBN 0-688-16365-3 (pa)   LC 87-24540
Young Christopher Chant, in training to become the
next Chrestomanci or head controller of magic in the
world, becomes a key figure in a battle with renegade
sorcerers because he has nine lives
"The author moves a large and captivating cast of
characters around with a choreographer's skill and gives
to an enchanter's apprenticeship the same homely qualities one might need to master driving a car. Although the
plot is almost labyrinthine and occasionally confusing,
the individual episodes are wonderfully entertaining."
Horn Book

The spellcoats. Greenwillow Bks. 1995 279p
$15; pa $4.95 (7 and up)   **Fic**
1. Fantasy fiction
ISBN 0-688-13362-2; 0-688-13401-7 (pa)
    LC 94-1507
First United States edition published 1979 by
Atheneum
This is the third title in the Dalemark quartet. Tanaqui
discovers she has the only means to conquer the evil
Kankredin who threatens her own people and the Hea-
thens who have invaded Dalemark
This is "written with great depth and drama and with
vivid characterizations." Horn Book Guide
Followed by The crown of Dalemark

Jordan, Sherryl

The raging quiet. Simon & Schuster Bks. for
Young Readers 1999 266p $17 (7 and up)   **Fic**
1. Prejudices—Fiction 2. Deaf—Fiction 3. Middle
ages—Fiction
ISBN 0-689-82140-9   LC 98-23283
Suspicious of sixteen-year-old Marnie, a newcomer to
their medieval village, the residents accuse her of witchcraft when she discovers that the village madman is not
crazy but deaf and she begins to communicate with him
through hand gestures
"Eloquent, descriptive prose draws readers into the period, and through memorable, well-defined characters,
Jordan effectively illustrates the timeless dangers of targeting individuals for being different." Booklist

Jukes, Mavis

Expecting the unexpected; sex ed with Mrs.
Gladys Furley, R.N. Delacorte Press 1996 132p
$15.95; pa $3.99   **Fic**
1. School stories 2. Family life—Fiction 3. Sisters—
Fiction
ISBN 0-385-32242-9; 0-440-41227-7 (pa)
    LC 96-2464
In subtitle, the words "human interaction" are crossed
out, and replaced by "sex ed"
Twelve-year-old River and her sixth-grade classmates
handle the information from their sex education class in
different ways, and it leads River to the mistaken conclusion that her older sister's unusual behavior is due to
pregnancy
"The characterizations . . . are fresh and vivid. Relentless jests about PMS, pubic hair and panty liners become a little forced, but nonetheless demonstrate how
well attuned Jukes . . . is to pre-adolescent concerns and
attitudes about puberty." Publ Wkly

Planning the impossible. Delacorte Press 1999
169p $14.95   **Fic**
1. School stories 2. Friendship—Fiction 3. Family
life—Fiction
ISBN 0-385-32243-7   LC 98-26222
Companion volume to Expecting the unexpected
As twelve-year-old River and some of her friends
work on a handbook for sixth-grade parents, they have
to deal with information from the candid Ms. Furley's
sex education lessons as well as the efforts of the class
flirt to break up several couples
"Jukes's multiring circus of classroom antics, preado-
lescent courtship and squabbles with parents and peers
entertainingly depicts the middle-school experience."
Publ Wkly

Karr, Kathleen

The great turkey walk. Farrar, Straus & Giroux
1998 197p $16   **Fic**
1. Turkeys—Fiction 2. West (U.S.)—Fiction
ISBN 0-374-32773-4   LC 97-38859
In 1860, a somewhat simple-minded fifteen-year-old
boy attempts to herd one thousand turkeys from Missouri
to Denver, Colorado, in hopes of selling them at a profit
"Based on an actual event, this is a lively and entertaining story." Horn Book Guide

Oh, those Harper girls! Farrar, Straus & Giroux
1992 181p $16; pa $4.95   **Fic**
1. Frontier and pioneer life—Fiction 2. Texas—Fiction
ISBN 0-374-35609-2; 0-374-45599-6 (pa)
    LC 91-34873
In West Texas in 1869, Lily and her five older sisters
participate in a series of misguided schemes to save their
father's ranch
The story "is told with tongue-in-cheek humor in this
high-spirited, rollicking western. Adventure, fun, and a
dash of history." Voice Youth Advocates

Katz, Welwyn Wilton

Out of the dark. Margaret K. McElderry Bks.
1996 176p $16   **Fic**
1. Mothers and sons—Fiction 2. Ships—Fiction
3. Vikings—Fiction 4. Newfoundland—Fiction
ISBN 0-689-80947-6   LC 96-2467
Also available in paperback from Publisher's Group
West

Thirteen-year-old Ben, unhappy with his new home in
Newfoundland and haunted by memories of his murdered
mother, becomes increasingly absorbed with the remains
of a Viking settlement which inspire him to build and
sail a model ship in her honor

"Fantasy and reality blend seamlessly into a well-
crafted coming-of-age story." Voice Youth Advocates

Keehn, Sally M., 1947-

I am Regina. Philomel Bks. 1991 240p $15.95;
pa $4.99   **Fic**
1. Indians of North America—Fiction 2. United
States—History—1755-1763, French and Indian
War—Fiction
ISBN 0-399-21797-5; 0-440-40754-0 (pa)
LC 90-20098
In 1755, as the French and Indian War begins, ten-
year-old Regina is kidnapped by Indians in western
Pennsylvania, and she must struggle to hold onto memo-
ries of her earlier life as she grows up under the name
of Tskinnak and starts to become Indian herself

"A first-person narrative based on [a] true story . . .
related with all the impact of a hard-hitting documentary." SLJ

Kehret, Peg

The blizzard disaster. Pocket Bks. 1998 137p
$14; pa $3.99   **Fic**
1. Blizzards—Fiction 2. Science fiction
ISBN 0-671-00963-X; 0-671-00962-1 (pa)
LC 98-229710
"A Minstrel hardcover"
"On a farm in Minnesota in 1940, Janis's father decides that her beloved pony must be put down because
of its failing eyesight. Then, on her way home from
school, Janis is lost in a fierce blizzard. . . . Meanwhile,
modern sixth graders Warren and Betsy utilize the Instant Commuter device to travel back in time to observe
the 1940 Armistice Day snowstorm as research for a
school assignment. . . . The two story lines come together in the middle of the blizzard as the time travelers risk
their chance of return to rescue Janis's little sister." SLJ
"The story is fast paced and exciting." Booklist

Cages. Cobblehill Bks. 1991 150p o.p.; Pocket
Bks. paperback available $3.99   **Fic**
1. Shoplifting—Fiction 2. Animal welfare—Fiction
ISBN 0-671-75879-9 (pa)   LC 90-21230
After losing an acting role and fighting with her alcoholic stepfather, Kit is arrested for shoplifting and ordered to work, as part of her sentence, at an animal shelter

"Kit is a bit too good to be true, but readers will relate to her anguish and her spirit and courage. Though
the outcome is neat and positive, the journey, which is
laced with humor as well as heartache, offers grist for
thought." Booklist

I'm not who you think I am. Dutton Children's
Bks. 1999 154p $15.99   **Fic**
1. Mentally ill—Fiction 2. Mothers and daughters—
Fiction
ISBN 0-525-46153-1   LC 98-33879
Ginger "is being stalked by a mentally ill woman who
believes that the 13-year-old is her daughter. Meanwhile,
Ginger's favorite teacher, Mr. Wren, is being harassed by
Mrs. Vaughn, an irate and influential parent who doesn't
like the way he is coaching the girls' basketball team.
. . . When the two plots converge in the final scenes,
everything is resolved satisfactorily. This enjoyable novel
will draw readers' interest and keep them turning pages."
SLJ

Searching for Candlestick Park. Cobblehill Bks.
1997 149p $14.99   **Fic**
1. Runaway children—Fiction 2. Cats—Fiction 3. Fathers and sons—Fiction
ISBN 0-525-65256-6   LC 97-11222
Determined to find his father and relive their good
times, twelve-year-old Spencer takes his cat, slips away
from home in Seattle, and sets out for San Francisco's
Candlestick Park

This is "a fast-paced, exciting adventure. A good
choice for reading aloud as well as starting class discussion." Booklist

Keillor, Garrison

The Sandy Bottom Orchestra; [by] Garrison
Keillor and Jenny Lind Nilsson. Hyperion Bks. for
Children 1996 263p $14.95; lib bdg $15.49; pa
$5.95   **Fic**
1. Violins—Fiction 2. Family life—Fiction
ISBN 0-7868-0173-5; 0-7868-2145-0 (lib bdg);
0-7868-1250-8 (pa)   LC 96-41404
Fourteen-year-old Rachel comes to terms with her ec-
centric family while taking refuge in her violin playing
"Filled with wry, affectionate descriptions of mid-
nineties lifestyles, this will amuse those who enjoy
Keillor's whimsical observations of personal quirks and
contemporary attitudes." Booklist

Keith, Harold, 1903-

Rifles for Watie. Crowell 1957 332p $14.89; pa
$4.95   **Fic**
1. Watie, Stand, 1806-1871—Fiction 2. United
States—History—1861-1865, Civil War—Fiction
ISBN 0-690-04907-2; 0-06-447030-X (pa)
Awarded the Newbery Medal, 1958
"Young Jeff Bussey longs for the life of a Union soldier during the Civil War, but before long he realizes the
cruelty and savagery of some men in the army situation.
The war loses its glamor as he sees his very young
friends die. When he is made a scout, his duties take him
into the ranks of Stand Watie, leader of the rebel troops
of the Cherokee Indian Nation, as a spy. He makes good
friends among the enemy troops and falls in love with
Lucy Washbourne, beautiful part-Cherokee girl and rebel
sympathizer." Stensland. Lit By & About the Am Indian
"An exceptionally well-written story of the Civil War
as it was fought in the western states." Bull Cent Child
Books

Keller, Beverly

The Amazon papers. Harcourt Brace & Co. 1996 150p $12; pa $5 (7 and up)   **Fic**

ISBN 0-15-201345-8; 0-15-201346-6 (pa)

LC 96-7756

Fifteen-year-old Iris gets into hilarious trouble when her mother goes on vacation and leaves her alone

"Full of situations that border on slapstick and peopled by a host of weird characters, the story is a delight." Booklist

Kerr, M. E., 1927-

Gentlehands. Harper & Row 1978 183p hardcover o.p. paperback available $4.95 (7 and up)   **Fic**

1. Grandfathers—Fiction 2. Social classes—Fiction 3. Criminals—Fiction

ISBN 0-06-447067-9 (pa)   LC 77-11860

"Buddy Boyle tries to impress rich, socially elite Skye Pennington by introducing her to his refined and cultured grandfather—and discovers that his grandfather is a Nazi war criminal." Booklist

"The author's skill in conveying the conversation and thought of this age is superb. The intrigue surrounding Buddy's grandfather offers suspense and excitement to the boy-meets-girl story line and adds some interesting questions to the end." Babbling Bookworm

Night kites. Harper & Row 1986 216p hardcover o.p. paperback available $4.95 (7 and up)   **Fic**

1. Homosexuality—Fiction 2. Brothers—Fiction 3. AIDS (Disease)—Fiction

ISBN 0-06-447035-0 (pa)   LC 85-45386

"A Charlotte Zolotow book"

"Seventeen-year-old Erick suddenly learns that his older brother, Pete, whom he admires and tries to emulate, is gay and sick with AIDS. He also struggles with his feelings for his best friend's girl, Nicki, a nonconformist with a 'fast' reputation. Pete and Nicki are the 'night kites' of the title—they dare to be different." BAYA Book Rev

"Pete and his methods of coping with his disease and its effects on himself, his friends, his family, and ultimately, his community, are sensitively and non-sentimentally drawn, and seem to be portrayed accurately. This is sure to be a popular title, and will be a natural for booktalks." Voice Youth Advocates

Kim, Helen, 1959-

The long season of rain. Holt & Co. 1996 275p $15.95 (7 and up)   **Fic**

1. Family life—Fiction 2. Orphans—Fiction 3. Korea—Fiction

ISBN 0-8050-4758-1   LC 96-16597

Also available in paperback from Fawcett

"Edge books"

When an orphan boy comes to live with her family, eleven-year-old Junehee begins to realize that the demands placed on Korean women can destroy their lives

"Kim's calmly but sharply observant narrative . . . affords insight into another culture. . . . A master of understatement, Kim conveys tremendous meaning between the lines." Publ Wkly

Kimmel, Elizabeth Cody

In the stone circle. Scholastic 1998 225p $15.95   **Fic**

1. Ghost stories 2. Wales—Fiction

ISBN 0-590-21308-3   LC 97-14737

While spending the summer in an old stone house in Wales, fourteen-year-old Cristyn comes to terms with the death of her mother while satisfying the request of a thirteenth-century princess

"Kimmel handles the history and the ghost of the girl Carwen with a deft naturalness that keeps both vivid, and the resolution of all the plots strands is satisfying without being overly pat." Booklist

Kincaid, Jamaica

Annie John. Farrar, Straus & Giroux 1985 148p $18.95; pa $10 (7 and up)   **Fic**

1. Antigua and Barbuda—Fiction

ISBN 0-374-10521-9; 0-614-27276-9 (pa)

Also available in paperback from New Am. Lib.

"Episodes from the young life of Annie John, aged 10 to 17, as she grows up on the Caribbean island of Antigua. This is a magical coming-of-age tale, ripe with the special ambience of its tropical setting and sustained by Annie's far from naive awareness of the world around her. Death, illness, and poverty intrude on the narrator's perceptive sensibility from time to time, but even these experiences instruct her and expand her understanding of life and its shifting reality. . . . A poetic and intensely moving work." Booklist

Kindl, Patrice, 1951-

Owl in love. Houghton Mifflin 1993 204p $15   **Fic**

1. Supernatural—Fiction 2. Owls—Fiction 3. Teachers—Fiction

ISBN 0-395-66162-5   LC 92-26952

Also available in paperback from Penguin Bks.

A fourteen-year-old girl, who can transform into an owl, has a crush on her science teacher which leads her into interesting new relationships with both humans and owls

"Kindl's prose is remarkably even in its wit, one of many virtues in this tautly plotted and touching novel." Publ Wkly

The woman in the wall. Houghton Mifflin 1997 185p $14.95   **Fic**

1. Shyness—Fiction

ISBN 0-395-83014-1   LC 96-24567

Also available in paperback from Penguin Bks.

Anna is "an extremely shy child who retreats behind the walls of her family's large, dilapidated house and lives alone in her secret rooms until she is 14 years old. Then . . . Anna finally comes out and faces the world. . . . This contemporary story is just on the edge of the surreal. . . . What makes you suspend disbelief is the authority of Anna's quirky, vulnerable narrative voice, which pulls you into a touching, dreamy story told with tender comedy." Booklist

Kirkpatrick, Katherine A., 1964-

Trouble's daughter; the story of Susanna Hutchinson, Indian captive; [by] Katherine Kirkpatrick. Delacorte Press 1998 247p $14.95   **Fic**

1. Hutchinson, Susanna, b. 1633—Fiction 2. United States—History—1600-1775, Colonial period—Fiction 3. Delaware Indians—Fiction 4. New York (State)—Fiction

ISBN 0-385-32600-9   LC 98-6030

When her family is massacred by Lenape Indians in 1643, nine-year-old Susanna, daughter of Anne Hutchinson, is captured and raised as a Lenape

"Based on actual events . . . this is the compelling story of a young girl torn by divided loyalties." Voice Youth Advocates

Klass, David

California Blue. Scholastic 1994 200p $13.95; pa $4.50 (7 and up)   **Fic**

1. Butterflies—Fiction 2. Environmental protection—Fiction

ISBN 0-590-46688-7; 0-590-46689-5 (pa)
    LC 93-13705

When seventeen-year-old John Rodgers discovers a new sub-species of butterfly which may necessitate closing the mill where his dying father works, they find themselves on opposite sides of the environmental conflict

"The absorbing first-person narration rings true, projecting the credible voice of a teenager just beginning to break free from his emotional ties at home, family and friends. The fears, excitement, anger and energy of this awkward psychological time are movingly captured here." Publ Wkly

Danger zone. Scholastic 1996 232p $16.95; pa $4.50 (7 and up)   **Fic**

1. Basketball—Fiction 2. Race relations—Fiction 3. African Americans—Fiction

ISBN 0-590-48590-3; 0-590-48591-1 (pa)
    LC 94-20234

When he joins a predominantly black "Teen Dream Team" that will be representing the United States in an international basketball tournament in Rome, Jimmy Doyle makes some unexpected discoveries about prejudice, racism, and politics

"The pace never lags, and Klass does a convincing job of capturing the feel of the game and depicting Doyle's attempts to be accepted by his teammates, as well as showing what happens when some terrorists add fear to the list of the team's opponents." Booklist

Klass, Sheila Solomon

Next stop, nowhere. Scholastic 1995 181p $14.95   **Fic**

1. Fathers and daughters—Fiction 2. Divorce—Fiction 3. Friendship—Fiction

ISBN 0-590-46686-0   LC 94-20235

When her mother remarries, fourteen-year-old Beth has to leave her familiar life in New York City and her new friend Josef to go live with her artisan father in Vermont

"Scenes set in New York City and Vermont are equal-

ly well drawn, giving a real sense of contrasting lifestyles. This is a light, humorous story with a sweet romantic subplot." Booklist

The uncivil war. Holiday House 1997 162p $15.95   **Fic**

1. School stories 2. Friendship—Fiction

ISBN 0-8234-1329-2   LC 95-15548

Also available in paperback from Bantam Bks.

Even with her father as principal, Asa Andersen is certain that sixth grade will be perfect, until a new boy in school starts making fun of her name and the baby her mother is expecting is born prematurely

"The novel not only is enjoyable but also explores issues to which many readers will relate." Booklist

Klause, Annette Curtis

Alien secrets. Delacorte Press 1993 227p $15.95; pa $4.99   **Fic**

1. Science fiction 2. Mystery fiction

ISBN 0-385-30928-7; 0-440-41061-4 (pa)
    LC 92-31326

On her journey to the distant planet where her parents are working, twelve-year-old Puck befriends a troubled alien and becomes involved in a dangerous mystery involving a precious artifact

"This fast-paced adventure novel features a smart heroine, an appealing alien, plenty of intrigue, and a noble mission that readers won't be able to resist." SLJ

The silver kiss. Delacorte Press 1990 198p hardcover o.p. paperback available $4.50 (7 and up)   **Fic**

1. Vampires—Fiction 2. Death—Fiction

ISBN 0-440-21346-0 (pa)   LC 89-48880

"One evening, when 17-year-old Zoë is sitting in the park contemplating her mother's imminent death due to cancer, her father's lack of support, and her best friend's move, she meets Simon. Simon is startlingly handsome and strangely compelling. As their friendship grows over time, Simon reveals to Zoë his true identity: he is a vampire, trying to kill his younger vampire brother." SLJ

"There's inherent romantic appeal in the vampire legend, and Klause weaves all the gory details into a poignant love story that becomes both sensuous and suspenseful." Booklist

Klise, Kate

Letters from camp; illustrated by M. Sarah Klise. Avon Bks. 1999 178p il $15   **Fic**

1. Camps—Fiction 2. Brothers and sisters—Fiction 3. Letters—Fiction

ISBN 0-380-97539-4   LC 98-52315

Sent to Camp Happy Harmony to learn how to get along with each other, pairs of brothers and sisters chronicle in letters home how they come to suspect the intentions of the singing family running the camp

This is a "delightfully wacky story. . . . The humor is very gentle and tongue-in-cheek. . . . An entirely satisfying camp adventure." Booklist

Koertge, Ronald

The Arizona kid; [by] Ron Koertge. Little, Brown 1988 228p o.p.; Avon Bks. paperback available $3.99 (7 and up)   **Fic**
    1. Rodeos—Fiction 2. Homosexuality—Fiction 3. Arizona—Fiction
    ISBN 0-380-70776-4 (pa)   LC 87-35361
    "Joy Street books"
    Sixteen-year-old Billy comes to terms with his own values when he is sent to live with his gay uncle in Tucson and is introduced to the world of rodeos where he falls in love with an outspoken racehorse rider named Cara
    This novel displays a "fine sensitivity to the insecurities of the adolescent male who's frequently called 'shorty,' the stresses of the gay lifestyle under the AIDS cloud of gloom, and the bittersweet playfulness of a summer romance." Voice Youth Advocates

Tiger, tiger, burning bright; a novel. Orchard Bks. 1994 179p $17.95; lib bdg $18.99   **Fic**
    1. Grandfathers—Fiction 2. Old age—Fiction 3. California—Fiction
    ISBN 0-531-06840-4; 0-531-08690-9 (lib bdg)
        LC 93-37758
    Also available in paperback from Avon Bks.
    "A Melanie Kroupa book"
    Worried that his mother will send his beloved grandfather to a nursing home "for his own good," Jesse and some of his eighth-grade classmates accompany Pappy into the mountains near their small California town to look for the tiger tracks he claims to have seen
    "Koertge has created a quirky, often hilarious, cast of characters in a small central California town. . . . The dialogue, whether between Jesse and his family members or between Jesse and his cronies, sounds exactly right." Book Rep

Koller, Jackie French

The Falcon. Atheneum Bks. for Young Readers 1998 181p $16 (7 and up)   **Fic**
    ISBN 0-689-81294-9   LC 97-34062
    "Luke Carver resents his school journaling assignment until he discovers that writing is a nonthreatening way to express his feelings—at least some of them. Those that are too painful he is only willing to begin exploring. And he is quick to abandon his explorations for tales of misadventures that always result in horrible consequences. When one such exploit lands him in a psychiatric ward, Luke must face an emotional demon that has haunted him for years. Instead of being a trite contrivance, the journaling serves as an integral stage of Luke's emotional evolution." Booklist

A place to call home. Atheneum Bks. for Young Readers 1995 204p $16; pa $4.50 (7 and up)
        Fic
    1. Abandoned children—Fiction 2. Foster home care—Fiction 3. Race relations—Fiction 4. Racially mixed people—Fiction
    ISBN 0-689-80024-X; 0-689-81395-3 (pa)
        LC 95-7559
    "Fifteen-year-old biracial Anna tries to care for her five-year-old sister and infant brother when her alcoholic mother disappears yet again. Anna discovers her mother's car in a nearby lake—evidence of her suicide. . . . In spite of the grimness and apparent hopelessness of Anna's situation, she finds help, love, friendship." Booklist
    "In this problem novel, the author reveals how racism, child molestation, alcoholism, child abuse, single parenting, adoption, foster care, and suicide impact the lives of children and youth. However, in Anna, the author creates a character who is intelligent, strong and determined to do what is the greater good for her family." Voice Youth Advocates

Konigsburg, E. L.

Journey to an 800 number. Atheneum Pubs. 1982 138p hardcover o.p. paperback available $4.99   **Fic**
    1. Fathers—Fiction 2. Parent and child—Fiction 3. Social classes—Fiction
    ISBN 0-689-82679-6 (pa)   LC 81-10829
    Also available in paperback from Dell
    Bo learns about kindness, love, loyalty, appearances, and pretense from the unusual characters he meets when he is sent to live with his father after his mother decides to remarry
    "With a fine display of irony yet without aiming over the heads of young readers, the author has written a splendid satire on modern American life and has peopled it with some of her most original and eccentric characters." Horn Book

A proud taste for scarlet and miniver; written and illustrated by E. L. Konigsburg. Atheneum Pubs. 1973 201p il $17   **Fic**
    1. Eleanor, of Aquitaine, Queen, consort of Henry II, King of England, 1122?-1204—Fiction
    ISBN 0-689-30111-1   LC 73-76320
    Also available in paperback from Dell
    This is an historical novel about the 12th century queen, Eleanor of Aquitaine, wife of kings of France and England and mother of King Richard the Lion Heart and King John. Impatiently awaiting the arrival of her second husband, King Henry II, in heaven, she recalls her life with the aid of some contemporaries
    The author "has succeeded in making history amusing as well as interesting. . . . The characterization is superb." Horn Book

The view from Saturday. Atheneum Bks. for Young Readers 1996 163p $16; pa $4.50   **Fic**
    1. School stories 2. Friendship—Fiction 3. Physically handicapped—Fiction
    ISBN 0-689-80993-X; 0-689-81721-5 (pa)
        LC 95-52624
    Awarded the Newbery Medal, 1997
    "A Jean Karl book"
    Four students, with their own individual stories, develop a special bond and attract the attention of their teacher, a paraplegic, who choses them to represent their sixth-grade class in the Academic Bowl competition
    "Glowing with humor and dusted with magic. . . . Wrought with deep compassion and a keen sense of balance." Publ Wkly

Korman, Gordon, 1963-
The chicken doesn't skate. Scholastic 1996 197p
$14.95; pa $4.50   **Fic**
1. Chickens—Fiction 2. School stories 3. Hockey—
Fiction
ISBN 0-590-85300-7; 0-590-85301-5 (pa)
    LC 96-2042
Wild things happen at the South Middle School when
Milo's science project, Henrietta the chicken, becomes
the hockey team's mascot and their only chance for a
winning season
"Korman has the voices of these middle-school kids
down cold; the silly chicken humor works because the
kids' reactions . . . are as real as the main plot is outrageous. This is a genuinely funny, refreshingly unpretentious novel." Booklist

The sixth grade nickname game. Hyperion Bks.
for Children 1998 154p $14.95; lib bdg $15.49; pa
$5.99   **Fic**
1. Nicknames—Fiction 2. School stories
ISBN 0-7868-0432-7; 0-7868-2382-8 (lib bdg);
0-7868-1335-0 (pa)   LC 98-12343
Eleven-year-old best friends Jeff and Wiley, who like
to give nicknames to their classmates, try to find the
right one for the new girl Cassandra, while adjusting to
the football coach who has become their new teacher
"This is a funny, fast-paced grade-school romp." Bull
Cent Child Books

Something fishy at Macdonald Hall. Scholastic
1995 198p $14.95   **Fic**
1. School stories
ISBN 0-590-25521-5   LC 95-2074
Just as the Headmaster of Macdonald Hall is on the
verge of retirement, a wave of practical jokes hits the
school, and roommates Bruno and Boots become prime
suspects
A "tale of madcap humor, peopled with some of the
funniest, most ridiculous adults in middle-grade fiction."
SLJ
Other available titles about Bruno and Boots are:
Beware the fish! (1980)
Go jump in the pool (1979)
This can't be happening at MacDonald Hall! (1978)
The Zucchini Warriors (1988)

The Twinkie Squad. Scholastic 1992 194p
$13.95; pa $3.99   **Fic**
1. School stories
ISBN 0-590-45249-5; 0-590-45250-9 (pa)
    LC 91-30382
Chaos spreads when Douglas, the most eccentric sixth
grader in Thaddeus G. Little Middle School, joins the
Twinkie Squad, a special counselling group for problem
students
This "story is a string of weird caricatures and sopho-
moric action gags, tied together with just enough plot to
make a kind of wacky sense." Booklist

Koss, Amy Goldman, 1954-
The Ashwater experiment. Dial Bks. for Young
Readers 1999 153p $16.99   **Fic**
1. Moving—Fiction 2. Friendship—Fiction 3. Califor-
nia—Fiction
ISBN 0-8037-2391-1   LC 98-23995

Twelve-year-old Hillary, who has traveled across the
country all her life with her parents who sell crafts, finds
herself facing a stay of nine whole months in Ashwater,
California
"Koss artfully sidesteps the predictable and crafts a
truly original piece of fiction brimming with humor and
insight." Horn Book Guide

Krensky, Stephen, 1953-
The printer's apprentice; illustrated by Madeline
Sorel. Delacorte Press 1995 103p il $13.95; pa
$3.99   **Fic**
1. Zenger, John Peter, 1697-1746—Fiction 2. New
York (N.Y.)—Fiction 3. United States—History—
1600-1775, Colonial period—Fiction
ISBN 0-385-32095-7; 0-440-41280-3 (pa)
    LC 94-36721
In 1735 in New York City, a young printer's apprentice learns about the importance of freedom of speech
when the printer Peter Zenger is arrested and tried for
writing articles criticizing the government
The author "creates a lively adventure story, making
skillful use of the boy's struggle of conscience to introduce the principle of freedom of the press. . . . Madeline
Sorel's humorous full-page pen drawings add a vigorous
sense of the time and place. An afterword further explains the historical events." Horn Book

Krisher, Trudy
Kinship. Delacorte Press 1997 299p $15.95; pa
$4.50 (7 and up)   **Fic**
1. Mothers and daughters—Fiction 2. Fathers and
daughters—Fiction 3. Georgia—Fiction
ISBN 0-385-32272-0; 0-440-22023-8 (pa)
    LC 96-35480
Companion volume to Spite fences
In 1961 fifteen-year-old Pert, who lives with her
mother in a trailer park in Kinship, Georgia, meets her
long-absent father and discovers the true meaning of
home
"Pert keeps a positive attitude toward life, lacing her
unvarnished views of the town with wonderfully ironic,
laugh-out-loud humor even while making heartbreaking
discoveries. A rich and remarkable story." SLJ

Spite fences. Delacorte Press 1994 283p
hardcover o.p. paperback available $4.50 (7 and
up)   **Fic**
1. Race relations—Fiction 2. Mothers and daughters—Fiction 3. Georgia—Fiction
ISBN 0-440-22016-5 (pa)   LC 94-8665
"This is the story of a thirteen-year-old girl as much
an outcast from her family as she is from her southern
town. Maggie Pugh is physically abused by her mother,
beaten and nearly raped by a violent neighbor, and re-
viled for her championship of African-American friends
who, during the summer of 1960, are challenging rural
Georgia racism with sit-ins and other forms of protest."
Bull Cent Child Books
"Characters emerge as complex individuals, not pawns
of a political agenda. Hearts will go out to Maggie as
she weathers various forms of physical and emotional
abuse; her final triumph is a tribute to all who have suffered for justice." Publ Wkly

Kurtz, Jane

The storyteller's beads. Harcourt Brace & Co.
1998 154p $15   **Fic**
  1. Friendship—Fiction   2. Prejudices—Fiction
3. Blind—Fiction 4. Ethiopia—Fiction
  ISBN 0-15-201074-2   LC 97-42312
  "Gulliver books"
  During the political strife and famine of the 1980's,
two Ethiopian girls, one Christian and the other Jewish
and blind, struggle to overcome many difficulties, including their prejudices about each other, as they make the
dangerous journey out of Ethiopia
  "The novel presents an involving portrait of Ethiopian
culture through the eyes of two well-defined characters."
Horn Book Guide

LaFaye, A., 1970-

Edith Shay. Viking 1998 183p $15.99 (7 and
up)   **Fic**
  1. United States—History—1865-1898—Fiction
  ISBN 0-670-87598-8   LC 98-16832
  Leaving her home in Wisconsin in 1865, sixteen-year-
old Katherine sets out for Chicago to prove to her family
that she can make a life for herself
  "LaFaye offers a multidimensional portrait of a young
woman in transition . . . revealed in poetic and poignant
language." Publ Wkly

Strawberry Hill. Simon & Schuster Bks. for
Young Readers 1999 272p $16.95   **Fic**
  1. Friendship—Fiction   2. Family life—Fiction
3. Maine—Fiction
  ISBN 0-689-82441-6   LC 98-26887
  During the summer of 1976 in Tidal, Maine twelve-
year-old Raleia Pendle feels like a misfit with her hippie
parents and begins a friendship with the eighty-eight-
year-old town recluse
  "With its easygoing yet imaginative style, this examination of a girl's search for her own time and place will
strike a chord with similarly inquisitive young readers."
Bull Cent Child Books

The year of the Sawdust Man. Simon &
Schuster Bks. for Young Readers 1998 220p $16
                                                       Fic
  1. Mothers and daughters—Fiction 2. Divorce—Fiction 3. Louisiana—Fiction
  ISBN 0-689-81513-1   LC 97-14501
  In 1934, when her mother leaves her and her father,
eleven-year-old Nissa tries to cope with the gossip of her
small Louisiana town and the changes in her own life
  "The author creates a believable set of characters and
a realistic environment, and sustains them well with a
lyrical and leisurely use of language." SLJ

Larson, Rodger

What I know now. Holt & Co. 1997 262p
$15.95 (7 and up)   **Fic**
  1. Homosexuality—Fiction 2. California—Fiction
  ISBN 0-8050-4869-3   LC 96-36723
  In 1957 in California, having fallen in love with a
young man who has come to his house to build a garden,
Dave, a fourteen-year-old gay boy finds his life and his

world view changing
  "This is a well-told story that depicts a gay protagonist as a real person who is able to provide a positive
male role model for a young man during a transitional
period in his life." SLJ

Lasky, Kathryn

Alice Rose & Sam; a novel. Hyperion Bks. for
Children 1998 252p $15.95; lib bdg $16.49; pa
$4.50   **Fic**
  1. Twain, Mark, 1835-1910—Fiction 2. Friendship—
Fiction 3. Nevada—Fiction
  ISBN 0-7868-0336-3; 0-7868-2277-5 (lib bdg);
0-7868-1222-2 (pa)   LC 97-40132
  Alice Rose, an irrepressible twelve-year-old, shares
adventures with Mark Twain, an outlandish reporter on
her father's newspaper in Virginia City, Nevada, during
the 1860s
  The author's "picturesque dialogue and precise, energetic characterizations more than make up for the book's
choppy flow." Publ Wkly

Beyond the burning time. Blue Sky Press (NY)
1994 272p $14.95; pa $4.50 (7 and up)   **Fic**
  1. Witchcraft—Fiction 2. Salem (Mass.)—Fiction
3. Mothers and daughters—Fiction
  ISBN 0-590-47331-X; 0-590-47332-8 (pa)
                    LC 94-5231
  When, in the winter of 1691, accusations of witchcraft
surface in her small New England village, twelve-year-
old Mary Chase fights to save her mother from execution
  "Well researched and documented with extensive
notes. . . . A readable, engrossing, and sometimes exciting tale of an important era in American history." SLJ

Beyond the divide. Macmillan 1983 254p $17;
pa $3.95 (7 and up)   **Fic**
  1. Overland journeys to the Pacific—Fiction
2. Amish—Fiction 3. Fathers and daughters—Fiction
  ISBN 0-02-751670-9; 0-689-80153-7 (pa)
                    LC 82-22867
  "When her father is shunned by their Amish community, Meribah Simon leaves with him to join the 1849
Gold Rush. As the journey west grows more desperate,
the two are abandoned by their fellow passengers. Her
father dies, but Meriban wins her struggle for survival.
Details in this engrossing novel are based upon journals
of the period; author's note provides additional background." Soc Educ

Dreams in the golden country; the diary of
Zipporah Feldman, a Jewish immigrant girl.
Scholastic 1998 188p il (Dear America) $11.95
                                                       Fic
  1. Jews—Fiction 2. Immigration and emigration—Fiction 3. New York (N.Y.)—Fiction
  ISBN 0-590-02973-8   LC 97-26213
  Twelve-year-old Zippy, a Jewish immigrant from Russia, keeps a diary account of the first eighteen months of
her family's life on the Lower East Side of New York
City in 1903-1904
  "The hopes and dreams of a young girl are beautifully
portrayed through Lasky's eloquent and engaging narrative." SLJ

Lasky, Kathryn—*Continued*

Elizabeth I; red rose of the House of Tudor. Scholastic 1999 237p il (Royal diaries) $10.95   **Fic**

1. Elizabeth I, Queen of England, 1533-1603—Fiction 2. Great Britain—History—1485-1603, Tudors—Fiction

ISBN 0-590-68484-1   LC 99-11178

In a series of diary entries, Princess Elizabeth, the eleven-year-old daughter of King Henry VIII, celebrates holidays and birthdays, relives her mother's execution, revels in her studies, and agonizes over her father's health

"Well written and captivating." Voice Youth Advocates

A journey to the New World; the diary of Remember Patience Whipple. Scholastic 1996 173p il map (Dear America) $9.95   **Fic**

1. Mayflower (Ship)—Fiction 2. Pilgrims (New England colonists)—Fiction 3. Massachusetts—History—1600-1775, Colonial period—Fiction

ISBN 0-590-50214-X   LC 95-25715

Twelve-year-old Mem presents a diary account of the trip she and her family made on the Mayflower in 1620 and their first year in the New World

"The format, with spaces between entries, will appeal to reluctant readers, while the lively writing will hold the attention of good readers. A historical note on the year 1620, maps, a diagram of the Mayflower, and reproductions of historical prints add to the social-studies value of the book." SLJ

Memoirs of a bookbat. Harcourt Brace & Co. 1994 216p $10.95; pa $6   **Fic**

1. Censorship—Fiction 2. Books and reading—Fiction

ISBN 0-15-215727-1; 0-15-201259-1 (pa)

LC 93-36402

Fourteen-year-old Harper, an avid reader of fantasy who must hide her books from her fundamentalist parents, comes to realize that their public promotion of censorship threatens her freedom to make her own choices

"In this very smart (and somewhat acerbic) book . . . Lasky combines fictional characters with real-life authors and religious groups (such as Operation Rescue) to create a credible and entertaining story of an emerging independent thinker." Publ Wkly

The night journey; with drawings by Trina Schart Hyman. Warne 1981 149p il o.p.; Penguin Bks. paperback available $4.99   **Fic**

1. Jews—Russia—Fiction 2. Russia—Fiction

ISBN 0-14-032048-2 (pa)   LC 81-2225

This novel "describes the escape of a Jewish family from the persecutions and pogroms of Tsarist Russia. . . . It is told as a story-within-a-story, as thirteen-year-old Rachel learns, bit by bit, what her great-grandmother went through as a child." Bull Cent Child Books

"The novel shifts back and forth from the dangerous journey out of Russia to Rachel's own casual, secure life at home and school. These transitions are handled with a smoothness that doesn't break the intrinsic tension of the story, and the contrast between the two lives demonstrates with poignant clarity the real meaning of freedom. The portrayal of warm, supportive families in both stories becomes a link between past and present." SLJ

True north; a novel of the underground railroad. Blue Sky Press (NY) 1996 267p $14.95; pa $4.99   **Fic**

1. Abolitionists—Fiction 2. Underground railroad—Fiction 3. Slavery—Fiction

ISBN 0-590-20523-4; 0-590-20524-2 (pa)

LC 95-2922

"Fourteen-year-old Lucy is the youngest daughter of a proper, upper-middle-class family living in Boston in 1858. Afrika, a young slave, doesn't know how old she is, but she knows it's time to make a run for freedom via the Underground Railroad. The girls' lives collide when Lucy discovers Afrika hiding in her grandfather's house. . . . Rich imagery and detail add to the suspenseful plot, and the characters, revealed in alternating perspectives, are vivid and believable." Booklist

Lawrence, Iain, 1955-

The smugglers. Delacorte Press 1999 183p $15.95   **Fic**

1. Smuggling—Fiction 2. Adventure fiction 3. Great Britain—History—1714-1837—Fiction

ISBN 0-385-32663-7   LC 98-41582

Sequel to The wreckers

As the nineteenth century begins, sixteen-year-old John Spencer sets out to sail his father's schooner, The Dragon, from Kent to London and becomes involved in smuggling and danger

"The book's nonstop action, fast-paced plot, and picturesque characters make for a real page-turner." SLJ

The wreckers. Delacorte Press 1998 196p $15.95; pa $4.99   **Fic**

1. Shipwrecks—Fiction 2. Adventure fiction 3. Great Britain—History—1714-1837—Fiction

ISBN 0-385-32535-5; 0-440-41545-4 (pa)

LC 97-31625

Also available Thorndike Press large print edition

"In 1799 fourteen-year-old John Spencer survives a shipwreck on the coast of Cornwall. To his horror, he soon learns that the villagers are not rescuers, but pirates who lure ships ashore in order to plunder their cargoes. . . . Lawrence creates an edge-of-the-chair survival/mystery story. Fast-moving, mesmerizing." Horn Book Guide

Lawrence, Louise, 1943-

Dream-weaver. Clarion Bks. 1996 231p $14.95; pa $6.95 (7 and up)   **Fic**

1. Science fiction

ISBN 0-395-71812-0; 0-395-92864-8 (pa)

LC 95-25856

"When her frightening dreams about a blue-eyed, alien boy come to the attention of the Dream-Weavers Guild, Eth is accepted for training even though she is unusually young. As she learns the arts of healing and weaving dreams that maintain harmony and stability in her society, a spaceship from Earth is carrying 3,000 colonists to her planet, among them 17-year-old Troy, who fears the colonists' intentions for their new world. . . . The action is intense with lots of twists and turns; Lawrence's characters are striking; and her conclusion is satisfying, though not what readers may expect. All in all, a first-rate piece of science fiction." Booklist

Layefsky, Virginia

Impossible things. Marshall Cavendish 1998 207p $14.95   **Fic**
1. Death—Fiction 2. Fathers and sons—Fiction 3. Mothers and sons—Fiction 4. Supernatural—Fiction
ISBN 0-7614-5038-6   LC 98-11459
On his twelfth birthday, Brady discovers an unusual egg in his own private cave on the beach near his house, and the creature that hatches from it helps him deal with his mother's death and his father's impending remarriage
Brady's voice "rings true as that of an early adolescent. His descriptions bring the other characters, settings, and situations to life, successfully blending fantasy and realism in a compelling story." SLJ

Le Guin, Ursula K., 1929-

A wizard of Earthsea. Atheneum Pubs. 1991 197p $16.95   **Fic**
1. Fantasy fiction
ISBN 0-689-31720-4   LC 90-23884
Also available in paperback from Bantam Bks.
"A Parnassus Press book"
A reissue of the title first published 1968 by Parnassus Press
"An imaginary archipelago is the setting for . . . [this] fantasy. . . . In a willful misuse of his limited powers, the novice wizard unleashes a shadowy, malevolent creature that endangers his life and the world of Earthsea." Booklist
A "powerful fantasy-allegory. Though set as prose, the rhythms of the langauge are truly and consistently poetical." Read Ladders for Hum Relat. 5th edition
Other available titles about Earthsea are:
The farthest shore (1984)
Tehanu (1990)
The tombs of Atuan (1988)

Lee, Marie G.

Necessary roughness. HarperCollins Pubs. 1996 228p $14.95; lib bdg $14.89; pa $4.95 (7 and up)
                                                      Fic
1. Korean Americans—Fiction 2. Prejudices—Fiction 3. Football—Fiction 4. Fathers and sons—Fiction
ISBN 0-06-025124-7; 0-06-025130-1 (lib bdg); 0-06-447169-1 (pa)   LC 96-34185
Sixteen-year-old Korean American Chan moves from Los Angeles to a small town in Minnesota, where he must cope not only with racism on the football team but also with the tensions in his relationship with his strict father
"Lee's tight characterizations lift this novel above the ordinary, and the football action will appeal to sports' fans." SLJ

L'Engle, Madeleine, 1918-

A ring of endless light. Farrar, Straus & Giroux 1980 324p o.p.; Dell paperback available $5.50
                                                      Fic
1. Death—Fiction 2. Dolphins—Fiction
ISBN 0-440-97232-9 (pa)   LC 79-27679
A Newbery Medal honor book, 1981

Vicky Austin, who appeared earlier in Meet the Austins (1960) and The moon by night (1963), "is now sixteen and saddened by the fact that her beloved grandfather has terminal cancer; her summer is further disturbed because a family friend has lost his life rescuing a would-be suicide, the latter a rich, unhappy young man who makes demands on Vicky's time and affections. She is, however, more responsive to Adam [a character who previously appeared in The arm of the starfish (1965)] who works at a marine biology station and who is the first to realize that Vicky has telepathic powers and can communicate with the dolphins he's using in experiments." Bull Cent Child Books

A wrinkle in time. Farrar, Straus & Giroux 1962 $17   **Fic**
1. Fantasy fiction
ISBN 0-374-38613-7
Also available G.K. Hall large print edition and in paperback from Dell
Awarded the Newbery Medal, 1963
"A brother and sister, together with a friend, go in search of their scientist father who was lost while engaged in secret work for the government on the tesseract problem. A tesseract is a wrinkle in time. The father is a prisoner on a forbidding planet, and after awesome and terrifying experiences, he is rescued, and the little group returns safely to Earth and home." Child Books Too Good To Miss
"It makes unusual demands on the imagination and consequently gives great rewards." Horn Book
Other available titles in this series are:
Many waters (1986)
A swiftly tilting planet (1978)
A wind in the door (1973)

Lester, Alison, 1952-

Quicksand pony. Houghton Mifflin 1998 c1997 136p $15   **Fic**
1. Horses—Fiction 2. Australia—Fiction
ISBN 0-395-93749-3   LC 98-6930
"Walter Lorraine books"
First published 1997 in Australia
After her pony Bella, trapped in quicksand, is rescued by a mysterious unseen person, ten-year-old Biddy follows the trail into the Australian bush and discovers the solution to a disappearance that happened years ago
"A multilayered story of survival, love, mystery, and family relationships." SLJ

Lester, Jim, 1945-

Fallout. Delacorte Press 1996 212p hardcover o.p. paperback available $3.99 (7 and up)   **Fic**
1. Fathers and sons—Fiction 2. School stories 3. Texas—Fiction
ISBN 0-440-22683-X (pa)   LC 95-21106
After transferring to a Texas prep school during his junior year, Kenny finds it difficult to live up to the reputation of his heroic father who died in the Vietnam War
"Lester's novel is entertaining, fast-paced, and comes alive with memorable characters." SLJ

Lester, Julius

Othello; a novel. Scholastic 1995 151p $14.95; pa $3.99 (7 and up)   **Fic**
ISBN 0-590-41967-6; 0-590-41966-8 (pa)
                                LC 94-12833
"An interpretation of Shakespeare's play in the form of a novel casts Othello, Iago, and Iago's wife as African immigrants in Elizabethan England. The first half of the book details the courtship and marriage of Othello and Desdemona; the second half closely follows the plot of the play and includes, in boldface, quotations and paraphrases from Shakespeare's play. An ambitious yet accessible reworking." Horn Book Guide

Levine, Gail Carson, 1947-

Ella enchanted. HarperCollins Pubs. 1997 232p $15.95; lib bdg $15.89; pa $4.95   **Fic**
1. Fantasy fiction
ISBN 0-06-027510-3; 0-06-027511-1 (lib bdg); 0-06-440705-5 (pa)   LC 96-30734
A Newberry Medal honor book, 1998
In this novel based on the story of Cinderella, Ella struggles against the childhood curse that forces her to obey any order given to her
"As finely designed as a tapestry, Ella's story both neatly incorporates elements of the original tale and mightily expands them." Booklist

The princess test; illustrated by Mark Elliott. HarperCollins Pubs. 1999 91p il (Princess tales) $9.95; lib bdg $8.89   **Fic**
1. Fairy tales
ISBN 0-06-028062-X; 0-06-028063-8 (lib bdg)
                                LC 98-27960
Also available in the Princess tale series: Cinderellis and the glass hill (2000); The fairy's mistake (1999); Princess Sonora and the long sleep (1999)
In this humorous retelling of Hans Christian Andersen's "The Princess and the Pea," Lorelei must pass many difficult tests in order to prove that she is a true princess and win the hand of Prince Nicholas
"Breezily told, with a wealth of comic detail, slyly comtemporary dialogue, and genuine affection for the genre that inspired [it]." Bull Cent Child Books

Levitin, Sonia, 1934-

Annie's promise. Atheneum Pubs. 1993 186p $15; pa $3.99   **Fic**
1. Camps—Fiction 2. World War, 1939-1945—Fiction 3. Family life—Fiction 4. Jews—Fiction
ISBN 0-689-31752-2; 0-689-80440-7 (pa)
                                LC 92-16819
Sequel to Silver days
This third book about the Platt family "is told from the point of view of Annie, the youngest of the three sisters. At twelve, Annie's personal issues of growing up are far more immediate to her than the world events of 1945. An opportunity to attend a summer camp becomes the catalyst for Annie to move beyond her home and family and find what she wants to do with her life." Horn Book
"This is a thoughtful book about blossoming and independence that possesses a particular poignancy due to its characters and time." Bull Cent Child Books

The cure. Harcourt Brace & Co. 1999 181p $16
                                Fic
1. Antisemitism—Fiction 2. Science fiction 3. Jews—Europe—Fiction 4. Middle Ages—Fiction
ISBN 0-15-201827-1   LC 98-33907
Gemm, a young boy living in 2407, collides with the past when he finds himself in Strasbourg in 1348 confronting the antisemitism that sweeps through Europe during the Black Plague
"Levitin weaves a chilling story linking two worlds." ALAN

Escape from Egypt; a novel. Little, Brown 1994 267p o.p.; Puffin Bks. paperback available $4.99 (7 and up)   **Fic**
1. Moses (Biblical figure)—Fiction 2. Bible stories 3. Jews—Fiction
ISBN 0-14-037537-6 (pa)   LC 93-29376
When Moses comes to lead the Israelites to the Promised Land, Jesse, a Hebrew slave, finds his life changed by his growing faith in God and his attraction to the half-Egyptian, half-Syrian Jennat
Levitin "has written a book that is troubling, moving, and sensual—and that forces its readers to think." Booklist

Journey to America; illustrated by Charles Robinson. Atheneum Pubs. 1993 c1970 150p il $16; pa $3.95   **Fic**
1. World War, 1939-1945—Fiction 2. Jewish refugees—Fiction 3. Family life—Fiction
ISBN 0-689-31829-4; 0-689-71130-1 (pa)
A reissue of the title first published 1970
"In a strong immigration story, Lisa Platt, the middle daughter, tells how her family is forced to leave Nazi Germany and make a new life in the United States. First their father leaves, then the others escape to Switzerland, where they endure harsh conditions. After months of separation, the family is reunited in New York." Rochman. Against borders
Followed by Silver days

The return. Atheneum Pubs. 1987 213p $16
                                Fic
1. Jews—Ethiopia—Fiction 2. Antisemitism—Fiction
ISBN 0-689-31309-8   LC 86-25891
Also available in paperback from Fawcett Bks.
"In a docunovel of a Jewish Ethiopian family's flight to Israel, Levitin focuses on an orphan, Desta, whose older brother, Joas, persuades her to leave the village where hunger and political recriminations constantly threaten their lives." Bull Cent Child Books
"A vivid and compelling book. . . . Levitin's tour de force is sensitively written; her command of the language is impressive and she uses Ethiopian terms effectively, interspersing them in ways readers will understand." Booklist

Silver days. Atheneum Pubs. 1989 185p hardcover o.p. paperback available $3.95   **Fic**
1. Immigration and emigration—Fiction 2. Jews—Fiction 3. World War, 1939-1945—Fiction 4. Family life—Fiction
ISBN 0-689-71570-6 (pa)   LC 88-27491
Sequel to Journey to America

Levitin, Sonia, 1934—_Continued_
In this second volume the Platt family "finds life difficult in Manhattan and moves to California, where Papa insists that he will be able to make a decent living. The story is told by the middle daughter (Lisa, 13) and the narration is punctuated by her italicized journal entries." Bull Cent Child Books
The "story moves forward easily through incident and detail. The sense of the times is strong, both in terms of the war's reaching shadow and the prejudices that are quickly displayed." Booklist
Followed by Annie's promise

The singing mountain. Simon & Schuster Bks. for Young Readers 1998 261p $17 (7 and up)
Fic
1. Jews—Fiction 2. Israel—Fiction
ISBN 0-689-80809-7   LC 97-33365
While traveling in Israel for the summer, seventeen-year-old Mitch decides to stay and pursue a life of Jewish orthodoxy, forcing him to make some important decisions about the family and life he is leaving in southern California
"This plot-driven novel bristles with questions about faith, love, family, acceptance, and self-determination." Booklist

Yesterday's child. Simon & Schuster Bks. for Young Readers 1997 248p $17; pa $4.99 (7 and up)
Fic
1. Mothers and daughters—Fiction 2. Homicide—Fiction 3. Mystery fiction
ISBN 0-689-80810-0; 0-689-82073-9 (pa)
LC 96-31649
After her mother's sudden death, high school student Laura starts hunting for information about her mother's mysterious past, and in searching, uncovers some terrible secrets
"An interesting premise and an engrossing story filled with multi-faceted characters and an exciting climax." Child Book Rev Serv

Levy, Marilyn, 1937-
Run for your life. Houghton Mifflin 1996 217p $15 (7 and up)
Fic
1. Track athletics—Fiction 2. African Americans—Fiction 3. California—Fiction
ISBN 0-395-74520-9   LC 95-24379
Also available in paperback from Putnam Pub. Group
While living in a housing project in Oakland, California, thirteen-year-old Kisha joins a track team which helps her discover that she can be a winner
"This is a highly readable and engrossing story." SLJ

Lewis, C. S. (Clive Staples), 1898-1963
The lion, the witch, and the wardrobe; illustrated by Pauline Baynes. HarperCollins Pubs. 1994 189p il $15.95; lib bdg $15.89; pa $8.95
Fic
1. Fantasy fiction
ISBN 0-06-023481-4; 0-06-023482-2 (lib bdg); 0-06-440499-4 (pa)   LC 93-8889
A reissue of the title first published 1950 by Macmillan

Four English schoolchildren find their way through the back of a wardrobe into the magic land of Narnia and assist Aslan, the golden lion, to triumph over the White Witch, who has cursed the land with eternal winter
This begins "the 'Narnia' stories, outstanding modern fairy tales with an underlying theme of good overcoming evil." Child Books Too Good to Miss
Other available titles about Narnia are:
The horse and his boy (1954)
The last battle (1956)
The magician's nephew (1956)
Prince Caspian (1951)
The silver chair (1953)
The voyage of the Dawn Treader (1952)

Lindquist, Susan Hart
Summer soldiers. Delacorte Press 1999 178p $14.95
Fic
1. World War, 1914-1918—Fiction 2. Ranch life—Fiction 3. California—Fiction
ISBN 0-385-32641-6   LC 98-47429
"This story about 11-year-old Joe Farrington, his three friends, and their families is set in a small California town during World War I. The fellowship between the four sheep-raising families is challenged when three of the fathers enlist in the army, while only Jim's father remains at home." SLJ
"Lindquist's characters contend with many thorny issues—friendship, bravery, and bullies—in a realistic yet upbeat manner." Booklist

Lipsyte, Robert
The brave. HarperCollins Pubs. 1991 195p hardcover o.p. paperback available $4.95 (7 and up)
Fic
1. Indians of North America—Fiction 2. Boxing—Fiction 3. New York (N.Y.)—Fiction
ISBN 0-06-447079-2 (pa)   LC 90-25396
Sequel to The contender
"A Charlotte Zolotow book"
Having left the Indian reservation for the streets of New York, seventeen-year-old boxer Sonny Bear tries to harness his inner rage by training with Alfred Brooks, who has left the sport to become a policeman
Lipsyte "avoids the inaccuracies so common to the genre and delivers a compelling and multidimensional story. His style is razor-sharp, and his imagery comes across with pounding clarity. The book fairly pulsates with energy, especially in the fight scenes, and ends with Sonny starting over in the grimy world of low-level professional boxing." SLJ
Followed by The chief

The chief. HarperCollins Pubs. 1993 226p hardcover o.p. paperback available $4.95 (7 and up)
Fic
1. Indians of North America—Fiction 2. Boxing—Fiction
ISBN 0-06-447097-0 (pa)   LC 92-54502
Sequel to The brave
This novel is "narrated by Marty Malcolm Witherspoon, a sensitive and earnest black aspiring writer who has become a confidant of (and publicist for) a half-Native American boxing hero, Sonny Bear. Lurking be-

Lipsyte, Robert—*Continued*

hind the action is a dispute involving political power and gambling that threatens to split the Moscondaga Indian Nation into warring factions. The major conflict is not who wins the boxing duels but how Sonny can use his hard-won fame to help his people resolve their problems." SLJ

"Dramatic doings, terse and thrilling language and deftly sketched characters produce a heart-pounding read." Publ Wkly

The contender. Harper & Row 1967 182p $14.89; pa $4.95 (7 and up)   **Fic**
1. Boxing—Fiction 2. Harlem (New York, N.Y.)—Fiction 3. African Americans—Fiction
ISBN 0-06-023920-4; 0-06-447039-3 (pa)

"After a street fight in which he is the chief target, Alfred wanders into a gym in his neighborhood. He decides not only to improve his physical condition but also to become a boxer. Because of this interest Alfred's life is completely changed. He assumes a more positive outlook on his immediate future, even within the confines of a black ghetto." Shapiro. Fic for Youth. 3d edition

Followed by The brave

One fat summer. Harper & Row 1977 152p hardcover o.p. paperback available $4.95 (7 and up)   **Fic**
1. Weight loss—Fiction 2. Obesity—Fiction
ISBN 0-06-447073-3 (pa)   LC 76-49746

"Bobby Marks is 14 and fat. How fat, he doesn't know because he jumps off the scale when it hits 200 pounds. In one action-packed summer Bobby learns that altered physical appearance can bolster self-esteem. He's not sure he likes his friend Joanie's new nose and new ego, but he's certainly pleased with his own svelte new image. The slimming is a result of his summer job; tending the grounds of the town miser." West Coast Rev Books

"The plot elements are nicely balanced and paced, the characterization is developed with insight, and the writing style is deft and polished." Bull Cent Child Books

Followed by Summer rules

Summer rules; a novel. Harper & Row 1981 150p hardcover o.p. paperback available $3.95 (7 and up)   **Fic**
1. Camps—Fiction
ISBN 0-06-447071-7 (pa)   LC 79-2816

Sequel to One fat summer

"An Ursula Nordstrom book"

Bobby Marks "is forced by his father to work as a camp counselor. Bobby finds his job much more difficult than he anticipated but he learns to cope while also dealing with his old enemy Willie, sex, and truth." Child Book Rev Serv

This "is a believable book, generously sprinkled with touches of humor. As a sequel it holds up nicely." ALAN

Followed by The summerboy (1982)

Lisle, Janet Taylor, 1947-

Forest. Orchard Bks. 1993 150p $15.95   **Fic**
1. Squirrels—Fiction 2. Fantasy fiction
ISBN 0-531-06803-X   LC 93-9630

Also available in paperback from Scholastic

"A Richard Jackson book"

Twelve-year-old Amber's invasion of an organized forest community of squirrels starts a war between humans and beasts, despite the protests of an unconventional and imaginative squirrel named Woodbine

"Lisle has created a world of innocence marked with heartache, truth infused with absurdity, and wisdom relinquished to recklessness—all in the guise of animal fantasy." Bull Cent Child Books

Littke, Lael

Haunted sister. Holt & Co. 1998 217p $16.95 (7 and up)   **Fic**
1. Near-death experiences—Fiction 2. Twins—Fiction 3. Sisters—Fiction 4. Supernatural—Fiction
ISBN 0-8050-5729-3   LC 98-12144

A sixteen-year-old girl suffers a near-death experience in which her twin sister, who died in an accident twelve years before, returns to forcibly share her body

"A twist at the end both surprises and satisfies. A positive family story with strong psychological overtones." Booklist

Little, Jean, 1932-

The belonging place. Viking 1997 124p $13.99   **Fic**
1. Orphans—Fiction 2. Immigration and emigration—Fiction 3. Scotland—Fiction 4. Canada—Fiction
ISBN 0-670-87593-7

This story focuses on "Elspet Mary whose mother is killed by a runaway horse. Elspet Mary stays with friends until her dad returns to take her to relatives in a nearby village. Elspet is welcomed and made one of the family. Her new father is not happy with their life in Scotland so he decides to take the family to Canada's unexplored frontier. Elspet Mary is not happy about the move. She encounters many adventures and tragedy along the way, but in the end finds where she truly belongs." Child Book Rev Serv

"Young readers will appreciate this quiet but strong little page-turner." Bull Cent Child Books

London, Jack, 1876-1916

The call of the wild   **Fic**
1. Dogs—Fiction 2. Alaska—Fiction

Various editions available

First published 1903

"The dog hero, Buck, is stolen from his comfortable home and pressed into service as a sledge dog in the Klondike. At first he is abused by both men and dogs, but he learns to fight ruthlessly and finally finds in John Thornton a master whom he can respect and love. When Thornton is murdered, he breaks away to the wilds and becomes the leader of a pack of wolves." Reader's Ency

White Fang   **Fic**
1. Dogs—Fiction 2. Alaska—Fiction

Various editions available

First published 1906

London, Jack, 1876-1916—*Continued*

White Fang "is about a dog, a cross-breed, sold to Beauty Smith. This owner tortures the dog to increase his ferocity and value as a fighter. A new owner Weedom Scott, brings the dog to California, and, by kind treatment, domesticates him. White Fang later sacrifices his life to save Scott." Haydn. Thesaurus of Book Dig

Lord, Bette Bao

In the Year of the Boar and Jackie Robinson; illustrations by Marc Simont. Harper & Row 1984 169p il hardcover o.p. paperback available $4.95
Fic
1. Chinese Americans—Fiction 2. School stories
ISBN 0-06-440175-8 (pa)   LC 83-48440
"In a story based in part on the author's experience as an immigrant, Shirley Temple Wong . . . arrives in Brooklyn and spends her first year in public school." Bull Cent Child Books
"Warm-hearted, fresh, and dappled with humor, the episodic book, which successfully encompasses both Chinese dragons and the Brooklyn Dodgers, stands out in the bevy of contemporary problem novels. And the unusual flavor of the text infiltrates the striking illustrations picturing the pert, pigtailed heroine making her way in 'Mei Guo'—her new 'Beautiful Country.'" Horn Book

Lowry, Lois

Anastasia Krupnik. Houghton Mifflin 1979 113p $16
Fic
1. Family life—Fiction
ISBN 0-395-28629-8
Also available in paperback from Dell and from Bantam Bks.
This book describes the tenth year in the life of fourth-grader Anastasia. As she "experiences rejection of a long labored-over poem, fights acceptance of the coming arrival of a baby sibling, deliberates about becoming Catholic (in order to change her name), has a crush on Washburn Cummings who constantly dribbles an imaginary basketball, and learns to understand her senile grandmother's inward eye, she grows and matures." Booklist
"Anastasia's father and mother—an English professor and an artist—are among the most humorous, sensible, and understanding parents to be found in . . . children's fiction, and Anastasia herself is an amusing and engaging heroine." Horn Book
Other available titles about Anastasia Krupnik and her family are:
All about Sam (1988)
Anastasia, absolutely (1995)
Anastasia again! (1981)
Anastasia, ask your analyst (1984)
Anastasia at this address (1991)
Anastasia at your service (1982)
Anastasia has the answers (1986)
Anastasia on her own (1985)
Anastasia's chosen career (1987)
Attaby, Sam! (1992)
See you around Sam! (1996)
Zooman Sam (1999)

Autumn Street. Houghton Mifflin 1980 188p $16
Fic
1. World War, 1939-1945—Fiction 2. Friendship—Fiction
ISBN 0-395-27812-0   LC 80-376
Also available in paperback from Dell
"Elizabeth, the teller of the story, feels danger around her when her father goes to fight in World War II. She, her older sister, and her pregnant mother go to live with her grandparents on Autumn Street. Tatie, the black cook-housekeeper, and her street-wise grandson Charley love Elizabeth and reassure her during this difficult time." Child Book Rev Serv
"Characters, dialogue, believable plot combine in this well written story to capture the mind and heart of all who read this memorable and touching book." Voice Youth Advocates

Find a stranger, say goodbye. Houghton Mifflin 1978 187p $16.95 (7 and up)
Fic
1. Mothers and daughters—Fiction 2. Adoption—Fiction
ISBN 0-395-26459-6   LC 78-1024
Also available in paperback from Dell
Seemingly a girl who has everything, Natalie, at seventeen, goes in pursuit of her real mother
"While Nat's history falls a bit too easily into place, her characterization is sensitive and credibly rendered and reinforced by a well-defined cast of subordinate characters and fine writing." Booklist

The giver. Houghton Mifflin 1993 180p $14.95
Fic
1. Science fiction
ISBN 0-395-64566-2   LC 92-15034
Also available Thorndike Press large print edition and in paperback from Dell
Awarded the Newbery Medal, 1994
Given his lifetime assignment at the Ceremony of Twelve, Jonas becomes the receiver of memories shared by only one other in his community and discovers the terrible truth about the society in which he lives
"A riveting, chilling story that inspires a new appreciation for diversity, love, and even pain. Truly memorable." SLJ

Number the stars. Houghton Mifflin 1989 137p $16
Fic
1. World War, 1939-1945—Fiction 2. Jews—Fiction 3. Friendship—Fiction 4. Denmark—Fiction
ISBN 0-395-51060-0   LC 88-37134
Also available in paperback from Dell
Awarded the Newbery Medal, 1990
"Best friends Annemarie Johansen and Ellen Rosen must suddenly pretend to be sisters one night when Ellen's parents go into hiding to escape a Nazi roundup in wartime Copenhagen. With the help of a young resistance fighter, the Johansens smuggle the Rosens aboard Annemarie's uncle's fishing boat bound for freedom in Sweden." Bull Cent Child Books
"The appended author's note details the historical incidents upon which Lowry bases her plot. . . . The message is so closely woven into the carefully honed narrative that the whole work is seamless, compelling, and memorable." Horn Book

Lowry, Lois—*Continued*
The one hundredth thing about Caroline.
Houghton Mifflin 1983 150p $16   **Fic**
1. Single parent family—Fiction 2. Brothers and sisters—Fiction
ISBN 0-395-34829-3   LC 83-12629
Also available in paperback from Dell

"Caroline, fascinated by dinosaurs, spends much of her free time prowling New York's Museum of Natural History; her best friend, Stacy, practices being an investigative reporter. The combination proves disastrous when Caroline's mother becomes interested in Frederick Fiske, the mysterious man in the fifth-floor apartment who looks, Caroline is convinced, like the evil 'Tyrannosaurus rex' and who seemingly wants to eliminate Caroline and her brother, J.P." Booklist

"Lowry's style is bright, fast-paced and funny, with skillfully-drawn, believable characters." SLJ

Followed by Switcharound

Rabble Starkey. Houghton Mifflin 1987 192p
$16   **Fic**
1. Friendship—Fiction 2. Mothers and daughters—Fiction
ISBN 0-395-43607-9   LC 86-27542
Also available G.K. Hall large print edition and in paperback from Dell

"Parable Starkey and her mother, Sweet Hosanna, move into the Bigelows' house to take charge of the children after Mrs. Bigelow's hospitalization for mental illness. . . . [This is] a smooth first-person narrative that quietly takes on class as well as individual differences. In the end, Lowry has managed to portray a large, diverse cast by carefully and consistently focusing the point of view as one of a maturing observer." Bull Cent Child Books

Stay! Keeper's story. Houghton Mifflin 1997
127p il $15   **Fic**
1. Dogs—Fiction
ISBN 0-395-87048-8   LC 97-1569
Also available in paperback from Dell

"The canine narrator is a mongrel with class, a poetically inclined, refined animal of good upbringing if not bloodlines. He leaves the relative safety of his first home (an alley outside a French restaurant) for the perils of the wide world in search of a human friend." Bull Cent Child Books

"The author proves she is as well versed in animal behavior as in human sensibilities. Her warm sense of humor and vivid imagination . . . accentuate Keeper's unorthodox perceptions of the world." Publ Wkly

A summer to die; illustrated by Jenni Oliver.
Houghton Mifflin 1977 154p il $16   **Fic**
1. Sisters—Fiction 2. Death—Fiction
ISBN 0-395-25338-1   LC 77-83
Also available in paperback from Bantam Bks.

"Meg, 13, envies her older sister's popularity and prettiness and finds it difficult to cope with Molly's degenerating illness and eventual death." Booklist

"As told by Meg, the chronicle of this experience is a sensitive exploration of the complex emotions underlying the adolescent's first confrontation with human mortality; the author suggests nuances of contemporary conversation and situations without sacrificing the finesse with which she limns her characters." Horn Book

Switcharound. Houghton Mifflin 1985 118p $16
Fic
1. Brothers and sisters—Fiction 2. Family life—Fiction
ISBN 0-395-39536-4   LC 85-14576
Also available in paperback from Dell

Sequel to The one hundredth thing about Caroline

Forced to spend a summer with their father and his "new" family, Caroline, age eleven, and J.P., age thirteen, are given unpleasant responsibilities for which they are determined to get revenge

"There is a bit too convenient an all-ends-tied final chapter, but the strong characterization, the humorous style and yeasty dialogue, and the change and development (including some shaking of stereotypical sex roles) in the two main characters give the story both substance and appeal." Bull Cent Child Books

Taking care of Terrific. Houghton Mifflin 1983
168p $16 (7 and up)   **Fic**
1. Babysitters—Fiction 2. Boston (Mass.)—Fiction
ISBN 0-395-34070-5   LC 82-23331
Also available in paperback from Dell

Fourteen-year-old Enid Crowley is "bored by the prospect of a Boston summer. That's before she begins taking care of a precocious . . . four-year-old, Joshua Warwick Cameron IV, who prefers to be called Tom Terrific, before she meets the friendly black musician in the Public Garden, or the bag ladies, before she discovers that that pest of a classmate, Seth, is really a very nice boy." Bull Cent Child Books

"Although the plot seems incredible, the book as a whole is somehow satisfying. The Boston setting is vividly evoked, and the diverse cast of characters adds variety and flavor to the narrative." Horn Book

Your move, J.P.! Houghton Mifflin 1990 122p
$15   **Fic**
1. School stories
ISBN 0-395-53639-1   LC 89-24707
Also available in paperback from Dell

Caroline's older brother, J.P. Tate who appeared in The one hundredth thing about Caroline and Switcharound, has a "crush on Angela Galsworthy, newly arrived at his private school from London, England. . . . Anxious to sustain Angela's interest, J.P. tells her that he is suffering from triple framosis, a rare but fatal disease. Angela believes him and J.P. is stuck with his lie." Bull Cent Child Books

"The author makes the most of the humor in J.P.'s antics but maintains a rueful sympathy throughout for his plight and for his eventual admission of truth." Horn Book

Lynch, Chris
Extreme Elvin. HarperCollins Pubs. 1999 230p
$14.95; lib bdg $14.89 (7 and up)   **Fic**
1. School stories
ISBN 0-06-028040-9; 0-06-028210-X (lib bdg)
LC 98-28820
Sequel to Slot machine

As he enters high school, fourteen-year-old Elvin continues to deal with his weight problem as he tries to find his place among his peers

"This is a funny, insightful, and wholly engaging novel." SLJ

Lynch, Chris—*Continued*

Iceman. HarperCollins Pubs. 1994 181p $15; lib bdg $14.89; pa $4.95 (7 and up)   **Fic**
1. Hockey—Fiction 2. Parent and child—Fiction
ISBN 0-06-023340-0; 0-06-023341-9 (lib bdg); 0-06-447114-4 (pa)   LC 93-7776
"Fourteen-year-old Eric is an ice hockey player who has a well-earned reputation for playing a rough game and being physically violent on the ice. He is encouraged by his father, a second-rate public relations man, who lives vicariously through the team's winning. Whereas, his mother, a former nun, has made saving his soul a priority." Child Book Rev Serv
"Much better than the usual sports novel, this is an unsettling, complicated portrayal of growing up in a dysfunctional family. Lynch is a wizard with game color, and he challenges the violence of the game throughout the story." Booklist

Mick. HarperCollins Pubs. 1996 146p (Blue-eyed son) hardcover o.p. paperback available $4.50 (7 and up)   **Fic**
1. Prejudices—Fiction 2. Irish Americans—Fiction 3. Boston (Mass.)—Fiction
ISBN 0-06-447121-7 (pa)   LC 94-18725
His friendship with two Hispanic students offers fifteen-year-old Mick an alternative to the drunken savagery of his brother and the narrow thinking of his Irish-American neighborhood in Boston
"With realistic street language and an in-your-face writing style that complements the plot, Lynch immerses readers in Mick's world of alcohol, racism, and dysfunction, out of which emerges a noble anti-hero who risks physical danger and alienation for the sake of doing what is right." SLJ
Other available titles in the Blue-eyed son trilogy are:
Blood relations (1996)
Dog eat dog (1996)

Political timber. HarperCollins Pubs. 1996 166p $14.95; lib bdg $14.89; pa $4.95 (7 and up)   **Fic**
1. Elections—Fiction 2. Grandfathers—Fiction
ISBN 0-06-027360-7; 0-06-027361-5 (lib bdg); 0-06-447141-1 (pa)   LC 96-5750
High school senior Gordon Foley runs for mayor at the behest of his grandfather, an old-style politician scheming to regain power while he's in prison for fraud
"Fresh, funny, and at times devastatingly frank. . . . The book is a great read that offers some discussion fodder as well." Horn Book Guide

Shadow boxer. HarperCollins Pubs. 1993 215p lib bdg $14.89; pa $4.50 (7 and up)   **Fic**
1. Boxing—Fiction 2. Brothers—Fiction 3. Fathers and sons—Fiction
ISBN 0-06-023028-2 (lib bdg); 0-06-447112-8 (pa)   LC 92-47490
"Fourteen-year-old George has felt responsible for his younger brother Monty ever since the death of his father, a heavyweight boxer. George passes on the boxing lessons Dad taught him and is equally intent on teaching Monty about life outside the ring. The fight sequences, fraternal dynamics, and memorable cast of eccentric characters make for some riveting episodes in the rough, tough-talking book." Horn Book Guide

Slot machine. HarperCollins Pubs. 1995 241p lib bdg $14.89; pa $4.95 (7 and up)   **Fic**
1. Camps—Fiction 2. Sports—Fiction 3. Friendship—Fiction
ISBN 0-06-023585-3 (lib bdg); 0-06-447140-3 (pa)   LC 94-48235
When overweight thirteen-year-old Elvin Bishop is sent to camp at St. Paul's Seminary Retreat Center, he and his two best friends are forced to try out various sports in order to find out where they belong
"The religious setting is used to heighten the irony. There is some beer drinking. Pornography is discussed and in one scene described in an inoffensive way. Likewise, there is a scene or two of adolescent male exhibitionism, again not graphically described, and finally it is implied that Frank undergoes hazing of a homosexual nature." Book Rep
Followed by Extreme Elvin

Whitechurch. HarperCollins Pubs. 1999 247p $14.95; lib bdg $14.89 (7 and up)   **Fic**
ISBN 0-06-028330-0; 0-06-028331-9 (lib bdg)   LC 98-54799
"Pauly and his friend Oakley are both in love with Lilly, who alone seems to have the power to leave the small town the three friends are trapped in." Horn Book Guide
"Told in first person by Oakley, chapters read like vignettes, with some comprised solely of poetry. . . . There are compelling sparks of perception, unique angles, disturbing moments, and even humor. . . . Situations and language make this novel appropriate for older teen readers . . . though savvy junior high readers could also handle it." Voice Youth Advocates

Lyons, Mary E.

Letters from a slave girl; the story of Harriet Jacobs. Scribner 1992 146p il $16; pa $3.95   **Fic**
1. Jacobs, Harriet A. (Harriet Ann), 1813-1896 or 7—Fiction 2. Slavery—Fiction 3. African Americans—Fiction
ISBN 0-684-19446-5; 0-689-80015-0 (pa)   LC 91-45778
A fictionalized version of the life of Harriet Jacobs, told in the form of letters that she might have written during her slavery in North Carolina and as she prepared for escape to the North in 1842
This "is historical fiction at its best. . . . Mary Lyons has remained faithful to Jacobs's actual autobiography throughout her readable, compelling novel. . . . Her observations of the horrors of slavery are concise and lucid. The letters are written in dialect, based on Jacobs's own writing and on other slave narrations of the period." Horn Book

MacGregor, Rob

Hawk moon. Simon & Schuster Bks. for Young Readers 1996 191p $16 (7 and up)   **Fic**
1. Mystery fiction 2. Hopi Indians—Fiction
ISBN 0-689-80171-8   LC 96-18981
Also available in paperback from Bantam Bks.
Companion volume to Prophecy rock (1995)
"High school star running back Will Lansa is back home in Aspen, Colorado, after having spent the summer

MacGregor, Rob—*Continued*

on the Hopi reservation in Arizona with his father, a tribal policeman. Shortly after his return, Will's girlfriend Myra disappears and is presumed dead. When Will's knife turns up with Myra's blood on the blade and traces of a designer drug on the hilt, Will becomes a murder suspect." Voice Youth Advocates

"A well-written, fast-moving murder mystery. . . . Interesting, believable teen and adult characters and fast-paced action make this novel a real bridge to adult murder mysteries." SLJ

Mackel, Kathy

Can of worms. Avon Bks. 1999 146p $15; pa $3.99   **Fic**

1. Extraterrestrial beings—Fiction 2. Science fiction
ISBN 0-380-97681-1; 0-380-80050-0 (pa)

            LC 98-53346

Bullied and unhappy at school, thirteen-year-old Mike, who has always thought that he might be an alien, sends a distress call into space asking to be rescued from the ignorance and cruelty of his life on Earth

"This humorous, fast-paced science-fiction adventure is set in the real world of adolescent angst, bullies, and first love." SLJ

MacLachlan, Patricia

Journey. Delacorte Press 1991 83p $14.95; pa $3.99   **Fic**

1. Family life—Fiction
ISBN 0-385-30427-7; 0-440-40809-1 (pa)

            LC 90-21052

When their mother goes off, leaving her two children with their grandparents, they feel as if their past has been erased until Grandfather finds a way to restore it to them

"This is a spellbinding tale, lean only in its length. The author's clipped dialogue and meticulously pared-down descriptions convey a deceptive simplicity—there are deep, intricate rumblings beneath the surface calm of MacLachlan's words." Publ Wkly

Maguire, Gregory

The good liar. Clarion Bks. 1999 129p $15

            Fic

1. World War, 1939-1945—Fiction 2. France—Fiction
ISBN 0-395-90697-0   LC 98-19981
First published 1995 in Ireland

Now an old man living in the United States, Marcel recalls his childhood in German-occupied France, especially the summer that he and his older brother Rene befriended a young German soldier

"At once poignant, thoughtful, and laced with humor, the book offers readers an unusual perspective on history." Horn Book Guide

Mahy, Margaret

Aliens in the family. Scholastic 1986 174p
hardcover o.p. paperback available $3.25   **Fic**

1. Science fiction 2. Stepfamily—Fiction
ISBN 0-590-44898-6 (pa)   LC 86-3908

"In a science fantasy set in New Zealand, Jacqueline (Jake) Raven comes to visit her father and the family he's acquired with a second marriage. His wife, Philippa, is fine, and her son Lewis isn't bad, but her daughter Dora is the ultra-feminine type Jake despises. What finally draws them together is the protective circle they feel they must draw around Bond, an extraterrestrial visitor whose identity must be hidden from their parents and whose time-travel project is threatened by the evil forces who pursue him." Bull Cent Child Books

"Using Bond and Jake as aliens in their own situations, Mahy has written a story of families learning to accept and believe in each other in spite of, and even because of, their differences." Voice Youth Advocates

The changeover; a supernatural romance. Atheneum Pubs. 1984 214p $16   **Fic**

1. Witchcraft—Fiction
ISBN 0-689-50303-2   LC 83-83446
Also available in paperback from Puffin Bks.
"A Margaret K. McElderry book"

"The protagonist is Laura, who cannot convince her mother that her little brother is dying because an evil wizard has taken possession of his body. As a last, desperate measure Laura agrees to a changeover: her friend Sorenson, his mother, and his grandmother are all witches and they induct her into their occult world so that she will have the power to take possession of the wizard and save her brother." Bull Cent Child Books

"Mahy tells a tale of whiteknuckle suspense in her elegant style, abating the terrors frequently with astringently witty observations. . . . The principals and supporting players in the cast are expertly individualized." Publ Wkly

The greatest show off earth; illustrated by Wendy Smith. Viking 1994 186p il $13.99; pa $4.99   **Fic**

1. Science fiction
ISBN 0-670-85736-X; 0-14-037926-6 (pa)

            LC 94-20287

Delphinium spends her tenth birthday aboard a traveling space circus, fighting against the dark forces who are bent on stamping out fun

"Mahy's inventiveness is rampant, and there's plenty of tongue-in-cheek suspense to keep the story rolling." Bull Cent Child Books

Manes, Stephen, 1949-

An almost perfect game. Scholastic 1995 162p $14.95; pa $3.99   **Fic**

1. Baseball—Fiction
ISBN 0-590-44432-8; 0-590-44433-6 (pa)

            LC 94-18192

As he and his grandmother keep score at the last game of the season for the local minor league team, Jake and his older brother begin to wonder if Jake's scorecard can control the outcome of the game

"Manes wonderfully evokes minor-league baseball at its most irrepressible, and the witty, first-person narration helps to carry the story along." SLJ

Marchetta, Melina, 1965-

Looking for Alibrandi. Orchard Bks. 1999 250p $16.95; lib bdg $17.99 (7 and up)   **Fic**
1. Fathers and daughters—Fiction 2. Australia—Fiction
ISBN 0-531-30142-7; 0-531-33142-3 (lib bdg)
LC 98-35804

During her senior year in a Catholic school in Sydney, Australia, seventeen-year-old Josie meets and must contend with the father she has never known

"What emerges from this delightful first-person narrative is a strong, fresh, adolescent female voice. . . . Lively, well-drawn characters and realistic teen concerns and situations." Booklist

Marino, Jan

The day that Elvis came to town; a novel. Little, Brown 1991 204p o.p.; Avon Bks. paperback available $3.50 (7 and up)   **Fic**
1. Presley, Elvis, 1935-1977—Fiction 2. African Americans—Fiction 3. Prejudices—Fiction 4. Alcoholism—Fiction 5. Georgia—Fiction
ISBN 0-380-71672-0 (pa)   LC 90-13493

Wanda feels betrayed when her parents' glamorous boarder doesn't introduce her to Elvis Presley, and it takes a near-tragedy to reunite them and to help her face the truth about her family and herself

"This novel teaches without being didactic, exploring both racism and alcoholism appropriately and powerfully. But most of all, the characters—even the most disagreeable ones—are drawn with affection." SLJ

For the love of Pete; a novel. Little, Brown 1993 197p o.p.; Avon Bks. paperback available $3.50   **Fic**
1. Household employees—Fiction 2. Fathers and daughters—Fiction
ISBN 0-380-72281-X (pa)   LC 92-36465

When her grandmother moves into a nursing home, twelve-year-old Phoebe sets out in the old family car with three of Gram's servants, on a search for the father who abandoned her at birth

This "is a poignant and, at times, hilarious adventure. The gentle coming-of-age story is carefully crafted and peopled with memorable characters." Horn Book Guide

Marsden, John, 1950-

Checkers. Houghton Mifflin 1998 122p $15 (7 and up)   **Fic**
1. Psychiatric hospitals—Fiction 2. Mental illness—Fiction 3. Australia—Fiction
ISBN 0-395-85754-6   LC 97-49405

An unnamed Australian "teenage girl describes her interactions with her fellow patients in a mental hospital and recalls the events that led to her institutionalization. Her memories center on her pet dog and on a financial scandal that involved her businessman father." Horn Book Guide

"Marsden's beautiful prose packs an emotional wallop. . . . This affecting account of a family under siege by the media is both an engaging read and a strong psychological exploration." Booklist

Letters from the inside. Houghton Mifflin 1994 c1991 146p $14.95 (7 and up)   **Fic**
1. Friendship—Fiction 2. Prisoners—Fiction 3. Australia—Fiction
ISBN 0-395-68985-6   LC 93-41185
Also available in paperback from Dell
First published 1991 in Australia

"Mandy and Tracey become penpals after Tracey places an ad for such in an Australian teen magazine. At first the missives are friendly and chatty . . . but gradually darker truths are revealed: Tracey is in prison, Mandy is becoming increasingly frightened of her older brother." Bull Cent Child Books

"The characters are vivid, each developed through her choice of language and response to the other girl's life. Marsden gives the reader a great deal to think about, exploring human responses to violence and victimization, Tracey's responsibility for her crime, and a justice system which abuses her." Horn Book

Tomorrow, when the war began. Houghton Mifflin 1995 286p $15 (7 and up)   **Fic**
1. War stories 2. Australia—Fiction
ISBN 0-395-70673-4   LC 94-29299
Also available in paperback from Bantam Bks.
First published 1993 in Australia

"Australian teenager Ellie and six of her friends return from a winter break camping trip to find their homes burned or deserted, their families imprisoned, and their country occupied by foreign military force in league with a band of disaffected Australians. As their shock wears off, the seven decide they must stick together if they are to survive." SLJ

"The novel is a riveting adventure through which Marsden explores the capacity for evil and the necessity of working together to oppose it." Horn Book

Other available titles in this series are:
Darkness be my friend (1999)
The dead of night (1997)
A killing frost (1998)

Matas, Carol, 1949-

After the war. Simon & Schuster Bks. for Young Readers 1996 116p map $16; pa $4.50 (7 and up)   **Fic**
1. Holocaust, 1933-1945—Fiction 2. Jews—Europe—Fiction
ISBN 0-689-80350-8; 0-689-80722-8 (pa)
LC 95-43613

After being released from Buchenwald at the end of World War II, fifteen-year-old Ruth risks her life to lead a group of children across Europe to Palestine

"Rich in texture and simple in its honesty, this story resonates with feeling." Voice Youth Advocates
Followed by The garden

The garden. Simon & Schuster Bks. for Young Readers 1997 102p $15; pa $4.50 (7 and up)   **Fic**
1. Israel-Arab War, 1948-1949—Fiction 2. Jews—Fiction
ISBN 0-689-80349-4; 0-689-80723-6 (pa)
LC 96-41405
Sequel to After the war

Matas, Carol, 1949—*Continued*

After leading a group of Jewish refugees to Israel after World War II, sixteen-year-old Ruth joins the Haganah, the Jewish Army, and helps her people fight to keep the land granted to them by the United Nations

"A riveting, relevant novel that raises tough questions—and provides no easy answers. . . . A truly good read." SLJ

Greater than angels. Simon & Schuster Bks. for Young Readers 1998 133p $16 (7 and up)   **Fic**
1. World War, 1939-1945—Fiction 2. Jews—France—Fiction 3. Holocaust, 1933-1945—Fiction 4. Jewish refugees—Fiction

ISBN 0-689-81353-8   LC 97-27565

Anna, a teenaged German refugee, relates how she and other Jewish children were cared for by the citizens of Le Chambon-sur-Lignon, France, during the German occupation

"This well-researched historical novel will make a good addition to middle-school collections." SLJ

In my enemy's house. Simon & Schuster Bks. for Young Readers 1999 167p $16 (7 and up)
      Fic
1. World War, 1939-1945—Fiction 2. Jews—Germany—Fiction 3. Holocaust, 1933-1945—Fiction

ISBN 0-689-81354-6   LC 98-16330

When German soldiers arrive in Zloczow during World War II, Marisa, a fifteen-year-old Jewish girl, must decide whether or not to conceal her identity and work for a Nazi in Germany in order to survive

"Although this is fiction, it has the immediacy and impact of a true story. Marisa's ordeal is compelling, moving—and deeply disturbing." SLJ

Matcheck, Diane

The sacrifice. Farrar, Straus & Giroux 1998 197p $16 (7 and up)   **Fic**
1. Crow Indians—Fiction 2. Orphans—Fiction

ISBN 0-374-36378-1   LC 97-36408

Also available in paperback from Puffin Bks.

When her father's death leaves her orphaned and an outcast among her Apsaalooka (Crow) people, fifteen-year-old Weak-one sets out to avenge his death and prove that she, not her dead twin brother, is destined to be the Great One

"An author's note . . . locates the book's time in the mid-eighteenth century and the setting as Montana, Wyoming, and Nebraska, including the Yellowstone region. Matcheck's descriptions are as breathtaking as the real-life scenery. Readers will not only have a sense of place, but they will also be gripped by many of the same emotions that seize Weak-one." Booklist

Mathis, Sharon Bell, 1937-

Listen for the fig tree. Viking 1974 175p hardcover o.p. paperback available $4.99 (7 and up)   **Fic**
1. African Americans—Fiction 2. Kwanzaa—Fiction 3. Blind—Fiction 4. Mothers and daughters—Fiction

ISBN 0-14-034364-4 (pa)

A sixteen-year-old black girl's first celebration of Kwanza gives her a sense of the past and strength to deal with her troubled mother and her own blindness

"Mathis has a talent for the music of black speech and for conveying the togetherness of black people. But she has a more important talent, characterization and the ability to describe delicate relationships." N Y Times Book Rev

Teacup full of roses. Viking 1972 125p hardcover o.p. paperback available $4.99 (7 and up)   **Fic**
1. African Americans—Fiction 2. Family life—Fiction 3. Drug abuse—Fiction

ISBN 0-14-32328-7 (pa)

"Because of the mother's especially protective concern for her eldest son, Paul, the world of the Brooks family revolves around him—to the detriment of the rest of the family. After a hospital stay for detoxification from heroin, Paul returns home. With him comes tragedy that destroys David, the youngest son, who had an 'outasight' basketball arm, and changes the life of the middle son, Joe, who had a gift for telling stories. This is an exploration of love and loyalty in a black inner-city family." Shapiro. Fic for Youth. 3d edition

Mazer, Harry, 1925-

The last mission. Delacorte Press 1979 182p o.p.; Dell paperback available $4.50 (7 and up)
      Fic
1. World War, 1939-1945—Fiction 2. Prisoners of war—Fiction 3. Jews—Fiction

ISBN 0-440-94797-9 (pa)   LC 79-50674

In 1944 a 15-year-old Jewish boy tells his family he will travel in the West but instead, enlists in the United States Air Corps and is subsequently taken prisoner by the Germans

"Told in a rapid journalistic style, occasionally peppered with barrack-room vulgarities, the story is a vivid and moving account of a boy's experience during World War II as well as a skillful, convincing portrayal of his misgivings as a Jew on enemy soil and of his ability to size up—in mature human fashion—the misery around him." Horn Book

Snow bound. Delacorte Press 1973 146p o.p.; Dell paperback available $4.50 (7 and up)   **Fic**
1. Wilderness survival—Fiction 2. Runaway children—Fiction

ISBN 0-440-96134-3 (pa)   LC 72-7958

Also available in hardcover from P. Smith

"Tony Laporte is angry when his parents will not allow him to keep a stray dog, so he takes off in his mother's old car. Driving without a license in the middle of a snowstorm that soon becomes a blizzard, Tony picks up a hitchhiker, Cindy Reichert. Trying to impress the slightly older girl with his driving skill, Tony wrecks the car, leaving the two stranded in a desolate area far from a main highway, with little likelihood of rescue for days." Shapiro. Fic for Youth. 3d edition

When the phone rang. Scholastic 1985 181p hardcover o.p. paperback available $4.50 (7 and up)   **Fic**
1. Death—Fiction 2. Brothers and sisters—Fiction

ISBN 0-590-44773-4 (pa)   LC 84-6098

Mazer, Harry, 1925——*Continued*

When their parents are killed in an airplane crash, three siblings try to keep the family together in the face of overwhelming personal and financial problems

The author "has written an intense (but not unrelieved), realistic portrayal of grief's effect on three young people—the anger, the adjustments, the growing in maturity, and the love and concern they each feel for the others." Booklist

Who is Eddie Leonard? Delacorte Press 1993 188p hardcover o.p. paperback available $3.99 (7 and up)   **Fic**
ISBN 0-440-21922-1 (pa)   LC 93-22114

"When 15-year-old Eddie Leonard's grandmother dies, he feels invisible, 'like a gray ghost,' searching for something, but not knowing what. Although his grandmother was often cruel, and her stories of how he came to live with her were vague, inconsistent, and dissatisfying, she provided the only constant in his life. When he sees a poster of a missing child, everything changes. Eddie believes he is Jason Diaz, a boy who has been missing for 12 years." Booklist

"Mazer has written a book teens will respond to, a story about the often painful search for self identity. Eddie Leonard will touch each reader who travels with him as he searches for and finds himself." Voice Youth Advocates

The wild kid. Simon & Schuster Bks. for Young Readers 1998 103p $15; pa $4.50   **Fic**
1. Mentally handicapped—Fiction 2. Wild children—Fiction 3. Runaway children—Fiction
ISBN 0-689-80751-1; 0-689-82289-8 (pa)
                                          LC 97-42578

Twelve-year-old Sammy, who is mildly retarded, runs away from home and becomes a prisoner of Kevin, a wild kid living in the woods

"A gripping survival story with flesh-and-blood characters." SLJ

Mazer, Norma Fox, 1931-

After the rain. Morrow Junior Bks. 1987 291p $16 (7 and up)   **Fic**
1. Grandfathers—Fiction 2. Death—Fiction
ISBN 0-688-06867-7   LC 86-33270
Also available G.K. Hall large print edition and in paperback from Avon Bks.

A Newbery Medal honor book, 1988

"Adolescent Rachel has always been a little afraid of Grandpa Izzy, her mother's father; sharp-tongued and irritable, the old man seems to have no kindness or softness in his nature. After the family learns that he has terminal cancer (which Izzy isn't told), Rachel begins to visit him and walk with him daily, and by the time he is near the end and hospitalized, she has come to love him." Bull Cent Child Books

"A powerful book, dealing with death and dying and the strength of family affection." Horn Book

Crazy Fish. Morrow Junior Bks. 1998 c1980 184p $15 (7 and up)   **Fic**
1. Friendship—Fiction 2. Uncles—Fiction 3. School stories
ISBN 0-688-16281-9   LC 98-10587
Also available in paperback from Avon Bks.

First published 1980 by Dutton with title Mrs. Fish, Ape, and me, the Dump Queen

A friendless girl, teased mercilessly at school because her uncle manages the town dump, finds a friend in Mrs. Fish, the school custodian, and gradually life becomes more bearable

"Written in a naturalistic style, this character study peeks into the hearts of those deemed 'different' and shows how an unlikely family is created." Horn Book Guide

Out of control. Morrow Junior Bks. 1993 217p $16 (7 and up)   **Fic**
1. Sexual harassment—Fiction 2. Friendship—Fiction
ISBN 0-688-10208-5   LC 92-32516
Also available in paperback from Avon Bks.

"An incident of sexual harassment occurring in a high school corridor dramatically alters the lives of two of the students involved. Of the three youths accused of assaulting sharp-tongued Valerie Michon, only Rollo, a junior, experiences twinges of guilt which evolve into a desperate need to be forgiven by his family as well as his victim. Meanwhile, bitter, fearful Valerie struggles to regain her independence and trust in men." Publ Wkly

"This is a work of real strength, a book in which every character, every facet of plot, suggests credibility and provokes introspection." Voice Youth Advocates

Silver. Morrow Junior Bks. 1988 261p $16 (7 and up)   **Fic**
1. Friendship—Fiction 2. Child sexual abuse—Fiction
ISBN 0-688-06865-0   LC 88-18652
Also available in paperback from Avon Bks.

"When Sarabeth Silver's mother moves the two of them to the far end of Roadview Trailer Park, she puts Sarabeth in the Drumlins school district and scores again in her relentless drive to ensure that her daughter will have better. . . . The relative insignificance of wealth becomes glaringly clear when her enigmatic friend, Patty, reveals that she is the victim of sexual abuse." Voice Youth Advocates

"Mazer's story unfolds smoothly. She has an ear for dialogue that gives her scenes an easy credibility, and the story's central drama of a girl's physical abuse is handled without oversensationalizing the plot." Booklist

The solid gold kid; a novel; by Norma Fox Mazer and Harry Mazer. Delacorte Press 1977 219p o.p.; Bantam Bks. paperback available $3.99 (7 and up)   **Fic**
1. Kidnapping—Fiction
ISBN 0-553-27851-7 (pa)   LC 76-47238
Derek Chapman hitches a ride and later realizes he has unwittingly assisted in what he has dreaded and anticipated—his own kidnapping

"A cliff-hanger. . . . There are credible relationships formed among the victims, including a romance, and the pace certainly doesn't lag." Booklist

Taking Terri Mueller. Morrow 1983 c1981 212p o.p.; Avon Bks. paperback available $4.50   **Fic**
1. Parental kidnapping—Fiction 2. Divorce—Fiction 3. Parent and child—Fiction
ISBN 0-380-79004-1 (pa)   LC 82-18849

Mazer, Norma Fox, 1931——_Continued_

"Thirteen-year-old Terri and her father, Phil, have an almost idyllic relationship. Together they travel across the country, moving wherever Phil's carpentry work takes him. Terri has no reason to doubt what her father has told her about her mother's death in an auto accident nine years before. No reason, that is, until she overhears a conversation indicating something is being kept from her. . . . For a book that begins so benignly, amazing emotional depths are reached." Booklist

McCaffrey, Anne

Black horses for the king. Harcourt Brace & Co. 1996 217p map $17 (7 and up)   **Fic**
1. Arthur, King—Fiction 2. Horses—Fiction 3. Great Britain—History—0-1066—Fiction
ISBN 0-15-227322-0   LC 95-36366
Also available in paperback from Ballantine Pub. Group

Galwyn, son of a Roman Celt, escapes from his tyrannical uncle and joins Lord Artos, later know as King Arthur, using his talent with languages and way with horses to help secure and care for the Libyan horses that Artos hopes to use in battle against the Saxons

"The Arthurian flavor is well maintained throughout, and both characterizations and events are totally convincing." Booklist

If wishes were horses. ROC 1998 85p $13.95 (7 and up)   **Fic**
1. Fantasy fiction
ISBN 0-451-45642-4   LC 98-23917

"Tirza helps her mother, Lady Talarrie, deal with the realities that befall their small village when war comes their way. . . . Tirza knows some of her mother's miracles come from the three crystals she always wears, and Tirza cannot wait until her sixteenth birthday when she earns her own crystal. . . . This is a short, easily-read fairy tale that any McCaffrey fan will enjoy." Voice Youth Advocates

Pegasus in flight. Ballantine Bks. 1990 290p hardcover o.p. paperback available $5.99 (7 and up)   **Fic**
1. Science fiction
ISBN 0-345-36897-5 (pa)   LC 90-92901
Sequel to To ride Pegasus (1990)
"A Del Rey book"
"As director of the Jerhatten Center for Parapsychic Talents, telepath Rhyssa Owen struggles to protect her psychically gifted people—called 'Talents'—from a world that both fears and wants to exploit their abilities." Libr J

[The Pern series] (7 and up)   **Fic**
1. Fantasy fiction

"The people of Pern are in danger of the Threads, and look to the tamed dragons for protection from the thread-like spores. . . . McCaffrey has created a vivid and believable world, alive with interesting characters and events. There is plenty of action, a good plot, and the writing is excellent." Roman. Sequences

Fantasy titles set on Pern are:
All the Weyrs of Pern (1991)
The chronicles of Pern: first fall (1993)
The dolphins of Pern (1994)
Dragondrums (1979)
Dragonflight (1968)
Dragonholder (1999)
Dragonquest (1971)
Dragonriders of Pern (1978)
Dragonsdawn (1988)
Dragonseye (1997)
Dragonsinger (1977)
Dragonsong (1976)
The masterharper of Pern (1998)
Moreta: Dragonlady of Pern (1983)
Nerilka's story (1986)
The Renegades of Pern (1989)
White dragon (1978)

McCaughrean, Geraldine, 1951-

The pirate's son. Scholastic 1998 c1996 294p $16.95 (7 and up)   **Fic**
1. Pirates—Fiction 2. Madagascar—Fiction 3. Adventure fiction
ISBN 0-590-20344-4   LC 97-45650
First published 1996 in the United Kingdom

Left penniless in eighteenth century England, fourteen-year-old Nathan Gull and his mousy sister Maud accompany Tamo, the son of a notorious pirate, to his homeland of Madagascar where they are all changed by their encounter with Tamo's dangerous past

"Readers will devour this riveting, thoughtful tale of both piracy and the clash of cultures." Horn Book Guide

McDonald, Joyce

Swallowing stones. Delacorte Press 1997 245p $15.95; pa $4.50 (7 and up)   **Fic**
1. Guilt—Fiction 2. Death—Fiction
ISBN 0-385-32309-3; 0-440-22672-4 (pa)
                    LC 97-1402

Dual perspectives reveal the aftermath of seventeen-year-old Michael MacKenzie's birthday celebration during which he discharges an antique Winchester rifle and unknowingly kills the father of high school classmate Jenna Ward

"This mesmerizing story largely derives its power from the respect McDonald demonstrates for these teens and their emotions, and her unwavering focus on their changing relationships in response to the tragedy." SLJ

McGraw, Eloise Jarvis

The moorchild; [by] Eloise McGraw. Margaret K. McElderry Bks. 1996 241p $16; pa $4.50
                    Fic
1. Fantasy fiction 2. Fairies—Fiction
ISBN 0-689-80654-X; 0-689-82033-X (pa)
                    LC 95-34107

Newbery Medal honor book, 1997

"Saaski, a half-human, half-Moorfolk child, is banished from the Mound and placed as a changeling in a human village, where she is regarded with suspicion and treated with scorn." Horn Book Guide

"Incorporating some classic fantasy motifs and icons, McGraw . . . conjures up an appreciably familiar world that, as evidence of her storytelling power, still strikes an original chord." Publ Wkly

McKay, Hilary

The exiles. Margaret K. McElderry Bks. 1992 217p $16; pa $4.50 **Fic**
1. Sisters—Fiction 2. Grandmothers—Fiction
ISBN 0-689-50555-8; 0-689-82013-5 (pa)
LC 91-38220

The four Conroy sisters spend a wild summer at the seaside with Big Grandma, who tries to break them of their reading habit by substituting fresh air and hard work for books and gets unexpected results

This is an "extremely and continuously funny book." Bull Cent Child Books

Other available titles about the Conroy sisters are:
The exiles at home (1994)
The exiles in love (1998)

McKillip, Patricia A., 1948-

The riddle-master of Hed. Atheneum Pubs. 1976 228p il o.p. (7 and up) **Fic**
1. Fantasy fiction
LC 76-5492

Riddle-master: the complete trilogy, which includes: The riddle-master of Hed; Heir of sea & fire (1977); and Harpist in the wind (1979), available in paperback from Ace Bks.

"Morgon, Prince of Hed, goes in pursuit of an explanation for the three stars on his forehead. Accompanied by Deth, the harpist, Morgon ultimately is led to the High One himself." Roman. Sequences

"Many of the elements and the names appear to be drawn from Welsh mythology, but the author has the ability to deal with familiar themes in a fresh manner and a poetic facility in description." Horn Book

McKinley, Robin

Beauty; a retelling of the story of Beauty & the beast. Harper & Row 1978 247p $15.95; pa $4.95 (7 and up) **Fic**
1. Fairy tales
ISBN 0-06-024149-7; 0-06-440477-3 (pa)
LC 77-25636

"McKinley's version of this folktale is embellished with rich descriptions and settings and detailed characterizations. The author has not modernized the story but varied the traditional version to attract modern readers. The values of love, honor, and beauty are placed in a magical setting that will please the reader of fantasy." Shapiro. Fic for Youth. 3d edition

The blue sword. Greenwillow Bks. 1982 272p $16 (7 and up) **Fic**
1. Fantasy fiction
ISBN 0-688-00938-7
LC 82-2895

Also available in paperback from Ace Bks.

"King Corlath kidnaps Homelander Harry Crewe because he senses that she has the power to help his people in their war against the Northerners. Harry soon grows to like and respect the kindly, sincere Hillmen, and after intense training she assumes a position among Corlath's special Riders. . . . The first in a projected series about the mythical kingdom of Damar." Child Book Rev Serv

"This is a zesty, romantic heroic fantasy with an appealingly stalwart heroine, a finely realized mythical kingdom, and a grounding in reality that enhances the tale's verve as a fantasy." Booklist

The hero and the crown. Greenwillow Bks. 1985 246p $16 (7 and up) **Fic**
1. Fantasy fiction
ISBN 0-688-02593-5
LC 84-4074

Also available in paperback from Ace Bks.

Awarded the Newbery Medal, 1985

"A prequel rather than sequel to 'The Blue Sword' McKinley's second novel set in the . . . mythical kingdom of Damar centers on Aerin, daughter of a Damarian king and his second wife, a witchwoman from the feared, demon-ridden North. The narrative follows Aerin as she seeks her birthright, becoming first a dragon killer and eventually the savior of the kingdom." Booklist

The author "has in this suspenseful prequel . . . created an utterly engrossing fantasy, replete with a fairly mature romantic subplot as well as adventure." N Y Times Book Rev

Rose daughter. Greenwillow Bks. 1997 306p $16 (7 and up) **Fic**
1. Fairy tales
ISBN 0-688-15439-5
LC 96-48783

Also available in paperback from Ace Bks.

"Nearly twenty years after the publication of *Beauty: A Retelling of the Story of Beauty and the Beast* McKinley has . . . produced another full-length novel retelling the same tale." Horn Book Guide

Compared to Beauty, this "is fuller bodied, with richer characterizations and a more mystical, darker edge. . . . There is more background on the Beast in this version . . . and Beauty's choice at the end, a departure from that in *Beauty*, is just so right. Readers will be enchanted, in the best sense of the word." Booklist

McKissack, Patricia C., 1944-

A picture of Freedom; the diary of Clotee, a slave girl. Scholastic 1997 192p il maps (Dear America) $9.95 **Fic**
1. Slavery—Fiction 2. Underground railroad—Fiction 3. African Americans—Fiction
ISBN 0-590-25988-1
LC 96-25673

In 1859 twelve-year-old Clotee, a house slave who must conceal the fact that she can read and write, records in her diary her experiences and her struggle to decide whether to escape to freedom

"McKissack brings Clotee alive through touching and sobering details of slave life." SLJ

Run away home. Scholastic 1997 160p $14.95 **Fic**
1. African Americans—Fiction 2. Apache Indians—Fiction 3. Alabama—Fiction
ISBN 0-590-46751-4
LC 96-43673

"This story of the young Apache who escaped from the train transporting Geronimo and his companions-in-exile from Florida to Alabama is rooted in the author's family history. The narrator is eleven-year-old Sarah Jane Crossman, who first befriends Sky when, sick and friendless, he seeks shelter in her family's barn." Horn Book

"Grabbing readers with wonderful characters, an engaging plot, and vital themes, McKissack weaves a compelling story of cultural clash, tragedy, accommodation, and ultimate triumph." SLJ

McLaren, Clemence, 1938-
Inside the walls of Troy; a novel of the women who lived the Trojan War. Atheneum Bks. for Young Readers 1996 199p $16 (7 and up)   **Fic**
1. Helen of Troy (Legendary character)—Fiction
2. Cassandra (Legendary character)—Fiction 3. Trojan War—Fiction
ISBN 0-689-31820-0   LC 93-8127
Also available in paperback from Bantam Bks.
The events surrounding the famous battle between the Greeks and the Trojans are told from the points of view of two women, the beautiful Helen and the prophetic Cassandra
"These ancient stories are made as fresh and vivid as any modern tale by the electrifying characters and sensual details." Booklist

Menick, Stephen
The muffin child. Philomel Bks. 1998 216p $17.99   **Fic**
1. Orphans—Fiction 2. Death—Fiction 3. Balkan Peninsula—Fiction
ISBN 0-399-23303-2   LC 97-51817
In this story "set in a small Balkan farming village, eleven-year-old Tanya's parents are swept away by a flooding river. Denying the loss, she continues to perform the daily chores and makes muffins each day in preparation for their return. Menick tells an engrossing story that examines basic human traits of greed, love, and self-preservation." Horn Book Guide

Merrill, Jean, 1923-
The pushcart war; with illustrations by Ronni Solbert. HarperCollins Pubs. 1992 c1964 222p il o.p.; Dell paperback available $5.99   **Fic**
1. Trucks—Fiction 2. New York (N.Y.)—Fiction
ISBN 0-440-91157-5 (pa)
A reissue of the title first published 1964 by W. R. Scott
In the near future, "arrogant, mammoth trucks threaten to crowd people, small cars, pushcarts, and peddlers off the streets of New York. When a truck contemptuously runs down a pushcart, the peddlers rebel and wage a guerrilla war against the trucks, using a primitive, but effective, secret weapon. Funny, dramatic, tongue-in-cheek satire on the sheer bigness which is overwhelming urban life but which is here, for once, defeated by the little people who 'are' the city." Moorachian. What is a City?

Metzger, Lois
Ellen's case. Atheneum Bks. for Young Readers 1995 189p $16 (7 and up)   **Fic**
1. Trials—Fiction   2. Cerebral   palsy—Fiction
3. Brothers and sisters—Fiction
ISBN 0-689-31934-7   LC 95-2707
Also available in paperback from Penguin Bks.
"A Jean Karl book"
"In this sequel to *Barry's Sister (1992)*, Ellen, 16, is reluctant to become involved in the malpractice trial against the doctor who delivered her brother Barry, now a four year old with cerebral palsy. But soon, she becomes infatuated with the charismatic and flamboyant lawyer, Jack Frazier." Book Rep
The author "creates riveting testimony and high suspense. . . . The complex psychology embedded in this sophisticated and poignant tale is quite remarkable." N Y Times Book Rev

Meyer, Carolyn
Drummers of Jericho. Harcourt Brace & Co. 1995 308p $11; pa $5 (7 and up)   **Fic**
1. Prejudices—Fiction 2. Jews—Fiction 3. Friendship—Fiction
ISBN 0-15-200441-6; 0-15-200190-5 (pa)
          LC 94-36105
"Gulliver books"
A fourteen-year-old Jewish girl goes to live with her father and stepmother in a small town and soon finds herself the center of a civil rights battle when she objects to the high school band marching in the formation of a cross
"This is a well-crafted and powerfully thought-provoking novel about religious persecution." Voice Youth Advocates

Gideon's people. Harcourt Brace & Co. 1996 297p $12; pa $6   **Fic**
1. Amish—Fiction 2. Jews—Fiction 3. Family life—Fiction
ISBN 0-15-200303-7; 0-15-200304-5 (pa)
          LC 95-37917
"Gulliver books"
"Twelve-year-old Isaac Litvak, an Orthodox Jew, wakes up after a wagon accident in the home of an Amish family. . . . Trouble begins when Gideon, the sixteen-year-old son in this kind Amish family, announces to his new-found friend, Isaac, that he is secretly planning to run away." ALAN
"Deft characterizations and juxtaposition of fathers and sons amplify similarities and differences between the families and cultures." SLJ

Jubilee journey. Harcourt Brace & Co. 1997 271p $13; pa $6   **Fic**
1. African Americans—Fiction 2. Race relations—Fiction 3. Racially mixed people—Fiction
ISBN 0-15-201377-6; 0-15-201591-4 (pa)
          LC 96-44563
"Gulliver books"
This story "takes place three generations after the story of Rose Lee Jefferson [in White lilacs]. . . . We meet Rose Lee's great-granddaughter, thirteen-year-old Emily Rose Chartier, who lives in Connecticut with her white father, black mother, and two brothers. . . . Emily Rose's image of herself is jolted . . . when she, her mother, and brothers go to Texas to visit her great-grandmother. . . . Jubilee journey has all the characteristics of a satisfying sequel. . . . It also succeeds as a stand-alone novel, with well-developed characters, especially the engaging protagonist. The author confronts difficult issues without becoming didactic." Voice Youth Advocates

Meyer, Carolyn—*Continued*

Where the broken heart still beats; the story of Cynthia Ann Parker. Harcourt Brace Jovanovich 1992 197p $16.95; pa $7 (7 and up)   **Fic**
1. Parker, Cynthia Ann, 1827?-1864—Fiction 2. Comanche Indians—Fiction
ISBN 0-15-200639-7; 0-15-295602-6 (pa)

LC 92-2578

"Gulliver books. Great episodes"

Having been taken as a child and raised by Comanche Indians, thirty-four-year-old Cynthia Ann Parker is forcibly returned to her white relatives, where she longs for her Indian life and her only friend is her twelve-year-old cousin Lucy

"A thoughtful and thought provoking book, this embroiders liberally but convincingly on the few facts known about the subject, a famous captive who was mother of the Comanche leader Quanah Parker." Bull Cent Child Books

White lilacs. Harcourt Brace Jovanovich 1993 242p il $13; pa $6   **Fic**
1. Race relations—Fiction 2. African Americans—Fiction 3. Texas—Fiction
ISBN 0-15-200641-9; 0-15-200626-5 (pa)

LC 92-30503

"Gulliver books"

In 1921 in Dillon, Texas, twelve-year-old Rose Lee sees trouble threatening her black community when the whites decide to take the land there for a park and forcibly relocate the black families to an ugly stretch of territory outside the town

"This bittersweet novel is poignant and tender, both in its spare vernacular dialogue and delicate description." Publ Wkly

Followed by Jubilee journey

Mikaelsen, Ben, 1952-

Stranded. Hyperion Bks. for Children 1995 247p $15.95; lib bdg $16.49; pa $4.95   **Fic**
1. Whales—Fiction 2. Physically handicapped—Fiction 3. Florida—Fiction
ISBN 0-7868-0072-0; 0-7868-2059-4 (lib bdg); 0-7868-1109-9 (pa)   LC 94-27069

Twelve-year-old Koby, who has lost a foot in an accident, sees a chance to prove her self-reliance to her parents when she tries to rescue two stranded pilot whales near her home in the Florida Keys

"This is a heartwarming story, believable and at the same time grist for fantasies of heroism and wonderful deeds." Voice Youth Advocates

Miklowitz, Gloria D., 1927-

Camouflage. Harcourt Brace & Co. 1998 166p $16   **Fic**
1. Fathers and sons—Fiction 2. Militia movements—Fiction
ISBN 0-15-201467-5   LC 97-18053

While visiting his father for the summer, fourteen-year-old Kyle finds himself gradually becoming enmeshed in a militia's plot to wage war on the federal government

This "is a thought provoking discussion-starter." SLJ

Masada; the last fortress; [by] Gloria Miklowitz. Eerdmans Bks. for Young Readers 1998 188p maps $16; pa $7 (7 and up)   **Fic**
1. Masada Site (Israel)—Fiction 2. Jews—Fiction
ISBN 0-8028-5165-7; 0-8028-5168-1 (pa)

LC 98-17756

As the Roman army marches inexorably across the Judean desert towards the fortress of Masada, Simon and his family and friends prepare, along with the rest of the Jewish Zealots, to fight and never surrender

"Recommended for historical fiction lovers, this story has obviously been thoroughly researched. . . . This is an exciting story in which everyday people must make some horrible wartime decisions." Voice Youth Advocates

Past forgiving. Simon & Schuster Bks. for Young Readers 1995 153p $16 (7 and up)   **Fic**
1. Date rape—Fiction
ISBN 0-671-88442-5   LC 94-13057

Fifteen-year-old Alexandra finds that her boyfriend Cliff demands all her time, isolates her by his jealousy, becomes physically abusive, and finally rapes her

"A realistic book about an important topic." Book Rep

Mills, Claudia, 1954-

Dinah for president. Macmillan 1992 126p $14; pa $3.95   **Fic**
1. School stories
ISBN 0-02-766999-8; 0-689-71854-3 (pa)

LC 91-34839

Dinah Seabrooke, featured in Dynamite Dinah (1990), now in her first year of middle school, struggles to become a big fish in what seems like an ocean—and in the process discovers the value of recycling and of friendship with the elderly

This book "features a refreshing true-to-life middle schooler, complete with wild enthusiasms and klutziness. The book is funny and appealing. It is sure to be popular with young middle schoolers." Voice Youth Advocates

Other available titles about Dinah are:
Dinah forever (1998)
Dinah in love (1993)

Standing up to Mr. O. Farrar, Straus & Giroux 1998 165p $16   **Fic**
1. Teachers—Fiction 2. School stories 3. Animal welfare—Fiction
ISBN 0-374-34721-2   LC 98-3843

Twelve-year-old Maggie comes to dread biology class because her favorite teacher is insisting that she dissect a worm, an assignment that makes her feel very squeamish and awakens her to the question of animal rights

"Maggie's strong sentiments are lightened by her sense of humor in this thought-provoking book." Horn Book Guide

You're a brave man, Julius Zimmerman. Farrar, Straus & Giroux 1999 152p $16   **Fic**
1. Mothers and sons—Fiction 2. Babysitters—Fiction 3. School stories
ISBN 0-374-38708-7   LC 98-50799

Sequel to Losers, Inc. (1997)

Mills, Claudia, 1954-—*Continued*

Twelve-year-old Julius has his hands full over the summer when his mother attempts to improve his grades and teach him responsibility by signing him up for a French class and getting him a job babysitting

The author's "humorously constructed scenes . . . are both touching and peppered with laugh-out-loud apercus. . . . Although the ending is a little bit neat, this novel as a whole rings satisfyingly true." Publ Wkly

Moon, Pat, 1946-

The spying game. Putnam 1999 c1993 200p $16.99   Fic
1. Death—Fiction 2. Fathers and sons—Fiction
ISBN 0-399-23354-7   LC 98-13069
First published 1993 in the United Kingdom

After his father is killed in a traffic accident, twelve-year-old Joe Harris becomes obsessed with punishing the man he thinks is responsible, but his plan gets out of control when he discovers that the man's son is a classmate

"Moon expertly weaves together the many strands of this novel, and she makes readers care for all of her characters." SLJ

Moore, Yvette

Freedom songs. Orchard Bks. 1991 168p o.p.; Puffin Bks. paperback available $4.99   Fic
1. African Americans—Fiction 2. Uncles—Fiction
ISBN 0-14-036017-4 (pa)   LC 88-43073

"Sheryl is a black fourteen-year-old who launches her narrative with an account of her family's trip to North Carolina on Easter of 1963. There she sees Jim Crow laws in action. . . . Back in Brooklyn, she organizes a concert to raise money for the freedom riders, one of whom, her Uncle Pete, is killed by a bomb at the school where he teaches black southerners registering to vote." Bull Cent Child Books

"Humorous details of typical adolescent concerns and escapades lighten the serious nature of a well-crafted story." Horn Book

Morgenstern, Susie Hoch

Secret letters from 0 to 10; [by] Susie Morgenstern; translated by Gill Rosner. Viking 1998 137p $15.99   Fic
1. Friendship—Fiction 2. School stories 3. Paris (France)—Fiction
ISBN 0-670-88007-8   LC 98-5559
Original French edition published 1996

Ten-year-old Ernest lives a boring existence in Paris with his grandmother until a lively girl named Victory enters his class at school

"Morgenstern has created extremely well-drawn, distinct, and sometimes quirky characters with eloquent dialogue." SLJ

Mori, Kyoko

Shizuko's daughter. Holt & Co. 1993 227p $15.95 (7 and up)   Fic
1. Suicide—Fiction 2. Mothers and daughters—Fiction 3. Remarriage—Fiction 4. Japan—Fiction
ISBN 0-8050-2557-X   LC 92-26956

Also available in paperback from Fawcett Bks.

"Yuki is 12 when her mother, Shizuko, commits suicide, leaving Yuki to a distant father and a self-serving stepmother. Forbidden by custom from seeing her mother's family, Yuki is left to fend for herself; and she does, falling back on the artistic talent she inherited from her mother." Booklist

"Mori paints beautiful pictures with words, creating visual images that can be as haunting and elliptical as poetry." Horn Book

Morpurgo, Michael

Escape from Shangri-La. Philomel Bks. 1998 178p $16.99   Fic
1. Grandfathers—Fiction 2. Old age—Fiction 3. Great Britain—Fiction
ISBN 0-399-23311-3   LC 98-4878

"Cessie has just begun to know her long-absent grandfather when Popsicle, as he is called, is placed in a nursing home. The eleven-year-old helps Popsicle escape from the nursing home and sail to France to find the woman who saved him when he participated in the evacuation of Dunkirk." Horn Book Guide

"Cessie's voice is beautifully realized. . . . The swift pace moves smoothly from incident to incident, and the characterizations of even minor figures are complex enough to add depth and reasonance." Bull Cent Child Books

Robin of Sherwood; illustrated by Michael Foreman. Harcourt Brace & Co. 1996 113p il $22
Fic
1. Robin Hood (Legendary character)—Fiction
ISBN 0-15-201315-6   LC 95-45740
First published 1966 in the United Kingdom

"Morpurgo recounts the story of Robin Hood as a tale within a tale. In the modern-day framework story, a boy tells of a storm that uprooted a massive, beloved oak tree. Among the roots he finds a silver arrowhead, a long curved stick, a horn, and a human skeleton. He faints and dreams of Robin, who flees to Sherwood when the Sheriff's men catch him poaching. Robin goes on to rescue his father from the Sheriff's prison, joins the Outcasts who live in Sherwood, marries Marion, who bears him a son, and has many other adventures. . . . [This] features Foreman's sensitive, dynamic line-and-watercolor artwork. A fine, original piece of storytelling, faithful in spirit to the legend of Robin Hood." Booklist

The war of Jenkins' ear. Philomel Bks. 1995 171p $16.95; pa $5.95   Fic
1. School stories 2. Christian life—Fiction 3. Great Britain—Fiction
ISBN 0-399-22735-0; 0-698-11550-3 (pa)
LC 94-7602

"It is the 1952 autumn term at England's Redlands Prep, and Toby Jenkins is back at a school he loathes. But Toby's feelings change with the arrival of Christopher, a new student who is not like other boys. . . . Then a war breaks out between the prep boy 'toffs' and the village 'oiks,' and Christopher's role as a peacemaker has a sacred aura about it. It comes almost as no surprise to Toby when Christopher confesses that he hears voices and that those voices have told him he is Jesus incarnate. . . . Morpurgo's reach is long, but he succeeds at almost

Morpurgo, Michael—*Continued*
every level. God and the mystery of faith are at the center of the story, yet both are fully grounded in the affairs of adolescent boys: rivalries, sports, even first love." Booklist

Morris, Gerald, 1963-
The squire, his knight, & his lady. Houghton Mifflin 1999 232p $15   **Fic**
1. Gawain (Legendary character)—Fiction 2. Knights and knighthood—Fiction 3. Great Britain—History—0-1066—Fiction
ISBN 0-395-91211-3   LC 98-28718
Sequel to The squire's tale
After several years at King Arthur's court, Terence, as Sir Gawain's squire and friend, accompanies him on a perilous quest that tests all their skills and whose successful completion could mean certain death for Gawain
"Laced with magic, humor, and chivalry, this reworking of 'Sir Gawain and the Green Knight,' in which Gawain learns humility and Terence discovers his true place in the world, provides an engaging introduction to the original tale." Horn Book

The squire's tale. Houghton Mifflin 1998 212p $15   **Fic**
1. Gawain (Legendary character)—Fiction 2. Knights and knighthood—Fiction 3. Great Britain—History—0-1066—Fiction
ISBN 0-395-86959-5   LC 97-12447
In medieval England, fourteen-year-old Terence finds his tranquil existence suddenly changed when he becomes the squire of the young Gawain of Orkney and accompanies him on a long quest, proving Gawain's worth as a knight and revealing an important secret about his own true identity
"Well-drawn characters, excellent, snappy dialogue, detailed descriptions of medieval life, and a dry wit put a new spin on this engaging tale of the characters and events of King Arthur's time." Booklist
Followed by The squire, his knight, & his lady

Mosier, Elizabeth
My life as a girl. Random House 1999 193p $17; lib bdg $18.99 (7 and up)   **Fic**
1. Prisoners—Fiction 2. Waiters and waitresses—Fiction 3. Arizona—Fiction
ISBN 0-679-89035-1; 0-679-99035-6 (lib bdg)
                                             LC 98-8688
During her last summer in Phoenix, Arizona, before going to an eastern college, eighteen-year-old Jaime works two waitress jobs and plans her escape from a life forever changed by her father's prison sentence
"Featuring lifelike dialogue, three-dimensional characters and an upbeat outcome, the novel also serves up glossy, attention-getting prose." Publ Wkly

Mowry, Jess, 1960-
Ghost train. Holt & Co. 1996 164p $14.95
                                                        Fic
1. Haitian Americans—Fiction 2. Supernatural—Fiction
ISBN 0-8050-4440-X   LC 96-10291

"On Remi DuMont's first night in his new home, a train thunders past his window and he watches a murder being committed. Remi, 13, is a recent immigrant from Haiti to Oakland, CA. . . . He soon realizes that the late-night train is a ghost train and the murder reenacted on it nightly actually happened more than 50 years ago. As the boy and his new friend Niya investigate, they put together the pieces of an unsolved crime and an unexplained disappearance. They then step into the past to try to right a long-standing wrong." SLJ
"Containing more substance than most thrillers for this age group, this horror story is underscored by strong social commentary on poverty, waste and materialism." Publ Wkly

Murphy, Jim, 1947-
The journal of James Edmond Pease, a Civil War Union soldier. Scholastic 1998 173p il (My name is America) $9.95   **Fic**
1. Orphans—Fiction 2. United States—History—1861-1865, Civil War—Fiction
ISBN 0-590-43814-X   LC 98-10738
James Edmond, a sixteen-year-old orphan, keeps a journal of his experiences and those of "G" Company which he joined as a volunteer in the Union Army during the Civil War
This "is very well written, and Pease's unassuming personality keeps him a vivid, accessible narrator throughout." Booklist

West to a land of plenty; the diary of Teresa Angelino Viscardi. Scholastic 1998 204p il maps (Dear America) $9.95   **Fic**
1. Frontier and pioneer life—Fiction 2. Italian Americans—Fiction
ISBN 0-590-73888-7   LC 97-23064
While traveling in 1883 with her Italian American family (including a meddlesome little sister) and other immigrant pioneers to a utopian community in Idaho, fourteen-year-old Teresa keeps a diary of her experiences along the way
"Engaging colorful characters abound. . . . Excellent archival photos and notes enhance the presentation of this historical novel." SLJ

Myers, Anna
The keeping room. Walker & Co. 1997 135p $15.95   **Fic**
1. United States—History—1775-1783, Revolution—Fiction 2. Fathers and sons—Fiction
ISBN 0-8027-8641-3   LC 97-2964
Left in charge of the family by his father who joins the Revolutionary War effort, thirteen-year-old Joey undergoes such great changes that he fears he may be betraying his beloved parent
"The story has plenty of action to keep it going and enough reflection to give it meaning." Booklist

Myers, Walter Dean, 1937-
Fallen angels. Scholastic 1988 309p $14.95; pa $4.99 (7 and up)   **Fic**
1. Vietnam War, 1961-1975—Fiction 2. African American soldiers—Fiction
ISBN 0-590-40942-5; 0-590-40943-3 (pa)
                                             LC 87-23236

Myers, Walter Dean, 1937-—*Continued*
Coretta Scott King award for text, 1989
"Black, seventeen, perceptive and sensitive, Richie (the narrator) has enlisted and been sent to Vietnam; in telling the story of his year of active service, Richie is candid about the horror of killing and the fear of being killed, the fear and bravery and confusion and tragedy of the war." Bull Cent Child Books
"Except for occasional outbursts, the narration is remarkably direct and understated; and the dialogue, with morbid humor sometimes adding comic relief, is steeped in natural vulgarity, without which verisimilitude would be unthinkable." Horn Book

Fast Sam, Cool Clyde, and Stuff. Viking 1975 190p hardcover o.p. paperback available $4.99 (7 and up)   **Fic**
1. Harlem (New York, N.Y.)—Fiction 2. African Americans—Fiction 3. Friendship—Fiction
ISBN 0-14-032613-8 (pa)   LC 74-32383
"In an affectionate, colloquial narrative, Stuff, now 18, recalls the time when he was 13, hanging out on 116th Street, and enjoying being part of a circle of dependable friends, the best of whom were Fast Sam and Cool Clyde." Booklist
"A funny, fast-paced story of teenagers in the ghetto. The characters are memorable. . . . The plot is an exciting one." Read Teach

Hoops; a novel. Delacorte Press 1981 183p hardcover o.p. paperback available $4.99 (7 and up)   **Fic**
1. Basketball—Fiction 2. Harlem (New York, N.Y.)—Fiction 3. African Americans—Fiction
ISBN 0-440-93884-8 (pa)   LC 81-65497
"Growing up in the streets of Harlem, seventeen-year-old Lonnie Jackson dreams of making a better life. He has a 'game,' and sees basketball as his way out of the ghetto." ALAN
"This story offers the reader some fast, descriptive basketball action, a love story between Lonnie and girlfriend Mary-Ann, peer friendship problems, and gangster intrigues. Most importantly, however, it portrays the growth of a trusting and deeply caring father-son relationship between [the coach] Cal and [fatherless] Lonnie." Voice Youth Advocates
Followed by The outside shot

The journal of Joshua Loper; a black cowboy. Scholastic 1999 158p il (My name is America) $10.95   **Fic**
1. Cowhands—Fiction 2. African Americans—Fiction 3. West (U.S.)—Fiction
ISBN 0-590-02691-7   LC 98-18661
In 1871 Joshua Loper, a sixteen-year-old black cowboy, records in his journal his experiences while making his first cattle drive under an unsympathetic trail boss
"With characteristic research, sensitivity, and insight, Myers offers a lively, youthful portrait of the life and times of this black cowboy." SLJ

The journal of Scott Pendleton Collins; a World War II soldier. Scholastic 1999 140p il (My name is America) $10.95   **Fic**
1. World War, 1939-1945—Fiction
ISBN 0-439-05013-8   LC 99-13615

A seventeen-year-old soldier from central Virginia records his experiences in a journal as his regiment takes part in the D-Day invasion of Normandy and subsequent battles to liberate France
"This brief novel presents an accurate depiction of the horror of battle. The narrative voice is engaging and believable." SLJ

Me, Mop, and the Moondance Kid; illustrated by Rodney Pate. Delacorte Press 1988 154p il hardcover o.p. paperback available $4.50   **Fic**
1. Baseball—Fiction 2. Adoption—Fiction 3. Friendship—Fiction
ISBN 0-440-40396-0 (pa)   LC 88-6503
"Eleven-year-old T. J. and his younger brother Billy, a.k.a. the Moondance Kid, have been living with their adoptive parents for about six months, and are settling in well. They are worried that their friend Mop, a girl who has not yet been adopted, may be transferred to an orphanage some distance away. Mop decides to join T. J.'s little league team in order to get close to the coach and his wife, whom she suspects are interested in adopting her." SLJ
"Myers's keen sense of humor, quick, natural dialogue and irresistible protagonists make this novel a winner." Publ Wkly
Followed by Mop, Moondance, and the Nagasaki Knights (1992)

Monster; illustrations by Christopher Myers. HarperCollins Pubs. 1999 281p il $14.95; lib bdg $14.89 (7 and up)   **Fic**
1. Trials—Fiction 2. Prisons—Fiction 3. African Americans—Fiction
ISBN 0-06-028077-8; 0-06-028078-6 (lib bdg)
     LC 98-40958
Coretta Scott King honor book text, 2000
While on trial as an accomplice to a murder, sixteen-year-old Steve Harmon records his experiences in prison and in the courtroom in the form of a film script as he tries to come to terms with the course his life has taken
"Balancing courtroom drama and a sordid jailhouse setting with flashbacks to the crime, Myers adeptly allows each character to speak for him or herself, leaving readers to judge for themselves the truthfulness of the defendants, witnesses, lawyers, and, most compellingly, Steve himself." Horn Book Guide

Motown and Didi; a love story. Viking Kestrel 1984 174p hardcover o.p. paperback available $4.50 (7 and up)   **Fic**
1. African Americans—Fiction 2. Harlem (New York, N.Y.)—Fiction 3. Drug abuse—Fiction
ISBN 0-440-95762-1 (pa)   LC 84-3632
Motown and Didi, two teenage loners in Harlem, become allies in a fight against Touchy, the drug dealer whose dope is destroying Didi's brother, and find themselves falling in love with each other
"What emerges from this grim and all-too believable milieu is a tender and touching love story and a common-man hero." Bull Cent Child Books

The Mouse rap. Harper & Row 1990 186p lib bdg $14.89; pa $4.95   **Fic**
1. African Americans—Fiction 2. Buried treasure—Fiction 3. Harlem (New York, N.Y.)—Fiction
ISBN 0-06-024344-9 (lib bdg); 0-06-440356-4 (pa)
     LC 89-36419

Myers, Walter Dean, 1937——*Continued*

During an eventful summer in Harlem, fourteen-year-old Mouse and his friends fall in and out of love and search for a hidden treasure from the days of Al Capone

"A crisp rap beat, an intriguing, intergenerational cast of characters, and the zaniness of events make this story of fourteen-year-old Mouse and his friends a very upbeat adventure." Horn Book Guide

The outside shot. Delacorte Press 1984 185p o.p.; Dell paperback available $4.50 (7 and up)

Fic

1. Basketball—Fiction 2. African Americans—Fiction 3. School stories

ISBN 0-440-96784-8 (pa)   LC 84-4271

Sequel to Hoops

Recruited by a small midwestern college to play basketball, Lonnie has many new experiences, including working with a child who needs physical therapy and dealing with corruption in college sports

"While the games are exciting and the gambling racket suspenseful, what sets this book apart from other sports stories is Lonnie's growth in his new environment. . . . Altogether, this is a deeply moving, believable story of a very American rite of passage into adulthood." SLJ

Scorpions. Harper & Row 1988 216p $14.95; lib bdg $14.89; pa $4.95   Fic

1. African Americans—Fiction 2. Juvenile delinquency—Fiction 3. Harlem (New York, N.Y.)—Fiction

ISBN 0-06-024364-3; 0-06-024365-1 (lib bdg); 0-06-447066-0 (pa)   LC 85-45815

A Newbery Medal honor book, 1989

Set in Harlem, this "story presents a brutally honest picture of the tragic influence of gang membership and pressures on a young black adolescent. Jamal Hicks, age twelve, reluctantly follows the orders of his older brother, now serving time in prison for robbery, and takes his place as leader of the Scorpions. When Jamal's leadership is challenged, disaster follows and Jamal learns some tragic lessons about friendship and owning a gun." Child Book Rev Serv

Slam! Scholastic 1996 266p $15.95; pa $4.99 (7 and up)   Fic

1. Basketball—Fiction 2. African Americans—Fiction 3. School stories

ISBN 0-590-48667-5; 0-590-48668-3 (pa)

LC 95-46647

Coretta Scott King Award for text, 1997

Seventeen-year-old "Slam" Harris is counting on his noteworthy basketball talents to get him out of the inner city and give him a chance to succeed in life, but his coach sees things differently

Myers "descriptions of Slam on the court . . . use crisp details, not flowery language, to achieve their muscular poetry, and Myers is equally vivid in relating the torment Slam feels as he stares at a page of indecipherable algebra formulas. . . . [This is an] admirably realistic coming-of-age novel." Booklist

Somewhere in the darkness. Scholastic 1992 168p $14.95; pa $3.50 (7 and up)   Fic

1. Fathers and sons—Fiction 2. Prisoners—Fiction

ISBN 0-590-42411-4; 0-590-42414-2 (pa)

LC 91-19295

A Newbery Medal honor book, 1993

A teenage boy accompanies his father, who has recently escaped from prison, on a trip that turns out to be a time of, often painful, discovery for them both

"This is one of Myer's most memorable pieces of writing: there is not an unnecessary word or phrase; the scenes are vivid and emotionally powerful; and the characters are heartbreakingly realistic. A page-turner elevated to a higher plane by its theme of the universal quest of a son for his father." Horn Book

Naidoo, Beverley

Chain of fire; illustrations by Eric Velasquez. Lippincott 1990 c1989 245p il $14; pa $4.95

Fic

1. South Africa—Fiction

ISBN 0-397-32426-X; 0-06-440468-4 (pa)

LC 89-27551

First published 1989 in the United Kingdom

"The political awakening of fifteen-year-old Naledi, who first appeared in *Journey to Jóburg*, is recounted with passion and eloquence as the author describes the resettling of Black villagers to their new and barren 'homeland'—the result of South Africa's policy of apartheid." Horn Book Guide

Journey to Jo'burg; a South African story; illustrations by Eric Velasquez. Lippincott 1986 80p il lib bdg $14.89; pa $4.95   Fic

1. South Africa—Fiction

ISBN 0-397-32169-4 (lib bdg); 0-06-440237-1 (pa)

LC 85-45508

"This touching novel graphically depicts the plight of Africans living in the horror of South Africa. Thirteen-year-old Maledi and her 9-year-old brother leave their small village, take the perilous journey to the city, and encounter, firsthand, the painful struggle for justice, freedom, and dignity in the 'City of Gold.' A provocative story with a message readers will long remember." Soc Educ

Followed by Chain of fire

No turning back; a novel of South Africa. HarperCollins Pubs. 1997 c1995 189p lib bdg $14.89; pa $4.95   Fic

1. Runaway children—Fiction 2. South Africa—Fiction

ISBN 0-06-027506-5 (lib bdg); 0-06-440749-7 (pa)

LC 96-28980

First published 1995 in the United Kingdom

When the abuse at home becomes too much for twelve-year-old Sipho, he runs away to the streets of Johannesburg and learns to survive in the post-apartheid world

"Charged with a rhythm that begins beating on the first page and carries through until the last, Naidoo's novel is a can't-put-it-down account." Horn Book

Namioka, Lensey

Den of the White Fox. Harcourt Brace & Co. 1997 216p $14; pa $6 (7 and up)   Fic

1. Japan—Fiction

ISBN 0-15-201282-6; 0-15-201283-4 (pa)

LC 96-34840

Namioka, Lensey—*Continued*

Earlier titles in this series are: The coming of the bear (1992), Island of ogres (1989), and Valley of the broken cherry trees (1980)

"Browndeer Press"

In medieval Japan, Matsuzo and Zenta, two out-of-work samurai warriors must use their fighting skills when they join a group of local boys, led by the mysterious White Fox, in resistance to a cruel occupying force

"Fans of earlier books about the duo and others intrigued by medieval Japan, samurai, and the art of jujitsu will follow the story's strong characters into its rousing period mystery." Booklist

Ties that bind, ties that break; a novel. Delacorte Press 1999 154p $15.95   **Fic**

1. Sex role—Fiction 2. China—Fiction

ISBN 0-385-32666-1   LC 98-27877

"In early twentieth-century China, Ailin's liberal father allows her to avoid the tradition of foot-binding, but a broken engagement makes her family fear for her future. Ailin's intelligence and hard work—and a lot of luck—lead her to a new life in America." Horn Book Guide

"In lyrical, descriptive prose, Namioka compassionately portrays a young girl's coming-of-age in a repressive, challenging time." Booklist

Napoli, Donna Jo, 1948-

Changing tunes. Dutton Children's Bks. 1998 130p $15.99   **Fic**

1. Divorce—Fiction

ISBN 0-525-45861-1   LC 98-10034

Ten-year-old Eileen's life changes drastically when her father separates from her mother and moves out, taking with him the piano on which she is used to practicing every day

The author explores "a painful situation with sensitivity and a generous dash of humor." Booklist

Song of the Magdalene. Scholastic 1996 240p $15.95; pa $4.99 (7 and up)   **Fic**

1. Mary Magdalene, Saint—Fiction 2. Christian saints—Fiction

ISBN 0-590-93705-7; 0-590-93706-5 (pa)   LC 96-7066

Tells the story of Miriam, a young girl being raised by her widowed father in ancient Israel, who grows up to be Mary Magdalene

"Napoli has taken a few Biblical facts about Mary Magdalene and created a possible past in a beautifully written story with well-developed characters." Book Rep

Spinners; [by] Donna Jo Napoli & Richard Tchen. Dutton Children's Bks. 1999 197p $15.99 (7 and up)   **Fic**

1. Fairy tales 2. Fathers and daughters—Fiction

ISBN 0-525-46065-9   LC 98-54640

A "tailor promises that he will clothe his bride in gold; to this end, he steals an elderly woman's spinning wheel and ends up obsessed, turning straw into gold but somehow 'rumpling' his leg—thus earning his lover's disdain and the hated sobriquet Rumpelstiltskin. The narrative then fast-forwards and shifts to Saskia, the miller's daughter (really Rumpelstiltskin's child), whose mother has died in childbirth." Publ Wkly

"A thoughtfully designed and well-woven interpretation of an ancient and disturbing tale." Bull Cent Child Books

Stones in water. Dutton Children's Bks. 1997 209p $15.99; pa $4.99   **Fic**

1. World War, 1939-1945—Fiction

ISBN 0-525-45842-5; 0-14-130600-9 (pa)   LC 97-14253

After being taken by German soldiers from a local movie theater along with other Italian boys including his Jewish friend, Roberto is forced to work in Germany, escapes into the Ukrainian winter, before desperately trying to make his way back home to Venice

This is a "gripping, meticulously researched story (loosely based on the life of an actual survivor)." Publ Wkly

Trouble on the tracks. Scholastic 1997 190p $14.95   **Fic**

1. Smuggling—Fiction 2. Brothers and sisters—Fiction 3. Railroads—Fiction 4. Australia—Fiction

ISBN 0-590-13447-7   LC 96-27934

While traveling across the Australian outback on a train, twelve-year-old Zach and his younger sister Eve uncover an endangered bird smuggling ring and try to save two trains from a full-speed collision

"The novel is exciting, yet funny. The book's real strength, however, and the heart of the story, is the interaction between the two youngsters." SLJ

Zel. Dutton Children's Bks. 1996 227p $15.99; pa $4.99 (7 and up)   **Fic**

1. Fairy tales 2. Mothers and daughters—Fiction

ISBN 0-525-45612-0; 0-14-130116-3 (pa)   LC 96-15135

Based on the fairy tale Rapunzel, the story is told in alternating chapters from the point of view of Zel, her mother, and the prince, and delves into the psychological motivations of the characters

"This version, with its Faustian overtones, will challenge readers to think about this old story on a deeper level. It begs for discussion in literature classes." SLJ

Naylor, Phyllis Reynolds, 1933-

Danny's Desert Rats. Atheneum Bks. for Young Readers 1998 134p $16; pa $4.50   **Fic**

1. Cats—Fiction 2. Brothers—Fiction 3. Clubs—Fiction

ISBN 0-689-81776-2; 0-689-83133-1 (pa)   LC 97-28006

Sequel to Being Danny's dog (1995)

T.R. and his twelve-year-old brother Danny join their friends in forming a group called the Desert Rats, and their major mission for the summer is helping Paul keep his beloved cat despite their townhouse development's rule against pets

"This novel is characterized by warm relationships and humorous dialogue." SLJ

The fear place. Atheneum Pubs. 1994 118p $16; pa $3.95   **Fic**

1. Brothers—Fiction 2. Pumas—Fiction 3. Camping—Fiction

ISBN 0-689-31866-9; 0-689-80442-3 (pa)   LC 93-38891

Naylor, Phyllis Reynolds, 1933— *Continued*

When he and his older brother Gordon are left camping alone in the Rocky Mountains, twelve-year-old Doug faces his fear of heights and his feelings about Gordon--with the help of a cougar

This is "a solid action story, tense and involving. . . . A satisfying wilderness adventure." Publ Wkly

Ice. Atheneum Bks. for Young Readers 1996 194p $16; pa $4.50   **Fic**
1. Family life—Fiction 2. Farm life—Fiction
ISBN 0-689-80005-3; 0-689-81872-6 (pa)
                                           LC 95-5279

"A Jean Karl book"

When thirteen-year-old Chrissa is sent to her paternal grandmother's farm, she learns more about her absent father and some of the reasons for her distant relationship with her mother

"Naylor is a master of strong adolescent characterizations. Just the right amount of adventure and suspense keeps the plot moving quickly without getting mired in emotional soul-searching." Book Rep

The keeper. Atheneum Pubs. 1986 212p $16
                                           Fic
1. Mental illness—Fiction 2. Fathers and sons—Fiction
ISBN 0-689-31204-0   LC 85-20029

Junior high school student Nick must face the fact that his father is plunging fast into serious mental illness

"The author gives us a meticulous description, almost a case history, of the terrifying transformation of Jacob Karpinski from a quiet, but loving and conscientious, husband and father into a paranoid, dangerous madman. . . . A book of considerable power." Horn Book

Reluctantly Alice. Atheneum Pubs. 1991 182p $16   **Fic**
1. School stories 2. Family life—Fiction
ISBN 0-689-31681-X   LC 90-37956

"A Jean Karl book"

Continuing the adventures of Alice McKinley begun in The agony of Alice (1985) and Alice in rapture, sort of (1989), this novel finds Alice setting out to be "Alice the likable" in her first year of junior high

"Naylor combines laugh-out-loud scenes with moments of sudden gentleness. . . . The characters are complex, the dialogue is droll, the junior high world authentic." Booklist

Other available titles about Alice are:
Achingly Alice (1998)
Alice in April (1993)
Alice in-between (1994)
Alice in lace (1996)
Alice on the outside (1999)
Alice the brave (1995)
All but Alice (1992)
Outrageously Alice (1997)

Sang Spell. Atheneum Bks. for Young Readers 1998 176p $16; pa $4.50 (7 and up)   **Fic**
1. Orphans—Fiction 2. Appalachian Region—Fiction
ISBN 0-689-82007-0; 0-689-82006-2 (pa)
                                           LC 97-34067

"A Jean Karl book"

When his mother is killed in an automobile accident, high-schooler Josh decides to hitchhike across country, and finds himself trapped in a mysterious village somewhere in the Appalachian Mountains, among a group of people who call themselves Melungeons

"Naylor's memorable story skillfully combines the real world with a haunting, fantasy one." Voice Youth Advocates

Shiloh. Atheneum Pubs. 1991 144p $15   **Fic**
1. Dogs—Fiction 2. West Virginia—Fiction
ISBN 0-689-31614-3   LC 90-603

Also available in paperback from Dell
Awarded the Newbery Medal, 1992

When he finds a lost beagle in the hills behind his West Virginia home, Marty tries to hide it from his family and the dog's real owner, a mean-spirited man known to shoot deer out of season and to mistreat his dogs

"A credible plot and characters, a well-drawn setting, and nicely paced narration combine in a story that leaves the reader feeling good." Horn Book

Other available titles in this series are:
Saving Shiloh (1997)
Shiloh season (1996)

Nelson, Theresa, 1948-

Earthshine; a novel. Orchard Bks. 1994 182p $16.95; lib bdg $17.99   **Fic**
1. AIDS (Disease)—Fiction 2. Fathers and daughters—Fiction 3. Homosexuality—Fiction
ISBN 0-531-06867-6; 0-531-08717-4 (lib bdg)
                                           LC 94-8793

Also available in paperback from Dell
"A Richard Jackson book"

"Slim—real name Margery—is twelve, living with her actor father and her father's lover, Larry; her father is dying of AIDS, and Slim participates in a church youth group for kids close to people with the disease." Bull Cent Child Books

"Major and minor charcters are real people and never case studies. And the author's use of language expresses both the action and underlying feelings while remaining true to the voice of the narrator. . . . This special book should find a wide audience." SLJ

The Empress of Elsewhere; a novel. DK Ink 1998 278p $17.95   **Fic**
1. Friendship—Fiction 2. Family life—Fiction 3. Monkeys—Fiction
ISBN 0-7894-2498-3   LC 98-13209

"A Richard Jackson book"

When he and his younger sister agree to help their wealthy, elderly neighbor care for the capuchin monkey that keeps getting away from her, Jimmy also helps the woman's troublesome granddaughter deal with secrets from her family's past

"By turns comic and heartrending, the story is propelled along by Jim's distinctive East Texan narration and populated by a cast of memorable characters." Horn Book Guide

Neufeld, John, 1938-

Boys lie; a novel. DK Ink 1999 165p $16.95 (7 and up)   **Fic**
ISBN 0-7894-2624-2   LC 98-34546

Neufeld, John, 1938——*Continued*
"A Richard Jackson book"

Eighth-grader Gina Smith is targeted as easy by some boys in her new school because of her physical development and an incident in her past in which she was assaulted in a public swimming pool

"Neufeld has written a sensitive, realistic novel about an all-too-common rite of passage." SLJ

Newman, Robert, 1909-1988
The case of the Baker Street Irregular; a Sherlock Holmes story. Atheneum Pubs. 1978 216p hardcover o.p. paperback available $4.95
Fic

1. Mystery fiction 2. London (England)—Fiction
ISBN 0-689-70766-5 (pa) LC 77-15463
Also available in hardcover from P. Smith

Brought to London under mysterious circumstances by his tutor, young Andrew Tillett seeks the help of Sherlock Holmes when his tutor is kidnapped and he himself is threatened with the same fate

"The author is as urbane and fluent as the legendary Mr. Holmes; he seems thoroughly comfortable with the characters, the atmosphere, and the turn-of-the century London setting; and the story moves along with unflagging energy." Horn Book

Newton, Suzanne, 1936-
I will call it Georgie's blues; a novel. Viking 1983 197p hardcover o.p. paperback available $5.99 (7 and up)
Fic

1. Family life—Fiction 2. Jazz music—Fiction 3. Clergy—Fiction
ISBN 0-14-034536-1 (pa) LC 83-5849

Because the Baptist minister's children in a small North Carolina town have difficulty conforming to the roles their father wishes them to play for public consumption, fifteen-year-old Neal feels he must hide his consuming interest in jazz music

"The author portrays the fishbowl life of a minister's family with painful accuracy. The novel unfolds too slowly to hold the attention of most teenagers, but it offers considerable rewards for the serious reader." Child Book Rev Serv

Nix, Garth, 1963-
Sabriel. HarperCollins Pubs. 1996 c1995 292p $15.95; lib bdg $15.89; pa $5.95 (7 and up)
Fic

1. Fantasy fiction
ISBN 0-06-027322-4; 0-06-027323-2 (lib bdg); 0-06-447183-7 (pa) LC 96-1295
First published 1995 in Australia

Sabriel, daughter of the necromancer Abhorsen, must journey into the mysterious and magical Old Kingdom to rescue her father from the Land of the Dead

"The final battle is gripping, and the bloody cost of combat is forcefully presented. The story is remarkable for the level of originality of the fantastic elements . . . and for the subtle presentation, which leaves readers to explore for themselves the complex structure and significance of the magic elements." Horn Book

Shade's children. HarperCollins Pubs. 1997 310p $15.95; lib bdg $15.89; pa $5.95 (7 and up)
Fic

1. Science fiction
ISBN 0-06-027324-0; 0-06-027325-9 (lib bdg); 0-06-447196-9 (pa) LC 97-3841

In a savage postnuclear world, four young fugitives attempt to overthrow the bloodthirsty rule of the Overlords with the help of Shade, their mysterious mentor

"Grim, unusual, and fascinating." Horn Book

Nixon, Joan Lowery, 1927-
A family apart. Bantam Bks. 1987 162p (Orphan train series) hardcover o.p. paperback available $4.50
Fic

1. Foster home care—Fiction 2. Brothers and sisters—Fiction 3. United States—History—1783-1865—Fiction
ISBN 0-440-91309-8 (pa) LC 87-12563

"The first volume in the *Orphan Train* series, this is based on a real program, the Children's Aid Society's placement of orphans who travelled from New York City to the West to be adopted by residents there. In this story, set in 1860, widowed Mrs. Kelley realizes she cannot support her six children and gives them up for adoption. The protagonist is the oldest girl, Frances, who disguises herself as a boy so that she can be paired with her baby brother for adoption, and they are indeed taken together by a very nice family." Bull Cent Child Books

"The plot is rational and well paced; the characters are real and believable; the time setting important to U.S. history, and the values all that anyone could ask for." Voice Youth Advocates

Other available titles in the Orphan train series are:
Caught in the act (1988)
Circle of love (1997)
A dangerous promise (1994)
In the face of danger (1988)
Keeping secrets (1995)
A place to belong (1989)

The haunting. Delacorte Press 1998 184p $15.95 (7 and up)
Fic

1. Ghost stories 2. Louisiana—Fiction
ISBN 0-385-32247-X LC 97-32658

When her mother inherits an old plantation house in the Louisiana countryside, fifteen-year-old Lia seeks to rid it of the evil spirit that haunts it

"This title has it all—a hint of romance, some really scary scenes, and a plucky heroine who successfully routs both outer and inner demons." Horn Book Guide

Murdered, my sweet. Delacorte Press 1997 200p $15.95; pa $4.50 (7 and up)
Fic
1. Mystery fiction
ISBN 0-385-32245-3; 0-440-22005-X (pa)
LC 96-43431

Jenny and her mother hunt a killer while fearing for their own safety, after the reading of their millionaire cousin's will leads to the murder of another cousin

"Another solid Nixon mystery without too much violence and lots of suspense." Booklist

Nixon, Joan Lowery, 1927-—*Continued*

Search for the Shadowman. Delacorte Press 1996 149p $15.95; pa $4.50 **Fic**
1. Genealogy—Fiction 2. Texas—Fiction 3. Mystery fiction
ISBN 0-385-32203-8; 0-440-41128-9 (pa)
LC 96-5740

While working on a genealogy project for his seventh grade history class, Andy Bonner becomes determined to solve the mystery surrounding a distant relative who was accused of stealing the family fortune

"Nixon has once again delivered a riveting tale of suspense set against a background of fascinating historical context, brought up to date through e-mail and the Internet." SLJ

Who are you? Delacorte Press 1999 184p $15.95 (7 and up) **Fic**
1. Art museums—Fiction 2. Mystery fiction
ISBN 0-385-32566-5
LC 98-43000

When the police discover that a man who has been shot has been keeping a file of her entire life, sixteen-year-old Kristi, an aspiring artist, suspects a connection with the possible theft of a painting from a museum

"Appealing characters, an interesting scenario, and a fascinating peek into the big-money art world will keep the pages turning." Booklist

Norton, Andre, 1912-

The monster's legacy; illustrated by Jody A. Lee. Atheneum Bks. for Young Readers 1996 151p il $17 (7 and up) **Fic**
1. Fantasy fiction
ISBN 0-689-80731-7
LC 95-80677
"A Byron Press book"

Sarita, apprentice to the Embroidier Dame Argalas, escapes from Earl Florian's enemies with the Earl's infant son and seeks refuge in the mountainous lair of the legendary beast, the Loden

"Mix in fast-paced adventure, a sense of constant danger, and a mystery about long-gone dragons and their legacy—and you have a very satisfying tale." Booklist

Witch World [series] (7 and up) **Fic**
1. Fantasy fiction 2. Witchcraft—Fiction

"'Witch World' was the first novel in a series which has become Norton's most highly regarded work, enjoyed by adults as well as teenagers. . . . It is basically a sword-and-sorcery series, even if it is not labelled as such. The first of these books is the tale of a man, a World War II veteran named Simon Tregarth, who is projected by magic into the rugged terrain of a mysterious parallel world. There he helps save the life of a young witch, and subsequently becomes a soldier on behalf of her beleaguered people." Pringle. Modern Fantasy
Available titles in the Witch World series are:
Ciara's song (1998)
Flight of vengeance (1992)
Gryphon's eyrie (1984)
On wings of magic (1994)
Songsmith (1992)
The warding of Witch World (1996)

Nye, Naomi Shihab

Habibi. Simon & Schuster Bks. for Young Readers 1997 259p $16; pa $4.99 **Fic**
1. Jewish-Arab relations—Fiction 2. Jerusalem—Fiction
ISBN 0-689-80149-1; 0-689-82523-4 (pa)
LC 97-10943

When fourteen-year-old Liyanne Abboud, her younger brother, and her parents move from St. Louis to a new home between Jerusalem and the Palestinian village where her father was born, they face many changes and must deal with the tensions between Jews and Palestinians

"Poetically imaged and leavened with humor, the story renders layered and complex history understandable through character and incident." SLJ

O'Brien, Robert C., 1918-1973

Mrs. Frisby and the rats of NIMH; illustrated by Zena Bernstein. Atheneum Pubs. 1971 223p il lib bdg $17; pa $4.50 **Fic**
1. Mice—Fiction 2. Rats—Fiction
ISBN 0-689-20651-8 (lib bdg); 0-689-71068-2 (pa)
LC 74-134818

Awarded the Newbery Medal, 1972

"Mrs. Frisby, a widowed mouse, is directed by an owl to consult with the rats that live under the rosebush about her problem of moving her sick son from the family's endangered home. Upon entering that rats' quarters, Mrs. Frisby discovers to her astonishment that the rats are not ordinary rodents, but highly intelligent creatures that escaped from an NIMH laboratory after being taught to read." Booklist

"The story is fresh and ingenious, the style witty, and the plot both hilarious and convincing." Saturday Rev

Followed by Racso and the rats of NIMH and R-T, Margaret, and the rats of NIMH by Jane Leslie Conly

Z for Zachariah. Atheneum Pubs. 1975 c1974 246p hardcover o.p. paperback available $4.50 (7 and up) **Fic**
1. Science fiction
ISBN 0-02-044650-0 (pa)

"Told in diary form by a 16-year-old girl, O'Brien's posthumous story is set in the future, after a nuclear war. Ann Burden believes she is the last person on earth. Her family has left her to look after their farm in a deep valley as they drive off to look for other survivors. They never return. One day, Ann sees the smoke from a campfire and watches as it comes closer. The reader is at first relieved but gradually frightened, like the heroine, as she finds that the man who arrives at her home is no friend but a deadly enemy." Publ Wkly

"The journal form is used by O'Brien very effectively, with no lack of drama and contrast, and the pace and suspense of the story are adroitly maintained until the dramatic and surprising ending." Bull Cent Child Books

O'Dell, Scott, 1898-1989

The black pearl; illustrated by Milton Johnson. Houghton Mifflin 1967 140p il $17 **Fic**
1. Pearl fisheries—Fiction 2. Baja California (Mexico: Peninsula)—Fiction
ISBN 0-395-06961-0
LC 67-23311
Also available in paperback from Dell

O'Dell, Scott, 1898-1989—*Continued*

"The people of Baja California feared a demon creature, a giant ray—El Manta Diablo. He was believed to live in a cave at the end of a lagoon. . . . Yet Ramón Salazar, goaded by the taunts of the greatest pearl diver of his father's fleet, dared to enter the cave to dive for a pearl even more wonderful than the one El Sevillano had boasted of. And he found it—the Paragon of Pearls, the Pearl of Heaven. Then came the encounter with the Manta." Horn Book

"The stark simplicity of the story and the deeper significance it holds in the triumph of good over evil add importance to the book, but even without that the book would be enjoyable as a rousing adventure tale with supernatural overtones and beautifully maintained tempo and suspense." Bull Cent Child Books

Island of the Blue Dolphins. Houghton Mifflin 1960 184p $16   Fic
1. Indians of North America—Fiction 2. Wilderness survival—Fiction 3. San Nicolas Island (Calif.)—Fiction
ISBN 0-395-06962-9
Also available in paperback from Dell
Awarded the Newbery Medal, 1961
"Unintentionally left behind by members of her California Native American tribe who fled a tragedy-ridden island, young Karana must construct a life for herself. Without bitterness or self-pity, she is able to extract joy and challenge from her eighteen years of solitude." Shapiro. Fic for Youth. 3d edition
Followed by Zia

Sarah Bishop. Houghton Mifflin 1980 184p $16   Fic
. 1. United States—History—1775-1783, Revolution—Fiction 2. American loyalists—Fiction 3. Wilderness survival—Fiction 4. New York (State)—Fiction
ISBN 0-395-29185-2   LC 79-28394
Also available in paperback from Scholastic
"Surrounded by war, prejudice, and fear, fifteen-year-old Sarah Bishop quietly determines to live her own kind of life in the wilderness that was Westchester County, New York, during the Revolution. Orphaned Sarah plucks up her courage when she is wrongfully dealt with by both the American and British forces, and she creates a home for herself and her animal friends in the forest near Long Pond." Child Book Rev Serv
"The story line is basically sharp and clear; O'Dell's messages about the bitterness and folly of war, the dangers of superstition, and the courage of the human spirit are smoothly woven into the story, as are the telling details of period and place." Bull Cent Child Books

The serpent never sleeps; a novel of Jamestown and Pocahontas; illustrations by Ted Lewin. Houghton Mifflin 1987 227p il $17   Fic
1. Pocahontas, d. 1617—Fiction 2. United States—History—1600-1775, Colonial period—Fiction
ISBN 0-395-44242-7   LC 87-3026
Also available in paperback from Fawcett Bks.
"Serena sails on the 'Sea Venture' to follow young Anthony Foxcroft, who is running away from prison. Serena is infatuated with him and is not over the infatuation until he dies. The background is Jamestown and Serena is involved with and befriends Pocahontas, but the

main focus is on Serena and her problems." Voice Youth Advocates

"The credibility of this novel lies not in the heroine, and far less in the immature hero, handsome Anthony Foxcroft, but rather in the stark grim reality of the sheer survival in the inhospitable Jamestown wilderness. O'Dell's portrayal relates the privations and dangers of every side." Booklist

Sing down the moon. Houghton Mifflin 1970 137p $17   Fic
1. Navajo Indians—Fiction
ISBN 0-395-10919-1
Also available in paperback from Dell
This story is told "through the eyes of a young Navaho girl as she sees the rich harvest in the Canyon de Chelly in 1864 destroyed by Spanish slavers and the subsequent destruction by white soldiers which forces the Navahos on a march to Fort Sumner." Publ Wkly
"There is a poetic sonority of style, a sense of identification, and a note of indomitable courage and stoicism that is touching and impressive." Saturday Rev

Streams to the river, river to the sea; a novel of Sacagawea. Houghton Mifflin 1986 191p il $16
                                    Fic
1. Sacagawea, b. 1786—Fiction 2. Lewis and Clark Expedition (1804-1806)—Fiction 3. Indians of North America—Fiction
ISBN 0-395-40430-4   LC 86-936
Also available G.K. Hall large print edition and in paperback from Fawcett Bks.
"This is the story of the Shoshone girl who served as an interpreter for the Lewis & Clark expedition. Sacagawea narrates the story, beginning with her abduction, as a young teenager, by the Minnetarees. " Voice Youth Advocates
"An informative and involving choice for American history students and pioneer-adventure readers." Bull Cent Child Books

Thunder rolling in the mountains; [by] Scott O'Dell and Elizabeth Hall. Houghton Mifflin 1992 128p map $17   Fic
1. Nez Percé Indians—Fiction
ISBN 0-395-59966-0   LC 91-15961
Also available in paperback from Dell
"Told from the point of view of Chief Joseph's daughter, this historical novel concerns the forced removal of the Nez Perce tribe from their homeland in 1877. Fourteen-year-old Sound of Running Feet describes her people's pain at leaving their beloved Wallowa Valley, their disagreements over whether to resist the government troops that plague them, and their suffering as every act of defense or defiance brings on a more devastating reaction." Booklist
"This is a sad, dark-hued story told in Mr. O'Dell's lean, affecting prose." Child Book Rev Serv

Zia. Houghton Mifflin 1976 179p $18   Fic
1. Indians of North America—Fiction 2. Christian missions—Fiction
ISBN 0-395-24393-9   LC 75-44156
Also available in paperback from Dell

O'Dell, Scott, 1898-1989—*Continued*

In this sequel to Island of the Blue Dolphins, the author invents a niece for Karana "in the character of Zia, a young Indian who lives at the Santa Barbara Mission and who dreams of sailing to the island to rescue her aunt. After one thwarted attempt to get there, and imprisonment for helping some fellow Indians flee the Mission, Zia finds her dream realized. A sea captain and a priest bring Karana from Dolphin Island—and haltingly, the two women are reunited." N Y Times Book Rev

"Zia is an excellent story in its own right, written in a clear, quiet, and reflective style which is in harmony with the plot and characterization." SLJ

Oppel, Kenneth

Silverwing. Simon & Schuster Bks. for Young Readers 1997 217p $16   **Fic**

1. Bats—Fiction

ISBN 0-689-81529-8   LC 97-10977

When a newborn bat named Shade but sometimes called "Runt" becomes separated from his colony during migration, he grows in ways that prepare him for even greater journeys

"Oppel's bats are fully developed characters who, if not quite cuddly, will certainly earn readers' sympathy and respect. In *Silverwing* the author has created an intriguing microcosm of rival species, factions, and religions." Horn Book

Orr, Wendy, 1953-

Peeling the onion. Holiday House 1997 c1996 166p $15.95 (7 and up)   **Fic**

1. Traffic accidents—Fiction 2. Hospitals—Fiction

ISBN 0-8234-1289-X   LC 96-42353

Also available in paperback from Dell

First published 1996 in Australia

Following an automobile accident in which her neck is broken, a teenage karate champion begins a long and painful recovery with the help of her family

"Grimly realistic . . . this story of gritty survival will grab even the most reluctant readers." SLJ

Orwell, George, 1903-1950

Animal farm (7 and up)   **Fic**

1. Animals—Fiction 2. Totalitarianism—Fiction

Various editions available

First published 1945 in the United Kingdom; first United States edition 1946

"The animals on Farmer Jones's farm revolt in a move led by the pigs, and drive out the humans. The pigs become the leaders, in spite of the fact that their government was meant to be 'classless.' The other animals soon find that they are suffering varying degrees of slavery. A totalitarian state slowly evolves in which 'all animals are equal but some animals are more equal than others.' This is a biting satire aimed at communism." Shapiro. Fic for Youth. 3d edition

Nineteen eighty-four (7 and up)   **Fic**

1. Totalitarianism—Fiction

Various editions available

First published 1949 by Harcourt, Brace

"A dictatorship called Big Brother rules the people in a collectivist society where Winston Smith works in the Ministry of Truth. The Thought Police persuade the people that ignorance is strength and war is peace. Winston becomes involved in a forbidden love affair and joins the underground to resist this mind control." Shapiro. Fic for Youth. 3d edition

Osborne, Mary Pope, 1949-

Standing in the light; the captive diary of Catherine Carey Logan, Delaware Valley, Pennsylvania, 1763. Scholastic 1998 184p il (Dear America) $9.95   **Fic**

1. United States—History—1600-1775, Colonial period—Fiction 2. Pennsylvania—Fiction 3. Delaware Indians—Fiction 4. Society of friends—Fiction

ISBN 0-590-13462-0   LC 97-40083

A Quaker girl's diary reflects her experiences growing up in the Delaware River Valley of Pennsylvania and her capture by Lenape Indians in 1763

"Osborne successfully sustains readers' attention with a strong story line while informing them about American history." SLJ

Oughton, Jerrie, 1937-

The war in Georgia. Houghton Mifflin 1997 183p $14.95 (7 and up)   **Fic**

1. Family life—Fiction 2. World War, 1939-1945—Fiction 3. Georgia—Fiction

ISBN 0-395-81568-1   LC 96-22029

Also available in paperback from Dell

Living in Georgia during World War II, thirteen-year-old Shanta sometimes feels that her family and neighborhood are more hopeless battlefields that those in foreign lands

"This story makes you believe in the love and laughter and friendship that give you hope in the worst of times." Booklist

Paterson, Katherine

Bridge to Terabithia; illustrated by Donna Diamond. Crowell 1977 128p $14.95; lib bdg $15.89; pa $4.95   **Fic**

1. Friendship—Fiction 2. Death—Fiction 3. Virginia—Fiction

ISBN 0-690-01359-0; 0-690-04635-9 (lib bdg); 0-06-440184-7 (pa)   LC 77-2221

Awarded the Newbery medal, 1978

The life of Jess, a ten-year-old boy in rural Virginia expands when he becomes friends with a newcomer who subsequently meets an untimely death trying to reach their hideaway, Terabithia, during a storm

"Jess and his family are magnificently characterized; the book abounds in descriptive vignettes, humorous sidelights on the clash of cultures, and realistic depictions of rural school life." Horn Book

The great Gilly Hopkins. Crowell 1978 148p $14.95; lib bdg $14.89; pa $4.95   **Fic**

1. Foster home care—Fiction

ISBN 0-690-03837-2; 0-690-03838-0 (lib bdg); 0-06-440201-0 (pa)   LC 77-27075

Paterson, Katherine—*Continued*

"Cool, scheming, and deliberately obstreperous, 11-year-old Gilly is ready to be her usual obnoxious self when she arrives at her new foster home. . . . But Gilly's old tricks don't work against the all-encompassing love of the huge, half-illiterate Mrs. Trotter. . . . Determined not to care she writes a letter full of wild exaggerations to her real mother that brings, in return, a surprising visit from an unknown grandmother." Booklist

"Paterson's development of the change in Gilly is brilliant and touching. . . . A well-structured story [this] has vitality of writing style, natural dialogue, deep insight in characterization, and a keen sense of the fluid dynamics in human relationships." Bull Cent Child Books

Jacob have I loved. Crowell 1980 216p $14.95; lib bdg $14.89; pa $4.95　　Fic
1. Twins—Fiction 2. Sisters—Fiction 3. Chesapeake Bay (Md. and Va.)—Fiction
ISBN 0-690-04078-4; 0-690-04079-2 (lib bdg); 0-06-440368-8 (pa)　　LC 80-668

"Sara Louise, called Wheeze, felt like the unloved twin in competition with her sister Caroline. On a small Chesapeake Bay island Louise is isolated and denied the opportunity to fulfill her hopes and goals while everyone caters to her twin sister. The return of an old captain after a 50-year absence, and the advent of the war, gives Louise a chance to grow toward maturity and achieve her wish to work alongside her father." Shapiro. Fic for Youth. 3d edition

Jip; his story. Lodestar Bks. 1996 181p $15.99; pa $4.99　　Fic
1. Slavery—Fiction 2. African Americans—Fiction 3. Vermont—Fiction 4. Racially mixed people—Fiction
ISBN 0-525-67543-4; 0-14-038674-2 (pa)　　LC 96-2680

While living on a Vermont poor farm during 1855 and 1856, Jip learns that his mother was a runaway slave, and that his father, the plantation owner, plans to reclaim him as property

"This historically accurate story is full of revelations and surprises, one of which is the return appearance of the heroine of *Lyddie*. . . . The taut, extremely readable narrative and its tender depictions of friendship and loyalty provide first-rate entertainment." Publ Wkly

Lyddie. Lodestar Bks. 1991 182p $15.99; pa $4.99　　Fic
1. United States—History—1815-1861—Fiction 2. Massachusetts—Fiction 3. Factories—Fiction
ISBN 0-525-67338-5; 0-14-034981-2 (pa)　　LC 90-42944

Also available Thorndike Press large print edition

Impoverished Vermont farm girl Lyddie Worthen is determined to gain her independence by becoming a factory worker in Lowell, Massachusetts, in the 1840s

"Not only does the book contain a riveting plot, engaging characters, and a splendid setting, but the language—graceful, evocative, and rhythmic—incorporates the rural speech patterns of Lyddie's folk, the simple Quaker expressions of the farm neighbors, and the lilt of fellow mill girl Bridget's Irish brogue. . . . A superb story of grit, determination, and personal growth." Horn Book

The master puppeteer; illustrated by Haru Wells. Crowell 1976 c1975 179p il hardcover o.p. paperback available $4.95　　Fic
1. Japan—Fiction 2. Puppets and puppet plays—Fiction
ISBN 0-06-440281-9 (pa)

"In 18th-century Osaka, Japan, Jiro, son of a starving puppetmaker, runs away from home to apprentice himself to Yoshida, the ill-tempered master of the Hanaza puppet theater. As Jiro works to learn the art of the puppeteer and travels among the savage, hunger-crazed bands of night rovers in search of his parents, he becomes aware of a mysterious connection between Saboro, a Robin Hood-like figure, and the Hanaza theater itself." SLJ

"The make-believe world of the Japanese puppet theatre merges excitingly with the hungry, desperate realities of 18th century Osaka in this better-than-average junior novel." Bull Cent Child Books

Of nightingales that weep; illustrated by Haru Wells. Crowell 1974 170p $14; pa $4.50　　Fic
1. Japan—Fiction
ISBN 0-690-00485-0; 0-06-440282-7 (pa)

"Takiko, daughter of a famous samurai killed in the wars, is taken into the court of the boy emperor Antoku as a musician and personal servant. Takiko's conflicting loyalties to the Heike-supported court, a dashing Genji warrior, and her physically grotesque but goodhearted peasant stepfather form the impetus for her internal development while the war rages around her." Booklist

"The battle scenes are vivid, the details of court life convincing, the characters drawn with some depth; this is unusual and stirring historical fiction." Bull Cent Child Books

Park's quest. Lodestar Bks. 1988 148p hardcover o.p. paperback available $4.99　　Fic
1. Farm life—Fiction 2. Vietnamese Americans—Fiction
ISBN 0-14-034262-1 (pa)　　LC 87-32422

Eleven-year-old Park makes some startling discoveries when he travels to his grandfather's farm in Virginia to learn about his father who died in the Vietnam War and meets a Vietnamese-American girl named Thanh

The author "confronts the complexity, the ambiguity, of the war and the emotions of those it involved with an honesty that young readers are sure to recognize and appreciate." N Y Times Book Rev

Paton, Alan

Cry, the beloved country (7 and up)　　Fic
1. Race relations—Fiction 2. South Africa—Fiction

Various editions available
First published 1948 by Scribner

"Reverend Kumalo, a black South African preacher, is called to Johannesburg to rescue his sister. There he learns that his son Absalom has been accused of murdering a young white attorney whose interests and sympathies had been with the natives. Despite this, the attorney's father comes to the aid of the minister to help the natives in their struggle to survive a drought." Shapiro. Fic for Youth. 3d edition

Paton Walsh, Jill, 1937-

Fireweed. Farrar, Straus & Giroux 1970 133p
$18.25; pa $3.50   Fic
1. World War, 1939-1945—Fiction 2. London (England)—Fiction
ISBN 0-374-32310-0; 0-374-42316-4 (pa)
During World War II, "Bill and Julie had found each
other by chance, each of them lurking around London after having started off with a group of children being
evacuated. Julie had money, Bill could cope, and together the two made a clandestine home in the rubble of a
building. Only when Julie was caught by a raid did Bill,
staring in anguish at the fresh ruins, realize how important she had become to him." Saturday Rev
"The development of a relationship . . . is one of the
two main achievements of this book. . . . The second
achievement is the setting, the picture given without
squeamishness or apparent over-emphasis of London in
the blitz—the humour, the fear, the misery, the sometimes uncanny normality." Times Lit Suppl

Grace. Farrar, Straus & Giroux 1992 255p $16;
pa $5.95   Fic
1. Darling, Grace—Fiction 2. Shipwrecks—Fiction
3. Great Britain—Fiction
ISBN 0-374-32758-0; 0-374-42792-5 (pa)
                                        LC 91-31054
After helping her father rescue the survivors of a shipwreck on the coast of England in 1838, Grace Darling
finds her quiet life crumbling around her as she is unwillingly fashioned into a national hero
"This true event, and much of the aftermath, have
been used by the author to blend fact and fiction with
consummate skill in creating a narrative that is powerfully dramatic in its initial impact and sharply observant in
describing the consequent events." Bull Cent Child
Books

A parcel of patterns. Farrar, Straus & Giroux
1983 136p hardcover o.p. paperback available
$3.95   Fic
1. Plague—Fiction 2. Great Britain—Fiction
ISBN 0-374-45743-3 (pa)   LC 83-48143
Also available in hardcover from P. Smith
Mall Percival tells how the plague came to her Derby-
shire village of Eyam in the year 1665, how the villagers
determined to isolate themselves to prevent further
spread of the disease, and how three-fourths of them died
before the end of the following year
"Historical in broad outline, the narrative blends superb characterizations, skillful plotting, and convincing
speech for a hauntingly memorable story that offers a
richly textured picture of the period." Child Book Rev
Serv

Paulsen, Gary

Alida's song. Delacorte Press 1999 88p $15.95
                                                     Fic
1. Grandmothers—Fiction 2. Farm life—Fiction
ISBN 0-385-32586-X   LC 98-37015
In this sequel to The cookcamp, "Grandma Alida once
again steps in at a troubled time in her grandson's life.
Now the boy is 14; living with violent, drunken parents.
. . . [A] letter arrives from his grandmother offering him
a summer job as a hired hand on a farm. . . . He accepts

the offer and experiences a season of hard work, music,
dancing, and hearty meals served up with warmth, love,
and understanding. . . . This beautifully written novella
is a quiet tribute to a loving relative." SLJ

Brian's return. Delacorte Press 1999 117p
$15.95   Fic
1. Wilderness survival—Fiction
ISBN 0-385-32500-2   LC 98-24278
Companion volume to Hatchet, and Brian's Winter
After having survived alone in the wilderness, Brian
finds that he can no longer live in the city but must return to the place where he really belongs
"This work is bold, confident and persuasive, its tran-
scendental themes powerfully seductive." Publ Wkly

Brian's winter. Delacorte Press 1996 133p
$15.95; pa $4.99   Fic
1. Survival after airplane accidents, shipwrecks, etc.—
Fiction
ISBN 0-385-32198-8; 0-440-22719-4 (pa)
                                        LC 95-41337
In this novel Paulsen presents an alternate scenario to
Hatchet, where Brian Robeson was rescued "after surviving a plane crash and summer alone in the north Canadian woods. Now . . . Paulsen shows what would have
happened if the 13-year-old boy had been forced to endure the harsh winter." SLJ
"Paulsen writes with the authoritative particularity of
someone who knows the woods. This docunovel is for
outdoors lovers and also for all of those adventurers snug
at home in a centrally heated high-rise. The facts are the
drama." Booklist

Canyons. Delacorte Press 1990 184p hardcover
o.p. paperback available $4.99   Fic
1. Apache Indians—Fiction 2. Texas—Fiction
ISBN 0-440-21023-2 (pa)   LC 90-2829
Finding a skull on a camping trip in the canyons outside El Paso, Texas, Brennan becomes involved with the
fate of a young Apache Indian who lived in the late
1800s
"Paulsen involves readers so deeply in the lives of
both characters, telling the story in alternating chapters
marked by the cadence and language distinctive to each
boy and his time and place, that the whole becomes a
compelling and dramatic experience that is powerful
stuff." SLJ

The cookcamp. Orchard Bks. 1991 115p $15.95
                                                     Fic
1. Grandmothers—Fiction 2. World War, 1939-
1945—Fiction
ISBN 0-531-05927-8   LC 90-7734
Also available in paperback from Dell
"A Richard Jackson book"
During World War II, a little boy is sent to live with
his grandma, a cook in a camp for workers building a
road through the wilderness
"Paulsen's simply told story strikes extraordinary emotional chords. . . . Those hungry for adventure stories, as
well as more introspective readers, will be spellbound by
this stirring novel." Publ Wkly
Followed by Alida's song

Paulsen, Gary—*Continued*

Dogsong. Bradbury Press 1985 177p $16; pa $4.50   **Fic**
1. Inuit—Fiction 2. Arctic regions—Fiction
ISBN 0-02-770180-8; 0-689-80409-1 (pa)
LC 84-20443

A fourteen-year-old Eskimo boy who feels assailed by the modernity of his life takes a 1400-mile journey by dog sled across ice, tundra, and mountains seeking his own "song" of himself

The author's "mystical tone and blunt prose style are well suited to the spare landscape of his story, and his depictions of Russell's icebound existence add both authenticity and color to a slick rendition of the vision-quest plot, which incorporates human tragedy as well as promise." Booklist

Harris and me; a summer remembered. Harcourt Brace & Co. 1993 157p $13.95   **Fic**
1. Farm life—Fiction 2. Cousins—Fiction
ISBN 0-15-292877-4
LC 93-19788
Also available in paperback from Dell

Sent to live with relatives on their farm because of his unhappy home life, an eleven-year-old city boy meets his distant cousin Harris and is given an introduction to a whole new world

"A hearty helping of old-fashioned, rip-roaring entertainment." Publ Wkly

Hatchet. Bradbury Press 1987 195p $16; pa $4.99   **Fic**
1. Survival after airplane accidents, shipwrecks, etc.—Fiction 2. Divorce—Fiction
ISBN 0-02-770130-1; 0-689-82699-0 (pa)
LC 87-6416
A Newbery Medal honor book, 1988

After a plane crash, thirteen-year-old Brian spends fifty-four days in the wilderness, learning to survive initially with only the aid of a hatchet given him by his mother, and learning also to survive his parents' divorce

"Paulsen's knowledge of our national wilderness is obvious and beautifully shared. Beyond that Paulsen grips Brian (and the reader) by the throat, shaking him into enlightenment and self-confidence after having endured several life-threatening events." Voice Youth Advocates

Followed by The river

The haymeadow; illustrated by Ruth Wright Paulsen. Delacorte Press 1992 195p il hardcover o.p. paperback available $4.50   **Fic**
1. Ranch life—Fiction 2. Sheep—Fiction 3. Wyoming—Fiction
ISBN 0-440-40923-3 (pa)
LC 91-36666
Fourteen-year-old John comes of age and gains self-reliance during the summer he spends up in the Wyoming mountains tending his father's herd of sheep

"The protagonist is clearly imagined; the style is both consciously simple and dramatic. . . . There's even a touch of humor." Bull Cent Child Books

The island. Orchard Bks. 1988 202p $17.95
    Fic
1. Islands—Fiction 2. Wisconsin—Fiction
ISBN 0-531-05749-6
LC 87-24761
Also available in paperback from Dell

"A Richard Jackson book"

"Wil Neuton moves with his parents from Madison, Wis., to a small house in the north woods, miles from the nearest village, because of his father's work with the state highway department. He then discovers a lake with a single island in the middle of it; or rather, he feels as though the island had discovered him and drawn him to it for some mysterious and important purpose." N Y Times Book Rev

"With humor and psychological genius, Paulsen develops strong adolescent characters who lend new power to youth's plea to be allowed to apply individual skills in their risk-taking. . . . Altogether an impressive and forceful work of reflective fiction." Voice Youth Advocates

The monument. Delacorte Press 1991 151p $15; pa $4.50   **Fic**
1. Artists—Fiction 2. Physically handicapped—Fiction
ISBN 0-385-30518-4; 0-440-40782-6 (pa)
LC 91-13919
Thirteen-year-old Rocky, self-conscious about the braces on her leg, has her life changed by the remarkable artist named Mick who comes to her small Kansas town to design a war memorial

"In sparse, sensitive, moving prose, Paulsen illuminates a small town and its inhabitants' beautiful and ugly sides to create a tribute to art." Voice Youth Advocates

Mr. Tucket. Delacorte Press 1994 166p $15.95; pa $4.50   **Fic**
1. Frontier and pioneer life—Fiction 2. West (U.S.)—Fiction
ISBN 0-385-31169-9; 0-440-41133-5 (pa)
LC 93-31180
In 1848, while on a wagon train headed for Oregon, fourteen-year-old Francis Tucket is kidnapped by Pawnee Indians and then falls in with a one-armed trapper who teaches him how to live in the wild

"Superb characterizations, splendidly evoked setting and thrill-a-minute plot make this book a joy to gallop through." Publ Wkly

Other available titles about Francis Tucket are:
Call me Francis Tucket (1995)
Tucket's gold (1999)
Tucket's ride (1997)

Nightjohn. Delacorte Press 1993 92p $15.95; pa $4.50 (7 and up)   **Fic**
1. Slavery—Fiction 2. Reading—Fiction 3. African Americans—Fiction
ISBN 0-385-30838-8; 0-440-21936-1 (pa)
LC 92-1222
Twelve-year-old Sarny's brutal life as a slave becomes even more dangerous when a newly arrived slave offers to teach her how to read

"Paulsen is at his best here: the writing is stark and bareboned, without stylistic pretensions of any kind. The narrator's voice is strong and true, the violence real but stylized with an almost mythic tone. . . . The simplicity of the text will make the book ideal for older reluctant readers." Bull Cent Child Books

Followed by Sarny

Paulsen, Gary—*Continued*

The rifle. Harcourt Brace & Co. 1995 105p $16 (7 and up)   **Fic**

1. Rifles—Fiction 2. United States—History—1775-1783, Revolution—Fiction

ISBN 0-15-292880-4   LC 95-730

Also available in paperback from Dell

"The centerpiece of the book is a flintlock rifle made in 1768 by a gifted American gunsmith named Cornish McManus. . . . The story follows . . . the life of the gun as it passes from McManus to a trapper/soldier to century-long storage to a 1993 gun nut and finally into the hands of a gas station owner, who mounts it over his fireplace. On Christmas Eve, a stray spark ignites the loaded weapon and the errant bullet kills a neighbor child." Voice Youth Advocates

"Paulsen's message is clear and cutting: a machine made for killing, no matter how lovingly crafted and benignly kept, remains a machine made for killing." Booklist

The river. Delacorte Press 1991 132p $15.95; pa $4.99   **Fic**

1. Survival after airplane accidents, shipwrecks, etc.—Fiction

ISBN 0-385-30388-2; 0-440-22750-X (pa)

    LC 90-49294

In this sequel to Hatchet "It's a year later, and Brian, now 15, is persuaded to repeat what he did in Hatchet—survive for a period in the Canadian wilderness. . . . Derek, a government psychologist, will take notes so that others can learn from Brian's experience. Everything goes well . . . until Derek is hit by lightning and lies in a coma. With no tools except a knife, Brian has to build a raft, navigate the river and the wild rapids, and haul Derek to the trading post about 100 miles downstream." Booklist

"The writing is clean and the survival action straightforward." Bull Cent Child Books

Sarny; a life remembered. Delacorte Press 1997 180p $15.95; pa $4.99 (7 and up)   **Fic**

1. Slavery—Fiction 2. African Americans—Fiction 3. Teachers—Fiction

ISBN 0-385-32195-3; 0-440-21973-6 (pa)

    LC 96-53842

This sequel to Nightjohn continues the adventures of Sarny, the slave girl Nightjohn taught to read, through the aftermath of the Civil War during which time she taught other Blacks and lived a full life until age ninety-four

The author "breathes life into a full and complex character that is guaranteed to remain in readers' hearts long after they finish her story." Voice Youth Advocates

The Schernoff discoveries. Delacorte Press 1997 103p $15.95; pa $4.50   **Fic**

1. Friendship—Fiction 2. School stories

ISBN 0-385-32194-5; 0-440-41463-6 (pa)

    LC 96-45390

Harold and his best friend, both hopeless geeks and societal misfits, try to survive unusual science experiments, the attacks of the football team, and other dangers of junior high school

"The tone is breezy, funny, and sometimes touching (but not too mushy) and bound to keep the most reluctant reader chuckling." Bull Cent Child Books

Soldier's heart; a novel of the Civil War. Delacorte Press 1998 106p $15.95 (7 and up)   **Fic**

1. United States—History—1861-1865, Civil War—Fiction 2. Post-traumatic stress disorder—Fiction

ISBN 0-385-32498-7   LC 98-10038

"Being the story of the enlistment and due service of the boy Charley Goddard in the First Minnesota Volunteers." Title page

Eager to enlist, fifteen-year-old Charley has a change of heart after experiencing both the physical horrors and mental anguish of Civil War combat

"This compelling and realistic depiction of war is based on a true story. . . . Paulsen's writing is crisp and fast-paced, and this soldier's story will haunt readers long after they finish reading the novel." Book Rep

The tent; a parable in one sitting. Harcourt Brace & Co. 1995 86p $14 (7 and up)   **Fic**

1. Fathers and sons—Fiction 2. Texas—Fiction 3. Religion—Fiction

ISBN 0-15-292879-0   LC 94-36103

Also available in paperback from Dell

"Motivated by financial need, Steven's father dons the guise of an itinerant preacher, and they travel the Southwest holding prayer meetings and 'healings.' Though the hoax brings wealth, both father and son begin to suffer pangs of guilt." Horn Book Guide

"While the setting and subject matter are atypical of Paulsen, the author's unique ability to pen a story is again demonstrated. . . . *The Tent* may surprise Paulsen's many fans, but it will not disappoint them." SLJ

The Transall saga. Delacorte Press 1998 248p $15.95; pa $5.50   **Fic**

1. Science fiction

ISBN 0-385-32196-1; 0-440-21976-0 (pa)

    LC 97-40773

While backpacking in the desert, thirteen-year-old Mark falls into a tube of blue light and is transported into a more primitive world, where he must use his knowledge and skills to survive

"A riveting tale of adventure and action." Voice Youth Advocates

The voyage of the Frog. Orchard Bks. 1989 141p $16.95   **Fic**

1. Sea stories

ISBN 0-531-05805-0   LC 88-15261

Also available Thorndike Press large print edition and in paperback from Dell

"A Richard Jackson book"

"David's beloved uncle Owen has just died of cancer, and David has inherited a sailboat, the *Frog*, which the two of them often sailed together. Now David takes the boat out to scatter his uncle's ashes, but he's caught in a storm and swept hundreds of miles southwest." Bull Cent Child Books

"The author, knowledgeable in sailing lore and lyrical and powerful in descriptions of either silken seas or crashing breakers, has made the ocean both a background and a protagonist in David's transition from boy to young man." Horn Book

Paulsen, Gary—*Continued*

The winter room. Orchard Bks. 1989 103p
$15.95; lib bdg $16.99   **Fic**
1. Farm life—Fiction 2. Minnesota—Fiction
ISBN 0-531-05839-5; 0-531-08439-6 (lib bdg)
            LC 89-42541
Also available in paperback from Dell
A Newbery Medal honor book, 1990
"A Richard Jackson book"
A young boy growing up on a northern Minnesota
farm describes the scenes around him and recounts his
old Norwegian uncle's tales of an almost mythological
logging past
"While this seems at first to be a collection of anecdotes organized around the progression of the farm calendar, Paulsen subtly builds a conflict that becomes apparent in the last brief chapters, forceful and well-
prepared. . . . Lyrical and only occasionally sentimental,
the prose is clean, clear, and deceptively simple." Bull
Cent Child Books

Peck, Richard, 1934-

Are you in the house alone? Viking 1976 156p
hardcover o.p. paperback available $4.99 (7 and
up)   **Fic**
1. Rape—Fiction
ISBN 0-440-90227-4 (pa)   LC 76-28810
"Gail is frightened by the obscene telephone calls she
receives and the notes that are left on her school locker.
It is after she has been raped by a classmate while she
is babysitting that she begins to understand the real
meaning of fear. Although she is a victim, she is doubted
by her family, friends, and the police. Most unendurable
is the fact that she is forced frequently to cross the path
of her attacker, the son of a prominent member of the
community." Shapiro. Fic for Youth. 3d edition

The great interactive dream machine; another
adventure in cyberspace. Dial Bks. for Young
Readers 1996 149p $14.99; pa $4.99   **Fic**
1. Computers—Fiction 2. Space and time—Fiction
3. School stories
ISBN 0-8037-1989-2; 0-14-038264-X (pa)
           LC 95-53263
Companion volume to Lost in cyberspace
Josh Lewis is unwillingly drawn into the computer experiments of Aaron, his friend and fellow classmate at an
exclusive New York private school, and the two find
themselves uncontrollably transported through space and
time
"Humor, fantasy, science fiction, and even a touch of
mystery all cleverly combine to make this book a guaranteed fun, fast-paced adventure." SLJ

The last safe place on earth. Delacorte Press
1995 161p $15.95; pa $4.50 (7 and up) **Fic**
1. Censorship—Fiction 2. Family life—Fiction
3. Christian fundamentalism—Fiction
ISBN 0-385-32052-3; 0-440-22007-6 (pa)
           LC 94-446
Fifteen-year-old Todd sees his perfect suburban world
start to unravel when his little sister has her mind poisoned by a member of a fundamentalist sect and he begins to notice signs of censorship in his community

"Peck writes with wit and warmth that will sweep
teens into a world they'll recognize. He has a sharp eye
for the poetic image that captures the contemporary
scene." Booklist

A long way from Chicago; a novel in stories.
Dial Bks. for Young Readers 1998 148p $15.99
           Fic
1. Grandmothers—Fiction 2. Great Depression, 1929-
1939—Fiction
ISBN 0-8037-2290-7   LC 98-10953
A Newbery Medal honor book, 1999
Joe recounts his annual summer trips to rural Illinois
with his sister during the Great Depression to visit their
larger-than-life grandmother
"The novel reveals a strong sense of place, a depth of
characterization, and a rich sense of humor." Horn Book

Lost in cyberspace. Dial Bks. for Young
Readers 1995 151p $14.99; pa $4.99   **Fic**
1. Space and time—Fiction 2. School stories
3. Brothers and sisters—Fiction
ISBN 0-8037-1931-0; 0-14-037856-1 (pa)
           LC 94-48330
Companion volume to The great interactive dream machine
While dealing with changes at home, sixth-grader Josh
and his friend Aaron use the computer at their New York
prep school to travel through time, learning some secrets
from the school's past and improving Josh's home situation
This "will appeal to today's computer literate generation while allowing their imaginations to soar. A time-
traveling journey that will keep the reader on the edge
of his seat—or computer." Child Book Rev Serv

Remembering the good times. Delacorte Press
1985 181p o.p.; Dell paperback available $4.50 (7
and up)   **Fic**
1. Suicide—Fiction 2. Friendship—Fiction
ISBN 0-440-97339-2 (pa)   LC 84-19962
This novel focuses on "both friendship and suicide as
a trio of adolescents becomes a pair when one of them
kills himself. Buck, Kate & Trav have been friends for
four years—since they were 12 or 13. . . . When Trav
first shoplifts and then commits suicide, Kate and Buck
wonder if they ever really knew him at all." Voice Youth
Advocates
"This is a sad book but not a morbid one, and it's
written with insight and a saving humor." Bull Cent
Child Books

Strays like us. Dial Bks. 1998 155p $15.99
           Fic
ISBN 0-8037-2291-5   LC 97-18575
When her drug-addict mother can no longer care for
her, twelve-year-old Molly comes to stay with her great-
aunt and slowly begins to realize that others in the small
town also feel as if they don't belong
This novel's "easy-flowing action readily absorbs the
reader into the lives of contemporary characters and a realistic, believable plot." Voice Youth Advocates

Peck, Richard, 1934-—*Continued*

Voices after midnight. Delacorte Press 1989
181p hardcover o.p. paperback available $4.50
Fic
1. Space and time—Fiction 2. Brothers and sisters—
Fiction 3. New York (N.Y.)—Fiction
ISBN 0-440-40378-2 (pa)   LC 89-1099
Living with their sister and parents in a rented house
in New York City during the summer, Chad and Luke
uncover a mystery involving the former tenants of the
house when the two brothers slip back in time to 1888
This is a "typical Peck page-turner, intelligently plotted, peopled with engagingly believable characters, and
filled with brand names, topical references, and slyly humorous send-ups of trendy teens." SLJ

Peck, Robert Newton, 1928-

Cowboy ghost. HarperCollins Pubs. 1999 200p
$15.95; lib bdg $15.89   **Fic**
1. Cowhands—Fiction 2. Brothers—Fiction 3. Fathers
and sons—Fiction 4. Florida—Fiction
ISBN 0-06-028168-5; 0-06-028211-8 (lib bdg)
LC 98-34915
Growing up without a mother and with an aloof father
on a cattle ranch in Florida in the first part of the 1900s
has made Titus very close to his older brother, Micah,
and determined to make Micah proud of him when the
two go on their first cattle drive together
"The imaginative metaphors, salty language, and winning protagonist will engage readers." Bull Cent Child
Books

A day no pigs would die. Knopf 1973 c1972
150p $24; pa $4.99   **Fic**
1. Shakers—Fiction 2. Farm life—Fiction 3. Vermont—Fiction
ISBN 0-394-48235-2; 0-679-85306-5 (pa)
"Rob lives a rigorous life on a Shaker farm in Vermont in the 1920s. Since farm life is earthy, this book
is filled with Yankee humor and explicit descriptions of
animals mating. A painful incident that involves the
slaughter of Rob's beloved pet pig is instrumental in urg-
ing him toward adulthood. The death of his father completes the process of his accepting responsibility." Shapiro. Fic for Youth. 3d edition

Nine man tree; a novel. Random House 1998
170p lib bdg $18.99   **Fic**
1. Family life—Fiction 2. Everglades (Fla.)—Fiction
ISBN 0-679-89257-5   LC 97-43624
In Depression-era Florida, eleven-year-old Yoolee assumes the responsibility of protecting his family from the
wild boarhog which is terrorizing the people of the Everglades
"Peck's descriptive prose, obvious respect for his characters, and reverence for untamed nature combine with
an authentic feel for the vernacular of the region to
transport readers smoothly to another time and place."
Booklist

Petry, Ann Lane

Tituba of Salem Village; [by] Ann Petry.
Crowell 1964 254p $14.95; pa $4.95   **Fic**
1. Tituba—Fiction 2. Salem (Mass.)—Fiction
3. Witchcraft—Fiction 4. African Americans—Fiction
ISBN 0-690-82677-X; 0-06-440403-X (pa)
LC 64-20691
"From the beauty of the island of Barbados, Tituba is
uprooted to the dreary, gray cold of Boston. As the slave
in the household of the minister, Samuel Parris, Tituba
cooks, nurses, and attends to his sickly wife, daughter,
and niece. When the minister moves to a new post in Salem Village, Tituba becomes the central figure in a
witchcraft trial." Shapiro. Fic for Youth. 3d edition

Pevsner, Stella

Sing for your father, Su Phan; by Stella Pevsner
and Fay Tang. Clarion Bks. 1997 107p $14   **Fic**
1. Vietnam—Fiction 2. Vietnam War, 1961-1975—
Fiction 3. Fathers and daughters—Fiction
ISBN 0-395-82267-X   LC 97-4290
This "is a fictionalized account of Tang's childhood in
Vietnam during the war and told through a young girl's
eyes. A once proud and affluent family is cast into poverty when the father is taken prisoner for failure to join
the Communist party. . . . The story of these courageous
people is told in a simple and moving way and will
serve as an introduction to the conflict in Vietnam for
the middle school reader." Book Rep

Would my fortune cookie lie? Clarion Bks.
1996 186p $14.95   **Fic**
1. Moving—Fiction 2. Mystery fiction 3. Family
life—Fiction
ISBN 0-395-73082-1   LC 95-36720
While worrying that her mom is plotting to move the
family from their Chicago home, thirteen-year-old Alexis
also wonders about the mysterious young man who
seems to be shadowing her and her friend
"The many sympathetic characters and the frequent
twists of plot will keep the pages turning. Graced with
an unusually appealing jacket, this novel will intrigue
and involve readers from beginning to end." Booklist

Pfeffer, Susan Beth, 1948-

The year without Michael. Bantam Bks. 1987
164p hardcover o.p. paperback available $4.50
Fic
1. Missing children—Fiction 2. Family life—Fiction
ISBN 0-553-27373-6 (pa)   LC 87-11474
"Thirteen year old Michael disappears on a Sunday afternoon. His family may never know what happened to
him but they will hope and search until he's found. It
falls upon Jody, Michael's older sister, to hold the family
together as the stress and uncertainty mount." BAYA
Book Rev
"This offers "taut structuring, sound characterization,
and honest dialogue." SLJ

Pfitsch, Patricia Curtis

Keeper of the light. Simon & Schuster Bks. for
Young Readers 1997 137p $16   **Fic**
1. Lighthouses—Fiction 2. Sex role—Fiction
3. Michigan—Fiction
ISBN 0-689-81492-5   LC 96-39745

Pfitsch, Patricia Curtis—Continued

After her father's death in 1872, Faith takes over his job as lighthouse keeper on Lake Superior, until her mother decides to move into town, where Faith finds herself stifled by the role society expects her to play

"The historical novel moves quickly, and Faith is a strong heroine who refuses to fit the model of femininity around her." Horn Book Guide

Philbrick, W. R. (W. Rodman)

The fire pony; [by] Rodman Philbrick. Blue Sky Press (NY) 1996 175p $14.95; pa $4.50   **Fic**
1. Brothers—Fiction 2. Horses—Fiction 3. Ranch life—Fiction
ISBN 0-590-55251-1; 0-590-56862-0 (pa)
                     LC 95-43330

Eleven-year-old Roy lets himself find a loving family and a new home on the horse ranch which he and his older half-brother happen to come upon

"Philbrick offers lots of interesting details about ranch life and training and racing horses, but it's the tension that will hook readers till the dramatic conclusion." Booklist

Freak the Mighty; [by] Rodman Philbrick. Blue Sky Press (NY) 1993 169p $14.95; pa $3.99   **Fic**
1. Learning disabilities—Fiction 2. Physically handicapped—Fiction 3. Friendship—Fiction
ISBN 0-590-47412-X; 0-590-47413-8 (pa)
                     LC 93-19913

"Large, awkward, learning-disabled Maxwell Kane, whose father is in prison for murdering his mother, and crippled, undersized Kevin are both mocked by their peers. . . . The boys establish a friendship—and a partnership. Kevin defends them with his intelligence, while Max is his friend's 'legs,' affording him a chance to participate in the larger world. Inspired by tales of King Arthur, they become knights fighting for good and true causes. But Kevin's illness progresses, and when he dies, Max is left with the memories of an extraordinary relationship and, perhaps, the insight to think positively about himself and his future." SLJ

"The story is both riveting and poignant, with solid characters, brisk pacing, and even a little humor to carry us along." Booklist

Followed by Max the Mighty

Max the Mighty; [by] Rodman Philbrick. Blue Sky Press (NY) 1998 166p $16.95; pa $3.99   **Fic**
1. Runaway teenagers—Fiction 2. Friendship—Fiction
ISBN 0-590-18892-5; 0-590-57964-9 (pa)
                     LC 97-11762

In this sequel to Freak the Mighty, fourteen-year-old Max helps a younger girl escape from her abusive stepfather by running away with her to the distant town of Chivalry, Montana, searching for her real father

"The book, like Max, possesses a rueful and rawboned sparkle that makes it engaging." Bull Cent Child Books

Pierce, Meredith Ann, 1958-

A gathering of gargoyles. Little, Brown 1984 263p o.p.; Harcourt Brace & Co. paperback available $6 (7 and up)   **Fic**
1. Fantasy fiction
ISBN 0-15-201801-8 (pa)   LC 84-12195
Sequel to The darkangel (1982)
"An Atlantic Monthly Press book"

In this second volume of the trilogy "the quest to defeat the darkangels and their evil creator continues as Aeriel and Irrylath, whom Aeriel rescued from his enchantment before his transformation from mortal to darkangel was complete, escape to Esternesse." Booklist

The author "is intensely visual, even poetic, in her descriptions and imaginative in her surprising plot turns. And she is strong in her overall conception of a courageous, loving girl who is both compassionate and determined." N Y Times Book Rev

Followed by The pearl of the soul of the world

The pearl of the soul of the world. Little, Brown 1990 243p o.p.; Harcourt Brace & Co. paperback available $6 (7 and up)   **Fic**
1. Fantasy fiction
ISBN 0-15-201800-X (pa)   LC 89-31647
"Joy Street books"

The third volume in the Darkangel trilogy. With the aid of a shimmering pearl, Ariel battles the White Witch to free her husband Irrylath

"The great strength of the story, besides the wraithlike, haunting heroine, is the style, with shimmering, fragile textures and delicate, shadowy descriptions." Horn Book

Pierce, Tamora, 1954-

Circle of magic: Briar's book. Scholastic Press 1999 258p $15.95   **Fic**
1. Fantasy fiction
ISBN 0-590-55359-3   LC 98-26148
Fourth in the Circle of magic fantasy series. Briar, a young mage-in-training, and his teacher Rosethorn must use their magic to fight a deadly plague that is ravaging Summersea

"An entirely satisfying, carefully crafted fantasy." Booklist

Circle of magic: Daja's book. Scholastic Press 1998 234p $15.95   **Fic**
1. Fantasy fiction
ISBN 0-590-55358-5   LC 97-44825
Third in the Circle of magic fantasy series. While at Gold Ridge castle to the north of Winding Circle, Daja and the three other mages-in-training who have become her friends develop their unique magical talents as they try to prevent a devastating forest fire from consuming everything in its path

"With lots of action, drama and excitement, vibrant characters and fascinating detail, this is a sure winner." Voice Youth Advocates

Circle of magic: Sandry's book. Scholastic 1997 252p $15.95   **Fic**
1. Fantasy fiction
ISBN 0-590-55356-9   LC 95-39540

Pierce, Tamora, 1954-—*Continued*

First in the The Circle of magic fantasy series. Sandry and three other young misfits find themselves living in a strictly disciplined community called Winding Circle Temple where they become friends while also learning to do crafts and to use their powers, especially magic

"Pierce has created an excellent new world where magic is a science and utterly believable and populated it with a cast of well-realized characters." Booklist

Circle of magic: Tris's book. Scholastic 1998 251p $15.95 **Fic**
1. Fantasy fiction
ISBN 0-590-55357-7   LC 97-8521

Second in the Circle of magic fantasy series. With the defenses of Winding Circle Temple seriously weakened by an earthquake, Tris and her fellow mages-in-training try to join their different magic powers to protect the Winding Circle community from a pirate attack

"While the plot has all the dashing derring-do fantasy readers yearn for . . . it is the depiction of the relationships among the four friends and their mentors that provides the emotional core that will hold readers." Bull Cent Child Books

First test. Random House 1999 216p (Protector of the small) $16; lib bdg $17.99; pa $4.99 **Fic**
1. Fantasy fiction
ISBN 0-679-88914-0; 0-679-98914-5 (lib bdg); 0-679-88917-5 (pa)   LC 98-30903

Set in the imaginary kingdom of Tortall, setting for the author's Lioness quartet and the Immortals series

First title in the projected Protector of the small series. Ten-year-old Keladry of Mindalen, daughter of nobles, serves as a page but must prove herself to the males around her if she is ever to fulfill her dream of becoming a knight

"Pierce spins a whopping good yarn, her plot balanced on a solid base of action and characterization." Bull Cent Child Books

Wolf-speaker. Atheneum Pubs. 1994 182p (Immortals) $16.95 **Fic**
1. Fantasy fiction
ISBN 0-689-31833-2   LC 93-21909

Also available in paperback from Random House

"A Jean Karl book"

With the help of her animal friends, Daine fights to save the kingdom of Tortall from ambitious mortals and dangerous immortals

"Pierce has created a story that combines the true elements of fantasy with well-developed characters and plot." Book Rep

Other available titles in the Immortals series are:
The Emperor Mage (1995)
The realms of the gods (1996)
Wild magic (1992)

Pinkney, Andrea Davis

Hold fast to dreams. Morrow Junior Bks. 1995 106p $16 **Fic**
1. Moving—Fiction 2. Prejudices—Fiction 3. African Americans—Fiction
ISBN 0-688-12832-7   LC 94-32909

Also available in paperback from Hyperion Bks.

"When 12-year-old Deirdre's father gets a new job in New York City, the family relocates from Baltimore to suburban Connecticut. There are few blacks in Wexford and the white kids whisper and stare. . . . Deirdre, however, pursues her interest in photography and makes a friend." SLJ

"Pinkney is candid about the pain and loss as well as the achievement, and the docunovel is enlivened by characters drawn with warmth and wit." Booklist

Raven in a dove house. Harcourt Brace & Co. 1998 208p $16 **Fic**
1. African Americans—Fiction 2. Cousins—Fiction
ISBN 0-15-201461-6   LC 97-36180

Also available in paperback from Hyperion Bks.

"Gulliver books"

While twelve-year-old Nell and her fourteen-year-old cousin struggle with the loss of parents and other hardships, both African American youths learn to rely on themselves

"Shifting moods, increasing tension, and a well-defined setting make this novel compelling and thought-provoking." SLJ

Pinkwater, Daniel Manus, 1941-

The education of Robert Nifkin; [by] Daniel Pinkwater. Farrar, Straus & Giroux 1998 167p $16 (7 and up) **Fic**
1. School stories 2. Chicago (Ill.)—Fiction
ISBN 0-374-31969-3   LC 97-32332

Set in the 1950s in Chicago, Robert Nifkin tells his highly unorthodox high school experiences in the form of a college application essay

"The novel literally crackles and the comedy is occasionally laugh-out-loud funny." Booklist

Plummer, Louise

The unlikely romance of Kate Bjorkman. Delacorte Press 1995 183p hardcover o.p. paperback available $4.50 (7 and up) **Fic**
ISBN 0-440-22704-6 (pa)   LC 94-49614

"Neither writing a romance novel nor starring in one is characteristic of Kate Bjorkman, she freely admits; yet she feels compelled to try both when her brother comes home from college for Christmas with the love of her life, a childhood friend of his. The intelligent, thoroughly entertaining romantic comedy contains many laugh-out-loud moments and shrewd asides on the writing process." Horn Book Guide

Powell, Randy

Tribute to another dead rock star. Farrar, Straus & Giroux 1999 215p $17 (7 and up) **Fic**
1. Mothers and sons—Fiction 2. Brothers—Fiction 3. Mentally handicapped—Fiction
ISBN 0-374-37748-0   LC 98-35522

For a tribute to his mother, a dead rock star, fifteen-year-old Grady returns to Seattle, where he faces his mixed feelings for his retarded younger half-brother Louie while pondering his own future

"The smoothly written novel depicts a real teen with unusual parentage and eloquently portrays the complexities and affections of family life." Horn Book Guide

Pullman, Philip, 1946-
Clockwork; or, All wound up; with illustrations by Leonid Gore. Levine Bks. 1998 c1996 112p il $14.95; pa $4.99   **Fic**
1. Supernatural—Fiction
ISBN 0-590-12999-6; 0-590-12998-8 (pa)
LC 97-27458
First published 1996 in the United Kingdom
Long ago in Germany, a storyteller's story and an apprentice clockwork-maker's nightmare meet in a menacing, lifelike figure created by the strange Dr. Kalmenius
"Pullman laces his tale with subtle humor while maintaining the suspense until the end. Misty, moody, and atmospheric black-and-white drawings by Leonid Gore make a perfect fit for this gothic gem." Voice Youth Advocates

Count Karlstein; decorative illustrations by Diana Bryan. Knopf 1998 c1982 243p $17; lib bdg $18.99; pa $4.99   **Fic**
1. Horror fiction 2. Switzerland—Fiction
ISBN 0-679-89255-9; 0-679-99255-3 (lib bdg); 0-375-80348-3 (pa)   LC 97-44160
First published 1982 in the United Kingdom
In the mountains of Switzerland the wicked Count Karlstein plots to abandon his two nieces in a hunting lodge as prey for the Demon Huntsman and his ghostly hounds
"Dashing, sparkling and wildly over-the-top fun." Publ Wkly

The ruby in the smoke. Knopf 1987 c1985 230p lib bdg $11.99; pa $4.99 (7 and up)   **Fic**
1. Mystery fiction 2. Orphans—Fiction 3. London (England)—Fiction
ISBN 0-394-98826-4 (lib bdg); 0-394-89589-4 (pa)
LC 86-20983
First published 1985 in the United Kingdom
This story "begins in 1872 on a 'cold, fretful' October afternoon in London. Sally Lockhart is the 16-year-old heroine who asks some innocent questions about her father's death that lead her into a world of stolen rubies and the opium trade." N Y Times Book Rev
"Pullman uses a cliff-hanger at the end of each chapter to keep readers enthralled in this fast-paced, intricate, and suspenseful novel. Sally's complex characterization as a resourceful, yet occasionally unsure, young woman, makes her both likable and memorable." Voice Youth Advocates
Followed by Shadow in the North

Shadow in the north. Knopf 1988 c1986 331p hardcover o.p. paperback available $4.99 (7 and up)   **Fic**
1. Mystery fiction 2. London (England)—Fiction
ISBN 0-394-82599-3 (pa)   LC 87-29846
First published 1986 in the United Kingdom with title: The shadow in the plate
Set in Victorian England, this is "a sequel to The Ruby in the Smoke which introduced the photographer Fred Garland and young Sally Lockhart, his financial adviser and partner. . . . A tight, exciting plot is built round the machinations of Bellman, a business man who has murdered his partner and stolen his invention. . . . Terrorism, blackmail and industrial fraud combine with

the romantic relations between Fred and Sally to make a novel of historical interest for technical detail and complex plot." Grow Point
Followed by The tiger in the well

The tiger in the well. Knopf 1990 407p hardcover o.p. paperback available $4.99 (7 and up)   **Fic**
1. Jews—Fiction 2. Mystery fiction 3. London (England)—Fiction
ISBN 0-679-82671-8 (pa)   LC 90-4159
"Sally Lockhart, first met in *Ruby in the Smoke* and *Shadow in the North* is now a young woman, left alone with a toddler since the death of her lover, Frederick Garland. Nothing prepares her for the shock of receiving a summons from a man she has never even heard of, suing her for divorce and the custody of her beloved Harriet. Two other figures emerge: Daniel Goldberg, a Jewish slum radical with a violent past; and the ironically titled Tzaddik (saint), who preys on helpless European Jewish immigrants." SLJ
"Pullman provides a suspenseful, textured mystery. Especially fine is his use of detail—nineteenth-century London comes alive here." Booklist

Qualey, Marsha
Thin ice. Delacorte Press 1997 261p $14.95; pa $4.99 (7 and up)   **Fic**
1. Brothers and sisters—Fiction 2. Orphans—Fiction
ISBN 0-385-32298-4; 0-440-22037-8 (pa)
LC 97-2083
Seventeen-year-old Arden has been raised by her older brother, Scott since their parents died when she was just six years old. When Scott is presumed drowned in a snowmobile accident, Arden is convinced he's really run away
"Hooked by Qualey's . . . full-bodied characters, expertly evoked rural setting and crackerjack pacing, readers will waver, wondering if Arden is on the right track or simply crazed by grief. An edge-of-the-seat adventure." Publ Wkly

Quintana, Anton
The baboon king; translated by John Nieuwenhuizen. Walker & Co. 1999 183p $15.95 (7 and up)   **Fic**
1. Baboons—Fiction 2. Kikuyu (African people)—Fiction 3. Masai (African people)—Fiction 4. Africa—Fiction
ISBN 0-8027-8711-8   LC 99-18322
Son of a Kikuyu mother and a Masai herdsman father, Morengáru the hunter lives on the edges of tribal society until an actual banishment forces him to make a life for himself among a troop of baboons
"The visceral descriptions, explorations of the animals' psychology, and realizations about his own humanity make this a memorable, even mystical novel." SLJ

Rabe, Berniece
Hiding Mr. McMulty. Harcourt Brace & Co. 1997 240p $18   **Fic**
1. Race relations—Fiction 2. Missouri—Fiction
ISBN 0-15-201330-X   LC 96-49144

Rabe, Berniece—*Continued*

"Browndeer Press"

In 1937 in southeastern Missouri, eleven-year-old Rass, son of a proud sharecropper, proves his worth when a flood destroys his family's home and forces his best friend, an elderly black man, into hiding from the Ku Klux Klan

"The edge-of-the-seat adventure is given substance by its exploration of what it means to be a decent human being." Horn Book Guide

Randle, Kristen D., 1952-

Breaking rank. Morrow Junior Bks. 1999 201p $15 (7 and up)   **Fic**

1. Gangs—Fiction 2. School stories

ISBN 0-688-16243-6   LC 98-27867

Seventeen-year-old Casey has some of her preconceived notions challenged when she begins to tutor Baby, a member of a ganglike non-conformist society called the Clan

"The alternating points of view and Randle's taut, poetic prose provide remarkable character depth and complexity. . . . Gritty, smart, and realistic, the novel perceptively explores issues of religion, sex and sexual abstinence, peer pressure, and integrity with grace and compassion." Booklist

Rapp, Adam

The buffalo tree. Front St. 1997 188p $15.95 (7 and up)   **Fic**

1. Juvenile delinquency—Fiction 2. Prisons—Fiction

ISBN 1-886910-19-7   LC 96-54698

While serving a six-month sentence at a juvenile detention center, thirteen-year-old Sura struggles to survive the experience with his spirit intact

"Rapp's prose is powerful, graphic, and haunting. . . . The world that Rapp portrays is often ugly, disturbing, and brutal. . . . An outstanding novel of redemption and survival." SLJ

Raskin, Ellen, 1928-1984

The Westing game. Dutton 1978 185p $15.99; pa $4.99   **Fic**

1. Mystery fiction

ISBN 0-525-42320-6; 0-14-034991-X (pa)

LC 77-18866

Awarded the Newbery medal, 1979

"This mystery puzzle . . . centers on the challenge set forth in the will of eccentric multimillionaire Samuel Westing. Sixteen heirs of diverse backgrounds and ages are assembled in the old 'Westing house,' paired off, and given clues to a puzzle they must solve—apparently in order to inherit." SLJ

"The rules of the game make eight pairs of the players; each oddly matched couple is given a ten thousand dollar check and a set of clues. The result is a fascinating medley of word games, disguises, multiple aliases and subterfuges—in a demanding but rewarding book." Horn Book

Rawlings, Marjorie Kinnan, 1896-1953

The yearling; with pictures by N. C. Wyeth. Scribner 1985 c1938 400p il $27; pa $5.95   **Fic**

1. Florida—Fiction 2. Deer—Fiction

ISBN 0-684-18461-3; 0-02-044931-3 (pa)

LC 85-40301

Also available G.K. Hall large print edition

Reissue of the title first published 1938; awarded Pulitzer Prize, 1939

"Young Jody Baxter lives a lonely life in the scrub forest of Florida until his parents unwillingly consent to his adopting an orphan fawn. The two become inseparable until the fawn destroys the meager crops. Then Jody realizes that this situation offers no compromise. In the sacrifice of what he loves best, he leaves his own yearling days behind." Read Ladders for Hum Relat. 5th edition

"With its excellent descriptions of Florida scrub landscapes, its skillful use of native vernacular, its tender relation between Jody and his pet fawn, The Yearling is a simply written, picturesque story of boyhood." Time

Rawls, Wilson, 1913-

Summer of the monkeys. Doubleday 1976 239p $15.95; pa $5.50 (7 and up)   **Fic**

1. Monkeys—Fiction 2. Oklahoma—Fiction

ISBN 0-385-11450-8; 0-553-29818-6 (pa)

LC 75-32295

"When Jay Berry Lee discovers a passel of valuable circus monkeys living in the river bottoms near his home, he thinks his fortune is made. Armed with his crippled sister's advice and his grandpa's ingenious traps, he sets out with the family hound dog to catch the critters, collect the reward, and buy himself the pony and the gun he's always wanted. Nobody, least of all Jay Berry, reckons on the comical problems 29 smart monkeys can make for a 14-year-old Oklahoma farm boy. . . . A heartwarming story that escapes a trite conclusion via a fine blend of folksy humor and delightful characterization." Booklist

Where the red fern grows; the story of two dogs and a boy. Bantam Bks. 212p $16.95; pa $5.50

Fic

1. Dogs—Fiction 2. Ozark Mountains—Fiction

ISBN 0-385-32330-1; 0-440-41267-6 (pa)

First published 1961 by Doubleday

"Looking back more than 50 years to his boyhood in the Ozarks, the narrator recalls how he achieved his heart's desire in the ownership of two redbone hounds, how he taught them all the tricks of hunting, and how they won the championship coon hunt before Old Dan was killed by a mountain lion and Little Ann died of grief. Although some readers may find this novel hackneyed and entirely too sentimental, others will enjoy the fine coonhunting episodes and appreciate the author's feelings for nature." Booklist

Reeder, Carolyn, 1937-

Across the lines. Atheneum Bks. for Young Readers 1997 220p $16   **Fic**

1. United States—History—1861-1865, Civil War—Fiction 2. African Americans—Fiction 3. Race relations—Fiction

ISBN 0-689-81133-0   LC 96-31068

Reeder, Carolyn, 1937—— *Continued*

Also available in paperback from Avon Bks.

Edward, the son of a white plantation owner, and his black house servant and friend Simon witness the siege of Petersburg during the Civil War

"Twelve-year-old Edward and his family flee to Petersburg just before the Yankees capture their Virginia plantation; Simon, Edward's former slave and companion, performs various jobs for Union troops advancing on the same city. During the span of a year, the boys make parallel journeys toward a deeper understanding of the complex nature of freedom and friendship. Told in the alternating voices of Edward and Simon, this thoughtful Civil War story resonates with authenticity." Horn Book Guide

Captain Kate. Avon Bks. 1999 210p $15 **Fic**
1. Canals—Fiction 2. Brothers and sisters—Fiction 3. United States—History—1861-1865, Civil War—Fiction
ISBN 0-380-97628-5 LC 98-24845

During the Civil War twelve-year-old Kate enlists the help of her stepbrother Seth in taking the family's coal-carrying barge down the Cumberland and Ohio Canal

"The story has plenty of action and detailed descriptions of boats and life along the waterway. Tension builds gradually and is released at exact moments." SLJ

Foster's war. Scholastic Press 1998 267p $16.95
Fic
1. World War, 1939-1945—Fiction 2. Fathers and sons—Fiction
ISBN 0-590-09846-2 LC 97-10682

When his older brother joins the army during World War II in order to escape the rages of an authoritarian father, eleven-year-old Foster fights his battles on the homefront

"An excellent evocation of life in America during the Second World War. Written in a simple, straightforward manner." Voice Youth Advocates

Shades of gray. Macmillan 1989 152p $15
Fic
1. Orphans—Fiction 2. Uncles—Fiction 3. United States—History—1861-1865, Civil War—Fiction
ISBN 0-02-775810-9 LC 89-31976
Also available in paperback from Avon Bks.

At the end of the Civil War, twelve-year-old Will, having lost all his immediate family, reluctantly leaves his city home to live in the Virginia countryside with his aunt and the uncle he considers a "traitor" because he refused to take part in the war

"Minor plot threads (Will's adjustment to rural life, his relationships with the local boys and his affection for his cousin Meg) provide changes of tone and tempo in a novel that has, despite an uneven pace, both momentum and nuance." Bull Cent Child Books

Rees, Douglas C.

Lightning Time; a novel; by Douglas Rees. DK Ink 1997 166p $15.95 **Fic**
1. Brown, John, 1800-1859—Fiction 2. Abolitionists—Fiction 3. Slavery—Fiction
ISBN 0-7894-2458-4 LC 97-31028
Also available in paperback from Puffin Bks.
"A Richard Jackson book"

Fourteen-year-old Theodore Worth struggles with the decision to leave his home in Boston and join the controversial abolitionist John Brown in the fight against slavery

"Rees has created a fine historical novel that explores the complexities of the abolitionist cause. The first-person narrative is fast-paced, the historical setting laid out only when necessary to the plot." Horn Book

Reiss, Kathryn

PaperQuake; a puzzle. Harcourt Brace & Co. 1998 264p $17 **Fic**
1. Sisters—Fiction 2. Earthquakes—Fiction 3. San Francisco (Calif.)—Fiction 4. Mystery fiction
ISBN 0-15-201183-8 LC 97-33217

Certain that she is being drawn by more than coincidences into the lives of people living nearly 100 years ago, Violet, who feels like the odd sister in a set of triplets, searches for clues to help her avert an imminent tragedy

"Themes of adventure and family relationships, heightened by an atmospheric sense of place, are deftly woven into this clever and skillfully written mystery." Horn Book Guide

Richter, Conrad, 1890-1968

The light in the forest. Knopf 1953 179p o.p.; Fawcett Bks. paperback available $4.99 **Fic**
1. Frontier and pioneer life—Fiction 2. Delaware Indians—Fiction
ISBN 0-449-70437-8 (pa) LC 52-12207
Also available in hardcover from Amereon
Companion volume to A country of strangers (1966)

"A boy stolen in early childhood and brought up by the Delawares is at fifteen suddenly returned to the family he has forgotten. He resents his loss of independence, hates the brutality of the white man's civilization, and longs only for a return to the Indians whom he remembers as peace-loving and kind. His return to the Delawares does not, however, bring him peace; rather, he must make a bitter choice between helping his Indian brothers kill a group of unsuspecting white men or helping the white men escape. This is both vivid re-creation of outdoor life and a provocative study in conflicting loyalties." Horn Book

Rinaldi, Ann, 1934-

An acquaintance with darkness. Harcourt Brace & Co. 1997 294p (Great episodes) $16; pa $6 (7 and up) **Fic**
1. Lincoln, Abraham, 1809-1865—Assassination—Fiction 2. Physicians—Fiction
ISBN 0-15-201294-X; 0-15-202197-3 (pa)
LC 96-51008

When her mother dies and her best friend's family is implicated in the assassination of President Lincoln, fourteen-year-old Emily Pigbush must go live with an uncle she suspects of being involved in stealing bodies for medical research

"The setting of this easy read is authentically described and skillfully intertwined with the story." Voice Youth Advocates

Rinaldi, Ann, 1934-—*Continued*

Cast two shadows; the American revolution in the South. Harcourt Brace & Co. 1998 281p (Great episodes) $16; pa $3.95 (7 and up)   **Fic**
1. United States—History—1775-1783, Revolution—Fiction 2. South Carolina—Fiction
ISBN 0-15-200881-0; 0-15-200882-9 (pa)
LC 98-4770
"Gulliver books"

In South Carolina in 1780, fourteen-year-old Caroline sees the Revolutionary War take a terrible toll among her family and friends and comes to understand the true nature of war

"Rinaldi has incorporated prodigious historical research and provocative themes to produce a deftly plotted and fast-paced novel." SLJ

The fifth of March; a story of the Boston Massacre. Harcourt Brace & Co. 1993 335p (Great episodes) $12; pa $6 (7 and up)   **Fic**
1. Adams family—Fiction 2. Boston Massacre, 1770—Fiction 3. United States—History—1600-1775, Colonial period—Fiction
ISBN 0-15-200343-6; 0-15-227517-7 (pa)
LC 93-17821
"Gulliver books"

Fourteen-year-old Rachel Marsh, an indentured servant in the Boston household of John and Abigail Adams, is caught up in the colonists' unrest that eventually escalates into the massacre of March 5, 1770

"The story moves along briskly, and details of life in 18th-century Boston are woven into the narrative." SLJ

Hang a thousand trees with ribbons; the story of Phillis Wheatley. Harcourt Brace & Co. 1996 336p $12; pa $6 (7 and up)   **Fic**
1. Wheatley, Phillis, 1753-1784—Fiction 2. African Americans—Fiction 3. Slavery—Fiction 4. United States—History—1600-1775, Colonial period—Fiction
ISBN 0-15-200876-4; 0-15-200877-2 (pa)
LC 96-872

A fictionalized biography of the eighteenth-century African woman who, as a child, was brought to New England to be a slave, and after publishing her first poem when a teenager, gained renown throughout the colonies as an important black American poet

"Rinaldi blends history, romance, and drama into an inspiring novel that will leave a lasting impression on readers and broaden their understanding of slavery in colonial America." Book Rep

In my father's house. Scholastic 1993 323p $14.95; pa $4.99 (7 and up)   **Fic**
1. United States—History—1861-1865, Civil War—Fiction 2. Stepfathers—Fiction
ISBN 0-590-44730-0; 0-590-44731-9 (pa)
LC 91-46839

"The story is told from the point of view of Osceola, Wilmer McLean's stepdaughter. Bull Run, the first battle of the war, is fought on the McLean's land and their home is damaged. Flashbacks review pre-War events and develop family characters. The narrative ends in 1865 at Appomattox Court House when Grant receives Lee's surrender in the parlor of the family's new home. . . . Even reluctant history students will enjoy learning about the Civil War by reading this work." Book Rep

Keep smiling through. Harcourt Brace & Co. 1996 188p $12; pa $6 (7 and up)   **Fic**
1. World War, 1939-1945—Fiction 2. German Americans—Fiction
ISBN 0-15-200768-7; 0-15-201072-6 (pa)
LC 95-31214

"Kay is a ten-year-old girl living in the country during World War II. . . . When Kay accidentally overhears a conversation between her grandfather and a local merchant, she learns that the German shopkeeper is loyal to Germany and is distributing pamphlets to American Germans for the Motherland. She fears invoking the wrath of her stepmother by getting her grandfather in trouble, but she feels that it is more important to tell the truth than to protect herself." Voice Youth Advocates

"Kay's vulnerability spills across the entire novel, bathing it in poignancy and enveloping the reader in its old-fashioned, bittersweet truths." Publ Wkly

Mine eyes have seen. Scholastic 1998 273p $16.95 (7 and up)   **Fic**
1. Brown, John, 1800-1859—Fiction 2. Harpers Ferry (W. Va.)—History—John Brown's Raid, 1859—Fiction 3. Abolitionists—Fiction 4. Fathers and daughters—Fiction
ISBN 0-590-54318-0
LC 97-10680

In the summer of 1859, fifteen-year-old Annie travels to the Maryland farm where her father, John Brown, is secretly assembling his provisional army prior to their raid on the United States arsenal at nearby Harpers Ferry

This "is a poignant and deeply moving tale based on extensive research into the life of the real Annie Brown." SLJ

The second bend in the river. Scholastic 1997 279p $15.95 (7 and up)   **Fic**
1. Tecumseh, Shawnee Chief, 1768-1813—Fiction 2. Shawnee Indians—Fiction 3. Frontier and pioneer life—Fiction
ISBN 0-590-74258-2
LC 96-25938

In 1798 Rebecca, a young settler in the Ohio territory, meets the Shawnee called Tecumseh and later develops a deep friendship with him

"Rinaldi weaves a powerfully romantic tale of two Americans from the colonial era. Her attention to period details . . . and careful separation of fact from fiction strengthen the credibility of the story without diminishing any of its appeal." Booklist

A stitch in time. Scholastic 1994 305p $13.95; pa $3.99 (7 and up)   **Fic**
1. Family life—Fiction 2. Quilting—Fiction 3. Frontier and pioneer life—Fiction
ISBN 0-590-46055-2; 0-590-46056-0 (pa)
LC 93-8964

This is the first volume of the Quilt trilogy

"The Chelmsfords of Massachusetts are a respected merchant family after the War of Independence. But there are shadows and silences that Hannah can't understand. Her father behaves unfairly toward her and sister Abigail while favoring a third daughter. The night before the sisters go their separate ways, they divide up fabrics intended for a family quilt." Publisher's note

Followed by Broken days (1995)

Rinaldi, Ann, 1934——_Continued_
Wolf by the ears. Scholastic 1991 252p $13.95;
pa $4.99 (7 and up)   **Fic**
1. Jefferson, Thomas, 1743-1826—Fiction 2. Slavery—Fiction 3. African Americans—Fiction
ISBN 0-590-43413-6; 0-590-43412-8 (pa)
                                        LC 90-40563
"Set at Monticello from 1819-1822, this provocative
historical novel deals with the conflicts of teenage Harriet Hemings, daughter of the slave Sally and allegedly of
Thomas Jefferson. A member of two worlds, Harriet is
confused about the truth of her parentage, her love of her
master, her need to leave home and people she loves,
and her eventual plan to pass as white." ALAN

Ritter, John H., 1951-
Choosing up sides. Philomel Bks. 1998 166p
$15.99   **Fic**
1. Left- and right-handedness—Fiction 2. Fathers and
sons—Fiction 3. Baseball—Fiction
ISBN 0-399-23185-4   LC 97-39779
"In 1921 Ohio, a minister's son is condemned by his
father because of his natural inclination for using his left
hand. Luke discovers he has a talent for playing baseball,
although Pa disdains sports—especially a game that utilizes Luke's 'evil' hand." Horn Book Guide
"This is an entertaining and thought-provoking coming-of-age story." Book Rep

Roberts, Willo Davis
The kidnappers. Atheneum Bks. for Young
Readers 1998 137p $15; pa $4.50   **Fic**
1. Kidnapping—Fiction 2. Wealth—Fiction 3. New
York (N.Y.)—Fiction
ISBN 0-689-81394-5; 0-689-81393-7 (pa)
                                        LC 96-53677
"A Jean Karl book"
No one believes eleven-year-old Joey, who has a repu-
tation for telling tall tales, when he claims to have wit-
nessed the kidnapping of the class bully outside their ex-
pensive New York City private school
"The combination of a witty narrative and a suspense-
ful plot makes this a good page-turner that will leave
even the most reluctant readers glued to their seats."
Booklist

Pawns. Atheneum Bks. for Young Readers 1998
154p $16   **Fic**
1. Mystery fiction 2. Orphans—Fiction 3. Death—
Fiction 4. Swindlers and swindling—Fiction
ISBN 0-689-81668-5   LC 97-36505
"A Jean Karl book"
After her mother's death and her father's suicide,
fourteen-year-old Teddi finds some stability when she
moves in with Mamie, her good-hearted next door neighbor—until the arrival of a woman claiming to be the
pregnant wife of Mamie's son who recently died in a
plane crash
"Roberts blends the elements of mystery and suspense,
a budding romance, and coming to terms with traumatic
events of the past into a taut, well-constructed plot." SLJ

Twisted summer. Atheneum Bks. for Young
Readers 1996 156p $15; pa $3.99   **Fic**
1. Mystery fiction
ISBN 0-689-80459-8; 0-689-80600-0 (pa)
                                          LC 95-585

"A Jean Karl book"
Fourteen-year-old Cici hopes for a romantic summer
at the beach but instead finds herself trying to solve a
murder which had occurred there the previous year
"The brisk pace of this suspenseful murder mystery
lures readers right to the gripping ending. . . . This is a
well-crafted, sophisticated story." SLJ

What are we going to do about David?
Atheneum Pubs. 1993 164p $16   **Fic**
1. Parent and child—Fiction 2. Grandmothers—Fiction
ISBN 0-689-31793-X   LC 92-4726
"A Jean Karl book"
Upset that his parents do not seem to pay any attention to him or care about him, eleven-year-old David becomes even more worried when they deposit him for the
summer with a grandmother he hardly knows so that
they can go about their own busy lives
"This first-person novel has convincing situations and
characters. . . . Fans of Roberts' popular mysteries will
appreciate the suspense that permeates this realistic story
about one boy's fate." Booklist

Robinet, Harriette Gillem, 1931-
Forty acres and maybe a mule. Atheneum Bks.
for Young Readers 1998 132p $16   **Fic**
1. African Americans—Fiction 2. Reconstruction
(1865-1876)—Fiction 3. United States—History—
1865-1898—Fiction
ISBN 0-689-82078-X   LC 97-39169
"A Jean Karl book"
Born with a withered leg and hand, Pascal, who is
about twelve years old, joins other former slaves in a
search for a farm and the freedom which it promises
"Robinet skillfully balances her in-depth historical
knowledge with the feelings of her characters, creating a
story that moves along rapidly and comes to a bittersweet conclusion." Booklist

Washington City is burning. Atheneum Bks. for
Young Readers 1996 149p map $16   **Fic**
1. Madison, Dolley, 1768-1849—Fiction 2. United
States—History—1812-1815, War of 1812—Fiction
3. Slavery—Fiction
ISBN 0-689-80773-2   LC 95-33382
"A Jean Karl book"
"Robinet has used some events of the War of 1812
and other historical facts as the background for this first-
person fictionalized narrative. Virginia, or Virgie as
Dolley Madison insists on calling her, recounts her life
as a young slave of James and Dolley Madison. . . .
Robinet evokes both empathy and dislike for her young
heroine as Virginia recounts how she foolishly reveals
secret information about slave escapes. . . . An above-
average choice for historical-fiction shelves." SLJ

Robinson, Barbara
The best Christmas pageant ever; pictures by
Judith Gwyn Brown. Harper & Row 1972 80p il
$14.95; lib bdg $14.89; pa $4.95   **Fic**
1. Christmas—Fiction 2. Pageants—Fiction
ISBN 0-06-025043-7; 0-06-025044-5 (lib bdg);
0-06-440275-4 (pa)   LC 72-76501

Robinson, Barbara—*Continued*

In this story the six Herdmans, "absolutely the worst kids in the history of the world," discover the meaning of Christmas when they bully their way into the leading roles of the local church nativity play

"Although there is a touch of sentiment at the end . . . the story otherwise romps through the festive preparations with comic relish, and if the Herdmans are so gauche as to seem exaggerated, they are still enjoyable, as are the not-so-subtle pokes at pageant-planning in general." Bull Cent Child Books

The best school year ever. HarperCollins Pubs. 1994 117p $14.95; lib bdg $14.89; pa $4.95 **Fic**
1. School stories
ISBN 0-06-023039-8; 0-06-023043-6 (lib bdg); 0-06-440492-7 (pa)   LC 93-50891

In this sequel to The best Christmas pageant ever, the horrible Herdmans, cause mayhem throughout the school year

This will "have children laughing out loud at the Herdmans' antics and believing that even such remarkably *bad* kids have some good qualities." Booklist

Rocklin, Joanne

For your eyes only! illustrations by Mark Todd. Scholastic 1997 136p il $14.95 **Fic**
1. School stories 2. Poetry—Fiction
ISBN 0-590-67447-1   LC 95-39532

The entries in the journals of two sixth grade students reveal much about their personal feelings, family lives, and a growing interest in poetry sparked by their new substitute teacher

"The journals move the plot quickly along and express a range of emotions. The entries adeptly show how the characters grow emotionally as well as artistically; the writing and situations are realistic and believable." SLJ

Rodgers, Mary, 1931-

Freaky Friday. Harper & Row 1972 145p $15.95; lib bdg $15.89; pa $4.95 **Fic**
1. Mothers and daughters—Fiction
ISBN 0-06-025048-8; 0-06-025049-6 (lib bdg); 0-06-080392-4 (pa)

"'When I woke up this morning, I found I'd turned into my mother.' So begins the most bizarre day in the life of 13-year old Annabel Andrews, who discovers one Friday morning she has taken on her mother's physical characteristics while retaining her own personality. Readers will giggle in anticipation as Annabel plunges madly from one disaster to another trying to cope with various adult situations." Publ Wkly

"There's nothing didactic here; the story bubbles along in fine style as Annabel sees herself as others see her . . . and adjusts to the rigors of her mother's problems and the inevitable complications of changed roles. A fresh, imaginative, and entertaining story." Bull Cent Child Books

Followed by A billion for Boris (1974)

Rodowsky, Colby F., 1932-

Hannah in between; [by] Colby Rodowsky. Farrar, Straus & Giroux 1994 151p $15 **Fic**
1. Alcoholism—Fiction 2. Mothers and daughters—Fiction
ISBN 0-374-32837-4   LC 93-35478

Also available in paperback from Troll

As she starts seventh grade, twelve-year-old Hannah can no longer ignore her mother's increasingly erratic behavior caused by drinking

"This heartrending novel offers a frank, sensitive depiction of alcoholism and its effects." Publ Wkly

Remembering Mog. Farrar, Straus & Giroux 1996 135p $14 (7 and up) **Fic**
1. Homicide—Fiction 2. Death—Fiction 3. Family life—Fiction
ISBN 0-374-34663-1   LC 95-30616

Also available in paperback from Avon Bks.

After graduating from a private high school in Baltimore, Annie comes to terms with the loss of her sister who had been murdered two years earlier

"Rodowsky touchingly depicts the barrenness, anger, and yearning that are part of bereavement; the authentic twist of Annie's guilt and confusion at growing beyond her older sister . . . sets this title apart from many on the subject." Bull Cent Child Books

The Turnabout Shop; [by] Colby Rodowsky. Farrar, Straus & Giroux 1998 135p $16 **Fic**
1. Mothers and daughters—Fiction 2. Death—Fiction 3. Orphans—Fiction
ISBN 0-374-37889-4   LC 97-33229

In "conversations" with her dead mother, fifth-grader Livvy records her adjustment to living in Baltimore with a woman she had never met, and she comes to see the wisdom of her mother's choice as she gets to know the woman's large, loving family

"The characters are all well developed and the situations are entirely believable. What stands out most here, though, is Livvy's voice. Its blend of humor and heartbreak makes this a very real and unforgettable novel." SLJ

Rostkowski, Margaret I., 1945-

After the dancing days; a novel. Harper & Row 1986 217p $14; lib bdg $14.89; pa $4.95 **Fic**
1. World War, 1914-1918—Fiction 2. Physically handicapped—Fiction
ISBN 0-06-025077-1; 0-06-025078-X (lib bdg); 0-06-440248-7 (pa)   LC 85-45810

"In the aftermath of World War I, 13-year-old Annie befriends a horribly burned and embittered young veteran at a veteran's hospital in Kansas, against the express wishes of her mother. A young girl's first steps into adulthood raise questions about peace, heroism, patriotism, and the physical and emotional casualties of war." Soc Educ

Rowling, J. K.

Harry Potter and the sorcerer's stone; illustrations by Mary Grandpré. Levine Bks. 1998 c1997 309p il $16.95; pa $5.99 **Fic**
1. Fantasy fiction 2. Witches—Fiction
ISBN 0-590-35340-3; 0-590-35342-X (pa)   LC 97-39059

Also available Thorndike Press large print edition

First published 1997 in the United Kingdom with title: Harry Potter and the philosopher's stone

Rowling, J. K.—*Continued*
Rescued from the outrageous neglect of his aunt and uncle, Harry, a young boy with a great destiny, proves his worth while attending Hogwarts School for Wizards and Witches
This "is a brilliantly imagined and beautifully written fantasy." Booklist
Other available titles about Harry Potter are:
Harry Potter and the Chamber of Secrets (1999)
Harry Potter and the goblet of fire (2000)
Harry Potter and the prisoner of Azkaban (1999)

Rubinstein, Gillian
Foxspell. Simon & Schuster Bks. for Young Readers 1996 219p $16   **Fic**
1. Foxes—Fiction 2. Supernatural—Fiction 3. Australia—Fiction
ISBN 0-689-80602-7   LC 96-11824
First published 1994 in Australia
Twelve-year-old Tod's mystical links with a spirit, half man and half fox, and with the natural world surrounding his grandmother's house in the Australian countryside challenge his attempt to adjust to the real world
"A complex, compelling tale of maturing and belonging." Voice Youth Advocates

Under the cat's eye; a tale of morph and mystery. Simon & Schuster Bks. for Young Readers 1998 204p $16   **Fic**
1. Supernatural—Fiction 2. School stories
ISBN 0-689-81800-9   LC 97-32643
Jai and his friends at a boarding school join forces with shape-shifters in their attempt to defeat the headmaster who steals the souls and futures of the students
"Rubinstein creates an intriguing series of universes, in each of which the rules of science/magic differ tellingly, and readers will be caught up by the story's interlocking plotlines." Booklist

Ruby, Lois, 1942-
Steal away home. Macmillan 1994 192p $16; pa $4.50   **Fic**
1. Slavery—Fiction 2. Underground railroad—Fiction 3. Society of Friends—Fiction
ISBN 0-02-777883-5; 0-689-82435-1 (pa)
LC 93-47300
"Twelve-year-old Dana discovers a skeleton in a secret room of the old house her family is restoring in Lawrence, Kansas. Dana also finds a small diary that tells the story of James Weaver and his Quaker family, the occupants of the house during the 1850s. James is sworn to secrecy in assisting his mother to help runaway slaves along the Underground Railroad. . . . The alternating chapters—moving between James's life and that of Dana and her friends . . . create a kind of thread weaving the historical reality into contemporary time. The skillfully rendered book will appeal to a wide audience." Horn Book

Ruckman, Ivy, 1931-
In care of Cassie Tucker. Delacorte Press 1998 166p $14.95   **Fic**
1. Frontier and pioneer life—Fiction 2. Family life—Fiction 3. Cousins—Fiction 4. Nebraska—Fiction
ISBN 0-385-32514-2   LC 97-44217
When her teenage cousin moves in with her family on their Nebraska farm in 1899, eleven-year-old Cassie learns a lot, including the meaning of "heathen" and "bigot"
"Ruckman's novel—inspired by the life of her grandmother—is an engaging re-creation of a frontier world." Booklist

Night of the twisters. Crowell 1984 153p lib bdg $14.89; pa $4.95   **Fic**
1. Tornadoes—Fiction 2. Nebraska—Fiction
ISBN 0-690-04409-7 (lib bdg); 0-06-440176-6 (pa)
LC 83-46168
"Twelve-year-old Dan describes the events leading up to the hour that his town was struck seven times by tornadoes. Alone at home, [in Grand Island, Nebraska] Dan, his baby brother, and his best friend Arthur ride out the storm huddled in the shower stall in Dan's basement and then begin the search for their parents." Sci Child
"Ruckman does a good job of creating and maintaining suspense, produces dialogue that sounds appropriate for a stress situation, and gives her characters some depth and differentiation." Bull Cent Child Books

Rylant, Cynthia
A fine white dust. Bradbury Press 1986 106p $16; pa $3.95   **Fic**
1. Religion—Fiction 2. Friendship—Fiction 3. Family life—Fiction
ISBN 0-02-777240-3; 0-689-80462-8 (pa)
LC 86-1003
A Newbery Medal honor book, 1987
The visit of the traveling Preacher Man to his small North Carolina town gives new impetus to thirteen-year-old Peter's struggle to reconcile his own deeply felt religious belief with the beliefs and non-beliefs of his family and friends
"Blending humor and intense emotion with a poetic use of language, Cynthia Rylant has created a taut, finely drawn portrait of a boy's growth from seeking for belief, through seduction and betrayal, to a spiritual acceptance and a readiness 'for something whole.'" Horn Book

The Heavenly Village. Blue Sky Press (NY) 1999 95p $15.95   **Fic**
1. Future life—Fiction 2. Death—Fiction
ISBN 0-439-04096-5   LC 98-48603
Undecided souls who have died while they are not quite ready to go to heaven find themselves in the halfway place known as the Heavenly Village
"This is a special book, probably not for everyone, but Rylant's graceful offering will move many young readers. . . . Rylant writes with unembellished eloquence." Booklist

The islander; a novel. DK Ink 1998 96p $14.95
Fic
1. Grandfathers—Fiction 2. Islands—Fiction 3. Mermaids and mermen—Fiction
ISBN 0-7894-2490-8   LC 97-36059
Also available in paperback from Bantam Bks.
Living with his grandfather on an island off British Columbia, ten-year-old Daniel feels deep loneliness until the night he meets a mermaid whose identity he tries to learn
"The novel reads quickly and easily, and the voice, though subdued, is compelling." Horn Book Guide

Rylant, Cynthia—*Continued*

Missing May. Orchard Bks. 1992 89p $14.95;
lib bdg $15.99   **Fic**
  1. Death—Fiction 2. West Virginia—Fiction
  ISBN 0-531-05996-0; 0-531-08596-1 (lib bdg)
                              LC 91-23303
Also available in paperback from Dell
Awarded the Newbery Medal, 1993
"A Richard Jackson book"
After the death of the beloved aunt who has raised
her, twelve-year-old Summer and her uncle Ob leave
their West Virginia trailer in search of the strength to go
on living
  "There is much to ponder here, from the meaning of
life and death to the power of love. That it all succeeds
is a tribute to a fine writer who brings to the task a natural grace of language, an earthly sense of humor, and a
well-grounded sense of the spiritual." SLJ

Sachar, Louis, 1954-
Holes. Farrar, Straus & Giroux 1998 233p $16
                                       Fic
  1. Juvenile delinquency—Fiction 2. Friendship—Fiction 3. Buried treasure—Fiction
  ISBN 0-374-33265-7   LC 97-45011
Awarded the Newbery Medal, 1999
"Frances Foster books"
As further evidence of his family's bad fortune which
they attribute to a curse on a distant relative, Stanley
Yelnats is sent to a hellish correctional camp in the Texas desert where he finds his first real friend, a treasure,
and a new sense of himself
  "This delightfully clever story is well-crafted and
thought-provoking, with a bit of a folklore thrown in for
good measure." Voice Youth Advocates

Sachs, Marilyn, 1927-
Surprise party. Dutton Children's Bks. 1998
164p $15.99   **Fic**
  1. Brothers and sisters—Fiction 2. Family life—Fiction 3. Parties—Fiction
  ISBN 0-525-45962-6   LC 98-10036
Despite her younger brother's knack for getting into
trouble, Gen involves him in planning a party for for
their parents' twenty-fifth anniversary—with truly surprising results
  "Relationships and feelings ring true from both sides
of the angel-devil equation in this well-constructed, believable story, written with a light touch." Booklist

Saint-Exupéry, Antoine de, 1900-1944
The little prince; written and illustrated by
Antoine de Saint-Exupery; translated from the
French by Richard Howard. Harcourt 2000 83p il
$18; pa $12   **Fic**
  ISBN 0-15-202398-4; 0-15-601207-3 (pa)
                                LC 99-50439
A new translation of the title first published 1943 by
Reynal & Hitchcock
  "This many-dimensional fable of an airplane pilot who
has crashed in the desert is for readers of all ages. The
pilot comes upon the little prince soon after the crash.
The prince tells of his adventures on different planets
and on Earth as he attempts to learn about the universe
in order to live peacefully on his own small planet. A
spiritual quality enhances the seemingly simple observations of the little prince." Shapiro. Fic for Youth. 3d edition

Salisbury, Graham, 1944-
Jungle dogs. Delacorte Press 1998 183p $15.95;
pa $4.95   **Fic**
  1. Wild dogs—Fiction 2. Brothers—Fiction 3. Hawaii—Fiction
  ISBN 0-385-32187-2; 0-440-41573-X (pa)
                                LC 98-5561
While worrying about the wild dogs that supposedly
lurk in the jungle along his paper route, Hawaiian sixth
grader Boy Regis also seeks to stop his older brother Da-
mon from fighting all his battles for him
  "The novel boasts a compelling narrative voice, a
sympathetic protagonist, and throws in enough drama to
bring the story to a satisfying end." ALAN

Shark bait. Delacorte Press 1997 151p $15.95;
pa $4.50   **Fic**
  1. Fathers and sons—Fiction 2. Friendship—Fiction
3. Hawaii—Fiction
  ISBN 0-385-32237-2; 0-440-22803-4 (pa)
                               LC 96-54708
Mokes is torn between obeying his father, the police
chief in the small town of Kailua, Hawaii, and being
with his friends who plan to go see a fight between an
island boy and a sailor
  "This fast-paced account of boys craving excitement
and seeking acceptance, not to mention direction, among
their peers when adult guidance isn't available expertly
re-creates its distinctive Hawaiian locale even as it explores universal themes." Horn Book Guide

Under the blood-red sun. Delacorte Press 1994
246p $15.95; pa $4.99   **Fic**
  1. Pearl Harbor (Oahu, Hawaii), Attack on, 1941—
Fiction 2. World War, 1939-1945—Fiction 3. Japanese Americans—Fiction 4. Hawaii—Fiction
  ISBN 0-385-32099-X; 0-440-41139-4 (pa)
                                LC 94-444
Tomikazu Nakaji's biggest concerns are baseball,
homework, and a local bully, until life with his Japanese
family in Hawaii changes drastically after the bombing
of Pearl Harbor in December 1941
  "Character development of major figures is good, the
setting is warmly realized, and the pace of the story
moves gently though inexorably forward." SLJ

Schmidt, Gary D.
Anson's way. Clarion Bks. 1999 213p $15
                                        Fic
  1. Fathers and sons—Fiction 2. Ireland—Fiction
  ISBN 0-395-91529-5   LC 98-29220
While serving as a British Fencible to maintain the
peace in Ireland, Anson finds that his sympathy for a
hedge master, a teacher devoted to teaching Irish children their forbidden language and culture, places him in
conflict with the law of King George II
  "Wonderfully descriptive, captivating prose and well-
defined characters draw readers into eighteenth-century
Ireland." Booklist

Schnur, Steven
The shadow children; illustrated by Herbert Tauss. Morrow Junior Bks. 1994 86p il $16; lib bdg $15.93   **Fic**
1. Holocaust, 1933-1945—Fiction 2. Ghost stories 3. France—Fiction
ISBN 0-688-13281-2; 0-688-13831-4 (lib bdg)
LC 94-5098
While spending the summer on his grandfather's farm in the French countryside, eleven-year-old Etienne discovers a secret dating back to World War II and encounters the ghosts of Jewish children who suffered a dreadful fate under the Nazis
"The prose is spare and beautiful, and the expressive charcoal illustrations move from the warm affection of the present to the shadowy horror that won't go away." Booklist

Scoppettone, Sandra, 1936-
Trying hard to hear you. Harper & Row 1974 264p o.p.; Alyson Publs. paperback available $9.95 (7 and up)   **Fic**
1. Homosexuality—Fiction 2. Friendship—Fiction
ISBN 1-55583-367-5 (pa)
Faced with the revelation that her best friend is a homosexual, a sixteen-year-old tries to cope with her own and her friends' reactions toward him
"Characterization is excellent and the story involving." Booklist

Seago, Kate
Matthew unstrung. Dial Bks. 1998 236p $16.99 (7 and up)   **Fic**
1. Mental illness—Fiction 2. Clergy—Fiction 3. Fathers and sons—Fiction 4. Brothers—Fiction
ISBN 0-8037-2230-3   LC 96-50159
"Studying at a Bible college for an ill-suited career in the clergy, Matthew caves under the demands of his unyielding minister father and suffers a nervous breakdown. Set in 1910, the novel presents a chilling depiction of mental illness in a less enlightened time. Matthew's eventual recovery at his brother's Colorado ranch is movingly portrayed." Horn Book Guide

Sebestyen, Ouida, 1924-
Far from home. Little, Brown 1980 191p $15.95
Fic
1. Family life—Fiction 2. Hotels and motels—Fiction
ISBN 0-316-77932-6   LC 80-18328
Also available in paperback from Dell
"An Atlantic Monthly Press book"
After the death of his mother, 13-year-old Salty goes to take her place working for the Buckley Arms boarding house where he begins to learn about the complexities of love and family
"Sebestyen's cast of strongly conceived characters compels the somewhat slender plot line forward to a dramatic and vivid conclusion that finds each personality altered after the confrontation." Booklist

Words by heart. Little, Brown 1979 162p $15.95   **Fic**
1. African Americans—Fiction 2. Race relations—Fiction 3. Family life—Fiction
ISBN 0-316-77931-8   LC 78-27847

Also available in paperback from Bantam Bks.
"An Atlantic Monthly Press book"
"It is 1910, and Lena's family is the only black family in her small Southwestern town. When Lena wins a scripture reciting contest that a white boy is supposed to win, her family is threatened. Lena's father tries to make her understand that by hating the people who did this, the problems that cause their behavior are not solved. Only more hatred and violence cause Lena and the village to understand the words of her father." ALAN
Followed by On fire (1987)

Seidler, Tor, 1952-
Mean Margaret; pictures by Jon Agee. Michael Di Capua Bks. 1997 165p il $14.95; lib bdg $14.89   **Fic**
1. Marmots—Fiction
ISBN 0-06-205090-7; 0-06-205091-5 (lib bdg)
This is the "story of a newly wed woodchuck couple who find a willful, wailing human toddler and take her into their home and into their hearts." SLJ
"Both hilarious and heartwarming, *Mean Margaret* is a delightful fantasy filled with memorably offbeat characters and situations. . . . Agee's black-and-white drawings match the text in wit and boundless good humor." Booklist

Service, Pamela F.
Weirdos of the universe, unite! Atheneum Pubs. 1992 136p o.p.; Fawcett Bks. paperback available $4.50   **Fic**
1. Fantasy fiction
ISBN 0-449-70429-7 (pa)   LC 91-18438
"A Jean Karl book"
Dedicated weirdos Mandy and Owen accidentally summon up five mythological beings, who need their aid in defending Earth from space invaders
"An enjoyable adventure story with more than a little humor. An easy choice to booktalk, particularly for classes studying mythology and folklore." Booklist

Seymour, Tres
The revelation of Saint Bruce. Orchard Bks. 1998 120p $16.95; lib bdg $17.99 (7 and up)
Fic
1. School stories 2. Friendship—Fiction
ISBN 0-531-30109-5; 0-531-33109-1 (lib bdg)
LC 98-13719
"Called 'Saint Bruce' because of his highly developed conscience and strict moral code, a high school senior is shunned by his friends after he tells a teacher that they got drunk in school." Horn Book Guide
"The author's voice sounds convincingly like a real teenager, and the central dilemma—loyalty to friends vs. personal ethics and morality—is one that many teens may find themselves confronting." Voice Youth Advocates

Sheldon, Dyan
Confessions of a teenage drama queen. Candlewick Press 1999 272p $16.99 (7 and up)
Fic
1. School stories
ISBN 0-7636-0822-X   LC 98-53914

Sheldon, Dyan—*Continued*

In her first year at a suburban New Jersey high school, Mary Elizabeth Cep, who now calls herself "Lola," sets her sights on the lead in the annual drama production, and finds herself in conflict with the most popular girl in school

"An exuberant and hilarious celebration of the ups and downs of high school life. . . . The story is off-beat, outrageous, and utterly charming." SLJ

Shelley, Mary Wollstonecraft, 1797-1851

Frankenstein (7 and up)   Fic

Various editions available
First published 1818
"The tale relates the exploits of Frankenstein, an idealistic Genevan student of natural philosophy, who discovers at the university of Ingolstadt the secret of imparting life to inanimate matter. Collecting bones from charnel-houses, he constructs the semblance of a human being and gives it life. The creature, endowed with supernatural strength and size and terrible in appearance, inspires loathing in whoever sees it." Oxford Companion to Engl Lit. 5th edition

Shusterman, Neal

The dark side of nowhere; a novel. Little, Brown 1997 185p $15.95   Fic
1. Extraterrestrial beings—Fiction 2. Science fiction
ISBN 0-316-78907-0   LC 96-19895
Also available in paperback from TOR Bks.
Fourteen-year-old Jason faces an identity crisis after discovering that he is the son of aliens who stayed on earth following a botched invasion mission
"Shusterman tells a fast-paced story, giving Jason many vivid, original turns of phrase, letting the plot get weird enough to keep readers enthralled, then coming back to the human emotions at the heart of it all." Booklist

Downsiders. Simon & Schuster Bks. for Young Readers 1999 246p $16   Fic
1. Subways—Fiction 2. New York (N.Y.)—Fiction
ISBN 0-689-80375-3   LC 98-38555
When fourteen-year-old Lindsay meets Talon and discovers the Downsiders world which had evolved from the subway built in New York in 1867 by Alfred Ely Beach, she and her new friend experience the clash of their two cultures
"Shusterman has invented an alternate world in the Downside that is both original and humorous." Voice Youth Advocates

The eyes of Kid Midas. Little, Brown 1992 185p o.p.; TOR Bks. paperback available $3.99
                     Fic
1. Magic—Fiction 2. Eyeglasses—Fiction
ISBN 0-8125-3460-3 (pa)   LC 92-17897
Kevin is entranced when he finds a pair of sunglasses that turn his desires into reality, but then things start to get out of control
"The novel features steady action with occasional touches of bizarre, inspired humor and is hypnotically readable." Libr J

Silverberg, Robert

Letters from Atlantis; illustrated by Robert Gould. Atheneum Pubs. 1990 136p il o.p.; Warner Bks. paperback available $4.99 (7 and up)   Fic
1. Science fiction 2. Atlantis—Fiction
ISBN 0-446-36286-7 (pa)   LC 90-562
"A Byron Preiss book"
While his body remains in deep sleep, Roy transfers his mind into the mind of a royal prince living in Atlantis 180 centuries ago
"Silverberg cleverly makes Atlantis itself one of the characters through detailed descriptions and finely tuned nuance. He also does an excellent job of juxtaposing modern, often witty prose against the stuff of legend." Booklist

Skolsky, Mindy Warshaw

Love from your friend, Hannah; a novel; with illustrations by Hannah herself. DK Ink 1998 246p il $17.95   Fic
1. Letters—Fiction 2. Great Depression, 1929-1939—Fiction 3. New York (State)—Fiction
ISBN 0-7894-2492-4   LC 97-29819
Also available in paperback from HarperCollins
Other titles about Hannah are: Carnival and kopeck and more about Hannah (1979), Hannah and the best father on route 9w (1982), and The whistling teakettle and other stories about Hannah (1977)
"A Richard Jackson book"
"Hannah is lonely after her best friend moves away from their Grand View, NY, neighborhood. Between September 1937 and July 1938, the girl writes volumes of letters to her new pen pal, Edward; her grandparents; Franklin D, and Eleanor Roosevelt; and White House secretary Margaret 'Missy' Lehand." SLJ
"Skolsky vividly shows readers what life was like during the Depression for one spunky heroine with a terrific sense of humor." Publ Wkly

Skurzynski, Gloria

Cliff hanger; by Gloria Skurzynski and Alane Ferguson. National Geographic Soc. 1999 147p il (National parks mystery) $15.95   Fic
1. Foster home care—Fiction 2. Mystery fiction
ISBN 0-7922-7036-3   LC 98-8716
Twelve-year-old Jack and his younger sister visit Mesa Verde National Park, where they delve into the park's history while gradually uncovering the mysterious past of their family's teenage foster child Lucky
"The authors do a fine job of integrating lots of material into an exciting story." Booklist
Other available titles in the National parks mystery series are:
Deadly waters (1999)
Rage of fire (1998)
Wolf stalker (1997)

Spider's voice. Atheneum Bks. for Young Readers 1999 200p $16.95 (7 and up)   Fic
1. Abelard, Peter, 1079-1142—Fiction 2. Héloïse, 1101-1164—Fiction 3. France—Fiction 4. Middle ages—Fiction
ISBN 0-689-82149-2   LC 98-7981

Skurzynski, Gloria—*Continued*

"In this story of the legendary Héloïse and Abelard, Abelard chooses twelve-year-old Aran to be his personal servant because he is mute and will not be able to speak of the lovers' trysts." Horn Book Guide

"The story is complicated and compelling, full of drama, love, and violence. . . . Skurzynski is masterful in her characterizations." SLJ

The virtual war. Simon & Schuster Bks. for Young Readers 1997 152p $16; pa $4.50   **Fic**
1. Virtual reality—Fiction 2. Science fiction
ISBN 0-689-81374-0; 0-689-82425-4 (pa)
             LC 96-35346

In a future world where global contamination has necessitated limited human contact, three young people with unique genetically engineered abilities are teamed up to wage a war in virtual reality

"Skurzynski's anti-war message is clear yet never didactic; her characters are complex and fully realized, the pacing brisk, and the story compelling." Bull Cent Child Books

Sleator, William

The beasties. Dutton Children's Bks. 1997 198p $15.99; pa $4.99 (7 and up)   **Fic**
1. Ecology—Fiction 2. Horror fiction
ISBN 0-525-45598-1; 0-14-130639-4 (pa)
             LC 97-6147

"In this horror tale, Doug and his sister are captured by the beasties who live in tunnels underneath the forest. Threatened and genetically mutated by the destruction of the wilderness, the beasties have taken to kidnapping people and amputating body parts they need. Sleator handles the ickier aspects of the story with aplomb, and the menacing atmosphere and suspense-serving pace are all they should be." Horn Book Guide

The boxes. Dutton Children's Bks. 1998 196p $15.99 (7 and up)   **Fic**
1. Science fiction
ISBN 0-525-46012-8   LC 98-9285

When she opens two strange boxes left in her care by her mysterious uncle, fifteen-year-old Annie discovers a swarm of telepathic creatures and unleashes a power capable of slowing down time

"Sleator has written a page-turner. . . . His writing is crisp and clean, letting the story speak for itself." Voice Youth Advocates

The boy who reversed himself. Dutton 1986 167p hardcover o.p. paperback available $4.99
                             Fic
1. Science fiction 2. Space and time—Fiction
ISBN 0-14-038965-2 (pa)   LC 86-19700

When Laura discovers that the unpopular boy living next door to her has the ability to go into the fourth dimension, she makes the dangerous decision to accompany him on his journeys there

"What follows is a terrifying trip into the fourth dimension, populated by some of Sleator's most unusual characters to date. An utterly fantastic and ultimately satisfying novel by a master storyteller." SLJ

The duplicate. Dutton 1988 154p hardcover o.p. paperback available $3.99 (7 and up)   **Fic**
1. Science fiction
ISBN 0-553-28634-X (pa)   LC 87-30562

Sixteen-year-old David, finding a strange machine that creates replicas of living organisms, duplicates himself and suffers the horrible consequences when the duplicate turns against him

"There are some points in the story when the roles of the clones (referred to as Duplicates A and B) become congested to the detriment of the book's pace, but fantasy fans will doubtless find the concept fresh enough and eerie enough to compensate for this, and Sleator is, as always, economical in casting and structuring his story." Bull Cent Child Books

House of stairs. Dutton 1974 166p hardcover o.p. paperback available $4.99 (7 and up)   **Fic**
1. Science fiction
ISBN 0-14-034580-9 (pa)

"Five 15-year-old orphans with widely ranging personality characteristics are involuntarily placed in a house of endless stairs and subjected to psychological experiments on conditioned human responses." Booklist

"The setting is bleak, dramatic and convincing; the interaction and development of the five young people as characters trapped in an abrasive situation are compelling. A very effective and provocative suspense story that can be read for plot alone or doubly enjoyed for the mystery and the message." Bull Cent Child Books

Interstellar pig. Dutton 1984 197p hardcover o.p. paperback available $3.99 (7 and up)   **Fic**
1. Science fiction
ISBN 0-553-25564-9 (pa)   LC 84-4132

"Solitary and bored, Barney is quickly attracted by the exotic appearance and protean personalities of Zena, Manny, and Joe, who have rented the summer house next door. The interest of the sophisticated adults in sixteen-year-old Barney at first flatters, then intrigues, and finally terrifies him as he becomes absorbed in their compulsion to possess 'The Piggy.' When he realizes that the talisman has power, the game expands in significance." Horn Book

The author "draws the reader in with intimations of danger and horror, but the climactic battle is more slapstick than horrific, and the victor's prize could scarcely be more ironic. Problematic as straight science fiction but great fun as a spoof on human-alien contact." Booklist

The night the heads came. Dutton Children's Bks. 1996 154p $15.99   **Fic**
1. Science fiction 2. Extraterrestrial beings—Fiction
ISBN 0-525-45463-2   LC 95-32321

When aliens abduct both Leo and his artist friend Tim, Leo tries to determine why these creatures from outer space want particularly to use his friend's talent

"This fast-paced science fiction romp is very entertaining and will keep readers turning the pages." SLJ

Others see us. Dutton Children's Bks. 1993 163p $14.99; pa $3.99 (7 and up)   **Fic**
1. Science fiction 2. Extrasensory perception—Fiction
ISBN 0-525-45104-8; 0-14-037514-7 (pa)
             LC 93-18940

Sleator, William—*Continued*
"After falling off his bicycle into a toxic waste dump, Jared develops the ability to read other people's thoughts. He is catapulted into psychic combat with his amoral grandmother and sociopathically manipulative cousin, both of whom are also mind-readers." Publ Wkly
"The story is most intriguing when the three mind-readers are struggling to protect their own thoughts while exploring the minds of those around them. A fascinating story compelling for the exemplary storytelling and the seductive nature of the fantasy." Horn Book

Rewind. Dutton Children's Bks. 1999 120p $15.99   **Fic**
1. Science fiction 2. Death—Fiction
ISBN 0-525-46130-2   LC 99-12260
"When Peter is mowed down by a car and killed after running into the street following a fight with his parents, he learns, in the 'great white light,' that he has another chance. In fact, he gets three chances to go back and change the events of his life so that the accident never occurs. . . . The premise is irresistible, and the suspense crackles." Horn Book

Singularity. Dutton 1985 170p hardcover o.p. paperback available $4.99 (7 and up)   **Fic**
1. Twins—Fiction 2. Science fiction
ISBN 0-14-037598-8 (pa)   LC 84-26075
Sixteen-year-old twins Harry and Barry stumble across a gateway to another universe, where a distortion in time and space causes a dramatic change in their competitive relationship
"The book has a title with a fine double entendre and is an unusual, suspenseful yarn told by a master storyteller." Horn Book

Strange attractors. Dutton 1990 169p hardcover o.p. paperback available $4.99   **Fic**
1. Space and time—Fiction 2. Science fiction
ISBN 0-14-034582-5 (pa)   LC 89-33840
"The strange attractors are people from a parallel universe: a brilliant scientist, Sylvan, and his beautiful daughter, Eve, whose reckless manipulation of time travel has plunged their timeline into chaos. Their search for a stable timeline brings them to our world, where they must destroy their doppelgängers, the 'real' Sylvan and Eve, or drag this world into chaos, too. Max, a teenage science student, is forced to become their unwilling ally or be destroyed himself." SLJ
"Sleator's talent for fascinating scientific manipulation is fully in evidence and exceptionally well conceived here. . . . Along with the clever science, Sleator turns in some good suspense." Booklist

Slepian, Jan, 1921-
The Broccoli tapes. Philomel Bks. 1989 157p $14.95   **Fic**
1. Cats—Fiction 2. Death—Fiction 3. Brothers and sisters—Fiction 4. Hawaii—Fiction
ISBN 0-399-21712-6   LC 88-25490
Also available in paperback from Scholastic
"Both 12-year-old Sara and her 13-year-old brother, Sam, have trouble adjusting to Hawaii during the five months that their family is living there. . . . When Sara and Sam rescue a wild cat (who is later named Broccoli),

they meet Eddie Nutt. At first Eddie is as suspicious and untrusting as Broccoli until the bonds of friendship gradually develop. The story unfolds through Sara's cassette tapes sent to her teacher and classmates back home." SLJ
"Slepian is a fine writer, and the elements of her story are smoothly meshed, the action and characterization mutually affective. The message that love is worth the chance of pain is given by the people in her story, not didactically imposed by the author." Bull Cent Child Books

The mind reader. Philomel Bks. 1997 132p $15.95   **Fic**
1. Telepathy—Fiction 2. Runaway children—Fiction
ISBN 0-399-23150-1   LC 97-10573
In 1930, while their families are performing in a traveling vaudeville show in San Francisco, ten-year-old Annie helps her best friend Connie when he decides to run away rather than use his mindreading abilities any longer
"This is an unusual adventure story that has a little of everything, and it is rich and full as, well, a vaudeville stage." Bull Cent Child Books

Smith, Roland, 1951-
The Sasquatch. Hyperion Bks. for Children 1998 188p $15.95; lib bdg $16.49; pa $5.99   **Fic**
1. Sasquatch—Fiction 2. Mount Saint Helens (Wash.)—Fiction
ISBN 0-7868-0368-1; 0-7868-2315-1 (lib bdg); 0-7868-1334-2 (pa)   LC 97-39650
Thirteen-year-old Dylan follows his father into the woods on the slopes of Mount St. Helens, which is on the brink of another eruption, in an attempt to protect the resident Sasquatch from ruthless hunters
"The prose is well written, the characters well defined, and the story gripping." Voice Youth Advocates

Thunder cave. Hyperion Bks. for Children 1995 250p $17.49; pa $5.95   **Fic**
1. Adventure fiction 2. Masai (African people)—Fiction 3. Kenya—Fiction
ISBN 0-7868-0068-2; 0-7868-1159-5 (pa)
LC 94-19714
"When his mother is fatally struck by a car, Jacob evades his stepfather's plan to have him go live with relatives in Nebraska by flying off to Kenya to find his father, a scientist researching the diminishing herds of elephants. Jacob's father is in the bush and incommunicado, and most of the book follows Jacob's . . . journey to find him." Bull Cent Child Books
"In superhero fashion, Jacob is far wiser than his years, but he does make some typical kid mistakes in his journey-quest. The Kenyan setting, the animal scenes and the depiction of the Masai's relationship to the land make this novel stand above the rest." Book Rep

Smith, Sherwood
Court duel; book II of the Crown & court duet. Harcourt Brace & Co. 1998 245p $18 (7 and up)
Fic
1. Fantasy fiction
ISBN 0-15-201609-0   LC 97-23879
Sequel to Crown duel

Smith, Sherwood—*Continued*

Brought to court by a mysterious letter, teenage Countess Meliara finds herself the subject of all sorts of courtly intrigues and attentions, including those of the deposed king's sister and an ardent, secret suitor

"Readers will enjoy immersing themselves in the subtleties of courtly life and love." SLJ

Crown duel; book I of the Crown & court duet. Jane Yolen Bks. 1997 214p $18 (7 and up) **Fic**

1. Fantasy fiction
ISBN 0-15-201608-2   LC 96-44193

To fulfill their father's dying wish, teenage Countess Meliara and her brother Branaric organize a revolution against a greedy king

"Smith tells a fast-moving tale of adventure, intrigue, and honor. . . . Characters and setting are well realized." Booklist

Followed by Court duel

Snyder, Zilpha Keatley

Cat running. Delacorte Press 1994 168p $15.95; pa $4.50   **Fic**

1. Great Depression, 1929-1939—Fiction 2. Running—Fiction
ISBN 0-385-31056-0; 0-440-41152-1 (pa)
     LC 94-447

"Sixth grader Cat Kinsey is sure she is the fastest runner in Brownwood School until Zane Perkins arrives barefoot and clothed in ragged overalls. He's an 'Okie,' and to most Californians during the Great Depression, that automatically translates to 'lazy, dirty, and shiftless.' When Cat's father forbids her to wear slacks because he feels they are unseemly, she ignores Zane's challenge and refuses to race during the school's annual Play Day. . . . This story is both appealing and informative. The characters are well drawn and beautifully motivated." SLJ

Gib rides home. Delacorte Press 1998 246p $15.95; pa $4.50   **Fic**

1. Orphans—Fiction 2. Horses—Fiction
ISBN 0-385-32267-4; 0-440-41257-9 (pa)
     LC 97-21486

Despite the harsh treatment he has endured at the Lovell House orphanage, ten-year-old Gib Whittaker manages to maintain his hopeful outlook when he is "farmed out" to help with the horses of a wealthy banker in 1908

"In a book inspired by the life of the author's father, the novel delivers an engaging glimpse of history as well as a compelling story." SLJ

Another title about Gib is:
Gib and the gray ghost (2000)

The runaways. Delacorte Press 1999 245p $15.95   **Fic**

1. Runaway children—Fiction 2. Nevada—Fiction
ISBN 0-385-32599-1   LC 98-22258

Twelve-year-old Dani hates living in the small desert town of Rattler Springs, Nevada, but her plans to run away get complicated when nine-year-old Stormy and an imaginative new girl named Pixie decide they want to go along

"The book is set in the 1950s, and the dying town and desperate people are very real and touching. The plight of these creative and neglected children will keep readers turning the pages." SLJ

Song of the gargoyle. Delacorte Press 1991 232p hardcover o.p. paperback available $4.50   **Fic**

1. Adventure fiction
ISBN 0-440-40898-9 (pa)   LC 90-3772

When mysterious men in black abduct his father, the court jester of Austerneve, thirteen-year-old Tymmon flees into the forest, where he acquires a strange animal companion and plots to rescue his father

"This tale, a mixture of magic and hard-won truths, is deeply layered and affecting." Booklist

Sonenklar, Carol

My own worst enemy. Holiday House 1999 151p $15.95   **Fic**

1. School stories 2. Family life—Fiction
ISBN 0-8234-1456-6   LC 98-41952

As she begins classes at a new middle school, Eve decides to try to fit in so that her father, who has just lost his job, will have less to worry about, but she finds that being true to herself is really the best thing to do

"While Sonenklar's . . . moral about being true to yourself is well-worn, her satirical execution of it is fresh, frank and entertaining." Publ Wkly

Soto, Gary

Buried onions. Harcourt Brace & Co. 1997 149p $17 (7 and up)   **Fic**

1. Violence—Fiction 2. Mexican Americans—Fiction
ISBN 0-15-201333-4   LC 96-53112

Also available in paperback from HarperCollins

When nineteen-year-old Eddie drops out of college, he struggles to find a place for himself as a Mexican American living in a violence-infested neighborhood of Fresno, California

"Soto has created a beautiful, touching, and truthful story. . . . The lyrical language and Spanish phrases add to the immediacy of setting and to the sensitivity the author brings to his character's life." Voice Youth Advocates

Off and running; illustrated by Eric Velasquez. Delacorte Press 1996 136p il hardcover o.p. paperback available $4.50   **Fic**

1. School stories 2. Mexican Americans—Fiction
ISBN 0-440-41432-6 (pa)   LC 95-36194

When they learn that Rudy Herrera and Alex Garcia, two fifth-grade class clowns, plan to run against them in the school elections, Miata and her friend Ana know that they face a difficult race

"This book offers an engaging look at student politics. But, more importantly, it is a realistic, warm portrayal of a Latino school in California." SLJ

The pool party; illustrated by Robert Casilla. Delacorte Press 1993 104p il $13.95; pa $3.50   **Fic**

1. Mexican Americans—Fiction 2. Family life—Fiction 3. California—Fiction
ISBN 0-385-30890-6; 0-440-41010-X (pa)
     LC 92-34407

Soto, Gary—*Continued*

While helping his father and grandfather work as gardeners in Fresno, California, ten-year-old Rudy sees some differences between his Mexican-American family and the wealthy families that live nearby

"A few elements make this story special: the poetic perfection Soto exhibits both in description and in authentic dialogue and the immersion of readers into the bosom of a loving, hard-working Mexican-American family." SLJ

Taking sides. Harcourt Brace Jovanovich 1991 138p $17; pa $8   **Fic**
1. Hispanic Americans—Fiction 2. Basketball—Fiction
ISBN 0-15-284076-1; 0-15-284077-4 (pa)
LC 91-11082
Fourteen-year-old Lincoln Mendoza, an aspiring basketball player, must come to terms with his divided loyalties when he moves from the Hispanic inner city to a white suburban neighborhood

This is a "light but appealing story. . . . Because of its subject matter and its clear, straightforward prose, it will be especially good for reluctant readers." SLJ

Southgate, Martha

Another way to dance. Delacorte Press 1996 179p $15.95; pa $4.50   **Fic**
1. Ballet—Fiction 2. Divorce—Fiction 3. African Americans—Fiction 4. New York (N.Y.)—Fiction
ISBN 0-385-32191-0; 0-440-21968-X (pa)
LC 95-53819
While spending the summer at the School of American Ballet in New York City, fourteen-year-old Vicki Harris must come to terms with the reality of her parents' divorce, her crush on Mikhail Baryshnikov, and the impact of being an African American on her future as a dancer

"Southgate offers a poignant account of self-discovery, convincingly hopeful and steadfast in its refusal to settle for easy solutions." Publ Wkly

Speare, Elizabeth George, 1908-1994

The sign of the beaver. Houghton Mifflin 1983 135p $16   **Fic**
1. Frontier and pioneer life—Fiction 2. Indians of North America—Fiction 3. Friendship—Fiction
ISBN 0-395-33890-5   LC 83-118
Also available in paperback from Dell
Left alone to guard the family's wilderness home in eighteenth-century Maine, Matt is hard-pressed to survive until local Indians teach him their skills

Matt "begins to understand the Indians' ingenuity and respect for nature and the devasting impact of the encroachment of the white man. In a quiet but not unsuspenseful story . . . the author articulates historical facts along with the adventures and the thoughts, emotions, and developing insights of a young adolescent." Horn Book

The witch of Blackbird Pond. Houghton Mifflin 1958 249p $16   **Fic**
1. Connecticut—History—1600-1775, Colonial period—Fiction 2. Witchcraft—Fiction 3. Puritans—Fiction
ISBN 0-395-07114-3

Also available in paperback from Dell
Awarded the Newbery Medal, 1959
"Headstrong and undisciplined, Barbados-bred Kit Tyler is an embarrassment to her Puritan relatives, and her sincere attempts to aid a reputed witch soon bring her to trial as a suspect." Child Books Too Good to Miss

"Three satisfactorily concluded romances run through this absorbing story [set in Connecticut]. The New England of colonial times—of candle-dipping, soap-boiling, and corn-husking bees—is realistically drawn as background for a solidly written character study." Horn Book

Spinelli, Jerry, 1941-

Crash. Knopf 1996 162p $16; lib bdg $17.99; pa $4.99   **Fic**
1. Football—Fiction   2. Grandfathers—Fiction
3. Friendship—Fiction
ISBN 0-679-87957-9; 0-679-97957-3 (lib bdg);
0-679-88550-1 (pa)   LC 95-30942
"Crash is a star football player. He torments Penn, a classmate who is everything Crash is not—friendly, small, and a pacifist. When his beloved grandfather comes to live with his family and suffers a debilitating stroke, Crash begins to see value in many of the things he has scorned." Horn Book Guide

"Readers will devour this humorous glimpse at what jocks are made of while learning that life does not require crashing helmet-headed through it." SLJ

Maniac Magee; a novel. Little, Brown 1990 184p $15.95   **Fic**
1. Orphans—Fiction 2. Homeless persons—Fiction
3. Race relations—Fiction
ISBN 0-316-80722-2   LC 89-27144
Also available Thorndike Press large print edition and in paperback from HarperCollins Pubs.
Awarded the Newbery Medal, 1991
"Orphaned at three, Jeffery Lionel Magee, after eight unhappy years with relatives, one day takes off running. A year later, he ends up 200 miles away in Two Mills, a highly segregated community. Part tall tale and part contemporary realistic fiction, this unusual novel magically weaves timely issues of homelessness, racial prejudice, and illiteracy into an energetic story that bursts with creativity enthusiasm, and hope for the future. In short, it's a celebration of life." Booklist

There's a girl in my hammerlock. Simon & Schuster Bks. for Young Readers 1991 199p $14; pa $4.50   **Fic**
1. Wrestling—Fiction 2. Sex role—Fiction 3. School stories
ISBN 0-671-74684-7; 0-671-86695-8 (pa)
LC 91-8765
Thirteen-year-old Maisie joins her school's formerly all-male wrestling team and tries to last through the season, despite opposition from other students, her best friend, and her own teammates

The author "tackles a meaty subject—traditional gender roles—with his usual humor and finesse. The result, written in a breezy, first-person style, is a rattling good sports story that is clever, witty and tightly written." Publ Wkly

Spinelli, Jerry, 1941-—*Continued*

Wringer. HarperCollins Pubs. 1997 228p $14.95;
lib bdg $14.89; pa $4.95   **Fic**
1. Courage—Fiction 2. Violence—Fiction 3. Pigeons—Fiction
ISBN 0-06-024913-7; 0-06-024914-5 (lib bdg);
0-06-440578-8 (pa)   LC 96-37897
A Newbery Medal honor book, 1998
"Joanna Cotler books"
"During the annual pigeon shoot, it is a town tradition
for 10-year-old boys to break the necks of wounded
birds. In this riveting story told with verve and suspense,
Palmer rebels." SLJ

Springer, Nancy

I am Mordred; a tale from Camelot. Philomel
Bks. 1998 184p $16.99 (7 and up)   **Fic**
1. Arthur, King—Fiction 2. Great Britain—History—
0-1066—Fiction 3. Fathers and sons—Fiction
ISBN 0-399-23143-9   LC 97-39740
"Mordred, the bad seed, the son of King Arthur and
his sister, spends his youth learning who he is and then
trying to deal with the prophecy made by Merlin that he
will kill his father." SLJ
"Springer humanizes Arthurian archvillain Mordred in
a thoroughly captivating and poignant tale." Booklist

Looking for Jamie Bridger. Dial Bks. for Young
Readers 1995 159p $14.99; lib bdg $14.89 (7 and
up)   **Fic**
1. Grandparents—Fiction 2. Homosexuality—Fiction
ISBN 0-8037-1773-3; 0-8037-1774-1 (lib bdg)
      LC 94-25484
"Fourteen-year-old Jamie Bridger has led a sheltered
life with her domineering grandfather and loving but passive
grandmother; her quest to know about her parentage
. . . becomes paramount when her grandfather dies. . . .
Jamie travels across Pennsylvania and New York to find
the man she believes to be her father. She does discover
her grandparents' estranged son (they threw him out
when they discovered he was gay), also named Jamie
Bridger, but she eventually finds out that he is not her
father but her brother, that she was in fact the daughter
of the people she knew as her grandparents." Bull Cent
Child Books
"Solid characters and tough issues, including religious
fanaticism, homosexuality, and mental illness, are encountered
and presented with balance and clarity." SLJ

Toughing it. Harcourt Brace & Co. 1994 119p
$10.95; pa $4.95 (7 and up)   **Fic**
1. Death—Fiction 2. Brothers—Fiction
ISBN 0-15-200008-9; 0-15-200011-9 (pa)
      LC 93-42231
Sixteen-year-old Shawn must deal with his loss and
anger after witnessing his older brother's murder
"Springer gives a clear picture of emotionally ragged
lives, with poverty accentuating the difficulty of mourning
and of finding one's identity. The book's language
and the depiction of Tuff's mother, who often seeks
comfort in men, are direct." Booklist

Stanley, Diane, 1943-

Time apart. Morrow Junior Bks. 1999 263p $16
     Fic
1. Mothers and daughters—Fiction 2. Fathers and
daughters—Fiction 3. Great Britain—Fiction
ISBN 0-688-16997-X   LC 99-13659
"When her divorced mother is diagnosed with breast
cancer, 13-year-old Ginny suddenly finds herself en route
to England, where her uncommunicative, seldom-seen father
is helping to run a reconstructed Iron Age settlement." SLJ
"This is a dynamic coming-of-age tale." Booklist

Staples, Suzanne Fisher

Dangerous skies. Farrar, Straus & Giroux 1996
231p $16 (7 and up)   **Fic**
1. African Americans—Fiction 2. Prejudices—Fiction
3. Friendship—Fiction
ISBN 0-374-31694-5   LC 95-45529
Also available in paperback from HarperCollins
"Frances Foster books"
"At twelve, white boy Buck and black girl Tunes
Smith are best friends. . . . The adolescents' idyllic
world of fishing and observing nature is shattered when
their much older friend Jorge Rodrigues is murdered, and
Tunes is accused of the crime. . . . Staples's beautifully
written and chilling tale of contemporary racism should
keep young adult readers turning pages until they reach
the heart-breaking end." Voice Youth Advocates

Haveli. Knopf 1993 259p $18; pa $4.99 (7 and
up)   **Fic**
1. Sex role—Fiction 2. Pakistan—Fiction
ISBN 0-679-84157-1; 0-679-86569-1 (pa)
      LC 92-29054
Sequel to Shabanu
Having relented to the ways of her people in Pakistan
and married the rich older man to whom she was
pledged against her will, Shabanu is now the victim of
his family's blood feud and the malice of his other wives
"Staples brews a potent mix here: the issue of a woman's
role in a traditional society, page-turning intrigue,
tough women characters, and a fluidity of writing that
blends it all together." Booklist

Shabanu; daughter of the wind. Knopf 1989
240p $18; lib bdg $18.99; pa $4.99 (7 and up)
     Fic
1. Sex role—Fiction 2. Pakistan—Fiction
ISBN 0-394-84815-2; 0-394-94815-7 (lib bdg);
0-679-81030-7 (pa)   LC 89-2714
When eleven-year old Shabanu, the daughter of a nomad
in the Cholistan Desert of present-day Pakistan, is
pledged in marriage to an older man whose money will
bring prestige to the family, she must either accept the
decision, as is the custom, or risk the consequences of
defying her father's wishes
"Interspersing native words throughout adds realism,
but may trip up readers, who must be patient enough to
find meaning through context. This use of language is,
however, an important element in helping Staples paint
an evocative picture of life in the desert that includes
references to the hard facts of reality." Booklist
Followed by Haveli

Steinbeck, John, 1902-1968

The pearl; with drawings by José Clemente Orozco. Viking 1947 90p hardcover o.p. paperback available $5.95 (7 and up)   **Fic**
1. Mexico—Fiction 2. Poverty—Fiction
ISBN 0-14-017737-X (pa)

"Kino, a poor pearl-fisher, lives a happy albeit spartan life with his wife and their child. When he finds a magnificent pearl, the Pearl of the World, he is besieged by dishonest pearl merchants and envious neighbors. Even a greedy doctor ties his professional treatment of their baby when it is bitten by a scorpion to the possible acquisition of the pearl. After a series of disasters, Kino throws the pearl away since it has brought him only unhappiness." Shapiro. Fic for Youth. 3d edition

The red pony. Viking 100p $15.95; pa $5.95
                                                    Fic
1. Horses—Fiction 2. Ranch life—Fiction 3. California—Fiction
ISBN 0-670-59184-X; 0-14-017736-1 (pa)
                                        LC 86-1610
Also available G.K. Hall large print edition and in paperback from Bantam Bks.

First published 1937

"Jody Tiflin, ten years old, begins to grow up in these four vignettes describing his life on a farm in California. He takes responsibility for his red pony and suffers when it dies. An old man arouses Jody's curiosity about what is beyond the mountains, and he anxiously awaits the birth of a colt. His grandfather's tales are a source of interest and wonder for Jody." Shapiro. Fic for Youth. 3d edition

Stevenson, James, 1929-

The unprotected witness. Greenwillow Bks. 1997 170p $15   **Fic**
1. Witnesses—Fiction 2. Organized crime—Fiction 3. Homicide—Fiction
ISBN 0-688-15133-7   LC 96-39130
Also available in paperback from Dell
Sequel to The bones in the cliff (1995)

After the murder of his father, who has been hiding under the Witness Protection Program, Pete finds himself the target of sinister men who seem to think he knows where a large sum of money is hidden

"The first-person narrative is fluid, with crisp, natural dialogue and minimal but effective description. Stevenson has . . . created a great read, accessible and thought-provoking." Horn Book

Stevenson, Robert Louis, 1850-1894

Dr. Jekyll and Mr. Hyde (7 and up)   **Fic**

Various editions available
First published 1886 with title: The strange case of Dr. Jekyll and Mr. Hyde
"The disturbing tale of the dual personality of Dr. Jekyll, a physician. A generous and philanthropic man, he is preoccupied with the problems of good and evil and with the possibility of separating them into two distinct personalities. He develops a drug that transforms him into the demonic Mr. Hyde, in whose person he exhausts all the latent evil in his nature. He also creates an anti-

dote that will restore him to his respectable existence as Dr. Jekyll. Gradually, however, the unmitigated evil of his darker self predominates, until finally he performs an atrocious murder. . . . The novel is of great psychological perception and strongly concerned with ethical problems." Reader's Ency. 4th edition

Kidnapped (7 and up)   **Fic**
1. Adventure fiction 2. Scotland—Fiction

Various editions available
First published 1886
This historical novel "deals with the adventures of David Balfour, the young hero, and Alan Breck, a Jacobite who is considered one of Stevenson's most interesting and best-drawn characters. A sequel, *Catriona*, was published in 1893." Reader's Ency. 4th edition

Treasure Island   **Fic**
1. Buried treasure—Fiction 2. Pirates

Various editions available
First published 1882
Young Jim Hawkins discovers a treasure map in the chest of an old sailor who dies under mysterious circumstances at his mother's inn. He shows it to Dr. Livesey and Squire Trelawney who agree to outfit a ship and sail to Treasure Island. Among the crew is the pirate Long John Silver and his followers who are in pursuit of the treasure
"A masterpiece among romances." Baker. Guide to the Best Fic

Stewart, Jennifer J.

If that breathes fire, we're toast! Holiday House 1999 118p $15.95   **Fic**
1. Dragons—Fiction 2. Arizona—Fiction
ISBN 0-8234-1430-2   LC 98-36883
When twelve-year-old Rick and his mother move from San Diego to Tucson he is not too happy about the change, but when they get a fire-breathing, time-traveling dragon to replace their broken furnace, his new life starts to get more interesting
"The sharp, funny phrasing and the likable, believable characters give the book freshness and zip." Booklist

Stolz, Mary, 1920-

Cezanne Pinto; a memoir. Knopf 1994 279p $16; pa $4.99   **Fic**
1. Slavery—Fiction 2. African Americans—Fiction 3. Underground railroad—Fiction
ISBN 0-679-84917-3; 0-679-88933-7 (pa)
                                        LC 92-46765
In his old age Cezanne Pinto recalls his youth as a slave on a Virginia plantation, his escape to a new life in Canada, his return to the U.S. to fight in the Civil War, and his life as a cowboy in Texas where he searches for his long-lost mother
"Stolz laces bits of history into the narrative, introducing facts where they fit. The text is conversational, with much of it in dialect. As Cezanne becomes committed to learning and speaking more formal English, his effort is reflected by subtly evolving language. He is revealed as a complex and rich character, filled with sorrow and fortitude. A compelling book." SLJ

541

Strasser, Todd, 1950-

The accident. Delacorte Press 1988 178p o.p.;
Dell paperback available $4.50 (7 and up)   **Fic**
1. Drunk driving—Fiction 2. Mystery fiction
ISBN 0-440-20635-9 (pa)   LC 87-37411

After four of his friends leave a beer party and suffer
a fatal accident, eighteen-year-old Matt senses something
peculiar about the police investigation and suspects a
cover-up to hide the identity of who was really responsible for the accident

"In addition to the narrative of the accident and its aftermath, Strasser . . . provides the reader with factual information about the lethal combination of drinking and
driving. He gives it to his readers straight and lets them
form their own conclusions." Voice Youth Advocates

Close call. Putnam 1999 118p $15.99   **Fic**
1. Friendship—Fiction 2. Baseball—Fiction
ISBN 0-399-23134-X   LC 98-36947

A group of fifth and sixth graders find a way to deal
with personal differences, family problems, and some
rock-throwing high school boys so that they can play
baseball

"Winning elements include fully formed characters,
snappy, credible dialogue and a quick-moving plot that
tackles real-life issues with a light touch." Publ Wkly

Hey, Dad, get a life! Holiday House 1996 164p
$15.95   **Fic**
1. Ghost stories 2. Fathers and daughters—Fiction
3. Sisters—Fiction
ISBN 0-8234-1278-4   LC 96-46839
Also available in paperback from Troll

When a supernatural presence begins doing favors for
twelve-year-old Kelly and her eight-year-old sister Sasha,
they realize that the ghost of their dead father has returned to watch over them

"Touching yet surprisingly cheerful, this is a compassionate and accessible tale of a family's adjustment to
loss." Bull Cent Child Books

How I spent my last night on earth. Simon &
Schuster Bks. for Young Readers 1998 169p
(Time Zone High series) $16 (7 and up)   **Fic**
1. School stories
ISBN 0-689-81113-6   LC 97-43473

When a rumor appears on the Internet that a giant asteroid is about to destroy Earth, Legs Hanover scrambles
to meet the boy of her dreams, elusive Andros Bliss

"The pace is as frantic as an Internet virus rumor.
This is Armageddon-lite, and just the thing to chase
away the winter blues." Bull Cent Child Books

Other available titles in the Time Zone High series are:
Girl gives birth to own prom date (1996)
How I changed my life (1995)

Sutcliff, Rosemary, 1920-1992

Flame-colored taffeta. Farrar, Straus & Giroux
1986 129p $11.95; pa $4.95   **Fic**
1. Smuggling—Fiction 2. Great Britain—History—0-
1066—Fiction
ISBN 0-374-32344-5; 0-374-42341-5 (pa)
     LC 86-18351

This is a "tale of a girl who rescues a mysterious,
wounded man. Twelve-year-old Damaris, who lives on a
seaside Sussex farm, discovers a young man who has
been shot in the leg. She and 13-year-old Peter hide the
man, who calls himself Tom Wildgoose, in their secret
meeting place—a half-ruined cottage in the forest." Publ
Wkly

"The suspenseful story involves its characters less in
historical events than in personal interplay. . . . Rosemary Sutcliff is still a superbly evocative storyteller, conveying a vibrant sense of seasons and of place." Horn
Book

Sword song. Farrar, Straus & Giroux 1998
c1997 271p $18 (7 and up)   **Fic**
1. Vikings—Fiction 2. Great Britain—History—0-
1066—Fiction
ISBN 0-374-37363-9   LC 98-16827
First published 1997 in the United Kingdom

At sixteen, Bjarni is cast out of the Norse settlement
in the Angles' Land for an act of oath-breaking and
spends five years sailing the west coast of Scotland and
witnessing the feuds of the clan chiefs living there

"This is a well-crafted story that will appeal to sophisticated readers." SLJ

Sweeney, Joyce, 1955-

Free fall. Delacorte Press 1996 229p $15.95; pa
$4.50 (7 and up)   **Fic**
1. Caves—Fiction 2. Brothers—Fiction 3. Friendship—Fiction
ISBN 0-385-32211-9; 0-440-21975-2 (pa)
     LC 95-41340

"Lost while exploring an obscure cave in Ocala National Forest, brothers Neil and David and two of their
friends, Randy and Terry, seek escape not only from the
cave, but from the anger and guilt still festering from a
tragic fire that killed Neil and David's younger sister."
Bull Cent Child Books

"In their anger and frustration at the situation, a lot of
obscenity is used. . . . A gripping, sometimes scary tale
of survival and brotherhood." Voice Youth Advocates

Shadow. Delacorte Press 1994 216p $15.95; pa
$3.99 (7 and up)   **Fic**
1. Extrasensory perception—Fiction 2. Brothers and
sisters—Fiction 3. Cats—Fiction
ISBN 0-385-32051-5; 0-440-21986-8 (pa)
     LC 93-32215

During the summer when her older brothers' fighting
escalates dangerously, thirteen-year-old Sarah becomes
increasingly aware of her ability to sense things that others cannot, including the presence of her beloved dead
cat

"This book offers a suspenseful examination of friendship, loss and perception. Sweeney has created fully-
dimensional characters, and she portrays troubling family
dynamics with realism and sensitivity. Some dialogue between Brian and Patrick, though a realistic presentation
of their rage, may be strong for less mature readers."
Book Rep

Swift, Jonathan, 1667-1745

Gulliver's travels (7 and up)   **Fic**
1. Fantasy fiction

Swift, Jonathan, 1667-1745—*Continued*
Various editions available
First published 1726
"In the account of his four wonder-countries Swift satirizes contemporary manners and morals, art and politics—in fact the whole social scheme—from four different points of view. The huge Brobdingnagians reduce man to his natural insignificance, the little people of Lilliput parody Europe and its petty broils, in Laputa philosophers are ridiculed, and finally all Swift's hatred and contempt find their satisfaction in degrading humanity to a bestial condition." Baker. Guide to the Best Fic

Talbert, Marc, 1953-
The Purple Heart. HarperCollins Pubs. 1992
135p $14.95; pa $3.50   **Fic**
1. Fathers and sons—Fiction 2. Vietnam war, 1961-1975—Fiction
ISBN 0-06-020428-1; 0-380-71985-1 (pa)
                                          LC 91-23084
"Willa Perlman books"
When his wounded father is sent home early from Vietnam, Luke finds it difficult to adjust to the troubled, emotionally shaken man who seems so unlike the fearless hero of his dreams
"Characters have integrity and depth, especially Luke, who is particularly convincing and well developed. Filled with subtle but significant emotional parallels . . . Talbert's portrayal of the relationship is deeply moving but never sentimental." Booklist

Tamar, Erika, 1934-
The junkyard dog. Knopf 1995 185p $15; pa $4.99   **Fic**
1. Dogs—Fiction 2. Stepfathers—Fiction
ISBN 0-679-87057-1; 0-679-88561-7 (pa)
                                          LC 94-22368
"Katie begins to accept her new stepfather when he is the only one who can help her save the junkyard dog she loves. Her love for the mistreated dog and her distrust of her stepfather are both strong, and these well-developed, believable emotions carry the accessible story. Katie is an appealing heroine, and her life in a struggling urban neighborhood is compelling." Horn Book Guide

Tashjian, Janet, 1956-
Multiple choice. Holt & Co. 1999 186p $15.95
                                              Fic
1. Obsessive-compulsive neurosis—Fiction
ISBN 0-8050-6086-3   LC 98-43349
Monica, a fourteen-year-old perfectionist and word game expert, tries to break free from all of the suffocating rules in her life by creating a game for living called Multiple Choice
"This eye-opening, multifaceted exploration of obsessive-compulsive disorder is effectively packaged in a creative, compelling story."

Taylor, Mildred D.
The friendship; pictures by Max Ginsburg. Dial Bks. for Young Readers 1987 53p il $15.99; lib bdg $13.89; pa $3.99   **Fic**
1. African Americans—Fiction 2. Race relations—Fiction 3. Mississippi—Fiction
ISBN 0-8037-0417-8; 0-8037-0418-6 (lib bdg); 0-14-038964-4 (pa)   LC 86-29309
Coretta Scott King Award for text, 1988
"A bitter short story about race relations in rural Mississippi during the Depression focuses on an incident between an old Black man, Mr. Tom Bee, and a white storekeeper, Mr. John Wallace. Indebted to Tom for saving his life as a young man, John had promised they would always be friends. But now, years later, John insists that Tom call him 'Mister' and shoots the old man for defiantly—and publicly—calling him by his first name. Narrator Cassie Logan and her brothers, characters from Taylor's previous books, are verbally abused by Wallace's villainous sons before witnessing the encounter." Bull Cent Child Books

The gold Cadillac; pictures by Michael Hays. Dial Bks. for Young Readers 1987 43p il $15.99; lib bdg $12.89; pa $3.99   **Fic**
1. African Americans—Fiction 2. Prejudices—Fiction 3. Race relations—Fiction
ISBN 0-8037-0342-2; 0-8037-0343-0 (lib bdg); 0-14-038963-6 (pa)   LC 86-11526
"The shiny gold Cadillac that Daddy brings home one summer evening marks a stepping stone in the lives of Wilma and 'lois, two black sisters growing up in Ohio during the fifties. At first neighbors and relatives shower them with attention. But when the family begins the long journey to the South to show off the car to their Mississippi relatives, the girls, for the first time, encounter the undisguised ugliness of racial prejudice." Horn Book
"Full-page sepia paintings effectively portray the characters, setting, and mood of the story events as Hays ably demonstrates his understanding of the social and emotional environments which existed for blacks during this period." SLJ

Let the circle be unbroken. Dial Bks. for Young Readers 1981 394p $16.99; pa $4.99   **Fic**
1. African Americans—Fiction 2. Mississippi—Fiction 3. Great Depression, 1929-1939—Fiction
ISBN 0-8037-4748-9; 0-14-034892-1 (pa)
                                          LC 81-65854
Also available in paperback boxed set with Roll of Thunder, hear my cry and The road to Memphis
Sequel to Roll of thunder, hear my cry
This continuation of the Logan family's story covers "a series of tangential events so that it is a family record, a picture of the depression years in rural Mississippi, and an indictment of black-white relations in the Deep South. A young friend is convicted of a murder of which he is innocent, a pretty cousin is insulted by some white boys and her father taunted because he married a white woman, an elderly neighbor tries to vote, the government pays farmers to plow their crops under, etc." Bull Cent Child Books
The author "provides her readers with a literal sense of witnessing important American history. . . . Moreover, [she] never neglects the details of her volatile 9-year-old heroine's interior life. The daydreams, the jeal-

Taylor, Mildred D.—*Continued*
ousy, the incredible ardor of that age come alive." N Y
Times Book Rev

Mississippi bridge; by Mildred Taylor; pictures
by Max Ginsburg. Dial Bks. for Young Readers
1990 62p il $15.99; lib bdg $13.89; pa $3.99
Fic
1. Race relations—Fiction 2. African Americans—
Fiction 3. Prejudices—Fiction 4. Mississippi—Fiction
ISBN 0-8037-0426-7; 0-8037-0427-5 (lib bdg);
0-553-15992-5 (pa)   LC 89-27898
In this story featuring the children of Mississippi's Logan family, "Jeremy Simms, a 10-year-old white neighbor, describes a harrowing incident after the Logans and
other blacks are ordered off the weekly bus in a foggy
rainstorm." N Y Times Book Rev
"Taylor has shaped this episode into a haunting meditation that will leave readers vividly informed about segregation practices and the unequal rights that prevailed in
that era . . . a telling piece of social history." Booklist

The road to Memphis; by Mildred Taylor. Dial
Bks. 1989 290p $15; pa $4.99   **Fic**
1. Race relations—Fiction 2. African Americans—
Fiction 3. Mississippi—Fiction
ISBN 0-8037-0340-6; 0-14-036077-8 (pa)
LC 88-33654
Also available in paperback boxed set with Let the
circle be unbroken and Roll of thunder, hear my cry
Coretta Scott King award for text, 1989
Sadistically teased by two white boys in 1940's rural
Mississippi, Cassie Logan's friend, Moe, severely injures
one of the boys with a tire iron and enlists Cassie's help
in trying to flee the state
"Reading the previous books of the series is not nec-
essary in order to understand and enjoy this volume.
Taylor's continued smooth, easy language provides readability for all ages, with a focus on universal human
pride, worthy values, and individual responsibility. This
action-packed drama is highly recommended." Voice
Youth Advocates

Roll of thunder, hear my cry. Dial Bks. for
Young Readers 1976 276p $15.99; pa $4.99 **Fic**
1. African Americans—Fiction 2. Mississippi—Fiction
ISBN 0-8037-7473-7; 0-14-034893-X (pa)
Also available in paperback boxed set with Let the
circle be unbroken and The road to Memphis
Awarded the Newbery Medal, 1977
"The time is 1933. The place is Spokane, Mississippi
where the Logans, the only black family who own their
own land, wage a courageous struggle to remain independent, displeasing a white plantation owner bent on
taking their land. But this suspenseful tale is also about
the story's young narrator, Cassie, and her three brothers
who decide to wage their own personal battles to maintain the self-dignity and pride with which they were
raised. . . . Ms. Taylor's richly textured novel shows a
strong, proud black family . . . resisting rather than suc-
cumbing to oppression." Child Book Rev Serv
Followed by Let the circle be unbroken

Song of the trees; pictures by Jerry Pinkney.
Dial Bks. for Young Readers 1975 48p il
hardcover o.p. paperback available $3.99   **Fic**
1. African Americans—Fiction 2. Great Depression,
1929-1939—Fiction 3. Mississippi—Fiction
ISBN 0-440-41396-6 (pa)
Eight-year-old Cassie Logan tells how her family
"leaving Mississippi during the Depression was cheated
into selling for practically nothing valuable and beautiful
giant old pines and hickories, beeches and walnuts in the
forest surrounding their house." Adventuring with Books

The well; David's story. Dial Bks. for Young
Readers 1995 92p $14.99; lib bdg $14.89   **Fic**
1. African Americans—Fiction 2. Race relations—
Fiction 3. Mississippi—Fiction
ISBN 0-8037-1802-0; 0-8037-1803-9 (lib bdg)
LC 94-25360
"David Logan (Cassie's father) tells this story from
his childhood. . . . There's a drought, and the Logans
possess the only well in the area that has not gone dry.
Black and white alike come for water freely given by the
family, but the Simms boys can't seem to stand the nec-
essary charity, and their resentment explodes when David's big brother Hammer beats Charlie Simms after
Charlie hits David." Bull Cent Child Books
This story "delivers an emotional wallop in a concentrated span of time and action. . . . This story reverberates in the heart long after the final paragraph is read."
Horn Book

Taylor, Theodore, 1921-
The cay. Doubleday 1969 137p $15.95   **Fic**
1. Race relations—Fiction 2. Caribbean region—Fiction 3. Survival after airplane accidents, shipwrecks,
etc.—Fiction 4. Blind—Fiction
ISBN 0-385-07906-0
Also available in paperback from Avon Bks.
"When the freighter which was to take Phillip and his
mother from wartime Curacao to the United States is tor-
pedoed, Phillip finds himself afloat on a small raft with
a hugh, old, very black West Indian man. Phillip becomes blind from injuries and resents his dependence
upon old Timothy. Through exciting adventures on a
very small cay (coral island), Phillip learns to overcome
his prejudice toward Timothy and to see him as a man
and a friend." Read Ladders for Hum Relat. 5th edition
"Starkly dramatic, believable and compelling." Saturday Rev
Followed by Timothy of the cay

Sweet Friday Island. Harcourt Brace & Co.
1994 173p $10.95; pa $5 (7 and up)   **Fic**
1. Survival after airplane accidents, shipwrecks, etc.—
Fiction 2. Fathers and daughters—Fiction 3. Baja California (Mexico: Peninsula)—Fiction 4. Islands—Fiction
ISBN 0-15-200009-7; 0-15-200012-7 (pa)
LC 93-32435
First published 1984 by Scholastic
"Teenage Peg and her father go on a camping vacation to a supposedly uninhabited island in the Sea of
Cortez. Ignoring the warnings of the mainland locals
. . . they arrive on the island only to become quickly
victimized by an unseen assailant they label Señor Psy-

Taylor, Theodore, 1921——*Continued*
cho." SLJ

"Lots of suspense, lots of tension with a father-daughter combination that is unique and believable. The adventure is plausible, fast moving and sure to please adventure fans." Voice Youth Advocates

Timothy of the cay. Harcourt Brace & Co. 1993 161p $13.95 **Fic**
1. Race relations—Fiction 2. Caribbean region—Fiction 3. Survival after airplane accidents, shipwrecks, etc.—Fiction 4. Blind—Fiction
ISBN 0-15-288358-4   LC 93-7898
Also available in paperback from Avon Bks.

In this sequel to The cay, "Taylor brings Timothy from his West Indian adolescence to his final voyage of the ill-fated SS Hato and Phillip from the rescue ship's sick bay, two months after Timothy's death, to the moment when he can return to the cay where it all began." Voice Youth Advocates

"Somewhat more thoughtful than its well-loved antecedent, this boldly drawn novel is no less commanding." Publ Wkly

The weirdo. Harcourt Brace Jovanovich 1991 289p $15.95 (7 and up) **Fic**
1. Bears—Fiction 2. Wildlife conservation—Fiction 3. North Carolina—Fiction
ISBN 0-15-294952-6   LC 91-55415
Also available in paperback from Avon Bks.

Seventeen-year-old Chip Clewt fights to save the black bears in the Powhaten National Wildlife Refuge

"Taylor weaves strong elements of natural history and human psychology into a long but absorbing suspense story. . . . The violence erupting in the disagreement between conservationists and hunters is timely, realistic, and chilling." Horn Book

Temple, Frances, 1945-1995

The Beduins' gazelle. Orchard Bks. 1996 150p $15.95; lib bdg $16.99 **Fic**
1. Bedouins—Fiction 2. Deserts—Fiction 3. Middle East—Fiction
ISBN 0-531-09519-3; 0-531-08869-3 (lib bdg)
LC 95-33530
Also available in paperback from HarperCollins
"A Richard Jackson book"

"In 1302, Atiyah and Halima, cousins betrothed at birth, are separated when Atiyah travels from the desert to Fez to study. . . . While in Fez, Atiyah meets and befriends Etienne, a French pilgrim who is studying Arabic, whom readers met in 'The Ramsay Scallop' . . . . When word travels to Atiyah that Halima is lost, he and Etienne return to the desert to find her. But Halima is rescued by another tribe whose sheikh wants her as his newest wife." Voice Youth Advocates

"Told in short, rapid chapters, Temple's briskly paced story is fueled by a cast of complex, emotionally resonant characters." Publ Wkly

Grab hands and run. Orchard Bks. 1993 165p $15.95; lib bdg $16.99 **Fic**
1. El Salvador—Fiction 2. Refugees—Fiction 3. Canada—Fiction
ISBN 0-531-05480-2; 0-531-08630-5 (lib bdg)
LC 92-34063

Also available in paperback from HarperCollins
"A Richard Jackson book"

After his father disappears, twelve-year-old Felipe, his mother, and his younger sister set out on a difficult and dangerous journey, trying to make their way from their home in El Salvador to Canada

"The taut and absorbing escape is made all the more real by the fully fleshed out characters and heart-stopping situations." SLJ

The Ramsay scallop; a novel. Orchard Bks. 1994 310p $18.95; lib bdg $19.99 **Fic**
1. Middle Ages—Fiction 2. Pilgrims and pilgrimages—Fiction
ISBN 0-531-06836-6; 0-531-08686-0 (lib bdg)
LC 93-29697
Also available in paperback from HarperCollins
"A Richard Jackson book"

At the turn of the fourteenth century in England, fourteen-year-old Elenor finds her betrothal to an ambitious lord's son launching her on a memorable pilgrimage to far-off Spain

"With a nod to *The Canterbury Tales*, the book highlights the stories that their fellow pilgrims share with Elenor and Thomas; the stories are sad, romantic, and instructive, and all help shape the journey into the special thing it becomes for the duo. . . . The leisurely pace of the pilgrimage allows the author to introduce a large cast of characters and to decorate her story with historical details that enlighten and intrigue." Booklist

Tonight, by sea; a novel. Orchard Bks. 1995 152p $15.95; lib bdg $16.99 **Fic**
1. Refugees—Fiction 2. Haiti—Fiction
ISBN 0-531-06899-4; 0-531-08749-2 (lib bdg)
LC 94-32167
Also available in paperback from HarperCollins
"A Richard Jackson book"

As governmental brutality and poverty become unbearable, Paulie joins with others in her small Haitian village to help her uncle secretly build a boat they will use to try to escape to the United States

"In an elegant prose style [the author] captures the lyrical cadence of Creole speech and paints an affecting portrait of a proud, resourceful people trying to survive in the face of lawlessness and tyranny." SLJ

Thesman, Jean

The ornament tree. Houghton Mifflin 1996 232p $16 (7 and up) **Fic**
1. Orphans—Fiction 2. Feminism—Fiction
ISBN 0-395-74278-1   LC 95-17102
Also available in paperback from Avon Bks.

"In 1914 in Seattle, 14-year-old orphan Bonnie moves to the boardinghouse of her independent-minded female relatives and becomes involved with the people who live and work there. . . . The focus is on the events of the times, including the end of World War I, the flu epidemic, the labor riots, the start of Prohibition, and, above all, the struggle for women's rights." Booklist

"The underlying issues are substantial, but the presentation is laced with humor and warmth—no small feat." Horn Book

Followed by The tree of bells

Thesman, Jean—*Continued*
The other ones. Viking 1999 181p $15.99 (7 and up)   **Fic**
1. Witchcraft—Fiction 2. School stories
ISBN 0-670-88594-0   LC 98-45711
High school sophomore Bridget Raynes has to decide whether or not to accept her powers of witchcraft, or abandon them and try to fit in as an ordinary teenager
"Thesman has created a quiet and thought-provoking coming-of-age story delightfully flavored with touches of humor, romance, and teenage angst." Voice Youth Advocates

The storyteller's daughter. Houghton Mifflin 1997 180p $16 (7 and up)   **Fic**
1. Fathers and daughters—Fiction 2. Great Depression, 1929-1939—Fiction 3. Family life—Fiction
ISBN 0-395-80978-9   LC 96-1756
Also available in paperback from Puffin Bks.
Fifteen-year-old Quinn, the middle child in a Depression-era working class family, learns some secrets about her beloved father, who has always been a source of strength and optimism for his family, friends, and neighbors
"Thesman describes the sights, smells, and sounds her characters experience so effectively that the reader quickly becomes absorbed in the story." Voice Youth Advocates

Summerspell. Simon & Schuster Bks. for Young Readers 1995 169p $15 (7 and up)   **Fic**
1. Runaway teenagers—Fiction
ISBN 0-671-50130-5   LC 94-25737
"When she runs away from home - and from her brother-in-law's unwanted sexual attentions - to her grandmother's cabin in the woods, Jocelyn is followed by friend Baily. Her attempts at escape and self-discovery are further complicated by the appearance of a nervous, suspicious stranger, who turns out to be a girl in disguise." Horn Book Guide
"There are many elements to this contemporary, realistic novel including environmental concerns; sexual abuse; dysfunctional families; and racial bigotry." SLJ

The tree of bells. Houghton Mifflin 1999 232p $15 (7 and up)   **Fic**
1. Feminism—Fiction
ISBN 0-395-90510-9   LC 98-27787
Sequel to The ornament tree
"Keeping secret her cousin Bonnie's plans to travel to China, sixteen-year-old Clare Harris contemplates her own future. . . . Clare becomes more interested in helping the underprivileged in 1920s Seattle and more involved in the small dramas taking place at her family's lively boarding house. For those who enjoyed the first book, this installment will more than satisfy." Horn Book Guide

Thompson, Julian F., 1927-
Brothers. Knopf 1998 217p $17; lib bdg $18.99 (7 and up)   **Fic**
1. Militia movements—Fiction 2. Brothers—Fiction 3. Mentally ill—Fiction
ISBN 0-679-89082-3; 0-679-99082-8 (lib bdg)   LC 98-11001

When his idolized older brother leaves college for a mental health facility and then disapppears, seventeen-year-old Chris follows him to the compound of an anti-government militia group and tries to rescue him
"With intriguing characters and a fast-moving plot, this book will grab readers." SLJ

The grounding of Group 6. Holt & Co. 1997 291p $15.95 (7 and up)   **Fic**
1. Horror fiction
ISBN 0-8050-5085-X   LC 96-38546
First published 1983 by Avon Bks.
Arriving at what they believe is an exclusive school, five sixteen-year olds are unaware that they have been sent there to be exterminated and that their teacher is a murderer for hire
"The satiric thriller is pure page-turning entertainment." Horn Book Guide

Thompson, Kate
Midnight's choice. Hyperion Bks. for Children 1999 236p $15.99; lib bdg $16.49; pa $5.99   **Fic**
1. Supernatural—Fiction
ISBN 0-7868-0381-9; 0-7868-2329-1 (lib bdg); 0-7868-1266-4 (pa)   LC 98-39546
Sequel to Switchers
Tess, who has the ability to change into animal form, must choose between good and evil as she tries to decide whether to "Switch" into a phoenix or a vampire for the rest of time
"Full of action and depth. . . . It is a mesmerizing and respectful look, through the lens of fantasy, at young people making the decisions that will shape their adult lives." SLJ

Switchers. Hyperion Bks. for Children 1998 219p $14.95; lib bdg $15.49; pa $5.99   **Fic**
1. Weather—Fiction 2. Supernatural—Fiction 3. Arctic regions—Fiction
ISBN 0-7868-0380-0; 0-7868-2328-3 (lib bdg); 0-7868-1266-4 (pa)   LC 97-33056
When freakish weather grips the Arctic regions and moves southward Tess and Kevin save the world from disaster through their ability to switch into animal forms
"A terrific read that's sure to keep youngsters turning pages. . . . This tale will incite imaginations and provide a launching pad for discussion." SLJ
Followed by Midnight's choice

Tolan, Stephanie S., 1942-
The face in the mirror. Morrow Junior Bks. 1998 214p $15   **Fic**
1. Ghost stories 2. Theater—Fiction
ISBN 0-688-15394-1   LC 97-48359
Joining his estranged father in a professional production of Shakespeare's "Richard III," Jared tries to cope with acting insecurities, his obnoxious half brother, and a theater ghost
"Drama buffs will especially enjoy this well-paced ghost story." Horn Book Guide

Welcome to the Ark. Morrow Junior Bks. 1996 250p $15; pa $4.95 (7 and up)   **Fic**
1. Gifted children—Fiction 2. Parapsychology—Fiction
ISBN 0-688-13724-5; 0-688-15861-7 (pa)   LC 96-10163

Tolan, Stephanie S., 1942—*Continued*

"Four troubled young people live in a group home: Doug, seventeen, Miranda, sixteen, Taryn, nine, and Elijah, eight. Formerly patients in a psychiatric hospital, they are chosen for the home because of their exceptional intelligence and psychic powers. . . . The kids 'connect' with each other through dreams and telepathy, and reach out to others like themselves all over the world via the Internet. . . . Tolan does a superb job depicting emotionally disturbed, gifted youth. . . . The book will be best appreciated by sophisticated readers who understand its subtleties." Voice Youth Advocates

Tolkien, J. R. R. (John Ronald Reuel), 1892-1973

The hobbit; or, There and back again; illustrated by the author. Houghton Mifflin 1938 310p il $14.95; pa $11.95   **Fic**
1. Fantasy fiction
ISBN 0-395-07122-4; 0-395-28265-9 (pa)
                                               LC 38-5859
Also available from Houghton Mifflin in an edition with illustrations by Michael Hague for $29.95 (ISBN 0-395-36290-3); paperback available from Ballantine Bks.
First published 1937 in the United Kingdom
"This fantasy features the adventures of hobbit Bilbo Baggins, who joins a band of dwarves led by Gandalf the Wizard. Together they seek to recover the stolen treasure that is hidden in Lonely Mountain and guarded by Smaug the Dragon." Shapiro. Fic for Youth. 3d edition
"The background of the story is full of authentic bits of mythology and magic and the book has the rare quality of style. It is written with a quiet humor and the logical detail in which children take delight. . . . But this is a book with no age limits." Horn Book
Followed by The lord of the rings trilogy

The lord of the rings. 2nd ed. Houghton Mifflin 1967 c1966 3v ea $21.95, pa $11.95 (7 and up)
                                               Fic
1. Fantasy fiction
                                               LC 76-12275
Also available in a boxed set for $75, pa $45.95 (ISBN 0-395-19395-8; 0-395-48907-5); also available in paperback from Ballantine Bks.
The trilogy was first published 1954-55 in the United Kingdom. This revised edition first published 1966 in the United Kingdom
Contents: v1 The fellowship of the ring (ISBN 0-395-48931-8; 0-395-27223-8); v2 The two towers (ISBN 0-395-48933-4; 0-395-27222-X); v3 The return of the king (0-395-48930-X; 0-395-27221-1)
"This is a tale of imaginary gnomelike creatures who battle against evil. Led by Frodo, the hobbits embark on a journey to prevent a magic ring from falling into the grasp of the powers of darkness. The forces of good succeed in their fight against the Dark Lord of evil, and Frodo and Sam bring the Ring to Mount Doom, where it is destroyed." Shapiro. Fic for Youth. 3d edition

Tomlinson, Theresa

Child of the May. Orchard Bks. 1998 120p $15.95; lib bdg $16.99   **Fic**
1. Maid Marian (Legendary character)—Fiction
2. Robin Hood (Legendary character)—Fiction
3. Great Britain—Fiction
ISBN 0-531-30118-4; 0-531-33118-0 (lib bdg)
                                               LC 98-15440
Sequel to The forestwife
Fifteen-year-old Magda helps Robin Hood's men rescue Lady Matilda and her daughter Isabelle from the clutches of the Sheriff of Nothingham's evil henchman
"Although the plot is well constructed, the novel's strength is in its fully realized setting and cast of strong-willed characters." Horn Book

The Forestwife. Orchard Bks. 1995 170p $16.95; lib bdg $17.99   **Fic**
1. Maid Marian (Legendary character)—Fiction
2. Robin Hood (Legendary character)—Fiction
3. Great Britain—Fiction
ISBN 0-531-09450-2; 0-531-08750-6 (lib bdg)
                                               LC 94-33007
Also available in paperback from Dell
In England during the reign of King Richard I, fifteen-year-old Marian escapes from an arranged marriage to live with a community of forest folk that includes a daring young outlaw named Robert
"This exciting book is based on Medieval folk tales of the Green Lady and Green Man and Robin Hood. . . . The book is full of strong, memorable characters, action, and vivid descriptions with an underlying love story." Voice Youth Advocates
Followed by Child of the May

Turner, Megan Whalen, 1965-

The thief. Greenwillow Bks. 1996 219p $15
                                               Fic
1. Adventure fiction 2. Thieves—Fiction
ISBN 0-688-14627-9   LC 95-41040
Also available in paperback from Puffin Bks.
A Newbery Medal honor book, 1997
"Gen languishes in prison for boasting of his skill as a thief. The magus—the king's powerful advisor—needing a clever thief to find an ancient ring that gives the owner the right to rule a neighboring country, bails Gen out. Their journey toward the treasure is marked by danger and political intrigue, and features a motley cast, tales of old gods, and the revelation of Gen's true identity." Publisher's note
"A tantalizing, suspenseful, exceptionally clever novel. . . . The author's characterization of Gen is simply superb." Horn Book

Twain, Mark, 1835-1910

The adventures of Huckleberry Finn   **Fic**
1. Mississippi River—Fiction 2. Missouri—Fiction

Various editions available
First published 1885. This is a companion volume to The adventures of Tom Sawyer
This novel "begins with Huck's escape from his drunken, brutal father to the river, where he meets up with Jim, a runaway slave. The story of their journey

Twain, Mark, 1835-1910—*Continued*
downstream, with occasional forays into the society
along the banks, is an American classic that captures the
smells, rhythms, and sounds, the variety of dialects and
the human activity of life on the great river. It is also a
penetrating social commentary that reveals corruption,
moral decay, and intellectual impoverishment through
Huck and Jim's encounters with traveling actors and con
men, lynch mobs, thieves, and southern gentility." Reader's Ency. 4th edition

The adventures of Tom Sawyer   **Fic**
1. Mississippi River—Fiction 2. Missouri—Fiction

Various editions available
First published 1876
The plot "is episodic, dealing in part with Tom's
pranks in school, Sunday school, and the respectable
world of his Aunt Polly, and in part with his adventures
with Huck Finn, the outcaste son of the local ne'er-do-
well. . . . Tom and Huck witness a murder and, in terror
of the murderer, Injun Joe, secretly flee to Jackson's island. They are searched for, are finally mourned for
dead, and return to town in time to attend their own funeral. Tom and his sweetheart, Becky Thatcher get lost
in a cave in which Injun Joe is hiding. . . . The story
closely follows incidents involving Twain and his friends
that occured in Hannibal, Mo." Benet's Reader's Ency of
Am Lit
Followed by two sequels Tom Sawyer abroad (1894)
and Tom Sawyer, detective, (1896)

A Connecticut Yankee in King Arthur's court
                              Fic
1. Arthur, King—Fiction 2. Chivalry—Fiction
3. Great Britain—History—0-1066—Fiction

Various editions available
First published 1889; published in the United Kingdom with title: Yankee at the court of King Arthur
This satiric novel is a "tale of a commonsensical Yankee who is carried back in time to Britain in the Dark
Ages, and it celebrates homespun ingenuity and democratic values in contrast to the superstitious ineptitude of
a feudal monarchy." Merriam-Webster's Ency of Lit

The prince and the pauper   **Fic**
1. Edward VI, King of England, 1537-1553—Fiction
2. Great Britain—History—1485-1603, Tudors—Fiction

Various editions available
First published 1881
"Edward VI of England and a little pauper change
places a few days before Henry VIII's death. The prince
wanders in rags, while Tom Canty suffers the horrors of
princedom. At the last moment, the mistake is rectified.
The book, dedicated to Twain's two daughters, is a favorite among children." Reader's Ency. 4th edition

Uchida, Yoshiko, 1921-1992
A jar of dreams. Atheneum Pubs. 1981 131p
$15; pa $3.95   **Fic**
1. Japanese Americans—Fiction 2. Family life—Fiction 3. Prejudices—Fiction 4. California—Fiction
ISBN 0-689-50210-9; 0-689-71041-0 (pa)
                                 LC 81-3480

"A Margaret K. McElderry book"
"A story of the Depression Era is told by eleven-year-
old Rinko, the only girl in a Japanese-American family
living in Oakland and suffering under the double burden
of financial pressure and the prejudice that had increased
with the tension of economic competition. Into the
household comes a visitor who is a catalyst for change."
Bull Cent Child Books
"Rinko in her guilelessness is genuine and refreshing,
and her worries and concerns seem wholly natural, honest, and convincing." Horn Book
Other available titles about Rinko Tsujimura and her
family are:
The best bad thing (1983)
The happiest ending (1985)

Journey home; illustrated by Charles Robinson.
Atheneum Pubs. 1978 131p il $16; pa $3.95
                                    Fic
1. Japanese Americans—Fiction 2. Prejudices—Fiction 3. Family life—Fiction
ISBN 0-689-50126-9; 0-689-70755-X (pa)
                                    LC 78-8792

Sequel to Journey to Topaz
"A Margaret K. McElderry book"
"The bittersweet story of a Japanese-American family's struggle to return to a normal life after their
relocation camp experience in Utah. . . . Seen through
the eyes of twelve-year-old Yuki, the plight of her parents, who want to return to California, the disillusion-
ment of her brother, who returns from the war with shattered dreams, and the despair of her friends, who want
to rebuild their lives in spite of the hostility outside the
camp, take on a special poignancy." Child Book Rev
Serv
"This book fills a great need in describing the cruel
treatment inflicted upon Japanese-Americans during
World War II by fellow Americans." SLJ

Journey to Topaz; a story of the
Japanese-American evacuation; illustrated by
Donald Carrick. Scribner 1971 149p il o.p.;
Creative Art Publs. paperback available $9.95
                                    Fic
1. Japanese Americans—Fiction
ISBN 0-916870-85-5 (pa)
This is the story of eleven-year-old Yuki, her eigh-
teen-year-old brother and her mother, who were uproot-
ed, evacuated and interned in Topaz, the War Relocation
Center in Utah during World War II
"This tragic herding of innocent people is described
with dignity and a sorrowful sense of injustice that never
becomes bitter." Saturday Rev
Followed by Journey home

Ure, Jean
Plague. Harcourt Brace Jovanovich 1991 218p
$16.95 (7 and up)   **Fic**
1. Epidemics—Fiction 2. London (England)—Fiction
ISBN 0-15-262429-5   LC 91-8714
Also available in paperback from Penguin Bks.
First published 1989 in the United Kingdom with title:
Plague 99

Ure, Jean—*Continued*

"Sixteen-year-old Fran returns from a four-week wilderness trip to find that London has suffered a terrible catastrophe that has left most of its inhabitants, including her parents, dead. She finds her now-orphaned best friend, Harriet, and they meet Shahid, a former schoolmate. The three band together to try to survive in the hostile, nearly deserted city. . . . A riveting and thought-provoking novel, sure to attract a wide audience." Booklist

Van Leeuwen, Jean

Blue sky, butterfly. Dial Bks. for Young Readers 1996 125p $14.99; pa $4.99   **Fic**
1. Divorce—Fiction 2. Family life—Fiction
ISBN 0-8037-1972-8; 0-14-038153-8 (pa)
LC 95-34511

"Twig, 11, is desolate at the unforseen collapse of her parents' marriage. Her mother, normally intelligent, loving, and active, retreats into a silent depression, giving up everyday routines like laundry, shopping, and cooking. Twig's older brother retreats into his room and his music. Her father is simply absent. . . . Twig's story is brief but intense, honest and effective." SLJ

Bound for Oregon; pictures by James Watling. Dial Bks. for Young Readers 1994 167p il map $14.99; lib bdg $14.89; pa $4.99   **Fic**
1. Todd, Mary Ellen, 1843-1924—Fiction 2. Overland journeys to the Pacific—Fiction 3. Oregon Trail—Fiction
ISBN 0-8037-1526-9; 0-8037-1527-7 (lib bdg); 0-14-038319-0 (pa)   LC 93-26709

A fictionalized account of the journey made by nine-year-old Mary Ellen Todd and her family from their home in Arkansas westward over the Oregon Trail in 1852

"The appealing narrator, the forthright telling, and the concrete details of life along the Oregon Trail will draw readers into the story." Booklist

Vanasse, Deb

Out of the wilderness. Clarion Bks. 1999 165p $15   **Fic**
1. Fathers and sons—Fiction 2. Brothers—Fiction 3. Wilderness survival—Fiction 4. Alaska—Fiction
ISBN 0-395-91421-3   LC 98-22692

Josh tries to endure living in the Alaskan wilderness with his father and half-brother Nathan, but Nathan's uncompromising reverence for nature and its wild creatures causes difficulties that reinforce Josh's determination to return to city life

"This story succeeds on several levels. The characters are believable and the reader appreciates the interwoven struggles Josh faces. . . . The beauty and danger of the Alaskan wilderness is lined in lyrical prose that rises above most tales of adventure." ALAN

Vande Velde, Vivian, 1951-

A coming evil. Houghton Mifflin 1998 213p $16   **Fic**
1. World War, 1939-1945—Fiction 2. France—Fiction
ISBN 0-395-90012-3   LC 97-32196

"Parisian 13-year-old Lizette is sent to live with her aunt in German-occupied rural France in the fall of 1940. There she meets Gerard, the ghost of a fourteenth-century Templar knight. . . . As she learns more about Gerard and the evils of his time, she comes to understand the true dangers of the Nazi occupation, and the importance of helping her aunt hide several Jewish and Gypsy children." Booklist

This is a "well-written novel. . . . The plot moves briskly and Vande Velde does a good job of creating the war-time atmosphere of fear and suspicion." SLJ

Ghost of a hanged man. Marshall Cavendish 1998 95p $14.95   **Fic**
1. Ghost stories 2. West (U.S.)—Fiction
ISBN 0-7614-5015-7   LC 97-23773

An outlaw condemned to be hanged threatens to wreak vengeance from the grave on those responsible for his death

"Fast-paced and delightfully creepy." Horn Book Guide

Never trust a dead man. Harcourt Brace & Co. 1999 194p $17   **Fic**
1. Mystery fiction
ISBN 0-15-201899-9   LC 98-39885

Wrongly convicted of murder and punished by being sealed in the tomb with the dead man, seventeen-year-old Selwyn enlists the help of a witch and the resurrected victim to find the true killer

"Filled with engaging characters, witty dialogue, and lots of action, this is an entertaining blend of fantasy, whodunit, and comedy." SLJ

Verne, Jules, 1828-1905

Around the world in eighty days   **Fic**
1. Voyages around the world—Fiction 2. Adventure fiction

Various editions available
Original French edition, 1873

"The hero, Phileas Fogg, undertakes his hasty world tour as the result of a bet made at his London club. He and his French valet Passepartout meet with some fantastic adventures, but these are overcome by the loyal servant and the endlessy inventive Fogg. The feat they perform is incredible for its day; Fogg wins his bet, having circled the world in only eighty days." Reader's Ency. 4th edition

A journey to the centre of the earth   **Fic**
1. Adventure fiction 2. Science fiction

Various editions available
Original French edition, 1864. Variant title: A trip to the center of the earth

"More than half the book is given to the preliminaries before the actual descent begins, the first two chapters relying on a standard point of departure, the discovery of a manuscript giving the location of the caverns in Iceland. The narrative shows Verne's intense care in presenting the latest scientific thought of his age, while the sighting of the plesiosaurus and the giant humanoid shepherding mammoths indicates how well he incorporated lengthy imaginary episodes to flesh out the factual report." Anatomy of Wonder 4

Verne, Jules, 1828-1905—*Continued*

Twenty thousand leagues under the sea   **Fic**
1. Submarines—Fiction 2. Sea stories 3. Science fiction

Various editions available
Original French edition, 1870
This romance is "remarkable for its prognostication of the invention of deep-sea submarines. The central characters of the tale, in the process of exploring marine disturbances, are captured by the megalomaniacal Captain Nemo. An undersea tour in a strange craft and their ensuing escape conclude the work." Reader's Ency. 4th edition

Voigt, Cynthia

Bad girls. Scholastic 1996 277p $16.95; pa $4.50   **Fic**
1. School stories 2. Friendship—Fiction
ISBN 0-590-60134-2; 0-590-60135-0 (pa)
LC 95-16168
After meeting on the first day in Mrs. Chemsky's fifth-grade class, Margalo and Mikey help each other in and out of trouble, as they try to maintain a friendship while each asserts her independence
"The talk is very funny . . . the action is nonstop; and the confrontations are dramatic, both verbal and physical." Booklist
Another available title about Margalo and Mikey is:
Bad, badder, baddest (1997)

Dicey's song. Atheneum Pubs. 1982 196p $17 (7 and up)   **Fic**
1. Grandmothers—Fiction
ISBN 0-689-30944-9   LC 82-3882
Also available in paperback from Fawcett Bks.
Awarded the Newbery Medal, 1983
Sequel to Homecoming
Dicey "had brought her siblings to the grandmother they'd never seen when their mother (now in a mental institution) had been unable to cope. This is the story of the children's adjustment to Gram (and hers to them) and to a new school and a new life—but with some of the old problems. Dicey, in particular, has a hard time since she must abandon her role of surrogate mother and share the responsibility with Gram." Bull Cent Child Books
"The vividness of Dicey is striking. . . . Unlike most sequels, this outdoes its predecessor by being more fully realized and consequently more resonant." Booklist

Homecoming. Atheneum Pubs. 1981 312p $18 (7 and up)   **Fic**
1. Brothers and sisters—Fiction 2. Abandoned children—Fiction
ISBN 0-689-30833-7   LC 80-36723
Also available in paperback from Fawcett Bks.
"When their momma abandons them in a shopping center, Dicey Tillerman and her three younger brothers and sisters set out on foot for where momma was ostensibly taking them—to Great-Aunt Cilla's in Bridgeport, Connecticut. They arrive to find only Cousin Eunice; Priscilla has died. Eunice, mindlessly religious and insensitive to their needs, agrees to look after them. But Dicey

knows she has to take another chance and another journey, this time to Crisfield, Maryland, where she hopes their unknown grandmother might provide a better home." Booklist
"The characterizations of the children are original and intriguing, and there are a number of interesting minor characters encountered in their travels." SLJ
Followed by Dicey's song

Izzy, willy-nilly. Atheneum Pubs. 1986 258p $17; pa $4.99 (7 and up)   **Fic**
1. Physically handicapped—Fiction
ISBN 0-689-31202-4; 0-689-80446-6 (pa)
LC 85-22933
"An amputee after a drunk-driving accident, Izzy struggles to accept what has happened and in doing so becomes not only a deeper, stronger person but also begins to see her family and friends in a new, revealing light." Booklist
"Voigt shows unusual insight into the workings of a 15-year-old girl's mind. . . . Just as Voigt's perceptive empathy brings Izzy to life, other characterizations are memorable, whether of Izzy's shallow former friends or of her egocentric 10-year-old sister." Publ Wkly

Jackaroo. Atheneum Pubs. 1985 291p $20 (7 and up)   **Fic**
1. Heroes and heroines—Fiction 2. Adventure fiction
ISBN 0-689-31123-0   LC 85-7954
Also available in paperback from Scholastic
"An Argo book"
"In a far-off feudal kingdom, where the people are hungry and oppressed by the lords, 16-year-old Gwyn, the innkeeper's daughter, takes on the identity of a masked legendary hero, Jackaroo, whose brave deeds for the poor have always inspired hope in harsh times." Booklist
"The style is fluid and consistent with the personalities of her characters; the setting is evoked through skillfully crafted description; the situations speak directly to the human condition. What is most notable, however, is the skill with which the social and political structures are described without interrupting the flow of the plot." Horn Book

On fortune's wheel. Atheneum Pubs. 1990 276p hardcover o.p. paperback available $4.99 (7 and up)   **Fic**
1. Adventure fiction
ISBN 0-689-82957-4 (pa)   LC 89-39010
Also available in paperback from Fawcett Bks.
Faced with the prospect of an unhappy life in the Kingdom, fourteen-year-old Birle accompanies a young runaway nobleman on a journey south and falls into slavery in the citadel of a cruel prince
"*On Fortune's Wheel,* set in the same imaginary world as *Jackaroo* is a lush narrative woven from elements of classic fairy tales and legends." Publ Wkly

A solitary blue. Atheneum Pubs. 1983 189p $16 (7 and up)   **Fic**
1. Divorce—Fiction 2. Parent and child—Fiction
ISBN 0-689-31008-0   LC 83-6007
Also available in paperback from Scholastic

Voigt, Cynthia—*Continued*

Jeff Greene, a minor character from Dicey's song, "is abandoned by his mother at age seven and suffers from the benign neglect of his college professor father. As a teenager, Jeff again sees and is charmed by his mother only to become disillusioned by her." Child Book Rev Serv

"This is the most mature and sophisticated of Voigt's novels. . . . Beautifully knit . . . compelling and intelligent." Bull Cent Child Books

Wallace, Bill, 1947-

Aloha summer. Holiday House 1997 168p $15.95　**Fic**
1. Moving—Fiction 2. Hawaii—Fiction
ISBN 0-8234-1306-3　LC 96-48778
In 1925 fourteen-year-old John, an Oklahoma farm boy, has to accept many changes in his life when his father takes a job on a pineapple plantation in Hawaii and the family moves there

"Honest, vulnerable John narrates this sweet yet unsentimental look at first love, the poison of prejudice, and plain folk who know what is right and what is not." Voice Youth Advocates

Eye of the great bear. Pocket Bks. 1999 162p $14　**Fic**
1. West (U.S.)—Fiction
ISBN 0-671-02504-X
"A face-to-face encounter with a big grizzly cures a jumpy 12-year-old of his fear of being afraid in this family adventure set in turn-of-the-century western Texas and Montana. . . . The tale is vigorously told, with uncomplicated situations, cliff-hangers at many chapter ends, and incidents both entertaining and suspenseful." Booklist

Wallace, Rich

Shots on goal. Knopf 1997 148p $17; lib bdg $18.99; pa $4.99 (7 and up)　**Fic**
1. Soccer—Fiction 2. Friendship—Fiction
ISBN 0-679-88670-2; 0-679-98670-7 (lib bdg); 0-679-88671-0 (pa)　LC 97-11310
While pursuing his goal of helping his Sturbridge, Pa. soccer team win the championship in the district playoffs, fifteen-year-old Bones tries to deal with his resentment of his best friend, on whose girlfriend he has a crush

"The soccer matches are fast, the interaction with girls unromantically realistic, and the voice is engaging, as Bones tells his story as a rueful eyewitness account." Bull Cent Child Books

Wrestling Sturbridge. Knopf 1996 135p $17; pa $4.99 (7 and up)　**Fic**
1. Wrestling—Fiction 2. Friendship—Fiction
ISBN 0-679-87803-3; 0-679-88555-2 (pa)　LC 95-20468
"Narrator Ben, a high school senior, doesn't want to be like his father and so many others in Sturbridge, Pa., who after graduating get a job at the cinder block plant. Seemingly his only alternative is to become a state wrestling champion and thus win an athletic scholarship. But his way is firmly blocked by his buddy Al, who reigns

supreme in their weight class." Publ Wkly
"The wresting scenes are thrilling. . . . Like Ben, whose voice is so strong and clear here, Wallace weighs his words carefully, making every one count in this excellent, understated first novel." Booklist

Walter, Mildred Pitts, 1922-

Second daughter; the story of a slave girl. Scholastic 1996 214p $15.95　**Fic**
1. Bett, Mum, 1744?-1829—Fiction 2. African Americans—Fiction 3. Slavery—Fiction 4. Massachusetts—History—1600-1775, Colonial period—Fiction
ISBN 0-590-48282-3　LC 95-4691
"In 1781, a slave named Elizabeth Freeman, also known as Mum Bet, successfully sued the Commonwealth of Massachusetts. This historical novel, narrated by her fictional sister Aissa, details their lives and describes eloquently their unquenchable desire for freedom. . . . Without being sensationalized, the narrative succeeds in exposing the horrors of slavery." SLJ

Walter, Virginia A.

Making up Megaboy; by Virginia Walter; graphics by Katrina Roeckelein. DK Pub. 1998 62p il $16.95　**Fic**
1. Violence—Fiction
ISBN 0-7894-2488-6　LC 97-36073
Also available in paperback from Bantam Bks.
"A Richard Jackson book"
When thirteen-year-old Robbie shoots an old man in a liquor store, everyone who knows the quiet, withdrawn youth struggles to understand this act of seemingly random violence

"The combination of first-person perspectives and computer-generated graphics is riveting, and the discussion possibilities are wide open." Booklist

Watkins, Yoko Kawashima

My brother, my sister, and I. Bradbury Press 1994 275p $17; pa $4.50　**Fic**
1. World War, 1939-1945—Fiction 2. Japan—Fiction
ISBN 0-02-792526-9; 0-689-80656-6 (pa)　LC 93-23535
Sequel to So far from the bamboo grove
Living as refugees in Japan in 1947 while trying to locate their missing father, thirteen-year-old Yoko and her older brother and sister must endure a bad fire, injury, and false charges of arson, theft, and murder

"Watkins's first-person narration is beautifully direct and emotionally honest." Publ Wkly

So far from the bamboo grove. Lothrop, Lee & Shepard Bks. 1986 183p hardcover o.p. paperback available $4.95　**Fic**
1. World War, 1939-1945—Fiction 2. Korea—Fiction 3. Japan—Fiction
ISBN 0-688-13115-8 (pa)　LC 85-15939
Also available in paperback from Penguin Bks.
A fictionalized autobiography in which eight-year-old Yoko escapes from Korea to Japan with her mother and sister at the end of World War II

"An admirably told and absorbing novel." Horn Book
Followed by My brother, my sister, and I

Wells, H. G. (Herbert George), 1866-1946

The war of the worlds (7 and up)   **Fic**
1. Science fiction

Various editions available
First published 1898
"The inhabitants of Mars, a loathsome though highly organized race, invade England, and by their command of superior weapons subdue and prey on the people." Baker. Guide to the Best Fic

Westall, Robert, 1929-1993

The kingdom by the sea. Farrar, Straus & Giroux 1991 175p $15; pa $3.95   **Fic**
1. World War, 1939-1945—Fiction 2. Great Britain—Fiction 3. Dogs—Fiction
ISBN 0-374-34205-9; 0-374-44060-3 (pa)
LC 91-12500
Also available Thorndike Press large print edition
During World War II twelve-year-old Harry and a stray dog travel through war-torn England in search of safety
This novel is "sparely written but rich in details of time and place and especially in character. Even minor characters are vividly depicted. Adult concerns Harry must contend with (the death-dealing destructiveness of war, potential child molestation) are handled appropriately for young readers. The plot is engrossing." SLJ

The machine gunners. Greenwillow Bks. 1976 c1975 186p hardcover o.p. paperback available $4.95   **Fic**
1. World War, 1939-1945—Fiction 2. Great Britain—Fiction
ISBN 0-688-15498-0 (pa)   LC 76-13630
First published 1975 in the United Kingdom
"Garmouth, England, is under constant bombing attack by the Germans in World War II. Charles McGill finds a machine gun in a downed German plane and, with that weapon as protection, he and his friends construct a fortress in preparation for an enemy attack. They capture a German soldier who becomes their friend. Instead of the expected Nazis, other gangs and their families become the enemy. An attack mistakenly thought to be by Nazis leaves their only ally, the German soldier, dead." Shapiro. Fic for Youth. 3d edition
Followed by Fathom five (1980)

The promise. Scholastic 1991 c1990 169p $13.95   **Fic**
1. Ghost stories 2. Death—Fiction 3. Great Britain—Fiction
ISBN 0-590-43760-7   LC 90-40564
First published 1990 in the United Kingdom
After his sort-of-girlfriend dies, teen-aged Bob is shocked to discover that their love was stronger than he thought, even strong enough to transcend death
"The story is set in England during World War II which adds some interesting historical information, but the setting and time period don't take away from the book which is a wonderful ghost story." Voice Youth Advocates

The stones of Muncaster Cathedral. Farrar, Straus & Giroux 1993 97p $11; pa $3.95   **Fic**
1. Horror fiction 2. Supernatural—Fiction 3. Great Britain—Fiction
ISBN 0-374-37263-2; 0-374-47119-3 (pa)
LC 92-55096
First published 1991 in the United Kingdom
Soon after steeplejack Joe Clarke begins work on one of the spires of Muncaster's medieval cathedral, terrible things start to happen and Joe realizes that there is a malevolent force connected to the spire's gargoyle
"The tower's secret is indeed a whopper, fittingly capping the unrelenting suspense that precedes its revelation." Publ Wkly

Time of fire. Scholastic 1997 c1994 172p $15.95   **Fic**
1. World War, 1939-1945—Fiction 2. Great Britain—Fiction
ISBN 0-590-47746-3   LC 96-37259
First published 1994 in the United Kingdom
In England during World War II, with his mother dead from a German bomb and his father off in training and action but keeping him informed by letter, Sonny tries to understand the darkest truths of war and retribution
"The story of Sonny's emotional crisis is poignant and believable, and it's blended seamlessly into the larger historical, strategic, and moral aspects of the account." Bull Cent Child Books

Westwood, Chris

Virtual world. Viking 1997 c1996 217p $15.99 (7 and up)   **Fic**
1. Virtual reality—Fiction 2. Computers—Fiction 3. Science fiction
ISBN 0-670-87546-5   LC 97-9388
First published 1996 in the United Kingdom
Fourteen-year-old Jack North finds himself literally drawn into the frightening world of what he thinks is a new virtual reality game
"Westwood is excellent at depicting the fascination and milieu of cyberculture; his slightly futuristic universe bumps things ahead just enough to make his inventions and changes credible but keeps things grounded enough in contemporary reality . . . to remain credible." Bull Cent Child Books

Whelan, Gloria

Goodbye, Vietnam. Knopf 1992 135p $13; lib bdg $13.99; pa $3.99   **Fic**
1. Refugees—Fiction 2. Vietnamese—Fiction
ISBN 0-679-82263-1; 0-679-92263-6 (lib bdg); 0-679-82376-X (pa)   LC 91-3660
Thirteen-year-old Mai and her family embark on a dangerous sea voyage from Vietnam to Hong Kong to escape the unpredictable and often brutal Vietnamese government
"While the book has the suspense and appeal of any good escape story, Whelan is neither melodramatic nor sentimental, and the sometimes horrific details of the scary voyage are plain but understated." Bull Cent Child Books

White, Ruth

Belle Prater's boy. Farrar, Straus & Giroux 1996 196p $16 **Fic**
1. Cousins—Fiction 2. Parent and child—Fiction 3. Virginia—Fiction 4. Appalachian region—Fiction
ISBN 0-374-30668-0 LC 94-43625
Also available in paperback from Dell
A Newbery Medal honor book, 1997
"Gypsy and her cousin Woodrow become close friends after Woodrow's mother disappears. Both sixth-graders feel deserted by their parents—Gypsy discovers that her father committed suicide—and need to define themselves apart from these tragedies. White's prose evokes the coal mining region of Virginia and the emotional quality of her characters' transformations." Horn Book Guide

White, T. H. (Terence Hanbury), 1906-1964

The once and future king. Putnam 1958 677p $25.95 **Fic**
1. Arthur, King—Fiction 2. Great Britain—History—0-1066—Fiction
ISBN 0-399-10597-2 LC 58-10760
Also available in paperback from Ace Bks.
An omnibus edition of four novels; The sword in the stone (1939), The witch in the wood (1939, now called The Queen of Air and Darkness) and The ill-made knight (1940) A number of alterations have been made in the earlier books. Previously unpublished, The candle in the wind "deals with the plotting of Mordred and his kinsmen of the house of Orkney, and their undying enmity to King Arthur." Times Lit Suppl
"White's contemporary retelling of Malory's *Le Morte d'Arthur* is both romantic and exciting." Shapiro. Fic for Youth. 3d edition

Wiesel, Elie, 1928-

Night, Dawn, The accident: three tales. Hill & Wang 1972 318p hardcover o.p. paperback available $11 (7 and up) **Fic**
1. Jews—Fiction
ISBN 0-374-52140-9 (pa)
In Dawn, Elisha, a young Jewish terrorist fighting for the creation of Israel in the 1940s is faced with an agonizing moral dilemma. He is to be the executioner of a British officer in reprisal for the hanging of a captured terrorist. A survivor of the concentration camps and a victim all of his life, Elisha considers whether he is any different from his oppressors if he can execute a helpless prisoner in cold blood. Night is a memoir. The accident concerns a survivor of Auschwitz who, recovering from a near-fatal accident, questions the meaning of man's existence and purpose, and death

Willey, Margaret

Facing the music. Delacorte Press 1996 183p hardcover o.p. paperback available $3.99 (7 and up) **Fic**
1. Death—Fiction 2. Brothers and sisters—Fiction 3. Bands (Music)—Fiction
ISBN 0-440-22680-5 (pa) LC 95-22187

Through her love of music and membership in her brother's band, sixteen-year-old Lisa learns to deal with her feelings of abandonment following her mother's death
"A fast-paced read that will keep kids turning pages and leave them with something to think about as well." SLJ

Williams, Carol Lynch, 1959-

If I forget, you remember. Delacorte Press 1998 201p $15.95 **Fic**
1. Grandmothers—Fiction 2. Alzheimer's disease—Fiction
ISBN 0-385-32534-7 LC 97-20582
Twelve-year-old Elyse's plan to write an award-winning novel during the summer is interrupted when her grandmother, who has Alzheimer's disease, moves in with the family
"The smooth writing, tenderness, and excellent pacing keep the reader engrossed." Voice Youth Advocates

My Angelica. Delacorte Press 1999 149p $15.95 **Fic**
1. Authorship—Fiction 2. Contests—Fiction 3. School stories
ISBN 0-385-32622-X LC 98-23139
Fifteen-year-old Sage is enthusiastic about submitting her historical romance novel to the school creative writing contest, but her would-be boyfriend George thinks that it is awful and tries to stop her
"The twists and turns of the plot, the way the 'real' characters interact, and the concern and caring underlying the humorous situations make this a truly enjoyable novel." SLJ

The true colors of Caitlynne Jackson. Delacorte Press 1997 168p $14.95; pa $3.99 **Fic**
1. Child abuse—Fiction 2. Abandoned children—Fiction 3. Mothers and daughters—Fiction 4. Sisters—Fiction
ISBN 0-385-32249-6; 0-440-41235-8 (pa) LC 96-24835
Twelve-year-old Caity and her younger sister Cara must fend for themselves when their abusive mother storms out of the house with a suitcase and doesn't come back
"Williams delineates her characters with great delicacy and weaves her theme of growth through hardship into a skillfully constructed text." Booklist

Williams-Garcia, Rita

Like sisters on the homefront. Lodestar Bks. 1995 165p $15.99 (7 and up) **Fic**
1. African Americans—Fiction 2. Family life—Fiction 3. Teenage mothers—Fiction
ISBN 0-525-67465-9 LC 95-3690
"It's bad enough that 14-year-old Gayle has one baby, but when she becomes pregnant again by another boy, Mama's had enough. She takes Gayle for an abortion and then ships her and her baby south to stay with religious relatives. . . . With the help of her dying great-grandmother, who leaves Gayle the family's African-American oral tradition, she begins to mature and understand her place in the family and her future." Child Book

Williams-Garcia, Rita—*Continued*
Rev Serv
"Beautifully written, the text captures the cadence and rhythm of New York street talk and the dilemma of being poor, black, and uneducated. This is a gritty, realistic, well-told story." SLJ

Wilson, Diane L.
I rode a horse of milk white jade; [by] Diane Lee Wilson. Orchard Bks. 1998 232p $17.95; lib bdg $18.99 (7 and up)   **Fic**
1. Horses—Fiction 2. Mongolia—Fiction
ISBN 0-531-30024-2; 0-531-33024-9 (lib bdg)
LC 97-23838
Also available in paperback from HarperCollins
Oyuna tells her granddaughter the story of how love for her horse enabled her to win a race and bring good luck to her family living in Mongolia in 1339
This "story is an exciting one that will reward diligent, proficient readers." SLJ

Wilson, Jacqueline
The suitcase kid; illustrated by Ying-Hwa Hu. Delacorte Press 1997 140p il $15.95; pa $4.50
    Fic
1. Divorce—Fiction 2. Family life—Fiction
ISBN 0-385-32311-5; 0-440-41371-0 (pa)
LC 96-29083
First published 1992 in the United Kingdom
Ten-year-old Andrea tries to deal with her parents' divorce and the presence of stepparents, stepsisters, and stepbrothers
"Wilson's frank portrayal of the realities of shared custody will ring true for young readers. . . . Andrea's attempts to cope with her challenging life are, at turns, funny, sad, and poignant." Booklist

Wisler, G. Clifton, 1950-
Caleb's choice. Lodestar Bks. 1996 154p $14.99; pa $4.99   **Fic**
1. Slavery—Fiction 2. Underground railroad—Fiction
ISBN 0-525-67526-4; 0-14-038256-9 (pa)
LC 96-2339
While living in Texas in 1858, fourteen-year-old Caleb faces a dilemma in deciding whether or not to assist fugitive slaves in their run for freedom
"This fast-paced, easy-to-read novel proves that history can be intriguing and exciting. Wisler draws readers into this masterful, and often humorous, tale." ALAN

The drummer boy of Vicksburg. Lodestar Bks. 1997 133p $15.99; pa $4.99   **Fic**
1. Howe, Orion P., d. 1930—Fiction 2. United States—History—1861-1865, Civil War—Fiction
ISBN 0-525-67537-X; 0-14-038673-4 (pa)
LC 96-21184
"This historical novel tells of a drummer boy who serves in the Union army during the Civil War. The author's appended note tells of his research on the life of the real-life hero, Orion Howe, whose experiences in the Fifty-fifth Illinois Infantry Regiment provide the framework for the book. . . . Details of the common soldier's lot provide readers with enough realism to believe in the story." Booklist

Red Cap. Lodestar Bks. 1991 160p hardcover o.p. paperback available $3.99   **Fic**
1. Powell, Ransom J., 1849-1899—Fiction 2. Andersonville Prison—Fiction 3. United States—History—1861-1865, Civil War—Fiction
ISBN 0-14-036936-8 (pa)   LC 90-21944
A young Yankee drummer boy displays great courage when he's captured and sent to Andersonville Prison
The author "presents a well-researched view of the war. He effectively interweaves the known facts of Powell's life with first-person accounts of other soldiers and prisoners to create an exciting story." SLJ

Wittlinger, Ellen
Hard love. Simon & Schuster Bks. for Young Readers 1999 224p $16.95 (7 and up)   **Fic**
1. Authorship—Fiction 2. Lesbians—Fiction
ISBN 0-689-82134-4   LC 98-6668
"John, cynical yet vulnerable, thinks he's immune to emotion until he meets bright, brittle Marisol, the author of his favorite zine. He falls in love, but Marisol, a lesbian, just wants to be friends. A love story of a different sort—funny, poignant, and thoughtful." Booklist

Wolff, Virginia Euwer
Bat 6. Scholastic 1998 230p $16.95   **Fic**
1. Softball—Fiction 2. Japanese Americans—Fiction 3. Prejudices—Fiction
ISBN 0-590-89799-3   LC 97-14742
"During a sixth-grade girls' softball game in 1949, a deeply troubled girl whose father was killed at Pearl Harbor attacks a Japanese-American girl whose family was interned. . . . Wolff's evocation of period and place is masterful, and the questions she raises about war, race, and cherished beliefs are difficult and honest." Horn Book Guide

Make lemonade. Holt & Co. 1993 200p $15.95
    Fic
1. Teenage mothers—Fiction 2. Babysitters—Fiction 3. Poverty—Fiction
ISBN 0-8050-2228-7   LC 92-41182
Also available Thorndike Press large print edition and in paperback from Scholastic
"Fourteen-year-old LaVaughn accepts the job of babysitting Jolly's two small children but quickly realizes that the young woman, a seventeen-year-old single mother, needs as much help and nurturing as her two neglected children. The four become something akin to a temporary family, and through their relationship each makes progress toward a better life. Sixty-six brief chapters, with words arranged on the page like poetry, perfectly echo the patterns of teenage speech." Horn Book Guide

The Mozart season. Holt & Co. 1991 249p o.p.; Scholastic paperback available $4.99   **Fic**
ISBN 0-439-16309-9 (pa)   LC 90-23635
Allegra spends her twelfth summer practicing a Mozart concerto for a violin competition and finding many significant connections in her world
"With a clear, fresh voice that never falters, Wolff gives readers a delightful heroine, a fully realized setting, and a slowly building tension that reaches a stunning climax." SLJ

Wolff, Virginia Euwer—*Continued*

Probably still Nick Swansen. Holt & Co. 1988 144p $14.95 (7 and up) **Fic**
1. Learning disabilities—Fiction
ISBN 0-8050-0701-6   LC 88-13175
Also available in paperback from Scholastic
Sixteen-year-old learning-disabled Nick struggles to endure a life in which the other kids make fun of him, he has to take special classes, his date for the prom makes an excuse not to go with him, and he is haunted by the memory of his older sister who drowned while he was watching
"It is a poignant, gentle, utterly believable narrative." Booklist

Wood, Frances

Becoming Rosemary. Delacorte Press 1997 247p hardcover o.p. paperback available $3.99 **Fic**
1. Family life—Fiction 2. North Carolina—Fiction
ISBN 0-440-41238-2 (pa)   LC 96-21698
While twelve-year-old Rosemary observes life in 1790 North Carolina, she knows that she can choose to be what she has to be and that doing so will make her different
"This is a gentle but realistic story of growing up and the choices that have to be made. Its unusual combination of historical setting and magic are an effective and remarkable way to present the traditional 'coming-of-age' story." Voice Youth Advocates

Wood, June Rae, 1946-

The man who loved clowns. Putnam 1992 224p $15.95 **Fic**
1. Down syndrome Fiction 2. Mentally handicapped—Fiction 3. Uncles—Fiction
ISBN 0-399-21888-2   LC 91-33861
Also available in paperback from Hyperion
Thirteen-year-old Delrita, whose unhappy life has caused her to hide from the world, loves her uncle Punky but sometimes feels ashamed of his behavior because he has Down's syndrome
"Wood's prose is strong and flowing, with a good balance of dialogue and narrative, and with several well-developed and memorable characters." SLJ
Followed by Turtle on a fence post

Turtle on a fence post. Putnam 1997 264p $16.95 **Fic**
1. Death—Fiction
ISBN 0-399-23184-6   LC 96-53622
Sequel to The man who loved clowns
A grumpy old veteran with his own history of grief helps fourteen-year-old Delrita release the pent-up emotions she holds following the death of her parents and uncle
"Those readers who became attached to Delrita in the first book will find plenty to enjoy here." SLJ

Woodruff, Elvira

Dear Austin; letters from the Underground Railroad; illustrated by Nancy Carpenter. Knopf 1998 137p il $16; lib bdg $17.99 **Fic**
1. Underground railroad—Fiction 2. Slavery—Fiction 3. African Americans—Fiction 4. Pennsylvania—Fiction
ISBN 0-679-88594-3; 0-679-98594-8 (lib bdg)
LC 98-5314
Sequel to Dear Levi (1994)
In 1853, in letters to his older brother, eleven-year-old Levi describes his adventures in the Pennsylvania countryside with his black friend Jupiter and his experiences with the Underground Railroad
"The smoothly written text is fast paced." Horn Book Guide

Woodson, Jacqueline

The house you pass on the way. Delacorte Press 1997 99p $14.95; pa $4.50 (7 and up) **Fic**
1. Lesbians—Fiction 2. Racially mixed people—Fiction 3. African Americans—Fiction
ISBN 0-385-32189-9; 0-440-22797-6 (pa)
LC 97-1620
When fourteen-year-old Staggerlee, the daughter of a racially mixed marriage, spends a summer with her cousin Trout, she begins to question her sexuality to Trout and catches a glimpse of her possible future self
"Woodson writes beautifully about feelings and issues, and this slim novel is packed with them. Racism is discussed clearly, family barriers are built and torn down, and sexuality and young women's coming-of-age are explored. . . . Woodson stops well short of being sexually explicit." Voice Youth Advocates

I hadn't meant to tell you this. Delacorte Press 1994 115p $15.95; pa $4.50 **Fic**
1. African Americans—Fiction 2. Friendship—Fiction 3. Incest—Fiction 4. Child sexual abuse—Fiction
ISBN 0-385-32031-0; 0-440-21960-4 (pa)
LC 93-8733
Marie, the only black girl in the eighth grade willing to befriend her white classmate Lena, discovers that Lena's father is doing horrible things to her in private
"Woodson's characters are deftly drawn, whole individuals; her spare prose and crystal images create a haunting, poetic novel." Horn Book Guide
Followed by Lena

If you come softly. Putnam 1998 181p $15.99 (7 and up) **Fic**
1. African Americans—Fiction 2. Race relations—Fiction 3. New York (N.Y.)—Fiction
ISBN 0-399-23112-9   LC 97-32212
After meeting at their private school in New York, fifteen-year-old Jeremiah, who is black and whose parents are separated, and Ellie, who is white and whose mother has twice abandoned her, fall in love and then try to cope with people's reactions
"The gentle and melancholy tone of this book makes it ideal for thoughtful readers and fans of romance." Voice Youth Advocates

Woodson, Jacqueline—*Continued*
Last summer with Maizon. Delacorte Press 1990
105p hardcover o.p. paperback available $3.99
                               Fic
1. Friendship—Fiction 2. African Americans—Fiction
3. Brooklyn (New York, N.Y.)—Fiction
ISBN 0-440-40555-6 (pa)   LC 89-23403
Eleven-year-old Margaret tries to accept the inevitable
changes that come one summer when her father dies and
her best friend Maizon goes away to a private boarding
school
"These are wonderfully rich and complex characters
who have a strong sense of community and look out for
each other." Voice Youth Advocates
Other available titles about Maizon and Margaret are:
Between Madison & Palmetto (1993)
Maizon at Blue Hill (1992)

Lena. Delacorte Press 1999 115p $15.95   **Fic**
1. Runaway teenagers—Fiction 2. Sisters—Fiction
ISBN 0-385-32308-5   LC 98-24317
In this sequel to I hadn't meant to tell you this, thirteen-year-old Lena and her younger sister Dion mourn
the death of their mother as they hitchhike from Ohio to
Kentucky while running away from their abusive father
"Soulful, wise and sometimes wrenching, this taut story never loses its grip on the reader." Publ Wkly

Wrede, Patricia C., 1953-
Dealing with dragons. Harcourt Brace
Jovanovich 1990 212p $17   **Fic**
1. Fantasy fiction 2. Dragons—Fiction
ISBN 0-15-222900-0   LC 89-24599
Also available in paperback from Scholastic
"A Jane Yolen book"
Bored with traditional palace life, a princess goes off
to live with a group of dragons and soon becomes in-
volved with fighting against some disreputable wizards
who want to steal away the dragons' kingdom
"A decidedly diverting novel with plenty of action and
many slightly skewed fairy-tale conventions that add to
the laugh-out-loud reading pleasure and give the story a
wide appeal. . . . This is book one in the Enchanted
Forest Chronicles." Booklist
Other available titles in the Enchanted Forest chronicles
series are:
Calling on dragons (1993)
Searching for dragons (1991)
Talking to dragons (1993)

Wright, Betty Ren
Out of the dark. Scholastic 1995 149p $13.95
                               Fic
1. Ghost stories 2. Grandmothers—Fiction
ISBN 0-590-43598-1   LC 93-48025
"Jessie and her parents have recently moved to her
grandmother's rural home, but her enjoyment of the
house is marred by nightmares that are chillingly real.
Her parents' frustrations with unemployment have put a
strain on the whole family, and she doesn't feel able to
share her terror as the threatening ghost of her dreams
begins to appear while she is awake. . . . Relationships
built on well-defined characters add realism to this supernatural tale. Effective and well crafted." SLJ

Wynne-Jones, Tim
Stephen Fair; a novel. DK Ink 1998 218p
$15.95 (7 and up)   **Fic**
1. Dreams—Fiction 2. Family life—Fiction
ISBN 0-7894-2495-9   LC 97-40328
Also available in paperback from HarperCollins
"A Melanie Kroupa book"
At the age of fifteen Stephen begins having nightmares like the ones that drove his older brother away
from home, and eventually the dreams lead to a discovery that is shocking but that ultimately allows his family
to come back together
"A couple of facile scenes don't detract from the
strong characterization, rich imagery, and well-crafted
writing of this ultimately redemptive mystery, which explores truth, deception, and the meaning of family." Horn
Book Guide

Yep, Laurence
The amah. Putnam 1999 181p $15.99   **Fic**
1. Family life—Fiction 2. Chinese Americans—Fiction
ISBN 0-399-23040-8   LC 98-49046
"When her mother becomes the amah (Chinese governess) for a wealthy white girl, twelve-year-old Amy
must skip her ballet classes—in which she is preparing
for the role of Cinderella's mean stepsister—to baby-sit
her siblings." Horn Book Guide
"An enjoyable book about friendship, family, and traditions." Voice Youth Advocates

The case of the Goblin Pearls. HarperCollins
Pubs. 1997 179p (Chinatown mystery) $14.95; lib
bdg $14.89; pa $4.95   **Fic**
1. Mystery fiction 2. Chinese Americans—Fiction
3. San Francisco (Calif.)—Fiction
ISBN 0-06-024444-5; 0-06-024446-1 (lib bdg);
0-06-440552-4 (pa)   LC 96-22924
Lily and her aunt, a Chinese American movie actress,
join forces to solve the theft of some priceless pearls and
stop the operator of a sweatshop in San Francisco's Chinatown
"With enough fun and intrigue to keep the pages turning, this is a worthwhile series title." SLJ
Other available titles in the Chinatown mystery series
are:
The case of the firecrackers (1999)
The case of the lion dance (1998)

Child of the owl. Harper & Row 1977 217p lib
bdg $14.89; pa $4.95   **Fic**
1. Chinese Americans—Fiction 2. Grandmothers—
Fiction 3. San Francisco (Calif.)—Fiction
ISBN 0-06-026743-7 (lib bdg); 0-06-440336-X (pa)
                               LC 76-24314
"Casey, a twelve-year-old Chinese American girl, is
more American than Chinese. When her father, a compulsive gambler, is hospitalized after a severe beating,
Casey moves in with her grandmother in San Francisco's
Chinatown. Although she is a street-smart child, Casey
finds that she is an outsider in this community. Her
grandmother teaches her something of her heritage and
what it means to be 'a child of the owl.'" Shapiro. Fic
for Youth. 3d edition

Yep, Laurence—*Continued*

The cook's family. Putnam 1998 184p $15.99; pa $4.99 **Fic**

1. Chinese Americans—Fiction 2. Grandmothers—Fiction

ISBN 0-03-992907-8; 0-698-11804-9 (pa)

LC 97-23892

Sequel to Ribbons

As her parents' arguments become more frequent, Robin looks forward to the visits that she and her grandmother make to Chinatown, where they pretend to be an elderly cook's family, giving Robin new insights into her Chinese heritage

"The sense of place is immediate. . . . This is a fun story . . . and a unique one that will appeal to readers on several levels." SLJ

Dragon of the lost sea. Harper & Row 1982 213p hardcover o.p. paperback available $4.95 **Fic**

1. Fantasy fiction

ISBN 0-06-440227-4 (pa)

LC 81-48644

"A Charlotte Zolotow book"

Shimmer, a renegade dragon princess, tries to redeem herself by capturing the evil Civet, with the help of a human boy named Thorn

This "is beautifully adapted to the grand scope of high fantasy, it is deftly structured, and it's lightened by wry humor." Bull Cent Child Books

Other available titles about Shimmer and her companions are:

Dragon cauldron (1991)
Dragon steel (1985)
Dragon war (1992)

Dragon's gate. HarperCollins Pubs. 1993 273p $14.95; pa $4.95 **Fic**

1. Chinese—United States—Fiction 2. Railroads—Fiction

ISBN 0-06-022971-3; 0-06-440489-7 (pa)

LC 92-43649

A Newbery Medal honor book, 1994

When he accidentally kills a Manchu, a fifteen-year-old Chinese boy is sent to America to join his father, an uncle, and other Chinese working to build a tunnel for the transcontinental railroad through the Sierra Nevada mountains in 1867

"Yep has succeeded in realizing the primary characters and the irrepressibly dramatic story. . . . The carefully researched details will move students to thought and discussion." Bull Cent Child Books

Other available titles in this family saga are:
Mountain light (1985)
The serpent's children (1984)

Dragonwings. Harper & Row 1975 248p lib bdg $14.89; pa $4.95 **Fic**

1. Chinese Americans—Fiction 2. San Francisco (Calif.)—Fiction 3. Fathers and sons—Fiction

ISBN 0-06-026738-0 (lib bdg); 0-06-440085-9 (pa)

LC 74-2625

"In 1903 Moon Shadow, eight years old, leaves China for the 'Land of the Golden Mountains,' San Francisco, to be with his father, Windrider, a father he has never seen. There, beset by the trials experienced by most for-

eigners in America, Moonrider shares his father's dream—to fly. This dream enables Windrider to endure the mockery of the other Chinese, the poverty he suffers in this hostile place—the land of the white demons—and his loneliness for his wife and his own country." Shapiro. Fic for Youth. 3d edition

Hiroshima; a novella. Scholastic 1995 56p $9.95; pa $2.99 **Fic**

1. Hiroshima (Japan)—Bombardment, 1945—Fiction

ISBN 0-590-20832-2; 0-590-20833-0 (pa)

LC 94-18195

"This moving and detailed narrative chronicles the dropping of the atomic bomb on Hiroshima and its effects on its citizens, especially on twelve-year-old Sachi. Based on true accounts, this book describes the horrors and sadness as well as the courage and hope that result from war." Soc Educ

Later, gator. Hyperion Bks. for Children 1995 122p $13.95; lib bdg $13.89; pa $4.50 **Fic**

1. Chinese Americans—Fiction 2. Brothers—Fiction 3. Alligators—Fiction

ISBN 0-7868-0059-3; 0-7868-2083-7 (lib bdg); 0-7868-1277-X (pa)

LC 94-11254

"Teddy resents his goody-goody brother, Bobby. Urged to get Bobby a suitable pet for his eighth birthday, Teddy buys an alligator instead. Bobby unexpectedly adores Oscar—sharp teeth, voracious appetite, and all. The challenge of feeding Oscar unites the boys, but also gets Teddy in trouble . . . again." Publisher's note

"The characterizations of the family and portrayal of the culture of San Francisco's Chinatown are plausible and likable. Yep acknowledges the peril and cruelty of exotic pet ownership in a brief afterword." Horn Book

Ribbons. Putnam 1996 179p $15.95; pa $5.99 **Fic**

1. Chinese Americans—Fiction 2. Grandmothers—Fiction 3. Ballet—Fiction

ISBN 0-399-22906-X; 0-698-11606-2 (pa)

LC 95-33488

Eleven-year-old Robin, a promising young ballet student cannot afford to continue lessons when her Chinese grandmother emigrates from Hong Kong, creating jealousy and conflict among the entire family

"An appealing story that draws readers into the world of ballet while offering an authentic and sometimes amusing look at the dynamics of Chinese-American family life." SLJ

Followed by The cook's family

The star fisher. Morrow Junior Bks. 1991 150p $16 **Fic**

1. Chinese Americans—Fiction 2. Moving—Fiction 3. Prejudices—Fiction

ISBN 0-688-09365-5

LC 90-23785

Also available in paperback from Penguin Bks.

Fifteen-year-old Joan Lee and her family find the adjustment hard when they move from Ohio to West Virginia in the 1920s

"Based on experiences from Laurence Yep's own family history, the story offers unique insight into the plight of ethnic minorities. It is disturbing but never depressing, poignant but not melancholy. . . . The book is a pleasure to read, entertaining its audience even as it educates their hearts." Horn Book

Yep, Laurence—*Continued*

Thief of hearts. HarperCollins Pubs. 1995 197p
lib bdg $14.89; pa $4.95   **Fic**
1. Chinese Americans—Fiction 2. Friendship—Fiction
3. San Francisco (Calif.)—Fiction 4. Racially mixed
people—Fiction
ISBN 0-06-025342-8 (lib bdg); 0-06-440591-5 (pa)
                                              LC 94-18703
"Stacy is not pleased that she's been elected by her
parents to show a new girl from China around school,
particularly when it turns out that Hong Ch'un is snotty
and difficult, even calling Stacy *t'ung chung,* 'mixed
seed.' Stacy's mother (whose story was told in *Child of
the Owl) . . .* is of Chinese descent, and her father Caucasian, and when Hong Ch'un is accused by the other
kids of stealing, Stacy feels torn between parental instruction, ethnic loyalty, and peer acceptance." Bull Cent
Child Books
"Told with candor and controlled emotion, this first-
person narrative presents a difficult topic in a manner accessible to a wide audience." Horn Book

Yolen, Jane

Armageddon summer; [by] Jane Yolen & Bruce
Coville. Harcourt Brace & Co. 1998 266p $17; pa
$6 (7 and up)   **Fic**
1. Cults—Fiction
ISBN 0-15-201767-4; 0-15-202268-6 (pa)
                                              LC 98-6920
Fourteen-year-old Marina and sixteen-year-old Jed accompany their parents' religious cult, the Believers, to
await the end of the world atop a remote mountain,
where they try to decide what they themselves believe
"Yolen and Coville, writing in alternating chapters
from Marina's and Jed's points of view, explore their
rich, thought-provoking theme with the perfect balance of
gripping adventure and understated pathos, leavened by
a dollop of humor." Booklist

Briar Rose. Doherty Assocs. 1992 190p (Fairy
tale series) $17.95; pa $4.99 (7 and up)   **Fic**
1. Holocaust, 1933-1945—Fiction 2. Fantasy fiction
ISBN 0-312-85135-9; 0-8125-5862-6 (pa)
                                              LC 92-25456
"A TOR book"
"Yolen takes the story of Briar Rose (commonly
known as Sleeping Beauty) and links it to the Holocaust.
. . . Rebecca Berlin, a young woman who has grown up
hearing her grandmother Gemma tell an unusual and
frightening version of the Sleeping Beauty legend, realizes when Gemma dies that the fairy tale offers one of
the very few clues she has to her grandmother's past.
. . . By interpolating Gemma's vivid and imaginative
story into the larger narrative, Yolen has created an engrossing novel." Publ Wkly

Children of the wolf; a novel. Viking 1984 136p
hardcover o.p. paperback available $4.99   **Fic**
1. Wild children—Fiction 2. India—Fiction
ISBN 0-14-036477-3 (pa)   LC 83-16979
"Focuses on Mohandas, an orphaned Indian boy, and
his task of 'civilizing' two feral girls who have been
raised by wolves." Child Book Rev Serv
"The characters are varied and true. . . . A vivid
piece that has the capacity to stir readers and to make
them think." Booklist

The devil's arithmetic. Viking Kestrel 1988
170p $15.99; pa $4.99   **Fic**
1. Jews—Fiction 2. Holocaust, 1933-1945—Fiction
ISBN 0-670-81027-4; 0-14-034535-3 (pa)
                                              LC 88-14235
"During a Passover Seder, 12-year-old Hannah finds
herself transported from America in 1988 to Poland in
1942, where she assumes the life of young Chaya. Within days the Nazis take Chaya and her neighbors off to
a concentration camp, mere components in the death factory. As days pass, Hannah's own memory of her past,
and the prisoners' future, fades until she is Chaya completely." Publ Wkly
"Yolen does a fine job of illustrating the importance
of remembering. She adds much to children's understanding of the effects of the Holocaust." SLJ

Dragon's blood; a fantasy. Delacorte Press 1982
243p o.p.; Harcourt Brace & Co. paperback
available $6   **Fic**
1. Dragons—Fiction 2. Fantasy fiction
ISBN 0-15-200866-7 (pa)   LC 81-69668
This is the first book in the Pit dragons trilogy set "on
the planet of Austar IV in the Erato Galaxy. Austar IV
is well-known for its dragon breeding and fighting. The
central character . . . is Jakkin, a bond slave, who
dreams of stealing a baby dragon to raise and train for
fighting in order to buy his bond and become his own
master. The book describes the carrying out of his plan
with the help of the girl, Akki, and Jakkin's own perseverance." Voice Youth Advocates
The author "has successfully created a believable society, a plucky young protagonist, a first love initiation,
detailed dragon lore, and lots of 'against the adult establishment' adventure." ALAN
Followed by Heart's Blood

The dragon's boy. Harper & Row 1990 120p
$14   **Fic**
1. Arthur, King—Fiction 2. Merlin (Legendary character)—Fiction
ISBN 0-06-026789-5   LC 89-24642
"This is a retelling of the education and coming of
age of 13-year-old Artos (Arthur). Old Linn (Merlin) is
to be his teacher, but, doubting he can command the
boy's attention, he constructs a fire-breathing dragon as
a façade." SLJ
"Scattered throughout the book are broad hints of
Artos's identity, but even children unfamiliar with the
legendary King Arthur should find the crisply told story
accessible and entertaining." Horn Book

Heart's Blood. Delacorte Press 1984 238p o.p.;
Harcourt Brace & Co. paperback available $6
                                                     Fic
1. Dragons—Fiction 2. Fantasy fiction
ISBN 0-15-200865-9 (pa)   LC 83-14978
Sequel to Dragon's blood
This is the second book in the Pit dragons trilogy.
Jakkin, now a free dragon trainer, has his plans abruptly
changed when he is asked to infiltrate rebel forces taking
hold on the planet
Followed by A sending of dragons

Yolen, Jane—*Continued*

Hobby; the young Merlin trilogy. Harcourt Brace & Co. 1996 90p $15 **Fic**
1. Merlin (Legendary character)—Fiction 2. Fantasy fiction
ISBN 0-15-200815-2   LC 95-36735
Also available in paperback from Scholastic
Sequel to Passager
Young Merlin is orphaned by a fire and joins a traveling pair of magicians who help him begin to discover his true powers
"The characters are well drawn and appealing." SLJ
Followed by Merlin

Merlin; the young Merlin trilogy, book three. Harcourt Brace & Co. 1997 91p $15 **Fic**
1. Merlin (Legendary character)—Fiction 2. Fantasy fiction
ISBN 0-15-200814-4   LC 96-11683
Also available in paperback from Scholastic
Sequel to Hobby
Merlin, now twelve years old, begins to come into his magic while being held captive by a band of wild folk
This book is "written in stark but poetic language that will challenge some readers." SLJ

Passager; the young Merlin trilogy, book one. Harcourt Brace & Co. 1996 76p $15 **Fic**
1. Merlin (Legendary character)—Fiction 2. Fantasy fiction
ISBN 0-15-200391-6   LC 94-27101
Also available in paperback from Scholastic
A foundling rediscovers his identity through the help of the falconer who adopts him
A "stark, poignant, and absorbing tale. . . . This 'skinny' book will entice reluctant readers, but its rich language and poetic phrasing make it compelling and challenging." SLJ
Followed by Hobby

The Pictish child. Harcourt Brace & Co. 1999 135p $16 **Fic**
1. Magic—Fiction 2. Fantasy fiction 3. Scotland—Fiction
ISBN 0-15-202261-9   LC 99-6303
"Book two of the Tartan Magic series, which began with the *Wizard's Map* . . . picks up just after Jennifer, Peter, and Molly's adventures with the evil wizard Michael Scot. . . . Molly is given a talisman that sets into motion a chain of mysterious events involving a young Pict girl who has slipped forward in time from ninth-century Britain. . . . Yolen . . . delivers enough action, as well as a good deal of information about early Pict life, to please fans of the earlier novel." Booklist

A sending of dragons. Delacorte Press 1987 189p il o.p.; Harcourt Brace & Co. paperback available $6 **Fic**
1. Dragons—Fiction 2. Fantasy fiction
ISBN 0-15-200864-0 (pa)   LC 87-6689
Sequel to Heart's blood
This is the third book in the Pit dragons trilogy "After the revolt on Austar IV, Jakkin and Akki are forced to hide with five young dragons, Heart's Blood's hatchlings, their only companions. The hatchlings are bonded

to the young couple in a special way. . . . Jakkin and Akki [are] able . . . to communicate telepathically with dragons." Voice Youth Advocates

The wizard's map. Harcourt Brace & Co. 1999 132p $15 **Fic**
1. Magic—Fiction 2. Fantasy fiction 3. Scotland—Fiction
ISBN 0-15-202067-5   LC 98-33889
This is the first book in the Tartan Magic series. Thirteen-year-old twins Jennifer and Peter Dyer and their younger sister Molly visit relatives in Scotland and become involved in the plans of a diabolical wizard
"The action never flags, making this a sure bet for fantasy and adventure fans." Booklist
Followed by The Pictish child

Young, Karen Romano

The Beetle and me; a love story. Greenwillow Bks. 1999 181p $15 (7 and up) **Fic**
1. Automobiles—Fiction 2. Family life—Fiction
ISBN 0-688-15922-2   LC 98-16327
Surrounded by her busy extended family and their many cars, fifteen-year-old Daisy pursues her goal of single-handedly restoring the car of her dreams, the old purple Volkswagen Beetle from her childhood
"An oddly endearing, 'tweaked' love story that touches on numerous teen concerns: following your dream; getting along with parents; and, of course, finding that perfect set of wheels." Booklist

Young, Ronder Thomas

Learning by heart. Houghton Mifflin 1993 172p $14.95 **Fic**
1. Race relations—Fiction 2. African Americans—Fiction 3. Family life—Fiction 4. Southern States—Fiction
ISBN 0-395-65369-X   LC 92-46887
Also available in paperback from Penguin Bks.
In the early 1960s, ten-year-old Rachel sees changes in her family and her small Southern town as she tries to sort out how she feels about her young black maid, racial prejudice, and her responsibility for her own life
"The story's subtle, quiet plot serves as a backdrop for beautifully rich characterizations." SLJ

Moving Mama to town. Orchard Bks. 1997 219p $17.95; lib bdg $18.99 **Fic**
1. Fathers and sons—Fiction 2. Family life—Fiction 3. Georgia—Fiction
ISBN 0-531-30025-0; 0-531-33025-7 (lib bdg)
    LC 96-38993
Also available in paperback from Dell
"A Melanie Kroupa book"
In 1947, his head filled with the advice and wisdom of his runaway father, thirteen-year-old Freddy moves his mother from their Georgia farm into town and takes on the challenge of holding his family together
"Young has a fine ear for regional speech and creates a strong and positive sense of time and place. Freddy is a likable hero who is forced to grow up way too soon." SLJ

Yumoto, Kazumi

The friends; translated by Cathy Hirano. Farrar, Straus & Giroux 1996 169p $15   **Fic**
1. Friendship—Fiction   2. Old   age—Fiction   3. Death—Fiction 4. Japan—Fiction
ISBN 0-374-32460-3   LC 96-11134
Also available in paperback from Dell
Original Japanese edition, 1992
Curious about death, three sixth-grade boys named Kiyama, Kawabe, and Yamashita decide to spy on an old man waiting for him to die, but they end up becoming his friends
"The translation from the Japanese is immediate, both lyrical and casual. The characters . . . are subtly drawn. Readers will be moved by the terror of death, the bond across generations, and the struggle of those whom society labels losers." Booklist

The spring tone; translated by Cathy Hirano. Farrar, Straus & Giroux 1999 165p $16 (7 and up)
                                          Fic
1. Family life—Fiction 2. Death—Fiction 3. Japan—Fiction
ISBN 0-374-37153-9   LC 98-35525
Original Japanese edition 1995
Plagued by headaches and nightmares, Tomomi tries to make sense of her grandmother's death, her little brother's obsession with saving sick and abandoned cats, and her fear that she is becoming a monster
"Somber, subtle, and intricately woven. . . . Yumoto's writing is lyrical as well as nitty-gritty and gives readers both a fascinating glimpse into Japanese urban living and a compassionate look at the difficulties inherent in family life." Booklist

Zemser, Amy Bronwen

Beyond the mango tree. Greenwillow Bks. 1998 166p $15   **Fic**
1. Mothers and daughters—Fiction 2. Diabetes—Fiction 3. Liberia—Fiction
ISBN 0-688-16005-0   LC 97-32268
Also available in paperback from HarperCollins
While living in Liberia with her possessive, diabetic mother and often-absent father, twelve-year-old Sarina longs for a friend with whom to experience the world beyond her yard
"Zemser's poetic, wrenching narrative transports readers to a foreign land, but the truths they uncover will surely hit home." Publ Wkly

Zindel, Paul

The Pigman; a novel. Harper & Row 1968 182p lib bdg $14.89 (7 and up)   **Fic**
ISBN 0-06-026828-X   LC 68-10784
Also available in paperback from Bantam Bks.
"John Conlan and Lorraine Jensen, high school sophomores, are both troubled young people who have problems at home. They become friendly with an elderly widower, Mr. Pignati, who welcomes them into his home and shares with them his simple pleasures, including his collection of ceramic pigs, of which he is proud. When the Pigman, as the young people call him, goes to the hospital after a heart attack, they take advantage of his house for a party that becomes destructive. The conse-

quences are tragic and propel the two young friends into more responsible behavior." Shapiro. Fic for Youth. 3d edition
Followed by The Pigman's legacy

The Pigman's legacy. Harper & Row 1980 183p o.p.; Bantam Bks. paperback available $5.50 (7 and up)   **Fic**
ISBN 0-553-26599-7 (pa)   LC 79-2684
Sequel to The Pigman
"Feeling guilty over Mr. Pignati's death, John and Lorraine try to make up for it by befriending another elderly man." Roman. Sequences

Raptor. Hyperion Bks. for Children 1998 170p $14.95; lib bdg $15.49; pa $4.95 (7 and up)
                                          Fic
1. Dinosaurs—Fiction 2. Horror fiction
ISBN 0-7868-0338-X; 0-7868-2374-7 (lib bdg); 0-7868-1224-9 (pa)   LC 98-5330
Zack and his Ute Indian friend, Uta, find themselves trapped in a cave with a living dinosaur—the deadly Utahraptor
"If readers can survive the violent opening scene, they will enjoy equally descriptive encounters throughout the rest of the book. Although gory, these vivid portrayals make the narrative effective. . . . The imaginative ending offers an opportunity for discussion about mutation and animal freedom." SLJ

Reef of death. HarperCollins Pubs. 1998 177p $14.95; lib bdg $14.89 (7 and up)   **Fic**
1. Australia—Fiction 2. Horror fiction
ISBN 0-06-024728-2; 0-06-024733-9 (lib bdg)
                                      LC 97-21864
Also available in paperback from Hyperion
While helping a beautiful Aboriginal girl search for her people's missing treasure near the Great Barrier Reef, seventeen-year-old PC finds himself fighting an evil scientist and a deadly underwater monster
"Few YA writers can spin a tale of terror with the deftness and macabre humor of Zindel." Booklist

The undertaker's gone bananas. Harper & Row 1978 239p o.p.; Bantam Bks. paperback available $4.50 (7 and up)   **Fic**
1. Mystery fiction
ISBN 0-553-27189-X (pa)   LC 78-54606
Two teenagers believe a neighbor, an undertaker, has murdered his wife but can't convince anyone else
"Although there are a few grisly scenes, the narrative is thoroughly entertaining and filled with genuine humor; it has all the ingredients of a suspenseful murder mystery, complete with the hero and heroine riding off together at the end." Horn Book

S C   Story Collections

Books in this class include collections of short stories by one author and collections by more than one author. Folklore is in class 398.2

Adams, Richard, 1920-

Tales from Watership Down; with decorations by John Lawrence. Knopf 1996 267p $23   **S C**
1. Rabbits—Fiction 2. Short stories
ISBN 0-679-45125-0   LC 96-17047

Adams, Richard, 1920——_Continued_
Also available in paperback from Avon Bks.

This collection of nineteen tales is the sequel to the novel Watership Down. It "is divided into three parts: traditional tales that help to explain how things came to be in the rabbit world; some of the adventures encountered by El-ahrairah (rabbit folk hero) and his comrades on their return trip home after defeating the Black Rabbit of Inle; and a continuation of the story of Watership Down and its many inhabitants." SLJ

Aiken, Joan, 1924-
A fit of shivers; tales for late at night. Delacorte Press 1992 c1990 147p hardcover o.p. paperback available $4.50   S C
1. Horror fiction 2. Short stories
ISBN 0-440-41120-3 (pa)   LC 92-6130
First published 1990 in the United Kingdom
Ten short stories with elements of horror or the supernatural
"Vengeful ghosts, shrieking doors, eerie dreams, weird and unexplainable somethings, and haunted houses abound and contribute a wonderfully creepy feeling. . . . With well-defined moods and settings, they are stories for good readers who enjoy scary tales with unusual plots." Booklist

A foot in the grave; [by] Joan Aiken and Jan Pieńkowski. Viking 1991 c1989 128p il hardcover o.p. paperback available $3.99   S C
1. Ghost stories 2. Short stories
ISBN 0-14-036111-1 (pa)   LC 92-156011
First published 1989 in the United Kingdom
"At Pienkowski's request, Aiken has written a series of ghost stories—sometimes spooky-funny and sometimes disturbingly eerie—to accompany the artist's stark, surrealistic paintings." Booklist

Give yourself a fright: thirteen tales of the supernatural. Delacorte Press 1989 180p hardcover o.p. paperback available $3.99   S C
1. Horror fiction 2. Short stories
ISBN 0-440-41014-2 (pa)   LC 88-20366
"A magic duck, ghosts, the devil, a confused muse, and human evil haunt these 13 unusual stories that hover between fantasy and reality; humor and psychological terror. The styles vary, giving an interesting texture to the collection." SLJ

Alexander, Lloyd
The foundling and other tales of Prydain. rev & expanded ed. Holt & Co. 1999 98p $17.95 S C
1. Fantasy fiction 2. Short stories
ISBN 0-8050-6130-4   LC 98-42807
First published 1973; this revised and expanded edition includes two additional stories: Coll and his white pig and The truthful harp first published separately 1965 and 1967 respectively
Eight short stories dealing with events that preceded the birth of Taran, the Assistant Pig-Keeper and key figure in the author's five works on the Kingdom of Prydain which began with The book of three
"The stories are written with vivid grace and humor." Chicago. Children's Book Center [review of 1973 edition]

American eyes; new Asian-American short stories for young adults; edited by Lori M. Carlson; introduction by Cynthia Kadohata. Holt & Co. 1994 144p $14.95 (7 and up)   S C
1. Asian Americans—Fiction 2. Short stories
ISBN 0-8050-3544-3   LC 94-22391
Also available in paperback from Fawcett Bks.

These ten stories reflect the conflict Asian Americans face in balancing an ancient heritage and an unknown future
"The stories are sensitive, realistic, humorous and eye-opening. The characters represent all facets of human behavior. . . . This well-balanced collection helps us see life through another's eyes no matter what our ancestry." Book Rep

American fairy tales; from Rip Van Winkle to the Rootabaga stories; compiled by Neil Philip; illustrated by Michael McCurdy; preface by Alison Lurie. Hyperion 1996 160p il $22.95; lib bdg $23.49; pa $12.95   S C
1. Fairy tales 2. Short stories
ISBN 0-7868-0207-3; 0-7868-2171-X (lib bdg); 0-7868-1093-9 (pa)   LC 95-49143
Among the authors represented in this story collection are Nathaniel Hawthorne, Frank Stockton, Howard Pyle, and Louisa May Alcott
"Brief, carefully honed introductions set each selection in context and analyze its peculiarly American aspects. . . . With appended source notes and selective bibliography, this collection will serve as a fine resource for American literary study and as a springboard for further exploration." Horn Book

Andersen, Hans Christian, 1805-1875
The little mermaid and other fairy tales; collected and with an introduction by Neil Philip; illustrated by Isabelle Brent. Viking 1998 137p il $21.99   S C
1. Fairy tales 2. Short stories
ISBN 0-670-87840-5   LC 98-60069
Includes seventeen fairy tales including the well known, such as The tinderbox and The emperor's new clothes, as well as the lesser known, such as Little Ida's flowers and The beetle
"This volume combines an informal storytelling voice and a glamorous design with lots of gold leaf and lavishly colored illustrations." Booklist

Asimov, Isaac, 1920-1992
I, robot. Gnome Press 1950 253p o.p.; Bantam Bks. paperback available $6.99 (7 and up) S C
1. Science fiction 2. Robots—Fiction 3. Short stories
ISBN 0-553-29438-5 (pa)
"These loosely connected stories cover the career of Dr. Susan Calvin and United States Robots, the industry that she heads, from the time of the public's early distrust of these robots to its later dependency on them. This collection is an important introduction to a theme often found in science fiction: the encroachment of technology on our lives." Shapiro. Fic for Youth. 3d edition

Avi, 1937-
What do fish have to do with anything? and
other stories; illustrated by Tracy Mitchell.
Candlewick Press 1997 202p il $16.99; pa $4.99
S C
1. Short stories
ISBN 0-7636-0329-5; 0-7636-0412-7 (pa)
LC 97-1354
"Willie believes a homeless man possesses a cure for
unhappiness. A minister dares his devilish son to be
good. Pet-obsessed Eve receives visitations from two deceased cats. . . . These are among seven . . . stories
dealing with communication in troubled relationships."
Publisher's note
"While Avi's endings are not tidy, they are effective:
each story brings its protagonist beyond childhood self-
absorption to the realization that one is an integral part
of a bigger picture." Horn Book

The **Book** of dragons; selected and illustrated by
Michael Hague. Morrow 1995 146p il $20
S C
1. Dragons—Fiction 2. Fantasy fiction 3. Short stories
ISBN 0-688-10879-2 LC 94-42958
"Excerpts from classic novels such as J. R. R. Tolkien's *The Hobbit*, C. S. Lewis's *Voyage of the Dawn
Treader*, and short stories such as Kenneth Grahame's
'The Reluctant Dragon' are included. In addition, there
are folktales from China, Italy, and Germany. Most of
the heroes are men, but occasionally children are the
only ones who can outsmart the dragon. . . . Hague's
beautiful full-page watercolors reflect the different moods
of the stories and the temperaments of the dragons depicted." SLJ

Bradbury, Ray, 1920-
The Martian chronicles (7 and up) S C
1. Science fiction 2. Short stories

Hardcover and paperback reprint editions available
from various publishers
First published 1950 by Doubleday
This book's "closely interwoven short stories, linked
by recurrent images and themes, tell of the repeated attempts by humans to colonize Mars, of the way they
bring their old prejudices with them, and of the repeated,
ambiguous meetings with the shape-changing Martians."
Sci Fic Ency

Brooke, William J.
Teller of tales. HarperCollins Pubs. 1994 170p
hardcover o.p. paperback available $5.95 S C
1. Fairy tales 2. Short stories
ISBN 0-06-440511-7 (pa) LC 93-43421
"The background story is that of an old man who is
learning to tell old stories through the new medium of
type; he is encouraged, taunted, and eventually loved as
a father by a tough and streetwise young girl whom he
takes into his home. Using these two characters sometimes as tale-telling mouthpieces and sometimes as folk-
loric *dramatis personae*, Brooke tells versions of 'The
Emperor's New Clothes,' 'Goldilocks,' 'Little Red Riding Hood,' and 'Rumpelstiltskin.'" Bull Cent Child
Books

A telling of the tales: five stories; drawings by
Richard Egielski. Harper & Row 1990 132p il
hardcover o.p. paperback available $5.95 S C
1. Short stories
ISBN 0-06-440467-6 (pa) LC 89-36588
A retelling of five classic folk/fairy tales, including
Cinderella, Sleeping Beauty, Paul Bunyan, John Henry,
and Jack and the Beanstalk, from a contemporary
perspective
"Brooke has succeeded in making these old familiar
tales his own, softening their make-believe, playing with
their meanings, but leaving their magic utterly intact.
. . . A perceptive and engaging collection that's ideal for
reading aloud." SLJ

Conford, Ellen
Crush; stories. HarperCollins Pubs. 1998 138p
$14.95; pa $4.95 (7 and up) S C
1. Dating (Social customs)—Fiction 2. Valentine's
Day—Fiction 3. Short stories
ISBN 0-06-025414-9; 0-06-440778-0 (pa)
LC 97-34335
A series of romantic episodes in the lives of B.J. and
other students at Cutter's Forge High as they plan for the
Valentine's Day Sweetheart Stomp
"Addressing such issues as peer pressure, self-esteem,
respect, alienation, greed, and heartbreak, the clever sto-
ries . . . show how much self-image can differ from outward appearance and reputation." Booklist

Conrad, Pam, 1947-1996
Our house; the stories of Levittown; illustrations
by Brian Selznick. Scholastic 1995 65p il $14.95
S C
1. Short stories 2. Levittown (N.Y.)—Fiction
ISBN 0-590-46523-6 LC 94-42126
Six stories, one from each decade from the 1940s to
the 1990s, about children growing up in Levittown, New
York
"Vivid descriptions and poignant observations leave
indelible impressions. . . . Conrad's fresh, imaginative
approach to the concept of 'home' makes this an ideal
starting point for discussion, creative writing, and other
class activities." Booklist

Coville, Bruce
Odder than ever; stories by Bruce Coville.
Harcourt Brace & Co. 1999 146p $16 S C
1. Horror fiction 2. Short stories
ISBN 0-15-201747-X LC 98-51102
A collection of nine short stories featuring a ghost, a
goblin, a giant, and other unusual creatures
"From light fantasy to more thought-provoking
themes, this has something for everyone." Booklist

Oddly enough; stories by Bruce Coville;
illustrations by Michael Hussar. Harcourt Brace &
Co. 1994 122p $15.95 S C
1. Horror fiction 2. Short stories
ISBN 0-15-200093-3 LC 94-16286
Also available in paperback from Pocket Bks.
"Jane Yolen books"

Coville, Bruce—*Continued*

A collection of nine short stories featuring an angel, unicorn, vampire, werewolf, and other unusual creatures

"The stories are well written. . . . The plots . . . are always clear and characterizations deftly drawn. . . . A worthwhile purchase, particularly for classroom discussions." SLJ

Crutcher, Chris, 1946-

Athletic shorts: six short stories. Greenwillow Bks. 1991 154p $16 (7 and up) **S C**

1. Short stories

ISBN 0-688-10816-4 LC 91-4418

Also available Thorndike Press large print edition and in paperback from Dell

"As the title suggests, athletics are part of the selections; and Crutcher, as usual, is best at accurately portraying the world of high school teammates and coaches—readers can practically smell the sweat. In the first story—a monologue by a fat guy who manages to keep his dignity—the author seamlessly blends humor with more serious elements. . . . The final entry, a gritty, no-holds-barred account of the fear surrounding AIDS, is especially effective. These *Athletic Shorts* will speak to YAs, touch them deeply, and introduce them to characters they'll want to know better." SLJ

Dickinson, Peter, 1927-

The lion-tamer's daughter and other stories. Delacorte Press 1997 298p $15.95; pa $4.99 (7 and up) **S C**

1. Supernatural—Fiction 2. Short stories

ISBN 0-385-32327-1; 0-440-22690-2 (pa)

LC 96 20022

Each of these stories touches on the idea of a twin, ghostly double of a live person, or a secret self

"The stories develop in credible directions, and in each justice is well served by the end. . . . Satisfying, richly imaginative writing." SLJ

Dirty laundry; stories about family secrets; edited by Lisa Rowe Fraustino. Viking 1998 181p $16.99 (7 and up) **S C**

1. Family life—Fiction 2. Short stories

ISBN 0-670-87911-8 LC 97-52309

Eleven short stories revealing the dark secrets of a variety of troubled families. M. E. Kerr, Chris Crutcher, Bruce Coville, and Richard Peck, are among the contributors

"Amusing, surprising, but most of all thought-provoking, these stories can serve as a springboard for class discussion as easily as they provide diversion on a lazy afternoon." Voice Youth Advocates

Don't read this! and other tales of the unnatural; [by] Margaret Mahy [et al.]; illustrations by The Tjong Khing. Front St. 1998 213p il $15.95

  S C

1. Ghost stories 2. Short stories

ISBN 1-886910-22-7 LC 98-3215

Published in the United Kingdom with title: Fingers on the back of the neck and other ghost stories

An international collection of ghost stories and spooky tales by such authors as Susan Cooper, Roberto Piumini, and Bjarne Reuter

"These are enjoyable, unsettling tales sans sex and gore—refreshing and recommended." Voice Youth Advocates

Doyle, Sir Arthur Conan, 1859-1930

Adventures of Sherlock Holmes (7 and up)

  S C

1. Mystery fiction 2. Short stories

Various editions available

First published 1892

Twelve of the famous cases successfully solved by the great detective and his partner, Dr. Watson

The complete Sherlock Holmes; with a preface by Christopher Morley. Doubleday 1960 c1930 1122p $25 (7 and up) **S C**

1. Mystery fiction 2. Short stories

ISBN 0-385-00689-6

Also available in a two-volume paperback edition from Bantam Bks.

First published 1930

Fifty-eight Sherlock Holmes stories which were originally published in nine separate volumes: A study in scarlet (1887); The sign of the four (1890); Adventures of Sherlock Holmes (1892); Memoirs of Sherlock Holmes (1894); The return of Sherlock Holmes (1905); The hound of the Baskervilles (1902); The valley of fear (1915); His last bow (1917); The case book of Sherlock Holmes (1927)

Dragons & dreams; a collection of new fantasy and science fiction stories; edited by Jane Yolen, Martin H. Greenberg and Charles G. Waugh. Harper & Row 1986 180p $12.95

  S C

1. Fantasy fiction 2. Science fiction 3. Short stories

ISBN 0-06-026792-5 LC 85-45384

"All originals, the tales are imaginative and gracefully written. A subway train that travels to the future, an angel who entrusts a precious box to a young boy, a girl whose dream characters go on strike, a baby 'hag' who seeks a name, and an irridescent glass ball that contains a secret are just a few of the nuggets these fantasies hold. Written by Patricia MacLachlan, Patricia McKillip, Diana Wynne Jones, Monica Hughes, Jane Yolen, and others, the 10 stories are handy read-aloud length for middle graders, intriguing come-ons for leading the uninitiated into fantasy, and satisfying rainy-or-any-other-day companions as read-alones." Booklist

Ellis, Sarah, 1952-

Back of beyond; stories of the supernatural. Margaret K. McElderry Bks. 1997 136p $15 **S C**

1. Supernatural—Fiction 2. Short stories

ISBN 0-689-81484-4 LC 97-6844

A collection of twelve otherworldly stories which blend reality and unreality

"The stories are consistently well written, and Ellis seems to have had a wonderful time creating 12 intriguing, completely different views of the supernatural—from the playfully weird to the truly eerie." Booklist

Fleischman, Paul

Graven images; 3 stories; illustrations by Andrew Glass. Harper & Row 1982 85p il hardcover o.p. paperback available $4.95   **S C**

1. Supernatural—Fiction 2. Short stories

ISBN 0-06-440186-3 (pa)   LC 81-48649

"A Charlotte Zolotow book"

Three stories about people whose lives are influenced by sculptured figures. In Saint Crispin's follower, "Nicholas, an apprentice cobbler, believes the statue of St. Crispin in his village square is guiding him to a successful courtship with a comely lass. . . . The other two tales are grim examples of retribution. A wooden figurehead, 'The Binnacle Boy,' unmasks a killer in an old whaling port, and a statue commissioned by a ghost proves that a father has murdered his son in 'The Man of Influence.'" Publ Wkly

Galloway, Priscilla, 1930-

Truly grim tales. Delacorte Press 1995 132p pa $4.99 (7 and up)   **S C**

1. Fairy tales 2. Short stories

ISBN 0-440-22728-3   LC 95-6037

A guilt-ridden prince with a foot fetish seeking his glass-slippered dance partner and a beauty contest winner as Snow White's murderous stepmother are featured in two of the original "grim" plots in this young adult collection loosely based on eight traditional fairy tales

"The interpretations are provocative and ingenious throughout, managing to add magic to the originals rather than allowing the new layers to diminish them." Bull Cent Child Books

A **Glory** of unicorns; compiled by Bruce Coville; illustrated by Alix Berenzy. Scholastic 1998 198p il $16.95; pa $4.50   **S C**

1. Unicorns—Fiction 2. Short stories

ISBN 0-590-95943-3; 0-439-06628-X (pa)
          LC 97-13689

Eleven stories and one poem, by such authors as Nancy Varian Berberick, Gregory Maguire, and Margaret Bechard, about unicorns in both mythical and contemporary settings

"Exciting and thought-provoking. Even readers who shy away from the science fiction/fantasy genres will enjoy these short tales and their special messages." Voice Youth Adovates

Gorog, Judith, 1938-

When nobody's home; fifteen baby-sitting tales of terror. Scholastic 1996 95p $15.95; pa $4.50   **S C**

1. Horror fiction 2. Short stories

ISBN 0-590-46862-6; 0-590-46874-X (pa)
          LC 93-34595

"The common theme is baby-sitting, and the stories depict bizarre and bloody happenings that occur when someone is responsible for children, pets, or houses." Booklist

"The normal made terrifying is the heart of good horror, and Gorog is a master. She takes the ordinary experience of babysitting and gives it a wrench to the dark side, infusing her clever writing with a crafty sense of humor." Voice Youth Advocates

The **Haunted** house: a collection of original stories; edited by Jane Yolen and Martin H. Greenberg; illustrated by Doron Ben-Ami. HarperCollins Pubs. 1995 88p il lib bdg $14.89; pa $3.95   **S C**

1. Ghost stories 2. Short stories

ISBN 0-06-024468-2 (lib bdg); 0-06-440646-6 (pa)
          LC 94-25136

"The premise is intriguing: over the years, seven families have moved into the house at 66 Brown's End, and each time, a child has discovered a different ghost. Yolen, Bruce Coville, Barbara Goldin, Mary Whittington, Janet Gill, and Anna and Gary Hines have loaded the house from basement to attic with spirits of all sorts—from abandoned ghost puppies to an insatiable gourmet ghost. The stories are all wonderful—eerie and unsettling enough to be satisfying, but lightened with humor." Booklist

Help wanted: short stories about young people working; selected by Anita Silvey. Little, Brown 1997 174p $15.45 (7 and up)   **S C**

1. Work—Fiction 2. Short stories

ISBN 0-316-79148-2   LC 96-34827

A collection of twelve short stories exploring the world of work, by such authors as Gary Soto, Norma Fox Mazer, and Ray Bradbury

"This enticing collection offers a little something for everyone." Publ Wkly

Henry, O., 1862-1910

The gift of the Magi and other stories; illustrated by Michael Dooling; afterword by Peter Glassman. Books of Wonder 1997 205p il $22 (7 and up)   **S C**

1. Short stories

ISBN 0-688-14581-7   LC 96-30639

An illustrated collection of fourteen short stories reflecting various aspects of American life at the turn of the nineteenth century

"This collection will work best when read aloud across generations. Dooling's exquisite color plates, one for each story, in shades of brown and red, are both low-key and warm, with a realistic style that captures the wry characterization of O. Henry's prose." Booklist

Jennings, Paul, 1943-

Unbearable! more bizarre stories. Viking 1995 c1990 116p $14.99; pa $3.99   **S C**

1. Fantasy fiction 2. Supernatural—Fiction 3. Short stories

ISBN 0-670-86262-2; 0-14-038595-9 (pa)
          LC 94-45198

First published 1990 in Australia

"A girl rummages in goat droppings while trying to recover the valuable opal the creature consumed. A boy uses his incredibly smelly feet to stop bullies from killing a two-hundred-year-old sea turtle. Jennings's stories entice readers with their off-the-wall, often disgusting, plot twists." Horn Book Guide

Uncovered! weird, weird stories. Viking 1996 c1995 134p $14.99   **S C**

1. Fantasy fiction 2. Supernatural—Fiction 3. Short stories

ISBN 0-670-86856-6   LC 95-46464

Jennings, Paul, 1943—_Continued_

First published 1995 in Australia

"In the opening selection, a dying boy's mentally disabled brother manages to grant his final wish to see a snowman, a sight normally impossible in their warm Australian home. In the collection's most risqué tale, 'Pubic Hare,' a boy exacts a gentle revenge on his classmates with the help of a dead friend whose ashes give him extraordinary powers of concentration. Other stories range from poignant to wacky, but all are united by the witty, engaging prose style that is Jennings's hallmark." SLJ

Undone! more mad endings. Viking 1995 c1993 117p $14.99; pa $3.99   S C
1. Fantasy fiction 2. Supernatural—Fiction 3. Short stories
ISBN 0-670-86005-0; 0-14-038398-0 (pa)
LC 94-34976
First published 1993 in Australia
A collection of eight stories about the scary, the supernatural, or the unusual, including a mysterious bottle whose contents let you read people's minds and homemade granola that turns a boy into an apple tree
"Sometimes clever, sometimes dark, and often quirky, the roundup offers good variety and lots of surprises." Booklist

Unmentionable! more amazing stories. Viking 1993 c1991 120p hardcover o.p. paperback available $3.99   S C
1. Fantasy fiction 2. Supernatural—Fiction 3. Short stories
ISBN 0-14-037399-3 (pa)   LC 92-25930
Also available companion volumes Unreal! (1991) and Uncanny! (1991)
First published 1991 in Australia
A collection of nine stories about the scary, the supernatural, or the unusual, including an ice maiden with a deadly kiss and a magic harmonica with the power to do good or evil
"Jennings occasionally salts his tales with things traditionally 'unmentionable.' But while he may be offbeat in his choice of subjects, he is never sensational. His curious, entertaining stories are sometimes sharp, sometimes creepy, often clever manipulations of the totally bizarre and the real." Booklist

Jiménez, Francisco, 1943-

The circuit: stories from the life of a migrant child. University of N.M. Press 1997 134p pa $10.95   S C
1. Mexican Americans—Fiction 2. Migrant labor—Fiction 3. Short stories
ISBN 0-8263-1797-9   LC 97-4844
Also available in hardcover from Houghton Mifflin
A collection of twelve short stories about Mexican American migrant farmworkers
"Each of these short stories builds quietly to a surprise that reveals the truth, and together the stories lead to the tearing climax." Booklist

Johnson, Angela, 1961-

Gone from home: short takes. DK Ink 1998 104p $15.95 (7 and up)   S C
1. Short stories
ISBN 0-7894-2499-1   LC 97-52097
A collection of short stories in which young people extend help to those around them while trying to find hopeful answers to life's problems
"Throughout this remarkable collection, Johnson reflects on the human soul in all its variety, and in all its goodness." Horn Book Guide

Join in; multiethnic short stories by outstanding writers for young adults; edited by Donald R. Gallo. Delacorte Press 1993 256p hardcover o.p. paperback available $5.50   S C
1. Short stories
ISBN 0-440-21957-4 (pa)   LC 92-43169
"The 17 stories cross the boundaries of race and culture and probe the universal themes of belonging, acceptance, family, and friendship." Booklist
"Uneven in quality, this will nevertheless offer grounds for discussion among young adults, who will appreciate the accessibility and brevity of the stories." Bull Cent Child Books

Kimmel, Eric A.

Sword of the samurai; adventure stories from Japan. Harcourt Brace & Co. 1999 114p $15
                                                  S C
1. Japan—Fiction 2. Adventure fiction 3. Short stories
ISBN 0-15-201985-5   LC 98-16633
"Browndeer Press"
Eleven short stories about samurai warriors, their way of life, courage, wit, and foolishness
"These selections offer something for everyone: humor, wisdom and adventure along with a gentle and graceful introduction to the code of ethics that continues to shape Japan today." Publ Wkly

Kipling, Rudyard, 1865-1936

The jungle books   S C
1. Animals—Fiction 2. India—Fiction 3. Short stories

Various editions available
A collection of fifteen animal stories first published 1894 and 1895 in two volumes by Macmillan with titles: The jungle book and The second jungle book. Both books also are available separately from various publishers
The central figure in the stories is the human Mowgli, brought up in the jungle in India by Mother Wolf

Lester, Julius

Long journey home: stories from black history. Dial Press (NY) 1972 147p $13.99; pa $4.99
                                                  S C
1. African Americans—Fiction 2. Short stories
ISBN 0-8037-4953-8; 0-14-038981-4 (pa)
Also available in paperback from Scholastic

Lester, Julius—*Continued*

"Six original short stories based on real characters and incidents depict the drama and tragedy of the black experience." Chicago Public Libr

"In a foreword, Julius Lester explains that he has chosen minor figures because the mass of people were the 'movers of history' while the great figures are their symbols. . . . The selections are diversified in their settings and alike in their sharply-etched effectiveness." Bull Cent Child Books

Mazer, Harry, 1925-

The dog in the freezer: three novellas. Simon & Schuster Bks. for Young Readers 1997 170p $16; pa $4.50 S C

1. Dogs—Fiction 2. Short stories
ISBN 0-689-80753-8; 0-689-80754-6 (pa)
LC 96-44833

"The first story is told by a dog that changes places with his boy. . . . In the second . . . a fatherless boy goes to live with his uncle and finds puppy love with an older girl and real love with his puppy. In the title tale, a teenager feels compelled to bury the dead dog of the meanest man in the building. Mazer's writing is bright and fine and often very funny and with lots of emotion. . . . A poem by Mazer's daughter has its own charm and makes a fitting finish to the book." Booklist

McKean, Thomas

Into the candlelit room and other strange tales. Putnam 1999 215p $17.99 S C

1. Supernatural—Fiction 2. Short stories
ISBN 0-399-23359-8 LC 98-13070

In a series of letters and diary entries, five young people describe their experiences with evil and the supernatural, including encounters with a demon, a ghost, and a fortuneteller

"McKean's ear for colloquial language, easy flowing narrative, suspenseful circumstances, and fine characterization combine to make this collection a page-turner." Voice Youth Advocates

McKinley, Robin

The door in the hedge. Greenwillow Bks. 1981 216p lib bdg $15 S C

1. Fairy tales 2. Short stories
ISBN 0-688-00312-5 LC 80-21903

The author "presents four romantic tales that elaborate—to a greater or lesser degree—upon the supernatural lore of fairy tale, myth, and legend. Two of the stories are original in plot and in characters. . . . The other two stories are literary recastings of Grimm tales, 'The Princess and the Frog' . . . [and] 'The Twelve Dancing Princesses.'" Horn Book

"These tales are well-written and enjoyable to read. It is too bad they lack illustrations." Child Book Rev Serv

A knot in the grain and other stories. Greenwillow Bks. 1994 195p $14 S C

1. Supernatural—Fiction 2. Short stories
ISBN 0-688-09201-2 LC 93-17557

Also available in paperback from HarperCollins

This "collection of five stories by a master storyteller deals mainly with love: true, enduring love between apparently ill-matched lovers. Four of the stories share the setting of *The Blue Sword* and *The Hero and the Crown* while the title story is contemporary. McKinley has at her command a clear, apparently effortless style; fresh, original ideas; a romantic outlook; and a remarkable ability to evoke wonder and belief." Horn Book Guide

McKissack, Patricia C., 1944-

The dark-thirty; Southern tales of the supernatural; illustrated by Brian Pinkney. Knopf 1992 122p il $16; lib bdg $17.99; pa $12 S C

1. Ghost stories 2. African Americans—Fiction 3. Short stories
ISBN 0-679-81863-4; 0-679-91863-9 (lib bdg); 0-679-88335-5 (pa) LC 92-3021

A Newbery Medal honor book, 1993; Coretta Scott King Award for text, 1993

A collection of ghost stories with African American themes, designed to be told during the Dark Thirty—the half hour before sunset—when ghosts seem all too believable

"Strong characterizations are superbly drawn in a few words. The atmosphere of each selection is skillfully developed and sustained to the very end." SLJ

Montgomery, L. M. (Lucy Maud), 1874-1942

Christmas with Anne and other holiday stories; edited by Rea Wilmshurst. Delacorte Press 1996 214p il $16.95 S C

1. Christmas—Fiction 2. Short stories
ISBN 0-385-32288-7 LC 96-11657

"Fourteen short stories published in magazines during the early 1900s and two Christmas episodes from *Anne of Green Gables* and *Anne of Windy Poplars* make up this collection of Christmas tales." Booklist

These stories "are filled with the formal language and exuberant descriptive passages so characteristic of the author's day. . . . A nice introduction to Montgomery and a welcome treat for fans." SLJ

Murphy, Jim, 1947-

Night terrors. Scholastic 1993 177p $13.95; pa $3.50 S C

1. Ghost stories 2. Supernatural—Fiction 3. Short stories
ISBN 0-590-45341-6; 0-590-45342-4 (pa) LC 92-27102

Gravedigger Digger Barnes shares chilling tales he's heard in his graveyard wanderings in the eastern states

"These selections build suspense from the very beginning. The contemporary nature of the settings makes the twists that come at the end of each one all the more frightening." SLJ

A **Newbery** Christmas; fourteen stories of Christmas by Newbery Award-winning authors; selected by Martin H. Greenberg and Charles G. Waugh; introduction by Carol-Lynn Rössel Waugh. Delacorte Press 1991 189p $19.95 S C

1. Christmas—Fiction 2. Short stories
ISBN 0-385-30485-4 LC 91-17124

A Newbery Christmas—*Continued*

This collection includes stories by such authors as Eleanor Estes, E. L. Konigsburg, Madeleine L'Engle, and Katherine Paterson

"This unique collection . . . celebrates Christmas as a time when magic becomes real and the impossible becomes possible. . . . . A book that should be a part of every library's holiday collection." SLJ

A Newbery Halloween; a dozen scary stories by Newbery Award-winning authors; selected by Martin H. Greenberg and Charles G. Waugh; introduction by Lloyd Alexander. Delacorte Press 1993 189p $16.95   S C
1. Halloween—Fiction 2. Short stories
ISBN 0-385-31028-5   LC 92-43877

A collection of short stories with a Halloween theme, by such Newbery Award-winning authors as E. L. Konigsburg, Beverly Cleary, Virginia Hamilton, and Paul Fleischman

"Greenberg and Waugh have done their choosing well. . . . This will serve the dual purposes of read-aloud and read-alone and serve them both well." Booklist

A Newbery zoo; a dozen animal stories by Newbery Award-winning authors; selected by Martin H. Greenberg and Charles G. Waugh; introduction by Betsy Byars. Delacorte Press 1995 179p $16.95   S C
1. Animals—Fiction 2. Short stories
ISBN 0-385-32263-1   LC 94-32712

This is a collection of animal stories by "authors such as Beverly Cleary, Betsy Byars, and Jean Craighead George. . . . Because the stories will appeal to readers of diverse ages, the book will be attractive for family sharing, but the collection may work best as a means for reaching children who think they don't like to read." Booklist

Night terrors; stories of shadow and substance; edited by Lois Duncan. Simon & Schuster Bks. for Young Readers 1996 175p $16 (7 and up)   S C
1. Horror fiction 2. Short stories
ISBN 0-689-80346-X   LC 95-44901

Contents: The monkey's wedding, by J. Aiken; Satan's shadow, by A. Ferguson; The chosen, by M. Harrah; The bogey man, by A. C. Klause; Bearing Paul, by C. Lynch; The beautiful thing, by H. Mazer; The house on Buffalo Street, by N. F. Mazer; The dark beast of death, by J. L. Nixon; Girl at the window, by R. Peck; The grind of an axe, by T. Taylor; Moon kill, by P. Windsor

"The stories deal with madness, witchcraft, homicide and incest. While the book should be popular with students, the subject matter may be too mature for some middle-schoolers." Voice Youth Advocates

A Nightmare's dozen; stories from the dark; edited by Michael Stearns; illustrated by Michael Hussar. Harcourt Brace & Co. 1996 239p il $17 (7 and up)   S C
1. Horror fiction 2. Short stories
ISBN 0-15-201247-8   LC 96-3382

Also available in paperback from Dell

Also available A wizard's dozen (1993) and A starfarer's dozen (1995)

"Jane Yolen books"

This collection includes stories by such authors as Jane Yolen, Vivian Vande Velde, Nancy Springer, and Martha Soukup

"This collection of 14 original psychological horror tales is short on the gory stuff, but long on the terrors of adolescence and family life. From ghostly alcoholic fathers killed in drunk-driving accidents to obnoxious siblings who are conveniently made to disappear in amusement parks, these stories will please those readers ready for more sophisticated material." SLJ

Ortiz Cofer, Judith, 1952-
An island like you; stories of the barrio. Orchard Bks. 1995 165p $15.95; lib bdg $16.99 (7 and up)   S C
1. Puerto Ricans—United States—Fiction 2. Short stories
ISBN 0-531-06897-8; 0-531-08747-6 (lib bdg)
                              LC 94-32496

"A Melanie Kroupa book"

"Twelve linked short stories explore teenage life in or about the Paterson, New Jersey barrio. . . . Cofer tells of various kids, such as a girl sent to spend the summer in Puerto Rico with her grandparents, a boy helped by his teacher to find unsuspected power in poetry, a girl uneasy about working with a mentally retarded man at her poolside summer job, a boy whose duty hour with his grandfather takes a suprising turn. . . . The combination of interweaving of characters, intensity of emotion, and deft control of language makes this a rewarding collection." Bull Cent Child Books

Paterson, Katherine
A midnight clear: stories for the Christmas season. Lodestar Bks. 1995 212p $16 (7 and up)   S C
1. Christmas—Fiction 2. Short stories
ISBN 0-525-67529-9   LC 95-12590

"These stories were originally written for the author's husband, a pastor, to read to his congregation on Christmas Eve. Among them are the story of a man on his way to his dying father's bedside who picks up a troubled young hitchhiker; a Girl Scout and an eccentric old woman in a nursing home who form an unlikely friendship; and a minister's daughter who plays the coveted part of Mary in the Sunday School pageant despite a series of humorous mishaps in previous years. . . . These stories celebrate the human spirit and will make good family fare." Horn Book

Places I never meant to be; original stories by censored writers; edited by Judy Blume. Atheneum Bks. for Young Readers 1999 198p $16.95 (7 and up)   S C
1. Short stories
ISBN 0-689-82034-8   LC 98-30343

"This collection of 11 original short stories and a reprint of the late Norma Klein's college writing is interspersed with personal essays about the authors' views on censorship and its effect upon their work. Among the authors included are Norma Fox Mazer, Jacqueline Woodson, Harry Mazer, and Susan Beth Pfeffer." SLJ

"The contributors are a stellar list of well-known YA

Places I never meant to be—*Continued*
authors. . . . The authors' notes about censorship add a thought-provoking dimension to the collection, as does Blume's introduction, and the stories themselves are emotionally intense." Bull Cent Child Books

Poe, Edgar Allan, 1809-1849
Tales of Edgar Allan Poe; illustrated by Barry Moser; afterword by Peter Glassman. Books of Wonder 1991 308p il $22   S C
1. Horror fiction 2. Short stories
ISBN 0-688-07509-6   LC 91-3277
This illustrated collection includes The gold bug; The tell-tale heart; The fall of the House of Usher and The pit and the pendulum
"Moser's watercolor paintings for 14 of Poe's best stories are both macabre and understated. The best of them make us further imagine the terrible things beyond the edge." Booklist

Potok, Chaim, 1929-
Zebra and other stories. Knopf 1998 146p $18; lib bdg $19.99 (7 and up)   S C
1. Short stories
ISBN 0-679-85440-1; 0-679-95440-6 (lib bdg)
          LC 98-4769
A collection of stories about six different young people who each experience a life-changing event
"Potok's ability to spin a tale is extraordinary and this collection will be devoured by those who loved his earlier works, and those lucky enough to stumble upon this one." Voice Youth Advocates

Read into the millennium; tales of the future; from the editors of Read magazine. Millbrook Press 1999 160p lib bdg $22.40   S C
1. Science fiction 2. Short stories
ISBN 0-7613-0962-4   LC 98-8390
"This collection of futuristic fiction features one of Isaac Asimov's early robot stories, a chilling and mythic look at life after the nuclear age by Stephen Vincent Benét, and a fast-paced tale by Robert Lipsyte. . . . Adaptations of *The Time Machine* and Frankenstein and . . . selections from *The Martian Chronicles* by Ray Bradbury and Lois Lowry's *The Giver*." Horn Book Guide

Reynolds, Marilyn, 1935-
Beyond dreams; true-to-life series from Hamilton High. Morning Glory Press 1995 190p $15.95; pa $8.95 (7 and up)   S C
1. School stories 2. Short stories
ISBN 1-885356-01-3; 1-885356-00-5 (pa)
          LC 95-17802
Includes six short stories that deal with crisis situations faced by teenagers, including racism, abuse, sense of failure, aging relatives, drunk driving, and abortion
"All the stories are interesting and well paced, and each has a slightly different style. . . . Young adults will certainly identify with the characters and their problems, and it is particularly useful to have these issues addressed . . . with alternate male and female narrators." Booklist

Rites of passage; stories about growing up by black writers from around the world; edited by Tonya Bolden; with a foreword by Charles Johnson. Hyperion Bks. for Children 1994 208p $16.95   S C
1. African Americans—Fiction 2. Blacks—Fiction 3. Short stories
ISBN 1-56282-688-3   LC 93-31304
"Seventeen 'growing up' stories by noted black writers from the U.S., the Caribbean, Central America, England, Africa, and Australia. . . . The adolescent protagonists are well drawn, and their coming-of-age stories offer meaningful anecdotes on coping with, adapting to, and interpreting life's experiences." SLJ

Singer, Isaac Bashevis, 1904-1991
The power of light; eight stories for Hanukkah; with illustrations by Irene Lieblich. Farrar, Straus & Giroux 1980 86p il $15; pa $7.95   S C
1. Hanukkah—Fiction 2. Jews—Fiction 3. Short stories
ISBN 0-374-36099-5; 0-374-45984-3 (pa)
          LC 80-20263
"The stories, bound together by recurring Hanukkah motifs—the lamp, the dreidel, and the pancakes, tell chiefly of events affecting the lives of Eastern European Jews. Ranging from such somber happenings as the drafting of small Jewish boys to serve in the Russian army during the nineteenth century through the bombing and burning of the Warsaw ghetto, the harrowing events are seen in the context of the celebration of Hanukkah." Horn Book

Sixteen: short stories by outstanding writers for young adults; edited by Donald R. Gallo. Delacorte Press 1984 179p hardcover o.p. paperback available $5.50 (7 and up)   S C
1. Short stories
ISBN 0-440-97757-6 (pa)   LC 84-3250
"This is a collection of sixteen short stories for young adults especially commissioned from such authors as Joan Aiken, M. E. Kerr, Richard Peck, and Norma and Harry Mazer. Divided into five sections ('Friendships', 'Turmoils', 'Loves', 'Decisions', and 'Families'), some of the stories are fantasies, some are realistic, others are funny, scary, or poignant, but all are choice examples of their genre." Child Book Rev Serv

Skinner, David, 1963-
Thundershine: tales of metakids; illustrated by Kevin Skinner. Simon & Schuster Bks. for Young Readers 1999 115p il $15   S C
1. Supernatural—Fiction 2. Short stories
ISBN 0-689-80556-X   LC 98-29250
A collection of four stories about young people with extraordinary powers, including a girl who talks with the planet Pluto, a girl who can alter reality by redrawing maps, and a girl who can change shape
"This well-written and unusual collection will probably generate some interesting discussions." Voice Youth Advocates

Sleator, William

Oddballs: stories. Dutton Children's Bks. 1993 134p $14.99; pa $3.99   S C
1. Family life—Fiction 2. Friendship—Fiction
3. Short stories
ISBN 0-525-45057-2; 0-14-037438-8 (pa)
LC 92-27666

A collection of stories based on experiences from the author's youth and peopled with an unusual assortment of family and friends

"Fresh, funny, and slightly gross, the quasi-autobiographical glimpses will grab the reader's attention." Horn Book Guide

Somehow tenderness survives; stories of Southern Africa; selected by Hazel Rochman. Harper & Row 1988 147p lib bdg $12.95; pa $4.95 (7 and up)   S C

1. Short stories 2. South Africa—Fiction
ISBN 0-06-025022-4 (lib bdg); 0-06-447063-6 (pa)
LC 88-916

A collection of eight short stories and two "autobiographical accounts which vividly evoke what it means to come of age in South Africa under apartheid. The contributors, including Doris Lessing and Nadine Gordimer, as well as lesser-known writers, are of various races and their stories cover a time span of 35 years. . . . This title should be in every YA collection. A glossary and notes on contributors are included." Voice Youth Advocates

Soto, Gary

Baseball in April, and other stories. Harcourt Brace Jovanovich 1990 111p $16; pa $6   S C
1. Mexican Americans—Fiction 2. California—Fiction 3. Short stories
ISBN 0-15-202573-1; 0-15-202567-7 (pa)
LC 89-36460

A collection of eleven short stories focusing on the everyday adventures of Hispanic young people growing up in Fresno, California

Each story "gets at the heart of some aspect of growing up. The insecurities, the embarrassments, the triumphs, the inequities of it all are chronicled with wit and charm. Soto's characters ring true and his knowledge of, and affection for, their shared Mexican-American heritage is obvious and infectious." Voice Youth Advocates

Local news. Harcourt Brace Jovanovich 1993 148p $13.95   S C
1. Mexican Americans—Fiction 2. California—Fiction 3. Short stories
ISBN 0-15-248117-6   LC 92-37905
Also available in paperback from Scholastic

A collection of thirteen short stories about the everyday lives of Mexican American young people in California's Central Valley

"These stories resonate with integrity, verve, and compassion." Horn Book

Petty crimes. Harcourt Brace & Co. 1998 157p $16   S C
1. Mexican Americans—Fiction 2. Short stories
ISBN 0-15-201658-9   LC 97-37114

A collection of short stories about Mexican American youth growing up in California's Central Valley

"A sense of family strength relieves the under-current of sadness in these raw stories." Horn Book Guide

Spinelli, Jerry, 1941-

The library card. Scholastic 1997 148p $15.95; pa $3.99   S C
1. Books and reading—Fiction 2. Short stories
ISBN 0-590-46731-X; 0-590-38633-6 (pa)
LC 96-18412

"A library card is the magical object common to each of these four stories in which a budding street thug, a television addict, a homeless orphan, and a lonely girl are all transformed by the power and the possibilities that await them within the walls of the public library. Spinelli's characters . . . are unusual and memorable; his writing both humorous and convincing." Horn Book Guide

Stay true: short stories for strong girls; compiled and edited by Marilyn Singer. Scholastic 1998 204p $16.95; pa $4.99 (7 and up)   S C

1. Girls—Fiction 2. Short stories
ISBN 0-590-36031-0; 0-590-36033-7 (pa)
LC 97-14709

A collection of short stories by various authors, including Andrea Davis Pinkney, M.E. Kerr, and Anne Mazer, about adolescent girls coming of age

"Funny, poignant, thought provoking." Voice Youth Advocates

Talking leaves; contemporary native American short stories; introduced and edited by Craig Lesley; associate editor, Katheryn Stavrakis. Dell 1991 xxvi, 385p pa $12.95   S C

1. Indians of North America—Fiction 2. Short stories
ISBN 0-385-31272-5   LC 92-139334
"A Laurel trade paperback"

This anthology includes contributions by such authors as Louise Erdrich, Diane Glancy, Michael Dorris, N. Scott Momaday, Paula Gunn Allen, and Mary Tallmountain

"All these stories have a strong sense of person and place and engagingly inform of the Native American condition." Libr J

Taylor, Theodore, 1921-

Rogue wave and other red-blooded sea stories. Harcourt Brace & Co. 1996 184p $16   S C
1. Sea stories 2. Short stories
ISBN 0-15-201408-X   LC 96-14585
Also available in paperback from Avon Bks.

This "collection comprises five stories previously published in the 1950s and 1960s in such magazines as Argosy and three original ones focusing on teenagers' sea adventures. . . . Juicy subjects such as sharks, a cruel captain, and the psychological battle between a captured German U-boat commander and a scholarly British officer are fleshed out in very masculine style, with lots of physical detail and excitement, and most of the stories end with the sort of punchy conclusion that characterizes the best short stories." Booklist

Trapped!: cages of mind and body; edited by Lois Duncan. Simon & Schuster 1998 228p $16 (7 and up)   **S C**
1. Short stories
ISBN 0-689-81335-X   LC 97-18049

"In a variety of stories, plus a brief play by Rita Williams-Garcia and a series of poems from Lois Duncan, 13 noted authors for young adults write about situations in which they feel trapped by their circumstances." Baya Book Rev

"A powerhouse collection of diverse, innovative, and captivating stories presented in a plethora of styles. . . . Each story offers a treasure not to be missed. Occasional coarse language and adult themes are discreetly handled." Booklist

Twelve shots: outstanding short stories about guns; edited by Harry Mazer. Delacorte Press 1997 229p $15.95; pa $4.99 (7 and up)   **S C**
1. Firearms—Fiction 2. Short stories
ISBN 0-385-32238-0; 0-440-22002-5 (pa)
     LC 96-37838

"This collection of 12 original short stories . . . range from the humorous to the tragic, and each has a theme involving youth and guns. The contributors include Chris Lynch, Harry Mazer, Richard Peck, Walter Dean Myers, and Rita Williams-Garcia. . . . The book makes for entertaining and thought-provoking reading." SLJ

Ultimate sports: short stories by outstanding writers for young adults; edited by Donald R. Gallo. Delacorte Press 1995 333p hardcover o.p. paperback available $5.99 (7 and up)   **S C**
1. Sports—Fiction 2. Short stories
ISBN 0-440-22707-0 (pa)   LC 94-49610

This anthology includes stories by: Chris Crutcher; Will Weaver; Norma Fox Mazer; Robert Lipsyte; Thomas J. Dygard and Chris Lynch

"There is a terrific mix of the serious and the light-hearted, female and male characters, and traditional and nontraditional games. A winning collection." SLJ

Vampires: a collection of original stories; edited by Jane Yolen and Martin H. Greenberg. HarperCollins Pubs. 1991 228p $15; pa $4.50 (7 and up)   **S C**
1. Vampires—Fiction 2. Short stories
ISBN 0-06-026800-X; 0-06-440485-4 (pa)
     LC 90-27888

A collection of thirteen original stories about vampires by a variety of authors

"In this collection of chilling, funny, and sensitive stories, the undead include piano teachers, mean old aunts, and even the girl next door." Booklist

Vande Velde, Vivian, 1951-

Curses, Inc. and other stories. Harcourt Brace & Co. 1997 226p $16   **S C**
1. Magic—Fiction 2. Short stories
ISBN 0-15-201452-7   LC 96-24856
Also available in paperback from Dell
"Jane Yolen books"

A collection of ten stories about magic
"The tone of the collection varies from funny to

haunting, from rueful to gothic, as Vande Velde roams from the familiar environs of fairy tales to the swamps of the plantation south. Give this one to readers who are ready for some sophisticated tales of the supernatural." Bull Cent Child Books

Tales from the Brothers Grimm and the Sisters Weird. Harcourt Brace & Co. 1995 128p il $17
     S C
1. Fairy tales 2. Short stories
ISBN 0-15-200220-0   LC 94-26341
Also available in paperback from Dell
"Jane Yolen Books"

This collection presents alternative versions of such familiar fairy tales as Rumpelstiltskin, Hansel and Gretel, and The Princess and the Pea

"Vande Velde challenges readers' notions of good, bad, and ugly. . . . Modern references and sensibilities . . . add to the humor (often the gallows variety). Entertaining and provocative, these selections make good read-alouds and can be used to spark discussion or creative writing exercises." SLJ

Visions: nineteen short stories by outstanding writers for young adults; edited by Donald R. Gallo. Delacorte Press 1987 228p hardcover o.p. paperback available $5.99 (7 and up)   **S C**
1. Short stories
ISBN 0-440-20208-6 (pa)   LC 87-6787

"Information about the authors follows each of nineteen original short stories, most of them impressive examples of the genre, all of them written by established men and women. Among the familiar names: Joan Aiken, M.E. Kerr, Walter Dean Myers, Richard Peck. The tales are grouped under such headings as 'Adjustments' or 'Kinships,' and include both realistic and fanciful writing, most of the work being of fine quality and the rest only slightly less so." Bull Cent Child Books

Vivelo, Jackie

Chills in the night; tales that will haunt you. DK Ink 1997 123p pa $14.95   **S C**
1. Supernatural—Fiction 2. Short stories
ISBN 0-7894-2463-0

"These eight spooky stories include a tale of a teacher exacting revenge on her misbehaving students and a . . . time-travel piece in which two cousins visit the past via a dumbwaiter." Horn Book Guide

These stories "are creepy and weird enough to appeal to readers, especially those who don't want something too scary. Vivelo turns everyday experiences into something strange and fearsome." Booklist

Westall, Robert, 1929-1993

Demons and shadows; the ghostly best stories of Robert Westall. Farrar, Straus & Giroux 1993 264p $16; pa $6.95 (7 and up)   **S C**
1. Ghost stories 2. Horror fiction 3. Short stories
ISBN 0-374-31768-2; 0-374-41701-6 (pa)
     LC 93-7949

"With a distinctive British flavor, and featuring primarily adult protagonists and emotionally complex situations, this collection demands a sophisticated reader who will discover here satisfying and well-wrought stories that linger in the memory." Booklist

Where angels glide at dawn; new stories from Latin America; edited by Lori M. Carlson and Cynthia L. Ventura; introduction by Isabel Allende; illustrations by José Ortega. Lippincott 1990 114p il $14; lib bdg $13.89; pa $4.50

S C

1. Latin America—Fiction 2. Short stories
ISBN 0-397-32424-3; 0-397-32425-1 (lib bdg); 0-06-440464-1 (pa)   LC 90-6697
"This collection of translated stories amplifies the richness of Latin American culture. . . . Bolstered by a glossary of terms and brief explanations of each entry's setting, these 10 tales are as accessible as they are intriguing." Publ Wkly

Who do you think you are? stories of friends and enemies; selected by Hazel Rochman and Darlene Z. McCampbell. Little, Brown 1993 170p hardcover o.p. paperback available $8.95 (7 and up)   S C

1. Friendship—Fiction 2. Short stories
ISBN 0-316-75320-3 (pa)   LC 93-314
"Joy Street books"
"Louise Erdrich, John Updike, Ray Bradbury, Joyce Carol Oates, Sandra Cisneros, Tim O'Brien, Richard Peck, and Maya Angelou are among the 15 writers represented in this anthology of stories [two prose excerpts and a poem] about friendship and loss of friendship." Booklist
"Meticulously chosen and arranged, these works crystalize moments of vulnerability, sorrow and understanding; together, they serve as an excellent introduction to modern American writing." Publ Wkly

Wrede, Patricia C., 1953-
Book of enchantments. Harcourt Brace & Co. 1996 234p $17   S C

1. Magic—Fiction 2. Short stories
ISBN 0-15-201255-9   LC 95-41036
Also available in paperback from Scholastic
"Jane Yolen books"
"This collection of original short stories uses archetypal fairy- and folktale motifs that feature strong female protagonists. Wrede's forte in firmly establishing characterization allows the reader to care about the outcome of each of the ten stories. Fine examples of new twists on ancient tales, the stories range in tone from witty to sad." Horn Book Guide

Wyeth, Sharon Dennis
Vampire bugs: stories conjured from the past; illustrated by Curtis E. James. Delacorte Press 1995 80p il $14.95; pa $3.99   S C

1. Supernatural—Fiction 2. African Americans—Fiction 3. Short stories
ISBN 0-385-32082-5; 0-440-41155-6 (pa)
LC 94-20315
"These six tales of young people transformed into lightning bugs, placed under spells, or visited by ghosts will raise goosebumps and serve as an accessible introduction to African-American folklore. Three of the stories were adapted from traditional folktales; the rest are fictional works that have some basis in historical events or characters." Horn Book Guide

Wynne-Jones, Tim
The book of changes; stories. Orchard Bks. 1995 c1994 143p $15.95   S C

1. Short stories
ISBN 0-531-09489-8   LC 95-6034
Also available in paperback from Penguin Bks.
"A Melanie Kroupa book"
First published 1994 in Canada
The stories "focus on what seem to be ordinary events. . . . Yet with his prowess for crafting each tale so that it neatly comes full circle, Wynne-Jones makes the quotidian well worth reading about. . . . The characters' on-target thoughts and banter attest to the author's familiarity with—and compassion for—today's kids." Publ Wkly

Lord of the Fries and other stories. DK Pub. 1999 214p $17.95   S C

1. Canada—Fiction 2. Short stories
ISBN 0-7894-2623-4   LC 98-41581
"'Lord of the Fries' features a pair of friends who try to penetrate the mysterious past of a legendarily cranky fast-food entrepreneur; 'The Fallen Angel' features a choirboy bedeviled by a new and problematic arrival in the choir loft; 'The Chinese Babies' bring together a Welsh-speaking English Canadian, a van full of French Canadians, several generations of moody family, and some important games of chess." Bull Cent Child Books
"Fresh dialogue, sympathetic and idiosyncratic protagonists, and surprises around every corner." Publ Wkly

Yee, Paul
Tales from Gold Mountain; stories of the Chinese in the New World; paintings by Simon Ng. Macmillan 1989 64p il o.p.; Groundwood Bks. reissue available $18.95   S C

1. Chinese—North America—Fiction 2. Short stories
ISBN 0-88899-098-7 (pa)   LC 89-12643
"The eight stories in this collection are . . . rooted in the real experiences of the Chinese who came to North America seeking the prosperity of Gold Mountain. Though Mr. Yee has drawn on tales he heard growing up in Vancouver's Chinatown and on research into the lives of the Chinese who settled in Canada, the stories contain many parallels with the experiences of the Chinese in the United States." Horn Book
These "brief, pithy tales strikingly reflect traditional Chinese beliefs and customs in new world circumstances. . . . Romance, family loyalty, and justice are important themes, and an element of surprise is never far away." Booklist

Yolen, Jane
Twelve impossible things before breakfast; stories. Harcourt Brace & Co. 1997 175p $17   S C

1. Fantasy fiction 2. Short stories
ISBN 0-15-201524-8   LC 97-667
This is "a collection of twelve fantasy stories, some altered favorites, others brand new." Voice Youth Advocates
"There is something here for everyone—tales that are scary, gross, or fanciful." SLJ

PART 2

AUTHOR, TITLE, SUBJECT, AND ANALYTICAL INDEX

AUTHOR, TITLE, SUBJECT, AND ANALYTICAL INDEX

This index to the books in the Classified Catalog includes author, title, subject, and analytical entries; added entries for publishers' series, for joint authors, and for editors of works entered under title; and name and subject cross-references; all arranged in one alphabet. This index also includes title and subject entries for works listed in the CD-ROM section.

The number or symbol in bold face type at the end of each entry refers to the Dewey Decimal Classification or to the Fiction or Story Collection Section where the main entry for the book will be found. Works classed in 92 will be found under the heading for the person written about. The notation "7 and up" indicates that the item is likely to be of interest to young people in grades seven and higher.

For further information about this index and for examples of entries, see Directions for Use of the Catalog.

4 x 4 vehicles. Carroll, J.   **629.22**

6th grade can really kill you. DeClements, B.   **Fic**

The **11:59**. McKissack, P. C.
In McKissack, P. C. The dark-thirty p35-42   **S C**

The **13th** floor. Fleischman, S.   **Fic**

A **16th** century mosque. Macdonald, F.   **297**

The **20th** century
In World history on file v4   **909**

20th century inventions [series]
Hoare, S. Digital revolution   **621.381**
Morgan, N. Lasers   **621.36**

21st century earth: opposing viewpoints (7 and up)   **303.49**

21st century health and wellness [series]
Little, M. Sexually transmitted diseases   **616.95**

33 things every girl should know (7 and up)   **810.8**

100 books for girls to grow on. Dodson, S.   **028.1**

100 most popular children's authors. McElmeel, S. L.   **810.3**

100 most popular scientists for young adults. Haven, K. F.   **920**

The **100** most popular young adult authors. Drew, B. A.   **810.9**

101 amazing optical illusions. Jennings, T.   **152.14**

101 essential tips [series]
Mills, D. Aquarium fish   **639.34**

101 stories of the great ballets. Balanchine, G.   **792.8**

101 things to do on the Internet. Wallace, M.   **004.6**

160 ways to help the world. Duper, L. L.   **361.3**

175 more science experiments to amuse and amaze your friends. Cash, T.   **507.8**

882 ½ amazing answers to your questions about the Titanic. Brewster, H.   **910.4**

1400-1499 (15th century) *See* Fifteenth century

1500-1599 (16th century) *See* Sixteenth century

1700-1799 (18th century) *See* Eighteenth century

1812: the war nobody won. Marrin, A.   **973.5**

The **1960s:** opposing viewpoints (7 and up)   **973.92**

2000-2099 (21st century) *See* Twenty-first century

2001: a space odyssey. Clarke, A. C.   **Fic**

A

A & E biography [series]
Briggs, C. S. Women in space   **920**
Finlayson, R. Nelson Mandela   **92**
Howard, M. Christopher Reeve   **92**
Howard, M. Madeleine Albright   **92**
Kite, L. P. Maya Angelou   **92**
Krohn, K. E. Princess Diana   **92**
Krohn, K. E. Rosie O'Donnell   **92**
Lazo, C. E. Arthur Ashe   **92**
Ruth, A. Louisa May Alcott   **92**
Ruth, A. Mother Teresa   **92**

A.B.C.'s *See* Alphabet

A.I.D.S. (Disease) *See* AIDS (Disease)

A+ projects in earth science, Janice VanCleave's. VanCleave, J. P.   **550**

A to Z of Native American women. Sonneborn, L.   **920.003**

A to Z of women in science and math. Yount, L.   **920.003**

AAAS *See* American Association for the Advancement of Science

AACR *See* Anglo-American cataloguing rules

Aaseng, Nathan, 1953-
Black inventors (7 and up)   **920**
Invertebrates (7 and up)   **592**
Navajo code talkers   **940.54**
Poisonous creatures   **591.6**
The Titanic (7 and up)   **910.4**
Twentieth-century inventors (7 and up)   **920**
Vertebrates   **596**
You are the juror   **345**

AASL *See* American Association of School Librarians

Adams, Samuel, 1722-1803
About
Fradin, D. B. Samuel Adams   **92**

Adams, Simon
Children's illustrated encyclopedia. See Children's illustrated encyclopedia   **031**
The DK visual timeline of the 20th century   **909.82**
Titanic   **910.4**

Adams family
Fiction
Rinaldi, A. The fifth of March (7 and up)   **Fic**

Adamson, Joy, 1910-1980
Born free: a lioness of two worlds   **599.75**
About
Neimark, A. E. Wild heart: the story of Joy Adamson, author of Born free (7 and up)   **92**

Adamson, Lynda G.
American historical fiction   **016.813**
Literature connections to American history, 7-12   **016.973**
Literature connections to world history, 7-12   **016.9**

ADD See Attention deficit disorder

Addams, Jane, 1860-1935
About
Harvey, B. C. Jane Addams   **92**

Addiction to alcohol See Alcoholism

Addictive behavior See Compulsive behavior

Addresses See Speeches

Adirondack Mountains (N.Y.)
Fiction
Bauer, J. Backwater (7 and up)   **Fic**

Adler, Bill, 1929-
(ed) Growing up black. See Growing up black   **920**

Adler, C. S. (Carole S.), 1932-
Not just a summer crush   **Fic**

Adler, Carole S. See Adler, C. S. (Carole S.), 1932-

Adler, David A., 1947-
The kids' catalog of Jewish holidays   **296.4**
We remember the Holocaust   **940.53**

Administration of criminal justice
Barr, R. Juvenile crime (7 and up)   **364.36**
Criminal justice: opposing viewpoints (7 and up)   **345**
Goodwin, W. Teen violence (7 and up)   **364.36**
See/See also pages in the following book(s):
Inequality: opposing viewpoints in social problems p119-62 (7 and up)   **305**

Admirable hare. McCaughrean, G.
In McCaughrean, G. The golden hoard: myths and legends of the world p49-51   **398.2**

Adoff, Arnold, 1935-
(ed) I am the darker brother. See I am the darker brother   **811.008**
(ed) My black me. See My black me   **811.008**

Adolescence
Daldry, J. The teenage guy's survival guide (7 and up)   **305.23**
Gravelle, K. What's going on down there?   **612.6**
Gray, H. M. Real girl/real world (7 and up)   **305.23**
Gurian, M. From boys to men   **305.23**
Jukes, M. Growing up: it's a girl thing   **612.6**
Jukes, M. It's a girl thing   **305.23**
Shandler, S. Ophelia speaks (7 and up)   **305.23**
Bibliography
Zvirin, S. The best years of their lives   **011.6**

Adolescent fathers See Teenage fathers

Adolescent mothers See Teenage mothers

Adolescent pregnancy See Teenage pregnancy

Adolescent prostitution See Juvenile prostitution

Adolescent psychology
Ng, G. Everything you need to know about self-mutilation (7 and up)   **616.85**

Adolescent rights. Greenberg, K. E.   **346**

Adolescents See Teenagers

Adoption
Kaminker, L. Everything you need to know about being adopted (7 and up)   **362.7**
See/See also pages in the following book(s):
The Family: opposing viewpoints (7 and up)   **306.8**
Warren, A. Orphan train rider   **362.7**
Fiction
Johnson, A. Heaven   **Fic**
Lowry, L. Find a stranger, say goodbye (7 and up)   **Fic**
Myers, W. D. Me, Mop, and the Moondance Kid   **Fic**

Adventure and adventurers
Explorers & discoverers   **920.003**
Platt, R. DK illustrated book of great adventurers   **910**
Fiction
See Adventure fiction

Adventure fiction
See also Science fiction; Sea stories
Alexander, L. The Beggar Queen   **Fic**
Alexander, L. The Illyrian adventure   **Fic**
Alexander, L. The iron ring   **Fic**
Alexander, L. The Kestrel   **Fic**
Alexander, L. The remarkable journey of Prince Jen   **Fic**
Alexander, L. Westmark   **Fic**
Campbell, E. The Shark Callers (7 and up)   **Fic**
Cross, G. The great American elephant chase   **Fic**
Fleischman, S. Bandit's moon   **Fic**
Fleischman, S. The whipping boy   **Fic**
Hobbs, W. Ghost canoe   **Fic**
Kimmel, E. A. Sword of the samurai   **S C**
Lawrence, I. The smugglers   **Fic**
Lawrence, I. The wreckers   **Fic**
McCaughrean, G. The pirate's son (7 and up)   **Fic**

Adventure fiction—*Continued*

Smith, R. Thunder cave **Fic**

Snyder, Z. K. Song of the gargoyle **Fic**

Stevenson, R. L. Kidnapped (7 and up) **Fic**

Turner, M. W. The thief **Fic**

Verne, J. Around the world in eighty days **Fic**

Verne, J. A journey to the centre of the earth **Fic**

Voigt, C. Jackaroo (7 and up) **Fic**

Voigt, C. On fortune's wheel (7 and up) **Fic**

The **adventure** of Black Peter. Doyle, Sir A. C.
In Doyle, Sir A. C. The complete Sherlock Holmes **S C**

The **adventure** of Charles Augustus Milverton. Doyle, Sir A. C.
In Doyle, Sir A. C. The complete Sherlock Holmes **S C**

The **adventure** of Shoscombe Old Place. Doyle, Sir A. C.
In Doyle, Sir A. C. The complete Sherlock Holmes **S C**

The **adventure** of the Abbey Grange. Doyle, Sir A. C.
In Doyle, Sir A. C. The complete Sherlock Holmes **S C**

The **adventure** of the Beryl Coronet. Doyle, Sir A. C.
In Doyle, Sir A. C. Adventures of Sherlock Holmes **S C**
In Doyle, Sir A. C. The complete Sherlock Holmes **S C**

The **adventure** of the blanched soldier. Doyle, Sir A. C.
In Doyle, Sir A. C. The complete Sherlock Holmes **S C**

The **adventure** of the Blue Carbuncle. Doyle, Sir A. C.
In Doyle, Sir A. C. Adventures of Sherlock Holmes **S C**
In Doyle, Sir A. C. The complete Sherlock Holmes **S C**

The **adventure** of the Bruce-Partington plans. Doyle, Sir A. C.
In Doyle, Sir A. C. The complete Sherlock Holmes **S C**

The **adventure** of the cardboard box. Doyle, Sir A. C.
In Doyle, Sir A. C. The complete Sherlock Holmes **S C**

The **adventure** of the copper beeches. Doyle, Sir A. C.
In Doyle, Sir A. C. Adventures of Sherlock Holmes **S C**
In Doyle, Sir A. C. The complete Sherlock Holmes **S C**

The **adventure** of the creeping man. Doyle, Sir A. C.
In Doyle, Sir A. C. The complete Sherlock Holmes **S C**

The **adventure** of the dancing men. Doyle, Sir A. C.
In Doyle, Sir A. C. The complete Sherlock Holmes **S C**

The **adventure** of the devil's foot. Doyle, Sir A. C.
In Doyle, Sir A. C. The complete Sherlock Holmes **S C**

The **adventure** of the dying detective. Doyle, Sir A. C.
In Doyle, Sir A. C. The complete Sherlock Holmes **S C**

The **adventure** of the empty house. Doyle, Sir A. C.
In Doyle, Sir A. C. The complete Sherlock Holmes **S C**

The **adventure** of the engineer's thumb. Doyle, Sir A. C.
In Doyle, Sir A. C. Adventures of Sherlock Holmes **S C**

The **adventure** of the golden pince-nez. Doyle, Sir A. C.
In Doyle, Sir A. C. The complete Sherlock Holmes **S C**

The **adventure** of the illustrious client. Doyle, Sir A. C.
In Doyle, Sir A. C. The complete Sherlock Holmes **S C**

The **adventure** of the lion's mane. Doyle, Sir A. C.
In Doyle, Sir A. C. The complete Sherlock Holmes **S C**

The **adventure** of the Mazarin stone. Doyle, Sir A. C.
In Doyle, Sir A. C. The complete Sherlock Holmes **S C**

The **adventure** of the missing three-quarter. Doyle, Sir A. C.
In Doyle, Sir A. C. The complete Sherlock Holmes **S C**

The **adventure** of the noble bachelor. Doyle, Sir A. C.
In Doyle, Sir A. C. Adventures of Sherlock Holmes **S C**
In Doyle, Sir A. C. The complete Sherlock Holmes **S C**

The **adventure** of the Norwood builder. Doyle, Sir A. C.
In Doyle, Sir A. C. The complete Sherlock Holmes **S C**

The **adventure** of the priory school. Doyle, Sir A. C.
In Doyle, Sir A. C. The complete Sherlock Holmes **S C**

The **adventure** of the red circle. Doyle, Sir A. C.
In Doyle, Sir A. C. The complete Sherlock Holmes **S C**

The **adventure** of the retired colourman. Doyle, Sir A. C.
In Doyle, Sir A. C. The complete Sherlock Holmes **S C**

The **adventure** of the second stain. Doyle, Sir A. C.
In Doyle, Sir A. C. The complete Sherlock Holmes **S C**

The **adventure** of the six Napoleons. Doyle, Sir A. C.
In Doyle, Sir A. C. The complete Sherlock Holmes   S C

The **adventure** of the solitary cyclist. Doyle, Sir A. C.
In Doyle, Sir A. C. The complete Sherlock Holmes   S C

The **adventure** of the speckled band. Doyle, Sir A. C.
In Doyle, Sir A. C. Adventures of Sherlock Holmes   S C
In Doyle, Sir A. C. The complete Sherlock Holmes   S C

The **adventure** of the Sussex vampire. Doyle, Sir A. C.
In Doyle, Sir A. C. The complete Sherlock Holmes   S C

The **adventure** of the three gables. Doyle, Sir A. C.
In Doyle, Sir A. C. The complete Sherlock Holmes   S C

The **adventure** of the three Garridebs. Doyle, Sir A. C.
In Doyle, Sir A. C. The complete Sherlock Holmes   S C

The **adventure** of the three students. Doyle, Sir A. C.
In Doyle, Sir A. C. The complete Sherlock Holmes   S C

The **adventure** of the veiled lodger. Doyle, Sir A. C.
In Doyle, Sir A. C. The complete Sherlock Holmes   S C

The **adventure** of Wisteria Lodge. Doyle, Sir A. C.
In Doyle, Sir A. C. The complete Sherlock Holmes   S C

Adventurers [series]
Holbrook, M. Snorkeling   **797.2**

Adventures in archaeology. McGowen, T.   **930.1**

The **adventures** of Blue Avenger. Howe, N.   **Fic**

The **adventures** of Eustace. Lewis, C. S.
In The Book of dragons p10-15   S C

The **adventures** of Huckleberry Finn. Twain, M.   **Fic**

The **Adventures** of Kivio
In The Dancing fox: Arctic folktales p3-11   **398.2**

Adventures of Sherlock Holmes. Doyle, Sir A. C.   S C
also in Doyle, Sir A. C. The complete Sherlock Holmes   S C

The **adventures** of Simon and Susanna. Lester, J.
In Lester, J. The last tales of Uncle Remus p151-56   **398.2**

The **adventures** of Sojourner. Wunsch, S. T.   **629.43**

The **adventures** of Tom Sawyer. Twain, M.   **Fic**

Advertising
Day, N. L. Advertising   **659.1**

Dunn, J. M. Advertising (7 and up)   **659.1**
See/See also pages in the following book(s):
Alcohol: opposing viewpoints p58-95 (7 and up)   **362.292**
Mass media: opposing viewpoints p58-87 (7 and up)   **302.23**

AECT *See* Association for Educational Communications and Technology

Aeken, Hieronymus van *See* Bosch, Hieronymus, d. 1516

Aeneas (Legendary character)
See/See also pages in the following book(s):
Hamilton, E. Mythology p319-42   **292**

Aeronautics
See also Airplanes; Flight; Rocketry
The Visual dictionary of flight   **629.133**
Accidents
See Aircraft accidents
Flights
Taylor, R. L. The first solo flight around the world   **629.13**
History
Freedman, R. The Wright brothers: how they invented the airplane   **92**
Nahum, A. Flying machine   **629.133**

Aesthetics
See also Art appreciation

AFDC (Aid to families with dependent children)
See Child welfare

Africa
Peoples of Africa   **960**
Biography—Dictionaries
African biography   **920.003**
Encyclopedias
Altman, S. The encyclopedia of African-American heritage   **305.8**
Encarta Africana 2000. See entry in CD-ROM section, Part 3
Fiction
Dickinson, P. AK (7 and up)   **Fic**
Quintana, A. The baboon king (7 and up)   **Fic**
Folklore
See Folklore—Africa
History
Haskins, J. African beginnings   **960**
Jones, C. Africa, 1500-1900 (7 and up)   **960**
See/See also pages in the following book(s):
The World in 1492 p67-95   **909**
Politics and government
Rasmussen, R. K. Modern African political leaders (7 and up)   **920**
Social life and customs—Dictionaries
Haskins, J. From Afar to Zulu   **960**

Africa, East *See* East Africa

Africa, South *See* South Africa

Africa, 1500-1900. Jones, C.   **960**

African-American achievers [series]
Banks, W. The Black Muslims   **297**
Chambers, V. The Harlem Renaissance   **700**
DeAngelis, G. The black cowboys   **978**
Stovall, T. The Buffalo Soldiers   **978**

African Americans—Fiction—*Continued*

McKissack, P. C. Let my people go   **221.9**

McKissack, P. C. A picture of Freedom   **Fic**

McKissack, P. C. Run away home   **Fic**

Meyer, C. Jubilee journey   **Fic**

Meyer, C. White lilacs   **Fic**

Moore, Y. Freedom songs   **Fic**

Myers, W. D. Fast Sam, Cool Clyde, and Stuff (7 and up)   **Fic**

Myers, W. D. Hoops (7 and up)   **Fic**

Myers, W. D. The journal of Joshua Loper   **Fic**

Myers, W. D. Monster (7 and up)   **Fic**

Myers, W. D. Motown and Didi (7 and up)   **Fic**

Myers, W. D. The Mouse rap   **Fic**

Myers, W. D. The outside shot (7 and up)   **Fic**

Myers, W. D. Scorpions   **Fic**

Myers, W. D. Slam! (7 and up)   **Fic**

Paterson, K. Jip   **Fic**

Paulsen, G. Nightjohn (7 and up)   **Fic**

Paulsen, G. Sarny (7 and up)   **Fic**

Petry, A. L. Tituba of Salem Village   **Fic**

Pinkney, A. D. Hold fast to dreams   **Fic**

Pinkney, A. D. Raven in a dove house   **Fic**

Reeder, C. Across the lines   **Fic**

Rinaldi, A. Hang a thousand trees with ribbons (7 and up)   **Fic**

Rinaldi, A. Wolf by the ears (7 and up)   **Fic**

Rites of passage   **S C**

Robinet, H. G. Forty acres and maybe a mule   **Fic**

Sebestyen, O. Words by heart   **Fic**

Southgate, M. Another way to dance   **Fic**

Staples, S. F. Dangerous skies (7 and up)   **Fic**

Stolz, M. Cezanne Pinto   **Fic**

Taylor, M. D. The friendship   **Fic**

Taylor, M. D. The gold Cadillac   **Fic**

Taylor, M. D. Let the circle be unbroken   **Fic**

Taylor, M. D. Mississippi bridge   **Fic**

Taylor, M. D. The road to Memphis   **Fic**

Taylor, M. D. Roll of thunder, hear my cry   **Fic**

Taylor, M. D. Song of the trees   **Fic**

Taylor, M. D. The well   **Fic**

Walter, M. P. Second daughter   **Fic**

Williams-Garcia, R. Like sisters on the homefront (7 and up)   **Fic**

Woodruff, E. Dear Austin   **Fic**

Woodson, J. The house you pass on the way (7 and up)   **Fic**

Woodson, J. I hadn't meant to tell you this   **Fic**

Woodson, J. If you come softly (7 and up)   **Fic**

Woodson, J. Last summer with Maizon   **Fic**

Wyeth, S. D. Vampire bugs: stories conjured from the past   **S C**

Young, R. T. Learning by heart   **Fic**

Folklore

Hamilton, V. The people could fly: American black folktales   **398.2**

Lester, J. The last tales of Uncle Remus   **398.2**

Talk that talk: an anthology of African-American storytelling (7 and up)   **398.2**

History

African American breakthroughs   **305.8**

The African-American experience on file   **305.8**

African Americans: opposing viewpoints (7 and up)   **305.8**

Bair, B. Though justice sleeps (7 and up)   **305.8**

Branch, M. M. Juneteenth   **394.26**

Cooper, M. L. Bound for the promised land   **305.8**

DeAngelis, G. The black cowboys   **978**

Dornfeld, M. The turning tide (7 and up)   **305.8**

Douglass, F. Frederick Douglass, in his own words (7 and up)   **305.8**

Frankel, N. Break those chains at last: African Americans, 1860-1880 (7 and up)   **305.8**

Golay, M. Reconstruction and reaction (7 and up)   **305.8**

Grossman, J. R. A chance to make good (7 and up)   **305.8**

Hansen, J. Breaking ground, breaking silence   **974.7**

Hull, M. Struggle and love, 1972-1997 (7 and up)   **305.8**

Isserman, M. Journey to freedom (7 and up)   **305.8**

Katz, W. L. Black pioneers (7 and up)   **920**

King, W. Toward the promised land (7 and up)   **305.8**

Littlefield, D. C. Revolutionary citizens (7 and up)   **305.8**

McGowen, T. African-Americans in the Old West   **978**

McKissack, P. C. The civil rights movement in America from 1865 to the present   **323.1**

McPherson, J. M. Marching toward freedom (7 and up)   **973.7**

Myers, W. D. Now is your time!   **305.8**

Nardo, D. Braving the New World, 1619-1784 (7 and up)   **305.8**

Patrick, D. The New York Public Library amazing African American history   **305.8**

Reef, C. Africans in America (7 and up)   **305.8**

Schlissel, L. Black frontiers   **978**

Spangenburg, R. The African-American experience (7 and up)   **917.3**

Thomas, V. M. Lest we forget (7 and up)   **326**

Trotter, J. W. From a raw deal to a New Deal? African Americans, 1929-1945 (7 and up)   **305.8**

White, D. G. Let my people go: African Americans, 1804-1860 (7 and up)   **305.8**

Yount, L. Frontiers of freedom (7 and up)   **978**

History—Chronology

Hornsby, A., Jr. Chronology of African American history (7 and up)   **305.8**

Ake, Anne, 1943-
The gorilla (7 and up)   **599.8**

Akiba's singing water. Wyeth, S. D.
In Wyeth, S. D. Vampire bugs: stories conjured from the past p65-74   **S C**

Akkadians (Sumerians) *See* Sumerians

Al Capone and the roaring twenties. King, D. C.
    92

Alabama
Davis, L. Alabama
In America the beautiful, second series
    973
Shirley, D. Alabama
In Celebrate the states   **973**
    Fiction
Capote, T. The Thanksgiving visitor   **Fic**
English, K. Francie   **Fic**
McKissack, P. C. Run away home   **Fic**

Alabiso, Vincent
(ed) Flash!: the Associated Press covers the
world. See Flash!: the Associated. Press covers the world   **070.4**

Aladdin. Philip, N.
In Philip, N. The Arabian nights p79-98
    398.2

Alamo (San Antonio, Tex.)
Carter, A. R. Last stand at the Alamo
    976.4

The **ALAN** Review   **028.505**

Alaska
Stefoff, R. Alaska
In Celebrate the states   **973**
Walsh Shepherd, D. Alaska
In America the beautiful, second series
    973
    Fiction
George, J. C. Water sky   **Fic**
London, J. The call of the wild   **Fic**
London, J. White Fang   **Fic**
Vanasse, D. Out of the wilderness   **Fic**

Albert Einstein and the frontiers of physics. Bernstein, J.   **92**

Albinos and albinism
Landau, E. Living with albinism   **616.5**

Albright, Madeleine Korbel, 1937-
    About
Hasday, J. L. Madeleine Albright   **92**
Howard, M. Madeleine Albright   **92**
See/See also pages in the following book(s):
Jones, V. B. Government & politics   **920**

Albyn, Carole Lisa, 1955-
The multicultural cookbook for students
    641.5

Alcatraz Island (Calif.)
    Fiction
Bunting, E. Someone is hiding on Alcatraz Island   **Fic**

The **alchemist**. McCaughrean, G.
In McCaughrean, G. The crystal pool: myths
and legends of the world p41-44
    398.2

Alcibiades, ca. 450-404 B.C.
See/See also pages in the following book(s):
Nardo, D. Leaders of ancient Greece (7 and up)
    920

Alcock, Vivien, 1924-
A change of aunts
In The Oxford book of scary tales p24-35
    808.8
Qwertyuiop
In Help wanted: short stories about young
people working   **S C**

Alcohol
    Physiological effect
See/See also pages in the following book(s):
Alcohol: opposing viewpoints p16-56 (7 and up)
    362.292

Alcohol and you. Miner, J. C.   **362.292**
Alcohol drug dangers. Clayton, L.   **362.292**
Alcohol: opposing viewpoints (7 and up)
    362.292

Alcoholic beverages
    See also Drinking of alcoholic beverages

Alcoholism
    See also Drinking of alcoholic beverages
Banfield, S. Inside recovery   **616.86**
Chemical dependency: opposing viewpoints (7
and up)   **362.29**
Chiu, C. Teen guide to staying sober (7 and up)
    362.292
Clayton, L. Alcohol drug dangers   **362.292**
Hanan, J. When someone you love is addicted
(7 and up)   **362.29**
Miner, J. C. Alcohol and you (7 and up)
    362.292
Mitchell, H. R. Teen alcoholism (7 and up)
    362.292
Pringle, L. P. Drinking   **362.292**
See/See also pages in the following book(s):
Alcohol: opposing viewpoints p97-157 (7 and
up)   **362.292**
Blue, R. Staying out of trouble in a troubled
family (7 and up)   **362.7**
    Fiction
Bauer, J. Rules of the road (7 and up)   **Fic**
Brooks, B. No kidding (7 and up)   **Fic**
Bruchac, J. The heart of a chief   **Fic**
Conly, J. L. Crazy lady!   **Fic**
Deaver, J. R. Chicago blues (7 and up)
    Fic
Hermes, P. Cheat the moon   **Fic**
Marino, J. The day that Elvis came to town (7
and up)   **Fic**
Rodowsky, C. F. Hannah in between   **Fic**

Alcoran *See* Koran

Alcott, Louisa May, 1832-1888
Rosy's journey
In American fairy tales p92-104   **S C**
    About
Meigs, C. L. Invincible Louisa   **92**
Ruth, A. Louisa May Alcott   **92**
See/See also pages in the following book(s):
Faber, D. Great lives: American literature p91-
99   **920**
Lyons, M. E. Keeping secrets (7 and up)
    920

All the names of Baby Hag. MacLachlan, P.
In Dragons & dreams p43-54   **S C**

All the Weyrs of Pern. McCaffrey, A. See note
under McCaffrey, A. [The Pern series]
    Fic

All through the night. Field, R.
In A Newbery Christmas p117-25   **S C**

Allaby, Michael, 1933-
Biomes of the world   **577**
Droughts (7 and up)   **551.57**
Floods (7 and up)   **551.48**
Temperate forests (7 and up)   **577.3**

Allan, Ross
Dog obedience training   **636.7**

Allegories
Adams, R. Watership down   **Fic**
Golding, W. Lord of the Flies (7 and up)
    Fic

Allen, John Logan, 1941-
(ed) Explorers. See Explorers   **920.003**

Allen, Judy
(ed) Anthology for the earth. See Anthology for
the earth   **808.8**

Allen, Karen Jordan
Mrs. Pomeroy
In A Nightmare's dozen   **S C**

Allen, Paula Gunn
Deer Woman
In Talking leaves   **S C**

Allen, Zita
Black women leaders of the civil rights movement (7 and up)   **323.1**

Allende, Isabel
See/See also pages in the following book(s):
Shirey, L. Latin American writers (7 and up)
    860.9

Allergy
Latta, S. L. Allergies (7 and up)   **616.97**

Alles, Gregory D.
(ed) The Encyclopedia of world religions. See
The Encyclopedia of world religions
    200.3

The **alley.** Romero, D.
In Join in p223-38   **S C**

Alligators
Dow, L. Alligators and crocodiles (7 and up)
    597.9
Patent, D. H. The American alligator   **597.9**
Fiction
Yep, L. Later, gator   **Fic**
The **alligators.** Updike, J.
In Who do you think you are? p64-72
    S C

Alligators and crocodiles. Dow, L.   **597.9**

Allison, Anthony
Hear these voices (7 and up)   **305.23**

Allison, Stephen, 1969-
(ed) Scientists. See Scientists   **920.003**

Allusions
Brewer's dictionary of phrase and fable
    803

Almanac of famous people   **920.003**

Almanacs
Information please almanac, atlas & yearbook
    031.02
The New York Times almanac   **031.02**
Rand McNally world facts & maps   **310.5**
Women's almanac   **305.4**
The World almanac and book of facts
    031.02
The World almanac for kids   **031.02**

Almond, David, 1951-
Skellig   **Fic**

An **almost** perfect game. Manes, S.   **Fic**

Aloha summer. Wallace, B.   **Fic**

Alomar, Roberto, 1968-
About
Macht, N. L. Roberto Alomar   **92**

Alone. McCaughrean, G.
In McCaughrean, G. The bronze cauldron:
myths and legends of the world p35-36
    398.2

Alonso, Karen
Korematsu v. United States (7 and up)
    323.1
Schenck v. United States (7 and up)   **342**

Alou, Felipe, 1935-
See/See also pages in the following book(s):
Morey, J. Famous Hispanic Americans p1-13
    920

Alou, Moises, 1966-
About
Muskat, C. Moises Alou   **92**

Alphabet
Samoyault, T. Alphabetical order   **411**

Alphabet art: thirteen ABCs from around the
world. Fisher, L. E.   **745.6**

Alphabet books *See* Alphabet

Alphabetical order. Samoyault, T.   **411**

Alphabets
    See also Lettering
Fisher, L. E. Alphabet art: thirteen ABCs from
around the world   **745.6**

Alter, Judy
The Santa Fe Trail   **978**

Alternative medicine
Facklam, H. Alternative medicine (7 and up)
    615.5
Kowalski, K. M. Alternative medicine (7 and
up)   **615.5**
Rattenbury, J. Understanding alternative medi-
cine (7 and up)   **615.5**

Altman, Linda Jacobs, 1943-
Arkansas
    In Celebrate the states   **973**
California
    In Celebrate the states   **973**
The creation of Israel (7 and up)   **956.94**
Forever outsiders   **909**
Genocide (7 and up)   **303.6**
Plague and pestilence   **614.4**
Slavery and abolition in American history
    973.7
Women inventors (7 and up)   **920**

Altman, Susan
The encyclopedia of African-American heritage **305.8**
Extraordinary black Americans: from colonial to contemporary times **920**

Alvarez, Julia
Daughter of invention
In Growing up Latino p3-15 **810.8**

Alvarez, Luis W.
See/See also pages in the following book(s):
Oleksy, W. G. Hispanic-American scientists (7 and up) **920**

Alvarez de Cabral, Pedro *See* Cabral, Pedro Alvares, 1460?-1526?

Alvin Ailey American Dance Theater
Mitchell, J. Alvin Ailey American Dance Theater: Jack Mitchell photographs (7 and up) **792.8**

Alzheimer's disease
Harmon, D. Life out of focus (7 and up) **616.8**
Landau, E. Alzheimer's disease (7 and up) **362.1**
Fiction
Williams, C. L. If I forget, you remember **Fic**

Am I blue?. Coville, B.
In Coville, B. Odder than ever **S C**

Amado, Jorge, 1912-
See/See also pages in the following book(s):
Shirey, L. Latin American writers (7 and up) **860.9**

The **amah.** Yep, L. **Fic**

Amanar, Simona
See/See also pages in the following book(s):
Rutledge, R. The best of the best in gymnastics **920**

Amanda and the wounded birds. Rodowsky, C. F.
In Visions: nineteen short stories by outstanding writers for young adults p78-86 **S C**

Amankamek. Bruchac, J.
In Bruchac, J. When the Chenno howls **398.2**

Amateur theater
See also Readers' theater
Ross, B. B. Junior Broadway **792.6**

Amazing bugs. Macquitty, M. **595.7**

Amazing facts **031.02**

Amazing grace. Paterson, K.
In Paterson, K. A midnight clear: stories for the Christmas season **S C**

The **Amazon** papers. Keller, B. **Fic**

The **Amazon** rainforest. Johnson, D. **577.3**

Amazon River valley
Goodman, S. Bats, bugs, and biodiversity **577.3**
Johnson, D. The Amazon rainforest (7 and up) **577.3**
Kallen, S. A. Life in the Amazon rainforest (7 and up) **981**

Amberland. Aiken, J.
In Aiken, J. A foot in the grave p115-128 **S C**

Amboseli National Park (Kenya)
Pringle, L. P. Elephant woman **599.67**

Ambrose, Alison *See* Cole, Alison

Ambush. O'Brien, T.
In Who do you think you are? p152-55 **S C**

Amerasians
Fiction
Garland, S. Song of the buffalo boy **Fic**

America
See also Latin America; South America
See/See also pages in the following book(s):
The World in 1492 p127-53 **909**
Antiquities
Bendick, J. Tombs of the ancient Americas **393**
Exploration
Haskins, J. Against all opposition **920**
Meltzer, M. Columbus and the world around him **92**
West, D. C. Braving the North Atlantic **970.01**
Exploration—Fiction
Dorris, M. Guests **Fic**
Dorris, M. Morning Girl **Fic**

America as story. Coffey, R. K. **016.813**

America at war [series]
Bosco, P. I. World War I **940.3**
Golay, M. The Civil War **973.7**
Greenblatt, M. The War of 1812 **973.5**
Isserman, M. The Korean War **951.9**
Isserman, M. World War II **940.53**

America in historical fiction. VanMeter, V. **016.813**

America in the 1960s. Kronenwetter, M. **973.92**

America in the Korean War. Dolan, E. F. **951.9**

America in World War I. Dolan, E. F. **940.3**

America the beautiful, second series **973**

American albums from the collections of the Library of Congress [series]
Behind the lines **973.7**
One nation again **973.8**
Presidents in a time of change **920**
Presidents of a divided nation **920**
Presidents of a growing country **920**
Presidents of a world power **920**
Presidents of a young republic **920**
The Road to Appomattox **973.7**

The **American** alligator. Patent, D. H. **597.9**

American art
Celebrate America in poetry and art **811.008**

American Association for the Advancement of Science
Science Books & Films. See Science Books & Films **016.5**

American Association of School Librarians
Information power **027.8**

American astronomers. Camp, C. A. **920**

American authors, 1600-1900 **920.003**

American poetry—Collections—*Continued*
The Oxford book of children's verse in America 811.008
The Oxford book of story poems 821.008
The Oxford treasury of classic poems (7 and up) 821.008
The Oxford treasury of time poems 821.008
The Place my words are looking for 811.008
Poetry from A to Z 808.1
Poetspeak: in their work, about their work (7 and up) 811.008
The Random House book of poetry for children 821.008
Reflections on a gift of watermelon pickle . . . and other modern verse 811.008
Singing America 811.008
Slam dunk: basketball poems 811.008
Three centuries of American poetry, 1623-1923 (7 and up) 811.008
Hispanic American authors—Collections
Cool salsa 811.008

American political leaders. O'Brien, S. 920.003

American profiles [series]
Aaseng, N. Black inventors 920
Aaseng, N. Twentieth-century inventors 920
Altman, L. J. Women inventors 920
Dubovoy, S. Civil rights leaders 920
Helmer, D. S. Women suffragists 920
Oleksy, W. G. Hispanic-American scientists 920
Yount, L. Asian-American scientists 920
Yount, L. Contemporary women scientists 920

American religious experience [series]
Williams, J. K. The Amish 289.7
Williams, J. K. The Christian Scientists 289.5
Williams, J. K. The Mormons 289.3
Williams, J. K. The Quakers 289.6
Williams, J. K. The Shakers 289
The **American** Revolution, 1763-1783. Collier, C. 973.3
The **American** revolutionaries: a history in their own words, 1750-1800 973.3
American science *See* Science—United States
American sculpture
Greenberg, J. The sculptor's eye 730.9
American Sign Language. Sternberg, M. L. A. 419
American Sign Language concise dictionary. See Sternberg, M. L. A. American Sign Language 419
American sign language dictionary, Random House. Costello, E. 419
American songs
See also Folk songs—United States
American sports poems 811.008
American troublemakers [series]
Haynes, R. M. Ida B. Wells, antilynching crusader 92

American war series
Stein, R. C. World War II in Europe 940.54
Stein, R. C. World War II in the Pacific 940.54

American women of achievement [series]
Biracree, T. Wilma Rudolph 92
Huber, P. W. Sandra Day O'Connor 92
IlgenFritz, E. Anne Hutchinson 92
Richmond, M. A. Phillis Wheatley 92
Weisberg, B. Susan B. Anthony 92
American women scientists. Reynolds, M. D. 920
The **Americana** annual. See The Encyclopedia Americana 031

Americanisms
Dictionary of American slang 427
The Doubleday Roget's thesaurus in dictionary form 423
Young, S. The new comprehensive American rhyming dictionary 423
America's forests. Staub, F. J. 577.3
America's greatest game. Buckley, J., Jr. 796.332
America's prairies. Staub, F. J. 577.4
America's prisons: opposing viewpoints (7 and up) 365
America's victims: opposing viewpoints (7 and up) 306
Ames, Lee J., 1921-
[Draw 50 series] 743
Drawing with Lee Ames 741.2
Ami, Miriam Bat- *See* Bat-Ami, Miriam, 1950-
Amish
Williams, J. K. The Amish (7 and up) 289.7
Fiction
Lasky, K. Beyond the divide (7 and up) Fic
Meyer, C. Gideon's people Fic
Amistad (Schooner)
Jurmain, S. Freedom's sons 326
Myers, W. D. Amistad: a long road to freedom 326

Ammon, Bette D.
More rip-roaring reads for reluctant teen readers 028.5

Among the hidden. Haddix, M. P. Fic
Amos Fortune, free man. Yates, E. 92
Amphetamines
See also Methamphetamine
Schleifer, J. Methamphetamine (7 and up) 362.29
Amphibians
See also Frogs
Behler, J. L. The Audubon Society field guide to North American reptiles and amphibians 597.9
Clarke, B. Amphibian 597.8
Silverstein, A. Snakes & such 639
Stebbins, R. C. A field guide to western reptiles and amphibians 597.9

Amundsen, Roald, 1872-1928
See/See also pages in the following book(s):
Lomask, M. Great lives: exploration p1-12
920

Amusements
See also Juggling

Anabolic steroids *See* Steroids

Anaesthetics *See* Anesthetics

Ananse the Spider in search of a fool. Bryan, A.
In Bryan, A. Ashley Bryan's African tales,
uh-huh p1-8 **398.2**

Anansi and the mind of god. McCaughrean, G.
In McCaughrean, G. The golden hoard: myths
and legends of the world p110-13
398.2

Anasazi culture *See* Pueblo Indians

Anastasia *See* Anastasiíâ Nikolaevna, Grand
Duchess, daughter of Nicholas II, Emperor of
Russia, 1901-1918

Anastasia, absolutely. Lowry, L. See note under
Lowry, L. Anastasia Krupnik **Fic**

Anastasia again!. Lowry, L. See note under Lowry, L. Anastasia Krupnik **Fic**

Anastasia, ask your analyst. Lowry, L. See note
under Lowry, L. Anastasia Krupnik **Fic**

Anastasia at this address. Lowry, L. See note under Lowry, L. Anastasia Krupnik **Fic**

Anastasia at your service. Lowry, L. See note under Lowry, L. Anastasia Krupnik **Fic**

Anastasia has the answers. Lowry, L. See note
under Lowry, L. Anastasia Krupnik **Fic**

Anastasia Krupnik. Lowry, L. **Fic**

Anastasia on her own. Lowry, L. See note under
Lowry, L. Anastasia Krupnik **Fic**

Anastasia's album. Brewster, H. **92**

Anastasia's chosen career. Lowry, L. See note under Lowry, L. Anastasia Krupnik **Fic**

**Anastasiíâ Nikolaevna, Grand Duchess, daugh-
ter of Nicholas II, Emperor of Russia,
1901-1918**
About
Brewster, H. Anastasia's album **92**

Anatomy
See also Musculoskeletal system; Physiology
Parker, S. The beginner's guide to animal autopsy **571.3**

Anatomy, Comparative *See* Comparative anatomy

Anatomy, Human *See* Human anatomy

Anaya, Rudolfo A.
The apple orchard
In Growing up Latino p292-304 **810.8**
Dead end
In Join in p101-09 **S C**

Ancient architecture
Jessop, J. The X-ray picture book of big buildings of the ancient world **720**

Ancient China. Cotterell, A. **931**

Ancient civilization
See also Classical civilization
Early humans **930.1**

McGowen, T. Adventures in archaeology
930.1
Stefoff, R. Finding the lost cities (7 and up)
930.1
The Visual dictionary of ancient civilizations
930

Ancient Egypt. Hart, G. **932**
Ancient Greece!. Hart, A. **938**
Ancient Greece and Rome **938**
Ancient Greeks. Baker, R. F. **938**
The **ancient** Hebrews. Mann, K. **909**

Ancient history
See also Classical dictionaries
Burrell, R. E. C. Oxford first ancient history
909
Corbishley, M. Rome and the ancient world
930
Pictorial works
Smithsonian timelines of the ancient world
930

The **ancient** Incas. Bingham, H. **985**
Ancient Rome. Corbishley, M. **937**
Ancient Rome. James, S. **937**
Ancient wonders. Wood, T. **930.1**
And justice for all. Nunez, S. J. **346**
And not afraid to dare. Bolden, T. **920**
And still the birds keep circling. Rubinstein, G.
In Trapped!: cages of mind and body p181-
201 **S C**
And the lights flickered. Goldin, B. D.
In The Haunted house: a collection of original
stories **S C**
And the rains came tumbling down. McCaughrean,
G.
In McCaughrean, G. The bronze cauldron:
myths and legends of the world p107-08
398.2
And the soul shall dance. Yamauchi, W.
In American dragons p144-54 **810.8**

Andersen, Hans Christian, 1805-1875
The little mermaid and other fairy tales
S C
Contents: The tinderbox; Little Ida's flowers; The little mermaid; The emperor's new clothes; The steadfast tin soldier; The
flying trunk; The sweethearts; The bell; The little match girl; The
collar; The goblin at the grocer's; In a thousand years' time; Five
peas from the same pod; The beetle; The toad; Dance, dance,
dolly mine!; The gardener and his master
The princess and the pea; adaptation. See
Levine, G. C. The princess test **Fic**

Anderson, Dave
The story of football **796.332**
The story of golf **796.352**

Anderson, Elizabeth Garrett, 1836-1917
See/See also pages in the following book(s):
Celebrating women in mathematics and science
p101-10 **920**

Anderson, Ivie, 1904-1949
See/See also pages in the following book(s):
Gourse, L. Swingers and crooners p78-80 (7 and
up) **781.65**

Anderson, Laurie Halse, 1961-
Passport
In Dirty laundry: stories about family secrets
p128-39 **S C**

Anthony, Piers
See/See also pages in the following book(s):
Reid, S. E. Presenting young adult science fiction p136-53 (7 and up)   **813.009**

Anthony, Susan B., 1820-1906
About
Weisberg, B. Susan B. Anthony   **92**
See/See also pages in the following book(s):
Helmer, D. S. Women suffragists (7 and up)   **920**

Anthony, Suzanne
West Indies   **972.9**

Anthropogeography *See* Human geography

Anthropologists
Mark, J. T. Margaret Mead (7 and up)   **92**
Poynter, M. The Leakeys   **92**
Fiction
Abelove, J. Go and come back (7 and up)   **Fic**

Anthropology
See also Forensic anthropology

Anti-war poetry *See* War poetry

Antigua and Barbuda
Fiction
Kincaid, J. Annie John (7 and up)   **Fic**

Antiquities
See also Bible—Antiquities; Archeology
McGowen, T. Adventures in archaeology   **930.1**
Moloney, N. The young Oxford book of archaeology (7 and up)   **930.1**
Wood, T. Ancient wonders   **930.1**

Antiquity of man *See* Human origins

Antisemitism
See also Jews—Persecutions
Fiction
Greenberg, J. I never promised you a rose garden (7 and up)   **Fic**
Irwin, H. Sarah with an H   **Fic**
Levitin, S. The cure   **Fic**
Levitin, S. The return   **Fic**

Antokoletz, Maria Adele de
See/See also pages in the following book(s):
Lucas, E. Contemporary human rights activists p51-63 (7 and up)   **920**

Antonio, Sam
See/See also pages in the following book(s):
Mendoza, P. M. Extraordinary people in extraordinary times p59-70 (7 and up)   **920**

Antonius, Marcus, ca. 83-30 B.C.
See/See also pages in the following book(s):
Brooks, P. S. Cleopatra p61-99 (7 and up)   **92**

Ants
Pascoe, E. Ants   **595.7**

Anzaldúa, Gloria, 1942-
People should not die in June in South Texas
In Growing up Latino p280-87   **810.8**

Anzovin, Steven, 1954-
(jt. auth) Kane, J. N. Famous first facts   **031.02**
(jt. auth) Podell, J. Old worlds to new   **920.003**

AP *See* Associated Press

Apache Indians
Golston, S. E. Changing woman of the Apache (7 and up)   **970.004**
Melody, M. E. The Apache
In Indians of North America series   **970.004**
Schwarz, M. Cochise, Apache chief   **92**
Schwarz, M. Geronimo, Apache warrior   **92**
See/See also pages in the following book(s):
Brown, D. A. Bury my heart at Wounded Knee p191-217, 392-413 (7 and up)   **970.004**
Ehrlich, A. Wounded Knee: an Indian history of the American West   **970.004**
Fiction
Burks, B. Walks Alone   **Fic**
McKissack, P. C. Run away home   **Fic**
Paulsen, G. Canyons   **Fic**
Wars
Aleshire, P. Reaping the whirlwind (7 and up)   **973.8**

Aparicio, Frances R.
(ed) Latino voices. See Latino voices   **860.8**

Apes
See also Chimpanzees; Gorillas
Saign, G. The great apes   **599.8**

Apiculture *See* Bees

Apollo, 1980-
Minimum wage
In Trapped!: cages of mind and body p205-27   **S C**

Apollo 11 (Spacecraft)
Green, J. Race to the moon   **629.45**

Apollo Project *See* Project Apollo

An **apology** to the moon furies. Vega, E.
In Growing up Latino p47-72   **810.8**

Appalachia. Rylant, C.   **974**

Appalachian Mountain region *See* Appalachian region

Appalachian region
Rylant, C. Appalachia   **974**
Fiction
Cleaver, V. Where the lilies bloom   **Fic**
Naylor, P. R. Sang Spell (7 and up)   **Fic**
White, R. Belle Prater's boy   **Fic**

Appalachian Trail
Andryszewski, T. Step by step along the Appalachian Trail   **796.51**

Apparitions. San Souci, R.
In San Souci, R. A terrifying taste of short & shivery p30-34   **398.2**

Appelfeld, Aharon *See* Appelfeld, Aron

Appelfeld, Aron
See/See also pages in the following book(s):
Mandell, S. L. Writers of the Holocaust (7 and up)   **940.53**

Appetite depressants
Barrett, C. The dangers of diet drugs and other weight-loss products   **615**
Clayton, L. Diet pill drug dangers   **615**

Appetite disorders *See* Eating disorders

Apple Computer Inc.
Kendall, M. E. Steve Wozniak (7 and up)   **92**

The **apple** of contentment. Pyle, H.
In American fairy tales p81-91   **S C**

The **apple** orchard. Anaya, R. A.
In Growing up Latino p292-304   **810.8**

Applegarth, Margaret T., 1886-1976
The legend of the black Madonna
In Christmas gif' p18-25   **810.8**

Appleseed, Johnny, 1774-1845
About
Lawlor, L. The real Johnny Appleseed   **92**
See/See also pages in the following book(s):
Calvert, P. Great lives: the American frontier
p81-92   **920**

Appomattox Campaign, 1865
The Road to Appomattox   **973.7**

Appraisal   **016.5**

Apprentices
Fiction
DeFelice, C. C. The apprenticeship of Lucas
Whitaker   **Fic**
Fleischman, P. Saturnalia   **Fic**

The **apprenticeship** of Lucas Whitaker. DeFelice,
C. C.   **Fic**

April 2000: the third expedition. Bradbury, R.
In Read into the millenium p73-102   **S C**

April Mendez. Spinelli, J.
In Spinelli, J. The library card   **S C**

April morning. Fast, H.   **Fic**

Aquanauts *See* Underwater exploration

Aquarium fish. Mills, D.   **639.34**

Aquariums
See also Marine aquariums
Mills, D. Aquarium fish   **639.34**

Aquatic animals *See* Marine animals

Aquatic plants *See* Marine plants

Aquino, Corazon
See/See also pages in the following book(s):
Price-Groff, C. Twentieth-century women politi-
cal leaders (7 and up)   **920**

Arab-Israel War, 1948-1949 *See* Israel-Arab War,
1948-1949

Arab-Israeli conflicts *See* Israel-Arab conflicts

Arab-Jewish relations *See* Jewish-Arab relations

The **Arabian** nights. Philip, N.   **398.2**

Arabs
See also Bedouins
Folklore
Philip, N. The Arabian nights   **398.2**
The Seven voyages of Sinbad the Sailor
    398.2

Palestine
See Palestinian Arabs

Arachnida *See* Spiders

Arafat, Yasir, 1929-
About
Ferber, E. Yasir Arafat   **92**

Arapaho Indians
Fowler, L. The Arapaho
In Indians of North America series
    970.004

See/See also pages in the following book(s):
Ehrlich, A. Wounded Knee: an Indian history of
the American West   **970.004**

Arawak Indians *See* Taino Indians

Arbitration, International *See* International arbitration

Arbuthnot, May Hill, 1884-1969
(jt. auth) Sutherland, Z. Children & books
    028.5

Archaeological detective. See entry in CD-ROM
section, Part 3

Archaeology *See* Archeology

The **archaeology** of North America. Snow, D. R.
In Indians of North America series
    970.004

Archbold, Rick, 1950-
Deep-Sea explorer: the story of Robert Ballard,
discoverer of the Titanic   **92**
(jt. auth) Ballard, R. D. The discovery of the Titanic   **910.4**
(jt. auth) Ballard, R. D. Ghost liners   **910.4**
(jt. auth) Ballard, R. D. Lost liners   **910.4**
(jt. auth) Bateman, R. Safari   **599**

Archeological specimens *See* Antiquities

Archeology
See also Bible—Antiquities; Antiquities;
Excavations (Archeology); Prehistoric peo-
ples; Rock drawings, paintings, and engrav-
ings; names of extinct cities; and names of
groups of people and of cities (except extinct
cities), countries, regions, etc., with the subdi-
vision Antiquities
Archaeological detective. See entry in CD-ROM
section, Part 3
Deem, J. M. Bodies from the bog   **930.1**
Ganeri, A. The search for tombs   **393**
Getz, D. Frozen man   **930.1**
Lauber, P. Tales mummies tell   **930.1**
Lessem, D. The iceman   **930.1**
McGowen, T. Adventures in archaeology
    930.1
McIntosh, J. Archeology   **930.1**
Moloney, N. The young Oxford book of archae-
ology (7 and up)   **930.1**
The mystery of the pipe wreck. See entry in
CD-ROM section, Part 3
Patent, D. H. Secrets of the ice man   **930.1**
Reinhard, J. Discovering the Inca Ice Maiden
    930.1
Stefoff, R. Finding the lost cities (7 and up)
    930.1
Tanaka, S. Discovering the Iceman   **930.1**

Archer, Jules
Special interests (7 and up)   **324**
They had a dream   **920**
To save the earth (7 and up)   **920**

Archimedes, ca. 287-212 B.C.
See/See also pages in the following book(s):
Nardo, D. Scientists of Ancient Greece p68-78
(7 and up)   **920**

Architects
Boulton, A. O. Frank Lloyd Wright, architect (7
and up)   **92**
Malone, M. Maya Lin   **92**

Armstrong, Jennifer, 1961- —*Continued*
Statue of Liberty factory
In Stay true: short stories for strong girls
S C
Steal away Fic
Jennings, P. The century for young people
909.82
(jt. auth) Opdyke, I. G. In my hands
940.53
Armstrong, Louis, 1900-1971
About
Old, W. Louis Armstrong 92
See/See also pages in the following book(s):
Gourse, L. Swingers and crooners p17-34 (7 and up) 781.65
Mour, S. I. American jazz musicians p19-27
920
Armstrong, Neil, 1930-
About
Bredeson, C. Neil Armstrong 92
Armstrong, Pam, 1961-
(ed) Sea searcher's handbook. See Sea searcher's handbook 577.7
Armstrong, William Howard, 1914-1999
Sounder Fic
Army life See Soldiers
Arnold, Benedict, 1741-1801
About
Fritz, J. Traitor: the case of Benedict Arnold
92
King, D. C. Benedict Arnold and the American Revolution 92
Arnold, Caroline, 1944-
City of the Gods 972
El Niño 551.6
Hawk highway in the sky 598
On the brink of extinction 598
Pelé: the king of soccer 92
Stories in stone 709.01
Arnosky, Jim
Sketching outdoors in spring 743
Sketching outdoors in summer 743
Arnsteen, Katy Keck, 1934-
(il) Bentley, N. The young journalist's book
070.1
Aronson, Billy
Meteors 523.5
Aronson, Marc
Art attack (7 and up) 700
(jt. auth) Leonard, T. M. Day by day: the seventies 909.82
(jt. auth) Meltzer, E. Day by day: the eighties
909.82
Aronson, Virginia
Venus Williams 92
Around the world in a hundred years. Fritz, J.
910.4
Around the world in eighty days. Verne, J.
Fic
Arrick, Fran
The good girls
In Visions: nineteen short stories by outstanding writers for young adults p107-20
S C

Arrowhead Finger. Bruchac, J.
In Bruchac, J. The girl who married the Moon: tales from Native North America p13-20 398.2
Art
Isaacson, P. M. A short walk around the Pyramids & through the world of art 700
Dictionaries
The Oxford dictionary of art (7 and up)
703
Encyclopedias
International encyclopedia of art 703
History
Art: a world history (7 and up) 709
Gardner's art through the ages (7 and up)
709
Janson, H. W. History of art for young people (7 and up) 709
Museums
See Art museums
Art, African *See* African art
Art, African American *See* African American art
Art, American *See* American art
Art, Hispanic American *See* Hispanic American art
Art, Indian *See* Indians of North America—Art
Art, Modern *See* Modern art
Art, Prehistoric *See* Prehistoric art
Art, Renaissance *See* Renaissance art
Art: a world history (7 and up) 709
Art and society
Aronson, M. Art attack (7 and up) 700
Art appreciation
Aronson, M. Art attack (7 and up) 700
Corrain, L. The art of the Renaissance
709.02
Greenberg, J. The sculptor's eye 730.9
Richardson, J. Looking at pictures 750
Sturgis, A. Optical illusions in art 750.1
Welton, J. Looking at paintings (7 and up)
750.1
Art around the world [series]
Finley, C. Aboriginal art of Australia
759.01
Finley, C. The art of African masks 391
Finley, C. Art of the Far North 704
Art attack. Aronson, M. 700
Art museums
See also names of individual art museums
Richardson, J. Looking at pictures 750
Thomson, P. The nine-ton cat: behind the scenes at an art museum 708
Fiction
Nixon, J. L. Who are you? (7 and up) Fic
The **art** of African masks. Finley, C. 391
The **art** of hand reading. Reid, L. 133.6
Art of jazz [series]
Gourse, L. Striders to beboppers and beyond
781.65
Gourse, L. Swingers and crooners 781.65
The **art** of making comic books. Pellowski, M.
741.5

Arts
History
Ochoa, G. The Wilson chronology of the arts (7 and up) **700**
Arts, African American *See* African American arts
Arts, Japanese *See* Japanese arts
Arts and crafts *See* Handicraft
Arts and crafts skills [series]
Bulloch, I. Cartoons & animation **741.5**
Arturo's flight. Ortiz Cofer, J.
In Ortiz Cofer, J. An island like you p27-40 **S C**

Arvey, Michael
Miracles: opposing viewpoints (7 and up) **231.7**
As ever, Gordy. Hahn, M. D. **Fic**
As true as she wants it. Skinner, D.
In Skinner, D. Thundershine: tales of metakids **S C**
Asch, Frank
Sawgrass poems **811**
Ash, Mary Kay
See/See also pages in the following book(s):
Lutz, N. J. Business & industry **920**
Ash, Russell
Fantastic book of 1001 lists **031.02**
Incredible comparisons **031.02**
The top 10 of everything 2000 **031.02**
The world in one day **031.02**
Ash. McCaughrean, G.
In McCaughrean, G. The silver treasure: myths and legends of the world p42-50 **398.2**
Ashabranner, Brent K., 1921-
Our beckoning borders **325.73**
Still a nation of immigrants **325.73**
Their names to live **959.704**
To seek a better world **305.8**
Ashby, Ruth
Elizabethan England **942.05**
(ed) Herstory: women who changed the world. See Herstory: women who changed the world **920**

Ashe, Arthur
About
Lazo, C. E. Arthur Ashe **92**
Martin, M. Arthur Ashe (7 and up) **92**
Asher, Sandra Fenichel, 1942-
See also Asher, Sandy, 1942-
The wise men of Chelm [play]
In Theatre for young audiences p217-43 **812.008**
Asher, Sandy, 1942-
See also Asher, Sandra Fenichel, 1942-
Great moves
In Visions: nineteen short stories by outstanding writers for young adults p130-40 **S C**
A hundred bucks of happy
In Visions: nineteen short stories by outstanding writers for young adults p141-48 **S C**

Workout!
In Center stage **812.008**
Ashes. Pfeffer, S. B.
In Places I never meant to be **S C**
Ashley Bryan's African tales, uh-huh. Bryan, A. **398.2**
The **Ashwater** experiment. Koss, A. G. **Fic**
Asia
See also names of individual countries, e.g. China
Asia inspirer 4.0. See entry in CD-ROM section, Part 3
Biography
Wakin, E. Asian independence leaders (7 and up) **920**
History
See/See also pages in the following book(s):
The World in 1492 p33-65 **909**
Asia inspirer 4.0. See entry in CD-ROM section, Part 3
Asian American experience [series]
Chiu, C. Lives of notable Asian Americans: literature and education **920**
Takaki, R. T. Strangers at the gates again **305.8**
The **Asian-American** experience on file **305.8**
Asian American literature *See* American literature—Asian American authors
Asian-American scientists. Yount, L. **920**
Asian American voices **815**
Asian Americans
The Asian-American experience on file **305.8**
Asian American voices **815**
Takaki, R. T. Strangers at the gates again (7 and up) **305.8**
Biography
Chiu, C. Lives of notable Asian Americans: literature and education (7 and up) **920**
Yount, L. Asian-American scientists (7 and up) **920**
Fiction
American eyes (7 and up) **S C**
Crew, L. Children of the river (7 and up) **Fic**
History
Asian Americans: opposing viewpoints (7 and up) **305.8**
Asian Americans: opposing viewpoints (7 and up) **305.8**
Asian independence leaders. Wakin, E. **920**
Asimov, Isaac, 1920-1992
Asimov's chronology of science and discovery **509**
Asimov's guide to the Bible **220.7**
I, robot (7 and up) **S C**
Contents: Robbie; Runaround; Reason; Catch that rabbit; Liar; Little lost robot; Escape; Evidence; The evitable conflict
Reason
In Read into the millenium p57 **S C**
Asimov's chronology of science and discovery. Asimov, I. **509**

Asimov's guide to the Bible. Asimov, I.
220.7

Ask the bones. Olson, A. N.
In Olson, A. N. Ask the bones: scary stories from around the world p30-36 **398.2**

Ask the bones: scary stories from around the world. Olson, A. N. **398.2**

ASPCA complete cat care manual. Edney, A. T. B. **636.8**

The **ass**. Philip, N.
In Philip, N. The Arabian nights p77-78
398.2

The **assault** on the record. Hoffius, S.
In Ultimate sports: short stories by outstanding writers for young adults p161-78
S C

Assisted suicide *See* Euthanasia

Assisted suicide (7 and up) **179.7**

Associated Press
Flash!: the Associated Press covers the world (7 and up) **070.4**

Association for Educational Communications and Technology
American Association of School Librarians. Information power **027.8**

Associations
See also Clubs

Asteroids
Kraske, R. Asteroids **523.4**

Asthma
Murphy, W. B. Asthma (7 and up) **616.2**
Silverstein, A. Asthma (7 and up) **616.2**

Astounding optical illusions. Joyce, K.
152.14

Astrology
Royer, M.-P. Astrology: opposing viewpoints
133.5
Schwartz, A. Telling fortunes **133.3**

Astronautics
See also Space flight
Baird, A. The U.S. Space Camp book of astronauts **629.45**
Briggs, C. S. Women in space **920**
Cole, M. D. Hubble Space Telescope **522**
English, J. Mission: Earth **550**
Johnstone, M. The history news in space
629.4
Stott, C. Space exploration **629.4**

Astronauts
See also Women astronauts
Baird, A. The U.S. Space Camp book of astronauts **629.45**
Bredeson, C. Neil Armstrong **92**
Burns, K. Black stars in orbit **920**
Cole, M. D. Astronauts **629.45**
Collins, M. Flying to the moon **629.45**
Kramer, B. John Glenn **92**
See/See also pages in the following book(s):
Haskins, J. Black eagles p138-71 **629.13**
Dictionaries
Cassutt, M. Who's who in space **920.003**

Astronomers
See also Women astronomers
Camp, C. A. American astronomers **920**
Datnow, C. L. Edwin Hubble **92**
Fisher, L. E. Galileo **92**
Fradin, D. B. The planet hunters **523.4**
Litwin, L. B. Benjamin Banneker **92**

Astronomy
See also Constellations; Stars
Astronomy (7 and up) **520**
Bond, P. DK guide to space **520**
Bramwell, M. Mapping the planets and space
520
Campbell, A. The New York Public Library amazing space **520**
Chartrand, M. R. The Audubon Society field guide to the night sky **523**
Cole, M. D. Hubble Space Telescope **522**
Dickinson, T. NightWatch (7 and up) **520**
Ford, H. The young astronomer **520**
Fradin, D. B. The planet hunters **523.4**
Lippincott, K. Astronomy **520**
Mitton, S. The young Oxford book of astronomy **520**
Outer space **520**
Pasachoff, J. M. A field guide to the stars and planets **523**
Redfern, M. The Kingfisher young people's book of space **520**
Ridpath, I. Facts on File stars & planets atlas
520
Stott, C. New astronomer (7 and up) **520**
The Universe (7 and up) **520**
See/See also pages in the following book(s):
Earth science on file **550**

Astronomy (7 and up) **520**

Asylum for Nightface. Brooks, B. **Fic**

At her majesty's request [biography of Sarah Forbes Bonetta] Myers, W. D. **92**

At issue [series]
Cloning **174**
Does capital punishment deter crime?
364.66
Welfare reform **361.6**

At the stomp. Conford, E.
In Conford, E. Crush p131-38 **S C**

Athens (Greece)
Antiquities
Macdonald, F. A Greek temple **938**

Athlete. Maguire, G.
In Trapped!: cages of mind and body p119-27
S C

Athletes
See also African American athletes; Women athletes
Lipsyte, R. Jim Thorpe **92**
O'Brien, E. Starving to win (7 and up)
616.85

Drug use
See also Steroids
Monroe, J. Steroid drug dangers **362.29**
Stewart, G. Drugs and sports (7 and up)
362.29

Athletes—Drug use—*Continued*
See/See also pages in the following book(s):
Currie, S. The Olympic games p67-83 (7 and up) **796.48**
Margolis, J. A. Violence in sports p76-93 (7 and up) **796**
Newton, D. E. Drug testing p81-92 (7 and up) **363.4**
Sports and athletes: opposing viewpoints p160-86 (7 and up) **796**

Athletic medicine *See* Sports medicine

Athletic shorts: six short stories. Crutcher, C.
S C

Athletics
See also Sports; Track athletics

Atkin, S. Beth
Voices from the fields **331.5**
Voices from the streets. See Voices from the streets **364.36**

Atkinson, Mary, 1938-
The Snake book. See The Snake book
597.9

Atlanta (Ga.)
Social conditions
See/See also pages in the following book(s):
Carter, J. Talking peace p148-62 (7 and up) **327.1**
Atlanta (7 and up) **973.7**

Atlanta Campaign, 1864
Atlanta (7 and up) **973.7**

Atlantis
Fiction
Silverberg, R. Letters from Atlantis (7 and up) **Fic**

Atlas of American history **911**
Atlas of American history. Ferrell, R. H. **911**
Atlas of American migration. Flanders, S. A. **304.8**
Atlas of ancient Egypt. Baines, J. **932**
The **Atlas** of endangered species **333.95**
Atlas of marine aquarium fishes. Dr. Burgess's. Burgess, W. **639.34**
The **atlas** of shipwrecks & treasure. Pickford, N. **910.4**
The **atlas** of the classical world. Bardi, P. **938**
Atlas of the world **912**

Atlases
Atlas of the world **912**
DK student atlas **912**
Encarta interactive world atlas 2000. See entry in CD-ROM section, Part 3
Explorer atlas of the world **912**
Geography on file **912**
Goode's world atlas **912**
Maps on file **912**
Millennium world atlas **912**
National Geographic atlas of the world **912**

Atlases, Historical *See* Historical atlases

Atler, Vanessa
See/See also pages in the following book(s):
Rutledge, R. The best of the best in gymnastics **920**

Atmosphere
See also Air

Atomic bomb
Cohen, D. The Manhattan Project (7 and up) **623.4**
Critical mass: America's race to build the atomic bomb. See entry in CD-ROM section, Part 3
Grant, R. G. Hiroshima and Nagasaki (7 and up) **940.54**

Atomic energy *See* Nuclear energy

Atomic power plants *See* Nuclear power plants

Atomic warfare *See* Nuclear warfare

Atomic weapons *See* Nuclear weapons

Atoms
Cooper, C. Matter **530**

Attaboy, Sam!. Lowry, L. See note under Lowry, L. Anastasia Krupnik **Fic**

The **attack** on Pearl Harbor. Rice, E. **940.54**

Attention deficit disorder
Beal, E. Everything you need to know about ADD/ADHD (7 and up) **616.85**
Fiction
Gantos, J. Joey Pigza swallowed the key **Fic**

Attention to detail. Haratani, R.
In American dragons p120-25 **810.8**

Attic treasure. Gould, J.
In The Big book of holiday plays p266-70 **812.008**

Attucks, Crispus, d. 1770
See/See also pages in the following book(s):
Haskins, J. One more river to cross **920**

Auch, Mary Jane
Frozen summer **Fic**
Journey to nowhere **Fic**

Audiobooks
Reviews
AudioFile **028.1**
AudioFile **028.1**

Audiovisual materials
Bibliography
Media review digest **016.3713**
See/See also pages in the following book(s):
Shulman, W. L. Resource guide **940.53**
Catalogs
Adamson, L. G. Literature connections to American history, 7-12 **016.973**
Adamson, L. G. Literature connections to world history, 7-12 **016.9**
Reviews
Media review digest **016.3713**
Science Books & Films **016.5**

Audubon Society *See* National Audubon Society

The **Audubon** Society field guide to North American butterflies. Pyle, R. M. **595.7**

The **Audubon** Society field guide to North American fishes, whales, and dolphins **597**

The **Audubon** Society field guide to North American insects and spiders. Milne, L. J. **595.7**

The **Audubon** Society field guide to North American mushrooms. Lincoff, G.   **579.5**

The **Audubon** Society field guide to North American reptiles and amphibians. Behler, J. L.   **597.9**

The **Audubon** Society field guide to North American rocks and minerals. Chesterman, C. W.   **549**

The **Audubon** Society field guide to North American seashells. Rehder, H. A.   **594**

The **Audubon** Society field guide to North American seashore creatures. Meinkoth, N. A.   **592**

The **Audubon** Society field guide to North American wildflowers: eastern region. Niering, W. A.   **582.13**

The **Audubon** Society field guide to North American wildflowers: western region. Spellenberg, R.   **582.13**

The **Audubon** Society field guide to the night sky. Chartrand, M. R.   **523**

Augenbraum, Harold
(ed) Growing up Latino. See Growing up Latino   **810.8**

Augustus, Emperor of Rome, 63 B.C.-14 A.D.
See/See also pages in the following book(s):
Nardo, D. Rulers of ancient Rome (7 and up)   **920**

Aung San, U, 1915-1947
See/See also pages in the following book(s):
Wakin, E. Asian independence leaders p127-41 (7 and up)   **920**

Aung San Suu Kyi
About
Stewart, W. Aung San Suu Kyi (7 and up)   **92**

See/See also pages in the following book(s):
Hacker, C. Nobel Prize winners p6-11   **920**
Lucas, E. Contemporary human rights activists p93-105 (7 and up)   **920**
Price-Groff, C. Twentieth-century women political leaders (7 and up)   **920**

Aunt Cyrilla's Christmas basket. Montgomery, L. M.
In Montgomery, L. M. Christmas with Anne and other holiday stories p45-59   **S C**

Aunt Horrible's last visit. Hecht, J.
In Vampires: a collection of original stories p187-201   **S C**

Aunt Millicent. Steele, M.
In Read all about it! p12-28   **808.8**

Aunt Moon's young man. Hogan, L.
In Talking leaves   **S C**

Aunt Parnetta's electric blisters. Glancy, D.
In Talking leaves   **S C**

Aunt Susan. Aiken, J.
In Aiken, J. Give yourself a fright: thirteen tales of the supernatural p147-56   **S C**

Aunts
Fiction
Bauer, J. Backwater (7 and up)   **Fic**
Brokaw, N. S. Leaving Emma   **Fic**

Couloumbis, A. Getting near to baby   **Fic**
Irwin, H. The original Freddie Ackerman   **Fic**

Auschwitz (Poland: Concentration camp)
Kinderlager (7 and up)   **940.53**

Australia
Heinrichs, A. Australia   **994**
Fiction
Baillie, A. Secrets of Walden rising   **Fic**
Lester, A. Quicksand pony   **Fic**
Marchetta, M. Looking for Alibrandi (7 and up)   **Fic**
Marsden, J. Checkers (7 and up)   **Fic**
Marsden, J. Letters from the inside (7 and up)   **Fic**
Marsden, J. Tomorrow, when the war began (7 and up)   **Fic**
Napoli, D. J. Trouble on the tracks   **Fic**
Rubinstein, G. Foxspell   **Fic**
Zindel, P. Reef of death (7 and up)   **Fic**
History
See/See also pages in the following book(s):
The World in 1492 p97-125   **909**
Natural history
See Natural history—Australia

Australian aborigines
Finley, C. Aboriginal art of Australia   **759.01**
Folklore
Oodgeroo. Dreamtime   **398.2**

Australian painting
Finley, C. Aboriginal art of Australia   **759.01**

Authoritarianism *See* Totalitarianism

Authors
See also Child authors; Literature—Bio-bibliography; Women authors
Gillespie, J. T. The Newbery companion   **028.5**
Junior DISCovering authors 2.0. See entry in CD-ROM section, Part 3
Newbery and Caldecott Medal books, 1966-1975   **028.5**
Newbery and Caldecott medal books, 1976-1985   **028.5**
Newbery Medal books, 1922-1955   **028.5**
Pauses   **028.5**
Read all about it!   **808.8**
Dictionaries
Authors & artists for young adults   **920.003**
Lives and works: young adult authors   **810.3**
Seventh book of junior authors & illustrators   **920.003**
Something about the author   **920.003**
Something about the author: autobiography series   **920.003**
Twentieth-century young adult writers   **920.003**
World authors, 1900-1950   **920.003**
World authors, 1950-1970   **920.003**
World authors, 1970-1975   **920.003**
World authors, 1975-1980   **920.003**
World authors, 1980-1985   **920.003**
World authors, 1985-1990   **920.003**
World authors, 1990-1995   **920.003**

Bard, Therese Bissen
  Student assistants in the school library media center **027.8**
Bard of Avon: the story of William Shakespeare. Stanley, D. **92**
Bardi, Piero
  The atlas of the classical world **938**
Barefoot dancer: the story of Isadora Duncan. O'Connor, B. **92**
Barghusen, Joan D., 1935-
  The bald eagle (7 and up) **598**
  Cults (7 and up) **291.9**
Barghusen, Laura, 1964-
  The bear (7 and up) **599.78**
Barker, Keith, d. 1998
  Outstanding books for children and young people **028.5**
Barkin, Carol, 1944-
  (jt. auth) James, E. How to write super school reports **808**
  (jt. auth) James, E. How to write terrific book reports **808**
  (jt. auth) James, E. Sincerely yours **808**
  (jt. auth) James, E. Social smarts **395**
Barmeier, Jim
  The brain (7 and up) **612.8**
The **barn**. Avi **Fic**
Barnes, Marian E.
  (ed) Talk that talk: an anthology of African-American storytelling. See Talk that talk: an anthology of African-American storytelling **398.2**
Barnes-Svarncy, Patricia
  The New York Public Library science desk reference **500**
  Zimbabwe **968.91**
Barnett, Ida B. Wells- See Wells-Barnett, Ida B., 1862-1931
Barnett, Paul, 1949-
  See also Grant, John, 1949-
Barnhart, Robert K.
  (ed) The Barnhart dictionary of etymology. See The Barnhart dictionary of etymology **422.03**
The **Barnhart** dictionary of etymology **422.03**
Barns. Johnson, A.
  In Johnson, A. Gone from home: short takes p13-19 **S C**
Barnum, P. T. (Phineas Taylor), 1810-1891
  About
  Andronik, C. M. Prince of Humbugs: a life of P.T. Barnum **92**
Barnum, Phineas Taylor See Barnum, P. T. (Phineas Taylor), 1810-1891
The **baron** of Petronia. Vizenor, G. R.
  In Talking leaves **S C**
Barr, Catherine
  (ed) From biography to history. See From biography to history **016.8**

Barr, Roger, 1951-
  Juvenile crime (7 and up) **364.36**
Barraclough, Geoffrey, 1908-1984
  The Times atlas of world history. See The Times atlas of world history **911**
Barrett, Cece
  The dangers of diet drugs and other weight-loss products **615**
Barrett, Tracy, 1955-
  Anna of Byzantium **Fic**
  Kentucky
    In Celebrate the states **973**
  Nat Turner and the slave revolt **92**
  Tennessee
    In Celebrate the states **973**
  Virginia
    In Celebrate the states **973**
Barron, Ann E.
  The Internet and instruction **004.6**
Barron, Kenny
  See/See also pages in the following book(s):
  Gourse, L. Striders to beboppers and beyond p130-33 (7 and up) **781.65**
Barron, Rachel
  Richard Nixon (7 and up) **92**
Barron, T. A.
  The fires of Merlin. See note under Barron, T. A. The lost years of Merlin **Fic**
  The lost years of Merlin (7 and up) **Fic**
  The Merlin effect **Fic**
  The mirror of Merlin. See note under Barron, T. A. The lost years of Merlin **Fic**
  The seven songs of Merlin. See note under Barron, T. A. The lost years of Merlin **Fic**
Barron's how to prepare for high school entrance examinations, SSAT, ISEE. See Peters, M. How to prepare for the SSAT, ISEE high school entrance examinations **373.1**
Barsosio, Sally
  See/See also pages in the following book(s):
  Rutledge, R. The best of the best in track & field p14-19 **920**
Bartlett, John, 1820-1905
  Familiar quotations **808.88**
Bartlett's Roget's thesaurus **423**
Bartoletti, Susan Campbell, 1958-
  Growing up in coal country **331.3**
  Kids on strike! **331.8**
  No man's land **Fic**
  Rice pudding days
    In Dirty laundry: stories about family secrets p18-39 **S C**
Barton, Clara, 1821-1912
  About
  Whitelaw, N. Clara Barton **92**
  See/See also pages in the following book(s):
  DeAngelis, G. Science & medicine **920**
Bas mitzvah See Bat mitzvah
Baseball
  See also Softball
  Aylesworth, T. G. The kids' world almanac of baseball (7 and up) **796.357**
  Brashler, W. The story of Negro league baseball **796.357**

Bathrooms
 Colman, P. Toilets, bathtubs, sinks, and sewers
 643

Bats
 Perry, P. J. Bats **599.4**
 Fiction
 Oppel, K. Silverwing **Fic**
Bats, bugs, and biodiversity. Goodman, S.
 577.3

Battered children *See* Child abuse
Battered women *See* Abused women
Battered women (7 and up) **362.82**
Battering of wives *See* Wife abuse
The **battle** of Chihaya Castle. Kimmel, E. A.
 In Kimmel, E. A. Sword of the samurai p53-
 62 **Fic**
The **battle** of the drums. McCaughrean, G.
 In McCaughrean, G. The bronze cauldron:
 myths and legends of the world p63-67
 398.2
The **Battle** of the Little Bighorn in American his-
 tory. Ferrell, N. W. **973.8**
Battles of World War II [series]
 Rice, E. The attack on Pearl Harbor
 940.54
Batty. Jennings, P.
 In Jennings, P. Undone! p1-17 **S C**
Bauer, Joan
 Backwater (7 and up) **Fic**
 Pancakes
 In Trapped!: cages of mind and body p131-47
 S C
 Rules of the road (7 and up) **Fic**
 Squashed (7 and up) **Fic**
 Sticks **Fic**
 Thwonk (7 and up) **Fic**
Bauer, Marion Dane, 1938-
 Face to face **Fic**
 On my honor **Fic**
 Our stories **808.3**
 A question of trust **Fic**
 A taste of smoke **Fic**
 What's your story? **808.3**
 A writer's story (7 and up) **92**
Bauermeister, Erica
 Let's hear it for the girls **028.1**
Baum, L. Frank (Lyman Frank), 1856-1919
 The glass dog
 In American fairy tales p105-15 **S C**
 About
 Carpenter, A. S. L. Frank Baum **92**
Baum, Lyman Frank *See* Baum, L. Frank
 (Lyman Frank), 1856-1919
Baumfree, Isabella *See* Truth, Sojourner, d. 1883
Bawden, Nina, 1925-
 Granny the Pag **Fic**
 Off the road **Fic**
 The outside child **Fic**
Bayard Rustin: behind the scenes of the civil
 rights movement. Haskins, J. **92**
Baylor, Elgin, 1934-
 See/See also pages in the following book(s):
 Bayne, B. C. Sky kings (7 and up)
 796.323

Bayne, Bijan C.
 Sky kings (7 and up) **796.323**
Bazler, Judith A.
 (ed) Science experiments on file. See Science
 experiments on file **507.8**
Be-ers and doers. Wilson, B.
 In Help wanted: short stories about young
 people working **S C**
Be not far from me. Kimmel, E. A. **221.9**
Beaches
 Fiction
 Adler, C. S. Not just a summer crush **Fic**
 Howe, J. The watcher (7 and up) **Fic**
The **beaded** moccasins. Durrant, L. **Fic**
Beal, Eileen
 Everything you need to know about
 ADD/ADHD (7 and up) **616.85**
 Ritalin (7 and up) **616.85**
Bean, Lowell John
 The Cahuilla
 In Indians of North America series
 970.004
Bean, Suzanne M., 1957-
 (jt. auth) Karnes, F. A. Girls & young women
 inventing **608**
 (jt. auth) Karnes, F. A. Girls and young women
 entrepreneurs **658**
Beans
 See/See also pages in the following book(s):
 Johnson, S. A. Tomatoes, potatoes, corn, and
 beans p26-37 **641.3**
The **bear** man. Brown, D. A.
 In Brown, D. A. Dee Brown's folktales of the
 Native American p18-22 **398.2**
The **Bear** Woman. Bruchac, J.
 In Bruchac, J. The girl who married the
 Moon: tales from Native North America
 p75-83 **398.2**
Beardance. Hobbs, W. **Fic**
Bearden, Romare, 1914-1988
 See/See also pages in the following book(s):
 Greenberg, J. The American eye p51-59
 920
 Haskins, J. One more river to cross **920**
Beardsley, John
 Pablo Picasso (7 and up) **92**
Bearing, Paul. Lynch, C.
 In Night terrors **S C**
Bearing witness (7 and up) **808.8**
Bears
 See also Grizzly bear; Polar bear
 Barghusen, L. The bear (7 and up) **599.78**
 Stonehouse, B. Bears **599.78**
 Ward, P. Wild bears of the world (7 and up)
 599.78
 Fiction
 Hobbs, W. Beardance (7 and up) **Fic**
 Taylor, T. The weirdo (7 and up) **Fic**
The **bear's** speech. Cortázar, J.
 In Where angels glide at dawn p3-5
 S C
Bearstone. Hobbs, W. **Fic**

Beast and Beauty. Vande Velde, V.
In Vande Velde, V. Tales from the Brothers
Grimm and the Sisters Weird p109-28
S C

The beast is in the labyrinth. Myers, W. D.
In Places I never meant to be   S C

The beasties. Sleator, W.   Fic

Beattie, Owen
Buried in ice   998

Beatty, Patricia, 1922-1991
Jayhawker   Fic

Beauties and beasts. Hearne, B. G.   398.2

The beautiful thing. Mazer, H.
In Night terrors   S C

Beauty. McKinley, R.   Fic

Beauty and the Beast
In Hearne, B. G. Beauties and beasts p3-13
398.2

Beauty and the beast. Willard, N.   398.2

Beauty lessons. Ortiz Cofer, J.
In Ortiz Cofer, J. An island like you p41-54
S C

The Beauty Way—the ceremony of White-Painted
Woman. Bruchac, J.
In Bruchac, J. The girl who married the
Moon: tales from Native North America
p84-89   398.2

Beaver face. Lelooska, D.
In Lelooska, D. Echoes of the elders p32-38
398.2

Becca's story. Forman, J. D.   Fic

Bechard, Margaret, 1953-
If it doesn't kill you (7 and up)   Fic

Beckelman, Laurie
The human body   612

Beckwourth, James Pierson, 1798-1866
See/See also pages in the following book(s):
Haskins, J. Against all opposition p31-39
920

Becoming Rosemary. Wood, F.   Fic

A bed of peas. Galloway, P.
In Galloway, P. Truly grim tales   S C

Bedouins
Fiction
Temple, F. The Beduins' gazelle   Fic

Bedtime snacks. Yep, L.
In Yep, L. The rainbow people p4-10
398.2

The Beduins' gazelle. Temple, F.   Fic

Bee, Robert L.
The Yuma
In Indians of North America series
970.004

The Bee-man of Orn. Stockton, F.
In American fairy tales p67-80   S C

Beech, Olive Ann, 1903-1993
See/See also pages in the following book(s):
Jeffrey, L. S. Great American businesswomen
p26-35   920

Beecher family
About
Fritz, J. Harriet Beecher Stowe and the Beecher
preachers   92

Been to yesterdays: poems of a life. Hopkins, L.
B.   811

Beers, Kylene
(ed) Into focus. See Into focus   028.1

Bees
Lavies, B. Killer bees   595.7

The beetle. Andersen, H. C.
In Andersen, H. C. The little mermaid and
other fairy tales p112-20   S C

The Beetle and me. Young, K. R.   Fic

Beezlebub's baby. Aiken, J.
In Aiken, J. A foot in the grave p40-47
S C

Before Thanksgiving. McKean, T.
In McKean T. Into the candlelit room and
other strange tales p171-87   S C

Before the storm. Lassieur, A.   970.004

Begay, Shonto
Navajo   811

The Beggar Queen. Alexander, L.   Fic

The beginner's guide to animal autopsy. Parker,
S.   571.3

Beginning life. Flanagan, G. L.   612.6

The beginning of something. Bridgers, S. E.
In Visions: nineteen short stories by outstand-
ing writers for young adults p213-28
S C

Beginning with the ears. Olson, A. N.
In Olson, A. N. Ask the bones: scary stories
from around the world p42-45   398.2

Behavior, Compulsive *See* Compulsive behavior

Behind the Blue and Gray. Ray, D.   973.7

Behind the lines   973.7

Behind the lines. Holland, I.   Fic

Behind the mask: the life of Queen Elizabeth I.
Thomas, J. R.   92

Behler, John L.
The Audubon Society field guide to North
American reptiles and amphibians   597.9
National Audubon Society first field guide: rep-
tiles   597.9

Beiderbecke, Bix, 1903-1931
About
Collins, D. R. Bix Beiderbecke (7 and up)
92

Beier, Ulli
(ed) The Penguin book of modern African poetry. See The Penguin book of modern African
poetry   896

Beil, Karen Magnuson
Fire in their eyes   628.9

Being analog. Crawford, W.   020

Belarus
Levy, P. M. Belarus   947.8

Belfast (Northern Ireland)
Fiction
Banks, L. R. Maura's angel   Fic
Social life and customs
McMahon, P. One Belfast boy   941.6

Belgium
Pateman, R. Belgium   949.3

Beliefs and cultures [series]
Ganeri, A. Buddhist   294.3

Benton, M. J. (Michael J.), 1956-
Dinosaurs   **567.9**

Benton, Michael, 1939-
Dinosaur and other prehistoric animal factfinder
   560

Benton, Michael J. *See* Benton, M. J. (Michael J.), 1956-

Benton, Thomas Hart, 1782-1858
See/See also pages in the following book(s):
Kennedy, J. F. Profiles in courage p85-105 (7 and up)   **920**

Benton, Thomas Hart, 1889-1975
See/See also pages in the following book(s):
Greenberg, J. The American eye p33-41
   920

Beowulf. Osborne, M. P.
In Osborne, M. P. Favorite medieval tales p8-16   **398.2**

Berberick, Nancy Varian
A song for Croaker Nordge
In A Glory of unicorns p127-43   **S C**

Berdan, Frances
The Aztecs
In Indians of North America series
   970.004

Bereavement
Death is hard to live with (7 and up)
   155.9
DiGiulio, R. C. Straight talk about death and dying (7 and up)   **155.9**
Fry, V. L. Part of me died, too   **155.9**
Gootman, M. E. When a friend dies (7 and up)
   155.9
Grollman, E. A. Straight talk about death for teenagers (7 and up)   **155.9**
Grosshandler, J. Coping when a parent dies (7 and up)   **155.9**
Hyde, M. O. Meeting death   **155.9**
Krementz, J. How it feels when a parent dies
   155.9
Schleifer, J. Everything you need to know when someone you know has been killed (7 and up)
   155.9
Weiss, S. Everything you need to know about dealing with losses (7 and up)   **155.9**
See/See also pages in the following book(s):
Death and dying: opposing viewpoints p98-146 (7 and up)   **155.9**

Berenice. Poe, E. A.
In Poe, E. A. Tales of Edgar Allan Poe p293-304   **S C**

Berg, Elizabeth, 1953-
Senegal   **966.3**

Berger, Gilda
Celebrate!   **296.4**

Berger, Laura Standley, 1963-
(ed) Twentieth-century young adult writers. See Twentieth-century young adult writers
   920.003

Berger, Pam
Internet for active learners   **004.6**

Bergin, Mark
(il) Macdonald, F. A 16th century mosque
   297

(jt. auth) Macdonald, F. A Greek temple
   938

Berlin (Germany)
   History
Westerfeld, S. The Berlin airlift   **943.087**
The **Berlin** airlift. Westerfeld, S.   **943.087**

Berlin Wall (1961-1989)
Grant, R. G. The Berlin Wall   **943.087**

Berman, Avis
James McNeill Whistler (7 and up)   **92**

Bernstein, Jeremy, 1929-
Albert Einstein and the frontiers of physics (7 and up)   **92**

The **Bermuda** Triangle. Wynne-Jones, T.
In Wynne-Jones, T. Lord of the Fries and other stories p69-90   **S C**

Berra, Yogi, 1925-
See/See also pages in the following book(s):
Gilbert, T. W. Damn Yankees (7 and up)
   796.357

Berries
   See also Strawberries

Berry, James
Ajeemah and his son   **Fic**

Berry, Louise A.
(jt. auth) Miller, C. G. Air alert   **363.7**

Bertie's New Year. Montgomery, L. M.
In Montgomery, L. M. Christmas with Anne and other holiday stories p199-211
   S C

Beshore, George W.
Science in ancient China   **509**
Science in early Islamic culture   **509**

Bess and Croc. Coatsworth, E. J.
In A Newbery zoo   **S C**

Bess Call. San Souci, R.
In San Souci, R. Cut from the same cloth p13-18   **398.2**

The **best** bad thing. Uchida, Y. See note under Uchida, Y. A jar of dreams   **Fic**

Best books
Best books for young adult readers   **011.6**
Book Links   **028.505**
Carter, B. Best books for young adults
   028.1
The Horn Book Magazine   **028.505**
National Council of Teachers of English. Committee on the Junior High and Middle School Booklist. Your reading   **011.6**
New York Public Library. Books for the teen age   **011.6**
Notable children's trade books in the field of social studies   **016.3**
Outstanding science trade books for children
   016.5

Best books for young adult readers   **011.6**
Best books for young adults. Carter, B.   **028.1**
The **best** Christmas pageant ever. Robinson, B.
   Fic
Best magic, Bill Severn's. Severn, B.   **793.8**
The **best** of Shakespeare. Nesbit, E.   **822.3**
The **best** of the best in gymnastics. Rutledge, R.
   920

Bibliographic instruction—*Continued*
Foundations for effective school library media programs **027.8**
Garrett, L. J. Teaching library skills in middle and high school **027.8**
Jweid, R. The library-classroom partnership **027.8**
Rankin, V. The thoughtful researcher **027.62**
Smith, J. B. Achieving a curriculum-based library media center program **027.8**
Thomas, N. P. Information literacy and information skills instruction **027.8**
Volkman, J. D. Cruising through research **025.5**
Yucht, A. H. Flip it! **025.5**

Bibliographical citations
Shields, N. E. Where credit is due (7 and up) **808**

Bibliography
See also Bibliographical citations; Books
Books in print **015.73**
Subject guide to Books in print **015.73**

Best books
See Best books

Bicenti. Walters, A. L.
In Talking leaves **S C**

Bicycle racing

Fiction
Christopher, M. Olympic dream **Fic**

Biegel, Paul, 1925-
The ivory door
In Don't read this! and other tales of the unnatural p110-31 **S C**

Bierhorst, John
The mythology of Mexico and Central America (7 and up) **299**
The mythology of North America (7 and up) **299**
The mythology of South America (7 and up) **299**

Bierman, John
Righteous gentile [biography of Raoul Wallenberg] (7 and up) **92**

Biesty, Stephen
Stephen Biesty's cross-sections: Castle **940.1**
Stephen Biesty's cross-sections: Man-of-war **359.1**
Stephen Biesty's incredible body **611**
Stephen Biesty's incredible everything **670**
Stephen Biesty's incredible explosions **741.6**

Big Annie of Calumet. Stanley, J. **331.8**
Big bang. Couper, H. **523.1**
Big bang cosmology *See* Big bang theory
Big bang theory
Couper, H. Big bang **523.1**
The **big** black umbrella. Leach, M.
In The Oxford book of scary tales p86-87 **808.8**
The **Big** book of holiday plays **812.008**

The **big** dinin'. Van Laan, N.
In Van Laan, N. With a whoop and a holler p27-31 **398**
Big foot *See* Sasquatch
Big game hunting *See* Hunting
Big Tree People. Bruchac, J.
In Bruchac, J. When the Chenoo howls **398.2**
The **Big** Wander. Hobbs, W. **Fic**
Bigfoot *See* Sasquatch
Bigger. Calvert, P. **Fic**
Biggest. McCaughrean, G.
In McCaughrean, G. The bronze cauldron: myths and legends of the world p97-101 **398.2**
BigWater. Sherman, C. W.
In Rites of passage p79-88 **S C**
The **bijli**. San Souci, R.
In San Souci, R. A terrifying taste of short & shivery p35-38 **398.2**
Bilbo Baggins and Smaug. Tolkien, J. R. R.
In The Book of dragons p39-46 **S C**
Bilingual books

English-Spanish
Cool salsa **811.008**
Herrera, J. F. Laughing out loud, I fly **811**
Mora, P. The desert is my mother. El desierto es mi madre **811**
The Tree is older than you are (7 and up) **860.8**

Bilingual education
See/See also pages in the following book(s):
Culture wars: opposing viewpoints p170-80 (7 and up) **306**
Bill, Buffalo *See* Buffalo Bill, 1846-1917
Bill Clinton and his presidency. Landau, E. **92**
Bill of rights (U.S.) *See* United States. Constitution. 1st-10th amendments
The **Bill** of Rights. Nardo, D. **342**
Bill Pickett: African-American rodeo star. Sanford, W. R. **92**
Bill Severn's best magic. Severn, B. **793.8**
Billy, the Kid
See/See also pages in the following book(s):
Glass, A. Bad guys **920**
Billy. Brooks, B. See note under Brooks, B. Zip **Fic**
Biloxi Indians
Brain, J. P. The Tunica-Biloxi
In Indians of North America series **970.004**
Bindweed. Aiken, J.
In Aiken, J. A foot in the grave p97-114 **S C**
Binge-purge behavior *See* Bulimia
Bingen, Hildegard von *See* Hildegard, von Bingen, Saint, 1098-1179
Bingham, Hiram, 1875-1956
The ancient Incas **985**
Bingo Brown and the language of love. Byars, B. C. See note under Byars, B. C. The burning questions of Bingo Brown **Fic**

Black, Wallace B.
Slaves to soldiers   **973.7**
Black Americans *See* African Americans
Black Americans of achievement [series]
  Adair, G. George Washington Carver   **92**
  Bisson, T. Nat Turner   **92**
  De Angelis, T. Louis Farrakhan   **92**
  Dolan, S. Bob Marley   **92**
  Frankl, R. Charlie Parker, musician   **92**
  Gentry, T. Paul Laurence Dunbar   **92**
  Hanley, S. A. Philip Randolph   **92**
  Hasday, J. L. Tina Turner   **92**
  Hill, A. E. Denzel Washington   **92**
  Jakoubek, R. E. Joe Louis   **92**
  Kliment, B. Billie Holiday   **92**
  Krass, P. Sojourner Truth   **92**
  Lawler, M. Marcus Garvey   **92**
  Norman, W. L. Lewis Latimer   **92**
  Palmer, L. Lena Horne   **92**
  Preston, K. K. Scott Joplin   **92**
  Rhodes, L. R. Coretta Scott King   **92**
  Stauffer, S. Will Smith   **92**
  Taylor, M. W. Harriet Tubman   **92**
  Urban, J. Richard Wright   **92**
Black art (Magic) *See* Witchcraft
Black authors
  See also African American authors
Black, blue, & gray. Haskins, J.   **973.7**
The **Black** Bull of Norroway
  In Hearne, B. G. Beauties and beasts p92-96
    398.2
The **black** cauldron. Alexander, L. *See* note under
  Alexander, L. The book of three   **Fic**
The **black** cowboys. DeAngelis, G.   **978**
Black death *See* Plague
The **Black** Death (7 and up)   **614.5**
The **Black** Death. Corzine, P.   **614.5**
Black diamond. McKissack, P. C.   **796.357**
Black eagles. Haskins, J.   **629.13**
Black Elk, 1863-1950
See/See also pages in the following book(s):
Krull, K. They saw the future p67-73
    133.3
Black fighting men. Reef, C.   **920**
The **black** fox. Byars, B. C.
  In A Newbery zoo   **S C**
The **black** fox. San Souci, R.
  In San Souci, R. A terrifying taste of short &
    shivery p137-40   **398.2**
Black frontiers. Schlissel, L.   **978**
Black hair. Martin, R.
  In Martin, R. Mysterious tales of Japan
    398.2
Black hands, white sails. McKissack, P. C.
    639.2
Black hearts in Battersea. Aiken, J. *See* note under
  Aiken, J. The wolves of Willoughby Chase
    Fic
Black holes (Astronomy)
  Couper, H. Black holes   **523.8**
Black hoops. McKissack, F.   **796.323**
Black horses for the king. McCaffrey, A.   **Fic**

Black Indians: a hidden heritage. Katz, W. L.
    305.8
Black inventors. Aaseng, N.   **920**
Black literature (American) *See* American litera-
  ture—African American authors
Black magic (Witchcraft) *See* Magic
Black music
  See also African American music
Black musicians
  See also African American musicians
Black Muslims
  Banks, W. The Black Muslims   **297**
  De Angelis, T. Louis Farrakhan   **92**
  Haskins, J. Louis Farrakhan and the Nation of
    Islam   **92**
  Myers, W. D. Malcolm X (7 and up)   **92**
The **black** pearl. O'Dell, S.   **Fic**
Black pioneers. Katz, W. L.   **920**
Black poetry (American) *See* American poetry—
  African American authors
Black powder. Wu, W. F.
  In American dragons p211-34   **810.8**
The **black** press and the struggle for civil rights.
  Senna, C.   **071**
Black ships before Troy. Sutcliff, R.   **883**
The **black** snake. Olson, A. N.
  In Olson, A. N. Ask the bones: scary stories
    from around the world p99-104
    398.2
Black stars [series]
  Haskins, J. African American entrepreneurs
    920
  Haskins, J. African American military heroes
    920
  Sullivan, O. R. African American inventors
    920
Black stars in orbit. Burns, K.   **920**
Black women leaders of the civil rights move-
  ment. Allen, Z.   **323.1**
Black women of the Old West. Katz, W. L.
    978
Blackburn, G. Meredith
  (comp) Index to poetry for children and young
  people. *See* Index to poetry for children and
  young people   **808.81**
Blackburn, Lorraine A.
  (comp) Index to poetry for children and young
  people. *See* Index to poetry for children and
  young people   **808.81**
The **Blackfeet.** Lacey, T. J.
  In Indians of North America series
    970.004
Blackfoot Indians *See* Siksika Indians
Blackmail. Soto, G.
  In Soto, G. Local news p1-13   **S C**
Blacks
    Biography
  See also African Americans—Biography
  Cameron, A. The kidnapped prince: the life of
    Olaudah Equiano   **92**
  Dolan, S. Bob Marley   **92**
  Katz, W. L. Proudly red and black   **920**

Blacks—Biography—*Continued*
Myers, W. D. Toussaint L'Ouverture   **92**
        Fiction
Bell, W. Zack (7 and up)   **Fic**
Rites of passage   **S C**
        History
Palmer, C. A. The first passage (7 and up)
   326
      Quotations
My soul looks back, 'less I forget   **808.88**
    United States
  See African Americans
Blacks in art
  See also African Americans in art
Feelings, T. The middle passage (7 and up)
   759.13
Blacks in literature
  See also African Americans in literature
The **blacksmith** and the Devil. Lester, J.
  In Lester, J. The last tales of Uncle Remus
  p141-47   **398.2**
Blacksmithing
See/See also pages in the following book(s):
Lyons, M. E. Catching the fire: Philip Simmons,
  blacksmith   **92**
Blackwell, Elizabeth, 1821-1910
See/See also pages in the following book(s):
Celebrating women in mathematics and science
  p89-100   **920**
DeAngelis, G. Science & medicine   **920**
Blackwood, Gary L.
Alien astronauts   **001.9**
Extraordinary events and oddball occurrences
   001.9
Life on the Oregon Trail (7 and up)   **979.5**
The Shakespeare stealer   **Fic**
Blair, Eric *See* Orwell, George, 1903-1950
Blake, Arthur
The Scopes trial   **345**
Blakeslee, Ann R.
A different kind of hero   **Fic**
Blashfield, Jean F.
Colorado
  In America the beautiful, second series
   973
Sparks of life [series]   **546**
Virginia
  In America the beautiful, second series
   973
Wisconsin
  In America the beautiful, second series
   973
Blassingame, Wyatt
The look-it-up book of presidents   **920**
Blauer, Ettagale
Morocco   **964**
South Africa   **968**
The **blaze** engulfs. Sherrow, V.   **940.53**
A **blaze** of glory. Coville, B.
  In Coville, B. Oddly enough p105-18
   S C
The **blessing**. Goldin, B. D.
  In Goldin, B. D. Journeys with Elijah p57-63
   222

Blind
Freedman, R. Out of darkness: the story of Lou-
  is Braille   **92**
Keller, H. The story of my life   **92**
St. George, J. Dear Dr. Bell—your friend, Helen
  Keller   **92**
      Fiction
Kurtz, J. The storyteller's beads   **Fic**
Mathis, S. B. Listen for the fig tree (7 and up)
   Fic
Taylor, T. The cay   **Fic**
Taylor, T. Timothy of the cay   **Fic**
The **Blind** boy and the loon
  In The Dancing fox: Arctic folktales p125-31
   398.2
Blishen, Edward, 1920-1996
Stand up Mr. Dickens (7 and up)   **823.009**
The **blizzard** disaster. Kehret, P.   **Fic**
Blizzards
      Fiction
Kehret, P. The blizzard disaster   **Fic**
Block, Francesca Lia
The box
  In Trapped!: cages of mind and body p35-45
   S C
I was a teenage fairy (7 and up)   **Fic**
The **block**. Hughes, L.   **811**
Blodgett, Katharine, 1898-1979
See/See also pages in the following book(s):
Altman, L. J. Women inventors p63-73 (7 and
  up)   **920**
Blonde. Min, K.
  In American eyes p3-7   **S C**
Blood
Ballard, C. The heart and circulatory system
   612.1
     Circulation
  See also Cardiovascular system
Silverstein, A. The circulatory system
   612.1
      Diseases
  See also Leukemia
Blood and bone. Galloway, P.
  In Galloway, P. Truly grim tales   **S C**
The **blood-ghoul** of Scarsdale. Friesner, E. M.
  In Vampires: a collection of original stories
  p81-78   **S C**
Blood kin. Sherman, D.
  In Vampires: a collection of original stories
  p35-63   **S C**
Blood libel. Hussey, L. A.
  In Vampires: a collection of original stories
  p157-86   **S C**
Blood on the forehead. Kerr, M. E.   **808.3**
Blood relations. Lynch, C. See note under Lynch,
  C. Mick   **Fic**
A **bloodthirsty** tale. McCaughrean, G.
  In McCaughrean, G. The silver treasure:
  myths and legends of the world p103-07
   398.2
The **bloody** country. Collier, J. L.   **Fic**
Bloom, Susan P.
Presenting Avi (7 and up)   **813.009**

Bodybuilding (Weight lifting) *See* Weight lifting

The **bogey** man. Klause, A. C.
   In Night terrors   **S C**

The **Boggart**. Cooper, S.   **Fic**

The **Boggart** and the monster. Cooper, S. See note
   under Cooper, S. The Boggart   **Fic**

Bogs *See* Wetlands

Bogues, Muggsy, 1965-
See/See also pages in the following book(s):
   Rappoport, K. Guts and glory   **920**

Bohl, Al
   Guide to cartooning   **741.5**

Bohr, Niels Henrik David, 1885-1962
See/See also pages in the following book(s):
   Henderson, H. Nuclear physics p34-54 (7 and
   up)   **539.7**

Boiko, Claire
   The case of the bewitched books
   In The Big book of holiday plays p78-86
      812.008

   Cinder-Riley
   In The Big book of holiday plays p271-78
      812.008

   The reform of Benjamin Scrimp
   In The Big book of holiday plays p119-30
      812.008

Boitano, Brian
   Boitano's edge   **92**

Boitano's edge. Boitano, B.   **92**

Bolden, Tonya
   And not afraid to dare   **920**
   (ed) 33 things every girl should know. See 33
   things every girl should know   **810.8**
   (ed) Rites of passage. See Rites of passage
      S C

Bolton, A. C.
   The friendly ghost
   In The Oxford book of scary tales p137-43
      808.8

Bolton, Jonathan
   Joseph Brant   **92**

Bolundeers. Yolen, J.
   In A Nightmare's dozen   **S C**
   In Yolen, J. Twelve impossible things before
   breakfast p87-99   **S C**

Bombaugh, Ruth J.
   Science fair success (7 and up)   **507.8**

**Bombing of the World Trade Center, New York
(N.Y.) 1993** *See* World Trade Center Bombing,
New York, N.Y., 1993

Bonafini, Hebe de
See/See also pages in the following book(s):
   Lucas, E. Contemporary human rights activists
   p51-63 (7 and up)   **920**

Bonafoux, Pascal, 1949-
   A weekend with Rembrandt   **92**

Bonaparte, Napoleon *See* Napoleon I, Emperor of
the French, 1769-1821

Bonar, Samantha
   Comets   **523.6**

Bond, Peter, 1948-
   DK guide to space   **520**

Bond, Ruskin
   Eyes of the cat
   In The Oxford book of scary tales p76-78
      808.8

Bone [excerpt] Ng, F. M.
   In American eyes p108-30   **S C**

Bone dance. Brooks, M.   **Fic**

The **bone** detectives. Jackson, D.   **614**

A **bone** from a dry sea. Dickinson, P.   **Fic**

Bones
   Parker, S. Skeleton   **573.7**
   Simon, S. Bones   **612.7**
   The Visual dictionary of the skeleton   **573.7**

Bones. Strasser, T.
   In Ultimate sports: short stories by outstanding writers for young adults p238-50
      S C

Bonetta, Sarah Forbes, b. 1843?
About
   Myers, W. D. At her majesty's request   **92**

Bonham-Boveé, Jonita Ruth, d. 1994
See/See also pages in the following book(s):
   Mendoza, P. M. Extraordinary people in extraor-
   dinary times p102-10 (7 and up)   **920**

Boni, Simone
   (il) Loria, S. Pablo Picasso   **92**

Bonney, William H. *See* Billy, the Kid

Bonnin, Gertrude Simmons *See* Zitkala-Ša, 1876-
1938

Bonson, Richard
   Disaster!   **363.34**

Bonvillain, Nancy
   The Hopi
   In Indians of North America series
      970.004

   The Huron
   In Indians of North America series
      970.004

   The Inuit
   In Indians of North America series
      970.004

   The Mohawk
   In Indians of North America series
      970.004

   Native American medicine
   In Indians of North America series
      970.004

   Native American religion
   In Indians of North America series
      970.004

   The Sac and Fox
   In Indians of North America series
      970.004

   The Santee Sioux
   In Indians of North America series
      970.004

   The Teton Sioux
   In Indians of North America series
      970.004

   The Zuni
   In Indians of North America series
      970.004

Boo, Michael
   The story of figure skating   **796.91**

Booth, John Wilkes, 1838-1865
About
Otfinoski, S. John Wilkes Booth and the Civil War 92

Boots See Shoes

Borges, Jorge Luis, 1899-1986
About
Lennon, A. Jorge Luis Borges 92
See/See also pages in the following book(s):
Shirey, L. Latin American writers (7 and up) 860.9

Borglum, Gutzon, 1867-1941
About
Curlee, L. Rushmore 730.9

Borkowska, Anna, d. 1988
See/See also pages in the following book(s):
Lyman, D. Holocaust rescuers 920

Borland, Hal, 1900-1978
When the legends die Fic

Born free: a lioness of two worlds. Adamson, J. 599.75

Born naked. Mowat, F. 92

Born worker. Soto, G.
In Soto, G. Petty crimes S C

The **borning** room. Fleischman, P. Fic

Bornstein, Harry
(ed) The Comprehensive signed English dictionary. See The Comprehensive signed English dictionary 419

Bosch, Hieronymus, d. 1516
About
Schwartz, G. Hieronymus Bosch (7 and up) 92

Boschung, Herbert T., Jr.
The Audubon Society field guide to North American fishes, whales, and dolphins. See The Audubon Society field guide to North American fishes, whales, and dolphins 597

Bosco, Peter I.
World War I (7 and up) 940.3

The **Boscombe** Valley mystery. Doyle, Sir A. C.
In Doyle, Sir A. C. Adventures of Sherlock Holmes S C
In Doyle, Sir A. C. The complete Sherlock Holmes S C

Boshblobberbosh. Lewis, J. P. 811

Bosnia and Hercegovina
See also Sarajevo (Bosnia and Hercegovina)
Black, E. Bosnia (7 and up) 949.7

Bosse, Malcolm J., 1934-
The examination (7 and up) Fic

Boston (Mass.)
Fiction
Fleischman, P. Saturnalia Fic
Forbes, E. Johnny Tremain Fic
Lowry, L. Taking care of Terrific (7 and up) Fic
Lynch, C. Mick (7 and up) Fic

Boston Children's Museum activity book [Series]
Zubrowski, B. Making waves 532

Zubrowski, B. Mirrors 535

Boston Massacre, 1770
Lukes, B. L. The Boston Massacre (7 and up) 973.3
Fiction
Rinaldi, A. The fifth of March (7 and up) Fic

Boston Tea Party, 1773
Hull, M. The Boston Tea Party in American history 973.3

The **Boston** Tea Party in American history. Hull, M. 973.3

Botany
See also Plants
Hershey, D. R. Plant biology science projects (7 and up) 580.7
Perry, P. J. Science fair success with plants (7 and up) 580.7
Silverstein, A. Plants 580
Taylor, B. Incredible plants 580
VanCleave, J. P. Janice VanCleave's plants 580

Botany, Medical See Medical botany

Boudicca See Boadicea, Queen, d. 62

Boulton, Alexander O.
Frank Lloyd Wright, architect (7 and up) 92

Bound for America. Haskins, J. 326

Bound for Oregon. Van Leeuwen, J. Fic

Bound for the promised land. Cooper, M. L. 305.8

A **bouquest** of flowers. McCaughrean, G.
In McCaughrean, G. The crystal pool: myths and legends of the world p24-26 398.2

Bourke-White, Margaret, 1904-1971
About
Rubin, S. G. Margaret Bourke-White (7 and up) 92
Welch, C. A. Margaret Bourke-White 92

Bourne, Joyce
(ed) Kennedy, M. The concise Oxford dictionary of music 780.3

Boveé, Jonita Ruth Bonham- See Bonham-Boveé, Jonita Ruth, d. 1994

Bowen, Gary
Stranded at Plimoth Plantation, 1626 974.4

Bowermaster, Jon, 1954-
(jt. auth) Steger, W. Over the top of the world 998

Bowie, James, 1799?-1836
See/See also pages in the following book(s):
Calvert, P. Great lives: the American frontier p15-28 920

Bowler, Tim
Midget (7 and up) Fic

Bowman-Kruhm, Mary
(jt. auth) Wirths, C. G. Coping with confrontations and encounters with the police 363.2

Bowman's store. Bruchac, J. 92

Brain, Jeffrey P.
The Tunica-Biloxi
In Indians of North America series
970.004

Brain
Barmeier, J. The brain (7 and up)   612.8
Brynie, F. H. 101 questions your brain has asked about itself but couldn't answer . . . until now   612.8
The Human mind explained (7 and up)
153
Simon, S. The brain   612.8

Brainstorm!. Tucker, T.   609

Brainwashing
See/See also pages in the following book(s):
Cohen, D. Cults p34-44 (7 and up)   291.9

Braly, David
The night watchman
In Read all about it! p244-51   808.8

Bramwell, Martyn
Mapping the planets and space   520
Polar exploration   998

Brancato, Robin F.
Fourth of July
In Sixteen: short stories by outstanding writers for young adults p102-12   S C
War of the words
In Center stage   812.008

Branch, Muriel Miller
Juneteenth   394.26

Brandenberg, Aliki *See* Aliki

Brandon and the aliens. Yolen, J.
In Yolen, J. Twelve impossible things before breakfast p109-23   S C

Brandt, Sue R., 1916-
State flags   929.9
State trees   582.16

Branston, Brian, 1914-
Gods and heroes from Viking mythology
293

Branston, Ronald Victor *See* Branston, Brian, 1914-

Brant, Beth, 1941-
Swimming upstream
In Talking leaves   S C

Brant, Joseph, 1742-1807
About
Bolton, J. Joseph Brant   92

Brashler, William
The story of Negro league baseball
796.357

The **brave.** Lipsyte, R.   Fic

Brave Bird, Mary
Lakota woman (7 and up)   92

Brave new world. Huxley, A.   Fic

Brave quest. McCaughrean, G.
In McCaughrean, G. The golden hoard: myths and legends of the world p29-38
398.2

Braving the New World, 1619-1784. Nardo, D.
305.8

Braving the North Atlantic. West, D. C.
970.01

Bray, Marian Flandrick, 1957-
Pale mare
In Stay true: short stories for strong girls
S C

Brazil
Bender, E. Brazil   981

A **break.** Johnson, A.
In Johnson, A. Gone from home: short takes p97-104   S C

Break those chains at last: African Americans, 1860-1880. Frankel, N.   305.8

Breaker's bridge. Yep, L.
In Yep, L. The rainbow people p124-34
398.2

Breaking ground, breaking silence. Hansen, J.
974.7

Breaking rank. Randle, K. D.   Fic

Breaking the chains: African-American slave resistance. Katz, W. L.   326

Breckinridge, Mary, 1881-1965
About
Wells, R. Mary on horseback   92

Bredeson, Carmen
Henry Cisneros   92
The moon   523.3
Neil Armstrong   92
Shannon Lucid   92
Texas
In Celebrate the states   973
Tide pools   577.6

Breedlove, Sarah *See* Walker, C. J., Madame, 1867-1919

Breen, Karen, 1943-
Index to collective biographies for young readers   920

Brenda. Spinelli, J.
In Spinelli, J. The library card   S C

Brenner, Barbara
If you were there in 1776   973.3

Brent, Linda *See* Jacobs, Harriet A. (Harriet Ann), 1813-1896 or 7

Brer Bear comes to the community. Lester, J.
In Lester, J. The last tales of Uncle Remus p25-28   398.2

Brer Bear exposes Brer Rabbit. Lester, J.
In Lester, J. The last tales of Uncle Remus p37-39   398.2

Brer Buzzard and Brer Crow. Lester, J.
In Lester, J. The last tales of Uncle Remus p138-41   398.2

Brer Fox and the white grapes. Lester, J.
In Lester, J. The last tales of Uncle Remus p94-98   398.2

Brer Possum's dilemma. Torrence, J.
In From sea to shining sea p249-51
810.8

Brer Rabbit and Aunt Nancy. Lester, J.
In Lester, J. The last tales of Uncle Remus p149-51   398.2

Brer Rabbit and Miss Nancy. Lester, J.
In Lester, J. The last tales of Uncle Remus p16-22   398.2

Brer Rabbit in Mr. Man's garden. Lester, J.
In From sea to shining sea p212-15
    810.8

Brer Rabbit, King Polecat, and the gingercakes.
Lester, J.
In Lester, J. The last tales of Uncle Remus
p123-28   **398.2**

Brer Rabbit teaches Brer Bear to comb his hair.
Lester, J.
In Lester, J. The last tales of Uncle Remus
p39-41   **398.2**

Brer Rabbit throws a party. Lester, J.
In Lester, J. The last tales of Uncle Remus
p62-63   **398.2**

Breuilly, Elizabeth
Religions of the world (7 and up)   **291**

Brewer, Ebenezer Cobham, 1810-1897
Brewer's dictionary of phrase and fable. See
Brewer's dictionary of phrase and fable
    803

Brewer's dictionary of phrase and fable   **803**

Brewster, Hugh
882 ½ amazing answers to your questions about
the Titanic   **910.4**
Anastasia's album   **92**
(jt. auth) Marschall, K. Inside the Titanic
    910.4

Brewster, Todd
(jt. auth) Jennings, P. The century for young
people   **909.82**

Brewton, John Edmund, 1898-
(comp) Index to children's poetry. See Index to
children's poetry   **808.81**

Brewton, Sara Westbrook
(comp) Index to children's poetry. See Index to
children's poetry   **808.81**
(comp) Index to poetry for children and young
people. See Index to poetry for children and
young people   **808.81**

Brian's return. Paulsen, G.   **Fic**

Brian's winter. Paulsen, G.   **Fic**

Briar Rose. Yolen, J.   **Fic**
Briar's book. See Pierce, T. Circle of magic: Briar's book   **Fic**

Bricktop, 1894-1984
See/See also pages in the following book(s):
Haskins, J. African American entrepreneurs p93-
96   **920**

The **bridal** gown. Olson, A. N.
In Olson, A. N. Ask the bones: scary stories
from around the world p125-28
    398.2

Bride price. Crew, L.
In Join in p111-26   **S C**

Brides, midwives, and widows. Bentley, J.
    978

The **bridge.** Vande Velde, V.
In Vande Velde, V. Tales from the Brothers
Grimm and the Sisters Weird p70-76
    S C

Bridge to Terabithia. Paterson, K.   **Fic**

Bridger, James, 1804-1881
See/See also pages in the following book(s):
Calvert, P. Great lives: the American frontier
p29-43   **920**

Bridgers, Jay
Everything you need to know about having an
addictive personality (7 and up)   **616.86**

Bridgers, Sue Ellen, 1942-
The beginning of something
In Visions: nineteen short stories by outstand-
ing writers for young adults p213-28
    S C

Bridges, Ruby
Through my eyes: the autobiography of Ruby
Bridges   **92**

The **bridge's** complaint. Yolen, J.
In Yolen, J. Twelve impossible things before
breakfast p101-08   **S C**

A **brief** moment in the life of Angus Bethune.
Crutcher, C.
In Crutcher, C. Athletic shorts: six short sto-
ries p3-25   **S C**

Briefcase. Myers, W. D.
In Twelve shots: outstanding short stories
about guns p7-24   **S C**

Briggs, Carole S., 1950-
Women in space   **920**

Bright Freedom's song. Houston, G.   **Fic**

Bright Thursdays. Senior, O.
In Rites of passage p50-70   **S C**

Brill, Marlene Targ
Illinois
In Celebrate the states   **973**
Indiana
In Celebrate the states   **973**
Michigan
In Celebrate the states   **973**

A **brilliant** streak: the making of Mark Twain.
Lasky, K.   **92**

Brimner, Larry Dane, 1949-
Rock climbing   **796.52**
Snowboarding   **796.9**
Voices from the camps (7 and up)   **940.53**

Bristow, M. J.
(ed) National anthems of the world. See National anthems of the world   **782.42**

Britain. Fuller, B.   **941**

British Library writers' lives [series]
Shellard, D. William Shakespeare   **822.3**

British Museum (Natural History) *See* Natural
History Museum (London, England)

Brittain, Bill
Dr. Dredd's wagon of wonders. See note under
Brittain, B. The wish giver   **Fic**
Professor Popkin's prodigious polish. See note
under Brittain, B. The wish giver   **Fic**
Shape-changer   **Fic**
The wish giver   **Fic**

Broadcast journalism
See also Television broadcasting of news
Garner, J. We interrupt this broadcast (7 and up)
    070.1
Wakin, E. How TV changed America's mind (7
and up)   **070.1**

The **Broccoli** tapes. Slepian, J.   **Fic**

Brock, Juliet Clutton- *See* Clutton-Brock, Juliet

Brockman, C. Frank (Christian Frank), 1902-
Trees of North America   **582.16**

Brockman, Christian Frank *See* Brockman, C. Frank (Christian Frank), 1902-

Brokaw, Nancy Steele
Leaving Emma   **Fic**

The **broken** blade. Durbin, W.   **Fic**

Broken bridge. Banks, L. R.   **Fic**

Broken chain. Soto, G.
In Read all about it! p29-39   **808.8**
In Soto, G. Baseball in April, and other stories p1-12   **S C**

Broncos (Football team) *See* Denver Broncos (Football team)

Bronwen and the crows. Leonard, A.
In The Oxford book of scary tales p98-105   **808.8**

The **bronze** cauldron [story] McCaughrean, G.
In McCaughrean, G. The bronze cauldron: myths and legends of the world p5-10   **398.2**

The **bronze** cauldron: myths and legends of the world. McCaughrean, G.   **398.2**

Brooke, William J.
Teller of tales   **S C**
Contents: The Emperor's clothes are news; Rumpelstiltskin by any other name; Gold in locks; Little Well-Read Riding Hood; Teller's tale; Tale of tellers
A telling of the tales: five stories   **S C**
Contents: The waking of the prince; The growin' of Paul Bunyan; The fitting of the slipper; The working of John Henry; The telling of a tale

Brooker, Kyrsten
(jt. auth) Krull, K. They saw the future   **133.3**

Brookfield, Karen
Book   **070.5**

Brooklyn (New York, N.Y.)
Fiction
Fisher, L. E. The jetty chronicles   **Fic**
Woodson, J. Last summer with Maizon   **Fic**

Brooks, Bruce, 1950-
Asylum for Nightface (7 and up)   **Fic**
Billy. See note under Brooks, B. Zip   **Fic**
Boot. See note under Brooks, B. Zip   **Fic**
Cody. See note under Brooks, B. Zip   **Fic**
Dooby. See note under Brooks, B. Zip   **Fic**
Midnight hour encores (7 and up)   **Fic**
The moves make the man (7 and up)   **Fic**
No kidding (7 and up)   **Fic**
Prince. See note under Brooks, B. Zip   **Fic**
Reed. See note under Brooks, B. Zip   **Fic**
Shark. See note under Brooks, B. Zip   **Fic**
Vanishing   **Fic**
Woodsie. See note under Brooks, B. Zip   **Fic**
Woodsie, again. See note under Brooks, B. Zip   **Fic**
Zip   **Fic**

Brooks, Garth
About
Howey, P. Garth Brooks   **92**

Brooks, Gwendolyn
See/See also pages in the following book(s):
Strickland, M. R. African-American poets p39-45   **920**

Brooks, Martha, 1944-
Bone dance (7 and up)   **Fic**
A boy and his dog
In Who do you think you are? p58-63   **S C**

Brooks, Philip *See* Wilkinson, Philip, 1955-

Brooks, Philip, 1963-
Extraordinary Jewish Americans   **920**

Brooks, Polly Schoyer
Cleopatra (7 and up)   **92**

Brooks, Terry, 1944-
See/See also pages in the following book(s):
MacRae, C. D. Presenting young adult fantasy fiction (7 and up)   **813.009**

Brooks Gollobin, Laurie
Selkie [play]
In Theatre for young audiences p579-604   **812.008**

Brother, can you spare a dime?. Meltzer, M.   **330.973**

Brother Imás. Hinojosa, R.
In Growing up Latino p250-58   **810.8**

Brother Rabbit sells corn. Winther, B.
In Winther, B. Plays from Hispanic tales   **812**

Brotherhood of Sleeping Car Porters
See/See also pages in the following book(s):
Hanley, S. A. Philip Randolph p60-78   **92**

Brothers
Fiction
Bloor, E. Tangerine (7 and up)   **Fic**
Bosse, M. J. The examination (7 and up)   **Fic**
Bowler, T. Midget (7 and up)   **Fic**
Cannon, A. E. The shadow brothers (7 and up)   **Fic**
Durrant, L. Echohawk   **Fic**
Dygard, T. J. River danger (7 and up)   **Fic**
Gregory, K. Orphan runaways   **Fic**
Hinton, S. E. Rumble fish (7 and up)   **Fic**
Hinton, S. E. Tex (7 and up)   **Fic**
Kerr, M. E. Night kites (7 and up)   **Fic**
Lynch, C. Shadow boxer (7 and up)   **Fic**
Naylor, P. R. Danny's Desert Rats   **Fic**
Naylor, P. R. The fear place   **Fic**
Peck, R. N. Cowboy ghost   **Fic**
Philbrick, W. R. The fire pony   **Fic**
Powell, R. Tribute to another dead rock star (7 and up)   **Fic**
Salisbury, G. Jungle dogs   **Fic**
Seago, K. Matthew unstrung (7 and up)   **Fic**
Springer, N. Toughing it (7 and up)   **Fic**
Sweeney, J. Free fall (7 and up)   **Fic**
Thompson, J. F. Brothers (7 and up)   **Fic**
Vanasse, D. Out of the wilderness   **Fic**
Yep, L. Later, gator   **Fic**

Brothers. Thompson, J. F.   **Fic**

Brothers and bone. Hamilton, V.
In Hamilton, V. The dark way p132-36   **398.2**

Brown, Rachel, 1898-1980
See/See also pages in the following book(s):
Altman, L. J. Women inventors p74-87 (7 and up)　　**920**

Brown, Risa W.
(jt. auth) Totten, H. L. Culturally diverse library collections for youth　　**011.6**

Brown, Roslind Varghese
Tunisia　　**961.1**

Brown, Travis, 1926-
Historical first patents (7 and up)　　**608**

Brown v. Board of Education. Tackach, J.　　**344**

Brown v. Board of Education (1954). Dudley, M. E.　　**344**

Brownian motion. Wolff, V. E.
In Ultimate sports: short stories by outstanding writers for young adults p207-36　　**S C**

Brownstone, David M.
(jt. auth) Franck, I. M. The Wilson chronology of women's achievements　　**305.4**

Bruce, Henry Clay, 1836-1902
See/See also pages in the following book(s):
Katz, W. L. Black pioneers p153-65 (7 and up)　　**920**

Bruce, Robert *See* Robert I, King of Scotland, 1274-1329

Bruce-Mitford, Miranda
The illustrated book of signs & symbols (7 and up)　　**302.2**

Bruchac, James
(jt. auth) Bruchac, J. When the Chenoo howls　　**398.2**

Bruchac, Joseph, 1942-
Bowman's store (7 and up)　　**92**
Four ancestors　　**398.2**
Includes the following stories: Greeting the sun, a Maushop story; The moon basket; The three hunters and the Great Bear; How Coyote stole fire; How the Earth began; Wihio and Grandfather Rock; Tacobud, the mountain that ate people; Clay Old Woman and Clay Old Man; Talking to the clay; The Cloud-Swallower giant; Gluskabe and the Snow Bird; Aglabem's dam; Raven and the tides; How the prairie became ocean; The bird whose wings made the wind; The whirlwind within; How Saynday tried to marry Whirlwind Girl; How the people pushed up the sky; The gift of stories, the gift of breath
The girl who married the Moon: tales from Native North America　　**398.2**
Contents: Arrowhead Finger; The abandoned girl; The girl and the Chenoo; The girl who escaped; Stonecoat; The girl who helped Thunder; The girl who married an Osage; The girl who almost married an owl; The poor Turkey Girl; The girl who gave birth to Water-Jar Boy; The Bear Woman; The Beauty Way—the ceremony of White-Painted Woman; How Pelican Girl was saved; Where the girl rescued her brother; Chipmunk Girl and Owl Woman; The girl who married the Moon
Going home
In Talking leaves　　**S C**
The heart of a chief　　**Fic**
Lasting echoes (7 and up)　　**970.004**
Turtle makes war on Man
In From sea to shining sea p252-55　　**810.8**
When the Chenoo howls　　**398.2**
Contents: The Stone Giant; The Flying Head; Ugly-face; Chenoo; Amankamek; Keewahkwee; Yakwawiak; Man Bear; The Spreaders; Aglebemu; Big Tree People; Toad Woman

Brundtland, Gro Harlem
See/See also pages in the following book(s):
Graham, K. Contemporary environmentalists p69-84 (7 and up)　　**920**
Price-Groff, C. Twentieth-century women political leaders (7 and up)　　**920**

Bruno, Leonard C.
Math and mathematicians　　**920**

Bruns, Roger
Jesse James　　**92**
Julius Caesar　　**92**

Bruun, Bertel
(jt. auth) Robbins, C. S. Birds of North America　　**598**

Bryan, Ashley, 1923-
Ashley Bryan's African tales, uh-huh　　**398.2**
Contents: The ox of the wonderful horns: Ananse the Spider in search of a fool; Frog and his two wives; Elephant and Frog go courting; Tortoise, Hare, and the sweet potatoes; The ox of the wonderful horns [story]
Beat the story-drum, pum-pum: Hen and Frog; Why Bush Cow and Elephant are bad friends; The husband who counted the spoonfuls; Why Frog and Snake never play together; How animals got their tails
Lion and the ostrich chicks: Lion and the ostrich chicks [story]; The son of the wind; Jackal's favorite game; The foolish boy
The cat's purr
In From sea to shining sea p260-63　　**810.8**

Bryan, Mike
(jt. auth) Ripken, C., Jr. Cal Ripken, Jr., my story　　**92**

Bryant, Barry, 1940-1997
(jt. auth) Pandell, K. Learning from the Dalai Lama　　**294.3**

Brynie, Faith Hickman, 1946-
101 questions your brain has asked about itself but couldn't answer . . . until now　　**612.8**

Bstan-'dzin-rgya-mtsho *See* Dalai Lama XIV, 1935-

Bubonic plague *See* Plague

Buchanan, James, 1791-1868
See/See also pages in the following book(s):
Presidents of a young republic　　**920**

Buck, Pearl S. (Pearl Sydenstricker), 1892-1973
See/See also pages in the following book(s):
Faber, D. Great lives: American literature p173-82　　**920**

Buckley, James, Jr.
America's greatest game　　**796.332**

Bud, not Buddy. Curtis, C. P.　　**Fic**

Buddha, Gautama *See* Gautama Buddha

Buddha. Demi　　**294.3**

The **Buddha** and the five hundred queens. Krishnaswami, U.
In Krishnaswami, U. Shower of gold: girls and women in the stories of India p24-30　　**398.2**

Buddhism
Demi. The Dalai Lama　　**92**
Ganeri, A. Buddhist　　**294.3**
Hewitt, C. Buddhism　　**294.3**
Pandell, K. Learning from the Dalai Lama　　**294.3**
Wangu, M. B. Buddhism (7 and up)　　**294.3**

Burg, David F.
The Great Depression (7 and up)   973.91
Burgan, Michael
Maryland
In America the beautiful, second series
973
Burgess, Warren
Dr. Burgess's atlas of marine aquarium fishes
639.34
Burgess Wise, David
The ultimate race car (7 and up)   796.72
The **burglar**. Kimmel, E. A.
In Kimmel, E. A. Sword of the samurai p73-
83   Fic
Burial
Colman, P. Corpses, coffins, and crypts (7 and
up)   393
Buried alive. Fletcher, R. J.   811
Buried in ice. Beattie, O.   998
Buried onions. Soto, G.   Fic
Buried treasure
Pickford, N. The atlas of shipwrecks & treasure
(7 and up)   910.4
Fiction
Barron, T. A. The Merlin effect   Fic
Ferris, J. All that glitters (7 and up)   Fic
Hamilton, V. The mystery of Drear House
Fic
Hobbs, W. Ghost canoe   Fic
Myers, W. D. The Mouse rap   Fic
Sachar, L. Holes   Fic
Stevenson, R. L. Treasure Island   Fic
Buried treasure. Hughes, M. S.   635
The **buried** treasure. Yep, L.
In Yep, L. The tree of dreams   398.2
Burke, Robert O'Hara, 1820-1861
See/See also pages in the following book(s):
Lomask, M. Great lives: exploration p24-32
920
Burks, Brian
Soldier boy   Fic
Walks Alone   Fic
Burleigh, Robert, 1936-
Hoops   811
Who said that?   808.88
Burma *See* Myanmar
Burnford, Sheila, 1918-1984
The incredible journey   Fic
Burnie, David
Bird   598
The concise encyclopedia of the human body
612
Dictionary of nature   570.3
Insects & spiders   595.7
Light   535
Plant   580
Tree   582.16
The **burning** questions of Bingo Brown. Byars, B.
C.   Fic
Burning up. Cooney, C. B.   Fic
Burns, Anthony, 1834-1862
About
Hamilton, V. Anthony Burns   92

Burns, Ken
(jt. auth) Ward, G. C. Shadow ball
796.357
Burns, Khephra
Black stars in orbit   920
Burr, Brooks M.
(jt. auth) Page, L. M. A field guide to freshwa-
ter fishes: North America north of Mexico
597
Burrell, R. E. C. (Roy Eric Charles), 1923-
Oxford first ancient history   909
Burrell, Roy Eric Charles *See* Burrell, R. E. C.
(Roy Eric Charles), 1923-
Burroughs, John, 1837-1921
About
Wadsworth, G. John Burroughs   92
Burt, William Henry, 1903-1987
A field guide to the mammals   599
Burton, John A.
(ed) The Atlas of endangered species. See The
Atlas of endangered species   333.95
Burton, Sir Richard Francis, 1821-1890
See/See also pages in the following book(s):
Lomask, M. Great lives: exploration p33-44
920
Bury my bones but keep my words. Fairman, T.
398.2
Bury my heart at Wounded Knee. Brown, D. A.
970.004
Burying grounds *See* Cemeteries
Busbey, Arthur Bresnahan, 1953-
Rocks & fossils. See Rocks & fossils   550
Busch, Frederick, 1941-
Custody
In Twelve shots: outstanding short stories
about guns p102-21   S C
Busenberg, Bonnie
Vanilla, chocolate, & strawberry   664
Bush, Barbara, 1925-
About
Greenberg, J. E. Barbara Pierce Bush, 1925-
92
Bush, George, 1924-
See/See also pages in the following book(s):
Presidents in a time of change   920
Bush lion. Scott, R.
In The Oxford book of scary tales p74-75
808.8
Bushman, Claudia L.
Mormons in America (7 and up)   289.3
Bushman, Richard L., 1931-
(jt. auth) Bushman, C. L. Mormons in America
289.3
Business & industry. Lutz, N. J.   920
Business and politics
Gay, K. Who's running the nation? (7 and up)
322
Business depression, 1929-1939 *See* Great De-
pression, 1929-1939
Business enterprises
See also Corporations
Karnes, F. A. Girls and young women entrepre-
neurs (7 and up)   658

C

El **caballito** of seven colors. Winther, B.
  In Winther, B. Plays from Hispanic tales
                              812

Cabeza de Vaca, Alvar Nuñez *See* Nuñez Cabeza de Vaca, Alvar, 16th cent.

The **cabinet**. Feinberg, B. S.   **352.24**

Cabinet officers
  Bredeson, C. Henry Cisneros   **92**
  Dolan, E. F. Shaping U.S. foreign policy (7 and up)   **327.73**
  Feinberg, B. S. The cabinet   **352.24**
  Hasday, J. L. Madeleine Albright   **92**
  Howard, M. Madeleine Albright   **92**

Cabot, John, 1450-1498
  See/See also pages in the following book(s):
  Fritz, J. Around the world in a hundred years p63-67   **910.4**
  Lomask, M. Great lives: exploration p57-61
                               920
  West, D. C. Braving the North Atlantic
                              970.01

Cabot, Sebastian, ca. 1474-1557
  See/See also pages in the following book(s):
  West, D. C. Braving the North Atlantic
                              970.01

Cabral, Pedro Alvares, 1460?-1526?
  See/See also pages in the following book(s):
  Fritz, J. Around the world in a hundred years p59-61   **910.4**

Cadnum, Michael
  Edge (7 and up)   **Fic**
  Heat (7 and up)   **Fic**
  In a dark wood (7 and up)   **Fic**
  Rundown (7 and up)   **Fic**
  Zero at the bone (7 and up)   **Fic**

Caesar, Julius, 100-44 B.C.
  About
  Bruns, R. Julius Caesar   **92**
  See/See also pages in the following book(s):
  Brooks, P. S. Cleopatra p26-60 (7 and up)
                               92
  Nardo, D. Rulers of ancient Rome (7 and up)
                              920

The **cage**. Sender, R. M.   **940.53**

Cage birds
  Zeaman, J. Birds   **636.5**

Cages. Kehret, P.   **Fic**

Cages. Myers, W. D.
  In Center stage   **812.008**

Cahuilla Indians
  Bean, L. J. The Cahuilla
    In Indians of North America series
                             970.004

Cairns, Conrad
  Medieval castles (7 and up)   **728.8**

Calabro, Marian
  The perilous journey of the Donner Party
                             978

Calamity Jane, 1852-1903
  About
  Faber, D. Calamity Jane   **92**

Sanford, W. R. Calamity Jane: frontier original
                               92
  See/See also pages in the following book(s):
  Calvert, P. Great lives: the American frontier p44-54   **920**

Calcium
  Farndon, J. Calcium
    In The Elements [Benchmark Bks.]   **546**

A **Caldecott** celebration. Marcus, L. S.   **741.6**

Caldecott Medal
  Marcus, L. S. A Caldecott celebration
                              741.6
  Newbery and Caldecott Medal books, 1966-1975
                              028.5
  Newbery and Caldecott medal books, 1976-1985
                              028.5
  Newbery and Caldecott medalists and honor book winners   **011.6**

Caleb's choice. Wisler, G. C.   **Fic**

Calendars
  Marks, D. F. Let's celebrate today   **394.26**

California
  Altman, L. J. California
    In Celebrate the states   **973**
  Heinrichs, A. California
    In America the beautiful, second series
                              973
              Fiction
  Cadnum, M. Edge (7 and up)   **Fic**
  Cooney, C. B. Flash fire (7 and up)   **Fic**
  Cottonwood, J. Quake!   **Fic**
  Hobbs, V. How far would you have gotten if I hadn't called you back? (7 and up)   **Fic**
  Holman, F. Real   **Fic**
  Koertge, R. Tiger, tiger, burning bright   **Fic**
  Koss, A. G. The Ashwater experiment   **Fic**
  Larson, R. What I know now (7 and up)
                              Fic
  Levy, M. Run for your life (7 and up)   **Fic**
  Lindquist, S. H. Summer soldiers   **Fic**
  Soto, G. Baseball in April, and other stories
                             S C
  Soto, G. Local news   **S C**
  Soto, G. The pool party   **Fic**
  Steinbeck, J. The red pony   **Fic**
  Uchida, Y. A jar of dreams   **Fic**
        Gold discoveries
  See/See also pages in the following book(s):
  Yount, L. Frontiers of freedom p39-52 (7 and up)   **978**
      Gold discoveries—Fiction
  Cushman, K. The ballad of Lucy Whipple
                              Fic
  Fleischman, S. Bandit's moon   **Fic**

California Blue. Klass, D.   **Fic**

The **California** condor. Silverstein, A.   **598**

California condors *See* Condors

Calisthenics *See* Gymnastics

Call me Francis Tucket. Paulsen, G. See note under Paulsen, G. Mr. Tucket   **Fic**

The **call** of the sea. McCaughrean, G.
  In McCaughrean, G. The crystal pool: myths and legends of the world p57-60
                              398.2

The **call** of the wild. London, J.   **Fic**

Canfield, Jack, 1944-
(comp) Chicken soup for the kid's soul. See
Chicken soup for the kid's soul **158**
(comp) Chicken soup for the teenage soul. See
Chicken soup for the teenage soul **158**

Cann, Kate, 1954-
Living in the world **158**

Cannibal village
In The Dancing fox: Arctic folktales p84-91
398.2

Cannon, A. E. (Ann Edwards)
The shadow brothers (7 and up) **Fic**

Cannon, Ann Edwards *See* Cannon, A. E. (Ann Edwards)

Cannon, Annie Jump, 1863-1941
See/See also pages in the following book(s):
Camp, C. A. American astronomers p36-43
920

Canoes and canoeing
Fiction
Conly, J. L. Trout summer **Fic**
Dygard, T. J. River danger (7 and up) **Fic**

Canterbury tales. Cohen, B. **821**

Canto familiar. Soto, G. **811**

Cantor, Georg, 1845-1918
See/See also pages in the following book(s):
Henderson, H. Modern mathematicians (7 and up) **920**

Cantor, Milton, 1925-
(ed) Documents of American history. See Documents of American history **973**

Canyons. Paulsen, G. **Fic**

Cape Town (South Africa)
Stein, R. C. Cape Town **968**

Capek, Michael, 1947-
Murals **751.7**

Caper, William
Whoopi Goldberg **92**

Capital punishment
The Death penalty: opposing viewpoints (7 and up) **364.66**
Does capital punishment deter crime? (7 and up) **364.66**
Herda, D. J. Furman v. Georgia (7 and up) **345**
Stewart, G. The death penalty (7 and up) **364.66**
Wolf, R. V. Capital punishment (7 and up) **364.66**
See/See also pages in the following book(s):
Nardo, D. The Bill of Rights p75-85 (7 and up) **342**

Capitalism
See also Entrepreneurship

Capitalists and financiers
Kent, Z. Andrew Carnegie **92**
Meltzer, M. The many lives of Andrew Carnegie (7 and up) **92**

Capone, Al, 1899-1947
About
King, D. C. Al Capone and the roaring twenties **92**

Capote, Truman, 1924-1984
The Thanksgiving visitor **Fic**

Captain Jack *See* Kintpuash, Modoc Chief, 1837?-1873

Captain Kate. Reeder, C. **Fic**

Caras, Roger A.
A most dangerous journey (7 and up)
599.67

Carbon
Sparrow, G. Carbon
In The Elements [Benchmark Bks.] **546**

Carbon 14 dating *See* Radiocarbon dating

Carbon dioxide greenhouse effect *See* Greenhouse effect

Carbone, Elisa Lynn, 1954-
Stealing freedom **Fic**

Card, Orson Scott
Children of the mind. See note under Card, O. S. Ender's game **Fic**
Ender's game (7 and up) **Fic**
Speaker for the Dead. See note under Card, O. S. Ender's game **Fic**
Xenocide. See note under Card, O. S. Ender's game **Fic**
See/See also pages in the following book(s):
Reid, S. E. Presenting young adult science fiction p36-52 (7 and up) **813.009**

Cardiovascular system
See also Blood—Circulation; Heart
Ballard, C. The heart and circulatory system
612.1
Johansson, P. Heart disease **616.1**
Simon, S. The heart **612.1**

Cardona, Manuel, 1934-
See/See also pages in the following book(s):
Oleksy, W. G. Hispanic-American scientists (7 and up) **920**

Cardús, David, 1922-
See/See also pages in the following book(s):
Oleksy, W. G. Hispanic-American scientists (7 and up) **920**

Care, Medical *See* Medical care

Care of the dying *See* Terminal care

Career discovery encyclopedia **331.7**

Career education *See* Vocational education

Career guidance *See* Vocational guidance

Careers *See* Occupations

The **Caribbean.** See Hodge, A. The West Indies
972.9

Caribbean region
See also West Indies
Antiquities
Macaulay, D. Ship **387.2**
Fiction
Taylor, T. The cay **Fic**
Taylor, T. Timothy of the cay **Fic**
History
See/See also pages in the following book(s):
Marrin, A. Terror of the Spanish Main: Sir Henry Morgan and his buccaneers (7 and up)
92

Caricatures *See* Cartoons and caricatures

Caring. McKean, T.
In McKean, T. Into the candlelit room and other strange tales p89-111 **S C**

Cartoons and caricatures—*Continued*
Tallarico, T. Drawing and cartooning monsters
743

Carver, George Washington, 1864?-1943
About
Adair, G. George Washington Carver   92
See/See also pages in the following book(s):
Hacker, C. Great African Americans in history
920
Haskins, J. Outward dreams p63-71   609

Carwardine, Mark
Whales, dolphins, and porpoises (7 and up)
599.5

Cary, Eve
The rights of students (7 and up)   344

Casalini, Max
(jt. auth) Ventura, P. Food   641.3

Casals, Pablo, 1876-1973
About
Garza, H. Pablo Casals   92

The **case** book of Sherlock Holmes. Doyle, Sir A. C.
In Doyle, Sir A. C. The complete Sherlock Holmes   S C

A **case** of identity. Doyle, Sir A. C.
In Doyle, Sir A. C. Adventures of Sherlock Holmes   S C
In Doyle, Sir A. C. The complete Sherlock Holmes   S C

The **case** of Roe v. Wade. Stevens, L. A.
344

The **case** of the Baker Street Irregular. Newman, R.   Fic

The **case** of the bewitched books. Boiko, C.
In The Big book of holiday plays p78-86   812.008

The **case** of the firecrackers. Yep, L. See note under Yep, L. The case of the Goblin Pearls   Fic

The **case** of the Goblin Pearls. Yep, L.   Fic

The **case** of the lion dance. Yep, L. See note under Yep, L. The case of the Goblin Pearls   Fic

Caseley, Judith, 1951-
Losing Louisa (7 and up)   Fic

Caselli, Giovanni
In search of Troy   939
In search of Tutankhamun   932

Casey Jones, railroad man. Cohn, A.
In From sea to shining sea p170-71   810.8

Cash, Terry
175 more science experiments to amuse and amaze your friends   507.8

The **cask** of Amontillado. Poe, E. A.
In Poe, E. A. Tales of Edgar Allan Poe p51-59   S C

Cassady, Marsh, 1936-
(ed) The Book of monologues for aspiring actors. See The Book of monologues for aspiring actors   808.82

Cassandra (Legendary character)
Fiction
McLaren, C. Inside the walls of Troy (7 and up)   Fic

Cassatt, Mary, 1844-1926
See/See also pages in the following book(s):
Glubok, S. Great lives: painting p1-9   920
Sills, L. Visions p6-19   920

Cassell's French dictionary: French-English, English-French   443

Cassell's German-English, English-German dictionary   433

Cassell's Italian dictionary: Italian-English, English-Italian   453

Cassell's Latin dictionary: Latin-English, English-Latin   473

Cassell's Spanish dictionary. See Cassell's Spanish-English, English-Spanish dictionary   463

Cassell's Spanish-English, English-Spanish dictionary   463

Cassie, Brian, 1953-
National Audubon Society first field guide: trees   582.16

Cassirer, Nadine Gordimer *See* Gordimer, Nadine, 1923-

Cassutt, Michael
Who's who in space   920.003

Cast two shadows. Rinaldi, A.   Fic

Castellanos, Rosario
See/See also pages in the following book(s):
Shirey, L. Latin American writers (7 and up)   860.9

Castle, Kate
Ballet   792.8
My ballet book   792.8

Castle at war. Langley, A.   940.1

Castle in the air. Jones, D. W.   Fic

The **castle** of Llyr. Alexander, L. See note under Alexander, L. The book of three   Fic

Castles
Biesty, S. Stephen Biesty's cross-sections: Castle   940.1
Cairns, C. Medieval castles (7 and up)   728.8
Day, M. The world of castles and forts   355.7
Gravett, C. Castle   728.8
Langley, A. Castle at war   940.1
Macaulay, D. Castle   728.8
Macdonald, F. A medieval castle   940.1
Nardo, D. The medieval castle (7 and up)   940.1
Steele, P. Castles   728.8

Castro, Chava
(jt. auth) Gravelle, K. What's going on down there?   612.6

Castro, Nick
(jt. auth) Gravelle, K. What's going on down there?   612.6

Caswell, Helen Rayburn, 1923-
Sedna, the sea goddess
In From sea to shining sea p18-22   810.8

Chavez, Cesar, 1927-1993
About
Cedeño, M. E. Cesar Chavez   92
Collins, D. R. Farmworker's friend: the story of Cesar Chavez   92
See/See also pages in the following book(s):
Morey, J. Famous Mexican Americans p1-13   920
Streissguth, T. Legendary labor leaders (7 and up)   920

Chávez, Denise, 1948-
The closet
In Growing up Latino p85-98   810.8

Cheap raw material. Meltzer, M.   331.3

Cheat the moon. Hermes, P.   Fic

Check, William A.
AIDS (7 and up)   616.97

Check. Ellis, S.
In Ellis, S. Back of beyond   S C

Checkers. Dickinson, P.
In Dickinson, P. The lion tamer's daughter and other stories p105-63   S C

Checkers. Marsden, J.   Fic

Cheetahs
MacMillan, D. M. Cheetahs   599.75
Thompson, S. E. Built for speed   599.75

Chemical dependency: opposing viewpoints (7 and up)   362.29

Chemical elements
The Elements [Benchmark Bks.]   546
Elements [Grolier]   546
Newton, D. E. Chemical elements   546

Chemical engineering
See also Biotechnology

Chemical pollution *See* Pollution

Chemical warfare
See/See also pages in the following book(s):
Weapons of mass destruction: opposing viewpoints (7 and up)   358

Chemistry
Challoner, J. The visual dictionary of chemistry   540
Gardner, R. Science projects about kitchen chemistry (7 and up)   540.7
Oxlade, C. Chemistry   540.7

Chemists
Hager, T. Linus Pauling and the chemistry of life (7 and up)   92
Pasachoff, N. E. Marie Curie and the science of radioactivity (7 and up)   92
Poynter, M. Marie Curie: discoverer of radium   92

Ch'en, Hsing-shen *See* Chern, Shiing-shen, 1911-

Chen, Mary F.
Knuckles
In American eyes p62-79   S C

Cheney, Glenn Alan
Nuclear proliferation (7 and up)   327.1

Cheng, Chen-sun
A young painter [biography of Wang Yani]   92

Cheng, Pang Guek, 1950-
Mongolia   951.7

Chenoo. Bruchac, J.
In Bruchac, J. When the Chenoo howls   398.2

Chern, Shiing-shen, 1911-
See/See also pages in the following book(s):
Henderson, H. Modern mathematicians (7 and up)   920

Cherokee Indians
Bial, R. The Cherokee   970.004
Klausner, J. Sequoyah's gift   92
Perdue, T. The Cherokee
In Indians of North America series   970.004
Schwarz, M. Wilma Mankiller   92
Shumate, J. Sequoyah   92
Sonneborn, L. Will Rogers, Cherokee entertainer   92

Cherokee Nation v. Georgia. Sherrow, V.   346

Chesapeake Bay (Md. and Va.)
Fiction
Paterson, K. Jacob have I loved   Fic

Chess
Keene, R. D. The Simon & Schuster pocket book of chess (7 and up)   794.1

The **chessmen** of doom. Bellairs, J. See note under Bellairs, J. The curse of the blue figurine   Fic

Chesterman, Charles W.
The Audubon Society field guide to North American rocks and minerals   549

Cheyenne Indians
Henry, C. E. Ben Nighthorse Campbell   92
Hoig, S. The Cheyenne
In Indians of North America series   970.004
Viola, H. J. It is a good day to die   973.8
See/See also pages in the following book(s):
Brown, D. A. Bury my heart at Wounded Knee p331-49 (7 and up)   970.004
Ehrlich, A. Wounded Knee: an Indian history of the American West   970.004

The **Cheyenne** prophet. Brown, D. A.
In Brown, D. A. Dee Brown's folktales of the Native American p46-59   398.2

Cheyenne revenge [excerpt] Trafzer, C. E.
In Talking leaves   S C

Chiappe, Luis M.
(jt. auth) Dingus, L. The tiniest giants   567.9

Chicago (Ill.)
Fiction
Cisneros, S. The house on Mango Street (7 and up)   Fic
Deaver, J. R. Say goodnight, Gracie (7 and up)   Fic
Pinkwater, D. M. The education of Robert Nifkin (7 and up)   Fic
Race relations
See/See also pages in the following book(s):
Cooper, M. L. Bound for the promised land p21-45   305.8
Social conditions
Harvey, B. C. Jane Addams   92

Chicago blues. Deaver, J. R.   Fic

Children—*Continued*
Abuse
See Child abuse
Adoption
See Adoption
Civil rights
Malaspina, A. Children's rights (7 and up)
305.23
See/See also pages in the following book(s):
Carter, J. Talking peace p163-69 (7 and up)
327.1

Employment
See also Moneymaking projects for children
Bartoletti, S. C. Growing up in coal country
331.3
Bartoletti, S. C. Kids on strike! **331.8**
Freedman, R. Kids at work **331.3**
Gay, K. Child labor (7 and up) **331.3**
Gourley, C. Good girl work **331.3**
Kuklin, S. Iqbal Masih and the crusaders against child slavery (7 and up) **331.3**
Meltzer, M. Cheap raw material (7 and up)
331.3
Parker, D. L. Stolen dreams **331.3**
Springer, J. Listen to us (7 and up) **331.3**
Law and legislation
Gold, S. D. In re Gault (1967) (7 and up)
345
Greenberg, K. E. Adolescent rights (7 and up)
346
Landau, E. Your legal rights (7 and up)
346
Malaspina, A. Children's rights (7 and up)
305.23
Nunez, S. J. And justice for all (7 and up)
346
United States
Greenberg, J. E. Young people's letters to the president **973**
United States—Social conditions
Child welfare: opposing viewpoints (7 and up)
362.7
Children, Retarded *See* Mentally handicapped children
Children & books. Sutherland, Z. **028.5**
Children and television *See* Television and children
Children of divorced parents
Schultz, M. A. Teens with single parents (7 and up) **306.8**
Children of God (Movement)
See/See also pages in the following book(s):
Cohen, D. Cults p118-31 (7 and up) **291.9**
Children of immigrants
Kosof, A. Living in two worlds (7 and up)
325.73
Children of single parents *See* Single parent family
Children of the Dust Bowl. Stanley, J. **371.9**
Children of the mind. Card, O. S. See note under Card, O. S. Ender's game **Fic**
Children of the river. Crew, L. **Fic**
Children of the wolf. Yolen, J. **Fic**

The **children** of Topaz. Tunnell, M. O.
940.53
Children of working parents
See/See also pages in the following book(s):
Working women: opposing viewpoints p35-43 (7 and up) **331.4**
Children's Book Council (New York, N.Y.)
Children's books: awards & prizes. See Children's books: awards & prizes **028.5**
Notable children's trade books in the field of social studies. See Notable children's trade books in the field of social studies **016.3**
Outstanding science trade books for children. See Outstanding science trade books for children **016.5**
Children's book review index **028.1**
Children's books and their creators **028.5**
Children's books: awards & prizes **028.5**
Children's books from other countries **028.5**
Children's books in children's hands **028.5**
Children's catalog **011.6**
Children's courts *See* Juvenile courts
Children's history of the 20th century **909.82**
Children's illustrated encyclopedia **031**
Children's libraries
See also Young adults' library services
Jay, M. E. Ready-to-go reading incentive programs for schools and libraries **028.5**
Minkel, W. Delivering Web reference services to young people **025.04**
Periodicals
Journal of Youth Services in Libraries
027.6205
Children's literature
See also Caldecott Medal; Carnegie medal; Fairy tales; Kate Greenaway medal; Newbery Medal; Picture books for children
Bibliography
Anderson, V. Fiction sequels for readers 10 to 16 **016.8**
Barker, K. Outstanding books for children and young people **028.5**
Bauermeister, E. Let's hear it for the girls
028.1
Children's books: awards & prizes **028.5**
Children's books from other countries
028.5
Children's catalog **011.6**
Cooper-Mullin, A. Once upon a heroine
028.1
Dodson, S. 100 books for girls to grow on
028.1
Gillespie, J. T. Guides to collection development for children and young adults **011.6**
Holsinger, M. P. The ways of war **016.8**
Kennemer, P. K. Using literature to teach middle grades about war **016.8**
National Council of Teachers of English. Committee on the Junior High and Middle School Booklist. Your reading **011.6**
Newbery and Caldecott medalists and honor book winners **011.6**
Odean, K. Great books for boys **028.1**
Odean, K. Great books for girls **028.1**

The **Chinese-American** experience. Wu, Dana
Y.-H.   **305.8**

The **Chinese** American family album. Hoobler, D.
                                           305.8

Chinese Americans
    See also Chinese—United States
    Hoobler, D. The Chinese American family al-
       bum   **305.8**
    Wu, Dana Y.-H. The Chinese-American experi-
       ence   **305.8**
    See/See also pages in the following book(s):
    Asian Americans: opposing viewpoints (7 and
       up)   **305.8**
    Takaki, R. T. Strangers at the gates again p43-
       55 (7 and up)   **305.8**
                  Biography
    Yep, L. The lost garden   **92**
                  Fiction
    Lord, B. B. In the Year of the Boar and Jackie
       Robinson   **Fic**
    Yep, L. The amah   **Fic**
    Yep, L. The case of the Goblin Pearls   **Fic**
    Yep, L. Child of the owl   **Fic**
    Yep, L. The cook's family   **Fic**
    Yep, L. Dragonwings   **Fic**
    Yep, L. Later, gator   **Fic**
    Yep, L. Ribbons   **Fic**
    Yep, L. The star fisher   **Fic**
    Yep, L. Thief of hearts   **Fic**

Chinese artists *See* Artists, Chinese

The **Chinese** babies. Wynne-Jones, T.
    In Wynne-Jones, T. Lord of the Fries and
       other stories p173-214   **S C**

Chinese civilization *See* China—Civilization

Chinese language
    Young, E. Voices of the heart   **179**

Chinese science *See* Science—China

Chinook Indians
    Trafzer, C. E. The Chinook
    In Indians of North America series
                                         970.004

A **chip** of glass ruby. Gordimer, N.
    In Somehow tenderness survives p105-18
                                             S C

Chipmunk Girl and Owl Woman. Bruchac, J.
    In Bruchac, J. The girl who married the
       Moon: tales from Native North America
       p108-15   **398.2**

Chippewa Indians *See* Ojibwa Indians

Chisholm, Shirley, 1924-
    See/See also pages in the following book(s):
    Haskins, J. One more river to cross   **920**

Chiu, Christina
    Lives of notable Asian Americans: literature and
       education (7 and up)   **920**
    Teen guide to staying sober (7 and up)
                                          362.292

Chivalry
    See also Medieval civilization
    Bulfinch, T. Bulfinch's Mythology   **291.1**
                  Fiction
    Twain, M. A Connecticut Yankee in King Ar-
       thur's court   **Fic**

Chocolate
    See/See also pages in the following book(s):
    Busenberg, B. Vanilla, chocolate, & strawberry
       p39-71   **664**
    Johnson, S. A. Tomatoes, potatoes, corn, and
       beans p95-109   **641.3**

The **chocolate** war. Cormier, R.   **Fic**

Choctaw Indians
    McKee, J. O. The Choctaw
    In Indians of North America series
                                         970.004
                  Fiction
    Harrell, B. O. Longwalker's journey   **Fic**

Choi, Sook Nyul
    Echoes of the white giraffe. See note under
       Choi, S. N. Year of impossible goodbyes
                                              Fic
    Gathering of pearls. See note under Choi, S. N.
       Year of impossible goodbyes   **Fic**
    Year of impossible goodbyes   **Fic**

Cholera
    See/See also pages in the following book(s):
    Farrell, J. Invisible enemies p167-92 (7 and up)
                                            614.4

Choosing up sides. Ritter, J. H.   **Fic**

Chopin, Kate, 1851-1904
    See/See also pages in the following book(s):
    Lyons, M. E. Keeping secrets (7 and up)
                                              920

Choreographers
    Freedman, R. Martha Graham, a dancer's life (7
       and up)   **92**
    Lewis-Ferguson, J. Alvin Ailey, Jr.: a life in
       dance   **92**

The **chosen**. Harrah, M.
    In Night terrors   **S C**

Chrisman, Arthur Bowie, 1889-1953
    Ah Tcha the sleeper
    In A Newbery Halloween p75-82   **S C**

Christ *See* Jesus Christ

Christian, Spencer
    Shake, rattle, and roll   **551.2**

Christian fiction
                  Bibliography
    Walker, B. J. Developing Christian fiction col-
       lections for children and adults   **025.2**

Christian fundamentalism
                  Fiction
    Peck, R. The last safe place on earth (7 and up)
                                              Fic

Christian life
                  Fiction
    Brooks, B. Asylum for Nightface (7 and up)
                                              Fic
    Coman, C. Tell me everything   **Fic**
    Morpurgo, M. The war of Jenkins' ear   **Fic**

Christian missionaries
    Dolan, S. Junípero Serra   **92**

Christian missions
                  Fiction
    O'Dell, S. Zia   **Fic**

Christian saints
    Armstrong, C. Lives and legends of the saints
                                              920

Church, Frederic Edwin, 1826-1900
See/See also pages in the following book(s):
Glubok, S. Great lives: painting p24-31
920

Church
See also Christianity
Church and state
Andryszewski, T. School prayer (7 and up)
344
Dudley, M. E. Engel v. Vitale (1962) (7 and up)
344
Gaustad, E. S. Church and state in America (7 and up) **322**
See/See also pages in the following book(s):
Civil liberties: opposing viewpoints p119-59 (7 and up) **323**
Church and state in America. Gaustad, E. S.
322
Church history
See also United States—Church history
The Rise of Christianity (7 and up) **270**
1517-1648, Reformation
See Reformation
Dictionaries
The Oxford dictionary of the Christian Church
270
Church of Christ, Scientist *See* Christian Science
Church of Jesus Christ of Latter-day Saints
Bushman, C. L. Mormons in America (7 and up) **289.3**
Nash, C. R. The Mormon Trail and the Latter-Day Saints in American history **289.3**
Williams, J. K. The Mormons (7 and up) **289.3**
Churchill, Sir Winston, 1874-1965
About
Severance, J. B. Winston Churchill **92**
Ciara's song. Norton, A. See note under Norton, A. Witch World [series] **Fic**
Cicero, Marcus Tullius, 106-43 B.C.
See/See also pages in the following book(s):
Nardo, D. Rulers of ancient Rome (7 and up)
920
Ciencin, Scott
Dinoverse **Fic**
Ciment, James
Scholastic encyclopedia of the American Indian
970.004
Cincinnati (Ohio)
History
See/See also pages in the following book(s):
Katz, W. L. Black pioneers p49-58 (7 and up)
920
Cinder-Riley. Boiko, C.
In The Big book of holiday plays p271-78
812.008
Cinderella (Ballet)
See/See also pages in the following book(s):
McCaughrean, G. The Random House book of stories from the ballet p36-47 **792.8**
Cinematography
Hamilton, J. Special effects in film and television **791.43**

Ciphers
Huckle, H. The secret code book **652**
Circle of love. Nixon, J. L. See note under Nixon, J. L. A family apart **Fic**
Circle of magic: Briar's book. Pierce, T. **Fic**
Circle of magic: Daja's book. Pierce, T. **Fic**
Circle of magic: Sandry's book. Pierce, T.
Fic
Circle of magic: Tris's book. Pierce, T. **Fic**
A **circle** unbroken. Hotze, S. **Fic**
The **circuit**. Jiménez, F.
In Help wanted: short stories about young people working **S C**
In Jiménez, F. The circuit: stories from the life of a migrant child p73-83 **S C**
In Leaving home: stories p53-62 **808.8**
The **circuit:** stories from the life of a migrant child. Jiménez, F. **S C**
Circulatory system *See* Cardiovascular system
The **circulatory** system. Silverstein, A. **612.1**
Circumnavigation *See* Voyages around the world
Circus
Andronik, C. M. Prince of Humbugs: a life of P.T. Barnum **92**
Granfield, L. Circus **791.3**
Cisneros, Henry
About
Bredeson, C. Henry Cisneros **92**
See/See also pages in the following book(s):
Morey, J. Famous Mexican Americans p14-26
920
Cisneros, Sandra
The house on Mango Street (7 and up) **Fic**
The monkey garden
In Growing up Latino p288-91 **810.8**
My Lucy friend who smells like corn
In Who do you think you are? p119-21
S C
About
Mirriam-Goldberg, C. Sandra Cisneros **92**
Citations, Bibliographical *See* Bibliographical citations
Cities and towns
Millard, A. A street through time **936**
Cities and towns, ruined, extinct, etc. *See* Extinct cities
Cities of the world [series]
Stein, R. C. Cape Town **968**
City: a story of Roman planning and construction. Macaulay, D. **711**
City life
Fiction
Fleischman, P. Seedfolks **Fic**
The **City** of Brass. Philip, N.
In Philip, N. The Arabian nights p24-32
398.2
The **city** of gold and lead. Christopher, J. See note under Christopher, J. The White Mountains
Fic
City of the Gods. Arnold, C. **972**

Classical dictionaries
The Oxford companion to classical civilization
938.003

Classical music *See* Music

Classical mythology

See also Eros (Greek deity); Psyche (Greek deity)
Craft, M. Cupid and Psyche   **292**
Fisher, L. E. Cyclops   **292**
Fleischman, P. Dateline: Troy (7 and up)
   292
Hamilton, E. Mythology   **292**
McCaughrean, G. Greek gods and goddesses
   292
Morley, J. Greek myths   **292**
Pickels, D. E. Egyptian kings and queens and classical deities   **930**
Dictionaries
Daly, K. N. Greek and Roman mythology A to Z   **292**

Classification

Books

See Books—Classification
Classification, Dewey Decimal *See* Dewey Decimal Classification

Classified catalogs
Children's catalog   **011.6**
Senior high school library catalog   **011.6**
Classroom Computer Learning. See Technology and Learning   **371.305**
Classroom Computer News. See Technology and Learning   **371.305**

Clay, Cassius *See* Ali, Muhammad, 1942-

Clay, Rebecca
Ukraine   **947**
Clay Old Woman and Clay Old Man. Bruchac, J.
In Bruchac, J. Four ancestors p45-47
   398.2
Clay v. United States. Freedman, S.   **343**

Clayton, L. (Lawrence)
Alcohol drug dangers   **362.292**
Diet pill drug dangers   **615**
Clayton, Lawrence *See* Clayton, L. (Lawrence)
Clean as a whistle. Coville, B.
In Coville, B. Oddly enough p43-59
   S C

Cleanliness
See also Sanitation
Clear as mud. Jennings, P.
In Jennings, P. Undone! p75-92   **S C**

Cleary, Beverly
The baddest witch in the world
In A Newbery Halloween p1-12   **S C**
Dear Mr. Henshaw   **Fic**
A girl from Yamhill: a memoir   **92**
Henry and Ribsy go fishing
In A Newbery zoo   **S C**
My own two feet   **92**
Ramona, the sheep suit, and the three wise persons
In A Newbery Christmas p163-84   **S C**
Strider   **Fic**

Cleaver, Bill
(jt. auth) Cleaver, V. Where the lilies bloom
   Fic
Cleaver, Vera
Where the lilies bloom   **Fic**
Clemenc, Ana K., 1888-1956
About
Stanley, J. Big Annie of Calumet   **331.8**
Clemens, Roger
About
Macht, N. L. Roger Clemens   **92**
Clemens, Samuel Langhorne *See* Twain, Mark, 1835-1910
Cleopatra, Queen of Egypt, d. 30 B.C.
About
Brooks, P. S. Cleopatra (7 and up)   **92**
Stanley, D. Cleopatra   **92**
See/See also pages in the following book(s):
Meltzer, M. Ten queens p11-23   **920**
Clergy
Fiction
Craven, M. I heard the owl call my name (7 and up)   **Fic**
Newton, S. I will call it Georgie's blues (7 and up)   **Fic**
Seago, K. Matthew unstrung (7 and up)
   Fic

Cleveland, Grover, 1837-1908
See/See also pages in the following book(s):
Presidents of a growing country   **920**
Cleveland (Ohio)
History
See/See also pages in the following book(s):
Katz, W. L. Black pioneers p72-82 (7 and up)
   920
Clever Mistress Murray. Jagendorf, M. A.
In From sea to shining sea p68-73   **810.8**
Click! fun with photography. Price, S.   **771**
Cliff hanger. Skurzynski, G.   **Fic**
Clifford, Nick
Incredible earth   **551.1**
Clifton, James A.
The Potawatomi
In Indians of North America series
   970.004

Climate
See also Greenhouse effect; Meteorology; United States—Climate; Weather
Arnold, C. El Niño   **551.6**
Encyclopedia of climate and weather   **551.6**
Climbing plants
Petrides, G. A. A field guide to trees and shrubs
   582.16
Climo, Shirley, 1928-
Magic & mischief   **398.2**
Includes the following stories: The giant of Castle Treen; The very old woman and the Piskey; The widow and the Spriggans of Trencrom Hill; Tom Treverrow and the Knackers; Pleasing Betty Stoggs; The changeling of Brea Vean; The bewitching of Sea Pink; The mermaid of Zennor; The cornish teeny-tiny; Duffy and the Bucca
Clinton, Bill, 1946-
About
Cwiklik, R. Bill Clinton   **92**
Kelly, M. Bill Clinton (7 and up)   **92**

Cocked & locked. Lynch, C.
In Twelve shots: outstanding short stories about guns p25-43   **S C**

Code deciphering *See* Cryptography

Codes *See* Ciphers

Cody, William Frederick *See* Buffalo Bill, 1846-1917

Cody. Brooks, B. See note under Brooks, B. Zip   **Fic**

Coe, Lewis, 1911-
The telegraph   **621.383**

Cofer, Judith Ortiz *See* Ortiz Cofer, Judith, 1952-

Coffey, Rosemary K.
America as story   **016.813**

Coffin, Tristram Potter, 1922-
(ed) The Folklore of American holidays. See The Folklore of American holidays   **394.26**

Cohabitation *See* Unmarried couples

Cohen, Barbara, 1932-1992
Canterbury tales   **821**
Contents: The nun's priest's tale; The pardoner's tale; The wife of Bath's tale; The franklin's tale

Cohen, Caron Lee
Sally Ann Thunder Ann Whirlwind Crockett meets Mike Fink, Snappin' Turkle
In From sea to shining sea p118-20   **810.8**

Cohen, Daniel, 1936-
Animal rights (7 and up)   **179**
Cloning (7 and up)   **571.8**
Cults (7 and up)   **291.9**
Dangerous ghosts   **133.1**
Ghostly warnings   **133.1**
Ghosts of the deep   **133.1**
Great conspiracies and elaborate cover-ups (7 and up)   **001.9**
The Manhattan Project (7 and up)   **623.4**
Prophets of doom (7 and up)   **133.3**
Real vampires   **398**
Werewolves   **398**

Cohen, Hennig
(ed) The Folklore of American holidays. See The Folklore of American holidays   **394.26**

Cohen, Richard M., 1938-
(jt. auth) Neft, D. S. The sports encyclopedia: baseball   **796.357**

Cohn, Amy
Casey Jones, railroad man
In From sea to shining sea p170-71   **810.8**

Jack and the two-bullet hunt
In From sea to shining sea p90-91   **810.8**
Strong as Annie Christmas
In From sea to shining sea p277-79   **810.8**

With a way, hey, Mister Stormalong
In From sea to shining sea p104-06   **810.8**

(comp) From sea to shining sea. See From sea to shining sea   **810.8**

Coil, Suzanne M.
Harriet Beecher Stowe (7 and up)   **92**

Robert Hutchings Goddard (7 and up)   **92**

Coincoin, Maria Theresa, 1742-1816
See/See also pages in the following book(s):
Haskins, J. African American entrepreneurs p7-11   **920**

Coins
Hughes, R. P. Fell's official know-it-all guide: coins   **737.4**

Colbert, Jan
(ed) Dear Dr. King. See Dear Dr. King   **323.1**

Colby, Vineta
(ed) World authors, 1975-1980. See World authors, 1975-1980   **920.003**
(ed) World authors, 1980-1985. See World authors, 1980-1985   **920.003**
(ed) World authors, 1985-1990. See World authors, 1985-1990   **920.003**

Cold harbour. Aiken, J.
In Aiken, J. A foot in the grave p7-26   **S C**

Cold Shoulder Road. Aiken, J. See note under Aiken, J. The wolves of Willoughby Chase   **Fic**

A **cold** stake. Karr, P. A.
In Vampires: a collection of original stories p134-56   **S C**

Cold war
Warren, J. A. Cold War (7 and up)   **327.73**
See/See also pages in the following book(s):
Grant, R. G. The Berlin Wall   **943.087**
Westerfeld, S. The Berlin airlift   **943.087**

Cole, Alison
The Renaissance (7 and up)   **709.02**

Cole, Brock, 1938-
Celine (7 and up)   **Fic**
The facts speak for themselves (7 and up)   **Fic**
The goats   **Fic**

Cole, Joanna
A frog's body   **597.8**

Cole, Michael D.
Astronauts   **629.45**
Galileo spacecraft   **629.43**
Hubble Space Telescope   **522**
Living on Mars   **629.4**
Moon base   **629.4**
TWA flight 800   **363.1**

Cole, Nat King, 1919?-1965
See/See also pages in the following book(s):
Gourse, L. Swingers and crooners p114-20 (7 and up)   **781.65**

Coleman, Bessie, 1896?-1926
About
Hart, P. S. Up in the air: the story of Bessie Coleman   **92**
See/See also pages in the following book(s):
Hart, P. S. Flying free p14-21   **629.13**
Haskins, J. Black eagles p17-48   **629.13**

Coleman, Lori
Fundamental soccer   **796.334**

Coleman, Michael
Weirdo's war   **Fic**

Cook, James, 1728-1779
See/See also pages in the following book(s):
Lomask, M. Great lives: exploration p90-102
    920

Cook, Scott
(il) Van Laan, N. With a whoop and a holler
    398

Cook-Lynn, Elizabeth
A visit from Reverend Tileston
In Talking leaves   **S C**

The **cookcamp**. Paulsen, G.   **Fic**

Cooking
Albyn, C. L. The multicultural cookbook for
students   **641.5**
Cobb, V. Science experiments you can eat
    507.8
Cook, D. F. The kids' multicultural cookbook
    641.5
D'Amico, J. The healthy body cookbook
    641.5
George, J. C. Acorn pancakes, dandelion salad
and 38 other wild recipes   **641.6**
Holiday cooking around the world   **641.5**
Perl, L. Hunter's stew and hangtown fry: what
pioneer America ate and why   **641.5**
Perl, L. Slumps, grunts, and snickerdoodles:
what Colonial America ate and why
    641.5
Plante, E. M. The American kitchen, 1700 to
the present (7 and up)   **643**
Vezza, D. S. Passport on a plate   **641.5**
Webb, L. S. Holidays of the world cookbook for
students   **641.5**
Wilder, L. I. The Laura Ingalls Wilder country
cookbook   **641.5**
Wilkes, A. Children's quick & easy cookbook
    641.5

Cooking. Medearis, A. S.   **641.5**

The **cook's** family. Yep, L.   **Fic**

Cool math. Maganzini, C.   **510.7**

Cool salsa   **811.008**

Coolidge, Calvin, 1872-1933
See/See also pages in the following book(s):
Presidents of a world power   **920**

Cooney, Caroline B., 1947-
Burning up (7 and up)   **Fic**
Driver's Ed (7 and up)   **Fic**
The face on the milk carton (7 and up)
    Fic
Flash fire (7 and up)   **Fic**
Flight #116 is down (7 and up)   **Fic**
Prisoner of time (7 and up)   **Fic**
The terrorist (7 and up)   **Fic**
The voice on the radio (7 and up)   **Fic**
What child is this? (7 and up)   **Fic**
Whatever happened to Janie? (7 and up)
    Fic

Cooney, Miriam P.
(ed) Celebrating women in mathematics and science. See Celebrating women in mathematics
and science   **920**

Cooper, Chris
Matter   **530**

Cooper, Dan
Enrico Fermi and the revolutions in modern
physics (7 and up)   **92**

Cooper, Ilene
The Dead Sea scrolls   **296.1**

Cooper, J. California
How, why to get rich
In Rites of passage p130-42   **S C**

Cooper, James Fenimore, 1789-1851
See/See also pages in the following book(s):
Faber, D. Great lives: American literature p3-10
    920

Cooper, Michael L., 1950-
Bound for the promised land   **305.8**
The double V campaign   **940.54**
Hell Fighters   **940.4**

Cooper, Susan, 1935-
The Boggart   **Fic**
The Boggart and the monster. See note under
Cooper, S. The Boggart   **Fic**
The dark is rising. See note under Cooper, S.
Over sea, under stone   **Fic**
Ghost story
In Don't read this! and other tales of the un-
natural p33-50   **S C**
Greenwitch. See note under Cooper, S. Over
sea, under stone   **Fic**
The grey king. See note under Cooper, S. Over
sea, under stone   **Fic**
Over sea, under stone   **Fic**
Silver on the tree. See note under Cooper, S.
Over sea, under stone   **Fic**

Cooper-Hewitt Museum
Tambini, M. The look of the century   **745.2**

Cooper-Mullin, Alison, 1954-
Once upon a heroine   **028.1**

Cooperative learning activities in the library media center. Farmer, L. S. J.   **027.8**

Copage, Eric V.
Kwanzaa (7 and up)   **641.5**

Coping when a parent dies. Grosshandler, J.
    155.9

Coping with an emotionally distant father.
Jamiolkowski, R. M.   **158**

Coping with braces and other orthodontic work.
Lee, J.   **617.6**

Coping with confrontations and encounters with
the police. Wirths, C. G.   **363.2**

Coping with diabetes. Kelly, P.   **616.4**

Coping with hereditary diseases. Jacobs, M. B.
    616

Coping with migraines and other headaches.
Votava, A.   **616.8**

Coping with scoliosis. Eisenpreis, B.   **616.7**

Coping with self-mutilation. Clarke, A.
    616.85

Coping with stress. Packard, G. K.   **155.9**

Coping with the dangers of tattooing, body piercing, and branding. Wilkinson, B.   **617.9**

Copley, Bob
The tall Mexican: the life of Hank Aguirre, all-
star pitcher, businessman, humanitarian (7 and
up)   **92**

Coville, Bruce
Aliens ate my homework   **Fic**
Aliens stole by body. See note under Coville, B.
   Aliens ate my homework   **Fic**
Biscuits of glory
   In The Haunted house: a collection of original
    stories   **S C**
The box
   In Dragons & dreams p1-11   **S C**
The guardian of memory
   In A Glory of unicorns p1-28   **S C**
I left my sneakers in dimension X. See note un-
   der Coville, B. Aliens ate my homework
                              Fic
Into the land of the unicorns   **Fic**
The Japanese mirror
   In A Nightmare's dozen   **S C**
Odder than ever   **S C**
Includes the following stories: The golden sail; The stinky
princess; The giants tooth; The metamorphosis of Justin Jones;
Biscuits of glory; There's nothing under the bed; I, Earthling;
Am I blue?; The Japanese mirror
Oddly enough   **S C**
Contents: The box; Duffy's jacket; Homeward bound; With his
head tucked underneath his arm; Clean as a whistle; The lan-
guage of blood; Old glory; The passing of the pack; A blaze of
glory
The search for Snout. See note under Coville, B.
   Aliens ate my homework   **Fic**
The secret of life, according to Aunt Gladys
   In The Dirty laundry: stories about family se-
    crets p1-17   **S C**
The skull of truth   **Fic**
William Shakespeare's A midsummer night's
   dream   **822.3**
William Shakespeare's Macbeth   **822.3**
(comp) A Glory of unicorns. See A Glory of
   unicorns   **S C**
(jt. auth) Yolen, J. Armageddon summer
                                Fic

Coville, Katherine
Story hour
   In A Glory of unicorns p97-112   **S C**
The cow of no color. Jaffe, N.
   In Jaffe, N. The cow of no color: riddle sto-
    ries and justice tales from around the
    world p10-13   **398.2**
The cow of no color: riddle stories and justice
   tales from around the world. Jaffe, N.
                               398.2
The **coward**. Kimmel, E. A.
   In Kimmel, E. A. Sword of the samurai p23-
    30   **Fic**
Cowboy. Murdoch, D. H.   **978**
Cowboy ghost. Peck, R. N.   **Fic**
Cowboys, Indians, and gunfighters. Marrin, A.
                               978
Cowboys of the wild West. Freedman, R.
                               978

Cowhands
DeAngelis, G. The black cowboys   **978**
Faber, D. Calamity Jane   **92**
Freedman, R. Cowboys of the wild West
                               978
Murdoch, D. H. Cowboy   **978**
Sanford, W. R. Bill Pickett: African-American
   rodeo star   **92**

Sanford, W. R. Calamity Jane: frontier original
                               92
See/See also pages in the following book(s):
Yount, L. Frontiers of freedom p87-103 (7 and
   up)   **978**
                 Fiction
Myers, W. D. The journal of Joshua Loper
                               Fic
Peck, R. N. Cowboy ghost   **Fic**
                  Songs
Songs of the Wild West   **782.42**
Cowles, Kathleen *See* Krull, Kathleen, 1952-
Cox, Clinton
Come all you brave soldiers   **973.3**
Fiery vision: the life and death of John Brown
   (7 and up)   **92**
The forgotten heroes   **978**
Mark Twain   **92**
Undying glory   **973.7**
Cox, Reginald H. W.
The seven wonders of the historic world
                             909.07
Coye, Jennifer Marmaduke
(jt. auth) Cooper-Mullin, A. Once upon a hero-
   ine   **028.1**
Coyote and the rolling rock. Brown, D. A.
   In Brown, D. A. Dee Brown's folktales of the
    Native American p109-11   **398.2**
Coyote helps decorate the night. Courlander, H.
   In From sea to shining sea p16-17   **810.8**
Cozic, Charles P., 1957-
(ed) AIDS: opposing viewpoints. See AIDS: op-
   posing viewpoints   **616.97**
(ed) America's prisons: opposing viewpoints.
   See America's prisons: opposing viewpoints
                                365
(ed) Illegal drugs. See Illegal drugs   **364.1**
(ed) Welfare reform. See Welfare reform
                                361.6
Crack (Drug)
Holmes, A. Psychological effects of cocaine and
   crack addiction (7 and up)   **362.29**
Robbins, P. R. Crack and cocaine drug dangers
                                362.29
Crack and cocaine drug dangers. Robbins, P. R.
                                362.29
Crack cocaine *See* Crack (Drug)
Cracker Jackson. Byars, B. C.   **Fic**
Craft, Ellen, ca. 1826-ca. 1897
See/See also pages in the following book(s):
Bolden, T. And not afraid to dare   **920**
Craft, Marie
Cupid and Psyche   **292**
Crafts (Arts) *See* Handicraft
Crafts from the past [series]
Chapman, G. The Egyptians   **745.5**
Chapman, G. The Greeks   **745.5**
Chapman, G. The Romans   **745.5**
Crain, Esther
(jt. auth) Katz, W. A. The Columbia Granger's
   guide to poetry anthologies   **016.80881**
Crane, Stephen, 1871-1900
The red badge of courage (7 and up)   **Fic**

The **crane** maiden. Martin, R.
  In Martin, R. Mysterious tales of Japan
        398.2

The **crane** wife [play] Carlisle, B.
  In Theatre for young audiences p453-77
        812.008

Cranes (Birds)
  DuTemple, L. A. North American cranes
        598
  Patent, D. H. The whooping crane   **639.9**

Crash. Spinelli, J.   **Fic**

Craven, Margaret
  I heard the owl call my name (7 and up)
        Fic

Crawford, Andy
  (il) Bull, J. Change your room   **747**

Crawford, Walt
  Being analog   **020**

Crayton, Pearl
  The day the world almost came to an end
    In Rites of passage p25-32   **S C**

Crazy as a daisy. Williams-Garcia, R.
  In Stay true: short stories for strong girls
        S C

Crazy Fish. Mazer, N. F.   **Fic**

Crazy Horse, Sioux Chief, ca. 1842-1877
      About
  Freedman, R. The life and death of Crazy Horse
        92

  See/See also pages in the following book(s):
  Calvert, P. Great lives: the American frontier
    p125-36   **920**
  Kallen, S. A. Native American chiefs and warriors (7 and up)   **920**

The **Crazy** Horse Electric game. Crutcher, C.
        Fic

Crazy lady!. Conly, J. L.   **Fic**

Creating the Constitution, 1787. Collier, C.
        342

Creation
  Hamilton, V. In the beginning: creation stories from around the world   **291.1**
  Lester, J. When the beginning began   **296.1**
      Study and teaching
  See Evolution—Study and teaching

The **creation** of Israel. Altman, L. J.   **956.94**

Creationism
  See also Evolution

Creative fire (7 and up)   **700**

Creative writing
  Bauer, M. D. Our stories   **808.3**
  Bauer, M. D. What's your story?   **808.3**
  Seuling, B. To be a writer   **808**
  The Writing trek language adventures: grades 6-8. See entry in CD-ROM section, Part 3
  Young, S. Writing with style   **808**

The **creatures** in the house. Westall, R.
  In Westall, R. Demons and shadows p183-208
        S C

Credit
  See also Consumer credit

Creech, Sharon
  Absolutely normal chaos   **Fic**

  Bloomability   **Fic**
  Chasing Redbird   **Fic**
  Walk two moons   **Fic**

Creed, Alexander
  Uganda   **967.61**

Creek Indians
  Green, M. D. The Creeks
    In Indians of North America series
        970.004

Creeps from the deep. Taylor, L. R.   **578.7**

The **cremation** of Sam McGee. Service, R. W.
        811

Crew, Gary, 1947-
  Tunnel rat dreaming
    In Trapped!: cages of mind and body p165-77
        S C

Crew, Linda
  Bride price
    In Join in p111-26   **S C**
  Children of the river (7 and up)   **Fic**
  Fire on the wind   **Fic**

Crews. Hinojosa, M.   **302.3**

Cribb, Joe
  Money   **332.4**

Crichton, Michael, 1942-
  Jurassic Park (7 and up)   **Fic**

Crick, Francis, 1916-
      About
  Edelson, E. James Watson and Francis Crick and the building blocks of life (7 and up)
        92

Cricket never does. Livingston, M. C.   **811**

Crickets
  Pascoe, E. Crickets and grasshoppers   **595.7**

Crickets and grasshoppers. Pascoe, E.   **595.7**

Crime
    See also Computer crimes; Hate crimes; Homicide; Trials; Victims of crimes; White collar crimes
  Bode, J. Hard time (7 and up)   **364.36**
  Gaines, A. Private investigators and bounty hunters (7 and up)   **363.2**
  Lane, B. Crime & detection   **364**
  Powell, P. Major unsolved crimes (7 and up)
        364.1
      Fiction
  Cadnum, M. Edge (7 and up)   **Fic**
  Ferris, J. Love among the walnuts (7 and up)
        Fic

Crime & detection. Lane, B.   **364**

Crime, justice, and punishment [series]
  Campbell, A. Forensic science   **363.2**
  D'Angelo, L. Hate crimes   **364.1**
  DeAngelis, G. Cyber crimes   **364.1**
  DeAngelis, G. White-collar crime   **364.1**
  Faherty, S. Victims and victims' rights
        362.88
  Gaines, A. Private investigators and bounty hunters   **363.2**
  Gaines, A. Terrorism   **364.1**
  Powell, P. Major unsolved crimes   **364.1**
  Wilker, J. Organized crime   **364.1**
  Wolf, R. V. Capital punishment   **364.66**

Crime syndicates *See* Organized crime

Crimean War, 1853-1856
Bachrach, D. The Crimean War (7 and up)
947

Crimes, Political *See* Political crimes and offenses

Crimes, White collar *See* White collar crimes

Criminal investigation
See also Forensic anthropology; Forensic sciences
Campbell, A. Forensic science (7 and up)
363.2
Jackson, D. The bone detectives **614**
Jones, C. F. Fingerprints and talking bones
363.2
Lane, B. Crime & detection **364**
Silverstein, H. Threads of evidence (7 and up)
363.2

Criminal justice, Administration of *See* Administration of criminal justice

Criminal justice: opposing viewpoints (7 and up)
345

Criminal procedure
Fireside, H. The Fifth Amendment (7 and up)
347

Criminalistics *See* Forensic sciences

Criminals
See also Thieves
Glass, A. Bad guys **920**
King, D. C. Al Capone and the roaring twenties
92
Dictionaries
MacNee, M. J. Outlaws, mobsters & crooks
920.003
Fiction
Kerr, M. E. Gentlehands (7 and up) **Fic**

Crippen, Cynthia
(jt. auth) Leonard, T. M. Day by day: the seventies **909.82**

Crisfield, Deborah
Winning volleyball for girls **796.325**

Crisman, Ruth, 1914-
Racing the Iditarod Trail **798.8**

Crist-Evans, Craig
Moon over Tennessee **Fic**

Criswell, Sara Dixon, 1945-
Homelessness (7 and up) **362.5**

Critical mass: America's race to build the atomic bomb. See entry in CD-ROM section, Part 3

Criticism
See also Books—Reviews

Crockett, Davy, 1786-1836
See/See also pages in the following book(s):
Calvert, P. Great lives: the American frontier p137-48 **920**

Crocodiles
See also Alligators
Dow, L. Alligators and crocodiles (7 and up)
597.9

Crook, George, 1829-1890
See/See also pages in the following book(s):
Ehrlich, A. Wounded Knee: an Indian history of the American West **970.004**

The **crooked** man. Doyle, Sir A. C.
In Doyle, Sir A. C. The complete Sherlock Holmes **S C**

Crooker waits. San Souci, R.
In San Souci, R. A terrifying taste of short & shivery p1-5 **398.2**

Crosby, Bing, 1904-1977
See/See also pages in the following book(s):
Gourse, L. Swingers and crooners p35-38 (7 and up) **781.65**

Crosher, Judith
Technology in the time of ancient Egypt
609
Technology in the time of ancient Greece
609
Technology in the time of the Maya **609**

Crosland, David W.
See/See also pages in the following book(s):
Powledge, F. We shall overcome p130-34
323.1

Cross, Gillian, 1945-
The great American elephant chase **Fic**
New World **Fic**

Cross cultural conflict *See* Culture conflict

Cross out where not applicable. Conford, E.
In Conford, E. Crush p101-06 **S C**

Crossing over. Storr, C.
In The Oxford book of scary tales p16-21
808.8

Crossing the Delaware. Peacock, L. **973.3**

Crossley-Holland, Kevin
Slam and the ghosts
In The Oxford book of scary tales p14-15
808.8

Crow & Weasel. Leonard, J.
In Theatre for young audiences p244-83
812.008

Crow and Hawk. Brown, D. A.
In Brown, D. A. Dee Brown's folktales of the Native American p148-50 **398.2**

Crow Dog, Mary *See* Brave Bird, Mary

Crow Indians
Hoxie, F. E. The Crow
In Indians of North America series
970.004
Fiction
Matcheck, D. The sacrifice (7 and up) **Fic**

Crow learns a lesson. Lester, J.
In Lester, J. When the beginning began p39-42 **296.1**

Crowe, Chris
Presenting Mildred D. Taylor (7 and up)
813.009

Crown duel. Smith, S. **Fic**

The **crown** of Dalemark. Jones, D. W. **Fic**

Crow's sun. Niatum, D.
In Talking leaves **S C**

Cruel sisters. Wrede, P. C.
In Wrede, P. C. Book of enchantments p184-203 **S C**

Cruelty to animals *See* Animal welfare

Cruise, Tom
    About
    Powell, P. Tom Cruise   **92**
Cruises *See* Ocean travel
Cruising through research. Volkman, J. D.
    025.5
The **cruncher** 2.0. See entry in CD-ROM section,
    Part 3
Crush. Conford, E.   **S C**
Crutcher, Chris, 1946-
    Athletic shorts: six short stories (7 and up)
        S C
    Contents: A brief moment in the life of Angus Bethune; The
    pin; The other pin; Goin' fishin'; Telephone man; In the time I
    get
    The Crazy Horse Electric game (7 and up)
        Fic
    Ironman (7 and up)   **Fic**
    Popeye the sailor
    In Dirty laundry: stories about family secrets
        p162-77   **S C**
    Running loose (7 and up)   **Fic**
    Staying fat for Sarah Byrnes   **Fic**
    Stotan! (7 and up)   **Fic**
    Superboy
    In Ultimate sports: short stories by outstand-
        ing writers for young adults p51-67
        S C
    About
    Davis, T. Presenting Chris Crutcher (7 and up)
        813.009
Crutchfield, Jimmie, 1910-1993
    See/See also pages in the following book(s):
    Brashler, W. The story of Negro league baseball
        796.357
Cruz, Bárbara
    José Clemente Orozco   **92**
Cry Baby. Jennings, P.
    In Jennings, P. Unmentionable! p70-84
        S C
Cry, the beloved country. Paton, A.   **Fic**
Cryptography
    Aaseng, N. Navajo code talkers   **940.54**
    Durrett, D. Unsung heroes of World War II (7
        and up)   **940.54**
    Huckle, H. The secret code book   **652**
Crystal, David, 1941-
    (ed) The Cambridge biographical encyclopedia.
    See The Cambridge biographical encyclopedia
        920.003
Crystal & gem. Symes, R. F.   **548**
The **crystal** garden. Grove, V.   **Fic**
The **crystal** pool. McCaughrean, G.
    In McCaughrean, G. The crystal pool: myths
        and legends of the world p79-81
        398.2
The **crystal** pool: myths and legends of the world.
    McCaughrean, G.   **398.2**
Crystallography *See* Crystals
Crystals
    Symes, R. F. Crystal & gem   **548**
Cuban Americans
    Hoobler, D. The Cuban American family album
        305.8

Cuchulain (Legendary character)
    See/See also pages in the following book(s):
    Ross, A. Druids, gods & heroes from Celtic my-
        thology p32-52   **299**
The **cuckoo's** child. Freeman, S. T.   **Fic**
Cuffe, Paul, 1759-1817
    See/See also pages in the following book(s):
    Haskins, J. African American entrepreneurs p12-
        16   **920**
    Katz, W. L. Proudly red and black p1-9
        920
Cuffie, Terrasita A., 1964-
    Maya Angelou (7 and up)   **92**
Cullen-DuPont, Kathryn
    Elizabeth Cady Stanton and women's liberty (7
        and up)   **92**
    The encyclopedia of women's history in Ameri-
        ca (7 and up)   **305.4**
    (jt. auth) Frost-Knappman, E. Women's rights
        on trial   **346**
    (jt. auth) Frost-Knappman, E. Women's suffrage
        in America   **324.6**
Cullinan, Bernice E.
    (ed) A Jar of tiny stars: poems by NCTE award-
        winning poets. See A Jar of tiny stars: poems
        by NCTE award-winning poets   **811.008**
Culloch and the big pig. McCaughrean, G.
    In McCaughrean, G. The crystal pool: myths
        and legends of the world p107-12
        398.2
Cults
    See also Satanism
    Barghusen, J. D. Cults (7 and up)   **291.9**
    Cohen, D. Cults (7 and up)   **291.9**
    Gay, K. Communes and cults (7 and up)
        291.9
    Porterfield, K. M. Straight talk about cults (7
        and up)   **291.9**
    Zeinert, K. Cults (7 and up)   **291.9**
    Fiction
    Haddix, M. P. Leaving Fishers (7 and up)
        Fic
    Yolen, J. Armageddon summer (7 and up)
        Fic
Cultural and geographical exploration [series]
    Bingham, H. The ancient Incas   **985**
    Building the Panama Canal   **972**
    Jerusalem and the Holy Land   **956.94**
    Robert E. Peary and the rush to the North Pole
        998
Cultural anthropology *See* Ethnology
Cultural atlas for young people [series]
    Corbishley, M. Ancient Rome   **937**
    Corbishley, M. The Middle Ages   **940.1**
Cultural pluralism *See* Multiculturalism
Culturally diverse library collections for youth.
    Totten, H. L.   **011.6**
Culture, Popular *See* Popular culture
Culture conflict
    Collier, C. Clash of cultures, prehistory-1638
        970.004
    Hull, M. Ethnic violence (7 and up)   **305.8**

Culture crafts [series]

Temko, F. Traditional crafts from Africa **745.5**

Temko, F. Traditional crafts from Mexico and Central America **745.5**

Culture shock *See* Culture conflict

Culture wars: opposing viewpoints (7 and up) **306**

Cultures of the past [series]

Ashby, R. Elizabethan England **942.05**
Hinds, K. The Incas **985**
Mann, K. The ancient Hebrews **909**
Millar, H. Spain in the age of exploration **946**

Cultures of the world [series]

Bassis, V. Ukraine **947.7**
Berg, E. Senegal **966.3**
Brown, R. V. Tunisia **961.1**
Cheng, P. G. Mongolia **951.7**
Dhilawala, S. Armenia **947.5**
Falconer, K. Peru **985**
Foley, E. Costa Rica **972.86**
Foley, E. Ecuador **986.6**
Fuller, B. Britain **941**
Gascoigne, I. Papua New Guinea **995.3**
Hassig, S. M. Somalia **967.73**
Heale, J. Democratic Republic of the Congo **967.51**
Heale, J. Madagascar **969.1**
Heale, J. Tanzania **967.8**
Hestler, A. Yemen **953.3**
Holmes, T. Zambia **968.94**
Jermyn, L. Uruguay **989.5**
Kagda, F. Algeria **965**
Kagda, F. Hong Kong **951.25**
Kagda, S. Lithuania **947.9**
Levy, P. M. Belarus **947.8**
Levy, P. M. Ghana **966.7**
Levy, P. M. Liberia **966.62**
Levy, P. M. Sudan **962.4**
Mansfield, S. Laos **959.4**
McGaffey, L. Honduras **972.83**
NgCheong-Lum, R. Tahiti **996**
O'Shea, M. Kuwait **953.67**
Pateman, R. Belgium **949.3**
Sheehan, P. Luxembourg **949.35**
Sheehan, S. Guatemala **972.81**
Sheehan, S. Lebanon **956.92**
Sioras, E. Czech Republic **943.7**
Smelt, R. New Zealand **993**
South, C. Jordan **956.95**
Spilling, M. Estonia **947.9**
Spilling, M. Georgia **947.5**
Whyte, M. Bangladesh **954.92**

Cummings, Pat, 1950-

(ed) Talking with artists [I-III] See Talking with artists [I-III] **741.6**

Cummings, Richard, 1931-

Simple makeup for young actors **792**

Cupid (Roman deity) *See* Eros (Greek deity)

Cupid and Psyche

In Hearne, B. G. Beauties and beasts p41-55 **398.2**

Cupid and Psyche. Craft, M. **292**

Cupid and Psyche. McCaughrean, G.

In McCaughrean, G. The bronze cauldron: myths and legends of the world p20-25 **398.2**

The **cure**. Levitin, S. **Fic**

Curie, Marie, 1867-1934

About

Pasachoff, N. E. Marie Curie and the science of radioactivity (7 and up) **92**
Poynter, M. Marie Curie: discoverer of radium **92**

See/See also pages in the following book(s):
Celebrating women in mathematics and science p111-24 **920**
DeAngelis, G. Science & medicine **920**
Hacker, C. Nobel Prize winners p12-17 **920**
Henderson, H. Nuclear physics p1-17 (7 and up) **539.7**

Curie, Pierre, 1859-1906

See/See also pages in the following book(s):
Henderson, H. Nuclear physics p1-17 (7 and up) **539.7**

Curiosities and wonders

See also Monsters; World records

Amazing facts **031.02**
Ash, R. Fantastic book of 1001 lists **031.02**
Ash, R. The top 10 of everything 2000 **031.02**
Ash, R. The world in one day **031.02**
Blackwood, G. L. Extraordinary events and oddball occurrences **001.9**
Drimmer, F. Incredible people **920**
Floyd, E. R. Great American mysteries (7 and up) **001.9**
Guinness book of records **032.02**
The Guinness book of records 1492 **031.02**
Simon, S. Strange mysteries from around the world **001.9**
Wilson, C. Mysteries of the universe **001.9**
Wood, T. Ancient wonders **930.1**

The **curious** honeybird. McCaughrean, G.

In McCaughrean, G. The crystal pool: myths and legends of the world p76-78 **398.2**

Curlee, Lynn, 1947-

Rushmore **730.9**

Curran, Christine Perdan

Sexually transmitted diseases (7 and up) **616.95**

Current biography yearbook **920.003**

Current controversies [series]

Assisted suicide **179.7**
Conserving the environment **333.7**
Guns and violence **363.3**
Illegal drugs **364.1**
Marriage and divorce **306.8**
The Rights of animals **179**
Smoking **362.29**
Youth violence **364.36**

Current events

Facts on File world news CD-ROM. See entry in CD-ROM section, Part 3

The **dark** way. Hamilton, V. **398.2**

Darkness be my friend. Marsden, J. See note under Marsden, J. Tomorrow, when the war began **Fic**

Darling, Grace
Fiction
Paton Walsh, J. Grace **Fic**

Darling, Jay Norwood, 1876-1962
See/See also pages in the following book(s):
Byrnes, P. Environmental pioneers (7 and up)
920

Darling, Kathy
Chameleons on location **597.9**
(jt. auth) Cobb, V. Don't try this at home!
507.8
(jt. auth) Cobb, V. You gotta try this!
507.8

The **darning** needle. Kimmel, E. A.
In From sea to shining sea p189-91
810.8

Darwin, Charles, 1809-1882
About
Parker, S. Charles Darwin and evolution
92
Stefoff, R. Charles Darwin and the evolution revolution (7 and up) **92**
See/See also pages in the following book(s):
Stefoff, R. Scientific explorers p102-14 **509**

Darwinism *See* Evolution

Dasch, E. Julius (Ernest Julius), 1932-
(ed) Explorers. See Explorers **920.003**

Dasch, Ernest Julius *See* Dasch, E. Julius (Ernest Julius), 1932-

Dash, Joan
We shall not be moved (7 and up) **331.4**

Dashing through the snow. Shahan, S. **798.8**

Data base management *See* Database management

Data explorer. See entry in CD-ROM section, Part 3

Data processing *See* Electronic data processing

Data storage and retrieval systems *See* Information systems

Data transmission systems
See also Computer networks

Database management
Jacsó, P. Build your own database **005.7**

Date rape
See/See also pages in the following book(s):
Rue, N. N. Everything you need to know about abusive relationships (7 and up) **362.7**
Fiction
Miklowitz, G. D. Past forgiving (7 and up)
Fic

Dateline: Troy. Fleischman, P. **292**

Dating (Social customs)
Rue, N. N. Everything you need to know about abusive relationships (7 and up) **362.7**
Drama
Soto, G. Novio boy (7 and up) **812**
Fiction
Conford, E. Crush (7 and up) **S C**

Poetry
Turner, A. W. A lion's hunger (7 and up)
811

Datnow, Claire L.
Edwin Hubble **92**

The **daughter-in-law** who got her way. Krishnaswami, U.
In Krishnaswami, U. Shower of gold: girls and women in the stories of India p31-35
398.2

Daughter of invention. Alvarez, J.
In Growing up Latino p3-15 **810.8**

A **daughter** of the sea. Wartski, M. C.
In Join in p86-96 **S C**

Daughters and fathers *See* Fathers and daughters

Daughters and mothers *See* Mothers and daughters

David, King of Israel
About
Eisler, C. T. David's songs **223**

David, Jacques-Louis, 1748-1825
See/See also pages in the following book(s):
Glubok, S. Great lives: painting p32-40
920

David, Jay *See* Adler, Bill, 1929-

David's songs. Eisler, C. T. **223**

Davidson, Sue, 1925-
Getting the real story: Nellie Bly and Ida B. Wells **92**

Davies, Judy, 1947-
(jt. auth) Doiron, R. Partners in learning
027.8

Davies, Rhys, 1903-1978
Fear
In Read all about it! p223-29 **808.8**

Davis, Benjamin O., Jr.
See/See also pages in the following book(s):
Haskins, J. Black eagles p75-108 **629.13**

Davis, Brangien
What's real, what's ideal (7 and up)
616.85

Davis, Jefferson, 1808-1889
About
Burch, J. J. Jefferson Davis **92**

Davis, Lee Allyn
Environmental disasters (7 and up) **363.7**

Davis, Lucile
Alabama
In America the beautiful, second series
973
Puerto Rico
In America the beautiful, second series
973

Davis, Miles
See/See also pages in the following book(s):
Mour, S. I. American jazz musicians p77-84
920

Davis, Stuart, 1892-1964
See/See also pages in the following book(s):
Greenberg, J. The American eye p42-50
920

Davis, Terry
Presenting Chris Crutcher (7 and up)
813.009

Dawes, Dominique, 1976-
See/See also pages in the following book(s):
Rutledge, R. The best of the best in gymnastics
920

Dawn. Wiesel, E.
In Wiesel, E. Night, Dawn, The accident: three tales **Fic**

Dawn. Wynne-Jones, T.
In Leaving home: stories p91-114 **808.8**
In Wynne-Jones, T. The book of changes p109-33 **S C**

Day, Malcolm
The world of castles and forts **355.7**

Day, Nancy
Animal experimentation **179**

Day, Nancy L.
Advertising **659.1**

Day, Trevor
Oceans (7 and up) **551.46**

Day by day: the eighties. Meltzer, E. **909.82**

Day by day: the seventies. Leonard, T. M.
909.82

Day by day: the sixties. Parker, T. **909.82**

The **day** Fort Sumter was fired on. Haskins, J.
973.7

A **day** in the country. Jacobson, D.
In Somehow tenderness survives p37-47
S C

A **day** no pigs would die. Peck, R. N. **Fic**

The **day** puffins netted Hid-Well. Norman, H.
In Norman, H. The girl who dreamed only geese, and other tales of the Far North
398.2

The **day** that Elvis came to town. Marino, J.
Fic

The **day** the Cisco Kid shot John Wayne. Candelaria, N.
In Growing up Latino p115-30 **810.8**

The **day** the women got the vote. Sullivan, G.
305.4

The **day** the world almost came to an end. Crayton, P.
In Rites of passage p25-32 **S C**

The **day** they came to arrest the book. Hentoff, N.
Fic

The **day** we went to see snow. Villanueva Collado, A.
In Where angels glide at dawn p27-33
S C

De Angelis, Therese
Louis Farrakhan **92**
Native Americans and the Spanish
In Indians of North America series
970.004

De Balboa, Vasco Núñez *See* Balboa, Vasco Núñez de, 1475-1519

De Bonafini, Hebe *See* Bonafini, Hebe de

De Chamorro, Violeta Barrios *See* Chamorro, Violeta Barrios de

De La Croix, Horst
Gardner's art through the ages. See Gardner's art through the ages **709**

De Lint, Charles, 1951-
Laughter in the leaves
In Dragons & dreams p95-107 **S C**
There's no such thing
In Vampires: a collection of original stories p8-18 **S C**

De Mejo, Oscar, 1911-1992
(il) Gellman, M. Does God have a big toe?
221.9

De Orellana, Francisco *See* Orellana, Francisco de, d. ca. 1546

De Pinna, Simon *See* Pinna, Simon de

De Sable, Jean Baptiste Pointe *See* Pointe de Sable, Jean Baptiste, 1745?-1818

De Saint-Exupéry, Antoine *See* Saint-Exupéry, Antoine de, 1900-1944

De San Martín, José *See* San Martín, José de, 1778?-1850

De Santa Anna, Antonio López *See* Santa Anna, Antonio López de, 1794?-1876

De Souza, Philip
(jt. auth) Langley, A. The Roman news
937

Dead end. Anaya, R. A.
In Join in p101-09 **S C**

Dead flies. Conrad, P.
In Conrad, P. Our house p22-28 **S C**

Dead letter. Byars, B. C. See note under Byars, B. C. The dark stairs **Fic**

The **dead** of night. Marsden, J. See note under Marsden, J. Tomorrow, when the war began
Fic

Dead Sea scrolls
Cooper, I. The Dead Sea scrolls **296.1**

Deadly waters. Skurzynski, G. See note under Skurzynski, G. Cliff hanger **Fic**

Deaf
Keller, H. The story of my life **92**
Landau, E. Deafness **617.8**
St. George, J. Dear Dr. Bell—your friend, Helen Keller **92**
Fiction
Armstrong, J. Mary Mehan awake (7 and up)
Fic
Jordan, S. The raging quiet (7 and up) **Fic**
Means of communication
See also Sign language

Deafness. Landau, E. **617.8**

Deal, Borden, 1922-1985
Anteaus
In Help wanted: short stories about young people working **S C**

Dealing with dragons. Wrede, P. C. **Fic**

Dean, Ruth, 1947-
Life in the American colonies (7 and up)
973.2
Teen prostitution (7 and up) **362.7**

DeAngelis, Gina
The black cowboys **978**
Cyber crimes (7 and up) **364.1**
Science & medicine **920**
White-collar crime (7 and up) **364.1**

Dear America [series]

Denenberg, B. When will this cruel war be over?   **Fic**

Gregory, K. The winter of red snow   **Fic**

Lasky, K. Dreams in the golden country   **Fic**

Lasky, K. A journey to the New World   **Fic**

McKissack, P. C. A picture of Freedom   **Fic**

Murphy, J. West to a land of plenty   **Fic**

Osborne, M. P. Standing in the light   **Fic**

Dear Austin. Woodruff, E.   **Fic**

Dear author   **028.5**

Dear dog. McCaughrean, G.

In McCaughrean, G. The crystal pool: myths and legends of the world p61-66   **398.2**

Dear Dr. Bell—your friend, Helen Keller. St. George, J.   **92**

Dear Dr. King   **323.1**

Dear Jane. Lavelle, S.

In The Oxford book of scary tales p8-13   **808.8**

Dear Mr. Henshaw. Cleary, B.   **Fic**

Dear Mrs. Parks. Parks, R.   **305.23**

Death

See also Terminal care

Death and dying: opposing viewpoints (7 and up)   **155.9**

Death is hard to live with (7 and up)   **155.9**

DiGiulio, R. C. Straight talk about death and dying (7 and up)   **155.9**

Fry, V. L. Part of me died, too   **155.9**

Gootman, M. E. When a friend dies (7 and up)   **155.9**

Grollman, E. A. Straight talk about death for teenagers (7 and up)   **155.9**

Grosshandler, J. Coping when a parent dies (7 and up)   **155.9**

Hyde, M. O. Meeting death   **155.9**

Krementz, J. How it feels when a parent dies   **155.9**

Schleifer, J. Everything you need to know when someone you know has been killed (7 and up)   **155.9**

See/See also pages in the following book(s):

Colman, P. Corpses, coffins, and crypts (7 and up)   **393**

Gellman, M. Lost & found p95-161   **155.9**

Fiction

Blume, J. Tiger eyes (7 and up)   **Fic**

Brooks, B. Vanishing   **Fic**

Coman, C. Tell me everything   **Fic**

Conly, J. L. Crazy lady!   **Fic**

Cooney, C. B. Driver's Ed (7 and up)   **Fic**

Cormier, R. The bumblebee flies anyway (7 and up)   **Fic**

Couloumbis, A. Getting near to baby   **Fic**

Craven, M. I heard the owl call my name (7 and up)   **Fic**

Creech, S. Walk two moons   **Fic**

Deaver, J. R. Say goodnight, Gracie (7 and up)   **Fic**

Deuker, C. Heart of a champion (7 and up)   **Fic**

Draper, S. M. Tears of a tiger (7 and up)   **Fic**

Fletcher, R. J. Flying solo   **Fic**

Fox, P. The eagle kite   **Fic**

Gilbert, B. S. Stone water (7 and up)   **Fic**

Haas, J. Unbroken   **Fic**

Hamilton, V. Cousins   **Fic**

Henkes, K. Sun & spoon   **Fic**

Hermes, P. Cheat the moon   **Fic**

Hesse, K. Phoenix rising   **Fic**

Johnson, A. Toning the sweep   **Fic**

Klause, A. C. The silver kiss (7 and up)   **Fic**

Layefsky, V. Impossible things   **Fic**

L'Engle, M. A ring of endless light   **Fic**

Lowry, L. A summer to die   **Fic**

Mazer, H. When the phone rang (7 and up)   **Fic**

Mazer, N. F. After the rain (7 and up)   **Fic**

McDonald, J. Swallowing stones (7 and up)   **Fic**

Menick, S. The muffin child   **Fic**

Moon, P. The spying game   **Fic**

Paterson, K. Bridge to Terabithia   **Fic**

Roberts, W. D. Pawns   **Fic**

Rodowsky, C. F. Remembering Mog (7 and up)   **Fic**

Rodowsky, C. F. The Turnabout Shop   **Fic**

Rylant, C. The Heavenly Village   **Fic**

Rylant, C. Missing May   **Fic**

Sleator, W. Rewind   **Fic**

Slepian, J. The Broccoli tapes   **Fic**

Springer, N. Toughing it (7 and up)   **Fic**

Westall, R. The promise   **Fic**

Willey, M. Facing the music (7 and up)   **Fic**

Wood, J. R. Turtle on a fence post   **Fic**

Yumoto, K. The friends   **Fic**

Yumoto, K. The spring tone (7 and up)   **Fic**

Poetry

Poe, E. A. Annabel Lee   **811**

Stopping for death (7 and up)   **808.81**

Death, **Apparent** *See* Near-death experiences

Death and dying: opposing viewpoints (7 and up)   **155.9**

Death be not proud [biography of his son] Gunther, J.   **92**

The **death** camps. Lace, W. W.   **940.53**

Death forgiven. Jiménez, F.

In Jiménez, F. The circuit: stories from the life of a migrant child p57-60   **S C**

Death is hard to live with (7 and up)   **155.9**

The **death** of El Cid. McCaughrean, G.

In McCaughrean, G. The golden hoard: myths and legends of the world p94-99   **398.2**

Death of the Iron Horse. Goble, P.

In From sea to shining sea p160-63   **810.8**

The **death** of wizards. Westall, R.

In Westall, R. Demons and shadows p209-25   **S C**

Death penalty *See* Capital punishment

The **death** penalty. Stewart, G.   364.66

The **Death** penalty: opposing viewpoints (7 and up)   364.66

Death's door. Byars, B. C. See note under Byars, B.C. The dark stairs   Fic

Deaver, Julie Reece
Chicago blues (7 and up)   Fic
Say goodnight, Gracie (7 and up)   Fic

The **debate** in sign language. Lieberman, S.
In From sea to shining sea p34-35   810.8

DeBruyne-Ammon, Bette *See* Ammon, Bette D.

Debs, Eugene V. (Eugene Victor), 1855-1926
See/See also pages in the following book(s):
Streissguth, T. Legendary labor leaders (7 and up)   920

Debts, Government *See* Public debts

Debts, Public *See* Public debts

Decision making
See also Problem solving

Decisions, decisions: the Constitution. See entry in CD-ROM section, Part 3

Declaration of Independence *See* United States. Declaration of Independence

DeClements, Barthe, 1920-
6th grade can really kill you   Fic
Liar, liar   Fic

Decoration, Interior *See* Interior design

DeCurtis, Anthony
(ed) The Rolling Stone illustrated history of rock & roll. See The Rolling Stone illustrated history of rock & roll   781.66

Dee Brown's folktales of the Native American. Brown, D. A.   398.2

The **deeds** and prophecies of Old Man. Brown, D. A.
In Brown, D. A. Dee Brown's folktales of the Native American p59-62   398.2

Deem, James M.
Bodies from the bog   930.1

Deep into it. Murphy, J.
In Murphy, J. Night terrors p125-32   S C

Deep-Sea explorer: the story of Robert Ballard, discoverer of the Titanic. Archbold, R.   92

Deep wizardry. Duane, D. See note under Duane, D. A wizard abroad   Fic

Deer
See also Elk
Patent, D. H. Deer and elk   599.64
Fiction
Rawlings, M. K. The yearling   Fic

Deer and elk. Patent, D. H.   599.64

The **deer** dance. Winther, B.
In Winther, B. Plays from Hispanic tales   812

Deer Woman. Allen, P. G.
In Talking leaves   S C

Deere, John, 1804-1886
See/See also pages in the following book(s):
Calvert, P. Great lives: the American frontier p161-76   920

DeFelice, Cynthia C.
The apprenticeship of Lucas Whitaker   Fic
The dancing skeleton
In From sea to shining sea p322-25   810.8
The ghost of Fossil Glen   Fic
Lostman's River   Fic
Nowhere to call home   Fic

The **defender**. Lipsyte, R.
In Ultimate sports: short stories by outstanding writers for young adults p180-92   S C

Defense mechanisms (Zoology) *See* Animal defenses

Defoe, Daniel, 1661?-1731
Robinson Crusoe (7 and up)   Fic

Degas, Edgar, 1834-1917
About
Skira-Venturi, R. A weekend with Degas   92

See/See also pages in the following book(s):
Glubok, S. Great lives: painting p41-48   920

Degas, Hilaire Germain Edgar *See* Degas, Edgar, 1834-1917

Deities *See* Gods and goddesses

Delacre, Lulu, 1957-
Golden tales   398.2
Contents: How the sea was born; Guanina; The eleven thousand Virgins; The laughing skull; Sención, the Indian girl; When the sun and the moon were children; How the rainbow was born; The miracle of Our Lady of Guadalupe; El Dorado; Manco Capac and the rod of gold; Kákuy; The courier

Delaware
Schuman, M. Delaware
In Celebrate the states   973

Delaware Indians
Grumet, R. S. The Lenapes
In Indians of North America series   970.004
Fiction
Curry, J. L. Dark Shade (7 and up)   Fic
Durrant, L. The beaded moccasins   Fic
Kirkpatrick, K. A. Trouble's daughter   Fic
Osborne, M. P. Standing in the light   Fic
Richter, C. The light in the forest   Fic

Delinquency, Juvenile *See* Juvenile delinquency

The **deliverers** of their country. Nesbit, E.
In The Book of dragons p50-66   S C

Delivering Web reference services to young people. Minkel, W.   025.04

Dellenbaugh, Frederick Samuel, 1853-1935
About
Maurer, R. The wild Colorado (7 and up)   979.1

Demi, 1942-
Buddha   294.3
The Dalai Lama   92

Democracy in action [series]
Dolan, E. F. Shaping U.S. foreign policy   327.73

Democratic Republic of the Congo. Heale, J.   967.51

Diehn, Gwen, 1943-
Making books that fly, fold, wrap, hide, pop up, twist, and turn **736**

Diet
See also Eating customs

Diet pill drug dangers. Clayton, L. **615**

Diet pills *See* Appetite depressants

Diets, Reducing *See* Weight loss

A **different** kind of hero. Blakeslee, A. R. **Fic**

Digestion
Ballard, C. The stomach and digestive system **612.3**

Digger in paradise. Murphy, J.
In Murphy, J. Night terrors p33-37 **S C**

Digger's good-bye. Murphy, J.
In Murphy, J. Night terrors p171-77 **S C**

Digger's promise. Murphy, J.
In Murphy, J. Night terrors p1-5 **S C**

The **digital** field trip to the rainforest. See entry in CD-ROM section, Part 3

The **digital** field trip to the wetlands. See entry in CD-ROM section, Part 3

Digital revolution. Hoare, S. **621.381**

DiGiulio, Robert C., 1949-
Straight talk about death and dying (7 and up) **155.9**

Dillon, Diane
(il) Bible. O.T. Ecclesiastes. To every thing there is a season **223**

Dillon, Leo, 1933-
(il) Bible. O.T. Ecclesiastes. To every thing there is a season **223**

DiMaggio, Joe
See/See also pages in the following book(s):
Gilbert, T. W. Damn Yankees (7 and up) **796.357**

A **dime** a dozen. Grimes, N. **811**

Dinah for president. Mills, C. **Fic**

Dinah forever. Mills, C. See note under Mills, C. Dinah for president **Fic**

Dinah in love. Mills, C. See note under Mills, C. Dinah for president **Fic**

Diner, Hasia R.
Jews in America (7 and up) **305.8**

Dingle, Derek T.
First in the field: baseball hero Jackie Robinson **92**

Dingus, Lowell
The tiniest giants **567.9**

Dinkins is dead. San Souci, R.
In San Souci, R. A terrifying taste of short & shivery p82-85 **398.2**

Dinosaur and other prehistoric animal factfinder. Benton, M. **560**

Dinosaur worlds. Lessem, D. **567.9**

Dinosaurs
Benton, M. J. Dinosaurs **567.9**
Dingus, L. The tiniest giants **567.9**
Facklam, M. Tracking dinosaurs in the Gobi **567.9**

Lambert, D. The ultimate dinosaur book **567.9**
Lessem, D. Dinosaur worlds **567.9**
Lessem, D. Jack Horner: living with dinosaurs **92**
Lindsay, W. Tyrannosaurus **567.9**
Patent, D. H. In search of the maiasaurs **567.9**
Tanaka, S. Graveyards of the dinosaurs **567.9**
The Visual dictionary of dinosaurs **567.9**
The Visual dictionary of prehistoric life **560**
Zallinger, P. Dinosaurs and other archosaurs **567.9**

Dictionaries
Benton, M. Dinosaur and other prehistoric animal factfinder **560**

Encyclopedias
Dinosaurs of the world **567.9**

Fiction
Ciencin, S. Dinoverse **Fic**
Crichton, M. Jurassic Park (7 and up) **Fic**
Foster, A. D. The Hand of Dinotopia **Fic**
Gurney, J. Dinotopia: a land apart from time **Fic**
Zindel, P. Raptor (7 and up) **Fic**

Dinosaurs and other archosaurs. Zallinger, P. **567.9**

Dinosaurs of the world **567.9**

Dinotopia: a land apart from time. Gurney, J. **Fic**

Dinotopia: first flight. Gurney, J. See note under Gurney, J. Dinotopia: a land apart from time **Fic**

Dinotopia lost. Foster, A. D. See note under Foster, A. D. The Hand of Dinotopia **Fic**

Dinotopia: the world beneath. Gurney, J. See note under Gurney, J. Dinotopia: a land apart from time **Fic**

Dinoverse. Ciencin, S. **Fic**

Diphtheria
Fiction
Haddix, M. P. Running out of time **Fic**

Direction (Motion pictures) *See* Motion pictures—Production and direction

Dirty laundry (7 and up) **S C**

Disabled *See* Handicapped

The **disappearance.** Guy, R. **Fic**

The **disappearance** of Lady Frances Carfax. Doyle, Sir A. C.
In Doyle, Sir A. C. The complete Sherlock Holmes **S C**

Disappearing acts. Byars, B. C. See note under Byars, B.C. The dark stairs **Fic**

Disarmament *See* Arms control

Disaster!. Bonson, R. **363.34**

Disasters
See also Accidents; Natural disasters
Davis, L. A. Environmental disasters (7 and up) **363.7**
Garner, J. We interrupt this broadcast (7 and up) **070.1**

Discover Mars. Skurzynski, G.   **523.4**

Discoveries (in geography) *See* Exploration

Discoveries and inventions [series]
Dale, R. Early cars   **629.222**

Discoveries library [series]
Burnie, D. Insects & spiders   **595.7**
Graham, I. How things work   **600**
Lynch, A. Great buildings   **720**
Parker, S. The human body   **612**
Wood, R. Great inventions   **609**

DISCovering biography. See entry in CD-ROM section, Part 3

Discovering graph secrets. Markle, S.   **001.4**

Discovering the Iceman. Tanaka, S.   **930.1**

Discovering the Inca Ice Maiden. Reinhard, J.
    930.1

The **discovery** of the Titanic. Ballard, R. D.
    910.4

Discrimination
    See also Hate crimes; Race discrimination; Sex discrimination
Discrimination: opposing viewpoints (7 and up)
    305.8

Discrimination in education
    See also Segregation in education
    Law and legislation
Banfield, S. The Bakke case (7 and up)
    344

Discrimination in employment
See/See also pages in the following book(s):
Working women: opposing viewpoints p47-103
(7 and up)   **331.4**

Discrimination in public accommodations
Fireside, H. Plessy v. Ferguson (7 and up)
    342

Discrimination: opposing viewpoints (7 and up)
    305.8

The **disease** book. Hyde, M. O.   **616**

Disease germs *See* Bacteria

Diseases
    See also Chickenpox; names of specific diseases and groups of diseases; and subjects with the subdivision *Diseases*
Hyde, M. O. The disease book   **616**
Jacobs, M. B. Coping with hereditary diseases
(7 and up)   **616**

Diseases and people [series]
Benowitz, S. I. Cancer   **616.99**
Carson, M. K. Epilepsy   **616.8**
Curran, C. P. Sexually transmitted diseases
    616.95
Johansson, P. Carpal tunnel syndrome and other repetitive strain injuries   **616.8**
Johansson, P. Heart disease   **616.1**
Latta, S. L. Allergies   **616.97**
Latta, S. L. Food poisoning and foodborne diseases   **615.9**
Majure, J. AIDS   **616.97**
Silverstein, A. Asthma   **616.2**
Silverstein, A. Chickenpox and shingles
    616.9
Silverstein, A. Depression   **616.85**
Silverstein, A. Measles and rubella   **616.9**

Silverstein, A. Sickle cell anemia   **616.1**
Veggeberg, S. Lyme disease   **616.9**
Willett, E. Meningitis   **616.8**

Dishonesty *See* Honesty

Disney, Walt, 1901-1966
    About
Finch, C. The art of Walt Disney   **791.43**
Walt Disney: his life in pictures   **92**

Disney (Walt) Company *See* Walt Disney Company

Disney (Walt) Productions *See* Walt Disney Productions

A **disorderly** table. Goldin, B. D.
    In Goldin, B. D. Journeys with Elijah p21-28
    222

Displaced persons *See* Refugees

Dissection
Parker, S. The beginner's guide to animal autopsy   **571.3**

Dissent
Kronenwetter, M. Protest! (7 and up)   **303.4**

Distinguished African American scientists of the 20th century (7 and up)   **920**

Dither farm. Hite, S. See note under Hite, S.
Those darn Dithers   **Fic**

Diversity, Biological *See* Biological diversity

Divination
Schwartz, A. Telling fortunes   **133.3**

Diving
    Fiction
Cadnum, M. Heat (7 and up)   **Fic**

Divorce
    See also Children of divorced parents; Remarriage
Goldentyer, D. Divorce   **306.89**
Marriage and divorce (7 and up)   **306.8**
Porterfield, K. M. Straight talk about divorce (7 and up)   **306.89**
Sanders, P. Divorce and separation   **306.89**
See/See also pages in the following book(s):
The Family: opposing viewpoints (7 and up)
    306.8

    Fiction
Caseley, J. Losing Louisa (7 and up)   **Fic**
Cleary, B. Dear Mr. Henshaw   **Fic**
Cleary, B. Strider   **Fic**
Cole, B. Celine (7 and up)   **Fic**
Danziger, P. The Divorce Express   **Fic**
Fine, A. Step by wicked step   **Fic**
Johnson, A. Songs of faith   **Fic**
Klass, S. S. Next stop, nowhere   **Fic**
LaFaye, A. The year of the Sawdust Man
    Fic
Mazer, N. F. Taking Terri Mueller   **Fic**
Napoli, D. J. Changing tunes   **Fic**
Paulsen, G. Hatchet   **Fic**
Southgate, M. Another way to dance   **Fic**
Van Leeuwen, J. Blue sky, butterfly   **Fic**
Voigt, C. A solitary blue (7 and up)   **Fic**
Wilson, J. The suitcase kid   **Fic**

Divorce and separation. Sanders, P.   **306.89**

The **Divorce** Express. Danziger, P.   **Fic**

Dixon, Jeane, 1918-1997
See/See also pages in the following book(s):
Krull, K. They saw the future p91-97
133.3

The **DK** art school series (7 and up) **751**

DK dictionary/thesaurus **423**

DK discoveries [series]
Bramwell, M. Polar exploration **998**
Langley, A. Castle at war **940.1**
Murdoch, D. H. Tutankhamun **932**
Platt, R. Aztecs **972**
Rice, M. Pompeii **937**
Stott, C. Moon landing **629.45**

The **DK** geography of the world **910**

DK guide to space. Bond, P. **520**

DK Millennium world atlas. See Millennium world atlas **912**

DK nature encyclopedia **508**

DK riding club [series]
Henderson, C. Horse & pony breeds **636.1**
Henderson, C. Horse & pony care **636.1**
Henderson, C. Horse & pony shows & events **798.2**
Henderson, C. Improve your riding skills **798.2**

The **DK** science encyclopedia **503**

DK student atlas **912**

DK ultimate sports lists. Meserole, M. **796**

DK ultimate visual dictionary 2000 **423**

DK ultimate visual dictionary of science. See Ultimate visual dictionary of science **503**

The **DK** visual timeline of the 20th century. Adams, S. **909.82**

Do not alight here. Aiken, J.
In Aiken, J. Give yourself a fright: thirteen tales of the supernatural p31-43 **S C**

Do people grow on family trees?. Wolfman, I. **929**

Do you want my opinion?. Kerr, M. E.
In Sixteen: short stories by outstanding writers for young adults p93-100 **S C**

Dobie, J. Frank (James Frank), 1888-1964
The mezcla man
In From sea to shining sea p30-32 **810.8**

Dobie, James Frank *See* Dobie, J. Frank (James Frank), 1888-1964

Dobyns, Henry F.
The Pima-Maricopa
In Indians of North America series **970.004**

Doctor Faust. McCaughrean, G.
In McCaughrean, G. The bronze cauldron: myths and legends of the world p31-34 **398.2**

Doctors *See* Physicians

A **doctor's** life. Storring, R. **610.69**

Documents of American history **973**

Dodson, Shireen
100 books for girls to grow on **028.1**

Does capital punishment deter crime? (7 and up) **364.66**

Does God have a big toe?. Gellman, M. **221.9**

Dog eat dog. Lynch, C. See note under Lynch, C. Mick **Fic**

The **dog** in the freezer. Mazer, H.
In Mazer, H. The dog in the freezer: three novellas p77-166 **S C**

The **dog** in the freezer: three novellas. Mazer, H. **S C**

A **dog** named Ransom. Vivelo, J.
In Vivelo, J. Chills in the night p36-54 **S C**

Dog obedience training. Allan, R. **636.7**

Dog racing
See also Iditarod Trail Sled Dog Race, Alaska; Sled dog racing

Doglicks. Gorog, J.
In Gorog, J. When nobody's home p9-15 **S C**

Dogs
Alderton, D. Dogs (7 and up) **636.7**
American Kennel Club. The complete dog book **636.7**
The Complete dog book for kids **636.7**
Paulsen, G. My life in dog years **92**
Paulsen, G. Puppies, dogs, and blue northers **798.8**

Fiction
Armstrong, W. H. Sounder **Fic**
Burnford, S. The incredible journey **Fic**
Calvert, P. Bigger **Fic**
Calvert, P. Sooner **Fic**
Cleary, B. Strider **Fic**
Fleischman, S. Jim Ugly **Fic**
Gipson, F. B. Old Yeller **Fic**
Henkes, K. Protecting Marie **Fic**
London, J. The call of the wild **Fic**
London, J. White Fang **Fic**
Lowry, L. Stay! **Fic**
Mazer, H. The dog in the freezer: three novellas **S C**
Naylor, P. R. Shiloh **Fic**
Rawls, W. Where the red fern grows **Fic**
Tamar, E. The junkyard dog **Fic**
Westall, R. The kingdom by the sea **Fic**

Training
Allan, R. Dog obedience training **636.7**

Dogs, Wild *See* Wild dogs

Dogsong. Paulsen, G. **Fic**

Dōhaku's head. Kimmel, E. A.
In Kimmel, E. A. Sword of the samurai p5-10 **Fic**

Doherty, Charles
Far Eastern art
In International encyclopedia of art **703**

Doherty, Kieran
William Penn **92**

Doiron, Ray
Partners in learning **027.8**

Dolan, Edward F., 1924-
America in the Korean War (7 and up) **951.9**
America in World War I **940.3**
The American Civil War **973.7**

The collections included and their contents are as follows: Adventures of Sherlock Holmes: A scandal in Bohemia; The Red-
headed League; A case of identity; The Boscombe Valley mystery; The five orange pips; The man with the twisted lip; The adventure of the Blue Carbuncle; The adventure of the speckled
band; The adventure of the engineer's thumb; The adventure of
the noble bachelor; The adventure of the Beryl Coronet; The adventure of the copper beeches

Memoirs of Sherlock Holmes: Silver Blaze; The yellow face;
The stock-broker's clerk; The 'Gloria Scott'; The Musgrave ritu-
al; The Reigate puzzle; The crooked man; The resident patient;
The Greek interpreter; The naval treaty; The final problem

The return of Sherlock Holmes: The adventure of the empty
house; The adventure of the Norwood builder; The adventure of
the dancing men; The adventure of the solitary cyclist; The adventure of the priory school; The adventure of Black Peter; The

adventure of Charles Augustus Milverton; The adventure of the
six Napoleons; The adventure of the three students; The adventure of the golden pince-nez; The adventure of the missing three-
quarter; The adventure of the Abbey Grange; The adventure of
the second stain

The valley of fear: The tragedy of Birlstone; The Scrowrers

His last bow: The adventure of Wisteria Lodge; The adventure
of the cardboard box; The adventure of the red circle; The adventure of the Bruce-Partington plans; The adventure of the
dying detective; The disappearance of Lady Frances Carfax; The
adventure of the Devil's foot; His last bow

The case book of Sherlock Holmes: The adventure of the illustrious client; The adventure of the blanched soldier; The adventure of the Mazarin stone; The adventure of the Three Gables;
The adventure of the Sussex vampire; The adventure of the three
Garridebs; The problem of Thor Bridge; The adventure of the
creeping man; The adventure of the lion's mane; The adventure
of the veiled lodger; The adventure of Shoscombe Old Place; The
adventure of the retired colourman

Draft resisters
   See also Conscientious objectors
Dragisic, Patricia
   How to write a letter (7 and up)   **808**
Draglia, Stacy
   See/See also pages in the following book(s):
   Rutledge, R. The best of the best in track & field p26-31   **920**
The **dragon** and the enchanted filly. Calvino, I.
   In The Book of dragons p1-9   **S C**
Dragon cauldron. Yep, L. See note under Yep, L.
   Dragon of the lost sea   **Fic**
Dragon of the lost sea. Yep, L.   **Fic**
Dragon steel. Yep, L. See note under Yep, L.
   Dragon of the lost sea   **Fic**
The **dragon** tamers. Nesbit, E.
   In The Book of dragons p128-46   **S C**
Dragon war. Yep, L. See note under Yep, L.
   Dragon of the lost sea   **Fic**
Dragondrums. McCaffrey, A. See note under McCaffrey, A. [The Pern series]   **Fic**
Dragonflight. McCaffrey, A. See note under McCaffrey, A. [The Pern series]   **Fic**
Dragonholder. McCaffrey, A. See note under McCaffrey, A. [The Pern series]   **Fic**
Dragonquest. McCaffrey, A. See note under McCaffrey, A. [The Pern series]   **Fic**
Dragonriders of Pern. McCaffrey, A. See note under McCaffrey, A. [The Pern series]
   Fic
Dragons
   See/See also pages in the following book(s):
   Nigg, J. Wonder beasts (7 and up)   **398**
   Fiction
   The Book of dragons   **S C**
   Fletcher, S. Dragon's milk (7 and up)   **Fic**
   Fletcher, S. Flight of the Dragon Kyn (7 and up)   **Fic**
   Fletcher, S. Sign of the dove (7 and up)
      Fic
   Stewart, J. J. If that breathes fire, we're toast!
      Fic
   Wrede, P. C. Dealing with dragons   **Fic**
   Yolen, J. Dragon's blood   **Fic**
   Yolen, J. Heart's Blood   **Fic**
   Yolen, J. A sending of dragons   **Fic**
Dragons & dreams   **S C**
Dragon's blood. Yolen, J.   **Fic**
The **dragon's** boy. Yolen, J.   **Fic**
Dragon's gate. Yep, L.   **Fic**
Dragon's milk. Fletcher, S.   **Fic**
Dragons to dine. McCaughrean, G.
   In McCaughrean, G. The bronze cauldron: myths and legends of the world p1-4
      398.2
Dragonsdawn. McCaffrey, A. See note under McCaffrey, A. [The Pern series]   **Fic**
Dragonseye. McCaffrey, A. See note under McCaffrey, A. [The Pern series]   **Fic**
Dragonsinger. McCaffrey, A. See note under McCaffrey, A. [The Pern series]   **Fic**
Dragonsong. McCaffrey, A. See note under McCaffrey, A. [The Pern series]   **Fic**

Dragonwings. Yep, L.   **Fic**
Drake, Sir Francis, 1540?-1596
   About
   Marrin, A. The sea king: Sir Francis Drake and his times (7 and up)   **92**
Drama
   See also Children's plays; One act plays
   Collections
   Great scenes for young actors   **808.82**
   Theatre for young audiences   **812.008**
   Indexes
   Karp, R. S. Plays for children and young adults
      808.82
Drama in education
   Shepard, A. Stories on stage   **812**
Drama of American history [series]
   Collier, C. The American Revolution, 1763-1783
      973.3
   Collier, C. Andrew Jackson's America, 1824-1850   **973.5**
   Collier, C. Building a new nation: the Federalist era, 1789-1801   **973.4**
   Collier, C. Clash of cultures, prehistory-1638
      970.004
   Collier, C. Creating the Constitution, 1787
      342
   Collier, C. The French and Indian War, 1660-1763   **973.2**
   Collier, C. Hispanic America, Texas, and the Mexican War, 1835-1850   **973.6**
   Collier, C. The Jeffersonian Republicans: the Louisiana Purchase and the war of 1812
      973.4
   Collier, C. The paradox of Jamestown, 1585-1700   **975.5**
   Collier, C. Pilgrims and Puritans, 1620-1676
      974.4
Dramatists
   Weitzman, D. L. Great lives: theater (7 and up)
      920
Dramatists, American
   McKissack, P. C. Young, black, and determined: a biography of Lorraine Hansberry   **92**
Dramatists, English
   Stanley, D. Bard of Avon: the story of William Shakespeare   **92**
Dramer, Kim
   Kublai Khan   **92**
   Native Americans and Black Americans
   In Indians of North America series
      970.004
   The Shoshone
   In Indians of North America series
      970.004
Draper, Sharon M. (Sharon Mills)
   Forged by fire (7 and up)   **Fic**
   Tears of a tiger (7 and up)   **Fic**
Draw 3-D. DuBosque, D.   **742**
[Draw 50 series]. Ames, L. J.   **743**
Draw insects. DuBosque, D.   **743**
Drawing
   Ames, L. J. [Draw 50 series]   **743**
   Ames, L. J. Drawing with Lee Ames   **741.2**
   Arnosky, J. Sketching outdoors in spring
      743

Drawing—*Continued*

Arnosky, J. Sketching outdoors in summer
743

DuBosque, D. Draw 3-D 742
DuBosque, D. Draw insects 743
Horton, J. An introduction to drawing
In The DK art school series 751
Smith, R. Drawing figures
In The DK art school series 751
Tallarico, T. Drawing and cartooning monsters
743
Welton, J. Drawing (7 and up) 741.2

Drawing and cartooning monsters. Tallarico, T.
743

Drawing figures. Smith, R.
In The DK art school series 751

A **drawing** in the sand. Butler, J. 704

Drawing with Lee Ames. Ames, L. J. 741.2

Dream flier. Yep, L.
In Yep, L. The rainbow people p154-60
398.2

Dream girl. Yep, L.
In Yep, L. The tree of dreams 398.2

Dream job. Sharmat, M. W.
In Visions: nineteen short stories by outstanding writers for young adults p23-29
S C

Dream journey. McCaughrean, G.
In McCaughrean, G. The silver treasure: myths and legends of the world p14-19
398.2

The **dream** keeper and other poems. Hughes, L.
811

The **dream** tree. Yep, L.
In Yep, L. The tree of dreams 398.2

Dream-weaver. Lawrence, L. Fic

Dreaming the sky down. Burford, B.
In Rites of passage p177-90 S C

Dreams

Fiction

Wynne-Jones, T. Stephen Fair (7 and up)
Fic
Yep, L. The tree of dreams 398.2

Dreams in the golden country. Lasky, K. Fic

The **dreams** of Mairhe Mehan. Armstrong, J.
Fic

Dreamtime. Oodgeroo 398.2

The **Dred** Scott case. Fleischner, J. 342

The **Dred** Scott decision. January, B. 342

Dreiser, Theodore, 1871-1945
See/See also pages in the following book(s):
Faber, D. Great lives: American literature p111-20
920

Dresang, Eliza T.
Radical change 028.5

Dressed for the occasion. Miller, B. M. 391

Dresselhaus, Mildred S., 1930-
See/See also pages in the following book(s):
Lindop, L. Scientists and doctors (7 and up)
920

Drew, Bernard A. (Bernard Alger), 1950-
The 100 most popular young adult authors
810.9

Drew, Charles Richard, 1904-1950
About
Talmadge, K. S. The life of Charles Drew
92
See/See also pages in the following book(s):
Haskins, J. One more river to cross 920

Drimmer, Frederick
Incredible people 920

Drinking. Pringle, L. P. 362.292

Drinking of alcoholic beverages
Alcohol: opposing viewpoints (7 and up)
362.292
Pringle, L. P. Drinking 362.292

Drinking problem *See* Alcoholism; Drinking of alcoholic beverages

The **dripping** cutlass. Olson, A. N.
In Olson, A. N. Ask the bones: scary stories from around the world p92-98 398.2

Drivers, Automobile *See* Automobile drivers

Driver's Ed. Cooney, C. B. Fic

Driver's test. Carter, A. R.
In Center stage 812.008

Driving under the influence of alcohol *See* Drunk driving

Drohan, Michele Ingber
Weight-loss programs (7 and up) 616.85

Drop Star. San Souci, R.
In San Souci, R. Cut from the same cloth p21-26 398.2

Dropouts
Stewart, G. Teen dropouts (7 and up)
362.7

Droughts
Allaby, M. Droughts (7 and up) 551.57
Fiction
Baillie, A. Secrets of Walden rising Fic

Drowned Ammet. Jones, D. W. Fic

Drucker, Malka, 1945-
Jacob's rescue Fic

Drug abuse
See also Solvent abuse
Banfield, S. Inside recovery 616.86
Bridgers, J. Everything you need to know about having an addictive personality (7 and up)
616.86
Chemical dependency: opposing viewpoints (7 and up) 362.29
Connelly, E. R. Through a glass darkly (7 and up) 362.29
Drug abuse: opposing viewpoints (7 and up)
362.29
Hanan, J. When someone you love is addicted (7 and up) 362.29
Holmes, A. Psychological effects of cocaine and crack addiction (7 and up) 362.29
Hyde, M. O. Mind drugs (7 and up)
616.86
Illegal drugs (7 and up) 364.1
Klein, W. Drugs and denial (7 and up)
362.29
Littell, M. A. Heroin drug dangers 362.29
Mass, W. Teen drug abuse (7 and up)
362.29
Monroe, J. Steroid drug dangers 362.29

Duane, Diane, 1952-—*Continued*
High wizardry. See note under Duane, D. A
  wizard abroad **Fic**
Midnight snack
  In Sixteen: short stories by outstanding writ-
    ers for young adults p22-30 **S C**
So you want to be a wizard. See note under
  Duane, D. A wizard abroad **Fic**
Uptown local
  In Dragons & dreams p151-78 **S C**
A wizard abroad **Fic**
DuBois, Graham
Prelude to victory
  In The Big book of holiday plays p254-65
    812.008
Prologue to adventure
  In The Big book of holiday plays p3-13
    812.008
DuBosque, Doug
Draw 3-D **742**
Draw insects **743**
Dubovoy, Sina
Civil rights leaders (7 and up) **920**
Dubulihasa. Fairman, T.
  In Fairman, T. Bury my bones but keep my
    words p130-41 **398.2**
Duder, Tessa
Sea changes
  In Ultimate sports: short stories by outstand-
    ing writers for young adults p252-72
    S C
Dudley, Mark E.
Brown v. Board of Education (1954) (7 and up)
    344
Engel v. Vitale (1962) (7 and up) **344**
Dudley, William, 1964-
(ed) The 1960s: opposing viewpoints. See The
  1960s: opposing viewpoints **973.92**
(ed) African Americans: opposing viewpoints.
  See African Americans: opposing viewpoints
    305.8
(ed) Asian Americans: opposing viewpoints. See
  Asian Americans: opposing viewpoints
    305.8
(ed) The Civil War: opposing viewpoints. See
  The Civil War: opposing viewpoints
    973.7
(ed) Endangered oceans: opposing viewpoints.
  See Endangered oceans: opposing viewpoints
    577.7
(ed) Epidemics: opposing viewpoints. See Epidemics: opposing viewpoints **614.4**
(ed) The Industrial revolution: opposing viewpoints. See The Industrial revolution: opposing viewpoints **330.973**
(ed) Media violence: opposing viewpoints. See
  Media violence: opposing viewpoints
    303.6
(ed) Native Americans: opposing viewpoints.
  See Native Americans: opposing viewpoints
    970.004
(ed) The Vietnam War: opposing viewpoints.
  See The Vietnam War: opposing viewpoints
    959.704

Duffy, Carol Ann
(ed) I wouldn't thank you for a valentine. See
  I wouldn't thank you for a valentine
    808.81
(ed) Stopping for death. See Stopping for death
    808.81
Duffy and the Bucca. Climo, S.
  In Climo, S. Magic & mischief p111-22
    398.2
Duffy's jacket. Coville, B.
  In Coville, B. Oddly enough p11-18
    S C
Duggleby, John
Story painter: the life of Jacob Lawrence
    92
Duke Ellington: giant of jazz. Old, W. **92**
**Dull Knife, Cheyenne Chief, ca. 1828-1879 or
1883**
See/See also pages in the following book(s):
Ehrlich, A. Wounded Knee: an Indian history of
  the American West **970.004**
Dumas, Alexandre, 1802-1870
The three musketeers (7 and up) **Fic**
Dunbar, Bonnie S.
See/See also pages in the following book(s):
Briggs, C. S. Women in space **920**
Dunbar, Paul Laurence, 1872-1906
The collected poetry of Paul Laurence Dunbar
    811
The complete poems of Paul Laurence Dunbar
  In Dunbar, P. L. The collected poetry of Paul
    Laurence Dunbar **811**
About
Gentry, T. Paul Laurence Dunbar **92**
See/See also pages in the following book(s):
Strickland, M. R. African-American poets p19-
27 **920**
Dunbar-Nelson, Alice Moore, 1875-1935
See/See also pages in the following book(s):
Lyons, M. E. Keeping secrets (7 and up)
    920
Duncan, Dayton
People of the West **978**
The West **978**
Duncan, Isadora, 1878-1927
About
O'Connor, B. Barefoot dancer: the story of Isa-
  dora Duncan **92**
Duncan, Lois, 1934-
Don't look behind you (7 and up) **Fic**
I know what you did last summer (7 and up)
    Fic
Killing Mr. Griffin (7 and up) **Fic**
Locked in time (7 and up) **Fic**
Psychic connections (7 and up) **133**
Stranger with my face (7 and up) **Fic**
Summer of fear (7 and up) **Fic**
The third eye (7 and up) **Fic**
The twisted window (7 and up) **Fic**
(ed) Night terrors. See Night terrors **S C**
(ed) Trapped!: cages of mind and body. See
  Trapped!: cages of mind and body **S C**
Duncan, Quince, 1940-
Swan song
  In Rites of passage p89-90 **S C**

Earth
  Gallant, R. A. Earth (7 and up)   550
  Lauber, P. Seeing Earth from space   525
  Taylor, B. Earth explained   550
Internal structure
  Clifford, N. Incredible earth   551.1
Earth. Daniels, P.   550
Earth always endures (7 and up)   897
Earth at risk [series]
  Catalano, J. Animal welfare   179
The **earth** atlas. Van Rose, S.   550
Earth explained. Taylor, B.   550
Earth keepers [series]
  Reef, C. Henry David Thoreau   92
Earth quest. See entry in CD-ROM section, Part
  3
Earth science on file   550
Earth sciences
  See also Geology
  Campbell, A. The New York Public Library in-
    credible Earth   550
  Daniels, P. Earth   550
  Earth quest. See entry in CD-ROM section, Part
    3
  Earth science on file   550
  English, J. Mission: Earth   550
  Lauber, P. Seeing Earth from space   525
  VanCleave, J. P. Janice VanCleave's A+
    projects in earth science (7 and up)   550
  The Visual dictionary of the earth   550
Dictionaries
  Farndon, J. Dictionary of the earth   550.3
Earth words. Simon, S.   363.7
Earth works. Dwyer, J. R.   016.3637
Earthenware *See* Pottery
Earthquake games. Levy, M.   551.2
Earthquakes
  Christian, S. Shake, rattle, and roll   551.2
  Levy, M. Earthquake games   551.2
  Silverstein, A. Plate tectonics   551.1
  Walker, S. M. Earthquakes   551.2
Fiction
  Cottonwood, J. Quake!   Fic
  Reiss, K. PaperQuake   Fic
Earthshine. Nelson, T.   Fic
Earthwitch. Wrede, P. C.
  In Wrede, P. C. Book of enchantments p71-
    95   S C
Earthworms. Pascoe, E.   592
Eason, Alethea
  The unicorns of Kabustan
  In A Glory of unicorns p115-24   S C
East *See* Asia
East (Near East) *See* Middle East
East Africa
History
  Wilson, T. H. City states of the Swahili coast
                                                 967.6
East Indians
United States
See/See also pages in the following book(s):
  Takaki, R. T. Strangers at the gates again p83-
    93 (7 and up)   305.8

East of the sun and west of the moon
  In Hearne, B. G. Beauties and beasts p66-75
                                                 398.2
Eastern Africa *See* East Africa
Eastern Europe
Fiction
  Dickinson, P. Shadow of a hero (7 and up)
                                                 Fic
The **Eastern** forest. Fielding, E.   577.3
Eastman, Charles Alexander, 1858-1939
About
  Badt, K. L. Charles Eastman   92
Eastman, Mary Huse, 1870-1963
  Index to fairy tales. See Index to fairy tales
                                                 398.2
Easy menu ethnic cookbooks [series]
  Holiday cooking around the world   641.5
Eat your enemy. Springer, N.
  In Twelve shots: outstanding short stories
    about guns p161-78   S C
Eat your words. Jones, C. F.   641.3
Eating customs
  See also Table etiquette
  Solheim, J. It's disgusting—and we ate it!
                                                 641.3
Eating disorders
  See also Anorexia nervosa; Bulimia
  Barrett, C. The dangers of diet drugs and other
    weight-loss products   615
  Bode, J. Food fight   616.85
  Clayton, L. Diet pill drug dangers   615
  Davis, B. What's real, what's ideal (7 and up)
                                                 616.85
  Drohan, M. I. Weight-loss programs (7 and up)
                                                 616.85
  Eating disorders (7 and up)   616.85
  Frankenberger, E. Food and love (7 and up)
                                                 616.85
  Frissell, S. Eating disorders and weight control
    (7 and up)   616.85
  O'Brien, E. Starving to win (7 and up)
                                                 616.85
  Vollstadt, E. W. Teen eating disorders (7 and
    up)   616.85
See/See also pages in the following book(s):
  Folkers, G. Taking charge of my mind & body
    (7 and up)   613
  Gray, H. M. Real girl/real world (7 and up)
                                                 305.23
  Schwager, T. The right moves p122-32 (7 and
    up)   613.7
Eating disorders (7 and up)   616.85
Eating disorders and weight control. Frissell, S.
                                                 616.85
The **ebony** horse. Philip, N.
  In Philip, N. The Arabian nights p65-76
                                                 398.2
Ecclesiastes, Book of *See* Bible. O.T. Ecclesiastes
Ecclesiastical rites and ceremonies *See* Rites and
  ceremonies
Echoes of the elders. Lelooska, D.   398.2
Echoes of the white giraffe. Choi, S. N. See note
  under Choi, S. N. Year of impossible
  goodbyes   Fic

Echohawk. Durrant, L.   **Fic**

Eckert, John Presper, 1919-1995
See/See also pages in the following book(s):
Northrup, M. American computer pioneers p37-45   **920**

Eckstine, Billy
See/See also pages in the following book(s):
Gourse, L. Swingers and crooners p105-07 (7 and up)   **781.65**

Ecological movement *See* Environmental movement

Ecology

> *See also* Biogeography; Biological diversity; Environmental protection; Food chains (Ecology); Habitat (Ecology); types of ecology, e.g. Marine ecology

Allaby, M. Biomes of the world   **577**
Exploring the Nardoo. See entry in CD-ROM section, Part 3
Fredericks, A. D. Exploring the oceans   **551.46**
Gardner, R. Science projects about the environment and ecology (7 and up)   **363.7**
Guiberson, B. Z. Exotic species   **577**
Kerrod, R. Facts on File wildlife atlas   **578**
Orr, R. Nature cross-sections   **577**
Patent, D. H. Fire: friend or foe   **577.2**
Sayre, A. P. Wetland   **577.6**
Scott, M. M. The young Oxford book of ecology   **577**
Snedden, R. The environment   **577**
VanCleave, J. P. Janice Vancleave's ecology for every kid   **577**
See/See also pages in the following book(s):
Patent, D. H. Biodiversity p41-51   **333.95**
Dictionaries
Simon, S. Earth words   **363.7**
Encyclopedias
Macmillan encyclopedia of the environment   **333.7**
Fiction
Sleator, W. The beasties (7 and up)   **Fic**

Ecology, Human *See* Human ecology

Ecology crafts for kids. Needham, B.   **745.5**

Ecosystem [series]
Allaby, M. Temperate forests   **577.3**
Day, T. Oceans   **551.46**

Ecosystems of North America [series]
Fielding, E. The Eastern forest   **577.3**
Katz, S. The Great Lakes   **577.6**
Mudd-Ruth, M. The deserts of the Southwest   **577.5**
Ormsby, A. The prairie   **577.4**

Ecuador
Foley, E. Ecuador   **986.6**

Eddy, Mary Baker, 1821-1910
About
Williams, J. K. The Christian Scientists (7 and up)   **289.5**

Edelman, Marian Wright
About
Old, W. Marian Wright Edelman (7 and up)   **92**
Siegel, B. Marian Wright Edelman   **92**

See/See also pages in the following book(s):
Lindop, L. Champions of equality (7 and up)   **920**

Edelson, Edward, 1932-
Gregor Mendel, and the roots of genetics (7 and up)   **92**
James Watson and Francis Crick and the building blocks of life (7 and up)   **92**

Edelson, Paula
Straight talk about teenage pregnancy (7 and up)   **362.7**
(jt. auth) Presma, F. Straight talk about today's families   **306.8**

Edgar, Kathleen J.
Everything you need to know about media violence   **303.6**

Edge, Rosalie
See/See also pages in the following book(s):
Byrnes, P. Environmental pioneers (7 and up)   **920**

Edge. Cadnum, M.   **Fic**

Edge books [series]
A Way out of no way   **810.8**

The edge of the sea. Carson, R.   **577.7**

Edible plants
George, J. C. Acorn pancakes, dandelion salad and 38 other wild recipes   **641.6**

Edison, Thomas A. (Thomas Alva), 1847-1931
InventorLabs: technology. See entry in CD-ROM section, Part 3
Parker, S. Thomas Edison and electricity   **92**

Edith Shay. LaFaye, A.   **Fic**

Edmo, Ed
After Celilo
In Talking leaves   **S C**

Edney, A. T. B.
ASPCA complete cat care manual   **636.8**

Edney, Andrew *See* Edney, A. T. B.

Education

> *See also* Schools; Teaching

See/See also pages in the following book(s):
The Information revolution: opposing viewpoints (7 and up)   **303.4**
Social aspects
Stanley, J. Children of the Dust Bowl   **371.9**
United States—Directories
The Handbook of private schools   **370.25**
United States—History
Loeper, J. J. Going to school in 1776   **370.9**

Education, Bilingual *See* Bilingual education

Education, Discrimination in *See* Discrimination in education

Education, Segregation in *See* Segregation in education

The education of Robert Nifkin. Pinkwater, D. M.   **Fic**

Educational counseling

> *See also* Vocational guidance

Educational media *See* Teaching—Aids and devices

El Greco, 1541-1614
See/See also pages in the following book(s):
Glubok, S. Great lives: painting p78-96
920

El-hi textbooks and serials in print **016.3713**
El Niño (Ocean current)
Arnold, C. El Niño **551.6**
El Salvador
Fiction
Temple, F. Grab hands and run **Fic**
Elderly
See also Old age
See/See also pages in the following book(s):
Inequality: opposing viewpoints in social problems p270-317 (7 and up) **305**
Eldin, Peter
Magic **793.8**
Eleanor, of Aquitaine, Queen, consort of Henry II, King of England, 1122?-1204
See/See also pages in the following book(s):
Meltzer, M. Ten queens p43-57 **920**
Fiction
Konigsburg, E. L. A proud taste for scarlet and miniver **Fic**
Elections
See/See also pages in the following book(s):
Carter, J. Talking peace p126-47 (7 and up)
327.1
Fiction
Lynch, C. Political timber (7 and up) **Fic**
Electric lines
See/See also pages in the following book(s):
Macaulay, D. Underground p67-77 **624**
Electricity
Parker, S. Electricity **537**
Pinna, S. de. Electricity **621.3**
Pollard, M. The light bulb and how it changed the world **621.3**
Electron microscopes
Tomb, H. Microaliens **502.8**
Electronic data processing
See also Artificial intelligence; Database management
Data explorer. See entry in CD-ROM section, Part 3
Dictionaries
Spencer, D. D. Illustrated computer dictionary for young people **004**
Electronic toys
See also Computer games
Electronics
Hoare, S. Digital revolution **621.381**
Elementary school libraries
See also Children's libraries
The **Elements** [Benchmark Bks.] **546**
Elements [Grolier] **546**
Elephant and Frog go courting. Bryan, A.
In Bryan, A. Ashley Bryan's African tales, uh-huh p13-19 **398.2**
Elephant woman. Pringle, L. P. **599.67**
Elephants
Caras, R. A. A most dangerous journey (7 and up) **599.67**

Levine, S. P. The elephant (7 and up)
599.67
Pringle, L. P. Elephant woman **599.67**
Redmond, I. Elephant **599.67**
Smith, R. In the forest with the elephants
599.67
Fiction
Cross, G. The great American elephant chase
Fic
The **elevator**. Sleator, W.
In Read all about it! p236-43 **808.8**
The **eleven** thousand Virgins. Delacre, L.
In Delacre, L. Golden tales p15-18 **398.2**
Elias (Biblical figure) *See* Elijah (Biblical figure)
Elijah (Biblical figure)
About
Goldin, B. D. Journeys with Elijah **222**
Elijah and the three brothers. Goldin, B. D.
In Goldin, B. D. Journeys with Elijah p39-47
222
Elijah Muhammad, 1897-1975
See/See also pages in the following book(s):
Banks, W. The Black Muslims **297**
Haskins, J. Louis Farrakhan and the Nation of Islam **92**
Elion, Gertrude B., 1918-1999
See/See also pages in the following book(s):
Yount, L. Contemporary women scientists (7 and up) **920**
Eliot Miles does not wish you a merry Christmas because . . . Konigsburg, E. L.
In A Newbery Christmas p51-53 **S C**
Elish, Dan, 1960-
Harriet Tubman and the underground railroad
92
James Meredith and school desegregation
92
Vermont
In Celebrate the states **973**
Washington, D.C.
In Celebrate the states **973**
Elizabeth I, Queen of England, 1533-1603
About
Stanley, D. Good Queen Bess: the story of Elizabeth I of England **92**
Thomas, J. R. Behind the mask: the life of Queen Elizabeth I (7 and up) **92**
See/See also pages in the following book(s):
Meltzer, M. Ten queens p73-83 **920**
Fiction
Lasky, K. Elizabeth I **Fic**
Elizabeth Cady Stanton and women's liberty. Cullen-DuPont, K. **92**
Elizabethan England. Ashby, R. **942.05**
Elk
Patent, D. H. Deer and elk **599.64**
Ella enchanted. Levine, G. C. **Fic**
Ellavich, Marie C.
(ed) Scientists. See Scientists **920.003**
Ellen's case. Metzger, L. **Fic**
Ellington, Duke, 1899-1974
About
Old, W. Duke Ellington: giant of jazz **92**

The **end** of the Young family feud. Montgomery, L. M.
In Montgomery, L. M. Christmas with Anne and other holiday stories p31-43
    S C

Endangered animals & habitats [series]
Ake, A. The gorilla   **599.8**
Barghusen, J. D. The bald eagle   **598**
Barghusen, L. The bear   **599.78**
DuTemple, L. A. Seals and sea lions
    599.79
Hull, M. The rhinoceros   **599.66**
Johnson, D. The Amazon rainforest   **577.3**
Levine, S. P. The elephant   **599.67**
Levine, S. P. The tiger   **599.75**
Mitchell, H. R. The wolf   **599.77**
Presnall, J. J. The giant panda   **599.78**
Price-Groff, C. The manatee   **599.5**
Woog, A. The shark   **597**
Woog, A. The whale   **599.5**
Wroble, L. A. The oceans   **577.7**
Endangered birds of North America. Sayre, A. P.
    598

Endangered in America [series]
Silverstein, A. The California condor   **598**
Silverstein, A. The grizzly bear   **599.78**
Silverstein, A. The mustang   **599.66**
Silverstein, A. The sea otter   **599.7**
Endangered mammals of North America. Sherrow, V.   **599**
Endangered oceans: opposing viewpoints (7 and up)   **577.7**
Endangered species
    See also Rare animals; Wildlife conservation
Ake, A. The gorilla (7 and up)   **599.8**
Arnold, C. On the brink of extinction   **598**
The Atlas of endangered species   **333.95**
Barghusen, J. D. The bald eagle (7 and up)
    598
Barghusen, L. The bear (7 and up)   **599.78**
DuTemple, L. A. Seals and sea lions (7 and up)
    599.79
Hull, M. The rhinoceros (7 and up)   **599.66**
Levine, S. P. The elephant (7 and up)
    599.67
Levine, S. P. The tiger (7 and up)   **599.75**
Mitchell, H. R. The wolf (7 and up)
    599.77
Patent, D. H. Back to the wild   **639.9**
Presnall, J. J. The giant panda (7 and up)
    599.78
Price-Groff, C. The manatee (7 and up)
    599.5
Roberts, R. Endangered species   **333.95**
Sayre, A. P. Endangered birds of North America
    598
Sherrow, V. Endangered mammals of North America   **599**
Silverstein, A. The grizzly bear   **599.78**
Silverstein, A. The sea otter   **599.7**
Woog, A. The shark (7 and up)   **597**
Woog, A. The whale (7 and up)   **599.5**
See/See also pages in the following book(s):
Endangered oceans: opposing viewpoints (7 and up)   **577.7**

Netzley, P. D. Issues in the environment p13-31 (7 and up)   **333.7**
Encyclopedias
The Grolier student encyclopedia of endangered species   **591.68**
Nagel, R. Endangered species   **333.95**
Ender's game. Card, O. S.   **Fic**
The **endless** steppe: growing up in Siberia. Hautzig, E. R.   **92**
Endrezze, Anita
The humming of stars and bees and waves
    In Talking leaves   S C
Endurance, Physical *See* Physical fitness
Endurance (Ship)
Armstrong, J. Shipwreck at the bottom of the world (7 and up)   **998**
Kimmel, E. C. Ice story   **998**
Energy *See* Force and energy
Energy. Challoner, J.   **621**
Energy forever? [series]
Graham, I. Solar power   **621.47**
Graham, I. Water power   **620.1**
Graham, I. Wind power   **621.4**
Energy resources
Challoner, J. Energy   **621**
Parker, S. Fuels for the future   **333.79**
Silverstein, A. Energy   **621**
The sun's joules. See entry in CD-ROM section, Part 3
Engel, Stephen
About
Dudley, M. E. Engel v. Vitale (1962) (7 and up)
    344
Engel v. Vitale (1962). Dudley, M. E.   **344**
Engelbert, Phillis
The complete weather resource   **551.5**
Technology in action   **603**
(ed) U.X.L science fact finder. See U.X.L science fact finder   **500**
Engelbreit, Mary
Hey, kids! Come craft with me   **745.5**
Engelmann, Jeanne
(jt. auth) Folkers, G. Taking charge of my mind & body   **613**
Engels, John Peffer- *See* Peffer-Engels, John, 1966-
Engfer, LeeAnne, 1963-
(jt. auth) Parker, D. L. Stolen dreams
    331.3
Engineering, Genetic *See* Genetic engineering
Engineering, Structural *See* Structural engineering
Engineers
Oleksy, W. G. Hispanic-American scientists (7 and up)   **920**
England
Lace, W. W. England (7 and up)   **942**
Lister, M. England   **942**
History
    See Great Britain—History
Social life and customs
Ashby, R. Elizabethan England   **942.05**
Sancha, S. The Luttrell village   **942.03**

Evaluating the school library media center.
Everhart, N.   027.8
Evans, Bill, 1929-1980
See/See also pages in the following book(s):
Gourse, L. Striders to beboppers and beyond
p102-05 (7 and up)   781.65
Evans, Craig Crist- *See* Crist-Evans, Craig
Evans, Eva Knox
Goat comes to the Christmas party
In Christmas gif' p26-31   810.8
Evans, Ivor H.
(ed) Brewer's dictionary of phrase and fable.
See Brewer's dictionary of phrase and fable
803
Evans, Lawrence Watt- *See* Watt-Evans, Lawrence, 1954-
Evans, Minnie, 1892-1987
About
Lyons, M. E. Painting dreams: Minnie Evans,
visionary artist   92
Everglades (Fla.)
Fiction
DeFelice, C. C. Lostman's River   Fic
George, J. C. The talking earth   Fic
Peck, R. N. Nine man tree   Fic
Poetry
Asch, F. Sawgrass poems   811
Everhart, Nancy
Evaluating the school library media center
027.8
Everlasting life. Hamilton, V.
In Hamilton, V. The dark way p73-75
398.2
Evers-Williams, Myrlie
See/See also pages in the following book(s):
Lindop, L. Champions of equality (7 and up)
920
Everson, Carrie J., 1842-1914
See/See also pages in the following book(s):
Altman, L. J. Women inventors p12-23 (7 and
up)   920
Everyday I sing the blues: the story of B.B. King.
Shirley, D.   92
Everyday living skills *See* Life skills
Everyday material science experiments [series]
Mebane, R. C. Air & other gases   530.4
Mebane, R. C. Metals   669
Mebane, R. C. Plastics & polymers   547
Mebane, R. C. Salts & solids   530.4
Mebane, R. C. Water & other liquids
530.4
Everything weather. See entry in CD-ROM section, Part 3
Everything you need to know about abusive relationships. Rue, N. N.   362.7
Everything you need to know about ADD/ADHD.
Beal, E.   616.85
Everything you need to know about being adopted. Kaminker, L.   362.7
Everything you need to know about conflict resolution. Nathan, A.   158
Everything you need to know about creating your
own support system. Kreiner, A.   158

Everything you need to know about dealing with
losses. Weiss, S.   155.9
Everything you need to know about dealing with
sexual assault. Kaminker, L.   362.883
Everything you need to know about going to the
gynecologist. Diamond, S. N.   618.1
Everything you need to know about having an addictive personality. Bridgers, J.   616.86
Everything you need to know about media violence. Edgar, K. J.   303.6
Everything you need to know about mononucleosis. Smart, P.   616.9
Everything you need to know about protecting
yourself and others from abduction. Wiloch,
T.   613.6
Everything you need to know about self-
mutilation. Ng, G.   616.85
Everything you need to know when a parent
doesn't speak English. Lakin, P.   306.4
Everything you need to know when someone you
know has been killed. Schleifer, J.   155.9
Evidence. Asimov, I.
In Asimov, I. I, robot   S C
The **evil** eye. Olson, A. N.
In Olson, A. N. Ask the bones: scary stories
from around the world p134-40
398.2
The **evitable** conflict. Asimov, I.
In Asimov, I. I, robot   S C
Evolution
Gallant, R. A. Early humans   599.93
Gamblin, L. Evolution   576.8
Gardner, R. Human evolution (7 and up)
599.93
Lindsay, W. Prehistoric life   560
Parker, S. Charles Darwin and evolution
92
Silverstein, A. Evolution   576.8
Stefoff, R. Charles Darwin and the evolution
revolution (7 and up)   92
See/See also pages in the following book(s):
Patent, D. H. Biodiversity p53-63   333.95
Study and teaching
Blake, A. The Scopes trial   345
Nardo, D. The Scopes trial (7 and up)   345
Thorndike, J. L. Epperson v. Arkansas (7 and
up)   345
Ewing, Maurice, 1906-1974
See/See also pages in the following book(s):
Polking, K. Oceanographers and explorers of the
sea p11-21   920
Ewing, W. Maurice *See* Ewing, Maurice, 1906-
1974
Ex poser. Jennings, P.
In Jennings, P. Unmentionable! p85-88
S C
Ex-service men *See* Veterans
The **examination.** Bosse, M. J.   Fic
Examinations
Gilbert, S. D. How to do your best on tests (7
and up)   371.2
Excavations (Archeology)
Goodman, S. Stones, bones, and petroglyphs
930.1

Exploring the Titanic. Ballard, R. D.   **910.4**

Express to Valley Forge. Dias, E. J.
In The Big book of holiday plays p241-53
812.008

Extinct animals
See also Prehistoric animals; Rare animals

Extinct cities
Stefoff, R. Finding the lost cities (7 and up)
930.1

The **extinguished** lights. Singer, I. B.
In Singer, I. B. The power of light p13-20
S C

Extraordinary American Indians. Avery, S.
920

Extraordinary black Americans: from colonial to contemporary times. Altman, S.   **920**

Extraordinary events and oddball occurrences. Blackwood, G. L.   **001.9**

Extraordinary explorers [series]
Stefoff, R. Scientific explorers   **509**

Extraordinary Hispanic Americans. Sinnott, S.
920

Extraordinary Jewish Americans. Brooks, P.
920

An **extraordinary** life. Pringle, L. P.   **595.7**

Extraordinary people [series]
Brooks, P. Extraordinary Jewish Americans
920
Gulotta, C. Extraordinary women in politics
920
Kent, D. Extraordinary people with disabilities
920
Price-Groff, C. Extraordinary women journalists
920
Stille, D. R. Extraordinary women of medicine
920

Extraordinary people in extraordinary times. Mendoza, P. M.   **920**

Extraordinary people with disabilities. Kent, D.
920

Extraordinary women in politics. Gulotta, C.
920

Extraordinary women journalists. Price-Groff, C.
920

Extraordinary women of medicine. Stille, D. R.
920

Extrasensory perception
See also Telepathy
See/See also pages in the following book(s):
Duncan, L. Psychic connections p1-13 (7 and up)   **133**
Paranormal phenomena: opposing viewpoints p119-55 (7 and up)   **133**
Fiction
Bowler, T. Midget (7 and up)   **Fic**
Duncan, L. The third eye (7 and up)   **Fic**
Sleator, W. Others see us (7 and up)   **Fic**
Sweeney, J. Shadow (7 and up)   **Fic**

Extraterrestrial beings
Kettelkamp, L. ETs and UFOs   **001.9**
Netzley, P. D. Alien abductions: opposing viewpoints (7 and up)   **001.9**
Wilson, C. UFOs and aliens   **001.9**

Fiction
Brittain, B. Shape-changer   **Fic**
Coville, B. Aliens ate my homework   **Fic**
Dexter, C. Alien game   **Fic**
Mackel, K. Can of worms   **Fic**
Shusterman, N. The dark side of nowhere
Fic
Sleator, W. The night the heads came   **Fic**

Extreme Elvin. Lynch, C.   **Fic**

Extreme skateboarding. Ryan, P.   **796.22**

Extreme sports [series]
Ryan, P. Extreme skateboarding   **796.22**

Exultate jubilate. Paterson, K.
In Paterson, K. A midnight clear: stories for the Christmas season   **S C**

Exum, J. Cheryl
(jt. auth) Bach, A. Miriam's well   **221.9**

Exupéry, Antoine de Saint- *See* Saint-Exupéry, Antoine de, 1900-1944

Exxon Valdez (Ship)
Markle, S. After the spill   **363.7**
Sherrow, V. The Exxon Valdez   **363.7**

Eye of the great bear. Wallace, B.   **Fic**

Eye of the storm. Kramer, S. P.   **778.9**

Eyeglasses
Fiction
Shusterman, N. The eyes of Kid Midas   **Fic**

The **eyes**. Pearson, K.
In Don't read this! and other tales of the unnatural p132-48   **S C**

Eyes knows. Jennings, P.
In Jennings, P. Unmentionable! p108-20
S C

Eyes of a stranger. Heisel, S. E.   **Fic**

The **eyes** of Kid Midas. Shusterman, N.   **Fic**

Eyes of the cat. Bond, R.
In The Oxford book of scary tales p76-78
808.8

The **eyes** of the killer robot. Bellairs, J. See note under Bellairs, J. The curse of the blue figurine   **Fic**

Eyes on the prize: America's civil rights years, 1954-1965. Williams, J.   **323.1**

Eyewitness art [series]
Cole, A. The Renaissance   **709.02**
Opie, M.-J. Sculpture   **730.9**
Welton, J. Drawing   **741.2**
Welton, J. Looking at paintings   **750.1**

Eyewitness books [series]
Adams, S. Titanic   **910.4**
Arthur, A. Shell   **594**
Bender, L. Invention   **609**
Brookfield, K. Book   **070.5**
Burnie, D. Bird   **598**
Burnie, D. Plant   **580**
Burnie, D. Tree   **582.16**
Byam, M. Arms & armor   **355.8**
Clarke, B. Amphibian   **597.8**
Clutton-Brock, J. Cat   **599.75**
Cotterell, A. Ancient China   **931**
Cribb, J. Money   **332.4**
Early humans   **930.1**
Grau, A. Dance   **792.8**

F

Facklam, Howard—*Continued*
Bacteria 579.3
Viruses 579.2
Facklam, Margery, 1927-
Tracking dinosaurs in the Gobi 567.9
(jt. auth) Facklam, H. Bacteria 579.3
(jt. auth) Facklam, H. Viruses 579.2
Factories
Fiction
Paterson, K. Lyddie Fic
Factory deluxe. See entry in CD-ROM section,
Part 3
Facts, Miscellaneous *See* Curiosities and wonders
Facts about the Congress. Christianson, S. G.
328.73
Facts about the presidents. Kane, J. N. 920
Facts about the states 973
The **Facts** on File atlas of stars and planets. See
Ridpath, I. Facts on File stars & planets atlas
520
Facts on File science sourcebooks [series]
Grady, S. M. Virtual reality 006
Thomas, P. Talking bones 614
Facts on File stars & planets atlas. Ridpath, I.
520
The **Facts** on File visual dictionary. Corbeil, J.-C.
423
Facts on File wildlife atlas. Kerrod, R. 578
Facts on File world news CD-ROM. See entry in
CD-ROM section, Part 3
The **facts** speak for themselves. Cole, B. Fic
Fader, Kim Brown, 1956-
Russia (7 and up) 947
Fagan, Eleanora *See* Holiday, Billie, 1915-1959
Faherty, Sara
Victims and victims' rights (7 and up)
362.88
Faidley, Warren
About
Kramer, S. P. Eye of the storm 778.9
Fair shares. Philip, N.
In Philip, N. The Arabian nights p22-23
398.2
Fairies
Encyclopedias
Rose, C. Spirits, fairies, gnomes, goblins (7 and
up) 398
Fiction
Block, F. L. I was a teenage fairy (7 and up)
Fic
McGraw, E. J. The moorchild Fic
Fairman, Tony
Bury my bones but keep my words 398.2
Contents: Nyar-upoko; Zazamankh; The man with a tree on his
head; The bag of money; The good herdboy; Karimirwa and
Musiguku; There's one day for the victim; Hare and the white
man; Hare and his friends; Dubulihasa; Omutugwa; The wise lit-
tle girl; The two swindlers
The **Fairy** serpent
In Hearne, B. G. Beauties and beasts p29-31
398.2
Fairy tale. Mujica, B. L.
In Where angels glide at dawn p77-97
S C

Fairy tale series
Yolen, J. Briar Rose Fic
Fairy tales
See also Fantasy fiction
American fairy tales S C
Andersen, H. C. The little mermaid and other
fairy tales S C
Brooke, W. J. Teller of tales S C
Galloway, P. Truly grim tales (7 and up)
S C
Hearne, B. G. Beauties and beasts 398.2
Levine, G. C. The princess test Fic
McKinley, R. Beauty (7 and up) Fic
McKinley, R. The door in the hedge S C
McKinley, R. Rose daughter (7 and up)
Fic
Napoli, D. J. Spinners (7 and up) Fic
Napoli, D. J. Zel (7 and up) Fic
Philip, N. The Arabian nights 398.2
The Seven voyages of Sinbad the Sailor
398.2
Vande Velde, V. Tales from the Brothers
Grimm and the Sisters Weird S C
Willard, N. Beauty and the beast 398.2
Indexes
Index to fairy tales 398.2
The **Falcon**. Koller, J. F. Fic
The **falcon**. Palmer, G.
In Theatre for young audiences p338-63
812.008
Falconer, Kieran, 1970-
Peru 985
Falcons
Arnold, C. Hawk highway in the sky 598
The **fall** of the House of Usher. Poe, E. A.
In Poe, E. A. Tales of Edgar Allan Poe p127-
52 S C
The **fallen** angel. Wynne-Jones, T.
In Wynne-Jones, T. Lord of the Fries and
other stories p116-49 S C
Fallen angels. Myers, W. D. Fic
Falling off the Empire State Building. Mazer, H.
In Ultimate sports: short stories by outstand-
ing writers for young adults p302-13
S C
Falling stars *See* Meteors
Falling up. Silverstein, S. 811
Fallout. Lester, J. Fic
Falsehood *See* Truthfulness and falsehood
The **Falsoms'** Christmas dinner. Montgomery, L.
M.
In Montgomery, L. M. Christmas with Anne
and other holiday stories p147-59
S C
Familiar quotations. Bartlett, J. 808.88
Family
See also types of family members
Blue, R. Staying out of trouble in a troubled
family (7 and up) 362.7
The **Family**: opposing viewpoints (7 and up)
306.8
Presma, F. Straight talk about today's families
(7 and up) 306.8

Famous trials [series]—*Continued*
Tackach, J. The trial of John Brown, radical abolitionist **345**

Fanaticism

Fiction
Brooks, B. Asylum for Nightface (7 and up) **Fic**

Fancy dress *See* Costume

Fang, Li-chih *See* Fang Lizhi

Fang Lizhi
See/See also pages in the following book(s):
Lucas, E. Contemporary human rights activists p65-77 (7 and up) **920**

The **fantastic** book of snow-boarding. McKenna, L. **796.9**

Fantastic fiction *See* Fantasy fiction

Fantastic films *See* Fantasy films

Fantasy fiction
See also Fairy tales; Science fiction
Alexander, L. The Arkadians **Fic**
Alexander, L. The book of three **Fic**
Alexander, L. The foundling and other tales of Prydain **S C**
Alexander, L. Gypsy Rizka **Fic**
Alexander, L. The high king **Fic**
Almond, D. Skellig **Fic**
Avi. Perloo the bold **Fic**
Barron, T. A. The lost years of Merlin (7 and up) **Fic**
Barron, T. A. The Merlin effect **Fic**
Bell, C. Ratha's challenge (7 and up) **Fic**
The Book of dragons **S C**
Bradbury, R. The Halloween tree **Fic**
Cooper, S. Over sea, under stone **Fic**
Coville, B. Into the land of the unicorns **Fic**
Coville, B. The skull of truth **Fic**
Dragons & dreams **S C**
Duane, D. A wizard abroad **Fic**
Farmer, N. The warm place **Fic**
Fleischman, S. The 13th floor **Fic**
Fletcher, S. Dragon's milk (7 and up) **Fic**
Fletcher, S. Flight of the Dragon Kyn (7 and up) **Fic**
Fletcher, S. Sign of the dove (7 and up) **Fic**
Foster, A. D. The Hand of Dinotopia **Fic**
Gurney, J. Dinotopia: a land apart from time **Fic**
Hite, S. Answer my prayer (7 and up) **Fic**
Ibbotson, E. Which witch? **Fic**
Jacques, B. Redwall **Fic**
Jennings, P. Unbearable! **S C**
Jennings, P. Uncovered! **S C**
Jennings, P. Undone! **S C**
Jennings, P. Unmentionable! **S C**
Jones, D. W. Cart and cwidder (7 and up) **Fic**
Jones, D. W. Castle in the air **Fic**
Jones, D. W. The crown of Dalemark (7 and up) **Fic**
Jones, D. W. Dark Lord of Derkholm (7 and up) **Fic**
Jones, D. W. Drowned Ammet (7 and up) **Fic**

Jones, D. W. Howl's moving castle **Fic**
Jones, D. W. The lives of Christopher Chant **Fic**
Jones, D. W. The spellcoats (7 and up) **Fic**
Le Guin, U. K. A wizard of Earthsea **Fic**
L'Engle, M. A wrinkle in time **Fic**
Levine, G. C. Ella enchanted **Fic**
Lewis, C. S. The lion, the witch, and the wardrobe **Fic**
Lisle, J. T. Forest **Fic**
McCaffrey, A. If wishes were horses (7 and up) **Fic**
McCaffrey, A. [The Pern series] (7 and up) **Fic**
McGraw, E. J. The moorchild **Fic**
McKillip, P. A. The riddle-master of Hed (7 and up) **Fic**
McKinley, R. The blue sword (7 and up) **Fic**
McKinley, R. The hero and the crown (7 and up) **Fic**
Nix, G. Sabriel (7 and up) **Fic**
Norton, A. The monster's legacy (7 and up) **Fic**
Norton, A. Witch World [series] (7 and up) **Fic**
Pierce, M. A. A gathering of gargoyles (7 and up) **Fic**
Pierce, M. A. The pearl of the soul of the world (7 and up) **Fic**
Pierce, T. Circle of magic: Briar's book **Fic**
Pierce, T. Circle of magic: Daja's book **Fic**
Pierce, T. Circle of magic: Sandry's book **Fic**
Pierce, T. Circle of magic: Tris's book **Fic**
Pierce, T. First test **Fic**
Pierce, T. Wolf-speaker **Fic**
Rowling, J. K. Harry Potter and the sorcerer's stone **Fic**
Service, P. F. Weirdos of the universe, unite! **Fic**
Smith, S. Court duel (7 and up) **Fic**
Smith, S. Crown duel (7 and up) **Fic**
Swift, J. Gulliver's travels (7 and up) **Fic**
Tolkien, J. R. R. The hobbit **Fic**
Tolkien, J. R. R. The lord of the rings (7 and up) **Fic**
Wrede, P. C. Dealing with dragons **Fic**
Yep, L. Dragon of the lost sea **Fic**
Yolen, J. Briar Rose (7 and up) **Fic**
Yolen, J. Dragon's blood **Fic**
Yolen, J. Heart's Blood **Fic**
Yolen, J. Hobby **Fic**
Yolen, J. Merlin **Fic**
Yolen, J. Passager **Fic**
Yolen, J. The Pictish child **Fic**
Yolen, J. A sending of dragons **Fic**
Yolen, J. Twelve impossible things before breakfast **S C**
Yolen, J. The wizard's map **Fic**

Encyclopedias
The Encyclopedia of fantasy **809.3**
The Ultimate encyclopedia of fantasy **809.3**

Fasts and feasts
Judaism
See Jewish holidays

The **fata**. San Souci, R.
In San Souci, R. A terrifying taste of short &
shivery p12-14   **398.2**

A **fate** totally worse than death. Fleischman, P.   **Fic**

Fathers
See also Teenage fathers

Jamiolkowski, R. M. Coping with an emotionally distant father (7 and up)   **158**

Fiction
Hermes, P. Cheat the moon   **Fic**

Konigsburg, E. L. Journey to an 800 number   **Fic**

Fathers, Single parent *See* Single parent family

Fathers and daughters
Fiction
Brooks, B. Midnight hour encores (7 and up)   **Fic**

Bunting, E. Spying on Miss Müller   **Fic**

Cadnum, M. Heat (7 and up)   **Fic**

Calvert, P. Glennis, before and after   **Fic**

Hamilton, V. Plain City   **Fic**

Hearne, B. G. Listening for Leroy   **Fic**

Henkes, K. Protecting Marie   **Fic**

Klass, S. S. Next stop, nowhere   **Fic**

Krisher, T. Kinship (7 and up)   **Fic**

Lasky, K. Beyond the divide (7 and up)   **Fic**

Marchetta, M. Looking for Alibrandi (7 and up)   **Fic**

Marino, J. For the love of Pete   **Fic**

Napoli, D. J. Spinners (7 and up)   **Fic**

Nelson, T. Earthshine   **Fic**

Pevsner, S. Sing for your father, Su Phan   **Fic**

Rinaldi, A. Mine eyes have seen (7 and up)   **Fic**

Stanley, D. Time apart   **Fic**

Strasser, T. Hey, Dad, get a life!   **Fic**

Taylor, T. Sweet Friday Island (7 and up)   **Fic**

Thesman, J. The storyteller's daughter (7 and
up)   **Fic**

Fathers and sons
Fiction
Avi. The barn   **Fic**

Bartoletti, S. C. No man's land   **Fic**

Bauer, M. D. Face to face   **Fic**

Bechard, M. If it doesn't kill you (7 and up)   **Fic**

Berry, J. Ajeemah and his son   **Fic**

Calvert, P. Bigger   **Fic**

Cormier, R. In the middle of the night (7 and
up)   **Fic**

Crist-Evans, C. Moon over Tennessee   **Fic**

Crutcher, C. Ironman (7 and up)   **Fic**

Deuker, C. Heart of a champion (7 and up)   **Fic**

Fenner, C. The king of dragons   **Fic**

Ferris, J. All that glitters (7 and up)   **Fic**

Fox, P. The eagle kite   **Fic**

Griffin, A. Sons of liberty   **Fic**

Hahn, M. D. Following my own footsteps   **Fic**

Hughes, M. The Golden Aquarians   **Fic**

Kehret, P. Searching for Candlestick Park   **Fic**

Layefsky, V. Impossible things   **Fic**

Lee, M. G. Necessary roughness (7 and up)   **Fic**

Lester, J. Fallout (7 and up)   **Fic**

Lynch, C. Shadow boxer (7 and up)   **Fic**

Miklowitz, G. D. Camouflage   **Fic**

Moon, P. The spying game   **Fic**

Myers, A. The keeping room   **Fic**

Myers, W. D. Somewhere in the darkness (7
and up)   **Fic**

Naylor, P. R. The keeper   **Fic**

Paulsen, G. The tent (7 and up)   **Fic**

Peck, R. N. Cowboy ghost   **Fic**

Reeder, C. Foster's war   **Fic**

Ritter, J. H. Choosing up sides   **Fic**

Salisbury, G. Shark bait   **Fic**

Schmidt, G. D. Anson's way   **Fic**

Seago, K. Matthew unstrung (7 and up)   **Fic**

Springer, N. I am Mordred (7 and up)   **Fic**

Talbert, M. The Purple Heart   **Fic**

Vanasse, D. Out of the wilderness   **Fic**

Yep, L. Dragonwings   **Fic**

Young, R. T. Moving Mama to town   **Fic**

Faulk, Odie B.
The Modoc
In Indians of North America series   **970.004**

Faulkner, William, 1897-1962
See/See also pages in the following book(s):
Faber, D. Great lives: American literature p193-
202   **920**

Faulkner, William J.
How the slaves helped each other
In From sea to shining sea p130-31   **810.8**

Favorite medieval tales. Osborne, M. P.   **398.2**

Favorite Norse myths. Osborne, M. P.   **293**

Favre, Brett
About
Gutman, B. Brett Favre   **92**

FBI *See* United States. Federal Bureau of Investigation

The **FBI** and law enforcement agencies of the
United States. Kronenwetter, M.   **363.2**

The **FDR** way. Morris, J. B.   **92**

Fear. Davies, R.
In Read all about it! p223-29   **808.8**

The **fear** place. Naylor, P. R.   **Fic**

Feast of Lights *See* Hanukkah

Feathertop. Hawthorne, N.
In American fairy tales p29-54   **S C**

Febold Feboldson, first citizen of Nebraska.
Schmidt, S.
In From sea to shining sea p178-79   **810.8**

Federal Bureau of Investigation (U.S.) *See* United States. Federal Bureau of Investigation

Finding the lost cities. Stefoff, R. **930.1**

Fine, Anne
   Flour babies   **Fic**
   Step by wicked step   **Fic**
   The Tulip touch   **Fic**

Fine, Edith Hope
   Barbara McClintock (7 and up)   **92**

Fine arts See Arts

A **fine** white dust. Rylant, C.   **Fic**

Finger, Charles Joseph, 1869-1941
   The magic ball
    In A Newbery Halloween p101-10   **S C**

Fingerprints and talking bones. Jones, C. F.
          363.2

Fingers on the back of the neck. Mahy, M.
    In Don't read this! and other tales of the un-
    natural p7-22   **S C**

Fingers on the back of the neck and other ghost
   stories. See Don't read this! and other tales of
   the unnatural   **S C**

Fink, Ida
   Splinter
    In Bearing witness p81-85   **808.8**
   See/See also pages in the following book(s):
   Mandell, S. L. Writers of the Holocaust (7 and
   up)   **940.53**

Finkelstein, Norman H., 1941-
   Remember not to forget   **940.53**
   The way things never were   **973.92**
   With heroic truth: the life of Edward R. Murrow
   (7 and up)   **92**

Finlayson, Reggie
   Nelson Mandela   **92**

Finley, Carol
   Aboriginal art of Australia   **759.01**
   The art of African masks   **391**
   Art of the Far North   **704**

Finn Mac Cumaill
   See/See also pages in the following book(s):
   Ross, A. Druids, gods & heroes from Celtic my-
   thology p53-64   **299**

Finn MacCool See Finn Mac Cumaill

Finn Maccoul. Osborne, M. P.
    In Osborne, M. P. Favorite medieval tales
   p1-7   **398.2**

Finnish Americans
              Fiction
   Holm, J. L. Our only May Amelia   **Fic**

Fire!. Masoff, J.   **628.9**

Fire!. See entry in CD-ROM section, Part 3

Fire fighters
   Beil, K. M. Fire in their eyes   **628.9**
   Masoff, J. Fire!   **628.9**

Fire fighting
   Gorrell, G. K. Catching fire   **628.9**

Fire: friend or foe. Patent, D. H.   **577.2**

A **fire** in her bones: the story of Mary Lyon.
   Rosen, D.   **92**

Fire in the forest. Pringle, L. P.   **577.2**

Fire in their eyes. Beil, K. M.   **628.9**

Fire into ice. Houston, J. A.   **748.2**

Fire on the wind. Crew, L.   **Fic**

The **fire** pony. Philbrick, W. R.   **Fic**

Firearms
              Fiction
   Fox, P. One-eyed cat   **Fic**
   Twelve shots: outstanding short stories about
   guns (7 and up)   **S C**
          Law and legislation
    See Gun control
   Hanson, F. O. The Second Amendment (7 and
   up)   **344**

Firebird (Ballet)
   See/See also pages in the following book(s):
   McCaughrean, G. The Random House book of
   stories from the ballet p85-94   **792.8**

Fireflies. Fleischman, P.
    In A Newbery zoo   **S C**

Fires
              Fiction
   Cooney, C. B. Flash fire (7 and up)   **Fic**
          Chicago (Ill.)
   Murphy, J. The great fire   **977.3**

The **fires** of Merlin. Barron, T. A. See note under
   Barron, T. A. The lost years of Merlin
              Fic

Fireside, Harvey, 1929-
   The Fifth Amendment (7 and up)   **347**
   New York Times v. Sullivan (7 and up)
              342
   Plessy v. Ferguson (7 and up)   **342**

The **Fireside** Book of Ghost Stories. Vivelo, J.
    In Vivelo, J. Chills in the night p89-101
              S C

A **firestorm** unleashed. Ayer, E. H.   **940.53**

Fireweed. Paton Walsh, J.   **Fic**

First book [series]
   Anderson, M. K. So proudly they served
              940.54
   Armbruster, A. The American flag   **929.9**
   Arnold, C. Pelé: the king of soccer   **92**
   Aronson, B. Meteors   **523.5**
   Bendick, J. Tombs of the ancient Americas
              393
   Black, W. B. Slaves to soldiers   **973.7**
   Bonar, S. Comets   **523.6**
   Bredeson, C. The moon   **523.3**
   Bredeson, C. Tide pools   **577.6**
   Brimner, L. D. Rock climbing   **796.52**
   Brimner, L. D. Snowboarding   **796.9**
   Brown, F. Special Olympics   **796**
   Carter, A. R. Last stand at the Alamo
              976.4
   Carter, A. R. The Spanish-American War
              973.8
   Conrad, D. C. The Songhay Empire   **966.2**
   Fitzgerald, K. The story of iron   **669**
   Fitzgerald, K. The story of oxygen   **546**
   Gallant, R. A. Limestone caves   **551.4**
   Gowell, E. T. Fountains of life   **577.7**
   Green, R. L. The empire of Ghana   **966.1**
   Green, R. King Henry VIII   **92**
   Green, R. Queen Victoria   **92**
   Green, R. Tutankhamun   **932**
   Green, R. William the Conqueror   **92**
   Greene, J. D. The Maya   **972**
   Haynes, J. Egyptian dynasties   **932**

First book [series]—*Continued*

Lampton, C. The World Wide Web   **004.6**

Landau, E. Bill Clinton and his presidency
  92

Landau, E. Joined at birth   **616**

Landau, E. Living with albinism   **616.5**

McGowen, T. World War II   **940.53**

Peffer-Engels, J. States of Ethiopia   **963**

Perry, P. J. Armor to venom   **591.47**

Perry, P. J. Bats   **599.4**

Perry, P. J. Hide and seek   **591.47**

Perry, P. J. Soaring   **797.5**

Quiri, P. R. The White House   **975.3**

Rauzon, M. J. Hummingbirds   **598**

Rauzon, M. J. Vultures   **598**

Saign, G. The African cats   **599.75**

Saign, G. The great apes   **599.8**

Van Steenwyk, E. Mathew Brady   **92**

Walsh Shepherd, D. The Klondike gold rush
  971.9

Williams, J. K. Matthew Henson, polar adventurer   **92**

Wilson, T. H. City states of the Swahili coast
  967.6

The **first** book of rhythms. See Hughes, L. The book of rhythms   **701**

The **first** day. Jones, E. P.
In Leaving home: stories p9-17   **808.8**

First generation children *See* Children of immigrants

First houses. Monroe, J. G.   **970.004**

First impressions [series]

Beardsley, J. Pablo Picasso   **92**

Berman, A. James McNeill Whistler   **92**

Greenfeld, H. Paul Gauguin   **92**

Kostenevich, A. G. Henri Matisse   **92**

Meryman, R. Andrew Wyeth   **92**

Rayfield, S. Pierre-Auguste Renoir   **92**

Rubin, S. G. Frank Lloyd Wright   **92**

Schwartz, G. Hieronymus Bosch   **92**

First in peace: George Washington, the Constitution, and the presidency. Rosenburg, J. M.
  92

First in the field: baseball hero Jackie Robinson. Dingle, D. T.   **92**

First job. Soto, G.
In Soto, G. Local news p26-34   **S C**

First Manassas (7 and up)   **973.7**

The **first** passage. Palmer, C. A.   **326**

First person America [series]

Brown, G. Conflict in Europe and the Great Depression   **973.9**

Brown, G. The struggle to grow   **973.8**

Steins, R. The nation divides   **973.7**

First snow. McCaughrean, G.
In McCaughrean, G. The golden hoard: myths and legends of the world p120-25
  398.2

The **first** solo flight around the world. Taylor, R. L.   **629.13**

First test. Pierce, T.   **Fic**

The **first** woman to vote in the state of California. Polese, C.
In From sea to shining sea p182-85
  810.8

The **First** World War. Kirchberger, J. H.
  940.3

The **fish** at dragon's gate. Mayo, M.
In Mayo, M. Mythical birds & beasts from many lands p46-54   **398.2**

Fish culture

See also Aquariums

The **fish** husband. Osborne, M. P.
In Osborne, M. P. Mermaid tales from around the world p33-36   **398.2**

A **fish** story. San Souci, R.
In San Souci, R. A terrifying taste of short & shivery p25-29   **398.2**

Fisher, Aileen Lucia, 1906-

Harriet Tubman—the second Moses
In Plays of black Americans p77-84
  812.008

I have a dream
In The Big book of holiday plays p178-86
  812.008

In Plays of black Americans p144-54
  812.008

Voting against the odds
In The Big book of holiday plays p54-62
  812.008

Fisher, Enid

Emotional ups and downs   **152.4**

Fisher, Leonard Everett, 1924-

Alexander Graham Bell   **92**

Alphabet art: thirteen ABCs from around the world   **745.6**

Cyclops   **292**

Galileo   **92**

The jetty chronicles   **Fic**

Niagara Falls   **971.3**

Number art: thirteen 1 2 3s from around the world   **513**

The Oregon Trail   **979.5**

To bigotry, no sanction   **296**

Fisher, Teresa

France   **641.5**

Fisheries

See/See also pages in the following book(s):
Endangered oceans: opposing viewpoints (7 and up)   **577.7**

The **fisherman** and the jinni. Philip, N.
In Philip, N. The Arabian nights p13-21
  398.2

Fishes

See also Aquariums; Tropical fish

Mills, D. Aquarium fish   **639.34**

North America

The Audubon Society field guide to North American fishes, whales, and dolphins
  597

Page, L. M. A field guide to freshwater fishes: North America north of Mexico (7 and up)
  597

Robins, C. R. A field guide to Atlantic coast fishes of North America   **597**

The **flight** of Red Bird. Rappaport, D.   92
Flight of the Dragon Kyn. Fletcher, S.   Fic
Flight of vengeance. Norton, A. See note under
    Norton, A. Witch World [series]   Fic
Flip it!. Yucht, A. H.   025.5
Flodin, Mickey
    (jt. auth) Butterworth, R. R. The Perigee visual
    dictionary of signing   419
The **flood**. Harjo, J.
    In Talking leaves   S C
Floods
    Allaby, M. Floods (7 and up)   551.48
Flores, Patrick Fernández, 1929-
    See/See also pages in the following book(s):
    Morey, J. Famous Mexican Americans p27-38
        920
Florida
    Chang, P. Florida
    In Celebrate the states   973
    Heinrichs, A. Florida
    In America the beautiful, second series
        973

Fiction
    Bloor, E. Tangerine (7 and up)   Fic
    Ferris, J. All that glitters (7 and up)   Fic
    Mikaelsen, B. Stranded   Fic
    Peck, R. N. Cowboy ghost   Fic
    Rawlings, M. K. The yearling   Fic
Flour babies. Fine, A.   Fic
The **flower** queen's daughter. Lang, A.
    In The Book of dragons p26-34   S C
Flowers, Helen F., 1931-
    Public relations for school library media pro-
    grams   021.7
Flowers
    See also State flowers; Wild flowers
Floyd, E. Randall
    Great American mysteries (7 and up)   001.9
Flu *See* Influenza
Fluek, Toby Knobel
    Memories of my life in a Polish village, 1930-
    1949 (7 and up)   92
Flutes
Fiction
    Hobbs, W. Kokopelli's flute   Fic
Flyairth. Adams, R.
    In Adams, R. Tales from Watership Down
        S C
Flyairth's departure. Adams, R.
    In Adams, R. Tales from Watership Down
        S C
Flyers. Hayes, D.   Fic
Flying *See* Flight
Flying away. Johnson, A.
    In Johnson, A. Gone from home: short takes
    p63-74   S C
The **Flying** Dutchman. Hamilton, V.
    In Hamilton, V. The dark way p38-42
        398.2
The **Flying** Dutchman. McCaughrean, G.
    In McCaughrean, G. The crystal pool: myths
    and legends of the world p123-27
        398.2

Flying free. Hart, P. S.   629.13
The **Flying** Head. Bruchac, J.
    In Bruchac, J. When the Chenoo howls
        398.2
Flying machine. Nahum, A.   629.133
Flying saucers *See* Unidentified flying objects
Flying solo. Fletcher, R. J.   Fic
Flying to the moon. Collins, M.   629.45
The **flying** trunk. Andersen, H. C.
    In Andersen, H. C. The little mermaid and
        other fairy tales p74-80   S C
Flynn, Jean
    Annie Oakley   92
Fodemski, Linda M.
    (jt. auth) Benson, A. C. Connecting kids and the
    Internet   004.6
Fog
    Dunn, A. Fog, mist, and smog   551.5
Fog, mist, and smog. Dunn, A.   551.5
Folcarelli, Ralph J.
    (jt. auth) Gillespie, J. T. Guides to collection de-
    velopment for children and young adults
        011.6
Foley, Erin, 1967-
    Costa Rica   972.86
    Ecuador   986.6
Foley, Mike
    Fundamental hockey   796.962
Folk lore *See* Folklore
Folk songs
United States
    From sea to shining sea   810.8
    Songs of the Wild West   782.42
Folk stories of the Hmong. Livo, N. J.   398.2
Folkers, Gladys, 1947-
    Taking charge of my mind & body (7 and up)
        613
Folklore
    See also Animals—Folklore; Dragons; Leg-
    ends; topics as themes in folklore and names
    of ethnic or national groups with the subdivi-
    sion *Folklore*
    The Folklore of world holidays   394.26
    Forest, H. Wisdom tales from around the world
        398.2
    Goddesses, heroes and shamans   291.1
    Hamilton, V. The dark way   398.2
    Hearne, B. G. Beauties and beasts   398.2
    Hughes, M. Popular superstitions   398
    Jaffe, N. The cow of no color: riddle stories and
    justice tales from around the world
        398.2
    Mayo, M. Mythical birds & beasts from many
    lands   398.2
    McCaughrean, G. The bronze cauldron: myths
    and legends of the world   398.2
    McCaughrean, G. The crystal pool: myths and
    legends of the world   398.2
    McCaughrean, G. The golden hoard: myths and
    legends of the world   398.2
    McCaughrean, G. The silver treasure: myths and
    legends of the world   398.2
    Olson, A. N. Ask the bones: scary stories from
    around the world   398.2

Forrester, Sandra, 1949-—_Continued_
Sound the jubilee   **Fic**

Forshay-Lunsford, Cin
Riding out the storm
_In_ Center stage   **812.008**
Saint Agnes sends the golden boy
_In_ Visions: nineteen short stories by outstanding writers for young adults p11-22
    S C

Forsyth, Elizabeth Held
(jt. auth) Hyde, M. O. The disease book
    616
(jt. auth) Hyde, M. O. The sexual abuse of children and adolescents   **362.7**

Fort, María Rosa
Tarma
_In_ Where angels glide at dawn p67-75
    S C

Forté-Escamilla, Kleya
Coming of age
_In_ Join in p230-37   **S C**

Forten, Charlotte L., 1837-1914
See/See also pages in the following book(s):
Lyons, M. E. Keeping secrets (7 and up)
    920

Forten, James, 1766-1842
See/See also pages in the following book(s):
Haskins, J. African American entrepreneurs p17-20   **920**

Fortification
Day, M. The world of castles and forts
    355.7
Gravett, C. Castle   **728.8**
Macaulay, D. Castle   **728.8**
Macdonald, F. A Roman fort   **355.7**

Fortune, Amos, 1709 or 10-1801
About
Yates, E. Amos Fortune, free man   **92**

Fortune, Timothy Thomas, 1856-1928
See/See also pages in the following book(s):
Senna, C. The black press and the struggle for civil rights p76-83 (7 and up)   **071**

Fortune cookie. Avi
_In_ Avi. What do fish have to do with anything? and other stories p175-203
    S C

Fortune teller. Nguyen, M. D.
_In_ American eyes p80-107   **S C**

Fortune telling
Schwartz, A. Telling fortunes   **133.3**

Forty acres and maybe a mule. Robinet, H. G.
    Fic

Fossey, Dian
About
Matthews, T. L. Light shining through the mist: a photobiography of Dian Fossey   **92**
See/See also pages in the following book(s):
Celebrating women in mathematics and science p195-206   **920**

Fossil hominids
Gallant, R. A. Early humans   **599.93**
The Visual dictionary of prehistoric life
    560

Fiction
Dickinson, P. A bone from a dry sea (7 and up)
    Fic

Fossil mammals
See also Mastodon
Giblin, J. The mystery of the mammoth bones
    569

Fossil reptiles
See also Dinosaurs
Lindsay, W. Tyrannosaurus   **567.9**

Fossils
See also Fossil mammals; Fossil reptiles; Prehistoric animals
Dingus, L. The tiniest giants   **567.9**
Facklam, M. Tracking dinosaurs in the Gobi
    567.9
The Historical atlas of the earth   **551.7**
Lessem, D. Dinosaur worlds   **567.9**
Lessem, D. Jack Horner: living with dinosaurs
    92
Lindsay, W. Prehistoric life   **560**
Patent, D. H. In search of the maiasaurs
    567.9
Rocks & fossils   **550**
Tanaka, S. Graveyards of the dinosaurs
    567.9
Taylor, P. D. Fossil   **560**
The Visual dictionary of prehistoric life
    560
Zallinger, P. Dinosaurs and other archosaurs
    567.9

Fiction
Dickinson, P. A bone from a dry sea (7 and up)
    Fic

Foster, Alan Dean, 1946-
Dinotopia lost. See note under Foster, A. D. The Hand of Dinotopia   **Fic**
The Hand of Dinotopia   **Fic**

Foster, Cecil
The scar
_In_ Rites of passage p11-24   **S C**

Foster, Jodie
See/See also pages in the following book(s):
Gaines, A. Entertainment & performing arts
    920

Foster, Leila Merrell
Iraq   **956.7**
Italy (7 and up)   **945**
Kuwait   **953.67**

Foster, Sarah Jane, 1839-1868
See/See also pages in the following book(s):
Lyons, M. E. Keeping secrets (7 and up)
    920

Foster home care
Fiction
Byars, B. C. The pinballs   **Fic**
Childress, A. Rainbow Jordan (7 and up)
    Fic
Cooney, C. B. What child is this? (7 and up)
    Fic
Guy, R. The disappearance   **Fic**
Hobbs, W. The maze (7 and up)   **Fic**
Hughes, D. Team picture   **Fic**
Johnston, J. Adam and Eve and Pinch-me (7 and up)   **Fic**

Foster home care—Fiction—*Continued*
Koller, J. F. A place to call home (7 and up)
    Fic
Nixon, J. L. A family apart   **Fic**
Paterson, K. The great Gilly Hopkins   **Fic**
Skurzynski, G. Cliff hanger   **Fic**
Foster's war. Reeder, C.   **Fic**
Foudray, Rita Schoch
Newbery and Caldecott medalists and honor book winners. See Newbery and Caldecott medalists and honor book winners   **011.6**
Foundations for effective school library media programs   **027.8**
Founding leaders: shapers of modern nations. See entry in CD-ROM section, Part 3
The **founding** of London. McCaughrean, G.
In McCaughrean, G. The bronze cauldron: myths and legends of the world p87-91
    398.2
The **foundling**. Alexander, L.
In Alexander, L. The foundling and other tales of Prydain p5-14   **S C**
The **foundling** and other tales of Prydain. Alexander, L.   **S C**
Fountain of youth. Talbert, M.
In Trapped!: cages of mind and body p67-83
    S C
Fountains of life. Gowell, E. T.   **577.7**
Four ancestors. Bruchac, J.   **398.2**
Four by four vehicles. See Carroll, J. 4 x 4 vehicles   **629.22**
The **four-footed** horror. Olson, A. N.
In Olson, A. N. Ask the bones: scary stories from around the world p37-41   **398.2**
Four perfect pebbles. Perl, L.   **940.53**
Four worlds and a broken stone. McCaughrean, G.
In McCaughrean, G. The crystal pool: myths and legends of the world p1-7
    398.2
The **Fourth** Amendment. Wetterer, C. M.
    345
Fourth of July. Brancato, R. F.
In Sixteen: short stories by outstanding writers for young adults p102-12   **S C**
Fowler, Loretta, 1944-
The Arapaho
In Indians of North America series
    970.004
Fox, Anne L., 1926-
Ten thousand children   **940.53**
Fox, Dan
Songs of the Wild West. See Songs of the Wild West   **782.42**
Fox, Mary Virginia
Douglas MacArthur (7 and up)   **92**
Fox, Paula
The eagle kite   **Fic**
Monkey island   **Fic**
One-eyed cat   **Fic**
The slave dancer   **Fic**
Fox hunt. Namioka, L.
In Join in p13-21   **S C**

The **fox** in the water. Adams, R.
In Adams, R. Tales from Watership Down
    S C
Fox Indians
Bonvillain, N. The Sac and Fox
In Indians of North America series
    970.004
The **Fox,** the goose, and the corn
In From sea to shining sea p259-63
    810.8
Foxes
Fiction
Rubinstein, G. Foxspell   **Fic**
Foxglove, Lady *See* Blue, Rose
Foxspell. Rubinstein, G.   **Fic**
Fractions. See entry in CD-ROM section, Part 3
Fradin, Dennis B.
The Connecticut colony   **974.6**
The planet hunters   **523.4**
Samuel Adams   **92**
Searching for alien life   **576.8**
"We have conquered pain"   **617.9**
The **fragrance** of paradise. Goldin, B. D.
In Goldin, B. D. Journeys with Elijah p49-56
    222
Frampton, David
(il) Chaikin, M. Clouds of glory   **296.1**
France
NgCheong-Lum, R. France   **944**
Fiction
Maguire, G. The good liar   **Fic**
Schnur, S. The shadow children   **Fic**
Skurzynski, G. Spider's voice (7 and up)
    Fic
Vande Velde, V. A coming evil   **Fic**
Folklore
See Folklore—France
History—1328-1589, House of Valois
Stanley, D. Joan of Arc   **92**
History—1328-1589, House of Valois—Fiction
Garden, N. Dove and sword (7 and up)
    Fic
History—1589-1789, Bourbons—Fiction
Dumas, A. The three musketeers (7 and up)
    Fic
History—1789-1799, Revolution
Banfield, S. The rights of man, the reign of terror: the story of the French Revolution (7 and up)   **944.04**
The French Revolution (7 and up)   **944.04**
History—1799-1815
Henderson, H. The age of Napoleon (7 and up)
    944.05
History—1940-1945, German occupation
Ungerer, T. Tomi: a childhood under the Nazis (7 and up)   **92**
Social life and customs
Fisher, T. France   **641.5**
France. Fisher, T.   **641.5**
Franceschetti, Donald R., 1947-
Biographical encyclopedia of mathematicians. See Biographical encyclopedia of mathematicians   **920.003**
Francie. English, K.   **Fic**

Freedom of the press—*Continued*
Herda, D. J. New York Times v. United States
(7 and up)   **342**
King, D. C. The right to speak out   **323.44**
Freedom Rides. Haskins, J.   **323.1**
Freedom songs. Moore, Y.   **Fic**
Freedom train. Sodaro, C.
In Plays of black Americans p3-18
  812.008
Freedom's children. Levine, E.   **323.1**
Freedom's sons. Jurmain, S.   **326**
Freeman, Cathy
See/See also pages in the following book(s):
Rutledge, R. The best of the best in track &
field p32-37   **920**
Freeman, Elizabeth *See* Bett, Mum, 1744?-1829
Freeman, Suzanne T.
The cuckoo's child   **Fic**
Freeman-Villalobos, Tina Marie
The way it was
In Talking leaves   **S C**
Fremon, David K.
The Great Depression in American history
  338.5
The Salem witchcraft trials in American history
  133.4
French, Michael, 1944-
(jt. auth) O'Grady, S. F. Basher five-two
  949.7
French and Indian War *See* United States—History—1755-1763, French and Indian War
The **French** and Indian War, 1660-1763. Collier,
C.   **973.2**
French artists *See* Artists, French
French cooking
Fisher, T. France   **641.5**
French language
Dictionaries
Cassell's French dictionary: French-English, English-French   **443**
Study and teaching
Tell me more pro: French version. See entry in
CD-ROM section, Part 3
The **French** Revolution (7 and up)   **944.04**
Fresco painting *See* Mural painting and decoration
Fresh meat. Koertge, R.
In Twelve shots: outstanding short stories
about guns p201-17   **S C**
Fresh paint. Fraustino, L. R.
In Dirty laundry: stories about family secrets
p98-127   **S C**
Fresh Prince *See* Smith, Will
Freud, Sigmund, 1856-1939
About
Muckenhoupt, M. Sigmund Freud (7 and up)
  92
Friedhoffer, Robert
Magic and perception   **793.8**
Physics lab in a hardware store   **530**
Physics lab in the housewares store   **530**
Science lab in a supermarket   **507.8**

Friedlander, Mark P.
The immune system (7 and up)   **616.07**
Friedman, Ina R.
The other victims   **940.53**
Friedman, Tova, 1938-
See/See also pages in the following book(s):
Kinderlager p5-53 (7 and up)   **940.53**
The **friendly** ghost. Bolton, A. C.
In The Oxford book of scary tales p137-43
  808.8
Friends, Society of *See* Society of Friends
The **friends**. Guy, R.   **Fic**
The **friends**. Yumoto, K.   **Fic**
The **friends** of Kwan Ming. Yee, P.
In Yee, P. Tales from Gold Mountain p25-31
  S C
Friends to die for. Giberga, J. S.   **Fic**
Friendship
Bode, J. Trust & betrayal (7 and up)   **158**
Romain, T. Cliques, phonies & other baloney
  158
Fiction
Blume, J. Here's to you, Rachel Robinson
  Fic
Blume, J. Just as long as we're together
  Fic
Brokaw, N. S. Leaving Emma   **Fic**
Brooks, B. The moves make the man (7 and up)
  Fic
Brooks, B. Zip   **Fic**
Byars, B. C. The pinballs   **Fic**
Carter, A. R. Bull catcher (7 and up)   **Fic**
Cole, B. The goats   **Fic**
Cormier, R. The bumblebee flies anyway (7 and
up)   **Fic**
Creech, S. Walk two moons   **Fic**
Crutcher, C. Staying fat for Sarah Byrnes
  Fic
Danziger, P. P.S. Longer letter later   **Fic**
Deaver, J. R. Say goodnight, Gracie (7 and up)
  Fic
DeClements, B. Liar, liar   **Fic**
Dessen, S. Someone like you (7 and up)
  Fic
Deuker, C. Heart of a champion (7 and up)
  Fic
Dygard, T. J. Running wild (7 and up)   **Fic**
Fenner, C. Randall's wall   **Fic**
Fine, A. The Tulip touch   **Fic**
Franklin, K. L. Nerd no more   **Fic**
Giff, P. R. Lily's crossing   **Fic**
Grove, V. The crystal garden   **Fic**
Guy, R. The friends   **Fic**
Hahn, M. D. Daphne's book   **Fic**
Hamilton, V. The planet of Junior Brown
  Fic
Hesse, K. Phoenix rising   **Fic**
Hite, S. Cecil in space (7 and up)   **Fic**
Jukes, M. Planning the impossible   **Fic**
Klass, S. S. Next stop, nowhere   **Fic**
Klass, S. S. The uncivil war   **Fic**
Konigsburg, E. L. The view from Saturday
  Fic
Koss, A. G. The Ashwater experiment   **Fic**
Kurtz, J. The storyteller's beads   **Fic**

Gallo, Donald R.—*Continued*
(ed) Sixteen: short stories by outstanding writers for young adults. See Sixteen: short stories by outstanding writers for young adults   **S C**
(ed) Ultimate sports: short stories by outstanding writers for young adults. See Ultimate sports: short stories by outstanding writers for young adults   **S C**
(ed) Visions: nineteen short stories by outstanding writers for young adults. See Visions: nineteen short stories by outstanding writers for young adults   **S C**

El **gallo** de bodas: the rooster on the way to the wedding. González, L. M.
In From sea to shining sea p364-65
   810.8

The **galloping** sleigh. Lofting, H.
In A Newbery Christmas p153-61   **S C**

Galloway, Priscilla, 1930-
Truly grim tales (7 and up)   **S C**
Contents: The name; Blood and bone; A bed of peas; The voice of love; The good mother; A taste for beauty; The woodcutter's wife; The prince

Galvin, Irene Flum
Japan   **952**

Galvin, Jack
(jt. auth) Pfetzer, M. Within reach: my Everest story   **796.52**

Gama, Vasco da, 1469-1524
See/See also pages in the following book(s):
Fritz, J. Around the world in a hundred years p51-57   **910.4**
Lomask, M. Great lives: exploration p113-19   **920**

Gambler's eyes. Yee, P.
In Yee, P. Tales from Gold Mountain p39-44   **S C**

Gamblin, Linda
Evolution   **576.8**

Gambling
Hjelmeland, A. Legalized gambling (7 and up)   **363.4**
Saunders, C. S. Straight talk about teenage gambling (7 and up)   **363.4**
Fiction
Hautman, P. Stone cold (7 and up)   **Fic**

A **game** of statues. Vivelo, J.
In Vivelo, J. Chills in the night p65-75   **S C**

Game plan. Dygard, T. J.   **Fic**

Game plan [series]
Owens, T. Hockey   **796.962**

Game protection
See also Birds—Protection

Games
See also Computer games; Sports; Word games; names of individual games
Loeffelbein, R. L. The recreation handbook   **793**

Games. Sleator, W.
In Sleator, W. Oddballs: stories p3-14   **S C**

Gammell, Stephen, 1943-
(il) Dancing teepees: poems of American Indian youth. See Dancing teepees: poems of American Indian youth   **897**

Gandhi, Indira, 1917-1984
See/See also pages in the following book(s):
Price-Groff, C. Twentieth-century women political leaders (7 and up)   **920**

Gandhi, Mahatma, 1869-1948
About
Mitchell, P. Gandhi   **92**
Severance, J. B. Gandhi, great soul   **92**
See/See also pages in the following book(s):
Wakin, E. Asian independence leaders p38-55 (7 and up)   **920**

Gandhi, Mohandas Karamchand See Gandhi, Mahatma, 1869-1948

Gandhi, great soul. Severance, J. B.   **92**

Ganeri, Anita, 1961-
Buddhist   **294.3**
Funny bones   **611**
The search for tombs   **393**
The story of communications   **384**
The story of writing and printing   **652**
The young person's guide to the orchestra   **784.2**

Gangs
Hinojosa, M. Crews (7 and up)   **302.3**
Stewart, G. Gangs (7 and up)   **364.36**
Voices from the streets (7 and up)   **364.36**
Fiction
Randle, K. D. Breaking rank (7 and up)   **Fic**

Gantos, Jack
Joey Pigza swallowed the key   **Fic**

Gaposchkin, Cecilia Helena Payne, 1900-1979
See/See also pages in the following book(s):
Camp, C. A. American astronomers p68-75   **920**

Garbage See Refuse and refuse disposal

Garbarino, Merwyn S.
The Seminole
In Indians of North America series   **970.004**

Garcia, Andy
See/See also pages in the following book(s):
Morey, J. Famous Hispanic Americans p53-63   **920**

Garcia, Mannie
(il) Lyons, M. E. Catching the fire: Philip Simmons, blacksmith   **92**

Garcia, Rita Williams- See Williams-Garcia, Rita

García de Paredes, Angel
(ed) Cassell's Spanish-English, English-Spanish dictionary. See Cassell's Spanish-English, English-Spanish dictionary   **463**

García Márquez, Gabriel, 1928-
About
Dolan, S. Gabriel García Márquez   **92**
See/See also pages in the following book(s):
Shirey, L. Latin American writers (7 and up)   **860.9**

Garden, Nancy
Dove and sword (7 and up)   **Fic**

George Washington and the birth of our nation.
Meltzer, M.   **92**

George Washington Carver. Hark, M.
In Plays of black Americans p39-65
    812.008

Georgia
Robinson Masters, N. Georgia
In America the beautiful, second series
    973

Fiction
Krisher, T. Kinship (7 and up)   **Fic**
Krisher, T. Spite fences (7 and up)   **Fic**
Marino, J. The day that Elvis came to town (7 and up)   **Fic**
Oughton, J. The war in Georgia (7 and up)
    Fic
Young, R. T. Moving Mama to town   **Fic**

Georgia (Republic)
Spilling, M. Georgia   **947.5**

Georgia (Soviet Union) *See* Georgia (Republic)

Geras, Adèle
The Random House book of opera stories
    792.5

Gerdes, Louise
(ed) Battered women. *See* Battered women
    362.82

Germ warfare *See* Biological warfare

Germain, Sophie, 1776-1831
See/See also pages in the following book(s):
Celebrating women in mathematics and science p37-46   **920**

The **German** American family album. Hoobler, D.
    305.8

German Americans
Hoobler, D. The German American family album   **305.8**

Fiction
Rinaldi, A. Keep smiling through (7 and up)
    Fic

German language
Dictionaries
Cassell's German-English, English-German dictionary   **433**

German prisoners of war
Fiction
Greene, B. Summer of my German soldier
    Fic

Germany
Ayer, E. H. Germany (7 and up)   **943**
History—1933-1945
Ayer, E. H. Parallel journeys (7 and up)
    940.53
Feldman, G. Understanding the Holocaust
    940.53
Koehn, I. Mischling, second degree: my childhood in Nazi Germany   **92**
Lace, W. W. The Nazis (7 and up)
    943.086
Politics and government—1933-1945
Byers, A. The Holocaust overview (7 and up)
    940.53
Feldman, G. Understanding the Holocaust
    940.53
The Rise of Nazi Germany (7 and up)
    943.086

Politics and government—1945-1990
Grant, R. G. The Berlin Wall   **943.087**

Germany's lightning war. McGowen, T.
    940.54

Germs *See* Bacteria

Geronimo, Apache Chief, 1829-1909
About
Schwarz, M. Geronimo, Apache warrior   **92**
See/See also pages in the following book(s):
Brown, D. A. Bury my heart at Wounded Knee p392-413 (7 and up)   **970.004**
Ehrlich, A. Wounded Knee: an Indian history of the American West   **970.004**
Kallen, S. A. Native American chiefs and warriors (7 and up)   **920**

Gerontology
See also Old age

Get on board: the story of the Underground Railroad. Haskins, J.   **326**

Getting Lincoln's goat. Goldman, E. M.   **Fic**

Getting near to baby. Couloumbis, A.   **Fic**

Getting started in science [series]
Gardner, R. Experiments with motion   **531**

Getting the facts of life. White, P. C.
In Rites of passage p91-102   **S C**

Getting the real story: Nellie Bly and Ida B. Wells. Davidson, S.   **92**

Gettysburg (Pa.), Battle of, 1863
Beller, S. P. To hold this ground   **973.7**
Gettysburg (7 and up)   **973.7**
Murphy, J. The long road to Gettysburg
    973.7
Fiction
Banks, S. H. Abraham's battle   **Fic**

Gettysburg (7 and up)   **973.7**

Getz, David, 1957-
Frozen man   **930.1**

Ghana
Levy, P. M. Ghana   **966.7**

Ghana Empire
Green, R. L. The empire of Ghana   **966.1**
McKissack, P. C. The royal kingdoms of Ghana, Mali, and Songhay   **966.2**

Gherman, Beverly
Robert Louis Stevenson, teller of tales   **92**

Ghost boy. Yolen, J.
In Yolen, J. Here there be ghosts p3-20
    810.8

Ghost canoe. Hobbs, W.   **Fic**

Ghost dance
See/See also pages in the following book(s):
Brown, D. A. Bury my heart at Wounded Knee p416-38 (7 and up)   **970.004**
Ehrlich, A. Wounded Knee: an Indian history of the American West   **970.004**

Ghost dancer. Wyeth, S. D.
In Wyeth, S. D. Vampire bugs: stories conjured from the past p36-48   **S C**

A **ghost** in the attic. Estes, E.
In A Newbery Halloween p37-51   **S C**

The **ghost** in the Tokaido Inn. Hoobler, D.
    Fic

Ghost liners. Ballard, R. D.   **910.4**

Ghost of a hanged man. Vande Velde, V.
                                   Fic

Ghost of Christmas past. Vivelo, J.
   In Vivelo, J. Chills in the night p76-88
                                   S C

The **ghost** of Eddy Longo. Wynne-Jones, T.
   In Wynne-Jones, T. The book of changes
   p83-108   S C

The **ghost** of El Castillo. Winther, B.
   In Winther, B. Plays from Hispanic tales
                                 812

The **ghost** of Fossil Glen. DeFelice, C. C.
                                     Fic

The **ghost** of Jean Lafitte. Schmidt, S.
   In From sea to shining sea p320-21
                               810.8

Ghost stories
   Aiken, J. A foot in the grave   S C
   Avi. Something upstairs: a tale of ghosts
                                     Fic
   Baillie, A. Secrets of Walden rising   Fic
   Bauer, M. D. A taste of smoke   Fic
   Conrad, P. Stonewords   Fic
   DeFelice, C. C. The ghost of Fossil Glen
                                     Fic
   Dickens, C. A Christmas carol (7 and up)
                                     Fic
   Don't read this! and other tales of the unnatural
                                     S C
   Hamilton, V. Sweet whispers, Brother Rush
                                     Fic
   The Haunted house: a collection of original stories   S C
   Kimmel, E. C. In the stone circle   Fic
   McKissack, P. C. The dark-thirty   S C
   Murphy, J. Night terrors   S C
   Nixon, J. L. The haunting (7 and up)   Fic
   San Souci, R. A terrifying taste of short & shivery   398.2
   Schnur, S. The shadow children   Fic
   Schwartz, A. More scary stories to tell in the dark   398.2
   Schwartz, A. Scary stories 3   398.2
   Schwartz, A. Scary stories to tell in the dark   398.2
   Strasser, T. Hey, Dad, get a life!   Fic
   Tolan, S. S. The face in the mirror   Fic
   Vande Velde, V. Ghost of a hanged man
                                     Fic
   Westall, R. Demons and shadows (7 and up)
                                   S C
   Westall, R. The promise   Fic
   Wright, B. R. Out of the dark   Fic
   Yolen, J. Here there be ghosts   810.8

Ghost story. Cooper, S.
   In Don't read this! and other tales of the unnatural p33-50   S C

A **ghost** story. Lester, J.
   In Lester, J. The last tales of Uncle Remus p33-36   398.2

Ghost train. Mowry, J.   Fic

Ghostly warnings. Cohen, D.   133.1

Ghosts
   Cohen, D. Dangerous ghosts   133.1
   Cohen, D. Ghostly warnings   133.1

Cohen, D. Ghosts of the deep   133.1
Wilson, C. Ghosts and the supernatural
                                   133.1
Wood, T. Ghosts of the West Coast 133.1
Woog, A. Poltergeists: opposing viewpoints (7 and up)   133.1
See/See also pages in the following book(s):
Duncan, L. Psychic connections p53-75 (7 and up)   133
                     Poetry
Yolen, J. Here there be ghosts   810.8

Ghosts and the supernatural. Wilson, C.
                                   133.1

The **ghost's** bride. Yep, L.
   In Yep, L. The rainbow people p54-59
                                   398.2

Ghosts of the deep. Cohen, D.   133.1

A **Giant** and her little son
   In The Dancing fox: Arctic folktales p20-25
                                   398.2

The **giant** of Castle Treen. Climo, S.
   In Climo, S. Magic & mischief p3-10
                                   398.2

Giant panda
   Presnall, J. J. The giant panda (7 and up)
                                 599.78
   See/See also pages in the following book(s):
   Ward, P. Wild bears of the world (7 and up)
                                 599.78

Giants
     See also Cyclopes (Greek mythology)

The **giant's** tooth. Coville, B.
   In Coville, B. Odder than ever   S C

Gib and the gray ghost. Snyder, Z. K. See note under Snyder, Z. K. Gib rides home   Fic

Gib rides home. Snyder, Z. K.   Fic

Gibbons, Thomas, 1757-1826
                    About
   Levinson, I. S. Gibbons v. Ogden (7 and up)
                                 343

Gibbons v. Ogden. Levinson, I. S.   343

Giberga, Jane Sughrue
   Friends to die for (7 and up)   Fic

Giblin, James, 1933-
   Charles A. Lindbergh   92
   Edith Wilson: the woman who ran the United States   92
   From hand to mouth   394.1
   Let there be light: a book about windows
                                   690
   The mystery of the mammoth bones   569
   The riddle of the Rosetta Stone   493

Gibson, Althea, 1927-
   See/See also pages in the following book(s):
   Gaines, A. Sports & athletics   920

Gibson, Josh, 1911-1947
   See/See also pages in the following book(s):
   Brashler, W. The story of Negro league baseball p95-109   796.357

Gibson, Robert O.
   The Chumash
   In Indians of North America series
                                 970.004

Gideon, Clarence Earl
About
Sherrow, V. Gideon v. Wainwright (7 and up)
                                                345
Gideon v. Wainwright. Sherrow, V.   345
Gideon's people. Meyer, C.   Fic
Giff, Patricia Reilly
Lily's crossing   Fic
Gifford, Douglas
Warriors, gods & spirits from Central & South
    American mythology   299
A **gift** for Pachacuti Inca. Winther, B.
    In Winther, B. Plays from Hispanic tales
                                            812
The **gift-giving**. Aiken, J.
    In Sixteen: short stories by outstanding writ-
    ers for young adults p134-46   S C
A **gift** of laughter. Sherman, A.
    In Leaving home: stories p27-33   808.8
The **gift** of stories, the gift of breath. Bruchac, J.
    In Bruchac, J. Four ancestors p92-93
                                            398.2
The **gift** of the Magi. Henry, O.
    In Henry, O. The gift of the Magi and other
    stories p191-201   S C
The **gift** of the Magi and other stories. Henry, O.
                                            S C
Gifted children
Fiction
Blume, J. Here's to you, Rachel Robinson
                                            Fic
Tolan, S. S. Welcome to the Ark (7 and up)
                                            Fic
Gifts from the sea. Westall, R.
    In Westall, R. Demons and shadows p168-82
                                            S C
The **gifts** of the mangy. Conford, E.
    In Conford, E. Crush p9-26   S C
Gilbert, Barbara Snow, 1954-
Stone water (7 and up)   Fic
Gilbert, Sara D.
How to do your best on tests (7 and up)
                                            371.2
Gilbert, Thomas W.
Damn Yankees (7 and up)   796.357
Gill, Sam D., 1943-
Dictionary of Native American mythology
                                            299
Gill-Lonergan, Janet
The gourmet ghost
    In The Haunted house: a collection of original
    stories   S C
Gilles de la Tourette's syndrome See Tourette
    syndrome
Gillespie, Dizzy, 1917-1993
See/See also pages in the following book(s):
Mour, S. I. American jazz musicians p57-66
                                            920
Gillespie, John Birks See Gillespie, Dizzy, 1917-
    1993
Gillespie, John Thomas, 1928-
Guides to collection development for children
    and young adults   011.6

Juniorplots 4   **028.5**
Middleplots 4   **028.5**
The Newbery companion   **028.5**
Gilman, Charlotte Perkins, 1860-1935
See/See also pages in the following book(s):
Lyons, M. E. Keeping secrets (7 and up)
                                            920
Ginger for the heart. Yee, P.
    In Yee, P. Tales from Gold Mountain p33-38
                                            S C
The **gingerbread** baby. McCaughrean, G.
    In McCaughrean, G. The bronze cauldron:
    myths and legends of the world p41-44
                                            398.2
The **gingi**. McKissack, P. C.
    In McKissack, P. C. The dark-thirty p95-110
                                            S C
Ginsburg, Ruth Bader
See/See also pages in the following book(s):
Lindop, L. Political leaders (7 and up)   920
Ginzberg, Louis, 1873-1953
Legends of the Bible. See Chaikin, M. Clouds
    of glory   296.1
Giotto, di Bondone, 1266?-1337
(il) L'Engle, M. The glorious impossible
                                            232.9
Giovanni, Nikki
Ego-tripping and other poems for young people
                                            811
(ed) Grand fathers. See Grand fathers
                                            810.8
(ed) Grand mothers. See Grand mothers
                                            810.8
(ed) Shimmy shimmy shimmy like my sister
    Kate. See Shimmy shimmy shimmy like my
    sister Kate   811.008
See/See also pages in the following book(s):
Strickland, M. R. African-American poets p65-
    73   920
Gipsies See Gypsies
Gipson, Frederick Benjamin, 1903-1973
Old Yeller   Fic
Giraffes
Fiction
Farmer, N. The warm place   Fic
Girard, Denis
Cassell's French dictionary: French-English, En-
    glish-French. See Cassell's French dictionary:
    French-English, English-French   443
Girl. Henry, O.
    In Henry, O. The gift of the Magi and other
    stories p122-32   S C
The **girl** and the Chenoo. Bruchac, J.
    In Bruchac, J. The girl who married the
    Moon: tales from Native North America
    p29-36   398.2
Girl at the window. Peck, R.
    In Night terrors   S C
A **girl** from Yamhill: a memoir. Cleary, B.
                                            92
Girl gives birth to own prom date. Strasser, T. See
    note under Strasser, T. How I spent my last
    night on earth   Fic
A **girl** named Disaster. Farmer, N.   Fic

Girl Scout badges and signs. Girl Scouts of the United States of America   **369.463**

Girl Scouts of the United States of America
Girl Scout badges and signs   **369.463**

The **girl** who almost married an owl. Bruchac, J.
In Bruchac, J. The girl who married the Moon: tales from Native North America p58-61   **398.2**

The **girl** who climbed to the sky. Brown, D. A.
In Brown, D. A. Dee Brown's folktales of the Native American p39-42   **398.2**

The **girl** who dreamed only geese. Norman, H.
In Norman, H. The girl who dreamed only geese, and other tales of the Far North   **398.2**

The **girl** who dreamed only geese, and other tales of the Far North. Norman, H.   **398.2**

The **girl** who escaped. Bruchac, J.
In Bruchac, J. The girl who married the Moon: tales from Native North America p37-43   **398.2**

The **girl** who gave birth to Water-Jar Boy. Bruchac, J.
In Bruchac, J. The girl who married the Moon: tales from Native North America p69-74   **398.2**

The **girl** who helped Thunder. Bruchac, J.
In Bruchac, J. The girl who married the Moon: tales from Native North America p51-54   **398.2**

The **girl** who married an Osage. Bruchac, J.
In Bruchac, J. The girl who married the Moon: tales from Native North America p55-57   **398.2**

The **girl** who married the Moon [story] Bruchac, J.
In Bruchac, J. The girl who married the Moon: tales from Native North America p116-22   **398.2**

The **girl** who married the Moon: tales from Native North America. Bruchac, J.   **398.2**

The **girl** who was swallowed by the earth. Hamilton, V.
In Hamilton, V. The dark way p108-12   **398.2**

The **girl** who watched in the nighttime. Norman, H.
In Norman, H. The girl who dreamed only geese, and other tales of the Far North   **398.2**

Girls
33 things every girl should know (7 and up)   **810.8**
Girls know best   **305.23**
Gray, H. M. Real girl/real world (7 and up)   **305.23**
Jukes, M. Growing up: it's a girl thing   **612.6**
Jukes, M. It's a girl thing   **305.23**
Shandler, S. Ophelia speaks (7 and up)   **305.23**

Books and reading
Bauermeister, E. Let's hear it for the girls   **028.1**

Cooper-Mullin, A. Once upon a heroine   **028.1**
Dodson, S. 100 books for girls to grow on   **028.1**
Odean, K. Great books for girls   **028.1**

Employment
See Children—Employment

Fiction
Stay true: short stories for strong girls (7 and up)   **S C**

Girls, Teenage *See* Teenagers

Girls & young women inventing. Karnes, F. A.   **608**

Girls and young women entrepreneurs. Karnes, F. A.   **658**

Girls know best   **305.23**

The **Girls** who wished for husbands
In The Dancing fox: Arctic folktales p39-45   **398.2**

Giselle (Ballet)
See/See also pages in the following book(s):
McCaughrean, G. The Random House book of stories from the ballet p29-35   **792.8**
Newman, B. The illustrated book of ballet stories p22-31   **792.8**

Give yourself a fright. Aiken, J.
In Aiken, J. Give yourself a fright: thirteen tales of the supernatural p160-80   **S C**

Give yourself a fright: thirteen tales of the supernatural. Aiken, J.   **S C**

The **giver**. Lowry, L.   **Fic**

The **giver** [excerpt] Lowry, L.
In Read into the millenium p139-46   **S C**

Glancy, Diane
Aunt Parnetta's electric blisters
In Talking leaves   **S C**

Glaser, Elizabeth
See/See also pages in the following book(s):
Lindop, L. Champions of equality (7 and up)   **920**

Glass, Andrew
Bad guys   **920**

The **glass** dog. Baum, L. F.
In American fairy tales p105-15   **S C**

Glassware
Houston, J. A. Fire into ice   **748.2**

Gleason, Katherine, 1960-
Native American literature   **897**

Gleeson, Brian
Ride 'em, round 'em, rope 'em: the story of Pecos Bill
In From sea to shining sea p286-88   **810.8**

Glenn, John, 1921-
About
Kramer, B. John Glenn   **92**

Glenn, Mel, 1943-
Foreign exchange (7 and up)   **811**
The taking of Room 114 (7 and up)   **811**

Glennis, before and after. Calvert, P.   **Fic**

Gliders (Aeronautics)
Perry, P. J. Soaring   **797.5**

Gliding and soaring
Perry, P. J. Soaring   **797.5**

Global profiles [series]
Graham, K. Contemporary environmentalists   **920**
Henderson, H. Modern mathematicians   **920**
Lucas, E. Contemporary human rights activists   **920**
Price-Groff, C. Twentieth-century women political leaders   **920**
Rasmussen, R. K. Modern African political leaders   **920**
Shirey, L. Latin American writers   **860.9**
Wakin, E. Asian independence leaders   **920**

Global warming *See* Greenhouse effect

Global warming: opposing viewpoints (7 and up)   **363.7**

Globe Theatre (London, England)
See also Shakespeare's Globe (London, England);
Aliki. William Shakespeare & the Globe   **792.09**
Morley, J. Shakespeare's theater   **792.09**

Gloria. Wynne-Jones, T.
In Wynne-Jones, T. The book of changes p134-43   **S C**

The **'Gloria** Scott'. Doyle, Sir A. C.
In Doyle, Sir A. C. The complete Sherlock Holmes   **. S C**

The **glorious** impossible. L'Engle, M.   **232.9**

A **Glory** of unicorns   **S C**

Glossaries *See* Encyclopedias and dictionaries

Glosskap and Wasis. Garner, A.
In From sea to shining sea p210-11   **810.8**

Glovemen. Sullivan, G.   **920**

Glover, David M.
The young Oxford book of the human being   **612**

Glubok, Shirley, 1933-
Great lives: painting   **920**
Olympic games in ancient Greece   **796.48**

Gluskabe and the Snow Bird. Bruchac, J.
In Bruchac, J. Four ancestors p57-61   **398.2**

Gnus
Lindblad, L. The Serengeti migration   **599.64**

Go and come back. Abelove, J.   **Fic**

Go for the goal. Hamm, M.   **796.334**

Go jump in the pool. Korman, G. See note under Korman, G. Something fishy at MacDonald Hall   **Fic**

Go tell it on the mountain. Baldwin, J.   **Fic**

Goat comes to the Christmas party. Evans, E. K.
In Christmas gif' p26-31   **810.8**

The **goats.** Cole, B.   **Fic**

Gobi Desert (Mongolia and China)
Facklam, M. Tracking dinosaurs in the Gobi   **567.9**

Goble, Paul
Death of the Iron Horse
In From sea to shining sea p160-63   **810.8**

The **goblin** at the grocer's. Andersen, H. C.
In Andersen, H. C. The little mermaid and other fairy tales p99-103   **S C**

God battles the Queen of the Waters. Lester, J.
In Lester, J. When the beginning began p7-10   **296.1**

God confronts Adam, the Woman, and the Snake. Lester, J.
In Lester, J. When the beginning began p87-92   **296.1**

God creates Adam. Lester, J.
In Lester, J. When the beginning began p59-63   **296.1**

God creates Woman. Lester, J.
In Lester, J. When the beginning began p64-68   **296.1**

God learns how to create. Lester, J.
In Lester, J. When the beginning began p1-5   **296.1**

God makes people. Lester, J.
In Lester, J. When the beginning began p49-57   **296.1**

God moves away. McCaughrean, G.
In McCaughrean, G. The silver treasure: myths and legends of the world p57-59   **398.2**

God returns to Heaven. Lester, J.
In Lester, J. When the beginning began p93-95   **296.1**

Godasiyo the woman chief. Brown, D. A.
In Brown, D. A. Dee Brown's folktales of the Native American p71-74   **398.2**

Goddard, Robert Hutchings, 1882-1945
About
Coil, S. M. Robert Hutchings Goddard (7 and up)   **92**
See/See also pages in the following book(s):
Aaseng, N. Twentieth-century inventors p27-38 (7 and up)   **920**
Maurer, R. Rocket!   **621.43**

The **goddess** and the buffalo demon. Krishnaswami, U.
In Krishnaswami, U. Shower of gold: girls and women in the stories of India p41-46   **398.2**

The **goddess** and the girl. Krishnaswami, U.
In Krishnaswami, U. Shower of gold: girls and women in the stories of India p11-15   **398.2**

Goddesses *See* Gods and goddesses

Goddesses, heroes and shamans   **291.1**

Godfrey, Neale S.
Neale S. Godfrey's ultimate kids' money book   **332.024**

Godmother. Mathis, S. B.
In Join in p173-99   **S C**

Gods & pharaohs from Egyptian mythology. Harris, G.   **299**

Goldman, E. M.
Getting Lincoln's goat (7 and up)   **Fic**
The night room (7 and up)   **Fic**
Goldman, Martin S.
Richard M. Nixon (7 and up)   **92**
Golem
Hamilton, V. Joseph Golem
In Hamilton, V. The dark way p87-96
    398.2
The **Golem**. McCaughrean, G.
In McCaughrean, G. The bronze cauldron:
myths and legends of the world p109-12
    398.2
The **golem**. Rogasky, B.   **398.2**
Golf
Anderson, D. The story of golf   **796.352**
    Biography
Lace, W. W. Tiger Woods   **92**
Uschan, M. V. Tiger Woods (7 and up)   **92**
Gollobin, Laurie Brooks *See* Brooks Gollobin,
Laurie
Golston, Sydele E.
Changing woman of the Apache (7 and up)
    970.004
Gompers, Samuel, 1850-1924
See/See also pages in the following book(s):
Streissguth, T. Legendary labor leaders (7 and
up)   **920**
Gone a-whaling. Murphy, J.   **639.2**
Gone from home: short takes. Johnson, A.
    S C
Gonen, Amiram
(ed) Peoples of the world. See Peoples of the
world   **306**
Gonzales, Doreen
Gloria Estefan   **92**
Gonzalez, Genaro, 1949-
Un hijo del sol
In Growing up Latino p38-46   **810.8**
Gonzalez, Gloria
The boy with yellow eyes
In Visions: nineteen short stories by outstand-
ing writers for young adults p204-12
    S C
Viva New Jersey
In Join in p51-60   **S C**
González, Lucía M.
El gallo de bodas: the rooster on the way to the
wedding
In From sea to shining sea p364-65
    810.8
Juan Bobo and the buñuelos
In From sea to shining sea p240-41
    810.8
Gooch, Anthony
(ed) Cassell's Spanish-English, English-Spanish
dictionary. See Cassell's Spanish-English, En-
glish-Spanish dictionary   **463**
Good Blanche, bad Rose, and the talking eggs.
Hamilton, V.
In Hamilton, V. Her stories p28-32
    398.2
Good girl work. Gourley, C.   **331.3**

The **good** girls. Arrick, F.
In Visions: nineteen short stories by outstand-
ing writers for young adults p107-20
    S C
Good grief. Bradbury, R.
In Who do you think you are? p3-13
    S C
Good health guides [series]
Fisher, E. Emotional ups and downs   **152.4**
The **good** herdboy. Fairman, T.
In Fairman, T. Bury my bones but not my
words p64-76   **398.2**
The **good** liar. Maguire, G.   **Fic**
Good morning! this is the future. Slesar, H.
In Read into the millenium p120-25   **S C**
The **good** mother. Galloway, P.
In Galloway, P. Truly grim tales   **S C**
Good news Bible. Bible   **220.5**
Good night, Jon; sleep tight, Jon. Murphy, J.
In Murphy, J. Night terrors p39-60   **S C**
Good Queen Bess: the story of Elizabeth I of Eng-
land. Stanley, D.   **92**
The **good** sword. Owen, R. B.
In The Book of dragons p110-20   **S C**
Goodall, Jane, 1934-
With love   **599.8**
See/See also pages in the following book(s):
Celebrating women in mathematics and science
p207-16   **920**
Goodbye, Vietnam. Whelan, G.   **Fic**
Goode, J. Paul, 1862-1932
Goode's world atlas. See Goode's world atlas
    912
Goode's school atlas. See Goode's world atlas
    912
Goode's world atlas   **912**
Goodman, Benny, 1909-1986
See/See also pages in the following book(s):
Mour, S. I. American jazz musicians p47-56
    920
Goodman, Joan E., 1950-
Hope's crossing   **Fic**
Goodman, Susan, 1952-
Bats, bugs, and biodiversity   **577.3**
Stones, bones, and petroglyphs   **930.1**
Ultimate field trip 3   **577.6**
The **goodness** of Matt Kaizer. Avi
In Avi. What do fish have to do with any-
thing? and other stories p35-59   **S C**
Goodnough, David
Pablo Neruda   **92**
Goodwin, William, 1943-
Mexico (7 and up)   **972**
Teen violence (7 and up)   **364.36**
Gootman, Marilyn E., 1944-
When a friend dies (7 and up)   **155.9**
GOP (Grand Old Party) *See* Republican Party
(U.S.)
Gordeeva, Ekaterina
    About
Shea, P. D. Ekaterina Gordeeva   **92**

The **great** interactive dream machine. Peck, R.
  Fic

Great inventions. Wood, R.   **609**

The **Great** Lakes. Katz, S.   **577.6**

The **great** little Madison. Fritz, J.   **92**

Great lives [series]
 Hurwitz, J. Sally Ride   **92**

Great lives: American literature. Faber, D.
  920

Great lives: exploration. Lomask, M.   **920**

Great lives: painting. Glubok, S.   **920**

Great lives: the American frontier. Calvert, P.
  920

Great lives: theater. Weitzman, D. L.   **920**

The **great** migration. Lawrence, J.   **759.13**

Great minds of science [series]
 Anderson, M. J. Carl Linnaeus   **92**
 Anderson, M. J. Isaac Newton   **92**
 Datnow, C. L. Edwin Hubble   **92**
 Klare, R. Gregor Mendel   **92**
 Poynter, M. The Leakeys   **92**
 Poynter, M. Marie Curie: discoverer of radium
  92
 Smith, L. W. Louis Pasteur   **92**
 Yount, L. Antoni van Leeuwenhoek   **92**

Great monologues for young actors   **808.82**

Great moves. Asher, S.
 In Visions: nineteen short stories by outstanding writers for young adults p130-40
  S C

Great mysteries [series]
 Arvey, M. Miracles: opposing viewpoints
  231.7
 Durrett, D. Angels: opposing viewpoints
  235
 Netzley, P. D. Alien abductions: opposing viewpoints
  001.9
 Royer, M.-P. Astrology: opposing viewpoints
  133.5
 Woog, A. Poltergeists: opposing viewpoints
  133.1

Great presidential decisions [series]
 Morris, J. B. The FDR way   **92**

Great scenes and monologues for children
  808.82

Great scenes for young actors   **808.82**

Great scenes for young actors from the stage. See Great scenes for young actors   **808.82**

The **great** shell of Kintyel. Brown, D. A.
 In Brown, D. A. Dee Brown's folktales of the Native American p28-39   **398.2**

The **Great** Swallowing Monster. McCaughrean, G.
 In The Oxford book of scary tales p64-69
  808.8

The **great** turkey walk. Karr, K.   **Fic**

Greatbatch, Wilson, 1919-
 See/See also pages in the following book(s):
 Aaseng, N. Twentieth-century inventors p103-15 (7 and up)   **920**

Greater than angels. Matas, C.   **Fic**

The **greatest** show off earth. Mahy, M.   **Fic**

Greco, El *See* El Greco, 1541-1614

Greece
Antiquities
See/See also pages in the following book(s):
 Burrell, R. E. C. Oxford first ancient history p96-205   **909**
Biography
 Baker, R. F. Ancient Greeks (7 and up)
  938
 Nardo, D. Leaders of ancient Greece (7 and up)
  920
Civilization
 Baker, R. F. Ancient Greeks (7 and up)
  938
 Bardi, P. The atlas of the classical world
  938
 Chapman, G. The Greeks   **745.5**
 Crosher, J. Technology in the time of ancient Greece   **609**
 Glubok, S. Olympic games in ancient Greece
  796.48
 Hart, A. Ancient Greece!   **938**
 Nardo, D. Greek and Roman sport (7 and up)
  796
 Powell, A. The Greek news   **938**
 See/See also pages in the following book(s):
 Macdonald, F. A Greek temple   **938**
Science
 See Science—Greece

The **greedy** man and the goat. Olson, A. N.
 In Olson, A. N. Ask the bones: scary stories from around the world p129-33
  398.2

Greek and Roman mythology A to Z. Daly, K. N.
  292

Greek and Roman science. Nardo, D.   **509**

Greek and Roman sport. Nardo, D.   **796**

Greek gods and goddesses. McCaughrean, G.
  292

The **Greek** interpreter. Doyle, Sir A. C.
 In Doyle, Sir A. C. The complete Sherlock Holmes   **S C**

Greek mythology *See* Classical mythology

Greek myths. Morley, J.   **292**

The **Greek** news. Powell, A.   **938**

Greek science *See* Science—Greece

A **Greek** temple. Macdonald, F.   **938**

The **Greeks**. Chapman, G.   **745.5**

Green, Carl R.
 (jt. auth) Sanford, W. R. Bill Pickett: African-American rodeo star   **92**
 (jt. auth) Sanford, W. R. Calamity Jane: frontier original   **92**

Green, Hannah *See* Greenberg, Joanne, 1932-

Green, Jen
 Race to the moon   **629.45**

Green, Lucinda
 The young rider   **798.2**

Green, Michael D., 1941-
 The Creeks
 In Indians of North America series
  970.004

Green, Rayna
 High cotton
 In Talking leaves   **S C**

Green, Rayna—*Continued*
Women in American Indian society
In Indians of North America series
970.004

Green, Rebecca L.
The empire of Ghana   966.1

Green, Robert, 1969-
China (7 and up)   951
King Henry VIII   92
Queen Victoria   92
Tutankhamun   932
William the Conqueror   92

Green Bay Packers (Football team)
Gutman, B. Brett Favre   92

The **green-clawed** thunderbird. Mayo, M.
In Mayo, M. Mythical birds & beasts from
many lands p37-45   398.2

Green ghosts. Yolen, J.
In Yolen, J. Here there be ghosts p86-94
810.8

Green willow. Martin, R.
In Martin, R. Mysterious tales of Japan
398.2

Greenaway, Theresa, 1947-
Jungle   577.3

Greenberg, Jan, 1942-
The American eye   920
Chuck Close, up close   92
The sculptor's eye   730.9

Greenberg, Joanne, 1932-
I never promised you a rose garden (7 and up)
Fic

Greenberg, Judith E.
Barbara Pierce Bush, 1925-   92
Young people's letters to the president   973

Greenberg, Keith Elliot, 1959-
Adolescent rights (7 and up)   346

Greenberg, Martin Harry
(ed) Dragons & dreams. See Dragons & dreams
S C
(ed) The Haunted house: a collection of original
stories. See The Haunted house: a collection
of original stories   S C
(comp) A Newbery Christmas. See A Newbery
Christmas   S C
(comp) A Newbery Halloween. See A Newbery
Halloween   S C
(comp) A Newbery zoo. See A Newbery zoo
S C
(ed) Vampires: a collection of original stories.
See Vampires: a collection of original stories
S C

Greenblatt, Miriam
The War of 1812   973.5

Greene, Bette, 1934-
An ordinary woman
In Sixteen: short stories by outstanding writ-
ers for young adults p125-32   S C
Summer of my German soldier   Fic

Greene, Jacqueline Dembar
The Maya   972

Greenfeld, Howard
Paul Gauguin (7 and up)   92

Greenfield, Eloise, 1929-
See/See also pages in the following book(s):
Strickland, M. R. African-American poets p83-
89   920

Greenfield, Jane
Books: their care and repair   025.7

Greenfield, Susan
(ed) The Human mind explained. See The Human mind explained   153

Greenhouse effect
Global warming: opposing viewpoints (7 and
up)   363.7
See/See also pages in the following book(s):
Miller, C. G. Air alert   363.7

Greensmith, Alan
(jt. auth) Harrison, C. Birds of the world
598

Greenwitch. Cooper, S. See note under Cooper, S.
Over sea, under stone   Fic

Greenwood histories of the modern nations [se-
ries]
Blumberg, A. The history of Israel   956.94

Greenwood library management collection
Young adults and public libraries   027.62

Greeting the Sun, a Maushop story. Bruchac, J.
In Bruchac, J. Four ancestors p9-11
398.2

Gregor Mendel, and the roots of genetics.
Edelson, E.   92

Gregory, Jean
See also Ure, Jean

Gregory, Kristiana
Orphan runaways   Fic
The winter of red snow   Fic

Gregory, Tony
The Dark Ages   909.07

Gretzky, Wayne
About
Santella, A. Wayne Gretzky   92
The **grey** king. Cooper, S. See note under Cooper,
S. Over sea, under stone   Fic

Gribbin, John R.
Time & space   530.1

Gribbin, Mary
(jt. auth) Gribbin, J. R. Time & space
530.1

Griffey, Ken, Jr.
About
Gutman, B. Ken Griffey, Jr.   92

Griffin, Adele
The other Shepards   Fic
Sons of liberty   Fic
Split just right   Fic

Griffin, Peni R.
Truth in the case of Eliza Mary Muller, by her-
self
In Stay true: short stories for strong girls
S C

Griffin, Robert, 1951-
(ed) The Folklore of world holidays. See The
Folklore of world holidays   394.26

Griggs, Jack L.
All the birds of North America   598

Grimes, Nikki
  A dime a dozen   **811**
  Hopscotch love   **811**
  Jazmin's notebook   **Fic**
Grimké, Angelina Emily, 1805-1879
About
  Todras, E. H. Angelina Grimké (7 and up)
    92
Grimké, Charlotte Forten, 1837-1914
See/See also pages in the following book(s):
  Bolden, T. And not afraid to dare   **920**
Grimm, Jacob, 1785-1863
  The devil and his grandmother
    In The Book of dragons p67-71   **S C**
The **grind** of an axe. Taylor, T.
  In Night terrors   **S C**
Grinnell, George Bird, 1849-1938
See/See also pages in the following book(s):
  Calvert, P. Great lives: the American frontier
    p177-92   **920**
Grisham, John
About
  Weaver, R. M. John Grisham (7 and up)
    92
Grizzly bear
  Patent, D. H. The way of the grizzly
    599.78
  Silverstein, A. The grizzly bear   **599.78**
Groff, Claire Price- *See* Price Groff, Claire
The **Grolier** children's encyclopedia. See The
  New Grolier children's encyclopedia   **031**
The **Grolier** library of women's biographies
    920.003
The **Grolier** multimedia encyclopedia. See Aca-
  demic American encyclopedia   **031**
Grolier multimedia encyclopedia, deluxe edition.
  See entry in CD-ROM section, Part 3
The **Grolier** student encyclopedia of endangered
  species   **591.68**
Grolier student library of explorers and explora-
  tion   **910.4**
Grollman, Earl A.
  Straight talk about death for teenagers (7 and
  up)   **155.9**
Gros Ventres of the Missouri *See* Hidatsa Indi-
  ans
Grosshandler, Janet
  Coping when a parent dies (7 and up)
    155.9
Grossman, James R.
  A chance to make good (7 and up)   **305.8**
Ground-hogs *See* Marmots
The **grounding** of Group 6. Thompson, J. F.
    Fic
Groups, Social *See* Social groups
Grove, Andrew S.
About
  Byman, J. Andrew Grove and the Intel Corpora-
  tion (7 and up)   **92**
Grove, Vicki
  The crystal garden   **Fic**
  Reaching Dustin   **Fic**
  The starplace   **Fic**

The **growin'** of Paul Bunyan. Brooke, W. J.
  In Brooke, W. J. A telling of the tales: five
    stories p37-48   **S C**
Growing up. Soto, G.
  In Soto, G. Baseball in April, and other sto-
    ries p97-107   **S C**
Growing up black   **920**
Growing up in coal country. Bartoletti, S. C.
    331.3
Growing up in the Great Depression. Wormser, R.
    973.91
Growing up: it's a girl thing. Jukes, M.
    612.6
Growing up Latino   **810.8**
Growth
  Parker, S. Reproduction and growth   **612.6**
  Parker, S. The reproductive system   **612.6**
Grumet, Robert Steven
  The Lenapes
    In Indians of North America series
    970.004
Gryphon's eyrie. Norton, A. See note under Nor-
  ton, A. Witch World [series]   **Fic**
Guanina. Delacre, L.
  In Delacre, L. Golden tales p7-12   **398.2**
The **guardian** of memory. Coville, B.
  In A Glory of unicorns p1-28   **S C**
Guatemala
  Sheehan, S. Guatemala   **972.81**
La **güera**. Soto, G.
  In Soto, G. Petty crimes   **S C**
Güereña, Salvador, 1952-
  (ed) Latino periodicals. See Latino periodicals
    011.6
Guess, George *See* Sequoyah, 1770?-1843
Guess who's back in town, dear?. Kerr, M. E.
  In Stay true: short stories for strong girls
    S C
Guests. Dorris, M.   **Fic**
Guiberson, Brenda Z.
  Exotic species   **577**
Guidance, Vocational *See* Vocational guidance
Guide to cartooning. Bohl, A.   **741.5**
Guide to popular U.S. government publications.
  Hoffmann, F. W.   **015.73**
Guide to reference books for school media cen-
  ters. See Safford, B. R. Guide to reference
  materials for school media centers   **011.6**
Guide to reference materials for school media cen-
  ters. Safford, B. R.   **011.6**
Guides to collection development for children and
  young adults. Gillespie, J. T.   **011.6**
Guilt
Fiction
  Cormier, R. In the middle of the night (7 and
  up)   **Fic**
  Fleischman, P. Whirligig (7 and up)   **Fic**
  McDonald, J. Swallowing stones (7 and up)
    Fic
Guinness book of records   **032.02**
The **Guinness** book of records 1492   **031.02**
Guinness book of world records. See Guinness
  book of records   **032.02**

Guitar solo. McCaughrean, G.
  In McCaughrean, G. The bronze cauldron: myths and legends of the world p11-13
  398.2
Gulf War, 1991 *See* Persian Gulf War, 1991
Gull-girl. McCaughrean, G.
  In McCaughrean, G. The crystal pool: myths and legends of the world p71-75
  398.2
Gulliver's travels. Swift, J.   **Fic**
Gulotta, Charles
  Extraordinary women in politics   **920**
Gun control
  Gun control: opposing viewpoints (7 and up)
  363.3
  Guns and violence (7 and up)   **363.3**
  Schwarz, T. Kids and guns (7 and up)
  363.3
Gun control: opposing viewpoints (7 and up)
  363.3
Guns and violence (7 and up)   **363.3**
Gunther, John, 1901-1970
  Death be not proud [biography of his son] (7 and up)   **92**
Gunther, John, 1929-1947
  About
  Gunther, J. Death be not proud (7 and up)
  92
Gurian, Michael
  From boys to men   **305.23**
Gurney, James, 1958-
  Dinotopia: a land apart from time   **Fic**
  Dinotopia: first flight. See note under Gurney, J. Dinotopia: a land apart from time   **Fic**
  Dinotopia: the world beneath. See note under Gurney, J. Dinotopia: a land apart from time
  Fic
Guthrie, Donna, 1946-
  Real world math (7 and up)   **332.024**
  (jt. auth) Hulme, J. N. How to write, recite, and delight in all kinds of poetry   **808.1**
Guthrie, Janet, 1938-
  See/See also pages in the following book(s):
  Gaines, A. Sports & athletics   **920**
Gutman, Bill
  Brett Favre   **92**
  Ken Griffey, Jr.   **92**
  Shooting stars   **796.323**
  Tae kwon do   **796.8**
Gutman, Dan
  Baseball's greatest games (7 and up)
  796.357
  Gymnastics   **796.44**
  Jackie and me   **Fic**
  The million dollar shot   **Fic**
  Virtually perfect   **Fic**
Guts and glory. Rappoport, K.   **920**
Guy, Rosa
  The disappearance   **Fic**
  The friends   **Fic**
  She
  In Sixteen: short stories by outstanding writers for young adults p147-53   **S C**

About
  Norris, J. Presenting Rosa Guy (7 and up)
  813.009
Gymnastics
  Bragg, L. W. Fundamental gymnastics
  796.44
  Durrett, D. Dominique Moceanu (7 and up)
  92
  Gutman, D. Gymnastics   **796.44**
  Jackman, J. The young gymnast   **796.44**
  Rutledge, R. The best of the best in gymnastics
  920
Gynecologists
  Diamond, S. N. Everything you need to know about going to the gynecologist (7 and up)
  618.1
Gynecology *See* Women—Health and hygiene
Gypsies
  Fiction
  Alexander, L. Gypsy Rizka   **Fic**
Gypsy Rizka. Alexander, L.   **Fic**

H

Haas, Jessie
  Unbroken   **Fic**
Habibi. Nye, N. S.   **Fic**
Habitat (Ecology)
  Kerrod, R. Facts on File wildlife atlas   **578**
  Lauber, P. Fur, feathers, and flippers   **591.7**
  Orr, R. Nature cross-sections   **577**
  VanCleave, J. P. Janice Vancleave's ecology for every kid   **577**
Habitats [series]
  Waterlow, J. Grasslands   **577.4**
Hacker, Carlotta
  Great African Americans in history   **920**
  Nobel Prize winners   **920**
Haddix, Margaret Peterson, 1964-
  Among the hidden   **Fic**
  Don't you dare read this, Mrs. Dunphrey (7 and up)   **Fic**
  Leaving Fishers (7 and up)   **Fic**
  Running out of time   **Fic**
Hagedorn, Jessica Tarahata, 1949-
  See/See also pages in the following book(s):
  Chiu, C. Lives of notable Asian Americans: literature and education p65-71 (7 and up)
  920
Hager, Thomas
  Linus Pauling and the chemistry of life (7 and up)   **92**
Hague, Michael, 1948-
  (comp) The Book of dragons. See The Book of dragons   **S C**
Hahn, Don
  Animation magic   **791.43**
Hahn, Kimiko, 1955-
  See/See also pages in the following book(s):
  Chiu, C. Lives of notable Asian Americans: literature and education p17-23 (7 and up)
  920
Hahn, Mary Downing, 1937-
  As ever, Gordy   **Fic**

Hahn, Mary Downing, 1937——_Continued_
Daphne's book — Fic
Following my own footsteps — Fic
Stepping on the cracks — Fic

Haiku
Livingston, M. C. Cricket never does — 811

Haile Selassie I, Emperor of Ethiopia, 1892-1975
See/See also pages in the following book(s):
Rasmussen, R. K. Modern African political leaders p1-15 (7 and up) — 920

The **hairy** hands. San Souci, R.
_In_ San Souci, R. A terrifying taste of short & shivery p52-57 — 398.2

Haiti
Hintz, M. Haiti — 972.94
Myers, W. D. Toussaint L'Ouverture — 92
Fiction
Temple, F. Tonight, by sea — Fic

Haitian Americans
Ashabranner, B. K. To seek a better world — 305.8
Fiction
Mowry, J. Ghost train — Fic

Hakim, Joy
A history of US — 973

Halberstam, David, 1934-
Playing for keeps: Michael Jordan and the world he made (7 and up) — 92

Hale, Clara
See/See also pages in the following book(s):
Bolden, T. And not afraid to dare — 920

Hale, Duane K.
The Chickasaw
_In_ Indians of North America series — 970.004

Hale, George Ellery, 1868-1938
See/See also pages in the following book(s):
Camp, C. A. American astronomers p44-51 — 920

Hall, Cally
Gemstones (7 and up) — 553.8

Hall, Donald, 1928-
(ed) The Oxford book of children's verse in America. See The Oxford book of children's verse in America — 811.008

Hall, Elizabeth, 1929-
(jt. auth) O'Dell, S. Thunder rolling in the mountains — Fic

Hall, Lynn, 1937-
If winter comes (7 and up) — Fic

Hall, Ruby Bridges _See_ Bridges, Ruby

Halley, Ned
Amazing facts. See Amazing facts — 031.02
Farm — 630.1

Halliburton, Warren J.
(comp) Historic speeches of African Americans. See Historic speeches of African Americans — 815

Halloween
Fiction
Bradbury, R. The Halloween tree — Fic
A Newbery Halloween — S C

A **Halloween** to remember. Konigsburg, E. L.
_In_ A Newbery Halloween p23-36 — S C
The **Halloween** tree. Bradbury, R. — Fic

Hallworth, Grace
The shiner
_In_ The Oxford book of scary tales p52-53 — 808.8

Halperin, Michael
(jt. auth) Drucker, M. Jacob's rescue — Fic

Hamanaka, Sheila
In search of the spirit — 920
The journey — 305.8

Hambly, Barbara
See/See also pages in the following book(s):
MacRae, C. D. Presenting young adult fantasy fiction (7 and up) — 813.009

Hamer, Fannie Lou Townsend, 1917-1977
See/See also pages in the following book(s):
Dubovoy, S. Civil rights leaders p101-12 (7 and up) — 920
Haskins, J. One more river to cross — 920

Hamer, Martin J., 1931-
The mountain
_In_ Rites of passage p45-49 — S C

Hamilton, Edith, 1867-1963
Mythology — 292

Hamilton, Jake
Special effects in film and television — 791.43

Hamilton, Lillian B.
(ed) The Comprehensive signed English dictionary. See The Comprehensive signed English dictionary — 419

Hamilton, Virginia, 1936-
Anthony Burns — 92
Cousins — Fic
The dark way — 398.2
Contents: The Banshee; Rolling Rio, the gray man, and Death; Baba Yaga, the terrible; The One-Inch Boy; Manabozo; The horned women; The Flying Dutchman; Medusa; The wicked stepmother; The tiny thing; The pretender; Childe Rowland and Burd Ellen; Everlasting life; Tanuki magic teakettle; Fenris, the wolf; Joseph Golem; The very large son; The free spirit; Bouki and Malice; The girl who was swallowed by the earth; The witch's boar; The argument; The magician's fellow; Brothers and bone; Yama, the God of Death; The witch's skinny

He Lion, Bruh Bear, and Bruh Rabbit
_In_ A Newbery zoo — S C
Her stories — 398.2
Includes the following stories: Little Girl and Buh Rabby; Lena and Big One Tiger; Marie and Redfish; Miz Hattie gets some company; Catskinella; Good Blanche, bad Rose, and the talking eggs; Mary Belle and the mermaid; Mom Bett and the little ones a-glowing; Who you!; Macie and boo hag; Lonna and Cat Woman; Malindy and little devil; Woman and Man started even; Luella and the tame parrot; The mer-woman out of the sea; Annie Christmas

The house of Dies Drear — Fic
In the beginning: creation stories from around the world — 291.1
Many thousand gone — 326
The mystery of Drear House — Fic
The peculiar such thing
_In_ From sea to shining sea p338-39 — 810.8

The people could fly [story]
_In_ From sea to shining sea p144-47 — 810.8

Hamilton, Virginia, 1936-—_Continued_
The people could fly: American black folktales
398.2
Plain City **Fic**
The planet of Junior Brown **Fic**
Second cousins **Fic**
Sweet whispers, Brother Rush **Fic**
The year Halloween happened one day early
_In_ A Newbery Halloween p167-82 **S C**
Hamley, Dennis, 1935-
Supermarket
_In_ The Oxford book of scary tales p106-11
808.8
Hamm, Mia, 1972-
Go for the goal (7 and up) **796.334**
Hammond, Susan Hazen- _See_ Hazen-Hammond, Susan
Hammond Explorer atlas of the world. See Explorer atlas of the world **912**
Hampton, Wilborn
Kennedy assassinated! **973.922**
Hanan, Jessica
When someone you love is addicted (7 and up)
362.29
Hanawalt, Barbara
The Middle Ages (7 and up) **909.07**
Hancock, Herbie, 1940-
See/See also pages in the following book(s):
Gourse, L. Striders to beboppers and beyond p106-10 (7 and up) **781.65**
Hand in hand **811.008**
The **hand** of death. Olson, A. N.
_In_ Olson, A. N. Ask the bones: scary stories from around the world p105-09
398.2
The **Hand** of Dinotopia. Foster, A. D. **Fic**
The **Handbook** of private schools **370.25**
Handedness See Left- and right-handedness
A **handful**. Johnson, A.
_In_ Johnson, A, Gone from home: short takes p51-57 **S C**
Handicapped
See also Mentally handicapped; Physically handicapped
Kent, D. Extraordinary people with disabilities **920**

Fiction
Crutcher, C. The Crazy Horse Electric game (7 and up) **Fic**
Handicapped children
See also Mentally handicapped children
Handicraft
Chapman, G. The Egyptians **745.5**
Chapman, G. The Greeks **745.5**
Chapman, G. The Romans **745.5**
Diehn, G. Making books that fly, fold, wrap, hide, pop up, twist, and turn **736**
Doney, M. Festivals **745.5**
Doney, M. Masks **745.59**
Doney, M. Puppets **745.592**
Engelbreit, M. Hey, kids! Come craft with me
745.5
Hart, A. Ancient Greece! **938**

Hart, A. Knights & castles **940.1**
Hendry, L. Making picture frames **745.5**
Holtschlag, M. Button crafts **745.5**
Needham, B. Ecology crafts for kids **745.5**
Stevens, B. S. Colonial American craftspeople
745.5
Temko, F. Traditional crafts from Africa
745.5
Temko, F. Traditional crafts from Mexico and Central America **745.5**
See/See also pages in the following book(s):
Sabbeth, A. Rubber-band banjos and a java jive bass **781**
The **handkerchief**. Olson, A. N.
_In_ Olson, A. N. Ask the bones: scary stories from around the world p73-77 **398.2**
Handler, Ruth, 1916-
See/See also pages in the following book(s):
Altman, L. J. Women inventors p100-12 (7 and up) **920**
Jeffrey, L. S. Great American businesswomen p36-45 **920**
The **handmaid** of the Lord. Paterson, K.
_In_ Paterson, K. A midnight clear: stories for the Christmas season **S C**
Hands, Rachel
Kiitos! Kiitos!
_In_ The Oxford book of scary tales p144-49
808.8
Hands in the darkness. Sieruta, P. D.
_In_ Help wanted: short stories about young people working **S C**
Haney, John
Vladimir Ilich Lenin **92**
Hang a thousand trees with ribbons. Rinaldi, A.
Fic
Hanley, Sally
A. Philip Randolph **92**
Hannah, Marc, 1956-
See/See also pages in the following book(s):
Northrup, M. American computer pioneers p83-92 **920**
Hannah in between. Rodowsky, C. F. **Fic**
Hansberry, Lorraine, 1930-1965
About
McKissack, P. C. Young, black, and determined: a biography of Lorraine Hansberry **92**
Hansen, Joyce
Breaking ground, breaking silence **974.7**
The captive **Fic**
Which way freedom? **Fic**
Women of hope **920**
Hansen, Mark Victor
(comp) Chicken soup for the teenage soul. See Chicken soup for the teenage soul **158**
Hanson, Freya Ottem, 1949-
The Second Amendment (7 and up) **344**
Hanukkah
Fiction
Singer, I. B. The power of light **S C**
A **Hanukkah** evening in my parents' house. Singer, I. B.
_In_ Singer, I. B. The power of light p3-9
S C

Hate crimes—*Continued*
  Hate groups: opposing viewpoints (7 and up)
      364.1

Hate groups: opposing viewpoints (7 and up)
      364.1

Hating Hansen. Taylor, T.
  In Taylor, T. Rogue wave and other red-
    blooded sea stories   **S C**

Haugen, David, 1969-
  The Civil War (7 and up)   **973.7**

Hauling gold. Taylor, T.
  In Taylor, T. Rogue wave and other red-
    blooded sea stories   **S C**

Haunted America [series]
  Wood, T. Ghosts of the West Coast   **133.1**

The **haunted** forest. Olson, A. N.
  In Olson, A. N. Ask the bones: scary stories
    from around the world p1-9   **398.2**

The **haunted** grove. San Souci, R.
  In San Souci, R. A terrifying taste of short &
    shivery p101-03   **398.2**

The **Haunted** house: a collection of original stories   **S C**

The **haunted** schoolhouse. Vivelo, J.
  In Vivelo, J. Chills in the night p19-35
      S C

Haunted sister. Littke, L.   **Fic**

The **haunting**. Nixon, J. L.   **Fic**

Hauser, Pierre
  Illegal aliens   **325.73**

Hautman, Pete, 1952-
  Stone cold (7 and up)   **Fic**

Hautzig, David
  (il) Krull, K. One nation, many tribes
      970.004

Hautzig, Esther Rudomin, 1930-
  The endless steppe: growing up in Siberia
      92

Have a heart. Conford, E.
  In Conford, E. Crush p27-50   **S C**

Haveli. Staples, S. F.   **Fic**

Havemann, Ernst
  A farm at Raraba
  In Somehow tenderness survives p119-34
      S C

Haven, Kendall F.
  100 most popular scientists for young adults (7
    and up)   **920**

Haviland, Virginia, 1911-1988
  Wiley and the Hairy Man
  In The Oxford book of scary tales p55-61
      808.8

Hawaii
  Goldberg, J. Hawaii
    In Celebrate the states   **973**
  Hintz, M. Hawaii
    In America the beautiful, second series
      973
        Fiction
  Salisbury, G. Jungle dogs   **Fic**
  Salisbury, G. Shark bait   **Fic**
  Salisbury, G. Under the blood-red sun   **Fic**
  Slepian, J. The Broccoli tapes   **Fic**

Wallace, B. Aloha summer   **Fic**
        History
  Linnea, S. Princess Ka'iulani   **92**
  Stanley, F. The last princess: the story of Prin-
    cess Ka'iulani of Hawai'i   **92**

Hawes, Charles Boardman, 1889-1923
  The tale of the poplar
  In A Newbery zoo   **S C**

The **hawk**. Gordon, J.
  In The Oxford book of scary tales p114-22
      808.8

Hawk highway in the sky. Arnold, C.   **598**

Hawk moon. MacGregor, R.   **Fic**

Hawking, S. W. (Stephen W.)
        About
  McDaniel, M. Stephen Hawking (7 and up)
      92

Hawking, Stephen W. *See* Hawking, S. W. (Stephen W.)

Hawks
  Arnold, C. Hawk highway in the sky   **598**

Hawthorne, Nathaniel, 1804-1864
  Feathertop
  In American fairy tales p29-54   **S C**
  See/See also pages in the following book(s):
  Faber, D. Great lives: American literature p21-
    30   **920**

Haycock, Ken
  (ed) Foundations for effective school library me-
    dia programs. See Foundations for effective
    school library media programs   **027.8**

Haycraft, Howard, 1905-1991
  (ed) American authors, 1600-1900. See
    American authors, 1600-1900   **920.003**

Hayden, Lewis, 1815-1889
        About
  Strangis, J. Lewis Hayden and the war against
    slavery (7 and up)   **92**

Hayes, Daniel, 1952-
  Flyers (7 and up)   **Fic**
  No effect   **Fic**

Hayes, Joe, 1945-
  La Llorona, the weeping woman
  In From sea to shining sea p331-35
      810.8

Hayes, Randy
  See/See also pages in the following book(s):
  Graham, K. Contemporary environmentalists
    p105-22 (7 and up)   **920**

Hayes, Rutherford B., 1822-1893
  See/See also pages in the following book(s):
  Presidents of a growing country   **920**

The **haymeadow**. Paulsen, G.   **Fic**

Haynes, Joyce
  Egyptian dynasties   **932**

Haynes, Richard M.
  Ida B. Wells, antilynching crusader   **92**

Haynes, Tricia
  Colombia   **986.1**

Haywood, Big Bill, 1869-1928
  See/See also pages in the following book(s):
  Streissguth, T. Legendary labor leaders (7 and
    up)   **920**

Haywood, William Dudley *See* Haywood, Big Bill, 1869-1928

Hazardous occupations

See also Industrial accidents

Hazelwood v. Kuhlmeier. Fuller, S. B.   **344**

Hazen, Elizabeth, 1885-1975

See/See also pages in the following book(s):

Altman, L. J. Women inventors p74-87 (7 and up)   **920**

Hazen-Hammond, Susan

Thunder Bear and Ko   **970.004**

He Lion, Bruh Bear, and Bruh Rabbit. Hamilton, V.

In A Newbery zoo   **S C**

Headache

Votava, A. Coping with migraines and other headaches (7 and up)   **616.8**

Heads of state

See also Kings and rulers; Presidents

Wakin, E. Asian independence leaders (7 and up)   **920**

Heale, Jay

Democratic Republic of the Congo   **967.51**

Madagascar   **969.1**

Tanzania   **967.8**

The **healer**. McKinley, R.

In McKinley, R. A knot in the grain and other stories p1-39   **S C**

Healing, Mental *See* Mental healing

The **healing** truth. Lay, K.

In A Glory of unicorns p145-62   **S C**

Health

See also Physical fitness

Folkers, G. Taking charge of my mind & body (7 and up)   **613**

Health on file   **613**

Environmental aspects

See Environmental health

Health, Public *See* Public health

Health care *See* Medical care

Health care personnel *See* Medical personnel

Health on file   **613**

The **healthy** body cookbook. D'Amico, J.   **641.5**

Hear these voices. Allison, A.   **305.23**

Hearing impaired

See also Deaf

Hearne, Betsy Gould

Beauties and beasts   **398.2**

Includes the following stories: Beauty and the Beast; The enchanted Tsarevitch; The princess and the pig; A bunch of laurel blooms for a present; The small-tooth dog; The fairy serpent; Monkey son-in-law; The lizard husband; Cupid and Psyche; The serpent and the grape-grower's daughter; The singing, soaring lark; East of the sun and west of the moon; Whitebear Whittington; The three daughters of King O'Hara; The Black Bull of Norroway; Bull-of-all-the-Land; Prince White Hog; The enchanted prince; The story of Five Heads; The ten serpents; Englè, Queen of Serpents; Sir Gawain and the loathly lady; The laidley worm of Spindleston Heughs; Kemp Owyne; Pinto Smalto; The dough prince; Old Man Coyote, the young man and two otter sisters

Listening for Leroy   **Fic**

Polaroid and other poems of view   **811**

Hearne, Elizabeth G. *See* Hearne, Betsy Gould

Hearst, Patricia Campbell

See/See also pages in the following book(s):

Aaseng, N. You are the juror   **345**

Heart

See also Blood—Circulation

Ballard, C. The heart and circulatory system   **612.1**

Silverstein, A. The circulatory system   **612.1**

Simon, S. The heart   **612.1**

The **heart** and circulatory system. Ballard, C.   **612.1**

Heart attack *See* Heart diseases

Heart diseases

Johansson, P. Heart disease   **616.1**

Heart of a champion. Deuker, C.   **Fic**

The **heart** of a chief. Bruchac, J.   **Fic**

A **heart** of stone. McCaughrean, G.

In McCaughrean, G. The silver treasure: myths and legends of the world p70-74   **398.2**

Heart's Blood. Yolen, J.   **Fic**

Heat

Gardner, R. Science projects about temperature and heat (7 and up)   **536**

Heat. Cadnum, M.   **Fic**

Heath, Alan

Windows on the world   **394.2**

Heaven. Johnson, A.   **Fic**

The **Heavenly** Village. Rylant, C.   **Fic**

Heavy Collar and the ghost woman. Brown, D. A.

In Brown, D. A. Dee Brown's folktales of the Native American p160-66   **398.2**

Hecht, Jeff

Aunt Horrible's last visit

In Vampires: a collection of original stories p187-201   **S C**

Heck, Alfons, 1928-

(jt. auth) Ayer, E. H. Parallel journeys   **940.53**

Heifetz, Aaron

(jt. auth) Hamm, M. Go for the goal   **796.334**

Heiligman, Deborah

The New York Public Library kid's guide to research   **025.5**

Heinemann, Sue, 1948-

The New York Public Library amazing women in American history   **305.4**

Heinrichs, Ann

Australia   **994**

California

In America the beautiful, second series   **973**

Florida

In America the beautiful, second series   **973**

Indiana

In America the beautiful, second series   **973**

Japan   **952**

Henson, Matthew Alexander, 1866-1955
About
Williams, J. K. Matthew Henson, polar adventurer   **92**
See/See also pages in the following book(s):
Hacker, C. Great African Americans in history   **920**
Haskins, J. Against all opposition p46-61   **920**
Haskins, J. One more river to cross   **920**
Hentoff, Nat
The day they came to arrest the book (7 and up)   **Fic**
Hepburn, Katharine, 1907-
See/See also pages in the following book(s):
Gaines, A. Entertainment & performing arts   **920**
Her Majesty's servants. Kipling, R.
In Kipling, R. The jungle books   **S C**
Her stories. Hamilton, V.   **398.2**
Heracles (Legendary character) *See* Hercules (Legendary character)
Herald, Diana Tixier
Teen genreflecting   **016.8**
Herald, Jacqueline
Fashions of a decade, The 1920s   **391**
Fashions of a decade, The 1970s   **391**
Herbal medicine *See* Medical botany
Herbal nightmare. Namioka, L.
In Center stage   **812.008**
Herbert, Janis, 1956-
Leonardo da Vinci for kids   **92**
Herbs
Goldish, M. The dangers of herbal stimulants   **615.9**
Hercegovina *See* Bosnia and Hercegovina
Hercules (Legendary character)
See/See also pages in the following book(s):
Hamilton, E. Mythology p224-43   **292**
Herda, D. J., 1948-
The Dred Scott case (7 and up)   **342**
Furman v. Georgia (7 and up)   **345**
New York Times v. United States (7 and up)   **342**
Here comes Eleanor [Roosevelt] Westervelt, V. V.   **92**
Here is my kingdom   **810.8**
Here there be ghosts. Yolen, J.   **810.8**
Heredity
See also Gene mapping
See/See also pages in the following book(s):
Kidd, J. S. Life lines p1-15 (7 and up)   **576.5**
Here's to you, Rachel Robinson. Blume, J.   **Fic**
Hermann, Spring
R.C. Gorman   **92**
Hermes, Patricia, 1936-
Calling me home   **Fic**
Cheat the moon   **Fic**
Mama, let's dance   **Fic**
Someone to count on   **Fic**

A **hero** ain't nothin' but a sandwich. Childress, A.   **Fic**
The **hero** and the crown. McKinley, R.   **Fic**
Heroes. Cormier, R.   **Fic**
Heroes and heroines
Mendoza, P. M. Extraordinary people in extraordinary times (7 and up)   **920**
Fiction
Voigt, C. Jackaroo (7 and up)   **Fic**
Heroes of the faith [series]
Booth, E. P. Martin Luther   **92**
Wellman, S. John Wesley   **92**
Heroin
Littell, M. A. Heroin drug dangers   **362.29**
Heroin drug dangers. Littell, M. A.   **362.29**
Heroines *See* Heroes and heroines
Heroism *See* Courage
Herons
Fiction
Avi. Blue heron   **Fic**
Herrera, Carolina
See/See also pages in the following book(s):
Morey, J. Famous Hispanic Americans p76-89   **920**
Herrera, Juan Felipe, 1948-
Laughing out loud, I fly   **811**
Herschel, Caroline Lucretia, 1750-1848
See/See also pages in the following book(s):
Celebrating women in mathematics and science p25-36   **920**
Hershele and Hanukkah. Singer, I. B.
In Singer, I. B. The power of light p63-72   **S C**
Hershey, David R.
Plant biology science projects (7 and up)   **580.7**
Herstory: women who changed the world (7 and up)   **920**
Herzegovina *See* Bosnia and Hercegovina
Hesse, Eva, 1936-1970
See/See also pages in the following book(s):
Greenberg, J. The American eye p98-105   **920**
Hesse, Karen
Letters from Rifka   **Fic**
The music of dolphins   **Fic**
Out of the dust   **Fic**
Phoenix rising   **Fic**
Hesser, Terry Spencer
Kissing doorknobs (7 and up)   **Fic**
Hestler, Anna
Yemen   **953.3**
Hewett, Lorri
Dancer (7 and up)   **Fic**
Hewitt, Catherine
Buddhism   **294.3**
Hewitt, Kathryn
(il) Krull, K. Lives of the presidents   **920**
Hexwood. Jones, D. W.   **Fic**
Hey, Dad, get a life!. Strasser, T.   **Fic**
Hey, kids! Come craft with me. Engelbreit, M.   **745.5**

Hines, Kim
Home on the mornin' train
In Theatre for young audiences p308-37
812.008
Hinojosa, Maria, 1961-
Crews (7 and up)   302.3
Hinojosa, Rolando, 1929-
Brother Imás
In Growing up Latino p250-58   810.8
Hinton, S. E.
The outsiders (7 and up)   Fic
Rumble fish (7 and up)   Fic
Taming the Star Runner (7 and up)   Fic
Tex (7 and up)   Fic
That was then, this is now (7 and up)   Fic
About
Daly, J. Presenting S.E. Hinton (7 and up)
813.009
Hintz, Martin, 1945-
Argentina   982
Haiti   972.94
Hawaii
In America the beautiful, second series
973
Iowa
In America the beautiful, second series
973
Louisiana
In America the beautiful, second series
973
Michigan
In America the beautiful, second series
973
Minnesota
In America the beautiful, second series
973
Missouri
In America the beautiful, second series
973
North Carolina
In America the beautiful, second series
973
Poland   943.8
Hipple, Theodore W.
(ed) Writers for young adults. See Writers for
young adults   920.003
Hiroshima (Japan)
Bombardment, 1945
Grant, R. G. Hiroshima and Nagasaki (7 and up)
940.54
Maruki, T. Hiroshima no pika   940.54
Bombardment, 1945—Fiction
Yep, L. Hiroshima   Fic
Hiroshima and Nagasaki. Grant, R. G.
940.54
Hiroshima no pika. Maruki, T.   940.54
Hirsch, E. D. (Eric Donald), 1928-
The dictionary of cultural literacy   031
Hirsch, Eric Donald *See* Hirsch, E. D. (Eric Donald), 1928-
Hirsch, Karen D.
(ed) Mind riot. See Mind riot   741.5
Hirunpidok, Visalaya
Yai
In American dragons p168-84   810.8

His last bow. Doyle, Sir A. C.
In Doyle, Sir A. C. The complete Sherlock
Holmes   S C
His last bow [short story] Doyle, Sir A. C.
In Doyle, Sir A. C. The complete Sherlock
Holmes   S C
Hispanic America, Texas, and the Mexican War,
1835-1850. Collier, C.   973.6
Hispanic American almanac [junior version]
305.8
Hispanic American art
Here is my kingdom   810.8
Hispanic American authors
Growing up Latino   810.8
Hispanic American poetry *See* American poetry—Hispanic American authors
Hispanic-American scientists. Oleksy, W. G.
920
Hispanic Americans
Garza, H. Pablo Casals   92
Gonzales, D. Gloria Estefan   92
Hispanic American almanac   305.8
Latino voices (7 and up)   860.8
Morey, J. Famous Hispanic Americans   920
Ochoa, G. The New York Public Library amazing Hispanic American history   305.8
Oleksy, W. G. Hispanic-American scientists (7 and up)   920
Sinnott, S. Extraordinary Hispanic Americans
920
Dictionaries
Meyer, N. E. The biographical dictionary of
Hispanic Americans   920.003
Fiction
Soto, G. Taking sides   Fic
Periodicals—Bibliography
Latino periodicals   011.6
Hispanic biographies [series]
Cruz, B. José Clemente Orozco   92
Gonzales, D. Gloria Estefan   92
Goodnough, D. Pablo Neruda   92
Mirriam-Goldberg, C. Sandra Cisneros   92
Hispanic heritage [series]
Cedeño, M. E. Cesar Chavez   92
Fernández, J. B. José de San Martín   92
Hispanics of achievement [series]
Dolan, S. Gabriel García Márquez   92
Dolan, S. Junípero Serra   92
Garza, H. Pablo Casals   92
Goldberg, J. Miguel de Cervantes   92
Lennon, A. Jorge Luis Borges   92
O'Brien, S. Antonio López de Santa Anna
92
O'Brien, S. Pancho Villa   92
Richardson, M. Francisco Goya   92
Stefoff, R. Plácido Domingo   92
Historians
Durden, R. F. Carter G. Woodson (7 and up)
92
Historic buildings
See also Literary landmarks; types of historic buildings
Lynch, A. Great buildings   720

Hitler-Jugend
See/See also pages in the following book(s):
Ayer, E. H. Parallel journeys (7 and up)
           940.53

Hitler Youth *See* Hitler-Jugend
Hitz, Demi *See* Demi, 1942-
Hitzeroth, Deborah, 1961-
 Golda Meir (7 and up)   **92**
HIV disease *See* AIDS (Disease)
HIV infection. Packer, K. L. **616.97**
HIV positive. Wolf, B.   **362.1**
Hjelmeland, Andy
 Legalized gambling (7 and up) **363.4**
Hmong (Asian people)
 Livo, N. J. Folk stories of the Hmong
           398.2
Ho, Chí Minh, 1890-1969
 See/See also pages in the following book(s):
 Wakin, E. Asian independence leaders p89-107
  (7 and up)   **920**
Ho, David D., 1952-
 See/See also pages in the following book(s):
 Yount, L. Asian-American scientists p85-93 (7
  and up)   **920**
Ho, Minfong
 The winter hibiscus
  In Join in p239-56   **S C**
Ho-Ichi the earless. Martin, R.
 In Martin, R. Mysterious tales of Japan
           398.2
Hoare, Stephen
 Digital revolution   **621.381**
The hobbit. Tolkien, J. R. R. **Fic**
Hobbs, Valerie
 How far would you have gotten if I hadn't
  called you back? (7 and up) **Fic**
Hobbs, Will
 Beardance (7 and up)   **Fic**
 Bearstone (7 and up)   **Fic**
 The Big Wander (7 and up) **Fic**
 Downriver (7 and up)   **Fic**
 Far North (7 and up)   **Fic**
 Ghost canoe   **Fic**
 Kokopelli's flute   **Fic**
 The maze (7 and up)   **Fic**
Hobby. Yolen, J.   **Fic**
The hobbyist. Lynch, C.
 In Ultimate sports: short stories by outstand-
  ing writers for young adults p315-33
           S C
Hobgood, Debby, 1964-
 (jt. auth) Pervola, C. How to get a job if you're
  a teenager   **650.14**
Hoboes *See* Tramps
Hobson, Archie, 1946-
 (ed) The Cambridge gazetteer of the United
  States and Canada. See The Cambridge gazet-
  teer of the United States and Canada
          917.3
Hockey
 Foley, M. Fundamental hockey **796.962**
 Owens, T. Hockey   **796.962**
 Stewart, M. Hockey (7 and up) **796.962**

Sullivan, G. All about hockey **796.962**
     Biography
 Santella, A. Wayne Gretzky **92**
     Fiction
 Brooks, B. Zip   **Fic**
 Korman, G. The chicken doesn't skate **Fic**
 Lynch, C. Iceman (7 and up) **Fic**
Hodge, Alison
 The West Indies   **972.9**
Hodges, David W.
 Classic racing cars   **629.228**
Hodges, Margaret
 Don Quíxote and Sancho Panza **Fic**
Hodges, Sarah Margaret *See* Hodges, Margaret
Hoei-shin, 5th cent.
 See/See also pages in the following book(s):
 Lomask, M. Great lives: exploration p127-30
           920
Hoffa, James Riddle *See* Hoffa, Jimmy
Hoffa, Jimmy
 See/See also pages in the following book(s):
 Streissguth, T. Legendary labor leaders (7 and
  up)   **920**
Hoffius, Stephen
 The assault on the record
  In Ultimate sports: short stories by outstand-
  ing writers for young adults p161-78
           S C
Hoffman, Frank W. *See* Hoffmann, Frank W.
 (Frank William), 1949-
Hoffman, Nancy, 1955-
 West Virginia
  In Celebrate the states **973**
Hoffman, Nina Kiriki
 Wonder never land
  In A Nightmare's dozen **S C**
Hoffmann, E. T. A. (Ernst Theodor Amadeus),
 1776-1822
 Nutcracker and the Mouse-King; dramatization.
  See Thane, A. The Christmas Nutcracker
Hoffmann, Ernst Theodor Amadeus *See* Hoff-
 mann, E. T. A. (Ernst Theodor Amadeus),
 1776-1822
Hoffmann, Frank W. (Frank William), 1949-
 Guide to popular U.S. government publications
          015.73
Hogan, Linda
 Aunt Moon's young man
  In Talking leaves   **S C**
Hogrogian, John G.
 Miranda v. Arizona (7 and up) **345**
Hoichi the earless. San Souci, R.
 In San Souci, R. A terrifying taste of short &
  shivery p118-22   **398.2**
Hoig, Stan
 The Cheyenne
  In Indians of North America series
          970.004
Holbrook, Mike
 Snorkeling   **797.2**
Hold fast to dreams. Pinkney, A. D. **Fic**
Hold your horses. Meltzer, M. **636.1**
Holding out. Sebestyen, O.
 In Center stage   **812.008**

The **hole** in the sky. Adams, R.
In Adams, R. Tales from Watership Down
         S C

Holes. Sachar, L.   **Fic**

Holford, David M.
Herbert Hoover   **92**

Holiday, Billie, 1915-1959
About
Kliment, B. Billie Holiday   **92**
See/See also pages in the following book(s):
Gourse, L. Swingers and crooners p57-63 (7 and up)   **781.65**

Holiday cooking around the world   **641.5**

Holidays
See also Christmas; Kwanzaa; Valentine's Day
The American book of days   **394.2**
The Folklore of American holidays   **394.26**
The Folklore of world holidays   **394.26**
Holidays, festivals, and celebrations of the world dictionary   **394.26**
Lizon, K. H. Colonial American holidays and entertainment   **394.26**
Marks, D. F. Let's celebrate today   **394.26**
Webb, L. S. Holidays of the world cookbook for students   **641.5**
Drama
The Big book of holiday plays   **812.008**

Holidays, Jewish *See* Jewish holidays

Holidays, festivals, and celebrations of the world dictionary   **394.26**

Holidays of the world cookbook for students. Webb, L. S.   **641.5**

Holland, Isabelle
Behind the lines   **Fic**
The man without a face   **Fic**

Holland, Kevin Crossley- *See* Crossley-Holland, Kevin

Holland *See* Netherlands

Hollander, John
(ed) Committed to memory. See Committed to memory   **821.008**

Hollerith, Herman
See/See also pages in the following book(s):
Northrup, M. American computer pioneers p9-17   **920**

Holliday, Doc *See* Holliday, John Henry, 1852?-1887

Holliday, John Henry, 1852?-1887
See/See also pages in the following book(s):
Glass, A. Bad guys   **920**

Hollywood and the pits. Lee, C.
In American dragons p34-47   **810.8**
In Help wanted: short stories about young people working   **S C**

Holm, Jennifer L.
Our only May Amelia   **Fic**

Holman, Felice
Real   **Fic**
Slake's limbo   **Fic**

Holmes, Ann
Psychological effects of cocaine and crack addiction (7 and up)   **362.29**

Holmes, Timothy
Zambia   **968.94**

Holocaust, 1933-1945
See also Holocaust survivors; World War, 1939-1945—Jews
Ayer, E. H. A firestorm unleashed   **940.53**
Ayer, E. H. Inferno   **940.53**
Ayer, E. H. Parallel journeys (7 and up)   **940.53**
Bachrach, S. D. Tell them we remember   **940.53**
Bearing witness (7 and up)   **808.8**
Bierman, J. Righteous gentile [biography of Raoul Wallenberg] (7 and up)   **92**
Byers, A. The Holocaust overview (7 and up)   **940.53**
Feldman, G. Understanding the Holocaust   **940.53**
Finkelstein, N. H. Remember not to forget   **940.53**
Gold, A. L. Memories of Anne Frank   **92**
Lace, W. W. The death camps (7 and up)   **940.53**
Leapman, M. Witnesses to war   **940.53**
Lyman, D. Holocaust rescuers   **920**
Meltzer, M. Never to forget: the Jews of the Holocaust   **940.53**
Meltzer, M. Rescue: the story of how Gentiles saved Jews in the Holocaust   **940.53**
Müller, M. Anne Frank (7 and up)   **92**
Opdyke, I. G. In my hands (7 and up)   **940.53**
People of the Holocaust   **920.003**
Rogasky, B. Smoke and ashes: the story of the Holocaust   **940.53**
Rol, R. van der. Anne Frank, beyond the diary   **92**
Sherrow, V. The blaze engulfs   **940.53**
Sherrow, V. The righteous gentiles (7 and up)   **940.53**
Sherrow, V. Smoke to flame   **940.53**
Spiegelman, A. Maus (7 and up)   **940.53**
Strahinich, H. The Holocaust (7 and up)   **940.53**
Wukovits, J. F. Anne Frank (7 and up)   **92**
See/See also pages in the following book(s):
Altman, L. J. Genocide p5-10, 49-73 (7 and up)   **303.6**
Bibliography
Shulman, W. L. Resource guide   **940.53**
Sullivan, E. T. The Holocaust in literature for youth   **016.94053**
Encyclopedias
The Holocaust   **940.53**
Fiction
Drucker, M. Jacob's rescue   **Fic**
Matas, C. After the war (7 and up)   **Fic**
Matas, C. Greater than angels (7 and up)   **Fic**
Matas, C. In my enemy's house (7 and up)   **Fic**
Schnur, S. The shadow children   **Fic**
Yolen, J. Briar Rose (7 and up)   **Fic**
Yolen, J. The devil's arithmetic   **Fic**

Holocaust, 1933-1945—*Continued*
Personal narratives
Adler, D. A. We remember the Holocaust
940.53
Ayer, E. H. In the ghettos (7 and up)
940.53
Bitton-Jackson, L. I have lived a thousand years
(7 and up) 940.53
Boas, J. We are witnesses (7 and up)
940.53
Fluek, T. K. Memories of my life in a Polish
village, 1930-1949 (7 and up) 92
Fox, A. L. Ten thousand children 940.53
Frank, A. The diary of a young girl 92
Frank, A. The diary of a young girl: the defini-
tive edition 92
Kinderlager (7 and up) 940.53
Kustanowitz, E. The hidden children of the
Holocaust (7 and up) 940.53
Lobel, A. No pretty pictures (7 and up) 92
Mandell, S. L. Writers of the Holocaust (7 and
up) 940.53
Perl, L. Four perfect pebbles (7 and up)
940.53
Rosenberg, M. B. Hiding to survive 940.53
Sender, R. M. The cage (7 and up) 940.53
Sender, R. M. To life (7 and up) 940.53
Siegal, A. Upon the head of the goat: a child-
hood in Hungary, 1939-1944 92
Voices and visions 940.53
We survived the Holocaust 940.53
The **Holocaust** 940.53
Holocaust [series]
Altman, L. J. Forever outsiders 909
Ayer, E. H. A firestorm unleashed 940.53
Ayer, E. H. Inferno 940.53
Chicoine, S. From the ashes 940.53
Sherrow, V. The blaze engulfs 940.53
Sherrow, V. Smoke to flame 940.53
Shulman, W. L. Resource guide 940.53
Voices and visions 940.53
The **Holocaust** in literature for youth. Sullivan, E.
T. 016.94053
Holocaust library [series]
Ayer, E. H. The survivors 940.53
Lace, W. W. The death camps 940.53
Lace, W. W. The Nazis 943.086
Sherrow, V. The righteous gentiles 940.53
Holocaust Museum (U.S.) *See* United States
Holocaust Memorial Museum
The **Holocaust** overview. Byers, A. 940.53
Holocaust remembered series
Byers, A. The Holocaust overview 940.53
Holocaust rescuers. Lyman, D. 920
Holocaust survivors
Ayer, E. H. Inferno 940.53
Ayer, E. H. The survivors 940.53
Bitton-Jackson, L. My bridges of hope (7 and
up) 92
Chicoine, S. From the ashes 940.53
Kinderlager (7 and up) 940.53
Rosenberg, M. B. Hiding to survive 940.53
Sender, R. M. To life (7 and up) 940.53
Voices and visions 940.53
We survived the Holocaust 940.53

Holsinger, M. Paul, 1938-
The ways of war 016.8
Holt, Kimberly Willis
My Louisiana sky Fic
Holtschlag, Margaret
Button crafts 745.5
Holtze, Sally Holmes
(ed) Seventh book of junior authors & illustra-
tors. See Seventh book of junior authors & il-
lustrators 920.003
The **Holy** Bible [King James Bible. Oxford Univ.
Press] Bible 220.5
The **Holy** Bible: new revised standard version. Bi-
ble 220.5
Holy Bible: the new King James Version. Bible
220.5
Holy Grail *See* Grail
Home. Johnson, A.
In Johnson, A. Gone from home: short takes
p25-37 S C
Home among the giants. Norman, H.
In Norman, H. The girl who dreamed only
geese, and other tales of the Far North
398.2
Home decoration *See* Interior design
Home life *See* Family life
Home now. Oba, R.
In American eyes p28-36 S C
Home on the mornin' train. Hines, K.
In Theatre for young audiences p308-37
812.008
Home run heroes: McGwire and Sosa. Stewart, M.
92
Home to El Building. Ortiz Cofer, J.
In Ortiz Cofer, J. An island like you p131-43
S C
Home video systems
See also Video recording
Homecoming. Voigt, C. Fic
The **homecoming**. Yep, L.
In Yep, L. The rainbow people p144-51
398.2
Homecooking. Woody, E.
In Talking leaves S C
Homeless persons
See also Refugees; Runaway children; Run-
away teenagers; Tramps
Criswell, S. D. Homelessness (7 and up)
362.5
Gottfried, T. Homelessness: whose problem is
it? (7 and up) 362.5
Stearman, K. Homelessness 362.5
Stewart, G. Homeless teens (7 and up)
362.5
Fiction
Fenner, C. The king of dragons Fic
Fox, P. Monkey island Fic
Spinelli, J. Maniac Magee Fic
Homeless teens. Stewart, G. 362.5
Homelessness. Criswell, S. D. 362.5
Homelessness. Stearman, K. 362.5
Homelessness: whose problem is it?. Gottfried, T.
362.5

Hop-frog. Poe, E. A.
In Poe, E. A. Tales of Edgar Allan Poe p81-93   S C

Hope. Gaeddert, L. B.   Fic

Hope's crossing. Goodman, J. E.   Fic

Hopi Indians
Bonvillain, N. The Hopi
In Indians of North America series
                                                             970.004
Fiction
MacGregor, R. Hawk moon (7 and up)   Fic

Hopke, William E.
(ed) The Encyclopedia of careers and vocational guidance. See The Encyclopedia of careers and vocational guidance   331.7

Hopkins, Lee Bennett, 1938-
Been to yesterdays: poems of a life   811
Pass the poetry, please!   372.6
(comp) Hand in hand. See Hand in hand
                                                             811.008
(comp) Lives: poems about famous Americans. See Lives: poems about famous Americans
                                                             811.008
(comp) Marvelous math. See Marvelous math
                                                             811.008
(comp) Pauses. See Pauses   028.5

Hopkins, Sarah Winnemucca, 1844?-1891
About
Scordato, E. Sarah Winnemucca   92

Hopper, Edward, 1882-1967
See/See also pages in the following book(s):
Greenberg, J. The American eye p25-32
                                                             920

Hopper, Grace
See/See also pages in the following book(s):
Celebrating women in mathematics and science p147-58   920
Northrup, M. American computer pioneers p29-36   920
Yount, L. Contemporary women scientists (7 and up)   920

Hopscotch love. Grimes, N.   811

Horlbeck, Barbara
(jt. auth) Steger, W. Over the top of the world
                                                             998

Hormones
See also Steroids

Horn, Maurice, 1931-
(ed) The World encyclopedia of comics. See The World encyclopedia of comics   741.5

The **Horn** Book guide interactive. See entry in CD-ROM section, Part 3

The **Horn** Book Guide to Children's and Young Adult Books   028.505

The **Horn** Book Magazine   028.505

Horn of plenty. Gotwalt, H. L. M.
In The Big book of holiday plays p87-100
                                                             812.008

Hornblower, Simon
(ed) The Oxford companion to classical civilization. See The Oxford companion to classical civilization   938.003

Horne, Gerald
Powell v. Alabama (7 and up)   345

Horne, Lena
About
Palmer, L. Lena Horne   92

The **horned** women. Hamilton, V.
In Hamilton, V. The dark way p32-37
                                                             398.2

Horner, Jack *See* Horner, John R.

Horner, John R.
About
Lessem, D. Jack Horner: living with dinosaurs
                                                             92
Patent, D. H. In search of the maiasaurs
                                                             567.9

Horning, Kathleen T.
From cover to cover   028.1

Hornsby, Alton, Jr.
Chronology of African American history (7 and up)   305.8

Horror fiction
Aiken, J. A fit of shivers   S C
Aiken, J. Give yourself a fright: thirteen tales of the supernatural   S C
Coville, B. Odder than ever   S C
Coville, B. Oddly enough   S C
Gorog, J. When nobody's home   S C
Night terrors (7 and up)   S C
A Nightmare's dozen (7 and up)   S C
Poe, E. A. Tales of Edgar Allan Poe   S C
Pullman, P. Count Karlstein   Fic
Schwartz, A. More scary stories to tell in the dark   398.2
Schwartz, A. Scary stories 3   398.2
Schwartz, A. Scary stories to tell in the dark
                                                             398.2
Sleator, W. The beasties (7 and up)   Fic
Thompson, J. F. The grounding of Group 6 (7 and up)   Fic
Westall, R. Demons and shadows (7 and up)
                                                             S C
Westall, R. The stones of Muncaster Cathedral
                                                             Fic
Zindel, P. Raptor (7 and up)   Fic
Zindel, P. Reef of death (7 and up)   Fic
History and criticism
Kies, C. N. Presenting young adult horror fiction (7 and up)   813.009

Horse, John, ca. 1812-ca. 1882
See/See also pages in the following book(s):
Katz, W. L. Proudly red and black p23-35
                                                             920

Horse & pony breeds. Henderson, C.   636.1

Horse & pony care. Henderson, C.   636.1

Horse & pony shows & events. Henderson, C.
                                                             798.2

The **horse** and his boy. Lewis, C. S. See note under Lewis, C. S. The lion, the witch, and the wardrobe   Fic

The **horse** of the War God. Coatsworth, E. J.
In A Newbery Halloween p157-65   S C

The **horse** that could fly. Mayo, M.
In Mayo, M. Mythical birds & beasts from many lands p11-21   398.2

Horseback riding *See* Horsemanship

How fear came. Kipling, R.
In Kipling, R. The jungle books   **S C**
How history is invented [series]
Wilson, L. L. The Salem witch trials   **133.4**
How I changed my life. Strasser, T. See note under Strasser, T. How I spent my last night on earth   **Fic**
How I got to be queen. Sarris, G.
In Talking leaves   **S C**
How I spent my last night on earth. Strasser, T.   **Fic**
How Ioscoda and his friends met the white men from the east and journeyed across the great waters. Brown, D. A.
In Brown, D. A. Dee Brown's folktales of the Native American p84-90   **398.2**
How it feels when a parent dies. Krementz, J.   **155.9**
How it works [series]
Ganeri, A. Funny bones   **611**
How many fools?. Philip, N.
In Philip, N. The Arabian nights p143-44   **398.2**
How men and women finally agreed. McCaughrean, G.
In McCaughrean, G. The golden hoard: myths and legends of the world p114-19   **398.2**
How music came to the world. Mayo, M.
In Mayo, M. Mythical birds & beasts from many lands p67-73   **398.2**
How music was fetched out of heaven. McCaughrean, G.
In McCaughrean, G. The golden hoard: myths and legends of the world p84-88   **398.2**
How Pelican Girl was saved. Bruchac, J.
In Bruchac, J. The girl who married the Moon: tales from Native North America p94-100   **398.2**
How Rabbit brought fire to the people. Brown, D. A.
In Brown, D. A. Dee Brown's folktales of the Native American p70-71   **398.2**
How Rabbit fooled Wolf. Brown, D. A.
In Brown, D. A. Dee Brown's folktales of the Native American p106-09   **398.2**
How rude!. Packer, A. J.   **395**
How Saynday tried to marry Whirlwind Girl. Bruchac, J.
In Bruchac, J. Four ancestors p83-84   **398.2**
How sex works. Fenwick, E.   **613.9**
How Sheherazade married the king. Philip, N.
In Philip, N. The Arabian nights p11-12   **398.2**
How the buffalo were released on earth. Brown, D. A.
In Brown, D. A. Dee Brown's folktales of the Native American p63-65   **398.2**
How the Earth began. Bruchac, J.
In Bruchac, J. Four ancestors p33-34   **398.2**

How the fairies became. McCaughrean, G.
In McCaughrean, G. The crystal pool: myths and legends of the world p113-14   **398.2**
How the first white men came to the Cheyennes. Brown, D. A.
In Brown, D. A. Dee Brown's folktales of the Native American p92-94   **398.2**
How the narwhal got its tusk. Norman, H.
In Norman, H. The girl who dreamed only geese, and other tales of the Far North   **398.2**
How the people pushed up the sky. Bruchac, J.
In Bruchac, J. Four ancestors p85-87   **398.2**
How the prairie became ocean. Bruchac, J.
In Bruchac, J. Four ancestors p71-74   **398.2**
How the rainbow was born. Delacre, L.
In Delacre, L. Golden tales p37-39   **398.2**
How the sea was born. Delacre, L.
In Delacre, L. Golden tales p3-5   **398.2**
How the slaves helped each other. Faulkner, W. J.
In From sea to shining sea p130-31   **810.8**
How the walls of the temple were built. Schwartz, H.
In Schwartz, H. Next year in Jerusalem p19-21   **296.1**
How the witch was caught. Lester, J.
In Lester, J. The last tales of Uncle Remus p66-70   **398.2**
How they broke away to go to the Rootabaga Country. Sandburg, C.
In American fairy tales p143-50   **S C**
How things work. Graham, I.   **600**
How things work [series]
Graham, I. Boats, ships, submarines, and other floating machines   **623.8**
How Tinktum Tidy recruited an army for the king. Lester, J.
In Lester, J. The last tales of Uncle Remus p82-88   **398.2**
How to do a science fair project. Tocci, S.   **507.8**
How-to-do-it manuals for librarians [series]
Developing an information literacy program K-12   **025.5**
Jones, P. Connecting young adults and libraries   **027.62**
Symons, A. K. Protecting the right to read   **323.44**
How-to-do-it manuals for school and public librarians [series]
Garrett, L. J. Teaching library skills in middle and high school   **027.8**
How to do your best on tests. Gilbert, S. D.   **371.2**
How to draw comic book bad guys and gals. Hart, C.   **741.5**
How to excel in science competitions. Krieger, M. J.   **507.8**
How to get a job if you're a teenager. Pervola, C.   **650.14**

Hull House (Chicago, Ill.)
Harvey, B. C. Jane Addams   **92**
Hulme, Joy N., 1922-
How to write, recite, and delight in all kinds of poetry   **808.1**
Hum it again, Jeremy. Okimoto, J. D.
In Center stage   **812.008**
Human anatomy
Beckelman, L. The human body   **612**
Biesty, S. Stephen Biesty's incredible body   **611**
Body works 6.0. See entry in CD-ROM section, Part 3
Burnie, D. The concise encyclopedia of the human body   **612**
Ganeri, A. Funny bones   **611**
Human body (7 and up)   **612**
Human body on file: anatomy   **611**
Human body on file: physiology   **612**
Parker, S. The body atlas   **611**
Parker, S. Human body   **612**
Parker, S. The human body   **612**
Rowan, P. Some body!   **611**
Under the microscope   **612**
The Visual dictionary of human anatomy   **611**
Williams, F. Human body   **611**
Human behavior
See also Risk-taking (Psychology)
Human beings
Glover, D. M. The young Oxford book of the human being   **612**
Human nature: opposing viewpoints (7 and up)   **128**
Human body (7 and up)   **612**
The **human body**. Beckelman, L.   **612**
Human body. Parker, S.   **612**
Human body. Williams, F.   **611**
Human body [series]
Ballard, C. The heart and circulatory system   **612.1**
Ballard, C. The skeleton and muscular system   **612.7**
Ballard, C. The stomach and digestive system   **612.3**
Parker, S. The lungs and respiratory system   **612.2**
Parker, S. The reproductive system   **612.6**
Human body on file: anatomy   **611**
Human body on file: physiology   **612**
Human body systems [series]
Silverstein, A. The circulatory system   **612.1**
Silverstein, A. The respiratory system   **612.2**
Human ecology
21st century earth: opposing viewpoints (7 and up)   **303.49**
Fyson, N. L. World population   **304.6**
Lewington, A. People of the rain forests   **577.3**
Human evolution. Gardner, R.   **599.93**

Human Genome Project
See/See also pages in the following book(s):
Kidd, J. S. Life lines p114-30 (7 and up)   **576.5**
Human geography
Encyclopedias
Junior Worldmark encyclopedia of world cultures   **306**
Human influence on nature
Davis, L. A. Environmental disasters (7 and up)   **363.7**
Macquitty, M. Desert   **577.5**
Roberts, R. Endangered species   **333.95**
See/See also pages in the following book(s):
Patent, D. H. Biodiversity p65-75   **333.95**
Human interaction with Mrs. Gladys Furley, R.N.
See Jukes, M. Expecting the unexpected   **Fic**
The **Human mind explained (7 and up)**   **153**
Human nature: opposing viewpoints (7 and up)   **128**
Human origins
See also Evolution; Fossil hominids; Prehistoric peoples
Gallant, R. A. Early humans   **599.93**
Gardner, R. Human evolution (7 and up)   **599.93**
Poynter, M. The Leakeys   **92**
See/See also pages in the following book(s):
Glover, D. M. The young Oxford book of the human being p8-25   **612**
Human relations
Bode, J. Trust & betrayal (7 and up)   **158**
Cann, K. Living in the world   **158**
Chicken soup for the kid's soul   **158**
Chicken soup for the teenage soul (7 and up)   **158**
Fisher, E. Emotional ups and downs   **152.4**
Girls know best   **305.23**
Kreiner, A. Everything you need to know about creating your own support system (7 and up)   **158**
Nathan, A. Everything you need to know about conflict resolution (7 and up)   **158**
Romain, T. Cliques, phonies & other baloney   **158**
Human rights
Human rights: opposing viewpoints (7 and up)   **323**
Lucas, E. Contemporary human rights activists (7 and up)   **920**
O'Connor, M. Equal rights   **323**
See/See also pages in the following book(s):
Carter, J. Talking peace p99-111 (7 and up)   **327.1**
Human rights: opposing viewpoints (7 and up)   **323**
The **humane societies. Sateren, S. S.**   **179**
Humboldt, Alexander, Freiherr von, 1769-1859
See/See also pages in the following book(s):
Stefoff, R. Scientific explorers p66-75   **509**
Humboldt, Friedrich Wilhelm Heinrich Alexander *See* Humboldt, Alexander, Freiherr von, 1769-1859

The **humming** of stars and bees and waves. Endrezze, A.
   In Talking leaves   **S C**

Humming whispers. Johnson, A.   **Fic**

Hummingbirds
   Rauzon, M. J. Hummingbirds   **598**

Humorous poetry
   Silverstein, S. Falling up   **811**
   Silverstein, S. A light in the attic   **811**
   Silverstein, S. Where the sidewalk ends
             811

Humphrey, Judy
   Genghis Khan   **92**

A **hundred** bucks of happy. Asher, S.
   In Visions: nineteen short stories by outstanding writers for young adults p141-48
             S C

The **hundred** dresses. Estes, E.
   In A Newbery Christmas p5-32   **S C**

The **hundredth** skull. San Souci, R.
   In San Souci, R. A terrifying taste of short & shivery p43-45   **398.2**

Hungary
   Steins, R. Hungary   **943.9**

Hunt, Irene, 1907-
   Across five Aprils   **Fic**
   Up a road slowly   **Fic**

Hunter, Clementine, 1886?-1988
   Talking with Tebé: Clementine Hunter, memory artist   **92**

Hunter, Elrose
   The story atlas of the Bible   **220.9**

Hunter, Mollie, 1922-
   The king's swift rider (7 and up)   **Fic**

The **hunter** and the Dakwa. Brown, D. A.
   In Brown, D. A. Dee Brown's folktales of the Native American p132-33   **398.2**

Hunter in the dark. Hughes, M.   **Fic**

Hunter's stew and hangtown fry: what pioneer America ate and why. Perl, L.   **641.5**

Hunting
           Fiction
   Hughes, M. Hunter in the dark (7 and up)
             Fic

Hunting bear. McColley, K.
   In Twelve shots: outstanding short stories about guns p44-71   **S C**

The **hunting** of Death. McCaughrean, G.
   In McCaughrean, G. The bronze cauldron: myths and legends of the world p113-15
             398.2

The **hunting** of the hind. McKinley, R.
   In McKinley, R. The door in the hedge p105-36   **S C**

Hunziker, Raymond E.
   (jt. auth) Burgess, W. Dr. Burgess's atlas of marine aquarium fishes   **639.34**

Hurley, Bobby
   See/See also pages in the following book(s):
   Rappoport, K. Guts and glory   **920**

Hurley, Jennifer A., 1973-
   Animal rights (7 and up)   **179**

   (ed) Child abuse: opposing viewpoints. See Child abuse: opposing viewpoints   **362.7**
   (ed) Teens at risk: opposing viewpoints. See Teens at risk: opposing viewpoints   **362.7**
   (ed) Weapons of mass destruction: opposing viewpoints. See Weapons of mass destruction: opposing viewpoints   **358**

Huron Indians
   Bonvillain, N. The Huron
   In Indians of North America series
           970.004

Hurricane Andrew. Sherrow, V.   **551.55**

Hurricanes
   See also Typhoons
   Lauber, P. Hurricanes   **551.55**
   Longshore, D. Encyclopedia of hurricanes, typhoons and cyclones (7 and up)   **551.55**
   Sherrow, V. Hurricane Andrew   **551.55**
           Fiction
   Garland, S. The silent storm   **Fic**

Hurston, Zora Neale, 1891-1960
   The talking mule
   In From sea to shining sea p224-25
           810.8
           About
   Lyons, M. E. Sorrow's kitchen: the life and folklore of Zora Neale Hurston   **92**

Hurwitz, Jane
   Sally Ride   **92**

Hurwitz, Sue, 1934-
   (jt. auth) Hurwitz, J. Sally Ride   **92**

Husain, Shahrukh *See* Shahrukh Husain, 1950-

The **husband** who counted the spoonfuls. Bryan, A.
   In Bryan, A. Ashley Bryan's African tales, uh-huh p70-80   **398.2**

Hush: an interview with America. Still, J.
   In Theatre for young audiences p395-428
           812.008

Hussey, Leigh Ann
   Blood libel
   In Vampires: a collection of original stories p157-86   **S C**

Hutchinson, Anne Marbury, 1591-1643
           About
   IlgenFritz, E. Anne Hutchinson   **92**

Hutchinson, Susanna, b. 1633
           Fiction
   Kirkpatrick, K. A. Trouble's daughter   **Fic**

Huxley, Aldous, 1894-1963
   Brave new world (7 and up)   **Fic**

Huynh, Quang Nhuong
   The land I lost: adventures of a boy in Vietnam
           92

Hwang, David Henry
   See/See also pages in the following book(s):
   Chiu, C. Lives of notable Asian Americans: literature and education p73-79 (7 and up)
           920

Hyams, Rachel, 1937-
   See/See also pages in the following book(s):
   Kinderlager p115-50 (7 and up)   **940.53**

Hyde, Lawrence E.
(jt. auth) Hyde, M. O. Meeting death
155.9

Hyde, Margaret Oldroyd, 1917-
The disease book 616
Meeting death 155.9
Mind drugs (7 and up) 616.86
Missing and murdered children (7 and up)
362.7
The sexual abuse of children and adolescents (7 and up) 362.7

Hydrogen
Farndon, J. Hydrogen
In The Elements [Benchmark Bks.] 546

Hydrothermal vents See Ocean bottom

Hygiene
See also Health

Hynes, Shona, 1975-
(jt. auth) Bulloch, I. Cartoons & animation
741.5

Hypatia, ca. 370-415
See/See also pages in the following book(s):
Celebrating women in mathematics and science
p1-6 920

Hyperactive children
See also Attention deficit disorder

The **hypnotist**. Sleator, W.
In Sleator, W. Oddballs: stories p43-55
S C

Hyzenthlay in action. Adams, R.
In Adams, R. Tales from Watership Down
S C

I

I am an American. Stanley, J. 940.53
I am an artichoke. Frank, L. K. Fic
I am Mordred. Springer, N. Fic
I am phoenix: poems for two voices. Fleischman, P. 811
I am Regina. Keehn, S. M. Fic
I am the cheese. Cormier, R. Fic
I am the darker brother 811.008
I am wings. Fletcher, R. J. 811
I am writing a poem about—a game of poetry
811.008

I, Earthling. Coville, B.
In Coville, B. Odder than ever S C
I feel a little jumpy around you (7 and up)
808.81
I hadn't meant to tell you this. Woodson, J.
Fic
I have a dream. Fisher, A. L.
In The Big book of holiday plays p178-86
812.008
In Plays of black Americans p144-54
812.008
I have a dream: the life and words of Martin Luther King, Jr. Haskins, J. 92
I have lived a thousand years. Bitton-Jackson, L.
940.53

I heard the owl call my name. Craven, M.
Fic
I, hungry Hannah Cassandra Glen . . . Mazer, N. F.
In Sixteen: short stories by outstanding writers for young adults p2-14 S C
I **know America** [series]
Johnson, L. C. Our Constitution 342
I know what you did last summer. Duncan, L.
Fic
I know why the caged bird sings [excerpt]
Angelou, M.
In Who do you think you are? p156-63
S C
I left my sneakers in dimension X. Coville, B. See note under Coville, B. Aliens ate my homework Fic
I like you, if you like me: poems of friendship
808.81
"I love you, Prime Minister!". McCaughrean, G.
In McCaughrean, G. The bronze cauldron: myths and legends of the world p102-06
398.2
I never promised you a rose garden. Greenberg, J.
Fic
—I never saw another butterfly— 741.9
I, robot. Asimov, I. S C
I rode a horse of milk white jade. Wilson, D. L.
Fic
I see the rhythm. Igus, T. 780.89
I, too, sing America 811.008
I was a teenage fairy. Block, F. L. Fic
I was born a slave: the story of Harriet Jacobs.
Fleischner, J. 92
I was dreaming to come to America 325.73
I **was there books** [series]
Tanaka, S. Discovering the Iceman 930.1
Tanaka, S. Graveyards of the dinosaurs
567.9
Tanaka, S. Lost temple of the Aztecs 972
I will call it Georgie's blues. Newton, S. Fic
I will not think of Maine. Kerr, M. E.
In Dirty laundry: stories about family secrets
p88-97 S C
I wouldn't have missed it: selected poems of Ogden Nash. Nash, O. 811
I wouldn't thank you for a valentine 808.81

Ibargüengoitia, Jorge, 1928-1983
Paletón and the musical elephant
In Where angels glide at dawn p51-55
S C

Ibbotson, Eva
Which witch? Fic

Ibo (African people) See Igbo (African people)

Ice. Naylor, P. R. Fic

Ice hockey See Hockey

Ice maiden. Jennings, P.
In Jennings, P. Unmentionable! p1-9
S C

Ice Man and the messenger of springtime. Brown, D. A.
  In Brown, D. A. Dee Brown's folktales of the Native American p79-80   **398.2**

Ice skating
  Boo, M. The story of figure skating   **796.91**
  Morrissey, P. The young ice skater   **796.91**

        Biography
  Baiul, O. Oksana: my own story   **92**
  Boitano, B. Boitano's edge   **92**
  Christopher, M. On the ice with—Tara Lipinski   **92**
  DuPont, L. H. Oksana Baiul   **92**
  Gatto, K. Michelle Kwan   **92**
  Kwan, M. Michelle Kwan, heart of a champion   **92**
  Poynter, M. Top 10 American women's figure skaters   **920**
  Shea, P. D. Ekaterina Gordeeva   **92**

Ice story. Kimmel, E. C.   **998**
The **ice** wolf. Kraus, J. H.
  In Theatre for young audiences p284-307   **812.008**
The **iceman**. Lessem, D.   **930.1**
Iceman. Lynch, C.   **Fic**
Ick. Wynne-Jones, T.
  In Wynne-Jones, T. Lord of the Fries and other stories p45-68   **S C**
Iconography *See* Religious art and symbolism
Idaho
  Stefoff, R. Idaho
  In Celebrate the states   **973**
Ida's New Year cake. Montgomery, L. M.
  In Montgomery, L. M. Christmas with Anne and other holiday stories p189-98   **S C**
Ideal states *See* Utopias
Identification
  See also Forensic anthropology
Idioms *See* English language—Idioms
Iditarod dream. Wood, T.   **798.8**
Iditarod Trail Sled Dog Race, Alaska
  Crisman, R. Racing the Iditarod Trail   **798.8**
  Dolan, E. M. Susan Butcher and the Iditarod Trail   **798.8**
  Paulsen, G. Winterdance   **798.8**
If I forget Thee, O Jerusalem. Wolf, B.   **956.94**
If I forget, you remember. Williams, C. L.   **Fic**
If it doesn't kill you. Bechard, M.   **Fic**
If that breathes fire, we're toast!. Stewart, J. J.   **Fic**
If the shoe fits. Soto, G.
  In Soto, G. Petty crimes   **S C**
If winter comes. Hall, L.   **Fic**
If wishes were horses. McCaffrey, A.   **Fic**
If you can't be lucky . . . Deuker, C.
  In Ultimate sports: short stories by outstanding writers for young adults p72-91   **S C**

If you come softly. Woodson, J.   **Fic**
If you were there in 1776. Brenner, B.   **973.3**
Igbo (African people)
  Nnoromele, S. Life among the Ibo women of Nigeria (7 and up)   **966.9**
Igloos
  Yue, C. The igloo   **728**
Igus, Toyomi, 1953-
  I see the rhythm   **780.89**
Iizuka, Shokansai
  See/See also pages in the following book(s):
  Hamanaka, S. In search of the spirit p15-19   **920**
Iktome and the ducks. Lame Deer, A. F.
  In From sea to shining sea p208-09   **810.8**
IlgenFritz, Elizabeth
  Anne Hutchinson   **92**
The **ill-made** knight. White, T. H.
  In White, T. H. The once and future king   **Fic**
The **ill-natured** muse. Aiken, J.
  In Aiken, J. Give yourself a fright: thirteen tales of the supernatural p89-108   **S C**
An **ill** wind. Aiken, J.
  In Aiken, J. A foot in the grave p71-96   **S C**
Illegal aliens
  Ashabranner, B. K. Our beckoning borders   **325.73**
  Hauser, P. Illegal aliens   **325.73**
Illegal drugs (7 and up)   **364.1**
Illinois
  Brill, M. T. Illinois
  In Celebrate the states   **973**
  Santella, A. Illinois
  In America the beautiful, second series   **973**

        Fiction
  Hunt, I. Across five Aprils   **Fic**
        History
  See/See also pages in the following book(s):
  Katz, W. L. Black pioneers p98-110 (7 and up)   **920**

Illiteracy *See* Literacy
Illness *See* Diseases
Illumination of books and manuscripts
  Wilson, E. B. Bibles and bestiaries   **745.6**
Illusions *See* Optical illusions
The **illustrated** book of ballet stories. Newman, B.   **792.8**
The **illustrated** book of myths. Philip, N.   **291.1**
The **illustrated** book of signs & symbols. Bruce-Mitford, M.   **302.2**
The **Illustrated** children's Bible   **220.5**
Illustrated computer dictionary for young people. Spencer, D. D.   **004**
Illustrated dictionary of mythology. Wilkinson, P.   **291.103**
Illustrated histories [series]
  McComb, D. G. Sports   **796**

Illustrated histories [series]—*Continued*
Schroeter, D. J. Israel   **956.94**

Illustrated history of the world [series]
Corbishley, M. Rome and the ancient world
    930
Gregory, T. The Dark Ages   **909.07**
Macdonald, F. The Middle Ages   **909.07**
Martell, H. M. The age of discovery
    909.08
Reynoldson, F. Conflict and change   **909.7**

Illustration of books
    See also Picture books for children
Biesty, S. Stephen Biesty's incredible explosions
    741.6
Marcus, L. S. A Caldecott celebration
    741.6
Talking with artists [I-III]   **741.6**

Illustrations, Humorous *See* Cartoons and caricatures

Illustrators
Lewin, T. Touch and go   **92**
Marcus, L. S. A Caldecott celebration
    741.6
Newbery and Caldecott Medal books, 1966-1975
    028.5
Newbery and Caldecott medal books, 1976-1985
    028.5
Pauses   **028.5**
Peet, B. Bill Peet: an autobiography   **92**
Talking with artists [I-III]   **741.6**
         Dictionaries
Seventh book of junior authors & illustrators
    920.003
Something about the author   **920.003**
Something about the author: autobiography series
    920.003

The **Illyrian** adventure. Alexander, L.   **Fic**

I'm not who you think I am. Kehret, P.   **Fic**

Immell, Myra
(ed) Eating disorders. See Eating disorders
    616.85

Immigrant experience [series]
Hauser, P. Illegal aliens   **325.73**

Immigrant experience. See entry in CD-ROM section, Part 3

Immigrants
Lakin, P. Everything you need to know when a parent doesn't speak English (7 and up)
    306.4

Immigration and emigration
    See also Children of immigrants; Immigrants; Refugees; names of countries with the subdivision *Immigration and emigration*; and names of nationality groups
         Fiction
Avi. Beyond the western sea   **Fic**
Hesse, K. Letters from Rifka   **Fic**
Lasky, K. Dreams in the golden country
    Fic
Levitin, S. Silver days   **Fic**
Little, J. The belonging place   **Fic**

Immigration: opposing viewpoints (7 and up)
    325.73

Immortality
    See also Future life

Immortals [series]
Pierce, T. Wolf-speaker   **Fic**

Immune system
Friedlander, M. P. The immune system (7 and up)   **616.07**

Immunization *See* Vaccination

Immunological system *See* Immune system

The **imp** of the perverse. Poe, E. A.
    In Poe, E. A. Tales of Edgar Allan Poe p9-17
    S C

Impact biography [series]
Anderson, M. K. Edgar Allan Poe   **92**
Coil, S. M. Harriet Beecher Stowe   **92**
Daily, R. Elvis Presley: the king of rock 'n' roll
    92
Goldberg, J. Albert Einstein   **92**
Gottfried, T. James Baldwin   **92**
Gourse, L. Mahalia Jackson: queen of gospel song   **92**
Martin, M. Arthur Ashe   **92**
McKissack, P. C. W.E.B. DuBois   **92**
Otfinoski, S. Scott Joplin   **92**
Shirley, D. Everyday I sing the blues: the story of B.B. King   **92**
Tessitore, J. Muhammed Ali   **92**

Impact books [series]
Cheney, G. A. Nuclear proliferation   **327.1**
Miner, J. C. Alcohol and you   **362.292**

Imperial Trans-Antarctic Expedition (1914-1917)
Armstrong, J. Shipwreck at the bottom of the world (7 and up)   **998**
Kimmel, E. C. Ice story   **998**

Importance of [series]
Cuffie, T. A. Maya Angelou   **92**
Fox, M. V. Douglas MacArthur   **92**
Hitzeroth, D. Golda Meir   **92**
Pratt, P. Ernest Hemingway   **92**
Presnall, J. J. Rachel Carson   **92**
Uschan, M. V. John F. Kennedy   **92**
Wukovits, J. F. Anne Frank   **92**
Wukovits, J. F. Martin Luther King, Jr.   **92**

Impossible things. Layefsky, V.   **Fic**

Improve your riding skills. Henderson, C.
    798.2

Impty-Umpty and the blacksmith. Lester, J.
    In Lester, J. The last tales of Uncle Remus p49-56   **398.2**

In a dark wood. Cadnum, M.   **Fic**

In a thousand years' time. Andersen, H. C.
    In Andersen, H. C. The little mermaid and other fairy tales p104-06   **S C**

In American history [series]
Altman, L. J. Slavery and abolition in American history   **973.7**
Ferrell, N. W. The Battle of the Little Bighorn in American history   **973.8**
Fremon, D. K. The Great Depression in American history   **338.5**
Fremon, D. K. The Salem witchcraft trials in American history   **133.4**

Indiana

Brill, M. T. Indiana
In Celebrate the states   973
Heinrichs, A. Indiana
In America the beautiful, second series
973

History

See/See also pages in the following book(s):
Katz, W. L. Black pioneers p83-97 (7 and up)
920

Indians

Bendick, J. Tombs of the ancient Americas
393
Woods, G. Science of the early Americas
509
See/See also pages in the following book(s):
Millard, A. Pyramids p43-55   909

Indians (of India) *See* East Indians

Indians of Central America

See also Mayas
See/See also pages in the following book(s):
Peoples of the Americas   970

Folklore

See/See also pages in the following book(s):
Delacre, L. Golden tales p1-27   398.2

Religion

Bierhorst, J. The mythology of Mexico and
Central America (7 and up)   299
Gifford, D. Warriors, gods & spirits from Central & South American mythology   299

Indians of Mexico

See also Aztecs; Mayas; Tarahumara Indians
Arnold, C. City of the Gods   972

Folklore

See/See also pages in the following book(s):
Delacre, L. Golden tales p29-43   398.2

Religion

Bierhorst, J. The mythology of Mexico and
Central America (7 and up)   299

Indians of North America

See also names of Indian peoples and linguistic families
Bruchac, J. Lasting echoes (7 and up)
970.004
Collier, C. Clash of cultures, prehistory-1638
970.004
Henry, C. E. Ben Nighthorse Campbell   92
Indians of North America series   970.004
Katz, W. L. Black Indians: a hidden heritage
305.8
Lassieur, A. Before the storm (7 and up)
970.004
Murdoch, D. H. North American Indian
970.004
Native Americans: opposing viewpoints (7 and
up)   970.004
Native North American almanac   970.004
Spangenburg, R. The American Indian experience (7 and up)   917.3
See/See also pages in the following book(s):
Katz, W. L. Black pioneers p11-18 (7 and up)
920
Peoples of the Americas   970

Antiquities

Arnold, C. Stories in stone   709.01

Snow, D. R. The archaeology of North America
In Indians of North America series
970.004

Art

The Serpent's tongue (7 and up)   970.004

Biography

American Indian biographies   920
Avery, S. Extraordinary American Indians
920
Freedman, R. Indian chiefs   920
Kallen, S. A. Native American chiefs and warriors (7 and up)   920
Katz, W. L. Proudly red and black   920

Dictionaries

Wolfson, E. From Abenaki to Zuni
970.004

Dwellings

Monroe, J. G. First houses   970.004

Encyclopedias

Ciment, J. Scholastic encyclopedia of the
American Indian   970.004
The Encyclopedia of North American Indians
970.004
The Gale encyclopedia of Native American
tribes   970.004
Pritzker, B. Native Americans   970.004
Waldman, C. Encyclopedia of Native American
tribes   970.004

Fiction

Brooks, M. Bone dance (7 and up)   Fic
Bruchac, J. The heart of a chief   Fic
Dorris, M. Sees Behind Trees   Fic
Hobbs, W. Kokopelli's flute   Fic
Holman, F. Real   Fic
Hotze, S. A circle unbroken   Fic
Jacobs, P. S. James Printer   Fic
Keehn, S. M. I am Regina   Fic
Lipsyte, R. The brave (7 and up)   Fic
Lipsyte, R. The chief (7 and up)   Fic
O'Dell, S. Island of the Blue Dolphins   Fic
O'Dell, S. Streams to the river, river to the sea
Fic
O'Dell, S. Zia   Fic
Speare, E. G. The sign of the beaver   Fic
Talking leaves   S C

Folklore

American Indian myths and legends   398.2
Brown, D. A. Dee Brown's folktales of the Native American   398.2
Bruchac, J. Four ancestors   398.2
Bruchac, J. The girl who married the Moon:
tales from Native North America   398.2
Bruchac, J. When the Chenoo howls   398.2
Lelooska, D. Echoes of the elders   398.2
Monroe, J. G. First houses   970.004

Games

Nicholson, L. The composite guide to lacrosse
796.34

Government relations

Kelly, L. C. Federal Indian policy
In Indians of North America series
970.004
Pevar, S. L. The rights of American Indians and
their tribes (7 and up)   342
Sherrow, V. Cherokee Nation v. Georgia (7 and
up)   346

Industrial design
Rubin, S. G. Toilets, toasters & telephones
683
Tambini, M. The look of the century (7 and up)
745.2
Industrial plants *See* Factories
Industrial revolution
Corrick, J. A. The Industrial Revolution (7 and up)
909.81
The Industrial revolution: opposing viewpoints (7 and up)
330.973
McCormick, A. L. The industrial revolution in American history
338
The **industrial** revolution in American history. McCormick, A. L.
338
The **Industrial** revolution: opposing viewpoints (7 and up)
330.973
Industries

History
See also Industrial revolution
Inequality *See* Equality
Inequality: opposing viewpoints in social problems (7 and up)
305
Infantile paralysis *See* Poliomyelitis
Infection and infectious diseases *See* Communicable diseases
Inferno. Ayer, E. H.
940.53
Influenza
See/See also pages in the following book(s):
Facklam, H. Viruses p38-41
579.2
Information finder. See The World Book encyclopedia
031
Information literacy and information skills instruction. Thomas, N. P.
027.8
Information literacy series
Rankin, V. The thoughtful researcher
027.62
Information networks
See also Computer networks; Internet
Information please almanac, atlas & yearbook
031.02
The **Information** please sports almanac
796
Information power. American Association of School Librarians
027.8
The **Information** revolution: opposing viewpoints (7 and up)
303.4
Information society
See also Information technology
The Information revolution: opposing viewpoints (7 and up)
303.4
Information storage and retrieval systems *See* Information systems
Information superhighway driver training course. See entry in CD-ROM section, Part 3
Information systems
See also Database management
Johnson, D. The indispensable librarian
027.8
Pappas, M. L. Searching electronic resources
025.04
Directories
Miller, E. B. The Internet resource directory for K-12 teachers and librarians
004.6

Information technology
Henderson, H. Issues in the information age (7 and up)
303.4
The Information revolution: opposing viewpoints (7 and up)
303.4
InfoTrac Junior Edition. See entry in CD-ROM section, Part 3
The **ingenious** Mr. Peale. Wilson, J.
92
Ingestion disorders *See* Eating disorders
Ingpen, Robert R.
A celebration of customs & rituals of the world
394.2
Ingram, Scott
Oregon
In America the beautiful, second series
973
The time machine
In Read into the millenium p116-33   S C
Ingram, William Scott *See* Ingram, Scott
Inhalant drug dangers. Monroe, J.
362.29
Inhalation abuse of solvents *See* Solvent abuse
Injuries *See* Accidents; Wounds and injuries
Inns *See* Hotels and motels
The **Innu** (The Montagnais-Naskapi). Armitage, P.
In Indians of North America series
970.004
Innuit *See* Inuit
Inoculation *See* Vaccination
Insane *See* Mentally ill
Hospitals
See Psychiatric hospitals
Insectivorous plants *See* Carnivorous plants
Insects
See also Ants; Butterflies; Grasshoppers; Moths
Burnie, D. Insects & spiders
595.7
Insects: little creatures in a big world. See entry in CD-ROM section, Part 3
Macquitty, M. Amazing bugs
595.7
Milne, L. J. The Audubon Society field guide to North American insects and spiders
595.7
Wilsdon, C. National Audubon Society first field guide: insects
595.7
Poetry
Fleischman, P. Joyful noise: poems for two voices
811
Insects & spiders. Burnie, D.
595.7
Insects in art
DuBosque, D. Draw insects
743
Insects: little creatures in a big world. See entry in CD-ROM section, Part 3
Inside government [series]
Feinberg, B. S. The cabinet
352.24
Sandak, C. R. The national debt
336.3
Inside guides [series]
Clifford, N. Incredible earth
551.1
Macquitty, M. Amazing bugs
595.7
Taylor, B. Animal homes
591.5
Taylor, B. Incredible plants
580
Wilkinson, P. Super structures
624
Williams, F. Human body
611

Internet—*Continued*
McCormick, A. L. The Internet (7 and up)
 004.6
Miller, E. B. The Internet resource directory for K-12 teachers and librarians **004.6**
Murray, L. K. Basic Internet for busy librarians **004.6**
Reese, J. Internet books for educators, parents, and students **004.6**
Rosner, M. A. Science fair success using the Internet (7 and up) **507.8**
Simpson, C. M. Internet for schools **004.6**
Smith, M. Neal-Schuman Internet policy handbook for libraries **025**
Wallace, M. 101 things to do on the Internet **004.6**
See/See also pages in the following book(s):
Civil liberties: opposing viewpoints p161-95 (7 and up) **323**
Henderson, H. Issues in the information age (7 and up) **303.4**
Mass media: opposing viewpoints p127-59 (7 and up) **302.23**
The **Internet** (7 and up) **004.6**
The **Internet** and instruction. Barron, A. E. **004.6**
The **Internet** and the First Amendment. Cate, F. H. **342**
Internet books for educators, parents, and students. Reese, J. **004.6**
Internet for active learners. Berger, P. **004.6**
Internet for schools. Simpson, C. M. **004.6**
The **Internet** resource directory for K-12 teachers and librarians. Miller, E. B. **004.6**
Internet technology for schools. Mambretti, C. **004.6**
Internment camps *See* Concentration camps
Interpersonal relations *See* Human relations
Interracial marriage
Nash, G. B. Forbidden love (7 and up) **305.8**
Fiction
Dorris, M. The window **Fic**
Interracial relations *See* Race relations
The **interrupted** wedding. San Souci, R.
In San Souci, R. A terrifying taste of short & shivery p91-94 **398.2**
Interstate commerce
Levinson, I. S. Gibbons v. Ogden (7 and up) **343**
Interstellar pig. Sleator, W. **Fic**
Intervention (International law)
See/See also pages in the following book(s):
War: opposing viewpoints p64-111 (7 and up) **355**
Intner, Sheila S., 1935-
Standard cataloging for school and public libraries **025.3**
Into focus **028.1**
Into the candlelit room. McKean, T.
In McKean, T. Into the candlelit room and other strange tales p1-87 **S C**
Into the candlelit room and other strange tales. McKean, T. **S C**

Into the deep forest with Henry David Thoreau. Murphy, J. **974.1**
Into the game. Williams-Garcia, R.
In Join in p3-11 **S C**
Into the gap. Garland, M.
In A Nightmare's dozen **S C**
Into the land of the unicorns. Coville, B. **Fic**
Into thin air. Kidd, J. S. **363.7**
Intoxicants *See* Stimulants
An **introduction** to acrylics. Smith, R.
In The DK art school series **751**
An **introduction** to drawing. Horton, J.
In The DK art school series **751**
An **introduction** to mixed media. Wright, M.
In The DK art school series **751**
An **introduction** to oil painting. Smith, R.
In The DK art school series **751**
An **introduction** to pastels. Wright, M.
In The DK art school series **751**
An **introduction** to perspective. Smith, R.
In The DK art school series **751**
An **introduction** to watercolor. Smith, R.
In The DK art school series **751**
Inuit
Bonvillain, N. The Inuit
In Indians of North America series **970.004**
Tiulana, P. Wise words of Paul Tiulana **92**
Yue, C. The igloo **728**
Art
Finley, C. Art of the Far North **704**
Fiction
George, J. C. Julie **Fic**
George, J. C. Julie of the wolves **Fic**
George, J. C. Water sky **Fic**
Houston, J. A. Frozen fire **Fic**
Paulsen, G. Dogsong **Fic**
Folklore
The Dancing fox: Arctic folktales **398.2**
Norman, H. The girl who dreamed only geese, and other tales of the Far North **398.2**
Social life and customs
Finley, C. Art of the Far North **704**
Invaders [series]
Facklam, H. Bacteria **579.3**
Facklam, H. Viruses **579.2**
Invasion of privacy *See* Right of privacy
Inventions
Aaseng, N. Black inventors (7 and up) **920**
Bender, L. Invention **609**
Erlbach, A. The kids' invention book **608**
Gates, P. Nature got there first **508**
Karnes, F. A. Girls & young women inventing **608**
Macaulay, D. The new way things work **600**
McKissack, P. C. African-American inventors **920**
Mount, E. Milestones in science and technology **509**
The new way things work. See entry in CD-ROM section, Part 3
Pollard, M. The light bulb and how it changed the world **621.3**

Irish Americans—Fiction—*Continued*

Clark, C. G. Nellie Bishop — Fic
Holland, I. Behind the lines — Fic
Lynch, C. Mick (7 and up) — Fic

Iron

Fitzgerald, K. The story of iron — 669
Sparrow, G. Iron
In The Elements [Benchmark Bks.] — 546

The **Iron** Moonhunter. Chang, K.
In From sea to shining sea p164-66 — 810.8

The **iron** ring. Alexander, L. — Fic

Ironman. Crutcher, C. — Fic

The **Iroquois**. Bial, R. — 970.004

Iroquois Indians

Bial, R. The Iroquois — 970.004
Graymont, B. The Iroquois
In Indians of North America series — 970.004

Irving, Washington, 1783-1859

The legend of Sleepy Hollow
In Irving, W. Rip Van Winkle & The legend of Sleepy Hollow — Fic
Rip Van Winkle
In American fairy tales p9-28 — S C
Rip Van Winkle and The legend of Sleepy Hollow — Fic
See/See also pages in the following book(s):
Faber, D. Great lives: American literature p31-39 — 920

Irwin, Hadley

The original Freddie Ackerman — Fic
Sarah with an H — Fic

Is anybody out there?. Couper, H. — 576.8

Is underground. Aiken, J. *See note under* Aiken, J. The wolves of Willoughby Chase — Fic

Isaac Newton and the scientific revolution. Christianson, G. E. — 92

Isaacson, Philip M., 1924-

Round buildings, square buildings, & buildings that wiggle like a fish — 720
A short walk around the Pyramids & through the world of art — 700

Isabel. Potok, C.
In Potok, C. Zebra and other stories p97-120 — S C

Isabella I, Queen of Spain, 1451-1504

See/See also pages in the following book(s):
Meltzer, M. Ten queens p56-71 — 920

Ishi

See/See also pages in the following book(s):
Drimmer, F. Incredible people p35-77 — 920

Isis and Osiris. McCaughrean, G.
In McCaughrean, G. The crystal pool: myths and legends of the world p50-56 — 398.2

Islam

Child, J. The rise of Islam — 297
Gordon, M. Islam (7 and up) — 297
Macdonald, F. A 16th century mosque — 297
The Muslim almanac — 297
Shahrukh Husain. What do we know about Islam? — 297
The Spread of Islam (7 and up) — 297

Wormser, R. American Islam (7 and up) — 297
See/See also pages in the following book(s):
Osborne, M. P. One world, many religions p25-34 — 291

Islamic countries

The Muslim almanac — 297

Civilization

Beshore, G. W. Science in early Islamic culture — 509

The **island**. Paulsen, G. — Fic

An **island** like you. Ortiz Cofer, J. — S C

Island of the Blue Dolphins. O'Dell, S. — Fic

Island of the lost children. Osborne, M. P.
In Osborne, M. P. Favorite medieval tales p25-33 — 398.2

Island Trees Public Schools (Levittown, N.Y.)

Gold, J. C. Board of Education v. Pico (1982) (7 and up) — 344

The **islander**. Rylant, C. — Fic

Islands

Fiction

Irwin, H. The original Freddie Ackerman — Fic
Paulsen, G. The island — Fic
Rylant, C. The islander — Fic
Taylor, T. Sweet Friday Island (7 and up) — Fic

Israel, Fred L.

(ed) Building the Panama Canal. *See* Building the Panama Canal — 972
(ed) Jerusalem and the Holy Land. *See* Jerusalem and the Holy Land — 956.94
(ed) Robert E. Peary and the rush to the North Pole. *See* Robert E. Peary and the rush to the North Pole — 998

Israel

See also Jerusalem

Fiction

Banks, L. R. Broken bridge — Fic
Levitin, S. The singing mountain (7 and up) — Fic

History

Altman, L. J. The creation of Israel (7 and up) — 956.94
Blumberg, A. The history of Israel (7 and up) — 956.94
Schroeter, D. J. Israel (7 and up) — 956.94
See/See also pages in the following book(s):
Ayer, E. H. The survivors p51-72 — 940.53
Chicoine, S. From the ashes — 940.53

Politics and government

Hitzeroth, D. Golda Meir (7 and up) — 92

Social life and customs

Jerusalem and the Holy Land — 956.94

Israel and the werewolf. San Souci, R.
In San Souci, R. A terrifying taste of short & shivery p114-17 — 398.2

Israel-Arab conflicts

Corzine, P. The Palestinian-Israeli accord (7 and up) — 956.94
See/See also pages in the following book(s):
Blumberg, A. The history of Israel (7 and up) — 956.94

Jackson, Colin
The young track and field athlete   **796.42**
Jackson, Donna, 1958-
The bone detectives   **614**
Jackson, Livia Bitton- *See* Bitton-Jackson, Livia
Jackson, Mahalia, 1911-1972
About
Gourse, L. Mahalia Jackson: queen of gospel song (7 and up)   **92**
Jackson, Sheila, 1956-
Costumes for the stage: a complete handbook for every kind of play   **792**
Jackson, Stonewall, 1824-1863
About
Fritz, J. Stonewall   **92**
Pflueger, L. Stonewall Jackson   **92**
See/See also pages in the following book(s):
Reger, J. P. Civil War generals of the Confederacy p46-61 (7 and up)   **920**
Shenandoah, 1862 (7 and up)   **973.7**
Jackson, Thomas Jonathan *See* Jackson, Stonewall, 1824-1863
Jacob have I loved. Paterson, K.   **Fic**
Jacobs, Harriet A. (Harriet Ann), 1813-1896 or 7
About
Fleischner, J. I was born a slave: the story of Harriet Jacobs   **92**
Fiction
Lyons, M. E. Letters from a slave girl   **Fic**
Jacobs, Marian B.
Coping with hereditary diseases (7 and up)   **616**
Jacobs, Paul Samuel
James Printer   **Fic**
Jacobs, Thomas A.
What are my rights? (7 and up)   **346**
Jacob's rescue. Drucker, M.   **Fic**
Jacobson, Dan, 1929-
A day in the country
In Somehow tenderness survives p37-47   **S C**
Jacques, Brian
The Bellmaker. See note under Jacques, B. Redwall   **Fic**
The legend of Luke. See note under Jacques, B. Redwall   **Fic**
The long patrol. See note under Jacques, B. Redwall   **Fic**
Mariel of Redwall. See note under Jacques, B. Redwall   **Fic**
Marlfox. See note under Jacques, B. Redwall   **Fic**
Martin the Warrior. See note under Jacques, B. Redwall   **Fic**
Mattimeo. See note under Jacques, B. Redwall   **Fic**
Mossflower. See note under Jacques, B. Redwall   **Fic**
The outcast of Redwall. See note under Jacques, B. Redwall   **Fic**
Pearls of Lutra. See note under Jacques, B. Redwall   **Fic**
Redwall   **Fic**

Salamandastron. See note under Jacques, B. Redwall   **Fic**
Jacsó, Péter
Build your own database   **005.7**
Jaffe, Nina
The cow of no color: riddle stories and justice tales from around the world   **398.2**
Contents: The cow of no color; The sound of work; Ximen Bao and the river spirit; The cloak; The thief and the pig; The testimony of the fly; Susannah and the elders; The jury; The magic seed; The bird lovers; An ounce of mud; The dance of Elegba; The three wives of Nenpetro; The flask; Kim Son Dal and the water-carriers; The land; Sharing the soup; A higher truth; The walnut and the pumpkin; The wise king; Josephus in the cave; The water pot and the necklace; The test
Jaffe, Steven H.
Who were the founding fathers? (7 and up)   **973.3**
Jagendorf, M. A. (Moritz Adolph), b. 1888
Clever Mistress Murray
In From sea to shining sea p68-73   **810.8**
The sad tale of three slavers
In From sea to shining sea p138-39   **810.8**
The sad tale of Tom the catfish
In From sea to shining sea p232-33   **810.8**
Jagendorf, Moritz Adolph *See* Jagendorf, M. A. (Moritz Adolph), b. 1888
Jakoubek, Robert E.
James Farmer and the freedom rides   **92**
Joe Louis   **92**
Jam!. Lee, J.   **781.65**
Jamaica
Fiction
Berry, J. Ajeemah and his son   **Fic**
James, Barbara, 1953-
Animal rights   **179**
James, Elizabeth
How to write super school reports   **808**
How to write terrific book reports   **808**
Sincerely yours   **808**
Social smarts   **395**
James, Henry, 1843-1916
See/See also pages in the following book(s):
Faber, D. Great lives: American literature p130-40   **920**
James, Jesse, 1847-1882
About
Bruns, R. Jesse James   **92**
James, John, 1959-
(jt. auth) Morley, J. A Roman villa   **937**
(il) Morley, J. Shakespeare's theater   **792.09**
James, Laura M.
(jt. auth) Kwan, M. Michelle Kwan, heart of a champion   **92**
James, Portia P.
The real McCoy (7 and up)   **609**
James, R. S.
Mozambique (7 and up)   **967.9**
James, Simon, 1957-
Ancient Rome   **937**
James, Will, 1892-1942
Tom and Jerry
In A Newbery zoo   **S C**

Japanese language—Dictionaries—*Continued*
Merriam-Webster's Japanese-English learner's dictionary   **495.6**
The Oxford-Duden pictorial Japanese and English dictionary   **495.6**
The **Japanese** mirror. Coville, B.
In Coville, B. Odder than ever   **S C**
In A Nightmare's dozen   **S C**
A **jar** of dreams. Uchida, Y.   **Fic**
A **Jar** of tiny stars: poems by NCTE award-winning poets   **811.008**
Jaramillo Levi, Enrique, 1944-
The cave
In Where angels glide at dawn p43-48
                                                  S C
Jason Kovak, the quick and the brave. Okimoto, J. D.
In Visions: nineteen short stories by outstanding writers for young adults p42-63
                                                  S C
Jawaharlal Nehru *See* Nehru, Jawaharlal, 1889-1964
Jay, Hilda L., 1921-
(jt. auth) Jay, M. E. Ready-to-go reading incentive programs for schools and libraries
                                                  028.5
(jt. auth) Yesner, B. L. Operating and evaluating school library media programs   **027.8**
Jay, M. Ellen
Ready-to-go reading incentive programs for schools and libraries   **028.5**
Jayhawker. Beatty, P.   **Fic**
Jazmin's notebook. Grimes, N.   **Fic**
Jazz music
See also Blues music
Collier, J. L. Jazz (7 and up)   **781.65**
Gourse, L. Striders to beboppers and beyond (7 and up)   **781.65**
Gourse, L. Swingers and crooners (7 and up)
                                                  781.65
Lee, J. Jam! (7 and up)   **781.65**
Mour, S. I. American jazz musicians   **920**
Fiction
Newton, S. I will call it Georgie's blues (7 and up)   **Fic**
Jazz musicians
Collins, D. R. Bix Beiderbecke (7 and up)
                                                  92
Frankl, R. Charlie Parker, musician   **92**
Gourse, L. Striders to beboppers and beyond (7 and up)   **781.65**
Kavanaugh, L. H. Quincy Jones   **92**
Mour, S. I. American jazz musicians   **920**
Old, W. Duke Ellington: giant of jazz   **92**
Old, W. Louis Armstrong   **92**
The **jealous** apprentice. Aiken, J.
In Aiken, J. Give yourself a fright: thirteen tales of the supernatural p56-69
                                                  S C
Jeanne d'Arc, Saint *See* Joan, of Arc, Saint, 1412-1431
The **Jedera** adventure. Alexander, L. See note under Alexander, L. The Illyrian adventure
                                                  Fic

Jefferis, David
Artificial intelligence   **629.8**
Cyberspace   **004.6**
Jefferson, Cathy A., 1952-
(jt. auth) Pappas, M. L. Searching electronic resources   **025.04**
Jefferson, Thomas, 1743-1826
About
Blumberg, R. What's the deal? Jefferson, Napoleon and the Louisiana Purchase (7 and up)
                                                  973.4
Meltzer, M. Thomas Jefferson (7 and up)
                                                  92
Severance, J. B. Thomas Jefferson (7 and up)
                                                  92
See/See also pages in the following book(s):
Collier, C. The Jeffersonian Republicans: the Louisiana Purchase and the war of 1812
                                                  973.4
Lindop, E. George Washington, Thomas Jefferson, Andrew Jackson   **920**
Fiction
Rinaldi, A. Wolf by the ears (7 and up)
                                                  Fic
The **Jeffersonian** Republicans: the Louisiana Purchase and the war of 1812. Collier, C.
                                                  973.4
Jeffrey, Laura S.
Christa McAuliffe   **92**
Great American businesswomen   **920**
Jemison, Mae C.
About
Yannuzzi, D. A. Mae Jemison   **92**
See/See also pages in the following book(s):
Bolden, T. And not afraid to dare   **920**
Briggs, C. S. Women in space   **920**
Lindop, L. Scientists and doctors (7 and up)
                                                  920
Jen, Gish
What means switch
In Who do you think you are? p96-118
                                                  S C
Jennings, Coleman A., 1933-
(ed) Theatre for young audiences. See Theatre for young audiences   **812.008**
Jennings, Paul, 1943-
Unbearable!   **S C**
Contents: Licked; Little black balls; Only gilt; Next time around; Nails; Yuggles; Granddad's gifts; Smelly feat
Uncovered!   **S C**
Contents: Forever; Too many rabbits; A mouthful; Listen ear; Picked bones; Just like me; Ringing wet; Backward step; Pubic Hare
Undone!   **S C**
Contents: Batty; Moonies; Noseweed; Wake up to yourself; Thought full; Clear as mud; What a woman; You be the judge
Unmentionable!   **S C**
Contents: Ice maiden; Birdman; Little squirt; The harmonica; The velvet throne; Cry Baby; Ex poser; Sloppy jalopy; Eyes knows
Jennings, Peter, 1938-
The century for young people   **909.82**
Jennings, Terry, 1938-
101 amazing optical illusions   **152.14**

Jennings, Thomas L., 1791-1859
See/See also pages in the following book(s):
Haskins, J. African American entrepreneurs p31-35   **920**

Jeremiah's song. Myers, W. D.
In Visions: nineteen short stories by outstanding writers for young adults p194-203   **S C**

Jericho. Hickman, J.   **Fic**

Jermyn, Leslie
Uruguay   **989.5**

Jernigan, Tamara, 1959-
See/See also pages in the following book(s):
Briggs, C. S. Women in space   **920**

Jerusalem
Schwartz, H. Next year in Jerusalem   **296.1**
Wolf, B. If I forget Thee, O Jerusalem   **956.94**
Fiction
Nye, N. S. Habibi   **Fic**
Poetry
Yolen, J. O Jerusalem   **811**

Jerusalem and the Holy Land   **956.94**

The **Jerusalem** Bible. See Bible. The new Jerusalem Bible   **220.5**

Jespersen, James
Mummies, dinosaurs, moon rocks   **930.1**

Jessop, Joanne
The X-ray picture book of big buildings of the ancient world   **720**
The X-ray picture book of big buildings of the modern world   **720**

Jesus Christ
About
L'Engle, M. The glorious impossible   **232.9**
Nativity
Bible. N.T. Selections. The Christmas story   **232.9**

The **jetty** chronicles. Fisher, L. E.   **Fic**

Jewels See Gems; Precious stones

The **Jewish** American family album. Hoobler, D.   **305.8**

Jewish-Arab relations
See also Israel-Arab conflicts
See/See also pages in the following book(s):
Carter, J. Talking peace p3-20 (7 and up)   **327.1**
Fiction
Banks, L. R. Broken bridge   **Fic**
Nye, N. S. Habibi   **Fic**

Jewish cooking
See/See also pages in the following book(s):
Adler, D. A. The kids' catalog of Jewish holidays   **296.4**

Jewish holidays
See also Hanukkah; Passover
Adler, D. A. The kids' catalog of Jewish holidays   **296.4**
Berger, G. Celebrate!   **296.4**
Yolen, J. Milk and honey   **296.4**

Jewish holocaust (1933-1945) See Holocaust, 1933-1945

Jewish legends
Chaikin, M. Clouds of glory   **296.1**

Goldin, B. D. Journeys with Elijah   **222**
Lester, J. When the beginning began   **296.1**
Patterson, J. Angels, prophets, rabbis & kings from the stories of the Jewish people   **296.1**
Rogasky, B. The golem   **398.2**
Schwartz, H. Next year in Jerusalem   **296.1**
Sobel, I. Moses and the angels   **296.1**

Jewish refugees
Ayer, E. H. The survivors   **940.53**
Fox, A. L. Ten thousand children   **940.53**
Fiction
Bat-Ami, M. Two suns in the sky (7 and up)   **Fic**
Levitin, S. Journey to America   **Fic**
Matas, C. Greater than angels (7 and up)   **Fic**

Jewish women
Biography
Taitz, E. Remarkable Jewish women (7 and up)   **920**

Jews
Biography
Mandell, S. L. Writers of the Holocaust (7 and up)   **940.53**
People of the Holocaust   **920.003**
Festivals
See Jewish holidays
Fiction
Cormier, R. Tunes for bears to dance to (7 and up)   **Fic**
Hesse, K. Letters from Rifka   **Fic**
Irwin, H. Sarah with an H   **Fic**
Lasky, K. Dreams in the golden country   **Fic**
Levitin, S. Annie's promise   **Fic**
Levitin, S. Escape from Egypt (7 and up)   **Fic**
Levitin, S. Silver days   **Fic**
Levitin, S. The singing mountain (7 and up)   **Fic**
Lowry, L. Number the stars   **Fic**
Matas, C. The garden (7 and up)   **Fic**
Mazer, H. The last mission (7 and up)   **Fic**
Meyer, C. Drummers of Jericho (7 and up)   **Fic**
Meyer, C. Gideon's people   **Fic**
Miklowitz, G. D. Masada (7 and up)   **Fic**
Pullman, P. The tiger in the well (7 and up)   **Fic**
Singer, I. B. The power of light   **S C**
Wiesel, E. Night, Dawn, The accident: three tales (7 and up)   **Fic**
Yolen, J. The devil's arithmetic   **Fic**
Folklore
Yolen, J. Milk and honey   **296.4**
History
Altman, L. J. Forever outsiders   **909**
Mann, K. The ancient Hebrews   **909**
Waldman, N. Masada   **933**
The Young reader's encyclopedia of Jewish history   **909**
See/See also pages in the following book(s):
Altman, L. J. The creation of Israel (7 and up)   **956.94**

Jews—*Continued*
Legends
See Jewish legends
Persecutions
See also Holocaust, 1933-1945; World War, 1939-1945—Jews—Rescue
Sherrow, V. Smoke to flame   **940.53**
Ethiopia—Fiction
Levitin, S. The return   **Fic**
Europe
Boas, J. We are witnesses (7 and up)
    940.53
Chicoine, S. From the ashes   **940.53**
Europe—Fiction
Levitin, S. The cure   **Fic**
Matas, C. After the war (7 and up)   **Fic**
France—Fiction
Matas, C. Greater than angels (7 and up)
    Fic
Germany
Ayer, E. H. Parallel journeys (7 and up)
    940.53
Koehn, I. Mischling, second degree: my childhood in Nazi Germany   **92**
Perl, L. Four perfect pebbles (7 and up)
    940.53
Germany—Fiction
Matas, C. In my enemy's house (7 and up)
    Fic
Hungary
Bierman, J. Righteous gentile [biography of Raoul Wallenberg] (7 and up)   **92**
Bitton-Jackson, L. I have lived a thousand years (7 and up)   **940.53**
Siegal, A. Upon the head of the goat: a childhood in Hungary, 1939-1944   **92**
Netherlands
Frank, A. The diary of a young girl   **92**
Frank, A. The diary of a young girl: the definitive edition   **92**
Gold, A. L. Memories of Anne Frank   **92**
Müller, M. Anne Frank (7 and up)   **92**
Reiss, J. The journey back   **92**
Reiss, J. The upstairs room   **92**
Rol, R. van der. Anne Frank, beyond the diary
    92
Wukovits, J. F. Anne Frank (7 and up)   **92**
Poland
Fluek, T. K. Memories of my life in a Polish village, 1930-1949 (7 and up)   **92**
Lobel, A. No pretty pictures (7 and up)   **92**
Poland—Fiction
Drucker, M. Jacob's rescue   **Fic**
Russia—Fiction
Lasky, K. The night journey   **Fic**
United States
Diner, H. R. Jews in America (7 and up)
    305.8
Fisher, L. E. To bigotry, no sanction   **296**
Hoobler, D. The Jewish American family album
    305.8
United States—Biography
Brooks, P. Extraordinary Jewish Americans
    920
Jews in America. Diner, H. R.   **305.8**

Jiang, Ji-li
Red scarf girl   **951.05**
Jie Ling
See/See also pages in the following book(s):
Rutledge, R. The best of the best in gymnastics
    920
Jijan. Honma, R.
In American dragons p203-10   **810.8**
Jim Ugly. Fleischman, S.   **Fic**
Jiménez, Francisco, 1943-
The circuit
    In Help wanted: short stories about young people working   **S C**
    In Leaving home: stories p53-62   **808.8**
The circuit: stories from the life of a migrant child   **S C**
    Contents: Under the wire; Soledad; Inside out; Miracle in Tent City; El angel de Oro; Christmas gift; Death forgiven; Cotton sack; The circuit; Learning the game; To have and to hold; Moving still
Jinnah, Mohamed Ali, 1876-1948
See/See also pages in the following book(s):
Wakin, E. Asian independence leaders p72-87 (7 and up)   **920**
Jip. Paterson, K.   **Fic**
Joan, of Arc, Saint, 1412-1431
About
Stanley, D. Joan of Arc   **92**
Fiction
Garden, N. Dove and sword (7 and up)
    Fic
Job, Amy G., 1942-
The school library media specialist as manager
    027.8
Job discrimination *See* Discrimination in employment
A **job** for Valentín. Ortiz Cofer, J.
    In Help wanted: short stories about young people working   **S C**
    In Ortiz Cofer, J. An island like you p112-30   **S C**
Job hunting
Pervola, C. How to get a job if you're a teenager (7 and up)   **650.14**
Job placement guidance *See* Vocational guidance
Jobs, Steven
See/See also pages in the following book(s):
Northrup, M. American computer pioneers p75-82   **920**
Jobs *See* Occupations
Joey Pigza swallowed the key. Gantos, J.   **Fic**
Johansson, Philip
Carpal tunnel syndrome and other repetitive strain injuries (7 and up)   **616.8**
Heart disease   **616.1**
John Barleycorn. McCaughrean, G.
    In McCaughrean, G. The golden hoard: myths and legends of the world p74-76
    398.2
John Brown's Raid, Harpers Ferry, W. Va., 1859 *See* Harpers Ferry (W. Va.)—History—John Brown's Raid, 1859
John Brown's Raid on Harpers Ferry in American history. Stein, R. C.   **973.7**

Journey to America. Levitin, S.   Fic

Journey to an 800 number. Konigsburg, E. L.   Fic

Journey to freedom. Isserman, M.   305.8

Journey to freedom [series]
Harper, J. E. Maya Angelou   92
Klingel, C. F. Coretta Scott King   92
Troy, D. W.E.B. DuBois   92

Journey to Jo'burg. Naidoo, B.   Fic

Journey to nowhere. Auch, M. J.   Fic

A journey to the centre of the earth. Verne, J.   Fic

A journey to the New World. Lasky, K.   Fic

Journey to Topaz. Uchida, Y.   Fic

A journey with Elijah. Goldin, B. D.
In Goldin, B. D. Journeys with Elijah p1-10   222

Journeys See Voyages and travels

Journeys with Elijah. Goldin, B. D.   222

The joy of signing. Riekehof, L. L.   419

Joyce, Katherine
Astounding optical illusions   152.14

Joyful noise: poems for two voices. Fleischman, P.   811

Joyner-Kersee, Jackie
See/See also pages in the following book(s):
Bolden, T. And not afraid to dare   920

Joyriding. Naughton, J.
In Ultimate sports: short stories by outstanding writers for young adults p4-19   S C

Juan Bobo and the buñuelos. González, L. M.
In From sea to shining sea p240-41   810.8

Jubilee journey. Meyer, C.   Fic

Judaism
Gates, F. C. Judaism (7 and up)   296
See/See also pages in the following book(s):
Osborne, M. P. One world, many religions p1-11   291

Customs and practices
See also Bar mitzvah; Bat mitzvah
Dictionaries
The Oxford dictionary of the Jewish religion   296.03

Judar and his brothers. Philip, N.
In Philip, N. The Arabian nights p42-64   398.2

Judges
See also Women judges
Kent, D. Thurgood Marshall and the Supreme Court   92
The Supreme Court justices   920.003

Juggling
Mitchelson, M. The most excellent book of how to be a juggler   793.8

Jukes, Mavis
Expecting the unexpected   Fic
Growing up: it's a girl thing   612.6
It's a girl thing   305.23
Planning the impossible   Fic

Julian, Hubert Fauntleroy
See/See also pages in the following book(s):
Hart, P. S. Flying free p40-45   629.13

Julian, Percy L., 1899-1975
See/See also pages in the following book(s):
Aaseng, N. Black inventors p113-24 (7 and up)   920
Haskins, J. Outward dreams p75+   609

Julie. George, J. C.   Fic

Julie of the wolves. George, J. C.   Fic

Julie's wolf pack. George, J. C.   Fic

Julius, Edward H., 1952-
Arithmetricks   513

July Saturday. Woodson, J.
In Places I never meant to be   S C

Jump ship to freedom. Collier, J. L.   Fic

Jumping the Nail. Bunting, E.   Fic

Juneteenth. Branch, M. M.   394.26

Jungalbook [play] Mast, E.
In Theatre for young audiences p478-517   812.008

Jungle. Greenaway, T.   577.3

The jungle books. Kipling, R.   S C

Jungle dogs. Salisbury, G.   Fic

Junior authors & illustrators series
Seventh book of junior authors & illustrators   920.003

Junior Broadway. Ross, B. B.   792.6

Junior chronicle of the 20th century   909.82

Junior DISCovering authors 2.0. See entry in CD-ROM section, Part 3

Junior high school libraries See High school libraries

Junior library of American Indians [series]
Gleason, K. Native American literature   897

Junior timelines on file. Tomaselli-Moschovitis, V.   902

Junior world biographies [series]
Nicholson, L. Booker T. Washington   92

Junior Worldmark encyclopedia of the Canadian provinces   971

Junior Worldmark encyclopedia of the states   973.03

Junior Worldmark encyclopedia of world cultures   306

Juniorplots 4. Gillespie, J. T.   028.5

The junkyard dog. Tamar, E.   Fic

Juno's Roman geese. McCaughrean, G.
In McCaughrean, G. The golden hoard: myths and legends of the world p66-73   398.2

Jupiter (Planet)
Exploration
Cole, M. D. Galileo spacecraft   629.43

Jurassic Park. Crichton, M.   Fic

Juratovac, Nicol
Dana's eyes
In American dragons p75-95   810.8

Jurmain, Suzanne
Freedom's sons   326

Jury
Aaseng, N. You are the juror   345

The **jury**. Jaffe, N.
In Jaffe, N. The cow of no color: riddle stories and justice tales from around the
world p47-51   **398.2**

Just, Ernest Everett, 1883-1941
See/See also pages in the following book(s):
Polking, K. Oceanographers and explorers of the
sea p23-31   **920**

Just as long as we're together. Blume, J.   **Fic**

Just like me. Jennings, P.
In Jennings, P. Uncovered! p75-82   **S C**

Just listen to this song I'm singing. Silverman, J.
                                                   782.42

Just once. Dygard, T. J.
In Ultimate sports: short stories by outstanding writers for young adults p196-205
                                                     S C

Just say yes. Murphy, J.
In Murphy, J. Night terrors p7-31   **S C**

Justice. McKissack, P. C.
In McKissack, P. C. The dark-thirty p22-34
                                                     S C

Justinian I, Emperor of the East, 483?-565
See/See also pages in the following book(s):
Nardo, D. Rulers of ancient Rome (7 and up)
                                                     920

Justinianus, Flavius Anicius Julianus *See* Justinian I, Emperor of the East, 483?-565

Juvenile courts
Gold, S. D. In re Gault (1967) (7 and up)
                                                     345

Juvenile crime. Barr, R.   **364.36**

Juvenile delinquency
See also Gangs
Barr, R. Juvenile crime (7 and up)   **364.36**
Bode, J. Hard time (7 and up)   **364.36**
Goodwin, W. Teen violence (7 and up)
                                                  364.36
Silverstein, H. Kids who kill (7 and up)
                                                   364.1
Youth violence (7 and up)   **364.36**
Zeinert, K. Victims of teen violence (7 and up)
                                                  362.88
See/See also pages in the following book(s):
Teens at risk: opposing viewpoints p63-105 (7
and up)   **362.7**
Fiction
Bunting, E. Someone is hiding on Alcatraz Is-
land   **Fic**
Cormier, R. We all fall down (7 and up)
                                                     Fic
Hinton, S. E. The outsiders (7 and up)   **Fic**
Hinton, S. E. Rumble fish (7 and up)   **Fic**
Hinton, S. E. That was then, this is now (7 and
up)   **Fic**
Myers, W. D. Scorpions   **Fic**
Rapp, A. The buffalo tree (7 and up)   **Fic**
Sachar, L. Holes   **Fic**

Juvenile prostitution
Dean, R. Teen prostitution (7 and up)
                                                    362.7

Jweid, Rosann, 1933-
The library-classroom partnership   **027.8**

K

Kaa's hunting. Kipling, R.
In Kipling, R. The jungle books   **S C**

Kadodwala, Dilip
Hinduism   **294.5**

Kadohata, Cynthia
Singing apples
In American eyes p49-61   **S C**

Kadono, Eiko, 1935-
The mirror
In Don't read this! and other tales of the un-
natural p85-109   **S C**

Kaffir boy [excerpt] Mathabane, M.
In Somehow tenderness survives p87-103
                                                     S C

Kafirs (African people) *See* Zulu (African people)

Kagda, Falaq
Algeria   **965**
Hong Kong   **951.25**

Kagda, Sakina, 1939-
Lithuania   **947.9**

Kahl, Jonathan D.
National Audubon Society first field guide:
weather   **551.5**

Kahlo, Frida, 1907-1954
About
Turner, R. M. Frida Kahlo   **92**
See/See also pages in the following book(s):
Sills, L. Inspirations p18-27   **920**

Kaiulani, Princess of Hawaii, 1875-1899
About
Linnea, S. Princess Ka'iulani   **92**
Stanley, F. The last princess: the story of Prin-
cess Ka'iulani of Hawai'i   **92**

Kákuy. Delacre, L.
In Delacre, L. Golden tales p59-63   **398.2**

Kalbag, Asha
Build your own Web site   **004.6**

Kali's curse. Krishnaswami, U.
In Krishnaswami, U. Shower of gold: girls
and women in the stories of India p104-
07   **398.2**

Kallen, Stuart A., 1955-
Egypt (7 and up)   **962**
Life in the Amazon rainforest (7 and up)
                                                     981
Native American chiefs and warriors (7 and up)
                                                     920
Rosie O'Donnell (7 and up)   **92**
The Salem witch trials (7 and up)   **133.4**

Kamen, Gloria, 1923-
Hidden music [biography of Fanny Cecile Mendelssohn Hensel]   **92**

Kamerman, Sylvia E.
(ed) The Big book of holiday plays. See The
Big book of holiday plays   **812.008**
(ed) Plays of black Americans. See Plays of
black Americans   **812.008**

Kaminker, Laura
Everything you need to know about being
adopted (7 and up)   **362.7**
Everything you need to know about dealing
with sexual assault (7 and up)   **362.883**

The **kids'** multicultural cookbook. Cook, D. F.
641.5

Kids on strike!. Bartoletti, S. C. **331.8**

Kids still having kids. Bode, J. **362.7**

The **kids'** volunteering book. Erlbach, A. **302**

Kids who kill. Silverstein, H. **364.1**

Kids who make a difference. Chandler, G.
363.7

The **kids'** world almanac of baseball. Aylesworth,
T. G. **796.357**

Kidsource. Voth, D. **507.8**

Kieler, Jørgen, 1919-
See/See also pages in the following book(s):
Lyman, D. Holocaust rescuers **920**

Kies, Cosette N., 1936-
Presenting young adult horror fiction (7 and up)
813.009

Kiitos! Kiitos!. Hands, R.
In The Oxford book of scary tales p144-49
808.8

Kikuyu (African people)
Quintana, A. The baboon king (7 and up)
Fic

Kilby, Jack St. Clair, 1923-
See/See also pages in the following book(s):
Northrup, M. American computer pioneers p57-
64 **920**

Kilcup, Rick
Randy, the red-horned rainmoose
In The Big book of holiday plays p168-77
812.008

Killer bees. Lavies, B. **595.7**

A **killing** frost. Marsden, J. See note under Marsden, J. Tomorrow, when the war began
Fic

Killing Mr. Griffin. Duncan, L. **Fic**

Killing the bear. Minty, J.
In Talking leaves **S C**

Kim, Helen, 1959-
The long season of rain (7 and up) **Fic**

Kim, Henny H., 1968-
(ed) Depression. See Depression **616.85**
(ed) Guns and violence. See Guns and violence
363.3
(ed) Youth violence. See Youth violence
364.36

Kim, Willyce, 1946-
See/See also pages in the following book(s):
Chiu, C. Lives of notable Asian Americans: literature and education p81-87 (7 and up)
920

Kim Son Dal and the water-carriers. Jaffe, N.
In Jaffe, N. The cow of no color: riddle stories and justice tales from around the
world p94-98 **398.2**

Kimberly, Gail
Child of Faerie
In A Glory of unicorns p165-82 **S C**

Kimmel, Elizabeth Cody
Ice story **998**
In the stone circle **Fic**

Kimmel, Eric A.
Bar mitzvah **296.4**

Be not far from me **221.9**
The darning needle
In From sea to shining sea p189-91
810.8
Sword of the samurai **S C**
Includes the following stories: Dōhaku's head; The samurai
and the dragon; The coward; Matajuro's training; The oxcart;
The battle of Chihaya Castle; Tomoe Gozen; The burglar; Devil
boy; The Rōnin and the tea master; No sword

Kimmens, Andrew C.
(ed) World authors, 1900-1950. See World authors, 1900-1950 **920.003**

Kincaid, Jamaica
Annie John (7 and up) **Fic**

Kinderlager (7 and up) **940.53**

Kindl, Patrice, 1951-
Owl in love **Fic**
The woman in the wall **Fic**

Kindred spirit: a biography of L. M. Montgomery,
creator of Anne of Green Gables. Andronik,
C. M. **92**

King, Ada *See* Lovelace, Ada King, Countess of,
1815-1852

King, B. B.
About
Shirley, D. Everyday I sing the blues: the story
of B.B. King (7 and up) **92**

King, Casey
Oh, freedom! **323.1**

King, Coretta Scott, 1927-
My life with Martin Luther King, Jr **92**
(ed) King, M. L. The words of Martin Luther
King, Jr. **323.1**
About
Klingel, C. F. Coretta Scott King **92**
Rhodes, L. R. Coretta Scott King **92**

King, Dave
My first photography book **771**

King, David C.
Al Capone and the roaring twenties **92**
Benedict Arnold and the American Revolution
92
Egypt **962**
Freedom of assembly **342**
Italy **945**
Kenya **967.62**
Peru **985**
The right to speak out **323.44**

King, Elizabeth, 1953-
Quinceañera **392**

King, F. Wayne
(jt. auth) Behler, J. L. The Audubon Society
field guide to North American reptiles and
amphibians **597.9**

King, Martin Luther, 1929-1968
The words of Martin Luther King, Jr.
323.1
About
Dear Dr. King **323.1**
Haskins, J. I have a dream: the life and words
of Martin Luther King, Jr. **92**
Haskins, J. The life and death of Martin Luther
King, Jr. **92**
King, C. S. My life with Martin Luther King, Jr
92

Kraus, Joanna Halpert, 1937-
The ice wolf
In Theatre for young audiences p284-307
812.008

Krecek, Joseph
See/See also pages in the following book(s):
Graham, K. Contemporary environmentalists
p123-138 (7 and up)   920

Kreiner, Anna
Everything you need to know about creating
your own support system (7 and up)   158

Krementz, Jill
How it feels when a parent dies   155.9

Krensky, Stephen, 1953-
The printer's apprentice   Fic

Kricher, John C.
Peterson first guide to seashores   577.7

Krieger, Melanie Jacobs
How to excel in science competitions
507.8
Means and probabilities (7 and up)   519.5

Krisher, Trudy
Kinship (7 and up)   Fic
Spite fences (7 and up)   Fic

Krishnaswami, Uma, 1956-
Shower of gold: girls and women in the stories
of India   398.2
Contents: The goddess and the girl; Savitri and the God of
Death; The Buddha and the five hundred queens; The daughter-
in-law who got her way; The mother of Karaikkal; The goddess
and the buffalo demon; Gotami and the mustard seed; Sita's story; The princess who wished to be beautiful; The warrior queen
of Jhansi; Vishnu's bride; The love story of Roopmati and Baz
Bahadur; The eight sons of Ganga; She who showers gold; The
magic tree; My name is Illusion; Kali's curse; Supriya's bowl

Kristina, Queen of Sweden, 1626-1689 *See*
Christina, Queen of Sweden, 1626-1689

Krizmanic, Judy
A teen's vegetarian cookbook (7 and up)
641.5

Krohn, Katherine E.
Princess Diana   92
Rosie O'Donnell   92

Kroll, Steven
Robert Fulton   92

Kronenwetter, Michael
America in the 1960s (7 and up)   973.92
The FBI and law enforcement agencies of the
United States (7 and up)   363.2
Protest! (7 and up)   303.4

Kronquist, Burleigh *See* Burleigh, Robert, 1936-

Krudop, Walter, 1966-
(il) Fletcher, R. J. Relatively speaking   811

Kruhm, Mary Bowman- *See* Bowman-Kruhm,
Mary

Krull, Kathleen, 1952-
Lives of the presidents   920
One nation, many tribes   970.004
Presenting Paula Danziger (7 and up)
813.009
They saw the future   133.3

Ku Klux Klan
See/See also pages in the following book(s):
D'Angelo, L. Hate crimes (7 and up)
364.1

Kublai Khan, 1216-1294
About
Dramer, K. Kublai Khan   92

Kuhn, Maggie, 1905-1995
See/See also pages in the following book(s):
Lindop, L. Champions of equality (7 and up)
920

Kuklin, Susan
After a suicide (7 and up)   362.7
Iqbal Masih and the crusaders against child
slavery (7 and up)   331.3

Kummer, Patricia K.
Côte d'Ivoire (Ivory Coast)   966.68

Kunitz, Stanley, 1905-
(ed) American authors, 1600-1900. See
American authors, 1600-1900   920.003

Kunkel, Dennis
(jt. auth) Tomb, H. Microaliens   502.8

Kurtz, Jane
The storyteller's beads   Fic

Kustanowitz, Esther
The hidden children of the Holocaust (7 and up)
940.53

Kuwait
Foster, L. M. Kuwait   953.67
O'Shea, M. Kuwait   953.67
History—1991, Persian Gulf War
See Persian Gulf War, 1991

Kwakiutl Indians
Walens, S. The Kwakiutl
In Indians of North America series
970.004
Fiction
Craven, M. I heard the owl call my name (7 and
up)   Fic

Kwan, Michelle
Michelle Kwan, heart of a champion   92
About
Gatto, K. Michelle Kwan   92

Kwanzaa
Copage, E. V. Kwanzaa (7 and up)   641.5
Walter, M. P. Kwanzaa: a family affair
394.26
Fiction
Mathis, S. B. Listen for the fig tree (7 and up)
Fic

Kyker, Keith
Wading the World Wide Web   004.6

L

An **L-shaped** grave. Aiken, J.
In Aiken, J. A fit of shivers p29-36   S C

La Salle, René Robert Cavelier *See* La Salle,
Robert Cavelier, sieur de, 1643-1687

La Salle, Robert Cavelier, sieur de, 1643-1687
See/See also pages in the following book(s):
Lomask, M. Great lives: exploration p138-45
920

La sylphide (Ballet)
See/See also pages in the following book(s):
McCaughrean, G. The Random House book of
stories from the ballet p48-56   792.8

Labor
> *See also* Agricultural laborers; Migrant labor; Work

Accidents
> *See* Industrial accidents

Labor disputes
> *See also* Strikes

Labor movement
> Stanley, J. Big Annie of Calumet   **331.8**
> Streissguth, T. Legendary labor leaders (7 and up)   **920**

Labor Statistics Bureau (U.S.) *See* United States. Bureau of Labor Statistics

Labor unions
> Dash, J. We shall not be moved (7 and up)   **331.4**

Laboratory animal experimentation *See* Animal experimentation

Lace, William W.
> The death camps (7 and up)   **940.53**
> England (7 and up)   **942**
> The Nazis (7 and up)   **943.086**
> Tiger Woods   **92**

Lacey, Theresa Jensen
> The Blackfeet
> *In* Indians of North America series
>   **970.004**
> The Pawnee
> *In* Indians of North America series
>   **970.004**

Lacrosse
> Nicholson, L. The composite guide to lacrosse
>   **796.34**

The **lad** and Luck's House. Bradley, W. H.
> *In* American fairy tales p129-42   **S C**

Ladner, Joyce A.
> *See/See also pages in the following book(s):*
> Powledge, F. We shall overcome p83-93
>   **323.1**

LaFaye, A., 1970-
> Edith Shay (7 and up)   **Fic**
> Strawberry Hill   **Fic**
> The year of the Sawdust Man   **Fic**

Lafferty, Peter
> Force & motion   **531**

LaFrance, Ron, d. 1996
> (jt. auth) Ciment, J. Scholastic encyclopedia of the American Indian   **970.004**

Lahr, Georgiana Lieder
> The kingdom of hearts
> *In* The Big book of holiday plays p236-40
>   **812.008**

The **Laidly** worm of Spindleston Heughs
> *In* Hearne, B. G. Beauties and beasts p139-42
>   **398.2**

Lake and pond. Sayre, A. P.   **577.6**

Lake ecology
> Katz, S. The Great Lakes   **577.6**
> Sayre, A. P. Lake and pond   **577.6**

The **lake** that flew away. McCaughrean, G.
> *In* McCaughrean, G. The golden hoard: myths and legends of the world p43-48
>   **398.2**

Lakin, Pat
> Everything you need to know when a parent doesn't speak English (7 and up)   **306.4**

Lakota Indians *See* Teton Indians

Lakota woman. Brave Bird, M.   **92**

Lamar, Lucius Quintus Cincinnatus, 1825-1893
> *See/See also pages in the following book(s):*
> Kennedy, J. F. Profiles in courage p159-85 (7 and up)   **920**

Lamb, Charles, 1775-1834
> Tales from Shakespeare   **822.3**

Lamb, Mary, 1764-1847
> (jt. auth) Lamb, C. Tales from Shakespeare
>   **822.3**

Lambert, David, 1932-
> The field guide to geology   **551**
> The ultimate dinosaur book   **567.9**

Lame Deer, Archie Fire, 1935-
> Iktome and the ducks
> *In* From sea to shining sea p208-09
>   **810.8**

The **lame** king. Aiken, J.
> *In* Aiken, J. Give yourself a fright: thirteen tales of the supernatural p44-55
>   **S C**

The **lame** warrior and the skeleton. Brown, D. A.
> *In* Brown, D. A. Dee Brown's folktales of the Native American p158-59   **398.2**

Lamia. McCaughrean, G.
> *In* McCaughrean, G. The crystal pool: myths and legends of the world p8-13
>   **398.2**

Lamm, C. Drew
> Stay true
> *In* Stay true: short stories for strong girls
>   **S C**

The **lamp** from the warlock's tomb. Bellairs, J.
> See note under Bellairs, J. The dark secret of Weatherend   **Fic**

Lampton, Christopher
> The World Wide Web   **004.6**

Lancaster, F. Wilfrid (Frederick Wilfrid), 1933-
> (jt. auth) Jacsó, P. Build your own database
>   **005.7**

Lancaster, Frederick Wilfrid *See* Lancaster, F. Wilfrid (Frederick Wilfrid), 1933-

Lancelot (Legendary character)
> Pyle, H. The story of Sir Launcelot and his companions (7 and up)   **398.2**

The **land.** Jaffe, N.
> *In* Jaffe, N. The cow of no color: riddle stories and justice tales from around the world p99-100   **398.2**

The **land** I lost: adventures of a boy in Vietnam. Huynh, Q. N.   **92**

The **Land** of the birds
> *In* The Dancing fox: Arctic folktales p63-69
>   **398.2**

Land of the free [series]
> King, D. C. Freedom of assembly   **342**
> King, D. C. The right to speak out   **323.44**

Land-otter. San Souci, R.
> *In* San Souci, R. A terrifying taste of short & shivery p20-24   **398.2**

Land use

See also Wetlands

Landau, Elaine

Alzheimer's disease (7 and up)	362.1
Bill Clinton and his presidency	92
Deafness	617.8
Epilepsy	616.8
Joined at birth	616
Living with albinism	616.5
Multiple births	618.2
Parkinson's disease (7 and up)	616.8
State birds	598
State flowers	582.13
Tourette syndrome (7 and up)	616.8
Tuberculosis (7 and up)	616.9
Your legal rights (7 and up)	346

(ed) We survived the Holocaust. See We survived the Holocaust **940.53**

Landau, Sidney I.

(ed) The Doubleday Roget's thesaurus in dictionary form. See The Doubleday Roget's thesaurus in dictionary form **423**

Landmark documents in American history 2.0. See entry in CD-ROM section, Part 3

Landmark Supreme Court cases [series]

Alonso, K. Korematsu v. United States	323.1
Alonso, K. Schenck v. United States	342
Banfield, S. The Bakke case	344
DeVillers, D. Marbury v. Madison	347
Farish, L. Tinker v. Des Moines	342
Fireside, H. New York Times v. Sullivan	342
Fireside, H. Plessy v. Ferguson	342
Freedman, S. Clay v. United States	343
Fuller, S. B. Hazelwood v. Kuhlmeier	344
Herda, D. J. The Dred Scott case	342
Herda, D. J. Furman v. Georgia	345
Herda, D. J. New York Times v. United States	342
Levinson, I. S. Gibbons v. Ogden	343
Miller, J. A. Texas v. Johnson	342
Persico, D. Mapp v. Ohio	345
Persico, D. New Jersey v. T.L.O.	345
Sherrow, V. Cherokee Nation v. Georgia	346
Sherrow, V. Gideon v. Wainwright	345
Thorndike, J. L. Epperson v. Arkansas	345
Trespacz, K. L. Ferrell v. Dallas I.S.D.	344

Landmarks, Literary See Literary landmarks

Lands and peoples **910.3**

Landscape drawing

Arnosky, J. Sketching outdoors in spring **743**

Arnosky, J. Sketching outdoors in summer **743**

Lane, Brian

Crime & detection **364**

Lang, Andrew, 1844-1912

The flower queen's daughter

In The Book of dragons p26-34 **S C**

Sigurd and Fafnir

In The Book of dragons p72-77 **S C**

Stan Bolovan

In The Book of dragons p96-109 **S C**

Lange, Dorothea, 1895-1965

About

Partridge, E. Restless spirit: the life and work of Dorothea Lange **92**

Langford, Michael John, 1933-

Photography (7 and up) **771**

Langhorne, Mary Jo

(ed) Developing an information literacy program K-12. See Developing an information literacy program K-12 **025.5**

Langley, Andrew

Castle at war	940.1
Medieval life	940.1
Renaissance	940.2
The Roman news	937

Langley, Myrtle

Religion **200**

Langston Hughes: poet of the people. Satchell, M.

In Plays of black Americans p19-38 **812.008**

Language and languages

See also Sign language

Language arts

See also Creative writing

The **language** of blood. Coville, B.

In Coville, B. Oddly enough p61-78 **S C**

The **language** of the birds. Schwartz, H.

In Schwartz, H. Next year in Jerusalem p14-18 **296.1**

Lansing, Sherry

See/See also pages in the following book(s):

Lutz, N. J. Business & industry **920**

Laos

Mansfield, S. Laos	959.4
Zickgraf, R. Laos	959.4

The **Laplander's** drum. Olson, A. N.

In Olson, A. N. Ask the bones: scary stories from around the world p53-59 **398.2**

Large fears, little demons. Malmgren, D.

In Center stage **812.008**

Large print books

Adams, R. Watership down	Fic
Avi. Nothing but the truth	Fic
Avi. The true confessions of Charlotte Doyle	Fic
Bauer, J. Squashed	Fic
Bible. Holy Bible: the new King James Version	220.5
Byars, B. C. The burning questions of Bingo Brown	Fic
Clarke, A. C. 2001: a space odyssey	Fic
Cormier, R. We all fall down	Fic
Crutcher, C. Athletic shorts: six short stories	S C
Crutcher, C. Staying fat for Sarah Byrnes	Fic
Dickinson, P. A bone from a dry sea	Fic
Kennedy, J. F. Profiles in courage	920
Lawrence, I. The wreckers	Fic
L'Engle, M. A wrinkle in time	Fic
Levine, E. Freedom's children	323.1

Learn to speak Spanish 8.0. See entry in CD-ROM section, Part 3

Learning, Art of See Study skills

Learning about—the Civil War. Stephens, E. C.
016.973

Learning and scholarship
   See also Education

Learning by heart. Young, R. T.   **Fic**

Learning disabilities
   See also Attention deficit disorder
      Fiction
DeClements, B. 6th grade can really kill you
                        Fic
Philbrick, W. R. Freak the Mighty   **Fic**
Wolff, V. E. Probably still Nick Swansen (7 and up)   **Fic**

Learning from the Dalai Lama. Pandell, K.
294.3

Learning resource centers See Instructional materials centers

Learning the game. Jiménez, F.
   In Jiménez, F. The circuit: stories from the life of a migrant child p84-95   **S C**

Learning Works meet the author series
   Markham, L. Lois Lowry   **92**
   Peters, S. T. Gary Paulsen   **92**

Leaves of grass. Whitman, W.   **811**

Leaving Emma. Brokaw, N. S.   **Fic**

Leaving Fishers. Haddix, M. P.   **Fic**

Leaving home: stories (7 and up)   **808.8**
Includes the following stories: The first day, by E. P. Jones; Dancer, by V. Sears; A gift of laughter, by A. Sherman; Rules of the game, by A. Tan; The circuit, by F. Jiménez; Bad influence, by J. Ortiz Cofer; Dawn, by T. Wynne-Jones; Trip in a summer dress, by A. Sanford; On the rainy river, by T. O'Brien; The setting sun and the rolling world, by C. Mungoshi; Zelzah: a tale from long ago, by N. F. Mazer; "Recitatif", by T. Morrison

Lebanon
   Sheehan, S. Lebanon   **956.92**

Lechón, Daniel
   (il) Mora, P. The desert is my mother. El desierto es mi madre   **811**

Lee, Cherylene
   Hollywood and the pits
      In American dragons p34-47   **810.8**
      In Help wanted: short stories about young people working   **S C**

Lee, Don L. See Madhubuti, Haki R.

Lee, Jeanne
   Jam! (7 and up)   **781.65**

Lee, Jordan
   Coping with braces and other orthodontic work
617.6

Lee, Li-Young, 1957-
   See/See also pages in the following book(s):
   Chiu, C. Lives of notable Asian Americans: literature and education p25-33 (7 and up)
920

Lee, Marie G.
   Necessary roughness (7 and up)   **Fic**
   Summer of my Korean soldier
      In American eyes p37-48   **S C**

See/See also pages in the following book(s):
Chiu, C. Lives of notable Asian Americans: literature and education p89-97 (7 and up)
920

Lee, Robert E. (Robert Edward), 1807-1870
      About
   Kerby, M. Robert E. Lee   **92**
   Marrin, A. Virginia's general: Robert E. Lee and the Civil War (7 and up)   **92**
   See/See also pages in the following book(s):
   Reger, J. P. Civil War generals of the Confederacy p20-45 (7 and up)   **920**

Lee, Spike
      About
   Haskins, J. Spike Lee (7 and up)   **92**
   McDaniel, M. Spike Lee   **92**
   See/See also pages in the following book(s):
   Haskins, J. African American entrepreneurs p151-55   **920**

Lee, Tsung Dao, 1926-
   See/See also pages in the following book(s):
   Yount, L. Asian-American scientists p13-24 (7 and up)   **920**

Leeming, David Adams, 1937-
   (ed) Myths, legends, and folktales of America. See Myths, legends, and folktales of America
398.2

Leeuwenhoek, Antoni van, 1632-1723
      About
   Yount, L. Antoni van Leeuwenhoek   **92**

Left- and right-handedness
      Fiction
   Ritter, J. H. Choosing up sides   **Fic**

The **left-over** reindeer. Gotwalt, H. L. M.
   In The Big book of holiday plays p144-60
812.008

The **legacy.** Aiken, J.
   In Aiken, J. A fit of shivers p134-47
S C

Legal aid
   Sherrow, V. Gideon v. Wainwright (7 and up)
345

Legalized gambling. Hjelmeland, A.   **363.4**

The **legend** of Jesse Owens. Nuwer, H.   **92**

The **legend** of Luke. Jacques, B. See note under Jacques, B. Redwall   **Fic**

The **legend** of Pin Oak. McKissack, P. C.
   In McKissack, P. C. The dark-thirty p3-16
S C

The **legend** of Sleepy Hollow. Irving, W.
   In Irving, W. Rip Van Winkle & The legend of Sleepy Hollow   **Fic**

The **legend** of the black Madonna. Applegarth, M. T.
   In Christmas gif' p18-25   **810.8**

Legendary heroes of the Wild West [series]
   Sanford, W. R. Bill Pickett: African-American rodeo star   **92**
   Sanford, W. R. Calamity Jane: frontier original
92

Legendary labor leaders. Streissguth, T.   **920**

Legends
      See also Folklore; Mythology
   Goddesses, heroes and shamans   **291.1**

Legends—*Continued*
Philip, N. Myths & legends (7 and up)
398.2
Indexes
Index to fairy tales 398.2
Switzerland
Early, M. William Tell 398.2
Legends, Jewish *See* Jewish legends
Legends of Charlemagne. Bulfinch, T.
In Bulfinch, T. Bulfinch's Mythology
291
Legends of the West [series]
Wukovits, J. F. Wyatt Earp 92
Legerdemain *See* Juggling
LeGuin, Ursula *See* Le Guin, Ursula K., 1929-
Lehtinen, Ileana Ros- *See* Ros-Lehtinen, Ileana, 1952-
Leidesdorff, William Alexander, 1810-1848
See/See also pages in the following book(s):
Haskins, J. African American entrepreneurs p36-40 920
Leif Eriksson, fl. 1000
See/See also pages in the following book(s):
Lomask, M. Great lives: exploration p103-12
920
Lelooska, Don
Echoes of the elders 398.2
Contents: The old Owl Witch; The boy and the loon; Raven & Sea Gull; Poogweese; Beaver face
Lemurs
See/See also pages in the following book(s):
Patent, D. H. Back to the wild p50-59
639.9
Lena. Woodson, J. Fic
Lena and Big One Tiger. Hamilton, V.
In Hamilton, V. Her stories p7-10 398.2
Lenape Indians *See* Delaware Indians
The **Lenapes**. Grumet, R. S.
In Indians of North America series
970.004
Lend me your ears 808.85
L'Engle, Madeleine, 1918-
A full house
In A Newbery Christmas p55-70 S C
The glorious impossible 232.9
Many waters. See note under L'Engle, M. A wrinkle in time Fic
Poor little Saturday
In A Newbery Halloween p53-74 S C
A ring of endless light Fic
A swiftly tilting planet. See note under L'Engle, M. A wrinkle in time Fic
A wind in the door. See note under L'Engle, M. A wrinkle in time Fic
A wrinkle in time Fic
Lenin, Vladimir Il´ich, 1870-1924
About
Haney, J. Vladimir Ilich Lenin 92
Lennon, Adrian
Jorge Luis Borges 92
Lenski, Lois, 1893-1974
The Christmas fake
In A Newbery Christmas p87-100 S C

Leon, Juan Ponce de *See* Ponce de Leon, Juan, 1460?-1521
Leonard, Alison
Bronwen and the crows
In The Oxford book of scary tales p98-105
808.8
Leonard, Jim
Crow & Weasel
In Theatre for young audiences p244-83
812.008
Leonard, Thomas M., 1937-
Day by day: the seventies (7 and up)
909.82
Leonardo, da Vinci, 1452-1519
About
Herbert, J. Leonardo da Vinci for kids 92
See/See also pages in the following book(s):
Glubok, S. Great lives: painting p94-105
920
Krull, K. They saw the future p43-49
133.3
Leonardo da Vinci for kids. Herbert, J. 92
Leon's story. Tillage, L. 92
The **leopard** in the rafters. Watts, M.
In The Oxford book of scary tales p132-36
808.8
Leopold, Aldo, 1886-1948
See/See also pages in the following book(s):
Byrnes, P. Environmental pioneers (7 and up)
920
Leprosy
See/See also pages in the following book(s):
Farrell, J. Invisible enemies p45-72 (7 and up)
614.4
Lerman, Louis
The Abolition Flyer
In Plays of black Americans p116-27
812.008
Lesbians
Mastoon, A. The shared heart (7 and up)
305.9
Fiction
Wittlinger, E. Hard love (7 and up) Fic
Woodson, J. The house you pass on the way (7 and up) Fic
Lesley, Craig
(ed) Talking leaves. See Talking leaves
S C
Lessem, Don
Dinosaur worlds 567.9
The iceman 930.1
Jack Horner: living with dinosaurs 92
Lessing, Doris May, 1919-
The old chief Mshlanga
In Somehow tenderness survives p19-35
S C
A **lesson** from the heart. Yabu, J.
In American dragons p161-65 810.8
Lest we forget. Thomas, V. M. 326
Lester, Alison, 1952-
Quicksand pony Fic
Lester, Jim, 1945-
Fallout (7 and up) Fic

Lester, Julius
  Brer Rabbit in Mr. Man's garden
  In From sea to shining sea p212-15
               810.8

  The child
  In Join in p142-49   **S C**
  From slave ship to freedom road   **326**
  Further tales of Uncle Remus. See note under
  Lester, J. The last tales of Uncle Remus
               398.2

  The last tales of Uncle Remus   **398.2**
  Contents: Why the cricket has elbows on his legs; Why the earth is mostly water; The origin of the ocean; Brer Rabbit and Miss Nancy; The old king and the new king; Brer Bear comes to the community; The snake; A ghost story; Brer Bear exposes Brer Rabbit; Brer Rabbit teaches Brer Bear to comb his hair; Why Brer Possum has no hair on his tail; Why Brer Possum loves peace; The baby who loved pumpkins; Impty-Umpty and the blacksmith; The angry woman; Brer Rabbit throws a party; Why Brer Fox's legs are black; How the witch was caught; The man who almost married a witch; Why dogs are tame; How Tinktum Tidy recruited an army for the king; Why guinea fowls are speckled; Why the Guineas stay awake; Brer Fox and the white grapes; Why the hawk likes to eat chickens; The little boy and his dogs; The man and the wild cattle; "Cutta cord-la"; Why Brer Bull growls and grumbles; Brer Rabbit, King Polecat, and the gingercakes; The fool; How Brer Lion lost his hair; The man and the boots; Why the goat has a short tail; Brer Buzzard and Brer Crow; The blacksmith and the Devil; Why chickens scratch in the dirt; Brer Rabbit and Aunt Nancy; The adventures of Simon and Susanna

  Long journey home: stories from black history
               S C
  Contents: Satan on my track; Louis; Ben; The man who was a horse; When freedom came; Long journey home
  More tales of Uncle Remus. See note under
  Lester, J. The last tales of Uncle Remus
               398.2

  Othello (7 and up)   **Fic**
  Spear
  In Places I never meant to be   **S C**
  The tales of Uncle Remus. See note under Lester, J. The last tales of Uncle Remus
               398.2
  To be a slave   **326**
  When the beginning began   **296.1**
  Contents: God learns how to create; God battles the Queen of the Waters; Sun and Moon; Strange creatures; The Angel of Death; Cat and Mouse; Leviathan and Fox; Crown learns a lesson; The grand parade; God makes people; God creates Adam; God creates Woman; Adam marries; The Snake; The Woman, Adam, and the fruit; God confronts Adam, the Woman, and the Snake; God returns to Heaven

Let my people go. McKissack, P. C. **221.9**
Let my people go: African Americans, 1804-1860.
  White, D. G.   **305.8**
Let the circle be unbroken. Taylor, M. D.
               Fic
Let there be life!. Baker, C. W. **778.5**
Let there be light: a book about windows. Giblin,
  J.   **690**
Let's celebrate today. Marks, D. F. **394.26**
Let's go fishing!. Schmidt, G. D. **799.1**
Let's hear it for the girls. Bauermeister, E.
               028.1
Let's visit Indonesia. See Lyle, G. Indonesia
               959.8

A **letter** from Santa Claus. Estes, E.
  In A Newbery Christmas p33-49   **S C**

Letter writing
  Dragisic, P. How to write a letter (7 and up)
               808
  James, E. Sincerely yours   **808**
Lettering
  See also Alphabets
  Fisher, L. E. Alphabet art: thirteen ABCs from around the world   **745.6**
Letters
  Dear author   **028.5**
           Fiction
  Danziger, P. P.S. Longer letter later **Fic**
  Klise, K. Letters from camp   **Fic**
  Skolsky, M. W. Love from your friend, Hannah
               Fic
Letters from a slave girl. Lyons, M. E. **Fic**
Letters from Atlantis. Silverberg, R. **Fic**
Letters from camp. Klise, K.   **Fic**
Letters from Leah. McKean, T.
  In McKean, T. Into the candlelit room and other strange tales p113-70 **S C**
Letters from Rifka. Hesse, K.   **Fic**
Letters from the inside. Marsden, J. **Fic**
Letting in the jungle. Kipling, R.
  In Kipling, R. The jungle books **S C**
Leukemia
          Fiction
  Hughes, M. Hunter in the dark (7 and up)
               Fic
LeVert, Suzanne
  Louisiana
  In Celebrate the states   **973**
  Massachusetts
  In Celebrate the states   **973**
Levi, Enrique Jaramillo *See* Jaramillo Levi, Enrique, 1944-
Levi, Primo, 1919-1987
  See/See also pages in the following book(s):
  Mandell, S. L. Writers of the Holocaust (7 and up)   **940.53**
Levi-Montalcini, Rita, 1909-
  See/See also pages in the following book(s):
  Lindop, L. Scientists and doctors (7 and up)
               920
Leviathan and Fox. Lester, J.
  In Lester, J. When the beginning began p34-38   **296.1**
Levine, Alan H.
  (jt. auth) Cary, E. The rights of students
               344
Levine, Ellen
  Anna Pavlova, genius of the dance **92**
  A fence away from freedom (7 and up)
              940.53
  Freedom's children   **323.1**
Levine, Gail Carson, 1947-
  Ella enchanted   **Fic**
  The princess test   **Fic**
Levine, Herbert M.
  Animal rights (7 and up)   **179**
Levine, Shar
  Fun with your microscope   **502.8**
  The microscope book   **502.8**

Levine, Stuart P., 1968-
The elephant (7 and up)   599.67
The tiger (7 and up)   599.75
Levinson, Isabel Simone
Gibbons v. Ogden (7 and up)   343
Levitin, Sonia, 1934-
Annie's promise   Fic
The cure   Fic
Escape from Egypt (7 and up)   Fic
Journey to America   Fic
The return   Fic
Silver days   Fic
The singing mountain (7 and up)   Fic
Yesterday's child (7 and up)   Fic
Levitt, Michael
(jt. auth) Conner, D. Learn to sail   797.1
Levittown (N.Y.)
Fiction
Conrad, P. Our house   S C
Levy, Marilyn, 1937-
Run for your life (7 and up)   Fic
Levy, Matthys
Earthquake games   551.2
Levy, Patricia Marjorie, 1951-
Belarus   947.8
Ghana   966.7
Liberia   966.62
Sudan   962.4
Lewin, Ted, 1935-
Touch and go   92
Lewington, Anna
People of the rain forests   577.3
Lewis, Barbara A., 1943-
What do you stand for?   170
Lewis, C. S. (Clive Staples), 1898-1963
The adventures of Eustace
  In The Book of dragons p10-15   S C
The horse and his boy. See note under Lewis,
  C. S. The lion, the witch, and the wardrobe
                                       Fic
The last battle. See note under Lewis, C. S. The
  lion, the witch, and the wardrobe   Fic
The lion, the witch, and the wardrobe Fic
The magician's nephew. See note under Lewis,
  C. S. The lion, the witch, and the wardrobe
                                       Fic
Prince Caspian. See note under Lewis, C. S.
  The lion, the witch, and the wardrobe
                                       Fic
The silver chair. See note under Lewis, C. S.
  The lion, the witch, and the wardrobe
                                       Fic
The voyage of the Dawn Treader. See note un-
  der Lewis, C. S. The lion, the witch, and the
  wardrobe   Fic
About
Gormley, B. C.S. Lewis   92
Lewis, Clive Staples *See* Lewis, C. S. (Clive Sta-
  ples), 1898-1963
Lewis, Edmonia, ca. 1843-ca. 1900
See/See also pages in the following book(s):
Katz, W. L. Proudly red and black p37-48
                                       920
Lewis, J. Patrick
Boshblobberbosh   811

Lewis, Jeffrey, 1972-
(jt. auth) Bulloch, I. Cartoons & animation
                                       741.5
Lewis, John L., 1880-1969
See/See also pages in the following book(s):
Streissguth, T. Legendary labor leaders (7 and
  up)   920
Lewis, Meriwether, 1774-1809
(jt. auth) Clark, W. Off the map   978
About
Blumberg, R. The incredible journey of Lewis
  and Clark   978
See/See also pages in the following book(s):
Calvert, P. Great lives: the American frontier
  p226-43   920
Lomask, M. Great lives: exploration p146-57
                                       920
Lewis, Reginald F.
See/See also pages in the following book(s):
Haskins, J. African American entrepreneurs
  p141-46   920
Lewis, Roland
Video (7 and up)   778.59
Lewis, Sinclair, 1885-1951
See/See also pages in the following book(s):
Faber, D. Great lives: American literature p240-
  49   920
Lewis and Clark Expedition (1804-1806)
Blumberg, R. The incredible journey of Lewis
  and Clark   978
Clark, W. Off the map   978
St. George, J. Sacagawea   92
See/See also pages in the following book(s):
Collier, C. The Jeffersonian Republicans: the
  Louisiana Purchase and the war of 1812 p30-
  44   973.4
Fiction
O'Dell, S. Streams to the river, river to the sea
                                       Fic
Lewis-Ferguson, Julinda, 1955-
Alvin Ailey, Jr.: a life in dance   92
Lewis Hayden and the war against slavery.
Strangis, J.   92
Lexington (Mass.), Battle of, 1775
Fiction
Fast, H. April morning (7 and up)   Fic
Li Chi slays the serpent. Pao, K.
  In The Book of dragons p35-38   S C
Liar. Asimov, I.
  In Asimov, I. I, robot   S C
Liar, liar. DeClements, B.   Fic
Liberia
Levy, P. M. Liberia   966.62
Fiction
Zemser, A. B. Beyond the mango tree   Fic
Liberty of speech *See* Freedom of speech
Librarians
Fiction
Bellairs, J. The dark secret of Weatherend
                                       Fic
Libraries
  See also Instructional materials centers;
  Public libraries

Lindop, Edmund—*Continued*
Woodrow Wilson, Franklin D. Roosevelt, Harry
S. Truman 920
Lindop, Laurie
Champions of equality (7 and up) 920
Political leaders (7 and up) 920
Scientists and doctors (7 and up) 920
Lindquist, Susan Hart
Summer soldiers Fic
Lindsay, William, 1956-
Prehistoric life 560
Tyrannosaurus 567.9
Ling, Mary
The Snake book. See The Snake book
597.9
Linnaeus, Carl *See* Linné, Carl von, 1707-1778
Linné, Carl von, 1707-1778
About
Anderson, M. J. Carl Linnaeus 92
Linnea, Sharon
Princess Ka'iulani 92
Linton, Patricia
(jt. auth) Bussell, D. The young dancer
792.8
Linus Pauling and the chemistry of life. Hager, T.
92
Lion and the ostrich chicks [story] Bryan, A.
In Bryan, A. Ashley Bryan's African tales,
uh-huh p115-34 398.2
The **lion** tamer's daughter. Dickinson, P.
In Dickinson, P. The lion tamer's daughter
and other stories p165-298 S C
The **lion-tamer's** daughter and other stories. Dick-
inson, P. S C
The **lion,** the witch, and the wardrobe. Lewis, C.
S. Fic
Lions
Adamson, J. Born free: a lioness of two worlds
599.75
A **lion's** hunger. Turner, A. W. 811
Lipinski, Tara
About
Christopher, M. On the ice with—Tara Lipinski
92
Lippincott, Gary, 1953-
(il) Coville, B. The skull of truth Fic
Lippincott, Kristen, 1954-
Astronomy 520
Lipsyte, Robert
The brave (7 and up) Fic
The chief (7 and up) Fic
The contender (7 and up) Fic
The defender
In Ultimate sports: short stories by outstand-
ing writers for young adults p180-92
S C
Future tense
In Read into the millenium p42-56 S C
In Sixteen: short stories by outstanding writ-
ers for young adults p60-70 S C
Jim Thorpe 92
Michael Jordan 92
One fat summer (7 and up) Fic

Summer rules (7 and up) Fic
Liquids
Mebane, R. C. Water & other liquids
530.4
Liquor problem *See* Drinking of alcoholic bever-
ages
Lisandrelli, Elaine Slivinski, 1951-
Ida B. Wells-Barnett (7 and up) 92
Ignacy Jan Paderewski (7 and up) 92
Lisle, Janet Taylor, 1947-
Forest Fic
List, Barbara A.
(jt. auth) Mount, E. Milestones in science and
technology 509
Listen ear. Jennings, P.
In Jennings, P. Uncovered! p41-56 S C
Listen for the fig tree. Mathis, S. B. Fic
Listen to us. Springer, J. 331.3
Listen up!. Trapani, M. 306.8
Listening for Leroy. Hearne, B. G. Fic
Lister, Maree
England 942
Literacy
Krashen, S. D. The power of reading 028
Literary landmarks
United States
Spangenburg, R. Literature and the arts (7 and
up) 917.3
Literary prizes
See also Caldecott Medal; Carnegie medal;
Kate Greenaway medal; Newbery Medal
Children's books: awards & prizes 028.5
Literary recreations
See also Word games
Literature
See also African Americans in literature;
Children's literature; Indians of North Ameri-
ca—Literature; War in literature; World War,
1939-1945—Literature and the war; Young
adult literature; names of national literatures,
e.g. *English literature*
Bio-bibliography
Authors & artists for young adults 920.003
World authors, 1950-1970 920.003
World authors, 1970-1975 920.003
World authors, 1975-1980 920.003
World authors, 1980-1985 920.003
World authors, 1985-1990 920.003
World authors, 1990-1995 920.003
Collections
Anthology for the earth 808.8
Bearing witness (7 and up) 808.8
The Necessary cat 808.8
The Oxford book of scary tales 808.8
Read all about it! 808.8
Dictionaries
Benet's reader's encyclopedia 803
Brewer's dictionary of phrase and fable
803
History and criticism
See also Authors
Masterpieces of world literature 809

Literature—*Continued*
Stories, plots, etc.
Gillespie, J. T. Juniorplots 4   **028.5**
Masterpieces of world literature   **809**
Study and teaching
Into focus   **028.1**
Literature and technology
Dresang, E. T. Radical change   **028.5**
Literature and the arts. Spangenburg, R.
    917.3
Literature connections to American history, 7-12.
    Adamson, L. G.   **016.973**
Literature connections to world history, 7-12.
    Adamson, L. G.   **016.9**
Literature for today's young adults. Donelson, K.
    L.   **028.5**
Literatures of the American Indian. Ruoff, A. L.
    B.
    In Indians of North America series
    970.004

Lithuania
    Kagda, S. Lithuania   **947.9**
Littell, Mary Ann
    Heroin drug dangers   **362.29**
Littke, Lael
    Haunted sister (7 and up)   **Fic**
Little, Jean, 1932-
    The belonging place   **Fic**
Little, Malcolm *See* Malcolm X, 1925-1965
Little, Marjorie
    Sexually transmitted diseases (7 and up)
    616.95
Little bear
    In The Dancing fox: Arctic folktales p98-104
    398.2
Little Bighorn, Battle of the, 1876
    Ferrell, N. W. The Battle of the Little Bighorn
    in American history   **973.8**
    Viola, H. J. It is a good day to die   **973.8**
Little black balls. Jennings, P.
    In Jennings, P. Unbearable! p7-21   **S C**
The **little** boy and his dogs. Lester, J.
    In Lester, J. The last tales of Uncle Remus
    p102-10   **398.2**
Little Crow, Sioux Chief, d. 1863
    See/See also pages in the following book(s):
    Brown, D. A. Bury my heart at Wounded Knee
    p38-65 (7 and up)   **970.004**
Little Girl and Buh Rabby. Hamilton, V.
    In Hamilton, V. Her stories p3-6   **398.2**
Little Ida's flowers. Andersen, H. C.
    In Andersen, H. C. The little mermaid and
    other fairy tales p27-34   **S C**
Little lost robot. Asimov, I.
    In Asimov, I. I, robot   **S C**
The **little** match girl. Andersen, H. C.
    In Andersen, H. C. The little mermaid and
    other fairy tales p91-94   **S C**
The **little** mermaid. Andersen, H. C.
    In Andersen, H. C. The little mermaid and
    other fairy tales p35-60   **S C**

The **little** mermaid. Osborne, M. P.
    In Osborne, M. P. Mermaid tales from around
    the world p71-77   **398.2**
The **little** mermaid and other fairy tales. Andersen,
    H. C.   **S C**
Little Mose. Wyeth, S. D.
    In Wyeth, S. D. Vampire bugs: stories con-
    jured from the past p8-18   **S C**
The **little** prince. Saint-Exupéry, A. de   **Fic**
Little scams. Soto, G.
    In Soto, G. Petty crimes   **S C**
Little squirt. Jennings, P.
    In Jennings, P. Unmentionable! p31-35
    S C
A **little** tiger in the Chinese night. Zhang, S. N.
    92
Little Well-Read Riding Hood. Brooke, W. J.
    In Brooke, W. J. Teller of tales p103-18
    S C
Littlefield, Daniel C.
    Revolutionary citizens (7 and up)   **305.8**
Litwin, Laura Baskes
    Benjamin Banneker   **92**
Liungman, Carl G., 1938-
    Dictionary of symbols (7 and up)   **302.2**
Liuzzo, Viola, 1925-1965
About
    Siegel, B. Murder on the highway: the Viola
    Liuzzo story   **92**
Lives and legends of the saints. Armstrong, C.
    920
Lives and works: young adult authors   **810.3**
The **lives** of Christopher Chant. Jones, D. W.
    Fic
Lives of North American birds. Kaufman, K.
    598
Lives of notable Asian Americans: literature and
    education. Chiu, C.   **920**
Lives of the presidents. Krull, K.   **920**
Lives: poems about famous Americans
    811.008
Living for the future [series]
    Fyson, N. L. World population   **304.6**
Living in the world. Cann, K.   **158**
Living in two worlds. Kosof, A.   **325.73**
Living lab: plants. See entry in CD-ROM section,
    Part 3
Living on Mars. Cole, M. D.   **629.4**
Living together *See* Unmarried couples
Living with albinism. Landau, E.   **616.5**
Living with the weather [series]
    Dunn, A. Fog, mist, and smog   **551.5**
Livingston, Myra Cohn
    Cricket never does   **811**
    (ed) I am writing a poem about—a game of po-
    etry. See I am writing a poem about—a game
    of poetry   **811.008**
    (ed) I like you, if you like me: poems of friend-
    ship. See I like you, if you like me: poems of
    friendship   **808.81**
    (comp) A Time to talk. See A Time to talk
    808.81

Livingston, Robert R., 1746-1813
See/See also pages in the following book(s):
Levinson, I. S. Gibbons v. Ogden (7 and up)
343

Livingstone, David, 1813-1873
See/See also pages in the following book(s):
Lomask, M. Great lives: exploration p158-69
920

Livo, Norma J., 1929-
Folk stories of the Hmong **398.2**
Includes the following stories: The beginning of the world; Legend of the rice seed; How seeds came again into the world and why dogs eat feces droppings; The origin of the shaman; Another age of happiness; Creation, flood, naming story; Why monkey and man do not live together; Why animals cannot talk; Why people eat three meals a day and why doodle bugs roll balls of dung; Why farmers have to work so hard; Why birds are never hungry; Why Hmong are forbidden to drink mother's milk; Why the Hmong live on mountains; Shoa and his fire; The story of the owl; A bird couple's vow; The monkeys and the grasshoppers; Sister-in-law Yer and the tiger: how a wise woman tricked the tiger; Zeej Choj Kim, the lazy man; Pumpkin seed and the snake; The handsome husband; Ngao Nao and Shee Na; The tiger steals Nkauj Ncoom; The orphan and the monkeys; The orphan boy and his wife; The tigers steal Nou Plai's wife, Ntxawm; Gwa and Uo and their two fish wives

The **Lizard** husband
In Hearne, B. G. Beauties and beasts p35-38
398.2

Lizon, Karen Helene
Colonial American holidays and entertainment
394.26

La **Llorona**, the weeping woman. Hayes, J.
In From sea to shining sea p331-35
810.8

Llosa, Mario Vargas *See* Vargas Llosa, Mario, 1936-

Lloyd, Elizabeth Jane
Watercolor still life
In The DK art school series **751**

Loans
See also Public debts

Lobbying
Archer, J. Special interests (7 and up) **324**
Seo, D. Generation react (7 and up) **303.4**

Lobel, Anita, 1934-
No pretty pictures (7 and up) **92**

Lobosco, Michael L.
Mental math workout **510.7**

Local news. Soto, G. **S C**

Locke, Ian
The wheel and how it changed the world
621.8

Locked in time. Duncan, L. **Fic**

Lockouts *See* Strikes

Loeffelbein, Robert L.
The recreation handbook **793**

Loeper, John J.
Going to school in 1776 **370.9**

Lofting, Hugh, 1886-1947
The galloping sleigh
In A Newbery Christmas p153-61 **S C**

Logan, John, 1923-1987
Christianity **200**

Logging *See* Lumber and lumbering

Lomask, Milton
Great lives: exploration **920**

London, Jack, 1876-1916
The call of the wild **Fic**
White Fang **Fic**
About
Dyer, D. Jack London (7 and up) **92**
See/See also pages in the following book(s):
Faber, D. Great lives: American literature p141-50 **920**

London (England)
Fiction
Cooney, C. B. The terrorist (7 and up) **Fic**
Newman, R. The case of the Baker Street Irregular **Fic**
Paton Walsh, J. Fireweed **Fic**
Pullman, P. The ruby in the smoke (7 and up)
Fic
Pullman, P. Shadow in the north (7 and up)
Fic
Pullman, P. The tiger in the well (7 and up)
Fic
Ure, J. Plague (7 and up) **Fic**

Lonergan, Janet Gill- *See* Gill-Lonergan, Janet

Long, Crawford W., 1815-1878
See/See also pages in the following book(s):
Fradin, D. B. "We have conquered pain"
617.9

Long journey home. Lester, J.
In Lester, J. Long journey home: stories from black history p129-47 **S C**

Long journey home: stories from black history. Lester, J. **S C**

The **long** patrol. Jacques, B. See note under Jacques, B. Redwall **Fic**

The **long** road to Gettysburg. Murphy, J.
973.7

The **long** season of rain. Kim, H. **Fic**

A **long** way from Chicago. Peck, R. **Fic**

The **longest** summer on record. Conrad, P.
In Conrad, P. Our house p29-39 **S C**

Longevity
See also Old age

Longfellow, Henry Wadsworth, 1807-1882
Henry Wadsworth Longfellow **811**
See/See also pages in the following book(s):
Faber, D. Great lives: American literature p40-48 **920**

Longshore, David
Encyclopedia of hurricanes, typhoons and cyclones (7 and up) **551.55**

Longstreet, James, 1821-1904
See/See also pages in the following book(s):
Reger, J. P. Civil War generals of the Confederacy p62-81 (7 and up) **920**

Longwalker
Fiction
Harrell, B. O. Longwalker's journey **Fic**

Longwalker's journey. Harrell, B. O. **Fic**

Lonna and Cat Woman. Hamilton, V.
In Hamilton, V. Her stories p56-60
398.2

Look at your body [series]
Parker, S. Reproduction and growth **612.6**

Look inside cross-sections [series]
Butterfield, M. Ships **623.8**

Lueders, Edward
(comp) Reflections on a gift of watermelon pickle . . . and other modern verse. See Reflections on a gift of watermelon pickle . . . and other modern verse **811.008**

Luella and the tame parrot. Hamilton, V.
In Hamilton, V. Her stories p75-77
398.2

Lukes, Bonnie L.
The Boston Massacre (7 and up) **973.3**

Lum, Darrell H. Y.
Yahk fahn, Auntie
In American dragons p5-13 **810.8**

Lum, Roseline NgCheong- *See* NgCheong-Lum, Roseline, 1962-

Lumbee Indians
Dial, A. The Lumbee
In Indians of North America series
970.004

Lumber and lumbering
Smith, R. In the forest with the elephants
599.67

Fiction
Crew, L. Fire on the wind **Fic**

Lunar bases
Cole, M. D. Moon base **629.4**

Lunar expeditions *See* Space flight to the moon

Lundy, Benjamin, 1789-1839
See/See also pages in the following book(s):
Lilley, S. R. Fighters against American slavery p25-35 (7 and up) **920**

Lungs
Parker, S. The lungs and respiratory system
612.2
The **lungs** and respiratory system. Parker, S.
612.2

Lunsford, Cin Forshay- *See* Forshay-Lunsford, Cin

Lupe and the forgetful family. Gorog, J.
In Gorog, J. When nobody's home p21-25
S C

Lurie, Jon
Fundamental snowboarding **796.9**

Lusane, Clarence, 1953-
No easy victories (7 and up) **323.1**

Lustig, Arnošt
See/See also pages in the following book(s):
Mandell, S. L. Writers of the Holocaust (7 and up) **940.53**

Luther, Martin, 1483-1546
About
Booth, E. P. Martin Luther (7 and up) **92**
The **lutin**. San Souci, R.
In San Souci, R. A terrifying taste of short & shivery p39-42 **398.2**

Lutkenhoff, Marlene
(ed) SPINAbilities. See SPINAbilities **616.8**
The **Luttrell** village. Sancha, S. **942.03**

Lutz, Norma Jean
Business & industry **920**

Luxembourg
Sheehan, P. Luxembourg **949.35**

Lyddie. Paterson, K. **Fic**

Lying *See* Truthfulness and falsehood

Lyle, Garry
Hong Kong **951.25**
Indonesia **959.8**

Lyman, Darryl, 1944-
Holocaust rescuers **920**

Lyme disease
Veggeberg, S. Lyme disease (7 and up)
616.9

Lynch, Anne, 1941-
Great buildings **720**

Lynch, Chris
Bearing, Paul
In Night terrors **S C**
Blood relations. See note under Lynch, C. Mick
Fic
Cocked & locked
In Twelve shots: outstanding short stories about guns p25-43 **S C**
Dog eat dog. See note under Lynch, C. Mick
Fic
Extreme Elvin (7 and up) **Fic**
The hobbyist
In Ultimate sports: short stories by outstanding writers for young adults p315-33
S C
Iceman (7 and up) **Fic**
Lie, no lie
In Places I never meant to be **S C**
Mick (7 and up) **Fic**
Political timber (7 and up) **Fic**
Shadow boxer (7 and up) **Fic**
Slot machine (7 and up) **Fic**
Whitechurch (7 and up) **Fic**

Lynch, Patricia Ann
Christianity (7 and up) **200**

Lynn, Elizabeth Cook- *See* Cook-Lynn, Elizabeth

Lyon, Mary, 1797-1849
About
Rosen, D. A fire in her bones: the story of Mary Lyon **92**

Lyons, Mary E.
Catching the fire: Philip Simmons, blacksmith
92
Keeping secrets (7 and up) **920**
Letters from a slave girl **Fic**
Painting dreams: Minnie Evans, visionary artist
92
Sorrow's kitchen: the life and folklore of Zora Neale Hurston **92**
Starting home: the story of Horace Pippin, painter **92**
Stitching stars: the story quilts of Harriet Powers **92**

M

Mabinogion
See/See also pages in the following book(s):
Bulfinch, T. Bulfinch's Mythology **291.1**
Ross, A. Druids, gods & heroes from Celtic mythology p65-81 **299**

MacArthur, Douglas, 1880-1964
About
Feinberg, B. S. Douglas MacArthur **92**

Magellan, Ferdinand, 1480?-1521
About
Macdonald, F. Magellan   910.4
See/See also pages in the following book(s):
Fritz, J. Around the world in a hundred years
p95-113   910.4
Lomask, M. Great lives: exploration p177-90
920

Magic
Fiction
Brittain, B. The wish giver   Fic
Hobbs, W. Kokopelli's flute   Fic
Ibbotson, E. Which witch?   Fic
Shusterman, N. The eyes of Kid Midas Fic
Vande Velde, V. Curses, Inc. and other stories
S C
Wrede, P. C. Book of enchantments   S C
Yolen, J. The Pictish child   Fic
Yolen, J. The wizard's map   Fic
Magic. Eldin, P.   793.8
Magic & mischief. Climo, S.   398.2
Magic and perception. Friedhoffer, R.   793.8
The **magic** ball. Finger, C. J.
In A Newbery Halloween p101-10   S C
Magic bow. Singer, M.
In Stay true: short stories for strong girls
S C
The **magic** seed. Jaffe, N.
In Jaffe, N. The cow of no color: riddle sto-
ries and justice tales from around the
world p55-58   398.2
The **magic-stealer**. Sherman, J.
In Vampires: a collection of original stories
p99-120   S C
The **magic** tree. Krishnaswami, U.
In Krishnaswami, U. Shower of gold: girls
and women in the stories of India p94-99
398.2

Magic tricks
Eldin, P. Magic   793.8
Friedhoffer, R. Magic and perception 793.8
Oxlade, C. Science magic with magnets
793.8
Severn, B. Bill Severn's best magic   793.8
Magicians
Eldin, P. Magic   793.8
Folklore
Sherman, J. Merlin's kin   398.2
The **magician's** fellow. Hamilton, V.
In Hamilton, V. The dark way p126-31
398.2
The **magician's** nephew. Lewis, C. S. See note
under Lewis, C. S. The lion, the witch, and
the wardrobe   Fic
Magill, Frank Northen, 1907-
(ed) Masterpieces of world literature. See Mas-
terpieces of world literature   809
Magill's choice [series]
American Indian biographies   920
Magnesium
Uttley, C. Magnesium
In The Elements [Benchmark Bks.]   546

Magnets
Oxlade, C. Science magic with magnets
793.8
Maguire, Gregory
Athlete
In Trapped!: cages of mind and body p119-27
S C
Beyond the fringe
In A Glory of unicorns p45-57   S C
The good liar   Fic
Mahony Miller, Bertha E. *See* Miller, Bertha E.
Mahony, 1882-1969
Mahy, Margaret
Aliens in the family   Fic
The changeover   Fic
Fingers on the back of the neck
In Don't read this! and other tales of the un-
natural p7-22   S C
The greatest show off earth   Fic
Maid Marian (Legendary character)
Fiction
Tomlinson, T. Child of the May   Fic
Tomlinson, T. The Forestwife   Fic
Maine
Kent, D. Maine
In America the beautiful, second series
973
Description
Murphy, J. Into the deep forest with Henry Da-
vid Thoreau   974.1
Fiction
Irwin, H. The original Freddie Ackerman
Fic
LaFaye, A. Strawberry Hill   Fic
Natural history
See Natural history—Maine
Maizon at Blue Hill. Woodson, J. See note under
Woodson, J. Last summer with Maizon
Fic
Major, Clarence
My mother and Mitch
In Rites of passage p191-202   S C
Major, John S., 1942-
The Silk Route   950
Major, Kevin, 1949-
Three people and two seals
In Sixteen: short stories by outstanding writ-
ers for young adults p113-24   S C
Major unsolved crimes. Powell, P.   364.1
Major world nations [series]
Anthony, S. West Indies   972.9
Barnes-Svarney, P. Zimbabwe   968.91
Bender, E. Brazil   981
Canesso, C. South Africa   968.06
Creed, A. Uganda   967.61
Dwyer, C. Chile   982
Haynes, T. Colombia   986.1
James, R. S. Mozambique   967.9
Lyle, G. Hong Kong   951.25
Lyle, G. Indonesia   959.8
McCulla, P. E. Tanzania   967.8
Rummel, J. Mexico   972
Stefoff, R. Japan   952.04
Stefoff, R. West Bank/Gaza Strip   956.95

Mammals—*Continued*

Whitaker, J. O., Jr. National Audubon Society field guide to North American mammals
599

Encyclopedias

Encyclopedia of mammals 599
National Geographic book of mammals 599
Mammals 599
Man *See* Human beings

Influence on nature

See Human influence on nature

Origin

See Human origins

Man, Fossil *See* Fossil hominids
Man, Prehistoric *See* Prehistoric peoples
The **man** and the boots. Lester, J.
In Lester, J. The last tales of Uncle Remus p133-36 398.2
The **man** and the wild cattle. Lester, J.
In Lester, J. The last tales of Uncle Remus p110-14 398.2
Man Bear. Bruchac, J.
In Bruchac, J. When the Chenoo howls
398.2
A **man** called Appleseed. Cochran, B. H.
In The Big book of holiday plays p290-99
812.008
The **man-child**. Rabin, A.
In Theatre for young audiences p364-94
812.008
The **man** I killed. O'Brien, T.
In Who do you think you are? p146-51
S C
The **man** in the ceiling. Feiffer, J. **Fic**
A **man** like Lincoln. McGowan, J.
In The Big book of holiday plays p196-208
812.008
The **man** of influence. Fleischman, P.
In Fleischman, P. Graven images p61-85
S C
In A Newbery Halloween p111-31 S C
Man-of-war, Stephen Biesty's cross-sections. Biesty, S. 359.1
The **man** who almost lived forever. McCaughrean, G.
In McCaughrean, G. The golden hoard: myths and legends of the world p100-02
398.2
The **man** who almost married a witch. Lester, J.
In Lester, J. The last tales of Uncle Remus p71-76 398.2
The **man** who loved clowns. Wood, J. R. **Fic**
The **man** who married a seagull. Norman, H.
In Norman, H. The girl who dreamed only geese, and other tales of the Far North
398.2
The **man** who was a horse. Lester, J.
In Lester, J. Long journey home: stories from black history p89-103 S C
The **man** who was Poe. Avi **Fic**
The **man** with a tree on his head. Fairman, T.
In Fairman, T. Bury my bones but keep my words p40-53 398.2

The **man** with the twisted lip. Doyle, Sir A. C.
In Doyle, Sir A. C. Adventures of Sherlock Holmes S C
In Doyle, Sir A. C. The complete Sherlock Holmes S C
The **man** without a face. Holland, I. **Fic**
Manabozo. Hamilton, V.
In Hamilton, V. The dark way p27-31
398.2
Mana's story. Dickinson, P. See note under Dickinson, P. Suth's story **Fic**
Manatees
Price-Groff, C. The manatee (7 and up)
599.5
Manco Capac and the rod of gold. Delacre, L.
In Delacre, L. Golden tales p55-57 398.2
Mandela, Nelson

About

Finlayson, R. Nelson Mandela 92
See/See also pages in the following book(s):
Rasmussen, R. K. Modern African political leaders p107-23 (7 and up) 920
Mandela, Winnie
See/See also pages in the following book(s):
Price-Groff, C. Twentieth-century women political leaders (7 and up) 920
Mandelbaum, Allen, 1926-
(ed) Three centuries of American poetry, 1623-1923. See Three centuries of American poetry, 1623-1923 811.008
Mandelbrot, Benoit B.
See/See also pages in the following book(s):
Henderson, H. Modern mathematicians (7 and up) 920
Mandell, Muriel, 1921-
Simple experiments in time with everyday materials 529
Mandell, Sherri Lederman
Writers of the Holocaust (7 and up)
940.53
Mandy. Yolen, J.
In Yolen, J. Here there be ghosts p73-83
810.8
Manes, Stephen, 1949-
An almost perfect game **Fic**
Manhattan Project
Cohen, D. The Manhattan Project (7 and up)
623.4
Maniac Magee. Spinelli, J. **Fic**
Manic-depressive illness
See also Depression (Psychology)
Mankiller, Wilma

About

Schwarz, M. Wilma Mankiller 92
See/See also pages in the following book(s):
Kallen, S. A. Native American chiefs and warriors (7 and up) 920
Lindop, L. Champions of equality (7 and up)
920
Price-Groff, C. Twentieth-century women political leaders (7 and up) 920

Marine animals—*Continued*
Parker, S. Seashore   **577.7**
Sea searcher's handbook   **577.7**
Taylor, L. R. Creeps from the deep   **578.7**

Marine aquariums
Burgess, W. Dr. Burgess's atlas of marine aquarium fishes   **639.34**

Marine biology
Gowell, E. T. Fountains of life   **577.7**
Bredeson, C. Tide pools   **577.6**
Carson, R. The edge of the sea (7 and up)   **577.7**
Erickson, J. Marine geology (7 and up)   **551.46**
Goodman, S. Ultimate field trip 3   **577.6**
Kricher, J. C. Peterson first guide to seashores   **577.7**
Meinkoth, N. A. The Audubon Society field guide to North American seashore creatures   **592**
Ricciuti, E. R. Ocean   **577.7**
Taylor, L. R. Creeps from the deep   **578.7**
World Book looks at the sea and its marvels   **577.7**

Marine ecology
Cerullo, M. M. Coral reef   **577.7**
Endangered oceans: opposing viewpoints (7 and up)   **577.7**
Fredericks, A. D. Exploring the oceans   **551.46**
Gowell, E. T. Fountains of life   **577.7**
Pringle, L. P. Coral reefs   **577.7**
Sayre, A. P. Coral reef   **577.7**
Sea searcher's handbook   **577.7**
Wroble, L. A. The oceans (7 and up)   **577.7**

Marine geology *See* Submarine geology
Marine geology. Erickson, J.   **551.46**

Marine mammals
   See also Dolphins; Porpoises; Seals (Animals); Whales

Marine plants
Parker, S. Seashore   **577.7**

Marine pollution
   See also Oil spills
Endangered oceans: opposing viewpoints (7 and up)   **577.7**
Wroble, L. A. The oceans (7 and up)   **577.7**

Mariners (Baseball team) *See* Seattle Mariners (Baseball team)

Marino, Jan
The day that Elvis came to town (7 and up)   **Fic**
For the love of Pete   **Fic**

Maris, Roger, 1934-1985
See/See also pages in the following book(s):
Gilbert, T. W. Damn Yankees (7 and up)   **796.357**

Marius, Gaius, ca. 157-86 B.C.
See/See also pages in the following book(s):
Nardo, D. Rulers of ancient Rome (7 and up)   **920**

Mark, Jan
No-good Claus
   In The Oxford book of scary tales p123-29   **808.8**

Mark, Joan T., 1937-
Margaret Mead (7 and up)   **92**
Mark Twain and Huckleberry Finn. Ross, S.   **92**
Mark Twain himself. Meltzer, M.   **92**
The **market** guide for young writers. Henderson, K.   **808**

Markham, Lois
Lois Lowry   **92**

Markle, Sandra, 1946-
After the spill   **363.7**
Discovering graph secrets   **001.4**

Markley, Oliver W.
(ed) 21st century earth: opposing viewpoints. See 21st century earth: opposing viewpoints   **303.49**

Markowitz, Harvey
(ed) American Indian biographies. See American Indian biographies   **920**

Marks, Alan
(il) Goodall, J. With love   **599.8**

Marks, Diana F.
Let's celebrate today   **394.26**

Marley, Bob
About
Dolan, S. Bob Marley   **92**
Marlfox. Jacques, B. See note under Jacques, B. Redwall   **Fic**

Marmots
Fiction
Seidler, T. Mean Margaret   **Fic**

Márquez, Gabriel García *See* García Márquez, Gabriel, 1928-

Marriage
   See also Divorce; Family; Remarriage; Weddings
Marriage and divorce (7 and up)   **306.8**

Marriage, Interracial *See* Interracial marriage

Marriage and divorce (7 and up)   **306.8**

Marrin, Albert, 1936-
1812: the war nobody won   **973.5**
Commander in Chief Abraham Lincoln and the Civil War (7 and up)   **973.7**
Cowboys, Indians, and gunfighters   **978**
Empires lost and won (7 and up)   **979**
Plains warrior: Chief Quanah Parker and the Comanches (7 and up)   **92**
The sea king: Sir Francis Drake and his times (7 and up)   **92**
Terror of the Spanish Main: Sir Henry Morgan and his buccaneers (7 and up)   **92**
Unconditional surrender (7 and up)   **973.7**
Virginia's general: Robert E. Lee and the Civil War (7 and up)   **92**

Mars (Planet)
Skurzynski, G. Discover Mars   **523.4**
Exploration
Cole, M. D. Living on Mars   **629.4**
Wunsch, S. T. The adventures of Sojourner   **629.43**

Masada Site (Israel)—*Continued*
Fiction
Miklowitz, G. D. Masada (7 and up)   **Fic**

Masai (African people)
Quintana, A. The baboon king (7 and up)
    Fic

Fiction
Smith, R. Thunder cave   **Fic**

Masih, Iqbal, d. 1995
About
Kuklin, S. Iqbal Masih and the crusaders against
  child slavery (7 and up)   **331.3**
See/See also pages in the following book(s):
Parker, D. L. Stolen dreams   **331.3**

Masks (Facial)
Doney, M. Masks   **745.59**
Finley, C. The art of African masks   **391**

Masoff, Joy, 1951-
Emergency!   **616.02**
Fire!   **628.9**

Mason, Bob
About
Montgomery, S. The snake scientist   **597.9**

Mason, Francis
(jt. auth) Balanchine, G. 101 stories of the great
  ballets   **792.8**

The **masque** of the Red Death. Poe, E. A.
  In Poe, E. A. Tales of Edgar Allan Poe p117-
  25   **S C**

Mass, Wendy, 1967-
Stonehenge (7 and up)   **936.2**
Teen drug abuse (7 and up)   **362.29**

Mass communication *See* Communication; Telecommunication

Mass media
Edgar, K. J. Everything you need to know about
  media violence   **303.6**
Mass media: opposing viewpoints (7 and up)
  302.23
Media violence: opposing viewpoints (7 and up)
  303.6
See/See also pages in the following book(s):
Teens at risk: opposing viewpoints p143-53 (7
  and up)   **362.7**

Mass media: opposing viewpoints (7 and up)
  302.23

Massachusetts
LeVert, S. Massachusetts
  In Celebrate the states   **973**
McNair, S. Massachusetts
  In America the beautiful, second series
  973
Fiction
Paterson, K. Lyddie   **Fic**
  History—1600-1775, Colonial period
Bowen, G. Stranded at Plimoth Plantation, 1626
  974.4
Collier, C. Pilgrims and Puritans, 1620-1676
  974.4
Pilgrim voices   **974.4**
See/See also pages in the following book(s):
IlgenFritz, E. Anne Hutchinson   **92**
History—1600-1775, Colonial period—Fiction
Jacobs, P. S. James Printer   **Fic**

Lasky, K. A journey to the New World
  Fic
Walter, M. P. Second daughter   **Fic**

Mast, Edward
Jungalbook [play]
  In Theatre for young audiences p478-517
  812.008

The **master** puppeteer. Paterson, K.   **Fic**
The **masterharper** of Pern. McCaffrey, A. See
  note under McCaffrey, A. [The Pern series]
  Fic
Masterpieces of world literature   **809**
Masters, Nancy Robinson *See* Robinson Masters,
  Nancy
Masters of art [series]
Corrain, L. The art of the Renaissance
  709.02
Loria, S. Pablo Picasso   **92**
Pozzi, G. Chagall   **92**

Mastodon
Giblin, J. The mystery of the mammoth bones
  569

Mastoon, Adam
The shared heart (7 and up)   **305.9**

Matajuro's training. Kimmel, E. A.
  In Kimmel, E. A. Sword of the samurai p31-
  39   **Fic**

Matas, Carol, 1949-
After the war (7 and up)   **Fic**
The garden (7 and up)   **Fic**
Greater than angels (7 and up)   **Fic**
In my enemy's house (7 and up)   **Fic**

Matcheck, Diane
The sacrifice (7 and up)   **Fic**

Materia medica
  See also Drugs

Math and mathematicians. Bruno, L. C.   **920**
Math for the real world. See entry in CD-ROM
  section, Part 3
Math games for middle school. Salvadori, M. G.
  510.7
Math wizardry for kids. Kenda, M.   **793.7**

Mathabane, Mark
Kaffir boy [excerpt]
  In Somehow tenderness survives p87-103
  S C

Mathematical models
  See also Computer simulation
Mathematical recreations
Kenda, M. Math wizardry for kids   **793.7**
Mathematicians
  See also Women mathematicians
Bruno, L. C. Math and mathematicians   **920**
Collier, B. Charles Babbage and the engines of
  perfection (7 and up)   **92**
Henderson, H. Modern mathematicians (7 and
  up)   **920**
Notable mathematicians (7 and up)   **920**
    Biography—Encyclopedias
Biographical encyclopedia of mathematicians
  920.003

Mayo, Edith
(ed) The Smithsonian book of the First Ladies.
See The Smithsonian book of the First Ladies
920

Mayo, Margaret, 1935-
Mythical birds & beasts from many lands
398.2
Contents: The horse that could fly; Don't ever look at a mermaid; The unicorn who walks alone; The green-clawed thunderbird; The fish at dragon's gate; Jamie and the biggest, first, and father of all sea serpents; How music came to the world; The one and only minotaur; Three fabulous eggs; Bird of the sun

The **maze.** Hobbs, W. **Fic**

Mazer, Anne, 1953-
Transformations of Cindy R.
In Stay true: short stories for strong girls
S C

Mazer, Harry, 1925-
The beautiful thing
In Night terrors **S C**
The dog in the freezer: three novellas **S C**
Contents: My life as a boy; Puppy love; The dog in the freezer
Falling off the Empire State Building
In Ultimate sports: short stories by outstanding writers for young adults p302-13
S C
Furlough—1944
In Sixteen: short stories by outstanding writers for young adults p83-92 **S C**
The last mission (7 and up) **Fic**
The rat children
In Places I never meant to be **S C**
Snow bound (7 and up) **Fic**
Until the day he died
In Twelve shots: outstanding short stories about guns p179-200 **S C**
When the phone rang (7 and up) **Fic**
Who is Eddie Leonard? (7 and up) **Fic**
The wild kid **Fic**
(jt. auth) Mazer, N. F. The solid gold kid
Fic
(ed) Twelve shots: outstanding short stories about guns. See Twelve shots: outstanding short stories about guns **S C**

Mazer, Norma Fox, 1931-
After the rain (7 and up) **Fic**
Carmella, Adelina, and Florry
In Help wanted: short stories about young people working **S C**
Crazy Fish (7 and up) **Fic**
Cutthroat
In Ultimate sports: short stories by outstanding writers for young adults p148-59
S C
Going fishing
In Stay true: short stories for strong girls
S C
The house on Buffalo Street
In Night terrors **S C**
I, hungry Hannah Cassandra Glen . . .
In Sixteen: short stories by outstanding writers for young adults p2-14 **S C**
Meeting the mugger
In Places I never meant to be **S C**
Out of control (7 and up) **Fic**
Silver (7 and up) **Fic**
The solid gold kid (7 and up) **Fic**

Taking Terri Mueller **Fic**
What happened in the cemetery
In Visions: nineteen short stories by outstanding writers for young adults p64-75
S C
Zelzah: a tale from long ago
In Leaving home: stories p179-99 **808.8**

McAuliffe, Christa
About
Jeffrey, L. S. Christa McAuliffe **92**

McCaffery, Laura Hibbets
Building an ESL collection for young adults
016.4

McCaffrey, Anne
All the Weyrs of Pern. See note under McCaffrey, A. [The Pern series] **Fic**
Black horses for the king (7 and up) **Fic**
The chronicles of Pern: first fall. See note under McCaffrey, A. [The Pern series] **Fic**
The dolphins of Pern. See note under McCaffrey, A. [The Pern series] **Fic**
Dragondrums. See note under McCaffrey, A. [The Pern series] **Fic**
Dragonflight. See note under McCaffrey, A. [The Pern series] **Fic**
Dragonholder. See note under McCaffrey, A. [The Pern series] **Fic**
Dragonquest. See note under McCaffrey, A. [The Pern series] **Fic**
Dragonriders of Pern. See note under McCaffrey, A. [The Pern series] **Fic**
Dragonsdawn. See note under McCaffrey, A. [The Pern series] **Fic**
Dragonseye. See note under McCaffrey, A. [The Pern series] **Fic**
Dragonsinger. See note under McCaffrey, A. [The Pern series] **Fic**
Dragonsong. See note under McCaffrey, A. [The Pern series] **Fic**
If wishes were horses (7 and up) **Fic**
The masterharper of Pern. See note under McCaffrey, A. [The Pern series] **Fic**
Moreta: Dragonlady of Pern. See note under McCaffrey, A. [The Pern series] **Fic**
Nerilka's story. See note under McCaffrey, A. [The Pern series] **Fic**
Pegasus in flight (7 and up) **Fic**
[The Pern series] (7 and up) **Fic**
Renegades of Pern. See note under McCaffrey, A. [The Pern series] **Fic**
White dragon. See note under McCaffrey, A. [The Pern series] **Fic**

McCall, Mary Reilly
(ed) Women's almanac. See Women's almanac
305.4

McCampbell, Darlene Z., 1942-
(ed) Bearing witness. See Bearing witness
808.8
(ed) Leaving home: stories. See Leaving home: stories **808.8**
(comp) Who do you think you are? See Who do you think you are? **S C**

McCarthy, Colin, 1951-
Reptile **597.9**

McDonald, Mary Ann, 1956——Continued
Rattlesnakes   597.9
McElmeel, Sharron L.
100 most popular children's authors   810.3
(jt. auth) Simpson, C. M. Internet for schools
004.6

McGaffey, Leta
Honduras   972.83
McGowan, Gary
(jt. auth) Hansen, J. Breaking ground, breaking
silence   974.7
McGowan, Jane
Bunnies and bonnets
In The Big book of holiday plays p279-89
812.008

A man like Lincoln
In The Big book of holiday plays p196-208
812.008

Mother for mayor
In The Big book of holiday plays p313-25
812.008

McGowan, Keith, 1968-
Sexual harassment (7 and up)   305.3
McGowen, Tom
Adventures in archaeology   930.1
African-Americans in the Old West   978
Germany's lightning war   940.54
The Korean War   951.9
Sink the Bismarck   940.54
World War II   940.53
McGraw, Eloise Jarvis
The moorchild   Fic
McGraw-Hill encyclopedia of world biography.
See Encyclopedia of world biography
920.003

McGreal, Elizabeth Yates See Yates, Elizabeth,
1905-
McGwire, Mark
                     About
Muskat, C. Mark McGwire   92
Stewart, M. Home run heroes: McGwire and
Sosa   92
Stewart, M. Mark McGwire   92
Thornley, S. Mark McGwire   92
McIlwraith, Maureen See Hunter, Mollie, 1922-
McIntosh, Jane
Archeology   930.1
McKay, Hilary
The exiles   Fic
The exiles at home. See note under McKay, H.
The exiles   Fic
The exiles in love. See note under McKay, H.
The exiles   Fic
McKean, Thomas
Into the candlelit room and other strange tales
S C

Contents: Into the candlelit room; Caring; Letters from Leah;
Before Thanksgiving; Lily
McKee, Jesse O.
The Choctaw
In Indians of North America series
970.004
McKee, Timothy Saunders, 1970-
(ed) No more strangers now. See No more
strangers now   968.06

McKenna, Lesley
The fantastic book of snow-boarding   796.9
McKenny, Margaret
(jt. auth) Peterson, R. T. A field guide to
wildflowers of northeastern and north-central
North America   582.13
McKillip, Patricia A., 1948-
Baba Yaga and the sorcerer's son
In Dragons & dreams p32-42   S C
The riddle-master of Hed (7 and up)   Fic
McKinley, Robin
Beauty (7 and up)   Fic
The blue sword (7 and up)   Fic
The door in the hedge   S C
Contents: The stolen princess; The princess and the frog; The
hunting of the hind; The twelve dancing princesses
The hero and the crown (7 and up)   Fic
A knot in the grain and other stories   S C
Contents: The healer; The stagman; Touk's house; Buttercups;
A knot in the grain
The outlaws of Sherwood   398.2
Rose daughter (7 and up)   Fic
McKinley, William, 1843-1901
See/See also pages in the following book(s):
Presidents of a growing country   920
St. George, J. In the line of fire   364.1
McKissack, Fredrick, 1939-
Black hoops   796.323
(jt. auth) McKissack, P. C. African-American inventors   920
(jt. auth) McKissack, P. C. African-American
scientists   920
(jt. auth) McKissack, P. C. Black diamond
796.357
(jt. auth) McKissack, P. C. Black hands, white
sails   639.2
(jt. auth) McKissack, P. C. Christmas in the big
house, Christmas in the quarters   394.26
(jt. auth) McKissack, P. C. The civil rights
movement in America from 1865 to the
present   323.1
(jt. auth) McKissack, P. C. Let my people go
221.9
(jt. auth) McKissack, P. C. Rebels against slavery   326
(jt. auth) McKissack, P. C. Red-tail angels: the
story of the Tuskegee airmen of World War
II   940.54
(jt. auth) McKissack, P. C. The royal kingdoms
of Ghana, Mali, and Songhay   966.2
(jt. auth) McKissack, P. C. Sojourner Truth:
ain't I a woman?   92
(jt. auth) McKissack, P. C. W.E.B. DuBois
92
(jt. auth) McKissack, P. C. Young, black, and
determined: a biography of Lorraine
Hansberry   92
McKissack, Pat See McKissack, Patricia C., 1944-
McKissack, Patricia C., 1944-
African-American inventors   920
African-American scientists   920
Black diamond   796.357
Black hands, white sails   639.2
Christmas in the big house, Christmas in the
quarters   394.26

Meltzer, Milton, 1915——*Continued*
(ed) The American revolutionaries: a history in their own words, 1750-1800. See The American revolutionaries: a history in their own words, 1750-1800   **973.3**
(ed) Lincoln, in his own words. See Lincoln, in his own words   **92**

Melville, Herman, 1819-1891
See/See also pages in the following book(s):
Faber, D. Great lives: American literature p49-58   **920**

Memoirs of a bookbat. Lasky, K.   **Fic**

Memoirs of Sherlock Holmes. Doyle, Sir A. C.
In Doyle, Sir A. C. The complete Sherlock Holmes   **S C**

Memories of Anne Frank. Gold, A. L.   **92**

Memories of my life in a Polish village, 1930-1949. Fluek, T. K.   **92**

The **men** in the moon. McCaughrean, G.
In McCaughrean, G. The silver treasure: myths and legends of the world p6-13   **398.2**

Menana of the waterfall. Osborne, M. P.
In Osborne, M. P. Mermaid tales from around the world p7-11   **398.2**

Menashe and Rachel. Singer, I. B.
In Singer, I. B. The power of light p31-39   **S C**

Menchú, Rigoberta
See/See also pages in the following book(s):
Lucas, E. Contemporary human rights activists p107-17 (7 and up)   **920**

Mendel, Gregor, 1822-1884
About
Edelson, E. Gregor Mendel, and the roots of genetics (7 and up)   **92**
Klare, R. Gregor Mendel   **92**

Mendel, Johann Gregor See Mendel, Gregor, 1822-1884

Mendelssohn, Fanny Cécile See Hensel, Fanny Cécile Mendelssohn, 1805-1847

Mendoza, Patrick M.
Extraordinary people in extraordinary times (7 and up)   **920**

Mendrinos, Roxanne Baxter
Using educational technology with at-risk students   **027.8**

Menick, Stephen
The muffin child   **Fic**

Meningitis
Willett, E. Meningitis (7 and up)   **616.8**

Mennonites
See also Amish
Kenna, K. A people apart   **289.7**

Menominee Indians
Ourada, P. K. The Menominee
In Indians of North America series   **970.004**

Menstruation
Gravelle, K. The period book   **612.6**
Jukes, M. Growing up: it's a girl thing   **612.6**
See/See also pages in the following book(s):
Jukes, M. It's a girl thing p10-32   **305.23**

Mental healing
See/See also pages in the following book(s):
Duncan, L. Psychic connections p202-19 (7 and up)   **133**

Mental illness
Fiction
Franklin, K. L. Dove song   **Fic**
Marsden, J. Checkers (7 and up)   **Fic**
Naylor, P. R. The keeper   **Fic**
Seago, K. Matthew unstrung (7 and up)   **Fic**

Mental math workout. Lobosco, M. L.   **510.7**

Mental suggestion
See also Brainwashing

Mental telepathy See Telepathy

Mentally handicapped
Fiction
Conly, J. L. Crazy lady!   **Fic**
Holt, K. W. My Louisiana sky   **Fic**
Mazer, H. The wild kid   **Fic**
Powell, R. Tribute to another dead rock star (7 and up)   **Fic**
Wood, J. R. The man who loved clowns   **Fic**

Mentally handicapped children
Fiction
Byars, B. C. The summer of the swans   **Fic**

Mentally ill
Fiction
Auch, M. J. Frozen summer   **Fic**
Greenberg, J. I never promised you a rose garden (7 and up)   **Fic**
Johnson, A. Humming whispers (7 and up)   **Fic**
Kehret, P. I'm not who you think I am   **Fic**
Thompson, J. F. Brothers (7 and up)   **Fic**

Institutional care
See also Psychiatric hospitals

The **mer-woman** out of the sea. Hamilton, V.
In Hamilton, V. Her stories p78-83   **398.2**

Mercier, Cathryn M.
(jt. auth) Bloom, S. P. Presenting Avi   **813.009**

Mercy killing See Euthanasia

Meredith, James
About
Elish, D. James Meredith and school desegregation   **92**

Merit badges. Paterson, K.
In Paterson, K. A midnight clear: stories for the Christmas season   **S C**

Merlin (Legendary character)
Fiction
Barron, T. A. The lost years of Merlin (7 and up)   **Fic**
Barron, T. A. The Merlin effect   **Fic**
Yolen, J. The dragon's boy   **Fic**
Yolen, J. Hobby   **Fic**
Yolen, J. Merlin   **Fic**
Yolen, J. Passager   **Fic**
The **Merlin** effect. Barron, T. A.   **Fic**
Merlin's kin. Sherman, J.   **398.2**

The **mermaid** in the millpond. Osborne, M. P.
In Osborne, M. P. Mermaid tales from around
the world p63-69   **398.2**
The **mermaid** of Zennor. Climo, S.
In Climo, S. Magic & mischief p89-95
     398.2
Mermaid tales from around the world. Osborne,
M. P.   **398.2**
Mermaids and mermen
Osborne, M. P. Mermaid tales from around the
world   **398.2**
Fiction
Rylant, C. The islander   **Fic**
The **mermaid's** revenge. Osborne, M. P.
In Osborne, M. P. Mermaid tales from around
the world p45-48   **398.2**
Merrell, James Hart, 1953-
The Catawbas
In Indians of North America series
     970.004
Merriam-Webster's dictionary of synonyms
     423
Merriam-Webster's geographical dictionary
     910.3
Merriam-Webster's Japanese-English learner's
dictionary   **495.6**
Merriam-Webster's school thesaurus   **423**
Merrill, Jean, 1923-
The pushcart war   **Fic**
The **merry** adventures of Robin Hood of great re-
nown in Notinghamshire. Pyle, H.   **398.2**
Meryman, Richard, 1926-
Andrew Wyeth (7 and up)   **92**
Meserole, Mike
DK ultimate sports lists   **796**
(ed) The Information please sports almanac. See
The Information please sports almanac
     796
Mesopotamia *See* Iraq
Meta human. Skinner, D.
In Skinner, D. Thundershine: tales of
metakids   **S C**
Metals
Mebane, R. C. Metals   **669**
Metalwork
See also Metals
Metamorphosis. Conford, E.
In Conford, E. Crush p51-68   **S C**
The **metamorphosis** of Justin Jones. Coville, B.
In Coville, B. Odder than ever   **S C**
Metaoomet, Sachem of the Wampanoags *See*
Philip, Sachem of the Wampanoags, d. 1676
Meteorology
See also Climate; Droughts; Weather
Elsom, D. M. Weather explained   **551.5**
Engelbert, P. The complete weather resource
     551.5
Everything weather. See entry in CD-ROM sec-
tion, Part 3
Kahl, J. D. National Audubon Society first field
guide: weather   **551.5**
Silverstein, A. Weather and climate   **551.5**

Meteors
Aronson, B. Meteors   **523.5**
Meth (Drug) *See* Methamphetamine
Methamphetamine
Schleifer, J. Methamphetamine (7 and up)
     362.29
Methodist Church
Wellman, S. John Wesley (7 and up)   **92**
Methylphenidate hydrochloride *See* Ritalin
Metoyer, Maria Theresa Coincoin *See* Coincoin,
Maria Theresa, 1742-1816
Metropolitan Museum of Art (New York, N.Y.)
Songs of the Wild West. See Songs of the Wild
West   **782.42**
Mettger, Zak
Reconstruction   **973.8**
Till victory is won   **973.7**
Metzger, Bruce Manning
(ed) The Oxford companion to the Bible. See
The Oxford companion to the Bible
     220.3
Metzger, Lois
Ellen's case (7 and up)   **Fic**
The **Mexican** American family album. Hoobler, D.
     305.8
The **Mexican-American** War. Nardo, D.
     973.6
Mexican Americans
Atkin, S. B. Voices from the fields   **331.5**
Bredeson, C. Henry Cisneros   **92**
Cedeño, M. E. Cesar Chavez   **92**
Collins, D. R. Farmworker's friend: the story of
Cesar Chavez   **92**
Hoobler, D. The Mexican American family al-
bum   **305.8**
Mirriam-Goldberg, C. Sandra Cisneros   **92**
Morey, J. Famous Mexican Americans   **920**
Drama
Soto, G. Novio boy (7 and up)   **812**
Fiction
Cisneros, S. The house on Mango Street (7 and
up)   **Fic**
Jiménez, F. The circuit: stories from the life of
a migrant child   **S C**
Soto, G. Baseball in April, and other stories
     S C
Soto, G. Buried onions (7 and up)   **Fic**
Soto, G. Local news   **S C**
Soto, G. Off and running   **Fic**
Soto, G. Petty crimes   **S C**
Soto, G. The pool party   **Fic**
Social life and customs
King, E. Quinceañera   **392**
Mexican artists *See* Artists, Mexican
Mexican, Central and South American art. Scott,
J. F.
In International encyclopedia of art   **703**
Mexican Indians *See* Indians of Mexico
Mexican literature
Collections
The Tree is older than you are (7 and up)
     860.8

Middle Ages—Fiction—*Continued*

Skurzynski, G. Spider's voice (7 and up)
             Fic

Temple, F. The Ramsay scallop   **Fic**

History

 See also Europe—History—476-1492

Pictorial works

Smithsonian timelines of the ancient world
             930

Middle East

Fiction

Temple, F. The Beduins' gazelle **Fic**

Poetry

The Space between our footsteps (7 and up)
           808.81

Middle East War, 1991 *See* Persian Gulf War, 1991

The **middle** passage. Feelings, T. **759.13**

Middle search plus. See entry in CD-ROM section, Part 3

Middleplots 4. Gillespie, J. T. **028.5**

Midget. Bowler, T.   **Fic**

A **midnight** clear. Paterson, K.

 In Paterson, K. A midnight clear: stories for the Christmas season **S C**

A **midnight** clear: stories for the Christmas season. Paterson, K. **S C**

Midnight hour encores. Brooks, B. **Fic**

Midnight snack. Duane, D.

 In Sixteen: short stories by outstanding writers for young adults p22-30 **S C**

Midnight's choice. Thompson, K. **Fic**

A **midsummer** night's dream, William Shakespeare's. Coville, B. **822.3**

Midwifery *See* Midwives

The **midwife's** apprentice. Cushman, K. **Fic**

Midwives

Fiction

Cushman, K. The midwife's apprentice **Fic**

Mighty math astro algebra. See entry in CD-ROM section, Part 3

Migrant labor

Atkin, S. B. Voices from the fields **331.5**

Cedeño, M. E. Cesar Chavez **92**

Collins, D. R. Farmworker's friend: the story of Cesar Chavez **92**

Stanley, J. Children of the Dust Bowl
           371.9

Fiction

Jiménez, F. The circuit: stories from the life of a migrant child **S C**

Migration *See* Immigration and emigration

Migration, Internal *See* Internal migration

Mikaelsen, Ben, 1952-

Stranded   **Fic**

Miklowitz, Gloria D., 1927-

Camouflage   **Fic**

The Fuller brush man

 In Visions: nineteen short stories by outstanding writers for young adults p100-06
           S C

Masada (7 and up)   **Fic**

Past forgiving (7 and up)   **Fic**

Miles, Patricia

Exit

 In The Oxford book of scary tales p152-[56]
           808.8

Miles, William, 1931-

(jt. auth) Burns, K. Black stars in orbit
           920

Milestones in black American history [series]

Dornfeld, M. The turning tide **305.8**

Hull, M. Struggle and love, 1972-1997
           305.8

King, W. Toward the promised land **305.8**

Nardo, D. Braving the New World, 1619-1784
           305.8

Milestones in discovery and invention [series]

Henderson, H. Nuclear physics **539.7**

Yount, L. Genetics and genetic engineering
           576.5

Milestones in science and discovery [series]

Henderson, H. Communications and broadcasting   **384**

Milestones in science and technology. Mount, E.
           509

Military aeronautics

 See also World War, 1939-1945—Aerial operations

Military art and science

Meltzer, M. Weapons & warfare **355**

Military intervention *See* Intervention (International law)

Military might [series]

McGowen, T. Germany's lightning war
          940.54

McGowen, T. Sink the Bismarck **940.54**

Military personnel

 See also Soldiers

Military policy

 See also National security

Military tanks

Harvey, I. Tanks   **623.7**

McGowen, T. Germany's lightning war
          940.54

Military uniforms

The Visual dictionary of military uniforms
          355.1

Militia movements

Hate groups: opposing viewpoints (7 and up)
          364.1

Stewart, G. Militias (7 and up) **322**

Fiction

Miklowitz, G. D. Camouflage **Fic**

Thompson, J. F. Brothers (7 and up) **Fic**

Militias. Stewart, G.   **322**

Milivojevic, JoAnn

Serbia   **949.7**

Milk and honey. Schwartz, H.

 In Schwartz, H. Next year in Jerusalem p48-56   **296.1**

Milk and honey. Yolen, J.   **296.4**

Millar, Heather, 1963-

Spain in the age of exploration **946**

Millard, Anne

Pyramids   **909**

Minorities

See also Discrimination; Ethnic relations

Discrimination: opposing viewpoints (7 and up) **305.8**

Katz, W. L. The Civil War to the last frontier, 1850-1880s **973.5**

Katz, W. L. The new freedom to the New Deal, 1913-1939 **973.91**

Katz, W. L. The westward movement and abolitionism, 1815-1850 **973.5**

Pascoe, E. Racial prejudice **305.8**

Piggins, C. A. A multicultural portrait of the Civil War (7 and up) **973.7**

Washburne, C. K. A multicultural portrait of colonial life **973.2**

Bibliography

Rochman, H. Against borders **011.6**

Totten, H. L. Culturally diverse library collections for youth **011.6**

Law and legislation

McDonald, L. The rights of racial minorities (7 and up) **342**

A **minority**. O'Connor, F.

In Bearing witness p86-97 **808.8**

Minty, Judith

Killing the bear

In Talking leaves **S C**

Mintz, Barbara

(jt. auth) Katan, N. J. Hieroglyphs, the writing of ancient Egypt **493**

The **miracle** at King David's tomb. Schwartz, H.

In Schwartz, H. Next year in Jerusalem p39-43 **296.1**

Miracle in Tent City. Jiménez, F.

In Jiménez, F. The circuit: stories from the life of a migrant child p27-44 **S C**

The **miracle** of Our Lady of Guadalupe. Delacre, L.

In Delacre, L. Golden tales p41-43 **398.2**

The **miracle** of Purun Bhagat. Kipling, R.

In Kipling, R. The jungle books **S C**

Miracles

Arvey, M. Miracles: opposing viewpoints (7 and up) **231.7**

Miranda, Ernesto

About

Gold, S. D. Miranda v. Arizona (1966) (7 and up) **345**

Hogrogian, J. G. Miranda v. Arizona (7 and up) **345**

Wice, P. B. Miranda v. Arizona (7 and up) **345**

Miranda v. Arizona. Hogrogian, J. G. **345**

Miranda v. Arizona. Wice, P. B. **345**

Miranda v. Arizona (1966). Gold, S. D. **345**

Miriam's well. Bach, A. **221.9**

Mirocha, Paul

(il) George, J. C. Acorn pancakes, dandelion salad and 38 other wild recipes **641.6**

Mirriam-Goldberg, Caryn

Sandra Cisneros **92**

The **mirror**. Kadono, E.

In Don't read this! and other tales of the unnatural p85-109 **S C**

The **mirror** crack'd. Christie, A. **Fic**

The **mirror** crack'd from side to side. See Christie, A. The mirror crack'd **Fic**

The **mirror** of Merlin. Barron, T. A. See note under Barron, T. A. The lost years of Merlin **Fic**

Mirrors

Zubrowski, B. Mirrors **535**

Miscegenation *See* Racially mixed people

Miscellaneous facts *See* Curiosities and wonders

The **mischief** makers. Swortzell, L.

In Theatre for young audiences p183-216 **812.008**

Mischling, second degree: my childhood in Nazi Germany. Koehn, I. **92**

Miss Butterfly. Mori, T.

In American dragons p26-33 **810.8**

Miss Emily's roses. Zambreno, M. F.

In Vampires: a collection of original stories p64-80 **S C**

Missing and murdered children. Hyde, M. O. **362.7**

Missing children

See also Runaway children

Hyde, M. O. Missing and murdered children (7 and up) **362.7**

Fiction

Pfeffer, S. B. The year without Michael **Fic**

Missing May. Rylant, C. **Fic**

Missing persons

See also Runaway teenagers

Fiction

Cadnum, M. Zero at the bone (7 and up) **Fic**

Mission: Earth. English, J. **550**

Missionaries, Christian *See* Christian missionaries

Missionaries of Charity

Morgan, N. Mother Teresa: saint of the poor **92**

Ruth, A. Mother Teresa **92**

Missions, Christian *See* Christian missions

Mississippi

George, C. Mississippi

In America the beautiful, second series **973**

Shirley, D. Mississippi

In Celebrate the states **973**

Fiction

Taylor, M. D. The friendship **Fic**

Taylor, M. D. Let the circle be unbroken **Fic**

Taylor, M. D. Mississippi bridge **Fic**

Taylor, M. D. The road to Memphis **Fic**

Taylor, M. D. Roll of thunder, hear my cry **Fic**

Taylor, M. D. Song of the trees **Fic**

Taylor, M. D. The well **Fic**

Race relations

Elish, D. James Meredith and school desegregation **92**

Walter, M. P. Mississippi challenge **323.1**

Mohawk Indians
Bolton, J. Joseph Brant   92
Bonvillain, N. The Mohawk
In Indians of North America series
                                                        970.004

Mohegan Indians
Fiction
Durrant, L. Echohawk   Fic
Durrant, L. Turtle clan journey   Fic
Mohican Indians *See* Mohegan Indians
Mohr, Nicholasa, 1935-
Mr. Mendelsohn
In Growing up Latino p131-46   810.8
Molecular biology
See/See also pages in the following book(s):
Edelson, E. James Watson and Francis Crick
and the building blocks of life (7 and up)
                                                            92

Molecules
Cooper, C. Matter   530
Molina, Mario, 1943-
See/See also pages in the following book(s):
Oleksy, W. G. Hispanic-American scientists (7
and up)   920
Mollusks
See also Slugs (Mollusks); Snails
Rehder, H. A. The Audubon Society field guide
to North American seashells   594
Molly Cottontail. San Souci, R.
In San Souci, R. Cut from the same cloth
p29-33   398.2
Moloney, N. (Norah)
The young Oxford book of archaeology (7 and
up)   930.1
Moloney, Norah *See* Moloney, N. (Norah)
Mom Bett and the little ones a-glowing. Hamilton,
V.
In Hamilton, V. Her stories p39-41
                                                         398.2
Momaday, N. Scott
She is beautiful in her whole being
In Talking leaves   S C
Mommy's baby. McCaughrean, G.
In McCaughrean, G. The crystal pool: myths
and legends of the world p45-49
                                                         398.2
Monarchs *See* Kings and rulers
Monarchs. Lasky, K.   595.7
Monarchy
See also Queens
Monasticism and religious orders for women
See also Nuns
Monerans & protists. Silverstein, A.   579
Monet, Claude, 1840-1926
See/See also pages in the following book(s):
Glubok, S. Great lives: painting p117-28
                                                            920
Money
Cribb, J. Money   332.4
Godfrey, N. S. Neale S. Godfrey's ultimate
kids' money book   332.024

Moneymaking projects for children
See/See also pages in the following book(s):
Otfinoski, S. The kid's guide to money p13-34
                                                        332.024
Mongolia
Cheng, P. G. Mongolia   951.7
Fiction
Wilson, D. L. I rode a horse of milk white jade
(7 and up)   Fic
Mongoose. Spinelli, J.
In Spinelli, J. The library card   S C
Monk, Thelonious, 1917-1982
See/See also pages in the following book(s):
Gourse, L. Striders to beboppers and beyond
p62-72 (7 and up)   781.65
Monkey do: the story of Hanuman. McCaughrean,
G.
In McCaughrean, G. The crystal pool: myths
and legends of the world p95-101
                                                         398.2
The **monkey** garden. Cisneros, S.
In Growing up Latino p288-91   810.8
Monkey island. Fox, P.   Fic
Monkey son-in-law
In Hearne, B. G. Beauties and beasts p32-34
                                                         398.2
Monkey stew. Van Laan, N.
In Van Laan, N. With a whoop and a holler
p11-12   398
Monkeys
See also Baboons
Fiction
Nelson, T. The Empress of Elsewhere   Fic
Rawls, W. Summer of the monkeys (7 and up)
                                                           Fic
The **monkey's** wedding. Aiken, J.
In Night terrors   S C
Mono (Disease) *See* Mononucleosis
Monologues
The Book of monologues for aspiring actors (7
and up)   808.82
Great monologues for young actors   808.82
Great scenes and monologues for children
                                                        808.82
Mononucleosis
Smart, P. Everything you need to know about
mononucleosis (7 and up)   616.9
Monroe, Jean Guard
First houses   970.004
Monroe, Judy
Inhalant drug dangers   362.29
Steroid drug dangers   362.29
Monseau, Virginia R., 1941-
Presenting Ouida Sebestyen (7 and up)
                                                        813.009
Monster. Myers, W. D.   Fic
The **monster** with emerald teeth. McCaughrean,
G.
In McCaughrean, G. The bronze cauldron:
myths and legends of the world p116-20
                                                         398.2
Monsters
Rovin, J. The encyclopedia of monsters (7 and
up)   001.9

Morgan, Kenneth O.
(ed) The Young Oxford history of Britain & Ireland. See The Young Oxford history of Britain & Ireland   **941**

Morgan, Nina
Lasers   **621.36**
Mother Teresa: saint of the poor   **92**

Morgan, Thomas Hunt, 1866-1945
See/See also pages in the following book(s):
Kidd, J. S. Life lines p16-24 (7 and up)
    576.5

Morgenstern, Susie Hoch
Secret letters from 0 to 10   **Fic**

Mori, Kyoko
Shizuko's daughter (7 and up)   **Fic**

Mori, Toshio, 1910-
Miss Butterfly
In American dragons p26-33   **810.8**

Moriguchi, Kakō, 1909-
See/See also pages in the following book(s):
Hamanaka, S. In search of the spirit p7-13
    920

Morin, Isobel V., 1928-
Our changing Constitution (7 and up)   **342**

Morley, Jacqueline
Greek myths   **292**
A Roman villa   **937**
Shakespeare's theater   **792.09**

Mormon Church *See* Church of Jesus Christ of Latter-day Saints

The **Mormon** Trail and the Latter-Day Saints in American history. Nash, C. R.   **289.3**

Mormons
Book of Mormon. The Book of Mormon
    289.3

Mormons in America. Bushman, C. L.   **289.3**

Morning Girl. Dorris, M.   **Fic**

Morocco
Blauer, E. Morocco   **964**

Morphine
See also Heroin

Morphology *See* Comparative anatomy

Morpurgo, Michael
Escape from Shangri-La   **Fic**
Robin of Sherwood   **Fic**
The war of Jenkins' ear   **Fic**

Morrice, Polly Alison
Iowa
In Celebrate the states   **973**

Morris, Gerald, 1963-
The squire, his knight, & his lady   **Fic**
The squire's tale   **Fic**

Morris, Jeffrey Brandon, 1941-
The FDR way   **92**

Morris, Juddi
Tending the fire: the story of Maria Martinez
    92

Morris, Mary, 1913-
(jt. auth) Morris, W. Morris dictionary of word and phrase origins   **422.03**

Morris, Neil
(jt. auth) Cox, R. H. W. The seven wonders of the historic world   **909.07**

Morris, William, 1913-1994
Morris dictionary of word and phrase origins
    422.03

Morris dictionary of word and phrase origins. Morris, W.   **422.03**

Morrison, Lillian, 1917-
(comp) Slam dunk: basketball poems. See Slam dunk: basketball poems   **811.008**

Morrison, Marion
Costa Rica   **972.86**

Morrison, Toni, 1931-
"Recitatif"
In Leaving home: stories p201-27   **808.8**
See/See also pages in the following book(s):
Bolden, T. And not afraid to dare   **920**
Hacker, C. Nobel Prize winners p30-35
    920

Morrissey, Peter, 1953-
The young ice skater   **796.91**

Morse, Samuel Finley Breese, 1791-1872
About
Coe, L. The telegraph   **621.383**

Morton, William Thomas Green, 1819-1868
See/See also pages in the following book(s):
Fradin, D. B. "We have conquered pain"
    617.9

Moschovitis, Valerie Tomaselli- *See* Tomaselli-Moschovitis, Valerie

Moser, Barry
(il) Lasky, K. A brilliant streak: the making of Mark Twain   **92**

Moser, Diane, 1944-
(jt. auth) Spangenburg, R. The African-American experience   **917.3**
(jt. auth) Spangenburg, R. The American Indian experience   **917.3**
(jt. auth) Spangenburg, R. Eleanor Roosevelt: a passion to improve   **92**
(jt. auth) Spangenburg, R. The history of science from the ancient Greeks to the scientific revolution   **509**
(jt. auth) Spangenburg, R. The history of science in the eighteenth century   **509**
(jt. auth) Spangenburg, R. The history of science in the nineteenth century   **509**
(jt. auth) Spangenburg, R. The history of science from 1895 to 1945   **509**
(jt. auth) Spangenburg, R. The history of science from 1946 to the 1990s   **509**
(jt. auth) Spangenburg, R. Literature and the arts   **917.3**
(jt. auth) Spangenburg, R. Political and social movements   **917.3**
(jt. auth) Spangenburg, R. Science and invention   **917.3**

Moses (Biblical figure)
About
Sobel, I. Moses and the angels   **296.1**
Fiction
Levitin, S. Escape from Egypt (7 and up)
    Fic

Moses and the angels. Sobel, I.   **296.1**

Mosier, Elizabeth
My life as a girl (7 and up)   **Fic**

Moslem countries *See* Islamic countries

Moslemism *See* Islam

Mosques
  Macdonald, F. A 16th century mosque   297

Moss, Carol (Carol Marie)
  Science in ancient Mesopotamia   509

Moss, Cynthia
  About
  Pringle, L. P. Elephant woman   599.67

Moss, Joyce, 1951-
  Profiles in American history   973

Moss, Kary L.
  The rights of women and girls (7 and up)   305.4

Mossflower. Jacques, B. See note under Jacques, B. Redwall   **Fic**

The **most** beautiful roof in the world. Lasky, K.   577.3

A **most** dangerous journey. Caras, R. A.   599.67

The **most** excellent book of how to be a juggler. Mitchelson, M.   793.8

Mostly harmless. Adams, D. See note under Adams, D. The Hitchhiker's Guide to the Galaxy   **Fic**

Motels *See* Hotels and motels

Mother and daughter. Soto, G.
  In Soto, G. Baseball in April, and other stories p60-68   **S C**

The **mother** and death. San Souci, R.
  In San Souci, R. A terrifying taste of short & shivery p141-45   398.2

Mother Earth, Father Sky. Lavender, D. S.   970.004

Mother for mayor. McGowan, J.
  In The Big book of holiday plays p313-25   812.008

Mother Jones *See* Jones, Mother, 1830-1930

Mother Nature's pharmacy. Kidd, J. S.   615

The **mother** of Karaikkal. Krishnaswami, U.
  In Krishnaswami, U. Shower of gold: girls and women in the stories of India p36-40   398.2

Mother Teresa *See* Teresa, Mother, 1910-1997

Mother Teresa's Mission of Charity *See* Missionaries of Charity

Mothers
  See also Surrogate mothers; Teenage mothers; Unmarried mothers

Mothers, Single parent *See* Single parent family

Mothers and daughters
  Fiction
  Brooks, B. Midnight hour encores (7 and up)   **Fic**
  Childress, A. Rainbow Jordan (7 and up)   **Fic**
  Cole, B. The facts speak for themselves (7 and up)   **Fic**
  Coman, C. Tell me everything   **Fic**
  Conrad, P. Zoe rising   **Fic**
  Deaver, J. R. Chicago blues (7 and up)   **Fic**

Frank, L. K. I am an artichoke (7 and up)   **Fic**
Griffin, A. Split just right   **Fic**
Grove, V. The crystal garden   **Fic**
Hermes, P. Someone to count on   **Fic**
Kehret, P. I'm not who you think I am   **Fic**
Krisher, T. Kinship (7 and up)   **Fic**
Krisher, T. Spite fences (7 and up)   **Fic**
LaFaye, A. The year of the Sawdust Man   **Fic**
Lasky, K. Beyond the burning time (7 and up)   **Fic**
Levitin, S. Yesterday's child (7 and up)   **Fic**
Lowry, L. Find a stranger, say goodbye (7 and up)   **Fic**
Lowry, L. Rabble Starkey   **Fic**
Mathis, S. B. Listen for the fig tree (7 and up)   **Fic**
Mori, K. Shizuko's daughter (7 and up)   **Fic**
Napoli, D. J. Zel (7 and up)   **Fic**
Rodgers, M. Freaky Friday   **Fic**
Rodowsky, C. F. Hannah in between   **Fic**
Rodowsky, C. F. The Turnabout Shop   **Fic**
Stanley, D. Time apart   **Fic**
Williams, C. L. The true colors of Caitlynne Jackson   **Fic**
Zemser, A. B. Beyond the mango tree   **Fic**

Mothers and sons
  Fiction
  Bauer, M. D. A question of trust   **Fic**
  Bennett, J. Sing me a death song (7 and up)   **Fic**
  Katz, W. W. Out of the dark   **Fic**
  Layefsky, V. Impossible things   **Fic**
  Mills, C. You're a brave man, Julius Zimmerman   **Fic**
  Powell, R. Tribute to another dead rock star (7 and up)   **Fic**

Mother's clothes. Soto, G.
  In Soto, G. Petty crimes   **S C**

Mothers on welfare. Stewart, G.   362.83

Mothers' pensions *See* Child welfare

Moths
  Pascoe, E. Butterflies and moths   595.7
  Whalley, P. E. S. Butterfly & moth   595.7

The **moths.** Viramontes, H. M.
  In Growing up Latino p32-37   810.8

Motion
  Gardner, R. Experiments with motion   531
  Lafferty, P. Force & motion   531

Motion picture actors *See* Actors

Motion picture cartoons *See* Animated films

Motion picture direction *See* Motion pictures—Production and direction

Motion picture photography *See* Cinematography

Motion picture producers and directors
  Haskins, J. Spike Lee (7 and up)   92
  Kramer, B. Ron Howard   92
  McDaniel, M. Spike Lee   92
  Rau, D. M. George Lucas   92
  Woog, A. Steven Spielberg   92

Motion picture production *See* Motion pictures— Production and direction

Motion pictures

See also Fantasy films; Musicals

Biography

Walt Disney: his life in pictures   92

History and criticism

Parkinson, D. The young Oxford book of the movies   791.43

Production and direction

O'Brien, L. Lights, camera, action!   791.43

Motivation (Psychology)

See also Wishes

Motorboats

Graham, I. Boats   623.8

Motown and Didi. Myers, W. D.   Fic

Motyer, Stephen, 1950-

Who's who in the Bible   220.9

Moulton, Carroll

(ed) Ancient Greece and Rome. See Ancient Greece and Rome   938

Mount, Ellis, 1921-

Milestones in science and technology   509

Mount Everest (China and Nepal)

Pfetzer, M. Within reach: my Everest story (7 and up)   796.52

Mount Holyoke College

Rosen, D. A fire in her bones: the story of Mary Lyon   92

Mount Rushmore National Memorial (S.D.)

Curlee, L. Rushmore   730.9

Mount Saint Helens (Wash.)

Lauber, P. Volcano: the eruption and healing of Mount St. Helens   551.2

Fiction

Smith, R. The Sasquatch   Fic

The **mountain**. Hamer, M. J.

In Rites of passage p45-49   S C

The **mountain**. Mungoshi, C.

In Don't read this! and other tales of the unnatural p23-32   S C

Mountain light. Yep, L. See note under Yep, L. Dragon's gate   Fic

Mountain lions *See* Pumas

The **mountain** that moved. Schwartz, H.

In Schwartz, H. Next year in Jerusalem p10-13   296.1

Mountaineering

Brimner, L. D. Rock climbing   796.52

Pfetzer, M. Within reach: my Everest story (7 and up)   796.52

Mountains

See also Adirondack Mountains (N.Y.); Catskill Mountains (N.Y.); Ozark Mountains

Simon, S. Mountains   551.4

Mour, Stanley I.

American jazz musicians   920

Mouse *See* Mice

The **Mouse** rap. Myers, W. D.   Fic

The **mousetrap**. Olson, A. N.

In Olson, A. N. Ask the bones: scary stories from around the world p78-84   398.2

A **mouthful**. Jennings, P.

In Jennings, P. Uncovered! p37-40   S C

Movable eyes. Aiken, J.

In Aiken, J. A foot in the grave p27-39   S C

The **moves** make the man. Brooks, B.   Fic

Moving

Fiction

Fletcher, R. J. Spider Boy   Fic

Koss, A. G. The Ashwater experiment   Fic

Pevsner, S. Would my fortune cookie lie?   Fic

Pinkney, A. D. Hold fast to dreams   Fic

Wallace, B. Aloha summer   Fic

Yep, L. The star fisher   Fic

Moving Mama to town. Young, R. T.   Fic

Moving pictures *See* Motion pictures

Moving still. Jiménez, F.

In Jiménez, F. The circuit: stories from the life of a migrant child p113-34   S C

Mowat, Farley

Born naked (7 and up)   92

Mowgli's brothers. Kipling, R.

In Kipling, R. The jungle books   S C

Mowry, Jess, 1960-

Ghost train   Fic

Mozambique

James, R. S. Mozambique (7 and up)   967.9

Fiction

Farmer, N. A girl named Disaster   Fic

The **Mozart** season. Wolff, V. E.   Fic

Mr. Mendelsohn. Mohr, N.

In Growing up Latino p131-46   810.8

Mr. Tucket. Paulsen, G.   Fic

Mr. Wilmer's strange Saturday. Lawson, R.

In A Newbery zoo   S C

Mrs. Ambroseworthy. Yolen, J.

In Yolen, J. Here there be ghosts p42-55   810.8

Mrs. Fish, Ape, and me, the Dump Queen. See Mazer, N. F. Crazy Fish   Fic

Mrs. Frisby and the rats of NIMH. O'Brien, R. C.   Fic

Mrs. Pomeroy. Allen, K. J.

In A Nightmare's dozen   S C

Ms. found in a bottle. Poe, E. A.

In Poe, E. A. Tales of Edgar Allan Poe p153-67   S C

Muckenhoupt, Margaret

Sigmund Freud (7 and up)   92

Mudd-Ruth, Maria

The deserts of the Southwest   577.5

The **muffin** child. Menick, S.   Fic

Mugabe, Robert Gabriel, 1924-

See/See also pages in the following book(s):

Rasmussen, R. K. Modern African political leaders p91-105 (7 and up)   920

Muhammad, Elijah *See* Elijah Muhammad, 1897-1975

Muhammedanism *See* Islam

Muir, J. (John), 1810-1882
See/See also pages in the following book(s):
Calvert, P. Great lives: the American frontier
p260-73   **920**
Muir, John *See* Muir, J. (John), 1810-1882
Muir, John, 1838-1914
About
Naden, C. J. John Muir, saving the wilderness
                                            92
See/See also pages in the following book(s):
Archer, J. To save the earth (7 and up)
                                            920
Byrnes, P. Environmental pioneers (7 and up)
                                            920
Mujica, Barbara Louise
Fairy tale
In Where angels glide at dawn p77-97
                                            S C
Mukherjee, Bharati
See/See also pages in the following book(s):
Chiu, C. Lives of notable Asian Americans: lit-
erature and education p99-105 (7 and up)
                                            920
Müller, Melissa
Anne Frank (7 and up)   **92**
Müller, V. K.
(comp) English-Russian dictionary. See English-
Russian dictionary   **491.7**
Mullin, Alison Cooper- *See* Cooper-Mullin, Ali-
son, 1954-
The **mulombe**. San Souci, R.
In San Souci, R. A terrifying taste of short &
shivery p95-100   **398.2**
Multicultural America. See entry in CD-ROM
section, Part 3
The **multicultural** cookbook for students. Albyn,
C. L.   **641.5**
Multicultural junior biographies [series]
Hermann, S. R.C. Gorman   **92**
Multicultural people *See* Racially mixed people
A **multicultural** portrait of America's music.
Press, D. P.   **781.64**
A **multicultural** portrait of colonial life.
Washburne, C. K.   **973.2**
A **multicultural** portrait of the American Revolu-
tion. Zell, F.   **973.3**
A **multicultural** portrait of the Civil War. Piggins,
C. A.   **973.7**
A **multicultural** portrait of the Great Depression.
Rensberger, S.   **973.91**
A **multicultural** portrait of World War I. Uschan,
M. V.   **940.4**
Multiculturalism
Heath, A. Windows on the world   **394.2**
See/See also pages in the following book(s):
Culture wars: opposing viewpoints p140-57 (7
and up)   **306**
Multimedia materials *See* Audiovisual materials
MultiMedia schools   **371.305**
Multiple birth
Landau, E. Multiple births   **618.2**
Multiple choice. Tashjian, J.   **Fic**

Mummies
Deem, J. M. Bodies from the bog   **930.1**
Getz, D. Frozen man   **930.1**
Lauber, P. Tales mummies tell   **930.1**
Lessem, D. The iceman   **930.1**
Patent, D. H. Secrets of the ice man   **930.1**
Perl, L. Mummies, tombs, and treasure: secrets
of ancient Egypt   **393**
Putnam, J. Mummy   **393**
Reinhard, J. Discovering the Inca Ice Maiden
                                            930.1
Tanaka, S. Discovering the Iceman   **930.1**
Mummies, dinosaurs, moon rocks. Jespersen, J.
                                            930.1
Mummies, tombs, and treasure: secrets of ancient
Egypt. Perl, L.   **393**
The **mummy**, the will and the crypt. Bellairs, J.
See note under Bellairs, J. The curse of the
blue figurine   **Fic**
Mungoshi, Charles
The mountain
In Don't read this! and other tales of the un-
natural p23-32   **S C**
The setting sun and the rolling world
In Leaving home: stories p157-64   **808.8**
Municipal planning *See* City planning
Munk, Walter H., 1917-
See/See also pages in the following book(s):
Polking, K. Oceanographers and explorers of the
sea p53-61   **920**
Muñoz, William, 1949-
(il) Patent, D. H. Fire: friend or foe   **577.2**
Mura, David
See/See also pages in the following book(s):
Chiu, C. Lives of notable Asian Americans: lit-
erature and education p45-51 (7 and up)
                                            920
Mural painting and decoration
Capek, M. Murals   **751.7**
Murals. Capek, M.   **751.7**
Murder *See* Homicide
Murder on the Calais Coach. See Christie, A.
Murder on the Orient Express   **Fic**
Murder on the highway: the Viola Liuzzo story.
Siegel, B.   **92**
Murder on the Orient Express. Christie, A.
                                            Fic
Murdered, my sweet. Nixon, J. L.   **Fic**
The **murders** in the Rue Morgue. Poe, E. A.
In Poe, E. A. Tales of Edgar Allan Poe p169-
216   **S C**
Murdoch, David Hamilton, 1937-
Cowboy   **978**
North American Indian   **970.004**
Tutankhamun   **932**
Murie, Margaret E., 1902-
See/See also pages in the following book(s):
Byrnes, P. Environmental pioneers (7 and up)
                                            920
Murie, Olaus Johan, 1889-1963
See/See also pages in the following book(s):
Byrnes, P. Environmental pioneers (7 and up)
                                            920

Murieta, Joaquín, d. 1853
Fiction
Fleischman, S. Bandit's moon   **Fic**

The **murky** secret. Olson, A. N.
  In Olson, A. N. Ask the bones: scary stories from around the world p10-16   **398.2**

Murphy, Barbara, 1933-
Eagle Cloud and Fawn
  In Join in p23-33   **S C**

Murphy, Bruce, 1962-
(ed) Benet's reader's encyclopedia. See Benet's reader's encyclopedia   **803**

Murphy, Jim, 1947-
Across America on an emigrant train   **92**
The boys' war   **973.7**
Gone a-whaling (7 and up)   **639.2**
The great fire   **977.3**
Into the deep forest with Henry David Thoreau   **974.1**
The journal of James Edmond Pease, a Civil War Union soldier   **Fic**
The long road to Gettysburg   **973.7**
Night terrors   **S C**
  <small>Contents: Digger's promise; Just say yes; Digger in paradise; Good night, Jon; sleep tight, Jon; Paradise lost; Like father, like son; The worst day of my life; The cat's-eye; Deep into it; Something always happens; Footprints in the snow; Digger's good-bye</small>
West to a land of plenty   **Fic**
A young patriot   **973.3**

Murphy, Wendy B.
Asthma (7 and up)   **616.2**

Murray, Laura K.
Basic Internet for busy librarians   **004.6**

Murray, Peter, 1952-
  See also Hautman, Pete, 1952-

Murrell, Kathleen Berton
Russia   **947**

Murrow, Edward R.
About
Finkelstein, N. H. With heroic truth: the life of Edward R. Murrow (7 and up)   **92**

Muscles
Simon, S. Muscles   **612.7**

Musculoskeletal system
  See also Bones; Muscles
Ballard, C. The skeleton and muscular system   **612.7**

Musée du Louvre
Louvre Museum. See entry in CD-ROM section, Part 3

Museum of Natural History (New York, N.Y.)
  See American Museum of Natural History

Museums
  See also Art museums

The **Musgrave** ritual. Doyle, Sir A. C.
  In Doyle, Sir A. C. The complete Sherlock Holmes   **S C**

Mushona (African people) *See* Shona (African people)

Mushrooms
  See also Fungi
Lincoff, G. The Audubon Society field guide to North American mushrooms   **579.5**

Music
Ardley, N. A young person's guide to music   **780**
Sabbeth, A. Rubber-band banjos and a java jive bass   **781**
Analysis, appreciation
  See Music appreciation
Dictionaries
Kennedy, M. The concise Oxford dictionary of music   **780.3**
History and criticism
The Kingfisher young people's book of music   **780.9**
Ventura, P. Great composers   **780.9**

Music, African *See* African music

Music, African American *See* African American music

Music. Medearis, A. S.   **780.89**

Music appreciation
  See also Music—History and criticism
Ganeri, A. The young person's guide to the orchestra   **784.2**

The **music** of dolphins. Hesse, K.   **Fic**

The **Music** of what happens   **811.008**

Musical instruments
Ganeri, A. The young person's guide to the orchestra   **784.2**
Hasday, J. L. Musical instruments from around the world   **784.19**
Sabbeth, A. Rubber-band banjos and a java jive bass   **781**
Dictionaries
Baines, A. The Oxford companion to musical instruments (7 and up)   **784.19**

Musical instruments from around the world. Hasday, J. L.   **784.19**

Musicals
Ross, B. B. Junior Broadway   **792.6**

Musicians
  See also Composers; Violoncellists
Dictionaries
Kennedy, M. The concise Oxford dictionary of music   **780.3**
Fiction
Brooks, B. Midnight hour encores (7 and up)   **Fic**
Fenner, C. Yolonda's genius   **Fic**
Frank, L. K. Will you be my Brussels sprout? (7 and up)   **Fic**

Musicians, African American *See* African American musicians

Muskat, Carrie
Mark McGwire   **92**
Moises Alou   **92**
Sammy Sosa   **92**

The **Muslim** almanac   **297**

Muslim countries *See* Islamic countries

Muslimism *See* Islam

Muslims, Black *See* Black Muslims

The **mustang.** Silverstein, A.   **599.66**

My Angelica. Williams, C. L.   **Fic**

My ballet book. Castle, K.   **792.8**

My black me **811.008**

My bridges of hope. Bitton-Jackson, L. **92**

My brother, my sister, and I. Watkins, Y. K. **Fic**

My brother Sam is dead. Collier, J. L. **Fic**

My Daniel. Conrad, P. **Fic**

My first photography book. King, D. **771**

My great-grandfather's grave-digging. Price, S.
In The Oxford book of scary tales p94-95 **808.8**

My guardian angel. Gorog, J.
In Gorog, J. When nobody's home p90-94 **S C**

My home is over Jordan. Forrester, S. **Fic**

My life as a boy. Mazer, H.
In Mazer, H. The dog in the freezer: three novellas p1-32 **S C**

My life as a girl. Mosier, E. **Fic**

My life in dog years. Paulsen, G. **92**

My life with Martin Luther King, Jr. King, C. S. **92**

My Louisiana sky. Holt, K. W. **Fic**

My Lucy. Gordon, H.
In Rites of passage p163-76 **S C**

My Lucy friend who smells like corn. Cisneros, S.
In Who do you think you are? p119-21 **S C**

My mother and 'Mitch. Major, C.
In Rites of passage p191-202 **S C**

My name is America [series]
Murphy, J. The journal of James Edmond Pease, a Civil War Union soldier **Fic**
Myers, W. D. The journal of Joshua Loper **Fic**
Myers, W. D. The journal of Scott Pendleton Collins **Fic**

My name is Illusion. Krishnaswami, U.
In Krishnaswami, U. Shower of gold: girls and women in the stories of India p100-03 **398.2**

My name is Joseph. Paterson, K.
In Paterson, K. A midnight clear: stories for the Christmas season **S C**

My own two feet. Cleary, B. **92**

My own worst enemy. Sonenklar, C. **Fic**

My pony book. Pritchard, L. **636.1**

My side of the mountain. George, J. C. **Fic**

My soul looks back, 'less I forget **808.88**

My sweet sixteenth. Wilkinson, B. S.
In Join in p128-40 **S C**

Myanmar
Smith, R. In the forest with the elephants **599.67**
Politics and government
Stewart, W. Aung San Suu Kyi (7 and up) **92**

Mycology *See* Fungi

Myers, Anna
The keeping room **Fic**

Myers, Christopher A.
(jt. auth) Myers, L. B. Galápagos: islands of change **508**

Myers, Jack
On the trail of the Komodo dragon and other explorations of science in action **590**

Myers, Lynne Born
Galápagos: islands of change **508**

Myers, Steve
(jt. auth) Sanders, P. Anorexia and bulimia **616.85**
(jt. auth) Sanders, P. Divorce and separation **306.89**

Myers, Walter Dean, 1937-
Amistad: a long road to freedom **326**
At her majesty's request [biography of Sarah Forbes Bonetta] **92**
The beast is in the labyrinth
In Places I never meant to be **S C**
Briefcase
In Twelve shots: outstanding short stories about guns p7-24 **S C**
Cages
In Center stage **812.008**
The escape
In Trapped!: cages of mind and body p101-16 **S C**
Fallen angels (7 and up) **Fic**
Fast Sam, Cool Clyde, and Stuff (7 and up) **Fic**
Harlem **811**
Hoops (7 and up) **Fic**
Jeremiah's song
In Visions: nineteen short stories by outstanding writers for young adults p194-203 **S C**
The journal of Joshua Loper **Fic**
The journal of Scott Pendleton Collins **Fic**
Malcolm X (7 and up) **92**
Me, Mop, and the Moondance Kid **Fic**
Monster (7 and up) **Fic**
Motown and Didi (7 and up) **Fic**
The Mouse rap **Fic**
Now is your time! **305.8**
One more river to cross (7 and up) **779**
The outside shot (7 and up) **Fic**
Scorpions **Fic**
Slam! (7 and up) **Fic**
Somewhere in the darkness (7 and up) **Fic**
Toussaint L'Ouverture **92**

Mysteries of the universe. Wilson, C. **001.9**

Mysterious tales of Japan. Martin, R. **398.2**

Mystery and detective stories *See* Mystery fiction

Mystery fiction
Avi. The man who was Poe **Fic**
Avi. Wolf rider: a tale of terror **Fic**
Bellairs, J. The curse of the blue figurine **Fic**
Bennett, J. Coverup (7 and up) **Fic**
Bennett, J. Sing me a death song (7 and up) **Fic**
Bennett, J. Skinhead (7 and up) **Fic**
Byars, B. C. The dark stairs **Fic**
Christie, A. The mirror crack'd (7 and up) **Fic**
Christie, A. Murder on the Orient Express (7 and up) **Fic**
Cooney, C. B. The terrorist (7 and up) **Fic**

N

Nacho loco. Soto, G.
   In Soto, G. Local news p91-101   S C
Naden, Corinne J.
   John Muir, saving the wilderness   92
   (jt. auth) Blue, R. Staying out of trouble in a
    troubled family   362.7
   (jt. auth) Gillespie, J. T. Juniorplots 4
        028.5
   (jt. auth) Gillespie, J. T. Middleplots 4
        028.5
   (jt. auth) Gillespie, J. T. The Newbery compan-
    ion   028.5
Nagasaki (Japan)
       Bombardment, 1945
   Grant, R. G. Hiroshima and Nagasaki (7 and up)
        940.54
Nagel, Rob
   Endangered species   333.95
Nahum, Andrew
   Flying machine   629.133
Naidoo, Beverley
   Chain of fire   Fic
   Journey to Jo'burg   Fic
   No turning back   Fic
Nailling, Lee, 1917-
       About
   Warren, A. Orphan train rider   362.7
Nails. Jennings, P.
   In Jennings, P. Unbearable! p50-68   S C
The name. Galloway, P.
   In Galloway, P. Truly grim tales   S C
Names
   See also Geographic names
Namioka, Lensey
   The all-American slurp
   In Visions: nineteen short stories by outstand-
    ing writers for young adults p32-41
        S C
   Den of the White Fox (7 and up)   Fic
   Fox hunt
   In Join in p13-21   S C
   Herbal nightmare
   In Center stage   812.008
   Ties that bind, ties that break   Fic
   Who's Hu? [excerpt]
   In American dragons p48-64   810.8
Nanji, Azim
   (ed) The Muslim almanac. See The Muslim al-
    manac   297
Nanticoke Indians
   Porter, F. W. The Nanticoke
   In Indians of North America series
        970.004
Nanye'hi *See* Ward, Nancy, 1738?-1822
Napoleon I, Emperor of the French, 1769-1821
       About
   Blumberg, R. What's the deal? Jefferson, Napo-
    leon and the Louisiana Purchase (7 and up)
        973.4
   Henderson, H. The age of Napoleon (7 and up)
        944.05

Napoleonic Wars *See* France—History—1799-
   1815
Napoli, Donna Jo, 1948-
   Changing tunes   Fic
   Song of the Magdalene (7 and up)   Fic
   Spinners (7 and up)   Fic
   Stones in water   Fic
   Trouble on the tracks   Fic
   Zel (7 and up)   Fic
Narcotic traffic *See* Drug traffic
Narcotics
   See also Cocaine; Heroin; Marijuana
Narcotics and teenagers *See* Teenagers—Drug
   use
Nardo, Don, 1947-
   The Bill of Rights (7 and up)   342
   Braving the New World, 1619-1784 (7 and up)
        305.8
   Greek and Roman science (7 and up)   509
   Greek and Roman sport (7 and up)   796
   Leaders of ancient Greece (7 and up)   920
   Life of a Roman slave (7 and up)   937
   The medieval castle (7 and up)   940.1
   The Mexican-American War (7 and up)
        973.6
   The Roman Colosseum (7 and up)   725
   Rulers of ancient Rome (7 and up)   920
   Scientists of Ancient Greece (7 and up)
        920
   The Scopes trial (7 and up)   345
   (ed) The Black Death. See The Black Death
        614.5
   (ed) The French Revolution. See The French
    Revolution   944.04
   (ed) The Rise of Christianity. See The Rise of
    Christianity   270
   (ed) The Rise of Nazi Germany. See The Rise
    of Nazi Germany   943.086
Narraganset Indians
   Simmons, W. S. The Narragansett
   In Indians of North America series
        970.004
       Fiction
   Fleischman, P. Saturnalia   Fic
Narrations *See* Monologues
Narrow escape. San Souci, R.
   In San Souci, R. A terrifying taste of short &
    shivery p130-36   398.2
Nash, Carol Rust
   The Mormon Trail and the Latter-Day Saints in
    American history   289.3
Nash, Diane, 1938-
   See/See also pages in the following book(s):
   Powledge, F. We shall overcome p163-73
        323.1
Nash, Gary B.
   Forbidden love (7 and up)   305.8
Nash, Ogden, 1902-1971
   I wouldn't have missed it: selected poems of
    Ogden Nash   811
Naskapi Indians
   Armitage, P. The Innu (The Montagnais-
    Naskapi)
   In Indians of North America series
        970.004

Nassau, Kurt
Experimenting with color (7 and up)   535.6
Nasser, Gamal Abdel, 1918-1970
See/See also pages in the following book(s):
Rasmussen, R. K. Modern African political
leaders p17-29 (7 and up)   920
Nastasia of the sea. Osborne, M. P.
In Osborne, M. P. Mermaid tales from around
the world p25-30   398.2
Nat Turner and the slave revolt. Barrett, T.
92
Nathan, Amy
Everything you need to know about conflict res-
olution (7 and up)   158
The **nation** divides. Steins, R.   973.7
Nation of Islam *See* Black Muslims
A **nation** torn. Ray, D.   973.7
National anthems of the world (7 and up)
782.42
National Audubon Society
The Audubon Society field guide to North
American fishes, whales, and dolphins. See
The Audubon Society field guide to North
American fishes, whales, and dolphins
597
Behler, J. L. The Audubon Society field guide
to North American reptiles and amphibians
597.9
Chartrand, M. R. The Audubon Society field
guide to the night sky   523
Chesterman, C. W. The Audubon Society field
guide to North American rocks and minerals
549
Lincoff, G. The Audubon Society field guide to
North American mushrooms   579.5
Milne, L. J. The Audubon Society field guide to
North American insects and spiders
595.7
Niering, W. A. The Audubon Society field
guide to North American wildflowers: eastern
region   582.13
Pyle, R. M. The Audubon Society field guide to
North American butterflies   595.7
Rehder, H. A. The Audubon Society field guide
to North American seashells   594
Spellenberg, R. The Audubon Society field
guide to North American wildflowers: western
region   582.13
National Audubon Society field guide to North
American birds, Eastern region. Bull, J. L.
598
National Audubon Society field guide to North
American mammals. Whitaker, J. O., Jr.
599
National Audubon Society first field guide: birds.
Weidensaul, S.   598
National Audubon Society first field guide: in-
sects. Wilsdon, C.   595.7
National Audubon Society first field guide: mam-
mals. Grassy, J.   599
National Audubon Society first field guide: rep-
tiles. Behler, J. L.   597.9
National Audubon Society first field guide: rocks
and minerals. Ricciuti, E. R.   552

National Audubon Society first field guide: trees.
Cassie, B.   582.16
National Audubon Society first field guide: weath-
er. Kahl, J. D.   551.5
National Audubon Society first field guide:
wildflowers. Hood, S.   582.13
National Basketball Association
Layden, J. NBA game day   796.323
Rappoport, K. Guts and glory   920
National Council for the Social Studies
Notable children's trade books in the field of
social studies. See Notable children's trade
books in the field of social studies   016.3
National Council of Teachers of English
A Jar of tiny stars: poems by NCTE award-
winning poets. See A Jar of tiny stars: poems
by NCTE award-winning poets   811.008
**National Council of Teachers of English. Com-
mittee on the Junior High and Middle
School Booklist**
Your reading   011.6
The **national** debt. Sandak, C. R.   336.3
National debts *See* Public debts
National emblems
Ultimate pocket flags of the world   929.9
National Endowment for the Arts
See/See also pages in the following book(s):
Culture wars: opposing viewpoints p181-93 (7
and up)   306
National Football League
Buckley, J., Jr. America's greatest game
796.332
National Gallery (Great Britain)
Richardson, J. Looking at pictures   750
National Gallery of Art (U.S.)
Thomson, P. The nine-ton cat: behind the scenes
at an art museum   708
National Geographic atlas of the world   912
National Geographic book of mammals   599
National Geographic maps. See entry in CD-ROM
section, Part 3
National Geographic nature library [series]
Daniels, P. Earth   550
National Geographic Society (U.S.)
Blumberg, R. What's the deal? Jefferson, Napo-
leon and the Louisiana Purchase   973.4
Historical atlas of the United States. See Histori-
cal atlas of the United States   911
Matthews, T. L. Always inventing: a
photobiography of Alexander Graham Bell
92
National Geographic book of mammals. See Na-
tional Geographic book of mammals   599
National Museum of American Art (U.S.)
Celebrate America in poetry and art. See Cele-
brate America in poetry and art   811.008
National parks and reserves
United States
Our national parks   917.3
National parks mystery [series]
Skurzynski, G. Cliff hanger   Fic

Nature cross-sections. Orr, R.   **577**
Nature got there first. Gates, P.   **508**
Nature study
  Andryszewski, T. Step by step along the Appa-
    lachian Trail   **796.51**
  Andryszewski, T. Step by step along the Pacific
    Crest Trail   **796.51**
        Encyclopedias
  Eyewitness encyclopedia of nature 2.0. See en-
    try in CD-ROM section, Part 3
Nature watch series
  Bailey, J. Birds of prey   **598**
Naughton, Jim, 1957-
  Joyriding
    In Ultimate sports: short stories by outstand-
      ing writers for young adults p4-19
                               S C
Nava. Potok, C.
  In Potok, C. Zebra and other stories p70-96
                               S C
Navaho Indians *See* Navajo Indians
Navajo. Begay, S.   **811**
The **Navajo.** Bial, R.   **970.004**
Navajo code talkers. Aaseng, N.   **940.54**
Navajo Indians
  Aaseng, N. Navajo code talkers   **940.54**
  Bial, R. The Navajo   **970.004**
  Durrett, D. Unsung heroes of World War II (7
    and up)   **940.54**
  Iverson, P. The Navajos
    In Indians of North America series
                         970.004
See/See also pages in the following book(s):
  Brown, D. A. Bury my heart at Wounded Knee
    p14-36 (7 and up)   **970.004**
  Ehrlich, A. Wounded Knee: an Indian history of
    the American West   **970.004**
              Fiction
  Cannon, A. E. The shadow brothers (7 and up)
                               Fic
  Hobbs, W. The Big Wander (7 and up)
                               Fic
  O'Dell, S. Sing down the moon   **Fic**
              Poetry
  Begay, S. Navajo   **811**
The **naval** treaty. Doyle, Sir A. C.
  In Doyle, Sir A. C. The complete Sherlock
    Holmes   **S C**
Naylor, Phyllis Reynolds, 1933-
  Achingly Alice. See note under Naylor, P. R.
    Reluctantly Alice   **Fic**
  Alice in April. See note under Naylor, P. R. Re-
    luctantly Alice   **Fic**
  Alice in-between. See note under Naylor, P. R.
    Reluctantly Alice   **Fic**
  Alice in lace. See note under Naylor, P. R. Re-
    luctantly Alice   **Fic**
  Alice on the outside. See note under Naylor, P.
    R. Reluctantly Alice   **Fic**
  Alice the brave. See note under Naylor, P. R.
    Reluctantly Alice   **Fic**
  All but Alice. See note under Naylor, P. R. Re-
    luctantly Alice   **Fic**
  Danny's Desert Rats   **Fic**
  The fear place   **Fic**

  Ice   **Fic**
  The keeper   **Fic**
  Outrageously Alice. See note under Naylor, P.
    R. Reluctantly Alice   **Fic**
  Reluctantly Alice   **Fic**
  Sang Spell (7 and up)   **Fic**
  Saving Shiloh. See note under Naylor, P. R.
    Shiloh   **Fic**
  Shiloh   **Fic**
  Shiloh season. See note under Naylor, P. R. Shi-
    loh   **Fic**
  The witch's eye
    In A Newbery Halloween p83-99   **S C**
              About
  Stover, L. T. Presenting Phyllis Reynolds
    Naylor (7 and up)   **813.009**
The **Nazis.** Lace, W. W.   **943.086**
Nazism *See* National socialism
NBA *See* National Basketball Association
NBA game day. Layden, J.   **796.323**
NCSS *See* National Council for the Social Studies
NCTE *See* National Council of Teachers of En-
  glish
NCTE bibliography series
  National Council of Teachers of En-
    glish/Committee on the Junior High and Mid-
    dle School Booklist. Your reading   **011.6**
Ndebele, Njabulo S. (Njabulo Simakahle)
  The test
    In Rites of passage p103-29   **S C**
NEA *See* National Endowment for the Arts
Neal-Schuman complete Internet companion for
  librarians. Benson, A. C.   **004.6**
Neal-Schuman Internet policy handbook for li-
  braries. Smith, M.   **025**
Neal-Schuman net-guide series
  Benson, A. C. Connecting kids and the Internet
                               004.6
  Benson, A. C. Neal-Schuman complete Internet
    companion for librarians   **004.6**
  Smith, M. Neal-Schuman Internet policy hand-
    book for libraries   **025**
Neale S. Godfrey's ultimate kids' money book.
  Godfrey, N. S.   **332.024**
Near-death experiences
              Fiction
  Littke, L. Haunted sister (7 and up)   **Fic**
Near East *See* Middle East
Nebraska
  McNair, S. Nebraska
    In America the beautiful second series
                               973
             Fiction
  Conrad, P. My Daniel   **Fic**
  Conrad, P. Prairie songs   **Fic**
  Hermes, P. Calling me home   **Fic**
  Ruckman, I. In care of Cassie Tucker   **Fic**
  Ruckman, I. Night of the twisters   **Fic**
The **Necessary** cat   **808.8**
Necessary roughness. Lee, M. G.   **Fic**
Need to know library [series]
  Beal, E. Everything you need to know about
    ADD/ADHD   **616.85**

Nevada—Fiction—*Continued*
Snyder, Z. K. The runaways   **Fic**

Never quite a Hollywood star. Revard, C.
In Talking leaves   **S C**

Never to forget: the Jews of the Holocaust.
Meltzer, M.   **940.53**

Never trust a dead man. Vande Velde, V.
    Fic

The **new** American Bible. Bible   **220.5**

New and selected poems. Soto, G.   **811**

New astronomer. Stott, C.   **520**

The **new** broom. Hark, M.
In The Big book of holiday plays p20-28
    812.008

The **New** Cassell's German dictionary. See
Cassell's German-English, English-German
dictionary   **433**

The **new** comprehensive American rhyming dictionary. Young, S.   **423**

New dictionary of American slang. See Dictionary
of American slang   **427**

New explorers
Pascoe, E. Virtual reality   **006**

New-Fangled Thanksgiving. Hark, M.
In The Big book of holiday plays p101-09
    812.008

The **new** freedom to the New Deal, 1913-1939.
Katz, W. L.   **973.91**

The **new** girl. Stewart, S.
In A Glory of unicorns p185-94   **S C**

The **New** Grolier children's encyclopedia   **031**

New Guinea
Fiction
Campbell, E. The Shark Callers (7 and up)
    Fic

New Hampshire
Otfinoski, S. New Hampshire
In Celebrate the states   **973**

New Jersey
Moragne, W. New Jersey
In Celebrate the states   **973**
Stein, R. C. New Jersey
In America the beautiful, second series
    973

New Jersey v. T.L.O. Persico, D.   **345**

The **new** Jerusalem Bible. Bible   **220.5**

New Mexico
Kent, D. New Mexico
In America the beautiful, second series
    973
McDaniel, M. New Mexico
In Celebrate the states   **973**
Fiction
Hobbs, W. Kokopelli's flute   **Fic**

New Orleans (La.)
Race relations
Bridges, R. Through my eyes: the autobiography
of Ruby Bridges   **92**

The **New** Oxford book of American verse (7 and
up)   **811.008**

New perspectives [series]
Grant, R. G. The Berlin Wall   **943.087**

Grant, R. G. Hiroshima and Nagasaki
    940.54

The **new** Prometheus. Shelley, M. W.
In Read into the millenium p34-40   **S C**

The **New** Rolling Stone encyclopedia of rock &
roll (7 and up)   **781.66**

New steps to service. Wasman, A.   **027.8**

The **new** Warren. Adams, R.
In Adams, R. Tales from Watership Down
    S C

The **new** way things work. Macaulay, D.   **600**

The **new** way things work. See entry in CD-ROM
section, Part 3

New World. Cross, G.   **Fic**

New Year's Eve. Soto, G.
In Soto, G. Local news p132-44   **S C**

New York (N.Y.)
Antiquities
Hansen, J. Breaking ground, breaking silence
    974.7
Fiction
Fox, P. Monkey island   **Fic**
Frank, L. K. I am an artichoke (7 and up)
    Fic
Frank, L. K. Will you be my Brussels sprout?
(7 and up)   **Fic**
Giberga, J. S. Friends to die for (7 and up)
    Fic
Griffin, A. The other Shepards   **Fic**
Holland, I. Behind the lines   **Fic**
Holman, F. Slake's limbo   **Fic**
Krensky, S. The printer's apprentice   **Fic**
Lasky, K. Dreams in the golden country
    Fic
Lipsyte, R. The brave (7 and up)   **Fic**
Merrill, J. The pushcart war   **Fic**
Peck, R. Voices after midnight   **Fic**
Roberts, W. D. The kidnappers   **Fic**
Shusterman, N. Downsiders   **Fic**
Southgate, M. Another way to dance   **Fic**
Woodson, J. If you come softly (7 and up)
    Fic
Race relations
See/See also pages in the following book(s):
Cooper, M. L. Bound for the promised land
p46-67   **305.8**

New York (State)
Heinrichs, A. New York
In America the beautiful, second series
    973
Schomp, V. New York
In Celebrate the states   **973**
Fiction
Armstrong, J. Mary Mehan awake (7 and up)
    Fic
Auch, M. J. Frozen summer   **Fic**
Auch, M. J. Journey to nowhere   **Fic**
Bat-Ami, M. Two suns in the sky (7 and up)
    Fic
Irving, W. Rip Van Winkle and The legend of
Sleepy Hollow   **Fic**
Kirkpatrick, K. A. Trouble's daughter   **Fic**
O'Dell, S. Sarah Bishop   **Fic**
Skolsky, M. W. Love from your friend, Hannah
    Fic

Nez Percé Indians—*Continued*
Trafzer, C. E. The Nez Perce
In Indians of North America series
970.004

See/See also pages in the following book(s):
Brown, D. A. Bury my heart at Wounded Knee
p315-30 (7 and up) 970.004
Freedman, R. Indian chiefs p91-113 920
Fiction
O'Dell, S. Thunder rolling in the mountains
Fic

NFL *See* National Football League
Ng, Fae Myenne, 1956-
Bone [excerpt]
In American eyes p108-30 S C
Ng, Gina
Everything you need to know about self-
mutilation (7 and up) 616.85
NgCheong-Lum, Roseline, 1962-
France 944
Tahiti 996
Nguyen, Longhang
Rain music
In American dragons p155-60 810.8
Nguyen, Minh Duc
Fortune teller
In American eyes p80-107 S C
Nguyen Tat Thành *See* Ho, Chí Minh, 1890-1969
Niagara Falls (N.Y. and Ont.)
Fisher, L. E. Niagara Falls 971.3
Niatum, Duane, 1938-
Crow's sun
In Talking leaves S C
Nicholls, Christine
(ed) Encyclopedia of biography. See Encyclope-
dia of biography 920.003
Nichols, C. Allen
(jt. auth) Rosenberg, J. K. Young people's
books in series: fiction and non-fiction, 1975-
1991 011.6
(ed) Young adults and public libraries. See
Young adults and public libraries 027.62
Nichols, Mary Anne, 1967-
(ed) Young adults and public libraries. See
Young adults and public libraries 027.62
Nichols, Terry Lynn
See/See also pages in the following book(s):
Sherrow, V. The Oklahoma City bombing
364.1
Nicholson, Jessie
Conversation piece
In The Big book of holiday plays p300-12
812.008
Nicholson, Lois, 1949-
Booker T. Washington 92
The composite guide to lacrosse 796.34
Nickel-a-pound plane ride. Soto, G.
In Soto, G. Local news p120-31 S C
Nicknames
Fiction
Korman, G. The sixth grade nickname game
Fic
Nicolle, David, 1944-
Medieval knights 940.1

Niehaus, Theodore F.
A field guide to Pacific states wildflowers
582.13
Niering, William A.
The Audubon Society field guide to North
American wildflowers: eastern region
582.13
Nieuwsma, Milton J.
(ed) Kinderlager. See Kinderlager 940.53
Nigeria
Social life and customs
Nnoromele, S. Life among the Ibo women of
Nigeria (7 and up) 966.9
Nigg, Joe
Wonder beasts (7 and up) 398
Night. Wiesel, E.
In Wiesel, E. Night, Dawn, The accident:
three tales Fic
Night, Dawn, The accident: three tales. Wiesel, E.
Fic
The **night** journey. Lasky, K. Fic
Night kites. Kerr, M. E. Fic
A **night** of terror. Olson, A. N.
In Olson, A. N. Ask the bones: scary stories
from around the world p60-65 398.2
Night of the twisters. Ruckman, I. Fic
The **night** out. Westall, R.
In Westall, R. Demons and shadows p90-106
S C
Night photograph. Conrad, P.
In Conrad, P. Our house p12-21 S C
The **night** room. Goldman, E. M. Fic
The **night** swimmers. Byars, B. C. Fic
Night terrors (7 and up) S C
Night terrors. Murphy, J. S C
The **night** the heads came. Sleator, W. Fic
The **night** watchman. Braly, D.
In Read all about it! p244-51 808.8
Night wolves. Yolen, J.
In The Haunted house: a collection of original
stories S C
In Yolen, J. Here there be ghosts p56-62
810.8
Nightbirds on Nantucket. Aiken, J. See note under
Aiken, J. The wolves of Willoughby Chase
Fic
Nighthorse, Ben *See* Campbell, Ben Nighthorse
Nightingale, Florence, 1820-1910
See/See also pages in the following book(s):
Celebrating women in mathematics and science
p77-88 920
Nightjohn. Paulsen, G. Fic
A **Nightmare's** dozen (7 and up) S C
NightWatch. Dickinson, T. 520
Nihancan and the dwarf's arrow. Brown, D. A.
In Brown, D. A. Dee Brown's folktales of the
Native American p114-15 398.2
Nihei, Judith
Koden
In American dragons p97-109 810.8
Nilsen, Aileen Pace
Presenting M.E. Kerr (7 and up) 813.009

Noseweed. Jennings, P.
  In Jennings, P. Undone! p30-44   **S C**
Nostradamus, 1503-1566
  See/See also pages in the following book(s):
  Krull, K. They saw the future p51-57
                                              133.3
Not just a summer crush. Adler, C. S.   **Fic**
The **not-just-anybody** family. Byars, B. C.
                                                Fic
Notable Americans [series]
  Barron, R. Richard Nixon   **92**
  Byman, J. Andrew Grove and the Intel Corpora-
    tion   **92**
  Collins, D. R. Bix Beiderbecke   **92**
Notable children's trade books in the field of so-
    cial studies   **016.3**
Notable mathematicians (7 and up)   **920**
Nothing but the truth. Avi   **Fic**
Notorious Americans and their times [series]
  King, D. C. Al Capone and the roaring twenties
                                                92
  King, D. C. Benedict Arnold and the American
    Revolution   **92**
  Otfinoski, S. John Wilkes Booth and the Civil
    War   **92**
  Sherrow, V. Joseph McCarthy and the Cold War
                                                92
Novello, Antonia
  See/See also pages in the following book(s):
  DeAngelis, G. Science & medicine   **920**
  Morey, J. Famous Hispanic Americans p102-14
                                               920
Novio boy. Soto, G.   **812**
Now is your time!. Myers, W. D.   **305.8**
Now you see it, now you don't. Simon, S.
                                             152.14
Nowhere to call home. DeFelice, C. C.   **Fic**
Nowhere to hide. Olson, A. N.
  In Olson, A. N. Ask the bones: scary stories
    from around the world p66-72   **398.2**
Noyce, Robert, 1927-1990
  See/See also pages in the following book(s):
  Northrup, M. American computer pioneers p57-
    64   **920**
Nuclear energy
  Critical mass: America's race to build the atom-
    ic bomb. See entry in CD-ROM section, Part
    3
  Kidd, J. S. Quarks and sparks (7 and up)
                                             621.48
Nuclear physics
  Henderson, H. Nuclear physics (7 and up)
                                              539.7
Nuclear power plants
      See also Nuclear energy
            Fiction
  Hesse, K. Phoenix rising   **Fic**
Nuclear proliferation. Cheney, G. A.   **327.1**
Nuclear warfare
            Fiction
  Hall, L. If winter comes (7 and up)   **Fic**

Nuclear weapons
      See also Atomic bomb
  Cheney, G. A. Nuclear proliferation (7 and up)
                                              327.1
  See/See also pages in the following book(s):
  Weapons of mass destruction: opposing view-
    points (7 and up)   **358**
Number art: thirteen 1 2 3s from around the
    world. Fisher, L. E.   **513**
Number Four, Bowstring Lane. Aiken, J.
  In Aiken, J. A fit of shivers p1-11   **S C**
Number the stars. Lowry, L.   **Fic**
Numerals
  Fisher, L. E. Number art: thirteen 1 2 3s from
    around the world   **513**
Numismatics
      See also Coins
Nunez, Sandra Joseph
  And justice for all (7 and up)   **346**
Nuñez Cabeza de Vaca, Alvar, 16th cent.
  See/See also pages in the following book(s):
  Duncan, D. People of the West p7-13   **978**
  Marrin, A. Empires lost and won p6-30 (7 and
    up)   **979**
Nunn, Laura Silverstein
  (jt. auth) Silverstein, A. AIDS   **616.97**
  (jt. auth) Silverstein, A. Asthma   **616.2**
  (jt. auth) Silverstein, A. The California condor
                                               598
  (jt. auth) Silverstein, A. Chickenpox and shin-
    gles   **616.9**
  (jt. auth) Silverstein, A. Clocks and rhythms
                                             571.7
  (jt. auth) Silverstein, A. Depression   **616.85**
  (jt. auth) Silverstein, A. Energy   **621**
  (jt. auth) Silverstein, A. Evolution   **576.8**
  (jt. auth) Silverstein, A. Food chains   **577**
  (jt. auth) Silverstein, A. The grizzly bear
                                             599.78
  (jt. auth) Silverstein, A. The mustang
                                             599.66
  (jt. auth) Silverstein, A. A pet or not?   **636**
  (jt. auth) Silverstein, A. Photosynthesis   **572**
  (jt. auth) Silverstein, A. Plate tectonics
                                             551.1
  (jt. auth) Silverstein, A. Sickle cell anemia
                                             616.1
  (jt. auth) Silverstein, A. Snakes & such
                                               639
  (jt. auth) Silverstein, A. Symbiosis   **577.8**
  (jt. auth) Silverstein, A. Weather and climate
                                             551.5
Nuns
  Morgan, N. Mother Teresa: saint of the poor
                                                92
  Ruth, A. Mother Teresa   **92**
The **nun's** priest's tale. Cohen, B.
  In Cohen, B. Canterbury tales   **821**
Nurses
  Wells, R. Mary on horseback   **92**
  Whitelaw, N. Clara Barton   **92**
Nutcracker (Ballet)
  See/See also pages in the following book(s):
  McCaughrean, G. The Random House book of
    stories from the ballet p57-69   **792.8**

Nutcracker (Ballet)—*Continued*
Newman, B. The illustrated book of ballet stories p52-61   **792.8**

Nutrition
See also Eating customs
D'Amico, J. The healthy body cookbook   **641.5**
See/See also pages in the following book(s):
Schwager, T. The right moves p43-114 (7 and up)   **613.7**

Nuts! Nuts! Nuts!. Van Laan, N.
In Van Laan, N. With a whoop and a holler p61-64   **398**

Nuwer, Hank
The legend of Jesse Owens (7 and up)   **92**

Nyar-upoko. Fairman, T.
In Fairman, T. Bury my bones but keep my words p13-30   **398.2**

Nye, Michael
(il) What have you lost? See What have you lost?   **808.81**

Nye, Naomi Shihab
Habibi   **Fic**
(comp) I feel a little jumpy around you. See I feel a little jumpy around you   **808.81**
(comp) The Space between our footsteps. See The Space between our footsteps   **808.81**
(comp) The Tree is older than you are. See The Tree is older than you are   **860.8**
(comp) What have you lost? See What have you lost?   **808.81**

Nyerere, Julius K., 1922-1999
See/See also pages in the following book(s):
Rasmussen, R. K. Modern African political leaders p61-73 (7 and up)   **920**

NYPL *See* New York Public Library

O

O Jerusalem. Yolen, J.   **811**

Oakley, Annie, 1860-1926
About
Flynn, J. Annie Oakley   **92**

Oates, Joyce Carol, 1938-
Where are you going, where have you been?
In Who do you think you are? p14-35   **S C**

Oba, Ryan
Home now
In American eyes p28-36   **S C**

Obedience. Brown, F.
In Read into the millenium p103-17   **S C**

Oberth, Hermann, 1894-1989
See/See also pages in the following book(s):
Maurer, R. Rocket!   **621.43**

Obesity
Control
See Weight loss
Fiction
Bennett, C. Life in the fat lane (7 and up)   **Fic**
Crutcher, C. Staying fat for Sarah Byrnes   **Fic**

Lipsyte, R. One fat summer (7 and up)   **Fic**

Object lesson. Queen, E.
In Read all about it! p53-66   **808.8**

Oblinger, Mattie, d. 1880
See/See also pages in the following book(s):
Duncan, D. People of the West p68-75   **978**

Oblinger, Uriah, d. 1901
See/See also pages in the following book(s):
Duncan, D. People of the West p68-75   **978**

O'Brien, Eileen, 1955-
Starving to win (7 and up)   **616.85**

O'Brien, Joanne, 1959-
(jt. auth) Breuilly, E. Religions of the world   **291**

O'Brien, Lisa, 1963-
Lights, camera, action!   **791.43**

O'Brien, Robert C., 1918-1973
Mrs. Frisby and the rats of NIMH   **Fic**
Z for Zachariah (7 and up)   **Fic**

O'Brien, Steven
American political leaders   **920.003**
Antonio López de Santa Anna   **92**
Pancho Villa   **92**

O'Brien, Tim, 1946-
Ambush
In Who do you think you are? p152-55   **S C**
The man I killed
In Who do you think you are? p146-51   **S C**
On the rainy river
In Leaving home: stories p133-56   **808.8**

Obscenity (Law)
See also Pornography

Obsessive-compulsive neurosis
Fiction
Hesser, T. S. Kissing doorknobs (7 and up)   **Fic**
Tashjian, J. Multiple choice   **Fic**

Ocampo, Adriana C., 1955-
See/See also pages in the following book(s):
Oleksy, W. G. Hispanic-American scientists (7 and up)   **920**

Occultism
See also Astrology; Divination; Fortune telling; Palmistry; Prophecies; Satanism

Occupational crimes *See* White collar crimes

Occupational guidance *See* Vocational guidance

Occupational outlook handbook. United States. Bureau of Labor Statistics   **331.7**

Occupational training
Unger, H. G. But what if I don't want to go to college (7 and up)   **331.7**

Occupations
Career discovery encyclopedia   **331.7**
The Encyclopedia of careers and vocational guidance   **331.7**
Encyclopedia of careers and vocational guidance. See entry in CD-ROM section, Part 3
Professional & technical careers (7 and up)   **331.7**

Offenses against the person
   See also Homicide; Kidnapping; Rape

Ogden, Aaron, 1756-1839
About
Levinson, I. S. Gibbons v. Ogden (7 and up)
   343

Oglala Indians
Freedman, R. The life and death of Crazy Horse
   92

See/See also pages in the following book(s):
Freedman, R. Indian chiefs p11-27   920

Oglesby, Carole A.
(ed) Encyclopedia of women and sport in America. See Encyclopedia of women and sport in America   796

O'Grady, Scott F.
Basher five-two   949.7

The **ogre's** arm. San Souci, R.
   In San Souci, R. A terrifying taste of short & shivery p46-51   398.2

Oh, freedom!. King, C.   323.1

Oh, those Harper girls!. Karr, K.   Fic

Ohio
Heinrichs, A. Ohio
   In America the beautiful, second series
   973
Sherrow, V. Ohio
   In Celebrate the states   973
Fiction
Fleischman, P. The borning room   Fic
Hamilton, V. The house of Dies Drear   Fic

Ohmi, Ayano, 1959-
(jt. auth) Hamanaka, S. In search of the spirit
   920

Ohrn, Dobrorah Gore
(ed) Herstory: women who changed the world. See Herstory: women who changed the world
   920

Oil painting *See* Painting

Oil painting portraits. Smith, R.
   In The DK art school series   751

Oil spills
DuTemple, L. A. Oil spills (7 and up)
   363.7
Markle, S. After the spill   363.7
Sherrow, V. The Exxon Valdez   363.7

Ojibwa Indians
Tanner, H. H. The Ojibwa
   In Indians of North America series
   970.004
Fiction
Erdrich, L. The birchbark house   Fic

O'Keeffe, Georgia, 1887-1986
See/See also pages in the following book(s):
Glubok, S. Great lives: painting p129-41
   920
Greenberg, J. The American eye p15-24
   920
Sills, L. Inspirations p6-17   920

Okheena, Mary
(il) The Dancing fox: Arctic folktales. See The Dancing fox: Arctic folktales   398.2

Okie, Susan
(jt. auth) Ride, S. K. To space & back
   629.45

Okimoto, Jean Davies, 1942-
Hum it again, Jeremy
   In Center stage   812.008
Jason Kovak, the quick and the brave
   In Visions: nineteen short stories by outstanding writers for young adults p42-63
   S C
Next month . . . Hollywood!
   In Join in p35-46   S C

Okita, Dwight, 1958-
See/See also pages in the following book(s):
Chiu, C. Lives of notable Asian Americans: literature and education p107-13 (7 and up)
   920

Oklahoma
Reedy, J. Oklahoma
   In America the beautiful, second series
   973
Fiction
Grove, V. The starplace   Fic
Hesse, K. Out of the dust   Fic
Rawls, W. Summer of the monkeys (7 and up)
   Fic

Oklahoma City (Okla.) bombing, 1995
Sherrow, V. The Oklahoma City bombing
   364.1

Oklahoma City Federal Building Bombing, Oklahoma City (Okla.), 1995 *See* Oklahoma City (Okla.) bombing, 1995

Oksana: my own story. Baiul, O.   92

Okutoro, Lydia Omolola
(comp) Quiet storm. See Quiet storm
   811.008

Ol' Gally Mander. Van Laan, N.
   In Van Laan, N. With a whoop and a holler p76-81   398

Ol' Master Biggety. Van Laan, N.
   In Van Laan, N. With a whoop and a holler p43-46   398

Olajuwon, Akeem *See* Olajuwon, Hakeem

Olajuwon, Hakeem
See/See also pages in the following book(s):
Rappoport, K. Guts and glory   920

Old, Wendie
Duke Ellington: giant of jazz   92
Louis Armstrong   92
Marian Wright Edelman (7 and up)   92

Old age
Fiction
Fleischman, P. Mind's eye   Fic
Bauer, J. Rules of the road (7 and up)   Fic
Hickman, J. Jericho   Fic
Koertge, R. Tiger, tiger, burning bright   Fic
Morpurgo, M. Escape from Shangri-La   Fic
Yumoto, K. The friends   Fic
The **old** chief Mshlanga. Lessing, D. M.
   In Somehow tenderness survives p19-35
   S C
Old glory. Coville, B.
   In Coville, B. Oddly enough p79-85
   S C

The **one** hundred most popular young adult authors. See Drew, B. A. The 100 most popular young adult authors **810.9**

One hundred one stories of the great ballets. See Balanchine, G. 101 stories of the great ballets **792.8**

One hundred seventy-five more science experiments to amuse and amaze your friends. See Cash, T. 175 more science experiments to amuse and amaze your friends **507.8**

The **one** hundredth thing about Caroline. Lowry, L. **Fic**

The **One-Inch** Boy. Hamilton, V.
In Hamilton, V. The dark way p23-26
398.2

One more river to cross. Haskins, J. **920**

One more river to cross. Myers, W. D. **779**

One nation again **973.8**

One nation, many tribes. Krull, K. **970.004**

One parent family *See* Single parent family

The **one** who watches. Ortiz Cofer, J.
In Ortiz Cofer, J. An island like you p72-81
S C

One world, many religions. Osborne, M. P.
291

O'Neal, Shaquille
About
Ungs, T. Shaquille O'Neal **92**

O'Neill, Eugene, 1888-1953
See/See also pages in the following book(s):
Faber, D. Great lives: American literature p250-58 **920**

O'Neill, Ruth
Stealing dreams
In A Glory of unicorns p59-73 **S C**

O'Neill, Terry, 1944-
Biomedical ethics (7 and up) **174**

O'Neill, William L.
World War II: a student companion (7 and up)
940.53

Only gilt. Jennings, P.
In Jennings, P. Unbearable! p22-34 **S C**

Only if you think so. Reynolds, M.
In Reynolds, M. Beyond dreams p9-36
S C

Oodgeroo, 1920-1993
Dreamtime **398.2**
Includes the following stories: The beginning of life; Biami and Bunyip; Mirrabooka; The midden; Burr-Nong; Wonga and Nudu; Curlew; Oodgeroo; Tuggan-Tuggan; Talwalpin and Kowinka; Pomera; Tia-Gam; Boonah; Mai

Opdyke, Irene Gut, 1921-
In my hands (7 and up) **940.53**
See/See also pages in the following book(s):
Lyman, D. Holocaust rescuers **920**

Opera
See/See also pages in the following book(s):
Steins, R. Leontyne Price, opera superstar
92

Stories, plots, etc.
Geras, A. The Random House book of opera stories **792.5**

Operating and evaluating school library media programs. Yesner, B. L. **027.8**

Operation Desert Storm *See* Persian Gulf War, 1991

Operetta
See also Musicals
Ophelia speaks. Shandler, S. **305.23**

Opie, Mary-Jane
Sculpture (7 and up) **730.9**

Oppel, Kenneth
Silverwing **Fic**

Oppenheimer, Sonya
(ed) SPINAbilities. See SPINAbilities **616.8**

Opposing viewpoints digests [series]
Currie, S. Slavery **326**
Haugen, D. The Civil War **973.7**
Hurley, J. A. Animal rights **179**
Nardo, D. The Bill of Rights **342**
Stewart, G. The death penalty **364.66**
Stewart, G. Gangs **364.36**
Torr, J. D. Euthanasia **179.7**

Opposing viewpoints juniors [series]
Steffens, B. Free speech **323.44**

Opposing viewpoints series
21st century earth: opposing viewpoints
303.49
Abortion: opposing viewpoints **363.46**
AIDS: opposing viewpoints **616.97**
Alcohol: opposing viewpoints **362.292**
America's prisons: opposing viewpoints
365
America's victims: opposing viewpoints
306
Animal rights: opposing viewpoints **179**
Biomedical ethics: opposing viewpoints **174**
Chemical dependency: opposing viewpoints
362.29
Child abuse: opposing viewpoints **362.7**
Child welfare: opposing viewpoints **362.7**
Civil liberties: opposing viewpoints **323**
Criminal justice: opposing viewpoints **345**
Culture wars: opposing viewpoints **306**
Death and dying: opposing viewpoints
155.9
The Death penalty: opposing viewpoints
364.66
Discrimination: opposing viewpoints **305.8**
Does capital punishment deter crime?
364.66
Drug abuse: opposing viewpoints **362.29**
Endangered oceans: opposing viewpoints
577.7
Epidemics: opposing viewpoints **614.4**
Euthanasia: opposing viewpoints **179**
The Family: opposing viewpoints **306.8**
Genetic engineering: opposing viewpoints
174
Global warming: opposing viewpoints
363.7
Gun control: opposing viewpoints **363.3**
Hate groups: opposing viewpoints **364.1**
Homosexuality: opposing viewpoints **305.9**
Human nature: opposing viewpoints **128**
Human rights: opposing viewpoints **323**
Immigration: opposing viewpoints **325.73**
Inequality: opposing viewpoints in social problems **305**

Orphan train series
Nixon, J. L. A family apart   Fic
The **Orphan** who became strong
    In The Dancing fox: Arctic folktales p46-54
          398.2

Orphans
Warren, A. Orphan train rider   **362.7**
           Fiction
Alder, E. The king's shadow (7 and up)
                 Fic
Blackwood, G. L. The Shakespeare stealer
                 Fic
Cleaver, V. Where the lilies bloom   Fic
Curtis, C. P. Bud, not Buddy   Fic
DeFelice, C. C. The apprenticeship of Lucas
    Whitaker   Fic
DeFelice, C. C. Nowhere to call home   Fic
Dickinson, P. Suth's story   Fic
Garland, S. The silent storm   Fic
Gregory, K. Orphan runaways   Fic
Haas, J. Unbroken   Fic
Kim, H. The long season of rain (7 and up)
                 Fic
Little, J. The belonging place   Fic
Matcheck, D. The sacrifice (7 and up)   Fic
Menick, S. The muffin child   Fic
Murphy, J. The journal of James Edmond Pease,
    a Civil War Union soldier   Fic
Naylor, P. R. Sang Spell (7 and up)   Fic
Pullman, P. The ruby in the smoke (7 and up)
                 Fic
Qualey, M. Thin ice (7 and up)   Fic
Reeder, C. Shades of gray   Fic
Roberts, W. D. Pawns   Fic
Rodowsky, C. F. The Turnabout Shop   Fic
Snyder, Z. K. Gib rides home   Fic
Spinelli, J. Maniac Magee   Fic
Thesman, J. The ornament tree (7 and up)
                 Fic

Orr, Richard
Nature cross-sections   **577**

Orr, Wendy, 1953-
Peeling the onion (7 and up)   Fic

Ortega, Kay
See/See also pages in the following book(s):
Morey, J. Famous Mexican Americans p98-105
              920

Orthodontics
Lee, J. Coping with braces and other orthodon-
    tic work   **617.6**
Rourke, A. C. Teeth and braces   **617.6**

Ortiz, Alfonso, 1939-1997
The Pueblo
    In Indians of North America series
             970.004
(ed) American Indian myths and legends. See
    American Indian myths and legends
             398.2

Ortiz Cofer, Judith, 1952-
American history
    In Who do you think you are? p36-46
             S C
Bad influence
    In Leaving home: stories p63-90   **808.8**

An island like you (7 and up)   **S C**
Contents: Bad influence; Arturo's flight; Beauty lessons; Catch
the moon; An hour with Abuelo; The one who watches; Matoa's
mirror; Don José of La Mancha; Abuela invents the zero; A job
for Valentín; Home to El Building; White balloons
A job for Valentín
    In Help wanted: short stories about young
    people working   **S C**

Orwell, George, 1903-1950
Animal farm (7 and up)   **Fic**
Nineteen eighty-four (7 and up)   **Fic**

Oryx multicultural folktale series
Hearne, B. G. Beauties and beasts   **398.2**

Osage Indians
Wilson, T. P. The Osage
    In Indians of North America series
             970.004

Osborne, Harold, 1905-1987
(ed) The Oxford dictionary of art. See The Ox-
    ford dictionary of art   **703**

Osborne, Linda Barrett, 1949-
(jt. auth) King, C. Oh, freedom!   **323.1**

Osborne, Mary Pope, 1949-
Favorite medieval tales   **398.2**
Contents: Finn Maccoul; Beowulf; The sword in the stone; Is-
land of the lost children; The song of Roland; The werewolf; Sir
Gawain and the Green Knight; Robin Hood and his merry men;
Chanticleer and the fox
Favorite Norse myths   **293**
George Washington   **92**
Mermaid tales from around the world
             398.2
Contents: The mystery of Melusine; Menana of the waterfall;
The sea nymph and the Cyclops; The enchanted cap; Nastasia of
the sea; The fish husband; The serpent and the Sea Queen; The
mermaid's revenge; The princess of the Tung Lake; The sea prin-
cess of Persia; The mermaid in the millpond; The little mermaid
One world, many religions   **291**
Paul Bunyan, the mightiest logger of them all
    In From sea to shining sea p280-83
             810.8
Standing in the light   **Fic**

The **Osbornes'** Christmas. Montgomery, L. M.
    In Montgomery, L. M. Christmas with Anne
    and other holiday stories p61-67
             S C

O'Shea, Maria
Kuwait   **953.67**

The **O'Tannenbaum** affair. Taylor, T.
    In Taylor, T. Rogue wave and other red-
    blooded sea stories   **S C**

Otfinoski, Steven, 1949-
Bulgaria (7 and up)   **949.9**
John Wilkes Booth and the Civil War   **92**
The kid's guide to money   **332.024**
New Hampshire
    In Celebrate the states   **973**
Scott Joplin (7 and up)   **92**
Speaking up, speaking out   **808.5**
Ukraine (7 and up)   **947.7**

Othello. Lester, J.   **Fic**

Other America [series]
Stewart, G. Homeless teens   **362.5**
Stewart, G. Mothers on welfare   **362.83**
Stewart, G. Teen addicts   **362.29**
Stewart, G. Teen dropouts   **362.7**

Overland journeys to the Pacific—*Continued*
Calabro, M. The perilous journey of the Donner Party   **978**
Fisher, L. E. The Oregon Trail   **979.5**
Lavender, D. S. Snowbound   **978**
The Oregon trail. See entry in CD-ROM section, Part 3

Fiction
Lasky, K. Beyond the divide (7 and up)   **Fic**
Van Leeuwen, J. Bound for Oregon   **Fic**

Ovsyanikov, Nikita
Polar bears (7 and up)   **599.78**

Owen, Ruth Bryan, 1885-1954
The good sword
In The Book of dragons p110-20   **S C**

Owens, Jesse, 1913-1980
About
Nuwer, H. The legend of Jesse Owens (7 and up)   **92**

Owens, Tom, 1960-
Collecting baseball cards   **769**
Collecting baseball memorabilia   **790.1**
Collecting basketball cards   **769**
Football   **796.332**
Hockey   **796.962**

Owl. Wolkstein, D.
In From sea to shining sea p266-67   **810.8**

Owl in love. Kindl, P.   **Fic**
The **owl** service. Garner, A.   **Fic**

Owls
Sattler, H. R. The book of North American owls   **598**

Fiction
Kindl, P. Owl in love   **Fic**

The **ox** of the wonderful horns [story] Bryan, A.
In Bryan, A. Ashley Bryan's African tales, uh-huh p27-39   **398.2**

The **oxcart**. Kimmel, E. A.
In Kimmel, E. A. Sword of the samurai p41-51   **Fic**

Oxford American children's encyclopedia   **031**

Oxford Book of American verse, The New   **811.008**

The **Oxford** book of children's verse in America   **811.008**

The **Oxford** book of scary tales   **808.8**

The **Oxford** book of story poems   **821.008**

The **Oxford** book of twentieth-century English verse (7 and up)   **821.008**

The **Oxford** book of war poetry (7 and up)   **808.81**

The **Oxford** companion to classical civilization   **938.003**

The **Oxford** companion to musical instruments. Baines, A.   **784.19**

The **Oxford** companion to the Bible   **220.3**

The **Oxford** dictionary of art (7 and up)   **703**

The **Oxford** dictionary of the Christian Church   **270**

The **Oxford** dictionary of the Jewish religion   **296.03**

The **Oxford-Duden** pictorial Japanese and English dictionary   **495.6**

Oxford first ancient history. Burrell, R. E. C.   **909**

Oxford portraits in science [series]
Bernstein, J. Albert Einstein and the frontiers of physics   **92**
Christianson, G. E. Isaac Newton and the scientific revolution   **92**
Collier, B. Charles Babbage and the engines of perfection   **92**
Cooper, D. Enrico Fermi and the revolutions in modern physics   **92**
Edelson, E. Gregor Mendel, and the roots of genetics   **92**
Edelson, E. James Watson and Francis Crick and the building blocks of life   **92**
Hager, T. Linus Pauling and the chemistry of life   **92**
Mark, J. T. Margaret Mead   **92**
Pasachoff, N. E. Marie Curie and the science of radioactivity   **92**
Stefoff, R. Charles Darwin and the evolution revolution   **92**

Oxford profiles [series]
Baker, R. F. Ancient Greeks   **938**
Keene, A. T. Peacemakers   **920.003**

Oxford student companions to American history [series]
O'Neill, W. L. World War II: a student companion   **940.53**

The **Oxford** treasury of classic poems (7 and up)   **821.008**

The **Oxford** treasury of time poems   **821.008**

Oxlade, Chris
Chemistry   **540.7**
Science magic with magnets   **793.8**
Weather   **551.5**

Oxygen
Farndon, J. Oxygen
In The Elements [Benchmark Bks.]   **546**
Fitzgerald, K. The story of oxygen   **546**

Ozark Mountains
Fiction
Rawls, W. Where the red fern grows   **Fic**

Ozick, Cynthia
The shawl
In Bearing witness p60-66   **808.8**

Ozone layer
Pringle, L. P. Vanishing ozone   **363.7**
See/See also pages in the following book(s):
Miller, C. G. Air alert   **363.7**

P

P.O.W.'s *See* Prisoners of war
P.S. Longer letter later. Danziger, P.   **Fic**
Pacific Crest Trail
Andryszewski, T. Step by step along the Pacific Crest Trail   **796.51**

Pawnee Indians
Lacey, T. J. The Pawnee
In Indians of North America series
        970.004

Pawns. Roberts, W. D.   **Fic**

Paying with shadows. Yep, L.
In Yep, L. The tree of dreams   **398.2**

Payton, Philip A., 1876-1917
See/See also pages in the following book(s):
Haskins, J. African American entrepreneurs p79-82   **920**

Peace
Carter, J. Talking peace (7 and up)   **327.1**
See/See also pages in the following book(s):
Keene, A. T. Peacemakers   **920.003**

Peace movements *See* Pacifism

Peacemakers. Keene, A. T.   **920.003**

Peacock, Louise
Crossing the Delaware   **973.3**

Peacock's ghost. San Souci, R.
In San Souci, R. A terrifying taste of short & shivery p109-13   **398.2**

Peale, Charles Willson, 1741-1827
About
Giblin, J. The mystery of the mammoth bones   **569**
Wilson, J. The ingenious Mr. Peale   **92**

Peanuts
See/See also pages in the following book(s):
Johnson, S. A. Tomatoes, potatoes, corn, and beans p51-63   **641.3**

Pear, Nancy
(ed) Explorers & discoverers. See Explorers & discoverers   **920.003**

Pearce, Philippa, 1920-
Who's afraid?
In Read all about it! p230-35   **808.8**

The **pearl.** Steinbeck, J.   **Fic**

Pearl fisheries
Fiction
O'Dell, S. The black pearl   **Fic**

Pearl Harbor (Oahu, Hawaii), Attack on, 1941
Rice, E. The attack on Pearl Harbor (7 and up)   **940.54**
Fiction
Salisbury, G. Under the blood-red sun   **Fic**

The **pearl** of the soul of the world. Pierce, M. A.   **Fic**

Pearls of Lutra. Jacques, B. See note under Jacques, B. Redwall   **Fic**

Pearson, Kit
The eyes
In Don't read this! and other tales of the unnatural p132-48   **S C**

Peary, Robert Edwin, 1856-1920
About
Dwyer, C. Robert Peary and the quest for the North Pole   **92**
Robert E. Peary and the rush to the North Pole (7 and up)   **998**
See/See also pages in the following book(s):
Lomask, M. Great lives: exploration p209-19   **920**

The **pebble** people. Jack, R.
In Talking leaves   **S C**

Peck, Richard, 1934-
Anonymously yours   **92**
Are you in the house alone? (7 and up)
          Fic
Girl at the window
In Night terrors   **S C**
The great interactive dream machine **Fic**
The last safe place on earth (7 and up) **Fic**
A long way from Chicago   **Fic**
Lost in cyberspace   **Fic**
Priscilla and the wimps
In Sixteen: short stories by outstanding writers for young adults p42-46   **S C**
In Who do you think you are? p92-95
          S C
Remembering the good times (7 and up)
          Fic
Shadows
In Visions: nineteen short stories by outstanding writers for young adults p2-10
          S C
Shotgun Cheatham's last night above ground
In Twelve shots: outstanding short stories about guns p122-37   **S C**
Strays like us   **Fic**
Voices after midnight   **Fic**
Waiting for Sebastian
In Dirty laundry: stories about family secrets p80-87   **S C**
About
Gallo, D. R. Presenting Richard Peck (7 and up)
          813.009

Peck, Robert Newton, 1928-
Cowboy ghost   **Fic**
A day no pigs would die   **Fic**
Nine man tree   **Fic**

The **peculiar** such thing. Hamilton, V.
In From sea to shining sea p338-39
          810.8

Pedagogy *See* Teaching

Pederson, Jay P.
(ed) African American breakthroughs. See African American breakthroughs **305.8**

Pedrode Urdemalas. Winther, B.
In Winther, B. Plays from Hispanic tales
          812

Peeling the onion   **808.81**

Peeling the onion. Orr, W.   **Fic**

Peer counseling
Nathan, A. Everything you need to know about conflict resolution (7 and up)   **158**

Peet, Bill
Bill Peet: an autobiography   **92**

Peffer-Engels, John, 1966-
States of Ethiopia   **963**

Pegasus in flight. McCaffrey, A.   **Fic**

Pelé, 1940-
About
Arnold, C. Pelé: the king of soccer   **92**

Pellant, Chris
Rocks and minerals   **549**

Peterson, Roger Tory, 1908-1996—*Continued*
A field guide to wildflowers of northeastern and north-central North America **582.13**

Peterson field guide series
Niehaus, T. F. A field guide to Pacific states wildflowers **582.13**
Pasachoff, J. M. A field guide to the stars and planets **523**
Peterson, R. T. A field guide to wildflowers of northeastern and north-central North America **582.13**
Petrides, G. A. A field guide to trees and shrubs **582.16**

Peterson field guides for young naturalists [series]
Latimer, J. P. Backyard birds **598**
Latimer, J. P. Birds of prey **598**
Latimer, J. P. Bizarre birds **598**
Latimer, J. P. Shorebirds **598**

Peterson first guide to birds of North America. See Peterson, R. T. A field guide to the birds **598**

Peterson first guide to seashores. Kricher, J. C. **577.7**

Peterson first guide to shells of North America. Douglass, J. L. **594**

Peterson first guide to the seashore. See Kricher, J. C. Peterson first guide to seashores **577.7**

Peterson first guide to wildflowers of northeastern and north-central North America. See Peterson, R. T. A field guide to wildflowers of northeastern and north-central North America **582.13**

Peterson natural history companions [series]
Kaufman, K. Lives of North American birds **598**

Peterson's summer opportunities for kids and teenagers **790.1**

Petrides, George A.
A field guide to trees and shrubs **582.16**

Petroglyphs *See* Rock drawings, paintings, and engravings

Petrouchka (Ballet)
See/See also pages in the following book(s):
McCaughrean, G. The Random House book of stories from the ballet p95-101 **792.8**

Petrushka (Ballet) *See* Petrouchka (Ballet)

Petry, Ann Lane
Tituba of Salem Village **Fic**

Pets
See also Domestic animals; names of animals, e.g. *Cats; Dogs;* etc.
George, J. C. A tarantula in my purse **92**
Silverstein, A. A pet or not? **636**

Pets. Avi
In Avi. What do fish have to do with anything? and other stories p121-50 **S C**

Pettit, Jayne
Michelangelo **92**

Petty crimes. Soto, G. **S C**

Pevar, Stephen L.
The rights of American Indians and their tribes (7 and up) **342**

Pevsner, Stella
Sing for your father, Su Phan **Fic**
Would my fortune cookie lie? **Fic**

Pfeffer, Susan Beth, 1948-
Ashes
In Places I never meant to be **S C**
Pigeon humor
In Sixteen: short stories by outstanding writers for young adults p32-41 **S C**
World affairs
In Center stage **812.008**
The year without Michael **Fic**

Pfetzer, Mark
Within reach: my Everest story (7 and up) **796.52**

Pfitsch, Patricia Curtis
Keeper of the light **Fic**

Pflueger, Lynda
Dolley Madison **92**
Jeb Stuart **92**
Stonewall Jackson **92**

Pharmacology
See also Drugs
Kidd, J. S. Mother Nature's pharmacy (7 and up) **615**

Pharmacy in the forest. Powledge, F. **615**

The **Philadelphia** adventure. Alexander, L. See note under Alexander, L. The Illyrian adventure **Fic**

Philanthropists
Kent, Z. Andrew Carnegie **92**
Meltzer, M. The many lives of Andrew Carnegie (7 and up) **92**

Philbrick, Rodman *See* Philbrick, W. R. (W. Rodman)

Philbrick, W. R. (W. Rodman)
The fire pony **Fic**
Freak the Mighty **Fic**
Max the Mighty **Fic**

Philip V, of Macedon, 238-179 B.C.
See/See also pages in the following book(s):
Nardo, D. Leaders of ancient Greece (7 and up) **920**

Philip, Sachem of the Wampanoags, d. 1676
See/See also pages in the following book(s):
Kallen, S. A. Native American chiefs and warriors (7 and up) **920**

Philip, Neil
The Arabian nights **398.2**
Contents: How Sheherazade married the king; The fisherman and the jinni; Fair shares; The City of Brass; The anklet; The wonderful bag; Judar and his brothers; The ebony horse; The ass; Aladdin; The speaking bird, the singing tree, and the golden water; True knowledge; Princess Nur al-Nihar, the three princes, and Peri-Banu; Ali Baba and the forty thieves; How many fools?; The keys of destiny
The illustrated book of myths **291.1**
Mythology **291.1**
Myths & legends (7 and up) **398.2**
Odin's family **293**
The story of Robin Hood **398.2**
The tale of Sir Gawain **398.2**

Physics

See also Nuclear physics; Relativity (Physics)

Challoner, J. The visual dictionary of physics   **530**

Friedhoffer, R. Physics lab in a hardware store   **530**

Friedhoffer, R. Physics lab in the housewares store   **530**

Gardner, R. Science projects about physics in the home (7 and up)   **507.8**

Study and teaching

Pinball science. See entry in CD-ROM section, Part 3

Physics lab in a hardware store. Friedhoffer, R.   **530**

Physics lab in the housewares store. Friedhoffer, R.   **530**

Physiology

See also Immune system

Body works 6.0. See entry in CD-ROM section, Part 3

Burnie, D. The concise encyclopedia of the human body   **612**

Human body (7 and up)   **612**

Human body on file: physiology   **612**

Parker, S. Human body   **612**

Parker, S. The human body   **612**

Under the microscope   **612**

See/See also pages in the following book(s):

Glover, D. M. The young Oxford book of the human being p28-83   **612**

Physique *See* Bodybuilding

Pianists

Gourse, L. Striders to beboppers and beyond (7 and up)   **781.65**

Lisandrelli, E. S. Ignacy Jan Paderewski (7 and up)   **92**

Reich, S. Clara Schumann   **92**

Picasso, Pablo, 1881-1973

About

Beardsley, J. Pablo Picasso (7 and up)   **92**

Loria, S. Pablo Picasso   **92**

Rodari, F. A weekend with Picasso   **92**

See/See also pages in the following book(s):

Glubok, S. Great lives: painting p142-58   **920**

Pick-Goslar, Hannah

About

Gold, A. L. Memories of Anne Frank   **92**

Picked bones. Jennings, P.

In Jennings, P. Uncovered! p57-74   **S C**

Pickels, Dwayne E.

Egyptian kings and queens and classical deities   **930**

Picketing *See* Strikes

Pickett, Bill, ca. 1860-1932

About

Sanford, W. R. Bill Pickett: African-American rodeo star   **92**

See/See also pages in the following book(s):

Katz, W. L. Proudly red and black p63-73   **920**

Pickford, Mary, 1893-1979

See/See also pages in the following book(s):

Gaines, A. Entertainment & performing arts   **920**

Pickford, Nigel

The atlas of shipwrecks & treasure (7 and up)   **910.4**

Picking up the pieces. Calvert, P.   **Fic**

Pico, Steven A.

About

Gold, J. C. Board of Education v. Pico (1982) (7 and up)   **344**

Picture books for children

Bibliography

Matulka, D. I. Picture this   **011.6**

Picture dictionaries

Corbeil, J.-C. The Facts on File visual dictionary   **423**

DK ultimate visual dictionary 2000   **423**

The Oxford-Duden pictorial Japanese and English dictionary   **495.6**

Picture frames and framing

Hendry, L. Making picture frames   **745.5**

A **picture** of Freedom. McKissack, P. C.   **Fic**

Picture this. Matulka, D. I.   **011.6**

Picture writing

See also Hieroglyphics

Liungman, C. G. Dictionary of symbols (7 and up)   **302.2**

The **Pied** Piper. McCaughrean, G.

In McCaughrean, G. The crystal pool: myths and legends of the world p27-31   **398.2**

Pieńkowski, Jan, 1936-

(jt. auth) Aiken, J. A foot in the grave   **S C**

Pierce, Franklin, 1804-1869

See/See also pages in the following book(s):

Presidents of a young republic   **920**

Pierce, Meredith Ann, 1958-

A gathering of gargoyles (7 and up)   **Fic**

The pearl of the soul of the world (7 and up)   **Fic**

See/See also pages in the following book(s):

MacRae, C. D. Presenting young adult fantasy fiction (7 and up)   **813.009**

Pierce, Tamora, 1954-

Circle of magic: Briar's book   **Fic**

Circle of magic: Daja's book   **Fic**

Circle of magic: Sandry's book   **Fic**

Circle of magic: Tris's book   **Fic**

The Emperor Mage. See note under Pierce, T. Wolf-speaker   **Fic**

First test   **Fic**

The realms of the gods. See note under Pierce, T. Wolf-speaker   **Fic**

Wild magic. See note under Pierce, T. Wolf-speaker   **Fic**

Wolf-speaker   **Fic**

Pierced by a ray of sun (7 and up)   **808.81**

Pietrusza, David, 1949-

Michael Jordan (7 and up)   **92**

The roaring twenties (7 and up)   **973.91**

Pietrzyk, Leslie
Maryland
In Celebrate the states   **973**
The **pig** goes courting. McCaughrean, G.
In McCaughrean, G. The silver treasure: myths and legends of the world p81-85
    398.2
Pigeon humor. Pfeffer, S. B.
In Sixteen: short stories by outstanding writers for young adults p32-41   **S C**
Pigeons
    Fiction
Spinelli, J. Wringer   **Fic**
Piggins, Carol Ann
A multicultural portrait of the Civil War (7 and up)   **973.7**
The **Pigman**. Zindel, P.   **Fic**
The **Pigman's** legacy. Zindel, P.   **Fic**
The **pilgrim** painting. Rawls, J.
In The Big book of holiday plays p110-18
    812.008
Pilgrim voices   **974.4**
Pilgrims (New England colonists)
Bowen, G. Stranded at Plimoth Plantation, 1626
    974.4
Collier, C. Pilgrims and Puritans, 1620-1676
    974.4
Pilgrim voices   **974.4**
    Fiction
Lasky, K. A journey to the New World
    Fic
Pilgrims and pilgrimages
    Fiction
Temple, F. The Ramsay scallop   **Fic**
Pilgrims and Puritans, 1620-1676. Collier, C.
    974.4
Pilots, Airplane *See* Air pilots
Pima Indians
Dobyns, H. F. The Pima-Maricopa
In Indians of North America series
    970.004
The **Pima-Maricopa**. Dobyns, H. F.
In Indians of North America series
    970.004
The **pimienta** pancakes. Henry, O.
In Henry, O. The gift of the Magi and other stories p55-71   **S C**
The **pin**. Crutcher, C.
In Crutcher, C. Athletic shorts: six short stories p27-49   **S C**
Pinball science. See entry in CD-ROM section, Part 3
The **pinballs**. Byars, B. C.   **Fic**
Pinch. Ellis, S.
In Ellis, S. Back of beyond   **S C**
The **pine** of Akoya. Martin, R.
In Martin, R. Mysterious tales of Japan
    398.2
The **pinhole** camera. Wynne-Jones, T.
In Wynne-Jones, T. Lord of the Fries and other stories p150-72   **S C**

Pinkney, Andrea Davis
Building bridges
In Stay true: short stories for strong girls
    S C
Hold fast to dreams   **Fic**
Raven in a dove house   **Fic**
Pinkwater, Daniel Manus, 1941-
The education of Robert Nifkin (7 and up)
    Fic
Pinkwater, Manus *See* Pinkwater, Daniel Manus, 1941-
Pinna, Simon de
Electricity   **621.3**
Pinto Smalto
In Hearne, B. G. Beauties and beasts p145-50
    398.2
Pioneer life *See* Frontier and pioneer life
Pioneers in health and medicine [series]
Kaye, J. The life of Daniel Hale Williams
    92
Kaye, J. The life of Florence Sabin   **92**
Talmadge, K. S. The life of Charles Drew
    92
Pious, Richard M., 1944-
Governments of the world (7 and up)
    320.3
Pipes, Rose
Rain forests   **577.3**
Pippen, Scottie
    About
McMane, F. Scottie Pippen   **92**
Pippin, Horace, 1888-1946
    About
Lyons, M. E. Starting home: the story of Horace Pippin, painter   **92**
Pirates
Marrin, A. Terror of the Spanish Main: Sir Henry Morgan and his buccaneers (7 and up)
    92
Platt, R. Pirate   **910.4**
Stevenson, R. L. Treasure Island   **Fic**
    Fiction
Fleischman, S. The 13th floor   **Fic**
McCaughrean, G. The pirate's son (7 and up)
    Fic
The **pirate's** son. McCaughrean, G.   **Fic**
Pisano, Vivian M.
(ed) Latino periodicals. See Latino periodicals
    011.6
The **pistachio** prescription. Danziger, P.   **Fic**
The **pit** and the pendulum. Poe, E. A.
In Poe, E. A. Tales of Edgar Allan Poe p95-115   **S C**
Pit dragons trilogy
Yolen, J. Dragon's blood   **Fic**
Yolen, J. Heart's Blood   **Fic**
Yolen, J. A sending of dragons   **Fic**
The **pitiful** encounter. Sleator, W.
In Sleator, W. Oddballs: stories p71-81
    S C
Pituh-plays. Sleator, W.
In Sleator, W. Oddballs: stories p103-12
    S C

Piumini, Roberto
Don't read this!
In Don't read this! and other tales of the un-
natural p51-70   **S C**
A **place** for winter. *See* Tiulana, P. Wise words of
Paul Tiulana   **92**
The **Place** my words are looking for   **811.008**
Place names *See* Geographic names
A **place** to belong. Nixon, J. L. *See* note under
Nixon, J. L. A family apart   **Fic**
A **place** to call home. Koller, J. F.   **Fic**
Places I never meant to be (7 and up)   **S C**
Plague
The Black Death (7 and up)   **614.5**
Corzine, P. The Black Death (7 and up)
                                              614.5
See/See also pages in the following book(s):
Farrell, J. Invisible enemies p73-100 (7 and up)
                                              614.4

Fiction
Paton Walsh, J. A parcel of patterns   **Fic**
Plague. Ure, J.   **Fic**
Plague 99. See Ure, J. Plague   **Fic**
Plague and pestilence. Altman, L. J.   **614.4**
A **plague** of crowders. Vivelo, J.
In Vivelo, J. Chills in the night p55-64
                                                  S C
Plain City. Hamilton, V.   **Fic**
Plains warrior: Chief Quanah Parker and the Co-
manches. Marrin, A.   **92**
Planes. Johnstone, M.   **629.133**
Planes and other flying things. Temko, F.
                                             745.592
The **planet** hunters. Fradin, D. B.   **523.4**
The **planet** of Junior Brown. Hamilton, V.
                                                  Fic
Planets
See also names of planets
Bramwell, M. Mapping the planets and space
                                              520
Fradin, D. B. The planet hunters   **523.4**
Ridpath, I. Facts on File stars & planets atlas
                                              520
Planned parenthood *See* Birth control
Planning the impossible. Jukes, M.   **Fic**
Plant biology science projects. Hershey, D. R.
                                              580.7
Plant diseases
See/See also pages in the following book(s):
Facklam, H. Viruses p48-54   **579.2**
Plantation life
Bial, R. The strength of these arms   **326**
Erickson, P. Daily life on a Southern plantation,
1853   **975**
McKissack, P. C. Christmas in the big house,
Christmas in the quarters   **394.26**
Plante, Ellen M.
The American kitchen, 1700 to the present (7
and up)   **643**
Plants
See also Climbing plants
Burnie, D. Plant   **580**

Gardner, R. Science projects about plants (7 and
up)   **580.7**
Hershey, D. R. Plant biology science projects (7
and up)   **580.7**
Kerrod, R. Facts on File wildlife atlas   **578**
Living lab: plants. *See* entry in CD-ROM sec-
tion, Part 3
Perry, P. J. Science fair success with plants (7
and up)   **580.7**
Silverstein, A. Plants   **580**
Taylor, B. Incredible plants   **580**
VanCleave, J. P. Janice VanCleave's plants
                                              580
The Visual dictionary of plants   **580**
Wildlife and plants of the world   **578**
Diseases
See Plant diseases
Plants, Edible *See* Edible plants
Plants, Industrial *See* Factories
Plants, Poisonous *See* Poisonous plants
Plastics
Mebane, R. C. Plastics & polymers   **547**
Plastics & polymers. Mebane, R. C.   **547**
Plate tectonics
Sattler, H. R. Our patchwork planet   **551.1**
Silverstein, A. Plate tectonics   **551.1**
Plato
See/See also pages in the following book(s):
Nardo, D. Scientists of Ancient Greece p36-45
(7 and up)   **920**
Platt, Richard, 1953-
Aztecs   **972**
DK illustrated book of great adventurers
                                              910
Inventions explained   **609**
Pirate   **910.4**
Shipwreck   **910.4**
Smithsonian visual timeline of inventions
                                              609
Spy   **327.12**
(jt. auth) Biesty, S. Stephen Biesty's cross-
sections: Castle   **940.1**
(jt. auth) Biesty, S. Stephen Biesty's incredible
body   **611**
(jt. auth) Biesty, S. Stephen Biesty's incredible
everything   **670**
(jt. auth) Biesty, S. Stephen Biesty's incredible
explosions   **741.6**
(jt. auth) Bonson, R. Disaster!   **363.34**
Play like a girl   **796**
Play production *See* Amateur theater
Playing for keeps: Michael Jordan and the world
he made. Halberstam, D.   **92**
Playing God. Sebestyen, O.
In Visions: nineteen short stories by outstand-
ing writers for young adults p87-99
                                                  S C
Plays *See* Drama—Collections; One act plays
Plays for children *See* Children's plays
Plays for children and young adults. Karp, R. S.
                                             808.82
Plays from Hispanic tales. Winther, B.   **812**
Plays of black Americans   **812.008**

Playwrights *See* Dramatists
Plazy, Gilles, 1942-
  A weekend with Rousseau   **92**
Pleasing Betty Stoggs. Climo, S.
  In Climo, S. Magic & mischief p49-55
      398.2

Plessy, Homer
About
Fireside, H. Plessy v. Ferguson (7 and up)
      342
Plessy v. Ferguson. Fireside, H.   **342**
PLO *See* Palestine Liberation Organization
Plugged in [series]
  Gurian, M. From boys to men   **305.23**
Plummer, Louise
  The unlikely romance of Kate Bjorkman (7 and
  up)   **Fic**
Pluralism (Social sciences) *See* Multiculturalism
Pocahontas, d. 1617
Fiction
O'Dell, S. The serpent never sleeps   **Fic**
Pocho. Villarreal, J. A.
  In Growing up Latino p165-92   **810.8**
Podell, Janet
  Old worlds to new   **920.003**
  (jt. auth) Kane, J. N. Famous first facts
      031.02
Podietz, Eva Abraham- *See* Abraham-Podietz,
  Eva
Poe, Edgar Allan, 1809-1849
  Annabel Lee   **811**
  Tales of Edgar Allan Poe   **S C**
  Contents: The imp of the perverse; The tell-tale heart; A de-
  scent into the maelstrom; The cask of Amontillado; The prema-
  ture burial; Hop-frog; The pit and the pendulum; The masque of
  the Red Death; The fall of the House of Usher; Ms. found in a
  bottle; The murders in the Rue Morgue; The purloined letter; The
  gold bug; Berenice
About
Anderson, M. K. Edgar Allan Poe (7 and up)
      92
That strange Mr. Poe. See entry in CD-ROM
  section, Part 3
See/See also pages in the following book(s):
Faber, D. Great lives: American literature p59-
  67   **920**
Fiction
Avi. The man who was Poe   **Fic**
Poem finder 95. See entry in CD-ROM section,
  Part 3
Poetics
Hulme, J. N. How to write, recite, and delight
  in all kinds of poetry   **808.1**
Janeczko, P. B. How to write poetry   **808.1**
The Place my words are looking for
      811.008
Poetry from A to Z   **808.1**
Poetry
    See also African poetry; American poetry;
  English poetry; Haiku; Indians of North
  America—Poetry; types of poetry; subjects
  with the subdivision *Poetry*
Collections
I feel a little jumpy around you (7 and up)
      808.81

I like you, if you like me: poems of friendship
      808.81
I wouldn't thank you for a valentine
      808.81
The Oxford book of war poetry (7 and up)
      808.81
Peeling the onion   **808.81**
Pierced by a ray of sun (7 and up)   **808.81**
The Space between our footsteps (7 and up)
      808.81
Step lightly (7 and up)   **808.81**
Stopping for death (7 and up)   **808.81**
Time is the longest distance (7 and up)
      808.81
A Time to talk (7 and up)   **808.81**
War and the pity of war   **808.81**
What have you lost? (7 and up)   **808.81**
Collections—Bibliography
Katz, W. A. The Columbia Granger's guide to
  poetry anthologies   **016.80881**
Fiction
Rocklin, J. For your eyes only!   **Fic**
Indexes
The Columbia Granger's Index to poetry in an-
  thologies   **808.81**
A Compilation of works listed in Granger's In-
  dex to poetry, 1904-1978   **808.81**
Index to children's poetry   **808.81**
Index to poetry for children and young people
      808.81
Poem finder 95. See entry in CD-ROM section,
  Part 3
Study and teaching
Hopkins, L. B. Pass the poetry, please!
      372.6
Poetry for young people [series]
Longfellow, H. W. Henry Wadsworth Longfel-
  low   **811**
Whitman, W. Walt Whitman   **811**
Poetry from A to Z   **808.1**
Poets
    See also Women poets
Poets, American
Dommermuth-Costa, C. Emily Dickinson
      92
Gentry, T. Paul Laurence Dunbar   **92**
Hill, C. M. Langston Hughes   **92**
The Invisible ladder (7 and up)   **811.008**
Meltzer, M. Langston Hughes   **92**
Reef, C. Walt Whitman (7 and up)   **92**
Richmond, M. A. Phillis Wheatley   **92**
Strickland, M. R. African-American poets
      920
Poets, Chilean
Goodnough, D. Pablo Neruda   **92**
Poetspeak: in their work, about their work (7 and
  up)   **811.008**
Pohaha. San Souci, R.
  In San Souci, R. Cut from the same cloth
  p87-91   **398.2**
Pointe de Sable, Jean Baptiste, 1745?-1818
  See/See also pages in the following book(s):
  Haskins, J. Against all opposition p15-23
      920

Poisonous animals
See also Rattlesnakes
Aaseng, N. Poisonous creatures   **591.6**
Poisonous creatures. Aaseng, N.   **591.6**
Poisonous plants
Dowden, A. O. T. Poisons in our path
    581.6
Poisons and poisoning
See also Food poisoning
Poisons in our path. Dowden, A. O. T.   **581.6**
Poland
Hintz, M. Poland   **943.8**
           Fiction
Drucker, M. Jacob's rescue   **Fic**
Polar bear
Ovsyanikov, N. Polar bears (7 and up)
    599.78
Polar exploration. Bramwell, M.   **998**
Polar regions
See also Antarctica; Arctic regions; North Pole
Bramwell, M. Polar exploration   **998**
Taylor, B. Arctic & Antarctic   **998**
Polaroid and other poems of view. Hearne, B. G.
    811
Polese, Carolyn, 1947-
The first woman to vote in the state of California
In From sea to shining sea p182-85
    810.8
Police
Wirths, C. G. Coping with confrontations and encounters with the police (7 and up)
    363.2
Police report. Yolen, J.
In Yolen, J. Here there be ghosts p22-26
    810.8
Poliomyelitis
See/See also pages in the following book(s):
Facklam, H. Viruses p33-6   **579.2**
Poliomyelitis vaccine
See/See also pages in the following book(s):
Sherrow, V. Jonas Salk   **92**
Political action committees *See* Lobbying
Political and social movements. Spangenburg, R.
    917.3
Political campaigns *See* Politics
Political crimes and offenses
Stewart, G. Militias (7 and up)   **322**
Political leaders. Lindop, L.   **920**
Political science
See also Comparative government
Countries of the world and their leaders yearbook   **910.2**
The Statesman's yearbook   **310.5**
Political timber. Lynch, C.   **Fic**
Politicians
See also Women politicians
Countries of the world and their leaders yearbook   **910.2**
           United States
Kennedy, J. F. Profiles in courage (7 and up)
    920

Schulman, A. Robert F. Kennedy (7 and up)
    92
           United States—Dictionaries
O'Brien, S. American political leaders
    920.003
Politics
See also Political science
Seo, D. Generation react (7 and up)   **303.4**
See/See also pages in the following book(s):
Mass media: opposing viewpoints p89-125 (7 and up)   **302.23**
Politics, Practical *See* Politics
Politics and business *See* Business and politics
Politics and students *See* Students—Political activity
Polk, James K. (James Knox), 1795-1849
See/See also pages in the following book(s):
Lindop, E. James K. Polk, Abraham Lincoln, Theodore Roosevelt   **920**
Presidents of a young republic   **920**
Polking, Kirk
Oceanographers and explorers of the sea
    920
Pollack, Jill S.
Women on the Hill (7 and up)   **328.73**
Pollard, Michael, 1931-
The clock and how it changed the world
    681.1
The light bulb and how it changed the world
    621.3
Pollock, Jackson, 1912-1956
See/See also pages in the following book(s):
Greenberg, J. The American eye p78-88
    920
Pollock, Paul Jackson *See* Pollock, Jackson, 1912-1956
Pollution
See also Air pollution; Environmental protection; Marine pollution; Water pollution
Biology concepts through discovery: Pollution. See entry in CD-ROM section, Part 3
Davis, L. A. Environmental disasters (7 and up)
    363.7
See/See also pages in the following book(s):
Conserving the environment p104-45 (7 and up)
    333.7
           Dictionaries
Simon, S. Earth words   **363.7**
Pollution control industry
See also Recycling
Polo, Marco, 1254-1323?
           About
Macdonald, F. Marco Polo   **92**
Stefoff, R. Marco Polo and the medieval explorers   **92**
See/See also pages in the following book(s):
Lomask, M. Great lives: exploration p220-29
    920
Poltergeists: opposing viewpoints. Woog, A.
    133.1
Polymers
Mebane, R. C. Plastics & polymers   **547**
Pometacom, Sachem of the Wampanoags *See* Philip, Sachem of the Wampanoags, d. 1676

Potatoes—*Continued*
See/See also pages in the following book(s):
Johnson, S. A. Tomatoes, potatoes, corn, and
beans p64-94 **641.3**

Potawatomi Indians
Clifton, J. A. The Potawatomi
In Indians of North America series
970.004

Potok, Chaim, 1929-
Zebra and other stories (7 and up) **S C**
Contents: Zebra; B.B.; Moon; Nava; Isabel; Max

Pottery
See/See also pages in the following book(s):
Morris, J. Tending the fire: the story of Maria
Martinez **92**

Pough, Frederick H. (Frederick Harvey), 1906-
A field guide to rocks and minerals **549**

Poultry
See also Turkeys

Poverty
Poverty: opposing viewpoints (7 and up)
362.5
See/See also pages in the following book(s):
Inequality: opposing viewpoints in social prob-
lems p73-117 (7 and up) **305**
Fiction
Conly, J. L. While no one was watching
Fic
Fenner, C. Randall's wall **Fic**
Steinbeck, J. The pearl (7 and up) **Fic**
Wolff, V. E. Make lemonade **Fic**
Poverty: opposing viewpoints (7 and up)
362.5

Powell, Anton
The Greek news **938**

Powell, Bud, 1924-1966
See/See also pages in the following book(s):
Gourse, L. Striders to beboppers and beyond
p72-78 (7 and up) **781.65**

Powell, Colin L.
About
Haskins, J. Colin Powell **92**
Hughes, L. Colin Powell: a man of quality (7
and up) **92**

Powell, Earl *See* Powell, Bud, 1924-1966

Powell, John A. (John Anthony)
(jt. auth) McDonald, L. The rights of racial minorities **342**

Powell, John Wesley, 1834-1902
About
Maurer, R. The wild Colorado (7 and up)
979.1
See/See also pages in the following book(s):
Calvert, P. Great lives: the American frontier
p295-310 **920**

Powell, Ozie
About
Horne, G. Powell v. Alabama (7 and up)
345

Powell, Phelan
Major unsolved crimes (7 and up) **364.1**
Tom Cruise **92**

Powell, Randy
Tribute to another dead rock star (7 and up)
Fic

Powell, Ransom J., 1849-1899
Fiction
Wisler, G. C. Red Cap **Fic**

Powell, William J., 1899-1942
See/See also pages in the following book(s):
Hart, P. S. Flying free p22-27 **629.13**
Haskins, J. Black eagles p51-58 **629.13**

Powell v. Alabama. Horne, G. **345**

Power (Mechanics)
See also Water power; Wind power
The **power** of light. Singer, I. B. **S C**
The **power** of light [story] Singer, I. B.
In Singer, I. B. The power of light p53-60
S C
The **power** of reading. Krashen, S. D. **028**

Power plants
See also Nuclear power plants
Power resources *See* Energy resources
Power tools. Valenza, J. K. **027.8**

Powers, Harriet, 1837-1911
About
Lyons, M. E. Stitching stars: the story quilts of
Harriet Powers **92**

Powhatan, ca. 1550-1618
See/See also pages in the following book(s):
Collier, C. The paradox of Jamestown, 1585-
1700 p42-59 **975.5**

Powhatan Indians
Feest, C. F. The Powhatan tribes
In Indians of North America series
970.004

Powledge, Fred
Pharmacy in the forest **615**
We shall overcome **323.1**

POWs *See* Prisoners of war

Poynter, Margaret
The Leakeys **92**
Marie Curie: discoverer of radium **92**
Top 10 American women's figure skaters
920

Pozzi, Gianni
Chagall **92**

The **prairie**. Ormsby, A. **577.4**

Prairie dogs
Patent, D. H. Prairie dogs **599.3**

Prairie ecology
Ormsby, A. The prairie **577.4**
Patent, D. H. Prairie dogs **599.3**
Sayre, A. P. Grassland **577.4**
Staub, F. J. America's prairies **577.4**
Prairie songs. Conrad, P. **Fic**

Pratt, Paula, 1959-
Ernest Hemingway (7 and up) **92**

Prayers in the public schools *See* Religion in the
public schools

Precious stones
See also Gems
Hall, C. Gemstones (7 and up) **553.8**
Symes, R. F. Crystal & gem **548**

Precipitation (Meteorology) *See* Rain

Predictions *See* Forecasting

Pregnancy

Flanagan, G. L. Beginning life   **612.6**
Fiction
Caseley, J. Losing Louisa (7 and up)   **Fic**

Dessen, S. Someone like you (7 and up)   **Fic**

Pregnancy, Teenage *See* Teenage pregnancy

Pregnancy, Termination of *See* Abortion

Prehistoric animals

   See also Dinosaurs

Zallinger, P. Dinosaurs and other archosaurs   **567.9**
Dictionaries
Benton, M. Dinosaur and other prehistoric animal factfinder   **560**

Prehistoric art

   See also Rock drawings, paintings, and engravings

Lauber, P. Painters of the caves   **759.01**

Patent, D. H. Mystery of the Lascaux Cave   **759.01**

Prehistoric life. Lindsay, W.   **560**

Prehistoric man *See* Fossil hominids

Prehistoric peoples

Deem, J. M. Bodies from the bog   **930.1**

Early humans   **930.1**

Getz, D. Frozen man   **930.1**

Lauber, P. Painters of the caves   **759.01**

Lessem, D. The iceman   **930.1**

Macdonald, F. The Stone Age news   **930.1**

Patent, D. H. Mystery of the Lascaux Cave   **759.01**

Patent, D. H. Secrets of the ice man   **930.1**

Tanaka, S. Discovering the Iceman   **930.1**
Fiction
Dickinson, P. Suth's story   **Fic**

Prejudices

   See also Antisemitism; Discrimination

D'Angelo, L. Hate crimes (7 and up)   **364.1**

Pascoe, E. Racial prejudice   **305.8**
Fiction
Bell, W. Zack (7 and up)   **Fic**

Blakeslee, A. R. A different kind of hero   **Fic**

Childress, A. Those other people (7 and up)   **Fic**

Conly, J. L. Crazy lady!   **Fic**

Cormier, R. Tunes for bears to dance to (7 and up)   **Fic**

Curtis, C. P. The Watsons go to Birmingham—1963   **Fic**

Fleischman, P. Saturnalia   **Fic**

Grove, V. The starplace   **Fic**

Irwin, H. Sarah with an H   **Fic**

Jordan, S. The raging quiet (7 and up)   **Fic**

Kurtz, J. The storyteller's beads   **Fic**

Lee, M. G. Necessary roughness (7 and up)   **Fic**

Lynch, C. Mick (7 and up)   **Fic**

Marino, J. The day that Elvis came to town (7 and up)   **Fic**

Meyer, C. Drummers of Jericho (7 and up)   **Fic**

Pinkney, A. D. Hold fast to dreams   **Fic**

Staples, S. F. Dangerous skies (7 and up)   **Fic**

Taylor, M. D. The gold Cadillac   **Fic**

Taylor, M. D. Mississippi bridge   **Fic**

Uchida, Y. A jar of dreams   **Fic**

Uchida, Y. Journey home   **Fic**

Wolff, V. E. Bat 6   **Fic**

Yep, L. The star fisher   **Fic**

Preller, James, 1961-

(jt. auth) Layden, J. NBA game day   **796.323**

Prelude to victory. DuBois, G.

   In The Big book of holiday plays p254-65   **812.008**

Prelutsky, Jack

(ed) The Random House book of poetry for children. See The Random House book of poetry for children   **821.008**

The **premature** burial. Poe, E. A.

   In Poe, E. A. Tales of Edgar Allan Poe p61-80   **S C**

Presenting Avi. Bloom, S. P.   **813.009**

Presenting Chris Crutcher. Davis, T.   **813.009**

Presenting Cynthia Voigt. Reid, S. E.   **813.009**

Presenting Kathryn Lasky. Brown, J.   **813.009**

Presenting M.E. Kerr. Nilsen, A. P.   **813.009**

Presenting Mildred D. Taylor. Crowe, C.   **813.009**

Presenting Ouida Sebestyen. Monseau, V. R.   **813.009**

Presenting Paula Danziger. Krull, K.   **813.009**

Presenting Phyllis Reynolds Naylor. Stover, L. T.   **813.009**

Presenting Richard Peck. Gallo, D. R.   **813.009**

Presenting Robert Cormier. Campbell, P. J.   **813.009**

Presenting Rosa Guy. Norris, J.   **813.009**

Presenting S.E. Hinton. Daly, J.   **813.009**

Presenting Ursula Le Guin. Reid, S. E.   **813.009**

Presenting young adult fantasy fiction. MacRae, C. D.   **813.009**

Presenting young adult horror fiction. Kies, C. N.   **813.009**

Presenting young adult science fiction. Reid, S. E.   **813.009**

Preservation of wildlife *See* Wildlife conservation

The **Presidency** A to Z   **352.23**

The **president** has been shot!. Jones, R. C.   **364.1**

Presidents

   See also Vice-presidents
Mexico
O'Brien, S. Antonio López de Santa Anna   **92**

Pullman, Philip, 1946——*Continued*
Count Karlstein	Fic
The ruby in the smoke (7 and up)	Fic
Shadow in the north (7 and up)	Fic
The tiger in the well (7 and up)	Fic

Pumas

Fiction
Naylor, P. R. The fear place	Fic

Pumping iron *See* Weight lifting

Puppets and puppet plays
Doney, M. Puppets	745.592

Fiction
Paterson, K. The master puppeteer	Fic

Puppies, dogs, and blue northers. Paulsen, G.
798.8

Puppy love. Mazer, H.
In Mazer, H. The dog in the freezer: three novellas p33-75   S C

Puritans
Collier, C. Pilgrims and Puritans, 1620-1676
974.4
IlgenFritz, E. Anne Hutchinson   92

Fiction
Speare, E. G. The witch of Blackbird Pond
Fic

The **purloined** letter. Poe, E. A.
In Poe, E. A. Tales of Edgar Allan Poe p217-42   S C

The **Purple** Heart. Talbert, M.   Fic

Push-up. Soto, G.
In Soto, G. Local news p47-59   S C

The **pushcart** war. Merrill, J.   Fic

Put on some antlers and walk like a moose. Sayre, A. P.   590.7

Putnam, James
Mummy	393
Pyramid	909

Pyle, Ernie, 1900-1945
About
O'Connor, B. The soldiers' voice: the story of Ernie Pyle   92

Pyle, Howard, 1853-1911
The apple of contentment
In American fairy tales p81-91   S C
The merry adventures of Robin Hood of great renown in Notinghamshire (7 and up)
398.2
The story of King Arthur and his knights (7 and up)   398.2
The story of Sir Launcelot and his companions (7 and up)   398.2
The story of the champions of the Round Table (7 and up)   398.2
The story of the Grail and the passing of Arthur (7 and up)   398.2

Pyle, Robert Michael
The Audubon Society field guide to North American butterflies   595.7

Pyramids
Macaulay, D. Pyramid	726
Millard, A. Pyramids	909
Putnam, J. Pyramid	909

Pyrrhus, King of Epirus, 318-272 B.C.
See/See also pages in the following book(s):
Nardo, D. Leaders of ancient Greece (7 and up)
920

Pytheas, of Massalia
See/See also pages in the following book(s):
Lomask, M. Great lives: exploration p229-33
920

Pythons
McDonald, M. A. Pythons   597.9

Q

Qoheleth *See* Bible. O.T. Ecclesiastes

Quake!. Cottonwood, J.   Fic

Quakers *See* Society of Friends

Qualey, Marsha
Thin ice (7 and up)   Fic

Quapaw Indians
Baird, W. D. The Quapaws
In Indians of North America series
970.004

Quarks and sparks. Kidd, J. S.   621.48

Quarterbacks!. Sullivan, G.   920

Queen, Ellery
Object lesson
In Read all about it! p53-66   808.8

Queen, J. Allen
Learn karate   796.8

Queen of diamonds. Dorris, M.
In Talking leaves   S C

Queens
See also names of queens and countries with the subdivision *Kings and rulers*
Brooks, P. S. Cleopatra (7 and up)	92
Green, R. Queen Victoria	92
Meltzer, M. Ten queens	920
Stanley, D. Cleopatra	92

Stanley, D. Good Queen Bess: the story of Elizabeth I of England   92
Thomas, J. R. Behind the mask: the life of Queen Elizabeth I (7 and up)   92

A **question** of arithmagic. McCaughrean, G.
In McCaughrean, G. The crystal pool: myths and legends of the world p14-17
398.2

A **question** of life and death. McCaughrean, G.
In McCaughrean, G. The silver treasure: myths and legends of the world p27-30
398.2

A **question** of trust. Bauer, M. D.   Fic

Questions & answers book of science facts. Graham, I.   500

Questions and answers
See also Examinations

Quicksand pony. Lester, A.   Fic

Quiet storm (7 and up)   811.008

Quilting
Bial, R. With needle and thread   746.46
Wilson, S. G. African American quilting
746.46

Quilting—*Continued*
Fiction
Rinaldi, A. A stitch in time (7 and up)   **Fic**
Quilts
Bial, R. With needle and thread   **746.46**
Lyons, M. E. Stitching stars: the story quilts of
  Harriet Powers   **92**
Quinceañera (Social custom)
King, E. Quinceañera   **392**
Quinlan, Kathryn A.
(jt. auth) Kent, D. Extraordinary people with
  disabilities   **920**
Quinlan, Susan E., 1954-
Puffins   **598**
Quintana, Anton
The baboon king (7 and up)   **Fic**
Quiquern. Kipling, R.
In Kipling, R. The jungle books   **S C**
Quiri, Patricia Ryon
The White House   **975.3**
Quotations
  See also Proverbs; subjects, classes of per-
  sons, and ethnic groups with the subdivision
  Quotations
Bartlett, J. Familiar quotations   **808.88**
Burleigh, R. Who said that?   **808.88**
My soul looks back, 'less I forget   **808.88**
Quotations for kids   **808.88**
Scholastic treasury of quotations for children
     808.88
Quotations for kids   **808.88**
Quran *See* Koran
Qwertyuiop. Alcock, V.
In Help wanted: short stories about young
  people working   **S C**

R

R-T, Margaret, and the rats of NIMH. Conly, J. L.
     Fic
Rabbi Nachman's chair. Schwartz, H.
In Schwartz, H. Next year in Jerusalem p44-
  47   **296.1**
Rabbits
Fiction
Adams, R. Tales from Watership Down
     S C
Adams, R. Watership down   **Fic**
The **rabbit's** ghost story. Adams, R.
In Adams, R. Tales from Watership Down
     S C
Rabble Starkey. Lowry, L.   **Fic**
Rabe, Berniece
Hiding Mr. McMulty   **Fic**
Rabies
See/See also pages in the following book(s):
Facklam, H. Viruses p26-9   **579.2**
Rabin, Arnold
The man-child
In Theatre for young audiences p364-94
     812.008
Raccoons
North, S. Rascal   **599.7**

Race discrimination
See/See also pages in the following book(s):
Sports and athletes: opposing viewpoints p93-
  124 (7 and up)   **796**
Law and legislation
McDonald, L. The rights of racial minorities (7
  and up)   **342**
Race relations
  See also Culture conflict; Ethnic relations;
  Multiculturalism; names of countries, cities,
  etc., with the subdivision *Race relations*
Fiction
Collier, J. L. With every drop of blood   **Fic**
Cooney, C. B. Burning up (7 and up)   **Fic**
English, K. Francie   **Fic**
Hearne, B. G. Listening for Leroy   **Fic**
Klass, D. Danger zone (7 and up)   **Fic**
Koller, J. F. A place to call home (7 and up)
     Fic
Krisher, T. Spite fences (7 and up)   **Fic**
Meyer, C. Jubilee journey   **Fic**
Meyer, C. White lilacs   **Fic**
Paton, A. Cry, the beloved country (7 and up)
     Fic
Rabe, B. Hiding Mr. McMulty   **Fic**
Reeder, C. Across the lines   **Fic**
Sebestyen, O. Words by heart   **Fic**
Spinelli, J. Maniac Magee   **Fic**
Taylor, M. D. The friendship   **Fic**
Taylor, M. D. The gold Cadillac   **Fic**
Taylor, M. D. Mississippi bridge   **Fic**
Taylor, M. D. The road to Memphis   **Fic**
Taylor, M. D. The well   **Fic**
Taylor, T. The cay   **Fic**
Taylor, T. Timothy of the cay   **Fic**
Woodson, J. If you come softly (7 and up)
     Fic
Young, R. T. Learning by heart   **Fic**
Race to the moon. Green, J.   **629.45**
Race to the top. McCaughrean, G.
In McCaughrean, G. The crystal pool: myths
  and legends of the world p36-40
     398.2
Races of people *See* Ethnology
Rachel and the angel. Westall, R.
In Westall, R. Demons and shadows p3-31
     S C
Racial balance in schools *See* School integration
Racial intermarriage *See* Interracial marriage
Racial prejudice. Pascoe, E.   **305.8**
Racially mixed people
Nash, G. B. Forbidden love (7 and up)
     305.8
What are you? (7 and up)   **305.8**
Fiction
Bell, W. Zack (7 and up)   **Fic**
Dorris, M. The window   **Fic**
Hamilton, V. Plain City   **Fic**
Koller, J. F. A place to call home (7 and up)
     Fic
Meyer, C. Jubilee journey   **Fic**
Paterson, K. Jip   **Fic**
Woodson, J. The house you pass on the way (7
  and up)   **Fic**
Yep, L. Thief of hearts   **Fic**

Racing the Iditarod Trail. Crisman, R.   **798.8**

Racism

  See also Race discrimination

Racso and the rats of NIMH. Conly, J. L.
                                Fic

Rader, Wendy *See* Dunn, Wendy

Radical change. Dresang, E. T.   **028.5**

Radicalism

  See also Militia movements

El **radio**. Soto, G.

  In Soto, G. Local news p35-46   **S C**

Radio journalism *See* Broadcast journalism

Radio programs

            Fiction

  Cooney, C. B. The voice on the radio (7 and up)   **Fic**

Radiocarbon dating

  Jespersen, J. Mummies, dinosaurs, moon rocks
                            930.1

Rafting (Sports)

  George, C. White-water rafting   **797.1**

            Fiction

  Bauer, M. D. Face to face   **Fic**

  Hobbs, W. Downriver (7 and up)   **Fic**

Rage of fire. Skurzynski, G. See note under
  Skurzynski, G. Cliff hanger   **Fic**

Ragged emperor. McCaughrean, G.

  In McCaughrean, G. The bronze cauldron: myths and legends of the world p71-77
                            398.2

The **raging** quiet. Jordan, S.   **Fic**

The **Raiders** jacket. Soto, G.

  In Soto, G. Local news p69-79   **S C**

Railroads

  Johnstone, M. Trains   **625.1**

            Fiction

  Napoli, D. J. Trouble on the tracks   **Fic**

  Yep, L. Dragon's gate   **Fic**

            History

  Blumberg, R. Full steam ahead   **385.09**

  Murphy, J. Across America on an emigrant train
                                92

  Stein, R. C. The Transcontinental Railroad in American history   **385.09**

Rain

  See also Acid rain; Droughts

  Gardner, R. Science project ideas about rain
                            551.57

Rain forest ecology

  Goodman, S. Bats, bugs, and biodiversity
                            577.3

  Greenaway, T. Jungle   **577.3**

  Johnson, D. The Amazon rainforest (7 and up)
                            577.3

  Lasky, K. The most beautiful roof in the world
                            577.3

  Lewington, A. People of the rain forests
                            577.3

  Pipes, R. Rain forests   **577.3**

  Sayre, A. P. Tropical rain forest   **577.3**

Rain forests

  The digital field trip to the rainforest. See entry in CD-ROM section, Part 3

The dynamic rainforest. See entry in CD-ROM section, Part 3

A field trip to the rainforest deluxe. See entry in CD-ROM section, Part 3

Rain forests. Pipes, R.   **577.3**

Rain music. Nguyen, L.

  In American dragons p155-60   **810.8**

Rainbow Jordan. Childress, A.   **Fic**

The **rainbow** people. Yep, L.   **398.2**

The **rainbow** people [story] Yep, L.

  In Yep, L. The rainbow people p178-90
                            398.2

Rainbow snake. McCaughrean, G.

  In McCaughrean, G. The golden hoard: myths and legends of the world p60-65
                            398.2

Rainfall *See* Rain

Raintree Steck-Vaughn interactive science encyclopedia. See entry in CD-ROM section, Part 3

Ramanujan Aiyangar, Srinivasa, 1887-1920

  See/See also pages in the following book(s):

  Henderson, H. Modern mathematicians (7 and up)   **920**

Ramírez, Blandina Cárdenas, 1944-

  See/See also pages in the following book(s):

  Morey, J. Famous Mexican Americans p106-18
                            920

Ramona, the sheep suit, and the three wise persons. Cleary, B.

  In A Newbery Christmas p163-84   **S C**

The **Ramsay** scallop. Temple, F.   **Fic**

Ranch life

            Fiction

  Hermes, P. Someone to count on   **Fic**

  Lindquist, S. H. Summer soldiers   **Fic**

  Paulsen, G. The haymeadow   **Fic**

  Philbrick, W. R. The fire pony   **Fic**

  Steinbeck, J. The red pony   **Fic**

Rand McNally Goode's world atlas. See Goode's world atlas   **912**

Rand McNally world facts & maps   **310.5**

Randall's wall. Fenner, C.   **Fic**

Randle, Kristen D., 1952-

  Breaking rank (7 and up)   **Fic**

Randolph, Asa Philip, 1889-1979

            About

  Hanley, S. A. Philip Randolph   **92**

  See/See also pages in the following book(s):

  Dubovoy, S. Civil rights leaders p57-71 (7 and up)   **920**

  Streissguth, T. Legendary labor leaders (7 and up)   **920**

Randolph, Jane Fitz- *See* Fitz-Randolph, Jane

Random House American sign language dictionary. Costello, E.   **419**

The **Random** House book of opera stories. Geras, A.   **792.5**

The **Random** House book of poetry for children
                            821.008

The **Random** House book of stories from the ballet. McCaughrean, G.   **792.8**

The **Random** House children's encyclopedia. See Children's illustrated encyclopedia   **031**

Random House dictionary of America's popular proverbs and sayings. Titelman, G. Y.
398.9

Random House library of knowledge [series]
Zallinger, P. Dinosaurs and other archosaurs
567.9

Random House unabridged dictionary. See Random House Webster's unabridged dictionary
423

Random House Webster's unabridged dictionary
423

Randy, the red-horned rainmoose. Kilcup, R.
In The Big book of holiday plays p168-77
812.008

Rankin, Jeannette, 1880-1973
See/See also pages in the following book(s):
Helmer, D. S. Women suffragists (7 and up)
920
Mendoza, P. M. Extraordinary people in extraordinary times p85-92 (7 and up)   **920**

Rankin, Virginia
The thoughtful researcher   **027.62**

The **ransom** of Red Chief. Henry, O.
In Henry, O. The gift of the Magi and other stories p28-46   **S C**

Rap music
Jones, K. M. Say it loud! (7 and up)
781.64

Rape
See also Date rape
Bode, J. Voices of rape (7 and up)
362.883
Kaminker, L. Everything you need to know about dealing with sexual assault (7 and up)
362.883

Fiction
Cadnum, M. Rundown (7 and up)   **Fic**
Childress, A. Those other people (7 and up)
Fic
Cole, B. The facts speak for themselves (7 and up)   **Fic**
Peck, R. Are you in the house alone? (7 and up)
Fic

Rapp, Adam
The buffalo tree (7 and up)   **Fic**

Rappaport, Doreen
Escape from slavery   **326**
The flight of Red Bird (7 and up)   **92**

Rappoport, Ken
Guts and glory   **920**

Raptor. Zindel, P.   **Fic**

Rare animals
See also Endangered species
Sayre, A. P. Endangered birds of North America
598

Rare plants
See also Endangered species

Rascal. North, S.   **599.7**

The **rascal** crow. Alexander, L.
In Alexander, L. The foundling and other tales of Prydian p41-50   **S C**

In A Newbery zoo   **S C**

Rashi, 1040-1105
Perush Rashi 'al ha-Torah. See Chaikin, M. Clouds of glory   **296.1**

Raskin, Ellen, 1928-1984
The Westing game   **Fic**

Rasmussen, R. Kent
Farewell to Jim Crow (7 and up)   **305.8**
Modern African political leaders (7 and up)
920
(ed) Encyclopedia of American government. See Encyclopedia of American government
320.03

The **rat** children. Mazer, H.
In Places I never meant to be   **S C**

Ratha's challenge. Bell, C.   **Fic**

Rationales for challenged books. See entry in CD-ROM section, Part 3

Rationalism
See also Enlightenment

Rats
Fiction
Conly, J. L. R-T, Margaret, and the rats of NIMH   **Fic**
Conly, J. L. Racso and the rats of NIMH
Fic
O'Brien, R. C. Mrs. Frisby and the rats of NIMH   **Fic**

Rattenbury, Jeanne
Understanding alternative medicine (7 and up)
615.5

The **rattle** and the drum. Sita, L.   **299**

Rattlesnakes
McDonald, M. A. Rattlesnakes   **597.9**

Rau, Christopher
(jt. auth) Rau, D. M. George Lucas   **92**

Rau, Dana Meachen, 1971-
George Lucas   **92**

Rauzon, Mark J.
Hummingbirds   **598**
Vultures   **598**

Raven & Sea Gull. Lelooska, D.
In Lelooska, D. Echoes of the elders p22-27
398.2

The **Raven** and the moon. McCaughrean, G.
In McCaughrean, G. The silver treasure: myths and legends of the world p114-17
398.2

The **raven** and the star fruit tree. Tran, V. D.
In From sea to shining sea p368-69
810.8

Raven and the tides. Bruchac, J.
In Bruchac, J. Four ancestors p67-69
398.2

Raven brings fresh water. Martin, F.
In From sea to shining sea p8-11   **810.8**

Raven in a dove house. Pinkney, A. D.   **Fic**

The **ravens.** Kordon, K.
In Don't read this! and other tales of the unnatural p71-84   **S C**

The **ravine.** Bradbury, R.
In Read all about it! p252-71   **808.8**

Rawlings, Marjorie Kinnan, 1896-1953
  The yearling   **Fic**
Rawls, James
  The pilgrim painting
    In The Big book of holiday plays p110-18
          812.008
Rawls, Wilson, 1913-
  Summer of the monkeys (7 and up)   **Fic**
  Where the red fern grows   **Fic**
Ray, Delia
  Behind the Blue and Gray   **973.7**
  A nation torn   **973.7**
Ray, G. Carleton
  (jt. auth) Robins, C. R. A field guide to Atlantic
    coast fishes of North America   **597**
Rayfield, Susan
  Pierre-Auguste Renoir (7 and up)   **92**
Raymond's run. Bambara, T. C.
  In Rites of passage p1-10   **S C**
  In Who do you think you are? p47-57
          S C
Rea, William R.
  African art
    In International encyclopedia of art   **703**
Reaching Dustin. Grove, V.   **Fic**
Read all about it!   **808.8**
The **read-aloud** handbook. Trelease, J.   **028.5**
Read into the millennium   **S C**
Read magazine
  Read into the millennium   **S C**
Reader's Digest explores [series]
  Astronomy   **520**
Reader's Digest pathfinders [series]
  Beckelman, L. The human body   **612**
Readers' guide abstracts full text mega edition.
  See entry in CD-ROM section, Part 3
Readers' guide for young people. See entry in
  CD-ROM section, Part 3
Readers' guide to periodical literature   **051**
Readers' theater
  Shepard, A. Stories on stage   **812**
Reading
  Into focus   **028.1**
  Krashen, S. D. The power of reading   **028**
        Fiction
  Paulsen, G. Nightjohn (7 and up)   **Fic**
Ready-to-go reading incentive programs for
  schools and libraries. Jay, M. E.   **028.5**
Reagan, Ronald, 1911-
  See/See also pages in the following book(s):
  Presidents in a time of change   **920**
Real. Holman, F.   **Fic**
Real girl/real world. Gray, H. M.   **305.23**
The **real** high school handbook. Lieberman, S. A.
          373
The **real** Johnny Appleseed. Lawlor, L.   **92**
The **real** McCoy. James, P. P.   **609**
Real vampires. Cohen, D.   **398**
Real world math. Guthrie, D.   **332.024**
Reality check. Trapani, M.   **306.8**

Really Rosie [play] Sendak, M.
  In Theatre for young audiences p72-98
          812.008
The **realms** of the gods. Pierce, T. See note under
  Pierce, T. Wolf-speaker   **Fic**
Reaping the whirlwind. Aleshire, P.   **973.8**
Reason. Asimov, I.
  In Asimov, I. I, robot   **S C**
  In Read into the millenium p57   **S C**
The **rebellion** of the magical rabbits. Dorfman, A.
  In Where angels glide at dawn p7-25
          S C
Rebels against slavery. McKissack, P. C.   **326**
Rebnord, Lisa
  (jt. auth) Hendry, L. Making picture frames
          745.5
Rebora, Piero
  (comp) Cassell's Italian dictionary: Italian-
    English, English-Italian. See Cassell's Italian
    dictionary: Italian-English, English-Italian
          453
Rebuilding the past [series]
  Burrell, R. E. C. Oxford first ancient history
          909
Recipes *See* Cooking
"Recitatif". Morrison, T.
  In Leaving home: stories p201-27   **808.8**
Recitations *See* Monologues
Reclamation of land
  See also Wetlands
Recommended books in Spanish for children and
  young adults, 1991-1995. Schon, I.   **011.6**
Recommended reference books for small and me-
  dium-sized libraries and media centers
          011
Reconstruction (1865-1876)
  Golay, M. Reconstruction and reaction (7 and
    up)   **305.8**
  January, B. Reconstruction   **973.8**
  Kirchberger, J. H. The Civil War and Recon-
    struction (7 and up)   **973.7**
  Mettger, Z. Reconstruction   **973.8**
  One nation again   **973.8**
  Presidents of a divided nation   **920**
  See/See also pages in the following book(s):
  Frankel, N. Break those chains at last: African
    Americans, 1860-1880 (7 and up)   **305.8**
  Senna, C. The black press and the struggle for
    civil rights p63-74 (7 and up)   **071**
        Fiction
  Robinet, H. G. Forty acres and maybe a mule
          Fic
Reconstruction and reaction. Golay, M.
          305.8
Recorded books *See* Audiobooks
Records, World *See* World records
Recreation
        Directories
  Peterson's summer opportunities for kids and
    teenagers   **790.1**
The **recreation** handbook. Loeffelbein, R. L.
          793

Rehder, Harald Alfred, 1907-1996
The Audubon Society field guide to North American seashells **594**

Reich, Susanna, 1954-
Clara Schumann **92**

Reid, Lori
The art of hand reading (7 and up) **133.6**

Reid, Suzanne Elizabeth
Presenting Cynthia Voigt (7 and up) **813.009**
Presenting Ursula Le Guin (7 and up) **813.009**
Presenting young adult science fiction (7 and up) **813.009**

Reid Banks, Lynne *See* Banks, Lynne Reid, 1929-

The **Reigate** puzzle. Doyle, Sir A. C.
In Doyle, Sir A. C. The complete Sherlock Holmes **S C**

Reincarnation
Fiction
Farmer, P. Penelope **Fic**

Reinhard, Johan
Discovering the Inca Ice Maiden **930.1**

Reiss, Johanna
The journey back **92**
The upstairs room **92**

Reiss, Kathryn
PaperQuake **Fic**

Relations among ethnic groups *See* Ethnic relations

Relatively speaking. Fletcher, R. J. **811**

Relativity (Physics)
See/See also pages in the following book(s):
Bernstein, J. Albert Einstein and the frontiers of physics (7 and up) **92**
Goldberg, J. Albert Einstein (7 and up) **92**

Religion
Langley, M. Religion **200**
Fiction
Paulsen, G. The tent (7 and up) **Fic**
Rylant, C. A fine white dust **Fic**
Social aspects
See/See also pages in the following book(s):
Culture wars: opposing viewpoints p36-51, 111-39 (7 and up) **306**

Religion and science
Science & religion: opposing viewpoints (7 and up) **215**

Religion in American life [series]
Bushman, C. L. Mormons in America **289.3**
Diner, H. R. Jews in America **305.8**
Gaustad, E. S. Church and state in America **322**
Martin, J. Native American religion **299**

Religion in the public schools
Andryszewski, T. School prayer (7 and up) **344**
Dudley, M. E. Engel v. Vitale (1962) (7 and up) **344**

Religions
See also Gods and goddesses
Birdseye, D. H. What I believe **200**

Breuilly, E. Religions of the world (7 and up) **291**
The Encyclopedia of world religions (7 and up) **200.3**
Gellman, M. How do you spell God? **200**
Osborne, M. P. One world, many religions **291**
Philip, N. Mythology **291.1**
Fiction
Blume, J. Are you there God? it's me, Margaret **Fic**

Religions of the world. Breuilly, E. **291**

Religious art and symbolism
Stories from the Old Testament **221.5**
See/See also pages in the following book(s):
Armstrong, C. Women of the Bible **220.9**

Religious ceremonies *See* Rites and ceremonies

Religious cults *See* Cults

Religious holidays
See also Jewish holidays

Religious literature
See also Christian fiction

Religious poetry
Yolen, J. O Jerusalem **811**
Yolen, J. Sacred places **811**

Relocation of Japanese Americans, 1942-1945
See Japanese Americans—Evacuation and relocation, 1942-1945

The **reluctant** dragon. Grahame, K.
In The Book of dragons p20-25 **S C**

Reluctantly Alice. Naylor, P. R. **Fic**

Remarkable Jewish women. Taitz, E. **920**

The **remarkable** journey of Prince Jen. Alexander, L. **Fic**

Remarriage
Fiction
Cole, B. Celine (7 and up) **Fic**
Mori, K. Shizuko's daughter (7 and up) **Fic**

Rembrandt Harmenszoon van Rijn, 1606-1669
About
Bonafoux, P. A weekend with Rembrandt **92**
See/See also pages in the following book(s):
Glubok, S. Great lives: painting p159-64 **920**

Remember me. Vande Velde, V.
In Vande Velde, V. Curses, Inc. and other stories p126-43 **S C**

Remember not to forget. Finkelstein, N. H. **940.53**

Remembering Mog. Rodowsky, C. F. **Fic**

Remembering the good times. Peck, R. **Fic**

Remington, Frederic, 1861-1909
See/See also pages in the following book(s):
Calvert, P. Great lives: the American frontier p311-27 **920**

Remstein, Henna, 1968-
Barbara Walters **92**

Renaissance
See also Fifteenth century; Sixteenth century

Ride, Sally K.
To space & back 629.45
About
Hurwitz, J. Sally Ride 92
See/See also pages in the following book(s):
Briggs, C. S. Women in space 920
Ride 'em, round 'em, rope 'em: the story of Pecos Bill. Gleeson, B.
In From sea to shining sea p286-88
810.8
A **ride** on the dumbwaiter. Vivelo, J.
In Vivelo, J. Chills in the night p102-23
S C
Rider Chan and the night river. Yee, P.
In Yee, P. Tales from Gold Mountain p51-56
S C
Riding *See* Horsemanship
Riding out the storm. Forshay-Lunsford, C.
In Center stage 812.008
Ridpath, Ian
Facts on File stars & planets atlas 520
Riekehof, Lottie L.
The joy of signing 419
The **rifle.** Paulsen, G. Fic
Rifles
Fiction
Paulsen, G. The rifle (7 and up) Fic
Rifles for Watie. Keith, H. Fic
Right- and left-handedness *See* Left- and right-handedness
The **right** moves. Schwager, T. 613.7
Right of assembly *See* Freedom of assembly
Right of privacy
Persico, D. Mapp v. Ohio (7 and up) 345
Persico, D. New Jersey v. T.L.O. (7 and up)
345
Wetterer, C. M. The Fourth Amendment (7 and up) 345
See/See also pages in the following book(s):
Civil liberties: opposing viewpoints p72-117 (7 and up) 323
Right to die
See also Euthanasia
Walker, R. A right to die? 179.7
See/See also pages in the following book(s):
Death and dying: opposing viewpoints p55-96 (7 and up) 155.9
The **right** to speak out. King, D. C. 323.44
Righteous gentile [biography of Raoul Wallenberg] Bierman, J. 92
The **righteous** gentiles. Sherrow, V. 940.53
Rights, Civil *See* Civil rights
Rights, Human *See* Human rights
The **rights** of American Indians and their tribes. Pevar, S. L. 342
Rights of animals *See* Animal rights
The **Rights** of animals (7 and up) 179
The **rights** of man, the reign of terror: the story of the French Revolution. Banfield, S.
944.04
The **rights** of racial minorities. McDonald, L.
342

The **rights** of students. Cary, E. 344
The **rights** of women and girls. Moss, K. L.
305.4
Rikiki and the wizard. Wrede, P. C.
In Wrede, P. C. Book of enchantments p1-8
S C
"Rikki-tikki-tavi". Kipling, R.
In Kipling, R. The jungle books S C
In Read all about it! p155-74 808.8
Riley, Dorothy Winbush
(ed) My soul looks back, 'less I forget. See My soul looks back, 'less I forget 808.88
Rillieux, Norbert, 1806-1894
See/See also pages in the following book(s):
Aaseng, N. Black inventors p9-19 (7 and up)
920
Haskins, J. Outward dreams p27-34 609
McKissack, P. C. African-American inventors p41-48 920
Rima's song. Marston, E.
In Join in p153-71 S C
Rinaldi, Ann, 1934-
An acquaintance with darkness (7 and up)
Fic
Cast two shadows (7 and up) Fic
The fifth of March (7 and up) Fic
Hang a thousand trees with ribbons (7 and up)
Fic
In my father's house (7 and up) Fic
Keep smiling through (7 and up) Fic
Mine eyes have seen (7 and up) Fic
The second bend in the river (7 and up)
Fic
A stitch in time (7 and up) Fic
Wolf by the ears (7 and up) Fic
A **ring** of endless light. L'Engle, M. Fic
Ringgold, Faith
See/See also pages in the following book(s):
Sills, L. Inspirations p40-51 920
Ringing wet. Jennings, P.
In Jennings, P. Uncovered! p83-99 S C
Riots
See/See also pages in the following book(s):
The 1960s: opposing viewpoints p182-94 (7 and up) 973.92
Rip Van Winkle. Irving, W.
In American fairy tales p9-28 S C
Rip Van Winkle. McCaughrean, G.
In McCaughrean, G. The silver treasure: myths and legends of the world p108-13
398.2
Rip Van Winkle and The legend of Sleepy Hollow. Irving, W. Fic
Ripken, Cal, Jr.
Cal Ripken, Jr., my story 92
About
Ripken, C., Jr. Cal Ripken, Jr., my story
92
Ripple, Jeff, 1963-
Sea turtles (7 and up) 597.9
The **Rise** of Christianity (7 and up) 270
The **rise** of Islam. Child, J. 297
The **Rise** of Nazi Germany (7 and up)
943.086

Risk-taking (Psychology)
Erlbach, A. Worth the risk   302
A **risky** prescription. Stiefer, S.   613.7
Ritalin
Beal, E. Ritalin (7 and up)   616.85
Rites and ceremonies
Ingpen, R. R. A celebration of customs & rituals of the world   394.2
Rites of passage   S C
Ritter, John H., 1951-
Choosing up sides   Fic
Ritter, Lawrence S.
The story of baseball   796.357
Ritual See Rites and ceremonies
The **river.** Paulsen, G.   Fic
River and stream. Sayre, A. P.   577.6
River danger. Dygard, T. J.   Fic
River ecology
Martin, P. A. F. Rivers and streams (7 and up)   577.6
Sayre, A. P. River and stream   577.6
Rivera, Diego, 1886-1957
See/See also pages in the following book(s):
Glubok, S. Great lives: painting p165-75   920
Rivera, Frida Kahlo See Kahlo, Frida, 1907-1954
Rivera, Tomás
On the road to Texas: Pete Fonseca
In Growing up Latino p147-54   810.8
Rivers
   See also Colorado River (Colo.-Mexico); Mississippi River
Exploring the Nardoo. See entry in CD-ROM section, Part 3
Rivers and streams. Martin, P. A. F.   577.6
Rivlin, Alice M.
See/See also pages in the following book(s):
Jeffrey, L. S. Great American businesswomen p46-73   920
Rizzo, Margaret
(jt. auth) Jweid, R. The library-classroom partnership   027.8
Roach, Marilynne K.
In the days of the Salem witchcraft trials   133.4
The **road** from home [biography of Veron Kherdian] Kherdian, D.   92
The **road** not taken. Frost, R.   811
The **Road** to Appomattox   973.7
The **road** to Camlann. Sutcliff, R.   398.2
The **road** to Memphis. Taylor, M. D.   Fic
Roads of destiny. Henry, O.
In Henry, O. The gift of the Magi and other stories p156-90   S C
Roanoke Island (N.C.)
Fiction
Forrester, S. Sound the jubilee   Fic
The **roaring** twenties. Pietrusza, D.   973.91
Robbers and outlaws See Thieves
Robbie. Asimov, I.
In Asimov, I. I, robot   S C

Robbins, Chandler S., 1918-
Birds of North America   598
Robbins, Paul R. (Paul Richard)
Crack and cocaine drug dangers   362.29
Roberson, John R., 1930-
Japan meets the world (7 and up)   952
Robert I, King of Scotland, 1274-1329
Fiction
Hunter, M. The king's swift rider (7 and up)   Fic
Robert, Henry Martyn, 1837-1923
The Scott, Foresman Robert's Rules of order newly revised   060.4
Robert, Sarah Corbin
(ed) Robert, H. M. The Scott, Foresman Robert's Rules of order newly revised   060.4
Robert E. Peary and the rush to the North Pole (7 and up)   998
Robert Frost: poems, life, legacy. See entry in CD-ROM section, Part 3
Robert Louis Stevenson, teller of tales. Gherman, B.   92
Robert Peary and the quest for the North Pole. Dwyer, C.   92
Robert the Bruce See Robert I, King of Scotland, 1274-1329
Roberts, Mickey
The Indian basket
In Talking leaves   S C
It's all in how you say it
In Talking leaves   S C
Roberts, Russell, 1953-
Endangered species   333.95
Roberts, Willo Davis
The kidnappers   Fic
Pawns   Fic
Twisted summer   Fic
What are we going to do about David?   Fic
Robert's Rules of order. Robert, H. M.   060.4
Robertshaw, Andrew
A soldier's life   355
Robertson, Oscar, 1938-
See/See also pages in the following book(s):
Bayne, B. C. Sky kings (7 and up)   796.323
Robeson, Paul, 1898-1976
About
Wright, D. K. Paul Robeson   92
Robin Hood (Legendary character)
McKinley, R. The outlaws of Sherwood   398.2
Philip, N. The story of Robin Hood   398.2
Pyle, H. The merry adventures of Robin Hood of great renown in Notinghamshire (7 and up)   398.2
Fiction
Cadnum, M. In a dark wood (7 and up)   Fic
Morpurgo, M. Robin of Sherwood   Fic
Tomlinson, T. Child of the May   Fic
Tomlinson, T. The Forestwife   Fic

Robin Hood and his merry men. Osborne, M. P.
In Osborne, M. P. Favorite medieval tales
p60-66 **398.2**

Robin Hood and the golden arrow. McCaughrean, G.
In McCaughrean, G. The golden hoard: myths and legends of the world p20-28 **398.2**

Robin of Sherwood. Morpurgo, M. **Fic**

Robinet, Harriette Gillem, 1931-
Forty acres and maybe a mule **Fic**
Washington City is burning **Fic**

Robinette, Joseph
Charlotte's web [play]
In Theatre for young audiences p7-45 **812.008**

Robins, C. Richard
A field guide to Atlantic coast fishes of North America **597**

Robinson, Barbara
The best Christmas pageant ever **Fic**
The best school year ever **Fic**

Robinson, Eddie
See/See also pages in the following book(s):
Haskins, J. One more river to cross **920**

Robinson, Heath *See* Robinson, William Heath, 1872-1944

Robinson, Jackie, 1919-1972
About
Dingle, D. T. First in the field: baseball hero Jackie Robinson **92**
Weidhorn, M. Jackie Robinson **92**
See/See also pages in the following book(s):
Brashler, W. The story of Negro league baseball p121-33 **796.357**
Fiction
Gutman, D. Jackie and me **Fic**

Robinson, Julia B., 1919-1985
See/See also pages in the following book(s):
Celebrating women in mathematics and science p159-72 **920**
Henderson, H. Modern mathematicians (7 and up) **920**

Robinson, William Heath, 1872-1944
Uncle Lubin and the dragon
In The Book of dragons p47-49 **S C**

Robinson Crusoe. Defoe, D. **Fic**

Robinson Masters, Nancy
Georgia
In America the beautiful, second series **973**
Kansas
In America the beautiful, second series **973**

Robotics *See* Robots

Robots
Jefferis, D. Artificial intelligence **629.8**
Fiction
Asimov, I. I, robot (7 and up) **S C**

Rochelle, Belinda
Witnesses to freedom **323.1**

Rochman, Hazel
Against borders **011.6**

(ed) Bearing witness. See Bearing witness **808.8**
(ed) Leaving home: stories. See Leaving home: stories **808.8**
(comp) Somehow tenderness survives. See Somehow tenderness survives **S C**
(comp) Who do you think you are? See Who do you think you are? **S C**

Rock & roll generation (7 and up) **973.91**

Rock and roll music *See* Rock music

Rock climbing. Brimner, L. D. **796.52**

Rock drawings, paintings, and engravings
Arnold, C. Stories in stone **709.01**

Rock music
The Rolling Stone illustrated history of rock & roll (7 and up) **781.66**
Woog, A. The history of rock and roll (7 and up) **781.66**
Encyclopedias
The New Rolling Stone encyclopedia of rock & roll (7 and up) **781.66**

Rock musicians
Daily, R. Elvis Presley: the king of rock 'n' roll (7 and up) **92**

Rock paintings *See* Rock drawings, paintings, and engravings

Rocket!. Maurer, R. **621.43**

Rocket boys. Hickam, H. H. **92**

Rocketry
Maurer, R. Rocket! **621.43**
Miller, R. The history of rockets **621.43**

Rocklin, Joanne
For your eyes only! **Fic**

Rocks
Chesterman, C. W. The Audubon Society field guide to North American rocks and minerals **549**
Pellant, C. Rocks and minerals **549**
Pough, F. H. A field guide to rocks and minerals **549**
Ricciuti, E. R. National Audubon Society first field guide: rocks and minerals **552**
Rocks & fossils **550**
Simon and Schuster's guide to rocks and minerals **549**
Symes, R. F. Rocks & minerals **549**
Zim, H. S. Rocks and minerals **549**

Rocks & fossils **550**

Rocks & minerals. Symes, R. F. **549**

Rocks and minerals. Pellant, C. **549**

Rocks and minerals. Zim, H. S. **549**

Rodari, Florian
A weekend with Picasso **92**

Roddick, Anita
See/See also pages in the following book(s):
Graham, K. Contemporary environmentalists p85-104 (7 and up) **920**

Rodents
Alderton, D. Rodents of the world (7 and up) **599.3**

Rodents of the world. Alderton, D. **599.3**

Rodeos
Fiction
Koertge, R. The Arizona kid (7 and up)
Fic

Rodgers, Marie E.
The Harlem Renaissance   016.7

Rodgers, Mary, 1931-
Freaky Friday   Fic

Rodowsky, Colby F., 1932-
Amanda and the wounded birds
In Visions: nineteen short stories by outstanding writers for young adults p78-86
S C
Hannah in between   Fic
Remembering Mog (7 and up)   Fic
The Turnabout Shop   Fic

Rodriguez, Matt, 1936-
See/See also pages in the following book(s):
Morey, J. Famous Hispanic Americans p142-55
920

Rodriguez, Paul
See/See also pages in the following book(s):
Morey, J. Famous Hispanic Americans p156-67
920

Roe, Jane *See* McCorvey, Norma
Roe v. Wade. Romaine, D. S.   344
Roe v. Wade (1973). Gold, S. D.   344
Roehm, Michelle, 1968-
(comp) Girls know best. See Girls know best
305.23

Rogasky, Barbara
The golem   398.2
Smoke and ashes: the story of the Holocaust
940.53

Rogers, Will, 1879-1935
About
Sonneborn, L. Will Rogers, Cherokee entertainer
92
Roget's II (7 and up)   423
Roget's international thesaurus   423
Roget's student thesaurus   423
Roget's thesaurus in dictionary form, The Doubleday   423
Roginski, James W., 1945-1993
(ed) Newbery and Caldecott medalists and honor book winners. See Newbery and Caldecott medalists and honor book winners   011.6
Rogue wave. Taylor, T.
In Taylor, T. Rogue wave and other red-blooded sea stories   S C
Rogue wave and other red-blooded sea stories. Taylor, T.   S C
Rohr, Janelle, 1963-
(ed) Science & religion: opposing viewpoints. See Science & religion: opposing viewpoints
215
Rol, Ruud van der
Anne Frank, beyond the diary   92
Roland and Horn Olivant. McCaughrean, G.
In McCaughrean, G. The silver treasure: myths and legends of the world p20-26
398.2

Roleff, Tamara L., 1959-
(ed) Abortion: opposing viewpoints. See Abortion: opposing viewpoints   363.46
(ed) AIDS: opposing viewpoints. See AIDS: opposing viewpoints   616.97
(ed) Biomedical ethics: opposing viewpoints. See Biomedical ethics: opposing viewpoints
174
(ed) Civil liberties: opposing viewpoints. See Civil liberties: opposing viewpoints   323
(ed) Global warming: opposing viewpoints. See Global warming: opposing viewpoints
363.7
(ed) Gun control: opposing viewpoints. See Gun control: opposing viewpoints   363.3
(ed) Hate groups: opposing viewpoints. See Hate groups: opposing viewpoints   364.1
(ed) Immigration: opposing viewpoints. See Immigration: opposing viewpoints   325.73
(ed) Marriage and divorce. See Marriage and divorce   306.8
(ed) The Rights of animals. See The Rights of animals   179
(ed) Suicide: opposing viewpoints. See Suicide: opposing viewpoints   362.28
(ed) Tobacco and smoking: opposing viewpoints. See Tobacco and smoking: opposing viewpoints   362.29
(ed) War: opposing viewpoints. See War: opposing viewpoints   355
Roll, William
(jt. auth) Duncan, L. Psychic connections
133
Roll of thunder, hear my cry. Taylor, M. D.
Fic
Rollerblading *See* In-line skating
Rolling Rio, the gray man, and Death. Hamilton, V.
In Hamilton, V. The dark way p5-13
398.2
The **Rolling** Stone encyclopedia of rock & roll. See The New Rolling Stone encyclopedia of rock & roll   781.66
The **Rolling** Stone illustrated history of rock & roll (7 and up)   781.66
Rollings, Willard H.
The Comanche
In Indians of North America series
970.004
Rollins, Charlemae, 1897-1979
(comp) Christmas gif'. See Christmas gif'
810.8
Romain, Trevor
Cliques, phonies & other baloney   158
Romaine, Deborah S., 1956-
Roe v. Wade (7 and up)   344
Roman architecture
Macaulay, D. City: a story of Roman planning and construction   711
The **Roman** Colosseum. Mann, E.   937
The **Roman** Colosseum. Nardo, D.   725
Roman emperors *See* Emperors—Rome
Roman Empire *See* Rome
A **Roman** fort. Macdonald, F.   355.7

Rosen, Dorothy
A fire in her bones: the story of Mary Lyon
92

Rosenberg, Ethel, 1915-1953
See/See also pages in the following book(s):
Kraft, B. H. Sensational trials of the 20th century p79-105 (7 and up)   **347**

Rosenberg, Judith K.
Young people's books in series: fiction and nonfiction, 1975-1991   **011.6**

Rosenberg, Julius, 1918-1953
See/See also pages in the following book(s):
Kraft, B. H. Sensational trials of the 20th century p79-105 (7 and up)   **347**

Rosenberg, Liz
(ed) The Invisible ladder. See The Invisible ladder   **811.008**

Rosenberg, Maxine B., 1939-
Hiding to survive   **940.53**

Rosenburg, John M.
First in peace: George Washington, the Constitution, and the presidency (7 and up)   **92**

Rosenthal, Ida Cohen, 1886-1973
See/See also pages in the following book(s):
Altman, L. J. Women inventors p50-62 (7 and up)   **920**

Roses by moonlight. Wrede, P. C.
In Wrede, P. C. Book of enchantments p27-48   **S C**

Rosetta stone
Giblin, J. The riddle of the Rosetta Stone   **493**

The **Rosetta** Stone: English I and English II (American). See entry in CD-ROM section, Part 3

Rosie the riveter. Colman, P.   **331.4**

Rosner, Marc Alan
Science fair success using the Internet (7 and up)   **507.8**

Rosow, La Vergne
Light 'n lively reads for ESL, adult, and teen readers   **011.6**

Ross, Anne
Druids, gods & heroes from Celtic mythology   **299**

Ross, Beverly B., 1931-
Junior Broadway   **792.6**

Ross, Bill
Straight from the bear's mouth   **580**

Ross, Edmund Gibson, 1826-1907
See/See also pages in the following book(s):
Kennedy, J. F. Profiles in courage p132-58 (7 and up)   **920**

Ross, Gayle
(jt. auth) Bruchac, J. The girl who married the Moon: tales from Native North America   **398.2**

Ross, Stewart
Causes and consequences of the Great Depression (7 and up)   **338.5**
Mark Twain and Huckleberry Finn   **92**

Rosteck, Mary Kay
(ed) People of the Holocaust. See People of the Holocaust   **920.003**

Rostkowski, Margaret I., 1945-
After the dancing days   **Fic**

Rosy's journey. Alcott, L. M.
In American fairy tales p92-104   **S C**

Rothfarb, Ed
In the land of the Taj Mahal (7 and up)   **954.02**

Rothman, Chuck
Curse of the undead
In Vampires: a collection of original stories p19-34   **S C**

Roughnecks. Cochran, T.   **Fic**

Round buildings, square buildings, & buildings that wiggle like a fish. Isaacson, P. M.   **720**

Rourke, Arlene C., 1944-
Teeth and braces   **617.6**

Rouse, Jeff, 1970-
The young swimmer   **797.2**

Rousseau, Henri Julien Félix, 1844-1910
About
Plazy, G. A weekend with Rousseau   **92**

Rovin, Jeff
The encyclopedia of monsters (7 and up)   **001.9**

Rowan, Peter
Some body!   **611**

Rowland-Warne, L.
Costume   **391**

Rowling, J. K.
Harry Potter and the Chamber of Secrets. See note under Rowling, J. K. Harry Potter and the sorcerer's stone   **Fic**
Harry Potter and the goblet of fire. See note under Harry Potter and the sorcerer's stone   **Fic**
Harry Potter and the prisoner of Azkaban. See note under Rowling, J. K. Harry Potter and the sorcerer's stone   **Fic**
Harry Potter and the sorcerer's stone   **Fic**

Royal Ballet School (Great Britain)
Bussell, D. The young dancer   **792.8**

Royal diaries [series]
Lasky, K. Elizabeth I   **Fic**

The **royal** kingdoms of Ghana, Mali, and Songhay. McKissack, P. C.   **966.2**

Royalty *See* Kings and rulers; Princesses; Queens

Roybal, Edward R., 1916-
See/See also pages in the following book(s):
Morey, J. Famous Mexican Americans p119-29   **920**

Royer, Mary-Paige, 1955-
Astrology: opposing viewpoints   **133.5**

Rubber-band banjos and a java jive bass. Sabbeth, A.   **781**

Rubella
Silverstein, A. Measles and rubella (7 and up)   **616.9**

Rubens, Sir Peter Paul, 1577-1640
See/See also pages in the following book(s):
Glubok, S. Great lives: painting p176-86   **920**

Russian Empire *See* Russia
Russian language
Dictionaries
English-Russian dictionary   **491.7**
Russian overture. Conford, E.
In Conford, E. Crush p85-93   **S C**
Rustin, Bayard, 1910-1987
About
Haskins, J. Bayard Rustin: behind the scenes of the civil rights movement   **92**
Rutberg, Becky
Mary Lincoln's dressmaker [biography of Elizabeth Keckley]   **92**
Ruth, Amy
Louisa May Alcott   **92**
Mother Teresa   **92**
Ruth, Babe, 1895-1948
See/See also pages in the following book(s):
Gilbert, T. W. Damn Yankees (7 and up)   **796.357**
Ruth, George Herman *See* Ruth, Babe, 1895-1948
Ruth, Maria Mudd- *See* Mudd-Ruth, Maria
Rutherford, Ernest, 1871-1937
See/See also pages in the following book(s):
Henderson, H. Nuclear physics p18-33 (7 and up)   **539.7**
Rutledge, Rachel
The best of the best in gymnastics   **920**
The best of the best in track & field   **920**
Ryan, Bryan
(ed) Hispanic American almanac. See Hispanic American almanac [junior version]   **305.8**
Ryan, Pat
Extreme skateboarding   **796.22**
Rybolt, Thomas R.
(jt. auth) Mebane, R. C. Air & other gases   **530.4**
(jt. auth) Mebane, R. C. Metals   **669**
(jt. auth) Mebane, R. C. Plastics & polymers   **547**
(jt. auth) Mebane, R. C. Salts & solids   **530.4**
(jt. auth) Mebane, R. C. Water & other liquids   **530.4**
Ryden, Hope
Wild horses I have known   **599.66**
Rylant, Cynthia
Appalachia   **974**
But I'll be back again   **92**
A fine white dust   **Fic**
The Heavenly Village   **Fic**
The islander   **Fic**
Missing May   **Fic**
Something permanent (7 and up)   **811**

S

S.O.R. losers. Avi   **Fic**
Saar, Betye, 1926-
See/See also pages in the following book(s):
Sills, L. Visions p32-45   **920**

Saar, David
The yellow boat
In Theatre for young audiences p535-78   **812.008**
Saari, Peggy
(ed) Explorers & discoverers. See Explorers & discoverers   **920.003**
(ed) Scientists. See Scientists   **920.003**
Saavedra, Miguel de Cervantes *See* Cervantes Saavedra, Miguel de, 1547-1616
Sabbeth, Alex, 1950-
Rubber-band banjos and a java jive bass   **781**
Sabin, Florence Rena, 1871-1953
About
Kaye, J. The life of Florence Sabin   **92**
Sabin vaccine *See* Poliomyelitis vaccine
Sable, Jean Baptiste Pointe de *See* Pointe de Sable, Jean Baptiste, 1745?-1818
Sabriel. Nix, G.   **Fic**
The **Sac** and Fox. Bonvillain, N.
In Indians of North America series   **970.004**
Sac Indians *See* Sauk Indians
Sacagawea, b. 1786
About
St. George, J. Sacagawea   **92**
See/See also pages in the following book(s):
Calvert, P. Great lives: the American frontier p328-38   **920**
Fiction
O'Dell, S. Streams to the river, river to the sea   **Fic**
Sacajawea *See* Sacagawea, b. 1786
Sacco, Nicola, 1891-1927
See/See also pages in the following book(s):
Kraft, B. H. Sensational trials of the 20th century p1-23 (7 and up)   **347**
Sachar, Louis, 1954-
Holes   **Fic**
Sachs, Marilyn, 1927-
Surprise party   **Fic**
Sacred fire. Wood, N. C.   **811**
Sacred places. Yolen, J.   **811**
The **sacrifice.** Matcheck, D.   **Fic**
The **sad** tale of three slavers. Jagendorf, M. A.
In From sea to shining sea p138-39   **810.8**
The **sad** tale of Tom the catfish. Jagendorf, M. A.
In From sea to shining sea p232-33   **810.8**
Sadko and the Tsar of the Sea. McCaughrean, G.
In McCaughrean, G. The bronze cauldron: myths and legends of the world p14-19   **398.2**
Safari. Bateman, R.   **599**
The **safe** zone. Chaiet, D.   **613.6**
Safety education
Chaiet, D. The safe zone   **613.6**
Wiloch, T. Everything you need to know about protecting yourself and others from abduction   **613.6**

Safford, Barbara Ripp
Guide to reference materials for school media
centers **011.6**

Safire, William
(comp) Lend me your ears. See Lend me your
ears **808.85**

Sagan, Carl, 1934-1996
See/See also pages in the following book(s):
Camp, C. A. American astronomers p84-91
920

Saign, Geoffrey, 1955-
The African cats **599.75**
The great apes **599.8**

Sailing
Conner, D. Learn to sail (7 and up) **797.1**

Sailors' life *See* Seafaring life

Saint Agnes sends the golden boy. Forshay-
Lunsford, C.
In Visions: nineteen short stories by outstand-
ing writers for young adults p11-22
S C

Saint Christopher. McCaughrean, G.
In McCaughrean, G. The silver treasure:
myths and legends of the world p53-56
398.2

Saint Crispin's follower. Fleischman, P.
In Fleischman, P. Graven images p25-59
S C

Saint-Exupéry, Antoine de, 1900-1944
The little prince **Fic**

Saint Helens, Mount (Wash.) *See* Mount Saint
Helens (Wash.)

Saint Valentine's Day *See* Valentine's Day

Saints
See also Christian saints

Sakyamuni *See* Gautama Buddha

Sal Fink. San Souci, R.
In San Souci, R. Cut from the same cloth
p51-55 **398.2**

Salamandastron. Jacques, B. See note under
Jacques, B. Redwall **Fic**

Salem (Mass.)
Fiction
Lasky, K. Beyond the burning time (7 and up)
Fic
Petry, A. L. Tituba of Salem Village **Fic**
History
Fremon, D. K. The Salem witchcraft trials in
American history **133.4**
Kallen, S. A. The Salem witch trials (7 and up)
133.4
Roach, M. K. In the days of the Salem witch-
craft trials **133.4**
Wilson, L. L. The Salem witch trials **133.4**
The **Salem** ghost ship. Shay, F.
In From sea to shining sea p113-14
810.8
The **Salem** witch trials. Kallen, S. A. **133.4**
The **Salem** witch trials. Wilson, L. L. **133.4**
The **Salem** witchcraft trials in American history.
Fremon, D. K. **133.4**

Salisbury, Graham, 1944-
Jungle dogs **Fic**

Shark bait **Fic**
In Ultimate sports: short stories by outstand-
ing writers for young adults p118-44
S C
Something like . . . love
In Dirty laundry: stories about family secrets
p140-61 **S C**
Under the blood-red sun **Fic**

Salish Coastal Indians *See* Coast Salish Indians

Salk, Jonas, 1914-1995
About
Sherrow, V. Jonas Salk **92**

Salk vaccine *See* Poliomyelitis vaccine

Sally Ann Thunder Ann Whirlwind Crockett meets
Mike Fink, Snappin' Turkle. Cohen, C. L.
In From sea to shining sea p118-20
810.8

Salmonson, Jessica Amanda
The ugly unicorn
In A Glory of unicorns p79-94 **S C**
The **saltcellar.** McCaughrean, G.
In McCaughrean, G. The silver treasure:
myths and legends of the world p121-26
398.2

Salts & solids. Mebane, R. C. **530.4**

Salvadori, Mario George, 1907-1997
Math games for middle school **510.7**
(jt. auth) Levy, M. Earthquake games
551.2

Salzman, Jack
(ed) Encyclopedia of African-American culture
and history. See Encyclopedia of African-
American culture and history **305.8**

Sammy Keyes and the curse of Moustache Mary.
Draanen, W. van See note under Draanen, W.
V. Sammy Keyes and the hotel thief **Fic**

Sammy Keyes and the hotel thief. Draanen, W.
van **Fic**

Sammy Keyes and the runaway elf. Draanen, W.
van See note under Draanen, W. V. Sammy
Keyes and the hotel thief **Fic**

Sammy Keyes and the Sisters of Mercy. Draanen,
W. van See note under Draanen, W. V.
Sammy Keyes and the hotel thief **Fic**

Sammy Keyes and the skeleton man. Draanen, W.
van See note under Draanen, W. V. Sammy
Keyes and the hotel thief **Fic**

Samoyault, Tiphaine
Alphabetical order **411**

Samuels, Barbara G.
(ed) Into focus. See Into focus **028.1**

The **samurai** and the dragon. Kimmel, E. A.
In Kimmel, E. A. Sword of the samurai p11-
21 **Fic**

San Francisco (Calif.)
Fiction
Reiss, K. PaperQuake **Fic**
Yep, L. The case of the Goblin Pearls **Fic**
Yep, L. Child of the owl **Fic**
Yep, L. Dragonwings **Fic**
Yep, L. Thief of hearts **Fic**

San Martín, José de, 1778?-1850
About
Fernández, J. B. José de San Martín **92**

Science and civilization—Continued
Moss, C. Science in ancient Mesopotamia
509
Nardo, D. Greek and Roman science (7 and up)
509
Stewart, M. Science in ancient India   **509**
Woods, G. Science in ancient Egypt   **509**
Woods, G. Science of the early Americas
509
Science and invention. Spangenburg, R.   **917.3**
Science and religion See Religion and science
Science and society [series]
Kidd, J. S. Into thin air   **363.7**
Kidd, J. S. Life lines   **576.5**
Kidd, J. S. Quarks and sparks   **621.48**
Kidd, J. S. Shades of green   **363.7**
Science Books & Films   **016.5**
Science Books, a quarterly review. See Science
Books & Films   **016.5**
Science concepts [series]
Silverstein, A. Clocks and rhythms   **571.7**
Silverstein, A. Plate tectonics   **551.1**
Science court: sound. See entry in CD-ROM section, Part 3
Science court: water cycle. See entry in CD-ROM section, Part 3
Science discoveries [series]
Parker, S. Benjamin Franklin and electricity
92
Parker, S. Charles Darwin and evolution
92
Parker, S. Thomas Edison and electricity
92
Science experiments on file   **507.8**
Science experiments you can eat. Cobb, V.
507.8
Science fair projects See Science projects
Science fair projects—planning, presenting, succeeding. Gardner, R.   **507.8**
Science fair success. Bombaugh, R. J.   **507.8**
Science fair success [series]
Krieger, M. J. How to excel in science competitions   **507.8**
Perry, P. J. Science fair success with plants
580.7
Rosner, M. A. Science fair success using the Internet   **507.8**
Science fair success using the Internet. Rosner, M. A.   **507.8**
Science fair success with plants. Perry, P. J.
580.7
Science fairs: ideas and activities   **507.8**
Science fiction
See also Fantasy fiction
Gutman, D. Jackie and me   **Fic**
Adams, D. The Hitchhiker's Guide to the Galaxy (7 and up)   **Fic**
Asimov, I. I, robot (7 and up)   **S C**
Bawden, N. Off the road   **Fic**
Bradbury, R. The Martian chronicles (7 and up)
S C
Brittain, B. Shape-changer   **Fic**
Card, O. S. Ender's game (7 and up)   **Fic**

Christopher, J. The White Mountains   **Fic**
Ciencin, S. Dinoverse   **Fic**
Clarke, A. C. 2001: a space odyssey (7 and up)
Fic
Coville, B. Aliens ate my homework   **Fic**
Crichton, M. Jurassic Park (7 and up)   **Fic**
Dexter, C. Alien game   **Fic**
Dickinson, P. Eva (7 and up)   **Fic**
Dragons & dreams   **S C**
Farmer, N. The Ear, the Eye, and the Arm
Fic
Gutman, D. Virtually perfect   **Fic**
Haddix, M. P. Among the hidden   **Fic**
Hughes, M. The Golden Aquarians   **Fic**
Hughes, M. Invitation to the game (7 and up)
Fic
Jones, D. W. Hexwood (7 and up)   **Fic**
Kehret, P. The blizzard disaster   **Fic**
Klause, A. C. Alien secrets   **Fic**
Lawrence, L. Dream-weaver (7 and up)   **Fic**
Levitin, S. The cure   **Fic**
Lowry, L. The giver   **Fic**
Mackel, K. Can of worms   **Fic**
Mahy, M. Aliens in the family   **Fic**
Mahy, M. The greatest show off earth   **Fic**
McCaffrey, A. Pegasus in flight (7 and up)
Fic
Nix, G. Shade's children (7 and up)   **Fic**
O'Brien, R. C. Z for Zachariah (7 and up)
Fic
Paulsen, G. The Transall saga   **Fic**
Read into the millennium   **S C**
Shusterman, N. The dark side of nowhere
Fic
Silverberg, R. Letters from Atlantis (7 and up)
Fic
Skurzynski, G. The virtual war   **Fic**
Sleator, W. The boxes (7 and up)   **Fic**
Sleator, W. The boy who reversed himself
Fic
Sleator, W. The duplicate (7 and up)   **Fic**
Sleator, W. House of stairs (7 and up)   **Fic**
Sleator, W. Interstellar pig (7 and up)   **Fic**
Sleator, W. The night the heads came   **Fic**
Sleator, W. Others see us (7 and up)   **Fic**
Sleator, W. Rewind   **Fic**
Sleator, W. Singularity (7 and up)   **Fic**
Sleator, W. Strange attractors   **Fic**
Verne, J. A journey to the centre of the earth
Fic
Verne, J. Twenty thousand leagues under the
sea   **Fic**
Wells, H. G. The war of the worlds (7 and up)
Fic
Westwood, C. Virtual world (7 and up)
Fic

History and criticism
Reid, S. E. Presenting young adult science fiction (7 and up)   **813.009**
Science for every kid series
VanCleave, J. P. Janice Vancleave's ecology for every kid   **577**
Science in ancient China. Beshore, G. W.
509
Science in ancient Egypt. Woods, G.   **509**
Science in ancient Greece. Gay, K.   **509**

Science projects [series]—*Continued*
Gardner, R. Science projects about weather
551.5

Science projects [Raintree series]
Oxlade, C. Chemistry **540.7**
Oxlade, C. Weather **551.5**
Pinna, S. de. Electricity **621.3**
Snedden, R. The environment **577**

Science projects about kitchen chemistry. Gardner, R. **540.7**

Science projects about physics in the home. Gardner, R. **507.8**

Science projects about plants. Gardner, R. **580.7**

Science projects about the environment and ecology. Gardner, R. **363.7**

Science projects about weather. Gardner, R. **551.5**

Science superstars [series]
Lessem, D. Jack Horner: living with dinosaurs **92**

The **Science** Teacher **507.05**

Scientific American sourcebooks [series]
Aaseng, N. Poisonous creatures **591.6**
McGowen, T. Adventures in archaeology **930.1**
Sayre, A. P. Endangered birds of North America **598**
Sherrow, V. Endangered mammals of North America **599**
Vogt, G. The solar system **523.2**

Scientific expeditions
See also Exploration
Stefoff, R. Scientific explorers **509**

Scientific experiments *See* Science—Experiments

Scientific explorers. Stefoff, R. **509**

Scientific recreations
Cash, T. 175 more science experiments to amuse and amaze your friends **507.8**
Cobb, V. Don't try this at home! **507.8**
Cobb, V. You gotta try this! **507.8**
Oxlade, C. Science magic with magnets **793.8**
See/See also pages in the following book(s):
Levy, M. Earthquake games **551.2**

Scientists
See also Environmentalists; Women scientists
Adair, G. George Washington Carver **92**
Anderson, M. J. Isaac Newton **92**
Christianson, G. E. Isaac Newton and the scientific revolution (7 and up) **92**
Coil, S. M. Robert Hutchings Goddard (7 and up) **92**
Distinguished African American scientists of the 20th century (7 and up) **920**
Edelson, E. James Watson and Francis Crick and the building blocks of life (7 and up) **92**
Haven, K. F. 100 most popular scientists for young adults (7 and up) **920**
Kozar, R. Inventors and their discoveries **920**

Lessem, D. Jack Horner: living with dinosaurs **92**
McKissack, P. C. African-American scientists **920**
Nardo, D. Scientists of Ancient Greece (7 and up) **920**
Oleksy, W. G. Hispanic-American scientists (7 and up) **920**
Polking, K. Oceanographers and explorers of the sea **920**
Sherrow, V. Jonas Salk **92**
Smith, L. W. Louis Pasteur **92**
Yount, L. Asian-American scientists (7 and up) **920**

Dictionaries
American men & women of science **920.003**
Podell, J. Old worlds to new **920.003**
Scientists **920.003**
Scientists and inventors **920.003**

Scientists **920.003**

Scientists and doctors. Lindop, L. **920**

Scientists and inventors **920.003**

Scientists of Ancient Greece. Nardo, D. **920**

Scoliosis
Eisenpreis, B. Coping with scoliosis (7 and up) **616.7**

Scopes, John Thomas
About
Blake, A. The Scopes trial **345**
Nardo, D. The Scopes trial (7 and up) **345**
See/See also pages in the following book(s):
Kraft, B. H. Sensational trials of the 20th century p24-47 (7 and up) **347**

The **Scopes** trial. Blake, A. **345**

The **Scopes** trial. Nardo, D. **345**

Scoppettone, Sandra, 1936-
Trying hard to hear you (7 and up) **Fic**

Scordato, Ellen
Sarah Winnemucca [Hopkins] **92**

Scorpions. Myers, W. D. **Fic**

Scotland
Fiction
Cooper, S. The Boggart **Fic**
Hunter, M. The king's swift rider (7 and up) **Fic**
Little, J. The belonging place **Fic**
Stevenson, R. L. Kidnapped (7 and up) **Fic**
Yolen, J. The Pictish child **Fic**
Yolen, J. The wizard's map **Fic**

Scott, Dred, ca. 1795-1858
About
Fleischner, J. The Dred Scott case **342**
Herda, D. J. The Dred Scott case (7 and up) **342**
January, B. The Dred Scott decision **342**

Scott, Elaine, 1940-
Close encounters **523**

Scott, John F., 1936-
Mexican, Central and South American art
In International encyclopedia of art **703**

Scott, Michael M.
The young Oxford book of ecology **577**

A **seat** in the garden. King, T.
   In Talking leaves   **S C**
Seattle Mariners (Baseball team)
   Gutman, B. Ken Griffey, Jr.   **92**
Sebestyen, Ouida, 1924-
   Far from home   **Fic**
   Holding out
     In Center stage   **812.008**
   Playing God
     In Visions: nineteen short stories by outstanding writers for young adults p87-99
                        S C
   Welcome
     In Sixteen: short stories by outstanding writers for young adults p47-59   **S C**
   Words by heart   **Fic**
          About
   Monseau, V. R. Presenting Ouida Sebestyen (7 and up)   **813.009**
The **Second** Amendment. Hanson, F. O.   **344**
The **second** bad thing. Conrad, P.
   In Conrad, P. Our house p49-63   **S C**
The **second** bend in the river. Rinaldi, A.   **Fic**
Second cousins. Hamilton, V.   **Fic**
Second daughter. Walter, M. P.   **Fic**
The **second** jungle book. See Kipling, R. The jungle books   **S C**
Second Manassas (7 and up)   **973.7**
Second stringer. Dygard, T. J.   **Fic**
Secondary school libraries *See* High school libraries
Secondary schools *See* High schools
The **secret** code book. Huckle, H.   **652**
The **secret** garden [play] Sterling, P.
   In Theatre for young audiences p99-141
                   812.008
Secret letters from 0 to 10. Morgenstern, S. H.
                   Fic
The **secret** of life, according to Aunt Gladys. Coville, B.
   In The Dirty laundry: stories about family secrets p1-17   **S C**
The **secret** of the underground room. Bellairs, J. See note under Bellairs, J. The curse of the blue figurine   **Fic**
The **secret** river. Adams, R.
   In Adams, R. Tales from Watership Down
                   S C
Secret service
     See also Espionage; Intelligence service; Spies
Secret writing *See* Cryptography
Secrets of the ice man. Patent, D. H.   **930.1**
Secrets of the unexplained [series]
   Blackwood, G. L. Alien astronauts   **001.9**
   Blackwood, G. L. Extraordinary events and oddball occurrences   **001.9**
Secrets of Walden rising. Baillie, A.   **Fic**
Seddon, Margaret Rhea *See* Seddon, Rhea, 1947-
Seddon, Rhea, 1947-
See/See also pages in the following book(s):
   Briggs, C. S. Women in space   **920**

Sedna, the sea goddess. Caswell, H. R.
   In From sea to shining sea p18-22   **810.8**
See through history [series]
   Howarth, S. The Middle Ages   **940.1**
   Nicolle, D. Medieval knights   **940.1**
   Wood, T. Ancient wonders   **930.1**
   Wood, T. The Renaissance   **940.2**
See you around Sam. Lowry, L. See note under Lowry, L. Anastasia Krupnik   **Fic**
Seedfolks. Fleischman, P.   **Fic**
Seeds
   Pascoe, E. Seeds and seedlings   **582**
Seeds and seedlings. Pascoe, E.   **582**
Seeing Earth from space. Lauber, P.   **525**
Sees Behind Trees. Dorris, M.   **Fic**
Segregation
     See also Discrimination
   See/See also pages in the following book(s):
   Levine, E. Freedom's children p3-16   **323.1**
       Law and legislation
   Fireside, H. Plessy v. Ferguson (7 and up)
                   342
Segregation in education
   Dudley, M. E. Brown v. Board of Education (1954) (7 and up)   **344**
   Haskins, J. Separate, but not equal   **379**
   Tackach, J. Brown v. Board of Education (7 and up)   **344**
   See/See also pages in the following book(s):
   Levine, E. Freedom's children p32-57
                   323.1
Seidler, Tor, 1952-
   Mean Margaret   **Fic**
Seismology *See* Earthquakes
Selassie, Emperor of Ethiopia *See* Haile Selassie I, Emperor of Ethiopia, 1892-1975
Selby, David
   (jt. auth) Willson, Q. The ultimate classic car book   **629.222**
Self-acceptance
   Sneddon, P. S. Body image (7 and up)
                 155.9
Self-defense
     See also Aikido
   Goedecke, C. J. Smart moves   **796.8**
Self-defense in animals *See* Animal defenses
Self-esteem
   Shepherd, K. R. Drugs and low self-esteem (7 and up)   **616.86**
Self-help programs *See* Twelve-step programs
Self-love (Psychology) *See* Self-esteem
Self-mutilation
   Clarke, A. Coping with self-mutilation (7 and up)   **616.85**
   Ng, G. Everything you need to know about self-mutilation (7 and up)   **616.85**
Self-perception
   Davis, B. What's real, what's ideal (7 and up)   **616.85**
   Sneddon, P. S. Body image (7 and up)
                 155.9
Self-respect *See* Self-esteem

Shakers—Fiction—*Continued*
Peck, R. N. A day no pigs would die   **Fic**
Shakespeare, William, 1564-1616
Macbeth; adaptation. See Coville, B. William Shakespeare's Macbeth   **822.3**
A midsummer night's dream; adaptation. See Coville, B. William Shakespeare's A midsummer night's dream   **822.3**
Othello; adaptation. See Lester, J. Othello   **Fic**
About
Aliki. William Shakespeare & the Globe   **792.09**
Morley, J. Shakespeare's theater   **792.09**
Shellard, D. William Shakespeare (7 and up)   **822.3**
Stanley, D. Bard of Avon: the story of William Shakespeare   **92**
Adaptations
Garfield, L. Shakespeare stories [I]-II   **822.3**
Lamb, C. Tales from Shakespeare   **822.3**
Nesbit, E. The best of Shakespeare   **822.3**
Williams, M. Tales from Shakespeare   **822.3**
Fiction
Blackwood, G. L. The Shakespeare stealer   **Fic**
The **Shakespeare** stealer. Blackwood, G. L.   **Fic**
Shakespeare's Globe (London, England)
Aliki. William Shakespeare & the Globe   **792.09**
Shakespeare's theater. Morley, J.   **792.09**
Shamanism
Wolfson, E. From the earth to beyond the sky   **970.004**
Shamir, Ilanah
(ed) The Young reader's encyclopedia of Jewish history. See The Young reader's encyclopedia of Jewish history   **909**
Shandler, Sara
Ophelia speaks (7 and up)   **305.23**
Shape
Ash, R. Incredible comparisons   **031.02**
Shape-changer. Brittain, B.   **Fic**
Shapes *See* Shape
Shaping U.S. foreign policy. Dolan, E. F.   **327.73**
Shapiro, Irwin, 1911-1981
Strong but quirky: the birth of Davy Crockett
In From sea to shining sea p85-87   **810.8**
Shapley, Harlow, 1885-1972
See/See also pages in the following book(s):
Camp, C. A. American astronomers p52-59   **920**
Shaq *See* O'Neal, Shaquille
The **shared** heart. Mastoon, A.   **305.9**
Sharing the crops. Courlander, H.
In From sea to shining sea p219-21   **810.8**
Sharing the soup. Jaffe, N.
In Jaffe, N. The cow of no color: riddle stories and justice tales from around the world p104-09   **398.2**

Shark. Brooks, B. See note under Brooks, B. Zip   **Fic**
Shark bait. Salisbury, G.   **Fic**
In Ultimate sports: short stories by outstanding writers for young adults p118-44   **S C**
The **Shark** Callers. Campbell, E.   **Fic**
Sharks
Macquitty, M. Shark   **597**
Woog, A. The shark (7 and up)   **597**
Fiction
Campbell, E. The Shark Callers (7 and up)   **Fic**
Sharmat, Marjorie Weinman, 1928-
Dream job
In Visions: nineteen short stories by outstanding writers for young adults p23-29   **S C**
May I have your autograph?
In Sixteen: short stories by outstanding writers for young adults p15-21   **S C**
Sharrar, Jack F., 1949-
(ed) Great monologues for young actors. See Great monologues for young actors   **808.82**
(ed) Great scenes and monologues for children. See Great scenes and monologues for children   **808.82**
(ed) Great scenes for young actors. See Great scenes for young actors   **808.82**
Shavit, Shelomoh
(ed) The Young reader's encyclopedia of Jewish history. See The Young reader's encyclopedia of Jewish history   **909**
Shavit, Shlomo *See* Shavit, Shelomoh
Shaw, Robert Gould, 1837-1863
About
Burchard, P. "We'll stand by the Union": Robert Gould Shaw and the Black 54th Massachusetts Regiment (7 and up)   **92**
The **shawl**. Ozick, C.
In Bearing witness p60-66   **808.8**
Shawnee Indians
Cwiklik, R. Tecumseh, Shawnee rebel   **92**
Hubbard-Brown, J. The Shawnee
In Indians of North America series   **970.004**
Stefoff, R. Tecumseh and the Shawnee confederation (7 and up)   **92**
Fiction
Rinaldi, A. The second bend in the river (7 and up)   **Fic**
Shay, Frank
The Salem ghost ship
In From sea to shining sea p113-14   **810.8**
She. Guy, R.
In Sixteen: short stories by outstanding writers for young adults p147-53   **S C**
She is beautiful in her whole being. Momaday, N. S.
In Talking leaves   **S C**

She who showers gold. Krishnaswami, U.
  In Krishnaswami, U. Shower of gold: girls
    and women in the stories of India p90-93
      398.2

Shea, Pegi Deitz, 1960-
  Ekaterina Gordeeva   **92**

Shearer, Barbara Smith
  (jt. auth) Shearer, B. F. State names, seals, flags,
    and symbols   **929.9**

Shearer, Benjamin F.
  State names, seals, flags, and symbols
                                                  929.9

Sheehan, Patricia, 1954-
  Luxembourg   **949.35**

Sheehan, Sean, 1951-
  Guatemala   **972.81**
  Lebanon   **956.92**

Sheep

Fiction

  Paulsen, G. The haymeadow   **Fic**

Sheep. Thomas, R.
  In Trapped!: cages of mind and body p19-31
                                                  S C

Shein, Lori, 1957-
  AIDS (7 and up)   **616.97**
  (jt. auth) Haugen, D. The Civil War   **973.7**
  (ed) Inequality: opposing viewpoints in social
    problems. See Inequality: opposing viewpoints
    in social problems   **305**

Sheldon, Dyan
  Confessions of a teenage drama queen (7 and
    up)   **Fic**

Shellard, Dominic
  William Shakespeare (7 and up)   **822.3**

Shelley, Mary Wollstonecraft, 1797-1851
  Frankenstein (7 and up)   **Fic**
  Frankenstein; adaptation. See The new Prome-
    theus

Shellfish

See also Mollusks

Shells
  Arthur, A. Shell   **594**
  Douglass, J. L. Peterson first guide to shells of
    North America   **594**
  Rehder, H. A. The Audubon Society field guide
    to North American seashells   **594**

Shenandoah, 1862 (7 and up)   **973.7**

Shenandoah, 1864 (7 and up)   **973.7**

Shenandoah Valley Campaign, 1862
  Shenandoah, 1862 (7 and up)   **973.7**

**Shenandoah Valley Campaign, 1864 (May-
August)**
  Shenandoah, 1864 (7 and up)   **973.7**

Shepard, Aaron
  Stories on stage   **812**

Shepherd, Donna Walsh *See* Walsh Shepherd,
  Donna, 1948-

Shepherd, K. R. (Kenneth Ronald)
  Drugs and low self-esteem (7 and up)
                                                  616.86

Shepherd, Kenneth Ronald *See* Shepherd, K. R.
  (Kenneth Ronald)

Sheptyts´kyĭ, Andriĭ, 1865-1944
  See/See also pages in the following book(s):
  Lyman, D. Holocaust rescuers   **920**

Sherman, Allan, 1924-1973
  A gift of laughter
    In Leaving home: stories p27-33   **808.8**

Sherman, Charlotte Watson, 1958-
  BigWater
    In Rites of passage p79-88   **S C**

Sherman, Delia
  Blood kin
    In Vampires: a collection of original stories
      p35-63   **S C**

Sherman, Gale W.
  (jt. auth) Ammon, B. D. More rip-roaring reads
    for reluctant teen readers   **028.5**

Sherman, Josepha
  The magic-stealer
    In Vampires: a collection of original stories
      p99-120   **S C**
  Merlin's kin   **398.2**

Sherrow, Victoria
  Bioethics and high-tech medicine (7 and up)
                                                  174
  The blaze engulfs   **940.53**
  Cherokee Nation v. Georgia (7 and up)
                                                  346
  Connecticut
    In Celebrate the states   **973**
  Endangered mammals of North America
                                                  599
  The Exxon Valdez   **363.7**
  Gideon v. Wainwright (7 and up)   **345**
  Hurricane Andrew   **551.55**
  Jonas Salk   **92**
  Joseph McCarthy and the Cold War   **92**
  Ohio
    In Celebrate the states   **973**
  The Oklahoma City bombing   **364.1**
  The righteous gentiles (7 and up)   **940.53**
  Smoke to flame   **940.53**
  The Titanic (7 and up)   **910.4**
  The World Trade Center bombing   **364.1**

Shields, Nancy E., 1928-
  Where credit is due (7 and up)   **808**

Shiloh (Tenn.), Battle of, 1862
  Shiloh (7 and up)   **973.7**

Shiloh (7 and up)   **973.7**

Shiloh. Naylor, P. R.   **Fic**

Shiloh season. Naylor, P. R. See note under
  Naylor, P. R. Shiloh   **Fic**

Shimmy shimmy shimmy like my sister Kate
                                                  811.008

Shimomura, Tsutomu
  See/See also pages in the following book(s):
  Yount, L. Asian-American scientists p95-103 (7
    and up)   **920**
The **shiner**. Hallworth, G.
  In The Oxford book of scary tales p52-53
                                                  808.8

Shingles (Disease)
  Silverstein, A. Chickenpox and shingles (7 and
    up)   **616.9**

Ship. Macaulay, D.   **387.2**

Short stories—Continued

Help wanted: short stories about young people working (7 and up)   S C

Henry, O. The gift of the Magi and other stories (7 and up)   S C

Jennings, P. Unbearable!   S C

Jennings, P. Uncovered!   S C

Jennings, P. Undone!   S C

Jennings, P. Unmentionable!   S C

Jiménez, F. The circuit: stories from the life of a migrant child   S C

Johnson, A. Gone from home: short takes (7 and up)   S C

Join in   S C

Kimmel, E. A. Sword of the samurai   S C

Kipling, R. The jungle books   S C

Leaving home: stories (7 and up)   **808.8**

Lester, J. Long journey home: stories from black history   S C

Mazer, H. The dog in the freezer: three novellas   S C

McKean, T. Into the candlelit room and other strange tales   S C

McKinley, R. The door in the hedge   S C

McKinley, R. A knot in the grain and other stories   S C

McKissack, P. C. The dark-thirty   S C

Montgomery, L. M. Christmas with Anne and other holiday stories   S C

Murphy, J. Night terrors   S C

A Newbery Christmas   S C

A Newbery Halloween   S C

A Newbery zoo   S C

Night terrors (7 and up)   S C

A Nightmare's dozen (7 and up)   S C

Ortiz Cofer, J. An island like you (7 and up)   S C

Paterson, K. A midnight clear: stories for the Christmas season (7 and up)   S C

Places I never meant to be (7 and up)   S C

Poe, E. A. Tales of Edgar Allan Poe   S C

Potok, C. Zebra and other stories (7 and up)   S C

Read into the millennium   S C

Reynolds, M. Beyond dreams (7 and up)   S C

Rites of passage   S C

Singer, I. B. The power of light   S C

Sixteen: short stories by outstanding writers for young adults (7 and up)   S C

Skinner, D. Thundershine: tales of metakids   S C

Sleator, W. Oddballs: stories   S C

Somehow tenderness survives (7 and up)   S C

Soto, G. Baseball in April, and other stories   S C

Soto, G. Local news   S C

Soto, G. Petty crimes   S C

Spinelli, J. The library card   S C

Stay true: short stories for strong girls (7 and up)   S C

Talking leaves   S C

Taylor, T. Rogue wave and other red-blooded sea stories   S C

Trapped!: cages of mind and body (7 and up)   S C

Twelve shots: outstanding short stories about guns (7 and up)   S C

Ultimate sports: short stories by outstanding writers for young adults (7 and up)   S C

Vampires: a collection of original stories (7 and up)   S C

Vande Velde, V. Curses, Inc. and other stories   S C

Vande Velde, V. Tales from the Brothers Grimm and the Sisters Weird   S C

Visions: nineteen short stories by outstanding writers for young adults (7 and up)   S C

Vivelo, J. Chills in the night   S C

Westall, R. Demons and shadows (7 and up)   S C

Where angels glide at dawn   S C

Who do you think you are? (7 and up)   S C

Wrede, P. C. Book of enchantments   S C

Wyeth, S. D. Vampire bugs: stories conjured from the past   S C

Wynne-Jones, T. The book of changes   S C

Wynne-Jones, T. Lord of the Fries and other stories   S C

Yee, P. Tales from Gold Mountain   S C

Yolen, J. Twelve impossible things before breakfast   S C

History and criticism

Short stories for students   **809.3**

Indexes

Short story index   **808.83**

Short stories for students   **809.3**

Short story index   **808.83**

A **short** walk around the Pyramids & through the world of art. Isaacson, P. M.   **700**

Shortelle, Dennis

(jt. auth) Gardner, R. The forgotten players   **796.357**

The **Shoshone**. Dramer, K.

In Indians of North America series   **970.004**

Shoshoni Indians

Dramer, K. The Shoshone

In Indians of North America series   **970.004**

St. George, J. Sacagawea   **92**

See/See also pages in the following book(s):

Freedman, R. Indian chiefs p73-89   **920**

Shostak, Jerome

(jt. auth) Peters, M. How to prepare for the SSAT, ISEE high school entrance examinations   **373.1**

Shotgun Cheatham's last night above ground. Peck, R.

In Twelve shots: outstanding short stories about guns p122-37   S C

Shots on goal. Wallace, R.   **Fic**

Shower of gold: girls and women in the stories of India. Krishnaswami, U.   **398.2**

The **shrieking** door. Aiken, J.

In Aiken, J. A fit of shivers p95-111   S C

Shrubs
Petrides, G. A. A field guide to trees and shrubs
582.16

Shulman, Fay Stanley *See* Stanley, Fay, 1925-1990

Shulman, William L.
Resource guide **940.53**
(comp) Voices and visions. See Voices and visions **940.53**

Shumate, Jane
Sequoyah **92**

Shurgin, Ann H., 1952-
(ed) The Folklore of world holidays. See The Folklore of world holidays **394.26**

Shusterman, Neal
The dark side of nowhere **Fic**
Downsiders **Fic**
The eyes of Kid Midas **Fic**

Shuttles, Space *See* Space shuttles

Shyness
Fiction
Kindl, P. The woman in the wall **Fic**

Siamese twins
Landau, E. Joined at birth **616**
See/See also pages in the following book(s):
Drimmer, F. Incredible people p78-108 **920**

Siberia (Russia)
Hautzig, E. R. The endless steppe: growing up in Siberia **92**

Siblings *See* Brothers and sisters

Sickle cell anemia
Silverstein, A. Sickle cell anemia (7 and up)
616.1

Sickness *See* Diseases

Siddhārtha *See* Gautama Buddha

Siegal, Aranka
Upon the head of the goat: a childhood in Hungary, 1939-1944 **92**

Siegel, Beatrice
Marian Wright Edelman **92**
Murder on the highway: the Viola Liuzzo story
92

Siegel, Dorothy Schainman
Dental health (7 and up) **617.6**

Sierra Club
Hart, J. Walking softly in the wilderness
796.51

Sierra i Fabra, Jordi, 1947-
Uninvited guests
In Don't read this! and other tales of the unnatural p197-213 **S C**

Sieruta, Peter D.
Hands in the darkness
In Help wanted: short stories about young people working **S C**

The **sight**. McKissack, P. C.
In McKissack, P. C. The dark-thirty p44-54
S C

Sign language
See also Indians of North America—Sign language
Butterworth, R. R. The Perigee visual dictionary of signing **419**

The Comprehensive signed English dictionary
419
Costello, E. Random House American sign language dictionary **419**
Riekehof, L. L. The joy of signing **419**
Sternberg, M. L. A. American Sign Language
419

The **sign** of the beaver. Speare, E. G. **Fic**
Sign of the dove. Fletcher, S. **Fic**
The **sign** of the four. Doyle, Sir A. C.
In Doyle, Sir A. C. The complete Sherlock Holmes **S C**

Signs and symbols
See also Sign language
Bruce-Mitford, M. The illustrated book of signs & symbols (7 and up) **302.2**
Liungman, C. G. Dictionary of symbols (7 and up) **302.2**

Signs of the times [series]
Ganeri, A. The story of communications
384
Ganeri, A. The story of writing and printing
652

Sigurd and Fafnir. Lang, A.
In The Book of dragons p72-77 **S C**

Sikhism
Kaur-Singh, K. Sikhism **294.6**

Siksika Indians
Lacey, T. J. The Blackfeet
In Indians of North America series
970.004

The **silent** storm. Garland, S. **Fic**
The **Silk** Route. Major, J. S. **950**

Sills, Leslie
Inspirations **920**
Visions **920**

Silver. Mazer, N. F. **Fic**
Silver Blaze. Doyle, Sir A. C.
In Doyle, Sir A. C. The complete Sherlock Holmes **S C**
The **silver** chair. Lewis, C. S. See note under Lewis, C. S. The lion, the witch, and the wardrobe **Fic**
Silver days. Levitin, S. **Fic**
The **silver** kiss. Klause, A. C. **Fic**
The **silver-miners**. McCaughrean, G.
In McCaughrean, G. The silver treasure: myths and legends of the world p1-5
398.2
Silver on the tree. Cooper, S. See note under Cooper, S. Over sea, under stone **Fic**
The **silver** treasure: myths and legends of the world. McCaughrean, G. **398.2**

Silverberg, Robert
Letters from Atlantis (7 and up) **Fic**

Silverman, Jerry
African roots **782.42**
Just listen to this song I'm singing **782.42**
Songs and stories from the American Revolution
782.42
Songs of protest and civil rights **782.42**

Silverman, Judith, 1933-
Breen, K. Index to collective biographies for young readers   920

Silverstein, Alvin
AIDS (7 and up)   616.97
Asthma (7 and up)   616.2
The California condor   598
Chickenpox and shingles (7 and up)   616.9
The circulatory system   612.1
Clocks and rhythms   571.7
Depression (7 and up)   616.85
Energy   621
Evolution   576.8
Food chains   577
Fungi   579.5
The grizzly bear   599.78
Invertebrates   592
Measles and rubella (7 and up)   616.9
Monerans & protists   579
The mustang   599.66
A pet or not?   636
Photosynthesis   572
Plants   580
Plate tectonics   551.1
The respiratory system   612.2
The sea otter   599.7
Sickle cell anemia (7 and up)   616.1
Snakes & such   639
Symbiosis   577.8
Vertebrates   596
Weather and climate   551.5

Silverstein, Herma
Kids who kill (7 and up)   364.1
Threads of evidence (7 and up)   363.2

Silverstein, Robert A.
(jt. auth) Silverstein, A. The circulatory system   612.1
(jt. auth) Silverstein, A. Fungi   579.5
(jt. auth) Silverstein, A. Invertebrates   592
(jt. auth) Silverstein, A. Measles and rubella   616.9
(jt. auth) Silverstein, A. Monerans & protists   579
(jt. auth) Silverstein, A. Plants   580
(jt. auth) Silverstein, A. The respiratory system   612.2
(jt. auth) Silverstein, A. The sea otter   599.7
(jt. auth) Silverstein, A. Vertebrates   596

Silverstein, Shel
Falling up   811
A light in the attic   811
Where the sidewalk ends   811

Silverstein, Virginia B.
(jt. auth) Silverstein, A. AIDS   616.97
(jt. auth) Silverstein, A. Asthma   616.2
(jt. auth) Silverstein, A. The California condor   598
(jt. auth) Silverstein, A. Chickenpox and shingles   616.9
(jt. auth) Silverstein, A. The circulatory system   612.1
(jt. auth) Silverstein, A. Clocks and rhythms   571.7
(jt. auth) Silverstein, A. Depression   616.85
(jt. auth) Silverstein, A. Energy   621

(jt. auth) Silverstein, A. Evolution   576.8
(jt. auth) Silverstein, A. Food chains   577
(jt. auth) Silverstein, A. Fungi   579.5
(jt. auth) Silverstein, A. The grizzly bear   599.78
(jt. auth) Silverstein, A. Invertebrates   592
(jt. auth) Silverstein, A. Measles and rubella   616.9
(jt. auth) Silverstein, A. Monerans & protists   579
(jt. auth) Silverstein, A. The mustang   599.66
(jt. auth) Silverstein, A. A pet or not?   636
(jt. auth) Silverstein, A. Photosynthesis   572
(jt. auth) Silverstein, A. Plants   580
(jt. auth) Silverstein, A. Plate tectonics   551.1
(jt. auth) Silverstein, A. The respiratory system   612.2
(jt. auth) Silverstein, A. The sea otter   599.7
(jt. auth) Silverstein, A. Sickle cell anemia   616.1
(jt. auth) Silverstein, A. Snakes & such   639
(jt. auth) Silverstein, A. Symbiosis   577.8
(jt. auth) Silverstein, A. Vertebrates   596
(jt. auth) Silverstein, A. Weather and climate   551.5

Silverwing. Oppel, K.   Fic

Silvey, Anita
(ed) Children's books and their creators. See Children's books and their creators   028.5
(comp) Help wanted: short stories about young people working. See Help wanted: short stories about young people working   S C

Simmons, Jake, 1901-1981
See/See also pages in the following book(s):
Haskins, J. African American entrepreneurs p97-100   920

Simmons, Philip
About
Lyons, M. E. Catching the fire: Philip Simmons, blacksmith   92

Simmons, William Scranton, 1938-
The Narragansett
In Indians of North America series   970.004

Simner, Janni Lee
Tearing down the unicorns
In A Glory of unicorns p31-42   S C

Simon, Seymour, 1931-
Bones   612.7
The brain   612.8
Earth words   363.7
The heart   612.1
Lightning   551.56
Mountains   551.4
Muscles   612.7
Now you see it, now you don't   152.14
Snakes   597.9
Strange mysteries from around the world   001.9
Wildfires   577.2

Simon & Schuster children's guide to sea creatures. Johnson, J.   591.7

The **Simon** & Schuster encyclopedia of animals
590.3

The **Simon** & Schuster pocket book of chess. Keene, R. D. **794.1**

Simon and Schuster's guide to rocks and minerals
549

Simple experiments in time with everyday materials. Mandell, M. **529**

Simple makeup for young actors. Cummings, R.
792

Simpson, Carol Mann, 1949-
Internet for schools **004.6**

Simpson, D. P.
Cassell's Latin dictionary: Latin-English, English-Latin. See Cassell's Latin dictionary: Latin-English, English-Latin **473**

Simpson, O. J.
See/See also pages in the following book(s):
Aaseng, N. You are the juror **345**
Kraft, B. H. Sensational trials of the 20th century p177-207 (7 and up) **347**

Simulation, computer *See* Computer simulation

Sinatra, Frank, 1915-1998
See/See also pages in the following book(s):
Gourse, L. Swingers and crooners p69-73 (7 and up) **781.65**

Sinbad the Sailor, The Seven voyages of
398.2

Sincerely yours. James, E. **808**

Sing down the moon. O'Dell, S. **Fic**

Sing for your father, Su Phan. Pevsner, S.
Fic

Sing me a death song. Bennett, J. **Fic**

Singer, Isaac Bashevis, 1904-1991
The power of light **S C**
Contents: A Hanukkah evening in my parents' house; The extinguished lights; The parakeet named Dreidel; Menashe and Rachel; The squire; The power of light; Hershele and Hanukkah; Hanukkah in the poorhouse

Singer, Marilyn, 1948-
Magic how
In Stay true: short stories for strong girls
S C
(comp) Stay true: short stories for strong girls. See Stay true: short stories for strong girls
S C

The **singer** above the river. McCaughrean, G.
In McCaughrean, G. The golden hoard: myths and legends of the world p77-83
398.2

The **singer** of seeds. Yolen, J.
In Yolen, J. Here there be ghosts p63-70
810.8

Singers
See also African American singers
Dolan, S. Bob Marley **92**
Gonzales, D. Gloria Estefan **92**
Gourse, L. Swingers and crooners (7 and up)
781.65
Howey, P. Garth Brooks **92**
Stefoff, R. Plácido Domingo **92**

Singh, Kanwaljit Kaur- *See* Kaur-Singh, Kanwaljit

Singing America **811.008**

Singing apples. Kadohata, C.
In American eyes p49-61 **S C**

The **singing** float. Hughes, M.
In Dragons & dreams p136-50 **S C**

The **singing** mountain. Levitin, S. **Fic**

The **Singing**, soaring lark
In Hearne, B. G. Beauties and beasts p60-65
398.2

Single parent family
See also Children of divorced parents; Unmarried mothers
Schultz, M. A. Teens with single parents (7 and up) **306.8**
Fiction
Byars, B. C. The night swimmers **Fic**
Griffin, A. Split just right **Fic**
Hamilton, V. Sweet whispers, Brother Rush
Fic
Lowry, L. The one hundredth thing about Caroline **Fic**

Singleton, Benjamin *See* Singleton, Pap, 1809-1892

Singleton, Pap, 1809-1892
See/See also pages in the following book(s):
Duncan, D. People of the West p94-101
978

Singularity. Sleator, W. **Fic**

Sink the Bismarck. McGowen, T. **940.54**

Sinnott, Susan
Extraordinary Hispanic Americans **920**

Sioras, Efstathia
Czech Republic **943.7**

Siouan Indians
See also Dakota Indians; Oglala Indians; Osage Indians

The **Sioux**. Bial, R. **970.004**

Sioux Indians *See* Dakota Indians

The **Sioux** who wrestled with a ghost. Brown, D. A.
In Brown, D. A. Dee Brown's folktales of the Native American p166-67 **398.2**

Sipes, Karen L., 1953-
(jt. auth) Closter, K. Fiction, food, and fun
028.5

Sir Galahad, Mr. Longfellow, and me. Horvath, B. F. **Fic**

Sir Gawain and the Green Knight. Osborne, M. P.
In Osborne, M. P. Favorite medieval tales p50-59 **398.2**

Sir Gawain and the loathly lady
In Hearne, B. G. Beauties and beasts p131-38
398.2

Sir Patrick Spens. McCaughrean, G.
In McCaughrean, G. The silver treasure: myths and legends of the world p118-20
398.2

SIRS government reporter. See entry in CD-ROM section, Part 3

SIRS Researcher. See entry in CD-ROM section, Part 3

Sis, Peter
Tibet **951**

Sister Fox and Brother Coyote. San Souci, R.
  In San Souci, R. Cut from the same cloth
    p93-99   **398.2**

Sisters

Fiction

Bauer, M. D. A taste of smoke   **Fic**
Couloumbis, A. Getting near to baby   **Fic**
Deaver, J. R. Chicago blues (7 and up)
      Fic
Dessen, S. That summer (7 and up)   **Fic**
Griffin, A. The other Shepards   **Fic**
Johnson, A. Humming whispers (7 and up)
      Fic
Jukes, M. Expecting the unexpected   **Fic**
Littke, L. Haunted sister (7 and up)   **Fic**
Lowry, L. A summer to die   **Fic**
McKay, H. The exiles   **Fic**
Paterson, K. Jacob have I loved   **Fic**
Reiss, K. PaperQuake   **Fic**
Strasser, T. Hey, Dad, get a life!   **Fic**
Williams, C. L. The true colors of Caitlynne
  Jackson   **Fic**
Woodson, J. Lena   **Fic**

Sisters (in religious orders, congregations, etc.)
  See Nuns

Sisters. Ellis, S.
  In Ellis, S. Back of beyond   **S C**

Sisters and brothers *See* Brothers and sisters

Sit!. Gorog, J.
  In Gorog, J. When nobody's home p41-45
      S C

Sit on a potato pan, Otis!. Agee, J.   **793.73**

Sita, Lisa, 1962-
  The rattle and the drum   **299**

Sita's story. Krishnaswami, U.
  In Krishnaswami, U. Shower of gold: girls
    and women in the stories of India p52-60
      398.2

A **sitter** and a find. Gorog, J.
  In Gorog, J. When nobody's home p83-89
      S C

Sitting Bull, Dakota Chief, 1831-1890
About
  St. George, J. To see with the heart: the life of
    Sitting Bull   **92**
  See/See also pages in the following book(s):
  Ehrlich, A. Wounded Knee: an Indian history of
    the American West   **970.004**
  Freedman, R. Indian chiefs p114-39   **920**

Sitting in Egypt. Gorog, J.
  In Gorog, J. When nobody's home p36-40
      S C

Sixteen: short stories by outstanding writers for
  young adults (7 and up)   **S C**

Sixteenth century
  Ashby, R. Elizabethan England   **942.05**

Sixteenth century mosque. Macdonald, F.
      297

Sixth grade can really kill you. See DeClements,
  B. 6th grade can really kill you   **Fic**

The **sixth** grade nickname game. Korman, G.
      Fic

The **sixty-two** curses of Caliph Arenschadd.
  Wrede, P. C.
  In Wrede, P. C. Book of enchantments p49-
    70   **S C**

Size
  Ash, R. Incredible comparisons   **031.02**

Size and shape *See* Shape

Sizzling summer reading programs for young
  adults. Kan, K.   **027.62**

Skaggs, Gayle, 1952-
  On display   **027.8**

Skateboards and skateboarding
  Ryan, P. Extreme skateboarding   **796.22**

Skating *See* Ice skating

Skeleton
  Ballard, C. The skeleton and muscular system
      612.7
  Parker, S. Skeleton   **573.7**
  Simon, S. Bones   **612.7**
  The Visual dictionary of the skeleton   **573.7**

The **skeleton** and muscular system. Ballard, C.
      612.7

Skellig. Almond, D.   **Fic**

Skelton, Olivia
  Vietnam   **959.7**

Sketching outdoors in spring. Arnosky, J.
      743

Sketching outdoors in summer. Arnosky, J.
      743

Skills, Life *See* Life skills

Skills for writers. See entry in CD-ROM section,
  Part 3

Skin deep. Vande Velde, V.
  In Vande Velde, V. Curses, Inc. and other
    stories p45-62   **S C**

Skin diving
  Holbrook, M. Snorkeling   **797.2**

The **skin** I'm in. Flake, S. G.   **Fic**

Skinhead. Bennett, J.   **Fic**

Skinner, David, 1963-
  Thundershine: tales of metakids   **S C**
  Contents: As true as she wants it; Walk this way; Poof Poof
  Ya does me a favor; Meta human
  The woeful princess
  In Trapped!: cages of mind and body p47-64
      S C

Skinner, Linda
  (jt. auth) Avery, S. Extraordinary American In-
    dians   **920**

Skinning out. McCaughrean, G.
  In McCaughrean, G. The golden hoard: myths
    and legends of the world p17-19
      398.2

Skira-Venturi, Rosabianca
  A weekend with Degas   **92**
  A weekend with Renoir   **92**
  A weekend with Van Gogh   **92**

Skolsky, Mindy Warshaw
  Love from your friend, Hannah   **Fic**

The **skull** of truth. Coville, B.   **Fic**

Skunk outwits Coyote. Brown, D. A.
  In Brown, D. A. Dee Brown's folktales of the
    Native American p111-13   **398.2**

Skurzynski, Gloria
 Cliff hanger   **Fic**
 Deadly waters. See note under Skurzynski, G.
  Cliff hanger   **Fic**
 Discover Mars   **523.4**
 Rage of fire. See note under Skurzynski, G.
  Cliff hanger   **Fic**
 Spider's voice (7 and up)   **Fic**
 The virtual war   **Fic**
 Wolf stalker. See note under Skurzynski, G.
  Cliff hanger   **Fic**
The **sky-blue** storybox. McCaughrean, G.
 In McCaughrean, G. The crystal pool: myths
  and legends of the world p128-33
                                                 398.2
Sky kings. Bayne, B. C.   **796.323**
Sky pioneer: a photobiography of Amelia Earhart.
 Szabo, C.   **92**
Skyscrapers
 Macaulay, D. Unbuilding   **690**
Slaight, Craig
 (ed) Great monologues for young actors. See
  Great monologues for young actors
                                                 808.82
 (ed) Great scenes and monologues for children.
  See Great scenes and monologues for children
                                                 808.82
 (ed) Great scenes for young actors. See Great
  scenes for young actors   **808.82**
Slake's limbo. Holman, F.   **Fic**
Slam!. Myers, W. D.   **Fic**
Slam and the ghosts. Crossley-Holland, K.
 In The Oxford book of scary tales p14-15
                                                 808.8
Slam dunk: basketball poems   **811.008**
Slater, Ann Tashi
 There's no reason to get romantic
  In American dragons p185-99   **810.8**
The **slave** dancer. Fox, P.   **Fic**
Slave trade
 Haskins, J. Bound for America   **326**
 Thomas, V. M. Lest we forget (7 and up)
                                                 326
See/See also pages in the following book(s):
 Reef, C. Africans in America p1-19 (7 and up)
                                                 305.8
  Fiction
 Fox, P. The slave dancer   **Fic**
Slavery
 Cameron, A. The kidnapped prince: the life of
  Olaudah Equiano   **92**
  Fiction
 Armstrong, J. Steal away   **Fic**
 Ayres, K. North by night   **Fic**
 Berry, J. Ajeemah and his son   **Fic**
 Carbone, E. L. Stealing freedom   **Fic**
 Collier, J. L. Jump ship to freedom   **Fic**
 Collier, J. L. War comes to Willy Freeman
                                                 Fic
 Collier, J. L. Who is Carrie?   **Fic**
 Forrester, S. Sound the jubilee   **Fic**
 Hansen, J. The captive   **Fic**
 Houston, G. Bright Freedom's song   **Fic**
 Lasky, K. True north   **Fic**

 Lyons, M. E. Letters from a slave girl   **Fic**
 McKissack, P. C. Let my people go   **221.9**
 McKissack, P. C. A picture of Freedom
                                                 Fic
 Paterson, K. Jip   **Fic**
 Paulsen, G. Nightjohn (7 and up)   **Fic**
 Paulsen, G. Sarny (7 and up)   **Fic**
 Rees, D. C. Lightning Time   **Fic**
 Rinaldi, A. Hang a thousand trees with ribbons
  (7 and up)   **Fic**
 Rinaldi, A. Wolf by the ears (7 and up)
                                                 Fic
 Robinet, H. G. Washington City is burning
                                                 Fic
 Ruby, L. Steal away home   **Fic**
 Stolz, M. Cezanne Pinto   **Fic**
 Walter, M. P. Second daughter   **Fic**
 Wisler, G. C. Caleb's choice   **Fic**
 Woodruff, E. Dear Austin   **Fic**
  History
 Haskins, J. Bound for America   **326**
 Palmer, C. A. The first passage (7 and up)
                                                 326
See/See also pages in the following book(s):
 Reef, C. Africans in America p1-48 (7 and up)
                                                 305.8
  Pictorial works
 Feelings, T. The middle passage (7 and up)
                                                 759.13
  Rome
 Nardo, D. Life of a Roman slave (7 and up)
                                                 937
  United States
 See also Abolitionists
 Altman, L. J. Slavery and abolition in American
  history   **973.7**
 Barrett, T. Nat Turner and the slave revolt
                                                 92
 Bial, R. The strength of these arms   **326**
 Bial, R. The underground railroad   **326**
 Bisson, T. Nat Turner   **92**
 Burchard, P. Lincoln and slavery (7 and up)
                                                 92
 Collier, C. The paradox of Jamestown, 1585-
  1700   **975.5**
 Currie, S. Slavery (7 and up)   **326**
 Douglass, F. Frederick Douglass, in his own
  words (7 and up)   **305.8**
 Erickson, P. Daily life on a Southern plantation,
  1853   **975**
 Fleischner, J. The Dred Scott case   **342**
 Fleischner, J. I was born a slave: the story of
  Harriet Jacobs   **92**
 Frankel, N. Break those chains at last: African
  Americans, 1860-1880 (7 and up)   **305.8**
 Golay, M. Reconstruction and reaction (7 and
  up)   **305.8**
 Gorrell, G. K. North star to freedom   **326**
 Hamilton, V. Anthony Burns   **92**
 Hamilton, V. Many thousand gone   **326**
 Haskins, J. Get on board: the story of the Un-
  derground Railroad   **326**
 Herda, D. J. The Dred Scott case (7 and up)
                                                 342
 January, B. The Dred Scott decision   **342**
 Jurmain, S. Freedom's sons   **326**

Slavery—United States—*Continued*
Katz, W. L. Breaking the chains: African-American slave resistance (7 and up)
326
King, W. Toward the promised land (7 and up)
305.8
Lester, J. From slave ship to freedom road
326
Lester, J. To be a slave 326
Marston, H. I. Isaac Johnson 92
McKissack, P. C. Christmas in the big house, Christmas in the quarters 394.26
McKissack, P. C. Rebels against slavery
326
Myers, W. D. Amistad: a long road to freedom
326
Nardo, D. Braving the New World, 1619-1784 (7 and up) 305.8
Rappaport, D. Escape from slavery 326
Sawyer, K. K. The underground railroad in American history 326
Schleichert, E. The Thirteenth Amendment (7 and up) 342
Steins, R. The nation divides 973.7
Tackach, J. The Emancipation Proclamation (7 and up) 973.7
Thomas, V. M. Lest we forget (7 and up)
326
White, D. G. Let my people go: African Americans, 1804-1860 (7 and up) 305.8
Yates, E. Amos Fortune, free man 92
See/See also pages in the following book(s):
Marrin, A. Commander in Chief Abraham Lincoln and the Civil War p39-65 (7 and up)
973.7
Tackach, J. The trial of John Brown, radical abolitionist (7 and up) 345
Yount, L. Frontiers of freedom p53-67 (7 and up) 978
Slavery and abolition in American history. Altman, L. J. 973.7
Slaves to soldiers. Black, W. B. 973.7
Sleator, William
The beasties (7 and up) Fic
The boxes (7 and up) Fic
The boy who reversed himself Fic
The duplicate (7 and up) Fic
The elevator
In Read all about it! p236-43 808.8
House of stairs (7 and up) Fic
Interstellar pig (7 and up) Fic
The night the heads came Fic
Oddballs: stories S C
Contents: Games; Frank's mother; The freedom fighters of Parkview; The hypnotist; The séance; The pitiful encounter; Leah's stories; Pituh-plays; Dad's cool; Oddballs
Others see us (7 and up) Fic
Rewind Fic
Singularity (7 and up) Fic
Strange attractors Fic
Sled dog racing
See also Iditarod Trail Sled Dog Race, Alaska
Paulsen, G. Puppies, dogs, and blue northers
798.8
Paulsen, G. Woodsong (7 and up) 796.5

Shahan, S. Dashing through the snow
798.8
Wood, T. Iditarod dream 798.8
Sleeping Beauty (Ballet)
See/See also pages in the following book(s):
McCaughrean, G. The Random House book of stories from the ballet p102-12 792.8
Newman, B. The illustrated book of ballet stories p10-21 792.8
The **sleeping** mountains. Winther, B.
In Winther, B. Plays from Hispanic tales
812
Sleight of hand *See* Juggling; Magic tricks
Slepian, Jan, 1921-
The Broccoli tapes Fic
The mind reader Fic
Slesar, Henry, 1927-
Good morning! this is the future
In Read into the millenium p120-25 S C
Slime, molds, and fungi. Pascoe, E. 579.5
Slippers. Yep, L.
In Yep, L. The rainbow people p162-68
398.2
SLJ/School Library Journal. See School Library Journal 027.805
Sloppy jalopy. Jennings, P.
In Jennings, P. Unmentionable! p89-107
S C
Slot machine. Lynch, C. Fic
Slote, Stanley J.
Weeding library collections 025.2
Slow learning children
See also Mentally handicapped children
Slugs (Mollusks)
Pascoe, E. Snails and slugs 594
Slumps, grunts, and snickerdoodles: what Colonial America ate and why. Perl, L. 641.5
Smale, Alan P.
The smooth man
In A Nightmare's dozen S C
Small business
See also Entrepreneurship
A **small** child and a large sitter. Gorog, J.
In Gorog, J. When nobody's home p16-20
S C
The **Small-tooth** dog
In Hearne, B. G. Beauties and beasts p25-28
398.2
Smallpox
See/See also pages in the following book(s):
Farrell, J. Invisible enemies p11-44 (7 and up)
614.4
Smallwood, Carol, 1939-
Insider's guide to school libraries 027.8
Smart, P. (Paul), 1957-
Everything you need to know about mononucleosis (7 and up) 616.9
Smart, Paul *See* Smart, P. (Paul), 1957-
Smart moves. Goedecke, C. J. 796.8
Smelly feat. Jennings, P.
In Jennings, P. Unbearable! p97-113
S C

Smoothey, Marion, 1943-
Graphs 001.4
The **smugglers**. Lawrence, I. Fic
Smuggling
Fiction
Lawrence, I. The smugglers Fic
Napoli, D. J. Trouble on the tracks Fic
Sutcliff, R. Flame-colored taffeta Fic
Smuggling of drugs See Drug traffic
Smyth, Ian
The young baseball player 796.357
Snails
Pascoe, E. Snails and slugs 594
Snails and slugs. Pascoe, E. 594
The **snake**. Lester, J.
In Lester, J. The last tales of Uncle Remus
p28-33 398.2
In Lester, J. When the beginning began p73-
80 296.1
The **Snake** book 597.9
Snake husband, Frog friend. Martin, R.
In Martin, R. Mysterious tales of Japan
398.2
The **snake** scientist. Montgomery, S. 597.9
Snake-spoke. Yep, L.
In Yep, L. The rainbow people p86-95
398.2

Snakes
See also Pythons; Rattlesnakes
Coborn, J. Snakes 639
Mattison, C. Snake 597.9
Montgomery, S. The snake scientist 597.9
Simon, S. Snakes 597.9
The Snake book 597.9
See/See also pages in the following book(s):
Byars, B. C. The moon and I 92
Snakes & such. Silverstein, A. 639
A **snap** of the fingers. San Souci, R.
In San Souci, R. A terrifying taste of short &
shivery p123-29 398.2
Snapshot. Czech, K. P. 770.9
Snatched away. TallMountain, M.
In Talking leaves S C
Snedden, Robert
The environment 577
Technology in the time of ancient Rome
609
Sneddon, Pamela Shires
Body image (7 and up) 155.9
Sneve, Virginia Driving Hawk
(comp) Dancing teepees: poems of American In-
dian youth. See Dancing teepees: poems of
American Indian youth 897
The **snooping** sitter. Gorog, J.
In Gorog, J. When nobody's home p5-8
S C
Snorkeling See Skin diving
Snorkeling. Holbrook, M. 797.2
Snow, Dean R., 1940-
The archaeology of North America
In Indians of North America series
970.004

Snow bound. Mazer, H. Fic
The **snow** husband. San Souci, R.
In San Souci, R. A terrifying taste of short &
shivery p58-61 398.2
The **snow** woman. Martin, R.
In Martin, R. Myterious tales of Japan
398.2
Snowboarding
Brimner, L. D. Snowboarding 796.9
Lurie, J. Fundamental snowboarding 796.9
McKenna, L. The fantastic book of snow-
boarding 796.9
Snowbound. Lavender, D. S. 978
Snyder, Zilpha Keatley
Cat running Fic
Gib and the gray ghost. See note under Snyder,
Z. K. Gib rides home Fic
Gib rides home Fic
The runaways Fic
Song of the gargoyle Fic
The three men
In Dragons & dreams p55-69 S C
So far from the bamboo grove. Watkins, Y. K.
Fic
So long, and thanks for all the fish. Adams, D.
See note under Adams, D. The Hitchhiker's
Guide to the Galaxy Fic
So proudly they served. Anderson, M. K.
940.54
So you want to be a wizard. Duane, D. See note
under Duane, D. A wizard abroad Fic
Soaring. Perry, P. J. 797.5
Sobel, Ileene
Moses and the angels 296.1
Soccer
Baddiel, I. Ultimate soccer 796.334
Coleman, L. Fundamental soccer 796.334
Hamm, M. Go for the goal (7 and up)
796.334
Scott, N. S. The thinking kid's guide to success-
ful soccer 796.334
Stewart, M. Soccer (7 and up) 796.334
Biography
Arnold, C. Pelé: the king of soccer 92
Fiction
Avi. S.O.R. losers Fic
Bloor, E. Tangerine (7 and up) Fic
Wallace, R. Shots on goal (7 and up) Fic
Soccer: the ultimate World Cup companion. See
Baddiel, I. Ultimate soccer 796.334
Social action
Chandler, G. Kids who make a difference
363.7
Duper, L. L. 160 ways to help the world
361.3
Social anthropology See Ethnology
Social classes
Fiction
Kerr, M. E. Gentlehands (7 and up) Fic
Konigsburg, E. L. Journey to an 800 number
Fic
Social customs See Manners and customs
Social drinking See Drinking of alcoholic bever-
ages

Social equality *See* Equality

Social ethics

> *See also* Bioethics
> Our country's founders (7 and up) **973.4**

Social groups

> Romain, T. Cliques, phonies & other baloney
> **158**

Social life and customs *See* Manners and customs

Social problems

> *See/See also pages in the following book(s):*
> Blue, R. Staying out of trouble in a troubled family (7 and up) **362.7**

Social sciences

> The other side. See entry in CD-ROM section, Part 3

> **Bibliography**
> Notable children's trade books in the field of social studies **016.3**

Social smarts. James, E. **395**

Societies

> *See also* Clubs

Society and art *See* Art and society

Society of Friends

> Doherty, K. William Penn **92**
> Williams, J. K. The Quakers (7 and up)
> **289.6**

> **Fiction**
> Osborne, M. P. Standing in the light **Fic**
> Ruby, L. Steal away home **Fic**

Sodaro, Craig

> Freedom train
> *In* Plays of black Americans p3-18
> **812.008**

Soekarno, 1901-1970

> *See/See also pages in the following book(s):*
> Wakin, E. Asian independence leaders p109 25 (7 and up) **920**

Softball

> Nitz, K. W. Fundamental softball **796.357**
> **Fiction**
> Wolff, V. E. Bat 6 **Fic**

Software, Computer *See* Computer software

The **Software** encyclopedia **005**

Soil ecology

> Lavies, B. Compost critters **591.5**

Sojourner Truth *See* Truth, Sojourner, d. 1883

Solar energy

> Graham, I. Solar power **621.47**

Solar power. Graham, I. **621.47**

Solar radiation

> *See also* Greenhouse effect

Solar system

> Vogt, G. The solar system **523.2**

Soldier boy. Burks, B. **Fic**

Soldier life (7 and up) **973.7**

Soldiers

> *See also* names of countries with the subdivision *Army—Military life*
> **History**
> Robertshaw, A. A soldier's life **355**

Soldier's heart. Paulsen, G. **Fic**

A **soldier's** life. Robertshaw, A. **355**

The **soldiers'** voice: the story of Ernie Pyle. O'Connor, B. **92**

Soledad. Jiménez, F.

> *In* Jiménez, F. The circuit: stories from the life of a migrant child p9-13 **S C**

Solheim, James

> It's disgusting—and we ate it! **641.3**

The **solid** gold kid. Mazer, N. F. **Fic**

Solids

> Mebane, R. C. Salts & solids **530.4**

A **solitary** blue. Voigt, C. **Fic**

Solomon ben Isaac *See* Rashi, 1040-1105

Solon, ca. 640-ca. 561 B.C.

> *See/See also pages in the following book(s):*
> Nardo, D. Leaders of ancient Greece (7 and up)
> **920**

Solvent abuse

> Monroe, J. Inhalant drug dangers **362.29**

Somalia

> Hassig, S. M. Somalia **967.73**

Some body!. Rowan, P. **611**

Somehow tenderness survives (7 and up)
> **S C**

Someone is hiding on Alcatraz Island. Bunting, E.
> **Fic**

Someone like you. Dessen, S. **Fic**

Someone to count on. Hermes, P. **Fic**

Somers, Jane *See* Lessing, Doris May, 1919-

Somerville, Louisa

> Rescue vehicles **629.04**

Somerville, Mary, 1780-1872

> *See/See also pages in the following book(s):*
> Celebrating women in mathematics and science p47-56 **920**

Something. Aiken, J.

> *In* Aiken, J. A fit of shivers p37-47 **S C**

Something about the author **920.003**

Something about the author: autobiography series
> **920.003**

Something always happens. Murphy, J.

> *In* Murphy, J. Night terrors p133-54 **S C**

Something fishy at Macdonald Hall. Korman, G.
> **Fic**

Something like . . . love. Salisbury, G.

> *In* Dirty laundry: stories about family secrets p140-61 **S C**

Something permanent. Rylant, C. **811**

Something upstairs: a tale of ghosts. Avi **Fic**

Something which is non-existent. Klein, N.

> *In* Places I never meant to be **S C**

Something wicked this way comes. Bradbury, R.
> **Fic**

Somewhere a puppy cries. Whittington, M. K.

> *In* The Haunted house: a collection of original stories **S C**

Somewhere in the darkness. Myers, W. D.
> **Fic**

The **son** of the wind. Bryan, A.

> *In* Bryan, A. Ashley Bryan's African tales, uh-huh p136-71 **398.2**

Sonenklar, Carol

> My own worst enemy **Fic**

A **song** for Croaker Nordge. Berberick, N. V.
In A Glory of unicorns p127-43 **S C**

The **song** of Roland. Osborne, M. P.
In Osborne, M. P. Favorite medieval tales p34-41 **398.2**

Song of the buffalo boy. Garland, S. **Fic**

Song of the gargoyle. Snyder, Z. K. **Fic**

Song of the Magdalene. Napoli, D. J. **Fic**

Song of the trees. Taylor, M. D. **Fic**

The **song** of the whales. Orlev, U.
In Don't read this! and other tales of the unnatural p174-96 **S C**

Songhai Empire
Conrad, D. C. The Songhay Empire **966.2**
McKissack, P. C. The royal kingdoms of Ghana, Mali, and Songhay **966.2**

The **Songhay** Empire. Conrad, D. C. **966.2**

Songs
See also National songs; Popular music
Johnson, J. W. Lift every voice and sing **782.42**
Silverman, J. African roots **782.42**
Silverman, J. Just listen to this song I'm singing **782.42**
Silverman, J. Songs of protest and civil rights **782.42**

Songs and stories from the American Revolution. Silverman, J. **782.42**

Songs of faith. Johnson, A. **Fic**

Songs of the Wild West **782.42**

Songsmith. Norton, A. See note under Norton, A. Witch World [series] **Fic**

Songwriters *See* Composers

Sonneborn, Liz
A to Z of Native American women **920.003**
Will Rogers, Cherokee entertainer **92**

Sons and daughters. Yee, P.
In Yee, P. Tales from Gold Mountain p17-23 **S C**

Sons and fathers *See* Fathers and sons

Sons and mothers *See* Mothers and sons

Sons of liberty. Griffin, A. **Fic**

Sonseray. Spinelli, J.
In Spinelli, J. The library card **S C**

Sooner. Calvert, P. **Fic**

Sorcery *See* Magic

Sorel, Madeline
(il) Krensky, S. The printer's apprentice **Fic**

Sorrow's kitchen: the life and folklore of Zora Neale Hurston. Lyons, M. E. **92**

SOS Titanic. Bunting, E. **Fic**

Sosa, Dan, 1923-
See/See also pages in the following book(s):
Morey, J. Famous Mexican Americans p130-39 **920**

Sosa, Sammy
About
Muskat, C. Sammy Sosa **92**
Stewart, M. Home run heroes: McGwire and Sosa **92**

Soto, Gary
Baseball in April, and other stories **S C**
Contents: Broken chain; Baseball in April; Two dreamers; Barbie; The no-guitar blues; Seventh grade; Mother and daughter; The Karate Kid; La Bamba; The marble champ; Growing up
Broken chain
In Read all about it! p29-39 **808.8**
Buried onions (7 and up) **Fic**
Canto familiar **811**
Local news **S C**
Contents: Blackmail; Trick-or-treating; First job; El radio; Push-up; The school play; The Raiders jacket; The challenge; Nacho loco; The squirrels; The mechanical mind; Nickel-a-pound plane ride; New Year's Eve
Neighborhood odes **811**
New and selected poems (7 and up) **811**
The no-guitar blues
In Help wanted: short stories about young people working **S C**
Novio boy (7 and up) **812**
Off and running **Fic**
Petty crimes **S C**
Contents: La güera; Mother's clothes; Try to remember; The boxing lesson; Your turn, Norma; The funeral suits; Little scams; If the shoe fits; Frankie the rooster; Born worker
The pool party **Fic**
Taking sides **Fic**

Soukup, Martha
Alita in the air
In A Nightmare's dozen **S C**

Soul looks back in wonder **811.008**

The **Soul** wanderer
In The Dancing fox: Arctic folktales p113-20 **398.2**

Souls. Johnson, A.
In Johnson, A. Gone from home: short takes p75-89 **S C**

Souls. Yolen, J.
In Yolen, J. Here there be ghosts p95-98 **810.8**

Sound
Sabbeth, A. Rubber-band banjos and a java jive bass **781**
Science court: sound. See entry in CD-ROM section, Part 3

The **sound** of work. Jaffe, N.
In Jaffe, N. The cow of no color: riddle stories and justice tales from around the world p14-17 **398.2**

Sound the jubilee. Forrester, S. **Fic**

Sounder. Armstrong, W. H. **Fic**

South, Coleman
Jordan **956.95**

South (U.S.) *See* Southern States

South Africa
Blauer, E. South Africa **968**
Canesso, C. South Africa **968.06**
No more strangers now **968.06**
Fiction
Naidoo, B. Chain of fire **Fic**
Naidoo, B. Journey to Jo'burg **Fic**
Naidoo, B. No turning back **Fic**
Paton, A. Cry, the beloved country (7 and up) **Fic**
Somehow tenderness survives (7 and up) **S C**

The **spring**. Dickinson, P.
   In Dickinson, P. The lion tamer's daughter
    and other stories p1-15   **S C**
The **spring** running. Kipling, R.
   In Kipling, R. The jungle books   **S C**
The **spring** tone. Yumoto, K.   **Fic**
Springer, Jane
   Listen to us (7 and up)   **331.3**
Springer, Nancy
   Eat your enemy
    In Twelve shots: outstanding short stories
     about guns p161-78   **S C**
   I am Mordred (7 and up)   **Fic**
   Looking for Jamie Bridger (7 and up)   **Fic**
   Toughing it (7 and up)   **Fic**
   Yeah, yeah
    In A Nightmare's dozen   **S C**
Springtime a la carte. Henry, O.
   In Henry, O. The gift of the Magi and other
    stories p144-55   **S C**
Sprug, Joseph W., 1922-
   (comp) Index to fairy tales. See Index to fairy
    tales   **398.2**
Spy. Platt, R.   **327.12**
Spy science. Wiese, J.   **363.2**
Spying *See* Espionage
The **spying** game. Moon, P.   **Fic**
Spying on Miss Müller. Bunting, E.   **Fic**
Squashed. Bauer, J.   **Fic**
The **squire**. Singer, I. B.
   In Singer, I. B. The power of light p43-50
        S C
The **squire**, his knight, & his lady. Morris, G.
        Fic
The **squire's** tale. Morris, G.   **Fic**
Squirrels

        Fiction
   Lisle, J. T. Forest   **Fic**
The **squirrels**. Soto, G.
   In Soto, G. Local news p102-12   **S C**
St. George, Judith, 1931-
   Dear Dr. Bell—your friend, Helen Keller
        92
   In the line of fire   **364.1**
   Sacagawea   **92**
   To see with the heart: the life of Sitting Bull
        92
St. George and the dragon. Kingston, W. H. G.
   In The Book of dragons p89-95   **S C**
St. Valentine's Day *See* Valentine's Day
Staal, Flossie Wong- *See* Wong-Staal, Flossie,
  1947-
Stage fright. Hines, A. G.
   In Dirty laundry: stories about family secrets
    p58-69   **S C**
Stagecoach Mary *See* Fields, Mary, 1832?-1914
The **stagman**. McKinley, R.
   In McKinley, R. A knot in the grain and oth-
    er stories p41-71   **S C**
Stallworthy, Jon
   (ed) The Oxford book of war poetry. See The
    Oxford book of war poetry   **808.81**

Stamina, Physical *See* Physical fitness
Stamp Act, 1765
   See/See also pages in the following book(s):
   Collier, C. The American Revolution, 1763-1783
    p22-31   **973.3**
Stamps, Postage *See* Postage stamps
Stan Bolovan. Lang, A.
   In The Book of dragons p96-109   **S C**
Stand up Mr. Dickens. Blishen, E.   **823.009**
Standard catalog for high school libraries. See Se-
  nior high school library catalog   **011.6**
Standard cataloging for school and public librar-
  ies. Intner, S. S.   **025.3**
Standing Bear, Ponca Chief, 1829?-1908
   See/See also pages in the following book(s):
   Brown, D. A. Bury my heart at Wounded Knee
    p352-66 (7 and up)   **970.004**
Standing in the light. Osborne, M. P.   **Fic**
Standing up to Mr. O. Mills, C.   **Fic**
Stanley, Diane, 1943-
   Bard of Avon: the story of William Shakespeare
        92
   Cleopatra   **92**
   Good Queen Bess: the story of Elizabeth I of
    England   **92**
   Joan of Arc   **92**
   Shaka, king of the Zulus   **92**
   Time apart   **Fic**
Stanley, Fay, 1925-1990
   The last princess: the story of Princess Ka'iulani
    of Hawai'i   **92**
Stanley, Jerry, 1941-
   Big Annie of Calumet   **331.8**
   Children of the Dust Bowl   **371.9**
   I am an American   **940.53**
Stanton, Elizabeth Cady, 1815-1902
        About
   Cullen-DuPont, K. Elizabeth Cady Stanton and
    women's liberty (7 and up)   **92**
   See/See also pages in the following book(s):
   Helmer, D. S. Women suffragists (7 and up)
        920
Staples, Suzanne Fisher
   Dangerous skies (7 and up)   **Fic**
   Haveli (7 and up)   **Fic**
   Shabanu (7 and up)   **Fic**
The **star** fisher. Yep, L.   **Fic**
Star lady. Paterson, K.
   In Paterson, K. A midnight clear: stories for
    the Christmas season   **S C**
The **Star** Maiden. San Souci, R.
   In San Souci, R. Cut from the same cloth p3-
    10   **398.2**
Star trek (Motion picture)
   See/See also pages in the following book(s):
   Reid, S. E. Presenting young adult science fic-
    tion p182-98 (7 and up)   **813.009**
Star Wars: episode I: incredible cross-sections.
  Reynolds, D. W.   **791.43**
Star Wars films
   Reynolds, D. W. Star Wars: episode I: incredi-
    ble cross-sections   **791.43**
   Reynolds, D. W. Star Wars: incredible cross
    sections   **791.43**

Stonecoat. Bruchac, J.
  In Bruchac, J. The girl who married the Moon: tales from Native North America p47-50   **398.2**
Stonecrop. Adams, R.
  In Adams, R. Tales from Watership Down   **S C**
Stonehenge (England)
  Mass, W. Stonehenge (7 and up)   **936.2**
Stonehouse, Bernard
  Bears   **599.78**
Stones, bones, and petroglyphs. Goodman, S.   **930.1**
Stones in water. Napoli, D. J.   **Fic**
The stones of Muncaster Cathedral. Westall, R.   **Fic**
Stoneware *See* Pottery
Stonewords. Conrad, P.   **Fic**
Stoplight. Yoon, S. C.-N.
  In American dragons p14-25   **810.8**
Stoppard, Miriam
  Sex ed (7 and up)   **613.9**
Stopping for death (7 and up)   **808.81**
Stores *See* Supermarkets
Stories from the Old Testament   **221.5**
Stories in stone. Arnold, C.   **709.01**
Stories on stage. Shepard, A.   **812**
Storms
  See also Dust storms; Hurricanes; Tornadoes
  Kramer, S. P. Eye of the storm   **778.9**
Storr, Catherine
  Crossing over
  In The Oxford book of scary tales p16-21   **808.8**
Storring, Rod
  A doctor's life   **610.69**
The story atlas of the Bible. Hunter, E.   **220.9**
Story hour. Coville, K.
  In A Glory of unicorns p97-112   **S C**
The story of baseball. Ritter, L. S.   **796.357**
The story of communications. Ganeri, A.   **384**
The story of figure skating. Boo, M.   **796.91**
The Story of Five Heads
  In Hearne, B. G. Beauties and beasts p115-19   **398.2**
The story of football. Anderson, D.   **796.332**
The story of golf. Anderson, D.   **796.352**
The story of iron. Fitzgerald, K.   **669**
The story of King Arthur and his knights. Pyle, H.   **398.2**
The story of King Fur-Rocious. Adams, R.
  In Adams, R. Tales from Watership Down   **S C**
The story of my life. Keller, H.   **92**
The story of Negro league baseball. Brashler, W.   **796.357**
The story of oxygen. Fitzgerald, K.   **546**
The story of Robin Hood. Philip, N.   **398.2**

Story of science [series]
  Gallant, R. A. Early humans   **599.93**
The story of Serah, who lived longer than Methuselah. Schwartz, H.
  In Schwartz, H. Next year in Jerusalem p26-31   **296.1**
The story of Sir Launcelot and his companions. Pyle, H.   **398.2**
The story of the Bat. Brown, D. A.
  In Brown, D. A. Dee Brown's folktales of the Native American p147   **398.2**
The story of the champions of the Round Table. Pyle, H.   **398.2**
The story of the comical field. Adams, R.
  In Adams, R. Tales from Watership Down   **S C**
The story of the Grail and the passing of Arthur. Pyle, H.   **398.2**
The story of the great marsh. Adams, R.
  In Adams, R. Tales from Watership Down   **S C**
The story of the terrible hay-making. Adams, R.
  In Adams, R. Tales from Watership Down   **S C**
The story of the three cows. Adams, R.
  In Adams, R. Tales from Watership Down   **S C**
The story of Wang Li. Coatsworth, E. J.
  In The Book of dragons p78-88   **S C**
The story of writing and printing. Ganeri, A.   **652**
Story painter: the life of Jacob Lawrence. Duggleby, J.   **92**
Story theater *See* Readers' theater
The storyteller's beads. Kurtz, J.   **Fic**
The storyteller's daughter. Thesman, J.   **Fic**
Storytelling
  Pellowski, A. The storytelling handbook   **372.6**
Fiction
  Fletcher, S. Shadow spinner   **Fic**
The storytelling handbook. Pellowski, A.   **372.6**
Stotan!. Crutcher, C.   **Fic**
Stott, Carole
  Moon landing   **629.45**
  New astronomer (7 and up)   **520**
  Space exploration   **629.4**
Stovall, TaRessa
  The Buffalo Soldiers   **978**
Stover, Lois T.
  Presenting Phyllis Reynolds Naylor (7 and up)   **813.009**
Stowe, Harriet Beecher, 1811-1896
About
  Coil, S. M. Harriet Beecher Stowe (7 and up)   **92**
  Fritz, J. Harriet Beecher Stowe and the Beecher preachers   **92**
  See/See also pages in the following book(s):
  Faber, D. Great lives: American literature p68-78   **920**

Stuart, Jeb, 1833-1864—About—*Continued*
See/See also pages in the following book(s):
Reger, J. P. Civil War generals of the Confederacy p82-101 (7 and up)   **920**

Stuart-Clark, Christopher
(comp) The Oxford book of story poems. See The Oxford book of story poems
821.008
(comp) The Oxford treasury of classic poems. See The Oxford treasury of classic poems
821.008

A **stubborn** sweetness. Paterson, K.
In Paterson, K. A midnight clear: stories for the Christmas season   **S C**

Student assistants in the school library media center. Bard, T. B.   **027.8**

Students
See also Dropouts
Civil rights
Cary, E. The rights of students (7 and up)
344
Law and legislation
Fuller, S. B. Hazelwood v. Kuhlmeier (7 and up)   **344**
Persico, D. New Jersey v. T.L.O. (7 and up)
345
Trespacz, K. L. Ferrell v. Dallas I.S.D. (7 and up)   **344**
Political activity
See/See also pages in the following book(s):
The 1960s: opposing viewpoints p115-25 (7 and up)   **973.92**

Study, Method of *See* Study skills

A **study** in scarlet. Doyle, Sir A. C.
In Doyle, Sir A. C. The complete Sherlock Holmes   **S C**

Study skills
Gilbert, S. D. How to do your best on tests (7 and up)   **371.2**
Wood, G. How to study (7 and up)   **371.3**

Sturgis, Alexander
Optical illusions in art   **750.1**

Subculture *See* Counter culture

Subject catalogs
Subject guide to Books in print   **015.73**
Subject guide to Children's books in print
015.73

Subject guide to Books in print   **015.73**

Subject guide to Children's books in print
015.73

Subject headings
Sears list of subject headings   **025.4**

Submarine exploration *See* Underwater exploration

Submarine geology
Erickson, J. Marine geology (7 and up)
551.46

Submarines
Fiction
Verne, J. Twenty thousand leagues under the sea   **Fic**

Substance abuse *See* Drug abuse

Subways
See/See also pages in the following book(s):
Macaulay, D. Underground p93-107   **624**
Fiction
Holman, F. Slake's limbo   **Fic**
Shusterman, N. Downsiders   **Fic**

Sucker. McCullers, C.
In Who do you think you are? p122-33
S C

Sudan
Levy, P. M. Sudan   **962.4**

Suffrage
See also African Americans—Suffrage; Women—Suffrage

Suffragists
Helmer, D. S. Women suffragists (7 and up)
920

Sugihara, Chiune *See* Sugihara, Sempo, 1900-1986

Sugihara, Sempo, 1900-1986
See/See also pages in the following book(s):
Lyman, D. Holocaust rescuers   **920**

Suicide
Kuklin, S. After a suicide (7 and up)
362.7
Suicide: opposing viewpoints (7 and up)
362.28
See/See also pages in the following book(s):
Fry, V. L. Part of me died, too p133-58
155.9
Fiction
Draper, S. M. Tears of a tiger (7 and up)
Fic
Mori, K. Shizuko's daughter (7 and up)
Fic
Peck, R. Remembering the good times (7 and up)   **Fic**

Suicide: opposing viewpoints (7 and up)
362.28

The **suitcase** kid. Wilson, J.   **Fic**

Sukarno *See* Soekarno, 1901-1970

Sullivan, Charles, 1933-
(ed) Here is my kingdom. See Here is my kingdom   **810.8**

Sullivan, Edward T.
The Holocaust in literature for youth
016.94053

Sullivan, George
All about hockey   **796.962**
The day the women got the vote   **305.4**
Glovemen   **920**
In the line of fire   **920**
Mathew Brady: his life and photographs   **92**
Quarterbacks!   **920**
To the bottom of the sea   **551.46**

Sullivan, Helen
Research reports (7 and up)   **808**

Sullivan, Irene F.
(jt. auth) Gill, S. D. Dictionary of Native American mythology   **299**

Sullivan, Kathryn D., 1953-
See/See also pages in the following book(s):
Polking, K. Oceanographers and explorers of the sea p103-11   **920**

Superstar lineup [series]—*Continued*
Lipsyte, R. Michael Jordan   92
Superstition
Hughes, M. Popular superstitions   398
Superstructures. See Corbishley, M. The world of
architectural wonders   720
Suppressants, Appetite *See* Appetite depressants
Supreme Court (U.S.) *See* United States. Su-
preme Court
The **Supreme** Court, A to Z (7 and up)   347
Supreme Court decisions [series]
Dudley, M. E. Brown v. Board of Education
(1954)   344
Dudley, M. E. Engel v. Vitale (1962)   344
Gold, J. C. Board of Education v. Pico (1982)
344
Gold, S. D. In re Gault (1967)   345
Gold, S. D. Miranda v. Arizona (1966)
345
Gold, S. D. Roe v. Wade (1973)   344
The **Supreme** Court justices   920.003
Supriya's bowl. Krishnaswami, U.
In Krishnaswami, U. Shower of gold: girls
and women in the stories of India p108-
12   398.2
Surgeons
Talmadge, K. S. The life of Charles Drew
92
Surprise party. Sachs, M.   Fic
Surrogate mothers
See/See also pages in the following book(s):
Biomedical ethics: opposing viewpoints p127-42
(7 and up)   174
**Survival after airplane accidents, shipwrecks,
etc.**
Fiction
Defoe, D. Robinson Crusoe (7 and up)   Fic
Golding, W. Lord of the Flies (7 and up)
Fic
Paulsen, G. Brian's winter   Fic
Paulsen, G. Hatchet   Fic
Paulsen, G. The river   Fic
Taylor, T. The cay   Fic
Taylor, T. Sweet Friday Island (7 and up)
Fic
Taylor, T. Timothy of the cay   Fic
The **survivors**. Ayer, E. H.   940.53
Susag, Dorothea M.
Roots and branches   810.9
Susan Butcher and the Iditarod Trail. Dolan, E.
M.   798.8
Susanna and Simon. San Souci, R.
In San Souci, R. Cut from the same cloth
p43-48   398.2
Susannah and the elders. Jaffe, N.
In Jaffe, N. The cow of no color: riddle sto-
ries and justice tales from around the
world p40-46   398.2
Sutcliff, Rosemary, 1920-1992
Black ships before Troy   883
Flame-colored taffeta   Fic
The light beyond the forest (7 and up)
398.2
The road to Camlann (7 and up)   398.2

The sword and the circle (7 and up)   **398.2**
Sword song (7 and up)   Fic
The wanderings of Odysseus   883
Sutherland, Zena, 1915-
Children & books   028.5
Suth's story. Dickinson, P.   Fic
Sutton, Dave *See* Woolls, E. Blanche
Suu Kyi *See* Aung San Suu Kyi
Svarney, Patricia Barnes- *See* Barnes-Svarney,
Patricia
Swain, William, 1821-1904
See/See also pages in the following book(s):
Duncan, D. People of the West p38-47
978
Swallowing stones. McDonald, J.   Fic
Swamps *See* Wetlands
Swan lake (Ballet)
See/See also pages in the following book(s):
McCaughrean, G. The Random House book of
stories from the ballet p7-17   792.8
Newman, B. The illustrated book of ballet sto-
ries p42-51   792.8
Swan song. Duncan, Q.
In Rites of passage p89-90   S C
Sweden
McNair, S. Sweden   948.5
Sweeney, Joyce, 1955-
Free fall (7 and up)   Fic
Shadow (7 and up)   Fic
Sweet Betsey from Pike. San Souci, R.
In San Souci, R. Cut from the same cloth
p57-64   398.2
Sweet Friday Island. Taylor, T.   Fic
Sweet Medicine
See/See also pages in the following book(s):
Duncan, D. People of the West p1-6   978
The **sweet** perfume of good-bye. Kerr, M. E.
In Visions: nineteen short stories by outstand-
ing writers for young adults p186-91
S C
Sweet whispers, Brother Rush. Hamilton, V.
Fic
The **sweethearts**. Andersen, H. C.
In Andersen, H. C. The little mermaid and
other fairy tales p81-83   S C
Sweetness. Johnson, A.
In Johnson, A. Gone from home: short takes
p1-11   S C
Swenson, May, 1919-1989
(comp) American sports poems. See American
sports poems   811.008
Swift, Jonathan, 1667-1745
Gulliver's travels (7 and up)   Fic
Swift-Runner and the trickster Tarantula. Brown,
D. A.
In Brown, D. A. Dee Brown's folktales of the
Native American p115-23   398.2
A **swiftly** tilting planet. L'Engle, M. See note un-
der L'Engle, M. A wrinkle in time   Fic
Swimming
Rouse, J. The young swimmer   797.2
Fiction
Crutcher, C. Stotan! (7 and up)   Fic

Swimming upstream. Brant, B.
In Talking leaves   S C
Swinburne, Stephen R.
Once a wolf   333.95
Swindlers and swindling
         Fiction
Roberts, W. D. Pawns   Fic
Swingers and crooners. Gourse, L.   781.65
Swisher, Clarice, 1933-
(ed) The Spread of Islam. See The Spread of Islam   297
Swisher, Karin, 1966-
(ed) Global warming: opposing viewpoints. See Global warming: opposing viewpoints   363.7
(ed) Violence: opposing viewpoints. See Violence: opposing viewpoints   303.6
Switcharound. Lowry, L.   Fic
Switchers. Thompson, K.   Fic
Switzerland
         Fiction
Creech, S. Bloomability   Fic
Pullman, P. Count Karlstein   Fic
         Legends
See Legends—Switzerland
Swoopes, Sheryl, 1971-
See/See also pages in the following book(s):
Gaines, A. Sports & athletics   920
The **sword.** Alexander, L.
In Alexander, L. The foundling and other tales of Prydian p53-62   S C
The **sword** and the circle. Sutcliff, R.   398.2
The **sword** in the stone. Osborne, M. P.
In Osborne, M. P. Favorite medieval tales p17-24   398.2
The **sword** in the stone. White, T. H.
In White, T. H. The once and future King   Fic
Sword of the samurai. Kimmel, E. A.   S C
The **sword-seller.** Wrede, P. C.
In Wrede, P. C. Book of enchantments p96-127   S C
Sword song. Sutcliff, R.   Fic
Swortzell, Lowell
The mischief makers
In Theatre for young audiences p183-216   812.008
Symbiosis
Silverstein, A. Symbiosis   577.8
Symbols *See* Signs and symbols
Symes, R. F.
Crystal & gem   548
Rocks & minerals   549
Symons, Ann K.
Protecting the right to read   323.44
Systems, Database management *See* Database management
Szabo, Corinne
Sky pioneer: a photobiography of Amelia Earhart   92
Szenes, Hannah *See* Senesh, Hannah, 1921-1944
Szeptycki, Andreas *See* Sheptyts´kyĭ, Andriĭ, 1865-1944

T

Table etiquette
Giblin, J. From hand to mouth   394.1
Tableware
Giblin, J. From hand to mouth   394.1
Tackach, James
Brown v. Board of Education (7 and up)   344
The Emancipation Proclamation (7 and up)   973.7
The trial of John Brown, radical abolitionist (7 and up)   345
Tacobud, the mountain that ate people. Bruchac, J.
In Bruchac, J. Four ancestors p43-44   398.2
Tadpoles *See* Frogs
Tadpoles. Pascoe, E.   597.8
Tae kwon do. Gutman, B.   796.8
Tafari Makonnen *See* Haile Selassie I, Emperor of Ethiopia, 1892-1975
Taft, Robert A., 1889-1953
See/See also pages in the following book(s):
Kennedy, J. F. Profiles in courage p221-35 (7 and up)   920
Taft, William H. (William Howard), 1857-1930
See/See also pages in the following book(s):
Presidents of a world power   920
Tagliaferro, Linda
Genetic engineering (7 and up)   576.5
Tahiti (French Polynesia)
NgCheong-Lum, R. Tahiti   996
Taiga. Sayre, A. P.   577.3
Taino Indians
         Fiction
Dorris, M. Morning Girl   Fic
Taitz, Emily
Remarkable Jewish women (7 and up)   920
Taiwan
Wee, J. Taiwan   951.24
Taj Mahal (Agra, India)
Moorcroft, C. The Taj Mahal   726
Takaki, Carol, 1930-
(jt. auth) Takaki, R. T. Strangers at the gates again   305.8
Takaki, Ronald T., 1939-
Strangers at the gates again (7 and up)   305.8
Taking care of business. Hill, K. S.
In Talking leaves   S C
Taking care of Terrific. Lowry, L.   Fic
Taking charge of my mind & body. Folkers, G.   613
The **taking** of Room 114. Glenn, M.   811
Taking risks *See* Risk-taking (Psychology)
Taking sides. Soto, G.   Fic
Taking Terri Mueller. Mazer, N. F.   Fic
Taking toll. Wentzien, M. de B.
In Stay true: short stories for strong girls   S C

Talab, Rosemary Sturdevant
Commonsense copyright   346.04
Talbert, Marc, 1953-
Fountain of youth
In Trapped!: cages of mind and body p67-83
    S C
The Purple Heart   Fic
The **tale** of Sir Gawain. Philip, N.   398.2
Tale of tellers. Brooke, W. J.
In Brooke, W. J. Teller of tales p149-70
    S C
Tale of the golden ball. Wyeth, S. D.
In Wyeth, S. D. Vampire bugs: stories con-
jured from the past p49-64   S C
The **tale** of the poplar. Hawes, C. B.
In A Newbery zoo   S C
Tales from Gold Mountain. Yee, P.   S C
Tales from Shakespeare. Lamb, C.   822.3
Tales from Shakespeare. Williams, M.   822.3
Tales from the Brothers Grimm and the Sisters
Weird. Vande Velde, V.   S C
Tales from Watership Down. Adams, R.   S C
Tales mummies tell. Lauber, P.   930.1
Tales of Edgar Allan Poe. Poe, E. A.   S C
The **tales** of Uncle Remus. Lester, J. See note un-
der Lester, J. The last tales of Uncle Remus
    398.2
Talk that talk: an anthology of African-American
storytelling (7 and up)   398.2
Talk to me. Avi
In Avi. What do fish have to do with any-
thing? and other stories p61-91   S C
Talk to the deaf. See Riekehof, L. L. The joy of
signing   419
Talking bones. Thomas, P.   614
Talking books See Audiobooks
The **talking** burro. Winther, B.
In Winther, B. Plays from Hispanic tales
    812
The **talking** earth. George, J. C.   Fic
Talking leaves   S C
The **talking** mule. Hurston, Z. N.
In From sea to shining sea p224-25
    810.8
Talking peace. Carter, J.   327.1
Talking points [series]
Grant, R. G. Genocide   303.6
James, B. Animal rights   179
Stearman, K. Homelessness   362.5
Talking to dragons. Wrede, P. C. See note under
Wrede, P. C. Dealing with dragons   Fic
Talking to the clay. Bruchac, J.
In Bruchac, J. Four ancestors p48-49
    398.2
Talking with artists [I-III]   741.6
Talking with Tebé: Clementine Hunter, memory
artist. Hunter, C.   92
The **tall** Mexican: the life of Hank Aguirre, all-star
pitcher, businessman, humanitarian. Copley,
B.   92
Tall Mountain, Mary See TallMountain, Mary,
1918-1994

Tall tales
San Souci, R. Cut from the same cloth
    398.2
Tallarico, Tony
Drawing and cartooning monsters   743
TallMountain, Mary, 1918-1994
Snatched away
In Talking leaves   S C
Talmadge, Katherine S.
The life of Charles Drew   92
Tamar, Erika, 1934-
The junkyard dog   Fic
The **tamarack** tree. Clapp, P.   Fic
Tamarin, Alfred
(jt. auth) Glubok, S. Olympic games in ancient
Greece   796.48
Tamarins
See/See also pages in the following book(s):
Patent, D. H. Back to the wild p40-49
    639.9
Tambini, Michael
Future   600
The look of the century (7 and up)   745.2
Taming the Star Runner. Hinton, S. E.   Fic
Tan, Amy
Rules of the game
In Leaving home: stories p35-52   808.8
See/See also pages in the following book(s):
Chiu, C. Lives of notable Asian Americans: lit-
erature and education p7-15 (7 and up)
    920
Tanaka, Shelley
Discovering the Iceman   930.1
Graveyards of the dinosaurs   567.9
Lost temple of the Aztecs   972
(jt. auth) Beattie, O. Buried in ice   998
Tang, Fay
(jt. auth) Pevsner, S. Sing for your father, Su
Phan   Fic
Tangerine. Bloor, E.   Fic
Tanks (Military science) See Military tanks
Tanner, Helen Hornbeck
The Ojibwa
In Indians of North America series
    970.004
Tansey, Richard G.
Gardner's art through the ages. See Gardner's
art through the ages   709
Tanuki magic teakettle. Hamilton, V.
In Hamilton, V. The dark way p76-81
    398.2
Tanzania
Heale, J. Tanzania   967.8
McCulla, P. E. Tanzania   967.8
Taoism
Hartz, P. Taoism (7 and up)   299
See/See also pages in the following book(s):
Osborne, M. P. One world, many religions p63-
69   291
Tarahumara Indians
Kennedy, J. G. The Tarahumara
In Indians of North America series
    970.004

Taran Wanderer. Alexander, L. See note under
Alexander, L. The book of three   **Fic**

A **tarantula** in my purse. George, J. C.   **92**

Tarling, D. H. (Donald Harvey)
(ed) The Historical atlas of the earth. See The
Historical atlas of the earth   **551.7**

Tarling, Donald Harvey See Tarling, D. H. (Donald Harvey)

Tarma. Fort, M. R.
In Where angels glide at dawn p67-75
     S C

Tarot says beware. Byars, B. C. See note under
Byars, B.C. The dark stairs   **Fic**

Tartan magic series
Yolen, J. The Pictish child   **Fic**
Yolen, J. The wizard's map   **Fic**

Tashjian, Janet, 1956-
Multiple choice   **Fic**

A **taste** for beauty. Galloway, P.
In Galloway, P. Truly grim tales   **S C**

A **taste** of smoke. Bauer, M. D.   **Fic**

Tate Gallery
Welton, J. Drawing   **741.2**

Tattooing
Wilkinson, B. Coping with the dangers of tattooing, body piercing, and branding (7 and
up)   **617.9**

Taussig, Helen Brooke, 1898-1986
See/See also pages in the following book(s):
Lindop, L. Scientists and doctors (7 and up)
     920
Yount, L. Contemporary women scientists (7
and up)   **920**

Taylor, Barbara, 1954-
Animal homes   **591.5**
Arctic & Antarctic   **998**
Earth explained   **550**
Incredible plants   **580**
(jt. auth) Cash, T. 175 more science experiments
to amuse and amaze your friends   **507.8**

Taylor, Cecil
See/See also pages in the following book(s):
Gourse, L. Striders to beboppers and beyond
p119-22 (7 and up)   **781.65**

Taylor, Glenhall
The perfect tribute
In The Big book of holiday plays p209-15
     812.008

Taylor, John Bigelow
(il) Pandell, K. Learning from the Dalai Lama
     294.3

Taylor, L. R. (Leighton R.)
Creeps from the deep   **578.7**

Taylor, Leighton R. See Taylor, L. R. (Leighton
R.)

Taylor, M. W. (Marian W.)
Chief Joseph   **92**
Harriet Tubman   **92**

Taylor, Marian W. See Taylor, M. W. (Marian
W.)

Taylor, Maureen, 1955-
Through the eyes of your ancestors   **929**

Taylor, Mildred D.
The friendship   **Fic**

The gold Cadillac   **Fic**
Let the circle be unbroken   **Fic**
Mississippi bridge   **Fic**
The road to Memphis   **Fic**
Roll of thunder, hear my cry   **Fic**
Song of the trees   **Fic**
The well   **Fic**

About
Crowe, C. Presenting Mildred D. Taylor (7 and
up)   **813.009**

Taylor, Paul D., 1953-
Fossil   **560**

Taylor, Richard L., 1933-
The first solo flight around the world
     629.13

Taylor, Theodore, 1921-
The cay   **Fic**
The grind of an axe
In Night terrors   **S C**
Rogue wave and other red-blooded sea stories
     S C
Contents: Rogue wave; Hauling gold; Wingman, fly me down;
Out there; Hating Hansen; The butcher; The schoolie; The
O'Tannenbaum Affair
Sweet Friday Island (7 and up)   **Fic**
Timothy of the cay   **Fic**
The weirdo (7 and up)   **Fic**

Taylor, Zachary, 1784-1850
See/See also pages in the following book(s):
Presidents of a young republic   **920**

Tchen, Richard
(jt. auth) Napoli, D. J. Spinners   **Fic**

Teacher tamer. Avi
In Avi. What do fish have to do with anything? and other stories p93-119
     S C

Teachers
See also Educators; Women teachers
Fiction
Adler, C. S. Not just a summer crush   **Fic**
Danziger, P. The cat ate my gymsuit   **Fic**
Flake, S. G. The skin I'm in   **Fic**
Kindl, P. Owl in love   **Fic**
Mills, C. Standing up to Mr. O   **Fic**
Paulsen, G. Sarny (7 and up)   **Fic**

Teaching
Aids and devices—Periodicals
Media & Methods   **371.305**
MultiMedia schools   **371.305**
Technology and Learning   **371.305**
TechTrends   **371.305**

Teaching library skills in middle and high school.
Garrett, L. J.   **027.8**

Teacup full of roses. Mathis, S. B.   **Fic**

Team picture. Hughes, D.   **Fic**

Teammates: Karl Malone and John Stockton.
Schnakenberg, R.   **92**

Tearing down the unicorns. Simner, J. L.
In A Glory of unicorns p31-42   **S C**

Tears of a tiger. Draper, S. M.   **Fic**

Technology
Barnes-Svarney, P. The New York Public Li-
brary science desk reference   **500**
Gates, P. Nature got there first   **508**

Temple, Charles A., 1947-
Children's books in children's hands. See Children's books in children's hands   **028.5**

Temple, Frances, 1945-1995
The Beduins' gazelle   **Fic**
Grab hands and run   **Fic**
The Ramsay scallop   **Fic**
Tonight, by sea   **Fic**

Temple, Lewis, 1800-1854
See/See also pages in the following book(s):
Aaseng, N. Black inventors p1-8 (7 and up)   **920**

Ten queens. Meltzer, M.   **920**
The **Ten** serpents
In Hearne, B. G. Beauties and beasts p120-23   **398.2**

Ten thousand children. Fox, A. L.   **940.53**

Tending the fire: the story of Maria Martinez. Morris, J.   **92**

Tenenbaum, Frieda, 1934-
See/See also pages in the following book(s):
Kinderlager p55-114 (7 and up)   **940.53**

Tennessee
Barrett, T. Tennessee
In Celebrate the states   **973**

Tennis
Douglas, P. Tennis (7 and up)   **796.342**
           Biography
Aronson, V. Venus Williams   **92**
Lazo, C. E. Arthur Ashe   **92**
Martin, M. Arthur Ashe (7 and up)   **92**

Tension (Psychology) See Stress (Psychology)
The **tent**. Paulsen, G.   **Fic**

Teotihuacán site (San Juan Teotihuacán, Mexico)
Arnold, C. City of the Gods   **972**
Tepee tales of the American Indian. See Brown, D. A. Dee Brown's folktales of the Native American   **398.2**

Terban, Marvin
Scholastic dictionary of idioms   **423**
Scholastic dictionary of spelling   **428**

Teresa, Mother, 1910-1997
           About
Morgan, N. Mother Teresa: saint of the poor   **92**
Ruth, A. Mother Teresa   **92**
See/See also pages in the following book(s):
Lucas, E. Contemporary human rights activists p1-11 (7 and up)   **920**

Tereshkova, Valentina, 1937-
See/See also pages in the following book(s):
Briggs, C. S. Women in space   **920**

Terezin (Czechoslovakia: Concentration camp)
—I never saw another butterfly—   **741.9**

Terkel, Susan Neiburg, 1948-
Colonial American medicine   **610.9**

Term paper writing See Report writing

Terminal care
           Ethical aspects
See/See also pages in the following book(s):
Death and dying: opposing viewpoints p16-53 (7 and up)   **155.9**

           Fiction
Cormier, R. The bumblebee flies anyway (7 and up)   **Fic**

Terrell, Mary Church, 1863-1954
See/See also pages in the following book(s):
Dubovoy, S. Civil rights leaders p31-43 (7 and up)   **920**
Helmer, D. S. Women suffragists (7 and up)   **920**

A **terrifying** taste of short & shivery. San Souci, R.   **398.2**

Terror of the Spanish Main: Sir Henry Morgan and his buccaneers. Marrin, A.   **92**

Terrorism
Gaines, A. Terrorism (7 and up)   **364.1**
Sherrow, V. The Oklahoma City bombing   **364.1**
Sherrow, V. The World Trade Center bombing   **364.1**
See/See also pages in the following book(s):
Weapons of mass destruction: opposing viewpoints p16-45 (7 and up)   **358**
           Fiction
Cooney, C. B. The terrorist (7 and up)   **Fic**
Cormier, R. After the first death (7 and up)   **Fic**

The **terrorist**. Cooney, C. B.   **Fic**

Tessitore, John
Muhammed Ali (7 and up)   **92**

The **test**. Jaffe, N.
In Jaffe, N. The cow of no color: riddle stories and justice tales from around the world p134-36   **398.2**

The **test**. Ndebele, N. S.
In Rites of passage p103-29   **S C**

The **testimony** of the fly. Jaffe, N.
In Jaffe, N. The cow of no color: riddle stories and justice tales from around the world p32-39   **398.2**

Testing for drug abuse See Drug testing

Tests See Examinations

Tet Offensive, 1968
Wills, C. A. The Tet offensive   **959.704**

Teton Indians
Bonvillain, N. The Teton Sioux
In Indians of North America series   **970.004**

The **Teton** Sioux. Bonvillain, N.
In Indians of North America series   **970.004**

Tetsunojo, Kanze
See/See also pages in the following book(s):
Hamanaka, S. In search of the spirit p35-41   **920**

Tex. Hinton, S. E.   **Fic**

Texas
Bredeson, C. Texas
In Celebrate the states   **973**
Heinrichs, A. Texas
In America the beautiful, second series   **973**
Turner, R. M. Texas traditions   **976.4**

Thieves—*Continued*
Fiction
Fleischman, S. Bandit's moon   **Fic**
Fleischman, S. The whipping boy   **Fic**
Turner, M. W. The thief   **Fic**
Thin ice. Qualey, M.   **Fic**
The **thing** that goes burp in the night. Webb, S.
   In Dragons & dreams p12-31   **S C**
Things that go bump in the night. Windham, K. T.
   In From sea to shining sea p340-41
     810.8
Thinkin' science zap!. See entry in CD-ROM section, Part 3
The **thinking** kid's guide to successful soccer. Scott, N. S.   **796.334**
The **third** eye. Duncan, L.   **Fic**
The **Thirteenth** Amendment. Schleichert, E.
     342
The **thirteenth** floor. See Fleischman, S. The 13th floor   **Fic**
Thirty three things every girl should know. See 33 things every girl should know   **810.8**
This boy's life [excerpt] Wolff, T.
   In Who do you think you are? p83-91
     S C
This can't be happening at MacDonald Hall!. Korman, G. See note under Korman, G. Something fishy at MacDonald Hall   **Fic**
Thomas, Debi
   See/See also pages in the following book(s):
   Gaines, A. Sports & athletics   **920**
Thomas, Jane Resh, 1936-
   Behind the mask: the life of Queen Elizabeth I (7 and up)   **92**
Thomas, Nancy P.
   Information literacy and information skills instruction   **027.8**
Thomas, Peggy
   Medicines from nature (7 and up)   **615**
   Talking bones (7 and up)   **614**
Thomas, Rob
   Sheep
   In Trapped!: cages of mind and body p19-31
     S C
   The war chest
   In Twelve shots: outstanding short stories about guns p138-60   **S C**
Thomas, Velma Maia
   Lest we forget (7 and up)   **326**
Thomas, Vickie, 1950-
   (jt. auth) Closter, K. Fiction, food, and fun
     028.5
Thomas Edison and electricity. Parker, S.   **92**
Thompson, Cliff
   (ed) World authors, 1990-1995. See World authors, 1990-1995   **920.003**
Thompson, Julian F., 1927-
   Brothers (7 and up)   **Fic**
   The grounding of Group 6 (7 and up)   **Fic**
Thompson, Kate
   Midnight's choice   **Fic**
   Switchers   **Fic**

Thompson, Ruth Plumly, 1893-1976
   The princess who could not dance
   In American fairy tales p120-128   **S C**
Thompson, Sharon Elaine, 1952-
   Built for speed   **599.75**
Thompson, Stephen P., 1953-
   (ed) Teenage pregnancy: opposing viewpoints. See Teenage pregnancy: opposing viewpoints
     362.7
   (ed) The War on drugs: opposing viewpoints. See The War on drugs: opposing viewpoints
     362.29
Thompson, Sue Ellen, 1948-
   (ed) Holidays, festivals, and celebrations of the world dictionary. See Holidays, festivals, and celebrations of the world dictionary
     394.26
Thompson, Wendy
   Franz Schubert   **92**
Thomson, Melissa
   (jt. auth) Dean, R. Life in the American colonies
     973.2
   (jt. auth) Dean, R. Teen prostitution   **362.7**
Thomson, Peggy, 1922-
   The nine-ton cat: behind the scenes at an art museum   **708**
Thoreau, Henry David, 1817-1862
About
   Murphy, J. Into the deep forest with Henry David Thoreau   **974.1**
   Reef, C. Henry David Thoreau   **92**
   See/See also pages in the following book(s):
   Faber, D. Great lives: American literature p79-88   **920**
Thorndike, Jonathan L., 1959-
   Epperson v. Arkansas (7 and up)   **345**
Thornley, Stew
   Mark McGwire   **92**
Thorpe, Jim, 1888-1953
About
   Lipsyte, R. Jim Thorpe   **92**
Those courageous women of the Civil War. Zeinert, K.   **973.7**
Those darn Dithers. Hite, S.   **Fic**
Those other people. Childress, A.   **Fic**
Those remarkable women of the American revolution. Zeinert, K.   **973.3**
Those three wishes. Gorog, J.
   In Read all about it! p475-78   **808.8**
Though justice sleeps. Bair, B.   **305.8**
Thought control See Brainwashing
Thought full. Jennings, P.
   In Jennings, P. Undone! p59-74   **S C**
Thought transference See Telepathy
The **thoughtful** researcher. Rankin, V.   **027.62**
A **thousand** cranes. Miller, K. S.
   In Theatre for young audiences p518-34
     812.008
Threads of evidence. Silverstein, H.   **363.2**
Threatened species See Endangered species
Three brothers. Gorog, J.
   In Gorog, J. When nobody's home p68-77
     S C

Three centuries of American poetry, 1623-1923 (7 and up) **811.008**

The Three daughters of King O'Hara
In Hearne, B. G. Beauties and beasts p84-91 **398.2**

Three fabulous eggs. Mayo, M.
In Mayo, M. Mythical birds & beasts from many lands p85-95 **398.2**

Three Foots. Van Laan, N.
In Van Laan, N. With a whoop and a holler p91-94 **398**

The three hunters and the Great Bear. Bruchac, J.
In Bruchac, J. Four ancestors p21-23 **398.2**

The three men. Snyder, Z. K.
In Dragons & dreams p55-69 **S C**

The three musketeers. Dumas, A. **Fic**

Three people and two seals. Major, K.
In Sixteen: short stories by outstanding writers for young adults p113-24 **S C**

The three wives of Nenpetro. Jaffe, N.
In Jaffe, N. The cow of no color: riddle stories and justice tales from around the world p84-87 **398.2**

Thro, Ellen
Volcanoes of the United States (7 and up) **551.2**

Through a glass darkly. Connelly, E. R. **362.29**

Through my eyes: the autobiography of Ruby Bridges. Bridges, R. **92**

Through the eyes of your ancestors. Taylor, M. **929**

Thunder and Smith. McCaughrean, G.
In McCaughrean, G. The crystal pool: myths and legends of the world p115-19 **398.2**

Thunder Bear and Ko. Hazen-Hammond, S. **970.004**

Thunder cave. Smith, R. **Fic**

Thunder rolling in the mountains. O'Dell, S. **Fic**

Thundershine: tales of metakids. Skinner, D. **S C**

Thurgood Marshall and the Supreme Court. Kent, D. **92**

Thwonk. Bauer, J. **Fic**

Tía Miseria. Loya, O.
In From sea to shining sea p202-05 **810.8**

Tibet (China)
Demi. The Dalai Lama **92**
Sis, P. Tibet **951**

Ticks
See also Lyme disease

Tide pools. Bredeson, C. **577.6**

Ties that bind, ties that break. Namioka, L. **Fic**

Tiger eyes. Blume, J. **Fic**

Tiger in the snow. Barber, D. W.
In The Oxford book of scary tales p36-43 **808.8**

The tiger in the well. Pullman, P. **Fic**

"Tiger! Tiger". Kipling, R.
In Kipling, R. The jungle books **S C**

Tiger, tiger, burning bright. Koertge, R. **Fic**

The tiger woman. San Souci, R.
In San Souci, R. A terrifying taste of short & shivery p104-08 **398.2**

Tigers
Levine, S. P. The tiger (7 and up) **599.75**

Till victory is won. Mettger, Z. **973.7**

Tillage, Leon, 1936-
Leon's story **92**

Time
Gardner, R. Experimenting with time (7 and up) **529**
Mandell, M. Simple experiments in time with everyday materials **529**
Pollard, M. The clock and how it changed the world **681.1**
See/See also pages in the following book(s):
Silverstein, A. Clocks and rhythms **571.7**
Poetry
The Oxford treasury of time poems **821.008**
Time is the longest distance (7 and up) **808.81**

Time & space. Gribbin, J. R. **530.1**

Time and space *See* Space and time

Time apart. Stanley, D. **Fic**

Time is the longest distance (7 and up) **808.81**

Time-Life Books
Atlanta. See Atlanta **973.7**
Chattanooga. See Chattanooga **973.7**
Chickamauga. See Chickamauga **973.7**
First Manassas. See First Manassas **973.7**
Gettysburg. See Gettysburg **973.7**
Leadership. See Leadership **920**
Rock & roll generation. See Rock & roll generation **973.91**
Second Manassas. See Second Manassas **973.7**
Shenandoah, 1862. See Shenandoah, 1862 **973.7**
Shenandoah, 1864. See Shenandoah, 1864 **973.7**
Shiloh. See Shiloh **973.7**
Soldier life. See Soldier life **973.7**
The Universe. See The Universe **520**

Time-Life student library [series]
Human body **612**
Mammals **599**
The Universe **520**

The time machine. Ingram, S.
In Read into the millenium p116-33 **S C**

Time of fire. Westall, R. **Fic**

Time quest book [series]
Beattie, O. Buried in ice **998**

A Time to talk (7 and up) **808.81**

Time Zone High series
Strasser, T. How I spent my last night on earth **Fic**

The timeline book of the arts. See Ochoa, G. The Wilson chronology of the arts **700**

Timelines of the ancient world. See Smithsonian timelines of the ancient world **930**

The **Times** atlas of world history **911**

Timmy. Prince, A.
In The Oxford book of scary tales p79-83 **808.8**

Timothy of the cay. Taylor, T. **Fic**

The **tinderbox.** Andersen, H. C.
In Andersen, H. C. The little mermaid and other fairy tales p19-26 **S C**

Ting, S. C. C. (Samuel Chao-chung), 1936-
See/See also pages in the following book(s):
Yount, L. Asian-American scientists p35-44 (7 and up) **920**

Ting, Samuel Chao-chung *See* Ting, S. C. C. (Samuel Chao-chung), 1936-

The **tiniest** giants. Dingus, L. **567.9**

Tinker, John Frederick
About
Farish, L. Tinker v. Des Moines (7 and up) **342**

Tinker v. Des Moines. Farish, L. **342**

The **tiny** thing. Hamilton, V.
In Hamilton, V. The dark way p54-59 **398.2**

Titanic (Steamship)
Aaseng, N. The Titanic (7 and up) **910.4**
Adams, S. Titanic **910.4**
Ballard, R. D. The discovery of the Titanic (7 and up) **910.4**
Ballard, R. D. Exploring the Titanic **910.4**
Brewster, H. 882 ½ amazing answers to your questions about the Titanic **910.4**
Marschall, K. Inside the Titanic **910.4**
Sherrow, V. The Titanic (7 and up) **910.4**
See/See also pages in the following book(s):
Archbold, R. Deep-Sea explorer: the story of Robert Ballard, discoverer of the Titanic **92**

Fiction
Bunting, E. SOS Titanic (7 and up) **Fic**

Titelman, Gregory Y.
Random House dictionary of America's popular proverbs and sayings **398.9**

Titian, ca. 1488-1576
See/See also pages in the following book(s):
Glubok, S. Great lives: painting p187-95 **920**

Tituba
Fiction
Petry, A. L. Tituba of Salem Village **Fic**

Tituba of Salem Village. Petry, A. L. **Fic**

Tiulana, Paul, 1921-1994
Wise words of Paul Tiulana **92**

Tiziano Vecelli *See* Titian, ca. 1488-1576

To be a slave. Lester, J. **326**
To be a writer. Seuling, B. **808**
To bigotry, no sanction. Fisher, L. E. **296**
To converse with the dumb beasts. Vande Velde, V.
In Vande Velde, V. Curses, Inc. and other stories p82-90 **S C**

To every thing there is a season. Bible. O.T. Ecclesiastes **223**

To have and to hold. Jiménez, F.
In Jiménez, F. The circuit: stories from the life of a migrant child p96-112 **S C**

To hold this ground. Beller, S. P. **973.7**
To life. Sender, R. M. **940.53**
To save the earth. Archer, J. **920**
To see with the heart: the life of Sitting Bull. St. George, J. **92**
To seek a better world. Ashabranner, B. K. **305.8**
To space & back. Ride, S. K. **629.45**
To the bottom of the sea. Sullivan, G. **551.46**

The **toad.** Andersen, H. C.
In Andersen, H. C. The little mermaid and other fairy tales p121-28 **S C**

Toad Woman. Bruchac, J.
In Bruchac, J. When the Chenoo howls **398.2**

Toads and slime. Gorog, J.
In Gorog, J. When nobody's home p46-51 **S C**

Tobacco and smoking: opposing viewpoints (7 and up) **362.29**

Tobacco habit
Ayer, E. H. Teen smoking (7 and up) **362.29**
McMillan, D. Teen smoking (7 and up) **362.29**
Pringle, L. P. Smoking **362.29**
Smoking (7 and up) **362.29**
Tobacco and smoking: opposing viewpoints (7 and up) **362.29**

Tobacco industry
Tobacco and smoking: opposing viewpoints (7 and up) **362.29**

Tocci, Salvatore
How to do a science fair project **507.8**

Todd, Mary Ellen, 1843-1924
Van Leeuwen, J. Bound for Oregon **Fic**

Todras, Ellen H., 1947-
Angelina Grimké (7 and up) **92**

The **toilet.** Mhlophe, G.
In Somehow tenderness survives p77-86 **S C**

Toilets, bathtubs, sinks, and sewers. Colman, P. **643**

Toilets, toasters & telephones. Rubin, S. G. **683**

Tolan, Stephanie S., 1942-
The face in the mirror **Fic**
Welcome to the Ark (7 and up) **Fic**

Tolkien, J. R. R. (John Ronald Reuel), 1892-1973
Bilbo Baggins and Smaug
In The Book of dragons p39-46 **S C**
The fellowship of the ring
In Tolkien, J. R. R. The lord of the rings **Fic**
The hobbit **Fic**
The lord of the rings (7 and up) **Fic**

Toussaint, Pierre, 1766-1853?
See/See also pages in the following book(s):
Haskins, J. African American entrepreneurs p21-24 **920**

Toussaint Louverture, 1743?-1803
About
Myers, W. D. Toussaint L'Ouverture **92**

Toward the promised land. King, W. **305.8**

The **Tower** of Babel. McCaughrean, G.
In McCaughrean, G. The silver treasure: myths and legends of the world p51-52 **398.2**

Town planning *See* City planning

Towns *See* Cities and towns

Toxic plants *See* Poisonous plants

A **trace** of blood. Olson, A. N.
In Olson, A. N. Ask the bones: scary stories from around the world p118-24 **398.2**

Track athletics
See also Running
Jackson, C. The young track and field athlete **796.42**
Macht, N. L. The composite guide to track & field **796.42**
Nuwer, H. The legend of Jesse Owens (7 and up) **92**
Rutledge, R. The best of the best in track & field **920**
Fiction
Levy, M. Run for your life (7 and up) **Fic**

Tracking dinosaurs in the Gobi. Facklam, M. **567.9**

Trade routes
Major, J. S. The Silk Route **950**

Trade unions *See* Labor unions

Trades *See* Occupations

Traditional black music [series]
Silverman, J. African roots **782.42**
Silverman, J. Songs of protest and civil rights **782.42**

Traditional crafts from Africa. Temko, F. **745.5**

Traditional crafts from Mexico and Central America. Temko, F. **745.5**

Traditions *See* Manners and customs

Traffic accidents
See also Drunk driving
Fiction
Orr, W. Peeling the onion (7 and up) **Fic**

Trafficking in drugs *See* Drug traffic

Trafzer, Clifford E.
Cheyenne revenge [excerpt]
In Talking leaves **S C**
The Chinook
In Indians of North America series **970.004**
The Nez Perce
In Indians of North America series **970.004**

The **tragedy** of Birlstone. Doyle, Sir A. C.
In Doyle, Sir A. C. The complete Sherlock Holmes **S C**

Trailblazers [series]
Collins, D. R. Farmworker's friend: the story of Cesar Chavez **92**
Ferris, J. What I had was singing: the story of Marian Anderson **92**
Hart, P. S. Up in the air: the story of Bessie Coleman **92**
McPherson, S. S. TV's forgotten hero: the story of Philo Farnsworth **92**
O'Connor, B. Barefoot dancer: the story of Isadora Duncan **92**
O'Connor, B. The soldiers' voice: the story of Ernie Pyle **92**
Rosen, D. A fire in her bones: the story of Mary Lyon **92**

The **train** room. Hines, G.
In The Haunted house: a collection of original stories **S C**

Training, Occupational *See* Occupational training

Trains, Railroad *See* Railroads

Trains. Johnstone, M. **625.1**

Traitor: the case of Benedict Arnold. Fritz, J. **92**

Tramps
Fiction
DeFelice, C. C. Nowhere to call home **Fic**

Tran, Van Dien
The raven and the star fruit tree
In From sea to shining sea p368-69 **810.8**

The **Transall** saga. Paulsen, G. **Fic**

The **Transcontinental** Railroad in American history. Stein, R. C. **385.09**

Transformations of Cindy R. Mazer, A.
In Stay true: short stories for strong girls **S C**

Transplantation of organs, tissues, etc.
See/See also pages in the following book(s):
Biomedical ethics: opposing viewpoints p51-107 (7 and up) **174**
O'Neill, T. Biomedical ethics p40-50 (7 and up) **174**

Transportation
Wilson, A. Dorling Kindersley visual timeline of transportation (7 and up) **629.04**

Trapani, Margi
Listen up! (7 and up) **306.8**
Reality check (7 and up) **306.8**

Trapped!: cages of mind and body (7 and up) **S C**

Travel
See also Ocean travel

Travels *See* Voyages and travels

The **Travels** of a fox
In From sea to shining sea p256-58 **810.8**

Travis, Dempsey, 1920-
See/See also pages in the following book(s):
Haskins, J. African American entrepreneurs p120-23 **920**

Treasure hunters [series]
Ganeri, A. The search for tombs **393**

Treasure Island. Stevenson, R. L. **Fic**

Twenty thousand leagues under the sea. Verne, J.
        Fic

The **Twinkie** Squad. Korman, G.   **Fic**

Twins

    See also Brothers and sisters

          Fiction

    Duncan, L. Stranger with my face (7 and up)
        Fic

    Littke, L. Haunted sister (7 and up)   **Fic**

    Paterson, K. Jacob have I loved   **Fic**

    Sleator, W. Singularity (7 and up)   **Fic**

Twins. Vande Velde, V.

    In Vande Velde, V. Tales from the Brothers Grimm and the Sisters Weird p88-106
        S C

The **Twist-mouth** family

    In From sea to shining sea p242-43
        810.8

Twisted summer. Roberts, W. D.   **Fic**

The **twisted** window. Duncan, L.   **Fic**

Two coins in the fountain. Conford, E.

    In Conford, E. Crush p69-84   **S C**

Two dreamers. Soto, G.

    In Soto, G. Baseball in April, and other stories p23-32   **S C**

Two dried fish

    In The Dancing fox: Arctic folktales p121-24
        398.2

Two sisters and their caribou husbands

    In The Dancing fox: Arctic folktales p55-62
        398.2

Two suns in the sky. Bat-Ami, M.   **Fic**

The **two** swindlers. Fairman, T.

    In Fairman, T. Bury my bones but keep my words p166-88   **398.2**

Two thousand and one: space odyssey. See Clarke, A. C. 2001: a space odyssey   **Fic**

The **two** towers. Tolkien, J. R. R.

    In Tolkien, J. R. R. The lord of the rings
        Fic

Tyler, John, 1790-1862

See/See also pages in the following book(s):

    Presidents of a young republic   **920**

Tyner, McCoy

See/See also pages in the following book(s):

    Gourse, L. Striders to beboppers and beyond p115-18 (7 and up)   **781.65**

Typhoons

    See also Hurricanes

    Longshore, D. Encyclopedia of hurricanes, typhoons and cyclones (7 and up)   **551.55**

Typography *See* Printing

Tyrannosaurus. Lindsay, W.   **567.9**

          U

U.F.O.'s *See* Unidentified flying objects

U.S. Holocaust Memorial Museum *See* United States Holocaust Memorial Museum

U.S.S.R. *See* Soviet Union

The **U.S.** Space Camp book of astronauts. Baird, A.   **629.45**

U-X-L biographies 2.0. See entry in CD-ROM section, Part 3

U-X-L science CD. See entry in CD-ROM section, Part 3

U.X.L science fact finder   **500**

Uchida, Yoshiko, 1921-1992

    The best bad thing. See note under Uchida, Y. A jar of dreams   **Fic**

    The happiest ending. See note under Uchida, Y. A jar of dreams   **Fic**

    The invisible thread   **92**

    A jar of dreams   **Fic**

    Journey home   **Fic**

    Journey to Topaz   **Fic**

Udvardy, Miklos D. F., 1919-1998

    National Audubon Society field guide to North American birds, Western region   **598**

UFOs *See* Unidentified flying objects

UFOs and aliens. Wilson, C.   **001.9**

Uganda

    Creed, A. Uganda   **967.61**

Ugly-face. Bruchac, J.

    In Bruchac, J. When the Chenoo howls
        398.2

The **ugly** unicorn. Salmonson, J. A.

    In A Glory of unicorns p79-94   **S C**

Uhle, Mary E.

    (jt. auth) Shields, N. E. Where credit is due
        808

Ukraine

    Bassis, V. Ukraine   **947.7**

    Clay, R. Ukraine   **947**

    Otfinoski, S. Ukraine (7 and up)   **947.7**

          History

    See/See also pages in the following book(s):

    Altman, L. J. Genocide p41-48 (7 and up)
        303.6

Ulam, Stanislaw M.

See/See also pages in the following book(s):

    Henderson, H. Modern mathematicians (7 and up)   **920**

The **ultimate** book of sports lists. See Meserole, M. DK ultimate sports lists   **796**

The **ultimate** classic car book. Willson, Q.
        629.222

The **ultimate** dinosaur book. Lambert, D.
        567.9

The **Ultimate** encyclopedia of fantasy   **809.3**

Ultimate field trip 1

    Goodman, S. Bats, bugs, and biodiversity
        577.3

Ultimate field trip 2

    Goodman, S. Stones, bones, and petroglyphs
        930.1

Ultimate field trip 3. Goodman, S.   **577.6**

Ultimate pocket flags of the world   **929.9**

The **ultimate** race car. Burgess Wise, D.
        796.72

Ultimate soccer. Baddiel, I.   **796.334**

Ultimate sports: short stories by outstanding writers for young adults (7 and up)   **S C**

Ultimate visual dictionary of science   **503**

United States—*Continued*
Immigration and emigration—Encyclopedias
American immigration   325.73
Local history
Facts about the states   973
Spangenburg, R. Early settlements (7 and up)
    917.3

Maps
See also United States—Historical geography—Maps
Military history
Gay, K. After the shooting stops (7 and up)
    355
Haskins, J. African American military heroes
    920
Military history—Encyclopedias
English, J. Scholastic encyclopedia of the United States at war   973.03
Military policy
See/See also pages in the following book(s):
War: opposing viewpoints p113-62 (7 and up)
    355
Moral conditions
America's victims: opposing viewpoints (7 and up)   306
National parks and reserves
See National parks and reserves—United States
National security
See National security—United States
Poetry
Celebrate America in poetry and art
    811.008
Politics and government
Christianson, S. G. Facts about the Congress (7 and up)   328.73
Spangenburg, R. Political and social movements (7 and up)   917.3
Tomaselli-Moschovitis, V. Government on file
    320.4
Politics and government—1783-1809
Collier, C. Building a new nation: the Federalist era, 1789-1801   973.4
Collier, C. Creating the Constitution, 1787
    342
Politics and government—1783-1865
Collier, C. The Jeffersonian Republicans: the Louisiana Purchase and the war of 1812
    973.4
Lindop, E. George Washington, Thomas Jefferson, Andrew Jackson   920
Politics and government—1815-1861
Collier, C. Andrew Jackson's America, 1824-1850   973.5
Lindop, E. James K. Polk, Abraham Lincoln, Theodore Roosevelt   920
Meltzer, M. Andrew Jackson and his America (7 and up)   92
Presidents of a young republic   920
Ray, D. A nation torn   973.7
Politics and government—1861-1865
Lindop, E. James K. Polk, Abraham Lincoln, Theodore Roosevelt   920
Presidents of a divided nation   920
Politics and government—1865-1898
January, B. Reconstruction   973.8

Mettger, Z. Reconstruction   973.8
One nation again   973.8
Presidents of a growing country   920
Politics and government—1898-1919
Lindop, E. James K. Polk, Abraham Lincoln, Theodore Roosevelt   920
Politics and government—1900-1999 (20th century)
Greenberg, J. E. Young people's letters to the president   973
Lindop, E. Woodrow Wilson, Franklin D. Roosevelt, Harry S. Truman   920
Presidents in a time of change   920
Presidents of a world power   920
Schulman, A. Robert F. Kennedy (7 and up)
    92
Politics and government—1945-1953
Sherrow, V. Joseph McCarthy and the Cold War
    92
Politics and government—1953-1961
Sherrow, V. Joseph McCarthy and the Cold War
    92
Politics and government—Encyclopedias
Encyclopedia of American government
    320.03
Politics and government—Handbooks, manuals, etc.
The United States government manual   353
Politics and government—Sources
American government. See entry in CD-ROM section, Part 3
SIRS government reporter. See entry in CD-ROM section, Part 3
Popular culture
See Popular culture—United States
Presidents
See Presidents—United States
Prisons
See Prisons—United States
Race relations
Birdseye, D. H. Under our skin   305.8
Bullard, S. Free at last (7 and up)   323.1
Cooper, M. L. The double V campaign
    940.54
Dear Dr. King   323.1
Dornfeld, M. The turning tide (7 and up)
    305.8
Dunn, J. M. The civil rights movement (7 and up)   323.1
Fireside, H. Plessy v. Ferguson (7 and up)
    342
Isserman, M. Journey to freedom (7 and up)
    305.8
King, C. Oh, freedom!   323.1
King, M. L. The words of Martin Luther King, Jr.   323.1
Levine, E. Freedom's children   323.1
Nash, G. B. Forbidden love (7 and up)
    305.8
Pascoe, E. Racial prejudice   305.8
Powledge, F. We shall overcome   323.1
Rasmussen, R. K. Farewell to Jim Crow (7 and up)   305.8
Rochelle, B. Witnesses to freedom   323.1
Senna, C. The black press and the struggle for civil rights (7 and up)   071

United States. Dept. of Commerce. Bureau of the Census *See* United States. Bureau of the Census

United States. Dept. of Justice. Federal Bureau of Investigation *See* United States. Federal Bureau of Investigation

United States. Dept. of Labor. Bureau of Labor Statistics *See* United States. Bureau of Labor Statistics

United States. Federal Bureau of Investigation
Kronenwetter, M. The FBI and law enforcement agencies of the United States (7 and up)
363.2

United States. National Endowment for the Arts *See* National Endowment for the Arts

United States. National Gallery of Art *See* National Gallery of Art (U.S.)

United States. National Museum of American Art *See* National Museum of American Art (U.S.)

United States. President (1861-1865: Lincoln)
Tackach, J. The Emancipation Proclamation (7 and up)
973.7

United States. Supreme Court
Constitution and the Supreme Court. See entry in CD-ROM section, Part 3
DeVillers, D. Marbury v. Madison (7 and up)
347
Huber, P. W. Sandra Day O'Connor
92
Kent, D. Thurgood Marshall and the Supreme Court
92
The Supreme Court, A to Z (7 and up)
347
The Supreme Court justices
920.003
The **United** States government manual
353

United States Holocaust Memorial Museum
Bachrach, S. D. Tell them we remember
940.53
—I never saw another butterfly—. See —I never saw another butterfly—
741.9

United States Naval Expedition to Japan (1852-1854)
Blumberg, R. Commodore Perry in the land of the Shogun
952

United States presidents [series]
Holford, D. M. Herbert Hoover
92
Malone, M. James Madison
92
Schraff, A. E. Woodrow Wilson
92
Spies, K. B. Franklin D. Roosevelt
92
United States stamps and stories. See Postal Service guide to U.S. stamps
769.56

Universal Negro Improvement Association
Lawler, M. Marcus Garvey
92

Universe
See also Cosmology
The **Universe** (7 and up)
520

The **unlikely** romance of Kate Bjorkman. Plummer, L.
Fic

Unmarried couples
See/See also pages in the following book(s):
Marriage and divorce (7 and up)
306.8

Unmarried fathers
See also Single parent family

Unmarried mothers
See also Single parent family
Stewart, G. Mothers on welfare (7 and up)
362.83

Fiction
Dessen, S. Someone like you (7 and up)
Fic

Unmentionable!. Jennings, P.
S C

The **unprotected** witness. Stevenson, J.
Fic

Unsung heroes of World War II. Durrett, D.
940.54

Until the day he died. Mazer, H.
In Twelve shots: outstanding short stories about guns p179-200
S C

Up a road slowly. Hunt, I.
Fic

Up from slavery: an autobiography. Washington, B. T.
92

Up in the air: the story of Bessie Coleman. Hart, P. S.
92

Up the airy mountain. Doyle, D.
In A Nightmare's dozen
S C

Updike, John
The alligators
In Who do you think you are? p64-72
S C

Uphill struggle. McCaughrean, G.
In McCaughrean, G. The bronze cauldron: myths and legends of the world p78-81
398.2

Upon the head of the goat: a childhood in Hungary, 1939-1944. Siegal, A.
92

Ups & downs. Klebanoff, S.
616.85

The **upstairs** room. Reiss, J.
92

Uptown local. Duane, D.
In Dragons & dreams p151-78
S C

Urashima Tarō. Martin, R.
In Martin, R. Mysterious tales of Japan
398.2

Urban, Joan, 1950-
Richard Wright
92

Urban areas *See* Cities and towns

Urban Indians. Fixico, D. L.
In Indians of North America series
970.004

Urban life *See* City life

Urban planning *See* City planning

Ure, Jean
Plague (7 and up)
Fic

Uruguay
Jermyn, L. Uruguay
989.5

Usborne computer guides series
Kalbag, A. Build your own Web site
004.6
Wallace, M. 101 things to do on the Internet
004.6

Uschan, Michael V., 1948-
John F. Kennedy (7 and up)
92
A multicultural portrait of World War I (7 and up)
940.4
Tiger Woods (7 and up)
92

Using educational technology with at-risk students. Mendrinos, R. B.
027.8

Using literature to teach middle grades about war. Kennemer, P. K.   **016.8**

Ute Indians
See/See also pages in the following book(s):
Brown, D. A. Bury my heart at Wounded Knee p367-89 (7 and up)   **970.004**
Fiction
Borland, H. When the legends die   **Fic**
Hobbs, W. Beardance (7 and up)   **Fic**
Hobbs, W. Bearstone (7 and up)   **Fic**

Utensile strength. Wrede, P. C.
In Wrede, P. C. Book of enchantments p204-23   **S C**

Uteritsoq and the duck-bill dolls. Norman, H.
In Norman, H. The girl who dreamed only geese, and other tales of the Far North   **398.2**

Utopias
Fiction
Huxley, A. Brave new world (7 and up)   **Fic**

Uttley, Colin
Magnesium
In The Elements [Benchmark Bks.]   **546**

V

V.C.R.'s *See* Video recording

V.D. *See* Sexually transmitted diseases

Vaca, Alvar Nuñez Cabeza de *See* Nuñez Cabeza de Vaca, Alvar, 16th cent.

Vaccination
See/See also pages in the following book(s):
Epidemics: opposing viewpoints p87-134 (7 and up)   **614.4**

Vagabonds *See* Tramps

Vagrants *See* Tramps

Vail, Rachel
Going sentimental
In Places I never meant to be   **S C**

Valdez, Luis
See/See also pages in the following book(s):
Morey, J. Famous Mexican Americans p140-52   **920**

Valdez (Ship) *See* Exxon Valdez (Ship)

Valentine's Day
Fiction
Conford, E. Crush (7 and up)   **S C**

Valenza, Joyce Kasman
Power tools   **027.8**

Vallejo, Mariano Guadalupe, 1808-1890
See/See also pages in the following book(s):
Duncan, D. People of the West p30-37   **978**

The **valley** of fear. Doyle, Sir A. C.
In Doyle, Sir A. C. The complete Sherlock Holmes   **S C**

Values
Lewis, B. A. What do you stand for?   **170**

Vampire bugs [story] Wyeth, S. D.
In Wyeth, S. D. Vampire bugs: stories conjured from the past p1-7   **S C**

Vampire bugs: stories conjured from the past. Wyeth, S. D.   **S C**

The **vampire** demon. Schwartz, H.
In Schwartz, H. Next year in Jerusalem p22-25   **296.1**

Vampires
Cohen, D. Real vampires   **398**
Fiction
Klause, A. C. The silver kiss (7 and up)   **Fic**
Vampires: a collection of original stories (7 and up)   **S C**

Vampires: a collection of original stories (7 and up)   **S C**

Van Allsburg, Chris
See/See also pages in the following book(s):
Marcus, L. S. A Caldecott celebration p31-37   **741.6**

Van Buren, Martin, 1782-1862
See/See also pages in the following book(s):
Presidents of a young republic   **920**

Van der Meer, Jan *See* Vermeer, Johannes, 1632-1675

Van der Rol, Ruud *See* Rol, Ruud van der

Van Deusen, Jean Donham, 1946-
Enhancing teaching and learning   **027.8**

Van Draanen, Wendelin *See* Draanen, Wendelin van

Van Gogh, Vincent *See* Gogh, Vincent van, 1853-1890

Van Laan, Nancy
With a whoop and a holler   **398**
Includes the following stories: One cold day; Monkey stew; Fool John; Possum plays dead; The big dinin'; The watermillion patch; Ol' Mister Biggety; How come Ol' Buzzard boards; Mister Grumpy rides the clouds; Nuts! Nuts! Nuts!; We hunted and we hollered; Ol' Gally Mander, Jack runs off, Three Foots

Van Leeuwen, Jean
Blue sky, butterfly   **Fic**
Bound for Oregon   **Fic**

Van Rose, Susanna
The earth atlas   **550**

Van Steenwyk, Elizabeth, 1928-
Mathew Brady   **92**

Vanasse, Deb
Out of the wilderness   **Fic**

VanCleave, Janice Pratt
Janice VanCleave's A+ projects in earth science (7 and up)   **550**
Janice Vancleave's ecology for every kid   **577**
Janice VanCleave's guide to the best science fair projects   **507.8**
Janice VanCleave's plants   **580**

Vande Velde, Vivian, 1951-
A coming evil   **Fic**
Curses, Inc. and other stories   **S C**
Contents: Curses, Inc.; Skin deep; Past sunset; To converse with the dumb beasts; Boy witch; Lost soul; Remember me; Witch-hunt; Cypress Swamp Granny; The witch's son
Cypress Swamp Granny
In A Nightmare's dozen   **S C**
Ghost of a hanged man   **Fic**
Never trust a dead man   **Fic**

Vande Velde, Vivian, 1951—_Continued_
Tales from the Brothers Grimm and the Sisters
Weird **S C**
Includes the following stories: Straw into gold; Frog; The
granddaughter; Jack; The bridge; Mattresses; Twins; Beast and
Beauty

Vanilla
See/See also pages in the following book(s):
Busenberg, B. Vanilla, chocolate, & strawberry
p15-37 **664**

Vanilla, chocolate, & strawberry. Busenberg, B.
664

Vanishing. Brooks, B. **Fic**

Vanishing ozone. Pringle, L. P. **363.7**

Vanishing species _See_ Endangered species

VanMeter, Vandelia
America in historical fiction **016.813**

Vanzetti, Bartolomeo, 1888-1927
See/See also pages in the following book(s):
Kraft, B. H. Sensational trials of the 20th
century p1-23 (7 and up) **347**

Vargas Llosa, Mario, 1936-
See/See also pages in the following book(s):
Shirey, L. Latin American writers (7 and up)
860.9

Vases
See also Glassware

Vaughan, Sarah, 1924-1990
See/See also pages in the following book(s):
Gourse, L. Swingers and crooners p101-07 (7
and up) **781.65**

Vaults (Sepulchral) _See_ Tombs

Vázquez de Coronado, Francisco, 1510-1549
See/See also pages in the following book(s):
Marrin, A. Empires lost and won p31-55 (7 and
up) **979**

VCRs _See_ Video recording

VD _See_ Sexually transmitted diseases

Vecelli, Tiziano _See_ Titian, ca. 1488-1576

Vega, Ed
An apology to the moon furies
_In_ Growing up Latino p47-72 **810.8**

Vegetables
See also names of vegetables
Johnson, S. A. Tomatoes, potatoes, corn, and
beans **641.3**

Vegetarian cooking
Krizmanic, J. A teen's vegetarian cookbook (7
and up) **641.5**

Veggeberg, Scott
Lyme disease (7 and up) **616.9**

Vehicles
See also Off-road vehicles
Somerville, L. Rescue vehicles **629.04**

Velásquez, William C.
See/See also pages in the following book(s):
Morey, J. Famous Mexican Americans p153-66
920

Velázquez, Diego, 1599-1660
See/See also pages in the following book(s):
Glubok, S. Great lives: painting p208-17
920

The **velvet** throne. Jennings, P.
_In_ Jennings, P. Unmentionable! p56-69
S C

Venereal diseases _See_ Sexually transmitted diseases

Vennema, Peter
(jt. auth) Stanley, D. Bard of Avon: the story of
William Shakespeare **92**
(jt. auth) Stanley, D. Cleopatra **92**
(jt. auth) Stanley, D. Good Queen Bess: the story of Elizabeth I of England **92**
(jt. auth) Stanley, D. Shaka, king of the Zulus
92

Ventura, Cynthia
(ed) Where angels glide at dawn. See Where angels glide at dawn **S C**

Ventura, Piero
Food **641.3**
Great composers **780.9**

Venturi, Rosabianca Skira- _See_ Skira-Venturi,
Rosabianca

Verhoeven, Rian
(jt. auth) Rol, R. van der. Anne Frank, beyond
the diary **92**

Vermeer, Johannes, 1632-1675
See/See also pages in the following book(s):
Glubok, S. Great lives: painting p218-22
920

Vermeer van Delft, Jan _See_ Vermeer, Johannes,
1632-1675

Vermont
Elish, D. Vermont
_In_ Celebrate the states **973**
Fiction
Paterson, K. Jip **Fic**
Peck, R. N. A day no pigs would die **Fic**

Verne, Jules, 1828-1905
Around the world in eighty days **Fic**
A journey to the centre of the earth **Fic**
Twenty thousand leagues under the sea **Fic**
See/See also pages in the following book(s):
Krull, K. They saw the future p59-65
133.3

Vertebrates
Aaseng, N. Vertebrates **596**
Silverstein, A. Vertebrates **596**
Encyclopedias
The Simon & Schuster encyclopedia of animals
590.3

Vertical file index **015.73**

The **very** large son. Hamilton, V.
_In_ Hamilton, V. The dark way p97-101
398.2

The **very** old woman and the Piskey. Climo, S.
_In_ Climo, S. Magic & mischief p15-20
398.2

Vespucci, Amerigo, 1451-1512
See/See also pages in the following book(s):
Fritz, J. Around the world in a hundred years
p69-75 **910.4**
Lomask, M. Great lives: exploration p234-40
920

Veterans
Fiction
Cormier, R. Heroes (7 and up) **Fic**

Vezza, Diane Simone
Passport on a plate **641.5**

Vinci, Leonardo da *See* Leonardo, da Vinci, 1452-1519

Vine, Allyn Collins, 1914-1994
See/See also pages in the following book(s):
Polking, K. Oceanographers and explorers of the sea p83-91   **920**

Viola, Herman J.
It is a good day to die   **973.8**

Violence
> *See also* Family violence

Bode, J. Hard time (7 and up)   **364.36**
Edgar, K. J. Everything you need to know about media violence   **303.6**
Goodwin, W. Teen violence (7 and up)   **364.36**
Guns and violence (7 and up)   **363.3**
Hull, M. Ethnic violence (7 and up)   **305.8**
Margolis, J. A. Violence in sports (7 and up)   **796**
Media violence: opposing viewpoints (7 and up)   **303.6**
Schwarz, T. Kids and guns (7 and up)   **363.3**
Violence: opposing viewpoints (7 and up)   **303.6**
Youth violence (7 and up)   **364.36**
Zeinert, K. Victims of teen violence (7 and up)   **362.88**
See/See also pages in the following book(s):
Mass media: opposing viewpoints p16-34 (7 and up)   **302.23**
Teens at risk: opposing viewpoints p63-105 (7 and up)   **362.7**

Fiction
Cadnum, M. Edge (7 and up)   **Fic**
Soto, G. Buried onions (7 and up)   **Fic**
Spinelli, J. Wringer   **Fic**
Walter, V. A. Making up Megaboy   **Fic**

Violence in sports. Margolis, J. A.   **796**

Violence: opposing viewpoints (7 and up)   **303.6**

Violinists, violoncellists, etc. *See* Violoncellists

Violins
Fiction
Keillor, G. The Sandy Bottom Orchestra   **Fic**

Violoncellists
Garza, H. Pablo Casals   **92**

Viramontes, Helena Maria, 1954-
The moths
In Growing up Latino p32-37   **810.8**

Virginia
Barrett, T. Virginia
In Celebrate the states   **973**
Blashfield, J. F. Virginia
In America the beautiful, second series   **973**
Fiction
Hite, S. Cecil in space (7 and up)   **Fic**
Hite, S. Those darn Dithers   **Fic**
Paterson, K. Bridge to Terabithia   **Fic**
White, R. Belle Prater's boy   **Fic**

Virginia's general: Robert E. Lee and the Civil War. Marrin, A.   **92**

Virtual reality
Grady, S. M. Virtual reality (7 and up)   **006**
Jefferis, D. Cyberspace   **004.6**
Pascoe, E. Virtual reality   **006**
Weiss, A. E. Virtual reality (7 and up)   **006**

Fiction
Cross, G. New World   **Fic**
Goldman, E. M. The night room (7 and up)   **Fic**
Skurzynski, G. The virtual war   **Fic**
Westwood, C. Virtual world (7 and up)   **Fic**

The **virtual** war. Skurzynski, G.   **Fic**
Virtual world. Westwood, C.   **Fic**
Virtually perfect. Gutman, D.   **Fic**
Virtue goes to town. Yep, L.
In Yep, L. The rainbow people p136-42   **398.2**

Viruses
> *See also* Chickenpox

Facklam, H. Viruses   **579.2**
Vishnu's bride. Krishnaswami, U.
In Krishnaswami, U. Shower of gold: girls and women in the stories of India p75-79   **398.2**

Vision disorders
Fiction
Dorris, M. Sees Behind Trees   **Fic**

Visions. Sills, L.   **920**
Visions: nineteen short stories by outstanding writers for young adults (7 and up)   **S C**
A **visit** from Reverend Tileston. Cook-Lynn, E.
In Talking leaves   **S C**
Visitors. Ellis, S.
In Ellis, S. Back of beyond   **S C**
The **Visual** dictionary of ancient civilizations   **930**
The **Visual** dictionary of animals   **591.4**
The **Visual** dictionary of buildings   **720**
The **visual** dictionary of chemistry. Challoner, J.   **540**
The **Visual** dictionary of dinosaurs   **567.9**
The **Visual** dictionary of flight   **629.133**
The **Visual** dictionary of human anatomy   **611**
The **Visual** dictionary of military uniforms   **355.1**
The **visual** dictionary of physics. Challoner, J.   **530**
The **Visual** dictionary of plants   **580**
The **Visual** dictionary of prehistoric life   **560**
The **Visual** dictionary of ships and sailing   **387.2**
The **Visual** dictionary of the earth   **550**
The **Visual** dictionary of the horse   **636.1**
The **Visual** dictionary of the skeleton   **573.7**

Vitale, William J.
About
Dudley, M. E. Engel v. Vitale (1962) (7 and up)   **344**

Viva New Jersey. Gonzalez, G.
  In Join in p51-60   **S C**
Vivelo, Jackie
  Chills in the night   **S C**
  Contents: When nothing's there at all; The haunted school-
  house; A dog named Ransom; A plague of crowders; A game of
  statues; Ghost of Christmas past; The Fireside Book of Ghost
  Stories; A ride on the dumbwaiter
Vizenor, Gerald Robert, 1934-
  The baron of Petronia
  In Talking leaves   **S C**
  China Browne
  In Talking leaves   **S C**
Vo, Quy
  See/See also pages in the following book(s):
  Graham, K. Contemporary environmentalists
  p37-52 (7 and up)   **920**
Vocational education
  Unger, H. G. But what if I don't want to go to
  college (7 and up)   **331.7**
Vocational guidance
  Career discovery encyclopedia   **331.7**
  The Encyclopedia of careers and vocational
  guidance   **331.7**
  Encyclopedia of careers and vocational guid-
  ance. See entry in CD-ROM section, Part 3
  Pervola, C. How to get a job if you're a
  teenager (7 and up)   **650.14**
  Professional & technical careers (7 and up)
       331.7
  Unger, H. G. But what if I don't want to go to
  college (7 and up)   **331.7**
  United States. Bureau of Labor Statistics. Occu-
  pational outlook handbook   **331.7**
Vocational training *See* Occupational training
Vocations *See* Occupations
Vogt, Gregory
  The solar system   **523.2**
The **voice** of love. Galloway, P.
  In Galloway, P. Truly grim tales   **S C**
Voice of Youth Advocates. See VOYA: Voice of
  Youth Advocates   **027.6205**
The **voice** on the radio. Cooney, C. B.   **Fic**
Voices after midnight. Peck, R.   **Fic**
Voices and visions   **940.53**
Voices from the camps. Brimner, L. D.
       940.53
Voices from the fields. Atkin, S. B.   **331.5**
Voices from the past [series]
  Gay, K. Persian Gulf War   **956.7**
  Gay, K. Revolutionary War   **973.3**
  Gay, K. Vietnam war   **959.704**
  Gay, K. World War I   **940.3**
  Gay, K. World War II   **940.53**
Voices from the streets (7 and up)   **364.36**
Voices from Vietnam. Denenberg, B.   **959.704**
Voices of Northern Ireland. Meyer, C.   **941.6**
Voices of rape. Bode, J.   **362.883**
Voices of the Civil War [series]
  Atlanta   **973.7**
  Chattanooga   **973.7**
  Chickamauga   **973.7**
  First Manassas   **973.7**
  Gettysburg   **973.7**

  Second Manassas   **973.7**
  Shenandoah, 1862   **973.7**
  Shenandoah, 1864   **973.7**
  Shiloh   **973.7**
  Soldier life   **973.7**
Voices of the heart. Young, E.   **179**
Voigt, Cynthia
  Bad, badder, baddest. See note under Voigt, C.
  Bad girls   **Fic**
  Bad girls   **Fic**
  Dicey's song (7 and up)   **Fic**
  Homecoming (7 and up)   **Fic**
  Izzy, willy-nilly (7 and up)   **Fic**
  Jackaroo (7 and up)   **Fic**
  On fortune's wheel (7 and up)   **Fic**
  A solitary blue (7 and up)   **Fic**
  About
  Reid, S. E. Presenting Cynthia Voigt (7 and up)
       813.009
Volavková, Hana
  (ed) —I never saw another butterfly—. See —I
  never saw another butterfly—   **741.9**
Volcano: the eruption and healing of Mount St.
  Helens. Lauber, P.   **551.2**
Volcanoes
  Christian, S. Shake, rattle, and roll   **551.2**
  Lauber, P. Volcano: the eruption and healing of
  Mount St. Helens   **551.2**
  Levy, M. Earthquake games   **551.2**
  Silverstein, A. Plate tectonics   **551.1**
  Thro, E. Volcanoes of the United States (7 and
  up)   **551.2**
  Walker, S. M. Volcanoes: earth's inner fire
       551.2
  Fiction
  Campbell, E. The Shark Callers (7 and up)
       Fic
Volcanoes of the United States. Thro, E.
       551.2
Volkman, John D.
  Cruising through research   **025.5**
Volleyball
  Crisfield, D. Winning volleyball for girls
       796.325
Vollstadt, Elizabeth Weiss, 1942-
  Teen eating disorders (7 and up)   **616.85**
Volunteer work
  Duper, L. L. 160 ways to help the world
       361.3
  Erlbach, A. The kids' volunteering book
       302
  Kids explore kids who make a difference
       302
Von Linné, Carl *See* Linné, Carl von, 1707-1778
Von Neumann, John, 1903-1957
  See/See also pages in the following book(s):
  Northrup, M. American computer pioneers p19-
  27   **920**
Vonnegut, Kurt, 1922-
  Harrison Bergeron
  In Read into the millenium p126-38   **S C**
The **voodoo** queen. Wyeth, S. D.
  In Wyeth, S. D. Vampire bugs: stories con-
  jured from the past p19-35   **S C**

Votava, Andrea
Coping with migraines and other headaches (7 and up)   **616.8**
Voth, Danna
Kidsource   **507.8**
Voting *See* Elections
Voting against the odds. Fisher, A. L.
In The Big book of holiday plays p54-62
812.008
VOYA: Voice of Youth Advocates   **027.6205**
The **voyage** of the Dawn Treader. Lewis, C. S.
See note under Lewis, C. S. The lion, the witch, and the wardrobe   **Fic**
The **voyage** of the Frog. Paulsen, G.   **Fic**
Voyages and travels
Macdonald, F. Marco Polo   **92**
Stefoff, R. Marco Polo and the medieval explorers   **92**
Voyages around the world
Macdonald, F. Magellan   **910.4**
Fiction
Verne, J. Around the world in eighty days
Fic
Vultures
Rauzon, M. J. Vultures   **598**

W

Waco (Tex.) cult siege, 1993
See/See also pages in the following book(s):
Cohen, D. Cults p7-13 (7 and up)   **291.9**
Wade, Henry, 1914-
About
Gold, S. D. Roe v. Wade (1973) (7 and up)
344
Romaine, D. S. Roe v. Wade (7 and up)
344
Stevens, L. A. The case of Roe v. Wade (7 and up)   **344**
Wading into marine biology. See Goodman, S.
Ultimate field trip 3   **577.6**
Wading the World Wide Web. Kyker, K.
004.6
Wadsworth, Ginger
John Burroughs   **92**
Waheenee, b. 1839?
See/See also pages in the following book(s):
Duncan, D. People of the West p102-15
978
Wainwright, Louie L.
About
Sherrow, V. Gideon v. Wainwright (7 and up)
345
Waiters and waitresses
Fiction
Mosier, E. My life as a girl (7 and up)
Fic
Waiting for Sebastian. Peck, R.
In Dirty laundry: stories about family secrets p80-87   **S C**
Waitresses *See* Waiters and waitresses
Wake up to yourself. Jennings, P.
In Jennings, P. Undone! p45-58   **S C**

Wakeman, John, 1928-
(ed) World authors, 1950-1970. See World authors, 1950-1970   **920.003**
(ed) World authors, 1970-1975. See World authors, 1970-1975   **920.003**
Wakin, Daniel, 1961-
(jt. auth) Wakin, E. Photos that made U.S. history   **973.9**
Wakin, Edward
How TV changed America's mind (7 and up)
070.1
Photos that made U.S. history   **973.9**
Wakin, Eric
Asian independence leaders (7 and up)   **920**
The **waking** of the prince. Brooke, W. J.
In Brooke, W. J. A telling of the tales: five stories p3-33   **S C**
Waldman, Carl
Encyclopedia of Native American tribes
970.004
Who was who in world exploration
920.003
Waldman, Neil, 1947-
Masada   **933**
Walens, Stanley, 1948-
The Kwakiutl
In Indians of North America series
970.004
Wales
Fiction
Garner, A. The owl service   **Fic**
Kimmel, E. C. In the stone circle   **Fic**
A **walk** on the wild side. Westall, R.
In Westall, R. Demons and shadows p48-79
S C
Walk this way. Skinner, D.
In Skinner, D. Thundershine: tales of metakids   **S C**
Walk two moons. Creech, S.   **Fic**
Walker, Barbara J.
Developing Christian fiction collections for children and adults   **025.2**
Walker, C. J., Madame, 1867-1919
About
Colman, P. Madam C.J. Walker   **92**
See/See also pages in the following book(s):
Aaseng, N. Black inventors p75-86 (7 and up)
920
Altman, L. J. Women inventors p36-49 (7 and up)   **920**
Haskins, J. African American entrepreneurs p63-66   **920**
Haskins, J. One more river to cross   **920**
Jeffrey, L. S. Great American businesswomen p16-25   **920**
Lutz, N. J. Business & industry   **920**
Walker, Kath *See* Oodgeroo, 1920-1993
Walker, Maggie Lena, 1867-1934
See/See also pages in the following book(s):
Haskins, J. African American entrepreneurs p69-73   **920**
Jeffrey, L. S. Great American businesswomen p8-15   **920**

The **War** of 1812. Greenblatt, M.   973.5
The **war** of Jenkins' ear. Morpurgo, M.   Fic
War of the words. Brancato, R. F.
   In Center stage   812.008
The **war** of the worlds. Wells, H. G.   Fic
The **War** on drugs: opposing viewpoints (7 and
   up)   362.29
War: opposing viewpoints (7 and up)   355
War poetry
   Granfield, L. In Flanders fields   811
   The Oxford book of war poetry (7 and up)
     808.81
   War and the pity of war   808.81
War stories
   Marsden, J. Tomorrow, when the war began (7
   and up)   Fic
      Bibliography
   Holsinger, M. P. The ways of war   016.8
Ward, Geoffrey C.
   Shadow ball   796.357
Ward, Nancy, 1738?-1822
   See/See also pages in the following book(s):
   Calvert, P. Great lives: the American frontier
   p339-51   920
Ward, Paul, 1959-
   Wild bears of the world (7 and up)   599.78
The **warding** of Witch World. Norton, A. See note
   under Norton, A. Witch World [series]
     Fic
Warhol, Andy, 1928?-1987
   See/See also pages in the following book(s):
   Greenberg, J. The American eye p89-97
     920
The **warm** place. Farmer, N.   Fic
Warne, L. Rowland- *See* Rowland-Warne, L.
Warner, J. F. (John F.), 1929-
   Colonial American home life   973.2
Warner, John F. *See* Warner, J. F. (John F.),
   1929-
Warren, Andrea
   Orphan train rider   362.7
Warren, Holly George- *See* George-Warren, Holly
Warren, James A.
   Cold War (7 and up)   327.73
The **warrior** queen of Jhansi. Krishnaswami, U.
   In Krishnaswami, U. Shower of gold: girls
   and women in the stories of India p68-74
     398.2
Warriors, gods & spirits from Central & South
   American mythology. Gifford, D.   299
Wartski, Maureen Crane, 1940-
   A daughter of the sea
   In Join in p86-96   S C
Washakie, Shoshone Chief, 1797-1900
   See/See also pages in the following book(s):
   Freedman, R. Indian chiefs p72-89   920
Washburne, Carolyn Kott, 1944-
   A multicultural portrait of colonial life
     973.2
Washington, Booker T., 1856-1915
   Up from slavery: an autobiography   92

      About
Nicholson, L. Booker T. Washington   92
See/See also pages in the following book(s):
Hacker, C. Great African Americans in history
     920
Washington, Denzel
      About
Hill, A. E. Denzel Washington (7 and up)
     92
Washington, George, 1732-1799
      About
Meltzer, M. George Washington and the birth of
   our nation   92
Osborne, M. P. George Washington   92
Peacock, L. Crossing the Delaware   973.3
Rosenburg, J. M. First in peace: George Wash-
   ington, the Constitution, and the presidency (7
   and up)   92
See/See also pages in the following book(s):
Collier, C. Building a new nation: the Federalist
   era, 1789-1801   973.4
Lindop, E. George Washington, Thomas Jeffer-
   son, Andrew Jackson   920
McPherson, S. S. Martha Washington   92
Washington, Martha, 1731-1802
      About
McPherson, S. S. Martha Washington   92
Washington (D.C.)
   Elish, D. Washington, D.C.
   In Celebrate the states   973
   Stein, R. C. Washington, D.C.
   In America the beautiful, second series
     973
      Fiction
   Armstrong, J. The dreams of Mairhe Mehan (7
   and up)   Fic
Washington (State)
   Stefoff, R. Washington
   In Celebrate the states   973
      Fiction
   Holm, J. L. Our only May Amelia   Fic
Washington City is burning. Robinet, H. G.
     Fic
Wasman, Ann
   New steps to service   027.8
Wasow, Omar, 1970-
   See/See also pages in the following book(s):
   Haskins, J. African American entrepreneurs
   p160-63   920
Waste products
     See also Recycling
The **watcher.** Howe, J.   Fic
Watchman, tell us of the night. Paterson, K.
   In Paterson, K. A midnight clear: stories for
   the Christmas season   S C
Water
   Mebane, R. C. Water & other liquids
     530.4
   Science court: water cycle. See entry in CD-
   ROM section, Part 3
   Williams, J. Water projects   532
Water & other liquids. Mebane, R. C.   530.4
Water animals *See* Marine animals

Water birds

See also Cranes (Birds); Herons; Puffins

Water pollution

Dolan, E. F. Our poisoned waters (7 and up)   **363.7**

McLeish, E. Keeping water clean   **363.7**

The **water** pot and the necklace. Jaffe, N.

In Jaffe, n. The cow of no color: riddle stories and justice tales from around the world p128-33   **398.2**

Water power

Graham, I. Water power   **620.1**

Water projects. Williams, J.   **532**

Water sky. George, J. C.   **Fic**

Water Spirit's gift of horses. Brown, D. A.

In Brown, D. A. Dee Brown's folktales of the Native American p99-101   **398.2**

Water sports

See also Rafting (Sports)

Water supply

McLeish, E. Keeping water clean   **363.7**

Watercolor color. Smith, R.

In The DK art school series   **751**

Watercolor landscape. Smith, R.

In The DK art school series   **751**

Watercolor still life. Lloyd, E. J.

In The DK art school series   **751**

Waterford, Helen, 1909-

(jt. auth) Ayer, E. H. Parallel journeys   **940.53**

Watergate Affair, 1972-1974

See/See also pages in the following book(s):

Barron, R. Richard Nixon (7 and up)   **92**

Goldman, M. S. Richard M. Nixon p97-127 (7 and up)   **92**

Kraft, B. H. Sensational trials of the 20th century p127-52 (7 and up)   **347**

Waterlow, Julia

Grasslands   **577.4**

The **watermillion** patch. Van Laan, N.

In Van Laan, N. With a whoop and a holler p33-38   **398**

Waters, Ethel, 1896-1977

See/See also pages in the following book(s):

Gourse, L. Swingers and crooners p38-43 (7 and up)   **781.65**

Watership down. Adams, R.   **Fic**

Watie, Stand, 1806-1871

Fiction

Keith, H. Rifles for Watie   **Fic**

Watkins, T. H. (Tom H.), 1936-2000

The Great Depression (7 and up)   **973.91**

Watkins, Tom H. *See* Watkins, T. H. (Tom H.), 1936-2000

Watkins, Yoko Kawashima

My brother, my sister, and I   **Fic**

So far from the bamboo grove   **Fic**

Watkyn, comma. Aiken, J.

In Aiken, J. A fit of shivers p77-94   **S C**

Watson, James D., 1928-

About

Edelson, E. James Watson and Francis Crick and the building blocks of life (7 and up)   **92**

Watson, Wenta Jean

Abe Lincoln and the runaways

In Plays of black Americans p105-15   **812.008**

The **Watsons** go to Birmingham—1963. Curtis, C. P.   **Fic**

Watt-Evans, Lawrence, 1954-

Richie

In Vampires: a collection of original stories p211-25   **S C**

What the cat dragged in

In A Nightmare's dozen   **S C**

Watts, James, 1955-

InventorLabs: technology. See entry in CD-ROM section, Part 3

Watts, Marilyn

The leopard in the rafters

In The Oxford book of scary tales p132-36   **808.8**

Watts history of sports [series]

Stewart, M. Baseball   **796.357**

Stewart, M. Basketball   **796.323**

Stewart, M. Football   **796.332**

Stewart, M. Hockey   **796.962**

Stewart, M. Soccer   **796.334**

Waugh, Charles G. (Charles Gordon), 1943-

(ed) Dragons & dreams. See Dragons & dreams   **S C**

(comp) A Newbery Christmas. See A Newbery Christmas   **S C**

(comp) A Newbery Halloween. See A Newbery Halloween   **S C**

(comp) A Newbery zoo. See A Newbery zoo   **S C**

Waves

Zubrowski, B. Making waves   **532**

The **way** it was. Freeman-Villalobos, T. M.

In Talking leaves   **S C**

The **way** of the grizzly. Patent, D. H.   **599.78**

A **Way** out of no way (7 and up)   **810.8**

Way people live [series]

Blackwood, G. L. Life on the Oregon Trail   **979.5**

Dean, R. Life in the American colonies   **973.2**

Kallen, S. A. Life in the Amazon rainforest   **981**

Nardo, D. Life of a Roman slave   **937**

Netzley, P. D. Life during the Renaissance   **940.2**

Nishi, D. Life during the Great Depression   **973.91**

Nnoromele, S. Life among the Ibo women of Nigeria   **966.9**

The **way** things never were. Finkelstein, N. H.   **973.92**

The **way** things work. See Macaulay, D. The new way things work   **600**

The **ways** of war. Holsinger, M. P.   **016.8**

We all fall down. Cormier, R.   **Fic**

We are all one. Yep, L.
   In Yep, L. The rainbow people p72-78
                    398.2

We are witnesses. Boas, J.   **940.53**

"We have conquered pain". Fradin, D. B.
                    617.9

We hunted and we hollered. Van Laan, N.
   In Van Laan, N. With a whoop and a holler
   p65   **398**

We interrupt this broadcast. Garner, J.   **070.1**

We organized. McKissack, P. C.
   In McKissack, P. C. The dark-thirty p17-21
                    S C

We remember the Holocaust. Adler, D. A.
                    940.53

We shall not be moved. Dash, J.   **331.4**

We shall overcome. Powledge, F.   **323.1**

We survived the Holocaust   **940.53**

Wealth
             Fiction
   Ferris, J. Love among the walnuts (7 and up)
                    Fic
   Giberga, J. S. Friends to die for (7 and up)
                    Fic
   Roberts, W. D. The kidnappers   **Fic**

Weapons
   See also Armor
   Byam, M. Arms & armor   **355.8**
   Meltzer, M. Weapons & warfare   **355**
   Weapons of mass destruction: opposing view-
   points (7 and up)   **358**
             History
   Weapons   **623.4**

Weapons   **623.4**

Weapons & warfare. Meltzer, M.   **355**

Weapons of mass destruction: opposing viewpoints (7 and up)   **358**

Weate, Jeremy
   A young person's guide to philosophy   **100**

Weather
   See also Meteorology
   Dunn, A. Fog, mist, and smog   **551.5**
   Elsom, D. M. Weather explained   **551.5**
   Encyclopedia of climate and weather   **551.6**
   Engelbert, P. The complete weather resource
                    551.5
   Everything weather. See entry in CD-ROM sec-
   tion, Part 3
   Gardner, R. Science projects about weather (7
   and up)   **551.5**
   Kahl, J. D. National Audubon Society first field
   guide: weather   **551.5**
   Oxlade, C. Weather   **551.5**
   Silverstein, A. Weather and climate   **551.5**
             Fiction
   Thompson, K. Switchers   **Fic**
             Statistics
   Weather almanac   **551.6**

Weather almanac   **551.6**

Weather and climate. Silverstein, A.   **551.5**

Weather explained. Elsom, D. M.   **551.5**

Weaver, Robyn M.
   Depression (7 and up)   **616.85**
   John Grisham (7 and up)   **92**

Weaver, Will
   Stealing for girls
   In Ultimate sports: short stories by outstand-
   ing writers for young adults p93-116
                    S C

The **weaver** of Yzad. Goldin, B. D.
   In Goldin, B. D. Journeys with Elijah p29-37
                    222

Web sites
   See/See also pages in the following book(s):
   Henderson, H. Issues in the information age (7
   and up)   **303.4**

Webb, C. Anne
   (ed) National Council of Teachers of English.
   Committee on the Junior High and Middle
   School Booklist. Your reading   **011.6**

Webb, Lois Sinaiko, 1922-
   Holidays of the world cookbook for students
                    641.5
   (jt. auth) Albyn, C. L. The multicultural cookbook for students   **641.5**

Webb, Sharon, 1936-
   The thing that goes burp in the night
   In Dragons & dreams p12-31   **S C**

Webster, Daniel, 1782-1852
   See/See also pages in the following book(s):
   Kennedy, J. F. Profiles in courage p64-84 (7
   and up)   **920**

Webster, David, 1930-
   (jt. auth) Gardner, R. Science project ideas
   about animal behavior   **591.5**
   (jt. auth) Gardner, R. Science projects about
   weather   **551.5**

Webster's dictionary of synonyms. See Merriam-
   Webster's dictionary of synonyms   **423**

Webster's geographical dictionary. See Merriam-
   Webster's geographical dictionary   **910.3**

Webster's student thesaurus. See Merriam-
   Webster's school thesaurus   **423**

Webster's third new international dictionary of the
   English language, unabridged   **423**

Weddings
             Fiction
   Dessen, S. That summer (7 and up)   **Fic**

Wee, Jessie
   The Philippines   **959.9**
   Taiwan   **951.24**

Weeding library collections. Slote, S. J.
                    025.2

A **weekend** with Degas. Skira-Venturi, R.   **92**

A **weekend** with Picasso. Rodari, F.   **92**

A **weekend** with Rembrandt. Bonafoux, P.
                    92

A **weekend** with Renoir. Skira-Venturi, R.   **92**

A **weekend** with Rousseau. Plazy, G.   **92**

A **weekend** with Van Gogh. Skira-Venturi, R.
                    92

A **weekend** with Winslow Homer. Beneduce, A.
                    92

Wentzien, Marion de Booy
Taking toll
In Stay true: short stories for strong girls
S C
Werblowsky, R. J. Zwi (Raphael Jehudah Zwi), 1924-
(ed) The Oxford dictionary of the Jewish religion. See The Oxford dictionary of the Jewish religion **296.03**
Werblowsky, Raphael Jehudah Zwi *See* Werblowsky, R. J. Zwi (Raphael Jehudah Zwi), 1924-
The **werewolf**. Osborne, M. P.
In Osborne, M. P. Favorite medieval tales p42-49 **398.2**
Werewolves
Cohen, D. Werewolves **398**
Werlin, Nancy, 1961-
War game
In Twelve shots: outstanding short stories about guns p88-101 S C
Wesley, John, 1703-1791
About
Wellman, S. John Wesley (7 and up) **92**
West, Cornel
(ed) Encyclopedia of African-American culture and history. See Encyclopedia of African-American culture and history **305.8**
West, Delno C., 1936-
Braving the North Atlantic **970.01**
West, Jean M.
(jt. auth) West, D. C. Braving the North Atlantic **970.01**
West, Margaret W. Denman- *See* Denman-West, Margaret W., 1926-
West (U.S.)
See/See also pages in the following book(s):
Faber, D. Calamity Jane **92**
Biography
Calvert, P. Great lives: the American frontier **920**
Exploration
See also Overland journeys to the Pacific
Blumberg, R. The incredible journey of Lewis and Clark **978**
Clark, W. Off the map **978**
See/See also pages in the following book(s):
St. George, J. Sacagawea **92**
Fiction
Blakeslee, A. R. A different kind of hero Fic
Fleischman, S. Jim Ugly Fic
Karr, K. The great turkey walk Fic
Myers, W. D. The journal of Joshua Loper Fic
Paulsen, G. Mr. Tucket Fic
Vande Velde, V. Ghost of a hanged man Fic
Wallace, B. Eye of the great bear Fic
History
Bentley, J. Brides, midwives, and widows **978**
Brown, D. A. Bury my heart at Wounded Knee (7 and up) **970.004**

Cox, C. The forgotten heroes **978**
DeAngelis, G. The black cowboys **978**
Duncan, D. People of the West **978**
Duncan, D. The West **978**
Ehrlich, A. Wounded Knee: an Indian history of the American West **970.004**
Freedman, R. Cowboys of the wild West **978**
Glass, A. Bad guys **920**
Jones, M. E. Daily life on the nineteenth century American frontier (7 and up) **978**
Katz, W. L. Black women of the Old West **978**
Marrin, A. Cowboys, Indians, and gunfighters **978**
McGowen, T. African-Americans in the Old West **978**
The Oregon trail. See entry in CD-ROM section, Part 3
Schlissel, L. Black frontiers **978**
Stovall, T. The Buffalo Soldiers **978**
Tunis, E. Frontier living **978**
Westward expansion **978**
Social life and customs
Patent, D. H. Homesteading **978**
West Bank
Stefoff, R. West Bank/Gaza Strip **956.95**
West Bank/Gaza Strip. Stefoff, R. **956.95**
West Indians
New York (N.Y.)—Fiction
Guy, R. The friends Fic
West Indies
Anthony, S. West Indies **972.9**
Hodge, A. The West Indies **972.9**
West to a land of plenty. Murphy, J. Fic
West Virginia
Hoffman, N. West Virginia
In Celebrate the states **973**
Fiction
Naylor, P. R. Shiloh Fic
Rylant, C. Missing May Fic
Westall, Robert, 1929-1993
Demons and shadows (7 and up) S C
Contents: Rachel and the angel; Graveyard shift; A walk on the wild side; The making of me; The night out; The Woolworth spectacles; A nose against the glass; Gifts from the sea; The creatures in the house; The death of wizards; The last day of Miss Dorinda Molyneaux
The kingdom by the sea Fic
The machine gunners Fic
The promise Fic
The stones of Muncaster Cathedral Fic
Time of fire Fic
Westerfeld, Scott
The Berlin airlift **943.087**
Western Europe *See* Europe
Western States *See* West (U.S.)
Westervelt, Virginia Veeder
Here comes Eleanor [Roosevelt] **92**
The **Westing** game. Raskin, E. Fic
Westmacott, Mary
See also Christie, Agatha, 1890-1976
Westmark. Alexander, L. Fic

What's your story?. Bauer, M. D.   **808.3**

Wheatley, Phillis, 1753-1784
    About
    Richmond, M. A. Phillis Wheatley   **92**
    See/See also pages in the following book(s):
    Strickland, M. R. African-American poets p11-17   **920**
    Fiction
    Rinaldi, A. Hang a thousand trees with ribbons (7 and up)   **Fic**

The **wheel** and how it changed the world. Locke, I.   **621.8**

Wheels
    Locke, I. The wheel and how it changed the world   **621.8**

Whelan, Gloria
    Goodbye, Vietnam   **Fic**

When a friend dies. Gootman, M. E.   **155.9**

When freedom came. Lester, J.
    In Lester, J. Long journey home: stories from black history p105-28   **S C**

When nobody's home. Gorog, J.   **S C**

When nothing matters anymore. Cobain, B.   **155.9**

When nothing's there at all. Vivelo, J.
    In Vivelo, J. Chills in the night p7-18   **S C**

When someone you love is addicted. Hanan, J.   **362.29**

When the beginning began. Lester, J.   **296.1**

When the Chenoo howls. Bruchac, J.   **398.2**

When the legends die. Borland, H.   **Fic**

When the phone rang. Mazer, H.   **Fic**

When the sun and the moon were children. Delacre, L.
    In Delacre, L. Golden tales p31-35   **398.2**

When the sun dies. Gallant, R. A.   **523.7**

When the train comes. Wicomb, Z.
    In Somehow tenderness survives p61-76   **S C**

When the Tripods came. Christopher, J. See note under Christopher, J. The White Mountains   **Fic**

When will this cruel war be over?. Denenberg, B.   **Fic**

Where angels glide at dawn   **S C**

Where are you going, where have you been?. Oates, J. C.
    In Who do you think you are? p14-35   **S C**

Where credit is due. Shields, N. E.   **808**

Where in the USA is Carmen Sandiego? 3.5. See entry in CD-ROM section, Part 3

Where in the world is Carmen Sandiego? 3.5. See entry in CD-ROM section, Part 3

Where the broken heart still beats. Meyer, C.   **Fic**

Where the girl rescued her brother. Bruchac, J.
    In Bruchac, J. The girl who married the Moon: tales from Native North America p101-07   **398.2**

Where the lilies bloom. Cleaver, V.   **Fic**

Where the red fern grows. Rawls, W.   **Fic**

Where the sidewalk ends. Silverstein, S.   **811**

Where will this shoe take you?. Lawlor, L.   **391**

Which way freedom?. Hansen, J.   **Fic**

Which witch?. Ibbotson, E.   **Fic**

While no one was watching. Conly, J. L.   **Fic**

The **whipping** boy. Fleischman, S.   **Fic**

Whipple, Laura
    (comp) Celebrating America. See Celebrating America   **811.008**

Whirligig. Fleischman, P.   **Fic**

Whistler, James McNeill, 1834-1903
    About
    Berman, A. James McNeill Whistler (7 and up)   **92**

    See/See also pages in the following book(s):
    Glubok, S. Great lives: painting p223-36   **920**

Whitaker, John O., Jr.
    National Audubon Society field guide to North American mammals   **599**

White, Deborah Gray
    Let my people go: African Americans, 1804-1860 (7 and up)   **305.8**

White, E. B. (Elwyn Brooks), 1899-1985
    See/See also pages in the following book(s):
    Faber, D. Great lives: American literature p278-86   **920**

White, Elwyn Brooks *See* White, E. B. (Elwyn Brooks), 1899-1985

White, George Henry, 1852-1918
    See/See also pages in the following book(s):
    Katz, W. L. Proudly red and black p49-61   **920**

White, Margaret Bourke- *See* Bourke-White, Margaret, 1904-1971

White, Paulette Childress, 1948-
    Getting the facts of life
    In Rites of passage p91-102   **S C**

White, Ruth
    Belle Prater's boy   **Fic**

White, T. H. (Terence Hanbury), 1906-1964
    The candle in the wind
    In White, T. H. The once and future king   **Fic**

    The ill-made knight
    In White, T. H. The once and future king   **Fic**

    The once and future king   **Fic**
    The sword in the stone
    In White, T. H. The once and future King   **Fic**

    The witch in the wood
    In White, T. H. The once and future king   **Fic**

White, Terence Hanbury *See* White, T. H. (Terence Hanbury), 1906-1964

White balloons. Ortiz Cofer, J.
    In Ortiz Cofer, J. An island like you p144-65   **S C**

White collar crimes
    DeAngelis, G. White-collar crime (7 and up)   **364.1**

White dragon. McCaffrey, A. See note under
  McCaffrey, A. [The Pern series]   **Fic**
White Fang. London, J.   **Fic**
White House (Washington, D.C.)
  Quiri, P. R. The White House   **975.3**
White lilacs. Meyer, C.   **Fic**
The White Mountains. Christopher, J.   **Fic**
White-out. Wolf, P.
  In Talking leaves   **S C**
The white seal. Kipling, R.
  In Kipling, R. The jungle books   **S C**
White-water rafting. George, C.   **797.1**
Whitebear Whittington
  In Hearne, B. G. Beauties and beasts p76-83
                                         398.2
Whitechurch. Lynch, C.   **Fic**
Whitelaw, Nancy
  Clara Barton   **92**
  Joseph Pulitzer and the New York World
                                         92
Whiteman, Roberta Hill, 1947-
  Summer girl
  In Talking leaves   **S C**
Whitman, Christine Todd
  See/See also pages in the following book(s):
  Lindop, L. Political leaders (7 and up) **920**
Whitman, Marcus, 1802-1847
  See/See also pages in the following book(s):
  Calvert, P. Great lives: the American frontier
    p352-71   **920**
Whitman, Narcissa Prentiss, 1808-1847
  See/See also pages in the following book(s):
  Calvert, P. Great lives: the American frontier
    p352-71   **920**
  Duncan, D. People of the West p22-29
                                         978
Whitman, Walt, 1819-1892
  Leaves of grass (7 and up)   **811**
  Walt Whitman (7 and up)   **811**
                 About
  Reef, C. Walt Whitman (7 and up)   **92**
  See/See also pages in the following book(s):
  Faber, D. Great lives: American literature p161-
    69   **920**
Whitney, Elinor *See* Field, Elinor Whitney, 1889-
  1980
Whittington, Mary K.
  Ahvel
  In Vampires: a collection of original stories
    p121-33   **S C**
  Somewhere a puppy cries
  In The Haunted house: a collection of original
    stories   **S C**
Who are you?. Nixon, J. L.   **Fic**
Who do you think you are? (7 and up)   **S C**
Who is Carrie?. Collier, J. L.   **Fic**
Who is Eddie Leonard?. Mazer, H.   **Fic**
Who ordered the jumbo shrimp? and other oxymo-
  rons. Agee, J.   **793.73**
Who said that?. Burleigh, R.   **808.88**
Who was who in world exploration. Waldman, C.
                                         920.003

Who were the founding fathers?. Jaffe, S. H.
                                         973.3
Who you!. Hamilton, V.
  In Hamilton, V. Her stories p45-50
                                         398.2
The **whooping** crane. Patent, D. H.   **639.9**
Whooping cranes *See* Cranes (Birds)
Who's afraid?. Pearce, P.
  In Read all about it! p230-35   **808.8**
Who's Hu? [excerpt] Namioka, L.
  In American dragons p48-64   **810.8**
Who's running the nation?. Gay, K.   **322**
Who's who in space. Cassutt, M.   **920.003**
Who's who in the Bible. Motyer, S.   **220.9**
Whose footprints?. McCaughrean, G.
  In McCaughrean, G. The golden hoard: myths
    and legends of the world p89-93
                                         398.2
Why alligator hates dog. Reneaux, J. J.
  In From sea to shining sea p46-49   **810.8**
Why Brer Bull growls and grumbles. Lester, J.
  In Lester, J. The last tales of Uncle Remus
    p119-23   **398.2**
Why Brer Fox's legs are black. Lester, J.
  In Lester, J. The last tales of Uncle Remus
    p64-66   **398.2**
Why Brer Possum has no hair on his tail. Lester,
  J.
  In Lester, J. The last tales of Uncle Remus
    p41-44   **398.2**
Why Brer Possum loves peace. Lester, J.
  In Lester, J. The last tales of Uncle Remus
    p44-46   **398.2**
Why Bush Cow and Elephant are bad friends.
  Bryan, A.
  In Bryan, A. Ashley Bryan's African tales,
    uh-huh p54-69   **398.2**
Why chickens scratch in the dirt. Lester, J.
  In Lester, J. The last tales of Uncle Remus
    p147-49   **398.2**
Why Coyote stopped imitating his friends. Brown,
  D. A.
  In Brown, D. A. Dee Brown's folktales of the
    Native American p150-53   **398.2**
Why dogs are tame. Lester, J.
  In Lester, J. The last tales of Uncle Remus
    p76-82   **398.2**
Why dogs have long tongues. Brown, D. A.
  In Brown, D. A. Dee Brown's folktales of the
    Native American p26-28   **398.2**
Why Frog and Snake never play together. Bryan,
  A.
  In Bryan, A. Ashley Bryan's African tales,
    uh-huh p81-92   **398.2**
Why guinea fowls are speckled. Lester, J.
  In Lester, J. The last tales of Uncle Remus
    p88-93   **398.2**
Why the cricket has elbows on his legs. Lester, J.
  In Lester, J. The last tales of Uncle Remus
    p3-8   **398.2**
Why the earth is mostly water. Lester, J.
  In Lester, J. The last tales of Uncle Remus
    p8-12   **398.2**

Why the goat has a short tail. Lester, J.
In Lester, J. The last tales of Uncle Remus
p136-38   **398.2**
Why the Guineas stay awake. Lester, J.
In Lester, J. The last tales of Uncle Remus
p93-94   **398.2**
Why the hawk likes to eat chickens. Lester, J.
In Lester, J. The last tales of Uncle Remus
p98-102   **398.2**
Why the rude visitor was flung by walrus. Norman, H.
In Norman, H. The girl who dreamed only
geese, and other tales of the Far North
                                           398.2
Whyte, Mariam
Bangladesh   **954.92**
Wice, Paul B.
Miranda v. Arizona (7 and up)   **345**
Wick, Walter
Walter Wick's optical tricks   **152.14**
The **wicked** stepmother. Hamilton, V.
In Hamilton, V. The dark way p49-53
                                           398.2
Wicomb, Zoë
When the train comes
In Somehow tenderness survives p61-76
                                           S C
Wide world [series]
Lewington, A. People of the rain forests
                                           577.3
The **widow** and the Spriggans of Trenscrom Hill.
Climo, S.
In Climo, S. Magic & mischief p25-30
                                           398.2
Wiese, Jim, 1948-
Spy science   **363.2**
Wiesel, Elie, 1928-
The accident
In Wiesel, E. Night, Dawn, The accident:
three tales   **Fic**
Dawn
In Wiesel, E. Night, Dawn, The accident:
three tales   **Fic**
Night
In Wiesel, E. Night, Dawn, The accident:
three tales   **Fic**
Night, Dawn, The accident: three tales (7 and
up)   **Fic**
See/See also pages in the following book(s):
Mandell, S. L. Writers of the Holocaust (7 and
up)   **940.53**
Wiesner, David
See/See also pages in the following book(s):
Marcus, L. S. A Caldecott celebration p38-45
                                           741.6
Wife abuse
See also Abused women
Fiction
Byars, B. C. Cracker Jackson   **Fic**
The **wife** of Bath's tale. Cohen, B.
In Cohen, B. Canterbury tales   **821**
Wigoder, Geoffrey, 1922-1999
(ed) The Holocaust. See The Holocaust
                                           940.53

(ed) The Oxford dictionary of the Jewish religion. See The Oxford dictionary of the Jewish
religion   **296.03**
The **wigwam** and the longhouse. Yue, C.
                                           970.004
Wihio and Grandfather Rock. Bruchac, J.
In Bruchac, J. Four ancestors p35-37
                                           398.2
Wild bears of the world. Ward, P.   **599.78**
Wild Boy of Aveyron, d. 1828
See/See also pages in the following book(s):
Drimmer, F. Incredible people p144-76   **920**
Wild cats
See also Cats; Cheetahs; Lions; Pumas; Tigers
Alderton, D. Wild cats of the world (7 and up)
                                           599.75
Clutton-Brock, J. Cat   **599.75**
Saign, G. The African cats   **599.75**
Wild cats of the world. Alderton, D.   **599.75**
Wild children
See/See also pages in the following book(s):
Drimmer, F. Incredible people p144-76   **920**
Fiction
Hesse, K. The music of dolphins   **Fic**
Mazer, H. The wild kid   **Fic**
Yolen, J. Children of the wolf   **Fic**
The **wild** Colorado. Maurer, R.   **979.1**
Wild dogs
Fiction
Salisbury, G. Jungle dogs   **Fic**
Wild flowers
Hood, S. National Audubon Society first field
guide: wildflowers   **582.13**
Niehaus, T. F. A field guide to Pacific states
wildflowers   **582.13**
Niering, W. A. The Audubon Society field
guide to North American wildflowers: eastern
region   **582.13**
Peterson, R. T. A field guide to wildflowers of
northeastern and north-central North America
                                           582.13
Spellenberg, R. The Audubon Society field
guide to North American wildflowers: western
region   **582.13**
Wild heart: the story of Joy Adamson, author of
Born free. Neimark, A. E.   **92**
Wild horses I have known. Ryden, H.   **599.66**
The **wild** kid. Mazer, H.   **Fic**
Wild magic. Pierce, T. See note under Pierce, T.
Wolf-speaker   **Fic**
Wild meat and the bully burgers [excerpt]
Yamanaka, L.-A.
In American eyes p8-12   **S C**
The **wild,** wild cookbook. See George, J. C. Acorn
pancakes, dandelion salad and 38 other wild
recipes   **641.6**
Wildebeests *See* Gnus
Wilder, Laura Ingalls, 1867-1957
The Laura Ingalls Wilder country cookbook
                                           641.5
About
Anderson, W. T. Laura Ingalls Wilder   **92**

Williams, Jean Kinney—*Continued*
The Christian Scientists (7 and up)   **289.5**
Matthew Henson, polar adventurer   **92**
The Mormons (7 and up)   **289.3**
The Quakers (7 and up)   **289.6**
The Shakers (7 and up)   **289**
South Korea (7 and up)   **951.95**

Williams, Joe
See/See also pages in the following book(s):
Gourse, L. Swingers and crooners p109-13 (7 and up)   **781.65**

Williams, John
Water projects   **532**

Williams, Juan
Eyes on the prize: America's civil rights years, 1954-1965 (7 and up)   **323.1**

Williams, Marcia, 1945-
Tales from Shakespeare   **822.3**

Williams, Mary E., 1960-
(ed) Culture wars: opposing viewpoints. See Culture wars: opposing viewpoints   **306**
(ed) Discrimination: opposing viewpoints. See Discrimination: opposing viewpoints   **305.8**
(ed) The Family: opposing viewpoints. See The Family: opposing viewpoints   **306.8**
(ed) Homosexuality: opposing viewpoints. See Homosexuality: opposing viewpoints   **305.9**
(ed) Human rights: opposing viewpoints. See Human rights: opposing viewpoints   **323**
(ed) Marriage and divorce. See Marriage and divorce   **306.8**
(ed) Tobacco and smoking: opposing viewpoints. See Tobacco and smoking: opposing viewpoints   **362.29**
(ed) Working women: opposing viewpoints. See Working women: opposing viewpoints   **331.4**

Williams, Mary Lou, 1910-1981
See/See also pages in the following book(s):
Gourse, L. Striders to beboppers and beyond p50-55 (7 and up)   **781.65**
Mour, S. I. American jazz musicians p39-46   **920**

Williams, Michael W. (Michael Warren)
(ed) The African American encyclopedia. See The African American encyclopedia   **305.8**

Williams, Myrlie Evers- *See* Evers-Williams, Myrlie

Williams, Phyllis S.
(jt. auth) Kenda, M. Math wizardry for kids   **793.7**

Williams, Tennessee, 1911-1983
See/See also pages in the following book(s):
Faber, D. Great lives: American literature p287-95   **920**

Williams, Thomas Lanier *See* Williams, Tennessee, 1911-1983

Williams, Venus
About
Aronson, V. Venus Williams   **92**

Williams-Garcia, Rita
About Russell
In Dirty laundry: stories about family secrets p70-79   **S C**
Chalkman
In Twelve shots: outstanding short stories about guns p218-26   **S C**
Crazy as a daisy
In Stay true: short stories for strong girls   **S C**
Into the game
In Join in p3-11   **S C**
Like sisters on the homefront (7 and up)   **Fic**

Williamson, Ray A., 1938-
(jt. auth) Monroe, J. G. First houses   **970.004**

Willis, Roy G.
(ed) World mythology. See World mythology   **291.1**

Wills, Charles A.
The Tet offensive   **959.704**

Willson, Quentin
Classic American cars (7 and up)   **629.222**
The ultimate classic car book (7 and up)   **629.222**

Wiloch, Thomas
Everything you need to know about protecting yourself and others from abduction   **613.6**

Wilsdon, Christina
National Audubon Society first field guide: insects   **595.7**

Wilson, Anthony, 1939-
Dorling Kindersley visual timeline of transportation (7 and up)   **629.04**

Wilson, Bernice
Art of the ancient Mediterranean world
In International encyclopedia of art   **703**

Wilson, Budge, 1927-
Be-ers and doers
In Help wanted: short stories about young people working   **S C**

Wilson, Claire
(jt. auth) Bolton, J. Joseph Brant   **92**

Wilson, Clive
(ed) The Kingfisher young people's book of music. See The Kingfisher young people's book of music   **780.9**

Wilson, Colin, 1931-
Ghosts and the supernatural   **133.1**
Mysteries of the universe   **001.9**
Psychic powers   **133.8**
UFOs and aliens   **001.9**

Wilson, Darryl Babe, 1939-
Diamond Island: Alcatraz
In Talking leaves   **S C**

Wilson, Diane L.
I rode a horse of milk white jade (7 and up)   **Fic**

Wilson, Edith Bolling Galt, 1872-1961
About
Flanagan, A. K. Edith Bolling Galt Wilson, 1872-1961   **92**

Winther, Barbara—*Continued*

Plays from Hispanic tales   **812**

Contents: El caballito of seven colors; The ghost of el castillo; The great hurricane; Brother Rabbit sells corn; Pedrode Urdemalas; Latino trio; The talking burro; A gift for Pachacuti Inca; The deer dance; The sleeping mountains; Macona, the honest warrior

Winthrop, John, 1588-1649

See/See also pages in the following book(s):

IlgenFritz, E. Anne Hutchinson p13-19, 69-97   **92**

Wirths, Claudine G.

Coping with confrontations and encounters with the police (7 and up)   **363.2**

Wisconsin

Blashfield, J. F. Wisconsin

In America the beautiful, second series   **973**

Zeinert, K. Wisconsin

In Celebrate the states   **973**

Fiction

Paulsen, G. The island   **Fic**

History

See/See also pages in the following book(s):

Katz, W. L. Black pioneers p136-42 (7 and up)   **920**

Wisdom tales from around the world. Forest, H.   **398.2**

Wise, David Burgess *See* Burgess Wise, David

The **wise** king. Jaffe, N.

In Jaffe, N. The cow of no color: riddle stories and justice tales from around the world p118-21   **398.2**

The **wise** little girl. Fairman, T.

In Fairman, T. Bury my bones but keep my words p153-65   **398.2**

The **wise** men of Chelm [play] Asher, S. F.

In Theatre for young audiences p217-43   **812.008**

Wise words of Paul Tiulana. Tiulana, P.   **92**

The **wish** giver. Brittain, B.   **Fic**

Wishes

Fiction

Brittain, B. The wish giver   **Fic**

Wisler, G. Clifton, 1950-

Caleb's choice   **Fic**

The drummer boy of Vicksburg   **Fic**

Red Cap   **Fic**

Wit and humor

See also Humorous poetry

Witch girl. Coatsworth, E. J.

In A Newbery Halloween p13-21   **S C**

Witch-hunt. Vande Velde, V.

In Vande Velde, V. Curses, Inc. and other stories p144-53   **S C**

The **witch** in the wood. White, T. H.

In White, T. H. The once and future king   **Fic**

The **witch** of Blackbird Pond. Speare, E. G.   **Fic**

Witchbirds. San Souci, R.

In San Souci, R. A terrifying taste of short & shivery p68-72   **398.2**

Witchcraft

See also Magic

Fremon, D. K. The Salem witchcraft trials in American history   **133.4**

Kallen, S. A. The Salem witch trials (7 and up)   **133.4**

Roach, M. K. In the days of the Salem witchcraft trials   **133.4**

Wilson, L. L. The Salem witch trials   **133.4**

See/See also pages in the following book(s):

Cohen, D. Cults p90-101 (7 and up)   **291.9**

Fiction

Duncan, L. Summer of fear (7 and up)   **Fic**

Ibbotson, E. Which witch?   **Fic**

Lasky, K. Beyond the burning time (7 and up)   **Fic**

Mahy, M. The changeover   **Fic**

Norton, A. Witch World [series] (7 and up)   **Fic**

Petry, A. L. Tituba of Salem Village   **Fic**

Speare, E. G. The witch of Blackbird Pond   **Fic**

Thesman, J. The other ones (7 and up)   **Fic**

Witches

Fiction

Rowling, J. K. Harry Potter and the sorcerer's stone   **Fic**

The **witch's** boar. Hamilton, V.

In Hamilton, V. The dark way p113-18   **398.2**

The **witch's** eye. Naylor, P. R.

In A Newbery Halloween p83-99   **S C**

The **witch's** head. San Souci, R.

In San Souci, R. A terrifying taste of short & shivery p77-81   **398.2**

The **witch's** skinny. Hamilton, V.

In Hamilton, V. The dark way p143-48   **398.2**

The **witch's** son. Vande Velde, V.

In Vande Velde, V. Curses, Inc. and other stories p180-217   **S C**

With a way, hey, Mister Stormalong. Cohn, A.

In From sea to shining sea p104-06   **810.8**

With a whoop and a holler. Van Laan, N.   **398**

With every drop of blood. Collier, J. L.   **Fic**

With heroic truth: the life of Edward R. Murrow. Finkelstein, N. H.   **92**

With his head tucked underneath his arm. Coville, B.

In Coville, B. Oddly enough p33-41   **S C**

With love. Goodall, J.   **599.8**

With my eyes closed. Arenas, R.

In Where angels glide at dawn p33-41   **S C**

With needle and thread. Bial, R.   **746.46**

Within reach: my Everest story. Pfetzer, M.   **796.52**

Witman, Kathleen

(ed) CD's, superglue, and salsa [series 2] *See* CD's, superglue, and salsa [series 2]   **670**

Witnesses
Fiction
Stevenson, J. The unprotected witness   **Fic**
Witnesses to freedom. Rochelle, B.   **323.1**
Witnesses to war. Leapman, M.   **940.53**
Wittlinger, Ellen
  Hard love (7 and up)   **Fic**
A **wizard** abroad. Duane, D.   **Fic**
A **wizard** of Earthsea. Le Guin, U. K.   **Fic**
The **wizard's** map. Yolen, J.   **Fic**
WNBA *See* Women's National Basketball Association
The **woeful** princess. Skinner, D.
  In Trapped!: cages of mind and body p47-64   **S C**
Wolf, Bernard, 1930-
  HIV positive   **362.1**
  If I forget Thee, O Jerusalem   **956.94**
Wolf, Phyllis
  White-out
  In Talking leaves   **S C**
Wolf, Robert V.
  Capital punishment (7 and up)   **364.66**
The **wolf.** Mitchell, H. R.   **599.77**
Wolf by the ears. Rinaldi, A.   **Fic**
Wolf Chief, d. 1934
See/See also pages in the following book(s):
  Duncan, D. People of the West p102-15   **978**
Wolf children *See* Wild children
Wolf rider: a tale of terror. Avi   **Fic**
Wolf-speaker. Pierce, T.   **Fic**
Wolf stalker. Skurzynski, G. See note under Skurzynski, G. Cliff hanger   **Fic**
Wolfbay Wings [series]
  Brooks, B. Zip   **Fic**
Wolff, Lisa, 1954-
  Teen depression (7 and up)   **616.85**
Wolff, Tobias, 1945-
  This boy's life [excerpt]
  In Who do you think you are? p83-91   **S C**
Wolff, Virginia Euwer
  Bat 6   **Fic**
  Brownian motion
  In Ultimate sports: short stories by outstanding writers for young adults p207-36   **S C**
  Make lemonade   **Fic**
  The Mozart season   **Fic**
  Probably still Nick Swansen (7 and up)   **Fic**
Wolfman, Ira
  Do people grow on family trees?   **929**
Wolfram, von Eschenbach, 12th cent.
  Parzival; adaptation. See Paterson, K. Parzival   **398.2**
Wolfson, Evelyn
  From Abenaki to Zuni   **970.004**
  From the earth to beyond the sky   **970.004**
Wolkstein, Diane
  Bye-bye
  In From sea to shining sea p367   **810.8**

Owl
  In From sea to shining sea p266-67   **810.8**
Wollstonecraft, Mary, 1759-1797
About
Miller, C. C. Mary Wollstonecraft and the rights of women (7 and up)   **92**
The **wolverine's** secret. Norman, H.
  In Norman, H. The girl who dreamed only geese, and other tales of the Far North   **398.2**
Wolves
  Mitchell, H. R. The wolf (7 and up)   **599.77**
  Smith, R. Journey of the red wolf   **599.77**
  Swinburne, S. R. Once a wolf   **333.95**
See/See also pages in the following book(s):
  Patent, D. H. Back to the wild p12-27   **639.9**
Fiction
George, J. C. Julie   **Fic**
George, J. C. Julie of the wolves   **Fic**
George, J. C. Julie's wolf pack   **Fic**
The **wolves** of Willoughby Chase. Aiken, J.   **Fic**
The **Woman,** Adam, and the fruit. Lester, J.
  In Lester, J. When the beginning began p81-85   **296.1**
Woman and Man started even. Hamilton, V.
  In Hamilton, V. Her stories p69-74   **398.2**
The **woman** in the snow. McKissack, P. C.
  In McKissack, P. C. The dark-thirty p55-65   **S C**
The **woman** in the wall. Kindl, P.   **Fic**
The **Woman** under the sea
  In The Dancing fox: Arctic folktales p12-19   **398.2**
The **woman** who left no footprints. McCaughrean, G.
  In McCaughrean, G. The bronze cauldron: myths and legends of the world p92-96   **398.2**
The **Woman** who lived by herself
  In The Dancing fox: Arctic folktales p78-83   **398.2**
The **woman** with the golden arm. Twain, M.
  In From sea to shining sea p342-43   **810.8**
Women
  See also Abused women; women of particular racial or ethnic groups, e.g. *African American women;* and women in various occupations and professions
Women's almanac   **305.4**
Biography
Gaines, A. Entertainment & performing arts   **920**
Hacker, C. Nobel Prize winners   **920**
Herstory: women who changed the world (7 and up)   **920**
Jones, V. B. Government & politics   **920**
Lindop, L. Champions of equality (7 and up)   **920**

World War, 1939-1945—*Continued*

Jews

See also Holocaust, 1933-1945

Adler, D. A. We remember the Holocaust
940.53

Boas, J. We are witnesses (7 and up)
940.53

Fluek, T. K. Memories of my life in a Polish village, 1930-1949 (7 and up) **92**

Koehn, I. Mischling, second degree: my childhood in Nazi Germany **92**

Lyman, D. Holocaust rescuers **920**

Reiss, J. The upstairs room **92**

Siegal, A. Upon the head of the goat: a childhood in Hungary, 1939-1944 **92**

Jews—Rescue

Bierman, J. Righteous gentile [biography of Raoul Wallenberg] (7 and up) **92**

Kustanowitz, E. The hidden children of the Holocaust (7 and up) **940.53**

Meltzer, M. Rescue: the story of how Gentiles saved Jews in the Holocaust **940.53**

Opdyke, I. G. In my hands (7 and up)
940.53

Sherrow, V. The righteous gentiles (7 and up)
940.53

Literature and the war—Bibliography

Holsinger, M. P. The ways of war **016.8**

Naval operations

McGowen, T. Sink the Bismarck **940.54**

Personal narratives

Dahl, R. Going solo **92**

Friedman, I. R. The other victims **940.53**

Hautzig, E. R. The endless steppe: growing up in Siberia **92**

Opdyke, I. G. In my hands (7 and up)
940.53

Reparations

Alonso, K. Korematsu v. United States (7 and up) **323.1**

Women

Anderson, M. K. So proudly they served
940.54

Germany

McGowen, T. Germany's lightning war
940.54

Japan

Maruki, T. Hiroshima no pika **940.54**

Poland

Opdyke, I. G. In my hands (7 and up)
940.53

United States

Brimner, L. D. Voices from the camps (7 and up) **940.53**

Colman, P. Rosie the riveter **331.4**

Hamanaka, S. The journey **305.8**

Houston, J. W. Farewell to Manzanar (7 and up) **940.53**

Isserman, M. World War II (7 and up)
940.53

Levine, E. A fence away from freedom (7 and up) **940.53**

Stanley, J. I am an American **940.53**

See/See also pages in the following book(s):

Trotter, J. W. From a raw deal to a New Deal? African Americans, 1929-1945 p87-109 (7 and up) **305.8**

World War, 1939-1945, in literature *See* World War, 1939-1945—Literature and the war

World War I. Bosco, P. I. **940.3**

World War I. Gay, K. **940.3**

World War II. Gay, K. **940.53**

World War II. Isserman, M. **940.53**

World War II. McGowen, T. **940.53**

World War II in Europe. Stein, R. C. **940.54**

World War II in the Pacific. Stein, R. C.
940.54

World War II: a student companion. O'Neill, W. L. **940.53**

World Wide Web

Jefferis, D. Cyberspace **004.6**

Kyker, K. Wading the World Wide Web
004.6

Lampton, C. The World Wide Web **004.6**

Minkel, W. Delivering Web reference services to young people **025.04**

World wide web sites *See* Web sites

World writers [series]

Miller, C. C. Mary Wollstonecraft and the rights of women **92**

Worldmark encyclopedia of cultures and daily life **306**

Worldmark encyclopedia of the nations
910.3

Worldmark encyclopedia of the states
973.03

Worms

Pascoe, E. Earthworms **592**

Worms and lice

In The Dancing fox: Arctic folktales p35-38
398.2

Wormser, Richard, 1933-

American Islam (7 and up) **297**

Growing up in the Great Depression (7 and up)
973.91

The **worst** day of my life. Murphy, J.

In Murphy, J. Night terrors p89-95 **S C**

Worth, Richard, 1945-

Women in combat (7 and up) **355**

Worth the risk. Erlbach, A. **302**

Wortis, Avi *See* Avi, 1937-

Woster, Alice

Hubbub on the bookshelf

In The Big book of holiday plays p63-77
812.008

Would my fortune cookie lie?. Pevsner, S.
Fic

Wounded Knee: an Indian history of the American West. Ehrlich, A. **970.004**

Wounded Knee Creek, Battle of, 1890

Streissguth, T. Wounded Knee, 1890 (7 and up)
973.8

The **wounded** wolf. George, J. C.

In A Newbery zoo **S C**

PART 3

SELECT LIST OF RECOMMENDED CD-ROMs

SELECT LIST OF RECOMMENDED CD-ROMs

AASL electronic library. 1999 edition. American Lib. Assn. 1 disc $30   **025.1**
1. School libraries
Windows

A searchable database of documents related to school library media including directories of organizations, book award lists, full-text articles and reports. Bibliographies of print and non-print resources are arranged thematically, and selected ERIC documents address trends and issues ranging from integrated library systems and the Internet, to assessment and copyright guidelines

American decades. Gale Res. 1998 1 disc $600   **973.9**
1. United States—History—1900-1999 (20th century)
2. United States—Civilization
Windows

"Provides 1500 essays, 200 primary source documents, 1000 biographies, and multimedia (more than 30 minutes of audio and video clips, and 1300 images) to engage students in learning about 20th century American history." SLJ

American government. ABC-CLIO Interactive 1998 1 disc $79   **973**
1. United States—Politics and government—Sources
Windows and MAC

Provides 1544 resources and primary source documents that can be used for research and to create multimedia slide presentations with tools included in the program. Resources include text, tables, graphics, photographs, and audio and video clips. Information can be located by topic, type of material, or keyword. Useful for government, American history, and civics courses

American history inspirer: The Civil War. Tom Snyder Productions, 80 Coolidge Hill Rd., Watertown, Mass. 02172-2817 1997 1 disc $79.95   **973.7**
1. United States—History—1861-1865, Civil War
Windows and MAC

Familiarizes students with early American history and geography and the distribution of ante-bellum resources and population through "trip planning" games. Strategy involves the consideration of factors such as dispersions of wealth, slaves, railroad track, industrial capacity, and staple crops; or shifts in population. Useful in one-computer classrooms since trip planning can be done offline

American leaders: profiles of great Americans. ABC-CLIO Interactive 1999 1 disc $129   **920**
1. United States—Biography
Windows and MAC

Information on the personal and professional lives of over 1200 Americans who have made outstanding contributions to American political, cultural, and social development. Men and women from diverse backgrounds are represented, including African-Americans, Hispanics, and Asians. A timeline feature represents biographees in relation to world events and other famous individuals

The **American** multimedia archive: the complete collection. Facts on File 1998 1 disc $299.95   **973**
1. United States—History
Windows

A collection of information, images, primary source documents, and multimedia that spans pre-Revolutionary America to the present based on the American Historical Images on File series. More than two thousand entries are organized into eleven eras. Topics within each era include Native Americans, African Americans, government, foreign affairs, and culture. Audio and video clips as well as a timeline are included for each of the time periods

Archaeological detective. Micro-Intel, 12000 Papinean Ave., Montreal, Que. Can. 42K 4RS 1997 1 disc $45   **930.1**
1. Archeology
Windows and MAC

Presents detailed information about the field of archaeology in a multimedia tutorial that explains the inquiry steps: preparations, excavating, analyzing data, interpreting findings, and sharing the information. In a series of five missions, users try to determine the identity of skeletal remains found at a site in Montreal. Clues are provided in the form of interactive puzzles, multiple-choice questions, video commentary by experts, and documents

Asia inspirer 4.0. Tom Snyder Productions 1998 1 disc $79.95   **950**
1. Asia
Windows and MAC

In this interactive adventure, students plan a path across Asia and collect various resources and commodities. Along the way, students learn about topics such as exports, natural resources, elevation, land area, population density, and regions

Biolab: fly. Pierian Spring Software, 5200 S.W. Macadam Ave., Suite 570, Portland, Or. 97201 1998 1 disc (Biolab series) $49   **595.7**
1. Flies
Windows and MAC

Three simulated experiments allow users to investigate dominant and recessive traits, hidden recessive genes, and sex-linked traits. From a menu, users choose from twenty-six traits to breed flies, and record results in a log. Progress is saved and can be viewed by teachers. Useful as an alternative to breeding real fruit flies, and for review and reinforcement of genetic concepts

Biolab: frog. Pierian Spring Software 1997 1 disc (Biolab series) $49   **597.8**
1. Frogs
Windows and MAC

This "real-life" dissection simulation provides an in-depth lab experience in the physiology of amphibians. Students can explore the frog's external mouth and its digestive, circulatory, reproductive, and skeletal systems

Biology concepts through discovery: Pollution. Educational Activities, P.O. Box 392, Freeport, N.Y. 11520 1997 1 disc $89   **363.7**
1. Pollution

Windows and MAC

This interactive program covers such topics as acid rain, endangered species, the effects of chemical and hazardous waste, the greenhouse effect, and ozone depletion. Scientific inquiry sections include video and writing activities that focus on biodegradability and air pollution. A list of words and terms as well as a review section with multiple choice questions and their answers are also provided

Body works 6.0. Learning Co., 7104 Ambassador Rd., Baltimore, Md. 21244-2732 1997 1 disc $69.95   **612**
1. Human anatomy 2. Physiology

Windows

This multimedia journey through the human body features 80 rotating virtual reality models (with 360-degree views); live-action videos and animations of body processes; x-rays, a sonogram and childbirth; audio pronunciations and definitions for more than 1,400 medical terms; over 400,000 words of text covering all aspects of anatomy and physiology. Includes a Web site index listing health-related resources

Book review digest. Wilson, H.W. 2000 1 disc apply to publisher for price   **028.1**
1. Books—Reviews

Windows and MAC

This work "provides excerpts from, and citations to, reviews of adult and juvenile fiction and nonfiction, trade books, and reference books. It currently covers reviews of almost 7,000 English-language publications each year that appear in 95 (26 recent additions) American, British, and Canadian periodicals in the humanities, social sciences, and general sciences, plus library review media. Entries, arranged alphabetically by author or title (as appropriate), give author, title, paging, price, publisher and year, ISBN, a descriptive introduction to the book, age or grade level (for juvenile works), suggested Sears subject headings, and LC card number. Reviewing information includes citations of reviews, name of reviewers, approximate length of each review, and up to four review excerpts chosen to provide a balance of opinion." Safford. Guide to Ref Materials for Sch Libr Media Cent. 5th edition

Boxer introductory algebra. Boxer Learning, 105 W. Main St., Suite A, Charlottesville, Va. 22902-5031 1997 1 disc (Boxer series) $49.98   **512**
1. Algebra

Windows

This program "uses guided interactive tutorials to introduce basic algebraic concepts. Content is divided into ten chapters that include lessons on topics such as integers; exponents; solving equations and inequalities; fractions and decimals; slope; and square roots." SLJ

Carmen Sandiego math detective. School edition. Broderbund, 7104 Ambassador Rd., Baltimore, Md. 21244-2732 1998 1 disc $59.95   **513**
1. Mathematics

Windows and MAC

This is an interactive CD-ROM challenging users to solve problems pertaining to numeration, geometry, measurement, and problem solving. The program is stimulating and exciting and offers a range of levels that can be individualized. It is an excellent resource for practicing math skills

Carmen Sandiego word detective. School edition. Broderbund 1997 1 disc $59.95   **420**
1. English language—Study and teaching 2. Word games

Windows and MAC

In this program students can "rescue the ACME agents who have been rendered speechless by Carmen's babble-on machine, [and] teachers can use the individual games separately to reinforce skills in grammar, spelling, alphabetizing, and vocabulary. Five independent activities are offered to accommodate a wide range of ages and abilities. Students can work on prefixes and suffixes to build new words or fill in missing parts of speech to complete stories reminiscent of the ever popular Mad-Libs games. Teacher components include a very helpful tracking section, customized spelling lists, tutorials, and lesson plans." Booklist

Chronicle encyclopedia of history. DK Interactive Learning 1997 1 disc $29.95   **902**
1. Historical chronology 2. World history

Windows

Also available school version

Presents highlights of history from prehistoric times to the modern era in "news of the day" format. Each of the fourteen eras have text that elaborates on a headline event, supplemented with captioned photos, narrated slides, and video. "History in the Making" provides overviews of the history and culture of twelve periods from Ancient Egypt to major wars in later centuries. Includes links to profiles of significant historical figures and to a Web site with updated information and top news stories

The **complete** National Geographic 110 years. Learning Co. 1998 32 discs $99.99   **910.5**
1. Geography—Periodicals

Windows

A complete file of 110 years of the National Geographic Magazine that includes articles, images, maps, etc. A powerful search engine makes it easy for students to locate specific articles by date, issue, topic or title

The **complete** reference collection. Learning Co. 1997 1 disc $49.95   **031**
1. Encyclopedias and dictionaries

Windows

Includes information from Compton's concise encyclopedia 1998; Webster's New World dictionary; Webster's New World thesaurus; Compton's world atlas; Merriam-Webster's geographical dictionary; World history: A Dictionary of important people, places, and events; Merriam-Webster's concise handbook for writers; The World Almanac and book of facts 1997; Compton's Internet directory; and The Columbia University complete home medical guide

Compton's encyclopedia deluxe. Learning Co. 2000 1 disc $69.95   **031**
1. Encyclopedias and dictionaries

Windows

Compton's encyclopedia deluxe—*Continued*

Includes over 40,000 articles, 700 sound clips, 150 videos and animations; a notebook and highlighter to track research findings; an up-to-date world atlas, dictionary, and thesaurus; a local, cultural resource guide based on the user's zip code; access to hundreds of full text newspapers, magazines, and news wires; and interactive timelines and links to more than 4,000 Web sites

Constitution and the Supreme Court. Primary Source Media (for sale by the Gale Group) 1997 1 disc (American journey: history in your hands) $149   **347.73**
1. United States. Supreme Court 2. United States. Constitution

Windows and MAC

"This CD-ROM offers a wealth of documents and pictures all relating to the U.S. Constitution and Supreme Court. Hyperlinked together with the original documents are signed essays that evaluate the source and put it in a historical context. Navigation is very simple, with an always present button menu at the bottom of the screen and blue hyperlinks within documents. The guide presents a list of the documents arranged by the Articles of the Constitution for easy integration into a history or government class, and a keyword search capability makes the program particularly useful for research." Booklist

Cornerstone mathematics. SkillsBank Corp., 7104 Ambassador Rd., Baltimore, Md. 21244-2732 1997 Each level 1 disc $249   **510**
1. Mathematics

Windows and MAC

CD-ROM designed as a comprehensive resource for identifying and meeting the needs of students in grades 3-8. The program offers review and practice in the content areas of number concepts, whole number computation and estimation, data and graphs, and decimals, fractions, and percents. Colorful graphics, animated characters, and lively music give this CD-ROM an entertaining twist. Level A grades 3-4; level B grades 5-6; level C grades 7-8

Critical mass: America's race to build the atomic bomb. Forest Technologies, 765 Industrial Dr., Cary, Ill. 60013 1998 1 disc $29.95   **621.48**
1. Atomic bomb 2. Nuclear energy

Windows and MAC

Also available school version

This interactive CD-ROM charts the development of the atomic bomb from its inception to its first explosion at the Trinity test site. Users meet many of the key people in the Manhattan Project, with illustrated biographies of scientists who were vital to the project

The cruncher 2.0. Knowledge Adventure, 19840 Pioneer Ave., Torrance, Calif. 90503 1999 1 disc $99.95   **005.7**
1. Graphic methods

Windows and MAC

This is a CD-ROM program that teaches students about the construction of spreadsheets. Spread over six tutorials, program users are introduced to basic concepts through the use of appealing graphics, cross-curricular projects, and friendly mentor guides. A project section has twenty activities that integrate spreadsheets into math, language arts, science, social studies, and art

Data explorer. Sunburst Communications 1998 1 disc $89.95   **005.7**
1. Statistics 2. Electronic data processing

Windows and MAC

Introduces statistics through the process of collecting data in spreadsheets; displaying the results in tables and graphs; and interpreting the results. Users can work with category data, number data, or mixed data. Includes directions for graphing and interpreting various types of graphs and sample surveys and directions for creating, recording, and printing survey information

Decisions, decisions: the Constitution. Tom Snyder Productions 1999 1 disc $149.95   **342**
1. Constitutional history—United States

Windows and MAC

This CD enables students to become familiar with the decision-making process involved in the formation of the U.S. Constitution. The program also provides an introduction to such topics as the balance of power, the ratification process, and the Great Compromise

The **digital** field trip to the rainforest. Educational version. Digital Frog International, 7377 Calfass Rd., Rural Route 2, Puslinch, Ont., Can. NOB 2JO 1997 1 disc $99   **577.34**
1. Rain forests

Windows and MAC

With this CD users take a virtual walking tour through the Blue Creek Rainforest Reserve in Belize. An extensive study of the rainforest is provided that can be used for research in biology, general science, and environmental studies. Narrated instructions on how to navigate are available from a "Quick Tour," and any word in the text can be clicked for a definition

The **digital** field trip to the wetlands. Digital Frog International 1996 1 disc $99   **577.63**
1. Wetlands

Windows and MAC

This exploration of the wetlands is notable for its use of pictures and an interface that simulates a field trip to a bog in Ontario. The program offers a fun experience supported by enough instructional information to make it an excellent teaching tool

DISCovering biography. Gale Group 1997 1 disc $500   **920**
1. Biography

Windows

This reference database covers 2000 of the most commonly studied people from ancient times to the present, from all areas of the world, and numerous fields of interest. This CD-ROM utilizes multimedia technology of images, sounds, illustrations, and photographs to enhance the presentation of the biographies

The **dynamic** rainforest. Learning Team, 84 Business Park Dr., Suite 309, Armonk, N.Y. 10504 1997 1 disc $49.95   **577.34**
1. Rain forests 2. Natural history—Australia

Windows and MAC

The dynamic rainforest—*Continued*
Introduces the intricacies of Australia's tropical rainforest. Videos and activities help students understand topics such as the evolution of the Australian Wet Tropics; how scientists identify trees and research species relationships; and how natural decomposition contributes to the recycling and regeneration of the rainforest. There are sections that highlight frogs, insects, and birds with sounds and photographs, and text windows introduce rainforest flora and fauna

Earth quest. DK Interactive Learning 1997 1 disc (Eyewitness virtual reality series) $29.95
550
1. Earth sciences
Windows and MAC
This CD-ROM allows the user to explore a cavernous, virtual reality museum within the earth. The program includes information on rocks, earthquakes, underground mining, valleys, canyons, coastlines, land masses, gemstones, and minerals

Ellis: intro and middle mastery. CALI, 1675 N. Freedom Blvd., Suite 2A, Provo, Utah 84606 1998 3 discs + 2 workbooks and 2 teacher's guides $995 (intro); $695 (middle mastery)
420
1. English language—Study and teaching 2. English as a second language
Windows
A variety of multimedia activities provide English-as-a-second-language (ESL) students with the opportunity to develop skills in areas such as listening, speaking, reading, and writing. The CD-ROM is suitable for novice-low to intermediate-high ESL learners and would be an asset for secondary classrooms or schools with an ESL student population

Encarta Africana 2000. Microsoft Corp., One Microsoft Way, Redmond, Wash. 98052 2 discs $69.95
960
1. Africa—Encyclopedias
Windows
This is a resource about African history, culture, and people of African descent. "Video, audio clips, photos, graphs and charts enhance articles. All of the resources may be easily accessed because navigation to the many sources of information is clearly delineated." SLJ

Encarta encyclopedia deluxe 2000. Microsoft Corp. 2 discs $69.95
031
1. Encyclopedias and dictionaries
Windows
This deluxe edition, contains over 40,000 articles, 14,000 photos and illustrations, 2,500 audio clips and 170 videos and animations. Other features include a multimedia collage section, 360-degree panoramic views, Web links, monthly updates, a curriculum guide, timeline and access to a news and periodical database

Encarta interactive world atlas 2000. Microsoft Corp. 2 discs $54.95
910
1. Atlases
Windows
Variant title: Encarta virtual globe

This version takes older students on three-dimensional virtual flights around the globe. The program uses articles and World Tours that combine text and multimedia to provide detailed interactive maps and cultural information. This CD-ROM also includes over 10,000 links to the Internet

Encarta reference suite 2000. Microsoft Corp. 5 discs $99.95
031
1. Encyclopedias and dictionaries
Windows
This set "includes Encarta's Deluxe Encyclopedia, Interactive World Atlas, and World English Dictionary (with Roget's Thesaurus, Encarta Book of Quotations, Computer Dictionary, Manual of Style, and Almanac). [Features include] 42,000 articles, 10,000 historical archive articles, more than 40 million words, 17,000 photos and illustrations, more than 170 videos and animations, 2,500 audio clips, 31,500 Web Links, a Timeline, and Curriculum Guide." Multimedia Sch

Encyclopaedia Britannica. Encyclopaedia Britannica Educ. Corp., 310 S. Michigan Ave., Chicago, Ill. 60604 2000 2 discs $59.95
031
1. Encyclopedias and dictionaries
Windows
Contains the full text of the 32-volume Encyclopaedia Britannica print set, the complete Merriam-Webster's Collegiate Dictionary, 10th Edition plus photos, interactive maps, timelines, and a research assistant

Encyclopedia of careers and vocational guidance. 2nd ed. Ferguson, J.G. 2000 1 disc $159.95
331.7
1. Occupations 2. Vocational guidance
Windows
An electronic version of the print title, providing articles on 500 careers in technical and professional fields, as well as descriptions of military jobs. There are addresses of organizations, scholarships, and internships with an option to create simple form letters to request additional information. Entries for the military cover physical demands, helpful attributes for interested candidates, training etc. Sixty articles on industries describe job opportunities

Encyclopedia of world biography. Gale Group 1999 1 disc $975
920
1. Biography
Windows
This CD-ROM presents biographical information on over 7,000 individuals. It provides an insight into each individual's life, contribution, and place in history and enables users to cross-reference information across time, place, and subject area

Europe inspirer 4.0. Tom Snyder Productions 1997 1 disc (Inspirer geography series) $79.95
914
1. Europe—Geography
Windows and MAC
Familiarizes students with maps of Europe as they plan routes in search of key resources. Students interpret maps and recognize geographic patterns as they learn about new countries of Eastern Europe, geographic locations of 48 countries, and natural resource distribution

Everything weather. Sunburst Communications, 101 Castleton St., Pleasantville, N.Y. 10570-9971 1996 1 disc $79.95 **551.5**
1. Weather 2. Meteorology
Windows and MAC

An aid to developing weather forecasting skills, this program allows students to observe and examine powerful weather phenomena. It teaches them how to identify cloud formations and their importance as signals of approaching weather and involves them in tracking hurricanes, inputting longitude and latitude, calculating the closeness of a thunderstorm, and creating weather charts

Exploring numbers. Pierian Spring Software 1998 1 disc (Odyssey of discovery series) $39
513
1. Mathematics
Windows and MAC

Five interactive modules explore major math concepts such as ordering and operations, decimals and integers, classification of real numbers, prime numbers, number patterns, exponents, square numbers and square roots, and scientific notation. The program adjusts the level of difficulty in response to correct answers. Includes a glossary with definitions of mathematical terms augmented with pronunciations and illustrations

Exploring the Nardoo. Learning Team 1997 1 disc $149.95 **994**
1. Ecology 2. Rivers
Windows and MAC

This CD-ROM uses interactive multimedia to allow students to study the environmental effects of urbanization on an imaginary pure Australian river system. The computer program provides students with practice in interpreting graphs, collecting quantitative data, analyzing media reports for bias, following correct scientific investigative technique, and organizing information for reports and presentations

Eyewitness encyclopedia of nature 2.0. DK Interactive Learning 1998 1 disc $29.95
503
1. Science—Encyclopedias 2. Nature study—Encyclopedias
Windows and MAC

Covers the behavior of animals in their natural habitat, the calls of birds of prey, environmental systems of the natural world, microscopic life, and the effects of climate. Introduces over 250 plants and animals through video sequences and sound clips

Eyewitness encyclopedia of science 2.0. DK Interactive Learning 1997 1 disc $29.95
503
1. Science—Encyclopedias
Windows and MAC

This CD-ROM contains all the references for physics, mathematics, earth science, and chemistry that could possibly be required. This extensive program is particularly suitable as a reference in a science laboratory or library media center at the middle level to college level

Eyewitness history of the world 2.0. DK Interactive Learning 1998 1 disc $29.95
902
1. Historical chronology 2. World history
Windows and MAC
Also available school version

This program allows viewers to select from ten time zones and four geographic areas. The articles are brief and engaging, while the maps, engaging photos, and sketches make the program visually stimulating. Includes a comprehensive U.S. history section and a Who's Who of over 200 biographies

Factory deluxe. Sunburst Communications 1998 1 disc $89.95 **513**
1. Mathematics
Windows and MAC

Five activities centered around a factory assembly line theme help students learn about shapes, rotations, angles and geometric attributes, perform computation with formulas; and utilize problem-solving strategies in five activities. There are nine levels of difficulty and teachers can monitor progress. Includes a calculator and journal feature

Facts on File world news CD-ROM. Facts on File News Services 2000 1 disc $1,150 per year with quarterly updates **031.02**
1. Current events 2. World history
Windows

This full-text database incorporates 20 years of Facts on File World News Digest, from January 1980 to the latest quarter and is enhanced with material from Today's Science on File, Issues and Controversies on File, and Funk and Wagnalls new encyclopedia. Also provided are country profiles, maps, news photos, biographies, and a collection of United States and international primary source documents

Famous first facts. Wilson, H.W. 2000 1 disc $150 **031.02**
1. Encyclopedias and dictionaries 2. United States—History
Windows

An electronic database compiled from the print edition of Famous first facts that covers a wide range of topics in American history, including noteworthy first events in science, the arts, health, and education. Searches can be refined by limiting to subject, name, city, date, or keywords

A **field** trip to the rainforest deluxe. Sunburst Communications 1998 1 disc $89.95
577.34
1. Rain forests
Windows and MAC

This CD-ROM allows students to journey through three major tropical rain forests in Africa, South America, and Southeast Asia. Student explorations on this virtual field trip are aided by the program's interactivity and high-quality graphics

Find it! science. Learning Team 1999 1 disc $149.95 **016.5**
1. Science—Bibliography
Windows and MAC

This is a searchable database of over 3,300 science books. The CD-ROM allows searches to be performed in nine areas and also includes facilities that enable searches to be narrowed. The topics covered in the database are relevant to elementary and middle school science curricula, and it is intended for use by students, teachers, and media specialists

Fire!. Tom Snyder Productions 1997 1 disc (Prime time math series) $79.95   **513**
1. Mathematics
Windows and MAC
Designed as a cooperative learning activity, this program applies problem solving to real-life experiences. Math skills involving formulas, basic algebra, measurement, order of operations, percents, rates, and the Pythagorean Theorem are used to assist fire fighters. Students collect data about water pressure, friction loss, hose and ladder lengths, size of nozzle tips, distance, rate, and building dimensions in order to complete the rescue. Correlated to NCTM Standards

Founding leaders: shapers of modern nations. ABC-CLIO Interactive 1998 1 disc $49
     920
1. Biography
Windows
Designed to provide an understanding of the genesis of countries and the men and women who were instrumental in these beginnings. There are lengthy biographies of over 300 political, intellectual, and military leaders, from the twelfth century to the present. Photos, links to related concepts and people, and maps are included when relevant

Fractions. Pierian Spring Software 1997 1 disc (Odyssey of discovery series) $39   **513**
1. Mathematics
Windows and MAC
Using a virtual reality format, this program engages users in practice with equivalent fractions; fraction calculations; ratios and percentages; and reducing, comparing, and ordering fractions. Each of the five interactive activities is introduced with brief text and a narrated overview. If errors are made by students in any activity, the level of difficulty is decreased and additional problems are displayed

Geometry inventor. Riverdeep Interactive Learning, 125 Cambridge Park Dr., Cambridge, Mass. 02140 1999 1 disc $99   **513**
1. Mathematics
Windows and MAC
Includes measurement tools for constructing geometry figures and for measuring length, angles, and area

Grolier multimedia encyclopedia, deluxe edition. Grolier Educ. 2000 2 discs $29.95   **031**
1. Encyclopedias and dictionaries
Windows and MAC
Offers all the features of the standard Grolier encyclopedia plus guided tours; interactive maps; and more. This "edition of GME boasts more than 16 hours of sound, Research Starters, a New Millennium Feature (focusing on the past 1000 years of world history), and 50 Historical Panoramas." Libr J

The **Horn** Book guide interactive. Heinemann (Portsmouth), 361 Hanover St., Portsmouth, N.H. 03801-3912 1998 1 disc $35   **028.505**
1. Children's literature—Periodicals 2. Books—Reviews
Windows and MAC
An electronic version of the print title with short reviews of books for children and young adults. Titles are rated on a scale from one to six. Searchable by title, author, subject, grade level, genre, etc.

Immigrant experience. Primary Source Media (for sale by the Gale Group) 1997 1 disc (American journey: history in your hands) $149
     325.73
1. United States—Immigration and emigration
Windows and MAC
This multimedia program studies immigration from the days of the early republic to present times. Immigration patterns are presented using documents, pictures, audio interviews, time lines, maps, and graphs

Information superhighway driver training course. Neal-Schuman 1997 1 disc + training guide package $49.95   **004.6**
1. Internet
Windows and MAC
A self-guide tutorial featuring a simulated environment that is designed to prepare students to use the Internet. The program begins with the history of the Internet; how a Web browser functions; and appropriate and inappropriate uses of the Internet. After taking a "Learner's Test," users learn about URLs; search engines and structuring searches; printing; bookmarking; and using E-mail with Pegasus Mail, Eudora Light, or Netscape Mail

InfoTrac Junior Edition. Gale Group 1999 1 disc $795 per year, updated quarterly   **051**
1. Periodicals—Indexes
Windows
Formerly SuperTom Junior
Provides coverage of the most recent thirty-six months of sixty-two general interest magazines (fifty-two full text), Information Please Almanacs, and thousands of articles from the Knight-Ridder/Tribune News Service. Magazines include Time, Newsweek, and U.S. News and World Report as well as popular titles such as Discover, Psychology Today, Current Biography, Popular Science, and Life. Topics span current events, social issues, the arts, science, health, etc.

Insects: little creatures in a big world. Learning Team 1997 1 disc $49.95   **595.7**
1. Insects
Windows and MAC
An extensive multimedia resource on eighteen species of insects. An "Insect Gallery" has data on the habitat, food, and life cycle of more than 600 insects, as well as photographs and audio recordings of singing insects. There are ten narrated videos and a variety of activities including an electron microscope feature to magnify details of insects

International inspirer 4.0. Tom Snyder Productions 1997 1 disc (Inspirer geography series) $79.95   **910**
1. Geography
Windows and MAC
Students move through 185 countries and investigate the geography, history, economics, demographics, politics, culture and daily life of each country

InventorLabs: technology. Houghton Mifflin Interactive (for sale by Sunburst Communications) 1997 1 disc $89.95   **609**
1. Edison, Thomas A. (Thomas Alva), 1847-1931 2. Bell, Alexander Graham, 1847-1922 3. Watts, James, 1955- 4. Inventions—History
Windows and MAC

InventorLabs: technology—*Continued*

Actors portraying the inventors Thomas Edison, Alexander Graham Bell, and James Watts introduce their virtual laboratories where users can explore personal objects and inventions. Nine interactive investigations cover heat and temperature, resistance of various metals, gear ratios, electrical circuits, sound waves, aerodynamics, lenses and light rays, pitch and frequency, and the use of magnets. An "Inventor Time Line" represents the contributions of the inventors in relation to historical events from 1840 to 1930

Junior DISCovering authors 2.0. Gale Group 1998 1 disc $400   **920**
1. Authors
Windows and MAC

Also known as U-X-L Junior DISCovering authors 2.0

Provides information on the lives and works of over 450 most-studied writers. Search options allow navigation by author, ethnicity, gender, title, subject, time period or character name. Includes plotlines of authors' best known works as well as author portraits

Landmark documents in American history 2.0. Facts on File 1998 1 disc $149.95   **973**
1. United States—History—Sources
Windows and MAC

Coverage includes Supreme Court decisions; treaties; essays; letters; legislation; speeches; government charters and constitutions; debates; party platforms; and all presidential inaugurals. Features introductions for every document, photos, video clips, biographies, and bibliographic information

Larson's leapfrog math intermediate 4. Meridian Creative Group, 2432 Shoreline Dr., Napa, Calif. 94558 1997 2 discs (Larson's leapfrog math series) $200   **513**
1. Mathematics
Windows and MAC

"Provides interactive practice in ten topics that align with National Council of Teachers of Mathematics (NCTM) Standards: number properties, multiplying mixed numbers, dividing fractions and mixed numbers, algebraic equations, geometry, ratios and proportions, percents, probability, and two sections on integers." SLJ

Larson's middle school math: an interactive approach. Meridian Creative Group 1998 4 discs (Larson's math series) $500   **513**
1. Mathematics
Windows and MAC

"Reinforces concepts covered in the middle school curriculum, based on NCTM Standards. The 20 modules include number concepts, number operations, percentage, fractions, probability, geometry, decimals, statistics, and basic Algebra." SLJ

Learn to speak Spanish 8.0. Learning Co. 1999 4 discs + cassette and textbook $49.95   **460**
1. Spanish language—Study and teaching
Windows and MAC

This is a comprehensive Spanish language instruction course that helps beginning learners to develop listening, reading, speaking, and writing skills and build grammar and vocabulary knowledge. Includes 30 lessons, audio and video clips of native speakers, cultural movies, and speech recognition technology

Library of Congress: eyes of the nation. SouthPeak Interactive, One Research Dr., Gary, N.C. 27513 1998 1 disc $39.95   **973**
1. United States—History
Windows

The world's largest library provides digital access to part of its collection with this program. Five sections incorporate over 3,000 images, text, and slide shows with narration. Time periods in American history are explored, as well as themes such as "The American Woman," "Arts," and "War." America can also be seen represented in daguerrotypes, panoramic maps, and other photography collections. Includes links to additional resources on the Library of Congress and History Channel Web sites

Living lab: plants. Mindplay, 160 W. Fort Lowell, Tucson, Ariz. 85705 1997 1 disc $79   **580**
1. Plants
Windows and MAC

This CD-ROM mixes three live-action videos with five interactive simulated laboratory experiments. Having viewed a video, students conduct botany experiments on the computer. These experiments combine scientific inquiry with narration, videos, tests, reviews and laboratory reports. This program is recommended as a basis for computer laboratory experiments and other related hands-on experiments in the classroom

Louvre Museum. Forest Technologies 1998 1 disc $29.95   **709**
1. Musée du Louvre
Windows and MAC

Provides a multimedia tour of approximately 150 works of art from the Louvre's collection. Activities and maps are included

Mapmaker's toolkit. Tom Snyder Productions 1999 1 disc $79.95   **526**
1. Maps
Windows and MAC

A library of more than 450 current and historical maps that allows students to research, customize, and publish their own maps. Layers can be applied to maps. Political features include regional and international boundaries, country names, cities, and continent names. Physical features include relief, grid, title, and water body labels. One hundred twenty-five historical maps correlated with major events, dates, locations, and topics are also available. Completed maps can be printed, displayed through the "Mapmakers Slide Show," or formatted and exported for use in other programs or on the Internet

Math for the real world. Knowledge Adventure 1997 1 disc $29.95   **513**
1. Mathematics
Windows and MAC

The premise of this game-type program is that users go on a road tour with a rock band, solving math problems and earning money to produce a music video. Players must keep an eye on their funds, the food meter, and the gas gauge. Money runs low from encountering road hazards and if math problems are not solved correctly. Over 4000 problems represent the categories of weight, volume, time, money, patterns, measurement, logic and critical thinking, fractions, and charts and graphs

Middle search plus. EBSCO Pub., 10 Estes St., Ipswich, Mass. 01938 1999 1 disc $899 per year includes monthly updates August thru May

051

1. Periodicals—Indexes

Windows and MAC

Contains indexing and abstracts for more than 180 periodicals with the full text of over 70 of these periodicals. Additional databases included with Middle Search Plus are Funk and Wagnalls new encyclopedia, 100 pamphlets, and EBSCO's Encyclopedia of animals. The information is stored on one current and one free backfile disc

Mighty math astro algebra. Edmark Corp., P.O. Box 97021, Redmond, Wash. 98073-9721 1997 1 disc (Mighty math series) $59.95

512

1. Algebra

Windows and MAC

This CD-ROM involves users signing in as captains of a spaceship and applying algebraic concepts to solve 92 missions that become more difficult as users automatically progress through the program. Topics covered include variables; functions and graphing; and fractions, decimals, and percents

Multicultural America. Primary Source Media (for sale by the Gale Group) 1997 1 disc (Documentary archives) $500

973

1. United States—History

Windows and MAC

Essays, photographs, and primary source materials introduce students to the multicultural history of America from early inhabitants to recent Asian and Hispanic immigrants. Themes explored include "Periods of contact between Native Americans and Europeans," "Newcomers since 1820," and "Legal obstacles to diversity." Includes more than 450 documents (some rare) and 400 images

The mystery of the pipe wreck. Sunburst Communications 1998 1 disc $99.95

930.1

1. Archeology 2. Shipwrecks

MAC

Interactive simulation of the exploration of an archaelogical site at the bottom of Monte Christi Bay in the Dominican Republic. Includes narrated text, photographs, sound, video clips, data tables, and charts. Students can explore six topics (pipes, jugs, ceramics, bones, "surprises," and timbers) that have narrated slide shows and videos with background information, problems to solve, and issues to examine

National Geographic maps. Mindscape (for sale by the Learning Co.) 1998 8 discs $119.95

912

1. Maps

Windows

This is an interactive program providing electronic access to every foldout map ever produced to accompany National Geographic Magazine. The CD-ROMs also provide multimedia presentations on topics related to the maps and the art of mapmaking

Native Americans: People of the desert. Rainbow Educational Media, 4540 Preslyn Dr., Raleigh, N.C. 27616-3177 1998 1 disc $99

970.004

1. Indians of North America—Southwestern States

Windows and MAC

Computer program that explores lives of Native Americans in the Southwestern States. It contains text, maps, slide shows, and video and audio tracks

Native Americans: People of the Plains. Rainbow Educational Media 1998 1 disc $99

970.004

1. Indians of North America—Great Plains

Windows and MAC

Uses text, narrated video, slide shows, and interactive elements to portray the history, culture, and accomplishments of the Plains Indians. There is information on the culture of early tribes; a video recreation of life in the 1800s from the perspective of a twelve-year-old boy; slides of 250 artifacts; a tour of the Knife River National Historic site in North Dakota; and a section on modern day Native Americans. Includes a reference section with photo and map archives, a map of Indian populations by state, a glossary, and five activities

The new way things work. DK Interactive Learning 1998 1 disc $29.95

600

1. Technology 2. Machinery 3. Inventions

Windows and MAC

This resource explains the workings of, and principles behind, more than 150 simple and complex machines and inventions. Includes more than 300 animations

NewsBank newsfile collection. NewsBank, 5020 Tamiami Trail N., Suite 110, Naples, Fla. 34103 1999 1 disc apply to publisher for price

051

1. Periodicals—Indexes

Windows and MAC

Consisting of over 500 regional, national, and international sources, this full-text news resource provides comprehensive coverage of current news, including social issues, economics, the environment, health and science, government and sports. Biographical articles on individuals, professions, and vocations, as well as reviews on theater, film, art, music, literature, and TV are also included

The Oregon trail. 4th ed. Learning Co. 1999 3 discs $39.95

979.5

1. Overland journeys to the Pacific 2. Oregon Trail 3. West (U.S.)—History

Windows and MAC

Also available school version

In this edition of the popular series, students blaze their own trail to Oregon, making choices at each juncture on the route. New character interaction allows students to communicate with characters along the way, learning about events and getting critical advice for their decision making. Includes 360-degree panning and full motion video; three levels of difficulty; and builds skills in map reading, decision making, reading comprehension, managing a budget, and critical thinking

The other side. Tom Snyder Productions 1999 1 disc $79.95

300

1. Social sciences

Windows and MAC

In this program students from around the country are allowed to experience global conflict-resolution skills in one classroom, between networked classrooms, or with other schools via the Internet. Two opposing groups must work to build a bridge between neighboring imaginary countries while maintaining security and the economy of their own nations

Photographer. Brighter Paths, 20200 Nine Mile Rd., St. Clair Shores, Mich. 48080 1997 1 disc $30   **771**
1. Photography
Windows

This is a computer program that helps the novice photographer to learn good photography. The program simulates the functions of virtually all good 35mm single-lens reflex cameras. Moreover, it takes and develops the shots and generates a critique of the resulting photographs

Pinball science. DK Interactive Learning 1998 1 disc $19.95   **530**
1. Physics—Study and teaching
Windows and MAC
Also available school version

Fosters problem-solving skills in learning the principles of kinetic and potential energy. Players rebuild three inventions that resemble pinball games by answering questions to unlock game components such as gears, faucets, springs, magnets, slingshot launchers, and black holes

Poem finder 95. Roth Pub., 175 Great Neck Rd., Great Neck, N.Y. 11021 1995 1 disc $300   **808.81**
1. Poetry—Indexes
DOS

Indexes 500,000 poems by 70,000 authors. Includes bibliographic information, author biographical data, and allows searching on multiple fields

Population ecology. CyberEd, P.O. Box 3037, Paradise, Calif. 95967-3037 1998 1 disc (Interactive biology multimedia courseware series) $99.95   **304**
1. Population
Windows and MAC

This software program explores patterns in population growth, reasons populations grow and stop growing and trends in human population. Graphs and diagrams depict core population concepts

Primary search. EBSCO Pub. 1999 1 disc $599 per year with quarterly updates   **051**
1. Periodicals—Indexes
Windows and MAC

Provides access to indexing and abstracts for articles from over 120 children's magazines; the full text of more than 17,000 articles for the current year; and over 500 charts, tables, and graphs. Also included are searchable full text for over 300 pamphlets, EBSCO's Encyclopedia of animals, the World Almanac, the World Almanac for kids, and Funk & Wagnalls new encyclopedia

Raintree Steck-Vaughn interactive science encyclopedia. Raintree Steck-Vaughn Pubs. 1997 1 disc $69.95   **503**
1. Science—Encyclopedias
Windows and MAC

A multimedia version of the Raintree Steck-Vaughn illustrated science encyclopedia. Eight topic areas such as living things, chemicals and materials, and earth and the universe have related sub-topics that lead to articles. There are 154 lab activities including science fair projects and twenty interactive experiments. Includes a note-taking feature

Rationales for challenged books. National Council of Teachers of English 1998 1 disc $39.95   **098**
1. Books—Censorship
Windows and MAC

This "is a compilation of more than 200 rationales for 170 titles that have been collected from organizations such as the American Library Association, the Long Island Coalition Against Censorship, and the Colorado Language Arts Society. . . . Some elementary level titles are included, but most of the works are targeted for middle and high school levels. They range from frequently challenged and classic works (*The Adventures of Huckleberry Finn, Daddy's Roommate, The Catcher in the Rye*) that have multiple rationale entries to lesser-known books. . . . There are also critical analyses from literary, educational, psychological, and child development perspectives; testimonials from young readers, parents, and authors themselves; and lists of references, review sources, awards for the works and authors, and publications in which titles are recommended." SLJ

Readers' guide abstracts full text mega edition. Wilson, H.W. 2000 2 discs apply to publisher for price   **051**
1. Periodicals—Indexes
Windows and MAC

Provides access to over 260 general interest periodicals and newspapers from the United States and Canada, including 137 full-text titles. In addition to news and current events, the database covers subjects such as politics, business, education, history, and science. Searches can be refined by limiting to fields such as author, title, journal, descriptor, and publication year. Users can view full records with comprehensive abstracts and descriptors or only the records with full-text articles

Readers' guide for young people. Wilson, H.W. 2000 1 disc apply to publisher for price   **051**
1. Periodicals—Indexes
Windows and MAC

Indexes and abstracts a database of over 75 periodicals, more than 60 of which have full text coverage. Titles include Current Biography, Time, Smithsonian, and U.S. News and World Report. Also included are 12 professional journals (8 full-text). Searches can be refined by limiting to fields such as author, title, journal, descriptor, and publication year

Robert Frost: poems, life, legacy. Holt & Co. 1997 1 disc $69.95   **92**
1. Frost, Robert, 1874-1963
Windows and MAC

This CD-ROM examines the life and work of Robert Frost, the four-time Pulitzer Prize winning poet. The CD-ROM dramatizes Frost's personal and artistic life with videos, photographs, manuscripts, and commentaries. Two collections of poetry are provided, with more than 60 poems featuring audio performances by Frost

The **Rosetta** Stone: English I and English II (American). Fairfield Language Technologies, 165 S. Main St., Harrisonburg, Va. 22801 1999 Each level includes data discs, an installation disc, a workbook and study guide (Rosetta Stone language library series) ea $295   **420**
1. English language—Study and teaching 2. English as a second language
Windows and MAC

The Rosetta Stone: English I and English II (American)—*Continued*

An ESL program that teaches basic vocabulary and grammatical structures. There are nineteen units, with ten or eleven chapters each, plus a review chapter. Each chapter builds on the previous one, and new vocabulary and grammar are integrated systematically. There are listening and reading activities and feedback is provided. Students can also record their own voice and compare their pronunciation with that of a native speaker

Science court: sound. Tom Snyder Productions 1997 1 disc (Science court series) $59.95
534
1. Sound
Windows and MAC

This program teaches the basic concepts of sound using an interactive format. Students work in groups to experiment with sound: discover properties of sound; observe properties of sound; review properties of sound; and access both oral and written presentation of the questions

Science court: water cycle. Tom Snyder Productions 1997 1 disc (Science court series) $59.95
553.7
1. Water
Windows and MAC

Simulates a court room drama to help students understand the principles of water science: accumulation, evaporation, condensation, and precipitation. In four court sessions, students interact in cooperative learning groups to analyze facts presented in the videos and conduct offline experiments to gather information

SIRS government reporter. SIRS Mandarin, P.O. Box 272348, Boca Raton, Fla. 33427-2348 2000 1 disc $800 per year, updated twice a year
973
1. United States—Politics and government—Sources
Windows and MAC

This database contains information published by and about our federal government. Coverage includes U.S. Government Documents, Historic Documents, U.S. Supreme Court Decisions, Justices' Directory, Congressional Directory, and the Federal Agency Directory

SIRS Researcher. SIRS Mandarin 2000 1 disc $1350 per year, updated three times a year
051
1. Periodicals—Indexes
Windows and MAC

This general reference database provides access to thousands of full-text articles from more than 1,200 newspapers, magazines, journals and government publications exploring social, scientific, historic, economic, political and global issues. Dating from 1989, many of the articles are accompanied by graphics, including charts, maps, diagrams and drawings

Skills for writers. Pierian Spring Software 1997 1 disc (Odyssey of discovery series) $39
808
1. English language—Study and teaching
MAC

This CD-ROM is aimed at sharpening writing skills among children. The program contains three specific activities displayed with clever eye-and-ear-catching graphics and sonics and offering opportunities for students of varying abilities and vocabularies

Space: a visual history of manned space flight. Sumeria, 100 Eucalyptus Dr., San Francisco, Calif. 94132 1998 1 disc $49.95
629.45
1. Outer space—Exploration 2. Space flight
Windows and MAC

A multimedia almanac tracing the history of manned space flight from the beginnings of the Mercury missions to space shuttle flights. Includes information on the technology and scientific principles of space flight and exploration, including the international space station, space-based science, satellites, space suits, and space walks. Video footage is drawn from NASA's film archive

The sun's joules. Learning Team 1997 1 disc $39.95
621
1. Energy resources
Windows and MAC
Also available school version

Eleven topics such as solar energy, biomass, photovoltaics, geothermal energy, and hydroelectric power help students learn about forms of energy and their effects on the environment. Information is presented in extensive text screens supplemented with photographs, graphics, and narrated videos. Each topic includes an activity. The program also has an annotated list of Web sites, a glossary, and bibliographies of related print resources

Tell me more pro: French version. Auralog, 2720 S. Hardy Dr., Suite 3, Tempe, Ariz. 85282 1998 3 discs $250
440
1. French language—Study and teaching
Windows

This set provides a voice recognition program allowing users to practice the major components of language acquisition. The CD-ROMs strengthen oral proficiency and reinforce vocabulary as well as other language skills

That strange Mr. Poe. Klise, Thomas S., P.O. Box 317, Waterford, Conn. 06385 1997 1 disc (Great American authors series) $62
92
1. Poe, Edgar Allan, 1809-1849
Windows and MAC

Explores Poe's personal and professional life through historical photographs, original artwork, and narrated text. Also includes information on literary contemporaries such as Emerson, Thoreau, Whitman, and Melville as well as historical events

Thinkin' science zap! School version. Edmark Corp. 1998 2 discs $59.95
530
1. Science
Windows and MAC

Covers the scientific principles of light, sound, and electric energy. Users explore the properties of physical science in simulated labs and apply the knowledge learned in order to create multimedia concepts that feature light and sound shows

U-X-L biographies 2.0. Gale Group 1999 1 disc $400
920
1. Biography
Windows and MAC

This database covers over 2500 full biographies of historical and contemporary persons from various ethnic groups and occupations. The entries vary in length and include information about early years, formative experiences, and careers. Many of the entries include fact boxes, photographs, portraits, and a list of books for further reading. The user can search by name, subject terms, personal data, picture gallery, or full text

U-X-L science CD. Gale Group 1997 1 disc $400
503
1. Science—Encyclopedias
Windows and MAC
Database of science articles ranging from acoustics to wildlife including conservation, technology, machines, and medicine. Some articles have photographs, videos, audio clips and hot-linked cross references. Includes biographies of scientists and a timeline for searching by year or scientific event

Ultimate word attack. Davidson, Box 2961, Torrance, Calif. 90503 1998 2 discs $29.95
372.6
1. English language—Study and teaching
Windows and MAC
This is a computer program that helps students build vocabulary through activities covering more than 4,000 words. The program's four different games reinforce both definition and use and give users ample opportunities to learn the vocabulary assigned. This program is excellent for individual vocabulary building and SAT preparation courses

Whales Web pack. Sunburst Communications 1998 1 disc $39.95
599.5
1. Whales
Windows and MAC
This CD serves as a pathfinder, organizing more than fifty links to appropriate sites and supporting activities related to whales, whaling, oceanography, marine biology, and conservation issues. Web sites are framed in concise instructional contexts that include suggested grade level ranges

What's the big idea, Ben Franklin? Scholastic 1999 2 discs (Curriculum connections learning) $29.95
92
1. Franklin, Benjamin, 1706-1790
Windows and MAC
Based on Jean Fritz's biography, the program encourages students to explore the life and times of one of the most eclectic founding figures of the country. A learning cube interface presents topical blocks that offer viewing, reading, and activity options. Topics cover Franklin's early years, inventions and ideas, travels, and political contributions

Where in the USA is Carmen Sandiego? 3.5. Broderbund 1998 1 disc $59.95
917.3
1. United States—Description
Windows and MAC
Students, tracking down Carmen and her gang through all 50 states and the District of Columbia, learn U.S. and state history, geography, economy, and culture. In addition, students' skills are also increased in electronic database research, almanac reference, deductive reasoning, and map reading

Where in the world is Carmen Sandiego? 3.5. Broderbund 1998 1 disc $59.95
910
1. Geography
Windows and MAC

This is a computer program that provides scenarios to help teach students about social studies and a wide range of other subjects. It can also introduce students to group learning processes and important research skills. The software features advanced, high resolution windowing; an abundance of geographical facts; and beautiful city scenes

Women in science. Tom Snyder Productions 1997 1 disc $79.95
920
1. Women scientists
Windows and MAC
Introduces the work of eight women scientists in the fields of biology, chemistry, geology, astronomy, and physics through biographies, multimedia, and interactive experiments. Biographical information includes educational background, career milestones, and achievements. Multimedia "Field Trips" provide tours of locations such as Antarctica and a dolphin pool. A separate section contains a database of 130 additional women scientists throughout history

World Book multimedia encyclopedia, deluxe edition. World Bk. 2000 2 discs $59.95
031
1. Encyclopedias and dictionaries
Windows and MAC
Also known as World Book Millennium 2000, deluxe edition
Provides electronic access to every article from the print version. Features include maps, pictures, illustrations, virtual reality bubble views, full-length video clips, charts, research wizards and homework helpers

Writing for readers. Pierian Spring Software 1997 1 disc (Odyssey of discovery series) $39
808
1. English language—Study and teaching
Windows and MAC
Presents four activities designed to provide practice in the fundamentals of creative writing. An "Incredible Story Machine" is used to develop character, plot, and setting. In other parts of the program, users hear six real writers share their motivation and process for writing; add dialogue and scene descriptions to cartoons; and get inspiration for writing from a palette of photos, sketches, and paintings

The **Writing** trek language adventures: grades 6-8. Sunburst Communications 1999 1 disc (Writing trek series) $89.95
372.6
1. English language—Study and teaching 2. Creative writing
Windows and MAC
"Provides interactive computer-based lessons, extension activities, and projects designed to improve and expand writing skills. From a fantasy village screen, the program allows students to access six 'Project Houses' that cover poetry, fiction, journalism, informational/persuasive writing, script writing, and using visual images with text. Each House follows the same format: presentation of concepts related to the mode of writing, two creative writing projects, and skill lessons." SLJ

PART 4

DIRECTORY OF PUBLISHERS AND DISTRIBUTORS

DIRECTORY OF PUBLISHERS AND DISTRIBUTORS

21st Cent. Bks. (Brookfield), 2 Old New Milford Rd., Brookfield, Conn. 06804 Tel 203-740-2220; 800-462-4703 Fax 203-740-2223

21st Cent. Bks. (NY): 21st Cent. Bks., 115 W. 18th St., New York, N.Y. 10011-4113 Tel 212-886-9200 Fax 212-633-0748

ABC-CLIO Inc., 130 Cremona Dr., P.O. Box 1911, Santa Barbara, Calif. 93116-1911 Tel 805-968-1911; 800-368-6868 (orders) Fax 805-685-9685 (orders)

Abrams: Harry N. Abrams Inc., 100 5th Ave., New York, N.Y. 10011 Tel 212-206-7715; 800-345-1359 Fax 212-645-8437

Addison Wesley Longman Inc., 1 Jacob Way, Reading, Mass. 01867 Tel 617-944-3700; 800-447-2226 Fax 617-944-9351

Aladdin Paperbacks, Simon & Schuster Bldg., 1230 Ave. of the Americas, New York, N.Y. 10020 Tel 212-698-7000; 800-223-2348; refer orders to Simon & Schuster Children's Ordering Dept., 200 Old Tappan Rd., Old Tappan, N.J. 07675 Tel 212-689-7000; 800-223-2336 (orders) Fax 800-445-6991

Alleyside Press, P.O. Box 800, Fort Atkinson, Wis. 53538-0800 Tel 920-563-9571; 800-558-2110 Fax 920-563-4801

Allyn & Bacon Inc., 160 Gould St., Needham Heights, Mass. 02194-2310 Tel 617-455-1200; 800-223-1360 Fax 617-455-1220; refer orders to Simon & Schuster, 200 Old Tappan Rd., Old Tappan, N.J. 07675 Tel 201-767-5937; 800-223-1360 Fax 800-445-6991

Alyson Publs. Inc., P.O. Box 4371, Los Angeles, Calif. 90078 Tel 213-871-1225; 800-525-9766 (orders only) Fax 213-467-6805

Amereon Ltd., 800 Wickham Ave., Mattituck, N.Y. 11952 Tel 631-298-5100 Fax 631-298-5631

American Assn. for the Advancement of Science, 1200 New York Ave. N.W., Washington, D.C. 20005 Tel 202-326-6400

American Bible Soc., 1865 Broadway, 7th Floor, New York, N.Y. 10023-7505 Tel 212-408-1200; 800-322-4253 Fax 212-408-1426; refer orders to P.O. Box 5656, Grand Central Station, New York, N.Y. 10163

American Lib. Assn., 50 E. Huron St., Chicago, Ill. 60611-2795 Tel 312-280-2425; 800-545-2433 (orders) Fax 312-280-3255; 312-826-9958 (orders)

American Soc. of Educators, 1429 Walnut St., Philadelphia, Pa. 19102

Andrews & McMeel Inc., 4520 Main St., Kansas City, Mo. 64111 Tel 816-932-6600; 800-826-4216 Fax 816-932-6706; refer orders to Ingram Bk. Co., 1 Ingram Blvd., La Vergne, Tenn. 37086-1986 Tel 615-793-5000; 800-937-8000 Fax 800-876-0186

Association for Educ. Communications & Technology, 1025 Vermont Ave. N.W., Suite 820, Washington, D.C. 20005 Tel 202-347-7834

Atheneum Bks. for Young Readers, Simon & Schuster Bldg., 1230 Ave. of the Americas, New York, N.Y. 10020 Tel 212-698-7000; 800-257-5755; refer orders to Simon & Schuster Children's Ordering Dept., 100 Front St., Riverside, N.J. 08075 Tel 800-223-2336 (orders) Fax 800-445-6991

Atheneum Pubs., 1230 Ave. of the Americas, New York, N.Y. 10020 Tel 212-698-7000; 800-223-2348 Fax 800-445-6991; refer orders to Simon & Schuster, 100 Front St., Riverside, N.J. 08075 Tel 800-223-2336 (orders) Fax 800-445-6991

AudioFile Publs., 37 Silver St., P.O. Box 109, Portland, Me. 04112-0109

August House Inc., 201 E. Markham St., Little Rock, Ark. 72201 Tel 501-372-5450; 800-284-8784 Fax 501-372-5579; refer orders to Ingram Bk. Co., 1 Ingram Blvd., La Vergne, Tenn. 37086-1986 Tel 615-793-5000; 800-937-8000 (orders only) Fax 800-876-0186

Avisson Press Inc., 3007 Taliaferro Rd., Greensboro, N.C. 27408 Tel 336-288-6989

Avon Bks., 1350 Ave. of the Americas, 2nd Floor, New York, N.Y. 10019 Tel 212-261-6800; 800-238-0658 Fax 212-261-6895; refer orders to HarperCollins Pubs., 1000 Keystone Ind. Park, Scranton, Pa. 18512-4621 Tel 800-242-7737 Fax 800-822-4090

Ballantine Bks., 201 E. 50th St., New York, N.Y. 10022 Tel 212-572-2620; 800-638-6460 Fax 212-872-8026; refer orders to Random House Inc., 400 Hahn Rd., Westminster, Md. 21157 Tel 410-848-1900; 800-733-3000

Bantam Bks. Inc., 1540 Broadway, New York, N.Y. 10036-4094 Tel 212-354-6500; 800-223-5780 (orders only) Fax 212-492-8941; refer orders to 2451 S. Wolf Rd., Des Plaines, Ill. 60018 Tel 312-827-1111; 800-323-9872 (orders)

Barron's Educ. Ser. Inc., 250 Wireless Blvd., Hauppauge, N.Y. 11788-3917 Tel 516-434-3311; 800-257-5729; 800-645-3476 (outside NY) Fax 516-434-3723

Beacon Press, 25 Beacon St., Boston, Mass. 02108-2892 Tel 617-742-2110 Fax 617-723-3097; refer orders to Random House Inc., 400 Hahn Rd., Westminster, Md. 21157 Tel 410-848-1900; 800-733-3000

Bedrick Bks.: Peter Bedrick Bks. Inc., 4255 W. Touhy Ave., Lincolnwood, Ill. 60646-1975 Tel 847-679-5500; 800-323-4900 (orders) Fax 847-679-2494; 800-998-3103 (orders)

Beech Tree Bks., 1350 Ave. of the Americas, New York, N.Y. 10019 Tel 212-261-6500; 800-237-0657 Fax 212-779-0965; refer orders to Wilmor Warehouse, P.O. Box 1219, 39 Plymouth St., Fairfield, N.J. 07007 Tel 973-227-7200; 800-237-0657

Behrman House Inc., 235 Watchung Ave., W. Orange, N.J. 07052 Tel 973-669-0447; 800-221-2755 Fax 973-669-9769

Benchmark Bks. (Tarrytown): Benchmark Bks., 99 White Plains Rd., P.O. Box 2001, Tarrytown, N.Y. 10591-9001 Tel 914-332-8888; 800-821-9881 Fax 914-332-1082

Berkley Pub. Group (The), 200 Madison Ave., New York, N.Y. 10016 Tel 212-951-8800; 800-631-8571 Fax 212-213-6706; refer orders to P.O. Box 506, E. Rutherford, N.J. 07073 Tel 800-847-5515 (orders) Fax 607-775-4829

Bernan Assocs., 4611-F Assembly Dr., Lanham, Md. 20706-4391 Tel 301-459-7666; 800-865-3457 Fax 301-459-0056; 800-865-3450

Beyond Words Pub. Inc., 20827 N.W. Cornell Rd., Suite 500, Hillsboro, Or. 97124-9808 Tel 503-531-8700; 800-284-9673 Fax 503-531-8773; refer orders to Publishers Group West, 1700 4th St., Berkeley, Calif. 94710 Tel 510-528-1444; 800-788-3123 Fax 510-528-3444

Blackbirch Press Inc., 260 Amity Rd., Woodbridge, Conn. 06525 Tel 203-387-7525; 800-831-9183 Fax 203-389-1596

Blue Sky Press (NY): Blue Sky Press, 555 Broadway, New York, N.Y. 10012-3999 Tel 212-343-6100 Fax 212-343-4535; refer orders to Penguin Putnam Inc., 405 Murray Hill Parkway, E. Rutherford, N.J. 07073 Tel 201-933-9292; 800-526-0275

Books of Wonder, 216 W. 18th St., Room 806, New York, N.Y. 10011 Tel 212-989-3475; 800-207-6968 Fax 212-989-1203; refer orders to HarperCollins Pubs., 1000 Keystone Ind. Park, Scranton, Pa. 18512-4621 Tel 800-242-7737 Fax 800-822-4090

Bowker: R.R. Bowker Co., 121 Chanlon Rd., New Providence, N.J. 07974 Tel 908-464-6800; 888-269-5372 (orders) Fax 908-508-7696; refer orders to P.O. Box 1001, Summit, N.J. 07902-1001

Boy Scouts of Am., P.O. Box 152079, 1325 W. Walnut Hill Lane, Irving, Tex. 75015-2079 Tel 972-580-2278 Fax 972-580-2502; refer orders to National Distr. Center, 2109 Westinghouse Blvd., P.O. Box 7143, Charlotte, N.C. 28241-7143 Tel 704-588-4260

Boyds Mills Press, 815 Church St., Honesdale, Pa. 18431 Tel 570-253-1164; 877-512-8366 (orders) Fax 570-253-0179

Bradbury Press Inc., 1230 Ave. of the Americas, New York, N.Y. 10020 Tel 212-698-7200; 800-223-2348; refer orders to Simon & Schuster Children's Order Dept., 100 Front St., Riverside, N.J. 08075 Tel 800-223-2336 Fax 800-445-6991

BridgeWater Bks., 100 Corporate Dr., Mahwah, N.J. 07430 Tel 201-529-4000; 800-929-8765 Fax 201-529-9347; refer orders to Penguin Putnam Inc., 405 Murray Hill Parkway, E. Rutherford, N.J. 07073 Tel 201-933-9292; 800-526-0275

Browndeer Press, 525 B St., Suite 1900, San Diego, Calif. 92101-4495 Tel 619-699-6707; 800-831-7799 Fax 619-699-6542; refer orders to Harcourt Inc., 6277 Sea Harbor Dr., Orlando, Fla. 32887 Tel 619-699-6707; 800-543-1918 (orders)

Callaway Eds. Inc., 70 Bedford St., New York, N.Y. 10014-4001 Tel 212-929-5212 Fax 212-929-8087

Cambridge Univ. Press, Edinburgh Bldg., Shaftesbury Rd., Cambridge CB2 2RU, Eng. Tel (01223) 312 393 Fax (01223) 315 052

Branch offices

U.S.: Cambridge Univ. Press, 40 W. 20th St., New York, N.Y. 10011-4211 Tel 212-924-3900; 800-872-7423; refer orders to 110 Midland Ave., Port Chester, N.Y. 10573-4930 Tel 914-937-9600; 800-872-7423 (orders only) Fax 914-937-4712

Camelot Pub. Co., P.O. Box 1357, Ormond Beach, Fla. 32175-1357 Tel 904-672-5672

Candlewick Press, 2067 Massachusetts Ave., Cambridge, Mass. 02140 Tel 617-661-3330 Fax 617-661-0565

Capstone Press Inc., 818 N. Willow St., Mankota, Minn. 56001 Tel 507-388-6650; 800-747-4992 Fax 507-625-4662; 888-262-0705

Carolrhoda Bks. Inc., 241 1st Ave. N., Minneapolis, Minn. 55401 Tel 612-332-3344; 800-328-4929 Fax 612-332-7615; 800-332-1132

Cartwheel Bks., 555 Broadway, New York, N.Y. 10012-3999 Tel 212-343-6100 Fax 212-343-4535; refer orders to Penguin Putnam Inc., 405 Murray Hill Parkway, E. Rutherford, N.J. 07073 Tel 201-933-9292; 800-526-0275

Checkmark Bks., 11 Penn Plaza, New York, N.Y. 10001-2006 Tel 212-967-8800; 800-322-8755 Fax 212-967-9196; 800-678-3633

Chelsea House Pubs., 1974 Sproul Rd., Suite 400, Broomall, Pa. 19008-0914 Tel 610-353-5166; 800-848-2665 Fax 610-359-1439

Chelsea Jrs., 1974 Sproul Rd., Suite 400, Broomall, Pa. 19008-0914 Tel 610-353-5166; 800-848-2665 Fax 610-359-1439

Chicago Review Press, 814 N. Franklin St., Chicago, Ill. 60610 Tel 312-337-0747; 800-888-4741 (orders only) Fax 312-337-5985; refer orders to Independent Pubs. Group, 814 N. Franklin, Chicago, Ill. 60610 Tel 312-337-0747; 800-888-4741 Fax 312-337-5985

Children's Bk. Council Inc., 568 Broadway, Suite 404, New York, N.Y. 10012 Tel 212-966-1990 Fax 212-966-2073

Children's Bk. Press, 246 1st St., Suite 101, San Francisco, Calif. 94105 Tel 415-995-2200 Fax 415-995-2222

Children's Press, 90 Sherman Turnpike, Danbury, Conn. 06816 Tel 203-797-3500; 800-621-1115 Fax 203-797-3143

Children's Science Bk. Review Com., 605 Commonwealth Ave., Boston, Mass. 02215

Child's World (The), P.O. Box 326, Chanhassen, Minn. 55317-0326 Tel 612-906-3939; 800-599-7323 Fax 612-906-3940

Christopher-Gordon Pubs. Inc., 1502 Providence Highway, Suite 12, Norwood, Mass. 02062-4643 Tel 781-762-5577; 800-934-8322 Fax 781-762-2110

Chronicle Bks., 85 2nd St., 6th Floor, San Francisco, Calif. 94105 Tel 415-537-3730; 800-722-6657 (orders only) Fax 415-537-4460; 800-858-7787; refer orders to Ingram Bk. Co., 1 Ingram Blvd., La Vergne, Tenn. 37086-1986 Tel 615-793-5000; 800-937-8000 (orders only) Fax 800-876-0186

Clarion Bks., 215 Park Ave. S., New York, N.Y. 10003 Tel 212-420-5800 Fax 212-420-5855; refer orders to Houghton Mifflin Co., 181 Ballardville St., Wilmington, Mass. 01887 Tel 508-661-1300; 800-225-3362

Cobblehill Bks., 375 Hudson St., New York, N.Y. 10014-3657 Tel 212-366-2000; 800-526-0275 (orders) Fax 212-366-2666; refer orders to Penguin Putnam Inc., 405 Murray Hill Parkway, E. Rutherford, N.J. 07073 Tel 201-933-9292; 800-526-0275

Columbia Univ. Press, 562 W. 113th St., New York, N.Y. 10025 Tel 212-666-1000 Fax 212-316-9422; refer orders to 136 S. Broadway, Irvington, N.Y. 10533 Tel 914-591-9111; 800-944-8648 Fax 914-591-9201; 800-944-1844

Conari Press, 2550 9th St., Suite 101, Berkeley, Calif. 94710 Tel 510-649-7175; 800-685-9595 (orders) Fax 510-649-7190; refer orders to Publishers Group West, 1700 4th St., Berkeley, Calif. 94710 Tel 510-528-1444; 800-788-3123 Fax 510-528-3444

Congressional Quarterly Inc., 1414 22nd St. N.W., Washington, D.C. 20037-1003 Tel 202-887-8500; 800-638-1710 (orders) Fax 202-887-6706

Contemporary Bks. Inc., 2 Prudential Plaza, Suite 1200, Chicago, Ill. 60601 Tel 312-540-4500; 800-621-1918 (orders only) Fax 312-540-4687

Copper Beech Bks., 2 Old New Milford Rd., Brookfield, Conn. 06804 Tel 203-740-2220; 800-462-4703 Fax 203-740-2223

Court Wayne Press, P.O. Box 19726, Boulder, Colo. 80308 Tel 877-929-6387

Coward-McCann Inc., 375 Hudson St., New York, N.Y. 10014 Tel 212-366-2000; 800-331-4624 Fax 212-213-6706; refer orders to Penguin Putnam Inc., Inside Sales Dept., 1 Grosset Dr., Kirkwood, N.Y. 13795 Tel 607-775-4829; 800-847-5515

Coward, McCann & Geoghegan See Coward-McCann

Crabtree Pub. Co., PMB 16A, 350 5th Ave., Suite 3308, New York, N.Y. 10118 Tel 212-496-5040; 800-387-7650 (orders) Fax 800-355-7166 (orders)

Creative Art Publs., 301 Riverland Rd., Fort Lauderdale, Fla. 33312 Tel 305-583-9207

Crestwood House Inc., 299 Jefferson Rd., Parsippany, N.J. 07054 Tel 973-739-8000; 800-858-7674 Fax 973-739-8053; 800-393-3156; refer orders to Silver Burdett Press, P.O. Box 2649, 4350 Equity Dr., Columbus, Ohio 43216 Tel 614-771-7398 Fax 614-771-7361

Crowell See HarperCollins Pubs.

Crown Pubs. Inc., 201 E. 50th St., New York, N.Y. 10022 Tel 212-751-2600; 800-733-3000 (orders only) Fax 301-857-9460

Delacorte Press, 1540 Broadway, New York, N.Y. 10036-4094 Tel 212-354-6500; 800-323-9872 Fax 212-765-3869

Dell Pub. Co. Inc., 1540 Broadway, New York, N.Y. 10036-4094 Tel 212-354-6500; 800-223-6834 Fax 212-492-9698

Dial Bks., 375 Hudson St., New York, N.Y. 10014 Tel 212-366-2000 Fax 212-366-2666; refer orders to Penguin Putnam Inc., 405 Murray Hill Parkway, E. Rutherford, N.J. 07073 Tel 201-933-9292; 800-526-0275

Dial Bks. for Young Readers, 375 Hudson St., New York, N.Y. 10014 Tel 212-366-2000 Fax 212-366-2666; refer orders to Penguin Putnam Inc., 405 Murray Hill Parkway, E. Rutherford, N.J. 07073 Tel 201-933-9292; 800-526-0275

Dial Press (NY): The Dial Press, 1540 Broadway, New York, N.Y. 10036-4094 Tel 212-354-6500; 800-223-6834 Fax 212-492-9698

Dillon Press, 299 Jefferson Rd., Parsippany, N.J. 07054 Tel 973-739-8000; 800-848-9500 Fax 973-739-8053; 800-393-3156; refer orders to Silver Burdett Press, P.O. Box 2649, 4350 Equity Dr., Columbus, Ohio 43216 Tel 614-771-7398 Fax 614-771-7361

Disney Press, 114 5th Ave., New York, N.Y. 10011 Tel 212-633-4400 Fax 212-633-4833; refer orders to Time Warner Trade Pub., Customer Service, 3 Center Plaza, Boston, Mass. 02108-2084 Tel 800-343-9204 Fax 800-286-9471

DK Ink, 95 Madison Ave., New York, N.Y. 10016 Tel 212-213-4800; 888-342-5357 Fax 212-213-5240; refer orders to Publishers Resources, 1224 Heil Quaker Blvd., La Vergne, Tenn. 37086-7001 Tel 615-793-5090; 800-937-5557 Fax 800-774-6733

DK Pub. Inc., 95 Madison Ave., New York, N.Y. 10016 Tel 212-213-4800; 888-342-5357 Fax 212-213-5240; refer orders to Publishers Resources, 1224 Heil Quaker Blvd., La Vergne, Tenn. 37086-7001 Tel 615-793-5090; 800-937-5557 Fax 800-774-6733

Doherty Assocs.: Tom Doherty Assocs. Inc., 175 5th Ave., New York, N.Y. 10010 Tel 212-388-0100; 800-221-7945 Fax 212-388-0191; refer orders to St. Martin's Press Inc., 175 5th Ave., Room 1715, New York, N.Y. 10010 Tel 212-674-5151; 800-221-7945 Fax 212-420-9314

Dolphin Bks. (NY): Dolphin Bks., 666 5th Ave., New York, N.Y. 10103 Tel 212-765-6500; 800-223-6834

Dorling Kindersley Ltd., 9 Henrietta St., London WC2E 8PS, Eng. Tel (0171) 836 5411 Fax (0171) 836 7570; refer orders to International Bk. Distributors (Hemel Hempstead) Ltd., Campus 400, Maylands Ave., Hemel Hempstead, Hertfordshire HP2 7EZ, Eng. Tel (01442) 881 900; 882 016 (orders) Fax (01442) 882 099; 882 288 (orders)
Branch offices
U.S.: DK Pub.

Doubleday, 1540 Broadway, New York, N.Y. 10036-4094 Tel 212-354-6500; 800-323-9872 (orders only) Fax 212-492-9700; 800-233-3294 (orders only); refer orders to Consumer Services, P.O. Box 5071, Des Plaines, Ill. 60017-5071

Doubleday Bks. for Young Readers, 1540 Broadway, New York, N.Y. 10036-4094 Tel 212-354-6500; 800-223-6834 Fax 212-492-8941; refer orders to 2451 S. Wolf Rd., Des Plaines, Ill. 60018 Tel 312-827-1111; 800-323-9872 (orders)

Dutton, 375 Hudson St., New York, N.Y. 10014-3657 Tel 212-366-2000; 800-526-0275 (orders) Fax 212-366-2666; refer orders to Penguin Putnam Inc., 405 Murray Hill Parkway, E. Rutherford, N.J. 07073 Tel 201-933-9292; 800-526-0275 Fax 201-933-2316

Dutton Children's Bks., 375 Hudson St., New York, N.Y. 10014-3657 Tel 212-366-2000; 800-526-0275 (orders) Fax 212-366-2666; refer orders to Penguin Putnam Inc., 405 Murray Hill Parkway, E. Rutherford, N.J. 07073 Tel 201-933-9292; 800-526-0275

EDC Pub., 10302 E. 55th Pl., Tulsa, Okla. 74146 Tel 918-622-4522; 800-331-4418; refer orders to P.O. Box 470663, Tulsa, Okla. 74147

Eerdmans: Wm. B. Eerdmans Pub. Co., 255 Jefferson Ave. S.E., Grand Rapids, Mich. 49503-4554 Tel 616-459-4591; 800-253-7521 (U.S. & Can. orders only) Fax 616-459-6540

Eerdmans Bks. for Young Readers, 255 Jefferson Ave. S.E., Grand Rapids, Mich. 49503-4554 Tel 616-459-4591; 800-253-7521 (U.S. & Can. orders only) Fax 616-459-6540

Enslow Pubs., 44 Fadem Rd., Springfield, N.J. 07081-0699 Tel 201-379-8890; 800-398-2504 Fax 201-379-7940

Facts on File Inc., 11 Penn Plaza, New York, N.Y. 10001-2006 Tel 212-967-8800; 800-322-8755 Fax 212-967-9196; 800-678-3633

Farrar, Straus & Giroux Inc., 19 Union Sq. W., New York, N.Y. 10003 Tel 212-741-6900 Fax 212-633-9385; refer orders to VHPS-Von Holtzbrinck Pub. Services, 16365 James Madison Highway (U.S. Route 15), Gordonsville, Va. 22942 Tel 540-672-7600; 888-330-8477 Fax 800-672-2054

Fawcett Bks., 201 E. 50th St., New York, N.Y. 10022 Tel 212-572-2713; 800-733-3000 (orders) Fax 212-572-6046; refer orders to Random House Inc., 400 Hahn Rd., Westminster, Md. 21157 Tel 410-848-1900; 800-733-3000

Fawcett Columbine, 201 E. 50th St., New York, N.Y. 10022 Tel 212-572-2620; 800-638-6460 Fax 212-872-8026; refer orders to Random House Inc., 400 Hahn Rd., Westminster, Md. 21157 Tel 410-848-1900; 800-733-3000

Fell: Frederick Fell Pub. Inc., 2131 Hollywood Blvd., Suite 305, Hollywood, Fla. 33020 Tel 954-925-5242; 800-771-3355 Fax 954-925-5244

Ferguson, J.G.: J.G. Ferguson Pub. Co., 200 W. Monroe, Suite 250, Chicago, Ill. 60606 Tel 312-580-5480 Fax 312-580-4948

Firefly Bks. (Buffalo): Firefly Bks., P.O. Box 1338, Ellicott Station, Buffalo, N.Y. 14205 Tel 800-387-5085

Fireside Bks., Simon & Schuster Bldg., 1230 Ave. of the Americas, New York, N.Y. 10020 Tel 212-698-7000; 800-223-2348; refer orders to Simon & Schuster Ordering Dept., 200 Old Tappan Rd., Old Tappan, N.J. 07675 Tel 800-223-2336 (orders) Fax 800-445-6991

Forest Press (Albany): Forest Press, 85 Watervliet Ave., Albany, N.Y. 12206-2082 Tel 518-489-8549 Fax 518-489-7804; 888-339-3921; refer orders to OCLC Forest Press, 6565 Frantz Rd., Dublin, Ohio 43017-3395

Foster Bks.: Frances Foster Bks., 19 Union Sq. W., New York, N.Y. 10003 Tel 212-741-6900; 888-330-8477 Fax 212-633-9385; refer orders to VHPS-Von Holtzbrinck Pub. Services, 16365 James Madison Highway (U.S. Route 15), Gordonsville, Va. 22942 Tel 540-672-7600; 888-330-8477 Fax 800-672-2054

Four Winds Press, 1230 Ave. of the Americas, New York, N.Y. 10020 Tel 212-698-7000; 800-257-5755; refer orders to Simon & Schuster Children's Ordering Dept., 200 Old Tappan Rd., Old Tappan, N.J. 07675 Tel 800-223-2336 (orders) Fax 800-445-6991

Free Spirit Pub. Inc., 400 1st Ave. N., Suite 616, Minneapolis, Minn. 55401-1730 Tel 612-338-2068; 800-735-7323 Fax 612-337-5050

Front St., 20 Battery Park Ave., Suite 403, Asheville, N.C. 28801 Tel 704-236-3097 Fax 704-236-3098; refer orders to Publishers Group West, 1700 4th St., Berkeley, Calif. 94710 Tel 510-528-1444; 800-788-3123 Fax 510-528-3444

Front St./Cricket Bks., 332 S. Michigan Ave., Suite 1100, Chicago, Ill. 60604-9968 Tel 312-939-1500

Fulcrum Resources, 350 Indiana St., Suite 350, Golden, Colo. 80401 Tel 303-277-1623; 800-992-2908 Fax 303-279-7111; 800-726-7112

Gale Res. Co., 27500 Drake Rd., Farmington Hills, Mich. 48331-3535 Tel 248-699-4253; 800-877-4253; refer orders to P.O. Box 9187, Farmington Hills, Mich. 48333-9187 Tel 800-877-4253 Fax 313-961-6083; 800-414-5043

Gallaudet College Press, 800 Florida Ave. N.E., Washington, D.C. 20002-3695 Tel 202-651-5488; 800-451-1073 Fax 202-651-5489

Garland Pub. Inc., 19 Union Sq. W., 8th Floor, New York, N.Y. 10003-3382 Tel 212-414-0650; 800-627-6273 Fax 212-414-0659; refer orders to Taylor & Francis Inc., 47 Runway Rd., Levittown, Pa. 19057-4700 Tel 215-269-0400; 800-821-8312 Fax 215-269-0363

Girl Scouts of the U.S.A., 420 5th Ave., New York, N.Y. 10018 Tel 212-852-8000 Fax 212-852-6511

Godine: David R. Godine Pub., 9 Lewis St., Lincoln, Mass. 01773 Tel 617-259-0700; 800-344-4771 Fax 617-259-9198

Golden Bks. (NY): Golden Bks., 850 3rd Ave., 7th Floor., New York, N.Y. 10022 Tel 212-753-8500; 800-558-5972 Fax 212-371-1091; refer orders to Western Pub. Co. Inc., 1220 Mound Ave., Racine, Wis. 53404 Tel 414-633-2431

Gospel Pub. House, 1445 Boonville Ave., Springfield, Mo. 65802-1894 Tel 417-831-8000; 800-641-4310 (orders only) Fax 800-328-0294

Granger Bk. Co. Inc., 11 Middle Neck Rd., Great Neck, N.Y. 11021 Tel 516-466-3676

Greenhaven Press Inc., P.O. Box 289009, San Diego, Calif. 92198-9009 Tel 858-485-7424; 800-231-5163 (orders) Fax 858-485-9549

Greenwillow Bks., 1350 Ave. of the Americas, New York, N.Y. 10019 Tel 212-261-6500 Fax 212-261-6619; 888-775-3260; refer orders to HarperCollins Pubs., 1000 Keystone Ind. Park, Scranton, Pa. 18512-4621 Tel 800-242-7737 Fax 800-822-4090

Greenwood Press, 88 Post Rd. W., P.O. Box 5007, Westport, Conn. 06881-5007 Tel 203-226-3571; 800-225-5800 (orders only) Fax 203-222-1502

Grolier Educ., 90 Old Sherman Turnpike, Danbury, Conn. 06816-0001 Tel 203-797-3500; 800-243-7256 Fax 203-797-3285

Grosset & Dunlap Pubs., 375 Hudson St., New York, N.Y. 10014 Tel 212-366-2000; 800-331-4624 Fax 212-213-6706; refer orders to Penguin Putnam Inc., Inside Sales Dept., 1 Grosset Dr., Kirkwood, N.Y. 13795 Tel 607-775-4829; 800-847-5515

Groundwood Bks. Ltd., 720 Bathurst St., Suite 500, Toronto, Ont., Can. M5S 2R4 Tel 416-537-2501 Fax 416-537-4647

Grove Weidenfeld See Grove/Atlantic, 841 Broadway, New York, N.Y. 10003-4793 Tel 212-614-7850; 800-638-6460 Fax 212-614-7886; refer orders to Publishers Group West, 1700 4th St., Berkeley, Calif. 94710 Tel 510-528-1444; 800-788-3123 Fax 510-528-3444

Hammond Inc., 515 Valley St., Maplewood, N.J. 07040 Tel 973-763-6000; 800-526-4953 Fax 973-763-7658; 888-763-7658

Harcourt Inc., 525 B St., Suite 1900, San Diego, Calif. 92101-4495 Tel 619-699-6707; 800-831-7799 Fax 619-699-6542; refer orders to 6277 Sea Harbor Dr., Orlando, Fla. 32887 Tel 619-699-6707; 800-543-1918 (orders)

Harcourt Brace & Co. See Harcourt

Harcourt Brace Jovanovich See Harcourt

Harmony Bks., 201 E. 50th St., New York, N.Y. 10022 Tel 212-751-2600; 800-733-3000 (orders only) Fax 301-857-9460

Harper & Row See HarperCollins Pubs.

HarperCollins Pubs., 10 E. 53rd St., New York, N.Y. 10022-5299 Tel 212-207-7000; 800-242-7737 Fax 212-207-7145; refer orders to 1000 Keystone Ind. Park, Scranton, Pa. 18512-4621 Tel 570-941-1500; 800-242-7737 Fax 800-822-4090

HarperPerennial, 10 E. 53rd St., New York, N.Y. 10022-5299 Tel 212-207-7000; 800-242-7737 Fax 212-207-7145; refer orders to HarperCollins Pubs., 1000 Keystone Ind. Park, Scranton, Pa. 18512-4621 Tel 570-941-1500; 800-242-7737 Fax 800-822-4090

Health Communications Inc., 3201 S.W. 15th St., Deerfield Beach, Fla. 33442-8124 Tel 954-360-0909; 800-851-9100 Fax 954-360-0034

Heinemann Interactive Lib., 1350 E. Touhy Ave., Suite 240 W., Des Plaines, Ill. 60018 Tel 847-390-2586; 888-844-5329 Fax 888-454-2279

Heinemann Lib., Halley Ct., Jordan Hill, Oxford OX2 8EJ, Eng. Tel (01865) 311 366 Fax (01865) 314 107
Branch offices
U.S.: Heinemann Lib., 1350 E. Touhy Ave., Suite 240 W., Des Plaines, Ill. 60018 Tel 847-390-2586; 888-844-5329 Fax 888-454-2279; refer orders to 500 Coventry Lane, Suite 200, Crystal Lake, Ill. 60014 Tel 815-477-3880; 800-822-8661 Fax 815-477-3997

Herald House, P.O. Box 1770, Independence, Mo. 64055-0770 Tel 816-252-5010; 800-767-8181 Fax 816-252-3976

Hill & Wang Inc., 19 Union Sq. W., New York, N.Y. 10003 Tel 212-741-6900; 888-330-8477 Fax 212-741-6973

Hill Bks.: Lawrence Hill Bks., 611 Broadway, Suite 530, New York, N.Y. 10012 Tel 212-260-0576 Fax 212-260-0853; refer orders to Independent Pubs. Group, 814 N. Franklin St., Chicago, Ill. 60610 Tel 312-337-0747; 800-888-4741 Fax 800-337-5985

Holiday House Inc., 425 Madison Ave., New York, N.Y. 10017 Tel 212-688-0085 Fax 212-421-6134

Holt & Co.: Henry Holt & Co., 115 W. 18th St., New York, N.Y. 10011 Tel 212-886-9200 Fax 212-645-5832; refer orders to VHPS-Von Holtzbrinck Pub. Services, 16365 James Madison Highway (U.S. Route 15), Gordonsville, Va. 22942 Tel 540-672-7600; 888-330-8477 Fax 800-672-2054

Horn Bk. Inc., 14 Beacon St., Boston, Mass. 02108 Tel 617-227-1555; 800-325-1170

Houghton Mifflin Co., 222 Berkeley St., Boston, Mass. 02116 Tel 617-351-5000 Fax 617-227-5409; refer orders to 181 Ballardville St., Wilmington, Mass. 01887 Tel 508-661-1300; 800-225-3362

Howell Bk. House Inc., 1633 Broadway, 7th Floor, New York, N.Y. 10019 Tel 212-654-8184 Fax 212-654-4784; refer orders to Macmillan Order Dept., 201 W. 103rd St., Indianapolis, Ind. 46290-1094 Tel 317-581-3500; 800-428-5331 (orders) Fax 800-882-8583

Hyperion, 114 5th Ave., New York, N.Y. 10011 Tel 212-633-4400 Fax 212-633-4833; refer orders to Time Warner Trade Pub., Customer Service, 3 Center Plaza, Boston, Mass. 02108-2084 Tel 800-759-0190 Fax 617-890-0875; 800-286-9471

Hyperion Bks. for Children, 114 5th Ave., New York, N.Y. 10011 Tel 212-633-4400 Fax 212-633-4833; refer orders to Time Warner Trade Pub., Customer Service, 3 Center Plaza, Boston, Mass. 02108-2084 Tel 800-759-0190 Fax 617-890-0875; 800-286-9471

Information Today Inc., 143 Old Marlton Pike, Medford, N.J. 08055-8750 Tel 609-654-6266; 800-300-9868 (orders) Fax 609-654-4309

Jane Yolen Bks., 525 B St., Suite 1900, San Diego, Calif. 92101-4495 Tel 619-699-6707; 800-831-7799 Fax 619-699-6542; refer orders to Harcourt Inc., 6277 Sea Harbor Dr., Orlando, Fla. 32887 Tel 619-699-6707; 800-543-1918 (orders)

Jewish Publ. Soc., 1930 Chestnut St., Philadelphia, Pa. 19103-4599 Tel 215-564-5925; 800-234-3151 (orders only) Fax 215-564-6640; refer orders to JPS Bks. Int., 22883 Quicksilver Dr., Dulles, Va. 20166 Tel 703-661-1500; 800-355-1165 Fax 703-661-1501

Jump at the Sun, 114 5th Ave., New York, N.Y. 10011 Tel 212-633-4400 Fax 212-633-4833; refer orders to Time Warner Trade Pub., Customer Service, 3 Center Plaza, Boston, Mass. 02108-2084 Tel 800-343-9204 Fax 800-286-9471

Kids Can Press, 585 1/2 Bloor St. W., Toronto, Ont., Can. M6G 1K5 Tel 416-534-6389 Fax 416-960-5437

Kingfisher (NY): Kingfisher, 95 Madison Ave., Suite 1205, New York, N.Y. 10016 Tel 212-686-1060; 800-497-1657 Fax 212-686-1082

Knopf: Alfred A. Knopf Inc., 201 E. 50th St., New York, N.Y. 10022 Tel 212-751-2600; 800-726-0600 Fax 212-572-2593; refer orders to Random House Inc., 400 Hahn Rd., Westminster, Md. 21157 Tel 410-848-1900; 800-733-3000

Lark Bks., 50 College St., Asheville, N.C. 28801 Tel 704-253-0467; 800-284-3388 Fax 704-253-7952

Learning Works Inc. (The), P.O. Box 6187, Santa Barbara, Calif. 93160 Tel 805-964-4220; 800-235-5767 Fax 805-964-1466

LearningExpress, 900 Broadway, Suite 604, New York, N.Y. 10003 Tel 212-995-2566; 800-543-7598 Fax 212-995-5512

Lee & Low Bks. Inc., 95 Madison Ave., New York, N.Y. 10016 Tel 212-779-4400 Fax 212-683-1894; refer orders to Publishers Group West, 1700 4th St., Berkeley, Calif. 94710 Tel 510-528-1444; 800-788-3123 Fax 510-528-3444

Lerner Publs. Co., 241 1st Ave. N., Minneapolis, Minn. 55401 Tel 612-332-3344; 800-328-4929 Fax 612-332-7615; 800-332-1132

Levine Bks.: Arthur A. Levine Bks., 555 Broadway, New York, N.Y. 10012-3999 Tel 212-343-6100 Fax 212-343-4535; refer orders to Penguin Putnam Inc., 405 Murray Hill Parkway, E. Rutherford, N.J. 07073 Tel 201-933-9292; 800-526-0275

Libraries Unlimited Inc., P.O. Box 6633, Englewood, Colo. 80155-6633 Tel 303-770-1200; 800-237-6124 Fax 303-220-8843

Linnet Bks., 2 Linsley St., North Haven, Conn. 06473-2517 Tel 203-239-2702 Fax 203-239-2568

Linnet Professional Publs., 2 Linsley St., North Haven, Conn. 06473-2517 Tel 203-239-2702 Fax 203-239-2568

Linworth Pub. Inc., 480 E. Wilson Bridge Rd., Suite L, Worthington, Ohio 43085 Tel 614-436-7107; 800-786-5017 Fax 614-436-9490

Lippincott See HarperCollins Pubs.

Little, Brown & Co. Inc., Time & Life Bldg., 1271 Ave. of the Americas, New York, N.Y. 10020 Tel 212-522-8700; 800-343-9204 Fax 212-522-2067; refer orders to Time Warner Trade Pub., Customer Service, 3 Center Plaza, Boston, Mass. 02108-2084 Tel 800-759-0190 Fax 617-890-0875; 800-286-9471

Lodestar Bks., 375 Hudson St., New York, N.Y. 10014-3657 Tel 212-366-2000; 800-526-0275 (orders) Fax 212-366-2666; refer orders to Penguin Putnam Inc., 405 Murray Hill Parkway, E. Rutherford, N.J. 07073 Tel 201-933-9292; 800-526-0275

Longman Group Ltd., Addison Wesley Longman Ltd., Edinburgh Gate, Harlow, Essex CM20 2JE, Eng. Tel (01279) 623 623 Fax (01279) 431 059; refer orders to P.O. Box 88, Harlow, Essex CM19 5SR, Eng. Tel (01279) 623 928 Fax (01279) 414 130
Branch offices
U.S.: Longman Pub., Longman Bldg., 10 Bank St., White Plains, N.Y. 10606-1951 Tel 914-993-5000; 800-862-7778 Fax 914-997-8115

Lothrop, Lee & Shepard Bks., 1350 Ave. of the Americas, New York, N.Y. 10019 Tel 212-261-6500; 800-237-0657 Fax 212-779-0965; refer orders to HarperCollins Pubs., 1000 Keystone Ind. Park, Scranton, Pa. 18512-4621 Tel 800-242-7737 Fax 800-822-4090

Lowell House Juvenile, 2020 Ave. of the Stars, No. 300, Los Angeles, Calif. 90067 Tel 310-552-7555 Fax 310-552-7573

Lucas Bks., P.O. Box 10667, San Rafael, Calif. 94912

Lucent Bks., 10911 Technology Pl., San Diego, Calif. 92127 Tel 619-485-7424; 800-231-5163 (orders) Fax 619-485-9549; refer orders to Greenhaven Press Inc., P.O. Box 289009, San Diego, Calif. 92198-9009 Tel 619-485-7424; 800-231-5163 Fax 619-485-9549

Macmillan, 909 Third Ave., New York, N.Y. 10022 Tel 212-884-5000; 646-497-9800; refer orders to IDG Books Worldwide, 10475 Crosspoint Blvd., Indianapolis, Ind. 46256 Tel 800-434-3422

Macmillan Lib. Ref. USA, 1633 Broadway, New York, N.Y. 10019 Tel 646-756-2500; refer orders to Gale Group, P.O. Box 9187, Farmington Hills, Mich. 48333-9187 Tel 248-699-4253; 800-877-4253 Fax 313-961-6083; 800-414-5043

Madison Bks., 4720 Boston Way, Lanham, Md. 20706 Tel 301-459-3366; 800-462-6420 Fax 301-459-2118; refer orders to National Bk. Network, 15200 NBN Way, P.O. Box 190, Blue Ridge Summit, Pa. 17214 Tel 800-462-6420 Fax 800-338-4550

Madison Press Bks., 40 Madison Ave., Toronto, Ont., Can. M5R 2S1 Tel 416-923-5027 Fax 416-923-7169

Magic Carpet Bks., 525 B St., Suite 1900, San Diego, Calif. 92101-4495 Tel 619-699-6707; 800-831-7799 Fax 619-699-6542; refer orders to Harcourt INC., 6277 Sea Harbor Dr., Orlando, Fla. 32887 Tel 619-699-6707; 800-543-1918 (orders)

Margaret K. McElderry Bks., 1230 Ave. of the Americas, New York, N.Y. 10020 Tel 212-698-7200; 800-257-5755

Marshall Cavendish Bks. Ltd., 119 Wardour St., London W1V 3TD, Eng. Tel (0171) 734 6710 Fax (0171) 734 6221
Branch offices
U.S.: Marshall Cavendish Corp., 99 White Plains Rd., P.O. Box 2001, Tarrytown, N.Y. 10591-9001 Tel 914-332-8888; 800-821-9881 Fax 914-332-1082

McFarland & Co. Inc. Pubs., P.O. Box 611, Jefferson, N.C. 28640-0611 Tel 910-246-4460; 800-253-2187 (orders only) Fax 910-246-5018

Meredith Bks., 1716 Locust St., Des Moines, Iowa 50309-3023 Tel 515-284-2415; 800-678-8091 Fax 515-284-3371

Merriam-Webster Inc., 47 Federal St., P.O. Box 281, Springfield, Mass. 01102 Tel 413-734-3134; 800-828-1880 Fax 413-731-5979

Messner: Julian Messner, 299 Jefferson Rd., Parsippany, N.J. 07054 Tel 973-739-8000; 800-848-9500 Fax 973-739-8053; 800-393-3156; refer orders to Silver Burdett Press, P.O. Box 2649, 4350 Equity Dr., Columbus, Ohio 43216 Tel 614-771-7398 Fax 614-771-7361

Metropolitan Mus. of Art, 1000 5th Ave., New York, N.Y. 10028 Tel 212-879-5500 Fax 212-472-8725; refer orders to Harry N. Abrams Inc., 100 5th Ave., New York, N.Y. 10011 Tel 212-206-7715; 800-345-1359 Fax 212-645-8437

Michael Di Capua Bks., 10 E. 53rd St., New York, N.Y. 10022-5299 Tel 212-207-7000; 800-242-7737 Fax 212-207-7145; refer orders to HarperCollins Pubs., 1000 Keystone Ind. Park, Scranton, Pa. 18512-4621 Tel 717-941-1500; 800-242-7737 Fax 800-822-4090

Mikaya Press, 12 Bedford St., New York, N.Y. 10014 Tel 212-647-1831 Fax 212-727-0236; refer orders to Firefly Bks. (Buffalo), P.O. Box 1338, Ellicott Station, Buffalo, N.Y. 14205 Tel 800-387-5085

Millbrook Press Inc. (The), 2 Old New Milford Rd., Brookfield, Conn. 06804 Tel 203-740-2220; 800-462-4703 Fax 203-740-2223

Miller Freeman Inc., 600 Harrison St., San Francisco, Calif. 94107 Tel 415-905-2470 Fax 415-848-5784; refer orders to Miller Freeman Distr. Center, 6600 Silacci Way, Gilroy, Calif. 95020 Tel 408-848-5296; 800-848-5594

Mint Pubs., 241 Lexington Ave., Mt. Kisco, N.Y. 10549

Mitchell Lane Pubs., 17 Matthew Bathon Ct., Elkton, Md. 21921 Tel 410-392-5036; 800-814-5484 Fax 410-392-4781

Modern Curriculum Press Inc., 13900 Prospect Rd., Cleveland, Ohio 44136 Tel 216-238-2222; 800-321-3106 Fax 216-238-0460

Monterey Bay Aquarium, 886 Cannery Row, Monterey, Calif. 93940 Tel 408-648-4841 Fax 408-644-7568

Morgan Reynolds Inc., 620 S. Elm St., Suite 384, Greensboro, N.C. 27406 Tel 910-275-1311 Fax 910-275-1152

Morning Glory Press, 6595 San Haroldo Way, Buena Park, Calif. 90620-3748 Tel 714-828-1998; 888-612-8254 Fax 714-828-2049; 888-327-4362

Morrow: William Morrow & Co. Inc., 1350 Ave. of the Americas, New York, N.Y. 10019 Tel 212-261-6500; 800-237-0657 Fax 212-779-0965; refer orders to HarperCollins Pubs., 1000 Keystone Ind. Park, Scranton, Pa. 18512-4621 Tel 800-242-7737 Fax 800-822-4090

Morrow Junior Bks., 1350 Ave. of the Americas, New York, N.Y. 10019 Tel 212-261-6500; 800-237-0657 Fax 212-779-0965; refer orders to HarperCollins Pubs., 1000 Keystone Ind. Park, Scranton, Pa. Tel 800-242-7737 Fax 800-822-4090

Muir Publs.: John Muir Publs., P.O. Box 613, Santa Fe, N.M. 87504-0613 Tel 505-982-4078; 800-888-7504 Fax 505-988-1680; refer orders to Publishers Group West, 1700 4th St., Berkeley, Calif. 94710 Tel 510-528-1444; 800-788-3123 Fax 510-528-3444

NAL/Dutton, 375 Hudson St., New York, N.Y. 10014-3657 Tel 212-366-2000; 800-526-0275 (orders) Fax 212-366-2666; refer orders to Penguin Putnam Inc., 405 Murray Hill Parkway, E. Rutherford, N.J. 07073 Tel 201-933-9292; 800-526-0275

National Council of Teachers of English, 1111 W. Kenyon Rd., Urbana, Ill. 61801-1096 Tel 217-328-3870; 800-369-6283 Fax 217-328-0977

National Council of Teachers of Mathematics, 1906 Association Dr., Reston, Va. 22091-1593 Tel 703-620-9840; 800-235-7566 (orders only) Fax 703-476-2970

National Geographic Soc., 1145 17th St. N.W., Washington, D.C. 20036 Tel 202-857-7000; 800-647-5463 Fax 301-921-1575; refer orders to Simon & Schuster Ordering Dept., 200 Old Tappan Rd., Old Tappan, N.J. 07675 Tel 800-223-2336 (orders) Fax 800-445-6991

National Science Teachers Assn., 1840 Wilson Blvd., Arlington, Va. 22201-3000 Tel 703-243-7100; 800-722-6782 (orders) Fax 703-243-7177

Neal-Schuman Pubs. Inc., 100 Varick St., New York, N.Y. 10013 Tel 212-925-8650 Fax 212-219-8916; 800-584-2414

Nelson, T.: Thomas Nelson Pubs., P.O. Box 141000, Nelson Pl. at Elm Hill Pike, Nashville, Tenn. 37214-1000 Tel 615-889-9000; 800-251-4000 Fax 615-391-5225; 800-448-8403

New Am. Lib. Inc. (The), 375 Hudson St., New York, N.Y. 10014-3657 Tel 212-366-2000; 800-526-0275 (orders) Fax 212-366-2666; refer orders to Penguin Putnam Inc., 405 Murray Hill Parkway, E. Rutherford, N.J. 07073 Tel 201-933-9292; 800-526-0275

New Amsterdam Bks., P.O. Box C, Franklin, N.Y. 13775-0303 Tel 607-829-2800; 800-944-4040 Fax 607-829-205; refer orders to National Bk. Network, 15200 NBN Way, P.O. Box 190, Blue Ridge Summit, Pa. 17214 Tel 800-462-6420 Fax 800-338-4550

New York Public Lib. Astor, Lenox & Tilden Foundations, 5th Ave. & 42nd St., New York, N.Y. 10018 Tel 212-512-0203; refer orders to Publications Office, 8 W. 40th St., 6th Floor, New York, N.Y. 10018 Tel 212-512-0202 Fax 212-704-8623

Newmarket Press, 18 E. 48th St., Suite 1501, New York, N.Y. 10017 Tel 212-832-3575; 800-669-3903 Fax 212-832-3629; refer orders to Random House Inc., 400 Hahn Rd., Westminster, Md. 21157 Tel 410-848-1900; 800-733-3000

North-South Bks., Industriestr. 8, 8625 Gossau, Zurich, Switzerland Tel (01) 9366868 Fax (01) 9366800

Branch offices

U.S.: North-South Bks., 1123 Broadway, Suite 800, New York, N.Y. 10010 Tel 212-463-9736; 800-722-6657 Fax 212-633-1004; refer orders to Chronicle Bks., 85 2nd St., 6th Floor, San Francisco, Calif. 94105 Tel 415-537-3730; 800-722-6657 (orders only) Fax 415-537-4460; 800-858-7787

Norton: W.W. Norton & Co. Inc., 500 5th Ave., New York, N.Y. 10110 Tel 212-354-5500; 800-233-4830 (orders) Fax 212-869-0856; 800-458-6515 (orders)

NTC Pub. Group, 4255 W. Touhy Ave., Lincolnwood, Ill. 60646-1975 Tel 847-679-5500; 800-323-4900 (orders) Fax 847-679-2494; 800-998-3103 (orders)

Oliver Press (Minneapolis): Oliver Press Inc., 5707 W. 36th St., Minneapolis, Minn. 55416-2510 Tel 612-926-8981 Fax 612-926-8965

Omnigraphics Inc., Penobscot Bldg., Detroit, Mich. 48226 Tel 313-961-1340; 800-234-1340 (orders) Fax 800-875-1340

Orchard Bks., 95 Madison Ave., 7th Floor, New York, N.Y. 10016 Tel 212-951-2600; 800-621-1115 Fax 212-213-6435

Oryx Press (The), 4041 N. Central Ave., 7th Floor, Phoenix, Ariz. 85012-3397 Tel 602-265-2651; 800-279-6799 Fax 602-265-6250; 800-279-4663

Overlook Press (The), 386 W. Broadway, 4th Floor, New York, N.Y. 10012 Tel 212-965-8400 Fax 212-965-9834; refer orders to 2568 Route 212, Woodstock, N.Y. 12498 Tel 914-679-6838 Fax 914-679-8571

Owl Bks. (Toronto): Owl Bks., 179 John St., Suite 500, Toronto, Ont., Can. M5T 3G5 Tel 416-971-5275 Fax 416-971-5294; refer orders to Firefly Bks. Ltd., 3680 Victoria Park Ave., Willowdale, Ont., Can. M2H 3K1 Tel 416-499-8412; 800-387-5085 Fax 800-565-6034

Oxford Univ. Press, Great Clarendon St., Oxford OX2 6DP, Eng. Tel (01865) 556 767 Fax (01865) 556 646
Branch offices
U.S.: Oxford Univ. Press Inc., 198 Madison Ave., New York, N.Y. 10016-4314 Tel 212-726-6000; 800-334-4249 Fax 212-725-2972; refer orders to 2001 Evans Rd., Cary, N.C. 27513 Tel 919-677 1303; 800-451-7556 Fax 919-677-1303

Pantheon Bks. Inc., 201 E. 50th St., New York, N.Y. 10022 Tel 212-572-2838; 800-638-0600 Fax 212-572-6030; refer orders to Random House Inc., 400 Hahn Rd., Westminster, Md. 21157 Tel 410-848-1900; 800-733-3000

Peel Productions, 512 Blanton St., Columbus, N.C. 28722 Tel 704-894-8838 Fax 704-894-8839; refer orders to Midpoint Trade Bks. Inc., 1263 Southwest Blvd., Kansas City, Kan. 66103 Tel 913-831-2233; 800-742-6139 Fax 913-362-7401

Pelican Pub. Co. Inc., 100 Burmaster St., P.O. Box 3110, Gretna, La. 70054 Tel 504-368-1175; 800-843-1724 (orders only) Fax 504-368-1195

Penguin Bks. Ltd., 27 Wrights Lane, London W8 5TZ, Eng. Tel (0171) 416 3000 Fax (0171) 416 3099; refer orders to P.O. Box 11, W. Drayton, Middlesex UB7 0DA, Eng. Tel (0181) 899 4000 Fax (0181) 899 4099
Branch offices
U.S.: Penguin Bks., 375 Hudson St., New York, N.Y. 10014-3657 Tel 212-366-2000; 800-331-4624 Fax 212-366-2666; refer orders to Penguin Putnam Inc., 405 Murray Hill Parkway, E. Rutherford, N.J. 07073 Tel 201-933-9292; 800-526-0275

Penguin Putnam Inc., 375 Hudson St., New York, N.Y. 10014-3657 Tel 212-366-2000; 800-331-4624 Fax 212-366-2666; refer orders to 405 Murray Hill Parkway, E. Rutherford, N.J. 07073 Tel 800-526-0275 Fax 800-227-9604

Perennial Lib., 10 E. 53rd St., New York, N.Y. 10022-5299 Tel 212-207-7000; refer orders to HarperCollins Pubs., Keystone Ind. Park, Scranton, Pa. 18512 Tel 800-982-4377; 800-242-7737 (outside Pa.)

Perlman Bks.: Willa Perlman Bks., 10 E. 53rd St., New York, N.Y. 10022-5299 Tel 212-207-7000; 800-242-7737 Fax 212-207-7145; refer orders to HarperCollins Pubs., 1000 Keystone Ind. Park, Scranton, Pa. 18512-4621 Tel 717-941-1500; 800-242-7737 Fax 800-822-4090

Peterson's Guides Inc., 202 Carnegie Center, Princeton, N.J. 08540 Tel 609-243-9111; 800-338-3282 (orders) Fax 609-243-9150; 452-0966 (orders)

Phi Delta Kappa Educ. Foundation, 408 N. Union, P.O. Box 789, Bloomington, Ind. 47402-0789 Tel 812-339-1156; 800-766-1156 Fax 812-339-0018

Philomel Bks., 375 Hudson St., New York, N.Y. 10014 Tel 212-366-2000; 800-331-4624 Fax 212-213-6706; refer orders to Penguin Putnam Inc., Inside Sales Dept., 1 Grosset Dr., Kirkwood, N.Y. 13795 Tel 607-775-4829; 800-847-5515

Pierian Press, P.O. Box 1808, Ann Arbor, Mich. 48106-1808 Tel 313-434-5530; 800-678-2435

Piñata Bks., Arte Público Press, Univ. of Houston, Houston, Tex. 77204-2090 Tel 713-743-2998; 800-633-2783 (orders only) Fax 713-743-2847

Plays Inc., 120 Boylston St., Boston, Mass. 02116 Tel 617-423-3157 Fax 617-423-2168

Pocket Bks., Simon & Schuster Bldg., 1230 Ave. of the Americas, New York, N.Y. 10020 Tel 212-698-7000; 800-223-2348; refer orders to Simon & Schuster Ordering Dept., 100 Front St., Riverside, N.J. 08075 Tel 800-223-2336 (orders) Fax 800-445-6991

PowerKids Press, 29 E. 21st St., New York, N.Y. 10010 Tel 212-777-3017; 800-237-9932 Fax 212-777-0277; 888-436-4643

Prentice-Hall Inc., 1 Lake St., Upper Saddle River, N.J. 07458-9925 Tel 201-236-7000; refer orders to Prentice-Hall/Allyn & Bacon, 200 Old Tappan Rd., Old Tappan, N.J. 07675 Tel 800-223-1360 Fax 800-445-6991

Prentice-Hall Int. Inc., 1 Lake St., Upper Saddle River, N.J. 07458-9925 Tel 201-236-7000; refer orders to Prentice-Hall/Allyn & Bacon, 200 Old Tappan Rd., Old Tappan, N.J. 07675 Tel 800-223-1360 Fax 800-445-6991

Price/Stern/Sloan Inc., 375 Hudson St., New York, N.Y. 10014 Tel 212-366-2000; 800-331-4624 Fax 212-213-6706; refer orders to Penguin Putnam Inc., Inside Sales Dept., 1 Grosset Dr., Kirkwood, N.Y. 13795 Tel 607-775-4829; 800-847-5515

Publishers Group West, 1700 4th St., Berkeley, Calif. 94710 Tel 510-528-1444; 800-788-3123 Fax 510-528-3444

Puffin Bks., 27 Wrights Lane, London W8 5TZ, Eng. Tel (0171) 416 3000 Fax (0171) 416 3099; refer orders to Penguin Bks. Ltd., P.O. Box 11, W. Drayton, Middlesex UB7 0DA, Eng. Tel (0181) 899 4000 Fax (0181) 899 4099
Branch offices
U.S.: Puffin Bks., 375 Hudson St., New York, N.Y. 10014-3657 Tel 212-366-2000 Fax 212-366-2666; refer orders to Penguin Putnam Inc., 405 Murray Hill Parkway, E. Rutherford, N.J. 07073 Tel 800-526-0275 Fax 800-227-9604

Putnam: G.P. Putnam's Sons, 375 Hudson St., New York, N.Y. 10014 Tel 212-366-2000; 800-331-4624 Fax 212-213-6706; refer orders to Penguin Putnam Inc., 405 Murray Hill Parkway, E. Rutherford, N.J. 07073 Tel 800-526-0275 Fax 800-227-9604

Putnam Pub. Group (The), 375 Hudson St., New York, N.Y. 10014 Tel 212-366-2000; 800-331-4624 Fax 212-213-6706; refer orders to Penguin Putnam Inc., 405 Murray Hill Parkway, E. Rutherford, N.J. 07073 Tel 800-526-0275 Fax 800-227-9604

Raintree Steck-Vaughn Pubs., 466 Southern Blvd., Chatham, N.J. 07928 Tel 973-514-1525; 888-363-4266 (orders) Fax 973-514-1612; 877-578-2638 (orders); refer orders to P.O. Box 26105, Austin, Tex. 78755 Tel 512-343-6854; 800-531-5015

Rand McNally, 8255 N. Central Park, Skokie, Ill. 60076-2970 Tel 847-329-8100 Fax 847-673-0813

Random House Inc., 201 E. 50th St., 22nd Floor, New York, N.Y. 10022 Tel 212-751-2600; 800-726-0600 Fax 800-659-2436; refer orders to 400 Hahn Rd., Westminster, Md. 21157 Tel 410-848-1900; 800-733-3000

Random House Value Pub. Inc., 40 Engelhard Ave., Avenel, N.J. 07001 Tel 908-827-2700; 800-223-6804 Fax 908-827-2641

Reader's Digest Assn. Inc. (The), 260 Madison Ave., New York, N.Y. 10016-2401 Tel 212-850-7100 Fax 212-850-7079; refer orders to Reader's Digest Rd., Pleasantville, N.Y. 10570 Tel 800-431-1246 Fax 914-238-7620

Reader's Digest Children's Bks., Reader's Digest Rd., Pleasantville, N.Y. 10570-7000 Tel 914-238-1000; 800-234-9000 Fax 914-244-4880; refer orders to Simon & Schuster Children's Ordering Dept., 200 Old Tappan Rd., Old Tappan, N.J. 07675 Tel 800-223-2336 (orders) Fax 800-445-6991

Rising Moon Bks. for Young Readers, P.O. Box 1389, Flagstaff, Ariz. 86002-1389 Tel 520-774-5251; 800-346-3257 Fax 520-774-0592; 800-257-9082

Riverfront Bks., 90 Sherman Turnpike, Danbury, Conn. 06816 Tel 203-797-3500; 800-621-1115 Fax 203-797-3143

Rizzoli Int. Publs. Inc., 300 Park Ave. S., 3rd Floor, New York, N.Y. 10010 Tel 212-387-3400 Fax 212-387-3535; refer orders to St. Martin's Press Inc., VHPS-Von Holtzbrinck Pub. Services, 16365 James Madison Highway (U.S. Route 15), Gordonsville, Va. 22942 Tel 540-672-7600; 888-330-8477 Fax 800-672-2054

ROC, 375 Hudson St., New York, N.Y. 10014-3657 Tel 212-366-2000; 800-526-0275 (orders) Fax 212-366-2666; refer orders to Penguin Putnam Inc., 405 Murray Hill Parkway, E. Rutherford, N.J. 07073 Tel 201-933-9292; 800-526-0275

Rosen Pub. Group Inc. (The), 29 E. 21st St., New York, N.Y. 10010 Tel 212-777-3017; 800-237-9932 Fax 212-777-0277; 888-436-4643

Rourke Publs., P.O. Box 3328, Vero Beach, Fla. 32964 Tel 561-234-6001 Fax 561-234-6622

Salem Press Inc., 131 North El Molino Ave., Suite 350, Pasadena, Calif. 91101 Tel 626-584-0106 Fax 626-584-1525; refer orders to Two University Plaza, Suite 121, Hackensack, N.J. 07601 Tel 800-221-1592 Fax 201-968-1411

Sargent Pubs.: Porter Sargent Pubs. Inc., 11 Beacon St., Suite 1400, Boston, Mass. 02108 Tel 617-523-1670 Fax 617-523-1021

Scarecrow Press Inc., 4720 Boston Way, Suite A, Lanham, Md. 20706-4310 Tel 301-459-3366; 800-462-6420 Fax 717-794-3803; 800-338-4550; refer orders to National Bk. Network, 15200 NBN Way, P.O. Box 190, Blue Ridge Summit, Pa. 17214 Tel 717-794-3800; 800-462-6420 Fax 800-338-4550

Schocken Bks. Inc., 201 E. 50th St., New York, N.Y. 10022 Tel 212-572-2559; 800-726-0600 Fax 212-572-6030; refer orders to Random House Inc., 400 Hahn Rd., Westminster, Md. 21157 Tel 410-848-1900; 800-733-3000

Scholastic Inc., 555 Broadway, New York, N.Y. 10012-3999 Tel 212-343-6100 Fax 212-343-4535; refer orders to HarperCollins Pubs., 1000 Keystone Ind. Park, Scranton, Pa. 18512-4621 Tel 800-242-7737 Fax 800-822-4090

Scholastic Press, 555 Broadway, New York, N.Y. 10012-3999 Tel 212-343-6100 Fax 212-343-4535; refer orders to HarperCollins Pubs., 1000 Keystone Ind. Park, Scranton, Pa. 18512-4621 Tel 800-242-7737 Fax 800-822-4090

Scholastic Ref., 555 Broadway, New York, N.Y. 10012-3999 Tel 212-343-6100 Fax 212-343-4535; refer orders to HarperCollins Pubs., 1000 Keystone Ind. Park, Scranton, Pa. 18512-4621 Tel 800-242-7737 Fax 800-822-4090

Scientific Am. Bks. for Young Readers, 41 Madison Ave., 37th Floor, New York, N.Y. 10010 Tel 212-576-9400 Fax 212-689-2383; refer orders to VHPS-Von Holtzbrinck Pub. Services, 16365 James Madison Highway (U.S. Route 15), Gordonsville, Va. 22942 Tel 540-672-7600; 888-330-8477 Fax 800-672-2054

Scott, Foresman & Co., 1900 E. Lake Ave., Glenview, Ill. 60025 Tel 708-729-3000 Fax 708-729-8910

Scott Pub. Co. (Sidney): Scott Pub. Co., 911 Vandemark Rd., Sidney, Ohio 45365 Tel 937-498-0802; refer orders to P.O. Box 828, Sidney, Ohio 45365 Tel 800-572-6885

Scribner: Charles Scribner's Sons, 1633 Broadway, New York, N.Y. 10019 Tel 646-756-2500; refer orders to Gale Group, P.O. Box 9187, Farmington Hills, Mich. 48333-9187 Tel 800-877-4253 Fax 313-961-6083; 800-414-5043

Seal Press (The), 3131 Western Ave., Suite 410, Seattle, Wash. 98121-1028 Tel 206-283-7844; 800-754-0271 Fax 206-285-9410; refer orders to Publishers Group West, 1700 4th St., Berkeley, Calif. 94710 Tel 510-528-1444; 800-788-3123 Fax 510-528-3444

Sierra Club Bks., 85 2nd St., 2nd Floor, San Francisco, Calif. 94105 Tel 415-291-1600 Fax 415-291-1602; refer orders to Random House Inc., 400 Hahn Rd., Westminster, Md. 21157 Tel 410-848-1900; 800-733-3000

Silver Burdett Press, 299 Jefferson Rd., Parsippany, N.J. 07054 Tel 973-739-8000; 800-848-9500 Fax 973-739-8053; 800-393-3156; refer orders to P.O. Box 2649, 4350 Equity Dr., Columbus, Ohio 43216 Tel 614-771-7398 Fax 614-771-7361

Silver Whistle Bks., 525 B St., Suite 1900, San Diego, Calif. 92101-4495 Tel 619-699-6707; 800-831-7799 Fax 619-699-6542; refer orders to Harcourt Inc., 6277 Sea Harbor Dr., Orlando, Fla. 32887 Tel 619-699-6707; 800-543-1918 (orders)

Simon & Schuster Inc. Pubs., Simon & Schuster Bldg., 1230 Ave. of the Americas, New York, N.Y. 10020 Tel 212-698-7000; 800-223-2348; refer orders to Simon & Schuster Ordering Dept., 100 Front St., Riverside, N.J. 08075 Tel 800-223-2336 (orders) Fax 800-445-6991

Simon & Schuster Bks. for Young Readers, Simon & Schuster Bldg., 1230 Ave. of the Americas, New York, N.Y. 10020 Tel 212-698-7000; 800-257-5755; refer orders to Simon & Schuster Children's Ordering Dept., 100 Front St., Riverside, N.J. 08075 Tel 800-223-2336 (orders) Fax 800-445-6991

Skira/Rizzoli, 300 Park Ave. S., 3rd Floor, New York, N.Y. 10010 Tel 212-387-3400 Fax 212-387-3535; refer orders to St. Martin's Press Inc., VHPS-Von Holtzbrinck Pub. Services, 16365 James Madison Highway (U.S. Route 15), Gordonsville, Va. 22942 Tel 540-672-7600; 888-330-8477 Fax 800-672-2054

Sleepy Hollow Press, 150 White Plains Rd., Tarrytown, N.Y. 10591 Tel 914-631-8200; refer orders to Fordham Univ. Press

Smith & Kraus Inc., P.O. Box 127, Lyme, N.H. 03768 Tel 603-643-6431; 800-895-4331 Fax 603-643-1831

Smith, P.: Peter Smith Pub., Inc., 5 Lexington Ave., Magnolia, Mass. 01930 Tel 508-525-3562

Smithsonian Institution Press, 470 L'Enfant Plaza, Suite 7100, Washington, D.C. 20560 Tel 202-287-3738 Fax 202-287-3184; refer orders to P.O. Box 960, Herndon, Va. 20172-0960 Tel 800-782-4612 Fax 703-689-0660

Somerville House Pub., 3080 Yonge St., Suite 5000, Toronto, Ont., Can. M4N 3N1 Tel 416-488-5938 Fax 416-488-5506

Sourcebooks Inc., 121 N. Washington St., Suite 2N, Naperville, Ill. 60540 Tel 630-961-3900; 800-727-8866 Fax 630-961-2168; refer orders to Login Pubs. Consortium, 1436 W. Randolph St., 2nd Floor, Chicago, Ill. 60607 Tel 312-432-7650; 800-626-4330 Fax 312-733-3107

St. James Press, c.o. Gale Group, 27500 Drake Rd., Farmington Hills, Mich. 48331-3535 Tel 248-699-4255; 800-877-4253 Fax 313-961-6083; 800-414-5043

St. Martin's Press Inc., 175 5th Ave., New York, N.Y. 10010-7842 Tel 212-674-5151; 800-221-7945 Fax 212-420-9314; refer orders to VHPS-Von Holtzbrinck Pub. Services, 16365 James Madison Highway (U.S. Route 15), Gordonsville, Va. 22942 Tel 540-672-7600; 888-330-8477 Fax 800-672-2054

Stackpole Bks. Inc., 5067 Ritter Rd., Mechanicsburg, Pa. 17055 Tel 717-796-0411; 800-732-3669 Fax 717-796-0412

Sterling Pub. Co. Inc., 387 Park Ave. S., New York, N.Y. 10016-8810 Tel 212-532-7160; 800-367-9692 Fax 212-213-2495; 800-542-7567

Stevens, G.: Gareth Stevens Inc., River Center Bldg., 1555 N. River Center Dr., Suite 201, Milwaukee, Wis. 53212 Tel 414-225-0333; 800-542-2595 Fax 414-225-0377

Stewart, Tabori & Chang Inc., 115 W. 18th St., 5th Floor, New York, N.Y. 10011 Tel 212-519-1200; 800-815-8328 Fax 212-519-1230; refer orders to U.S. Media Holdings Inc., Raritan Plaza III, 101 Fieldcrest Ave., Edison, N.J. 08837 Tel 732-225-4900; 800-932-0070 Fax 732-225-7588

Superintendent of Docs., U.S. Govt. Ptg. Office, Washington, D.C. 20402

T.F.H. Publs. Inc., 211 W. Sylvania Ave., Neptune City, N.J. 07753 Tel 908-988-8400; 800-631-2188 Fax 908-988-5466

Teacher Ideas Press, P.O. Box 6633, Englewood, Colo. 80155-6633 Tel 303-770-1200; 800-237-6124 Fax 303-220-8843

Ticknor & Fields, 215 Park Ave. S., New York, N.Y. 10003 Tel 212-420-5800; 800-225-3362 Fax 212-420-5855; refer orders to Houghton Mifflin Co., Wayside Rd., Burlington, Mass. 01803 Tel 617-272-1500; 800-225-3362

Time-Life Bks. Inc., 2000 Duke St., Alexandria, Va. 22314 Tel 703-838-7000; 800-621-7026 Fax 703-684-5224; refer orders to 1450 E. Parham Rd., Richmond, Va. 23280 Tel 800-621-7026

Times Bks., 201 E. 50th St., 22nd Floor, New York, N.Y. 10022 Tel 212-751-2600; 800-726-0600 Fax 800-659-2436; refer orders to Random House Inc., 400 Hahn Rd., Westminster, Md. 21157 Tel 410-848-1900; 800-733-3000

TOR Bks., 175 5th Ave., New York, N.Y. 10010 Tel 212-388-0100; 800-321-9299 Fax 212-388-0191; refer orders to St. Martin's Press Inc., VHPS-Von Holtzbrinck Pub. Services, 16365 James Madison Highway (U.S. Route 15), Gordonsville, Va. 22942 Tel 540-672-7600; 888-330-8477 Fax 800-672-2054

Tundra Bks. Inc., 481 University Ave., Suite 802, Toronto, Ont., Can. M5G 2E9 Tel 416-598-4786 Fax 416-598-0247
Subsidiaries
U.S.: Tundra Bks. of Northern N.Y., P.O. Box 1030, Plattsburgh, N.Y. 12901 Tel 416-598-4786 Fax 416-598-0247

Twayne Pubs., 1633 Broadway, New York, N.Y. 10019; refer orders to Gale Group, P.O. Box 9187, Farmington Hills, Mich. 48333-9187 Tel 248-699-4255; 800-877-4253 Fax 313-961-6083; 800-414-5043

U.S. Govt. Ptg. Office, USGPO Stop SSMB, Washington, D.C. 20401 Tel 202-512-1705 Fax 202-512-1655; refer orders to Superintendent of Docs., P.O. Box 371954, Pittsbugh, Pa. Tel 202-512-1800 Fax 202-512-2250

U.S. Postal Service, Philatelic Marketing Div., 475 L'Enfant Plaza S.W., Washington, D.C. 20260

U.X.L, 27500 Drake Rd., Farmington Hills, Mich. 48331-3535 Tel 248-699-4255; 800-877-4253 (orders) Fax 313-961-6083; 800-414-5043 (orders)

University of Ill. Press, 1325 S. Oak St., Champaign, Ill. 61820 Tel 217-333-0950 Fax 217-244-8082; refer orders to P.O. Box 4856, Baltimore, Md. 21211 Tel 800-545-4703 Fax 410-516-6969

University of N.M. Press, 1720 Lomas Blvd. N.E., Albuquerque, N.M. 87131-1591 Tel 505-277-4810; 800-249-7737 (orders) Fax 505-277-3350; 800-622-8667; refer orders to Order Dept., 3721 Spirit Dr., Albuquerque, N.M. 87106-5631

University Press of Va., P.O. Box 3608, University Station, Charlottesville, Va. 22903-0608 Tel 804-924-3468; 800-831-3406 Fax 877-288-6400

Viking, 375 Hudson St., New York, N.Y. 10014-3657 Tel 212-366-2000; 800-331-4624 Fax 212-366-2666; refer orders to Penguin Putnam Inc., 405 Murray Hill Parkway, E. Rutherford, N.J. 07073 Tel 201-933-9292; 800-526-0275

Viking Kestrel, 375 Hudson St., New York, N.Y. 10014-3657 Tel 212-366-2000; 800-331-4624 Fax 212-366-2666; refer orders to Penguin Putnam Inc., 405 Murray Hill Parkway, E. Rutherford, N.J. 07073 Tel 201-933-9292; 800-526-0275

Voyageur Press, 123 N. 2nd St., Stillwater, Minn. 55082 Tel 612-430-2210; 800-888-9653 (orders) Fax 612-430-2211

Walker & Co., 435 Hudson St., New York, N.Y. 10014 Tel 212-727-8300; 800-289-2553 Fax 212-727-0984

Warne: Frederick Warne Pubs. Ltd., 27 Wrights Lane, London W8 5TZ, Eng. Tel (0171) 416 3000 Fax (0171) 416 3199; refer orders to Penguin Bks. Ltd., P.O. Box 11, W. Drayton, Middlesex UB7 0DA, Eng. Tel (0181) 899 4000 Fax (0181) 899 4099
Branch offices
U.S.: Warne, 375 Hudson St., New York, N.Y. 10014-3657 Tel 212-366-2000; 800-526-0275 Fax 212-366-2666; refer orders to Penguin Putnam Inc., 405 Murray Hill Parkway, E. Rutherford, N.J. 07073 Tel 201-933-9292; 800-526-0275

Warner Bks., Time & Life Bldg., 1271 Ave. of the Americas, New York, N.Y. 10020 Tel 212-522-8700; 800-343-9204 Fax 212-522-2067; refer orders to Time Warner Trade Pub., Customer Service, 3 Center Plaza, Boston, Mass. 02108-2084 Tel 800-343-9204 Fax 800-286-9471

Watson-Guptill Publs., 1515 Broadway, New York, N.Y. 10036 Tel 212-536-5110; 800-278-8477 Fax 212-536-5359; refer orders to Distribution Center, 1695 Oak St., Lakewood, N.J. 08701 Tel 908-363-4511; 800-451-1741 Fax 908-363-0338

Watts: Franklin Watts Inc., 90 Sherman Turnpike, Danbury, Conn. 06816 Tel 203-797-3500; 800-621-1115 Fax 203-797-3143

Whitman, A.: Albert Whitman & Co., 6340 Oakton St., Morton Grove, Ill. 60053 Tel 847-581-0033; 800-255-7675 Fax 847-581-0039

Wiley: John Wiley & Sons Inc., 605 3rd Ave., New York, N.Y. 10158-0012 Tel 212-850-6000; 800-225-5945 Fax 212-850-6088; refer orders to 1 Wiley Dr., Somerset, N.J. 08875-1272 Tel 908-469-4400; 800-225-5945 Fax 908-302-2300

Williamson Pub. Co., Church Hill Rd., P.O. Box 185, Charlotte, Vt. 05445 Tel 802-425-2102; 800-234-8791 (orders) Fax 802-425-2199; 800-304-7224 (orders)

Wilson, H.W.: The H.W. Wilson Co., 950 University Ave., Bronx, N.Y. 10452 Tel 718-588-8400; 800-367-6770 Fax 718-590-1617; 800-590-1617

Wings Bks., 201 E. 50th St., 22nd Floor, New York, N.Y. 10022 Tel 212-751-2600; 800-726-0600 Fax 800-659-2436; refer orders to Random House Inc., 400 Hahn Rd., Westminster, Md. 21157 Tel 410-848-1900; 800-733-3000

Woodbine House, 6510 Bells Mill Rd., Bethesda, Md. 20817 Tel 301-897-3570; 800-843-7323 Fax 301-897-5838

Wordsong, 815 Church St., Honesdale, Pa. 18431 Tel 570-253-1164; 877-512-8366 (orders) Fax 570-253-0179 (orders)

Workman Pub. Co. Inc., 708 Broadway, New York, N.Y. 10003 Tel 212-254-5900; 800-722-7202 Fax 212-254-8098; 800-521-1832 (orders)

World Almanac, 1 International Blvd., Suite 444, Mahwah, N.J. 07495-0017 Tel 201-529-6900 Fax 201-529-6901

World Bk. Inc., 525 W. Monroe, 20th Floor, Chicago, Ill. 60661 Tel 312-258-3700; 800-621-8202 Fax 312-258-3950

Writer's Digest Bks., 1507 Dana Ave., Cincinnati, Ohio 45207 Tel 513-531-2222; 800-289-0963 Fax 513-531-4082

Zino Press Children's Bks., 2348 Pinehurst Dr., Middleton, Wis. 53562 Tel 608-836-6660; 800-356-2303 Fax 608-831-1570; 800-618-1570